COMICS VALUES ANNUAL: 1996 EDITION
The Comics Books Price Guide

by Alex G. Malloy

edited by Stuart Wells III

Antique Trader Books
Dubuque, Iowa

Designed by Stuart W. Wells III

Manufactured in the United States of America

ISBN: 0-930625-35-8
ISSN: 1062-4503

**Other books and magazines published by
Antique Trader Publications:**
Antiques & Collectibles Annual Price Guide
American & European Art Pottery Price Guide
American Pressed Glass & Bottles Price Guide
American & European Decorative & Art Glass Price Guide
Ceramics Price Guide
American & European Furniture Price Guide
Maloney's Antiques & Collectibles Resource Directory
The Antique Trader Weekly
Collector Magazine & Price Guide
Toy Trader Magazine
Postcard Collector Magazine
Discoveries Magazine
Big Reel Magazine
Military Trader Magazine
Baby Boomer Collectibles Magazine

**To order additional copies of this book or
other publications listed above, contact:
Antique Trader Publications
P.O. Box 1050
Dubuque, Iowa 52004
1-800-334-7165**

Contents

PREFACE

By Alex G. Malloy

The comic industry is currently in a state of great upheaval due to dramatic changes in the direct comic distribution service to comic shops. In the past, almost all comics and comic related merchandise was sold to comic shops by several major comic distributors who all carried essentially the same products, distinguishing themselves by the services and discounts they offered. Recently Marvel comics bought Heroes World, one of the several distributors, and now sells its comics exclusively through them. Similarly, Diamond Comic Distributors, Inc. has obtained exclusive distribution rights for DC comics, while Capitol City Distribution has bought out several smaller distributors. Comic shops have been caught in the middle of these changes, unable to receive the usual discounts. To make matters worse, new comic sales are reported down everywhere. Back issue sales on comics issued in the last two years are also very quiet, with the exception of certain hot titles.

In response to these recent changes, some dealers have opted to no longer carry new titles and trade only in back issues. Other dealers have expanded into the volatile game card phenomenon headed by *Magic the Gathering* game cards, while Pogs sell well for dealers in certain areas. Sales of comic related merchandise, especially comic cards, have also slowed down, with the exception of action figures.

On the bright side, Golden Age and Silver Age comics have been going up in value substantially. In fact, Golden age comics are the hottest they have ever been. Dealers around the country who handle early comics are reporting increased business. Action #1 was sold recently for $137,500 while the mile-high example of Whiz Comics reportedly sold for a whopping $176,000. The mile-high collection was formed by Edgar Church in Denver, Colorado and most examples in his collection came down to us in mint to near mint condition, resulting in the most sought-after provenance in comics.

Of the current hot titles, the exploits of various bad girls and their counterparts are the talk of the day. Lady Death, Shi, Vampirella, Wonder Woman and Lady Rawhide are all gathering steam, but The X-Men still rule the roost. Newer titles such as Spawn, Gen-13, X-Files and Lady Death also have a substantial following.

A few words on using this book are appropriate at this point. As you may have already noticed, we have segmented our listings just as the industry itself is segmented: DC, Marvel, Golden Age, Other Publishers (Color), Other Publishers

(Black & White), Classics Illustrated, and Underground Comix; each has its own section complete with comprehensive listing of each particular title. This year we have made separate sections for the four largest publishers (after DC and Marvel): Acclaim (Valiant), Dark Horse, Image and Malibu, located right at the beginning of the other publishers section. We hope this will enable you to find your favorite titles easily. If not, all 6,500 titles and their page locations are listed alphabetically in the index at the back.

Wherever necessary, cross-referencing has been provided. This style of listing greatly enhances the ease of usage of *Comic Values Annual*. When seeking information about a particular title, simply turn to the section indicated, follow alphabetically and you'll find prices, artist listing and any other significant information you may need. All abbreviations used in our listings are found at the end of this section, immediately preceding the first comics listings.

The values listed are the **retail price** for comics found in **near-mint** condition. Prices for comics in true mint condition, or in lesser grades, must be adjusted. An adjustment table can be found inside the book's cover. These prices are what a retailer or auction house will ask for the comic. A dealer will traditionally pay 50% of the retail price or more if he needs certain stock or thinks he can resell it quickly. However, he will often pay much less if he is overstocked, it's a slow moving title, or he is not really interested in buying.

Special thanks to Mark Haverty, Don Bouchard, El Curiouso, Jeremy Shorr, Meredith Woodwell, Mark Brown, Howard Harris, Stephen Passarelli, Carl Bridgers, John Pearce, Steve Sorbo, Bryan Ash, John Dacey, Dennis Shamp, Ray Rappaport, Michael Shippey, Don Bettis, Pat Callanan, Mike Salvo and Tim Fredrick for their assistance in producing this book.

Special thanks to Carey Hall, the editor of Comics Values Monthly for his input. I must also mention Harry Rinker, Robert J. Sodaro, Buddy Scalera, Neal Adams, Chris Adams, Debbie Monroe and Bea Andrews for guidance and talents in making this annual possible.

Last, but not least, to all the writers, artists, letterers, colorists, editors, and all at DC, Marvel, Dark Horse, Image, Malibu, Acclaim-Valiant, Entity Comics, Topps, Warp Graphics, Teckno Comics, Continuity.. Hearty Thanks!

REGIONAL REPORTS

**Meredith S.
Woodwell
Zanadu Comics
Seattle, WA**
Northwest

1995 will go down as the year the comics industry was turned on its head. Changing consumer tastes, rising cover prices and changes in comics distribution have all combined to create an atmosphere of uncertainty throughout the comics field.

Increased comic costs and the proliferation of character "family" titles and spin-offs have caused almost everyone to re-evaluate their comics-buying habits. Publisher loyalty disappeared several years ago, but now we're also seeing a weakening in character loyalty, as it has become prohibitively expensive for collectors to purchase every appearance of their favorite character. The same goes for those who purchase every new #1 issue or foil embossed, die-cut, gatefold, hologram cover.

Today's comics reader is developing a savvy ability to read through publisher hype to glean the best from today's comics pickings. They are aided in this endeavor by the many new, professional comics magazines, such as *Wizard*, that offer intra-industry critique and previews over a wide range of comics titles; new Internet connections, such as DC Online and the Tekno Comics Prodigy site; and a willingness by more publishers to collect their best stories into the more accessible trade paperback format.

QUALITY has become the demand word from today's comics consumers. Many fans now follow their favorite writers and artists from project to project, regardless of character or publisher — witness the rise of "creator owned" imprints at Dark Horse and Acclaim and the continued success of Image Comics, not to mention the successes of such self-publishing ventures as David Lapham's *Stray Bullets* or Steven R. Bissette's *Tyrant*. In fact, most self-published and/or non-superhero titles are experiencing rising popularity. Diversity is probably now at its greatest point since the Wertham trials at the beginning of the Silver Age.

The resurgent popularity of fine writing, meaningful storylines and tight characterization has boosted sales in all comic genres, including Manga (*Ranma 1/2, Oh My Goddess, Ghost in the Shell*), humor (*Bone, Grog, Scud: Disposable Assassin*),

fantasy (*Elfquest, Thieves & Kings, Poison Elves*), westerns (*Jonah Hex, Lone Ranger and Tonto*), crime (*Sin City, Stray Bullets*), mature readers (*VERTIGO, Spectre, Starman*), "underground" (*Hate, Eightball, Naughty Bits*), media tie-ins (*Star Wars, Star Trek, X-Files, Harlan Ellison's Dream Corridor*), and many other comics which refuse to be pigeon-holed (*Acme Novelty Library, Strangers in Paradise, Cerebus*).

Of course, even with these changes in reader's priorities, faddish trends still survive. Beginning with *Vengeance of Vampirella* and *Shi*, the "bad girl" comic has blossomed into an eye–(among other things)–popping universe filled by *Lady Death, Ghost, Lady Rawhide, Nira X: Cyberangel, Razor* and *Dawn*, among others. Eventually this "beauty" will fad(e)-away, but there's no telling how long this may take. As for other, passing fads, we've now come to the end of the "grim and gritty" era. Grim for grimness sake is on the way out, and in its wake we're seeing the re-emergence of the fun/teen hero. DC leads the way here with its *Impulse, Legionnaires* and *Superboy* titles; while these kids still have problems to face, they do so with a positive attitude and a sense of adventure that has been sorely missed for the past decade.

What else does the future hold? Look for more media crossovers, both from movies, TV and mass market novelists into comics and from comics to other mass media. Harlan Ellison, Andrew Vacchs and Joe R. Lansdale already pen their own successful comics, what other popular writers may soon join them? "Star Wars" and "The X-Files" are thriving in the comics market; might we also someday be reading copies of "Melrose Place," "Baywatch" or "My So Called Life?" And while many comics (*Batman, Superman, Judge Dredd, X-Men, Spider-Man, The Maxx, The Tick*) have already gained heightened exposure through TV, film and novelizations, watch for many many more to join them over the next few years, with enough licensed merchandise to gag the Ultimate Nullifier.

The comics industry has had a rough couple of years, and I expect it will remain the same through the end of 1995, but, to paraphrase a popular song, the future looks so bright, I think we're all gonna need shades!

Dennis Schamp
& Ray Rappaport
The Comic Gallery
San Diego, CA
Southwest

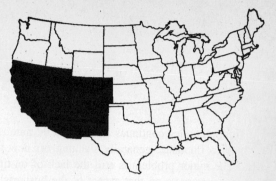

Welcome once again to sunny San Diego, and our impressions of the comic industry. Hope all of you have weathered the storms.

Marveloution. The one word on everyone's lips during the last part of 1994 and the first half of 1995. It seemed to be the one thing that actually brought competing retailers together. Even our customers, with access to the net, were coming to our store with questions such as "How will this affect your business?" I was glad to find out my customers were concerned for our welfare.

Now that the "BIG CHANGE" has happened, we can only watch and react. We still carry Marvel comics — we'd be foolish not to. But we are taking tighter reign on what we order. A few more of the better books, not so much of the chaff. Now, if only they could get their consumer order forms to ship on a timely manner.

The story lines themselves are picking up. We have noticed increases on the Spider-Man family of titles. I'm not sure if it's the clone thing or not. I do know the writing is some of the best (in my opinion) Marvel has had in the past few years. In the aftermath of the "Age of Apocalypse" story, the X-Men family sales have returned to pre-storyline numbers. I'm not sure what was accomplished, as we don't seem to have added any new readers, and have actually alienated some. Most readers are still unclear on the Edge family concept. Most titles already have a core following, and don't seem to be picking up any new readers. The 2099 family seems to be fading fast. Three titles are already cancelled for 1995. And, where the heck is Iron Man 2099?!?!?

DC-loution. Or should that be DC's solution? Either way, it's just another change retailers have to face. Is this a knee-jerk reaction to Major Comp.? DC says no. At least, DC has been more open than Marvel to the retailer for information sharing. All of my questions have been answered, all of our problems resolved quickly. Personally, I am a big fan of their comics, so I might be slightly biased, but in dealing with both companies during their transition phases, I can honestly say DC has provided more help and information than Marvel. But who can predict what the coming year will bring...

On the sales side, it seems that DC is slowing. Most of our numbers have been reduced 10%–15% from last quarter. Right now, the Batman and Superman families have enjoyed the most steady readership. Long storylines and tight plotting seem to

be keeping the reader's interests. The Milestone group, sadly, is one of our slowest sellers. We try to point these quality books out to our customers regularly, but most of them just don't bite. Any suggestions? The Vertigo group still keeps its readers riveted, sometimes using actual rivets. The mix of intense writing and innovative artwork is still a winning combination. The balance of DC's line of comics has a steady readership, and flourishes by constant word of mouth. I hope you all read the *Legion* and *Green Lantern*.

Image comics continues its push to be number two in the comic world. Sales continue to fluctuate, generally slacking off new titles by issue number 3 in most cases. The major problem is still the lack of on-time shipping. I still feel that they need to concentrate on that aspect of the business before taking on any more large projects. While the books are good and generate a huge amount of money, the lack of on-time product puts many retailers in a financial bind. I would rather see five to eight books every week, rather than 16 or so at the end of the month.

Dark Horse is running a close second to Image in the race of the "big six." With its movie and TV tie-ins, it stands at the brink of becoming a strong contender. We have noticed increased sales on its big books, as well as its smaller titles. We have big hopes for them in the coming year.

Malibu/Marvel is still trying to find its corner in the comic world. I do hope the merging of the major characters breathes some new life into this beast. The "Black September" storyline will be the turning point for the company. Unfortunately, we'll never know if they could have survived without it.

Acclaim/Valiant/Armada/Windjammer. Boom. Gone. Our sales have dropped to subscribers-only on all but one or two books. If Jim Shooter had stayed.....

With regards to the bountiful small presses, we have always done what we could to promote them. We have carried many titles other stores in our area would or could not carry. We even carry a selection of home grown, garage printed comics. This continues to be the starting ground for so much of our now popular talent. As a consumer, you owe it to yourself to give these books a read. I think you will be pleased.

What do I recommend? Glad you asked. *Cerebus, Wandering Star, Poison Elves, FemForce, Deadworld, Oz Squad, Three, High Speed Dirt, Airlock, Savage Henry,* and *Draculina*. There are others, but you have to discover them yourself.

Additional Comments: You, as a consumer, have a responsibility. It is only through your continued support that comics, and comic book stores, continue to exist. If you enjoy shopping at a particular store, tell them so. And tell them why. Positive feedback is a wonderful thing in the business world. On the flip side, if you don't enjoy shopping at that store, tell them so. And definitely tell them why. Don't just disappear. Give the store the chance to make things better for you. Chances are your suggestion will benefit others in the process. I would like to say thank you to all of our customers for choosing The Comic Gallery as your store. If you visit San Diego, be sure to stop by for the friendliest service in town. And, we always play killer tunes.

Pat Callanan
Cave Comics
Newtown, CT
Northeast

1995 could be best described as the year of change. There were fundamental changes in the way retailers order comics and the audience they now serve. The crash of the last few years seems to have bottomed out. New comic sales are slowly beginning to recover, but the customers have changed. The after–school rush of kids is gone, now its the after–work rush of adults. The kids were becoming tiny Trumps, more interested in what their books were worth than whether or not they enjoyed them. The adults, brought back by the recent Batman and Superman stories, were back for fun. They remember how much they enjoyed comics as kids and now they still can enjoy them as adults — a strange role reversal. The new exclusive distribution deals for Marvel and DC can only hurt comics. Lack of competition between distributors will result in higher wholesale prices to retailers and less market access to smaller publishers. This is not good.

So what's hot and what's not. 1995 is turning out to be the year of the bad girl. Shi, Dawn, Razor, Lady Death and even Wonder Woman are riding high in the sales charts. Newcomers Cynder and Kabuki are also picking up strength. Marvel sales are down across the board. The only bright spot was the Age of Apocalypse storyline; new costumes, fancy covers and clones were ignored.

DC held steady. *Batman* and *Superman* have dropped off somewhat, but that was balanced off by the rise of *Flash, Green Lantern, Wonder Woman, Catwoman* and *Robin. Impulse, Starman* and *Preacher* are books to watch. The Vertigo line has generally remained strong.

Its been an up and down year for Image. The old guard, *Shadowhawk, Savage Dragon, Cyberforce* and *Wetworks*, are down, but *Glory, Deathblow, The Maxx, Team 7* and *Backlash* are up. *Spawn* still is the best seller of all the Image titles, but it is only a third of what it was two years ago.

The largest growth in sales has been in small press independents. Chaos! Comics' *Lady Death* and *Evil Ernie, Strangers in Paradise, Stray Bullets, Bone* (which has recently joined Image), *Tyrant* and *Poison Elves* lead a very strong field. Others to watch for are *Strange Attractors, Thieves and Kings*, and *Hate*. I look for *Strangers in Paradise* and *Stray Bullets* to have big years this year.

In back issues, its been a nostalgia year. The returning adults are buying up the books they grew up with. Silver-age DC titles are by far the biggest sellers.

Superman, Batman, Challengers of the Unknown, Brave and the Bold, Showcase, and *The Flash* sell as fast as I get them. DC war comics, such as *G.I. Combat* and *Star Spangled War Stories* are instant sales but Marvel's *Sgt. Fury* just sits there. The Spider-Man and X-Men families are the only Marvel back issues in demand.

Current era titles that are moving are sandman, Peter David's *Hulk* and *Aquaman, Gen 13, Angela, The Tick, Gargoyles, Spawn, WildC.A.T.S* and *Wonder Woman.* So what's next? Hopefully slow but steady growth in the market, More women being brought in to the fan base. Less dark brooding stories. Storyline being valued over art. Cover prices that have less than four digits. We can only hope.

Jeremy Shorr
Titan Comics
Dallas, TX
South Central

Another year gone by and what a year it was! Titles cancelled, companies closing, creators changing titles and, oh yes, a few changes in the distribution arena. Nothing much to write home about, now was it?

The end result of this whole process is nowhere in sight. Image, Dark Horse and all the other "uncommitted" publishers are being courted right and left while all the other small press are scrambling for cash flow and market share. The individual retailer is faced with the problem of who to order what from, and how much to commit to which distributor, and whether they will pick up their books or have them drop-shipped, not to mention a bewildering array of order packs to choose between and customers who expect everything to be seamless regardless of the circumstances. Not too much to worry about in between paying the bills I suppose.

But enough about that, lets talk about the individual publishers for a moment:

MARVEL: Cancelled a lot of titles that not too many people will miss (good for them). Had a very well received "what if" in the Age of Apocalypse stories which sold very well, thank you. Their problem seems to be where they go from here with the X-Men. All the people that started reading with the Age of Apocalypse titles are now somewhat confused with the old X-universe and Marvel doesn't seem to be doing anything to help them out. Spider-Man has been, shall we say, slightly schizoid recently and people are starting to get burned out. With the upcoming departure of Peter and the Scarlet Spider taking over, things should calm down a lot. All in all, Marvel seems to be well positioned for the next year or so.

DC: Clark Kent's "death" was a non-event, maybe the trial of Superman will be a little more interesting—but how can someone who left the planet as an infant be responsible for the destruction of the whole place? Batman is back, his new uniform is slick, the movie was a hit, Bane is on the horizon and all is well. Will Hal Jordan be the next super-villain? His fans certainly don't like the idea, but DC seems to be setting him up that way. Byrne's on Wonder Woman and she looks great. He should take her into even higher levels than those she's recently been in.

Image: Each segment of the imprint has its own following and there doesn't seem to be much crossover. The best example is Spawn's appearance in *ShadowHawk* #18. No one noticed. *Wildstorm Rising* didn't get anyone reading any other titles than before. The individual titles are healthy and continue onward. Unfortunately, the stories in the books are still a little bare, but there are distinct signs of improvement. With the right guidance, Image could catch Marvel in market share before the end of the year.

Others: Valiant has their core readership, but little else. Can they make it through another year with the status quo? Even Acclaim doesn't have that much money. Chaos, Sirius and London Nights put out good product, but not enough to do more than cause ripples every couple of months. Verotik is making quite an impact with what product gets out; they need to be more consistent with shipping. Dark Horse has a solid and growing support base. Since most of their product is licensed material, they have a hard time gaining real strength in the marketplace. Maybe their Dark Horse Heroes line will make a difference in the near future.

The report card for the year? B+ overall. Even with all the confusion going on, good stories are still being told, artists are being given the opportunity to draw their best and people are still being intrigued by the whole process. I thing 1996 will be a major uptick year for the industry as a whole. An exciting time to be in comics.

Superman's Dead, Batman's Crippled, and I Don't Feel So Well Myself

With the Industry Reeling from a Series of One-Two Punches from Both Internal (the Revamping of Numerous "Classic" Characters) and External (the "Business" Side of The Hobby) Sources, it's High Time We Sat Back and Took Stock of what Brought Us Here in the First Place.

By Robert J. Sodaro

I'm thinking what I'm doing. I'm thinking what I've done. I'm thinking about a woman who never thought I'd come quite this far from nowhere, to see my work get done, but I still haven't forgotten; I used to do it all for fun[1]. For me, the so-called "fun" days of comics were way back when I first discovered them, some three-plus decades ago (yeah, that makes me old enough to be yer father, you whiny, investment-seeking, fanboy; so siddown an' shaddup whilst I like wax nostalgic for a couple o' pages. This is—after all—an annual we're puttin' together, an' I'm supposed to do stuff like that).

Back when I first discovered this wondrous hobby of ours (yes, dear boy, it was in fact wondrous at one time), I remember marking down on my calendar the approximate date of the next issue of *The Amazing Spider-Man* was due to hit the rack at my local drug store. (This was in those dark days before the direct market, before specialty shops, and before the Webbed-one had umpteen-bazillion titles that shipped every other day.) I would hop on my bike and peddle the couple or three miles into town to find out if the latest Spidey was there. Sometimes I got it right, and sometimes, I would have to ride back again the following week to score his book.

As the years went by, I graduated to a car, shifted the destination of my weekly ride once or thrice, winding up at a magazine stand where the owner literally held one copy of every comic that arrived (only a dozen or so each week), so my then-roommate and I could sift through and pull out what we wanted (returning the rest to the shelf). It was sometime in the early '80s that I made the jump to a direct-sales shop (Space Travelers in Derby, CT), where I remained until the owner was forced to close his doors some 10 years later. It seemed that a number of his customers saw what a way-cool cushy life he was living, and decided that if he could do it, so could they, and suddenly there were five or six comic shops operating in a rural area where there had been one. Needless to say, not only did they (inadvertently) drive their "mentor" our business, but they all wound up driving each other out of business as well proving that, while it don't take a rocket scientist to run a funnybook shop, it takes more than a long-time fan with a dream to do so.

---

[1] With apologies to singer/songwriter Meline

This is a business…I say this is a **business** ol' son, and it takes a **business**man to successfully operate a specialty shop. At any rate, I subsequently bounced around to a couple of specialty shops, eventually settling in at the original Dream factory in Norwalk, CT. The home base for a growing chain of comic shops—or so I thought. As I sit here writing this, the shop hasn't received comics in some five or six weeks, and I'm currently shopping around for a new place to buy my books. Still, locating a place to buy comics is merely the tip of an ever-emerging iceberg these days; what with Marvelution, Distributor Wars, Exclusive Agreements, Emerging Technologies, Buy-Outs, Company Failures, and the wholesale abandonment of the industry by the fast-buck, gimmick-laden, triple-Mylar-bagging, investor/collectors; and we haven't even discussed what's going on with the comics themselves!

For many, the feeding frenzy and the beginning of the end began when he who is our spiritual Godfather passed into the great beyond. No, I'm not talking about the death of Jack "King" Kirby, but the death of Superman. While he may not have been the first-ever superhero, he has certainly been not only the anchor of our industry, but the bedrock upon which it rested as well. Even the generic term "Superman" is a lexicon that has come to mean more than that red, blue, and yellow-clad figure soaring through the heavens. Superman is who we all really want to be.

I won't bore you with a load of pop, psycho-babble, clap-trap about our great Id's deep-dark, secret desires (partially because that's not where I'm going with all of this, but mostly because I not only really-and-truly have an honest-to Stan life (complete with wife, kids, cat, mortgage, career, In-Laws, et. ad. nauseam), but because I no longer give a right, royal leap into Long Island Sound about all that fanboy nonsense. (Siddown an' let me finish sonny!) When I point out that we all want to be superman, I don't mean that we want to bend steel in our bare hands, leap tall buildings, or even use our X-ray vision to see through girls skirts, I mean we all want to look good for our parents, girlfriends, wives, kids, etc. We want to be the best of the best…we want to be superman.

When DC had the temerity to kill off Big Blue, they proved beyond the shadow of a doubt what the six founding fathers of Image had been saying all along: all the old rules were gone, and we were now in virgin territory. When the Image six vocally split, first from Marvel, and then from Malibu (all at the very peak of their collective forms), they stated with finality an axiom that flew in the face of conventional (read: corporate) wisdom; that the creators were not only more important than we had previously imagined, but more important than we possibly could have imagined.

Then, if there were any doubters still remaining in the bleachers, the final few nails were hammered into the standard superhero's coffin when one, after another, all our superheroes were lined up at the recycling plant, ready to be reprocessed like so much #1 plastic. (Anyone remember that scene toward the end of *Soylent Green* when Charlton Heston's character was watching the steady stream of recently-deceased human carcasses that were being mulched down into food supplements? Holy pre-cognitive Org Batman!) The list of heroes who have been re-cast into tricked-up, posturing, media-grabbing, hollow poseurs of themselves is a near -endless litany of classic characters. In no particular order:

Superman (killed and brought back as a '90s hero—whatever the Hell that means); Batman (crippled, then hobbled with a full-fledged, gonzo, nut-case, bizzarro stand-in); Spider-Man (forced to confront his clone—an old odd-ball story long since

forgotten—if ever remembered—by most of the buying public); Green Lantern (sent 'round the twist and knocked off the edge of sanity, becoming the galaxy's greatest mass murder); Iron Man (first healed of his bad heart, then crippled, then turned into a raging lush, then you-fill-in-the-affliction); Aquaman (has hand lopped off and replaced with a hook—hey, even Earth-Prime has the technology for robotic prosthetics, what gives?); the Flash (Barry Allen killed, Wally West M.I.A. during *Zero Hour*); Robin #2 (Jason Todd. killed by a poorly conceived, badly mismanaged, fan phone-in murder conspiracy plot); Prof. X and the X-Men (in the most twisted application of retro-fit continuity, the Prof. gets his poor self whacked, and his students are shunted sideways into Earth-Weird: the Twilight Zone, then brought back into the here-and-now, only the here-and-now ain't no longer like it was—hey, don't ask me, I still haven't worked up the nerve to actually wade through all that rumpled-up, fanboy, pseudo-quantum-physics, cross-continuity—I just ate lunch); Captain America (dying); The Punisher ("killed" and replaced on the roster by four Frankie-come-latelies—what a novel idea); the joint deaths of Reed Richards and Dr. Doom…and these are just the ones I remember.

Some feel that the beginning of the end was heralded by the muchly-hyped *Death of Superman*, while some of the events listed in the previous occurred prior to that, they could be said to have served as darkling harbingers of things to come. There is no doubt that *The Death of Superman* certainly opened up the floodgates of superhero mass-mutilations. Still, this writer contends that Supes' death was merely the most-publicized link in a chain of events that began some 20 years ago. For me, the luster of pure comicbook-reading enjoyment began to fade when Gwen Stacy died. To be sure, I didn't perhaps realize it at the time, but as I look back, that is truly when I first began to lose some of my emotional attachment to my beloved hobby.

You see, for those of us who grew up bespeckeled and nerdish, Gwen Stacy was the ultimate in babeology. these days, it's so much a babe-*de jour* forum, but back then, there was only Gwen. I mean, here was this world-class looker who was head-over-heals in love with the Charlie Brown of the long-underwear set. Sure John Romita, Sr.'s Peter Parker has shed much of his Ditko-inspired geekiness, and was looking mighty buff in those days, but he was still (as Stan wrote him), essentially a nice-guy loser putz. Just imagine, if you will, an Elle MacPherson or a Anna Nicole Smith walking past the Brad Pitts and the Tom Cruises of the world, coming right up to you and saying, "You, yeah you. The one with the bad skin and goofy sweater you mom makes you wear. I want you!"

That's who Gwen Stacy was (and not just to me, but to all of us comicbook ultra-nerds). I distinctly remember reading news of her impending demise as if it were a rumor of sorts in some fan mag or other. I was dumbstruck. I wanted to write in and beg them not to do it, but I was afraid that if it was just a rumor, and I wrote in decrying it, it would plant the idea in their heads, and they would do it anyway. To this day, some 20 years hence, every time I think back about reading the ending of *Amazing Spider-Man* #121 (*The night Gwen Stacy Died*), I still get a queasy feeling in the pit of my stomach. (Good Lord, the simple fact that I remember that Gwen died in issue #121 without looking it up, but continue to misremember the names of my nephews proves that, in spite of any protests to the contrary, I'm still the consummate, aging, fanboy, geek—welcome to what passes for my life).

Unavoidable aside; a short time after Gwen's untimely demise-cum-murder, I

attended a NYC Con and ran across JRSR, who was doling out sketches. Proudly wearing my Spidey T-shirt, I (politely) elbowed my way into the clutch of fans (this was in the days before the need of hour-long lines presided over ominous-looking T-shirted thugs who bore a more-than-passing resemblance to what a gorilla would look like if you shaved it and put in a pair of Levi's and Reeboks). JR looked up, saw my Spidey shirt, smiled and reached past four or five others (who were probably there before me), and asked "Who would you like me to draw?"

Without hesitating, I breathily sighed "Gwen Stacy." "I can only draw her face," he responded. "That's okay," I replied. He then set about the task, and in mere moments, he had, once again, rendered her lovely features, and autographed it. Yet, as I reached over to take it back, he hovered over the drawing for a moment, and then drew in a word balloon and wrote "You did it Gerry C!" (The Gerry in question was none other than Gerry Conway, the scribe who had penned her demise.) JR, the fans at the table, and I all got a good laugh, and I thought the incident over. About a half-hour later, I espied Conway himself, and buttonholed him for his own "John Hancock". He agreed, and I nonchalantly flipped my program book to the very page on which Romita had drawn.

Spotting the accusation he chuckled, signed his name, and wrote "Yeah, and I'm glad I did!" For me, this served to somewhat soften the blow of her death a tad That old program book is one of my most cherished comicbook momentos.

Gwen was dead, but still the world went on...of so I thought. Flash forward a decade and a half to the skimpiest of news items in *CBG*. It was a brief blurb (probably transcribed verbatim from a Marvel press release), about the impending crippling of Tony Stark. As I recall the item, Stark was going to be the victim of a stalker. Some jilted girlfriend was going to snap and, *Fatal Instinct*-like, pump a round into his spine. According to the piece (and I'll never forget it), some unidentified spokesperson stated, "If the fans like it, we'll leave him crippled." You could have knocked me over with one of Hawkeye's arrow feathers.

"If the fans like it, we'll leave him crippled." What in the name of the hoary hosts of Asgard and the eternal Visanti was going on here? I kept wondering if I had missed a memo or something, stating that the new national sport was brutalizing U.S. heroes. I couldn't imagine that people who picked up and read (and enjoyed), the adventures of Tony (IM) Stark, would actually enjoy seeing him confined to a wheelchair. Apparently I was not only the only one who was disgusted by this dirty bit of nasty businesses and saw it as a dark harbinger of things to come. Forget Dark Phoenix, forget Clark with a ponytail, let's talk about the fact that people might actually like this. Let's talk about that somebody, somewhere, conceived of this little bit of Mad Barber of Fleet Street melodrama as being something that the fans might actually enjoy. Now I know we're all twisted.

All of which brings us kicking and screaming (not to mention bound up in black spandex, red lace, and black leather, draped head to toe with chains, spiked hair, safety pins through our eyelids, lips and (frontal) lobes while moshing to the reverberating sounds of Nine-Inch Nails, D Generation, and Green Day), to today's here-and-now (although, now that I think about it, there does seem to be a Rod Serling-like twist to my recent personal timeline, it I could only remember...damn, it's gone).

The whole world **is** different Jock'o, there's no use in denying the. We stand on the precipice of tomorrow, wondering what the dawning of the new day will bring.

Knowing all this, there are some who sit petrified, and ever waiting for the proverbial "other shoe" to drop; others scramble madly, in a blind-panic effort to duck and weave, in an ever-frenetic attempt to not be under that shoe when it hits the hardwood; others still, meeting behind closed doors in the ever-smoke-filled room all the while bragging about inking mysterious deals (hey, I was in a smoke-filed room once, the building was on fire, I left); then there are those who sit calmly on the sidelines, never moving from their comfy Laz-E-Boys, channel surfing, nursing a warmed-over brew, and smugly smart-mouthing "See, I told you so!" (no matter what they actually said, or what actually occurs).

This leaves only two final groups. One (the largest), that will follow lemming-like, whatever occurs, and a second which will, no matter what occurs, will still seek to find some good and continue to work within the system in a (perhaps ever-increasingly) futile attempt to preserve some vestige of lost glory to the medium we so dearly love. I like to think that I'm part of this last group. One of those who realizes that things change, and when they do, we must either adapt or die. I like to believe that I'm one of those "Lead, follow, or get the bloody Hell out of the way, but by ghod and the late-great King, don't just sit there on your freckled butt and say "You can't do that. Everyone and everything has to remain the same as it always was!" Sorry Charlie, it just ain't so.

And at the risk of deflating your already punctured bubble, it ain't never gonna be the way it used to be. Not ever again. So stop whining, and get with the program. If youse ain't working towards a solution (**any** solution), then youse part of the problem. In spite of (or perhaps because of), everything that's going on in the industry today, I firmly believe that we **will** survive. Sure, sure, comic shops, distributors, and publishers will fold up, be bought out or pursue negative agendas, and some creators will return to commercial art or have to go back to wearing their hair in a fishnet and asking, "You want fries with that?", but the industry itself will survive, and there **will** be comicbooks, places to buy them companies to publish them and creators to write, draw, and color them when my kids are old enough to read and enjoy them.

They might not be reading Spider-Man, Superman, or even Spawn, the comics might not be produced by Milestone, Valiant, or Dark Horse, and they might not be written and/or drawn by Claremont, Moore, Byrne, Miller, Liefeld or McFarlane; Hell, there might not even be superheroes around by that time, but I promise you that there will always be comics. I know this for sure because I'm working my damnedest to make it so, and so should you.

A dozen years after I stopped marking on my calendar when the next Spidey would be in, I was in a shop when a kid walked in, picked up the latest copy of *Transformers*, looked up and proudly stated that he had walked five miles from home to pick up the comic. "What a goofball," I remarked to the store owner after the kid departed with his purchase. A couple of weeks ago, as I write this, my 4-year-old son excitedly picked up the latest copy of *The Mighty Morphin' Power Rangers* off the rack and said "We don't have this one." At that moment is suddenly occurred to me that it doesn't really matter what comicbook you're waiting on, the fact that it gets you excited enough to wait for it makes it all worth while.

Superman revived, Batman healed, and I feel a little better myself, thanks.

Neal Adams' Exceptional Journey

To Some, Life is a Series Of Goals;
to Comicbook Grandmaster Neal Adams, The Journey's the Thing

To those of us who grew up reading comics in the late '60s and early '70s, you couldn't avoid the work of Neal Adams. His work on **Batman, Green Lantern/Green Arrow, Deadman, The Avengers** *(The Kree/Skrull War), and the final few issues of the original* **X-Men**, *seemed to lift the medium up, and catapult it to a new level of achievement. Always a critic of the status quo, and a staunch proponent for creator-rights, Adams always chose to exist at the outer marker of what was defined at the market. He has worked in commercial art, comic strips, and has even dabbled in theater and film. Always a trailblazer, Adams' work been as a beacon of light, illuminating the path for others to follow.*

In 1971 he and Dick Giordano founded Continuity Associates, a studio which has probably produced more major stars than any other. Adams and Continuity took chances, and went on to produce comics, not for the mainstream, but for the independent market including Atlas, Pacific, and ultimately its own publishing house, Continuity Comics. Currently Continuity has withdrawn its own imprint from the market, and the studio is producing comics for Acclaim's Windjammer imprint. As this edition of **CVA** *was going to press, Adams took time out of his hectic day to chat about his career, the nature of the industry, and his influence on it.*

****

CVA: How long have you been drawing comics?

Neal: I guess I started when I was 18 years old. I started drawing Archie Comics.

CVA: When you drew Archie Comics, did it look like Neal Adams artwork we're familiar seeing?

Neal: It looked exactly like Archie. Archie Comic artists are asked to be basically, rubber stamps of each other.

CVA: Too bad; it would be interesting to see Archie come out looking like *Batman* or *Deadman*.

Neal: It would be interesting.

CVA: In addition to your art career, you've been known for your ardent support of creator rights.

Neal: You could say kind of.

CVA: What would you say has been the single most important event in the last five years for the positive forward movement of creators' rights?

Neal: I think probably the most important thing that has happened [is that] Image Comics was created. It is a creator-owned company. It's not owned by businessmen who then make associations with the creators, it is owned by the creators. As we know, creators are too stupid to have their own

CVA: It seems that they proved that, yes we all want to see Spider-Man and X-Men, but we really want also want to see the creators, the guys who are drawing it probably just as much.

Neal: I don't know the answer to the question that poses. What do we want to see? Essentially, I don't know what we want to see, or what people want to see, or what they don't want to see. What I care about is potential. I sort of like the idea that when you're on a path going somewhere, it's not necessary to know the destination. It's important to be on the path. Because if you're not on the path, you'll never know what the destination is. So the potential for the industry was closed for a long, long time, because the creators never got the opportunity to say what they had to say. As much as I defend the creators, and I encourage creators to be as much a part of their creation as possible, I have said to the creators at various times, "Look buddy, put up or shut up. Here's your opportunity. Knock something out that turns people's heads." The question of whether or not they do have that ability has now been tested. Some of them do, some of them don't. A lot of them have just really big mouths, and they turn out dreck. But so what? You'll never know in an industry until you turn your creators loose to see what they can do. Sort of like the movie business 20 years ago. It wasn't until the people who were in the movies started making movies, that we got to see what the potential was; and although there was crap, there was also very good stuff. We have come to a different time in the movie business now—even though crap has been done and good stuff has been done—where we look at the product and say, in general, the product has been approved. I don't look to the magic formula being—give the creator the ability to create his own stuff and he will create his own stuff and he will create a gem every time. I say give them the opportunity to create their own stuff and we'll see what they do.

CVA: When the Image guys first came out they were slammed as pretty boys making pretty pictures, but it seems to me that, upon reflection, a lot of them were producing visual images of the kind you were producing 10 or 15 years earlier with the *X-Men* and with other stuff you were doing.

Neal: Well, this is true. I think possibly if you look at what I've done in the past, or what contribution I've made, is more like a pathfinder. To go out there and say, "Okay this is possible to do. This is possible to do. This is possible to do..." Here are five more things that are possible to do. Now I'll just sit here on this rock and wait for you to catch up so that we can move forward together.

CVA: Was it your intention all along to be that pathfinder? Or were you just finding your own voice?

Neal: I don't think my intentions were that clear. I've never really operated out of crystal clear intentions. I came into an industry that was basically in the Dark Ages. I recognized it, because I had, previous to coming into the

superhero comicbook[1] business, I was an illustrator, I was a syndicated comic strip artist. I did commercial art in many areas. I did storyboards, comps, theatrical design, all kinds of stuff. When I came into comics—which I dearly loved when I got here—it was like stepping back in time. None of the techniques of comicbooks, none of the aspects of comicbooks were consistent with modern times. In those days, we're talking about the '60s.

CVA: Why do you think that was?

Neal: Because of what happened in the '50s; Fredric Wertham wrote that book and comicbooks were attacked by congress, and everybody stepped back like the miserable cowards that they are, instead up stepping up and defending themselves. They got back out of the way of the onrush of events. The companies were so bitter at one another, that they continued in their bitterness to try to destroy one another. Not dissimilarly to the way they are doing it now. In Europe, where Fredric Wertham did not essentially exist, comicbooks, although they were inferior to American comicbooks, moved forward with time. By the time we were in the '60s, and we started to rediscover comicbooks, in Europe there were graphic novels. In Europe you could walk into a bookstore in Paris and buy a comicbook, but you would buy it in the bookstore, you wouldn't buy it on the comicbook rack. There were American superhero comicbooks, but there were also what is called, *abande essenee*, graphic novels and there were all kinds of wonderful things happening. In America, we were held back for 10 years. Many of our greatest most talented artists were put aside. If you think of Frank Frazetta, who through that time, was working for Al Capp doing penciling for the **Li'l Abner** comic strip. That's a tremendous waste. For nine years Frank Frazetta penciled it. Al Williamson became an assistant, did various jobs for various people. This was the Al Williamson of DC Comics, the tremendous Al Williamson. Wally Wood became a spot illustrator for **If** science fiction and various magazines around but could hardly get any regular work. Jack Davis got involved in commercial art and had to back off the comicbooks. Now, maybe he did it by choice, but basically we lost Jack Davis. George Evans, perhaps not the greatest, but certainly an effective EC comicbook artist was forced into commercial art. All these guys, Reed Krandal ended the back end of his life as a night watchman. Reed Krandal, a tremendously good artist. An incredible artist. The industry basically deserted its creators and its talent. They were put in the woodshed.

CVA: Getting back to you as being the pathfinder—either actively or

---

1. In the intro to Les Daniels' book *Marvel: Five Fabulous Decades of the World's Greatest Comics* Stan Lee explains his use of the word "comicbooks" over the more generally used "comic books." The author of this article subscribes wholeheartedly to Stan's theory, and thus has determined to utilize comicbook as one word rather than two, for—as Stan stated—comicbooks have become a legitimate medium unto them themselves, and are not merely "books" that are "comical."

	inadvertently—a number of creators cite your work, or having worked with you, as a major influence on their careers. It seems like quite a number of people came through your studios.
Neal:	I didn't make it easy for them either.
CVA:	That's what they all say.
Neal:	I am a difficult person to work with, but on the other hand, I consider this to be an important medium. I don't like crap. For me, from my point of view, I don't care if you're not the greatest artist in the world, what I care about is that an artist, and/or a writer does the best they can. This is the framework of what they're doing. I don't like hack. I really don't like people hacking out stuff. I like them to do work that means something to them. After all, that's what people remember.
CVA:	You've had your share of adversity. When things weren't going the way you felt they should be going, did you back off in comics?
Neal:	I can handle adversity, don't worry about me.
CVA:	Well, you certainly didn't have to become a night watchman.
Neal:	I've made a lot more money doing other things than comics. For example, for those of your readers who may remember or care, one of my favorite comicbooks was a comicbook called *Superman vs. Mohammed Ali*. Not necessarily because it was the greatest subject in the world—although I personally believe it was a good subject—but because I put a tremendous amount of work into that. I was paid for that comicbook $55 a page for the pencils. $55 a page, I can do a 1½" x 2" storyboard frame for an advertising agency in about eight minutes for that same amount of money. If you look at those pages, and you contemplate how much work was put into those pages I was losing money. It was a pleasure to lose that money. It was a pleasure because it meant more to me than that stupid little storyboard frame. That stupid little storyboard frame kept my family fed and taken care of, but that page fed the inner person.
CVA:	So you balanced yourself between paying the bills and making yourself happy?
Neal:	I have, but to me life is an experiment. I don't believe in goals, I believe in the road. I like the idea of the road. Even when I do storyboards or commercial art, I feel I'm learning something, and that contribution can go back later for whatever it comes back to, and make a difference. Now I may be wrong, but I've probably influenced more people than most in this industry by making the broad approach seem valuable to other people. So they look at it and say, "Hmmm, I wonder what it's like to use photographs. I wonder what it's like to experiment in reproduction techniques. I wonder what it's like to be smart at least one hour during the day."
CVA:	Do you sight your commercial art experience as influencing your comicbook art?
Neal:	I don't consider comicbook art to be an art form. I consider comicbook art

---

Samuree and Dragon © *Neal Adams*

to be the end that all art can go to. In other words, if somebody where to say to me, well, comicbooks aren't art, I would say to them, if you take the greatest artist that has ever lived, and the greatest writer that has ever lived, and had them write and draw a comicbook, would that then be art? What I'm saying essentially is that the "art" tends to hide what you're doing, because it puts a definition on it that it doesn't need to have. Comicbooks are, if you think of the broad stroke of history, and you think about the various forms of media that artists are able to work in; murals, frescos, panels, magazine illustration, all those various things. Comicbooks, strangely enough, since the days of cave paintings, have the potential to give the artist and the creator the greatest amount of freedom to create and communicate that creation to the greatest amount of people that has ever existed in the world, ever. It is, in its own way, the greatest artform that has ever existed. A film for example, is close to a comicbook, except that it takes a multitude of people to create it. A comicbook can be, certainly in the case of Jack Kirby, created by one person. The work that you see in that comicbook would take 40–100 million dollars to produce as a film. And only now that the technology has become available could it be done. One single artist by himself, in a month's time, can create realms of imagination that you cannot only read about, but see, and have it printed in a comicbook and disseminated to hundreds of thousands of people. This has never existed in history. We cannot look at this with too narrow a vision. The potential for comicbooks is greater than the potential for any form I have ever seen in my life. Just objectively. I'm not saying this is my opinion. I'm not talking about opinions here, I'm talking about facts.

CVA: Do you think the business of comicbooks and the distributor wars, and the buy-outs, and the crumbling of publishers are—at this point in time—in danger of destroying this medium?

Neal: It's very hard to know. Watching what's going on in the comicbook business is like watching what's happening in the film business, or watching any evolutionary process. I've had people say to me, 'Neal you started this whole thing. Now look what's happened.' My job was to start the ball rolling. If it crushes things on the way down the hill, that's the way it goes. That's too bad. I can't be responsible for that. Otherwise, the ball never starts to roll. So, I can't be responsible for what it does, I simply want to see it moving. I want to see something happen. I don't want to sit like the *status quo*, I want to see it moving forward. I'm just like everybody else. I'm watching an evolutionary process. There is history to look at. To say well, no matter what kind of a doomsayer you are, the fact of the matter is, history will tell you that it will recover. One way or another it will get back to itself. Many people may be hurt, many people may lose income, or have to do other things. All kinds of things will happen. But evolutionary-wise, we've seen in the film business, which is a perfect example for us in the publishing business as well, that in the end the process will cause the fittest to survive, and they will produce the best work, or something will happen. Whatever the evolution that takes place. It won't be exactly like the film business, but it will be similar to the film

business, and in the end we will all get to see what happens. I don't know what's going to happen. I have to look at it just like everybody else and say, 'Wow, this is really interesting. I hope too many people don't get hurt.' But too many people have jumped in, too many people have invested too much money. Too many people have managed to abuse the business so badly. Too many people have taken it too personally. Too people are yelling and are bitching at other people, and making themselves ridiculous in the process.

CVA: I don't want to sound unsympathetic, but it seems that quite a few people got into this business with that Mickey Rooney attitude of, 'Well my father's got a garage.' 'I have a guitar.' 'We can put a dance.' These people are comicbook fans, but their not businessmen, and they're not running their end of the business like it's a business.

Neal: So true. And, there has to be an evolutionary process to the way you run a business. After all, that's how comicbooks started. That's how all businesses started. 'Wow, you have an instrument, I have an instrument, let's start a band.' Some of those bands survive, and they become DC Comics, or Marvel Comics, or whatever. Some of those bands don't survive, because they didn't learn along the way to move with the times.

CVA: Not every band can be the Rolling Stones after 40 years.

Neal: It's interesting that there is the Rolling Stones and they are playing music after 40 years.

CVA: There are slews of one-hit-wonders. Not everybody can produce a *Watchman* or a *Deadman*.: which is, by the way, is one of my personal favorites of your work.

Neal: Do you know how many people pick a point out in history, and point out that was when I was at my best. There are people who use to read my *Ben Casey* comic strip and decided that's the best work I ever did.

CVA: I didn't say it was the best thing you ever did, I just said it's one of the things that I best remember of the work that you did. He's one of my favorite characters.

Neal: Well, I think it was a pretty good job. I particularly liked the writing.

CVA: Is there any work that you've done that doesn't wear well to you?

Neal: The first couple of issues of *Deadman* I didn't much like. I was working faster than I ought to, but you know, I've always considered it in a way to be a junk medium. I've changed my approach in different stories and where a might see a particular approach, I have to admit to myself that I did it consciously. If I flicker through a particular job, it's probably because I intended to flicker through a job. Not because I'm just a slob, but because I was looking to find something new. I don't look at these things, to be perfectly honest, as finished work. I look at them as experiments along the way. My journey is a journey of finding things out. My journey is not a journey of creating art.

CVA: You were one of the first people who actively tried to push the comic

medium beyond where it was.

Neal: That fight has just begun.

CVA: You've taken the comic motif outside the standard four-color superheroes stuff we see on the racks. I saw the comics your studio did for Wendy's. They were a pure delight.

Neal: Did you like the 3-D quality of them?

CVA: That was amazing. Was that something you developed?

Neal: That was Valiant Vision.

CVA: I thought so.

Neal: Not only was it Valiant Vision, but I tried to convince Valiant at the time that they were underrating what it is they were doing and treating it in a very off-handed way, and there were greater depths they could go to if they experimented with it. We got the opportunity. They wanted to do standard 3-D comics. We offered to do this Valiant Vision version. They went for it. We got to do an experiment that in fact, if those comicbooks were sold, were probably the best selling comicbooks in history, because there were nine million of them. We didn't, unfortunately, sell them.

CVA: You've always been a proponent of licensing e characters out. Creating characters is fine but once you create them you can license them beyond comics.

Neal: Yes. In fact, it's not until *Jurassic Park* that I've begun to take this aspect of doing comicbook-related material for film and television seriously. I have not been a proponent of doing the *Batman* television show. Although some of the movies that have come along have interested me, and made me interested in the medium. It wasn't until *Jurassic Park* was done that I really felt it was time for me to step out into the film and television business. So that's sort of what I'm doing. I'm trying to create a very similar kind of thing for film and television. Unfortunately I can't give you any previews right now, because certain things are in various stages of preparation and negotiation. You will find some things are going to be happening very soon.

CVA: You're also working for Windjammer; Acclaim Comic's creator-owned line.

Neal: Those are our regular comicbooks done in short series. Part of that is because we got hit so badly during the crash. At least we didn't go bankrupt like certain people did. It got to be very tough for a lot of people. I backed off just at the right time. There are companies now, who if they weren't backed or financed by major companies, would have been out of business three months ago. I took our little amount of money, and remember Continuity has never been supported by a major company. We've been supported by the money that we make. At that particular time when things got hairy, or just before they too got hairy, I backed off and said, 'Look we're going to close this thing down and come back later, because I don't want to go bankrupt on this market that's gone insane.' We found

other ways to do it. That hasn't stopped us from producing what I consider to be very terrific artwork. In this case we're publishing it under Windjammer. We may continue, we may do it with somebody else. We may publish ourselves. I don't know for sure exactly how we're going to do it in the future, but right now we're cranking stuff out, and we're doing Windjammer, and it's a happy situation. But, other things are popping up.

CVA: We mentioned that earlier. There's the business end of, yes you're an artist, and yes, you want to do what you want to do, but you still have to be smart enough to do business and say, 'Yeah, I'd love to keep doing *Knighthawk* and Continuity, but if I keep doing it I'll lose my shirt.' Which do you feel is more important? Producing the comic or feeding your family?

Neal: I think what you find is that you can actually do both. I have found that I can do both. Not necessarily exactly the way I want to all the time, but I have found tremendous opportunities along the way. If anybody has followed my career, there isn't a given amount of time that goes by, if they have a broad enough view, there isn't a given amount of time when I haven't done something very new, very different, very radical, not necessarily where they want me to do it. Those five comicbooks for Wendy's is a good example. Comicbook fans don't necessarily want me to do those Wendy's comicbooks, but those five Wendy's comicbooks made a statement, a major statement in the career of myself. And, other people in the industry who may now look at those things and say, 'Hmmm...is there something here for me? Is there something here I can build on? What's this all about?'

CVA: I've always enjoyed the concept of giveaway comicbooks. Marvel has got a whole slew of them. DC has certainly done a bunch of them. The tie-ins, the packaging, not just the stuff where you get Marvel comic packed in with a Marvel toy.

Neal: Let me give you a slightly broader example. A number of years ago, I told people that I was interested in being in the film business. I went out and made a film. I went to NYU to learn how to make film, and before the semester was over, I had started to shoot a film, and a year later I sold it to Troma: the worst distributor around. It wasn't a very good film, I admit, but interestingly enough I learned how to make film. That's one of the skills I have in my back pocket. So now I know how to make film. I don't know that there is any other publisher in the business that knows how to make film. So when the day comes, and it's coming very, very rapidly, when I have a license to sell to a film company, and the interest is there to make a film. I don't hand the thing over and say, go ahead make the film. For good or for bad, I can step in and say, I made a film. It wasn't that good. But, I intend to be part of the production staff. Whether I'm the director is immaterial. That I'd be part of the production staff, and that Continuity's participate in the making of this film is very important to me. I will then have taken the one giant step that all of us want to take, all of us think is impossible, mixing these two media together, because I will enter it with the brain of a comicbook artist. That hasn't really been done.

That doesn't mean that people who think like comicbook artists are not in the film business. Cameron is. Lucas is. Speilberg is. But there has never been a comicbook artist who has entered it, short of, well I guess you would have to give Felini a little bit of an edge there. He did actually do some comicbook work when he was a young man. Not very successfully. So, here is, forget the Wendy's thing. Here is Neal Adam's first film, what's it going to be? Or, maybe it's going to be Frank Miller's first film. What's it going to be? We're started to move out in the field, and bring in the things that we've learned, in our imagination into those areas. While not deserting the comicbook field. The future looks bright ahead. It's going to be very, very interesting.

CVA: When you talk about the film industry, there are so many films that have been described as being a comicbook plot or cartoony. It's always negative.

Neal: There are always opposite of what they are, to me, they're cartoons. And that's not what comicbooks are all about. Comicbooks are about serious stories, just one step beyond other stories. One of the things I point out to some of my Hollywood friends is that people think, first of all, that there is such a thing as Science Fiction in film, of course they're not. They are just adventures that take place in the future. There is hardly any Science Fiction. But also, people think, well we're already doing comicbooks in film. I point out for example, *Star Wars*. *Star Wars* was a wonderful film. I saw it three times. I thought that's a big next step. When they made *Star Wars* into a comicbook then all you really got was space ships flying around, guys in white plastic uniform shooting ray guns at one another, the kind of stuff that comicbooks deserted 40 years ago or more. When we created *Superman*, or when Jerry Seigel and Joe Shuster created *Superman*, we stepped into a whole new plain of imagination. That's what comicbooks are about. We're just starting to get a taste of that. I don't see too many people taking it very seriously. When I say seriously, I don't mean, 'We have to take this seriously.' I mean let's do it like guys want to do it in comicbooks. Turn it into real story that you can really watch, that still involves realms of the artists and writers imaginations. Go way beyond a normal story.

CVA: But if you ask somebody in the film industry if they did comicbooks, they would say, 'Yeah, we did *The Punisher*. we did *Captain America*.' Well no, you just bought the names and did a movie.

Neal: It's completely horse shit. Cameron comes the closest, to me, to producing a comicbook on film. He is way out in front of most everybody else. There are other people who do a very similar thing. Cameron is trying to do comicbooks on film. He was trying to do a Spider-Man movie. He is trying to do an X-Men movie. He's trying to do this sort of thing. And by God, I consider Cameron to be one of those people who has deserved the right to go ahead and do that sort of thing. The people that did *Judge Dredd*, they're doing tremendous work. But, we still haven't got it in its real form. The point of it is, that I feel we're on the threshold of doing some interesting things. Basically, my job earlier on was to get us at least to the

threshold way, way back in the Dark Ages. Now we're closer to the threshold. We're printing on good paper, we're printing with good reproduction methods. We're doing all these kinds of things we should be doing, and we're sort of catching up to the film business. The question is, what are we going to do as we move forward? I don't care about what we've done in the past, I just care about what we're going to do in the future.

Batman © DC Comics, Inc.

MAKING
THE GRADE

When comic collecting established itself as a source of income for savvy investors, it became clear that it was necessary to institute guidelines. Among these guidelines was the practice of grading comics fairly and evenly. Comic book values are established by a number of criteria, including scarcity, condition, and popularity. Grading is necessary in determining the true value of a particular issue.

For the purpose of brevity (and sanity), we shall explore the eight standard comic grades: mint, near mint, very fine, fine, very good, good, fair, and poor. Clearly, these eight grades could be split into even finer categories when haggling over an exceptionally rare or coveted Golden Age comic. In most cases, however, comic books can be evaluated using the eight standard grades.

New comic book collectors benefit most from learning how to assess the prospective value of a comic. These collectors protect themselves from being fleeced by unscrupulous dealers or hucksters. Yet, a majority of dealers, especially store owners, can be considered reliable judges of comic grade. Because comic retail may be their primary source of income, certain dealers are particularly adept at noticing comic book imperfections, especially in issues they intend to purchase. As such, hobbyists and collectors must understand that dealers need to make a minimum profit on their investments. Buying collectible comics entails certain risks. Therefore, dealers must scrutinize a comic to determine if the particular book will stand a chance of resale. Well-preserved comics are invariably more desirable to dealers because they are more desirable to collectors.

Despite the pop subcultural craze of comic book collecting, very old, well-preserved comics remain coveted collector's items. There are basically two reasons for this. The primary reason is that, in most cases, many people did not save their comic books for future generations. They read them and discarded them. Comic books were considered harmless ephemera for children. When these children outgrew their comics, their parents often threw them away. If everybody kept all of their comics, comics would not be valuable because everybody would have them scattered about the house!

The second reason that comics are collectible is because of their condition. This is a basic tenet of all collectibles. A car is more valuable with its original paint. A baseball card is more valuable if it has not been marred by bicycle spokes. Coke bottles, stamps, coins, and toys in good condition are all more valuable than their abused counterparts. Comic books are no exception.

It is a sad but basic fact of life that nothing lasts forever. Not metal nor rubber nor uranium! Everything has a shelf life, so to speak, and paper is no exception. The fact that paper comes from trees makes its life especially short by comparison. Paper is sensitive to light, heat, moisture, draught, pressure, impact, and just about every force of nature or man. Although paper has been a longtime tool of man, it is still downright delicate.

In spite of its shortcomings, paper has always been one of man's favorite inventions. Paper is cheap and plentiful, which are two cornerstones of effective capitalism. It is also a nearly perfect medium for written or drawn mass communications, which is why it is used for comic books. As mentioned, comic books were not designed to be preserved for fifty or more years. Rather, they were intended as unpretentious entertainment. As such, comic books were printed on rather cheap paper, usually the stock used for newspapers. Only the covers were privy to special glossy paper stocks.

Mint

Finding old comics in mint condition is rare or almost impossible. Mint condition comics usually fetch prices higher than price guide listings. Mint comics can sell for 120% or more of *Comics Values Annual* listed prices. The reason for this is the strict criteria reserved for mint comics.

Mint comics are perfect comics and allow no room for imperfections. Pages and covers must be free of discoloration, wear, and wrinkles. A mint comic is one that looks like it just rolled off the press. Staples and spine must meet perfectly without cover "rollover." The cover must be crisp, bright, and trimmed perfectly. The staples must not be rusted and the cover should not have any visible creases.

The interior pages of a mint comic are equally crisp and new. A mint comic must not show any signs of age or decay. Because of the paper stock used on many older comics, acid and oxygen cause interior pages to yellow and flake. It is much harder to find pre-1970 mint comics because of inferior storage techniques and materials. In the early days of collecting, few people anticipated that the very boxes and bags in which they stored their comics were contributing to decay. Acid from bags, backing boards, and boxes ate away at many comics.

Near Mint

A near mint comic and a mint comic are close siblings, with their differences slight, even to an experienced eye. Most of the new comics on the shelf of the local comic shop are in near mint condition. These are comics that have been handled gingerly to preserve the original luster of the book.

Near mint comics are bright, clean copies with no major or minor defects. Slight stress lines near the staples and perhaps a very minor printing defect are permissible. Corners must still be sharp and devoid of creases. Interior pages of newsprint stock should show almost no discernible yellowing. Near mint comics usually trade for 100% of the suggested *Comics Values Annual* listed prices.

Very Fine

A very fine comic is one that is routinely found on the shelves and back issue bins of most good direct market comic shops. This grade comic has few defects, none of them major. Stress around the staples of a very fine comic are visible but not yet radical enough to create wrinkles. Both the cover and interior pages should still be crisp and sharp, devoid of flaking and creases. Interior pages may be slightly yellowed from age.

Most high-quality older comics graded as very fine can obtain 80-90% of *Comics*

Values Annual listed prices. Newer comics graded as very fine get about 70-85% because many near mint copies probably exist. Despite that, very fine comics are desirable for most collectors.

Fine

Fine comics are often issues that may have been stored carefully under a bed or on a shelf by a meticulous collector. This grade of comic is also very desirable because it shows little wear and retains much of its original sharpness. The cover may be slightly off center from rollover. The cover retains less of its original gloss and may even possess a chip or wrinkle. The comers should be sharp but may also have a slight crease. Yellowing begins to creep into the interior pages of a comic graded as fine.

Fine comics are respectable additions to collections and sell for about 40-60% of the listed prices.

Very Good

A very good comic may have been an issue passed around or read frequently. This grade is the common condition of older books. Its cover will probably have lost some luster and may have two or three creases around the staples or edges. The corners of the book may begin to show the beginnings of minor rounding and chipping, but it is by no means a damaged or defaced comic. Comics in very good condition sell for about 30-40% of *Comics Values Annual* listed prices.

Good

A good comic is one that has been well read and is beginning to show its age. Although both front and back covers are still attached, a good grade comic may have a number of serious wrinkles and chips. The corners and edges of this grade comic may show clear signs of rounding and flaking. There should be no major tears in a good comic nor should any pages be clipped out or missing. Interior pages may be fairly yellowed and brittle. Good comics sell for about 15-25% of the *Comics Values Annual* listed prices.

Fair

A fair comic is one that has definitely seen better days and has considerably limited resale value for most collectors. This comic may be soiled and damaged on the cover and interior. Fair comics should be completely intact and may only be useful as a comic to lend to friends. Fair comics sell for about 10-20% of the *Comics Values Annual* listed prices.

Poor

Comics in poor condition are generally unsuitable for collecting or reading because they range from damaged to unrecognizable. Poor comics may have been water damaged, attacked by a small child, or worse, perhaps, gnawed on by the family pet! Interior and exterior pages may be cut apart or missing entirely. A poor comic sells for about 5-15% of the *Comics Values Annual* listed price.

Sniffing Out Grades

Despite everything that is mentioned about comic grading, the process remains relative to the situation. A comic that seems to be in very good condition may actually be a restored copy. A restored copy is generally considered to be in between the grade it was previous to restoration and the grade it has become. Many collectors avoid restored comics entirely.

Each collector builds his collection around what he believes is important. Some want every issue of a particular series or company. Others want every issue of a favorite artist or writer. Because of this, many collectors will purchase lower-grade comics to fill out a series or to try out a new series. Mint and near mint comics are usually much more desirable to hard-core collectors. Hobbyists and readers may find the effort and cost of collecting only high-grade comics financially prohibitive.

Getting artists or writers to autograph comics has also become a source of major dispute. Some collectors enjoy signed comics and others consider those very comics defaced! The current trends indicate that most collectors do enjoy signed comics. A signature does not usually change the grade of the comic.

As mentioned, comic grading is a subjective process that must be agreed upon by the buyer and seller. Buyers will often be quick to note minor defects in order to negotiate a better price. Sellers are sometimes selectively blind to their comic's defects. *Comics Values Annual: 1996* provides this grading guide as a protection for both parties.

Art work © Neal Adams

Name	Abbr.
Abel, Jack	**JA**
Abell, Dusty	DAb
Abnett, Dan	DAn
Abrams, Paul	PlA
Adams, Art	AAd
Adams, Neal	NA
Addeo, Stephen	StA
Adkins, Dan	DA
Adlard, Charlie	CAd
Albano, John	JAo
Albrecht, Jeff	JAl
Alcala, Alfredo	AA
Alcazar, Vincent	VAz
Alexander, Chris	CAx
Alibaster, Jo	JoA
Allred, Michael	MiA
Alstaetter, Karl	KlA
Amendola, Sal	Sal
Amaro, Gary	GyA
Ammerman, David	DvA
Anderson, Bill	BAn
Anderson, Brent	BA
Anderson, Murphy	MA
Andriola, Alfred	AlA
Andru, Ross	RA
Aparo, Jim	JAp
Althorp, Brian	BAp
Aragones, Sergio	SA
Ashe, Edd	EA
Austin, Terry	TA
Avison, Al	AAv
Ayers, Dick	DAy
Bachalo, Chris	**CBa**
Badger, Mark	MBg
Bagley, Mark	MBa
Baikie, Jim	JBa
Bailey, Bernard	BBa
Bair, Michael	MlB
Baker, Kyle	KB
Baker, Matt	MB
Balent, Jim	JBa
Barks, Carl	CB
Baron, Mike	MBn
Barr, Mike	MiB
Barreiro, Mike	MkB
Barreto, Ed	EB
Barras, John	DBs
Barry, Dan	DBa
Batista, Chris	CsB
Battlefield, D.	DB
Beauvais, Denis	DB
Beeston, John	JBe
Belardinelli, M.	MBe
Bell, Bob Boze	BBB
Bell, George	GBl
Bell, Julie	JuB
Benefiel, Scott	ScB
Bennett, Richard	RiB
Benson, Scott	StB
Berger, Charles	ChB
Bernstein, Robert	RbB
Biggs, Geoffrey	GB
Binder, Jack	JaB
Bingham, Jerry	JBi
Birch, JJ	JJB
Biro, Charles	CBi
Bisley, Simon	SBs
Bissette, Stephen	SBi
Blaisdell, Tex	TeB
Blasco, Jesus	JBl
Blevins, Bret	BBl
Blum, Alex	AB
Bode, Vaughn	VB
Bogdanove, Jon	JBg
Bolland, Brian	BB
Bolle, Frank	FBe

Name	Abbr.
Boller, David	DdB
Bolton, John	JBo
Bond, Philip	PBd
Booth, Brett	BBh
Boring, Wayne	WB
Bossart, William	WmB
Boxell, Tim	TB
Bradstreet, Tim	TBd
Braithwaite, Doug	DBw
Brasfield, Craig	CrB
Braun, Russell	RsB
Breeding, Brett	BBr
Brereton, Daniel	DlB
Brewster, Ann	ABr
Breyfogle, Norm	NBy
Bridwell, E. Nelson	ENB
Briefer, Dick	DBr
Bright, Mark	MBr
Brigman, June	JBr
Broderick, Pat	PB
Brodsky, Allyn	AyB
Broom, John	JBm
Broome, Matt	MtB
Brothers, Hernandez	HB
Brown, Bob	BbB
Browne, Dick	DkB
Brunner, Frank	FB
Bryant, Rick	RkB
Buckingham, Mark	MBu
Buckler, Rich	RB
Budget, Greg	GBu
Bugro, Carl	CBu
Bulanadi, Danny	DBl
Burgard, Tim	TmB
Burke, Fred	FBk
Burns, John	JBn
Burns, Robert	RBu
Burroughs, W.	WBu
Buscema, John	JB
Buscema, Sal	SB
Busiek, Kurt	KBk
Butler, Jeff	JBt
Butler, Steve	SBt
Buzz	Buzz
Byrne, John	JBy
Calafiore, Jim	**JCf**
Caldes, Charles	CCa
Callahan, Jim	JiC
Calnan, John	JCa
Cameron, Lou	LC
Campenella, Robert	RbC
Campbell, Stan	StC
Capullo, Greg	GCa
Cardy, Nick	NC
Carpenter, Brent D	BDC
Carrasco, Dario	DoC
Carter, Joe	JCt
Case, Richard	RCa
Castellaneta, Dan	DaC
Chadwick, Paul	PC
Chan, Ernie	ECh
Chang, Bernard	BCh
Charest, Travis	TC
Chase, Bobbie	BCe
Chaykin, Howard	HC
Check, Sid	SC
Chen, Mike	MCh
Chen, Sean	SCh
Chestney, Lillian	LCh
Chiarello, Mark	MCo
Chichester, D.G.	DGC
Chiodo, Joe	JCh
Christopher, Tom	TmC
Choi, Brandon	BCi
Chua, Ernie	Chu
Churchill, Ian	IaC

Name	Abbr.
Cirocco, Frank	FC
Citron, Sam	SmC
Claremont, Chris	CCl
Clark, Mike	MCl
Clark, Scott	ScC
Cockrum, Dave	DC
Colan, Gene	GC
Colby, Simon	SCy
Cole, Jack	JCo
Cole, Leonard B.	LbC
Colletta, Vince	ViC
Collins, Mike	MC
Collins, Nancy	NyC
Colon, Ernie	EC
Conway, Gerry	GyC
Cooper, Dave	DvC
Cooper, John	JCp
Corben, Richard	RCo
Costanza, Peter	PrC
Cowan, Denys	DCw
Cox, Jeromy	JCx
Craig, Johnny	JCr
Crandall, Reed	RC
Chriscross	Ccs
Crumb, Robert	RCr
Cruz, E. R.	ERC
Cruz, Jerry	JCz
Culdera, Chuck	CCu
Cullins, Paris	PCu
Currie, Andrew	ACe
Daniel, Tony	**TnD**
Danner, Paul	PuD
Darrow, Geof	GfD
David, Peter	PDd
Davis, Alan	AD
Davis, Jack	JDa
Davis, Guy	GyD
Day, Dan	Day
Day, Gene	GD
DeFalco, Tom	TDF
Deitch, Kim	KDe
Delano, Jamie	JaD
DeLaRosa, Sam	SDR
Delgado, Richard	DRd
DeMatteis, J. M.	JMD
DeMulder, Kim	KDM
DeZuniga, M.	MDb
DeZuniga, Tony	TD
Diaz, Paco	PaD
Dillin, Dick	DD
Dillon, Glyn	GlD
Dillon, Steve	SDi
Ditko, Steve	SD
Dixon, Chuck	CDi
Dixon, John	JDx
Dobbyn, Nigel	ND
Dodson, Terry	TyD
Doherty, Peter	PD
Dominguez, Luis	LDz
Doran, Colleen	CDo
Dorey, Mike	MDo
Dorman, Dave	DvD
Drake, Stan	SDr
Dresser, Larry	LDr
Drucker, Mort	MD
DuBerkr, Randy	RDB
Duffy, Jo	JDy
Dumm, Gary	GDu
Duursema, Jan	JD
Dwyer, Kieron	KD
Eaton, Scott	**SEa**
Edlund, Ben	BEd
Eisner, Will	WE
Elder, Bill	BE
Elias, Lee	LE
Elliot, D.	DE

Name	Abbr.
Ellison, Harlan	HaE
Emberlin, Randy	RyE
Englehart, Steve	SEt
Ennis, Garth	GEn
Epting, Steve	SEp
Erskine, Gary	GEr
Erwin, Steve	StE
Esposito, Mike	ME
Estrada, Ric	RE
Evans, George	GE
Everett, Bill	BEv
Ewins, Brett	BEw
Ezquerra, Carlos	CE
Fabry, Glenn	**GF**
Fago, Al	AFa
Farmer, Mark	MFm
Fegredo, Duncan	DFg
Feldstein, Al	AF
Fine, Lou	LF
Fingeroth, Danny	DFr
Finnocchiaro, Sal	SF
Fleisher, Michael	MFl
Flemming, Homer	HFl
Foreman, Dick	DiF
Forte, John	JF
Forton, Gerald	GFo
Fosco, Frank	FFo
Fox, Gardner	GaF
Fox, Gill	GFx
Fox, Matt	MF
Franchesco	Fso
Frank, Gary	GFr
Frazetta, Frank	FF
Freeman, John	JFr
Freeman, Simon	SFr
Frenz, Ron	RF
Friedrich, Mike	MkF
Frolechlich, A.	AgF
Fujitani(Fuje), Bob	BF
Furman, Simon	SFu
Gaiman, Neil	**NGa**
Galan, Manny	MaG
Gallant, Shannon	ShG
Gammill, Kerry	KGa
Garcia, Dave	DaG
Garney, Ron	RG
Garzon, Carlos	CG
Gascoine, Phil	PGa
Gaughan, Jack	JGa
Gecko, Gabe	GG
Geggan	Ggn
Gerber, Steve	SvG
Giacoia, Frank	FrG
Giarrano, Vince	VGi
Gibbons, Dave	DGb
Gibson, Ian	IG
Giella, Joe	JoG
Giffen, Keith	KG
Giordano, Dick	DG
Glanzman, Sam	SG
Gonzalez, Jorge	JGz
Goodman, Till	TGo
Goodwin, Archie	AGw
Golden, Michael	MGo
Gordon, Al	AG
Gottfredson, Floyd	FG
Gould, Chester	ChG
Grant, Alan	AlG
Grant, Steve	StG
Grau, Peter	PGr
Green, Dan	DGr
Greene, Sid	SGe
Grell, Mike	MGr
Griffith, Bill	BG
Griffiths, Martin	MGs
Grindberg, Tom	TGb

Name	Abbr.	Name	Abbr.	Name	Abbr.	Name	Abbr.
Gross, Peter	PrG	Jones, Kelley	KJo	Macchio, Ralph	RMc	Musial, Joe	JoM
Grossman, R.	RGs	Jones, Malcolm	MJ	Mackie, Howard	HMe	Muth, Jon J.	JMu
Gruenwald, Mark	MGu	Jones, R.A.	RAJ	Madureira, Joe	JMd	Mychaels, Marat	MMy
Grummett, Tom	TG	Jurgens, Dan	DJu	Maggin, Elliot S.	ESM	Naifeh, Ted	TNa
Guardineer, Frank	FG	Jusko, Joe	JJu	Maguire, Kevin	KM	Neary, Paul	PNe
Guay, Rebecca	RGu	Kaluta, Mike	MK	Magyar, Rick	RM	Nebres, Rudy	RN
Guice, Jackson	JG	Kamen, Jack	JKa	Mahlstedt, Larry	LMa	Nelson	Nel
Guichet, Yvel	YG	Kaminski, Len	LKa	Mahnke, Doug	DoM	Netzer, Mike	MN
Gulacy, Paul	PG	Kane & Romita	K&R	Mandrake, Tom	TMd	Newton, Don	DN
Gustovich, Mike	MG	Kane, Bob	Bka	Maneely, Joe	JMn	Nguyen, Hoang	HNg
Ha, Gene	GeH	Kane, Gil	GK	Manley, Mike	MM	Nichols, Art	ANi
Hall, Bob	BH	Kanigher, Bob	BbK	Mann, Roland	Man	Nicieza, Fabian	FaN
Halsted, Ted	TeH	Karounos, Paris T.	PaK	Manning, Russ	RsM	Nino, Alex	AN
Hama, Larry	LHa	Katz, Jack	JKz	Marais, Raymond	RdM	Nocenti, Ann	ANo
Hamilton, Tim	TH	Kavanagh, Terry	TKa	Maroto, Esteban	EM	Nocon, Cedric	CNn
Hamner, Cully	CHm	Kelly, Walt	WK	Marrinan, Chris	ChM	Nodell, Martin	MnN
Hampton, Bo	BHa	Kennedy, Cam	CK	Martin, Gary	GyM	Nolan, Graham	GN
Hampton, Scott	SHp	Keown, Dale	DK	Martin, Joe	JMt	Norem, Earl	EN
Hannigan, Ed	EH	Kerschl, Karl	KlK	Martinez, Henry	HMz	Nostrand, Howard	HN
Hanna, Scott	SHa	Kesel, Babara	BKs	Marz, Ron	RMz	Novick, Irv	IN
Harras, Bob	BHs	Kesel, Karl	KK	Marzan, Jose	JMz	Nowlan, Kevin	KN
Harris, Tim	THa	Kieth, Sam	SK	Mason, Tom	TMs	Olbrich, Dave	DO
Harris, Tony	TyH	King, Hannibal	HbK	Matsuda, Jeff	JMs	Olliffe, Patrick	PO
Harrison, Lou	LuH	Kinsler, Everett R.	EK	Mayer, Sheldon	ShM	O'Neil, Denny	DON
Harrison, Simon	SHn	Kirby, Jack	JK	Mayerik, Val	VMk	O'Neill, Kevin	KON
Hart, Ernest	EhH	Kisniro, Yukito	YuK	Mazzucchelli, David	DM	Ordway, Jerry	JOy
Hathaway, Kurt	KtH	Kitson, Barry	BKi	McCarthy, Brendon	BMy	Orlando, Joe	JO
Haynes, Hugh	HH	Kobasic, Kevin	KoK	McCorkindale, B	BMC	Ortiz, Jose	JOt
Hazlewood, Douglas	DHz	Kolins, Scott	ScK	McDaniel, Scott	SMc	Oskner, Bob	BO
Heath, Russ	RH	Krenkel, Roy	RKu	McDaniel, Walter	WMc	Ostrander, John	JOs
Hebbard, Robert	RtH	Krigstein, Bernie	BK	McDonnell, Luke	LMc	Pacella, Mark	MPa
Heck, Don	DH	Kubert, Adam	AKu	McFarlane, Todd	TM	Palais, Rudy	RP
Henry, Flint	FH	Kubert, Andy	NKu	McGregor, Don	DMG	Palmer, Tom	TP
Herman, Jack	JH	Kubert, Joe	JKu	McKean, Dave	DMc	Palmiotti, Jimmy	JP
Hempel, Mark	MaH	Kupperberg, Paul	PuK	McKenna, Mike	MkK	Pamai, Gene	GPi
Herrera,Ben	BHr	Kurtzman, Harvey	HK	McKeever, Ted	TMK	Panalign, Noly	NPI
Hester, Phil	PhH	Kwitney, Alisa	AaK	McKone, Mike	MMK	Panosian, Dan	DPs
Hewlett, Jamie	JHw	Lago, Ray	RyL	McLaughlin, Frank	FMc	Parkhouse, Annie	APh
Hibbard, E.E.	EHi	Lanning, Andy	ALa	McLeod, Bob	BMc	Parkhouse, Steve	SvP
Hicklenton, John	JHk	Lansdale, Joe	JLd	McMahon, M.	MMc	Parobeck, Mike	MeP
Higgins, Graham	GHi	Lapham, Dave	DL	McManus, Shawn	SwM	Pascoe, James	JmP
Higgins, John	JHi	Larkin, Bob	BLr	McWilliams, Al	AMc	Patterson, Bruce	BrP
Hitch, Bryan	BHi	LaRocque, Greg	GrL	Medina, Angel	AMe	Pearson, Jason	JPn
Hobbs, Bill	BlH	Larroca, Salvador	SvL	Medley, Linda	LiM	Pelletier, Paul	PaP
Hoberg, Rick	RHo	Larsen, Erik	EL	Mercadoocasio, Harvey	HMo	Pence, Eric	ErP
Hoffer, Mike	MkH	Lashley, Ken	KeL	Meskin, Mort	MMe	Pennington, Mark	MPn
Hogarth, Burne	BHg	Lavery, Jim	JLv	Messner-Loebs, Bill	BML	Pensa, Shea Anton	SAP
Hopgood, Kevin	KHd	Lawlis, Dan	DLw	Michelinie, David	DvM	Perez, George	GP
Hoover, Dave	DHv	Lawrence, Terral	TLw	Miehm, Grant	GtM	Perham, James	JPh
Horie, Richard	RHe	Lawson, Jim	JmL	Mighten, Duke	DMn	Perlin, Don	DP
Howell, Rich	RHo	Layton, Bob	BL	Mignola, Michael	MMi	Perryman, Edmund	EP
Hughes, Adam	AH	Leach, Garry	GL	Miki, Danny	DaM	Peterson, Brandon	BPe
Hudnall, James	JHI	Leach, Rick	RkL	Milgrom, Al	AM	Phillips, Joe	JoP
Hund, Dave	DeH	Lee, Jae	JaL	Miller, Frank	FM	Phillips, Sean	SeP
Hunt, Chad	CH	Lee, Jim	JLe	Miller, Steve	SM	Pini, Wendy	WP
Immonen, Stuart	SI	Lee, Stan	StL	Milligan, Peter	PrM	Platt, Stephen	SPa
Infantino, Carmine	CI	Leeke, Mike	MLe	Minor, Jason	JnM	Pleece, Warren	WaP
Ingles, Graham	GrI	Leialoha, Steve	SL	Mitchel, Barry	BM	Ploog, Mike	MP
Iorio, Medio	MI	Leon, John Paul	JPL	Moebius	Moe	Pollack, Rachel	RaP
Isherwood, Geoff	GI	Leonardi, Rick	RL	Moench, Doug	DgM	Pollard, Keith	KP
Ivie, Larry	LI	Levins, Rik	RLe	Moeller, Chris	CsM	Pollina, Adam	AdP
Ivy, Chris	CIv	Lieber, Larry	LLi	Montano, Steve	SeM	Porch, David	DPo
Jackson, Julius	JJn	Liefeld, Rob	RLd	Mooney, Jim	JM	Portacio, Whilce	WPo
Janke, Dennis	DJa	Lightle, Steve	SLi	Moore, Alan	AMo	Post, Howard	HwP
Janson, Klaus	KJ	Lim, Ron	RLm	Moore, Jeff	JMr	Potts, Carl	CP
Javinen, Kirk	KJa	Livingstone, R.	RLv	Moore, Jerome	JeM	Powell, Bob	BP
Jenney, Robert	RJ	Lloyd, David	DvL	Moore, John Francis	JFM	Power, Dermot	DPw
Jensen, Dennis	DJ	Lobdell, Scott	SLo	Morales, Rags	RgM	Pratt, George	GgP
Jimminiz, Phil	PJ	Locke, Vince	VcL	Morgan, Tom	TMo	Prosser, Jerry	JeP
Johnson, Dave	DvJ	Lopez, Jose	JL	Moretti, Mark	MMo	Pugh, Steve	StP
Johnson, Jeff	JJ	Lopresti, Aaron	AaL	Morisi, Pete	PMo	Pulido, Brian	BnP
Johnson, Paul	PuJ	Louapre, Dave	DLp	Morosco, Vincent	VMo	Quesada, Joe	JQ
Johnson, Todd	TJn	Lowe, John	Low	Morrison, Grant	GMo	Quinones, Peter	PQ
Jones, Casey	CJ	Lubbers, Bob	BLb	Morrow, Gray	GM	Quinn, David	DQ
Jones, Gerard	GJ	Luzniak, Greg	GLz	Mortimer, Win	WMo	Raboy, Mac	MRa
Jones, Jeff	JeJ	Lyle, Tom	TL	Murray, Brian	BrM	Ramos, Humberto	HuR

Name	Abbr.	Name	Abbr.	Name	Abbr.	Name	Abbr.
Ramos, Rodney	RyR	Sekowsky, Mike	MSy	Strazewski, Len	LeS	Wagner,Ron	RoW
Randall, Ron	RoR	Semeiks, Val	VS	Stroman, Larry	LSn	Walker, Kevin	KeW
Raney, Tom	TR	Senior, Geoff	GSr	Sullivan, Lee	LS	Ward, Bill	BWa
Rankin, Rich	RRa	Serpe, Jerry	JyS	Sutton, Tom	TS	Warner, Chris	CW
Rapmund, Norm	NRd	Severin, John	JSe	Swan, Curt	CS	Watkiss, John	JWk
Raymond, Alex	AR	Shanower, Eric	EiS	Sweetman, Dan	DSw	Washington 3, Robert	3RW
Redondo, Nestor	NR	Shamray, Gerry	GSh	**Taggart, Tom**	**TTg**	Weeks, Lee	LW
Reed, David	DvR	Sharp, Liam	LSh	Takezaki, Tony	ToT	Wein, Len	LWn
Reinhold, Bill	BR	Sherman, Jim	JSh	Talbot, Bryan	BT	Welch, Larry	LyW
Richards, Ted	TR	Shoemaker, Terry	TSr	Tallarico, Tony	TyT	Wendel, Andrew	AdW
Richardson, Mike	MRi	Shooter, Jim	JiS	Tanghal, Romeo	RT	Weringo, Mike	MeW
Rico, Don	DRi	Shuster, Joe	JoS	Tappin, Steve	SeT	West, Kevin	KWe
Ridgeway, John	JRy	Siegel & Shuster	S&S	Taylor, David	DTy	Weston, Chris	CWn
Rieber, John Ney	JNR	Sienkiewicz, Bill	BSz	Taylor, R.G.	RGT	Wheatley, Mark	MkW
Riley, John	JnR	Silvestri, Eric	EcS	Templeton, Ty	TTn	Whitney, Ogden	OW
Riply	Rip	Silvestri, Mark	MS	Teney, Tom	TmT	Wiacek, Bob	BWi
Robinson, James	JeR	Sim, Dave	DS	Tenney, Mark	MaT	Wildey, Doug	DW
Robbins, Frank	FR	Simon & Kirby	S&K	Texeira, Mark	MT	Wildman, Andrew	Wld
Robbins, Trina	TrR	Simon, Joe	JSm	Thibert, Art	ATi	Williams, Anthony	AWi
Robertson,Darrick	DaR	Simonson, Louise	LSi	Thomas, Dann	DTs	Williams, David	DdW
Rodier, Denis	DRo	Simonson, Walt	WS	Thomas, Roy	RTs	Williams, Kent	KW
Rogers, Marshall	MR	Simpson, Howard	HSn	Thomason, Derek	DeT	Williams, Scott	SW
Romita, John	JR	Simpson, Will	WSm	Thompson, Jill	JIT	Williamson, Al	AW
Romita, John Jr.	JR2	Sinnott, Joe	JSt	Thorne, Frank	FT	Williamson, Skip	SWi
Rosenberger, J.	JRo	Smith, Barry W.	BWS	Tinker, Ron	RnT	Willingham, Bill	BWg
Ross, Alex	AxR	Smith, Cam	CaS	Torres, Angelo	AT	Willis, Damon	DaW
Ross, David	DR	Smith, John	JnS	Toth, Alex	ATh	Wilshire, Mary	MW
Roth, Werner	WR	Smith, Malcolm	MSt	Totleben, John	JTo	Wilson, Colin	CWi
Royle, Jim	JRl	Smith, Paul	PS	Trimpe, Herb	HT	Wilson, Gahan	GW
Royle, John	JRe	Smith, Robin	RSm	Truog, Chas	ChT	Wilson, Keith S.	KSW
Rubi, Melvin	MvR	Smith, Ron	RS	Truman, Timothy	TT	Woch, Stan	SnW
Rubinstein, Joe	JRu	Snejbjerg, Peter	PSj	Tucci, Bill	BiT	Woggin, Bill	BWo
Rude, Steve	SR	Spark	Spk	Turner, Dwayne	DT	Wojtkiewicz, Chuck	Woj
Ruffner, Sean	SRf	Sparling, Jack	JkS	Tuska, George	GT	Wolf, Chance	CWf
Russell, P. Craig	CR	Spiegle, Dan	DSp	**Ulm, Chris**	**CU**	Wolfman, Marv	MWn
Ryan, Matt	MRy	Spiegelman, Art	ASp	**Vachss, Andrew**	**AVs**	Wolverton, Basil	BW
Ryan, Paul	PR	Spinks, Frank	FrS	Valentino, Jim	JV	Wood, Bob	BoW
Ryder, Tom	TmR	Springer, Frank	FS	Vallejo, Boris	BV	Wood, Wally	WW
St.Pierre, Joe	**JSP**	Starlin, Jim	JSn	Vancata, Brad	BVa	Wright, Greg	GWt
Sakai, Stan	SS	Starr, Leonard	LSt	Van Fleet, John	JVF	Wrightson, Berni	BWr
Salmons, Tony	TSa	Staton, Joe	JSon	VanHook, Kevin	KVH	Wyman, M.C.	MCW
Saltares, Javier	JS	Steacy, Ken	KSy	Vargas, Vagner	VV	**Yaep, Chap**	**CYp**
Sanders, Jim III	JS3	Steffan, Dan	DnS	Veitch, Rick	RV	Yeates, Tom	TY
Sasso, Mark	MSo	Stelfreeze, Brian	BSf	Velez, Ivan, Jr.	IV	Yeowell, Steve	SY
Saviuk, Alex	AS	Steranko, Jim	JSo	Velluto, Sal	SaV	**Zachary, Dean**	**DZ**
Schaffenberger, Kurt	KS	Stephenson, Eric	ErS	Vess, Charles	CV	Zaffino, Jorge	JZ
Schane, Tristan	TnS	Stern, Roger	RSt	Vey, Al	AV	Zeck, Mike	MZ
Schiller, Fred	FdS	Stevens, Dave	DSt	Vigil, Tim	TV	Zick, Bruce	BZ
Schmitz, Mark	MaS	Stiles, Steve	SvS	Vokes, Neil	NV	Zulli, Michael	MZi
Scott, Jeffery	JSc	Story, Karl	KlS	Von Eeden, Trevor	TVE	Zyskowski, Joseph	JZy
Scott, Trevor	TvS	Stout, William	WiS	Vosburg, Mike	MV	Zyskowski, Steven	SZ
Sears, Bart	BS	Stradley, Randy	RSd	**Wagner, Matt**	**MWg**		

GENERAL ABBREVIATIONS FOR COMICS LISTINGS

Adaptation	Adapt.	Giant Size	G-Size	Plotter	(pl)
Anniversary	Anniv.	Golden Age	G.A.	Prestige Format	PF
Annual	Ann.#	Graphic Album	GAm	Preview	Prev.
Appearance of	A:	Graphic Novel	GNv	Reprinted issue	rep.
Artist	(a)	Hardcover	HC	Retold	rtd.
Art & Plot	(a&pl)	Identy Revealed	IR:	Return/Revival of	R:
Art & Script	(a&s)	Inks by	(i)	Silver Age	S.A.
Back-Up Story	BU:	Introduction of	I:	Scripted/Written By	(s)
Beginning of	B:	Joins of	J:	Script & inks	(s&i)
Birth	b:	King Size	K-Size	Softcover	SC
Cameo by	C:	Leaving of	L:	Special	Spec.
Cover	(c)	New Costume	N:	Team Up	T.U.
Cover and Script	(c&s)	No issue Number	N#	Trade Paperback	TPB
Crossover with	x-over	Origin of	O:	Versus	V:
Death/Destruction of	D:	Painted Cover	P(c)	Wedding of	W:
Edition	Ed.	Part	pt.	With	w/
Ending of	E:	Pencils by	(p)	Without	w/o
Features	F:	Photographic cover	Ph(c)		

Abbr.	Name	Abbr.	Name	Abbr.	Name	Abbr.	Name
3RW	Robert Washington 3	BlH	Bill Hobbs	DaR	arrick Robertson	EC	Ernie Colon
AA	Alfredo Alcala	BLr	Bob Larkin	DaW	Damon Willis	ECh	Ernie Chan
AAd	Art Adams	BM	Barry Mitchel	Day	Dan Day	EcS	Eric Silvestri
AaK	Alisa Kwitney	BMc	Bob McLeod	DAy	Dick Ayers	EH	Ed Hannigan
AaL	Aaron Lopresti	BMC	B. McCorkindale	DB	D. Battlefield	EhH	Ernest Hart
AAv	Al Avison	BML	Bill Messner-Loebs	DB	Denis Beauvais	EHi	E.E. Hibbard
AB	Alex Blum	BMy	Brendon McCarthy	DBa	Dan Barry	EiS	Eric Shanower
ABr	Ann Brewster	BnP	Brian Pulido	DBl	Danny Bulanadi	EK	Everett R. Kinsler
ACe	Andrew Currie	BO	Bob Oskner	DBr	Dick Briefer	EL	Erik Larsen
AD	Alan Davis	BoW	Bob Wood	DBs	John Barras	EM	Esteban Maroto
AdP	Adam Pollina	BP	Bob Powell	DBw	Doug Braithwaite	EN	Earl Norem
AdW	Andrew Wendel	BPe	Brandon Peterson	DC	Dave Cockrum	ENB	E. Nelson Bridwell
AF	Al Feldstein	BR	Bill Reinhold	DCw	Denys Cowan	EP	Edmund Perryman
AFa	Al Fago	BrM	Brian Murray	DD	Dick Dillin	ERC	E.R. Cruz
AG	Al Gordon	BrP	Bruce Patterson	DdB	David Boller	ErP	Eric Pence
AgF	A. Frolechlich	BS	Bart Sears	DdW	David Williams	ErS	Eric Stephenson
AGw	Archie Goodwin	BSf	Brian Stelfreeze	DE	D. Elliot	ESM	Elliot S. Maggin
AH	Adam Hughes	BSz	Bill Sienkiewicz	DeH	Dave Hund	FaN	Fabian Nicieza
AIA	Alfred Andriola	BT	Bryan Talbot	DeT	Derek Thomason	FB	Frank Brunner
AKu	Adam Kubert	BV	Boris Vallejo	DFg	Duncan Fegredo	FBe	Frank Bolle
ALa	Andy Lanning	BVa	Brad Vancata	DFr	Danny Fingeroth	FBk	Fred Burke
AIG	Alan Grant	BW	Basil Wolverton	DG	Dick Giordano	FC	Frank Cirocco
AM	Al Milgrom	BWa	Bill Ward	DGb	Dave Gibbons	FdS	Fred Schiller
AMc	Al McWilliams	BWg	Bill Willingham	DGC	D.G. Chichester	FF	Frank Frazetta
AMe	Angel Medina	BWi	Bob Wiacek	DgM	Doug Moench	FFo	Frank Fosco
AMo	Alan Moore	BWo	Bill Woggin	DGr	Dan Green	FG	Frank Guardineer
AN	Alex Nino	BWr	Berni Wrightson	DH	Don Heck	FG	Floyd Gottfredson
ANi	Art Nichols	BWS	Barry Windsor-Smith	DHv	Dave Hoover	FH	Flint Henry
ANo	Ann Nocenti	BZ	Bruce Zick	DHz	Douglas Hazlewood	FM	Frank Miller
APh	Annie Parkhouse	Buzz	Buzz	DiF	Dick Foreman	FMc	Frank McLaughlin
AR	Alex Raymond	CAd	Charlie Adlard	DJ	Dennis Jensen	FR	Frank Robbins
AS	Alex Saviuk	CaS	Cam Smith	DJa	Dennis Janke	FrG	Frank Giacoia
ASp	Art Spiegelman	CAx	Chris Alexander	DJu	Dan Jurgens	FrS	Frank Spinks
AT	Angelo Torres	CB	Carl Barks	DK	Dale Keown	FS	Frank Springer
ATh	Alex Toth	CBa	Chris Bachalo	DkB	Dick Browne	Fso	Franchesco
ATi	Art Thibert	CBi	Charles Biro	DL	Dave Lapham	FT	Frank Thorne
AV	Al Vey	CBu	Carl Bugro	DlB	Daniel Brereton	GaF	Gardner Fox
AVs	Andrew Vachss	CCa	Charles Caldes	DLp	Dave Louapre	GB	Geoffrey Biggs
AW	Al Williamson	CCl	Chris Claremont	DLw	Dan Lawlis	GBl	George Bell
AWi	Anthony Williams	Ccs	Chriscross	DM	David Mazzucchelli	GBu	Greg Budget
AxR	Alex Ross	CCu	Chuck Culdera	DMc	Dave McKean	GC	Gene Colan
AyB	Allyn Brodsky	CDi	Chuck Dixon	DMG	Don McGregor	GCa	Greg Capullo
BA	Brent Anderson	CDo	Colleen Doran	DMn	Duke Mighten	GD	Gene Day
BAn	Bill Anderson	CE	Carlos Ezquerra	DN	Don Newton	GDu	Gary Dumm
BAp	Brian Althorp	CG	Carlos Garzon	DnS	Dan Steffan	GE	George Evans
BB	Brian Bolland	CH	Chad Hunt	DO	Dave Olbrich	GeH	Gene Ha
BBa	Bernard Bailey	ChB	Charles Berger	DoC	Dario Carrasco	GEn	Garth Ennis
BbB	Bob Brown	ChG	Chester Gould	DoM	Doug Mahnke	GEr	Gary Erskine
BBB	Bob Boze Bell	ChM	Chris Marrinan	DON	O'Neil, Denny	GF	Glenn Fabry
BBh	Brett Booth	CHm	Cully Hamner	DP	Don Perlin	GfD	Geof Darrow
BbK	Bob Kanigher	ChT	Chas Truog	DPo	Porch, David	GFo	Gerald Forton
BBl	Bret Blevins	Chu	Ernie Chua	DPs	Dan Panosian	GFr	Gary Frank
BBr	Brett Breeding	CI	Carmine Infantino	DPw	Power, Dermot	GFx	Gill Fox
BCe	Bobbie Chase	CIv	Chris Ivy	DQ	David Quinn	GG	Gabe Gecko
BCh	Bernard Chang	CJ	Casey Jones	DR	Ross, David	Ggn	Geggan
BCi	Brandon Choi	CK	Cam Kennedy	DRd	Richard Delgado	GgP	George Pratt
BDC	Brent D Carpenter	CNn	Cedric Nocon	DRi	Don Rico	GHi	Graham Higgins
BE	Bill Elder	CP	Carl Potts	DRo	Denis Rodier	GI	Geoff Isherwood
BEd	Ben Edlund	CR	P. Craig Russell	DS	Dave Sim	GJ	Gerard Jones
BEv	Bill Everett	CrB	Craig Brasfield	DSp	Dan Spiegle	GK	Gil Kane
BEw	Brett Ewins	CS	Curt Swan	DSt	Dave Stevens	GL	Garry Leach
BF	Bob Fujitani(Fuje)	CsB	Chris Batista	DSw	Dan Sweetman	GlD	Glyn Dillon
BG	Bill Griffith	CsM	Chris Moeller	DT	Dwayne Turner	GLz	Greg Luzniak
BH	Bob Hall	CU	Chris Ulm	DTs	Dann Thomas	GM	Gray Morrow
BHa	Bo Hampton	CV	Charles Vess	DTy	David Taylor	GMo	Grant Morrison
BHg	Burne Hogarth	CW	Chris Warner	DvA	David Ammerman	GN	Graham Nolan
BHi	Bryan Hitch	CWf	Chance Wolf	DvC	Dave Cooper	GP	George Perez
BHr	Ben Herrera	CWi	Colin Wilson	DvD	Dave Dorman	GPi	Gene Pamai
BHs	Bob Harras	CWn	Chris Weston	DvJ	Dave Johnson	GrI	Graham Ingles
BiT	Bill Tucci	CYp	Chap Yaep	DvL	David Lloyd	GrL	Greg LaRocque
BK	Bernie Krigstein	DA	Dan Adkins	DvM	David Michelinie	GSh	Gerry Shamray
Bka	Bob Kane	DAb	Dusty Abell	DvR	David Reed	GSr	Geoff Senior
BKi	Barry Kitson	DaC	Dan Castellaneta	DW	Doug Wildey	GT	George Tuska
BKs	Babara Kesel	DaG	Dave Garcia	DZ	Dean Zachary	GtM	Grant Miehm
BL	Bob Layton	DaM	Danny Miki	EA	Edd Ashe	GW	Gahan Wilson
BLb	Bob Lubbers	DAn	Dan Abnett	EB	Ed Barreto	GWt	Greg Wright

Abbr	Name
GyA	Gary Amaro
GyC	Gerry Conway
GyD	Guy Davis
GyM	Gary Martin
HaE	**Harlan Ellison**
HB	Hernandez Brothers
HbK	Hannibal King
HC	Howard Chaykin
HFl	Homer Flemming
HH	Hugh Haynes
HK	Harvey Kurtzman
HMe	Howard Mackie
HMo	Harvey Mercadoocasio
HMz	Henry Martinez
HN	Howard Nostrand
HNg	Hoang Nguyen
HSn	Howard Simpson
HT	Herb Trimpe
HuR	Humberto Ramos
HwP	Howard Post
IaC	**Ian Churchhill**
IG	Ian Gibson
IN	Irv Novick
IV	Ivan Velez, Jr.
JA	**Jack Abel**
JaB	Jack Binder
JaD	Jamie Delano
JaL	Jae Lee
JAl	Jeff Albrecht
JAo	John Albano
JAp	Jim Aparo
JB	John Buscema
JBa	Jim Balent
JBa	Jim Baikie
JBe	John Beeston
JBg	Jon Bogdanove
JBi	Jerry Bingham
JBl	Jesus Blasco
JBm	John Broom
JBn	John Burns
JBo	John Bolton
JBr	June Brigman
JBt	Jeff Butler
JBy	John Byrne
JCa	John Calnan
JCf	Jim Calafiore
JCh	Joe Chiodo
JCo	Jack Cole
JCp	John Cooper
JCr	Johnny Craig
JCt	Joe Carter
JCx	Jeromy Cox
JCz	Jerry Cruz
JD	Jan Duursema
JDa	Jack Davis
JDx	John Dixon
JDy	Jo Duffy
JeJ	Jeff Jones
JeM	Jerome Moore
JeP	Jerry Prosser
JeR	James Robinson
JF	John Forte
JFM	John Francis Moore
JFr	John Freeman
JG	Jackson Guice
JGa	Jack Gaughan
JGz	Jorge Gonzalez
JH	Jack Herman
JHi	John Higgins
JHk	John Hicklenton
JHl	James Hudnall
JHw	Jamie Hewlett
JiC	Jim Callahan
JiS	Jim Shooter
JJ	Jeff Johnson
JJB	JJ Birch
JJn	Julius Jackson
JJu	Joe Jusko
JK	Jack Kirby
JKa	Jack Kamen
JkS	Jack Sparling
JKu	Joe Kubert
JKz	Jack Katz
JL	Jose Lopez
JLd	Joe Lansdale
JLe	Jim Lee
JIT	Jill Thompson
JLv	Jim Lavery
JM	Jim Mooney
JMd	Joe Madureira
JMD	J.M. DeMatteis
JmL	Jim Lawson
JMn	Joe Maneely
JmP	James Pascoe
JMr	Jeff Moore
JMs	Jeff Matsuda
JMt	Joe Martin
JMu	Jon J. Muth
JMz	Jose Marzan
JnM	Jason Minor
JnR	John Riley
JNR	John Ney Rieber
JnS	John Smith
JO	Joe Orlando
JoA	Jo Alibaster
JoG	Joe Giella
JoM	Joe Musial
JoP	Joe Phillips
JoS	Joe Shuster
JOs	John Ostrander
JOt	Jose Ortiz
JOy	Jerry Ordway
JP	Jimmy Palmiotti
JPh	James Perham
JPL	John Paul Leon
JPn	Jason Pearson
JQ	Joe Quesada
JR	John Romita
JR2	John Romita, Jr.
JRe	John Royle
JRl	John Royle
JRo	J. Rosenberger
JRu	Joe Rubinstein
JRy	John Ridgeway
JS	Javier Saltares
JS3	Jim Sanders III
JSc	Jeffery Scott
JSe	John Severin
JSh	Jim Sherman
JSm	Joe Simon
JSn	Jim Starlin
JSo	Jim Steranko
JSon	Joe Staton
JSP	Joe St. Pierre
JSt	Joe Sinnott
JTo	John Totleben
JuB	Julie Bell
JV	Jim Valentino
JVF	John Van Fleet
JWk	John Watkiss
JyS	Jerry Serpe
JZ	Jorge Zaffino
JZy	Joseph Zyskowski
K&R	**Kane & Romita**
KB	Kyle Baker
KBk	Kurt Busiek
KD	Kieron Dwyer
KDe	Kim Deitch
KDM	Kim DeMulder
KeL	Ken Lashley
KeW	Kevin Walker
KG	Keith Giffen
KGa	Kerry Gammill
KHd	Kevin Hopgood
KJ	Klaus Janson
KJa	Kirk Javinen
KJo	Kelley Jones
KK	Karl Kesel
KIA	Karl Alstaetter
KlK	Karl Kerschl
KIS	Karl Story
KM	Kevin Maguire
KN	Kevin Nowlan
KoK	Kevin Kobasic
KON	Kevin O'Neill
KP	Keith Pollard
KS	Kurt Schaffenberger
KSW	Keith S. Wilson
KSy	Ken Steacy
KtH	Kurt Hathaway
KVH	Kevin VanHook
KW	Kent Williams
KWe	Kevin West
LbC	**Leonard B. Cole**
LC	Lou Cameron
LCh	Lillian Chestney
LDr	Larry Dresser
LDz	Luis Dominguez
LE	Lee Elias
LeS	Len Strazewski
LF	Lou Fine
LHa	Larry Hama
LI	Larry Ivie
LiM	Linda Medley
LKa	Len Kaminski
LLi	Larry Lieber
LMa	Larry Mahlstedt
LMc	Luke McDonnell
Low	John Lowe
LS	Lee Sullivan
LSh	Liam Sharp
LSi	Louise Simonson
LSn	Larry Stroman
LSt	Leonard Starr
LuH	Lou Harrison
LW	Lee Weeks
LWn	Len Wein
LyW	Larry Welch
MA	**Murphy Anderson**
MaG	Manny Galan
MaH	Mark Hempel
Man	Roland Mann
MaS	Mark Schmitz
MaT	Mark Tenney
MB	Matt Baker
MBa	Mark Bagley
MBe	M. Belardinelli
MBg	Mark Badger
MBn	Mike Baron
MBr	Mark Bright
MBu	Mark Buckingham
MC	Mike Collins
MCh	Mike Chen
MCl	Mike Clark
MCo	Mark Chiarello
MCW	M.C. Wyman
MD	Mort Drucker
MDb	M. DeZuniga
MDo	Mike Dorey
ME	Mike Esposito
MeP	Mike Parobeck
MeW	Mike Weringo
MF	Matt Fox
MFl	Michael Fleisher
MFm	Mark Farmer
MG	Mike Gustovich
MGo	Michael Golden
MGr	Mike Grell
MGs	Martin Griffiths
MGu	Mark Gruenwald
MI	Medio Iorio
MiA	Michael Allred
MiB	Mike Barr
MJ	Malcolm Jones
MK	Mike Kaluta
MkB	Mike Barreiro
MkF	Mike Friedrich
MkH	Mike Hoffer
MkK	Mike McKenna
MkW	Mark Wheatley
MlB	Michael Bair
MLe	Mike Leeke
MM	Mike Manley
MMc	M. McMahon
MMe	Mort Meskin
MMi	Michael Mignola
MMK	Mike McKone
MMo	Mark Moretti
MMy	Marat Mychaels
MN	Mike Netzer
MnN	Martin Nodell
Moe	Moebius
MP	Mike Ploog
MPa	Mark Pacella
MPn	Mark Pennington
MR	Marshall Rogers
MRa	Mac Raboy
MRi	Mike Richardson
MRy	Matt Ryan
MS	Mark Silvestri
MSo	Mark Sasso
MSt	Malcolm Smith
MSy	Mike Sekowsky
MT	Mark Texeira
MtB	Matt Broome
MV	Mike Vosburg
MvR	Melvin Rubi
MW	Mary Wilshire
MWg	Matt Wagner
MWn	Marv Wolfman
MZ	Mike Zeck
MZi	Michael Zulli
NA	**Neal Adams**
NBy	Norm Breyfogle
NC	Nick Cardy
ND	Nigel Dobbyn
Nel	Nelson
NGa	Neil Gaiman
NKu	Andy Kubert
NPl	Noly Panalign
NR	Nestor Redondo
NRd	Norm Rapmund
NV	Neil Vokes
NyC	Nancy Collins
OW	**Ogden Whitney**
PaD	**Paco Diaz**
PaK	Paris T. Karounos
PaP	Paul Pelletier
PB	Pat Broderick
PBd	Philip Bond
PC	Paul Chadwick
PCu	Paris Cullins
PD	Peter Doherty
PDd	Peter David
PG	Paul Gulacy
PGa	Phil Gascoine
PGr	Peter Grau
PHm	Phil Hester
PJ	Phil Jimminiz
PlA	Paul Abrams
PMo	Pete Morisi
PNe	Paul Neary
PO	Patrick Olliffe
PQ	Peter Quinones

PR	Paul Ryan	RRa	Rich Rankin
PrC	Peter Costanza	RS	Ron Smith
PrG	Peter Gross	RsB	Russell Braun
PrM	Peter Milligan	RSd	Randy Stradley
PS	Paul Smith	RsM	Russ Manning
PSj	Peter Snejbjerg	RSm	Robin Smith
PuD	Paul Danner	RSt	Roger Stern
PuJ	Paul Johnson	RT	Romeo Tanghal
PuK	Paul Kupperberg	RtH	Robert Hebbard
RA	**Ross Andru**	RTs	Roy Thomas
RAJ	R.A. Jones	RV	Rick Veitch
RaP	Rachel Pollack	RyE	Randy Emberlin
RB	Rich Buckler	RyL	Ray Lago
RbB	Robert Bernstein	RyR	Rodney Ramos
RbC	Robert Campenella	**S&K**	**Simon & Kirby**
RBu	Robert Burns	S&S	Siegel & Shuster
RC	Reed Crandall	SA	Sergio Aragones
RCa	Richard Case	Sal	Sal Amendola
RCo	Richard Corben	SAP	Shea Anton Pensa
RCr	Robert Crumb	SaV	Sal Velluto
RDB	Randy DuBerkr	SB	Sal Buscema
RdM	Raymond Marais	SBi	Stephen Bissette
RE	Ric Estrada	SBs	Simon Bisley
RF	Ron Frenz	SBt	Steve Butler
RG	Ron Garney	SC	Sid Check
RgM	Rags Morales	ScB	Scott Benefiel
RGs	R. Grossman	ScC	Scott Clark
RGT	R.G. Taylor	SCh	Sean Chen
RGu	Rebecca Guay	ScK	Scott Kolins
RH	Russ Heath	SCy	Simon Colby
RHe	Richard Horie	SD	Steve Ditko
RHo	Rick Hoberg	SDi	Steve Dillon
RHo	Rich Howell	SDr	Stan Drake
RiB	Richard Bennett	SDR	Sam DeLaRosa
Rip	Riply	SEa	Scott Eaton
RJ	Robert Jenney	SeM	Steve Montano
RkB	Rick Bryant	SeP	Sean Phillips
RkL	Rick Leach	SEp	Steve Epting
RKu	Roy Krenkel	SeT	Steve Tappin
RL	Rick Leonardi	SEt	Steve Englehart
RLd	Rob Liefeld	SF	Sal Finnocchiaro
RLe	Rik Levins	SFr	Simon Freeman
RLm	Ron Lim	SFu	Simon Furman
RLv	R. Livingstone	SG	Sam Glanzman
RM	Rick Magyar	SGe	Sid Greene
RMc	Ralph Macchio	SHa	Scott Hanna
RMz	Ron Marz	ShG	Shannon Gallant
RN	Rudy Nebres	ShM	Sheldon Mayer
RnT	Ron Tinker	SHn	Simon Harrison
RoR	Ron Randall	SHp	Scott Hampton
RoW	on Wagner	SI	Stuart Immonen
RP	Rudy Palais	SK	Sam Kieth

SL	Steve Leialoha	TMs	Tom Mason
SLi	Steve Lightle	TmT	Tom Teney
SLo	Scott Lobdell	TNa	Ted Naifeh
SM	Steve Miller	TnD	Tony Daniel
SmC	Sam Citron	TnS	Tristan Schane
SMc	Scott McDaniel	ToT	Tony Takezaki
SnW	Stan Woch	TP	Tom Palmer
SPa	Stephen Platt	TR	Tom Raney
Spk	Spark	TR	Ted Richards
SR	Steve Rude	TrR	Trina Robbins
SRf	Sean Ruffner	TS	Tom Sutton
SS	Stan Sakai	TSa	Tony Salmons
StA	Stephen Addeo	TSr	Terry Shoemaker
StB	Scott Benson	TT	Timothy Truman
StC	Stan Campbell	TTg	Tom Taggart
StE	Steve Erwin	TTn	Ty Templeton
StG	Steve Grant	TV	Tim Vigil
StL	Stan Lee	TVE	Trevor Von Eeden
StP	Steve Pugh	TvS	Trevor Scott
SvG	Steve Gerber	TY	Tom Yeates
SvL	Salvador Larroca	TyD	Terry Dodson
SvP	Steve Parkhouse	TyH	Tony Harris
SvS	Steve Stiles	TyT	Tony Tallarico
SW	Scott Williams	**VAz**	**Vincent Alcazar**
SWi	Skip Williamson	VB	Vaughn Bode
SwM	Shawn McManus	VcL	Vince Locke
SY	Steve Yeowell	VGi	Vince Giarrano
SZ	Steven Zyskowski	ViC	Vince Colletta
TA	**Terry Austin**	VMk	Val Mayerik
TB	Tim Boxell	VMo	Vincent Morosco
TBd	Tim Bradstreet	VS	Val Semeikis
TC	Travis Charest	VV	Vagner Vargas
TD	Tony DeZuniga	**WaP**	**Warren Pleece**
TDF	Tom DeFalco	WB	Wayne Boring
TeB	Tex Blaisdell	WBu	W. Burroughs
TeH	Ted Halsted	WE	Will Eisner
TG	Tom Grummett	WiS	William Stout
TGb	Tom Grindberg	WK	Walt Kelly
TGo	Till Goodman	Wld	Andrew Wildman
TH	Tim Hamilton	WmB	William Bossart
THa	Tim Harris	WMc	Walter McDaniel
TJn	Todd Johnson	WMo	Win Mortimer
TKa	Terry Kavanagh	Woj	Chuck Wojtkiewicz
TL	Tom Lyle	WP	Wendy Pini
TLw	Terral Lawrence	WPo	Whilce Portacio
TM	Todd McFarlane	WR	Werner Roth
TmB	Tim Burgard	WS	Walt Simonson
TmC	Tom Christopher	WSm	Will Simpson
TMd	Tom Mandrake	WW	Wally Wood
TMK	Ted McKeever	**YG**	**Yvel Guichet**
TMo	Tom Morgan	YuK	Yukito Kisniro
TmR	Tom Ryder		

GENERAL ABBREVIATIONS FOR COMICS LISTINGS

A:	Appearance of	GAm	Graphic Album	Prev.	Preview
(a)	Artist	GNv	Graphic Novel	pt.	Part
Adapt.	Adaptation	G-Size	Giant Size	rep.	Reprinted issue
Anniv.	Anniversary	HC	Hardcover	R:	Return/Revival of
Ann.#	Annual	I:	Introduction of	rtd.	Retold
(a&pl)	Art & Plot	(i)	Inks by	(s)	Scripted/Written By
(a&s)	Art & Script	IR:	Idenity Revealed	S.A.	Silver Age
B:	Beginning of	J:	Joins of	SC	Softcover
b:	Birth	K-Size	King Size	(s&i)	Script & inks
BU:	Back-Up Story	L:	Leaving of	Spec.	Special
C:	Cameo by	N:	New Costume	TPB	Trade Paperback
(c)	Cover	N#	No issue Number	T.U.	Team Up
(c&s)	Cover and Script	O:	Origin of	V:	Versus
D:	Death/Destruction of	P(c)	Painted Cover	W:	Wedding of
Ed.	Edition	(p)	Pencils by	w/	With
E:	Ending of	PF	Prestige Format	w/o	Without
F:	Features	Ph(c)	Photographic cover	x-over	Crossover with
G.A.	Golden Age	(pl)	Plotter		

THE ONLY ONE YOU'VE TRUSTED SINCE 1986!

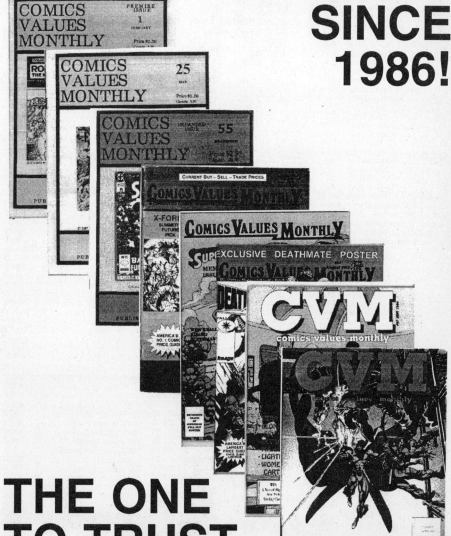

THE ONE TO TRUST IN 1996!

ABSOLUTE VERTIGO
Ashcan: Invisibles, other samples   1.00

Action Comics #1 © DC Comics, Inc.

ACTION
June, 1938
1 JoS,I&O:Superman;Rescues Evelyn
  Curry from electric chair   130,000.00
2 JoS,V:Emil Norvell 8,500.00
3 JoS,V:Thorton Blakely 7,500.00
4 JoS,V:Coach Randall 4,500.00
5 JoS,Emergency of
  Vallegho Dam 4,200.00
6 JoS,I:Jimmy Olsen,
  V:Nick Williams 4,200.00
7 JoS,V:Derek Niles 6,000.00
8 JoS,V:Gimpy 4,000.00
9 JoS,A:Det.Captain Reilly . . 3,800.00
10 JoS,Superman fights
  for prison reform 5,500.00
11 JoS,Disguised as
  Homer Ramsey 2,000.00
12 JoS,Crusade against
  reckless drivers 2,000.00
13 JoS,I:Ultra Humanite 3,000.00
14 JoS,BKa,V:Ultra Humanite,
  B:Clip Carson 2,000.00
15 JoS,BKa,Superman in
  Kidtown 2,500.00
16 JoS,BKa,Crusade against
  Gambling 1,500.00
17 JoS,BKa,V:Ultra Humanite   2,300.00
18 JoS,BKa,V:Mr.Hamilton
  O:Three Aces 1,500.00
19 JoS,BKa,V:Ultra Humanite
  B:Superman (c) 2,000.00
20 JoS,BKa,V:Ultra Humanite   1,800.00
21 JoS,BKa,V:Ultra Humanite   1,200.00
22 JoS,BKa,War between Toran
  and Galonia 1,200.00
23 JoS,BKa,SMo,I:Lex Luthor   3,000.00
24 JoS,BKa,BBa,SMo,FG,Meets
  Peter Carnahan 1,100.00
25 JoS,BKa,BBa,SMo,V:Medini 1,100.00
26 JoS,BKa,V:Clarence Cobalt 1,100.00
27 JoS,BKa,V:Mr & Mrs.Tweed 1,000.00
28 JoS,BKa,JBu,V:Strongarm
  Bandit 1,000.00
29 JoS,BKa,V:Martin 1,000.00

30 JoS,BKa,V:Zolar 1,000.00
31 JoS,BKa,JBu,V:Baron
  Munsdorf 800.00
32 JoS,BKa,JBu,I:Krypto Ray Gun
  V:Mr.Preston 800.00
33 JoS,BKa,JBu,V:Brett Hall,
  O:Mr. America 800.00
34 JoS,BKa,V:Jim Laurg 750.00
35 JoS,BKa,V:Brock Walter . . . 750.00
36 JoS,BKa,V:StuartPemberton   700.00
37 JoS,BKa,V:Commissioner
  Kennedy, O:Congo Bill 700.00
38 JoS,BKa,V:Harold Morton . . 700.00
39 JoS,BKa,Meets Britt Bryson   700.00
40 JoS,BKa,Meets Nancy
  Thorgenson 700.00
41 JoS,BKa,V:Ralph Cowan,
  E:Clip Carson 650.00
42 V:Lex Luthor,I&O:Vigilante   1,000.00
43 V:Dutch O'Leary,Nazi(c) . . . 700.00
44 V:Prof. Steffens,Nazi(c) . . . 700.00
45 V:Count Von Henzel,
  I:Stuff,Nazi(c) 700.00
46 V:The Domino 650.00
47 V:Lex Luthor—1st app. w/super
  powers,I:Powerstone 700.00
48 V:The Top 650.00
49 I:Puzzler 700.00
50 Meets Stan Doborak 650.00
51 I:Prankster 650.00
52 V:Emperor of America 650.00
53 JBu,V:Night-Owl 650.00
54 JBu,Meets Stanley
  Finchcomb 450.00
55 JBu,V:Cartoonist Al Hatt . . . 450.00
56 V:Emil Loring 450.00
57 V:Prankster 450.00
58 JBu,V:Adonis 450.00
59 I:Susie Thompkins,Lois
  Lane's niece 400.00
60 JBu,Lois Lane-Superwoman!   500.00
61 JBu,Meets Craig Shaw 400.00
62 JBu,V:Admiral Von Storff . . . 400.00
63 JBu,V:Professor Praline 400.00
64 I:Toyman 450.00
65 JBu,V:Truman Treadwell . . . 400.00
66 JBu,V:Mr.Annister 400.00
67 JBu,Superman School for
  Officer's Training 400.00
68 A:Susie Thompkins 400.00
69 V:Prankster 400.00
70 JBu,V:Thinker 400.00
71 Superman Valentine's
  Day Special 350.00
72 V:Mr. Sniggle 350.00
73 V:Lucius Spruce 350.00
74 Meets Adelbert Dribble 350.00
75 V:Johnny Aesop 350.00
76 A Voyage with Destiny 350.00
77 V:Prankster 350.00
78 The Chef of Bohemia 350.00
79 JBu,A:J. Wilbur Wolfingham   350.00
80 A:Mr. Mxyzptlk (2nd App) . . 550.00
81 Meets John Nicholas 350.00
82 JBu,V:Water Sprite 350.00
83 I:Hocus and Pocus 350.00
84 JBu,V:Dapper Gang 350.00
85 JBu,V:Toyman 350.00
86 JBu,V:Wizard of Wokit 350.00
87 V:Truck Hijackers 350.00
88 A:Hocus and Pocus 350.00
89 V:Slippery Andy 350.00
90 JBu,V:Horace Rikker and the
  Amphi-Bandits 350.00
91 JBu,V:Davey Jones 325.00

Action Comics #75 © DC Comics, Inc.

92 JBu,V:Nowmie Norman 325.00
93 Superman Christmas story . 325.00
94 JBu,V:Bullwer 'Bull' Rylie . . 325.00
95 V:Prankster 325.00
96 V:Mr. Twister 325.00
97 A:Hocus and Pocus 325.00
98 V:Mr. Mxyzptlk, A:Susie
  Thompkins 325.00
99 V:Keith Langwell 325.00
100 I:Inspector ErskineHawkins   750.00
101 V:Specs Dour,A-Bomb(c) . 450.00
102 V:Mr. Mxyzptlk 300.00
103 V:Emperor Quexo 300.00
104 V:Prankster 300.00
105 Superman Christmas story   300.00
106 Clark Kent becomes Baron
  Edgestream 300.00
107 JBu,A:J.Wilbur Wolfingham 300.00
108 JBu,V:Vince Vincent 300.00
109 V:Prankster 300.00
110 A:Susie Thompkins 300.00
111 Cameras in the Clouds . . . 300.00
112 V:Mr. Mxyzptlk 300.00
113 Just an Ordinary Guy 300.00
114 V:Mike Chesney 300.00
115 Meets Arthur Parrish 300.00
116 A:J. Wilbur Wolfingham . . . 300.00
117 Superman Christmas story   300.00
118 The Execution of Clark Kent 300.00
119 Meets Jim Banning 300.00
120 V:Mike Foss 300.00
121 V:William Sharp 300.00
122 V:Charley Carson 300.00
123 V:Skid Russell 300.00
124 Superman becomes
  radioactive 325.00
125 V:Lex Luthor 350.00
126 V:Chameleon 300.00
127 JKu,Superman on Truth or
  Consequences 350.00
128 V:'Aces' Deucey 300.00
129 Meets Gob-Gob 300.00
130 V:Captain Kidder 300.00
131 V:Lex Luthor 300.00
132 Superman meets George
  Washington 300.00
133 V:Emma Blotz 300.00
134 V:Paul Strong 300.00
135 V:John Morton 300.00

---

136 Superman Show-Off! 300.00
137 Meets Percival Winter 300.00
138 Meets Herbert Hinkle ... 300.00
139 Clark Kent...Daredevil! ... 300.00
140 Superman becomes Hermit 300.00
141 V:Lex Luthor 300.00
142 V:Dan the Dip 300.00
143 Dates Nikki Larve 300.00
144 O:Clark Kent reporting for
    Daily Planet 350.00
145 Meets Merton Gloop 300.00
146 V:Luthor 300.00
147 V:'Cheeks' Ross 300.00
148 Superman, Indian Chief . 300.00
149 The Courtship on Krypton! 300.00
150 V:Morko 300.00
151 V:Mr.Mxyzptlk,Lex Luthor
    and Prankster 300.00
152 I:Metropolis Shutterbug
    Society 300.00

Action Comics #106 © DC Comics, Inc.

153 V:Kingpin 300.00
154 V:Harry Reed 300.00
155 V:Andrew Arvin 300.00
156 Lois Lane becomes Super-
    woman,V:Lex Luthor 300.00
157 V:Joe Striker 300.00
158 V:Kane Korrell
    O:Superman (retold) 600.00
159 Meets Oswald Whimple .. 275.00
160 I:Minerva Kent 275.00
161 Meets Antara 275.00
162 V:'ITI' 275.00
163 Meets Susan Semple .. 275.00
164 Meets Stefan Andriessen . 275.00
165 V:Crime Czar 275.00
166 V:Lex Luthor 275.00
167 V:Prof. Nero 275.00
168 O:Olaf 275.00
169 Caveman Clark Kent! ... 275.00
170 V:Mad Artist of Metropolis . 275.00
171 The Secrets of Superman . 275.00
172 Lois Lane..Witch! 275.00
173 V:Dragon Lang 275.00
174 V:Miracle Twine Gang ... 275.00
175 V:John Vinden 275.00
176 V:Billion Dollar Marvin
    Gang 275.00

177 V:General 275.00
178 V:Prof. Sands 275.00
179 Superman in Mapleville ... 275.00
180 V:Syndicate of Five 225.00
181 V:Diamond Dave Delaney . 225.00
182 The Return from Planet
    Krypton 225.00
183 V:Lex Luthor 225.00
184 Meets Donald Whitmore .. 225.00
185 V:Issah Pendleton 225.00
186 The Haunted Superman .. 225.00
187 V:Silver 225.00
188 V:Cushions Raymond gang 225.00
189 Meets Mr.&Mrs. John
    Vandeveir 225.00
190 V:Mr. Mxyzptlk 225.00
191 V:Vic Vordan 225.00
192 Meets Vic Vordan 225.00
193 V:Beetles Brogan 225.00
194 V:Maln 225.00
195 V:Tiger Woman 225.00
196 Superman becomes Mental
    Man 225.00
197 V:Stanley Stark 225.00
198 The Six Lives of Lois Lane 225.00
199 V:Lex Luthor 225.00
200 V:Morwatha 225.00
201 V:Benny the Brute 225.00
202 Lois Lane's X-Ray Vision . 225.00
203 Meets Pietro Paresca 225.00
204 Meets Sam Spulby 225.00
205 Sergeant Superman 225.00
206 Imaginary story featuring
    Lois Lane 225.00
207 Four Superman Medals! .. 225.00
208 V:Mr. Mxyzptlk 225.00
209 V:'Doc' Winters 225.00
210 V:Lex Luthor,I:Superman
    Land 225.00
211 Superman Spectaculars .. 200.00
212 V:Thorne Varden 200.00
213 V:Paul Paxton 200.00
214 Superman,Sup.Destroyer! . 200.00
215 I:Superman of 2956 .... 200.00
216 A:Jor-El 200.00
217 Meets Mr&Mrs.Roger Bliss 200.00
218 I:Super-Ape from Krypton . 200.00
219 V:Art Shaler 200.00
220 The Interplanetary
    Olympics 200.00
221 V:Jay Vorrell 150.00
222 The Duplicate Superman . 150.00
223 A:Jor-El 150.00
224 I:Superman Island 150.00
225 The Death of Superman .. 175.00
226 V:Lex Luthor 150.00
227 The Man with the Triple
    X-Ray Eyes 150.00
228 A:Superman Museum 150.00
229 V:Dr. John Haley 150.00
230 V:Bart Wellins 150.00
231 Sir Jimmy Olsen, Knight of
    Metropolis 150.00
232 Meets Johnny Kirk 150.00
233 V:Torm 150.00
234 Meets Golto 150.00
235 B:Congo Bill,
    B:Tommy Tomorrow 120.00
236 A:Lex Luthor 120.00
237 V:Nebula Gang 120.00
238 I:King Krypton,the Gorilla . 120.00
239 'Superman's New Face' .. 120.00
240 V:Superman Sphinx 120.00
241 WB,A:Batman,Fortress of
    Solitude (Fort Superman) .. 115.00

242 I&O:Brainiac 800.00
243 Lady and the Lion 100.00
244 CS,A:Vul-Kor,Lya-La 100.00
245 WB,V:Kak-Kul 100.00
246 WB,A:Krypton Island 100.00
247 WB,Superman Lost Parents 100.00
248 B&I:Congorilla 100.00
249 AP,A:Lex Luthor 100.00
250 WB,'The Eye of Metropolis' 100.00
251 AP,E:Tommy Tomorrow . 100.00
252 I&O:Supergirl 1,000.00
253 B:Supergirl 175.00
254 I:Adult Bizarro 185.00
255 I:Bizarro Lois 110.00
256 'Superman of the Future' .. 65.00
257 WB,JM,V:Lex Luthor ... 65.00
258 A:Cosmic Man 65.00
259 A:Lex Luthor,Superboy ... 65.00
260 A:Mighty Maid 65.00
261 I:Streaky,E:Congorilla ... 65.00

Action Comics #346 © DC Comics, Inc.

262 A:Bizarro 45.00
263 O:Bizarro World 70.00
264 V:Bizarro 45.00
265 A:Hyper-Man 45.00
266 A:Streaky,Krypto 45.00
267 JM,3rd A:Legion,I:Invisible
    Kid 300.00
268 WB,A:Hercules 45.00
269 A:Jerro 45.00
270 CS,JM,A:Batman 55.00
271 A:Lex Luthor 45.00
272 A:Aquaman 40.00
273 A:Mr.Mxyzptlk 40.00
274 A:Superwoman 40.00
275 WB,JM,V:Braimiac 40.00
276 JM,6th A:Legion,I:Braniac 5,
    Triplicate Girl,Bouncing Boy 135.00
277 CS,JM,V:Lex Luthor ... 40.00
278 CS,Perry White Becomes
    Master Man 40.00
279 JM,V:Hercules,Samson .. 40.00
280 CS,JM,V:Braniac,
    A:Congorilla 40.00
281 JM,A:Krypto 40.00
282 JM,V:Mxyzptlk 40.00
283 CS,JM,A:Legion of Super

Outlaws 55.00	355 WB,JM,V:Lex Luthor 8.00
284 A:Krypto,Jerro 50.00	356 WB,JM,V:Jr. Annihilitor 8.00
285 JM,Supergirl Existence Revealed,	357 WB,JM,V:Annihilitor 8.00
C:Legion (12th app.) 60.00	358 NA(c),CS,JM,A:Superboy . . . 8.00
286 CS,JM,V:Lex Luthor 28.00	359 NA(c),CS,KS,C:Batman 8.00
287 JM,A:Legion 28.00	360 CS(c),A:Supergirl, 80pgs. . . 10.00
288 JM,A:Mon-El 25.00	361 NA(c),A:Parasite 7.00
289 JM,A:Adult Legion 25.00	362 RA,KS,V:Lex Luthor 7.00
290 JM,C:Phantom Girl 25.00	
291 JM,V:Mxyzptlk 20.00	
292 JM,I:Superhorse 22.00	
293 JM,O:Comet-Superhorse . . . 50.00	
294 JM,V:Lex Luthor 20.00	
295 CS,JM,V:Lex Luthor 22.00	
296 V:Super Ants 20.00	
297 CS,JM,A:Mon-El 20.00	
298 CS,JM,V:Lex Luthor 20.00	
299 O:Superman Robots 20.00	
300 JM,A:Mxyzptlk 35.00	
301 CS(c),JM,O:Superhorse . . . 15.00	
302 CS(c),JM,O:Superhorse . . . 15.00	
303 CS(c),Red Kryptonite story . 14.00	
304 CS,JM,I&O:Black Flame . . . 16.00	
305 CS(c),O:Supergirl 14.00	
306 JM,C:Mon-El,Braniac 5 . . . 14.00	
307 CS,JM,A:Saturn Girl 14.00	
308 CS(c),V:Hercules 14.00	
309 CS,A:Batman,JFK,Legion . . 17.00	
310 CS,JM,I:Jewel Kryptonite . . 14.00	
311 CS,JM,O:Superhorse 13.00	
312 CS,JM,V:Metallo-Superman 13.00	
313 JM,A:Supergirl,Lex Luthor,	
Batman 13.00	
314 JM,A:Justice League 13.00	
315 JM,V:Zigi,Zag 13.00	
316 JM,A:Zigi,Zag,Zyra 13.00	Action Comics #364 © DC Comics, Inc.
317 JM,V:Lex Luthor 13.00	
318 CS,JM,A:Brainiac 13.00	363 RA,KS,V:Lex Luthor 7.00
319 CS,JM,A:Legion,V:L.Luthor . 13.00	364 RA,KS,V:Lex Luthor 7.00
320 CS,JM,V:Atlas,Hercules . . . 13.00	365 A:Legion & J.L.A. 7.00
321 CS,JM,A:Superhorse 13.00	366 RA,KS,A:J.L.A. 7.00
322 JM,'Coward of Steel' 13.00	367 NA(c),CS,KS,A:Supergirl . . . 7.00
323 JM,A:Superhorse 13.00	368 CS,KS,V:Mxyzptlk 7.00
324 JM,A:Abdul 13.00	369 CS,KS,Superman's Greatest
325 CS,JM,Skyscraper Superman 13.00	Blunder 7.00
326 CS,JM,V:Legion of Super	370 NA(c),CS,KS 7.00
Creatures 13.00	371 NA(c),CS,KS 7.00
327 CS,JM,C:Brainiac 13.00	372 NA(c),CS,KS 7.00
328 JM,Hands of Doom 13.00	373 A:Supergirl, (giant size) 9.00
329 JM,V:Drang 13.00	374 NA(c),CS,KS,V:Super Thief . . 6.00
330 CS,JM,Krypto 13.00	375 CS,KS,The Big Forget 6.00
331 CS,V:Dr.Supernatural 13.00	376 CS,KS,E:Supergirl 6.00
332 CS,A:Brainiac 13.00	377 CS,KS,B:Legion 6.00
333 CS(c),A:Lex Luthor 13.00	378 CS,KS,V:Marauder 6.00
334 JM(c),A:Lex Luthor,80pgs . . 19.00	379 CS,JA,MA,V:Eliminator 6.00
335 CS,V:Lex Luthor 10.00	380 KS,Confessions of Superman 6.00
336 CS,O:Akvar 10.00	381 CS,Dictators of Earth 6.00
337 CS,V:Tiger Gang 10.00	382 CS,Clark Kent-Magician 6.00
338 CS,JM,V:Muto 10.00	383 CS,The Killer Costume 6.00
339 CS,V:Muto,Brainiac 10.00	384 CS,The Forbidden Costume . 6.00
340 JM,I:Parasite 12.00	385 CS,The Mortal Superman . . . 6.00
341 CS,V:Vakox,A:Batman 9.00	386 CS,Home For Old Supermen 6.00
342 WB,JM,V:Brainiac 9.00	387 CS,A:Legion,Even
343 WB,V:Eterno 9.00	Supermen Die 6.00
344 WB,JM,A:Batman 9.00	388 CS,A:Legion,Puzzle of
345 CS(c),A:Allen Funt 9.00	The Wild Word 6.00
346 WB,JM 9.00	389 A:Legion,The Kid Who
347 CS(c),A:Supergirl, 80pgs. . . 11.00	Struck Out Superman 6.00
348 WB,JM,V:Acid Master 8.00	390 CS,'Self-Destruct Superman' . 6.00
349 WB,JM,V:Dr.Kryptonite 8.00	391 CS,Punishment of
350 A:JLA 8.00	Superman's Son 6.00
351 WB,I:Zha-Vam 8.00	392 CS,E:Legion 6.00
352 WB,V:Zha-Vam 8.00	393 CS,MA,RA,A:Super Houdini . 4.50
353 WB,JM,V:Zha-Vam 8.00	394 CS,MA 4.50
354 JM,A:Captain Incredible 8.00	395 CS,MA,A:Althera 4.50
	396 CS,MA 4.50

397 CS,MA,Imaginary Story 4.50	
398 NA(c),CS,MA,I:Morgan Edge . 5.00	
399 NA(c),CS,MA,A:Superbaby . . 4.50	
400 NA(c),CS,MA,Kandor Story . . 5.00	
401 CS,MA,V:Indians 4.00	
402 NA(c),CS,MA,V:Indians 4.00	
403 CS,MA,Vigilante rep. 4.00	
404 CS,MA,Aquaman rep 4.00	
405 CS,MA,Vigilante rep. 4.00	
406 CS,MA,Atom & Flash rep. . . . 4.00	
407 CS,MA,V:Lex Luthor 4.00	
408 CS,MA,Atom rep. 4.00	
409 CS,MA,T.Tommorrow rep. . . . 4.00	
410 CS,MA,T.Tommorrow rep. . . . 4.00	
411 CS,MA,O:Eclipso rep. 6.00	
412 CS,MA,Eclipso rep. 4.00	
413 CS,MA,V:Brainiac 3.50	
414 CS,MA,B:Metamorpho 3.50	
415 CS,MA,V:Metroplis Monster . 3.50	
416 CS,MA 3.50	
417 CS,MA,V:Luthor 3.50	
418 CS,MA,V:Luthor,	
E:Metamorpho 3.50	
419 CS,MA,CI,DG,I:HumanTarget 7.00	
420 CS,MA,DG,V:Towbee 3.50	
421 CS,MA,B:Green Arrow 4.00	
422 CS,DG,O:Human Target 3.50	
423 CS,MA,DG,A:Lex Luthor 3.50	
424 CS,MA,Green Arrow 4.00	
425 CS,DD,NA,DG,B:Atom 8.00	
426 CS,MA,Green Arrow 3.50	
427 CS,MA,DD,DG,Atom 3.50	
428 CS,MA,DG,Luthor 3.50	
429 CS,BO,DG,C:JLA 3.50	
430 CS,MA,DD,DG,Atom 2.50	
431 CS,MA,Green Arrow 3.25	
432 CS,MA,DG,Toyman 3.00	
433 CS,BO,DD,DG,A:Atom 3.00	
434 CS,DD,Green Arrow 3.25	
435 FM(c),CS,DD,DG,Atom 3.00	
436 CS,DD,Green Arrow 3.25	
437 CS,DG,Green Arrow	
(100 page giant) 5.00	
438 CS,BO,DD,Atom 3.00	
439 CS,BO,DD,Atom 3.00	
440 1st MGr Green Arrow 7.50	
441 CS,BO,MGr,A:Green Arrow,	
Flash,R:Krypto 6.00	
442 CS,MS,MGr,Atom 3.50	
443 CS,A:JLA(100 pg.giant) 4.50	
444 MGr,Green Arrow 4.00	
445 MGr,Green Arrow 4.00	
446 MGr,Green Arrow 4.00	
447 CS,BO,RB,KJ,Atom 3.00	
448 CS,BO,DD,JL,Atom 3.00	
449 CS,BO 3.00	
450 MGr,Green Arrow 3.50	
451 MGr,Green Arrow 3.50	
452 CS,MGr,Green Arrow 3.50	
453 CS,Atom 3.00	
454 CS,E:Atom 3.50	
455 CS,Green Arrow 3.50	
456 CS,MGr,Green Arrow 3.50	
457 CS,MGr,Green Arrow 3.50	
458 CS,MGr,I:Black Rock 3.50	
459 CS,BO,Blackrock 3.00	
460 CS,I:Karb-Brak 3.00	
461 CS,V:Karb-Brak 3.00	
462 CS,V:Karb-Brak 3.00	
463 CS,V:Karb-Brak 3.00	
464 CS,KS,V:Pile-Driver 3.00	
465 CS,FMc,Luthor 3.00	
466 NA(c),CS,V:Luthor 3.00	
467 CS,V:Mzyzptlk 3.00	
468 NA(c),CS,FMc,V:Terra-Man . 3.00	

469 CS,TerraMan 3.00
470 CS,Flash Green Lantern . . 3.00
471 CS,V:Phantom Zone Female . 3.00
472 CS,V:Faora Hu-Ul 3.00
473 NA(c),CS,Phantom Zone
   Villians 3.00
474 KS,V:Doctor Light 3.00
475 KS,V:Karb-Brak,A:Vartox . . . 3.00
476 KS,V:Vartox 3.00
477 CS,DD,Land Lords of Earth . . 3.00
478 CS,Earth's Last 3.00
479 CS 3.00
480 CS,A:JLA,V:Amazo 3.00
481 CS,A:JLA,V:Amazo 3.00
482 CS,Amazo 3.00
483 CS,Amazo,JLA 3.00
484 CS,W:Earth 2 Superman
   & Lois Lane 3.25
485 NA(c),CS,rep.Superman#233 3.50
486 GT,KS,V:Lex Luthor 3.00
487 CS,AS,O:Atom 3.50
488 CS,AS,A:Air Wave 3.00
489 CS,AS,A:JLA,Atom 3.00
490 CS,Brainiac 3.00
491 CS,A:Hawkman 3.00
492 CS,'Superman's After Life' . 3.00
493 CS,A:UFO 3.00
494 CS 3.00
495 CS 3.00
496 CS,A:Kandor 3.00
497 CS 3.00
498 CS,Vartox 3.00
499 CS,Vartox 3.00
500 CS,Superman's Life Story
   A:Legion 5.00
501 KS 2.00
502 CS,A:Supergirl,Gal.Golem . 2.00
503 CS,'A Save in Time' 2.00
504 CS,'The Power and Choice' . 2.00
505 CS 2.00
506 CS 2.00
507 CS,A:Jonathan Kent 2.00
508 CS,A:Jonathan Kent 2.00
509 CS,JSn,DG 2.25
510 CS,Luthor 2.00
511 CS,AS,V:Terraman,
   A:Air Wave 2.00
512 CS,RT,V:Luthor,A:Air Wave . 2.00
513 CS,RT,V:Krell,A:Air Wave . . 2.00
514 CS,RT,V:Brainiac,A:Atom . . 2.00
515 CS,AS,A:Atom 2.00
516 CS,AS,V:Luthor,A:Atom . . . 2.00
517 CS,DH,A:Aquaman 2.00
518 CS,DH,A:Aquaman 2.00
519 CS,DH,A:Aquaman 2.00
520 CS,DH,A:Aquaman 2.00
521 CS,AS,I:Vixen,A:Atom 2.00
522 CS,AS,A:Atom 2.00
523 CS,AS,A:Atom 2.00
524 CS,AS,A:Atom 2.00
525 JSon,FMc,AS,I:Neutron,
   A:Air Wave 2.00
526 JSon,AS,V:Neutron 2.00
527 CS,AS,I:Satanis,A:Aquaman . 2.50
528 CS,AS,V:Brainiac,A:Aq'man . 2.00
529 GP(c),CS,DA,AS,A:Aquaman,
   V:Brainiac 2.00
530 CS,DA,Brainiac 2.00
531 JSon,FMc,AS,A:Atom 2.00
532 CS,C:New Teen Titans 2.00
533 CS,V:The. 2.00
534 CS,AS,V:Satanis,A:Air Wave . 2.00
535 GK(c),JSon,AS,
   A:Omega Men 2.00
536 JSon,AS,FMc,A:Omega Men . 2.00

537 IN,CS,AS,V:Satanis
   A:Aquaman 2.00
538 IN,AS,FMc,V:Satanis,
   A:Aquaman 2.00
539 KG(c),GK,AS,DA,A:Flash,
   Atom,Aquaman 2.00
540 GK,AS,V:Satanis 2.00
541 GK,V:Satanis 2.00
542 AS,V:Vandal Savage 2.00
543 CS,V:Vandal Savage 2.00
544 CS,MA,GK,GP,45th Anniv.
   D:Ardora,Lexor 3.00
545 GK,Brainiac 2.00
546 GK,A:JLA,New Teen Titans . 2.00
547 GK(c),CS 2.00
548 GK(c),AS,Phantom Zone . . 2.00
549 GK(c),AS 2.00
550 AS(c),GT 2.00
551 GK,Starfire becomes
   Red Star 2.00
552 GK,Forgotten Heroes
   (inc.Animal Man) 10.00
553 GK,Forgotten Heroes(inc.
   Animal Man) 9.00
554 GK(a&c) 2.00
555 CS,A:Parasite (X-over
   Supergirl #20) 2.00
556 CS,KS,C:Batman 2.00
557 CS,Terra-man 2.00
558 KS 2.00
559 KS,AS 2.00
560 AS,KG,BO,A:Ambush Bug . 2.00
561 KS,WB,Toyman 2.00
562 KS,Queen Bee 2.00
563 AS,KG,BO,A:Ambush Bug . 2.00
564 AS,V:Master Jailer 2.00
565 KG,BO,A:Ambush Bug 2.00
566 BO(i),MR 2.00
567 KS,AS,PB 2.00
568 CS,AW,AN 2.00
569 IN 2.00
570 KS 2.00
571 BB(c),AS,A:Thresh 222 . . . 2.00
572 WB,BO 2.00
573 KS,BO,AS 2.00
574 KS 2.00
575 KS,V:Intellax 2.00
576 KS,Earth's Sister Planet . . . 2.00
577 KG,BO,V:Caitlin 2.00
578 KS,Parasite 2.00
579 KG,BO,Asterix Parody 2.00
580 GK(c),KS,Superman's Failure 2.00
581 DCw(c),KS,Superman
   Requires Legal aid 2.00
582 AS,KS,Superman's Parents
   Alive 2.00
583 CS,KS,AMo(s),Last Pre
   Crisis Superman 10.00
584 JBy,DG,A:NewTeenTitans,
   I:Modern Age Superman. . . 3.00
585 JBy,DG,Phantom Stranger . . 2.50
586 JBy,DG,Legends,V:New
   Gods,Darkseid 2.50
587 JBy,DG,Demon 2.50
588 JBy,DG,Hawkman 2.50
589 JBy,DG,Gr.Lant.Corp. 2.50
590 JBy,DG,Metal Men 2.50
591 JBy,V:Superboy,A:Legion . . 2.50
592 JBy,Big Barda 2.50
593 JBy,Mr. Miracle 2.50
594 JBy,A:Booster Gold 2.50
595 JBy,A:M.Manhunter,
   I:Silver Banshee 2.50
596 JBy,A:Spectre,Millenium . . . 2.50
597 JBy,L.Starr(i),Lois V:Lana . 2.50

Action Comics #583 © DC Comics, Inc.

598 JBy,TyT,I:Checkmate 3.50
599 RA,JBy(i),A:MetalMen,
   BonusBook 2.50
600 JBy,GP,KS,JOy,DG,CS,MA,
   MMi,A:Wonder Woman;
   Man-Bat,V:Darkseid 8.00
Becomes:
ACTION WEEKLY
601 GK,DSp,CS,DJu,TD,
   B:Superman,Gr.Lantern,
   Blackhawk,Deadman,Secret
   Six,Wilddog 2.00
602 GP(c),GK,DSp,CS,DJu,TD . 1.75
603 GK,CS,DsP,DJu,TD 1.75
604 GK,DSp,CS,DJu,TD 1.75
605 NKu/AKu(c),GK,DSp,CS,
   DJu,TD 1.75
606 DSp,CS,DJu,TD 1.75
607 SLi(c),TD,DSp,CS,DJu 1.75
608 DSp,CS,DJu,TD,E:Blackhawk 1.75
609 BB(c),DSp,DJu,TD,CS,
   E:Wild Dog,B:Black Canary . 1.75
610 KB,DJu,CS,DSp,TD,CS
   A:Phantom Stranger 2.00
611 AN(c),DJu,DSp,CS,BKi,TD,
   BKi,B:Catwoman 3.00
612 PG(c),DSp,CS,BKi,TD,
   E:Secret Six,Deadman 2.50
613 MK(c),BKi,CS,MA,TGr,
   Nightwing,B:Phantom Stranger 2.50
614 TG,CS,Phantom Stranger
   E:Catwoman 2.50
615 MMi(c),CS,MA,BKi,TGr,
   Blackhawk,B:Wild Dog 1.75
616 ATh(c),CS,MA,E:Bl.Canary . 1.75
617 CS,MA,JO,A:Ph.Stranger . . 1.75
618 JBg(c),CS,MA,JKo,TD,
   B:Deadman,E:Nightwing 1.75
619 CS,MA,FS,FMc,KJo,TD,FMc,
   B:Sinister Six. 1.75
620 CS,MA,FS,FMc,KJo,TD 1.75
621 JO(c),CS,MA,FS,FMc,KJo,
   TD,MBr,E:Deadman 1.75
622 RF(c),MBr,TL,CS,MA,FS,
   FMc,A:Starman,E:Wild
   Dog,Blackhawk 1.75

623 MBr,TD,CS,MA,FS,FMc,JL,
  JKo,A:Ph.Stranger,
  B:Deadman,Shazam 1.75
624 AD(c),MBr,FS,FMc,CS,MA,
  TD,B:Black Canary 1.75
625 MBr,FS,FMc,CS,MA,
  TD,FMc 1.50
626 MBr,FS,FMc,CS,MA,JKo,TD,
  E:Shazam,Deadman 1.50
627 GK(c),MBr,RT,FS,FMc,CS,
  MA,TMd,B:Nightwing,Speedy . 1.75
628 TY(c),MBr,RT,TMd,CS,MA,
  FS,FMc,B:Blackhawk 1.50
629 CS,MA,MBr,RT,FS,FMc,TMd . 1.50
630 CS,MA,MBr,RT,FS,FMc,TMd,
  E:Secret Six 1.50
631 JS(c),CS,MA,MBr,RT,TMd,
  B:Phantom Stranger 1.50
632 TGr(c),CS,MA,MBr,RT,TMd . 1.50
633 CS,MA,MBr,RT,TMd 1.50
634 CS,MA,MBr,RT,TMd,E:Ph.Stranger,
  Nightwing/Speedy,Bl.hawk . . . 1.50
635 CS,MA,MBr,RT,EB,E:Black
  Canary,Green Lantern 1.50
636 DG(c),CS,MA,NKu,MPa,FMc,
  B:Demon,Wild Dog,Ph.Lady,
  Speedy,A:Phantom Stranger . . 1.75
637 CS,MA,KS,FMc,MPa,
  B:Hero Hotline 1.50
638 JK(c),CS,MA,KS,FMc,MPa . . 1.50
639 CS,MA,KS,FMc,MPa 1.50
640 CS,KS,MA,FS,FMc,MPa,
  E:Speedy,Hero Hotline 1.50
641 CS,MA,JL,DG,MPa,E:Demon,
  Phant.Lady,Superman,Wild Dog,
  A:Ph.Stranger,Hum.Target . . . 1.75
642 GK,SD,ATi,CS,JAp,JM,CI,KN,
  Green Lantern,Superman 1.50

Becomes:

ACTION COMICS

643 B:RSt(s),GP,BBr,V:Intergang . 2.50
644 GP,BBr,V:Matrix 2.00
645 GP,BBr,I:Maxima 2.00
646 KG,V:Alien Creature,
  A:Brainiac 2.00
647 GP,KGa,BBr,V:Brainiac 2.00
648 GP,KGa,BBr,V:Brainiac 2.00
649 GP,KGa,BBr,V:Brainiac 2.00
650 JOy,BBr,CS,BMc,GP,KGa,
  ATi,DJu,A:JLA,C:Lobo 3.00
651 GP,KGa,BBr,Day of Krypton
  Man #3,V:Maxima 3.00
652 GP,KGa,BBr,Day of Krypton
  Man #6,V:Eradicator 3.00
653 BMc,BBr,D:Amanda 2.00
654 BMc,BBr,A:Batman Pt.3 . . . . 2.50
655 BMc,BBr,V:Morrisson,Ma
  Kent's Photo Album 2.00
656 BMc,BBr,Soul Search #1,
  V:Blaze 2.00
657 KGa,BBr,V:Toyman 2.00
658 CS,Sinbad Contract #3 . . . . . 2.00
659 BMc,BBr,K.Krimson
  Kryptonite #3 . . . . 3.50
660 BMc,BBr,D:Lex Luthor 2.00
661 BMc,BBr,A:Plastic Man 2.00
662 JOy,JM,TG,BMc,V:Silver
  Banshee,Clark tells
  Lois his identity 3.00
662a 2nd printing 2.00
663 BMc,Time & Time Again,pt.2,
  A:JSA,Legion 2.00
664 BMc,Time & Time Again,pt.5 . 2.00
665 TG,V:Baron Sunday 2.00
666 EH,Red Glass Trilogy,pt.3 . . . 2.00

Action Annual #5
© DC Comics, Inc.

667 JOy,JM,TG,ATi,DJu,Revenge
  of the Krypton Man,pt.4 . . . . 2.25
668 BMc,Luthor confirmed dead . 2.00
669 BMc,V:Intergang,A:Thorn . . . 2.00
670 BMc,A:Waverider,JLA,JLE . . 2.00
671 KD,Blackout,pt.2 . . . . 2.00
672 BMc,Superman Meets Lex
  Luthor II 2.00
673 BMc,V:Hellgramite 2.00
674 BMc,Panic in the Sky (Prologue)
  R:Supergirl(Matrix) 3.50
675 BMc,Panic in the Sky #4,
  V:Brainiac 3.00
676 B:KK(s),JG,A:Supergirl,Lex
  Luthor II 1.75
677 JG,Supergirl V:Superman . . . 1.75
678 JG,O:Lex Luthor II 1.75
679 JG,I:Shellshock 1.75
680 JG,Blaze/Satanus War,pt.2 . . 1.75
681 JG,V:Hellgramite 1.75
682 DAb,TA,V:Hi-Tech 1.75
683 JG,I:Jackal,C:Doomsday . . . 6.00
683a 2nd printing 1.50
684 JG,Doomsday Pt.4 . . . . 10.00
684a 2nd printing 1.75
685 JG,Funeral for a Friend#2 . . . 4.00
686 JG,Funeral for a Friend#6 . . . 4.00
687 JG,Reign of Superman #1,Direct
  Sales,Die-Cut(c),Mini-Poster,
  F:Last Son of Krypton 3.00
687a newsstand Ed. 1.75
688 JG,V:Guy Gardner 2.00
689 JG,V:Man of Steel,A:Superboy,
  Supergirl,R:Real Superman . . 5.00
690 JG,Cyborg Vs. Superboy . . . 2.50
691 JG,A:All Supermen,V:Cyborg
  Superman,Mongul 3.50
692 JG,A:Superboy,Man of Steel . 1.75
693 JG,A:Last Son of Krypton . . . 1.75
694 JG,Spilled Blood#2,V:Hi-Tech 1.75
695 JG,Foil(c),I:Cauldron,A:Lobo . 2.75
695a Newsstand Ed. 1.75
696 JG,V:Alien,C:Doomsday 3.00
697 JG,Bizarro's World#3,
  V:Bizarro 1.75
698 JG,A:Lex Luthor 1.75
699 JG,A:Project Cadmus 1.50
700 JG,Fall of Metropolis#1 . . . . . 3.25

700a Platinum Edition 20.00
701 JG,Fall of Metropolis#5,
  V:Luthor 1.75
702 JG,DvM,B:DyM(s),R:Bloodsport1.75
703 JG,DvM,Zero Hour 1.75
704 JG,DvM,Eradicator 1.50
705 JG,DvM,Supes real? 1.50
706 JG,DvM,A:Supergirl 1.50
707 JG,DvM,V:Shado Dragon . . . 1.50
708 JG,DvM,R:Deathtrap 1.50
709 JG,DvM,A:Guy Gardner,
  Warrior 1.50
710 JG,DvM,Death of Clark Kent,pt.3
  [new Miraweb format begins] . . 1.95
711 JG,DvM,Death of Clark
  Kent,pt.7 . . . . 1.95
Ann.#1 AAd,DG,A:Batman 8.00
Ann.#2 MMi,CS,GP,JOy,DJu,BBr,
  V:Mongul 5.00
Ann.#3 TG,Armageddon X-over . . 3.00
Ann.#4 Eclipso,A:Captain
  Marvel 3.00
Ann.#5 MZ(c),Bloodlines,I:Loose
  Cannon 2.75
Ann.#6 Elseworlds,JBy(a&S) . . . 3.00
Gold.Ann.rep.#1 . . . . 1.50
#0 Peer Pressure,pt.4 . . . . 2.00

ADAM STRANGE

1 NKu,A.Strange on Rann 5.00
2 NKu,Wanted:Adam Strange . . 4.50
3 NKu,final issue 4.50

ADVANCED DUNGEONS & DRAGONS

1 JD,I:Onyx,Priam,Timoth,
  Cybriana,Vajra,Luna 12.00
2 JD,V:Imgig Zu,I:Conner 10.00
3 JD,V:Imgig Zu,I:Kyriani 9.00
4 JD,V:Imgig Zu,I:Kyriani 7.00
5 JD,Spirit of Myrrth I 7.00
6 JD,Spirit of Myrrth II 7.00
7 JD,Spirit of Myrrth III 5.50
8 JD,Spirit of Myrrth IV 5.50
9 JD,Catspawn Quartet I 5.50
10 JD,Catspawn Quartet II 4.50
11 JD,Catspawn Quartet III 4.50
12 JD,Catspawn Quartet IV 4.50
13 JD,Spell Games I 4.50
14 JD,Spell Games II 4.50
15 JD,Spell Games III 4.00
16 JD,Spell Games IV 4.00
17 JD,RM,Kyriani's Story I 4.00
18 JD,RM,Kyriani's Story II 4.00
19 JD,RM,Luna I 4.00
20 JD,RM,Luna II 4.00
21 JD,RM,Luna III 4.00
22 JD,RM,Luna IV 4.00
23 TMd,RM,Siege Dragons I . . . 3.00
24 Scavengers 2.50
25 JD,RM,Centaur Village 2.00
26 JD,Timoth the Centaur 2.00
27 JD,Kyriani,Dragons Eye #1 . . 2.00
28 JD,Dragons Eye #2 . . . . 2.00
29 JD,RM,Dragons Eye #3 . . . . 2.00
30 JD,RM,Carril's Killer
  Revealed 2.00
31 TMd,Onyx'Father,pt.1 . . . . . . 2.00
32 TMd,Onyx'Father,pt.2 . . . . . . 2.00
33 JD,Waterdeep,pt.1 . . . . 2.00
34 JD,Waterdeep,pt.2 . . . . 2.00
35 JD,RM,Waterdeep,pt.3 . . . . . 1.75
36 JD,RM,final issue 1.75
Ann.#1 JD,RM,Tmd 5.50

ADVENTURE COMICS
November 1938
[Prev: New Comics]

32 CF(c)	2,000.00
33	1,000.00
34 FG(c)	1,000.00
35 FG(c)	1,000.00
36 Giant Snake(c)	1,000.00
37 Rampaging Elephant(c)	1,000.00
38 Tiger(c)	1,000.00
39 Male Bondage(c)	1,000.00
40 CF(c),1st app. Sandman	24,000.00
41 Killer Shark(c)	2,500.00
42 CF,Sandman(c)	3,200.00
43 CF(c)	1,800.00
44 CF,Sandman(c)	3,100.00
45 FG(c)	1,800.00
46 CF,Sandman(c)	2,400.00
47 Sandman (c)	2,200.00
48 1st app.& B:Hourman	12,000.00
49	1,400.00

Adventure Comics #48
© DC Comics, Inc.

50 Hourman(c)	1,400.00
51 BBa(c),Sandman(c)	1,500.00
52 BBa(c),Hourman(c)	1,500.00
53 BBa(c),1st app. Minuteman	1,000.00
54 BBa(c),Hourman(c)	1,000.00
55 BBa(c),same	1,000.00
56 BBa(c),same	1,000.00
57 BBa(c),same	1,000.00
58 BBa(c),same	1,000.00
59 BBa(c),same	1,000.00
60 Sandman(c)	1,500.00
61 CF(c),JBu,Starman(c)	7,500.00
62 JBu(c),JBu,Starman(c)	1,000.00
63 JBu(c),JBu,same	1,000.00
64 JBu(c),JBu,same	1,000.00
65 JBu(c),JBu,same	1,000.00
66 JBu(c),JBu,O:Shining Knight, Starman(c)	1,100.00
67 JBu(c),JBu,O:Mist	1,000.00
68 JBu(c),JBu,same	1,000.00
69 JBu(c),JBu,1st app. Sandy, Starman(c)	1,100.00
70 JBu(c),JBu,Starman(c)	1,000.00
71 JBu(c),JBu,same	850.00
72 JBu(c),S&K,JBu,Sandman	6,500.00
73 S&K(c),S&K,I:Manhunter	6,500.00
74 S&K(c),S&K,You can't Escape your Fate-The Sandman	1,100.00

75 S&K(c),S&K,Sandman and Sandy Battle Thor in 'Villian from Valhalla'	1,100.00
76 S&K(c),Sandman(c),S&K	1,100.00
77 S&K,(c),S&K,same	1,100.00
78 S&K(c),S&K,same	1,100.00
79 S&K(c),S&K,Manhunter in 'Cobras of the Deep'	1,100.00
80 S&K(c),Sandman(c),S&K	1,100.00
81 S&K(c),MMe,S&K,same	900.00
82 S&K(c),S&K,Sandman X-Mas story	900.00
83 S&K(c),S&K,Sandman Boxing(c),E:Hourman	900.00
84 S&K(c),S&K	900.00
85 S&K(c),S&K,Sandman in 'The Amazing Dreams of Gentleman Jack'	900.00
86 S&K(c),Sandman(c)	900.00
87 S&K(c),same	900.00
88 S&K(c),same	900.00
89 S&K(c),same	900.00
90 S&K(c),same	900.00
91 S&K(c),JK	750.00
92 S&K(c)	550.00
93 S&K(c),Sandman in 'Sleep for Sale'	550.00
94 S&K(c),Sandman(c)	550.00
95 S&K(c),same	550.00
96 S&K(c),same	550.00
97 S&K(c),same	550.00
98 JK(c),Sandman in 'Hero of Dreams'	550.00
99 JK(c)	550.00
100	750.00
101 S&K(c)	500.00
102 S&K(c)	500.00
103 B:Superboy stories,(c),BU: Johnny Quick,Aquaman,Shining Knight,Green Arrow	1,800.00
104 S&S,ToyTown USA	650.00
105 S&S,Palace of Fantasy	450.00
106 S&S,Weather Hurricane	450.00
107 S&S,The Sky is the Limit	450.00
108 S&S,Proof of the Proverbs	450.00
109 S&S,You Can't Lose	450.00
110 S&S,The Farmer Takes it Easy	450.00
111 S&S,The Whiz Quiz Club	400.00
112 S&S,Super Safety First	400.00
113 S&S,The 33rd Christmas	400.00
114 S&S,Superboy Spells Danger	400.00
115 S&S,The Adventure of Jaguar Boy	400.00
116 S&S,JBu,Superboy Toy Tester	400.00
117 S&S,JBu,Miracle Plane	400.00
118 S&S,JBu,The Quiz Biz Broadcast	400.00
119 WMo,JBu,Superboy Meets Girls	400.00
120 S&S,JBu,A:Perry White; I:Ringmaster	450.00
121 S&S,Great Hobby Contest	350.00
122 S&S,Superboy-Super-Magician	350.00
123 S&S,Lesson For a Bully	350.00
124 S&S,Barbed Wire Boys Town	350.00
125 S&S,The Weight Before Christmas	350.00
126 S&S,Superboy:Crime Fighting Poet	350.00
127 MMe,O:Shining Knight;	

Super Bellboy	350.00
128 WMo,How Clark Kent Met Lois Lane'	350.00
129 WMo,Pupils of the Past	350.00
130 WMo,Superboy Super Salesman	350.00
131 WMo,The Million Dollar Athlete	300.00
132 WMo,Superboy Super Cowboy	300.00
133 WMo,Superboy's Report Card	300.00
134 WMo,Silver Gloves Sellout	300.00
135 WMo,The Most Amazing of All Boys	300.00
136 WMo,My Pal Superboy	300.00
137 WMo,Treasure of Tondimo	300.00
138 WMo,Around the World in Eighty Minutes	300.00
139 WMo,Telegraph Boy	300.00
140 Journey to the Moon	300.00

Adventure Comics #79
© DC Comics, Inc.

141 WMo,When Superboy Lost His Powers	300.00
142 WMo,The Man Who Walked With Trouble	350.00
143 WMo,The Superboy Savings Bank,A:Wooden Head Jones	350.00
144 WMo,The Way to Stop Superboy	350.00
145 WMo,Holiday Hijackers	350.00
146 The Substitute Superboy	350.00
147 Clark Kent,Orphan	350.00
148 Superboy Meets Mummies	350.00
149 Fake Superboys	350.00
150 FF,Superboy's Initiation	400.00
151 FF,No Hunting(c)	400.00
152 Superboy Hunts For a Job	350.00
153 FF,Clark Kent,Boy Hobo	400.00
154 The Carnival Boat Crimes	250.00
155 FF,Superboy-Hollywood Actor	350.00
156 The Flying Peril	250.00
157 FF,The Worst Boy in Smallville	350.00
158 The Impossible Task	250.00
159 FF,Superboy Millionaire?	350.00
160 Superboy's Phoney Father	250.00
161 FF	350.00
162 'The Super-Coach of	

Smallville High!' 250.00
163 FF,'Superboy's Phoney
  Father' 350.00
164 Discovers the Secret of
  a Lost Indian Tribe! 250.00
165 'Superboy's School for
  Stunt Men!' 250.00
166 'The Town That Stole
  Superboy' 250.00
167 'Lana Lang, Super-Girl!' .. 250.00
168 'The Boy Who Out Smarted
  Superboy' 250.00
169 'Clark Kent's Private
  Butler' 250.00
170 'Lana Lang's Big Crush' .. 225.00
171 'Superboy's Toughest
  Tasks!' 225.00
172 'Laws that Backfired' 225.00
173 'Superboy's School of
  Hard Knocks' 225.00
174 'The New Lana Lang!' 225.00
175 'Duel of the Superboys' ... 225.00
176 'Superboy's New Parents!' 225.00
177 'Hot-Rod Chariot Race!' .. 225.00
178 'Boy in the Lead Mask' ... 225.00

Adventure Comics #267
© DC Comics, Inc.

179 'The World's Whackiest
  Inventors' 225.00
180 Grand Prize o/t Underworld 225.00
181 'Mask for a Hero' 225.00
182 The Super Hick from
  Smallville' 200.00
183 'Superboy and Cleopatra' . 200.00
184 'The Shutterbugs of
  Smallville' 200.00
185 'The Mythical Monster' ... 200.00
186 .... 200.00
187 '25th Century Superboy' .. 200.00
188 'The Bull Fighter from
  Smallville' 200.00
189 Girl of Steel(Lana Lang) .. 200.00
190 The Two Clark Kents 200.00
191 .... 200.00
192 'The Coronation of
  Queen Lana Lang' 200.00
193 'Superboy's Lost Costume' 200.00

194 'Super-Charged Superboy' 200.00
195 'Lana Lang's Romance
  on Mars!' 200.00
196 'Superboy vs. King Gorilla' 200.00
197 V:Juvenile Gangs 200.00
198 'The Super-Carnival
  from Space' 200.00
199 'Superboy meets Superlad' 200.00
200 'Superboy and the Apes!' . 350.00
201 'Safari in Smallville!' 250.00
202 'Superboy City, U.S.A.' ... 250.00
203 'Uncle Superboy!' 300.00
204 'The Super-Brat of
  Smallville' 250.00
205 'The Journey of the
  Second Superboy!' 250.00
206 'The Impossible Creatures' 250.00
207 'Smallville's Worst
  Athlete' 250.00
208 'Rip Van Winkle of
  Smallville?' 250.00
209 'Superboy Week!' 250.00
210 I:Krypto,'The Superdog
  from Krypton' 2,400.00
211 'Superboy's Most
  Amazing Dream!' 200.00
212 'Superboy's Robot Twin' .. 200.00
213 'The Junior Jury of
  Smallville!' 200.00
214 A:Krypto 200.00
215 'The Super-Hobby of
  Superboy' 200.00
216 'The Wizard City' 200.00
217 'Superboy's Farewell
  to Smallville' 200.00
218 'The Two World's of
  Superboy' 200.00
219 The Rip Van Wrinkle of
  Smallville 200.00
220 The Greatest Show on Earth
  A:Krypto 200.00
221 'The Babe of Steel' 150.00
222 'Superboy's Repeat
  Performance' 150.00
223 'Hercules Junior' 150.00
224 'Pa Kent Superman' 150.00
225 'The Bird with
  Super-Powers' 150.00
226 'Superboy's Super Rival!' . 150.00
227 'Good Samaritan of
  Smallville' 150.00
228 'Clark Kent's Body Guard' . 150.00
229 .... 150.00
230 'The Secret of the
  Flying Horse' 150.00
231 'The Super-Feats of
  Super-Baby!' 150.00
232 'The House where
  Superboy was Born' 150.00
233 'Joe Smith, Man of Steel!' . 150.00
234 'The 1,001 Rides of
  Superboy!' 150.00
235 'The Confessions of
  Superboy!' 150.00
236 'Clark Kent's Super-Dad!' . 150.00
237 Robot War of Smallville! .. 150.00
238 'The Secret Past of
  Superboy's Father' 150.00
239 'The Super-Tricks of
  the Dog of Steel' 150.00
240 'The Super Teacher
  From Krypton' 150.00
241 'The Super-Outlaw of
  Smallville' 150.00
242 'The Kid From Krypton' ... 150.00

243 'The Super Toys From
  Krypton' 150.00
244 'The Poorest Family in
  Smallville' 150.00
245 'The Mystery of Monster X' 150.00
246 'The Girl Who Trapped
  Superboy!' 150.00
247 I&O:Legion 3,600.00
248 Green Arrow 120.00
249 CS,Green Arrow 120.00
250 JK,Green Arrow 120.00
251 JK,Green Arrow 120.00
252 JK,Green Arrow 120.00
253 JK,1st Superboy &
  Robin T.U 175.00
254 JK,Green Arrow 120.00
255 JK,Green Arrow 120.00
256 JK,O:Green Arrow 425.00
257 CS,LE,A:Hercules,Samson 100.00
258 LE,Aquaman,Superboy ... 100.00
259 I:Crimson Archer 100.00
260 1st S.A. O:Aquaman 480.00
261 GA,A:Lois Lane 75.00
262 O:Speedy 80.00
263 GA,Aquaman,Superboy ... 75.00
264 GA,A:Robin Hood 75.00
265 GA,Aquaman,Superboy ... 75.00
266 GA,I:Aquagirl 75.00
267 N:Legion(2nd app.) 800.00
268 I:Aquaboy 75.00
269 I:Aqualad,E:Green Arrow . 160.00
270 2nd A:Aqualad,B:Congorilla . 75.00
271 O:Lex Luthor rtd 150.00
272 I:Human Flying Fish 56.00
273 Aquaman,Superboy 56.00
274 Aquaman,Superboy 56.00
275 O:Superman/Batman
  T.U. rtd 115.00

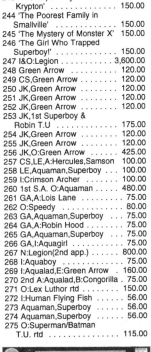

Adventure Comics #377
© DC Comics, Inc.

276 Superboy,3rd A:Metallo 50.00
277 Aquaman,Superboy 50.00
278 Aquaman,Superboy 50.00
279 CS,Aquaman,Superboy 50.00
280 CS,A:Lori Lemaris 50.00
281 Aquaman,Superboy
  E:Congorilla 50.00

---

282 5th A:Legion,I:Starboy	150.00
283 I:Phantom Zone	75.00
284 CS,JM,Aquaman,Superboy	32.00
285 WB,B:Bizarro World	70.00
286 I:Bizarro Mxyzptlk	75.00
287 I:Dev-Em,Bizarro Perry White, Jimmy Olsen	45.00
288 A:Dev-Em	45.00
289 Superboy	35.00
290 8th A:Legion,O&J:Sunboy, I:Brainiac 5	100.00
291 A:Lex Luthor	32.00
292 Superboy,I:Bizarro Lucy Lane, Lana Lang	32.00
293 CS,O&I:Marv-El,I:Bizarro Luthor	65.00
294 I:Bizarro M.Monroe,JFK	65.00
295 I:Bizarro Titano	35.00
296 A:Ben Franklin,George Washington	30.00
297 Lana Lang Superboy Sister	30.00
298 The Fat Superboy	30.00
299 I:Gold Kryptonite	35.00
300 B:Legion,J:Mon-El, E:Bizarro World	310.00
301 CS,O:Bouncing Boy	85.00
302 CS,Legion	50.00
303 I:Matter Eater Lad	55.00
304 D:Lightning Lad	55.00
305 A:Chameleon Boy	50.00
306 I:Legion of Sub.Heroes	40.00

Adventure Comics #426
© DC Comics, Inc.

307 I:Element Lad	45.00
308 I:Light Lass	45.00
309 I:Legion of Super Monsters	40.00
310 A:Mxyzptlk	40.00
311 CS,V:Legion of Substitue Heroes	30.00
312 R:Lightning Lad	32.00
313 CS,J:Supergirl	30.00
314 A:Hitler	30.00
315 A:Legion of Substitute Heroes	30.00
316 O:Legion	28.00
317 I&J:Dreamgirl	28.00
318 Legion	28.00

319 Legion	26.00
320 A:Dev-Em	26.00
321 I:Time Trapper	27.00
322 JF,A:Legion of Super Pets	22.00
323 JF,BU:Kypto	22.00
324 JF,I:Legion of Super Outlaws	22.00
325 JF,V:Lex Luthor	22.00
326 BU:Superboy	22.00
327 I&J:Timber Wolf	30.00
328 Legion	20.00
329 I:Legion of Super Bizarros	22.00
330 Legion	22.00
331 Legion	17.00
332 Legion	17.00
333 Legion	17.00
334 Legion	16.00
335 Legion	16.00
336 Legion	15.00
337 Legion	15.00
338 Legion	16.00
339 Legion	16.00
340 I:Computo	18.00
341 CS,D:Triplicate Girl (becomes Duo Damsel)	13.00
342 CS,Star Boy expelled	11.00
343 CS,V:Lords of Luck	11.00
344 CS,Super Stalag,pt.1	11.00
345 CS,Super Stalag,pt.2	11.00
346 CS,I&J:Karate Kid,Princess Projectra,I:Nemesis Kid	13.00
347 CS,Legion	11.00
348 I:Dr.Regulus	12.00
349 CS,I:Rond Vidar	11.00
350 CS,I:White Witch	12.00
351 CS,R:Star Boy	10.00
352 CS,I:Fatal Fire	10.00
353 CS,D:Ferro Lad	15.00
354 CS,Adult Legion	10.00
355 CS,J:Insect Queen	10.00
356 CS,Five Legion Orphans	9.00
357 CS,I:Controller	9.00
358 I:Hunter	9.00
359 CS,Outlawed Legion,pt.1	9.00
360 CS,Outlawed Legion,pt.2	9.00
361 I:Dominators (30th century)	10.00
362 I:Dr.Mantis Morto	9.00
363 V:Dr.Mantis Morlo	9.00
364 A:Legion of Super Pets	9.00
365 CS,I:Shadow Lass, V:Fatal Five	9.00
366 CS,J:Shadow Lass	7.00
367 N:Legion H.Q.,I:Dark Circle	9.00
368 CS	7.00
369 CS,JAb,I:Mordru	8.00
370 CS,JAb,V:Mordru	7.00
371 CS,JAb,I:Chemical King	9.00
372 CS,JAb,J:Timber Wolf, Chemical King	9.00
373 I:Tornado Twins	7.00
374 WM,I:Black Mace	7.00
375 I:Wanderers	8.00
376 Execution of Cham.Boy	7.00
377 Heroes for Hire	7.00
378 Twelve Hours to Live	7.00
379 Burial In Space	7.00
380 The Amazing Space Odyssey of the Legion,E:Legion	7.00
381 The Supergirl Gang C:Batgirl,B:Supergirl	4.50
382 NA(c),The Superteams Split Up,A:Superman	4.00
383 NA(c),Please Stop my Funeral, A:Superman,Comet,Streaky	5.00
384 KS,The Heroine Haters,	

A:Superman	4.00
385 Supergirl's Big Sister	4.00
386 The Beast That Loved Supergirl	4.00
387 Wolfgirl of Stanhope; A:Superman;V:Lex Luthor	4.00
388 Kindergarten Criminal; V:Luthor,Brainiac	4.00
389 A:Supergirl's Parents, V:Brainiac	4.00
390 Linda Danvers Superstar (80 page giant)	7.50
391 The Super Cheat;A:Comet	3.25
392 Supergirls Lost Costume	3.25
393 KS,Unwanted Supergirl	3.25
394 KS,Heartbreak Prison	3.25
395 Heroine in Haunted House	3.25
396 Mystery o/t Super Orphan	3.25
397 Now Comes Zod,N:Supergirl, V:Luthor	3.25
398 Maid of Doom,A:Superman, Streaky,Krypto,Comet	3.25
399 CI,Johnny Dee,Hero Bum	3.25
400 MSy,35th Anniv.,Return of the Black Flame	3.50
401 MSy,JAb,The Frightened Supergirl,V:Lex Luthor	2.50
402 MSy,JAb,TD,I:Starfire, Dr.Kangle	2.50
403 68 page giant	6.00
404 MSy,JAb,V:Starfire	2.50
405 V:Starfire,Dr.Kangle	2.50
406 MSy,JAb,Suspicion	2.50
407 MSy,JAb,Suspicion Confirmed N:Supergirl	2.50
408 The Face at the Window	2.50
409 MSy,DG,Legion rep.	2.50
410 N:Supergirl	2.50
411 CI,N:Supergirl	2.50
412 rep.Strange Adventures #180 (I:Animal Man).	5.00
413 GM,JKu,rep.Hawkman	2.25
414 Animal Man rep.	4.00
415 BO,GM,CI,Animal Man rep.	3.00
416 CI,All women issue,giantsize	3.50
417 GM,inc.rep.Adventure #161, Frazetta art.	2.25
418 ATh,Black Canary	2.25
419 ATh,Black Canary	2.25
420 Animal Man rep.	3.25
421 MSy,Supergirl	2.25
422 MSy,Supergirl	2.25
423 MSy,Supergirl	2.25
424 MSy,E:Supergirl,A:JLA	2.25
425 AN,ATh,I:Captain Fear	2.25
426 MSy,DG,JAp,Vigilante	2.25
427 TD	7.50
428 TD,I:Black Orchid	6.00
429 TD,AN,Black Orchid	5.00
430 A:Black Orchid	3.50
431 JAp,ATh,B:Spectre	2.50
432 JAp,AN,A:Spectre,Capt.Fear	2.50
433 JAp,AN	2.50
434 JAp	2.50
435 MGr(1st work),JAp,Aquaman	3.50
436 JAp,MGr,Aquaman	3.00
437 JAp,MGr,Aquaman	3.00
438 JAp,HC,DD,7 Soldiers	1.75
439 JAp	1.75
440 JAp,O:New Spectre	1.75
441 JAp,B:Aquaman	1.75
442 JAp,A:Aquaman	1.75
443 JAp	1.75
444 JAp	1.75
445 JAp,RE,JSon,Creeper	1.75

Adventure Comics #480
© DC Comics, Inc.

446 JAp,RE,JSon,Creeper 1.75
447 JAp,RE,JSon,Creeper 1.75
448 JAp,Aquaman 1.75
449 JAp,MN,TA,Jonn J'onz 1.50
450 JAp,MN,TA,Supergirl 1.50
451 JAp,MN,TA,Hawkman 1.50
452 JAp,Aquaman 1.50
453 MA,CP,JRu,B:Superboy
& Aqualad 1.50
454 CP,DG,A:Kryptonite Kid 1.50
455 CP,DG,A:Kryptonite Kid
E:Aqualad 1.50
456 JSon,JA 1.50
457 JSon,JA,JO,B:Eclipso 3.50
458 JSon,JAp,JO,BL,E:Superboy
& Eclipso 3.00
459 IN,FMc,JAp,JSon,DN,JA,A:Wond.
Woman,New Gods,Green Lantern,
Flash,Deadman,(giant size) . . . 2.00
460 IN,FMc,JAp,DN,DA,JSon,JA,
D:Darkseid 1.75
461 IN,FMc,JAp,JSon,DN,JA,
B:JSA & Aquaman 2.50
462 IN,FMc,DH,JL,DG,JA,
D:Earth 2,Batman 4.00
463 DH,JL,JSon,FMc 1.50
464 DH,JAp,JSon,DN,DA,
Deadman 1.75
465 DN,JSon,DG,JL 1.50
466 MN,JL,JSon,DN,DA 1.50
467 JSon,SD,RT,I:Starman
B:Plastic Man 1.50
468 SD,JSon 1.50
469 SD,JSon,O:Starman 1.50
470 SD,JSon,O:Starman 1.50
471 SD,JSon,I:Brickface 1.50
472 SD,RT,JSon 1.50
473 SD,RT,JSon 1.50
474 SD,RT,JSon 1.50
475 BB(c),SD,RT,JSon,DG,
B:Aquaman 1.50
476 SD,RT,JSon,DG 1.50
477 SD,RT,JSon,DG 1.50
478 SD,RT,JSon,DG 1.50
479 CI,DG,JSon,Dial H For Hero,
E:Starman and Aquaman 1.50
480 CI,DJ,B:Dial H for Hero 1.50
481 CI,DJ 1.50

482 CI,DJ,DH 1.50
483 CI,DJ,DH 1.50
484 GP(c),CI,DJ,DH 1.50
485 GP(c),CI,DJ 1.50
486 GP(c),DH,RT,TVE 1.50
487 CI,DJ,DH 1.50
488 CI,DJ,TVE 1.50
489 CI,FMc,TVE 1.50
490 GP(c),CI,E:Dial H for Hero . . 1.50
491 KG(c),DigestSize,DN,
Shazam,rep.other material . . 1.50
492 KG(c),DN,E:Shazam 1.50
493 KG(c),GT,B:Challengers of
the Unknown,reprints 1.50
494 KG(c),GT,Challengers,
reprints 1.50
495 ATh,reprints,Challengers 1.75
496 GK(c),ATh,reprints,
Challengers 1.75
497 ATh,DA,reps.,E:Challengers . . 1.75
498 GK(c),reprints,Rep.Legion . . . 1.50
499 GK(c),reprints,Rep 1.50
500 KG(c),Legion reprints,Rep . . . 1.50
501 reprints,Rep 1.50
502 reprints,Rep 1.50
503 reprints,final issue 1.50

ADVENTURES OF ALAN LADD
October-November, 1949

1 Ph(c) 500.00
2 Ph(c) 350.00
3 Ph(c) 250.00
4 Ph(c) 250.00
5 Ph(c),inc.Destination Danger 200.00
6 Ph(c) 200.00
7 . . . . 200.00
8 Grand Duchess takes over . 200.00
9 Deadlien in Rapula,
February-March, 1951 . . . . 200.00

Bob Hope #11 © DC Comics, Inc.

ADVENTURES OF BOB HOPE
February-March, 1951

1 Ph(c) 900.00
2 Ph(c) 400.00
3 Ph(c) 275.00
4 Ph(c) 250.00
5 thru 10 . . . . @200.00

11 thru 20 . . . . @125.00
21 thru 40 . . . . @85.00
41 thru 90 . . . . @50.00
91 thru 93 . . . . @20.00
94 C:Aquaman 22.00
95 thru 105 . . . . @20.00
106 NA 30.00
107 NA 30.00
108 NA 30.00
109 NA 30.00

ADVENTURES OF DEAN MARTIN AND JERRY LEWIS
July-August, 1952

1 . . . . 500.00
2 . . . . 250.00
3 thru 10 . . . . @125.00
11 thru 20 . . . . @75.00
21 thru 40 . . . . @50.00
Becomes:

ADVENTURES OF JERRY LEWIS

41 thru 55 . . . . @35.00
56 thru 69 . . . . @25.00
70 thru 87 . . . . @15.00
88 A:Bob Hope 18.00
89 thru 91 . . . . @15.00
92 C:Superman 30.00
93 thru 96 . . . . @15.00
97 A:Batman & Joker 30.00
98 thru 100 . . . . @15.00
101 thru 104 NA . . . . @25.00
105 A:Superman 20.00
106 thru 111 . . . . @8.00
112 A:Flash 15.00
113 thru 116 . . . . @8.00
117 A:Wonder Woman 10.00
118 thru 124 . . . . @6.00

ADVENTURES OF FORD FAIRLANE

1 DH,DG 1.50
2 DH 1.50
3 DH 1.50
4 DH 1.50

ADVENTURES OF THE OUTSIDERS
(see BATMAN & THE OUTSIDERS)

ADVENTURES OF OZZIE AND HARRIET
October-November, 1949

1 Ph(c) 450.00
2 . . . . 250.00
3 . . . . 200.00
4 . . . . 200.00
5 June-July, 1950 . . . . 200.00

ADVENTURES OF REX, THE WONDERDOG
January-February, 1952

1 ATh 600.00
2 ATh 300.00
3 ATh 250.00
4 . . . . 175.00
5 . . . . 175.00
6 thru 11 . . . . @125.00
12 thru 20 . . . . @75.00
21 thru 46 . . . . @50.00

ADVENTURES OF SUPERBOY
(See: SUPERBOY)

ADVENTURES OF SUPERMAN
(See: SUPERMAN)

AGENT LIBERTY SPECIAL
1 DAb,O:Agent Liberty 2.00

ALIEN NATION
1 JBi,movie adaption 2.50

ALL-AMERICAN COMICS
April, 1939
1 B:Hop Harrigan,Scribbly,Mutt&Jeff,
  Red,White&Blue,Bobby Thatcher,
  Skippy,Daiseybelle,Mystery Men
  of Mars,Toonerville 3,200.00
2 B:Ripley's Believe It or Not 1,000.00
3 Hop Harrigan (c) 750.00
4 Flag(c) 750.00
5 B:The American Way 750.00
6 ShM(c),Fredric Marchin in
  'The American Way' 600.00

All-American Comics #4
© DC Comics, Inc.

7 E:Bobby Thatcher,C.H.
  Claudy's 'A Thousand Years
  in a Minute' 600.00
8 B:Ultra Man 1,000.00
9 . . . . 650.00
10 ShM(c),E:The American Way,
  Santa-X-Mas(c) 600.00
11 Ultra Man(c) 600.00
12 E:Toonerville Folks 600.00
13 'The Infra Red Des'Royers' . 600.00
14 . . . . 600.00
15 E:Tippie and Reg'lar Fellars 600.00
16 O&1st App:Green Lantern,
  B:Lantern(c) 50,000.00
17 SMo(c) 9,000.00
18 SMo(c) 5,800.00
19 SMo(c),O&1st App: Atom,
  E:Ultra Man 8,500.00
20 I:Atom's costume,Hunkle

All-American Comics #23
© DC Comics, Inc.

becomes Red Tornado . . . 2,400.00
21 E:Wiley of West Point
  & Skippy 1,400.00
22 . . . . 1,500.00
23 E:Daieybelle 1,500.00
24 E:Ripley's Believe It or Not 1,700.00
25 O&1st App:Dr. Mid-Nite . . 5,800.00
26 O&I:Sargon the Sorcerer . 2,000.00
27 I:Doiby Dickles 2,400.00
28 . . . . 1,000.00
29 ShM(c) 1,000.00
30 ShM(c) 1,000.00
31 . . . . 1,000.00
32 . . . . 650.00
33 . . . . 650.00
34 . . . . 650.00
35 Doiby discovers Lantern's ID 650.00
36 . . . . 650.00
37 . . . . 650.00
38 . . . . 650.00
39 . . . . 650.00
40 . . . . 650.00
41 . . . . 600.00
42 . . . . 600.00
43 . . . . 600.00
44 'I Accuse the Green Lantern!' 600.00
45 . . . . 600.00
46 . . . . 600.00
47 Hop Harrigan meets the
  Enemy,(c) 600.00
48 . . . . 600.00
49 . . . . 600.00
50 E:Sargon 600.00
51 'Murder Under the Stars' . . . 500.00
52 . . . . 500.00
53 Green Lantern delivers
  the Mail 500.00
54 . . . . 500.00
55 'The Riddle of the
  Runaway Trolley' 500.00
56 V:Elegant Esmond 500.00
57 V:The Melancholy Men 500.00
58 . . . . 500.00
59 'The Story of the Man Who
  Couldn't Tell The Truth' . . . 500.00
60 . . . . 500.00
61 O:Soloman Grundy,'Fighters
  Never Quit' 2,200.00
62 'Da Distrik Attorney' 400.00

63 . . . . 400.00
64 'A Bag of Assorted Nuts!' . . 400.00
65 'The Man Who Lost
  Wednesday' 400.00
66 'The Soles of Manhattan!' . . 400.00
67 V:King Shark 400.00
68 Meets Napoleon&Joe Safeen 400.00
69 'Backwards Man!' 400.00
70 JKu,I:Maximillian O'Leary,
  V:Colley, the Leprechaun . . 400.00
71 E:Red,White&Blue,'The
  Human Bomb' 350.00
72 B:Black Pirate 350.00
73 B:Winkey,Blinky&Noddy,
  'Mountain Music Mayhem' . . 350.00
74 . . . . 350.00
75 . . . . 350.00
76 'Spring Time for Doiby' 350.00
77 Hop Harrigan(c) 350.00
78 . . . . 350.00
79 . . . . 350.00
80 . . . . 350.00
81 . . . . 350.00
82 . . . . 350.00
83 . . . . 350.00
84 'The Adventure of the Man
  with Two Faces' 350.00
85 . . . . 325.00
86 V:Crime of the Month Club . 325.00

All-American Comics #53
© DC Comics, Inc.

87 'The Strange Case of
  Professor Nobody' 325.00
88 'Canvas of Crime' 325.00
89 O:Harlequin 325.00
90 O:Icicle 325.00
91 'Wedding of the Harlequin' . 325.00
92 'The Icicle goes South' 325.00
93 'The Double Crossing Decoy' 325.00
94 A:Harlequin 325.00
95 'The Unmasking of the
  Harlequin' 325.00
96 ATh(c),'Solve the Mystery
  of the Emerald Necklaces!' . 325.00
97 ATh(c),'The Country Fair
  Crimes' 325.00
98 ATh,ATh(c),'End of Sports!' . 325.00
99 ATh,ATh(c),E:Hop Harrigan 325.00
100 ATh,I:Johnny Thunder . . . 750.00
101 ATh,ATh(c),E:Mutt and Jeff 600.00

102 ATh,ATh(c),E:Green Lantern 800.00
Becomes:

ALL-AMERICAN WESTERN

103 A:Johnny Thunder,'The City
 Without Guns,'All Johnny
 Thunder stories 250.00
104 ATh(c),'Unseen Allies' 200.00
105 ATh(c),'Hidden Guns' 150.00
106 ATh(c),'Snow Mountain
 Ambush' 125.00
107 ATh(c),'Cheyenne Justice' . 150.00
108 ATh(c),'Vengeance of
 the Silver Bullet' 125.00
109 ATh(c),'Secret of
 Crazy River' 125.00
110 ATh(c),'Ambush at
 Scarecrow Hills' 125.00
111 ATh(c),'Gun-Shy Sheriff' . . 125.00
112 ATh(c),'Double Danger' . . . 125.00
113 ATh(c),'Johnny Thunder
 Indian Chief' 150.00
114 ATh(c),'The End of
 Johnny Thunder' 125.00
115 ATh(c),'Cheyenne Mystery' 125.00
116 ATh(c),'Buffalo Raiders
 of the Mesa' 125.00
117 ATh(c),V:Black Lightnin . . . 100.00
118 ATh(c),'Challenge of
 the Aztecs' 100.00
119 GK(c),'The Vanishing
 Gold Mine' 100.00
120 GK(c),'Ambush at
 Painted Mountain' 100.00
121 ATh(c),'The Unmasking of
 Johnny Thunder' 100.00
122 ATh(c),'The Real
 Johnny Thunder' 100.00
123 GK(c),'Johnny Thunder's
 Strange Rival' 100.00
124 ATh(c),'The Iron Horse's
 Last Run' 100.00
125 ATh(c),'Johnny Thunder's
 Last Roundup' 100.00
126 ATh(c),'Phantoms of the
 Desert' 100.00
Becomes:

ALL-AMERICAN MEN OF WAR

127 (0) 450.00
128 (1) 350.00
2 JGr(c),Killer Bait 300.00
3 Pied Piper of Pyong-Yang . . 300.00
4 JGr(c),The Hills of Hate 300.00
5 One Second to Zero 175.00
6 IN(c),Jungle Killers 175.00
7 IN(c),Beach to Hold 175.00
8 IN(c),Sgt. Storm Cloud 175.00
9 . . . . 175.00
10 . . . . 175.00
11 JGr(c),Dragon's Teeth 175.00
12 . . . . 150.00
13 JGr(c),Lost Patrol 150.00
14 IN(c),Pigeon Boss 150.00
15 JGr(c),Flying Roadblock . . . 150.00
16 JGr(c),The Flying Jeep 150.00
17 JGr(c),Booby Trap Ridge . . 150.00
18 JKu(c),The Ballad of
 Battling Bells 150.00
19 JGr(c),IN,Torpedo Track . . . 125.00
20 JGr(c),JKu,Lifenet to
 Beach Road 125.00
21 JGr(c),IN,RH,The
 Coldest War 125.00

22 JGr(c),IN,JKu,Snipers Nest . 125.00
23 JGr(c),The Silent War 125.00
24 JGr(c),The Thin Line 125.00
25 JGr(c),IN,For Rent-One
 Foxhole 125.00
26 . . . . 125.00
27 JGr(c),RH,Fighting Pigeon . 125.00

All-American Men of War #8
© *DC Comics, Inc.*

28 JGr(c),RA,JKu,Medal
 for A Dog 125.00
29 IN(c),JKu,Battle Bridges . . . 135.00
30 JGr(c),RH,Frogman Hunt . . 125.00
31 JGr(c),Battle Seat 135.00
32 JGr(c),RH,Battle Station . . . 135.00
33 JGr(c),IN,Sky Ambush 125.00
34 JGr(c),JKu,No Man's Alley . 125.00
35 JGr(c),IN, Battle Call 90.00
36 JGr(c),JKu,Battle Window . . 90.00
37 JGr(c),JKu,The Big Stretch . . 90.00
38 JGr(c),RH,JKu,The
 Floating Sentinel 90.00
39 JGr(c),JKu,The Four Faces
 of Sgt. Fay 90.00
40 JGr(c),IN,Walking Helmet . . . 90.00
41 JKu(c),RH,JKu,The 50-50 War 75.00
42 JGr(c),JKu,Battle Arm 75.00
43 JGr(c),JKu,Command Post . . 75.00
44 JKu(c),The Flying Frogman . . 75.00
45 JGr(c),RH,Combat Waterboy . 75.00
46 JGr(c),IN,RH,Tank Busters . . 75.00
47 JGr(c),JKu,MD,Battle Freight . 75.00
48 JGr(c),JKu,MD,Roadblock . . 75.00
49 JGr(c),Walking Target 75.00
50 IN,RH,Bodyguard For A Sub . 75.00
51 JGr(c),RH,Bomber's Moon . . 50.00
52 JKu(c),RH,MD,Back
 Seat Driver 50.00
53 JKu(c),JKu,Night Attack 50.00
54 JKu(c),IN,Diary of a
 Fighter Pilot 50.00
55 JKu(c),RH,Split-Second Target 50.00
56 JKu,IN,RH,Frogman Jinx . . . 50.00
57 Pick-Up for Easy Co. 50.00
58 JKu(c),RH,MD,A Piece of Sky 50.00
59 JGr(c),JKu,The Hand of War . 50.00
60 JGr(c),The Time Table 50.00
61 JGr(c),IN,MD,Blind Target . . . 50.00
62 JGr(c),RH,RA,No(c) 50.00
63 JGr(c),JKu,Frogman Carrier . 50.00

64 JKu(c),JKu,RH,The Other
 Man's War 50.00
65 JGr(c),JKu,MD,Same
 Old Sarge 50.00
66 JGr(c),The Walking Fort 50.00
67 JGr(c),RH,A:Gunner&Sarge,
 The Cover Man 100.00
68 JKu(c),Gunner&Sarge,
 The Man & The Gun 50.00
69 JKu(c),A:Tank Killer,

All-American Men of War #13
© *DC Comics, Inc.*

 Bazooka Hill 50.00
70 JKu(c),IN,Pigeon
 Without Wings 50.00
71 JGr(c),A:Tank Killer,Target
 For An Ammo Boy 50.00
72 JGr(c),A:Tank Killer,T.N.T.
 Broom 50.00
73 JGr(c),JKu,No Detour 50.00
74 The Minute Commandos 50.00
75 JKu(c),Sink That Flattop 50.00
76 JKu(c),A:Tank Killer,
 Just One More Tank 50.00
77 JKu(c),IN,MD,Big Fish-
 little Fish 50.00
78 JGr(c),Tin Hat for an
 Iron Man 50.00
79 JKu(c),RA,Showdown Soldier 50.00
80 JKu(c),RA,The Medal Men . . 50.00
81 JGr(c),IN,Ghost Ship of
 Two Wars 25.00
82 IN(c),B:Johnny Cloud,
 The Flying Chief 25.00
83 IN(c),Fighting Blind 25.00
84 IN(c),Death Dive 25.00
85 RH(c),Battle Eagle 25.00
86 JGr(c),Top-Gun Ace 25.00
87 JGr(c),Broken Ace 25.00
88 JGr(c),The Ace of Vengeance 25.00
89 JGr(c),The Star Jockey 25.00
90 JGr(c),Wingmate of Doom . . 25.00
91 RH(c),Two Missions To Doom 25.00
92 JGr(c),The Battle Hawk 25.00
93 RH(c),The Silent Rider 25.00
94 RH(c),Be Brave-Be Silent . . . 25.00
95 RH(c),Second Sight
 For a Pilot 25.00
96 RH(c),The Last Flight
 of Lt. Moon 25.00

All comics prices listed are for *Near Mint* **condition.**   **CVA Page 11**

97 IN(c),A 'Target' Called
   Johnny 25.00
98 The Time-Bomb Ace 25.00
99 IN(c),The Empty Cockpit 25.00
100 RH(c),Battle o/t Sky Chiefs . 25.00
101 RH(c),Death Ship of
   Three Wars 15.00
102 JKu(c),Blind Eagle-Hungry
   Hawk 15.00
103 IN(c),Battle Ship-
   Battle Heart 15.00
104 JKu(c),The Last Target 15.00
105 IN(c),Killer Horse-Ship 15.00
106 IN(c),Death Song For
   A Battle Hawk 15.00
107 IN(c),Flame in the Sky 15.00
108 IN(c),Death-Dive of the Aces 15.00
109 IN(c),The Killer Slot 15.00
110 RH(c),The Co-Pilot was Death 15.00
111 RH(c),E:Johnny Cloud, Tag–
   You're Dead 15.00
112 RH(c),B:Balloon Buster,Lt.
   Steve Savage-Balloon Buster 15.00
113 JKu(c),The Ace of
   Sudden Death 15.00
114 JKu(c),The Ace Who
   Died Twice 15.00
115 IN(c),A:Johnny Cloud,
   Deliver One Enemy Ace-
   Handle With Care 15.00
116 IN(c),A:Baloon Buster,
   Circle of Death 15.00
117 September-October, 1966 .. 15.00

All-Flash #19 © DC Comics, Inc.

ALL-FLASH
Summer, 1941

1 EHi,O:Flash,I:The Monocle 7,200.00
2 EHi,The Adventure of Roy
   Revenge 1,400.00
3 EHi,The Adventure of
   Misplaced Faces 1,000.00
4 EHi,Tale of the Time Capsule 900.00
5 EHi,The Case of the Patsy
   Colt! Last Quarterly 700.00
6 EHi,The Ray that Changed
   Men's Souls 550.00
7 EHi,Adventures of a Writers
   Fantasy, House of Horrors . 550.00
8 EHi,Formula to Fairyland! .. 550.00

9 EHi,Adventure of the Stolen
   Telescope 550.00
10 EHi,Case of the Curious Cat 550.00
11 EHi,Troubles come
   in Doubles 450.00
12 EHi,Tumble INN to Trouble,
   Becomes Quarterly on orders
   from War Production Board
   O:The Thinker 450.00
13 EHi,I:The King 450.00
14 EHi,I:Winky,Blinky & Noddy
   Green Lantern (c) 550.00
15 EHi,Secrets of a Stranger .. 450.00
16 EHi,A:The Sinister 450.00
17 Tales of the Three Wishes .. 400.00
18 A:Winlky,Blinky&Noddy
   B:Mutt & Jeff reprints ... 400.00
19 No Rest at the Rest Home . 400.00
20 A:Winky, Blinky & Noddy .. 400.00
21 I:Turtle 350.00
22 The Money Doubler,E:Mutt
   & Jeff reprints 350.00
23 The Bad Men of Bar Nothing 350.00
24 I:Worry Wart,3 Court
   Clowns Get Caught 350.00
25 I:Slapsy Simmons,
   Flash Jitterbugs 350.00
26 I:The Chef,The Boss,Shrimp
   Coogan,A:Winky, Blinky &
   Noddy 375.00
27 A:The Thinker,Gangplank
   Gus story 350.00
28 A:Shrimp Coogan,Winky,
   Blinky & Noddy 350.00
29 The Thousand-Year Old Terror,
   A:Winky,Blinky & Noddy ... 350.00
30 The Vanishing Snowman .. 350.00
31 A:Black Hat,The Planet
   of Sport 350.00
32 I:Fiddler,A:Thinker
   December-January, 1947 .. 500.00

ALL FUNNY COMICS
Winter, 1943

1 Genius Jones 225.00
2 same 100.00
3 same 75.00
4 same 75.00
5 thru 10 .... @75.00
11 Genius Jones 40.00
12 same 40.00
13 same 40.00
14 .... 30.00
15 .... 40.00
16 A:DC Superheroes 125.00
17 .... 30.00
18 .... 30.00
19 .... 30.00
20 .... 30.00
21 .... 30.00
22 .... 30.00
23 May-June, 1948 .... 30.00

ALL-STAR COMICS
Summer, 1940

1 B:Flash,Hawkman,Hourman,Sandman,
   Spectre,Red White & Blue 9,000.00
2 B:Green Lantern and Johnny
   Thunder 3,500.00
3 First meeting of Justice Society
   with Flash as Chairman . 26,000.00
4 First mission of JSA 3,500.00
5 V:Mr. X,I:Hawkgirl 3,100.00
6 Flash leaves 2,100.00

All-Star Comics #3 © DC Comics, Inc.

7 Green Lantern becomes Chairman,
   L:Hourman, C:Superman,
   Batman & Flash 2,400.00
8 I:Wonder Women;Starman and
   Dr. Mid-Nite join,Hawkman
   becomes chairman 10,000.00
9 JSA in Latin America 2,000.00
10 C:Flash & Green Lantern,
   JSA Time Travel story .. 1,900.00
11 Wonder Women joins;
   I:Justice Battalion 1,700.00
12 V:Black Dragon society .. 1,700.00
13 V:Hitler 1,600.00
14 JSA in occupied Europe .. 1,600.00
15 I:Brain Wave,A:JSA's
   Girl Friends 1,500.00
16 Propaganda/relevance issue 1,200.00
17 V:Brain Wave 1,200.00
18 I:King Bee 1,300.00
19 Hunt for Hawkman 1,200.00
20 I:Monster 1,200.00
21 Time travel story 1,100.00
22 Sandman and Dr. Fate leave,
   I:Conscience, the Good Fairy 1,100.00
23 I:Psycho-Pirate 1,100.00
24 Propaganda/relevance issue,
   A:Conscience&Wildcat,Mr.Terrific;
   L:Starman & Spectre; Flash
   & Green Lantern return . 1,100.00
25 JSA whodunit issue 1,000.00
26 V:Metal Men from Jupiter . 1,000.00
27 Handicap issue,A:Wildcat . 1,000.00
28 Ancient curse comes to life . 900.00
29 I:Landor from 25th century . 900.00
30 V:Brain Wave 900.00
31 V:Zor 900.00
32 V:Psycho-Pirate 900.00
33 V:Soloman Grundy,A:Doiby
   Dickles, Last appearance
   Thunderbolt 1,800.00
34 I:Wizard 750.00
35 I:Per Degaton 750.00
36 A:Superman and Batman . 1,800.00
37 I:Injustice Society of
   the World 1,000.00
38 V:Villains of History,
   A:Black Canary 1,200.00
39 JSA in magic world,

All-Star Comics #42 © DC Comics, Inc.

ALL-STAR COMICS
1976–78

58 RE,WW,R:JSA,I:Power Girl	. . .	2.50
59 RE,WW,Brain Wave	. . . .	2.25
60 KG,WW,I:Vulcan	. . . .	2.25
61 KG,WW,V:Vulcan	. . . .	2.25
62 KG,WW,A:E-2 Superman	. . . .	2.25
63 KG,WW,A:E-2 Superman,		
Solomon Grundy	. . . .	2.25
64 WW,Shining Knight	. . . .	2.25
65 KG,WW,E-2 Superman,		
Vandal Savage	. . . .	2.25
66 JSon,BL,Injustice Society	. . .	2.25
67 JSon,BL	. . . .	2.25
68 JSon,BL	. . . .	2.25
69 JSon,BL,A:E-2 Superman,		
Starman,Dr.Mid-Nite	. . . .	2.25
70 JSon,BL,Huntress	. . . .	2.25
71 JSon,BL	. . . .	2.00
72 JSon,A:Golden.Age Huntress	.	2.00
73 JSon	. . . .	2.00
74 JSon	. . . .	2.00

Johnny Thunder leaves	. . . . 750.00
40 A:Black Canary,Junior Justice	
Society of America	. . . . 750.00
41 Black Canary joins,A:Harlequin,	
V:Injustice Society	
of the World	. . . . 750.00
42 I:Alchemist	. . . . 800.00
43 V:Interdimensional gold men	800.00
44 I:Evil Star	. . . . 800.00
45 Crooks develop stellar	
JSA powers	. . . . 750.00
46 Comedy issue	. . . . 750.00
47 V:Billy the Kid	. . . . 750.00
48 Time Travel story	. . . . 750.00
49 V:Comet-being invaders	. . . 750.00
50 V:College classmate of Flash	800.00
51 V:Diamond men from center	
of the Earth	. . . . 750.00
52 JSA disappears from	
Earth for years	. . . . 750.00
53 Time Travel issue	. . . . 750.00
54 Circus issue	. . . . 750.00
55 JSA fly to Jupiter	. . . . 750.00
56 V:Chameleons from	
31st Century	. . . . 750.00
57 I:Key	. . . . 800.00

Becomes:
ALL STAR WESTERN
April-May 1951

58 Trigger Twins	. . . . 250.00
59	. . . . 125.00
60	. . . . 125.00
61 thru 64 ATh	. . . . 100.00
65	. . . . 100.00
66	. . . . 100.00
67 GK,B:Johnny Thunder	. . . . 125.00
68 thru 81	. . . . @55.00
82 thru 98	. . . . @45.00
99 FF	. . . . 60.00
100	. . . . 50.00
101 thru 104	. . . . @35.00
105 O:JSA, March, 1987	. . . . . 35.00
106 and 107	. . . . @30.00
108 O:Johnny Thunder	. . . . . . 85.00
109 thru 116	. . . . @30.00
117 CI,O:Super-Chief	. . . . 50.00
118	. . . . 30.00
119	. . . . 25.00

All-Star Squadron #65 © DC Comics, Inc.

ALL STAR SQUADRON

1 RB,JOy,JSA,I:Degaton	. . . .	1.75
2 RB,JOy,Robotman	. . . .	1.50
3 RB,JOy,Robotman	. . . .	1.50
4 RB,JOy,Robotman	. . . .	1.50
5 RB/JOy,I:Firebrand(Dannette)	.	1.50
6 JOy,Hawkgirl	. . . .	1.50
7 JOy,Hawkgirl	. . . .	1.50
8 DH/JOy,A:Steel	. . . .	1.50
9 DH/JOy,A:Steel	. . . .	1.50
10 JOy,V:Binary Brotherhood	. . .	1.50
11 JOy,V:Binary Brotherhood	. . .	1.50
12 JOy,R:Dr.Hastor O:Hawkman	.	1.50
13 JOy,photo(c)	. . . .	1.50
14 JOy,JLA crossover	. . . .	1.50
15 JOy,JLA crossover	. . . .	1.50
16 I&D:Nuclear	. . . .	1.50
17 Trial of Robotman	. . . .	1.50
18 V:Thor	. . . .	1.50
19 V:Brainwave	. . . .	1.50
20 JOy,V:Brainwave	. . . .	1.50
21 JOy,I:Cyclotron (1st JOy		
Superman)	. . . .	1.75
22 JOy,V:Deathbolt,Cyclotron	. .	1.50

23 JOy,I:Amazing-Man	. . . .	1.50
24 JOy,I:Brainwave,Jr..	. . . . . .	3.50
25 JOy,I:Infinity Inc.	. . . .	3.00
26 JOy,Infinity Inc.	. . . .	2.50
27 Spectre	. . . .	1.50
28 JOy,Spectre	. . . .	1.50
29 JOy,retold story	. . . .	1.50
30 V:Black Dragons	. . . .	1.50
31 All-Star gathering	. . . .	1.50
32 O:Freedom Fighters	. . . .	1.50
33 Freedom Fighters,I:Tsunami	. .	1.50
34 Freedom Fighters	. . . .	1.50
35 RB,Shazam family	. . . .	1.50
36 Shazam family	. . . .	1.50
37 A:Shazam Family	. . . .	1.50
38 V:The Real American	. . . . . .	1.50
39 V:The Real American	. . . . . .	1.50
40 D:The Real American	. . . . . .	1.50
41 O:Starman	. . . .	1.50
42 V:Tsunami,Kung	. . . .	1.50
43 V:Tsunami,Kung	. . . .	1.50
44 I:Night & Fog	. . . .	1.50
45 I:Zyklon	. . . .	1.50
46 V:Baron Blitzkrieg	. . . .	1.50
47 TM,O:Dr.Fate	. . . .	3.50
48 A:Blackhawk	. . . .	1.25
49 A:Dr.Occult	. . . .	1.25
50 Crisis	. . . .	2.00
51 AA,Crisis	. . . .	1.25
52 Crisis	. . . .	1.25
53 Crisis,A:The Dummy	. . . .	1.25
54 Crisis,V:The Dummy	. . . .	1.25
55 Crisis,V:Anti-Monitor	. . . . . .	1.25
56 Crisis	. . . .	1.25
57 A:Dr.Occult	. . . .	1.25
58 I:Mekanique	. . . .	1.25
59 A:Mekanique,Spectre	. . . . . .	1.25
60 Crisis 1942, conclusion	. . . .	1.25
61 O:Liberty Belle	. . . .	1.25
62 O:The Shining Knight	. . . . . .	1.25
63 O:Robotman	. . . .	1.25
64 WB/TD,V:Funny Face	. . . . . .	1.25
65 DH/TD,O:Johnny Quick	. . . . .	1.25
66 TD,O:Tarantula	. . . .	1.25
67 TD,Last Issue,O:JSA	. . . . . .	1.25
Ann.#1 JOy,O:G.A.,Atom	. . . . . .	1.25
Ann.#2 JOy,Infinity Inc.	. . . .	1.50
Ann.#3 WB,JOy,KG,GP,DN	. . . . .	1.25

ALL STAR WESTERN
(see WEIRD WESTERN TALES)

AMBUSH BUG
June, 1985

1 KG,I:Cheeks	. . . .	1.25
2 KG	. . . .	1.00
3 KG	. . . .	1.00
4 KG,September,1985	. . . .	1.00
STOCKING STUFFER		
1 KG,R:Cheeks	. . . .	1.25

AMBUSH BUG
NOTHING SPECIAL

1 KG,A:Sandman,Death	. . . .	2.50

AMERICA vs.
JUSTICE SOCIETY
January, 1985

1 AA,R,Thomas Script	. . . .	1.50
2 AA	. . . .	1.25
3 AA	. . . .	1.25
4 AA,April,1985	. . . .	1.25

AMERICAN FREAK: A TALE OF THE UN-MEN
Vertigo
1 B:DLp,(s),VcL,R:Un-Men 2.25
2 VcL,A:Crassus 2.25
3 VcL,A:Scylla 2.25
4 VcL,A:Scylla 2.25
5 VcL,Final Issue 2.25

AMETHYST
[Limited Series]
May, 1983
1 Origin 1.25
2 thru 7 EC .... @1.00
8 EC,O:Gemworld 1.00
9 EC 1.00
10 EC 1.00
11 EC 1.00
12 EC,May, 1984 .... 1.00
Spec.#1 KG 1.25
[Regular Series]
January, 1985
1 thru 12 EC .... @1.00
13 EC,Crisis,A:Dr.Fate 1.00
14 EC 1.00
15 EC,Castle Amethyst Destroyed 1.00
16 EC,August, 1986 .... 1.00
Spec.#1 EM 1.25
[Mini-Series]
November, 1987
1 EM 1.25
2 EM 1.25
3 EM 1.25
4 EM,O:Mordru,Feb., 1988 .... 1.25

ANGEL & THE APE
1 Apes of Wrath,pt.1 .... 1.00
2 Apes of Wrath,pt.2,
A:G.Gardner 1.00
3 Apes of Wrath,pt.3,
A: Inferior Five 1.00
4 Apes of Wrath,pt.4,
A: Inferior Five, final issue 1.00

ANIMA
Vertigo
1 R:Anima 2.00

Animal Antics #11 © DC Comics, Inc.

2 V:Scarecrow 2.00
3 V:Scarecrow 2.00
4 A:Nameless one 2.00
5 CI,V:Arkana 2.00
6 CI,V:Arkana 2.00
7 Zero Hour 2.00
8 Nameless One 2.00
9 Superboy & Nameless One ... 2.00
10 A:Superboy 2.00
11 V:Nameless One 2.00
12 A:Hawkman,V:Shrike 1.95
13 A:Hawkman,Shrike 1.95
14 Return to Gotham City 1.95
15 V:Psychic Vampire, final issue 2.25

ANIMAL ANTICS
1946
1 .... 275.00
2 .... 150.00
3 thru 10 .... @90.00
11 thru 23 .... @65.00

ANIMAL-MAN
1 BB(c),B:GMo(s),ChT,DHz,
B:Animal Rights,I:Dr.Myers .. 15.00
2 BB(c),ChT,DHz,A:Superman . 10.00
3 BB(c),ChT,DHz,A:B'wana Beast 5.00
4 BB(c),ChT,DHz,V:B'wana Beast,
E:Animal Rights 5.00
5 BB(c),ChT,DHz,
I&D:Crafty Coyote 6.00
6 BB(c),ChT,DHz,A:Hawkman . 3.50
7 BB(c),ChT,DHz,D:Red Mask . 3.50
8 BB(c),ChT,DHz,V:Mirror Master 3.50
9 BB(c),DHz,TG,A:Martian
Manhunter 3.50
10 BB(c),ChT,DHz,A:Vixen,
B:O:Animal Man 3.50
11 BB(c),ChT,DHz,I:Hamed Ali,
Tabu,A:Vixen 3.50
12 BB(c),D:Hamed Ali,A:Vixen,
B'wanaBeast 3.50
13 BB(c),I:Dominic Mndawe,R:B'wana
Beast,Apartheid 3.50
14 BB(c),TG,SeM,A:Future Animal
Man,I:Lennox 3.50
15 BB(c),ChT,DHz,A:Dolphin . 3.50
16 BB(c),ChT,DHz,A:JLA ... 3.50
17 BB(c),ChT,DHz,A:Mirr.Master . 3.50
18 BB(c),ChT,DHz,A:Lennox ... 3.50
19 BB(c),ChT,DHz,D:Ellen,
Cliff,Maxine 3.50
20 BB(c),ChT,DHz,I:Bug-Man . 3.50
21 BB(c),ChT,DHz,N&V:Bug-Man 3.50
22 BB(c),PCu,SeM,A:Rip Hunter . 3.50
23 BB(c),A:Phantom Stranger . 3.00
24 BB(c),V:Psycho Pirate 2.50
25 BB(c),ChT,MFm,I:Comic
Book Limbo 2.50
26 BB(c),E:GMo(s),ChT,MFm,
A:Grant Morrison 2.50
27 BB(c),B:PMi(s),ChT,MFm ... 2.50
28 BB(c),ChT,MFm,I:Nowhere Man,
I&D:Front Page 2.50
29 ChT,SDi,V:National Man 2.50
30 BB(c),ChT,MFm,V:Angel Mob . 2.50
31 BB(c),ChT,MFm 2.50
32 BB(c),E:PMi(s),ChT,MFm 2.50
33 BB(c),B:TV(s),SDi,A:Travis
Cody 2.50
34 BB(c),SDi,Requiem 2.50
35 BB(c),SDi,V:Radioactive Dogs . 2.50
36 BB(c),SDi,A:Mr.Rainbow ... 2.50
37 BB(c),SDi,Animal/Lizard Man . 2.50
38 BB(c),SDi,A:Mr.Rainbow 2.00

39 BB(c),TMd,SDi,Wolfpack in
San Diego 2.00
40 BB(c),SDi,War of the Gods
x-over 2.00
41 BB(c),SDi,V:Star Labs
Renegades,I:Winky 2.00
42 BB(c),SDi,V:Star Labs
Renegades 2.00
43 BB(c),SDi,I:Tristess,A:Vixen . . 2.00
44 BB(c),SDi,A:Vixen 2.00
45 BB(c),StP,SDi,I:L.Decker . . 2.00
46 BB(c),SDi,I:Frank Baker 2.00
47 BB(c),SDi,I:Shining Man,
(B'wana Beast) 2.00
48 BB(c),SDi,V:Antagon 2.00
49 BB(c),SDi,V:Antagon 2.00
50 BB(c),E:TV(s),SDi,I:Metaman . 3.50
51 BB(c),B:JaD(s),StP,B:Flesh
and Blood 2.50
52 BB(c),StP,Homecoming 2.50
53 BB(c),StP,Flesh and Blood .. 2.50
54 BB(c),StP,Flesh and Blood ... 2.50
55 BB(c),StP,Flesh and Blood .. 2.50
56 BB(c),StP,E:Flesh and Blood,
Double-sized 5.00

Animal Man #60 © DC Comics, Inc.

Vertigo
57 BB(c),StP,B:Recreation,
Ellen in NY 2.50
58 BB(c),StP,Wild Side 2.50
59 BB(c),RsB,GHi(i),Wild Town . . 2.50
60 RsB,GHi(i),Wild life 2.50
61 BB(c),StP,Tooth and Claw#1 . 2.50
62 BB(c),StP,Tooth and Claw#2 .. 2.50
63 BB(c),V:Leviathan 2.50
64 DIB(c),WSm,DnS(i),
Breath of God 2.50
65 RDB(c),WSm,
Perfumed Garden 2.25
66 A:Kindred Spirit 2.25
67 StP,Mysterious Ways #1 ..... 2.25
68 StP,Mysterious Ways #2 ..... 2.25
69 Animal Man's Family 2.25
70 GgP(c),StP 2.25
71 GgP(c),StP,Maxine Alive? 2.25
72 StP 2.25
73 StP,Power Life Church 2.25
74 StP,Power Life Church 2.25
75 StP,Power Life Church 2.25
76 StP,Pilgrimage problems 2.00

77 Cliff shot	2.00
78 StP,Animal Man poisoned	2.00
79 New Direction	2.00
80 New Direction	2.00
81 Wild Type,pt.1	2.00
82 Wild Type,pt.2	2.00
83 Wild Type,pt.3	2.00
84 F:Maxine,SupernaturalDreams	2.00
85 Animal Mundi,pt.1	2.25
Ann.#1 BB(c),JaD,TS(i),RIB(i), Children Crusade,F:Maxine	4.25
TPB Rep.#1 thru #10	19.95

ANIMANIACS
1 F:Yakko,Wakko,Dot	1.50
2 Health Spa	1.50
3 Travel back in time	1.50
Christmas Spec.	1.50

ANTHRO
1 HwP	26.00
2 HwP	18.00
3 HwP	18.00
4 HwP	18.00
5 HwP	18.00
6 HwP,WW(c&a)	18.00

AQUAMAN
January-February, 1962
[1st Regular Series]
1 NC,I:Quisp	375.00
2 NC,V:Captain Sykes	165.00
3 NC,Aquaman from Atlantis	100.00
4 NC,A:Quisp	90.00
5 NC,The Haunted Sea	85.00
6 NC,A:Quisp	70.00
7 NC,Sea Beasts of Atlantis	70.00
8 NC,Plot to Steal the Seas	70.00
9 NC,V:King Neptune	70.00
10 NC,A:Quisp	70.00
11 I: Mera	56.00
12 NC,The Cosmic Gladiators	50.00
13 NC,Invasion of the Giant Reptiles	50.00
14 NC,AquamanSecretPowers	50.00
15 NC,Menace of the Man-Fish	50.00
16 NC,Duel of the Sea Queens	45.00
17 NC,Man Who Vanquished Aquaman	45.00
18 W:Aquaman & Mera	50.00
19 NC,Atlanteans For Sale	42.00
20 NC,Sea King's DoubleDoom	42.00
21 NC,I:Fisherman	35.00
22 NC,The Trap of the Sinister Sea Nymphs	35.00
23 NC,I:Aquababy	35.00
24 NC,O:Black Manta	28.00
25 NC,Revolt of Aquaboy	28.00
26 NC,I:O.G.R.E.	28.00
27 NC,Battle of the Rival Aquamen'	28.00
28 NC,Hail Aquababy,King of Atlantis	28.00
29 I:Ocean Master	29.00
30 NC,C:JLA	22.00
31 NC,V:O.G.R.E.	22.00
32 NC,V:Tryton	22.00
33 NC,I:Aquagirl	40.00
34 NC,I:Aquabeast	25.00
35 I:Black Manta	25.00
36 NC,What Seeks the Awesome Threesome?	25.00
37 I:Scavenger	25.00
38 NC,I:Liquidator	25.00

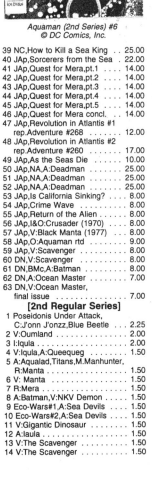

Aquaman (2nd Series) #6
© DC Comics, Inc.

39 NC,How to Kill a Sea King	25.00
40 JAp,Sorcerers from the Sea	22.00
41 JAp,Quest for Mera,pt.1	14.00
42 JAp,Quest for Mera,pt.2	14.00
43 JAp,Quest for Mera,pt.3	14.00
44 JAp,Quest for Mera,pt.4	14.00
45 JAp,Quest for Mera,pt.5	14.00
46 JAp,Quest for Mera concl.	14.00
47 JAp,Revolution in Atlantis #1 rep.Adventure #268	12.00
48 JAp,Revolution in Atlantis #2 rep.Adventure #260	17.00
49 JAp,As the Seas Die	10.00
50 JAp,NA,A:Deadman	25.00
51 JAp,NA,A:Deadman	25.00
52 JAp,NA,A:Deadman	25.00
53 JAp,Is California Sinking?	8.00
54 JAp,Crime Wave	8.00
55 JAp,Return of the Alien	8.00
56 JAp,I&O:Crusader (1970)	8.00
57 JAp,V:Black Manta (1977)	8.00
58 JAp,O:Aquaman rtd	9.00
59 JAp,V:Scavenger	8.00
60 DN,V:Scavenger	8.00
61 DN,BMc,A:Batman	8.00
62 DN,A:Ocean Master	7.00
63 DN,V:Ocean Master, final issue	7.00

[2nd Regular Series]
1 Poseidonis Under Attack, C:J'onn J'onzz,Blue Beetle	2.25
2 V:Oumland	2.00
3 I:Iqula	2.00
4 V:Iqula,A:Queequeg	1.50
5 A:Aqualad,Titans,M.Manhunter, R:Manta	1.50
6 V: Manta	1.50
7 R:Mera	1.50
8 A:Batman,V:NKV Demon	1.50
9 Eco-Wars#1,A:Sea Devils	1.50
10 Eco-Wars#2,A:Sea Devils	1.50
11 V:Gigantic Dinosaur	1.50
12 A:Iaula	1.50
13 V:The Scavenger	1.50
14 V:The Scavenger	1.50

Aquaman (3rd Series) #7
© DC Comics, Inc.

[3rd Regular Series]
0 B:PDd(s),Paternal secret	1.50
1 PDd(s),R:Aqualad,I:Charybdis	1.75
2 V:Charybdis	1.50
3 B:PDd(s),Superboy	1.50
4 B:PDd(s),Lobo	1.50
5 New Costume	1.50
6 V:The Deep Six	1.50
7 Kako's Metamorphosis	1.50
8 V:Corona and Naiad	1.50
9 JSP(c&a),V:Deadline,A:Koryak	1.75
10 A:Green Lantern,Koryak	1.75
Ann.#1 Year One Annual, V:Triton, A:Superman,Mera	3.50

AQUAMAN
[1st Limited Series]
February, 1986
1 V:Ocean Master	5.50
2 V:Ocean Master	3.00
3 V:Ocean Master	3.00
4 V:Ocean Master	3.00

[2nd Limited Series]
1 CS,Atlantis Under Siege	3.00
2 CS,V:Invaders	1.75
3 CS,Mera turned Psychotic	1.50
4 CS,Poseidonis Under Siege	1.50
5 CS,Last Stand,final issue	1.50
Spec#1 MPa,Legend o/Aquaman	2.00

AQUAMAN: TIME & TIDE
1 PDd(s),O:Aquaman	2.00
2 and 3 PDd(s),O:Aquaman cont@	1.75
4 PDd(s),O:Aquaman,final issue.	1.75

ARAK
September, 1981
1 EC,O:Ara	1.50
2 EC	1.00
3 EC,I:Valda	1.00
4 thru 10 EC	@1.00
11 EC,AA	1.00
12 EC,AA,I:Satyricus	1.00
13 thru 19 AA	@1.00
20 AA,O:Angelica	1.00
21 thru 23 AA	1.00
24 Double size	1.50

25 thru 30 . . . . @1.00	
31 D Arak,becomes shaman 1.00	
32 thru 48 . . . . @1.00	
49 CI/TD 1.00	
50 TD,November, 1985 . . . . 1.25	
Ann.#1 . . . . 1.00	

ARCANA: THE BOOKS OF MAGIC
Vertigo

Ann.#1 JBo(c),JNR(s),PrG,Children's
Crusade,R:Tim Hunter,
A:Free Country 6.00

ARGUS
[Mini-Series]

1 R:Argus,I:Raver 1.50
2 Blinded by metahuman hitmen . 1.75
3 Spy Satellite 1.75

ARION
November, 1982

1 JDu 1.50
2 JDu 1.00
3 JDu 1.00
4 JDu,O:Arion 1.00
5 JDu 1.00
6 JDu 1.00
7 thru 12 . . . . @1.00
13 JDu 1.00
14 JDu 1.00
15 JDu 1.00
16 thru 35, Oct. 1985 . . . . @1.00
Spec. 1.25

ARION THE IMMORTAL

1 RWi,R:Arion 1.75
2 RWi,V:Garffon 1.50
3 RWi,V:Garn Daanuth 1.50
4 RWi,V:Garn Daanuth 1.50
5 RWi,Darkworlet 1.50
6 RWi,MG,A:Power Girl 1.50

ARMAGEDDON 2001
May 1991

1 DJu,DG,I&O:Waverider 6.00
1a 2nd printing 3.00
1b 3rd printing (silver) 2.00
2 DJu,ATi,Monarch revealed as Hawk,
D:Dove,L:Capt Atom(JLE) 3.00
Spec.#1 MR 1.75

ARMAGEDDON 2001 ARMAGEDDON: THE ALIEN AGENDA

1 DJu,JOy,A:Monarch,Capt.Atom 1.75
2 V:Ancient Romans 1.25
3 JRu(i),The Old West 1.25
4 DG,GP,V:Nazi's,last issue 1.25

ARMAGEDDON: INFERNO

1 TMd,LMc,A:Creeper,Batman,
Firestorm 1.75
2 AAd,LMc,WS,I:Abraxis,A:Lobo . 1.50
3 AAd,WS,LMc,TMd,MN,R:Justice
Society 1.50
4 AAd,WS,LMc,TMd,MN,DG,
V:Abraxis,A:Justice Society . . . 1.50

ATARI FORCE

January, 1984
1 JL,I:TempestDart 1.50
2 JL 1.00
3 JL 1.00
4 RA/JL/JO 1.00
5 RA/JL/JO 1.00
6 thru 12 JL . . . . @1.00
13 KG 1.00
14 thru 20 EB . . . . @1.00
21 EB August, 1985 . . . . 1.00

ATLANTIS CHRONICLES

1 EM,Atlantis 50,000 years ago . 3.50
2 EM,Atlantis Sunk 3.25
3 EM,Twin Cities of Poseidonis
& Tritonis 3.25
4 EM,King Orin's Daughter
Cora Assumes Throne 3.25
5 EM,Orin vs. Shalako 3.25
6 EM,Contact with Surface
Dwellers 3.25
7 EM,Queen Atlanna gives Birth to
son(Aquaman)48 pg.final issue 3.25

Atom #2 © DC Comics, Inc.

ATOM, THE
June-July, 1962

1 MA,GK,I:Plant Master 750.00
2 MA,GK,V:Plant Master 275.00
3 MA,GK,I:Chronos 200.00
4 MA,GK,Snapper Carr 110.00
5 MA,GK 100.00
6 MA,GK 100.00
7 MA,GK,1st Atom & Hawkman
team-up 200.00
8 MA,GK,A:JLA,V:Doctor Light . 80.00
9 MA,GK 80.00
10 MA,GK 80.00
11 MA,GK 60.00
12 MA,GK 60.00
13 MA,GK 60.00
14 MA,GK 60.00
15 MA,GK 50.00
16 MA,GK 50.00
17 MA,GK 50.00
18 MA,GK 50.00
19 MA,GK,A:Zatanna 50.00
20 MA,GK 50.00
21 MA,GK 35.00

22 MA,GK 35.00
23 MA,GK 35.00
24 MA,GK,V:Jason Woodrue . . . 35.00
25 MA,GK 35.00
26 GK 35.00
27 GK 35.00
28 GK 35.00
29 GK,A:E-2 Atom,Thinker. . . . 125.00
30 GK 35.00
31 GK,A:Hawkman 30.00
32 GK 30.00
33 GK 30.00
34 GK,V:Big Head 30.00
35 GK 30.00
36 GK,A:Golden Age Atom 50.00
37 GK,I:Major Mynah 30.00
38 "Sinister stopover Earth"
Aug.-Sept., 1968 . . . . 30.00
Becomes:

ATOM & HAWKMAN
October-November, 1968

39 MA, V:Tekla 25.00
40 DD,JKu,MA 25.00
41 DD,JKu,MA 25.00
42 MA,V:Brama 25.00
43 MA,I:Gentleman Ghost 25.00
44 DD 25.00
45 DD, Oct.-Nov., 1969 . . . . 25.00

ATOM SPECIAL

1 SDi,V:Chronos 3.00
2 Zero Hour Atom 3.00

AVATAR

1 A:Midnight & Allies 8.00
2 Search for Tablets 6.00
3 V:Cyric, Myrkul, final issue 6.00

AZRAEL

1 I:New Azreal,Brian Bryan 2.25
2 A:Batman,New Azreal 1.95
3 V:Order of St. Dumas 1.95
4 The System 1.95
5 BKi(c&a),R:Ra's al Ghul,Talia
[new Miraweb format begins] . . 1.95
6 BKi(c&a),Ra's al Ghul,Talia . . . 1.95

BABYLON 5

1 From TV series 2.25
2 From TV series 1.95
3 Mysterious Assassin 1.95
4 V:Mysterious Assassin 1.95
5 Shadows of the Present,pt.1 . . 2.50
6 Shadows of the Present,pt.2 . . 2.50

BATGIRL

Spec.#1 V: Cormorant,I:Slash . . . 8.00

BATMAN
Spring, 1940

1 I:Joker,Cat(Catwoman),V:Hugo
Strange . . 45,000.00
2 V:Joker/Catwoman team . . 7,500.00
3 V:Catwoman 5,500.00
4 V:Joker 4,500.00
5 V:Joker 3,000.00
6 V:'Clock Maker' 2,200.00
7 V:Joker 2,200.00
8 V:Joker 2,200.00
9 V:Joker 2,200.00
10 V:Catwoman 2,200.00
11 V:Joker,Penguin 2,500.00
12 V:Joker 1,800.00

Batman #7 © DC Comics, Inc.

13 V:Joker	1,700.00
14 V:Penguin;Propaganda sty	1,900.00
15 V:Catwoman	1,700.00
16 I:Alfred,V:Joker	3,500.00
17 V:Penguin	1,100.00
18 V:Tweedledum & Tweedledee	1,100.00
19 V:Joker	1,100.00
20 V:Joker	1,100.00
21 V:Penguin	900.00
22 V:Catwoman,Cavalier	900.00
23 V:Joker	1,300.00
24 I:Carter Nichols, V:Tweedledum &Tweedledee	1,000.00
25 V:Joker/Penguin team	1,300.00
26 V:Cavalier	900.00
27 V:Penguin	900.00
28 V:Joker	1,000.00
29 V:Scuttler	900.00
30 V:Penguin,I:Ally Babble	900.00
31 I:Punch and Judy	650.00
32 O:Robin,V:Joker	700.00
33 V:Penguin,Jackall	750.00
34 A:Ally Babble	650.00
35 V:Catwoman	650.00
36 V:Penguin,A:King Arthur	650.00
37 V:Joker	850.00
38 V:Penguin	650.00
39 V:Catwoman,Christmas Story	650.00
40 V:Joker	800.00
41 V:Penguin	550.00
42 V:Catwoman	525.00
43 V:Penguin	525.00
44 V:Joker,A:Carter Nichols,Meets ancester Silas Wayne	750.00
45 V:Catwoman	525.00
46 V:Joker,A:Carter Nichols, Leonardo Da Vinci	500.00
47 O:Batman,V:Catwoman	1,700.00
48 V:Penguin, Bat-Cave story	600.00
49 I:Mad Hatter & Vicki Vale	850.00
50 I:Two-Face,A:Vicki Vale	550.00
51 V:Penguin	500.00
52 V:Joker	550.00
53 V:Joker	550.00
54 V:'The Treasure Hunter'	500.00
55 V:Joker	550.00
56 V:Penguin	500.00
57 V:Joker	550.00
58 V:Penguin	500.00

59 I:Deadshot	500.00
60 V:'Shark' Marlin	500.00
61 V:Penguin	575.00
62 O:Catwoman,I:Knight & Squire	650.00
63 V:Joker	400.00
64 V:Killer Moth	400.00
65 I:Wingman,V:Catwoman	425.00
66 V:Joker	425.00
67 V:Joker	425.00
68 V:Two-Face,Alfred story	375.00
69 I:King of the Cats, A:Catwoman	425.00
70 V:Penguin	400.00
71 V:Mr. Cipher	400.00
72 'The Jungle Batman'	400.00
73 V:Joker,A:Vicki Vale	500.00
74 V:Joker	400.00
75 I:The Gorilla Boss	400.00
76 V:Penguin	400.00
77 'The Crime Predictor'	400.00
78 'The Manhunter from Mars'	500.00
79 A:Vicki Vale	400.00
80 V:Joker	400.00

Batman #40 © DC Comics, Inc.

81 V:Two-Face	400.00
82 'The Flying Batman'	350.00
83 V:'Fish' Frye	350.00
84 V:Catwoman	400.00
85 V:Joker	350.00
86 V:Joker	350.00
87 V:Joker	350.00
88 V:Mr. Mystery	350.00
89 I:Aunt Agatha	350.00
90 I:Batboy	275.00
91 V:Blinky Grosset	275.00
92 I:Ace, the Bat-Hound	275.00
93 'The Caveman Batman'	275.00
94 Alfred has Amnesia	275.00
95 'The Bat-Train'	275.00
96 'Batman's College Days'	275.00
97 V:Joker	275.00
98 A:Carter Nichols,Jules Verne	275.00
99 V:Penguin,A:Carter Nichols, Bat Masterson	275.00
100 'Great Batman Contest'	1,200.00
101 'The Great Batman Hunt'	250.00
102 V:Mayne Mallok	250.00
103 A:Ace, the Bat-Hound	250.00
104 V:Devoe	250.00

105 A:Batwoman	325.00
106 V:Keene Harper gang	250.00
107 V:Daredevils	250.00
108 Bat-cave story	250.00
109 'The 1,000 Inventions of Batman'	250.00
110 V:Joker	275.00
111	200.00
112 I:Signalman	200.00
113 I:Fatman	200.00
114	200.00
115	200.00
116	200.00
117	200.00
118	200.00
119	200.00
120	200.00
121 I:Mr.Freeze	140.00
122	140.00
123 A:Joker	150.00
124 "Mystery Seed from Space"	140.00
125	140.00
126	140.00
127 A:Superman & Joker	150.00
128	120.00
129 O:Robin(Retold)	170.00
130	120.00
131 I:2nd Batman	95.00
132	95.00
133	95.00
134	95.00
135	95.00
136 A:Joker,Bat-Mite	140.00
137 V:Mr.Marvel,The Brand	95.00
138 A:Bat-Mite	95.00
139 I:Old Batgirl	95.00
140 A:Joker	100.00
141 V:Clockmaster	95.00
142 Batman robot story	95.00
143 A:Bathound	95.00
144 A:Joker,Bat-Mite,Bat-Girl	95.00
145 V:Mr.50,Joker	110.00
146 A:Bat-Mite,Joker	80.00
147 Batman becomes Bat-Baby	70.00
148 A:Joker	100.00
149 V:Maestro	70.00
150 V:Biff Warner,Jack Pine	70.00

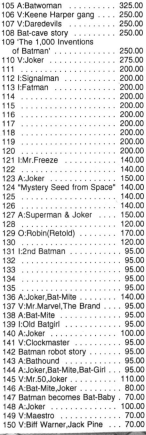

Batman © DC Comics, Inc.

151 V:Harris Boys	50.00
152 A:Joker	60.00
153 Other Dimension story	50.00
154 V:Dr. Dorn	50.00
155 1st S.A. Penguin	210.00
156 V:Gorilla Gang	50.00
157 V:Mirror Man	50.00
158 A:Bathound,Bat-Mite	50.00
159 A:Joker,Clayface	60.00
160 V:Bart Cullen	50.00
161 A:Bat-Mite	50.00
162 F:Robin	50.00
163 A:Joker	55.00
164 CI,A:Mystery Analysts,new Batmobile	40.00
165 V:The Mutated Man	40.00
166 Escape story	40.00
167 V:Karabi & Hydra, the Crime Cartel	40.00
168 V:Mr. Mammoth	40.00
169 A:Penguin	85.00
170 V:Getaway Genius	40.00
171 CI,1st S.A. Riddler	340.00
172 V:Flower Gang	32.00
173 V:Elwood Pearson	32.00
174 V:Big Game Hunter	32.00
175 V:Eddie Repp	32.00
176 Giant rep.A:Joker,Catwom.	50.00
177 BK,A:Elongated Man,Atom	30.00
178 CI	30.00
179 CI,2nd Riddler(Silver)	100.00
180 BK,A:Death-Man	40.00
181 CI,I:Poison Ivy	40.00
182 A:Joker,(giant size rep).	35.00
183 CI,A:Poison Ivy	32.00
184 CI,Mystery of the Missing Manhunters	32.00
185 Giant rep.	35.00
186 A:Joker	30.00
187 Giant rep.A:Joker	35.00
188 CI,A:Eraser	20.00
189 CI,A:Scarecrow	35.00
190 CI,A:Penguin	26.00
191 CI,The Day Batman Soldout	20.00
192 CI,The Crystal ball that betrayed Batman	20.00
193 Giant rep.	30.00
194 MSy,BK,A:Blockbuster,Mystery Analysts of Gotham City	20.00
195 CI	20.00
196 BK,Psychic Super-Sleuth	20.00
197 MSy,A:Bat Girl,Catwoman	50.00
198 A:Joker,Penguin,Catwoman, O:Batman rtd,(G-Size rep)	50.00
199 CI,'Peril o/t Poison Rings'	20.00
200 NA(c),O:rtd,A:Joker,Pengiun, Scarecrow	130.00
201 A:Batman Villians	22.00
202 BU:Robin	18.00
203 NA(c),(giant size)	18.00
204 FR(s),IN,JG	13.00
205 FR(s),IN,JG	13.00
206 FR(s),IN,JG	13.00
207 FR(s),IN,JG	13.00
208 GK,new O:Batman, A:Catwoman	22.00
209 FR(s),IN,JG	13.00
210 A:Catwoman	14.00
211 FR(s),IN,JG	13.00
212 FR(s),IN,JG	13.00
213 RA,30th Anniv.Batman,new O: Robin,rep.O:Alfred,Joker	38.00
214 IN,A:Batgirl	12.00
215 IN,DG	12.00
216 IN,DG,I:DaphnePennyworth	12.00

217 NA(c)	13.00
218 NA(c),giant	15.00
219 NA,IN,DG,Batman Xmas	25.00
220 NA(c),IN	12.00
221 IN,DG	12.00
222 IN,Rock'n Roll story	25.00
223 NA(c),giant	15.00
224 NA(c)	11.00
225 NA(c),IN,DG	11.00
226 IN,DG I:10-Eyed Man	11.00
227 IN,DG,A:Daphne Pennyworth	11.00
228 giant Deadly Traps rep.	12.00
229 IN	11.00
230 NA(c),Robin	11.00
231 F:Ten-Eyed Man	11.00
232 DON(s),NA,DG, I:Ras al Ghul	35.00
233 giant Bruce Wayne iss.	15.00
234 NA,DG,IN,1stS.A.Two-Face	75.00
235 CI,V:Spook	8.00
236 NA	15.00
237 NA	25.00
238 NA,JC,JKu,giant	15.00
239 NA,RB	12.00
240 NA(c),RB,giant,R-Ghul	10.00
241 IN,DG,RB,A:Kid Flash	8.00
242 RB,MK	8.00

Batman #251 © DC Comics, Inc.

243 NA,DG,Ras al Ghul	22.00
244 NA,Ras al Ghul	22.00
245 NA,IN,DG,FMc,Ras al Ghul	17.00
246	8.00
247 Deadly New Year	8.00
248	8.00
249 'Citidel of Crime'	8.00
250 IN,DG	8.00
251 NA,V:Joker	40.00
252	8.00
253 AN,DG,A:Shadow	8.00
254 NA,GK,B:100 page issues	18.00
255 GK,CI,NA,DG,I:CrazyQuilt	15.00
256 Catwoman	14.00
257 IN,DG,V:Penguin	15.00
258 IN,DG	9.00
259 GK,IN,DG,A:Shadow	9.00
260 IN,DG,Joker	20.00
261 CI,GK,E:100 page issues	12.00

262 A:Scarecrow	6.50
263 DG(i),A:Riddler	7.50
264 DON(s),DG,A:Devil Dayre	6.50
265 RB,BWr	7.00
266 DG,Catwoman(old Costume)	8.50
267 DG	6.50
268 DON(s),IN,TeB,V:Sheikh	6.50
269 A:Riddler	7.50
270 B:DvR(s)	6.50
271 IN,FMc	6.50
272 JL	6.50
273 V:Underworld Olympics/76	6.50
274	6.50
275	6.50
276	6.50
277	6.50
278	6.50
279 A:Riddler	7.50
280	6.50
281	6.50
282	6.50
283 V:Camouflage	6.50
284 JA,R:Dr.Tzin Tzin	6.50
285	6.00
286 V:Joker	8.00
287 BWi,MGr,Penguin	7.50
288 BWi,MGr,Penguin	7.50
289 MGr, V:Skull	6.50
290 MGr,V:Skull Dagger	6.50
291 B:Underworld Olympics #1, A:Catwoman	7.00
292 A:Riddler	6.50
293 A:Superman & Luthor	6.00
294 E:DvR(s),E:Underworld Olympics,A:Joker	7.00
295 GyC(s),MGo,JyS,V:Hamton	6.50
296 B:DvR(s),V:Scarecrow	6.50
297 RB,Mad Hatter	6.50
298 JCA,DG,V:Baxter Bains	6.50
299 DG	6.50
300 WS,DG,A:Batman E-2, Robin E-2	12.00
301 JCa,TeB	6.00
302 JCa,DG,V:Human Dynamo	6.00
303 JCa,DG	6.00
304 E:DvR(s),V:Spook	6.00
305 GyC,JCa,DeH,V:Thanatos	6.50
306 JCa,DeH,DN,V:Black Spider	6.50
307 B:LWn(s),JCa,DG, I:Limehouse Jack	6.50
308 JCa,DG,V:Mr.Freeze	6.50
309 E:LWn(s),JCa,FMc, V:Blockbuster	6.50
310 IN,DG,A:Gentleman Ghost	6.50
311 SEt,FMc,IN,Batgirl, V:Dr.Phosphorus	6.50
312 WS,DG,Calenderman	6.50
313 IN,FMc,VTwo-Face	6.50
314 IN,FMc,V:Two-Face	6.50
315 IN,FMc,V:Kiteman	6.50
316 IN,FMc,F:Robin, V:Crazy Quilt	6.50
317 IN,FMc,V:Riddler	7.00
318 IN,I:Fire Bug	6.50
319 JKu(c),IN,DG,A:Gentleman Ghost,E:Catwoman	6.50
320 BWr(c)	6.00
321 DG,WS,A:Joker,Catwoman	8.00
322 V:Cap.Boomerang,Catwoman	6.50
323 IN,A:Catwoman	6.50
324 IN,A:Catwoman	6.50
325	6.00
326 A:Catwoman	6.50
327 IN,A:Proffessor.Milo	6.00
328 A:Two-Face	6.00

329 IN,A:Two-Face	6.00
330	6.00
331 DN,FMc,V:Electrocutioner	6.00
332 IN,DN,Ras al Ghul.1st solo Catwoman story	7.00
333 IN,DN,A:Catwoman, Ras al Ghul	6.00
334 FMc,Ras al Ghul,Catwoman	6.00
335 IN,FMc,Catwoman,Ras al Ghul	6.00
336 JL,FMc,Loser Villains	5.50
337 DN,V:Snow Man	5.50
338 DN,Deathsport	5.50
339 A:Poison Ivy	5.50
340 GC,A:Mole	5.50
341 A:Man Bat	5.50
342 V:Man Bat	5.50
343 GC,KJ,I:The Dagger	5.50
344 GC,KJ,Poison Ivy	5.50
345 I:New Dr.Death,A:Catwoman	5.50
346 DN,V:Two Face	5.50
347 A:Alfred	5.50
348 GC,KJ,Man-Bat,A:Catwoman	6.00
349 GC,AA,A:Catwoman	6.00
350 GC,TD,A:Catwoman	6.00
351 GC,TD,A:Catwoman	6.00
352 Col Blimp	5.50
353 JL,DN,DA,A:Joker	8.00
354 DN,AA,V:HugoStrange,A: Catwoman	5.50
355 DN,AA:A:Catwoman	5.50
356 DG,DN,Hugo Strange	5.00
357 DN,AA,I:Jason Todd	7.00
358 A:King Croc	5.00
359 DG,O:King Croc,Joker	7.00
360 I:Savage Skull	5.00
361 DN,Man-Bat,I:Harvey Bullock	5.00
362 V:Riddler	5.00
363 V:Nocturna	5.00
364 DN,AA,J.Todd 1st full solo story (cont'd Detective #531)	5.00
365 DN,AA,C:Joker	5.00
366 DN,AA,Joker,J.Todd in Robin Costume	26.00
367 DN,AA,PoisonIvy	7.00
368 DN,AA,I:2nd Robin (Jason Todd)	20.00
369 DN,AA,I:Dr.Fang,V:Deadshot	5.00
370 DN,AA	4.00
371 DN,AA,V:Catman	4.50
372 DN,AA,A:Dr.Fang	4.00
373 DN,AA,V:Scarecrow	4.00
374 GC,AA,V:Penguin	5.00
375 GC,AA,V:Dr.Freeze	4.00
376 DN,Halloween issue	4.00
377 DN,AA,V:Nocturna	4.00
378 V:Mad Hatter	4.00
379 V:Mad Hatter	4.00
380 AA,V:Nocturna	4.00
381 V:Batman	4.00
382 A:Catwoman	4.50
383 GC	4.00
384 V:Calender Man	4.00
385 V:Calender Man	4.00
386 I:Black Mask	4.00
387 V:Black Mask	4.00
388 V:Capt.Boomerang & Mirror Master	4.00
389 V:Nocturna,Catwoman	4.50
390 V:Nocturna,Catwoman	4.50
391 V:Nocturna,Catwoman	4.50
392 A:Catwoman	4.50
393 PG,V:Cossack	3.50
394 PG,V:Cossack	3.50
395 V:Film Freak	3.50

Batman #476 © DC Comics, Inc.

396 V:Film Freak	3.50
397 V:Two-Face,Catwoman	4.00
398 V:Two-Face,Catwoman	4.00
399 HaE(s),Two-Face	3.50
400 BSz,AAd,GP,BB,A:Joker	20.00
401 JBy(c),TVE,Legends, A:Magpie	3.50
402 JSn,Fake Batman	3.50
403 DCw,Batcave discovered	3.50
404 DM,FM(s),B:Year 1,I:Modern Age Catwoman	15.00
405 FM,DM,Year 1	8.00
406 FM,DM,Year 1	8.00
407 FM,DM,E:Year 1	8.00
408 CW,V:Joker, new O:Jason Todd	5.00
408a 2nd printing	1.00
409 DG,RA,V:Crime School	4.00
409a 2nd printing	1.00
410 DC,Jason Todd	4.00
411 DC,DH,V:Two Face	3.00
412 DC,DH,I:Mime	3.00
413 DC,DH	3.00
414 JAp,Slasher	3.00
415 JAp,Millenium Week #2	3.00
416 JAp,1st Batman/Nightwing T.U.	3.00
417 JAp,B:10 Nights,I:KGBeast	12.00
418 JAp,V:KGBeast	10.00
419 JAp,V:KGBeast	10.00
420 JAp,E:10 Nights,D:KGBeast	10.00
421 DG	3.50
422 MBr,V:Dumpster Slayer	3.00
423 TM(c),DC,Who is Batman	4.00
424 MBr,Robin	3.00
425 MBr,Gordon Kidnapped	3.00
426 JAp,B:Death in the Family, V:Joker	12.00
427 JAp,V:Joker	9.00
428 JAp,D:2nd Robin	8.00
429 JAp,A:Superman, E:Death in the Family	6.00
430 JAp,JSn,V:Madman	5.00
431 JAp,Murder Investigation	2.75
432 JAp	2.75
433 JBy,JAp,Many Deaths of the Batman #1	5.00
434 JBy,JAp,Many Deaths #2	4.00
435 JBy,Many Deaths #3	4.00

436 PB,B:Year#3,A:Nightwing,I:Tim Drake as child	8.00
436a 2ndPrint(green DC logo)	2.00
437 PB,year#3	3.00
438 PB,year#3	2.50
439 PB,year#3	2.50
440 JAp,Lonely Place of Dying #1, A:Tim Drake (face not shown)	4.00
441 JAp,Lonely Place Dying	4.00
442 JAp,I:3rd Robin(Tim Drake)	6.00
443 JAp,I:Crimesmith	2.00
444 JAp,V:Crimesmith	2.00
445 JAp,I:K.G.Beast Demon	2.00
446 JAp,V:K.G.Beast Demon	2.00
447 JAp,D:K.G.Beast Demon	2.00
448 JAp,A:Penguin#1	2.50
449 MBr,A:Penguin#3	2.50
450 JAp,I:Joker II	2.00
451 JAp,V:Joker II	2.00
452 KD,Dark Knight Dark City#1	2.00
453 KD,Dark Knight Dark City#2	2.00
454 KD,Dark Knight Dark City#3	2.00
455 Identity Crisis#1, A:Scarecrow	3.00
456 IdentityCrisis#2	4.00
457 V:Scarecrow,A:Robin, New Costume	8.00
457a 2nd printing	2.00
458 R:Sarah Essen	2.00
459 A:Sarah Essen	2.00
460 Sisters in Arms,pt.1 A:Catwoman	3.00
461 Sisters in Arms,pt.2 Catwoman V:Sarah.Essen	3.00
462 Batman in San Francisco	1.75

Batman #480 © DC Comics, Inc.

463 Death Valley	1.75
464 V:Two-Hearts	1.75
465 Batman/Robin T.U.	3.00
466 Robin Trapped	2.00
467 Shadowbox #1(sequel to Robin Mini-Series)	2.50
468 Shadowbox #2	2.00
469 Shadowbox #3	2.00
470 War of the Gods x-over	1.75
471 V:Killer Croc	1.75
472 The Idiot Root,pt.1	1.75
473 The Idiot Root,pt.3	1.75
474 Destroyer,pt.1 (LOTDK#27)	2.25
475 R:Scarface,A:VickiVale	1.75

476 A:Scarface	1.75
477 Ph(c),Gotham Tale,pt.1	1.75
478 Ph(c),Gotham Tale,pt.2	1.75
479 TMd,I:Pagan	1.75
480 JAp,To the father I never	
knew	1.75
481 JAp,V:Maxie Zeus	1.75
482 JAp,V:Maxie Zeus	1.75
483 JAp,I:Crash & Burn	1.75
484 JAp,R:Black Mask	1.75
485 TGr,V:Black Mask	1.75
486 JAp,I:Metalhead	1.75
487 JAp,V:Headhunter	1.75
488 JAp,N:Azrael	10.00
489 JAp,Bane vs Killer Croc,	
I:Azrael as Batman	13.00
489a 2nd Printing	2.00
490 JAp,Bane vs.Riddler	7.00
490a 2nd Printing	1.75
490b 3rd Printing	1.50
491 JAp,V:Joker,A:Bane	6.00
491a 2nd Printing	1.50
492 B:DgM(s),NB,Knightfall#1,	
V:Mad Hatter,A:Bane	9.00
492a Platinum Ed.	55.00
492b 2nd Printing	1.50
493 NB,Knightfall,#3,Mr.Zsasz	5.00
494 JAp,TMd,Knightfall #5,A:Bane,	
V:Cornelius,Stirk,Joker	4.00
495 NB,Knightfall#7,V:Poison	
Ivy,A:Bane	3.50
496 JAp,JRu,Knightfall#9,V:Joker,	
Scarecrow,A:Bane	3.50
497 JAp,DG,Knightfall#11,V:Bane,	
Batman gets back broken	7.50
497a 2nd Printing	1.50
498 JAp,JRu,Knightfall#15,A:Bane,	
Catwoman,Azrael Becomes	
Batman	2.50
499 JAp,SHa,Knightfall#17,	
A:Bane,Catwoman	2.50
500 JQ(c),JAp,MM,Die Cut(c),	
Direct Market,Knightfall#19,	
V:Bane,N:Batman	5.00
500a JKo(c),Newstand Ed.	3.50
501 MM,I:Mekros	2.00
502 MM,V:Mekros	2.00
503 MM,V:Catwoman	2.00
504 MM,V:Catwoman	1.75
505 MM,V:Canibal	1.75
506 KJo(c),MM,A:Ballistic	1.75
507 KJo(c),MM,A:Ballistic	1.75
508 KJo(c),MM,V:Abattior	1.75
509 KJo(c),MM,KnightsEnd#1,	
A:Shiva	5.00
510 KJo(c),MM,Knights End #7,	
V:Azrael	1.75
511 Zero Hour, A:Batgirl	1.75
512 Killer Croc sewer battles	2.00
513 Two-Face and convicts	1.75
514 Identity Crisis	1.75
515 KJo,Return of Bruce Wayne,	
Troika,pt.1	1.75
515 Collector's Edition	2.50
516 V:The Sleeper	1.75
517 V:The Sleeper	1.75
518 V:The Black Spider	1.50
519 KJo,V:The Black Spider	
[new Miraweb format begins]	1.95
520 EB,A:James Gordon	1.95
Ann.#1 CS	350.00
Ann.#2	200.00
Ann.#3 A:Joker	150.00
Ann.#4	75.00
Ann.#5	70.00

Ann.#6	65.00
Ann.#7	60.00
Ann.#8 TVE,A:Ras al Ghul	8.00
Ann.#9 JOy,AN,PS	7.00
Ann.#10 DCw,DG,V:HugoStrange	7.00
Ann.#11 JBy(c),AMo(s),V:Penguin	8.00
Ann.#12 RA,V:Killer	5.00
Ann.#13 A:Two-Face	4.00
Ann.#14 O:Two-Face	3.00
Ann.#15 Armageddon,pt.3	6.00
Ann.#15a 2nd printing(silver)	2.50
Ann.#16 SK(c),Eclipso,V:Joker	3.00
Ann.#17 EB,Bloodline#8,	
I:Decimator	3.00
Ann.#18 Elseworld Story	3.25
PF Batman Returns:Movie Adaption,	
SE,JL	6.00
Newsstand Format	4.00
Spec.#1 MGo,I:Wrath	4.00
TPB, Many Deaths of the Batman;	
rep. #433-#435	3.95
TPB, Death in the Family;reprints	
Batman #426-#429	6.50
2nd printing	4.00
3rd printing	4.00
TPB Batman: Knight's End, rep.	
Batman #509-#510, Shadow of the	
Bat #29-#30, Detective #676-#677,	
Legends #62-#63, Catwoman #12,	
Robin #8-#9	14.95
TPB Knightfall rep. #1-#11	12.95
TPB Knightfall rep. #12-#19	12.95
TPB Venom	9.95
TPB Ten Knights of the Beast	5.95
TPB Year One FM(s)	12.95
TPB Year Two	9.95
Batman Archives Vol.3	39.95
Batman JOy,Movie adaptation	3.00
Perfect Bound	6.00
Batman: Arkham Asylum,DMc	28.00
Batman: Blind Justice	7.50
Batman: The Blue,The Grey,and	
The Bat;JL (Elseworlds)	5.95
Batman: Bride of the Demon,TGr,	
V:Ra's Al Ghul	21.00
Batman: Castle of the Bat,	
Elseworlds Story	5.95
Batman: Dark Joker KJo	26.00
Batman/Houdini: The Devil's	
Workshop	6.50
Batman: Digital Justice	26.00
Batman: Full Circle AD,A:Reaper	7.00
Batman Gallery,collection of past	
(c),posters,pin-ups,JQ(c)	4.00
Batman: Holy Terror	6.50
Batman: Gotham By Gaslight,MMi,	
V:Jack the Ripper	6.00
Batman: In Darkest Knight	
MiB(s),JBi	5.50
Batman/Judge Dredd: Judgement on	
Gotham,SBs,V:Scarecrow,Judge	
Death	9.00
Batman: The Killing Joke,BB,AMo(s),	
O:Joker,Batgirl paralyzed	18.00
2nd thru 6th Printings	@5.00
Batman: The Last Angel, F:Catwoman	
V:Aztec bat-god	12.95
Batman: Master of the Future,EB,	
Sequel to Goth.by Gaslight	6.00
Batman: Night Cries,SHa	30.00
Batman/Dracula:Red Rain KJo,MJ,	
Batman becomes Vampire,	
HC, Elseworlds Story	50.00
SC	12.00
Batman: Bloodstorm,KJo,V:Joker,	

Vampires, (sequel to Red Rain)	
HC	24.95
TPB	12.95
Batman: Seduction of the Gun,	
V:Illegal Gun Control	3.00
Batman: Son of the Demon,JBi,	
HC	55.00
SC	17.00
2nd thru 4th printings	@8.95
Two-Face Strikes Twice#1	5.25
Two-Face Strikes Twice#2	5.25
Batman: Vengeance of Bane,	
GN,I:Bane	30.00
2nd Printing	5.00
Batman: Year One Rep. Batman	
#404-#407	14.00
2nd Printing	9.95
3rd Printing	9.95

Batman Adventures #3
© DC Comics, Inc.

BATMAN ADVENTURES
(Based on TV cartoon series)

1 MeP,V:Penguin	7.00
2 MeP,V:Catwoman	6.00
3 MeP,V:Joker	5.00
4 MeP,V:Scarecrow	4.00
5 MeP,V:Scarecrow	4.00
6 MeP,A:Robin	4.00
7 MeP,V:Killer Croc,w/card	8.00
8 MeP,Larceny my Sweet	3.00
9 MeP,V:Two Face	3.00
10 MeP,V:Riddler	4.00
11 MeP,V:Man-Bat	2.50
12 MeP,F:Batgirl	2.50
13 MeP,V:Talia	2.50
14 MeP,F:Robin	2.00
15 MeP,F:Commissioner Gordon	2.00
16 MeP,V:Joker	2.00
17 MeP,V:Talia	2.00
18 MeP,R:Batgirl	1.75
19 MeP,V:Scarecrow	1.75
20 MeP,V:Mastermind,Mr.Nice,	
Perfessor	1.75
21 MeP,V:Man-Bat,Tygrus	1.75
22 MeP,V:Two-Face	1.75
23 MEP,V:Poison Ivy	1.75
24 MeP,I:Kyodi Ken	1.75
25 MeP,dbl.size,Superman	2.50

26 MeP,A:Robin,Batgirl 1.75
27 MeP,I:Doppleganger 1.75
28 Joker 1.75
29 A:Talia 1.50
30 O:Mastermind, Mr. Nice 1.50
31 I:Anarcky 1.50
32 Criminals dressed as
Napoleonic Soldiers 1.75
33 Bruce and date mugged 1.75
Ann.#2 JBa,BBI,DG,TG,SHa,BKi,MM,
GN,JRu,V:Demon,Ra's al
Ghul,Etrigan 3.50
Holiday Special 2.95
Spec. Mad Love 3.95
TPB Collected Adventures #1 . . . 5.95
TPB Collected Adventures #2 . . . 5.95

BATMAN & OUTSIDERS
August, 1983

1 B:MiB(s),JAp,O:Outsiders,
O:Geo Force 3.00
2 JAp,V:Baron Bedlam 2.50
3 JAp,V:Agent Orange 2.00
4 JAp,V:Fearsome Five 2.00
5 JAp,A:New Teen Titans 2.50
6 JAp,V:Cryonic Man 1.50
7 JAp,V:Cryonic Man 1.50
8 JAp,A:Phantom Stranger 1.50
9 JAp,I:Master of Disaster 1.50
10 JAp,A:Master of Disaster 1.50
11 JAp,V:Takeo 1.50
12 JAp,DG,O:Katana 1.50
13 JAp,Day,O:Batman 1.50
14 BWg,Olympics,V:Maxi Zeus . . 1.50
15 TVE,Olympics,V:Maxi Zeus . . . 1.50
16 JAp,L:Halo 1.50
17 JAp,V:Ahk-Ton 1.50
18 JAp,V:Ahk-Ton 1.50
19 JAp,A:Superman 1.50
20 JAp,V:Syonide,R:Halo 1.50
21 TVE,JeM,Solo Stories 1.50
22 AD,O:Halo,I:Aurakles 1.50
23 AD,O:Halo,V:Aurakles 1.50
24 AD,C:Kobra 1.50
25 AD,V:Kobra 1.50
26 AD 1.50
27 AD,V:Kobra 1.50
28 AD,I:Lia Briggs(Looker) 1.50
29 AD,V:Metamorpho 1.50
30 AD,C:Looker 1.50
31 AD,I&J:Looker 1.50
32 AD,L:Batman 1.50
Ann.#1 JA:Geo-Force,
I:Force of July 1.75
Ann.#2 V:Tremayne,W:Metamorpho
& Sapphire Stagg 1.50

Becomes:
ADVENTURES OF
THE OUTSIDERS
May, 1986

33 AD,V:Baron Bedlam 1.50
34 AD,Masters of Disaster 1.50
35 AD,V:Adolph Hitler 1.50
36 AD,A:Masters of Disaster . . . 1.50
37 . . . . 1.50
38 . . . . 1.50
39 thru 47 JAp,reprints
Outsiders #1-#9 . . . . @1.50

BATMAN CHRONICLES
1 CDi,LW,BSz 2.95

BATMAN: THE CULT
1 JSn,BWr,V:Deacon Blackfire . 10.00
2 JSn,BWr,V:Deacon Blackfire . . 7.00
3 JSn,BWr,V:Deacon Blackfire . . 6.00
4 JSn,BWr,V:Deacon Blackfire . . 6.00

BATMAN: THE DARK
KNIGHT RETURNS
1 FM,KJ,V:Two-Face 25.00
1a 2nd printing 5.00
1b 3rd printing 3.00
2 FM,KJ,V:Sons of the Batman . 11.00
2a 2nd printing 3.00
2b 3rd printing 2.50
3 FM,KJ,D:Joker 7.00
3a 2nd printing 3.00
4 FM,KJ,Batman vs.Superman,
A:Green Arrow,D:Alfred 6.00
HC 60.00
Paperback book 20.00
Warner paperback 17.00
HC,sign/num. 350.00
2nd-8th printing 12.95

BATMAN: A DEATH IN
THE FAMILY
1 rep. Batman #426-429 . . . . . . 8.00
1a 2nd printing 5.00
1b 3rd printing 4.00

BATMAN FAMILY
September-October, 1975

1 MGr,NA(rep.) Batgirl &
Robin begins,giant 7.50
2 V:Clue Master 4.50
3 Batgirl & Robin reveal ID 5.00
4 . . . . 4.50
5 . . . . 4.50
6 Joker Daughter 6.00
7 CS,A:Sportsmaster,
G.A.Huntress 3.50
8 First solo Robin story,
C:Joker's Daughter 3.00
9 Joker's Daughter 5.50
10 R:B'woman,1st solo Batgirl sty 4.00
11 MR,Man-Bat begins 5.00
12 MR 5.00
13 MR,DN,BWi 5.00
14 HC/JRu,Man-Bat 4.00
15 MGo,Man-Bat 3.00
16 MGo,Man-Bat 3.00
17 JA,DH,MG,Batman, B:Huntress
A:Demon,MK(c),A:Catwoman . 6.00
18 MGo,JSon,BL,Huntress,BM . . 3.00
19 MGo,JSon,BL,Huntress,BM . . 3.00
20 MGo,JSon,DH,A:Ragman,
ElongatedMan, Oct.-Nov.,1978 4.00

BATMAN:
GOTHAM NIGHTS
1 Gotham City Mini-series 2.00
2 Lives of Gotham Citizens 2.00
3 Lives of Gotham Citizens 2.00
4 Lives of Gotham Citizens 2.00

BATMAN:
GOTHAM NIGHTS II
1 Sequel to Gotham Nights 1.95
2 F:Carmine Sansone 1.95
3 Fire 1.95
4 JQ(c) Decisions 1.95

BATMAN: JAZZ
[Mini-Series]
1 I:Blue Byrd 2.50
2 V:Brotherhood of Bop 2.50
3 F:Blue Byrd 2.50

*Batman: Legends of the Dark
Knight #18 © DC Comics, Inc.*

BATMAN: LEGENDS OF
THE DARK KNIGHT
1 EH,Shaman of Gotham,pt.1,
Yellow(c) 7.00
1a Blue,Orange or Pink(c) 7.00
2 EH,Shaman of Gotham,pt.2 . . . 5.00
3 EH,Shaman of Gotham,pt.3 . . . 4.00
4 EH,Shaman of Gotham,pt.4 . . . 4.00
5 EH,Shaman of Gotham,pt.5 . . . 4.00
6 KJ,Gothic,pt.1 . . . . 4.50
7 KJ,Gothic,pt.2 . . . . 4.00
8 KJ,Gothic,pt.3 . . . . 4.00
9 KJ,Gothic,pt.4 . . . . 4.00
10 KJ,Gothic,pt.5 . . . . 4.00
11 PG,TA,Prey,pt.1 . . . . 4.00
12 PG,TA,Prey,pt.2 . . . . 4.00
13 PG,TA,Prey,pt.3 . . . . 4.00
14 PG,TA,Prey,pt.4 . . . . 4.00
15 PG,TA,Prey,pt.5 . . . . 4.00
16 TVE,Venom,pt.1 . . . . 12.00
17 TVE,JL,Venom,pt.2 . . . . 10.00
18 TVE,JL,Venom,pt.3 . . . . 10.00
19 TVE,JL,Venom,pt.4 . . . . 10.00
20 TVE,JL,Venom,pt.5 . . . . 10.00
21 BS,Faith,pt.1 . . . . 2.50
22 BS,Faith,pt.2 . . . . 2.50
23 BS,Faith,pt.3 . . . . 2.50
24 GK,Flyer,pt.1 . . . . 2.50
25 GK,Flyer,pt.2 . . . . 2.50
26 GK,Flyer,pt.3 . . . . 2.50
27 Destroyer,pt.2 (Batman#474) . 3.00
28 MWg,Faces,pt.1,V:Two-Face . 4.00
29 MWg,Faces,pt.2,V:Two-Face . 4.00
30 MWg,Faces,pt.3,V:Two-Face . 4.00
31 BA,Family 2.50
32 Blades,pt.1 . . . . 2.50
33 Blades,pt.2 . . . . 2.50
34 Blades,pt.3 . . . . 2.50

---

35 BHa,Destiny Pt.1 . . . . 2.50
36 BHa,Destiny Pt.2 . . . . 2.50
37 I:Mercy,V:The Cossack 2.50
38 KON,R:Bat-Mite 2.50
39 BT,Mask#1 . . . . 2.50
40 BT,Mask#2 . . . . 2.50
41 Sunset 2.25
42 CR,Hothouse #1 . . . . 2.25
43 CR,Hothouse #2,V:Poison Ivy . 2.25
44 SMc,Turf #1 . . . . 2.25
45 Turf#2 . . . . 2.25
46 RH,A:Catwoman,V:Catman . . . 2.50
47 RH,A:Catwoman,V:Catman . . . 2.50
48 RH,A:Catwoman,V:Catman . . . 2.50
49 RH,A:Catwoman,V:Catman . . . 2.50
50 BBI,JLe,KN,KM,WS,MZ,BB,
    V:Joker 6.00
51 JKu,A:Ragman 2.25
52 Tao #1,V:Dragon 2.25
53 Tao #2,V:Dragon 2.25
54 MMi 2.00
55 B:Watchtower 2.00
56 CDi(s),V:Battle Guards 2.00
57 CDi(s),E:Watchtower 2.00
58 Storm 2.00
59 DON(s),RoW,B:Qarry 2.00
60 RoW,V:Asp 2.00
61 RoW,V:Asp 2.00
62 RoW,KnightsEnd#4,A:Shiva,
    Nightwing 1.75
63 Knights End #10,V:Azrael 2.00
64 CBa 1.95
65 Joker 1.95
66 Joker 1.95
67 Going Sane,pt.3 . . . . 1.95
68 Going Sane,pt.4 . . . . 1.95
69 Criminals,pt.1 . . . . 1.95
70 Criminals,pt.2 . . . . 1.95
71 Werewolf,pt.1 . . . . 1.95
72 JWk(c&a),Werewolf,pt.2
    [new Miraweb format begins] . . 1.95
73 JWk(c&a),Werewolf,pt.3 . . . . . 1.95
Ann.#1 JAp,KG,DSp,TL,JRu,
    MGo,JQ,'Duel',C:Joker 5.50
Ann.#2 MN,LMc,W:Gordn&Essen . 4.00
Ann.#3 MM,I:Cardinal Sin 3.75
Ann.#4 JSon(c),Elseworlds Story . 3.75
Ann.#5 CDi(s)Year One Annuals,
    O:Man-Bat 3.95
Halloween Spec.I 6.95
Halloween Spec.II 4.95
TPB Batman: Gothic, rep.Legends of
    the Dark Knight #6–#10 . . . . . 12.95
TPB Prey,rep.Legends of the Dark
    Knight #11–#15 . . . . . . 12.95
Collected Legends of the Dark Knight
    BB(c),rep.#32-#34,#38,
    #42-#43 . . . . 12.95
TPB Shaman rep.#1–#5 . . . . 12.95

BATMAN: MASK OF THE PHANTASM
1 Movie Adapt. 5.25
1a Newstand Ed. 3.25

BATMAN: MITEFALL
1 V:Bane Mite 4.95

BATMAN RECORD COMIC
1966
1 . . . . 1.00

BATMAN: RUN, RIDDLER RUN
1 MBg,Batman V:Riddler 5.50
2 MBg,Batman V:Riddler 5.25
3 MBg,V:Perfect Securities 5.25

BATMAN: SHADOW OF THE BAT
1 NB,Last Arkham Pt.1 . . . . 3.50
1a Collector set,w/posters,pop-up 5.50
2 NB,Last Arkham Pt.2 . . . . 3.00
3 NB,Last Arkham Pt.3 . . . . 3.00
4 NB,Last Arkham Pt.4 . . . . 3.00
5 NB,A:Black Spider 2.50
6 NB,I:Chancer 2.50
7 Misfits Pt.1 . . . . 2.50
8 Misfits Pt.2 . . . . 2.50
9 Misfits Pt.3 . . . . 2.50
10 MC,V:Mad Thane of Gotham . 2.00
11 V:Kadaver 2.00
12 V:Kadaver,A:Human Flea . . . 2.00
13 NB,'The Nobody' 2.00
14 NB,Gotham Freaks#1 . . . . . . 2.00
15 NB,Gotham Freaks#2 . . . . . . 2.00
16 BBI,MM,A:Anarchy,Scarecrow . 2.00
17 BBI,V:Scarecrow 2.00
18 BBI,A:Anarchy,Scarecrow 2.00
19 BBI,Knightquest:The Crusade,pt.2,
    V:Gotham criminals 2.00
20 VGi,Knightquest:The Crusade,
    V:Tally Man 2.00
21 BBI,Knightquest:The Search,
    V:Mr.Asp 2.00
22 BBI,Knightquest:The Search,
    In London 2.00
23 BBI,Knightquest:The Search . . 2.00
24 BBI,Knightquest:The Crusade . 2.00
25 BSf(c),BBI,Knightquest: Crusade,
    A:Joe Public,V:Corrosive Man . 2.00
26 BSf(c),BBI,Knightquest: Crusade,
    V:Clayface 2.00
27 BSf(c),BBI,Knightquest: Crusade,
    I:Clayface Baby 2.00
28 BSf(c),BBI 2.00
29 BSf(c),BBI,KnightsEnd#2,
    A:Nightwing 3.50
30 BSf(c),BBI,KnightsEnd#8,
    V:Azrael 2.25
31 Zero Hour, V:Butler 1.95
32 Ventriloquist,Two-Face 1.95
33 Two-Face 1.95
34 V:Tally Man 1.95
35 BKi,Return of Bruce Wayne,
    Troika,pt.2 . . . . 1.95
35a Collectors Edition 2.95
36 Black Canary 1.95
37 Joker Hunt 1.95
38 V:The Joker 1.95
39 BSf(c),R:Solomon Grundy
    [new Miraweb format begins] . 1.95
40 BSf(c), F:Anarky 1.95
Ann.#1 TVE,DG,Bloodlines#3,
    I:Joe Public 3.75
Ann.#2 Elseworlds story 3.95

BATMAN: SWORD OF AZRAEL
1 JQ,KN,I:Azrael 20.00
2 JQ,KN,A:Azrael 15.00
3 JQ,KN,V:Biis,A:Azrael 15.00
4 JQ,KN,V:Biis,A:Azrael 15.00
TPB rep.#1–#4 . . . . 13.00
TPB Platinum 50.00

BATMAN/ GREEN ARROW: THE POISON TOMORROW
1 MN,JRu,V:Poison Ivy 6.25

BATMAN/GRENDEL: DEVIL'S MASQUE & DEVIL'S RIDDLE
1 MWg,Batman meets Grendel . . 5.25
2 MWg,Batman Vs. Grendel 5.25

BATMAN/JUDGE DREDD: VENDETTA IN GOTHAM
1 AlG(s),V:Ventriliquist 5.25

BATMAN/PUNISHER LAKE OF FIRE
1 DON(s),BKI,A:Punisher,
    V:Jigsaw 5.25

BATMAN/SPAWN: WAR DEVIL
1 DgM,CDi,AlG(s),KJ,V:Croatoan 6.00

BATMAN vs. PREDATOR
1 NKu,AKu,inc.8 trading cards
    bound in (Prestige) 7.00
1a Newssnand 5.00
2 NKu,AKu,Inc. pinups (prestige) 6.00
2a Newsstand 4.00
3 NKu,AKu,conclusion,inc.
    8 trading cards (Prestige) 6.00
3a Newsstand 4.00
TPB,rep.#1–#3 . . . . 5.95

BATMAN vs. PREDATOR II BLOODMATCH
1 R:Predators 2.75
2 A:Huntress 2.50
3 Assassins 2.50
4 V:Head Hunters 2.50

BATTLE CLASSICS
September-October, 1978
1 JKu, reprints 1.50

BEAUTIFUL STORIES FOR UGLY CHILDREN
Piranha Press
1 thru 11 . . . . @2.00
12 thru 14 . . . . @2.50
15 Blood Day 2.50
16 thru 23 . . . . @2.50

BEOWOLF
April-May, 1975
1 thru 5 . . . . @1.00
6 February-March, 1976 . . . . . . 1.00

BEST OF THE BRAVE & THE BOLD
1 JL(c),NA,rep.B&B #85. . . . . . . 2.50
2 JL(c),NA,rep.B&B #81 . . . . 2.50
3 JL(c),NA,rep.B&B #82 . . . . 2.50
4 JL(c),NA,rep.B&B #80 . . . . 2.50
5 JL(c),NA,rep.B&B #93 . . . . 2.50
6 JL(c),NA,rep.B&B #83 . . . . 2.50

BEWARE THE CREEPER
May-June, 1968

1	12.00
2	7.50
3	7.50
4	7.50
5	7.50
6 March-April, 1969	7.50

BIG ALL-AMERICAN COMIC BOOK
December, 1944

1 JKu	7,000.00

BIG BOOK OF FUN COMICS
Spring , 1936

1	7,500.00

BLACK CANARY
[Limited Series]

1 TVE/DG,New Wings,pt.1	2.25
2 TVE/DG,New Wings,pt.2	2.00
3 TVE/DG,New Wings,pt.3	2.00
4 TVE/DG,New Wings,pt.4,Conc	2.00

[Regular Series]

1 TVE,Hero Worship,pt.1	2.25
2 TVE,Hero Worship,pt.2	2.00
3 TVE,Hero Worship,pt.3	2.00
4 TVE,V:Whorrsman	2.00
5	2.00
6 Blynde Woman's Bluff	2.00
7 TVE,V:Maniacal Killer	2.00
8	1.75
9 A:Huntress	1.75
10 TVE,A:Nightwing,Huntress	1.75
11 TVE,A:Nightwing	1.75
12 final issue	1.75

BLACK CONDOR

1 I&O:Black Condor	1.25
2 V:Sky Pirate	1.25
3 V:Sky Pirate	1.25
4 V:The Shark	1.25
5 V:Mind Force	1.25
6 V:Mind Force	1.25
7 Forest Fire	1.25
8 MG,In Jail	1.25
9 A:The Ray	1.25
10	1.25
11 O:Black Condor	1.25

BLACKHAWK
Prev: Golden Age

108 DD,CCu,DD&CCu(c),The Threat from the Abyss A:Blaisie	350.00
109 DD,CCu,DD&CCu(c),The Avalanche Kid	125.00
110 DD,CCu,DD&CCu(c),Mystery of Tigress Island	125.00
111 DD,CCu,DD&CCu(c),Menace of the Machines	125.00
112 DD,CCu,DD(c),The Doomed Dog Fight	125.00
113 DD,CCu,CCu(c),Volunteers of Doom	125.00
114 DD,CCu,DD&CCu(c),Gladiators of Blackhawk Island	125.00
115 DD,CCu,DD&CCu(c),The Tyrant's Return	125.00
116 DD,CCu,DD&CCu(c),Prisoners	

of the Black Island	125.00
117 DD,CCu,DD&CCu(c),Menace of the Dragon Boat	125.00
118 DD,CCu,DD&SMo(c),FF,The Bandit With 1,000 Nets	135.00
119 DD,CCu,DD&SMo(c), V:Chief Blackhawk	75.00
120 DD,CCu,DD&SMo(c),The Challenge of the Wizard	75.00
121 DD,CCu,DD&CCu(c),Secret Weapon of the Archer	75.00
122 DD,CCu,DD&CCu(c),The Movie That Backfired	75.00
123 DD,CCu,DD&CCu(c),The Underseas Gold Fort	75.00
124 DD,CCu,DD&CCu(c),Thieves With A Thousand Faces	75.00
125 DD,CCu,DD&CCu(c),Secrets o/t Blackhawk Time Capsule	75.00
126 DD,CCu,DD&CCu(c),Secret of the Glass Fort	75.00
127 DD,CCu,DD&CCu(c),Blackie-The Winged Sky Fighter	75.00
128 DD,CCu,DD&CCu(c),The Vengeful Bowman	75.00
129 DD,CCu,DD&CCu(c),The Cavemen From 3,000 B.C.	75.00
130 DD,CCu,DD&SMo(c),The Mystery Missle From Space	75.00
131 DD,CCu,DD&CCu(c),The Return of the Rocketeers	60.00
132 DD,CCu,DD&CCu(c),Raid of the Rocketeers	60.00
133 DD,CCu,DD&CCu(c),Human Dynamo	60.00
134 DD,CC,DD&CC(c),The Sinister Snowman	60.00
135 DD,CCu,DD&CCu(c),The Underworld Supermarket	60.00
136 DD,CCu,DD&CCu(c),The Menace of the Smoke-Master	60.00
137 DD,CCu,DD&CCu(c),The Weapons That Backfired	60.00
138 DD,CCu,DD&SMo(c),The Menace of the Blob	60.00
139 DD,CCu,DD&CCu(c),The Secret Blackhawk	60.00
140 DD,CCu,DD&CCu(c),The Space Age Marauders	60.00
141 DD,CCu,DD&CCu(c),Crimes of the Captive Masterminds	50.00
142 DD,CCu,DD&CCu(c),Alien Blackhawk Chief	50.00
143 DD,SMo,DD&CCu(c),Lady Blackhawk's Rival	50.00
144 DD,CCu,DD&CCu(c),The Underworld Sportsmen	50.00
145 DD,CCu,DD&CCu(c),The Deadly Lensman	50.00
146 DD,CCu,DD&CCu(c),The Fantastic Fables of Blackhawk	50.00
147 DD,SMo,DD&CCu(c),The Blackhawk Movie Queen	50.00
148 DD,CCu,DD&CCu(c),Four Dooms For The Blackhawks	50.00
149 DD,CCu,DD&CCu(c),Masks of Doom	50.00
150 DD,CCu,DD&SMo(c), Blackhawk Mascot from Space	35.00
151 DD,CCu,DD&CCu(c),Lost City	35.00
152 DD,CCu,DD&SMo(c),Noah's Ark From Space	35.00
153 DD,CCu,DD&SMo(c), Boomerang Master	35.00
154 DD,CCu,DD&SMo(c),The	

Beast Time Forgot	35.00
155 DD,CCu,DD&CCu(c),Killer Shark's Land Armada	35.00
156 DD,CCu,DD&SMo(c),Peril of the Plutonian Raider	35.00
157 DD,CCu,DD&SMo(c),Secret of the Blackhawk Sphinx	35.00
158 DD,CCu,DD&SMo(c),Bandit Birds From Space	35.00
159 DD,CCu,DD&SMo(c),Master of the Puppet Men	35.00
160 DD,CCu,DD&CCu(c),The Phantom Spy	35.00
161 DD,SMo,DD&SMo(c),Lady Blackhawk's Crime Chief	35.00
162 DD,CCu,DD&CCu(c),The Invisible Blackhawk	35.00
163 DD,CCu,DD&SMo(c), Fisherman of Crime	35.00
164 DD,O:Blackhawk retold	35.00
165 DD,V:League of Anti Blackhawks	30.00
166 DD,A:Lady Blackhawk	30.00
167 DD,The Blackhawk Bandits	30.00
168 DD,Blackhawk Time Travelers	25.00
169 DD,Sinister Hunts of Mr. Safari	25.00
170 DD,A:Lady Blackhawk,V:Killer Shark	25.00
171 DD,Secret of Alien Island	25.00
172 DD,Challenge of the GasMaster	20.00
173 DD,The Super Jungle Man	20.00
174 DD,Andre's Impossible World	20.00
175 DD,The Creature with Blackhawk's Brain	20.00
176 DD,Stone Age Blackhawks	15.00
177 DD,Town that time Forgot	15.00
178 DD,Return of the Scorpions	15.00
179 DD,Invisible Dr.Dunbar	14.00
180 DD,Son of Blackhawk	15.00
181 DD,I:Tom Thumb Blackhawk	9.00
182 DD,A:Lady Blackhawk	9.00
183 DD,V:Killer Shark	9.00
184 DD,Island of Super Monkeys	9.00
185 DD,Last 7 days of the Blackhawks	9.00
186 DD,A:Lady Blackhawk	9.00
187 DD,V:Porcupine	9.00
188 DD,A:Lady Blackhawk	9.00
189 DD:O:rtd	9.00
190 DD,FantasticHumanStarfish	10.00
191 DD,A:Lady Blackhawk	7.00
192 DD,V:King Condor	6.00
193 DD,The Jailer's Revenge	6.00
194 DD,The Outlaw Blackhawk	6.00
195 DD,A:Tom Thumb Blackhawk	6.00
196 DD,Blackhawk WWII Combat Diary story	6.00
197 DD:new look	5.00
198 DD:O:rtd	8.00
199 DD,Attack with the Mummy Insects	5.00
200 DD,A:Lady Blackhawk, I:Queen Killer Shark	6.00
201 DD,Blackhawk Detached Diary Story,F:Hendrickson	5.00
202 DD,Combat Diary,F:Andre	5.00
203 DD:O:Chop-Chop	5.00
204 DD,A:Queen Killer Shark	5.00
205 DD,Combat Diary story	5.00
206 DD,Combat Diary, F:Olaf	5.00

All comics prices listed are for _Near Mint_ condition.

207 DD,Blackhawk Devil Dolls . . . 5.00
208 DD,Detached service diary
   F:Chuck 5.00
209 DD,V:King Condor 5.00
210 DD,Danger..Blackhawk Bait
   rep.Blackhawk #139. . . . . 4.00
211 DD,GC,Detached service
   diary 5.00
212 DD,Combat Diary,
   F:Chop-Chop 5.00
213 DD,Blackhawk goes
   Hollywood 5.00
214 DD,Team of Traitors 5.00
215 DD,Detached service diary
   F:Olaf 5.00
216 DD,A:Queen Killer Shark . . . 5.00
217 DD,Detached service diary
   F:Stanislaus 5.00
218 DD,7 against Planet Peril . . . 5.00
219 DD,El Blackhawk Peligroso . . 5.00
220 DD,The Revolt of the
   Assembled Man 5.00
221 DD,Detach service diary
   F:Hendrickson 3.50
222 DD,The Man from E=MC2 . . . 3.50
223 DD,V:Mr.Quick CHange 3.50
224 DD,Combat Diary,
   F:Stanislaus 3.50
225 DD,A:Queen Killer Shark . . . 3.50
226 DD,Secret Monster of
   Blackhawk Island 3.50
227 DD,Detached Service diary
   F:Chop-Chop 3.50
228 DD (1st art on JLA characters)
   Blackhawks become super-heroes,
   Junk-Heap heroes #1(C:JLA) . 3.50
229 DD,Junk-Heap Heroes #2
   (C:JLA) 3.50
230 DD,Junk-Heap Heroes concl.
   (C:JLA) 3.50
231 DD,A:Lady Blackhawk 3.50
232 DD,A:Lady Blackhawk 3.50
233 DD,Too Late,The Leaper . . . 3.50
234 DD,The Terrible Twins 3.50
235 DD,A Coffin for
   a Blackhawk 3.50
236 DD,Melt,Mutant, Melt 3.50
237 DD,Magnificent 7 Assassins . 3.50
238 DD,Walking Booby-Traps . . . 3.50
239 DD,The Killer That Time
   Forgot 3.50
240 DD,He Who Must Die 3.50
241 DD,A Blackhawk a Day 3.50
242 Blackhawks back in blue &
   black costumes 3.50
243 Mission Incredible (1968) . . . 3.50
244 GE,new costumes,Blackhawks
   become mercenaries (1976) . . 1.50
245 GE,Death's Double Deal 1.50
246 RE,GE,Death's Deadly Dawn 1.50
247 RE,AM,Operation:Over Kill . . 1.50
248 JSh,Vengeance is Mine!..
   Sayeth the Cyborg 1.50
249 RE,GE,V:Sky-Skull 1.50
250 RE,GE,FS,D:Chuck(1977) . . . 1.50
251 DSp,Back to WWII(1982) . . . 1.50
252 thru 258 DSp . . . . @1.50
259 . . . . 1.50
260 HC,ATh 1.50
261 thru 271 DSp . . . . @1.50
272 . . . . 1.50
273 DSp 1.50
274 DSp 1.50
     [2nd Series]
1 HC Mini-series,Blackhawk accused

of communism 4.50
2 HC,visits Soviet Union 3.50
3 HC,Atom Bomb threat to N.Y. . 3.50
     [3rd Series]
1 All in color for a Crime,pt.1
   I:The Real Lady Blackhawk . . . 1.50
2 All in color for a Crime,pt.2 . . . 1.50
3 Agent Rescue Attempt in Rome 1.50
4 Blackhawk's girlfriend murdered 1.50
5 I:Circus Organization 1.50
6 Blackhawks on false mission . . 1.50
7 V:Circus,A:Suicide Squad, rep.
   1st Blackhawk story 2.50
8 Project: Assimilation 1.50
9 V:Grundfest 1.50
10 Blackhawks Attacked 1.50
11 Master plan revealed 1.50
12 Raid on BlackhawkAirwaysHQ 1.50
13 Team Member Accused of . . . 1.75
14 Blackhawk test pilots 1.75
15 Plans for independence 1.75
16 Independence, final issue 1.75
Ann.#1 Hawks in Albania 2.95
Spec.#1 Assassination of JFK
   to Saigon,1975 . . . . 3.50

BLACK HOOD
Impact

1 O:Black Hood 1.25
2 Nick Cray becomes Black Hood 1.00
3 New Year's Eve,A:Creeptures . 1.00
4 Nate Cray become Black Hood,
   Dr.M.Harvey becomes Ozone . 1.00
5 E:Nate Cray as Black Hood
   V:Ozone 1.00
6 New Black Hood 1.00
7 History of Seaside City 1.25
8 V:Hit Coffee 1.25
9 V:Hit Coffee 1.25
10 Slime of Your Life #1 . . . . 1.25
11 Slime of Your Life #2 . . . . 1.25
12 Final Issue 1.25
Ann#1 Earthquest,w/trading card . 2.50

BLACK LIGHTNING
April, 1977

1 TVE,FS,I&O:Black Lightning . 3.50
2 TVE,FS,A:Talia 2.00
3 TVE,I:Tobias Whale 2.00
4 TVE,A:Jimmy Olsen 2.00
5 TVE,A:Superman 2.00
6 TVE,I:Syonide 2.00
7 TVE,V:Syonide 2.00
8 TVE,V:Tobias Whale 2.00
9 TVE,V:Annihilist 2.00
10 TVE,V:Trickster 2.00
11 TVE,The Ray back-up story,
   September-October, 1978 . . . . 2.50
     [2nd Series]
1 He's Back 1.95
2 V:Painkiller 1.95
3 V:Painkiller 1.95
4 V:Painkiller,Royal Family 1.95
5 Flashbacks of Past 1.95
6 V:Gangbuster 2.25

BLACK MASK

1 I:Black Mask 5.00
2 V:Underworld 5.00
3 V:Valentine 5.00

BLACK ORCHID
1 DMc,O:Black Orchid,
   A:Batman,Luthor,Poison Ivy . . 8.00

2 DMc,O:cont,Arkham Asylum . . 7.00
3 DMc,A:SwampThing,conc. 7.00
TPB rep. #1 thru #3 . . . . 20.00
     Vertigo
1 DMc(c),B:DiF(s),JIT, SnW,I:Sherilyn
   Somers,I:Logos,F:Walt Brody . 2.50
1a Platinum Ed. 30.00
2 JIT,SnW,Uprooting,V:Logos . . 2.25
3 JIT,SnW,Tainted Zone,
   V:Fungus 2.25
4 JIT,SnW,I:Nick & Orthia 2.25
5 DMc(c),JIT,SnW,
   A:Swamp Thing 2.25
6 JIT,BMc(i),God in the Cage . . . 2.25
7 JIT,RGu,SnW,
   Upon the Threshold 2.25
8 DMc(c),RGu,A:Silent People . . 2.25
9 DMc(c),RGu 2.25
10 DMc(c),RGu 2.25
11 DMc(c),RGu,In Tennessee . . . 1.95
12 DMc(c),RGu 2.25
13 DMc(c),RGu,F:Walt Brody . . . 2.25
14 DMc(c),RGu,Black Annis 1.95
15 DMc(c),RGu,Kobolds 1.95
16 DMc(c),RGu,Suzy,Junkin 1.95
17 Twisted Season,pt.1 . . . . 1.95
18 Twisted Season,pt.2 . . . . 1.95
19 Twisted Season,pt.3 . . . . 1.95
20 Twisted Season,pt.4 . . . . 1.95
21 Twisted Season,pt.5 . . . . 1.95
22 Twisted Season,pt.6, final iss. . 2.25
Ann.#1 DMc(c),DiF(s),GyA,JnM,F:Suzy,
   Childrens Crusade,BU:retells
   Adventure Comics#430 . . . . . 4.25

BLASTERS SPECIAL
1 A:Snapper Carr, Spider Guild . 2.00

BLOODBATH
1 A:Superman 3.75
2 A:New Heroes 3.75

BLOODPACK
[Mini-Series]
1 I:Blood Pack, V:Demolition . . . 1.50
2 A:Superboy 1.50
3 Loira's Corpse 1.50
4 Real Heroes Final Issue 1.50

Blood Syndicate #8 © DC Comics, Inc.

BLOOD SYNDICATE
(Milestone)
1 I:Blood Syndicate,Rob Chaplick,
  Dir.Mark.Ed.,w/B puzzle piece,
  Skybox card,Poster 4.00
1a Newstand Ed. 1.75
2 I:Boogieman,Tech-9 Vs.
  Holocaust 1.75
3 V:S.Y.S.T.E.M.,I:Mom,D:Tech-9 1.75
4 V:S.Y.S.T.E.M. 1.75
5 I:John Wing,Kwai,Demon Fox . 1.75
6 V:John Wing 1.75
7 I:Edmund,Cornelia 1.75
8 V:Demon Fox 1.75
9 O:Blood Syndicate,I:Templo . . 1.75
10 WS(c),Ccs,Shadow War,I:Iota,
  Sideshow,Rainsaw,Slag,Ash,
  Bad Betty,Oro 1.75
11 IV(s),Ccs,A:Aquamaria 1.75
12 IV(s),Ccs,V:Dinosaur 1.75
13 IV(s),Ccs,B:Roach War 1.75
14 IV(s),Ccs,V:Roaches 1.75
15 IV(s),Ccs,E:Roach War 1.75
16 IV(s),Ccs,Worlds Collide#6,
  A:Superman 1.75
17 Ccs,Worlds Collide#13,V:Rift . 1.75
18 Ccs,V:S.Y.S.T.E.M. 1.75
19 . . . . 1.75
20 . . . . 1.75
21 . . . . 1.75
22 . . . . 1.75
23 F:Boogieman 1.75
24 L:Third Rail,Brickhouse 1.75
25 R:Tech-9 . . . . 2.95
26 Return of the Dead 1.75
27 R:Masquerade 1.75
28 Tech-9 takes control 2.50

Blue Beetle #3 © DC Comics, Inc.

BLUE BEETLE
June, 1986
1 O:Blue Beetle 2.00
2 V:Fire Fist 1.00
3 V:Madmen 1.00
4 V:Doctor Alchemy 1.00
5 A:Question 1.00
6 V:Question 1.00
7 A:Question 1.00
8 A:Chronos 1.00

9 A:Chronos 1.00
10 Legends, V:Chronos 1.00
11 A:New Teen Titans 1.00
12 A:New Teen Titans 1.00
13 A:New Teen Titans 1.00
14 Pago Island,I:Catalyst 1.00
15 RA:V:Carapax 1.00
16 RA,Chicago Murders 1.00
17 R:Dan Garrett/Blue Beetle . . 1.00
18 D:Dan Garrett 1.00
19 RA,R:Dr. Cyber 1.00
20 RA,Millennium,A:JLI 1.00
21 RA,A:Mr.Miracle,
  Millennium tie in 1.00
22 RA,Prehistoric Chicago 1.00
23 DH,V:The Madmen 1.00
24 DH,final issue 1.00

BLUE DEVIL
June, 1984
1 O:Blue Devil 2.50
2 . . . . 1.50
3 A:Superman 1.50
4 A:JLA 1.50
5 . . . . 1.50
6 EC,I:Bolt 1.00
7 KG 1.00
8 GV 1.00
9 thru 16 . . . . @1.00
17 Crisis 1.25
18 Crisis 1.25
19 . . . . 1.00
20 RM,Halloween 1.00
21 RM,I:Roadmaster 1.00
22 RM,A:Jorj & Lehni 1.00
23 A:Jorj & Lehni 1.00
24 V:Blue Devil Toys 1.00
25 Mary Frances Cassidy 1.00
26 Special Baseball issue 1.00
27 Godfrey Goose 1.00
28 real live fan guest star 1.00
29 . . . . 1.00
30 Double sized 1.25
31 BSz,V:Seraph,December,1986 1.25
Ann.#1 . . . . 1.50

BOB, THE GALACTIC BUM
[Mini-Series]
1 A:Lobo 1.95
2 Planet Gnulp,A:Lobo 1.95
3 V:Khunds 1.95
4 Rando's Coronation 1.95

BOMBA, THE JUNGLE BOY
September-October, 1967
1 CI,MA,I:Bomba 15.00
2 thru 6 . . . . @10.00
7 September-October, 1968 . . 10.00

BOOKS OF MAGIC
[Limited Series]
1 B:NGa(s),JBo,F:Phantom Stranger,
  A:J.Constantine,Tim Hunter,
  Doctor Occult,Mister E 10.00
2 SHp,F:J.Constantine,A:Spectre,
  Dr.Fate,Demon,Zatanna 9.00
3 CV,F:Doctor Occult,
  A:Sandman 7.00
4 E:NGa(s),PuJ,F:Mr.E,A:Death . 7.00
TPB rep.#1-#4 . . . . 19.95
[Regular Series]
Vertigo

1 MkB,B:Bindings,R:Tim Hunter . 3.50
1a Platinum Edition 22.00
2 CV(c),MkB,V:Manticore 2.25
3 CV(c),MkB,E:Bindings 3.00
4 CV(c),MkB,A:Death 4.00
5 CV(c),I:Khara 2.25
6 Sacrifices,pt.I 1.95
7 Sacrifices,pt.II 1.95
8 Tim vs. evil Tim 1.95
9 Artificial Heart,pt.1 . . . . 1.95
10 Artificial Heart,pt.2 . . . . 1.95
11 Artificial Heart,pt.3 . . . . 1.95
12 Small Glass Worlds,pt.1 . . . . . 1.95
13 Small Glass Worlds,pt.2 . . . . . 1.95
14 CV(c),A:The Wobbly 2.50

BOOSTER GOLD
February, 1986
1 DJ,V:Blackguard 3.00
2 DJ,V:Minddancer 2.50
3 DJ,V:Minddancer 2.00
4 DJ,V:Minddancer 1.50
5 DJ,V:Fascinator 1.50
6 DJ,A:Superman 1.00
7 DJ,A:Superman 1.00
8 DJ,A:Braniac 5,Cham.Boy,
  Ultra Boy,pt.1 . . . . 1.25
9 DJ,A:Braniac 5,Cham.Boy,
  Ultra Boy,pt.2 . . . . 1.25
10 DJ,V:1000 . . . . 1.00
11 DJ,V:Shockwave 1.00
12 DJ,Booster Weakening 1.00
13 DJ,I:Rip Hunter(modern) 1.00
14 DJ,Rip Hunter 1.00
15 DJ,Rip Hunter 1.00
16 DJ,Boosters new company . . . 1.00
17 DJ,A:Cheshire & Hawk 1.00
18 DJ,V:Broderick 1.00
19 DJ,V:Rainbow Raider 1.00
20 DJ,V:Rainbow Raider 1.00
21 DJ,Goldstar captured by aliens 1.00
22 DJ,A:J.L.I.,D:Goldstar 1.00
23 DJ,A:Superman & Luthor 1.25
24 DJ,Millenium 1.00
25 DJ,last issue 1.00

BOY COMMANDOS
Winter, 1942–43
1 S&K,O:Liberty Belle;Sandman
  & Newsboy Legion 2,800.00
2 S&K 850.00
3 S&K 600.00
4 . . . . 400.00
5 . . . . 400.00
6 S&K 350.00
7 S&K 275.00
8 S&K 275.00
9 . . . . 275.00
10 S&K 275.00
11 Infinity(c) 275.00
12 thru 16 . . . . @150.00
17 Science Fiction(c) 165.00
18 . . . . 150.00
19 . . . . 150.00
20 . . . . 150.00
21 . . . . 100.00
22 . . . . 100.00
23 S&K,S&K,(c) 125.00
24 . . . . 110.00
25 . . . . 110.00
26 Science Fiction(c) 125.00
27 . . . . 100.00
28 . . . . 100.00
29 S&K story 110.00
30 Baseball Storm 110.00

---

31 . . . . 100.00	63 F:Supergirl&WonderWoman . 20.00	134 JAp,F:Green Lantern 4.00
32 A:Dale Evans(c) 110.00	64 F:Batman,V:Eclipso 60.00	135 JAp,F:Metal Men 4.00
33 . . . . 100.00	65 DG,FMc,F:Flash & Doom	136 JAp,F:Metal Men,Green Arr. . 4.00
34 I:Wolf 100.00	Patrol 20.00	137 F:Demon 4.00
35 . . . . 100.00	66 F:Metamorpho & Metal Men . 20.00	138 JAp,F:Mr.Miracle 4.00
36 November-December, 1949 . 125.00	67 CI,F:Batman & Flash 30.00	139 JAp,F:Hawkman 4.00
	68 F:Batman,Metamorpho,Joker,	140 JAp,F:Wonder Woman. 4.00
BRAVE AND THE BOLD	Riddler,Penguin 57.00	141 JAp,F:Bl.Canary,A:Joker . . . 10.00
August-September, 1955	69 F:Batman & Green Lantern . . 25.00	142 JAp,F:Aquaman 3.00
1 JKu,RH,IN,I:VikingPrince,Golden	70 F:Batman & Hawkman 25.00	143 O:Human Target 3.25
Gladiator,Silent Knight . . . 1,700.00	71 F:Batman & Green Arrow . . . 25.00	144 JAp,F:Green Arrow 3.25
2 F:Viking Prince 700.00	72 CI,F:Spectre & Flash 20.00	145 JAp,F:Phantom Stranger 3.00
3 F:Viking Prince 400.00	73 F:Aquaman & Atom 20.00	146 JAp,F:E-2 Batman 3.00
4 F:Viking Prince 400.00	74 B:Batman T.U.,A:Metal Men . 20.00	
5 B:Robin Hood 425.00	75 F:Spectre 20.00	
6 JKu,F:Robin Hood,E:Golden	76 F:Plastic Man 20.00	
Gladiator 300.00	77 F:Atom 20.00	
7 JKu,F:Robin Hood 300.00	78 F:Wonder Woman 20.00	
8 JKu,F:Robin Hood 300.00	79 NA,F:Deadman 30.00	
9 JKu,F:Robin Hood 300.00	80 NA,DG,F:Creeper 27.00	
10 JKu,F:Robin Hood 300.00	81 NA,F:Flash 27.00	
11 JKu,F:Viking Prince . . 220.00	82 NA,F:Aquaman,O:Ocean	
12 JKu,F:Viking Prince . . 210.00	Master 27.00	
13 JKu,F:Viking Prince . . 210.00	83 NA,F:Teen Titans 40.00	
14 JKu,F:Viking Prince . . 210.00	84 NA,F:Sgt.Rock 27.00	
15 JKu,F:Viking Prince . . 210.00	85 NA,F:Green Arrow 27.00	
16 JKu,F:Viking Prince . . 175.00	86 NA,F:Deadman 27.00	
17 JKu,F:Viking Prince . . 175.00	87 F:Wonder Woman 18.00	
18 JKu,F:Viking Prince . . 175.00	88 F:Wildcat 18.00	
19 JKu,F:Viking Prince . . 175.00	89 RA,F:Phantom Stranger 18.00	
20 JKu,F:Viking Prince . . 175.00	90 F:Adam Strange 18.00	
21 JKu,F:Viking Prince . . 175.00	91 F:Black Canary 18.00	
22 JKu,F:Viking Prince . . 175.00	92 F:Bat Squad 18.00	
23 JKu,O:Viking Prince 260.00	93 NA,House of Mystery 27.00	
24 JKu,E:Viking Prince,Silent	94 NC,F:Teen Titans 12.00	
Knight 190.00	95 F:Plastic Man 9.00	
25 RA,I&B:Suicide Squad 500.00	96 F:Sgt.Rock 9.00	
26 F:Suicide Squad 235.00	97 NC(i),F:Wildcat 9.00	
27 Creature of Ghost Lake . . . 220.00	98 JAp,F:Phantom Stranger 9.00	
28 I:Justice League of	99 NC,F:Flash 9.00	
America,O:Snapper Carr . . 4,400.00	100 NA,F:Green Arrow 27.00	147 JAp,A:Supergirl 3.00
29 F:Justice League 1,700.00	101 JA,F:Metamorpho 6.00	148 JSon,JAp,F:Plastic Man 3.00
30 F:Justice League 1,500.00	102 NA,JA,F:Teen Titans 12.00	149 JAp,F:Teen Titans 3.50
31 F:Cave Carson 225.00	103 FMc,F:Metal Men 5.50	150 JAp,F:Superman 3.00
32 F:Cave Carson 110.00	104 JAp,F:Deadman 5.50	151 JAp,F:Flash 3.50
33 F:Cave Carson 110.00	105 JAp,F:Wonder Woman 5.50	152 JAp,F:Atom 3.00
34 JKu,I&O:S.A. Hawkman . . 1,550.00	106 JAp,F:Green Arrow 5.50	153 DN,F:Red Tornado 3.00
35 JKu:F:Hawkman 400.00	107 JAp,F:Black Canary 5.50	154 JAp,F:Metamorpho 3.00
36 JKu:F:Hawkman 400.00	108 JAp,F:Sgt.Rock 5.50	155 JAp,F:Green Lantern 3.00
37 F:Suicide Squad 160.00	109 JAp,F:Demon 5.50	156 DN,F:Dr.Fate 3.00
38 F:Suicide Squad 150.00	110 JAp,F:Wildcat 5.50	157 JAp,F:Kamandi 3.00
39 F:Suicide Squad 150.00	111 JAp,F:Joker 12.50	158 JAp,F:Wonder Woman 3.00
40 JKu,F:Cave Carson 90.00	112 JAp,F:Mr.Miracle. 7.50	159 JAp,A:Ras al Ghul 3.00
41 F:Cave Carson 90.00	113 JAp,F:Metal Men 7.50	160 JAp,F:Supergirl 3.00
42 JKu,F:Hawkman 240.00	114 JAp,O:Viking Prince 7.50	161 JAp,F:Adam Strange 3.00
43 JKu,O:Hawkman 275.00	115 JAp,F:Spectre 7.50	162 JAp,F:Sgt.Rock 3.00
44 JKu,F:Hawkman 200.00	116 JAp,F:Sgt.Rock 7.50	163 DG,F:Black Lightning 3.00
45 CI,F:Strange Sports 35.00	117 JAp,F:Sgt.Rock 7.50	164 JL,F:Hawkman 3.00
46 CI,F:Strange Sports 35.00	118 JAp,F:Wildcat,V:Joker 11.00	165 DN,F:Man-bat 3.00
47 CI,F:Strange Sports 35.00	119 JAp,F:Man-Bat 4.50	166 DG,TA,DSp,F:Black Canary
48 CI,F:Strange Sports 35.00	120 JAp,F:Kamandi 4.50	A:Penguin,I:Nemesis 3.00
49 CI,F:Strange Sports 35.00	121 JAp,F:Metal Men 4.50	167 DC,DA,F:Blackhawk 3.00
50 F:GreenArrow & JonnJ'onzz . 95.00	122 JAp,F:Swamp Thing 4.50	168 JAp,DSp,F:Green Arrow 3.25
51 F:Aquaman & Hawkman . . . 120.00	123 JAp,F:Plastic Man 4.50	169 JAp,DSp,F:Zatanna 3.00
52 JKu,F:Sgt.Rock 80.00	124 JAp,F:Sgt.Rock 4.50	170 JA,F:Nemesis 3.00
53 ATh,F:Atom & Flash 35.00	125 JAp,F:Flash 4.50	171 JL,DSp,V:Scalphunter 3.00
54 I&O:Teen Titans 225.00	126 JAp,F:Aquaman 4.50	172 CI,F:Firestorm 3.00
55 F:Metal Man & Atom 30.00	127 JAp,F:Wildcat 4.50	173 JAp,F:Guardians 3.00
56 F:Flash & J'onn J'onzz 30.00	128 JAp,F:Mr.Miracle 4.50	174 JAp,F:Green Lantern 3.00
57 I&O:Metamorpho 100.00	129 F:Green Arrow,V:Joker 11.00	175 JAp,A:Lois Lane 3.00
58 F:Metamorpho 45.00	130 F:Green Arrow,V:Joker 11.00	176 JAp,F:Swamp Thing 3.00
59 F:Batman & Green Lantern . . 70.00	131 JAp,F:WonderWoman,	177 JAp,F:Elongated Man 3.00
60 A:Teen Titans,I:Wonder Girl . 70.00	A:Catwoman 5.00	
61 MA,O:Starman,BlackCanary . 60.00	132 JAp,F:King Fu Foom 4.00	
62 MA,O:Starman,BlackCanary . 60.00	133 JAp,F:Deadman 4.00	

Brave and the Bold #200
© DC Comics, Inc.

178 JAp,F:Creeper 3.00
179 EC,F:Legion o/Superheroes . 3.00
180 JAp,F:Spectre,Nemesis 3.00
181 JAp,F:Hawk & Dove 3.00
182 JAp,F:E-2 Robin 3.00
183 CI,V:Riddler 3.50
184 JAp,A:Catwoman 4.00
185 F:Green Arrow 3.25
186 JAp,F:Hawkman 3.00
187 JAp,F:Metal Men 3.00
188 JAp,F:Rose & Thorn 3.00
189 JAp,A:Thorn 3.00
190 JAp,F:Adam Strange 3.00
191 JAp,V:Joker,Penguin 7.50
192 JAp,F:Superboy 3.00
193 JAp,D:Nemesis 3.00
194 CI,F:Flash 3.00
195 JA,I:Vampire 3.00
196 JAp,F:Ragman 3.00
197 JSon,W:Earth II Batman &
    Catwoman 4.00
198 F:Karate Kid 3.00
199 RA,F:Spectre 3.00
200 DGb,JAp,A:Earth-2 Batman,I:
    Outsiders (GeoForce,Katana,Halo),
    E:Batman T.U.,final issue . . . 12.00
[Limited Series]
1 SAP,Green Arrow/Butcher T.U. 2.00
2 SAP,A:Black Canary,Question . 2.00
3 SAP,Green Arrow/Butcher 2.00
4 SAP,GA on Trial;A:Black
    Canary 2.00
5 SAP,V:Native Canadians,I.R.A. 2.00

BREATHTAKER
1 I:Breathtaker(Chase Darrow) . . 6.00
2 Chase Darrow captured 6.00
3 O:Breathtaker 6.00
4 V:The Man, final issue 4.95

BROTHER POWER, THE GEEK
September-October, 1968
1 . . . . 25.00
2 November-December, 1968 . . 20.00

The Butcher #1 © DC Comics

BUGS BUNNY
1 A:Bugs,Daffy,Search for Fudd
    Statues 1.00
2 Search for Statues cont.
    V:WitchHazel 1.00
3 Bugs&Co.in outer space, final . 1.50

BUTCHER, THE
[Limited Series]
1 MB,I:John Butcher 5.00
2 MB,in San Francisco 3.50
3 MB,V:Corporation 3.00
4 MB,A:Green Arrow 2.50
5 MB,A:Corvus,final issue 2.25

BUZZY
Winter, 1944
1 . . . . 165.00
2 . . . . 75.00
3 thru 5 . . . . @40.00
6 thru 10 . . . . @35.00
11 thru 15 . . . . @25.00
16 thru 25 . . . . @25.00
26 thru 35 . . . . @20.00
36 thru 45 . . . . @15.00
46 thru 76 . . . . @15.00
77 October, 1958 . . . . 15.00

CAMELOT 3000
December, 1982
1 BB,O:Arthur,Merlin 4.50
2 BB,A:Morgan LeFay 3.50
3 BB,J:New Knights 3.50
4 BB,V:McAllister 3.50
5 BB,O:Morgan Le Fay 3.50
6 BB,TA,W:Arthur 3.50
7 BB,TA,R:Isolde 3.50
8 BB,TA,D:Sir Kay 3.50
9 BB,TA,L:Sir Percival 3.50
10 BB,TA,V:Morgan Le Fay 3.50
11 BB,TA,V:Morgan Le Fay 3.50
12 BB,TA,D:Arthur 3.50

CAPTAIN ACTION
{Based on toy}
October-November, 1968
1 WW,I:Captain Action,Action
    Boy,A:Superman 45.00
2 GK,WW, V:Krellik 25.00
3 GK,I:Dr.Evil 25.00
4 GK,A:Dr.Evil 25.00
5 GK,WW,A:Matthew Blackwell,
    last issue 25.00

CAPTAIN ATOM
March, 1987
1 PB,O:Captain Atom 3.00
2 PB,C:Batman 2.00
3 PB,O:Captain Atom 1.75
4 PB,A:Firestorm 1.75
5 PB,A:Firestorm 1.75
6 PB,Dr.Spectro 1.75
7 R:Plastique 1.75
8 PB,Capt.Atom/Plastique 1.75
9 V:Bolt 1.75
10 PB,A:JLI 2.00
11 PB,A:Firestorm 1.50
12 PB,I:Major Force 1.50
13 PB,Christmas issue 1.50
14 PB,A:Nightshade 1.50
15 PB,Dr.Spectro, Major Force . 1.50
16 PB,A:JLI,V:Red Tornado 1.75
17 V:Red Tornado;A:Swamp

Thing,JLI 1.75
18 PB,A:Major Force 1.50
19 PB,Drug War 1.50
20 FMc,BlueBeetle 1.50
21 PB,A:Plastique,Nightshade . . . 1.50
22 PB,A:MaxLord,Nightshade,
    Plastique 1.50
23 PB,V:The Ghost 1.50
24 PB,Invasion X-over 1.50
25 PB,Invvasion X-over 1.50
26 A:JLA,Top Secret,pt.1 . . . . . . 1.75
27 A:JLA,Top Secret,pt.2 . . . . . 1.75
28 V:Ghost, Top Secret,pt.3 . . . 1.50
29 RT,Captain Atom cleared
    (new direction) 1.50
30 Janus Directive #11,V:Black
    Manta 1.50
31 RT,Capt.Atom's Powers,
    A:Rocket Red 1.50
32 Loses Powers 1.50
33 A:Batman 2.00
34 C:JLE 1.50
35 RT,Secret o/f Silver Shield,
    A:Major Force 1.50
36 RT,Las Vegas Battle,A:Major
    Force 1.50
37 I:New Atomic Skull 1.25
38 RT,A:Red Tornado,
    Black Racer 1.25
39 RT,A:Red Tornado 1.25
40 RT,V:Kobra 1.25
41 RT,A:Black Racer,
    Red Tornado 1.25
42 RT,A:Phantom Stranger,Red
    Tornado,Black Racer,
    Death from Sandman 1.25
43 RT,V:Nekron 1.25
44 RT,V:Plastique 1.25
45 RT,A:The Ghost,I:Ironfire 1.25
46 RT,A:Superman 1.25
47 RT,A:SupermanV:Ghost 1.25
48 RT,R:Red Tornado 1.25
49 RT,Plastique on trial 1.25
50 RT,V:The Ghost,DoubleSize . . 2.50
51 RT 1.25
52 RT,Terror on RTE.91' 1.25
53 RT,A:Aquaman 1.25
54 RT,A:Rasputin,Shadowstorm . . 1.25
55 RT,Inside Quantum Field 1.25
56 RT,Quantum Field cont. 1.25
57 RT,V:ShadowStorm,
    Quantum.Field 1.25
Ann.#1 I:Maj.Force 1.50
Ann.#2 A:RocketRed,Maj.Force . . 1.50

CAPTAIN CARROT
March, 1982
1 RA,A:Superman,Starro 1.25
2 AA 1.00
3 thru 19 . . . . @1.00
20 A:Changeling,November, 1983 1.00

CAPTAIN STORM
May-June, 1964
1 IN(c),Killer Hunt 18.00
2 IN(c),First Shot-Last Shot . . . 10.00
3 JKu,Death of a PT Boat 10.00
4 IN(c),First Command-Last
    Command 10.00
5 IN(c), Killer Torpedo 10.00
6 JKu,IN(c),Medals For An Ocean10.00
7 IN(c),A Bullet For The General 10.00
8 IN(c),Death of A Sub 10.00
9 IN(c),Sink That Flattop 10.00
10 IN(c),Only The Last Man Lives 10.00

11 IN(c),Ride a Hot Torpedo ... 10.00
12 JKu(c),T.N.T. Tea Party Abroad
   PT 47 .... 10.00
13 JKu,Yankee Banzai 10.00
14 RH(c),Sink Capt. Storm 10.00
15 IN(c),My Enemy-My Friend .. 10.00
16 IN(c),Battle of the Stinging
   Mosquito 10.00
17 IN(c),First Shot for a Dead Man 10.00
18 March-April, 1967 .... 10.00

CATWOMAN
[Limited Series]
1 O:Catwoman 11.00
2 Catwoman'sSister kidnapped .. 8.00
3 Battle 6.00
4 Final,V:Batman 6.00
[Regular Series]
0 JBa,O:Catwoman 1.50
1 B:JDy(s),JBa,DG,A:Bane 4.00
2 JBa,DG,A:Bane 2.75
3 JBa,DG,at Santa Prisca 2.50
4 JBa,DG,Bane's Secret 2.50
5 JBa,V:Ninjas 2.00
6 JBa,A:Batman 1.75
7 JBa,A:Batman 1.75
8 JBa,V:Zephyr 1.75
9 JBa,V:Zephyr 1.75
10 JBa,V:Arms Dealer 1.75
11 JBa 1.75
12 JBa,Knights End #6,A:Batman 1.50
13 JBa,Knights End,Aftermath#2 . 1.75
14 JBa,Zero Hour 1.50
15 JBa,new path 1.50
16 JBa,Island forterss 1.50
17 .... 1.50
18 .... 1.50
19 Amazonia 1.50
20 Hollywood 1.50
21 JBa(c&a)V:Movie Monster
   [new Miraweb format begins] .. 1.95
22 JBa(c&a) Family Ties,pt.1 ... .95
Ann.#1 Elseworlds Story,A:Ra's Al
   Ghul 2.95
Ann.#2 JBa(c&a) Year One Annuals,
   Young Selina Kyle 3.95

CATWOMAN DEFIANT
1 TGr,DG,V:Mr.Handsome 6.00

CENTURIONS
June, 1987
1 DH,V:Doc Terror 1.00
2 DH,O:Centurions 1.00
3 DH,V:Doc Terror 1.00
4 DH,September, 1987 .... 1.00

CHAIN GANG WAR
1 I:Chain Gang 2.50
2 V:8-Ball 1.75
3 C:Deathstroke 1.75
4 C:Deathstroke 1.75
5 Embossed(c),A:Deathstroke .. 2.50
6 A:Deathstroke,Batman 1.75
7 V:Crooked Man 1.75
8 B:Crooked Man 1.75
9 V:Crooked Man 1.75
10 A:Deathstroke,C:Batman 1.75
11 A:Batman 1.75
12 E:Crooked Man,D:Chain Gang,
   Final Issue 1.75

CHALLENGERS OF THE UNKNOWN
April-May, 1958
1 JK&JK(c),The Man Who
   Tampered With Infinity ... 1,650.00
2 JK&JK(c),The Monster Maker 500.00
3 JK&JK(c),The Secret of the
   Sorcerer's Mirror 500.00
4 JK,WW,JK(c),The Wizard of
   Time 420.00
5 JK, WW&JK(c),The Riddle of
   the Star-Stone 420.00
6 JK,WW,JK(c),Captives of
   the Space Circus 420.00
7 JK,WW,JK(c),The Isle of
   No Return 420.00
8 JK,WW,JK&WW(c),The
   Prisoners of the Robot Planet 420.00
9 The Plot To Destroy Earth .. 200.00
10 The Four Faces of Doom .. 200.00
11 The Creatures From The
   Forbidden World 100.00
12 The Three Clues To Sorcery 100.00
13 The Prisoner of the
   Tiny Space Ball 100.00
14 O: Multi Man 100.00
15 The Lady Giant and the Beast 100.00
16 Prisoners of the Mirage World 100.00
17 The Secret of the
   Space Capsules 100.00
18 The Menace of Mystery Island 100.00
19 The Alien Who Stole a Planet 100.00
20 Multi-Man Strikes Back 100.00
21 Weird World That Didn't Exist 100.00
22 The Thing In
   Challenger Mountain 100.00
23 The Island In The Sky 60.00
24 The Challengers Die At Dawn 60.00
25 Captives of the Alien Hunter . 60.00
26 Death Crowns the
   Challenge King 60.00
27 Master of the Volcano Men .. 60.00
28 The Riddle of the
   Faceless Man 60.00
29 Four Roads to Doomsday ... 60.00
30 Multi-Man...Villain Turned
   Hero 60.00
31 O:Challengers 65.00
32 One Challenger Must Die ... 30.00
33 Challengers Meet Their Master 30.00
34 Beachhead, USA 30.00
35 War Against The Moon Beast 30.00
36 Giant In Challenger Mountain 30.00
37 Triple Terror of Mr. Dimension 30.00
38 Menace the Challengers Made 30.00
39 Phantom of the Fair 30.00
40 Super-Powers of the
   Challengers 30.00
41 The Challenger Who Quit ... 12.00
42 The League of
   Challenger-Haters 12.00
43 New look begins 12.00
44 The Curse of the Evil Eye ... 12.00
45 Queen of the
   Challenger-Haters 12.00
46 Strange Schemes of the
   Gargoyle 12.00
47 The Sinister Sponge 12.00
48 A:Doom Patrol 15.00
49 Tyrant Who Owned the World 12.00
50 Final Hours for the
   Challengers 12.00
51 A:Sea Devil 12.00
52 Two Are Dead - Two To Go . 12.00
53 Who is the Traitor Among Us? 12.00

54 War of the Sub-Humans 12.00
55 D:Red Ryan 12.00
56 License To Kill 12.00
57 Kook And The Kilowatt Killer . 12.00
58 Live Till Tomorrow 12.00
59 Seekeenakee - The Petrified
   Giant 12.00
60 R:Red Ryan 10.00
61 Robot Hounds of Chang 10.00
62 Legion of the Weird 10.00
63 None Shall Escape the
   Walking Evil 10.00
64 JKu(c),Invitation to a Hanging 10.00
65 The Devil's Circus 6.00
66 JKu(c),Rendezvous With
   Revenge 6.00
67 NA(c),The Dream Killers 6.00
68 NA(c),One of Us is a Madman 6.00
69 JKu(c),I:Corinna 6.00
70 NA(c),Scream of Yesterdays .. 6.00
71 NC(c),When Evil Calls 6.00
72 NA(c),A Plague of Darkness .. 6.00
73 NC(c),Curse of the Killer
   Time Forgot 6.00
74 GT&NA(c),A:Deadman 12.00
75 JK(c),Ultivac Is Loose 4.50
76 JKu(c),The Traitorous
   Challenger 4.50
77 JK(c),Menace of the
   Ancient Vials 4.50
78 JK(c),The Island of No Return . 4.50
79 JKu(c),The Monster Maker ... 4.50
80 NC(c),The Day The Earth
   Blew Up 4.50
81 MN&NA(c),Multi-Man's
   Master Plan 4.50
82 MN&NA(c),Swamp Thing 4.50
83 Seven Doorways to Destiny . 4.50
84 To Save A Monster 4.50
85 The Creature From The End
   Of Time 4.50
86 The War At Time's End 4.50
87 July, 1978 .... 4.50

CHALLENGERS OF THE UNKNOWN
1 BB(c) In The Spotlight 1.75
2 .... 1.75
3 Challengers 'Split Up' 1.75
4 'Separate Ways' 1.75
5 Moffet 1.75
6 GK(c),Challengers reunited ... 1.75
7 AAd(c),June pregnant 1.75
8 final issue 1.75

CHECKMATE
April, 1988
1 From Vigilante & Action Comics 3.75
2 Chicago Bombings cont. 2.50
3 V:Terrorist Right 2.00
4 V:Crime Lords Abroad,B.U.Story
   'Training of a Knight' begins .. 2.00
5 Renegade nation of Quarac .. 2.00
6 Secret Arms Deal 1.75
7 Checkmate Invades Quarac ... 1.75
8 Consequences-Quarac Invasion 1.75
9 Checkmate's security in doubt . 1.75
10 V:Counterfeiting Ring 1.75
11 Invasion X-over 1.75
12 Invasion Aftermath extra 1.75
13 CommanderH.Stein's vacation 1.75
14 R:Blackthorn 1.75
15 Janus Directive #1 .... 1.75
16 Janus Directive #3 .... 1.75

17 Janus Directive #6 . . . . 1.75
18 Janus Directive #9 . . . . 1.75
19 Reorganization of Group 1.75
20 'Shadow of Bishop'
   A:Peacemaker,pt.1 . . . . 1.75
21 Peacemaker behind Iron
   Curtain,pt.2 . . . . 1.75
22 Mystery of Bishop Cont.,pt.3 . . 1.75
23 European Scientists
   Suicides,pt.4 . . . . 1.75
24 Bishop Mystery cont.,pt.5 . . . . 1.50
25 Bishop's Identity Revealed 1.50
26 Mazarin kidnaps H.Stein's kids 1.50
27 Stein rescue attempt,I:Cypher . 1.50
28 A:Cypher, Bishop-Robots 1.50
29 A:Cypher,Blackthorn 1.50
30 Irish Knight W.O'Donnell/British
   Knight L.Hawkins team-up . . . 1.50
31 V:Cypher International 2.00
32 V:Cypher International 2.00
33 final issue (32 pages) 2.00

CHIAROSCURO: THE PRIVATE LIVES OF LEONARDO DaVINCI
Vertigo
1 Biographical, Adult 2.50

CHILDREN'S CRUSADE
Vertigo
1 NGa(s),CBa,MkB(i),F:Rowland,
   Payne (From Sandman) . . . 4.75
2 NGa(s),AaK(s),JaD(s),PSj,A:Tim
   Hunter,Suzy,Maxine,final issue 4.50

CHRISTMAS WITH THE SUPER-HEROES
1 JBy(c) 2.95
2 PC,GM,JBy,NKu,DG A:Batman
   Superman,Deadman,(last
   Supergirl appearance) 2.95

CINDER & ASHE
March, 1988
1 JL,I:Cinder & Ashe 2.00
2 JL,Viet Nam Flashbacks 2.00
3 JL,Truth About Lacey revealed 2.00
4 JL,final issue, June, 1988 . . . . 2.00

CLASH
1 AKu,I:Joe McLash(b/w) 4.95
2 AKu,Panja-Rise to Power 4.95
3 AKu,V:Archons,conclusion 4.95

CLAW THE UNCONQUERED
May-June, 1975
1 . . . . 2.00
2 . . . . 1.50
3 Nudity panel 1.25
4 . . . . 1.00
5 . . . . 1.00
6 . . . . 1.00
7 . . . . 1.00
8 KG 1.00
9 KG/BL,Origin 1.00
10 KG 1.00
11 KG 1.00
12 KG/BL,Aug.-Sept., 1978 . . . . 1.00

The Comet #16 © DC Comics, Inc.

COMET, THE
Impact
1 TL,I&O:Comet I:Applejack, Victoria
   Johnson, Ben Lee 1.50
2 TL,A:Applejack,Lance Perry . . . 1.25
3 TL,V:Anti-nuclear terrorists . . . 1.25
4 TL,I&V:Black Hood,I:Inferno . . . 1.25
5 V:Cyborg Soldier 1.25
6 TL,I:The Hangman 1.25
7 'Press Problems' 1.25
8 TL,Comet ID discovered 1.25
9 TL,'Bad Judgment' 1.25
10 Fly/Comet T.U.,V:Dolphus 1.25
11 V:Inferno 1.25
12 V:Inferno 1.25
13 O:Comet's Powers 1.25
14 O:Comet's Powers Pt.2 . . . . . 1.25
15 Rob finds his mother 1.25
16 V:Aliens 1.25
17 "Shocking Truth" 1.25
18 Last Issue 1.25
Ann.#1 Earthquest,w/trading card . 2.25

COMIC CAVALCADE
1942–43
1 Green Lantern, Flash,
   Wildcat, Wonder Woman,
   Black Pirate 5,500.00
2 ShM,B:Mutt & Jeff 1,300.00
3 ShM, B:HotHarrigan, Sorcerer,000.00
4 Gay Ghost, A:Scribby,
   A:Red Tornado 850.00
5 Green Lantern, Flash
   Wonder Woman 850.00
6 Flash, Wonder Woman
   Green Lantern 750.00
7 A:Red Tornado, E:Scribby . . 750.00
8 Flash, Wonder Woman
   Green Lantern 750.00
9 Flash, Wonder Woman
   Green Lantern 750.00
10 Flash, Wonder Woman
   Green Lantern 750.00
11 Flash, Wonder Woman
   Green Lantern 600.00
12 E:Red, White & Blue 600.00
13 A:Solomon Grundy 1,000.00
14 Flash, Wonder Woman,

   Green Lantern 600.00
15 B:Johnny Peril 600.00
16 Flash, Wonder Woman,
   Green Lantern 600.00
17 Flash, Wonder Woman,
   Green Lantern 600.00
18 Flash, Wonder Woman,
   Green Lantern 600.00
19 Flash, Wonder Woman,
   Green Lantern 600.00
20 Flash, Wonder Woman,
   Green Lantern 600.00
21 Flash, Wonder Woman,
   Green Lantern 600.00
22 A:Atom 600.00
23 A:Atom 600.00
24 A:Solomon Grundy 700.00
25 A:Black Canary 400.00
26 ATh, E:Mutt & Jeff 400.00
27 ATh,ATh(c) 400.00
28 ATh E:Flash, Wonder Woman
   Green Lantern 400.00
29 E:Johnny Peril 450.00
30 RG,B:Fox & Crow 300.00
31 thru 39 RG . . . . @150.00
40 RG,ShM 150.00
41 thru 49 RG,ShM . . . . @100.00
50 thru 62 RG,ShM . . . . @125.00
63 RG,ShM, July 1954 . . . . . . 200.00

CONGO BILL
August-September, 1954
1 . . . . 400.00
2 . . . . 350.00
3 thru 6 . . . . 300.00
7 Aug.-Sept.,1955 . . . . @300.00

CONGORILLA
1 R:Congo Bill 2.00
2 BB(c),V:Congo Bill 1.75
3 BB(c),V:Congo Bill 1.75

COOL WORLD
1 Prequel to Movie 1.75
2 Movie Adaption 1.75
3 Movie Adaption 1.75

COPS
1 PB,O:Cops,double-size 2.50
2 PB,V:Big Boss 1.50
3 PB,RT,V:Dr.Bad Vibes 1.25
4 BS,A:Sheriff Sundown 1.25
5 PB,Blitz the Robo-Dog 1.25
6 PB,A:Ms.Demeaner 1.25
7 PB,A:Tramplor 1.25
8 PB,V:BigBoss & Ally 1.25
9 PB,Cops Trapped 1.25
10 PB,Dr.Bad Vibes becomes
   Dr.Goodvibes 1.25
11 PB,V:Big Boss 1.25
12 PB,V:Dr.Badvibe's T.H.U.G.S 1.25
13 Berserko/Ms.Demeanor
   marriage proposal 1.25
14 A:Buttons McBoom-Boom . . . 1.25
15 Cops vs. Crooks, final issue . . 1.25

COSMIC BOY
December, 1986
1 KG,EC,Legends tie-in 2.00
2 KG,EC,'Is History Destiny' 1.25
3 KG,EC,'Past,Present,Future' . . 1.25
4 KG,EC,Legends 1.25

COSMIC ODYSSEY
1 MMi,A:Superman,Batman,John
  Stewart,Starfire,J'onnJ'onzz,
  NewGods,Demon,JSn story . . 6.00
2 MMi,'Disaster'(low dist) 6.50
3 MMi,Return to New Genesis . . 5.00
4 MMi,A:Dr.Fate, final 4.00

CRIMSON AVENGER
1 Mini-series 1.00
2 V:Black Cross 1.00
3 'V:Killers of the Dark Cross' . . . 1.00
4 'V:Dark Cross,final issue 1.00

CRISIS ON
INFINITE EARTHS
April, 1985
1 B:MWn(s),GP,DG,I:Pariah,I&O:Alex
  Luthor,D:Crime Syndicate . . . 10.00
2 GP,DG,V:Psycho Pirate,
  A:Joker,Batman 6.00
3 GP,DG,D:Losers 5.00
4 GP,D:Monitor,I:2nd Dr.Light . . 5.00
5 GP,JOy,I:Anti-Monitor 5.00
6 GP,JOy,I:2nd Wildcat,A:Fawcett,
  Quality & Charlton heroes . . . 5.00
7 GP,JOy,DG,D:Supergirl 8.00
8 GP,JOy,D:1st Flash 11.00
9 GP,JOy,D:Aquagirl 5.00
10 GP,JOy,D:Psimon,A:Spectre . . 5.00
11 GP,JOy,D:Angle Man 6.00
12 E:MWn(s),GP,JOy,D:Huntress,Kole,
  Kid Flash becomes 2nd Flash,
  D:Earth 2 . . . . 8.00

Crucible #6 © DC Comics, Inc.

CRUCIBLE
Impact
1 JQ,F:The Comet 1.25
2 JQ,A:Black Hood,Comet 1.50
3 JQ,Comet Vs.Black Hood 1.50
4 JQ,V:Tomorrow Men 1.50
5 JQ,Black Hod vs Shield 1.25
6 JQ,V:The Crucible 1.25

Crusaders #6 © DC Comics, Inc.

CRUSADERS
Impact
May, 1992
1 DJu(c),I:Crusaders,inc Trading
  cards 1.25
2 V:Kalathar 1.00
3 V:Kalathar 1.00
4 Crusaders form as group 1.00
5 V:Cyber-Punks 1.25
6 V:Cyborg Villains 1.25
7 Woj,Low,F:Fireball 1.25
8 Last Issue 1.25

DALE EVANS COMICS
September-October, 1948
1 Ph(c),ATh,B:Sierra Smith . . . 400.00
2 Ph(c),ATh 200.00
3 ATh 150.00
4 thru 11 . . . . @150.00
12 thru 23 . . . . @75.00
24 July-August, 1952 . . . . 75.00

DAMAGE
1 I:Damage,V:Metallo 2.00
2 V:Symbolix 2.00
3 V:Troll 2.00
4 V:Troll 2.00
5 A:New Titans,V:Baron 2.25
6 Zero Hour,A:New Titans 2.25
7 Trial 1.95
8 Fragments,pt.1 . . . . 1.95
9 Fragments,pt.2 . . . . 1.95
10 Fragments,pt.3 . . . . 1.95
11 Fragments,pt.4 . . . . 1.95
12 Fragments,pt.5 . . . . 1.95
13 Picking Up The Pieces,pt.1 . . 2.25
14 Picking Up The Pieces,pt.2
  A:The Ray 2.25

DANGER TRAIL
July-August, 1950
1 Cl,Ath,I:King For A Day . . . 550.00
2 ATh 400.00
3 ATh 550.00
4 ATh 350.00
5 March-April, 1951 . . . . 350.00

DANGER TRAIL
1 thru 4 Cl,FMc,F:King Faraday
  V:Cobra 2.00

DARK MANSION OF
FORBIDDEN LOVE, THE
September-October, 1971
1 . . . . 6.00
2 and 4 March-April, 1972 . . . @3.50

DARKSTARS
1 TC(c),LSn,I:Darkstars 3.50
2 TC(c),LSn,F:Ferin Colos 2.50
3 LSn,J:Mo,Flint,V:Evil Star 2.00
4 TC,V:Evilstar 4.00
5 TC,A:Hawkman,Hawkwoman . . 3.00
6 TC,A:Hawkman 2.50
7 TC,V:K'llash 2.00
8 F:Ferris Colos 2.00
9 Colos vs K'lassh 2.00
10 V:Con Artists 2.00
11 TC,Trinity#4,A:Green Lantern,
  L.E.G.I.O.N. 2.00
12 TC(c),Trinity#7,A:Green Lantern,
  L.E.G.I.O.N. 2.00
13 TC(c),V:Alien Underworld 2.00
14 I:Annihilator 2.00
15 V:Annihilator 2.00
16 V:Annihilator 2.00
17 Murders 2.00
18 B:Eve of Destruction 2.00
19 A:Flash 2.00
20 E:Eve of Destruction 2.00
21 A:John Stewart,Donna Troy . . 2.00
22 A:Controllers 2.00
23 Donna Troy is new Darkstar . . 2.25
24 Zero Hour,V:HalJordan,Entropy 2.25
25 Stewart 2.25
26 Alien criminals 2.25
27 and 28 . . . . @1.95
29 V:Alien Syndicate 1.95
30 A:Green Lantern 1.95
31 V:Darkseid 2.25
32 Crimelord/Syndicate War,pt.3,
  A:New Titans,Supergirl,
  Deathstroke 2.25

DC CHALLENGE
November, 1985
1 GC,Batman 4.00
2 Superman 1.50
3 Cl,Adam Strange 1.50
4 GK/KJ,Aquaman 1.50
5 DGb,Dr.Fate,Capt.Marvel 1.50
6 Dr. 13 . . . . 1.50
7 Gorilla Grodd 1.50
8 DG,Outsiders, New Gods 1.50
9 New Teen Titans,JLA 1.50
10 CS,New Teen Titans,JLA 1.50
11 KG,Outsiders 1.50
12 DCw,TMd,DSp,New Teen Titans,
  October, 1986 . . . . 2.50

DC COMICS PRESENTS
July-August, 1978
[all have Superman]
1 JL,DA,F:Flash 3.50
2 JL,DA,F:Flash 2.50
3 JL,F:Adam Strange 1.75
4 JL,F:Metal Men,A:Mr.IQ 1.75
5 MA,F:Aquaman 1.75
6 CS,F:Green Lantern 1.75
7 DD,F:Red Tornado 1.75

8 MA,F:Swamp Thing 1.75
9 JSon,JA,RH,F:Wonder Woman 1.75
10 JSon,JA,F:Sgt.Rock 1.75
11 JSon,F:Hawkman 1.75
12 RB,DG,F:Mr.Miracle 1.75
13 DD,DG,F:Legion 2.00
14 DD,DG,F:Superboy 1.50
15 JSon,F:Atom,C:Batman 1.50
16 JSon,F:Black Lightning 1.50
17 JL,F:Firestorm 1.50
18 DD,F:Zatanna 1.50
19 JSon,F:Batgirl 2.00

DC Comics Presents #49
© DC Comics, Inc.

20 JL,F:Green Arrow 1.50
21 JSon,JSa,F:Elongated Man . . . 1.50
22 DD,FMc,F:Captain Comet . . . 1.50
23 JSon,F:Dr.Fate 1.50
24 JL,F:Deadman 1.50
25 DD,FMc,F:Phantom Stranger . 1.50
26 GP,DG,JSn,I:New Teen Titans,
  Cyborg,Raven,Starfire
  A:Green Lantern 12.00
27 JSn,RT,I:Mongul 3.00
28 JSn,RT,GK,F:Mongul 2.00
29 JSn,RT,AS,F:Spectre 2.00
30 CS,AS,F:Black Canary 1.50
31 JL,DG,AS,F:Robin 1.50
32 KS,AS,F:Wonder Woman . . . 1.50
33 RB,DG,AS,F:Captain Marvel . 1.50
34 RB,DG,F:Marvel Family 1.50
35 CS,GK,F:Man-bat 1.50
36 JSn,F:Starman 2.00
37 JSn,AS,F:Hawkgirl 1.50
38 GP(c),DH,AS,DG,D:Crimson
  Avenger,F:Flash 1.50
39 JSon,AS,F:PlasticMan,Toyman 1.50
40 IN,FMc,AS,F:Metamorpho 1.50
41 JL,FMc,GC,RT,I:New Wonder
  Woman,A:Joker 5.00
42 IN,FMc,F:Unknown Soldier . . . 1.50
43 BB(c),CS,F:Legion 1.50
44 IN,FMc,F:Dial H for Hero . . . 2.00
45 RB,F:Firestorm 1.50
46 AS,I:Global Guardians 1.50
47 CS,I:Masters of Universe 1.50
48 GK(c),AA,IN,FMc,F:Aquaman . 1.50
49 RB,F:Shazam!,V:Black Adam . 1.50
50 KS,CS,F:Clark Kent 1.50
51 AS,FMc,CS,F:Atom,Masters

of the Universe 1.50
52 KG,F:Doom Patrol,
  I:Ambush Bug 1.50
53 CS,TD,RA,DG,I:Atari Force . . 1.50
54 DN,DA,F:Gr.Arrow,Bl.Canary . 1.50
55 AS,F:Air Wave,A:Superboy . 1.50
56 GK(c),F:Power Girl 1.50
57 AS,FMc,F:Atomic Knights . . . 1.50
58 GK(c),AS,F:Robin,Elongated
  Man 1.50
59 KG,KS,F:Ambush Bug 1.50
60 GK(c),IN,TD,F:Guardians . . . 1.50
61 GP,F:Omac 1.50
62 GK(c),IN,F:Freedom Fighters . 1.50
63 AS,EC,F:Amethyst 1.50
64 GK(c),AS,FMc,F:Kamandi . . . 1.50
65 GM,F:Madame Xanadu 1.50
66 JKu,F:Demon 1.50
67 CS,MA,F:Santa Claus 1.50
68 GK(c),CS,MA,F:Vixen 1.50
69 IN,DJ,F:Blackhawk 1.50
70 AS,TD,F:Metal Men 1.50
71 CS,F:Bizarro 1.50
72 AS,DG,F:Phant.Stranger,Joker 3.50
73 CI,F:Flash 1.50
74 AS,RT,F:Hawkman 1.50
75 TMd,F:Arion 1.50
76 EB,F:Wonder Woman 1.50
77 CS,F:Forgotten Heroes 3.50
78 CS,F:Forgotten Villains 3.50
79 CS,AW,F:Legion 1.50
80 CS,F:Clark Kent 1.50
81 KG,BO,F:Ambush Bug 1.50
82 KJ,F:Adam Strange 1.50
83 IN,F:Batman/Outsiders 1.50
84 JK,ATh,MA,F:Challengers . . . 1.50
85 RV,AW,AMo(s),
  F:Swamp Thing 4.00
86 Crisis,F:Supergirl 1.50
87 CS,AW,Crisis,I:Earth Prime
  Superboy 1.50
88 KG,Crisis,F:Creeper 1.50
89 MMi(c),AS,F:Omega Men . . . 1.50
90 DCw,F:Firestorm,Capt.Atom . 1.50
91 CS,F:Captain Comet 1.50
92 CS,F:Vigilante 1.50
93 JSn(c),AS,KS,F:Elastic Four . 1.50
94 GP(c),TMd,DH,Crisis,F:Lady
  Quark,Pariah,Harbinger 1.50
95 MA(i),F:Hawkman 1.50
96 JSon,KS,F:Blue Devil 1.50
97 RV,F:Phantom Zone Villians,
  final issue,double-sized 1.50
Ann.#1,RB,F:Earth 2 Superman . 1.50
Ann.#2 GK(c),KP,I:Superwoman . 1.25
Ann.#3 GK,F:Captain Marvel . . 1.25
Ann.#4 EB,JOy,F:Superwoman . 1.25

DC/MARVEL
CROSSOVER CLASSICS
TPB, rep. all x-overs 17.95

DC GRAPHIC NOVEL
November, 1983
1 JL,Star Raiders 6.00
2 Warlords 6.00
3 EC,Medusa Chain 6.00
4 JK,Hunger Dogs 6.00
5 Me and Joe Priest 7.00
6 Space Clusters 7.00

DC S.F. GRAPHIC NOVEL
1 KG,Hell on Earth 6.00
2 Nightwings 6.00

3 Frost and Fire 6.00
4 Merchants of Venus 6.00
5 Metalzoic 6.00
6 MR,Demon-Glass Hand 6.00
7 Sandkings 6.00

DC SPECIAL
October-December, 1968
[All reprint]
1 CI,F:Flash,Batman,Adam Strange,
  (#1 thru #21 reps) 8.00
2 F:Teen Titans 5.00
3 GA,F:Black Canary 5.00
4 Mystery 5.00
5 JKu,F:Viking Prince/Sgt.Rock . 5.00
6 Wild Frontier 5.00
7 F:Strange Sports 5.00
8 Wanted 5.00
9 . . . . 5.00
10 LAW 5.00
11 NA,BWr,F:Monsters 5.00
12 JKu,F:Viking Prince 5.00
13 F:Strange Sports 5.00
14 Wanted,F:Penguin/Joker 6.00
15 GA,F:Plastic Man 6.00
16 F:Super Heroes & Gorillas . . . 3.50
17 F:Green Lantern 3.50
18 Earth Shaking Stories 3.50
19 F:War Against Gianta 3.50
20 Green Lantern 3.50
21 F:War Against Monsters 3.50
22 Three Musketeers 3.50
23 Three Musketeers 3.50
24 Three Musketeers 3.50
25 Three Musketeers 3.50
26 F:Enemy Ace(rep) 3.50
27 RB,JR,F:Captain Comet 3.50
28 DN,DA,Earth disasters 3.50
29 JSon,BL,O:JSA 4.00

DC SPECIAL SERIES
September, 1977
1 MN,DD,IN,FMc,JSon,JA,BMc,
  JRu,F:Batman,Flash,Green
  Lantern,Atom,Aquaman 5.00
2 BWr(c),BWr,F:Swamp Thing rep. 4.00
3 JKu(c),F:Sgt.Rock 3.00
4 AN,RT,Unexpected Annual . . . 3.00
5 CS,F:Superman 3.25
6 BMc(i),Secret Society Vs.JLA . 3.00
7 AN,F:Ghosts 3.00
8 RE,DG,F:Brave&Bold,Deadman 3.50
9 SD,RH,DAy,F:Wonder Woman . 3.00
10 JSon,MN,DN,TA,Secret Origins,
  O:Dr.Fate 3.00
11 JL,KS,MA,IN,WW,AS,F:Flash . 3.50
12 MK(c),RT,RH,TS,Secrets of
  Haunted House 3.00
13 JKu(c),RT,SBi,RE,F:Sgt.Rock . 3.00
14 BWr(c),F:Swamp Thing rep. . . 3.50
15 MN,JRu,MR,DG,MGo,
  F:Batman 4.50
16 RH,D:Jonah Hex 3.25
17 F:Swamp Thing rep. 3.50
18 JK(c),digest,F:Sgt.Rock rep. . 3.00
19 digest,Secret Origins
  O:Wonder Woman 3.50
20 BWr(c),F:Swamp Thing rep. . 3.50
21 FM,JL,DG,RT,DA,F:Batman,
  Legion 18.00
22 JKu(c),F:G.I.Combat 3.25
23 digest size,F:Flash 3.25
24 F:Worlds Finest 3.25
25 F:Superman II,Photo Album . 3.50
26 RA,F:Superman's Fortress . . 4.00

27 JL,DG,F:Batman vs.Hulk 7.50

DC SUPER-STARS
1 F:Teen Titans rep. 4.00
2 F:DC Super-Stars of Space . . . 1.50
3 CS,F:Superman,Legion 2.50
4 DC,MA,F:Super-Stars of Space 1.50
5 CI,F:Flash rep. 1.50
6 MA,F:Super-Stars of Space . . . 1.50
7 F:Aquaman rep. 1.50
8 CI,MA,F:Adam Strange 4.00
9 F:Superman rep. 1.50
10 DD,FMc,F:Superhero Baseball
   Special,A:Joker 5.50
11 GM,Super-Stars of Magic 1.50
12 CS,MA,F:Superboy 1.50
13 SA 1.50
14 RB,BL,JA,JRu,Secret Origins . 1.50
15 JKu(c),RB,RT(i),War Heroes . . 1.50
16 DN,BL,I:Star Hunters 1.50
17 JSon,MGr,BL,I&O:Huntress,O:Gr.
   Arrow,D:EarthII Catwoman . . 3.50
18 RT,DG,BL,F:Deadman,Phantom
   Stranger 2.50

DC UNIVERSE: TRINITY
1 TC,GeH,BKi,F:Darkstars,Green
  Lantern,L.E.G.I.O.N.,V:Triarch . 3.50
2 BKi,SHa,F:Darkstars,Green Lantern,
  L.E.G.I.O.N.,V:Triarch 3.50

DEADMAN
May, 1985
1 CI,NA,rep 5.00
2 NA,rep. 4.00
3 NA,rep. 3.00
4 NA,rep. 3.00
5 NA,rep. 3.00
6 NA,rep. 3.00
7 NA,rep.November, 1985. . . . . . 3.00
[Mini-Series]
March, 1986
1 JL,A:Batman 3.00
2 JL,V:Sensei,A:Batman 2.50
3 JL,D:Sensei 2.00
4 JL,V:Jonah, final issue 2.00

DEADMAN: EXORCISM
[Limited-Series]
1 KJo,A:Phantom Stranger 5.25
2 KJo,A:Phantom Stranger 5.25

DEADMAN: LOST SOULS
TPB Mike Baron, Kelly Jones . . 19.95

DEADMAN: LOVE AFTER DEATH
1 KJo,Circus of Monsters 4.25
2 KJo,Circus of Monsters 4.25

DEATH: THE HIGH COST OF LIVING
Vertigo
1 B:NGa(s),CBa,MBu(i),Death
  becomes Human,A:Hettie 5.00
1a Platinum Ed. 45.00
2 CBa,MBu(i),V:Eremite,A:Hettie . 4.50
3 E:NGa(s),CBa,MBu(i),V:Eremite,
  A:Hettie 3.50
3a Error Copy 7.00
HC 19.95
TPB w/Tori Amos Intro 12.95

DEADSHOT
1 LMc,From Suicide Squad . . 2.00
2 LMc,Search for Son 2.00
3 LMc,V:Pantha 1.50
4 LMc,final issue 1.50

DEATH GALLERY
Vertigo
1 DMc(c),NGa Death Sketch
  Various Pinups 3.50

Deathstroke the Terminator #17
© DC Comics, Inc.

DEATHSTROKE: THE TERMINATOR
1 MZ(c),(from New Teen Titans)
  SE,I:2nd Ravager 6.00
1a Second Printing,Gold 3.00
2 MZ(c),SE,Quraci Agents 4.00
3 SE,V:Ravager 3.50
4 SE,D:2ndRavager(Jackel) 3.50
5 Winter Green Rescue Attempt . 3.00
6 MZ(c),SE,B:City of Assassins,
  A:Batman 3.00
7 MZ(c),SE,A:Batman 2.50
8 MZ(c),SE,A:Batman 2.00
9 MZ(c),SE,E:City of Assassins,
  A:Batman;I:2nd Vigilante 2.00
10 MZ(c),ANi,GP,A:2nd Vigilante . 2.00
11 MZ(c),ANi,GP,A:2nd Vigilante . 2.00
12 MGo,Short Stories re:Slade . . 2.00
13 SE,V:Gr.Lant.,Flash,Aquaman . 2.00
14 ANi,Total Chaos#1,A:New Titans,
  Team Titans,V:Nightwing 2.00
15 ANi,Total Chaos#4,A:New Titans,
  Team Titans,I:Sweet Lili 2.00
16 ANi,Total Chaos#7 . . . . 2.00
17 SE,Titans Sell-Out #2
  A:Brotherhood of Evil 2.00
18 SE,V:Cheshire,R:Speedy 2.00
19 SE,V:Broth.of Evil,A:Speedy . . 2.00
20 SE,MZ(c),V:Checkmate 2.00
21 SE,MZ(c),A:Checkmate 2.00
22 MZ(c),Quality of Mercy#1 . . . 2.00
23 MZ(c),Quality of Mercy#2 . . . 2.00
24 MZ(c),V:The Black Dome 2.00
25 MZ(c),V:The Black Dome 2.00
26 MZ(c),SE,in Kenya 2.00
27 MZ(c),SE,B:World Tour,

  in Germany 2.00
28 MZ(c),SE,in France 2.00
29 KM(c),SE,in Hong Kong 2.00
30 SE,A:Vigilante 2.00
31 SE,in Milwaukie 2.00
32 SE,in Africa 2.00
33 SE,I:Fleur de Lis 2.00
34 SE,E:World Tour 2.00
35 V:Mercenaries 2.00
36 V:British General 2.00
37 V:Assassin 2.00
38 A:Vigilante 2.25
39 A:Vigilante 2.25
40 Wedding in Red 2.25
Ann.#1 Eclipso,A:Vigilante 3.75
Ann.#2 SE,I:Gunfire 3.50
Ann.#3 Elseworlds Story 4.25
TPB Full Circle rep#1-#4,
  New Titans#70 . . . . 12.95
Becomes:
DEATHSTROKE: THE HUNTED
0 Slade 2.50
41 Bronze Tiger 2.25
42 Wounded 2.25
43 . . . . 1.95
44 . . . . 1.95
45 A:New Titans 1.95
Becomes:
DEATHSTROKE
46 Checkmate,Wintergreen 1.95
47 I:New Vigilante 1.95
48 Crimelord/Syndicate War,pt.1 . 2.25
49 Crimelord/Syndicate War,pt.4
  A:Supergirl, New Titans, Hawkman
  Blood Pack 2.25

DEATHWISH
1 New mini-series 1.75
2 F:Rahme 2.50
3 . . . . 2.50
4 V:Boots 2.50

DEMOLITION MAN
1 thru 4 Movie Adapt 1.75

DEMON
[1st Regular Series]
1 JK,I:Demon 30.00
2 JK 18.00
3 JK 12.00
4 JK 12.00
5 JK 12.00
6 JK 11.00
7 JK 11.00
8 JK 11.00
9 JK 11.00
10 JK 9.00
11 JK 9.00
12 JK 9.00
13 JK 9.00
14 JK 9.00
15 JK 9.00
16 JK 9.00
[Limited Series]
0 Relationships 1.95
1 MWg,B:Jason Blood's Case . . . 5.00
2 MWg,Fight to Save Gotham . . . 3.00
3 MWg,Fight to Save Gotham . . . 2.50
4 MWg,final issue 2.50
[2nd Regular Series]
1 VS,A:Etrigan (32 pages) 4.00
2 VS,V:TheCrone 2.50

Demon (2nd Series) #53
© DC Comics, Inc.

3 VS,A:Batman	2.25
4 VS,A:Batman	2.25
5 VS,ThePit	2.25
6 VS,In Hell	2.25
7 VS,Etrigan-King of Hell	2.25
8 VS,Klarion the Witch Boy	2.25
9 VS,Jason Leaves Gotham	2.25
10 VS,A:PhantomStranger	2.25
11 VS,A:Klarion,C:Lobo	3.00
12 VS:Etrigan Vs. Lobo	2.50
13 VS:Etrigan Vs. Lobo	2.50
14 VS,V:Odd Squad,A:Lobo	2.50
15 VS,Etrigan Vs.Lobo	2.50
16 VS,Etrigan & Jason Blood switch bodies	2.00
17 VS, War of the Gods x-over	2.00
18 VS,V:Wotan,A:Scape Goat	2.00
19 VS,O:Demon,Demon/Lobo pin-up	3.00
20 VS,V:Golden Knight	2.00
21 VS,Etrigan/Jason, A:Lobo,Glenda	2.00
22 MWg,V:Mojo & Hayden	2.25
23 VS,A:Robin	2.00
24 VS,A:Robin	2.00
25 VS,V:Gideon Ryme	2.00
26 VS,B:America Rules	2.00
27 VS,A:Superman	2.00
28 VS,A:Superman	2.00
29 VS,E:America Rules	2.00
30 R:Asteroth	2.00
31 VS(c),A:Lobo	2.00
32 VS(c),A:Lobo,W.Woman	2.00
33 VS(c),A:Lobo,V:Asteroth	2.00
34 A:Lobo	2.00
35 A:Lobo,V:Belial	2.00
36 A:Lobo,V:Belial	2.00
37 A:Lobo,Morax	2.00
38 A:Lobo,Morax	2.00
39 A:Lobo	2.00
40 New Direction,B:GEn(s)	4.00
41 V:Mad Bishop	2.50
42 V:Demons	2.25
43 A:Hitman	2.00
44 V:Gotho-Demon,A:Hitman	2.00
45 V:Gotho-Demon,A:Hitman	2.00
46 R:Haunted Tank	2.50

47 V:Zombie Nazis	2.00
48 A:Haunted Tank,V:Zombie Nazis	2.00
49 b:Demon's Son,A:Joe Gun	1.95
50 GEn(s)	2.50
51 GEn(s),Son & Lovers	2.25
52 Etrigan & son	1.95
53 Glenda & child	1.95
54 Suffer the Children	1.95
55 Rebellion	1.95
56 F:Etrigan	1.95
57 Last Stand	1.95
58 Last issue	1.95
Ann.#1 Eclipso,V:Klarion	3.25
Ann.#2 I:Hitman	3.75

DETECTIVE COMICS
March, 1937

1 I:Slam Bradley	38,000.00
2 JoS	10,000.00
3 JoS	7,000.00
4 JoS	4,500.00
5 JoS	4,000.00
6 JoS	3,000.00
7 JoS	3,000.00
8 JoS,Mr. Chang(c)	3,400.00
9 JoS	3,000.00
10	3,000.00
11	2,200.00
12	2,200.00
13	2,200.00
14	2,200.00
15	2,200.00
16	2,200.00
17 I:Fu Manchu	2,200.00
18 Fu Manchu(c)	2,200.00
19	1,900.00
20 I:Crimson Avenger	3,500.00
21	1,800.00
22	2,200.00
23	1,800.00
24	1,800.00
25	1,800.00
26	1,800.00
27 BK,I:Batman	120,000.00
28 BK,V:Frenchy Blake	9,000.00
29 BK,I:Doctor Death	17,000.00
30 BK,V:Dr. Death	3,800.00
31 BK,I:Monk	17,000.00
32 BK,V:Monk	3,500.00
33 O:Batman,V:Scarlet Horde	24,000.00
34 V:Due D'Orterre	3,500.00
35 V:Sheldon Lenox	5,000.00
36 I:Hugo Strange	3,600.00
37 V:Count Grutt, last Batman solo	3,500.00
38 I:Robin, the Boy Wonder	22,000.00
39 V:Green Dragon	3,000.00
40 I:Clayface (Basil Karlo)	3,800.00
41 V:Graves	2,000.00
42 V:Pierre Antal	1,300.00
43 V:Harliss Greer	1,300.00
44 Robin Dream Story	1,300.00
45 V:Joker	2,000.00
46 V:Hugo Strange	1,100.00
47 Meets Harvey Midas	1,100.00
48 Meets Henry Lewis	1,100.00
49 V:Clayface	1,100.00
50 V:Three Devils	1,100.00
51 V:Mindy Gang	900.00
52 V:Loo Chung	900.00
53 V:Toothy Hare gang	900.00
54 V:Hook Morgan	900.00
55 V:Dr. Death	900.00
56 V:Mad Mack	900.00

Detective Comics #27
© DC Comics, Inc.

57 Meet Richard Sneed	900.00
58 I:Penguin	2,300.00
59 V:Penguin	1,100.00
60 V:Joker,I:Air Wave	1,000.00
61 The Three Racketeers	900.00
62 V:Joker	1,200.00
63 I:Mr. Baffle	800.00
64 I:Boy Commandos,V:Joker	2,200.00
65 Meet Tom Bolton	1,800.00
66 I:Two-Face	1,800.00
67 V:Penguin	1,200.00
68 V:Two-Face	1,000.00
69 V:Joker	1,000.00
70 Meet the Amazing Carlo	750.00
71 V:Joker	800.00
72 V:Larry the Judge	650.00
73 V:Scarecrow	650.00
74 I:Tweedledum & Tweedledee	650.00
75 V:Robber Baron	650.00
76 V:Joker	1,000.00
77 V:Dr. Matthew Thorne	650.00
78 V:Baron Von Luger	650.00
79 'Destiny's' Auction	650.00
80 V:Two-Face	750.00
81 I:Cavalier	550.00
82 V:Blackee Blondeen	550.00
83 V:Dr. Goodwin	600.00
84 V:Ivan Krafft	550.00
85 V:Joker	700.00
86 V:Gentleman Jim Jewell	500.00
87 V:Penguin	550.00
88 V:Big Hearted John	500.00
89 V:Cavalier	500.00
90 V:Capt. Ben	500.00
91 V:Joker	600.00
92 V:Braing Bulow	475.00
93 V:'Tiger' Ragland	475.00
94 V:Lefty Goran	475.00
95 V:The Blaze	475.00
96 F:Alfred	475.00
97 V:Nick Petri	475.00
98 Meets Casper Thurbridge	475.00
99 V:Penguin	750.00
100 V:Digger	750.00
101 V:Joe Bart	450.00
102 V:Joker	625.00
103 Meet Dean Gray	450.00
104 V:Fat Frank gang	450.00
105 V:Simon Gurlan	450.00

All comics prices listed are for *Near Mint* condition.

Detective Comics #68
© DC Comics, Inc.

106 V:Todd Torrey	450.00
107 V:Bugs Scarpis	450.00
108 Meet Ed Gregory	450.00
109 V:Joker	600.00
110 V:Prof. Moriarty	450.00
111 'Coaltown, USA'	450.00
112 'Case Without A Crime'	450.00
113 V:Blackhand	450.00
114 V:Joker	600.00
115 V:Basil Grimes	450.00
116 A:Carter Nichols, Robin Hood	450.00
117 'Steeplejack's Slowdown'	450.00
118 V:Joker	600.00
119 V:Wiley Derek	450.00
120 V:Penguin	700.00
121 F:Commissioner Gordon	450.00
122 V:Catwoman	450.00
123 V:Shiner	450.00
124 V:Joker	550.00
125 V:Thinker	450.00
126 V:Penguin	450.00
127 V:Dr. Agar	450.00
128 V:Joker	550.00
129 V:Diamond Dan mob	450.00
130	450.00
131 V:'Trigger Joe'	350.00
132 V:Human Key	350.00
133 Meets Arthur Loom	350.00
134 V:Penguin	375.00
135 A:Baron Frankenstein, Carter Nichols	350.00
136 A:Carter Nichols	350.00
137 V:Joker	450.00
138 V:Joker,O:Robotman	700.00
139 V:Nick Bailey	350.00
140 I:Riddler	2,500.00
141 V:'Blackie' Nason	400.00
142 V:Riddler	750.00
143 V:Pied Piper	400.00
144 A:Kay Kyser (radio personality)	400.00
145 V:Yellow Mask mob	400.00
146 V:J.J. Jason	400.00
147 V:Tiger Shark	400.00
148 V:Prof. Zero	400.00
149 V:Joker	500.00
150 V:Dr. Paul Visio	400.00
151 I&O:Pow Wow Smith	425.00

152 V:Goblin	425.00
153 V:Slits Danton	425.00
154 V:Hatch Marlin	425.00
155 A:Vicki Vale	425.00
156 'The Batmobile of 1950'	425.00
157 V:Bart Gillis	400.00
158 V:Dr. Doom	400.00
159 V:T. Worthington Chubb	400.00
160 V:Globe-Trotter	400.00
161 V:Bill Waters	425.00
162 Batman on railroad	425.00
163 V:Slippery Jim Elgin	425.00
164 Bat-signal story	425.00
165 'The Strange Costumes of Batman'	425.00
166 Meets John Gillen	425.00
167 A:Carter Nichols, Cleopatra	425.00
168 O:Joker	3,000.00
169 V:'Squint' Tolmar	425.00
170 Batman teams with Navy and Coast Guard	425.00
171 V:Penguin	550.00
172 V:Paul Gregorian	400.00
173 V:Killer Moth	400.00
174 V:Dagger	400.00
175 V:Kangaroo Kiley	400.00
176 V:Mr. Velvet	400.00
177 Bat-Cave story	350.00
178 V:Baron Swane	350.00
179 'Mayor Bruce Wayne'	350.00
180 V:Joker	375.00
181 V:Human Magnet	350.00
182 V:Maestro Dorn	350.00
183 V:John Cook	350.00
184 I:Firefly(Garfield Lynns)	350.00
185 'Secret's of Batman's Utility Belt'	350.00
186 'The Flying Bat-Cave'	350.00
187 V:Two-Face	350.00
188 V:William Milden	350.00
189 V:Styx	350.00
190 Meets Dr. Sampson, O:Batman	450.00
191 V:Executioner	325.00
192 V: Nails Riley	325.00
193 V:Joker	325.00
194 V:Sammy Sabre	325.00
195 Meets Hugo Marmon	325.00
196 V:Frank Lumardi	325.00
197 V:Wrecker	325.00
198 Batman in Scotland	325.00
199 V:Jack Baker	325.00
200 V:Brand Keldon	400.00
201 Meet Human Target	300.00
202 V:Jolly Roger	300.00
203 V:Catwoman	325.00
204 V:Odo Neral	300.00
205 O:Bat-Cave	400.00
206 V:Trapper	300.00
207 Meets Merko the Great	300.00
208 V:Groff	300.00
209 V:Inventor	300.00
210 V:'Brain' Hobson	300.00
211 V:Catwoman	300.00
212 Meets Jonathan Bard	300.00
213 V:Mirror-Man	350.00
214 'The Batman Encyclopedia'	250.00
215 I:Ranger, Legionairy, Gaucho & Musketeer,A:Knight & Squire (See World's Finest 89)	250.00
216 A:Brane Taylor	250.00
217 Meets Barney Barrows	250.00
218 V:Dr. Richard Marston	250.00
219 V:Marty Mantee	250.00
220 A:Roger Bacon, historical	

scientist/philosopher	250.00
221 V:Paul King	250.00
222 V:'Big Jim' Jarrell	250.00
223 V:'Blast' Varner	250.00
224	250.00
225 I&O:Martian Manhunter (J'onn J'onzz)	3,700.00
226 O:Robin's costume, A:J'onn J'onzz	850.00
227 A:Roy Raymond, J'onn J'onzz	350.00
228 A:Roy Raymond, J'onnJ'onz	325.00
229 A:Roy Raymond, J'onnJ'onz	325.00
230 A:Martian Manhunter,I:Mad Hatter	375.00
231 A:Batman,Jr.,Roy Raymond J'onn J'onzz	225.00
232 A:J'onn J'onzz	210.00
233 I&O:Batwoman	950.00
234 V:Jay Caird	225.00
235 O:Batman's Costume	360.00
236 V:Wallace Walby	235.00
237 F:Robin	210.00
238 V:Checkmate(villain)	210.00
239 Batman robot story	210.00
240 V:Burt Weaver	210.00
241 The Rainbow Batman	210.00
242 Batcave story	165.00
243 V:Jay Vanney	165.00
244 O:Batarang	165.00
245 F:Comm.Gordon	165.00
246	165.00
247 I:Professor Milo	165.00

Detective Comics #166
© DC Comics, Inc.

248	165.00
249 V:Collector	165.00
250 V:John Stannor	165.00
251 V:Brand Ballard	155.00
252 Batman in a movie	155.00
253 I:Terrible Trio	155.00
254 A:Bathound	155.00
255 V:Fingers Nolan	155.00
256 Batman outer-space story	155.00
257 Batman sci-fi story	155.00

258 Batman robot story 155.00
259 I:Calendar Man 155.00
260 Batman outer space story . 155.00
261 I:Dr. Double X 110.00
262 V:Jackal-Head 110.00
263 V:The Professor 110.00
264 . . . . 110.00
265 O:Batman retold 200.00
266 V:Astro 110.00
267 I&O:Bat-Mite 130.00
268 V:"Big Joe" Foster 110.00
269 V:Director 110.00
270 Batman sci-fi story 120.00
271 V:Crimson Knight,O:Martian
    Manhunter(retold) 120.00
272 V:Crystal Creature 120.00
273 A:Dragon Society 105.00
274 V:Nails Lewin 100.00
275 A:Zebra-Man 90.00
276 A:Batmite 90.00
277 Batman Monster story 90.00
278 A:Professor Simms 90.00
279 Batman robot story 90.00
280 A:Atomic Man 90.00
281 Batman robot story 71.00
282 Batman sci-fi story 71.00
283 V:Phantom of Gotham City . 71.00
284 V:Hal Durgan 71.00
285 V:Harbin 71.00
286 A:Batwoman 71.00
287 A:Bathound 71.00
288 V:Multicreature 71.00
289 A:Bat-Mite 71.00
290 Batman's robot story 71.00
291 Batman sci-fi story 71.00
292 Last Roy Raymond 71.00
293 A:Aquaman,J'onnJ'onzz . . . 71.00
294 V:Elemental Men,
    A:Aquaman 71.00
295 A:Aquaman 71.00
296 A:Aquaman 71.00
297 A:Aquaman 71.00
298 I:Clayface(Matt Hagen) . . . 130.00
299 Batman sci-fi stories 66.00
300 I:Mr.Polka-dot,E:Aquaman . 70.00
301 A:J'onnJ'onzz 50.00
302 A:J'onnJ'onz 40.00
303 A:J'onnJ'onnz 40.00
304 A:Clayface,J'onnJ'onz 40.00
305 Batman sci-fi story 40.00
306 A:J'onnJ'onnz 40.00
307 A:J'onnJ'onnz 40.00
308 A:J'onnJ'onnz 40.00
309 A:J'onnJ'onnz 40.00
310 A:Bat-Mite,J'onnJ'onnz . . . 40.00
311 I:Cat-Man,Zook 45.00
312 A:Clayface,J'onnJ'onnz . . . 35.00
313 A:J'onnJ'onnz 35.00
314 A:J'onnJ'onnz 35.00
315 I:Jungle Man 38.00
316 A:Dr.DoubleX,J'onnJ'onz . . 35.00
317 A:J'onnJ'onnz 35.00
318 A:Cat-Man,J'onnJ'onnz . . . 35.00
319 A:J'onnJ'onnz 35.00
320 A:Vicki Vale 35.00
321 I:Terrible Trio 38.00
322 A:J'onnJ'onnz 35.00
323 I:Zodiac Master,
    A:J'onn J'onnz 35.00
324 A:Mad Hatter,J'onnJ'onnz . . 35.00
325 A:Cat-Man,J'onnJ'onnz . . . 35.00
326 Batman sci-fi story 35.00
327 CI,25th ann,symbol change . 52.00
328 D:Alfred,I:WayneFoundation 70.00
329 A:Elongated Man 30.00

Detective Comics #277
© DC Comics, Inc.

330 "Fallen Idol of Gotham" 30.00
331 A:Elongated Man 26.00
332 A:Joker 30.00
333 A:Gorla 25.00
334 . . . . 25.00
335 . . . . 25.00
336 . . . . 25.00
337 "Deep Freeze Menace 25.00
338 . . . . 25.00
339 . . . . 25.00
340 . . . . 25.00
341 A:Joker 30.00
342 . . . . 25.00
343 BK,CI,Elongated Man 20.00
344 . . . . 20.00
345 CI,I:Blockbuster 20.00
346 . . . . 20.00
347 CI,Elongated Man 20.00
348 Elongated Man 20.00
349 BK(c),CI,Blockbuster 20.00
350 Elongated Man 20.00
351 CI,A:Elongated Man,
    I:Cluemaster 20.00
352 BK,Elongated Man 20.00
353 . . . . 20.00
354 BK,Elongated Man,I:Dr.
    Tzin-Tzin 20.00
355 CI,Elongated Man 20.00
356 BK,Outsider,Alfred 20.00
357 . . . . 20.00
358 BK,Elongated Man 20.00
359 I:new Batgirl 35.00
360 . . . . 20.00
361 CI 20.00
362 CI,Elongated Man 20.00
363 CI,Elongated Man 20.00
364 BK,Elongated Man 20.00
365 A:Joker 32.00
366 Elongated Man 20.00
367 Elongated Man 20.00
368 BK,Elongated Man 20.00
369 CA,Elongated Man,
    Catwoman 35.00
370 BK,Elongated Man 20.00
371 BK,Elongated Man 16.00

372 BK,Elongated Man 13.00
373 BK,Elongated Man 13.00
374 BK,Elongated Man 13.00
375 CI,Elongated Man 13.00
376 . . . . 13.00
377 MA,Elongated Man,
    V:Riddler 15.00
378 Elongated Man 13.00
379 CI,Elongated Man 13.00
380 Elongated Man 13.00
381 GaF,Marital Bliss Miss 13.00
382 FR(s),BbB,JoG,GaF(s),SGe 13.00
383 FR(s),BbB,JoG,GaF(s),SGe 13.00
384 FR(s),BbB,JoG,GaF(s),SGe,
    BU:Batgirl 13.00
385 E:FR(s),BbB,JoG,NA(c),GK,MA,
    MkF,BU:Batgirl 13.00
386 BbK,MkF,BbB,JoG,
    BU:Batgirl 13.00
387 RA,rep.Detective #27 . . . . . 35.00
388 JBr(s),BbB,JoG,
    GK,MA,FR(s) 20.00
389 FR(s),BbB,JoG,GK,MA 15.00
390 FR(s),BbB,JoG,GK,MA,
    A:Masquerader 15.00
391 FR(s),NA(c),BbB,
    JoG,GK,MA 11.00
392 FR(s),BbB,JoG,I:Jason Bard 11.00
393 FR(s),BbB,JoG,GK,MA 11.00
394 FR(s),BbB,JoG,GK,MA 11.00
395 FR(s),NA,DG,GK,MA 15.00
396 FR(s),BbB,JoG,GK,MA 11.00
397 DON(s),NA,DG,GK,MA 15.00
398 FR(s),BbB,JoG,GK,ViC 11.00
399 NA(c),DON(s),BbB,JoG,
    GK,ViC,Robin 12.00
400 FR(s),NA,DG,GK,I:Man-Bat . 30.00
401 NA(c),FR(s),JoG,
    BbB,JoG,GK,ViC 10.00
402 FR(s),NA,DG,V:Man-Bat . . . 15.00
403 FR(s),BbB,JoG,NA(c),GK,ViC,
    BU:Robin 11.00
404 NA,GC,GK,A:Enemy Ace . . 15.00
405 IN,GK,I:League of Assassins 10.00
406 DON(s),NA,DG,GK,MA 10.00
407 FR(s),NA,DG,V:Man-bat . . . 15.00
408 MWn(s),LWn(s),NA,DG,
    V:DrTzin Tzin 15.00
409 B:FR(s),BbB,FrG,DH,DG . . . 10.00
410 DON(s),FR(s),NA,DG,DH . . 10.00
411 NA(c),DON(s),BbB,DG,DH . 11.00
412 NA(c),BbB,DG,DH 11.00
413 NA(c),BbB,DG,DH 11.00
414 DON(s),IN,DG,DH 10.00
415 BbB,DG,DH 10.00
416 DH 10.00
417 BbB,DG,DH,BU:Batgirl 10.00
418 DON(s),DH,IN,DG,A:Creeper 10.00
419 DON(s),DH 10.00
420 DH 10.00
421 DON(s),BbB,DG,DH,A:Batgirl 9.00
422 BbB,DG,DH,Batgirl 9.00
423 BbB,DG,DH 9.00
424 BbB,DG,DH,Batgirl 9.00
425 BWr(c),DON(s),IN,DG,DH . . 10.00
426 LWn(s),DG,A:Elongated Man 9.00
427 IN,DG,DH,BU:Batgirl 9.00
428 BbB,DG,ENB(s),DD,JoG,
    BU:Hawkman 9.00
429 DG,JoG,V:Man-Bat 9.00
430 BbB,NC,ENS(s),DG,
    A:Elongated Man 9.00
431 DON(s),IN,MA 9.00
432 MA,A:Atom 9.00
433 DD,DG,MA 9.00

434 IN,DG,ENB(s),RB,DG 9.00	
435 E:FR(s),DG,IN 9.00	
436 MA,(i),DG,A:Elongated Man . 9.00	
437 JA,WS,I:Manhunter 17.00	
438 JA,WS,Manhunter 14.00	
439 DG,WS,O:Manhunter,Kid	
Eternity rep. 12.50	
440 JAp,WS 12.50	
441 HC,WS 12.50	
442 ATh,WS 12.50	
443 WS,D:Manhunter 15.00	
444 JAp,B:Bat-Murderer,	
A:Ra's Al Ghul 9.00	
445 JAp,MGr,A:Talia 9.00	
446 JAp,last giant 9.00	
447 DG(i),A:Creeper 8.00	
448 DG(i),E:Bat-Murderer,	
A:Creeper,Ra's Al Ghul 8.00	
449 'Midnight Rustler in Gotham' . 9.00	
450 WS 10.00	

Detective Comics #572
© DC Comics, Inc.

451 . . . . 8.00	
452 . . . . 8.00	
453 . . . . 8.00	
454 . . . . 8.00	
455 MGr,A:Hawkman,V:Vampire . 7.50	
456 V:Ulysses Vulcan 7.50	
457 O:Batman rtd 10.00	
458 A:Man Bat 7.50	
459 A:Man Bat 7.50	
460 . . . . 7.50	
461 V:Capt.Stingaree 7.50	
462 V:Capt.Stingaree,A:Flash . . 7.50	
463 MGr,Atom,I:Calc.,Bl.Spider . 7.50	
464 MGr,TA,BlackCanary 7.50	
465 TA,Elongated Man 7.50	
466 MR,TA,V:Signalman 14.00	
467 MR,TA 14.00	
468 MR,TA,A:JLA 14.00	
469 WS,I:Dr.Phosphorus 7.50	
470 WS,AM,V:Dr.Phosphorus . . . 7.50	
471 MR,TA,A:Hugo Strange . . . 12.00	
472 MR,TA,A:Hugo Strange . . . 12.00	
473 MR,TA,R:Deadshot 12.00	
474 MR,TA,A:Penguin,	
N:Deadshot 13.50	

475 MR,TA,A:Joker 20.00	
476 MR,TA,A:Joker 20.00	
477 MR,DG,rep.NA 12.00	
478 MR,DG,I:3rd Clayface 12.00	
479 MR,DG,A:3rd Clayface . . . 12.00	
480 DN,MA 8.00	
481 JSt,CR,DN,DA,MR,	
A:ManBat 10.00	
482 HC,MGo,DG,A:Demon 7.00	
483 DN,DA,SD,A:Demon,	
40 Anniv. 9.00	
484 DN,DA,Demon,O:1st Robin . 6.00	
485 DN,DA,D:Batwoman,A:Demon	
A:Ras al Ghul 5.00	
486 DN,DA,DG,I:Odd Man,	
V:Scarecrow 5.00	
487 DN,DA,A:Ras Al Ghul 5.00	
488 DN,V:Spook,Catwoman . . . 6.50	
489 IN,DH,DN,DA,Ras Al Ghul . . 5.00	
490 DN,DA,PB,FMc,A:Black	
Lightning;A:Ras Al Ghul 5.00	
491 DN,DA,PB,FMc,A:Black	
Lightning;V:Maxie Zeus 5.00	
492 DN,DA,A:Penguin 6.50	
493 DN,DA,A:Riddler 6.00	
494 DN,DA,V:Crime Doctor 5.00	
495 DN,DA,V:Crime Doctor 5.00	
496 DN,DA,A:Clayface I 5.00	
497 DN,DA 5.00	
498 DN,DA,V:Blockbuster . . 5.00	
499 DN,DA,V:Blockbuster . . 5.00	
500 DG,CI,WS,TY,JKu,Dead-	
man,Hawkman,Robin 12.00	
501 DN,DA 5.00	
502 DN,DA 5.00	
503 DN,DA,Batgirl,Robin,	
V:Scarecrow 5.00	
504 DN,DA,Joker 7.00	
505 DN,DA 5.00	
506 DN,DA 5.00	
507 DN,DA 5.00	
508 DN,DA,V:Catwoman 5.00	
509 DN,DA,V:Catman,Catwoman . 7.00	
510 DN,DA,V:Madhatter 5.00	
511 DN,DA,I:Mirage 5.00	
512 GC,45th Anniv. 5.00	
513 V:Two-Face 5.00	
514 . . . . 5.00	
515 . . . . 5.00	
516 . . . . 5.00	
517 . . . . 5.00	
518 V:Deadshot 5.00	
519 . . . . 5.00	
520 A:Hugo Strange,Catwoman . . 6.00	
521 IN,TVE,A:Catwoman,B:BU:Green	
Arrow 6.50	
522 D:Snowman 5.00	
523 V:Solomon Grundy 5.00	
524 2nd A:J.Todd 6.00	
525 J.Todd 5.00	
526 DN,AA,A:Joker,Catwoman	
500th A:Batman 15.00	
527 V:Man Bat 4.00	
528 Green Arrow,Ozone 4.00	
529 I:Night Slayer,Nocturna 4.00	
530 V:Nocturna 4.00	
531 GC,AA,Chimera,J.Todd (see	
Batman #364) 4.00	
532 GC,Joker 7.00	
533 . . . . 4.00	
534 GC,A:Gr.Arrow,V:PoisonIvy . . 4.00	
535 GC,A:Gr.Arrow,V:Crazy Quitt	
2nd A:New Robin 6.00	
536 GC,A:Gr.Arrow,V:Deadshot . . 4.00	
537 GC,A:Gr.Arrow 4.00	

538 GC,A:Gr.Arrow,V:Catman . . . 4.00	
539 GC,A:Gr.Arrow 4.00	
540 GC,A:Gr.Arrow,V:Scarecrow . 4.00	
541 GC,A:Gr.Arrow,V:Penguin . . . 5.50	
542 GC,A:Gr.Arrow 4.00	
543 GC,A:Gr.Arrow,V:Nightslayer . 4.00	
544 GC,A:Gr.Arrow,V:Nightslayer	
Nocturna 4.00	
545 . . . . 4.00	
546 . . . . 4.00	
547 . . . . 4.00	
548 PB 4.00	
549 PB,KJ,AMo(s),Gr.Arrow . . . 4.50	
550 KJ,AMo(s),Gr.Arrow 4.50	
551 PB,V:Calendar Man 4.00	
552 V:Black Mask 4.00	
553 V:Black Mask 4.00	
554 KJ,N:Black Canary 4.00	
555 GC,DD,GreenArrow 4.00	
556 GC,Gr.Arrow,V:Nightslayer . . 4.00	
557 V:Nightslayer 4.00	
558 GC,Green Arrow 4.00	
559 GC,Green Arrow 4.00	
560 GC,A:Green Arrow 4.00	

Detective Comics #624
© DC Comics, Inc.

561 . . . . 4.00	
562 GC,V:Film Freak 4.00	
563 V:Two Face 4.00	
564 V:Two Face 4.00	
565 GC,A:Catwoman 5.50	
566 GC,Joker 7.00	
567 GC,HarlanEllison 5.00	
568 KJ,Legends tie-in,A:Penguin . 5.50	
569 AD,V:Joker 9.00	
570 AD,EvilCatwoman,A:Joker . . . 9.00	
571 AD,V:Scarecrow 5.00	
572 AD,CI,A:Elongated Man,Sherlock	
Holmes,SlamBradley,50thAnn . 5.00	
573 AD,V:Mad Hatter 5.00	
574 AD,End old J.Todd/Robin sty . 5.00	
575 AD,Year 2,pt.1,I:Reaper . . . 16.00	
576 TM,AA,Year 2,pt.2,	
R:Joe Chill 13.00	
577 TM,AA,Year 2,pt.3,V:Reaper 13.00	
578 TM,AA,Year 2,pt.4,	
D:Joe Chill 13.00	

579 I:NewCrimeDoctor 3.00	
580 V:Two Face 3.00	
581 V:Two Face 3.00	
582 Millenium X-over 3.00	
583 I:Ventriloquist 3.00	
584 V:Ventriloquist 3.00	
585 I:Rat Catcher 3.00	
586 V:Rat Catcher 3.00	
587 NB,V:Corrosive Man 3.00	
588 NB,V:Corrosive Man 3.00	
589 Bonus Book #5 .... 4.00	
590 NB,V:Hassan 3.00	
591 NB,V:Rollo 3.00	
592 V:Psychic Vampire 3.00	
593 NB,V:Stirh 3.00	
594 NB,A:Mr.Potato 3.00	
595 IN,bonus book #11 .... 3.00	
596 V:Sladek 3.00	
597 V:Sladek 3.00	
598 DCw,BSz,Blind Justice #1 .. 8.00	
599 DCw,BSz,Blind Justice #2 .. 4.00	
600 DCw,BSz,Blind Justice #3,	
50th Anniv.(double size) 5.00	
601 NB,I:Tulpa 3.00	
602 NB,A:Jason Blood 2.50	
603 NB,A:Demon 2.50	
604 NB,MudPack #1,V:Clayface,	
poster insert 2.50	
605 NB,MudPack #2,V:Clayface . 2.50	
606 NB,MudPack #3,V:Clayface . 2.50	
607 NB,MudPack #4,V:Clayface,	
poster insert 2.50	
608 NB,I:Anarky 2.00	
609 NB,V:Anarky 2.00	
610 NB,V:Penguin 3.00	
611 NB,V:Catwoman,Catman .. 3.00	
612 NB,A:Vicki Vale 1.75	
613 Search for Poisoner 1.75	
614 V:Street Demons 1.75	
615 NB,Return Penguin #2 (see	
Batman #448-#449) 2.75	
616 NB 1.75	
617 A:Joker 1.75	
618 NB,DG,A:Tim Drake 1.75	
619 NB,V:Moneyspider 1.75	
620 NB,V:Obeah,Man 1.75	
621 NB,SM,Obeah,Man 1.75	
622 Demon Within,pt.1 .... 2.00	
623 Demon Within,pt.2 .... 2.00	
624 Demon Within,pt.3 .... 2.00	
625 JAp,I:Abattior 1.75	
626 JAp,A:Electrocutioner 1.75	
627 600th issue w/Batman,rep.	
Detective #27 .... 4.00	
628 JAp,A:Abattoir 1.75	
629 JAp,'The Hungry Grass' 1.75	
630 JAp,I:Stiletto 1.75	
631 JAp,V:Neo-Nazi Gangs 1.75	
632 JAp,V:Creature 1.75	
633 TMd,Fake Batman? 1.75	
634 'The Third Man' 1.75	
635 Video Game,pt.1 .... 1.75	
636 Video Game,pt.2 .... 1.75	
637 Video Game,pt.3 .... 1.75	
638 JAp,Walking Time Bomb 1.75	
639 JAp,The Idiot Root,pt.2 .... 1.75	
640 JAp,The Idiot Root,pt.4 .... 1.75	
641 JAp,Destroyer,pt.3	
(see LOTDK#27) 2.00	
642 JAp,Faces,pt.2 .... 1.75	
643 JAp,'Librarian of Souls' 1.75	
644 TL,Electric City,pt.1	
A:Electrocutioner 1.75	
645 TL,Electric City,pt.2 ...... 1.75	
646 TL,Electric City,pt.3 ...... 1.75

647 TL,V:Cluemaster 1.75	
648 MWg(c),TL,V:Cluemaster ... 1.75	
649 MWg(c),TL,V:Cluemaster ... 1.75	
650 TL,A:Harold,Ace 1.75	
651 TL,'A Bullet for Bullock' 1.75	
652 GN,R:Huntress 1.75	
653 GN,A:Huntress 1.75	
654 MN,The General,pt.1 ...... 1.75	
655 MN,The General,pt.2 ...... 2.00	
656 MN,The General,pt.3,C:Bane 5.00	
657 MN,A:Azrael,I:Cypher 10.00	
658 MN,A:Azrael 8.00	
659 MN,Knightfall#2,	
V:Ventriloquist,A:Bane 7.50	
660 Knightfall#4,Bane Vs.	
Killer Croc 5.00	
661 GN,Knightfall#6,V:Firefly,	
Joker,A:Bane 4.00	
662 GN,Knightfall#8,V:Firefly,	
Joker,A:Huntress,Bane 3.50	
663 GN,Knightfall#10,V:Trogg,	
Zombie,Bird,A:Bane 3.00	
664 GN,Knightfall#12,A:Azrael ... 3.00	
665 GN,Knightfall#16,A:Azrael ... 3.00	
666 GN,SHa,A:Azrael,Trogg,	
Zombie,Bird 2.25	
667 GN,SHa,Knightquest:Crusade,	
V:Trigger Twins 2.00	
668 GN,SHa,Knightquest:Crusade,	
Robin locked out of Batcave .. 2.00	
669 GN,SHa,Knightquest:Crusade,	
V:Trigger Twins 2.00	
670 GN,SHa,Knightquest:Crusade,	
F:Rene Montoya 2.00	
671 GN,SHa,V:Joker 2.00	
672 KJ(c),GN,SHa,Knightquest:	
Crusade,V:Joker 2.00	
673 KJ(c),GN,SHa,Knightquest:	
Crusade,V:Joker 2.00	
674 KJ(c),GN,SHa,Knightquest:	
Crusade 2.00	
675 Foil(c),KJ(c),GN,SHa,Knightquest:	
Crusade,V:Gunhawk,foil(c) ... 3.25	
675a Newsstand ed. 1.75	
676 KJ(c),GN,SHa,Knights End #3,	
A:Nightwing 4.00	
677 KJ(c),GN,SHa,Knights End #9	
V:Azrael 3.00	
678 GN,SHa,Zero Hour 2.00	
679 Ratcatcher 2.00	
680 Batman,Two-Face 1.75	
681 CDi,GN,KJ,Jean-Paul Valley . 1.75	
682 CDi,GN,SHa,Return of Bruce	
Wayne,Troika,pt.3 .... 1.75	
682a Collector's Edition 2.50	
683 R:Penguin,I:Actuary 1.75	
684 Daylight Heist 1.75	
685 Chinatown War 1.75	
686 V:King Snake,Lynx 1.95	
687 CDi,SHa,V:River Pirate 1.95	
Ann.#1 KJ,TD,A:Question,Talia,	
V:Penguin 6.00	
Ann.#2 VS,A:Harvey Harris 6.00	
Ann.#3 DJu,DG,Batman in Japan . 2.50	
Ann.#4 Armageddon,pt.10 ..... 3.00	
Ann.#5 SK(c),TMd,Eclipso,V:The	
Ventriloquist,Joker 3.00	
Ann.#6 JBa,I:Geist 2.75	
Ann.#7 CDi,Elseworlds Story ... 3.25	
Ann.#8 CDi,KD(c) Year One Annual	
O:The Riddler 3.95	

DOC SAVAGE
November, 1985
1 AKu/NKu,D:Orig. Doc Savage . 3.00

2 AKu/NKu,V:Nazi's 2.50	
3 AKu/NKu,V:Nazi's 2.50	
4 AKu/NKu,V:Heinz 2.50	

Doc Savage (2nd Series) #1
© DC Comics, Inc.

[2nd Series]

1 'Five in the Sky'(painted cov.) . 3.00	
2 Chip Lost in Himalayas 2.25	
3 Doc declares war on USSR ... 2.25	
4 DocSavage/Russian team-up .. 2.25	
5 V:The Erisians 2.25	
6 U.S.,USSR,China Alliance	
vs. Erisians 2.25	
7 Mind Molder,pt.1, I:Pat Savage 2.25	
8 .... 2.25	
9 In Hidalgo 2.25	
10 V:Forces of the Golden God .. 2.25	
11 Sunlight Rising,pt.1 .... 2.25	
12 Sunlight Rising,pt.2 .... 2.25	
13 Sunlight Rising,pt.3 .... 2.25	
14 Sunlight Rising,pt.4 .... 2.25	
15 SeaBaron #1 .... 2.25	
16 EB,Shadow & Doc Savage ... 2.25	
17 EB,Shadow & Doc Savage ... 2.25	
18 EB,Shadow/DocSavage conc. . 2.25	
19 All new 1930's story 2.25	
20 V:Airlord & his Black Zepplin .. 2.25	
21 Airlord (30's story conc.) 2.25	
22 Doc Savages Past,pt.1 ..... 2.25	
23 Doc Savages Past,pt.2 ..... 2.25	
24 Doc Savages Past,pt.3 (final) . 2.25	
Ann.#1 1956 Olympic Games .. 4.50	

DOCTOR FATE
July, 1987

1 KG,V:Lords of Chaos 3.00	
2 KG,New Dr. Fate 2.50	
3 KG,A:JLI 2.50	
4 KG,V:Lords of Chaos Champion 2.50	

[2nd Series]

1 New Dr.Fate,V:Demons 3.50	
2 A:Andrew Bennett(I,Vampire) .. 3.00	
3 A:Andrew Bennett(I,Vampire) .. 2.50	
4 V:I,Vampire 2.00	
5 Dr.Fate & I,Vampire in Europe . 2.00	

---

6 A:Petey 2.00
7 Petey returns home dimension . 2.00
8 Linda become Dr.Fate again . . 2.00
9 Eric's Mother's Ghost,
   A:Deadman 2.00
10 Death of Innocence,pt.1 . . . . . 2.00
11 Return of Darkseid, Death of
   Innocence,pt.2 . . . . 2.00
12 Two Dr.Fates Vs.Darkseid,
   Death of Innocence,pt.3 . . . . . 2.00
13 Linda in the Astral Realm,
   Death of Innocence,pt.4 . . . . . 2.00
14 Kent & Petey vs. Wotan 2.00
15 V:Wotan,A:JLI 2.00
16 Flashback-novice Dr.Fate . . . 1.75
17 Eric's Journey thru afterlife . . 1.75
18 Search for Eric 1.75
19 A:Dr.Benjamin Stoner, Lords of
   Chaos, Phantom Stranger,
   Search for Eric continued . . . 1.75
20 V:Lords of Chaos,Dr.Stoner,
   A:Phantom Stranger 1.75
21 V:Chaos,A:PhantomStranger . . 1.75
22 A:Chaos and Order 1.75
23 Spirits of Kent & Inza Nelson . 1.75
24 L:Dr.Fate Characters 1.75
25 I:New Dr. Fate 1.75
26 Dr.Fate vs. Orig.Dr.Fate 1.75
27 New York Crime 1.75
28 'Diabolism' 1.75
29 Kent Nelson 1.75
30 'Resurrection' 1.75
31 'Resurrection' contd. 1.75
32 War of the Gods x-over 1.75
33 War of the Gods x-over 1.75
34 A:T'Gilian 1.75
35 Kent Nelson in N.Y. 1.75
36 Search For Inza,A:Shat-Ru . . . 1.75
37 Fate Helmet Powers revealed . 1.75
38 'The Spirit Motor,'Flashback . . 1.75
39 U.S.Senate Hearing 1.75
40 A:Wonder Woman 1.75
41 O:Chaos and Order,last issue . 1.75
Ann.#1 TS,R:Eric's dead mother . 2.95

DOOM FORCE
Spec.#1 MMi(c),RCa,WS,PCu,KSy,
   I:Doom Force 2.75

DOOM PATROL
[1st series]
(see MY GREATEST ADVENTURE)

DOOM PATROL
[2nd Regular Series]
October, 1987
1 SLi,R:Doom Patrol,plus Who's Who
   background of team, I:Kalki . . . 3.00
2 SLi,V:Kalki 1.75
3 SLi,I:Lodestone 1.75
4 SLi,I:Karma 1.75
5 SLi,R:Chief 1.75
6 B:PuK(s),EL,GyM(i),
   I:Scott Fischer 2.00
7 EL,GyM(i),V:Shrapnel 1.75
8 EL,GyM(i),V:Shrapnel 1.75
9 E:PuK(s),EL,GyM(i),V:Garguax,
   & Bonus Book 1.75
10 EL,A:Superman 2.00
11 EL,R:Garguax 1.75
12 EL,A:Garguax 1.75
13 EL,A:Power Girl 1.75
14 EL,A:Power Girl 1.75
15 EL,Animal-Veg-.Mineral Man . . 1.75

Doom Patrol #9 © DC Comics, Inc.

16 V:GenImmotus,Animal-Veg.-
   Mineral Man 1.75
17 D:Celsius,A:Aquaman & Sea
   Devils, Invasion tie-in 4.00
18 Invasion 1.50
19 B:GMo(s),New Direction,
   I:Crazy Jane 11.00
20 I:Rebis(new Negative-Being),
   A:CrazyJane,Scissormen 8.00
21 V:Scissormen 5.00
22 City of Bone,V:Scissormen . . . 5.00
23 A:RedJack,Lodestone kidnap . 5.00
24 V:Red Jack 5.00
25 Secrets of New Doom Patrol . . 5.00
26 I:Brotherhood of Dada 4.00
27 V:Brotherhood of Dada 4.00
28 Trapped in nightmare,V:Dada . 4.00
29 Trapped in painting,
   A:Superman 4.00
30 SBs(c),V:Brotherhood of Dada 4.00
31 SBs(c),A:The Pale Police 4.00
32 SBs(c),V:Cult of
   Unwritten Book 4.00
33 SBs(c),V:Cult,A:Anti-God
   the DeCreator 3.00
34 SBs(c),Robotman vs. his brain,
   R:The Brain & Mr.Mallah 3.00
35 SBs(c),A:Men from
   N.O.W.H.E.R.E. 3.00
36 SBs(c),V:Men from
   N.O.W.H.E.R.E. 3.25
37 SBs(c),Rhea Jones Story 2.50
38 SBs(c),V:Aliens 2.50
39 SBs(c),V:Aliens 2.50
40 SBs(c),Aliens 2.50
41 SBs(c),Aliens 2.50
42 O:Flex Mentallo 2.50
43 SBs(c),V:N.O.W.H.E.R.E. 2.50
44 SBs(c),V:N.O.W.H.E.R.E. 2.50
45 . . . . 2.50
46 SBs(c),RCa,MkK,A:Crazy Jane,
   Dr.Silence 2.50
47 Scarlet Harlot (Crazy Jane) . . 2.50
48 V:Mr.Evans 2.50
49 TTg(c),RCa,MGb,I:Mr.Nobody . 2.50
50 SBs(c),V:Brotherhood of Dada
   & bonus artists portfolio 3.00

51 SBs(c),Mr.Nobody Runs for
   President 2.50
52 SBs(c),Mr.Nobody saga conc . 2.50
53 SBs(c),Parody Issue,A:Phantom
   Stranger,Hellblazer,Mr.E 2.50
54 Rebis'Transformation 2.50
55 SBs(c),V:Crazy Jane,
   Candle Maker 2.50
56 SBs(c),RCa,V:Candle Maker . . 2.50
57 SBs(c),RCa,V:Candle Maker,
   O:Team,Double-sized 4.00
58 SBs(c),V:Candle Maker 2.25
59 TTg(c),RCa,SnW(i),A:Candlemaker
   D:Larry Trainor 2.25
60 JHw(c),RCa,SnW(i),
   V:Candlemaker,A:Magnus 2.25
61 TTg(c),RCa,SnW(i),A:Magnus
   D:Candlemaker 2.25
62 DFg(c),RCa,SnW(i),
   V:Nanomachines 2.25
63 E:GMo(s),RCa,R:Crazy Jane,
   V:Keysmiths,BU:Sliding from the
   Wreckage 2.25

Vertigo
64 BB(c),B:RaP(s),RCa,SnW(i),
   B:Sliding from the Wreckage,
   R:Niles Caulder 2.25
65 TTg(c),RCa,SnW(i),Nannos . . 2.25
66 RCa,E:Sliding from the
   Wreckage 2.25
67 TTg(c),LiM,GHi(i),New HQ,I:Charlie,
   George,Marion,V:Wild Girl 2.25
68 TTg(c),LiM,GHi(i),I:Identity
   Addict 2.25
69 TTg(c),LiM,GHi(i),V:Identity
   Addict 2.25
70 TTg(c),SEa,TS(i),I:Coagula,
   V:Codpiece 2.25
71 TTg(c),LiM,TS(i),Fox & Crow . 2.25
72 TTg(c),LiM,TS(i),Fox vs Crow . 2.25
73 LiM,GPi(i),Head's Nightmare . . 2.25
74 LiM,TS(i),Bootleg Steele 2.25
75 BB(c),TMK,Teiresias Wars#1,
   Double size 2.25
76 Teiresias Wars#2 . . . . 2.25
77 BB(c),TMK,N:Cliff 2.25
78 BB(c),V:Tower of Babel 2.25
79 BB(c),E:Teiresias Wars 2.25
80 V:Yapping Dogs 1.95
81 B:Masquerade 2.25
82 E:Masquerade 2.25
83 False Memory 1.95
84 The Healers 1.95
85 Charlie the Doll 1.95
86 Imagine Ari's Friends 1.95
87 KB(c),Imagine Ari's
   Friends,pt.4,final issue 1.95
Ann.#1 A:Lex Luthor 2.00
Ann.#2 RaP(s),MkW,Children's
   Crusade,F:Dorothy,A:Maxine . . 4.25
Doom Patrol/Suicide Squad #1 EL,
   D:Mr.104,Thinker,Psi,Weasel . 2.50
TPB Crawling From the Wreckage,
   SBs(c),rep.#19-#25 . . . . 19.95

DOORWAY TO NIGHTMARE
January-February, 1978
1 I:Madame Xanadu 1.00
2 . . . . 1.00
3 . . . . 1.00
4 JCr 1.00
5 September-October, 1978 . . . . 1.00

DOUBLE ACTION COMICS
January, 1940
2 Pre-Hero DC 7,000.00

DRAGONLANCE
1 Krynn's Companion's advent. . . 5.00
2 Vandar&Riva vs.Riba's brother   4.00
3 V:Takhesis,Queen of Darkness   3.50
4 V:Lord Soth & Kitiara 3.50
5 V:Queen of Darkness 3.50
6 Gnatch vs. Kalthanan 3.50
7 Raistlin's Evil contd. 3.50
8 Raistlin's Evil concl. 2.00
9 Journey to land o/t Minotaurs
   A:Tanis, Kitiara 2.00
10 Blood Sea,'Arena of Istar' . . . 2.00
11 Cataclysm of Krynn Revealed
   'Arena of Istar' contd. 2.00
12 Horak vs.Koraf, Arena contd. . 2.00
13 Test of High Sorcery #1 . . . . 2.00
14 Test of High Sorcery #2 . . . . 2.00
15 Test of High Sorcery #3 . . . . 2.00
16 Test of High Sorcery #4 . . . . 2.00
17 Winter'sKnight:DragonkillPt.1 . 2.00
18 Winter'sKnight:DragonkillPt.1 . 2.00
19 Winter'sKnight:DragonkillPt.1 . 2.00
20 Winter'sKnight:DragonkillPt.1 . 2.00
21 Move to New World 2.00
22 Taladas,pt.1,A:Myrella 2.00
23 Taladas,pt.2,Riva vs. Dragon . 2.00
24 Taladas,pt.3,V:Minotaur Lord . 2.00
25 Taladas,pt.4,V:Axantheas . . . 2.00
26 Rune Discovery,V:Agents
   of Eristem 2.00
27 V:Agents of Eristem 2.00
28 Riva continued. 2.00
29 Riva continued 2.00
30 Dwarf War,pt.1 . . . . 1.75
31 Dwarf War,pt.2 . . . . 1.75
32 Dwarf War,pt.3 . . . . 1.75
33 Dwarf War,pt.4 . . . . 1.75
34 conc., last issue 1.75
Ann.#1 Myrella o/t Robed Wizards 2.95

DYNAMIC CLASSICS
Sept-October 1978
1 Rep. Detective 395 & 438 . . . . 3.00

ECLIPSO
1 BS,MPn,V:South American
   Drug Dealers 2.50
2 BS,MPn,A:Bruce Gordon 2.00
3 BS,MPn,R:Amanda Waller 2.00
4 BS,A:Creeper,Cave Carson . . . 3.00
5 A:Creeper,Cave Carson 3.00
6 LMc,V:Bruce Gordon 3.00
7 London,1891 . . . . 3.50
8 A:Sherlock Holmes 1.50
9 I:Johnny Peril 1.50
10 CDo,V:Darkseid 1.50
11 A:Creeper,Peacemaker,Steel . 1.50
12 V:Shadow Fighters 1.50
13 D:Manhunter,Commander Steel,
   Major Victory,Peacemaker,
   Wildcat,Dr.Midnight,Creeper . 1.75
14 A:JLA 1.50
15 A:Amanda Waller 1.50
16 V:US Army 1.50
17 A:Amanda Waller,Martian
   Manhunter,Wonder Woman,Flash,
   Bloodwynd,Booster Gold 1.75
18 A:Spectre,JLA,final issue 2.00
Ann.#1 I:Prism 2.50

Eclipso #5 © DC Comics, Inc.

ECLIPSO: THE DARKNESS WITHIN
1 BS,Direct w/purple diamond,
   A:Superman,Creeper 4.00
1a BS,Newstand w/out diamond . 3.00
2 BS,MPn,DC heroes V:Eclipso,
   D:Starman 3.00

80 PAGE GIANTS
August, 1964
1 Superman 325.00
2 Jimmy Olsen 135.00
3 Lois Lane 135.00
4 Golden Age-Flash 125.00
5 Batman 135.00
6 Superman 110.00
7 JKu&JKu(c),Sgt. Rock's Prize
   Battle Tales 105.00
8 Secret Origins,O:JLA,Aquaman,
   Robin,Atom, Superman . . . 225.00
9 Flash 110.00
10 Superboy 110.00
11 Superman,A:Lex Luthor . . . 110.00
12 Batman 110.00
13 Jimmy Olsen 100.00
14 Lois Lane 110.00
15 Superman & Batman 115.00
16 JLA #39 . . . . 75.00
17 Batman #176 . . . . 40.00
18 Superman #183 . . . . 18.00
19 Our Army at War #164 . . . . 10.00
20 Action #334 . . . . 16.00
21 Flash #160 . . . . 30.00
22 Superboy #129 . . . . 7.00
23 Superman #187 . . . . 13.00
24 Batman #182 . . . . 26.00
25 Jimmy Olsen #95 . . . . 10.00
26 Lois Lane #68 . . . . 10.00
27 Batman #185 . . . . 35.00
28 World's Finest #161 . . . . . . 11.00
29 JLA #48 . . . . 16.00
30 Batman #187 . . . . 35.00
31 Superman #193 . . . . 13.00
32 Our Army at War #177 . . . . . 8.00
33 Action #347 . . . . 11.00
34 Flash #169 . . . . 30.00

35 Superboy #138 . . . . 6.00
36 Superman #197 . . . . 12.00
37 Batman #193 . . . . 16.00
38 Jimmy Olsen #104 . . . . 5.00
39 Lois Lane #77 . . . . 6.00
40 World's Finest #170 . . . . . . 10.00
41 JLA #58 . . . . 12.00
42 Superman #202 . . . . 12.00
43 Batman #198 . . . . 24.00
44 Our Army at War #190 . . . . 5.00
45 Action #360 . . . . 8.00
46 Flash #178 . . . . 18.00
47 Superboy #147 . . . . 7.00
48 Superman #207 . . . . 12.00
49 Batman #203 . . . . 14.00
50 Jimmy Olsen #113 . . . . 5.00
51 Lois Lane #86 . . . . 6.00
52 World's Finest #179 . . . . . . 6.00
53 JLA #67 . . . . 8.00
54 Superman #212 . . . . 12.00
55 Batman #208 . . . . 13.00
56 Our Army at War #203 . . . . 5.00
57 Action #373 . . . . 8.00
58 Flash #187 . . . . 13.00
59 Superboy #156 . . . . 6.00
60 Superman #217 . . . . 10.00
61 Batman #213 . . . . 35.00
62 Jimmy Olsen #122 . . . . 5.00
63 Lois Lane #95 . . . . 5.00
64 World's Finest #188 . . . . . . 6.00
65 JLA #76 . . . . 7.00
66 Superman #222 . . . . 10.00
67 Batman #218 . . . . 13.00
68 Our Army at War #216 . . . . 5.00
69 Adventure #390 . . . . 6.00
70 Flash #196 . . . . 12.00
71 Superboy #165 . . . . 6.00
72 Superman #227 . . . . 10.00
73 Batman #223 . . . . 14.00
74 Jimmy Olsen #131 . . . . 5.00
75 Lois Lane #104 . . . . 4.00
76 World's Finest #197 . . . . . . 5.00
77 JLA #85 . . . . 6.00
78 Superman #232 . . . . 10.00
79 Batman #228 . . . . 12.00
80 Our Army at War #229 . . . . 5.00
81 Adventure #403 . . . . 6.00
82 Flash #205 . . . . 9.00
83 Superboy #174 . . . . 5.00
84 Superman #239 . . . . 10.00
85 Batman #233 . . . . 12.00
86 Jimmy Olsen #140 . . . . 5.00
87 Lois Lane #113 . . . . 4.00
88 World's Finest #206 . . . . . . 5.00
89 JLA #93 . . . . 6.00

EL DIABLO
1 I:El Diablo, double-size 2.50
2 V:Crime Lord Benny Contreras   2.00
3 'Day of the Dead' Celebration . 2.00
4 Storm #1 . . . . 2.25
5 Storm #2 . . . . 2.25
6 Storm #3 . . . . 2.25
7 Storm #4 . . . . 2.25
8 V:Car-Theft Ring 2.00
9 V:Crime Lord of Dos Rios 2.00
10 The Franchise #1 . . . . 2.00
11 The Franchise #2 . . . . 2.00
12 A:Greg Sanders (golden age) . 2.00
13 The River #1 . . . . 2.00
14 The River #2 . . . . 2.00
15 The River #3 . . . . 2.00
16 Final Issue 2.00

All comics prices listed are for *Near Mint* condition.

ELECTRIC WARRIOR
1 SF series,I:Electric Warriors	2.50
2 'Bloodstalker Mode'	2.00
3 Rogue Warrior vs. Z-Primes	2.00
4 Primmies vs. Electric Warriors	2.00
5 Lek 0-03 Rebels	2.00
6 Lek 0-03 vs. Masters	1.75
7 Lek'sFate,Derek Two-Shadows	1.75
8 Derek Two-Shadows Betrayed	1.75
9 Fate of Derek Two-Shadows	1.75
10 Two-Shadows as one	1.75
11 Rebellion	1.75
12 Rebellion continued	1.75
13 V:Prime One	1.75
14 Mutants Join Rebellion	1.75
15 Invaders Arrival	1.75
16 Unified Warriors vs. Invaders	1.75
17 V:Terrans, O:Electric Warriors	1.75
18 Origin continued, final issue	1.75

ELONGATED MAN
1 A:Copperhead	1.00
2 Modora,A:Flash,I:Sonar	1.00
3 A:Flash,V:Wurst Gang	1.00

ELVIRA
1 DSp,BB(c)	3.25
2 thru 9	@1.00
10	2.00
11 DSt(c)Find Cain	2.50

ENIGMA
Vertigo
1 B:PrM(s),DFg,I:Enigma,Michael Smith,V:The Head	3.50
2 DFg,I:The Truth	3.25
3 DFg,V:The Truth,I:Envelope Girl, Titus Bird	3.00
4 DFg,D:The Truth,I:Interior League	3.00
5 DFg,I:Enigma's Mother	3.00
6 DFg,V:Envelope Girl	3.00
7 DFg,V:Enigma's Mother,D:Envelope Girl,O:Enigma	3.00
8 E:PrM(s),DFg,final issue	3.00

EXTREME JUSTICE
0 New Group	1.50
1 V:Captain Atom	1.50
2 V:War Cyborgs	1.50
3 V:Synge	1.50
4 R:Firestorm the Nuclear Man	1.50
5 Firestorm & Elementals	1.75
6 Monarch,Captain Atom, Booster Gold, Maxima	1.75

EXTREMIST
Vertigo
1 B:PrM(s),TMK,I:The Order, Extremist(Judy Tanner)	2.50
1a Platinum Ed.	45.00
2 TMK,D:Extremist(Jack Tanner)	2.25
3 TMK,V:Patrick	2.25
4 E:PrM(s),TMK,D:Tony Murphy	2.25

FACE, THE
GN DFg,PrM	4.95

FAMILY MAN
Paradox
1 I:Family Man	4.95
2 V:Brother Charles	4.95

FATE
1 Dr. Fate	1.95
2 Nabu,Astral plane	1.95
3 Bloodstain	1.95
4 Decisions	1.95
5 Judged by Enclave	1.95
6 V:Grimoire	1.95
7 V:Dark Agent	1.95
8 V:Dark Agent	2.25
9 Tries to change his destiny	2.25

FIGHTING AMERICAN
1 GrL,R:Fighting American	1.75
2 GrL,Media Circus	1.75
3 GrL,I&V:Gross Nation Product, Def Iffit	1.75
4 GrL,V:Gross Nation Product, Def Iffit	1.75
5 GrL,PhorOptor	1.75
6 Final Issue	1.75

FIRESTORM
March, 1978
1 AM,JRu,I&O:Firestorm	4.00
2 AM,BMc,A:Superman	2.50
3 AM,I:Killer Froat	2.50
4 AM,BMc,I:Hyena	2.50
5 AM,BMc,Hyena	2.50

FIRESTORM, THE NUCLEAR MAN
(see FURY OF FIRESTORM)

FIRST ISSUE SPECIAL
April, 1975
1 JK,Atlas	3.00
2 Green Team	2.50
3 Metamorpho	2.50
4 Lady Cop	2.50
5 JK,Manhunter	2.75
6 JK,Dingbats	2.50
7 SD,Creeper	2.50
8 MGr,Warlord	15.00
9 WS,Dr.Fate	3.00
10 Outsiders(not Batman team)	2.50
11 NR,AM Code:Assassin	2.50
12 new Starman	2.50
13 return of New Gods	3.50

FLASH COMICS
January, 1940
1 SMo,SMo(c),O:Flash,Hawkman,The Whip & Johnny Thunder,B:Cliff Cornwall,Minute Movies	35,000.00
2 B:Rod Rain	4,000.00
3 SMo,SMo(c),B:The King	3,000.00
4 SMo,SMo(c),F:The Whip	2,500.00
5 SMo,SMo(c),F:The King	2,300.00
6 F:Flash	2,600.00
7 Hawkman(c)	1,500.00
8 Male bondage(c)	1,400.00
9 Hawkman(c)	1,400.00
10 SMo,SMo(c),Flash(c)	1,400.00
11 SMo,SMo(c)	1,000.00
12 SMo,SMo(c),B:Les Watts	1,000.00
13 SMo,SMo(c)	950.00
14 SMo,SMo(c)	950.00
15 SMo,SMo(c)	950.00
16 SMo,SMo(c)	950.00
17 SMo,SMo(c),E:Cliff Cornwall	950.00
18 SMo,SMo(c)	950.00
19 SMo,SMo(c)	950.00
20 SMo,SMo(c)	950.00

21 SMo(c)	800.00
22 SMo,SMo(c)	800.00
23 SMo,SMo(c)	800.00
24 SMo,SMo(c),Flash V:Spider-Men of Mars,A:Hawkgirl	1,100.00
25 SMo,SMo(c)	650.00
26 SMo,SMo(c)	650.00
27 SMo,SMo(c)	650.00
28 SMo,SMo(c),Flash goes to Hollywood	650.00
29 SMo,SMo(c)	650.00
30 SMo,SMo(c),Flash in'Adventure of the Curiosity Ray!'	650.00
31 SMo,SMo(c),Hawkman(c)	625.00
32 SMo,SM(c),Flash in'Adventure of the Fictious Villians'	600.00
33 SMo,SMo(c)	600.00

Flash Comics #47 © DC Comics, Inc.

34 SMo,SMo(c),Flash in 'The Robbers of the Round Table'	600.00
35 SMo,SMo(c)	600.00
36 SMo,SMo(c),Flash in'The Mystery of the Doll Who Walks Like A Man'	600.00
37 SMo,SMo(c)	600.00
38 SMo,SMo(c)	600.00
39 SMo,SMo(c)	600.00
40 SMo,SMo(c),Flash in 'The Man Who Could Read Man's Souls!'	600.00
41 SMo,SMo(c)	550.00
42 SMo,SMo(c),Flash V:The Gangsters Baby!	550.00
43 SMo,SMo(c)	550.00
44 SMo,SMo(c),Flash V:The Liars Club	550.00
45 SMo,SMo(c),F:Hawkman,Big Butch Makes Hall of Fame	550.00
46 SMo,SMo(c)	550.00
47 SMo,SMo(c),Hawkman in 'Crime Canned for the Duration'	550.00
48 SMo,SMo(c)	550.00
49 SMo,SMo(c)	550.00
50 SMo,SMo(c),Flash in 'Tale o/t 1,000 Dollar Bill'	550.00
51 SMo,SMo(c)	500.00
52 SMo,SMo(c),Flash in 'Case of the Machine that Thinks Like A Man'	500.00
53 SMo,SMo(c),Hawkman in	

'Simple Simon Met the
Hawkman' 500.00
54 SMo,SMo(c),Flash in
'Mysterious Bottle from
the Sea' 500.00
55 SMo,SMo(c),Hawkman in
'The Riddle of the
Stolen Statuette! 3 . . . . 500.00
56 SMo,SMo(c) 500.00
57 SMo,SMo(c),Hawkman in
'Adventure of the Gangster
and the Ghost' 500.00
58 SMo,SMo(c),'Merman meets
the Flash' 500.00
59 SMo,SMo(c),Hawkman
V:Pied Piper 500.00
60 SMo,SMo(c),Hawkman
V:The Wind Master 500.00
61 SMo,SMo(c),Hawkman
V:The Beanstalk 500.00
62 JKu,Flash in 'High Jinks
on the Rinks' 600.00
63 JKu(c),Hawkman in 'The
Tale of the Mystic Urn' 450.00
64 . . . . 450.00
65 JKu(c),Hawkman in 'Return
of the Simple Simon' 450.00
66 . . . . 450.00
67 JKu(c) 450.00
68 Flash in 'The Radio that
Ran Wild' 450.00
69 . . . . 450.00
70 JKu(c) 450.00
71 JKu(c),Hawkman in 'Battle
of the Birdmen' 450.00
72 JKu 450.00
73 JKu(c) 450.00
74 JKu(c) 450.00
75 JKu(c),Hawkman in 'Magic
at the Mardi Gras' 450.00
76 A:Worry Wart 450.00
77 Hawkman in 'The Case of
the Curious Casket' 450.00
78 . . . . 450.00
79 Hawkman in 'The Battle
of the Birds' 450.00
80 Flash in 'The Story of
the Boy Genius' 450.00
81 JKu(c),Hawkman's Voyage
to Venus 450.00
82 A:Walter Jordan 450.00
83 JKu,JKu(c),Hawkman in
'Destined for Disaster' 450.00
84 Flash V:'The Changeling' . . 450.00
85 JKu,JKu(c),Hawkman in
Hollywood 450.00
86 JKu,1st Black Canary,Flash
V:Stone Age Menace 1,300.00
87 Hawkman meets the Foil . . 600.00
88 JKu,Flash in 'The Case
of the Vanished Year!' 600.00
89 I:The Thorn 600.00
90 Flash in 'Nine Empty
Uniforms' 600.00
91 Hawkman V:The Phantom
Menace 700.00
92 1st full-length Black
Canary story 1,500.00
93 Flash V:Violin of Villainy . . . 700.00
94 JKu(c) 700.00
95 . . . . 700.00
96 . . . . 700.00
97 Flash in 'The Dream
that Didn't Vanish' 700.00
98 JKu(c),Hawkman in

'Crime Costume!' 700.00
99 Flash in 'The Star Prize
of the Year' 700.00
100 Hawkman in 'The Human
-Fly Bandits!' 1,600.00
101 . . . . 1,400.00
102 Hawkman in 'The Flying
Darkness' 1,400.00
103 . . . . 1,500.00
104 JKu,Hawkman in 'Flaming
Darkness' February, 1949 . 3,400.00

Flash Comics #185 © DC Comics, Inc.

FLASH
February-March, 1959
105 CI,O:Flash,I:Mirror
Master 4,200.00
106 CI,I&O:Gorilla Grodd,
O:Pied Piper 950.00
107 CI,A:Grodd 475.00
108 CI,A:Grodd 465.00
109 CI,A:Mirror Master 400.00
110 CI,MA,I:Kid Flash,
Weather Wizard 950.00
111 CI,A:Kid Flash,The Invasion
Of the Cloud Creatures 275.00
112 CI,I&O:Elongated Man,
A:Kid Flash 300.00
113 CI,I&O:Trickster 250.00
114 CI,A:Captain Cold 220.00
115 CI,A:Grodd 175.00
116 CI,A:Kid Flash,The Man
Who Stole Central City 175.00
117 CI,MA,I:Capt.Boomerang . 200.00
118 CI,MA 145.00
119 CI,W:Elongated Man 145.00
120 CI,A:Kid Flash,Land of
Golden Giants 145.00
121 CI,A:Trickster 125.00
122 CI,I&O:The Top 125.00
123 I:Earth 2,R:G.A.Flash 760.00
124 CI,A:Capt.Boomerang 100.00
125 CI,A:Kid Flash,The
Conquerors of Time 80.00
126 CI,A:Mirror Master 80.00
127 CI,A:Grodd 80.00
128 CI,O:Abra Kadabra 80.00

129 CI,A:Capt.Cold,Trickster,A:Gold.
Age Flash,C:JLA (flashback) 200.00
130 CI,A:Mirror Master,
Weather Wizard 80.00
131 CI,A:Green Lantern 75.00
132 CI,A:Daphne Dean 75.00
133 CI,A:Abra Kadabra 75.00
134 CI,A:Captain Cold 75.00
135 CI,N:Kid Flash 75.00
136 CI,A:Mirror Master 75.00
137 CI,Vandal Savage,R:JSA,
A:G.A.Flash 350.00
138 CI,A:Pied Piper 70.00
139 CI,I&O:Prof.Zoom(Reverse
Flash) 100.00
140 CI,O:Heat Wave 70.00
141 CI,A:Top 45.00
142 CI,A:Trickster 45.00
143 CI,A:Green Lantern 45.00
144 CI,A:Man Missile,Kid Flash . 45.00
145 CI,A:Weather Wizard 45.00
146 CI,A:Mirror Master 43.00
147 CI,A:Mr.Element,A:Reverse
Flash 43.00
148 CI,A:Capt.Boomerang 43.00
149 CI,A:Abra Kadabra 43.00
150 CI,A:Captain Cold 43.00
151 CI,A:Earth II Flash,
The Shade 67.00
152 CI,V:Trickster 40.00
153 CI,A:Mr.Element,Rev.Flash . 40.00
154 CI,The Day Flash Ran Away
with Himself 40.00
155 CI,A:MirrorMaster,Capt.Cold,Top
Capt. Boomerang,Grodd . . . 40.00
156 CI,A:Kid Flash,The Super Hero
who Betrayed the World . . . 40.00
157 CI,A:Doralla Kon,The Top . . 40.00
158 CI,V:The Breakaway Bandit
A:The Justice League 40.00
159 CI,A:Kid Flash 40.00
160 CI,giant 50.00
161 CI,A:Mirror Master 32.00
162 CI,Who Haunts the Corridor
of Chills 32.00
163 CI,A:Abra kadabra 32.00
164 CI,V:Pied Piper,A:KidFLash . 32.00
165 CI,W:Flash,Iris West 35.00
166 CI,A:Captain Cold 30.00
167 CI,O:Flash,I:Mopee 30.00
168 CI,A:Green Lantern 30.00
169 CI,O:Flash rtd,giant 45.00
170 CI,A:Abra Kadabra,
G.A.Flash 30.00
171 CI,A:Dexter Myles,Justice
League,Atom;V:Dr Light 24.00
172 CI,A:Grodd 24.00
173 CI,A:Kid Flash,EarthII Flash
V:Golden Man 24.00
174 CI,A:Mirror Master,Top
Captain Cold 24.00
175 2nd Superman/Flash race,
C:Justice League o/America 125.00
176 giant-size 35.00
177 RA,V:The Trickster 24.00
178 CI,(giant size) 35.00
179 RA,Fact or Fiction 24.00
180 RA,V:Baron Katana 24.00
181 RA,V;Baron Katana 12.00
182 A:Abra Kadabra 12.00
183 RA,V:The Frog 12.00
184 RA,V:Dr Yom 12.00
185 RA,Threat of the High Rise
Buildings 12.00
186 RA,A:Sargon 12.00

187 CI,AbraKadabra,giant 25.00	256 FMc,V:Top 3.50	B.U.Creeper 3.00
188 A:Mirror Master 12.00	257 FMc,A:Green Glider 3.50	324 CI,D:Reverse Flash 4.00
189 JKu(c),RA,A:Kid Flash 12.00	258 FMc,A:Black Hand 3.50	325 CI,A:Rogues Gallery 3.00
190 JKu(c),RA,A:Dexter Myles . . 12.00	259 FMc,IN 3.50	326 CI,A:Weather Wizard 3.00
191 JKu(c),RA,A:Green Lantern . 12.00	260 FMc,IN 3.50	327 CI,A:JLA,G.Grodd 3.00
192 RA;V:Captain Vulcan 12.00	261 FMc,IN,V:Golden Glider 3.50	328 CI 3.00
193 A:Captain Cold 12.00	262 FMc,IN,V:Golden Glider 3.50	329 CI,A:J.L.A.,G.Grodd 3.00
194 . . . . 12.00	263 FMc,IN,V:Golden Glider 3.50	330 CI,FMc,V:G.Grodd 3.00
195 GK,MA 12.00	264 FMc,IN,V:Golden Glider 3.50	331 CI,FMc,V:G.Grodd 3.00
196 CI,giant 25.00	265 FMc,IN 3.50	332 CI,FMc,V:Rainbow Raider . . . 3.00
197 GK 12.00	266 FMc,IN,V:Heat Wave 3.50	333 CI,FMc,V:Pied Piper 3.00
198 GK 12.00	267 FMc,IN,V:Heat Wave 3.50	334 CI,FMc,V:Pied Piper 3.00
199 GK 12.00	268 FMc,IN,A:E2 Flash 3.50	335 CI,FMc,V:Pied Piper 3.00
200 IN,MA 14.00	269 FMc,IN,A:Kid Flash 3.50	336 CI,FMc,V:Pied Piper 3.00
201 IN,MA,A:G.A. Flash 7.50	270 FMc,IN,V:Clown 3.50	337 CI,FMc,V:Pied Piper 3.00
202 IN,MA,A:Kid Flash 7.50	271 RB,V:Clown 3.50	338 CI,FMc,I:Big Sir 3.00
203 IN 7.50	272 RB,V:Clown 3.50	339 CI,FMc,A:Big Sir 3.00
204 . . . . 7.50	273 RB 3.50	340 CI,FMc,Trial,A:Big Sir 3.00
205 giant 12.00	274 RB 3.50	341 CI,FMc,Trial,A:Big Sir 3.00
206 A:Mirror Master 7.50	275 AS,D:Iris West,PCP story . . . 4.00	342 CI,FMc,Trial,V:RogueGallery . 3.00
207 . . . . 7.50	276 AS,A:JLA 3.50	343 CI,FMc,Trial,A:GoldFace 3.00
208 . . . . 7.50	277 AS,FMc,A:JLA,	344 CI,O:Kid Flash,Trial 3.00
209 A:Capt.Boomerang,Grodd	V:MirrorMaster 3.50	345 CI,A:Kid Flash,Trial 3.00
Trickster 7.50	278 A:Captain.Boomerang	346 CI,FMc,Trial,V:AbraKadabra . 3.00
210 CI 7.50	& Heatwave 3.50	347 CI,FMc,Trial,V:AbraKadabra . 3.00
211 O:Flash 10.00	279 A:Captain.Boomerang	348 CI,FMc,Trial,V:AbraKadabra . 3.00
212 A:Abra Kadabra 7.50	& Heatwave 3.50	349 CI,FMc,Trial,V:AbraKadabra . 3.00
213 CI 7.50	280 DH 3.50	350 CI,FMc,Trial,V:AbraKadabra . 7.00
214 CI,rep.Showcase #37	281 DH,V:Reverse Flash 4.00	Ann.#1 O:ElongatedMan,
(O:Metal Men),giant size. . . 12.00	282 DH,V:Reverse Flash 4.00	G.Grodd 280.00
215 IN,FMc,rep.Showcase #14 . 14.00	283 DH,V:Reverse Flash 4.00	
216 A:Mr.Element 7.50	284 DH,Flash's life story	
217 NA,A:Gr.Lant,Gr.Arrow 13.00	I:Limbo Lord 3.50	
218 NA,A:Gr.Lant,Gr.Arrow 13.00	285 DH,V:Trickster 3.50	
219 NA,L:Greeen Arrow 13.00	286 DH,I:Rainbow Raider 3.50	
220 IN,DG,A:KidFlash,Gr.Lantern . 7.50	287 DH,V:Dr.Alchemy 3.50	
221 IN 7.50	288 DH,V:Dr.Alchemy 3.50	
222 IN 7.50	289 DH,GP,1st GP DC art; V:Dr.	
223 DG,Green Lantern 7.50	Alchemy;B:B.U.Firestorm 8.00	
224 IN,DG,A:Green Lantern 7.50	290 GP 3.00	
225 IN,DG,A:Gr.Lant,Rev.Flash . 8.50	291 GP,DH,V:Sabretooth 3.00	
226 NA,A:Capt. Cold 10.00	292 GP,DH,V:Mirror Master 3.00	
227 IN,FMc,DG,Capt.Boomerang,	293 GP,DH,V:Pied Piper 3.00	
Green Lantern 7.50	294 GP,DH,V:Grodd 3.00	
228 IN 7.50	295 CI,JSn,V:Grodd 3.00	
229 IN,FMc,A:Green Arrow,	296 JSn,A:Elongated Man 3.00	
V:Rag Doll (giant size) 10.00	297 CI,A:Captain Cold 3.00	
230 A:VandalSavage,Dr.Alchemy . 7.50	298 CI,V:Shade,Rainbowraider . . 3.00	
231 FMc 7.50	299 CI,V:Shade,Rainbowraider . . 3.00	
232 giant 10.00	300 A:New Teen Titans 5.00	
233 giant 10.00	301 CI,A:Firestorm 3.00	
234 V:Reverse Flash 5.00	302 CI,V:Golden Glider 3.00	
235 . . . . 4.00	303 CI,V:Golden Glider 3.00	
236 MGr 4.00	304 CI,PB,I:Col.Computron;E:B.U.	*Flash Comics (2nd Series)#6*
237 IN,FMc,MGr,A:Prof Zoom,	Firestorm 3.00	*© DC Comics, Inc.*
Green Lantern 4.50	305 KG,CI,A:G.A.Flash,B:Dr.Fate . 4.00	
238 MGr 4.00	306 CI,KG,V:Mirror Master 4.00	**FLASH**
239 . . . . 4.00	307 CI,KG,V:Pied Piper 3.00	**[2nd Series]**
240 MGr 4.00	308 CI,KG 3.00	**October, 1985**
241 A:Mirror Master 4.00	309 CI,KG 4.00	1 JG,Legends,C:Vandal Savage 11.00
242 MGr,D:Top 4.00	310 CI,KG,V:Capt.Boomerang . . 3.00	2 JG,V:Vandal Savage 6.00
243 IN,FMc,MGr,TA,O:Top,	311 CI,KG,V:Capt.Boomerang . . 3.00	3 JG,I:Kilgore 4.00
A:Green Lantern 4.00	312 CI,A:Heatwave 3.00	4 JG,A:Cyborg 4.00
244 IN,FMc,A:Rogue's Gallery . . 4.00	313 KG,A:Psylon,E:Dr.Fate 3.00	5 JG,V:Speed Demon 4.00
245 IN,FMc,DD,TA,I:PlantMaster . 4.00	314 CI,I:Eradicator 3.00	6 JG,V:Speed Demon 4.00
246 IN,FMc,DD,TA,I:PlantMaster . 4.00	315 CI,V:Gold Face 3.00	7 JG,V:Red Trinity 4.00
247 . . . . 4.00	316 CI,V:Gold Face 3.00	8 JG,V:BlueTrinity,Millenium . . . 4.00
248 FMc,IN,I:Master 4.00	317 CI,V:Gold Face 3.00	9 JG,I:Chunk,Millenium 4.00
249 FMc,IN,V:Master 4.00	318 CI,DGb,V:Eradicator;B:	10 V:Chunk,Chunks World 3.00
250 IN,FMc,I:Golden Glider 4.00	B.U.Creeper 3.00	11 Return to Earth 3.00
251 FMc,IN,V:Golden Glider 3.50	319 CI,DGb,V:Eradicator 3.00	12 Velocity 9 . . . . 3.00
252 FMc,IN,I:Molder 3.50	320 CI,V:Eradicator 3.00	
253 FMc,IN,V:Molder 3.50	321 CI,D:Eradicator 3.00	
254 FMc 3.50	322 CI,V:Reverse Flash 3.00	
255 FMc,A:MirrorMaster 3.50	323 CI,V:Reverse Flash;E:	

13 Vandal Savage,V:Velocity 9	
Adicts	3.00
14 V:Vandal Savage	3.00
15 A:Velocity 9 Junkies	3.00
16 C:V.Savage,SpeedMcGeePt.1	3.00
17 GLa,Speed McGee,pt.2	3.00
18 GLa,SpeedMcGeePt.3,	
V:V.Savage	2.25
19 JM:+bonus book,R:Rogue	
Gallery,O:Blue/Red Trinity	2.25
20 A:Durlan	2.25
21 A:Manhunter,Invasion x-over	2.25
22 A:Manhunter,Invasion x-over	2.25
23 V:Abrakadabra	2.25
24 GLa,FlashRegainsSpeed,	
A:L.Lane	2.25
25 GLa,Search for Flash	2.25
26 GLa,I:Porcupine Man	2.25
27 GLa,Porcupine Man as Flash	2.25
28 GLa,A:Golden Glider,	
Capt.Cold	2.25
29 A:New Phantom Lady	2.25
30 GLa,Turtle Saga,pt.1	2.25
31 GLa,Turtle Saga,pt.2	2.00
32 GLa,Turtle Saga,pt.3,	
R:G.A.Turtle	2.00
33 GLa,Turtle Saga,pt.4	2.00
34 GLa,Turtle Saga,pt.5	2.00
35 GLa,Turtle Saga,pt.6,	
D:G.A.Turtle	2.00
36 GLa,V:Cult	2.00
37 GLa,V:Cult	2.00
38 GLa,V:Cult	2.00
39 GLa,V:Cult	2.00
40 GLa,A:Dr.Alchemy	2.00
41 GLa,A:Dr.Alchemy	2.00
42 GLa,MechanicalTroubles	2.00
43 GLa,V:Kilgore	2.00
44 GLa,V:Velocity	2.00
45 V:Gorilla Grod	2.00
46 V:Gorilla Grod	2.00
47 V:Gorilla Grod	2.00
48	2.00
49 A:Vandal Savage	2.00
50 N:Flash (double sz)V:Savage	4.00
51 I:Proletariat	2.00
52 I.R.S. Mission	1.75
53 A:Superman,Race to Save	
Jimmy Olsen	1.75
54 Terrorist Airline Attack	1.75
55 War of the Gods x-over	1.75
56 The Way of a Will,pt.1	1.75
57 The Way of a Will,pt.2	1.75
58 Meta Gene-activated Homeless	1.75
59 The Last Resort	1.75
60 Love Song of the Chunk	1.75
61 Wally's Mother's Wedding Day	1.75
62 GLa,Year 1,pt.1	2.25
63 GLa,Year 1,pt.2	1.75
64 GLa,Year 1,pt.3	1.75
65 GLa,Year 1,pt.4	1.75
66 A:Aq'man,V:Marine Marauder	1.75
67 GLa,V:Abra Kadabra	1.75
68 GLa,V:Abra Kadabra	1.75
69 GLa,Gorilla Warfare#2	1.75
70 Gorilla Warfare#4	1.75
71 GLa,V:Dr.Alchemy	1.75
72 GLa,V:Dr.Alchemy,C:Barry	
Allen	2.50
73 GLa,Xmas Issue,R:Barry Allen	2.50
74 GLa,A:Barry Allen?	2.25
75 GLa,A:Reverse Flash,V:Mob	
Violence	2.50
76 GLa,A:Reverse Flash	2.25
77 GLa,G.A.Flash vs	

Reverse Flash	2.25
78 GLa,V:Reverse Flash	2.25
79 GLa,V:Reverse Flash,48 pgs.	3.25
80 AD(c),V:Frances Kane	3.00
80a Newstand Ed	2.00
81 AD(c)	2.00
82 AD(c),A:Nightwing	2.00
83 AD(c),A:Nightwing,Starfire	2.00
84 AD(c),I:Razer	2.00
85 AD(c),V:Razer	2.00
86 AD(c),A:Argus	2.00
87 Chrismas issue	2.00
88	2.00
89 On Trial	2.00
90 On Trial#2	2.00
91 Out of Time	5.00
92 I:3rd Flash	5.00
93 A:Impulse	5.00
94 Zero Hour	5.00
95 Terminal Velocity,pt.1	1.75
96 Terminal Velocity,pt.2	1.75
97 Terminal Velocity,pt.3	1.75
98 Terminal Velocity,pt.4	1.75
99 Terminal Velocity,pt.5	1.75
100 I:New Flash	2.50
100a Collector's Edition	3.50
101 Velocity Aftermath	1.50
102 V:Mongul	1.75
103 Supernatural threat from	
Linda's Past Secret	1.75
Ann.#1 JG,The Deathtouch	4.00
Ann.#2 A:Wally's Father	3.00
Ann.#3 Roots	2.50
Ann.#4 Armageddon,pt7	2.50
Ann.#5 TC(1st Full Work),Eclipso,	
V:Rogue's Gallery	10.00
Ann.#6 Bloodlines#4,I:Argus	2.75
Ann.#7 Elseworlds story	2.95
Spec #1,IN,DG,CI,50th Anniv.,	
Three Flash's	4.50
T.V. Spec.#1,JS,w/episode guide	4.25

FLASH GORDON

1 DJu,I:New Flash Gordon	2.50
2 DJu,A:Lion-Men,Shark-Men	2.00
3 DJu,V:Shark-Men	1.50
4 DJu,Dale Kidnapped by Voltan	1.50
5 DJu,Alliance Against Ming	1.50

The Fly #12 © DC Comics, Inc.

6 DJu,Arctic City	1.50
7 DJu,Alliance vs. Ming	1.50
8 DJu,Alliance vs. Ming	1.50
9 DJu,V:Ming, final issue	1.50

FLY, THE
Impact

1 I&O:Fly I:Arachnus,Chromium	1.50
2 V:Chromium	1.25
3 O:Arachnus, I:Lt.Walker Odell	1.00
4 A:Black Hood, V:Arachnus	1.00
5 V:Arachnus	1.00
6 I:Blackjack	1.00
7 Oceanworld,V:Dolphus	1.00
8 A:Comet,Dolphus	1.00
9 F:Fireball, with trading card	1.00
10 V:General Mechanix	1.00
11 Suicide Issue	1.25
12 V:Agent from WEB	1.25
13 I:Tremor	1.25
14 V:Domino	1.25
15 V:Domino	1.25
16 V:Arachnus	1.25
17 Final Issue	1.25
Ann.#1 Earthquest,pt.4,w/card	2.25

FORBIDDEN TALES
OF DARK MANSION
May-June, 1972

5 thru 15 Feb.-March, 1974	@1.50

FOREVER PEOPLE

1 Return of Forever People	1.75
2 'Return of Earth of Yesterday'	1.25
3 A:Mark Moonrider	1.25
4 The Dark controlls M.Moonrider	1.25
5 R:MotherBox,Infinity Man	1.25
6 Donny's Fate, final issue	1.25

FORGOTTEN REALMS

1 A:RealmsMaster,PriamAgrivar	8.00
2 Mystic Hand of Vaprak,	
A:Ogre Mage	6.00
3 Mystic Hand of Vaprak contd.	5.50
4 Ogre Mage vs.Omen the Wizard	5.50
5 Dragon Reach #1	5.50
6 Dragon Reach #2	4.50
7 Dragon Reach #3	3.50
8 Dragon Reach #4	3.00
9 V:Giant Squid	2.50
10 'Head Cheese'	2.50
11 Triangles #1	2.50
12 Triangles #2	2.50
13 Triangles #3	2.50
14 A:Lich Viranton the Mage	2.00
15 Avatar Comics tie-in	2.00
16 Mad Gods and Paladins,pt.1	2.00
17 Mad Gods and Paladins,pt.2	2.00
18 Mad Gods and Paladins,pt.3	2.00
19 Mad Gods and Paladins,pt.4	2.00
20 Realms Master Crew captured	2.00
21 Catewere Tribe	2.00
22 V:The Akri	1.75
23 A:Sandusk the Leprechaun	1.75
24 'Everybody wants to rule	
the realms'	1.75
25 The Wake, final issue	1.75
Ann.#1 V:Advanced D&D crew	2.95

FOUR STAR BATTLE
TALES
February-March, 1973

1 thru 5, Nov.-Dec.,1973	@1.50

All comics prices listed are for *Near Mint* condition.

FOUR STAR SPECTACULAR
March-April, 1976

1	1.50
2 thru 6	@1.25

Fox and the Crow #4
© DC Comics, Inc.

FOX AND THE CROW
December-January, 1951

1	600.00
2	300.00
3	175.00
4	175.00
5	165.00
6 thru 10	@125.00
11 thru 20	@100.00
21 thru 40	@100.00
41 thru 60	@40.00
61 thru 80	@30.00
81 thru 94	@20.00
95	25.00
96 thru 99	@10.00
100	14.00
101 thru 108	@10.00

Becomes:

STANLEY & HIS MONSTER

109 thru 112 Oct.Nov.,1968	@10.00

FREEDOM FIGHTERS
March-April, 1976

1 Freedom Fighters go to Earth 1	1.50
2	1.25
3	1.25
4	1.25
5 A:Wonder Woman	1.25
6	1.25
7	1.25
8	1.25
9	1.25
10 O:Doll Man	1.25
11 O:Ray	1.25
12 O:Firebrand	1.25
13 O:Black Condor	1.25
14 A:Batgirl	1.25
15 O:Phantom Lady	1.25

FROM BEYOND THE UNKNOWN
October-November, 1969

1 JKu,CI	70.00
2 MA(c),CI,ATh	18.00
3 NA(c),CI	15.00
4 MA(c),CI	15.00
5 MA(c),CI	15.00
6 NA(c),I:Glen Merrit	18.00
7 CI,JKu(c)	15.00
8 NA(c),CI	18.00
9 NA(c),CI	18.00
10 MA(c),CI	15.00
11 MA(c),CI	12.00
12 JKu(c),CI	15.00
13 JKu(c),CI,WW	20.00
14 JKu(c),CI	15.00
15 MA(c),CI	12.00
16 MA(c),CI	12.00
17 MA(c),CI	12.00
18 MK(c),CI	10.00
19 MK(c),CI	10.00
20	10.00
21	10.00
22 MA(c)	12.00
23 CI,Space Museum	10.00
24 CI	10.00

FUNNY STOCKING STUFFER
March, 1985

1	1.00

FUNNY STUFF
Summer, 1944

1 B:3 Mousketeer Terrific Whatzit	450.00
2	225.00
3	150.00
4	140.00
5	140.00
6 thru 10	@85.00
11 thru 20	@50.00
21	40.00
22 C:Superman	140.00
23 thru 30	@40.00
31 thru 78	@30.00
79 July-August, 1954	30.00

FURY OF FIRESTORM
June, 1982

1 PB,I:Black Bison	3.00
2 PB,V:Black Bison	2.00
3 PB,V:Pied Piper, Killer Frost	2.00
4 PB,A:JLA,Killer Frost	2.00
5 PB,V:Pied Piper	2.00
6 V:Pied Piper	2.00
7 I:Plastique	2.00
8 V:Typhoon	2.00
9 V:Typhoon	2.00
10 V:Hyena	2.00
11 V:Hyena	2.00
12 PB,V:Hyena	2.00
13	2.00
14 PB,I:Enforcer,A:Multiplex	2.00
15 V:Multiplex	2.00
16 V:Multiplex	2.00
17 I:2000 Committee,Firehawk	2.00
18 I:Tokamak,A:Multiplex	2.00
19 GC,V:Goldenrod	2.00
20 A:Killer Frost	2.00
21 D:Killer Frost	2.50

22 O:Firestorm	2.50
23 I:Bug & Byte	2.00
24 I:Blue Devil,Bug & Byte	2.50
25 I:Silver Deer	2.00
26 V:Black Bison	2.00
27 V:Black Bison	2.00
28 I:Slipknot	2.00
29 I:2000 C'tee,I:Breathtaker	2.00
30 V:2000 Committee	2.00
31 V:2000 Committee	2.00
32 Phantom Stranger	2.00
33 A:Plastique	2.00
34 I:Killer Frost 2	2.00
35 V:K.Frost/Plastique,I:Weasel	2.00
36 V:Killer Frost & Plastique	2.00
37	2.00
38 V:Weasel	2.00
39 V:Weasel	2.00
40	2.00
41 Crisis	2.00
42 Crisis,A:Firehawk	2.00
43 V:Typhoon	2.00
44 V:Typhoon	2.00
45 V:Multiplex	2.00
46 A:Blue Devil	2.00
47 A:Blue Devil	2.00
48 I:Moonbow	2.00
49 V:Moonbow	2.00
50 W:Ed Raymond	2.00
51 A:King Crusher	2.00
52 A:King Crusher	2.00
53 V:Steel Shadow	2.00
54 I:Lava	2.00
55 Legends,V:World's Luckiest Man	2.00
56 Legends,A:Hawk	2.00
57	2.00
58 I:Parasite II	2.00
59	2.00
60 Secret behind Hugo's accident	2.00
61 V:Typhoon	2.00
61a Superman Logo	55.00
62 A:Russian 'Firestorm'	2.00
63 A:Capt.Atom	2.00
64 A:Suicide Squad	2.00
Ann.#1 EC,A:Firehawk, V:Tokamak	2.25
Ann.#2	2.25
Ann.#3	2.25
Ann.#4 KG,CS,GC,DG	2.25

Becomes:

FIRESTORM, THE NUCLEAR MAN
November, 1987

65 A:New Firestorm	2.00
66 A:Green Lantern	2.00
67 Millenium	2.00
68 Millenium	2.00
69 V:Zuggernaut,Stalnivolk USA	2.00
70 V:Flying Dutchman	2.00
71 Trapped in the Timestream	2.00
72 V:Zuggernaut	2.00
73 V:Stalnivolk & Zuggernaut	2.00
74 Quest for Martin Stein	2.00
75 Return of Martin Stein	2.00
76 Firestorm & Firehawk vs Brimstone	2.00
77 Firestorm & Firehawk in Africa	2.00
78 'Exile From Eden',pt.1	2.00
79 'Exile From Eden',pt.2	2.00
80 A:Power Girl,Starman,Invasion x-over	2.00
81 A:Soyuz,Invasion aftermath	2.00
82 Invasion Aftermath	2.00

---

83 V:Svarozhich	2.00
84	2.00
85 Soul of Fire,N:Firestorm	2.00
86 TMd,Janus Directive #7	2.00
87 TMd	2.00
88 TMd,E:Air Wave B:Maser	2.00
89 TMd,V:Firehawk,Vandermeer	
Steel	2.00
90 TMd,Elemental War #1	2.00
91 TMd,Elemental War #2	2.00
92 TMd,Elemental War #3	2.00
93 TMd	2.00
94 TMd,A:Killer Frost	2.00
95 TMd,V:Captains of Industry	2.00
96 TMd,A:Shango,African God &	
Obatala,Lord o/t White Cloth	2.00
97 TMd,A:Obatala,V:Shango	2.00
98 TMd,A:Masar	2.00
99 TMd,A:Brimstone,PlasmaGiant	2.00
100 TMd,AM,V:Brimstone (Firestorm	
back-up story) final issue	3.00
Ann.#5 JLI,Suicide Squad	
I:New Firestorm	2.50

GAMMARAUDERS

1 I:Animal-Warrior Bioborgs	2.00
2 V:The Slugnoids	2.00
3 V:Slugnoids,I:Squawk the	
Penguinoid	2.00
4 V:Slugnoids	1.50
5 V:Bioborg/Podnoid	1.50
6 Slash vs.Sassin,A:RadicalDebs	1.50
7 Jok findsSword that was broken	2.00
8 Jok's search for KirkwardDerby	2.00
9 Jok the Congressman	2.00
10 The Big Nada, final issue	2.00

GANG BUSTERS
December-January, 1947–48

1	400.00
2	200.00
3	125.00
4	125.00
5	125.00
6	125.00
7	125.00
8	125.00
9 Ph(c)	135.00
10 Ph(c)	135.00
11 Ph(c)	100.00
12 Ph(c)	100.00
13 Ph(c)	100.00
14 Ph(c),FF	175.00
15	70.00
16	70.00
17	160.00
18	60.00
19	60.00
20	60.00
21 thru 25	@50.00
26 JK	45.00
27 thru 40	@40.00
41 thru 44	@35.00
45 Comics Code	35.00
46 thru 50	35.00
51 MD	38.00
52 thru 66	@38.00
67 December-January, 1958–59	38.00

GHOSTDANCING
Vertigo
[Mini-Series]

1 I:Snake,Ghost Dancing	1.95
2 Secrets	1.95

3 I:Father Craft	2.50
4 Coyote prisoner	2.50

GHOSTS
September-October, 1971

1 JAp,NC(c),Death's Bridegroom!	12.00
2 WW,NC(c),Mission	
Supernatural	10.00
3 TD,NC(c),Death is my Mother	6.00
4 GT,NC(c),The Crimson Claw	6.00
5 NC(c),Death, The Pale	
Horseman	6.00
6 NC(c),A Specter Poured	
The Potion	4.00
7 MK(c),Death's Finger Points	4.00
8 NC(c),The Cadaver In	
The Clock	4.00
9 AA,NC(c),The Last Ride	
Of Rosie The Wrecker	4.00
10 NC(c),A Specter Stalks Saigon	4.00
11 NC(c),The Devils Lake	4.00
12 NC(c),The Macabre Mummy	
Of Takhem-Ahtem	4.00
13 NC(c),Hell Is One Mile High	4.00
14 NC(c),The Bride Wore	
A Shroud	4.00
15 AA,NC(c),The Ghost That	
Wouldn't Die	4.00
16 NC(c),Death's Grinning Face	4.00
17 NC(c),Death Held the	
Lantern High	4.00
18 AA,NC(c),Graveyard of	
Vengeance	4.00
19 AA,NC(c),The Dead Live On	4.00
20 NC(c),The Haunting Hussar	
Of West Point	4.00
21 NC(c),The Ghost In The	
Devil's Chair	3.50
22 NC(c),The Haunted Horns	
Of Death	3.50
23 NC(c),Dead Is My Darling!	3.50
24 AA,NC(c),You Too, Will Die	3.50
25 AA,NC(c),Three Skulls On	
The Zambezi	3.50
26 DP,NC(c),The Freaky Phantom	
Of Watkins Glen	3.50
27 NC(c),Conversation With	
A Corpse	3.50
28 DP,NC(c),Flight Of The	
Lost Phantom	3.50
29 NC(c),The Haunted Lady	
Of Death	3.50
30 NC(c),The Fangs of	
the Phantom	3.50
31 NC(c),Blood On The Moon	3.50
32 NC(c),Phantom Laughed Last	3.50
33 NC(c),The Hangman of	
Haunted Island	3.50
34 NC(c),Wrath of the Ghost Apes	3.50
35 NC(c),Feud with a Phantom	3.50
36 NC(c),The Boy Who Returned	
From The Gave	3.50
37 LD(c),Fear On Ice	3.50
38 LD(c),Specter In The Surf	3.50
39 LD(c),The Haunting Hitchhicker	3.50
40 LD(c),The Nightmare That	
Haunted The World	3.50
41 LD(c),Ship of Specters	3.50
42 LD(c),The Spectral Sentries	3.50
43 LD(c),3 Corpses On A Rope	3.50
44 LD(c),The Case of the	
Murdering Specters	3.50
45 LD(c),Bray of the	
Phantom Beast	3.50
46 LD(c),The World's Most	

Famous Phantom	3.50
47 LD(c),Wrath of the	
Restless Specters	3.50
48 DP,LD(c),The Phantom Head	3.50
49 The Ghost in the Cellar	3.50
50 Home Is Where The Grave Is	3.50
51 The Ghost Who Would Not Die	3.50
52 LD(c),The Thunderhead	
Phantom	3.50
53 LD(c),Whose Spirit Invades Me	3.50
54 LD(c),The Deadly Dreams	
Of Ernie Caruso	3.50
55 LD(c),The House That Was	
Built For Haunting	3.50
56 LD(c),The Triumph Of The	
Teen-Age Phantom	3.50
57 LD(c),The Flaming Phantoms	
of Oradour	3.50
58 LD(c),The Corpse in the Closet	3.50
59 LD(c),That Demon Within Me	3.50
60 LD(c),The Spectral Smile	
of Death	3.50
61 LD(c),When Will I Die Again	3.00
62 LD(c),The Phantom Hoaxer!	3.00
63 LD(c),The Burning Bride	3.00
64 LD(c),Dead Men Do Tell Tales	3.00
65 LD(c),The Imprisoned Phantom	3.00
66 LD(c),Conversation With A	
Corpse	3.00
67 LD(c),The Spectral Sword	3.00
68 LD(c),The Phantom of the	
Class of '76	3.00
69 LD(c),The Haunted Gondola	3.00
70 LD(c),Haunted Honeymoon	3.00
71 LD(c),The Ghost Nobody Knew	3.00
72 LD(c),The Ghost of	
Washington Monument	3.00
73 LD(c),The Specter Of The	
Haunted Highway	3.00
74 LD(c),The Gem That Haunted	
the World!	3.00
75 LD(c),The Legend Of The	
Lottie Lowry	3.00
76 LD(c),Two Ghosts of	
Death Row	3.00
77 LD(c),Ghost, Where Do	
You Hide?	3.00
78 LD(c),The World's Most	
Famous Phantom	3.00
79 LD(c),Lure of the Specter	3.00
80 JO(c),The Winged Specter	3.00
81 LD(c),Unburied Phantom	3.00
82 LD(c),The Ghost Who	
Wouldn't Die	3.00
83 LD(c),Escape From the Haunt	
of the Amazon Specter	3.00
84 LD(c),Torment of the	
Phantom Face	3.00
85 LD(c),The Fiery Phantom	
of Faracutin	3.00
86 LD(c),The Ghostly Garden	3.00
87 LD(c),The Phantom Freak	3.00
88 LD(c),Harem In Hell	3.00
89 JKu(c),Came The Specter	
Shrouded In Seaweed	3.00
90 The Ghost Galleon	3.00
91 LD(c),The Haunted Wheelchair	3.00
92 DH(c),Double Vision	3.00
93 MK(c),The Flaming Phantoms	
of Nightmare Alley	3.00
94 LD(c),Great Caesar's Ghost	3.00
95 All The Stage Is A Haunt	3.00
96 DH(c),Dread of the	
Deadly Domestic	3.00
97 JAp(c),A Very Special Spirit	

All comics prices listed are for *Near Mint* condition.

A:Spectre 8.00
98 JAp(c),The Death of a Ghost
    A:Spectre 8.00
99 EC(c),Till Death Do Us Join
    A:Spectre 8.00
100 EC&DG(c),The Phantom's
    Final Debt 2.00
101 MK(c),The Haunted Hospital . 2.00
102 RB&DG(c),The Fine Art
    Of Haunting 2.00
103 RB&DG(c),Visions and
    Vengeance 2.00
104 LD(c),The First Ghost 2.00
105 JKu(c) 2.00
106 JKu(c) 2.00
107 JKu(c) 2.00
108 JKu(c) 2.00
109 EC(c) 2.00
110 EC&DG(c) 2.00
111 JKu(c) 2.00
112 May, 1982 . . . . 2.00

G.I. COMBAT
January, 1957
Prev: Golden Age
44 RH,JKu,The Eagle and
    the Wolves 250.00
45 RH,JKu,Fireworks Hill 125.00
46 JKu,The Long Walk
    To Wansan 80.00
47 RH, The Walking Weapon . 80.00
48 No Fence For A Jet 80.00
49 Frying Pan Seat 80.00
50 Foxhole Pilot 80.00
51 RH,The Walking Grenade . . . 55.00

G.I. Combat #288 © DC Comics, Inc.

52 Jku,JKu(c),Call For A Tank . . 55.00
53 JKu,The Paper Trap 55.00
54 RH,JKu,Sky Tank 55.00
55 Call For A Gunner 55.00
56 JKu,JKu(c),The D.I.-And the
    Sand Fleas 55.00
57 RH,Live Wire For Easy 55.00
58 JKu(c),Flying Saddle 55.00
59 JKu,Hot Corner 55.00
60 RH,Bazooka Crossroads 55.00
61 JKu(c),The Big Run 35.00

62 RH,JKu,Drop An Inch 35.00
63 MD,JKu(c),Last Stand 35.00
64 MD,RH,JKu,JKu(c),The
    Silent Jet 35.00
65 JKu,Battle Parade 35.00
66 MD,The Eagle of Easy
    Company 35.00
67 JKu(c),I:Tank Killer 50.00
68 JKu,RH,The Rock 35.00
69 JKu,RH,The Steel Ribbon . . . 35.00
70 JKu,Bull's-Eye Bridge 35.00
71 MD,JKu(c),Last Stand 40.00
72 MD,JKu(c),Ground Fire 40.00
73 RH,JKu(c),Window War 40.00
74 RH,A Flag For Joey 40.00
75 RH,Dogtag Hill 40.00
76 MD,RH,JKu,Bazooka For
    A Mouse 40.00
77 RH,JKu,H-Hour For A Gunner 40.00
78 MD,RH,JKu(c),Who Cares
    About The Infantry 40.00
79 JKu,RH,Big Gun-Little Gun . . 40.00
80 JKu,RH(c),Flying Horsemen . 40.00
81 Jump For Glory 35.00
82 IN,Get Off My Back 35.00
83 Too Tired To Fight 40.00
84 JKu(c),Dog Company
    Is Holding 35.00
85 IN,JKu(c),The T.N.T. Trio . . . 35.00
86 JKu,RH(c),Not Return 35.00
87 RH(c),I:Haunted Tank 100.00
88 RH,JKu(c),Haunted Tank Vs.
    Ghost Tank 35.00
89 JA,RH,IN,Tank With Wings . 35.00
90 JA,IN,RH,Tank Raiders 35.00
91 IN,RH,The Tank and the Turtle 25.00
92 JA,IN,The Tank of Doom . . . 25.00
93 RH(c),JA,No-Return Mission . 25.00
94 IN,RH(c),Haunted Tank Vs.
    The Killer Tank 25.00
95 JA,RH(c),The Ghost of
    the Haunted Tank 25.00
96 JA,RH(c),The Lonesome Tank 25.00
97 IN,RH(c),The Decoy Tank . . . 25.00
98 JA,RH(c),Trap of Dragon's
    Teeth 25.00
99 JA,JKu,RH(c),Battle of the
    Thirsty Tanks 25.00
100 JA,JKu,Return of the
    Ghost Tank 25.00
101 JA,The Haunted Tank Vs.
    Attila's Battle Tiger 20.00
102 JKu(c),Haunted Tank
    Battle Window 20.00
103 JKu,JA,RH(c),Rabbit Punch
    For A Tiger 20.00
104 JA,JKu,RH(c),Blind
    Man's Radar 20.00
105 JA,JKu(c),Time Bomb Tank . 20.00
106 JA,JKu(c),Two-Sided War . . 20.00
107 JKu(c),The Ghost Pipers . . . 20.00
108 JKu(c),The Wounded
    Won't Wait,I:Sgt.Rock 22.00
109 JKu(c),Battle of the Tank
    Graveyard 20.00
110 IN,JKu(c),Choose Your War 20.00
111 JA,JKu(c),Death Trap 20.00
112 JA,JKu(c),Ghost Ace 15.00
113 JKu,RH(c),Tank Fight In
    Death Town 15.00
114 JA,RH(c),O:Haunted Tank . . 50.00
115 JA,RH(c),Medals For Mayhem 15.00
116 IN,JA,JKu(c),Battle Cry
    For A Dead Man 15.00
117 JA,RH,JKu(c),Tank In

The Ice Box 15.00
118 IN,JA,RH(c),My Buddy-
    My Enemy 15.00
119 IN,RH(c),Target For
    A Firing Squad 15.00
120 IN,JA,RH(c),Pull ATiger'sTail 15.00
121 RH(c),Battle of Two Wars . . 15.00
122 JA,JKu(c),Who Dies Next? . 15.00
123 IN,RH(c),The Target of Terror 15.00
124 IN,RH(c),Scratch That Tank . 15.00
125 RH(c),Stay Alive-Until Dark . 15.00
126 JA,RH(c),Tank Umbrella . . . 15.00
127 JA,JKu(c),Mission-Sudden
    Death 15.00
128 RH(c),The Ghost of
    the Haunted Tank 15.00
129 JA,RH(c),Hold That Town
    For A Dead Man 15.00
130 RH(c),Battle of the Generals 15.00
131 JKu&RH(c),Devil For Dinner 15.00
132 JA,JKu(c),The Executioner . 15.00
133 JKu(c),Operation:Death Trap 15.00
134 MD,JKu(c),Desert Holocaust 15.00
135 GE,JKu(c),Death is the Joker 15.00
136 JKu(c),Kill Now-Pay Later . . 15.00
137 JKu(c),We Can't See 15.00
138 JKu(c),I:The Losers 18.00
139 JKu(c),Corner of Hell 15.00
140 RH,MD,JKu(c),The LastTank 15.00
141 MD,JKu(c),Let Me Live..
    Let Me Die 5.00
142 RH,JKu(c),Checkpoint-Death 5.00
143 RH,JKu(c),The Iron Horseman 5.00
144 RH,MD,JKu(c),Every
    Man A Fort 5.00
145 MD,JKu(c),Sand,Sun
    and Death 5.00
146 JKu(c),Move the World 5.00
147 JKu(c),Rebel Tank 5.00
148 IN,JKu(c),The Gold-Plated
    General 5.00
149 JKu(c),Leave The
    Fighting To Us 5.00
150 JKu(c),The Death of the
    Haunted Tank 5.00
151 JKu(c),A Strong Right Arm . 5.00
152 JKu(c),Decoy Tank 5.00
153 JKu(c),The Armored Ark . . . 5.00
154 JKu(c),Battle Prize 5.00
155 JKu(c),The Long Journey . . 5.00
156 JKu(c),Beyond Hell 5.00
157 JKu(c),The Fountain 5.00
158 What Price War 5.00
159 JKu(c),Mission Dead End . . 5.00
160 JKu(c),Battle Ghost 5.00
161 JKu(c),The Day of the Goth . 5.00
162 JKu(c),The Final Victor 5.00
163 A Crew Divided 5.00
164 Siren Song 5.00
165 JKu(c),Truce,Pathfinder . . . 5.00
166 Enemy From Yesterday . . . 5.00
167 JKu(c),The Finish Line 5.00
168 NA(c),The Breaking Point . . 5.00
169 WS(c),The Death of the
    Haunted Tank 5.00
170 Chain of Vengeance 5.00
171 JKu(c),The Man Who
    Killed Jeb Stuart 5.00
172 RH(c),At The Mercy of
    My Foes 5.00
173 JKu(c),The Final Crash 5.00
174 JKu(c),Vow To A Dead Foe . 5.00
175 JKu(c),The Captive Tank . . . 5.00
176 JKu(c),A Star Can Cry 5.00
177 JKu(c),The Tank That

Missed D-Day	5.00
178 JKu(c),A Tank Is Born	5.00
179 JKu(c),One Last Charge	5.00
180 JKu(c),The Saints Go Riding On	5.00
181 JKu(c),The Kidnapped Tank	5.00
182 JKu(c),Combat Clock	5.00
183 JKu(c),6 Stallions To Hell- And Back	5.00
184 JKu(c),Battlefield Bundle	5.00
185 JKu(c),No Taps For A Tank	5.00
186 JKu(c),Souvenir From A Headhunter	5.00
187 JKu(c),The General Died Twice	5.00
188 The Devil's Pipers	5.00
189 The Gunner is a Gorilla	5.00
190 The Tiger and The Terrier	5.00
191 Decoy For Death	5.00
192 The General Has Two Faces	5.00
193 JKu(c),The War That Had To Wait	5.00
194 GE(c),Blitzkrieg Brain	5.00
195 JKu(c),The War That Time Forgot	5.00
196 JKu(c),Dead Men Patrol	5.00
197 JKu(c),Battle Ark	5.00
198 JKu(c),The Devil Rides A Panzer	5.00
199 JKu(c),A Medal From A Ghost	5.00
200 JKu(c),The Tank That Died	5.00
201 NA&RH(c),The Rocking Chair Soldiers	3.50
202 NA&RH(c),Walking Wounded Don't Cry	3.50
203 JKu(c),To Trap A Tiger	3.50
204 JKu(c),A Winter In Hell	3.50
205 JKu(c),A Gift From The Emperor	3.50
206 JKu(c),A Tomb For A Tank	3.50
207 JKu(c),Foxhole for a Sherman	3.50
208 JKu(c),Sink That Tank	3.50
209 JKu(c),Ring Of Blood	3.50
210 JKu(c),Tankers Also Bleed	3.50
211 JKu(c),A Nice Day For Killing	3.50
212 JKu(c),Clay Pigeon Crew	3.50
213 JKu(c),Back Door To War	3.50
214 JKu(c),The Tanker Who Couldn't Die	3.50
215 JKu(c),Last Stand For Losers	3.50
216 JKu(c),Ghost Squadron	3.50
217 JKu(c), The Pigeon Spies	3.50
218 JKu(c), 48 Hours to Die	3.50
219 thru 288	@3.50

GILGAMESH II

1 JSn,O:Gilgamesh	5.00
2 JSn,V:Nightshadow	4.50
3 JSn,V:Robotic Ninja	4.50
4 JSn,final issue	3.95

GODDESS
Vertigo
[Mini-Series]

1 I:Rosie Nolan	2.95
2 Rosie arrested	2.95

GOLDEN AGE
Elseworld

1 PS,F:JSA,All-Star Squadron	10.00
2 PS,I:Dynaman	8.00
3 PS,IR:Mr. Terrific is Ultra-Humanite	8.00
4 PS,D:Dynaman,Mr. Terrific	6.00

GREATEST STORIES EVER TOLD

Greatest Superman Stories Ever Told:

HC	75.00
SC	15.95

Greatest Batman Stories Ever Told:

HC	60.00
SC	16.00
Vol.#2 Catwoman & Penguin	16.95

Greatest Joker Stories Ever Told:

HC	45.00
SC BBo(c)	16.00

Greatest Flash Stories Ever Told:

HC	30.00
SC	15.00

Greatest Golden Age Stories Ever Told:

HC	25.00
SC	15.00

Greatest Fifties Stories Ever Told:

HC	30.00
SC	15.00

Greatest Team-Up Stories Ever Told:

HC	25.00
SC	15.00

GREEN ARROW
[Limited Series]

1 TVE,DG,O:Green Arrow	5.00
2 TVE,DG,A:Vertigo	3.50
3 TVE,DG,A:Vertigo	3.50
4 TVE,DG,A:Black Canary	3.50

[Regular Series]

1 EH,DG,V:Muncie	10.00
2 EH,DG,V:Muncie	6.00
3 EH,DG,FMc,V:Fyres	4.50
4 EH,DG,FMc,V:Fyres	4.50
5 EH,DG,FMc,Gauntlet	4.50
6 EH,DG,FMc,Gauntlet	4.50
7 EB,DG,A:Black Canary	4.50
8 DG,Alaska	4.00
9 EH,DG,FMc,R:Shado	4.00
10 EH,DG,FMc,A:Shado	4.00
11 EH,DG,FMc,A:Shado	4.00
12 EH,DG,FMc,A:Shado	3.00
13 DJu,DG,FMc,Moving Target	3.00
14 EH,DG,FMc	3.00
15 EH,DG,FMc,Seattle And Die	3.00
16 EH,DG,FMc,Seattle And Die	3.00
17 DJu,DG,FMc,The Horse Man	2.50
18 DJu,DG,FMc,The Horse Man	2.50
19 EH,DG,FMc,A:Hal Jordan	2.50
20 EH,DG,FMc,A:Hal Jordan	2.50
21 DJu,DG,B:Blood of Dragon, A:Shado	2.50
22 DJu,DG,A:Shado	2.50
23 DJu,DG,A:Shado	2.50
24 DJu,DG,E:Blood of Dragon	2.50
25 TVE,Witch Hunt #1	2.25
26 Witch Hunt #2	2.25
27 DJu,DG,FMc,R:Warlord	2.25
28 DJu,DG,FMc,A:Warlord	2.25
29 DJu,DG,FMc,Coyote Tears	2.25
30 DJu,DG,FMc,Coyote Tears	2.25
31 FMc,V:Drug Dealers	2.25
32 FMc,V:Drug Dealers	2.25
33 DJu,FMc,Psychology Issue	2.25
34 DJu,DG,A:Fryes,Arrested	2.25
35 B:Black Arrow Saga,A:Shade	2.25
36 Black Arrow Saga,A:Shade	2.25
37 Black Arrow Saga,A:Shade	2.25
38 E:Black Arrow Saga,A:Shade	2.25
39 DCw,Leaves Seattle	2.25
40 MGr,Spirit Quest,A: Indian Shaman	2.25

Green Arrow #77 © DC Comics, Inc.

41 DCw,I.R.A	2.25
42 DCw,I.R.A	2.25
43 DCw,I.R.A	2.25
44 DCw,Rock'n'Runes,pt.1	2.25
45 Rock'n'Runes,pt.2	2.25
46 DCw,Africa	2.25
47 DCw,V:Trappers	2.25
48 DCw,V:Trappers	2.25
49 V:Trappers	2.25
50 MGr(c),50th Anniv.,R:Seattle	3.00
51 Tanetti's Murder,pt.1	2.00
52 Tanetti's Murder,pt.2	2.00
53 The List,pt.1,A:Fyres	2.00
54 The List,pt.2,A:Fyres	2.00
55 Longbow Hunters tie-in	2.00
56 A:Lt. Cameron	2.00
57 And Not A Drop to Drink,pt.1	2.00
58 And Not A Drop to Drink,pt.2	2.00
59 Predator,pt.1	2.00
60 Predator,pt.2	2.00
61 FS,F:Draft Dodgers	2.00
62 FS	2.00
63 FS,B:Hunt for Red Dragon	2.00
64 FS,Hunt for Red Dragon	2.00
65 MGr(c),Hunt for Red Dragon	2.00
66 MGr(c),E:Hunt for Red Dragon	2.00
67 MGr(c),FS,V:Rockband Killer	2.00
68 MGr(c),FS,BumRap	2.00
69 MGr(c),Reunion Tour #1	2.00
70 Reunion Tour #2	2.00
71 Wild in the Streets #1	2.00
72 MGr(c),Wild in the Streets#2	2.00
73 MGr(c),F:Vietnam Vet	2.00
74 SAP,MGr(c),V:Sniper	2.00
75 MGr(c),A:Speedy Shado, Black Canary	3.00
76 MGr(c),R:Eddie Fyers	2.00
77 MGr(c),A:Eddie Fyers	2.00
78 MGr(c),V:CIA	2.00
79 MGr(c),V:CIA	2.00
80 MGr(c),E:MGr(s),V:CIA	2.00
81 B:CDi(s),JAp,V:Shrapnel, Nuklon	2.00
82 JAp,I:Rival	2.00
83 JAp,V:Yakuza	2.00
84 E:CDi(s),JAp,In Las Vegas	2.00
85 AlG(s),JAp,A:Deathstroke	2.00
86 DgM(s),JAp,A:Catwoman	2.00
87 JAp,V:Factory Owner	2.00

All comics prices listed are for *Near Mint* condition.   **CVA Page 47**

88 JAp,A:M.Manhunter,Bl.Beetle . 2.00
89 JAp,A:Anarky 2.25
90 Zero Hour 2.25
91 Hitman 2.25
92 Partner attacked 2.25
93 Secrets of Red File 2.25
94 I:Camo Rouge 2.25
95 V:Camo Rouge 2.25
96 I:Slyfox,A:Hal Jordan 1.95
97 Where Angels Fear to
    Tread,pt.2 . . . . 2.25
98 Where Angels Fear to
    Tread,pt.3, A:Arsenal 2.25
Ann.#1 A:Question,FablesII 3.50
Ann.#2 EH,DG,FMc,A:Question . . 3.00
Ann.#3 A:Question 2.50
Ann.#4 'The Black Alchemist' 3.25
Ann.#5 TVE,FS,Eclipso,Batman . 3.25
Ann.#6 JBa(c),I:Hook 3.50
Spec. #0 Return 2.00

GREEN ARROW LONGBOW HUNTERS
August, 1987
1 MGr,N:GreenArrow,I:Shado . . 12.00
1a 2nd printing 3.00
2 MGr,'Shadow' Revealed 9.00
2a 2nd printing 3.00
3 MGr,Tracking Snow 9.00
TPB, rep. #1-#3 . . . . 12.95

GREEN ARROW: THE WONDER YEARS
1 MGr,GM,B:New O:Green Arrow 2.50
2 MGr,GM,I:Brianna Stone 2.00
3 MGr,GM,A:Brianna Stone 2.00
4 MGr,GM,Conclusion 2.00

GREEN LANTERN
Autumn, 1941
1 O:Green Lantern, V:Master of
    Light, Arson in the Slums 18,000.00
2 V:Baldy,Tycoon's Legacy . . 3,800.00
3 . . . . 2,800.00
4 Doiby and Green Lantern
    join the Army 2,200.00
5 V:Nazis and Black
    Prophet,A:General Prophet 1,500.00
6 V:Nordo & Hordes of War Hungry
    Henchmen,Exhile of Exiles,
    A:Shiloh 1,100.00
7 The Wizard of Odds 1,100.00
8 The Lady and Her Jewels,
    A:Hop Harrigan 1,100.00
9 V:The Whistler, The School
    for Vandals 1,000.00
10 V:Vandal Savage,The Man Who
    Wanted the World,O:Vandal
    Savage 1,000.00
11 The Distardly Designs of
    Doiby Dickles' Pals 850.00
12 O:The Gambler 850.00
13 A:Angela Van Enters 850.00
14 Case of the Crooked Cook . 850.00
15 V:Albert Zero, One...Two...
    Three...Stop Thinking 850.00
16 V:The Lizard 850.00
17 V:Kid Triangle, Reward for
    Green Lantern 850.00
18 V:The Dandy,The Connoisseur of
    crime,X-mas(c) 1,000.00
19 V:Harpies, Sing a Song of
    Disaster A:Fate 750.00
20 A:Gambler 750.00

21 V:The Woodman,The Good
    Humor Man 750.00
22 A:Dapper Dan Crocker 750.00
23 Doiby Dickles Movie
    Ajax Pictures 750.00
24 A:Mike Mattson, Once A Cop 750.00
25 The Diamond Magnet 750.00
26 The Scourge of the Sea . . . 750.00
27 V:Sky Pirate 750.00
28 The Tricks of the
    Sports Master 750.00
29 Meets the Challange of
    the Harlequin 750.00
30 I:Streak the Wonder Dog . . 750.00
31 The Terror of the Talismans 600.00
32 The Case of the
    Astonishing Juggler 600.00
33 Crime goes West 600.00
34 Streak meets the Princess . 600.00
35 V:The Three-in-One Criminal 600.00
36 The Mystery of the
    Missing Messanger 750.00
37 A:Sargon 750.00
38 Double Play,May-June, 1949 750.00

GREEN LANTERN
1 GK,O:Green Lantern 2,400.00
2 GK,I:Qward,Pieface 600.00
3 GK,V:Qward 340.00
4 GK,Secret of GL Mask 275.00
5 GK,I:Hector Hammond 275.00
6 GK,I:Tomar-Re 210.00
7 GK,I&O:Sinestro 185.00
8 GK,1st Story in 5700 A.D. . . 185.00
9 GK,A:Sinestro 185.00
10 GK,O:Green Lantern's Oath 185.00
11 GK,V:Sinestro 170.00
12 GK,Sinestro,I:Dr.Polaris . . . 170.00
13 GK,A:Flash,Sinestro 170.00
14 GK,I&O:Sonar,1st Jordan
    Brothers story 130.00
15 GK,Zero Hour story 125.00
16 GK,MA,I:Star Saphire,
    O:Abin Sur 150.00
17 GK,V:Sinestro 120.00
18 GK 120.00
19 GK,A:Sonar 120.00
20 GK,A:Flash 130.00
21 GK,O:Dr.Polaris 100.00
22 GK,A:Hector Hammond,Jordan
    Brothers story 100.00
23 GK,I:Tattooed Man 100.00
24 GK,O:Shark 100.00
25 GK,V:Sonar,HectorHammond 100.00
26 GK,A:Star Sapphire 100.00
27 GK 100.00
28 GK,I:Goldface 100.00
29 GK,I:Black Hand 110.00
30 GK,I:Katma Tui 100.00
31 GK,Jordan brothers story . . . 75.00
32 GK 75.00
33 GK,V:Dr. Light 75.00
34 GK,V:Hector Hammond 75.00
35 GK,I:Aerialist 75.00
36 GK 75.00
37 GK,I:Evil Star 75.00
38 GK,A:Tomar-Re 75.00
39 GK,V:Black Hand 75.00
40 GK,O:Guardians,A:Golden
    Age Green Lantern 400.00
41 GK,A:Star Sapphire 50.00
42 GK,A:Zatanna 50.00
43 GK,A:Major Disaster 50.00
44 GK,A:Evil Star 50.00
45 GK,I:Prince Peril,A:Golden

Green Lantern #10 © DC Comics, Inc.

    Age Green Lantern 80.00
46 GK,V:Dr.Polaris 55.00
47 GK,5700 A.D. V:Dr.Polaris . . 55.00
48 GK,I:Goldface 55.00
49 GK,I:Dazzler 55.00
50 GK,V:Thraxon the Powerful . . 55.00
51 GK,Green Lantern's Evil
    Alter-ego 35.00
52 GK,A:Golden Age Green
    Lantern Sinestro 40.00
53 GK,CI,Jordon brothers story . 32.00
54 GK,Menace in the Iron Lung . 32.00
55 GK,Cosmic Enemy #1 . . . . . 32.00
56 GK 32.00
57 GK,V:Major Disaster 32.00
58 GK,Perils of the Powerless
    Green Lantern 32.00
59 GK,I:Guy Gardner(imaginary
    story) 190.00
60 GK,I:Lamplighter 22.00
61 GK,A:Gold.Age Gr.Lantern . . 25.00
62 Steel Small,Rob Big 20.00
63 NA(c),This is the Way the
    World Ends 20.00
64 MSy,We Vow Death to Green
    Lantern 20.00
65 MSy,Dry up and Die 20.00
66 MSy,5700 AD story 20.00
67 DD,The First Green Lantern . 20.00
68 GK,I Wonder where the
    Yellow Went? 20.00
69 GK,WW,If Earth Fails the
    Test.. It Means War 20.00
70 GK,A Funny Thing Happened
    on the way to Earth 20.00
71 GK,DD,MA,Jordan brothers . . 16.00
72 GK,Phantom o/t SpaceOpera 16.00
73 GK,MA,A:Star Sapphire,
    Sinestro 16.00
74 GK,MA,A:Star Sapphire,
    Sinestro 15.00
75 GK,Qward 15.00
76 NA,Gr.Lantern & Gr.Arrow
    team-up begins 125.00
77 NA,Journey to Desolation . . . 50.00
78 NA:A:Black Canary,A Kind of
    Loving..A Way to Death 50.00
79 NA,DA,A:Black Canary,Ulysses
    Star is Still Alive 40.00

Green Lantern © DC Comics, Inc.

80 NA,DG,Even an Immortal
can die 40.00
81 NA,DG,A:Black Canary,Death
be my Destiny 28.00
82 NA,DG,A:Black Canary,
V:Sinestro,(BWr 1 page) . . . 28.00
83 NA,DG,A:BlackCanary,Gr.Lantern
reveals I.D. to Carol Ferris . 28.00
84 NA,BWr,V:Black Hand 28.00
85 NA,Speedy on Drugs,pt.1,
rep.Green Lantern #1 . . . . . 40.00
86 NA,DG,Speedy on Drugs,pt.2,
ATh(rep)Golden Age G.L. . . 40.00
87 NA,DG,I:John Stewart,
2nd Guy Gardner app. 31.00
88 all reprints. 7.50
89 NA,And Through Him Save
the World 27.00
90 MGr,New Gr.Lantern rings . . . 6.00
91 MGr,V:Sinestro 5.00
92 MGr,V:Sinestro 5.00
93 MGr,TA,War Against the
World Builders 4.00
94 MGr,TA,DG,Green Arrow
Assassin,pt.1 . . . . 4.00
95 MGr,Gr.Arrow Assassin,pt.2 . . 4.00
96 MGr,A:Katma Tui 4.00
97 MGr,V:Mocker 4.00
98 MGr,V:Mocker 4.00
99 MGr,V:Mocker 4.00
100 MGr,AS,I:Air Wave 6.00
101 MGr,A:Green Arrow 5.50
102 AS,A:Green Arrow 4.50
103 AS,Earth-Asylum for an Alien 3.50
104 AS,A:Air Wave 5.00
105 AS,Thunder Doom 5.00
106 MGr,Panic..In High Places
& Low 5.00
107 AS,Green Lantern Corp.story 5.00
108 MGr,BU:G.A.Green Lantern,
V:Replikon 6.00
109 MGr,Replicon#2,GA.GL.#2 . 5.00
110 MGr,GA.GL.#3 . . . . 5.00
111 AS,O:Green Lantern,
A:G.A.Green Lantern 6.00
112 AS,O&A:G.A. Green Lantern . 7.00
113 AS,Christmas story 4.00

114 AS,I:Crumbler 4.00
115 AS,V:Crumbler 4.00
116 Guy Gardner as Gr.Lantern . 26.00
117 JSon,I:KariLimbo,V:Prof.Ojo . 4.00
118 AS,V:Prof.Ojo 4.00
119 AS,G.L.& G.A.solo storys . . . 3.50
120 DH,A:Kari,V:El Espectro 3.50
121 DH,V:El Espectro 3.50
122 DH,A:Guy Gardner,Superman 6.00
123 JSon,DG,E:Green Lantern/Green
Arrow T.U.,A:G.Gardner,
V:Sinestro 6.50
124 JSon,V:Sinestro 3.50
125 JSon,FMc,V:Sinestro 3.50
126 JSon,FMc,V:Shark 3.50
127 JSon,FMc,V:Goldface 3.50
128 JSon,V:Goldface 3.50
129 JSon,V:Star Sapphire 3.50
130 JSon,FMc,A:Sonar,B:Tales of the
Green Lantern Corps 3.00
131 JSon,AS,V:Evil Star 3.00
132 JSon,AS,E:Tales of GL Corps
B:B.U.Adam Strange 3.00
133 JSon,V:Dr.Polaris 2.50
134 JSon,V:Dr.Polaris 2.50
135 JSon,V:Dr.Polaris 2.50
136 JSon,A:Space Ranger,
Adam Strange 2.50
137 JSon,CI,MA,I:Citadel,A:Space
Ranger,A.Strange 2.50
138 JSon,A&O:Eclipso 4.00
139 JSon,V:Eclipso 3.00
140 JSon,I:Congressman Block
Adam Strange 2.50
141 JSon,I:OmegaMen 6.00
142 JSon,A:OmegaMen 4.00
143 JSon,A:OmegaMen 4.00
144 JSon,D:Tattooed Man,Adam
Strange 2.50
145 JSon,V:Goldface 2.50
146 JSon,CI,V:Goldface
E:B.U.Adam Strange 2.50
147 JSon,CI,V:Goldface 2.50
148 JSon,DN,DA,V:Quardians . . . 2.50
149 JSon,A:GL.Corps 2.50
150 JSon,anniversary 3.50
151 JSon,GL.Exiled in space 2.50
152 JSon,CI,GL Exile #2 . . . . . . 2.50
153 JSon,CI,Gr.Lantern Exile #3 . 2.50
154 JSon,Gr.Lantern Exile #4 . . . 2.50
155 JSon,Gr.Lantern Exile #5 . . . 2.50
156 GK,Gr.Lantern Exile #6 . . . . 2.50
157 KP,IN,Gr.Lantern Exile #7 . . . 2.50
158 KP,IN,Gr.Lantern Exile #8 . . . 2.50
159 KP,Gr.Lantern Exile #9 . . . . 2.50
160 KP,Gr.Lantern Exile #10 . . . . 2.50
161 KP,A:Omega Men,Exile #11 . 2.50
162 KP,Gr.Lantern Exile #12 . . . . 2.50
163 KP,Gr.Lantern Exile #13 . . . . 2.50
164 KP,A:Myrwhidden,Exile #14 . 2.50
165 KP,A:John Stewart & Gr.Lantern
Green Lantern Exile #15 . . . . 2.00
166 GT,FMc,DGi,Exile #16 . . . . . 2.00
167 GT,FMc,G.L.Exile #17 . . . . . 2.00
168 GT,FMc,G.L. Exile #18 . . . . . 2.00
169 Green Lantern Exile #19 . . . . 2.00
170 GT,MSy,GreenLanternCorps . 2.00
171 ATh,TA,DGb,Green Lantern
Exile #20 . . . . 2.00
172 DGb,E:Gr.Lant.Exile 2.00
173 DGb,I:Javelin,A:Congressman
Bloch 2.00
174 DGb,V:Javelin 2.00
175 DGb,A:Flash 2.25
176 DGb,V:The Shark 2.00

177 DGb,rep. Gr.Lant #128 . . .
178 DGb,A:Monitor,V:Demolition
Team 2.00
179 DGb,I:Predator 2.00
180 DGb,A:JLA 2.00
181 DGi,Hal Jordan quits as GL . 2.75
182 DGi,John Stewart taks over
V:Major Disaster 2.50
183 DGi,V:Major Disaster 2.50
184 DGb,Rep. Gr.Lant. #59 . . . . . 3.50
185 DGi,DH,V:Eclipso 4.00
186 DGi,V:Eclipso 4.00
187 BWi,John Stewart meets
Katma Tui 2.25
188 JSon,C:GrArrow,V:Sonar,John
Stewart reveals I.D. to world . 3.50
189 JSon,V:Sonar 2.00
190 JSon,A:Green Arrow/Black
Canary,Guy Gardner 2.00
191 JSon,IR:Predator is Star
Sapphire 2.00
192 JSon,O:Star Sapphire 2.00
193 JSon,V:Replikon,
A:G.Gardner 2.50
194 JSon,Crisis,R:G.Gardner 6.00
195 JSon,Guy Gardner as Green
Lantern,develops attitude . . 13.00
196 JSon,V:Shark,Hal Jordan
regains ring 4.00
197 JSon,V:Shark,Sonar,
Goldface 3.50
198 JSon,D:Tomar-Re,Hal returns as
Green Lantern,(double size) . . 3.00
199 JSon,V:Star Sapphire 2.00
200 JSon,final Gr.Lantern issue . . 2.50
Becomes:

GREEN LANTERN
CORPS

201 JSon,I:NewGr.LantCorps,V:Star
Sapphire, Sonar, Dr.Polaris . . 2.00
202 JSon,set up headquarters . . . 2.00
203 JSon,tribute to Disney 2.00
204 JSon,Arisia reaches puberty . 2.00
205 JSon,V:Black Hand 2.00
206 JSon,V:Black Hand 2.00
207 JSon, Legneds crossover . . . 2.00
208 JSon,I:Rocket Red Brigade,
Green Lanterns in Russia#1 . . 2.00
209 JSon,In Russia #2 . . . . 2.00
210 JSon,In Russia #3 . . . . 2.00
211 JSon,John Stewart proposes
to Katma Tui 1.75
212 JSon,W:J.Stewart&KatmaTui . 1.75
213 Json,For Want of a Male 1.75
214 IG,5700 A.D. Story 1.75
215 IG,Salaak and Chip quit . . . 1.75
216 IG,V:Carl 1.75
217 JSon,V:Sinestro 1.75
218 BWg,V:Sinestro 1.75
219 BWg,V:Sinestro 1.75
220 JSon,Millenium,pt.3 . . . . . . 1.75
221 JSon,Millenium 1.75
222 JSon,V:Sinestro 1.75
223 GK,V:Sinestro 1.75
224 GK,V:Sinestro 2.00
Ann.#1 GK 2.00
Ann.#2 JSa,BWg,S:AnM 2.50
Ann.#3 JBy,JL,JR 2.00
Spec.#1 A:Superman 2.00
Spec.#2 MBr,RT,V:Seeker 2.00
TPB rep.#84-#87,#89,Flash
#217-#219 . . . . 12.95
TPB rep. reprints of #1-#7 . . . . . 8.95

GREEN LANTERN
[2nd Regular Series]
1 PB,A:Hal Jordan,John Stuart,
Guy Gardner 5.00
2 PB,A:Tattooed Man 3.00
3 PB,Jordan vs.Gardner 4.00
4 PB,Vanishing Cities 2.00
5 PB Return to OA 2.00
6 PB 3GL'sCaptive 2.00
7 PB R:Guardians 2.00
8 PB R:Guardians 2.00
9 JSon,G.Gardner,pt.1 . . . . 3.00
10 JSon,G.Gardner,pt.2 . . . . 3.00
11 JSon,G.Gardner,pt.3 . . . . 3.00
12 JSon,G.Gardner,pt.4 . . . . 3.00
13 Jordan,Gardner,Stuart(giant) . . 2.50
14 PB,Mosaic,pt.1 . . . . 2.00
15 RT,Mosaic,pt.2 . . . . 2.00
16 MBr,RT,Mosaic,pt.3 . . . . 2.00
17 MBr,RT,Mosaic,pt.4 . . . . 2.00
18 JSon,JRu,G.Gardner,
A:Goldface 2.00

Green Lantern (2nd Series) #3
© DC Comics, Inc.

19 MBr,PB,JSon,A:All Four G.L.'s,
O:Alan Scott,A:Doiby Dickles
(D.Size-50th Ann.Iss.) 3.00
20 PB,RT,Hal Jordan G.L. Corp
story begins, A:Flicker 1.75
21 PB,RT,G.L. Corp.,pt.2,
V:Flicker 1.75
22 PB,RT,G.L. Corp.,pt.3,
R:Star Sapphire 1.75
23 PB,RT,V:Star Sapphire,
A:John Stuart 1.75
24 PB,RT,V:Star Sapphire 1.75
25 MBr,JSon,RT,Hal Vs.Guy,
A:JLA 2.75
26 MBr,V:Evil Star,Starlings 1.50
27 MBr,V:Evil Star,Starlings 1.50
28 MBr,V:Evil Star,Starlings 1.50
29 MBr,RT,R:Olivia Reynolds 1.50
30 MBr,RT,Gorilla Warfare#1 . . . . 1.50
31 MBr,RT,Gorilla Warfare#3 . . . . 1.50
32 RT(i),A:Floro,Arisia 1.50
33 MBr,RT,Third Law#1,
A;New Guardians 1.50

34 MBr,RT,Third Law#2,I:Entropy 1.50
35 MBr,RT,Third Law#3,V:Entropy 1.50
36 V:Dr.Light 1.50
37 MBg,RT,A:Guy Gardner 1.50
38 MBr,RT,A:Adam Strange 1.50
39 MBr,RT,A:Adam Strange 1.50
40 RT(i),A:Darkstar,
V:Reverse Flash 1.75
41 MBr,RT,V:Predator,
C:Deathstroke 1.50
42 MBr,RT,V:Predator,
Deathstroke 1.50
43 RT(i),A:Itty 1.50
44 RT(i),Trinity#2,A:L.E.G.I.O.N . . 1.75
45 GeH,Trinity#5,A:L.E.G.I.O.N.,
Darkstars 1.75
46 MBr,A:All Supermen,
V:Mongul 9.00
47 A:Green Arrow 7.00
48 KM(c),B:Emerald Twilight,I:Kyle
Rayner (Last Green Lantern) . . 8.00
49 KM(c),GJ(s),A:Sinestro 7.00
50 KM(c),GJ(s),D:Sinestro,Kiliwog,
Guardians,I:Last Green
Lantern (in Costume) 6.00
51 V:Ohm,A:Mongul 3.00
52 V:Mongul 2.00
53 A:Superman,V:Mongul 1.75
54 D:Alex,V:Major Force 1.75
55 Zero Hour,A:Alan Scott,
V:Major Force 1.75
56 Green Lantern and ring 1.50
57 Psimon 1.50
58 Donna Troy,Felix Faust 1.50
59 V:Dr. Polaris 1.50
60 Capital Punishment,pt.3 . . . . . 1.50
61 V:Kalibak,A:Darkstar 1.50
62 V:Duality,R:Ganthet 1.50
63 Parallax View: The Resurrection
of Hal Jordan,pt.1 . . . . 1.50
64 Parallax View,pt.2,A:Superman,
Flash,V:Parallax 1.75
Ann.#1 Eclipso,V:Star Sapphire . . 2.75
Ann.#2 Bloodlines#7,I:Nightblade . 2.50
Ann.#3 Elseworlds Story 2.95
TPB Emerald Twilight 6.25

GREEN LANTERN
CORPS QUARTERLY
1 DAb,JSon,FH,PG,MBr,F:Alan
Scott G'nort 3.00
2 DAb,JSon,PG,AG,Alan Scott . . 2.75
3 DAb,RT,F:Alan Scott,G'Nort . . 2.75
4 TA,AG(i),F:H.Jordan,G'Nort . . 2.75
5 F:Alan Scott,I:Adam 2.75
6 JBa,TC,F:Alan Scott 3.25
7 Halloween Issue 3.25
8 GeH,SHa,final issue 3.25

GREEN LANTERN:
EMERALD DAWN
[1st Limited Series]
1 MBr,RT,I:Mod.Age.Gr.Lantern . 8.00
2 MBr,RT,I:Legion (not group) . . 6.00
3 MBr,RT,V:Legion 4.00
4 MBr,RT,A:Green Lantern Corps 3.50
5 MBr,RT,V:Legion 3.00
6 MBr,RT,V:Legion 3.00
TPB rep#1-#6 . . . . 5.50
[2nd Limited Series]
1 MBr,A:Sinestro,Guy Gardner . . 2.50
2 MBr,RT,V:Alien Aliance 1.75
3 MBr,RT,Sinestro's Home Planet 1.75
4 MBr,RT,Korugar Revolt 1.75

5 MBr,RT,A:G.Gardner 1.75
6 MBr,RT,Trial of Sinestro 1.75

GREEN LANTERN:
GANTHET'S TALE
1 JBy,O:Guardians 7.00

GREEN LANTERN/
GREEN ARROW
1 NA rep. 5.00
2 NA,DG rep. 4.00
3 NA,DG rep. 4.00
4 NA,DG rep. 4.00
5 NA,DG rep. 4.00
6 NA,DG rep. 4.00
7 NA,DG rep. 4.00
TPB Roadback 8.95

GREEN LANTERN:
MOSAIC
1 F:John Stewart 2.00
2 D:Ch'p 1.75
3 V:Sinestro 1.50
4 F:The Children on Oa 1.50
5 V:Hal Jordan 1.50
6 A:Kilowog 1.50
7 V:Alien Faction 1.50
8 V:Ethereal Creatures 1.50
9 Christmas issue 1.50
10 V:Guardians 1.50
11 R:Ch'p 1.50
12 V:KKK 1.50
13 V:KKK,Racism 1.50
14 A:Salaak,Ch'p 1.50
15 A:Katma Tui,Ch'p 1.50
16 LMc,A:JLA,Green Lantern . . . 1.50
17 A:JLA 1.50
18 final issue 1.50

GREGORY III
Bookshelf Ed. 4.95
Platinum Ed. 30.00

GRIFFIN
1 I:Matt Williams as Griffin 5.50
2 V:Carson 5.25
3 A:Mary Wayne 5.25
4 A:Mary Wayne 5.25
5 Face to Face with Himself 5.25
6 Final Issue 5.25

GUARDIANS
OF METROPOLIS
1 Kirby characters 1.50
2 Donovan's creations 1.50
3 . . . . 1.50
4 Female Furies 1.50

GUNFIRE
1 B:LWn(s),StE,I:Ricochet 2.00
2 StE,V:Ricochet 2.00
3 StE,I:Purge 2.00
4 StE,V:Maraud 3 . . . . 2.00
5 StE,I:Exomorphic Man 1.95
6 New costume 1.95
7 Ragnarok 1.95
8 V:Tattoo 1.95
9 V:Ragnarock 1.95
10 V:Yakuza 1.95
11 V:Yakuza 1.95
12 I:New Weapon 1.95
13 A:JLA,V:Ragnarok, final issue . 2.25

GUY GARDNER

1 JSon,A:JLA,JLE	2.00
2 JSon,A:Kilowog	1.50
3 JSon,V:Big,Ugly Alien	1.50
4 JSon,G.Gardner vs Ice	1.50
5 JSon,A:Hal Jordan,V:Goldface	1.50
6 JSon,A:Hal Jordan,V:Goldface	1.50
7 JSon,V:Goldface	1.50
8 JSon,V:Lobo	1.50
9 JSon,Boodikka	1.50
10 JSon,V:Boodikka	1.50
11 JSon,B:Year One	1.50
12 JSon,V:Batman,Flash,Green Lantern	1.50
13 JSon,Year One#3	1.50
14 JSon,E:Year One	1.50
15 V:Bad Guy Gardner	1.50
16 B:CDi(s),MaT,V:Guy's Brother	1.75

Becomes:

GUY GARDNER: WARRIOR

17 V:Militia	2.00
18 B:Emerald Fallout,N:Guy Gardner, V:Militia	7.00
19 A:G.A.Green Lantern,V:Militia	2.00
20 A:JLA,Darkstars	2.00
21 E:Emerald Fallout,V:H.Jordan	2.00
22 I:Dementor	1.75
23 A:Buck Wargo	1.50
24 Zero Hour	1.50
25 A:Buck Wargo	2.50
26 Zero Hour	1.50
27 Capital Punishment	1.50
28 Capital Punishment,pt.2	1.50
29 I:Warriors Bar	1.50
29a Collector's Edition	2.95
30 V:Superman,Supergirl	1.50
31 A:Sentinel,Supergirl, V:Dementor	1.75
32 Way of the Warrior,pt.1,A:JLA	1.75
Ann.#1 Year One Annual, Leechun vs. Vuldarians	3.50

GUY GARDNER: REBORN

1 JSon,JRu,V:Goldface,C:Lobo	6.00
2 JSon,JRu,A:Lobo,V:Weaponers of Qward	5.50
3 JSon,JRu,A:Lobo,N:G.Gardner V:Qwardians	5.50

HACKER FILES

1 TS,Soft Wars#1,I:Jack Marshall	2.25
2 TS,Soft Wars#2	1.95
3 TS,Soft Wars#3	1.95
4 TS,Soft Wars#4	1.95
5 TS,A:Oracle(Batgirl)	1.95
6 TS,A:Oracle,Green Lantern	1.95
7 TS,V:Digitronix	1.95
8 TS,V:Digitronix	1.95
9 TS,V:Digitronix	1.75
10 V:Digitronix	1.95
11 TS,A:JLE	1.95
12 TS,V:Digitronix,final issue	1.95

HAMMERLOCKE

1 I:Hammerlocke	2.50
2 V:Tharn the Iron Spider	1.75
3 V:Tharn the Iron Spider	1.75
4 O:Hammerlocke	1.75
5 V:Sahara Skyhawk	1.75
6 V:Tharn the Iron Spider	1.75
7 V:Tharn	1.75
8 CSp,V:Iron Spider	1.75

HARDWARE
(Milestone)

1 DCw,I:Hardware,Edwin Alva,Reprise, Dir.Mark.Ed.,w/A puzzle piece, Skybox Card,Poster	5.00
1a NewsstandEd.	2.00
1b Platinum Ed.	35.00
2 DCw,V:Reprise,I:Barraki Young	2.00
3 DCw,O:EDwin Alva, I:S.Y.S.T.E.M.	2.00
4 DCw,V:S.Y.S.T.E.M.	2.00
5 DCw,I:Deathwish	2.00
6 DCw,V:Deathwish	1.75
7 DCw,O:Deathwish	1.75
8 DCw(c),O:Hardware	1.75
9 DCw(c),I:Technique	1.75
10 DCw(c),I:Harm,Transit	1.75
11 WS(c),DCw,Shadow War, I:Iron Butterfly,Dharma	1.75
12 RB,V:Harm	1.75
13 DCw,A:Reprise	1.75
14 DCw	1.75
15 DCw(c),HuR,V:Alva	1.75
16 Die-Cut(c),JBy(c),DCw, N:Hardware	4.25
16a Newsstand ED.	2.25
17 Worlds Collide,pt.2,A:Steel	1.75
18 Worlds Collide,pt.9,V:Rift	2.00
19 I:Evan,Tetras	1.75
20	1.75
21 Arcana,Helga	1.75
22 Curt & Assistant	1.75
23	1.75
24	1.75
25 V:Death Row, Sanction	2.95
26 Hunt For Deathwish,pt.1	1.75
27 Hunt For Deathwish,pt.2	1.75
28 Hunt For Deathwish,pt.3	1.75
29 Long Hot Summer, A:The Blood Syndicate, spec.low price	.99

HAWK & DOVE
[1st Regular Series]
August 1968

1 SD	40.00
2 SD	30.00
3 GK	25.00
4 GK	25.00
5 GK,C:Teen Titans	30.00
6 GK	25.00

[Limited Series]

1 RLd,I:New Dove	6.00
2 RLd,V:Kestrel	5.00
3 RLd,V:Kestrel	4.50
4 RLd,V:Kestrel	4.50
5 RLd,V:Kestrel,O:New Dove	4.50
TPB rep. #1-#5	9.95

[2nd Regular Series]

1 A:Superman,Green Lantern Hawkman	2.00
2 V:Aztec Goddess	1.75
3 V:Aztec Goddess	1.75
4 I:The Untouchables	1.50
5 I:Sudden Death, A:1st Dove's Ghost	1.50
6 A:Barter,Secrets o/Hawk&Dove	1.25
7 A:Barter,V:Count St.Germain	1.25
8 V:Count St.Germain	1.25
9 A:Copperhead	1.25
10 V:Gauntlet & Andromeda	1.25
11 A:New Titans,V:M.A.C., Andromeda Gauntlet	1.25
12 A:New Titans,V:Scarab	1.50
13 1960's,I:Shellshock	1.50

14 Prelue to O:Hawk & Dove, V:Kestrel	1.50
15 O:Hawk & Dove begins	1.50
16 HawkV:Dove,V:Lord of Chaos	1.50
17 V:Lords-Order & Chaos	1.50
18 The Creeper #1	1.50
19 The Creeper #2	1.50
20 KM,DG,Christmas Story	1.50
21 Dove	1.50
22 V:Sudden Death	1.50
23 A:Velv.Tiger,SuddenDeath	1.50
24 A:Velv.Tiger,SuddenDeath	1.50
25 Recap 1st 2 yrs.(48 pg)	2.00
26 Dove's past	1.50
27 The Hunt for Hawk	1.50
28 War of the Gods,A:Wildebeest A:Uncle Sam,final issue, double size	2.00
Ann.#1 In Hell	2.00
Ann.#2 CS,KGa,ArmageddonPt.5	2.00

HAWKMAN
April-May, 1964
[1st Regular Series]

1 MA,V:Chac	425.00
2 MA,V:Tralls	160.00
3 MA,V:Sky Raiders	95.00
4 MA,I&O:Zatanna	110.00
5 MA	85.00
6 MA	63.00
7 MA,V:I.Q.	63.00
8 MA	63.00
9 MA,V:Matter Master	63.00
10 MA,V:Caw	63.00
11 MA	45.00
12 MA	45.00
13 MA	45.00
14 GaF,MA,V:Caw	45.00
15 GaF,MA,V:Makkar	45.00
16 GaF,MA,V:Ruthvol	45.00
17 GaF,MA,V:Raven	45.00
18 GaF,MA,A:Adam Strange	35.00
19 GaF,MA,A:Adam Strange	35.00

Hawkman (3rd Series) #10
© DC Comics, Inc.

20 GaF,MA,V:Lionmane	32.00
21 GaF,MA,V:Lionmane	32.00
22 V:Falcon	32.00
23 V:Dr.Malevolo	32.00

All comics prices listed are for *Near Mint* condition.

24 Robot Raiders from
    Planet Midnight 32.00
25 DD,V:Medusa,G.A.Hawkman   32.00
26 RdM,CCu,DD 32.00
27 DD,JKu(c),V:Yeti 32.00

[2nd Regular Series]

1 DH,A:Shadow Thief 3.00
2 DH,V:Shadow Thief 2.00
3 DH,V:Shadow Thief 1.50
4 DH A:Zatanna 1.50
5 DH,V:Lionmane 1.50
6 DH,V:Gentleman Ghost,
    Lionmane 1.50
7 DH,Honor Wings 1.50
8 DH,Shadow War contd. 1.50
9 DH,Shadow War contd. 1.50
10 JBy(c),D:Hyatis Corp 1.50
11 End of Shadow War 1.25
12 Hawks on Thanagar 1.25
13 DH,Murder Case 1.25
14 DH,Mystery o/Haunted Masks . 1.25
15 DH,Murderer Revealed 1.25
16 DH,Hawkwoman lost 1.25
17 EH,DH,final issue 1.25
TPB rep.Brave & Bold apps. . . . 19.95

[3rd Regular Series]

1 B:JOs(s),JD,R:Hawkman,
    V:Deadline 4.00
2 JD,A:Gr.Lantern,V:Meta-Tech . 2.50
3 JD,I:Airstryke 2.25
4 JD,RM 2.00
5 JD(c),V:Count Viper 2.00
6 JD(c),A:Eradicator 2.00
7 JD(c),PuK(s),LMc,B:King of the
    Netherworld 2.00
8 LMc,E:King of the Netherworld . 2.00
9 BML(s) 2.00
10 I:Badblood 2.00
11 V:Badblood 2.00
12 V:Hawkgod 2.25
13 V:Hawkgod 2.25
14 New abilities,pt.1 . . . . 1.95
15 New abilities,pt.2 . . . . 1.95
16 Eyes of the Hawk,pt.3 . . . . . 1.95
17 Eyes of the Hawk,pt.4 . . . . . 1.95
18 Seagle,Ellis, Pepoy 1.95
19 F:Hawkman 1.95
21 RLm,V:Shadow Thief,
    Gentleman Ghost 2.25
22 Way of the Warrior,pt.3
    A:Warrior,JLA 2.25
Ann.#1 JD,I:Mongrel 3.75

HAWKWORLD

1 TT,Hawkman, Origin retold . . . 8.00
2 TT,Katar tried for treason 6.00
3 TT,Hawkgirl's debut 6.00

[1st Regular Series]

1 GN,Byth on Earth,R:Kanjar Ro . 4.00
2 GN,Katar & Shayera in Chicago 3.00
3 GN,V:Chicago Crime 2.00
4 GN,Byth's Control Tightens . . . 2.00
5 GN,Return of Shadow Thief . . . 2.00
6 GN,Stolen Thanagarian Ship . . 2.00
7 GN,V:Byth 2.00
8 GN,Hawkman vs. Hawkwoman . 2.00
9 GN,Hawkwoman in Prison 2.00
10 Shayera returns to Thanagar . 2.00
11 GN,Blackhawk,Express 2.00
12 GN,Princess Treska 2.00
13 TMd,A:Firehawk,V:Marauder . . 2.00
14 GN,Shayera's Father 2.00
15 GN,War of the Gods X-over . . 2.00
16 GN War of the Gods X-over . . 2.00

17 GN,Train Terrorists 2.00
18 GN,V:Atilla 2.00
19 GN,V:Atilla 2.00
20 V:Smir'Beau 2.00
21 GN,Thanagar Pt.1,
    A:J.S.A. Hawkman 2.00
22 GN,Thanagar Pt.2 . . . . 2.00
23 GN,Thanagar Pt.3 . . . . 2.00
24 GN,Thanagar Pt.4 . . . . 2.00
25 GN,Thanagar Pt.5 . . . . 2.00
26 GN,V:Attilla battle armor 2.00
27 JD,B:Flight's End 2.00
28 JD,Flight's End #2 . . . . 2.00
29 TT(c),JDu,Flight's End #3 . . . . 2.00
30 TT,Flight's End #4 . . . . 2.00
31 TT,Flight's End #5 . . . . 2.00
32 TT,V:Count Viper,final issue . . 2.50
Ann.#1 A:Flash 4.50
Ann.#2 Armageddon,pt.6 . . . . . 4.00
Ann.#2a reprint (Silver) 3.50
Ann.#3 Eclipso tie-in 3.25

HEART OF THE BEAST

GNv SeP 19.95

The Heckler #6 © DC Comics, Inc.

HECKLER, THE

1 KG,MJ,I:The Heckler 1.25
2 KG,MJ,V:The Generic Man . . . 1.25
3 KG,MJ,V:Cosmic Clown 1.25
4 KG,V:Bushwacker 1.25
5 KG,Theater Date 1.25
6 KG,I:Lex Concord 1.25
7 KG,V:Cuttin'Edge 1.25

HELLBLAZER
January, 1988

1 B:JaD(s),JRy,F:John
    Constantine 25.00
2 JRy,I:Papa Midnight 20.00
3 JRy,I:Blathoxi 12.00
4 JRy,I:Resurrection Crusade,
    Gemma 10.00
5 JRy,F:Pyramid of Fear 10.00
6 JRy,V:Resurrection Crusade,
    I:Nergal 10.00
7 JRy,V:Resurrection Crusade,
    I:Richie Simpson 8.00

8 JRy,AA,Constantine receives
    demon blood,V:Nergal 9.00
9 JRy,A:Swamp Thing 8.00
10 JRy,V:Nergal 8.00
11 MBu,Newcastle Incident,pt.1 . 7.00
12 JRy,D:Nergal 7.00
13 JRy,John has a Nightmare . . . 6.00
14 JRy,B:The Fear Machine,
    I:Mercury,Marj,Eddie 6.00
15 JRy,Shepard's Warning. 5.00
16 JRy,Rough Justice 5.00
17 MkH,I:Mr. Wester 5.00
18 JRy,R:Zed 5.00
19 JRy,I:Simon Hughes 5.00
20 JRy,F:Mr.Webster 5.00
21 JRy,I:Jallakuntilliokan 5.00
22 JRy,E:The Fear Machine. . . . 5.00
23 I&D:Jerry O'Flynn 4.00
24 E:JaD(s),I:Sammy Morris . . . 4.00
25 GMo(s),DvL,Early Warning . . . 4.00
26 GMo(s) 4.00
27 NGa(s),DMc,Hold Me 9.00
28 B:JaD(s),RnT,KeW,F:S.Morris . 4.00
29 RnT,KeW,V:Sammy Morris . . . 3.50
30 RnT,KeW,D:Sammy Morris . . . 3.50
31 E:JaD(s),SeP,Constantine's
    Father's Funeral 3.50
32 DiF(s),StP,I&D:Drummond . . . 3.00
33 B:JaD(s),MPn,I:Pat McDonell . 3.00
34 SeP,R:Mercury,Marj 3.00
35 SeP,Constantine's Past 3.00
36 Future Death,(preview of
    World Without End) 3.00
37 Journey to England's Secret
    Mystics 3.00
38 Constantine's Journey contd. . 3.00
39 Journey to Discovery 3.00
40 DMc,I:2nd Kid Eternity 6.00
41 B:GEn(s),WSm,MPn,Dangerous
    Habits 7.00
42 Dangerous Habits 6.00
43 I:Chantinelle 6.00
44 Dangerous Habits 6.00
45 Dangerous Habits 6.00
46 Dangerous Habits epilogue,
    I:Kit(John's girlfriend) 6.00
47 SnW(i),Pub Where I Was Born   3.00
48 Love Kills 3.00
49 X-mas issue,Lord o/t Dance . . 3.00
50 WSm,Remarkable Lives,A:Lord of
    Vampires (48pgs) 4.00
51 JnS,SeP,Laundromat-
    Possession 3.00
52 GF(c),WSm, Royal Blood . . . 3.00
53 GF(c),WSm, Royal Blood . . . 3.00
54 GF(c),WSm, Royal Blood . . . 3.00
55 GF(c),WSm, Royal Blood . . . 3.00
56 GF(c),B:GEn(s),DvL,
    V:Danny Drake 2.50
57 GF(c),SDi,Mortal Clay#1,
    V:Dr. Amis 2.50
58 GF(c),SDi,Mortal Clay#2,
    V:Dr. Amis 2.50
59 GF(c),WSm,MkB(i),KDM,B:Guys &
    Dolls 2.50
60 GF(c),WSm,MkB(i),F:Tali,
    Chantinelle 2.50
61 GF(c),WSm,MkB(i),E:Guys & Dolls,
    V:First of the Fallen 2.50
62 GF(c),SDi,End of the Line,I:Gemma,
    AIDS storyline insert w/Death . 2.50

Vertigo

63 GF(c),SDi,C:Swamp Thing,Zatanna
    Phantom Stranger 2.50
64 GF(c),SDi,B:Fear & Loathing,

A:Gabriel (Racism) 2.75
65 GF(c),SDi,D:Dez 2.50
66 GF(c),SDi,E:Fear and Loathing 2.50
67 GF(c),SDi,Kit leaves John 2.50
68 GF(c),SDi,F:Lord of Vampires,
Darius,Mary 2.50
69 GF(c),SDi,D:Lord of Vampires . 2.25
70 GF(c),SDi,Kit in Ireland 2.25
71 GF(c),SDi,A:WWII Fighter Pilot 2.25
72 GF(c),SDi,B:Damnation's
Flame,A:Papa Midnight 2.25
73 GF(c),SDi,Nightmare NY,
A:JFK 2.25
74 GF(c),SDi,I:Cedella,A:JFK 2.25
75 GF(c),SDi,E:Damnation'sFlame 2.25
76 GF(c),SDi,R:Brendan 2.25
77 Returns to England 2.25
78 GF(c),SDi,B:Rake at the
Gates of Hell 2.25
79 GF(c),SDi,In Hell 2.25
80 GF(c),SDi,In London 2.25
81 GF(c),SDi 2.25
82 Kit 1.95
83 Rake,Gates of Hell 1.95
84 John's past 1.95
85 Warped Notions,pt.1 . . . . 1.95
86 Warped Notions,pt.2 . . . . 1.95
87 Warped Notions,pt.3 . . . . 1.95
88 Warped Notions,pt.4 . . . . 1.95
89 Dreamtime 2.25
90 Dreamtime,pt.2 . . . . 2.25
91 Visits Battlefield 2.25
Ann.#1 JaD(s),BT,Raven Scar . . . 7.00
Spec.#1 GF(c),GEn(s),SDi,John
Constantine's teenage years . . 4.50
TPB Original Sins,rep.#1–#9 . . . 19.95
TPB Dangerous Habits,
rep.#41–#46 . . . . 14.95

HERCULES UNBOUND
October-November, 1975
1 thru 11 . . . . @1.25
12 August-September, 1977 . . . . 1.25

HEROES AGAINST HUNGER
1 NA,DG,JBy,CS,AA,BWr,BS,
Superman,Batman 3.50

HERO HOTLINE
1 thru 6, Mini-series . . . . @1.75

HEX
September, 1985
1 MT,I:Hex 2.50
2 MT 2.00
3 MT,V:Conglomerate 2.00
4 MT,V:Conglomerate 2.00
5 MT,A:Chainsaw Killer 2.00
6 MT,V:Conglomerate 2.00
7 MT,Tries to Return to own era . 2.00
8 MT,The Future 2.50
9 MT,Future Killer Cyborgs 1.50
10 MT,V:Death Cult 1.50
11 MT,V:The Batman 3.00
12 MT,A:Batman,V:Terminators . . 3.00
13 MT,I:New Supergroup 2.50
14 MT,A:The Dogs of War 1.50
15 KG,V:Chainsaw Killer 1.50
16 KG,V:Dogs of War 1.50
17 KG,Hex/Dogs of War T.U.
V:XXGG 1.50
18 KGr,Confronting the Past,final
Issue 1.50

HISTORY OF DC UNIVERSE
September, 1986
1 GP, From start to WWII 5.00
2 GP, From WWII to present . . . 5.00

HITCHHIKER'S GUIDE TO THE GALAXY
1 Based on the book 7.00
2 Based on the book 6.50
3 Based on the book 6.50

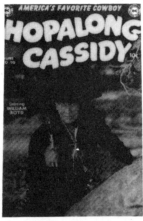

Hopalong Cassidy #90
© DC Comics, Inc.

HOPALONG CASSIDY
February, 1954
86 GC,Ph(c):William Boyd & Topper,
'The Secret o/t Tattooed
Burro' 175.00
87 GC,Ph(c),'The Tenderfoot
Outlaw' 100.00
88 Ph(c),GC,'15 Robbers of Rimfire
Ridge' 75.00
89 GC,Ph(c),'One-Day
Boom Town' 75.00
90 GC,Ph(c),'Cowboy Clown
Robberies' 50.00
91 GC,Ph(c),'The Riddle of
the Roaring R Ranch' 55.00
92 GC,Ph(c),'The Sky-Riding
Outlaws' 55.00
93 GC,Ph(c),'The Silver Badge
of Courage' 55.00
94 GC,Ph(c),'Mystery of the
Masquerading Lion' 55.00
95 GC,Ph(c),'Showdown at the
Post-Hole Bank' 55.00
96 GC,Ph(c),'Knights of
the Range' 55.00
97 GC,Ph(c),'The Mystery of
the Three-Eyed Cowboy' 55.00
98 GC,Ph(c),'Hopalong's
Unlucky Day' 55.00
99 GC,Ph(c),'Partners in Peril' . . 55.00
100 GC,Ph(c),'The Secrets
of a Sheriff' 75.00
101 GC,Ph(c),'Way Out West
Where The East Begins' 45.00

102 GC,Ph(c),'Secret of the
Buffalo Hat' 45.00
103 GC,Ph(c),'The Train-Rustlers
of Avalance Valley' 45.00
104 GC,Ph(c),'Secret of the
Surrendering Outlaws' 45.00
105 GC,Ph(c),'Three Signs
to Danger' 45.00
106 GC,Ph(c),'The Secret of
the Stolen Signature' 45.00
107 GC,Ph(c),'The Mystery Trail
to Stagecoach Town' 45.00
108 GC,Ph(c),'The Mystery
Stage From Burro Bend' 45.00
109 GC,'The Big Gun on Saddletop
Mountain' 45.00
110 GC,'The Dangerous Stunts
of Hopalong Cassidy' 35.00
111 GC,'Sheriff Cassidy's
Mystery Clue' 35.00
112 GC,'Treasure Trail to
Thunderbolt Ridge 35.00
113 GC,'The Shadow of the
Toy Soldier' 35.00
114 GC,'Ambush at
Natural Bridge' 35.00
115 GC,'The Empty-Handed
Robberies' 35.00
116 GC,'Mystery of the
Vanishing Cabin' 35.00
117 GC,'School for Sheriffs' 35.00
118 GC,'The Hero of
Comanche Ridge' 35.00
119 GC,'The Dream Sheriff of
Twin Rivers' 35.00
120 GC,'Salute to a Star-Wearer' 35.00
121 GC,'The Secret of the
Golden Caravan' 35.00
122 GC,'The Rocking
Horse Bandits' 35.00
123 GK,'Mystery of the
One-Dollar Bank Robbery' . . 35.00
124 GK,'Mystery of the
Double-X Brand' 35.00
125 GK,'Hopalong Cassidy's
Secret Brother' 35.00
126 GK,'Trail of the
Telltale Clues' 35.00
127 GK,'Hopalong Cassidy's
Golden Riddle' 35.00
128 GK,'The House That
Hated Outlaws' 35.00
129 GK,'Hopalong Cassidy's
Indian Sign' 35.00
130 GK,'The Return of the
Canine Sheriff' 35.00
131 GK&GK(c),'The Amazing
Sheriff of Double Creek' 35.00
132 GK,'Track of the
Invisible Indians' 35.00
133 GK,'The Golden Trail
to Danger' 35.00
134 GK,'Case of the
Three Crack-Shots' 35.00
135 GK,May-June, 1959 . . . . . . 35.00

HOT WHEELS
March-April, 1970
1 ATh 25.00
2 thru 5 ATh . . . . @20.00
6 NA 30.00

HOUSE OF MYSTERY
December-January, 1952
1 I Fell In Love With A Monster,200.00

2 The Mark of X	500.00
3	400.00
4 The Man With the Evil Eye	300.00
5 The Man With the Strangler Hands!	300.00
6 The Monster in Clay!	250.00
7 Nine Lives of Alger Denham!	250.00
8	250.00
9	250.00
10 The Wishes of Doom	250.00
11 Deadly Game of G-H-O-S-T	200.00
12 The Devil's Chessboard	200.00
13 The Theater Of A Thousand Thrills!	200.00
14	200.00
15 The Man Who Could Change the World	200.00
16 Dead Men Tell No Tales!	175.00
17	150.00
18	150.00
19	150.00
20 The Beast Of Bristol	150.00
21 Man Who Could See Death	150.00
22 The Phantom's Return	150.00
23	150.00
24 Kill The Black Cat	150.00
25 The Man With Three Eyes!	150.00
26	100.00
27 Fate Held Four Aces!	100.00
28 The Wings Of Mr. Milo!	100.00
29	100.00
30	100.00
31 The Incredible Illusions!	100.00
32 Pied Piper of the Sea	100.00
33 Mr. Misfortune!	100.00
34 The Hundred Year Duel	100.00
35	100.00

House of Mystery #26
© DC Comics, Inc.

36 The Treasure of Montezuma!	85.00
37 MD,The Statue That Came to Life	85.00
38 The Voyage Of No Return	85.00
39	85.00
40 The Coins That Came To Life	85.00
41 The Impossible Tricks!	85.00
42 The Stranger From Out There	85.00
43	85.00
44 The Secret Of Hill 14	85.00
45	85.00

46 The Bird of Fate	85.00
47 The Robot Named Think	85.00
48 The Man Marooned On Earth	85.00
49 The Mysterious Mr. Omen	85.00
50	75.00
51 Man Who Stole Teardrops	65.00
52 The Man With The Golden Shoes	65.00
53 The Man Who Hated Mirrors	65.00
54 The Woman Who Lived Twice	65.00
55 I Turned Back Time	65.00
56 The Thing In The Black Box	65.00
57 The Untamed	65.00
58	65.00
59 The Tomb Of Ramfis	65.00
60 The Prisoner On Canvas	65.00
61 JK,Superstition Day	65.00
62 The Haunting Scarecrow	50.00
63 JK,The Lady and The Creature	60.00
64 The Golden Doom	50.00
65 JK,The Magic Lantern	60.00
66 JK,Sinister Shadow	60.00
67 The Wizard Of Water	50.00
68 The Book That Bewitched	50.00
69 The Miniature Disasters	50.00
70 JK,The Man With Nine Lives	60.00
71 The Menace o/t Mole Man	50.00
72 JK,Dark Journey	60.00
73 Museum That Came to Life	42.00
74 Museum That Came To Life	42.00
75 Assignment Unknown!	42.00
76 JK,Prisoners Of The Tiny Universe	55.00
77 The Eyes That Went Berserk	45.00
78 JK(c),The 13th Hour	50.00
79 JK(c),The Fantastic Sky Puzzle	50.00
80 Man With Countless Faces!	40.00
81 The Man Who Made Utopia	40.00
82 The Riddle of the Earth's Second Moon	40.00
83 The Mystery of the Martian Eye	40.00
84 JK,BK,The 100-Century Doom	55.00
85 JK(c),Earth's Strangest Salesman	50.00
86 The Baffling Bargains	40.00
87 The Human Diamond	40.00
88 Return of the Animal Man	40.00
89 The Cosmic Plant!	40.00
90 The Invasion Of the Energy Creatures!	40.00
91 DD&SMo(c),The Riddle of the Alien Satellite	40.00
92 DD(c),Menace of the Golden Globule	40.00
93 NC(c),I Fought The Molten Monster	40.00
94 DD&SMo(c),The Creature In Echo Lake	40.00
95 The Wizard's Gift	40.00
96 The Amazing 70-Ton Man	40.00
97 The Alien Who Change History	40.00
98 DD&SMo(c),The Midnight Creature	40.00
99 The Secret of the Leopard God	40.00
100 The Beast Beneath Earth	32.00
101 The Magnificent Monster	22.00
102 Cellmate to a Monster	22.00
103 Hail the Conquering Aliens	22.00
104 I was the Seeing-Eye Man	22.00
105 Case of the Creature X-14	22.00
106 Invaders from the Doomed	

Dimension	22.00
107 Captives o/t Alien Fisherman	22.00
108 RMo,Four Faces of Frank Forbes	22.00
109 ATh,JKu,Secret of the Hybrid Creatures	22.00
110 Beast Who Stalked Through Time	22.00
111 Operation Beast Slayer	22.00
112 Menace of Craven's Creatures	22.00
113 RMo,Prisoners of Beast Asteroid	22.00
114 The Movies from Nowhere	22.00
115 Prisoner o/t Golden Mask	22.00
116 RMo,Return of the Barsfo Beast	22.00
117 Menace of the Fire Furies	15.00
118 RMo,Secret o/SuperGorillas	15.00
119 Deadly Gift from the Stars	15.00
120 ATh,Catman of KarynPeale	15.00
121 RMo,Beam that Transformed Men	15.00
122 Menace fo the Alien Hero	15.00
123 RMo,Lure o/t Decoy Creature	15.00
124 Secret of Mr. Doom	15.00
125 Fantastic Camera Creature	15.00
126 The Human Totem Poles	15.00
127 RMo,Cosmic Game o/Doom	15.00
128 NC,The Sorcerer's Snares	15.00
129 Man in the Nuclear Trap	15.00
130 The Alien Creature Hunt	15.00
131 Vengeance o/t GeyserGod	13.00
132 MMe,Beware My Invisible Master	13.00
133 MMe,Captive Queen of Beast Island	13.00
134 MMe,Secret Prisoner of Darkmore Dungeon	13.00
135 MMe,Alien Body Thief	13.00
136 MMe,Secret o/t StolenFace	13.00
137 MMe,Tunnel to Disaster	13.00
138 MMe,Creature Must Die	13.00
139 MMe,Creatures of Vengeful Eye	13.00
140 I&Only app.:Astro	13.00
141 MMe,The Alien Gladiator	13.00
142 MMe,The Wax Demons	13.00
143 J'onn J'onzz begins	175.00
144 J'onn J'onzz on Weird World of Gilgana	80.00
145 J'onn J'onzz app	45.00
146 BP,J'onn J'onzz	45.00
147 J'onn J'onzz	45.00
148 J'onn J'onzz	45.00
149 ATh,J'onn J'onzz	45.00
150 MMe,J'onn J'onzz	45.00
151 J'onn J'onzz	45.00
152 MMe,J'onn J'onzz	45.00
153 J'onn J'onzz	45.00
154 J'onn J'onzz	45.00
155 J'onn J'onzz	45.00
156 JM,I:Dial H for Hero (Giantboy Cometeer,Mole)J.J'onzz sty	55.00
157 JM,Dial H for Hero (Human Bullet,Super Charge,Radar Sonar Man) J'onn J'onnzz sty	50.00
158 JM,Dial H for Hero (Quake MasterSquid)J'onn J'onzz sty	45.00
159 JM,Dial H for Hero (Human Starfish,Hypno Man,Mighty Moppet) J'onn J'onzz sty	45.00
160 JM,Dial H for Hero (King Kandy	

A:Plastic Man,I:Marco Xavier (J'onn
  J'onzz new secret I.D.) 75.00
161 JM,Dial H for Hero (Magneto,
  Hornet Man,Shadow Man) .. 35.00
162 JM,Dial H for Hero (Mr.Echo,
  Future Man) J'onnJ'onzz sty . 35.00
163 JM,Dial H for Hero(Castor&Pollux,
  King Coil) J'onnJ'onzz sty ... 35.00
164 JM,Dial H for Hero (Super Nova
  Zip Tide) J'onnJ'onzz sty ... 35.00
165 JM,Dial H for Hero (Whoozis,
  Whatsis,Howzis) J'onn J'onzz
  story 35.00
166 JM,Dial H for Hero (Yankee
  Doodle Kid,Chief Mighty Arrow)
  J'onn J'onzz sty 35.00
167 JM,Dial H for Hero (Balloon Boy,
  Muscle Man,Radar Sonar Man)
  J'onn J'onzz sty 35.00
168 JM,Dial H for Hero (Thunderbolt,
  Mole,Cometeer,Hoopster)
  J'onn J'onzz sty 35.00
169 JM,I:Gem Girl in Dial H for
  Hero,J'onnJ'onzz sty 35.00
170 JM,Dial H for Hero (Baron
  BuzzSaw,Don Juan,Sphinx
  Man) J'onn J'onzz sty .. 35.00
171 JM,Dial H for Hero (King Viking
  Whirl-I-Gig) J'onnJ'onzz sty . . 35.00
172 JM,Dial H for Hero 35.00
173 E:Dial H for Hero,F:J'onn
  Jonzz 35.00
174 New direction,SA pg.13 ... 10.00
175 I:Cain 10.00
176 SA,Cain's Game Room 10.00
177 Curse of the Car 10.00
178 NA,The Game 15.00
179 BWr,NA,JO,Widow'sWalk .. 45.00
180 GK,WW,BWr,SA,Room 13 . 11.00
181 BWr,The Siren of Satan ... 11.00
182 ATh,The Devil's Doorway . . 10.00
183 BWr,WW(i),DeadCanKill .. 12.00
184 ATh,GK,WW,Eye o/Basilisk . 10.00
185 AW,The Beautiful Beast ... 12.00
186 BWr,NA,Nightmare 12.00
187 ATh,Mask of the Red Fox . . 7.00
188 TD,BWr,House of Madness . 12.00
189 WW(i),Eyes of the Cat 6.00
190 ATh,Fright 9.00
191 BWr,TD,Christmas Story,. ... 9.00
192 JAp,GM,DH,Garnener
  of Eden 5.00
193 BWr................. 11.00
194 ATh,NR,RH(rep),JK(rep)
  Born Loser 8.00
195 NR,BWr,ThingsOld..Things
  Forgotten 12.00
196 GM,GK,ATh(rep)A Girl &
  Her Dog 4.00
197 DD,NR,House of Horrors ... 4.00
198 MSy,NC,Day of the Demon . . 4.00
199 WW,RB,Sno'Fun 5.00
200 MK,TD,The Beast's Revenge 4.00
201 JAp,The Demon Within 4.00
202 MSy,GC(rep),SA,The Poster
  Plague,John Prentice? 4.00
203 NR,Tower of Prey 4.00
204 BWr,AN,All in the Family 9.00
205 The Coffin Creature 4.00
206 MSy,TP,The Burning 4.00
207 JSn,The Spell 9.00
208 Creator of Evil 4.00
209 AA,JAp,Tomorrow I Hang ... 8.00
210 The Immortal 4.00
211 NR,Deliver Us From Evil 7.50

212 MA,AN,Ever After 4.00
213 AN,Back from the Realm of
  the Damned 7.50
214 NR,The Shaggy Dog 7.50
215 The Man Who Wanted Power
  over Women 4.00
216 TD,Look into My Eyes & Kill . 4.00
217 NR,AA,Swamp God 7.50
218 FT,An Ice Place to Visit 4.00
219 AA,NR,Pledge to Satan 4.00
220 AA,AN,They Hunt Butterflies
  Don't They? 4.00

House of Mystery #221
© DC Comics, Inc.

221 FT,BWr,MK,He Who Laughs
  Last 8.00
222 AA,Night of the Teddy Bear . 4.00
223 Demon From the Deep 4.00
224 FR,AA,SheerFear,B:100pg . 11.00
225 AA,FT,AN,See No Evil 6.00
226 AA,FR,NR,SA,Monster in House
  Tour of House of Mystery ... 8.00
227 NR,AA,The Carriage Man .. 6.00
228 FR,NA(i),The Rebel 7.00
229 NR,Nightmare Castle,
  last 100 page 7.00
230 Experiment In Fear 4.00
231 Cold,Cold Heart 6.00
232 Last Tango in Hell 4.00
233 FR,Cake! 4.00
234 AM,Lafferty's Luck 4.00
235 NR,Wings of Black Death ... 4.00
236 SD,NA(i)Death Played a
  Sideshow 8.00
237 FT,Night of the Chameleon . 4.00
238 .... 4.00
239 Day of the Witch 4.00
240 The Murderer 4.00
241 FR,NR,DeathPulls theStrings 4.00
242 FR,The Balloon Vendor ... 4.00
243 Brother Bear 4.00
244 FT,Kronos..Zagros-Eborak . 4.00
245 AN,Check the J.C.Demon
  Catalogue Under...Death 4.00
246 DeathVault of Eskimo Kings . 4.00
247 SD,Death Rides the Waves . 4.00
248 NightJamieGaveUp theGhost 4.00
249 Hit Parade of Death 4.00
250 AN,Voyage to Hell 4.00
251 WW,AA,theCollector,68 pgs . 5.00

252 DP,RT,AA,FR,AN,ManKillers . 5.00
253 TD,AN,GK,KJ,Beware the
  Demon Child 3.50
254 SD,AN,MR,TheDevil's Place . 4.00
255 RE,GM,SometimesLeopards . 7.50
256 DAy,AN,Museum of Murders . 7.50
257 RE,MGo,TD(i),MBr,Xmas iss. 3.00
258 SD,RB,BMc,DG(i),The Demon
  and His Boy 3.00
259 RE,RT,MGo,DN,BL,'Hair Today,
  Gone Tomorrow,last giant 3.50
260 Go to Hades 3.00
261 The Husker 3.00
262 FreedFrom Infernos of Hell . . 3.00
263 JCr,Is There Vengeance
  After Death? 3.00
264 Halloween Issue 3.00
265 The Perfect Host 3.00
266 The Demon Blade 3.00
267 A Strange Way to Die 3.00
269 Blood on the Grooves 3.00
270 JSh,JRu,JBi,Black Moss 3.00
271 TS,HellHmoor of
  Brackenmoor 3.00
272 DN,DA,theSorcerer's Castle . 3.00
273 The Rites of Inheritance 3.00
274 MR,JBi,Hell Park 3.00
275 JCr,'Final Installment' 3.00
276 SD,MN,'Epode' 3.00
277 HC,AMi,'Limited
  Engagement' 3.00
278 'TV or Not TV' 3.00
279 AS,Trial by Fury 3.00
280 VMK,DAy,Hungry Jaws
  of Death 3.00
281 Now Dying in this Corner ... 3.00
282 JSw,DG,Superman/Radio
  Shack ins 3.00
283 RT,AN'Kill Me Gently' 3.00
284 KG,King and the Dragon 3.00
285 Cold Storage 3.00
286 Long Arm of the Law 3.00
287 NR,AS,BL,Legend o/t Lost . 3.00
288 DSp,Piper at Gates of Hell . . 3.00
289 Brother Bobby's Home for
  Wayward Girls & Boys 3.00
290 TS,I:I..Vampire 3.00
291 TS,DAy,I..Vampire #2 ..... 3.00
292 TS,MS,TD,RE,DSp,Wendigo . 3.00
293 GT,TS,A:I..Vampire #3 .... 3.00
294 CI,TY,GT,TD,The Darkness .. 3.00
295 TS,TVE,JCr,I..Vampire #4 ... 3.00
296 CI,BH,Night Women 3.00
297 TS,DCw,TD,I..Vampire #5 ... 3.00
298 TS,'Stalker on a Starless
  Night' 3.00
299 TS,DSp,I..Vampire #6 ..... 3.00
300 GK,DA,JSon,JCr,DSp,Anniv. . 3.00
301 JDu,TVE,KG,TY '...Virginia' . . 3.00
302 TS,NR,DSp,I..Vampire #7 ... 3.00
303 TS,DSp,I..Vampire #8 ..... 3.00
304 EC,RE,I..Vampire #9 ...... 3.00
305 TVE,EC,I..Vampire #10 .... 3.00
306 TS,TD,I..Vampire #11,
  A:Jack the Ripper 3.00
307 TS,I..Vampire #12 .... 3.00
308 TS,MT,NR,I..Vampire #13 . . 3.00
309 TS,I..Vampire #14 .... 3.00
310 TS(i),I..Vampire #15 ...... 3.00
311 I..Vampire #16 .... 3.00
312 TS(i),I..Vampire #17 ..... 3.00
313 TS(i),CI,I..Vampire #18 .... 3.00
314 TS,I..Vampire #19 .... 3.00
315 TS(i),TY,I..Vampire #20 .... 3.00
316 TS(i),GT,TVE,I..Vampire #21 . 3.00

---

317 TS(i),I..Vampire #22 ...... 3.00
318 TS(i),I..Vampire #23 ...... 3.00
319 TS,JOy,I..Vampire conc. 3.00
320 GM,Project: Inferior 3.00
321 final issue 3.00

HOUSE OF SECRETS
November-December, 1956

1 MD,JM,The Hand of Doom . 700.00
2 JPr,RMo,NC,Mask of Fear . 275.00
3 JM,JK,MMe,The Three
    Prophecies 275.00
4 JM,JK,MMe,Master of
    Unknown 200.00
5 MMe,The Man Who
    Hated Fear 110.00
6 NC,MMe,Experiment 1000 . 110.00
7 RMo,Island o/t Enchantress . 110.00
8 JK,RMo,The Electrified Man 110.00
9 JM,JSt,The Jigsaw Creatures 90.00
10 JSt,NC,I was a Prisoner
    of the Sea 90.00
11 KJ(c),NC,The Man who
    couldn't stop growing ... 90.00
12 JK,The Hole in the Sky 100.00
13 The Face in the Mist 65.00
14 MMe,The Man who Stole Air . 65.00
15 The Creature in the Camera . 65.00
16 NC,We matched wits with a
    Gorilla genius 50.00
17 DW,Lady in the Moon 50.00
18 MMe,The Fantastic
    Typewriter 50.00
19 MMe,NC,Lair of the
    Dragonfly 50.00
20 Incredible FireballCreatures . 50.00
21 Girl from 50,000 Fathoms ... 50.00
22 MMe,Thing from Beyond 50.00
23 MMe,I&O:Mark Merlin ... 120.00
24 NC,Mark Merlin story 50.00
25 MMe,Mark Merlin story 45.00
26 NC,MMe, Mark Merlin story .. 45.00
27 MME,Mark Merlin 45.00
28 MMe,Mark Merlin 45.00
29 NC,MMe,Mark Merlin 45.00
30 JKu,MMe,Mark Merlin 45.00
31 DD,MMe,RH,Mark Merlin ... 30.00
32 MMe,Mark Merlin 30.00
33 MMe,Mark Merlin 30.00
34 MMe,Mark Merlin 30.00
35 MMe,Mark Merlin 30.00
36 MMe,Mark Merlin 30.00
37 MMe,Mark Merlin 30.00
38 MMe,Mark Merlin 30.00
39 JKu,MMe,Mark Merlin 30.00
40 NC,MMe,Mark Merlin 30.00
41 MMe,Mark Merlin 30.00
42 MMe,Mark Merlin 30.00
43 RMo,MMe,CI,Mark Merlin ... 30.00
44 MMe,Mark Merlin 30.00
45 MMe,Mark Merlin 30.00
46 MMe,Mark Merlin 30.00
47 MMe,Mark Merlin 30.00
48 ATh,MMe,Mark Merlin 35.00
49 MMe,Mark Merlin 30.00
50 MMe,Mark Merlin 30.00
51 MMe,Mark Merlin 25.00
52 MMe,Mark Merlin 25.00
53 CI,Mark Merlin 25.00
54 RMo,MMe,Mark Merlin 25.00
55 MMe,Mark Merlin 25.00
56 MMe,Mark Merlin 25.00
57 MMe,Mark Merlin 25.00
58 MMe,O:Mark Merlin 25.00
59 MMe,Mark Merlin 25.00

60 MMe,Mark Merlin 25.00
61 I:Eclipso,A:Mark Merlin 155.00
62 MMe,Eclipso,Mark Merlin .. 65.00
63 GC,ATh,Eclipso,Mark Merlin . 45.00
64 MMe,ATh,M Merlin,Eclipso .. 45.00
65 MMe,ATh,M Merlin,Eclipso .. 45.00
66 MMe,ATh,M Merlin,Eclipso . 110.00
67 MMe,ATh,M Merlin,Eclipso .. 45.00
68 MMe,Mark Merlin,Eclipso .. 45.00
69 MMe,Mark Merlin,Eclipso .. 45.00
70 MMe,Mark Merlin,Eclipso .. 45.00
71 MMe,Mark Merlin,Eclipso .. 45.00
72 MMe,Mark Merlin,Eclipso .. 45.00
73 MMe,D:Mark Merlin,I:Prince
    Ra-Man; Eclipso 45.00
74 MMe,Prince Ra-Man,Eclipso . 45.00
75 MMe,Prince Ra-Man,Eclipso . 45.00
76 MMe,Prince Ra-Man,Eclipso . 45.00
77 MMe,Prince Ra-Man,Eclipso . 45.00
78 MMe,Prince Ra-Man,Eclipso . 45.00
79 MMe,Prince Ra-Man,Eclipso . 45.00
80 MMe,Prince Ra-Man,Eclipso . 45.00
81 I:Abel, new mystery format
    Don't Move It 8.00
82 DD,NA,One & only, fully guaran
    teed super-permanent 100% .. 5.00
83 ATh,The Stuff that Dreams
    are Made of 4.00
84 DD,If I had but world enough
    and time 4.00
85 DH,GK,NA,Second Chance .. 5.00
86 GT,GM,Strain 5.00
87 DD,DG,RA,MK,The Coming
    of Ghaglan 5.00
88 DD,The Morning Ghost 4.00
89 GM,DH,Where Dead MenWalk 4.00
90 GT,RB,NA,GM,The Symbionts 7.00
91 WW,MA,The Eagle's Talon .. 6.00
92 BWr,TD(i),I:Swamp Thing
    (Alex Olson) 400.00
93 JAp,TD,ATh(rep.)Lonely in
    Death 6.50
94 TD,ATh(rep.)Hyde.and
    go Seek 6.50
95 DH,NR,The Bride of Death ... 4.00
96 DD,JAb,WW, the Monster ... 8.00
97 JAp,Divide and Murder 4.00
98 MK,ATh(rep),Born Losers 4.50
99 NR,TD(i),Beyond His
    Imagination 4.00
100 TP,TD,AA,Rest in Peace ... 4.00
101 AN,Small Invasion 3.00
102 NR,A Lonely Monstrosity 3.00
103 AN,Village on Edge o/Forever 5.00
104 NR,AA,GT,Ghosts Don't
    Bother Me...But... ...... 3.00
105 JAp,AA,An Axe to Grind ... 3.00
106 AN,AA,This Will Kill You ... 5.00
107 AA,The Night of the Nebbish . 5.00
108 A New Kid on the Block 3.00
109 AA,AN...And in Death, there
    is no Escape 3.00
110 Safes Have Secrets, Too ... 2.50
111 TD,Hair-I-Kari 2.50
112 Case of the Demon Spawn .. 2.50
113 MSy,NC,NR,Spawns
    of Satan 2.50
114 FBe,Night Game 2.50
115 AA,AN,Nobody Hurts My
    Brother 2.50
116 NR,Like Father,Like Son 2.50
117 AA,AN,Revenge for the Deadly
    Dummy 2.50
118 GE,Very Last Picture Show .. 2.50
119 A Carnival of Dwarves 2.50

120 TD,AA,The Lion's Share 2.50
121 Ms.Vampire Killer 2.50
122 AA,Requiem for Igor 2.50
123 ATh,A Connecticut Ice Cream
    Man in King Arthur's Court ... 3.00
124 Last of the Frankensteins .. 2.50
125 AA,FR,Instant Re-Kill 2.50
126 AN,On Borrowed Time 2.50
127 MSy,A Test of Innocence ... 2.50
128 AN,Freak Out! 2.50
129 Almost Human 2.50
130 All Dolled Up! 2.50
131 AN,Point of No Return 2.50
132 Killer Instinct 2.50
133 Portraits of Death 2.50
134 NR,Inheritance of Blood 2.50
135 The Vegitable Garden 3.50
136 Last Voyage of Lady Luck ... 2.00
137 The Harder They Fall 2.00
138 Where Dreams are Born ... 3.50
139 SD,NR,A Real Crazy Kid ... 2.50
140 NR,O:Patchwork Man 2.50
141 You Can't Beat the Devil .. 3.00
142 Playmate 2.00
143 The Evil Side 2.00
144 The Vampire of Broadway .. 2.25
145 Operation wasSuccessful,But 2.00
146 Snake's Alive 2.00
147 AN,The See-Through Thief .. 2.00
148 SD,Sorcerer's Apprentice .. 2.00
149 The Evil One 2.00
150 A:PhantomStranger & Dr.13 . 2.25
151 MGo,Nightmare 2.50
152 Sister Witch 2.00
153 VM,AN,Don't Look Now ... 2.00
154 JL,Last issue 2.00

Human Target Spec.#1
© DC Comics, Inc.

HUMAN TARGET SPECIAL

1 DG(i),Prequel to T.V. Series .. 2.00

HUNTRESS, THE

1 JSon/DG 2.00
2 JSon,Search for Family's

Murderer 2.00	
3 JSon,A:La Bruja 1.50	
4 JSon,Little Italy/Chinatown	
Gangs 1.50	
5 JSon,V:Doctor Mandragora . . . 1.50	
6 JSon,Huntress'secrets revealed 1.50	
7 JSon,V:Serial Killer 1.50	
8 JSon,V:Serial Killer 1.50	
9 JSon,V:Serial Killer 1.50	
10 JSon,Nuclear Terrorists in NY . 1.50	
11 JSon,V:Wyvern,Nuclear	
Terrorists contd. 1.50	
12 JSon,V:Nuclear Terrorists cont 1.50	
13 JSon,Violence in NY 1.50	
14 JSon,Violence contd.,New	
Mob boss 1.50	
15 JSon,I:Waterfront Warrior . . . 1.50	
16 JSon,Secret of Waterfront	
Warrior revealed 1.50	
17 JSon,Batman+Huntress#1 . . . 1.25	
18 JSon,Batman+Huntress#2 . . . 1.25	
19 JSon,Batman+Huntress#3,final	
issue 1.25	

HUNTRESS
[Limited Series]
1 CDi(s),MN,V:Redzone 1.75
2 MN,V:Redzone 1.50
3 MN,V:Redzone 1.75
4 MN,V:Spano,Redzone 1.50

Icon #4 © Milestone Media, Inc.

ICON
Milestone
1 Direct Market Ed.,MBr,MG,I:Icon,
  Rocket,S.H.R.E.D.,w/poster,
  card,C puzzle piece 3.25
1a Newsstand Ed. 2.00
2 MBr,MG,I:Payback 1.75
3 MBr,MG,V:Payback 1.75
4 MBr,MG,Teen Pregnancy Issue 1.75
5 MBr,MG,V:Blood Syndicate . . . 1.75
6 MBr,MG,V:Blood Syndicate . . . 1.75
7 MBr,MG 1.75
8 MBr,MG,O:Icon 1.75
9 WS(c),MBr,MG,Shadow War,
  I:Donner,Blitzen 1.75
10 MBr,MG,V:Holocaust 1.75
11 MBr,Hero Worship 1.75

12 Sanctimony 1.75	
13 MBr,Rocket & Static T.U. 1.75	
14 JBy(c) 1.75	
15 Worlds Collide,pt.4,A:Superboy 1.75	
16 Worlds Collide,pt.11,	
V:Superman,Rift 1.75	
17 Mothership Connection 1.75	
18 Mothership Connection,pt.2 . . 1.75	
19 Mothership Connection,pt.3 . . 1.75	
20 Rocket 1.75	
21 . . . . 1.75	
22 . . . . 1.75	
23 New Rocket 1.75	
24 F:Buck Wild 1.75	
25 V:Oblivion 2.95	
26 V:Oblivion 1.75	
27 Move to Paris Island projects . 2.50	

IMMORTAL DR. FATE
1 WS,KG,rep. 1.75
2 KG,rep. 1.25
3 KG,rep. 1.25

IMPACT WINTER SPECIAL
Impact
1 CI/MR/TL,A:All Impact Heros,
  President Kidnapped 2.50

IMPULSE
1 Young Flash Adventures 1.75
2 V:Terrorists 1.75
3 In School 1.75
4 V:White Lightning 1.75

INFERIOR FIVE
March-April, 1967
1 MSy 45.00
2 MSy,A:Plastic Man 25.00
3 . . . . 15.00
4 . . . . 15.00
5 . . . . 15.00
6 . . . . 15.00
7 . . . . 15.00
8 . . . . 15.00
9 . . . . 15.00
10 A:Superman 15.00
11 JO(c&a) 15.00
12 JO(c&a) 15.00

INFINITY, INC.
March, 1984
1 JOy,O:Infinity Inc. 4.00
2 JOy,End of Origin 3.00
3 JOy,O:Jade 2.50
4 JOy,V:JSA 2.50
5 JOy,V:JSA 2.50
6 JOy,V:JSA 2.50
7 JOy,V:JSA 2.50
8 JOy,V:Ultra Humanite 2.50
9 JOy,V:Ultra Humanite 2.50
10 JOy,V:Ultra Humanite 2.00
11 DN,GT,O:Infinity Inc. 2.00
12 Infinity Unmasks,I:Yolanda
  Montez (New Wildcat) 2.00
13 DN,V:Rose & Thorn 2.00
14 1st TM DC art,V:Chroma 4.00
15 TM,V:Chroma 3.00
16 TM,I:Helix (Mr. Bones) 3.00
17 TM,V:Helix 3.00
18 TM,Crisis 3.00
19 TM,JSA,JLA x-over,
  I:Mekanique 3.00

20 TM,Crisis 3.00	
21 TM,Crisis,I:HourmanII,	
Dr.Midnight 3.00	
22 TM,Crisis 3.00	
23 TM,Crisis 3.00	
24 TM,Crisis 3.00	
25 TM,Crisis,JSA 3.00	
26 TM,V:Carcharo 3.00	
27 TM,V:Carcharo 3.00	
28 TM,V:Carcharo 3.00	
29 TM,V:Helix 3.00	
30 TM,Mourning of JSA 3.00	
31 TM,V:Psycho Pirate 3.00	
32 TM,V:Psycho Pirate 3.00	
33 TM,O:Obsidian 3.00	
34 TM,A: Global Guardians 3.00	
35 TM,V:Infinitors 3.00	
36 TM,V:Injustice Unl. 3.00	
37 TM,TD,O:Northwind 3.00	
38 Helix on Trial 1.75	

Infinity, Inc. #37 © DC Comics, Inc.

39 O:Solomon Grundy 1.75
40 V:Thunderbolt 1.75
41 Jonni Thunder 1.75
42 TD,V:Hastor,L:Fury 1.75
43 TD,V:Hastor,Silver Scarab . . . 1.75
44 TD,D:Silver Scarab 1.75
45 MGu,A:New Teen Titans,
  V:Ultra-Humanite 1.75
46 TD,Millenium,V:Floronic Man . . 1.75
47 TD,Millenium,V:Harlequin 1.75
48 TD,O:Nuklon 1.75
49 Silver Scarab becomes
  Sandman 2.00
50 TD,V:The Wizard,O:Sandman . 3.00
51 W:Fury & Sandman,D:Skyman 1.75
52 V:Helix 1.75
53 V:Justice Unlimited,last issue . 1.75
Ann.#1 TM,V:Thorn 4.00
Ann.#2 V:Degaton,x-over Young
  All-Stars Annual #1 . . . . 2.00
Spec.#1 TD,A:Outsiders,V:Psycho
  Pirate 1.50

INVASION!
1 TM,I:Vril Dox,Dominators
  (20th century) 4.50

2 TM,KG,DG,I:L.E.G.I.O.N. 4.00
3 BS,DG,I:Blasters 3.50
Daily Planet-Invasion! 16p 2.00

INVISIBLES
Vertigo
1 GMo(s) 3.25
2 GMo(s),Down & Out,pt.1 . . . . . 2.25
3 GMo(s),Down & Out,pt.2 . . . . . 2.25
4 GMo(s),Down & Out,pt.3 . . . . . 2.25
5 Arcadia,pt.1 . . . . 2.00
6 Arcadia,pt.2 . . . . 2.00
7 Arcadia,pt.3 . . . . 2.00
8 Arcadia,pt.4 . . . . 2.00
9 SeP(c),L:Dane 2.50
10 SeP(c),CWn,Jim Crow v.
  Zombies 2.50

IRONWOLF
1 HC,rep. 2.00

IRONWOLF: FIRES OF THE REVOLUTION
Hardcov.GN MMi,CR,R:Ironwolf . 29.95

ISIS
October-November, 1976
1 RE/WW 5.00
2 MN 1.25
3 thru 6 . . . . @1.25
7 O:Isis 1.25
8 Dec.-Jan., 1977–78 . . . . 1.25

IT'S GAMETIME
September-October, 1955
1 . . . . 400.00
2 . . . . 350.00
3 . . . . 350.00
4 March-April, 1956 . . . . 350.00

JACKIE GLEASON AND THE HONEYMOONERS
June-July, 1956
1 Based on TV show 500.00
2 . . . . 350.00
3 . . . . 300.00
4 . . . . 300.00
5 . . . . 300.00
6 . . . . 300.00
7 . . . . 300.00
8 . . . . 300.00
9 . . . . 300.00
10 . . . . 300.00
11 . . . . 300.00
12 April-May, 1958 . . . . 350.00

JAGUAR
Impact
1 I&O:Jaguar I: Timon De Guzman,
  Maxx 13,Prof.Ruiz, Luiza
  Timmerman 1.25
2 Development of Powers 1.25
3 A:Maxx-13 . . . . 1.25
4 A:Black Hood 1.25
5 V:Void,The Living Black Hole . . 1.25
6 'The Doomster',A:Maxx-13 . . . . 1.25
7 Jaguar Secret Discovered,
  V:Void 1.25
8 V:Aryan League 1.25
9 I:Moonlighter(w/trading cards) . 1.25
10 V:Invisible Terror 1.25
11 Defending Comedienne 1.25

The Jaguar #6 © DC Comics, Inc.

12 V:The Bodyguard 1.25
13 V:Purge 1.25
14 'Frightmare in Rio',last iss. . . 1.25
Ann.#1 Earthquest,w/trading card . 2.50

JEMM, SON OF SATURN
September, 1984
1 GC/KJ mini-series 1.50
2 GC 1.25
3 GC,Origin 1.25
4 A:Superman 1.25
5 Kin 1.25
6 . . . . 1.25
7 thru 12 GC, Aug. 1985 . . . . @1.25

JIMMY WAKELY
September-October, 1949
1 Ph(c),ATh,The Cowboy
  Swordsman 500.00
2 Ph(c),ATh,The Prize Pony . . 275.00
3 Ph(c),ATh,The Return of
  Tulsa Tom 275.00
4 Ph(c),ATh,FF,HK,Where's
  There'sSmokeThere'sGunfire 300.00
5 ATh,The Return of the
  Conquistadores 225.00
6 ATh,Two Lives of
  Jimmy Wakely 225.00
7 The Secret of Hairpin Canyon 225.00
8 ATh,The Lost City of
  Blue Valley 225.00
9 ATh,The Return of the
  Western Firebrands 200.00
10 ATh,Secret of Lantikin's Light 200.00
11 ATh,Trail o/a Thousand Hoofs200.00
12 ATh,JKU,The King of Sierra
  Valley 200.00
13 ATh,The Raiders of Treasure
  Mountain 200.00
14 ATh(c),JKu,The Badmen
  of Roaring Flame Valley . . . 200.00
15 GK(c),Tommyguns on the
  Range 200.00
16 GK(c),The Bad Luck Boots . 175.00
17 GK(c),Terror atThunderBasin 175.00
18 July-August, 1952 . . . . 200.00

JOHNNY THUNDER
February-March, 1973
1 ATh 5.00
2 GK,MD 4.00
3 ATh,GK,MD,July-August, 1973 . 4.00

JOKER, THE
1 IN,DG,A:TwoFace 22.00
2 IN,JL WillieTheWeeper 13.00
3 JL,A:Creeper 12.00
4 JL,A:GreenArrow 10.00
5 . . . . 10.00
6 V:Sherlock Holmes 10.00
7 IN,A:Luthor 10.00
8 . . . . 10.00
9 A:Catwoman 12.00

JONAH HEX
March-April, 1977
1 'Vengeance For A Fallen
  Gladiator' 40.00
2 'The Lair of the Parrot' 18.00
3 'The Fugitive' 14.00
4 'The Day of Chameleon' 14.00
5 'Welcome to Paradise' 14.00
6 'The Lawman' 14.00
7 'Son of the Apache' 10.00
8 O:Jonah Hex 9.00
9 BWr(c) 9.00
10 GM(c),'Violence at Vera Cruz' . 9.00
11 'The Holdout' 7.00
12 JS(c) 7.00
13 'The Railroad Blaster' 7.00
14 'The Sin Killer' 7.00
15 'Saw Dust and Slow Death' . . . 7.00
16 'The Wyandott Verdict!' 5.00
17 . . . . 5.00
18 . . . . 5.00
19 'The Duke of Zarkania!' 5.00
20 'Phantom Stage to William
  Bend' 5.00
21 'The Buryin'!' 5.00
22 'Requiem For A Pack Rat' . . . 5.00
23 'The Massacre of the
  Celestials!' 5.00
24 'Minister of the Lord' 5.00
25 'The Widow Maker' 5.00
26 'Death Race to Cholera Bend!' . 4.00
27 'The Wooden Six Gun!' 4.00
28 'Night of the Savage' 4.00
29 'The Innocent' 4.00
30 O:Jonah Hex 4.50
31 A:Arbee Stoneham 4.00
32 A:Arbee Stoneham 4.00
33 'The Crusador' 4.00
34 'Christmas in an Outlaw Town' 4.00
35 'The Fort Charlotte Brigade' . . 4.00
36 'Return to Fort Charlotte' 4.00
37 DAy,A:Stonewall Jackson 4.00
38 . . . . 4.00
39 'The Vow of a Samurai!' 4.00
40 DAy 4.00
41 DAy,'Two for the Hangman!' . . 4.00
42 'Wanted for Murder' 4.00
43 JKu(c) 4.00
44 JKu(c),DAy 4.00
45 DAy,Jonah gets married 4.00
46 JKu(c),DAy 4.00
47 DAy,'Doom Rides the Sundown
  Town' 4.00
48 DAy,A:El Diablo 4.00
49 DAy 4.00
50 DAy,'The Hunter' 4.00
51 DAy,'The Comforter' 3.50

52 DAy,'Rescue'	3.50
53 DAy	3.50
54	3.50
55 'Trail of Blood'	3.50
56 DAy,'The Asylum'	3.50
57 B:El Diablo backup story	3.50
58 DAy,'The Treasure of Catfish Pond'	3.50
59 DAy,'Night of the White Lotus'	3.50
60 DAy,'Domain of the Warlord'	3.50
61 DAy, 'In the Lair of the Manchus!'	3.50
62 DAy,'The Belly of the Malay Tiger!'	3.50
63 DAy	3.50
64 DAy,'The Pearl!'	3.50
65 DAy,'The Vendetta!'	3.50
66 DAy'Requiem for a Coward'	3.50
67 DAy,'Deadman's Hand!'	3.50
68 DAy,'Gunfight at Gravesboro!'	3.50
69 DAy,'The Gauntlet!'	3.50
70 DAy	3.50
71 DAy,'The Masquerades'	3.50
72 DAy,'Tarantula'	3.50
73 DAy,Jonah in a wheel chair	3.50
74 DAy,A:Railroad Bill	3.50
75 DAy,JAp,A:Railroad Bill	3.50
76 DAy,Jonah goes to Jail	3.00
77 DAy,'Over the Wall'	3.00
78 DAy,Me Ling returns	3.00
79 DAy,'Duel in the Sand'	3.00
80 A:Turnbull	3.00
81 DAy	3.00
82 DAy	3.00
83 thru 89 DAy	@3.00
90 thru 92	@3.00
92 August, 1985	3.00

JONAH HEX AND OTHER WESTERN TALES
September-October, 1979

1	2.00
2 NA,ATh,SA,GK	3.00
3 January-February, 1980	1.75

JONAH HEX: RIDERS OF THE WORM AND SUCH
Vertigo
[Mini-Series]

1 R:Ronah Hex	2.95
2 At Wildes West Ranch	2.95
3 History Lesson	2.95
4 I:Autumn Brothers	2.95
5 V:Big worm, final issue	2.95

JONAH HEX: TWO-GUN MOJO
Vertigo

1 B:JLd(s),TT,SG(i),R:Jonah Hex, I:Slow Go Smith	8.00
1a Platinum Ed.	50.00
2 TT,SG(i),D:Slow Go Smith,I:Doc Williams,Wild Bill Hickok	6.00
3 TT,SG(i),Jonah captured	5.00
4 TT,SG(i),O:Doc Williams	5.00
5 TT,SG(i),V::Doc Williams	5.00

JONNI THUNDER
February, 1985

1 DG,origin issue	1.25
2 DG	1.25
3 DG	1.25

JUDGE DREDD

1 R:Judge Dredd	2.50
2 Silicon Dreams	2.25
3 Terrorists	2.50
4 Mega-City One crisis	2.25
5 Solitary Dredd	2.25
6 V:Richard Magg	2.25
7	2.25
8 V:Ministry of Fear	2.25
9 V:Mister Synn	2.25
10 D:Judge Dredd	2.25
11 Mega-City One Chaos	2.25
12 V:Wally Squad	2.25

JUDGE DREDD: LEGENDS OF THE LAW

1 Organ Donor,pt.1	2.50
2 Organ Donor,pt.2	2.25
3 Organ Donor,pt.3	2.25
4 Organ Donor,pt.4	2.25
5 Trial By Gunfire,pt.1	2.25
6 Trial By Gunfire,pt.2	2.25
7 JHi(c) Trial By Gunfire,pt.3	2.25
8 JBy(s) Fall From Grace,pt.1	2.25

JUSTICE, INC.
May-June, 1975

1 AMc,JKu(c),O:Avenger	3.00
2 JK	1.25
3 JK	1.25
4 JK,JKu(c),November-December, 1975	1.25

[Mini-Series]

1 PerfectBound 'Trust & Betrayal'	3.95
2 PerfectBound	3.95

JUSTICE LEAGUE AMERICA
(see JUSTICE LEAGUE INTERNATIONAL)

JUSTICE LEAGUE EUROPE

1 BS,A:Wonder Woman	4.00
2 BS,Search for Nazi-Killer	3.00
3 BS,A:Jack O'Lantern, Queen Bee	2.50
4 BS,V:Queen Bee	2.50
5 JRu,BS,Metamorpho's Baby, A:Sapphire Starr	2.50
6 BS,V:Injustice League	2.00
7 BS,Teasdale Imperative#2, A:JLA	2.00
8 BS,Teasdale Imperative#4, A:JLA	2.00
9 BS,ANi,A:Superman	2.00
10 BS,V:Crimson Fox	2.00
11 BS,C:DocMagnus&Metal Men	2.00
12 BS,A:Metal Men	2.00
13 BS,V:One-Eyed Cat, contd from JLA #37	2.00
14 I:VCR	2.00
15 BS,B:Extremists Vector saga, V:One-Eyed Cat,A:BlueJay	2.00
16 BS,A:Rocket Reds, Blue Jay	2.25
17 BS,JLI in Another Dimension	2.25
18 BS,Extremists Homeworld	2.25
19 BS,E:Extremist Vector Saga	2.25
20 MR,I:Beefeater,V:Kilowog	1.75
21 MR,JRu,New JLE embassy in London,A:Kilowog	1.50
22 MR,JLE's Cat stolen	1.50
23 BS,O:Crimson Fox	1.50

24 BS,Worms in London	1.50
25 BS,V:Worms	1.50
26 BS,V:Starro	1.50
27 BS,JLE V:JLE,A:JLA,V:Starro	1.50
28 BS, JLE V:JLE,A:J'onnJ'onzz, V:Starro	1.50
29 BS,Breakdowns #2,V:Global Guardians	1.75
30 Breakdowns#4,V:J.O'Lantern	1.50
31 Breakdowns #6,War of the Gods tie-in	1.50
32 Breakdowns #8,A:Chief(Doom Patrol)	1.50
33 Breakdowns #10,Lobo vs. Despero	1.50
34 Breakdowns #12,Lobo vs.Despero	1.50
35 Breakdowns #14,V:Extremists, D:Silver Sorceress	1.50
36 Breakdowns #16,All Quit	1.50
37 B:New JLE,I:Deconstructo	1.75
38 V:Deconstructo,A:Batman	1.50
39 V:Deconstructo,A:Batman	1.50
40 J:Hal Jordan,A:Metamorpho	1.50
41 A:Metamorpho,Wond.Woman	1.50
42 A:Wonder Woman,V:Echidna	1.50
43 V:Amos Fortune	1.50
44 V:Amos Fortune	1.50
45 Red Winter#1,V:Rocket Reds	1.50

Justice League Europe #44
© DC Comics, Inc.

46 Red Winter#2	1.50
47 Red Winter#3,V:Sonar	1.50
48 Red Winter#4,V:Sonar	1.50
49 Red Winter #5,V:Sonar	1.50
50 Red Winter#6,Double-sized, V:Sonar,J:Metamorpho	3.25
Ann.#1 A:Global Guardians	2.00
Ann.#2 MR,CS,ArmageddonPt.7	3.00
Ann.#3 RT(i),Eclipso tie-in	2.75
Justice League Spectacular JLE(c) New Direction	1.50

Becomes: Justice League International
[2nd Series]

JUSTICE LEAGUE INTERNATIONAL
[1st Series]

1 KM,TA,New Team,I:Max. Lord . 9.00
2 KM,AG,A:BlueJay & Silver
  Sorceress 6.00
3 KM,AG,J:Booster Gold, V:Rocket
  Lords 5.00
3a Superman Logo 75.00
4 KM,AG,V:Royal Flush 4.00
5 KM,AG,A:The Creeper 3.00
6 KM,AG,A:The Creeper 3.00
7 KM,AG,L:Dr.Fate,Capt.Marvel,
  J:Rocket Red,Capt.Atom
  (Double size) 3.00
8 KM,AG,KG,Move to Paris Embassy,
  I:C.Cobert,B.U.Glob.Guardians. 2.50
9 KM,AG,KG,Millenium,Rocket
  Red-Traitor 2.50
10 KG,KM,AG,A:G.L.Corps,
  Superman,I:G'Nort 2.50
11 KM,AG,V:Construct,C:Metron . 2.50
12 KG,KM,AG,O:Max Lord 2.50
13 KG,KM,A:Suicide Squad 2.50
14 SL,AG,J:Fire&Ice,L:Ron,
  I:Manga Kahn 2.50
15 SL,AG,V:Magna Kahn 2.00
16 KM,AG,I:Queen Bee 2.00
17 KM,AG,V:Queen Bee 2.00
18 KM,AG,MPn,A:Lobo,Guy Gardner
  (bonus book) 4.00
19 KM,JRu,A:Lobo vs.Guy Gardner,
  J:Hawkman & Hawkwoman . . 3.00
20 KM,JRu(i),A:Lobo,G.Gardner . 2.00
21 KM,JRu(i),A:Lobo vs.Guy
  Gardner 2.00
22 KM,JRu,Imskian Soldiers . . . 2.00
23 KM,JRu,I:Injustice League . . 2.00
24 KM,JRu,DoubleSize + Bonus
  Bk#13,I:JusticeLeagueEurope . 3.00
25 KM(c),JRu(i),Vampire story . . 2.00
Ann.#1 BWg,DG,CR 2.00
Ann.#2 BWg,JRu,A:Joker 3.00
Ann.#3 KM(c),JRu,JLI Embassies 2.50
Spec.#1 Mr.Miracle 2.00
Spec.#2,The Huntress 2.95
TPB new beginning,rep.#1-#7 . 12.95
TPB The Secret Gospel of Maxwell
  Lord Rep. #8-#12, Ann.#1 . . 12.95
Becomes:

JUSTICE LEAGUE AMERICA

26 KM(c),JRu(i),Possessed Blue
  Beetle 2.50
27 KM(c),JRu,DG(i),'Exorcist',
  (c)tribute 2.00
28 KM(c),JRu(i), A:Black Hand . . 2.00
29 KM(c),JRu(i),V:Mega-Death . . 2.00
30 KM(c),BWg,JRu,J:Huntress,
  D:Mega-Death 2.00
31 ANi,AH,JRu,Teasdale Imperative
  #1,N:Fire,Ice,A:JLE 3.00
32 ANi,AH,Teasdale Imperative
  #3, A:JLE 3.00
33 ANi,AH,GuyGardner vs.Kilowog 2.50
34 ANi,AH,'Club JLI,'A:Aquaman . 2.50
35 ANi,JRu,AH,A:Aquaman 2.50
36 Gnort vs. Scarlet Skier 2.00
37 ANi,AH,L:Booster Gold 2.00
38 JRu,AH,R:Desparo,D:Steel . . . 2.00
39 JRu,AH,V:Desparo,D:Mr.Miracle,
  Robot 2.00
40 AH,Mr.Miracle Funeral 2.00
41 MMc,MaxForce 2.00

Justice League America #87
© *DC Comics, Inc.*

42 MMc,J:L-Ron 2.00
43 AH,KG,The Man Who Knew Too
  Much #1 . . . . 2.00
44 AH,Man Knew Too Much #2 . . 2.00
45 AH,MJ,JRu,Guy & Ice's 2nd
  date 2.00
46 Glory Bound #1,I:Gen.Glory . . 2.00
47 Glory Bound #2,J:Gen.Glory . . 2.00
48 Glory Bound #3,V:DosUberbot 2.00
49 Glory Bound #4 . . . . 2.00
50 Glory Bound #5 (double size) . 2.50
51 JRu,AH,V:BlackHand,
  R:Booster Gold 2.00
52 TVE,Blue Beetle Vs. Guy Gardner
  A:Batman 2.00
53 Breakdowns #1, A:JLE 2.00
54 Breakdowns #3, A:JLE 2.00
55 Breakdowns #5,V:Global
  Guardians 2.00
56 Breakdowns #7, U.N. revokes
  JLA charter 2.00
57 Breakdowns #9,A:Lobo,
  V:Despero 2.00
58 BS,Breakdowns #11,Lobo
  Vs.Despero 2.00
59 BS,Breakdowns #13,
  V:Extremists 2.00
60 KM,TA,Breakdowns #15,
  End of J.L.A. 2.00
61 DJu,I:Weapons Master,B:New
  JLA Line-up,I:Bloodwynd 3.00
62 DJu,V:Weapons Master 2.00
63 DJu,V:Starbreaker 2.00
64 DJu,V:Starbreaker 2.00
65 DJu,V:Starbreaker 2.00
66 DJu,Superman V:Guy Gardner 2.00
67 DJu,Bloodwynd mystery 2.00
68 DJu,V:Alien Land Baron 2.00
69 DJu, Doomsday Pt.1-A 16.00
69a 2nd printing 2.00
70 DJu,Funeral for a Friend#1 . . 10.00
70a 2nd printing 2.00
71 DJu,J:Agent Liberty,Black Condor,
  The Ray,Wonder Woman 6.00
71a Newsstand ed. 4.00
71b 2nd Printing 1.50
72 DJu,A:Green Arrow,Black
  Canary,Atom,B:Destiny's Hand 5.00

73 DJu,Destiny's Hand #2 . . . . . . 4.00
74 DJu,Destiny's Hand #3 . . . . . . 3.00
75 DJu,E:Destiny's Hand #4,Martian
  Manhunter as Bloodwynd 2.00
76 DJu,Blood Secrets#1,
  V:Weaponmaster 1.50
77 DJu,Blood Secrets#2,
  V:Weaponmaster 1.50
78 MC,V:The Extremists 1.50
79 MC,V:The Extremists 1.50
80 KWe,N:Booster Gold 1.50
81 KWe,A:Captain Atom 1.50
82 KWe,A:Captain Atom 1.50
83 KWe,V:Guy Gardner 1.50
84 KWe,A:Ice 1.75
85 KWe,V:Frost Giants 1.75
86 B:Cults of the Machine 1.75
87 N:Booster Gold 1.75
88 E:Cults of the Machine 1.75
89 Judgement Day#1,
  V:Overmaster 1.75
90 Judgement Day#4 . . . . 1.50
91 Aftershocks #1 . . . . 1.75
92 Zero Hour,I:Triumph 1.50
93 Power Girl and child 1.50
94 Scarabus 1.50
95 . . . . 1.50
96 Funeral 1.50
97 I:Judgment 1.50
98 J:Blue Devil, Ice Maiden 1.50
99 V:New Metahumes 1.50
100 GJ,Woj,V:Lord Havok,dbl.size 2.95
100a Collector's Edition 3.95
101 GJ,Woj,Way of the
  Warrior,pt.2 . . . . 1.75
Ann.#4 KM(c),I:JL Antartica 3.00
Ann.#5 MR,KM,DJu,Armageddon . 4.00
Ann.#5a 2nd Printing,silver 2.00
Ann.#6 DC,Eclipso 2.75
Ann.#7 I:Terrorsmith 2.75
Ann.#8 Elseworlds Story 2.95
Justice League Spectacular DJu,
  JLA(c) New Direction 2.00

JUSTICE LEAGUE INTERNATIONAL
[2nd Regular Series]
Prev: Justice League Europe

51 Aztec Cult 1.50
52 V:Aztec Cult 1.50
53 R:Fox's Husband 1.50
54 RoR,A:Creator 1.50
55 RoR,A:Creator 1.50
56 RoR,V:Terrorists 1.50
57 RoR,V:Terrorists 1.50
58 RoR,V:Aliens 1.50
59 RoR,A:Guy Gardner 1.50
60 GJ(s),RoR 1.75
61 GJ(s),V:Godfrey 1.75
62 GJ(s),N:Metamorpho,V:Godfrey 1.75
63 GJ(s),In Africa 1.75
64 GJ(s),V:Cadre 1.75
65 JudgmentDay#3,V:Overmaster 1.75
66 JudgmentDay#6,V:Overmaster 1.50
Ann.#4 Bloodlines#9,I:Lionheart . 2.75
Ann.#5 . . . . 3.25
Ann.#6 Elseworlds Story 2.95

JUSTICE LEAGUE INTERNATIONAL
QUARTERLY

1 I:Conglomerate 4.00
2 MJ(i),R:Mr.Nebula 3.50

3 V:Extremists,C:Original JLA . . . 3.50
4 KM(c),MR,CR,A:Injustice
  League. 3.00
5 KM(c),Superhero Attacks 3.00
6 EB,Elongated Man,B.U.Global
  Guardians,Powergirl,B.Beetle . 3.00
7 EB,DH,MR.Global Guardians . . 3.00
8 . . . . 3.00
9 DC,F:Power Girl,Booster Gold . 3.50
10 F:Flash,Fire & Ice 3.50
11 F:JL Women 3.50
12 F:Conglomerate 3.50
13 V:Ultraa 3.50
14 MMi(c),PuK(s),F:Captain Atom,Blue
  Beetle,Nightshade,Thunderbolt 3.75
15 F:Praxis 3.50
16 F:Gen Glory 3.50
17 Final Issue 3.50

Justice League of America #11
© DC Comics, Inc.

JUSTICE LEAGUE
OF AMERICA
October-November, 1960

1 MSy,I&O:Despero 2,700.00
2 MSy,A:Merlin 675.00
3 MSy,I&O:Kanjar Ro 500.00
4 MSy,J:Green Arrow 350.00
5 MSy,I&O:Dr.Destiny 250.00
6 MSy,Prof. Fortune 200.00
7 MSy,Cosmic Fun-House 200.00
8 MSy,For Sale-Justice League 200.00
9 MSy,O:JLA 350.00
10 MSy,I:Felix Faust 195.00
11 MSy,A:Felix Faust 145.00
12 MSy,I&O:Dr Light 145.00
13 MSy,A:Speedy 145.00
14 MSy,J:Atom 145.00
15 MSy,V:Untouchable Aliens . 135.00
16 MSy,I:Maestro 110.00
17 MSy,A:Tornado Tyrant 110.00
18 MSy,V:Terrane,Ocana 110.00
19 MSy,A:Dr.Destiny 110.00
20 MSy,V:Metal Being 110.00
21 MSy,R:JSA,1st S.A Hourman,
  Dr.Fate 250.00
22 MSy,R:JSA 225.00
23 MSy,I:Queen Bee 55.00
24 MSy,A:Adam Strange 55.00

25 MSy,I:Draad,the Conqueror . . 55.00
26 MSy,A:Despero 55.00
27 MSy,V:I,A:Amazo 55.00
28 MSy,I:Headmaster Mind,
  A:Robin 55.00
29 MSy,I:Crime Syndicate,A:JSA,
  1st S.A. Starman 70.00
30 MSy,V:Crime Syndicate,
  A:JSA 70.00
31 MSy,J:Hawkman 40.00
32 MSy,I&O:Brain Storm 34.00
33 MSy,I:Endless One 30.00
34 MSy,A:Dr.Destiny,Joker 35.00
35 MSy,A:Three Demons 30.00
36 MSy,A:Brain Storm,
  Handicap story 30.00
37 MSy,A:JSA,x-over,
  1st S.A.Mr.Terrific 55.00
38 MSy,A:JSA,Mr.Terrific 55.00
39 Giant 60.00
40 MSy,A:Shark,Penguin 28.00
41 MSy,I:Key 28.00
42 MSy,A:Metamorpho 18.00
43 MSy,I:Royal Flush Gang 18.00
44 MSy,A:Unimaginable 18.00
45 MSy,I:Shaggy Man 18.00
46 MSy,A:JSA,Blockbuster,Solomon
  Grundy,1st S.A Sandman . . . 85.00
47 MSy,A:JSA,Blockbuster,
  Solomon Grundy 30.00
48 Giant 26.00
49 MSy,A:Felix Faust 15.00
50 MSy,A:Robin 15.00
51 MSy,A:Zatanna,Elong.Man . . 15.00
52 MSy,A:Robin,Lord of Time . . . 15.00
53 MSy,A:Hawkgirl 15.00
54 MSy,A:Royal Flush Gang 15.00
55 MSy,A:JSA,E-2 Robin 35.00
56 MSy,A:JSA,E-2 Robin 25.00
57 MSy,Brotherhood 15.00
58 Reprint(giant size). 15.00
59 MSy,V:Impossibles 15.00
60 MSy,A:Queen Bee,Batgirl . . . 15.00
61 MSy,A:Lex Luthor,Penguin . . 15.00
62 MSy,V:Bulleteers 12.00
63 MSy,A:Key 12.00
64 DD,I:Red Tornado,A:JSA . . . 14.00
65 DD,A:JSA 14.00
66 DD,A:Demmy Gog 12.00
67 MSy,Giant reprints 12.00
68 DD,V:Choas Maker 13.00
69 DD,L:Wonder Woman 9.00
70 DD,A:Creeper 9.00
71 DD,L:J'onn J'onnz 9.00
72 DD,A:Hawkgirl 9.00
73 DD,A:JSA 10.00
74 DD,D:Larry Lance,A:JSA . . . 10.00
75 DD,J:Black Canary 9.00
76 Giant,MA,two page pin-up . . . 7.00
77 DD,A:Joker,L:Snapper Carr . . 8.00
78 DD,R:Vigilante 6.00
79 DD,A:Vigilante 6.00
80 DD,A:Tomar-Re,Guardians . . . 6.00
81 DD,V:Jest-Master 6.00
82 DD,A:JSA 7.50
83 DD,A:JSA,Spectre 7.50
84 DD,Devil in Paradise 6.00
85 Giant reprint 7.50
86 DD,V:Zapper 6.00
87 DD,A:Zatanna,I:Silver
  Sorceress,Blue Jay 6.00
88 DD,A:Mera 6.00
89 DD,A:Harlequin Ellis,
  (i.e. Harlan Ellison) 6.00
90 CI(c),MA(ci),DD,V:Pale People 6.00

91 DD,A:JSA,V:Solomon Grundy . 6.00
92 DD,A:JSA,V:Solomon Grundy . 7.00
93 DD:A:JSA,(giant size) 7.00
94 DD,NA,O:Sandman,rep.
  Adventure #40 . . . . 23.00
95 DD,rep.More Fun Comics #67,
  All American Comics #25 . . . . 7.00
96 DD,I:Starbreaker 7.00
97 DD,MS,O:JLA 6.00
98 DD,A:Sargon,Gold.Age reps . . 5.00
99 DD,G.A. reps. 5.00
100 DD,A:JSA,Metamorpho,
  R:7 Soldiers of Victory 8.00
101 DD,A:JSA,7 Soldiers 7.00
102 DD,DG,A:JSA,7 Soldiers
  D:Red Tornado 7.00
103 DD,DG,Halloween issue,
  A:Phantom Stranger 4.00
104 DD,DG,A:Shaggy Man,
  Hector Hammond 4.00
105 DD,DG,J:ElongatedMan 4.00
106 DD,DG,J:RedTornado 4.00
107 DD,DG,I:Freedom Fighters,
  A:JSA 7.50
108 DD,DG,A:JSA,
  Freedom Fighters 7.00
109 DD,DG,L:Hawkman 4.00
110 DD,DG,A:John Stewart,
  Phantom Stranger 4.00
111 DD,DG,I:Injustice Gang 4.00
112 DD,DG,A:Amazo 4.00
113 DD,DG,A:JSA 6.00
114 DD,DG,A:SnapperCarr 4.00
115 DD,FMc,A:J'onnJ'onnz 4.00
116 DD,FMc,I:Golden Eagle 5.00
117 DD,FMc,R:Hawkman 3.50
118 DD,FMc 3.50
119 DD,FMc,A:Hawkgirl 3.50
120 DD,FMc,A:Adam Strange . . . 3.50
121 DD,FMc,W:Adam Strange . . . 3.50
122 DD,FMc,JLA casebook story
  V:Dr.Light 3.50
123 DD,FMc,A:JSA 5.50
124 DD,FMc,A: JSA 5.50
125 DD,FMc,A:Two-Face 3.50
126 DD,FMc,A:Two-Face 3.50
127 DD,FMc,V:Anarchist 3.50
128 DD,FMc,J:W.Woman 3.50
129 DD,FMC,D:RedTornado 3.00
130 DD,FMc,O:JLASatellite 3.00
131 DD,FMc,V:Queen Bee,Sonar . 3.00
132 DD,FMc,A:Supergirl 3.00
133 DD,FMc,A:Supergirl 3.00
134 DD,FMc,A:Supergirl 3.00
135 DD,FMc,A:Squad.of Justice . . 3.00
136 DD,FMc,A:E-2Joker 3.50
137 DD,FMc,Superman vs.
  Capt. Marvel 4.00
138 NA(c),DD,FMc,A:Adam
  Strange 3.00
139 NA(c),DD,FMc,A:AdamStrange,
  Phantom Stranger,doub.size . 3.50
140 DD,FMc,Manhunters 3.00
141 DD,FMc,Manhunters 3.00
142 DD,FMc,F:Aquaman,Atom,
  Elongated Man 3.00
143 DD,FMc,V:Injustice Gang . . . 3.50
144 DD,FMc,O:JLA 3.00
145 DD,FMc,A:Phant.Stranger . . 3.00
146 J:Red Tornado,Hawkgirl 3.00
147 DD,FMc,A:Legion 3.00
148 DD,FMc,A:Legion 3.00
149 DD,FMc,A:Dr.Light 3.00
150 DD,FMc,A:Dr.Light 3.00
151 DD,FMc,A:Amos Fortune . . . 2.50

Justice League of America #30
© DC Comics, Inc.

152 DD,FMc	2.50
153 GT,FMc,I:Ultraa	2.50
154 MK(c),DD,FMc	2.50
155 DD,FMc	2.50
156 DD,FMc	2.50
157 DD,FMc,W:Atom	2.50
158 DD,FMc,A:Ultraa	2.50
159 DD,FMc,A:JSA,Jonah Hex, Enemy Ace	3.00
160 DD,FMc,A:JSA,Jonah Hex, Enemy Ace	3.00
161 DD,FMc,J:Zatanna	2.50
162 DD,FMc	2.50
163 DD,FMc,V:Mad Maestro	2.50
164 DD,FMc,V:Mad Maestro	2.50
165 DD,FMc	2.50
166 DD,FMc,V:Secret Society	2.50
167 DD,FMc,V:Secret Society	2.50
168 DD,FMc,V:Secret Society	2.50
169 DD,FMc,A:Ultraa	2.50
170 DD,FMc,A:Ultraa	2.50
171 DD,FMc,A:JSA,D:Mr.Terrific	2.50
172 DD,FMc,A:JSA,D:Mr.Terrific	2.50
173 DD,FMc,A:Black Lightning	2.50
174 DD,FMc,A:Black Lightning	2.50
175 DD,FMc,V:Dr.Destiny	2.50
176 DD,FMc,V:Dr.Destiny	2.00
177 DD,FMc,V:Desparo	2.00
178 JSn(c),DD,FMc,V:Desparo	2.00
179 JSn(c),DD,FMc,J:Firestorm	2.50
180 JSn(c),DD,FMc,V:Satin Satan	2.00
181 DD,FMc,L:Gr.Arrow,V:Star	3.50
182 DD,FMc,A:Green Arrow, V:Felix Faust	3.00
183 JSn(c),DD,FMc,A:JSA, NewGods	3.00
184 GP,FMc,A:JSA,NewGods	3.00
185 JSn(c),GP,FMc,A:JSA, New Gods	3.00
186 FMc,GP,V:Shaggy Man	2.00
187 DH,FMc,N:Zatanna	2.00
188 DH,FMc,V:Proteus	2.00
189 BB(c),RB,FMc,V:Starro	2.00
190 BB(c),RB,LMa,V:Starro	2.00
191 RB,V:Amazo	2.00

192 GP,O:Red Tornado	2.00
193 GP,RB,JOy,I:AllStarSquad	2.50
194 GP,V:Amos Fortune	2.00
195 GP,A:JSA,V:Secret Society	3.00
196 GP,RT,A:JSA,V:Secret Soc.	3.00
197 GP,RT,KP,A:JSA,V:Secret Society	3.00
198 DH,BBr,A:J.Hex,BatLash	2.00
199 GP(c),DH,BBr,A:Jonah Hex, BatLash	2.00
200 GP,DG,BB (1st Batman),PB,TA, BBr,GK,CI,JAp,JKu,Anniv.,A:Adam Strange,Phantom Stranger, J:Green Arrow	4.50
201 GP(c),DH,A:Ultraa	2.00
202 GP(c),DH,BBr,JLA in Space	2.00
203 GP(c),DH,RT,V:Royal Flush Gang	2.00
204 GP(c),DH,RT,V:R.FlushGang	2.00
205 GP(c),DH,RT,V:R.FlushGang	2.00
206 DH,RT,A:Demons 3	2.00
207 GP(c),DH,RT,A:All Star Squadron,JSA	2.50
208 GP(c),DH,RT,A:All Star Squadron,JSA	2.50
209 GP(c),DH,RT,A:All Star Squadron,JSA	2.50
210 RB,RT,JLA casebook #1	2.00
211 RB,RT,JLA casebook #2	2.00
212 GP(c),RB,PCu,RT,c.book #3	2.00
213 GP(c),DH,RT	2.00
214 GP(c),DH,RT,I:Siren Sist.h'd	2.00
215 GP(c),DH,RT	2.00
216 DH	2.00
217 GP(c),RT(i)	2.00
218 RT(i),A:Prof.Ivo	2.00
219 GP(c),RT(i),A:JSA	2.25
220 GP(c),RT,O:Bl.Canary,A:JSA	2.25
221 Beasts #1	2.00
222 RT(i),Beasts #2	2.00
223 RT(i),Beasts #3	2.00
224 DG(i),V:Paragon	2.00
225 V:Hellrazor	2.00
226 FMc(i),V:Hellrazor	2.00
227 V:Hellrazor,I:Lord Claw	2.00
228 GT,AN,R:J'onnJonzz,War of the Worlds,pt.1	2.00
229 War of the Worlds,pt.2	2.00
230 War of the Worlds conc.	2.00
231 RB(i),A:JSA,Supergirl	2.25
232 A:JSA Supergirl	2.25
233 New JLA takes over book, B:Rebirth,F:Vibe	2.00
234 F:Vixen	2.00
235 F:Steel	2.00
236 E:Rebirth,F:Gypsy	2.00
237 A:Superman,Flash,WWoman	2.00
238 A:Superman,Flash,WWoman	2.00
239 V:Ox	2.00
240 MSy,TMd	2.00
241 GT,V:Amazo	2.00
242 GT,V:Amazo,Mask(Toy tie-in) insert	2.00
243 GT,L:Aquaman,V:Amazo	2.00
244 JSon,Crisis,A:InfinityInc,JSA	2.00
245 LMc,Crisis,N:Steel	2.00
246 LMc,JLA leaves Detroit	2.00
247 LMc,JLA returns to old HQ	2.00
248 LMc,F:J'onn J'onzz	2.00
249 LMc,Lead-in to Anniv.	2.00
250 LMc,Anniv.,A:Superman, Green Lantern,Green Arrow, Black Canary,R:Batman	2.75
251 LMc,V:Despero	1.75
252 LMc,V:Despero,N:Elongated	

Man	1.75
253 LMc,V:Despero	1.75
254 LMc,V:Despero	1.75
255 LMc,O:Gypsy	1.75
256 LMc,Gypsy	1.75
257 LMc,A:Adam,L:Zatanna	1.75
258 LMc,Legends x-over,D:Vibe	1.75
259 LMc,Legends x-over	1.75
260 LMc,Legends x-over,D:Steel	1.75
261 LMc,Legends,final issue	4.00
Ann.#1 DG(i),A:Sandman	3.00
Ann.#2 I:NewJLA	2.00
Ann.#3 MG(i),Crisis	2.00

Justice League Task Force #12
© DC Comics, Inc.

JUSTICE LEAGUE TASK FORCE

1 F:Mart.Manhunter,Nightwing, Aquaman,Flash,Gr.Lantern	2.50
2 V:Count Glass,Blitz	1.75
3 V:Blitz,Count Glass	1.75
4 DG,F:Gypsy,A:Lady Shiva	1.75
5 JAl,Knightquest:Crusade,F:Bronze Tiger,Green Arrow,Gypsy	2.00
6 JAl,Knightquest:Search,F:Bronze Tiger,Green Arrow,Gypsy	1.75
7 PDd(s),F:Maxima,Wonder Woman, Dolphin,Gypsy,Vixen,V:Luta	1.75
8 PDd(s),SaV,V:Amazons	1.75
9 GrL,V:Wildman	1.75
10 Purification Plague#1	1.75
11 Purification Plague#2	1.75
12 Purification Plague#3	1.75
13 Jugdement Day#2, V:Overmaster	1.75
14 Jugdement Day#5, V:Overmaster	1.75
15 Aftershocks #2	1.75
16 Zero Hour,A:Triumph	1.75
17 Savage	1.50
18 Savage	1.50
19 Martian Manhunter	1.50
20 Savage Legacy,pt.4	1.50
21 F:Martian Manhunter	1.50
22 F:Triumph	1.50
23 V:Vampire	1.50
24 F:Von Mauler, Gypsy	1.50
25 A:Impulse & Damage, V:Mystek	1.75

JUSTICE SOCIETY
OF AMERICA
[Limited Series]
1 B:Veng.From Stars,A:Flash . . . 2.00
2 A:BlackCanary,V:Solomon Grundy,
  C:G.A.Green Lantern. 1.75
3 A:G.A.Green Lantern,Black Canary,
  V:Sol.Grundy 1.75
4 A:G.A.Hawkman,C:G.A.Flash . . 1.75
5 A:G.A.Hawkman,Flash 1.75
6 FMc(i),A:Bl.Canary,G.A.Gr.Lantern,
  V:Sol.Grundy,V.Savage 1.75
7 JSA united,V:Vandal Savage . . 1.75
8 E:Veng.FromStar,V:V.Savage,
  Solomon Grundy 1.75
Spec.#1 DR,MG,End of JSA 2.00
[Regular Series]
1 V:The New Order 1.75
2 V:Ultra Gen 1.50
3 R:Ultra-Humanite 1.50
4 V:Ultra-Humanite 1.50
5 V:Ultra-Humanite 1.50
6 F:Johnny Thunderbolt 1.50
7 ..Or give me Liberty 1.50
8 Pyramid Scheme 1.50
9 V:Kulak 1.50
10 V:Kulak,final issue 1.50

Kamandi: At Earth's End #2
© DC Comics, Inc.

KAMANDI, THE LAST
BOY ON EARTH
October-November, 1972
1 JK,O:Kamandi 22.00
2 JK 14.00
3 JK 9.00
4 JK,I:Prince Tuftan 9.00
5 JK 9.00
6 JK 9.00
7 JK 8.00
8 JK 8.00
9 JK 8.00
10 JK 8.00
11 JK 8.00
12 JK 8.00
13 thru 24 JK . . . . @6.00
25 thru 28 JK . . . . @3.00
29 A:Superman 3.00
30 JK 3.00
31 . . . . 3.00

32 Double size 4.00
33 thru 57 . . . . @3.00
58 A:Karate Kid 3.00
59 JSn,A:Omac, Sept.-Oct,1978 . 5.00

KAMANDI: AT
EARTH'S END
[Mini-Series]
1 R:Kamandi 2.00
2 V:Kingpin,Big Q 2.00
3 A:Sleeper Zom,Saphira 2.00
4 A:Superman 2.00
5 A:Superman,V:Ben Boxer 2.00
6 final issue 2.00

KARATE KID
March-April, 1976
1 I:Iris Jacobs,A:Legion 1.50
2 A:Major Disaster 1.25
3 . . . . 1.25
4 . . . . 1.25
5 . . . . 1.25
6 thru 10 . . . . @1.25
11 A:Superboy/Legion 1.25
12 A:Superboy/Legion 1.25
13 A:Superboy/Legion 1.25
14 A:Robin 1.25
15 July-August, 1978 . . . . 1.25

KID ETERNITY
1 GMo(s),DFg,O:Kid Eternity . . . 5.50
2 GMo(s),DFg,A:Mr.Keeper 5.50
3 GMo(s),DFg,True Origin revealed,
  final issue. 5.50

KID ETERNITY
Vertigo
1 B:ANo(s),SeP,R:Kid Eternity,
  A:Mdm.Blavatsky,Hemlock . . . 2.75
2 SeP,A:Sigmund Freud,Carl Jung,
  A:Malocchio 2.50
3 SeP,A:Malocchio,I:Dr.Pathos . . 2.25
4 SeP,A:Neal Cassady 2.25
5 SeP,In Cyberspace 2.25
6 SeP,A:Dr.Pathos,Marilyn
  Monroe 2.25
7 SeP,I:Infinity 2.25
8 SeP,In Insane Asylum 2.25
9 SeP,Asylum,A:Dr.Pathos 2.25
10 SeP,Small Wages 2.25
11 ANi(s),I:Slap 2.25
12 SeP,A:Slap 2.25
13 SeP,Date in Hell,pt.1 . . . . . . 2.25
14 SeP,Date in Hell,pt.2 . . . . . . 2.25
15 SeP,Date in Hell,pt.3 . . . . . . 2.25
16 SeP,The Zone 2.25

KILL YOUR BOYFRIEND
Vertigo
GNv PBd(c) 4.95

KISSYFUR
1 . . . . 2.00

KOBALT
Milestone
1 JBy(c),I:Kobalt,Richard Page . . 2.25
2 . . . . 1.75
3 I:Slick,Volt,Red Light 2.00
4 I:Slick,Volt,Red Light 2.00
5 Richard Page 1.75
6 Volt 1.75

7 Static 1.75
8 A:Hardward 1.75
9 . . . . 1.75
10 A:Harvest 1.75
11 V:St.Cloud 1.75
12 V:Rabid 1.75
13 V:Harvester 1.75
14 Long Hot Summer, V:Harvester 2.50

KOBRA
1 JK,I:Kobra & Jason Burr 2.00
2 I:Solaris 1.50
3 KG/DG,TA,V:Solaris 1.75

4 V:Servitor 1.25
5 RB/FMc,A:Jonny Double 1.25
6 MN/JRu,A:Jonny Double 1.25
7 MN/JRu,A:Jonny Double last iss 1.25

KONG THE UNTAMED
June-July, 1975
1 thru 4 . . . . @1.25
5 February-March, 1976 . . . . . . 1.25

KRYPTON CHRONICLES
1 CS,A:Superman 1.50
2 CS,A:Black Flame 1.25
3 CS,O:Name of Kal-El 1.25

LAST DAYS OF THE
JUSTICE SOCIETY
1 . . . . 3.00

LAST ONE
Vertigo
1 B:JMD(s),DSw,I:Myrwann,Patrick
  Maguire's Story 3.25
2 DSw,Pat's Addiction to Drugs . 3.00
3 DSw,Pat goes into Coma 3.00
4 DSw,In Victorian age 3.00
5 DSw,Myrwann Memories 3.00
6 E:JMD(s),DSw,final Issue 3.00

LEADING COMICS
Winter, 1941–42
1 O:Seven Soldiers of Victory,
  B:Crimson Avenger,Green Arrow
  & Speedy,Shining Knight,
  A:The Dummy 2,200.00
2 MMe,V:Black Star 750.00
3 V:Dr. Doome 650.00
4 'Seven Steps to Conquest',
  V:The Sixth Sense 500.00
5 'The Miracles that Money
  Couldn't Buy' 500.00
6 'The Treasure that Time
  Forgot' 450.00
7 The Wizard of Wisstark 450.00
8 Seven Soldiers Go back
  through the Centuries 450.00
9 V:Mr. X,'Chameleon of Crime' 450.00
10 King of the Hundred Isles . . 450.00
11 'The Hard Luck Hat!' 350.00
12 'The Million Dollar
  Challenge!' 350.00
13 'The Trophies of Crime' . . . 350.00
14 Bandits from the Book' 350.00
15 (fa) 90.00
16 thru 22 (fa) . . . . @45.00
23 (fa),I:Peter Porkchops 100.00
24 thru 30 (fa) . . . . @45.00
31 (fa) 30.00
32 (fa) 30.00

All comics prices listed are for *Near Mint* condition.

33 (fa) 50.00
34 thru 40 (fa) . . . . @30.00
41 (fa),February-March, 1950 . . 30.00

LEAVE IT TO BINKY
February-March, 1948

1 . . . . 175.00
2 . . . . 70.00
3 . . . . 60.00
4 . . . . 60.00
5 thru 14 . . . . @30.00
15 SM,Scribbly 40.00
16 thru 60 . . . . @15.00
61 thru 71 . . . . @7.50

LEGEND OF THE SHIELD
Impact

1 I:Shield,V:Mann-X,I:Big Daddy,
Lt.Devon Hall,Arvell Hauser,Mary
Masterson-Higgins 1.50
2 Shield in Middle East 1.25
3 Shield Goes A.W.O.L. 1.25
4 Hunt for Shield 1.25
5 A:Shield's Partner Dusty 1.25
6 O:Shield, V:The Jewels 1.25
7 Shield/Fly team-up 1.25
8 V:Weapon 1.25
9 Father Vs. Son 1.25
10 Arvell Hauser 1.25
11 inc,Trading cards 1.25
12 . . . . 1.25
13 Shield court martialed 1.25
14 Mike Barnes becomes Shield . 1.25
15 Shield becomes a Crusader . . 1.25
16 V:Soviets,final issue 1.25
Ann.#1 Earthquest,w/trading card . 2.25

LEGEND OF WONDER WOMAN

1 Return of Atomia 1.25
2 A:Queens Solalia & Leila 1.25
3 Escape from Atomia 1.25
4 conclusion 1.25

Legends of Daniel Boone #7
© DC Comics, Inc.

LEGENDS

1 JBy,V:Darkseid 3.50
2 JBy,A:Superman 2.50
3 JBy,I:Suicide Squad 2.50
4 JBy,V:Darkseid 2.50
5 JBy,A:Dr. Fate 2.50
6 JBy,I:Justice League 7.50
TPB rep.#1-#6 JBy(c) 9.95

LEGENDS OF DANIEL BOONE, THE
Oct., 1955–Jan., 1957

1 . . . . 450.00
2 . . . . 300.00
3 thru 8 . . . . 250.00

LEGENDS OF THE DARK KNIGHT
(see BATMAN)

LEGENDS OF THE WORLD FINEST

1 WS(s),DIB,V:Silver Banshee,Blaze,
Tullus,Foil(c) 5.25
2 WS(s),DIB,V:Silver Banshee,Blaze,
Tullus,Foil(c) 5.25
3 WS(s),DIB,V:Silver Banshee,Blaze,
Tullus,Foil(c) 5.25

L.E.G.I.O.N. '89-94

1 BKi,V:Computer Tyrants 4.00
2 BKi,V:Computer Tyrants 3.00
3 BKi,V:Computer Tyrants,
A:Lobo 4.00
4 BKi,V: Lobo 4.00
5 BKi,J:Lobo(in the rest of the
series),V:Konis-Biz 3.00
6 BKi,V:Konis-Biz 3.00
7 BKi,Stealth vs Dox 3.00
8 BKi,R:Dox 3.00
9 BKi,J:Phase (Phantom Girl) . . . 2.50
10 BKi,Stealth vs Lobo 2.50
11 BKi,V:Mr.Stoorr 2.50
12 BKi,V:Emerald Eye 2.50
13 BKi,V:Emerald Eye 2.50
14 BKi,V:Pirates 2.50
15 BKi,V:Emerald Eye 2.50
16 BKi,J:LarGand 2.50
17 BKi,V:Dragon-Ro 2.50
18 BKi,V:Dragon-Ro 2.50
19 V:Lydea,L:Stealth 2.50
20 Aftermath 2.50
21 D:Lyrissa Mallor,V:Mr.Starr . . . 2.50
22 V:Mr.Starr 2.50
23 O:R.J.Brande(double sized) . . 3.50
24 BKi,V:Khunds 2.50
25 BKi,V:Khunds 2.50
26 BKi,V:Khunds 2.50
27 BKi,J:Lydea Mallor 2.50
28 KG,Birth of Stealth's Babies . . 2.50
29 BKi,J:Capt.Comet,Marij'n Bek . 2.50
30 BKi,R:Stealth 2.50
31 Lobo vs.Capt.Marvel 3.50
32 V:Space Biker Gang 2.00
33 A:Ice-Man 2.00
34 MPn,V:Ice Man 2.00
35 Legion Disbanded 2.00
36 Dox proposes to Ignea 2.00
37 V:Intergalactic Ninjas 2.00
38 BKi,Lobo V:Ice Man 2.00
39 BKi,D:G'odd,V:G'oddSquad . . 2.00
40 BKi,V:Kyaltic Space Station . . 2.00
41 BKi,A:Stealth'sBaby 2.00

42 BKi,V:Yeltsin-Beta 2.00
43 BKi,V:Yeltsin-Beta 2.00
44 V:Yeltsin-Beta,C:Gr.Lantern . . 2.00
45 . . . . 2.00
46 BKi,A:Hal Jordan 2.00
47 BKi,Lobo vs Hal Jordan 2.00
48 BKi,R:Ig'nea 2.00
49 BKi,V:Ig'nea 2.00
50 BKi,V:Ig'nea,A:Legion'67 . . . . 3.75
51 F:Lobo,Telepath 2.00
52 BKi,V:Cyborg Skull of Darius . . 2.00
53 BKi,V:Shadow Creature 2.00
54 BKi,V:Shadow Creature 2.00
55 BKi,V:Shadow Beast 2.00
56 BKi,A:Masked Avenger 2.00
57 BKi,Trinity,V:Green Lantern . . . 2.00
58 BKi,Trinity#6,A:Green Lantern,
Darkstar 2.00
59 F:Phase 2.00
60 V:Phantom Riders 2.00
61 Little Party 2.00
62 A:R.E.C.R.U.I.T.S. 2.00
63 A:Superman 2.00
64 BKi(c),V:Mr.B 2.00
65 BKi(c),V:Brain Bandit 2.00
66 Stealth and Dox name child . . 2.00
67 F:Telepath 2.00
68 . . . . 1.75
69 . . . . 2.00
70 Zero Hour, last issue 2.50
Ann.#1 A:Superman,V:Brainiac . 5.50
Ann.#2 Armageddon 2001 . . . . 3.50
Ann.#3 Eclipso tie-in 3.25
Ann.#4 SHa(i),I:Pax 3.75
Ann.#5 Elseworlds story 3.50

LEGION OF SUBSTITUTE HEROES

Spec.#1 KG 1.50

LEGION OF SUPER-HEROES
[Reprint Series]

1 rep. Tommy Tomorrow 10.00
2 rep. Tommy Tomorrow 6.00
3 rep. Tommy Tomorrow 6.00
4 rep. Tommy Tomorrow 6.00

[1st Regular Series]
Prev: SUPERBOY (& LEGION)

259 JSon,L:Superboy 6.00
260 RE,I:Circus of Death 4.00
261 RE,V:Circus of Death 3.50
262 JSh,V:Engineer 3.50
263 V:Dagon the Avenger 3.50
264 V:Dagon the Avenger 3.50
265 JSn,DG,Superman/Radio Shack
insert 3.50
266 R:Bouncing Boy,Duo Damsel 3.00
267 SD,V:Kantuu 3.00
268 SD,BWi,V:Dr.Mayavale 3.00
269 V:Fatal Five 3.00
270 V:Fatal Five 3.00
271 V:Tharok (Dark Man) 2.50
272 CI,SD,O:J:Blok, I:New
Dial 'H' for Hero 2.50
273 V:Stargrave 2.50
274 SD,V:Captain Frake 2.50
275 V:Captain Frake 2.50
276 SD,V:Mordru 2.50
277 A:Reflecto(Superboy) 2.50
278 A:Reflecto(Superboy) 2.50
279 A:Reflecto(Superboy) 2.50
280 R:Superboy 2.50
281 SD,V:Time Trapper 2.50

282 V:Time Trapper 2.50
283 O:Wildfire 2.50
284 PB,V:Organleggor 2.50
285 PB,KG(1st Legion)V:Khunds . 4.00
286 PB,KG,V:Khunds 3.00
287 KG,V:Kharlak 5.00
288 KG,V:Kharlak 3.00
289 KG,Stranded 3.00

Legion of Super-Heroes #270
© DC Comics, Inc.

290 KG,B:Great Darkness Saga,
　　J:Invisible Kid II 3.00
291 KG,V:Darkseid's Minions . . . 2.00
292 KG,V:Darkseid's Minions 2.00
293 KG,Daxam destroyed 2.00
294 KG,E:Great Darkness Saga,
　　V:Darkseid,A:Auron,Superboy . 2.00
295 KG,A:Green Lantern Corps . 1.75
296 KG,D:Cosmic Boys family . 1.75
297 KG,O:Legion,A:Cosmic Boy . 1.75
298 KG,EC,I:Amethyst 1.75
299 KG,R:Invisible Kid I 1.75
300 KG,CS,JSon,DC,KS,DG 2.00
301 KG,R:Chameleon Boy 1.75
302 KG,A:Chameleon Boy 1.75
303 KG,V:Fatal Five 1.75
304 KG,V:Fatal Five 1.75
305 KG,V:Micro Lad 1.75
306 KG,CS,RT,O:Star Boy 1.75
307 KG,GT,Omen 1.75
308 KG,V:Omen 1.75
309 KG,V:Omen 1.75
310 KG,V:Omen 1.75
311 KG,GC,New Headquarters . . 1.75
312 KG,V:Khunds 1.75
313 KG,V:Khunds 1.75
Ann.#1 IT,KG,I:Invisible Kid 3.50
Ann.#2 DGb,W:Karate Kid and
　　Princess Projectra 2.00
Ann.#3 CS,RT,A:Darkseid 2.00
Ann.#4 reprint 2.00
Ann.#5 reprint 1.50
Legion Archives Vol 1 HC 39.95
Legion Archives Vol 2 HC 39.95
Legion Archives Vol 3 HC 39.95
Legion Archives Vol 4 HC 39.95
Becomes:

TALES OF LEGION OF SUPER HEROES

LEGION OF SUPER-HEROES
[3rd Regular Series]

1 KG,V:Legion of Super-Villians . 4.00
2 KG,V:Legion of Super-Villians . 2.50
3 KG,V:Legion of Super-Villians . 2.50
4 KG,D:Karate Kid 2.50
5 KG,D:Nemesis Kid 2.50
6 JO,F:Lightning Lass 2.25
7 SLi,A:Controller 2.25
8 SLi,V:Controller 2.25
9 SLi,V:Sklarians 2.25
10 V:Khunds 2.25
11 EC,KG,L:Orig 3 members 2.00
12 SLi,EC,A:Superboy 2.00
13 SLi,V:Lythyls,F:TimberWolf . . . 2.00
14 SLi,J:Sensor Girl (Princess
　　Projectra),Quislet,Tellus,Polar
　　Boy,Magnetic Kid 2.00
15 GLa,V:Dr. Regulus 2.00
16 SLi,Crisis tie-in,F:Braniac5 . . . 2.00
17 GLa,O:Legion 2.00
18 GLa,Crisis tie-in,V:InfiniteMan . 2.00
19 GLa,V:Controller 2.00
20 GLa,V:Tyr 2.00
21 GLa,V:Emerald Empress 1.75
22 GLa,V:Restorer,A:Universo . . 1.75
23 SLi,GLa,A:Superboy,
　　Jonah Hex 1.75
24 GLa,NBi,A:Fatal Five 1.75
25 GLa,V:FatalFive 1.75
26 GLa,V:FatalFive,O:SensorGirl . 1.75
27 GLa,GC,A:Mordru 1.75
28 GLa,L:StarBoy 1.75
29 GLa,V:Starfinger 1.75
30 GLa,V:Universo 1.75
31 GLa,A:Ferro Lad,Karate Kid . 1.75
32 GLa,V:Universo,I:Atmos 1.75
33 GLa,V:Universo 1.75
34 GLa,V:Universo 1.75
35 GLa,V:Universo,R:Saturn Girl . 1.75
36 GLa,R:Cosmic Boy 1.75
37 GLa,V:Universo,I:Superboy
　　(Earth Prime) 11.00
38 GLa,V:TimeTrapper,
　　D:Superboy 11.00
39 CS,RT,O:Colossal Boy 1.75
40 GLa,I:New Starfinger 1.75
41 GLa,V:Starfinger 1.75
42 GLa,Millenium,V:Laurel Kent . 1.75
43 GLa,Millenium,V:Laurel Kent . 1.75
44 GLa,O:Quislet 1.75
45 GLa,CS,MGr,DC,30th Ann. . 3.50
46 GLa,Conspiracy 1.75
47 GLa,PB,V:Starfinger 1.75
48 GLa,Conspiracy,A:Starfinger . 1.75
49 PB,Conspiracy,A:Starfinger . 1.75
50 KG,V:Time Trapper,A:Infinite
　　Man,E:Conspiracy 3.00
51 KG,V:Gorak,L:Brainiac5 . . . . 1.75
52 KG,V:Gil'Dishpan 1.75
53 KG,V:Gil'Dishpan 1.75
54 KG,V:Gorak 1.75
55 KG,EC,JL,EL,N:Legion 1.75
56 EB,V:Inquisitor 1.75
57 KG,V:Emerald Empress 1.75
58 KG,V:Emerald Empress 1.75
59 KG,MBr,F:Invisible Kid 1.75
60 KG,B:Magic Wars 1.75
61 KG,Magic Wars 1.75
62 KG,D:Magnetic Lad 1.75
63 KG,E:Magic Wars #4,final iss. . 1.75
Ann.#1 KG,Murder Mystery 2.50
Ann.#2 KG,CS,O:Validus,
　　A:Darkseid 3.00
Ann.#3 GLa,I:2nd Karate Kid 2.50
Ann.#4 BKi,V:Starfinger 2.50
Ann #5 I:2nd Legion Sub.Heroes . 2.50

Legion of Super-Heroes #31
© DC Comics, Inc.

[4th Regular Series]
1 KG,R:Cosmic Boy, Chameleon 3.25
2 KG,R:Ultra Boy,I:Kono 2.50
3 KG,D:Block,V:Roxxas 2.50
4 KG,V:Time Trapper 2.50
5 KG,V:Mordru,A:Glorith 2.50
6 KG,I:Laurel Gand 2.50
7 KG,V:Mordru 2.25
8 KG,O:Legion 2.25
9 KG,O:Laurel Gand 2.25
10 KG,V:Roxxas 2.25
11 KG,V:Roxxas 2.00
12 KG,I:Kent Shakespeare 2.00
13 KG,V:Dominators,posters . . . 2.00
14 KG,J:Tenzil Kem 2.00
15 KG,Khund Invasion 2.00
16 KG,V:Khunds 2.00
17 KG,V:Khunds 2.00
18 KG,V:Khunds 2.00
19 KG,cont.from Adv.of Superman
　　#478,A:Original Dr. Fate 2.25
20 KG,V:Dominators 2.00
21 KG,B:Quiet Darkness,
　　A:Lobo,Darkseid 3.00
22 KG,A:Lobo,Darkseid 2.50
23 KG,A:Lobo,Darkseid 2.50
24 KG,E:Quiet Darkness,A:Lobo,
　　Darkseid,C:Legionairres 2.75
25 DAb,I:Legionairres 3.00
26 JPn,B:Terra Mosaic,V:B.I.O.N . 2.00
27 JPn,V:B.I.O.N. 2.00
28 JPn,O:Sun Boy 2.00
29 JPn,I:Monica Sade 2.00
30 JPn,V:Dominators 2.00
31 CS,AG,F:Shvaughn as man . . 2.00
32 JPn,D:Karate Kid,Prin.Projectra,
　　Chameleon Boy(Legionaires) . 2.00
33 R:Kid Quantum 2.00
34 R:Sun Boy 2.00
35 JPN,V:Dominators 2.00
36 JPn,E:Terra Mosaic 2.00

---

37 JBr,R:Star Boy,Dream Girl . . . 2.00
38 JPn,Earth is destroyed 5.00
39 SI,A:Legionnaires 2.00
40 SI,Legion meets Legionnaires . 2.00
41 SI,F:The Legionnaires 2.25
42 SI,V:Glorith 2.00
43 SI,B:Mordru Arises 2.00
44 SI,R:Karate Kid 2.00
45 SI,R:Roxxas 2.00
46 SI, ... 2.00
47 SI, ... 2.00
48 SI,E:Mordru Arises 2.00
49 F:Matter Eater Lad 2.00
50 W:Tenzil & Saturn Queen,
   R:Wildfire,V:B.I.O.N. 3.75
51 R:Kent,Celeste,Ivy,V:Grimbor . 2.00
52 F:Timber Wolf 2.00
53 SI,V:Glorith 2.25
54 SI,Foil,Die-Cut(c),
   N:L.E.G.I.O.N 3.25
55 SI,On Rimbor 2.50
56 SI,R:Espionage Squad 2.00
57 SI,R:Khund Legionnaires 2.00
58 SI,D:Laurel Gand 2.00
59 SI,R:Valor,Dawnstar 2.25
60 SI,End of an Era#3 . . . . 2.25
61 SI,End of an Era#6 . . . . 2.25
62 I:New Team 1.95
63 Alien Attack 1.95
64 . . . . 1.95
65 . . . . 1.95
66 I:New Team Members 1.95
67 F:Leviathan 1.95
68 F:Leviathan 1.95
69 V:Durlan 2.25
70 A:Andromeda, Brainiac 5 . . . . 2.25
Ann.#1 O:Ultra Boy,V:Glorith . . . 3.50
Ann.#2 O:Valor 3.50
Ann.#3 N:Timberwolf 4.00
Ann.#4 I:Jamm 3.50
Ann.#5 SI(c),CDo,MFm,TMc,
   Elseworlds Story 3.75
Ann.#6 Year One Annual + pin-ups 3.95
TPB Great Darkness Saga 17.95
TPB Legion Archives, rep.#1-#3 . 39.95
TPB Legion Archives, rep.#4 . . . 49.95

Legionnaires #18 © DC Comics, Inc.

LEGIONNAIRES
1 CSp,V:Mano and the Hand,Bagged
   w/SkyBox promo card 3.50

1a w/out card 2.50
2 CSp,V:Mano 2.00
3 CSp,I:2nd Emerald Empress . . 2.00
4 CSp,R:Fatal Five 2.00
5 CSp,V:Fatal Five 2.00
6 CSp,V:Fatal Five 1.75
7 AH,V:Devil Fish 1.75
8 CDo,F:Brainiac 5 . . . . 1.75
9 CSp,A:Kid Quantum 1.75
10 CSp,A:Kono,I:2nd Kid Psycho 1.75
11 CSp,J:2nd Kid Pyscho 1.75
12 CSp,A:2nd Kid Pyscho 1.75
13 FFo,V:Grimbor 1.75
14 V:Grimbor 1.75
15 V:Grimbor 1.75
16 In Time 1.75
17 End of An Era #1 . . . . 1.75
18 Zero Hour, LSH 1.75
19 Problems 1.50
20 Moon Battle 1.50
21 and 22 . . . . @1.50
23 Saturday Night 1.50
24 F:Triad 1.50
25 F:Chameleon 1.50
26 F:Apparition, Ultra Boy 1.75
27 V:The Dayamites 2.25
Ann.#1 Elseworlds Story 2.95

LEGIONAIRRES THREE
1 EC,Saturn Girl,Cosmic Boy . . . 4.00
2 EC,V:Time Trapper,pt.1 . . . . . . 3.00
3 EC,V:Time Trapper,pt.2 . . . . . . 3.00
4 EC,V:Time Trapper,pt.3 . . . . . . 2.75

LIMITED COLLECTORS EDITION
Summer, 1973
21 Shazam 10.00
22 Tarzan 7.00
23 House of Mystery 7.00
24 Rudolph, the Red-nosed
   Reindeer 4.00
25 NA,NA(c),Batman 10.00
27 Shazam 7.00
29 Tarzan 4.00
31 NA,O:Superman 8.00
32 Ghosts 4.00
33 Rudolph 3.00
34 X-Mas with Superheroes 5.00
35 Shazam 5.00
36 The Bible 4.00
37 Batman 10.00
38 Superman 8.00
39 Secret Origins 8.00
40 Dick Tracy 4.00
41 ATh,Super Friends 6.00
42 Rudolph 3.00
43 X-mas with Super-Heroes 4.00
44 NA,Batman 10.00
45 Secret Origins-Super Villians . . 3.00
46 ATh,JLA 5.00
47 Superman 4.00
48 Superman-Flash Race 4.00
49 Superboy & Legion of
   Super-Heroes 4.00
50 Rudolph 3.00
51 NA,NA(c),Batman 10.00
52 NA,NA(c),The Best of DC . . . 6.00
57 Welcome Back Kotter 3.00
59 NA,BWr,Batman,1978 . . . . . 12.00

LITTLE SHOP OF HORRORS
1 GC 2.50

LOBO
[1st Limited Series]
1 SBs,Last Czarnian #1 . . . . 7.00
1a 2nd Printing 3.00
2 SBs,Last Czarnian #2 . . . . 5.00
3 SBs,Last Czarnian #3 . . . . 4.00
4 SBs,Last Czarnian #4 . . . . 4.00
Ann.#1 Bloodlines#1,I:Layla 3.75
Lobo Paramilitary X-Mas SBs . . . 5.50
Lobo:Blazing Chain of Love,DCw . 1.50
TPB Last Czarnian,rep.#1-#4 . . . 9.95
TPB Lobo's Greatest Hits 12.95
[Regular Series]
1 VS,Foil(c),V:Dead Boys 3.25
2 VS 2.00
3 VS 2.00
4 VS,Quigly Affair 2.00
5 V:Bludhound 2.00
6 I:Bim Simms 2.00
7 A:Losers 2.00
8 A:Losers 2.25
9 V:Lobo 2.25
10 Preacher 1.95
11 Goldstar vs. Rev.Bo 1.95
12 . . . . 1.95
13 . . . . 1.95
14 Lobo, P.I. 1.95
15 Lobo, P.I.,pt.2 . . . . 1.95
16 Lobo, P.I.,pt.3 . . . . 1.95
17 Lobo, P.I.,pt.4 . . . . 2.25
Ann.#2 Elseworlds Story 3.50

LOBO'S BIG BABE SPRING BREAK SPECIAL
1 Miss Voluptuous Contest 1.95

LOBO BOUNTY HUNTING FOR FUN AND PROFIT
1 F:Fanboy 4.95

LOBO: A CONTRACT ON GAWD
1 AIG(s),KD 2.00
2 AIG(s),KD,A:Dave 2.00
3 AIG(s),KD 1.75
4 AIG(s),KD,Final Issue 1.75

LOBO CONVENTION SPECIAL
1 Lobo at Comic Convention . . . 2.00

LOBO'S BACK
1 SBs,w/3(c) inside,V:Loo 4.50
1a 2nd printing 1.50
2 SBs,Lobo becomes a woman . 2.50
3 SBs,V:Heaven 2.50
4 SBs,V:Heaven 2.50
TPB GF(c),rep.#1-#4 . . . . 9.95

LOBO: INFANTICIDE
1 KG,V:Su,Lobo Bastards 2.00
2 Lobo at Boot Camp 1.75
3 KG,Lobo Vs.his offspring 1.75
4 KG,V:Lobo Bastards 1.75

LOBO IN THE CHAIR
1 AIG(s) 2.25

LOBO: PORTRAIT OF A VICTIM
1 VS,I:John Doe 2.00

Lobo: A Contract on Gawd #4
© DC Comics, Inc.

LOBO: UNAMERICAN GLADIATORS

1 CK,V:Satan's Brothers	2.00
2 CK,V:Jonny Caesar	2.00
3 CK,MMi(c),V:Satan Brothers	2.00
4 CK,MMi(c),V:Jonny Caeser	2.00

LOBOCOP

1 StG(s)	2.25

LOIS AND CLARK: THE NEW ADVENTURES OF SUPERMAN

TPB	9.95

LOIS LANE
August, 1986

1 and 2 GM	@1.50

LONG HOT SUMMER, THE
Milestone
[Mini-Series]

1 Blood Syndicate v. G.R.I.N.D.	2.95

LOONEY TUNES MAG.

1 thru 6	@1.95

LOONEY TUNES

1 thru 6 Warner Bros. cartoons	@1.75
7 thru 11 Warner Bros.	@1.75
12 The Cotton Tail Club	1.50
13 F:Tasmanian Devil	1.50
14 Football Season	1.50
15 Jewel Thief	1.50
16 F:Yosemite Sam,Speedy Gonzales	1.50

LOOSE CANNON
[Mini-Series]

1 AdP,V:Bounty Hunters	1.75
2 V:Bounty Hunters & The Eradicator	1.75

LORDS OF THE ULTRAREALM

1 PB	3.50
2 PB	2.00
3 PB	1.50
4 PB	1.50
5 PB	1.50
6 PB	1.50
Spec.#1 PB,DG,Oneshot	2.25

LOSERS SPECIAL

1 Crisis,D:Losers	1.25

MADAME XANADU

1 MR/BB	2.00

MAN-BAT

1 SD,AM,A:Batman	9.00
2 V:The Ten-Eyed Man	8.00
Reprint NA(c)	4.00

MAN-BAT vs. BATMAN

1 NA,DG,reprint	4.00

MANHUNTER

1 from Millenium-Suicide Squad	1.50
2 in Tokyo,A:Dumas	1.25
3 The Yakuza,V:Dumas	1.25
4 Secrets Revealed-Manhunter, Dumas & Olivia	1.25
5 A:Silvia Kandery	1.25
6 A:Argent,contd.Suicide Squad Annual #1	1.25
7 Vlatavia, V:Count Vertigo	1.25
8 FS,A:Flash,Invasion x-over	1.25
9 FS,Invasion Aftermath extra (contd from Flash #22)	1.25
10 Salvage,pt.1	1.25
11 Salvage,pt.2	1.25
12	1.25
13	1.25
14 Janus Directive #5	1.25
15 I:Mirage	1.25
16 V:Outlaw	1.25
17 In Gotham,A:Batman	1.50
18 Saints & Sinners,pt.1,R:Dumas	1.25
19 Saints & Sinners,pt.2,V:Dumas	1.25
20 Saints & Sinners,pt.3,V:Dumas	1.25
21 Saints & Sinners,pt.4, A:Manhunter Grandmaster	1.25
22 Saints & Sinners,pt.5, A:Manhunter Grandmaster	1.25
23 Saints & Sinners,pt.6,V:Dumas	1.25
24 DG,Showdown, final issue	1.25
[2nd Series]	
0	1.95
1	1.95
2 N:Wild Huntsman	1.95
3 V:Malig	1.95
4 Necrodyne	1.95
5 V:Skin Walker	1.95
6 V:Barbarian,Incarnate	1.95
7 V:Incarnate,A:White Lotus & Capt. Atom	2.25
8 V:Butcher Boys	2.25

MAN OF STEEL

1 JBy,DG,I:Modern Superman	4.50
1a 2nd edition	3.00
2 JBy,DG,R:Lois Lane	3.00
3 JBy,DG,A:Batman	3.00
4 JBy,DG,V:Lex Luthor	3.00
5 JBy,DG,I:Modern Bizarro	3.00

6 JBy,DG,A:Lana Lang	3.00
TPB rep. Man of Steel #1–#6	12.95
TPBa 2nd printing	7.95

MANY LOVES OF DOBIE GILLIS
May-June, 1960

1	150.00
2	75.00
3	65.00
4	65.00
5 thru 9	@40.00
10 thru 25	@28.00
26 October, 1964	28.00

MARTIAN MANHUNTER

1 A:JLI	1.75
2 A:JLI,V:Death God	1.50
3 V:Death God,A:Dr.Erdel	1.50
4 A:JLI,final issue	1.50
[Mini-Series]	
1 EB,American Secrets #1	5.25
2 EB,American Secrets #2	4.95
3 EB,American Secrets #3	4.95

MASK
December, 1985

1 HC(c),TV tie-in,I:Mask Team	2.00
2 HC(c),In Egypt,V:Venom	1.75
3 HC(c),'Anarchy in the U.K.'	1.75
4 HC(c),V:Venom, final issue, March, 1986	1.00
[2nd Series]	
February, 1987	
1 CS/KS,reg.series	1.25
2 CS/KS,V:Venom	1.00
3 CS/KS,V:Venom	1.00
4 CS/KS,V:Venom	1.00
5 CS/KS,Mask operatives hostage	1.00
6 CS/KS,I:Jacana	1.00
7 CS/KS,Mask gone bad?	1.00
8 CS/KS,Matt Trakker,V:Venom	1.00
9 CS/KS,V:Venom, last issue, October, 1987	1.00

MASTERS OF THE UNIVERSE
May, 1986

1 GT,AA,O:He-Man	1.50
2 GT,AA,V:Skeletor	1.25
3 GT,V:Skeletor	1.25

MASTERWORKS SERIES OF GREAT COMIC BOOK ARTISTS
May, 1983

1	2.50
2	2.50
3 December, 1983	2.50

'MAZING MAN
January, 1986

1 I:Maze	1.00
2	1.00
3	1.00
4	1.00
5	1.00
6 Shea Stadium	1.00
7 Shea Stadium	1.00
8 Cat-Sitting	1.00
9 Bank Hold-up	1.00
10	1.00

All comics prices listed are for *Near Mint* condition.

11 Jones Beach	1.00
12 FM(c),last issue, Dec., 1986	1.00
Spec.#1	2.25
Spec.#2	2.25
Spec.#3 KB/TM	2.25

MEN OF WAR
August, 1977

1 I:Gravedigger,Code Name: Gravedigger,I:Enemy Ace	1.50
2 JKu(c),The Five-Walled War	1.25
3 JKu(c),The Suicide Strategem	1.25
4 JKu(c),Trail by Fire	1.25
5 JKu(c),Valley of the Shadow	1.25
6 JKu(c),A Choice of Deaths	1.25
7 JKu(c),Milkrun	1.25
8 JKu(c),Death-Stroke	1.25
9 JKu(c),Gravedigger-R.I.P.	1.25
10 JKu(c),Crossroads	1.25
11 JKu(c),Berkstaten	1.25
12 JKu(c),Where Is Gravedigger?	1.25
13 JKu(c),Project Gravedigger - Plus One	1.25
14 JKu(c),The Swirling Sands of Death	1.25
15 JKu(c),The Man With the Opened Eye	1.25
16 JKu(c),Hide and Seek The Spy	1.25
17 JKu(c),The River of Death	1.25
18 JKu(c),The Amiens Assault	1.25
19 JKu(c),An Angel Named Marie	1.25
20 JKu(c),Cry:Jerico	1.25
21 JKu(c),Home-Is Where The Hell Is	1.25
22 JKu(c),Blackout On The Boardwalk	1.25
23 JKu(c),Mission: Six Feet Under	1.25
24 JKu&DG(c),The Presidential Peril	1.25
25 GE(c),Save the President	1.25
26 March, 1980	1.25

MERCY
Vertigo
Graphic Novel I:Mercy	8.00

METAL MEN
April-May, 1965
[1st Regular Series]

1 RA,I:Missile Men	375.00
2 RA,Robot of Terror	135.00
3 RA,Moon's Invisible Army	80.00
4 RA,Bracelet of Doomed Hero	80.00
5 RA,Menace of the Mammoth Robots	80.00
6 RA,I:Gas Gang	65.00
7 RA,V:Solar Brain	55.00
8 RA,Playground of Terror	55.00
9 RA,A:Billy	55.00
10 RA,A:Gas Gang	55.00
11 RA,The Floating Furies	45.00
12 RA,A:Missile Men	40.00
13 RA,I:Nameless	40.00
14 RA,A:Chemo	40.00
15 RA,V:B.O.L.T.S.	40.00
16 RA,Robots for Sale	40.00
17 JKu(c),RA,V:Bl.Widow Robot	40.00
18 JKu(c),RA	40.00
19 RA,V:Man-Horse of Hades	40.00
20 RA,V:Dr.Yes	40.00
21 RA,C:Batman & Robin,Flash Wonder Woman	25.00
22 RA,A:Chemo	25.00
23 RA,A:Sizzler	25.00

24 RA,V:Balloonman	25.00
25 RA,V:Chemo	25.00
26 RA,V:Metal Men	25.00
27 RA,O:Metal Men,rtd	46.00
28 RA	25.00
29 RA,V:Robot Eater	25.00
30 RA,GK,in the Forbidden Zone	25.00
31 RA,GK	23.00
32 RA,Robot Amazon Blues	18.00
33 MS,The Hunted Metal Men	18.00
34 MS	18.00
35 MS	18.00
36 MS,The Cruel Clowns	18.00
37 MS,To walk among Men	18.00
38 MS	18.00
39 MS,Beauty of the Beast	18.00
40 MS	18.00
41 MS	18.00
42 RA,reprint	10.00
43 RA,reprint	10.00
44 RA,reprint,V:Missile Men	10.00
45 WS	10.00
46 WS,V:Chemo	10.00
47 WS,V:Plutonium Man	10.00
48 WS,A:Eclipso	15.00
49 WS,A:Eclipso	15.00
50 WS,JSa	10.00
51 JSn,V:Vox	10.00
52 JSn,V:Brain Children	10.00
53 JA(c),V:Brain Children	10.00
54 JSn,A:Green Lantern	10.00
55 JSn,A:Green Lantern	10.00
56 JSn,V:Inheritor	10.00

[Limited Series]
1 DJu,BBr,Foil(c)	8.00
2 DJu,BBr,O:Metal Men	5.00
3 DJu,BBr,V:Missile Men	3.50
4 DJu,BBr,final issue	3.00

Metamorpho (Limited Series) #1
© DC Comics, Inc.

METAMORPHO
July-August, 1965
[Regular Series]

1 A:Kurt Vornok	85.00
2 Terror from the Telstar	45.00
3 Who stole the USA	45.00
4 V:Cha-Cha Chaves	28.00

5 V:Bulark	28.00
6	28.00
7	20.00
8	20.00
9	20.00
10 I:Element Girl	28.00
11 thru 17 March-April, 1968	@15.00

[Limited Series]
1 GN,V:The Orb of Ra	1.75
2 GN,A:Metamorpho's Son	1.75
3 GN,V:Elemental Man	1.75
4 GN,final Issue	1.75

METROPOLIS S.C.U.
1 Special Police unit	1.50
2 Eco-terror in Metropolis	1.50
3 Superman	1.50
4 final issue	1.50

MILLENIUM
January, 1988
1 JSa,SEt, The Plan	1.75
2 JSa,SEt, The Chosen	1.75
3 JSa,SEt, Reagen/Manhunters	1.75
4 JSa,SEt, Mark Shaw/Batman	1.75
5 JSa,SEt, The CHosen	1.75
6 JSa,SEt, Superman	1.75
7 JSa,SEt, Boster Gold	1.75
8 JSa,SEt,I:New Guardians	1.75

MISTER E
1 (From Books of Magic)	1.75
2 A:The Shadower	1.75
3 A:The Shadower	1.75
4 A:Tim Hunter, Dr. Fate, Phantom Stranger, final issue	1.75

MISTER MIRACLE
1 JK,I:Mr.Miracle	35.00
2 JK,I:Granny Goodness	20.00
3 JK,'Paraniod Pill'	10.00
4 JK,I:Barda	8.00
5 JK,I:Vermin Vundabar	8.00
6 JK,I:Female Furies	8.00
7 JK,V:Kanto	8.00
8 JK,V:Lump	8.00
9 JK,O:Mr.Miracle,C:Darkseid	7.00
10 JK,A:Female Furies	6.00
11 JK,V:Doctor Bedlum	6.00
12 JK	6.00
13 JK	6.00
14 JK	6.00
15 JK,O:Shilo Norman	6.00
16 JK	6.00
17 JK	6.00
18 JK,W:Mr.Miracle & Barda	6.00
19 MR,NA,DG,TA,JRu,AM	6.00
20 MR	4.00
21 MR	4.00
22 MR	4.00
23 MG	4.00
24 MG,RH	4.00
25 MG,RH	4.00
Spec.#1 SR	2.50

[2nd Series]
1 IG	2.50
2 IG	1.75
3 IG,A:Highfather,Forever People	1.50
4 IG,A:The Dark,Forever People	1.50
5 IG,V:TheDark,A:ForeverPeople	1.50
6 A:G.L. Gnort	1.25
7 A:Blue Beetle,Booster Gold	1.25
8 RM,A:Blue Beetle,Booster Gold	1.25
9 I:Maxi-Man	1.25

All comics prices listed are for *Near Mint* condition.

Mister Miracle #17
© DC Comics, Inc.

10 V:Maxi-Man 1.25
11 . . . . 1.25
12 . . . . 1.25
13 Manga Khan Saga begins,
  A:L-Ron,A:Lobo 3.00
14 A:Lobo 3.00
15 Manga Khan contd 1.25
16 MangaKhan cont.,JLA#39tie-in 1.25
17 On Apokolips,A:Darkseid 1.25
18 On Apokolips 1.25
19 Return to Earth, contd
  from JLA#42 . . . . 1.25
20 IG,Oberon 1.25
21 Return of Shilo 1.25
22 New Mr.Miracle revealed 1.25
23 Secrets of the 2 Mr. Miracles
  revealed, A:Mother Box 1.25
24 . . . . 1.25
25 . . . . 1.25
26 Monster Party,pt.1 . . . . 1.25
27 Monster Party,pt.2,
  A:Justice League 1.25
28 final issue 1.25

MR. DISTRICT ATTORNEY
January-February, 1948
1 The Innocent Forger 600.00
2 The Richest Man In Prison . 225.00
3 The Honest Convicts 175.00
4 The Merchant of Death 175.00
5 The Booby-Trap Killer 175.00
6 The D.A. Meets Scotland Yard150.00
7 The People vs. Killer Kane . 150.00
8 The Rise and Fall of 'Lucky'
  Lynn 150.00
9 The Case of the Living
  Counterfeit 150.00
10 The D.A. Takes a Vacation . 125.00
11 The Game That Has
  No Winners 125.00
12 Fake Accident Racket 125.00
13 The Execution of Caesar
  Larsen 125.00
14 The Innocent Man In
  Murderers' Row 125.00
15 Prison Train 125.00

16 The Wire Tap Crimes 125.00
17 The Bachelor of Crime 125.00
18 The Case of the Twelve
  O'Clock Killer 125.00
19 The Four King's Of Crime . . 125.00
20 You Catch a Killer 125.00
21 I Was A Killer's Bodyguard . . 85.00
22 The Marksman of Crime 85.00
23 Diary of a Criminal 85.00
24 The Killer In The Iron Mask . . 85.00
25 I Hired My Killer 85.00
26 The Case of the Wanted
  Criminals 85.00
27 The Case of the Secret Six . . 85.00
28 Beware the Bogus Beggars . 85.00
29 The Crimes of Mr. Jumbo . . . 85.00
30 Man of a Thousand Faces . . 85.00
31 The Hot Money Gang 85.00
32 The Case o/t Bad Luck Clues 85.00
33 A Crime Is Born 85.00
34 The Amazing Crimes of Mr. X 85.00
35 This Crime For Hire 85.00
36 The Chameleon of Crime . . . 85.00
37 Miss Miller's Big Case 85.00
38 The Puzzle Shop For Crime . 85.00
39 Man Who Killed Daredevils . . 85.00
40 The Human Vultures 85.00
41 The Great Token Take 85.00
42 Super-Market Sleuth 85.00
43 Hotel Detective 85.00
44 S.S. Justice,B:Comics Code . 75.00
45 Miss Miller, Widow 75.00
46 Mr. District Attorney,
  Public Defender 75.00
47 The Missing Persons Racket . 75.00
48 Manhunt With the Mounties . 75.00
49 The TV Dragnet 75.00
50 The Case of Frank Bragan,
  Little Shot 75.00
51 The Big Heist 75.00
52 Crooked Wheels of Fortune . 75.00
53 The Courtroom Patrol 75.00
54 The Underworld Spy Squad . 75.00
55 The Flying Saucer Mystery . . 75.00
56 The Underworld Oracle 75.00
57 The Underworld Employment
  Agency 75.00
58 The Great Bomb Scare 75.00
59 Great Underworld Spy Plot . . 75.00
60 The D.A.'s TV Rival 75.00
61 SMo(c),Architect of Crime . . 75.00
62 A-Bombs For Sale 75.00
63 The Flying Prison 75.00
64 SMo(c),The Underworld
  Treasure Hunt 75.00
65 SMo(c),World Wide Dragnet . 75.00
66 SMo(c),The Secret of the
  D.A.'s Diary 75.00
67 January-February, 1959 . . . . 75.00

MR. PUNCH
HC DMc,NGa,Nightmarish
  tale, 1994 . . . . 24.95

MOBFIRE
1 WaP,Gangsters in London 2.50
2 WaP, ... 2.50
3 WaP,The Bocor 2.50
4 WaP,V:Bocor 2.50
5 WaP,Voice in My Head 2.50
6 WaP,Genetic Babies, final issue 2.50

MODESTY BLAISE
1 DG,V:Gabriel 4.95

2 DG,V:Gabriel 4.95
GN Spy Thriller 19.95

MOONSHADOW
Vertigo
1 JMD(s),JMu,rep. 2.25
2 JMD 2.25
3 JMD 2.25
4 JMD 2.25
5 fully painted 2.25
6 . . . . 2.25
7 F:Shady Lady 2.25
8 Rep. Search for Ira 2.25
9 JMD,JMu,A:Tittletat Twins 2.25
10 JMD,JMu,Interplanetary
  Prostitutes 2.25
11 JMu,Ira's life story 2.25

MORE FUN COMICS
(See: NEW FUN COMICS)

MOVIE COMICS
April, 1939
1 'Gunga Din' 2,000.00
2 Stagecoach 1,400.00
3 East Side of Heaven 1,000.00
4 Captain Fury,B:Oregon Trail 800.00
5 Man in the Iron Mask 800.00
6 September, 1939 . . . . 1,000.00

MS. TREE QUARTERLY
1 MGr,A:Batman 3.50
2 A:Butcher 2.95
3 A:Butcher 2.95
4 'Paper Midnight' 3.95
5 Murder/Rape Investigation 3.95
6 Gothic House 3.95
7 . . . . 3.95
8 CI,FMc,Ms Tree Pregnant(c),
  B.U. King Faraday 3.95
9 Child Kidnapped 3.95
10 V:International Mob 3.50

MUTT AND JEFF
1939
1 . . . . 800.00
2 . . . . 400.00
3 . . . . 300.00
4 and 5 . . . . @250.00
6 thru 10 . . . . @130.00
11 thru 20 . . . . @110.00
21 thru 30 . . . .@67.00
31 thru 50 . . . .@35.00
51 thru 70 . . . .@30.00
71 thru 80 . . . .@25.00
81 thru 99 . . . .@20.00
100 . . . . 25.00
101 thru 103 . . . . @20.00
104 thru 148 . . . . @15.00

MY GREATEST ADVENTURE
January-February, 1955
1 LSt,I Was King Of
  Danger Island 900.00
2 My Million Dollar Dive 450.00
3 I Found Captain
  Kidd's Treasure 300.00
4 I Had A Date With Doom . . . 300.00
5 I Escaped From Castle Morte 275.00
6 I Had To Spend A Million . . . 250.00
7 I Was A Prisoner On Island X 225.00
8 The Day They Stole My Face 225.00

---

9 I Walked Through The Doors
of Destiny 225.00
10 We Found A World Of
Tiny Cavemen 225.00
11 LSt(c),My Friend, Madcap
Manning 175.00
12 MMe(c),I Hunted Big Game
in Outer Space 175.00
13 LSt(c),I Hunted Goliath
The Robot 175.00
14 LSt,I Had the Midas
Touch of Gold 175.00
15 JK, I Hunted the Worlds
Wildest Animals 175.00
16 JK,I Died a Thousand Times 175.00
17 JK,I Doomed the World . . . 175.00
18 JK(c),We Discovered The
Edge of the World 175.00
19 I Caught Earth's
Strangest Criminal 175.00
20 JK,I Was Big-Game
on Neptune 175.00
21 JK,We Were Doomed By
The Metal-Eating Monster . . 175.00
22 I Was Trapped In The
Magic Mountains 125.00
23 I Was A Captive In
Space Prison 125.00
24 NC(c),I Was The Robinson
Crusoe of Space 125.00
25 I Led Earth's Strangest
Safari! 125.00
26 NC(c),We Battled The
Sand Creature 125.00
27 I Was the Earth's First Exile 125.00
28 I Stalked the Camouflage
Creatures 150.00
29 I Tracked the
Forbidden Powers 125.00
30 We Cruised Into the
Supernatural! 125.00
31 I Was A Modern Hercules . . . 75.00
32 We Were Trapped In A Freak
Valley! 75.00
33 I Was Pursued by
the Elements 75.00
34 DD,We Unleashed The Cloud
Creatures 75.00
35 I Solved the Mystery of
Volcano Valley 75.00
36 I Was Bewitched
By Lady Doom 75.00
37 DD&SMo(c),I Hunted the
Legendary Creatures! 75.00
38 DD&SMo(c),I Was the Slave
of the Dream-Master 75.00
39 DD&SMo(c),We were Trapped
in the Valley of no Return . . 75.00
40 We Battled the Storm Creature 75.00
41 DD&SMo(c),I Was Tried
by a Robot Court 50.00
42 DD&SMo(c),My Brother
Was a Robot 50.00
43 DD&SMo(c),I Fought the
Sonar Creatures 50.00
44 DD&SMo(c),We Fought the
Beasts of Petrified Island . . 50.00
45 DD&SMo(c),We Battled the
Black Narwahl 50.00
46 DD&SMo(c),We Were Prisoners
of the Sundial of Doom 50.00
47 We Became Partners of the
Beast Brigade 50.00
48 DD&SMo(c),I Was Marooned
On Earth 50.00

49 DD&SMo(c),I Was An Ally
Of A Criminal Creature 50.00
50 DD&SMo(c),I Fought the
Idol King 50.00
51 DD&SMo(c),We Unleashed
the Demon of the Dungeon . . 45.00
52 DD&SMo(c),I Was A
Stand-In For an Alien 45.00
53 DD&SMo(c),I, Creature Slayer 45.00
54 I Was Cursed With
an Alien Pal 45.00
55 DD&SMo(c),I Beacame The
Wonder-Man of Space 45.00
56 DD&SMo(c),My Brother-The
Alien 45.00
57 DD&SMo(c),Don't Touch Me
Or You'll Die 45.00
58 DD&SMo(c),I was Trapped
in the Land of L'Oz 50.00
59 DD&SMo(c),Listen Earth-I
Am Still Alive 50.00
60 DD&SMo(c),ATh,I Lived in
Two Worlds 50.00
61 DD&SMo(c),ATh,I Battled For
the Doom-Stone 50.00
62 DD&SMo(c),I Fought For
An Alien Enemy 35.00
63 DD&SMo(c),We Braved the
Trail of the Ancient Warrior . . 35.00
64 DD&SMo(c),They Crowned My
Fiance Their King! 35.00
65 DD&SMo(c),I Lost the Life
or Death Secret 35.00
66 DD&SMo(c),I Dueled with
the Super Spirits 35.00
67 I Protected the Idols
of Idoro! 35.00
68 DD&SMo(c),My Deadly Island
of Space 35.00
69 DD&SMo(c),I Was A Courier
From the Past 35.00
70 DD&SMo(c),We Tracked the
Fabled Fish-Man! 35.00
71 We Dared to open the Door
of Danger Dungeon 35.00
72 The Haunted Beach 35.00
73 I Defeiller Mountain 35.00
74 GC(c),We Were Challenged
By The River Spirit 35.00
75 GC(c),Castaway Cave-Men
of 1950 . . . . 35.00
76 MMe(c),We Battled the
Micro-Monster 35.00
77 ATh,We Found the Super-
Tribes of Tomorrow 40.00
78 Destination-'Dead Man's Alley' 35.00
79 Countdown in Dinosaur Valley 35.00
80 BP,I:Doom Patrol 350.00
81 BP,ATh,I:Dr. Janus 125.00
82 BP,F:Doom Patrol 110.00
83 BP,F:Doom Patrol 110.00
84 BP,V:General Immortus 110.00
85 BP,ATh,F:Doom Patrol 110.00
Becomes:

DOOM PATROL
March, 1964
86 BP,I:Brogherhood of Evil 80.00
87 BP,O:Negative Man 55.00
88 BP,O:Chief 50.00
89 BP,I:Animal-Veg.-MineralMan 50.00
90 BP,A:Brotherhood of Evil 50.00
91 BP,I:Manto, Gargvax 50.00
92 BP,I:Dr.Tyme, A:Mento 50.00
93 BP,A:Brotherhood of Evil 50.00
94 BP,I:Dr.Radich, The Claw . . . 50.00

95 BP,A:Animal-Vegetable
-Mineral Man 50.00
96 BP,A:General Immortus,
Brotherhood of Evil 46.00
97 BP,A:General Immortus,
Brotherhood of Evil 46.00
98 BP,I:Mr.103 . . . . 46.00
99 I:Beast Boy 50.00
100 BP,O:Beast Boy,Robotman . 60.00
101 BP,A:Beast Boy 28.00
102 BP,A:Beast Boy,Challengers
of the Unknown 27.00
103 BP,A:Beast Boy 27.00
104 BP,W:Elasti-Girl,Mento,
C:JLA,Teen Titans 27.00
105 BP,A:Beast Boy 27.00
106 BP,O:Negative Man 27.00
107 BP,A:Beast Boy, I:Dr.Death . 27.00
108 BP,A:Brotherhood of Evil . . . 27.00
109 BP,I:Mandred 27.00
110 BP,A:Garguax,Mandred,
Brotherhood of Evil 25.00
111 BP,I:Zarox-13,A:Brotherhood
of Evil 25.00
112 BP,O:Beast Boy,Madame
Rouge 25.00
113 BP,A:Beast Boy,Mento 25.00
114 BP,A:Beast Boy 25.00
115 BP,A:Beast Boy 25.00
116 BP,A:Madame Rouge 25.00
117 BP,I:Black Vulture 25.00
118 BP,A:Beast Boy 25.00
119 BP,A:Madam Rouge 25.00
120 I:Wrecker 25.00
121 JO,D:Doom Patrol 75.00
122 rep.Doom Patrol #89 . . . . . 5.00
123 rep.Doom Patrol #95 . . . . . 5.00
124 rep.Doom Patrol #90 . . . . . 5.00
[2nd Series]
See: DOOM PATROL

MY NAME IS CHAOS
1 JRy,Song Laid Waste to Earth . 4.95
2 JRy,Colonization of Mars 4.95
3 JRy,Search for Eternal Beings . 4.95
4 JRy,final issue 4.95

MY NAME IS HOLOCAUST
Milestone
[Mini-Series]
1 F:Holocaust (Blood Syndicate) . 1.75
2 V:Cantano 1.75
3 A:Blood Syndicate 1.75

MYSTERY IN SPACE
April-May, 1951
1 CI&FrG(c),FF,B:Knights of the
Galaxy,Nine Worlds to
Conquer 1,800.00
2 CI(c),MA,A:Knights of the
Galaxy, Jesse James-
Highwayman of Space 700.00
3 CI(c),A:Knights of the
Galaxy, Duel of the Planets . 600.00
4 CI(c),S&K,MA,A:Knights of the
Galaxy, Master of Doom . . . 600.00
5 CI(c),A:Knights of the Galaxy,
Outcast of the Lost World . . 600.00
6 CI(c),A:Knights of the Galaxy,
The Day the World Melted . 450.00
7 GK(c),ATh,A:Knights of the Galaxy,
Challenge o/t Robot Knight . 450.00
8 MA,It's a Women's World . . 450.00
9 MA(c),The Seven Wonders

of Space 450.00
10 MA(c),The Last Time I
   Saw Earth 450.00
11 GK(c),Unknown Spaceman . 250.00
12 MA,The Sword in the Sky . . 250.00
13 MA(c),MD,Signboard
   in Space 250.00
14 MA,GK(c),Hollywood
   in Space 250.00
15 MA(c),Doom from Station X 250.00
16 MA(c),Honeymoon in Space 250.00
17 MA(c),The Last Mile of Space 250.00
18 MA(c),GK,Chain Gang
   of Space 250.00
19 MA(c),The Great
   Space-Train Robbery 275.00

Mystery in Space #20
© *DC Comics, Inc.*

20 MA(c),The Man in the
   Martian Mask 200.00
21 MA(c),Interplanetary
   Merry- Go-Round 200.00
22 MA(c),The Square Earth . . . 200.00
23 MA(c),Monkey-Rocket
   to Mars 200.00
24 MA(c),A:Space Cabby,
   Hitchhiker of Space 200.00
25 MA(c),Station Mars on the Air 150.00
26 GK(c),Earth is the Target . . 150.00
27 The Human Fishbowl 150.00
28 The Radio Planet 150.00
29 GK(c),Space-Enemy
   Number One 150.00
30 GK(c),The Impossible
   World Named Earth 150.00
31 GK(c),The Day the Earth
   Split in Two 135.00
32 GK(c),Riddle of the
   Vanishing Earthmen 135.00
33 The Wooden World War . . . 135.00
34 GK(c),The Man Who
   Moved the World 135.00
35 The Counterfeit Earth 135.00
36 GK(c),Secret of the
   Moon Sphinx 135.00
37 GK(c),Secret of the
   Masked Martians 135.00
38 GK(c),The Canals of Earth . 135.00
39 GK(c),Sorcerers of Space . . 135.00
40 GK(c),Riddle of the

Runaway Earth 135.00
41 GK(c),The Miser of Space . 135.00
42 GK(c),The Secret of the
   Skyscraper Spaceship 135.00
43 GK(c),Invaders From the
   Space Satellites 135.00
44 GK(c),Amazing Space Flight
   of North America 135.00
45 GK(c),MA,Flying Saucers
   Over Mars 135.00
46 GK(c),MA,Mystery of the
   Moon Sniper 135.00
47 GK(c),MA,Interplanetary Tug
   of War 135.00
48 GK(c),MA,Secret of the
   Scarecrow World 135.00
49 GK(c),The Sky-High Man . . 135.00
50 GK(c),The Runaway
   Space-Train 135.00
51 GK(c),MABattle of the
   Moon Monsters 135.00
52 GK(c),MSy,Mirror Menace
   of Mars 135.00
53 GK(c),B:Adam Strange stories,
   Menace o/t Robot Raiders 1,200.00
54 GK(c),Invaders of the
   Underground World 300.00
55 GK(c),The Beast From
   the Runaway World 225.00
56 GK(c),The Menace of
   the Super-Atom 125.00
57 GK(c),Mystery of the
   Giant Footsteps 125.00
58 GK(c),Chariot in in the Sky . 125.00
59 GK(c),The Duel of the
   Two Adam Stranges 125.00
60 GK(c),The Attack of the
   Tentacle World 125.00
61 CI&MA(c),Threat of the
   Tornado Tyrant 80.00
62 CI&MA(c),The Beast with
   the Sizzling Blue Eyes 80.00
63 The Weapon that
   Swallowed Men 80.00
64 The Radioactive Menace . . . 80.00
65 Mechanical Masters of Rann . 80.00
66 Space-Island of Peril 80.00
67 Challenge of the
   Giant Fireflies 80.00
68 CI&MA(c),Fadeaway Doom . . 80.00
69 CI&MA(c),Menace of the
   Aqua-Ray Weapon 80.00
70 CI&MA(c),Vengeance of
   the Dust Devil 80.00
71 CI&MA(c),The Challenge of
   the Crystal Conquerors 80.00
72 The Multiple Menace Weapon 75.00
73 CI&MA(c),The Invisible
   Invaders of Rann 60.00
74 CI&MA(c),The Spaceman
   Who Fought Himself 60.00
75 CI&MA(c),The Planet That
   Came to a Standstill 200.00
76 CI&MA(c),Challenge of
   the Rival Starman 60.00
77 CI&MA(c),Ray-Gun in the Sky 60.00
78 CI&MA(c),Shadow People
   of the Eclipse 60.00
79 CI&MA(c),The Metal
   Conqueror of Rann 60.00
80 CI&MA(c),The Deadly
   Shadows of Adam Strange . . 60.00
81 CI&MA(c),The Cloud-Creature
   That Menaced Two Worlds . . 45.00
82 CI&MA(c),World War on

Earth and Rann 45.00
83 CI&MA(c),The Emotion-Master
   of Space 45.00
84 CI&MA(c),The Powerless
   Weapons of Adam Strange . . 45.00
85 CI&MA(c),Riddle of the
   Runaway Rockets 45.00
86 CI&MA(c),Attack of the
   Underworld Giants 45.00
87 MA(c),The Super-Brain of
   Adam Strange,B:Hawkman . 180.00
88 CI&MA(c),The Robot Wraith
   of Rann 125.00
89 MA(c),Siren o/t Space Ark . 125.00
90 CI&MA(c),Planets and
   Peril, E:Hawkman 125.00
91 CI&MA(c),Puzzle of
   the Perilous Prisons 20.00
92 DD&SMo(c),The Alien Invasion
   From Earth,B:Space Ranger . 25.00
93 DD&SMo(c),The Convict
   Twins of Space 25.00
94 DD&SMo(c),The Adam
   Strange Story 25.00
95 The Hydra-Head From
   Outer Space 25.00
96 The Coins That Doomed
   Two Planets 25.00
97 The Day Adam Strange
   Vanished 25.00
98 The Wizard of the Cosmos . . 25.00
99 DD&SMo(c),The World-
   Destroyer From Space 25.00
100 DD&SMo(c),GK,The Death
   of Alanna 25.00
101 GK(c),The Valley of
   1,000 Dooms 25.00
102 GK,The Robot World of Rann 25.00
103 The Billion-Dollar Time-
   Capsule(Space Ranger),I:Ultra
   the Multi-Agent 25.00
104 thru 109 . . . . @10.00
110 Sept. 1966 . . . . 10.00
111 JAp,SD,MR,DSp,Sept. 1980 10.00
112 JAp,TS,JKu(c) 10.00
113 JKu(c),MGo 10.00
114 JKu(c),JCr,SD,DSp 10.00
115 JKu(c),SD,GT,BB 10.00
116 JSn(c),JCr,SD 10.00
117 DN,GT,March, 1981 . . . . . . 10.00

MYSTERY PLAY
Vertigo
HC GMo(s),JMu 19.95

NATHANIEL DUSK
February, 1984
1 GC(p) 1.50
2 GC(p) 1.25
3 GC(p) 1.25
4 GC(p), May 1984 . . . . 1.25

NATHANIEL DUSK II
October, 1985
1 thru 4 GC,January, 1986 . . . @2.00

NAZZ, THE
1 Michael'sBook 5.50
2 Johnny'sBook 4.95
3 Search for Michael Nazareth . . 4.95
4 V:Retaliators,final issue 4.95

All comics prices listed are for *Near Mint* condition.

NEW ADVENTURES OF SUPERBOY
(See: SUPERBOY)

NEW BOOK OF COMICS
1937
1 Dr.Occult	9,500.00
2 Dr.Occult	6,500.00

NEW COMICS
1935
1	10,000.00
2	5,000.00
3 thru 6	@3,500.00
7 thru 11	@3,000.00

Becomes:

NEW ADVENTURE COMICS
January, 1937
12 S&S	3,000.00
13 thru 20	@2,500.00
21	2,500.00
22 thru 31	@2,200.00

Becomes:

ADVENTURE COMICS

More Fun Comics #32
© DC Comics, Inc.

NEW FUN COMICS
February, 1935
1 B:Oswald the Rabbit, Jack Woods	30,000.00
2	10,000.00
3	6,000.00
4	6,000.00
5	6,000.00
6 S&S,B:Dr.Occult, Henri Duval	10,000.00

Becomes:

MORE FUN COMICS
7 S&S,WK	3,600.00
8 S&S,WK	3,200.00
9 S&S,E:Henri Duval	3,200.00
10 S&S	2,200.00
11 S&S,B:Calling all Girls	2,200.00
12 S&S	1,800.00
13 S&S	1,800.00

14 S&S,Color,Dr.Occult	8,500.00
15 S&S	3,500.00
16 S&S,Christmas(c)	3,500.00
17 S&S	3,300.00
18 S&S	1,300.00
19 S&S	1,300.00
20 HcK,S&S	1,300.00
21 S&S	1,200.00
22 S&S	1,200.00
23 S&S	1,200.00
24 S&S	1,200.00
25 S&S	1,000.00
26 S&S	1,100.00
27 S&S	1,100.00
28 S&S	1,100.00
29 S&S	1,100.00
30 S&S	1,100.00
31 S&S	1,100.00

More Fun Comics #38
© DC Comics, Inc.

32 S&S,E:Dr. Occult	1,100.00
33	1,100.00
34	1,100.00
35	1,100.00
36 B:Masked Ranger	1,100.00
37 thru 40	@1,100.00
41 E:Masked Ranger	900.00
42 thru 50	@900.00
51 I:The Spectre	2,600.00
52 O:The Spectre,pt.1, E:Wing Brady	35,000.00
53 O:The Spectre,pt.2, B:Capt.Desmo	22,000.00
54 E:King Carter,Spectre(c)	6,000.00
55 I:Dr.Fate,E:Bulldog Martin, Spectre(c)	8,500.00
56 B:Congo Bill,Dr.Fate(c)	2,200.00
57 Spectre(c)	2,200.00
58 Spectre(c)	2,200.00
59 A:Spectre	2,500.00
60 Spectre(c)	2,000.00
61 Spectre(c)	1,700.00
62 Spectre(c)	1,700.00
63 Spectre(c),E:St.Bob Neal	1,700.00
64 Spectre(c),B:Lance Larkin	1,700.00
65 Spectre(c)	1,700.00
66 Spectre(c)	1,700.00
67 Spectre(c),O:Dr. Fate, E:Congo Bill,Biff Bronson	4,400.00
68 Dr.Fate(c),B:Clip Carson	1,300.00

69 Dr.Fate(c)	1,300.00
70 Dr.Fate(c),E:Lance Larkin	1,300.00
71 Dr.Fate(c),I:Johnny Quick	3,800.00
72 Dr. Fate has Smaller Helmet, E:Sgt. Carey,Sgt.O'Malley	1,100.00
73 Dr.Fate(c),I:Aquaman,Green Arrow,Speedy	6,500.00
74 Dr.Fate(c),A:Aquaman	1,300.00
75 Dr.Fate(c)	1,200.00
76 Dr.Fate(c),MMe,E:Clip Carson, B:Johnny Quick	1,200.00
77 MMe,Green Arrow(c)	1,200.00
78 MMe,Green Arrow(c)	1,200.00
79 MMe,Green Arrow(c)	1,200.00
80 MMe,Green Arrow(c)	1,200.00
81 MMe,Green Arrow(c)	750.00
82 MMe,Green Arrow(c)	750.00
83 MMe,Green Arrow(c)	750.00
84 MMe,Green Arrow(c)	750.00
85 MMe,Green Arrow(c)	750.00
86 MMe	750.00
87 MMe,E:Radio Squad	750.00
88 MMe,Green Arrow(c)	750.00
89 MMe,O:Gr.Arrow&Speedy	1,000.00
90 MMe,Green Arrow(c)	750.00
91 MMe,Green Arrow(c)	550.00
92 MMe,Green Arrow(c)	550.00
93 MMe,B:Dover & Clover	550.00
94 MMe,Green Arrow(c)	550.00
95 MMe,Green Arrow(c)	550.00
96 MMe,Green Arrow(c)	550.00
97 MMe,JKu,E:Johnny Quick	550.00
98 E:Dr. Fate	550.00
99 Green Arrow(c)	550.00
100	750.00
101 O&I:Superboy, E:The Spectre	5,800.00
102 A:Superboy	900.00
103 A:Superboy	700.00
104 Superboy(c)	550.00
105 Superboy(c)	550.00
106	550.00
107 E:Superboy	550.00
108 A:Genius Jones,'Genius Meets Genius'	125.00
109 A:Genius Jones, The Disappearing Deposits	125.00
110 A:Genius Jones, Birds, Brains and Burglary	125.00
111 A:Genius Jones, Jeepers Creepers	125.00
112 A:Genius Jones, The Tell-Tale Tornado	125.00
113 A:Genius Jones, Clocks and Shocks	125.00
114 A:Genius Jones, The Milky Way	125.00
115 A:Genius Jones,Foolish Questions	125.00
116 A:Genius Jones,Palette For Plunder	125.00
117 A:Genius Jones,Battle of the Pretzel Benders	125.00
118 A:Genius Jones,The Sinister Siren	125.00
119 A:Genius Jones,A Perpetual Jackpot	125.00
120 A:Genius Jones,The Man in the Moon	125.00
121 A:Genius Jones,The Mayor Goes Haywire	100.00
122 A:Genius Jones,When Thug-Hood Was In Floor	100.00
123 A:Genius Jones,Hi Diddle Diddle, the Cat and the Fiddle	100.00

More Fun Comics #107
© DC Comics, Inc.

124 A:Genius Jones, The Zany Zoo	100.00
125 Genius Jones, Impossible But True	500.00
126 A:Genius Jones,The Case of the Gravy Spots	100.00
127 November-December, 1947	200.00

NEW GODS, THE
February-March, 1971

1 JK,I:Orion	25.00
2 JK	17.00
3 JK	14.00
4 JK,O:Manhunter, rep.	14.00
5 JK,I:Fastbak & Black Racer	14.00
6 JK	14.00
7 JK,O:Orion	14.00
8 JK	14.00
9 JK,I:Forager	14.00
10 JK	14.00
11 JK	14.00
12 DN,DA,R:New Gods	5.00
13 DN,DA	5.00
14 DN,DA	5.00
15 RB,BMc	5.00
16 DN,DA	5.00
17 DN,DA	5.00
18 DN,DA	5.00
19 DN,DA	4.00

NEW GODS
(Reprints)

1 JK reprint	2.25
2 JK reprint	2.00
3 JK reprint	2.00
4 JK reprint	2.00
5 JK reprint	2.00
6 JK rep.+NewMaterial	2.00

NEW GODS
[2nd Series]

1 From Cosmic Odyssey	2.00
2 A:Orion of New Genesis	1.50
3 A:Orion	1.50
4 Renegade Apokolyptian Insect Colony	1.50
5 Orion vs. Forager	1.50

6 A:Eve Donner, Darkseid	1.50
7 Bloodline #1	1.50
8 Bloodline #2	1.50
9 Bloodline #3	1.50
10 Bloodline #4	1.50
11 Bloodline #5	1.50
12 Bloodlines #6	1.50
13 Back on Earth	1.50
14 I:Reflektor	1.50
15 V:Serial Killer	1.50
16 A:Fastbak & Metron	1.50
17 A:Darkseid, Metron	1.50
18 A:YugaKhan,Darkseid, Moniters	1.50
19 V:Yuga Khan	1.50
20 Darkseid Dethroned, V:Yuga Khan	1.50
21 A:Orion	1.50
22 A:Metron	1.50
23 A:Forever People	1.50
24 A:Forever People	1.50
25 The Pact #1,R:Infinity Man	1.50
26 The Pact #2	1.50
27 Asault on Apokolips,Pact#3	1.50
28 Pact #4, final issue	1.50

NEW GUARDIANS

1 JSon,from Millenium series	2.50
2 JSon,Colombian Drug Cartel	1.75
3 JSon,in South Africa, V:Janwillem's Army	1.25
4 JSon,V:Neo-Nazi Skinheads in California	1.25
5 JSon,Tegra Kidnapped	1.25
6 JSon, In China, Invasion x-over	1.25
7 JSon, Guardians Return Home	1.25
8 JSon, V:Janwillem	1.25
9 JSon, A:Tome Kalmaku, V:Janwillem	1.25
10 JSon, A:Tome Kalmaku	1.25
11 PB,Janwillem's secret	1.25
12 PB,New Guardians Future revealed, final issue	1.25

NEW TEEN TITANS
November, 1980

1 GP,RT,V:Gordanians (see DC Comics Presents #26	14.00
2 GP,RT,I:Deathstroke the Terminator, I&D:Ravager	18.00
3 GP,I:Fearsome Five	7.00
4 GP,RT,A:JLA,O:Starfire	8.00
5 CS,RT,O:Raven,I:Trigon	7.00
6 GP,V:Trigon,O:Raven	5.00
7 GP,RT,O:Cyborg	6.00
8 GP,RT,A Day in the Life	5.00
9 GP,RT,A:Terminator, V:Puppeteer	6.00
10 GP,RT,A:Terminator	9.00
11 GP,RT,V:Hyperion	3.50
12 GP,RT,V:Titans of Myth	3.50
13 GP,RT,R:Robotman	3.00
14 GP,RT,I:New Brotherhood of Evil,V:Zahl and Rouge	3.00
15 GP,RT,D:Madame Rouge	3.00
16 GP,RT,I:Captain Carrot	3.00
17 GP,RT,I:Frances Kane	3.00
18 GP,RT,A:Orig.Starfire	3.00
19 GP,RT,A:Hawkman	3.00
20 GP,RT,V:Disruptor	3.00
21 GP,RT,GC,I:Brother Blood, Night Force	3.00
22 GP,RT,V:Brother Blood	2.50
23 GP,RT,I:Blackfire	2.50
24 GP,RT,A:Omega Men,I:X-hal	2.50

25 GP,RT,A:Omega Men	2.50
26 GP,RT,I:Terra,Runaway #1	2.50
27 GP,RT,A:Speedy,Runaway #2	2.50
28 GP,RT,V:Terra	3.50
29 GP,RT,V:Broth.of Evil	2.00
30 GP,RT,V:Broth.of Evil,J:Terra	2.00
31 GP,RT,V:Broth.of Evil	1.50
32 GP,RT,I:Thunder & Lightning	1.50
33 GP,I:Trident	1.50
34 GP,V:The Terminator	3.00
35 KP,RT,V:Mark Wright	1.50
36 KP,RT,A:Thunder & Lightning	1.50
37 GP,RT,A:Batman/Outsiders(x-over	

New Teen Titans #10
© DC Comics, Inc.

BATO#5),V:Fearsome Five	2.00
38 GP,O:Wonder Girl	1.50
39 GP,Grayson quits as Robin	5.00
40 GP,A:Brother Blood	1.50
Ann.#1 GP,RT,Blackfire	3.50
Ann.#2 GP,I:Vigilante	3.00
Ann.#3 GP,DG,D:Terra,A:Deathstroke V:The H.I.V.E.	3.50
Ann.#4 rep.Direct Ann.#1	1.25
TPB Judas Contract rep.#39-#44, Ann.#3,new GP(c)	14.95

[Special Issues]

Keebler:GP,DG,Drugs	3.00
Beverage:Drugs,RA	3.00
IBM:Drugs	4.00

Becomes:

TALES OF THE TEEN TITANS

41 GP,A:Brother Blood	2.00
42 GP,DG,V:Deathstroke	5.00
43 GP,DG,V:Deathstroke	5.00
44 GP,DG,I:Nightwing,O:Deathstroke Joe Wilson becomes Jericho	8.00
45 GP,A:Aqualad,V:The H.I.V.E.	2.00
46 GP,A:Aqualad,V:The H.I.V.E.	2.00
47 GP,A:Aqualad,V:The H.I.V.E.	2.00
48 SR,V:The Recombatants	2.00
49 GP,CI,V:Dr.Light,A:Flash	2.00
50 GP/DG W:Wonder Girl & Terry Long,C:Batman,	

All comics prices listed are for *Near Mint* condition.   **CVA Page 73**

Wonder Woman 2.50
51 RB,A:Cheshire 2.00
52 RB,A:Cheshire 2.00
53 RB,I:Ariel,A:Terminator 2.50
54 RB,A:Terminator 2.50
55 A:Terminator 2.50
56 A:Fearsome Five 1.75
57 A:Fearsome Five 1.75
58 E:MWn(s),A:Fearsome Five 1.75
59 rep. DC presents #26 . . . . . . 1.50
60 thru 99 rep. . . . . @1.50
[Limited Series]
1 GP,O:Cyborg 2.00
2 GP,O:Raven 2.00
3 GD,O:Changling 2.00
4 GP/EC,O:Starfire 2.00

NEW TEEN TITANS
[Direct sales series]
August, 1984
1 B:MWn(s),GP,L:Raven 5.00
2 GP,D:Azareth,A:Trigon 3.50
3 GP,V:Raven 3.00
4 GP,V:Trigon,Raven 3.00
5 GP,D:Trigon,Raven disappears 3.00
6 GP,A:Superman,Batman 2.50
7 JL,V:Titans of Myth 2.50
8 JL,V:Titans of Myth 2.50
9 JL,V:Titans of Myth,I:Kole . . . 2.50
10 JL,O:Kole 2.50
11 JL,O:Kole 2.50
12 JL,Ghost story 2.50
13 EB,Crisis 2.25
14 EB,Crisis 2.25
15 EB,A:Raven 2.25
16 EB,A:OmegaMen 2.25
17 EB,V:Blackfire 2.25
18 E:MWn(s),EB,V:Blackfire 2.25
19 EB,V:Mento 2.25
20 GP(c),EB,V:Cheshire,J.Todd . 2.25
21 GP(c),EB,V:Cheshire,J.Todd . 2.25
22 GP(c),EB,V:Blackfire,Mento,
Brother Blood 2.25
23 GP(c),V:Blackfire 2.25
24 CB,V:Hybrid 2.25
25 EB,RT,V:Hybrid,Mento,A:Flash 2.25
26 KGa,V:Mento 2.00
27 KGa,Church of Br.Blood 2.00
28 EB,RT,V:BrotherBlood,A:Flash 2.00
29 EB,RT,V:Brother Blood,
A:Flash,Robin 2.00
30 EB,Batman,Superman 2.25
31 EB,RT,V:Brother Blood,A:Flash
Batman,Robin,Gr.Lantern Corps
Superman 2.00
32 EB,RT,Murder Weekend 2.00
33 EB,V:Terrorists 2.00
34 EB,RT,V:Mento,Hybird 2.00
35 PB,RT,V:Arthur & Eve 2.00
36 EB,RT,I:Wildebeest 2.50
37 EB,RT,V:Wildebeest 2.00
38 EB,RT,A:Infinity 2.00
39 EB,RT,F:Raven 2.00
40 EB,RT,V:Gentleman Ghost . . . 2.00
41 EB,V:Wildebeest,A:Puppeteer,
Trident,Wildebeest 2.00
42 EB,RT,V:Puppeteer,Gizmo,
Trident,Wildebeest 2.00
43 CS,RT,V:Phobia 2.00
44 RT,V:Godiva 2.00
45 EB,RT,A:Dial H for Hero 2.00
46 EB,RT,A:Dial H for Hero 2.00
47 O:Titans,C:Wildebeest 2.00
48 EB,RT,A:Red Star 2.00
49 EB,RT,A:Red Star 2.00

Ann.#1 A:Superman,V:Brainiac . . 2.50
Ann.#2 JBy,JL,O:Brother Blood . . 3.00
Ann.#3 I:Danny Chase 2.50
Ann.#4 V:Godiva 2.50
Becomes:

NEW TITANS
50 B:MWn(s),GP,BMc,B:Who is
Wonder Girl? 5.00
51 GP,BMc 3.00
52 GP,BMc 3.00
53 GP,RT 3.00
54 GP,RT,E:Who is Wonder Girl? . 3.00
55 GP,RT,I:Troia 3.00
56 MBr,RT,Tale of Middle Titans . 2.50
57 GP,BMc,V:Wildebeast 2.50
58 GP,TG,BMc,V:Wildebeast . . . 2.50
59 GP,TG,BMc,V:Wildebeast 2.50
60 GP,TG,BMc,3rd A:Tim Drake
(Face Revealed),Batman 5.00
61 GP,TG,BMc,A:Tim Drake,
Batman 5.00
62 TG,AV,A:Deathstroke 4.00
63 TG,AV,A:Deathstroke 4.00
64 TG,AV,A:Deathstroke 4.00
65 TG,AV,A:Deathstroke,Tim Drake,
Batman 4.00
66 TG,AV,V:Eric Forrester 2.50
67 TG,AV,V:Eric Forrester 2.50
68 SE,V:Royal Flush Gang 2.50
69 SE,V:Royal Flush Gang 2.50
70 SE,A:Deathstroke 4.00
71 TG,AV,B:Deathstroke,
B:Titans Hunt 7.00

New Titans #97 © DC Comics, Inc.

72 TG,AV,D:Golden Eagle 5.00
73 TG,AV,I:Phantasm 5.00
74 TG,AV,I:Pantha 4.00
75 TG,AV,IR:Jericho/Wildebeast . 4.00
76 TG,AV,V:Wildebeests 3.00
77 TG,AV,A:Red Star,N:Cyborg . . 3.00
78 TG,AV,V:Cyborg 3.00
79 TG,AV,I:Team Titans 4.00
80 KGa,PC,A:Team Titans 3.00
81 CS,AV,War of the Gods 3.00
82 TG,AV,V:Wildebeests 3.00
83 TG,AV,D:Jericho 3.50
84 TG,AV,E:Titans Hunt 3.00

85 TG,AV,I:Baby Wildebeest 2.50
86 CS,AV,E:Deathstroke. 2.50
87 TG,AV,A:Team Titans 2.50
88 TG,AV,CS,V:Team Titans 2.50
89 JBr,I:Lord Chaos 2.50
90 TG,AV,Total Chaos#2,A:Team
Titans,D'stroke,V:Lord Chaos . 2.00
91 TG,AV,Total Chaos#5,A:Team
Titans,D'stroke,V:Lord Chaos . 2.00
92 E:MWn(s),TG,AV,Total Chaos#8,
A:Team Titans,V:Lord Chaos . 2.00
93 TG,AV,Titans Sell-Out#3 . . . . . 2.00
94 PJ,F:Red Star & Cyborg 2.00
95 PJ,Red Star gains new powers 2.00
96 PJ,I:Solar Flare,
V:Konstantine 2.00
97 TG,AV,B:The Darkening,R:Speedy
V:Brotherhood of Evil 2.00
98 TG,AV,V:Brotherhood of Evil . . 2.00
99 TG,AV,I:Arsenal (Speedy) 2.00
100 TG,AV,W:Nightwing&Starfire,
V:Deathwing,Raven,A:Flash,Team
Titans,Hologram(c) 4.00
101 AV(i),L:Nightwing 2.00
102 AV(i),A:Prester John 2.00
103 AV(i),V:Bro. of Evil 2.00
104 Terminus #1 . . . . 2.00
105 Terminus #2 . . . . 2.00
106 Terminus #3 . . . . 2.00
107 Terminus #4 . . . . 2.00
108 A:Supergirl,Flash 2.00
109 F:Starfire 2.00
110 A:Flash,Serg.Steele 2.00
111 A:Checkmate 2.00
112 A:Checkmate 2.00
113 F:Nightwing 2.25
114 L:Starfire, Nightwing,Panthra,
Wildebeest 1.95
115 A:Trigon 1.95
116 Changling 1.95
117 V:Psimon 1.95
118 V:Raven + Brotherhood 1.95
119 Suffer the Children,pt.1 . . . . . 1.95
120 Forever Evil,pt.2 . . . . 1.95
121 Forever Evil,pt.3 . . . . 1.95
122 Crimelord/Syndicate War,pt.2
J:Supergirl 2.25
123 MWn(s),RRa,O:Minion 2.25
Ann.#5 O:Children of the Sun . . . 4.00
Ann.#6 CS,F:Starfire 4.00
Ann.#7 Armageddon 2001,I:Future
Teen Titans 6.00
Ann.#8 PJ,Eclipso,V:Deathstroke . 3.75
Ann.#9 Bloodlines#5,I:Anima . . . 3.75
Ann.#10 Elseworlds story 3.75
Ann.#11 Year One Annual 3.95
#0 Spec. Zero Hour,new team . . 1.95

NEW TITANS SELL-OUT SPECIAL
1 SE,AV,AH,I:Teeny Titans,
w/Nightwing poster 3.75

NEW YORK WORLD'S FAIR
1 1939 . . . . 12,000.00
2 1940 . . . . 7,000.00

NIGHT FORCE
August, 1982
1 GC,1:Night Force 1.25
2 thru 13 GC . . . . @1.25
14 GC,September,1983 . . . . 1.25

New York World's Fair Comics #2(nn)
© DC Comics, Inc.

NUTSY SQUIRREL
September-October, 1954
61 SM		40.00
62 thru 71		@25.00
72 November, 1957		25.00

OMAC
September-October, 1974
1 JK,I&O:Omac		11.00
2 JK,I:Mr.Big		9.00
3 JK,100,000 foes		8.00
4 JK,V:Kafka		8.00
5 JK,New Bodies for Old		8.00
6 JK,The Body Bank		8.00
7 JK,The Ocean Stealers		8.00
8 JK,Last issue		8.00

[2nd Series]
1 JBy,B&W prestige		5.00
2 JBy,The Great Depression era		4.50
3 JBy,'To Kill Adolf Hitler'		4.50
4 JBy,D:Mr.Big		4.50

OMEGA MEN
December, 1982
1 KG,V:Citadel		2.50
2 KG,O:Broot		2.00
3 KG,I:Lobo		8.00
4 KG,D:Demonia,I:Felicity		1.50
5 KG,V:Lobo		5.00
6 KG,V:Citadel,D:Gepsen		2.00
7 O:Citadel,L:Auron		2.00
8 R:Nimbus,I:H.Hokum		2.00
9 V:HarryHokum,A:Lobo		5.00
10 A:Lobo (First Full Story)		7.00
11 V:Blackfire		1.50
12 R:Broots Wife		1.50
13 A:Broots Wife		1.50
14 Karna		1.50
15 Primus Goes Mad		1.50
16 Spotlight Issue		1.50
17 V:Psions		1.50
18 V:Psions		1.50
19 V:Psions,C:Lobo		3.00
20 V:Psions,A:Lobo		5.00
21 Spotlight Issue		1.50
22 Nimbus		1.50
23 Nimbus		1.50

Omega Men #5 © DC Comics, Inc.

24 Okaara		1.50
25 Kalista		1.50
26 V:Spiderguild		1.50
27 V:Psions		1.50
28 V:Psions		1.50
29 V:Psions		1.50
30 R:Primus,I:Artin		1.50
31 Crisis tie-in		1.50
32 Felicity		1.50
33 Regufe World		1.50
34 A:New Teen Titans		1.50
35 A:New Teen Titans		1.50
36 Last Days of Broot		1.50
37 V:Spiderguild,A:Lobo		4.00
38 A:Tweener Network		1.25
Ann.#1 KG,R:Harpis		2.25
Ann.#2 KG,O:Primus		2.25

OUR ARMY AT WAR
August, 1952
1 CI(c),Dig Your Foxhole Deep		750.00
2 CI(c),Champ		400.00
3 GK(c),No Exit		300.00
4 IN(c),Last Man		300.00
5 IN(c),T.N.T. Bouquet		250.00
6 IN(c),Battle Flag		250.00
7 IN(c),Dive Bomber		250.00
8 IN(c),One Man Army		250.00
9 GC(c),Undersea Raider		250.00
10 IN(c),Soldiers on the High Wire		250.00
11 IN(c),Scratch One Meatball		250.00
12 IN(c),The Big Drop		200.00
13 BK(c),Ghost Ace		200.00
14 Drummer of Waterloo		200.00
15 IN(c),Thunder in the Skies		200.00
16 IN(c),A Million To One Shot		200.00
17 IN(c),The White Death		200.00
18 IN(c),Frontier Fighter		200.00
19 IN(c),The Big Ditch		200.00
20 IN(c),Abandon Ship		200.00
21 IN(c),Dairy of a Flattop		150.00
22 IN(c),Ranger Raid		150.00
23 IN(c),Jungle Navy		150.00
24 IN(c),Suprise Landing		150.00
25 JGr(c),Take 'Er Down		150.00

26 JGr(c),Sky Duel		150.00
27 IN(c),Diary of a Frogman		150.00
28 JGr(c),Detour-War		150.00
29 IN(c),Grounded Fighter		150.00
30 JGr(c),Torpedo Raft		150.00
31 IN(c),Howitzer Hill		150.00
32 JGr(c),Battle Mirror		125.00
33 JGr(c),Fighting Gunner		125.00
34 JGr(c),Point-Blank War		125.00
35 JGr(c),Frontline Tackle		125.00
36 JGr(c),Foxhole Mascot		125.00
37 JGr(c),Walking Battle Pin		125.00
38 JGr(c),Floating Pillbox		125.00
39 JGr(c),Trench Trap		125.00
40 RH(c),Tank Hunter		125.00
41 JGr(c),Jungle Target		125.00
42 IN(c),Shadow Targets		100.00
43 JGr(c),A Bridge For Billy		100.00
44 JGr(c),Thunder In The Desert		100.00
45 JGr(c),Diary of a Fighter Pilot		100.00
46 JGr(c),Prize Package		100.00
47 JGr(c),Flying Jeep		100.00
48 IN(c),Front Seat		100.00
49 JKu(c),Landing Postponed		100.00
50 JGr(c),Mop-Up Squad		100.00
51 JGr(c),Battle Tag		75.00
52 JGr(c),Pony Express Pilot		75.00
53 JGr(c),One Ringside-For War		75.00
54 JKu(c),No-Man Secret		75.00
55 JGr(c),No Rest For A Raider		75.00
56 JKu(c),You're Next		75.00
57 JGr(c),Ten-Minute Break		75.00
58 JKu(c),The Fighting Snow Bird		75.00
59 JGr(c),The Mustang Had My Number		75.00
60 JGr(c),Ranger Raid		75.00
61 JGr(c),A Pigeon For Easy Co.		85.00
62 JKu(c),Trigger Man		85.00
63 JGr(c),The Big Toss		85.00
64 JKu(c),Tank Rider		85.00
65 JGr(c),Scramble-War Upstairs		85.00
66 RH(c),Gunner Wanted		85.00
67 JKu(c),Boiling Point		85.00
68 JKu(c),End of the Line		85.00
69 JGr(c),Combat Cage		85.00
70 JGr(c),Torpedo Tank		85.00
71 JGr(c),Flying Mosquitoes		85.00
72 JGr(c),No. 1 Pigeon		85.00
73 JKu(c),Shooting Gallery		85.00
74 JGr(c),Ace Without Guns		85.00
75 JGr(c),Blind Night Fighter		85.00
76 JKu(c),Clipped Hellcat		85.00
77 JGr(c),Jets Don't Dream		85.00
78 IN(c),Battle Nurse		85.00
79 JGr(c),What's the Price of a B-17?		85.00
80 JGr(c),The Sparrow And The...Hawk		85.00
81 JGr(c),Sgt. Rock in The Rock of Easy Co.		950.00
82 JGr(c),Gun Jockey		200.00
83 JGr(c),B:Sgt.Rock Stories, The Rock and the Wall		400.00
84 JKu(c),Laughter On Snakehead Hill		125.00
85 JGr(c),Ice Cream Soldier		150.00
86 RH(c),Tank 711		125.00
87 RH(c),Calling Easy Co.		125.00
88 JGr(c),The Hard Way		125.00
89 RH(c),No Shoot From Easy		125.00
90 JKu(c),3 Stripes Hill		125.00
91 JGr(c),No Answer from Sarge		125.00
92 JGr(c),Luck of Easy		85.00
93 JGr(c),Deliver One Airfield		85.00
94 JKu(c),Target-Easy Company		85.00

Our Army at War #8 © DC Comics, Inc.

95 JKu(c),Battle Of The Stripes . 85.00
96 JGr(c),Last Stand For Easy . . 85.00
97 JKu(c),What Makes A
   Sergeant Run? 85.00
98 JKu(c),Soldiers Never Die . . . 85.00
99 JKu(c),Easy's Hardest Battle . 85.00
100 JKu(c),No Exit For Easy 85.00
101 JKu(c),End Of Easy 50.00
102 JKu(c),The Big Star 50.00
103 RH(c),Easy's Had It 50.00
104 JKu(c),A New Kind Of War . 50.00
105 JKu(c),T.N.T. Birthday 50.00
106 JKu(c),Meet Lt. Rock 50.00
107 JKu(c),Doom Over Easy . . . 50.00
108 JGr(c),Unknown Sergeant . . 50.00
109 JKu(c),Roll Call For Heroes . 50.00
110 JKu(c),That's An Order 50.00
111 JKu(c),What's The Price
   Of A Dog Tag 50.00
112 JKu(c),Battle Shadow 50.00
113 JKu(c),Eyes Of A
   Blind Gunner 50.00
114 JKu(c),Killer Sergeant 50.00
115 JKu(c),Rock's Battle Family . 50.00
116 JKu(c),S.O.S. Sgt. Rock . . . 50.00
117 JKu(c),Snafu Squad 45.00
118 RH(c),The Tank Vs. The
   Tin Soldier 45.00
119 JKu(c),A Bazooka For
   Babyface 45.00
120 JGr(c),Battle Tags
   For Easy Co. 25.00
121 JKu(c),New Boy In Easy . . . 25.00
122 JKu(c),Battle of the
   Pajama Commandoes 25.00
123 JGr(c),Battle Brass Ring . . . 25.00
124 JKu(c),Target-Sgt. Rock . . . 25.00
125 JKu(c),Hold-At All Costs . . . 25.00
126 RH(c),The End Of
   Easy Company 25.00
127 JKu(c),4 Faces of Sgt. Rock 25.00
128 JKu(c),O:Sgt. Rock 125.00
129 JKu(c),Heroes Need Cowards 25.00
130 JKu(c),No Hill For Easy . . . 25.00
131 JKu(c),One Pair of
   Dogtags For Sale 25.00
132 JKu(c),Young Soldiers
   Never Cry 25.00
133 JKu(c),Yesterday's Hero . . . 25.00

134 JKu(c),The T.N.T. Book . . . 25.00
135 JKu(c),Battlefield Double . . . 25.00
136 JKu(c),Make Me A Hero . . . 25.00
137 JKu(c),Too Many Sergeants 25.00
138 JKu(c),Easy's Lost Sparrow 25.00
139 JKu(c),A Firing Squad
   For Easy 25.00
140 JKu(c),Brass Sergeant 25.00
141 JKu(c),Dead Man's Trigger . 25.00
142 JKu(c),Easy's New Topkick . 25.00
143 JKu(c),Easy's T.N.T. Crop . . 25.00
144 JKu(c),The Sparrow And
   The Tiger 25.00
145 JKu(c),A Feather For
   Little Sure Shot 25.00
146 JKu(c),The Fighting Guns
   For Easy 25.00
147 JKu(c),Book One:Generals
   Don't Die 25.00
148 JKu(c),Book Two:Generals
   Don't Die:Generals Are
   Sergeants With Stars 25.00
149 JKu(c),Surrender Ticket . . . 25.00
150 JKu(c),Flytrap Hill 25.00
151 JKu(c),War Party,
   I:Enemy Ace 125.00
152 Jku(c),Last Man-Last Shot . 30.00
153 JKu(c),Easy's Last Stand . 25.00
154 JKu(c),Boobytrap Mascot . 25.00
155 JKu(c),No Stripes For Me . 25.00
156 JKu(c),The Human Tank Trap 25.00
157 JKu(c),Nothin's Ever
   Lost In War 25.00
158 JKu(c),Iron Major-Rock
   Sergeant 25.00
159 JKu(c),The Blind Gun 25.00
160 JKu(c),What's The Color
   Of Your Blood 25.00
161 JKu(c),Dead End
   For A Dogface 25.00
162 JKu(c),The Price and
   The Sergeant 25.00
163 JKu(c),Kill Me-Kill Me 25.00
164 JKu(c),No Exit For Easy,
   reprint from #100 . . . . 25.00
165 JKu(c),The Return of the
   Iron Major 15.00
166 JKu(c),Half A Sergeant 15.00
167 JKu(c),Kill One-Save One . . 15.00
168 JKu(c),I Knew The
   Unknown Soldier 15.00
169 JKu(c),Nazi On My Back . . . 15.00
170 JKu(c),Buzzard Bait Hill . . . 15.00
171 JKu(c),The Sergeant Must Die 15.00
172 JKu(c),A Slug For A Sergeant 15.00
173 JKu(c),Easy's Hardest Battle,
   reprint from #99 . . . . 15.00
174 JKu(c),One Kill Too Many . . 15.00
175 JKu(c),T.N.T. Letter 15.00
176 JKu(c),Give Me Your Stripes 15.00
177 JKu(c),Target-Easy Company,
   reprint from #94 . . . . 15.00
178 JKu(c),Only One Medal
   For Easy 15.00
179 JKu(c),A Penny Jackie
   Johnson 15.00
180 JKu(c),You Can't
   Kill A General 15.00
181 RH(c),Monday's Coward-
   Tuesday's Hero 15.00
182 NA,RH(c),The Desert Rats
   of Easy 18.00
183 NA,JKu(c),Sergeants Don't
   Stay Dead 18.00
184 JKu(c),Candidate For A

   Firing Squad 15.00
185 JKu(c),Battle Flag For A G.I. 15.00
186 NA,JKu(c),3 Stripes Hill
   reprint from #90 . . . . 18.00
187 JKu(c),Shadow of a Sergeant 10.00
188 JKu(c),Death Comes for Easy 10.00
189 JKu(c),The Mission Was
   Murder 10.00
190 JKu(c),What Make's A
   Sergeant Run?, reprint
   from #97 . . . . 10.00
191 JKu(c),Death Flies High,
   A:Johnny Cloud 10.00
192 JKu(c),A Firing Squad
   For A Sergeant 10.00
193 JKu(c),Blood In the Desert . 10.00
194 JKu(c),A Time For Vengeance 10.00
195 JKu(c),Dead Town 10.00
196 JKu(c),Stop The War-I Want
   To Get Off 10.00
197 JKu(c),Last Exit For Easy . . 10.00
198 JKu(c),Plugged Nickel 10.00
199 JKu(c),Nazi Ghost Wolf 10.00
200 JKu(c),The Troubadour . . . 15.00
201 JKu(c),The Graffiti Writer . . 10.00
202 JKu(c),The Sarge Is Dead . . . 6.00
203 JKu(c),Easy's Had It,
   reprint from # 103 . . . . 8.00
204 JKu(c) 6.00
205 JKu(c) 6.00
206 JKu(c),There's A War On . . . 6.00
207 JKu(c),A Sparrow's Prayer . 6.00
208 JKu(c),A Piece of Rag...And
   A Hank of Hair 6.00
209 JKu(c),I'm Still Alive 6.00
210 JKu(c),I'm Kilroy 6.00
211 JKu(c),The Treasure of
   St. Daniel 6.00
212 JKu(c),The Quiet War 6.00
213 JKu(c),A Letter For Bulldozer 6.00
214 JKu(c),Where Are You? . . . 6.00
215 JKu(c),Pied Piper of Peril . . 6.00
216 JKu(c),Doom Over Easy,
   reprint from # 107 . . . . 6.00
217 JKu(c),Surprise Party 6.00
218 JKu(c),Medic! 6.00
219 JKu(c),Yesterday's Hero . . . 5.00
220 JKu(c),Stone-Age War 5.00
221 JKu(c),Hang-Up 5.00
222 JKu(c),Dig In, Easy 5.00
223 JKu(c),On Time 5.00
224 JKu(c),One For The Money . 5.00
225 JKu(c),Face Front 5.00
226 JKu(c),Death Stop 5.00
227 JKu(c),Traitor's Blood 5.00
228 JKu(c),It's A Dirty War 5.00
229 JKu(c),The Battle of the
   Sergeants, reprint from #128 . . 6.00
230 JKu(c),Home Is The Hunter . . 6.00
231 JKu(c),My Brother's Keeper . 5.00
232 JKu(c),3 Men In A Tub 5.00
233 JKu(c),Head Count 5.00
234 JKu(c),Summer In Salerno . . 5.00
235 JKu(c),Pressure Point 5.00
236 JKu(c),Face The Devil 5.00
237 JKu(c),Nobody Cares 5.00
238 JKu(c),I Kid You Not 5.00
239 JKu(c),The Soldier 5.00
240 JKu(c),NA 8.00
241 JKu(c),War Story 5.00
242 JKu(c),Infantry 5.00
243 JKu(c),24 Hour Pass 5.00
244 JKu(c),Easy's First Tiger 5.00
245 JKu(c),The Prisoner 5.00
246 JKu(c),Naked Combat 5.00

247 JKu(c),The Vision 5.00
248 JKu(c),The Firing Squad 5.00
249 JKu(c),The Luck of Easy,WW   8.00
250 JKu(c),90 Day Wonder 5.00
251 JKu(c),The Iron Major 5.00
252 JKu(c),The Iron Hand 5.00
253 JKu(c),Rock and Iron 5.00
254 JKu(c),The Town 5.00
255 JKu(c),What's It Like 5.00
256 JKu(c),School For Sergeants . 5.00
257 JKu(c),The Castaway 5.00
258 JKu(c),The Survivors 5.00
259 JKu(c),Lost Paradise 5.00
260 JKu(c),Hell's Island 5.00
261 JKu(c),The Medal That
  Nobody Wanted 5.00
262 JKu(c),The Return 5.00
263 JKu(c),The Cage 5.00
264 JKu(c),The Hunt 5.00
265 JKu(c),The Brother 5.00
266 JKu(c),The Evacuees 5.00
267 JKu(c),A Bakers Dozen 5.00
268 JKu(c),The Elite 5.00
269 JKu(c) 5.00
270 JKu(c),Spawn of the Devil . . 5.00
271 JKu(c),Brittle Harvest 5.00
272 JKu(c),The Bloody Flag 5.00
273 JKu(c),The Arena 5.00
274 JKu(c),Home Is The Hero . . . 5.00
275 JKu(c),Graveyard Battlefield . 5.00
276 JKu(c),A Bullet For Rock 5.00
277 JKu(c),Gashouse Gang 5.00
278 JKu(c),Rearguard Action 5.00
279 JKu(c),Mined City 5.00
280 JKu(c),Mercy Mission 5.00
281 JKu(c),Dead Man's Eyes . . . 5.00
282 JKu(c),Pieces of Time 5.00
283 JKu(c),Dropouts 5.00
284 JKu(c),Linkup 5.00
285 JKu(c),Bring Him Back 5.00
286 JKu(c),Firebird 5.00
287 JKu(c),The Fifth Dimension . . 5.00
288 JKu(c),Defend-Or Destroy . . . 5.00
289 JKu(c),The Line 5.00
290 JKu(c),Super-Soldiers 5.00
291 JKu(c),Death Squad 5.00
292 JKu(c),A Lesson In Blood . . . 5.00
293 JKu(c),It Figures 5.00
294 JKu(c),Coffin For Easy 5.00
295 JKu(c),The Devil in Paradise . 5.00
296 JKu(c),Combat Soldier 5.00
297 JKu(c),Percentages 5.00
298 JKu(c),Return to Chartres . . . 5.00
299 JKu(c),Three Soldiers 5.00
300 JKu(c),300th Hill 5.00
301 JKu(c),The Farm 5.00
Becomes:
SGT. ROCK
302 JKu(c),Anzio-The Bloodbath,
  part I 8.00
303 JKu(c),Anzio, part II 6.00
304 JKu(c),Anzio, part III 6.00
305 JKu(c),Dead Man's Trigger,
  reprint from #141 . . . . 6.00
306 JKu(c),The Last Soldier 6.00
307 JKu(c),I'm Easy 6.00
308 JKu(c),One Short Step 6.00
309 JKu(c),Battle Clowns 6.00
310 JKu(c),Hitler's Wolf Children . 6.00
311 JKu(c),The Sergeant and
  the Lady 6.00
312 JKu(c),No Name Hill 6.00
313 JKu(c),A Jeep For Joey 6.00
314 JKu(c),Gimme Sky 6.00
315 JKu(c),Combat Antenna 6.00

316 JKu(c),Another Hill... . . . . 6.00
317 JKu(c),Hell's Oven 6.00
318 JKu(c),Stone-Age War 6.00
319 JKu(c),To Kill a Sergeant . . . 6.00
320 JKu(c),Never Salute a
  Sergeant 6.00
321 JKu(c),It's Murder Out Here . 5.00
322 JKu(c),The Killer 5.00
323 JKu(c),Monday's Hero 5.00
324 JKu(c),Ghost of a Tank 5.00
325 JKu(c),Future Kill, part I 5.00
326 JKu(c),Future Kill, part II 5.00
327 JKu(c),Death Express 5.00
328 JKu(c),Waiting For Rock 5.00
329 JKu(c),Dead Heat 5.00
330 JKu(c),G.I. Trophy 5.00
331 JKu(c),The Sons of War 5.00
332 JKu(c),Pyramid of Death 5.00
333 JKu(c),Ask The Dead 5.00
334 JKu(c),What's Holding Up
  The War 5.00
335 JKu(c),Killer Compass 5.00
336 JKu(c),The Red Maple Leaf . 5.00
337 JKu(c),A Bridge Called Charlie 5.00
338 JKu(c),No Escape From
  the Front 5.00
339 JKu(c),I Was Here Before . . . 5.00
340 JKu(c),How To Win A War . . 5.00
341 JKu(c),High-Flyer 5.00
342 JKu(c),The 6 sides of
  Sgt. Rock 5.00
343 thru 350 . . . . @5.00
351 thru 422 . . . . @2.00

OUR FIGHTING FORCES
October-November, 1954
1 IN,JGr(c),Human Booby Trap 500.00
2 RH,IN,IN(c),Mile-Long Step . 250.00
3 RA,JKu(c),Winter Ambush . . 200.00
4 RA,JGr(c),The Hot Seat . . . 150.00
5 IN,RA,JGr(c),The Iron Punch 150.00
6 IN,RA,JGr(c),The Sitting Tank 125.00
7 RA,JKu,JGr(c),Battle Fist . . . 125.00
8 IN,RA,JGr(c),No War
  For A Gunner 125.00
9 JKu,RH,JGr(c),Crash-
  Landing At Dawn 125.00
10 WW,RA,JGr(c),Grenade
  Pitcher 150.00
11 JKu,JGr(c),Diary of a Sub . . 100.00
12 IN,JKu,JGr(c),Jump Seat . . 100.00
13 RA,JGr(c),Beach Party 100.00
14 JA,RA,IN,JGr(c),Unseen War 100.00
15 RH,JKu,JGr(c),Target For
  A Lame Duck 100.00
16 RH,JGr(c),Night Fighter 100.00
17 RA,JGr(c),Anchored Frogman 100.00
18 RH,JKu,JGr(c),Cockpit Seat   100.00
19 RA,JKu(c),Straighten ThatLine100.00
20 RA,MD,JGr(c),The
  Floating Pilot 100.00
21 RA,JKu(c),The Bouncing
  Baby of Company B 65.00
22 JKu,RA,JGr(c),3 Doorways
  To War 65.00
23 RA,IN,JA,JGr(c),Tin Fish Pilot 65.00
24 RA,RH,JGr(c),Frogman Duel . 65.00
25 RA,JKu(c),Dead End 65.00
26 IN,RH,JKu(c),Tag Day 65.00
27 MD,RA,JKu(c),TNT Escort . . 65.00
28 RH,MD,JKu(c),All Quiet at C.P.65.00
29 JKu,JKu(c),Listen To A Jet . . 65.00
30 IN,RA,JKu(c),Fort
  For A Gunner 65.00
31 MD,RA,JKu(c),Silent Sub . . . 55.00

32 RH,MD,RH(c),PaperWorkWar 55.00
33 RH,JKu,JKu(c),Frogman
  In A Net 55.00
34 JA,JGr,JKu(c),Calling U-217 . 55.00
35 JA,JGr,JKu(c),Mask of
  a Frogman 55.00
36 MD,JA,JKu(c),Steel Soldier . . 55.00
37 JA,JGr,JGr(c),Frogman
  In A Bottle 55.00
38 RH,RA,JA,JGr(c),Sub Sinker . 55.00
39 JA,RH,RH(c),Last Torpedo . . 55.00
40 JGr,JA,JKu,JKu(c),The
  Silent Ones 55.00
41 JGr,RH,JA,JKu(c),Battle
  Mustang 75.00
42 RH,MD,JGr(c),Sorry-
  Wrong Hill 45.00
43 MD,JKu,JGr(c),Inside Battle . 25.00
44 MD,RH,RA,JGr(c),Big Job
  For Baker 45.00
45 RH,RA,JGr(c),B:Gunner and
  Sarge, Mop-Up Squad 175.00
46 RH,RA,JGr(c),Gunner's Squad 45.00
47 RH,JKu(c),TNT Birthday 45.00
48 JA,RH,JGr(c),A Statue
  For Sarge 45.00
49 RH,MD,JGr(c),Blind Gunner . 45.00
50 JA,RH,JGr(c),I:Pooch,My
  Pal, The Pooch 45.00
51 RA,JA,RH(c),Underwater
  Gunner 25.00
52 MD,JKu,JKu(c),The Gunner
  and the Nurse 25.00
53 JA,RA,JGr(c),An Egg
  For Sarge 25.00
54 . . . . 25.00
55 MD,RH,JGr(c),The Last Patrol 25.00
56 RH,RA,JGr(c),Bridge of Bullets 25.00
57 JA,IN,JGr(c),A Tank For Sarge 25.00
58 JA,JGr(c),Return of the Pooch 25.00
59 RH,JA,JGr(c),Pooch-Patrol
  Leader 25.00
60 RH,JA,JGr(c),Tank Target . . . 25.00
61 JA,JGr(c),Pass to Peril 25.00
62 JA,JGr(c),The Flying Pooch . 25.00
63 JA,RH,JGr(c),Pooch-Tank
  Hunter 25.00
64 JK,RH,JGr(c),A Lifeline
  For Sarge 25.00
65 IN,JA,JGr(c),Dogtag Patrol . . 25.00
66 JKu,JA,JGr(c),Trail of the
  Ghost Bomber 25.00
67 IN,JA,JGr(c),Purple Heart
  For Pooch 25.00
68 JA,JGr(c),Col. Hakawa's
  Birthday Party 25.00
69 JA,JKu,JGr(c),
  Destination Doom 25.00
70 JA,JKu(c),The Last Holdout . 25.00
71 JA,JGr(c),End of the Marines . 20.00
72 JA,JGr(c),Four-Footed Spy . . 15.00
73 IN,JGr(c),The Hero Maker . . . 15.00
74 IN,JGr(c),Three On A T.N.T.
  Bull's-Eye 15.00
75 JKu(c),Purple Heart Patrol . . 15.00
76 JKu(c),The T.N.T. Seat 15.00
77 JKu(c),No Foxhole-No Home . 15.00
78 JGr(c),The Last Medal 15.00
79 JA,JGr(c),Backs to the Sea . . 15.00
80 JA,JGr(c),Don't Come Back . 15.00
81 JA,JGr(c),Battle of
  the Mud Marines 15.00
82 JA,JGr(c),Battle of the
  Empty Helmets 15.00
83 RA,JKu(c),Any Marine

Can Do It	15.00
84 JA,JKu(c),The Gun of Shame	15.00
85 Ja,JKu(c),The TNT Pin-Points	15.00
86 JKu(c),3 Faces of Combat .	15.00
87 JKu(c),Battle o/t Boobytraps	15.00
88 GC,JKu(c),Devil Dog Patrol . .	15.00
89 JKu(c),TNT Toothache	15.00
90 JKu(c),Stop the War	15.00
91 JKu(c),The Human Shooting	
Gallery	8.00
92 JA,JKu(c),The Bomb That	
Stopped The War	8.00
93 IN,JKu(c),The Human Sharks .	8.00
94 RH(c),E:Gunner,Sarge & Pooch,	
The Human Blockbusters . .	8.00
95 GC,RH(c),B:The Fighting Devil	
Dog, Lt. Rock, The	
Fighting Devil Dog	8.00
96 JA,RH(c),Battle of Fire	8.00
97 IN(c),Invitation To A	
Firing Squad	8.00
98 IN(c),E:The Fighting Devil	
Dog, Death Wore A Grin	8.00
99 JA,JKu(c),B:Capt. Hunter,	
No Mercy in Vietnam	8.00
100 GC,IN(c),Death Also	
Stalks the Hunter	6.00
101 JA,RH(c),Killer of Vietnam . . .	6.00
102 RH,JKu(c),Cold Steel	
For A Hot War	6.00
103 JKu(c),The Tunnels of Death .	6.00
104 JKu(c),Night Raid In Vietnam	6.00
105 JKu(c),Blood Loyality	6.00
106 IN(c),Trail By Fury	6.00
107 IN(c),Raid Of The Hellcats . .	6.00
108 IN(c),Kill The Wolf Pack	6.00
109 IN(c),Burn, Raiders, Burn . . .	6.00
110 IN(c),Mountains Full of Death	6.00
111 IN(c),Train of Terror	6.00
112 IN(c),What's In It For	
The Hellcats?	6.00
113 IN(c),Operation-Survival	6.00
114 JKu(c),No Loot For The	
Hellcats	6.00
115 JKu(c),Death In The Desert . .	6.00
116 JKu(c),Peril From the Casbah	6.00
117 JKu(c),Colder Than Death . .	6.00
118 JKu(c),Hell Underwater	6.00
119 JKu(c),Bedlam In Berlin	6.00
120 JKu(c),Devil In The Dark	6.00
121 JKu(c),Take My Place	6.00
122 JKu(c),24 Hours To Die	6.00
123 JKu(c),B:Born Losers,No	
Medals No Graves	6.00
124 JKu(c),Losers Take All	6.00
125 Daughters of Death	6.00
126 JKu(c),Lost Town	6.00
127 JKu(c),Angels Over Hell's	
Corner	6.00
128 JKu(c),7 11 War	6.00
129 JKu(c),Ride The Nightmare . .	6.00
130 JKu(c),Nameless Target	6.00
131 JKu(c),Half A Man	6.00
132 JKu(c),Pooch, The Winner . .	6.00
133 JKu(c),Heads or Tails	6.00
134 JKu(c),The Real Losers	6.00
135 JKu(c),Death Picks A Loser .	6.00
136 JKu(c),Decoy For Death	6.00
137 JKu(c),God Of The Losers . .	6.00
138 JKu(c),The Targets	6.00
139 JKu(c),The Pirate	6.00
140 JKu(c),Lost...One Loser	6.00
141 JKu(c),Bad Penny, The	6.00
142 JKu(c), 1/2 A Man	6.00
143 JKu(c),Diamonds Are	

For Never	6.00
144 JKu(c),The Lost Mission	6.00
145 JKu(c),A Flag For Losers . . .	6.00
146 JKu(c),The Forever Walk . . .	6.00
147 NA(c),The Glory Road	6.00
148 JKu(c),The Last Charge	6.00
149 FT(c),A Bullet For	
A Traitor	6.00
150 JKu(c),Mark Our Graves . . .	6.00
151 JKu(c),Kill Me With Wagner .	6.00
152 JK(c),A Small Place In Hell . .	6.00
153 JK(c),Big Max	6.00
154 JK(c),Bushido,Live By The	
Code, Die By The Code	6.00
155 JK(c),The Captives	6.00
156 JK(c),Good-Bye Broadway . .	6.00
157 JK(c),Panama Fattie	6.00
158 JK(c),Bombing Out On	
The Panama Canal	6.00
159 JK(c),Mile-A-Minute Jones . .	6.00
160 JKu(c),Ivan	6.00
161 JKu(c),The Major's Dream . .	6.00
162 Gung-Ho	6.00
163 JKu(c),The Unmarked Graves	6.00
164 JKu(c),A Town Full Of Losers	6.00
165 LD(c),The Rowboat Fleet . . .	6.00
166 LD(c),Sword of Flame	6.00
167 LD(c),A Front Seat In Hell . . .	6.00
168 LD(c),A Cold Day To Die .	6.00
169 JKu(c),Welcome Home-And	
Die	6.00
170 JKu(c),A Bullet For	
The General	6.00
171 JKu(c),A Long Day...	
A Long War	6.00
172 JKu(c),The Two-Headed Spy	6.00
173 JKu(c),An Appointment	
With A Direct Hit	6.00
174 JKu(c),Winner Takes-Death .	6.00
175 JKu(c),Death Warrant	6.00
176 JKu(c),The Loser Is A	
Teen-Ager	6.00
177 JKu(c),This Loser Must Die . .	6.00
178 JKu(c),Last Drop For Losers .	6.00
179 JKu(c),The Last Loser	6.00
180 JKu(c),Hot Seat In A	
Cold War	6.00
181 JKu(c),Sept.-Oct., 1978	6.00

OUTCASTS
October, 1987

1	2.00
2 thru 10	@1.75
11 final issue	1.75

OUTLAWS

1 LMc,I:Hood	1.95
2 LMc,O:Hood	1.95
3 LMc,V:Evil King	1.95
4 LMc,V:Lord Conductor	1.95
5 LMc,Archery contest	1.95
6 LMc,Raid on King's Castle . . .	1.95
7 LMc,Refuge, V:Lord Conductor	1.95

OUTSIDERS, THE
November, 1985
[1st Regular Series]

1 JAp,I:Looker	3.50
2 JAp,V:Nuclear Family	2.50
3 JAp,V:Force of July	2.00
4 JAp,V:Force of July	2.00
5 JAp,Christmas Issue	2.00
6 JAp,V:Duke of Oil	2.00
7 JAp,V:Duke of Oil	2.00

The Outsiders #19
© *DC Comics, Inc.*

8 JAp,Japan	2.00
9 JAp/SD/JOp,BlkLightning	2.00
10 JAp,I:Peoples Heroes	2.00
11 JAp,Imprisoned in death camp	1.75
12 JAp,Imprisoned in death camp	1.75
13 JAp,desert island	1.75
14 JAp,Looker/murder story	1.75
15 DJu,V:Bio-hazard	1.75
16 Halo vs.Firefly	1.75
17 JAp,J:Batman	1.75
18 JAp,BB,V:Eclipso	2.00
19 JAp,V:Windfall	1.75
20 JAp,Masters of Disaster	1.75
21 JAp,V:Kobra,I:Clayface IV	1.75
22 JAp,V:Strike Force Kobra	1.75
23 Return of People's Heroes . . .	1.75
24 TVE,JAp,V:Skull,A:Duke of Oil	1.75
25 JAp,V:Skull	1.75
26 JAp,in Markovia	1.75
27 EL,Millenium	1.75
28 EL,Millenium,final issue	1.75
Ann.#1,KN,V:Skull,A:Batman . . .	2.50
Spec.#1,A:Infinity,Inc	1.75

[2nd Regular Series]

1 Alpha,TC(c),B:MiB(s),PaP,	
I:Technocrat,Faust,Wylde . . .	3.50
1a Omega,TC(c),PaP,V:Vampires	3.50
2 PaP,V:Sanction	2.00
3 PaP,V:Eradicator	2.00
4 PaP,A:Eradicator	2.00
5 PaP,V:Atomic Knight,A:Jihad . .	2.00
6 PaP,V:Jihad	2.00
7 PaP,C:Batman	2.00
8 PaP,V:Batman,I:Halo	2.00
9 PaP,V:Batman	1.75
10 PaP,B:Final Blood, R:Looker .	2.25
11 PaP,Zero Hour,E:Final Blood .	1.95
12 PaP	1.95
13 New base	1.95
14 Martial Arts Spectacular	1.95
15 V:New Year's Evil	1.95
16 R:Windfall	1.95
17 A:Green Lantern	1.95
18 Sins of the Father	1.95
19 Sins of the Father, pt.2	2.25
20 DvA,V:Metamorpho	2.25

PEACEMAKER
January, 1988
1 A:Dr.Tzin-Tzin 1.25
2 . . . . 1.25
3 . . . . 1.25
4 . . . . 1.25

PENGUIN TRIUMPHANT
1 JSon,A:Batman,Wall Street . . . 6.00

Peter Cannon: Thunderbolt #2
© DC Comics, Inc.

PETER CANNON: THUNDERBOLT
1 thru 6 MC . . . . @1.50
7 MC,'Battleground' 1.50
8 MC,Cairo Kidnapped 1.50
9 MC 1.50
10 MC,A:JLA 1.50
11 MC,V:Havoc,A:Checkmate . . . 1.50
12 MC,final Issue 1.25

PETER PANDA
August-September, 1953
1 . . . . 165.00
2 . . . . 95.00
3 thru 9 . . . . @60.00
10 August-September, 1958 . . . 60.00

PETER PORKCHOPS
November-December, 1949
1 . . . . 175.00
2 . . . . 105.00
3 thru 10 . . . . @80.00
11 thru 30 . . . . @40.00
31 thru 61 . . . . @20.00
62 October-December, 1960 . . . 20.00

PHANTOM, THE
October, 1987
1 JO,A:Modern Phantom,13th
  Phantom 2.00
2 JO,Murder Trial in Manhattan . 1.50
3 JO,A:Chessman 1.50

4 JO,V:Chessman,final issue . . . 1.50

PHANTOM, THE
1 LMc,V:Gun Runners 2.50
2 LMc,V:Gun Runners 2.00
3 LMc,V:Drug Smugglers 1.75
4 LMc,In America,A:Diana Palner 1.75
5 LMc,Racial Riots 1.50
6 LMc,in Africa,Toxic Waste
  Problem 1.50
7 LMc,'Gold Rush' 1.50
8 LMc,'Train Surfing' 1.50
9 LMc,'The Slave Trade' 1.50
10 LMc,Famine in Khagana 1.50
11 LMc,Phantom/Diana Wedding
  proposal 1.50
12 LMc,Phantom framed for
  murder 1.50
13 W:Phantom & Diana Palner
  C:Mandrake last issue 1.50

PHANTOM STRANGER
August-September, 1952
1 . . . . 950.00
2 . . . . 600.00
3 . . . . 500.00
4 . . . . 500.00
5 . . . . 500.00
6, June-July, 1953 . . . . 500.00

PHANTOM STRANGER
May-June, 1969
1 CI rep.&new material 60.00
2 CI rep.&new material 25.00
3 CI rep.&new material 23.00
4 NA,I:Tala,1st All-new issue . . 30.00
5 MSy,MA,A:Dr.13 . . . . 18.00
6 MSy,A:Dr.13 . . . . 18.00
7 JAp,V:Tala 18.00
8 JAp,A:Dr.13 . . . . 18.00
9 JAp,A:Dr.13 . . . . 18.00
10 JAp,I:Tannarak 18.00
11 JAp,V:Tannarak 14.00
12 JAp,TD,Dr.13 solo story 14.00
13 JAp,TD,Dr.13 solo 14.00
14 JAp,TD,Dr.13 solo 14.00
15 JAp,ATh(rep),TD,Iron Messiah 9.00
16 JAp,TD,MMes(rep)Dr.13 solo . 9.00
17 JAp,I:Cassandra Craft 9.00
18 TD,Dr.13 solo 9.00
19 JAp,TD,Dr.13 solo 9.00
20 JAp,'And A Child
  Shall Lead Them' 9.00
21 JAp,TD,Dr.13 solo 6.00
22 JAp,TD,I:Dark Circle 6.00
23 JAp,MK,I:Spawn-Frankenstein . 6.00
24 JAp,MA,Spawn Frankenstein . 6.50
25 JAp,MA,Spawn Frankenstein . 6.00
26 JAp,A:Frankenstein 6.00
27 V:Dr. Zorn 6.00
28 BU:Spawn of Frankenstein . . . 6.00
29 V:Dr.Zorn 6.00
30 E:Spawn of Frankenstein 6.00
31 B:BU:Black Orchid 7.00
32 NR,BU:Black Orchid 7.00
33 MGr,A:Deadman 6.50
34 BU:Black Orchid 7.00
35 BU:Black Orchid 7.00
36 BU:Black Orchid 7.00
37 BU:Black Orchid 7.00
38 BU:Black Orchid 7.00
39 A:Deadman 6.00
40 A:Deadman 6.00
41 A:Deadman 6.00

PHANTOM STRANGER
October, 1987
1 MMi,CR,V:Eclipso 3.00
2 MMi,CR,V:Eclipso 2.25
3 MMi,CR,V:Eclipso 2.25
4 MMi,CR,V:Eclipso, Jan. 1988 . . 2.25

PHANTOM ZONE, THE
January, 1982
1 GD/TD,A:Jax-Ur 1.25
2 GC/TD,A:JLA 1.25
3 GC/TD,A:Mon-El 1.25
4 GC/TD 1.25

PICTURE STORIES FROM THE BIBLE
Autumn, 1942–43
1 thru 4 Old Testament . . . @125.00
1 thru 3 New Testament . . . @150.00

PLASTIC MAN
[1st Series]
November-December, 1966
1 GK,I:Dr.Drome(1966 series
  begins) 60.00
2 V:The Spider 20.00
3 V:Whed 20.00
4 V:Dr.Dome 20.00
5 1,001 Plassassins 20.00
6 V:Dr.Dome 20.00
7 O:Plastic Man Jr.,A:Original
  Plastic Man,Woozy Winks . . . 20.00
8 V:The Weasel 10.00
9 V:Joe the Killer Pro 10.00
10 V:Doll Maker(series ends) . . . 10.00
11 (1976 series begins) 6.00
12 I:Carrot-Man 6.00
13 A:Robby Reed 6.00
14 V:Meat By-Product & Sludge . . 6.00
15 I:Snuffer,V:Carrot-Man 6.00
16 V:Kolonel Kool 6.00
17 O:Plastic Man 6.00
18 V:Professor Klean 6.00
19 I&Only App.Marty Meeker . . . 6.00
20 V:Snooping Sneetches
  October-November, 1977 . . . . 6.00

PLASTIC MAN
1 Mini-series,Origin retold 1.25
2 V:The Ooze Brothers 1.25
3 In Los Angeles 1.25
4 End-series,A:Superman 1.25

PLOP!
September-October, 1973
1 SA-AA,GE,ShM 5.00
2 AA,SA 4.00
3 AA,SA 4.00
4 BW,SA 4.00
5 MA,MSy,SA 4.00
6 MSy,SA 4.00
7 SA 3.50
8 SA 3.50
9 SA 3.50
10 SA 3.50
11 ATh,SA 4.00
12 SA 3.50
13 WW(c),SA 5.00
14 WW,SA 5.00
15 WW(c),SA 5.00
16 SD,WW,SA 5.00
17 SA 3.50
18 SD,WW,SA 5.00

19 WW,SA	5.00
20 SA,WW	5.00
21 JO,WW	5.00
22 JO,WW,BW	5.00
23 BW,WW	3.00
24 SA,WW,Nov.-Dec., 1976	2.00

POWER GIRL
[Mini-Series]

1	1.00
2 A:The Weaver, mongo Krebs	1.00
3 V:The Weaver	1.00
4 V:Weaver, final issue	1.00

POWER OF SHAZAM!

1 R:Captain Marvel	2.00
2 V:Arson Fiend	1.50
3 V:Ibac	1.50
4 JOy,R:Mary Marvel,Tawky, Tawny	1.75
5 JOy(c&a),F:Mary Marvel, V:Black Adam	1.75
HC JOy(a&s),O:Captain Marvel	22.00
GNv JOy(a&s),O:Captain Marvel	9.95

POWER OF THE ATOM

1 1st Issue, Origin retold	1.25
2 Return of Powers	1.25
3 I:Strobe	1.25
4 A:Hawkman+bonus book #8	1.25
5 DT,A:Elongated Man	1.25
6 JBy,V:Chronos	1.25
7 GN,Invasion,V:Khunds,Chronos	1.25
8 GN,Invasion,V:Chronos	1.25
9 GN,A:Justice League	1.25
10 GN,I:Humbug	1.25
11 GN,V:Paul Hoben	1.25
12 GN,V:Edg the Destroyer	1.25
13 GN,Blood Stream Journey	1.25
14 GN,V:Humbug	1.25
15 GN,V:Humbug	1.25
16 GN,V:The CIA	1.25
17 GN,V:The Sting	1.25
18 GN,V:The CIA, last issue	1.25

PREACHER
Vertigo

1 I:Jesse Custer, Genesis	3.50
2 Saint of Killers	2.50
3 GF(c),I:Angels	2.50
4 GF(c),V:Saint of Killers	2.50

PREZ
August-September, 1973

1 I:Prez (from Sandman #54)	15.00
2 thru 4 F:Prez	11.00

PRIMAL FORCE

O New Team	1.95
1 Claw	1.95
2 Cataclysm	1.95
3	1.95
4 Claw	1.95
5 V:Demons	1.95
6 V:The Four Beasts	1.95
7 Trip to the Past	1.95
8 N.Choles(p),I:New Team	2.25
9 Maltis worsens, Tornado speaks	2.25

PRINCE
Piranha Press

1 DCw,KW,based on rock star	10.00
1a Second printing	2.50

1b 3rd printing	2.00

PRISONER, THE

1 Based on TV series	5.00
2 'By Hook or by Crook'	5.00
3 'Confrontation'	5.00
4 'Departure' final issue	5.00

PSYBA-RATS, THE
[Mini-Series]

1 CDi,A:Robin	2.50
2 CDi,A:Robin	1.50
3 CDi,F:Razorsharp,final issue	1.50

PSYCHO

1 I:Psycho	5.25
2 Sonya Rescue	4.95
3 'Psycho against the World'	4.95

QUESTION, THE
February, 1987

1 DCw,R:Question,I:Myra,A:Shiva	3.50
2 DCw,A:Batman,Shiva	2.00
3 DCw,I:Mayor Firman	2.00
4 DCw,V:Hatch	2.00
5 DCw,Hub City fall Apart	2.00
6 DCw,Abuse story	2.00
7 DCw,V:Mr.Volk	2.00
8 DCw,I:Mikado	2.00
9 DCw,O:Rodor	2.00
10 DCw,O:Rodor cont.	2.00
11 DCw,Transformation	2.00
12 DCw,Poisoned Ground	2.00
13 DCw,V:The Spartans	2.00
14 DCw,V:The Spartans	2.00
15 DCw,The Klan in Hub City	2.00
16 DCw,'Butch Cassidy & Sundance Kid'	2.00
17 DCw,A:Green Arrow	2.50
18 DCw,A:Green Arrow	2.50
19 DCw,V:Terrorists	2.00
20 DCw,Travelling Circus	2.00
21 DCw,V:Junior Musto	2.00
22 DCw,Election Night	2.00
23 DCw,Election Night contd	2.00
24 DCw,Election Night contd	2.00
25 DCw,Myra Critically Ill	2.00
26 A:Riddler	2.00
27 DCw	2.00
28 DCw,A:Lady Shiva	2.00
29 DCw,V:Lady Shiva	2.00
30 DCw,A:Lady Shiva	2.00
31 DCw,Hub City Chaos contd	2.00
32 DCw,Identity Crisis	2.00
33 DCw,Identity Crisis contd	2.00
34 DCw,Identity Crisis contd	2.00
35 DCw,Fate of Hub City	2.00
36 DCw,final issue (contd.G.A.Ann#3 Question Quarterly #1)	2.00
Ann.#1 DCw,A:Batman,G.A.	3.00
Ann.#2 A:Green Arrow	4.00

QUESTION QUARTERLY

1 DCw	4.50
2 DCw	3.95
3 DCw(c) Film	2.95
4 DCw,MM,'Waiting for Phil'	2.95
5 DCw,MMi,MM,last issue	2.95

RAGMAN
[1st Limited Series]

1 I&O:Ragman	5.00
2 I:Opal	3.50

3 V:Mr. Big	3.00
4 JKu(1st interior on character)	3.00
5 JKu,O:Ragman,final issue	3.00

[2nd Limited Series]

1 PB,O:Ragman	3.50
2 PB,O:Ragman Powers	3.00
3 PB,Original Ragman	2.75
4 PB,Gang War	2.75
5 PB,V:Golem	2.75
6 PB,V:Golem,A:Batman	2.75
7 PB,V:Golem,A:Batman	2.75
8 PB,V:Golem,A:Batman	2.75

RAGMAN: CRY OF THE DEAD

1 JKu(c),R:Ragman	2.00
2 JKu(c),A:Marinette	2.00
3 JKu(c),V:Marinette	2.00
4 JKu(c),Exorcism	2.00
5 JKu(c),V:Marinette	2.00
6 JKu(c),final issue	2.00

THE RAY
[Limited Series]

1 JQ,ANi,I&O:Ray(Ray Torril)	14.00
2 JQ,ANi,I:G.A. Ray	10.00
3 JQ,ANi,A:G.A. Ray	8.00
4 JQ,ANi,V:Dr.Polaris	8.00
5 JQ,ANi,V:Dr.Polaris	6.00
6 JQ,ANi,C:Lobo,final issue	6.00
TPB In A Blaze of Power	9.95

[Regular Series]

1 JQ(c),RPr,V:Brinestone, A:Superboy	3.50
1a Newsstand Ed.	1.75
2 RPr,V:Brinestone,A:Superboy	1.75
3 RPr,I:Death Masque	1.75
4 JQ(c),RPr,I:Death Masque, Dr. Polaris	2.00
5 JQ(c),RPr,V:G.A.Ray	1.95
6 JQ(c),RPr,V:Black Canary	1.95
7 JQ(c),RPr,V:Canary/Ray	1.95
8 V:Lobo,Black Canary	1.95
9 Ray Undoes the past	1.95
10 F:Happy Terril	1.95
11 30 years in future	1.95
12 V:Mystech	1.95
13 V:Death Masque	2.25
14 The Ray needs help, V:Death Masque	2.25
Ann.#1 Year One Annual	3.95

REAL FACT COMICS
March-April, 1946

1 S&K,Harry Houdini story	350.00
2 S&K, Rin-Tin-Tin story	250.00
3 H.G. Wells story	175.00
4 Jimmy Stewart story,B:Just Imagine	250.00
5 Batman & Robin(c)	1,100.00
6 O:Tommy Tomorrow	750.00
7 'The Flying White House'	100.00
8 VF,A:Tommy Tomorrow	400.00
9 S&K,Glen Miller story	175.00
10 'The Vigilante' by MMe	175.00
11 EK,'How the G-Men Capture Public Enemies!'	125.00
12 'How G-Men are Trained'	125.00
13 Dale Evans story	300.00
14 Will Rogers story,'Diary of Death'	90.00
15 A:The Master Magician- Thurston	95.00

16 A:Four Reno Brothers,
  T.Tommorrow 300.00
17'I Guard an Armored Car' 90.00
18 'The Mystery Man of
  Tombstone' 90.00
19 'The Weapon that Won the
  West' 90.00
20 JKu 100.00
21 JKu,July-August, 1949 . . . . 100.00

REAL SCREEN COMICS
Spring, 1945
1 B:Fox & the Crow,Flippity
  & Flop 650.00
2 (fa) 350.00
3 (fa) 175.00
4 thru 7 (fa) . . . . @140.00
8 thru 11 (fa) . . . . @100.00
12 thru 20 (fa) . . . . @80.00
21 thru 30 (fa) . . . . @60.00
31 thru 40 (fa) . . . . @40.00
41 thru 128 (fa) . . . . @30.00
Becomes:
TV SCREEN CARTOONS
129 thru 137 . . . . @40.00
138 January-February, 1961 . . 40.00

R.E.B.E.L.S '94
0 New team 1.95
1 L.E.G.I.O.N.,Green Lantern . . . 1.95
2 Dissent 1.95
3 . . . . 1.95
4 Ship goes Insane 1.95
R.E.B.E.L.S '95
5 F:Dox 1.95
6 Dox Defeated 1.95
7 John Sin 1.95
8 V:Galactic Bank 2.25
9 F:Dox,Ignea,Garv,Strata 2.25

RED TORNADO
1 Cl/FMc 1.25
2 Cl/FMc,A:Superman 1.25
3 Cl/FMc 1.25
4 Cl/FMc 1.25

RESTAURANT AT THE END OF THE UNIVERSE
1 Adapt. 2nd book in Hitchhikers'
  Guide to the Galaxy,
  I:The Restaurant 5.95
2 V:The Meal 6.95
3 Final issue 6.95

RICHARD DRAGON, KUNG FU FIGHTER
April-May, 1975
1 O:Richard Dragon 1.50
2 JSn/AM 1.50
3 JK 1.25
4 RE/WW 1.25
5 RE/WW 1.25
6 RE/WW 1.25
7 RE/WW 1.25
8 RE/WW 1.25
9 RE 1.25
10 RE 1.25
11 RE 1.25
12 RE 1.25
13 thru 17 RE . . . . @1.25
18 November-December, 1977 . . 1.25

RIMA, THE JUNGLE GIRL
April-May, 1974
1 NR,I:Rima,O:Pt. 1 . . . . 2.00
2 NR,O:Pt.2 . . . . 1.50
3 NR,O:Pt.3 . . . . 1.25
4 NR,O:Pt.4 . . . . 1.25
5 NR 1.25
6 NR 1.25
7 April-May, 1975 . . . . 1.25

RING, THE
1 GK,Opera Adaption 12.00
2 GK,Sigfried's Father's Sword . . 7.00
3 GK,to save Brunhilde 6.00
4 GK, final issue 6.00
TPB rep.#1 thru #4 . . . . 19.95

RIP HUNTER, TIME MASTER
March-April, 1961
1 . . . . 350.00
2 . . . . 150.00
3 thru 5 . . . . @70.00
6 and 7 Ath . . . . @70.00
8 thru 15 . . . . @45.00
16 thru 20 . . . . @45.00
21 thru 28 . . . . @45.00
29 November-December, 1965 . 45.00

ROBIN
[1st Limited Series]
1 TL,BB(c),Trial,pt.1(&Poster) . . . 5.00
1a 2nd printing 2.50
1b 3rd printing 1.50
2 TL,BB(c) Trial,pt.2 . . . . 3.00
2a 2nd printing 1.50
3 TL,BB(c) Trial,pt.3 . . . . 2.00
4 TL,Trial,pt.4 . . . . 2.00
5 TL,Final issue,A:Batman 2.00
TPB BB(c),rep.#1–#5,Batman
  #455–#457 . . . . 7.95
[2nd Limited Series]
1 Direct,Hologram(c)Joker face . . 2.00
1a (c)Joker straightjacket 2.00
1b (c)Joker standing 2.00
1c (c)Batman 2.00
1d Newsstand(no hologram) . . . 1.00
1e collectors set,extra holo. . . . 12.00
2 Direct,Hologram(c) Robin/Joker
  Knife 1.50
2a (c)Joker/Robin-Dartboard 1.50
2b (c)Robin/Joker-Hammer 1.50
2c Newsstand(no hologram) 1.00
2d collectors set,extra holo. 8.00
3 Direct,Holo(c)Robin standing . . 1.50
3a (c)Robin swinging 1.50
3b Newsstand(no hologram) 1.50
3c collectors set,extra holo. 6.00
4 Direct,Hologram 1.50
4a Newsstand (no hologram) . . . 1.25
4b collectors set,extra holo. 1.50
Collectors set (#1 thru #4) 30.00
[3rd Limited Series]
1 TL,A:Huntress,Collector's Ed.
  movable(c),poster 3.00
1a MZ(c),Newsstand Ed. 1.50
2 TL,V:KGBeast,A:Huntress 2.75
2a MZ(c),Newsstand Ed 1.50
3 TL,V:KGBeast,A:Huntress 2.75
3a MZ(c),newsstand Ed. 1.50
4 TL,V:KGBeast,A:Huntress 2.75
4a MZ(c),newsstand Ed. 1.50

5 TL,V:KGBeast,A:Huntress 2.75
5a MZ(c),newsstand Ed. 1.50
6 TL,V:KGBeast,King Snake,
  A:Huntress. 2.75
6a MZ(c),Newsstand Ed. 1.50

Robin (Regular Series) #1
© DC Comics, Inc.

[Regular Series]
1 B:CDi(s),TG,SHa,V:Speedboyz   4.00
1a Newstand Ed. 2.00
2 TG,V:Speedboyz 2.00
3 TG,V:Cluemaster,
  Electrocutioner 1.75
4 TG,V:Cluemaster,Czonk,
  Electrocutioner 1.75
5 TG,V:Cluemaster,Czonk,
  Electrocutioner 1.75
6 TG,A:Huntress 1.75
7 TG,R:Robin's Father 1.75
8 TG,KnightsEnd#5,A:Shiva 3.00
9 TG,Knights End:Aftermath 2.25
10 TG,Zero Hour,V:Weasel 1.50
11 New Batman 1.50
12 Robin vs. thugs 1.50
13 V:Steeljacket 1.50
14 CDi(s),TG,Return of Bruce
  Wayne,Troika,pt.4 . . . . 1.75
14a Collector's edition 2.50
15 Cluemaster Mystery 1.50
16 F:Spoiler 1.50
17 I:Silver Monkey,V:King Snake,Lynx
  [New Miraweb format begins] . 1.95
18 Gotham City sabotaged 1.95
TPB A Hero Reborn,JAp,TL 4.95
TPB Tragedy and Triumph,
  TL,NBy 9.95
Ann.#1 TL,Eclipso tie-in,V:Anarky   3.00
Ann.#2 KD,JL,Bloodlines#10,
  I:Razorsharp 2.75
Ann.#3 Elseworlds Story 3.25
Ann.#4 Year One Annual 2.95

ROBIN 3000
1 CR,Elseworlds,V:Skulpt 5.25
2 CR,Elseworlds,V:Skulpt 5.25

All comics prices listed are for *Near Mint* condition.

ROBIN HOOD TALES
Jan.-Feb., 1957–Mar.-Apr., 1958
7 . . . . 120.00
8 thru 14 . . . . @120.00

ROBOTECH DEFENDERS
1 MA,mini-series 3.50
2 MA 3.00

ROGAN GOSH
Vertigo
1 PF PrM(s) (From Revolver) . . . 7.25

RONIN
July, 1983
1 FM,1:Billy 7.00
2 FM,I:Casey 5.00
3 FM,V:Agat 5.00
4 FM,V:Agat 5.00
5 FM,V:Agat 6.00
6 FM,D:Billy 8.00
Paperback, FM inc. Gatefold . . 12.00

Roots of the Swamp Thing #2
© DC Comics, Inc.

ROOTS OF THE SWAMP THING
July, 1986
1 BWr,rep.SwampThing#1&#2 . . 3.00
2 BWr,rep.SwampThing#3&#4 . . 3.00
3 BWr,rep.SwampThing#5&#6 . . 3.00
4 BWr,rep.SwampThing#7&#8 . . 3.00
5 BWr,rep.SwampThing#9&#10,
  H.O.S. #92, final issue 3.00

RUDOLPH THE RED -NOSED REINDEER
December, 1950
1950 . . . . 50.00
1951 thru 1954 . . . . @35.00
1955 thru 1962 Winter . . . . . @20.00

SAGA OF RAS AL GHUL
1 NA,DG,reprints 5.00

2 rep. 4.00
3 rep.Batman #242&#243 . . . . . . 4.00
4 rep.Batman #244&#245,
  Detective #410 . . . . 4.00
TPB reps. 17.95

SAGA OF THE SWAMP THING
May, 1982
1 JmP(s),TY,DSp,O:Swamp Thing,
  BU:PhantomStranger 4.00
2 Ph(c),TY,DSp,I:Grasp 2.00
3 TY,DSp,V:Vampires 2.00
4 TY,TD,V:Demon 2.00
5 TY 2.00
6 TY,I:General Sunderland 2.00
7 TY 2.00
8 TY 2.00
9 TY 2.00
10 TY 2.00
11 TY,I:Golem 2.00
12 LWn(s),TY 2.00
13 TY,D:Grasp 2.00
14 A:Phantom Stranger 2.00
15 . . . . 2.00
16 SBi,JTo 2.00
17 I:Matthew Cable 4.00
18 JmP(s),LWn(s),SBi,JTo,BWr,
  R:Arcane 2.00
19 JmP(s),SBi,JTo,V:Arcane 2.00
20 B:AMo(s),Day,JTo(i),D:Arcane
  (Original incarnation) 22.00
21 SBi,JTo,O:Swamp Thing,I:Floronic
  Man,D:General Sunderland . . 18.00
22 SBi,JTo,O:Floronic Man 12.00
23 SBi,JTo,V:Floronic Man 12.00
24 SBi,JTo,V:Floronic Man,A:JLA,
  In Arkham 12.00
25 SBi,A:Jason Blood,I:Kamara . 10.00
26 SBi,A:Demon,
  D:Matthew Cable 10.00
27 SBi,D:Kamara,A:Demon 8.00
28 SwM,Burial of Alec Holland . . . 8.00
29 SBi,JTo,R:Arcane 8.00
30 SBi,AA,D:Abby,C:Joker,
  V:Arcane 10.00
31 RV,JTo,D:Arcane 7.00
32 SwM,Tribute to WK Pogo strip . 7.00
33 rep.H.O.S.#92,A:Cain & Abel . 7.00
34 SBi,JTo,Swamp Thing & Abby
  Fall in Love 11.00
35 SBi,JTo,Nukeface,pt.1 . . . . . . 5.00
36 SBi,JTo,Nukeface,pt.2 . . . . . . 5.00
37 RV,JTo,I:John Constantine,
  American Gothic,pt.1 . . . . . . 20.00
38 SnW,JTo,V:Water-Vampires
  (Pt.1) A:J.Constantine 10.00
39 SBi,JTo,V:Water-Vampires
  (Pt.2) A:J.Constantine 7.00
40 SBi,JTo,C:J.Constantine,
  The Curse 5.00
41 SBi,AA,Voodoo Zombies #1 . . 3.00
42 SBi,JTo,RoR,
  Voodoo Zombies #2 . . . . 3.00
43 SnW,RoR,Windfall,
  I:Chester Williams 3.00
44 SBi,JTo,RoR,V:Serial Killer,
  C:Batman,Constantine,Mento . 5.00
45 SnW,AA,Ghost Dance 3.00
Ann.#1 MT,TD,Movie Adaption . . 2.00
Ann.#2 AMo(s),E:Arcane,A:Deadman,
  Phantom Stranger,Spectre,
  Demon,Resurrection of Abby . . 7.00
Ann.#3 AMo(s),Ape issue 4.00
TPB rep.#21-#27 . . . . 12.95

TPB rep.#28-#34,Ann.#2 . . . . . 14.95
Becomes:
SWAMP THING
46 B:AMo(s) cont'd,SBi,JTo,Crisis,
  A:John Constantine,Phantom
  Stranger 3.00
47 SBi,Parliment of Trees,Full
  origin,A:Constantine 3.00
48 SBi,JTo,V:Brujeria,
  A:Constantine. 3.00
49 SBi,AA,A:Constantine,Demon,Ph.
  Stranger,Spectre,Deadman . . . 3.00
50 SBi,RV,JTo,concl.American
  Gothic,D:Zatara&Sargon,
  Double Size 6.00
51 RV,AA,L:Constantine 3.00
52 RV,AA,Arkham Asylum,A:Flor.
  Man,Lex Luthor,C:Joker,
  2-Face,Batman 4.00
53 JTo,V:Batman,Swamp Thing
  Banished to Space 4.00
54 JTo script,RV,AA,C:Batman . . 3.00
55 RV,AA,JTo,A:Batman,. 3.00
56 RV,AA,My Blue Heaven 3.00
57 RV,AA,A:Adam Strange 3.00
58 RV,AA,A:Adam Strange,GC,
  Spectre preview 3.00
59 JTo,RV,AA,D:Patchwork Man . 3.00
Direct Sales Only
60 JTo,Loving the Alien 3.00
61 RV,AA,All Flesh is Grass
  G.L.Corps X-over 3.00
62 RV(&script),AA,Wavelength,
  A:Metron,Darkseid 3.00
63 RV,AA,Loose Ends(reprise) . . 3.00
64 E:AMo(s),SBi,TY,RV,AA,
  Return of the Good Gumbo . . . 3.00
65 RV,JTo,A:Constantine 3.50
66 RV,Elemental Energy 2.50
67 RV,V:Solomon Grundy,
  Hellblazer preview 5.00
68 RV,O:Swamp Thing 2.50
69 RV,O:Swamp Thing 2.50
70 RV,AA,Quest for SwampThing . 2.50
71 RV,AA,Fear of Flying 2.50
72 RV,AA,Creation 2.50
73 RV,AA,A:John Constantine . . . 3.00
74 RV,AA,Abbys Secret 2.50
75 RV,AA,Plant Elementals 2.50
76 RV,AA,A:John Constantine . . . 3.00
77 TMd,AA,A:John Constantine . . 3.00
78 TMd,AA,Phantom Pregnancy . 2.50
79 RV,AA,A:Superman,Luthor . . . 2.50
80 RV,AA,V:Aliends 2.50
81 RV,AA,Invasion x-over 2.50
82 RV,AA,A:Sgt.Rock & Easy Co. . 2.50
83 RV,AA,A:Enemy Ace 2.50
84 RV,AA,A:Sandman 10.00
85 RV,TY,Time Travel contd. 2.50
86 RV,TY,A:Tomahawk 2.50
87 RV,TY,Camelot,A:Demon 2.50
88 RV,TY,A:Demon,Golden
  Gladiator 2.50
89 MM,AA,The Dinosaur Age . . . 2.50
90 BP,AA,Birth of Abbys Child
  (Tefe) 2.75
91 PB,AA,Abbys Child (New
  Elemental) 2.50
92 PB,AA,Ghosts of the Bayou . . 2.50
93 PB,AA,New Power 2.50
94 PB,AA,Ax-Murderer 2.50
95 PB,AA,Toxic Waste Dumpers . 2.50
96 PB,AA,Tefes Powers 2.50
97 PB,AA,Tefe,V:Nergal,
  A:Arcane 2.50

98 PB,AA,Tefe,in Hell 2.50
99 PB,AA,Tefe,A:Mantago,
John Constantine 3.00
100 PB,AA,V:Angels of Eden,
(48 pages) 3.50
101 AA,A:Tefe 2.50
102 V:Mantagos Zombies,inc. prev.
of Worlds Without End 2.50
103 Green vs. Grey 2.50
104 Quest for Elementals,pt.1 .. 2.50
105 Quest for Elementals,pt.2 .. 2.50
106 Quest for Elementals,pt.3 .. 2.50
107 Quest for Elementals,pt.4 .. 2.50
108 Quest for Elementals,pt.5 .. 2.50
109 Quest for Elementals,pt.6 .. 2.50
110 TMd,A:Father Tocsin 2.50
111 V:Ghostly Zydeco Musician .. 2.50
112 TMd,B:Swamp Thing
for Governor 2.50
113 E:Swamp Thing for Governor 2.50
114 TMd,Hellblazer 2.75
115 TMd,A:Hellblazer,V:Dark
Conrad 2.75
116 From Body of Swamp Thing . 2.25
117 JD,The Lord of Misrule,
Mardi Gras 2.25
118 A Childs Garden,A:Matthew
the Raven 2.25
119 A:Les Perdu 2.25
120 F:Lady Jane 2.25
121 V:Sunderland Corporation ... 2.25
122 I:The Needleman 2.25
123 V:The Needleman 2.25
124 In Central America 2.25
125 V:Anton Arcane,20th Anniv. . 3.75
126 Mescalito 2.25
127 Project Proteus #1 .... 2.25
128 Project proteus #2 .... 2.25

Vertigo
129 CV(c),B:NyC(s),SEa,KDM(i),
Sw.Thing's Deterioration .. 2.25
130 CV(c),SEa,KDM(i),A:John
Constantine,V:Doctor Polygon . 2.25
131 CV(c),SEa,KDM(i),I:Swamp
Thing's,Doppleganger,
F:The Folk 2.25
132 CV(c),SEa,KDM(i),
V:Doppleganger 2.25
133 CV(c),SEa,KDM(i),R:General
Sunderland,V:Thunder Petal .. 2.25
134 CV(c),SEa,KDM(i),Abby Leaves,
C:John Constantine 2.25
135 CV(c),SEa,KDM(i),A:J.Constantine,
Swamp Thing Lady Jane meld 2.25
136 CV(c),RsB,KDM(i),A:Lady Jane,
Dr.Polygon,John Constantine . 2.25
137 CV(c),E:NyC(s),RsB,KDM(i),
IR:Sunderland is Anton Arcane,
A:J.Constantine 2.25
138 CV(c),DiF(s),RGu,KDM,B:Mind
Fields 2.25
139 CV(c),DiF(s),RGu,KDM,A:Black
Orchid,cont'd fr.Black Orchid #5 ..... 2.25
140 B:Bad Gumbo 2.50
140a Platinum Ed. 30.00
141 A:Abigail Arcane 2.25
142 Bad Gumbo#3 .... 2.25
143 E:Bad Gumbo 2.25
144 In New York City 2.25
145 In Amsterdam 2.25
146 V:Nelson Strong 2.25
147 Hunter 1.95
148 Sargon 1.95
149 Sargon 1.95

150 V:Sargon 1.95
151 .... 1.95
152 River Run,pt.1 .... 1.95
153 River Run 1.95
154 River Run 2.25
155 River Run 2.25
156 PJ,River Run 2.25
Ann.#4 PB/AA,A:Batman 2.75
Ann.#5 A:BrotherPower Geek ... 3.25
Ann.#6 Houma 3.50
Ann.#7 CV(c),NyC(s),MBu(i),Childrens
Crusade,F:Tefe,A:Maxine,BU:
Beautyand the Beast 4.25

SANDMAN
[1st Regular Series]
1 JK,I&O:Sandman,I:General
Electric 9.00
2 V:Dr.Spider 5.00
3 Brain that Blanked
out the Bronx 5.00
4 JK,Panic in the Dream Stream . 5.00
5 JK,Invasion of the Frog Men .. 5.00
6 JK,WW,V:Dr.Spider 6.00

[2nd Regular Series]
1 B:NGa(s),SK,I:2nd Sandman . 70.00
2 SK,A:Cain,Abel 40.00
3 SK,A:John Constantine 35.00
4 SK,A:Demon 30.00
5 SK,A:Mr.Miracle,J'onnJ'onzz . 25.00
6 V:Doctor Destiny 20.00
7 V:Doctor Destiny 17.00
8 Sound of her wings,F:Death . 55.00
8a Guest Ed.Pin Up Covr 200.00
9 Tales in the Sand,Doll's House
prologue 15.00
10 B:Doll's House,A:Desire
& Despair,I:Brut & Glob 14.00
11 MovingIn,A:2ndS-man 14.00
12 Play House,D;2ndS'man 14.00
13 Men of Good Fortune,A:Death,
Lady Constantine 14.00
14 Collectors,D:Corinthian 15.00
15 Into' Night,DreamVortex 13.00
16 E:Doll's House,Lost Hearts .. 13.00
17 Calliope 11.00
18 Dream of a 1000 Cats 11.00
19 Midsummer Nights Dream .. 10.00
19a error copy 55.00
20 Strange Death Element Girl,
A:Death 10.00
21 Family Reunion,B:Season
of Mists 12.00
22 Season of Mists,I:Daniel Hall 15.00
23 Season of Mists 10.00
24 Season of Mists 10.00
25 Season of Mists 10.00
26 Season of Mists 9.00
27 E:Season of Mists 9.00
28 Ownership of Hell 9.00
29 A:Lady J.Constantine 7.00
30 Ancient Rome;A:Death,Desire . 8.00
31 Ancient Rome,pt.2 .... 7.00
32 B:The Game of You 8.00
33 The Game of You 7.00
34 The Game of You 6.00
35 The Game of You 6.00
36 The Game of You,48pgs 7.00
37 The Game of You,Epilogue ... 6.00
38 Convergence 5.00
39 Convergence,A:Marco Polo ... 5.00
40 Convergence,A:Cain,Abel,Eve,
Matthew the Raven 5.00
41 JIT,VcL,(i),B:Brief Lives,
F:Endless 6.00

Sandman (1st Regular Series) #1
© DC Comics, Inc.

42 JIT,VcL,(i),F:Delirium,Dream .. 5.00
43 JIT,VcL,(i),A:Death,Etain 5.00
44 JIT,VcL,(i),R:Corinthian,
Destruction 4.50
45 JIT,VcL,(i),F:Tiffany,
Ishtar(Belli) 4.50
46 JIT,VcL,(i),F:Morpheus/Bast,A:AIDS
insert story,F:Death 4.50

Vertigo
47 JIT,VcL,(i),A:Endless 3.50
48 JIT,VcL,(i),L:Destruction 3.50
49 JIT,VcL,(i),E:Brief Lives,
F:Orpheus 3.50
50 DMc(c),CR,Tales of Baghdad,
pin-upsby TM,DMc,MK 4.00
50a Gold Ed. 70.00
51 BT,MBu(i),B:Inn at the end of the
World,Gaheris' tale 3.00
52 BT,MBu(i),JWk,Cluracan's
Story 3.00
53 BT,DG,MBu(i),MZi,Hob's
Leviathan 3.00
54 BT,MiA,MBu(i),R:Prez 3.00
55 SAp,VcL,BT,MBu(i),F:Klaproth,
Cerements's Story 3.00
56 BT,MBu(i),DG,SLi(i),GyA,TyH(i),
E:Inn at the end of the World,
C:Endless 3.00
57 MaH,B:Kindly Ones,Inc.American
Freak Preview 2.50
58 MaH,Kindly Ones,pt.2,
A:Lucifer 2.50
59 MaH,Kindly Ones,pt.3,R:Fury . 2.50
60 MaH,Kindly Ones,pt.4 ...... 2.50
61 MaH,Kindly Ones,pt.5 ...... 2.25
62 Kindly Ones,pt.6,Murder 2.25
63 MaH,Kindly Ones,pt.7,
A:Rose Walker 2.25
64 Kindly Ones,pt.8 .... 2.25
65 MaH,Kindly Ones,pt.9,Dream
Kingdom 2.25
66 MaH,Kindly Ones,pt.10 ...... 2.25
67 MaH,Kindly Ones,pt.11 ...... 2.25
68 MaH,Kindly Ones,pt.12 ...... 2.25
69 MaH,Kindly Ones finale 2.25

All comics prices listed are for *Near Mint* condition.

TPB Dream Country,Rep.#17-#20 15.00
TPB The Dolls House,Rep.#8-#16 15.00
Fables and Reflections,HC,rep. . 29.95
TPB Preludes & Nocturnes,
  Rep.#1-#8 . . . . 15.00
Season of Mists,HC,rep.#21-#28 40.00
Season of Mists,SC 19.95
Spec.BT,Glow in the Dark(c),The
  Legend of Orpheus,
  (inc. Portrait Gallery) 6.00
HC A Game of You,rep.#32-#37 32.00
HC Brief Lives 29.95
TPB Brief Lives 19.95
TPB Sandman:A Game of You . 19.95
TPB Fables & Reflections 19.95
TPB World's End DMc(c) 19.95

SANDMAN MYSTERY THEATRE
Vertigo
1 B:MWg(s),GyD,R:G.A.Sandman,
  B:Tarantula,I:Mr.Belmont,
  Dian Belmont 3.50
2 GyD,V:Tarantula 3.00
3 GyD,V:Tarantula 2.50
4 GyD,E:Tarantula 2.50
5 JWk,B:The Face 2.25
6 JWk,The Face #2 . . . . 2.25
7 JWk,The Face #3 . . . . 2.25
8 JWk,E:The Face 2.25
9 RGT,B:The Brute,I:Rocket
  Ramsey 2.25
10 RGT,The Brute#2 . . . . 2.25
11 RGT,The Brute#3 . . . . 2.25
12 RGT,E:The Brute 2.25
13 GyD,B:The Vamp 2.25
14 GyD,The Vamp#2 . . . . 2.25
15 GyD,The Vamp#3 . . . . 2.25
16 GyD,E:The Vamp 2.25
17 GyD,B:The Scorpion 2.25
18 GyD,The Scorpion,pt.2 . . . . . 2.25
19 GyD,The Scorpion,pt.3 . . . . . 2.25
20 GyD,The Scorpion,pt.4 . . . . . 2.25
21 Dr. Death 2.25
22 Dr. Death,pt.2 . . . . 2.25
23 Dr. Death,pt.3 . . . . 2.25
24 Dr. Death,pt.4 . . . . 2.25
25 The Butcher,pt.1 . . . . 2.25
26 The Butcher,pt.2 . . . . 2.25
27 The Butcher,pt.3 . . . . 2.25
28 The Butcher,pt.4 . . . . 2.25
Ann.#1 . . . . 3.95
TPB The Tarantula 14.95

SCARAB
Vertigo
1 GF(c),B:JnS(s),SEa,MkB(i),
  R&O:Scarab,V:Halaku-umid . . 2.25
2 GF(c),SEa,MkB(i),A:Phantom
  Stranger 2.25
3 GF(c),SEa,MkB(i),in North
  Carolina 2.25
4 GF(c),SEa,MkB(i),V:Rathoroch . 2.25
5 GF(c),SEa,MkB(i) 2.25
6 GF(c),SEa,MkB(i),V:Gloryboys . 2.25
7 GF(c),SEa,MkB(i),V:Scientists . 2.25
8 GF(c),SEa,MkB(i),Final Issue . . 2.25

SCARLETT
1 I:Scarlett,Blood o/t Innocent . . . 2.00
2 Blood of the Innocent cont. . . . 1.75
3 Blood of the Innocent cont. . . . 1.75
4 V:The Nomads 1.75
5 GM,O:Nomads 1.75

Scarlett #14 © DC Comics, Inc.

6 thru 8 GM,Blood of the Damned 1.75
9 GM,V:Undead 1.75
10 B:Blood of the City 1.75
11 I:Afterburn 1.75
12 V:Sligoth 1.75
13 V:Gearsman 1.75
14 final issue 1.75

SCRIBBLY
August-September, 1948
1 SM 600.00
2 . . . . 400.00
3 . . . . 300.00
4 . . . . 300.00
5 . . . . 300.00
6 thru 10 . . . . @250.00
11 thru 15, Dec-Jan.1951–52 @200.00

SEA DEVILS
September-October, 1961
1 RH 375.00
2 RH 175.00
3 RH 125.00
4 RH 125.00
5 RH 125.00
6 thru 10 RH . . . . @65.00
11 . . . . 45.00
12 . . . . 45.00
13 JKu,GC,RA 45.00
14 thru 20 . . . . @45.00
21 I:Capt X,Man Fish 30.00
22 thru 35, May-June, 1967 . . @30.00

SEBASTIAN O
Vertigo
1 GMo(s),SY,I:Sebastian O,A:Lord
  Lavender,Roaring Boys 2.50
2 GMo(s),SY,V:Roaring Boys,
  Assassins,A:Abbe 2.50
3 GMo(s),SY,D:Lord Lavender . . 2.50

SECRET HEARTS
September-October, 1949
1 'Make Believe Sweetheart' . . 250.00
2 ATh,'Love Is Not A Dream' . 125.00
3 'Sing Me A Love Song' 110.00
4 ATh 110.00
5 ATh 110.00

6 . . . . 110.00
7 . . . . 110.00
8 . . . . 75.00
9 . . . . 75.00
10 thru 20 . . . . @70.00
21 thru 26 . . . . @50.00
27 B:Comics Code 35.00
28 thru 30 . . . . @35.00
31 thru 70 . . . . @25.00
71 thru 110 . . . . @20.00
111 thru 120 . . . . @15.00
121 thru 150 . . . . @5.00
151 thru 153, July 1971 . . . . . . @3.00

SECRET ORIGINS
February-March, 1973
1 O:Superman,Batman,Ghost,
  Flash 8.00
2 O:Green Lantern,Atom,
  Supergirl 5.00
3 O:Wonder Woman,Wildcat 4.00
4 O:Vigilante by MMe 4.00
5 O:The Spectre 3.00
6 O:Blackhawk,Legion of Super
  Heroes 3.00
7 O:Robin, Aquaman,October-
  November, 1974 . . . . 3.00

SECRET ORIGINS
April, 1986
1 JOy,WB,F:Superman 4.00
2 GK,F:Blue Beetle 3.50
3 JBi,F:Captain Marvel 3.00
4 GT,F:Firestorm 2.75
5 GC,F:Crimson Aventer 3.00
6 DG,MR,F:Batman 5.00
7 F:Sandman, Guy Gardner 3.50
8 MA,F:Shadow Lass,Dollman . . 2.50
9 GT,F:Skyman,Flash 2.50
10 JL,JO,JA,F:Phantom Stranger . 2.25
11 LMc,TD,F:Hawkman,Powergirl 2.00
12 F:Challengers of the Unknown
  I:G.A. Fury 2.00
13 EL,F:Nightwing 3.00
14 F:Suicide Squad 2.25
15 KMo,DG,F:Deadman,Spectre . 2.25
16 AKu,F:Hourman,Warlord 2.00
17 KGi,F:Green Lantern 2.25
18 . . . . 2.00
19 JM(c),MA 2.00
20 RL,DG,F:Batgirl 3.00
21 GM,MA,F:Jonah Hex 2.00
22 F:Manhunter,Millenium tie-in . . 2.00
23 F:Manhunter,Millenium tie-in . . 2.00
24 F:Dr.Fate,Blue Devil 2.00
25 F:The Legion 2.00
26 F:Black Lightning 2.00
27 F:Zatanna,Zatara 1.75
28 RLd,GK,F:Nightshade,Midnight 1.75
29 F:Atom,Red Tornado 1.75
30 F:Elongated Man 1.75
31 F:Justice Society of America. . 1.75
32 F:Justice League America. . . . 3.00
33 F:Justice League Inter.. . . . . . 2.00
34 F:Justice League Inter. 2.00
35 KSu,F:Justice League Inter. . . 2.00
36 F:Green Lantern 3.00
37 F:Legion of Subst. Heroes . . . 1.75
38 F:Green Arrow,Speedy 2.00
39 F:Batman,Animal Man 3.50
40 F:Gorilla City 1.75
41 F:Flash Villains 2.50
42 DC,F:Phantom Girl 1.75
43 TVE,TT,F:Hawk & Dove 1.75
44 F:Batman,Clayface tie-in 3.00

Secret Origin #29
© DC Comics, Inc.

45 F:Blackhawk,El Diablo	1.75
46 CS,F:All Headquarters	1.75
47 CS,F:The Legion	1.75
48 KG,F:Ambush Bug	1.75
49 F: The Cadmus Project	2.50
50 GP,CI,DG,F:Batman,Robin, Flash,Black Canary	5.00
Ann.#1 JBy,F:Doom Patrol	3.00
Ann.#2 CI,MA,F:Flash	2.00
Ann.#3 F:The Teen Titans	3.00
Spec.#1 SK,PB,DG,F:Batman's worst Villians,A:Penguin	4.00
TPB DG,New Origin Batman	4.50

SECRET SOCIETY OF SUPER-VILLAINS
May-June, 1976

1 A:Capt.Boomerang, Grodd, Sinestro	2.50
2 R:Capt.Comet,A:Green Lantern	2.50
3 A:Mantis, Darkseid	2.00
4 A:Kalibak,Darkseid,Gr.Lantern	2.00
5 RB,D:Manhunter,A:JLA	2.00
6 RB/BL,A:Black Canary	1.50
7 RB/BL,A:Hawkgirl,Lex Luthor	1.50
8 RB/BL,A:Kid Flash	1.50
9 RB/BMc,A:Kid Flash, Creeper	1.50
10 DAy/JAb,A:Creeper	1.25
11 JO,N:Wizard	1.25
12 BMc,A:Blockbuster	1.25
13 A:Crime Syndicate of America	1.00
14 A:Crime Syndicate of America	1.00
15 A:G.A.Atom, Dr. Mid Nite	1.25

SECRETS OF HAUNTED HOUSE
April-May, 1975

1 LD(c),Dead Heat	2.00
2 ECh(c),A Dead Man	1.50
3 ECh(c),Pathway To Purgatory	1.50
4 LD(c),The Face of Death	1.50
5 BWr(c),Gunslinger!	1.50
6 JAp(c),Deadly Allegiance	1.50
7 JAp(c),It'll Grow On You	1.50
8 MK(c),Raising The Devil	1.50
9 LD(c),The Man Who Didn't Believe in Ghosts	1.50

10 MK(c),Ask Me No Questions	1.50
11 MK(c),Picasso Fever!	1.25
12 JO&DG(c),Yorick's Skull	1.25
13 JO&DG(c),The Cry of the Warewolf	1.25
14 MK(c),Selina	1.25
15 LD(c),Over Your Own Dead Body	1.25
16 MK(c),Water, Water Every Fear	1.25
17 LD(c),Papa Don	1.25
18 LD(c),No Sleep For The Dying	1.25
19 LD(c),The Manner of Execution	1.25
20 JO(c),The Talisman of the Serpent	1.25
21 LD(c),The Death's Head Scorpion	1.25
22 LD(c),See How They Die	1.25
23 LD(c),The Creeping Red Death	1.25
24 LD(c),Second Chance To Die	1.25
25 LD(c),The Man Who Cheated Destiny	1.25
26 MR(c),Elevator to Eternity	1.25
27 DH(c),Souls For the Master	1.25
28 DH(c),Demon Rum	1.25
29 MK(c),Duel of Darkness	1.25
30 JO(c),For the Love of Arlo	1.25
31 I:Mister E	2.00
32 The Legend of the Tiger's Paw	1.25
33 In The Attic Dwells Dark Seth	1.25
34 Double Your Pleasure	1.25
35 Deathwing, Lord of Darkness	1.25
36 RB&DG(c),Sister Sinister	1.25
37 RB&DG(c),The Third Wish Is Death	1.25
38 RB&DG(c),Slaves of Satan	1.25
39 RB&DG(c),The Witch-Hounds of Salem	1.25
40 RB&DG(c),The Were-Witch of Boston	1.25
41 JKu(c),House at Devil's Tail	1.25
42 JKu(c),Mystic Murder	1.25
43 JO(c),Mother of Invention	1.25
44 BWr(c),Halloween God	1.25
45 EC&JO(c),Star-Trakker	1.25
46 March, 1982	1.25

SINISTER HOUSE OF SECRET LOVE
October-November, 1971

1	1.50
2 JJ(c)	1.50
3 ATh	1.25
4 April-May, 1972	1.25

Becomes:

SECRETS OF SINISTER HOUSE
June-July, 1972

5	2.00
6	1.25
7 NR	1.25
8	1.25
9	1.25
10 NA(i)	4.00
11	1.25
12	1.25
13	1.25
14	1.25
15	1.25
16	1.25
17 DBa	1.25
18 June-July, 1974	1.25

SECRETS OF THE LEGION OF SUPER-HEROES
January, 1981

1 O:Legion	1.50
2 O:Brainiac 5	1.00
3 March, 1981,O:Karate Kid	1.00

SENSATION COMICS
January, 1942

1 I:Wonder Woman,Wildcat	10,000.00
2 I:Etta Candy & the Holiday Girls, Dr. Poison	2,000.00
3 Diana Price joins Military Intelligence	1,200.00
4 I:Baroness PaulaVonGunther	1,000.00
5 V:Axis Spies	750.00
6 Wonder Woman receives magic lasso,V:Baroness Gunther	750.00
7 V:Baroness Gunther	600.00
8 Meets Gloria Bullfinch	600.00
9 A:The Real Diana Prince	600.00
10 V:Ishti	600.00
11 I:Queen Desira	600.00
12 V:Baroness Gunther	500.00
13 V:Olga,Hitler(c)	600.00
14	500.00
15 V:Simon Slikery	500.00
16 V:Karl Schultz	500.00
17 V:Princess Yasmini	500.00
18 V:Quito	500.00
19 Wonder Woman goes berserk	500.00
20 V:Stoffer	500.00
21 V:American Adolf	400.00
22 V:Cheetah	400.00
23 'War Laugh Mania'	400.00
24 I:Wonder Woman's mental radio	400.00
25	400.00
26 A:Queen Hippolyte	400.00
27 V:Ely Close	400.00
28 V:Mayor Prude	400.00
29 V:Mimi Mendez	400.00
30 V:Anton Unreal	400.00
31 'Grow Down Land'	300.00
32 V:Crime Chief	300.00
33 Meets Percy Pringle	300.00
34 I:Sargon	325.00
35 V:Sontag Henya in Atlantis	250.00
36 V:Bedwin Footh	250.00
37 A:Mala((1st app. All-Star #8)	250.00
38 V:The Gyp	250.00
39 V:Nero	250.00
40 I:Countess Draska Nishki	250.00
41 V:Creeper Jackson	225.00
42 V:Countess Nishki	225.00
43 Meets Joel Heyday	225.00
44 V:Lt. Sturm	225.00
45 V:Jose Perez	225.00
46 V:Lawbreakers Protective League	225.00
47 V:Unknown	225.00
48 V:Topso and Teena	225.00
49 V:Zavia	225.00
50 V:'Ears' Fellock	225.00
51 V:Boss Brekel	200.00
52 Meets Prof. Toxino	200.00
53 V:Wanta Wynn	200.00
54 V:Dr. Fiendo	200.00
55 V:Bughumans	200.00
56 V:Dr. Novel	200.00
57 V:Syonide	200.00
58 Meets Olive Norton	200.00

All comics prices listed are for *Near Mint* condition.

59 V:Snow Man	200.00
60 V:Bifton Jones	200.00
61 V:Bluff Robust	200.00
62 V:Black Robert of Dogwood	200.00
63 V:Prof. Vibrate	200.00
64 V:Cloudmen	200.00
65 V:Lim Slait	200.00
66 V:Slick Skeener	200.00
67 V:Daredevil Dix	200.00
68 'Secret of the Menacing Octopus'	225.00
69 V:Darcy Wells	200.00
70 Unconquerable Woman of Cocha Bamba	200.00
71 V:Queen Flaming	200.00

Sensation Comics #37
© DC Comics, Inc.

72 V:Blue Seal Gang	200.00
73 Wonder Woman time travel story.	200.00
74 V:Spug Spangle	200.00
75 V:Shark	200.00
76 V:King Diamond	200.00
77 V:Boss Brekel	200.00
78 V:Furiosa	200.00
79 Meets Leila and Solala	200.00
80 V:Don Enrago	200.00
81 V:Dr. Frenzi	225.00
82 V:King Lunar	175.00
83 V:Prowd	175.00
84 V:Duke Daxo	175.00
85 Meets Leslie M. Gresham	175.00
86 'Secret of the Amazing Bracelets'	175.00
87 In Twin Peaks(in Old West)	175.00
88 Wonder Woman in Holywood	175.00
89 V:Abacus Rackeett gang	175.00
90 'The Secret of the Modern Sphinx'	175.00
91	175.00
92 V:Duke of Deceptions	150.00
93 V:Talbot	150.00
94 Girl Isue	225.00
95	200.00
96	200.00
97	200.00
98 'Strange Mission'	200.00
99 I:Astra	200.00
100	275.00
101 'Battle for the Atom World'	200.00

102 'Queen of the South Seas'	200.00
103 V:Robot Archers	200.00
104 'The End of Paradise Island'	200.00
105 'Secret of the Giant Forest'	200.00
106 E:Wonder Woman	200.00
107 ATh,Mystery issue	350.00
108 ATh,I:Johnny Peril	300.00
109 Ath,A:Johnny Peril	325.00

Becomes:

SENSATION MYSTERY

110 B:Johnny Peril	200.00
111 'Spectre in the Flame'	175.00
112 'Death has 5 Guesses'	175.00
113	175.00
114 GC,'The Haunted Diamond'	175.00
115 'The Phantom Castle'	175.00
116 'The Toy Assassins', July-August, 1953	175.00

SERGEANT BILKO
May-June, 1957

1 Based on TV show	400.00
2	225.00
3	200.00
4	175.00
5	175.00
6 thru 17	@150.00
18 March-April, 1960	150.00

SERGEANT BILKO'S PVT. DOBERMAN
June-July, 1958

1	225.00
2	150.00
3	100.00
4	100.00
5	100.00
6 thru 10	@75.00
11 February-March, 1960	75.00

SGT. ROCK
(See: OUR ARMY AT WAR)

SGT. ROCK SPECIAL
October, 1988

#1 rep.Our Army at War#162-#63	2.00
#2 rep.Brave & Bold #52	2.00
#3 rep.Showcase #45	2.00
#4 rep.Our Army at War#147-#48	2.00
#5 rep.Our Army at War#81&#103	2.00
#6 rep.Our Army at War #160	2.00
#7 rep.Our Army at War #85	2.00
#8 rep.	2.00
#9	2.00
#10 thru #20 reprints.	@2.00

SGT. ROCK'S PRIZE BATTLE TALES
Winter, 1964

1	125.00

SGT. ROCK SPECIAL

1 TT,MGo,JKu,CR,(new stories)	2.95

SHADE
June-July, 1977
[1st Regular Series]

1 SD,I&O: Shade	4.00
2 SD,V:Form	3.25
3 SD,V:The Cloak	2.75

4 SD,Return to Meta-Zone	2.75
5 SD,V:Supreme Decider	2.75
6 SD,V:Khaos	2.75
7 SD,V:Dr.Z.Z.	2.75
8 SD,last issue	2.75

Shade, The Changing Man #35
© DC Comics, Inc.

SHADE, THE CHANGING MAN
July, 1990

1 B:PrM(s),CBa,MPn,I:Kathy George, I&D:Troy Grezer	7.00
2 CBa,MPn,Who Shot JFK#1	5.00
3 CBa,MPn,Who Shot JFK#2	4.00
4 CBa,MPn,V:American Scream	3.00
5 CBa,MPn,V:Hollywood Monsters	3.00
6 CBa,MPn,V:Ed Loot	3.00
7 CBa,MPn,I:Arnold Major	2.75
8 CBa,Mpn,I:Lenny	2.75
9 CBa,MPn,V:Arnold Major	2.75
10 CBa,MPn,Paranioa	2.75
11 CBa,MPn,R:Troy Grezer	2.50
12 CBa,MPn,V:Troy Grezer	2.50
13 CBa,MPn,I:Fish Priest	2.50
14 CBa,MPn,V:Godfather of Guilt	2.50
15 CBa,MPn,I:Spirit	2.50
16 CBa,MPn,V:American Scream	2.50
17 RkB(i),V:Rohug	2.50
18 MPn,E:American Scream	2.50
19 MPn,V:Dave Messiah Seeker	2.50
20 JD,CBa,MPn,RkB,R:Roger	2.50
21 MPn,The Road,A:Stringer	2.25
22 The Road,Childhood	2.25
23 The Road	2.25
24 The Road	2.25
25 The Road	2.25
26 MPn(i),F:Lenny	2.25
27 MPn(i),Shade becomes female	2.25
28 MPn(i),Changing Woman#2	2.25
29 MPn(i),Changing Woman#3	2.25
30 Another Life	2.25
31 Ernest & Jim#1	2.25
32 Ernest & Jim#2	2.25

Vertigo

33 CBa,B:Birth Pains	2.25
34 CBa,RkB(i),GID(i),A:Brian Juno,	

Garden of Pain 2.25	
35 CBa,RkB(i),E:Birth Pains,	
V:Juno 2.25	
36 CBa,PrG(i),RkB(i),B:Passion child,	
I:Miles Laimling 2.25	
37 CBa,RkB(i),Shade/Kathy 2.25	
38 CBa,RkB(i),Great American	
Novel 2.25	
39 CBa,SEa,RkB(i),Pond Life . . . 2.25	
40 PBd,at Hotel Shade 2.25	
41 GID,Pandora's Story,Kathy is	
pregnant 2.25	
42 CBa,RkB(i),SY,B:History Lesson,	
A:John Constantine 2.50	
43 CBa,RkB(i),PBd,Trial of William	
Matthieson,A:J.Constantine . . 2.50	
44 CBa,RkB(i),E:History Lesson,	
D:William Matthieson,A:John	
Constantine 2.50	
45 CBa,B:A Season in Hell 2.25	
46 CBa(c),GID,Season in Hell#2 . 2.25	
47 CBa(c),GID,A:Lenny 2.25	
48 CBa(c),GID 2.25	
49 CBa(c),GID,Kathy's Past 2.25	
50 GID,BBl,MiA,pin-up gallery . . . 3.25	
51 GID,BBl,MiA,Masks,pt.1 . . . . 3.25	
52 GID,BBl,MiA,Masks,pt.2 . . . . 3.25	
53 GID,BBl,MiA,Masks,pt.3 . . . . 3.25	
54 Meeting 1.95	
55 . . . . 1.95	
56 . . . . 1.95	
57 MBu,PrM,F:George 1.95	
58 PrM,Michael Lark 1.95	
59 MBu,PrM,Nasty Infections,pt.1 2.25	
60 MBu,PrM,Nasty Infections,pt.2 2.25	
61 MBu,PrM,Nasty Infections,pt.3 2.25

SHADO, SONG OF THE DRAGON
1 GM(i),From G.A. Longbow	
Hunters 5.50	
2 GM(i),V:Yakuza 4.95	
3 GM(i),V:Yakuza 4.95	
4 GM(i),V:Yakuza 4.95

SHADOW, THE
October-November, 1973
[1st Regular Series]
1 MK,The Doom Puzzle 30.00	
2 MK,V:Freak Show Killer 22.00	
3 MK,BWr 24.00	
4 MK,Ninja Story 22.00	
5 FR 12.00	
6 MK 22.00	
7 FR 11.00	
8 FR 11.00	
9 FR 11.00	
10 . . . . 11.00	
11 A:Avenger 11.00	
12 . . . . 11.00

[Limited Series]
1 HC,R:Shadow 6.00	
2 HC,O:Shadow 4.00	
3 HC,V:Preston Mayrock 3.00	
4 HC,V:Preston Mayrock 3.00	
TPB rep. #1 thru #4 . . . . 12.95

[2nd Regular Series]
1 BSz,Shadows & Light,pt.1 . . . . 3.50	
2 BSz,Shadows & Light,pt.2 . . . . 3.50	
3 BSz,Shadows & Light,pt.3 . . . . 3.50	
4 BSz,Shadows & Light,pt.4 . . . . 3.50	
5 BSz,Shadows & Light,pt.5 . . . . 3.50	
6 BSz,Shadows & Light,pt.6 . . . . 3.50	
7 MR,KB,Harold Goes to

Washington 2.00	
8 KB,Seven Deadly Finns,pt.1 . . 2.00	
9 KB,Seven Deadly Finns,pt.2 . . 2.00	
10 KB,Seven Deadly Finns,pt.3 . . 2.00	
11 KB,Seven Deadly Finns,pt.4 . . 2.00	
12 KB,Seven Deadly Finns,pt.5 . . 2.00	
13 KB,Seven Deadly Finns,pt.6 . . 2.00	
14 KB,Body And Soul,pt.1 . . . . . 2.00	
15 KB,Body And Soul,pt.2 . . . . . 2.00	
16 KB,Body And Soul,pt.3 . . . . . 2.00	
17 KB,Body And Soul,pt.4 . . . . . 2.00	
18 KB,Body And Soul,pt.5 . . . . . 2.00	
19 KB,Body And Soul,pt.6 . . . . . 2.00	
Ann.#1 JO,AA,Shadows & Light	
prologue 3.00	
Ann.#2 KB,Agents 2.50

SHADOW CABINET
Milestone
0 WS(c),3RL,Shadow War,Foil(c),A:All	
Milestone characters 3.00	
1 JBy(c),3RW,I&D:Corpsickle . . 2.00	
2 3RW,V:Arcadian League 1.75	
3 3RW,F:Sideshow 2.00	
4 3RW,F:Sideshow 2.00	
5 . . . . 1.75	
6 . . . . 1.75	
7 . . . . 1.75	
8 New Cabinet 1.75	
9 R:Old Cabinet 1.75	
10 V:Red Dog 1.75	
11 Death Issue 1.75	
12 SYSTEM 1.75	
13 A:Hardware,Starlight 1.75	
14 Long Hot Summer, Iron Butterfly	
Starlight 2.50

SHADOW OF BATMAN
1 reprints of Detective Comics . 10.00	
2 . . . . 7.50	
3 . . . . 7.50	
4 . . . . 7.50

SHADOW OF THE BATMAN
December, 1985
1 WS,AM,MR,rep. 10.00	
2 MR,TA,rep.A:Hugo Strange . . . 7.50	
3 MR,TA,rep.A:Penguin 7.50	
4 MR,TA,rep.A:Joker 8.50	
5 MR,DG,rep. 7.50

SHADOWS FALL
1 JVF,Voyage of self-discovery . . 2.95	
2 JVF,More of tale 2.95	
3 JVF,Shen confronts shadow . . 2.95	
4 JVF,Gale wounded 2.95	
5 JVF,Shadow goes Berserk . . . 2.95	
6 JVF,F:Warren Gale,final issue . 2.95

SHADOW STRIKES!, THE
September, 1989
1 EB,Death's Head 3.00	
2 EB,EB,PoliticalKiller,V:Rasputin 2.50	
3 EB,V:Mad Monk,V:Rasputin . . 2.00	
4 EB,D:Mad Monk,V:Rasputin . . 2.00	
5 EB,Shadow & Doc Savage#1 . . 2.00	
6 Shadow & Doc Savage #3 . . . . 2.00	
7 RM,A:Wunderkind,O:Shadow's	
Radio Show 2.00	
8 EB,A:Shiwan Khan 2.00	
9 Fireworks#2 . . . . 2.00	
10 EB,Fireworks#3 . . . . 2.00

11 EB,O:Margo Lane 2.00	
12 EB,V:Chicago Mob 2.00	
13 EB,V:Chicago Mob 2.00	
14 EB,V:Chicago Mob 2.00	
15 EB,V:Chicago Mob 2.00	
16 Assassins,pt.1 . . . . 2.00	
17 Assassins,pt.2 . . . . 2.00	
18 Shrevvie 2.00	
19 NY,NJ Tunnel 2.00	
20 Shadow+Margo Vs.Nazis . . . 2.00	
21 V:Shiwan Khan 2.00	
22 V:Shiwan Khan 2.00	
23 V:Shiwan Khan 2.00	
24 Search for Margo Lane 2.00	
25 In China 2.00	
26 V:Shiwan Khan 2.00	
27 V:Shiwan Khan,Margo	
Rescued 2.00	
28 SL,In Hawaii 2.00	
29 DSp,'Valhalla',V:Nazis 2.00	
30 The Shadow Year One,pt.1 . . 2.00	
31 The Shadow Year One,pt.2 . . 2.00	
Ann.#1 DSp 'Crimson Dreams' . . 4.00

SHADOW WAR OF HAWKMAN
May, 1985
1 AA,V:Thangarians 1.50	
2 AA,V:Thangarians 1.25	
3 AA,V:Thangarians,A:Aquaman,	
Elong.Man 1.25	
4 AA,V:Thangarians 1.25	
Spec.#1 V:Thangarians 1.25

Shazam! #1 © DC Comics, Inc.

SHAZAM!
February, 1973
[1st Regular Series]
1 B:DON(s),CCB,O:Capt.Marvel . 4.50	
2 CCB,A:Mr.Mind 2.50	
3 CCB,V:Shagg Naste 2.00	
4 E:DON(s),CCB,V:Ibac 2.00	
5 B:ESM(s),CCB,A:Leprechaun . . 2.00	
6 B:DON(s),CCB,Dr,Sivana 2.00	
7 CCB,A:Capt Marvel Jr. 2.00	
8 CCB,O:Marvel Family 2.00	
9 E:DON(S)DC,CCB,A:Mr.Mind,

Captain Marvel Jr.	2.00
10 ESM(s)CCB,BO	2.00
11 VICKS,BO,rep.	2.00
12 BO,DG	2.00
13 BO,KS,A:Luthor	2.00
14 KS,A:Monster Society	2.00
15 KS,BO,Luthor	2.00
16 KS,BO	2.00
17 KS,BO	2.00
18 KS,BO	2.00
19 KS,BO,Mary Marvel	2.00
20 KS,A:Marvel Family	2.00
21 reprint	2.00
22 reprint	2.00
23 reprint	2.00
24 reprint	2.00
25 KS,DG,I&O:Isis	2.00
26 KS	2.00
27 KS,A:KidEternity	2.50
28 KS	2.00
29 KS	2.00
30 KS	2.00
31 KS,A:MinuteMan	2.00
32 KS	2.00
33 KS	2.00
34 O:Capt.Marvel Jr.	2.00
35 DN,KS,A:Marvel Family	2.00

[Limited Series]

1 O:Shazam&Capt.Marvel	1.50
2 V:Black Adam	1.25
3 V:Black Adam	1.25
4 V:Black Adam	1.25

SHAZAM ARCHIVES
1 Rep.Whiz Comics#2-#15	49.95

SHAZAM, THE NEW BEGINNING
April, 1987

1 O:Shazam & Capt.Marvel	1.50
2 V:Black Adam	1.25
3 V:Black Adam	1.25
4 V:Black Adam	1.25

SHERLOCK HOLMES
September-October, 1975

1	1.00

SHOWCASE
March-April, 1956

1 F:Fire Fighters	2,000.00
2 JKu,F:Kings of Wild	600.00
3 F:Frogmen	580.00
4 CI,JKu,I&O:S.A. Flash (Barry Allen)	18,500.00
5 F:Manhunters	700.00
6 JK,I&O:Challengers of the Unknown	2,700.00
7 JK,F:Challengers	1,300.00
8 CI,F:Flash,I:Capt.Cold	6,000.00
9 F:Lois Lane	2,800.00
10 F:Lois Lane	1,700.00
11 JK(c),F:Challengers	1,200.00
12 JK(c),F:Challengers	1,100.00
13 CI,F:Flash,Mr.Element	2,700.00
14 CI,F:Flash,Mr.Element	2,600.00
15 I:Space Ranger	1,200.00
16 F:Space Ranger	650.00
17 GK(c),I:Adam Strange	1,650.00
18 GK(c),F:Adam Strange	800.00
19 GK(c),F:Adam Strange	950.00
20 I:Rip Hunter	550.00
21 F:Rip Hunter	325.00

DC Showcase #12 © DC Comics, Inc.

22 GK,I&O:S.A. Green Lantern (Hal Jordan)	4,000.00
23 GK,F:Green Lantern	1,250.00
24 GK,F:Green Lantern	1,200.00
25 JKu,F:Rip Hunter	200.00
26 JKu,F:Rip Hunter	200.00
27 RH,I:Sea Devils	575.00
28 RH,F:Sea Devils	300.00
29 RH,F:Sea Devils	300.00
30 O:Aquaman	500.00
31 GK(c),F:Aquaman	300.00
32 F:Aquaman	300.00
33 F:Aquaman	300.00
34 GK,MA,I&O:S.A. Atom	1,200.00
35 GK,MA,F:Atom	650.00
36 GK,MA,F:Atom	500.00
37 RA,I:Metal Man	450.00
38 RA,F:Metal Man	350.00
39 RA,F:Metal Man	260.00
40 RA,F:Metal Man	235.00
41 F:Tommy Tomorrow	95.00
42 F:Tommy Tomorrow	95.00
43 F:Dr.No(James Bond 007)	350.00
44 F:Tommy Tomorrow	80.00
45 JKu,O:Sgt.Rock	150.00
46 F:Tommy Tomorrow	60.00
47 F:Tommy Tomorrow	60.00
48 F:Cave Carson	35.00
49 F:Cave Carson	35.00
50 MA,CI,F:I Spy	35.00
51 MA,CI,F:I Spy	35.00
52 F:Cave Carson	35.00
53 JKu(c),RH,F:G.I.Joe	35.00
54 JKu(c),RH,F:G.I.Joe	35.00
55 MA,F:Dr.Fate,Spectre,1st S.A. Green Lantern,Solomon Grundy	200.00
56 MA,F:Dr.Fate	55.00
57 JKu,F:Enemy Ace	80.00
58 JKu,F:Enemy Ace	70.00
59 F:Teen Titans	75.00
60 MA,F:Spectre	150.00
61 MA,F:Spectre	80.00
62 JO,I:Inferior 5	55.00
63 JO,F:Inferior 5	29.00
64 MA,F:Spectre	75.00
65 F:Inferior 5	29.00

DC Showcase #39 © DC Comics, Inc.

66 I:B'wana Beast	13.00
67 F:B'wana Beast	13.00
68 I:Maniaks	13.00
69 F:Maniaks	13.00
70 I:Binky	13.00
71 F:Maniaks	13.00
72 JKu,ATH,F:Top Gun	13.00
73 SD,I&O:Creeper	90.00
74 I:Anthro	50.00
75 SD,I:Hawk & Dove	70.00
76 NC,I:Bat Lash	35.00
77 BO,I:Angel & Ape	35.00
78 I:Jonny Double	17.00
79 I:Dolphin	28.00
80 NA(c),F:Phantom Stranger	13.00
81 I:Windy & Willy	13.00
82 I:Nightmaster	45.00
83 BWr,MK,F:Nightmaster	42.00
84 BWr,MK,F:Nightmaster	42.00
85 JKu,F:Firehair	12.00
86 JKu,F:Firehair	12.00
87 JKu,F:Firehair	12.00
88 F:Jason's Quest	6.00
89 F:Jason's Quest	6.00
90 F:Manhunter	5.00
91 F:Manhunter	5.00
92 F:Manhunter	5.00
93 F:Manhunter	5.00
94 JA,JSon,I&O:2nd Doom Patrol	10.00
95 JA,JSon,F:2nd Doom Patrol	9.00
96 JA,JSon,F:2nd Doom Patrol	9.00
97 JO,JSon,O:Power Girl	5.00
98 JSon,DG,Power Girl	5.00
99 JSon,DG,Power Girl	5.00
100 JSon,all star issue	6.00
101 JKu(c),AM,MA,Hawkman	5.00
102 JKu(c),AM,MA,Hawkman	5.00
103 JKu(c),AM,MA,Hawkman	5.00
104 RE,OSS Spies	5.00
TPB Rep.1956-59	19.95

SHOWCASE' 93
1 AAd(c),EH,AV,F:Catwoman, Blue Devil,Cyborg	5.50
2 KM(c),EH,AV,F:Catwoman, Blue Devil,Cyborg	4.00
3 KM(c),EH,TC,F:Catwoman, Blue Devil,Flash	3.50

4 F:Catwoman,Blue Devil,
  Geo-Force 2.50
5 F:KD,DG,BHi,F:Robin,Blue
  Devil,Geo-Force 2.50
6 MZ(c),KD,DG,F:Robin,Blue
  Devil,Deathstroke 2.50
7 BSz(c),KJ,Knightfall#13,F:Two-
  Face,Jade&Obsidian 5.00
8 KJ,Knightfall#14,F:Two-Face,
  Peacemaker,Fire and Ice 4.00
9 F:Huntress,Peacemaker,Shining
  Knight 2.50
10 BWg,SI,F:Huntress,Batman,
  Dr.Light,Peacemaker,Deathstroke,
  Katana,M.Manhunter 2.50
11 GP(c),F:Robin,Nightwing,
  Peacemaker,Deathstroke,Deadshot,
  Katana,Dr.Light,Won.Woman . 2.50
12 AD(c),BMc,F:Robin,Nightwing,
  Green Lantern,Creeper 2.50

SHOWCASE '94
1 KN,F:Joker,Gunfire,Orion,Metro 2.25
2 KON(c),E:Joker,B:Blue Beetle . 2.25
3 MMi(c),B:Razorsharpe 2.25
4 AIG(s),DG,F:Arkham Asylum inmates
  E:Razorsharpe,Blue Bettle . . . 2.25
5 WS(c),CDi(s),PJ,B:Robin & Huntress,
  F:Bloodwynd,Loose Cannon . . 2.25
6 PJ,KK(s),F:Robin & Huntress . 2.25
7 JaL(c),PDd(s),F:Comm. Gordon 2.25
8 AIG(s),O:Scarface,Ventriloquist,
  F:Monarch,1st Wildcat 1.95
9 AIG(s),DJ,O:Scarface,Ventriloquist,
  F:Monarch,Waverider 2.75
10 JQ(c),AIG(s),F:Azrael,Zero Hour,
  B:Black Condor 2.25
11 Black Condor, Man-Bat 1.95
12 Barbara Gordon 1.95

SHOWCASE '95
1 Supergirl 1.95
2 . . . . 1.95
3 F:Eradicator,Claw 1.95
4 A:Catwoman,Hawke 2.50
5 F:Thorne,Firehawk 2.95
6 DRo(c&a),F:Lobo,Bibbo 2.25

SILVER AGE
DC CLASSICS
Action #252(rep) 1.50
Adventure #247(rep) 1.50
Brave and Bold #28 (rep) 1.50
Detective #225 (rep) 1.50
Detective #327 (rep) 1.50
Green Lantern #76 (rep) 1.50
House of Secrets #92 (rep) 2.00
Showcase #4 (rep) 1.75
Showcase #22 (rep) 1.50
Sugar & Spike #99(1st printing) . . 1.50

SILVER BLADE
September, 1987
1 KJ,GC,maxi-series 1.50
2 thru 12 GC . . . . @1.50

SKIN GRAFT
Vertigo
1 B:JeP(s),WaP,I:John Oakes,
  A:Tattooed Man(Tarrant) 3.25
2 WaP,V:Assassins 3.00
3 WaP,In Kyoto,I:Mizoguchi Kenji 3.00
4 E:JeP(s),WaP,V:Tarrant,Kenji . 3.00

SKREEMER
May, 1989
1 . . . . 1.50
2 thru 6 . . . . @2.00

SKULL AND BONES
1 EH,I&O:Skull & Bones 4.95
2 EH,V:KGB 4.95
3 EH,V:KGB 4.95

SLASH MARAUD
November, 1987
1 PG 2.25
2 PG 2.00
3 thru 10 PG . . . . @2.00

SONIC DISRUPTORS
1 thru 10 . . . . @1.75

SON OF AMBUSH BUG
July, 1986
1 . . . . 1.00
2 thru 6 KG . . . . @1.00

SOVEREIGN SEVEN
1 CCI(s),DT,I:Sovereign Seven,
  V:Female Furies,A:Darkseid . . 1.95

SPANNER'S GALAXY
December, 1984
1 mini-series 1.50
2 thru 6 . . . . @1.00

Spectre (2nd Series) #28
© DC Comics, Inc.

SPECTRE, THE
November-December, 1967
1 MA,V:Captain Skull 80.00
2 NA,V:Dirk Rawley 55.00
3 NA,A:Wildcat 50.00
4 NA 50.00
5 NA 50.00
6 MA 30.00
7 MA,BU:Hourman 30.00
8 MA,Parchment of Power

Perilous 30.00
9 BWr(2nd BWr Art) 35.00
10 MA 30.00
[2nd Regular Series]
April, 1987
1 GC,O:Spectre 3.50
2 GC,Cult of BRM 3.00
3 GC,Fashion Model Murders . . 2.00
4 GC 2.00
5 GC,Spectre's Murderer 2.00
6 GC,Spectre/Corrigan separated 2.00
7 A:Zatanna,Wotan 2.00
8 A:Zatanna,Wotan 2.00
9 GM,Spectre's Revenge 2.00
10 GM,A:Batman,Millenium 2.25
11 GM,Millenium 2.00
12 GM,The Talisman,pt.1 . . . . . 1.75
13 GM,The Talisman,pt.2 . . . . . 1.75
14 GM,The Talisman,pt.3 . . . . . 1.75
15 GM,The Talisman,pt.4 . . . . . 1.75
16 Jim Corrigan Accused 1.75
17 New Direction,'Final Destiny' . 1.75
18 Search for Host Body 1.75
19 'Dead Again' 1.75
20 Corrigan Detective Agency . . 1.75
21 A:Zoran 1.50
22 BS,Sea of Darkness,A:Zoran . 1.50
23 A:Lords of Order,
  Invasion x-over 1.50
24 BWg,Ghosts i/t Machine#1 . . . 1.50
25 Ghosts in the Machine #2 . . . 1.50
26 Ghosts in the Machine #3 . . . 1.50
27 Ghosts in the Machine #4 . . . 1.50
28 Ghosts in the Machine #5 . . . 1.50
29 Ghosts in the Machine #6 . . . 1.50
30 Possession 1.50
31 Spectre possessed, final issue 1.50
Ann.#1, A:Deadman 2.75
[3rd Regular Series]
1 B:JOs(s),TMd,R:Spectre,
  Glow in the dark(c) 8.00
2 TMd,Murder Mystery 5.00
3 TMd,O:Spectre 4.00
4 TMd,O:Spectre 4.00
5 TMd,BB(c),V:Kidnappers 3.50
6 TMd,Spectre prevents evil . . . 3.50
7 TMd 3.50
8 TMd,Glow in the dark(c) 5.00
9 TMd,MWg(c),V:The Reaver . . 3.00
10 TMd,V:Michael 2.50
11 TMd,V:Azmodeus 2.50
12 V:Reaver 2.50
13 TMd,V:Count Vertigo,
  Glow in the Dark(c) 3.00
14 JoP,A:Phantom Stranger . . . 2.00
15 TMd,A:Phantom Stranger,Demon,
  Doctor Fate,John Constantine . 2.00
16 JAp,V:I.R.A. 2.00
17 TT(c),TMd,V:Eclipso 2.00
18 TMd,D:Eclipso 2.00
19 TMd,V:Hate 2.00
20 A:Lucien 2.00
21 V:Naiad,C:Superman 2.50
22 A:Superman 2.25
23 Book of Judgment, pt.1 . . . . . 1.95
24 Book of Judgment, pt.2 . . . . . 1.95
25 Book of Judgment, pt.3 . . . . . 1.95
26 . . . . 1.95
27 R:Azmodus 1.95
28 V:Azmodus 1.95
29 V:Azmodus 1.95
30 V:Azmodus 1.95
31 Descent into Pandemonium . . 2.25
TPB Punishment and Crimes . . . 9.95

Spelljammer #14 © DC Comics, Inc.

SPELLJAMMER
September, 1990
1 RogueShip#1	3.00
2 RogueShip#2	2.50
3 RogueShip#3	2.00
4 RogueShip#4	2.00
5 New Planet	1.75
6 Tember, Planet contd	1.75
7 Planet contd	1.75
8 conclusion	1.75
9 Meredith Possessed	1.75
10 Tie-in w/Dragonlance #33&34	1.75
11 Dwarf Citidel	1.75
12 Kirstig Vs. Meredith	1.75
13 Tember to the Rescue	1.75
14 Meredith's Son #1	1.75
15 Meredith's Son #2	1.75

STANLEY & HIS MONSTER
(see FOX AND THE CROW)

STANLEY & HIS MONSTER
1 R:Stanley	1.25
2 I:Demon Hunter	1.25
3 A:Ambrose Bierce	1.25
4 final issue	1.25

S.T.A.R. CORPS
1 A:Superman	2.00
2 I:Fusion,A:Rampage	1.75
3 I:Brainstorm	1.75
4 I:Ndoki	1.75
5 I:Trauma	1.75
6 I:Mindgame	1.75

STAR HUNTERS
October-November, 1977
1 DN&BL	1.00
2 LH&BL	1.00
3 MN&BL,D:Donovan Flint	1.00
4 thru 7	@1.00

STARMAN
October, 1988
1 TL,I&O:New Starman	3.00

2 TL,V:Serial Killer,C:Bolt	2.00
3 TL,V:Bolt	1.50
4 TL,V:Power Elite	1.50
5 TL,Invasion,A:PowerGirl, Firestorm	1.50
6 TL,Invasion,A:G.L.,Atom	1.50
7 TL,Soul Searching Issue	1.50
8 TL,V:LadyQuark	1.50
9 TL,A:Batman,V:Blockbuster	2.00
10 TL,A:Batman,V:Blockbuster	2.00
11 TL,V:Power Elite	1.50
12 TL,V:Power Elite,A:Superman	1.50
13 TL,V:Rampage	1.50
14 TL,A:A:Superman,V:Parasite	1.50
15 TL,V:Deadline	1.50
16 TL,O:Starman	1.50
17 TL,V:Dr.Polaris,A:PowerGirl	1.50
18 TL,V:Dr.Polaris,A:PowerGirl	1.50
19 TL,V:Artillery	1.50
20 TL,FireFighting	1.50
21 TL,Starman Quits	1.50
22 TL,V:Khunds	1.50
23 TL,A:Deadline	1.50
24 TL,A:Deadline	1.50
25 TL,V:Deadline	1.50
26 V:The Mist	1.50
27 V:The Mist	1.50
28 A:Superman	7.00
29 V:Plasmax	1.50
30 Seduction of Starman #1	1.50
31 Seduction of Starman #2	1.50
32 Seduction of Starman #3	1.50
33 Seduction of Starman #4	1.50
34 A:Batman	1.50
35 A:Valor,Mr.Nebula,ScarletSkier	1.50
36 A:Les Mille Yeux	1.50
37 A:Les Mille Yeux	1.50
38 War of the Gods X-over	1.50
39 V:Plasmax	1.50
40 V:Las Vegas	1.50
41 V:Maaldor	1.50
42 Star Shadows,pt.1,A:Eclipso	3.00
43 Star Shadows,pt.2,A:Lobo, Eclipso	2.50
44 Star Shadows,pt.3,A:Eclipso V:Lobo	2.50
45 Star Shadows,pt.4, V:Eclipso	2.50

STARMAN
0 New Starman	2.50
1 Threat of the Mist	2.25
2	2.25
3 V:Son of the Mist	2.25
4	2.25
5 V:Starman	2.25
6 Times Past Features	2.25
7 Sinister Circus	1.95
8 TyH(c),Sinister Circus	2.25
9 TyH(c),Mist's daughter breaks out of prison	2.25

STAR SPANGLED COMICS
October, 1941
1 O:Tarantula,B:Captain X of the R.A.F.,Star Spangled Kid, Armstrong of the Army	2,400.00
2 V:Dr. Weerd	900.00
3	550.00
4 V:The Needle	550.00
5 V:Dr. Weerd	550.00
6 E:Armstrong	350.00
7 S&K,O&1st app:The Guardian, B:Robotman,The Newsboy	

Legion, TNT	4,400.00
8 O:TNT & Dan the Dyna-Mite	1,200.00
9	1,100.00
10	1,100.00
11	850.00
12 Newsboy Legion stories, 'Prevue of Peril!'	850.00
13 'Kill Dat Story!'	850.00
14 'The Meanest Man on Earth!'	850.00

Star Spangled Comics #6 © DC Comics, Inc.

15 'Playmates of Peril'	850.00
16 'Playboy of Suicide Slum!'	850.00
17 V:Rafferty Mob	850.00
18 O:Star Spangled Kid	1,000.00
19 E:Tarantula	750.00
20 B:Liberty Belle	800.00
21	650.00
22 'Brains for Sale'	650.00
23 'Art for Scrapper's Sake'	650.00
24	650.00
25 'Victuals for Victory'	650.00
26 'Louie the Lug goes Literary'	650.00
27 'Turn on the Heat!'	650.00
28 'Poor Man's Rich Man'	650.00
29 'Cabbages and Comics'	650.00
30	350.00
31 'Questions Please!'	350.00
32	350.00
33	350.00
34 'From Rags to Run!'	350.00
35 'The Proud Poppas'	350.00
36 'Cowboy of Suicide Slum'	350.00
37	350.00
38	350.00
39 'Two Guardians are a Crowd'	350.00
40	350.00
41 Back the 6th War Loan(c)	300.00
42	300.00
43 American Red Cross(c)	300.00
44	300.00
45 7th War Loan (c)	300.00
46	300.00
47	300.00
48	300.00
49	300.00
50	300.00
51 A:Robot Robber	300.00
52 'Rehearsal for Crime'	300.00
53 'The Poet of Suicide Slum'	300.00

Star Spangled Comics #40
© DC Comics, Inc.

54 'Dead-Shot Dade's Revenge' 300.00
55 'Gabby Strikes a Gusher' . . 300.00
56 'The Treasuer of Araby' . . . 300.00
57 'Recruit for the Legion' 300.00
58 'Matadors of Suicide Slum' . 300.00
59 . . . . 300.00
60 . . . . 300.00
61 . . . . 300.00
62 'Prevue of Tomorrow' 300.00
63 . . . . 300.00
64 'Criminal Cruise' 300.00
65 B:Robin,(c) & stories 1,000.00
66 V:No Face 600.00
67 'The Castle of Doom 450.00
68 . . . . 450.00
69 'The Stolen Atom Bomb' . . . 700.00
70 V:The Clock 450.00
71 'Perils of the Stone Age' . . . 450.00
72 'Robin Crusoe' 450.00
73 V:The Black Magician 450.00
74 V:The Clock 450.00
75 The State vs. Robin 450.00
76 V:The Fence 450.00
77 'The Boy who Wanted Robin
for Christmas' 450.00
78 'Rajah Robin' 450.00
79 'V:The Clock,'The Tick-Tock
Crimes' 450.00
80 'The Boy Disc Jockey' 450.00
81 'The Seeing-Eye Dog Crimes' 375.00
82 'The Boy who Hated Robin' . 350.00
83 'Who is Mr. Mystery',B:Captain
Compass backup story 350.00
84 How can we Fight Juvenile
Delinquency?' 500.00
85 'Peril at the Pole' 350.00
86 . . . . 400.00
87 V:Sinister Knight 500.00
88 Robin Declares War on
Batman, B:Batman app. . . .
89 'Batman's Utility Belt?' 400.00
90 'Rancho Fear!' 400.00
91 'Cops 'n' Robbers?' 400.00
92 'Movie Hero No. 1?' 400.00
93 . . . . 400.00
94 'Underworld Playhouse' 400.00
95 'The Man with the Midas Touch',
E:Robin(c),Batman story . . . 400.00

96 B:Tomahawk(c) & stories . . 300.00
97 'The 4 Bold Warriors' 275.00
98 . . . . 250.00
99 'The Second Pocahontas' . . 275.00
100 'The Frontier Phantom' . . . 275.00
101 Peril on the High Seas . . . 200.00
102 . . . . 200.00
103 'Tomahawk's Death Duel!' . 200.00
104 'Race with Death!' 200.00
105 'The Unhappy Hunting
Grounds' 200.00
106 'Traitor in the War Paint' . . 200.00
107 'The Brave who Hunted
Tomahawk' 200.00
108 'The Ghost called Moccasin
Foot!' 200.00
109 'The Land Pirates of
Jolly Roger Hill!' 200.00
110 'Sally Raines Frontier Girl' 225.00
111 'The Death Map of Thunder
Hill' 225.00
112 . . . . 250.00
113 FF,V:'The Black Cougar' . . 300.00
114 'Return of the Black Cougar' 275.00
115 'Journey of a Thousand
Deaths' 250.00
116 'The Battle of Junction Fort' 250.00
117 'Siege?' 250.00
118 V:Outlaw Indians 200.00
119 'The Doomed Stockade?' . . 175.00
120 'Revenge of Raven Heart!' . 175.00
121 'Adventure in New York!' . . 175.00
122 'I:Ghost Breaker,(c)& stories 200.00
123 'The Dolls of Doom' 150.00
124 'Suicide Tower' 150.00
125 'The Hermit's Ghost Dog!' . 150.00
126 'The Phantom of Paris!' . . . 150.00
127 'The Supernatural Alibi!' . . 150.00
128 C:Batman,'The Girl who
lived 5,000 Years!' 150.00
129 'The Human Orchids' 175.00
130 'The Haunted Town',
July, 1952 . . . . 200.00

Becomes:

STAR SPANGLED
WAR STORIES
August, 1952

131 CS&StK(c),I Was A Jap
Prisoner of War 500.00
132 CS&StK(c),The G.I. With
The Million-Dollar Arm 375.00
133 CS&StK(c),Mission-San
Marino 350.00
3 CS&StK(c),Hundred-Mission
Mitchell 200.00
4 CS&StK(c),The Hot Rod Tank 200.00
5 LSt(c),Jet Pilot 200.00
6 CS(c),Operation Davy Jones 200.00
7 CS(c),Rookie Ranger,The . . 150.00
8 CS(c),I Was A
Holywood Soldier 150.00
9 CS&StK(c),Sad Sack Squad 150.00
10 CS,The G.I. & The Gambler 150.00
11 LSt(c),The Lucky Squad . . . 135.00
12 CS(c),The Four Horseman of
Barricade Hill 135.00
13 No Escape 135.00
14 LSt(c),Pitchfork Army 135.00
15 The Big Fish 135.00
16 The Yellow Ribbon 135.00
17 IN(c),Prize Target 135.00
18 IN(c),The Gladiator 135.00
19 IN(c),The Big Lift 135.00

20 JGr(c),The Battle of
the Frogmen 135.00
21 JGr(c),Dead Man's Bridge . . 125.00
22 JGr(c),Death Hurdle 125.00
23 JGr(c),The Silent Frogman . 125.00
24 JGr(c),Death Slide 125.00
25 JGr(c),S.S. Liferaft 125.00
26 JGr(c),Bazooka Man 125.00
27 JGr(c),Taps for a Tail Gunner 125.00
28 JGr(c),Tank Duel 125.00
29 JGr(c),A Gun Called Slugger 125.00
30 JGr(c),The Thunderbolt Tank 125.00
31 IN(c),Tank Block 75.00
32 JGr(c),Bridge to Battle 75.00
33 JGr(c),Pocket War 75.00
34 JGr(c),Fighting...Snowbirds . . 75.00
35 JGr(c),Zero Hour 75.00
36 JGr(c),A G.I. Passed Here . . 75.00
37 JGr(c),A Handful of T.N.T. . . 75.00
38 RH(c),One-Man Army 75.00
39 JGr(c),Flying Cowboy 75.00
40 JGr(c),Desert Duel 75.00
41 IN(c),A Gunner's Hands 50.00
42 JGr(c),Sniper Alley 50.00
43 JGr(c),Top Kick Brother 50.00
44 JGr(c),Tank 711
Doesn't Answer 50.00
45 JGr(c),Flying Heels 50.00
46 JGr(c),Gunner's Seat 50.00
47 JGr(c),Sidekick 50.00
48 JGr(c),Battle Hills 50.00
49 JGr(c),Payload 50.00
50 JGr(c),Combat Dust 50.00
51 JGr(c),Battle Pigeon 45.00
52 JGr(c),Cannon-Man 45.00
53 JGr(c),Combat Close-Ups . . . 45.00
54 JGr(c),Flying Exit 45.00
55 JKu(c),The Burning Desert . . 45.00
56 JKu(c),The Walking Sub 45.00
57 JGr(c),Call For a Frogman . . 45.00
58 JGr(c),MD,Waist Punch 45.00
59 JGr(c),Kick In The Door 45.00
60 JGr(c),Hotbox 45.00
61 JGr(c),MD,Tow Pilot 45.00
62 JGr(c),The Three GIs 45.00
63 JGr(c),Flying Range Rider . . 45.00
64 JGr(c),MD,Frogman Ambush . 45.00
65 JGr(c),JSe,Frogman Block . . 45.00
66 JGr(c),Flattop Pigeon 45.00
67 RH(c),MD,Ashcan Alley 45.00
68 JGr(c),The Long Step 45.00
69 JKu(c),Floating Tank, The' . . 45.00
70 JKu(c),No Medal For
Frogman 40.00
71 JKu(c),Shooting Star 40.00
72 JKu(c),Silent Fish 40.00
73 JGr(c),MD,The Mouse &
the Tiger 40.00
74 JGr(c),MD,Frogman Bait 40.00
75 JGr(c),MD,Paratroop
Mousketeers 40.00
76 MD,JKu(c),Odd Man 40.00
77 MD,JKu(c),Room to Fight . . . 40.00
78 MD,JGr(c),Fighting Wingman . 40.00
79 MD,JKu(c),Zero Box 40.00
80 MD,JGr(c),Top Gunner 40.00
81 MD,RH(c),Khaki Mosquito . . . 40.00
82 MD,JKu(c),Ground Flier 40.00
83 MD,JGr(c),Jet On
My Shoulder 40.00
84 MD,IN(c),O:Mademoiselle
Marie 100.00
85 IN(c),A Medal For Marie 75.00
86 JGr(c),A Medal For Marie . . . 75.00
87 JGr(c),T.N.T. Spotlight 50.00

---

88 JGr(c),The Steel Trap	50.00
89 IN(c),Trail of the Terror	50.00
90 RA(c),Island of Armored Giants	225.00
91 JGr(c),The Train of Terror	35.00
92 Last Battle of the Dinosaur Age	75.00
93 Goliath of the Western Front	35.00
94 JKu(c),The Frogman and the Dinosaur	75.00
95 Guinea Pig Patrol,Dinosaurs	75.00
96 Mission X,Dinosaur	75.00
97 The Sub-Crusher, Dinosaur	75.00
98 Island of Thunder, Dinosaur	75.00
99 The Circus of Monsters, Dinosaur	75.00
100 The Volcano of Monsters, Dinosaur	125.00
101 The Robot and the Dinosaur	75.00
102 Punchboard War,Dinosaur	75.00
103 Doom at Dinosaur Island, Dinosaur	75.00
104 The Tree of Terror, Dinosaurs	75.00
105 The War of Dinosaur Island	75.00
106 The Nightmare War, Dinosaurs	75.00
107 Battle of the Dinosaur Aquarium	75.00
108 Dinosaur D-Day	75.00
109 The Last Soldiers	75.00
110 thru 133	@75.00
134 NA	85.00
135	60.00
136	60.00
137 Dinosaur	60.00
138 Enemy Ace	50.00
139	35.00
140	35.00
141	35.00
142	15.00
143	15.00
144 NA,JKu	20.00
145	15.00
146	15.00
147	15.00
148	15.00
149	15.00
150 JKu,Viking Prince	15.00
151 I:Unknown Soldier	30.00
152	10.00
153	10.00
154 O:Unknown Soldier	20.00
155	10.00
156 I:Battle Album	8.00
157 thru 160	6.00
161 E:Enemy Ace	6.00
162 thru 170	@10.00
171 thru 200	@8.00
201 thru 204	@2.50

Becomes:
UNKNOWN SOLDIER
April-May, 1977

205 thru 247	@1.25
248 and 249 O:Unknown Soldier	@1.25
250	1.25
251 B:Enemy Ace	1.25
252 thru 268	@1.25

STAR TREK
February, 1984
[1st Regular Series]

1 TS,The Wormhole Connection	15.00
2 TS,The Only Good Klingon	8.00
3 TS,Errand of War	7.00
4 TS,Deadly Allies	7.00
5 TS,Mortal Gods	7.00
6 TS,Who is Enigma?	6.00
7 EB,O:Saavik	6.00
8 TS,Blood Fever	6.00
9 TS,Mirror Universe Saga #1	6.00
10 TS,Mirror Universe Saga #2	6.00
11 TS,Mirror Universe Saga #3	6.00
12 TS,Mirror Universe Saga #4	6.00
13 TS,Mirror Universe Saga #5	5.00
14 TS,Mirror Universe Saga #6	5.00
15 TS,Mirror Universe Saga #7	5.00
16 TS,Mirror Universe Saga end	5.00
17 TS,The D'Artagnan Three	5.00
18 TS,Rest & Recreation	5.00
19 DSp,W.Koenig story	5.00
20 TS,Girl	5.00
21 TS,Dreamworld	5.00
22 TS,The Wolf #1	5.00
23 TS,The Wolf #2	4.00

Star Trek #1 © DC Comics, Inc.

24 TS,Double Blind #1	4.00
25 TS,Double Blind #2	4.00
26 TSV:Romulans	4.00
27 TS,Day in the Life	4.00
28 GM,The Last Word	4.00
29 Trouble with Bearclaw	4.00
30 CI,F:Uhura	4.00
31 TS,Maggie's World	4.00
32 TS,Judgment Day	4.00
33 TS,20th Anniv.	4.50
34 V:Romulans	2.50
35 GM,Excelsior	2.50
36 GM,StarTrek IV tie-in	2.50
37 StarTrek IV tie-in	2.50
38 AKu,The Argon Affair	2.50
39 TS,A:Harry Mudd	2.50
40 TS,A:Harry Mudd	2.50
41 TS,V:Orions	2.50
42 TS,The Corbomite Effect	2.50
43 TS,Paradise Lost #1	2.50
44 TS,Paradise Lost #2	2.50
45 TS,Paradise Lost #3	2.50
46 TS,Getaway	2.50
47 TS,Idol Threats	2.50
48 TS,The Stars in Secret Influence	2.50

49 TS,Aspiring to be Angels	2.50
50 TS,Anniv.	3.50
51 TS,Haunted Honeymoon	2.50
52 TS,'Hell in a Hand Basket'	2.50
53 'You're Dead,Jim'	2.50
54 Old Loyalties	2.50
55 TS,Finnegan's Wake	2.50
56 GM,Took place during 5 year Mission	2.50
Ann.#1 All Those Years Ago	4.00
Ann.#2 DJw,The Final Voyage	3.00
Ann.#3 CS,F:Scotty	3.00
Star Trek III Adapt.TS	2.50
Star Trek IV Adapt. TS	2.50
StarTrek V Adapt.	2.50

[2nd Regular Series]
October, 1989

1 The Return	8.00
2 The Sentence	5.00
3 Death Before Dishonor	3.50
4 Reprocussions	3.50
5 Fast Friends	3.50
6 Cure All	3.50
7 Not Sweeney!	3.50
8 Going,Going	3.00
9 ...Gone	3.00
10 Trial of James Kirk #1	3.00
11 Trial of James Kirk #2	3.00
12 Trial of James Kirk #3	3.00
13 Return of Worthy #1	3.00
14 Return of Worthy #2	3.00
15 Return of Worthy #3	3.00
16 Worldsinger	2.50
17 Partners? #1	2.50
18 Partners? #2	2.50
19 Once A Hero	2.50
20	2.50
21 Kirk Trapped	2.25
22 A:Harry Mudd	2.25
23 The Nasgul,A:Harry Mudd	2.25
24 25th Anniv.,A:Harry Mudd	3.50
25 Starfleet Officers Reunion	2.25
26 Pilkor 3	2.25
27 Kirk Betrayed	2.25
28 V:Romulans	2.25
29 Mediators	2.25
30 Veritas #1	2.25
31 Veritas #2	2.25
32 Veritas #3	2.25
33 Veritas #4	2.25
34 JD,F:Kirk,Spock,McCoy	2.25
35 Tabukan Syndrome#1	2.25
36 Tabukan Syndrome#2	2.25
37 Tabukan Syndrome#3	2.25
38 Tabukan Syndrome#4	2.25
39 Tabukan Syndrome#5	2.25
40 Tabukan Syndrome#6	2.25
41 Runaway	2.25
42 Helping Hand	2.25
43 V:Binzalans	2.25
44 Acceptable Risk	2.25
45 V:Trelane	2.25
46 V:Captain Klaa	2.25
47 F:Spock & Saavik	2.25
48 The Neutral Zone	2.25
49 weapon from Genesis	2.25
50 "The Peacemaker"	3.75
51 "The Price"	2.00
52 V:Klingons	2.00
53 Timecrime #1	2.00
54 Timecrime #2	2.00
55 Timecrime #3	2.00
56 Timecrime #4	2.00
57 Timecrime #5	2.00
58 F:Chekov	2.00

---

59 Uprising	2.00
60 Hostages	2.00
61 On Talos IV	2.25
62 Alone,pt.1, V:aliens	2.25
63 Alone,pt.2	2.25
64 Kirk	2.25
65 Kirk in Space	2.25
66 Spock	2.25
67 Ambassador Stonn	2.25
68	2.25
69 Wolf in Cheap Clothing,pt.1	2.25
70 Wolf in Cheap Clothing,pt.2	2.25
71 Wolf in Cheap Clothing,pt.3	2.50
72 Wolf in Cheap Clothing,pt.4	2.50
73 Star-crossed,pt.1	2.50
Ann.#1 GM,sty by G.Takei(Sulu)	4.00
Ann.#2 Kirks 1st Yr At Star Fleet Academy	4.00
Ann #3 KD,F:Ambassador Sarek	3.50
Ann.#4 F:Spock on Pike's ship	3.50
Spec.#1 PDd(s),BSz	3.75
Spec.#2 The Defiant	3.95
Debt of Honor,AH,CCl(s),HC	27.00
Debt of Honor SC	14.95
Spec. 25th Anniv.	6.95
Star Trek VI,movie adapt(direct)	5.95
Star Trek VI,movie(newsstand)	2.95
TPB Best of Star Trek reps.	19.95
TPB Who Killed Captain Kirk?, rep.Star Trek#49-#55	16.95
TPB The Ashes of Eden, Shatner novel adapt.	14.95

STAR TREK: MODULA IMPERATIVE

1 Planet Modula	6.00
2 Modula's Rebels	4.50
3 Spock/McCoy rescue Attempt	4.00
4 Rebel Victory	4.00
TPB reprints both minis	19.95

STAR TREK: NEXT GENERATION
February, 1988
[1st Regular Series]

1 based on TV series,Where No Man Has Gone Before	15.00
2 Spirit in the Sky	10.00
3 Factor Q	8.00
4 Q's Day	8.00
5 Q's Effects	8.00
6 Here Today	8.00

[2nd Regular Series]

1 Return to Raimon	14.00
2 Murder Most Foul	8.50
3 Derelict	7.50
4 The Hero Factor	7.50
5 Serafin's Survivors	6.00
6 Shadows in the Garden	6.00
7 The Pilot	5.00
8 The Battle Within	5.00
9 The Pay Off	5.00
10 The Noise of Justice	5.00
11 The Imposter	4.00
12 Whoever Fights Monsters	4.00
13 The Hand of the Assassin	4.00
14 Holiday on Ice	4.00
15 Prisoners of the Ferengi	3.50
16 I Have Heard the Mermaids Singing	3.50
17 The Weapon	3.50
18 MM,Forbidden Fruit	3.50
19 The Lesson	3.50
20 Lost Shuttle	3.50

21 Lost Shuttle cont.	3.50
22 Lost Shuttle cont.	3.50
23 Lost Shuttle cont.	3.50
24 Lost Shuttle conc.	3.50
25 Okona S.O.S.	3.50
26 Search for Okona	3.00
27 Worf,Data,Troi,Okona trapped on world	3.00
28 Worf/K'Ehleyr story	3.00
29 Rift,pt.1	3.00
30 Rift,pt.2	3.00
31 Rift conclusion	3.00
32	3.00
33 R:Mischievous Q	3.00
34 V:Aliens,F:Mischievous Q	3.00
35 Way of the Warrior	2.50
36 Shore Leave in Shanzibar#1	2.50
37 Shore Leave in Shanzibar#2	2.50
38 Shore Leave in Shanzibar#3	2.50
39 Divergence #1	2.50
40 Divergence #2	2.50
41 V:Strazzan Warships	2.50
42 V:Strazzans	2.50
43 V:Strazzans	2.50
44 Disrupted Lives	2.50
45 F:Enterprise Surgical Team	2.50
46 Deadly Labyrinth	2.50
47 Worst of Both World's#1	2.50
48 Worst of Both World's#2	2.50
49 Worst of Both World's#3	2.50
50 Double Sized,V:Borg	4.00
51 V:Energy Beings	2.25
52 in the 1940's	2.25
53 F:Picard	2.25
54 F:Picard	2.25
55 Data on Trial	2.25
56 Abduction	2.25
57 Body Switch	2.25
58 Body Switch	2.25
59 B:Children in Chaos	2.25
60 Children in Chaos#2	2.25
61 E:Children in Chaos	2.25
62 V:Stalker	2.25
63 A:Romulans	2.25
64 Geordie	2.25
65 Geordie	2.25
66	2.25
67 Friends/Strangers	2.25
68 Friends/Strangers,pt.2	2.25
69 Friends/Strangers,pt.3	2.25
70 Friends/Strangers,pt.4	2.25
71 War of Madness,pt.1	2.50
72 War of Madness,pt.2	2.50
73 War of Madness,pt.3	2.50
Ann.#1 A:Mischievous Q	3.50
Ann.#2 BP,V:Parasitic Creatures	3.50
Ann.#3	2.50
Ann.#4 MiB(s),F:Dr.Crusher	3.50
Series Finale	4.25
Spec.#1	3.75
Spec.#2 CCl(s)	4.00
Star Trek N.G.:Sparticus	5.00
TPB Beginnings, BSz(c) rep.	19.95

STAR TREK N.G.: DEEP SPACE

1 Crossover with Malibu	2.50
2	2.50

STAR TREK N.G.: MODULA IMPERATIVE

1 A:Spock,McCoy	6.00
2 Modula Overrun by Ferengi	5.00
3 Picard,Spock,McCoy & Troi	

trapped	4.00
4 final issue	4.00

STAR TREK N.G.: SHADOWHEART

1	2.25
2	2.25
3	2.25
4 Worf Confront Nikolai	2.25

Static #13 © Milestone Media, Inc.

STATIC
Milestone

1 JPL,I:Static,Hotstreak,Frieda Goren, w/poster,card,D puzzle piece	4.00
1a Newstand Ed.	2.00
1b Platinum Ed.	40.00
2 JPL,V:Hotstreak,I:Tarmack	2.00
3 JPL,V:Tarmack	1.75
4 JPL,A:Holocaust,I:Don Cornelius	1.75
5 JPL,I:Commando X	1.75
6 JPL,V:Commando X	1.75
7 3RW,V:Commando X	1.75
8 WS(c),3RW,Shadow War,I:Plus	1.75
9 3RW,I:Virus	1.75
10 3RW,I:Puff,Coil	1.75
11 3RW,V:Puff,Coil	1.75
12 3RW,I:Joyride	1.75
13 I:Shape Changer	1.75
14 Worlds Collide,V:Rift	2.75
15 V:Paris Bloods	1.75
16 Revelations	1.75
17 Palisade	1.75
18 Princess Nightmare	1.75
19	1.75
20	1.75
21 A:Blood Syndicate	1.75
22 V:Rabis	1.75
23 A:Boogieman	1.75
24 A:Dusk	1.75
25 Long Hot Summer, V:Dusk, 48pgs	3.95

STEEL

1 JBg(c),B:LSi(s),CsB,N:Steel	3.00
2 JBg(c),CsB,V:Toastmaster	2.00
3 JBg(c),CsB,V:Amertek	2.00
4 JBg(c),CsB	2.00
5 JBg(c),CsB,V:Sister's Attacker	2.00

All comics prices listed are for *Near Mint* condition.

Steel #14
© *DC Comics, Inc.*

6 JBg(c),CsB,Worlds Collide,pt.5 . 2.00
7 Worlds Collide,pt.6 . . . . 1.75
8 Zero Hour,I:Hazard 1.75
9 F:Steel 1.50
10 F:Steel 1.50
11 . . . . 1.50
12 . . . . 1.50
13 A:Maxima 1.50
14 A:Superman 1.50
15 R:White Rabbit 1.50
16 V:White Rabbit
   [new Miraweb format begins] . . 1.95
17 Steel controls armor powers . . 1.95
Ann.#1 Elseworlds story 2.95

STEEL, THE
INDESTRUCTIBLE MAN
March, 1978

1 DH,I:Steel 1.00
2 DH 1.00
3 DH 1.00
4 DH 1.00
5 October-November, 1978 . . . . 1.00

STRANGE ADVENTURES
August-September, 1950

1 The Menace of the Green
  Nebula 1,900.00
2 S&K,JM(c),Doom From
  Planet X 900.00
3 The Metal World 600.00
4 BP,The Invaders From the
  Nth Dimension 550.00
5 The World Inside the Atom . . 500.00
6 The Confessions of a Martian 500.00
7 The World of Giant Ants . . . 500.00
8 MA,ATh,Evolution Plus 500.00
9 MA,B:Captain Comet,The
  Origin of Captain Comet . . 1,000.00
10 MA,CI,The Air Bandits
   From Space 500.00
11 MA,CI,Day the Past
   Came Back 350.00
12 MA,CI,GK(c),The Girl From
   the Diamond Planet 350.00
13 MA,CI,GK(c),When the Earth
   was Kidnapped 350.00
14 MA,CI,GK(c),Destination

Doom 350.00
15 MA,CI,GK(c),Captain Comet-
   Enemy of Earth 325.00
16 MA,CI,GK(c),The Ghost of
   Captain Comet 325.00
17 MA,CI,GK(c),Beware the
   Synthetic Men 325.00
18 CI,MA(c),World of Flying Men 325.00
19 CI,MA(c),Secret of the
   Twelve Eternals 325.00
20 CI,Slaves of the Sea Master 325.00
21 CI,MA(c),Eyes of the
   Other Worlds 250.00
22 CI,The Guardians of the
   Clockwork Universe 250.00
23 CI,MA(c),The Brain Pirates
   of Planet X 250.00
24 CI,MA(c),Doomsday on Earth 250.00
25 CI,GK(c),The Day
   That Vanished 250.00
26 CI,Captain Vs. Miss Universe 250.00
27 CI,MA(c),The Counterfeit
   Captain Comet 250.00
28 CI,Devil's Island in Space . . 250.00
29 CI,The Time Capsule From
   1,000,000 B.C. 250.00
30 CI,MA(c),Menace From the
   World of Make-Believe 225.00
31 CI,Lights Camera Action . . . 225.00
32 CI,MA(c),The Challenge of
   Man-Ape the Mighty 225.00
33 CI,MA(c),The Human Beehive 225.00
34 CI,MA(c) 225.00
35 CI,MA(c),Cosmic Chessboard 225.00
36 CI,MA(c),The Grab-Bag
   Planet 225.00
37 CI,MA(c),The Invaders From
   the Golden Atom 225.00
38 CI,MA(c),Seeing-Eye Humans 225.00
39 CI,MA(c),The Guilty Gorilla . 300.00
40 CI,MA(c),The Mind Monster . 225.00
41 CI,MA(c),The Beast From Out
   of Time 225.00
42 CI,MD,MA(c),The Planet of
   Ancient Children 225.00
43 CI,MD,MA(c),The Phantom
   Prize Fighter 225.00
44 CI,MA(c),The Planet That
   Plotted Murder 225.00
45 CI,MD,MA(c),Gorilla World . 225.00
46 CI,MA(c),E:Captain Comet
   Interplanetary War Base . . . 225.00
47 CI,MA(c),The Man Who Sold
   the Earth 225.00
48 CI,MA(c),Human Phantom . 225.00
49 CI,MA(c),The Invasion
   from Indiana 225.00
50 CI,MA(c),The World Wrecker 175.00
51 CI,MA(c),The Man Who
   Stole Air 175.00
52 CI,MA(c),Prisoner of the
   Parakeets 175.00
53 CI,MA(c),The Human Icicle . 175.00
54 CI,MA(c),The Electric Man . 125.00
55 CI,MA(c),The Gorilla Who
   Challanged the World,pt.I . . 125.00
56 CI,The Jungle Emperor,pt.II 125.00
57 CI,The Spy from Saturn . . . 125.00
58 CI,I Hunted the Radium Man 125.00
59 CI,The Ark From Planet X . . 125.00
60 CI,Across the Ages 125.00
61 CI,The Mirages From Space 125.00
62 CI,The Fireproof Man 125.00
63 CI,I Was the Man in the Moon 125.00
64 CI,GK(c),Gorillas In Space . 125.00

65 CI,GK(c),Prisoner From Pluto 125.00
66 CI,GK(c),The Human Battery 125.00
67 CI,GK(c),Martian Masquerader 125.00
68 CI,The Man Who Couldn't
   Drown 125.00
69 CI,Gorilla Conquest of Earth 125.00
70 CI,Triple Life of Dr. Pluto . . 125.00
71 CI,MSy,Zero Hour For Earth . 75.00
72 CI,The Skyscraper That Came
   to Life 75.00
73 CI,The Amazing Rain of Gems 75.00
74 CI,The Invisible Invader
   From Dimension X 75.00
75 CI,Secret of the Man-Ape . . . 75.00
76 CI,B:Darwin Jones,The Robot
   From Atlantis 75.00
77 CI,A:Darwin Jones,The World
   That Slipped Out of Space . . 75.00
78 CI,The Secret of the Tom
   Thumb Spaceman 75.00
79 CI,A:Darwin Jones,Invaders
   from the Ice World 75.00
80 CI,Mind Robbers of Venus . . 75.00
81 CI,The Secret of the
   Shrinking Twins 75.00
82 CI,Giants of the Cosmic Ray . 70.00
83 CI,Assignment in Eternity . . . 70.00

Strange Adventures #13
© *DC Comics, Inc.*

84 CI,Prisoners of the Atom
   Universe 70.00
85 CI,The Amazing Human Race 70.00
86 CI,The Dog That Saved the
   Earth 70.00
87 CI,New Faces For Old 70.00
88 CI,A:Darwin Jones,The Gorilla
   War Against Earth 70.00
89 CI,Earth For Sale 70.00
90 CI,The Day I Became a
   Martian 70.00
91 CI,Midget Earthmen of Jupiter 70.00
92 CI,GK(c),The Amazing Ray
   of Knowledge 70.00
93 CI,GK(c),A:Darwin Jones,
   Space-Rescue By Proxy 70.00
94 MA,CI,GK(c),Fisherman of
   Space 70.00
95 CI,The World at my Doorstep 70.00
96 CI,MA(c),The Menace of
   Saturn's Rings 70.00
97 CI,MA(c),MSy,Secret of the

Space-Giant 70.00
98 CI,GK(c),MSy,Attack on Fort
Satellite 70.00
99 CI,MSy,GK(c),Big Jump Into
Space 70.00
100 CI,MSy,The Amazing Trial
of John (Gorilla) Doe 100.00
101 CI,MSy,GK(c),Giant From
Beyond 60.00
102 MSy,GK(c),The Three Faces

Strange Adventures #235
© DC Comics, Inc.

of Barry Morrell 65.00
103 GK(c),The Man Who
Harpooned Worlds 65.00
104 MSy,GK(c),World of Doomed
Spacemen 65.00
105 MSy,GK(c),Fisherman From
the Sea 65.00
106 MSy,CI,GK(c),Genie in the
Flying Saucer 65.00
107 MSy,CI,GK(c),War of the
Jovian Bubble-Men 65.00
108 MSy,CI,GK(c),The Human
Pet of Gorilla Land 65.00
109 MSy,CI,GK(c),The Man Who
Weighted 100 Tons 65.00
110 MSy,CI,GK(c),Hand From
Beyond 65.00
111 MSy,CI,GK(c),Secret of
the Last Earth-Man 60.00
112 MSy,CI,GK(c),Menace of
the Size-Changing Spaceman 60.00
113 MSy,CI,GK(c),Deluge From
Space 60.00
114 MSy,CI,GK(c),Secret of the
Flying Buzz Saw 60.00
115 MSy,CI,GK(c),The Great
Space-Tiger Hunt 60.00
116 MSy,CI,RH,GK(c),Invasion
of the Water Warriors 60.00
117 MSy,CI,GK(c),I:Atomic
Knights 400.00
118 MSy,CI,The Turtle-Men of
Space 100.00
119 MSy,CI,MA(c),Raiders
From the Giant World 70.00

120 MSy,CI,MA,Attack of the Oil
Demons 175.00
121 MSy,CI,MA(c),Invasion of the
Flying Reptiles 45.00
122 MSy,CI,MA(c),David and the
Space-Goliath 45.00
123 MSy,CI,MA(c),Secret of the
Rocket-Destroyer 45.00
124 MSy,CI,MA(c),The Face-Hunter
From Saturn 45.00
125 MSy,CI,The Flying Gorilla
Menace 45.00
126 MSy,CI,MA(c),Return of the
Neanderthal Man 45.00
127 MSy,CI,MA(c),Menace
From the Earth-Globe 45.00
128 MSy,CI,MA(c),The Man
With the Electronic Brain 45.00
129 MSy,CI,MA(c),The Giant
Who Stole Mountains 45.00
130 MSy,CI,MA.War With the
Giant Frogs 45.00
131 MSy,CI,MA(c),Emperor
of the Earth 45.00
132 MSy,CI,MA(c),The Dreams
of Doom 45.00
133 MSy,CI,MA(c),The Invisible
Dinosaur 45.00
134 MSy,CI,MA(c), The Aliens
Who Raided New York 45.00
135 MSy,CI,MA(c),Fishing Hole
in the Sky 45.00
136 MSy,CI,MA(c),The Robot
Who Lost Its Head 30.00
137 MSy,CI,MA(c),Parade of the
Space-Toys 30.00
138 MSy,CI,MA(c),Secret of the
Dinosaur Skeleton 45.00
139 MSy,CI,MA(c),Space-Roots
of Evil 30.00
140 MSy,CI,MA(c),Prisoner of
the Space-Patch 30.00
141 MSy,CI,MA(c),Battle Between
the Two Earths 45.00
142 MSy,CI,MA(c),The Return of
the Faceless Creature 30.00
143 MSy,CI,MA(c),The Face in
the Atom-Bomb Cloud 30.00
144 MSy,CI,MA(c),A:Atomic
Knights, When the Earth
Blacked Out 45.00
145 MSy,CI,MA,The Man Who
Lived Forever 30.00
146 MSy,CI,MA(c),Perilous Pet
of Space 30.00
147 MSy,CI,MA(c),The Dawn-
World Menace 45.00
148 MSy,CI,MA(c),Earth Hero,
Number One 30.00
149 MSy,CI,MA(c),Raid of
the Rogue Star 30.00
150 MSy,CI,MA(c),When Earth
Turned into a Comet 35.00
151 MSy,CI,MA(c),Invasion Via
Radio-Telescope 28.00
152 MSy,MA(c),The Martian
Emperor of Earth 28.00
153 MSy,MA(c),Threat of the
Faceless Creature 28.00
154 CI,MSy,MA,GK(c),Earth's
Friendly Invaders 28.00
155 MSy,MA,GK(c),Prisoner
of the Undersea World 28.00
156 MSy,CI,MA(c),The Man
With the Head of Saturn 28.00

157 MSy,CI,MA(c),Plight of
the Human Cocoons 28.00
158 MSy,CI,MA(c),The Mind
Masters of Space 28.00
159 MSy,CI,MA(c),The Maze
of Time 28.00
160 MSy,CI,MA(c),A:Atomic
Knights, Here Comes the
Wild Ones 28.00
161 MSy,CI,MA(c),Earth's Frozen
Heat Wave,E:Space Museum 22.00
162 CI,MA(c),Mystery of the
12 O'Clock Man 20.00
163 MA(c),The Creature in
the Black Light 22.00
164 DD&SMo(c),I Became
a Robot 20.00
165 DD&SMo(c),I Broke the
Supernatural Barrier 20.00
166 DD&SMo(c),I Lived in
Two Bodies 20.00
167 JkS(c),The Team That
Conquered Time 20.00
168 JkS(c),I Hunted Toki
the Terrible 18.00
169 DD&SMo(c),The Prisoner
of the Hour Glass 18.00
170 DD&SMo(c),The Creature
From Strange Adventures . . . 18.00
171 The Diary o/t 9-Planet Man? 18.00
172 DD&SMo(c),I Became
the Juggernaut Man 18.00
173 The Secret of the
Fantasy Films 18.00
174 JkS(c),The Ten Ton Man . . 18.00
175 Danger: This Town is
Shrinking 18.00
176 DD&SMo(c),The Case of
the Cosmonik Quartet 18.00
177 I Lived a Hundred Lives,
O:Immortal Man 20.00
178 JkS(c),The Runaway Comet 18.00
179 JkS(c),I Buried Myself Alive . 18.00
180 CI,I:Animal Man,'I Was the
Man With Animal Powers . . 250.00
181 The Man of Two Worlds . . . 12.00
182 JkS(c),The Case of the
Blonde Bombshell 12.00
183 JM(c),The Plot to Destroy
the Earth 12.00
184 GK(c),A:Animal Man,The
Return of the Man With
Animal Powers 135.00
185 JkS(c),Ilda-Gangsters Inc. . . 12.00
186 Beware the Gorilla Witch . . . 12.00
187 JkS(c),O:The Enchantress . 20.00
188 SD,JkS(c),I Was the
Four Seasons 12.00
189 SD,JkS(c),The Way-Out
Worlds of Bertram Tilley 12.00
190 CI,A:Animal Man,A-Man-the
Hero with Animal Powers . . 150.00
191 JkS(c),Beauty vs. the Beast 12.00
192 Freak Island 12.00
193 The Villian Maker 12.00
194 JkS(c),The Menace of the
Super- Gloves 12.00
195 JkS(c),Secret of the Three
Earth Dooms,A:Animal Man . 80.00
196 JkS(c),Mystery of the
Orbit Creatures 12.00
197 The Hostile Hamlet 10.00
198 JkS(c),Danger! Earth
is Doomed 10.00
199 Robots of the Round Table . 10.00

200	10.00
201 JkS,Animal Man	50.00
202	10.00
203	10.00
204	10.00
205 CI,I&O:Deadman	50.00
206 NA,MSy	45.00
207 NA	35.00
208 NA	35.00
209 NA	35.00
210 NA	35.00
211 NA	35.00
212 NA	35.00
213 NA	35.00
214 NA	35.00
215 NA	35.00
216 NA	35.00
217 MA,MSy,A:Adam Strange	10.00
218 MA,CI,MSy	8.00
219 CI,JKu	8.00
220 CI,JKu	8.00
221 CI	8.00
222 MA,New Adam Strange	12.00
223 MA,CI	8.00
224 MA,CI	8.00
225 MA,JKu	8.00
226 MA,JKu,New Adam Strange	12.00
227 JKu	10.00
228 NA(c)	25.00
229	8.00
230 GM(c)	8.00
231 E:Atomic Knights	8.00
232 JKu	6.00
233 JKu	6.00
234 JKu	6.00
235 NA(c)	20.00
236	6.00
237	6.00
238 MK(c)	6.00
239	6.00
240 MK(c)	6.00
241	6.00
242 MA	6.00
243	6.00
244 October-November, 1974	6.00

STREETS

1 Tenderloin	4.95
2 Procurement	4.95
3	4.95

SUGAR & SPIKE
April-May, 1956

1 SM	650.00
2 SM	350.00
3 SM	275.00
4 SM	230.00
5 SM	230.00
6 thru 10 SM	@150.00
11 thru 20 SM	@125.00
21 thru 29 SM	@65.00
30 SM,A:Scribbly	80.00
31 thru 50 SM	@65.00
51 thru 70 SM	@50.00
71 thru 79 SM	@20.00
80 SM,I:Bernie the Brain	30.00
81 thru 97 SM	@20.00
98 SM,October-November, 1971	20.00

SUICIDE SQUAD
May, 1987

1 LMc,Legends,I:Jihad	2.50
2 LMc,V:The Jihad	2.00
3 LMc,V:Female Furies	1.75

4 LMc,V:William Hell	1.75
5 LM,A:Penguin	2.50
6 LM,A:Penguin	2.50
7 LMc,V:Peoples Hero	1.50
8 LMc,O:SquadMembers	1.50
9 LMc,Millenium	1.50
10 LMc,A:Batman	1.50
11 LMc,A:Vixen,Speedy	1.50
12 LMc,Enchantress, V:Nightshade	1.50
13 LMc,X-over,JLI#13	2.00
14 Nightshade Odyssey #1	1.50
15 Nightshade Odyssey #2	1.50
16 R:Shade	3.00
17 LMc,V:The Jihad	1.25
18 LMc,V:Jihad	1.25
19 LMc,Personal Files 1988	1.25
20 LMc,V:Mirror Master	1.25
21 LMc,bonus book #10	1.25
22 LMc,D:Senator Cray	1.25
23 LMc,Invasion	1.25
24 LMc,V:Guerillas	1.25
25 L:Nightshade	1.25
26 D:Rick Flag,Jihad	1.25
27 Janus Directive #2	1.25
28 Janus Directive #4	1.25
29 Janus Directive #8	1.25
30 Janus Directive #10	1.25

Suicide Squad #54 © DC Comics, Inc.

31 Personal Files 1989	1.25
32 V:Female Furies	1.25
33 GI,V:Female Furies	1.25
34 GI,V:Granny Goodness	1.25
35 LMc,GI,V:Female Furies	1.25
36 GI,D:Original Dr.Light	1.25
37 GI,A:Shade,The Changing Man,V:Loa	1.50
38 LMc,GI,O:Bronze Tiger	1.25
39 GI,D:Loa	1.25
40 Phoenix Gambit #1,A:Batman Int. Poster	1.50
41 Phoenix Gambit #2	1.25
42 Phoenix Gambit,A:Batman	1.25
43 Phoenix Gambit,A:Batman	1.25
44 I:New Atom,O:Captain Boomerang	1.25
45 A:Kobra	1.00
46 A:Kobra	1.00
47 GI,A:Kobra,D:Ravan	1.00
48 GI,New Thinker	1.00

49 GI,New Thinker	1.00
50 GI,50 Years of S.Squad	2.00
51 A:Deadshot	1.00
52 R:Docter Light	1.00
53 GI,The Dragon's Horde #1	1.00
54 GI,The Dragon's Horde #2	1.00
55 GI,The Dragon's Horde #3	1.00
56 GI,The Dragon's Horde #4	1.00
57 GI,The Dragon's Horde conc.	1.00
58 GI,War of the Gods x-over	1.00
59 GI,A:Superman, Batman, Aquaman,A:Jihad, Hayoth	1.25
60 GI,A:Superman,Batman, Aquaman,Jihad,The Hayoth	1.25
61 GI,A:Superman,Batman, Aquaman,V:Jihad	1.25
62 GI,R:Ray Palmer,A:Batman Superman,Aquaman	1.25
63 GI,I:Gvede, Lord of Death	1.25
64 GI,A:Task Force X	1.25
65 GI,Bronze Tiger	1.25
66 GI,Final Iss.E:Suicide Squad	1.25
Ann.#1 GN,V:Argent,A:Manhunter	1.75

SUPERBOY
March 1949

1 Superman (c)	5,000.00
2 'Superboy Day'	1,200.00
3	900.00
4 The Oracle of Smallville	650.00
5 Superboy meets Supergirl, Pre-Adventure #252	600.00
6 I:Humpty Dumpty,the Hobby Robber	525.00
7 WB,V:Humpty Dumpty	525.00
8 CS,I:Superbaby,V:Humpty Dumpty	500.00
9 V:Humpty Dumpty	475.00
10 CS,I:Lana Lang	500.00
11 CS,2nd Lang,V:Humpty Dumpty	400.00
12 CS,The Heroes Club	400.00
13 CS,Scout of Smallville	400.00
14 CS,I:Marsboy	400.00
15 CS,A:Superman	400.00
16 CS,A:Marsboy	300.00
17 CS,Superboy's Double	300.00
18 CS,Lana Lang-Hollywood Star	300.00
19 CS,The Death of Young Clark Kent	300.00
20 CS,The Ghost that Haunted Smallville	300.00
21 CS,Lana Lang-Magician	225.00
22 CS,The New Clark Kent	225.00
23 CS,The Super Superboy	225.00
24 CS,The Super Fat Boy of Steel	225.00
25 CS,Cinderella of Smallville	225.00
26 CS,A:Superbaby	225.00
27 CS,Clark Kent-Runaway.	235.00
28 CS,The Man Who Defeated Superboy	225.00
29 CS,The Puppet Superboy	225.00
30 CS,I:Tommy Tuttle	175.00
31 CS,The Amazing Elephant Boy From Smallville	175.00
32 CS,His Majesty King Superboy	175.00
33 CS,The Crazy Costumes of the Boy of Steel	175.00
34 CS,Hep Cats o/Smallville	175.00
35 CS,The Five Superboys	175.00
36	175.00
37 CS,I:Thaddeus Lang	175.00

Superboy #25 © DC Comics, Inc.

38 CS,Public Chimp #1 ...... 175.00
39 CS,Boy w/Superboy Powers 175.00
40 CS,The Magic Necklace ... 125.00
41 CS,Superboy Meets
   Superbrave 125.00
42 CS,Gaucho of Smallville ... 125.00
43 CS,Super-Farmer o/Smallville 125.00
44 The Amazing Adventure of
   Superboy's Costume 125.00
45 A Trap For Superboy 125.00
46 The Battle of Fort Smallville 125.00
47 CS,A:Superman 125.00
48 CS,Boy Without Super-Suit . 125.00
49 I:Metallo (Jor-El's Robot) .. 150.00
50 The Super-Giant of Smallville 125.00
51 I:Krypto 100.00
52 CS,The Powerboy from Earth 100.00
53 CS,A:Superman 100.00
54 CS,The Silent Superboy ... 100.00
55 CS,A:Jimmy Olson 100.00
56 CS,A:Krypto 100.00
57 CS,One-Man Baseball Team 100.00
58 CS,The Great Kryptonite
   Mystery 100.00
59 CS,A:Superbaby 100.00
60 The 100,000 Cowboy 100.00
61 The School For Superboys .. 75.00
62 I:Gloria Kent 75.00
63 CS,The Two Boys of Steel .. 75.00
64 CS,A:Superboy 75.00
65 Superboy's Moonlight Spell .. 75.00
66 The Family with X-Ray Eyes . 75.00
67 I:Klax-Ar 75.00
68 O&I:Bizarro 400.00
69 How Superboy Learned
   To Fly 55.00
70 O:Superboy's Glasses 55.00
71 A:Superbaby 55.00
72 The Flying Girl of Smallville . 55.00
73 CS,A:Superbaby 55.00
74 A:Jor-El & Lara 55.00
75 A:Superbaby 55.00
76 I:Super Monkey 55.00
77 Superboy's Best Friend 55.00
78 O:Mr.Mzyzptik 100.00
79 A:Jar-El & Lara 55.00
80 Superboy meets Supergirl ... 85.00
81 The Weakling From Earth ... 45.00
82 A:Bizarro Krypto 45.00

83 I:Kryptonite Kid 45.00
84 A:William Tell 45.00
85 Secret of Mighty Boy 45.00
86 I:PeteRoss,A:Legion 90.00
87 I:Scarlet Jungle of Krypton .. 40.00
88 The Invader from Earth 40.00
89 I:Mon-El 200.00
90 A:Pete Ross 40.00
91 CS,Superboy in Civil War ... 40.00
92 CS,I:Destructo,A:Lex Luthor . 40.00
93 A:Legion 45.00
94 I:Superboy Revenge Squad,
   A:Pete Ross 25.00
95 Imaginary Story,The Super
   Family From Krypton 25.00
96 A:Pete Ross,Lex Luther 25.00
97 Krypto Story 22.00
98 Legion,I&O:Ultraboy 40.00
99 O: The Kryptonite Kid 22.00
100 I:Phantom Zone 135.00
101 The Handsome Hound
   of Steel 12.00
102 O:Scarlet Jungle of Krypton 12.00
103 CS,A:King Arthur,Jesse James
   Red Kryptonite 12.00
104 O:Phantom Zone 16.00
105 CS,'The Simpleton of Steel' 12.00
106 CS,A:Brainiac 12.00
107 CS,I:Superboy Club of
   Smallville 15.00
108 The Kent's First Super Son . 12.00
109 The Super Youth of Bronze . 12.00
110 A:Jor-El 12.00
111 Red Kryptonite Story 12.00
112 CS,A:Superbaby 12.00
113 'The Boyhood of Dad Kent' . 12.00
114 A:Phantom Zone,
   Mr.Mxyzptlk 12.00
115 A:Phantom Zone,Lex Luthor 12.00
116 'The Wolfboy of Smallville' . 12.00
117 A:Legion 12.00
118 CS,'The War Between
   Superboy and Krypto' 11.00
119 V:Android Double 10.00
120 A:Mr.Mxyzptlk 10.00
121 CS,A:Jor-El,Lex Luthor 8.00
122 Red Kryptonite Story 8.00
123 CS,The Curse of the
   Superboy Mummy 8.00
124 I:Insect Queen 8.00
125 O:Kid Psycho 8.00
126 O:Krypto 8.00
127 A:Insect Queen 6.00
128 A:Phantom Zone,Kryptonite
   Kid,Dev En 6.00
129 rep.A:Mon-El,SuperBaby ... 11.00
130 .... 6.00
131 A:Lex Luthor,Mr.Mxyzptlk,I:
   Space Canine Patrol Agents .. 6.00
132, CS,A:Space Canine
   Patrol Agents 6.00
133 A:Robin, repr. 6.00
134 'The Scoundrel of Steel' 6.00
135 A:Lex Luthor 6.00
136 A:Space Canine Agents 6.00
137 Mysterious Mighty Mites 6.00
138 giant, Superboy's Most
   Terrific Battles 10.00
139 'The Samson of Smallville' .. 6.00
140 V:The Gambler 6.00
141 No Mercy for a Hero 6.00
142 A:Super Monkey 6.00
143 NA(c),'The Big Fall' 6.00
144 'Superboy's Stolen Identity' .. 6.00
145 NA(c)Kents become young .. 6.00

146 NA(c),CS,'The Runaway' ... 6.00
147 giant O:Legion 10.00
148 NA(c),CS,C:PolarBoy 5.50
149 NA(c),A:Bonnie & Clyde ... 5.50
150 JAb,V:Mr.Cipher 5.50
151 NA(c),A:Kryptonite Kid 5.50
152 NA(c),WW 5.50
153 NA(c),WW,A:Prof Mesmer ... 6.00
154 WW(i),A:Jor-El & Lara
   'Blackout For Superboy' 5.50
155 NA(c),WW,'Revolt of the
   Teenage Robots' 5.50
156 giant 8.00
157 WW 5.50
158 WW,A:Jor-El & Lara 5.50
159 WW(i),A:Lex Luthor 5.50
160 WW,'I Chose Eternal Exile' .. 5.50
161 WW,'The Strange Death of
   Superboy' 5.50
162 A:Phantom Zone 4.00
163 NA(c),'Reform School Rebel' . 4.00
164 NA(c),'Your Death Will
   Destroy Me' 4.00
165 giant 8.00
166 NA(c),A:Lex Luthor 4.00
167 NA(c),MA,A:Superbaby 4.00
168 NA(c),MA,Hitler 4.00
169 MA,A:Lex Luthor 3.00
170 MA,A:Genghis Khan 3.00
171 MA,A:Aquaboy 3.00
172 MA(i),GT,A:Legion,
   O:Lightning Lad,Yango 5.00
173 NA(c),GT,DG,O:CosmicBoy . 4.00
174 giant 8.00
175 NA(c),MA,Rejuvenation of
   Ma & Pa Kent 4.00
176 NA(c),MA,GT,WW,A:Legion . 4.00
177 MA,A:Lex Luthor 2.00
178 NA(c),MA,Legion Reprint ... 3.00
179 MA,A:Lex Luthor 2.00
180 MA,O:Bouncing Boy 2.00
181 MA 2.00
182 MA,A:Bruce Wayne 2.00
183 MA,GT,CS(rep),A:Legion ... 3.00
184 MA,WW,O:Dial H rep. 3.50
185 A:Legion 3.00
186 MA 2.00
187 MA 2.00
188 MA,DC,O:Karkan,A:Legn ... 2.00
189 MA 2.00
190 MA,WW 2.50
191 MA,DC O:SunBoy retold 2.00
192 MA 2.00
193 MA,WW,N:Chameleon Boy,
   Shrinking Violet 2.50
194 MA 2.00
195 MA,WW,I:Wildfire,
   N:Phantom Girl 2.50
196 last Superboy solo 2.00
197 DC,Legion begins, New
   Costumes,I:Tyr 6.00
198 DC N:Element Lad,
   Princess Projectra 3.00
199 DC,A:Tyr, Otto Orion 3.00
200 DC,M:Bouncing Boy
   & Duo Damsel 5.00
201 DC,Wildfire returns 3.00
202 N:Light Lass 3.00
203 MGr,D:Invisible Kid 3.00
204 MGr,A:Supergirl 3.00
205 MGr,CG,100 pages 4.00
206 MGr,A:Ferro Lad 3.00
207 MGr,O:Lightning Lad 3.00
208 MGr,CS,68pp,Legion of
   Super Villains 3.00

Superboy #168 © DC Comics, Inc.

209 MGr,N:Karate Kid 3.00
210 MGr,O:Karate Kid 3.00
211 MGr 2.50
212 MGr,L:Matter Eater Lad 2.50
213 MGr,V:Benn Pares 2.50
214 MGr,V:Overseer 2.50
215 MGr,A:Emerald Empress . . . 2.50
216 MGr,I:Tyroc 2.50
217 MGr,I:Laurel Kent 2.50
218 J:Tyroc,A:Fatal Five 2.50
219 MGr,A:Fatal Five 2.50
220 MGi,BWi 2.50
221 MGr,BWi,I:Grimbor 2.50
222 MGr,BWi,MN,BL,A:Tyroc . . . 2.50
223 MGr,BWi 2.50
224 MGr,BWi,V:Pulsar Stargrave . 2.50
225 MGr(c),BWi,JSh,MN 2.50
226 MGr(c),MN,JSh,JA,
    I:Dawnstar 2.75
227 MGr(c),JSon,JA,V:Stargrave . 2.50
228 MGr(c),JSh,JA,
    D:Chemical King 2.50
229 MGr(c),JSh,JA,V:Deregon . . 2.00
230 MGr(c),JSh,V:Sden 2.00

Becomes:

SUPERBOY & THE
LEGION OF
SUPER-HEROES

231 MGr(c),JSh,MN,JA,doub.size
    begins,V:Fatal Five 2.00
232 MGr(c),JSh,RE,JA,V:
    Dr.Regulus 2.00
233 MGr(c),JSh,BWi,MN,BL,
    I:Infinite Man 2.00
234 MGr(c),RE,JA,V:Composite
    Creature 2.00
235 MGr,GT 2.00
236 MGr(c),BMc,JSh,MN,JRu,
    V:Khunds 2.00
237 MGr(c),WS,JA 2.50
238 JSn(c),reprint 2.00
239 MGR(c),JSn,JRu,Ultra Boy
    accused 2.50
240 MGr(c),HC,BWi,JSh,BMc,
    O:Dawnstar;V:Grimbor 2.00
241 JSh,BMc,A:Ontir 2.00

242 JSh,BMc,E:Double Size 2.00
243 MGr(c),JA,JSon 2.00
244 JSon,V:Dark Circle 2.00
245 MA,JSon,V:Mordu 2.00
246 MGr(c),JSon,DG,MA,
    V:Fatal Five 2.00
247 JSon,JA,anniv.issue 2.00
248 JSon 2.00
249 JSon,JA 2.00
250 JSn,V:Omega 2.50
251 JSn,Brainiac 5 goes insane . . 2.50
252 JSon,V:Starburst bandits 2.00
253 JSon,I:Blok,League of
    Super Assassins 2.00
254 JSon,V:League of Super
    Assassins 2.00
255 JSon,A:Jor-El 2.00
256 JSon 2.00
257 SD,JSon,DA,V:Psycho
    Warrior 2.00
258 JSon,V:Psycho Warrior 2.00

Becomes:

Legion of Super Heroes
[2nd Series]

[NEW ADVENTURES OF]
SUPERBOY
January, 1980

1 KS 1.50
2 KS 1.25
3 KS 1.25
4 KS 1.25
5 KS 1.25
6 KS 1.25
7 KS,JSa 1.25
8 thru 33 KS . . . . @1.25
34 KS,I:Yellow Peri 1.25
35 thru 44 KS . . . . @1.25
45 KS,I:Sunburst 1.25
46 KS,A:Sunburst 1.25
47 KS,A:Sunburst 1.25
48 KS 1.25
49 KS,A:Zatara 1.25
50 KS,KG,A:Legion 1.50
51 KS,FM(c)In Between Years . . . 1.25
52 KS 1.25
53 KS 1.25
54 KS 1.25

SUPERBOY
February, 1990

1 TV Tie-in,JM,photo(c) 1.25
2 JM,T.J.White Abducted 1.25
3 JM,'Fountain of Youth' 1.25
4 JM,'Big Man on Campus' 1.25
5 JM,Legion Homage 1.25
6 JM,Luthor 1.25
7 JM,Super Boy Arrested 1.25
8 JM,AAd(i),Bizarro 1.25
9 JM/CS,PhantomZone#1 . . . . . . 1.25
10 JM/CS,PhantomZone#2 . . . . . 1.25
11 CS 1.25
12 CS,X-Mas in Smallville 1.25

Becomes:

ADVENTURES OF
SUPERBOY

13 A:Mr.Mxyzptlk 1.75
14 CS,A:Brimstone 1.25
15 CS,Legion Homage 1.25
16 CS,Into the Future 1.25
17 CS,A:Luthor 1.25
18 JM,'At the Movies' 1.25
19 JM,Blood Transfusion 1.25

20 JM,O:Nicknack,(G.Gottfried
    script) 1.25
21 V:Frost Monster 1.25
22 . . . . 1.25
Spec.#1 CS,A:Ma Kent 1.75

*Superboy (2nd Series) #1
© DC Comics, Inc.*

SUPERBOY
[2nd Series]

1 B:KK(s),TG,DHz,V:Sidearm . . . 3.00
2 TG,DHz,I:Knockout 2.50
3 TG,DHz,I:Scavenger 2.00
4 TG,DHz,MeP,I:Lock n' Load . . . 2.00
5 TG,DHz,I:Silver Sword 2.00
6 TG,DHz,Worlds Collide,pt.3
    C:Rocket 1.75
7 Worlds Collide, pt.8,V:Rift 1.75
8 Zero Hour,A:Superboy 1.50
9 Silican Dragon 1.50
10 Monster 1.50
11 Techno 1.50
12 Copperhead 1.50
13 Watery Grave,pt.1 . . . . 1.50
14 Watery Grave,pt.2 . . . . 1.50
15 Watery Grave,pt.3 . . . . 1.50
16 TG,DHz,KK,V:Loose Cannon
    [New Miraweb format begins] . 1.95
17 TG,DHz,KK Looking for
    Roxy Leech 1.95
Ann.#1 Elseworlds Story 3.25

SUPER FRIENDS
November, 1976

1 ECh(c),JO,RE,'Fury of the
    Superfoes',A:Penguin 2.50
2 RE,A:Penguin 1.50
3 RF(c),RF,A:JLA 1.50
4 RF,V:Riddler,I:Skyrocket 1.50
5 RF(c),RF,V:Greenback 1.50
6 RF(c),RF,A:Atom 1.50
7 RF(c),RF,I:Zan & Jana,
    A:Seraph 1.50
8 RF(c),RF,A:JLA 1.50
9 RF(c),RF,A:JLA,I:Iron Maiden . 1.50
10 RF(c),RF'TheMonkeyMenace' . 1.50
11 RF(c),RF 1.50
12 RF(c),RF,A:TNT 1.50
13 RF(c),RF 1.50

14 RF(c),RF 1.50
15 RF(c),RF, A:The Elementals . . 1.50
16 RF(c),RF,V:The Cvags 1.50
17 RF(c),RF,A:Queen Hippolyte . . 1.50
18 KS(c),V:Tuantra,Time Trapper . 1.50
19 RF(c),RF,V:Menagerie Man . . . 1.50
20 KS(c),KS,V:Frownin' Fritz 1.50
21 RF(c),RF,V:Evil Superfriends
    Doubles 1.50
22 RF(c),RF,V:Matador Mob 1.50
23 FR(c),RF,V:Mirror Master 1.50
24 RF(c),RF,V:Exorians 1.50
25 RF(c),RF,V:Overlord,
    A:Green Lantern, Mera 1.50
26 RF(c),RF,A:Johnny Jones 1.50
27 RF(c),RF,'The Spaceman Who
    Stole the Stars 1.50
28 RF(c),RF,A:Felix Faust 1.50
29 RF(c),RF,B.U.KS,'Scholar From
    the Stars 1.50
30 RF(c),RF,V:Grodd & Giganta . 1.50
31 RF(c),RF,A:Black Orchid 1.50
32 KS(c),KS,A:Scarecrow 1.50
33 RF(c),RF,V:Menagerie Man . . 1.50
34 RF(c)RF,'The Creature That
    Slept a Million Years' 1.50
35 RT,'Circus o/t Super Stars . . . 1.50
36 RF(c),RF,A:Plastic Man
    & Woozy 1.50
37 RF(c),RF,A:Supergirl;
    B.U. A:Jack O'Lantern 1.50
38 RF(c),RF,V:Grax;
    B.U. A:Serpah 1.50
39 RF(c),RF,A:Overlord;
    B.U. A:Wonder Twins 1.50
40 RF(c),RF,V:The Monacle;
    B.U. Jack O'Lantern 1.50
41 RF(c),RF,V:Toyman;
    B.U. A:Seraph 1.50
42 RT,A:Flora,V:Flame; B.U.Wonder
    Twins' Christmas Special 1.50
43 KS(c),RT,V:Futuro; B.U.JSon
    A:Plastic Man 1.50
44 KS(c),RT,'Peril o/t Forgotten
    Identities'; B.U.Jack O'Lantern . 1.50
45 KS(c),RT,A:Bushmaster,
    Godiva, Rising Sun, Olympian,
    Little Mermaid, Wild Huntsman;
    B.U. Plastic Man,V: Sinestro . . 1.50
46 RT,V:The Conqueror;
    B.U. BO,Seraph 1.50
47 KS(c),RT,A:Green Fury
    August 1981 . . . . 1.50

SUPERGIRL
[1st Regular Series]
November, 1972

1 'Trail of the Madman';
    Superfashions From Fans;
    B:B.U. DG,Zatanna 2.50
2 BO(c)A:Prof.Allan,Bottle
    City of Kandor 1.50
3 BO(c),'The Garden of Death' . . 1.50
4 V:Super Scavanger 1.50
5 BO(c),A:Superman,V:Dax; B.U.
    MA:Rep.Hawkman #4 . . . . 1.50
6 BO(c),'Love & War' 1.50
7 BO(c),A:Zatanna 1.50
8 BO(c),A:Superman,Green Lantern
    Hawkman 1.50
9 BO(c),V:Sharkman 1.50
10 A:Prey,V:Master Killer
    September 1974 . . . . 1.50

[DARING NEW
ADVENTURES OF]
SUPERGIRL
[2nd Regular Series]
November 1982

1 CI,BO,I:Psi; B:B.U.Lois Lane . 1.50
2 CI,BO,C:Decay 1.50
3 CI,BO,V:Decay,'Decay Day' . . 1.50
4 CI,BO,V:The Gang 1.50
5 CI,BO,V:The Gang 1.50
6 CI,BO,V:The Gang 1.50
7 CI,BO,V:The Gang 1.50
8 CI,BO,A:Doom Patrol 1.50
9 CI,BO,V:Reactron
    A:Doom Patrol 1.50
10 CI,BO,'Radiation Fever' 1.50
11 CI,BO,V:Chairman 1.50
12 CI,BO,V:Chairmann 1.50
13 CI,BO,N:Supergirl,A:Superman
    V:Blackstarr 1.50

Becomes:

SUPERGIRL
December, 1983

14 GK(c),CI,BO,V:Blackstarr
    A:Rabbi Nathan Zuber 1.50
15 CI,BO,V:Blackstarr,
    A:Blackstarr's Mom 1.50
16 KG/BO(c),CI,BO,
    A:Ambush Bug 1.50
17 CI/DG(c),CI,BO,V:Matrix
    Prime 1.50
18 DG(c),CI,BO, V:Kraken 1.50
19 EB/BO(c),CI,BO,'Who Stole
    Supergirl's Life' 1.50
20 CI,BO,C:JLA,Teen Titans:
    Teh Parasite 1.50
21 EB/BO(c),EB,Kryptonite Man . . 1.50
22 EB(c),CI,BO,'I Have Seen the
    Future & it is Me' 1.50
23 EB(c),CI,BO,'The Future
    Begins Today'
    September 1984 . . . . 1.50
Spec.#1 JL/DG(c),GM,Movie Adapt.1.50
Spec.#1 AT,Honda give-away . . . 1.50

[Limited Series]

1 KGa(c),B:RSt(s),JBr,O:Supergirl 2.00
2 KGa(c),JBr 1.75
3 KGa(c),JBr,D:Clones 1.75
4 KGa(c),RSt(s),JBr,final Issue . 1.75

SUPERGIRL/TEAM
LUTHOR SPECIAL

1 JBr,F:Supergirl,Lex Luthor 4.00

SUPER HEROES
BATTLE SUPER GORILLA
Winter, 1976

1 Superman Flash rep. 1.00

SUPERMAN
Summer 1939

1 JoS,O:Superman,reprints Action
    Comics #1-#4 . . . . 85,000.00
2 JoS,I:George Taylor 7,000.00
3 JoS,V:Superintendent
    Lyman 4,500.00
4 JoS,V:Lex Luthor 3,500.00
5 JoS,V:Lex Luthor 2,400.00
6 JoS,V:'Brute' Bashby 1,900.00
7 JoS,I:Perry White 2,000.00
8 JoS,V:Jackal 1,800.00
9 JoS,V:Joe Gatson 1,800.00

10 JoS,V:Lex Luthor 1,700.00
11 JoS,V:Rolf Zimba 1,200.00
12 JoS,V:Lex Luthor 1,200.00
13 JoS,I:Jimmy Olsen,V:Lex
    Luthor,'The Archer' 1,200.00
14 JoS,I:Lightning Master . . . 1,200.00
15 JoS,V:The Evolution King . 1,100.00
16 JoS,V:Mr. Sinus 1,000.00
17 JoS,V:Lex Luthor,Lois Lane first
    suspects Clark is Superman 1,000.00
18 JoS,V:Lex Luthor 950.00
19 JoS,V:Funnyface,
    1st Imaginary story 950.00
20 JoS,V:Puzzler,Leopard . . . 950.00
21 JoS,V:Sir Gauntlet 800.00

Superman #55 © DC Comics, Inc.

22 JoS,V:Prankster 750.00
23 JoS,Propaganda story 750.00
24 V:Cobra King 850.00
25 Propaganda story 750.00
26 I:J.Wilbur Wolfingham,
    A:Mercury 700.00
27 V:Toyman 700.00
28 V:J.Wilbur Wolfingham,
    A:Hercules 700.00
29 V:Prankster 700.00
30 I&O:Mr. Mxyztplk 1,100.00
31 V:Lex Luthor 650.00
32 V:Toyman 650.00
33 V:Mr. Mxyztptlk 650.00
34 V:Lex Luthor 650.00
35 V:J.Wilbur Wolfingham 650.00
36 V:Mr. Mxyztptlk 650.00
37 V:Prankster,A:Sinbad 650.00
38 V:Lex Luthor 650.00
39 V:J.Wilbur Wolfingham 650.00
40 V:Mr. Mxyzptlk,A:Susie
    Thompkins 650.00
41 V:Prankster 500.00
42 V:J.Wilbur Wolfingham 500.00
43 V:Lex Luthor 500.00
44 V:Toyman,A:Shakespeare . . 500.00
45 A:Hocus & Pocus,Lois Lane
    as Superwoman 500.00
46 V:Mr. Mxyzptlk,Lex Luthor,
    Superboy flashback 500.00
47 V:Toyman 500.00
48 V:Lex Luthor 500.00
49 V:Toyman 500.00
50 V:Prankster 500.00

---

51 V:Mr. Mxyzptlk	400.00
52 V:Prankster	400.00
53 WB,O:Superman	1,500.00
54 V:Wrecker	400.00
55 V:Prankster	400.00
56 V:Prankster	400.00
57 V:Lex Luthor	400.00
58 V:Tiny Trix	400.00
59 V:Mr.Mxyzptlk	400.00
60 V:Toyman	400.00
61 I:Kryptonite,V:Prankster	800.00
62 V:Mr.Mxyzptlk,A:Orson Welles	400.00
63 V:Toyman	400.00
64 V:Prankster	400.00
65 V:Mala,Kizo and U-Ban	400.00
66 V:Prankster	400.00
67 A:Perry Como,I:Brane Taylor	400.00
68 V:Lex Luthor	400.00
69 V:Prankster,A:Inspector Erskine Hawkins	400.00
70 V:Prankster	400.00
71 V:Lex Luthor	350.00
72 V:Prankster	350.00
72a giveaway	500.00
73 Flashback story	350.00
74 V:Lex Luthor	350.00
75 V:Prankster	350.00
76 A:Batman (Superman & Batman revel each other's identities)	1,000.00
77 A:Pocahontas	350.00
78 V:Kryptonian snagriff, A:Lana Lang	350.00
79 V:Lex Luthor,A:Inspector Erskine Hawkins	350.00
80 A:Halk Kar	350.00
81 V:Lex Luthor	350.00
82 V:Mr. Mxyzptlk	300.00
83 V:'The Brain'	300.00
84 Time-travel story	300.00
85 V:Lex Luthor	300.00
86 V:Mr.Mxyzptlk	300.00
87 WB,V:The Thing from 40,000 AD'	300.00
88 WB,V:Lex Luthor,Toyman, Prankster team	350.00
89 V:Lex Luthor	300.00
90 V:Lex Luthor	325.00
91 'The Superman Stamp'	300.00
92 Goes back to 12th Century England	300.00
93 V:'The Thinker'	300.00
94 'Clark Kent's Hillbilly Bride'	300.00
95 A:Susie Thompkins	300.00
96 V:Mr. Mxyzptlk	250.00
97 'Superboy's Last Day In Smallville'	250.00
98 'Clark Kent, Outlaw!'	250.00
99 V:Midnite gang	250.00
100 F:Superman-Substitute Schoolteacher	1,200.00
101 A:Lex Luthor	200.00
102 I:Superman Stock Company	200.00
103 A:Mr.Mxyzptlk	200.00
104 F:Clark Kent,Jailbird	200.00
105 A:Mr.Mxyzptlk	200.00
106 A:Lex Luthor	200.00
107 F:Superman In 30th century (pre-Legion)	200.00
108 I:Perry White Jr.	200.00
109 I:Abner Hokum	200.00
110 A:Lex Luthor	200.00

111 Becomes Mysto the Great	160.00
112 A:Lex Luthor	160.00
113 A:Jor-El	160.00
114 V:The Great Mento	160.00
115 V:The Organizer	160.00
116 Return to Smallville	160.00
117 A:Lex Luthor	160.00
118 F:Jimmy Olsen	160.00
119 A:Zoll Orr	160.00
120 V:Gadget Grim	160.00
121 I:XL-49 (Futureman)	130.00
122 In the White House	130.00
123 CS,pre-Supergirl tryout A:Jor-El & Lara	150.00
124 F:Lois Lane	125.00
125 F:Superman College Story	125.00
126 F:Lois Lane	125.00
127 WB,I&O:Titano	160.00
128 V:Vard & Boka	125.00
129 WB,I&O:Lori Lemaris	125.00

Superman #89 © DC Comics, Inc.

130 A:Krypto,the Superdog	160.00
131 A:Mr. Mxyzptlk	100.00
132 A:Batman & Robin	100.00
133 F:Superman Joins Army	100.00
134 A:Supergirl & Krypto	100.00
135 A:Lori Lemaris,Mr.Mxyzptlk	100.00
136 O:Discovery Kryptonite	100.00
137 CS,I:Super-Menace	100.00
138 A:Titano,Lori Lemaris	100.00
139 CS,O:Red Kryptonite	100.00
140 WB,I:Bizarro Jr,Bizarro Supergirl,Blue Kryptonite	125.00
141 I:Lyla Lerrol,A:Jor-EL & Lara	80.00
142 WB,CS,A:Al Capone	80.00
143 WB,F:Bizarro meets Frankenstein	80.00
144 O:Superboy's 1st Public Appearance	80.00
145 F:April Fool's Issue	80.00
146 F:Superman's life story	100.00
147 CS,I:Adult Legion	90.00
148 CS,V:Mxyzptlk	80.00
149 CS:A:Luthor,C:JLA	85.00
150 CS,KS,V:Mxyzptlk	40.00
151 CS	35.00
152 A:Legion	35.00

153 CS	35.00
154 CS,V:Mzyzptlk	35.00
155 WB,CS,V:Cosmic Man	35.00
156 CS,A:Legion,Batman	35.00
157 CS,I:Gold kryptonite	40.00
158 CS,I:Nightwing&Flamebird	35.00
159 CS,Imaginary Tale F:Lois Lane	35.00
160 CS,F:Perry White	35.00
161 D:Ma & Pa Kent	40.00
162 A:Legion	25.00
163 CS	24.00
164 CS,Luthor,I:Lexor	24.00
165 CS,A:Saturn Woman	24.00
166 CS	24.00
167 CS,I:Ardora,Brainiac	48.00
168 CS	24.00
169 Great DC Contest	24.00
170 CS,A:J.F.Kennedy,Luthor	24.00
171 CS,Mxyzptlk	24.00
172 CS,Luthor,Brainiac	24.00
173 CS,A:Batman	24.00
174 Mxyzptlk	24.00
175 CS,Luthor	24.00
176 CS,Green Kryptonite	24.00
177 Fortress of Solitude	24.00
178 CS, Red Kryptonite	24.00

Superman #259 © DC Comics, Inc.

179 CS,Clark Kent in Marines	24.00
180 CS	24.00
181 Superman 2965	24.00
182 CS,Toyman	24.00
183 giant	24.00
184 Secrets of the Fortress	20.00
185 JM,Superman's Achilles Heel	20.00
186 CS,The Two Ghosts of Superman	20.00
187 giant	20.00
188 V:Zunial,The Murder Man	15.00
189 WB,The Mystery of Krypton's Second Doom	18.00
190 WB,I:Amalak	20.00
191 The Prisoner of Demon	20.00
192 CS,Imaginary Story, I:Superman Jr.	20.00
193 giant	22.00
194 CS,Imaginary,A:Supes Jr.	20.00

195 CS,V:Amalak	20.00
196 WB,reprint	20.00
197 giant	22.00
198 CS,F:The Real Clark Kent	20.00
199 CS,F:Superman/Flash race, A:JLA	150.00
200 WB,A:Brainiac	20.00
201 CS,F:Clark Kent Abandons Superman	12.00
202 A:Bizarro,(giant size)	18.00
203 F:When Superman Killed His Friends	12.00
204 NA(c),RA,A:Lori Lemaris	12.00
205 NA(c),I:Black Zero	12.00
206 NA(c),F:The Day Superman Became An Assistant	12.00
207 CS,F:The Case Of the Collared Crimefighter	16.00
208 NA(c),CS	9.00
209 CS,F:The Clark Kent Monster	12.00
210 CS,F:Clark Kent's Last Rites	12.00
211 CS,RA	12.00
212 giant	16.00
213 CS,JA,V:Luthor,C:Brainiac 5	10.00
214 NA(c),CS,JA,F:The Ghosts That Haunted Superman	10.00
215 NA(c),CS,JA,V:Luthor, Imaginary Story	10.00
216 JKu(c),RA,Superman in Nam	10.00
217 CS,A:Mr.Mxyzptlk	16.00
218 CS,JA,A:Mr.Mxyzptlk	10.00
219 CS,F:Clark Kent-Hero, Superman Public Enemy	10.00
220 CS,A:Flash	10.00
221 CS,F:The Two Ton Superman	10.00
222 giant	16.00
223 CS,A:Supergirl	10.00
224 CS,Imaginary Story	10.00
225 CS,F:The Secret of the Super Imposter	10.00
226 CS,F:When Superman Became King Kong	10.00
227 Krypton,(giant)	16.00
228 CS,DA	10.00
229 WB,CS	10.00
230 CS,DA,Luthor	10.00
231 CS,DA,Luthor	10.00
232 F:Krypton,(giant)	16.00
233 CS,MA,I:Quarrum	10.00
234 NA(c),CS,MA	10.00
235 CS,MA	10.00
236 CS,MA,DG,A:Green Arrow	10.00
237 NA(c),CS,MA	10.00
238 CS,MA,GM	10.00
239 giant	16.00
240 CS,DG,MK,A:I-Ching	7.00
241 CS,MA,A:Wonder Woman	6.00
242 CS,MA,A:Wonder Woman	6.00
243 CS,MA	5.00
244 CS,MA	5.00
245 100 pg reprints	8.00
246 CS,MA,RB,I:S.T.A.R. Labs	4.00
247 CS,MA,Guardians o/Universe	4.00
248 CS,MA,A:Luthor,I:Galactic Golem	4.00
249 CS,MA,DD,NA,I:Terra-Man	7.50
250 CS,MA,Terraman	4.00
251 CS,MA,RB	4.00
252 NA(c),rep.100pgs	8.00
253 CS,MA	4.00
254 CS,MA,NA	7.50
255 CS,MA,DG	3.00
256 CS,MA	3.00
257 CS,MA,DD,DG,A:Tomar-Re	3.00
258 CS,MA,DC	3.00

259 CS,MA,A:Terra-Man	3.00
260 CS,DC,I:Valdemar	3.00
261 CS,MA,V:Star Sapphire	3.00
262 CS,MA	3.00
263 CS,MA,DD,FMc	3.00
264 DC,CS,I:SteveLombard	3.00
265 CS,MA	3.00
266 CS,MA,DD,V:Snowman	3.00
267 CS,MA,BO	3.00
268 CS,BO,DD,MA,A:Batgirl	3.00
269 CS,MA	3.00
270 CS,MA,V:Valdemar	3.00
271 CS,BO,DG,V:Brainiac	3.00
272 100pg.reprints	5.00
273 CS,DG	2.50
274 CS	2.50
275 CS,DG,FMc	2.50
276 CS,BO,I&O:Captain Thunder	2.50

Superman #292 © DC Comics, Inc.

277 CS	2.50
278 CS,BO,Terraman,100page	5.00
279 CS,Batgirl,Batman	3.00
280 CS,BO	2.50
281 CS,BO,I:Vartox	2.50
282 CS,KS,N:Luthor	2.50
283 CS,BO,Mxyzptlk	2.50
284 CS,BO,100p reprint	5.00
285 CS,BO	2.50
286 CS,BO	2.50
287 CS,BO,R:Krypto	2.50
288 CS,BO	2.50
289 CS,BO,JL	2.50
290 CS,V:Mxyzptlk	2.50
291 CS,BO	2.50
292 CS,BO,AM,O:Luthor	2.50
293 CS,BO	2.50
294 CS,JL,A:Brain Storm	2.50
295 CS,BO	2.50
296 CS,BO,Identity Crisis #1	2.50
297 CS,BO,Identity Crisis #2	2.50
298 CS,BO,Identity Crisis #3	2.50
299 CS,BO,Identity Crisis #4 A:Luthor,Brainiac,Bizarro	2.50
300 CS,BO,2001,anniversary	5.50
301 BO,JL,V:Solomon Grundy	2.50
302 JL,BO,V:Luthor,A:Atom	2.50
303 CS,BO,I:Thunder&Lightning	2.50
304 CS,BO,V:Parasite	2.50

305 CS,BO,V:Toyman	2.50
306 CS,BO,V:Bizarro	2.50
307 NA(c),JL,FS,A:Supergirl	2.50
308 NA(c),JL,FS,A:Supergirl	2.50
309 JL,FS,A:Supergirl	2.25
310 CS,V:Metallo	2.25
311 CS,FS,A:Flash	2.25
312 CS,FS,A:Supergirl	2.25
313 NA(c),CS,DA,A:Supergirl	2.25
314 NA(c),CS,DA,A:Gr.Lantern	2.25
315 CS,DA,V:Blackrock	2.25
316 CS,DA,V:Metallo	2.25
317 NA(c),CS,DA,V:Metallo	2.25
318 CS	2.00
319 CS,V:Solomon Grundy	2.00
320 CS,V:Solomon Grundy	2.00
321 CS,V:Parasite	2.00
322 CS,V:Solomon Grundy	2.00
323 CS,DA,I:Atomic Skull	2.00
324 CS,A:Atomic Skull	2.00
325 CS	2.00
326 CS,V:Blackrock	2.00
327 CS,KS,V:Kobra,C:JLA	2.00
328 CS,KS,V:Kobra	2.00
329 KS,CS	2.00
330 CS,F:glasses explained	2.00
331 CS,I:Master Jailer	2.00
332 CS,V:Master Jailer	2.00
333 CS,V:Bizarro	2.00
334 CS	2.00
335 CS,W:Mxyzptlk	2.00
336 CS,V:Rose And Thorn	2.00
337 CS,A:Brainiac,Bizarro	2.00
338 CS,F:Kandor enlarged	2.00
339 CS,I.N.R.G.X	2.00
340 CS,V:N.R.G.X	2.00
341 CS,F:Major Disaster	2.00
342 CS,V:Chemo	2.00
343 CS	2.00
344 CS,A:Phantom Stranger	2.00
345 CS,'When time ran backward'	2.00
346 CS,'Streak of Bad Luck'	2.00
347 JL	2.00
348 CS	2.00
349 CS,V:Mxyzptlk	2.00
350 CS,'Clark Kent's Vanishing Classmate'	2.00
351 CS,JL,A:Mxyzptlk	2.00
352 CS,RB	2.00
353 CS,origin	2.00
354 CS,JSon,I:Superman 2020	2.00
355 CS,JSon,F:Superman 2020	2.00
356 CS,V:Vartox	2.00
357 CS,DCw,F:Superman 2020	2.00
358 CS,DG,DCw	2.00
359 CS	2.00
360 CS,AS,F:World of Krypton	2.00
361 CS,AS	2.00
362 CS,KS,DA	2.00
363 CS,RB,C:Luthor	2.00
364 GP(c),RB,AS	2.00
365 CS,KS	2.00
366 CS,KS	2.00
367 CS,GK,F:World of Krypton	2.00
368 CS,AS	2.00
369 RB,FMc,V:Parasite	2.00
370 CS,KS,FMc,A:Chemo	2.00
371 CS	2.00
372 CS,GK,F:Superman 2021	2.00
373 CS,V:Vartox	2.00
374 GK(c),CS,DA,KS,V:Vartox	2.00
375 CS,DA,GK,V:Vartox	2.00
376 CS,DA,CI,BO,SupergirlPrev.	1.75
377 GK(c),CS,V:Terra-Man	1.75
378 CS	1.75

All comics prices listed are for *Near Mint* condition.　　　**CVA Page 101**

379 CS,V:Bizarro	1.75
380 CS	1.75
381 GK(c),CS	1.75
382 GK(c),CS	1.75
383 CS	1.75
384 GK(c),CS	1.75
385 GK(c),CS,V:Luthor	1.75
386 GK(c),CS,V:Luthor	1.75
387 GK(c),CS	1.75
388 GK(c),CS	1.75
389 GK(c),CS	1.75
390 GK(c),CS,V:Vartox	1.75
391 GK(c),CS,V:Vartox	1.75
392 GK(c),CS,V:Vartox	1.75
393 IN,DG,V:Master Jailer	1.75
394 CS,V:Valdemar	1.75
395 CS,V:Valdemar	1.75
396 CS	1.75
397 EB,V:Kryptonite Man	1.75
398 CS,AS,DJ	1.75
399 CS,BO,EB	1.75
400 HC(c),FM,AW,JO,JSo,MR, TA,WP,MK,KJ,giant	4.00
401 CS,BO,V:Luthor	1.75
402 CS,BO,WB	1.75
403 CS,BO,AS	1.75
404 CI,BO,V:Luthor	1.75
405 KS,KK,AS,F:Super-Batman	1.75
406 IN,AS,KK	1.75
407 IN,V:Mxyzptlk	1.75
408 CS,AW,JRu,F:Nuclear Holocaust	1.75
409 CS,AW,KS	1.75
410 CS,AW,V:Luthor	1.75
411 CS,MA,F:End Earth-Prime	1.75
412 CS,AW,V:Luthor	1.75
413 CS,AW,V:Luthor	1.75
414 CS,AW,Crisis tie-in	2.00
415 CS,AW,Crisis,W:Super Girl	2.00
416 CS,AW,Luthor	1.75
417 CS,V:Martians	1.75
418 CS,V:Metallo	1.75
419 CS,V:Iago	1.75
420 CS,F:Nightmares	1.75
421 CS,V:Mxyzptlk	1.75
422 BB(c),CS,TY,LMa,V:Werewolf	1.75
423 AMo(s),CS,GP,F:Last Superman	10.00
Ann.#1 I:Supergirl Rep	500.00
Ann.#2 I&O:Titano	250.00
Ann.#3 I:Legion	200.00
Ann.#4 O:Legion	150.00
Ann.#5 A:Krypton	125.00
Ann.#6 A:Legion	100.00
Ann.#7 O:Superman,Silver Anniv.	75.00
Ann.#8 F:Secret origins	50.00
Ann.#9 GK(c),ATh,TA,CS, A:Batman	6.00
Ann.#10 CS,MA,F:Sword of Superman	5.00
Ann.#11 AMo(s),DGb,A:Batman, Robin,Wonder Woman	6.00
Ann.#12 BB(c),AS,A:Lex Luthor, Last War Suit	3.00
Game Give-away	10.00
Giveaway CS,AT	2.00
Pizza Hut 1977	6.00
Radio Shack 1980 JSw,DG	5.00
Radio Shack 1981 CS	5.00
Radio Shack 1982 CS	5.00
Spec.#1 GK	3.50
Spec.#2 GK,V:Brainiac	3.50
Spec.#3 IN,V:Amazo	3.50
Superman III Movie,CS	1.50
Superman IV Movie,DH,DG,FMc	1.50

Becomes:
ADVENTURES OF SUPERMAN

424 JOy,I:Man O'War	3.00
425 JOy,Man O'War	2.50
426 JOy,Legends,V:Apokolips	2.50
427 JOy,V:Qurac	2.50
428 JOy,V:Qurac,I:JerryWhite	2.50
429 JOy,V:Concussion	2.50
430 JOy,V:Fearsome Five	2.50
431 JOy,A:Combattor	2.00
432 JOy,I:Jose Delgado	2.00
433 JOy,V:Lex Luthor	2.00
434 JOy,I:Gang Buster	2.50
435 JOy,A:Charger	2.00
436 JOy,Millenium x-over	2.00
437 JOy,Millenium X-over	2.00
438 JOy,N:Brainiac	2.50
439 JOy,R:Superman Robot	2.00

The Adventures of Superman #485
© DC Comics, Inc.

440 JOy,A:Batman,Wond.Woman	2.00
441 JOy,V:Mr.Mxyzptlk	2.00
442 JOy,V:Dreadnaught,A:JLI	2.00
443 JOy,DHz,I:Husque	2.00
444 JOy,Supergirl SagaPt.2	2.00
445 JOy,V:Brainiac	2.00
446 JOy,A:Gangbuster, A:Luthor's Old Costume	2.00
447 JOy,A:Gangbuster	2.00
448 JOy,I:Dubbilex,A:Gangbuster	2.00
449 JOy,Invasion X-over	2.00
450 JOy,Invasion X-over	2.00
451 JOy,'Superman in Space'	2.00
452 DJu,V:Wordbringer	2.00
453 JOy,DJu,A:Gangbuster	2.00
454 JOy,DJu,V:Mongul	2.50
455 DJu,ATb,A:Eradicator	6.00
456 DJu,ATb,V:Turmoil	2.00
457 DJu,V:Intergang	2.00
458 DJu,KJ,R:Elastic Lad (Jimmy Olsen)	2.00
459 DJu,V:Eradicator	3.00
460 DJu,NKu,V:Eradicator	3.00
461 DJu,GP,V:Eradicator	3.00
462 DJu,ATb,Homeless Christmas Story	2.00

463 DJu,ATb,Superman Races Flash	3.00
464 DJu,ATb,Day of Krypton Man #2,A:Lobo	3.50
465 DJu,ATb,Day of Krypton Man #5,V:Draaga	3.00
466 DJu,DG,V:Team Excalibur Astronauts,I:Hank Henshaw (becomes Cyborg Superman)	10.00
467 DJu,ATb,A:Batman	2.50
468 DJu,ATb,Man Of Steel's Journal,V:Hank Henshaw	8.00
469 DJu,ATb,V:Dreadnaught	2.00
470 DJu,ATb,Soul Search #3, D:Jerry White	2.00
471 CS,Sinbad Contract #2	2.00
472 DJu,ATb,Krisis of Krimson Kryptonite #2	3.00
473 DJu,ATb,A:Green Lantern, Guy Gardner	2.00
474 DJu,ATb,Drunk Driving issue	2.00
475 DJu,ATb,V:Kilgrave,Sleez	2.00
476 DJu,BBr,Time & Time Again,pt.1, A:Booster Gold,Legion	2.00
477 DJu,BBr,T & T Again,pt.4, A:Legion	2.00
478 DJu,BBr,T & T Again,pt.7, A:Legion,Linear Man	2.00
479 EH,Red Glass Trilogy#2	2.00
480 JOy,DJu,BMc,TG,BBr,CS, Revenge of the Krypton Man,pt.3	3.00
481 1st TG Supes,DHz,V:Parasite	2.00
482 TG,DHz,V:Parasite	2.00
483 TG,DHz,V:Blindspot	2.00
484 TG,Blackout #1,V:Mr.Z	2.00
485 TG,DHz,Blackout #5,A:Mr.Z	2.00
486 TG,V:Purge	2.00
487 TG,DHz,X-mas,A:Agent Liberty	2.00
488 TG,Panic in the Sky,pt.3, V:Brainiac	3.00
489 TG,Panic in the Sky,Epilope	3.00
490 TG,A:Agent Liberty,Husque	1.75
491 TG,DHz,V:Cerberus,Metallo	1.75
492 WS(c),V:Sons of Liberty, A:Agent Liberty	1.75
493 TG,Blaze/Satanus War,pt.1	1.75
494 TG,DHz,I:Kismet	1.75
495 TG,DHz,A:Forever People, Darkseid	1.75
496 V:Mr.Mxyzptlk,C:Doomsday	5.00
496a 2nd printing	1.50
497 TG,Doomsday Pt.3,A:Maxima, Bloodwynd	10.00
497a 2nd printing	1.75
498 TG,Funeral for a Friend#1	5.00
498a 2nd Printing	1.25
499 TG,DHz,Funeral for a Friend#5	3.50
500 JOy(c),B:KK(s),TG,DJu,JBg,JG, BBr,Bagged,Superman in limbo, I:Four Supermen,Direct Sales	3.50
500a Newsstand Ed.	3.00
500b Platinum Ed.	70.00
501 TG,Reign of Supermen#2,Direct Sales,Die-Cut(c),Mini-poster F:Superboy	2.50
501a Newstand Ed.	2.00
502 TG,A:Supergirl,V:Stinger	2.00
503 TG,Cyborg Superman Vs. Superboy	2.50
504 TG,DHz,A:All Supermen, V:Mongul	3.00
505 TG,DHz,Superman returns to	

Adventures of Superman #499
© DC Comics, Inc.

Metropolis,Holografx(c) 3.00
505a Newstand Ed. 2.00
506 TG,DHz,A:Guardian 1.75
507 Spilled Blood#1,V:Bloodsport   1.75
508 BKi,A:Challengers of the
  Unknown 1.75
509 BKi,A:Auron 1.75
510 BKi,Bizarro's World#2,
  V:Bizarro 1.75
511 BKi,A:Guardian 1.75
512 BKi,V:Parasite 1.75
513 BKi,Battle for Metropolis #4 . . 1.75
514 BKi,Fall of Metropolis #4 . . . . 1.75
515 BKi,Massacre in Metropolis . . 1.75
516 BKi,Zero Hour,I:Alpha
  Centurion 1.50
517 BKi,deathtrap 1.50
518 BKi 1.50
519 KK,BKi,Secret of Superman's
  Tomb 1.50
520 SI,KK,JMz,100 crimes at
  midnight 1.50
521 SI,KK,R:Thorn 1.50
522 SI,KKIdentity known 1.50
523 SI,KK,Death of C.Kent,pt.2 . . 1.50
524 SI,KK,Death of C.Kent,pt.6
  [New Miraweb format begins] . 1.95
525 SI,KK 1.95
Ann.#1 JSn(c),DJu,I:Word Bringer 3.00
Ann.#2 CS/JBy,KGa/DG,BMc,
  A:L.E.G.I.O.N.'90 (Lobo) 5.50
Ann.#3 BHi,JRu,DG,
  Armageddon 2001. . . . . 3.00
Ann.#4 BMc,A:Lobo,Guy Gardner,
  Eclipso tie-in 3.00
Ann.#5 TG,I:Sparx 2.75
Ann.#6 MMi(c),Elseworlds Story . 3.00
Superman Archives HC rep 39.95

SUPERMAN'S BUDDY
1954
1 w/costume 1,000.00
1 w/out costume 400.00

SUPERMAN'S CHRISTMAS ADVENTURE
1 (1940) 2,000.00
2 (1944) 675.00

SUPERMAN AND THE GREAT CLEVELAND FIRE
1948
1 for Hospital Fund 400.00

SUPERMAN (miniature)
1942
1 Py-Co-Pay Tooth Powder
  Give- Away 600.00
2 CS,Superman Time Capsule 400.00
3 CS,Duel in Space 250.00
4 CS,Super Show in Metropolis 250.00

SUPERMAN RECORD COMIC
1966
1 w/record 100.00
1 w/out record 35.00

SUPERMAN-TIM STORE PAMPHLETS
1942
Superman-Tim store Monthly
  Membership Pamphlet, 16
  pages of stories, games,
  puzzles (1942), each 100.00
Superman-Tim store Monthly
  Membership Pamphlet, 16
  pages of stories, games,
  puzzles (1943), each 100.00
Superman-Tim store Monthly
  Membership Pamphlet, 16
  pages of stories, games,
  puzzles (1944), each 100.00
Superman-Tim store Monthly
  Membership Pamphlet, 16
  pages of stories, games,
  puzzles (1945), each 100.00
Superman-Tim store Monthly
  Membership Pamphlet, 14-16
  pages of stories, games,
  puzzles, 5"x8" color(c),
  (1946), each 100.00
Superman-Tim stamp
  album, 1946 . . . . 150.00
Superman-Tim store Monthly
  Membership Pamphlet, 14-16
  pages of stories, games,
  puzzles, 5"x8" color(c),
  (1947), each 100.00
Superman-Tim stamp album,
  Superman story, 1947 . . . . 175.00
Superman-Tim store Monthly
  Membership Pamphlet, 14-16
  pages of stories, games,
  puzzles, 5"x8" color(c),(1948),
  each 100.00
Superman-Tim stamp
  album, 1948 . . . . 125.00
Superman-Tim store Monthly
  Membership Pamphlet, 14-16
  pages of stories, games,
  puzzles, 5"x8" color(c),
  (1949), each 100.00
Superman-Tim store Monthly
  Membership Pamphlet, 14-16
  pages of stories, games,

puzzles, 5"x8" color(c)
(1950), each 100.00

Superman (2nd Regular Series) #1
© DC Comics, Inc.

SUPERMAN
[2nd Regular Series]
January, 1987
1 JBy,TA,I:Metallo 5.00
2 JBy,TA,V:Luthor 3.00
3 JBy,TA,Legends tie-in 2.50
4 JBy,KK,V:Bloodsport 2.25
5 JBy,KK,V:Host 2.00
6 JBy,KK,V:Host 2.00
7 JBy,KK,V:Rampage 2.00
8 JBy,KK,A:Superboy,Legion . . . 2.00
9 JBy,KK,V:Joker 3.50
10 JBy,KK,V:Rampage 2.00
11 JBy,KK,V:Mr.Mxyzptlk 2.00
12 JBy,KK,A:Lori Lemaris 2.00
13 JBy,KK,Millenium 2.00
14 JBy,KK,A:Green Lantern 2.00
15 JBy,KK,I:New Prankster 2.00
16 JBy,KK,A:Prankster 2.00
17 JBy,KK,O:Silver Banshee . . . 2.00
18 MMi,KK,A:Hawkman 2.00
19 JBy,V:Skyhook 2.00
20 JBy,KK,A:Doom Patrol 2.50
21 JBy,A:Supergirl 2.00
22 JBy,A:Supergirl 2.00
23 MMi,CR,O:Silver Banshee . . . 2.00
24 KGa,V:Rampage 2.00
25 KGa,V:Brainiac 2.00
26 KGa,BBr,V:Baron Sunday 2.00
27 KGa,BBr,V:Guardian 2.00
28 KGa,BBr,Supes Leaves Earth . 2.00
29 DJu,BBr,V:Word Bringer 2.00
30 KGa,DJu,A:Lex Luthor 2.00
31 DJu,PCu,V:Mxyzptlk 2.00
32 KGa,V:Mongul 2.00
33 KGa,A:Cleric 2.00
34 KGa,V:Skyhook 2.00
35 CS,KGa,A:Brainiac 2.00
36 JOy,V:Prankster 2.00
37 JOy,A:Guardian 2.00
38 JOy,Jimmy Olsen Vanished . . 2.00
39 JOy,KGa,V:Husque 2.00

40 JOy,V:Four Armed Terror 2.00
41 JOy,Day of Krypton Man #1,
A:Lobo 3.50
42 JOy,Day of Krypton Man #4,
V:Draaga 3.50
43 JOy,V:Krypton Man 2.00
44 JOy,A:Batman 2.00
45 JOy,F:Jimmy Olsen's Dairy . . 2.00
46 DJu,JOy,A:Jade, Obsidian,
I:New Terra-Man 2.00
47 JOy,Soul Search #2,V:Blaze . 2.00
48 CS,Sinbad Contract #1 . . . . . 2.00
49 JOy,Krisis of K.Kryptonite#1 . . 3.00
50 JBy,KGa,DJu,JOy,BBr,CS,Krisis
of Krimson Kryptonite #4,
Clark Proposes To Lois 6.00
50a 2nd printing 1.50
51 JOy,I:Mr.Z 1.75
52 KGa,V:Terra-Man 1.75
53 JOy,Superman reveals i.d. . . . 3.50
53a 2nd Printing 1.25
54 JOy,KK,Time & Time Again#3 . 1.75
55 JOy,KK,Time & Time Again#6 . 1.75
56 EH,KK,Red Glass Trilogy#1 . . 1.75
57 JOy,DJu,BBr,ATi,JBg,BMc,TG,
Revenge o/t Krypton Man #2 . . 3.50
58 DJu,BBr,I:Bloodhounds 1.75
59 DJu,BBr,A:Linear Men 1.75
60 DJu,EB,I:Agent Liberty,
V:Intergang 2.00
61 DJu,BBr,A:Waverider,
V:Linear Men 1.75
62 DJu,BBr,Blackout #4,A:Mr.Z . . 1.75
63 DJu,A:Aquaman 1.75
64 JG,Christmas issue 1.75
65 DJu,Panic in the Sky#2,
I:New Justice League 3.50
66 DJu,Panic in the Sky#6,
V:Brainiac 4.00
67 DJu,Aftermath 1.75
68 DJu,V:Deathstroke 1.75
69 WS(c),DJu,A:Agent Liberty . . . 1.75
70 DJu,BBr,A:Robin,V:Vampires . 1.75
71 DJu,Blaze/Satanus War 1.75
72 DJu,Crisis at Hand#2 . . . . 1.75
73 DJu,A:Waverider,V:Linear
Men,C:Doomsday 6.00
73a 2nd printing 1.50
74 DJu,V:Doomsday,A:JLA . . . 12.00
74a 2nd printing 1.75
75 DJu,V:Doomsday,D:Superman,
Collectors Ed. 22.00
75a newstand Ed. 9.00
75b 2nd printing 4.00
75c 3rd printing 1.50
75d 4th Printing 1.25
75e Platinum Ed. 150.00
76 DJu,BBr,Funeral for Friend#4 . 3.00
77 DJu,BBr,Funeral for Friend#8 . 3.00
78 DJu,Reign of Supermen#3,
Die-Cut(c),Mini poster,F:Cyborg
Supes,A:Doomsday 2.50
78a Newstand Ed. 2.00
79 DJu,BBr,Memorial Service for
Clark 2.00
80 DJu,BBr,Coast City Blows up,
V:Mongul 4.00
81 DJu,O:Cyborg Superman 3.50
82 DJu,Chromium(c),A:All Supermen,
V:Cyborg Superman 5.00
82a Newstand Ed. 2.25
83 DJu,A:Batman 1.75
84 DJu,V:Toyman 1.75
85 DJu,V:Toyman 1.75
86 DJu,A:Sun Devils 1.75

87 DJu(c&s),SI,JRu,Bizzaro's World#1
R:Bizarro 1.75
88 DJu(c&s),SI,JRu,Bizzaro's World#5
D:Bizarro 1.75
89 DJu(c&s),V:Cadmus Project . . 1.75
90 DJu(c&s),Battle for
Metropolis#3 . . . . 1.75
91 DJu(c&s),Fall of Metropolis#3 . 1.75
92 Massacre in Metropolis 1.75
93 Zero Hour,A:Batman 1.75
94 Conduit 1.75
95 Brainiac 1.75
96 Virtual Reality 1.75
97 Shadow Dragon 1.75
98 R:Shadow Strike 1.75
99 R:Agent Liberty 1.75
100 BBr,DJu,Death of C.Kent,pt.1 2.95
100a Collectors Edition 3.95
101 Death of Clark Kent,pt.5
[New Miraweb format begins] . 1.95
102 DJu,A:Captain Marvel 1.95
Ann.#1 RF,BBr,A:Titano 2.00
Ann.#2 RF,BBr,R:Newsboy Legion
& Guardian 3.00
Ann.#3 DAb(1st Work),TA,DG,
Armageddon 2001. . . . . 9.00
Ann.#3a 2nd printing(silver) 2.00
Ann.#4 Eclipso 2.75
Ann.#5 Bloodlines#6,DL,I:Myriad . 2.75
Ann.#6 Elseworlds Story 2.95
Ann.#7 WS(c),Year One Annual
A:Dr. Occult 3.95
Earth Day 1991 KGa 5.50
Earth Stealers JBy,CS,JOy 2.95
Legacy of Superman#1 WS,JG,F:
Guardian,Waverider,Sinbad . . . 4.00
Newstime-The Life and Death of
the Man of Steel-Magazine,
DJu,BBr,JOy,JG,JBg 3.25
Spec#1 WS,V:L.Luthor,'Sandman' . 6.00
Speeding Bullets EB 8.00
Under a Yellow Sun KGa,EB 5.95
TPB Panic in the Sky rep.
Panic in the Sky 9.95
TPB Return of Superman rep.Reign
of Superman 14.95
TPB Time and Time Again 7.50
TPB World Without Superman . . . 7.50

SUPERMAN, EARTH DAY 1991
1 KGa,Metropolis 'Clean-Up' 5.50

SUPERMAN/DOOMSDAY: HUNTER/PREY
1 DJu(a&s),BBr,R:Doomsday,R:Cyborg
Superman,A:Darkseid 5.50
2 DJu(a&s),BBr,V:Doomsday,Cyborg
Superman,A:Darkseid 5.25
3 DJu(a&s),BBr,V:Doomsday . . . 5.25

SUPERMAN FAMILY
Prev: Superman's Pal,
Jimmy Olsen
April-May, 1974
164 KS,NC(c),Jimmy Olsen:'Death
Bites with Fangs of Stone' . . . 2.50
165 KS,NC(c),Supergirl:'Princess
of the Golden Sun' 2.00
166 KS,NC(c),Lois Lane:'The
Murdering Arm of Metropolis' . 2.00
167 KS,NC(c),Jimmy Olsen:'A
Deep Death for Mr. Action' . . . 2.00
168 NC(c):Supergirl:'The Girl

Superman/Doomsday #3
© DC Comics, Inc.

with the See-Through Mind' . . 2.00
169 NC(c),Lois Lane:'Target of
the Tarantula' 2.00
170 KS(c),Jimmy Olsen:'The Kid
Who Adopted Jimmy Olsen' . . 2.00
171 ECh(c),Supergirl:'Cleopatra-
Queen of America' 2.00
172 KS(c),Lois Lane:'The Cheat
the Whole World Cheered' . . . 2.00
173 KS(c),Jimmy Olsen:'Menace
of the Micro-Monster' 2.00
174 KS(c),Supergirl:'Eyes of
the Serpent' 2.00
175 KS(c),Lois Lane:'Fadeout
For Lois' 2.00
176 KS(c),Jimmy
Olsen:'Nashville, Super-Star' . . 2.00
177 KS(c),Supergirl:'Bride
of the Stars' 1.50
178 KS(c),Lois Lane:'The Girl
With the Heart of Steel' 1.50
179 KS(c),Jimmy Olsen:'I Scared
Superman to Death' 1.50
180 KS,Supergirl:'The Secret of
the Spell-Bound Supergirl' . . . 1.50
181 ECh(c),Lois Lane:'The Secret
Lois Lane Could Never Tell' . . 1.50
182 CS&NA(c),Jimmy Olsen:
'Death on Ice' 1.50
183 NA(c),Supergirl:'Shadows
of Phantoms' 1.50
184 NA(c),Supergirl:'The
Visitors From The Void' 1.50
185 NA(c),Jimmy Olsen: The
Fantastic Fists and Fury
Feet of Jimmy Olsen' 1.50
186 JL&DG(c),Jimmy Olsen:
'The Bug Lady' 1.50
187 JL(c),Jimmy Olsen:'The
Dealers of Death' 1.50
188 JL&DG(c),Jimmy Olsen:
'Crisis in Kandor' 1.50
189 JL(c),Jimmy Olsen:'The
Night of the Looter' 1.50
190 Jimmy Olsen:'Somebody
Stole My Town' 1.50

191 Superboy:'The Incredible
  Shrinking Town' 1.50
192 RA&DG(c),Superboy:'This
  Town For Plunder' 1.50
193 RA&DG(c),Superboy:'Menace
  of the Mechanical Monster' . . . 1.50
194 MR,Superboy:'When
  the Sorcerer Strikes' 1.50
195 RA&DG(c),Superboy:'The Curse
  of the Un-Secret Identity' 1.50
196 JL&DG(c),Superboy:'The
  Shadow of Jor-El' 1.50
197 JL(c),Superboy:'Superboy's
  Split Personality' 1.50
198 JL(c),Superboy:'Challenge
  of the Green K-Tastrophe' 1.50
199 RA&DG(c),Supergirl:'The
  Case of Cape Caper' 1.50
200 RA&DG(c),Lois Lane:
  'Unhappy Anniversary' 1.50
201 RA&DG(c),Supergirl:'The
  Face on Cloud 9' 1.50
202 RA&DG(c),Supergirl:'The
  Dynamic Duel' 1.50
203 RA&DG(c),Supergirl:'The
  Supergirl From Planet Earth' . . 1.50
204 RA&DG(c),Supergirl:'The
  Earth-quake Enchantment' . . . 1.50
205 RA&DG(c),Supergirl:'Magic
  Over Miami' 1.50
206 RA&DG(c),Supergirl:'Strangers
  at the Heart's Core' 1.50
207 RA&DG(c),Supergirl:'Look
  Homeward, Argonian' 1.50
208 RA&DG(c),Supergirl:'The
  Super-Switch to New York' . . . 1.50
209 Supergirl:'Strike Three-
  You're Out' 1.50
210 Supergirl:'The Spoil Sport
  of New York' 1.50
211 RA&DG(c),Supergirl:'The Man
  With the Explosive Mind' 1.50
212 RA&DG(c),Supergirl:'Payment
  on Demand' 1.50
213 thru 222 Sept., 1982 . . . . . @1.50

SUPERMAN: KAL
1 Medieval Superman 5.95

SUPERMAN:
THE MAN OF STEEL
1 B:LSi(s),DJu,BMc,JOy,BBr,TG,
  Revenge o/t Krypton Man#1 . 5.50
2 JBg,V:Cerberus 3.00
3 JBg,War of the Gods X-over . 2.50
4 JBg,V:Angstrom 2.50
5 JBg,CS,V:Atomic Skull 2.50
6 JBg,Blackout#3,A:Mr.Z 2.50
7 JBg,V:Cerberus 2.50
8 KD,V:Jolt,Blockhouse 2.50
9 JBg,Panic in the Sky#1,
  V:Brainiac. 3.00
10 JBg,Panic in the Sky#5,
  D:Draaga 2.50
11 JBg,V:Flashpoint 2.00
12 JBg,V:Warwolves 2.00
13 JBg,V:Cerberus 2.00
14 JBg,A:Robin,V:Vampires 2.00
15 KG,KGa,Blaze/Satanus War . 2.00
16 JBg,Crisis at Hand#1 . . . . . . 2.00
17 JBg,V:Underworld,
  C:Doomsday. 7.00
17a 2nd printing 1.50
18 JBg,I:Doomsday,V:Underworld 9.00

18a 2nd printing 4.00
18b 3rd printing 2.00
19 JBg,Doomsday,pt.5 . . . . 8.00
19a 2nd printing 2.00

Superman: The Man of Steel #12
© DC Comics, Inc.

20 JBg,Funeral for a Friend#3 . . 4.00
21 JBg,Funeral for a Friend#7 . . 4.00
22 JBg,Reign of Supermen#4,Direct
  Sales,Die-Cut(c),mini-poster,
  F:Man of Steel 2.50
22a Newsstand Ed. 1.75
23 JBg,V:Superboy 2.00
24 JBg,V:White Rabbit,A:Mongul . 2.00
25 JBg,A:Real Superman 5.00
26 JBg,A:All Supermen,V:Mongul,
  Cyborg Superman 2.50
27 JBg,A:Superboy,Lex Luthor . . 2.00
28 JBg(c),A:Steel 1.75
29 LSi(s),JBg,Spilled Blood#3,
  V:Hi-Tech,Blood Thirst 1.75
30 LSi(s),JBg,V:Lobo,Vinyl(c) . . 3.00
30a Newstand Ed. 1.75
31 MBr,A:Guardian 1.75
32 MBr,Bizarro's World#4,
  V:Bizarro 1.75
33 MBr,V:Parasite 1.75
34 JBg,A:Lex Men,Dubbile Men . 1.75
35 JBg,Worlds Collide#1,
  I:Fred Bentson 1.75
36 JBf,Worlds Collide,pt.10,V:Rift
  A:Icon 1.75
37 JBg,Zero Hour,A:Batman . . . 1.75
38 Mystery 1.50
39 JBg,Luthor 1.50
40 . . . . 1.50
41 Locke 1.50
42 F:Locke 1.50
43 V:Deathtrap 1.50
44 Prologue to Death 1.50
45 JGb,DJa,Death of Clark Kent,pt.4
  [New Miraweb format begins] . 1.95
46 JBg,DJa,A:Shadowdragon . . . 1.95
Ann.#1 Eclipso tie-in,A:Starman . 2.75
Ann.#2 Bloodlines#2,I:Edge 2.75
Ann.#3 MBr,Elseworlds Story . . . 2.95
Ann.#4 Year One Annual 2.95

SUPERMAN:
THE MAN OF TOMORROW
1 TGu,BBr,RSt(s),V:Lex Luthor . . 1.95

SUPERMAN'S GIRL
FRIEND, LOIS LANE
March-April, 1958
1 CS,KS 2,200.00
2 CS,KS 550.00
3 CS,KS,spanking panel shown 350.00
4 CS,KS 325.00
5 CS,KS 300.00
6 CS,KS 250.00
7 CS,KS 250.00
8 CS,KS 225.00
9 CS,KS, A:Pat Boone 225.00
10 CS,KS 225.00
11 CS,KS 175.00
12 CS,KS 175.00
13 CS,KS 150.00
14 KS,'Three Nights in the
  Fortress of Solitude' 125.00
15 KS,I:Van-Zee 125.00
16 KS, Lois' Signal-Watch 125.00
17 KS,CS,A:Brainiac 125.00
18 KS,A:Astounding Man 125.00
19 KS,'Superman of the Past' . 100.00
20 KS,A:Superman 100.00
21 KS,A:Van-Zee 90.00
22 KS,A:Robin Hood 90.00
23 KS,A:Elastic Lass, Supergirl . 90.00
24 KS,A:Van-Zee, Bizarro 90.00
25 KS,'Lois Lane's
  Darkest Secret' 75.00
26 KS,A:Jor-El 75.00
27 KS,CS,A:Bizarro 75.00
28 KS,A:Luthor 75.00
29 CS,A:Aquaman,Batman,Green
  Arrow 75.00
30 KS,A:Krypto,Aquaman 50.00
31 KS,A:Lori Lemaris 35.00
32 KS,CS,A:Bizarro 35.00
33 KS,CS,A:Phantom Zone,Lori
  Lemaris, Mon-El 40.00

Superman's Girl Friend, Lois Lane #11
© DC Comics, Inc.

34 KS,A:Luthor,Supergirl 35.00
35 KS,CS,A:Supergirl 35.00
36 KS,CS,Red Kryptonite Story . 35.00

All comics prices listed are for *Near Mint* condition.

37 KS,CS,'The Forbidden Box' . 35.00
38 KS,CS,A:Prof.Potter,
  Supergirl 35.00
39 KS,CS,A:Supergirl,Jor-El,
  Krypto, Lori Lemaris 35.00
40 KS,'Lois Lane, Hag!' 35.00
41 KS,CS,'The Devil and
  Lois Lane' 35.00
42 KS,A:Lori Lemaris 35.00
43 KS,A:Luthor 35.00
44 KS,A:Lori Lemaris,Braniac,
  Prof. Potter 35.00
45 KS,CS,'The Superman-Lois
  Hit Record' 35.00
46 KS,A:Luthor 35.00
47 KS,'The Incredible Delusion' . 35.00
48 KS,A:Mr. Mxyzptlk 35.00
49 KS,The Unknown Superman . 35.00
50 KS,A:Legion 30.00
51 KS,A:Van-Zee & Lori Lemaris 25.00
52 KS,'Truce Between Lois
  Lane and Lana Lang' 25.00
53 KS,A:Lydia Lawrence 25.00
54 KS,CS,'The Monster That
  Loved Lois Lane' 25.00
55 KS,A:Supergirl 25.00
56 KS,'Lois Lane's
  Super-Gamble!' 28.00
57 KS,'The Camera From
  Outer Space' 25.00
58 KS,'The Captive Princess' . . 25.00
59 KS,CS,A:Jor-El & Batman . . 25.00
60 KS,'Get Lost,Superman!' 25.00
61 KS,A:Mxyzptlk 25.00
62 KS,A:Mxyzptlk 25.00
63 KS,'The Satanic Schemes
  of S.K.U.L.' 25.00
64 KS,A:Luthor 25.00
65 KS,A:Luthor 25.00
66 KS,'They Call Me the Cat!' . . 25.00
67 KS,'The Bombshell of
  the Boulevards' 25.00
68 . . . . 30.00
69 KS,Lois Lane's Last Chance . 20.00
70 KS,I:Silver Age Catwoman,
  A:Batman,Robin,Penguin . . 165.00
71 KS,A:Catwoman,Batman,
  Robin,Penguin 110.00
72 KS,CS,A:Ina Lemaris 12.00
73 KS,'The Dummy and
  the Damsell' 12.00
74 KS,A:Justice League & Bizarro
  World,I:Bizarro Flash 28.00
75 KS,'The Lady Dictator' 12.00
76 KS,A:Hap-El 12.00
77 giant size 12.00
78 KS,Courtship,Kryptonian Style 15.00
79 KS,B:NA(c) 9.00
80 KS,'Get Out of My Life,
  Superman' 9.00
81 KS,'No Witnessesin
  Outerspace' 9.00
82 GT,A:Brainiac&Justice League 9.00
83 GT,'Witch on Wheels' 9.00
84 GT,KS,'Who is Lois Lane?' . . . 9.00
85 GT,KS,A:Kandorians 9.00
86 giant size 9.00
87 GT,KS,A:Cor-Lar 9.00
88 GT,KS,'Through a Murderer's
  Eyes' 9.00
89 CS,A:Batman & Batman Jr. . . 10.00
90 GT,A:Dahr-nel 8.00
91 GT,A:Superlass 8.00
92 GT,A:Superhorse 8.00
93 GT,A:Wonder Woman 8.00

94 GT,KS,A:Jor 8.00
95 giant size 10.00
96 GT,A:Jor 6.00
97 GT,KS,A:Lori Lemaris,
  Luma Lynai,Lyla Lerrol 6.00
98 GT,A:Phantom Zone 6.00
99 GT,KS,A:Batman 7.00
100 GT,A:Batman 7.00
101 GT,KS,'The Super-Reckless
  Lois Lane' 6.00
102 GT,KS,When You're Dead,
  You're Dead 6.00
103 GT,KS,A:Supergirl 6.00
104 giant size 9.00
105 RA,I&O:Rose & Thorn 5.00
106 WR,'I am Curious Black!' . . . 5.00
107 WR,The Snow-Woman Wept . 5.00
108 WR,The Spectre Suitor 5.00
109 WR,'I'll Never Fall
  in Love Again' 5.00
110 WR,'Indian Death Charge!' . . 5.00
111 WR,A:Justice League 5.00
112 WR,KS,A:Lori Lemaris 3.00
113 giant size 7.00
114 WR,KS,A:Rose & Thorn 4.00
115 WR,A:The Black Racer 3.00
116 WR,A:Darkseid & Desaad . . 3.00
117 WR,'S.O.S From Tomorrow!' . 3.00
118 WR,A:Darkseid & Desaad . . 3.00
119 WR,A:Darkseid & Lucy Lane . 3.00
120 WR,'Who Killed Lucy Lane?' . 3.00
121 WR,A:The Thorn 3.00
122 WR,A:The Thorn 3.00
123 JRo,'Ten Deadly Division
  of the 100' 3.00
124 JRo,'The Hunters' 3.00
125 JRo,'Death Rides Wheels!' . . 3.00
126 JRo,'The Brain Busters' . . . 3.00
127 JRo,'Curse of the Flame' . . . 3.00
128 JRo,A:Batman & Aquaman . 3.00
129 JRo,'Serpent in Paradise' . . 3.00
130 JRo,'The Mental Murster' . . . 3.00
131 JRo,Superman–Marry Me!' . 3.00
132 JRo,Zatanna B.U. 3.00
133 JRo,'The Lady is a Bomb' . . 3.00
134 JRo,A:Kandor 3.00
135 JRo,'Amazing After-Life
  of Lois Lane' 3.00
136 JRo,A:Wonder Woman 3.00
137 JRo,'The Stolen Subway'
  Sept.-Oct.,1974 . . . . 4.00
Ann.#1 . . . . 80.00
Ann.#2 . . . . 50.00

SUPERMAN'S PAL, JIMMY OLSEN
September-October, 1954
1 CS,'The Boy of 100 Faces!' 2,700.00
2 CS,The Flying Jimmy Olsen 700.00
3 CS,'The Man Who Collected
  Excitement 500.00
4 CS,'King For A Day!' 300.00
5 CS,'The Story of Superman's
  Souvenirs 300.00
6 CS,Kryptonite story 250.00
7 CS,'The King of Marbles' . . . 250.00
8 CS,'Jimmy Olsen, Crooner' . 250.00
9 CS,'The Missile of Steel' . . 250.00
10 CS,'Jungle Jimmy Olsen' . . 250.00
11 CS,'TNT.Olsen,The Champ' 200.00
12 CS,'Invisible Jimmy Olsen' . 200.00
13 CS,'Jimmy Olsen's
  Super Issue' 150.00
14 CS,'The Boy Superman' . . . 150.00
15 CS,'Jimmy Olsen,Speed

Superman's Pal, Jimmy Olsen #55
© DC Comics, Inc.

  Demon' 150.00
16 CS,'The Boy Superman' . . 150.00
17 CS,J.Olsen as cartoonist . . 150.00
18 CS,A:Superboy 150.00
19 CS,'Supermam's Kid Brother 150.00
20 CS,'Merman of Metropolis' . 150.00
21 CS,'The Wedding of Jimmy
  Olsen' 100.00
22 CS,'The Super Brain of
  Jimmy Olsen' 100.00
23 CS,'The Adventure of
  Private Olsen' 100.00
24 CS,'The Gorilla Reporter' . . 100.00
25 CS,'The Day There Was
  No Jimmy Olsen 100.00
26 CS,'Bird Boy of Metropolis' . . 75.00
27 CS,'The Outlaw Jimmy Olsen' 75.00
28 CS,'The Boy Who Killed
  Superman' 75.00
29 CS,A:Krypto 75.00
30 CS,'The Son of Superman' . . 75.00
31 CS,I:Elastic Lad 55.00
32 CS,A:Prof.Potter 55.00
33 CS,'Human Flame Thrower' . 55.00
34 CS,'Superman's Pal of Steel' 55.00
35 CS,'Superman's Enemy' 55.00
36 CS,I:Lois Lane,O:Jimmy Olsen
  as Superman's Pal 55.00
37 CS,O:Jimmy Olsen's SignalWatch,
  A:Elastic Lad(Jimmy Olsen) . 55.00
38 CS,'Olsen's Super-Supper' . . 55.00
39 CS,'The Super-Lad of Space' 55.00
40 CS,A:Supergirl,Hank White
  (Perry White's son) 55.00
41 CS,'The Human Octopus' . . . 55.00
42 CS,'Jimmy The Genie' 35.00
43 WB,CS,'Jimmy Olsen's Private
  Monster' 35.00
44 CS,'Miss Jimmy Olsen' 35.00
45 CS,A:Kandor 35.00
46 CS,A:Supergirl,Elastic Lad . . 35.00
47 CS,'Monsters From Earth!' . . 35.00
48 CS,I:Superman Emergency
  Squad 35.00
49 CS,A:Congorilla & Congo Bill 35.00

Superman's Pal, Jimmy Olsen #107
© DC Comics, Inc.

50 CS,A:Supergirl,Krypto,Bizarro 35.00
51 CS,A:Supergirl 20.00
52 CS,A:Mr. Mxyzptlk,
 Miss Gzptlsnz 20.00
53 CS,A:Kandor,Lori Lemaris,
 Mr.Mxyztlk 20.00
54 CS,A:Elastic Lad 20.00
55 CS,A:Aquaman,Thor 20.00
56 KS,Imaginary story 20.00
57 KS,A:Supergirl,Imaginary story 15.00
58 CS,C:Batman 15.00
59 CS,A:Titano 15.00
60 CS,'The Fantastic Army of
 General Olsen' 15.00
61 CS,Prof. Potter 15.00
62 CS,A:Elastic Lad,Phantom
 Zone 15.00
63 CS,A:Supergirl,Kandor 12.00
64 CS,'Jimmy Olsen's
 Super-Romance 10.00
65 CS,A:Miss Gzptlsnz 10.00
66 CS,KS,A:Mr. Mxyzptlk 10.00
67 CS,'The Dummy That Haunted
 Jimmy Olsen' 10.00
68 CS,'The Helmet of Hate' 10.00
69 CS,A:Nightwing,Flamebird .. 10.00
70 A:Supergirl,Lori Lemaris,
 Element Lad 10.00
71 CS,A:Mr. Mxyzptlk 8.00
72 CS,A:Legion of Super-Heroes,
 Jimmy Olsen becomes honorary
 member 10.00
73 A:Kandor 10.00
74 CS,A:Mr. Mxyzptlk,Lex Luthor . 8.00
75 CS,A:Supergirl 8.00
76 CS,A:Legion of Super-Heroes 10.00
77 CS,Jimmy Olsen becomes
 Colossal Boy, A:Titano 8.00
78 CS,A:Aqualad 8.00
79 CS,'The Red-Headed Beetle
 of 1,000 B.C.' 8.00
80 CS,A:Bizarro 8.00
81 CS,KS,A:Lori Lemaris,I&O
 only A:Mighty Eagle 8.00
82 CS,'The Unbeatable Jimmy

Olsen' 8.00
83 CS,A:Kandor 8.00
84 CS,A:Titano 8.00
85 CS,C:Legion of Super-Heroes 10.00
86 CS,A:Congorilla,Braniac 6.00
87 A:Lex Luthor,Brainiac,Legion
 of Super-Villians 10.00
88 C:Legion of Super-Heroes ... 7.50
89 I:Agent Double-Five,C:John F.
 Kennedy 6.00
90 CS,A:Mr. Mxyzptlk 6.00
91 CS,C:Batman & Robin 5.00
92 JM,A:Batman,Robin,Supergirl . 5.00
93 'The Batman-Superman of
 Earth-XI' 5.00
94 O:Insect Queen retold 5.00
95 Giant 13.00
96 I:Tempus 5.00
97 A:Fortress of Solitude 4.00
98 'The Bride of Jungle Jimmy' . 4.00
99 A:Legion of Super-Heroes ... 4.00
100 A:Legion of Super-Heroes ... 7.50
101 A:Jor-El and Lara 4.00
102 'Superman's Greatest Double
 Cross!' 4.00
103 'The Murder of Clark Kent!' .. 4.00
104 Giant 8.00
105 V:Tempus 3.50
106 CS,A:Legion of Super-Heroes 3.50
107 A:Krypto 3.50
108 CS,'The Midas of Metropolis' . 3.50
109 A:Lex Luthor 3.50
110 CS,'Jimmy Olsen's Blackest
 Deeds!' 3.50
111 .... 3.50
112 .... 3.50
113 V:Magnaman 5.00
114 'The Wrong Superman!' 3.50
115 A:Aquaman 3.50
116 A:Brainiac 3.50
117 'Planet of the Capes' 3.50
118 A:Lex Luthor 3.50
119 'Nine Lives Like a Cat!' 3.50
120 V:Climate King 3.50
121 thru 125 .... @3.50
126 CS,Riddle of Kryptonite Plus . 3.50
127 CS,Jimmy in Revolutionary
 War 3.50
128 I:Mark Olsen(Jimmy's Father) 3.50
129 MA,A:Mark Olsen 3.50
130 MA,A:Robin,Brainiac 3.50
131 .... 5.00
132 MA,When Olsen Sold out
 Superman 3.50
133 JK,B:New Newsboy Legion,
 I:Morgan Edge 8.00
134 JK,I:Darkseid 12.00
135 JK,I:New Guardian 7.50
136 JK,O:New Guardian,
 I:Dubbilex 6.00
137 JK,I:Four Armed Terror 5.00
138 JK,V:Four Armed Terror 5.00
139 JK,A:Don Rickles,I:Ugly
 Mannheim 5.00
140 .... 5.00
141 JK,A:Don Rickles,Lightray
 B:Newsboy Legion rep 5.00
142 JK,I:Count Dragorian 5.00
143 JK,V:Count Dragorian 5.00
144 JK,A Big Thing in a Deep
 Scottish Lake 5.00
145 JK,Brigadoon 5.00
146 JK,Homo Disastrous 5.00
147 JK,Superman on New
 Genesis,A:High Father,

I:Victor Volcanium 5.00
148 JK,V:Victor Volcanium,
 E:Newsboy Legion rep 5.00
149 BO(i),The Unseen Enemy,
 B:Plastic Man rep 3.50
150 BO(i) A Bad Act to Follow ... 3.50
151 BO(i),A:Green Lantern 3.50
152 MSy,BO,I:Real Morgan Edge 3.50
153 MSy,Murder in Metropolis ... 3.50
154 KS,The Girl Who Was Made
 of Money 3.50
155 KS,Downfall of Judas Olsen . 3.50
156 KS,Last Jump for
 a Skyjacker 3.50
157 KS,Jimmy as Marco Polo ... 3.50
158 KS,A:Lena Lawrence
 (Lucy Lane) 3.50
159 KS,Jimmy as Spartacus 3.50
160 KS,A:Lena Lawrence
 (Lucy Lane) 3.50
161 KS,V:Lucy Lane 3.50
162 KS,A:Lex Luthor 3.50
163 KS,Jimmy as Marco Polo
 February 1974 .... 3.50

SUPERMAN
SPECTACULAR
1982
1 A:Luthor & Terra-Man 2.50

SUPERMAN,
THE SECRET YEARS
February, 1985
1 CS,KS,FM(c) 1.50
2 CS,KS,FM(c) 1.25
3 CS,KS,FM(c) 1.25
4 CS,KS,FM(c), May 1985 ..... 1.25

SUPERMAN VS.
AMAZING SPIDER-MAN
April, 1976
1 RA/DG,oversized 10.00
1a 2nd printing, signed 15.00

SUPERMAN WORKBOOK
1945
1 rep. Superman #14 ...... 750.00

SUPER POWERS
July, 1984
[Kenner Action Figures]
1 A:Batman & Joker 1.75
2 A:Batman & Joker 1.25
3 A:Batman & Joker 1.00
4 A:Batman & Joker 1.00
5 JK(c),JK,A:Batman & Joker ... 1.25
[2nd Series]
1 JK,'Seeds of Doom' 1.00
2 JK,'When Past & Present Meet' 1.00
3 JK,'Time Upon Time' 1.00
4 JK,There's No Place Like Rome 1.00
5 JK,'Once Upon a Tomorrow' .. 1.00
6 JK,'Darkkseid o/t Moon' 1.00
[3rd Series]
1 CI,'Threshold' 1.00
2 CI,'Escape' 1.00
3 CI,'Machinations' .... .75
4 CI,'A World Divided' .... .75

SUPER-TEAM FAMILY
October-November, 1975
1 rep. 1.00

---

2 Creeper/Wildcat 1.00
3 RE/WW,Flash & Hawkman . . . 1.00
4 . . . . 1.00
5 . . . . 1.00
6 . . . . 1.00
7 . . . . 1.00
8 JSh,Challengers 1.00
9 JSh,Challengers 1.00
10 JSh,Challengers 1.00
11 Supergirl,Flash,Atom 1.00
12 Green Lantern,Hawkman 1.00
13 Aquaman, Capt. Comet 1.00
14 Wonder Woman,Atom 1.00
15 Flash & New Gods,
March-April, 1978 . . . . . 1.00

SWAMP THING
[1st Regular Series]
October-November, 1972

1 B:LWn(s),BWr,O:Swamp Thing 60.00
2 BWr,I:Arcane 32.00
3 BWr,I:Patchwork Man 20.00
4 BWr 20.00
5 BWr 15.00
6 BWr 15.00
7 BWr,A:Batman 20.00
8 BWr,Lurker in Tunnel 13 . . . . 14.00
9 BWr 14.00
10 E:BWr,A;Arcane 14.00
11 thru 22 NR . . . . @6.00
23 NR,reverts to Dr.Holland 6.00
24 NR 6.00
TPB rep.#1-#10,House of Secrets
#92,Dark Genesis Saga 19.95

SWAMP THING
(see SAGA OF THE SWAMP THING)

SWORD OF SORCERY
February-March, 1973

1 MK(c),HC 10.00
2 BWv,NA,Hc 15.00
3 BWv,HC,MK,WS 10.00
4 HC,WS 5.00
5 November-December, 1973 . . 5.50

SWORD OF THE ATOM
September, 1983

1 GK 1.50
2 GK 1.25
3 GK 1.25
4 GK 1.25
Spec.#1 GK 1.25
Spec.#2 GK 1.25
Spec.#3 PB 1.50

TAILGUNNER JO
September, 1988

1 . . . . 1.25
2 . . . . 1.25
3 . . . . 1.25
4 . . . . 1.25
5 . . . . 1.25
6 . . . . 1.25

TALES OF THE GREEN
LANTERN CORPS
May, 1981

1 JSon,FMc,O:Green Lantern . . . 1.50
2 JSon,FMc 1.25
3 JSon,FMc 1.25

TALES OF THE LEGION
OF SUPER HEROES
August, 1984
(Previously:
Legion of Super Heroes)

314 KG,V:Ontiir 1.50
315 KG(i),V:Dark Circle 1.50
316 KG(i),O:White Witch 1.50
317 KG(i),V:Dream Demon 1.50
318 KG(i),V:Persuader 1.50
319 KG(i),V:Persuader,
A:Superboy 1.50
320 DJu,V:Magpie 1.50
321 DJu,Exile,V:Kol 1.50
322 DJu,Exile,V:Kol 1.50
323 DJu,Exile,V:Kol 1.50
324 DJu,EC,V:Dev-Em 1.50
325 DJu,V:Dark Circle 1.50
326 reprint of Baxter #1 . . . . 1.00
327 reprint of Baxter #2 . . . . 1.00
328 reprint of Baxter #3 . . . . 1.00
329 reprint of Baxter #4 . . . . 1.00
330 reprint of Baxter #5 . . . . 1.00
331 reprint of Baxter #6 . . . . 1.00
332 reprint of Baxter #7 . . . . 1.00
333 reprint of Baxter #8 . . . . 1.00
334 reprint of Baxter #9 . . . . 1.00
335 reprint of Baxter #10 . . . . . . 1.00
336 reprint of Baxter #11 . . . . . . 1.00
337 reprint of Baxter #12 . . . . . . 1.00
338 reprint of Baxter #13 . . . . . . 1.00
339 reprint of Baxter #14 . . . . . . 1.00
340 reprint of Baxter #15 . . . . . . 1.00
341 reprint of Baxter #16 . . . . . . 1.00
342 reprint of Baxter #17 . . . . . . 1.00
343 reprint of Baxter #19 . . . . . . 1.00
344 reprint of Baxter #19 . . . . . . 1.00
345 reprint of Baxter #20 . . . . . . 1.00
346 reprint of Baxter #21 . . . . . . 1.00
347 reprint of Baxter #22 . . . . . . 1.00
348 reprint of Baxter #23 . . . . . . 1.00
349 reprint of Baxter #24 . . . . . . 1.00
350 reprint of Baxter #25 . . . . . . 1.00
351 reprint of Baxter #26 . . . . . . 1.00
352 reprint of Baxter #27 . . . . . . 1.00
353 reprint of Baxter #28 . . . . . . 1.00
354 reprint of Baxter #29 . . . . . . 1.00
Ann.#4 rep. Baxter Ann.#1 . . . . 1.00
Ann.#5 rep. Baxter Ann.#2 . . . . 1.00

TALES OF THE
NEW TEEN TITANS
June, 1982

1 GP, O:Cyborg 2.00
2 GP, O:Raven 2.00
3 GD, O:Changling 2.00
4 GP/EC,O:Starfire 2.00

TALES OF THE
TEEN TITANS
(see NEW TEEN TITANS)

TALES OF THE
UNEXPECTED
February-March, 1956

1 The Out-Of-The-World Club . 850.00
2 . . . . 400.00
3 . . . . 275.00
4 Seven Steps to the Unknown 275.00
5 . . . . 275.00
6 'The Girl in the Bottle' 200.00
7 NC(c),Pen That Never Lied . 200.00

Tales of the Unexpected #2
© DC Comics, Inc.

8 . . . . 200.00
9 LSt(c),The Amazing Cube . . 200.00
10 MMe(c),The Strangest Show
On Earth 200.00
11 LSt(c),Who Am I? 125.00
12 JK,Four Threads of Doom . . 125.00
13 JK(c),Weapons of Destiny . . 125.00
14 SMo(c),The Forbidden Game 100.00
15 JK,MMe,Three Wishes
to Doom 125.00
16 JK,The Magic Hammer 125.00
17 JK,Who Is Mr. Ashtar? 125.00
18 JK(c),MMe,A Man Without A
World 125.00
19 NC,Man From Two Worlds . 100.00
20 NC(c),The Earth Gladiator . 100.00
21 JK,The Living Phantoms . . 100.00
22 JK(c),The Man From Robot
Island 100.00
23 JK,The Invitation From Mars! 100.00
24 LC,The Secret Of Planetoid
Zero! 100.00
25 The Sorcerer's Asteroid! . . . 100.00
26 MMe,The Frozem City 100.00
27 MMe,The Prison In Space . 100.00
28 The Melting Planet 100.00
29 The Phantom Raider 100.00
30 The Jinxed Planet 100.00
31 RH,Keep Off Our Planet . . . 90.00
32 Great Space Cruise Mystery . 90.00
33 The Man Of 1,000 Planets . . 90.00
34 Ambush In Outer Space 90.00
35 MMe,I Was A Space Refugee! 90.00
36 The Curse Of The
Galactic Goodess 90.00
37 The Secret Prisoners
Of Planet 13 . . . . 90.00
38 The Stunt Man Of Space . . . 90.00
39 The Creatures From The
Space Globe 90.00
40 B:Space Ranger,The Last
Days Of Planet Mars! 750.00
41 SMo(c),The Destroyers From
The Stars! 250.00
42 The Secret Of The
Martian Helmet 250.00
43 The Riddle Of The Burning
Treasures,I:Space Ranger . 600.00

44 DD&SMo(c),The Menace Of
The Indian Aliens 150.00
45 DD&SMo(c),The Sheriff
From Jupiter 150.00
46 DD&SMo(c),The
Duplicate Doom! 150.00
47 DD(c),The Man Who Stole
The Solar System 125.00
48 Bring 'Em Back Alive-
From Space 125.00
49 RH,The Fantastic Lunar-Land 125.00
50 MA,King Barney The Ape . . 125.00
51 Planet Earth For Sale 100.00
52 Prisoner On Pluto 100.00
53 Interplanetary Trouble Shooter 100.00
54 The Ugly Sleeper Of Klanth,
Dinosaur 125.00
55 The Interplanetary
Creature Trainer 100.00
56 B:Spaceman At Work,Invaders
From Earth 100.00
57 The Jungle Beasts Of Jupiter 100.00
58 The Boss Of The
Saturnian Legion 100.00
59 The Man Who Won A World 100.00
60 School For Space Sleuths . 100.00
61 The Mystery Of The
Mythical Monsters 75.00
62 The Menace Of The Red
Snow Crystals 75.00
63 Death To Planet Earth 75.00
64 Boy Usurper Of Planet Zonn . 75.00
65 The Creature That
Couldn't Exist 75.00
66 MMe,Trap Of The Space
Convict 75.00
67 The Giant That
Devoured A Village 75.00
68 Braggart From Planet Brax . . 40.00
69 Doom On Holiday Asteroid . . 40.00
70 The Hermit Of Planetoid X . . 40.00
71 Manhunt In Galaxy G-2! 40.00
72 The Creature Of 1,000 Dooms 40.00
73 The Convict Defenders
Of Space! 40.00
74 Prison Camp On Asteroid X-3! 40.00
75 The Hobo Jungle Of Space . . 40.00
76 The Warrior Of Two Worlds! . 40.00
77 Dateline-Outer Space 40.00
78 The Siren Of Space 40.00
79 Big Show On Planet Earth! . . 40.00
80 The Creature Tamer! 40.00
81 His Alien Master! 40.00
82 Give Us Back Our Earth!,
E:Space Ranger 40.00
83 DD&SMo(c),The Anti-Hex
Merchant! 30.00
84 DD&SMo(c),The Menace Of
The 50-Fathom Men 30.00
85 JkS(c),The Man Who Stole My
Powers,B:Green Glob 30.00
86 DD&SMo(c),They'll Never
Take Me Alive! 25.00
87 JkS(c),The Manhunt Through
Two Worlds 25.00
88 DD&SMo(c),GK,The Fear
Master 25.00
89 DD,SMo(c),Nightmare on Mars 25.00
90 JkS(c),The Hero Of 5,000 BC 25.00
91 JkS(c),The Prophetic Mirages,
I:Automan 25.00
92 The Man Who Dared To Die! 25.00
93 JkS(c),Prisoners Of Hate
Island 25.00
94 The Monster Mayor - USA . . 25.00

95 The Secret Of Chameleo-Man 25.00
96 Wanted For Murder...1966...
6966 . . . . 25.00
97 One Month To Die 25.00
98 Half-Man/Half Machine 25.00
99 JkS(c),Nuclear Super-Hero! . 25.00
100 Judy Blonde, Secret Agent! . 25.00
101 The Man in The Liquid Mask! 22.00
102 Bang!Bang! You're Dead . . 22.00
103 JA,ABC To Disaster 22.00
104 NA(c),Master Of The
Voodoo Machine 22.00

Becomes:

UNEXPECTED, THE

February-March, 1968

105 The Night I Watched
Myself Die 18.00
106 B:Johnny Peril,The Doorway
Into Time 12.00
107 MD,JkS(c),The Whip Of Fear! 15.00
108 JkS(c),Journey To
A Nightmare 12.00
109 JkS(c),Baptism By Starfire! . 12.00
110 NA(c),Death Town, U.S.A.! . 18.00
111 NC(c),Mission Into Eternity . 18.00
112 NA(c),The Brain Robbers! . . 18.00
113 NA(c),The Shriek Of
Vengeance 18.00
114 NA(c),My Self-My Enemy! . . 18.00
115 BWr,NA(c),Diary Of
A Madman 18.00
116 NC(c),Express Train
To Nowhere! 12.00
117 NC(c),Midnight Summons
The Executioner! 12.00
118 NA(c),A:Judge Gallows,Play
A Tune For Treachery 18.00
119 BWr,NC(c),Mirror,Mirror
On The Wall 15.00
120 NC(c),Rambeau's Revenge . 12.00
121 BWr,NA(c),Daddy's
Gone-A-Hunting 20.00
122 WW,DG(c),The Phantom
Of The Woodstock Festival . . 15.00
123 NC(c),Death Watch! 12.00
124 NA(c),These Walls Shall
Be Your Grave 18.00
125 NC(c),Screech Of Guilt! . . . 10.00
126 ATh,NC(c),You Are Cordially
Invited To Die! 12.00
127 GT,JK,ATh,NC(c),Follow The
Piper To Your Grave 12.00
128 DW,BWr,NC(c),Where Only
The Dead Are Free! 15.00
129 NC(c),Farewell To A
Fading Star 10.00
130 NC(c),One False Step 10.00
131 NC(c),Run For Your Death! . 10.00
132 MD,GT,NC(c),The Edge Of
Madness 10.00
133 WW,JkS(c),A:Judge Gallows,
Agnes Doesn't Haunt Here
Anymore! 12.00
134 GT,NC(c),The Restless Dead 10.00
135 NC(c),Death, Come
Walk With Me! 8.00
136 SMo,GT,NC(c),An Incident
of Violence 10.00
137 WW,NC(c),Dark Vengeance! 12.00
138 WW,NC(c),Strange Secret of
the Huan Shan Idol 12.00
139 GT,NC(c),The 2 Brains of
Beast Bracken! 10.00
140 JkS(c),The Anatomy of Hate . 8.00
141 NC(c),Just What Did Eric See? 8.00

142 NC(c),Let The Dead Sleep! . . 8.00
143 NC(c),Fear is a Nameless
Voice 8.00
144 NC(c),The Dark Pit of
Dr. Hanley 8.00
145 NC(c),Grave of Glass 6.00
146 NC(c),The Monstrosity! 6.00
147 NC(c),The Daughter of
Dr. Jekyll 6.00
148 NC(c),Baby Wants Me Dead! 6.00
149 NC(c),To Wake the Dead . . . 6.00
150 NC(c),No One Escapes From
Gallows Island 6.00
151 NC(c),Sorry, I'm Not Ready
To Die! 6.00
152 GT,NC(c),Death Wears Many
Faces 8.00
153 NC(c),Who's That Sleeping
In My Grave? 6.00
154 NC(c),Murder By Madness . . 6.00
155 NC(c),Non-Stop Journey
Into Fear 6.00
156 NC(c),A Lunatic Is Loose
Among Us! 6.00
157 NC(c),The House of
the Executioner 6.00
158 NC(c),Reserved for Madmen
Only 6.00
159 NC(c),A Cry in the Night 6.00
160 NC(c),Death of an Exorcist . . 6.00
161 BWr,NC(c),Has Anyone
Seen My Killer 10.00
162 JK,NC(c),I'll Bug You
To Your Grave 7.00
163 DD,LD(c),Room For Dying . . 5.00
164 House of the Sinister Sands . 5.00
165 LD(c),Slayride in July 5.00
166 LD(c),The Evil Eyes of Night . 5.00
167 LD(c),Scared Stiff 5.00
168 LD(c),Freak Accident 5.00
169 LD(c),What Can Be Worse
Than Dying? 5.00
170 LD(c),Flee To Your Grave . . . 5.00
171 LD(c),I.O.U. One Corpse . . . 5.00
172 LD(c),Strangler in Paradise . . 5.00
173 LD(c),What Scared Sally? . . . 5.00
174 LD(c),Gauntlet of Fear 5.00
175 LD(c),The Haunted Mountain 5.00
176 JkS(c),Having A
Wonderful Crime 5.00
177 ECh(c),Reward for the Wicked 5.00
178 LD(c),Fit To Kill! 5.00
179 LD(c),My Son, The Mortician . 5.00
180 GT,LD(c),The Loathsome
Lodger of Nightmare Inn 7.00
181 LD(c),Hum of the Haunted . . 5.00
182 LD(c),Sorry, This Coffin
is Occupied 5.00
183 LD(c),The Dead Don't
Always Die 5.00
184 LD(c),Wheel of Misfortune! . . 5.00
185 LD(c),Monsters from a
Thousand Fathoms 5.00
186 LD(c),To Catch a Corpse . . . 5.00
187 LD(c),Mangled in Madness . . 5.00
188 LD(c),Verdict From The Grave 5.00
189 SD,LD(c),Escape From the
Grave 6.00
190 LD(c),The Jigsaw Corpse . . . 4.00
191 MR,JO(c),Night of the Voodoo
Curse 6.00
192 LD(c),A Killer Cold & Clammy 4.00
193 DW,LD(c),Don't Monkey the
Murder 4.00
194 LD(c),Have I Got a Ghoul

All comics prices listed are for *Near Mint* condition.

For You 4.00
195 JCr,LD(c),Whose Face is at
    My Window 6.00
196 LD(c),The Fear of Number 13 4.00
197 LD(c),Last Laugh of a Corpse 4.00
198 JSn(c),Rage of the
    Phantom Brain 4.00
199 LD(c),Dracula's Daughter . . . 4.00
200 GT,RA&DG(c),A:Johnny Peril,
    House on the Edge of Eternity 6.00
201 Do Unto Others 4.00
202 JO,LD(c),Death Trap 4.00
203 MK(c),Hang Down Your
    Head, Joe Mundy 4.00
204 DN,JKu(c),Twinkle, Twinkle
    Little Star 4.00
205 JkS,A:Johnny Peril,The Second
    Possession of Angela Lake . . . 4.00
206 JkS,A:Johnny Peril,The
    Ultimate Assassin 4.00
207 JkS,A:Johnny Peril,Secret of
    the Second Star 4.00
208 JkS,A:Johnny Peril,Factory
    of Fear 4.00
209 JkS,Game for the Ghastly . . . 4.00
210 Vampire of the Apes,Time
    Warp 4.00
211 A:Johnny Peril,The Temple
    of the 7 Stars 4.00
212 JkS,MK(c),A:Johnny Peril,The
    Adventure of the Angel's Smile 4.00
213 A:Johnny Peril,The Woman
    Who Died Forever 4.00
214 JKu(c),Slaughterhouse Arena 4.00
215 JKu(c),Is Someone
    Stalking Sandra 4.00
216 GP,JKu(c),Samurai Nightmare 4.00
217 ShM,DSp,EC(c),Dear Senator 4.00
218 KG,ECh&DG(c),I'll Remember
    You Yesterday 4.00
219 JKu(c),A Wild Tale 4.00
220 ShM,JKu(c),The Strange
    Guide 4.00
221 SD,ShM,JKu(c),Em the
    Energy Monster 4.00
222 KG,SD(c),May, 1982 . . . . . . 4.00

TALES OF THE
WILDERNESS
1 GK,special 2.00

TANK GIRL
1 Movie Adaptation 5.95

TANK GIRL:
THE ODYSSEY
Vertigo
1 New Limited Series 2.25
2 BBo(c),Land of Milk & Honey . . 2.25

TARZAN
April, 1972
(Previously published by Gold Key)
207 JKu,O:Tarzan,pt.1 . . . . 5.00
208 thru 210 JKu,O:Tarzan,pt.2–4 3.00
211 thru 258 February, 1977 . . @2.00

TARZAN FAMILY
November-December, 1975
(Formerly: Korak, Son of Tarzan)
60 B:Korak 1.25
61 thru 66 Nov.-Dec.,1976 . . . . @1.25

TEAM TITANS
1 KM,Total Chaos#3,A:New Titans,
    Deathstroke,V:Lord Chaos,
    BU:KGa,Killowat 2.50
1a BU:AV(i),Mirage 2.50
1b BU:MN,GP,Nightrider 2.50
1c BU:AH,Redwing 2.50
1d BU:GP(i),Terra 2.50
2 KM,Total Chaos#6,A:New
    Titans, V:Chaos,C:Battalion . . . 2.00
3 KM,Total Chaos#9,V:Lord
    Chaos, A:New Titans 2.00
4 KM,Titans Sell-Out#4,
    J:Battalion, Troia 2.00
5 KM,A:Battalion 2.00
6 ANi,A:Battalion 2.00
7 PJ,I:Nightwing of 2001 . . . . . . 2.00
8 PJ,A:Raven 2.00
9 PJ,V:Bloodwing 2.00
10 PJ,V:Vampiric Creatures 2.00
11 PJ,F:Battalion 2.00
12 PJ,F:Battalion 2.00
13 PJ,New Direction 2.00
14 PJ,V:Clock King,Chronos,Calander
    Man,Time Commander 2.00
15 PJ 2.00
16 PJ,F:Nightrider 2.00
17 PJ,A:Deathwing 2.00
18 IR:Leader 2.00
19 V:Leader 2.00
20 PJ,V:Lazarium 2.00
21 PJ,V:US Government 2.00
22 PJ,A:Chimera 2.25
23 PJ,I:Warhawk(Redwing) 2.25
24 PJ,Zero Hour,R.Kole,last issue 2.25
Ann.#1 I:Chimera 3.50
Ann.#2 PJ,Elseworlds Story 3.75

TEEN BEAT
November-December, 1967
1 Monkees photo 17.00
Becomes:

TEEN BEAM
2 Monkees 14.00

TEEN TITANS
[1st Series]
January, 1966
1 NC,Titans join Peace Corps . 165.00
2 NC,I:Garn Akaru 75.00
3 NC,I:Ding Dong Daddy 40.00
4 NC,A:Speedy 40.00
5 NC,I:Ant 40.00
6 NC,A:Beast Boy 30.00
7 NC,I:Mad Mod 30.00
8 IN/JAb,I:Titans Copter 30.00
9 NC,A:Teen Titan Sweatshirts . 30.00
10 NC,I:Bat-Bike 30.00
11 IN/NC A:Speedy 26.00
12 NC,in Spaceville 21.00
13 NC,Christmas story 21.00
14 NC,I:Gargoyle 21.00
15 NC,I:Capt. Rumble 21.00
16 NC,I:Dimension X 21.00
17 NC,A:Mad Mod 21.00
18 NC,1:Starfire (Russian) 25.00
19 GK,WW,J:Speedy 21.00
20 NA,NC J:Joshua 23.00
21 NA,NC,A:Hawk,Dove 23.00
22 NA,NC,O:Wondergirl 23.00
23 GK,NC,N:Wondergirl 12.00
24 GK,NC 12.00
25 NC,I:Lilith,A:J.L.A 12.00
26 NC,I:Mal 14.00

27 NC 12.00
28 NC,A:Ocean Master 12.00
29 NC,A:Ocean Master 12.00
30 NC,A:Aquagirl 12.00
31 NC,GT,A:Hawk,Dove 12.00
32 NC,I:Gnarrk 9.00
33 GT,NS,A:Gnarrk 9.00
34 GT,NC 9.00
35 GT,NC,O:Mal 9.00
36 GT,NC,JAp,V:Hunchback 9.00
37 GT,NC 9.00
38 GT,NC 9.00
39 GT,NC,Rep.Hawk & Dove 9.00
40 NC,A:Aqualad 9.00
41 NC,DC,Lilith Mystery 9.00
42 NC 9.00
43 NC,Inherit the Howling Night . . 9.00
44 C:Flash 9.00

Teen Titans (1st Series) #45
© DC Comics, Inc.

45 IN,V:Fiddler 9.00
46 IN,A:Fiddler 12.00
47 C:Two-Face 6.00
48 I:Bumblebee,Harlequin,
    A:Two-Face 11.00
49 R:Mal As Guardian 6.00
50 DH,I:Teen Titans West 10.00
51 DH,A:Teen Titans West 6.00
52 DH,A:Teen Titans West 6.00
53 O:Teen Titans, A:JLA 8.00

TEEN TITANS
SPOTLIGHT
August, 1986
1 DCw,DG,Starfire "Apartheid" . . 1.50
2 DCw,DG,Starfire Apartheid#2 . 1.00
3 RA,Jericho 1.00
4 RA,Jericho 1.00
5 RA,Jericho 1.00
6 RA,Jericho 1.00
7 JG,Hawk 1.50
8 JG,Hawk 1.00
9 Changeling 1.00
10 EL,Aqualad And Mento 1.50
11 JO,Brotherhood of Evil 1.00
12 EC,Wondergirl 1.00
13 Cyborg 1.00

*Teen Titans Spotlight #9
© DC Comics, Inc.*

14 1stNightwing/Batman
 Team-up 2.50
15 EL,Omega Men 1.50
16 Thunder And Lightning 1.00
17 DH,Magennta 1.00
18 ATi,Aqualad,A:Aquaman 1.50
19 Starfire,A:Harbinger,Millenium
 X-over 1.00
20 RT(i),Cyborg 1.00
21 DSp,Flashback sty w/orig.Teen
 Titans 1.25

TEMPUS FUGITIVE
1990
1 KSy,Time Travel,I:Ray 27 . . . . 4.95
2 KSy,Viet Nam 4.95
3 KSy,World War I 4.95
4 KSy,final issue 4.95

3-D BATMAN
1953, 1966
1 rep.Batman #42 & #48 . . . . 700.00
1a A:Tommy Tomorrow (1966) 250.00

THRILLER
November, 1983
1 TVE 1.75
2 TVE,O:Thriller 1.50
3 TVE 1.50
4 TVE 1.50
5 TVE,DG,Elvis satire 1.50
6 TVE,Elvis satire 1.50
7 TVE 1.50
8 TVE 1.50
9 TVE 1.50
10 TVE 1.50
11 AN 1.50
12 AN 1.50

TIMBER WOLF
1 AG(i),V:Thrust 2.00
2 V:Captain Flag 1.50
3 AG(i),V:Creeper 1.50
4 AG(i),V:Captain Flag 1.50
5 AG(i),V:Dominators,Capt.Flag . 1.50

Timber Wolf #4 © DC Comics, Inc.

TIME MASTERS
February, 1990
1 ATi,O:Rip Hunter,A:JLA 2.50
2 ATi,A:Superman 2.00
3 ATi,A:Jonah Hex, Cave Carson 2.00
4 ATi,Animal Man #22 x-over . . . 2.00
5 ATi,A:Viking Prince 2.00
6 ATi,A:Dr.Fate 2.00
7 ATi,A:GrLantern,Arion 2.00
8 ATi,V:Vandal Savage 2.00

TITANS SELL-OUT SPECIAL
1 SE,AV,I:Teeny Titans,
 w/Nightwing poster 3.75

TIME WARP
October-November, 1979
1 JAp,RB,SD,MK(c),DN,TS 15.00
2 DN,JO,TS,HC,SD,MK(c),GK . 10.00
3 DN,SD,MK(c),TS 10.00
4 MN,SD,MK(c),DN 10.00
5 DN,MK(c),July 1980 . . . . 1.00

TOMAHAWK
September-October, 1950
1 Prisoner Called Tomahawk . 700.00
2 FF(4pgs),Four Boys
 Against the Frontier 350.00
3 Warpath 225.00
4 Tomahawk Wanted: Dead
 or Alive 225.00
5 The Girl Who Was Chief . . . 225.00
6 Tomahawk-King of the Aztecs 175.00
7 Punishment of Tomahawk . . 175.00
8 The King's Messenger 175.00
9 The Five Doomed Men 175.00
10 Frontied Sabotage 175.00
11 Girl Who Hated Tomahawk . 150.00
12 Man From Magic Mountain . 150.00
13 Dan Hunter's Rival 150.00
14 The Frontier Tinker 150.00
15 The Wild Men of
 Wigwam Mountain 150.00
16 Treasure of the Angelique . . 150.00
17 Short-Cut to Danger 150.00
18 Bring In M'Sieur Pierre 150.00
19 The Lafayette Volunteers . . 150.00
20 NC(c),The Retreat of

Tomahawk 150.00
21 NC(c),The Terror of the
 Wrathful Spirit 100.00
22 CS(c),Admiral Tomahawk . . 100.00
23 CS(c),The Indian Chief
 From Oxford 100.00
24 NC(c),Adventure In the
 Everglades 100.00
25 NC(c),The Star-Gazer of
 Freemont 100.00
26 NC(c),Ten Wagons For
 Tomahawk 100.00
27 NC(c),Frontier Outcast 100.00
28 I:Lord Shilling 125.00
29 The Conspiracy of Wounded
 Bear 150.00
30 The King of the Thieves . . . 100.00
31 NC(c),The Buffalo Brave
 From Misty Mountain 75.00
32 NC(c),The Clocks That
 Went to War 75.00
33 The Paleface Tribe 75.00
34 The Capture of General
 Washington 75.00
35 Frontier Feud 75.00
36 NC(c),A Cannon for Fort
 Reckless 75.00
37 NC(c),The Feathered Warriors 75.00
38 The Frontier Zoo 75.00
39 The Redcoat Trickster 75.00
40 Fearless Fettle-Daredevil . . . 75.00
41 The Captured Chieftain 75.00
42 The Prisoner Tribe 75.00
43 Tomahawk's Little Brother . . . 75.00
44 The Brave Named Tomahawk 75.00
45 The Last Days of Chief Tory . 75.00
46 The Chief With 1,000 Faces . 50.00
47 The Frontier Rain-Maker 50.00
48 Indian Twin Trouble 50.00
49 The Unknown Warrior 50.00
50 The Brave Who Was Jinxed . 50.00
51 General Tomahawk 50.00
52 Tom Thumb of the Frontier . . 50.00
53 The Four-Footed Renegade . . 50.00
54 Mystery of the 13th Arrows . . 50.00
55 Prisoners of the Choctaw . . . 50.00
56 The Riddle of the
 Five Little Indians 50.00
57 The Strange Fight
 at Fort Bravo 75.00
58 Track of the Mask 35.00
59 The Mystery Prisoner of
 Lost Island 35.00
60 The Amazing Walking Fort . . 35.00
61 Tomahawk's Secret Weapons 35.00
62 Strongest Man in the World . 35.00
63 The Frontier Super Men 35.00
64 The Outcast Brave 35.00
65 Boy Who Wouldn't Be Chief . 35.00
66 DD&SMo(c),A Trap For
 Tomahawk 35.00
67 DD&SMo(c),Frontier Sorcerer 35.00
68 DD&SMo(c),Tomahawk's
 Strange Ally 35.00
69 DD&SMo(c),Tracker-King
 of the Wolves 35.00
70 DD&SMo(c),Three Tasks
 for Tomahawk 35.00
71 DD&SMo(c),The Boy Who
 Betrayed His Country 35.00
72 DD&SMo(c),The Frontier Pupil 35.00
73 DD&SMo(c),The Secret of
 the Indian Sorceress 35.00
74 DD&SMo(c),The Great
 Paleface Masquerade 35.00

75 DD&SMo(c),The Ghost of
    Lord Shilling 35.00
76 DD&SMo(c),The Totem-Pole
    Trail 35.00
77 DD&SMo(c),The Raids of
    the One-Man Tribe 35.00
78 DD&SMo(c),The Menace
    of the Mask 35.00
79 DD&SMo(c),Eagle Eye's
    Debt of Honor 35.00
80 DD&SMo(c),The Adventures
    of Tracker 25.00
81 The Strange Omens of
    the Indian Seer 25.00
82 The Son of the Tracker 25.00
83 B:Tomahawk Rangers,20
    Against the Tribe 25.00
84 There's a Coward Among
    the Rangers 25.00
85 The Wispering War 25.00
86 Rangers vs. King Colossus . . 15.00
87 The Secrets of Sgt.
    Witch Doctor 15.00
88 The Rangers Who Held
    Back the Earth 15.00
89 The Terrible Tree-Man 15.00
90 The Prisoner In The Pit 15.00
91 The Tribe Below the Earth . . 15.00
92 The Petrified Sentry of
    Peaceful Valley 15.00
93 The Return of King Colosso . 15.00
94 Rip Van Ranger 15.00
95 The Tribe Beneath the Sea . . 15.00

Tomahawk #6 © DC Comics, Inc.

96 The Ranger Killers 15.00
97 The Prisoner Behind the
    Bull's-Eye 15.00
98 The Pied Piper Rangers 15.00
99 The Rangers vs. Chief Cobweb 15.00
100 The Weird Water-Tomahawk . 15.00
101 Tomahawk, Enemy Spy . . . 10.00
102 The Dragon Killers 10.00
103 The Frontier Frankenstein . . 10.00
104 The Fearful Freak of
    Dunham's Dungeon 10.00
105 The Attack of the Gator God 10.00
106 The Ghost of Tomahawk . . . 10.00
107 Double-Cross of the
    Gorilla Ranger 10.00
108 New Boss For the Rangers . 10.00

109 The Caveman Ranger 10.00
110 Tomahawk Must Die 10.00
111 Vengeance of the Devil-Dogs 6.00
112 The Rangers vs. Tomahawk . 6.00
113 The Mad Miser of
    Carlisle Castle 6.00
114 The Terrible Power of
    Chief Iron Hands 6.00
115 The Deadly Flaming Ranger . 6.00
116 NA(c),The Last Mile of
    Massacre Trail 6.00
117 NA(c),Rangers'Last Stand . . . 6.00
118 NA(c),Tomahawk, Guilty
    of Murder 6.00
119 NA(c),Bait For a Buzzard . . . 6.00
120 NC(c),The Coward Who,
    Lived Forever 6.00
121 NA(c),To Kill a Ranger 6.00
122 IN(c),Must the Brave Die 6.00
123 NA(c),The Stallions of Death . 6.00
124 NA(c),The Valley of
    No Return 6.00
125 NA(c),A Chief's Feather
    For Little Bear 6.00
126 NA(c),The Baron of
    Gallows Hill 6.00
127 NA(c),The Devil is Waiting . . 6.00
128 NA(c),Rangers-Your 9
    Lives For Mine 6.00
129 NA(c),Treachery at
    Thunder Ridge 6.00
130 NA(c),Deathwatch at
    Desolation Valley 6.00
131 JKu(c),B:Son of Tomahawk,
    Hang Him High 6.00
132 JKu(c),Small Eagle...Brother
    Hawk 3.00
133 JKu(c),Scalp Hunter 3.00
134 JKu(c),The Rusty Ranger . . . 3.00
135 JKu(c),Death on Ghost
    Mountain 3.00
136 JKu(c),A Piece of Sky 3.00
137 JKu(c),Night of the Knife 3.00
138 JKu(c),A Different Kind
    of Christmas 3.00
139 JKu(c),Death Council 3.00
140 Jku(c),The Rescue,
    May-June, 1972 . . . . 3.00

TOR
May-June, 1975
1 JKu,O:Tor 1.25
2 thru 6, Tor reprints . . . . @1.25

TOTAL RECALL
1 Movie Adaption 3.00

TRIUMPH
[Mini-Series]
1 and 2 From Zero Hour 1.75

TSR WORLDS
TSR
1 I:SpellJammer 4.50

TV SCREEN CARTOONS
(see REAL SCREEN COMICS)

TWILIGHT
1 JL,Last Frontier 5.50
2 JL,K.SorensenVs.T.Tomorrow . 4.95
3 JL,K.SorensenVs.T.Tomorrow
    (Conclusion) 4.95

UNAUTHORIZED BIO OF LEX LUTHOR
1 EB 3.95

UNDERWORLD
December, 1987
1 EC,New Yorks Finest 1.25
2 EC,A:Black Racer 1.25
3 EC,V:Black Racer 1.25
4 EC,final issue 1.25

UNEXPECTED, THE
(see TALES OF THE UNEXPECTED)

UNKNOWN SOLDIER
(see STAR SPANGLED)

UNKNOWN SOLDIER
April, 1977
1 True Origin revealed,Viet
    Nam 1970 . . . . 1.50
2 Origin contd.,Iran 1977 . . . . . 1.50
3 Origin contd.Afghanistan1982 . 1.50
4 Nicaragua 1.50
5 Nicaragua contd. 1.50
6 . . . . 1.50
7 Libia 1.50
8 Siberia, U.S.S.R. 1.75
9 North Korea 1952 . . . . 1.75
10 C.I.A. 1.75
11 C.I.A., Army Intelligence 1.75
12 final issue,Oct.1982 . . . . 1.75

UNTOLD LEGEND OF BATMAN
July, 1980
1 JA,JBy,(1st DC work)O:Batman 6.00
2 JA,O:Joker&Robin 4.50
3 JA,O:Batgirl 4.50

V
(TV Adaptation)
February, 1985
1 CI/TD 1.35
2 CI/TD 1.25
3 CI/TD 1.25
4 CI/TD 1.25
5 CI/TD 1.25
6 CI/TD 1.25
7 CI/TD 1.25
8 CI/TD 1.25
9 CI/TD 1.25
10 CI/TD 1.25
11 CI/TD 1.25
12 CI/TD 1.25
13 CI/TD 1.25
14 CI/TD 1.25
15 CI/TD 1.25
16 CI/TD 1.25
17 DG 1.25
18 DG 1.25

V FOR VENDETTA
September, 1988
1 Reps.Warrior Mag(U.K.),I:V,
    A:M.Storm (Moore scripts) . . 5.00
2 Murder Spree 3.50
3 Govt. Investigators close in . . 3.00
4 T.V. Broadcast take-over 3.00
5 Govt.Corruption Expose 3.00

6 Evey in Prison 3.00
7 Evey released 2.50
8 Search for V,A:Finch 2.50
9 V:Finch 2.50
10 D:V 2.50
TPB 1990 . . . . 14.95

Valor #20 © DC Comics, Inc.

VALOR

1 N:Valor,A:Lex Luthor Jr 2.00
2 MBr,AG,V:Supergirl 1.50
3 MBr,AG,V:Lobo 1.50
4 MBr,AG,V:Lobo 1.50
5 MBr,A:Blasters 1.50
6 A:Blasters,V:Kanjar Ru 1.50
7 A:Blasters 1.50
8 AH(c),V:The Unimaginable . . . 1.50
9 AH(c),PCu,A:Darkstar 1.50
10 AH(c),V:Unimaginable 1.50
11 A:Legionnaires 1.50
12 AH(c),B:D.O.A. 4.00
13 AH(c),D:Valor's Mom 3.50
14 AH(c),A:JLA,Legionnaires . . . 2.50
15 SI(c),D.O.A #4. . . . . 2.00
16 CDo,D.O.A #5. . . . . 2.00
17 CDo,LMc,D:Valor 1.75
18 A:Legionnaires 1.75
19 CDo,A:Legionnaires,V:Glorith . 1.75
20 CDo,A:Wave Rider 1.75
21 . . . . 1.75
22 End of an Era,pt.2 . . . . 1.75
23 Zero Hour 1.75

VAMPS
Vertigo

1 BB(c) 3.00
2 BB(c) 2.50
3 thru 5 BB(c) . . . . @2.25
6 BB(c),last issue 2.25

VERTIGO JAM

1 GF(c),NGa(s),ANo(s),PrM(s),GEn(s),
JaD(s),KN,SDi,SEa,NyC(s),EiS,PhH,
KDM(i),SeP,MiA,RaP(s),MPn(i),
Vertigo Short Stories 4.50

VERTIGO PREVIEW

Preview of new Vertigo titles,
new Sandman story 1.75

VERTIGO VISIONS: DR. OCCULT

1 F:Dr. Occult 3.95

VERTIGO VISIONS: THE GEEK

1 RaP(s),MiA,V:Dr.Abuse 4.25

VERTIGO VISIONS: PHANTOM STRANGER

1 AaK(s),GyD,The Infernal House 3.75

VIGILANTE, THE
October, 1983

1 KP,DG,F:Adrian Chase 3.50
2 KP 3.00
3 KP,Cyborg 2.50
4 DN,V:Exterminator 2.50
5 KP 2.50
6 O:Vigilante 3.00
7 O:Vigilante 3.00
8 RA,V:Electrocutioner 2.50
9 RA,V:Electrocutioner 2.50
10 RA,DG,avenges J.J. 2.50
11 RA,V:Controller 2.00
12 GK,"Journal" 2.00
13 GK,"Locke Room Murder" . . . 2.00
14 RA,V:Hammer 2.00
15 RA,V:Electrocutioner 2.00
16 RA 2.00
17 Moore 3.00
18 Moore 3.00
19 RA 2.00
20 A:Nightwing 2.50
21 A:Nightwing 2.50
22 . . . . 2.00
23 V:Electrocutioner 2.00
24 "Mother's Day" 2.00
25 RM,V:Police Torturers 2.00
26 V:Electrocutioner 2.00
27 V:Electrocutioner 2.00
28 New Vigilante 2.00
29 RM,New Vigilante 2.00
30 RM,D:Glitz Jefferson 2.00
31 RM,New York Violence 2.00
32 RM,New York Violence 2.00
33 RM,V:Rapist 2.00
34 . . . . 2.00
35 JBy(c),O:MadBomber 2.00
36 MGr(c),V:Peacemaker 2.25
37 MGr,RM,V:Peacemaker 2.25
38 MGr,PeaceMaker 2.25
39 White Slavery 2.00
40 HC(c),White Slavery 2.00
41 . . . . 2.00
42 A:Peacemaker,V:Terrorists . . . 2.00
43 V:PeaceMaker 2.00
44 DC,V:Qurac 2.00
45 I:Black Thorn 2.00
46 Viigilante in Jail 2.00
47 A:Batman 2.50
48 I:Homeless Avenger 2.00
49 . . . . 2.00
50 KSy(c)D:Vigilante 2.50
Ann.#1 . . . . 3.00
Ann.#2 V:Cannon 2.50

VIPER

1 Based on the TV Show 2.25
2 . . . . 2.00
3 . . . . 1.95
4 final issue 1.95

WANDERERS
June, 1988

1 I:New Team 1.25
2 V:The Performer 1.25
3 A:Legion of Superheroes 1.25
4 V:Controller Hunters 1.25
5 O:Wanderers 1.25
6 V:Terrorists 1.25
7 V:Medtorians 1.25
8 O:Psyche 1.25
9 O:Psyche 1.25
10 F:Quantum Queen 1.25
11 F:Quantum Queen 1.25
12 V:Aliens 1.25
13 V:Dinosaurs 1.25

WANTED: THE WORLD'S MOST DANGEROUS VILLIANS
July-August, 1972

1 rep. Batman,Green Lantern . . . 4.00
2 Batman/Joker/Penguin 5.00
3 . . . . 3.00
4 . . . . 3.00
5 . . . . 3.00
6 . . . . 3.00
7 . . . . 3.00
8 . . . . 3.00
9 . . . . 3.00

WARLORD
January, 1976

1 MGr,O:Warlord 16.00
2 MGr,I:Machiste 9.00
3 MGr,'War Gods of Skartaris' . . . 7.00
4 MGr,'Duel of the Titans' 6.50
5 MGr,'The Secret of Skartaris' . . 6.50
6 MGr,I:Mariah,Stryker 6.00
7 MGr,O:Machiste 5.50
8 MGr,A:Skyra 5.50
9 MGr,N:Warlord 5.50
10 MGr,I:Ashiya 6.00
11 MGr,rep.1st Issue special #8 . 5.00
12 MGr,I:Aton 5.00
13 MGr,D:Stryker 5.00
14 MGr,V:Death 5.00
15 MGr,I:Joshua 5.00
16 MGr,I:Saaba 5.00
17 MGr,'Citadel of Death' 5.00
18 MGr,I:Shadow 5.00
19 MGr,'Wolves of the Steppes' . . 5.00
20 MGr,I:Joshua clone 5.00
21 MGr,D:Joshua clone,Shadow . 3.00
22 MGr'Beast in the Tower' 3.00
23 MGr,'Children of Ba'al' 3.00
24 MGr,I:Iigia 3.00
25 MGr,I:Ahir 3.00
26 MGr,'The Challenge' 3.00
27 MGr,'Atlantis Dying' 3.00
28 MGr,I:Wizard World' 3.00
29 MGr,I:Mongo Ironhand' 3.00
30 MGr,C:Joshua 3.00
31 MGr,'Wing over Shamballah' . . 3.00
32 MGr,I:Shakira 3.00
33 MGr,Birds of Prey,A:Shakira . . 3.00
34 MGr,Sword of the Sorceror,
   I:Hellfire 3.00
35 MGr,C:Mike Grell 3.00
36 MGr,'Interlude' 3.00
37 MGr,JSn,I:Firewing,B:Omac . . 6.00
38 MGr,I:Jennifer,A:Omac 3.00
39 MGr,JSn,'Feast of Agravar' . . . 4.00
40 MGr,N:Warlord 3.00
41 MGr,A:Askir 2.50

---

42 MGr,JSn,A:Tara,Omac 3.50
43 MGr,JSn,'Berserk'A:Omac .. 3.50
44 MGr,'The Gamble' 3.00
45 MGr,'Nightmare in Vista
    Vision',A:Omac 3.00
46 MGr,D:Shakira 3.00
47 MGr,I:Mikola,E:Omac 3.00
48 MGr,EC,TY,I:Arak,Claw(B) .. 3.00
49 MGr,TY,A:Shakira,E:Claw ... 2.50
50 MGr,'By Fire and Ice' 2.50
51 MGr,TY,rep.#1,
    I(B):Dragonsword 2.00
52 MGr,TY,'Back in the U.S.S.R. . 2.50
53 MT,TY,'Sorcerer's Apprentice' . 2.00
54 MT,'Sorceress Supreme',
    E:Dragonsword 2.00
55 MT,'Have a Nice Day' 2.00
56 MT,JD,I:Gregmore,(B):Arion . 2.00
57 MT,'The Two Faces of
    Travis Morgan' 2.00
58 MT,O:Greamore 2.00
59 MGr,A:Joshua 2.00
60 JD,'Death Dual' 2.00
61 JD,A:Greamore 2.00
62 JD,TMd,A:Mikola,E:Arion ... 2.00
63 JD,RR,I(B):Barren Earth 2.00
64 DJu,RR'Elsewhere' 2.00
65 DJu,RR,A:Wizard World,
    No Barren Earth 2.00
66 DJu'Wizard World',
    No Barren Earth 2.00
67 DJu,RR,'The Mark' 2.00
68 DJu,RR 2.00
69 DJu,RR 2.00
70 DJu,'Outback' 2.00
71 DJu/DA,'The Journey Back'
    No Barren Earth 2.00
72 DJu,DA,I:Scarhart,No Barren
    Earth 2.00
73 DJ,DA,'Cry Plague' 2.00
74 DJu,No Barren Earth 2.00
75 DJu,'All Dreams Must Pass'
    No Barren Earth 2.00
76 DJu,DA,RR,A:Sarga 2.00
77 DJu,DA,RR,Let My People Go 2.00
78 DJu,RR,'Doom's Mouth' 2.00
79 PB,RM,'Paradox',No Barren
    Earth 2.00
80 DJu,DA,RR,'Future Trek' ... 2.00
81 DJu,DA,RR,'Thief's Magic' ... 2.00
82 DJu,DA,RR,'Revolution' 2.00
83 DJu,RR,'All the President's
    Men' 2.00
84 DJu,DA,RR,'Hail to the Chief' . 2.00
85 DJu,RR,'The Price of Change' . 2.00
86 DJ,DA,No Barren Earth 2.00
87 DJu,RB,RR,I:Hawk 2.00
88 DJu,RB,RR,I:Patch,E:Barren
    Earth 2.00
89 RB,I:Sabertooth 2.00
90 RB,'Demon's of the Past' ... 2.00
91 DJu,DA,I:Maddox,O:Warlord
    O:Jennifer 1.75
92 NKu,'Evil in Ebony' 2.00
93 RR,A:Sabertooth 1.75
94 'Assassin's Prey' 1.75
95 AKu,'Dragon's Doom' 2.00
96 'Nightmare Prelude' 1.75
97 RB,A:Saaba,D:Scarhart 1.75
98 NKu,Crisis tie-in 2.00
99 NKu'Fire and Sword' 2.00
100 AKu,D:Greamore,Sabertooth 2.00
101 MGr,'Temple of Demi-god' .. 1.75
102 I:Zuppara,Error-Machiste
    with two hands 1.75

103 JBi,'Moon Beast' 1.75
104 RR,'Dragon Skinner' 1.75
105 RR,'Stalilers of Skinner' ... 1.75
106 RR,I:Daimon 1.75
107 RR,'Bride of Yano' 1.75
108 RR,I:Mortella 1.75
109 RR,A:Mortella 1.75
110 RR,A:Skyra III 1.75
111 RR,'Tearing o/t Island Sea' .. 1.75
112 RR,'Obsession' 1.75
113 RR,'Through Fiends
    Destroy Me' 1.75
114 RR,'Phenalegeno Dies' 1.75
115 RR,'Citadel of Fear' 1.75
116 RR,'Revenge of the Warlord' . 1.75
117 RR,A:Power Girl 1.75
118 RR,A:Power Girl 1.75
119 RR,A:Power Girl 1.75
120 ATb,A:Power Girl 1.75
121 ATb,A:Power Girl 1.75
122 ATb,A:Power Girl 1.75
123 JD,TMd,N:Warlord 1.75
124 JD,TMd,I:Scavenger 1.75
125 JD,TMd,D:Tara 1.75
126 JD,TMd,A:Machiste 1.75
127 JD,'The Last Dragon' 1.75
128 JD,I:Agife 1.75
129 JD,Vision of Quest 1.75
130 JD,A:Maddox 1.75
131 JD,RLd,'Vengeful Legacies' .. 5.00
132 'A New Beginning' 1.75
133 JD,final issue (44pg) 2.00
Ann.#1 MGr,A:Shakira 3.00
Ann.#2 I:Krystovar 1.75
Ann.#3 DJu,'Full Circle' 1.75
Ann.#4 A:New Gods,
    Legends tie-in 1.75
Ann.#5 AKu,Hellfire 1.75
TPB Warlord:Savage Empire,
    Rep.#1-#10,#12,Special #8 . 19.95

[Limited Series]
1 Travis Morgan retrospective ... 1.75
2 Fate of T. Morgan revealed ... 1.75
3 Return of Deimos 1.75
4 V:Deimos 1.75
5 MGr(c),Skartaros at War 1.75

WAR OF THE GODS
1 GP,A:Lobo,Misc.Heroes,Circe
    (direct) 1.75
2 GP,A:Misc.Heroes,V:Circe,
    w/poster 1.75
2a (Newsstand) 1.75
3 GP,A:Misc.Heroes,V:Circe,
    w/poster 1.75
3a Newsstand 1.75
4 GP,A:Misc.Heroes,V:Circe,
    w/poster 1.75
4a Newsstand 1.75

WASTELAND
December, 1987
1 Selection of Horror stories 1.75
2 .... 1.75
3 .... 1.75
4 .... 1.75
5 'The big crossover story' 1.75
6 .... 1.75
7 'Great St.Louis Electrical
    Giraffe Caper' 1.75
8 'Dead Detective' 1.75
9 .... 1.75
10 TT,African Folk Tale 1.75
11 'Revenge o/t Swamp Creature' 1.75

Wasteland #6 © DC Comics, Inc.

12 JO,'After the Dead Detective' . 1.75
13 TT(c),JO 2.00
14 JO,RM,'Whistling Past the
    Graveyard' 2.00
15 JO,RM 2.00
16 JO 2.00
17 JO 2.00
18 JO,RM,final issue 2.00

WATCHMEN
September, 1986
1 B:AMo,DGb,D:Comedian 7.50
2 DGb,Funeral for Comedian ... 6.00
3 DGb,F:Dr.Manhattan 5.00
4 DGb,O:Dr.Manhattan 5.00
5 DGb,F:Rorschach 5.00
6 DGb,O:Rorschach 5.00
7 DGb,F:Nite Owl 5.00
8 DGb,F:Silk Spectre 5.00
9 DGb,O:Silk Spectre 5.00
10 DGb,A:Rorschach 5.00
11 DGb,O:Ozymandius 5.00
12 DGb,D:Rorsharch 5.00
TPB rep.#1-#12 .... 14.95

WEB
Impact
1 I:Gunny, Bill Grady, Templar .. 1.25
2 O:The Web, I:Brew, Jump,
    Sunshine Kid 1.00
3 Minions of Meridian, I:St.James 1.00
4 Agent Jump vs. UFO 1.00
5 Agent Buster/Fly team-up
    V:Meridian 1.00
6 I:Posse,A:Templar 1.00
7 V:Meridian's Forces 1.00
8 R: Studs 1.00
9 Earthquest,pt.1 .... 2.50
10 V:Templar 1.25
11 V:Templar 1.25
12 "The Gauntlet",A:Shield 1.25
13 Frenzy#1 .... 1.25
14 Frenzy#2 .... 1.25
Ann.#1 Earthquest,w/trading card . 2.50

WEIRD, THE
April, 1988

1 BWr,A:JLI 4.00
2 BWr,A:JLI 3.00
3 BWr,V:Jason 3.00
4 final issue 2.50

WEIRD WAR TALES
September-October, 1971

1 JKu(c),JKu,RH,Fort which
  Did Not Return 6.00
2 JKu,MD,Military Madness 5.00
3 JKu(c),RA,The Pool 5.00
4 JKu(c),Ghost of Two Wars 4.00
5 JKu(c),RH,Slave 4.00
6 JKu(c),Pawns, The Sounds
  of War 4.00
7 JKu(c),JKu,RH,Flying Blind . . 4.00
8 NA(c),The Avenging Grave . . . 6.00
9 NC(c),The Promise 4.00
10 NC(c),Who is Haunting
  the Haunted Chateau 4.00
11 NC(c),ShM,October 30, 1918:
  The German Trenches, WWI . . 3.00
12 MK(c),God of Vengeance 2.00
13 LD(c),The Die-Hards 2.00
14 LD(c),ShM,The Ghost of
  McBride's Woman 2.00
15 LD(c),Ace King Just Flew
  In From Hell 2.00
16 LD(c),More Dead Than Alive . . 2.00
17 GE(c),Dead Man's Hands 3.00
18 GE(c),Captain Dracula 3.00
19 LD(c),The Platoon That
  Wouldn't Die 2.00
20 LD(c),Operation Voodoo 2.00
21 LD(c),One Hour To Kill 2.00
22 LD(c),Wings of Death 2.00
23 LD(c),The Bird of Death 2.00
24 LD(c),The Invisible Enemy . . . 2.00
25 LD(c),Black Magic...White
  Death 2.00
26 LD(c),Jump Into Hell 2.00
27 LD(c),Survival of the
  Fittest 2.00
28 LD(c),Isle of Forgotten
  Warriors 2.00
29 LD(c),Breaking Point 2.00
30 LD(c),The Elements of Death . 2.00
31 LD(c),Death Waits Twice 2.00
32 LD(c),The Enemy, The Stars . . 2.00
33 LD(c),Pride of the Master
  Race 2.00
34 LD(c),The Common Enemy . . . 2.00
35 LD(c),The Invaders 2.00
36 JKu(c),Escape 2.00
37 LD(c),The Three Wars of
  Don Q 2.00
38 JKu(c),Born To Die 2.00
39 JKu(c),The Spoils of War 2.00
40 ECh(c),Back From The Dead . 2.00
41 JL(c), The Dead Draftees of
  Regiment Six 2.00
42 JKu(c),Old Soldiers Never
  Die 2.00
43 ECh(c),Bulletproof 2.00
44 JKu(c),ShM,The Emperor
  Weehawken 2.00
45 JKu(c),The Battle of Bloody
  Valley 2.00
46 Kill Or Be Killed 2.00
47 JKu(c),Bloodbath of the Toy
  Soldiers 2.00
48 JL(c),Ultimate Destiny 2.00
49 The Face Of The Enemy 2.00

50 ECh(c),-An Appointment With
  Destiny 2.00
51 JKu(c),Secret Weapon 2.00
52 JKu(c),The Devil Is A
  Souvenir Hunter 2.00
53 JAp(c), Deadly Dominoes 2.00
54 GM(c),Soldier of Satan 2.00
55 JKu(c),A Rebel Shall Rise
  From The Grave 2.00
56 AM(c),The Headless Courier . . 2.00
57 RT(c),Trial By Combat 2.00
58 JKu(c),Death Has A Hundred
  Eyes 2.00
59 The Old One 2.00
60 JKu(c),Night Flight 2.00
61 HC(c),Mind War 2.00
62 JKu(c),The Grubbers 2.00
63 JKu(c),Battleground 2.00
64 JKu(c),Deliver Me For D-Day . 2.00
65 JKu(c),The Last Cavalry
  Charge 2.00
66 JKu(c),The Iron Star 2.00
67 JKu(c),The Attack of the
  Undead 2.00
68 FM,JKu(c),The Life and Death of
  Charlie Golem 2.00
69 JKu(c),The Day After Doomsday 2.00
70 LD(c),The Blood Boat 2.00
71 LD(c),False Prophet 2.00
72 JKu(c),Death Camp 2.00
73 GE(c),The Curse of Zopyrus . . 2.00
74 GE(c),March of the Mammoth . 2.00
75 JKu(c),The Forgery 2.00
76 JKu(c),The Fire Bug 2.00
77 JKu(c),Triad 2.00
78 JKu(c),Indian War In Space . . 2.00
79 JKu(c),The Gods Themselves . 2.00
80 JKu(c),An Old Man's Profession 2.00
81 JKu(c),It Takes Brains To
  Be A Killer 2.00
82 GE(c),Funeral Fire 2.00
83 GE(c),Prison of the Mind 2.00
84 JKu(c),Devil's Due 2.00
85 thru 124 June 1983 . . . . . . @2.00

ALL STAR WESTERN

1 NA(c),CI 12.00
2 NA(c),GM,B:Outlaw 5.00
3 NA(c),GK,O:El Diablo 4.00
4 NA(c),GK,JKu,GM 4.00
5 NA(c),JAp,E:Outlaw 4.00
6 GK,B:Billy the Kid 4.00
7 . . . . 4.00
8 E:Billy the Kid 4.00
9 FF 6.00
10 GM,I:Jonah Hex 110.00
11 GM,A:Jonah Hex 50.00
Becomes:

WEIRD WESTERN TALES
June-July, 1972

12 NA,BWr,JKu 6.00
13 . . . . 6.00
14 ATh 3.00
15 NA(c),GK 6.00
16 thru 28 . . . . @2.00
29 O:Jonah Hex 8.00
30 . . . . 2.00
31 thru 38 . . . . @2.00
39 I&O:Scalphunter 2.00
40 thru 70 . . . . @2.00

WEIRD WORLDS
August-September, 1971

1 JO,MA,John Carter 10.00

2 NA,JO(c),MA,BWr 15.00
3 MA,NA 12.00
4 MK(c),MK 5.00
5 MK(c),MK 5.00
6 MK(c),MK 5.00
7 John Carter ends 5.00
8 HC,I:Iron Wolf 4.00
9 HC 4.00
10 HC,Last issue 4.00

Western Comics #6 © DC Comics, Inc.

WESTERN COMICS
January-February, 1948

1 MMe,B:Vigilante,Podeo Rick,
  WyomingKid,CowboyMarshal 450.00
2 MMe,Vigilante vs. Dirk Bigger 225.00
3 MMe,Vigilante vs. Pecos Kid 175.00
4 MMe,Vigilante as Pecos Kid 175.00
5 I:Nighthawk 150.00
6 Wyoming Kid vs. 'The
  Murder Mustang' 125.00
7 Wyoming Kid in 'The Town
  That Was Never Robbed . . 125.00
8 O:Wyoming Kid 150.00
9 Wyoming Kid vs. Jack
  Slaughter 125.00
10 Nighthawk in 'Tunnel ofTerror'125.00
11 Wyoming Kid vs. Mayor Brock100.00
12 Wyoming Kid vs. Baldy Ryan 100.00
13 I:Running Eagle 100.00
14 Wyoming Kid in 'The Siege
  of Praire City 100.00
15 Nighthawk in 'Silver, Salt
  and Pepper 100.00
16 Wyoming Kid vs. Smilin' Jim 100.00
17 BP,Wyoming Kid vs. Prof.
  Penny 100.00
18 LSt on Nighthawk,WyomingKid
  in 'Challenge of the Chiefs' . 100.00
19 LSt,Nighthawk in 'The
  Invisible Rustlers 100.00
20 LSt,Nighthawk in 'The Mystery
  Mail From Defender Dip' . . . 75.00
21 LSt,Nighthawk in 'Rattlesnake
  Hollow' 75.00
22 LSt,I:Jim Pegton 75.00
23 LSt,Nighthawk reveals
  ID to Jim 75.00
24 The $100,000 Impersonation . 75.00
25 V:Souix Invaders 75.00

26 The Storming of the Sante Fe Trail	75.00
27 The Looters of Lost Valley	75.00
28 The Thunder Creek Rebellion	75.00
29 Six Guns of the Wyoming Kid	75.00
30 V:Green Haired Killer	75.00
31 The Sky Riding Lawman	75.00
32 Death Rides the Stage Coach	75.00
33	75.00
34 Prescription For Killers	75.00
35 The River of Rogues	75.00
36 Nighthawk(c),Duel in the Dark	55.00
37 The Death Dancer	65.00
38 Warpath in the Sky	65.00
39 Death to Fort Danger	65.00
40 Blind Man's Bluff	65.00
41 thru 60	@55.00
61 thru 85	@40.00

WHO'S WHO

1	2.00
2 thru 9	@1.50
10 inc.	1.25
11 inc. Infinity Inc.	1.25
12 inc. Kamandi	1.25
13 inc. Legion of Super Heroes/ Villains	1.25
14 inc.	1.25
15 inc. Metal Men	1.25
16 inc. New Gods	1.25
17 inc. Outsiders	1.25
18 inc. Power Girl	1.25
19 inc. Robin	1.25
20 inc.	1.25
21 inc. The Spectre	1.25
22 inc. Superman	1.25
23 inc. Teen Titans	1.25
24 inc. Unknown Soldier	1.25
25 inc.	1.25
26 inc.	1.25

WHO'S WHO
(PACKET)

1 inc. Superman	6.00
1a 2nd printing	5.50
2 inc. Flash	5.50
2a 2nd printing	5.00
3 inc. Green Lantern	5.50
4 inc. Wonder Woman	5.50
5 inc. Batman	5.50
6 inc. Hawkman	5.50
7 inc. Shade	5.50
8 inc. Lobo	6.00
9 inc. Legion of Super-Heroes	5.50
10 inc. Robin	5.50
11 inc. L.E.G.I.O.N. '91	5.50
12 inc. Aquaman	5.50
13 Villains issue, inc. Joker	6.00
14 inc. New Titans	5.50
15 inc. Doom Patrol	5.50
16 inc. Catwoman,final issue	5.00

WHO'S WHO
IN IMPACT

1 Shield	4.95
2 Black Hood	4.95

WHO'S WHO
IN THE LEGION

1 History/Bio of Legionnaires	1.25
2 inc. Dream Girl	1.25
3 inc. Karate Kid	1.25
4 inc. Lightning Lad	1.25

5 inc. Phantom Girl	1.25
6 inc. Timber Wolf	1.25
7 wraparound(c)	1.25

WHO'S WHO
IN STAR TREK

1 HC(c)	1.50
2 HC(c)	1.50

WHO'S WHO
UPDATE '87

1 inc. Blue Beetle	1.50
2 inc. Catwoman	1.25
3 inc. Justice League	1.25
4	1.25
5 inc. Superboy	1.25

WHO'S WHO
UPDATE '88

1 inc. Brainiac	1.25
2 inc. JusticeLeagueInternational	1.25
3 inc. Shado	1.25
4 inc. Zatanna	1.25

WHO'S WHO UPDATE '93

1 F:Eclipso,Azrael	5.25

WILD DOG
September, 1987

1 mini series DG(i),I:Wild Dog	1.00
2 DG(i),V:Terrorists	1.00
3 DG(i)	1.00
4 DG(i),O:Wild Dog, final issue	1.00
Spec.#1	2.50

WINDY & WILLY
May-June, 1969

1 thru 4	@1.00

Witch Craft #1
© DC Comics, Inc.

WITCHCRAFT
Vertigo

1 CV(c),Three Witches from Sandman	4.00
2 F:Mildred	3.50
3 Final issue	3.25

WONDER WOMAN
Summer, 1942

1 O:Wonder Woman,A:Paula Von Gunther	8,500.00
2 I:Earl of Greed,Duke of Deception and Lord Conquest, A:Mars	1,500.00
3 Paula Von Gunther reforms	1,000.00
4 A:Paula Von Gunther	750.00
5 I:Dr. Psycho,A:Mars	750.00
6 I:Cheetah	600.00
7	600.00
8 I:Queen Clea	600.00
9 I:Giganto	600.00
10 I:Duke Mephisto Saturno	600.00
11 I:Hypnoto	450.00
12 I:Queen Desira	450.00
13 V:King Rigor & the Seal Men	450.00

Wonder Woman #10
© DC Comics, Inc.

14 I:Gentleman Killer	450.00
15 I:Solo	450.00
16 I:King Pluto	450.00
17 Wonder Woman goes to Ancient Rome	450.00
18 V:Dr. Psycho	450.00
19 V:Blitz	450.00
20 V:Nifty and the Air Pirates	450.00
21 I:Queen Atomia	400.00
22 V:Saturno	400.00
23 V:Odin and the Valkyries	400.00
24 I:Mask	400.00
25 V:Purple Priestess	400.00
26 I:Queen Celerita	400.00
27 V:Pik Socket	400.00
28 V:Cheetah,Clea,Dr. Poison, Giganta,Hypnata,Snowman, Zara (Villainy,Inc.)	325.00
29 V:Paddy Gypso	325.00
30 'The Secret of the Limestone Caves'	325.00
31 V:Solo	250.00
32 V:Uvo	250.00
33 V:Inventa	250.00
34 V:Duke of Deception	250.00
35 'Jaxo,Master of Thoughts'	250.00
36 V:Lord Cruello	250.00
37 A:Circe	250.00
38 V:Brutex	250.00
39 'The Unmasking of Wonder Woman'	250.00

40 'Hollywood Goes To Paradise Island' 250.00	
41 'Wonder Woman,Romance Editor' 225.00	
42 V:General Vertigo 225.00	
43 'The Amazing Spy Ring Mystery' 225.00	
44 V:Master Destroyer 225.00	
45 'The Amazon and the Leprachaun' 350.00	
46 V:Prof. Turgo 225.00	
47 V:Duke of Deception 225.00	
48 V:Robot Woman 225.00	
49 V:Boss 225.00	
50 V:Gen. Voro 225.00	

40 'Hollywood Goes To Paradise
Island' 250.00
41 'Wonder Woman,Romance
Editor' 225.00
42 V:General Vertigo 225.00
43 'The Amazing Spy Ring
Mystery' 225.00
44 V:Master Destroyer 225.00
45 'The Amazon and the
Leprachaun' 350.00
46 V:Prof. Turgo 225.00
47 V:Duke of Deception 225.00
48 V:Robot Woman 225.00
49 V:Boss 225.00
50 V:Gen. Voro 225.00
51 V:Garo 175.00
52 V:Stroggo 175.00
53 'Crime Master of Time .. 175.00
54 A:Merlin 175.00
55 'The Chessmen of Doom' .. 175.00
56 V:Plotter Gang 175.00
57 V:Mole Men 175.00
58 V:Brain 175.00
59 V:Duke Dozan 175.00
60 A:Paula Von Gunther 175.00
61 'Earth's Last Hour' 125.00
62 V:Angles Andrews 125.00
63 V:Duke of Deception 125.00
64 V:Thought Master 125.00
65 V:Duke of Deception 125.00
66 V:Duke of Deception 125.00
67 'Confessions of a Spy' 125.00
68 'Landing of the Flying
Saucers' 125.00
69 'Johann Gutenberg,Chris.
Columbus, Paul Revere
and the Wright Brothers ... 125.00
70 I:Angle Man 125.00
71 'One-Woman Circus' 100.00
72 V:Mole Goldings 100.00
73 V:Prairie Pirates 100.00
74 'The Carnival of Peril' 100.00
75 V:Angler 100.00
76 .... 100.00
77 V:Smokescreen gang 100.00
78 V:Angle Man 100.00
79 V:Spider 100.00
80 V:Machino 100.00
81 V:Duke of Deception,
Angle Man 100.00
82 A:Robin Hood 100.00
83 'The Boy From Nowhere' .. 100.00
84 V:Duke of Deception,
Angle Man 100.00
85 V:Capt. Virago 100.00
86 V:Snatcher 100.00
87 'The Day the Clocks Stopped' 100.00
88 V:Duke of Deception 100.00
89 'The Triple Heroine' 100.00
90 Wonder Woman on Jupiter . 100.00
91 'The Interplanetary Olympics' 75.00
92 V:Angle Man 75.00
93 V:Duke of Deception 75.00
94 V:Duke of Deception,
A:Robin Hood 75.00
95 O:Wonder Woman's tiara ... 85.00
96 V:Angle Man 75.00
97 'The Runaway Time Express' 75.00
98 .... 75.00
99 V:Silicons 75.00
100 Anniversary Issue 70.00
101 V:Time Master 50.00
102 F:Steve Trevor 50.00
103 V:Gadget-Maker 50.00
104 A:Duke of Deception 50.00

105 O,I:Wonder Woman 275.00
106 W.Woman space adventure 50.00
107 Battles space cowboys 50.00
108 Honored by U.S. Post Off. . 50.00
109 V:Slicker 50.00
110 I:Princess 1003 .... 50.00
111 I:Prof. Menace 50.00
112 V:Chest of Monsters 40.00
113 A:Queen Mikra 40.00
114 V:Flying Saucers 40.00
115 A:Angle Man 40.00
116 A:Professor Andro 40.00
117 A:Etta Candy 40.00
118 A:Merman 40.00
119 A:Mer Boy 40.00
120 A:Hot & Cold Alien 40.00
121 A:Wonder Woman Family .. 25.00
122 I:Wonder Tot 25.00
123 A:Wonder Girl,Wonder Tot . 25.00
124 A:Wonder Girl,Wonder Tot . 25.00
125 WW-Battle Prize 25.00
126 I:Mr.Genie 25.00
127 Suprise Honeymoon 15.00
128 O:InvisiblePlane 15.00
129 A:WonderGirl,WonderTot .. 15.00
130 A:Angle Man 15.00
131 .... 8.00
132 V:Flying Saucer 8.00
133 A:Miss X 8.00
134 V:Image-Maker 8.00

Wonder Woman #35
© DC Comics, Inc.

135 V:Multiple Man 8.00
136 V:Machine Men 8.00
137 V:Robot Wonder Woman ... 8.00
138 V:Multiple Man 8.00
139 Amnesia revels Identity 8.00
140 A:Morpheus,Mr.Genie 8.00
141 A:Angle Man 8.00
142 A:Mirage Giants 8.00
143 A:Queen Hippolyte 8.00
144 I:Bird Boy 8.00
145 V:Phantom Sea Beast 8.00
146 $1,000 Dollar Stories 8.00
147 Wonder Girl becomes Bird Girl
and Fish Girl 8.00
148 A:Duke of Deception 8.00
149 Last Day of the Amazons ... 8.00
150 V:Phantome Fish Bird 8.00
151 F:1st Full Wonder Girl story . 7.00
152 F:Wonder Girl 7.00

153 V:Duke of Deception 7.00
154 V:Boiling Man 7.00
155 I married a monster 7.00
156 V:Brain Pirate 7.00
157 A:Egg Fu,the First 7.00
158 A:Egg Fu,the First 7.00
159 Origin 8.00
160 A:Cheetah,Dr. Psycho 6.00
161 A:Angle Man 6.00
162 O:Diana Prince 6.00
163 A:Giganta 6.00
164 A:Angle Man 6.00
165 A:Paper Man,Dr.Psycho 6.00
166 A:Egg Fu,The Fifth 6.00
167 A:Crimson Centipede 6.00
168 RA,ME,V:Giganta 6.00
169 RA,ME,Crimson Centipede .. 6.00
170 RA,ME,V:Dr.Pyscho 6.00
171 A:Mouse Man 5.00
172 IN,A:Android Wonder Woman 5.00
173 A:Tonia 5.00
174 A:Angle Man 5.00
175 V:Evil Twin 5.00
176 A:Star Brothers 5.00
177 A:Super Girl 5.00
178 MSy,DG,I:New Wonder
Woman 5.00
179 D:Steve Trevor,I:Ching 4.00
180 MSy,DG,wears no costume
I:Tim Trench 4.00
181 MSy,DG,A:Dr.Cyber 3.00
182 MSy,DG

Wonder Woman #53
© DC Comics, Inc.

183 MSy,DG,V:War 4.00
184 MSy,DG,A:Queen Hippolyte . 4.00
185 MSy,DG,V:Them 3.00
186 MSy,DG,I:Morgana 3.00
187 MSy,DG,A:Dr.Cyber 3.50
188 MSy,DG,A:Dr.Cyber 3.00
189 MSy,DG 3.00
190 MSy,DG 3.00
191 MSy,DG 3.00
192 MSy,DG 3.00
193 MSy,DG 3.00
194 MSy,DG 3.00
195 MSy,WW 3.50
196 MSy,DG,giant,Origin rep. ... 4.50
197 MSy,DG 3.50
198 MSy,DG 3.50
199 JJ(c),DG 7.00

All comics prices listed are for *Near Mint* condition.   **CVA Page 117**

200	JJ(c),DG	7.00	243		1.50
201	DG,A:Catwoman	4.00	244		1.50
202	DG,A:Catwoman,I:Fafhrd		245		1.50
	& the Gray Mouser	4.00	246		1.50
203	DG,Womens lib	2.00	247		1.50
204	DH,BO,rewears costume	1.75	248	D:Steve Trevor	1.50
205	DH,BO	1.75	249	A:Hawkgirl	1.50
206	DH,O:Wonder Woman	2.50	250	I:Orana	1.50
207	RE	1.75	251	O:Orana	1.50
208	RE	1.75	252		1.50
209	RE	1.75	253		1.50
210	RE	1.75	254		1.50
211	RE,giant	3.00	255	V:Bushmaster	1.50
212	CS,A:Superman,tries to		256	V:Royal Flush Gang	1.50
	rejoin JLA	1.75			
213	IN,A:Flash	1.75			
214	CS,giant,A:Green Lantern	3.00			
215	A:Aquaman	1.50			
216	A:Black Canary	1.50			
217	DD,A:Green Arrow	2.00			
218	KS,Red Tornado	1.50			
219	CS,A:Elongated Man	1.50			
220	DG,NA,A:Atom	2.00			
221	CS,A:Hawkman	1.50			
222	A:Batman	2.00			
223	R:Steve Trevor	1.50			
224		1.50			
225		1.50			
226		1.50			
227		1.50			
228	B:War stories	1.50			
229		1.50			
230	V:Cheetah	1.50			
231		1.50			

Wonder Woman #202
© DC Comics, Inc.

Wonder Woman #278
© DC Comics, Inc.

232	MN,A:JSA	1.50	257		1.50
233	GM	1.50	258		1.50
234		1.50	259		1.50
235		1.50	260		1.50
236		1.50	261		1.50
237	RB(c),O:Wonder Woman	1.75	262	RE,A:Bushmaster	1.50
238	RB(c)	1.50	263		1.50
239	RB(c)	1.50	264		1.50
240		1.50	265		1.50
241	JSon,DG,A:Spectre	1.50	266		1.50
242		1.50	267	R:Animal Man	18.00
			268	A:Animal Man	15.00
			269	WW(i),Rebirth of Wonder	
				Woman,pt.1	1.50
			270	Rebirth,pt.2	1.50
			271	JSon,B:Huntress,Rebirth,pt.3	1.50
			272	JSon	1.50
			273	JSon,A:Angle Man	1.50
			274	JSon,I:Cheetah II	1.50
			275	JSon,V:Cheetah II	1.50
			276	JSon,V:Kobra	1.50
			277	JSon,V:Kobra	1.50
			278	JSon,V:Kobra	1.50
			279	JSon,A:Demon,Catwoman	2.50
			280	JSon,A:Demon,Catwoman	2.50
			281	JSon,Earth 2 Joker	2.50
			282	JSon,Earth 2 Joker	2.50
			283	Earth 2 Joker	2.50
			284		1.50
			285	JSon,V:Red Dragon	1.50
			286		1.50

287	DH,RT,JSon,Teen Titans	2.25
288	GC,RT,New Wonder Woman	1.50
289	GC,RT,JSon,New W.Woman	1.50
290	GC,RT,JSon,New W.Woman	1.50
291	GC,FMc,A:Zatanna	1.50
292	GC,FMc,RT,Supergirl	1.50
293	GC,FMc,Starfire,Raven	1.50
294	GC,FMc,JSon,V:Blockbuster	1.50
295	GC,FMc,JSon,Huntress	1.50
296	GC,Fmc,JSon	1.50
297	MK(c),GC,FMc,JSon	1.50
298	GC,FMc,JSon	1.50
299	GC,FMc,JSon	1.50
300	GC,FMc,RA,DG,KP,RB,KG	
	C:New Teen Titans	3.25
301	GC,FMc	1.50
302	GC,FMc,V:Artemis	1.50
303	GC,FMc,Huntress	1.50
304	GC,FMc,Huntress	1.50
305	GC,Huntress,I:Circe	1.50
306	DH,Huntress	1.50
307	DH,Huntress,Black Canary	1.50
308	DH,Huntress,Black Canary	1.50
309	DH,Huntress	1.50
310	DH,Huntress	1.50
311	DH,Huntress	1.50
312	DH,DSp,A:Gremlins	1.50
313	DH,V:Circe	1.50
314	DH,Huntress	1.50
315	DH,Huntress	1.50
316	DH,Huntress	1.50
317	DH,V:Cereberus	1.50
318	DH,V:Space Aliens	1.50
319	DH,V:Dr.Cyber	1.50
320	DH	1.50
321	DH,Huntress	1.50
322	IN	1.50
323	DH,A:Cheetah, Angle Man	1.50
324	DH	1.50
325	DH	1.50
326	DH	1.50
327	DH,Crisis	1.50
328	DH,Crisis	1.50
329	DH,Crisis, giant	2.00

WONDER WOMAN
[2nd Regular Series]
February, 1987

1	GP,O:Amazons,Wonder Woman	5.00
2	GP,I:Steve Trevor	3.00
3	GP,I:Julia Vanessa	2.50
4	GP,V:Decay	2.00
5	GP,V:Deimos,Phobos	2.00
6	GP,V:Ares	1.50
7	GP,I:Myndi Mayer	1.50
8	GP,O:Legends,A:JLA,Flash	1.50
9	GP,I:New Cheetah	1.50
10	GP,V:Seven Headed Hydra,	
	Challenge of the Gods,pt.1,	
	gatefold(c)	1.50
10a	regular(c)	1.50
11	GP,V:Echidna,Challenge	
	of the Gods,pt.3	1.50
12	GP,Millenium,V:Pan, Challenge	
	of the Gods,pt.3,	
	Millenium x-over	1.50
13	GP,Millenium,A:Ares,Challenge	
	of the Gods,pt.4	1.50
14	GP,A:Hercules	1.50
15	GP,I:New Silver Swan	1.50
16	GP,V:Silver Swan	1.50
17	GP,DG,V:Circe	1.50
18	GP,DG,V:Circe,+Bonus bk#4	1.50
19	GP,FMc,V:Circe	1.50
20	GP,BMc,D:Myndi Mayer	1.50

21 GP,BMc,L:Greek Gods,
   Destruction of Olympus 1.50
22 GP,BMc,F:Julia, Vanessa 1.50
23 GP,R:Hermes,V:Phobos,
   Prelude to New Titans #50 . . . 1.50
24 GP,V:Ixion, Phobos 1.50
25 CMa,Invasion,A:JLA 1.25
26 CMa,Invasion,V:Capt.Atom . . . 1.25
27 CMa,V:Khunds,A:Cheetah . . . 1.25
28 CMa,V:Cheetah 1.25
29 CMa,V:Cheetah 1.25
30 CMa,V:Cheetah 1.25
31 CMa,V:Cheetah 1.25
32 TG,V:Amazons,A:Hermes 1.25
33 CMa,V:Amazons,Cheetah 1.25
34 CMa,I:Shim'Tar 1.25
35 CMa,V:Shim'Tar 1.25
36 CMa,A:Hermes 1.25
37 CMa,V:Discord,A:Superman . . 1.25
38 CMa,V:Eris 1.25
39 CMa,V:Eris,A:Lois Lane 1.25
40 CMa,V:Eris,A:Lois Lane 1.25
41 CMa,RT,F:Julia,Ties that Bind . 1.25
42 CMa,RT,V:Silver Swan 1.25
43 CMA,RT,V:Silver Swan 1.25
44 CMa,RT,V:SilverSwan 1.25

Wonder Woman (2nd Regular
Series) #68 © DC Comics, Inc.

45 CM,RT,Pandora's Box 1.25
46 RT,Suicide Issue,D:Lucy 1.50
47 RT,A:Troia 1.25
48 RTP,A:Troia 1.25
49 recap of 1st four years 1.25
50 RT,SA,BB,AH,CM,KN,PCR,MW
   A:JLA,Superman 2.00
51 RT,V:Mercury 1.25
52 CM,KN,Shards,V:Dr.Psycho . . 1.25
53 RT,A:Pariah 1.25
54 RT,V:Dr.Psycho 1.25
55 RT,V:Dr.Psycho 1.25
56 RT,A:Comm.Gordon 1.25
57 RT,A:Clark Kent,Bruce Wayne   1.25
58 RT,War of the Gods,V:Atlas . . 2.00
59 RT,War of the Gods,
   A:Batman Robin 2.00
60 RT,War of the Gods,
   A:Batman, Lobo 2.00

61 RT,War of the Gods,V:Circe . . 2.00
62 War o/t Gods,Epilogue. 1.50
63 BB(c)A:Deathstroke,Cheetah . . 1.75
64 BB(c),Kidnapped Child 1.50
65 BB(c),PCu,V:Dr.Psycho 1.50
66 BB(c),PCu,Exodus In Space#1 1.50
67 BB(c),PCu,Exodus In Space#2 1.50
68 BB(c),PCu,Exodus In Space#3 1.50
69 PCu, Exodus In Space#4 . . . . 1.50
70 PCu,Exodus In Space#5 . . . . . 1.50
71 BB(c),DC,RT,Return fr.space . 1.50
72 BB(c),O:retold 1.75
73 BB(c),Diana gets a job 1.50
74 BB(c),V:White Magician 1.50
75 BB(c),A:The White Magician . . 1.50
76 BB(c),A:Doctor Fate 1.50
77 BB(c) 1.50
78 BB(c),A:Flash 1.50
79 BB(c),V:Mayfly,A:Flash 1.50
80 BB(c),V:Ares Buchanan 1.50
81 BB(c),V:Ares Buchanan 1.50
82 BB(c),V:Ares Buchanan 1.50
83 BB(c),V:Ares Buchanan 1.50
84 BB(c),V:Ares Buchanan 1.75
85 BB(c) 2.00
86 BB(c),Turning Point 2.50
87 BB(c),No Quarter,NoSanctuary 2.50
88 BB(c),A:Superman 5.00
89 BB(c),A:Circle 3.50
90 New Direction 3.25
91 Choosing Wonder Woman 3.25
92 New Wonder Woman 3.25
93 New Wonder Woman 3.25
94 . . . . 2.00
95 V:Cheetah 1.75
96 V:The Joker 1.75
97 V:The Joker 1.75
98 BB(c),F:Artemis 1.75
99 BB(c),A:White Magician 1.75
100 BB(c) White Magician defeats
    Artemis 2.95
100a Collector's ed., holo(c) 3.95
Ann.#1,GP,AAd,RA,BB,JBo,JL,CS
    Tales of Paradise Island 2.00
Ann.#2 CM,F:Mayer Agency . . . 2.50
Ann.#3 Eclipso tie-in 2.50
Spec #1 A:Deathstroke,Cheetah . 2.25
Spec.#0 History of Amazons 5.00
TPB The Contest, rep. #90,#0
    #91-#93 . . . . 9.95

WORLD OF KRYPTON
July, 1979
1 HC/MA.O:Jor-El 1.50
2 HC/MA,A:Superman 1.00
3 HC 1.00
[2nd Series]
1 MMi,John Byrne script 1.00
2 MMi,John Byrne script 1.00
3 MMi,John Byrne script 1.00
4 MMi,A:Superman 1.00

WORLD OF METROPOLIS
1988
1 DG(i),O:Perry White 1.00
2 DG(i),O:Lois Lane 1.00
3 DG(i),Clark Kent 1.00
4 DG(i),O:Jimmy Olsen 1.00

WORLD OF SMALLVILLE
1988
1 KS/AA,Secrets of Ma&Pa Kent 1.25
2 KS/AA,'Stolen Moments' 1.25
3 KS/AA,Lana Lang/Manhunter . 1.25

4 KS/AA,final issue 1.25

WORLDS COLLIDE
1 MBr(c),3RW,CsB,Ccs,DCw,
   TG,A:Blood Syndicate,Icon,
   Hardware,Static,Superboy,
   Superman,Steel,Vinyl Cling(c) . 4.25
1a Newsstand Ed. 2.75

WORLD'S BEST COMICS
Spring, 1941
1 Superman vs. the Rainmaker,
   Batman vs. Wright 9,500.00
Becomes:
WORLD'S FINEST COMICS
2 Superman V:'The Unknown X',
   Batman V:Ambrose Taylor 2,400.00
3 I&O:Scarecrow 2,200.00

World's Finest Comics #24
© DC Comics, Inc.

4 Superman V:Dan Brandon,
   Batman V:Ghost Gang . . . 1,500.00
5 Superman V:Lemuel P.Potts,
   Batman V:Brains Kelly . . . 1,500.00
6 Superman V:Metalo,Batman
   meets Scoop Scanlon 1,100.00
7 Superman V:Jenkins,Batman
   V:Snow Man Bandits 1,100.00
8 Superman:'Talent Unlimited'
   Batman V:Little Nap Boyd,
   B:Boy Commandos 1,000.00
9 Superman:'One Second to
   Live',Batman V:Bramwell B.
   Bramwell 1,000.00
10 Superman V:The Insect Master,
   Batman reforms Oliver Hunt 900.00
11 Superman V:Charlie Frost,
   Batman V:Rob Calendar . . . 850.00
12 Superman V:Lynx,Batman:
   'Alfred Gets His Man' 850.00
13 Superman V:Dice Dimant,
   Batman,V:Swami Pravhoz . . 850.00
14 Superman V:Al Bandar,Batman
   V:Jib Buckler 850.00
15 Superman V:Derby Bowser,
   Batman V:Mennekin 850.00
16 Superman:'Music for the Masses,
   Batman V:Nocky Johnson . . 850.00
17 Superman:'The Great Godini',

Batman V:Dr.Dreemo 750.00	Hated Reporters 325.00	B:Tommy Tomorrow 100.00
18 Superman:'The Junior Reporters,	48 A:Joker 325.00	103 'The Secrets of the
Batman V:Prof.Brane 700.00	49 Superman meets the	Sorcerer's Treasure 100.00
19 A:The Joker 700.00	Metropolis Shutterbug	104 A:Lex Luthor 100.00
20 A:Toyman 700.00	Society, A:Penguin 325.00	105 V:Khalex 100.00
21 Superman:'Swindle in	50 'Superman Super Wrecker' . 325.00	106 V:Duplicate Man 100.00
Sweethearts!' 550.00	51 Superman:'The Amazing	107 'The Secret of the Time
22 Batman V:Nails Finney 550.00	Talents of Lois Lane' 325.00	Creature' 100.00
23 Superman:'The Colossus	52 A:J.Wilbur Wolfingham 325.00	108 'The Star Creatures' ... 100.00
of Metropolis' 550.00	53 Superman V:Elias Toomey . 325.00	109 V:Fangan 100.00
24 .... 550.00	54 'The Superman Who Avoided	110 'The Alien Who Doomed
25 Superman V:Ed Rook,Batman:	Danger!' 325.00	Robin!' 100.00
'The Famous First Crimes' . 550.00	55 A:Penguin 325.00	111 V:Floyd Frisby 100.00
26 'Confessions of Superman' . 550.00	56 Superman V:Dr.Vallin,Batman	112 .... 100.00
27 'The Man Who Out-Supered	V:Big Dan Hooker 325.00	113 1st Bat-Mite/Mr.Mxyzptlk
Superman 550.00	57 'The Artificial Superman' ... 325.00	team-up 100.00
28 A:Lex Luther,Batman V:Glass	58 Superman V:Mr.Fenton ... 325.00	114 'Captives o/t Space Globes' 100.00
Man 550.00	59 A:Lex Luthor,Joker 325.00	115 The Curse That Doomed
	60 A:J.Wilbur Wolfingham 325.00	Superman 65.00
	61 A:Joker,'Superman's	116 V:Vance Collins 65.00
	Blackout' 250.00	117 A:Batwoman,Lex Luthor ... 65.00
	62 A:Lex Luthor 250.00	118 V:Vath-Gar 65.00
	63 Superman:'Clark Kent,	
	Gangster' 250.00	
	64 Superman:'The Death of Lois	
	Lane,Batman:'Bruce Wayne...	
	Amateur Detective' 250.00	
	65 'The Confessions of Superman',	
	Batman V:The Blaster 350.00	
	66 'Superman,Ex-Crimebuster;	
	Batman V:Brass Haley 300.00	
	67 Superman:'Metropolis-Crime	
	Center!' 300.00	
	68 Batman V:The Crimesmith . 300.00	
	69 A:Jor-El,Batman	
	V:Tom Becket 300.00	
	70 'The Two Faces of Superman',	
	Batman:'Crime Consultant' . 300.00	
	71 B:Superman/Batman	
	team-ups 650.00	

World's Finest Comics #33
© DC Comics, Inc.

29 Superman:'The Books that	72 V:Heavy Weapon gang 450.00	
couldn't be Bound' 550.00	73 V:Fang 450.00	
30 Superman:'Sheriff Clark Kent',	74 'The Contest of Heroes' ... 400.00	
Batman V:Joe Coyne 550.00	75 V:The Purple Mask Mob ... 350.00	
31 'Superman's Super-Rival',Batman:	76 'When Gotham City	
'Man with the X-Ray Eyes' . 450.00	Challenged Metropolis 250.00	
32 Superman visits	77 V:Prof.Pender 250.00	
Ancient Egypt 450.00	78 V:Varrel mob 250.00	
33 'Superman Press, Inc.',	79 A:Aladdin 250.00	
Batman V:James Harmon .. 450.00	80 V:Mole 250.00	
34 'The Un-Super Superman' .. 450.00	81 Meet Ka Thar from future .. 200.00	
35 Daddy Superman,A:Penguin 450.00	82 A:Three Musketeers 200.00	
36 Lois Lane,Sleeping Beauty . 450.00	83 'The Case of the Mother	
37 'The Superman Story',Batman	Goose Mystery' 200.00	119 V:General Grambly 65.00
V:T-Gun Jones 450.00	84 V:Thad Linnis gang 200.00	120 V:Faceless Creature 65.00
38 If There were No Superman 450.00	85 Meet Princess Varina 200.00	121 I:Miss Arrowette 65.00
39 Superman V:Big Jim Martin,	86 V:Henry Bartle 200.00	122 V:Klor 30.00
Batman V:J.J.Jason 450.00	87 V:Elton Craig 200.00	123 A:Bat-Mite & Mr. Mxyzptlk .. 30.00
40 Superman V:Check,Batman:'4	88 1st team-up Luthor & Joker . 225.00	124 V:Hroguth,E:Tommy
Killers Against Fate!' 450.00	89 I:Club of Heroes 200.00	Tomorrow 30.00
41 I:Supermanium,	90 A:Batwoman 200.00	125 V:Jundy,B:Aquaman 30.00
E:Boy Commandos 350.00	91 V:Rohtul,descendent of Lex	126 A:Lex Luthor 30.00
42 Superman goes to Uranus,	Luthor 150.00	127 V:Zerno 30.00
A:Marco Polo & Kubla Khan 325.00	92 Ist & only A:Skyboy 125.00	128 V:Moose Morans 30.00
43 A:J.Wilbur Wolfingham 325.00	93 V:Victor Danning 150.00	129 Joker/Luthor T.U. 40.00
44 Superman:'The Revolt of the	94 O:Superman/Batman team,	130 .... 25.00
Thought Machine' 325.00	A:Lex Luthor 425.00	131 V:Octopus 25.00
45 Superman:'Lois Lane and Clark	95 'Battle o/t Super Heroes' ... 100.00	132 V:Denny Kale,Shorty Biggs . 25.00
Kent,Private Detectives 325.00	96 'Super-Foes from Planet X' . 100.00	133 .... 25.00
46 Superman V:Mr. 7 .... 325.00	97 V:Condor Gang 100.00	134 V:Band of Super-Villians .. 25.00
47 Superman:'The Girl Who	98 I:Moonman 100.00	135 V:The Future Man 25.00
	99 JK,V:Carl Verril 100.00	136 The Batman Nobody
	100 A:Kandor, Lex Luthor 225.00	Remembered 25.00
	101 A:Atom Master 100.00	137 A:Lex Luthor 25.00
	102 V:Jo-Jo Groff gang,	138 V:General Grote 25.00
		139 V:Sphinx Gang,E:Aquaman . 25.00

World's Finest Comics #63
© DC Comics, Inc.

140 CS,V:Clayface 25.00
141 CS,A:Jimmy Olsen 25.00
142 CS,O:Composite Man 25.00
143 CS,A:Kandor,I:Mailbag 18.00
144 CS,A:Clayface,Brainiac 18.00
145 CS,Prison for Heroes 18.00
146 CS,Batman,Son of Krypton . 18.00
147 CS,A:Jimmy Olsen 18.00
148 CS,A:Lex Luthor,Clayface . . 18.00
149 CS,The Game of the
    Secret Identities 18.00
150 CS,V:Rokk and Sorban 15.00
151 CS,A:Krypto,BU:Congorilla . 12.00
152 CS,A:The Colossal Kids,Bat-
    mite,V:Mr.Mxyzptlk 12.00
153 CS,V:Lex Luthor 12.00
154 CS,The Sons of Batman &
    Superman(Imaginary) 12.00
155 CS,The 1000th Exploit of
    Batman & Superman 12.00
156 CS,I:BizarroBatman,V:Joker 65.00
157 CS,The Abominable Brats
    (Imaginary story) 12.00
158 CS,V:Brainiac 12.00
159 CS,A:Many Major villians,I:Jim
    Gordon as Anti-Batman & Perry
    White as Anti-Superman 12.00
160 V:Dr Zodiac. 12.00
161 CS,80 page giant 18.00
162 V:The Jousting Master 10.00
163 CS,The Court of No Hope . . 10.00
164 CS,I:Genia,V:Brainiac 10.00
165 CS,The Crown of Crime . . . 10.00
166 CS,V:Muto & Joker 14.00
167 CS,The New Superman &
    Batman(Imaginary) V:Luthor . 10.00
168 CS,R:Composite Superman 10.00
169 The Supergirl/Batgirl Plot;
    V:Batmite,Mr.Mxyzptlk 11.00
170 80 page giant,reprint 10.00
171 CS,V:The Executioners 9.00
172 CS,Superman & Batman
    Brothers (Imaginary) 9.00
173 CS,The Jekyll-Hyde Heroes . 9.00
174 CS,Secrets of the Double
    Death Wish 9.00
175 NA(1st Batman),C:Flash . . . 12.00
176 NA,A:Supergirl & Batgirl . . . 10.00
177 V:Joker & Luthor 9.00
178 The Has-Been Superman . . 6.00
179 CS,giant 8.00
180 RA,ME,Supermans Perfect
    Crime 6.00
181 RA,ME 6.00
182 RA,ME,The Mad Manhunter . 6.00
183 RA,ME,Supermans Crimes
    of the Ages 6.00
184 RA,ME,A:JLA,Robin 6.00
185 CS,The Galactic Gamblers . . 6.00
186 RA,ME,The Bat Witch 6.00
187 RA,ME,Demon Superman . . 6.00
188 giant,reprint 8.00
189 RA,ME,V:Lex Luthor 8.00
190 RA,V:Lex Luthor 5.00
191 RA,A:Jor-El,Lara 5.00
192 RA,The Prison of No Escape 5.00
193 The Breaking of Batman
    and Superman 5.00
194 RA,ME,Inside the Mafia 5.00
195 RA,ME,Dig Now-Die Later . . . 5.00
196 CS,The Kryptonite Express,
    E:Batman 5.00
197 giant 6.00
198 DD,B:Superman T.U.,
    A:Flash 60.00

199 DD,Superman & Flash race 60.00
200 NA(c),DD,Prisoners of the
    Immortal World; A:Robin 5.00
201 NA(c),DD,A Prize of Peril,
    A:Green Lantern,Dr. Fate. . . . 3.50
202 NA(c),DD,Vengeance of the
    Tomb Thing,A:Batman 4.00
203 NA(c),DD,Who's Minding the
    Earth,A:Quamar 4.00
204 NA(c),DD,Journey to the
    End of Hope,A:Wonder Woman 4.00
205 NA(c),DD,The Computer that
    Captured a Town,Frazetta Ad,
    A:Teen Titans 6.00
206 DD,giant reprint 8.00
207 DD,Superman,A:Batman,
    V:Dr.Light 4.00
208 NA(c),DD,A:Dr Fate 4.00
209 NA(c),DD,A:Green Arrow,
    Hawkman,I&V:The Temper . . 4.00
210 NA(c),DD,A:Batman 4.00
211 NA(c),DD,A:Batman 4.00
212 CS(c),And So My World
    Begins,A:Martian Manhunter . . 4.00
213 DD,Peril in a Very Small
    Place,A:The Atom 4.00
214 DD,A:Vigilante 4.00
215 DD,Saga of the Super Sons
    (Imaginary story) 4.00
216 DD,R:Super Sons,Little Town
    with a Big Secret 4.00
217 DD,MA,Heroes with
    Dirty Hands 4.00
218 DD,DC,A:Batman,
    BU:Metamorpho 4.00
219 DD,Prisoner of Rogues Rock;
    A:Batman 4.00
220 DD,MA,Let No Man Write My
    Epitaph,BU:Metamorpho 4.00
221 DD,Cry Not For My Forsaken
    Son; R:Super Sons 4.00
222 DD,Evil In Paradise 4.00
223 DD,giant,A:Deadman,Aquaman
    Robotman 7.00
224 DD,giant,A:Super Sons,
    Metamorpho,Johnny Quick . . 7.00
225 giant,A:Rip Hunter,Vigilante,
    Black Canary,Robin 4.00
226 A:Sandman,Metamorpho,
    Deadman,Martian Manhunter . 5.00
227 MGr,BWi,A:The Demonic Duo,
    Vigilante,Rip Hunter,Deadman,
    I:Stargrave 4.00
228 ATh,A:Super Sons,Aquaman,
    Robin,Vigilante 4.00
229 I:Powerman,A:Metamorpho . 3.00
230 A:Super-Sons,Deadman,
    Aquaman 4.00
231 A:Green Arrow,Flash 3.00
232 DD,The Dream Bomb 3.00
233 A:Super-Sons 3.00
234 CS,Family That Fled Earth . 3.00
235 DD,V:Sagitaurus 3.00
236 DD,A:The Atom 3.00
237 Intruder from a Dead World . . 3.00
238 DD,V:Luthor,A:Super-Sons. . 3.00
239 CS,A:Gold(from Metal Men) . 3.00
240 DD,A:Kandor 3.00
241 Make Way For a New World . 3.00
242 EC,A:Super-Sons 3.00
243 CS,AM,A:Robin 3.00
244 NA(c),JL,MA,MN,TA,giant
    B:Green Arrow 5.00
245 NA(C),CS,MA,MN,TA,
    GM,JSh,BWi,giant 5.00

246 NA(c),KS,MA,MN,TA,GM,
    DH,A:JLA 4.00
247 KS,GM,giant 5.00
248 KS,GM,DG,TVE,A:Sgt.Rock . 4.00
249 KS,SD,TVE,A:Phantom
    Stranger,B:Creeper 5.00
250 GT,SD,Superman,Batman,
    Wonder Woman,Green Arrow,
    Black Canary,team-up 3.00
251 GT,SD,JBi,BL,TVE,RE,
    JA,A:Poison Ivy,Speedy,
    I:CountVertigo 3.00
252 GT,TVE,SD,JA,giant 3.00
253 KS,DN,TVE,SD,B:Shazam . . 3.00

World's Finest #172
© DC Comics, Inc.

254 GT,DN,TVE,SD,giant 3.00
255 JL,DA,TVE,SD,DN,KS,
    E:Creeper 3.00
256 MA,DN,KS,DD,Hawkman,Black
    Lightning,giant 3.00
257 DD,FMc,DN,KS,GT,RB,
    RT,giant 3.00
258 NA(c),RB,JL,DG,DN,KS,RT,
    giant 3.00
259 RB,DG,MR,MN,DN,KS 3.00
260 RB,DG,MN,DN 2.50
261 RB,DG,AS,RT,EB,DN,
    A:Penguin, Terra Man 4.00
262 DG,DN,DA,JSon,RT,
    Aquaman 2.50
263 RB,DG,DN,TVE,JSh,Aquaman,
    Adam Strange 2.50
264 RB,DG,TVE,DN,Aquaman . . . 2.50
265 RB,DN,RE,TVE 2.50
266 RB,TVE,DN 2.50
267 RB,DG,TVE,AS,DN,
    A:Challengers of the Unknown 2.50
268 DN,TVE,BBr,RT,AS 2.50
269 RB,FMc,TVE,BBr,AS,DN,DA . 2.50
270 NA(c),RB,RT,TVE,AS,
    DN,LMa 2.50
271 GP(c),RB,FMc,O:Superman/
    Batman T.U. 2.75
272 RB,DN,TVE,BBr,AS 2.50
273 TVE,LMa,JSon,AS,DN,DA,
    A:Plastic Man 2.50
274 TVE,LMa,BBr,GC,AS,DN,
    Green Arrow 2.50
275 RB,FMc,TVE,LMa,DSp,AS,

DN,DA,A:Mr.Freeze 2.50
276 GP(c),RB,TVE,LMa,DSp,CI,
    DN,DA 2.50
277 GP(c),RT,TVE,DSp,AS,DN,
    DH,V:Dr.Double X 2.50
278 GP(c),RB,TVE,LMa,DSp,DN . 2.50
279 KP,TVE,LMa,AS,DN,
    B:Kid Eternity 2.50
280 RB,TVE,LMa,AS,DN 2.50
281 GK(c),IN,TVE,LMa,AS,DN . . . 2.50
282 IN,FMc,GK,CI,last giant
    E:Kid Eternity 2.50
283 GT,FMc,GK 2.25
284 GT,DSp,A:Legion,E:G.Arrow . 2.50
285 FM(c),RB,A:Zatanna 2.25
286 RB,A:Flash 2.50
287 TVE,A:Flash 2.50

World's Finest #291
© DC Comics, Inc.

288 A:JLA 2.25
289 GK(c),Kryll way of Dying 2.25
290 TD(i),I:Stalagron 2.25
291 WS(c),TD(i),V:Stalagron 2.25
292 . . . . 2.25
293 . . . . 2.25
294 . . . . 2.25
295 FMc(i) 2.25
296 RA 2.25
297 GC,V:Pantheon 2.25
298 V:Pantheon 2.25
299 GC,V:Pantheon 2.25
300 RA,GP,KJ,MT,FMc,A:JLA . . . 2.25
301 Rampage 2.25
302 DM,NA(rep) 2.25
303 Plague 2.25
304 SLi,O:Null&Void 2.25
305 TVE,V:Null&Void 2.25
306 SLi,I:Swordfish & Barracuda . 2.25
307 TVE,V:Null&Void 2.25
308 GT,Night and Day 2.25
309 MT,AA,V:Quantum 2.25
310 I:Sonik 2.25
311 A:Monitor 2.25
312 AA,I:Network 2.25
313 AA(i),V:Network 2.25
314 AA(i),V:Executrix 2.25
315 V:Cathode 2.25

316 LSn,I:Cheapjack 2.25
317 LSn,V:Cheapjack 2.25
318 AA(i),A:Sonik 2.25
319 AA(i),I:REM 2.25
320 AA(i),V:REM 2.25
321 AA,V:Chronos 2.25
322 KG,The Search 2.25
323 AA(i),final issue 2.25

WORLD'S FINEST
[Limited Series]
1 SR,KK,Worlds Apart 8.00
2 SR,KK,Worlds Collide 6.00
3 SR,KK,Worlds At War 6.00
TPB rep.#1-#3 . . . . 19.95

WORLD'S GREATEST SUPER-HEROES
1977
1 A:Batman,Robin 2.50

WORLD WITHOUT END
1990
1 The Host, I:Brother Bones 5.00
2 A:Brother Bones 3.50
3 . . . . 3.50
4 House of Fams 2.50
5 Female Fury 2.50
6 conclusion 2.50

WRATH OF THE SPECTRE
May, 1988
1 JAp,rep.Adventure #431-#433 . 2.50
2 JAp,rep.Adventure #434-#436 . 2.50
3 JAp,rep.Adventure #437-#440 . 2.50
4 JAp,reps.,final issue 2.50

XENOBROOD
0 New team 1.50
1 Battles 1.50
2 Bestiary 1.50
3 A:Superman 1.50
4 V:Bestiary 1.50
5 V:Vimian 1.50
6 final issue 1.50

XOMBI
Milestone
0 WS(c),DCw,Shadow War,Foil(c),
    I:Xombi,Twilight 2.50
1 JBy(c),B:Silent Cathedrals 2.00
1a Platinum ed. 15.00
2 I:Rabbi Simmowitz,Golms,Liam
    Knight of the Spoken Fire . . . 1.75
3 A:Liam 2.00
4 Silent Cathedrals 2.00
5 Silent Cathedrals 1.75
6 Silent Cathedrals 1.75
7 School of Anguish 1.75
8 School of Anguish,pt.2 . . . . . . 1.75
9 School of Anguish,pt.3 . . . . . . 1.75
10 School of Anguish,pt.4 . . . . . . 1.75
11 School of Anguish,pt.5 . . . . . . 1.75
12 Truth and Surprises 1.75
13 V:Kinderessen 1.75
14 Long Hot Summer, A:Cheryl
    Saltz 2.50

YOUNG ALL STARS
June, 1987
1 I:IronMunro&FlyingFox,D:TNT . 4.50

2 V:Axis Amerika 2.50
3 V:Axis Amerika 2.00
4 I:The Tigress 1.50
5 I:Dyna-mite,O:Iron Munro 1.50
6 . . . . 1.50
7 Baseball Game,A:Tigress 1.25
8 Millenium 1.25
9 Millenium 1.25
10 Hugo Danner 1.25
11 'Birth of Iron Munro' 1.25
12 'Secret of Hugo Danner' 1.25
13 'V:Deathbolt,Ultra-Humanite . . 1.25
14 Fury+Ultra Humanite 1.25
15 IronMunro At high school 1.25
16 Ozyan Inheritance 1.25
17 Ozyan Inheritance 1.25
18 Ozyan Inheritance 1.25
19 Ozyan 1.50
20 O:Flying Fox 1.50
21 Atom & Evil#1 . . . . 1.50
22 Atom & Evil#2 . . . . 1.50
23 Atom & Evil#3 . . . . 1.50
24 Atom & Evil#4 . . . . 1.50
25 . . . . 1.50
26 End of the All Stars? 1.75
27 'Sons of Dawn' begins 1.75
28 Search for Hugo Danner 1.75
29 A:Hugo Danner 1.75
30 V:Sons of Dawn 1.75
31 V:Sons of Dawn,last issue . . . 1.75
Ann.#1 MG,V:Mekanique 2.25

YOUNG LOVE
September-October, 1963
39 . . . . 8.00
40 thru 50 . . . . @5.00
51 thru 70 . . . . @4.00
71 thru 80 . . . . @3.00
81 thru 126 . . . . @1.50

ZATANNA
1987
1 R:Zatanna 2.25
2 N:Zatanna 2.25
3 Come Together 2.25
4 V:Xaos 2.25

ZERO HOUR: CRISIS IN TIME
4 DJu(a&s),JOy,A:All DC Heroes,
    D;2nd Flash 1.50
3 DJu(a&S),JOy,D:G.A.Sandman,
    G:A.Atom,Dr.Fate,1st Wildcat
    IR:Time Trapper is Rokk Krinn,
    Hawkmen merged 1.50
2 DJu(a&s),Joy 1.50
1 DJu(a&s),JOy,b:Power Gir's
    Child 1.50
0 DJu(A&s),JOy,Gatefold(c),Extant
    vs. Spectre 1.50

ABRAHAM STONE
1 JKu, Early 20th century 6.95

ACTION FORCE
March, 1987
1 U.K. G.I. Joe Series 1.50
2 thru 39 .... @1.00
40 1988 .... 1.00

ACTUAL CONFESSIONS
See: LOVE ADVENTURES

ACTUAL ROMANCES
October, 1949
1 .... 35.00
2 Photo Cover 20.00

ADVENTURE INTO FEAR
See: FEAR

ADVENTURE INTO MYSTERY
Atlas
May, 1956
1 BEv(c),Future Tense 165.00
2 Man on the 13th Floor 100.00
3 Next Stop Eternity 75.00
4 AW, The Hex 100.00
5 BEv,The People Who Weren't 75.00
6 The Wax Man 75.00
7 May, 1957 .... 75.00

ADVENTURES INTO TERROR
See: JOKER COMICS

Adventures into Weird Worlds #27
© Marvel Entertainment Group

ADVENTURES INTO WEIRD WORLDS
January, 1952
1 RH,GT,The Walking Death . 225.00
2 The Thing In the Bottle 150.00
3 The Thing That Waited 100.00
4 BEv,RH,TheVillageGraveyard 100.00
5 BEv,I Crawl Thru Graves ... 100.00

6 The Ghost Still Walks 100.00
7 Monsters In Disguise 100.00
8 Nightmares 100.00
9 Do Not Feed 100.00
10 BEv,Down In The Cellar ... 100.00
11 Phantom 75.00
12 Lost In the Graveyard 75.00
13 Where Dead Men Walk 75.00
14 A Shriek In the Night 75.00
15 Terror In Our Town 75.00
16 The Kiss of Death 75.00
17 RH,He Walks With A Ghost . 75.00
18 Ivan & Petroff 75.00
19 It Happened One Night 75.00
20 The Doubting Thomas 75.00
21 What Happened In the Cave . 85.00
22 RH,The Vampire's Partner .. 60.00
23 The Kiss of Death 60.00
24 Halfway Home 60.00
25 BEv,JSt,The Mad Mamba ... 60.00
26 Good-Bye Earth 60.00
27 The Dwarf of Horror Moor .. 150.00
28 DW,Monsters From the Grave 75.00
29 Bone Dry 45.00
30 JSt,The Impatient Ghost;
    June, 1954 .... 45.00

ADVENTURES OF CAPTAIN AMERICA
September, 1991
1 KM,JRu,O:Capt. America 5.75
2 KM,KWe,TA,O:Capt.America .. 5.50
3 KM,KWe,JRu,D:Lt.Col.Fletcher 5.50
4 KWe,JRu,V:Red Skull 5.50

ADVENTURES OF CYCLOPS & PHOENIX
1 SLo(s),GeH,AV,O:Cable 4.00
2 SLo(s),GeH,AV,O:Cable 3.25
3 SLo(s),GeH,AV,O:Cable 3.25
4 SLo(s),GeH,AV,O:Cable 3.25

ADVENTURES OF HOMER GHOST
Atlas
June, 1957
1 .... 25.00
2 August, 1957 .... 20.00

ADVENTURES OF PINKY LEE
Atlas
July, 1955
1 .... 125.00
2 .... 65.00
3 .... 54.00
4 .... 54.00
5 .... 54.00

ADVENTURES ON THE PLANET OF THE APES
October, 1975
1 GT,Planet of the Apes Movie
    Adaptation 2.50
2 GT,Humans Captured 2.50
3 GT,Man Hunt 2.50
4 GT,Trial By Fear 2.50
5 GT, Fury in the
    Forbidden Zone 2.50
6 GT,The Forbidden Zone,Cont'd 2.50
7 AA,Man Hunt Cont'd 2.50
8 AA,Brent & Nova Enslaved ... 2.50

9 AA,Mankind's Demise 2.50
10 AA,When Falls the Lawgiver .. 2.50
11 AA,The Final Chapter;
    December, 1976 .... 2.50

ADVENTURES OF THE THING
1 rep. Marvel 2 in 1 #50 ...... 2.50
2 rep. Marvel 2 in 1 #80
    B.U. Ghost Rider 1.50
3 rep. Marvel 2 in 1 #51 ...... 1.50
4 rep. Marvel 2 in 1 #77 ...... 1.50

AIRTIGHT GARAGE
Epic
1 thru 4 rep.Moebius GNv ... @2.50

AKIRA
Epic
September, 1988
1 The Highway,I:Kaneda,Tetsuo,
    Koy,Ryu,Colonel,Takaski ... 15.00
1a 2nd printing 4.50
2 Pursuit,I:Number27,(Masaru) . 10.00
2a 2nd printing 4.50
3 Number 41,V:Clown Gang ... 10.00
4 King of Clowns,V:Colonel ... 10.00
5 Cycle Wars,V:Clown Gang .. 10.00
6 D:Yamagota 6.50
7 Prisoners and Players,I:Miyo . 6.50
8 Weapon of Vengeance 6.00
9 Stalkers 6.50
10 The Awakening 6.50
11 Akira Rising 6.50
12 Enter Sakaki 6.50
13 Desperation 6.50
14 Caught in the Middle 6.50
15 Psychic Duel 6.50
16 Akira Unleashed 6.50
17 Emperor of Chaos 6.50
18 Amid the Ruins 5.00
19 To Save the Children 5.00
20 Revelations 5.00
21 .... 5.00
22 .... 5.00
23 .... 5.00
24 Clown Gang 5.00
25 Search For Kay 5.00
26 Juvenile A Project 5.00
27 Kay and Kaneda 5.00
28 Tetsuo 5.00
29 Tetsuo 5.00
30 Tetsuo,Kay,Kaneda 5.00
31 D:Kaori,Kaneda,Vs.Tetsuo ... 5.00
32 Tetsuo'sForces vs.U.S.Forces . 5.00
33 Tetsuo V:Kaneda 5.00
34 .... 5.00
TPB Akira:Reprints#1-#3 ...... 13.95
TPB Akira:Reprints#4-#6 ...... 13.95
TPB Akira:Reprints#7-#9 ...... 13.95
TPB Akira:Reprints#10-#12 .... 14.95
TPB Akira:Reprints#13-#15 .... 14.95
TPB Akira:Reprints#16-#18 .... 14.95
TPB Akira:Reprints#19-#21 .... 16.95
TPB Akira:Reprints#22-#24 .... 16.95
TPB Akira:Reprints#25-#27 .... 16.95
TPB Akira:Reprints#28-#30 .... 17.95

ALADDIN
1 .... 1.50
2 .... 1.50
3 .... 1.50
4 .... 1.50

5 A:Queen Tatiana 1.50
6 A:Zena 1.50
7 Genie Convention 1.50
8 Body Switch 1.50
9 Archery Contest 1.50
10 Genie winds back his powers . 1.50
TPB rep. #1–#4 . . . . 9.95

ALF
Star
March, 1988

1 Photo Cover 2.00
1a 2nd printing 1.00
2 Alf Causes trouble 1.50
3 More adventures 1.50
4 Willie on Melmac 1.50
5 I:Alf's evil twin 1.50
6 Photo Cover 1.50
7 Pygm-Alien 1.50
8 Ochmoneks' Garage 1.25
9 Alf's Independence Day 1.25
10 Alf goes to College 1.25
11 Halloween special 1.00
12 Alf loses memory 1.00
13 Racetrack of my Tears 1.00
14 Night of the Living Bread 1.25
15 Alf on the Road 1.00
16 More Adventures 1.00
17 Future vision 1.00
18 More Adventures 1.00
19 The Alf-strologer 1.00
20 Alf the Baby Sitter,pt.1 . . . . . 1.00
21 Alf the Baby Sitter,pt.2 . . . . . 1.00
22 X-Men parody 1.00
23 Alf visits Australia 1.00
24 Rhonda visits Earth 1.00
25 More Adventures 1.00
26 Alf gets a job 1.00
27 Alf lost 1.00
28 Alf's Amnesia 1.00
29 Alf/Brian reporters 1.00
30 Shakespeare Baby 1.00
31 Alf's Summer Camp 1.00
32 Arnold Schwarzemeimac . . . 1.00
33 Dungeons & Dragons Spoof . 1.00
34 Alf-Red & Alf-Blue(2 Alfs) 1.00
35 Gone with the Wind 1.00
36 More Adventures 1.00
37 Melmacian Gothic 1.00
38 Boundtree Hunters 1.00
39 Pizarro Alf 1.00
40 A:Zoreo 1.00
41 TV 1.00
42 V:Alf 1.00
43 House Break-in 1.00
44 A:Fantastic Fur 1.00
45 Melmenopaus 1.00
46 Goes to Center of Earth 1.00
47 Meteor Bye-Products,pt.1 . . . 1.00
48 Meteor Bye-Products,pt.2 . . . . 1.00
49 1st Rhonda solo story 1.00
50 Final Issue, giant size 1.75
Ann.#1 Evol.War 3.00
Ann.#2 . . . . 1.75
Spring Spec.#1 . . . . 1.75
Holiday Spec.#2 . . . . 2.00

ALIEN LEGION
Epic
April, 1984

1 FC,TA,I:Sarigar,Montroc 2.25
2 FC,TA,CP,V:Harkilons 2.25
3 FC,TA,CW,V:Kroyzo 2.25
4 FC,TA,CW,F:Skob 2.25

5 FC,CW,D:Skob 2.25
6 FC,CW,WPo,V:Harkilons 2.25

Alien Legion #7
© Marvel Entertainment Group

7 CW,WPo,I:Lora 2.25
8 CW,WPo,V:Harkilons 2.25
9 CW,V:Harkilons 2.25
10 CW,LSn,V:Harkilons 2.25
11 CW,LSn,V:Harkilons 2.25
12 LSn,A:Aob-Sin 2.25
13 LSn,F:Montroc 2.25
14 LSn,V:Cordar 2.25
15 LSn,V:Alphor,Betro,&Gamoid . 2.25
16 LSn,J:Tomaro 2.25
17 LSn,Durge on Drugs 2.25
18 LSn,V:Dun 2.25
19 LSn,A:GalarcyScientist 2.25
20 LSn,L:Skilene 2.25

[2nd Series]

1 LSn,I:Guy Montroc 2.00
2 LSn,V:Quallians 2.00
3 LSn,Hellscope 2.00
4 LSn,V:Harkillons 2.00
5 LSn,F:JuggerGrimrod 2.00
6 LSn,F:JuggerGrimrod 2.00
7 LSn,A:Guy Montroc 2.00
8 LSn,I:Nakhira 2.00
9 LSn,V:Harkilons 2.00
10 LSn,V:Harkilons 2.00
11 LSn,V:Harkilons 2.00
12 LSn,Tamara Pregnant 2.00
13 LSn,V:MomojianKndrel 2.00
14 LSn,J:Saravil 2.00
15 LSn,J:Spellik 2.00
16 LSn,D:Jugger's Father 2.00
17 LSn,O:JuggerGrimrod 2.00
18 LSn,O:JuggerGrimrod 2.00

ALIEN LEGION: ONE
PLANET AT A TIME

1 HNg,CDi,One Planet at a Time 4.95
2 HNg,CDi 4.95
3 HNg,CDi 4.95

ALIEN LEGION:
ON THE EDGE
Epic

1 LSn,V:B'Be No N'ngth 4.95

2 LSn,V:B'Be No N'ngth 4.95
3 LSn,V:B'Be No N'ngth 4.95
4 LSn,V:B'Be No N'ngth 4.95

ALIEN LEGION
TENANTS OF HELL
Epic

1 LSn,Nomad Squad On
　Combine IV 4.50
2 LSn,L:Torie Montroc,I:Stagg . . 4.50
TPB Alien Legion:Slaughterworld . 9.95

ALL-SELECT COMICS
Fall, 1943
Timely (Daring Comics)

1 B:Capt.America,Sub-Mariner,
　Human Torch;WWII 3,200.00
2 A:Red Skull,V:Axis Powers . . 1,400.00
3 B:Whizzer,V:Axis 1,000.00
4 V: Axis 1,700.00
5 E:Sub-Mariner,V:Axis 700.00
6 A:The Destroyer,V:Axis 600.00
7 E:Whizzer,V:Axis 600.00
8 V:Axis Powers 600.00
9 V:Axis Powers 600.00
10 E:Capt.America,Human Torch;
　A:The Destroyer 600.00
11 I:Blonde Phantom,A:Miss
　America 1,000.00

Becomes:

BLONDE PHANTOM

12 B:Miss America;The Devil's
　Playground 650.00
13 B:Sub-Mariner;Horror In
　Hollywood 400.00
14 E:Miss America;Horror At
　Haunetd Castle 325.00
15 The Man Who Deserved
　To Die 325.00
16 A:Capt.America,Bucky;
　Modeled For Murder 500.00
17 Torture & Rescue 300.00
18 Jealously,Hate & Cruelty . . . 300.00
19 Killer In the Hospital 300.00
20 Blonde Phantom's Big Fall . 300.00
21 Murder At the Carnival 300.00
22 V: Crime Bosses 300.00

Lovers #23
© Marvel Entertainment Group

Becomes:

LOVERS

23 Love Stories	50.00
24 My Dearly Beloved	25.00
25 The Man I Love	30.00
26 thru 29	@15.00
30	30.00
31 thru 36	@15.00
37	34.00
38	34.00
39	14.00
40	14.00
41	14.00
42 thru 65	@14.00
66	12.00
67 ATh	35.00
68 thru 85	@12.00
86 August, 1957	12.00

ALL SURPRISE
Timely
Fall, 1943

1 (fa),F:Super Rabbit,Gandy, Sourpuss	110.00
2	50.00
3	35.00
4 thru 10	@35.00
11 HK	50.00
12 Winter, 1946	35.00

ALL-TRUE CRIME
See: OFFICIAL TRUE CRIME CASES

ALL WINNERS COMICS
Summer, 1941

1 S&K,BEv,B:Capt.America & Bucky, Human Torch & Toro,Sub-Mariner A:The Angel,Black Marvel	8,500.00
2 S&K,B:Destroyer,Whizzer	2,300.00
3 BEv,Bucky & Toro Captured	1,500.00
4 BEv,Battle For Victory For America	1,700.00
5 V:Nazi Invasion Fleet	1,000.00
6 V:Axis Powers,A: Black Avenger	1,000.00

All Winners #10
© Marvel Entertainment Group

7 V:Axis Powers	750.00
8 V:Axis Powers	750.00
9 V:Nazi Submarine Fleet	750.00
10 V:Nazi Submarine Fleet	750.00
11 V: Nazis	550.00
12 A:Red Skull,E:Destroyer; Jap P.O.W. Camp	600.00
13 V:Japanese Fleet	550.00
14 V:Japanese Fleet	550.00
15 Japanese Supply Train	550.00
16 In Alaska V:Gangsters	550.00
17 V:Gansters;Atomic Research Department	550.00
18 V:Robbers;Internal Revenue Department	600.00
19 I:All Winners Squad, Fall, 1946	1,500.00
21 A:All-Winners Squad;Riddle of the Demented Dwarf	1,400.00

Becomes:

ALL TEEN COMICS

20 F:Georgie,Willie, Mitzi,Patsy Walker	40.00

Becomes:

TEEN COMICS

21 A:George,Willie,Mitzi, Patsy Walker	48.00
22 A:George,Willie,Margie, Patsy Walker	30.00
23 A:Patsy Walker,Cindy,George	30.00
24	45.00
25	30.00
26	40.00
27	30.00
28	45.00
29	45.00
30	45.00
31 thru 34	@30.00
35 May, 1950	30.00

Becomes:

JOURNEY INTO UNKNOWN WORLDS
Atlas

36(1) RH,End of the Earth	1,000.00
37(2) BEv,GC,When Worlds Collide	500.00
38(3) GT,Land of Missing Men	450.00
4 MS,RH,Train to Nowhere	275.00
5 MS,Trapped in Space	275.00
6 GC,RH,World Below the Atlantic	275.00
7 BW,RH,House That Wasn't	425.00
8 RH,The Stone Thing	275.00
9 MS,JSt,The People Who Couldn't Exist	300.00
10 THe Undertaker	275.00
11 BEv,Frankie Was Afraid	200.00
12 The Last Voice You Hear	200.00
13 The Witch Woman	135.00
14 BW,BEv,CondemnedBuilding	350.00
15 They Crawl By Night	350.00
16 Scared to Death	175.00
17 BEv,GC,RH,The Ice Monster Cometh	175.00
18 The Broth Needs Somebody	200.00
19 GC,The Long Wait	200.00
20 GC,RH,The Race That Vanished	175.00
21 thru 25	@125.00
26 thru 35	@100.00
36 thru 44	@75.00
45 AW,SD	85.00
46	60.00

47	60.00
48 GW	60.00
49	60.00
50 JDa,RC	75.00
51 WW,SD,JSe	75.00
52	50.00
53 RC,BP	70.00
54 AT,BP	65.00
55 AW,RC,BEv	70.00
56 BEv	65.00
57 JO	55.00
58 MO	55.00
59 AW,August, 1957	70.00

ALL WINNERS COMICS
[2nd Series]
August, 1948

1 F:Blonde Phantom,A:Capt.America Sub-Mariner,Human Torch	8,500.00

Becomes:

ALL WESTERN WINNERS

2 B,I&O:Black Rider,B:Two-Gun Kid, Kid-Colt	325.00
3 Black Rider V: Satan	200.00
4 Black Rider Unmasked	200.00

Becomes:

WESTERN WINNERS

5 I Challenge the Army	200.00
6 The Mountain Mystery	175.00
7 Ph(c) Randolph Scott	175.00

Becomes:

BLACK RIDER

8 Ph(c),B:Black Rider;Valley of Giants	250.00
9 Wrath of the Redskin	125.00
10 O:Black Rider	150.00
11 Redmen on the Warpath	75.00
12 GT,The Town That Vanished	75.00
13 The Terrified Tribe	75.00
14 The Tyrant of Texas	75.00
15 Revolt of the Redskins	60.00
16	60.00
17	60.00
18	60.00
19 SSh,GT,A:Two-Gun Kid	60.00
20 GT	75.00
21 SSh,GT,A:Two-Gun Kid	65.00
22 SSh,A:Two-Gun Kid	65.00
23 SSh,A:Two-Gun Kid	65.00
24 SSh,JSt	65.00
25 SSh,JSt,A:Arrowhead	65.00
26 SSh,A:Kid-Colt	65.00
27 SSh,A:Kid-Colt	70.00

Becomes:

WESTERN TALES OF BLACK RIDER

28 JSe,D:Spider	80.00
29	60.00
30	60.00
31	60.00

Becomes:

GUNSMOKE WESTERN

32 F:Kid Colt,Billy Buckskin	60.00
33	57.00
34	28.00
35	57.00
36	57.00
37	30.00
38	23.00
39	23.00
40	40.00

All comics prices listed are for *Near Mint* condition.

41 .... 20.00
42 .... 20.00
43 .... 20.00
44 .... 23.00
45 .... 23.00
46 thru 55 .... @20.00
56 .... 23.00
57 thru 76 .... @18.00
77 July, 1963 .... 16.00

ALPHA FLIGHT
August, 1983

1 JBy,I:Puck,Marrina,Tundra 6.00
2 JBy,I:Master,Vindicator Becomes
   Guardian,B:O:Marrina 3.00
3 JBy,O:Master,A:Namor,Invisible
   Girl, ... 2.50
4 JBy,A:Namor,Invisible Girl,
   E:O:Marrina,A:Master 2.50
5 JBy,B:O:Shaman,F:Puck 2.50
6 JBy,E:O:Shaman,I:Kolomag ... 2.50
7 JBy,B:O:Snowbird,I:Delphine
   Courtney & Deadly Ernest 2.50
8 JBy,E:O:Snowbird,O:Deadly
   Ernest,I:Nemesis 2.50
9 JBy,O:Aurora,A:Wolverine,
   Super Skrull 3.50
10 JBy,O:Northstar,V:SuperSkrull . 3.00
11 JBy,I:Omega Flight,Wild Child
   O:Sasquatch 2.50
12 JBy,D:Guardian,V:Omega
   Flight 3.00
13 JBy,C:Wolverine,Nightmare .. 10.00
14 JBy,V:Genocide 2.00
15 JBy,R:Master 2.00
16 JBy,BWi,V:Master,C:Wolverine
   I:Madison Jeffries 3.00
17 JBy,BWi,A:Wolverine,X-Men .. 7.00
18 JBy,BWi,J:Heather,I:Ranaq .. 2.00
19 JBy,I:Talisman,V:Ranaq 2.00
20 JBy,I:Gilded Lily,N:Aurora 2.00
21 JBy,BWi,O:Gilded Lily,Diablo . 2.00
22 JBy,BWi,I:Pink Pearl 2.00
23 JBy,BWi,D:Sasquatch,
   I:Tanaraq 2.00
24 JBy,BWi,V:Great Beasts,J:Box 2.50
25 JBy,BWi,V:Omega Flight
   I:Dark Guardian 2.00
26 JBy,BWi,A:Omega Flight,Dark
   Guardian 2.00
27 JBy,V:Omega Flight 2.00
28 JBy,Secret Wars II,V:Omega
   Flight,D:Dark Guardian 2.00
29 MMi,V:Hulk,A:Box 2.00
30 MMi,I&O:Scramble,R:Deadly
   Ernest 2.00
31 MMi,D:Deadly Ernest,
   O:Nemesis 2.00
32 MMi(c),JBg,O:Puck,I:2nd
   Vindicator 2.00
33 MMi(c),SB,X-Men,I:Deathstrike 6.00
34 MMi(c),SB,Wolverine,V:
   Deathstrike 7.00
35 DR,R:Shaman 2.00
36 MMi(c),DR,A:Dr.Strange 2.00
37 DR,O:Pestilence,N:Aurora 2.00
38 DR,A:Namor,V:Pestilence 2.00
39 MMi(c),DR,WPo,A:Avengers .. 2.50
40 DR,WPo,W:Namor & Marrina . 2.50
41 DR,WPo,I:Purple Girl,
   J:Madison Jeffries 2.50
42 DR,WPo,I:Auctioneer,J:Purple Girl,
   A: Beta Flight 2.50
43 DR,WPo,V:Mesmero,Sentinels 2.50
44 DR,WPo,D:Snowbird,

Alpha Flight #128
© *Marvel Entertainment Group*

A:Pestilence 2.50
45 JBr,WPo,R:Sasquatch,
   L:Shaman 2.50
46 JBr,WPo,I:2nd Box 2.50
47 MMi,WPo,TA,Vindicator solo . 2.50
48 SL(i),I:Omega 2.50
49 JBr,WPo,I:Manikin,D:Omega .. 2.50
50 WS(c),JBr,WPo,L:Northstar,Puck,
   Aurora,A:Loki,Double size 2.75
51 JLe(1st Marv),WPo(i),V:Cody 10.00
52 JBr,WPo(i),I:Bedlam,
   A:Wolverine 5.00
53 JLe,WPo(i),I:Derangers,Goblin
   D&V:Bedlam,A:Wolverine .. 6.00
54 WPo(i),O&J:Goblyn 2.00
55 JLe,TD,V:Tundra 4.00
56 JLe,TD,V:Bedlamites 4.00
57 JLe,TD,V:Crystals,
   C:Dreamqueen 4.00
58 JLe,AM,V:Dreamqueen 4.00
59 JLe,AM,I:Jade Dragon,R:Puck . 4.00
60 JLe,AM,V:J.Dragon,D.Queen . 4.00
61 JLe,AM,on Trial
   (1st JLe X-Men) 4.00
62 JLe,AM,V:Purple Man 4.00
63 MG,V:U.S.Air Force 2.00
64 JLe,AM,V:Great Beasts 4.00
65 JLe(c),AM(i),Dream Issue 2.00
66 JLe(c),I:China Force 2.00
67 JLe(c),O:Dream Queen 2.00
68 JLe(c),V:Dream Queen 2.00
69 JLe(c),V:Dream Queen 2.00
70 MM(i),V:Dream Queen 2.00
71 MM(i),I:Sorcerer 2.00
72 V:Sorcerer 2.00
73 MM(i),V:Sorcerer 2.00
74 MM(i),Alternate Earth 2.00
75 JLe(c),MMi(i),Double Size ... 3.00
76 MM(i),V:Sorcerer. 2.00
77 MM(i),V:Kingpin 2.00
78 MM(i),A:Dr.Strange,Master ... 2.00
79 MM(i),AofV:Scorpion,Nekra . 2.00
80 MM(i),AofV,V:Scorpion,Nekra . 2.00
81 JBy(c),MM(i),B:R:Northstar ... 2.00
82 JBy(c),MM(i),E:R:Northstar ... 2.00
83 JSh 2.00
84 MM(i),Northstar 2.00
85 MM(i) 2.00

86 MBa,MM,V:Sorcerer 2.00
87 JLe(c),MM(i),A:Wolverine 7.00
88 JLe(c),MM(i),A:Wolverine 6.00
89 JLe(c),MM(i),R:Guardian,A:
   Wolverine 5.00
90 JLe(c),MM(i),A:Wolverine 5.00
91 MM(i),A:Dr.Doom 2.00
92 Guardian vs.Vindicator 2.00
93 MM(i),A:Fant.Four,I:Headlok .. 2.00
94 MM(i),V:Fant.Four,Headlok .. 2.00
95 MM(i),Lifelines 2.00
96 MM(i),A:Master 2.00
97 B:Final Option,A:Her 2.00
98 A:Avengers 2.00
99 A:Avengers 2.00
100 JBr,TMo,DR,LMa,E:Final Option
   A:Galactus,Avengers,D:
   Guardian,G-Size 2.50
101 TMo,Final Option Epilogue,
   A:Dr.Strange,Avengers 2.00
102 TMo,I:Weapon Omega, ... 2.00
103 TMo,V:Diablo,U.S.Agent 2.00
104 TMo,N:Alpha Flight,Weapon
   Omega is Wild Child 2.00
105 TMo,V:Pink Pearl 2.00
106 MPa,Aids issue,Northstar
   acknowledges homosexuality . 6.00
106a 2nd printing 3.00
107 A:X-Factor,V:Autopsy 2.50
108 A:Soviet Super Soldiers 2.00
109 V:Peoples Protectorate 2.00
110 PB,Infinity War,I:2nd Omega
   Flight,A:Wolverine 2.00
111 PB,Infinity War,V:Omega
   Flight,A:Wolverine 2.00
112 PB,Infinity War,V:Master 2.00
113 V:Mauler 2.00
114 A:Weapon X 2.00
115 PB,I:Wyre,A:Weapon X 2.00
116 PB,I:Rok,V:Wyre 2.00
117 PB,V:Wyre 2.00
118 PB,V:Thunderball 2.00
119 PB,V:Wrecking Crew 2.00
120 PB,10th Anniv.,V:Hardliners,
   w/poster 2.50
121 PCu,V:Brass Bishop,A:Spider-
   Man,Wolverine,C:X-Men 2.00
122 PB,BKi,Inf.Crusade 2.00
123 PB,BKi,Infinity Crusade 2.00
124 PB,BKi,Infinity Crusade 2.00
125 PB,V:Carcass 2.00
126 V:Carcass 2.00
127 SFu(s),Infinity Crusade 2.00
128 B:No Future 2.00
129 C:Omega Flight 2.00
130 E:No Future,last issue,
   Double Sized 2.50
Ann.#1 LSn,V:Diablo,Gilded Lily . 2.25
Ann.#2 JBr,BMc 1.75
Spec.#1 PB,A:Wolverine,
   O:First Team,V:Egghead 3.75
Spec.#1 Newsstand ver.of #97 .. 1.50
Spec.#2 Newsstand ver.of #98 .. 1.50
Spec.#3 Newsstand ver.of #99 .. 1.50
Spec.#4 Newsstand ver.of #100 . 2.00

AMAZING ADVENTURES
June, 1961

1 JK,SD,O&B:Dr.Droom;Torr . 850.00
2 JK,SD,This is Manoo 350.00
3 JK,SD,Trapped in the
   Twilight World 350.00
4 JK,SD, I Am X 350.00
5 JK,SD, Monsteroso 350.00
6 JK,SD,E:Dr.Droom; Sserpo . 350.00

Amazing Adventures #3
© Marvel Entertainment Group

Becomes:

AMAZING ADULT FANTASY
December, 1961

7 SD,Last Man on Earth 450.00
8 SD,The Coming of the Krills 400.00
9 SD,The Terror of Tim Boo Ba 325.00
10 SD,Those Who Change . . . 325.00
11 SD,In Human Form 325.00
12 SD,Living Statues 325.00
13 SD,At the Stroke of Midnight 325.00
14 SD,Beware of the Giants . . 350.00

Becomes:

AMAZING FANTASY
August, 1962

15 JK(c),SD,I:Spider-Man,
I:Aunt May, Flash Thompson,
Burglar, I&D:Uncle Ben . . 20,000.00

AMAZING ADVENTURES
August, 1970
[1st Regular Series]

1 JK,JB,B:Inhumans,Bl.Widow . 17.00
2 JK,JB,A:Fantastic Four 11.00
3 JK,GC,BEv,V:Mandarin 10.00
4 JK,GC,BEv,V:Mandarin 10.00
5 NA,TP,DH,BEv,V:Astrologer . 12.00
6 NA,DH,SB,V:Maximus 10.00
7 NA,DH,BEv 10.00
8 NA,DH,BEv,E:Black Widow,
A:Thor,(see Avengers #95) . . 10.00
9 MSy,BEv,V:Magneto 12.00
10 GK(c),MSy,V:Magneto,
E:Inhumans 12.00
11 GK(c),TS,B:O:New Beast,
A:X-Men 17.00
12 GK(c),TS,MP,A:Iron Man . . . 13.00
13 JR(c),TS,V:New Br'hood
Evil Mutants,I:Buzz Baxter
(Mad Dog) 10.00
14 GK(c),TS,JM,V:Quasimodo . . 10.00
15 JSn(c),TS,A:X-Men,V:Griffin . 10.00
16 JSn(c),FMc(i),V:Juggernaut . . 10.00
17 JSn,A:X-Men,E:Beast 10.00
18 HC,NA,B:Killraven 10.00
19 HC,Sirens on 7th Avenues . . . 5.00

20 Coming of the Warlords 5.00
21 Cry Killraven 5.00
22 Killraven 5.00
23 Killraven 5.00
24 New Year Nightmare-2019AD . 5.00
25 RB,V:Skar 5.00
26 GC,V:Ptson-Rage Vigilante . . . 5.00
27 CR,JSn,V:Death Breeders . . . 5.00
28 JSn,CR,V:Death Breeders . . . 5.00
29 CR,Killraven 5.00
30 CR,Killraven 5.00
31 CR,Killraven 5.00
32 CR,Killraven 5.00
33 CR,Killraven. 5.00
34 CR,D:Hawk 5.00
35 KG,Killraven Continued. 5.00
36 CR,Killraven Continued. 5.00

Amazing Adventures #8
© Marvel Entertainment Group

37 CR,O:Old Skull 5.00
38 CR,Killraven Continued. 5.00
39 CR,E:Killraven 5.00

[2nd Regular Series]

1 rep.X-Men#1,38,Professor X . 6.00
2 rep.X-Men#1,39,O:Cyclops . . 5.00
3 rep.X-Men#2,40,O:Cyclops . . 5.00
4 rep.X-Men#2,41,O:Cyclops . . 5.00
5 rep.X-Men#3,42,O:Cyclops . . 5.00
6 JBy(c),rep.X-Men#3,43,Cyclops 5.00
7 rep.X-Men#4,44,O:Iceman . . . 5.00
8 rep.X-Men#4,45,O:Iceman . . . 5.00
9 JBy(c),X-Men#5,46,O:Iceman . 5.00
10 rep.X-Men#5,47,O:Iceman . . 5.00
11 rep.X-Men#6,48,Beast 5.00
12 rep.X-Men#6,Str.Tales#168 . . 5.00
13 rep.X-Men #7 . . . . 5.00
14 rep.X-Men #8 . . . . 5.00

AMAZING COMICS
Timely Comics
Fall, 1944

1 F:Young Allies,Destroyer,
Whizzer, Sergeant Dix . . . 1,000.00

Becomes:

COMPLETE COMICS

2 F:Young Allies,Destroyer,Whizzer

Sergeant Dix; Winter'44-5 . . 550.00

AMAZING DETECTIVE CASES
Atlas
November, 1950

3 Detective/Horror Stories . . . 125.00
4 Death of a Big Shot 60.00
5 . . . . 60.00
6 Danger in the City 60.00
7 . . . . 45.00
8 . . . . 45.00
9 GC, The Man Who Wasn't . . 45.00
10 GT 45.00
11 The Black Shadow 75.00
12 MS,BK, Harrigan's Wake . . . 75.00
13 BEv,JSt, ... 100.00
14 Hands Off; September, 1952 . 75.00

AMAZING HIGH ADVENTURE
August, 1984

1 BSz,JSo,JS 3.00
2 PS,AW,BSz,TA,MMi,BBl,CP,CW 2.50
3 MMi,VM,JS 2.50
4 JBo,JS,SBi 2.50
5 JBo; October, 1986 . . . . 2.50

AMAZING SPIDER-MAN
March, 1963

1 JK(c),SED,I:Chameleon,J.Jonah &
John Jameson,A:F.Four . 15,000.00
2 SD,I:Vulture,Tinkerer
C:Mysterio(disguised) 2,800.00
3 SD,I&O:Dr.Octopus 1,600.00
4 SD,I&O:Sandman,I:Betty
Brant,Liz Allen 1,100.00
5 SD,V:Dr.Doom,C:Fant.Four . 875.00
6 SD,I&O:Lizard,The Connors . 950.00
7 SD,V:Vulture 650.00
8 SD,JK,I:Big Brain,V:Human
Torch,A:Fantastic Four 625.00
9 SD,I&O:Electro 665.00
10 SD,I:Enforcers,Big Man . . . 550.00
11 SD,V:Dr.Octopus,
D:Bennett Brant 420.00
12 SD,V:Dr.Octopus 400.00

Amazing Spider-Man #4
© Marvel Entertainment Group

---

13 SD,I:Mysterio 450.00
14 SD,I:Green Goblin,
   V:Enforcers, Hulk 1,300.00
15 SD,I:Kraven,A:Chameleon . 400.00
16 SD,A:Daredevil,
   V:Ringmaster 300.00
17 SD,2nd A:Green Goblin,
   A:Human Torch 400.00
18 SD,V:Sandman,Enforcers,
   C:Avengers,F.F.,Daredevil . 275.00
19 SD,V:Sandman,I:Ned Leeds
   A:Human Torch 250.00
20 SD,I&O:Scorpion 280.00
21 SD,A:Beetle,Human Torch . 200.00
22 SD,V:The Clown,Masters of
   Menace 175.00
23 SD,V:GreenGoblin(3rd App.) 250.00
24 SD,V:Mysterio 160.00
25 SD,I:Spider Slayer,Spencer
   Smythe,C:Mary Jane 180.00
26 SD,I:CrimeMaster,V:Green
   Goblin 200.00
27 SD,V:CrimeMaster,
   Green Goblin 180.00
28 SD,I:Molten Man,Peter Parker
   Graduates High School,rare
   in near-mint condition 275.00
29 SD,V:Scorpion 135.00

Amazing Spider-Man #48
© Marvel Entertainment Group

30 SD,I:Cat Burglar 135.00
31 SD,I:Gwen Stacy,Harry Osborn
   Prof.Warren,V:Dr.Octopus . 175.00
32 SD,V:Dr.Octopus 110.00
33 SD,V:Dr.Octopus 110.00
34 SD,V:Kraven 110.00
35 SD,V:Molten Man 110.00
36 SD,I:The Looter 110.00
37 SD,V:Professor Stromm,
   I:Norman Osborn 135.00
38 SD,V:Joe Smith(Boxer) 110.00
39 JR,IR:Green Goblin is Norman
   Osborn 175.00
40 JR,O:Green Goblin 240.00
41 JR,I:Rhino,C:Mary Jane . . . 120.00
42 JR,V:John Jameson,I:Mary
   Jane (Face Revealed) 120.00
43 JR,O:Rhino 78.00
44 JR,V:Lizard(2nd App.) 78.00
45 JR,V:Lizard 78.00

46 JR,I&O:Shocker 82.00
47 JR,V:Kraven 78.00
48 JR,I:Fake Vulture,A:Vulture . . 78.00
49 JR,V:Fake Vulture,Kraven . . 78.00
50 JR,I:Kingpin,Spidey Quits,
   C:Johnny Carson 350.00
51 JR,V:Kingpin 120.00
52 JR,V:Kingpin,I:Robbie
   Robertson,D:Fred Foswell . . 65.00
53 JR,V:Dr.Octopus 60.00
54 JR,V:Dr.Octopus 55.00
55 JR,V:Dr.Octopus 55.00
56 JR,V:Dr.Octopus,I:Capt.Stacy 55.00
57 JR,DH,A:Kazar 55.00
58 JR,DH,V:Spencer Smythe,
   Spider Slayer 55.00
59 JR,DH,V:Kingpin 60.00
60 JR,DH,V:Kingpin 55.00
61 JR,DH,V:Kingpin 60.00
62 JR,DH,V:Medusa 48.00
63 JR,DH,V:1st & 2nd
   Vulture 48.00
64 JR,DH,V:Vulture 48.00
65 JR,JM,V:Prisoners 48.00
66 JR,DH,V:Mysterio 48.00
67 JR,JM,V:Mysterio,I:Randy
   Robertson 48.00
68 JR,JM,V:Kingpin 50.00
69 JR,JM,V:Kingpin 50.00
70 JR,JM,V:Kingpin 50.00
71 JR,JM,V:Quicksilver,C:Scarlet
   Witch,Toad,A:Vision 45.00
72 JR,JB,JM,V:Shocker 40.00
73 JR,JB,JM,I:Man Mountain Marko,
   Silvermane 40.00
74 JR,JM,V:Silvermane 38.00
75 JR,JM,V:Silvermane,A:Lizard 36.00
76 JR,JM,V:Lizard,A:H.Torch . . 36.00
77 JR,JM,V:Lizard,A:H.Torch . . . 36.00
78 JR,JM,I&O:Prowler 40.00
79 JR,JM,V:Prowler 35.00
80 JR,JB,JM,V:Chameleon 35.00
81 JR,JB,JM,I:Kangaroo 35.00
82 JR,JM,V:Electro 35.00
83 JR,I:Richard Fisk(as Schemer),
   Vanessa(Kingpin's wife)
   V:Kingpin 40.00
84 JR,JB,JM,V:Schemer,Kingpin 35.00
85 JR,JB,JM,V:Schemer,Kingpin 35.00
86 JR,JM,V:Black Widow, C:Iron
   Man, Hawkeye 32.00
87 JR,JM,Reveals ID to his
   friends,changes mind 32.00
88 JR,JM,V:Dr.Octopus 32.00
89 GK,JR,V:Dr.Octopus 32.00
90 GK,JR,V:Dr.Octopus
   D:Capt.Stacy 42.00
91 GK,JR,I:Bullit 32.00
92 GK,JR,V:Bullit,A:Iceman . . . 32.00
93 JR,V:Prowler 32.00
94 JR,SB,V:Beetle,O:Spider-Man 50.00
95 JR,SB,London,V:Terrorists . . 32.00
96 GK,JR,A:Green Goblin,Drug
   Mention,No Comic Code . . . 75.00
97 GK,V:Green Goblin,Drugs . . . 75.00
98 GK,V:Green Goblin,Drugs . . . 75.00
99 GK,Prison Riot,A:Carson . . . 32.00
100 JR(c),GK,Spidey gets four
   arms from serum 150.00
101 JR(c),GK,I:Morbius,the
   Living Vampire,A:Lizard . . 175.00
101a Reprint,Metallic ink 2.50
102 JR(c),GK,O:Morbius,
   V:Lizard 135.00
103 GK,V:Kraven,A:Kazar 27.00

104 GK,V:Kraven,A:Kazar 27.00
105 GK,V:Spenser Smythe,
   Spider Slayer 27.00
106 JR,V:Spenser Smythe,
   Spider Slayer 25.00
107 JR,V:Spenser Smythe,
   Spider Slayer 25.00
108 JR,R:Flash Thompson,
   I:Sha-Shan,V:Vietnamese . . . 25.00
109 JR,A:Dr.Strange,
   V:Vietnamese 25.00
110 JR,I:The Gibbon 25.00
111 JR,V:The Gibbon,Kraven . . 25.00
112 JR,Spidey gets an Ulcer . . . 25.00
113 JSn,JR,I:Hammerhead
   V:Dr.Octopus 27.00
114 JSn,JR,V:Hammerhead,Dr.
   Octopus,I:Jonas Harrow 27.00
115 JR,V:Hammerhead,
   Dr.Octopus 25.00
116 JR,JM,V:The Smasher 25.00
117 JR,JM,V:Smasher,Disruptor . 25.00

Amazing Spider-Man #56
© Marvel Entertainment Group

118 JR,JM,V:Smasher,Disruptor 25.00
119 JR,A:Hulk 36.00
120 GK,JR,V:Hulk 36.00
121 GK,JR,V:Green Goblin
   D:Gwen Stacy,Drugs 115.00
122 GK,JR,D:Green Goblin . . . 135.00
123 GK,JR,A:Powerman 21.00
124 GK,JR,I:Man-Wolf 23.00
125 RA,JR,O:Man-Wolf 22.00
126 JM(c),RA,JM,V:Kangaroo,
   A: Human Torch 21.00
127 JR(c),RA,V:3rd Vulture,
   A:Human Torch 21.00
128 JR(c),RA,V:3rd Vulture 21.00
129 K&R(c),RA,I:Punisher,
   Jackal 275.00
129a reprint,Marv.Milestone 2.95
130 JR(c),RA,V:Hammerhead,
   Dr.Octopus,I:Spider-Mobile . 18.00
131 GK(c),RA,V:Hammerhead,
   Dr.Octopus 18.00
132 GK(c),JR,V:Molten Man . . . 17.00
133 JR(c),RA,V:Molten Man . . . 17.00

134 JR(c),RA,I:Tarantula,C:
   Punisher(2nd App.) 27.00
135 JR(c),RA,V:Tarantula,
   A:Punisher 67.00
136 JR(c),RA,I:2nd GreenGoblin 50.00
137 GK(c),RA,V:Green Goblin . . 38.00
138 K&R(c),RA,V:Green Goblin . . 25.00
139 K&R(c),RA,I:Grizzly,V:Jackal 25.00
140 GK(c),RA,I:Gloria Grant,
   V:Grizzly,Jackal 25.00
141 JR(c),RA,V:Mysterio 25.00
142 JR(c),RA,V:Mysterio 25.00
143 K&R(c),RA,I:Cyclone 25.00
144 K&R(c),RA,V:Cyclone 25.00
145 K&R(c),RA,V:Scorpion 25.00
146 RA,JR,V:Scorpion 25.00
147 JR(c),RA,V:Tarantula 25.00
148 GK(c),RA,V:Tarantula,IR:Jackal
   is Prof.Warren 40.00
149 K&R(c),RA,D:Jackal 130.00
150 GK(c),RA,V:SpenserSmythe 65.00
151 RA,JR,V:Shocker 55.00
152 K&R(c),RA,V:Shocker 16.00
153 K&R(c),RA,V:Paine 16.00
154 JR(c),SB,V:Sandman 16.00
155 JR(c),SB,V:Computer 15.00
156 JR(c),RA,I:Mirage,W:Ned
   Leeds & Betty Brant 15.00
157 JR(c),RA,V:Dr.Octopus 15.00
158 JR(c),RA,V:Dr.Octopus 15.00
159 JR(c),RA,V:Dr.Octopus 15.00
160 K&R(c),RA,V:Tinkerer 15.00
161 K&R(c),RA,A:Nightcrawler,
   C:Punisher 18.00
162 JR(c),RA,Nightcrawler,
   Punisher,I:Jigsaw 20.00
163 JR(c),RA,Kingpin 11.00
164 JR(c),RA,Kingpin 11.00
165 JR(c),RA,Lizard 11.00
166 JR(c),RA,Lizard 11.00
167 JR(c),RA,V:Spiderslayer,
   I:Will-o-the Wisp 11.00
168 JR(c),KP,V:Will-o-the Wisp . 14.00
169 RA,V:Dr.Faustas 11.00
170 RA,V:Dr.Faustas 11.00
171 RA,A:Nova 12.00
172 RA,V:Molten Man 11.00
173 JR(c),RA,JM,V:Molten Man . 11.00
174 RA,TD,JM,A:Punisher 18.00
175 RA,JM,A:Punisher,D:Hitman 16.00
176 RA,TD,V:Green Goblin 16.00
177 RA,V:Green Goblin 16.00
178 RA,JM,V:Green Goblin 16.00
179 RA,V:Green Goblin 16.00
180 RA,IR&V:Green Goblin is Bart
   Hamilton) 16.00
181 GK(c),SB,O:Spider-Man.. . 10.00
182 RA,A:Rocket Racer 9.00
183 RA,BMc,V:Rocket Racer . . . 9.00
184 RA,V:White Tiger 9.00
185 RA,V:White Tiger 9.00
186 KP,A:Chameleon,Spidey
   cleared by police of charges . . 9.00
187 JSn,BMc,A:Captain
   America,V:Electro 10.00
188 KP,A:Jigsaw 9.00
189 JBy,JM,A:Man-Wolf 10.00
190 JBy,JM,A:Man-Wolf 10.00
191 KP,V:Spiderslayer 8.00
192 KP,JM,V:The Fly 8.00
193 KP,JM,V:The Fly 8.00
194 KP,I:Black Cat 16.00
195 KP,AM,JM,O:Black Cat 9.00
196 AM,JM,D:Aunt May,A:Kingpin 8.00
197 KP,JM,V:Kingpin 8.00

Amazing Spider-Man #229
© *Marvel Entertainment Group*

198 SB,JM,V:Mysterio 8.00
199 SB,JM,V:Mysterio 8.00
200 JR(c),KP,JM,D:Burglar,Aunt May
   alive,O:Spider-Man 27.00
201 KP,JM,A:Punisher 18.00
202 KP,JM,A:Punisher 18.00
203 FM(c),KP,A:Dazzler 9.00
204 JR2(c),KP,V:Black Cat 8.00
205 KP,JM,V:Black Cat 8.00
206 JBy,GD,V:Jonas Harrow . . . 10.00
207 JM,V:Mesmero 8.00
208 JR2,AM,BBr,V:Fusion(1stJR2
   SpM art),I:Lance Bannon . . . 11.00
209 KJ,BMc,JRu,BWi,AM,
   I:Calypso, V:Kraven 9.00
210 JR2,JSt,I:Madame Web 7.50
211 JR2,JM,A:Sub-mariner 7.50
212 JR2,JM,I:Hydro-Man 7.50
213 JR2,JM,V:Wizard 7.50
214 JR2,JM,V:Frightful Four,
   A: Namor,Llyra 7.50
215 JR2,JM,V:Frightful Four,
   A: Namor,Llyra 7.50
216 JR2,JM,A:Madame Web 7.50
217 JM,V:Sandman,
   Hydro-Man 7.50
218 FM(c),JR2,JM,AM,V:Sandman
   Hydro-Man 7.50
219 FM(c),LMc,JM,V:Grey
   Gargoyle,A:Matt Murdock . . . 7.50
220 BMc,A:Moon Knight 7.50
221 JM(i),A:Ramrod 7.00
222 WS(c),BH,JM,I:SpeedDemon 7.00
223 JR2,AM,A:Red Ghost 7.00
224 JR2,V:Vulture 7.00
225 JR2,BWi,V:Foolkiller 7.00
226 JR2,JM,A:Black Cat 7.00
227 JR2,JM,A:Black Cat 7.00
228 RL,Murder Mystery 7.00
229 JR2,JM,V:Juggernaut 8.50
230 JR2,JM,V:Juggernaut 8.50
231 JR2,AM,V:Cobra 7.00
232 JR2,JM,V:Mr.Hyde 7.00
233 JR2,JM,V:Tarantula 7.00
234 JR2,DGr,V:Tarantula 7.00

235 JR2,V:Tarantula,C:Deathlok
   O:Will-o-the Wisp 7.00
236 JR2,D:Tarantula 7.00
237 BH,A:Stilt Man 7.00
238 JR2,JR,I:Hobgoblin (inc.
   Tattoo transfer) 70.00
238a w/out Tattoo 25.00
239 JR2,V:Hobgoblin 40.00
240 JR2,BL,Vulture 6.00
241 JR2,O:Vulture 6.00
242 JR2,Mad Thinker 6.00
243 JR2,Peter Quits School 6.00
244 JR2,KJ,V:Hobgoblin 12.00
245 JR2,V:Hobgoblin 17.00
246 JR2,DGr,Daydreams issue . . 6.00
247 JR2,JR,V:Thunderball 6.00
248 JR2,BBr,RF,TA,V:Thunderball,
   Kid who Collects Spider-Man . 6.00
249 JR2,DGr,V:Hobgoblin,
   A:Kingpin 14.00
250 JR2,KJ,V:Hobgoblin 14.00
251 RF,KJ,V:Hobgoblin,Spidey
   Leaves in Secret Wars 15.00
252 RF,BBr,returns from Secret
   Wars,N:Spider-Man 23.00
253 RL,I:Rose 10.00
254 RL,JRu,V:Jack O'Lantern . . . 7.00
255 RF,JRu,Red Ghost 6.50
256 RF,JRu,I:Puma,A:Black Cat . 8.00
257 RF,JRu,V:Puma,
   A:Hobgoblin 10.00
258 RF,JRu,A:Black Cat,Fant.Four,
   Hobgoblin,V:Black Costume . 15.00
259 RF,JRu,A:Hobgoblin,O:
   Mary Jane 16.00
260 RF,JRu,BBr,V:Hobgoblin . . 12.00
261 CV(c),RF,JRu,V:Hobgoblin . 12.00
262 Ph(c),BL,Spidey Unmasked . 8.00
263 RF,BBr,I:Spider-Kid 5.00
264 Paty,V:Red Nine 5.00
265 RF,JRu,V:Black Fox,
   I:Silver Sable 15.00
265a 2nd printing 1.50
266 RF,JRu,I:Misfits,Toad 5.00
267 BMc,PDd(s),A:Human Torch . 5.00
268 JBy(c),RF,JRu,Secret WarsII . 5.00
269 RF,JRu,V:Firelord 5.00
270 RF,BMc,V:Firelord,
   A:Avengers,I:Kate Cushing . . 5.00
271 RF,JRu,A:Crusher Hogan,
   V:Manslaughter 5.00
272 SB,KB,I&O:Slyde 5.00
273 RF,JRu,Secret Wars II,
   A:Puma 5.00
274 TMo,JR,Secret Wars II,
   Beyonder V:Mephisto,A:1st
   Ghost Rider 10.00
275 RF,JRu,V:Hobgoblin,O:Spidey
   (From Amaz.Fantasy#15) . . . 13.00
276 RF,BBr,V:Hobgoblin 10.00
277 RF,BL,CV,A:Daredevil,
   Kingpin 8.00
278 A:Hobgoblin,V:Scourge,
   D:Wraith 6.00
279 RL,A:Jack O'Lantern,
   2nd A:Silver Sable 7.00
280 RF,BBr,V:Sinister Syndicate,
   A:Silver Sable,Hobgoblin,
   Jack O'Lantern 6.00
281 RF,BBr,V:Sinister Syndicate,
   A:Silver Sable,Hobgoblin,
   Jack O'Lantern 11.00
282 RL,BL,A:X-Factor 5.50
283 RF,BL,V:Titania,Absorbing
   Man,C:Mongoose 6.50

All comics prices listed are for *Near Mint* condition.

284 RF,BBr,JRu,B:Gang War,
  A: Punisher,Hobgoblin 13.00
285 MZ(c),A:Punisher,Hobgoblin 18.00
286 ANi(i),V:Hobgoblin,A:Rose . 10.00
287 EL,ANi,A:Daredevil,Hobgoblin 8.00
288 E:Gang War,A:Punisher,
  Falcon,Hobgoblin,Daredevil,
  Black Cat, Kingpin 9.00
289 TMo,IR:Hobgoblin is Ned Leeds,
  I:2nd Hobgoblin (Jack O'
  Lantern) 20.00
290 JR2,Peter Proposes 8.00
291 JR2,V:Spiderslayer 8.00
292 AS,V:Spiderslayer,Mary
  Jane Accepts proposal 8.00
293 MZ,BMc,V:Kraven 12.00
294 MZ,BMc,D:Kraven 12.00
295 BSz(c),KB(i),Mad Dog,pt.#2 . 8.00
296 JBy(c),AS,V:Dr.Octopus 7.00
297 AS,V:Dr.Octopus 7.00
298 TM,BMc,V:Chance,C:Venom
  (not in costume) 40.00
299 TM,BMc,V:Chance,I:Venom 30.00
300 TM,O:Venom 70.00
301 TM,A:Silver Sable 18.00
302 TM,V:Nero,A:Silver Sable .. 18.00
303 TM,A:Silver Sable,Sandman 18.00
304 TM,JRu,V:Black Fox,Prowler
  I:Jonathan Caesar 16.00
305 TM,JRu,V:BlackFox,Prowler 16.00
306 TM,V:Humbug,Chameleon . 13.00
307 TM,O:Chameleon 13.00
308 TM,V:Taskmaster,J.Caesar . 13.00
309 TM,I:Styx & Stone 13.00
310 TM,V:Killershrike 13.00
311 TM,Inferno,V:Mysterio 13.00
312 TM,Inferno,Hobgoblin V:
  Green Goblin 16.00
313 TM,Inferno,V:Lizard 14.00
314 TM,X-mas issue,V:J.Caesar 14.00
315 TM,V:Venom,Hydro-Man ... 20.00
316 TM,V:Venom 20.00
317 TM,V:Venom,A:Thing 20.00
318 TM,V:Scorpion 10.00
319 TM,V:Scorpion,Rhino 10.00
320 TM,B:Assassin Nation Plot
  A:Paladin,Silver Sable 10.00
321 TM,A:Paladin,Silver Sable ... 8.00
322 TM,A:Silver Sable,Paladin ... 8.00
323 TM,A:Silver Sable,Paladin,
  Captain America 8.00
324 TM(c),EL,AG,V:Sabretooth,A:
  Capt.America,Silver Sable ... 17.00
325 TM,E:Assassin Nation Plot,
  V:Red Skull,Captain America,
  Silver Sable 8.00
326 V:Graviton,A of V 5.00
327 EL,AG,V:Magneto,A of V. . . . 6.00
328 TM,V:Hulk,A of V. 12.00
329 EL,V:Tri-Sentinel 6.00
330 EL,A:Punisher,Black Cat 6.00
331 EL,A:Punisher,C:Venom 8.00
332 EL,V:Venom,Styx & Stone . 12.00
333 EL,V:Venom,Styx & Stone . 12.00
334 EL,B:Sinister Six,A:Iron Man . 6.00
335 EL,TA,A:Captain America ... 6.00
336 EL,D:Nathan Lubensky,
  A:Dr.Strange,Chance 5.00
337 WS(c),EL,TA,A:Nova 5.00
338 EL,A:Jonathan Caesar 5.00
339 EL,JR,E:Sinister Six,A:Thor
  D:Jonathan Caesar 5.00
340 EL,V:Femme Fatales 4.00
341 EL,V:Tarantula,Powers Lost . 4.00
342 EL,A:Blackcat,V:Scorpion ... 4.00

343 EL,Powers Restored,
  C:Cardiac,V:Chameleon 4.00
344 EL,V:Rhino,I:Cardiac,Cletus
  Kassady(Carnage),A:Venom . 10.00
345 MBa,V:Boomerang,C:Venom,
  A:Cletus Kassady(infected w/
  Venom-Spawn) 15.00
346 EL,V:Venom 10.00
347 EL,V:Venom 10.00
348 EL,A:Avengers 4.00
349 EL,A:Black Fox 4.00

Amazing Spider-Man #298
© Marvel Entertainment Group

350 EL,V:Doctor Doom,Black Fox 5.00
351 MBa,A:Nova,V:Tri-Sentinel .. 5.00
352 MBa,A:Nova,V:Tri-Sentinel . 4.00
353 MBa,B:Round Robin:The Side
  Kick's Revenge,A:Punisher,
  Nova,Moon Knight,Darkhawk . 4.00
354 MBa,A:Nova,Punisher,
  Darkhawk,Moon Knight 4.00
355 MBa,A:Nova,Punisher,
  Darkhawk,Moon Knight 4.00
356 MBa,A:Moon Knight,
  Punisher,Nova 4.00
357 MBa,A:Moon Knight,
  Punisher,Darkhawk,Nova 4.00
358 MBa,E:Round Robin:The Side
  Kick's Revenge,A:Darkhawk,
  Moon Knight,Punisher,Nova,
  Gatefold(c) 4.00
359 CMa,A:Cardiac,C:Cletus
  Kasady (Carnage) 6.00
360 CMa,V:Cardiac,C:Carnage .. 7.00
361 MBa,I:Carnage 16.00
361a 2nd printing 3.00
362 MBa,V:Carnage,Venom 11.00
362a 2nd printing 3.00
363 MBa,V:Carnage,Venom 9.00
364 MBa,V:Shocker 3.00
365 MBa,JR,V:Lizard,30th Anniv.,
  Hologram(c),w/poster,Prev.of
  Spider-Man 2099 by RL 6.00
366 JBi,A:Red Skull,Taskmaster . 3.00
367 JBi,A:Red Skull,Taskmaster . 3.00
368 MBa,B:Invasion of the Spider
  Slayers #1,BU:Jonah Jameson 2.50
369 MBa,V:Electro,BU:Green
  Goblin 2.50

370 MBa,V:Scorpion,BU:A.May .. 2.00
371 MBa,V:Spider-Slayer,
  BU:Black Cat 2.50
372 MBa,V:Spider-Slayer 2.50
373 MBa,V:Sp.-Slayer,BU:Venom 3.00
374 MBa,V:Venom 3.00
375 MBa,V:Venom,30th Anniv.,Holo
  graphx(c) 5.00
376 V:Styx&Stone,A:Cardiac ... 2.00
377 V:Cardiac,O:Styx&Stone ... 2.00
378 MBa,Total Carnage#3,V:Shriek,
  Carnage,A:Venom,Cloak 2.00
379 MBa,Total Carnage#7,
  V:Carnage,A:Venom 2.00
380 MBa,Maximum Carnage#11 . 2.00
381 MBa,V:Dr.Samson,A:Hulk .. 1.75
382 MBa,V:Hulk,A:Dr.Samson ... 1.75
383 MBa,V:Jury 1.75
384 MBa,AM,V:Jury 1.75
385 B:DvM(s),MBa,RyE,V:Jury .. 1.50
386 MBa,RyE,B:Lifetheft,V:Vulture 4.00
387 MBa,RyE,V:Vulture 4.00
388 Blue Foil(c),MBa,RyE,RLm,TP,
  E:Lifetheft,D:Peter's Synthetic
  Parents,BU:Venom,Cardiac,
  Chance, ... 4.00
388a Newsstand Ed. 2.50
389 MBa,RyE,E:Pursuit,
  V:Chameleon, ... 1.75
390 MBa,RyE,B:Shrieking,
  A:Shriek,w/cel 3.25
390a Newsstand Ed. 1.75
391 MBa,RyE,V:Shriek,Carrion .. 1.75
392 MBa,RyE,V:Shriek,Carrion .. 1.75
393 MBa,RyE,E:Shrieking,
  V:Shriek,Carrion 1.75
394 MBa,RyE,Power & Responsibility,
  pt.2,V:Judas Traveller, ... 1.75
394a w/flip book,2 covers 3.25
395 MBa,RyE,R:Puma 1.50
396 MBa,RyE,A:Daredevil,
  V:Vulture, Owl 1.50
397 MBa,Web of Death,pt.1,V:Stunner,
  Doc Ock 1.50
398 MBa,Web of Death,pt.3 ..... 1.50
399 MBa,Smoke and Mirrors,pt.2 . 1.50
400 MBa,Death of a Parker 2.95
400a die-cut cover 3.95
401 MBa,The Mark of Kaine,pt.2 . 1.50
402 MBa,R:Judas Travellor 1.50
403 MBa,JMD,LMa The Trial of
  Peter Parker, pt.2 .... 1.50
Ann.#1 SD,I:Sinister Six 450.00
Ann.#2 SD,A:Dr.Strange 235.00
Ann.#3 JR,DH,A:Avengers 80.00
Ann.#4 A:H.Torch,V:Mysterio,
  Wizard 80.00
Ann.#5 JR(c),A:Red Skull,I:Peter
  Parker's Parents 90.00
Ann.#6 JR(c),Rep.Ann.#1,Fant.
  Four #1,SpM #8 .... 25.00
Ann.#7 JR(c),Rep.#1,#2,#38 .. 21.00
Ann.#8 Rep.#46,#50 .... 21.00
Ann.#9 JR(c),Rep.Spec.SpM #2 . 23.00
Ann.#10 JR(c),GK,V:Human Fly . 13.00
Ann.#11 GK(c),DP,JM,JR2,AM, . 13.00
Ann.#12 JBy(c),KP,Rep.#119,
  #120 .... 13.00
Ann.#13 JBy,TA,V:Dr.Octopus . 14.00
Ann.#14 FM,TP,A:Dr.Strange,
  V:Dr.Doom,Dormammu 15.00
Ann.#15 FM,KJ,BL,Punisher ... 22.00
Ann.#16 JR2,JR,I:New Captain
  Marvel,A:Thing 9.00
Ann.#17 EH,JM,V:Kingpin 7.00

Ann.#18 RF,BL,JG,V:Scorpion . . . 7.00
Ann.#19 JR(c),MW,V:Spiderslayer 7.00
Ann.#20 BWi(i),V:Iron Man 2020 . 7.00
Ann.#21 JR(c),PR,W:SpM,direct 16.00
Ann.#21a W:SpM,news stand . . 15.00
Ann.#22 JR(c),MBa(1stSpM),SD,
  JG,RLm,TD,Evolutionary War,
  I:Speedball,New Men 9.00
Ann.#23 JBy(c),RLd,MBa,RF,
  AtlantisAttacks#4,A:She-Hulk . 9.00
Ann.#24 GK,SD,MZ,DGr,
  A:Ant Man 5.00
Ann.#25 EL(c),SB,PCu,SD,
  Vibranium Vendetta#1,Venom . 6.00
Ann.#26 Hero Killers#1,A:New
  Warriors,BU:Venom,Solo 6.00
Ann.#27 TL,I:Annex,w/card 3.50
Ann.#28 SBt(s),V:Carnage,BU:Cloak &
  Dagger,Rhino 3.25
G-Size Superheroes #1 GK,
  A:Morbius,Man-Wolf 55.00
G-Size #1 JR(c),RA,DH,
  A:Dracula 25.00
G-Size #2 K&R(c),RA,AM,
  A:Master of Kung Fu 18.00
G-Size #3 GK(c),RA,DocSavage 18.00
G-Size #4 GK(c),RA,Punisher . 55.00
G-Size #5 GK(c),RA,V:Magnum . 15.00
G-Size #6 Rep.Ann.#4 . . . . . . 10.00
G-Size Spec.#1 O:Symbiotes 3.95
GNv Fear Itself RA,A:S.Sable . . 12.95
GNv Spirits of the Earth CV,Scotland,
  V:Hellfire Club 25.00
Milestone rep.#149 . . . . 2.95
TPB Assassination Plot,
  rep.#320-325 . . . . 14.95
TPB Carnage,rep.#361-363 . . . . . 6.95
TPB Cosmic Adventures rep.
  Amaz.SpM #327-329,Web #59
  61,Spec.SpM #158-160 . . . . 19.95
TPB Kraven's Last Hunt, Reps. AS
  #293,294,Web.#31,32,P.Parker
  #131,132,SC 15.95
  HC 19.95
TPB Origin of the Hobgoblin rep.#238,
  239,244,245,249-251 . . . . . 14.95
TPB Saga of the Alien Costume,reps.
  #252-259 . . . . 9.95
TPB Spider-Man Vs. Venom,reps.
  A.SpM#298-300,315-317 . . . 10.00
TPB Venom Returns rep.Amaz.SpM.
  #331-333,344-347 . . . . 12.95
TPB The Wedding,Reps.A.S.
  #290-292,Ann#21 . . . . 12.95
Nothing Can Stop the Juggernaut,
  reps.#229,230 . . . . 3.95
Sensational Spider-Man,reps.
  Ann.#14,15; 4.95
Skating on Thin Ice(Canadian) . 15.00
Skating on Thin Ice(US) 1.50
Soul of the Hunter MZ,BMc,
  R:Kraven 7.00
Unicef:Trial of Venom,
  A:Daredevil,V:Venom 50.00
See Also:
PETER PARKER;
SPECTACULAR SPIDER-MAN;
WEB OF SPIDER-MAN

AMAZING SPIDER-MAN INDEX
SEE: OFFICIAL MARVEL INDEX TO THE AMAZING SPIDER-MAN

AMAZING SPIDER-MAN COLLECTION
1 Mark Bagley card set 2.95
2 from card set 2.95
3 MBa, card set art 2.95

AMERICAN TAIL II
December, 1991
1 movie adaption 1.00
2 movie adaption 1.00

ANIMAX
Star Comics
December, 1986
1 Based on Toy Line 1.00
2 . . . . 1.00
3 . . . . 1.00
4 June, 1987 . . . . 1.00

ANNEX
December, 1994
1 WMc,I:Brace 2.00
2 WMc,V:Brace 1.75
3 . . . . 1.75
4 final issue 1.95

ANNIE
(Treasury Edition)
October, 1982
1 Movie Adaptation 1.25
2 November, 1982 . . . . 1.25

ANNIE OAKLEY
Atlas
Spring, 1948
1 A:Hedy Devine 250.00
2 CCB,I:Lana,A:Hedy Devine . 150.00
3 . . . . 125.00
4 . . . . 125.00
5 . . . . 75.00
6 . . . . 60.00
7 . . . . 60.00
8 . . . . 60.00
9 AW, ... 60.00
10 . . . . 45.00
11 June, 1956 . . . . 45.00

A-1
1 The Edge 5.95
2 Cheeky,Wee Budgie Boy 5.95
3 King Leon 5.95
4 King Leon 5.95

APOCALYPSE STRIKEFILES
1 After Xavier special 2.50

ARIZONA KID
Atlas
March, 1951
1 RH,Coming of the Arizons Kid 100.00
2 RH,Code of the Gunman . . . 45.00
3 RH(c) 42.00
4 . . . . 42.00
5 . . . . 40.00
6 January, 1952 . . . . 40.00

ARRGH!
December, 1974
Satire
1 Vampire Rats 3.75
2 . . . . 2.00

3 Beauty And the Big Foot 2.00
4 The Night Gawker 2.00
5 September, 1975 . . . . 2.00

ARROWHEAD
April, 1954
1 Indian Warrior Stories 65.00
2 . . . . 45.00
3 . . . . 45.00
4 November, 1954 . . . . 45.00

ASTONISHING
See: MARVEL BOY

Astonishing Tales #26
© Marvel Entertainment Group

ASTONISHING TALES
August, 1970
1 BEv(c),JK,WW,KaZar,Dr.Doom 20.00
2 JK,WW,Ka-Zar,Dr.Doom . . . 12.00
3 BWS,WW,Ka-Zar,Dr.Doom . 18.00
4 BWS,WW,Ka-Zar,Dr.Doom . 18.00
5 BWS,GT,Ka-Zar,Dr.Doom . . 18.00
6 BWS,BEv,GT,I:Bobbi Morse . 18.00
7 HT,GC,Ka-Zar,Dr.Doom . . . 11.00
8 HT,TS,GT,GC,TP,Ka-Zar . . . 11.00
9 GK(c),JB,Ka-Zar,Dr.Doom . . 7.00
10 GK(c),BWS,SB,Ka-Zar . . . 10.00
11 GK,O:Kazar 7.00
12 JB,DA,NA,V:Man Thing 8.00
13 JB,RB,DA,V:Man Thing 3.00
14 GK(c),rep. Kazar 3.00
15 GK,TS,Kazar 3.00
16 RB,AM,A:Kazar 3.00
17 DA,V:Gemini 3.00
18 JR(c),DA,A:Kazar 3.00
19 JR(c),DA,JSn,JA,I:Victorious . . 3.00
20 JR(c),A:Kazar 3.00
21 RTs(s),DAy,B:It 3.00
22 RTs(s),DAy,V:Granitor 3.00
23 RTs(s),DAy,A:Fin Fang Foom . 3.00
24 RTs(s),DAy,E:It 3.00
25 RB(a&s),B:I&O:Deathlok,
  GP(1st art) 50.00
26 RB(a&s),I:Warwolf 15.00
27 RB(a&s),I:Warwolf 12.00
28 RB(a&s),V:Warwolf 12.00
29 rep.Marv.Super Heroes #18 . 18.00
30 RB(a&s),KP, ... 12.00

31 RB(a&s),BW,KP,V:Ryker ... 12.00
32 RB(a&s),KP,V:Ryker 10.00
33 RB(a&s),KJ,I:Hellinger 10.00
34 RB(a&s),KJ,V:Ryker 10.00
35 RB(a&s),KJ,I:Doomsday-Mech 10.00
36 RB(a&s),KP,E:Deathlok,
    I:Godwulf 12.00

A-TEAM
March, 1984

1 .... 1.00
2 .... 1.00
3 May, 1984 .... 1.00

ATOMIC AGE
Epic
November, 1990

1 AW 4.50
2 AW 4.50
3 AW,February, 1991 .... 4.50

Avengers #1
© Marvel Entertainment Group

AVENGERS
September, 1963

1 JK,O:Avengers,V:Loki 2,000.00
1a rep.Marvel Milestone 2.95
2 JK,V:Space Phantom 570.00
3 JK,V:Hulk,Sub-Mariner 400.00
4 JK,R&J:Captain America .. 1,100.00
5 JK,L:Hulk,V:Lava Men 230.00
6 JK,I:Masters of Evil 180.00
7 JK,V:Baron Zemo,
    Enchantress 180.00
8 JK,I:Kang 190.00
9 JK(c),DH,I&D:Wonder Man . 215.00
10 JK(c),DH,I:Immortus 175.00
11 JK(c),DH,A:Spider-Man,
    V:Kang 155.00
12 JK(c),DH,V:Moleman,
    Red Ghost 95.00
13 JK(c),DH,I:Count Nefaria .. 100.00
14 JK,DH,V:Count Nefaria 95.00
15 JK,DH,D:Baron Zemo 80.00
16 JK,J:Hawkeye,Scarlet Witch,
    Quicksilver 80.00

Avengers #20
© Marvel Entertainment Group

16a Marvel Milestone 2.95
17 JK(c),DH,V:Mole Man,A:Hulk 75.00
18 JK(c),DH,V:The Commisar .. 75.00
19 JK(c),DH,I&O:Swordsman,
    O:Hawkeye 80.00
20 JK(c),DH,WW,V:Swordsman,
    Mandarin 50.00
21 JK(c),DH,WW,V:Power Man
    (not L.Cage),Enchantress ... 50.00
22 JK(c),DH,WW,V:Power Man . 50.00
23 JK(c),DH,JR,V:Kang 40.00
24 JK(c),DH,JR,V:Kang 40.00
25 JK(c),DH,V:Dr.Doom 40.00
26 DH,V:Attuma 40.00
27 DH,V:Attuma,Beetle 40.00
28 JK(c),DH,I:1st Goliath,
    I:Collector 42.00
29 DH,V:Power Man,Swordsman 40.00
30 JK(c),DH,V:Swordsman 40.00
31 DH,V:Keeper of the Flame . 40.00
32 DH,I:Bill Foster 30.00
33 DH,V:Sons of the Serpent
    A:Bill Foster 30.00
34 DH,V:Living Laser 30.00
35 DH,V:Mandarin 30.00
36 DH,V:The Ultroids 30.00
37 GK(c),DH,V:Ultroids 30.00
38 GK(c),DH,V:Enchantress,
    Ares,J:Hercules 30.00
39 DH,V:Mad Thinker 30.00
40 DH,V:Sub-Mariner 30.00
41 JB,V:Dragon Man,Diablo .. 20.00
42 JB,V:Dragon Man,Diablo .. 20.00
43 JB,V:Red Guardian 20.00
44 JB,V:Red Guardian,
    O:Black.Widow 20.00
45 JB,V:Super Adoptoid 20.00
46 JB,V:Whirlwind 20.00
47 JB,GT,V:Magneto 25.00
48 GT,I&O:New Black Knight ... 25.00
49 JB,V:Magneto 25.00
50 JB,V:Typhon 20.00
51 JB,GT,R:Iron Man,Thor
    V:Collector 20.00
52 JB,J:Black Panther,
    I:Grim Reaper 22.00
53 JB,GT,A:X-Men; x-over
    X-Men #45 .... 30.00

54 JB,GT,V:Masters of Evil
    I:Crimson Cowl(Ultron) 19.00
55 JB,I:Ultron,V:Masters of Evil . 16.00
56 JB,D:Bucky retold,
    V:Baron Zemo 16.00
57 JB,I:Vision,V:Ultron 65.00
58 JB,O&J:Vision 33.00
59 JB,I:Yellowjacket 20.00
60 JB,W:Yellowjacket & Wasp .. 18.00
61 JB,A:Dr.Strange,x-over
    Dr. Strange #178 .... 17.00
62 JB,I:Man-Ape,A:Dr.Strange .. 17.00
63 GC,I&O:2nd Goliath(Hawkeye)
    V:Egghead 16.00
64 GC,V:Egghead,O:Hawkeye .. 16.00
65 GC,V:Swordsman,Egghead .. 16.00
66 BWS,I:Ultron 6,Adamantium . 17.00
67 BWS,V:Ultron 6 .... 17.00
68 SB,V:Ultron 13.00
69 SB,I:Nighthawk,Grandmaster,
    Squadron Supreme, V:Kang . 15.00
70 SB,O:Squadron Supreme
    V:Kang 13.00
71 SB,I:Invaders,V:Kang 20.00
72 SB,A:Captain Marvel,
    I:Zodiac 13.00
73 HT(i),V:Sons of Serpent 13.00
74 JB,TP,V:Sons of Serpent,
    IR:Black Panther on TV 13.00
75 JB,TP,I:Arkon 14.00
76 JB,TP,V:Arkon 13.00
77 JB,TP,V:Split-Second Squad . 13.00
78 SB,TP,V:Lethal Legion 13.00
79 JB,TP,V:Lethal Legion 13.00
80 JB,TP,I&O:Red Wolf 14.00
81 JB,TP,A:Red Wolf 13.00
82 JB,TP,V:Ares,A:Daredevil ... 13.00
83 JB,TP,I:Valkyrie,
    V:Masters of Evil 14.00
84 JB,TP,V:Enchantress,Arkon . 13.00
85 JB,V:Squadron Supreme ... 13.00
86 JB,JMA:Squad Supreme ... 13.00
87 SB(i),O:Black Panther,
    V: A.I.M. 24.00
88 SB,JM,V:Psyklop,A:Hulk,
    Professor.X 13.00
89 SB,B:Kree/Skrull War 13.00
90 SB,V:Sentry #459,Ronan,
    Skrulls 13.00
91 SB,V:Sentry #459,Ronan,
    Skrulls 13.00
92 SB,V:Super Skrull,Ronan, ... 14.00
93 NA,TP,V:Super-Skrull,G-Size 55.00
94 NA,JB,TP,V:Super-Skrull,
    I:Mandroids 35.00
95 NA,TP,V:Maximus,Skrulls,
    A:Inhumans,O:Black Bolt ... 35.00
96 NA,TP,V:Skrulls,Ronan 35.00
97 GK&BEv(c),JB,TP,E:Kree-Skrull
    War,I:Annihilus,Ronan,Skrulls,
    A:Golden Age Heroes 17.00
98 BWS,SB,V:Ares,R:Hercules,
    R&N:Hawkeye 24.00
99 BWS,TS,V:Ares 24.00
100 BWS,JSr,V:Ares & Kratos .. 60.00
101 RB,DA,A:Watcher 9.00
102 RB,JSt,V:Grim Reaper,
    Sentinels 9.00
103 RB,JSt,V:Sentinels 9.00
104 RB,JSt,V:Sentinels 9.00
105 JB,JM,V:Savage Land
    Mutates; A:Black Panther .. 9.00
106 GT,DC,RB,V:Space Phantom 9.00
107 GT,DC,JSn,V:Space
    Phantom, Grim Reaper 11.00

108 DH,DC,JSt,V:Space
 Phantom,Grim Reaper 9.00
109 DH,FMc,V:Champion,
 L:Hawkeye 9.00
110 DH,V:Magneto,A:X-Men ... 17.00
111 DH,J:Bl.Widow,A:Daredevil,
 X-Men,V:Magneto 17.00
112 DH,I:Mantis,V:Lion-God,
 L:Black Widow 10.00

Avengers #93
© Marvel Entertainment Group

113 FBe(i),V:The Living Bombs .. 8.00
114 JR(c),V:Lion-God,J:Mantis,
 Swordsman 7.50
115 JR(c),A:Defenders,V:Loki,
 Dormammu 10.00
116 JR(c),A:Defenders,S.Surfer
 V:Loki,Dormammu 10.00
117 JR(c),FMc(i),A:Defenders,Silv.
 Surfer,V:Loki,Dormammu .. 10.00
118 JR(c),A:Defenders,S.Surfer
 V:Loki,Dormammu 10.00
119 JR(c),DH(i),V:Collector 7.00
120 JSn(c),DH(i),V:Zodiac 7.00
121 JR&JSn(c),JB,DH,V:Zodiac .. 7.00
122 K&R(c),V:Zodiac 7.00
123 JR(c),DH(i),O:Mantis 7.00
124 JR(c),JB,DC,V:Kree,O:Mantis 7.00
125 JR(c),JB,DC,V:Thanos 14.00
126 DC(i),V:Klaw,Solarr 10.00
127 GK(c),SB,JSon,A:Inhumans,
 V:Ultron,Maximus 10.00
128 K&R(c),SB,JSon,V:Kang 7.00
129 SB,JSon,V:Kang 7.00
130 GK(c),SB,JSon,V:Slasher,
 Titanic Three 7.00
131 GK(c),SB,JSon,V:Kang,
 Legion of the Unliving 6.00
132 SB,JSon,Kang,Legion
 of the Unliving 6.00
133 GK(c),SB,JSon,O:Vision 6.00
134 K&R(c),SB,JSon,O:Vision .. 6.00
135 JSn&JR(c),GT,O:Mantis,
 Vision,C:Thanos 7.50
136 K&R(c),rep Amazing Adv#12 . 6.00
137 JR(c),GT,J:Beast,
 Moondragon 7.50

138 GK(c),GT,V:Toad 6.00
139 K&R(c),GT,V:Whirlwind 6.00
140 K&R(c),GT,V:Whirlwind 6.00
141 GK(c),GP,V:Squad.Sinister . 5.00
142 K&R(c),GP,V:Squadron
 Sinister,Kang 5.00
143 GK(c),GP,V:Squadron
 Sinister,Kang 5.00
144 GP,GK(c),V:Squad.Sinister,
 O&J:Hellcat,O:Buzz Baxter ... 5.00
145 GK(c),DH,V:Assassin 5.00
146 GK(c),DH,KP,V:Assassin ... 5.00
147 GP,V:Squadron Supreme .. 5.00
148 JK(c),GP,V:Squad.Supreme . 5.00
149 GP,V:Orka 5.00
150 GP,JK,rep.Avengers #16 .... 5.00
151 GP,new line-up,
 R:Wonder Man 4.50
152 JB,JSt,I:New Black Talon .. 5.00
153 JB,JSt,V:L.Laser,Whizzer .. 4.50
154 GP,V:Attuma 4.50
155 SB,V:Dr.Doom,Attuma 4.50
156 SB,I:Tyrak,V:Attuma 4.50
157 DH,V:Stone Black Knight .. 4.50
158 JK(c),SB,I&O:Graviton, ... 4.50
159 JK(c),SB,V:Graviton, ... 4.50
160 GP,V:Grim Reaper 4.50
161 GP,V:Ultron,A:Ant-Man 4.50
162 GP,V:Ultron,I:Jocasta 4.50
163 GT,A:Champions,V:Typhon .. 4.50
164 JBy,V:Lethal Legion 6.00
165 JBy,V:Count Nefario 6.00
166 JBy,V:Count Nefario 6.00
167 GP,A:Guardians,A:Nighthawk,
 Korvac,V:Porcupine 4.00
168 GP,A:Guardians,V:Korvac,
 I:Gyrich 4.00
169 SB,I:Eternity Man 4.00
170 GP,R:Jocasta,C:Ultron,
 A:Guardians 4.00
171 GP,V:Ultron,A:Guardians,
 Ms Marvel 4.00
172 SB,KJ,V:Tyrak 4.00
173 SB,V:Collector 4.00
174 GP(c),V:Collector 4.00
175 V&O:Korvac,A:Guardians ... 4.00
176 V:Korvac,A:Guardians 4.00
177 DC(c),D:Korvac,A:Guardians . 4.00
178 CI,V:Manipulator 4.00
179 JM,AG,V:Stinger,Bloodhawk . 4.00
180 JM,V:Monolith,Stinger,
 D:Bloodhawk 4.00
181 JBy,GD,I:Scott Lang 5.50
182 JBy,KJ,V:Maximoff 5.00
183 JBy,KJ,J:Ms.Marvel 5.00
184 JBy,KJ,J:Falcon,
 V:Absorbing Man 5.00
185 JBy,DGr,O:Quicksilver & Scarlet
 Witch,I:Bova,V:Modred 5.00
186 JBy,DGr,V:Modred,Chthon .. 5.00
187 JBy,DGr,V:Chthon,Modred .. 5.00
188 JBy,DGr,V:The Elements ... 5.00
189 JBy,DGr,V:Deathbird 5.00
190 JBy,DGr,V:Grey Gargoyle,
 A:Daredevil 5.00
191 JBy,DGr,V:Grey Gargoyle,
 A:Daredevil 5.00
192 I:Inferno 3.00
193 FM(c),SB,DGr,O:Inferno ... 3.00
194 GP,JRu,J:Wonder Man 3.00
195 GP,JRu,A:Antman,
 I&C:Taskmaster 4.00
196 GP,JA,A:Antman,
 V:Taskmaster, ... 4.00
197 CI,JAb,V:Red Ronin 3.00

198 GP,DGr,V:Red Ronan 3.00
199 GP,DGr,V:Red Ronan 3.00
200 GP,DGr,V:Marcus,
 L:Ms.Marvel 4.00
201 GP,DGr,F:Jarvis 3.00
202 GP,V:Ultron 3.00
203 CI,V:Crawlers,F:Wonderman . 2.50
204 DN,DGr,V:Yellow Claw 2.50
205 DGr,V:Yellow Claw 2.50
206 GC,DGr,V:Pyron 2.50
207 GC,DGr,V:Shadowlord 2.50
208 GC,DGr,V:Berserker 2.50
209 DGr,A:Mr.Fantastic,V:Skrull .. 2.50
210 GC,DGr,V:Weathermen 2.50
211 GC,DGr,Moon Knight,J:Tigra . 2.50
212 DGr,V:Elfqueen 2.50
213 BH,DGr,L:Yellowjacket 2.50
214 BH,DGr,V:Gh.Rider,A:Angel . 4.00
215 DGr,A:Silver Surfer,
 V:Molecule Man 3.00
216 DGr,A:Silver Surfer,
 V:Molecule Man 3.00
217 BH,DGr,V:Egghead,
 R:Yellowjacket,Wasp 2.50
218 DP,V:M.Hardy 2.50
219 BH,A:Moondragon,Drax 3.50
220 BH,DGr,D:Drax,V:MnDragon . 3.50
221 J:She Hulk 2.50
222 V:Masters of Evil 2.50
223 A:Antman 2.50
224 AM,A:Antman 2.50
225 A:Black Knight 2.50
226 A:Black Knight 2.50
227 J:2nd Captain Marvel,
 O:Avengers 2.50
228 V:Masters of Evil 2.50
229 JSi,V:Masters of Evil 2.50
230 A:Cap.Marvel,L:Yellowjacket . 2.50
231 AM,JSi,J:2nd Captain Marvel,
 Starfox 2.50
232 AM,JSi 2.50
233 JBy,V:Annihilus 2.50
234 AM,JSi,O:ScarletWitch 2.50
235 AM,JSi,V:Wizard 2.50
236 AM,JSi,A:SpM,V:Lava Men . 2.50
237 AM,JSi,A:SpM,V:Lava Men . 2.50
238 AM,JSi,V:Moonstone,
 O:Blackout 2.50
239 AM,JSi,A:David Letterman .. 2.50
240 AM,JSi,A:Dr.Strange 2.50
241 AM,JSi,V:Morgan LeFey ... 2.50
242 AM,JSi,Secret Wars 2.50
243 AM,JSi,Secret Wars 2.50
244 AM,JSi,V:Dire Wraiths 2.50
245 AM,JSi,V:Dire Wraiths 2.50
246 AM,JSi,V:Eternals 2.50
247 AM,JSi,A:Eternals,V:Deviants 2.50
248 AM,JSi,A:Eternals,V:Deviants 2.50
249 AM,JSi,A:Maelstrom 2.50
250 AM,JSi,A:W.C.A.
 V:Maelstrom 3.00
251 BH,JSi,A:Paladin 2.50
252 BH,JSi,J:Hercules
 V:Blood Brothers 2.50
253 BH,JSi,J:Black Knight 2.50
254 BH,JSi,A:W.C.A. 2.50
255 TP,p(c),JB,Legacy of
 Thanos/Sanctuary II 2.50
256 JB,TP,A:Kazar 2.50
257 JB,TP,D:Savage Land,
 I:Nebula 3.00
258 JB,TP,A:SpM,Firelord,Nebula 2.50
259 JB,TP,V:Nebula 2.50
260 JB,TP,SecretWarsII,
 IR:Nebula is Thanos' Grand

daughter 2.50
261 JB,TP,Secret Wars II 2.50
262 JB,TP,J:Submariner 2.50
263 JB,TP,X-Factor tie-in,
   Rebirth,Marvel Girl,pt.1 . . . 5.00
264 JB,TP,I:2nd Yellow Jacket . . . 2.50
265 JB,TP,Secret Wars II 2.50
266 JB,TP,Secret Wars II,A:
   Silver Surfer 2.50
267 JB,TP,V:Kang 2.50
268 JB,TP,V:Kang 2.50
269 JB,TP,V:Kang,A:Immortus . . . 2.50
270 JB,TP,V:Moonstone 2.50
271 JB,TP,V:Masters of Evil 2.50
272 JB,TP,A:Alpha Flight 2.50
273 JB,TP,V:Masters of Evil 2.50
274 JB,TP,V:Masters of Evil 2.50
275 JB,TP,V:Masters of Evil 2.50
276 JB,TP,V:Masters of Evil 2.50
277 JB,TP,V:Masters of Evil 2.50
278 JB,TP,V:Tyrok,J:Dr.Druid . . . 2.50
279 JB,TP,new leader 2.50
280 BH,KB,O:Jarvis 2.50
281 JB,TP,V:Olympian Gods 2.50
282 JB,TP,V:Cerberus 2.50
283 JB,TP,V:Olympian Gods 2.50
284 JB,TP,V:Olympian Gods 2.50
285 JB,TP,V:Zeus 2.50
286 JB,TP,V:Fixer 2.50
287 JB,TP,V:Fixer 2.50
288 JB,TP,V:Sentry 459 . . . . 2.50
289 JB,TP,J:Marrina 2.50
290 JB,TP,V:Adaptoid 2.50
291 JB,TP,V:Marrina 2.50
292 JB,TP,V:Leviathon 2.50
293 JB,TP,V:Leviathon 2.50
294 JB,TP,V:Nebula 2.50
295 JB,TP,V:Nebula 2.50
296 JB,TP,V:Nebula 2.50
297 JB,TP,V:Nebula 2.50
298 JB,TP,Inferno,Edwin Jarvis . . 2.50
299 JB,TP,Inferno,V:Orphan
   Maker,R:Gilgemesh 2.50
300 JB,TP,WS,Inferno,V:Kang,
   O:Avengers,J:Gilgemesh,
   Mr.Fantastic,Invis.Woman . . 3.50
301 BH,DH,A:SuperNova 2.25
302 RB,TP,V:SuperNova,
   A:Quasar 2.25
303 RB,TP,V:SuperNova,A:FF . . 2.00
304 RB,TP,V:U-Foes,Puma 2.00
305 PR,TP,V:Lava Men 2.25
306 PR,TP,O:Lava Men 2.00
307 PR,TP,V:Lava Men 2.00
308 PR,TP,A:Eternals,J:Sersi . . . 2.00
309 PR,TP,V:Blastaar 2.00
310 PR,TP,V:Blastaar 2.00
311 PR,TP,Acts of Veng.,V:Loki . . 3.00
312 PR,TP,Acts of Vengeance,
   V:Freedom Force 3.00
313 PR,TP,Acts of Vengeance,
   V:Mandarin,Wizard 3.00
314 PR,TP,J:Sersi,A:Spider-Man,
   V:Nebula 4.50
315 PR,TP,A:SpM,V:Nebula 3.00
316 PR,TP,A:Spider-Man 3.00
317 PR,TP,A:SpM,V:Nebula 3.00
318 PR,TP,A:SpM,V:Nebula 3.00
319 PR,B:Crossing Line 2.00
320 PR,TP,A:Alpha Flight 2.00
321 PR,Crossing Line#3 . . . . 2.00
322 PR,TP,Crossing Line#4 . . . . . 2.00
323 PR,TP,Crossing Line#5 . . . . . 2.00
324 PR,TP,E:Crossing Line 2.00
325 V:MotherSuperior,

Machinesmith 2.00
326 TP,I:Rage 5.00
327 TP,V:Monsters 2.00
328 TP,O:Rage 4.00
329 TP,J:Sandman,Rage 2.75
330 TP,V:Tetrarch of Entropy . . . 2.00
331 TP,J:Rage,Sandman 2.00
332 TP,V:Dr.Doom 2.00
333 HT,V:Dr.Doom 2.00
334 NKu,TP,B:Collector,
   A:Inhumans 2.00
335 RLm(c),SEp,TP,V:Thane
   Ector,A:Collector. 1.75
336 RLm(c),SEp,TP 1.75
337 RLm(c),SEp,TP,V:ThaneEctor 1.75
338 RLm(c),SEp,TP,A:Beast. . . . 1.75
339 RLm(c),SEp,TP,E:Collector . . 1.75
340 RLm(c),F:Capt.Amer.,Wasp . . 1.75
341 SEp,TP,A:New Warriors,V:Sons
   of Serpents 1.75
342 SEP,TP,A:New Warriors,
   V:Hatemonger 1.75
343 SEp,TP,J:Crystal,C&I:2nd
   Swordsman,Magdalene 2.00
344 SEp,TP,I:Proctor 3.00
345 SEp,TP,Oper. Galactic Storm
   Pt.5,V:Kree,Shiar 1.75
346 SEp,TP,Oper. Galactic Storm
   Pt.12,I:Star Force 1.75
347 SEp,TP,Oper. Galactic Storm
   Pt.19,D:Kree Race,Conclusion 2.00
348 SEp,TP,F:Vision 1.75
349 SEp,TP,V:Ares 1.75
350 SEp,TP,rep.Avengers#53,A:Prof.
   X,Cyclops,V:StarJammers . . . 3.00
351 KWe,V:Star Jammers 1.75
352 V:Grim Reaper 1.75
353 V:Grim Reaper 1.75
354 V:Grim Reaper 1.75
355 BHs(s),SEp,I:Gatherers,
   Coal Tiger 2.00
356 B:BHs(s),SEp,TP,A:Bl.Panther
   D:Coal Tiger 1.75
357 SEp,TP,A:Watcher 1.75
358 SEp,TP,V:Arkon 1.75
359 SEp,TP,A:Arkon 1.75
360 SEp,TP,V:Proctor,double-size,
   bronze foil(c) 6.00
361 SEp,I:Alternate Vision 2.00
362 SEp,TP,V:Proctor 2.00
363 SEp,TP,V:Proctor,D:Alternate
   Vision,C:Deathcry,Silver Foil(c),
   30th Anniv., ... 4.50
364 SEp,TP,I:Deathcry,V:Kree . . 1.75
365 SEp,TP,V:Kree 1.75
366 SEp,TP,V:Kree,N:Dr.Pym,Gold
   Foil(c) 4.50
367 F:Vision 1.75
368 SEp,TP,Bloodties#1,
   A:X-Men 4.00
369 SEp,TP,E:BHs(s),Bloodties#5,
   D:Cortez,V:Exodus,Platinum
   Foil(c) 3.50
370 SEp(c),TP(c),GI,V:Deviants,
   A:Kro,I:Delta Force 1.75
371 GM,TP,V:Deviants,A:Kro 1.75
372 B:BHs(s),SEp,TP,I:2nd
   Gatherers,A:Proctor 1.75
373 SEp,TP,I:Alternate Jocasta,
   V:Sersi 1.75
374 SEp,TP,O&I:Proctor is Alternate
   Black Knight 1.75
375 SEp,TP,Double Sized,D:Proctor,
   L:Sersi,Black Knight 2.75
376 F:Crystal,I:Terrigen 1.75

377 F:Quicksilver 1.50
378 TP,I:Butcher 1.50
379 TP,Hercules,V:Hera 1.50
379a Avengers Double Feature #1
   flip-book with Giant-Man #1 . . . 2.50
380 Hera 1.50
380a Avengers Double Feature #2
   flip-book with Giant Man #2 . . . 2.50
381 Quicksilvr, Scarlet Witch 1.50
381a Avengers Double Feature #3
   flip-book with Giant Man #3 . . . 2.50
382 Wundagore 1.50
382a Avengers Double Feature #4
   flip-book with Giant Man #4 . . 2.50
383 A:Fantastic Force,V:Arides . . 1.50
384 Hercules Vs. Stepmom 1.50
385 V:Red Skull 1.50
386 F:Black Widow 1.50
387 Taking A.I.M.,pt.2 . . . . 1.50
388 Taking A.I.M.,pt.4 . . . . 1.50

Avengers Ann. #22
© *Marvel Entertainment Group*

Ann.#1 DH,V:Mandarin,
   Masters of Evil 42.00
Ann.#2 DH,JB,V:Scar.Centurion . 15.00
Ann.#3 rep.#4,T.ofSusp.#66-68 . 16.00
Ann.#4 rep.#5,#6 . . . . 8.00
Ann.#5 JK(c),rep.#8,#11 . . . . . . 8.00
Ann.#6 GP,HT,V:Laser,Nuklo,
   Whirlwind 6.00
Ann.#7 JSn,JRu,V:Thanos,A:Captain
   Marvel,D:Warlock(2nd) 34.00
Ann.#8 GP,V:Dr.Spectrum 6.00
Ann.#9 DN,V:Arsenal 5.00
Ann.#10 MGo,A:X-Men,Spid.Woman,
   I:Rogue,V:Br.o/Evil Mutants . . 12.00
Ann.#11 DP,V:Defenders 5.00
Ann.#12 JG,V:Inhumans,Maximus 4.00
Ann.#13 JBy,V:Armin Zola 4.00
Ann.#14 JBy,KB,V:Skrulls 4.00
Ann.#15 SD,KJ,V:Freedom Force 4.00
Ann.#16 RF,BH,TP,JR2,BSz,KP,AW,
   MR,BL,BWi,JG,KN,A:Silver
   Surfer,Rebirth Grandmaster . 4.50
Ann.#17 MBr,MG,Evol.Wars,J:2nd
   Yellow Jacket 4.00
Ann.#18 MBa,MG,Atlan.Attack#8,

J:Quasar	3.00
Ann.#19 HT,Terminus Factor	2.50
Ann.#20 Subterran.Odyssey#1	2.50
Ann.#21 Citizen Kang#4	2.50
Ann.#22 I:Bloodwraith,w/card	3.25
Ann.#23 JB	3.25
G-Size#1 JR(c),RB,DA,I:Nuklo	6.00
G-Size#2 JR(c),DC,O:Kang,	
D:Swordsman,O:Rama-Tut	5.00
G-Size#3 GK(c),DC,V:Kang,Legion	
of the Unliving	5.00
G-Size#4 K&R(c),DH,W:Scarlet Witch	
&Vision,O:Mantis,Moondragon	5.00
G-Size#5 rep,Annual #1.	3.00
GNv Death Trap:The Vault RLm,	
A:Venom	20.00
Milestone #1,Rep.#1	2.95
Milestone #2 rep.#16	2.95
TPB Greatest Battles of the	
Avengers	15.95
TPB Korvac Saga,rep.#167-177	12.95
TPB Yesterday Quest,Rep.#181,182	
185-187	6.95

AVENGERS INDEX
SEE: OFFICIAL MARVEL
INDEX TO THE AVENGERS

AVENGERS LOG
1 GP(c),History of the Avengers	2.25

AVENGERS SPOTLIGHT
August, 1989
Formerly: Solo Avengers

21 AM,DH,TMo,JRu,Hawkeye,	
Starfox	1.25
22 AM,DH,Hawkeye,O:Swordsman	1.25
23 AM,DH,KD,Hawkeye,Vision	1.25
24 AM,DH,Hawkeye,O:Espirita	1.25
25 AM,TMo,Hawkeye,Rick Jones	1.25
26 A of V,Hawkeye,Iron Man	1.25
27 A of V,AM,DH,DT,Hawkeye,	
Avengers	1.25
28 A of V,AM,DH,DT,Hawkeye,	
Wonder Man,Wasp	1.25
29 A of V,DT,Hawkeye,Iron Man	1.25
30 AM,DH,Hawkeye,New Costume	1.25
31 AM,DH,KW,Hawkeye,US.Agent	1.25
32 AM,KW,Hawkeye,U.S.Agent	1.25
33 AM,DH,KW,Hawkeye,US.Agent	1.25
34 AM,DH,KW,SLi(c),Hawkeye	
U.S.Agent	1.25
35 JV,Gilgamesh	1.25
36 AM,DH,Hawkeye	1.25
37 BH,Dr.Druid	1.25
38 JBr,Tigra	1.25
39 GCo,Black Knight	1.25
40 Vision,Last Issue	1.25

AVENGERS STRIKEFILE
1 BHa(s),Avengers Pin-ups	2.00

AVENGERS: THE
TERMINATRIX OBJECTIVE
1 B:MGu(s),MG,Holografx(c),	
V:Terminatrix	2.75
2 MG,V:Terminatrix,A:Kangs	2.00
3 MG,V:Terminatrix,A:Kangs	2.00
4 MG,Last issue	2.00

AVENGERS WEST COAST
September, 1989
Prev: West Coast Avengers

47 JBy,V:J.Random	2.50
48 JBy,V:J.Random	2.50
49 JBy,V:J.Random,W.Man	2.50
50 JBy,R:G.A.Human Torch	2.50
51 JBy,R:Iron Man	2.50
52 JBy,V:MasterPandmonum	2.50
53 JBy,Acts ofVeng.,V:U-Foes	2.50
54 JBy,Acts ofVeng.,V:MoleMan	2.50
55 JBy,Acts ofVeng.finale,V:Loki	
Magneto kidnaps Sc.Witch	3.00
56 JBy,V:Magneto	3.00
57 JBy,V:Magneto	3.00
58 V:Vibro,	2.00
59 TMo,V:Hydro-Man,A:Immortus	2.00
60 PR,V:Immortus,	2.00
61 PR,V:Immortus	2.00
62 V:Immortus	2.00
63 PR,I:Living Lightning	2.00
64 F:G.A.Human Torch	2.00
65 PR,V:Ultron,Grim Reaper	2.00
66 PR,V:Ultron,Grim Reaper	2.00
67 PR,V:Ultron,Grim Reaper	2.00
68 PR,V:Ultron	2.00
69 PR,USAgent vs Hawkeye,	
I:Pacific Overlords	3.00
70 DR,V:Pacific Overlords	1.75
71 DR,V:Pacific Overlords	1.75
72 DR,V:Pacific Overlords	1.75
73 DR,V:Pacific Overlords	1.75
74 DR,J:Living Lightning,Spider	
Woman,V:Pacific Overlords.	1.75
75 HT,A:F.F,V:Arkon,double	2.00
76 DR,Night Shift,I:Man-Demon	1.50
77 DR,A:Satannish & Nightshift	1.50
78 DR,V:Satannish & Nightshift	1.50
79 DR,A:Dr.Strange,V:Satannish	1.50
80 DR,Galactic Storm,pt.2	1.50
81 DR,Galactic Storm,pt.9	1.50
82 DR,Galactic Storm,pt.16	
A:Lilandra	1.50
83 V:Hyena	1.50
84 DR,I:Deathweb,A:SpM,	
O:Spider-Woman	1.75
85 DR,A:SpM,V:Death Web	1.50
86 DR,A:SpM,V:Death Web	1.50
87 DR,A:Wolverine,V:Bogatyri	1.75
88 DR,A:Wolverine,V:Bogatyri	1.75
89 DR,V:Ultron	1.50
90 DR,A:Vision,V:Ultron	1.50
91 DR,V:Ultron,I:War Toy	1.50
92 DR,V:Goliath(Power Man)	1.50
93 DR,V:Doctor Demonicus	1.50
94 DR,J:War Machine	1.75
95 DR,A:Darkhawk,V:Doctor	
Demonicus	1.50
96 DR,Inf.Crusade	1.50
97 ACe,Inf.Crusade,V:Power	
Platoon	1.50
98 DR,I:4th Lethal Legion	1.50
99 DR,V:4th Lethal Legion	1.50
100 DR,D:Mockingbird,V:4th Lethal	
Legion,Red Foil(c)	4.50
101 DR,Bloodties#3,V:Exodus	5.00
102 DR,L:Iron Man,Spider-Woman,	
US Agent,Scarlet Witch,War	
Machine,last issue	5.00
Ann.#4 JBy,TA,MBa,Atlan.Attacks	
#12,V:Seven Brides of Set	4.00
Ann.#5 Terminus Factor	3.50
Ann.#6 Subterranean Odyssey#5	2.50
Ann.#7 Assault on Armor City#4	2.25
Ann.#8 DR,I:Raptor w/card	3.25

BALDER THE BRAVE
November, 1985

1 WS,SB,V:Frost Giants	1.50
2 WS,SB,V:Frost Giants	1.25
3 WS,SB,V:Frost Giants	1.25
4 WS,SB,V:Frost Giants;Feb,1986	1.25

BARBARIANS, THE
Atlas
June, 1975

1 O: Andrax,A: Iron Jaw	1.75

BARBIE
January, 1991

1 polybagged with Credit Card	3.00
2	1.50
3	1.50
4 Ice Skating	1.50
5 Sea Cruise	1.50
6 Sun Runner Story	1.50
7 Travel issue	1.50
8 TV Commercial	1.50
9 Music Tour Van	1.50
10 Barbie in Italy	1.50
11 Haunted Castles	1.50
12 Monkey Bandit	1.50
13 MW,A:Skipper,Ken	1.50
14 Country Fair	1.50
15 Barbie in Egypt,pt.1	1.50
16 Barbie in Egypt,pt.2	1.50
17 Weightwatchers/Art issue	1.50
18 V:heavy Metal Band	1.50
19 A:Surfer Pal	1.50
20 Skipper at Special Olympics	1.25
21 I:Whitney,female fire fighter	1.25
22 Barbie in Greece	1.25
23 thru 27	@1.25
28 Valentine's Day Issue	1.25
29 Skipper babysits	1.25
30 Cowgirls on the Range	1.25
31 Rest and Relaxation	1.25
32 A:Dandy the Gorilla	1.25
33 thru 41	@1.25
42 thru 49	@1.50
50 Anniv. issue, Disney World(c)	2.25
51 Vet's assistant	1.50
52 Valentines Day Special	1.50
53 Marooned	1.50
54 Female Inventors	1.50
55 in Nashville	1.50

BARBIE FASHION
January, 1991

1 polybagged with dorknob hanger	2.00
2 thru 55	@1.25

BATTLE
Atlas
March, 1951

1 They called Him a Coward	100.00
2 The War Department Secrets	45.00
3 The Beast of the Bataan	30.00
4 I:Buck Private O'Toole	30.00
5 Death Trap Of Gen. Wu.	30.00
6 RH	30.00
7 Enemy Sniper	30.00
8 A Time to Die	30.00
9 RH	35.00
10	30.00
11 thru 20	@25.00
21	35.00
22	25.00
23	35.00
24	25.00
25	25.00
26 JR	25.00

All comics prices listed are for *Near Mint* **condition.**

27	25.00
28 JSe	25.00
29	25.00
30	25.00
31 RH	27.00
32 JSe,GT	25.00
33 GC,JSe,JSt	25.00
34 JSe	25.00
35	25.00
36 BEv	27.00
37 RA,JSt	25.00
38	20.00
39	20.00
40	20.00
41	22.00
42 thru 46	@20.00
47 JO	20.00
48	20.00
49	20.00
50 BEv	20.00
51	20.00
52 GWb	20.00
53	20.00
54	20.00
55 GC	35.00
56	20.00
57	20.00
58	22.00
59	20.00
60 A:Combat Kelly	20.00
61 A:Combat Kelly	20.00
62 A:Combat Kelly	20.00
63	26.00
64	26.00
65	26.00
66 JSe,JK	32.00
67 JSe,JK	32.00
68 JSe,JK	24.00
69 RH,JSe,JK	24.00
70 BEv,SD; June, 1960	24.00

BATTLE ACTION
Atlas
February, 1952

1	100.00
2	40.00
3	28.00
4	28.00
5	25.00
6	28.00
7	28.00
8	35.00
9	28.00
10	28.00
11 thru 15	@20.00
16 thru 26	@18.00
27	25.00
28	18.00
29	18.00
30 August, 1957	25.00

BATTLE BRADY
See: MEN IN ACTION

BATTLEFIELD
Atlas
April, 1952

1 RH, Slaughter on Suicide Ridge	75.00
2	40.00
3 Ambush Patrol	40.00
4	40.00
5 Into the Jaws of Death	40.00
6 thru 10	@20.00

11 GC,May, 1953	20.00

BATTLEFRONT
Atlas
June, 1952

1 RH(c),Operation Killer	125.00
2	55.00
3 Spearhead	40.00
4 Death Trap of General Chun	40.00
5 Terror of the Tank Men	35.00
6 A:Combat Kelly	35.00
7 A:Combat Kelly	35.00
8 A:Combat Kelly	35.00
9 A:Combat Kelly	35.00
10 A:Combat Kelly	35.00
11 thru 20	@20.00
21 thru 39	@16.00
40 AW	35.00
15	16.00
16 AW	35.00
43 thru 48 August,1957	@16.00

BATTLEGROUND
Atlas
September, 1954

1	85.00
2 JKz	40.00
3 thru 8	@25.00
9	35.00
10	25.00
11	35.00
12	20.00
13	35.00
14	30.00
15	20.00
16	20.00
17	20.00
18	35.00
19	20.00
20 August, 1957	20.00

BATTLESTAR GALACTICA
March, 1979

1 EC,B:TV Adaptation; Annihalation	3.00
2 EC,Exodus	2.50
3 EC,Deathtrap	2.50
4 WS,Dogfight	2.50
5 WS,E:TV Adaptation;Ambush	2.50
6 Nightmare	1.50
7 Commander Adama Trapped	1.50
8 Last Stand	1.50
9 Space Mimic	1.50
10 This Planet Hungers	1.50
11 WS,Starbuck's Dilemma	1.50
12 WS,Memory Ends	1.50
13 WS,All Out Attack	1.50
14 Radiation Threat	1.50
15 Ship of Crawling Death	1.50
16	1.50
17 Animal on the Loose	1.50
18 Battle For the Forbidden Fruit	1.50
19 Starbuck's Back	1.50
20 Duel to the Death	1.50
21 To Slay a Monster..To Deatroy a World	1.50
22 WS,A Love Story?	1.50
23 December, 1981	1.50

BATTLETIDE

1 thru 4 F: Death's Head II and Killpower	@1.75

BATTLETIDE II

1 Foil embossed cover	2.95
2 thru 8 F: Death's Head II and Killpower	@1.75

BEAUTY AND THE BEAST
January, 1985

1 DP,Beast & Dazzler,direct	4.00
1a DP,Beast & Dazzler,UPC	2.00
2 DP,Beast & Dazzler	2.00
3 DP,Beast & Dazzler	2.00
4 DP,Beast & Dazzler	2.00

BEAUTY AND THE BEAST

1	1.50
2 Wardrobe's birthday party	1.50
3	1.50
4	1.50
5	1.50
6 Lumiere takes Cogsworth's job	1.50
7 Belle & Chip caught in snow	1.50
8	1.50
9 Can Beast prove his love?	1.50
10 Chip & Belle have a snow ball	1.50
11 History of Beast's Castle	1.50

BEST WESTERN
June, 1949

58 A:KidColt,BlackRider,Two-Gun Kid;Million DollarTrainRobbery	100.00
59 A:BlackRider,KidColt,Two-Gun Kid;The Black Rider Strikes	90.00

Becomes:

WESTERN OUTLAWS & SHERIFFS

60 PH(c),Hawk Gaither	100.00
61 Ph(c),Pepper Lawson	75.00
62 Murder at Roaring House Bridge	75.00
63 thru 65	@75.00
66	50.00
67	70.00
68 thru 72	@50.00
73 June, 1952	40.00

BEAVIS & BUTT-HEAD

1 Based on the MTV Show	8.00
1a 2nd Printing	2.50
2 Dead from the Neck up	3.50
3 Break out at Burger World	3.00
4 Tattoo Parlor	2.25
5 Field Day	2.25
6 Revulsion	2.25
7 Oldies bot	2.25
8 Be a clown	2.25
9 Makin' movies	2.25
10 Halloween	2.25
11	1.95
12	1.95
13	1.95
14 Join Biker Gang	1.95
15 Spring Break	1.95
16 Capture The Flag	1.95
17 with video camera	1.95
TPB Greatest Hits, rep.#1–#4	12.95
TPB Holidazed and Confused	12.95

BEWARE
March, 1973

1 Reprints	4.50
2 thru 8	@2.50

Becomes:

TOMB OF DARKNESS
9 Reprints 2.00
10 thru 22 . . . . @1.00
23 November, 1976 . . . . 2.00

BIKER MICE FROM MARS
1 I:Biker Mice 1.50
2 thru 3 . . . . 1.50

BILL & TED'S BOGUS JOURNEY
November, 1991
1 Movie Adaption 3.25

BILL & TED'S EXCELLENT COMICS
December, 1991
1 From Movie; Wedding Reception 1.25
2 Death Takes a Vacation 1.25
3 'Daze in the Lives' 1.25
4 Station Plague 1.25
5 Bill & Ted on Trial 1.25
6 Time Trial 1.25
7 Time Trial, Concl 1.25
8 History Final 1.25
9 I:Morty(new Death) 1.25
10 'Hyperworld' 1.25
11 Lincoln assassination 1.25
12 Last issue 1.25

BILLY BUCKSKIN WESTERN
Atlas
November, 1955
1 MD,Tales of the Wild Frontier 70.00
2 MD,Ambush 45.00
3 MD,AW, Thieves in the Night 45.00
Becomes:

2-GUN KID
4 SD,A: Apache Kid 60.00
Becomes:

TWO-GUN WESTERN
5 B:Apache Kid,Doc Holiday, Kid Colt Outlaw 55.00
6 . . . . 30.00
7 . . . . 30.00
8 RC 40.00
9 AW 40.00
10 . . . . 30.00
11 AW 40.00
12 September, 1957,RC 40.00

BISHOP
1 Mountjoy, foil cover 4.50
2 foil stamped cover 4.00
3 JOs 3.50
4 V:Mountjoy 3.50

BIZARRE ADVENTURES
See: MARVEL PREVIEW

BLACK AXE
1 JR2(c),A:Death's Head II 2.00
2 JR2(2),A:Sunfire,V:The Hand . . 2.00
3 A:Death's Head II,V:Mesphisto . 2.00
4 in ancient Egypt 2.00
5 KJ(c),In Wakanda 2.00
6 KJ(c),A:Black Panther 2.00
7 KJ(c),A:Black Panther 1.75
8 . . . . 1.75
9 . . . . 1.75

10 . . . . 1.75
11 . . . . 1.75
12 . . . . 1.75
13 . . . . 1.75

BLACK CAT
Limited Series]
1 Wld,A:Spider-Man,V:Cardiac, I:Faze 1.75
2 Wld,V:Faze 1.50
3 Wld,Cardiac 1.50
4 Wld,V:Scar 1.50

BLACK DRAGON
Epic
May 1985
1 JBo 6.00
2 JBo 4.00
3 JBo 3.00
4 JBo 3.00
5 JBo 3.00
6 JBo 3.00

BLACK GOLIATH
Feb., 1976—Nov., 1976
1 GT,O:Black Goliath,Cont's From Powerman #24 . . . . 5.00
2 GT,V:Warhawk 4.00
3 GT,D:Atom-Smasher 4.00
4 KP,V:Stilt-Man 4.00
5 D:Mortag 4.00

BLACK KNIGHT, THE
Atlas
May, 1955—April, 1956
1 O: Crusader;The Black Knight Rides 500.00
2 Siege on Camelot 400.00
3 Blacknight Unmasked 300.00
4 Betrayed 300.00
5 SSh,The Invincible Tartar . . 300.00

BLACK KNIGHT
June, 1990—Sept., 1990
1 TD,R:Original Black Knight . . . 2.00
2 TD,A:Dreadknight 1.75
3 RB,A:Dr.Strange 1.75

Black Panther #10
© Marvel Entertainment Group

4 RB,TD,A:Dr Strange, Valkyrie . 1.75

BLACK PANTHER
[1st Series]
Jan., 1977—May, 1979
1 JK,V:Collectors 8.00
2 JK,V:Six Million Year Man 4.00
3 JK,V:Ogar 3.50
4 JK,V:Collectors 3.50
5 JK,V:Yeti 3.50
6 JK,V:Ronin 3.50
7 JK,V:Mister Little 3.50
8 JK,D:Black Panther 3.50
9 JK,V:Jakarra 3.50
10 JK,V:Jakarra 3.50
11 JK,V:Kilber the Cruel 3.50
12 JK,V:Kilber the Cruel 3.50
13 JK,V:Kilber the Cruel 3.50
14 JK,A:Avengers,V:Klaw 3.50
15 JK,A:Avengers,V:Klaw 3.50

BLACK PANTHER
July 1988—Oct. 1988
[1st Mini-Series]
1 I:Panther Spirit 3.50
2 V:Supremacists 3.00
3 A:Malaika 2.50
4 V:Panther Spirit 2.00
[2nd Mini-Series]
PANTHER'S PREY
May, 1991
1 DT,A:W'Kabi,V:Solomon Prey . 4.95
2 DT,V:Solomon Prey 4.95
3 DT,V:Solomon Prey 4.95
4 DT,V:Solomon Prey 4.95

BLACK RIDER
See: ALL WINNERS COMICS

BLACK RIDER RIDES AGAIN
Atlas
Sept., 1957
1 JK,Treachery at Hangman's Ridge 135.00

BLACKSTONE, THE MAGICIAN
May, 1948—Sept., 1948
2 B:Blonde Phantom 350.00
3 . . . . 250.00
4 Bondage(c) 250.00

BLACKWULF
1 AMe,Embossied(c),I:Mammoth, Touchstone,Toxin,D:Pelops, V:Tantalus, ... 2.50
2 AMe,I:Sparrow,Wildwind 1.75
3 AMe,I:Scratch 1.50
4 AMe,I:Giant-man 1.50
5 AMe 1.50
6 AMe,Tantalus 1.50
7 AMe,V:Tantalus 1.50
8 AMe 1.50
9 Seven Worlds of Tantalus,pt.1 A:Daredevil 1.50
10 Seven Worlds of Tantalus,pt.2, last issue 1.50

BLADE,
THE VAMPIRE HUNTER
1 Foil(c),Clv(i),R:Dracula 3.25
2 Clv(i),V:Dracula 1.95
3 Clv(i) 1.95
4 Clv(i) 1.95
5 Clv(i) 1.95
6 Clv(i) 1.95
7 Clv(i) 1.95
8 Bible John, Morbius 1.95
9 .... 1.95
10 R:Dracula 1.95
11 Dracula Untombed,pt.2 ...... 1.95

BLADE RUNNER
October, 1982
1 AW, Movie Adaption 1.50
2 AW, ... 1.50

BLAZE
[Limited Series]
1 HMe(s),RoW,A:Clara Menninger 2.00
2 HMe(s),RoW,I:Initiate 2.00
3 HMe(s),RoW, ... 2.00
4 HMe(s),RoW,D:Initiate,Last
   issue 2.00
[Regular Series]
1 HMz,LHa,foil (c) 3.25
2 HMz,LHa,I:Man-Thing 2.25
3 HMz,LHa,V:Ice Box Bob 1.95
4 HMz,LHa,Apache Autumn,pt.1 1.95
5 HMz,LHa,Apache Autumn,pt.2 1.95
6 Apache Autumn,pt.3 .... 1.95
7 Carnivale Quintano 1.95
8 A:Arcae 1.95
9 Clara's Eyeballs 1.95
10 Undead M.C. 1.95
11 A:Punisher 1.95
12 reunited with children, final iss. 1.95

BLAZE CARSON
September, 1948
1 SSh(c),Fight,Lawman
   or Crawl 125.00
2 Guns Roar on Boot Hill 75.00
3 A:Tex Morgan 85.00
4 A:Two-Gun Kid 75.00
5 A:Tex Taylor 75.00
Becomes:
REX HART
6 CCB,Ph(c),B:Rex Hart,
   A:Black Rider 125.00
7 Ph(c),Mystery at Bar-2 Ranch 100.00
8 Ph(c),The Hombre Who
   Killed His Friends 100.00
Becomes:
WHIP WILSON
9 Ph(c),B:Whip Wilson,O:Bullet;
   Duel to the Death 350.00
10 Ph(c),Wanted for Murder .. 250.00
11 Ph(c) 250.00
Becomes:
GUNHAWK, THE
12 The Redskin's Revenge 75.00
13 GT,The Man Who Murdered
   Gunhawk 60.00
14 .... 60.00
15 .... 60.00
16 .... 60.00
17 .... 60.00
18 December, 1951 .... 60.00

BLAZE, THE WONDER
COLLIE
October, 1949
2 Ph(c),Blaze-Son of Fury ... 125.00
3 Ph(c), Lonely Boy;Feb.,1950 100.00

BLONDE PHANTOM
See: ALL-SELECT COMICS

BLOOD
Feb., 1988—April, 1988
1 .... 6.00
2 .... 5.00
3 .... 5.00
4 .... 5.00

BLOOD & GLORY
1 KJ Cap & the Punisher 5.95
2 KJ Cap & the Punisher 5.95
3 KJ Cap & the Punisher 5.95

BLOODLINES
Epic
1 F:Kathy Grant-Peace Corps ... 5.95

BLOODSEED
1 LSh,I:Bloodseed 2.25
2 LSh,V:Female Bloodseed 2.25

BOOK OF THE DEAD
1 thru 4 Horror rep .... @2.00
5 and 6 .... @1.75

BOZZ CHRONICLES, THE
Epic
December, 1985
1 thru 5 .... @1.75
6 May, 1986 .... 1.75

BRATS BIZARRE
Epic
1 .... 3.25
2 thru 4 .... @2.50

BREAK THE CHAIN
1 KB,KRS-One,w/audio tape 7.00

BRUTE FORCE
August, 1990
1 JD/JSt 1.00
2 .... 1.00
3 .... 1.00
4 November, 1990 .... 1.00

BUCK DUCK
Atlas
June, 1953
1 (fa)stories 36.00
2 and 3 .... @21.00
4 December, 1953 .... 21.00

BUCKAROO BANZAI
December, 1984
1 Movie Adaption 2.00
2 Conclusion, February, 1985 ... 2.00

BULLWINKLE & ROCKY
Star
November, 1987
1 EC&AM,Based on 1960's TV

Series 3.00
2 EC&AM, ... 2.00
3 EC&AM,Rumpled Mudluck
   Thyme Mag 2.00
4 EC&AM,Boris and Natasha ... 2.00
5 EC&AM, ... 2.00
6 EC&AM,Wassamatta Me 2.00
7 EC&AM,Politics,Moose V:Boris 2.00
8 EC&AM,Superhero, March,1989 2.00
9 EC 2.00

BULLWINKLE &
ROCKY COLLECTION
TPB, AM,early stories 4.95

Cable #1
© *Marvel Entertainment Group*

CABLE
[Limited Series]
1 JR2,DGr,V:Mutant Liberation
Front,A:Weapon X 4.00
2 JR2,DGr,V:Stryfe,O:Weapon X 3.00
[Regular Series]
1 B:FaN(s),ATi,O:Cable,V:New
Canaanites,A:Stryfe,foil(c) .. 5.00
2 ATi,V:Stryfe 2.50
3 ATi,A:Six Pack 2.25
4 ATi,A:Six Pack 2.25
5 DaR,V:Sinsear 2.25
6 DT,A:Tyler,Zero,Askani,
Mr.Sinister,C:X-Men 2.50
7 V:Tyler,A:Askani,X-Men,Domino 2.25
8 O:Cable,V:Tyler,A:X-Men,Cable is
Nathan Summers 2.25
9 MCW,B:Killing Field,A:Excalibur,
V:Omega Red 2.25
10 MCW,A:Acolytes,Omega Red . 2.25
11 MCW,E:Killing Field,D:Katu ... 2.25
12 SLo(s),B:Fear & Loathing,
V:Senyaka 2.25
13 V:D'Spayre 2.00
14 V:S'yM 2.25
15 A:Thorn 2.25
16 Foil(c),Dbl-size,A:Jean,Scott
Logan,V:Phalanx 4.50
16a Newsstand ed. 2.50

17 Deluxe ed.	1.95
17a Newsstand ed.	1.50
18 Deluxe ed.	1.95
18a Newsstand ed.	1.50
19 Deluxe ed.	1.95
19a Newsstand ed.	1.50
20 V:Legion, Deluxe ed. w/card . .	1.95
20a Newsstand ed.	1.50
21 Cable makes tough decisions, A:Domino	1.50
TPB Cable,rep.New Mutants #87-94	15.95

CADILLACS & DINOSAURS
Epic
November, 1990

1 Rep.Xenozoic Tales	3.00
2 Rep.Xenozoic Tales	2.50
3 Rep.Xenozoic Tales	2.50
4 Rep.Xenozoic Tales	2.50
5 Rep.Xenozoic Tales	2.50
6 Rep.Xenozoic Tales, April,1991	2.50

Cage #1 © Marvel Entertainment Group

CAGE

1 DT,R:Luke Cage,I:Hardcore, . .	1.75
2 DT,V:Hammer	1.50
3 DT,A:Punisher,V:Untouchables	1.50
4 DT,A:Punisher,V:Untouchables	1.50
5 DT,I:New Power Man	1.50
6 DT,V:New Power Man	1.50
7 DT,A:Avengers West Coast . .	1.50
8 DT,V:Steele,Wonder Man	1.50
9 V:Rhino,A:Hulk	1.50
10 DT,V:Hulk,Rhino	1.50
11 DT,V:Rapidfire	1.50
12 A:Iron Fist,double size	2.00
13 V:The Thinker	1.50
14 PCu,I:Coldfire	1.50
15 DT,For Love Nor Money#2, A:Silver Sable,Terror	1.50
16 DT,For Love Nor Money#5, A:Silver Sable,Terror	1.50
17 DT,Infinty Crusade	1.50
18 A:Dred,V:Creed	1.50
19 A:Dakota North	1.50

20 Last issue	1.50

CAMP CANDY
May, 1990

1 thru 6, Oct. 1990	@1.00

CAPTAIN AMERICA COMICS
Timely/Atlas
May, 1941

1 S&K,Hitler(c),I&O:Capt.America & Bucky,A:Red Skull,B:Hurricane, Tuk the Caveboy	48,000.00
2 S&K,RC,AAv,Hitler(c), I:Circular Shield;Trapped in the Nazi Stronghold . . .	7,000.00
3 S&K,RC,AAv,Stan Lee's 1st Text, A:Red Skull,Bondage(c) . .	5,000.00
4 S&K,AAv,Ringmaster's .	3,500.00
5 S&K,AAv,Ringmaster's Wheel of Death	3,000.00
6 S&K,AAv,O:Father Time, E:Tuk	2,500.00
7 S&K,A: Red Skull	3,000.00
8 S&K, The Tomb	2,300.00
9 S&K,RC,V:Black Talon . . .	2,200.00
10 S&K,RC,Chamber of Horrors	2,200.00
11 AAv,E:Hurricane;Feuding Mountaneers	1,700.00
12 AAv,B:Imp,E:Father Time; Pygmie's Terror	1,700.00
13 AAv,O:Secret Stamp;All Out For America	1,800.00
14 AAv,V:Japs;Pearl Harbor Symbol cover	1,700.00
15 AAv,Den of Doom	1,700.00
16 AAv,A:R.Skull;CapA Unmasked	2,000.00
17 AAv,I:Fighting Fool; Graveyard	1,500.00
18 AAv,V:Japanese	1,300.00
19 AAv,V:Ghouls, B:Human Torch	1,200.00
20 AAv,A:Sub-Mariner,V:Nazis	1,200.00
21 SSh(c),Bucky Captured . .	1,000.00
22 SSh(c),V:Japanese	1,100.00
23 SSh(c),V:Nazis	1,100.00
24 SSh(c),V:Black Dragon Society	1,100.00
25 SSh(c),V:Japs;Drug Story .	1,100.00
26 ASh(c),V:Nazi Fleet	1,000.00
27 ASh(c)CapA&Russians V:Nazis, E:Secret Stamp . .	1,000.00
28 ASh(c),NaziTortureChamber	1,000.00
29 ASh(c),V:Nazis;French Underground	1,000.00
30 SSh(c),Bucky Captured . .	1,000.00
31 ASh(c),Bondage(c)	900.00
32 SSh(c),V: Japanese Airforce	900.00
33 ASh(c),V:Nazis;Brenner Pass	900.00
34 SSh(c),Bondage(c)	900.00
35 SSh(c),CapA in Japan . .	900.00
36 Sh(c),V:Nazis;Hitler(c) . .	1,100.00
37 ASh(c),CapA in Berlin, A:Red Skull	1,000.00
38 ASh(c),V:Japs;Bondage(c)	1,000.00
39 ASh(c),V:Japs;Boulder Dam	1,000.00
40 SSh(c),V:Japs;Ammo Depot	1,000.00
41 ASh(c),FinalJapaneseWar(c)	800.00
42 ASh(c),V:Bank Robbers . .	800.00
43 ASh(c),V:Gangsters	800.00
44 ASh(c),V:Gangsters	800.00
45 ASh(c),V:Bank Robbers . .	800.00

46 ASh(c),Holocaust(c)	800.00
47 ASh(c),Final Nazi War(c) . .	800.00
48 ASh(c),V:Robbers	750.00
49 ASh(c),V:Sabatuers	800.00
50 ASh(c),V:Gorilla Gang	800.00
51 ASh(c),V:Gangsters	750.00
52 ASh(c),V:Atom Bomb Thieves	750.00
53 ASh(c),V:Burglars	750.00
54 ASh(c),TV Studio, V:Gangsters	750.00
55 V:Counterfeiters	750.00
56 SSh(c),V:Art Theives	750.00
57 Symbolic CapA(c)	750.00
58 ASh(c),V:Bank Robbers . . .	750.00
59 SSh(c)O:CapA Retold;Private Life of Captain America . .	1,200.00
60 V:The Human Fly	750.00
61 SSh(c),V:Red Skull; Bondage(c)	1,100.00
62 SSh(c),Kingdom of Terror . .	750.00
63 SSh(c),I&O:Asbestos Lady; The Parrot Strikes	800.00
64 Diamonds Spell Doom	750.00
65 When Friends Turn Foes . .	750.00
66 O:Golden Girl;Bucky Shot . .	850.00
67 E:Toro(in Human Torch); Golden Girl Team-Up	750.00
68 A:Golden Girl;Riddle of the Living Dolls	750.00
69 Weird Tales of the Wee Males, A:Sun Girl	750.00
70 A:Golden Girl,Sub-Mariner, Namora;Worlds at War	750.00
71 A:Golden Girl; Trapped . . .	750.00
72 Murder in the Mind	750.00
73 The Outcast of Time	750.00
74 A:Red Skull;Capt.America's Weird Tales	1,400.00
75 Thing in the Chest	750.00
76 JR(c),CapA CommieSmasher	750.00
77 CapA Commie Smasher . . .	500.00
78 JR(c),V:Communists; September, 1954	500.00

Captain America #102
© Marvel Entertainment Group

CAPTAIN AMERICA
Prev: **Tales of Suspense**
April, 1968

100 JK,A:Avengers	325.00
101 JK,I:4th Sleeper	90.00
102 JK,V:Red Skull,4th Sleeper	45.00
103 JK,V:Red Skull	45.00
104 JK,DA,JSo,V:Red Skull	45.00
105 JK,DA,A:Batroc	45.00
106 JK,Cap.Goes Wild	45.00
107 JK,Red Skull	45.00
108 JK,Trapster	45.00
109 JK,O:Captain America	50.00
110 JSo,JSt,A:Hulk,Rick Jones in Bucky Costume	60.00
111 JSo,JSt,I:Man Killer	55.00
112 JK,GT,Album	30.00
113 JSo,TP,Avengers, D:Madame Hydra	55.00
114 JR,SB,C:Avengers	25.00
115 JB,SB,A:Red Skull	25.00
116 GC,JSt,A:Avengers	25.00
117 JR(c),GC,JSt,I:Falcon	45.00
118 JR(c),GC,JSt,A:Falcon	20.00
119 GC,JSt,O:Falcon	20.00
120 GC,JSt,A:Falcon	20.00
121 GC,JSt,V:Man Brute	18.00
122 GC,JSt,Scorpion	15.00
123 GC,JSt,A:NickFury, V:Suprema	15.00
124 GC,JSt,I:Cyborg	15.00
125 GC,Mandarin	15.00
126 JK&BEv(c),GC,A:Falcon	15.00
127 GC,WW,A:Nick Fury	15.00
128 GC,V:Satan's Angels	15.00
129 GC,Red Skull	15.00
130 GC,I:Batroc	17.00
131 GC,V:Hood	13.00
132 GC,A:Bucky Barnes	13.00
133 GC,O:Modok,B:Capt.America/ Falcon Partnership	13.00
134 GC,V:Stone Face	13.00
135 JR(c),GC,TP,A:Nick Fury	13.00
136 GC,BEv,V:Tyrannus	13.00
137 GC,BEv,A:Spider-Man	15.00
138 JR,A:Spider-Man	14.00
139 JR,Falcon solo	10.00
140 JR,O:Grey Gargoyle	10.00
141 JR,JSt,V:Grey Gargoyle	10.00
142 JR,JSt,Nick Fury	10.00
143 JR,Red Skull	9.00
144 GM,JR,N:Falcon,V:Hydra	9.00
145 GK,JR,V:Hydra	9.00
146 JR(c),SB,V:Hydra	8.00
147 GK(c),SB,V:Hydra	8.00
148 SB,JR,Red Skull	8.00
149 GK(c),SB,JM,V:Batroc	8.00
150 K&R(c),SB,V:The Stranger	8.00
151 SB,V:Mr.Hyde	8.00
152 SB,V:Scorpion,Mr.Hyde	8.00
153 SB,JM,V:50's Cap	8.00
154 SB,V:50's Cap	8.00
155 SB,FMc,O:50's Cap	8.00
156 SB,FMc,V:50's Cap	8.00
157 SB,I:The Viper	8.00
158 SB,V:The Viper	7.00
159 SB,V:PlantMan,Porcupine	7.00
160 SB,FMc,V:Solarr	7.00
161 SB,V:Dr.Faustus	7.00
162 JSn(c),SB,V:Dr.Faustus	8.00
163 SB,I:Serpent Squad	8.00
164 JR(c),I:Nightshade	8.00
165 SB,FMc,V:Yellow Claw	7.00
166 SB,FMc,V:Yellow Claw	7.00
167 SB,V:Yellow Claw	7.00

Captain America #109
© Marvel Entertainment Group

168 SB,I&O:Phoenix (2nd Baron Zemo)	8.00
169 SB,FMc,C:Black Panther	7.00
170 K&R(c),SB,C:Black Panther	7.00
171 JR(c),SB,A:Black Panther	7.00
172 GK(c),SB,C:X-Men	16.00
173 GK(c),SB,A:X-Men	17.00
174 GK(c),SB,A:X-Men	17.00
175 SB,A:X-Men	17.00
176 JR(c),SB,O:Capt.America	1000
177 JR(c),SB,A:Lucifer,Beast	6.00
178 SB,A:Lucifer	6.00
179 SB,A:Hawkeye	6.00
180 GK(c),SB,I:1st Nomad(Cap)	8.00
181 GK(c),SB,I&O:New Cap	7.00
182 FR,Madam Hydra	7.00
183 GK(c),FR,R:Cap,D:New Cap	10.00
184 K&R(c),HT,A:Red Skull	6.00
185 GK(c),SB,FR,V:Red Skull	6.00
186 GK(c),FR,O:Falcon	7.00
187 K&R(c),FR,V:Druid	6.00
188 GK(c),SB,V:Druid	6.00
189 GK(c),FR,V:Nightshade	6.00
190 GK(c),FR,A:Nightshade	6.00
191 FR,A:Stilt Man,N.Fury	6.00
192 JR(c),FR,A:Dr.Faustus	6.00
193 JR(c),JK,'Mad Bomb'	6.00
194 JK,I:Gen.Heshin	6.00
195 JK,1984	6.00
196 JK,Madbomb	6.00
197 JK,Madbomb	6.00
198 JK,Madbomb	6.00
199 JK,Madbomb	6.00
200 JK,Madbomb	7.00
201 JK,Epilogue	5.00
202 JK,Night People	5.00
203 JK,Night People	5.00
204 JK,I:Argon	5.00
205 JK,V:Argon	5.00
206 JK,I:Swine	5.00
207 JK,V:Swine	5.00
208 JK,I:Arnim Zola,D:Swine	5.00
209 JK,O:Arnim Zola,I:Primus	5.00
210 JK,A:Red Skull	5.00
211 JK,A:Red Skull	5.00

212 JK,A:Red Skull	5.00
213 JK,I:Night Flyer	5.00
214 JK,D:Night Flyer	5.00
215 GT,Redwing	5.00
216 Reprint,JK	5.00
217 JB, I:Quasar(Marvel Boy) I:Vamp	6.00
218 SB,A:Iron Man	5.00
219 SB,JSt,V:TheCorporation	5.00
220 SB,D:L.Dekker	5.00
221 SB,Ameridroid	5.00
222 SB,I:Animus(Vamp)	5.00
223 SB,Animus	5.00
224 MZ,V:Animus	5.00
225 SB,A:Nick Fury	5.00
226 SB,A:Nick Fury	5.00
227 SB,A:Nick Fury	5.00
228 SB,Constrictor	5.00
229 SB,R:SuperAgents of Shield	5.00
230 SB,A:Hulk	5.00
231 SB,DP,A:Grand Director	5.00
232 SB,DP,V:Grand Director	5.00
233 SB,DP,D:Sharon Carter	5.00
234 SB,DP,A:Daredevil	5.50
235 SB,FM,A:Daredevil	5.50
236 SB,V:Dr.Faustus	5.00
237 SB,'From the Ashes'	5.00
238 SB,V:Hawk Riders	5.00
239 JBy(c),SB,V:Hawk Riders	5.00
240 SB,V:A Guy Named Joe	5.00
241 A:Punisher	50.00
242 JSt,A:Avengers	4.00
243 GP(c),RB,V:Adonis	4.00
244 TS,'A Monster Berserk'	4.00
245 CI,JRn,Nazi Hunter	4.00
246 GP(c),JBi,V:Joe	4.00
247 JBy,V:BaronStrucker	5.50
248 JBy,JRu,Dragon Man	5.50
249 JBy,O:Machinesmith, A:Air-Walker	5.50
250 JBy,Cap for Pres	5.50
251 JBy,V:Mr.Hyde	5.50
252 JBy,V:Batrok	5.50
253 JBy,V:Baron Blood	5.50
254 JBy,D:B.Blood,UnionJack,I:3rd Union Jack	5.50
255 JBy,40th Anniv.,O:Cap	5.50
256 GC,V:Demon Druid	3.50
257 A:Hulk	3.50
258 MZ,V:Blockbuster	3.50
259 MZ,V:Dr. Octopus	3.50
260 AM,In Jail	3.50
261 MZ,A:Nomad	4.00
262 MZ,V:Ameridroid	3.50
263 MZ,V:Red Skull	3.50
264 MZ,X-Men	5.00
265 MZ,A:Spider-Man,N.Fury	4.00
266 MZ,A:Spider-Man	4.00
267 MZ,V:Everyman	3.50
268 MZ,A:Defenders(x-over from Def.#106)	3.50
269 MZ,A:Team America	3.50
270 MZ,V:Tess-One	3.50
271 MZ,V:Mr.X	3.50
272 MZ,I:Vermin	4.50
273 MZ,A:Nick Fury	3.50
274 MZ,D:SamSawyer	3.50
275 MZ,V:Neo-Nazis	3.50
276 MZ,V:Baron Zemo	3.50
277 MZ,V:Baron Zemo	3.50
278 MZ,V:Baron Zemo	3.50
279 MZ,V:Primus	3.50
280 MZ,V:Scarecrow	3.50
281 MZ,A:Spider Woman, R:'50's Bucky	3.50

Captain America #310
© Marvel Entertainment Group

282 MZ,I:2nd Nomad 8.50
282a (second primting) 2.00
283 MZ,A:Viper 4.00
284 SB,Nomad 3.50
285 MZ,V:Porcupine 3.50
286 MZ,V:Deathlok 6.00
287 MZ,V:Deathlok 6.00
288 MZ,V:Deathlok,D:Hellinger .. 6.00
289 MZ,A:Red Skull 3.50
290 JBy(c),RF,A:Falcon 3.50
291 JBy(c),HT,V:Tumbler 3.50
292 I&O:Black Crow 3.50
293 V:Mother Superior 3.50
294 R:Nomad 3.50
295 V:Sisters of Sin 3.50
296 V:Baron Zemo 3.50
297 O:Red Skull 3.50
298 V:Red Skull 3.50
299 V:Red Skull 3.50
300 D:Red Skull 5.00
301 PNe,A:Avengers 2.50
302 PNe,I:Machete,V:Batroc 2.50
303 PNe,V:Batroc 2.50
304 PNe,V:Stane Armor 2.50
305 PNe,A:Capt.Britain,V:Modred 2.75
306 PNe,A:Capt.Britain,V:Modred 2.75
307 PNe,I:Madcap 2.50
308 PNe,I:Armadillo,
     Secret WarsII 2.50
309 PNe,V:Madcap 2.50
310 PNe,V:Serpent Society,I:Cotton
     Mouth,Diamondback 3.50
311 PNe,V:Awesome Android ... 2.50
312 PNe,I:Flag Smasher 2.50
313 PNe,D:Modok 2.50
314 PNe,A:Nighthawk 2.50
315 PNe,V:Serpent Society 2.50
316 PNe,A:Hawkeye 2.50
317 PNe,I:Death-Throws 2.50
318 PNe,V&D:Blue Streak 2.50
319 PNe,V:Scourge,D:Vamp 2.50
320 PNe,V:Scourge 2.50
321 PNe,V:Flagsmasher,
     I:Ultimatum 2.50
322 PNe,V:Flagsmasher 2.50

323 PNe,I:Super Patriot
     (US Agent) 5.00
324 PNe,V:Whirlwind,Trapster ... 2.50
325 I:Slug,A:Nomad 2.50
326 V:Dr.Faustus 2.50
327 MZ(c)V:SuperPatriot 4.00
328 MZ(c),I:Demolition Man 2.50
329 MZ(c),A:Demolition Man 2.50
330 A:Night Shift,Shroud 2.50
331 A:Night Shift,Shroud 2.50
332 BMc,Rogers resigns 11.00
333 B:John Walker Becomes
     6th Captain America 10.00
334 I:4th Bucky 6.00
335 V:Watchdogs 5.00
336 A:Falcon 3.50
337 TMo,I:The Captain 3.50
338 KD,AM,V:Professor Power .. 3.50
339 KD,TD,Fall of Mutants,
     V:Famine 3.50
340 KD,AM,A:Iron Man, ... 3.00
341 KD,AM,I:Battlestar,A:Viper .. 2.50
342 KD,AM,A:D-Man,Falcon,
     Nomad,Viper 2.50
343 KD,AM,A:D-Man,Falcon,
     Nomad 2.50
344 KD,AM,A:D-Man,Nomad 3.00
345 KD,AM,V:Watchdogs 2.50
346 KD,AM,V:Resistants 2.50
347 KD,AM,V:RWinger&LWinger . 2.50
348 KD,AM,V:Flag Smasher 2.50
349 KD,AM,V:Flag Smasher 2.50
350 KD,AM,doub-size,Rogers Ret.
     as Captain Am,V:Red Skull,
     E:6th Cap 5.00
351 KD,AM,A:Nick Fury 2.50
352 KD,AM,I:Supreme Soviets ... 2.50
353 KD,AM,V:Supreme Soviets .. 2.50
354 KD,AM,I:USAgent,
     V:Machinesmith 4.00
355 RB,AM,A:Falcon,Battlestar .. 2.50
356 AM,V:Sisters of Sin 2.50
357 KD,AM,V:Sisters of Sin
     Baron Zemo,Batroc 2.50
358 KD,B:Blood Stone Hunt 2.50
359 KD,V:Zemo,C:Crossbones .. 2.00
360 KD,I:Crossbones 2.75
361 KD,V:Zemo,Batroc 2.00
362 KD,V:Zemo,Crossbones 2.00
363 KD,E:Blood Stone Hunt,
     V:Crossbones,C:Wolverine ... 2.00
364 KD,V:Crossbones 2.00
365 KD,Acts of Vengeance,
     V:SubMariner,Red Skull 2.00
366 1st RLm Capt.Amer.,Acts of
     Vengeance,V:Controller 2.50
367 KD,Acts of Vengeance,
     Magneto Vs. Red Skull 3.00
368 RLm,V:Machinesmith 2.00
369 RLm,I:Skeleton Crew 2.00
370 RLm,V:Skeleton Crew 2.00
371 RLm,V:Trump,Poundcakes .. 2.00
372 RLm,B:Streets of Poison,
     Cap on Drugs,C:Bullseye ... 2.50
373 RLm,V:Bullseye,V:Bl.Widow . 2.00
374 RLm,V:Bullseye,A:Daredevil . 2.00
375 RLm,A:Daredevil 2.00
376 RLm,A:Daredevil 2.00
377 RLm,V:Crossbones,Bullseye . 2.00
378 RLm,E:Streets of Poison,Red
     Skull vs Kingpin,V:Crossbones 2.00
379 RLm(c),V:Serpent Society ... 2.00
380 RLm,V:Serpent Society 2.00
381 RLm,V:Serpent Society 2.00
382 RLm,V:Serpent Society 2.00

383 RLm(c),RLm,50th Anniv.
     64Pages 5.00
384 RLm,A:Jack Frost 2.00
385 RLm,A:USAgent 2.00
386 RLm,Cap./USAgent T.U. 2.00
387 B:Superia Strategem 2.00
388 A:Paladin 2.00
389 Superia Strategem #3 ...... 2.00
390 Superia Strategem #4 ...... 2.00
391 Superia Strategem #5 ...... 2.00
392 E:Superia Strategem 2.00
393 V:Captain Germany 1.75
394 A:Red Skull,Diamondback ... 1.75
395 A:Red Skull,Crossbones 1.75
396 I:2nd Jack O'Lantern 2.00
397 V:Red Skull,X-Bones,Viper .. 1.75
398 Operation:Galactic Storm
     Pt.1,V:Warstar 2.00
399 Operation Galactic Storm
     Pt.8,V:Kree Empire 1.75
400 Operation Galactic Storm
     Pt.15,BU:rep.Avengers #4 .... 3.50
401 R:D-Man,A:Avengers 1.75
402 RLe,B:Man & Wolf,
     A:Wolverine 2.00
403 RLe,A:Wolverine 2.00
404 RLe,A:Wolverine 2.00
405 RLe,A:Wolverine 2.00
406 RLe,A:Wolverine 2.00
407 RLe,A:Wolverine,Cable 2.00
408 RLe,E:Man & Wolf 1.75
409 RLe,V:Skeleton Crew 1.50
410 RLe,V:Crossbones,Skel.Crew . 1.50
411 RLe,V:Snapdragon 1.50
412 RLe,V:Batroc,A:Shang-Chi .. 1.50
413 A:Shang-Chi,V:Superia 1.50
414 RLe,A:Kazar,Black Panther .. 1.50
415 Rle,A:Black Panther,Kazar .. 1.50
416 RLe,Savage Land Mutates,
     A:Black.Panther,Kazar 1.50
417 RLe,A:Black Panther,Kazar,
     V:AIM 1.50
418 RLe,V:Night People 1.50
419 RLe,V:Viper 1.50
420 RLe,I:2nd Blazing Skull,
     A:Nightshift 2.95
421 RLe,V:Nomad 1.50
422 RLe,I:Blistik 1.50
423 RTs(s),MCW,V:Namor 1.50
424 MGv(s),A:Sidewinder 1.50
425 B:MGu(s),DHv,Embossed(c),I:2nd
     Super Patriot,Dead Ringer .. 3.25
426 DHv,A:Super Patriot,Dead Ringer,
     V:Resistants 1.50
427 DHv,V:Super Patriot,Dead
     Ringer 1.75
428 DHv,I:Americop 1.75
429 DHv,V:Kono 1.75
430 Daemon Dran, Americop 1.75
431 DHv,I:Free Spirit 1.50
432 DHv,Fighting Chance 1.50
433 DHv,Baron Zemo 1.50
434 DHv,A:Fighting Spirit,
     V:King Cobra 1.50
435 DHv,Fighting Chance 1.50
436 V:King Cobra, Mister Hyde,
     Fighting Chance conclusion .. 1.50
437 Cap in a Coma 1.50
438 I:New Body Armor 1.50
439 Dawn's Early Light,pt.2 ..... 1.50
440 Taking A.I.M.,pt.1 .... 1.50
441 Taking A.I.M.,pt.3 .... 1.50
Ann.#1 rep. 16.00
Ann.#2 rep. 11.00
Ann.#3 JK 5.00

Captain America Ann. #8
© Marvel Entertainment Group

Ann.#4 JK,V:Magneto,I:Mutant
  Force 10.00
Ann.#5 'Deathwatcher' 4.00
Ann.#6 A:Contemplator 4.00
Ann.#7 O:Shaper of Worlds 4.00
Ann.#8 MZ,A:Wolverine 48.00
Ann.#9 MBa,SD,Terminus Factor
  #1,N:Nomad 4.50
Ann.#10 MM,Baron Strucker,pt.3
  (see Punisher Ann.#4) 2.50
Ann.#11 Citizen Kang#1 . . . . . . 2.50
Ann.#12 I:Bantam,w/card 3.25
Ann.#13 RTs(s),MCW, ... 3.25
Drug Wars PDd(s),SaV,A:New
  Warriors 2.00
G-Size#1 GK(c),rep.O:Cap.Amer. 12.00
HC vol.Slipcase Rep.#1
  thru #10 (From 1940's) 75.00
Medusa Effect RTs(s),MCW,RB,
  V:Master Man 2.95
Movie Adapt 2.00
Spec.#1 Rep.Cap.A #110,#111 . . 2.00
Spec.#2 Rep.Cap.A.#113
  & Strange Tales #169 . . . . . . 2.00
TPB Bloodstone Hunt,rep.
  #357-364 . . . . 15.95
TPB Streets of Poison,
  rep. #372–#377
TPB War and Remembrance,
  rep. #247–#255 . . . . 12.95
Collector's Preview 1.95
Ashcan 75

CAPTAIN BRITAIN
CLASSICS
1 AD rep. 2.50

CAPTAIN CONFEDERACY
Epic
November, 1991
1 I:Capt.Confederacy,Kid Dixie . . 2.25
2 Meeting of Superhero Reps . . . 2.25
3 Framed for Murder 2.25
4 Superhero conference,final iss. 2.25

CAPTAIN JUSTICE
March, 1988
1 Based on TV Series 1.00
2 April, 1988 . . . . 1.00

CAPTAIN MARVEL
May, 1968
1 GC,O:retold,V:Sentry#459 . . 110.00
2 GC,V:Super Skrull 32.00
3 GC,V:Super Skrull 20.00
4 GC,Sub-Mariner 20.00
5 DH,I:Metazoid 20.00
6 DH,I:Solam 12.00
7 JR(c),DH,V:Quasimodo 12.00
8 DH,I:Cuberex 12.00

Captain Marvel #2
© Marvel Entertainment Group

9 DH,D:Cuberex 12.00
10 DH,V:Number 1 . . . . 11.00
11 BWS(c),I:Z0 . . . . 11.00
12 K&R(c),I:Man-Slayer 8.00
13 FS,V:Man-Slayer 8.00
14 FS,Iron Man 8.00
15 TS,DA,Z0 . . . . 7.50
16 DH,Ronan 7.50
17 GK,DA,O:R.Jones ret,N:Capt.
  Marvel 8.50
18 GK,JB,DA,I:Mandroid 7.50
19 GK,DA,Master.of.MM 7.50
20 GK,DA,I:Rat Pack 7.50
21 GK,DA,Hulk 7.50
22 GK(c),WB,V:Megaton 7.50
23 GK(c),WB,FMc,V:Megaton . . 7.50
24 GK(c),WB,ECh,I:L.Mynde . . . 7.50
25 1st JSn,Cap.Marvel,Cosmic
  Cube Saga Begins 30.00
26 JSn,DC,Thanos(2ndApp.)
  A:Thing 35.00
27 JSn,V:Thanos,A:Mentor,
  Starfox, I:Death 25.00
28 JSn,DGr,Thanos Vs.Drax,
  A:Avengers 25.00
29 JSn,AM,O:Zeus,C:Thanos
  I:Eon,O:Mentor 14.00
30 JSn,AM,Controller,C:Thanos . 14.00
31 JSn,AM,Avengers,
  Thanos,Drax,Mentor 15.00
32 JSn,AM,DGr,O:Drax,
  Moondragon,A:Thanos 15.00

Captain Marvel #60
© Marvel Entertainment Group

33 JSn,KJ,E:Cosmic Cube Saga
  1st D:Thanos 25.00
34 JSn,JA,V:Nitro(leads to
  his Death) 8.00
35 GK(c),AA,Ant Man 4.00
36 AM,Watcher,Rep.CM#1 . . . . . 6.00
37 AM,KJ,Nimrod 4.00
38 AM,KJ,Watcher 4.00
39 AM,KJ,Watcher 4.00
40 AM,AMc,Watcher 4.00
41 AM,BWr,CR,BMc,TA,Kree . . . 4.50
42 AM,V:Stranger,C:Drax 4.50
43 AM,V:Drax 4.50
44 GK(c),AM,V:Drax 4.50
45 AM,I:Rambu 4.00
46 AM,TA,D:Fawn 4.00
47 AM,TA,A:Human Torch 4.00
48 AM,TA,I:Chetah 4.00
49 AM,V:Ronan,A:Cheetah 4.00
50 AM,TA,Avengers,
  V:Super Adaptiod 4.00
51 AM,TA,V:Mercurio,4-D Man . . 4.00
52 AM,TA,V:Phae-dor 4.00
53 AM,TA,A:Inhumans 4.00
54 PB,V:Nitro 4.00
55 PB,V:Death-grip 4.00
56 PB,V:Death-grip 4.00
57 PB,V:Thor,A:Thanos 8.00
58 PB,Drax/Titan 4.00
59 PB,Drax/Titan,I:Stellarax . . . 4.00
60 PB,Drax/Titan 4.00
61 PB,V:Chaos 4.00
62 PB,V:Stellarax 4.00
G-Size #1 reprints 8.00

CAPTAIN MARVEL
1989
1 MBr,I:Powerkeg,V:Moonstone . 3.00
1 DyM(s),MBr,V:Skinhead(1993) . 2.00
PF Death of Captain Marvel 7.95

CAPTAIN PLANET
October, 1991
1 I&O:Captain Planet 1.00
2 V:Dr.Blights' Smog Monster . . . 1.00
3 V:Looten Plunder 1.00
4 'Pollutionland' 1.25

---

5 V:Duke Nukem 1.25
6 A:Capt.Pollution,Eco-Villains . . 1.25
7 thru 9 . . . . @1.25
10 V:Litterbug 1.25
11 BHi,V:Greedly 1.25
12 V:Looten Plunder,last issue . . . 1.25

CAPT. SAVAGE & HIS LEATHERNECK RAIDERS
January, 1968
1 SSh(c),C:Sgt Fury;The Last
Bansai 12.50
2 SSh(c),O:Hydra;Return of Baron
Strucker 6.00
3 SSh,Two Against Hydra 6.00
4 SSh,V:Hydra;The Fateful Finale 6.00
5 SSh,The Invincible Enemy . . . 6.00
6 Mission;Save a Howler 6.00
7 SSh,Objective:Ben Grimm . . . 6.50
8 Mission:Foul Ball 6.00
Becomes:

CAPT. SAVAGE & HIS BATTLEFIELD RAIDERS
9 . . . . 6.00
10 To the Last Man 5.00
11 A:Sergeant Fury 5.00
12 V:The Japanese 3.75
13 The Junk Heap Juggernauts . . 5.00
14 Savage's First Mission 5.00
15 Within the Temple Waits Death 5.00
16 V:The Axis Powers 5.00
17 V:The Axis Powers 5.00
18 V:The Axis Powers 5.00
19 March, 1970 . . . . 5.00

CARE BEARS
Star
November, 1985
1 . . . . 1.50
2 thru 14 . . . . @1.00
Marvel
15 thru 20 . . . . @1.00

CARTOON KIDS
Atlas
1957
1 A:Dexter the Demon,Little
Zelda,Willie,Wise Guy 25.00

CAR WARRIORS
Epic
1990
1 Based on Roll Playing Game . . 2.25
2 Big Race Preparations 2.25
3 Ft.Delorean-Lansing Race begin 2.25
4 Race End, Final issue 2.25

CASEY–CRIME PHOTOGRAPHER
August, 1949
1 Ph(c),Girl on the Docks 90.00
2 Ph(c),Staats Cotsworth 55.00
3 Ph(c),He Walked With Danger 55.00
4 Ph(c),Lend Me Your Life . . . 55.00
Becomes:
TWO GUN WESTERN
[1st Series]
5 JB,B,I&O:Apache Kid 125.00
6 The Outcast 75.00
7 Human Sacrifice 75.00
8 JR,DW,A:Kid Colt,Texas Kid,

Doc Holiday 75.00
9 A:Kid Colt,Marshall"Frosty"
Bennet Texas Kid 75.00
10 . . . . 75.00
11 thru 13 . . . . @60.00
14 June, 1952 . . . . 60.00

CAT, THE
Nov., 1972—June 1973
1 JM,I&O:The Cat 11.00
2 JM,V:The Owl 7.00
3 BEv,V:Kraken 7.00
4 JSn,V:Man-Bull 7.00

CHAMBER OF CHILLS
November, 1972
1 SSh,A Dragon Stalks By
Night,(H.Ellison Adapt.) 5.00
2 FB,BEv,SD,Monster From the
Mound,(RE Howard Adapt.) . . 3.00
3 FB,BEv,SD, Thing on the Roof 3.00
4 FB,BEv,SD, Opener of the
Crypt,(J.Jakes,E.A.Poe Adapt) 3.00
5 FB,BEv,SD, Devils Dowry 3.00
6 FB,BEv,SD, Mud Monster 3.00
7 thru 24 FB,BEv,SD . . . . . . @3.00
25 FB,BEv,SD November, 1976 . . 3.00

CHAMBER OF DARKNESS
October, 1969
1 JB, Tales of Maddening Magic 35.00
2 NA(script),Enter the Red Death 13.00
3 JK,BWS,JB, Something Lurks
on Shadow Mountain 15.00
4 BWS,JK Monster Man Came
Walking 42.00
5 JK,SD, And Fear Shall Follow
(Lovecraft Adapt.) 7.00
6 SD 7.00
7 SD,JK,BWr, Night of the
Gargoyle 20.00
8 DA,BEv, Beast that Walks Like
a Man Special, 5 Tales of
Maddening Magic,Jan. 1972 . . 7.00
Becomes:
MONSTERS ON THE PROWL
9 SAD,BWS,Monster Stories
Inc,Gorgilla 7.50
10 JK,Roc 5.00
11 JK,A Titan Walks the Land . . . 5.00
12 HT,JK,Gomdulla The Living
Pharoah 5.00
13 HT,JK,Tragg 5.00
14 JK,SD,Return of the Titan 5.00
15 FrG,JK,The Thing Called It . . . 5.00
16 JSe,SD,JK, Serpent God of
Lost Swamp,A:King Kull 5.00
17 JK,SD,The Coming of Colossus 5.00
18 JK,SD,Bruttu 5.00
19 JK,SD,Creature From the
Black Bog 5.00
20 JK,SD,Oog Lives Again 5.00
21 JK,SD,A Martian Stalks
the City 5.00
22 JK,SD,Monster Runs Amok . . . 3.00
23 JK,SD,The Return of Grogg . . . 3.00
24 JK,SD, Magnetor 3.00
25 JK,Colossus Lives Again 3.00
26 JK,SD,The Two Headed Thing 3.00
27 JK,Sserpo 3.00
28 JK,The Coming of Monsteroso 3.00
29 JK,SD Monster at my Window . 3.00

30 JK,Diablo Demon from the 5th
Dimension, October, 1974 . . . . 3.00

Champions #1
© *Marvel Entertainment Group*

CHAMPIONS
June, 1986
1 GK(c),DH,I&O:Champions . . . 20.00
2 DH,O:Champions 14.00
3 GT,Assault on Olympus 13.00
4 GT,'Murder at Malibu' 12.00
5 DH,I:Rampage 12.00
6 JK(c),GT,V:Rampage 12.00
7 GT,O:Black Widow,I:Darkstar . 12.00
8 BH,O:Black Widow 12.00
9 BH,BL,V:Crimson Dynamo . . . 12.00
10 BH,BL,V:Crimson Dynamo . . . 12.00
11 JBy,A:Black Goliath,Hawkeye 13.00
12 JBy,BL,V:Stranger 13.00
13 JBy,BL,V:Kamo Tharn 13.00
14 JBy,I:Swarm 13.00
15 JBy,V:Swarm 13.00
16 BH,A:Magneto,Dr.Doom,
Beast 12.00
17 GT,JBy,V:Sentinels,last issue 13.00

CHILDREN OF THE VOYAGE
1 F:Sam Wantling 3.25
2 Counterfeit Man 2.25
3 V:Voyager 2.25
4 Last Issue 2.25

CHILI
May, 1969
1 . . . . 18.00
2 . . . . 10.00
3 . . . . 9.00
4 . . . . 9.00
5 . . . . 9.00
6 thru 15 . . . . @7.00
16 thru 20 . . . . @6.00
21 thru 25 . . . . @5.00
26 December, 1973 . . . . 5.00
Spec.#1,1971 . . . . 10.00

CHUCK NORRIS
Star
January, 1987

1 SD		1.00
2		1.00
3		1.00
4		1.00
5 September, 1987		1.00

CINDY COMICS
See: KRAZY COMICS

CLANDESTINE

Preview issue, Intro		1.50
1 MFm,AD,foil(c)		2.95
2		2.50
3 I:Argent,Kimera		2.50
4 R:Adam		2.50
5 MFm,AD,O:Adam Destine		2.50
6 A:Spider-Man		2.50
7 A:Spider-Man		2.50
8 A:Dr.Strange		2.50
9 Training Time		2.50
10 A:Britanic		2.50

CLASSIC CONAN
See: CONAN SAGA

CLASSIC X-MEN
See: X-MEN

CLIVE BARKER'S
BOOK OF THE DAMNED
Epic
November, 1991

1 JBo,Hellraiser companion		4.95
2 MPa,Hellraiser Companion		4.95

CLIVE BARKER'S
HELLRAISER
Epic

1 BWr,DSp		9.00
2		8.00
3		6.50
4		6.25
5		6.25
6		6.25
7 The Devil's Brigade #1		6.25
8 The Devil's Brigade #2&3		6.25
9 The Devil's Brigade #4&5		6.25
10 The Devil's Brigade #6&7 foil Cover		5.50
11 The Devil's Brigade #8&9		4.50
12 The Devil's Brigade #10-12		4.50
13 MMi,RH,Devil's Brigade #13		4.50
14 The Devil's Brigade #14		4.95
15 The Devil's Brigade #15		4.95
16 E:Devil's Brigade		4.95
17 BHa,DR,The Harrowing		4.95
18 O:Harrowers		4.95
19 A:Harrowers		4.95
20 NGa(s),DMc,Last Laugh		4.95

CLOAK & DAGGER
(Limited Series)
October, 1983

1 RL,TA,I:Det.O'Reilly, Father Delgado		2.50
2 RL,TA,V:Duane Hellman		2.00
3 RL,TA,V:Street Gang		2.00
4 RL,TA,O:Cloak & Dagger,		2.00

CLOAK & DAGGER
[1st Regular Series]
July 1985

1 RL,Pornography		2.00
2 RL,Dagger's mother		1.50
3 RL,A:Spider-Man		2.00
4 RL,Secret Wars II		1.50
5 RL,I:Mayhem		1.25
6 RL,A:Mayhem		1.25
7 RL,A:Mayhem		1.25
8 TA, Drugs		1.50
9 AAd,TA,A:Mayhem		3.00
10 BBI,TA,V:Dr. Doom		1.25
11 BBI,TA,Last Issue		1.25

[Mutant Misadventures of]
CLOAK & DAGGER
[2nd Regular Series]
October, 1988

1 CR(i),A:X-Factor		3.00
2 CR(i),C:X-Factor,V:Gromitz		2.50
3 SW(i),JLe(c),A:Gromitz		2.00
4 TA(i),Inferno,R:Mayhem		2.00
5 TA(i),R:Mayhem		2.00
6 TA(i),A:Mayhem		1.75
7 A:Crimson Daffodil,V:Ecstacy		1.75
8 Acts of Vengeance prelude		1.75
9 Acts of Vengeance		2.00
10 Acts of Vengeance,"X-Force" name used,Dr.Doom		2.50
11		1.50
12 A:Dr.Doom		1.50
13 A:Dr.Doom		1.50
14 RL		1.50
15 RL		1.50
16 RL,A:Spider-Man		2.50
17 A:Spider-Man,		2.50
18 Inf.Gauntlet X-over, A:Spider-Man, Ghost Rider		3.00
19 O:Cloak & Dagger,final issue		2.50
GNv Predator and Prey		14.95

CODENAME: GENETIX

1 PGa,A:Wolverine		2.00
2 PGa,V:Prime EvilA:Wolverine		2.00
3		2.00
4 A:Wolverine,Kazar		2.00

CODE NAME: SPITFIRE
See: SPITFIRE AND
THE TROUBLESHOOTERS

COLOSSUS:
GOD'S COUNTRY

PF V:Cold Warriors		6.95

COMBAT
Atlas
June, 1952

1 War Stories, Bare Bayonets		75.00
2 Break Thru,(Dedicated to US Infantry)		35.00
3		25.00
4		40.00
5 thru 10		@25.00
11 April, 1953		25.00

COMBAT CASEY
See: WAR COMBAT

COMBAT KELLY AND
THE DEADLY DOZEN
Atlas
November, 1951

1 RH,Korean war stories		100.00
2 Big Push		50.00
3 The Volunteer		30.00
4 V:Communists		30.00
5 OW,V:Communists		30.00
6 V:Communists		30.00
7 V: Communists		30.00
8 Death to the Reds		30.00
9		30.00
10		30.00
11		25.00
12 thru 16		@25.00
17 A:Combat Casey		35.00
18 A:Battle Brady		15.00
19 V:Communists		15.00
20 V:Communists		15.00
21 Transvestite Cover		30.00
22 thru 40		@15.00
41 thru 44 August, 1957		@15.00

COMBAT KELLY
June, 1972

1 JM, Stop the Luftwaffe		3.00
2 The Big Breakout		2.00
3 O:Combat Kelly		2.00
4 Mutiny,A:Sgt.Fury and the Howling Commandoes		2.00
5 Escape or Die		2.00
6 The Fortress of Doom		2.00
7 Nun Hostage,V:Nazis		2.00
8 V:Nazis		2.00
9 October, 1973		2.00

COMET MAN
February, 1987

1 BSz(c),I:Comet Man		1.50
2 BSz(c),A:Mr.Fantastic		1.00
3 BSz(c),A:Hulk		1.00
4 BSz(c),A:Fantistic Four		1.00
5 BSz(c),A:Fantastic Four		1.00
6 BSz(c),Last issue, July,1987		1.00

COMIX BOOK
(black & white magazine)
1974

1		7.50
2		4.50
3		5.00
4		3.75
5 1976		3.75

COMMANDO
ADVENTURES
Atlas
June, 1957

1 Seek, Find and Destroy		35.00
2 MD, Hit 'em and Hit 'em Hard, August,1957		30.00

COMPLETE COMICS
See: AMAZING COMICS

COMPLETE MYSTERY
August, 1948

1 Seven Dead Men		175.00
2 Jigsaw of Doom		125.00
3 Fear in the Night		125.00
4 A Squealer Dies Fast		125.00

Becomes:

TRUE COMPLETE
MYSTERY

5 Rice Mancini,
   The Deadly Dude 110.00
6 Ph(c),The Frame-up that Failed 90.00
7 Ph(c),Caught 90.00
8 Ph(c),The Downfall of Mr.
   Anderson, October, 1949 ... 90.00

CONAN
THE ADVENTURER

1 RT(s),RK,Red Foil(c) 3.00
2 RT(s),RK 1.75
3 RT(s),RK 1.50
4 .... 1.50
5 .... 1.50
6 .... 1.50
7 .... 1.50
8 .... 1.50
9 .... 1.50
10 .... 1.50
11 Torture Chamber 1.50
12 Abominations of Yondo 1.50
13 Seven Warriors 1.50
14 RTs,Young Conan,last issue .. 1.50

Conan the Barbarian #1
© Marvel Entertainment Group

CONAN THE BARBARIAN
October, 1979

1 BWS/DA,O:Conan,A:Kull ... 220.00
2 BWS/SB,Lair o/t Beast-Men .. 85.00
3 BWS,SB,Grey God Passes . 160.00
4 BWS,SB,Tower o/t Elephant . 60.00
5 BWS,Zukala's Daughter 60.00
6 BWS,SB,Devil Wings Over
   Shadizar 40.00
7 BWS,SB,DA,C:Thoth-Amon,
   I:Set 40.00
8 BWS,TS,TP,Keepers o/t Crypt 40.00
9 BWS,SB,Garden of Fear 40.00
10 BWS,SB,JSe,Beware Wrath of
   Anu;BU:Kull 45.00
11 BWS,SB,Talons of Thak 45.00
12 BWS,GK,Dweller in the Dark,

   Blood of the Dragon B.U. ... 28.00
13 BWS,SB,Web o/t Spider-God 28.00
14 BWS,SB,Green Empress of
   Melnibone 45.00
15 BWS,SB 45.00
16 BWS,Frost Giant's Daughter . 25.00
17 GK,Gods of Bal-Sagoth,
   A:Fafnir 13.00
18 GK,DA,Thing in the Temple,
   A:Fafnir 13.00
19 BWS,DA,Hawks from
   the Sea 25.00
20 BWS,DA,Black Hound of
   Vengeance,A:Fafnir 25.00
21 BWS,CR,VM,DA,SB, Monster
   of the Monoliths 20.00
22 BWS,DA,rep.Conan #1 ..... 24.00
23 BWS,DA,Shadow of the
   Vulture,I:Red Sonja 35.00
24 BWS,Song of Red Sonja ... 32.00
25 JB,SB,JSe,Mirrors of Kharam
   Akkad,A:Kull 12.00
26 JB,Hour of the Griffin 7.00
27 JB,Blood of Bel-Hissar 6.00
28 JB,Moon of Zembabwei 6.00
29 JB,Two Against Turan 6.00
30 JB,The Hand of Nergal 6.00
31 JB,Shadow in the Tomb 4.00
32 JB,Flame Winds of Lost Khitai 4.00
33 JB,Death & 7 Wizards 4.00
34 JB,Temptress in the Tower
   of Flame 4.00
35 JB,Hell-Spawn of Kara-Shehr . 4.00
36 JB,Beware of Hyrkanians
   bearing Gifts 4.00
37 NA,Curse of the Golden Skull . 8.00
38 JB,Warrior & Were-Woman ... 3.50
39 JB,Dragon from the
   Inland Sea 3.50
40 RB,Fiend from Forgotten City . 3.50
41 JB,Garden of Death & Life ... 3.50
42 JB,Night of the Gargoyle 3.50
43 JB,Tower o/Blood,A:RedSonja 3.50
44 JB,Flame&Fiend,A:RedSonja . 5.00
45 JB,Last Ballad of Laza-Lanti .. 5.00
46 JB,JSt,Curse of the Conjurer .. 3.50
47 JB,DA,Goblins in the
   Moonlight 3.50
48 JB,DG,DA,Rats Dance at Raven
   gard,BU:Red Sonja 3.50
49 JB,DG,Wolf-Woman 3.50
50 JB,DG,Dweller in the Pool ... 3.50
51 JB,DG,Man Born of Demon .. 3.00
52 JB,TP,Altar and the Scorpion . 3.00
53 JB,FS,Brothers of the Blade .. 3.00
54 JB,TP,Oracle of Ophir 3.00
55 JB,TP,Shadow on the Land .. 3.00
56 JB,High Tower in the Mist ... 3.00
57 MP,Incident in Argos 3.00
58 JB,Queen o/tBlackCoast,
   2nd A:Belit 4.00
59 JB,Ballad of Belit,O:Belit 3.00
60 JB,Riders o/t River Dragons . 3.00
61 JB,She-Pirate,I:Amra 2.50
62 JB,Lord of the Lions,O:Amra .. 2.50
63 JB,Death Among Ruins,
   V&D:Amra 2.50
64 JSon,AM,rep.Savage Tales#5 . 2.50
65 JB,Fiend o/tFeatheredSerpent . 2.50
66 JB,Daggers & Death Gods,
   C:Red Sonja 2.50
67 JB,Talons of the Man-Tiger,
   A:Red Sonja 2.50
68 JB,Of Once & Future Kings,
   V:KingKull,A:Belit,Red Sonja . 2.50

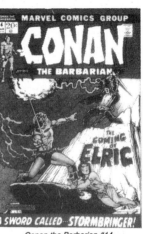

Conan the Barbarian #14
© Marvel Entertainment Group

69 VM,Demon Out of the Deep .. 2.50
70 JB,City in the Storm 2.50
71 JB,Secret of Ashtoreth 2.50
72 JB,Vengeance in Asgalun 2.50
73 JB,...In the Well of Skelos 2.50
74 JB,Battle at the Black Walls
   C:Thoth-Amon 2.50
75 JB,Hawk-Riders of Harakht ... 2.50
76 JB,Swordless in Stygia 2.50
77 JB,When Giants Walk
   the Earth 2.50
78 JB,rep.Savage Sword #1,
   A:Red Sonja 2.50
79 HC,Lost Valley of Iskander ... 2.50
80 HC,Trial By Combat 2.50
81 HC,The Eye of the Serpent ... 2.00
82 HC,The Sorceress o/t Swamp . 2.00
83 HC,The Dance of the Skull ... 2.00
84 JB,Two Against the Hawk-City,
   I:Zula 2.00
85 JB,Of Swordsmen & Sorcerers,
   O:Zulu 2.00
86 JB,Devourer of the Dead 2.00
87 TD, rep. Savage Sword #3... 2.00
88 JB,Queen and the Corsairs ... 2.00
89 JB,Sword & the Serpent,
   A:Thoth-Amon 2.00
90 JB,Diadem of the Giant-Kings . 2.00
91 JB,Savage Doings in Shem ... 2.00
92 JB,The Thing in the Crypt 2.00
93 JB,Of Rage & Revenge 2.00
94 JB,BeastKing ofAbombi,L:Zulu 2.00
95 JB,The Return of Amra 2.00
96 JB,Long Night of Fang
   & Talon,pt.1 .... 2.00
97 JB,Long Night of Fang
   & Talon,pt.2 .... 2.00
98 JB,Sea-Woman 2.00
99 JB,Devil Crabs o/t Dark Cliffs . 2.00
100 JB,Death on the Black Coast,
   D:Belit (double size) 3.50
101 JB,The Devil has many Legs . 1.75
102 JB,The Men Who
   Drink Blood 1.75
103 JB,Bride of the Vampire 1.75
104 JB,The Vale of Lost Women . 1.75
105 JB,Whispering Shadows 1.75
106 JB,Chaos in Kush 1.75

All comics prices listed are for *Near Mint* condition.

107 JB,Demon of the Night 1.75
108 JB,Moon-Eaters of Darfar . . . 1.75
109 JB,Sons o/t Bear God 1.75
110 JB,Beward t/Bear o/Heaven . 1.75
111 JB,Cimmerian Against a City . 1.75
112 JB,Buryat Besieged 1.75
113 JB,A Devil in the Family 1.75
114 JB,The Shadow of the Beast . 1.75
115 JB,A War of Wizards, A:Red
    Sonja Double size 10th Anniv.
    (L:Roy Thomas script) 2.50
116 JB,NA,Crawler in the Mist . . 1.75
117 JB,Corridor of Mullah-Kajar . . 1.75
118 JB,Valley of Forever Night . . 1.75
119 JB,Voice of One Long Gone . 1.75
120 JB,The Hand of Erlik 1.75
121 JB,BMc,Price of Perfection . . 1.75
122 JB,BMc,The City Where Time
    Stood Still 1.75
123 JB,BMc,Horror Beneath the
    Hills 1.75
124 JB,BMc,the Eternity War 1.75
125 JB,BMc,the Witches ofNexxx . 1.75
126 JB,BMc,Blood Red Eye
    of Truth 1.75
127 GK,Snow Haired Woman
    of the Wastes 1.75
128 GK,And Life Sprang Forth
    From These 1.75
129 GK,The Creation Quest 1.75
130 GK,The Quest Ends 1.75

131 GK,The Ring of Rhax 1.75
132 GK,Games of Gharn 1.75
133 GK,The Witch of Widnsor . . . 1.75
134 GK,A Hitch in Time 1.75
135 MS,JRu,The Forest o/t Night . 1.75
136 JB,The River of Death 1.75
137 AA,Titans Gambit 1.75
138 VM,Isle of the Dead 1.75
139 VM,In the Lair of
    the Damned 1.75
140 JB,Spider Isle 1.75
141 JB,The Web Tightens 1.75
142 JB,The Maze,the Man,
    the Monster 1.75
143 JB,Life Among the Dead 1.75
144 JB,The Blade & the Beast . . . 1.75
145 Son of Cimmeria 1.75
146 JB,Night o/t Three Sisters . . 1.75
147 JB,Tower of Mitra 1.75
148 JB,The Plague of Forlek 1.75
149 JB,Deathmark 1.75
150 JB,Tower of Flame 1.75
151 JB,Vale of Death 1.50
152 JB,Dark Blade of
    Jergal Zadh 1.50
153 JB,Bird Men of Akah Ma'at . . 1.50
154 JB,the Man-Bats of
    Ur-Xanarrh 1.50
155 JB,SL,The Anger of Conan . . 1.50
156 JB,The Curse 1.50
157 JB,The Wizard 1.50
158 JB,Night of the Wolf 1.50
159 JB,Cauldron of the Doomed . 1.50
160 Veil of Darkness 1.50
161 JB,House of Skulls,A:Fafnir . 1.50
162 JB,Destroyer in the Flame,
    A:Fafnir 1.50
163 JB,Cavern of the Vines of
    Doom,A:Fafnir 1.50
164 The Jeweled Sword of Tem . 1.50
165 JB,V:Nadine 1.50
166 JB,GI,Blood o/t Titan,A:Fafnir 1.50
167 JB,Creature From Time's

Conan the Barbarian #83
© Marvel Entertainment Group

    Dawn,A:Fafnir 1.50
168 JB,Bird Woman & the Beast . 1.50
169 JB,Tomb of the Scarlet Mage 1.50
170 JB,Dominion of the Dead,
    A&D:Fafnir 1.50
171 JB,Barbarian Death Song . . 1.50
172 JB,Reavers in Borderland . . . 1.50
173 JB,Honor Among Thieves . . . 1.50
174 JB,V:Tetra 1.50
175 JB,V:Spectre ofDeath 1.50
176 JB,Argos Rain 1.50
177 JB,V:Nostume 1.50
178 JB,A:Tetra,Well of Souls 1.50
179 JB,End of all there is,A:Kiev . 1.50
180 JBV:AnitRenrut 1.50
181 JB,V:KingMaddoc II 1.50
182 JB,V:King of Shem 1.50
183 JB,V:Imhotep 1.50
184 JB,V:Madoc 1.50
185 JB,R:Tetra 1.50
186 JB,The Crimson Brotherhood 1.50
187 JB,V:Council of Seven 1.50
188 JB,V:Devourer-Souls 1.50
189 JB,V:Devourer-Souls 1.50
190 JB,Devourer-Souls 1.50
191 Deliverance 1.50
192 JB,V:TheKeeper 1.50
193 Devourer-Souls 1.50
194 V:Devourer-Souls 1.50
195 Blood of Ages 1.50
196 V:Beast 1.50
197 A:Red Sonja 1.50
198 A:Red Sonja 1.50
199 O:Kaleb 1.50
200 JB,D.sizeV:Dev-Souls 2.00
201 NKu,GI,Thulsa Doom 1.50
202 . . . . 1.50
203 V:Thulsa Doom 1.50
204 VS,GI,A:Red Sonja,I:Strakkus 1.50
205 A:Red Sonja 1.50
206 VS,GI,Heku trilogy,pt.1 . . . . . 1.50
207 VS,GI,Heku,pt.2,O:Kote 1.50
208 VS,GI,Heku,pt.3 . . . . 1.50
209 VS,GI,Heku epilogue 1.50
210 VS,GI,V:Sevante 1.50
211 VS,GI,V:Sevante 1.50
212 EC,GI 1.50
213 V:Ghamud Assassins 1.50

214 AA 1.50
215 VS,AA,Conan Enslaved 1.50
216 V:Blade of Zed 1.50
217 JLe(c),V:Blade of Zed 1.50
218 JLe(c),V:Picts 1.50
219 JLe(c),V:Forgotten Beasts . . 1.50
220 Conan the Pirate 1.50
221 Conan the Pirate 1.50
222 AA,DP,Revenge 1.50
223 AA,Religious Cult 1.50
224 AA,Cannibalism 1.50
225 AA,Conan Blinded 1.50
226 AA,Quest for Mystic Jewel . . 1.50
227 AA,Mystic Jewel,pt.2 . . . . 1.50
228 AA,Cannibalism,pt.1 . . . . 1.50
229 AA,Cannibalism,pt.2 . . . . 1.50
230 FS,SDr,Citadel,pt.1 . . . . 1.50
231 FS,DP,Citadel,pt.2 . . . . 1.50
232 RLm,Birth of Conan 3.00
233 RLm,DA,B:Conan as youth . 2.00
234 RLm,DA 2.00
235 RLm,DA 2.00
236 RLm,DA 2.00
237 DA,V:Jormma 1.50
238 DA,D:Conan 1.50
239 Conan Possessed 1.50
240 Conan Possessed 1.50
241 TM(c),R:RoyThomasScript . 3.50
242 JLe(c),A:Red Sonja 2.50
243 WPo(c),V:Zukala 2.00
244 A:Red Sonja,Zula 1.50
245 A:Red Sonja,V:King
    of Vampires 1.50
246 A:Red Sonja,V:MistMonster . . 1.50
247 A:Red Sonja,Zula 1.50
248 V:Zulu 1.50
249 A:Red Sonja,Zula 1.50
250 A:RedSonja,Zula,V:Zug
    double size. 2.00
251 Cimmeria,V:Shumu Gorath . . 1.50
252 ECh 1.50
253 ECh,V:Kulan-Goth(X-Men
    Villain) 1.50
254 ECh,V:Shuma-Gorath (Dr.
    Strange Villain) 1.50
255 ECh,V:Shuma-Gorath 1.50
256 ECh,D:Nemedia's King 1.50
257 ECh,V:Queen Vammator 1.50
258 AA(i),A:Kulan Gath 1.50
259 V:Shuma-Gorath 1.50
260 AA(i),V:Queen Vammatar . . . 1.50
261 V:Cult of the Death Goddess . 1.50
262 V:The Panther 1.50
263 V:Malaq 1.50
264 V:Kralic 1.50
265 V:Karlik 1.50
266 Conan the Renegade(adapt) . 1.50
267 adaption of Tor 1.50
268 adaption of Tor 1.50
269 V:Agohoth,Prince Borin 1.50
270 Devourer of the Dead 1.50
271 V:Devourer of Souls 1.50
272 V:Devourer 1.50
273 V:Purple Lotus 1.50
274 V:She-Bat 1.50
275 RTs(s),Last Issue cont. in
    Savage Sword of Conan 5.00
Giant#1 GK,TS,Hour of the
    Dragon, inc.rep.Conan#3,
    I:Belit 8.00
Giant#2 GK,TS,Conan Bound,
    inc. rep Conan #5 . . . . 5.00
Giant#3 GK,TS,To Tarantia
    & the Tower,inc.rep.Conan#6 . 5.00
Giant#4,GK,FS,Swords of the

Conan the Barbarian #178
© Marvel Entertainment Group

South,inc.rep.Conan #7 . . . . . 5.00
Giant#5 rep.Conan #14,#15
  & Back-up story #12 . . . . 5.00
KingSz.#1 rep.Conan #2,#4 . . . . 13.00
Ann.#2 BWS,Phoenix on the Sword
  A:Thoth-Amon 4.00
Ann.#3 JB,HC,Mountain of
  the Moon God, B.U.Kull story . 2.00
Ann.#4 JB,Return of the
  Conqueror,A:Zenobia 2.00
Ann.#5 JB,W:Conan/Zenobia 2.00
Ann.#6 GK,King of the
  Forgotten People 2.00
Ann.#7 JB,Red Shadows
  & Black Kraken 1.50
Ann.#8 VM,Dark Night of the
  White Queen 1.50
Ann.#9 . . . . 1.50
Ann.#10 Scorched Earth
  (Conan #176 x-over) 1.50
Ann.#11 . . . . 1.50
Conan-Barbarian Movie Spec.#1 . 1.25
Conan-Barbarian Movie Spec.#2 . 1.25
Conan-Destroyer Movie Spec.#1 . 1.25
Red Nails Special Ed.BWS 4.00
Conan & Ravagers Out of Time . . 9.95
Conan the Reaver 9.95
Conan the Rogue, JB,V:Romm . . 9.95
Horn of Azroth 9.95
Skull of Set 9.95

CLASSIC CONAN
June, 1987

1 BWS,rep. 2.00
2 BWS,rep. 2.00
3 BWS,rep. 2.00
Becomes:
CONAN SAGA
4 rep. 3.50
5 rep. 3.50
6 rep. 3.50
7 rep. 3.50
8 rep. 3.50
9 rep. 3.50
10 rep. 3.50

11 rep. 3.00
12 rep. 3.00
13 rep. 3.00
14 rep.Savage Sword #5 . . . . 3.00
15 rep.Savage Sword #7 . . . . 3.00
16 rep.Savage Sword #12 . . . . . . 3.00
17 rep.Savage Sword 3.00
18 rep.Savage Sword 3.00
19 rep.Savage Sword #28 . . . . . . 3.00
20 rep.Savage Sword #25 . . . . . . 3.00
21 rep.Savage Sword 3.00
22 rep.Giant Size Conan #1&2 . . 3.00
23 rep.Hour of the Dragon 3.00
24 rep.Hour of the Dragon 3.00
25 rep.Savage Sword 3.00
26 rep.Savage Sword #11 . . . . . . 3.00
27 rep.Savage Sword #15 . . . . . . 3.00
28 rep.Savage Sword #16 . . . . . . 2.25
29 rep.Savage Sword #17 . . . . . . 2.25
30 rep.Savage Sword #18 . . . . . . 2.25
31 rep.Savage Sword #19 . . . . . . 2.25
32 rep.Savage Sword #5 . . . . 2.25
33 rep.Savage Sword #5 . . . . 2.25
34 rep.Savage Sword # 2.25
35 rep.Savage Sword #32 . . . . . . 2.25
36 rep.Savage Sword #12 . . . . . . 2.25
37 rep.Savage Sword #34 . . . . . . 2.25
38 rep.Conan #94&#95 . . . . 2.25
39 rep.Conan #96&#97 . . . . 2.25
40 rep.Savage Sword #26 . . . . . . 2.25
41 rep.Savage Sword #27 . . . . . . 2.25
42 rep.Savage Sword #40 . . . . . . 2.25
43 rep.Savage Sword #41 . . . . . . 2.25
44 rep.Savage Sword #42 . . . . . . 2.25
45 rep.Savage Sword #43 . . . . . . 2.25
46 rep.Savage Sword #15 . . . . . . 2.25
47 rep.Savage Sword #22 . . . . . . 2.25
48 rep.Savage Sword #23 . . . . . . 2.25
49 rep.Sav.Sword Super Spec#2 . 2.25
50 rep.Conan #58 . . . . 2.25
51 rep.Conan #59&#60 . . . . 2.25
52 rep.Conan #61 . . . . 2.25
53 thru 63 rep.Savage Sword . @2.25
64 thru 93 rep. . . . . @2.25
94 . . . . 2.25
95 D:Belit 2.25
96 . . . . 2.25
97 Red Sonja rep. 2.25
98 rep. #106–#108 . . . . 2.25

CONAN CLASSICS
1 rep. Conan #1 . . . . 2.00
2 rep. Conan #2 . . . . 2.00
3 rep. Conan #3 . . . . 1.75
4 rep. Conan #4 . . . . 1.50
5 rep. Conan #5 . . . . 1.50
6 rep. Conan #6 . . . . 1.50
7 rep. Conan #7 . . . . 1.50
8 rep. 1.50
9 Garden of Fear 1.50
10 V:Anu 1.50
11 New Sword Manuever 1.50

KING CONAN
March, 1980
1 JB,ECh,I:Conn,V:Thoth-Amon . 4.00
2 JB,Black Sphinx of Nebthu . . . 2.50
3 JB,Dragon Wings Over
  Zembabwei 2.50
4 JB,V:Thoth-Amon 2.50
5 JB,The Sorcerer in the Realm
  of Madness 2.50
6 JB,The Lady's Name Is..Trouble 2.50
7 PS,JB 2.75
8 A:Queen Reclaimed 2.75

9 JB,V:Medusa Monster 2.25
10 V:Sea Monster 2.25
11 V:Giant Totem Monster 1.75
12 V:Monster 1.75
13 V:Monster 1.75
14 V:Demon 1.75
15 V:Sea Monster 1.75
16 Conan Into Battle 1.75
17 A:Conn 1.75
18 King of the Freaks? 1.75
19 MK(c),Skull & X-Bones cover . 1.75
Becomes:
CONAN THE KING
20 MS,The Prince is Dead 2.00
21 MS,Shadows 2.00
22 GI/MS,The Black Dragons,Prince
  Conan II back-up story begins . 2.00
23 MS/GI,Ordeal 2.00
24 GI/MS,Fragments:AWitch'sTale 2.00
25 MS/GI,Daggers 2.00
26 MS/GI,PrinceConanII B.U.ends 2.00
27 MS/GI,A Death in Stygia 2.00
28 MS/GI,Call of the Wild,
  A:Red Sonja 2.00
29 MS,The Sleeping Lion 2.00
30 GI,Revenge on the Black River 2.00
31 GI,Force of Arms 2.00
32 GI,Juggernaut 2.00
33 . . . . 2.00
34 . . . . 2.00
35 . . . . 2.00
36 . . . . 2.00
37 AW,Sack of Belverus 2.00
38 MM,A:Taurus,Leora 2.00
39 The Tower 2.00
40 . . . . 2.00
41 V:Leora 2.00
42 Thee Armada,A:Conn 2.00
43 . . . . 2.00
44 . . . . 2.00
45 V:Caliastros 2.00
46 V:Caliastros 2.00
47 TD,V:Caliastros 2.00
48 . . . . 2.00
49 . . . . 2.00
50 GI,50th Anniversary issue 2.00
51 GI,Death of Prince Conn 2.00
52 GI,Prince Conn story contd . . . 2.00
53 GI,A:Thoth-Amon 2.00
54 GI,V:Thoth-Amon 2.00
55 GI,Sorcerers Ring,final issue . . 2.00

CONEHEADS
1 Based SNL 2.00
2 Based SNL 2.00
3 Based SNL 1.75

CONTEST OF CHAMPIONS
June, 1982
1 JR2,Grandmaster vs. Mistress
  Death, A:Alpha Flight 8.00
2 JR2,Grandmaster vs. Mistress
  Death, A:X-Men 6.00
3 JR2,D:Grandmaster, Rebirth
  Collector, A:X-Men 6.00

COPS: THE JOB
1 MGo(c),V:Serial killer 1.50
2 MGo(c) 1.25
3 MGo(c),V:Eviscerator 1.25
4 MGo(c),D:Eviscerator,Nick 1.25

COSMIC POWERS
1 RMz(s),RLm,JP,F:Thanos 2.75
2 RMz(s),JMr,F:Terrax 2.75
3 RMz(s),F:Jack of Hearts 2.50
4 RMz(s),RLm,F:Legacy 2.50
5 RMz(s),F&O:Morg 2.50
6 RMz(s),F&O:Tyrant 2.50

COSMIC POWERS UNLIMITED
1 Surfer vs. Thanos 3.95

COUNT DUCKULA
Star
November, 1988
1 O:CountDuckula,B:DangerMouse1.25
2 A:Danger Mouse 1.00
3 thru 15 .... @1.00

COWBOY ACTION
See: WESTERN THRILLERS

COWBOY ROMANCES
October, 1949
1 Ph(c),Outlaw and the Lady . 125.00
2 Ph(c),William Holden/Mona
Freeman,Streets of Laredo . . 75.00
3 Phc,Romance in
Roaring Valley 50.00
Becomes:
YOUNG MEN
4 A Kid Names Shorty 85.00
5 Jaws of Death 55.00
6 Man-Size 55.00
7 The Last Laugh 55.00
8 Adventure stories continued . . 55.00
9 Draft Dodging story 55.00
10 US Draft Story 55.00
11 Adventure stories continued . 40.00
12 B:On the Battlefield,
inc.Spearhead 40.00
13 RH,Break-through 40.00
14 RH,Fox Hole 40.00
15 Battlefield stories cont, ... 40.00
16 Sniper Patrol 40.00
17 Battlefield stories cont, ... 40.00
18 BEv,Warlord 40.00
19 BEv 40.00
20 BEv,E:On the Battlefield . 40.00
21 B:Flash Foster and his High
Gear Hot Shots 40.00
22 Screaming Tires 40.00
23 E:Flash Foster and his High
Gear Hot Shots 40.00
24 BEv,B:Capt. America,Human
Torch,Sub-Mariner,O:Capt.
America,Red Skull 450.00
25 BEv,JR, Human Torch,Capt.
America,Sub-Mariner 350.00
26 BEv,Human Torch, Capt.
America,Sub Mariner 350.00
27 Bev, Human Torch/Toro
V:Hypnotist 350.00
28 E:Human Torch, Capt.America,
Sub Mariner,June, 1954 ... 350.00

COWGIRL ROMANCES
See: DARING MYSTERY

COYOTE
Epic
June, 1983
1 SL, ... 1.50
2 SL 1.50
3 BG 1.50
4 SL 1.50
5 SL 1.50
6 SL 1.50
7 SL,SD 1.50
8 SL 1.50
9 SL,SD 1.50
10 SL 1.50
11 FS,1st TM art,O:Slash 6.00
12 TM 3.00
13 TM 3.00
14 FS,TM,A:Badger 3.50
15 SL 1.50
16 SL,A:Reagan,Gorbachev ... 1.50

CRASH RYAN
Epic
October, 1984
1 War Story 1.75
2 Doomsday 1.50
3 Fortress Japan 1.50
4 January, 1985 .... 1.50

CRAZY
Atlas
December, 1953
1 BEv,satire, Frank N.Steins
Castle 100.00
2 BEv,Beast from 1000 Fathoms 75.00
3 Bev,Madame Knockwurst's
Whacks Museum 65.00
4 BEv,I Love Lucy satire 65.00
5 BEv,Censorship satire 65.00
6 BEv,satire 65.00
7 BEv,satire,July, 1954 ..... 65.00

CRAZY
February, 1973
1 Not Brand Echh reps, ...
Forbushman 4.50
2 Big,Batty Love and Hisses issue 3.00
3 Stupor-Man,A:Fantastical
Four, June 1973 .... 3.00

CRAZY
(Black and white magazine)
October, 1973
1 Satire,parody 3.50
2 .... 2.00
3 thru 81 .... @1.50
82 X-Men(c) 1.50
83 thru 93 .... @1.00

CREATURES ON THE LOOSE
See: TOWER OF SHADOWS

CRIME CAN'T WIN
See: KRAZY COMICS

CRIME FIGHTERS
April, 1948—Nov., 1949
1 Police Stories 125.00
2 Jewelry robbery 50.00
3 The Nine who were Doomed . 50.00
4 Human Beast at Bay 40.00
5 V:Gangsters 40.00

6 Pickpockets 40.00
7 True Cases, Crime Can't Win 40.00
8 True Cases, Crime Can't Win 40.00
9 Ph(c),It Happened at Night .. 40.00
10 Ph(c),Killer at Large 40.00
Atlas
Sept., 1954—Jan., 1955
11 V:Gangsters 35.00
12 V:Gangsters 35.00
13 Clay Pidgeon 35.00

CRITICAL MASS
Epic
Jan., 1990—July, 1990
1 KS,GM,BSzF:ShadowlineSaga . 4.95
2 .... 4.95
3 GM,SDr,JRy 4.95
4 .... 4.95
5 JZ 4.95
6 .... 4.95
7 July, 1990 .... 4.95

CROSSOVER CLASSICS
TPB Marvel and D.C. GP(c),reprints
both Spider-Man/Superman,the
Batman/Hulk and the X-Men/New
Teen Titans Battles 17.95

CRYPT OF SHADOWS
January, 1973
1 BW,RH,Midnight on Black
Mountain 5.50
2 Monster at the Door 2.50
3 Dead Man's Hand 2.50
4 Cl,Secret in the Vault 2.50
5 JM,The Graveyard Ghoul 2.50
6 BEv,Don't Bury Me Deep 2.50
7 JSt,The Haunting of Bluebeard 2.50
8 How Deep my Grave 2.50
9 Beyond Death 2.50
10 A Scream in the Dark 2.50
11 The Ghouls in my Grave 2.00
12 Behind the Locked Door 2.00
13 SD,Back From the Dead 2.00
14 The Thing that Creeps 2.00
15 My Coffin is Crowded 2.00
16 .... 2.00
17 In the Hands of Shandu 2.00
18 SD,Face of Fear 2.00
19 SD,Colossus that Challenged
the World 2.00
20 A Monster walks Among Us . . 2.00
21 SD,Death Will Be Mine,
November 1975 .... 2.00

CUPID
December, 1949
1 Ph(c),Cora Dod's Amazing
Decision 60.00
2 Ph(c),Betty Page, Mar. 1950 125.00

CURSE OF THE WEIRD
1 thru 4 SD,rep. 50's Sci-Fi 1.50

CYBERSPACE 3000
1 A:Dark Angel,Galactus,V:Badoon,
Glow in the dark(c) 3.25
2 SeT,A:Galactus, Dark Angel ... 2.00
3 SeT,A:Galactus,Keeper 2.00
4 SeT,A:Keeper 2.00
5 SeT,A:Keeper 2.00
6 SeT,A:Warlock 2.00
7 SeT,I:Gamble 2.00

8 SeT,A:Warlock	2.00
9 SeT	1.75
10 SeT	1.75
11 SeT	1.75

DAKOTA NORTH
1986

1 (Now in Cage)	1.50
2	1.25
3	1.25
4	1.25
5 February, 1987	1.25

DAMAGE CONTROL
May, 1989

1 EC/BWi;A:Spider-Man	3.00
2 EC/BWi;A:Fant.Four	2.00
3 EC/BWi;A:Iron Man	2.00
4 EC/BWi;A:X-Men	2.00

[2nd Series]

1 EC,A:Capt.America&Thor	3.00
2 EC,A:Punisher	2.50
3 EC	2.00
4 EC,Punisher	2.00

[3rd Series]

1 Clean-up Crew Returns	1.50
2 A:Hulk,New Warriors	1.50
3 A:Avengers W.C.,Wonder Man, Silver Surfer	1.50
4 A:SilverSurfer & others	1.50

DANCES WITH DEMONS

1 CAd	2.95
2 CAd,V:Manitou	1.95
3 CAd,V:Manitou	1.95
4 CAd,last issue	1.95
5 Okay, there's more!	1.95
6	1.95

Daredevil #1
© *Marvel Entertainment Group*

DAREDEVIL
April, 1964

1 B:StL(s),JK(c),BEv, I&O:Daredevil,I:Karen Page, Foggy Nelson	1,450.00

2 JK(c),JO,V:Electro	450.00
3 JK(c),JO,I&O:The Owl	265.00
4 JK(c),JO,I&O:Killgrave	200.00
5 JK(c),WW,V:Masked Matador	185.00
6 WW,I&O Original Mr. Fear	125.00
7 WW,I:Red Costume,V:Namor	190.00
8 WW,I&O:Stiltman	110.00
9 WW(i),Killers Castle	100.00
10 WW(i),V:Catman	100.00
11 WW(i),R:Cat	90.00
12 JK,JR,2nd A:Kazar	85.00
13 JK,JR,O:Ka-Zar	75.00
14 JR,If This Be Justice	75.00
15 JR,A:Ox	75.00
16 JR,A:Spider-Man, I:Masked Marauder	85.00
17 JR,A:Spider-Man	85.00
18 JR,A:Gladiator	60.00
19 JR,V:Gladiator	60.00
20 JR(c),GC,V:Owl	50.00
21 GC,BEv,V:Owl	38.00
22 GC,V:Tri-man	38.00
23 GC,V:Tri-man	38.00
24 GC,A:Ka-Zar	38.00
25 GC,V:Leapfrog	30.00
26 GC,V:Stiltman	30.00
27 GC,Spider-Man	35.00
28 GC,V:Aliens	30.00
29 GC,V:The Boss	30.00
30 BEv(c),GC,A:Thor	30.00
31 GC,V:Cobra	28.00
32 GC,V:Cobra	28.00
33 GC,V:Beetle	28.00
34 BEv(c),GC,O:Beetle	28.00
35 BEv(c),GC,A:Susan Richards	28.00
36 GC,A:FF	28.00
37 GC,V:Dr.Doom	28.00
38 GC,A:FF	28.00
39 GC,GT,V:Unholy Three	28.00
40 GC,V:Unholy Three	28.00
41 GC,D:Mike Murdock	30.00
42 GC,DA,I:Jester	28.00
43 JK(c),GC,A:Capt.America	24.00
44 JSo(c),GC,V:Jester	20.00
45 GC,V:Jester	20.00
46 GC,V:Jester	20.00
47 GC,'Brother Take My Hand'	20.00
48 GC,V:Stiltman	20.00
49 GC,V:Robot,I:Starr Saxon	20.00
50 JR(c),BWS,JCr,V:Robot	25.00
51 B:RTs(s),BWS,V:Robot	25.00
52 BWS,JCr,A:Black Panther	25.00
53 GC,O:Daredevil	27.00
54 GC,V:Mr.Fear,A:Spidey	20.00
55 GC,V:Mr.Fear	16.00
56 GC,V:Death Head	16.00
57 GC,V:Death Head	16.00
58 GC,V:Stunt Master	15.00
59 GC,V:Torpedo	15.00
60 GC,V:Crime Wave	15.00
61 GC,V:Cobra	15.00
62 GC,O:Night Hawk	15.00
63 GC,V:Gladiator	15.00
64 GC,A:Stuntmaster	15.00
65 GC,V:BrotherBrimstone	15.00
66 GC,V:BrotherBrimstone	15.00
67 BEv(c),GC,Stiltman	15.00
68 AC,V:Kragg Blackmailer, a:Bl.Panther,DD'sID Rev.	15.00
69 E:RTs(s),GC,V:Thunderbolts, A:Bl.Panther(DD's ID Rev)	15.00
70 GC,V:Terrorists	15.00
71 RTs(s),GC,V:Terrorists	15.00
72 GyC(s),GC,Tagak,V:Quother	12.00
73 GC,V:Zodiac	12.00

74 B:GyC(s),GC,I:Smasher	12.00
75 GC,V:El Condor	12.00
76 GC,TP,V:El Condor	12.00
77 GC,TP,V:Manbull	12.00
78 GC,TP,V:Manbull	12.00
79 GC,TP,V:Manbull	12.00
80 GK(c),GC,TP,V:Owl	12.00
81 GK(c),GC,JA,A:Black Widow	12.00
82 GK(c),GC,JA,V:Scorpion	12.00
83 JR(c),BWS,BEv,V:Mr.Hyde	14.00
84 GK(c),GC,Assassin	10.00
85 GK(c),GC,A:Black Widow	10.00
86 GC,TP,V:Ox	10.00
87 GC,TP,V:Electro	10.00
88 GC(c),GC,TP,O:Black Widow	10.00
89 GC,TP,A:Black Widow	10.00
90 E:StL(s),GK(c),GC,TP,V:Ox	10.00
91 GK(c),GC,TP,I:Mr. Fear	10.00
92 GK(c),GC,TP,A:BlackPanther	10.00
93 GK(c),GC,TP,A:Black Widow	10.00
94 GK(c),GC,TP,V:Damon Dran	10.00
95 GK(c),GC,TP,V:Manbull	10.00
96 GK(c),GC,ECh,V:Manbull	10.00
97 GK(c),V:Dark Messiah	10.00
98 E:GyC(s),GC,ECh,V:Dark Messiah	10.00
99 B:SvG(s),JR(c),V:Hawkeye	10.00
100 GC,V:Angar the Screamer	25.00
101 RB,A:Angar the Screamer	9.00
102 A:Black Widow	7.00
103 JR(c),DH,A:Spider-Man	7.00
104 GK(c),DH,V:Kraven	7.00
105 DH,JSn,DP,C:Thanos	12.00
106 JR(c),DH,A:Black Widow	7.00
107 JSn(c),JB(i),A:Capt.Marvel	7.00
108 K&R(c),PG(i),V:Beetle	7.00
109 GK(c),DH(i),V:Beetle	7.00
110 JR(c),GC,A:Thing,O:Nekra	7.00
111 JM(i),I:Silver Samurai	8.50
112 GK(c),GC,V:Mandrill	7.00
113 JR(c),V:Gladiator	7.00
114 GK(c),I:Death Stalker	7.00
115 V:Death Stalker	6.00
116 GK(c),GC,V:Owl	6.00
117 E:SvG(s),K&R(c),V:Owl	6.00
118 JR(c),DH,I:Blackwing	6.00
119 GK(c),DH(i),V:Crusher	6.00
120 GK(c),V:Hydra,I:El Jaguar	6.00
121 GK(c),A:Shield	5.00
122 GK(c),V:Blackwing	5.00
123 V:Silvermane,I:Jackhammer	5.00
124 B:MWn(s),GK(c),GC,KJ, I:Copperhead	5.00
125 GK(c),KJ(i),V:Copperhead	5.00
126 GK(c),KJ(i),D: 2nd Torpedo	5.00
127 GK(c),KJ(i),V:3rd Torpedo	5.00
128 GK(c),KJ(i),V:Death Stalker	5.00
129 KJ(i),V:Man Bull	5.00
130 KJ(i),V:Brother Zed	5.00
131 KJ(i),I&O:2nd Bullseye	24.00
132 KJ(i),V:Bullseye	6.00
133 JM(i),GK(c),V:Jester	4.00
134 JM(i),V:Chamelon	4.00
135 JM(i),V:Jester	4.00
136 JB,JM,V:Jester	4.00
137 JB,V:Jester	4.00
138 JBy,A:Ghost Rider	15.00
139 SB,V:A Bomber	4.00
140 SB,V:Gladiator	4.00
141 GC,Bullseye	4.00
142 GC,V:Cobra	4.00
143 E:MWn(s),GC,V:Cobra	4.00
144 GT,V:Manbull	4.00
145 GT,V:Owl	4.00
146 GC,V:Bullseye	5.00

Daredevil #163
© Marvel Entertainment Group

147 GC,V:Killgrave	3.50
148 GC,V:Deathstalker	3.50
149 KI,V:Smasher	3.50
150 GC,KJ,I:Paladin	4.50
151 GC,Daredevil Unmasked	3.50
152 KJ,V:Paladin	3.50
153 GC,V:Cobra	3.50
154 GC,V:Mr. Hyde	3.50
155 V:Avengers	3.50
156 GC,V:Death Stalker	3.50
157 GC,V:Death Stalker	3.50
158 FM,V:Death Stalker	56.00
159 FM,V:Bullseye	30.00
160 FM,Bullseye	20.00
161 FM,V:Bullseye	20.00
162 SD,JRu,'Requiem'	5.00
163 FM,V:Hulk,I:Ben Urich	16.00
164 FM,KJ,A:Avengers	16.00
165 FM,KJ,V:Dr.Octopus	16.00
166 FM,KJ,V:Gladiator	16.00
167 FM,KJ,V:Mauler	16.00
168 FM,KJ,I&O:Elektra	50.00
169 FM,KJ,V:Bullseye	17.00
170 FM,KJ,V:Bullseye	17.00
171 FM,KJ,V:Kingpin	9.00
172 FM,KJ,V:Bullseye	9.00
173 FM,KJ,V:Gliadator	9.00
174 FM,KJ,V:Gladiator	9.00
175 FM,KJ,A:Elektra,V:Hand	20.00
176 FM,KJ,A:Elektra	15.00
177 FM,KJ,A:Stick	9.00
178 FM,KJ,V:PowerMan&I.Fist	9.00
179 FM,KJ,V:Elektra	12.00
180 FM,KJ,V:Kingpin	10.00
181 FM,KJ,V:Bullseye,D:Elektra, A:Punisher	18.00
182 FM,KJ,A:Punisher	9.00
183 FM,KJ,V:PunisherDrug	9.00
184 FM,KJ,V:PunisherDrug	9.00
185 FM,KJ,V:King Pin	6.00
186 FM,KJ,V:Stiltman	6.00
187 FM,KJ,A:Stick	6.00
188 FM,KJ,A:Black Widow	6.00
189 FM,KJ,A:Stick,A:BlackWidow	6.00
190 FM,KJ,R:Elektra	8.00
191 FM,TA,A:Bullseye	6.00
192 KJ,V:Kingpin	4.00
193 KJ,Betsy	4.00

194 KJ,V:Kingpin	4.00
195 KJ,Tarkington Brown	4.00
196 KJ,A:Wolverine	8.00
197 V:Bullseye	3.00
198 V:Dark Wind	3.00
199 V:Dark Wind	3.00
200 JBy(c),V:Bullseye	3.50
201 JBy(c),A:Black Widow	2.50
202 I:Micah Synn	2.50
203 JBy(c),I:Trump	2.50
204 BSz(c),V:Micah Synn	2.50
205 I:Gael	2.50
206 V:Micah Synn	2.50
207 BSz(c),A:Black Widow	2.50
208 Harlan Ellison	3.00
209 Harlan Ellison	3.00
210 DM,V:Micah Synn	2.50
211 DM,V:Micah Synn	2.50
212 DM,V:Micah Synn	2.50
213 DM,V:Micah Synn	2.50
214 DM,V:Micah Synn	2.50
215 DM,A:Two-Gun Kid	2.50
216 DM,V:Gael	2.50
217 BS(c),V:Gael	2.50
218 KP,V:Jester	2.50
219 FM,JB	3.00
220 DM,D:Heather Glenn	2.50
221 DM,Venice	2.50
222 DM,A:Black Widow	2.50
223 DM,Secret Wars II	2.50
224 DM,V:Sunturion	2.50
225 DM,V:Vulture	2.50
226 FM(plot),V:Gladiator	3.00
227 FM,Kingpin,Kar.Page	8.00
228 FM,DM,V:Kingpin	5.00
229 FM,Kingpin,Turk	5.00
230 R:Matt's Mother	5.00
231 FM,DM,V:Kingpin	5.00
232 FM,V:Kingpin,Nuke	5.00
233 FM,Kingpin,Nuke,Capt.Am.	5.00
234 SD,KJ,V:Madcap	2.00
235 SD,KJ,V:Mr. Hyde	2.00
236 BWS,A:Black Widow	5.00
237 AW(i),V:Klaw	2.00
238 SB,SL,AAd(c)V:Sabretooth	9.00
239 AAd(c),AW,GI(i),V:Rotgut	2.00
240 AW,V:Rotgut	2.00
241 MZ(c),TM,V:Trixter	4.00
242 KP,V:Caviar Killer	2.00
243 AW,V:Nameless One	2.00
244 TD(i),V:Nameless One	2.00
245 TD(i),A:Black Panther	2.00
246 TD(i),V:Chance	2.00
247 KG,A:Black Widow	2.00
248 RL,AW,A:Wolverine, V:Bushwhacker	11.00
249 RL,AW,V:Wolverine, Bushwhacker	10.00
250 JR2,AW,I:Bullet	3.50
251 JR2,AW,V:Bullet	3.00
252 JR2,AW,Fall o/Mutants	4.50
253 JR2,AW,V:Kingpin	3.00
254 JR2,AW,I:Typhoid Mary	18.00
255 JR2,AW,A:Kingpin,TMary	8.00
256 JR2,AW,A:Kingpin,TMary	8.00
257 JR2,AW,A:Punisher	10.00
258 RLm,V:Bengal	3.50
259 JR2,AW,V:TyphoidMary	5.00
260 JR2,AW,V:T.Mary,K.pin	5.00
261 JR2,AW,HumanTorch	2.50
262 JR2,AW,Inferno	2.50
263 JR2,AW,Inferno	2.50
264 SD,AW,MM,V:The Owl	2.50
265 JR2,AW,Inferno	2.50
266 JR2,AW,V:Mephisto	2.50

Daredevil #226
© Marvel Entertainment Group

267 JR2,AW,V:Bullet	2.50
268 JR2,AW,V:TheMob	2.50
269 JR2,AW,V:Pyro&Blob	2.50
270 JR2,AW,A:Spider-Man, I:Blackheart	3.00
271 JR2,AW,I:Number9	2.50
272 JR2,AW,I:Shotgun	3.00
273 JR2,AW,V:Shotgun	2.50
274 JR2,AW,V:Inhumans	2.50
275 JR2,AW,ActsOfVen.,V:Ultron	2.50
276 JR2,AW,ActsOfVen.,V:Ultorn	2.50
277 RL,AW,Vivian's Story	1.75
278 JR2,AW,V:Blackheart, A:Inhumans	2.50
279 JR2,AW,V:Mephisto, A:Inhumans	2.50
280 JR2,AW,V:Mephisto, A:Inhumans	2.50
281 JR2,AW,V:Mephisto, A:Inhumans	2.50
282 JR2,AW,V:Mephisto, A:Silver Surfer, Inhumans	2.50
283 MBa,AW,A:Captain America	2.00
284 LW,AW,R:Bullseye	1.75
285 LW,AW,B:Bullseye become DD#1	1.75
286 LW,AW,GCa,Fake Daredevil #2	1.75
287 LW,AW,Fake Daredevil #3	1.75
288 LW,AW,A:Kingpin	1.75
289 LW,AW,A:Kingpin	1.75
290 LW,AW,E:Fake Daredevil	1.75
291 LW,AW,V:Bullet	1.75
292 LW,A:Punisher,V:Tombstone	2.50
293 LW,A:Punisher,V:Tombstone	2.00
294 LW,V:The Hand	1.75
295 LW,V:The Hand, A:GhostRider	1.75
296 LW,AW,V:The Hand	1.75
297 B:DGC(s),LW,AW,B:Last Rites, V:Typhoid Mary,A:Kingpin	3.50
298 LW,AW,A:Nick Fury,Kingpin	2.50
299 LW,AW,A:Nick Fury,Kingpin	2.50
300 LW,AW,E:Last Rites,	4.50
301 V:The Owl	1.75
302 V:The Owl	1.75
303 V:The Owl	1.75
304 AW,Non-action issue	1.75

305 AW,A:Spider-Man 1.75
306 AW,A:Spider-Man 1.75
307 1st SMc DD,Dead Man's Hand #1,
　A:Nomad 3.00
308 SMc,Dead Man's Hand #5,
　A:Punisher,V:Silvermane 2.00
309 SMc,Dead Man's Hand#7,
　A:Nomad,Punisher 2.00
310 SMc,Inf.War,V:Calipso 2.00
311 SMc,V:Calypso 2.00
312 Firefighting issue 1.75
313 SMc,V:Pyromaniac 2.00
314 SMc,V:Mr.Fear,I:Shock 2.00
315 SMc,V:Mr.Fear 2.00
316 Goes Underground 1.75
317 SMc,Comedy Issue 2.00

Daredevil #257
© *Marvel Entertainment Group*

318 SMc,V:Taskmaster 2.00
319 SMc,Fall from Grace Prologue,
　A:Silver Sable,Garrett,Hand . 22.00
319a 2nd Printing 10.00
320 SMc,B:Fall from Grace,
　V:Crippler,S.Sable,A:Stone . . 18.00
321 SMc,N:Daredevil,A:Venom,
　Garret, V:Hellspawn,Glow
　in the Dark(c) 9.00
321a Newsstand Ed. 6.00
322 SMc,A:Venom,Garret,Siege . 6.00
323 SMc,Venom,A:Siege,Garret,
　I:Erynys 4.00
324 SMc,A:Garret,R:Elektra,
　A:Stone, Morbius 3.50
325 SMc,E:Fall from Grace, A:Garret,
　Siege,Elektra,Morbius,V:Hand,
　D:Hellspawn,Double size 4.00
326 SMc,B:Tree of Knowledge,
　I:Killobyte,A:Capt.America 2.00
327 E:DGC(s),SMc,A:Capt.Amer. . 1.75
328 GtW(s),V:Wirehead,A:Captain
　America,S.Sable,Wild Pack . . . 1.75
329 B:DGC(s),SMc,A:Captain
　America, S.Sable,Iron Fist 1.75
330 SMc,A:Gambit 1.75
331 SMc,A:Captain America,
　VLHydra 1.75
332 A:Captain America,Gambit . . 1.75
333 TGb,GWt 1.75
334 TGb,GWt 1.75
335 . . . . 1.75

336 . . . . 1.50
337 V:Kingpin,A:Blackwulf 1.50
338 Wages of Sin,pt.1 . . . . 1.50
339 Wages of Sin,pt.2 . . . . 1.50
340 R:Kingpin 1.50
341 Kingpin 1.50
342 DGc,KP,V:Kingpin 1.50
Ann.#1 GC 30.00
Ann.#2 reprints. 8.00
Ann.#3 reprints 8.00
Ann.#4 (1976)GT,A:Black
　Panther,Namor 6.00
Ann.#5 (1989)MBa,JLe,JR2,KJ,
　WPo,AM,Atlantis Attacks,
　A:Spider-Man 5.00
Ann.#6 TS,Lifeform#2,A:Typhoid
　Mary 2.75
Ann.#7 JG,JBr,Von Strucker
　Gambit,pt.1,A:Nick Fury 2.50
Ann.#8 Sys.Bytes#2,A:Deathlok . 2.75
Ann.#9 MPa,I:Devourer,w/card,tie-in
　to "Fall From Grace" 5.00
Ann.#10 I:Ghostmaker,A:Shang
　Chi, Elektra 3.25
G-Size #1 GK(c),reprints 12.00
TPB Born Again,rep.#227-#233 . 10.95
TPB Fall of the Kingpin,
　rep.#297-300 . . . . 15.95
TPB Gangwar,Reprints
　#169-#172,#180 . . . . 12.95
TPB Marked for Death,reps#159-
　161,163,164 . . . . 9.95
Daredevil/Punisher:Child's Play
　reprints#182-#184 . . . . 7.00

DAREDEVIL: THE MAN WITHOUT FEAR

1 B:FM(s),JR2,AW,O:Daredevil,
　A:Stick,D:Daredevil's Father . . 9.00
2 JR2,AW,A:Stick,Stone,Elektra . 8.00
3 JR2,AW,A:Elektra,Kingpin 7.00
4 JR2,AW,A:Kingpin,I:Mickey . . 6.00
5 JR2,AW,A:Mickey,Last Issue . . 5.00
TPB rep.#1#5 . . . . 15.95

DARING MYSTERY COMICS

Timely
Jan., 1940

1 ASh(c),JSm,O:Fiery Mask,
　A:Monako John Steele,Doc Doyle,
　Flash FosterBarney Mullen,
　Sea Rover, Bondage (c) . 12,000.00
2 ASh(c),JSm,O:Phantom Bullet
　A:Zephyr Jones & K4,Laughing
　Mask Mr.E,B:Trojak 4,000.00
3 ASh(c),JSm,A:Phantom
　Reporter,Marvex,Breeze
　Barton, B:Purple Mask . . . 2,500.00
4 ASh(c),A:G-Man Ace,K4,Monako,
　Marvex,E:Purple Mask,
　B:Whirlwind Carter 1,500.00
5 JSm,B:Falcon,A:Fiery Mask,K4,
　Little Hercules,Bondage(c) 1,500.00
6 S&K,O:Marvel Boy,A:Fiery
　Mask, Flying Fame,Dynaman,
　Stuporman,E:Trojak 2,000.00
7 S&K,O:Blue Diamond,A:The Fin,
　Challenger,Captain Daring,
　Silver Scorpion,Thunderer . 1,900.00
8 S&K,O:Citizen V,A:Thunderer,
　Fin Silver Scorpion,Captain
　Daring Blue Diamond 1,500.00
Becomes:

DARING COMICS

9 ASh(c),B:Human Torch,Toro,
　Sub Mariner 600.00
10 ASh(c),A:The Angel 500.00
11 ASh(c),A:The Destroyer . . . 500.00
12 E:Human Torch,Toro,Sub-
　Mariner, Fall, 1945 . . . . 500.00
Becomes:

JEANIE COMICS

13 B:Jeanie,Queen of the
　Teens Mitzi,Willie 70.00
14 Baseball(c) 40.00
15 Schoolbus(c) 40.00
16 Swimsuit(c) 56.00
17 HK,Fancy dress party(c),
　Hey Look 37.00
18 HK,Jeanie'sDate(c),Hey Look 37.00
19 Ice-Boat(c),Hey Look 37.00
20 Jukebox(c) 30.00
21 . . . . 30.00
22 HK,Hey Look 37.00
23 . . . . 30.00
24 . . . . 30.00
25 . . . . 30.00
26 . . . . 30.00
27 E:Jeanie,Queen of Teens . . . 30.00
Becomes:

COWGIRL ROMANCES

28 Ph(c),Mona Freeman/MacDonald
　Carey,Copper Canyon 120.00

DARK ANGEL
See: HELL'S ANGEL

DARK CRYSTAL
April, 1983
1 movie adaption 1.00
2 movie adaption,May 1983 . . . . 1.00

DARK GUARD

1 A:All UK Heroes 2.95
2 A:All UK Heroes 1.75
3 V:Leader,MyS-Tech 1.75
4 V:MyS-Tech 1.75

Darkhawk #20
© *Marvel Entertainment Group*

5 . . . . 1.75
6 . . . . 1.75
7 . . . . 1.75

DARKHAWK
March, 1991
1 MM,I&O:Darkhawk,
  A:Hobgoblin 8.00
2 MM,A:SpiderMan,V:Hobgoblin . 6.00
3 MM,A:SpiderMan,V:Hobgoblin . 4.00
4 MM,I:Savage Steel 3.00
5 MM,I:Portal 3.00
6 MM,A:Cap.Am,D.D.,Portal,
  V:U-Foes 3.00
7 MM,I:Lodestone 2.00
8 MM,V:Lodestone 2.00
9 MM,A:Punisher,V:Savage Steel 2.00
10 MM,A&N:Tombstone 2.00
11 MM,V:Tombstone 2.00
12 MM,V:Tombstone,R:Dark
  Hawks'Father 2.00
13 MM,V:Venom 4.00
14 MM,V:Venom,D:Dark
  Hawks Father 3.00
15 MM,Heart of the Hawk,concl . . 2.00
16 MM,V:Terrorists 2.00
17 MM,I:Peristrike Force 2.00
18 MM,V:Mindwolf 2.00
19 MM,R:Portal,A:Spider-Man,V:The
  Brotherhood of Evil Mutants . . 2.00
20 MM,A:Spider-Man,Sleepwalker,
  V:Brotherhood of Evil Mutants . 2.00
21 MM,B:Return to Forever 1.75
22 MM,A:Ghost Rider 1.75
23 MM,I:Evilhawk 1.75
24 V:Evilhawk 1.50
25 MM,O:Darkhawk,V:Evilhawk,
  Holo-graphx(c) 3.00
26 A:New Warriors 1.50
27 A:New Warriors,V:Zarrko 1.50
28 A:New Warriors,Zarrko 1.50
29 A:New Warriors 1.50
30 I:Purity 1.50
31 Infinity Crusade 1.50
32 R:Savage Steel 1.50
33 I:Cuda 1.50
34 V:Cuda 1.50
35 DFr(s),V:Venom 1.50
36 DFr(s),V:Scokers,A:Venom . . . 1.50
37 DFr(s),V:Venom 1.50
38 DFr(s),N:Darkhawk 1.50
39 DFr(s) 1.50
40 DFr(s) 1.75
41 DFr(s) 1.75
42 DFr(s), V:Portal,I:Shaper 1.75
43 DFr(s) 1.75
44 DFr(s) 1.75
45 DFr(s),A:Portal 1.75
46 DFr(s) 1.75
47 . . . . 1.50
48 R:Darkhawk,V:Mahari 1.50
49 V:Overhawk 1.50
50 V:Overhawk 2.50
Ann.#1 MM,Assault on ArmorCity. 3.25
Ann.#2 GC,AW,I:Dreamkiller,
  w/Trading card 3.25
Ann.#3 I:Damek 2.95

DARKHOLD
1 RCa,I:Redeemers,Polybagged
  w/poster,A:Gh.Rider,Blaze . . . 3.25
2 RCa,R:Modred 2.50
3 A:Modred,Scarlet Witch 2.00
4 V:Sabretooth,N'Garai 2.00
5 A:Punisher, Ghost Rider 2.00

6 RCa,V:Dr.Strange 2.00
7 A:Dr.Strange,V:Japanese Army 2.00
8 Betrayal #1 . . . . 2.00
9 Diabolique 2.00
10 V:Darkholders 2.00
11 Midnight Massacre#3,D:Modred,
  Vicki 2.50
12 V:Chthon 2.00
13 V:Missing Link 2.00
14 Vicki's Secret revealed 2.00
15 Siege of Darkness,pt.#4 . . . . 2.00
16 Siege of Darkness,pt.#12 . . . . 2.00

DARK MAN
MOVIE ADAPTION
September, 1990
1 BH/MT/TD 2.25
2 BH/TD 1.50
3 BH/TD,final issue 1.50

DARKMAN
September, 1990
1 JS,R:Darkman 3.95
2 JS,V:Witchfinder 2.95
3 JS,Witchfinder 2.95
4 JS,V:Dr.West 2.95
5 JS,Durant 2.95
6 JS,V:Durant 2.95

DATE WITH MILLIE
Atlas
October, 1956
[1st Series]
1 . . . . 110.00
2 . . . . 60.00
3 thru 7 . . . . @40.00

[2nd Series]
October, 1959
1 . . . . 50.00
2 thru 7 . . . . @30.00
Becomes:

LIFE WITH MILLIE
8 . . . . 30.00
9 . . . . 23.00
10 . . . . 23.00
11 thru 20 . . . . @19.00
Becomes:

MODELING WITH MILLIE
21 . . . . 30.00
22 thru 53 . . . . @17.00
54 June, 1967 . . . . 17.00

DATE WITH PATSY
September, 1957
1 A:Patsy Walker 35.00

DAZZLER
March, 1981
1 AA,JR2,A:X-Men,Spm,
  O:Dazzler 3.50
2 WS,JR2,AA,X-Men,A:SpM 2.50
3 JR2,Dr.Doom 1.50
4 FS,Dr.Doom 1.50
5 FS,I:Blue Shield 1.50
6 FS,Hulk 1.50
7 FS,Hulk 1.50
8 FS,Quasar 1.50
9 FS,D:Klaw 1.50
10 FS,Galactus 1.50
11 FS,Galactus 1.50
12 FS,The Light That Failed 1.50
13 FS,V:Grapplers 1.50

Dazzler #24
© Marvel Entertainment Group

14 FS,She Hulk 1.50
15 FS,BSz,Spider Women 1.50
16 FS,BSz,Enchantress 1.50
17 FS,Angel,V:Doc Octopus 1.50
18 FS,BSz,A:Fantastic Four,Angel,
  V:Absorbing Man 1.50
19 FS,Blue Bolt,V:Absorbing Man 1.50
20 FS,V:Jazz and Horn 1.50
21 FS,A:Avengers,F.F.,C:X-Men,
  (double size) 1.50
22 FS,V:Rogue,Mystique 2.00
23 FS,V:Rogue,A:Powerman,
  Iron Fist 2.00
24 FS,V:Rogue,A:Powerman,
  Iron Fist 1.75
25 FS,'The Jagged Edge' 1.50
26 FS,Lois London 1.50
27 FS,Fugitive 1.50
28 FS,V:Rogue 2.00
29 FS,Roman Nekoboh 1.50
30 FS,Moves to California 1.50
31 FS,The Last Wave 1.50
32 FS,A:Inhumans 1.50
33 Chiller 1.50
34 FS,Disappearance 1.50
35 FS,V:Racine Ramjets 1.50
36 JBy(c),FS,V:Tatterdemalion . . 1.50
37 JBy(c),FS 1.50
38 PC,JG,X-Men 5.00
39 PC,JG,Caught in the grip of
  death 1.50
40 PC,JG,Secret Wars II 1.75
41 PC,JG,A:Beast 1.50
42 PC,JG,A:Beast,last issue 2.00

DEADLIEST HEROES OF KUNG FU
(magazine)
Summer, 1975
1 . . . . 3.50

DEADLY FOES OF SPIDERMAN
May, 1991

1 AM,KGa,V:Sinister Syndicate	5.00
2 AM,Boomerang on Trial	3.50
3 AM,Deadly Foes Split	3.50
4 AM,Conclusion	3.50
TPB rep. #1–#4	12.95

DEADLY HANDS OF KUNG FU
April, 1974

1 NA(c),JSa,JSon,O:Sons of the Tiger, B:Shang-Chi, Bruce Lee Pin-up	5.00
2 NA(c),JSa	2.50
3 NA(c),JSon,A:Sons of the Tiger	2.50
4 NA(Bruce Lee)(c),JSon,Bruce Lee biography	4.00
5	3.00
6 GP,JSon,A:Sons of the Tiger	3.00
7 GP,JSon,A:Sons of the Tiger	3.00
8 GP,JSon,A:Sons of the Tiger	3.00
9 GP,JSon,A:Sons of the Tiger	3.00
10 GP,JSon,A:Sons of the Tiger	3.00
11 NA(c),GP,JSon,A:Sons of the Tiger	3.00
12 NA(c),GP,JSon,A:Sons of the Tiger	3.00
13 GP,JSon,A:Sons of the Tiger	3.00
14 NA(c),GP,JSon,A:Sons of the Tiger	3.00
15 JSa,Annual #1	5.00
16 JSon,A:Sons of the Tiger	2.00
17 NA9c),JSon,KG,A:Sons of the Tiger	2.00
18 JSon,A:Sons of the Tiger	2.00
19 JSon,I:White Tiger	2.00
20 GP,O:White Tiger	3.00
21	2.00
22 KG	2.00
23 GK	2.00
24 KG	2.00
25	2.00
26	2.00
27	2.00
28 JSon,O:Jack of Hearts	4.00
29	2.00
30	2.00
31 JSon	2.00
32 MR,JSon	2.00
33 MR,February, 1977	2.00
Special Album Edition,NA, Summer 1974	3.00

DEAD OF NIGHT
December, 1973

1 JSt,Horror reprints,A Haunted House is not a Home	5.00
2 BEv(c),House that Fear Built	3.00
3 They Lurk Below	3.00
4 Warewolf Beware	3.00
5 Deep Down	3.00
6 Jack the Ripper	3.00
7 SD,The Thirteenth Floor	3.00
8 Midnight Brings Dark Madness	3.00
9 Deathride	3.00
10 SD,I Dream of Doom	3.00
11 GK/BWr(c),I:Scarecrow, Fires of Rebirth,Fires of Death August, 1975	3.00

DEADPOOL

1 B:FaN(s),JMd,MFm(i), V:Slayback,Nyko	6.00
2 JMd,MFm(i),V:Black Tom Cassidy,Juggernaut	5.00
3 JMd,MFm(i),I:Comcast, Makeshift,Rive,A:Slayback	4.00
4 E:FaN(s),JMd,MFm(i), A:Slayback,Kane	3.50

DEATH³

1 I:Death Metal,Death Wreck	2.95
2 V:Ghost Rider	1.75
3 A:Hulk,Cable,Storm,Thing	1.75
4 Last issue	1.75

DEATHLOK
July, 1990
[Limited Series]

1 JC,SW,I:Michael Colins (2nd Deathlok)	8.00
2 JC,SW,V:Wajler	6.00
3 DCw,SW,V:Cyberants	5.00
4 DCw,SW,V:Sunfire,final issue	5.00

[Regular Series]

1 DCw,MM,V:Warwolf	4.00
2 DCw,MM,A:Dr.Doom,Machine Man, Forge	3.25
3 DCw,MM,V:Dr.Doom, A:Mr.Fantastic	3.00
4 DCw,MM,A:X-Men,F.F.,Vision, O:Mechadoom	3.00
5 DCw,MM,V:Mechadoom, A:X-Men,Fantastic Four	3.00
6 DCw,MM,A:Punisher, V:Silvermane	2.50
7 DCw,MM,A:Punisher, V:Silvermane	2.50
8 A:Main Frame,Ben Jacobs	2.00
9 DCw,MM,A:Ghost Rider, V:Nightmare	2.50
10 DCw,MM,A:GhR,V:Nightmare	2.50
11 DCw,MM,V:Moses Magnum	2.00
12 DCw,MM,Biohazard Agenda	2.00
13 DCw,MM,Biohazard Agenda	2.00
14 DCw,MM,Biohazard Agenda	2.00
15 DCw,MM,Biohazard Agenda	2.00
16 DCw,MM,Inf.War,V:Evilok	2.00
17 WMc,MM,B:Cyberwar	2.00
18 WMc,A:Silver Sable	2.00
18a Newstand Ed.	1.75
19 SMc,Cyberwar#3	2.00
20 SMc,Cyberwar#4	2.00
21 E:Cyberwar,A:Cold Blood Nick Fury	2.00
22 V:Moses Magnum, A:Black Panther	2.00
23 A:Bl.Panther,V:Phreak,Stroke	2.00
24 V:MosesMagnum,A:Bl.Panther	2.00
25 WMc,V:MosesMagnum,A:Black Panther,holo-grafx(c)	3.25
26 V:Hobogoblin	2.00
27 R:Siege	2.00
28 Infinty Crusade	2.00
29 Inner Fears	2.00
30 KHd,V:Hydra	2.00
31 GWt(s),KoK,B:Cyberstrike, R:1st Deathlok	2.00
32 GWt(s),KoK,A:Siege	2.00
33 GWt(s),KoK,V:Justice Peace	2.00
34 GWt(s),KoK,E:Cyberstrike,V:Justice Peace,final issue	2.00
Ann.#1 JG,I:Timestream	2.75
Ann.#2 I:Tracer,w/card	2.95

DEATHLOK SPECIAL

1 Rep.MiniSeries	4.00
2 Rep.MiniSeries	2.50
3 Rep.MiniSeries	2.50
4 Rep.MiniSeries, final issue	2.50

DEATH METAL

1 JRe,I:Argon,C:Alpha Flight	1.95
2 JRe,V:Alpha Flight	1.95
3 JRe,I:Soulslug	1.95
4 Re,Last Issue	1.95

DEATH METAL VS. GENETIX

1 PaD,w/card	2.95
2 PaD,w/card	2.95

Death's Head #1
© Marvel Entertainment Group

DEATH'S HEAD
December, 1988

1 V:Backbreaker	1.00
2 A:Dragons Claws	6.00
3	4.00
4 V:Plague Dog	3.00
5 V:Big Shot	3.00
6 V:Big Shot	3.00
7	3.00
8	3.00
9 A:Fantastic Four	4.00
10 A:Iron Man	4.00
TPB Reprints#1-#10	12.95

DEATH'S HEAD
[Limited Series]

1 A:'Old' Death's Head	1.95

DEATH'S HEAD II
March, 1992
[Limited Series]

1 LSh,I:2nd Death's Head, D:1st Death's Head	19.00
1a 2nd printing,Silver	3.50
2 LSh,A:Fantastic Four	6.00
2a 2nd printing,Silver	3.00

All comics prices listed are for *Near Mint* condition.

3 LSh,I:Tuck 5.00
4 LSh,A:Wolverine,Spider-Man,
  Punisher 4.00
[Regular Series]
1 LSh,A:X-Men,I:Wraithchilde . . . 3.00
2 LSh,A:X-Men 2.25
3 LSh,A:X-Men,V:Raptors 2.25
4 LSh,A:X-Men,V:Wraithchilde . . 2.25
5 V:UnDeath's Head II,
  A:Warheads 2.25
6 R:Tuck,V:Major Oak 2.25
7 V:Major Oak 2.25
8 V:Wizard Methinx 2.25
9 BHi,V:Cybernetic Centaurs . . . 2.25
10 DBw,A:Necker 2.25
11 SCy,R:Charnel 2.25
12 DAn(s),SvL,V:Charnel 2.25
13 SvL,A:Liger 2.25
14 SvL,Brain Dead Cold,Blue
  Foil(c) 3.25
15 SvL,V:Duplicates 2.25
16 SvL,DAn 2.25
17 SvL,DAn 1.95
18 SvL,DAn 1.95
Spec. Gold Ed. LSh(a&s) 3.95

DEATH'S HEAD II/DIE CUT
1 I:Die Cut 3.25
2 O:Die Cut 1.75

DEATH'S HEAD II/
KILLPOWER: BATTLETIDE
[1st Limited Series]
1 GSr,A:Wolverine 2.50
2 thru 4 GSr,A:Wolverine . . . . @2.00
[2nd Limited Series]
1 A:Hulk 3.25
2 V:Hulk 1.75
3 A:Hulk 1.75
4 last issue 1.75

DEATH-WRECK
1 A:Death's Head II 1.95
2 V:Gangsters 1.95
3 A:Dr.Necker 1.95
4 last issue 1.95

DEEP, THE
November, 1977
1 Cl,Movie Adaption 2.00

DEFENDERS
August, 1972
1 SB,I&D:Necrodames 60.00
2 SB,V:Calizuma 35.00
3 GK(c),SB,JM,V:UndyingOne . 30.00
4 SB,FMc,Bl.Knight,V:Valkyrie . 30.00
5 SB,FMc,D:Omegatron 30.00
6 SB,FMc,V:Cyrus Black 23.00
7 SB,FBe,A:Hawkeye 23.00
8 SB,FBe,Avengers,SilverSurfer 23.00
9 SB,FMc,Avengers 23.00
10 SB,FBe,Thor vs. Hulk 30.00
11 SB,FBe,A:Avengers 15.00
12 SB,JA,Xemnu 14.00
13 GK(c),SB,KJ,J:Night Hawk . . 14.00
14 SB,DGr,O:Hyperion 14.00
15 SB,KJ,A:Professor X,V:Magneto,
  Savage Land Mutates 23.00
16 GK(c),SB,Professor X,V:Magneto,
  Savage Land Mutates 23.00
17 SB,DGr,Power Man 10.00
18 GK(c),SB,DGr,A:Power Man . 10.00

Defenders #13
© Marvel Entertainment Group

19 GK(c),SB,KJ,A:Power Man . . 10.00
20 K&R(c),SB,A:Thing 10.00
21 GK(c),SB,O:Valkyrie 8.00
22 GK(c),SB,V:Sons o/t Serpent . 8.00
23 GK(c),SB,A:Yellow Jacket . . . 8.00
24 GK(c),SB,BMc,A:Daredevil . . 8.00
25 GK(c),SB,JA,A:Daredevil 8.00
26 K&R(c),SB,A:Guardians 13.00
27 K&R(c),SB,A:Guardians
  C:Starhawk 13.00
28 K&R(c),SB,A:Guardians
  I:Starhawk 14.00
29 K&R(c),SB,A:Guardians 13.00
30 JA(i),A:Wong 6.00
31 GK(c),SB,JM,Nighthawk 6.00
32 GK(c),SB,JM,O:Nighthawk . . 6.00
33 GK(c),SB,JM,V:Headmen . . . 6.00
34 SB,JM,V:Nebulon 6.00
35 GK(c),SB,KJ,I:Red Guardian . 6.00
36 GK(c),SB,KJ,A:Red Guardian . 6.00
37 GK(c),SB,KJ,J:Luke Cage . . . 6.00
38 SB,KJ,V:Nebulon 6.00
39 SB,KJ,V:Felicia 6.00
40 SB,KJ,V:Assassin 6.00
41 KG,KJ,Nighthawk 6.00
42 KG,KJ,V:Rhino 6.00
43 KG,KJ,Cobalt Man,Egghead . . 6.00
44 KG,KJ,J:Hellcat,V:Red Rajah . 6.00
45 KG,KJ,Valkyrie V:Hulk 6.00
46 KG,KJ,L:DrStrange,LukeCage . 6.00
47 KG,KJ,Moon Knight 6.00
48 KG,A:Wonder Man 6.00
49 KG,O:Scorpio 6.00
50 KG,Zodiac,D:Scorpio 6.00
51 KG,Moon Knight 6.00
52 KG,Hulk,V:Sub Mariner 6.00
53 KG,DC,MG,TA,C&I:Lunatik . . . 5.00
54 MG,Nigh Fury 5.00
55 Cl,O:Red Guardian 5.00
56 Cl,KJ,Hellcat,V:Lunatik 5.00
57 DC,Ms.Marvel 5.00
58 Return of Dr.Strange 5.00
59 I:Belathauzer 5.00
60 V:Vera Gemini 5.00
61 Spider-Man,A:Lunatik 6.00
62 Hercules,C:Polaris 5.00
63 Mutli Heroes 5.00
64 Mutli Heroes 5.00

65 Red Guardian 5.00
66 JB,Valkyrie I 5.00
67 Valkryie II 5.00
68 HT,When Falls the Mountain . . 5.00
69 HT,A:The Anything Man 5.00
70 HT,A:Lunatik 5.00
71 HT,O:Lunatik 5.00
72 HT,V:Lunatik 5.00
73 HT,Foolkiller,V:WizardKing . . . 6.00
74 HT,Foolkiller,L:Nighthawk 6.00
75 HT,Foolkiller 5.00
76 HT,O:Omega 3.00
77 HT,Moon Dragon 3.00
78 HT,Yellow Jacket 3.00
79 HT,Tunnel World 3.00
80 HT,DGr,Nighthawk 3.00
81 HT,Tunnel World 3.00
82 DP,JSt,Tunnel World 3.00
83 DP,JSt,Tunnel World 3.00
84 DP,JSt,Black Panther 3.00
85 DP,JSt,Black Panther 3.00
86 DP,JSt,Black Panther 3.00
87 DP,JSt,V:Mutant Force 3.00
88 DP,JSt,Matt Mardock 3.00
89 DP,JSt,D:Hellcat's
  Mother, O:Mad-Dog 3.00
90 DP,JSt,Daredevil 3.00
91 DP,JSt,Daredevil 3.00
92 DP,JSt,A:Eternity,
  Son of Satan 4.00
93 DP,JSt,Son of Satan 4.00
94 DP,JSt,I:Gargoyle 3.00
95 DP,JSt,V:Dracula,O:Gargoyle . 3.00
96 DP,JSt,Ghost Rider 4.50
97 DP,JSt,False Messiah 3.00
98 DP,JSt,A:Man Thing 3.00
99 DP,JSt,Conflict 3.00
100 DP,JSt,DoubleSize,V:Satan . 4.00
101 DP,JSt,Silver Surfer 3.00
102 DP,JSt,Nighthawk 3.00
103 DP,JSt,I:Null 3.00
104 DP,JSt,Devilslayer,J:Beast . . 3.00
105 DP,JSt,V:Satan 3.00
106 DP,Daredevil,D:Nighthawk . . 3.00
107 DP,JSt,Enchantress,A:D.D. . . 3.00
108 DP,A:Enchantress 3.00
109 DP,A:Spider-Man 3.50
110 DP,A:Devilslayer 3.00
111 DP,A:Hellcat 3.00
112 DP,A:SquadronSupreme 3.00
113 DP,A:SquadronSupreme 3.00
114 DP,A:SquadronSupreme 3.00
115 DP,A:Submariner 3.00
116 DP,Gargoyle 3.00
117 DP,Valkyrie 3.00
118 DP,V:Miracleman 3.00
119 DP,V:Miracleman 3.00
120 DP,V:Miracleman 3.00
121 DP,V:Miracleman 3.00
122 DP,A:Iceman 3.00
123 DP,I:Cloud,V:Secret Empire . 3.00
124 DP,V:Elf 3.00
125 DP,New Line-up:Gargoyle,Moon
  dragon,Valkyrie,Iceman,Beast,
  Angel,W:Son of Satan & Hellcat
  I:Mad Dog 5.00
126 DP,A:Nick Fury 3.00
127 DP,V:Professor Power 3.00
128 DP,V:Professor Power 3.00
129 DP,V:Professor Power,New
  Mutants X-over 3.00
130 DP,V:Professor Power 3.00
131 DP,V:Walrus,A:Frogman . . . 3.00
132 DP,V:Spore Monster 3.00
133 DP,V:Spore Monster 3.00

134 DP,I:Manslaughter 3.00
135 DP,V:Blowtorch Brand 3.00
136 DP,V:Gargoyle 3.00
137 DP,V:Gargoyle 3.00
138 DP,O:Moondragon 3.00

Defenders #100
© *Marvel Entertainment Group*

139 DP,A:Red Wolf,V:Trolls 3.00
140 DP,V:Asgardian Trolls 3.00
141 DP,All Flesh is Grass 3.00
142 DP,V:M.O.N.S.T.E.R. 3.00
143 DP,I:Andromeda,Runner 3.00
144 DP,V:Moondragon 3.00
145 DP,V:Moondragon 3.00
146 DP,Cloud 3.00
147 DP,A:Andromeda,I:Interloper . 3.00
148 DP,A:Nick Fury 3.00
149 DP,V:Manslaughter,O:Cloud . 3.00
150 DP,O:Cloud,double-size 3.50
151 DP,A:Interloper 3.00
152 DP,Secret Wars II,D:Moon-
    dragon,Valkyrie,Gargoyle 4.00
Giant#1 GK(c),JSn,AM,O:Hulk . . 12.00
Giant#2 GK,KJ,Son of Satan 8.00
Giant#3 JSn,DA,JM,DN,A:D.D.. . . 6.00
Giant#4 GK(c),DH,A:YellowJack . . 6.00
Giant#5 K&R(c),DH,A:Guardians . 6.00
Ann.#1 SB,KJ 6.00

DEFENDERS OF
DYNATRON CITY
1 FC,I:Defenders of Dynatron City
   (from video game & TV ser.) . . 1.25
2 FC,O:Defender of D.City 1.25
3 FC,A:Dr Mayhem 1.25
4 FC 1.25
5 FC,V:Intelligent Fleas 1.25
6 FC,V:Dr.Mayhem 1.25

DEFENDERS OF
THE EARTH
Jan., 1987—Sept., 1984
1 AS,Flash Gordon & Mandrake . 2.00
2 AS,Flash Gordon & Mandrake . 2.00
3 AS,O:Phantom 2.00
4 AS,O:Mandrake 2.00

DELLA VISION
Atlas
April, 1955
1 The Television Queen 80.00
2 . . . . 55.00
3 . . . . 55.00
Becomes:
PATTY POWERS
4 . . . . 35.00
5 . . . . 22.00
6 . . . . 22.00
7 October, 1956 . . . . 22.00

DENNIS THE MENACE
November, 1981
1 . . . . 1.25
2 thru 12 . . . . @1.00
13 November, 1982 . . . . 1.00

DESTROYER, THE
November 1989
1 Black & White Mag. 3.50
2 thru 9 . . . . @2.25
10 June 1990 . . . . 2.25
TPB rep. B/w mag(color) 9.95

THE DESTROYER:
TERROR
December, 1991
1 V:Nuihc 1.95
2 V:Nuihc 1.95
3 GM,V:Nuihc 1.95
4 DC,'The Last Dinosaur' 1.95

DEVIL DINOSAUR
April, 1978—Dec., 1978
1 JK,I:Devil Dinosaur,Moon Boy . 4.00
2 JK,War With the Spider God . . 3.00
3 JK,Giant 3.00
4 JK,Objects From the Sky 3.00
5 JK,The Kingdom of the Ants . . 3.00
6 JK,The Fall 3.00
7 JK,Prisoner of the Demon Tree . 3.00
8 JK,V:Dino Riders 3.00
9 JK,Lizards That Stand 3.00

DEVIL-DOG DUGAN
Atlas
July, 1956
1 War Stories 50.00
2 . . . . 35.00
3 . . . . 25.00
Becomes:
TALE OF THE MARINES
4 BP,War Stories 25.00
Becomes:
MARINES AT WAR
5 War Stories 15.00
6 . . . . 15.00
7 The Big Push,August, 1957 . 15.00

DEXTER THE DEMON
See: MELVIN THE MONSTER

DIE-CUT
1 A:Beast 2.50
2 V:X-Beast 1.75
3 A:Beast,Prof.X 1.75
4 V:Red Skull 1.75

DIE-CUT VS. G-FORCE
1 SFr(s),LSh(c),I:G-Force 2.75
2 SFr(s),LSh(c),Last issue 2.75

DIGITEK
1 DPw,I:Digitek,C:Deathlok 2.25
2 DPw,A:Deathlok,V:Bacillicons . 2.25
3 DPw,A:Deathlok,V:Bacillicons . 2.25
4 DPw,V:Bacillicons 2.25

DINO RIDERS
February, 1989
1 Based on Toys 1.00
2 . . . . 1.00
3 May, 1989 . . . . 1.00

DINOSAURS: A
CELEBRATION
Epic
Horns and Heavy Armor 4.95
Bone-Heads and Duck-Bills 4.95
Terrible Claws and Tyrants 4.95
Egg Stealers and Earth Shakers . 4.95

DISNEY AFTERNOON
1 DarkwingDuck vs.FearsomeFive 1.50
2 . . . . 1.50
3 . . . . 1.50
4 DarkwingDuck:Gum w/t Wind . 1.50
5 F:Baloo, Mrs. Cunningham . . . 1.50
6 . . . . 1.50
7 F:Darkwing Duck 1.50
8 . . . . 1.50
9 DarkwingDuck:Borsht to Death 1.50

DOC SAVAGE
October, 1972
1 JM,Pulp Adapts,Death Eighty
   Stories High 8.50
2 JSo(c),The Feathered Serpent
   Strikes 6.00
3 JSo(c),Silver Death's Head . . 6.00
4 JSo(c),The Hell Diver 5.00
5 GK(c),Night of the Monsters . . 5.00
6 JSo(c),Where Giants Walk . . . 5.00
7 JSo(c),Brand of the Werewolfs . 5.00
8 In the Lair of the Werewolf
   January, 1974 . . . . 5.00
Giant#1 thru #2 Reprints 4.50

DOC SAVAGE
August, 1975
(black & white magazine)
1 JB,Ph(c),Ron Ely 5.75
2 JB 3.25
3 JB 3.25
4 . . . . 3.25
5 thru 7 . . . . @3.25
8 Spring 1977 . . . . 3.25

DOCTOR WHO
October, 1984
1 BBC TV Series,UK reprints,
   Return of the Daleks 4.50
2 Star Beast 3.00
3 Transformation 3.00
4 A:K-9,Daleks 3.00
5 V:Time Witch,Colin Baker
   interview 3.00
6 B:Ancient Claw saga 3.00
7 . . . . 3.00
8 The Collector 3.00

All comics prices listed are for *Near Mint* condition.

9 The Life Bringer 3.00
10 This is your Life 3.00
11 The Deal 3.00
12 End of the Line 3.00
13 V:The Cybermen 3.00
14 Clash of the Neutron Knight . . 3.00
15 B:Peter Davison-Dr. Who 3.00
16 Into the Realm of Satan, ... 3.00
17 Peter Davison Interview 3.00
18 A:Four Dr.Who's 3.00
19 A:The Sontarans 3.00
20 The Stockbridge Horror 3.00
21 The Stockbridge Horror 3.00
22 The Stockbridge Horror 3.00
23 The Unearthly Child,
   August 1984 . . . . 3.00

DOPEY DUCK COMICS
Timely
Fall, 1945
1 A:Casper Cat,Krazy Krow . . . 75.00
2 A:Casper Cat,Krazy Krow . . . 72.00
Becomes:
WACKY DUCK
3 Paperchase(c) 65.00
4 Wacky Duck(c) 90.00
5 Duck & Devil(c) 57.00
6 Cliffhanger(c) 57.00
1 Baketball(c) 40.00
2 Traffic Light(c) 40.00
Becomes: JUSTICE COMICS

Dr. Strange #178
© Marvel Entertainment Group

DR. STRANGE
[1st Series]
Prev: Strange Tales
June, 1968
169 DA,O:Dr.Strange 125.00
170 DA,A:Ancient One 55.00
171 TP,DA,V:Dormammu 38.00
172 GC,TP,V:Dormammu 38.00
173 GC,TP,V:Dormammu 38.00
174 GC,TP,I:Satannish 38.00
175 GC,TP,I:Asmodeus 38.00
176 GC,TP,V:Asmodeus 38.00
177 GC,TP,D:Asmodeus,
    N:Dr.Strange 38.00

178 GC,TP,A:Black Knight 38.00
179 BWS(c),rep.AmazSpM
    Ann.#2 . . . . 38.00
180 GC,TP,V:Nightmare 38.00
181 FB(c),GC,TP,I:Demons of
    Despair 38.00
182 GC,TP,V:Juggernaut 39.00
183 BEv(c),GC,TP,
    I:Undying Ones 36.00
[2nd Regular Series]
1 FB,DG,I:Silver Dagger 35.00
2 FB,DG,I:Soul Eater 20.00
3 FB,A:Dormammu 12.00
4 FB,DG,V:Death 9.00
5 FB,DG,A:Silver Dagger 9.00
6 FB(c),GC,KJ,A:Umar,I:Gaea . . 8.00
7 GC,JR,A:Dormammu 8.00
8 GK(c),GC,TP,O:Clea 8.00
9 GK(c),GC,A:Dormammu,O:Clea 8.00
10 B:MWn(s),GK(c),GC,A:Eternity 8.00
11 JR(c),GC,TP,A:Eternity 6.00
12 GC,TP,A:Eternity 6.00
13 GC,TP,A:Eternity 6.00
14 GC,TP,A:Dracula 7.00
15 GC,TP,A:Devil 6.00
16 GC,TP,A:Devil 6.00
17 GC,TP,A:Styggro 6.00
18 GC,A:Styggro 6.00
19 GC,AA,I:Xander 6.00
20 A:Xander 6.00
21 DA,O:Dr.Strange 5.00
22 I:Apalla 5.00
23 E:MWn(s),JSn,A:Wormworld . 5.00
24 JSn,A:Apalla,I:Visamajoris . . . 5.00
25 AM,V:Dr.Strange Yet 5.00
26 JSn,A:The Ancient One 5.00
27 TS,A:Stygyro,Sphinx 4.00
28 TS,A:Ghost Rider,
    V:In-Betweener 5.00
29 TS,A:Nighthawk 4.00
30 I:Dweller 3.50
31 TS,A:Sub Mariner 3.50
32 A:Sub Mariner 3.50
33 TS,A:The Dreamweaver 3.50
34 TS,A:Nightmare,D:CyrusBlack . 3.50
35 TS,V:Dweller,I:Ludi 3.50
36 Thunder of the Soul 3.50
37 Fear,the Final Victor 3.50
38 GC,DG,A:Baron Mordo 3.50
39 GC,DG,A:Baron Mordo 3.50
40 GC,A:Asrael 3.50
41 GC,A:Man Thing 3.00
42 GC,A:Black Mirror 3.00
43 V:Shadow Queen 3.00
44 GC,A:Princess Shialmar 3.00
45 GC,A:Demon in the Dark 3.00
46 FM,A:Sibylis 3.00
47 MR,TA,I:Ikonn 3.00
48 MR,TA,Brother Voodoo 3.00
49 MR,TA,A:Baron Mordo 3.00
50 MR,TA,A:Baron Mordo 3.00
51 MR,TA,A:Sgt. Fury,
    V:Baron Mordo 3.00
52 MR,TA,A:Nightmare 2.50
53 MR,TA,A:Nightmare,Fantastic
    Four,V:Rama-Tut 2.50
54 PS,V:Tiboro 2.50
55 MGo,TA,V:Madness 2.50
56 PS,TA,O:Dr.Strange 4.00
57 KN,TA,A:Dr.Doom 2.50
58 DGr,TA,V:Dracula 2.50
59 DGr,TA,V:Dracula 2.50
60 DGr,TA,Scarlet Witch 2.50
61 DGr,TA,V:Dracula 2.50
62 SL,V:Dracula 2.50

Doctor Strange (2nd Series) #24
© Marvel Entertainment Group

63 CP,V:Topaz 2.50
64 TSa,'Art Rage' 2.50
65 PS,Charlatan 2.50
66 PS,'The Cosen One' 2.50
67 SL,A:Jessica Drew,Shroud . . . 2.50
68 PS,A:Black Knight 2.25
69 PS,A:Black Knight 2.25
70 BBI,V:Umar 2.25
71 DGr,O:Dormammu 2.25
72 PS,V:Umar 2.25
73 PS,V:Umar 2.25
74 MBg,Secret Wars II 2.25
75 A:Fantastic Four 2.25
76 A:Fantastic Four 2.25
77 A:Topaz 2.25
78 A:Cloak,I:Ecstacy 3.00
79 A:Morganna 2.00
80 A:Morganna,C:Rintah 2.00
81 V:Urthona,I:Rintah 2.00
Ann.#1 CR,'Doomworld' 4.50
G-Size#1 K&R(c),reps Strange
    Tales#164-#168 . . . . 6.00
[3rd Regular Series]
1 V:Dorammu 7.50
2 V:Dorammu 4.00
3 I:Dragon Force 3.00
4 EL(c),A:Dragon Force 3.00
5 JG,V:Baron Mordo 4.00
6 JG,I:Mephista 3.00
7 JG,V:Agamotto,Mephisto 3.00
8 JG,V:Mephisto & Satanish 3.00
9 JG,O:Dr.Strange 3.00
10 JG,V:Morbius 4.00
11 JG,A of V,V:Hobgoblin,
    C:Morbius 5.00
12 JG,A of V,V:Enchantress 2.75
13 JG,A of V,V:Arkon 2.75
14 JG,B:Vampiric Verses,
    A:Morbius 3.50
15 JG,A:Morbius,Amy Grant(C) . . 5.00
16 JG,A:Morbius,Brother Voodoo . 3.50
17 JV,TD,A:Morbius,Br.Voodoo . . 3.50
18 JG,E:Vampiric Verses,A:Morbius,
    Brother Voodoo,R:Varnae . . . 3.50
19 GC,A:Azrael 2.50
20 JG,TD,A:Morbius,V:Zom 3.50
21 JG,TD,B:Dark Wars,
    R:Dormammu 2.50

---

22 JG,TD,LW,V:Dormammu 2.50
23 JG,LW,V:Dormammu 2.50
24 JG,E:Dark Wars,V:Dormammu 2.50
25 RLm,A:Red Wolf, Black Crow . 2.50
26 GI,V:Werewolf By Night 2.50
27 GI,V:Werewolf By Night 2.50
28 X-over Ghost Rider #12,
    V:Zodiac 4.00
29 A:Baron Blood 2.50
30 Topaz' Fate 2.50
31 TD,Inf.Gauntlet,A:Silver Surfer 3.00
32 Inf.Gauntlet,A:Warlock,Silver
    Surfer,V:Silver Dagger 2.50
33 Inf.Gauntlet,V:Thanos,
    Zota,A:Pip 2.50
34 Inf.Gauntlet,V:Dr.Doom,
    A:Pip,Scarlet Witch 2.50
35 Inf.Gauntlet,A:Thor,Pip,
    Scarlet Witch 2.50
36 Inf.Gauntlet,A:Warlock(leads
    into Warlock&Inf.Watch#1) ... 3.00
37 GI,V:Frankensurfer 2.00
38 GI,Great Fear #1 .... 2.00
39 GI,Great Fear #2 .... 2.00
40 GI,Great Fear #3,A:Daredevil . 2.00
41 GI,A:Wolverine 3.00
42 GI,Infinity War,V:Galactus,A:
    Silver Surfer 2.25
43 GI,Infinity War,Galactus Vs.
    Agamotto,A:Silver Surfer ... 2.00
44 GI,Infinity War,V:Juggernaut .. 2.00
45 GI,Inf.War,O:Doctor Strange . 2.00
46 GI,Inf.War,R:old costume ... 2.00
47 GI,Inf.War,V:doppleganger ... 2.00
48 GI,V:The Vishanti 2.00
49 GI,R:Dormammu 2.00
50 GI,A:Hulk,Ghost Rider,Silver
    Surfer,V:Dormammu(leads into
    Secret Defenders)holo-grafx(c) 4.25
51 GI,V:Religious Cult 2.00
52 GI,A:Morbius 2.00
53 GI,Closes Mansion,L:Wong ... 2.00
54 GI,Infinity Crusade 2.00
55 GI,Inf.Crusade 2.00
56 GI,Inf.Crusade 2.00
57 A:Kyllian,Urthona 2.00
58 V:Urthona 2.00
59 GI,V:Iskelior 2.00
60 B:DQ(s),Siege of
    Darkness,pt.#7 .... 5.00
61 Siege of Darkness,pt.#15 ... 3.25
62 V:Dr.Doom 2.25
63 JJ(c),V:Morbius 2.00
64 MvR,V:Namor 2.00
65 MvR,V:Namor,Vengeance 2.25
66 A:Wong 2.25
67 R:Clea 2.25
68 MvR 1.95
69 MvR 1.95
70 A:Hulk 1.95
71 V:Hulk 1.95
72 Metallic(c),Last Rites,pt.1 ... 1.95
73 Last Rites,pt.2 .... 1.95
74 SY,DQ,Last Rites,pt.3 .... 1.95
75 Prismatic cover 3.50
76 I:New Costume 1.95
77 Mob Clean-up 1.95
78 R:Chton 1.95
79 Doc;s new Asylum 1.95
Ann #2 Return of Defenders,Pt4 . 5.00
Ann #3 GI,I:Killiam,w/card 3.25
Ann.#4 V:Salome 2.95
GNv Triumph and Torment MBg,
    F:Dr. Strange & Dr.Doom 9.95
    HC 14.95

DR. STRANGE CLASSICS
March, 1984
1 SD,Reprints 1.75
2 .... 1.75
3 .... 1.75
4 June, 1984 .... 1.75

DR. STRANGE VS. DRACULA
1 rep. MWn(s),GC 2.00

DR. STRANGE/GHOST RIDER SPECIAL
1 Newsstand vers. of Dr.Str.#28 . 6.00

DR. ZERO
Epic
April, 1988
1 BSz,DCw,I:Dr.Zero 2.00
2 BSz,DCw 1.50
3 BSz,DCw 1.50
4 thru 6 .... @1.50
7 DSp 1.50
8 End series, August, 1989 .... 1.50

DOLLY DILL
1945
1 Newstand 70.00

DOOM 2099
1 PB,I:Doom 2099,V:Tiger Wylde,
    foil(c) 5.00
2 I:Rook Seven 3.00
3 PB,V:Tiger Wylde 2.50
4 PB,V:Tiger Wylde 2.00
5 PB,I:Fever 2.00
6 I:Duke Stratosphear 2.00
7 PB,I:Paloma,V:Duke,Fever Haze 2.00
8 PB,C:Ravage 2.00
9 EC,V:Jack the Ripper 2.00
10 PB,w/Poster 2.00
11 PB,I:Thandaza 1.75
12 PB,V:Thandaza 1.75
13 PB(c),JFm(s),V:Necrotek 1.75
14 RLm(c),PB,Fall o/t Hammer#4 . 1.75
15 PB,I:Radian 1.75
16 EC(a&s), ... 1.75
17 PB,V:Radian,w/card 1.75
18 PB, ... 1.75
19 PB,C:Bloodhawk 1.75
20 PB,A:Bloodhawk 1.75
21 PB,Shadow King 1.75
22 PB,R:Duke Stratosphere 1.50
23 PB,R:Tyger Wylde 1.50
24 PB 1.50
25 PB 2.25
25a foil cover 2.95
26 .... 1.50
27 Revolution 1.50
28 Prologue to D-Day 1.50
Becomes:

DOOM 2099 A.D.
29 Doom Invades America ... 1.95
29a Chromium Cover 3.50
30 D:Corporate Head 1.95
31 PB,One Nation Under Doom .. 1.95

DOUBLE DRAGON
July, 1991
1 I:Billy&Jimmy Lee 1.00
2 Dragon Statue Stolen,V:Stelth . 1.00
3 Billy Vs. Jimmy 1.00

4 Dragon Force out of control ... 1.00
5 V:Stealth 1.00
6 V:Nightfall, final issue 1.00

D.P. 7
November, 1986
1 O:DP7 .... 1.00
2 V:Headhunter 1.00
3 RT,Headhunters 1.00
4 RT,V:Wompus 1.00
5 RT,Exorcist 1.00
6 RT,I:The Sweat Shop 1.00
7 RT,V:Clinic 1.00
8 RT,V:Clinic 1.00
9 RT,AW,I:New Paranormals 1.00
10 RT,I:Mysterious People 1.00
11 AW(i)V:Regulator 1.00
12 O:Randy 1.00
13 O:Charly 1.00
14 AW 1.00
15 .... 1.00
16 V:BlackPower 1.00
17 .... 1.00
18 Pitt tie-in 1.00
19 .... 1.25
20 Spitfire 1.25
21 .... 1.25
22 .... 1.25
23 A:PsiForce 1.25
24 A:Mastodon 1.25
25 V:Famileech 1.50
26 V:Famileech 1.50
27 The Pitt 1.25
28 V:The Candidate 1.50
29 Deadweight 1.25
30 V:Para-troop 1.50
31 A:Chrome 1.50
32 I:The Cure,last issue,
    June 1989 .... 1.50
Ann.#1,I:Witness 1.00

DRACULA LIVES
1973—July, 1975
(black & white magazine)
1 .... 10.00
2 O:Dracula 7.50
3 .... 6.00
4 MP 5.00
5 thru 12 .... @4.00
13 July, 1975 .... 4.00

DRAFT, THE
1988
1 Sequel to The Pit 3.75

DRAGON LINES
[1st Limited Series]
1 RLm,V:Terrorist on Moon,
    Embossed(c) 3.00
2 RLm,V:Kuei Emperor 2.25
3 RLm,V:Spirit Boxer 2.25
4 RLm,K:Kuei Emperor 2.25
[Regular Series]
1 B:PQ(s),RLm,I:Tao 2.50
2 RLm, ... 2.50

DRAGONSLAYER
October, 1981
1 Movie adapt. 1.25
2 Movie adapt,November, 1981 . 1.25

DRAGON STRIKE
1 Based on TSR Game 1.50

DRAGON'S TEETH/ DRAGON'S CLAWS
July, 1988

1 GSr,I:Mercy Dragon,
  Scavenger,Digit Steel 1.75
2 GSr,V:Evil Dead 1.50
3 GSr,Go Home 1.50
4 GSr 1.50
5 GSr,I:Death's Head 18.00
6 thru 10 GSr .... @1.75

DREADLANDS
Epic

1 Post-Apocalyptic Mini-series .. 3.95
2 Trapped in Prehistoric Past ... 3.95
3 V:Alien Time Travelers 3.95
4 Final Issue 3.95

Dreadstar (Epic)
© Marvel Entertainment Group

DREADSTAR
Epic
November, 1982

1 JSn,I:Lord Papal 5.00
2 JSn,O:Willow 2.50
3 JSn,V:Lord Papal 2.25
4 JSn,I:Z 2.25
5 JSn,V:Teutun 2.25
6 JSn,BWr,Interstellar Toybox ... 2.25
7 JSn,BWr,V:Dr.Mezlo 2.25
8 JSn,V:Z 2.25
9 JSn,V:Z 2.25
10 JSn,V:Z 2.25
11 JSn,O:Lord Papal 2.00
12 JSn,I:Dr.Delphi 2.00
13 JSn,V:Infra Red & Ultra Violet . 2.00
14 JSn,V:Lord Papal 2.00
15 JSn,new powers 2.00
16 JSn,V:Lord Papal 2.00
17 JSn,V:Willows father 2.00
18 JSn,V:Dr.Mezlo 2.00
19 JSn,V:Dr Mezlo 2.00
20 JSn,D:Oedi 2.00
21 JSn,D:Dr.Delphi 2.00
22 JSn,V:Lord Papal 2.00
23 JSn,V:Lord Papal 2.00
24 JSn,JS,V:Lord Papal 2.00
25 JSn,V:Lord Papal 2.00

26 JSn,R:Oedi 2.00
Ann.#1 JSn,The Price 2.50
See OTHER PUB. section

DREADSTAR & COMPANY
July, 1985

1 JSo,reprint 1.25
2 JSo,rep. 1.00
3 JSo,rep. 1.00
4 JSo,rep. 1.00
5 JSo,rep,December, 1985. .... 1.00

DROIDS
Star
April, 1986

1 JR 3.00
2 AW 3.00
3 JR/AW 3.00
4 AW 3.00
5 AW 3.00
6 EC/AW,A:Luke Skywalker ... 3.00
7 EC/AW,A:Luke Skywalker 3.00
8 EC/AW,A:Luke Skywalker 3.00

DRUID

1 R:Dr. Druid Surprise!!! 2.50
2 F:Nekra 1.95
3 deranged canibal wisemen ... 1.95

DUNE
April, 1985

1 Movie Adapt,Rep. Marvel
  Super Spec,BSz 1.50
2 Movie Adapt,BSz 1.50
3 Movie Adapt,BSz,June, 1985 . 1.50

DYNOMUTT
November, 1977

1 Based on TV series 1.00
2 thru 5 .... @1.00
6 September, 1978 .... 1.00

ECTOKID
Razorline

1 I:Dex Mungo,BU:Hokum & Hex 2.75
2 O:Dex 2.00
3 I:Ectosphere 2.00
4 I:Brothers Augustine 2.00
5 A:Saint Sinner 2.00
6 Highway 61 Revisited 2.00
7 .... 2.00
8 V:Ice Augustine 1.75
9 Love is like a Bullet 1.95
10 .... 1.95
Ectokid Unleashed 2.95

ELECTRIC UNDERTOW
December, 1989

1 MBa,Strike Force 3.95
2 MBa, Will Deguchis 3.95
3 MBa, Alien Invaders 3.95
4 MBa,Attack on Beijing 3.95
5 MBa, Morituri defeated,March,
1990 .... 3.95

ELEKTRA: ASSASSIN
August, 1986

1 FM,BSz,V:Shield 8.00
2 FM,BSz,I:Garrett 7.00
3 FM,BSz,V:Shield,A:Garrett ... 6.00
4 FM,BSz,V:Shield,A:Garrett 6.00
5 FM,BSz,I:Chastity,A:Garrett .. 6.00

6 FM,BSz,A:Nick Fury,Garrett ... 6.00
7 FM,BSz,V:Ken Wind,A:Garrett . 6.00
8 FM,BSz,V:Ken Wind,A:Garrett . 8.00
TPB Rep #1-8 .... 12.95

ELEKTRA LIVES AGAIN
Graphic Novel FM,R:Elektra,A:Matt
  Murdock,V:The Hand 30.00

ELEKTRA: ROOT OF EVIL
1 V:Snakeroot 2.95
2 V:Snakeroot 2.95
3 Elektra's Brother 2.95
4 V:The Hand 2.95

ELEKTRA: SAGA
February, 1984

1 FM,rep.Daredevil 7.00
2 FM,rep.Daredevil 7.00
3 FM,rep.Daredevil 7.00
4 FM,rep.Daredevil 7.00
TPB Reprints#1-#4 .... 16.95

ELFQUEST
August, 1985

1 WP,reprints 6.00
2 WP 3.00
3 WP 3.00
4 WP 3.00
5 WP 3.00
6 WP,Young Cutter V:Mad Coil .. 3.00
7 WP,Young Cutter V:Mad Coil .. 2.50
8 WP 2.50
9 WP 2.50
10 WP,A:Cutter, Skywise 2.50
11 WP,I:Two Edge 2.50
12 WP,The Mysterious Forest .. 2.50
13 WP,The Forest, A:Leetah ... 2.50
14 WP,A:The Bone Woman 2.50
15 WP,The Forest, continued ... 2.50
16 WP,Forbidden Grove 2.00
17 WP,Blue Mountain 2.00
18 WP,Secrets 2.00
19 WP,Twisted Gifts 2.00
20 WP,Twisted Gifts 2.00
21 WP 2.00
22 WP,A:Winnowill 2.00
23 WP,Blue Mountain,A:Winnowill 2.00
24 WP,The Quest Usurped 2.00
25 WP,Northern Wastelands 2.00
26 WP,Rayeks Story 2.00
27 WP,Battle Preparations 2.00
28 WP,Elves vs. Trolls 2.00
29 WP,Battle Beneath Blue
  Mountain 2.00
30 and 31 WP .... @2.00
32 WP,Conclusion, March 1988 .. 2.00

ELSEWHERE PRINCE
Epic
May, 1990

1 thru 5 .... @2.00
6 October, 1990 .... 2.00

ELVIRA
October, 1988
Spec.Black & White,Movie Adapt. 2.00

EPIC
1 Wildcards,Hellraiser 4.95
2 Nightbreed,Wildcards 4.95
3 DBw,MFm,Alien Legion, ... 4.95
4 Stalkers,Metropol,Wildcards ... 4.95

EPIC GRAPHIC NOVEL

Moebius 1: Upon a Star	10.00
Moebius 2: Arzach	10.00
Moebius 3: Airtight Garage	10.00
Moebius 4: Long Tomorrow	10.00
Moebius 5:	10.00
Moebius 6: Pharadonesia	10.00
Last of Dragons	7.00
The Incal 1 Moebius	11.00
The Incal 2 Moebius	11.00
The Incal 3 Moebius	11.00
JBo,Someplace Strange	7.00
MZ,Punisher	16.95

EPIC ILLUSTRATED
Spring, 1980

1 Black and White/Color Mag.	6.00
2 thru 10	@4.50
11 thru 15	@3.50
16	4.00
17 thru 20	@3.00
21 thru 25	@3.00
26 thru 34, March, 1986	@5.50

EPIC LITE
Epic
November, 1991

One-shot short stories	3.95

Eternals (2nd Series) #1
© Marvel Entertainment Group

ETERNALS
[1st Series]
July, 1976

1 JK,I:Ikaris	4.50
2 JK,I:Ajak	3.50
3 JK,I:Sersi	5.00
4 JK,Night of the Demons	2.50
5 JK,I:Makarri,Zuras Thena,Domo	2.50
6 JK,Gods & Men at City College	2.50
7 JK,V:Celestials	2.50
8 JK,I:Karkas, Reject	2.50
9 JK,I:Sprite,Reject vs. Karkas	2.50
10 JK,V:Celestials	2.50
11 JK,I:Kingo Sunen	2.50
12 JK,I:Uni-Mind	2.50

13 JK,I:FOrgottenOne(Gilgamesh)	2.50
14 JK,V:Hulk	2.50
15 JK,V:Hulk	2.50
16 JK,I:Dromedan	2.50
17 JK,I:Sigmar	2.50
18 JK,I:Nerve Beast	2.50
19 JK,Secret o/t Pyramid	2.50
Ann.#1 JK,V:Timekillers	3.00

ETERNALS, THE
[2nd Series]
October, 1985

1 SB,I:Cybele	1.50
2 SB,V:Deviants	1.50
3 SB,V:Deviants	1.50
4 SB,V:Deviants	1.50
5 SB,V:Deviants	1.50
6 SB,V:Deviants	1.50
7 SB,V:Deviants	1.50
8 WS,SB,V:Deviants	1.50
9 WS,SB,V:Deviants	1.50
10 WS,SB,V:Deviants	1.50
11 WS,KP,V:Deviants	1.50
12 WS,KP,V:Deviants	1.50

ETERNALS:
HEROD FACTOR
November, 1991

1 MT/BMc,A:Sersi (giant size)	2.50

EVERYMAN
Epic
One Shot.Supernatural Story
(Animated Cel Artwork) | 4.50

EWOKS
Star
June, 1985—Sept., 1987

1 Based on TV Series	3.00
2	2.50
3	2.50
4 A:Foonars	2.50
5 Wicket vs. Ice Demon.	2.50
6 Mount Sorrow, A:Teebo	2.50
7 A:Logray,V:Morag	2.50
8	2.50
9 Lost in Time	2.50
10 Lost in Time	1.50
11 Kneesaa Shrunk,A:Fleebogs	1.50
12	1.50
13	1.50
14 Teebo- King for a Day	1.50
15	1.50

EXCALIBUR
April, 1988

1 AD,Special,O:Excalibur,	
V:Technet	15.00
1a 2nd Printing	5.00
1b 3rd Printing	4.50
2 AAd,Mojo Mayhem,A:X-Babies	6.00
3 Air Apparent Spec.RLm,KJ,JG,TP,	
RL,EL,JRu,A:Coldblood	5.25

[Regular Series]

1 B:CCl(s),AD,V:Warwolves,	
I:Widget	12.00
2 AD,V:Warwolves,I:Kylun	7.50
3	5.00
4 AD,V:Arcade,Crazy Gang	4.00
5 AD,V:Arcade	4.00
6 AD,Inferno,I:Alistaire Stuart	4.00
7 AD,Inferno	4.00
8 RLm,JRu,A:New Mutants	4.00

9 AD,I:Nazi-Excalibur	4.00
10 MR,V:Nazi-Excalibur	4.00
11 MR,V:Nazi-Excalibur	4.00
12 AD,Fairy Tale Dimension	4.00
13 AD,The Prince,N:Capt.Britian	4.00
14 AD,Too Many Heroes	3.50
15 AD,I:US James Braddock	3.50
16 AD,V:Anjulie	3.50
17 AD,C:Prof.X,Starjammers	3.50
18 DJ,DA,V:Jamie Braddock	3.50
19 RL,TA,AM,V:Jamie Braddock	3.50
20 RLm,JRu,V:Demon Druid	3.50
21 I:Crusader X	3.00
22 V:Crusader X	3.00
23 AD,V:Magik	3.00
24 AD,Return Home,C:Galactus	3.00
25 E:CCl(s),AM,A:Galactus,Death,	
Watcher	3.00
26 RLm,JRu,V:Mastermind	3.00
27 BWS,BSz,A:Nth Man	4.00
28 BBl,Night at Bar	2.50
29 JRu,V:Nightmare,A:PowerPack	2.50
30 DR,AM,A:Doctor Strange	2.50
31 DR,AM,V:Son of Krakoa	2.50
32 V:Mesmero	2.50
33 V:Mesmero	2.50
34 V:Mesmero	2.50
35 AM,Missing Child	2.50
36 AM,V:Silv.Sable,Sandman	2.50
37 A:Avengers W.C.,Dr.Doom	2.50
38 A:Avengers W.C.,Dr.Doom	2.50
39 A:Avengers W.C.,Dr.Doom	2.50
40 O:Excalibur,Trial-Lockheed	2.50
41 V:Warwolves,V:Cable	3.00
42 AD,Team Broken Up	4.00
43 AD,Nightcrawler,V:Capt.Brit	3.00
44 AD,Capt.Britain On Trial	3.00
45 AD,I:N-Men	3.00
46 AD,Return of Kylun,C:Cerise	3.00
47 AD,I:Cerise	3.00
48 AD,A:Anti-Phoenix	3.00
49 AD,MFm,V:Necrom,R:Merlyn	3.00
50 AD,Phoenix,V:Necrom,Merlyn	4.00
51 V:Giant Dinosaurs	2.00
52 O:Phoenix,A:Prof X,MarvGirl	2.00
53 A:Spider-Man,V:The Litter	2.00
54 AD,MFm,V:Crazy Gang	2.50
55 AD,MFm,A:Psylocke	2.50
56 AD,MFm,A:Psylocke,	
V:Saturyne,Jamie Braddock	2.50
57 A:X-Men,Alchemy,V:Trolls	2.75
58 A:X-Men,Alchemy,V:Trolls	2.75
59 A:Avengers	2.00
60 A:Avengers	2.00
61 AD,MFm,Phoenix Vs.Galactus	2.25
62 AD,MFm,A:Galactus	2.25
63 AD,MFm,V:Warpies	2.25
64 AD,MFm,V:RCX,R:Rachel	2.25
65 AD,MFm,R:Dark Phoenix	2.25
66 AD,MFm,V:Ahab,Sentinels,	
O:Widget	2.25
67 AD,MFm,V:Ahab,Sentinels	2.25
68 V:Starjammers	2.00
69 A:Starjammers	2.00
70 A:Starjammers	2.00
71 DaR,Hologram(c),N:Excalibur	6.00
72 KeL,V:Siena Blaze	2.00
73 TSr,V:Siena Blaze	2.00
74 InC,A:Mr.Sinster,Siena Blaze	2.00
75 SLo(s),KeL,I:Daytripper(Amanda	
Sefton),Britannic(Capt.Britain),	
BU:Nightcrawler	3.50
75a Newstand Ed.	2.25
76 KeL,V:D'spayre	2.00
77 KeL,R:Doug Ramsey	2.00

78 A:Zero,Doug Ramsey	2.25
79 A:Zero,Doug Ramsey	2.25
80 A:Zero,Doug Ramsey	2.25
81 Doug Ramsey	2.25
82	2.50
82a foil(c)	3.50
83 regular ed.	1.50
83a Deluxe ed. Kitty,Nightcrawler	2.25
84 regular ed.	1.50
84a Deluxe ed.	2.25
85 regular ed.	1.50
85a Deluxe ed.	2.25
86 regular ed.	1.50
86a Deluxe ed.	2.25
87 KeL,Secrets of the Genoshan Mutate Technology	1.95
Ann.#1 I:Khaos,w/card	3.25
Spec #1 The Possession	4.00
Spec #2 RLm,DT,JG,RL, A:Original X-Men	2.75
PF Cold Blood	4.95
GN Weird War III	9.95
TPB Wild, Wild Life	5.95

FACTOR X

1 After Xavier	3.50
2 Scott vs. Alex Summers	2.25
3 Cyclops vs. Havok	2.25
4 Jean & Scott	1.95

FAFHRD AND THE GRAY MOUSER
Epic
October, 1990

1 MMi	5.00
2 & 3 MMi	@5.00
4 MMi, February 1991	5.00

FAITHFUL
November, 1949

1 Ph(c),I Take This Man	65.00
2 Ph(c),Love Thief,Feb.,1950	50.00

FALCON
November, 1983

Falcon #4
© Marvel Entertainment Group

1 PS,V:Nemesis	2.00
2 V:Sentinels	1.50
3 V:Electro	1.50
4 A:Capt.America, February, 1984	1.50

FALLEN ANGELS
April, 1987

1 KGa,TP,A:Sunspot,Warlock	4.00
2 KGa,TP,I:Gomi,Fallen Angels	3.00
3 KGa,TP,A:X-Factor	3.00
4 KGa,TP,A:Moon Boy, Devil Dinosaur	3.00
5 JSon,D:Angel,Don	3.00
6 JSon,Coconut Grove	3.00
7 KGa,Captured in CoconutGrove	3.00
8 KGa,L:Sunspot,Warlock	2.50

FANTASTIC FORCE

1 Foil stamped cover	2.50
2 Moses	1.75
3	1.75
4 A:Captain America	1.75
5 I:Dreadface	1.75
6 F:Vibraxis	1.75
7 V:Doom	1.75
8 V:Crimson Cadre	1.75
9 Atlantis Rising	1.75

FANTASTIC FOUR
November, 1961

1 JK,I&O:Mr.Fantastic,Thing Invisible Girl,Human Torch Mole Man	13,000.00
2 JK,I:Skrulls	2,500.00
3 JK,I:Miracleman	1,600.00
4 JK,R:Submariner	2,000.00
5 JK,JSt,I&O:Doctor Doom	2,100.00
6 JK,V:Doctor Doom	1,100.00
7 JK,I:Kurrgo	600.00
8 JK,I:Alicia Masters,I&O: Puppet Master	600.00
9 JK,V:Submariner	550.00
10 JK,V:Doctor Doom,I:Ovoids	550.00
11 JK,I:Impossible Man	425.00
12 JK,V:Hulk	700.00
13 JK,SD,I&O:Red Ghost, I:Watcher	350.00
14 JK,SD,V:Submariner	250.00
15 JK,I:Mad Thinker	250.00
16 JK,V:Doctor Doom	250.00
17 JK,V:Doctor Doom	250.00
18 JK,I:Super Skrull	250.00
19 JK,I&O:Rama Tut	250.00
20 JK,I:Molecule Man	250.00
21 JK,I:Hate Monger	175.00
22 JK,V:Mole Man	175.00
23 JK,V:Doctor Doom	175.00
24 JK,I:Infant Terrible	175.00
25 JK,Thing vs.Hulk	300.00
26 JK,V:Hulk,A:Avengers	300.00
27 JK,A:Doctor Strange	130.00
28 JK,1st X-Men x-over	165.00
29 JK,V:Red Ghost	120.00
30 JK,I&O:Diablo	120.00
31 JK,V:Mole Man	100.00
32 JK,V:Superskrull	100.00
33 JK,I:Attuma	100.00
34 JK,I:Gideon	100.00
35 JK,I:Dragon Man,A:Diablo	100.00
36 JK,I:Medusa,Frightful Four	100.00
37 JK,V:Skrulls	90.00
38 JK,V:Frightful Four,I:Trapster	90.00
39 JK,WW,A:Daredevil	90.00
40 JK,A:Daredevil,Dr.Doom	90.00

Fantastic Four #3
© Marvel Entertainment Group

41 JK,V:Fright.Four,A:Medusa	76.00
42 JK,V:Frightful Four	76.00
43 JK,V:Frightful Four	76.00
44 JK,JSt,I:Gorgon, V:Dragon Man	80.00
45 JK,JSt,I:Inhumans(Black Bolt, Triton,Lockjaw,Crystal, Karnak)	90.00
46 JK,JSt,V:Seeker	74.00
47 JK,JSt,I:Maximus,Attilan, Alpha Primitives	60.00
48 JK,JSt,I:Silver Surfer, C:Galactus	750.00
49 JK,JSt,A:Silver Surfer, V:Galactus	200.00
50 JK,JSt,V:Galactus,Silver Surfer,I:Wyatt Wingfoot	250.00
51 JK,JSt,I:Negative Zone	50.00
52 JK,JSt,I:Black Panther	100.00
53 JK,JSt,I:Klaw,Vibranium	60.00
54 JK,JSt,I:Prester John	45.00
55 JK,JSt,A:Silver Surfer	70.00
56 JK,JSt,O:Klaw,A:Inhumans, C:Silver Surfer	58.00
57 JK,JSt,V:Doc Doom, A:Silver Surfer	58.00
58 JK,JSt,V:Doc Doom, A:Silver Surfer	58.00
59 JK,JSt,V:Doc Doom, A:Silver Surfer	58.00
60 JK,JSt,V:Doc Doom, A:Silver Surfer	58.00
61 JK,JSt,V:Sandman, A:Silver Surfer	58.00
62 JK,JSt,I:Blastaar	40.00
63 JK,JSt,V:Blastaar	38.00
64 JK,JSt,I:The Kree,Sentry	38.00
65 JK,JSt,I:Ronan,Supreme Intelligence	43.00
66 JK,JSt,O:Him,A:Crystal	82.00
67 JK,JSt,I:Him	95.00
68 JK,JSt,V:Mad Thinker	38.00
69 JK,JSt,V:Mad Thinker	35.00
70 JK,JSt,V:Mad Thinker	35.00
71 JK,JSt,V:Mad Thinker	35.00

Fantastic Four #13
© Marvel Entertainment Group

72 JK,JSt,A:Watcher,S.Surfer . . 50.00
73 JK,JSt,A:SpM,DD,Thor . . . 30.00
74 JK,JSt,A:Silver Surfer 45.00
75 JK,JSt,A:Silver Surfer 45.00
76 JK,JSt,V:Psycho Man,S.Surf . 40.00
77 JK,JSt,V:Galactus,S.Surfer . . 40.00
78 JK,JSt,V:Wizard 30.00
79 JK,JSt,A:Crystall,V:Mad
   Thinker 30.00
80 JK,JSt,A:Crystal 30.00
81 JK,JSt,J:Crystal,V:Wizard . . . 30.00
82 JK,JSt,V:Maximus 30.00
83 JK,JSt,V:Maximus 30.00
84 JK,JSt,V:Doctor Doom 25.00
85 JK,JSt,V:Doctor Doom 25.00
86 JK,JSt,V:Doctor Doom 25.00
87 JK,JSt,V:Doctor Doom 25.00
88 JK,JSt,V:Mole Man 25.00
89 JK,JSt,V:Mole Man 25.00
90 JK,JSt,V:Skrulls 20.00
91 JK,JSt,V:Skrulls,I:Torgo 20.00
92 JK,JSt,V:Torgo,Skrulls 20.00
93 JK,V:Torgo,Skrulls 20.00
94 JK,JSt,I:Agatha Harkness . . . 20.00
95 JK,JSt,I:Monocle 22.00
96 JK,JSt,V:Mad Thinker 20.00
97 JK,JSt,V:Monster from
   Lost Lagoon 20.00
98 JK,JSt,V:Kree Sentry 20.00
99 JK,JSt,A:Inhumans 20.00
100 JK,JSt,V:Puppetmaster 70.00
101 JK,JSt,V:Maggia 16.00
102 JK,JSt,V:Magneto 18.00
103 JR,V:Magneto 18.00
104 JR,V:Magneto 18.00
105 JR,L:Crystal 12.00
106 JR,JSt,'Monster's Secret' . . 12.00
107 JB,JSt,V:Annihilus 12.00
108 JK,JB,JR,JSt, V:Annihilus . . 12.00
109 JB,JSt,V:Annihilus 12.00
110 JB,JSt,V:Annihilus 12.00
111 JB,JSt,A:Hulk 12.00
112 JB,JSt,Thing vs. Hulk 32.00
113 JB,JSt,I:Overmind 10.00
114 JR(c),JB,V:Overmind 8.00

115 JR(c),JB,JSt,I:Eternals 10.00
116 JB,JSt,O:Stranger 10.00
117 JB,JSt,V:Diablo 8.00
118 JR(c),JB,JM,V:Diablo 8.00
119 JB,JSt,V:Klaw 8.00
120 JB,JSt,I:Gabriel(Airwalker)
   (Robot) 8.00
121 JB,JSt,V:Silver Surfer,D:
   Gabriel Destroyer 15.00
122 JR(c),JB,JSt,V:Galactus,
   A:Silver Surfer 15.00
123 JB,JSt,V:Galactus,
   A:Silver Surfer 14.00
124 JB,JSt,V:Monster 7.00
125 E:StL(s),JB,JSt,V:Monster . . . 7.00
126 B:RTs(s),JB,JSt,
   O:FF,MoleMan 7.00
127 JB,JSt,V:Mole Man 7.00
128 JB,JSt,V:Mole Man 10.00
129 JB,JSt,I:Thundra,
   V:Frightful Four 7.00
130 JSo(c),JB,JSt,V:Frightful Four 6.00
131 JSo(c),JB,JSt,V:QuickSilver . . 6.00
132 JB,JSt,J:Medusa 6.00
133 JSt(i),V:Thundra 6.00
134 JB,JSt,V:Dragon Man 6.00
135 JB,JSt,V:Gideon 6.00
136 JB,JSt,A:Shaper 6.00
137 JB,JSt,A:Shaper 6.00
138 JB,JSt,O:Miracle Man 6.00
139 JB,V:Miracle Man 6.00
140 JB,JSt,O:Annihilus 6.00
141 JR(c),JB,JSt,V:Annihilus 6.00
142 RB,JSt,A:Doc Doom 6.00
143 GK(c),RB,V:Doc Doom 6.00
144 RB,JSt,V:Doc Doom 6.00
145 JSt&GK(c),RA,I:Ternak 6.00
146 RA,JSt,V:Ternak 6.00
147 RB,JSt,V:Subby 6.00
148 RB,JSt,V:Frightful Four 6.00
149 RB,JSt,V:Sub-Mariner 6.00
150 GK(c),RB,JSt,W:Crystal &
   Quicksilver,V:Ultron 7.00
151 RB,JSt,O:Thundra 5.00
152 JR(c),RB,JM,A:Thundra 5.00
153 GK(c),RB,JSt,A:Thundra 5.00
154 GK(c),rep.Str.Tales #127 . . . 5.00
155 RB,JSt,A:Surfer 8.00
156 RB,JSt,A:Surfer,V:Doom 8.00
157 RB,JSt,A:Surfer 8.00
158 RB,JSt,V:Xemu 5.00
159 RB,JSt,V:Xemu 5.00
160 K&R(c),JB,V:Arkon 4.50
161 RB,JSt,V:Arkon 4.50
162 RB,DA,JSt,V:Arkon 4.50
163 RB,JSt,V:Arkon 4.50
164 JK(c),GP,JSt,V:Crusader,R:
   Marvel Boy,I:Frankie Raye . . 4.50
165 GP,JSt,O:Crusader,
   O&D:Marvel Boy 4.50
166 GP,V:Hulk 6.00
167 JK(c),GP,JSt,V:Hulk 6.00
168 RB,JSt,J:Luke Cage 5.00
169 RB,JSt,V:Puppetmaster 5.00
170 GP,JSt,L:Luke Cage 5.00
171 JK(c),RB,GP,JSt,I:Gor 4.00
172 JK(c),GP,JSt,V:Destroyer . . . 4.00
173 JB,JSt,V:Galactus,O:Heralds . 4.00
174 JB,V:Galactus 4.00
175 JB,A:High Evolutionary 4.00
176 GP,JSt,V:Impossible Man . . . 4.00
177 JP,JS,A:Frightful Four
   I:Texas Twister,Capt.Ultra 3.50
178 GP,V:Frightful Four,Brute . . . 3.50
179 JSt,V:Annihilus 3.50

Fantastic Four #67
© Marvel Entertainment Group

180 reprint #101 . . . . 3.50
181 E:RTs(s),JSt,V:Brute,
   Annihilus 3.50
182 SB,JSt,V:Brute,Annihilus 3.50
183 SB,JSt,V:Brute,Annihilus 3.50
184 GP,JSt,V:Eliminator 3.50
185 GP,JSt,V:Nich.Scratch 3.50
186 GP,JSi,I:Salem's Seven 3.50
187 GP,JSt,V:Klaw,Molecule Man 3.50
188 GP,JSt,V:Molecule Man 3.50
189 reprint FF Annual #4 . . . . . . 3.50
190 SB,O:Fantastic Four 4.00
191 GP,JSt,V:Plunderer,
   Team Breaks Up 3.50
192 GP,JSt,V:Texas Twister 3.50
193 KP,JSt,V:Darkoth,Diablo 3.50
194 KP,V:Darkoth,Diablo 3.50
195 KP,A:Sub-Mariner 3.50
196 KP,V:Invincible Man (Reed),
   A:Dr.Doom,Team Reunited . . 3.50
197 KP,JSt,Red Ghost 3.50
198 KP,JSt,V:Doc Doom 3.50
199 KP,JSt,V:Doc Doom 3.50
200 KP,JSt,V:Doc Doom 6.00
201 KP,JSt,FF's Machinery 3.00
202 KP,JSt,V:Quasimodo 3.00
203 KP,JSt,V:Mutant 3.00
204 KP,JSt,V:Skrulls 3.00
205 KP,JSt,V:Skrulls 3.00
206 KP,JSt,V:Skrulls,A:Nova 3.00
207 SB,JSt,V:Monocle,A:SpM . . . 4.00
208 SB,V:Sphinx,A:Nova 2.50
209 JBy,JSt,I:Herbie,A:Nova 5.00
210 JBy,JS,A:Galactus 4.00
211 JBy,JS,I:Terrax,A:Galactus . . 5.00
212 JBy,JSt,V:Galactus,Sphinx . . 4.00
213 JBy,JSt,V:Terrax,Galactus
   Sphinx 4.00
214 JBy,JSt,V:Skrull 4.00
215 JBy,JSt,V:Blastaar 4.00
216 JBy,V:Blastaar 4.00
217 JBy,JSt,A:Dazzler 4.50
218 JBy,JSt,V:FrightfulFour,
   A:Spider-Man 4.00
219 BSz,JSt,A:Sub-Mariner 3.00

220 JBy,JSt,A:Vindicator 3.50	252 JBy,1st sideways issue,V:	298 JB,SB,V:Umbra-Sprite 2.50
221 JBy,JSt,V:Vindicator 3.50	Ootah,A:Annihilus,w/tattoo . . . 4.50	299 JB,SB,She-Hulk,V:Thing,
222 BSz,JSt,V:Nicholas Scratch . . 2.75	252a w/o tattoo 2.00	A:Spider-Man,L:She-Hulk 2.50
223 BSz,JSt,V:Salem's Seven . . . 2.75	253 JBy,V:Kestorans,A:Annihilus . 3.00	300 JB,SB,W:Torch & Fake Alicia
224 BSz,A:Thor 2.75	254 JBy,V:Mantracora,	(Lyja),A:Puppet-Master,Wizard,
225 BSz,A:Thor 2.75	A:She-Hulk,Wasp 3.00	Mad Thinker,Dr.Doom 3.00
226 BSz,A:Shogun 2.75	255 JBy,A:Daredevil,Annihilus,	301 JB,SB,V:Wizard,MadThinker . 2.25
227 BSz,JSt,V:Ego-Spawn 2.75	V:Mantracora 3.00	302 JB,SB,V:Project Survival 2.25
228 BSz,JSt,V:Ego-Spawn 2.75	256 JBy,A:Avengers,Galactus,	303 JB,RT,A:Thundra,V:Machus . 2.25
229 BSz,JSt,I:Firefrost,Ebon	V:Annihilus,New Costumes . . . 3.00	304 JB,JSt,V:Quicksilver,
Seeker 3.00	257 JBy,A:Galactus,Death,Nova,	A:Kristoff 2.25
230 BSz,JSt,A:Avengers,	Scarlet Witch 3.50	305 JB,JSt,V:Quicksilver,
O:Firefrost & Ebon Seeker . . . 2.75	258 JBy,V:Dr.Doom,D:Hauptmann 3.00	J:Crystal,A:Dr.Doom 2.25
231 BSz,JSt,V:Stygorr 2.75	259 JBy,V:Terrax,Dr.Doom,	306 JB,JSt,A:Capt.America,
232 JBy,New Direction,V:Diablo . 5.00	C:Silver Silver 3.00	J:Ms.Marvel,V:Diablo 2.25
233 JBy,V:Hammerhead 3.50	260 JBy,V:Terrax, Dr.Doom,	307 JB,JSt,L:Reed&Sue,V:Diablo . 2.25
234 JBy,V:Ego 3.50	A:Silver Surfer,Sub-Mariner . . 5.00	308 JB,JSt,I:Fasaud 2.25
235 JBy,O:Ego 3.50	261 JBy,A:Sub-Mariner,Marrina,	309 JB,JSt,V:Fasaud 2.25
236 JBy,V:Dr.Doom,A:Puppet	Silver Surfer,Sc.Witch,Lilandra 5.00	310 KP,JSt,V:Fasaud,N:Thing
Master, 20th Anniv. 4.50	262 JBy,O:Galactus,A:Odin,	& Ms.Marvel 2.25
237 JBy,V:Solons 3.50	(J.Byrne in story) 3.50	311 KP,JSt,A:Black Panther,
	263 JBy,V:Messiah,A:Mole Man . . 3.00	Dr.Doom,V:THRob 2.25
	264 JBy,V:Messiah,A:Mole Man . . 3.00	312 KP,JSt,A:Black Panther,
	265 JBy,A:Trapster,Avengers,	Dr.Doom,X-Factor 2.25
	J:She-Hulk,Secret Wars 4.50	313 SB,JSt,V:Lava Men,
	266 KGa,JBy,A:Hulk,Sasquatch,	A:Moleman 2.00
	V:Karisma 3.00	314 KP,JSt,V:Belasco 2.00
	267 JBy,A:Hulk,Sasquatch,Morbius,	315 KP,JSt,V:Mast.Pandem. 2.00
	V:Dr.Octopus,Sue miscarries . . 4.00	316 KP,JSt,A:CometMan 2.00
	268 JBy,V:Doom's Mask 3.00	317 KP,JSt,L:Crystal 2.00
	269 JBy,R:Wyatt Wingfoot,	318 KP,JSt,V:Dr.Doom 2.00
	I:Terminus 3.00	319 KP,JSt,G-Size,O:Beyonder . . 2.25
	270 JBy,V:Terminus 3.00	320 KP,JSt,Hulk vs Thing 2.50
	271 JBy,V:Gormuu 3.00	321 RLm,RT,A:She-Hulk 2.00
	272 JBy,I:Warlord (Nathaniel	322 KP,JSt,Inferno,V:Graviton . . . 2.00
	Richards) 3.00	323 KP,JSt,RT,Inferno A:Mantis . . 2.00
	273 JBy,V:Warlord 3.00	324 KP,JSt,RT,A:Mantis 2.00
	274 JBy,AG,cont.from Thing#19,	325 RB,RT,A:Silver Surfer,
	A:Spider-Man's Black Costume 3.00	D:Mantis 2.50
	275 JBy,AG,V:T.J.Vance 3.00	326 KP,RT,I:New Frightful Four . . 2.00
	276 JBy,JOy,V:Mephisto,	327 KP,RT,V:Frightful Four 2.00
	A:Dr.Strange 3.00	328 KP,RT,V:Frightful Four 2.00
	277 JBy,JOy,V:Mephisto,	329 RB,RT,V:Mole Man 2.00
	A:Dr.Strange,R:Thing 3.00	330 RB,RT,V:Dr.Doom 2.00
	278 JBy,JOy,O:Dr.Doom,A:Kristoff	331 RB,RT,V:Ultron 2.00
	(as Doom) 3.00	332 RB,RT,V:Aron 2.00
	279 JBy,JOy,V:Dr.Doom(Kristoff),	333 RB,RT,V:Aron,Frightful Four . 2.00
	I:New Hate-Monger 3.00	334 RB,Acts of Vengeance 2.00
	280 JBy,JOy,I:Malice,	335 RB,RT,Acts of Vengeance . . 2.00
	V:Hate-Monger 3.00	336 RLm,Acts of Vengeance, . . . 2.00
	281 JBy,JOy,A:Daredevil,V:Hate	337 WS,A:Thor,Iron Man,
	Monger,Malice 3.00	B:Timestream saga 5.00
	282 JBy,JOy,A:Power Pack,Psycho	338 WS,V:Deathshead,A:Thor,
	Man,Secret Wars II 3.00	Iron Man 3.00
	283 JBy,JOy,V:Psycho-Man 3.00	339 WS,V:Gladiator 2.50
	284 JBy,JOy,V:Psycho-Man 3.00	340 WS,V:Black Celestial 2.50
	285 JBy,JOy,Secret Wars II	341 WS,A:Thor,Iron Man 2.50
	A:Beyonder 3.00	342 A:Rusty,C:Spider-Man 2.50
	286 JBy,TA,R:Jean Grey,	343 WS,V:Stalin 2.50
	A:Hercules Capt.America 4.50	344 WS,V:Stalin 2.50
	287 JBy,JSt,A:Wasp,V:Dr.Doom . 3.00	345 WS,V:Dinosaurs 2.50
	288 JBy,JSt,V:Dr.Doom,Secret	346 WS,V:Dinosaurs 2.50
	Wars II 3.00	347 AAd,ATI(i)A:Spider-Man,
	289 JBy,AG,D:Basilisk,V:Blastaar,	GhostRider,Wolverine,Hulk . . . 7.00
	R:Annihilus 3.00	347a 2nd printing 4.50
	290 JBy,AG,V:Annihilus 3.00	348 AAd,ATI(i)A:Spider-Man,
	291 JBy,CR,A:Nick Fury 3.00	GhostRider,Wolverine,Hulk . . . 5.50
	292 JBy,AG,A:Nick Fury,V:Hitler . 3.00	348a 2nd printing 4.00
	293 JBy,AG,A:Avengers.W.C. . . . 3.00	349 AAd,ATI(i),AM(i)A:Spider-Man,
	294 JOy,AG,V:FutureCentralCity . 2.50	Wolverine,GhostRider,Hulk,
	295 JOy,AG,V:Fut.Central City . . . 2.50	C:Punisher 5.50
	296 BWS,KGa,RF,BWi,AM,KJ,JB,	350 WS,Am(i),R:Ben Grimm as
	SL,MS,JRu,JOy,JSt,25th	Thing.(48p) 3.25
	Anniv.,V:MoleMan 4.00	351 MBa,Kubic 2.50
	297 JB,SB,V:Umbra-Sprite 2.50	352 WS,Reed Vs.Dr.Doom 2.50

Fantastic Four #140
© *Marvel Entertainment Group*

238 JBy,O:Frankie Raye,	
new Torch 3.50	
239 JBy,I:Aunt Petunia,	
Uncle Jake 4.50	
240 JBy,A:Inhumans,b:Luna 3.50	
241 JBy,A:Black Panther 3.50	
242 JBy,A:Daredevil,Thor,Iron Man	
Spider-Man,V:Terrax 3.50	
243 JBy,A:Daredevil,Dr.Strange,	
Spider-Man,Avengers,V:Galactus,	
Terrax 4.00	
244 JBy,A:Avengers,Dr.Strange,	
Galactus, Frankie Raye	
Becomes Nova 5.00	
245 JBy,V:Franklin Richards 3.50	
246 JBy,V:Dr.Doom,	
A:Puppet Master 3.50	
247 JBy,A:Dr.Doom,I:Kristoff,	
D:Zorba 3.50	
248 JBy,A:Inhumans 3.50	
249 JBy,V:Gladiator 3.50	
250 JBy,A:Capt.America,SpM	
V:Gladiator 4.00	
251 JBy,A:Annihilus 3.00	

353 WS,E:Timestream Saga,
A:Avengers, ... 2.50
354 WS,Secrets of the Time
Variance Authority 2.50
355 AM,V:Wrecking Crew 2.00
356 B:TDF(s),PR,A:New Warriors,
V:Puppet Master 2.00
357 PR,V:Mad Thinker,
Puppetmaster, ... 2.00
358 PR,AAd,30th Anniv.,1st Marv. Die
Cut(c),D:Lyja,V:Paibok,BU:
Dr.Doom 5.00
359 PR,I:Devos the Devastator . . 2.00
360 PR,V:Dreadface 2.00
361 PR,V:Dr.Doom,X-masIssue . . 2.00
362 PR,A:Spider-Man,
I:WildBlood 2.00
363 PR,I:Occulus,A:Devos 2.00
364 PR,V:Occulus 2.00
365 PR,V:Occulus 2.00
366 PR,Infinity War,R:Lyja 2.00
367 PR,Inf.War,A:Wolverine 2.00
368 PR,V:Infinity War X-Men 2.00
369 PR,Inf.War,R:Malice,
A:Thanos 2.00
370 PR,Inf.War,V:Mr.Fantastic
Doppleganger 2.00
371 PR,V:Lyja,foil(c) 6.00
371a 2nd Printing 3.00
372 PR,A:Spider-Man,Silver
Sable 2.00
373 PR,V:Aron,Silver sable 2.00
374 PR,V:Secret Defenders 2.00
375 V:Dr.Doom,A:Inhumans,Lyja,
Holo-Grafix(c) 4.50
376 PR,A:Nathan Richards,V:Paibok,
Devos,w/Dirt Magazine 3.75
376a w/out Dirt Magazine 2.00
377 PR,V:Paibok,Devos,Klaw,
I:Huntara 2.00
378 PR,A:Sandman,SpM,DD 2.00
379 PR,V:Ms.Marvel 2.00
380 PR,A:Dr.Doom,V:Hunger 2.00
381 PR,D:Dr.Doom,Mr.Fantastic,
V:Hunger 10.00
382 PR,V:Paibok,Devos,Huntara . 4.00
383 PR,V:Paibok,Devos,Huntara . 2.00
384 PR,A:Ant-Man,V:Franklin
Richards 2.00
385 PR,A:Triton,Tiger Shark,
Starblast#7 . . . . 2.00
386 PR,Starblast#11,A:Namor,Triton,
b:Johnny & Lyja child 1.75
387 Die-Cut & Foil (c),PR,N:Invisible
Woman,J:Ant-Man,A:Namor . . 3.25
387a Newsstand Ed. 1.75
388 PR,I:Dark Raider,V:FF,
Avengers,w/cards 2.00
389 PR,I:Raphael Suarez,A:Watcher,
V:Collector 2.00
390 PR,A:Galactus 2.00
391 PR,I:Vibraxas 1.75
392 Dark Raider 1.75
393 . . . . 1.75
394 Neon(c) w/insert print 2.95
394a Newsstand ed.,no bag/inserts 1.75
395 Thing V:Wolverine 1.75
396 . . . . 1.75
397 Resurrection,pt.1 . . . . 1.75
398 regular edition 1.50
398a Enhanced cover 2.75
399 Watcher's Lie 1.75
399a Foil stamped cover 2.50
400 Watcher's Lie,pt.3 . . . . 3.95
401 V:Tantalus 1.50

402 Atlantis Rising,Namor
vs. Black Bolt 1.50
Ann.#1 JK,SD,I:Atlantis,Dorma,
Krang,V:Namor,O:FF 500.00
Ann.#2 JK,JSt,O:Dr.Doom . . . 325.00
Ann.#3 JK,W:Reed and Sue . . . 130.00
Ann.#4 JK,JSt,I:Quasimodo 70.00
Ann.#5 JK,JSt,A:Inhumans,Silver
Surfer,Black Panther,
I:Psycho Man 100.00
Ann.#6 JK,JSt,I:Annihilus,
Franklin Richards 40.00
Ann.#7 JK(c),reprints 23.00
Ann.#8 JR(c),reprints 12.00
Ann.#9 JK(c),reprints. 12.00
Ann.#10 reprints Ann.#3 . . . . . . 12.00
Ann.#11 JK(c),JB,A:The Invaders . 8.00
Ann.#12 A:The Invaders 7.00
Ann.#13 V:The Mole Man 7.00
Ann.#14 GP,V:Salem's Seven . . . 7.00
Ann.#15 GP,V:Dr.Doom,Skrulls . . 5.00
Ann.#16 V:Dragonlord 5.00
Ann.#17 JBy,V:Skrulls 5.00
Ann.#18 KGa,V:Skrulls,W:Black
Bolt and Medusa,A:Inhumans . 5.00
Ann.#19 JBy,V:Skrulls 5.00
Ann.#20 TD(i),V:Dr.Doom 4.00
Ann.#21 JG,JSt,Evol.Wars 4.00
Ann.#22 RB,Atlantis Attacks,
A:Avengers 4.00
Ann.#23 JG,GCa,Days of Future
Present #1 . . . . 5.00
Ann.#24 JG,AM,Korvac Quest #1,
A:Guardians of the Galaxy . . . 3.00
Ann.#25 Citizen Kang #3 . . . . . . 2.50
Ann.#26 HT,I:Wildstreak,
V:Dreadface,w/card 3.25
Ann.#27 MGu,V:Justice Peace . . 3.25
G-Size#1 RB,Thing/Hulk 15.00
G-Size#2 K&R(c),JB,Time to Kill . 9.00
G-Size#3 RB,JSt,Four Horseman . 9.00
G-Size#4 JB,JSt,I:Madrox 10.00
G-Size#5 JK(c),V:Psycho Man,
Molecule Man 7.00
G-Size#6 V:Annihilus 7.00
Spec.#1 Rep.Ann.#1 JBy(c) 2.00
TPB Rep.#347-349 . . . . 5.95
TPB Nobody Gets Out Alive, rep.
Fant.Four #387–#392 + new. 15.95
TPB Trial of Galactus,reprints
#242-244,#257-262 . . . . 9.95
Milestone rep. #1 . . . . 2.95
Ashcan .75

FANTASTIC FOUR:
ATLANTIS RISING

1 B:Atlantis Rising 3.95
2 TDF,MCW,finale, acetate(c) . . . 3.95

FANTASTIC FOUR INDEX
SEE: OFFICIAL MARVEL
INDEX TO THE
FANTASTIC FOUR

FANTASTIC FOUR ROAST

1 FH/MG/FM/JB/MA/TA,May,1982 5.00

FANTASTIC FOUR
UNLIMITED

1 HT,A:Bl.Panther,V:Klaw 4.50
2 HT,JQ(c),A:Inhumans 4.25
3 HT,V:Blastaar,Annihilus 4.25
4 RTs(s),HT,V:Mole Man,A:Hulk . 4.25

5 RTs(s),HT,V:Frightful Four 4.25
6 RTs(s),HT,V:Namor 3.95
7 HT,V:Monsters 3.95
8 . . . . 3.95
9 A:Antman 3.95
10 RTs,HT,V:Maelstrom,A:Eternals 3.95

FANTASTIC FOUR
vs. X-MEN
February, 1987

1 JBg,TA,V:Dr.Doom 5.00
2 JBg,TA,V:Dr.Doom 3.50
3 JBg,TA,V:Dr.Doom 3.50
4 JBg,TA,V:Dr.Doom, June 1987 3.50
TPB Reprints Mini-series 12.95

FANTASTIC WORLD OF
HANNA-BARBERA
December, 1977

1 . . . . 1.00
2 . . . . 1.00
3 June, 1978 . . . . 1.00

Fantasy Masterpieces #11
© Marvel Entertainment Group

FANTASY MASTERPIECES
February, 1966

1 JK/DH/SD,reprints 35.00
2 JK,SD,DH,Fin Fang Foom . . . 14.00
3 GC,DH,JK,SD,Capt.A rep. . . . 12.00
4 JK,Capt.America rep. 12.00
5 JK,Capt.America rep. 12.00
6 JK,Capt.America rep. 12.00
7 SD,Sub Mariner rep. 12.00
8 H.Torch & Sub M.rep. 15.00
9 SD,MF,O:Human Torch Rep . 15.00
10 rep.All Winners #19 . . . . 12.00
11 JK,(rep),O:Toro 12.00
Becomes:
   MARVEL SUPER-HEROES

FANTASY MASTERPIECES
[Volume 2]
December, 1979

1 JB,JSt,Silver Surfer rep. 6.00

2 JB,JSt,Silver Surfer rep. 6.00
3 JB,JSt,Silver Surfer rep. 6.00
4 JB,JSt,Silver Surfer rep. 6.00
5 JB,JSt,Silver Surfer rep. 6.00
6 JB,JSt,Silver Surfer rep. 6.00
7 JB,JSt,Silver Surfer rep. 6.00
8 JB/JSn,Warlock rep.Strange
　　Tales #178 . . . . 5.00
9 JB,JSn,rep.StrangeTales#179 . 5.00
10 JB,JSn,rep.StrangeTales#180 . 5.00
11 JB,JSn,rep.StrangeTales#181 . 5.00
12 JB,JSn,rep.Warlock #9 . . . . . 5.00
13 JB,JSn,rep.Warlock #10 . . . . 5.00
14 JB,JSn,rep.Warlock #11 . . . . 5.00

FAREWELL TO WEAPONS
1 DirtBag,W/Nirvana Tape 3.50

FEAR
November, 1970
1 1950's Monster rep. B:I Found
　　Monstrum,The Dweller
　　in the Black Swamp 10.00
2 X The Thing That Lived 5.00
3 Zzutak, The Thing That
　　Shouldn't Exist 5.00
4 I Turned Into a Martian 5.00
5 I Am the Gorilla Man 4.00
6 The Midnight Monster 4.00
7 I Dream of Doom 4.00
8 It Crawls By Night! 4.00
9 Dead Man's Escape 4.00

Fear #3
© Marvel Entertainment Group

Becomes:
ADVENTURE INTO FEAR
10 GM,B:Man-Thing 8.00
11 RB,I:Jennifer Kale,Thog 5.00
12 JSn,RB 5.00
13 VM,Where World's Collide . . . 3.00
14 VM,Plague o/t Demon Cult . . . 3.00
15 VM,Lord o/t Dark Domain . . . 3.00
16 VM,ManThing in Everglades . . 3.00
17 VM,I:Wundarr(Aquarian) 3.00
18 VM 3.00
19 VM,FMc,I:Howard the Duck,
　　E:Man-Thing 12.00
20 PG,B:Morbius 25.00
21 GK,V:Uncanny Caretaker . . . 12.00

22 RB,V:Cat-Demond 10.00
23 1st CR art,A World He
　　Never Made 10.00
24 CR,V:Blade 10.00
25 You Always Kill the One
　　You Love 9.00
26 V:Uncanny Caretaker 9.00
27 V:Simon Stroud 9.00
28 Doorway Down into Hell 9.00
29 Death has a Thousand Eyes . . 9.00
30 Bloody Sacrifice 9.00
31 last issue,December 1975 . . . 9.00

FEUD
Epic
1 I:Skids,Stokes,Kite 2.50
2 V:Grunts,Skide,Stockers 2.25
3 . . . . 2.25
4 . . . . 2.25

FIGHT MAN
1 I:Fight Man 2.00

FIRESTAR
March, 1986
1 MW,SL,O:Firestar,A:X-Men,
　　New Mutants 5.00
2 MW,BWI,A:New Mutants 5.00
3 AAd&BSz(c),MW,SL,
　　A:White Queen 3.00
4 MW,SL,V:White Queen 3.00

FISH POLICE
1 V:S.Q.U.I.D,Hook 1.25
2 V:Hook 1.25
3 V:Hook 1.25
4 V:Hook 1.25
5 V:Goldie Prawn 1.25
6 Shark Bait #1 . . . . 1.25

FLASH GORDON
1 R:Flash Gordon 2.00
2 AW,final issue 2.95

FLINTSTONE KIDS
Star Comics
August, 1987
1 thru 10 . . . . @1.00
11 April, 1989 . . . . 1.00

FLINTSTONES
October, 1977
1 From TV Series 1.50
2 . . . . 1.25
3 . . . . 1.25
4 A:Jetsons 1.25
5 . . . . 1.25
6 . . . . 1.25
7 February, 1979 . . . . 1.25

FOOLKILLER
October, 1990
1 I:Kurt Gerhardt
　　(Foolkiller III) 4.00
2 O:Foolkiller I & II 3.50
3 Old Costume 3.00
4 N:Foolkiller 2.50
5 Body Count 2.50
6 Fools Paradise 2.00
7 Who the Fools Are 2.00
8 Sane Must Inherit Earth,A:SpM 2.00
9 D:Darren Waite 2.00

10 New Identity, July 1991 . . . . . 2.00

FOORFUR
Star Comics
August, 1987
1 thru 6 . . . . @1.00

FORCE WORKS
1 TmT,Pop-up(c),I:Century,V:Kree,
　　N:US Agent 4.75
2 TmT,V:Scatter 1.75
3 TmT,V:Scatter 1.50
4 Civil War 1.50
5 regular cover 1.50
5a Neon(c),bagged w/print 2.95
6 Hands of the Mandarin,pt.1 . . 1.50
7 Hands of the Mandarin,pt.2 . . 1.50
8 DAn,ALa,Christmas Party 1.50
9 I:Dream Guard 1.50
10 V:Dream Guard 1.50
11 F:War Machine 1.50
12 V:Recorder 2.50
13 DAn,Ala,A:Avengers 1.50

FOR YOUR EYES ONLY
1 HC,James Bond rep. 2.00
2 HC,James Bond rep. 2.00

FRAGGLE ROCK
1 thru 8 . . . . @1.00
[Volume 2]
April, 1988
1 thru 5 . . . . @1.00
6 September, 1988 . . . . 1.00

FRANCIS, BROTHER
OF THE UNIVERSE
(one shot) 1980
1 . . . . 2.50

FRANKENSTEIN
See: MONSTER OF
FRANKENSTEIN

FRED HEMBECK
DESTROYS THE
MARVEL UNIVERSE
1 . . . . 2.00

FRIGHT
June, 1975
1 . . . . 1.50

FRONTIER WESTERN
February, 1956
1 RH, ... 100.00
2 AW,GT 65.00
3 MD 65.00
4 MD 40.00
5 RC 50.00
6 AW, ... 60.00
7 JR 30.00
8 RC 30.00
9 . . . . 30.00
10 August, 1957 . . . . 30.00

FUNNY FROLICS
Summer, 1945
1 (fa) 86.00
2 . . . . 46.00
3 . . . . 38.00

4 .... 38.00
5 HK 45.00

FURY
1 MCW,O:Fury,A:S.A. Heroes . . . 3.25

FURY OF S.H.I.E.L.D.
1 Foil etched cover 2.50
2 A:Iron Man 1.95
3 J:Hydra 1.95
4 w/decoder card 2.50

GALACTIC GUARDIANS
1 KWe,C:Woden 1.75
2 KWe,I:Hazmat,Savant,Ganglia . 1.50
3 KWe 1.50
4 KWe,final issue 1.50

GAMBIT
1 HMe(c),LW,KJ,Embossed(c),D:Henri
  LeBeau,V:Assassin's Guild . . 6.50
1a Gold Ed. 30.00
2 LW,KJ,C:Gideon,A:Rogue . . . 5.00
3 LW,KJ,A:Candra,Rogue,
  D:Gambit's Father 4.50
4 LW,KJ,A:Candra,Rogue,D:Tithe
  Collector 4.00

GAMBIT AND
THE X-TERNALS
1 X-Force after Xavier 3.50
2 V:Deathbird,Starjammers 1.95
3 V:Imperial Guard 1.95
4 Charles Kidnapped 1.95

GARGOYLE
June, 1985
1 BWr(c),from 'Defenders' 2.00
2 .... 1.50
3 .... 1.50
4 .... 1.50

GARGOYLES
1 TV Series 2.50
2 TV Series 1.50
3 F:Broadway 1.50
4 V:Statues 1.50
5 Humanoid Gargoyles 1.50
6 Medusa Project concl. 1.50

GENE DOGS
1 I:Gene DOGS,w/cards 2.75
2 V:Genetix 2.00
3 V:Hurricane 2.00
4 last issue 1.75

GENERATION X
1 CBa,Banshee & White Queen . 5.00
2 CBa,SLo 2.00
2a Deluxe edition 3.00
3 CBa 1.50
3a Deluxe edition 1.95
4 CBa,V:Nanny,Orphanmaker .. 1.50
4a Deluxe edition 1.95
5 SLo,CBa,MBu,two new young
  mutants at the Academy 1.95

GENERIC COMIC
1 .... 1.50

GENETIX
1 B:ALa(s),w/cards 2.75
2 I:Tektos 2.00
3 V:Tektos 1.75
4 PGa,V:MyS-Tech 1.75
5 PGa,V:MyS-Tech 1.75
6 V:Tektos 1.95

GEORGIE COMICS
Spring, 1945
1 Georgie stories begin 120.00
2 Pet Shop (c) 55.00
3 Georgie/Judy(c) 40.00
4 Wedding Dress(c) 40.00
5 Monty/Policeman(c) 40.00
6 Classroom(c) 40.00
7 Fishing(c) 45.00
8 Soda Jerk(c) 35.00
9 Georgie/Judy(c),HK,Hey Look 45.00
10 Georgie/Girls(c),HK,Hey Look 45.00
11 Table Tennis(c),A:Margie,Millie 30.00
12 Camping(c) 30.00
13 Life Guard(c),HK,Hey Look .. 40.00
14 Classroom(c),HK,Hey Look .. 45.00
15 Winter Sports(c) 25.00
16 .... 25.00
17 HK,Hey Look 25.00
18 .... 25.00
19 Baseball(c) 25.00
20 Title change to Georgie
  & Judy Comics 25.00
21 Title change to Georgie
  & Judy Comics 20.00
22 Georgie comics 20.00
23 .... 20.00
24 .... 20.00
25 .... 40.00
26 .... 20.00
27 .... 20.00
28 .... 20.00
29 .... 35.00
30 thru 38 .... @20.00
39 October, 1952 .... 20.00

GETALONG GANG
May, 1985—March, 1986
1 thru 6 .... @1.00

GHOST RIDER
[1st Regular Series]
September, 1973
1 GK,JSt,C:Son of Satan 70.00
2 GK,I:Son of Satan,A:Witch
  Woman 30.00
3 JR,D:Big Daddy Dawson,
  new Cycle 18.00
4 GK,A:Dude Jensen 18.00
5 GK,JR,I:Roulette 18.00
6 JR,O:Ghost Rider 16.00
7 JR,A:Stunt Master 16.00
8 GK,A:Satan,I:Inferno 15.00
9 GK,TP,O:Johnny Blaze 16.00
10 JSt,A:Hulk 16.00
11 GK,KJ,SB,A:Hulk 13.00
12 GK,KJ,FR,A:Phantom Eagle . 12.00
13 GK,JS,GT,A:Trapster 12.00
14 GT,A:The Orb 12.00
15 SB,O:The Orb 12.00
16 DC,GT,Blood in the Water . 12.00
17 RB,FR,I:Challenger 12.00
18 RB,FR,A:Challenger,
  Spider-Man 13.00
19 GK,FR,A:Challenger 12.00
20 GK,KJ,JBy,A:Daredevil 15.00

Ghost Rider #1
© Marvel Entertainment Group

21 A:Gladiator,D:Eel 9.00
22 AM,DH,KP,JR,A:Enforcer 9.00
23 JK,DH,DN,I:Water Wiz. 9.00
24 GK,DC,DH,A:Enforcer 9.00
25 GK,DH,A:Stunt Master 9.00
26 GK,DP,A:Dr. Druid 9.00
27 SB,DP,A:Hawkeye 9.00
28 DP,A:The Orb 9.00
29 RB,DP,A:Dormammu 9.00
30 DP,A:Dr.Strange 9.00
31 FR,DP,BL,A:Bounty Hunt. ... 7.00
32 KP,BL,DP,A:Bounty Hunt. 7.00
33 DP,I:Dark Riders 7.00
34 DP,C:Cyclops 7.00
35 JSn,AM,A:Death 8.00
36 DP,Drug Mention 7.00
37 DP,I:Dick Varden 6.00
38 DP,A:Death Cult 6.00
39 DP,A:Death Cult 6.00
40 DP,I:Nuclear Man 6.00
41 DP,A:Jackal Gang 6.00
42 DP,A:Jackal Gang 6.00
43 CI:Crimson Mage 6.00
44 JAb,CI,A:Crimson Mage 6.00
45 DP,I:Flagg Fargo 6.00
46 DP,A:Flagg Fargo 6.00
47 AM,DP 6.00
48 BMc,DP 6.00
49 DP,I:The Manitou 6.00
50 DP,A:Night Rider 9.00
51 AM,PD,A:Cycle Gang 5.00
52 AM,DP 5.00
53 DP,I:Lord Asmodeus 5.00
54 DP,A:The Orb 5.00
55 DP,A:Werewolf By Night 5.50
56 DP,A:Moondark,I:Night Rider . 5.00
57 AM,DP,I:The Apparition 5.00
58 DP,FM,A:Water Wizard 5.00
59 V:Water Wizard,Moon Dark . . 5.00
60 DP,HT,A:Black Juju 5.00
61 A:Arabian Knight 5.00
62 KJ,A:Arabian Knight 5.00
63 LMc,A:The Orb 5.00
64 BA,V:Azmodeus 5.00
65 A:Fowler 5.00
66 BL,A:Clothilde 5.00
67 DP,A:Sally Stantop 5.00
68 O:Ghost Rider 6.00

69	5.00
70 I:Jeremy	5.00
71 DP,I:Adam Henderson	5.00
72 A:Circus of Crime	5.00
73 A:Circus of Crime	5.00
74 A:Centurions	5.00
75 I:Steel Wind	5.50
76 DP,A:Mephisto,I:Saturnine	5.00
77 O:Ghost Rider's Dream	6.00
78 A:Nightmare	5.00
79 A:Man Cycles	5.00
80 A:Centurions	5.00
81 D:Ghost Rider	11.00

[2nd Regular Series]

1 JS,MT,I:2nd Ghost Rider, Deathwatch	20.00
1a 2nd printing	6.00
2 JS,MT,I:Blackout	11.00
3 JS,MT,A:Kingpin,V:Blackout, Deathwatch	10.00
4 JS,MT,V:Mr.Hyde	15.00
5 JLe(c),JS,MT,A:Punisher	11.00
5a rep.Gold	5.00
6 JS,MT,A:Punisher	7.00
7 MT,V:Scarecrow	6.00
8 JS,MT,V:H.E.A.R.T	6.00
9 JS,MT,A:Morlocks,X-Factor	4.50
10 JS,MT,O:Zodiac	4.50
11 LSn,MT,V:Nightmare, A:Dr.Strange	4.00
12 JS,MT,A:Dr.Strange	4.00
13 MT,V:Snow Blind,R:J.Blaze	4.00
14 MT,Blaze Vs.Ghost Rider	4.00
15 MT,A:Blaze,V:Blackout Glow in Dark(c)	8.00
15a 2nd printing (gold)	3.00
16 MT,A:Blaze,Spider-Man, V:Hobgoblin	3.00
17 MT,A:Spider-Man,Blaze, V:Hobgoblin	3.00
18 MT,V:Reverend Styge	2.50
19 MT,A:Mephisto	2.50
20 MT(i),O:Zodiac	2.50
21 MT(i),V:Snowblind, A:Deathwatch	2.50
22 MT,A:Deathwatch,Ninjas	2.50
23 MT,I:Hag & Troll,A:Deathwatch	2.50
24 MT,V:Deathwatch,D:Snowblind, C:Johnny Blaze	2.50
25 V:Blackout (w/Center spread pop-up)	4.00
26 A:X-Men,V:The Brood	4.00
27 A:X-Men,V:The Brood	4.00
28 NKu,JKu,Rise of the Midnight Sons#1,V:Lilith,w/poster	3.00
29 NKu,JKu,A:Wolverine,Beast	3.00
30 NKu,JKu,V:Nightmare	2.50
31 NKu,JKu,Rise o/t Midnight Sons#6, A:Dr.Strange,Morbius, Nightstalkers,Redeemers, V:Lilith,w/poster	2.50
32 BBi,A:Dr.Strange	2.25
33 BBi,AW,V:Madcap (inc.Superman tribute on letters page)	2.25
34 BBi,V:Deathwatchs' ninja	2.00
35 BBi,AW,A:Heart Attack	2.00
36 BBi,V:Mr.Hyde,A:Daredevil	2.00
37 BBi,A:Archangel,V:HeartAttack	2.00
38 MM,V:Scarecrow	2.00
39 V:Vengeance	2.00
40 Midnight Massacre#2, D:Demogblin	2.50
41 Road to Vengeance#1	2.00
42 Road to Vengeance#2	2.00
43 Road to Vengeance#3	2.00

44 Siege of Darkness,pt.#2	2.00
45 Siege of Darkness,pt.#10	2.00
46 HMe(s),New Beginning	2.00
47 HMe(s),RG,	2.00
48 HMe(s),RG,A:Spider-Man	2.00
49 HMe(s),RG,A:Hulk,w/card	2.25
50 Red Foil(c),AKu,SMc,A:Blaze, R:2nd Ghost Rider	3.25
50a Newsstand Ed.	2.75
51 SvL	2.25
52 SvL	1.95
53 SvL,V:Blackout	1.95
54 SvL,V:Blackout	1.95
55 V:Mr. Hyde	1.95
56 The Next Wave	1.95
57 A:Wolverine	1.95
58 HMe,SvL,Betrayal,pt.1	1.95
59 Betrayal,pt.2	1.95
60 Betrayal,pt.3	1.95
61 Betrayal,pt.4	1.95
62 In Chains,pt.1, A:Fury	1.95
63 In Chains,pt.2	1.95
Ann.#1 I:Night Terror,w/card	3.25
Ann.#2 F:Scarecrow	2.95
TPB Midnight Sons,rep.GhR#28,31, Morbius#1,Darkhold#1,Spirits of Vengeance#1,Nightstalkers#1	19.95
TPB Resurrected rep.#1-#7	12.95
TPB Ghost Rider/Wolverine/Punisher: Dark Design	5.95
Hearts of Darkness	4.95
Poster Book	4.95

GHOST RIDER AND BLAZE: SPIRITS OF VENGEANCE

1 AKu,polybagged w/poster,V:Lilith, Rise of the Midnight Sons#2	4.50
2 AKu,V:Steel Wind	2.50
3 AKu,CW,V:The Lilin	2.00
4 AKu,V:Hag & Troll,C:Venom	3.00
5 AKu,BR,Spirits of Venom#2, A:Venom,Spidey,Hobgoblin	5.00
6 AKu,Spirits of Venom#4,A:Venom, Spider-Man,Hobgoblin	3.50
7 AKu,V:Steel Vengeance	2.00
8 V:Mephisto	2.00
9 I:Brimstone	2.00
10 AKu,V:Vengeance	2.00
11 V:Human Spider Creature	2.00
12 AKu,BR,Vengeance,glow in the dark(c)	3.25
13 AKu,Midnight Massacre#5	2.50
14 Missing Link#2	2.00
15 Missing Link#3	2.00
16 V:Zarathos,Lilith	2.00
17 HMe(s),Siege/Darkness,pt.8	2.00
18 HMe(s),Siege/Darkness,pt.13	2.00
19 HMe(s),HMz,V:Vampire	2.00
20 HMe(s),A:Steel Wind	2.00
21 HMe(s),HMz,V:Werewolves	2.00
22 HMe(s),HMz,V:Cardiac	2.25
23 HMe(s),HMz,A:Steel Wind	1.95

GHOST RIDER/CAPTAIN AMERICA: FEAR

1 GN, AW, V:Scarecrow	6.25

GHOST RIDER 2099

1 Holografx(c),LKa,CBa,MBu,I:Ghost Rider 2099,w/card	2.75
1a Newsstand Ed.	1.75
2 LKa,CBa,MBu,	1.75

3 LKa,CBa,MBu,I:Warewolf	1.75
4 LKa,CBa,MBu,V:Warewolf	1.75
5 LKa,CBa,MBu	1.75
6 LKa,CBa,MBu	1.75
7 LKa,CBa,MBu	1.75
8 LKa,CBa,MBu	1.75
9	1.50
10	1.50
11 V:Bloodsport Society	1.50
12 I:Coda	1.50

Becomes:

GHOST RIDER 2099 A.D.

13 F:Doom	1.95
14 Deputized by Doom	1.95
15 One Nation Under Doom	1.95

G.I. Joe #44
© Marvel Entertainment Group

G.I. JOE
June, 1982

1 HT,BMc,Baxter paper	5.00
2 DP,JAb,North Pole	6.00
3 HT,JAb,Trojan Robot	2.50
4 HT,JAb,Wingfield	2.50
5 DP,Central Park	2.50
6 HT,V:Cobra	2.50
7 HT,Walls of Death	2.50
8 HT,Sea Strike	2.50
9 The Diplomat	2.50
10 Springfield	2.50
11 Alaska Pipeline	2.50
12 V:Snake Eyes	3.00
13 Rio Lindo	2.50
14 V:Destro	2.50
15 A:Red Eye	2.50
16 V:Cobra	2.50
17 Loose Ends	2.50
18 V:Destro	2.50
19 D:General Kwinn	2.50
20 JBy(c),GI,Clutch	2.50
21 SL(i),Silent Interlude	2.50
22 V:Destro	2.50
23 I:Duke	2.00
24 RH,I:Storm Shadow	2.50
25 FS,I:Zartan	2.50
26 SL(i),O:Snake Eyes	3.00
27 FS,O:Snake Eyes	2.50

28 Swampfire	2.50
29 FS,V:Destro	2.50
30 JBy(c),FS,V:Dreddnoks	2.50
31 V:Destro	2.00
32 FS,V:Dreddnoks	2.50
33 FS,Celebration	2.00
34 Shakedown	2.00
35 JBy(c),MBr,V:Dreddnoks	2.00
36 MBr,Shipwar	2.00
2a to 36a 2nd printings	**@1.00**
37 FS,Twin Brothers,I:Flint	2.00
38 V:Destro	2.00
39 Jungle	2.00
40 Hydrofoil	2.00
41	2.00
42 A:Stormshadow	2.00
43 Death Issue,New Joe	2.00
44 V:Cobra	2.00
45 V:Cobra	2.00
46 V:Cobra	2.00
47 V:Cobra,D:Stormshadow	2.00
48 V:Cobra	2.00
49 V:Cobra,I:Serpentor	2.00
50 I:G.I.Joe Missions,R:S'shadow	2.25
51 V:Cobra Emperor	1.50
52 V:Stormshadow	1.50
53 Hawk V:Cobra	1.50
54 V:Destro	1.50
55 The Pit	1.50
56 V:Serpentor	1.50
57 V:Destro	1.50
58 V:Cobra	1.50
59 Armor	1.50
60 TM,I:Zanzibar	2.50
61 MR,D:Cobra Commander	1.25
62 Trial	1.25
63 A:GI Joe Snow Job	1.25
64 V:Baroness	1.25
65 V:Cobra	1.25
66 Stalker Rescued	1.25
67	1.25
68 I:Battleforce 2000	1.25
69 TSa	1.25
70 V:Destro	1.25
71	1.25
72	1.25
73	1.25
74	1.25
75 MR	1.25
76 D:Serpentor	1.25
77 MR,V:Cobra	1.25
78 V:Cobra	1.25
79 MR,V:Dreadnoks	1.25
80 V:Cobra	1.25
81 MR,V:Dreadnoks	1.00
82 MR,V:Cobra	1.00
83 I:RoadPig	1.00
84 MR,O:Zartan	1.00
85 Storm Shadow,Vs.Zartan	1.00
86 MR,25th Anniv.	1.00
87 TSa,V:Cobra	1.00
88 TSa,V:Python Patrol	1.00
89 MBr,V:Road Pig	1.00
90 MBr,R:Red Ninjas	1.00
91 TSa,V:Red Ninjas,D:Blind Masters	1.00
92 MBr,V:Cobra Condor	1.00
93 MBr,V:Baroness	1.00
94 MBr,A:Snake Eyes	1.00
95 MBr,A:Snake Eyes	1.00
96 MBr,A:Snake Eyes	1.00
97	1.00
98 MBr,R:Cobra Commander	1.00
99 HT	1.00
100 MBr	1.50

101 MBr	1.00
102 MBr	1.00
103 MBr,A:Snake Eyes	1.00
104 MBr,A:Snake Eyes	1.00
105 MBr,A:Snake Eyes	1.00
106 MBr,StormShadowStalker	1.00
107	1.00
108 I:G.I.Joe Dossiers	1.00
109 Death Issue	1.00
110 Mid-East Crisis	1.00
111 A:Team Ninjas	1.00
112 A:Team Ninjas	1.00
113 V:Cobra	1.00
114 V:Cobra	1.00
115 Story Concl.Dusty Dossier	1.00
116 Destro:Search&Destroy #1	1.00
117 Destro:Search&Destroy #2	1.00
118 Destro:Search&Destroy #3	1.00
119 HT,Android Dopplegangers	1.00
120 V:Red Ninjas,Slice & Dice	1.00
121 V:Slice & Dice	1.25
122 V:Slice & Dice	1.25
123 I:Eco-Warriors,A:Big Man	1.25
124 V:Headman	1.25
125 V:Headhunters	1.25
126 R:Firefly	1.25
127 R:Original G.I.Joe	1.25
128 V:Firefly	1.25
129 V:Cobra Commander	1.25
130 V:Cobra Commander	1.25
131 V:Cobra Commander	1.25
132 V:Cobra	1.25
133 V:Cobra	1.25
134 V:Red Ninjas, Firefly, Hostilities	1.25
135 V:Cobra Ninja w/card	1.75
136 w/Trading Card	1.75
137 V:Night Creepers,w/card	1.75
138 V:Night Creepers,w/card	1.75
139 R:Transformers,V:Cobra	1.25
140 A:Transformers	1.25
141 A:Transformers	1.25
142 A:Transformers	1.25
143 F:Scarlet	1.25
144 O:Snake Eyes	1.25
145 V:Cobra	1.25
146 F:Star Brigade	1.25
147 F:Star Brigade	1.25
148 F:Star Brigade	1.25
149	1.25
150 Cobra Commander vs. Snake Eyes	2.00
151 V:Cobra	1.50
152 First G.I. Joe	1.50
153 V:Cobra	1.50
154	1.50
155 final issue	1.50
SC GI Joe and the Transformers	4.95
Spec. TM rep.#61	1.50
Ann.#1	3.00
Ann.#2	2.00
Ann.#3	2.00
Ann.#4	2.00
Ann.#5	2.00

G.I. JOE EUROPEAN MISSIONS
June, 1988

1 British rep.	1.25
2	1.50
3	1.50
4	1.50
5 thru 15	@1.75

G.I. JOE SPECIAL MISSIONS
October, 1986

1 HT,New G.I. Joe	1.75
2 HT	1.50
3 HT	1.50
4 HT	1.50
5 HT	1.50
6 HT,Iron Curtain	1.50
7 HT	1.50
8 HT	1.50
9 HT	1.50
10 thru 21 HT	@1.00
22	1.00
23 HT	1.00
24	1.00
25 HT	1.00
26 HT	1.00
27	1.00
28 HT,final	1.00

G.I. JOE VS. TRANSFORMERS

1 HT,mini-series	1.75
2 HT,Cobra	1.50
3 HT,Cobra,Deceptions	1.00
4 HT,Cobra,Deceptions	1.00

G.I. JOE UNIVERSE

1 Biographies rep.#1	2.50
2	2.00
3 MZ(c)	2.00
4	1.25

G.I. JOE YEARBOOK

1 Biographies	2.50
2 MG	2.00
3 MZ(c)	2.00
4	2.00

G.I. TALES
See: SERGEANT BARNEY BARKER

GIRL COMICS
Atlas
November, 1949

1 Ph(c),True love stories,I Could Escape From Love	125.00
2 Ph(c),JKu,Blind Date	65.00
3 BEv,Ph(c),Liz Taylor	90.00
4 PH(c),Borrowed Love	45.00
5 Love stories	45.00
6 same	45.00
7 same	45.00
8 same	45.00
9 same	45.00
10 The Deadly Double-Cross	45.00
11 Love stories	45.00
12 BK,The Dark Hallway	50.00

Becomes:

GIRL CONFESSIONS

13	50.00
14	30.00
15	30.00
16 BEv	35.00
17 BEv	35.00
18 BEv	35.00
19	25.00
20	25.00
21 thru 34	@17.00
35 August, 1954	17.00

All comics prices listed are for *Near Mint* condition.

GIRLS' LIFE
Atlas
January, 1954

1	50.00
2	25.00
3	20.00
4	20.00
5	20.00
6 November, 1954	20.00

Godzilla #23
© Marvel Entertainment Group

GODZILLA
August, 1977

1 HT,JM,Based on Movie Series	9.00
2 HT,FrG,GT,Seattle Under Seige	6.00
3 HT,TD,A;Champions	4.00
4 TS,TD,V;Batragon	4.00
5 TS,KJ,Isle of the Living Demons	6.00
6 HT,A Monster Enslaved	6.00
7 V:Red Ronin	6.00
8 V:Red Ronin	6.00
9 Las Gamble in Las Vegas	6.00
10 V:Yetrigar	6.00
11 V;Red Ronin,Yetrigar	4.00
12 Star Sinister	4.00
13 V:Mega-Monster	4.00
14 V:Super-Beasts	4.00
15 Stampede	4.00
16 Jaws of Fear	4.00
17 Godzilla Shrunk	4.00
18 Battle Beneath Eighth Avenue	4.00
19 Panic on the Pier	4.00
20 A;Fantastic Four	4.50
21 V;Devil Dinosaur	4.00
22 V:Devil Dinosaur	4.00
23 A;Avengers	4.50
24 July, 1979	4.00

GROO CHRONICLES
Epic
1989

1 SA	8.00
2 SA	4.00
3 SA	4.00
4 SA	4.00
5 SA	4.00
6 SA	3.50

GROO, THE WANDERER
(see Pacific, Eclipse)
Epic

1 SA,I:Minstrel	12.00
2 SA,A:Minstrel	8.00
3 SA,Medallions	7.00
1013 SA,Airship	6.00
5 SA,Slavers	6.00
6 SA,The Eye of the Kabala	5.00
7 SA,A:Sage	5.00
8 SA,A:Taranto	6.00
9 SA,A:Sage	5.00
10 SA,I:Arcadio	5.00
11 SA,A:Arcadio	5.00
12 SA,Groo Meets the Thespians	4.00
13 SA,A:Sage	4.00
14 SA	4.00
15 SA,Monks	4.00
16 SA,A:Taranto	4.00
17 SA,Pirannas	4.00
18 SA,I:Groo Ella	4.00
19 SA,A:Groo Ella	3.00
20 SA,A:Groo Ella	3.00
21 SA,I:Arba,Dakarba	3.00
22 SA,Ambassador	3.00
23 SA,I:Pal,Drumm	3.00
24 SA,Arcadio's	3.00
25 SA,Taranto	3.00
26 SA,A:Arba,Taranto	3.00
27 SA,A:Minstrel,Sage	3.00
28 SA	3.00
29 SA,I:Ruferto	4.00
30 SA,A:Ruferto	3.00
31 SA,A:Pal,Drumm	2.00
32 SA,C:Sage	2.00
33 SA,Pirates	2.00
34 SA,Wizard's amulet	2.00
35 SA,A:Everybody	2.00
36 SA,A:Everybody	2.00
37 SA,A:Ruferto	2.00
38 SA,Dognappers	2.00
39 SA,A:Pal,Drumm	2.00
40 SA	2.00
41 SA,I:Granny Groo	2.00
42 SA,A:Granny Groo	2.00
43 SA,A:Granny Groo	2.00
44 SA,A:Ruferto	2.00
45 SA	2.00
46 SA,New Clothes	2.00
47 SA,A:Everybody	2.00
48 SA,A:Ruferto	2.00
49 SA,C:Chakaal	2.00
50 SA,double size	3.00
51 SA,A:Chakaal	2.00
52 SA,A:Chakaal	2.00
53 SA,A:Chakaal	2.00
54 SA,A:Ahak	2.00
55 SA,A:Ruferto	2.00
56 SA,A:Minstrael	2.00
57 SA,A:Ruferto	2.00
58 SA,A:Idol	2.00
59 SA	2.00
60 SA,A:Ruferto	2.00
61 SA,A:Horse	2.00
62 SA,A:Horse	1.75
63 SA,A:Drumm	1.75
64 SA,A:Artist	1.75
65 SA	1.75
66 SA	1.75
67 SA	1.75
68 SA	1.75
69 SA	1.75
70 SA	1.50
71 SA	1.50
72 SA	1.50

73 SA,Amnesia,pt1	1.50
74 SA,Amnesia,pt2	1.50
75 SA,Memory Returns	1.50
76 SA	1.50
77 SA	1.50
78 SA,R:Weaver,Scribe	1.50
79 SA,Groo the Assassin	1.50
80 SA,I:Thaiis,pt.1	1.50
81 SA,Thaiis,pt.2	1.50
82 SA,Thaiis,pt.3	1.50
83 SA,Thaiis,pt.4	1.50
84 SA,Thaiis Conclusion	1.50
85 SA,Groo turns invisible	1.50
86 SA,Invisible Groo	1.50
87 SA,Groo's Army	1.50
88 SA,V:Cattlemen,B.U. Sage	2.50
89 SA,New Deluxe Format	2.25
90 SA,Worlds 1st Lawyers	2.25
91 SA,Bonus Pages	2.25
92 SA,Groo Becomes Kid Groo	2.25
93 SA,Groo destroys glacier	2.25
94 SA	2.25
95 SA,Endangered Species	2.25
96 SA,Wager of the Gods#1	2.25
97 SA,Wager of the Gods#2	2.25
98 SA,Wager of the Gods#3	2.25
99 SA,E:Wager of the Gods	2.25
100 SA,Groo gets extra IQ points	2.75
101 SA,Groo loses intelligence	2.25
102 SA,F:Newly literate Groo	2.25
103 SA,General Monk	2.25
104 SA,F:Oso,Ruferto	2.25
105 SA,V:Minotaurs	2.25
106 SA,B:Man of the People	2.25
107 SA,Man of the People#2	2.25
108 SA,Man of the People#3	2.25
109 SA,E:Man of the People	2.25
110 SA,Mummies	2.25
111 SA,The Man who Killed Groo	2.25
112 SA,Rufferto Avenged	2.25
113 SA	2.25
114 SA,V:Vultures	2.25
115 SA	2.25
116 SA,Early unto Morning	2.25
117 SA	2.25
118 SA	2.25
119 SA	2.25
120 Groo hangs up swords	2.25
GNv Death of Groo	8.00
GNv 2nd print	8.00
TPB Groo Adventures	8.95
TPB Groo Carnival	8.95
TPB Groo Expose	8.95
TPB GRoo Festival	8.95
TPB Groo Garden	10.95

GROOVY
March, 1968—July, 1968

1 Monkeys,Ringo Starr,Photos	50.00
2 Cartoons,Gags,Jokes	40.00
3	40.00

GUARDIANS OF THE GALAXY
June, 1990

1 B:JV(a&s),I:Taserface,R:Aleta	9.00
2 MZ(c),JV,V:Stark,C:Firelord	6.00
3 JV,V:Stark,I:Force,C:Firelord	5.00
4 JV,V:Stark,A:Force,Firelord	4.00
5 JV,TM(c),V:Force,I:Mainframe (Vision)	4.00
6 JV,V:Force,Vance Possesses Capt.America Shield	4.00
7 GP(c),JV,I:Malevolence,	

Guardians of the Galaxy #1
© Marvel Entertainment Group

O:Starhawk 4.50
8 SLi(c),JV,V:Yondu,C:Rancor . . 5.00
9 RLd(c),JV,I:Replica,Rancor . . . 6.00
10 JLe(c),JV,V:Rancor,The Nine
    I&C:Overkill(Taserface) 5.00
11 BWi(c),JV,V:Rancor,I:Phoenix . 5.00
12 ATb(c),JV,V:Overkill
    A:Firelord 3.00
13 JV,A:Ghost Rider,Force,
    Malevolence 4.00
14 JS(c),JV,A:Ghost Rider,Force,
    Malevolence 4.00
15 JSn(c),JV,I:Protege,V:Force . . 3.00
16 JV,V:Force,A:Protege,
    Malevolence,L:Vance Astro . . . 3.25
17 JV,V:Punishers(Street Army),
    L:Martinex,N:Charlie-27, ... 3.00
18 JV,V:Punishers,I&C:Talon,A:
    Crazy Nate 4.00
19 JV,V:Punishers,A:Talon 3.00
20 JV,I:Major Victory (Vance Astro)
    J:Talon & Krugarr 3.00
21 JV,V:Rancor 2.50
22 JV,V:Rancor 2.50
23 MT,V:Rancor,C:Silver Surfer . . 2.50
24 JV,A:Silver Surfer 3.50
25 JV, Prismatic Foil(c)
    V:Galactus,A:SilverSurfer 5.00
25a 2nd printing,Silver 2.50
26 JV,O:Guardians(retold) 2.00
27 JV,Infinity War,O:Talon,
    A:Inhumans 2.00
28 JV,Inf.War,V:Various Villians . . 2.00
29 HT,Inf.War,V:Various Villians . . 2.00
30 KWe,A:Captain America 2.00
31 KWe,V:Badoon,A:Capt.A. 1.75
32 KWe,V:Badoon Gladiator 1.75
33 KWe,A:Dr.Strange,R:Aleta . . . 1.50
34 KWe,J:Yellowjacket II 1.50
35 KWe,A:Galatic Guardians,
    V:Bubonicus 1.50
36 KWe,A:Galatic Guardians,
    V:Dormammu 1.50
37 KWe,V:Dormammu,A:Galatic
    Guardians 1.50

38 KWe,N:Y.jacket,A:Beyonder . . 1.50
39 KWe,Rancor Vs. Dr.Doom,Holo-
    grafx(c) 3.25
40 KWe,V:Loki,Composite 1.50
41 KWe,V:Loki,A:Thor 1.50
42 KWe,I:Woden 1.50
43 KWe,A:Woden,V:Loki 1.50
44 KWe,R:Yondu 1.50
45 KWe,O:Starhawk 1.50
46 KWe,N:Major Victory 1.50
47 KWe,A:Beyonder,Protoge,
    Overkill 1.50
48 KWe,V:Overkill 1.75
49 KWe,A:Celestial 1.75
50 Foil(c),R:Yondu,Starhawk sep-
    arated,BU:O:Guardians 3.25
51 KWe,A:Irish Wolfhound 1.50
52 KWe,A:Drax 1.50
53 KWe,V:Drax 1.50
54 KWe,V:Sentinels 1.50
55 KWe,Ripjack 1.50
56 Ripjack 1.50
57 R:Keeper 1.50
58 . . . . 1.50
59 A:Keeper 1.50
60 F:Starhawk 1.50
61 F:Starhawk 1.50
62 Guardians Stop War of the Worlds
    last issue 1.50
Ann.#1 Korvac Quest #4,I:Krugarr 3.00
Ann.#2 HT,I:Galactic Guardians,
    System Bytes #4 . . . . 3.00
Ann.#3 CDo,I:Irish Wolfhound,
    w/Trading card 3.25
Ann.#4 V:Nine 3.25
TPB rep #1 thru #6 . . . . 12.95

GUNHAWK, THE
See: BLAZE CARSON

GUNHAWKS
October, 1972

1 SSh,B:Reno Jones & Kid
    Cassidy Two Rode Together . . 4.00
2 Ride out for Revenge 2.75
3 Indian Massacre 2.75
4 Trial by Ordeal 2.75
5 The Reverend Mr. Graves 2.75
6 E:Reno Jones & Kid Cassidy
    D:Kid Cassidy 2.75
7 A Gunhawks Last Stand
    A;Reno Jones, October, 1973   2.75

GUNRUNNER

1 I:Gunrunner,w/trading cards . . . 2.95
2 A:Ghost Rider 2.00
3 V:Cynodd 2.00
4 . . . . 2.00
5 A:Enhanced 2.00
6 final issue 1.75

GUNSLINGER
See: TEX DAWSON,
GUNSLINGER

GUNSMOKE WESTERN
See: ALL WINNERS COMICS

HARROWERS

1 MSt(s),GC,F:Pinhead 3.25
2 GC,AW(i), ... 2.75
3 GC,AW(i), ... 2.75
4 GC,AW(i), ... 2.75

5 GC,AW(i),Devil's Pawn#1 . . . . 2.75
6 GC,AW(i),Devil's Pawn#2 . . . . 2.75

HARVEY
October, 1970

1 . . . . 6.00
2 thru 5 . . . . @4.00
6 December, 1972 . . . . 4.00

HAVOK & WOLVERINE
Epic
March, 1988

1 JMu,KW,V:KGB,Dr.Neutron . . . 7.00
2 JMu,KW,V:KGB,Dr.Neutron . . . 5.00
3 JMu,KW,V:Meltdown 5.00
4 JMu,KW,V:Meltdown,Oct.1989 . 5.00
TPB rep.#1-4 . . . . 16.95

Hawkeye Limited Series #4
© Marvel Entertainment Group

HAWKEYE
September, 1983
[1st Limited Series]

1 A:Mockingbird 3.00
2 I:Silencer 2.50
3 I:Bombshell,Oddball 2.00
4 V:Crossfire,W:Hawkeye &
    Mockingbird, (Dec. 1983) 2.00
[2nd Limited Series]
1 B:CDi(s),ScK,V:Trickshot,
    I:Javelynn,Rover 2.00
2 ScK,V:Viper 2.00
3 ScK,A:War Machine,N:Hawkeye,
    V:Secret Empire 2.00
4 E:CDi(s),ScK,V:Trickshot,Viper,
    Javelynn 2.00

HEADMASTERS
STAR
July, 1987

1 FS,Transformers 1.25
2 and 3 . . . . @1.00
4 January, 1988 75

HEARTS OF DARKNESS

One Shot JR2/KJ,F:Ghost Rider,
    Punisher,Wolverine,V:Blackheart,
    (double Gatefold Cover) 5.50

HEATHCLIFF
Star
April, 1985
1 thru 16 .... @1.00
17 Masked Moocher 1.00
18 thru 49 .... @1.00
50 Double-size 1.00
51 thru 55 .... @1.00

HEATHCLIFF'S FUNHOUSE
Star
May, 1987
1 thru 9 .... @1.00
10 1988 .... 1.00

HEAVY HITTERS
Ann.#1 .... 4.00

HEDY DEVINE COMICS
Aug., 1947—Sept., 1952
22 I:Hedy Devine 60.00
23 BW,Beauty and the Beach,
   HK,Hey Look 65.00
24 High Jinx in Hollywood,
   HK, Hey Look 65.00
25 Hedy/Bull(c),HK,Hey Look ... 70.00
26 Skating(c),HK,Giggles&Grins . 50.00
27 Hedy at Show(c),HK,Hey Look 60.00
28 Hedy/Charlie(c),HK,Hey Look 60.00
29 Tennis(c),HK,Hey Look 60.00
30 .... 60.00
31 thru 34 .... @30.00
35 thru 50 .... @30.00

HEDY WOLFE
Atlas
August, 1957
1 Patsy Walker's Rival 35.00

HELLHOUND
1 Hellhound on my Trial 2.50
2 Love in Vain 2.50
3 Last Fair Deal Gone Down ... 2.25

HELLRAISER
See: CLIVE BARKER'S HELLRAISER

HELLRAISER III HELL ON EARTH
1 Movie Adaptation,(prestige) ... 4.95
1a Movie Adapt.(magazine) 2.95

HELLSTORM
1 R:Daimon Hellstrom,
   Parchment(c) 3.50
2 A:Dr.Strange,Gargoyle 3.00
3 O:Hellstorm. 2.75
4 V:Ghost Rider 2.75
5 MB, ... 2.50
6 MB,V:Dead Daughter 2.50
7 A:Armaziel 2.50
8 Hell is where the heart is 2.25
9 LKa(s),Highway to Heaven ... 2.25
10 LKa(s),Heaven's Gate 2.25
11 LKa(s),PrG,Life in Hell 2.25
12 Red Miracles 2.25
13 Red Miracles Sidewalking 2.25
14 Red Miracles Murder is Easy . 2.25
15 Cigarette Dawn 2.75

16 Down Here 2.25
17 The Saint of the Pit 2.00
18 .... 2.00
19 .... 2.00
20 .... 2.00
21 final issue 2.00

Hell's Angel #4
© Marvel Entertainment Group

HELL'S ANGEL
1 GSr,A:X-Men,O:Hell's Angel .. 3.00
2 GSr,A:X-Men,V:Psycho Warriors 2.50
3 GSr,A:X-Men,V:MyS-Tech 2.00
4 GSr,A:X-Men,V:MyS-Tech 2.00
5 GSr,A:X-Men,V:MyS-Tech 2.00
6 Gfr,A:X-Men,V:MyS-Tech 2.00
7 DMn,A:Psylocke,V:MyS-Tech .. 2.00
Becomes:
DARK ANGEL
8 DMn,A:Psylocke 2.00
9 A:Punisher 2.00
10 MyS-Tech Wars tie-in 2.00
11 A:X-Men,MyS-Tech wars tie-in 2.00
12 A:X-Men 2.00
13 A:X-Men,Death's Head II 2.00
14 Aftermath#2 .... 1.75
15 Aftermath#3 .... 1.75
16 SvL,E:Aftermath,last issue .. 1.75

HERCULES PRINCE OF POWER
September, 1982
1 BL,I:Recorder 3.00
2 BL,I:Layana Sweetwater 2.00
3 BL,V:The Brothers,C:Galactus . 2.00
4 BL,A:Galactus 2.00
[2nd Series]
March, 1984
1 BL,I:Skyypi 2.50
2 BL,A:Red Wolf 1.50
3 BL,A:Starfox 1.50
4 BL,D:Zeus, June, 1984 ...... 1.50

HERO
May, 1990
1 .... 2.50

2 .... 2.00
3 .... 1.50
4 RH 1.50
5 RH 1.50
6 October, 1990 .... 1.50

HERO FOR HIRE
June, 1972
1 GT,JR,I&O:Power Man 36.00
2 GT,A:Diamond Back 15.00
3 GT,I:Mace 12.00
4 V:Phantom of 42nd St. 12.00
5 GT,A:Black Mariah 12.00
6 V:Assassin 7.00
7 GT,Nuclear Bomb issue 7.00
8 GT,A:Dr.Doom 7.00
9 GT,A:Dr.Doom,Fant.Four 7.00
10 GT,A:Dr.Death,Fant.Four 7.00
11 GT,A:Dr.Death 6.00
12 GT,C:Spider-Man 6.00
13 A:Lion Fang 6.00
14 V:Big Ben 6.00
15 Cage Goes Wild 6.00
16 O:Stilletto,D:Rackham 6.00
Becomes: POWER MAN

HEROES FOR HOPE
1 TA/JBy/HC/RCo/BWr,A:XMen . 6.00

HOKUM & HEX
Razorline
1 BU:Saint Sinner 2.75
2 I:Analyzer 2.00
3 I:Wrath 2.00
4 I:Z-Man 2.00
5 V:Hyperkind 2.00
6 B:Bloodshed 2.00
7 V:Bloodshed 2.00
8 V:Bloodshed 2.00
9 E:Bloodshed,final issue 2.25

HOLIDAY COMICS
January, 1951
1 LbC(c),Christmas(c) 125.00
2 LbC(c),Easter Parade(c) ... 125.00
3 LbC(c),4th of July(c) 85.00
4 LbC(c),Summer Vacation 65.00
5 LbC(c),Christmas(c) 70.00
6 LbC(c),Birthday(c) 80.00
7 LbC(c),Rodeo (c) 65.00
8 LbC(c),Christmas(c)
   October, 1952 .... 65.00

HOLLYWOOD SUPERSTARS
Epic
November, 1990
1 DSp 2.00
2 thru 4 DSp .... @2.25
5 DSp, March, 1991 .... 2.25

HOMER, THE HAPPY GHOST
March, 1955
1 .... 45.00
2 .... 25.00
3 .... 16.00
4 thru 15 .... @16.00
16 thru 22 .... @14.00
[2nd Series]
November, 1969
1 .... 8.00

2 thru 5 . . . . @7.50

HOOK
1 JRy,GM,movie adaption 1.00
2 JRy,Return to Never Land 1.00
3 Peter Pans Magic 1.00
4 conclusion 1.00
Hook Super Spec.#1 . . . . 2.95

HORRORS, THE
Jan., 1953—April, 1954
11 LbC(c),The Spirit of War . . . 125.00
12 LbC(c),Under Fire 90.00
13 LbC(c),Terror Castle 90.00
14 LbC(c),Underworld Terror . . . 90.00
15 LbC(c),The Mad Bandit 90.00

HOUSE II
1 1987, Movie Adapt. 2.00

Howard the Duck #7
© Marvel Entertainment Group

HOWARD THE DUCK
January, 1976
1 FB,SL,A:SpiderMan,I:Beverly . . 7.00
2 FB,V:TurnipMan&Kidney Lady . 2.00
3 JB,Learns Quack Fu 1.50
4 GC,V:Winky Man 1.50
5 GC,Becomes Wrestler 1.50
6 GC,V:Gingerbread Man 1.50
7 GC,V:Gingerbread Man 1.50
8 GC,A:Dr.Strange,ran for Pres. . 1.50
9 GC,V:Le Beaver 1.25
10 GC,A:Spider-Man 2.00
11 GC,V:Kidney Lady 1.25
12 GC,I:Kiss 4.00
13 GC,A:Kiss 4.00
14 GC,Howard as Son of Satan . 2.00
15 GC,A:Dr.Strange,A:Dr.Bong . 1.25
16 GC,DC,JB,DG,TA,
   V:Incredible Creator 1.25
17 GC,D:Dr.Bong 1.25
18 GC,Howard the Human #1 . . 1.25
19 GC,Howard the Human #2 . . 1.25
20 GC,V:Sudd 1.25
21 GC,V:Soofi 1.25
22 A:ManThing,StarWars Parody . 1.25
23 A:ManThing,StarWars Parody . 1.25
24 GC,NightAfter..SavedUniverse 1.25

25 GC,V:Circus of Crime 1.25
26 GC,V:Circus of Crime 1.25
27 GC,V:Circus of Crime 1.25
28 GC,Cooking With Gas 1.25
29 Duck-Itis Poster Child 1978 . . . 1.25
30 Iron Duck,V:Dr. Bong 1.25
31 Iron Duck,V:Dr. Bong 1.25
32 V:Gopher 1.25
33 BB(c),The Material Duck 1.25
Ann.#1, V:Caliph of Bagmom . . . 1.25

HOWARD THE DUCK MAGAZINE
October, 1979
(black & white)
1 . . . . 2.50
2 . . . . 1.50
3 . . . . 1.50
4 Beatles,Elvis,Kiss 5.00
5 . . . . 1.50
6 . . . . 1.50
7 . . . . 2.00
8 . . . . 1.50
9 March, 1981 . . . . 1.50

HUGGA BUNCH
Star Comics
Oct., 1986—Aug., 1987
1 . . . . 1.25
2 thru 6 . . . . @1.00

HULK 2099
1 GJ,Foil(c),V:Draco 2.50
2 GJ,V:Draco 1.50
3 I:Golden Boy 1.50
4 . . . . 1.50
5 Ultra Hulk 1.50
Becomes:
HULK 2099 A.D.
6 Gamma Ray Scientist 1.50
7 A:Doom,Dr.Apollo 1.95
8 One Nation Under Doom 1.95

HUMAN FLY
July, 1987
1 I&O:Human Fly,A:Spider-Man . 5.00

Human Fly #3
© Marvel Entertainment Group

2 A:Ghost Rider 7.50
3 DC,JSt(c),DP,'Fortress of Fear' 1.75
4 JB/TA(c),'David Drier' 1.75
5 V:Makik 1.75
6 Fear in Funland 1.75
7 ME,Fury in the Wind 1.75
8 V:White Tiger 1.75
9 JB/TA(c),ME,V:Copperhead,A:
   White Tiger,Daredevil 1.75
10 ME,Dark as a Dungeon 1.75
11 ME,A:Daredevil 1.75
12 ME,Suicide Sky-Dive 1.75
13 BLb/BMc(c),FS,V:Carl Braden . 1.75
14 BLb/BMc(c),SL,Fear Over
   Fifth Avenue 1.75
15 BLb/BMc(c),War in the
   Washington Monument 1.75
16 BLb/BMc(c),V:Blaze Kendall . . 1.75
17 BLb,DP,Murder on the Midway 1.75
18 V:Harmony Whyte 1.75
19 BL(c),V:Jacopo Belbo
   March, 1979 . . . . 1.75

RED RAVEN COMICS
Timely Comics
August, 1940
1 JK,O:Red Raven,I:Magar,A:Comet
   Pierce & Mercury,Human Top,
   Eternal Brain 7,000.00
Becomes:
HUMAN TORCH
Fall, 1940
2 (#1)ASh(c),BEv,B:Sub-Mariner
   A:Fiery Mask,Falcon,Mantor,
   Microman 16,000.00
3 (#2)Ash(c),BEv,V:Sub-
   Mariner,Bondage(c) 3,000.00
4 (#3)ASh(c),BEv,O:Patriot . 2,300.00
5 (#4)V:Nazis,A:Patriot,Angel
   crossover 1,600.00
5a(#5)ASh(c),V:Sub-Mariner . 2,750.00
6 ASh(c),Doom Dungeon . . . 1,000.00
7 ASh(c),V:Japanese 1,000.00
8 ASh(c),BW,V:Sub-Mariner . 1,700.00
9 ASh(c),V:General Rommel . 1,000.00
10 ASh(c),BW,V:Sub-Mariner . 1,200.00
11 ASh(c),Nazi Oil Refinery . . . 800.00
12 ASh(c),V:Japanese,
   Bondage(c) 800.00
13 ASh(c),V:Japanese,
   Bondage(c) 800.00
14 ASh(c),V:Nazis 800.00
15 ASh(c),Toro Trapped 800.00
16 ASh(c),V:Japanese 600.00
17 ASh(c),V:Japanese 600.00
18 ASh(c),V:Japanese,
   MacArthurs HQ 600.00
19 ASh(c),Bondage(c) 600.00
20 ASh(c),Last War Issue 600.00
21 ASh(c),V:Organized Crime . 600.00
22 ASh(c),V:Smugglers 600.00
23 ASh(c),V:Giant Robot 600.00
24 V:Mobsters 600.00
25 The Masked Monster 600.00
26 Her Diary of Terror 600.00
27 SSh(c),BEv,V:The Asbestos
   Lady 600.00
28 BEv,The Twins Who Weren't 600.00
29 You'll Die Laughing 600.00
30 BEv,The Stranger,A:Namora 500.00
31 A:Namora 450.00
32 A:Sungirl,Namora 450.00
33 Capt.America crossover . . . 500.00
34 The Flat of the Land 450.00

35 A;Captain America,Sungirl . 500.00
36 A:Submariner 375.00
37 BEv,A:Submariner 375.00
38 BEv,A:Submariner,
Final Issue,August, 1954 . . . 375.00

Human Torch #3
© Marvel Entertainment Group

HUMAN TORCH
September, 1974
1 JK,rep.StrangeTales #101 . . . . 6.00
2 rep.Strange Tales #102 . . . . . . 4.00
3 rep.Strange Tales #103 . . . . . . 4.00
4 rep.Strange Tales #104 . . . . . . 4.00
5 rep.Strange Tales #105 . . . . . . 4.00
6 rep.Strange Tales #106 . . . . . . 4.00
7 rep.Strange Tales #107 . . . . . . 4.00
8 rep.Strange Tales #108 . . . . . . 4.00

HYPERKIND
Razorline
1 I:Hyperkind,BU:EctoKid 2.75
2 I:Bliss 2.00
3 V:Living Void 2.00
4 FBk(s),I:Paragon John 2.00
5 V:Paragon John 2.00
6 Vetus Unleashed 2.00
7 . . . . 2.00
8 I:Tempest 2.00
9 I:Lazurex,w/card 2.25

HYPERKIND UNLEASHED
1 BU,V:Thermakk 2.95

ICEMAN
December, 1984
1 DP,mini-series 2.00
2 DP,V:Kali 1.50
3 DP,A;Original X-Men,Defenders
Champions 1.50
4 DP,Oblivion,June, 1985 . . . . . . 1.50

IDEAL
Timely
July, 1948
1 Antony and Cleopatra 175.00
2 The Corpses of Dr.Sacotti . 150.00
3 Joan of Arc 125.00

4 Richard the Lionhearted
A:The Witness 200.00
5 Phc,Love and Romance 70.00
Becomes:
LOVE ROMANCES
6 Phc,I Loved a Scoundrel . . . 40.00
7 . . . . 30.00
8 . . . . 35.00
9 thru 20 . . . . @20.00
21 . . . . 35.00
22 . . . . 20.00
23 . . . . 20.00
24 . . . . 35.00
25 . . . . 35.00
26 thru 34 . . . . @18.00
35 . . . . 18.00
36 . . . . 30.00
37 . . . . 18.00
38 . . . . 30.00
39 . . . . 18.00
40 thru 44 . . . . @16.00
45 . . . . 19.00
46 . . . . 15.00
47 . . . . 15.00
48 . . . . 10.00
49 . . . . 29.00
50 . . . . 10.00
51 . . . . 10.00
52 . . . . 10.00
53 . . . . 29.00
54 . . . . 10.00
55 . . . . 10.00
56 . . . . 10.00
57 . . . . 19.00
58 thru 74 . . . . @10.00
75 . . . . 18.00
76 . . . . 10.00
77 . . . . 10.00
78 . . . . 18.00
79 . . . . 10.00
80 . . . . 10.00
81 . . . . 10.00
82 JK(c) 18.00
83 . . . . 10.00
84 JK 20.00
85 . . . . 23.00
86 thru 95 . . . . @8.00
96 JK 18.00
97 . . . . 10.00
98 JK 30.00
99 JK 18.00
100 . . . . 10.00
101 . . . . 10.00
102 . . . . 10.00
103 . . . . 10.00
104 . . . . 10.00
105 JK 18.00
106 JKJuly, 1963 . . . . 18.00

IDEAL COMICS
Timely
Fall, 1944
1 B:Super Rabbit,Giant Super
Rabbit V:Axis(c) 100.00
2 Super Rabbit at Fair(c) 56.00
3 Beach Party(c) 45.00
4 How to Catch Robbers 45.00
Becomes:
WILLIE COMICS
5 B:Willie,George,Margie,Nellie
Football(c) 58.00
6 Record Player(c) 30.00
7 Soda Fountain(c),HK,Hey Look 42.00
8 Fancy Dress(c) 30.00

9 . . . . 30.00
10 HK,Hey Look 40.00
11 HK,Hey Look 40.00
12 . . . . 25.00
13 . . . . 35.00
14 thru 18 . . . . @24.00
19 . . . . 35.00
20 Li'L Willie Comics 24.00
21 Li'L Willie Comics 24.00
22 . . . . 24.00
23 May, 1950 . . . . 24.00

IDOL
Epic
1 I:Idol 2.95
2 Phantom o/t Set 2.95
3 Conclusion 2.95

IMMORTALIS
1 A:Dr.Strange 1.95
2 A:Dr.Strange 1.95
3 A:Dr.Strange,V:Vampires 1.95
4 Mephisto, final issue 1.75

IMPOSSIBLE MAN SUMMER VACATION
1 GCa,DP 2.50
2 . . . . 2.00

INCAL, THE
Epic
November, 1988
1 Moebius,Adult 2.50
2 Moebius,Adult 2.00
3 Moebius,Adult, January, 1989 . 2.00

INCOMPLETE DEATH'S HEAD
1 thru 10 rep.Death's Head #1
thru #10 . . . . @2.00
11 rep.Death's Head #11 . . . . . . 1.75

INCREDIBLE HULK
May, 1962
1 JK,I:Hulk(Grey Skin),Rick Jones,
Thunderbolt Ross,Betty Ross,
Gremlin,Gamma Base . . . 7,500.00
2 JK,SD,O:Hulk,(Green skin) 1,800.00
3 JK,O:rtd.,I:Ring Master,
Circus of Crime 1,200.00
4 JK,V:Mongu 1,000.00
5 JK,I:General Fang 1,000.00
6 SD,I:Metal Master 1,500.00
See: Tales to Astonish #59-#101
April, 1968
102 MSe,GT,O:Retold 175.00
103 MSe,I:Space Parasite 90.00
104 MSe,O&N:Rhino 75.00
105 MSe,GT,I:Missing Link 55.00
106 MSe,HT,GT 50.00
107 HT,V:Mandarin 50.00
108 HT,JMe,A:Nick Fury 50.00
109 HT,JMe,A:Ka-Zar 50.00
110 HT,JMe,A:Ka-Zar 50.00
111 HT,DA,I:Galaxy Master 28.00
112 HT,DA,O:Galaxy Master . . . 28.00
113 HT,DA,V:Sandman 28.00
114 HT,DA 28.00
115 HT,DA,A:Leader 28.00
116 HT,DA,V:Super Humanoid . . 28.00
117 HT,DA,A:Leader 28.00
118 HT,V:Sub-Mariner 28.00

119 HT,V:Maximus 18.00	160 HT,V:Tiger Shark 6.00	228 SB,BMc,I:Moonstone,V:Doc
120 HT,V:Maximus 18.00	161 HT,V:Beast 8.00	Samson 3.50
121 HT,I:The Glob 18.00	162 HT,I:Wendigo I 9.50	229 SB,O:Moonstone,V:Doc
122 HT,V:Thing 22.00	163 HT,I:Gremlin 6.00	Samson 3.50
123 HT,V:Leader 18.00	164 HT,I:Capt.Omen 6.00	230 JM,BL,A:Bug Thing 3.50
124 HT,SB,V:Rhino,Leader 18.00	165 HT,I:Aquon 6.00	231 SB,I:Fred Sloan 3.50
125 HT,V:Absorbing Man 18.00	166 HT,I:Zzzax 6.00	232 SB,A:Capt.America 3.50
126 HT,A:Dr.Strange 18.00	167 HT,JAb,V:Modok 6.00	233 SB,A:Marvel Man 3.50
127 HT,Moleman vs.Tyrannus	168 HT,JAb,I:Harpy 6.00	234 SB,Marvel Man Changes name
I:Mogol 10.00	169 HT,JAb,I:Bi-Beast 6.00	to Quasar 3.50
128 HT,A:Avengers 10.00	170 HT,JAb,V:Volcano 6.00	235 SB,A:Machine Man 3.50
129 HT,V:Glob 10.00	171 HT,JAb,A:Abomination,Rhino .. 6.00	236 SB,A:Machine Man 3.50
130 HT,Banner Vs Hulk 10.00	172 HT,JAb,X:X-Men 7.00	237 SB,A:Machine Man 3.50
131 HT,A:Iron Man 9.00	173 HT,V:Cobolt Man 6.00	238 SB,JAb,Jimmy Carter 3.50
132 HT,JSe,V:Hydra 9.00	174 HT,V:Cobolt Man 6.00	239 SB,I:Gold Bug 3.50
133 HT,JSe,I:Draxon 9.00	175 JAb,V:Inhumans 6.00	240 SB,Eldorado 3.50
134 HT,SB,I:Golem 9.00	176 HT,JAb,A:Man-Beast,C:Warlock	241 SB,A:Tyrannus 3.00
135 HT,SB,V:Kang 9.00	Crisis on Counter-Earth .. 17.00	242 SB,Eldorado 3.00
	177 HT,JAb,D:Warlock 20.00	243 SB,A:Gammernon 3.00
	178 HT,JAb,Warlock Lives 20.00	244 SB,A:It 3.00
	179 HT,JAb, ... 6.00	245 SB,A:Super Mandroid 3.00
	180 HT,JAb,I:Wolverine	246 SB,V:Capt.Marvel 3.00
	V:Wendigo I 110.00	247 SB,A:Bat Dragon 3.00
	181 HT,JAb,A:Wolverine (1st	248 SB,V:Gardener 3.00
	Full Story),V:Wendigo II ... 350.00	249 SD,R:Jack Frost 3.00
	182 HT,JAb,I&D:Crackajack	250 SB,A:Silver Surfer 12.00
	Jackson,C:Wolverine 65.00	251 MG,A:3-D Man 3.00
	183 HT,V:Zzzaz 5.00	252 SB,A:Woodgod 3.00
	184 HT,V:Living Shadow 5.00	253 SB,A:Woodgod 3.00
	185 HT,V:General Ross 5.00	254 SB,I:U-Foes 3.00
	186 HT,I:Devastator 5.00	255 SB,V:Thor 3.00
	187 HT,JSt,V:Gremlin 5.00	256 SB,I&O:Sabra 3.00
	188 HT,JSt,I:Droog 5.00	257 SB,I&O:Arabian Knight 3.00
	189 HT,JSt,I:Datrine 5.00	258 I:Soviet Super Soldiers 3.00
	190 HT,MSe,Toadman 5.00	259 SB,A:Soviet Super-Soldiers
	191 HT,JSt,Toadman,I:Glorian ... 5.00	O:Darkstar 3.00
	192 HT,V:The Lurker 5.00	260 SB,Sugata 3.00
	193 HT,JSt,Doc.Samson regains	261 SB,V:Absorbing Man 3.00
	Powers 5.00	262 SB,I:Glazer 3.00
	194 SB,JSt,V:Locust 5.00	263 SB,A:Avalanche 3.00
	195 SB,JSt,V:Abomination 5.00	264 SB,A:Corruptor 3.00
	196 SB,JSt,V:Army 5.00	265 SB,I:Rangers 3.50
	197 BWr(c),SB,JSt,A:Man-Thing . 5.00	266 SB,V:High Evolutionary 2.50
	198 SB,JSt,A:Man-Thing 5.00	267 SB,V:Rainbow,O:Glorian ... 2.50

Incredible Hulk #141
© Marvel Entertainment Group

136 HT,SB,I:Xeron 9.00	199 SB,JSt,V:Shield,Doc Samson 5.00	268 SB,I:Pariah 2.50
137 HT,V:Abomination 9.00	200 SB,JSt,Multi,Hulk in Glenn	269 SB,I:Bereet 2.50
138 HT,V:Sandman 9.00	Talbots Brain 33.00	270 SB,A:Abomination 2.50
139 HT,V:Leader 9.00	201 SB,JSt,V:Fake Conan 4.00	271 SB,I:Rocket Raccoon,
140 HT,V:Psyklop 9.00	202 SB,JSt,A:Jarella 4.00	20th Anniv. 2.50
141 HT,JSe,I&O:Doc Samson .. 10.00	203 SB,JSt,A:Jarella 4.00	272 SB,C:X-Men,I:Wendigo III ... 4.00
142 HT,JSe,V:Valkyrie,A:Doc	204 SB,JStI:Kronus 4.00	273 SB,A:Alpha Flight 4.00
Samson 7.50	205 SB,JSt,D:Jarella 4.00	274 SB,Beroct 2.50
143 DA,JSe,V:Dr.Doom 7.50	206 SB,JSt,C:Dr.Strange 4.00	275 SB,JSt,I:Megalith 2.50
144 DA,JSe,V:Dr.Doom 7.50	207 SB,JSt,A:Dr.Strange 4.00	276 SB,JSt,V:U-Foes 2.50
145 HT,JSe,O:Retold 9.00	208 SB,JSt,V:Absorbing Man ... 4.00	277 SB,JSt,U-Foes 2.50
146 HT,JSe,Leader 6.00	209 SB,JSt,V:Absorbing Man ... 4.00	278 SB,JSt,C:X-Men,
147 HT,JSe,Doc Samson loses	210 SB,A:Dr.Druid,O:Merlin II ... 4.00	Avengers,Fantastic Four 2.50
Powers 6.00	211 SB,A:Dr.Druid 4.00	279 SB,JSt,C:X-Men,
148 HT,JSe,I:Fialan 6.00	212 SB,I:Constrictor 4.50	Avengers,Fantastic Four 2.50
149 HT,JSe,I:Inheritor 6.00	213 SB,TP,I:Quintronic Man 4.00	280 SB,JSt,Jack Daw 2.50
150 HT,JSe,I:Viking,A:Havoc ... 11.00	214 SB,Jack of Hearts 4.00	281 SB,JSt,Trapped in Space ... 2.50
151 HT,JSe,C:Ant Man 6.00	215 SB,V:Bi-Beast 3.50	282 SB,JSt,A:She Hulk 2.50
152 HT,DA,Many Cameos 6.00	216 SB,Gen.Ross 3.50	283 SB,JSt,A:Avengers 2.50
153 HT,JSe,C:Capt.America 6.00	217 SB,I:Stilts,A:Ringmaster ... 3.50	284 SB,JSt,A:Avengers 2.50
154 HT,JSe,A:Ant Man,	218 SB,KP,Doc Samson versus	285 SB,JSt,Northwind,V:Zzzax ... 2.50
V:Chameleon 6.00	Rhino 3.50	286 SB,JSt,V:Soldier 2.50
155 HT,JSe,I:Shaper of Worlds .. 6.00	219 SB,V:Capt.Barravuda 3.50	287 SB,JSt,V:Soldier 2.50
156 HT,V:Hulk 6.00	220 SB,Robinson Crusoe 3.50	288 SB,JSt,V:Abomination 2.50
157 HT,I:Omnivac,Rhino 6.00	221 SB,AA,A:Sting Ray 3.50	289 SB,JSt,V:Modok 2.50
158 HT,C:Warlock,V:Rhino 6.00	222 JSn,AA,Cavern of Bones ... 3.50	290 SB,JSt,V:Modok 2.50
159 HT,V:Abomination,Rhino 6.00	223 SB,V:Leader 3.50	291 SB,JSt,V:Thunderbolt Ross .. 2.50
	224 SB,V:The Leader 3.50	292 SB,JSt,V:Dragon Man 2.50
	225 SB,V:Leader,A:Doc Samson . 3.50	293 SB,V:Nightmare 2.50
	226 SB,JSt,A:Doc Samson 3.50	294 SB,V:Boomerang 2.50
	227 SB,JK,A:Doc Samson 3.50	295 SB,V:Boomerang 2.50

Incredible Hulk #177
© Marvel Entertainment Group

296 SB,A:Rom 2.50
297 SB,V:Nightmare 2.50
298 KN(c),SB,V:Nightmare 2.50
299 SB,A:Shield 2.50
300 SB,A:Spider-Man,Avengers
    Doctor Strange 6.00
301 SB,Crossroads 2.50
302 SB,Crossroads 2.50
303 SB,V:The Knights 2.50
304 SB,V:U-Foes 2.50
305 SB,V:U-Foes 2.50
306 SB,V:Klaatu 2.50
307 SB,V:Klaatu 2.50
308 SB,V:Puffball Collective 2.50
309 SB,V:Goblin & Glow 2.50
310 Crossroads 2.50
311 Crossroads 2.50
312 Secret Wars II,O:Bruce 3.50
313 A:Alpha Flight 2.50
314 JBy,V:Doc Samson 6.00
315 JBy,A:Doc Samson,Banner
    & Hulk Separated 3.00
316 JBy,A:Avengers,N:Doc
    Samson 3.00
317 JBy,I:Hulkbusters,A:Doc
    Samson 3.00
318 JBy,A:Doc Samson 3.00
319 JBy,W:Bruce & Betty 5.00
320 AM,A:Doc Samson 2.50
321 AM,A:Avengers 2.50
322 AM,A:Avengers 2.50
323 AM,A:Avengers 2.50
324 AM,R:Grey Hulk(1st since #1),
    A:Doc Samson 11.00
325 AM,Rick Jones as Hulk 3.50
326 A:Rick Jones,New Hulk 6.00
327 AM,F:General Ross 2.50
328 AM,1st PDd(s),Outcasts 7.00
329 AM,V:Enigma 5.00
330 1st TM Hulk,D:T-bolt Ross . 22.00
331 TM,V:Leader 18.00
332 TM,V:Leader 12.00
333 TM,V:Leader 12.00
334 TM,I:Half-life 12.00
335 HorrorIssue 5.00

336 TM,A:X-Factor 10.00
337 TM,A:X-Factor,
    A:Doc Samson 10.00
338 TM,I:Mercy,V:Shield 10.00
339 TM,A:RickJones 10.00
340 TM,Hulk vs Wolverine 40.00
341 TM,V:Man Bull 9.00
342 TM,V:Leader 9.00
343 TM,V:Leader 9.00
344 TM,V:Leader 9.00
345 TM,V:Leader,Double-Size . . 11.00
346 TM,EL,L:Rick Jones 7.00
347 In Las Vegas,I:Marlo Chandler,
    V:Absorbing Man 5.00
348 V:Absorbing Man 4.00
349 A:Spider-Man 4.50
350 Hulk vs Thing,A:Beast
    V:Dr.Doom 5.00
351 R:Jarella's World 4.00
352 V:Inquisitor 4.00
353 R:Bruce Banner 4.00
354 V:Maggia 4.00
355 V:Glorian 4.00
356 V:Glorian,Cloot 4.00
357 V:Glorian,Cloot 4.00
358 V:Glorian,Cloot 4.00
359 JBy(c),C:Wolverine(illusion) . . 5.00
360 V:Nightmare & Dyspare 4.00
361 A:Iron Man,V:Maggia 4.00
362 V:Werewolf By Night 4.00
363 Acts of Vengeance 4.00
364 A:Abomination,B:Countdown . 4.00
365 A:Fantastic Four 4.00
366 A:Leader,I:Riot Squad 4.00
367 1st DK Hulk,I:Madman(Leader's
    brother),E:Countdown 18.00
368 SK,V:Mr.Hyde 10.00
369 DK,V:Freedom Force 9.00
370 DK,R:Original Defenders 9.00
371 DK,BMc,A:Orig.Defenders . . 7.00
372 DK,R:Green Hulk 16.00
373 DK,Green Hulk & Grey Hulk . 7.00
374 DK,BMc,Skrulls,
    R:Rick Jones 7.00
375 DK,BMc,V:Super Skrull 7.00
376 DK,BMc,Green Hulk,Grey
    Hulk & Banner fight 8.00
377 DK,BMc,New Green Hulk,
    combination of green,grey, and
    Bruce Banner,A:Ringmaster . 20.00
377a 2nd printing (gold) 8.50
378 V:Rhino,Christmas Issue 4.00
379 DK,MFm,I:Pantheon 10.00
380 A:Nick Fury,D:Crazy-8 . . . . . 4.00
381 DK,MFm,Hulk J:Pantheon . . 6.00
382 DK,MFm,A:Pantheon 6.00
383 DK,MFm,Infinity Gauntlet . . . 6.00
384 DK,MFm,Infinity Gauntlet . . . 6.00
385 DK,MFm,Infinity Gauntlet . . . 6.00
386 DK,MFm,V:Sabra,A:Achilles . 5.00
387 DK,MFm,A:Sabra,A:Achilles . 5.00
388 DK,MFm,I:Speed Freak,Jim
    Wilson,revealed to have AIDS . 5.00
389 1st Comic art By Gary Barker
    (Garfield),A:Man-Thing,Glob . . 4.00
390 DK,MFm,B:War & Pieces,
    C:X-Factor 5.00
391 DK,MFm,V:X-Factor 5.00
392 DK,MFm,E:War & Pieces,
    A:X:Factor 5.00
393 DK,MFm,R:Igor,A:Soviet Super
    Soldiers,30th Anniv.,Green
    foil(c) 8.00
393a 2nd printing,Silver 2.50
394 MFm(i),F:Atalanta,I:Trauma . 3.00

395 DK,MFm,A:Punisher,
    I:Mr.Frost 4.00
396 DK,MFm,A:Punisher,
    V:Mr.Frost 4.00
397 DK,MFm,B:Ghost of the
    Past,V:U-Foes,A:Leader 4.00
398 DK,MFm,D:Marlo,V:Leader . . 4.00
399 JD,A:FF,Dr.Strange 3.00
400 JD,MFm,E:Ghost of the Past,
    V:Leader,1st Holo-grafx(c),1st
    GFr Hulk(pin-up) 5.00
400a 2nd Printing 2.50
401 JDu,O:Agememnon 2.00
402 JDu,V:Juggernaut 2.00
403 GFr,V:Red Skull,Avengers . 4.00
404 GFr,V:Red Skull,Juggernaut,
    A:Avengers 3.50
405 GFr,Ajax Vs. Achilles 2.75
406 GFr,V:Captain America 2.00
407 GFr,I:Piecemeal,A:Madman,
    B:O:Ulysses 2.00
408 GFr,V:Madman,Piecemeal,
    D:Perseus,A:Motormouth,
    Killpower 1.75
409 GFr,A:Motormouth,Killpower,
    V:Madman 1.75
410 GFr,A:Nick Fury,S.H.I.E.L.D.,
    Margo agrees to marry Rick . . 1.75
411 GFr,V:Nick Fury,S.H.I.E.L.D. . 1.75
412 PaP,V:Bi-Beast,A:She-Hulk . . 1.75
413 GFr,CaS,B:Troyjan War,
    I:Cassiopea,Armageddon,
    V:Trauma 1.75
414 GFr,CaS,V:Trauma,C:S.Surfer 1.75
415 GFr,CaS,V:Trauma,A:Silver
    Surfer,Starjammers 1.75
416 GFr,CaS,E:Troyjan War,D:Trauma,
    A:S.Surfer,Starjammers 1.75
417 GFr,CaS,Rick's/Marlo's Bachelor/
    Bachelorette Party 1.75
418 GFr,CaS,W:Rick & Marlo,
    A:Various Marvel persons,
    Die Cut(c) 2.75
418a Newsstand Ed. 1.75
419 CaS,V:Talos 1.75
420 GFr,CaS,AIDS Story,
    D: Jim Wilson 1.75
421 CaS,B:Myth Conceptions . . . 1.75
422 GFr,Myth Conceptions,pt.2 . . 1.75
423 GFr,CaS,MythConcept.,pt.3 . 1.50
424 B:Fall of the Hammer 1.50
425 Enhanced cover 3.50
426 PDa,LSh,R:Mercy 1.50
426a deluxe edition 1.95
427 A:Man-Thing 1.50
427a deluxe edition 1.95
428 Suffer The Children 1.95
429 Abortion Issue 1.95
430 A:Speed Freak 1.95
431 PDa,LSh R:Abomination 1.95
Ann.#1,A:Inhumans 56.00
Ann.#2 rep.O:Hulk,A:Leader . . 35.00
Ann.#3 rep.A:Leader 10.00
Ann.#4 IR:Hulk/Banner 8.00
Ann.#5 V:Xemnu,Diablo 6.00
Ann.#6 HT,A:Dr.Strange,I:Paragon
    (Her) 4.00
Ann.#7 JBy,BL,A:Angel,Iceman
    A:Doc Samson 7.00
Ann.#8 Alpha Flight 6.00
Ann.#9 Checkmate 3.00
Ann.#10,A:Captain Universe . . . 3.00
Ann.#11 RB,JSt,A:Spider-Man,
    Avengers,V:Unis 4.00
Ann.#12 . . . . 3.00

Ann.#13 . . . . 3.00	
Ann.#14 JBy,SB 3.00	
Ann.#15 V:Abomitation 3.00	
Ann.#16 HT,Life Form #3,	
A:Mercy 3.00	
Ann.#17 Subterran.Odyssey #2 . . 3.00	
Ann #18 KM,TA,TC(1st Work),Return	
of the Defenders,Part 1 . . . . . . 7.00	
Ann.#19 I:Lazarus,w/card 3.25	
Ann.#20 SvL,SI 1.75	
G-Size #1 rep.Greatest Foes . . . 10.00	
TPB Ground Zero rep.#340-345 . 12.95	

INCREDIBLE HULK: FUTURE IMPERFECT
1 GP,V:Maestro 12.00
2 GP,V:Maestro 10.00

INCREDIBLE HULK vs. WOLVERINE
October, 1986
1 HT,rep #181 B:,V:Wolverine. . 14.00

[Further Adventures of] INDIANA JONES
January, 1983
1 JBy/TA 2.00
2 JBy/TA 1.50
3 . . . . 1.50
4 KGa 1.50
5 KGa 1.50
6 HC/TA 1.50
7 thru 24 KGa . . . . @1.50
25 SD,What Lurks Within the Tomb 1.50
26 SD 1.50
27 SD 1.50
28 SD 1.50
29 SD 1.50
30 SD 1.50
31 SD,The Summit Meeting 1.50
32 SD,Fly the Friendly Skies 1.50
33 SD 1.50
34 SD, March, 1986 . . . . 1.50

INDIANA JONES AND THE LAST CRUSADE
1 B&W,Mag.,movie adapt, 1989. . 2.95
[Mini-Series]
1 Rep,Movie adapt, 1989. . . . . . 1.25
2 Rep,Movie adapt. 1.25
3 Rep,Movie adapt 1.25
4 Rep,Movie adapt. 1.25

INDIANA JONES AND THE TEMPLE OF DOOM
1 Movie adapt, 1984 . . . . 1.25
2 Movie adapt. 1.25
3 Movie adapt. 1.25

INFINITY CRUSADE
1 RLm,AM,I:Goddess,A:Marvel
Heroes,foil(c) 4.00
2 RLm,AM,V:Goddess 3.00
3 RLm,AM,V:Goddess,Mephisto . 3.00
4 RLm,AM,V:Goddess,A:Magnus 3.00
5 RLm,AM,V:Goddess 3.00
6 RLm,AM,V:Goddess 3.00

INFINITY GAUNTLET
July, 1991
1 GP,O:Infinity Gauntlet 19.00

2 GP,JRu,2ndRebirth:Warlock . . 7.00
3 GP,JRu,I:Terraxia 6.00
4 GP,JRu,RLm,V:Thanos 6.00
5 JRu,RLm,V:Thanos,D:Terraxia . 6.00
6 RLm,JRu,V:Nebula 6.00
TPB rep. #1 thru 6 . . . . 24.95

INFINITY WAR
1 RLm,AM,R:Magus,Thanos 6.00
2 RLm,AM,V:Magus,A:Everyone . 4.00
3 RLm,AM,V:Magus,A:Everyone . 3.50
4 RLm,AM,Magus gets Gauntlet . 3.50
5 RLm,AM,V:Magus 3.50
6 RLm,AM,V:Magus 3.50

INHUMANOIDS
Star
Jan., 1987—July, 1987
1 Hasbro Toy 1.25
2 O:Inhumanoids 1.25
3 V:D'Compose 1.25
4 A:Sandra Shore 1.25

Inhumans #1
© Marvel Entertainment Group

INHUMANS
October, 1975
1 GP,V:Blastaar 4.00
2 GP,V:Blastaar 2.50
3 GP,I:Kree S 2.00
4 GK,Maximus 2.00
5 GK,V:Maximus 2.00
6 GK,Maximus 2.00
7 GK,DP,I:Skornn 2.00
8 GP,DP,Skornn 2.00
9 reprint,V:Mor-Tog 2.00
10 KP,D:Warkon 2.00
11 KP,JM,I:Pursuer 2.00
12 KP,Hulk 2.00
Spec#1(The Untold Saga),
O:Inhumans 2.00
Spec. Atlantis Rising story 2.95

INTERFACE
Epic
December, 1989

1 ESP 2.50
2 thru 7 . . . . @2.00
8 . . . . 2.25

INVADERS
August, 1975
1 FR,JR(c),A:Invaders,
A:Mastermind 9.00
2 FR,JR(c)I:Brain Drain 7.00
3 FR,JR(c),I:U-Man 6.00
4 FR,O&V:U-Man 5.00
5 RB,JM,V:Red Skull 5.00
6 FR,V:Liberty Legion 5.00
7 FR,I:Baron Blood,
1st Union Jack 5.00
8 FR,FS,J:Union Jack 5.00
9 FR,FS,O:Baron Blood 5.00
10 FR,FS,rep.Captain
America Comics#22 . . . . 5.00
11 FR,FS,I:Blue Bullet 4.00
12 FR,FS,I:Spitfire 4.00
13 FR,FS,GK(c),I:Golem,
Half Face 4.00
14 FR,FS,JK(c),I:Crusaders 4.00
15 FR,FS,JK(c),V:Crusaders 4.00
16 FR,JK(c),V:Master Man 4.00
17 FR,FS,GK(c),I:Warrior Woman 4.00
18 FR,FS,GK(c),R:1st Destroyer . 4.00
19 FR,FS,V:Adolph Hitler 4.00
20 FR,FS,GK(c),I&J:2nd Union Jack
BU:rep.Marvel Comics #1 . . 7.50
21 FR,FS,GK(c),BU:rep.Marvel
Mystery #10 . . . . 5.50
22 FR,FS,GK(c),O:Toro 3.00
23 FR,FS,GK(c),I:Scarlet Scarab . 3.00
24 FR,FS,GK(c),rep.Marvel
Mystery #17 . . . . 4.00
25 FR,FS,GK(c),V:Scarlet Scarab 3.00
26 FR,FS,GK(c),V:Axis Agent . . . 3.00
27 FR,FS,GK(c),V:Axis Agent . . . 3.00
28 FR,FS,I:2nd Human Top,
Golden Girl,Kid Commandos . . 3.00
29 FR,FS,I:Teutonic Knight 3.00
30 FR,FS,V:Teutonic Knight 3.00
31 FR,FS,V:Frankenstein 3.00
32 FR,FS,JK(c),A:Thor 4.50
33 FR,FS,JK(c),A:Thor 4.50
34 FR,FS,V:Master Man 3.00
35 FR,FS,I:Iron Cross 3.00
36 FR,FS,O:Iron Cross 3.00
37 FR,FS,V:Iron Cross 3.00
38 FR,FS,V:Lady Lotus 3.00
39 FR,FS,O:Lady Lotus 3.00
40 FR,FS,V:Baron Blood 3.00
41 E:RTs(s)FR,FS,V:Super Axis,
double-size 4.00
Ann.#1 A:Avengers,R:Shark 5.00
G-Size#1 FR,rep.Submariner#1 . . 5.00
[Limited Series]
1 R:Invaders 2.00
2 V:Battle Axis 2.00
3 R:Original Vison (1950's) 2.00
4 V:The Axis 2.00

IRON FIST
November, 1975
1 JBy,A:Iron Man 40.00
2 JBy,V:H'rythl 20.00
3 JBy,KP,KJ,V:Ravager 16.00
4 JBy,V:Radion 16.00
5 JBy,V:Scimitar 16.00
6 JBy,O:Misty Knight 12.50
7 JBy,V:Khimbala Bey 12.50
8 JBy,V:Chaka 12.50

All comics prices listed are for *Near Mint* condition.

9 JBy,V:Chaka 12.50
10 JBy,DGr,A:Chaka 12.50
11 JBy,V:Wrecking Crew 12.50
12 JBy,DGr,V:Captain America . 12.50
13 JBy,A:Boomerang 12.50
14 JBy,I:Sabretooth 175.00
14a reprint,Marv.Milestone 4.00
15 JBy,A&N:Wolverine,A:X-Men
   September 1977 . . . . 45.00

IRONJAW
Atlas
January, 1975

1 NA(c),MSy 2.00
2 NA(c) 1.50
3 . . . . 1.25
4 July, 1975 O:IronJaw 1.25

Iron Man #26
© Marvel Entertainment Group

IRON MAN
May, 1968

1 B:StL,AGw(s),JCr,GC,
   I:Mordius 375.00
2 JCr,I:Demolisher 125.00
3 JCr,V:The Freak 100.00
4 JCr,A:Unicorn 80.00
5 JCr,GT,I:Cerebos 65.00
6 JCr,GT,V:Crusher 75.00
7 JCr,GT,V:Gladiator 50.00
8 JCr,GT,O:Whitney Frost 45.00
9 JCr,GT,A:Mandarin 42.00
10 JCr,GT,V:Mandarin 42.00
11 JCr,GT,V:Mandarin 37.00
12 JCr,GT,I:Controller 37.00
13 JCr,GT,A:Nick Fury 37.00
14 JCr,V:Night Phantom 37.00
15 JCr,GT,A:Red Ghost 37.00
16 JCr,GT,V:Unicorn 27.00
17 JCr,GT,I:Madam Masque,
   Midas 29.00
18 JCr,GT,V:Madame Masque . 27.00
19 JCr,GT,V:Madame Masque . 27.00
20 JCr,I:Charlie Gray 27.00
21 JCr,I:Eddie 22.00
22 JCr,D:Janice Cord 22.00
23 JCr,I:Mercenary 24.00

24 JCr,GT,V:Madame Masque . . 22.00
25 JCr,A:Sub-Mariner 24.00
26 JCr,DH,J:Val-Larr 20.00
27 JCr,DH,I:Firebrand 20.00
28 E:AGw(s),JCr,DH,
   V:Controller 20.00
29 B:StL,AyB(s),DH,V:Myrmidon 22.00
30 DH,I:Monster Master 22.00
31 DH,I:Mastermind 18.00
32 GT,I:Mechanoid 17.00
33 DH,I:Spy Master 17.00
34 DH,A:Spy Master 17.00
35 DH,A:Daredevil,Spymaster . 17.00
36 E:AyB(s),DH,I:RamRod 17.00
37 DH,A:Ramrod 17.00
38 GT,Jonah 17.00
39 HT,I:White Dragon 15.00
40 GT,A:White Dragon 15.00
41 GT,JM,I:Slasher 15.00
42 GT,I:Mikas 15.00
43 GT,JM,A:Mikas,I:Guardsmen 15.00
44 GT,A:Capt.America 15.00
45 GT,A:Guardsman 15.00
46 GT,D:Guardsman 15.00
47 BS,JM,O:Iron Man 22.00
48 GT,V:Firebrand 14.00
49 GT,V:Adaptoid 14.00
50 B:RTs(s),GT,V:Prin.Python . 14.00
51 GT,C:Capt.America 14.00
52 GT,I:Raga 14.00
53 GT,JSn,I:BlackLama 12.00
54 GT,BEv,Sub-Mariner,I:Madame
   MacEvil (Moondragon) 14.00
55 JSn,I:Destroyer,Thanos,Mentor
   Starfox(Eros),Blood Bros. . 110.00
55a reprint,Marv.Milestone 2.95
56 JSn,I:Fangor 25.00
57 GT,R:Mandarin 10.00
58 GT,V:Mandarin 10.00
59 GT,A:Firebrand 10.00
60 GT,C:Daredevil 10.00
61 GT,Marauder 10.00
62 whiplash 10.00
63 GT,A:Dr.Spectrum 10.00
64 GT,I:Rokk 10.00
65 GT,O:Dr.Spectrum 10.00
66 GT,V:Thor 10.00
67 GT,V:Freak 10.00
68 GT,O:Iron Man 12.00
69 GT,V:Mandarin 9.00
70 GT,A:Sunfire 9.00
71 GT,V:Yellow Claw 7.50
72 E:RTs(s),GT,V:Black Lama . . 7.50
73 B:LWn(s),KP,JM,V:Titanic
   Three 7.50
74 KP,V:Modok 7.50
75 V:Black Lama 7.50
76 Rep,A:Hulk 7.50
77 V:Thinker 7.50
78 GT,V:Viet Cong 7.50
79 GT,I:Quasar(not Current one) . 7.50
80 JK(c),O:Black Lama 7.50
81 A:Black Lama 6.00
82 MSe,A:Red Ghost 6.00
83 E:LWn(s),HT,MSe,Red Ghost . 6.00
84 HT,A:Dr.Ritter 6.00
85 HT,MSe,A:Freak 6.00
86 B:MWn(s),GT,I:Blizzard 7.00
87 GT,V:Blizzard 6.00
88 E:MWn(s),GT,
   V:Blood Brothers 6.00
89 GT,A:D.D.,Blood Bros. 6.00
90 JK(c),GT,Controller,A:Thanos . 7.50
91 GT,BL,A:Controller 6.00
92 JK(c),GT,V:Melter 6.00

93 JK(c),HT,V:Kraken 6.00
94 JK(c),HT,V:Kraken 6.00
95 JK(c),GT,PP,V:Ultimo 6.00
96 GT,DP,V:Ultimo 6.00
97 GT,DP,I:Guardsman II 6.00
98 GT,DP,A:Sunfire 6.00
99 GT,V:Mandarin 6.00
100 JSn(c),GT,V:Mandarin 14.00
101 GT,I:Dread Knight 5.00
102 GT,O:Dread Knight 5.00
103 GT,V:Jack of Hearts 5.00
104 GT,V:Midas 5.00
105 GT,V:Midas 5.00
106 GT,V:Midas 5.00
107 KP,V:Midas 5.00
108 CI,A:Growing Man 5.00
109 JBy(c),CI,V:Van Guard 5.00
110 KP,I:C.Arcturus 5.00
111 KP,O:Rigellians 5.00
112 AA,KP,V:Punisher from
   Beyond 5.00
113 KP,HT,V:Unicorn,Spymaster . 5.50
114 KG,I:Arsenal 5.00
115 JR2,O:Unicorn,V:Ani-men . . 5.00
116 JR2,BL,V:MadameMasque . . 5.00
117 BL,JR2,1st Romita Jr 6.00
118 JBy,BL,A:Nick Fury 7.00
119 BL,JR2,Alcholic Plot 6.00
120 JR2,BL,A:Sub-Mariner,
   I:Rhodey(becomes War Machine),
   Justin Hammer 10.00
121 BL,JR2,A:Submariner 5.00
122 DC,CI,BL,O:Iron Man 5.00
123 BL,JR2,V:Blizzard 5.00
124 BL,JR2,A:Capt.America . . . 4.00
125 BL,JR2,A:Ant-Man 4.00
126 BL,JR2,V:Hammer 4.00
127 BL,JR2,Battlefield 4.00
128 BL,JR2,Alcohol 6.00
129 SB,A:Dread Night 3.50
130 BL,V:Digital Devil 3.50
131 BL,V:Hulk 3.50
132 BL,V:Hulk 3.50
133 BL,A:Hulk,Ant-Man 3.50
134 BL,V:Titanium Man 3.50
135 BL,V:Titanium Man 3.50
136 V:Endotherm 3.50
137 BL,Fights oil rig fire 3.50
138 BL,Dreadnought,Spymaster . . 3.50
139 BL,Dreadnought,Spymaster . . 3.50
140 BL,V:Force 3.50
141 BL,JR2,V:Force 3.50
142 BL,JR2,Space Armor 3.50
143 BL,JR2,V:Sunturion 3.50
144 BL,JR2,Sunturion,O:Rhodey . 3.50
145 BL,JR2,A:Raiders 3.50
146 BL,JR2,I:Black Lash 3.50
147 BL,JR2,V:Black Lash 3.00
148 BL,JR2,V:Terrorists 3.00
149 BL,JR2,V:Dr.Doom 3.00
150 BL,JR2,V:Dr.Doom,Dble . . . 5.00
151 TA,BL,A:Antman 3.00
152 BL,JR2,New Armor 3.00
153 BL,JR2,V:Living Laser 3.00
154 BL,JR2,V:Unicorn 3.00
155 JR2,V:Back-Getters 3.00
156 JR2,I:Mauler 3.25
157 V:Spores 3.00
158 CI,AM,Iron Man Drowning . . 3.00
159 PS,V:Diablo 3.00
160 SD,V:Serpent'sSquad 3.00
161 A:Moon Knight 3.00
162 V:Space Ships 3.00
163 V:Chessmen 3.00
164 LMc,A:Bishop 3.00

Iron Man #87
© *Marvel Entertainment Group*

165 LMc,Meltdown 3.00
166 LMc,V:Melter 2.50
167 LMc,Alcholic Issue 2.50
168 LMc,A:Machine Man 2.50
169 LMc,B:Rhodey as 2nd
  Ironman 12.00
170 LMc,2nd Ironman 10.00
171 LMc,2nd Ironman 3.00
172 LMc,V:Firebrand 3.00
173 LMc,Stane International 3.00
174 LMc,Alcoholism 3.50
175 LMc,Alcoholism 3.50
176 LMc,Alcoholism 3.50
177 LMc,Alcoholism 3.00
178 LMc,V:Wizard 3.00
179 LMc,V:Mandarin 2.75
180 LMc,V:Mandarin 2.75
181 LMc,V:Mandarin 2.75
182 LMc,Secret Wars 2.75
183 LMc,Turning Point 2.75
184 LMc,Moves to California 2.75
185 LMc,V:Zodiac Field 2.75
186 LMc,I:Vibro 2.75
187 LMc,V:Vibro 2.75
188 LMc,I:New Brother's Grimm . 2.75
189 LMc,I:Termite 3.00
190 LMc,O:Termite,A:Scar.Witch . 3.00
191 LMc,New Grey Armor 5.00
192 LMc,V:Iron Man(Tony Stark) . 5.00
193 LMc,V:Dr.Demonicus 2.75
194 LMc,I:Scourge,A:West Coast
  Avengers 2.75
195 LMc,A:Shaman 2.75
196 LMc,V:Dr.Demonicus 2.75
197 LMc,Secret Wars II 2.75
198 SB,V:Circuit Breaker 2.50
199 LMc,E:Rhodey as 2nd Ironman,
  V:Obadiah Stone 2.75
200 LMc,D:Obadiah Stone 5.00
201 MBr,V:Madam Masque 2.00
202 A:Kazar 2.00
203 MBr,A:Hank Pym 2.00
204 MBr,V:Madame Masque 2.00
205 MBr,V:A.I.M. 2.00
206 MBr,V:Goliath 2.00

207 MBr,When t/Sky Rains Fire . . 2.00
208 MBr,V:A.I.M. 2.00
209 V:Living Laser 2.00
210 MBr,V:Morgan Le Fey 2.00
211 AS,V:Living Laser 2.00
212 DT,V:Iron Monger 2.00
213 A:Dominic Fortune 2.00
214 A:Spider-Woman 2.00
215 BL,AIM 2.00
216 BL,MBr,D:Clymenstra 2.00
217 BL,MRr,V:Hammer 2.00
218 BL,MBr,Titanic 2.00
219 BL,V:The Ghost 2.00
220 BL,MBr,V:The Ghost,
  D:Spymaster 2.00
221 BL,MBr,V:The Ghost 2.00
222 BL,MBr,R:Abrogast 2.00
223 BL,MBr,V:Blizzard,Beetle . . . 2.00
224 BL,V:Justin Hammer,Force . . 2.00
225 BL,MBr,B:Armor Wars 6.00
226 BL,MBr,V:Stingray 4.50
227 BL,MBr,V:Mandroids 4.00
228 BL,MBr,V:Guardsmen 4.00
229 BL,D:Titanium Man 4.00
230 V:Firepower, ... 4.00
231 V:Firepower,N:Iron Man 4.00
232 BWS,Nightmares,E:Armor
  Wars 4.50
233 JG,BL,A:AntMan 2.00
234 JG,BL,A:Spider-Man 3.00
235 JG,BL,V:Grey Gargoyle 2.00
236 JG,BL,V:Grey Gargoyle 2.00
237 JG,BL,V:SDI Monster 2.00
238 JG,BL,V:Rhino,D:M.Masque . 2.00
239 JG,BL,R:Ghost 2.00
240 JG,BL,V:Ghost 2.00
241 BL,V:Mandarin 2.00
242 BL,BWS,V:Mandarin 3.00
243 BL,BWS,Stark Paralyzed . . . 3.00
244 BL,V:Fixer,A:Force(D.Size) . . 5.00
245 BL(c),V:Dreadnaughts 2.00
246 BL,HT,V:A.I.M.,Maggia 2.00
247 BL,A:Hulk 2.25
248 BL,Tony Stark Cured 2.25
249 BL,V:Dr.Doom 2.00
250 BL,V:Dr.Doom,A of V 2.00
251 HT,AM,V:Wrecker,A of V . . . 2.00
252 HT,AM,V:Chemistro,A of V . . 2.00
253 BL,V:Slagmire 2.00
254 BL,V:Spymaster 2.00
255 HT,V:Devestator
  I:2nd Spymaster 2.00
256 JR2,V:Space Station 2.00
257 V:Samurai Steel 2.00
258 JR2,BWi,B:Armor Wars II,V:
  Titanium Man 2.25
259 JR2,BWi,V:Titanium Man . . . 2.00
260 JR2,BWi,V:Living Laser 2.00
261 JR2,BWi,A:Mandarin 1.75
262 JR2,BWi,A:Mandarin 1.75
263 JR2,BWi,A:Wonderman,
  V:Living Laser 1.75
264 JR2,BWi,A:Mandarin 1.75
265 JR2,BWi,V:Dewitt 1.50
266 JR2,BWi,E:Armor Wars II . . . 1.50
267 PR,BWi,B:New O:Iron Man,
  Mandarin,V:Vibro 1.75
268 PR,BWi,E:New O:Iron Man. . 1.75
269 PR,BWi,A:Black Widow 1.75
270 PR,BWi,V:Fin Fang Foom . . . 1.75
271 PR,BWi,V:Fin Fang Foom . . . 1.75
272 PR,BWi,O:Mandarin 1.75
273 PR,BWi,V:Mandarin 1.75
274 MBr,BWi,V:Mandarin 1.75
275 PR,BWi,A:Mandarin,Fin Fang

Foom (Double size) 2.00
276 PR,BWi,A:Black Widow 1.75
277 PR,BWi,A:Black Widow 1.75
278 BWi,Galactic Storm,pt.6
  A:Capt.America,V:Shatterax . . 1.75
279 BWi,Galactic Storm,pt.13,
  V:Ronan,A:Avengers 1.75
280 KHd,V:The Stark 1.75
281 KHd,I&V:Masters of Silence,
  C:War Machine Armor 3.50
282 KHd,I:War Machine Armor,
  V:Masters of Silence 3.50
283 KHd,V:Masters of Silence . . . 2.50
284 KHd,Stark put under Cryogenic
  Freeze,B:Rhodey as Iron Man . 3.00
285 KHd,BWi(i),Tony's Funeral . . 2.00
286 KHd,V:Avengers West Coast . 1.75
287 KHd,I:New Atom Smasher . . 1.75
288 KHd,30th Anniv.,V:Atom
  Smasher,foil(c) 4.50
289 KHd,V:Living Laser,
  R:Tony Stark 1.50
290 KHd,30th Anniv.,N:Iron Man,
  Gold foil(c) 4.50
291 KHd,E:Rhodey as Iron Man,
  Becomes War Machine 2.00
292 KHd,Tony reveals he is alive . 1.50
293 KHd,V:Controller 1.50
294 KHd,Infinity Crusade 1.50
295 KHd,Infinity Crusade 1.50
296 KHd,V:Modam,A:Omega Red 1.50
297 KHd,V:Modam,A:Omega Red . 1.50
298 KHd(c),I:Earth Mover 1.50
299 KHd(c),R:Ultimo 1.50
300 KHd,TMo,N:Iron Man,I:Iron Legion,
  Foil(c),A:W.Machine,V:Ultimo . 4.25
300a Newstand Ed. 2.75
301 KHd,B:Crash and Burn,
  A:Deathlok,C:Venom 1.50
302 KHd,V:Venom 1.75
303 KHd,V:New Warriors,
  C:Thundrstrike 1.75
304 KHd,C:Hulk,V:New Warriors,
  Thundrstrike,N:Iron Man 1.75
305 KHd,V:Hulk 1.75
306 KHd,E:Stark Enterprise 1.75
307 TMo,I:Vor/Tex,R:Mandarin . . 1.50
308 TMo,Vor/Tex 1.50
309 TMo,Vor/Tex 1.50
310 regular 1.50
310a Neon(c),with insert print . . . 2.95
311 V:Mandarin 1.50
312 . . . . 1.50
313 LKa,TMo,AA Meeting 1.50
314 LKa,TMo,new villain 1.50
315 A:Black Widow 1.50
316 I:Slag,A:Crimson Dynamo . . . 1.50
317 In Dynamos Armor 1.50
318 LKa,TMo,V:Slag 1.50
G-Size #1 Reprints 8.00
Ann.#1 rep.Iron Man #25 . . . . . 20.00
Ann.#2 rep.Iron Man #6 . . . . . . 10.00
Ann.#3 SB,Manthing 6.00
Ann.#4 DP,GT,V:Modok,
  A:Champions 4.00
Ann.#5 JBr,A:Black Panther 2.50
Ann.#6 A:Eternals,V:Brother
  Tode 2.50
Ann.#7 LMc,A:West Coast
  Avengers, I:New Goliath 2.50
Ann.#8 A:X-Factor 3.00
Ann.#9 V:Stratosfire,A:Sunturion . 2.50
Ann.#10 PS,BL,Atlantis Attacks #2
  A:Sub-Mariner 3.00
Ann.#11 SD,Terminus Factor #2 . 2.00

Iron Man #187
© Marvel Entertainment Group

Ann.#12 Subterran.Odyssey #4 . . 2.00
Ann.#13 GC,AW,Assault on Armor
  City,A:Darkhawk 2.50
Ann.#14 TMo,I:Face Theif,w/card,
  BU:War Machine 3.25
Ann.#15 GC,V:Controller 3.25
Spec.#1 rep. 20.00
Spec.#2 rep. 8.00
PB Iron Man 2020 . . . . 5.95
TPB Armor Wars rep.#225-#232 12.95
TPB Many Armors of Iron Man . 15.95
TPB Power of Iron Man 9.95
TPB JR2,BL,Iron Man vs. Dr. Doom
  rep. #149-#150,#249-#250 . . 12.95
Iron Manual BSz(c),guide to Iron
  Man's technology 2.00

IRON MAN/
FORCE WORKS
COLLECTORS' PREVIEW
1 Neon wrap-around(c), double
  size, X-over preview 1.95

IRON MAN &
SUBMARINER
1 GC,April, 1968 . . . . 225.00

IRON MANUAL
1 BSz(c),Guide to Iron Man's
  technology 1.75

ISLAND OF DR. MOREAU
October, 1977
1 GK(c),movie adapt. 2.00

IT'S A DUCK'S LIFE
February, 1950
1 F,Buck Duck,Super Rabbit . . 60.00
2 . . . . 30.00
3 thru 10 . . . . @20.00
11 February, 1952 . . . . 20.00

JACK OF HEARTS
January, 1984
1 Mini series 1.50

2 O:Jack of Hearts 1.00
3 . . . . 1.00
4 Final issue,April 1984 . . . . 1.00

JAMES BOND JR.
1 I&O:JamesBondJr.(TVseries) . . 3.00
2 Adventures Contd. 1.50
3 V:Goldfinger,Odd Job 1.50
4 thru 6 . . . . @1.50
  V:Scumlord 1.50
8 V:Goldfinger,Walter D.Plank . . 1.50
9 V:Dr.No in Switzerland 1.50
10 V:Robot,Dr.DeRange 1.50
11 V:S.C.U.M. 1.50
12 V:Goldfinger,Jaws 1.50

JANN OF THE JUNGLE
See: JUNGLE TALES

JEANIE COMICS
See: DARING MYSTERY

JIHAD
Epic
1 Cenobites vs. Nightbreed 4.50
2 E:Cenobites vs. Nightbreed 4.50

JOHN CARTER,
WARLORD OF MARS
June, 1977
1 GK,DC,O:John Carter,Created
  by Edgar Rice Burroughs 5.00
2 GK/DC(c),GK,RN, White Apes
  of Mars 3.00
3 GK,RN,Requiem for a Warlord . 3.00
4 GK,RN, Raiding Party 3.00
5 GK,RN,Giant Battle Issue 3.00
6 GK/DC(c),GK,Alone Against a
  World 3.00
7 GK,TS,Showdown 3.00
8 GK,RN,Beast With Touch of
  Stone 3.00
9 GK,RN,Giant Battle Issue 3.00
10 GK,The Death of Barsoom? . . 3.00
11 RN,O:Dejah Thoris 2.00
12 RN,City of the Dead 2.00
13 RN,March of the Dead 2.00
14 RN,The Day Helium Died 2.00
15 RN,GK,Prince of Helium
  Returns 2.00
16 RN,John Carters Dilemna 2.00
17 BL,What Price Victory 5.00
18 FM,Tars Tarkas Battles Alone . 1.50
19 RN(c),War With the Wing Men . 1.50
20 RN(c),Battle at the Bottom
  of the World 1.50
21 RN(c),The Claws of the Banth 1.50
22 RN(c),The Canyon of Death . . 1.50
23 Murder on Mars 1.50
24 GP/TA(c),Betrayal 1.50
25 Inferno 1.50
26 Death Cries the Guild of
  Assassins 1.50
27 Death Marathon 1.50
28 Guardians of the Lost
  City October, 1979 . . . . 2.50
Ann.#1 RN(c),GK,Battle
  story 2.00
Ann.#2 RN(c),GK,Outnumbered . . 2.00
Ann.#3 RN(c),GK,Battle
  story 2.00

JOKER COMICS
Timely
April, 1942
1 BW,I&B:Powerhouse Pepper,
  A:Stuporman 1,100.00
2 BW,I:Tessie the Typist 450.00
3 BW,A:Tessie the Typist,
  Squat Car Squad 300.00
4 BW,Squat Car (c) 300.00
5 BW,same 300.00
6 BW, ... 200.00
7 BW 200.00
8 BW 200.00
9 BW 200.00
10 BW,Shooting Gallery (c) . . . 200.00
11 BW 175.00
12 BW 175.00
13 BW 175.00
14 BW 175.00
15 BW 175.00
16 BW 175.00
17 BW 175.00
18 BW 175.00
19 BW 175.00
20 BW 175.00
21 BW 150.00
22 BW 150.00
23 BW,HK,'Hey Look' 150.00
24 BW,HK,'Laff Favorites' 150.00
25 BW,HK,same 150.00
26 BW,HK,same 150.00
27 BW 150.00
28 . . . . 35.00
29 BW 150.00
30 BW 150.00
31 BW 125.00
32 B:Millie,Hedy 35.00
33 HK 50.00
34 . . . . 35.00
35 HK 50.00
36 HK 50.00
37 . . . . 35.00
38 . . . . 35.00
39 . . . . 35.00
40 . . . . 35.00
41 A:Nellie the Nurse 35.00
42 I:Patty Pin-up 50.00
Becomes:
ADVENTURES INTO
TERROR
43(1)AH,B:Horror Stories 225.00
44(2)AH,'Won't You Step Into
  My Palor' 175.00
3 GC,'I Stalk By Night' 125.00
4 DR,'The Torture Room' 125.00
5 GC,DR,'The Hitchhiker' . . . 150.00
6 RH,'The Dark Room' 100.00
7 GT(c),BW,'Where Monsters
  Dwell' 300.00
8 JSt,'Enter... the Lizard' 100.00
9 RH(c),JSt,'The Dark
  Dungeon' 110.00
10 'When the Vampire Calls' . . . 110.00
11 JSt,'Dead Man's Escape' . . . 75.00
12 BK,'The Man Who Cried
  Ghost' 110.00
13 BEv(c),'The Hands of Death' . 75.00
14 GC,'The Hands' 75.00
15 'Trapped by the Tarantula' . . 75.00
16 RH(c),'Her Name Is Death' . . 75.00
17 'I Die Too Often',Bondage(c) . 75.00
18 'He's Trying to Kill Me' 75.00
19 'The Girl Who Couldn't Die' . . 75.00
20 . . . . 75.00

21 . . . . 60.00
22 . . . . 60.00
23 . . . . 60.00
24 MF,GC 85.00
25 thru 30 . . . . @60.00
31 May, 1954 . . . . 60.00

Journey Into Mystery #83
© Marvel Entertainment Group

JOURNEY INTO MYSTERY
June, 1952
1 RH(c),B:Mystery/Horror
  stories 1,650.00
2 'Don't Look' 600.00
3 'I Didn't See Anything' 450.00
4 RH,BEv(c),'I'm Drowning,'
  severed hand (c) 450.00
5 RH,BEv(c),'Fright' 300.00
6 BEv(c),'Till Death Do
  Us Part' 300.00
7 BEv(c),'Ghost Guard' 300.00
8 'He Who Hesitates' 300.00
9 BEv(c),'I Made A Monster' . 300.00
10 'The Assassin of Paris' . . . 300.00
11 RH,GT,'Meet the Dead' . . . 250.00
12 'A Night At Dragmoor Castle' 250.00
13 'The Living and the Dead' . . 250.00
14 DAy,RH,'The Man Who
  Owned A World' 250.00
15 RH(c),'Till Death Do
  Us Part' 250.00
16 DW,'Vampire Hand' 250.00
17 SC,'Midnight On Black
  Mountain' 250.00
18 'He Wouldn't Stay Dead' . . . 250.00
19 JF,'The Little Things' 250.00
20 BEv,BP,'After Man, What' . . 250.00
21 JKu,'The Man With No Past' 250.00
22 'Haunted House' 225.00
23 GC,'Gone, But Not Forgotten' 150.00
24 'The Locked Drawer' 150.00
25 'The Man Who Lost Himself' 150.00
26 'The Man From Out There' . 150.00
27 'BP,JSe,'Masterpiece' 150.00
28 'The Survivor' 150.00
29 'Three Frightened People' . . 150.00
30 JO,'The Lady Who Vanished' 150.00
31 'The Man Who Had No Fear' 150.00

32 'Elevator In The Sky' 150.00
33 SD,AW,'There'll Be Some
  Changes Made' 175.00
34 BP,BK,'The Of The
  Mystic Ring' 150.00
35 LC,JF,'Turn Back The Clock' 150.00
36 'I, The Pharaoh' 150.00
37 BEv(c),'The Volcano' 150.00
38 SD,'Those Who Vanish' . . . 150.00
39 BEv(c),DAy,WW,'The
  Forbidden Room' 150.00
40 BEv(c),JF,'The Strange
  Secret Of Henry Hill' 150.00
41 BEv(c),GM,RC,'I Switched
  Bodies' 125.00
42 BEv(c),GM,'What Was
  Farley's Other Face 125.00
43 AW,'Ghost Ship' 125.00
44 thru 50 SD,JK . . . . @125.00
51 thru 55 SD,JK . . . . @125.00
56 thru 61 SD,JK . . . . @125.00
62 SD,JK,I:Xemnu 175.00
63 thru 68 SD,JK . . . . @100.00
69 thru 82 . . . . @100.00
83 JK,SD,I&O:Thor 3,100.00
84 JK,SD,DH,I:Executioner . . . 750.00
85 JK,SD,I:Loki,Heimdall,Balder,
  Tyr,Odin,Asgard 425.00
86 JK,SD,DH,V:Tomorrow Man 280.00
87 JK,SD,V:Communists 225.00
88 JK,SD,V:Loki 225.00
89 JK,SD,O:Thor(rep) 235.00
90 SD,I:Carbon Copy 150.00
91 JSt,SD,I:Sandu 120.00
92 JSt,SD,V:Loki,I:Frigga 120.00
93 DAy,JK,SD,I:Radioactive
  Man 125.00
94 JSt,SD,V:Loki 100.00
95 JSt,SD,I:Duplicator 100.00
96 JSt,SD,I:Merlin II 100.00
97 JK,I:Lava Man,O:Odin 130.00
98 DH,JK,I&O:Cobra 90.00
99 DH,JK,I:Mr.Hyde,Surtur . . . 85.00
100 DH,JK,V:Mr.Hyde 85.00
101 JK,V:Tomorrow Man 60.00
102 JK,I:Sif,Hela 65.00
103 JK,I:Enchantress,
  Executioner 65.00
104 JK,Giants 60.00
105 JK,V:Hyde,Cobra 60.00
106 JK,O:Balder 60.00
107 JK,I:Grey Gargoyle,Karnilla . 60.00
108 JK,A:Dr.Strange 55.00
109 JK,V:Magneto 70.00
110 JK,V:Hyde,Cobra,Loki 55.00
111 JK,V:Hyde,Cobra,Loki . . . 50.00
112 JK,V:Hulk,O:Loki 135.00
113 JK,V:Grey Gargoyle 55.00
114 JK,I&O:Absorbing Man . . . 50.00
115 JK,O:Loki,V:Absorbing Man . 70.00
116 JK,V:Loki,C:Daredevil 50.00
117 JK,V:Loki 50.00
118 JK,I:Destroyer 50.00
119 JK,V:Destroyer,I:Hogun,
  Fandrall,Volstagg 50.00
120 JK,A:Avengers,Absorbing
  Man 50.00
121 JK,V:Absorbing Man 50.00
122 JK,V:Absorbing Man 50.00
123 JK,V:Absorbing Man 50.00
124 JK,A:Hercules 50.00
125 JK,A;Hercules 50.00
Annual #1, JK,I:Hercules 125.00
Becomes: THOR

JOURNEY INTO MYSTERY
[2nd series]
October, 1972
1 GK,TP,MP,'Dig Me No Grave' . 8.00
2 GK,'Jack the Ripper' 4.00
3 JSn,TP,'Shambler From
  the Stars' 4.00
4 GC,DA,'Haunter of the Dark',
  H.P. Lovecraft adaptation 4.00
5 RB,FrG,'Shadow From the
  Steeple',R. Bloch adaptation . 4.00
6 Mystery Stories 3.00
7 thru 19 . . . . @3.00

JOURNEY INTO UNKNOWN WORLDS
See: ALL WINNERS COMICS

JUNGLE ACTION
Atlas
October, 1954
1 JMn,JMn(c),B:Leopard Girl . 160.00
2 JMn,JMn(c) 125.00
3 JMn,JMn(c) 100.00
4 JMn,JMn(c) 100.00
5 JMn,JMn(c) 100.00
6 JMn,JMn(c),August, 1955 . . 100.00

JUNGLE ACTION
Oct., 1972–Nov., 1976
1 JB(c),Lorna,Tharn,Jann
  reprints 8.50
2 GK(c),same 4.50
3 JSn(c),same 4.50
4 GK(c),same 4.50
5 JR(c),JB,B:Black Panther,
  V:Man-Ape 7.50
6 RB/FrG(c),RB,V:Kill-Monger . 4.50
7 RB/KJ(c),RB,V:Venomn 4.50
8 RB/KJ(c),RB,GK,
  O:Black Panther 4.50
9 GK/KJ(c),RB,V:Baron Macabre 4.50
10 GK/FrG(c),V:King Cadaver . . . 4.50
11 GK(c),V:Baron Macabre,Lord
  Karnaj 4.50
12 RB/KJ(c),V:Kill Monger 4.00
13 GK/JK(c),V:White Gorilla,
  Sombre 4.00
14 GK(c),V:Prehistoric
  Monsters 4.00
15 GK(c),V:Prehistoric
  Monsters 4.00
16 GK(c),V:Venomm 4.00
17 GK(c),V:Kill Monger 4.00
18 JKu(c),V:Madame Slay 4.00
19 GK(c),V:KKK,'Sacrifice
  of Blood' 4.00
20 V:KKK,'Slaughter In The
  Streets' 4.00
21 V:KKK,'Cross Of Fire, Cross
  Of Death' 3.50
22 JB(c),V:KKK,Soul Stranger . . 3.50
23 JBy(c),V:KKK 3.50
24 GK(c),I:Wind Eagle 3.50

JUNGLE TALES
Atlas
September, 1954
1 B:Jann of the Jungle,Cliff
  Mason,Waku 125.00
2 GT,Jann Stories cont. 75.00

---

3 Cliff Mason,White Hunter,
   Waku Unknown Jungle 75.00
4 Cliff Mason,Waku,Unknown
   Jungle 75.00
5 RH(c),SSh,Cliff Mason,Waku,
   Unknown Jungle 75.00
6 DH,SSh,Cliff Mason,Waku,
   Unknown Jungle 75.00
7 DH,SSh,Cliff Mason,Waku,
   Unknown Jungle 75.00

Becomes:

JANN OF THE
JUNGLE
8 SH,SSh,'The Jungle Outlaw' 125.00
9 'With Fang and Talons' 50.00
10 AW,'The Jackal's Lair' 60.00
11 'Bottonless Pit' 50.00
12 'The Lost Safari' 50.00
13 'When the Trap Closed' 50.00
14 V:Hunters 50.00
15 BEv(c),DH,V:Hunters 50.00
16 BEv(c),AW,'Jungle Vengeance' 70.00
17 BEv(c),DH,AW,June, 1957 .. 70.00

JUSTICE
November, 1986
1 I:Justice 1.25
2 .... 1.00
3 Yakuza Assassin 1.00
4 thru 8 .... @1.00
9 KG 1.00
10 thru 18 .... @1.00
19 thru 31 .... @1.25
32 Last issue,A:Joker 1.50

JUSTICE COMICS
Atlas
Fall, 1947
7(1) B:FBI in Action,'Mystery of
   White Death' 125.00
8(2),HK,'Crime is For Suckers' . 75.00
9(3),FBI Raid 70.00
4 Bank Robbery 70.00
5 Subway(c) 50.00
6 E:FBI In Action 50.00
7 Symbolic(c) 50.00
8 Funeral(c) 50.00
9 B:'True Cases Proving Crime
   Can't Win' 50.00
10 Ph(c),Bank Hold Up 50.00
11 Ph(c),Behind Bars 50.00
12 Ph(c),The Crime of
   Martin Blaine 40.00
13 Ph(c),The Cautiouc Crook ... 50.00
14 Ph(c) 50.00
15 Ph(c) 45.00
16 F:"Ears"Karpik-Mobster 35.00
17 'The Ragged Stranger' 35.00
18 'Criss-Cross' 35.00
19 'Death Of A Spy' 35.00
20 'Miami Mob' 35.00
21 'Trap' 35.00
22 'The Big Break' 35.00
23 thru 51 .... @30.00
52 'Flare Up' 35.00

Becomes:

TALES OF JUSTICE
May, 1955—Aug., 1957
53 BEv,'Keeper Of The Keys' .. 75.00
54 thru 57 .... @50.00
58 BK 60.00
59 BK 60.00
60 thru 63 .... @40.00

64 RC,DW,JSe 50.00
65 RC 50.00
66 JO,AT 50.00
67 DW 50.00

JUSTICE:
FOUR BALANCE
1 A:Thing, Yancy Street Gang .. 1.75
2 V:Hate Monger 1.75
3 the story continues... .... 1.75
4 ...to its conclusion 1.75

KATHY
Atlas
Oct., 1959—Feb., 1964
1 'Teenage Tornado' 35.00
2 .... 20.00
3 thru 15 .... @15.00
16 thru 27 .... @8.00

Ka-Zar #16
© Marvel Entertainment Group

KA-ZAR
[1st Series]
January, 1974
1 O:Savage Land 3.50
2 DH,JA,A:Shanna The She-Devil 2.50
3 DH,V:Man-God,A:El Tigre 2.50
4 DH,V:Man-God 2.50
5 DH,D:El-Tigre 2.50
6 JB/AA,V:Bahemoth 2.00
7 JB/BMc'Revenge of the
   River-Gods' 2.00
8 JB/AA,'Volcano of
   Molten Death' 2.00
9 JB,'Man Who Hunted Dinosaur' 2.00
10 JB,'Dark City of Death' 2.00
11 DH/FS,'Devil-God of Sylitha' . 1.50
12 RH,'Wizard of Forgotten
   Death' 1.50
13 V:Lizard Men 1.50
14 JAb,V:Klaw 1.50
15 VM,V:Klaw,'Hellbird' 1.50
16 VM,V:Klaw 1.50
17 VM,V:Klaw 1.50
18 VM,V:Klaw,Makrum 1.50
19 VM,V:Klaw,Raknor the Slayer . 1.50
20 VM,V:Klaw,'Fortress of Fear' .. 1.50

[2nd Series]
1 BA,O:Ka-Zar 2.00
2 thru 7 BA .... @1.50
8 BA,Kazar Father 1.50
9 BA 1.50
10 BA,Direct D 1.50
11 BA/GK,Zabu 1.50
12 BA,Panel Missing 1.50
12a Scarce Reprint 2.00
13 BA 2.00
14 BA/GK,Zabu 1.50
15 BA 1.50
16 .... 1.50
17 Detective 1.50
18 .... 1.50
19 .... 1.50
20 A:Spiderman 2.00
21 .... 2.00
22 A:Spiderman 2.00
23 A:Spiderman 2.00
24 A:Spiderman 2.00
25 A:Spiderman 2.00
26 A:Spiderman 2.00
27 A:Buth 1.50
28 Pangea 1.50
29 W:Kazar & Shanna, Doub.Size 2.00
30 V:Pterons 1.50
31 PangeaWarII 1.50
32 V:Plunderer 1.50
33 V:Plunderer 1.50
34 Last Issue Doub.Size 2.00

[1970 Reprints Series]
August, 1970
1 X-Men ID 14.00
2 Daredevil 12, 13 .... 10.00
3 DDH,Spiderman,March, 1971 10.00

KELLYS, THE
See: KID KOMICS

KENT BLAKE OF THE
SECRET SERVICE
May, 1951—July, 1953
1 U.S. Govt. Secret Agent
   stories,Bondage cover 75.00
2 JSt,Drug issue,'Man with
   out A Face 50.00
3 'Trapped By The Chinese
   Reds' 30.00
4 Secret Service Stories 30.00
5 RH(c),'Condemned To Death' 30.00
6 Cases from Kent Blake files . 30.00
7 RH(c),Behind Enemy Lines .. 30.00
8 V:Communists 30.00
9 thru 14 .... @30.00

KICKERS INC.
November, 1986
1 SB,O:Kickers 1.25
2 SB 1.00
3 RF,Witches 1.00
4 RF,FIST 1.00
5 RF,A:D.P.7 .... 1.00
6 RF 1.00
7 RF 1.00
8 RF 1.00
9 .... 1.00
10 TD 1.00
11 .... 1.00
12 October, 1987 .... 1.00

KID & PLAY
1 Based on Rap Group 1.25

2 Drug Issue	1.25
3 At your Friends Expense	1.25
4	1.25
5	1.25
6 Record Contract	1.25
7 Fraternity Pledging	1.25
8 Kid and Cindy become an item	1.25
9 C:Marvel Heroes	1.25

KID COLT OUTLAW
Atlas
August, 1948

1 B:Kid Colt,A:Two-Gun Kid	500.00
2 'Gun-Fighter and the Girl'	275.00
3 'Colt-Quick Killers For Hire'	200.00

Kid Colt Outlaw #114
© Marvel Entertainment Group

4 'Wanted',A:Tex Taylor	200.00
5 'Mystery of the Misssing Mine',A:Blaze Carson	200.00
6 A:Tex Taylor,'Valley of the Warewolf'	150.00
7 B:Nimo the Lion	150.00
8	150.00
9	135.00
10 'The Whip Strikes',E:Nimo the Lion	160.00
11 O:Kid Colt	150.00
12	90.00
13 DRi	90.00
14	90.00
15 'Gun Whipped in Shotgun City'	90.00
16	90.00
17	90.00
18 DRi	90.00
19	75.00
20 'The Outlaw'	75.00
21 thru 30	@75.00
31	60.00
32	60.00
33 thru 45 A:Black Rider	@40.00
46 RH(c)	35.00
47 DW	35.00
48 RH(c),JKu	38.00
49	35.00
50	35.00
51 thru 56	@30.00

57 AW	38.00
58 AW	38.00
59 AW	38.00
60 AW	38.00
61	20.00
62	20.00
63	20.00
64	25.00
65	25.00
66 thru 78	@20.00
79 Origin Retold	25.00
80 thru 86	@20.00
87 JDa(reprint)	25.00
88 AW	30.00
89 AW,Matt Slade	30.00
90 thru 99	@12.00
100	19.00
101	14.00
102	10.00
103 'The Great Train Robbery'	10.00
104 JKu(c),DH,'Trail of Kid Colt'	10.00
105 DH,V:Dakota Dixon	10.00
106 JKu(c),'The Circus of Crime'	10.00
107	10.00
108 BEv	10.00
109 DAy,V:The Barracuda	10.00
110 GC,V:Iron Mask	10.00
111 JKu(c),V:Sam Hawk, The Man Hunter	10.00
112 JKu(c),V:Mr. Brown	10.00
113 JKu(c),GC,V:Bull Barton	10.00
114 JKu(c),Return of Iron Mask	10.00
115 JKu(c),V:The Scorpion	10.00
116 JKu(c),GC,V:Dr. Danger & Invisible Gunman	10.00
117 JKu(c),GC,V:The Fatman & His Boomerang	10.00
118 V:Scorpion,Bull Barton, Dr. Danger	10.00
119 DAy(c),JK,V:Bassett The Badman	10.00
120 'Cragsons Ride Again'	10.00
121 A:Rawhide Kid,Iron Mask	7.50
122 V:Rattler Ruxton	7.50
123 V:Ringo Barker	7.50
124 A:Phantom Raider	7.50
125 A:Two-Gun Kid	7.50
126 V:Wes Hardin	6.00
127 thru 129	@6.00
130 O:Kid Colt	6.00
131 thru 150	@6.00
151 thru 200 reprints	@4.00
201 thru 228 reprints	@2.00
229 April, 1979	2.00

KID FROM DODGE CITY
Atlas
July, 1957—Sept., 1957

1	50.00
2	25.00

KID FROM TEXAS
Atlas
June, 1957—Aug, 1957

1	50.00
2	25.00

KID KOMICS
Timely
February, 1943

1 SSh(c),BW,O:Captain Wonder & Tim Mulrooney I:Whitewash,

Knuckles,Trixie Trouble, Pinto Pete Subbie	2,000.00
2 AsH(c),F:Captain Wonder Subbie, B:Young Allies, B:Red Hawk,Tommy Tyme	800.00
3 ASh(c),A:The Vision & Daredevils	600.00
4 ASh(c),B:Destroyer,A:Sub-Mariner, E:Red Hawk,Tommy Tyme	500.00
5 ASh(c),V:Nazis	400.00
6 ASh(c),V:Japanese	400.00
7 ASh(c),B;Whizzer	400.00
8 ASh(c),V:Train Robbers	400.00
9 ASh(c),V:Elves	400.00
10 ASh(c),E:Young Allies, The Destoyer,The Whizzer	400.00

Becomes:
KID MOVIE KOMICS

11 F:Silly Seal,Ziggy Pig HK,Hey Look	150.00

Rusty #14
© Marvel Entertainment Group

Becomes:
RUSTY COMICS

12 F:Rusty,A:Mitzi	75.00
13 Do not Disturb(c)	42.00
14 Beach(c),BW,HK,Hey Look	67.00
15 Picnic(c),HK,Hey Look	56.00
16 Juniors Grades,HK,HeyLook	56.00
17 John in Trouble,HK,HeyLook	56.00
18 John Fired	30.00
19 Fridge raid(c),HK	30.00
20 And Her Family,HK	57.00
21 And Her Family,HK	90.00
22	90.00

Becomes:
KELLYS, THE

23 F:The Kelly Family(Pop, Mom,Mike,Pat & Goliath)	60.00
24 Mike's Date,A:Margie	40.00
25 Wrestling(c)	40.00

Becomes:
SPY CASES

26(#1) Spy stories	125.00
27(#2) BEv,Bondage(c)	75.00
28(#3) Sabotage,A:Douglas Grant Secret Agent	75.00
4 The Secret Invasion	50.00

5 The Vengeance of Comrade
    de Casto 50.00
6 A:Secret Agent Doug Grant . 50.00
7 GT,A:Doug Grant 50.00

Spy Cases #9
© *Marvel Entertainment Group*

8 Atom Bomb(c),Frozen
    Horror 60.00
9 Undeclared War 50.00
10 Battlefield Adventures 35.00
11 Battlefield Adventures 30.00
12 Battlefield Adventures 30.00
13 Battlefield Adventures 30.00
14 Battlefield Adventures 30.00
15 Doug Grant 30.00
16 Doug Grant 30.00
17 Doug Grant 30.00
18 Contact in Ankara 30.00
19 Final Issue,October, 1953 . . . 30.00

KID SLADE GUNFIGHTER
See: MATT SLADE

KILLFRENZY

1 . . . . 1.95
2 Castle Madspike 1.95

KILLPOWER:
THE EARLY YEARS

1 B:MiB,Goes on Rampage 3.25
2 thru 3 O:Killpower 2.00
4 E:MiB,last issue 2.00

KING ARTHUR & THE
KNIGHTS OF JUSTICE

1 Based on Cartoon 1.25
2 Based on Cartoon 1.25
3 Based on Cartoon 1.25

KING CONAN:
See: CONAN THE KING

KITTY PRIDE
& WOLVERINE
November, 1984

1 AM,V:Ogun 8.00
2 AM,V:Ogun 6.00

3 thru 5 AM,V:Ogun . . . . @5.00
6 AM,D:Ogun, April, 1985 . . . . . . 5.50

KNIGHTS OF
PENDRAGON
July, 1990
[1st Regular Series]

1 GEr 2.75
2 thru 7 . . . . @2.25
8 inc.SBi Poster 2.25
9 V:Bane Fisherman 2.25
10 Cap.Britain/Union Jack 2.25
11 A:Iron Man 2.25
12 A:Iron Man,Union Jack 2.25
13 O:Pendragon 2.25
14 A:Mr.Fantastic,Invisible Woman
    Black Panther 2.25
15 BlackPanther/Union Jack T.U. . 2.25
16 A:Black Panther 2.25
17 D:Albion, Union Jack,
    A:Black Panther 2.25
18 A:Iron Man,Black Panther 2.25

[2nd Regular Series]

1 GEr,A:Iron Man,R:Knights of
    Pendragon,V:MyS-TECH 2.25
2 A:Iron Man,Black Knight 2.00
3 PGa,A:Iron Man,Black Knight . . 2.00
4 Gawain Vs. Bane 2.00
5 JRe,V:Magpie 2.00
6 A:Spider-Man 2.00
7 A:Spider-Man,V:Warheads 2.00
8 JRe,A:Spider-Man 2.00
9 A:Spider-Man,Warheads 2.00
10 V:Baron Blood 2.00
11 . . . . 2.00
12 MyS-TECH Wars,V:Skire 2.00
13 A:Death's Head II 2.00
14 A:Death's Head II 2.00
15 D:Adam,A:Death's Head II . . . 2.00

KRAZY KOMICS
Timely
July, 1942

1 B:Ziggy Pig,Silly Seal 200.00
2 Toughy Tomcat(c) 115.00
3 Toughy Tomcat/Bunny(c) 62.00
4 Toughy Tomcat/Ziggy(c) 62.00
5 Ziggy/Buzz Saw(c) 62.00
6 Toughy/Cannon(c) 62.00
7 Cigar Store Indian(c) 62.00
8 Toughy/Hammock(c) 62.00
9 Hitler(c) 62.00
10 Newspaper(c) 80.00
11 Canoe(c) 44.00
12 Circus(c) 75.00
13 Pirate Treasure(c) 44.00
14 Fishing(c) 44.00
15 Ski-Jump(c) 45.00
16 Airplane(c) 33.00
17 Street corner(c) 33.00
18 Mallet/Bell(c) 33.00
19 Bicycle(c) 33.00
20 Ziggy(c) 33.00
21 Toughy's date(c) 33.00
22 Crystal Ball(c) 33.00
23 Sharks in bathtub(c) 33.00
24 Baseball(c) 33.00
25 HK,Krazy Krow(c) 48.00
26 Super Rabbit(c) 33.00
Becomes:
CINDY COMICS

27 HK,B:Margie,Oscar 75.00
28 HK,Snow sled(c) 50.00

29 . . . . 50.00
30 . . . . 50.00
31 HK 50.00
32 . . . . 30.00
33 A;Georgie 30.00
34 thru 40 . . . . @30.00
Becomes:
CRIME CAN'T WIN

41 Crime stories 90.00
42 . . . . 45.00
43 GT,Horror story 60.00
4 thru 11 . . . . @35.00
12 September, 1953 . . . . 35.00

KRAZY KOMICS
Timely
[2nd Series]
August, 1948

1 BW,HK,B:Eustice Hayseed . 225.00
2 BW,O:Powerhouse Pepper
    November, 1948 . . . . 150.00

KRAZY KROW
Summer, 1945

1 B:Krazy Krow 92.00
2 . . . . 55.00
3 Winter, 1945-46 . . . . 55.00

Kree-Skrull War #1
© *Marvel Entertainment Group*

KREE-SKULL WAR
September, 1983

1 JB,NA,reprints 5.00
2 JB,NA,October, 1983 . . . . 5.00

KRULL
November, 1983

1 Ph(c),BBI,movie adapt 1.00
2 BBI,reprint,Marvel Super
    Special,December, 1983 . . . . . 1.00

KULL
[1st Series]
June, 1971

1 MSe,RA,WW,A King Comes
    Riding,O:Kull 10.00
2 MSe,JSe,Shadow Kingdom . . . 5.00

---

3 MSe,JSe,Death Dance of
  Thulsa Doom 5.00
4 MSe,JSe,Night o/t Red Slayers 3.00
5 MSe,JSe,Kingdom By the Sea . 3.00
6 MSe,JSe,Lurker Beneath
  the Sea 2.00
7 MSe,JSe,Delcardes'Cat,
  A:Thulsa Doom 2.00
8 MSe,JSe,Wolfshead 2.00
9 MSe,JSe,The Scorpion God . . 2.00
10 MSe,Swords o/t White Queen . 2.00
11 MP,King Kull Must Die, O:Kull
  cont.,A:Thulsa Doom 2.00
12 MP,SB,Moon of Blood,V:Thulsa
  Doom,B:SD,B.U.stories 2.00
13 MP,AM,Torches From Hell,
  V:Thulsa Doom 2.00
14 MP,JA,The Black Belfry,
  A:Thulsa Doom 2.00
15 MP,Wings o/t Night-Beast,
  E:SD,B.U.stories 2.00
16 EH,Tiger in the Moon,
  A:Thulsa Doom 2.00
17 AA,EH,Thing from Emerald
  Darkness 2.00
18 EH,AA,Keeper of Flame
  & Frost 2.00
19 EH,AA,The Crystal Menace . . 2.00
20 EH,AA,Hell Beneath Atlantis . . 2.00
21 City of the Crawling Dead 1.75
22 Talons of the Devil-Birds 1.75
23 Demon Shade 1.75
24 Screams in the Dark 1.75
25 A Lizard's Throne 1.75
26 Into Death's Dimension 1.75
27 The World Within 1.75
28 Creature and the Crown,
  A:Thulsa Doom 1.75
29 To Sit the Topaz Throne,
  V:Thulsa Doom, final issue . . . 1.75
[2nd Series]
1 JB,Brule 2.50
2 Misareenia 2.00
[3rd Series]
May, 1983
1 JB,BWi,DG,Iraina 1.50
2 JB,Battle to the Death 1.25
3 JB 1.00
4 JB 1.00
5 JB 1.00
6 JB 1.00
7 JB,Masquerade Death 1.00
8 JB 1.00
9 JB 1.00
10 JB,June, 1985 . . . . 1.00

KULL AND THE BARBARIANS
May, 1975
1 NA,GK,reprint Kull #1 . . . . . . 5.00
2 BBI,reprint,December, 1983 . . . 2.00
3 NA,HC,O:Red Sonja 3.00

LABRYNTH
May, 1986
1 Movie adapt 2.00
2 . . . . 1.50
3 January, 1987 . . . . 1.50

LAFF-A-LYMPICS
March, 1978
1 F;Hanna Barbera 2.00
2 thru 5 . . . . @1.50
6 thru 13, March 1979 . . . . . . @1.00

LANA
August, 1948
1 F:Lana Lane The Show Girl,
  A:Rusty,B:Millie 85.00
2 HK,Hey Look,A:Rusty 50.00
3 Show(c),B:Nellie 30.00
4 Ship(c) 30.00
5 Audition(c) 30.00
6 Stop sign(c) 30.00
7 Beach(c) 30.00
Becomes:

LITTLE LANA
8 Little Lana(c) 26.00
9 Final Issue,March, 1950 . . . . 26.00

LANCE BARNES: POST NUKE DICK
1 I:Lance Barnes 2.50
2 Cigarettes 2.50
3 Warring Mall Tribe 2.50
4 V:Ex-bankers,last issue 2.50

LAST AMERICAN
Epic
December, 1990
1 . . . . 3.50
2 . . . . 3.00
3 . . . . 2.50
4 Final issue, March, 1991. . . . . 2.25

LAST STARFIGHTER, THE
October, 1984
1 JG(c),BBI,Movie adapt 1.00
2 Movie adapt 1.00
3 BBI,December, 1984 . . . . 1.00

LAWBREAKERS ALWAYS LOSE!
Spring, 1948
1 Partial Ph(c),Adam and Eve,
  HK,Giggles and Grins 125.00
2 FBI V:Fur Theives 60.00
3 . . . . 50.00
4 Asylum(c) 50.00
5 . . . . 50.00
6 Pawnbroker(c) 55.00
7 Crime at Midnight 125.00
8 Prison Break 40.00
9 Ph(c),He Prowled at Night . . 40.00
10 Phc(c),I Met My Murderer
  October, 1949 . . . . 40.00

LAWDOG
1 B:CDi(s),FH,I:Lawdog 2.50
2 FH,V:Vocal-yokel Cultist 2.25
3 FH,Manical Nazis 2.25
4 FH,V:Zombies 2.25
5 FH 2.25
6 FH 2.25
7 FH,V:Zombies 2.25
8 FH,w/card 2.25
9 FH,w/card 2.25
10 last issue, w/card 2.25

LAWDOG & GRIMROD: TERROR AT THE CROSSROADS
1 . . . . 3.50

LEGION OF MONSTERS
September, 1975
(black & white magazine)
1 NA(c),GM,I&O:Legion of
  Monsters,O:Manphibian 30.00

LEGION OF NIGHT
October, 1991
1 WPo/SW,A:Fin Fang Foom . . . 5.50
2 WPo,V:Fin Fang Foom 5.50

LETHAL FOES OF SPIDER-MAN
1 B:DFr(s),SMc,R:Stegron 2.00
2 SMc,A:Stegron 2.00
3 SMc,V:Spider-Man 2.00
4 E:DFr(s),SMc,Last Issue 2.00

Life of Captain Marvel #3
© Marvel Entertainment Group

LIFE OF CAPTAIN MARVEL
August, 1985
1 rep.Iron Man #55,
  Capt.Marvel #25,26 . . . . 9.00
2 rep.Capt.Marvel#26-28 . . . . . 6.50
3 rep.Capt.Marvel#28-30
  Marvel Feature #12 . . . . 6.00
4 rep.Marvel Feature #12,Capt.
  Marvel #31,32,Daredevil#105 . 6.00
5 rep.Capt.Marvel #32-#34 . . . . 6.00

LIFE OF CHRIST
1 Birth of Christ 3.00
2 MW,The Easter Story 3.00

LIFE OF POPE JOHN-PAUL II
1 JSt, January, 1983 . . . . 5.00
1a Special reprint 3.00

LIFE WITH MILLIE
See: DATE WITH MILLIE

LIGHT AND DARKNESS WAR
Epic
October, 1988
1 . . . . 4.00
2 . . . . 3.00
3 thru 6 December, 1989 . . . . @2.50

LINDA CARTER, STUDENT NURSE
Atlas
September, 1961
1 . . . . 24.00
2 thru 9, January, 1963 . . . . @15.00

LION KING
1 based on Movie 2.75

LI'L KIDS
August, 1970
1 . . . . 7.50
2 thru 11 . . . . @4.50
12 June, 1973 . . . . 4.50

LI'L PALS
September, 1972
1 . . . . 2.50
2 thru 5, May, 1973 . . . . @2.50

LITTLE ASPRIN
July, 1949
1 HK,A;Oscar 66.00
2 HK 38.00
3 December, 1949 . . . . 20.00

LITTLE LANA
See: LANA

LITTLE LENNY
June, 1949
1 . . . . 40.00
2 . . . . 22.00
3 November, 1949 . . . . 22.00

LITTLE LIZZIE
June, 1949
1 Roller Skating(c) 44.00
2 Soda(c) 25.00
3 Movies(c) 25.00
4 Lizzie(c) 25.00
5 Lizzie/Swing(c) April,1950 . . . 25.00
[2nd Series]
September, 1953
1 . . . . 30.00
2 . . . . 20.00
3 January, 1954 . . . . 20.00

LITTLE MERMAID, THE
1 . . . . 1.50
2 Reception for Pacifica royalty . . 1.50
3 TrR,Ariel joins fish club 1.50
4 . . . . 1.50
5 . . . . 1.50
6 TrR,Ariel decorates coral"tree" . 1.50
7 TrR,Flogglefish banished 1.50
8 . . . . 1.50
9 Annual Sea Horse Tournament 1.50
10 TrR,Annual Blowfish Tournament1.50
11 TrR,Sharkeena,King Triton . . . 1.50

Logan's Run #6
© Marvel Entertainment Group

LOGAN'S RUN
January, 1977
1 GP,From Movie 4.00
2 GP,Cathedral Kill 2.50
3 GP,Lair of Laser Death 2.50
4 GP,Dread Sanctuary 2.50
5 GP,End Run 2.50
6 MZ,B.U.Thanos/Drax 12.00
7 TS,Cathedral Prime 2.50

LONGSHOT
September, 1985
1 AAd,WPo(i),BA,I:Longshot . . . 15.00
2 AAd,WPo(i),I:RicoshetRita . . . 12.00
3 AAd,WPo(i),I:Mojo,Spiral 12.00
4 AAd,WPo(i),A:Spider-Man . . . 10.00
5 AAd,WPo(i),A:Dr. Strange . . . 10.00
6 AAd,WPo(i),A:Dr. Strange . . . 12.00
TPB Reprints #1-#6 . . . . 16.95

LOOSE CANNONS
1 DAn 2.50
2 DAn 2.50
3 DAn 2.75

LORNA, THE JUNGLE GIRL
Atlas
July, 1953
1 Terrors of the Jungle,O:Lorna 150.00
2 Headhunter's Strike
    I:Greg Knight 65.00
3 . . . . 50.00
4 . . . . 50.00
5 . . . . 50.00
6 RH(c),GT 40.00
7 RH(c) 40.00
8 Jungle Queen Strikes Again . 40.00
9 . . . . 40.00
10 White Fang 40.00
11 Death From the Skies 40.00
12 Day of Doom 30.00
13 thru 17 . . . . @30.00
18 AW(c) 45.00

19 thru 25 . . . . @30.00
26 August, 1957 . . . . 30.00

LOVE ADVENTURES
Atlas
October, 1949
1 Ph(c) 60.00
2 Ph(c),Tyrone Power/Gene
Tierney 55.00
3 thru 12 . . . . @26.00
Becomes:
ACTUAL CONFESSIONS
13 . . . . 16.00
14 December, 1952 . . . . 16.00

LOVE DRAMAS
October, 1949
1 Ph(c),JKa 75.00
2 January, 1950 . . . . 50.00

LOVE ROMANCES
See: IDEAL

LOVERS
See: ALL-SELECT COMICS

LOVE SECRETS
October, 1949
1 . . . . 50.00
2 January, 1950 . . . . 35.00

MACHINE MAN
April, 1978
1 JK,From 2001 . . . . 4.00
2 JK 3.00
3 JK,V:Ten-For,The Mean
Machine 3.00
4 JK,V:Ten-For,Battle on A
Busy Street 3.00
5 JK,V:Ten-For,Day of the
Non-Hero 2.50
6 JK,V:Ten-For 2.50
7 JK,With A Nation Against Him . 2.50
8 JK,Escape:Impossible 2.50
9 JK,In Final Battle 2.50
10 SD,Birth of A Super-Hero 2.50
11 SD,V;Binary Bug 2.50
12 SD,"Where walk the Gods" . . 2.50
13 SD,Xanadu 2.50
14 SD,V:Machine Man 2.50
15 SD,A:Thing,Human Torch . . . 2.50
16 SD,I:Baron Brimstone And the
Satan Squad 2.50
17 SD,Madam Menace 2.50
18 A:Alpha Flight 6.50
19 I:Jack o'Lantern 20.00

MACHINE MAN
[Limited-Series]
October, 1984
1 HT,BWS,V:Baintronics 5.00
2 HT,BWS,C:Iron Man of 2020 . . 5.00
3 HT,BWS,I:Iron Man of 2020 . . . 6.00
4 HT,BWS,V:Iron Man of 2020 . 4.50
TPB rep.#1-4 . . . . 5.95

MACHINE MAN 2020
1 rep. limited series #1–#2 . . . . . 2.00
2 rep. limited series #3–#4 . . . . . 2.00

MAD ABOUT MILLIE
April, 1969

1	23.00
2 thru 16	@12.50
17 December, 1970	12.50
Ann.#1	10.00

MADBALLS
Star
September, 1986

1 Based on Toys	1.25
2 thru 9	@1.00
10 June, 1988	1.00

MAD DOG

1 from Bob TV Show	1.50
2 V:Trans World Trust Corp.	1.25
3 V:Cigarette Criminals	1.25
4 V:Dogs of War	1.25
5 thru 6	@1.95

MAGIK
December, 1983

1 JB,TP,F:Storm and Illyana	4.00
2 JB,TP,A:Belasco,Sym	3.50
3 TP,A:New Mutants,Belasco	3.50
4 TP,V:Belasco,A:Sym	3.50

MAGNETO

0 JD,JBo,rep. origin stories.	8.00
0a Gold ed.	30.00
0b Platinum ed.	40.00

MAN COMICS
Atlas
December, 1949

1 GT,Revenge	100.00
2 GT,Fury in his Fists	50.00
3 Mantrap	40.00
4 The Fallen Hero	40.00
5 Laugh,Fool,Laugh	40.00
6 Black Hate	30.00
7 The Killer	30.00
8 BEv,An Eye For an Eye	35.00
9 B:War Issues,Here Comes Sergeant Smith	25.00
10 Korean Communism	25.00
11 RH,Cannon Fodder	25.00
12 The Black Hate	25.00
13 GC,RH,Beach Head	25.00
14 GT,No Prisoners	40.00
15	25.00
16	20.00
17 RH	20.00
18 thru 20	@20.00
21 GC	20.00
22 BEv,BK,JSt	60.00
23 thru 26	@20.00
27 E:War Issues	20.00
28 Where Mummies Prowl, Sept., 1953	20.00

MANDRAKE

1 fully painted series	2.95
2 V:Octon	2.95
3 final issue	2.95

MAN FROM ATLANTIS
February, 1978

1 TS,From TV Series,O:Mark Harris	1.50
2 FR,FS,The Bermuda Triangle	

Trap	1.25
3 FR,FS,Undersea Shadow	1.25
4 FR,FS,Beware the Killer Spores	1.25
5 FR,FS,The Ray of the Red Death	1.25
6 FR,FS,Bait for the Behemoth	1.25
7 FR,FS,Behold the Land Forgotten, August, 1978	1.25

Man Thing #1
© Marvel Entertainment Group

MAN-THING
[1st Series]
January, 1974

1 FB,JM,A:Howard the Duck	17.00
2 VM,ST,Hell Hath No Fury	8.00
3 VM,JA,I:Original Foolkiller	8.00
4 VM,JA,O&D:Foolkiller	5.00
5 MP,Night o/t Laughing Dead	4.00
6 MP,V:Soul-Slayers,Drug Issue	4.00
7 MP,A Monster Stalks Swamp	4.00
8 MP,Man Into Monster	4.00
9 MP,Deathwatch	4.00
10 MP,Nobody Dies Forever	4.00
11 MP,Dance to the Murder	4.00
12 KJ,Death-Cry of a Dead Man	4.00
13 TS,V:Captain Fate	4.00
14 AA,V:Captain Fate	4.00
15 A Candle for Saint Cloud	4.00
16 JB,TP,Death of a Legend	4.00
17 JM,Book Burns in Citrusville	4.00
18 JM,Chaos on the Campus	4.00
19 JM,FS,I:Scavenger	4.00
20 JM,A:Spider-Man,Daredevil, Shang-Chi,Thing	4.50
21 JM,O:Scavenger,Man Thing	4.00
22 JM,C:Howard the Duck	4.00
G-Size #1 MP,SD,JK,rep.TheGlob	5.00
G-Size #2 JB,KJ,The Monster Runs Wild	4.00
G-Size #3 AA,A World He Never Made	4.00
G-Size #4 FS,EH,inc.Howard the Duck vs.Gorko	4.00
G-Size #5 DA,EH,inc.Howard the Duck vs.Vampire	6.00

MAN-THING
[2nd Series]
Nov., 1979—July, 1981

1 JM,BWi	2.00
2 BWi,JM,Himalayan Nightmare	1.50
3 BWi.JM,V:Snowman	1.50
4 BWi,DP,V:Mordo,A:Dr Strange	1.50
5 DP,BWi,This Girl is Terrified	1.50
6 DP,BWi,Fraternity Rites	1.25
7 BWi,DP Return of Captain Fate	1.25
8 BWi,DP,V:Captain Fate	1.25
9 BWi(c),Save the Life of My Own Child	1.25
10 BWi,DP,Swampfire	1.25
11 Final issue	1.25

MARINES AT WAR
See: DEVIL-DOG DUGAN

MARINES IN ACTION
Atlas
June, 1955

1 B:Rock Murdock,Boot Camp Brady	35.00
2 thru 13	@16.00
14 September, 1957	16.00

MARINES IN BATTLE
Atlas
August, 1954

1 RH,B:Iron Mike McGraw	60.00
2	30.00
3 thru 6	@25.00
7	35.00
8	25.00
9	25.00
10	25.00
11 thru 16	@20.00
17	35.00
18 thru 22	@20.00
23	35.00
24	20.00
25 September, 1958	25.00

MARSHALL LAW
Epic
October, 1987

1	4.50
2	3.00
3	2.50
4	2.50
5	2.25
6 May, 1989	1.95

MARVEL ACTION HOUR: FANTASTIC FOUR

1 regular	1.50
1a bagged with insert print from animated series	3.25
2 V:Puppet Master	1.50
3	1.50
4 V:Sub-Mariner	1.50
5	1.50
6 R:Skrulls	1.50
7 V:Doctor Doom	1.50
8 Wanted by the Law	1.50

MARVEL ACTION HOUR: IRON MAN

1 regular	1.50
1a bagged with insert print from animated series	3.25

All comics prices listed are for *Near Mint* condition.

2 V:War Machine 1.50
3 V:Ultimo 1.50
4 A:Force Works, Hawkeye,
  War Machine 1.50
5 . . . . 1.50
6 V:Fing Fang Foom 1.50
7 V:Mandarin 1.50
8 V:Robots 1.50

MARVEL ACTION UNIVERSE
TV Tie-in
January, 1989
1 Rep.Spider-Man & Friends . . . 2.50

MARVEL ADVENTURES
STARRING DAREDEVIL
December, 1975
1 Rep,Daredevil #22 . . . . 2.00
2 thru 5, Rep,Daredevil #23-26 @1.25
6 DD #27 October, 1976 . . . . . . 1.25

MARVEL & DC PRESENTS
November, 1982
1 WS,TA,X-Men & Titans,A:Darkseid,
  Deathstroke(3rd App.), ... 18.00

MARVEL BOY
December, 1950
1 RH,O:Marvel Boy,Lost World 450.00
2 BEv,The Zero Hour 400.00
Becomes:
ASTONISHING
3 BEv,Marvel Boy,V:Mr Death 450.00
4 BEv,Stan Lee,The
  Screaming Tomb 300.00
5 BEv,Horro in the Caves of
  Doom 300.00
6 BEv,My Coffin is Waiting
  E:Marvel Boy 300.00
7 JR,Nightmare 125.00
8 RH,Behind the Wall 125.00
9 RH(c),The Little Black Box . 125.00
10 BEv,Walking Dead 125.00
11 BF,JSt.Mr Mordeau 100.00
12 GC,BEv,Horror Show 100.00
13 BK,MSy,Ghouls Gold 100.00
14 BK,The Long Jump Down . . 100.00
15 BEv(c),Grounds for Death . . . 85.00
16 BEv(c),DAy,SSh,Don't Make
  a Ghoul of Yourself 100.00
17 Who Was the Wilmach
  Werewolf? 85.00
18 BEv(c),JR,Vampire at my
  Window 125.00
19 BK,Back From the Grave . . 100.00
20 GC,Mystery at Midnight . . . 85.00
21 Manhunter 75.00
22 RH(c),Man Against Werewolf 75.00
23 The Woman in Black 85.00
24 JR,The Stone Face 75.00
25 RC,I Married a Zombie 85.00
26 RH(c),I Died Too Often 70.00
27 . . . . 70.00
28 No Evidence 70.00
29 BEv(c),GC,Decapitation(c) . . 70.00
30 Tentacled eyeball story . . . 100.00
31 . . . . 60.00
32 A Vampire Takes a Wife . . . 60.00
33 SMo 60.00
34 Transformation 60.00
35 . . . . 60.00

36 Pithecanthrope Giant 60.00
37 BEv,Poor Pierre 60.00
38 The Man Who Didn't Belong . 50.00
39 . . . . 50.00
40 . . . . 50.00
41 . . . . 50.00
42 . . . . 50.00
43 . . . . 50.00
44 RC 60.00
45 BK 60.00
46 . . . . 50.00
47 BK 60.00
48 . . . . 50.00
49 . . . . 50.00
50 . . . . 50.00
51 . . . . 50.00
52 . . . . 50.00
53 . . . . 55.00
54 . . . . 55.00
55 . . . . 65.00
56 . . . . 50.00
57 . . . . 75.00
58 . . . . 40.00
59 . . . . 40.00
60 . . . . 55.00
61 . . . . 40.00
62 . . . . 45.00
63 August, 1957 . . . . 45.00

MARVEL CHILLERS
October, 1975
1 GK(c),I:Mordred the Mystic . . . 4.00
2 E:Mordred 2.50
3 HC/BWr(c),B:Tigra,The Were
  Woman 2.50
4 V:Kraven The Hunter 2.50
5 V:Rat Pack,A:Red Wolf 2.50
6 RB(c),JBy,V:Red Wolf 2.50
7 JK(c),GT,V:Super Skrull
  E:Tigra,October, 1976 . . . . . 2.50

MARVEL CHRISTMAS SPECIAL
1 DC/AAd/KJ/SB/RLm,A:Ghost Rider
  X-Men,Spider-Man 2.25

MARVEL CLASSICS COMICS
1976
1 GK/DA(c),B:Reprints from
  Pendulum Illustrated Comics
  Dr.Jekyll & Mr. Hyde 5.00
2 GK(c),AN,Time Machine 3.50
3 GK/KJ(c) The Hunchback of
  Notre Dame 3.50
4 GK/DA(c),20,000 Leagues–
  Beneath the Sea 3.50
5 GK(c),RN,Black Beauty 3.50
6 GK(c),Gullivers Travels 3.50
7 GK(c),Tom Sawyer 3.50
8 GK(c),AN,Moby Dick 3.50
9 GK(c),NR,Dracula 3.50
10 GK(c),Red Badge of Courage . 3.50
11 GK(c),Mysterious Island 3.50
12 GK/DA(c),AN,Three Musketeers 3.50
13 GK(c),Last of the Mohicans . . . 3.50
14 GK(c),War of the Worlds 3.50
15 GK(c),Treasure Island 3.50
16 GK(c),Ivanhoe 3.00
17 JB/ECh(c),The Count of
  Monte Cristo 3.00
18 ECh(c),The Odsyssey 3.00
19 JB(c),Robinson Crusoe 3.00
20 Frankenstein 3.00

21 GK(c),Master of the World . . . 3.00
22 GK(c),Food of the Gods 3.00
23 Moonstone 3.00
24 GK/RN(c),She 3.00
25 The Invisible Man 3.00
26 JB(c),The Illiad 3.00
27 Kidnapped 3.00
28 MGo(1st art) The Pit and
  the Pendulum 10.00
29 The Prisoner of Zenda 3.00
30 The Arabian Nights 3.00
31 The First Men in the Moon . . . 3.00
32 GK(c),White Fang . . . .'. 3.00
33 The Prince and the Pauper . . . 3.00
34 AA,Robin Hood 3.00
35 FBe,Alice in Wonderland 3.00
36 A Christmas Carol
  December, 1978 . . . . 3.00

MARVEL COLLECTORS ITEM CLASSICS
February, 1965
1 SD,JK,reprint FF #2 . . . . 46.00
2 SD,JK,reprint FF #3 . . . . 25.00
3 SD,JK,reprint FF #4 . . . . 25.00
4 SD,JK,reprint FF #7 . . . . 25.00
5 SD,JK,reprint FF #8 . . . . 12.00
6 SD,JK,reprint FF #9 . . . . 12.00
7 SD,JK,reprint FF #13 . . . . . . 12.00
8 SD,JK,reprint FF #10 . . . . . . 12.00
9 SD,JK,reprint FF #14 . . . . . . 12.00
10 SD,JK,reprint FF #15 . . . . . . 12.00
11 SD,JK,reprint FF #16 . . . . . . 10.00
12 SD,JK,reprint FF #17 . . . . . . 10.00
13 SD,JK,reprint FF #18 . . . . . . 10.00
14 SD,JK,reprint FF #20 . . . . . . 10.00
15 SD,JK,reprint FF #21 . . . . . . 10.00
16 SD,JK,reprint FF #22 . . . . . . 10.00
17 SD,JK,reprint FF #23 . . . . . . 10.00
18 SD,JK,reprint FF #24 . . . . . . 10.00
19 SD,JK,reprint FF #27 . . . . . . 10.00
20 SD,JK,reprint FF #28 . . . . . . 10.00
21 SD,JK,reprint FF #29 . . . . . . 10.00
22 SD,JK,reprint FF #30 . . . . . . 10.00
Becomes:
MARVEL'S GREATEST COMICS
23 SD,JK,reprint FF#31 . . . . 4.00
24 SD,JK,reprint FF#32 . . . . 4.00
25 SD,JK,reprint FF#33 . . . . 4.00
26 SD,JK,reprint FF#34 . . . . 4.00
27 SD,JK,reprint FF#35 . . . . 4.00
28 SD,JK,reprint FF#36 . . . . 4.00
29 JK,reprint FF#37 . . . . 4.00
30 JK,reprint FF#38 . . . . 4.00
31 JK,reprint FF#40 . . . . 4.00
32 JK,reprint FF#42 . . . . 4.00
33 JK,reprint FF#44 . . . . 4.00
34 JK,reprint FF#47 . . . . 4.00
35 JK,reprint FF#48 . . . . 8.50
36 JK,reprint FF#49 . . . . 7.00
37 JK,reprint FF#50 . . . . 7.00
38 JK,reprint FF#51 . . . . 4.00
39 JK,reprint FF#52 . . . . 3.00
40 JK,reprint FF#53 . . . . 3.00
41 JK,reprint FF#54 . . . . 3.00
42 JK,reprint FF#55 . . . . 3.00
43 JK,reprint FF#56 . . . . 3.00
44 JK,reprint FF#61 . . . . 3.00
45 JK,reprint FF#62 . . . . 3.00
46 JK,reprint FF#63 . . . . 3.00
47 JK,reprint FF#64 . . . . 3.00
48 JK,reprint FF#65 . . . . 3.00
49 JK,reprint FF#66 . . . . 6.00

50 JK,reprint FF#67 .... 6.00
51 thru 75 JK,reprint FF ..... @1.75
76 thru 82 JK,reprint FF ..... @1.25
83 thru 95 Reprint FF .... @1.25
96 Reprint FF#, January, 1981 .. 1.25

MARVEL COMICS
October-November, 1939
1 FP(c),BEv,CBu,O:Sub-Mariner
   I&B:The Angel,A:Human Torch,
   Kazar,Jungle Terror,
   B:The Masked Raider .. 90,000.00
Becomes:
MARVEL MYSTERY COMICS
2 CSM(c),BEv,CBu,PGn,
   B:American, Ace,Human
   Torch,Sub-Mariner,Kazar 12,000.00

Marvel Mystery Comics #10
© Marvel Entertainment Group

3 ASh(c),BEv,CBu,PGn,
   E:American Ace 5,200.00
4 ASh(c),BEv,CBu,PGn,
   I&B:Electro,The Ferret,
   Mystery Detective 4,500.00
5 ASh(c),BEv,CBu,PGn,
   Human Torch(c) 10,000.00
6 ASh(c),BEv,CBu,PGn,
   Angel(c) 2,700.00
7 ASh(c),BEv,CBu,PGn,
   Bondage(c) 3,000.00
8 ASh(c),BEv,CBu,PGn,Human
   TorchV:Sub-Mariner 3,200.00
9 ASh(c),BEv,CBu,PGn,Human
   Torch V:Sub-Mariner(c) . 10,000.00
10 ASh(c),BEv,CBu,PGn,B:Terry
   Vance Boy Detective 2,500.00
11 ASh(c),BEv,CBu,PGn,
   Human Torch V:Nazis(c) .. 2,000.00
12 ASh(c),BEv,CBu,
   PGn,Angel(c) 1,800.00
13 ASh(c),BEv,CBu,PGn,S&K,
   I&B:The Vision 2,100.00
14 ASh(c),BEv,CBu,PGn,S&K,
   Sub-Mariner V:Nazis 1,200.00
15 ASh(c),BEv,CBu,PGn,S&K,
   Sub-Mariner(c) 1,300.00
16 ASh(c),BEv,CBu,PGn,S&K,Human
   Torch/Nazi Airbase (c) ... 1,100.00

17 ASh(c),BEv,CBu,PGn,S&K
   Human Torch/Sub-Mariner 1,300.00
18 ASh(c),BEv,CBu,PGn,S&K,
   Human Torch & Toro(c) .. 1,100.00
19 ASh(c),BEv,CBu,PGn,S&K,
   O:Toro,E:Electro 1,100.00
20 ASh(c),BEv,CBu,PGn,S&K,
   O:The Angel 1,200.00
21 ASh(c),BEv,CBu,PGn,S&K,
   I&B:The Patriot 1,100.00
22 ASh(c),BEv,CBu,PGn,S&K,
   Toro/Bomb(c) 900.00
23 ASh(c),BEv,CBu,PGn,S&K,
   O:Vision,E:The Angel 900.00
24 ASh(c),BEv,CBu,S&K,
   Human Torch(c) 900.00
25 ASh(c),BEv,CBu,S&K,Nazi(c) 900.00
26 ASh(c),BEv,CBu,S&K,
   Sub-Mariner(c) 800.00
27 ASh(c),BEv,CBu,
   S&K,E:Kazar 800.00
28 ASh(c),BEv,CBu,S&K,Bondage
   (c),B:Jimmy Jupiter 800.00
29 ASh(c),BEv,CBu,Bondage(c) 800.00
30 BEv,CBu,Pearl Harbor(c) .. 800.00
31 BEv,CBu,HUman Torch(c) . 800.00
32 CBu,I:The Boboes 800.00
33 ASHc(c),CBu,Japanese(c) . 800.00
34 ASh(c),CBu,V:Hitler 900.00
35 ASh(c),Beach Assault(c) ... 800.00
36 ASh(c),Nazi Invasion of
   New York(c) 800.00
37 SSh(c),Nazi(c) 800.00
38 SSh(c),Battlefield(c) 800.00
39 ASh(c),Nazis/U.S(c) 800.00
40 ASh(c),Zeppelin(c) 800.00
41 ASh(c),JapaneseCommand(c) 700.00
42 ASh(c),Japanese Sub(c) ... 700.00
43 ASh(c),Destroyed Bridge(c) . 700.00
44 ASh(c),Nazi Super Plane(c) 700.00
45 ASh(c),Nazi(c) 700.00
46 ASh(c),Hitler Bondage(c) .. 700.00
47 ASh(c),Ruhr Valley Dam(c) . 700.00
48 ASh(c),E:Jimmy Jupiter,
   Vision,Allied Invasion(c) ... 700.00
49 ASh(c),O:Miss America,
   Bondage(c) 1,000.00
50 ASh(c),Bondage(c),Miss
   Patriot 700.00
51 ASh(c),Nazi Torture(c) 600.00
52 ASh(c),Bondage(c) 600.00
53 ASh(c),Bondage(c) 600.00
54 ASh(c),Bondage(c) 600.00
55 ASh(c),Bondage(c) 600.00
56 ASh(c),Bondage(c) 600.00
57 ASh(c),Torture/Bondage(c) . 600.00
58 ASH(c),Torture(c) 600.00
59 ASh(c),Testing Room(c) ... 600.00
60 ASh(c),Japanese Gun(c) .. 600.00
61 Torturer Chamber(c) 600.00
62 ASh(c),Violent(c) 600.00
63 ASh(c),NaziHighCommand(c) 600.00
64 ASh(c),Last Nazi(c) 600.00
65 ASh(c),Bondage(c) 600.00
66 ASh(c),Last Japanese(c) ... 600.00
67 ASh(c),Treasury raid(c) 600.00
68 ASh(c),Torture Chamber(c) . 500.00
69 ASh(c),Torture Chamber(c) . 500.00
70 Cops & Robbers(c) 500.00
71 ASh(c),Egyptian(c) 500.00
72 Police(c) 500.00
73 Werewolf Headlines(c) 500.00
74 ASh(c),Robbery(c),E:The
   Patriot 500.00
75 Tavern(c),B:Young Allies .. 500.00

76 ASh(c),Shoot-out(c),B:Miss
   America 500.00
77 Human Torch/Sub-Mariner(c) 500.00
78 Safe Robbery(c) 500.00
79 Super Villians(c),E:The
   Angel 505.00
80 I:Capt.America(in Marvel) . 700.00
81 Mystery o/t Crimson Terror . 550.00
82 I:Sub-Mariner/Namora Team-up
   O:Namora,A:Capt.America 1,000.00
83 The Photo Phantom,E;Young
   Allies 500.00
84 BEv,B:The Blonde Phantom 700.00
85 BEv,A:Blonde Phantom,
   E;Miss America 500.00
86 BEv,Blonde Phantom ID
   Revealed,E:Bucky 600.00
87 BEv,I:Capt.America/Golden
   Girl Team-up 625.00
88 BEv,E:Toro 550.00
89 BEv,I:Human Torch/Sun Girl
   Team-up 600.00
90 BEv,Giant of the Mountains 600.00
91 BEv,I:Venus,E:Blonde
   Phantom,Sub-Mariner 600.00
92 BEv,How the Human Torch was
   Born,D:Professor Horton,I:The
   Witness,A:Capt.America .. 1,000.00
92a Marvel #33(c)rare,reprints 6,000.00
Becomes:
MARVEL TALES
August, 1949
93 The Ghoul Strikes 550.00
94 BEv,The Haunted Love 400.00
95 The Living Death 300.00
96 MSy,The Monster Returns . 300.00
97 DRi,MSy,The Wooden Horror 300.00
98 BEv,BK,MSy,The Curse of
   the Black Cat 300.00
99 DRi,The Secret of the Wax
   Museum 300.00
100 The Eyes of Doom 300.00
101 The Man Who Died Twice . 300.00
102 BW,A Witch Among Us .. 400.00
103 RA,A Touch of Death 275.00
104 RH(c),BW,BEv,The Thing
   in the Mirror 375.00
105 RH(c),GC,JSt,The Spider . 250.00
106 RH(c),BK,BEv,In The Dead of
   the Night 250.00
107 GC,OW,BK,The Thing in the
   Sewer 250.00
108 RH(c),BEv,JR,Horror in the
   Moonlight 150.00
109 BEv(c),A Sight for Sore Eyes150.00
110 RH,SSh,A Coffin for Carlos 150.00
111 BEv,Horror Under the Earth 150.00
112 The House That Death Built 150.00
113 RH,Terror Tale 150.00
114 BEv(c),GT,JM,2 for Zombie 150.00
115 The Man With No Face ... 150.00
116 JSt 150.00
117 BEv(c),GK,Terror in the
   North 150.00
118 RH,DBr,GC,A World
   Goes Mad 150.00
119 RH,They Gave Him A Grave 150.00
120 GC,Graveyard(c) 150.00
121 GC,Graveyard(c) 150.00
122 JKu,Missing One Body ... 150.00
123 No Way Out 150.00
124 He Waits at the Tombstone 150.00
125 JF,Horror House 150.00
126 DW,It Came From Nowhere 100.00
127 BEv(c),GC,MD,Gone is the

Gargoyle	100.00
128 Emily,Flying Saucer(c) . . .	100.00
129 You Can't Touch Bottom .	100.00
130 RH(c),JF,The Giant Killer .	100.00
131 GC,BEv,Five Fingers	100.00
132	75.00
133	75.00
134 BK,JKu,Flying Saucer(c) . . .	90.00
135 thru 141	@75.00
142	75.00
143	75.00
144	80.00
145	75.00
146	50.00
147	75.00
148	50.00
149	50.00
150	50.00
151	50.00
152	75.00
153	85.00
154	50.00
155	50.00
156	50.00
157	75.00
158	50.00
159 August, 1957	75.00

Marvel Comics Presents #44
© Marvel Entertainment Group

MARVEL COMICS PRESENTS
September, 1988

1 WS(c),B:Wolverine(JB,KJ),Master of Kung Fu(TS),Man-Thing(TGr,DC) F:Silver Surfer(AM) 12.00
2 F:The Captain(AM) 7.50
3 JR2(c),F:The Thing(AM) 6.00
4 F:Thor(AM) 6.00
5 F:Daredevil(DT,MG) 6.00
6 F:Hulk 5.00
7 F:Submariner(SD) 5.00
8 CV(c),E:Master of Kung Fu,F: Iron Man(JS) 5.00
9 F:Cloak,El Aquila 5.00
10 E:Wolverine,B:Colossus(RL,CR), F:Machine Man(SD,DC) 5.00
11 F:Ant-Man(BL),Slag(RWi) 3.00
12 E:Man-Thing,F:Hercules(DH),

Namorita(FS) 3.00
13 B:Black Panther(GC,TP),F: Shanna,Mr.Fantastic & Invisible Woman 3.00
14 F:Nomad(CP),Speedball(SD) . 3.00
15 F:Marvel Girl(DT,MG),Red Wolf(JS) 3.00
16 F:Kazar(JM),Longshot(AA) . . . 3.00
17 E:Colossus,B:Cyclops(RLm), F:Watcher(TS) 4.00
18 F:She-Hulk(JBy,BWi),Willie Lumpkin(JSt) 3.00
19 RLd(c)B:Dr.Strange(MBg), I:Damage Control(EC,AW) . . . 3.00
20 E:Dr.Strange,F:Clea(RLm) . . . 3.00
21 F:Thing,Paladin(RWi,DA) 3.00
22 F:Starfox(DC),Wolfsbane & Mirage 3.00
23 F:Falcon(DC),Wheels(RWi) . . . 3.00
24 E:Cyclops,B:Havok(RB,JRu), F:Shamrock(DJ,DA) 3.00
25 F:Ursa Major,I:Nth Man 4.00
26 B&I:Coldblood(PG),F:Hulk . . . 2.50
27 F:American Eagle(RWi) 2.50
28 F:Triton(JS) 2.50
29 F:Quasar(PR) 2.50
30 F:Leir(TMo) 2.50
31 EL,E:Havok,B:Excalibur (EL,TA) 4.00
32 TM(c),F:Sunfire(DH,DC) 3.00
33 F:Namor(JLe) 4.00
34 F:Captain America(JsP) 3.00
35 E:Coldblood,F:Her(EL,AG) . . . 4.00
36 BSz(c),F:Hellcat(JBr) 4.00
37 E:Bl.Panther,F:Devil-Slayer . . . 3.00
38 E:Excalibur,B:Wonderman(JS), Wolverine(JB),F:Hulk(MR,DA) . 5.00
39 F:Hercules(BL),Spider-Man . . . 3.50
40 F:Hercules(BL),Overmind(DH) . 3.50
41 F:Daughters of the Dragon(DA), Union Jack(KD) 3.50
42 F:Iron Man(MBa),Siryn(LSn) . . 3.50
43 F:Iron Man(MBa),Siryn(LSn) . . 3.50
44 F:Puma(BWi),Dr.Strange 3.50
45 E:Wonderman,F:Hulk(HT), Shooting Star 3.50
46 RLd(c),B:Devil-Slayer,F:Namor, Aquarian 3.50
47 JBy(c),E:Wolverine,F:Captain America,Arabian Knight(DP) . . 3.50
48 B:Wolverine&Spider-Man(EL), F:Wasp,Storm&Dr.Doom 5.00
49 E:Devil-Slayer,F:Daredevil(RWi), Gladiator(DH) 5.00
50 E:Wolverine&Spider-Man,B:Comet Man(KJo),F:Captain Ultra(DJ), Silver Surfer(JkS) 5.00
51 B:Wolverine(RLd),F:Iron Man (MBr,DH),Le Peregrine 4.00
52 F:Rick Jones(RWi,TMo) . . 4.00
53 E:Wolverine,Comet Man,F: Silver Sable&Black Widow (RLd,BWi),B:Stingray 4.00
54 B:Wolverine&Hulk(DR), Werewolf,F:Shroud(SD,BWi) . . 5.00
55 F:Collective Man(GLa) 5.00
56 E:Stingray,F:Speedball(SD) . . . 5.00
57 DK(c),B:Submariner(MC,MFm), Black Cat(JRu) 5.00
58 F:Iron Man(SD) 5.00
59 E:Submariner,Werewolf, F:Punisher 5.00
60 B:Poison,Scarlet Witch, F:Captain America(TL) 5.00
61 E:Wolverine&Hulk,

F:Dr.Strange 5.00
62 F:Wolverine(PR),Deathlok(JG) 5.00
63 F:Wolverine(PR),E:Scarlet Witch,Thor(DH) 4.00
64 B:Wolverine&Ghost Rider(MT), Fantastic Four(TMo),F:Blade . . 4.00
65 F:Starfox(ECh) 3.50
66 F:Volstagg 3.50
67 E:Poison,F:Spider-Man(MG) . . 3.50
68 B:Shanna(PG),E:Fantastic Four F:Lockjaw(JA,AM) 3.50
69 B:Daredevil(DT),F:Silver Surfer 3.50
70 F:BlackWidow&Darkstar(AM) . 3.50
71 E:Wolverine&Ghost Rider,F: Warlock(New Mutants)(SMc) . 3.50
72 B:Weapon X(BWS),E:Daredevil, F:Red Wolf(JS) 7.00
73 F:Black Knight(DC), Namor(JM) 5.00
74 F:Constrictor(SMc),Iceman & Human Torch(JSon,DA) 5.00
75 F:Meggan & Shadowcat, Dr.Doom(DC) 5.00
76 F:Death's Head(BHi,MFm), A:Woodgod(DC) 5.00
77 E:Shanna,B:Sgt.Fury&Dracula (TL,JRu),F:Namor 4.00
78 F:Iron Man(KSy),Hulk&Selene . 4.00
79 E:Sgt.Fury&Dracula,F:Dr.Strange, Sunspot(JBy) 4.00
80 F:Daughters of the Dragon,Mister Fantastic(DJ),Captain America (SD,TA) 4.00
81 F:Captain America(SD,TA), Daredevil(MR,AW),Ant-Man . . 3.50
82 B:Firestar(DT),F:Iron Man(SL), Power Man 3.50
83 F:Hawkeye,Hum.Torch(SD,EL) 3.00
84 E:Weapon X 3.00
85 B:Wolverine(SK),Beast(RLd,JaL- 1st Work),F:Speedball(RWi), I:Cyber 10.00
86 F:PaladinE:RLd on Beast 5.00
87 E:Firestar,F:Shroud(RWi) 5.00
88 F:Solo,Volcana(BWi) 5.00
89 F:Spitfire(JSn),Mojo(JMa) 5.00
90 B:Ghost Rider & Cable,F: Nightmare 4.50
91 F:Impossible Man 3.50
92 E:Wolverine,Beast, F:Northstar(JMa) 3.50
93 SK(c),B:Wolverine,Nova, F:Daredevil 3.00
94 F:Gabriel 3.00
95 SK(c),E:Wolverine,F:Hulk 3.00
96 B:Wolverine(TT),E:Nova, F:Speedball 3.00
97 F:Chameleon,Two-Gun Kid, E:Ghost Rider/Cable 3.00
98 E:Wolverine,F:Ghost Rider, Werewolf by Night 2.50
99 F:Wolverine,Ghost Rider, Mary Jane,Captain America. . . 2.50
100 SK,F:Ghost Rider,Wolverine, Dr.Doom,Nightmare 3.00
101 SK(c),B:Ghost Rider&Doctor Strange,Young Gods,Wolverine &Nightcrawler,F:Bar With No Name 2.00
102 RL,GC,AW,F:Speedball 2.00
103 RL,GC,AW,F:Puck 2.00
104 RL,GC,AW,F:Lockheed 2.00
105 RL,GC,AW,F:Nightmare 2.00
106 RL,GC,AW,F:Gabriel,E:Ghost Rider&Dr.Strange 2.00

107 GC,AW,TS,B:Ghost Rider&
  Werewolf 2.00
108 GC,AW,TS,SMc,E:Wolverine&
  Nightcrawler,B:Thanos 2.00
109 SLi,TS,SMc,B:Wolverine&
  Typhoid Mary,E:Young Gods . . 2.00
110 SLi,SMc,F:Nightcrawler 2.00
111 SK(c),SLi,RWi,F:Dr.Strange,
  E:Thanos 2.00
112 SK(c),SLi,F:Pip,Wonder Man,
  E:Ghost Rider&Werewolf 2.00
113 SK(c),SLi,B:Giant Man,
  Ghost Rider&Iron Fist 1.75
114 SK(c),SLi,F:Arabian Knight . . 1.75
115 SK(c),SLi,F:Cloak&Dagger . . 1.75
116 SK(c),SLi,E:Wolverine &
  Typhoid Mary 1.75
117 SK,PR,B:Wolverine&Venom,
  I:Ravage 2099 . . . . 4.00
118 SK,PB,RWi,E:Giant Man,
  I:Doom 2099 . . . . 3.00
119 SK,GC,B:Constrictor,E:Ghost
  Rider&Iron Fist,F:Wonder Man 3.00
120 SK,GC,E:Constrictor,B:Ghost
  Rider/Cloak & Dagger,
  F:Spider-Man 2.00
121 SK,GC,F:Mirage,Andromeda . 2.50
122 SK(c),GK,E:Wolverine&Venom,
  Ghost Rider&Cloak&Dagger,F:
  Speedball&Rage,Two-Gun Kid 2.50
123 SK(c),DJ,SLi,B:Wolverine&Lynx,
  Ghost Rider&Typhoid Mary,
  She-Hulk,F:Master Man 1.75
124 SK(c),DJ,MBa,SLi,F:Solo . . . 1.75
125 SLi,SMc,DJ,B:Iron Fist 1.75
126 SLi,DJ,E:She-Hulk 1.75
127 SLi,DJ,DP,F:Speedball 1.75
128 SLi,DJ,RWi,F:American Eagle 1.75
129 SLi,DJ,F:Ant Man 1.75
130 DJ,SLi,RWi,E:Wolverine&Lynx,
  Ghost Rider&Typhoid Mary,Iron
  Fist,F:American Eagle 1.75
131 MFm,B:Wolverine,Ghost Rider&
  Cage,Iron Fist&Sabretooth,
  F:Shadowcat 1.75
132 KM(c),F:Iron Man 1.75
133 F:Cloak & Dagger 1.75
134 SLi,F:Vance Astro 1.75
135 SLi,F:Daredevil 1.75
136 B:Gh.Rider&Masters of Silence,
  F:Iron Fist,Daredevil 1.75
137 F:Ant Man 1.75
138 B:Wolverine,Spellbound 1.75
139 F:Foreigner 1.75
140 F:Captain Universe 1.75
141 BCe(s),F:Iron Fist 1.75
142 E:Gh.Rider&Masters of Silence,
  F:Mr.Fantastic 1.75
143 Siege of Darkness,pt.#3,
  B:Werewolf,Scarlet Witch,
  E:Spellbound 2.00
144 Siege of Darkness,pt.#6,
  B:Morbius 2.00
145 Siege of Darkness,pt.#11 . . . 2.00
146 Siege of Darkness,pt.#14 . . . 1.75
147 B:Vengeance,F:Falcon,Masters of
  Silence,American Eagle 1.75
148 E:Vengeance,F:Capt.Universe,
  Black Panther 1.75
149 F:Daughter o/t Dragon,Namor,
  Vengeance,Starjammers 1.75
150 ANo(s),SLi,F:Typhoid Mary,DD,
  Vengeance,Wolverine 1.75
151 ANo(s),F:Typhoid Mary,DD,
  Vengeance 1.75

152 CDi(s),PR,B:Vengeance,Wolverine,
  War Machine,Moon Knight . . . 1.75
153 CDi(s),A:Vengeance,Wolverine,
  War Machine,Moon Knight . . . 1.75
154 CDi(s),E:Vengeance,Wolverine,
  War Machine,Moon Knight . . . 1.75
155 CDi(s),B:Vengeance,Wolverine,
  War Machine,Kymaera 1.75
156 B:Shang Chi,F:Destroyer . . . 1.50
157 F:Nick Fury 1.50
158 AD,I:Clan Destine,E:Kymaera,
  Shang Chi,Vengeance 1.75
159 B:Hawkeye, New Warriors,
  F:Fun,E:Vengeance 1.75
160 B:Vengeance,Mace 2.00
161 E:Hawkeye 1.75
162 B:Tigra,E:Mace 1.75
163 E:New Warriors 1.75
164 Tigra, Vengeance 1.75
165 Tigra, Vengeance 1.75
166 Turbo, Vengeance 1.75

167 Turbo, Vengeance 1.75
168 Thing, Vengeance 1.75
169 Mandarin, Vengeance 1.75
170 Force, Vengeance 1.75
171 Nick Fury 1.75
172 Lunatik 1.75
173 . . . . 1.75
174 . . . . 1.75
175 . . . . 1.75
TPB Ghost Rider & Cable,rep
  #90-97 . . . . 3.95
TPB Save the Tyger,rep.Wolverine
  story from #1-10 . . . . 3.95

MARVEL COMICS
SUPER SPECIAL
[Magazine, 1977]
1 JB,WS,Kiss,Features &Photos 75.00
2 JB,Conan(1978) 6.00
3 WS,Close Encounters 5.00
4 GP,KJ,Beatles story 15.00
Becomes:
MARVEL SUPER SPECIAL
5 Kiss 1978 . . . . 40.00
6 GC,Jaws II 3.00
7 Does Not Exist
8 Battlestar Galactica(Tabloid) . . 3.00
9 Conan 4.00
10 GC,Starlord 3.00
11 JB,RN,Weirdworld, ... 3.00
12 JB,Weirdworld, ... 3.00
13 JB,Weirdworld, ... 3.00
14 GC,Meteor,adapt 3.00
15 Star Trek 6.00
15a Star Trek 9.00
16 AW,B:Movie Adapts,Empire
  Strikes Back 7.00
17 Xanadu 2.00
18 HC(c),JB,Raiders of the Lost
  Ark 2.00
19 HC,For Your Eyes Only 5.00
20 Dragonslayer 2.50
21 JB,Conan 1.00
22 JSo(c),AW,Bladerunner 2.00
23 Annie 2.00
24 Dark Crystal 2.00
25 Rock and Rule 2.00
26 Octopussy 2.50
27 AW,Return of the Jedi 6.00
28 PH(c),Krull 2.00
29 DSp,Tarzan of the Apes 2.00
30 Indiana Jones and the Temple

  of Doom 2.50
31 The Last Star Fighter 2.00
32 Muppets Take Manhattan . . . 2.00
33 Buckaroo Banzai 2.00
34 GM,Sheena 2.00
35 JB,Conan The Destroyer 2.00
36 Dune 2.00
37 2010 . . . . 2.00
38 Red Sonja 2.00
39 Santa Claus 2.00
40 JB,Labrynth 2.00
41 Howard the Duck,Nov.,1986 . . 2.00

MARVEL DOUBLE
FEATURE
December, 1973
1 JK,GC,B:Tales of Suspense
  Reprints,Capt.America,
  Iron-Man 5.00
2 JK,GC ,A:Nick Fury 2.50
3 JK,GC 2.50
4 JK,GC,Cosmic Cube 2.50
5 JK,GC,V:Red Skull 2.50
6 JK,GC,V:Adaptoid 2.50
7 JK,GC,V:Tumbler 2.50
8 JK,GC,V:Super Adaptoid 2.50
9 GC,V:Batroc 2.50
10 GC 2.50
11 GC,Capt.America Wanted 2.50
12 GC,V:Powerman,Swordsman . 2.50
13 GC,A:Bucky 2.50
14 GC,V:Red Skull 2.50
15 GK,GC,V:Red Skull 2.50
16 GC,V:Assassin 2.50
17 JK,GC,V:Aim,Iron Man &
  Sub-Mariner #1 . . . . 4.00
18 JK,GC,V:Modok,Iron Man #1 . 5.00
19 JK,GC,E:Capt.America 5.00
20 JK(c) 2.50
21 Capt.America,Black Panther
  March, 1977 . . . . 2.50

MARVEL FANFARE
March, 1972
1 MG,TA,PS,F:Spider-Man,

Marvel Fanfare #21
© Marvel Entertainment Group

Daredevil,Angel	12.00
2 MG,SM,FF,TVe,F:SpM,Ka-Zar	10.00
3 DC,F:X-Men	8.00
4 PS,TA,MG,F:X-Men,Deathlok	8.00
5 MR,F:Dr.Strange	4.00
6 F:Spider-Man,Scarlet Witch	4.50
7 F:Hulk/Daredevil	3.00
8 CI,TA,GK,F:Dr.Strange	3.00
9 GM,F:Man Thing	3.00
10 GP,B:Black Widow	3.50
11 GP,D:M.Corcoran	3.50
12 GP,V:Snapdragon	3.50
13 GP,E:B.Widow,V:Snapdragon	3.50
14 F:Fantastic Four,Vision	2.75
15 BWS,F:Thing,Human Torch	3.00
16 DC,JSt,F:Skywolf	2.50
17 DC,JSt,F:Skywolf	2.50
18 FM,JRu,F:Captain America	3.00
19 RL,F:Cloak and Dagger	2.50
20 JSn,F:Thing&Dr.Strange	3.00
21 JSn,F:Thing And Hulk	3.00
22 KSy,F:Iron Man	2.50
23 KSy,F:Iron Man	2.50
24 F:Weird World	3.00
25 F:Weird World	2.50
26 F:Weird World	2.50
27 F:Daredevil	2.50
28 KSy,F:Alpha Flight	2.50
29 JBy,F:Hulk	3.00
30 BA,AW,F:Moon Knight	2.50
31 KGa,F:Capt.America, Yellow Claw	2.50
32 KGa,PS,F:Capt.America, Yellow Claw	2.50
33 JBr,F:X-Men	5.00
34 CV,F:Warriors Three	2.50
35 CV,F:Warriors Three	2.50
36 CV,F:Warriors Three	2.50
37 CV,F:Warriors Three	2.50
38 F:Captain America	2.50
39 JSon,F:Hawkeye,Moon Knight	2.50
40 DM,F:Angel,Storm,Mystique	3.00
41 DGb,F:Dr.Strange	2.50
42 F:Spider-Man	4.00
43 F:Sub-Mariner,Human Torch	2.50
44 KSy,F:Iron Man vs.Dr.Doom	2.50
45 All Pin-up Issue,WS,AAd,MZ, JOy,BSz,KJ,HC,PS,JBy	4.00
46 F:Fantastic Four	2.50
47 MG,F:Spider-Man,Hulk	3.00
48 KGa,F:She-Hulk	2.50
49 F:Dr.Strange	2.50
50 JSon,JRu,F:Angel	3.00
51 JB,JA,GC,AW,F:Silver Surfer	4.00
52 F:Fantastic Four	2.50
53 GC,AW,F:Bl.Knight,Dr.Strange	2.50
54 F:Black Knight,Wolverine	3.50
55 F:Powerpack,Wolverine	3.50
56 CI,DH,F:Shanna t/She-Devil	2.50
57 BBI,AM,F:Shanna,Cap.Marvel	2.50
58 BBI,F:Shanna,Vision/Sc.Witch	2.50
59 BBI,F:Shanna,Hellcat	2.50
60 PS,F:Daredevil,Capt.Marvel	2.50

MARVEL FEATURE
[1st Regular Series]
December, 1971

1 RA,BE,NA,I&O:Defenders & Omegatron	75.00
2 BEv,F:The Defenders	40.00
3 BEv,F:The Defenders	38.00
4 F:Antman	15.00
5 F:Antman	10.00
6 F:Antman	8.00
7 CR,F:Antman	8.00

Marvel Feature #9
© Marvel Entertainment Group

8 JSc,CR,F:Antman,O:Wasp	8.00
9 CR,F:Antman	8.00
10 CR,F:Antman	8.00
11 JSn,JSt,F:Thing & Hulk	15.00
12 JSn,JSt,F:Thing,Iron Man, Thanos,Blood Brothers	12.00

[2nd Regular Series]
(All issues feature Red Sonja)

1 DG,The Temple of Abomination	3.50
2 FT,Blood of the Hunter	2.00
3 FT,Balek Lives	2.00
4 FT,Eyes of the Gorgon	2.00
5 FT,The Bear God Walks	2.00
6 FT,C:Conan,Belit	2.00
7 FT,V:Conan,A:Belit,Conan#68	2.00

MARVEL FRONTIER COMICS SPECIAL

1 All Frontier Characters	3.25
1994	2.95

MARVEL FUMETTI BOOK
April, 1984

1 NA(c),Stan Lee, All photos	1.25

MARVEL GRAPHIC NOVEL
1982

1 JSn,D:Captain Marvel,A:Most Marvel Characters	32.00
1a 2nd printing	10.00
1b 3rd-5th printing	7.00
2 F:Elric,Dreaming City	12.00
2a 2nd printing	7.00
3 JSn,F:Dreadstar	12.00
3a 2nd-3rd printing	7.00
4 BMc,I:New Mutants,Cannonball Sunspot,Psyche,Wolfsbane	22.00
4a 2nd printing	10.00
4b 3rd-4th printing	8.00
5 BA,F:X-Men	17.00
5a 2nd printing	9.00
5b 3rd-5th printing	7.00
6 WS,F:Starslammers	10.00
6a 2nd printing	7.00

7 CR,F:Killraven	7.00
8 RWi,AG,F:Super Boxers	8.00
8a 2nd printing	7.00
9 DC,F:Futurians	12.00
9a 2nd printing	7.00
10 RV,F:Heartburst	8.00
10a 2nd printing	6.00
11 VM,F:Void Indigo	12.00
12 F:Dazzler the Movie	10.00
12a 2nd printing	6.00
13 MK,F:Starstruck	7.00
14 JG,F:SwordsofSwashbucklers	6.00
15 CV,F:Raven Banner	6.00
16 GLa,F:Alladin Effect	6.00
17 MS,F:Living Monolith	7.00
18 JBy,F:She-Hulk	10.00
18 later printings	8.95
19 F:Conan	6.00
20 F:Greenberg the Vampire	6.00
21 JBo,F:Marada the She-wolf	6.00
22 BWr,Hooky,F:Spider-Man	12.00
23 DGr,F:Dr.Strange	6.00
24 FM,BSz,F:Daredevil	10.00
25 F:Dracula	8.00
26 FC,TA,F:Alien Legion	6.00
27 BH,F:Avengers	6.00
28 JSe,F:Conan the Reaver	6.50
29 BWr,F:Thing & Hulk	8.00
30 F:A Sailor's Story	6.00
31 F:Wolf Pack	6.00
32 SA,F:Death of Groo	10.00
33 F:Thor	6.00
34 AW,F:Cloak & Dagger	6.00
35 MK/RH,F:The Shadow	13.00
36 F:Willow movie adaption	7.00
37 BL,F:Hercules	7.00
38 JB,F:Silver Surfer	16.00
39 F:Iron Man,Crash	14.50
40 JZ,F:The Punisher	15.00
41 F:Roger Rabbit	7.00
42 F:Conan of the Isles	9.00
43 EC,F:Ax	6.00
44 BJ,F:Arena	6.00
45 JRy,F:Dr.Who	9.00
46 TD,F:Kull	7.00
47 GM,F:Dreamwalker	7.00
48 F:Sailor's Storm II	7.00
49 MBd,F:Dr.Strange&Dr.Doom	18.00
50 F:Spider-Man,Parallel Lives	9.00
51 F:Punisher,Intruder	12.00
52 DSp,F:Roger Rabbit	9.00
53 PG,F:Conan	6.95
54 HC,F:Wolverine & Nick Fury	17.00

MARVEL HOLIDAY SPECIAL

1 StG(s),PDd(s),SLo(s),RLm,PB,	3.25

MARVEL MASTERPIECES COLLECTION

1 Joe Jusko Masterpiece Cards	3.25
2 F:Wolverine,Thanos,Apocalypse	3.25
3 F:Gambit,Venom,Hulk	3.25
4 F:Wolverine Vs. Sabretooth	3.25

MARVEL MASTERPIECES II COLLECTION

1 thru 3 w/cards	@2.95

MARVEL MILESTONE EDITION

1 X-Men #1 rep.	2.95
2 Fantastic Four #1, Rep.	2.95

3 Amazing Fantasy #15 rep. 2.95
4 Incredible Hulk #1 . . . . 2.95
5 Amazing Spider-Man #1 . . . . . 2.95

MARVEL MINI-BOOKS
1966
(black & white)
1 F:Capt.America,Spider-Man,Hulk
Thor,Sgt.Fury 12.00
2 thru 6 same . . . . @12.00

MARVEL MOVIE PREMIERE
1975
(black & white magazine)
1 Land That Time Forgot,
Burroughs adapt 5.00

MARVEL MOVIE SHOWCASE FEATURING STAR WARS
November, 1982
1 Rep,Stars Wars #1-6 . . . . 4.00
2 December, 1982 . . . . 4.00

MARVEL MOVIE SPOTLIGHT FEATURING RAIDERS OF THE LOST ARK
November, 1982
1 Rep,Raiders of Lost Ark#1-3 . . 3.00

MARVEL MYSTERY COMICS
See: MARVEL COMICS

MARVEL NO-PRIZE BOOK
January, 1983
1 MGo(c),Stan Lee as
Dr Doom(c) 3.00

MARVEL: PORTRAITS OF A UNIVERSE
1 Fully painted moments 2.95
2 Fully painted moments 2.95
3 F:Death of Elektra 2.95
4 final issue 2.95

MARVEL PREMIERE
April, 1972
1 GK,O:Warlock,Receives Soul Gem,
Creation of Counter Earth . . . 50.00
2 GK,JK,F:Warlock 30.00
3 BWS,F:Dr.Strange 30.00
4 FB,BWS,F:Dr.Strange 15.00
5 MP,CR,F:Dr.Strange,I:Sligguth 10.00
6 MP,FB,F:Dr.Strange 10.00
7 MP,CR,F:Dr.Strange,I:Dagoth 10.00
8 JSn,F:Dr.Strange 10.00
9 NA,FB,F:Dr.Strange 10.00
10 FB,F:Dr.Strange,
D:Ancient One 11.00
11 NA,FB,F:Dr.Strange,I:Shuma 10.00
12 NA,FB,F:Dr.Strange 10.00
13 NA,FB,F:Dr.Strange 10.00
14 NA,FB,F:Dr.Strange 10.00
15 GK,DG,I&O:Iron Fist,pt.1 . . 65.00
16 DG,O:Iron Fist,pt.2,V:Scythe . 28.00
17 DG,'Citadel on the
Edge of Vengeance' 15.00

MARVEL COMICS GROUP
MARVEL PREMIERE
FEATURING
THE POWER OF...
WARLOCK
RHODAN AND THE HOUNDS OF HELIOS!

Marvel Premiere #2
© Marvel Entertainment Group

18 DG,V:Triple Irons 15.00
19 DG,A:Ninja 13.00
20 I:Misty Knight 13.00
21 V:Living Goddess 13.00
22 V:Ninja 13.00
23 PB,V:Warhawk 13.00
24 PB,V:Monstroid 13.00
25 1st JBy,AMc,E:Iron Fist 20.00
26 JK,GT,F:Hercules 3.00
27 F:Satana 3.00
28 F:Legion Of Monsters,A:Ghost
Rider,Morbius,Werewolf. 25.00
29 JK,I:Liberty Legion,
O:Red Raven 3.00
30 JK,F:Liberty Legion 3.00
31 JK,I:Woodgod 3.00
32 HC,F:Monark 3.00
33 HC,F:Solomon Kane 3.00
34 HC,F:Solomon Kane 3.00
35 I&O:Silver Age 3-D Man 3.00
36 F:3-D Man 3.00
37 F:3-D Man 3.00
38 AN,MP,I:Weird World 3.00
39 AM,I:Torpedo(1st solo) 3.00
40 AM,F:Torpedo 3.00
41 TS,F:Seeker 3000 . . . . 3.00
42 F:Tigra 3.00
43 F:Paladin 3.00
44 KG,F:Jack of Hearts(1stSolo) . 3.00
45 GP,F:Manwolf 3.00
46 GP,F:Manwolf 3.00
47 JBy,I:2nd Antman(Scott Lang) . 5.00
48 JBy,F:2nd Antman 4.00
49 F:The Falcon 2.50
50 TS,TA,F:Alice Cooper 7.00
51 JBi,F:Black Panther,V:Klan . . 2.50
52 JBi,F:B.Panther,V:Klan 2.50
53 JBi,F:B.Panther,V:Klan 2.50
54 GD,TD,I:Hammer 2.50
55 JSt,F:Wonderman(1st solo) . . 3.50
56 HC,TA,F:Dominic Fortune . . . 2.50
57 WS(c),I:Dr.Who 3.50
58 TA(c),FM,F:Dr.Who 2.50
59 F:Dr.Who 2.50
60 WS(c),DGb,F:Dr.Who 2.50

61 TS,F:Starlord 2.50

MARVEL PRESENTS
December, 1985
1 BMc,F:Bloodstone 7.50
2 BMc,O:Bloodstone 6.00
3 AM,B:Guardians/Galaxy 22.00
4 AM,I:Nikki 14.00
5 AM,'Planet o/t Absurd' 14.00
6 AM,V:Karanada 14.00
7 AM,'Embrace the Void' 14.00
8 AM,JB,JSt,reprint.S.Surfer#2 . 20.00
9 AM,O:Starhawk 14.00
10 AM,O:Starhawk 14.00
11 AM,D:Starhawk's Children . . 14.00
12 AM,E:Guardians o/t Galaxy . 14.00

MARVEL PREVIEW
February, 1975
(black & white magazine)
1 NA,AN,Man Gods From
Beyond the Stars 5.00
2 GM(c),O:Punisher 200.00
3 GM(c),Blade the Vampire Slayer 3.00
4 GM(c),I&O:Starlord 4.00
5 Sherlock Holmes 3.00
6 Sherlock Holmes 3.00
7 KG,Satana,A:Sword in the Star 4.00
8 GM,MP,Legion of Monsters . 12.00
9 Man-God,O:Starhawk 3.00
10 JSn,Thor the Mighty 4.00
11 JBy,I:Starlord 6.00
12 MK,Haunt of Horror 3.50
13 JSn(c),Starhawk 5.00
14 JSn(c),Starhawk 5.00
15 MK(c),Starhawk 3.50
16 GC,Detectives 3.00
17 GK,Black Mask 3.00
18 GC,Starlord 3.00
19 Kull 3.00
20 HC,NA,GP,Bizarre Adventures 5.00
21 SD,Moonlight 5.00
22 JB,King Arthur 3.00
23 JB,GC,FM,Bizarre Adventures . 5.00
24 Debut Paradox 3.00
Becomes:
BIZARRE ADVENTURES
25 MG,TA,MR,Lethal Ladies 3.00
26 JB(c),King Kull 3.00
27 JB,AA,GP,Phoenix,A:Ice-Man . 7.50
28 MG,TA,FM,NA,The Unlikely
Heroes,Elektra 5.00
29 JB,WS,Horror 3.50
30 JB,Tomorrow 3.00
31 JBy,After the Violence Stops . . 3.50
32 Gods 3.00
33 Ph(c),Horror 3.00
34 PS,Christmas Spec,Son of Santa
Howard the Duck,Feb.,1983 . . 4.00

MARVEL PREVIEW 1993
Preview of 1993 . . . . 3.95

MARVEL SAGA
December, 1985
1 JBy,Fantastic Four,Wolv. 2.50
2 Hulk 1.50
3 Spider-Man 2.50
4 X-Men 2.50
5 Thor 1.50
6 Fantastic Four 1.50
7 Avengers 1.50

All comics prices listed are for *Near Mint* condition.   **CVA Page 191**

8 X-Men 2.00
9 Angel 1.50
10 X-Men 2.00
11 X-Men 2.00
12 O:Capt. America 1.50
13 O:Daredevil,Elektra 1.50
14 O:Green Goblin 2.00
15 Avengers 1.50
16 Daredevil,X-Men 2.00
17 Kazar,X-Men 2.00
18 Hawkeye-Quicksilver 1.50
19 SpM,Thor,Daredevil 2.00
20 Daredevil,Giant Man 1.50
21 FF,V:Frightful Four 1.50
22 Wedding 1.50
23 . . . . 1.50
24 . . . . 1.50
25 O:Silver Surfer,Dec.,1987 . . . 2.25

MARVEL SPECTACULAR
August, 1973
1 JK,rep Thor #128 . . . . 2.50
2 JK,rep Thor #129 . . . . 2.00
3 JK,rep Thor #130 . . . . 2.00
4 JK,rep Thor #133 . . . . 2.00
5 JK,rep Thor #134 . . . . 2.00
6 JK,rep Thor #135 . . . . 1.75
7 JK,rep Thor #136 . . . . 1.75
8 JK,rep Thor #137 . . . . 1.75
9 JK,rep Thor #138 . . . . 1.75
10 JK,rep Thor #139 . . . . 1.75
11 JK,rep Thor #140 . . . . 1.75
12 JK,rep Thor #141 . . . . 1.75
13 JK,rep Thor #142 . . . . 1.75
14 JK,rep Thor #143 . . . . 1.75
15 JK,rep Thor #144 . . . . 1.75
16 JK,rep Thor #145 . . . . 1.75
17 JK,rep Thor #146 . . . . 1.75
18 JK,rep Thor #147 . . . . 1.75
19 JK,rep Thor#148,Nov.,1975 . . 1.75

MARVEL SPOTLIGHT
November, 1971
[1st Regular Series]
1 NA(c)WW,F:Red Wolf 30.00
2 MP,BEv,NA,I&O:Werewolf . . . 35.00
3 MP,F:Werewolf 18.00
4 SD,MP,F:Werewolf 18.00
5 SD,MP,I&O:Ghost Rider . . . 120.00
6 MP,TS,F:Ghost Rider 40.00
7 MP,TS,F:Ghost Rider 40.00
8 JM,MB,F:Ghost Rider 40.00
9 TA,F:Ghost Rider 28.00
10 SD,JM,F:Ghost Rider 28.00
11 SD,F:Ghost Rider 28.00
12 SD,2nd A:Son of Satan 28.00
13 F:Son of Satan 25.00
14 JM,F:Son of Satan,I:Ikthalon . 25.00
15 JM, F:Son of Satan,
   I:Baphomet 15.00
16 JM,F:Son of Satan 15.00
17 JM,F:Son of Satan 15.00
18 F:Son of Satan, I:Allatou . . . 15.00
19 F:Son of Satan 15.00
20 F:Son of Satan 15.00
21 F:Son of Satan 15.00
22 F:Son of Satan, Ghost Rider . 20.00
23 F:Son of Satan 15.00
24 JM,F:Son of Satan 15.00
25 GT,F:Sinbad 4.00
26 F:The Scarecrow 4.00
27 F:The Sub-Mariner 4.00
28 F:Moon Knight (1st full solo). . 12.00
29 F:Moon Knight 11.00

30 JSt,JB,F:Warriors Three 4.00
31 HC,JSn,F:Nick Fury 4.00
32 I:Spiderwoman, Jessica Drew . 9.00
33 F:Deathlok, I:Devilslayer 8.00

MARVEL SPOTLIGHT
[2nd Regualar Series]
July, 1979
1 PB,F:Captain Marvel 2.50
1a No'1' on Cover 4.00
2 FM(c),F:Captain Marvel,A:Eon . 2.00
3 PB,F:Captain Marvel 2.00
4 PB,F:Captain Marvel 2.00
5 FM(c),SD,F:Dragon Lord 2.00
6 F:Star Lord 2.00
7 FM(c),F:StarLord 2.00
8 FM,F:Captain Marvel 2.50
9 FM(c),SD,F:Captain Universe . 2.00
10 SD,F:Captain Universe 2.00
11 SD,F:Captain Universe 2.00

MARVEL SPOTLIGHT ON CAPTAIN AMERICA
1 thru 4, Captain America rep. @2.95

MARVEL SPOTLIGHT ON DR. STRANGE
1 thru 4, Dr. Strange, rep. . . . @2.95

MARVEL SPOTLIGHT ON SILVER SURFER
1 thru 4, Silver Surfer, rep. . . . @2.95

MARVEL SUPER ACTION
(One-Shot)
January, 1976
1 TD,GE,FS,MP,HC,F:Punisher,
   Weirdworld,Dominic Fortune,
   I:Huntress(Mockingbird) . . . 100.00

MARVEL SUPER ACTION
May, 1977
1 JK,reprint,Capt.America #100 . 3.50
2 JK,reprint,Capt.America #101 . 2.00
3 JK,reprint,Capt.America #102 . 2.00
4 BEv,RH,reprint,Marvel Boy #1 . 2.00
5 JK,reprint,Capt.America #103 . 2.00
6 JK,reprint,Capt.America #104 . 2.00
7 JK,reprint,Capt.America #105 . 2.00
8 JK,reprint,Capt.America #106 . 2.00
9 JK,reprint,Capt.America #107 . 2.00
10 JK,reprint,Capt.America #108 . 2.00
11 JK,reprint,Capt.America #109 . 2.00
12 JSo,reprint,Capt.America #110 . 2.00
13 JSo,reprint,Capt.America #111 . 2.00
14 JB,reprint,Avengers #55 . . . . . 2.00
15 JB,reprint,Avengers #56 . . . . . 2.00
16 Reprint,Avengers,annual #2 . . 2.00
17 Reprint,Avengers # 2.00
18 JB(c),reprint,Avengers #57 . . 2.00
19 JB(c),reprint,Avengers #58 . . 2.00
20 JB(c),reprint,Avengers #59 . . 2.00
21 Reprint,Avengers #60 . . . . . . 1.50
22 JB(c),reprint,Avengers #61 . . 1.50
23 Reprint,Avengers #63 . . . . . . 1.50
24 Reprint,Avengers #64 . . . . . . 1.50
25 Reprint,Avengers #65 . . . . . . 1.50
26 Reprint,Avengers #66 . . . . . . 1.50
27 BWS,Reprint,Avengers #67 . . 1.50
28 BWS,Reprint,Avengers #68 . . 1.50
29 Reprint,Avengers #69 . . . . . . 1.50
30 Reprint,Avengers #70 . . . . . . 1.50

31 Reprint,Avengers #71 . . . . . . 1.50
32 Reprint,Avengers #72 . . . . . . 1.50
33 Reprint,Avengers #73 . . . . . . 1.50
34 Reprint,Avengers #74 . . . . . . 1.50
35 JB(c),Reprint,Avengers #75 . . 1.50
36 JB(c),Reprint,Avengers #75 . . 1.50
37 JB(c),Reprint,Avengers #76
   November, 1981 . . . . 1.50

MARVEL SUPERHEROES
October, 1966
(One-Shot)
1 Rep. D.D. #1, Avengers #2,
   Marvel Mystery #8 . . . . 75.00

MARVEL SUPER-HEROES
[1st Regular Series]
(Prev.: Fantasy Masterpieces)
12 GC,I&O:Captain Marvel . . 125.00
13 GC,2nd A:Captain Marvel . . 65.00
14 F:Spider-Man 110.00
15 GC,F:Medusa 25.00
16 I:Phantom Eagle 25.00
17 O:Black Knight 25.00
18 GC,I:Guardians o/t Galaxy . . 70.00
19 F:Kazar 20.00
20 F:Dr.Doom,Diablo 20.00
21 thru 31 reprints . . . . @10.00
32 thru 55 rep. Hulk/Submariner
   from Tales to Astonish . . . @2.00
56 reprints Hulk #102 . . . . 3.50
57 thru 105 reps.Hulk issues . . @1.50

MARVEL SUPERHEROES
May, 1990
[2nd Regular Series]
1 RLm,F:Hercules,Moon Knight,
   Magik,Bl.Panther,Speedball . . . 4.00
2 . . . . 3.50
3 F:Captain America,Hulk,Wasp . 4.50
4 AD,F:SpM,N.Fury,D.D.,Speedball
   Wond.Man,Spitfire,Bl.Knight . 3.50
5 F:Thor,Thing,Speedball,
   Dr.Strange 3.50
6 RB,SD,F:X-Men,Power Pack,
   Speedball,Sabra 3.00
7 RB,F:X-Men,Cloak & Dagger . 2.75
8 F:X-Men,Iron Man,Namor 2.50
9 F:Avengers W.C,Thor,Iron Man 3.00
10 DH,F:Namor,Fantastic Four,
   Ms.Marvel#24 . . . . 3.50
11 F:Namor,Ms.Marvel#25 . . . . 3.00
12 F:Dr.Strange,Falcon,Iron Man . 3.00
13 F:Iron Man 2.75
14 BMc,RWi,F:Iron Man,
   Speedball, Dr.Strange 2.75
15 KP,DH,F:Thor,Iron Man,Hulk . 2.75
Holiday Spec.#1 AAd,DC,JRu,F:FF,
   X-Men,Spider-Man,Punisher . . 3.25
Holiday Spec.#2 AAd(c),SK,MGo,
   RLm,SLi,F:Hulk,Wolverine,
   Thanos,Spider-Man 3.25
Fall Spec.RB,A:X-Men,Shroud,
   Marvel Boy,Cloak & Dagger . . 2.25

MARVEL SUPERHEROES MEGAZINE
1 thru 6 rep. . . . . @2.95

MARVEL SUPER SPECIAL
See: MARVEL COMICS

MARVEL TAILS
November, 1983
1 ST,Peter Porker 2.00

Marvel Tales #98
© Marvel Entertainment Group

MARVEL TALES
1964
1 All reprints,O:Spider-Man . . . 250.00
2 rep.Avengers #1,X-Men #1,
  Hulk #3 . . . . 75.00
3 rep.Amaz.SpM.#6 . . . . 40.00
4 rep.Amaz.SpM.#7 . . . . 20.00
5 rep.Amaz.SpM.#8 . . . . 20.00
6 rep.Amaz.SpM.#9 . . . . 20.00
7 rep.Amaz.SpM.#10 . . . . 20.00
8 rep.Amaz.SpM.#13 . . . . 15.00
9 rep.Amaz.SpM.#14 . . . . 20.00
10 rep.Amaz.SpM.#15 . . . . 18.00
11 rep.Amaz.SpM.#16 . . . . 18.00
12 rep.Amaz.SpM.#17 . . . . 18.00
13 rep.Amaz.SpM.#18
  rep.1950's Marvel Boy 12.00
14 rep.Amaz.SpM.#19,
  reps.Marvel Boy 7.50
15 rep.Amaz.SpM.#20,
  reps.Marvel Boy 7.50
16 rep.Amaz.SpM.#21,
  reps.Marvel Boy 7.50
17 thru 22 rep.Amaz.SpM.
  #22-#27 . . . . @5.50
23 thru 27 rep.Amaz.SpM.
  #30-#34 . . . . @5.50
28 rep.Amaz.SpM.#35&36 . . . . . 5.00
29 rep.Amaz.SpM.#39&40 . . . . . 5.00
30 rep.Amaz.SpM.#58&41 . . . . . 5.00
31 rep.Amaz.SpM.#42 . . . . 5.00
32 rep.Amaz.SpM.#43&44 . . . . . 5.00
33 rep.Amaz.SpM.#45&47 . . . . . 5.00
34 rep.Amaz.SpM.#48 . . . . 4.00
35 rep.Amaz.SpM.#49 . . . . 4.00
36 thru 41 rep.
  Amaz.SpM.#51-#56 . . . . @4.00
42 thru 53 rep.
  Amaz.SpM.#59-#70 . . . . . . @4.00
54 thru 80 rep.
  Amaz.SpM.#73-#99 . . . . . . @4.00

81 rep.Amaz.SpM.#103 . . . . 4.00
82 rep.Amaz.SpM.#103-4 . . . . . . 4.50
83 thru 97 rep.
  Amaz.SpM#104-#118 . . . . @4.00
98 rep.Amaz.SpM.#121 . . . . 5.00
99 rep.Amaz.SpM.#122 . . . . 4.50
100 rep.Amaz.SpM.#123,BU:Two
  Gun Kid,Giant-Size 3.50
101 thru 105 rep.Amaz.
  SpM.#124-#128 . . . . @3.00
106 rep.Amaz.SpM.#129,
  (I:Punisher) 9.00
107 thur 110 rep.Amaz.
  SpM.#130-133 . . . . @2.00
111 Amaz.SpM#134,A:Punisher . . 4.00
112 Amaz.SpM#135,A:Punisher . . 3.00
113 thru 125 rep.Amaz.Spider
  Man #136-#148 . . . . @2.00
126 rep.Amaz.Spider-Man#149 . . 4.00
127 rep.Amaz.Spider-Man#150 . . 3.00
128 rep.Amaz.Spider-Man#151 . . 4.00
129 thru 136 rep.Amaz.Spider
  Man #152-#159 . . . . @2.50
137 rep.Amaz.Fantasy#15 . . . . . 7.00
138 rep.Amaz.SpM.#1 . . . . 7.00
139 thru 149 rep.
  AmazSpM#2-#12 . . . . @2.50
150 rep.AmazSpM Ann#1 . . . . . . 2.50
151 rep.AmazSpM#13 . . . . 2.50
152 rep.AmazSpM#14 . . . . 4.00
153 thru 190
  rep.AmazSpM#15-52 . . . . . . @2.00
191 rep. #96-98 . . . . 2.25
192 rep. #121-122 . . . . 2.25
193 thru 198 rep.Marv.Team
  Up#59-64 . . . . @2.00
199 . . . . 2.00
200 rep. SpM Annual 14 . . . . . . 2.00
201 thru 206 rep.Marv.
  Team Up#65-70 . . . . @2.00
207 . . . . 2.00
208 . . . . 2.00
209 MZ(c),rep.SpM#129,Punisher 6.00
210 MZ(c),rep.SpM#134 . . . . 5.00
211 MZ(c),rep.SpM#135 . . . . 5.00
212 MZ(c),rep.Giant-Size#4 . . . . 5.00
213 MZ(c),rep.Giant-Size#4 . . . . 5.00
214 MZ(c),rep.SpM#161 . . . . 5.00
215 MZ(c),rep.SpM#162 . . . . 3.00
216 MZ(c),rep.SpM#174 . . . . 3.00
217 MZ(c),rep.SpM#175 . . . . 3.00
218 MZ(c),rep.SpM#201 . . . . 3.00
219 MZ(c),rep.SpM#202 . . . . 3.00
220 MZ(c),rep.Spec.SpM #81 . . . 3.00
221 MZ(c),rep.Spec.SpM #82 . . . 3.00
222 MZ(c),rep.Spec.SpM #83 . . . 2.00
223 thru 227 TM(c),rep.
  SpM #88-92 . . . . @2.25
228 TM(c),rep.Spec.SpM#17 . . . . 2.00
229 TM(c),rep.Spec.SpM#18 . . . . 2.00
230 TM(c),rep.SpM #203 . . . . . . 2.00
231 TM(c),rep.Team-Up#108 . . . . 2.00
232 TM(c),rep. 2.00
233 TM(c),rep. X-Men 2.00
234 TM(c),rep. X-Men 2.00
235 TM(c),rep. X-Men 2.00
236 TM(c),rep. X-Men 2.00
237 TM(c),rep. 2.00
238 TM(c),rep. 2.00
239 TM(c),rep.SpM,Beast 2.00
240 rep.SpM,Beast,MTU#90 . . . . 1.50
241 rep.MTU#124 . . . . 1.50
242 rep.MTU#89,Nightcrawler . . . 1.50
243 rep.MTU#117,SpM,Wolverine 1.50
244 MR(c),rep. 1.50

245 MR(c),rep. 1.50
246 MR(c),rep. 1.50
247 MR(c),rep.MTU Annual #6 . . 1.50
248 MR(c),rep. 1.50
249 MR(c),rep.MTU #14 . . . . 1.50
250 MR(c),rep.MTU #100 . . . . . . 1.50
251 rep.Amaz.SpM.#100 . . . . . . 1.50
252 rep.Amaz.SpM.#101 . . . . . . 3.50
253 rep.Amaz.SpM.#102 . . . . . . 3.00
254 rep.MTU #15,inc.2 Ghost
  Rider pin-ups by JaL 3.00
255 SK(c),rep.MTU #58,
  BU:Ghost Rider 1.75
256 rep. MTU 1.50
257 rep.Amaz.SpM.#238 . . . . . . 1.50
258 rep.Amaz.SpM.#239 . . . . . . 1.50
259 thru 261 rep.Amaz.SpM.#249
  thru 251 . . . . 1.50
262 rep Marvel Team-Up #53 . . 1.25
263 rep Marvel Team-Up #54 . . 1.25
264 rep.B:Amaz.SpM.Ann.#5 . . 1.25
265 rep.E:Amaz.SpM.Ann.#5 . . 1.25
266 thru 274 rep.Amaz.SpM#252
  thru #260 . . . . @1.25
275 rep.Amaz.SpM#261 . . . . . . 1.25
276 rep.Amaz.SpM#263 . . . . . . 1.25
277 rep.Amaz.SpM#265 . . . . . . 1.25
278 thru 282 rep.Amaz.SpM#268
  thru 272 . . . . 1.25
283 rep.Amaz.SpM#273 . . . . . . 1.25
284 rep.Amaz.SpM#275 . . . . . . 1.25
285 rep.Amaz.SpM#276 . . . . . . 1.25
286 rep.Amaz.SpM#277 . . . . . . 1.25
287 rep.Amaz.SpM#278 . . . . . . 1.25
288 rep.Amaz.SpM#280 . . . . . . 1.50
289 rep.Amaz.SpM#281 . . . . . . 1.25
290 rep.Amaz.SpM 1.50
291 rep.Amaz.SpM 1.50

MARVEL TALES
See: MARVEL COMICS

MARVEL TEAM-UP
March, 1972
(Spider-Man in all,unless *)
1 RA,F:Hum.Torch,V:Sandman . 75.00
2 RA,F:Hum.Torch,V:Sandman . 30.00
3 F:Human Torch,V:Morbius . . 50.00
4 GK,F:X-Men,A:Morbius 50.00
5 GK,F:Vision 14.00
6 GK,F:Thing,O:Puppet Master,
  V:Mad Thinker 14.00
7 RA,F:Thor 14.00
8 JM,F:The Cat 14.00
9 RA,F:Iron Man 14.00
10 JM,F:Human Torch 14.00
11 JM,F:The Inhumans 10.00
12 RA,F:Werewolf 11.00
13 GK,F:Captain America 9.00
14 GK,F:Sub-Mariner 9.00
15 RA,F:Ghostrider 15.00
16 GK,JM,F:Captain Marvel 8.00
17 GK,F:Mr.Fantastic,
  A:Capt.Marvel 8.00
18 *F:Hulk,Human Torch 8.00
19 SB,F:Ka-Zar 8.00
20 SB,F:Black Panther 9.00
21 SB,F:Dr.Strange 6.00
22 SB,F:Hawkeye 6.00
23 *F:Human Torch,Iceman,
  C:Spider-Man,X-Men 7.00
24 JM,F:Brother Voodoo 6.00
25 JM,F:Daredevil 6.00
26 *F:H.Torch,Thor,V:Lavamen . 6.00

Marvel Team-Up #25
© *Marvel Entertainment Group*

27 JM,F:The Hulk	6.00
28 JM,F:Hercules	6.00
29 *F:Human Torch,Iron Man	6.00
30 JM,F:The Falcon	7.00
31 JM,F:Iron Fist	7.00
32 *F:Hum.Torch,Son of Satan	5.00
33 SB,F:Nighthawk	5.00
34 SB,F:Valkyrie	5.00
35 SB,*F:H.Torch,Dr.Strange	5.00
36 SB,F:Frankenstein	6.00
37 SB,F:Man-Wolf	5.00
38 SB,F:Beast	5.00
39 SB,F:H.Torch,I:Jean Dewolff	5.00
40 SB,F:Sons of the Tiger	5.00
41 SB,F:Scarlet Witch	5.00
42 SB,F:Scarlet Witch,Vision	5.00
43 SB,F:Dr.Doom	5.00
44 SB,F:Moon Dragon	5.00
45 SB,F:Killraven	7.00
46 SB,F:Deathlok	7.00
47 F:The Thing	5.00
48 SB,F:Iron Man,I:Wraith	5.00
49 SB,F:Iron Man	5.00
50 SB,F:Dr.Strange	5.00
51 SB,F:Iron Man	4.00
52 SB,F:Captain America	4.00
53 1st JBy New X-Men,F:Hulk	15.00
54 JBy,F:Hulk,V:Woodgod	6.00
55 JBy,F:Warlock,I:Gardener	8.00
56 SB,F:Daredevil	4.00
57 SB,F:Black Widow	4.00
58 JBy,F:Ghost Rider,V:Trapster	6.00
59 JBy,F:Yellowjacket,V:Equinox	5.00
60 JBy,F:Wasp,V:Equinox	5.00
61 JBy,F:Human Torch	5.00
62 JBy,F:Ms.Marvel	5.00
63 JBy,F:Iron Fist	5.50
64 JBy,F:Daughters o/t Dragon	5.00
65 JBy,I:Captain Britain(U.S.) I:Arcade	7.50
66 JBy,F:Captain Britain	6.00
67 JBy,F:Tigra,V:Kraven	5.00
68 JBy,F:Man-Thing,I:D'Spayre	5.00
69 JBy,F:Havok	6.00
70 JBy,F:Thor	5.00

71 F:The Falcon,V:Plantman	4.00
72 F:Iron Man	4.00
73 F:Daredevil	4.00
74 BH,F:Not ready for prime time players(Saturday Night Live)	5.00
75 JBy,F:Power Man	4.00
76 HC,F:Dr.Strange	4.00
77 HC,F:Ms.Marvel	4.00
78 DP,F:Wonderman	4.00
79 JBy,TA,F:Red Sonja	5.00
80 SpM,F:Dr.Strange,Clea	4.00
81 F:Satana	4.00
82 SB,F:Black Widow	4.00
83 SB,F:Nick Fury	4.00
84 SB,F:Master of Kung Fu	4.00
85 SB,F:Bl.Widow,Nick Fury	4.00
86 BMc,F:Guardians o/t Galaxy	5.00
87 GC,F:Black Panther	3.50
88 SB,F:Invisible Girl	3.50
89 RB,F:Nightcrawler	4.50
90 BMc,F:The Beast	4.00
91 F:Ghost Rider	4.00
92 Cl,F:Hawkeye,I:Mr.Fear IV	3.50
93 Cl,F:Werewolf I:Tatterdemalion (named)	5.00
94 MZ,F:Shroud	3.50
95 I:Mockingbird(Huntress)	4.00
96 F:Howard the Duck	3.50
97 *F:Hulk,Spiderwoman	3.50
98 F:Black Widow	3.50
99 F:Machine Man	3.50
100 FM,JBy,F:F.F.,I:Karma, BU:Storm & Bl.Panther	12.00
101 F:Nighthawk	3.00
102 F:Doc Samson,Rhino	3.00
103 F:Antman	3.00
104 *F:Hulk,Ka-zar	3.00
105 *F:Powerman,Iron Fist,Hulk	3.00
106 HT,F:Captain America	3.00
107 HT,F:She-Hulk	3.00
108 HT,F:Paladin	3.00
109 HT,F:Dazzler	3.00
110 HT,F:Iron Man	3.00
111 HT,F:Devil Slayer	3.00
112 HT,F:King Kull	3.00
113 HT,F:Quasar,V:Lightmaster	3.00
114 HT,F:Falcon	3.00
115 HT,F:Thor	3.00
116 HT,F:Valkyrie	3.00
117 HT,F:Wolv,V:Prof Power	15.00
118 HT,F:Professor X	4.00
119 KGa,F:Gargoyle	3.00
120 KGa,F:Dominic Fortune	3.00
121 KGa,F:Human Torch,I:Leap Frog(Frog Man)	3.00
122 KGa,F:Man-Thing	3.00
123 KGa,F:Daredevil	3.00
124 KGa,F:Beast	3.50
125 KGa,F:Tigra	3.00
126 BH,F:Hulk	3.00
127 KGa,F:Watcher,X-mas issue	3.00
128 Ph(c)KGa,F:Capt.America.	3.00
129 KGa,F:The Vision	3.00
130 KGa,F:The Scarlet Witch	3.00
131 KGa,F:Leap Frog	3.00
132 KGa,F:Mr.Fantastic	3.00
133 KGa,F:Fantastic Four	3.00
134 F:Jack of Hearts	3.00
135 F:Kitty Pryde	3.00
136 F:Wonder Man	3.00
137 *F:Aunt May & F.Richards	3.00
138 F:Sandman,I:New Enforcers	3.00
139 F:Sandman,Nick Fury	3.00
140 F:Black Widow	3.00
141 SpM(2nd App Black Costume)	

F:Daredevil	4.00
142 F:Captain Marvel(2nd one)	3.00
143 F:Starfox	3.00
144 F:M.Knight,V:WhiteDragon	3.00
145 F:Iron Man	3.00
146 F:Nomad	3.50
147 F:Human Torch	3.00
148 F:Thor	3.00
149 F:Cannonball	3.50
150 F:X-Men,V:Juggernaut	5.50
Ann.#1 SB,F:New X-Men	16.00
Ann.#2 F:The Hulk	5.00
Ann.#3 F:Hulk,PowerMan	4.00
Ann.#4 F:Daredevil,Moon Knight	3.00
Ann.#5 F:Thing,Scarlet Witch, Quasar,Dr.Strange	3.00
Ann.#6 F:New Mutants,Cloak & Dagger(cont.New Mutants#22)	4.00
Ann.#7 F:Alpha Flight	3.00

MARVEL TEAM-UP INDEX
SEE: OFFICIAL MARVEL
INDEX TO
MARVEL TEAM-UP

MARVEL
Treasury Edition
September, 1974

1 SD,Spider-Man,I:Contemplator	7.00
2 JK,F:Fant.Four,Silver Surfer	6.00
3 F:Thor	4.00
4 BWS,F:Conan	4.50
5 O:Hulk	4.00
6 GC,FB,SD,F:Dr.Strange	4.00
7 JB,JK,F:The Avengers	4.50
8 F:X-Mas stories	5.00
9 F:Super-Hero Team-Up	4.00
10 F:Thor	4.00
11 F:Fantastic Four	4.00
12 F:Howard the Duck	4.00
13 F:X-Mas stories	4.00
14 F:Spider-Man	4.00
15 BWS,F:Conan,Red Sonja	4.50
16 F:Defenders	3.00
17 F:The Hulk	3.00
18 F:Spider Man,X-Men	5.00
19 F:Conan	4.50
20 F:Hulk	3.00
21 F:Fantastic Four	3.00
22 F:Spider-Man	3.50
23 F:Conan	3.00
24 F:The Hulk	2.50
25 F:Spider-Man,Hulk	3.00
26 GP,F:Hulk,Wolverine,Hercules	9.00
27 HT,F:Hulk,Spider-Man	3.50
28 JB,JSt,F:SpM:Superman	6.00

MARVEL TREASURY
OF OZ
1975
(oversized)

1 JB,movie adapt.	4.00

MARVEL TREASURY
SPECIAL

1 Vol. I Spiderman,1974	4.00
2 Vol. II Capt. America,1976	3.50

MARVEL TWO-IN-ONE
January, 1974
(Thing in all, unless *)

1 GK,F:Man-Thing	27.00

Marvel Two-In-One #10
© Marvel Entertainment Group

2 GK,JSt,F:Namor,Namorita . . . 10.00
3 F:Daredevil 10.00
4 F:Capt.America,Namorita 10.00
5 F:Guardians of the Galaxy . . . 17.00
6 F:Dr.Strange 15.00
7 F:Valkyrie 7.00
8 F:Ghost Rider 10.00
9 F:Thor 6.00
10 KJ,F:Black Widow 6.00
11 F:Golem 4.00
12 F:Iron Man 4.00
13 F:Power Man 4.00
14 F:Son of Satan 8.00
15 F:Morbius 9.00
16 F:Ka-zar 4.00
17 F:Spider-Man 4.50
18 F:Spider-Man 4.50
19 F:Tigra 4.00
20 F:The Liberty Legion 4.00
21 F:Doc Savage 3.50
22 F:Thor,Human Torch 3.50
23 F:Thor,Human Torch 3.50
24 SB,F:Black Goliath 3.50
25 F:Iron Fist 4.00
26 F:Nick Fury 3.00
27 F:Deathlok 6.00
28 F:Sub-Mariner 3.00
29 F:Master of Kung Fu 3.00
30 JB,F:Spiderwoman 5.00
31 F:Spiderwoman 3.00
32 F:Invisible girl 3.00
33 F:Modred the Mystic 3.00
34 F:Nighthawk,C:Deathlok 3.50
35 F:Skull the Slayer 3.00
36 F:Mr.Fantastic 3.00
37 F:Matt Murdock 3.00
38 F:Daredevil 3.00
39 F:The Vision 3.00
40 F:Black Panther 3.00
41 F:Brother Voodoo 3.00
42 F:Captain America 3.00
43 JBy,F:Man-Thing 5.00
44 GD,F:Hercules 3.00
45 GD,F:Captain Marvel 4.50
46 F:The Hulk 5.00
47 GD,F:Yancy Street Gang,
    I:Machinesmith 3.00
48 F:Jack of Hearts 3.00

49 GD,F:Dr.Strange 3.00
50 JBy,JS,F:Thing & Thing 4.00
51 FM,BMc,F:Wonderman,Nick
    Fury, Ms.Marvel 5.00
52 F:Moon Knight,I:Crossfire 3.00
53 JBy,JS,F:Quasar,C:Deathlok . . 3.50
54 JBy,JS,D:Deathlok,
    I:Grapplers 10.00
55 JBy,JS,I:New Giant Man 3.00
56 GP,GD,F:Thundra 2.50
57 GP,GD,F:Wundarr 2.50
58 GP,GD,I:Aquarian,A:Quasar . . 2.50
59 F:Human Torch 2.50
60 GP,GD,F:Impossible Man,
    I:Impossible Woman 2.50
61 GD,F:Starhawk,I&O:Her 3.00
62 GD,F:Moondragon 3.00
63 GD,F:Warlock 3.00
64 DP,GD,F:Stingray,
    I:Serpent Squad 2.50
65 GP,GD,F:Triton 2.50
66 GD,F:Scarlet Witch,
    V:Arcade 2.50
67 F:Hyperion,Thundra 2.50
68 F:Angel,V:Arcade 2.50
69 GD,F:Guardians o/t Galaxy . . . 5.00
70 F:The Inhumans 2.50
71 F:Mr.Fantastic,I:Deathurge,
    Maelstrom 2.50
72 F:Stingray 2.50
73 F:Quasar 2.50
74 F:Puppet Master,Modred 2.50
75 F:The Avengers,O:Blastaar . . . 2.50
76 F:Iceman,O:Ringmaster 2.50
77 F:Man-Thing 2.50
78 F:Wonder Man 2.50
79 F:Blue Diamond,I:Star Dancer . 2.50
80 F:Ghost Rider 4.00
81 F:Sub-Mariner 2.00
82 F:Captain America 2.00
83 F:Sasquatch 3.00
84 F:Alpha Flight 3.00
85 F:Giant-Man 2.00
86 O:Sandman 2.25
87 F:Ant-Man 2.00
88 F:She-Hulk 2.00
89 F:Human Torch 2.00
90 F:Spider-Man 2.25
91 V:Sphinx 2.00
92 F:Jocasta,V:Ultron 2.00
93 F:Machine Man,D:Jocasta 2.25
94 F:Power Man,Iron Fist 2.00
95 F:Living Mummy 2.00
96 F:Sandman,C:Marvel Heroes . 2.00
97 F:Iron Man 2.00
98 F:Franklin Richards 2.00
99 JBy(c),F:Rom 2.00
100 F:Ben Grimm 2.50
Ann.#1 SB,F:Liberty Legion 5.00
Ann.#2 JSn,2nd D:Thanos,A:Spider
    Man,Avengers,Capt.Marvel,
    I:Lord Chaos,Master Order . . 35.00
Ann.#3 F:Nova 4.00
Ann.#4 F:Black Bolt 3.50
Ann.#5 F:Hulk,V:Pluto 3.00
Ann.#6 I:American Eagle 3.00
Ann.#7 I:Champion,A:Hulk,Thor,
    DocSamson,Colossus,Sasquatch,
    WonderMan 3.50

OFFICIAL HANDBOOK OF THE
MARVEL UNIVERSE
January, 1983
1 Abomination-Avengers'
    Quintet 7.50

2 BaronMordo-Collect.Man 6.00
3 Collector-Dracula 5.00
4 Dragon Man-Gypsy Moth 5.00
5 Hangman-Juggernaut 5.00
6 K-L 5.00
7 Mandarin-Mystique 4.00
8 Na,oria-Pyro 4.00
9 Quasar to She-Hulk 4.00
10 Shiar-Sub-Mariner 4.00
11 Subteraneans-Ursa Major 4.00
12 Valkyrie-Zzzax 4.00
13 Book of the Dead 4.00
14 Book of the Dead 4.00
15 Weaponry 4.00
[2nd Series]
1 Abomination-Batroc 5.00
2 Beast-Clea 4.00
3 Cloak & D.-Dr.Strange 4.00
4 Dr.Strange-Galactus 4.00
5 Gardener-Hulk 4.00
6 Human Torch-Ka-Zar 3.25
7 Kraven-Magneto 3.25
8 Magneto-Moleman 3.25
9 Moleman-Owl 3.25
10 . . . . 3.25
11 . . . . 2.50
12 S-T 2.50
13 . . . . 2.50
14 V-Z 2.50
15 . . . . 2.50
16 Book of the Dead 2.50
17 Handbook of the Dead,inc.
    JLe illus. 2.50
18 . . . . 2.50
19 . . . . 2.50
20 Inc.RLd illus. 2.50
Marvel Universe Update
1 thru 8 . . . . @1.75
Marvel Universe Packet
1 inc. Spider-Man 5.50
2 inc. Captain America 4.50
3 inc. Ghost Rider 5.00
4 inc. Wolverine 4.50
5 inc. Punisher 4.25
6 inc. She-Hulk 3.95
7 inc. Daredevil 3.95
8 inc. Hulk 3.95
9 inc. Moon Knight 3.95
10 inc. Captain Britain 3.95
11 inc. Storm 3.95
12 inc. Silver Surfer 3.95
13 inc. Ice Man 4.50
14 inc. Thor 4.50
15 thru 22 . . . . @4.50
23 inc. Cage 4.50
24 inc. Iron Fist 4.50
25 inc.Deadpool,Night Thrasher . . 4.50
26 inc. Wonderman 4.95
27 inc.Beta Ray Bill,Pip 4.95
28 inc.X-Men 4.95
29 inc.Carnage 4.95
30 thru 36 . . . . @4.95

MARVEL X-MEN
COLLECTION
1 thru 3 JL from the 1st series
    X-Men Cards 3.25

MARVELS
1 B:KBk(s),AxR,I:Phil Sheldon,
    A:G.A.Heroes,Human Torch Vs
    Namor 15.00
2 AxR,A:S.A.Avengers,FF,X-Men 13.00
3 AxR,FF vs Galactus 10.00

4 AxR,Final issue 9.00
HC rep.#1-#4 . . . . 34.95

MARVIN MOUSE
Atlas
September, 1957
1 BEv,F:Marvin Mouse 30.00

Master of Kung Fu #100
© Marvel Entertainment Group

MASTER OF KUNG FU, SPECIAL MARVEL ED.
April, 1974
Prev: SPECIAL MARVEL EDITION
17 JSn,I:Black Jack Tarr 18.00
18 PG,1st Gulacy Art 14.00
19 PG,A:Man-Thing 11.00
20 GK(c),PG,AM,V:Samurai 11.00
21 AM,Season of Vengeance..
  Moment of Death 7.00
22 PG,DA,Death 7.00
23 AM,KJ,River of Death 7.00
24 JSn,WS,AM,ST,Night of the
  Assassin 7.00
25 JSt(c),PG,ST,Fists Fury...
  Rites of Death 6.00
26 KP,ST,A:Daughter of
  Fu Manchu 5.00
27 SB,FS,A:Fu Manchu 5.00
28 EH,ST,Death of a Spirit 5.00
29 PG,V:Razor-Fist 5.50
30 PG,DA,Pit of Lions 5.50
31 GK&DA(c),PG,DA,Snowbuster 2.50
32 GK&ME(c),SB,ME,Assault on an
  Angry Sea 5.00
33 PG,Messenger of Madness,
  I:Leiko Wu 5.00
34 PG,Captive in A Madman's
  Crown 5.00
35 PG,V:Death Hand 5.00
36 The Night of the Ninja's 4.00
37 V:Darkstrider & Warlords of
  the Web 4.00
38 GK(c),PG,A:The Cat 4.00
39 GK(c),PG,A:The Cat 4.00
40 PG,The Murder Agency 4.00

41 . . . . 4.00
42 GK(c),PG,TS,V:Shockwave . . . 4.00
43 PG,V:Shockwave 4.00
44 SB(c),PG,V:Fu Manchu 4.00
45 GK(c),PG,Death Seed 4.00
46 PG,V:Sumo 4.00
47 PG,The Cold White
  Mantle of Death 4.00
48 PG,Bridge of a 1,000 Dooms . 4.00
49 PG,V:Shaka Kharn,The
  Demon Warrior 4.00
50 PG,V:Fu Manchu 4.00
51 PG(c),To End...To Begin 4.00
52 Mayhem in Morocco 2.50
53 . . . . 2.50
54 JSn(c),Death Wears Three
  Faces 2.50
55 PG(c),The Ages of Death 2.50
56 V:The Black Ninja 2.50
57 V:Red Baron 2.50
58 Behold the Final Mask 2.50
59 GK(c),B:Phoenix Gambit,
  Behold the Angel of Doom . . . 2.50
60 A:Dr.Doom,Doom Came 2.50
61 V:Skull Crusher 2.50
62 Coast of Death 2.50
63 GK&TA(c),Doom Wears
  Three Faces 2.50
64 PG(c),To Challenge a Dragon . 2.50
65 V:Pavane 2.50
66 V:Kogar 2.50
67 PG(c),Dark Encounters 2.50
68 Final Combats,V:The Cat 2.50
69 . . . . 2.50
70 A:Black Jack Tarr,Murder
  Mansion 2.50
71 PG(c),Ying & Yang (c) 2.50
72 V:Shockwave 2.50
73 RN(c),V:Behemoths 2.50
74 TA(c),A:Shockwave 2.50
75 Where Monsters Dwell 2.50
76 GD,Battle on the Waterfront . . 3.00
77 GD,I:Zaran 3.00
78 GD,Moving Targets 3.00
79 GD,This Side of Death 3.00
80 GD,V:Leopard Men 3.00
81 GD,V:Leopard Men 3.00
82 GD,Flight into Fear 3.00
83 GD, ... 3.00
84 GD,V:Fu Manchu 3.00
85 GD,V:Fu Manchu 3.00
86 GD,V:Fu Manchu 3.00
87 GD,V:Zaran, ... 3.00
88 GD,V:Fu Manchu 3.00
89 GD,D:Fu Manchu 3.00
90 MZ,Death in Chinatown 3.00
91 GD,Gang War,drugs 4.00
92 GD,Shadows of the Past 3.00
93 GD,Cult of Death 3.00
94 GD,V:Agent Synergon 3.00
95 GD,Raid 3.00
96 GD,I:Rufus Carter 3.00
97 GD,V:Kung Fu's Dark Side . . . 3.00
98 GD,Fight to the Finish 3.00
99 GD,Death Boat 3.00
100 GD,Doublesize 4.00
101 GD,Not Smoke,Nor Beads,
  Nor Blood 2.50
102 GD,Assassins,1st GD(p) 4.00
103 GD,V:Assassins 2.50
104 GD,Fight without Reason,
  C:Cerberus 2.50
105 GD,I:Razor Fist 2.50
106 GD,C:Velcro 2.50
107 GD,A:Sata 2.50

108 GD 2.50
109 GD,Death is a Dark Agent . . 2.50
110 GD,Perilous Reign 2.50
111 GD 2.50
112 GD(c),Commit and Destroy . . 2.25
113 GD(c),V:Panthers 2.25
114 Fantasy o/t Autumn Moon . . . 2.25
115 GD 2.50
116 GD 2.50
117 GD,Devil Deeds Done
  in Darkness 2.50
118 GD,D:Fu Manchu,double 2.50
119 GD 2.50
120 GD,Dweller o/t Dark Stream . 2.50
121 Death in the City of Lights' . . 2.00
122 . . . . 2.00
123 V:Ninjas 2.00
124 . . . . 2.00
125 . . . . 2.00
Giant#1,CR,PG 3.00
Giant#2 PG,V:Yellow Claw 2.00
Giant#3 . . . . 2.00
Giant#4 JK,V:Yellow Claw 2.00
Spec.#1 Bleeding Black 3.25

MASTER OF KUNG FU: BLEEDING BLACK
1 V:ShadowHand,1991 . . . . 2.95

MASTERS OF TERROR
July, 1975
1 GM(c),FB,BWS,JSn,NA 3.00
2 JSn(c),GK,VM,September, 1975 2.00

MASTERS OF THE UNIVERSE
Star
May, 1986—March, 1988
1 I:Hordak 1.50
2 thru 12 . . . . @1.00
Movie #1 GT 2.00

MATT SLADE, GUNFIGHTER
Atlas
May, 1956
1 AW,AT,F:Matt Slade,Crimson
  Avenger 80.00
2 AW,A:Crimson Avenger 50.00
3 A:Crimson Avenger 35.00
4 A:Crimson Avenger 35.00
Becomes:

KID SLADE GUNFIGHTER
5 F:Kid Slade 40.00
6 . . . . 21.00
7 AW,Duel in the Night 45.00
8 July, 1957 . . . . 21.00

MELVIN THE MONSTER
Atlas
July, 1956
1 . . . . 60.00
2 thru 6 . . . . @40.00
Becomes:

DEXTER THE DEMON
September, 1957
7 . . . . 25.00

MEMORIES
Epic
1 Space Adventures 2.50

MENACE
Atlas
May, 1953
1 RH,BEv,GT,One Head Too
  Many 250.00
2 RH,BEv,GT,JSt,Burton's Blood175.00
3 BEv,RH,JR,The Werewolf . . 125.00
4 BEv,RH,The Four Armed Man 125.00
5 BEv,RH,GC,GT,I&O:Zombie 200.00
6 BEv,RH,JR,The Graymoor
  Ghost 125.00
7 JSt,RH,Fresh out of Flesh . . 100.00
8 RH,The Lizard Man 100.00
9 BEv,The Walking Dead . . . 110.00
10 RH(c),Half Man,Half... . . . . . 100.00
11 JKz,JR,Locked In,May, 1954 100.00

MEN IN ACTION
Atlas
April, 1952
1 Sweating it Out 60.00
2 US Infantry stories 30.00
3 RH 20.00
4 War stories 20.00
5 Squad Charge 20.00
6 War stories 20.00
7 RH(c),BK,No Risk Too Great 40.00
8 JRo(c),They Strike By Night . 20.00
9 SSh(c),Rangers Strike Back . 20.00
Becomes:

BATTLE BRADY
10 SSh(c),F:Battle Brady 50.00
11 SSh(c) 28.00
12 SSh(c),Death to the Reds . . . 20.00
13 . . . . 20.00
14 Final Issue,June, 1953 . . . . . 20.00

MEN'S ADVENTURES
See: TRUE WESTERN

MEPHISTO vs.
FOUR HEROES
April, 1987
1 JB,BWi,A:Fantastic Four 2.50
2 JB,BWi,A:X-Factor 2.25
3 JB,AM,A:X-Men 2.25
4 JB,BWi,A:Avengers,July, 1987 . 2.00

MERC
November, 1986
1 GM,O:Mark Hazard 1.50
2 GM 1.00
3 M,Arab Terrorists 1.00
4 GM 1.00
5 GM 1.00
6 GM 1.00
7 GM 1.00
8 GM 1.00
9 NKu/AKu 1.00
10 . . . . 1.00
11 . . . . 1.00
12 October, 1987 . . . . 1.00
Ann.#1 D:Merc 1.25

METEOR MAN
1 R:Meteor Man 1.25
2 V:GhostStrike,Malefactor,Simon 1.25
3 A:Spider-Man 1.25
4 A:Night Thrasher 1.25
5 Exocet 1.25
6 final issue 1.25

[TED McKEEVER'S]
METROPOL
Epic
1 Ted McKeever 2.95
2 . . . . 2.95
3 . . . . 2.95
4 . . . . 2.95
5 . . . . 2.95
6 . . . . 2.95
7 . . . . 2.95
8 Return of Eddy Current 2.95
9 'Wings of Silence' 2.95
10 'Rotting Metal,Rusted Flesh' . . 2.95
11 'Diagram of the Heart' 2.95
12 . . . . 2.95

METROPOL A.D.
Epic
1 R:The Angels 3.50
2 V:Demons 3.50
3 V:Nuclear Arsenal 3.50

Micronauts #1
© *Marvel Entertainment Group*

MICRONAUTS
[1st Series]
January, 1979
1 MGo,JRu,O:Micronauts 3.00
2 MGo,JRu,Earth 2.50
3 MGo,JRu 2.00
4 MGo 2.00
5 MGo,V:Prometheus 2.00
6 MGo 2.00
7 MGo,A:Man Thing 2.00
8 MGo,BMc,I:Capt. Univ. 2.50
9 MGo,I:Cilicia 2.00
10 MGo 2.00
11 MGo 2.00
12 MGo 2.00
13 HC,F:Bug 1.50
14 HC,V:Wartstaff 1.50
15 HC,AM,A:Fantastic Four 1.50
16 HC,AM,A:Fantastic Four 1.50
17 HC,AM,A:Fantastic Four 1.50
18 HC,Haunted House Issue 1.50

19 PB,V:Odd John 1.50
20 PB,A:Antman 1.50
21 PB,I:Microverse 1.50
22 PB 1.50
23 PB,V:Molecule Man 1.50
24 MGo,V:Computrex 1.50
25 PB,A:Mentallo 1.50
26 PB,A:Baronkarza 1.25
27 PB,V:Hydra,A:Shield 1.25
28 PB,V:Hydra,A:Shield 1.25
29 PB,Doc Samson 1.25
30 PB,A:Shield 1.25
31 PB,A:Dr.Strange 1.25
32 PB,A:Dr.Strange 1.25
33 PB,A:Devil of Tropica 1.25
34 PB,A:Dr.Strange 1.25
35 O:Microverse 1.50
36 KG,Dr.Strange 1.50
37 KG,Nightcrawler 3.50
38 GK,1st direct 2.50
39 SD 1.75
40 GK,A:FF 1.75
41 GK,Dr.Doom 1.25
42 GK 1.25
43 . . . . 1.25
44 . . . . 1.25
45 Arcade 1.25
46 . . . . 1.25
47 . . . . 1.25
48 JG 2.00
49 JG,V:BaronKarza 1.50
50 JG,V:BaronKarza 1.50
51 JG 1.50
52 JG 1.50
53 JG,V:Untouchables 1.50
54 JG,V:Tribunal 1.50
55 JG,V:KarzaWorld 1.50
56 JG,Kaliklak 1.50
57 JG,V:BaronKarza 1.50
58 JG,V:BaronKarza 1.50
59 JG,V:TheMakers 1.50
Ann.#1,SD 2.00
#2 SD 1.50
[2nd Series]
1 V:The Makers 1.50
2 AAd(c),V:The Makers 1.50
3 Huntar'sEgg 1.00
4 V:The Makers 1.00
5 The Spiral Path 1.00
6 L:Bug 1.00
7 Acroyear 1.00
8 V:Scion 1.00
9 R:Devil 1.00
10 V:Enigma Force 1.00
11 V:Scion 1.00
12 V:Scion 1.00
13 V:Dark Armada 1.00
14 V:Keys of the Zodiac 1.00
15 O:Marionette 1.00
16 Secret Wars II 1.50
17 V:Scion 1.00
18 Acroyear 1.00
19 R:Baron Karza 1.00
20 Last Issue 1.25

MICRONAUTS
(Special Edition)
December, 1983
1 MGo/JRu,rep. 2.00
2 MGo/JRu,rep. 2.00
3 Rep.MG/JRu 2.00
4 Rep.MG/JRu 2.00
5 Rep.MG/JRu,April, 1984 . . . . . 2.00

MIDNIGHT MEN
1 HC,I:Midnight Men 2.75
2 HC,J:Barnett 2.25
3 HC,Pasternak is Midnight Man . 2.25
4 HC,Last issue 2.25

MIDNIGHT SONS UNLIMITED
1 JQ,JBi,MT(c),A:Midnight Sons . 4.25
2 BSz(c),F:Midnight Sons 4.25
3 JR2(c),JS,A:SpiderMan 4.25
4 Siege of Darkness #17,
  D:2nd Ghost Rider 4.25
5 DQ(s),F:Mordred,Vengeance,
  Morbius,Werewolf,Blaze,
  I:Wildpride 4.25
6 DQ(s),F:Dr.Strange 3.95
7 DQ(s),F:Man-Thing 3.95
8 . . . . 3.95
9 J:Mighty Destroyer 3.95

MIGHTY MARVEL WESTERN
October, 1968
1 JK,All reprints,B:Rawhide Kid
  Kid Colt,Two-Gun Kids . . . 7.50

2 JK,DAy,Beware of the Barker
  Brothers 5.00
3 HT(c),JK,DAy,Walking Death . . 5.00
4 HT(c),DAy 5.00
5 HT(c),DAy,Ambush 5.00
6 HT(c),DAy Doom in the Desert 5.00
7 DAy,V:Murderous Masquerader 5.00
8 HT(c),DAy,Rustler's on the
  Range 5.00
9 JSe(c),JK,DAy,V:Dr Danger . . 5.00
10 OW,DH,Cougar 5.00
11 V:The Enforcers 2.00
12 JK,V:Blackjack Bordon 2.00
13 V:Grizzly 2.00
14 JK.V:The Enforcers 2.00
15 Massacre at Medicine Bend . . 2.00
16 JK,Mine of Death 2.00
17 Ambush at Blacksnake Mesa . 2.00
18 Six-Gun Thunderer 2.00
19 Reprints cont 2.00
20 same 2.00
21 same 1.50
22 . . . . 1.50
23 same 1.50
24 JDa,E:Kid Colt 1.50
25 B:Matt Slade 1.50
26 thru 31 Reprints . . . . . . @1.50
32 JK,AW,Ringo Kid #23 . . . . . . 1.25
33 thru 36 Reprints . . . . . . @1.25
37 JK,AW Two-Gun #51 . . . . . . 1.25
38 thru 45 Reprints . . . . . . @1.25
46 same,September, 1976 . . . . . . 1.25

MIGHTY MOUSE
Fall, 1946
[1st Series]
1 Terytoons Presents 650.00
2 . . . . 350.00
3 . . . . 250.00
4 Summer, 1947 . . . . 250.00

MIGHTY MOUSE
October, 1990
1 EC,Dark Mite Returns 3.00
2 EC,V:The Glove 2.00
3 EC/JBr(c)Prince Say More 1.50

4 EC/GP(c)Alt.Universe #1 . . . . . 1.50
5 EC,Alt.Universe #2 . . . . 1.50
6 'Ferment',A:MacFurline' 1.50
7 EC,V:Viral Worm 1.25
8 EC,BAT-BAT:Year One,
  O:Bug Wonder 1.25
9 EC,BAT-BAT:Year One,
  V:Smoker 1.25
10 'Night o/t Rating Lunatics' 1.25

Millie the Model #3
© Marvel Entertainment Group

MILLIE THE MODEL
Winter, 1945
1 O:Millie the Model,
  Bowling(c) 375.00
2 Totem Pole(c) 250.00
3 Anti-Noise(c) 125.00
4 Bathing Suit(c) 125.00
5 Blame it on Fame 125.00
6 Beauty and the Beast 125.00
7 Bathing Suit(c) 125.00
8 Fancy Dress(c),HK,Hey Look 125.00
9 Paris(c),BW 135.00
10 Jewelry(c),HK,Hey Look . . . 125.00
11 HK,Giggles and Grins 75.00
12 A;Rusty,Hedy Devine 65.00
13 A;Hedy Devine,HK,Hey Look 75.00
14 HK,Hey Look 75.00
15 HK,Hey Look 45.00
16 . . . . 75.00
17 thru 20 . . . . @60.00
21 thru 30 . . . . @50.00
31 thru 75 . . . . @30.00
76 thru 99 . . . . @20.00
100 . . . . 22.00
101 thru 126 . . . . @15.00
127 Millie/Clicker 20.00
128 A:Scarlet Mayfair 15.00
129 The Truth about Agnes 15.00
130 thru 153 . . . . @15.00
154 B:New Millie 15.00
155 thru 206 . . . . @15.00
207 December, 1973 . . . . 15.00
Ann.#1 How Millie Became
  a Model 125.00
Ann.#2 Millies Guide to
  the world of Modeling 75.00
Ann.#3 Many Lives of Millie 50.00

Ann.#4 Many Lives of Millie 30.00

MISS AMERICA COMICS
1944
1 Miss America(c),pin-ups . . . 750.00

MISS AMERICA MAGAZINE
Nov., 1944—Nov. 1958
2 Ph(c),Miss America costume
  I;Patsy Walker,Buzz Baxter,
  Hedy Wolfe 750.00
3 Ph(c),A:Patsy Walker,Miss
  America 300.00
4 Ph(c),Betty Page,A:Patsy
  Walker,Miss America 300.00
5 Ph(c),A:Patsy Walker,Miss
  America 300.00
6 Ph(c),A:Patsy Walker 50.00
7 Patsy Walker stories 30.00
8 same 30.00
9 same 30.00
10 same 30.00
11 same 30.00
12 same 30.00
13 thru 18 . . . . @30.00
21 . . . . 35.00
22 thru 45 . . . . @25.00
46 thru 93 . . . . @20.00

MISS FURY COMICS
Timely
Winter, 1942-43
1 Newspaper strip reprints,
  ASh(c) O:Miss Fury 1,800.00
2 V:Nazis(c) 900.00
3 Hitler/Nazi Flag(c) 700.00
4 ASh(c),Japanese(c) 550.00
5 ASh(c),Gangster(c) 550.00
6 Gangster(c) 550.00
7 Gangster(c) 550.00
8 Atom-Bomb Secrets(c)
  Winter, 1946 . . . . 550.00

MISTY
Star
December, 1985
1 F:Millie the Models Niece 1.50
2 thru 5 . . . . @1.00
6 May, 1986 . . . . 1.00

MITZI COMICS
Timely
Spring, 1948
1 HK:Hey Look,Giggles
  and Grins 75.00
Becomes:

MITZI'S BOYFRIEND
2 F:Chip,Mitzi/Chip(c) 33.00
3 Chips adventures 25.00
4 thru 7 same . . . . @25.00
Becomes:

MITZI'S ROMANCES
8 Mitzi/Chip(c) 32.00
9 . . . . 25.00
10 December, 1949 . . . . 25.00

MODELING WITH MILLIE
See: DATE WITH MILLIE

MOEBIUS
Epic
October, 1987

1	12.00
2	12.00
3	15.00
4	12.00
5	12.00
6 1988	12.00

MOLLY MANTON'S ROMANCES
September, 1949

1 Ph(c),Dare Not Marry	50.00
2 Ph(c),Romances of	35.00

Becomes:
ROMANTIC AFFAIRS

3 Ph(c)	27.00

MONSTER OF FRANKENSTEIN
January, 1973

1 MP,Frankenstein's Monster	18.00
2 MP,Bride of the Monster	9.00
3 MP,Revenge	9.00
4 MP,Monster's Death	9.00
5 MP,The Monster Walks Among Us	9.00

Becomes:
FRANKENSTEIN

6 MP,Last of the Frankensteins	5.00
7 JB,The Fiend and the Fury	5.00
8 JB,A:Dracula	10.00
9 JB,A:Dracula	10.00
10 JB,Death Strikes Frankenstein	5.00
11 Carnage at Castle Frankenstein	3.75
12 Frankenstein's Monster today	3.75
13 Undying Fiend	3.75
14 Fury of the Night Creature	3.75
15 Trapped in a Nightmare	3.75
16 The Brute and the Berserker	3.75
17 Phoenix Aflame	3.75
18 Children of the Damned September, 1975	3.75

MONSTERS ON THE PROWL
See: CHAMBER OF DARKNESS

MONSTERS UNLEASHED
July, 1973

1 GM(c),GC,DW,Black&White Mag	6.00
2 JB,FB,BEv,B:Frankenstein	8.00
3 NA(c),GK,GM,GT,B:Man-Thing	4.00
4 JB,GC,BK,I:Satana	4.00
5 JB	5.00
6 MP	4.00
7 AW	4.00
8 GP,NA	4.00
9 A:Wendigo	5.00
10 O:Tigra	4.00
11 FB(C),April, 1975	4.00
Ann.#1 GK	4.00

MOON KNIGHT
[1st Regular Series]
November, 1980

1 BSz,O:Moon Knight	6.00
2 BSz,V:Slasher	3.50
3 BSz,V:Midnight Man	3.00

4 BSz,V:Committee of 5	3.00
5 BSz,V:Red Hunter	3.00
6 BSz,V:White Angels	3.00
7 BSz,V:Moon Kings	3.00
8 BSz,V:Moon Kings, Drug	2.75
9 BSz,V:Midnight Man	2.75
10 BSz,V:Midnight Man	2.75
11 BSz,V:Creed (Angel Dust)	2.75
12 BSz,V:Morpheus	2.75
13 BSz,A:Daredevil & Jester	2.75
14 BSz,V:Stained Glass Scarlet	2.75
15 FM(c),BSz,1st Direct	4.00
16 V:Blacksmith	2.50
17 BSz,V:Master Sniper	2.50
18 BSz,V:Slayers Elite	2.50
19 BSz,V:Arsenal	2.50
20 BSz,V:Arsenal	2.50
21 A:Bother Voodoo	2.25
22 BSz,V:Morpheus	2.25
23 BSz,V:Morpheus	2.25
24 BSz,V:Stained Glass Scarlet	2.25
25 BSz,Black Specter	2.25
26 KP,V:Cabbie Killer	2.00
27 A:Kingpin	2.00
28 BSz,"Spirits in the Sands"	2.00
29 BSz,V:Werewolf	3.00
30 BSz,V:Werewolf	3.00
31 TA,V:Savage Studs	2.00
32 KN,Druid Walsh	2.00
33 KN,V:Druid Walsh	2.00
34 KN,Marc Spector	2.00
35 KN,X-Men,FF,V:The Fly DoubleSized	3.00
36 A:Dr.Strange	2.00
37 V:Zohar	2.00
38 V:Zohar	2.00

[2nd Regular Series]

1 O:Moon Knight,DoubleSize	2.50
2 Yucatan	2.00
3 V:Morpheus	2.00
4 A:Countess	2.00
5 V:Lt.Flint	2.00
6 GI,LastIssue	2.00

[3rd Regular Series]

1 V:Bushmaster	5.00
2 A:Spider-Man	4.00
3 V:Bushmaster	2.50
4 RH,A:Midnight,Black Cat	2.50
5 V:Midnight,BlackCat	2.50
6 A:BrotherVoodoo	2.50
7 A:BrotherVoodoo	2.50
8 TP,A:Punisher,A of V	4.00
9 TP,A:Punisher,A of V	4.00
10 V:Killer Shrike,A of V	2.00
11 TP,V:Arsenal	2.00
12 TP,V:Bushman,A:Arsenal	2.00
13 TP,V:Bushman	2.00
14 TP,V:Bushman	2.00
15 TP,Trial o/Marc Spector #1,A: Silv.Sable,Sandman,Paladin	3.00
16 TP,Trial o/Marc Spector #2,A: Silv.Sable,Sandman,Paladin	3.00
17 TP,Trial o/Marc Spector #3	3.00
18 TP,Trial o/Marc Spector #4	3.00
19 RLd(c),TP,SpM,Punisher	4.00
20 TP,A:Spider-Man,Punisher	3.00
21 TP,Spider-Man,Punisher	3.00
22 I:Harbinger	2.00
23 Confrontation	2.00
24 A:Midnight	2.00
25 MBa,TP,A:Ghost Rider	3.00
26 BSz(c),TP,B:Scarlet Redemption V:Stained Glass Scarlet	2.00
27 TP,V:Stained Glass Scarlet	2.00
28 TP,V:Stained Glass Scarlet	2.00

29 TP,V:Stained Glass Scarlet	2.00
30 TP,V:Stained Glass Scarlet	2.00
31 TP,E:Scarlet Redemption, A:Hobgoblin	2.50
32 TP,V:Hobgoblin,SpM(in Black)	4.00
33 TP,V:Hobgoblin,A:Spider-Man	4.00
34 V:Killer Shrike	2.00
35 TP,Return of Randall Spector Pt.1,A:Punisher	2.00
36 TP,A:Punisher,Randall	2.00
37 TP,A:Punisher,Randall	2.00
38 TP,A:Punisher,Randall	2.00
39 TP,N:Moon Knight,A:Dr.Doom	2.00
40 TP,V:Dr.Doom	2.00
41 TP,Infinity War,I:Moonshade	2.00
42 TP,Infinity War,V:Moonshade	2.00
43 TP(i),Infinity War	2.00
44 Inf.War,A:Dr.Strange.FF	2.00
45 V:Demogoblin	2.00
46 V:Demogoblin	2.00
47 Legacy Quest Scenario	2.00
48 I:Deadzone	2.00
49 V:Deadzone	2.00
50 A:Avengers,I:Hellbent, Die-cut(c)	3.50
51 A:Gambit,V:Hellbent	2.00
52 A:Gambit,Werewolf	2.00
53 "Pang"	2.00
54	2.00
55 SPa,V:Sunstreak	18.00
56 SPa,V:Seth	12.00
57 SPa,Inf.Crusade	10.00
58 SPa(c),A:Hellbent	4.00
59 SPa(c),	4.00
60 E:TKa(s),SPa,D:Moonknight	6.00
Spec.#1 ANi,A:Shang-Chi	2.50

MOON KNIGHT
(Special Edition)
November, 1983

1 BSz,reprints	2.00
2 BSz,reprints	2.00
3 BSz,reprints,January, 1984	2.00

MOON KNIGHT: DIVIDED WE FALL

1 DCw,V:Bushman	4.95

MOONSHADOW
Epic
May, 1985

1 JMu,O:Moonshadow	6.00
2 JMu,Into Space	4.00
3 JMu,The Looney Bin	3.50
4 JMu,Fights Ira	3.50
5 JMu,Prisoner	3.50
6 JMu,Hero of War	3.50
7 JMu,UnkshussFamily	3.50
8 JMu,Social Outcast	3.50
9 JMu,Search For Ira	3.50
10 JMu,Internat.House of T	3.50
11 JMu,UnkshussFamily	3.50
12 JMu,UnkshussFamily,Feb.1987	3.50

MONSTER MENACE

1 thru 4 SD,rep.	1.25

MORBIUS

1 V:Lilith,Lilin,A:Blaze,Gh.Rider Rise o/t Midnight Sons #3, polybagged w/poster	4.00
2 V:Simon Stroud	2.50
3 A:Spider-Man	2.00

All comics prices listed are for *Near Mint* condition.

Morbius #2
© Marvel Entertainment Group

4 I:Dr.Paine,C:Spider-Man 2.00
5 V:Basilisk,(inc Superman tribute
    on letters page) 2.00
6 V:Basilisk 2.00
7 V:Vic Slaughter 2.00
8 V:Nightmare 2.00
9 V:Nightmare 2.00
10 Two Tales 2.00
11 A:Nightstalkers 2.00
12 Midnight Massacre#4 .... 2.50
13 R:Martine,A:Lilith 2.00
14 RoW,V:Nightmare,A:Werewolf . 2.00
15 A:Ghost Rider,Werewolf 2.00
16 GWt(s),Siege of Darkness#5 .. 2.00
17 GWt(s),Siege of Darkness#17 . 2.00
18 GWt(s),A:Deathlok 2.00
19 GWt(s),A:Deathlok 2.00
20 GWt(s),I:Bloodthirst 2.00
21 B:Dance of the Hunter,A:SpM . 2.25
22 A:Spider-Man 2.25
23 E:Dance of the Hunter,A:SpM . 2.25
24 Return of the Dragon 2.25
25 RoW 2.50
26 .... 1.95
27 .... 1.95
28 A:Werewolf 1.95
29 .... 1.95
30 New Morbius 1.95
31 A:Mortine 1.95
32 Another Kill 1.95

MORBIUS REVISITED
1 WMc,rep.Fear #20 .... 1.95
2 WMc,rep.Fear #28 .... 1.95
3 WMc,rep.Fear #29 .... 1.95
4 WMc,rep.Fear #30 .... 1.95
5 WMc,rep.Fear #31 .... 1.95

MORT THE DEAD TEENAGER
1 LHa(s),I:Mort 1.75
2 thru 3 LHa(s), ... 1.75
4 LHa(s),last issue 1.75

MOTHER TERESA
1984
1 Mother Teresa Story 2.00

MOTOR MOUTH
1 GFr,A:Nick Fury,I:Motor
    Mouth,Killpower 4.00
2 GFr,A:Nick Fury, ... 2.50
3 GFr,V:Killpower,A:Punisher ... 2.50
4 GFr,A:Nick Fury,Warheads,
    Hell's Angel,O:Killpower 2.50
5 GFr,A:Excalibur,Archangel 2.50
6 GFr,A:Cable,Punisher 2.50
7 EP,A:Cable,Nick Fury 2.00
8 JFr,A:Cable,Nick Fury 2.00
9 JFr,A:Cable,N.Fury,V:Harpies . 2.00
10 V:Red Sonja 2.00
11 V:Zachary Sorrow 2.00
12 A:Death's Head II 2.00
13 A:Death's Head II 2.00

Ms. Marvel #14
© Marvel Entertainment Group

MS. MARVEL
January, 1977
1 JB,O:Ms Marvel 5.00
2 JB,JSt,V:Scorpion 4.00
3 JB,JSt,V:Doomsday Man 3.00
4 JM,JSt,V:Destructor 3.00
5 JM,JSt,A:V:Vision 3.00
6 JM,JSt,V:Grotesk 3.00
7 JM,JSt,V:Modok 3.00
8 JM,JSt,V:Grotesk 3.00
9 KP,JSt,I:Deathbird 5.00
10 JB,TP,V:Deathbird,Modok 3.00
11 V:Elementals 2.00
12 V:Hecate 2.00
13 Bedlam in Boston 2.00
14 V:Steeplejack 2.00
15 V:Tigershark 2.00
16 V:Tigershark,A:Beast 2.00
17 .... 2.00
18 I:Mystique,A;Avengers 6.50
19 A:Captain Marvel 3.00
20 V:Lethal Lizards,N:Ms.Marvel . 2.00
21 V:Lethal Lizards 2.00

22 V:Deathbirds 2.00
23 The Woman who Fell to Earth
    April, 1979 .... 2.00

MUPPET BABIES
Star
August, 1984
1 thru 10 .... @1.00
11 thru 20 .... @1.00
21 thru 25 July, 1989 .... @1.00

MUPPETS TAKE MANHATTAN
1 movie adapt,November, 1984 . 1.00
2 movie adapt 1.00
3 movie adapt,January, 1985 ... 1.00

MUTANTS: THE AMAZING X-MEN
1 X-Men After Xavier 3.50
2 Exodus, Dazzler,V:Abyss 2.25
3 F:Bishop 1.95
4 V:Apocalypse 1.95

MUTANTS: THE ASTONISHING X-MEN
1 Uncanny X-Men 3.50
2 V:Holocaust 2.25
3 V:Abyss 1.95
4 V:Beast,Infinities 1.95

MUTANTS: GENERATION NEXT
1 Generation X Ax 3.50
2 Genetic Slave Pens 2.25
3 V:Sugar Man 1.95
4 V:Sugar Man 1.95

MUTATIS
Epic
1 I:Mutatis 2.25
2 O:Mutatis 2.25
3 A:Mutatis 2.25

MY DIARY
December, 1949
1 Ph(c),The Man I Love 50.00
2 Ph(c),I Was Anybody's Girl
    March, 1950 .... 45.00

MY LOVE
July, 1949
1 Ph(c),One Heart to Give 50.00
2 Ph(c),Hate in My Heart 30.00
3 Ph(c), ... 30.00
4 Ph(c),Betty Page, April, 1950 115.00

MY LOVE
September, 1969
1 Love story reprints 7.50
2 thru 9 .... @4.00
10 .... 5.00
11 thru 38 .... @3.00
39 March, 1976 .... 3.00

MY ROMANCE
September, 1948
1 Romance Stories 50.00
2 .... 27.00
3 .... 27.00

Becomes:

MY OWN ROMANCE

4 Romance Stories Continue	47.00
5 thru 10	@25.00
11 thru 20	@18.00
21 thru 50	@15.00
51 thru 54	@11.00
55	30.00
56 thru 60	@11.00
61 thru 70	@6.00
71	55.00
72 thru 76	@10.00

Becomes:

TEENAGE ROMANCE

77 Romance Stories Continue	10.00
78 thru 85	@10.00
86 March, 1962	10.00

MYS-TECH WARS

1 BHi,A:FF,X-Men,Avengers	2.00
2 A:FF,X-Men,X-Force	2.00
3 BHi,A:X-Men,X-Force	2.00
4 A:Death's Head II	2.00

MYSTERY TALES
Atlas
March, 1952

1 GC,Horror Strikes at Midnight	350.00
2 BK,BEv,OW,The Corpse is Mine	200.00
3 RH,GC,JM, The Vampire Strikes	150.00
4 Funeral of Horror	150.00
5 Blackout at Midnight	150.00
6	150.00
7 JRo,The Ghost Hunter	150.00
8 BEv	150.00
9 BEv(c),the Man in the Morgue	150.00
10 BEV(c),GT,What Happened to Harry	150.00
11 BEv(c)	125.00
12 GT,MF	125.00
13	100.00
14 BEv(c),GT	100.00
15 RH(c),EK	100.00
16	100.00
17 RH(c)	100.00
18 AW,DAy,GC	125.00
19	100.00
20 Electric Chair	100.00
21 JF,MF,Decapitation	125.00
22 JF,MF	125.00
23 thru 27	@90.00
28	75.00
29 thru 32	@80.00
33 BEv	75.00
34	75.00
35 BEv	75.00
36	80.00
37 DW	75.00
38	75.00
39 BK	80.00
40	80.00
41 thru 43	@75.00
44 AW	85.00
45 SD	80.00
46 RC,SD,JP	85.00
47 DAy	80.00
48	65.00
49 GM,AT	65.00
50 JO,AW	80.00
51 DAy	80.00
52	60.00

53	60.00
54 RC,August, 1957	75.00

MYSTICAL TALES
Atlas
June, 1956

1 BEv,BP,JO,Say the Magical Words	200.00
2 BEv(c),JO,Black Blob	100.00
3 BEv(c),RC,Four Doors To	120.00

Mystical Tales #1
© Marvel Entertainment Group

4 BEv(c).The Condemned	100.00
5 AW,Meeting at Midnight	110.00
6 BK,AT,He Hides in the Tower	85.00
7 BEv,JF,JO,AT,FBe,The Haunted Tower	80.00
8 BK,SC, Stone Walls Can't Stop Him,August, 1957	85.00

MYSTIC COMICS
Timely
March, 1940
[1st Series]

1 ASh(c),O:The Blue Blaze,Dynamic Man,Flexo,B:Dakor the Magician A:Zephyr Jones,3X's,Deep Sea Demon,Bondage(c)	9,000.00
2 ASh(c),B:The Invisible Man Mastermind,	2,200.00
3 ASh(c),O:Hercules	1,600.00
4 ASh(c),O:Thin Man,Black Widow E:Hercules,Blue Blazes,Dynamic Man,Flexo,Invisible Man	1,800.00
5 ASh(c)O:The Black Marvel, Blazing Skull,Super Slave Terror,Sub-Earth Man	1,700.00
6 ASh(c),O:The Challenger, B:The Destroyer	1,700.00
7 S&K(c),B:The Witness,O:Davey and the Demon,E;The Black Widow,Hitler(c)	1,600.00
8 Bondage(c)	1,000.00
9 MSy,DRi,Hitler/Bondage(c)	1,000.00
10 E:Challenger,Terror	1,000.00

[2nd Series]
October, 1944

1 B:The Angel,Human Torch, Destroyer,Terry Vance,	

Tommy Tyme,Bondage(c)	1,000.00
2 E:Human Torch,Terry Vance,Bondage(c)	600.00
3 E:The Angel,Tommy Tyme Bondage(c)	500.00
4 ASh(c),A:Young Allies Winter, 1944-45	475.00

MYSTIC
[3rd Series]
March, 1951

1 MSy,Strange Tree	325.00
2 MSy,Dark Dungeon	200.00
3 GC,Jaws of Creeping Death	175.00
4 BW,MSy,The Den of the Devil Bird	300.00
5 MSy,Face	125.00
6 BW,She Wouldn't Stay Dead	300.00
7 GC,Untold Horror waits in the Tomb	125.00
8 DAy(c),BEv,GK,A Monster Among Us	125.00
9 BEv	125.00
10 GC	125.00
11 JR,The Black Gloves	100.00
12 GC	100.00
13 In the Dark	100.00
14 The Corpse and I	100.00
15 GT,JR,House of Horror	100.00
16 A Scream in the Dark	100.00
17 BEv,Behold the Vampire	100.00
18 BEv(c),The Russian Devil	100.00
19 Swamp Girl	100.00
20 RH(c)	100.00
21 BEv(c),GC	75.00
22 RH(c)	75.00
23 RH(c),RA,Chilling Tales	75.00
24 GK,How Many Times Can You Die	75.00
25 RH(c),RA,E.C.Swipe	75.00
26 Severed Head(c)	100.00
27 Who Walks with a Zombie	85.00
28 DW,Not Enough Dead	85.00
29 SMo,The Unseen	85.00
30 RH(c),DW	85.00
31 SC,JKz	85.00
32 The Survivor	85.00
33 thru 36	@85.00
37 thru 51	@75.00
52	85.00
53 thru 57	@75.00
58 thru 60	@80.00
61	75.00

'NAM, THE
December, 1986

1 MGo,Vietnam War	4.00
1a 2nd printing	1.50
2 MGo,Dust Off	2.50
3 MGo,Three Day Pass	2.00
4 MGo,TV newscrew	2.00
5 MGo,Top Sgt.	2.00
6 MGo,Monsoon	2.00
7 MGo,Cedar Falls	2.00
8 MGo,5th to the 1st	2.00
9 MGo,ActionIssue	2.00
10 MGo,Saigon	2.00
11 MGo,Christmas	1.75
12 MGo,AgentOrange	1.75
13 MGo	1.75
14	1.75
15 ReturningVets	1.75
16	1.75
17 Vietcong	1.75

All comics prices listed are for *Near Mint* condition.

The 'Nam #2
© Marvel Entertainment Group

18	1.75
19	1.75
20	1.75
21	1.75
22 Thanksgiving	1.75
23 XmasTruce of'67	1.75
24 TetOffensive	1.75
25 TetOffensive-KheSanh	1.75
26 HomefrontIssue	1.75
27 Candle in the Wind	1.75
28 Borderline	1.75
29 PeaceTalks	1.75
30 TheBunker	1.75
31 Fire and Ice	1.75
32 Nam in America	1.75
33 SpecialistDaniels	1.75
34 OperationPhoenix	1.75
35 Xmas-BobHope	1.75
36 RacialTension	1.75
37 Colorblind	1.75
38 Minefields	1.75
39	1.75
40	1.75
41 ,A:Thor,Iron Man, Cap.Am	1.75
42	1.75
43	1.75
44 SDr	1.75
45	1.75
46	1.75
47 TD	1.75
48 TD	1.75
49 Donut Dolly #1	1.75
50 HT,Donut Dolly #2 DoubSz	2.00
51 HT,Donut Dolly #3	1.75
52 Frank Castle(Punisher)#1	3.00
52a 2nd printing	2.00
53 Punisher #2	2.00
54 Death of Joe Hallen #1	1.75
55 TD,Death of Joe Hallen #2	1.50
56 TD,Death of Joe Hallen #3	1.50
57 TD,Death of Joe Hallen #4	1.50
58 TD,Death of Joe Hallen #5	1.50
59 P.O.W. Story #1	1.50
60 P.O.W. Story #2	1.50
61 P.O.W. Story #3	1.50

62 Speed & Ice,pt.1	1.50
63 Speed & Ice,pt.2	1.50
64 Speed & Ice,pt.3	1.50
65 Speed & Ice,pt.4	1.75
66 RH,Speed & Ice,pt.5	1.75
67 A:Punisher	2.00
68 A:Punisher	2.00
69 A:Punisher	2.00
70 Don Lomax writes	1.75
71 Vietnamese Point of View	1.75
72 The trials of war	1.75
73 War on the Homefront	1.75
74 Seige at An Loc	1.75
75 My Lai Massacre	2.25
76 R:Rob Little	1.75
77 Stateside	1.75
78	1.75
79 Beginning of the End#1	1.75
80 MGo(c),'68 Tet Offensive	1.75
81 MGo(c),TET Offensive ends	1.75
82 TET Offensive	1.75
83 thru 84 Last issue	1.75

'NAM MAGAZINE, THE
August, 1988
(black & white)

1 Reprints	3.00
2 thru 9	@2.50
10 May, 1989	2.50

NAMORA
Fall, 1948

1 BEv,DR	560.00
2 BEv,A:Sub-Mariner,Blonde Phantom	480.00
3 BEv,A:Sub-Mariner,Dec.,1948	430.00

NAMOR THE SUB-MARINER
April, 1990

1 JBy,BWi,I:Desmond & Phoebe Marrs	6.00
2 JBy,BWi,V:Griffin	4.00
3 JBy,BWi,V:Griffin	3.50
4 JBy,A:Reed & Sue Richards, Tony Stark	3.00
5 JBy,A:FF,IronMan,C:Speedball	3.00
6 JBy,V:Sluj	3.00
7 JBy,V:Sluj	3.00
8 JBy,V:Headhunter,R:D.Rand	3.00
9 JBy,V:Headhunter	3.00
10 JBy,V:Master Man,Warrior Woman	2.50
11 JBy,V:Mast.Man,War.Woman	2.50
12 JBy,R:Invaders,Spitfire	2.50
13 JBy,Namor on Trial,A:Fantastic Four,Captain America,Thor	2.50
14 JBy,R:Lady Dorma,A:Kazar Griffin	2.50
15 JBy,A:Iron Fist	2.50
16 JBy,A:Punisher,V:Iron Fist	2.50
17 JBy,V:Super Skrull(Iron Fist)	2.50
18 JBy,V:SuperSkrull,A:Punisher	2.50
19 JBy,V:Super Skrull,D:D.Marrs	2.50
20 JBy,Search for Iron Fist, O:Namorita	2.50
21 JBy,Visit to K'un Lun	2.50
22 JBy,Fate of Iron Fist, C:Wolverine	2.50
23 JBy,BWi,Iron Fist Contd., C:Wolverine	2.50
24 JBy,BWi,V:Wolverine	3.00
25 JBy,BWi,V:Master Khan	2.50
26 JaL,BWi,Search For Namor	9.00

27 JaL,BWi,V:Namorita	7.00
28 JaL,BWi,A:Iron Fist	6.00
29 JaL,BWi,After explosion	4.00
30 JaL,A:Doctor Doom	3.00
31 JaL,V:Doctor Doom	3.00
32 JaL,V:Doctor Doom, Namor regains memory	3.00
33 JaL,V:Master Khan	2.50
34 JaL,R:Atlantis	2.50
35 JaL,V:Tiger Shark	2.00
36 JaL,I:Suma-Ket,A:Tiger Shark	2.00
37 JaL,Blue Holo-Grafix,Altantean Civil War,N:Namor	3.00
38 JaL,O:Suma-Ket	2.00
39 A:Tigershark,V:Suma-Ket	1.50
40 V:Suma-Ket	1.50
41 V:War Machine	1.50
42 MCW,A:Stingray,V:Dorcas	1.50
43 MCW,V:Orka,Dorcas	1.50
44 I:Albatross	1.50
45 GI,A:Sunfire,V:Attuma	1.50
46 GI,	1.50
47 GI,Starblast #2	1.50
48 GI,Starblast #9,A:FF	1.50
49 GI,A:Ms. Marrs	1.50
50 GI,Holo-grafx(c),A:FF	3.25
50a Newsstand Ed.	2.00
51 AaL,	1.75
52 GI,I:Sea Leopard	1.75
53 GI,V:Sea Leopard	1.75
54 GI,I:Llyron	1.50
55 GI,V:Llyron	1.50
56 GI,V:Llyron	1.50
57 A:Capt. America, V:Llyron	1.50
58	1.50
59 GI,V:Abomination	1.50
60 A:Morgan Le Fay	1.50
61 Atlantis Rising	1.50
62 V:Triton	1.50
Ann.#1 Subterran.Odyssey #3	2.00
Ann.#2 Return o/Defenders,pt.3	4.00
Ann.#3 I:Assassin,A:Iron Fist, w/Trading card	3.25
Ann.#4 V:Hydra	2.95

NAVY ACTION
August, 1954

1 US Navy War Stories	60.00
2 Navy(c)	30.00
3 thru 17	@20.00
18 August, 1957	20.00

NAVY COMBAT
Atlas
June, 1955

1 DH,B;Torpedo Taylor	65.00
2 DH	30.00
3 DH	25.00
4 DH	25.00
5 DH	25.00
6 A:Battleship Burke	25.00
7 thru 10	@25.00
11 MD	20.00
12 RC	35.00
13	20.00
14	25.00
15	20.00
16	20.00
17 AW	35.00
18	20.00
19	20.00
20 October, 1958	20.00

NAVY TALES
Atlas
January, 1957

1 BEv(c),BP,Torpedoes	55.00
2 AW,RC,One Hour to Live	50.00
3 JSe(c)	40.00
4 JSe(c),GC,JSt,RC,July, 1957	40.00

NELLIE THE NURSE
Atlas
1945

1 Beach(c)	175.00
2 Nellie's Date(c)	85.00
3 Swimming Pool(c)	60.00
4 Roller Coaster(c)	60.00
5 Hospital(c),HK,Hey Look	65.00
6 Bedside Manner(c)	45.00
7 Comic book(c)A:Georgie	45.00
8 Hospital(c),A:Georgie	45.00
9 BW,Nellie/Swing(c)A:Millie	55.00
10 Bathing Suit(c),A:Millie	40.00
11 HK,Hey Look	60.00
12 HK,Giggles 'n' Grins	40.00
13 HK	35.00
14 HK	60.00
15 HK	60.00
16 HK	60.00
17 HK.A:Annie Oakley	35.00
18 HK	55.00
19	35.00
20	35.00
21	30.00
22	30.00
23	30.00
24	30.00
25	30.00
26	30.00
27	30.00
28 HK,Rusty Reprint	32.00
29 thru 35	@25.00
36 October, 1952	25.00

NEW ADVENTURES OF
CHOLLY & FLYTRAP
Epic

1	4.95
2	3.95
3	3.95

NEW MUTANTS, THE
March, 1983

1 BMc,MG,O:New Mutants	13.00
2 BMc,MG,V:Sentinels	8.00
2a Ltd.Test Cover 75c	55.00
3 BMc,MG,V:Brood Alien	7.00
4 SB,BMc,A:Peter Bristow	6.00
5 SB,BMc,A:Dark Rider	6.00
6 SB,AG,V:Viper	6.00
7 SB,BMc,V:Axe	6.00
8 SB,BMc,I:Amara Aquilla	6.00
9 SB,TMd,I:Selene	5.00
10 SB,BMc,C:Magma	5.00
11 SB,TMd,I:Magma	5.00
12 SB,TMd,J:Magma	5.00
13 SB,TMd,I:Cypher(Doug Ramsey) A:Kitty Pryde,Lilandra	6.00
14 SB,TMd,J:Magik,A:X-Men	5.00
15 SB,TMd,Mass.Academy	4.00
16 SB,TMd,V:Hellions,I:Warpath I:Jetstream	8.00
17 SB,TMd,V:Hellions,A:Warpath	5.00
18 BSz,V:Demon Bear,I:New Warlock,Magus	11.00

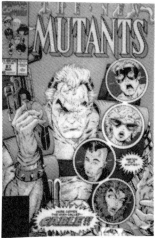

New Mutants #14
© Marvel Entertainment Group

19 BSz,V:Demon Bear	4.00
20 BSz,V:Demon Bear	4.00
21 BSz,O&J:Warlock,doub.sz	13.00
22 BSz,A:X-Men	4.50
23 BSz,Sunspot,Cloak & Dagger	4.00
24 BSz,A:Cloak & Dagger	4.00
25 BSz,A:Cloak & Dagger	9.00
26 BSz,I:Legion(Prof.X's son)	10.00
27 BSz,V:Legion	7.00
28 BSz,O:Legion	7.00
29 BSz,V:Gladiators,I:Guido (Strong Guy)	6.00
30 BSz,A:Dazzler	4.00
31 BSz,A:Shadowcat	4.00
32 SL,V:Karma	3.50
33 SL,V:Karma	3.50
34 SL,V:Amahl Farouk	3.50
35 BSz,J:Magneto	4.00
36 BSz,A:Beyonder	3.50
37 BSz,D:New Mutants	3.50
38 BSz,A:Hellions	3.50
39 BSz,A:White Queen	3.50
40 JG,KB,V:Avengers	3.50
41 JG,TA,Mirage	3.50
42 JG,KB,A:Dazzler	3.50
43 SP,V:Empath,A:Warpath	3.50
44 JG,V:Legion	3.50
45 JG,A:Larry Bodine	3.50
46 JG,KB,Mutant Massacre	5.00
47 JG,KB,V:Magnus	3.50
48 JG,CR,Future	3.50
49 VM,Future	3.50
50 JG,V:Magus,R:Prof.X	4.00
51 KN,A:Star Jammers	3.50
52 RL,DGr,Limbo	3.50
53 RL,TA,V:Hellions	3.50
54 SB,TA,N:New Mutants	3.50
55 BBI,TA,V:Aliens	3.00
56 JBr,TA,V:Hellions,A:Warpath	3.00
57 BBI,TA,I&J:Bird-Boy	3.00
58 BBI,TA,Bird-Boy	4.00
59 BBI,TA,Fall of Mutants, V:Dr.Animus	5.00
60 BBI,TA,F.of M.,D:Cypher	5.50
61 BBI,TA,Fall of Mutants	5.00

62 JMu,A:Magma,Hellions	3.00
63 BHa,JRu,Magik	3.50
64 BBI,TA,R:Cypher	3.00
65 BBI,TA,V:FreedomForce	3.00
66 BBI,TA,V:Forge	3.00
67 BBI,I:Gosamyr	3.00
68 BBI,V:Gosamyr	3.00
69 BBI,AW,I:Spyder	3.00
70 TSh,AM,V:Spyder	3.00
71 BBI,AW,V:N'Astirh	3.50
72 BBI,A,Inferno	3.50
73 BBI,W,A:Colossus	3.50
74 BBI,W,A:X-Terminators	3.00
75 JBy,Mc,Black King,V:Magneto	4.50
76 RB,TP,J:X-Terminators	3.00
77 RB,V:Mirage	3.00
78 RL,AW,V:FreedomForce	3.00
79 BBI,AW,V:Hela	3.00
80 BBI,AW,Asgard	3.00
81 LW,TSh,JRu,A:Hercules	3.00
82 BBI,AW,Asgard	3.00
83 BBI,Asgard	3.00
84 TSh,AM,V:QueenUla	3.00
85 RLd&TMc(c),BBI,V:Mirage	3.00
86 RLd,BWi,V:Vulture,C:Cable	12.00
87 RLd,BWi,I:Mutant Liberation Front,Cable	35.00
87a 2nd Printing	2.00
88 RLd,2nd Cable,V:Freedom Force	13.00
89 RLd,V:Freedom Force	9.00
90 RLd,A:Caliban,V:Sabretooth	9.00
91 RLd,A:Caliban,Masque, V:Sabretooth	9.00
92 RLd(c),BH,V:Skrulls	5.00
93 RLd,A:Wolverine,Sunfire, V:Mutant Liberation Front	11.00
94 RLd,A:Wolverine,Sunfire, V:Mutant Liberation Front	10.00
95 RLd,Extinction Agenda,V:Hodge A:X-Men,X-Factor,D:Warlock	10.00
95a 2nd printing(gold)	5.00
96 RLd,ATb,JRu,Extinction Agenda V:Hodge,A:X-Men,X-Factor	9.00
97 E:LSi(s),RLd(c),JRu,Extinction Agenda,V:Hodge	9.00

New Mutants #87
© Marvel Entertainment Group

98 FaN(s),RLd,I:Deadpool,Domino,
   Gideon,L:Rictor 12.00
99 FaN(s),RLd,I:Feral,Shatterstar,
   L:Sunspot,J:Warpath 9.00
100 FaN(s),RLd,J:Feral,Shatterstar,
   I:X-Force,V:Masque,Imperial
   Protectorate,A:MLF 9.00
100a 2nd Printing(Gold) 7.00
100b 3rd Printing(Silver) 3.50
Ann.#1 BMc,TP,L.Cheney 7.00
Ann.#2 AD,V:Mojo,I:Psylocke,Meggan
   (American App.) 7.00
Ann.#3 AD,PN,V:Impossible Man . 3.00
Ann.#4 JBr,BMc,Evol.Wars 6.00
Ann.#5 RLd,JBg,MBa,KWi,Atlantis
   Attacks,A:Namorita,I:Surf ... 15.00
Ann.#6 RLd(c),Days o/Future Present
   V:FranklinRichards,(Pin-ups) . 6.00
Ann.#7 JRu,RLd,Kings of Pain,
   I:Piecemeal & Harness,
   Pin-ups X-Force 5.00
Spec #1,AAd,TA,Asgard War 6.00
Summer Spec.#1 BBl,Megapolis . 3.50
TPB Demon Bear,rep.#18-21 ... 9.00

NEW MUTANTS:
DEMON BEAR
CCl/BSz,Rep.DemonBear 8.95

NEW WARRIORS
July, 1990
1 B:FaN(s),MBa,AW,V:Terrax,
   O:New Warriors 14.00
1a Gold rep. 4.50
2 FaN(s),MBa,AW,I:Midnight's Fire,
   Silhouette 9.00
3 MBa,LMa(i),V:Mad Thinker .. 7.00
4 MBa,LMa(i),I:Psionex 7.00
5 MBa,LMa(i),V:Star Thief,
   C:White Queen 6.00
6 MBa,LMa(i),V:StarThief,
   A:Inhumans 5.50
7 MBa,LMa(i),V:Bengal,
   C:Punisher 5.50
8 MBa,LMa(i),V:Punisher,
   I:Force of Nature 7.00
9 MBa,LMa(i),V:Punisher,Bengal,
   Force of Nature 6.00
10 MBa,LMa(i),V:Hellions,White
   Queen,I:New Sphinx 5.00
11 MBa,LMa(i),V:Sphinx,
   B:Forever Yesterday 4.00
12 MBa,LMa(i),V:Sphinx 4.00
13 MBa,LMa(i),V:Sphinx,
   E:Forever Yesterday 4.00
14 MBa,LMa(i),A:Namor,
   Darkhawk 3.00
15 MBa,LMa(i),V:Psionex,
   R:Terrax,N:Nova 3.00
16 MBa,LMa(i),A:Psionex,
   V:Terrax 3.00
17 MBa,LMa(i),A:Silver Surfer,Fant.
   Four,V:Terrax,I:Left Hand .. 3.00
18 MBa,LMa(i),O:Night Thrasher . 2.50
19 MBa,LMa(i),V:Gideon 2.50
20 MBa,LMa(i),V:Clan Yashida,
   Marvel Boy kills his father 2.50
21 MBa,LMa(i),I:Folding Circle .. 2.50
22 MBa,LMa(i),A:Darkhawk,Rage . 2.50
23 MBa,LMa(i),V:Folding Circle . 2.50
24 LMa(i),V:Folding Circle 2.50
25 MBa,LMa(i),Die-Cut(c),Marvel Boy
   found guilty of murder,D:Tai,
   O:Folding Circle 4.00

26 DaR,LMa(i),V:Guardsmen 2.00
27 DaR,LMa(i),Inf.War,Speedball Vs.
   his doppelganger,N:Rage 2.00
28 DaR,LMa(i),I:Turbo,Cardinal .. 2.00
29 DaR,LMa(i),V:Trans-Sabal ... 2.00
30 DaR,LMa(i),V:Trans Sabal ... 2.00
31 DaR,LMa(i)A:Cannonball,Warpath,
   Magma,O&N:Firestar 2.00
32 DaR,LMa(i),B:Forces of Darkness,
   Forces of Light,A:Spider-Man,
   Archangel,Dr.Strange 1.75
33 DaR,LMa(i),A:Cloak & Dagger,
   Turbo,Darkhawk 1.75
34 DaR,LMa(i),A:Avengers,SpM,
   Thing,Torch,Darkhawk,
   C:Darkling 1.75
35 DaR,LMa(i),A:Turbo 1.75
36 DaR,LMa(i),A:Turbo 1.75
37 F:Marvel Boy,V:Wizard 1.75
38 DaR,LMa(i),D:Rage's granny,
   V:Poison Memories 1.75
39 DaR,LMa(i),L:Namorita 1.75
40 DaR,LMa(i),B:Starlost,
   V:Supernova 2.50
40a Newsstand Ed. 1.50
41 DaR,LMa(i),V:Supernova 1.75
42 DaR,LMa(i),E:Starlost,N:Nova,
   V:Supernova 1.75
43 DaR,LMa(i),N&I:Justice
   (Marvel Boy) 1.75
44 Ph(c),DaR,LMa(i),N&I:Kymaera
   (Namorita) 1.75
45 DaR,LMa(i),Child's Play#2,
   N:Silhouette,Speedball,
   V:Upstarts 1.75
46 DaR,LMa(i),Child's Play#4,
   V:Upstarts 1.75
47 DaR,LMa(i),Time&TimeAgain,pt.1,
   A:Sphinx,I:Powerpax 1.75
48 DaR,LMa(i),Time&TimeAgain,pt.4,
   J:Cloak&Dagger,Darkhawk,Turbo,
   Powerpax,Bandit 1.75
49 DaR,LMa(i),Time&TimeAgain,pt.8
   V:Sphinx 1.75
50 reg. (c) 2.00
50a Glow-in-the-dark(c),V:Sphinx . 3.25
51 revamp 1.50
52 R:Psionex 1.50
53 V:Psionex 1.50
54 V:Speedball 1.50
55 V:Soldiers of Misfortune 1.50
56 V:Soldiers 1.50
57 A:Namor 1.50
58 F:Sabra 1.50
59 F:Speedball 1.50
60 Nova Omega,pt.2 .... 2.50
61 Warriors decimated! 1.50
Ann.#1 MBa,A:X-Force,V:Harness,
   Piecemeal,Kings of Pain #2 .. 5.00
Ann.#2 Hero Killers #4,V:Sphinx . 2.75
Ann.#3 LMa(i),E:Forces of Light,
   Forces of Darkness,I:Darkling
   w/card 3.25
Ann.#4 DaR(s),V:Psionex 3.25
TPB New Beginnings rep.Thor #411,
   412,New Warriors #1-4 .... 12.95

NFL SUPERPRO
1 .... 8.00
Spec.#1 reprints 2.00
(Regular Series)
October, 1991
1 A:Spider-Man,I:Sanzionaire .. 2.50
2 V:Quickkick 1.25
3 I:Instant Replay 1.00

4 V:Sanction 1.00
5 A:Real NFL Player 1.25
6 Racism Iss.,recalled by Marvel . 6.00
7 thru 11 .... @1.25
12 V:Nefarious forces of evil 1.25

NICK FURY, AGENT
OF S.H.I.E.L.D.
June, 1968
[1st Regular Series]
1 JSo/JSt,I:Scorpio 40.00
2 JSo,A:Centaurius 25.00

Nick Fury #2
© Marvel Entertainment Group

3 JSo,DA,V:Hell Hounds 21.00
4 FS,O:Nick Fury 20.00
5 JSo,V:Scorpio 25.00
6 FS,"Doom must Fall" 11.00
7 FS,V:S.H.I.E.L.D. 11.00
8 FS,Hate Monger 7.00
9 FS,Hate Monger 7.00
10 FS,JCr,Hate Monger 7.00
11 BS(c),FS,Hate Monger 7.00
12 BS 9.00
13 .... 6.00
14 .... 5.00
15 I:Bullseye 24.00
16 JK,rep. 4.00
17 JK,rep. 4.00
18 JK,rep. 4.00

[Limited Series]
1 JSo,rep. 3.00
2 JSo,rep. 2.00

[2nd Regular Series]
1 BH,I:New Shield,V:Death's
   Head(not British hero) 3.00
2 KP,V:Death's Head 2.00
3 KP,V:Death's Head 1.50
4 KP,V:Death's Head 1.50
5 KP,V:Death's Head 1.50
6 KP,V:Death's Head 1.50
7 KP,Chaos Serpent #1 ...... 1.50
8 KP,Chaos Serpent #2 ...... 1.50
9 KP,Chaos Serpent #3 ...... 1.50
10 KP,Chaos Serpent ends,
   A:Capt.America 1.50

11 D:Murdo MacKay 1.50
12 Hydra Affair #1 . . . . 1.50
13 Hydra Affair #2 . . . . 1.50
14 Hydra Affair #3 . . . . 1.50
15 Apogee of Disaster #1 . . . . . . 1.50
16 Apogee of Disaster #2 . . . . . . 1.50
17 Apogee of Disaster #3 . . . . . . 1.50
18 Apogee of Disaster #4 . . . . . . 1.50
19 Apogee of Disaster #5 . . . . . . 1.50
20 JG,A:Red Skull 2.50
21 JG,R:Baron Strucker 2.00
22 JG,A:Baron Strucker,R:Hydra . 2.00
23 JG,V:Hydra 2.00
24 A:Capt.Am,Thing,V:Mandarin . 1.75
25 JG,Shield Vs. Hydra 2.00
26 JG,A:Baron Strucker,
   C:Wolverine 2.50
27 JG,V:Hydra,A:Wolverine 2.50
28 V:Hydra,A:Wolverine 2.50
29 V:Hydra,A:Wolverine 2.50
30 R:Leviathan,A:Deathlok 2.00
31 A:Deathlok,V:Leviathan 2.00
32 V:Leviathan 2.00
33 Super-Powered Agents 2.00
34 A:Bridge(X-Force),V:Balance
   of Terror 2.00
35 A:Cage,V:Constrictor 2.00
36 . . . . 2.00
37 . . . . 2.00
38 Cold War of Nick Fury #1 . . . . 2.00
39 Cold War of Nick Fury #2 . . . . 2.00
40 Cold War of Nick Fury #3 . . . . 2.00
41 Cold War of Nick Fury #4 . . . . 2.00
42 I:Strike Force Shield 2.00
43 R:Clay Quatermain 2.00
44 A:Captain America 2.00
45 A:Bridge 2.00
46 V:Gideon,Hydra 2.00
47 V:Baron Strucker,last issue . . 2.00
TPB Death Duty V:Night Raven . . 5.95
TPB Captain America 5.95
TPB Scorpion Connection 7.95
Ashcan 75

NICK FURY, VERSUS S.H.I.E.L.D.
June, 1988

1 JSo(c),D:Quartermail 12.00
2 BSz(c),Into The Depths 15.00
3 Uneasy Allies 8.00
4 V:Hydra 6.00
5 V:Hydra 6.00
6 V:Hydra, December, 1988 . . . 6.00
TPB Reprints #1-#6 . . . . 15.95

NIGHTBREED
Epic
April, 1990

1 . . . . 5.50
2 . . . . 3.50
3 . . . . 3.00
4 . . . . 2.50
5 JG 2.50
6 BBI,Blasphemers,pt.1 . . . . 2.50
7 JG,Blasphemers,pt.2 . . . . 2.50
8 BBI,MM,Blasphemers,pt.3 . . . . 2.50
9 BBI,Blasphemers,pt.4 . . . . 2.50
10 BBI,Blasphemers,pt.5 . . . . 2.50
11 South America,pt.1 . . . . 2.25
12 South America,pt.2 . . . . 2.25
13 Emissaries o/Algernon Kinder . 2.25
14 Rawhead Rex Story 2.25
15 Rawhead Rex 2.25
16 Rawhead Rex 2.25

17 KN(i),V:Werewolves 2.25
18 V:Werewolves 2.25
19 V:Werewolves 2.25
20 Trapped in the Forest 2.25
21 V:Ozymandias 2.50
22 V:Ozymandias 2.50
23 F:Peloquin 2.50
24 Search for New Midian 2.50
25 Search for New Midian 2.50
Nightbreed:Genesis, Rep.#1-#4 . . 9.95

NIGHTCAT

1 DCw,I&O:Night Cat 4.50

NIGHTCRAWLER
November, 1985

1 DC,A;Bamfs 5.00
2 DC 3.00
3 DC,A:Other Dimensional X-Men 3.00
4 DC,A:Lockheed,V:Dark Bamf
   February, 1986 . . . . 3.00

NIGHTMARE

1 ANo, ... 1.95
2 ANo 1.95
3 ANo 1.95

NIGHTMARE ON ELM STREET
October, 1989

1 RB/TD/AA.,Movie adapt 3.00
2 AA,Movie adapt,Dec., 1989 . . . 2.25

NIGHTMASK
November, 1986

1 O:Night Mask 1.25
2 V:Gnome 1.00
3 V:Mistress Twilight 1.00
4 EC,D:Mistress Twilight 1.00
5 EC,Nightmare 1.00
6 EC 1.00
7 EC 1.00
8 EC 1.00
9 . . . . 1.00
10 Lucian 1.00
11 and 12, Oct. 1987 . . . . @1.00

NIGHT NURSE
November, 1972

1 The Making of a Nurse 4.00
2 Moment of Truth 2.50
3 . . . . 2.00
4 Final Issue,May, 1973 . . . . . . 2.00

NIGHT RIDER
October, 1974

1 Reprint Ghost Rider #1 . . . . . . 5.00
2 Reprint Ghost Rider #2 . . . . . . 2.00
3 Reprint Ghost Rider #3 . . . . . . 2.00
4 Reprint Ghost Rider #4 . . . . . . 2.00
5 Reprint Ghost Rider #5 . . . . . . 2.00
6 Reprint Ghost Rider #6
   August, 1975 . . . . 2.00

NIGHTSTALKERS

1 TP(i),Rise o/t Midnight Sons#5
   A:GR,J.Blaze,I:Meatmarket,
   polybagged w/poster 3.00
2 TP(i),V:Hydra 2.50
3 TP(i),V:Dead on Arrival 2.00
4 TP(i),V:Hydra 2.00
5 TP(i),A:Punisher 2.00

6 TP(i),A:Punisher 2.00
7 TP(i),A:Ghost Rider 2.00
8 Hannibal King vs Morbius 2.00
9 MPa,A:Morbius 2.00
10 Midnight Massacre#1,D:Johnny
   Blaze,Hannibal King 2.50
11 O:Blade 2.00
12 V:Vampires 2.00
13 V:Vampires 2.00
14 Wld,Siege of Darkness#1 . . . . 2.00
15 Wld,Siege of Darkness#9 . . . . 2.00
16 V:Dreadnought 2.00
17 F:Blade 2.00
18 D:Hannibal King,Frank Drake,
   last issue 2.00

Night Thrasher #1
© Marvel Entertainment Group

NIGHT THRASHER
[Limited Series]

1 B:FaN(s),DHv,N:Night Thrasher,
   V:Bengal 2.50
2 DHv,I:Tantrium 2.25
3 DHv,V:Gideon 2.25
4 E:FaN(s),DHv,A:Silhoutte 2.25
[Regular Series]
1 B:FaN(s),MBa,JS,V:Poison
   Memories 3.25
2 JS,V:Concrete Dragons 2.00
3 JS(c),I:Aardwolf,A:Folding Circle 2.00
4 JS(c),V:Aardwolf,I:Air Force . . . 2.00
5 JS,V:Air Force 2.00
6 Face Value,A:Rage 2.00
7 DdB,V:Bandit 2.00
8 DdB,V:Bandit 2.00
9 DdB,A:Tantrum 2.00
10 DdB,A:Iron Man,w/card 2.25
11 DdB,Time & Time Again,pt.2 . . 2.25
12 DdB,Time & Time Again,pt.5 . . 2.25
13 Lost in the Shadows,pt.1 . . . . . 1.95
14 Lost in the Shadows,pt.2 . . . . . 1.95
15 Money Don't Buy,pt.1 . . . . 1.95
16 A:Prowler 1.95
17 . . . . 1.95
18 . . . . 1.95
19 V:Tantrum 1.95
20 . . . . 1.95
21 Rage vs. Grind 1.95

NIGHTWATCH

1 RLm,I:Salvo,Warforce Holo(c) . 3.25
1a Newsstand ed. 1.75
2 RLm,AM,I:Flashpoint 1.50
3 RLm,AM,V:Flashpoint 1.50
4 RLm,A:Warrent,V:Gauntlet . . . 1.75
5 I:Sunstreak,A:Venom 1.50
6 V:Venom 1.50
7 I:Cardiaxe 1.50
8 V:Cardiaxe 1.50
9 origins 1.50
10 . . . . 1.50
11 . . . . 1.50
12 . . . . 1.50

NOCTURNE

1 DAn, in London 1.50

NO ESCAPE

1 Movie adapt. 1.50
2 Movie adapt. 1.50

NOMAD
November, 1990
[Limited Series]

1 B:FaN(s),A:Capt.America 4.00
2 A:Capt.America 3.00
3 A:Capt.America 2.50
4 A:Capt.America, final issue,
  February 1989 . . . . 2.50

[Regular Series]

1 B:FaN(s),R:Nomad,[Gatetfold(c),
  map] 3.00
2 V:Road Kill Club 2.50
3 V:U.S.Agent 2.00
4 DeadMan's Hand#2,V:Deadpool 2.00
5 DeadMan's Hand#4,V:Punisher 2.00
6 DeadMan's Hand#8,A:Punisher,
  Daredevil 2.00
7 Infinity War,V:Gambit,
  Doppleganger 2.00
8 L.A.Riots 2.00
9 I:Ebbtide 2.00
10 A:Red Wolf 2.00
11 in Albuquerque 2.00
12 In Texas 2.00
13 AIDS issue 2.00
14 Hidden in View 2.00
15 Hidden in View 2.00
16 A:Gambit 2.00
17 Bucky Kidnapped 2.00
18 A:Captain America,Slug 2.00
19 FaN(s),Faustus Affair 2.00
20 A:Six Pack 2.00
21 A:Man-Thing 2.00
22 American Dreamers#1,V:Zaran 2.00
23 American Dreamers#2 . . . . . . 2.00
24 American Dreamers#3 . . . . . . 2.00
25 American Dreamers#4,
   final issue 2.00

NORTHSTAR

1 SFr,DoC,V:Weapon:P.R.I.M.E. . 2.00
2 SFr,DoC,V:Arcade 2.00
3 SFr,DoC,V:Arcade 2.00
4 SFr,DoC,final issue 2.00
N Presents James O'Barr 2.50

NOT BRAND ECHH
August, 1967

1 JK(c),BEv,Forbush Man(c) . . 30.00
2 MSe,FrG,Spidey-Man,Gnat-Man
  & Rotten 15.00

3 MSe(C),JK,FrG,O:Charlie
  America 15.00
4 GC,JTg,TS,Scaredevil,
  ECHHs-Men 15.00
5 JK,TS,GC,I&O:Forbush Man . 15.00
6 MSe(c),GC,TS,W:Human Torch 15.00
7 MSe(c),GC,TS,O:Fantastical
  Four,Stupor Man 15.00
8 MSe(c),GC,TS,C:Beatles . . . 17.00
9 Bulk V:Sunk-Mariner 17.00
10 JK,The Worst of... . . . . 17.00
11 King Kong 17.00
12 Frankenstein,A:Revengers . . 17.00
13 Stamp Out Trading Cards(c) . 17.00

NOTHING CAN STOP THE JUGGERNAUT
1989

1 JR2,rep.SpM#229&#230 . . . . . 3.95

Nova #25
© *Marvel Entertainment Group*

NOVA
September, 1976
[1st Regular Series]

1 B:MWn(s),JB,JSt,I&O:Nova . 12.00
2 JB,JSt,I:Condor,Powerhouse . . 7.00
3 JB,JSt,I:Diamondhead 5.00
4 SB,TP,A:Thor,I:Corruptor 5.00
5 SB,V:Earthshaker 5.00
6 SB,V:Condor,Powerhouse,
  Diamondhead,I:Sphinx 5.00
7 SB,War in Space,O:Sphinx . . . 5.00
8 V:Megaman 5.00
9 V:Megaman 5.00
10 V:Condor,Powerhouse,
   Diamond-head Sphinx 5.00
11 V:Sphinx 4.50
12 A:Spider-Man 5.00
13 I:Crimebuster,A:Sandman . . . 4.50
14 A:Sandman 4.00
15 CI,C:Spider-Man, Hulk 4.00
16 CI,A:Yellow Claw 4.00
17 A:Yellow Claw 3.50
18 A:Yellow Claw, Nick Fury . . . 3.50
19 CI,TP,I:Blackout 3.50
20 What is Project X? 3.50
21 JB,BMc,JRu 3.50
22 CI,I:Comet 3.50

23 CI,V:Dr.Sun 3.50
24 CI,I:New Champions,V:Sphinx . 3.50
25 E:MWn(s),CI,A:Champions,
   V:Sphinx 3.50
[2nd Regular Series]
1 B:FaN(s),ChM,V:Gladiator,Foil
  Embossed(c) 3.25
2 ChM,V:Tail Hook Rape 2.00
3 ChM,A:Spider-Man,Corruptor . 2.00
4 ChM,I:NovaO:O 2.00
5 ChM,R:Condor,w/card 2.25
6 ChM,Time & Time Again,pt.3 . . 2.25
7 ChM,Time & Time Again,pt.6 . . 2.25
8 ChM,I:Shatterforce 2.25
9 ChM,V:Shatterforce 1.95
10 ChM,V:Diamondhead 1.95
11 ChM,V:Diamondhead 1.95
12 ChM,A:Inhumans 1.95
13 ChM,A:Inhumans 1.95
14 A:Condor 1.95
15 V:Brethern of Zorr 1.95
16 Countdown Conclusion 1.95
17 Nova Loses Powers 1.96
18 Nova Omega,pt.1 . . . . 1.95

Nth MAN
August, 1989

1 . . . . 2.00
2 thru 7 . . . . @1.00
8 DK 2.00
9 thru 15 . . . . @1.00
16 final issue,September, 1990 . . 1.00

OBNOXIO THE CLOWN
April, 1983

1 X-Men 2.00

OFFCASTES

1 I:Offcastes 2.50
2 V:Kaoro 1.95
3 Last Issue 1.95

OFFICIAL MARVEL INDEX:
1985–88
TO THE AMAZING SPIDER-MAN

Index 1 . . . . 3.00
Index 2 thru 9 . . . . @2.50
TO THE AVENGERS
Index 1 thru 7 . . . . @2.50
TO THE FANTASTIC FOUR
Index 1 thru 12 . . . . @2.25
TO MARVEL TEAM-UP
Index 1 thru 6 . . . . @1.75
TO THE X-MEN
Index 1 thru 7 . . . . @2.95
[Vol. 2] 1994
Index 1 thru 5 . . . . @1.95

OFFICIAL TRUE CRIME CASES
Fall, 1947

24 (1)SSh(c),The Grinning Killer 125.00
25 (2)She Made Me a Killer,HK . 85.00
Becomes:
ALL-TRUE CRIME
26 SSh(c),The True Story of Wilbur
   Underhill 100.00
27 Electric Chair(c),Robert Mais . 70.00
28 Cops V:Gangsters(c) 25.00
29 Cops V:Gangsters(c) 25.00

30 He Picked a Murderous Mind	25.00
31 Hitchiking Thugs(c)	25.00
32 Jewel Thieves(c)	25.00
33 The True Story of Dinton Phillips	25.00
34 Case of the Killers Revenge	25.00
35 Ph(c),Date with Danger	25.00
36 Ph(c)	25.00
37 Ph(c),Story of Robert Marone	25.00
38 Murder Weapon,Nick Maxim	25.00
39 Story of Vince Vanderee	25.00
40	25.00
41 Lou "Lucky" Raven	25.00
42 BK,Baby Face Nelson	35.00
43 Doc Channing Paulson	25.00
44 Murder in the Big House	25.00
45 While the City Sleeps	25.00
46	25.00
47 Gangster Terry Craig	25.00
48 GT,They Vanish By Night	25.00
49 BK,Squeeze Play	35.00
50 Shoot to Kill	25.00
51 Panic in the Big House	25.00
52 Prison Break, Sept., 1952	25.00

OLYMPIANS
Epic
July, 1991

1 Spoof Series	3.95
2 Conclusion	3.95

OMEGA THE UNKNOWN
March, 1976

1 JM,I:Omega	4.25
2 JM,A:Hulk	2.50
3 JM,A:Electro	2.00
4 JM,V:Yellow Claw	2.00
5 JM,V:The Wrench	2.00
6 JM,V:Blockbuster	2.00
7 JM,V:Blockbuster	2.00
8 JM,C:New Foolkiller,V:Nitro	6.00
9 JM,A:New Foolkiller, D:Blockbuster	7.50
10 JM,D:Omega the Unknown	2.00

ONE, THE
Epic
July, 1985

1 thru 5	@1.75
6 February, 1986	1.75

ONYX OVERLORD
Epic

1 JBi,Sequel to Airtight Garage	3.00
2 JBi,The Joule	2.75
3 JBi,V:Overlord	2.75
4 V:Starbilliard	2.75

OPEN SPACE
December, 1989

1	6.00
2	5.25
3	5.25
4 August, 1990,last issue	5.25

ORIGINAL GHOST RIDER

1 MT(c),rep Marvel Spotlight#5	2.25
2 rep.Marvel Spotlight#6	2.00
3 rep.Marvel Spotlight#7	2.00
4 JQ(c),rep.Marvel Spotlight#8	2.00
5 KM(c),rep.Marvel spotlight#9	2.00
6 rep.Marvel Spotlight#10	2.00
7 rep.Marvel Spotlight#11	2.00

8 rep.Ghost Rider#1	2.00
9 rep.Ghost Rider#2	2.00
10 rep.Marvel Spotlight#12	2.00
11 rep.Ghost Rider#3	2.00
12 rep.Ghost Rider#4	2.00
13 rep.Ghost Rider#38	2.00
14 thru 18 rep.Ghost Rider#6-10	@1.75
19 rep.Ghost Rider#11	1.75
20 rep.Ghost Rider#12	1.75
21 rep.Ghost Rider#13	1.75
22 rep.Ghost Rider#14	1.75
23 rep.Ghost Rider#15	1.95

ORIGINAL GHOST RIDER RIDES AGAIN
July, 1991

1 rep.GR#68+#69(O:JohnnyBlaze)	3.00
2 rep.G.R. #70,#71	2.00
3 rep.G.R. #72,#73	2.00
4 rep.G.R. #74,#75	2.00
5 rep.G.R. #76,#77	2.00
6 rep.G.R. #78,#79	2.00
7 rep.G.R. #80,#81	2.00

OUR LOVE
September, 1949

1 Ph(c),The Guilt of Nancy Crane	55.00
2 Ph(c),My Kisses Were Cheap	35.00

Becomes:
TRUE SECRETS

3 Love Stories,continued	50.00
4	24.00
5	24.00
6 BEv	30.00
7	24.00
8	24.00
9	24.00
10	24.00
11 thru 21	@18.00
22 BEv	30.00
23 thru 39	@12.00
40 September, 1956	12.00

OUR LOVE STORY
October, 1969

1	7.50
2	5.00
3	5.00
4	5.00
5 JSo	15.00
6 thru 13	@5.00
14 Gary Friedrich &Tarpe Mills	7.50
15 thru 37	@2.00
38 February, 1976	2.00

OUTLAW FIGHTERS
Atlas
August, 1954

1 GT,Western Tales	55.00
2 GT	35.00
3	35.00
4 A;Patch Hawk	35.00
5 RH, Final Issue,April, 1955	35.00

OUTLAW KID
Atlas
September, 1954

1 SSh,DW,B&O:Outlaw Kid,A;Black Rider	125.00
2 DW,A:Black Rider	55.00
3 DW,AW,GWb	50.00
4 DW(c),Death Rattle	35.00
5	35.00

6	35.00
7	35.00
8 AW,DW	45.00
9	35.00
10	45.00
11 thru 17	@25.00
18 AW	40.00
19 September, 1957	25.00

[2nd series]
August, 1970

1 JSe(c),DW,Jo,Showdown,rep	5.00
2 DW,One Kid Too Many	5.00
3 HT(c),DW,Six Gun Double Cross	3.00
4 DW	2.00
5 DW	2.00
6 DW	2.00
7 HT(c),DW,Treachery on the Trail	2.00
8 HT(c),DW,RC,Six Gun Pay Off	2.00
9 JSe(c),DW,GWb,The Kids Last Stand	3.00
10 GK(c),DAy,NewO:Outlaw Kid	1.50
11 GK(c),Thunder Along the Big Iron	1.50
12 The Man Called Bounty Hawk	1.50
13 The Last Rebel	1.50
14 The Kid Gunslingers of Calibre City	1.50
15 GK(c),V:Madman of Monster Mountain	1.50
16 The End of the Trail	1.50
17 thru 29	@1.50
30 October, 1975	1.50

PARAGON

1 I:Paragon,Nightfire	5.00

PATSY & HEDY
Atlas
February, 1952

1 B:Patsy Walker&Hedy Wolfe	75.00
2 Skating(c)	35.00
3 Boyfriend Trouble	30.00
4 Swimsuit(c)	30.00
5 Patsy's Date(c)	30.00
6 Swimsuit/Picnic(c)	30.00

Patsy and Her Pals #3
© Marvel Entertainment Group

---

7 Double-Date(c) 30.00
8 The Dance 30.00
9 .... 30.00
10 .... 30.00
11 thru 25 .... @20.00
26 thru 50 .... @15.00
51 thru 60 .... @10.00
61 thru 109 .... @6.00
110 February, 1967 .... 6.00

PATSY & HER PALS
May, 1953

1 MWs(c),F:Patsay Walker ... 60.00
2 MWs(c),Swimsuit(c) 30.00
3 MWs(c),Classroom(c) 22.00
4 MWs(c),Golfcourse(c) 22.00
5 MWs(c).Patsy/Buzz(c) 22.00
6 thru 10 .... @22.00
11 thru 28 .... @15.00
29 August, 1957 .... 15.00

PATSY WALKER
1945

1 F:Patsy Walker Adventures 250.00
2 Patsy/Car(c) 125.00
3 Skating(c) 75.00
4 Perfume(c) 75.00
5 Archery Lesson(c) 75.00
6 Bus(c) 75.00
7 Charity Drive(c) 75.00
8 Organ Driver Monkey(c) 75.00
9 Date(c) 75.00
10 Skating(c),Wedding Bells . 75.00
11 Date with a Dream 50.00
12 Love in Bloom,Artist(c) 50.00
13 Swimsuit(c),There Goes My
   Heart;HK,Hey Look 60.00
14 An Affair of the Heart,
   HK,Hey Look 60.00
15 Dance(c) 50.00
16 Skating(c) 50.00
17 Patsy's Diary(c),HK,Hey Look 60.00
18 Autograph(c) 50.00
19 HK,Hey Look 60.00
20 HK,Hey Look 60.00
21 HK,Hey Look 60.00
22 HK,Hey Look 60.00
23 .... 40.00
24 .... 40.00
25 HK,Rusty 65.00
26 .... 30.00
27 .... 30.00
28 .... 30.00
29 .... 30.00
30 HK,Egghead Double 45.00
31 .... 30.00
32 thru 57 .... @20.00
58 thru 99 .... @15.00
100 .... 15.00
101 thru 123 .... @8.00
124 December, 1965 .... 8.00
Fashion Parade #1 .... 40.00

PETER PARKER,
THE SPECTACULAR
SPIDER-MAN
December, 1976

1 SB,V:Tarantula 50.00
2 SB,V:Kraven,Tarantula 25.00
3 SB,I:Lightmaster 18.00
4 SB,V:Vulture,Hitman 15.00
5 SB,V:Hitman,Vulture 15.00
6 SB,V:Morbius,rep.M.T.U.#3 .. 20.00
7 SB,V:Morbius,A:Human Torch 25.00

8 SB,V:Morbius 25.00
9 SB,I:White Tiger 10.00
10 SB,A:White Tiger 10.00
11 JM,V:Medusa 9.00
12 SB,V:Brother Power 9.00
13 SB,V:Brother Power 9.00
14 SB,V:Brother Power 9.00
15 SB,V:Brother Power 9.00
16 SB,V:The Beetle 9.00
17 SB,A:Angel & Iceman
   Champions disbanded 10.00
18 SB,A:Angel & Iceman 10.00
19 SB,V:The Enforcers 9.00
20 SB,V:Lightmaster 9.00
21 JM,V:Scorpion 9.00
22 MZ,A:Moon Knight,V:Cyclone . 9.00
23 A:Moon Knight,V:Cyclone 9.00
24 FS,A:Hypno-Hustler 6.00
25 JM,FS,I:Carrion 8.00

Peter Parker #1
© Marvel Entertainment Group

26 JM,A:Daredevil,V:Carrion ... 7.00
27 DC,FM,I:Miller Daredevil,
   V:Carrion 22.00
28 FM,A:Daredevil,V:Carrion .. 18.00
29 JM,FS,V:Carrion 7.00
30 JM,FS,V:Carrion 7.00
31 JM,FS,D:Carrion 7.00
32 BL,JM,FS,V:Iguana 5.50
33 JM,FS,O:Iguana 5.50
34 JM,FS,V:Iguana,Lizard 5.50
35 V:Mutant Mindworm 5.50
36 JM,V:Swarm 5.50
37 DC,MN,V:Swarm 5.50
38 SB,V:Morbius 8.00
39 JM,JR2,V:Schizoid Man 5.50
40 FS,V:Schizoid Man 5.50
41 JM,V:Meteor Man,A:GiantMan . 5.00
42 JM,A:Fant.Four,V:Frightful 4 .. 5.00
43 JBy(c),MZ,V:The Ringer,
   V:Belladonna 5.00
44 JM,V:The Vulture 5.00
45 MSe,V:The Vulture 5.00
46 FM(c),MZ,V:Cobra 5.00
47 MSe,A:Prowler II 5.00
48 MSe,A:Prowler II 5.00
49 MSe,I:Smuggler 5.00

50 JR2,JM,V:Mysterio 5.00
51 MSe&FM(c),V:Mysterio 5.00
52 FM(c),D:White Tiger 5.00
53 JM,FS,V:Terrible Tinkerer 5.00
54 FM,WS,MSe,V:Silver Samurai . 5.00
55 LMc,JM,V:Nitro 5.00
56 FM,JM,V:Jack-o-lantern 13.00
57 JM,V:Will-o-the Wisp 5.00
58 JBy,V:Ringer,A:Beetle 6.00
59 JM,V:Beetle 5.00
60 JM&FM(c),O:Spider-Man,
   V:Beetle 5.50
61 JM,V:Moonstone 4.50
62 JM,V:Goldbug 4.50
63 JM,V:Molten Man 4.50
64 JM,I:Cloak&Dagger 10.00
65 BH,JM,V:Kraven,Calypso ... 4.50
66 JM,V:Electro 4.00
67 AMb,V:Boomerang 4.00
68 LMc,JM,V:Robot of Mendell
   Stromm 4.00
69 AM,A:Cloak & Dagger 8.00
70 A:Cloak & Dagger 8.00
71 JM,Gun Control issue 4.00
72 AM,V:Dr.Octopus 4.00
73 AM,JM,V:Dr.Octopus,A:Owl . 4.00
74 AM,JM,V:Dr.Octopus,R:Bl.Cat . 4.00
75 AM,JM,V:Owl,Dr.Octopus ... 4.50
76 AM,Black Cat on deathbed ... 3.50
77 AM,V:Gladiator,Dr.Octopus .. 3.50
78 AM,V:Dr.Octopus,C:Punisher . 3.50
79 AM,V:Dr.Octopus,A:Punisher . 4.00
80 AM,F:J.Jonah Jameson 3.50
81 A:Punisher 7.00
82 A:Punisher 7.00
83 A:Punisher 7.00
84 AM,F:Black Cat 3.50
85 AM,O:Hobgoblin powers
   (Ned Leeds) 22.00
86 FH,V:Fly 3.50
87 AM,Reveals I.D.to Black Cat . 3.50
88 AM,V:Cobra,Mr.Hyde 3.50
89 AM,Secret Wars,A:Kingpin ... 3.50
90 AM,Secret Wars 4.00
91 AM,V:Blob 3.50
92 AM,I:Answer 3.50

Peter Parker #50
© Marvel Entertainment Group

93 AM,V:Answer 3.50	
94 AM,A:Cloak & Dagger,V:	
Silver Mane 3.50	
95 AM,A:Cloak & Dagger,V:	
Silvermane 3.50	
96 AM,A:Cloak & Dagger,V:	
Silvermane 3.50	
97 HT,JM,A:Black Cat 3.50	
98 HT,JM,I:Spot 3.50	
99 HT,JM,V:Spot 3.50	
100 AM,V:Kingpin,C:Bl.Costume . 5.00	
101 JBy(c),AM,V:Killer Shrike . . 3.00	
102 JBy(c),AM,V:Backlash 3.00	
103 AM,V:Blaze;Not John Blaze . 3.00	
104 JBy(c),AM,V:Rocket Racer . . 3.00	
105 AM,A:Wasp 3.00	
106 AM,A:Wasp 3.00	
107 RB,D:Jean DeWolf,I:SinEater 5.00	
108 RB,A:Daredevil,V:Sin-Eater . . 4.00	
109 RB,A:Daredevil,V:Sin-Eater . . 4.00	
110 RB,A:Daredevil,V:Sin-Eater . . 4.00	
111 RB,Secret Wars II 3.00	
112 RB,A:Santa Claus,Black Cat . 3.00	
113 RB,Burglars,A:Black Cat 3.00	
114 BMc,V:Lock Picker 3.00	
115 BMc,A:Black Cat,Dr.Strange,	
I:Foreigner 3.50	
116 A:Dr.Strange,Foreigner,Black	
Cat,Sabretooth 8.00	
117 DT,C:Sabretooth,A:Foreigner,	
Black Cat,Dr.Strange 5.00	
118 MZ,D:Alexander,V:SHIELD . . 3.00	
119 RB,BMc,V:Sabretooth,	
A:Foreigner,Black Cat 7.00	

Peter Parker #116
© Marvel Entertainment Group

120 KG 3.00	
121 RB,BMc,V:Mauler 3.00	
122 V:Mauler 3.00	
123 V:Foreigner,Black Cat 3.00	
124 V:Dr.Octopus 3.00	
125 V:Wr.Crew,A:Spiderwoman . . 3.00	
126 JM,A:Sp.woman,V:Wrecker . . 3.00	
127 AM,V:Lizard 3.00	
128 C:DDevil,A:Bl.Cat,Foreigner . 3.50	
129 A:Black Cat,V:Foreigner 3.00	
130 A:Hobgoblin 6.00	
131 MZ,BMc,V:Kraven 9.00	
132 MZ,BMc,V:Kraven 9.00	
133 BSz(c),Mad Dog,pt.3 . . . . . . 8.00	

Ann.#1 RB,JM,V:Dr.Octopus 5.00
Ann.#2 JM,I&O:Rapier 4.50
Ann.#3 JM,V:Manwolf 4.50
Ann.#4 AM,O:Aunt May,A:Bl.Cat . 5.00
Ann.#5 I:Ace,Joy Mercado 4.50
Ann.#6 V:Ace 4.50
Ann.#7 Honeymoon iss,A:Puma . . 4.50
Becomes:
SPECTACULAR SPIDER-MAN

PETER PORKER
Star
May, 1985

1 Parody 2.50
2 . . . . 1.50
3 . . . . 1.50
4 . . . . 1.50
5 V:Senior Simians 1.50
6 A Blitz in Time 1.50
7 . . . . 1.50
8 Kimono My House 1.25
9 Uncouth my Tooth 1.25
10 Lost Temple of the Golden
   Retriever 1.25
11 Dog Dame Afternoon 1.25
12 The Gouda,Bad & Ugly 1.25
13 Halloween issue 1.25
14 Heavy Metal Issue 1.25
15 . . . . 1.25
16 Porker Fried Rice,Final Issue . 1.25
17 September, 1987 . . . . 1.25

PETER, THE LITTLE PEST
November, 1969

1 F:Peter 6.00
2 Rep,Dexter & Melvin 5.00
3 Rep,Dexter & Melvin 5.00
4 Rep,Dexter & Melvin,
   May, 1970 . . . . 5.00

PHANTOM
1 Lee Falk's Phantom 2.95
2 V:General Babalar 2.95
3 final issue 2.95

PHANTOM 2040
1 Based on cartoon 1.50
2 V:alloy 1.50
3 MPa centerfold 1.50

PHOENIX
(UNTOLD STORY)
April, 1984
1 JBy,O:Phoenix (R.Summers) . 12.00

PILGRIM'S PROGRESS
1 adapts John Bunyans novel . . 10.00

PINHEAD
1 Red Foil(c),from Hellraiser 2.95
2 DGC(s),V:Cenobites 2.50
3 DGC(s),V:Cenobites 2.50
4 DGC(s),V:Cenobites 2.50
5 DGC(s),Devil in Disguise 2.50
6 DGC(s), ... 2.50

PINHEAD VS.
MARSHALL LAW
1 KON,In Hell 2.95
2 KON 2.95

PINOCHIO & THE
EMPEROR OF THE NIGHT
March, 1988
1 Movie adapt. 1.25

PIRATES OF
DARK WATERS
November, 1991
1 based on T.V. series 1.00
2 Search for 13 Treasures 1.00
3 V:Albino Warriors,Konk 1.00
4 A:Monkey Birds 1.25
5 Tula Steals 1st Treasuer 1.25
6 thru 9 . . . . @1.25

PITT, THE
March, 1988
1 SB,SDr,A:Spitfire 4.50

PLANET OF THE APES
August, 1974
(black & white magazine)
1 MP 6.00
2 MP 4.00
3 . . . . 3.00
4 . . . . 5.00
5 . . . . 5.00
6 thru 10 . . . . @2.50
11 thru 20 . . . . @2.00
21 thru 28 . . . . @1.50
29 February, 1977 . . . . 1.50

PLANET TERRY
Star
April, 1985
1 thru 11 . . . . @1.00
12 March, 1986 . . . . 1.00

PLASMER
1 A:Captain America 3.50
2 A:Captain Britain,Black Knight . 2.25
3 A:Captain Britain 2.25
4 A:Captain Britain 2.25
5 thru 7 . . . . 1.95

PLASTIC FORKS
Epic
1990
1 . . . . 5.50
2 thru 5 . . . . @5.25

POLICE ACADEMY
November, 1989
1 Based on TV Cartoon 1.25
2 . . . . 1.00
3 . . . . 1.00
4 and 5 . . . . @1.00
6 February, 1990 . . . . 1.00

POLICE ACTION
January, 1954
1 JF,GC,Riot Squad 85.00
2 JF,Over the Wall 45.00
3 . . . . 35.00
4 DAy 35.00
5 DAy 35.00
6 . . . . 35.00
7 BPNovember, 1954 . . . . 35.00

POLICE BADGE
See: SPY THRILLERS

All comics prices listed are for _Near Mint_ condition.

POPPLES
Star
December, 1986
1 Based on Toys 1.00
2 . . . . 1.00
3 . . . . 1.00
4 . . . . 1.00
5 August, 1987 . . . . 1.00

POWDERED TOAST-MAN
Spec. F:Powder Toast-Man 3.25

POWERHOUSE PEPPER COMICS
1943—Nov., 1948
1 BW,Movie Auditions(c) 900.00
2 BW,Dinner(c) 500.00
3 BW,Boxing Ring(c) 400.00
4 BW,Subway(c) 400.00
5 BW,Bankrobbers(c) 500.00

POWER LINE
Epic
May, 1988
1 BMc(i) 2.25
2 Aw(i) 2.00
3 A:Dr Zero 2.00
4 . . . . 2.00
5 thru 7 GM . . . . @2.00
8 GM September, 1989 . . . . . . 2.00

POWER MAN
Prev: Hero for Hire
February, 1974
17 GT,A:Iron Man 10.00
18 GT,V:Steeplejack 7.50
19 GT,V:Cottonmouth 7.50
20 GT,Heroin Story 7.50
21 V:Original Power Man 5.00
22 V:Stiletto & Discus 5.00
23 V:Security City 5.00
24 GT,I:BlackGoliath(BillFoster) . . 5.00
25 A:Circus of Crime 5.00
26 GT,V:Night Shocker 5.00
27 GP,AMc,V:Man Called X 5.00
28 V:Cockroach 5.00
29 V:Mr.Fish 5.00
30 RB,KJ,KP,I:Piranha 5.00
31 SB,NA(i),V:Piranha 5.00
32 JSt,FR,A:Wildfire 3.50
33 FR,A:Spear 3.50
34 FR,A:Spear,Mangler 3.50
35 DA,A:Spear,Mangler 3.50
36 V:Chemistro 3.50
37 V:Chemistro 3.50
38 V:Chemistro 3.50
39 KJ,V:Chemistro,Baron 3.50
40 V:Baron 3.50
41 TP,V:Thunderbolt,Goldbug . . 3.50
42 V:Thunderbolt,Goldbug 3.50
43 AN,V:Mace 3.50
44 TP,A:Mace 3.50
45 JSn,A:Mace 4.00
46 GT,I:Zzzax(recreated) 3.50
47 BS,A:Zzzax 4.00
48 JBy,A:Iron Fist 5.00
49 JBy,A:Iron Fist 5.00
Becomes:
POWER MAN & IRON FIST
50 JBy,I:Team-up with Iron Fist . . 4.00
51 MZ,Night on the Town 2.50
52 MZ,V:Death Machines 2.50

53 SB,O:Nightshade 2.50
54 TR,O:Iron Fist 3.50
55 Chaos at the Coliseum 2.50
56 Mayhem in the Museum 2.50
57 X-Men,V:Living Monolith 7.00
58 1st El Aguila(Drug) 2.00
59 BL(c),TVE,V:Big Apple
   Bomber 1.75
60 BL(c),V:Terrorists 1.75
61 BL(c),V:The Maggia 1.75
62 BL(c),KGa,V:Man Mountain
   D:Thunerbolt 1.75
63 BL(c),Cage Fights Fire 1.75
64 DGr&BL(c),V:Suetre,Muerte . . 1.75
65 BL(c),A:El Aquila, ... 1.75
66 FM(c),Sabretooth(2nd App.) . . 50.00
67 V:Bushmaster 1.75
68 FM(c),V:Athur Nagan 2.00
69 V:Soldier 2.00
70 FM(c)V:El Supremo 1.75
71 FM(c),I:Montenegro 1.75
72 FM(c),V:Chako 1.75
73 FM(c),V:Rom 1.75
74 FM(c),V:Ninja 1.75
75 KGa,O:IronFist 2.50
76 KGa,V:Warhawk 2.50
77 KGa,A:Daredevil 2.50
78 KGa,A:El Aguila,Sabretooth
   (Slasher)(3rd App.) 20.00
79 V:Dredlox 1.75
80 KJ(c),V:Montenegro 1.75
81 V:Black Tiger 1.75
82 V:Black Tiger 1.75
83 V:Warhawk 1.75
84 V:Constrictor,A:Sabertooth
   (4th App.) 20.00
85 KP,V:Mole Man 1.75
86 A:Moon Knight 1.75
87 A:Moon Knight 1.75
88 V:Scimtar 1.75
89 V:Terrorists 1.75
90 V:Unus BS(c) 1.75
91 "Paths and Angles" 1.75
92 V:Hammeread,I:New Eel 1.75
93 A:Chemistro 1.75

94 V:Chemistro 1.75
95 Danny Rand 1.75
96 V,Chemistro 1.75
97 K'unlun,A:Fera 1.75
98 V:Shades & Commanche 1.75
99 R:Daught.of Dragon 1.75
100 O:K'unlun,DoubleSize 1.75
101 A:Karnak 1.75
102 V:Doombringer 1.75
103 O:Doombringer 1.75
104 V:Dr.Octopus,Lizard 1.75
105 F:Crime Buster 1.75
106 Luke Gets Shot 1.75
107 JBy(c),Terror issue 1.75
108 V:Inhuman Monster 1.75
109 V:The Reaper 1.75
110 V:Nightshade,Eel 1.75
111 I:Captain Hero 1.75
112 JBy(c),V:Control7 . . . . 1.75
113 JBy(c),A:Capt.Hero 1.75
114 JBy(c),V:Control7 . . . . 1.75
115 JBy(c),V:Stanley 1.75
116 JBy(c),V:Stanley 1.75
117 R:K'unlun 1.75
118 A:Colleen Wing 1.75
119 A:Daught.of Dragon 1.75
120 V:Chiantang 1.75
121 Secret Wars II 1.75
122 V:Dragonkin 1.75
123 V:Race Killer 1.75
124 V:Yellowclaw 1.75
125 MBr,LastIssue;D:Iron Fist . . . 3.00
Giant#1 reprints 4.00
Ann.#1 Earth Shock 5.00

POWER PACHYDERMS
September, 1989
1 Elephant Superheroes 1.50

POWER PACK
August, 1984
1 JBr,BWi,I&O:Power Pack,
   I:Snarks 3.00
2 JBr,BWi,V:Snarks 2.00
3 JBr,BWi,V:Snarks 2.00

---

4 JBr,BWi,V:Snarks	2.00
5 JBr,BWi,V:Bogeyman	2.00
6 JBr,BWi,A:Spider-Man	2.00
7 JBr,BWi,A:Cloak & Dagger	2.00
8 JBr,BWi,A:Cloak & Dagger	2.00
9 BA,BWi,A:Marrina	1.50
10 BA,BWi,A:Marrina	1.50
11 JBr,BWi,V:Morlocks	2.00
12 JBr,BWi,A:X-Men,V:Morlocks	3.00
13 BA,BWi,Baseball issue	1.50
14 JBr,BWi,V:Bogeyman	1.50
15 JBr,BWi,A:Beta Ray Bill	1.50
16 JBr,BWi,I&O:Kofi,J:Tattletale (Franklin Richards)	2.00
17 JBr,BWi,V:Snarks	1.50
18 BA,SW,Secret Wars II, V:Kurse	2.00
19 BA,SW,Doub.size,Wolverine	9.00
20 BMc,A:NewMutants	1.50
21 BA,TA,C:Spider-Man	1.50
22 JBg,BWi,V:Snarks	1.50
23 JBg,BWi,V:Snarks,C:FF	1.50
24 JBg,BWi,V:Snarks,C:Cloak	2.00
25 JBg,BWi,A:FF,V:Snarks	1.25
26 JBg,BWi,A:Cloak & Dagger	1.25
27 JBg,AG,A:Wolverine,X-Factor, V:Sabretooth	9.00
28 A:Fantastic Four,Hercules	1.25
29 JBg,DGr,A:SpM,V:Hobgoblin	2.00
30 VM,Crack	1.25
31 JBg,I:Trash	1.25
32 JBg,V:Trash	1.25
33 JBg,A:Sunspot,Warlock, C:Spider-Man	1.75
34 TD,V:Madcap	1.25
35 JBg,A:X-Factor,D:Plague	1.75
36 JBg,V:Master Mold	1.25
37 SDr(i),I:Light-Tracker	1.25
38 SDr(i),V:Molecula	1.25
39 V:Bogeyman	1.25
40 A:New Mutants,V:Bogeyman	1.75
41 SDr(i),V:The Gunrunners	1.25
42 JBg,SDr,Inferno,V:Bogeyman	2.00
43 JBg,SDr,AW,Inferno, V:Bogeyman	2.00
44 JBr,Inferno,A:New Mutants	2.25
45 JBr,End battle w/Bogeyman	1.50
46 WPo,A:Punisher,Dakota North	2.00
47 JBg,I:Bossko	1.50
48 JBg,Toxic Waste #1	1.50
49 JBg,JSh,Toxic Waste #2	1.50
50 AW(i),V:Snarks	1.50
51 GM,I:Numinus	1.50
52 AW(i),V:Snarks,A:Numinus	1.50
53 EC,A of V,A:Typhoid Mary	1.50
54 JBg,V:Mad Thinker	1.50
55 DSp,V:Mysterio	1.50
56 TMo,A:Fant.Four,Nova	1.50
57 TMo,A:Nova,V:Star Stalker	1.50
58 TMo,A:Galactus,Mr.Fantastic	1.50
59 TMo,V:Ringmaster	1.50
60 TMo,V:Puppetmaster	1.50
61 TMo,V:Red Ghost & Apes	1.50
62 V:Red Ghost & Apes (last issue)	1.50
Holiday Spec.JBr,Small Changes	2.25

PRINCE NAMOR, THE SUB-MARINER
September, 1984

1 I:Dragonrider, Dara	2.50
2 I:Proteus	1.50
3	1.25
4 December, 1984	1.25

PRINCE VALIANT

1 JRy,CV,Thule, Camelot and the Misty Isles	4.00
2 JRy,CV	4.00
3 JRy,CV	4.00
4 JRy,CV, final issue	4.00

PRIVATE EYE
Atlas
January, 1951

1	85.00
2	55.00
3 GT	55.00
4	40.00
5	40.00
6 JSt	40.00
7	40.00
8 March, 1952	40.00

PROWLER

1 beginning of miniseries	1.75
2 V:Nightcreeper	1.75
3	1.75
4 V:Vulture	1.75

PSI FORCE
November, 1986

1 MT,O:PSI Force	1.25
2 MT	1.00
3 MT,CIA	1.00
4 MT,J:Network	1.00
5 MT	1.00
6 MT(c)	1.00
7 MT(c)	1.00
8 MT	1.00
9 MT(c)	1.00
10 PSI Hawk	1.00
11	1.00
12 MT(c)	1.00
13	1.00
14 AW	1.00
15	1.00
16 RLm	1.25
17 RLm	1.25
18 RLm	1.25
19 RLm	1.25
20 RLm,V:Medusa Web;Rodstvow	1.50
21 RLm	1.50
22 RLm,A:Nightmask	1.50
23 A:D.P.7	1.50
24	1.50
25	1.25
26	1.25
27 thru 31	@1.50
32 June, 1989	1.50
Ann.#1	1.25

PSYCHONAUTS
Epic

1 thru 4 War in the Future	4.95

PUNISHER
January, 1986
[Limited Series]

1 MZ,Circle of Blood,double size	25.00
2 MZ,Back to the War	12.00
3 MZ,V:The Right	8.00
4 MZ,V:The Right	7.00
5 V:Jigsaw,end Mini-Series	7.00

[Regular Series]

1 KJ,V:Wilfred Sobel,Drugs	15.00
2 KJ,V:General Trahn,Bolivia	9.00
3 KJ,V:Colonel Fryer	6.00

Punisher Limited Series #1
© Marvel Entertainment Group

4 KJ,I:The Rev,Microchip Jr.	6.00
5 KJ,V:The Rev	6.00
6 DR,KN,V:The Rosettis	6.00
7 DR,V:Ahmad,D:Rose	6.00
8 WPo,SW(1st Punisher), V:Sigo & Roky	10.00
9 WPo,SW,D:MicrochipJr,V:Sigo	9.00
10 WPo,SW,A:Daredevil (x-over w/Daredevil #257)	15.00
11 WPo,SW,O:Punisher	5.00
12 WPo,SW,V:Gary Saunders	5.00
13 WPo,SW,V:Lydia Spoto	5.00
14 WPo,SW,I:McDowell,Brooks	5.00
15 WPo,SW,V:Kingpin	5.00
16 WPo,SW,V:Kingpin	4.00
17 WPo,SW,V:Kingpin	4.00
18 WPo,SW,V:Kingpin,C:X-Men	4.00
19 LSn,In Australia	3.00
20 WPo(c),In Las Vegas	3.00
21 EL,SW,Boxing Issue	3.00
22 EL,SW,I:Saracen	3.00
23 EL,SW,V:Scully	3.00
24 EL,SW,A:Shadowmasters	3.00
25 EL,AW,A:Shadowmasters	3.00
26 RH,Oper.Whistle Blower#1	2.50
27 RH,Oper.Whistle Blower#2	2.50
28 BR,A:Dr.Doom,A of Veng.	2.50
29 BR,A:Dr.Doom,A of Veng.	2.50
30 BR,V:Geltrate	2.50
31 BR,V:Bikers #1	2.50
32 BR,V:Bikers #2	2.50
33 BR,V:The Reavers	2.50
34 BR,V:The Reavers	2.50
35 BR,MF,Jigsaw Puzzle #1	2.50
36 MT,MF,Jigsaw Puzzle #2	2.50
37 MT,Jigsaw Puzzle #3	2.50
38 BR,MF,Jigsaw Puzzle #4	2.50
39 JSh,Jigsaw Puzzle #5	2.50
40 BR,JSh,Jigsaw Puzzle #6	2.50
41 BR,TD,V:Terrorists	2.50
42 MT,V:Corrupt Mili. School	2.50
43 BR,Border Run	2.00
44 Flag Burner	2.00
45 One Way Fare	2.00
46 HH,Cold Cache	2.00

All comics prices listed are for *Near Mint* condition.

47 HH,Middle East #1 . . . . 2.00
48 HH,Mid.East #2,V:Saracen . . . 2.00
49 HH,Punisher Hunted 2.00
50 HH,MGo(c),I:Yo Yo Ng 3.00
51 Chinese Mafia 2.00
52 Baby Snatchers 2.00
53 HH,in Prison 2.50
54 HH,in Prison 2.50
55 HH,in Prison 2.50
56 HH,in Prison 2.50
57 HH,in Prison 2.50
58 V:Kingpin's Gang,A:Micro 3.00
59 MT(c),V:Kingpin 2.00
60 VM,AW,Black Punisher,
   A:Luke Cage 2.00
61 VM,A:Luke Cage 2.00
62 VM,AW,A:Luke Cage 1.50
63 MT(c),VM,V:Thieves 1.50
64 Eurohit #1 . . . . 1.50
65 thru 70 Eurohit . . . . @1.50
71 AW(i) 1.50
72 AW(i) 1.50
73 AW(i),Police Action #1 . . . . . . 1.50
74 AW(i),Police Action #2 . . . . . . 1.50
75 AW(i),Police Action #3,foil(c),
   double size 3.25
76 LSn,in Hawaii 1.50
77 VM,Survive#1 . . . . 1.50
78 VM,Survive#2 . . . . 1.50
79 VM,Survive#3 . . . . 1.50
80 Goes to Church 1.50
81 V:Crooked Cops 1.50
82 B:Firefight 1.50
83 Firefight#2 . . . . 1.50
84 E:Firefight 1.50
85 Suicide Run 2.00
86 Suicide Run#3,Foil(c), ... 3.25
87 Suicide Run#6 . . . . 1.50
88 LSh(c),Suicide Run#9 . . . . . . 1.50
89 . . . . 1.75
90 Hammered 1.75
91 Silk Noose 1.75
92 Razor's Edge 1.75
93 Killing Streets 1.75
94 B:No Rules 1.50
95 No Rules 1.50
96 . . . . 1.50
97 CDi 1.50
98 . . . . 1.50
99 . . . . 1.50
100 New Punisher 2.95
100a Enhanced ed. 3.95
101 CC,Raid's Franks Tomb 1.50
102 A:Bullseye 1.50
103 Countdown 4 . . . . 1.50
104 CDi,Countdown 1, V:Kingpin,
   final issue 1.50
Ann.#1 MT,A:Eliminators,
   Evolutionary War. 8.00
Ann.#2 JLe,Atlantis Attacks #5,
   A:Moon Knight 5.00
Ann.#3 LS,MT,Lifeform #1 . . . . . 4.00
Ann.#4 Baron Strucker,pt.2
   (see D.D.Annual #7) 3.00
Ann.#5 System Bytes #1 . . . . . . 2.50
Ann.#6 I:Eradikator,w/card 3.25
GNv 8.00
Summer Spec #1 VM,MT 3.50
Summer Spec #2 SBs(c) 2.50
Summer Spec #3 V:Carjackers . . 2.50
Summer Spec #4 . . . . 3.25
Punisher:No Escape A:USAgent,
   Paladin 6.00
Movie Spec.BA 5.95
Punisher: The Prize 5.50

Punisher Limited Series #2
© Marvel Entertainment Group

Punisher:Bloodlines DC 6.25
Punisher:Blood on the Moors . . . 16.95
Punisher:G-Force 5.25
Punisher:Origin of Mirco Chip #1,
   O:Mirco Chip 2.00
Punisher:Origin of Mirco Chip #2
   V:The Professor 2.00
Classic Punisher rep early
   B/w magazines 7.00
Punisher:Back To School Spec.
   #1 JRy,short stories 3.25
   #2 BSz 2.95
Punisher:Die Hard in the Big
   Easy Mardi Gras 5.25
Holiday Spec.#1 V:Young
   Mob Capo 3.25
Holiday Spec #2 . . . . 2.95
Punisher:Ghosts o/t Innocent#1
   TGr, V:Kingpin's Dead Men . . 5.95
Punisher:Ghosts o/t Innocent#2
   TGr, V:Kingpin,Snake 5.95
Punisher: Eye For An Eye 9.95

PUNISHER/
CAPTAIN AMERICA:
BLOOD AND GLORY
1 thru 3 KJ,V:Drug Dealers . . . @6.25

PUNISHER ARMORY
July, 1990
1 JLe(c) 6.00
2 JLe(c) 3.00
3 . . . . 2.50
4 thru 6 . . . . @2.25
7 thru 10 . . . . @2.00

CLASSIC PUNISHER
1 TDz 4.95

PUNISHER/DAREDEVIL
1 Rep.Daredevil 6.00

PUNISHER MAGAZINE
October, 1989
1 MZ,rep.,Punisher #1 . . . . 2.50
2 MZ,rep 2.25
3 thru 13 KJ,rep. . . . . @2.25
14 rep. PWJ #1&#2 . . . . 2.25
15 rep. PWJ 2.25
16 rep.,1990 . . . . 2.25

PUNISHER
MEETS ARCHIE
1 JB 4.25
1a newsstand ed. 3.25

PUNISHER MOVIE COMIC
November, 1989
1 Movie adapt. 1.50
2 Movie adapt. 1.50
3 Movie adapt,December, 1989 . 1.50

PUNISHER MOVIE
SPECIAL
1 Movie Adapt.BA,1989 . . . . 5.95

PUNISHER: NO ESCAPE
OneShot A:USAgent,Paladin,1990 5.50

PUNISHER P.O.V.
July, 1991
1 BWr,Punisher/Nick Fury 6.00
2 BWr,A:Nick Fury,Kingpin 5.50
3 BWr,V:Mutant Monster,
   A:Vampire Slayer 5.50
4 BWr,A:Nick Fury 5.25

PUNISHER: THE PRIZE
1 1990 . . . . 4.95

PUNISHER 2099
1 TMo,Jake Gallows family
   Killed, foil(c) 2.50
2 TMo,I:Fearmaster,Kron,Multi
   Factor 2.25
3 TMo,V:Frightening Cult 2.25
4 TMo,V:Cyber Nostra 1.75
5 TMo,V:Cyber Nostra,Fearmaster 1.75
6 TMo,V:Multi-Factor 1.75
7 TMo,Love and Bullets#1 . . . . . 1.75
8 TMo,Love and Bullets#2 . . . . . 1.75
9 TMo,Love and Bullets#3 . . . . . 1.75
10 TMo,I:Jigsaw 1.50
11 TMo,V:Jigsaw 1.50
12 TMo,A:Spider-Man 2099 . . . . 1.50
13 TMo,Fall of the Hammer#5 . . . 1.50
14 WSm, ... 1.50
15 TMo,V:Fearmaster,
   I:Public Enemy 1.50
16 TMo,V:Fearmaster,
   Public Enemy 1.75
17 TMo,V:Public Enemy 1.75
18 TMo,I:Goldheart 1.75
19 TMo,I:Vendetta 1.50
20 . . . . 1.50
21 . . . . 1.50
22 V:Hotwire 1.50
23 I:Synchron,V:Hotwire 1.50
24 V:Synchron 1.50
25 Enhanced cover 2.95
25a newsstand ed. 2.25
26 V:Techno-Shaman 1.50
27 R:Blue Max 1.50
Becomes:

PUNISHER 2099 A.D.
28 Minister of Punishment 1.95
29 Minister of Punishment 1.95
30 One Nation Under Doom 1.95

Punisher War Journal #9
© Marvel Entertainment Group

PUNISHER WAR JOURNAL
November, 1988
1 CP,JLe,O:Punisher 9.00
2 CP,JLe,A:Daredevil 7.00
3 CP,JLe,A:Daredevil 7.00
4 CP,JLeV:The Sniper 6.00
5 CP,JLe,V:The Sniper 6.00
6 CP,JLe,A:Wolverine 9.00
7 CP,JLe,A:Wolverine 9.00
8 JLe,I:Shadowmasters 4.00
9 JLe,A:Black Widow 4.00
10 JLe,V:Sniper 4.00
11 JLe,Shock Treatment 4.00
12 JLe,AM,V:Bushwacker 4.00
13 JLe(c),V:Bushwacker 3.50
14 JLe(c),DR,RH,A:Spider-Man . . 4.00
15 JLe(c),DR,RH,A:Spider-Man . . 4.00
16 MT(i),Texas Massacre 3.00
17 JLe,AM,Hawaii 3.50
18 JLe,AM,Kahuna,Hawaii 3.50
19 JLe,AM,Traume in Paradise . . 3.50
20 AM 3.00
21 TSm,AM 2.50
22 TSm,AM,Ruins #1 .... 2.50
23 TSm,AM,Ruins #2 .... 2.50
24 .... 2.50
25 MT 3.00
26 MT,A:Saracen 3.00
27 MT,A:Saracen 3.00
28 MT 3.00
29 MT,A:Ghostrider 3.00
30 MT,A:Ghostrider 3.00
31 NKu,Kamchatkan
  Konspiracy#1 .... 2.50
32 Kamchatkan Konspiracy #2 . . . 2.25
33 Kamchatkan Konspiracy #3 . . . 2.25
34 V:Psycho 2.25
35 Movie Stuntman 2.25
36 Radio Talk Show #1 .... 2.25
37 Radio Talk Show #2 .... 2.25
38 .... 2.25

39 DGr,V:Serial Killer 2.25
40 MWg 2.00
41 Armageddon Express 2.00
42 Mob run-out 2.00
43 JR2(c) 2.00
44 Organ Donor Crimes 2.00
45 Dead Man's Hand #3,V:Viper . 2.25
46 Dead Man's Hand #6,V:Chainsaw
  and the Praetorians 2.00
47 Dead Man's Hand #7,A:Nomad,
  D.D,V:Hydra,Secret Empire . . . 2.00
48 B:Payback 2.00
49 JR2(c),V:Corrupt Cop 2.00
50 MT,V:Highjackers,I:Punisher
  2099 .... 2.50
51 E:Payback 2.00
52 A:Ice(from The'Nam) 2.00
53 A:Ice(from the Nam) 2.00
54 Hyper#1 .... 2.00
55 Hyper#2 .... 2.00
56 Hyper#3 .... 2.00
57 A:Ghost Rider,Daredevil 2.00
58 A:Ghost Rider,Daredevil 2.00
59 F:Max the Dog 2.00
60 CDi(s),F:Max the Dog 2.00
61 CDi(s),Suicide Run#1,Foil(c) . . 3.25
62 CDi(s),Suicide Run#4 ...... 2.00
63 CDi(s),Suicide Run#7 ...... 2.00
64 CDi(s),Suicide Run#10 ...... 3.25
64a Newsstand Ed. 2.50
65 B:Pariah 2.00
66 A:Captain America 2.25
67 Pariah#3 .... 2.25
68 A:Spider-Man 2.25
69 E:Pariah 1.95
70 .... 1.95
71 .... 1.95
72 V:Fake Punisher 1.95
73 E:Frank Castle 1.95
74 .... 1.95
75 MT(c) 2.50
76 First Entry 1.95
77 R:Stone COld 1.95
78 V:Payback,Heathen 1.95
79 Countdown 3 .... 1.95
80 Countdown 0, A:Nick Fury,
  V:Bullseye, final issue 1.95
TPB reprints #6,7 .... 4.95

PUNISHER WAR ZONE
1 JR2,KJ,Punisher As Johnny Tower
  Die-Cut Bullet Hole(c) 4.00
2 JR2,KJ,Mafia Career 3.00
3 JR2,KJ,Punisher/Mafia,contd . . 3.00
4 JR2,KJ,Cover gets Blown 3.00
5 JR2,KJ,A:Shotgun 3.00
6 JR2,KJ,A:Shotgun 3.00
7 JR2,V:Rapist in Central Park . . 2.00
8 JR2,V:Rapist in Central Park . . 2.00
9 JR2,V:Magnificent Seven 2.00
10 JR2,V:Magnificent Seven 2.00
11 JR2,MM,V:Magnificent Seven . 2.00
12 Punisher Married 2.00
13 Self-Realization 2.00
14 Psychoville#3 .... 2.00
15 Psychoville#4 .... 2.00
16 Psychoville#5 .... 2.00
17 Industrial Esponiage 2.00
18 Jerico Syndrome#2 .... 2.00
19 Jerico Syndrome#3 .... 2.00
20 B:2 Mean 2 Die 2.00
21 2 Mean 2 Die#2 .... 2.00
22 A:Tyger Tyger 2.00
23 Suicide Run#2,Foil(c) 3.25
24 Suicide Run#5, ... 2.00

Punisher War Zone #1
© Marvel Entertainment Group

25 Suicide Run#8, ... 2.50
26 CDi(s),JB,Pirates 2.00
27 CDi(s),JB, ... 2.25
28 CDi(s),JB,Sweet Revenge . . . 2.25
29 CDi(s),JB,The Swine 2.25
30 CDi(s),JB 1.95
31 CDi(s),JB,River of Blood,pt.1 . 1.95
32 CDi(s),JB,River of Blood,pt.2 . 1.95
33 CDi(s),JB,River of Blood,pt.3 . 1.95
34 CDi(s),JB,River of Blood,pt.4 . 1.95
35 River of Blood,pt.5 .... 1.95
36 River of Blood,pt.6 .... 1.95
37 O:Max 1.95
38 Dark Judgment,pt.1 .... 1.95
39 Dark Judgment,pt.2 .... 1.95
40 In Court 1.95
41 CDi,Countdown 2, final issue . 1.95
Ann.#1 Jb,MGo,(c),I:Phalanx,
  w/Trading card 3.25
Ann.#2 CDi(s),DR 2.95

PUNISHER: YEAR ONE
1 O:Punisher 2.50
2 O:Punisher 2.50
3 O:Punisher 2.50
4 finale 2.50

PUSSYCAT
October, 1968
(black & white magazine)
1 BEv,BWa,WW 125.00

QUASAR
October, 1989
1 O:Quasar 2.75
2 V:Deathurge,A:Eon 2.00
3 A:Human Torch,V:The Angler . 2.00
4 Acts of Vengeance,A:Aquarian . 2.00
5 A of Veng,V:Absorbing Man . . . 2.00
6 V:Klaw,Living Laser,Venom,
  Red Ghost 5.00
7 MM,A:Cosmic SpM,V:Terminus 3.50
8 MM,A:New Mutants,BlueShield 2.00
9 MM,A:Modam 2.00

---

10 MM,A:Dr.Minerva	2.00
11 MM,A:Excalibur,A:Modred	2.00
12 MM,A:Makhari,Blood Bros.	1.75
13 JLe(c)MM,J.into Mystery #1	1.75
14 TM(c)MM,J.into Mystery #2	2.00
15 MM,Journey into Mystery #3	1.75
16 MM,Double sized	2.25
17 MM,Race,A:Makkari,Whizzer, Quicksilver,Capt.Marv,Super Sabre,Barry Allen Spoof	2.50
18 GCa,N:Quasar	1.75
19 GCa,B:Cosmos in Collision, C:Thanos	2.50
20 GCa,A:Fantastic Four	2.50
21 GCa,V:Jack of Hearts	2.50
22 GCa,D:Quasar,A:Ghost Rider	2.50
23 GCa,A:Ghost Rider	2.50
24 GCa,A:Thanos,Galactus, D:Maelstrom	2.50
25 GCa,A:Eternity & Infinity,N:Quasar, E:Cosmos Collision	2.50
26 GCa,Inf.Gauntlet,A:Thanos	3.00
27 GCa,Infinity Gauntlet,I:Epoch	2.50
28 GCa,A:Moondragon,Her, X-Men	2.00
29 GCa,A:Moondragon,Her	1.50
30 GCa,What If? tie-in	1.50
31 GCa,R:New Universe	1.50
32 GCa,Op.GalacticStorm,pt.3	1.50
33 GCa,Op.GalacticStorm,pt.10	1.50
34 GCa,Op.GalacticStorm,pt.17	1.50
35 GCa,Binary V:Her	1.50
36 GCa,V:Soul Eater	1.50
37 GCa,V:Soul Eater	1.50
38 GCa,Inf.War,V:Warlock	1.50
39 SLi,Inf.War,V:Deathurge	1.50
40 SLi,Inf.War,V:Deathurge	1.50
41 R:Marvel Boy	1.50
42 V:Blue Marvel	1.50
43 V:Blue Marvel	1.50
44 V:Quagmire	1.50
45 V:Quagmire,Antibody	1.50
46 Neutron,Presence	1.50
47 1st Full Thunderstrike Story	1.50
48 A:Thunderstrike	1.50
49 Kalya Vs. Kismet	1.50
50 A:Man-Thing,Prism(c)	3.25
51 V:Angler,A:S.Supreme	1.50
52 V:Geometer	1.50
53	1.50
54 MGu(s),Starblast #2	1.50
55 MGu(s),A:Stranger	1.50
56 MGu(s),Starblast #10	1.50
57 MGu(s),A:Kismet	1.50
58	1.50
59 A:Thanos,Starfox	1.50
60 final issue	1.50

QUESTPROBE
August, 1984

1 JR,A:Hulk,I:Chief Examiner	2.00
2 AM,JM,A:Spider-Man	1.75
3 JSt,A:Thing & Torch	1.50

QUICK-TRIGGER WESTERN
See: WESTERN THRILLERS

RAIDERS OF THE LOST ARK
September, 1981

1 JB/KJ,movie adaption	2.00
2 JB/KJ,	1.75

3 JB/KJ,November,1981	1.75

RAVAGE 2099

1 PR,I:Ravage	2.50
2 PR,V:Deathstryk	2.00
3 PR,V:Mutroids	2.00
4 PR,V:Mutroids	1.50
5 PR,Hellrock	1.50
6 PR,N:Ravage	1.50
7 PR,new Powers	1.50
8 V:Deathstryke	1.50
9 PR,N:Ravage	1.50
10 V:Alchemax	1.50
11 A:Avatarr	1.50
12 Ravage Transforms	1.50
13 V:Fearmaster	1.50
14 V:Punisher 2099	1.50
15 Fall of the Hammer #2	1.50
16 I:Throwback	1.50
17 GtM,V:Throwback,O:X-11	1.50
18 GtM,w/card	1.75
19 GtM,	1.75
20 GtM,V:Hunter	1.50
21 Savage on the Loose	1.50
22 Exodus	1.50
23 Blind Justice	1.50
24 Unleashed	1.50
25 Flame Bearer	2.25
25a Deluxe ed.	2.95
26 V:Megastruck	1.50
27 V:Deathstryke	1.50
28 R:Hela	1.50
29 V:Deathstryke	1.50
30 King Ravage	1.50

Becomes:
RAVAGE 2099 A.D.

31 V:Doom	1.95
32 One Nation Under Doom	1.95

RAWHIDE KID
Atlas
March, 1955—May, 1979

1 B:Rawhide Kid & Randy, A:Wyatt Earp	450.00
2 Shoot-out(c)	175.00
3 V:Hustler	100.00
4 Rh(c)	100.00
5 GC	100.00
6 Six-Gun Lesson	75.00
7 AW	75.00
8	75.00
9	75.00
10 thru 16	@60.00
17 JK,O:Rawhide Kid	60.00
18 thru 20	@50.00
21	40.00
22	40.00
23 JK,O:Rawhide Kid Retold	85.00
24 thru 30	@40.00
31 JK,DAy,No Law in Mesa	35.00
32 JK,DAy,Beware of the Parker Brothers	35.00
33 JK(c),JDa,V:Jesse James	40.00
34 JDa,JK,V:Mister Lightning	40.00
35 JK(c),GC,JDa,I&D:The Raven	40.00
36 DAy,A Prisoner in Outlaw Town	35.00
37 JK(c),DAy,GC,V:The Rattler	35.00
38 DAy.V:The Red Raven	35.00
39 DAy	35.00
40 JK(c),DAy,A:Two Gun Kid	35.00
41 JK(c),The Tyrant of Tombstone Valley	35.00
42 JK	35.00

43 JK	35.00
44 JK(c),V:The Masked Maverick	35.00
45 JK(c),O:Rawhide Kid Retold	40.00
46 JK(c),ATh	30.00
47 JK(c),The Riverboat Raiders	25.00
48 GC,V:Marko the Manhunter	22.00
49 The Masquerader	22.00
50 A;Kid Colt,V:Masquerader	22.00
51 DAy,Trapped in the Valley of Doom	22.00
52 DAy,Revenge at Rustler's Roost	22.00
53 Guns of the Wild North	22.00
54 DH,BEv,The Last Showdown	22.00
55	22.00
56 DH,JTgV:The Peacemaker	22.00
57 V:The Scorpion	22.00
58 DAy	22.00
59 V:Drako	22.00
60 DAy,HT,Massacre at Medicine Bend	22.00
61 DAy,TS,A:Wild Bill Hickok	20.00
62 Gun Town,V:Drako	20.00
63 Shootout at Mesa City	20.00
64 HT,Duel of the Desparadoes	20.00
65 JTg,HT,BE	20.00
66 JTg,BEv,Death of a Gunfighter	20.00
67 Hostage of Hungry Hills	20.00
68 JB,V:The Cougar	20.00
69 JTg,The Executioner	20.00
70 JTg,The Night of the Betrayers	15.00
71 JTg,The Last Warrior	15.00
72 JTg,The Menace of Mystery Valley	15.00
73 JTg,The Manhunt	15.00
74 JTg,The Apaches Attack	15.00
75 JTg,The Man Who Killed The Kid	15.00
76 JTg,V:The Lynx	15.00
77 JTg,The Reckoning	15.00
78 JTg	15.00
79 JTg,AW,The Legion of the Lost	15.00
80 Fall of a Hero	15.00
81 thru 85	@15.00
86 JK,O:Rawhide Kid retold	15.00
87 thru 99	@9.00
100 O:Rawhide Kid retold	12.00
101 thru 135	@10.00
126 thru 151	@8.00

RAWHIDE KID
August, 1985

1 JSe,mini-series	1.50
2	1.25
3	1.25
4	1.25

RAZORLINE FIRST CUT
Razorline

1 Intro Razorline	1.00

REAL EXPERIENCES
See: TESSIE THE TYPIST

RED RAVEN
See: HUMAN TORCH

RED SONJA
[1st Series]
January, 1977

1 FT,O:Red Sonja,'Blood of the Unicorn'	3.50
2 FT,'Demon of the Maze'	2.50

Red Sonja #1
© Marvel Entertainment Group

3 FT,'The Games of Gita' 2.00
4 FT,'The Lake of the Unknown' . 2.00
5 FT,'Master of the Bells' 2.00
6 FT,'The Singing Tower' 1.25
7 FT,'Throne of Blood' 1.25
8 FT,Vengeance o/t Golden Circle 1.25
9 FT,'Chariot o/t Fire-Stallions' . . 1.25
10 FT,Red Lace,pt.1 . . . . 1.25
11 FT,Red Lace,pt.2 . . . . 1.25
12 JB/JRu,'Ashes & Emblems' . . 1.25
13 JB/AM,'Shall Skranos Fall' . . . 1.25
14 SB/AM,'Evening on the Border' 1.25
15 JB/TD,'Tomb of 3 Dead Kings'
May, 1979 . . . . 1.25
[2nd Series]
February, 1983
1 TD,GC 1.25
2 GC, March,1983 . . . . 1.00
[3rd Series]
August, 1983
1 . . . . 1.25
2 . . . . 1.25
3 thru 13 . . . . @1.25
1 movie adaption, 1985 . . . . . . 1.25
2 movie adaption, 1985 . . . . . . 1.25

RED WARRIOR
Atlas
January, 1951
1 GT,Indian Tales 80.00
2 GT(c),The Trail of the Outcast 50.00
3 The Great Spirit Speaks 40.00
4 O:White Wing 40.00
5 . . . . 40.00
6 Final Issue,December, 1951 . 40.00

RED WOLF
May, 1972
1 SSh(c),GK,JSe,F:Red Wolf
& Lobo 5.50
2 GK(c),SSh,Day of the Dynamite
Doom 3.00
3 SSh,War of the Wolf Brothers . 3.00
4 SSh,V:Man-Bear 3.00

5 GK(c),SSh 3.00
6 SSh,JA,V;Devil Rider 3.00
7 SSh,JA,Echoes from a Golden
Grave 3.00
8 SSh,Hell on Wheels 3.00
9 DAy,To Die Again,O:Lobo
September, 1973 . . . . 3.00

REN AND STIMPY SHOW
1 Polybagged w/Air Fowlers,
Ren(c) 22.00
1a Stimpy(c) 22.00
1b 2nd Printing 5.00
1c 3rd Printing 2.00
2 Frankenstimpy 15.00
2a 2nd Printing 2.00
3 Christmas issue 12.00
3a 2nd Printing 2.00
4 Where's Stimpy? 7.00
5 Teacher Bingo 6.00
6 A:SpM,V:Powdered Toast Man 6.00
7 F:Offical Yak Shaving Day 4.00
8 F:Bun Boy Burger Bunny 3.00
9 Untamed World 3.00
10 Bug Out 3.00
11 Ren's Peaceful Place 3.00
12 Teacher Bingo 3.00
13 Halloween issue 2.50
14 Mars needs Vecro 2.50
15 Christmas Spec. 2.25
16 . . . . 2.25
17 This Year's Model 2.25
18 U.S. Ohhhhh No! 2.25
19 Minimalist issue 2.25
20 F:Muddy Mudskipper 2.25
21 I'm The Cat 2.25
22 Badtime Stories 1.95
23 Athletics 1.95
24 Halloween 1.95
25 regular (c) 1.95
25a die-cut(c),A new addition . . . 2.95
26 . . . . 1.95
27 . . . . 1.95
28 Filthy the Monkey 1.95
29 Loch Ness Mess 1.95
30 Pinata game 1.95
31 Sausage Castle 1.95
32 Join Circus, UFO Abduction . . 1.95
TPB Running Joke,rep.#1-4,w/new
material 12.95
Spec. Virtual Stupidity #5 . . . . . 2.95

RETURN OF THE JEDI
1 AW,movie adapt 3.00
2 AW,movie adapt 3.00
3 AW,movie adapt 3.00
4 AW,movie adapt 3.00

REX HART
See: BLAZE CARSON

RICHIE RICH
1 Movie Adaptation 2.95

RINGO KID
January, 1970
[2nd Series]
1 AW,Reprints 3.00
2 JSe,Man Trap 2.00
3 JR,the Man From the Panhandle 1.50
4 HT(c),The Golden Spur 2.00
5 JMn,Ambush 2.00
6 Capture or Death 2.00

7 HT(c),JSe,JA,Terrible Treasure
of Vista Del Oro 2.00
8 The End of the Trail 2.00
9 JSe,Mystery of the Black
Sunset 2.00
10 Bad day at Black Creek 2.00
11 Bullet for a Bandit 1.50
12 A Badge to Die For 1.50
13 DW,Hostage at Fort Cheyenne 1.50
14 Showdown in the Silver
Cartwheel 1.50
15 Fang,Claw, and Six-Gun 1.50
16 Battle of Cattleman's Bank . . . 1.50
17 Gundown at the Hacienda . . . 1.50
18 . . . . 1.50
19 Thunder From the West 1.50
20 AW 1.50
21 thru 29 . . . . @1.50
30 November, 1973 . . . . 1.50

RINGO KID WESTERN
Atlas
August, 1954
1 JSt,O:Ringo Kid,B:Ringo Kid 160.00
2 I&O:Arab,A:Black Rider 80.00
3 . . . . 50.00
4 . . . . 50.00
5 . . . . 50.00
6 . . . . 55.00
7 . . . . 55.00
8 JSe 55.00
9 . . . . 30.00
10 JSe(c),AW 40.00
11 JSe(c) 30.00
12 JO 30.00
13 AW 40.00
14 thru 20 . . . . @30.00
21 September, 1957 . . . . 30.00

ROBOCOP
March, 1990
1 LS,I:Nixcops 9.00
2 LS,V:Nixcops 5.00
3 LS 3.50
4 LS 3.00
5 LS,WarzonePt1 . . . . 3.00
6 LS,WarzonePt2 . . . . 3.00
7 LS 2.50
8 LS,V:Gang-5 . . . . 2.50
9 LS,V:Vigilantes 2.50
10 LS 2.50
11 HT 2.50
12 LS,Robocop Army #1 . . . . . . 2.00
13 LS,Robocop Army #2 . . . . . . 2.00
14 LS,Robocop Army #3 . . . . . . 2.00
15 LS,Robocop Army #4 . . . . . . 2.00
16 TV take over 2.00
17 LS,V:The Wraith 2.00
18 LS,Mindbomb #1 . . . . 2.00
19 LS,Mindbomb #2 . . . . 2.00
20 In Detroit 2.00
21 LS,Beyond the Law,pt.1 . . . . 2.00
22 LS,Beyond the Law,pt.2 . . . . 2.00
23 LS,Beyond the Law,pt.3,final . . 2.00
Robocop Movie Adapt 4.95
Robocop II Movie Adapt 4.95

ROBOCOP II
August, 1990
1 MBa,rep.Movie Adapt 2.00
2 MBa,rep.Movie Adapt 1.50
3 MBa,rep.Movie Adapt 1.50

ROBOTIX
February, 1986
1 Based on toys 1.00

ROCKET RACCOON
May, 1985—Aug., 1985
1 thru 4 MM . . . . @1.50

ROCKO'S MODERN LIFE
1 and 2 . . . . @2.25
3 and 4 . . . . @1.95

ROGUE
1 Enhanced cover 4.50
2 A:Gambit 4.00
3 Gamtit or Rogue? 2.95
4 final issue 2.95

ROM
December, 1979
1 SB,I&O:Rom 3.00
2 FM(c),SB,V:Dire Wraiths 2.50
3 FM(c),SB,I:Firefall 2.50
4 SB,A:Firefall 2.00

Rom #41
© *Marvel Entertainment Group*

5 SB,A:Dr.Strange 2.00
6 SB,V:Black Nebula 1.50
7 SB,V:Dark Nebula 1.50
8 SB,V:Dire Wraiths 1.50
9 SB,V:Serpentyne 1.50
10 SB,V:U.S.Air Force 1.50
11 SB,V:Dire Wraiths 1.50
12 SB,A:Jack O' Hearts 1.75
13 SB,V:Plunderer 1.25
14 SB,V:Mad Thinker 1.25
15 SB,W:Brandy and Dire Wraith . 1.25
16 SB,V:Watchwraith 1.25
17 SB,A:X-Men 3.00
18 SB,A:X-Men 3.00
19 SB,JSt,C:X-Men 1.50
20 SB,JSt,A:Starshine 1.25
21 SB,JSt,A:Torpedo 1.25
22 SB,JSt,A:Torpedo 1.25
23 SB,JSt,A:Powerman,Iron Fist. . 1.25
24 SB,JSt,A:Nova 1.25

25 SB,JSt,Double-Sized 1.50
26 SB,JSt,V:Galactus 1.00
27 SB,JSt,V:Galactus 1.00
28 SB,JSt,D:Starshine 1.00
29 SB,Down in the Mines 1.00
30 SB,JSt,A:Torpedo 1.00
31 SB,JSt,V:Evil Mutants,Rogue . 2.00
32 SB,JSt,V:Evil Mutants 2.00
33 SB,V:Sybil 1.00
34 SB,A:Sub-Mariner 1.00
35 SB,A:Sub-Mariner 1.00
36 SB,V:Scarecrow 1.00
37 SB,A:Starshine 1.00
38 SB,A:Master of Kung Fu 1.00
39 SB,A:Master of Kung Fu 1.00
40 SB,A:Torpedo 1.00
41 SB,A:Dr.Strange 1.00
42 SB,A:Dr.Strange 1.00
43 SB,Rom Becomes Human . . . 1.00
44 SB,A:Starshine,O:Gremlin . . . 1.00
45 SB,V:Soviet Super Soldiers . . . 1.00
46 SB,V:Direwraiths 1.00
47 SB,New Look for Wraiths 1.00
48 SB,V:Dire Wraiths 1.00
49 SB,V:Dire Wraiths 1.00
50 SB,D:Torpedo,V:Skrulls 1.25
51 SB,F:Starshine 1.00
52 BSz(c),SB,V:Dire Wraiths 1.00
53 SB,BSz,V:Dire Wraiths 1.00
54 V:Dire Wraiths 1.00
55 V:Dire Wraihs 1.00
56 A:Alpha Flight 2.00
57 A:Alpha Flight 2.00
58 JG(c),A:Antman 1.00
59 SD,BL,V:Microbe Menace 1.00
60 SD,TP,V:Dire Wraiths 1.00
61 SD,V:Wraith-Realm 1.00
62 SD,A:Forge 1.25
63 SD,V:Dire Wraiths 1.00
64 SD,V:Dire Wraiths 1.00
65 SD,A:X-Men,Avengers 1.25
66 SD,Rom leaves Earth 1.25
67 SD,V:Scorpion 1.00
68 BSz(c)SD,Man & Machine 1.00
69 SD,V:Ego 1.00
70 SD 1.00
71 SD,V:Raak 1.00
72 SD,Secret Wars II 1.25
73 SD,JSt 1.00
74 SD,JBy,Code of Honor 1.00
75 SD,CR,Doublesize,last issue . . 1.50
Ann.#1 PB,A:Stardust 1.50
Ann.#2 I:Knights of Galador 1.25
Ann.#3 A:New Mutants 2.00
Ann.#4 V:Gladiator 1.25

ROMANCE DIARY
December, 1949
1 . . . . 65.00
2 March, 1950 . . . . 60.00

ROMANCES OF THE WEST
November, 1949
1 Ph(c),Calamity Jane,
 Sam Bass 100.00
2 March, 1950 . . . . 65.00

ROMANCE TALES
October, 1949
(no #1 thru 6)
7 . . . . 50.00
8 . . . . 35.00
9 March, 1950 . . . . 30.00

ROMANTIC AFFAIRS
See: MOLLY MANTON'S ROMANCES

ROYAL ROY
Star
May, 1985
1 thru 5 . . . . @1.00
6 March, 1986 . . . . 1.00

RUGGED ACTION
Atlas
December, 1954
1 Man-Eater 55.00
2 JSe,DAy.Manta-Ray 35.00
3 DAy 35.00
4 . . . . 35.00
Becomes:

STRANGE STORIES OF SUSPENSE
5 RH,The Little Black Box . . . 150.00
6 BEv,The Illusion 75.00
7 JSe(c),BEv,Old John's House 85.00
8 AW,BP,TYhumbs Down 85.00
9 BEv(c),Nightmare 75.00
10 RC,MME,AT 85.00
11 . . . . 65.00
12 . . . . 65.00
13 . . . . 60.00
14 AW 65.00
15 BK 60.00
16 August, 1957 . . . . 60.00

RUSTY COMICS
See: KID KOMICS

SABRETOOTH
[Limited Series]
1 B:LHa(s),MT,A:Wolverine 7.00
2 MT,A:Mystique,C:Wolverine . . . 5.00
3 MT,A:Mystique,Wolverine 4.50
4 E:LHa(s),MT,D:Birdy 4.00
TPB rep. #1-#4 . . . . 12.95

SABRETOOTH CLASSICS
1 rep. Power Man/Iron Fist #66 . . 1.75
2 rep. Power Man/Iron Fist #78 . . 1.75
3 rep. Power Man/Iron Fist #84 . . 1.75
4 rep. Spider-Man #116 . . . . 1.75
5 rep. Spider-Man #119 . . . . 1.50
6 reprints 1.50
7 reprints 1.50
8 reprints 1.50
9 reprints 1.50
10 Morlock Massacre 1.50
11 rep. Daredevil #238 . . . . 1.50
12 rep. V:Wolverine 1.50
13 rep. 1.50
14 A:Mauraders 1.50
15 Mutant Massacre, rep.
 Uncanny X-Men #221 . . . . . . 1.50

SACHS & VIOLENS
Epic
1 GP,PDd(s) 5.00
2 GP,PDd(s),V:Killer 3.25
3 GP,PDd(s),V:White Slavers . . 2.25
4 GP,PDd(s),D:Moloch 2.25

SAGA OF CRYSTAR
May, 1983

1 O:Crystar	2.25
2 A:Ika	1.50
3 A:Dr.Strange	1.50
4	1.50
5	1.50
6 A:Nightcrawler	2.00
7 I:Malachon	1.50
8	1.50
9	1.50
10 Chaos	1.50
11 Alpha Flight,February, 1985	2.00

SAGA OF ORIGINAL HUMAN TORCH

1 RB,O:Original Human Torch	3.00
2 RB,A:Toro	2.50
3 RB,V:Adolph Hitler	2.50
4 RB,Torch vs. Toro	2.50

ST. GEORGE
Epic
June, 1988

1 KJ,Shadow Line	1.25
2 KJ,I:Shrek	1.25
3 KJ	1.50
4 KJ	1.50
5	1.50
6	1.50
7 DSp	1.50
8 October, 1989	1.50

SAINT SINNER
Razorline

1 I:Phillip Fetter	2.75
2 F:Phillip Fetter	2.00
3 in Vertesque	2.00
4	2.00
5 Arcadia	2.00
6	2.00
7 The Child Stealer	2.00
8	1.95

SAM & MAX GO TO THE MOON

1 Dirtbag Special,w/Nirvana Tape	4.00

[Regular Series]

1 MMi,AAd,F:Skull Boy	3.25
2 AAd,MMi	2.95
3	2.95

SAMURAI CAT
Epic

1 I:MiaowaraTomokato	2.25
2 I:Con-Ed,V:Thpaghetti-Thoth	2.25
3 EmpireStateStrikesBack	2.25

SAVAGE COMBAT TALES
February, 1975

1 F:Sgt Strykers Death Squad	1.25
2 ATh,A:Warhawk	1.25
3 July, 1975	1.25

SAVAGE SWORD OF CONAN
August, 1974
(black & white magazine)

1 BWS,JB,NA,GK,O:Blackmark, 3rdA:Red Sonja,Boris(c)	75.00
2 NA(c),HC,GK,'Black Colossus,' B.U.King Kull;B.U.Blackmark	35.00
3 JB,BWS,GK,'At The Mountain of the Moon God;B.U.s: Kull;Blackmark	30.00
4 JB,RCo,GKIron Shadows in the Moon B.U.Blackmark,Boris(c)	15.00
5 JB,A WitchShall beBorn,Boris(c)	15.00
6 AN,'Sleeper 'Neath the Sands'	12.50
7 JB,Citadel at the Center of Time Boris(c)	12.50
8 inc.GK,'Corsairs against Stygia	12.50
9 Curse of the Cat-Goddess, Boris(c),B.U.King Kull	12.50
10 JB,'Sacred Serpent of Set' Boris(c)	10.00
11 JB,'The Abode of the Damned'	10.00
12 JB,Haunters of Castle Crimson Boris(c)	10.00
13 GK,The Thing in the Temple, B.U. Solomon Kane	10.00
14 NA,Shadow of Zamboula, B.U.Solomon Kane	10.00
15 JB,Boris(c),'Devil in Iron'	10.00
16 JB,BWS,People of the Black Circle,B.U.Bran Mak Morn	10.00
17 JB,'On to Yimsha!, B.U.Bran Mak Morn	10.00
18 JB,'The Battle of the Towers' B.U. Solomon Kane	10.00
19 JB,'Vengeance in Vendhya' B.U. Solomon Kane	10.00
20 JB,'The Slithering Shadow' B.U. Solomon Kane	10.00
21 JB,'Horror in the Red Tower'	10.00
22 JB,'Pool o/t Black One' B.U. Solomon Kane	10.00
23 JB,FT,'Torrent of Doom' B.U. Solomon Kane	10.00
24 JB,BWS,'Tower of the Elephant'B.U.Cimmeria	10.00
25 DG,SG,Jewels of Gwahlur, B.U.Solomon Kane.	10.00
26 JB/TD,Beyond the Black River, B.U.Solomon Kane	8.00
27 JB/TD,Children of Jhebbal Sag	8.00
28 JB/AA,Blood of the Gods	8.00
29 ECh,FT,Child of Sorcery, B.U. Red Sonja	8.00
30 FB,The Scarlet Citadel	8.00
31 JB/TD,The Flaming Knife,pt.1	8.00
32 JB/TD,Ghouls of Yanaldar,pt.2	8.00
33 GC,Curse of the Monolith, B.U.Solomon Kane	8.00
34 CI/AA,MP,Lair o/t Ice Worm;B.U. Solomon Kane,B.U.King Kull	8.00
35 ECh,Black Tears	8.00
36 JB,AA,Hawks over Shem	8.00
37 SB,Sons of the White Wolf B.U. Solomon Kane	8.00
38 JB/TD,The Road of the Eagles	8.00
39 SB/TD,The Legions of the Dead, B.U.Solomon Kane concl.	8.00
40 JB/TD,A Dream of Blood	8.00
41 JB/TD,Quest for the Cobra Crown A:Thoth-Amon,B.U.Sol.Kane	8.00
42 JB/TD,Devil-Tree of Gamburu, A:Thoth-Amon,B.U.Sol.Kane	8.00
43 JB/TD,King Thoth-Amon, B.U.King Kull	8.00
44 SB/TD,The Star of Khorala	8.00
45 JB/TD,The Gem in the Tower, B.U. King Kull	8.00
46 EC/TD,Moon of Blood, B.U. Hyborian Tale	8.00
47 GK/JB/JRu,Treasure of Tranicos	

Savage Sword of Conan #24
© Marvel Entertainment Group

C:Thoth-Amon	8.00
48 JB/KJ,A Wind Blows from Stygia C:Thoth-Amon	8.00
49 JB/TD,When Madness Wears the Crown, B.U.Hyborian Tale	6.00
50 JB/TD,Swords Across the Alimane	6.00
51 JB/TD,Satyrs' Blood	6.00
52 JB/TD,Conan the Liberator	6.00
53 JB,The Sorcerer and the Soul, B.U. Solomon Kane	6.00
54 JB,The Stalker Amid the Sands, B.U. Solomon Kane	6.00
55 JB,Black Lotus & Yellow Death B.U. King Kull	6.00
56 JB/TD,The Sword of Skelos	6.00
57 JB/TD,Zamboula	6.00
58 JB/TD,KGa,For the Throne of Zamboula,B.U.OlgerdVladislav	6.00
59 AA,ECh,City ofSkulls,B.U.Gault	6.00
60 JB,The Ivory Goddess	6.00
61 JB,Wizard Fiend of Zingara	6.00
62 JB/ECh,Temple of the Tiger, B.U. Solomon Kane	6.00
63 JB/ECh,TP/BMc,GK,Moat of Blood I:Chane of the Elder Earth	6.00
64 JB/ECh,GK,Children of Rhan, B.U. Chane	6.00
65 GK,JB,Fangs of the Serpent, B.U. Bront	6.00
66 thru 75	@6.00
76 thru 80	@5.00
81 JB/ECh,Palace of Pleasure, B.U. Bront	5.00
82 AA,BWS,Devil in the Dark.Pt.1 B.U.repConan#24,Swamp Gas	5.00
83 AA,MW,NA,ECh,Devil in the Dark Pt.2,B.U. Red Sonja,Sol.Kane	5.00
84 VM,Darksome Demon of Rabba Than	5.00
85 GK,Daughter of the God King	5.00
86 GK,Revenge of the Sorcerer	5.00
87	5.00
88 JB,Isle of the Hunter	5.00
89 AA,MW,Gamesman of Asgalun, B.U. Rite of Blood	5.00
90 JB,Devourer of Souls	5.00
91 JB,VM,Forest of Friends,	

B.U. The Beast,The Chain ... 5.00	
92 JB,The Jeweled Bird 5.00	
93 JB/ECh,WorldBeyond the Mists 5.00	
94 thru 101 .... @5.00	
102 GD,B.U.Bran Mac Morn 4.00	
103 GD,White Tiger of Vendhya,	
B.U. Bran Mac Morn 4.00	
104 .... 4.00	
105 .... 4.00	
106 Feud of Blood 4.00	
107 thru 118 .... @4.00	
119 ECh,A:Conan's Sister 4.00	
120 Star of Thama-Zhu 4.00	
121 .... 4.00	
122 .... 4.00	
123 ECh,Secret of the GreatStone 4.00	
124 ECh,Secret of the Stone 4.00	
125 Altar of the Goat God 4.00	
126 The Mercenary 4.00	
127 Reunion in Scarlet,Return	
of Valeria 4.00	
128 .... 4.00	
129 .... 4.00	
130 Reavers of the Steppes 4.00	
131 GI,Autumn of the Witch 4.00	
132 ECh,Masters o/t Broadsword . 4.00	
133 .... 4.00	
134 Conan the Pirate 4.00	
135 Conan the Pirate 4.00	
136 NKu,Stranded on DesertIsland 4.00	
137 ECh,The Lost Legion 4.00	
138 ECh,Clan o/t Lizard God 4.00	
139 ECh,A:Valeria 4.00	
140 ECh,The Ghost's Revenge .. 4.00	
141 ECh 4.00	
142 ECh,V:Warlord 4.00	
143 ECh 4.00	
144 ECh 4.00	
145 ECh 4.00	
146 ECh 4.00	
147 ECh 4.00	
148 BMc 4.00	
149 TGr,BMc,Conan Enslaved ... 4.00	
150 ECh 4.00	
151 ECh 4.00	
152 ECh,Valley Beyond the Stars 4.00	
153 Blood on the Sand,Pt.1 .... 4.00	
154 Blood on the Sand,Pt.2 ..... 4.00	
155 ECh,V:Vampires 4.00	
156 V:Corinthian Army 4.00	
157 V:Hyborians 4.00	
158 ECh,The Talisman-Gem 4.00	
159 Conan Enslaved 4.00	
160 .... 4.00	
161 V:Magician/Monsters 4.00	
162 AW,Horned God,B.U.Sol.Kane 3.00	
163 V:Picts 3.00	
164 Conan's Revenge 3.00	
165 B.U. King Kull 3.00	
166 ECh,Conan in New World,Pt.1 3.00	
167 ECh,Conan in New World,Pt.2 3.00	
168 ECh,Conan in New	
World,concl 3.00	
169 .... 3.00	
170 AW,A:Red Sonja,Valeria	
B.U. Solomon Kane 3.00	
171 TD,Conan Youth Story 2.50	
172 JS,JRu,Haunted Swamp,	
B.U.King Kull,Valeria,	
Red Sonja 2.50	
173 ECh,Under Siege 2.50	
174 AA,Red Stones of	
Rantha Karn 2.50	
175 The Demonslayer Sword 2.50	
176 FH,TT,V:Wizard,B.U. Witch	

Queen,Dagon,Ghouls 2.50	
177 LMc,TD,ECh,Conan the Prey,	
B.U.King Conan,Red Sonja ... 2.50	
178 AA,The Dinosaur God 2.50	
179 ECh,A:Red Sonja,Valeria,	
B.U.Conan 2.50	
180 ECh,Sky-God Bardisattva,	
B.U. King Kull 2.50	
181 TD,Conan the Pagan God?,	
B.U. Voodoo Tribe 2.50	
182 RB/RT,V:Killer Ants 2.50	
183 ECh,V:Kah-Tah-Dhen,	
B.U.King Kull 2.50	
184 AA,Return of Sennan 2.50	
185 The Ring of Molub 2.50	
186 AW,A:Thulsa Doom 2.50	
187 ECh,A:Conan's Brother? 2.50	
188 V:Kharban the Sorcerer 2.50	
189 A:Search Zukala for Gem ... 2.50	
190 JB/TD,Skull on the Seas,pt.1 . 2.25	
191 JB/ECh,Skull on the Seas,pt.2	
Thulsa Doom Vs.Thoth-Amon . 2.25	
192 JB/ECh,Skull on the Seas,pt.3	
B.U. King Kull 2.25	
193 JB/ECh,Skull on the Seas concl.	
V:Thulsa Doom & Thoth-Amon 2.25	
194 JB/ECh,Wanted for Murder,	
B.U. Li-Zya 2.25	
195 JB/ECh,V:Yamatains,	
Giant Tortoise 2.25	
196 JB/ECh,Treasure of the Stygian	
Prince-Toth-Mekri,A:Valeria ... 2.25	
197 RTs,JB,EC,Red Hand 2.25	
198 RTs,JB,EC,Red Hand 2.25	
199 RTs,JB,EC,V:Black Zarona .. 2.25	
200 RTs,JB,ECh,JJu(c),The Barbarian	
from Cross Plains 2.25	
201 RTs,MCW,return to Tarantia . 2.25	
202 RTs,JB,ECh,Conan in the City	
City of Magicians,pt.1 .... 2.25	
203 RTs,JB,ECh,Conan in the City	
City of Magicians,pt.2 .... 2.25	
204 RTs,JB,ECh,Conan in the City	
City of Magicians,pt.3 .... 2.25	
205 RTs,JB,ECh,Conan in the City	
City of Magicians,pt.4 .... 2.25	
206 RTs,JB,ECh,BLr(c),Conan in the	
City of Magicians,concl. 2.25	
207 RTs,JB,ECh,MK(c), Conan and	
the Spider God, pt.1 .... 2.25	
208 RTs,JB,ECh, Conan and the	
Spider God, pt.2 .... 2.25	
209 RTs,JB,Conan and the	
Spider God,pt.3 .... 2.25	
210 RTs,Conan and the	
Spider God,pt.4 .... 2.25	
211 RTs,Conan and the Gods of	
the Mountain,pt.1 .... 2.25	
212 RTs,Conand and the Gos of	
the Mountain,pt.2 .... 2.25	
213 RTs,Conan and the Gods of	
the Mountain,pt.3 .... 2.25	
214 RTs,Conan and the Gods of	
the Mountain,pt.4 .... 2.25	
215 RTs,JuB(c),Conan and the Gods	
of the Mountain,concl.. ...... 2.25	
216 RTs,AA,Vengeance of Nitocris 2.25	
217 RTs,Conan theMercenary,pt.1 2.25	
218 RTs,Conan theMercenary,pt.2 2.25	
219 RTs,A:Solomon Kane 2.25	
220 RTs,V:Skull Out of Time 2.25	
221 RTs,C.L.Moore story adapt. . 2.25	
222 RTs,The Haunter of the Towers	
B.U.JB,Conan Barbarian #1 .. 2.25	
223 RTs,A:Tuzune Thune 2.25	

224 RTs,JWk,The Dwellers Under the
Tombs,adapt. B.U.V:Dinosaurs 2.25
225 .... 2.25
226 RTs,EN(c),The Four Ages
of Conan, A:Red Sonja 2.25
227 RTs,JBu, besieged in a lost
city, B.U. Kull,Red Sonja 2.25
228 RTs,AN,Conan in chains! ... 2.25
229 RTs 2.25
230 RTs, Acheron falls, Ring of
Tkrubu,pt.2, R:Kull 2.25
231 RTs, V:Tuzoun Thune, B.U.
EM,Red Sonja 2.25
232 RTs 2.25
233 A:Juma the Black, Kull 2.25
234 RTs,JBu, A:Nefartari;
A:Red Sonja, Zula 2.25
235 RTs,JBu,The Daughter of
Raktauanishi, final issue 2.25
Ann.#1 SB,BWS,inc.'Beware the
Wrath of Anu',B.U. King
Kull Vs.Thulsa Doom 2.25

SAVAGE TALES
May, 1971
(black & white magazine)
1 GM,BWS,JR,I&O:Man-Thing,
B:Conan,Femizons,A:Kazar 100.00
2 GM,FB,BWS,AW,BWr,A:King
Kull rep,Creatures on
the Loose #10 .... 40.00
3 FB,BWS,AW,JSo 25.00
4 NA(c),E:Conan 16.00
5 JSn,JB,B:Brak the Barbarian 16.00
6 NA(c),JB,AW,B:Kazar 8.00
7 GM,NA 6.00
8 JB,A:Shanna,E:Brak 5.00
9 MK,A:Shanna 5.00
10 RH,NA,AW,A:Shanna 5.00
11 RH 5.00
12 Summer, 1975 .... 5.00
Ann.#1 GM,GK,BWS,O:Kazar ... 6.00

SAVAGE TALES
November, 1985
(black & white magazine)
1 MGo,I:The 'Nam 2.00
2 MGo 4.00
3 MGo 4.00
4 MGo 4.00
5 MGo 4.00
6 MGo 3.00
7 MGo 3.00
8 MGo 3.00
9 MGo,March, 1987 .... 3.00

SCARLET WITCH
1 ALa(s),DAn(s),JH,I:Gargan,
C:Master Pandemonium 2.00
2 C:Avengers West Coast 2.00
3 A:Avengers West Coast 2.00
4 V:Lore,last issue 2.00

SCOOBY-DOO
October, 1977
1 B:DynoMutt 1.50
2 thru 8 .... @1.00
9 February, 1979 .... 1.00

SECRET DEFENDERS
1 F:Dr.Strange(in all),Spider
Woman,Nomad,Darkhawk,
Wolverine,V:Macabre 3.25
2 F:Spider Woman,Nomad,Darkhawk,

Wolverine,V:Macabre 2.50
3 F:Spider Woman,Nomad,Darkhawk,
  Wolverine,V:Macabre 2.00
4 F:Namorita,Punisher,
  Sleepwalker,V:Roadkill 2.00
5 F:Naromita,Punisher,
  Sleepwalker, V:Roadkill 2.00
6 F:Spider-Man,Scarlet Witch,Captain
  America,V:Suicide Pack 2.00
7 F:Captain America,Scarlet Witch,
  Spider-Man 2.00
8 F:Captain America,Scarlet Witch,
  Spider-Man 2.00
9 F:War Machine,Thunderstrike,
  Silver Surfer 2.00
10 F:War Machine,Thunderstrike,
  Silver Surfer 2.00
11 TGb,F:Hulk,Nova,Northstar . . 2.00
12 RMz(s),TGb,F:Thanos 2.75
13 RMz(s),TGb,F:Thanos,Super Skrull,
  Rhino,Nitro,Titanium Man 2.00
14 RMz(s),TGb,F:Thanos,Super Skrull,
  Rhino,Nitro,Titanium Man,
  A:Silver Surfer 2.00
15 F:Dr.Druid,Cage,Deadpool . . . 2.25
16 F:Dr.Druid,Cage,Deadpool . . . 2.25
17 F:Dr.Druid,Cage,Deadpool . . . 2.25
18 F:Iron Fist,Giant Man 2.25
19 F:Dr.Druid,Cadaver,
  Shadowoman 1.95
20 V:Venom 1.95
21 V:Slaymaker 1.95
22 Final Defense,pt.1 . . . . 1.95
23 Final Defense,pt.2 . . . . 1.95
24 Final Defense,pt.3 . . . . 1.95
25 V:Dr.Druid 1.95

SECRET WARS
May, 1984
1 MZ,A:X-Men,Fant.Four,Avengers,
  Hulk,SpM in All,I:Beyonder . . . 4.00
2 MZ,V:Magneto 2.50
3 MZ,I:Titania & Volcana 2.50
4 BL,V:Molecule Man 2.50
5 BL,F:X-Men 2.50
6 MZ,V:Doctor Doom 2.00
7 MZ,I:New Spiderwoman 3.00
8 MZ,I:Alien Black Costume
  (for Spider-Man) 15.00
9 MZ,V:Galactus 2.00
10 MZ,V:Dr.Doom 2.00
11 MZ,V:Dr.Doom 2.00
12 MZ,Beyonder Vs. Dr.Doom . . . 2.50
TPB rep #1-#12 . . . . 19.95

SECRET WARS II
July, 1985
1 AM,SL,A:X-Men,New Mutants . 2.00
2 AM,SL,A:Fantastic Four 1.50
3 AM,SL,A:Daredevil 1.50
4 AM,I:Kurse 1.50
5 AM,SL,I:Boom Boom 2.50
6 AM,SL,A:Mephisto 1.50
7 AM,SL,A:Thing 1.50
8 AM,SL,A:Hulk 1.50
9 AM,SL,A:Everyone,double-size 2.00

SECTAURS
June, 1985
1 Based on toys 1.50
2 thru 10 1986 . . . . @1.00

SEMPER FI
December, 1988
1 JSe 2.00
2 JSe 1.50
3 JSe 1.50
4 JSe 1.50
5 JSe 1.50
6 . . . . 1.50
7 . . . . 1.00
8 . . . . 1.00
9 August, 1989,final issue 1.00

SENSATIONAL SPIDERMAN
1 KM/TP/KJ,Rep. 5.95

SERGEANT BARNEY BARKER
August, 1956
1 JSe,Comedy 70.00
2 JSe,Army Inspection(c) 50.00
3 JSe,Tank(c) 50.00
Becomes:

G.I. TALES
4 JSe,At Grips with the Enemy 35.00
5 . . . . 20.00
6 JO,BP,GWb, July, 1957 . . . . 25.00

Sgt. Fury #13
© *Marvel Entertainment Group*

SGT. FURY & HIS HOWLING COMMANDOS
May, 1963
1 Seven Against the Nazis . . 700.00
2 JK,Seven Doomed Men . . . 250.00
3 JK,Midnight on Massacre
  Mountain 150.00
4 JK,V:Lord Ha-Ha,D:Junior
  Juniper 150.00
5 JK,V:Baron Strucker 150.00
6 JK,The Fangs of the Fox . . 100.00
7 JK,Fury Court Martial 100.00
8 JK,V:Dr Zemo,I:Percival
  Pinkerton 100.00
9 DAy,V:Hitler 100.00
10 DAy,On to Okinwawa,I:Capt.
  Savage 100.00

11 DAy,V:Capt.Flint 50.00
12 DAy,Howler deserts 50.00
13 DAy,JK,A;Capt.America . . . 135.00
14 DAy,V:Baron Strucker 50.00
15 DAy,SD,Too Small to Fight
  Too Young to Die 50.00
16 DAy,In The Desert a Fortress
  Stands 50.00
17 DAy,While the Jungle Sleeps 50.00
18 DAy,Killed in Action 50.00
19 DAy,An Eye for an Eye 50.00
20 DAy,V:the Blitz Squad 50.00
21 DAy,To Free a Hostage 40.00
22 DAy,V:Bull McGiveney 40.00
23 DAy,The Man who Failed . . . 40.00
24 DAy,When the Howlers Hit
  the Home Front 40.00
25 DAy,Every Man my Enemy . . 40.00
26 DAy,Dum Dum Does it the
  Hard Way 40.00
27 DAy,O:Fury's Eyepatch 40.00
28 DAy,Not a Man Shall Remain
  Alive 40.00
29 DAy,V:Baron Strucker 40.00
30 DAy,Incident in Italy 40.00
31 Day,Into the Jaws of Death . . 25.00
32 DAy,A Traitor in Our Midst . . 25.00
33 DAy,The Grandeur That was
  Greece 25.00
34 DAy,O:Howling Commandoes 25.00
35 DAy,Berlin Breakout,J:Eric
  Koenig 25.00
36 DAy,My Brother My Enemy . . 25.00
37 DAy,In the Desert to Die 25.00
38 This Ones For Dino 25.00
39 Into the Fortress of Fear 25.00
40 That France Might be Free . 25.00
41 V:The Blitzers 25.00
42 Three Were AWOL 25.00
43 Scourge of the Sahara,A:Bob
  Hope,Glen Miller 25.00
44 JSe,The Howlers First Mission 25.00
45 JSe,I:The War Lover 25.00
46 DAy,They Also Serve 25.00
47 Tea and Sabotage 25.00
48 A:Blitz Squad 25.00
49 On to Tarawa 25.00
50 The Invasion Begins 25.00
51 The Assassin 25.00
52 Triumph at Treblinka 25.00
53 To the Bastions of Bavaria . . 25.00
54 Izzy Shoots the Works 25.00
55 Cry of Battle, Kiss of Death . . 20.00
56 Gabriel Blow Your Horn 20.00
57 TS,The Informer 20.00
58 Second Front 20.00
59 D-Day for Dum Dum 20.00
60 Authorised Personnel Only . 20.00
61 The Big Breakout 20.00
62 The Basic Training of Fury . . 20.00
63 V:Nazi Tanks 20.00
64 The Peacemonger,A:Capt
  Savage 20.00
65 Eric Koenig,Traitor 20.00
66 Liberty Rides the Underground 20.00
67 With a Little Help From My
  Friends 20.00
68 Welcome Home Soldier 20.00
69 While the City Sleeps 20.00
70 The Missouri Marauders 20.00
71 Burn,Bridge,Burn 20.00
72 Battle in the Sahara 20.00
73 Rampage on the
  Russian Front 20.00
74 Each Man Alone 20.00

All comics prices listed are for *Near Mint* condition.

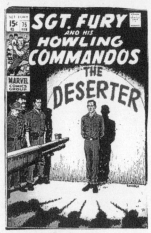

Sgt. Fury #75
© *Marvel Entertainment Group*

75 The Deserter 15.00
76 He Fought the Red Baron . . . 15.00
77 A Traitor's Trap,A:Eric Koenig 15.00
78 Escape or Die 15.00
79 Death in the High Castle 15.00
80 To Free a Hostage 15.00
81 The All American 15.00
82 Howlers Hit The
   Home Front,rep 15.00
83 Dum DumV:Man-Mountain
   McCoy 15.00
84 The Devil's Disciple 15.00
85 Fury V:The Howlers 15.00
86 Germ Warfare 15.00
87 Dum Dum does it...rep 15.00
88 Save General Patton 15.00
89 O:Fury's eyepatch,rep 15.00
90 The Chain That Binds 15.00
91 Not A Man...rep 12.00
92 Some Die Slowly 12.00
93 A Traitor...rep 12.00
94 GK(c),Who'll Stop the Bombs 12.00
95 7 Doomed Men, rep 12.00
96 GK(c),Dum-Dum Sees it
   Through 12.00
97 Till the Last Man Shall Fail . . 12.00
98 A:Deadly Dozen 12.00
99 Guerillas in Greece 12.00
100 When a Howler Falls 12.00
101 Pearl Harbor 7.00
102 Death For A Dollar 7.00
103 Berlin Breakout 7.00
104 The Tanks Are Coming 7.00
105 My Brother,My Enemy 7.00
106 Death on the Rhine 7.00
107 Death-Duel in the Desert . . . 7.00
108 Slaughter From the Skies . . . 7.00
109 This Ones For Dino,rep 7.00
110 JSe(c),The Reserve 7.00
111 V:Colonel Klaw 7.00
112 V:Baron Strucker 7.00
113 That France Might
    Be Free,rep 7.00
114 Jungle Bust Out 7.00
115 V:Baron Strucker 7.00
116 End of the Road 7.00
117 Blitz Over Britain 7.00
118 War Machine 7.00

118 War Machine 7.00
119 They Strike by Machine 7.00
120 Trapped in the Compound of
    Death 7.00
121 An Eye for an Eye 5.00
122 A;The Blitz Squad 5.00
123 To Free a Hostage 5.00
124 A:Bull McGiveney 5.00
125 The Man Who Failed 5.00
126 When the Howlers Hit Home.. 5.00
127 Everyman My Enemy,rep . . . 5.00
128 Dum Dum does it...rep 5.00
129 O:Fury's Eyepatch 5.00
130 A:Baron Strucker 5.00
131 Armageddon 5.00
132 Incident in Italy 5.00
133 thru 140 . . . . @5.00
141 thru 150 . . . . @5.00
151 thru 160 . . . . @4.00
161 thru 166 . . . . @4.00
167 December, 1981 . . . . 4.00
Ann.#1 Korea #4,#5 . . . . 80.00
Ann.#2 This was D-Day 40.00
Ann.#3 Vietnam 25.00
Ann.#4 Battle of the Bulge 15.00
Ann.#5 Desert Fox 7.50
Ann.#6 Blaze of Battle 7.50
Ann.#7 Armageddon 7.50

SEVEN BLOCK
Epic
1990
1 . . . . 2.50

SHADOWMASTERS
October, 1989
1 RH 11.00
2 . . . . 7.00
3 . . . . 6.00
4 January, 1990 . . . . 5.00

SHADOWRIDERS
1 I:Shadowriders,A:Cable,GR . . . 2.00
2 A:Ghost Rider 2.00
3 A:Cable 2.00
4 A:Cable 2.00

SHANNA, THE SHE-DEVIL
December, 1972
1 GT,F:Shanna 7.50
2 RA,The Dungeon of Doom . . . 5.00
3 RA,The Hour of the Bull 3.00
4 RA,Mandrill 3.00
5 JR(c),RA,V:Nekra, Aug., 1973   3.00

SHEENA
December, 1984
1 Movie Adapt 1.00
2 February, 1985 . . . . 1.00

SHE-HULK
February, 1980
[1st Regular Series]
1 JB,BWi,I&O:She-Hulk 4.00
2 BWi,D:She-Hulk's best friend . . 2.50
3 BWi,Wanted for Murder 2.50
4 BWi,V:Her Father 2.50
5 BWi,V:Silver Serpent 2.50
6 A:Iron Man 2.00
7 BWi,A:Manthing 2.00
8 BWi,A:Manthing 2.00
9 BWi,Identity Crisis 2.00
10 V:The Word 2.00

11 BWi,V:Dr.Morbius 2.00
12 V:Gemini 2.00
13 V:Man-Wolf 1.50
14 V:Hellcat 1.50
15 V:Lady Kills 1.50
16 She Hulk Goes Berserk 1.50
17 V:Man-Elephant 1.50
18 V:Grappler 1.50
19 V:Her Father 1.50
20 A:Zapper 1.50
21 V:Seeker 1.50
22 V:Radius 1.50
23 V:Radius 1.50
24 V:Zapper 1.50
25 Double-sized,last issue 2.00
[2nd Regular Series]
1 JBy,V:Ringmaster 2.50
2 JBy 2.25
3 JBy,A:Spider-Man 2.25
4 JBy,I:Blond Phantom 2.25
5 JBy 2.25
6 JBy,A:U.S.1,Razorback 2.25
7 JBy,A:U.S.1,Razorback 2.25
8 JBy,A:Saint Nicholas 2.25
9 AM(i) 2.00
10 AM(i) 2.00
11 . . . . 2.00
12 . . . . 2.00
13 SK(c) 2.00
14 MT(c),A:Howard the Duck . . . 2.00
15 SK(c) 2.00
16 SK(c) 2.00
17 SK(c),V:Dr.Angst 2.00
18 SK(c) 2.00
19 SK(c),V:Nosferata 2.00
20 SK(c),Darkham Asylum 2.00
21 SK(c),V:Blonde Phantom 2.00
22 SK(c),V:Blonde Phantom,A:All
   Winners Squad 2.00
23 V:Blonde Phantom 2.00
24 V:Deaths'Head 4.00
25 A:Hercules,Thor 2.00
26 A:Excalibur 2.00
27 Cartoons in N.Y. 2.00
28 Game Hunter Stalks She-Hulk   2.00
29 A:Wolv.,Hulk,SpM,Venom . . . 2.50
30 MZ(c),A:Silver Surfer,Thor
   Human Torch 2.25
31 JBy,V:Spragg the Living Hill . . 2.50
32 JBy,A:Moleman,V:Spragg . . . 2.00
33 JBy,A:Moleman,V:Spragg . . . 2.00
34 JBy,Returns to New York 2.00
35 JBy,V:X-Humed Men 2.00
36 JBy,X-mas issue (#8 tie-in) . . . 2.00
37 JBy,V:Living Eraser 2.00
38 JBy,V:Mahkizmo 2.00
39 JBy,V:Mahkizmo 2.00
40 JBy,V:Spraggs,Xemnu 2.00
41 JBy,V:Xemnu 2.00
42 JBy,V:USArcher 2.00
43 JBy,V:Xemnu 2.00
44 JBy,R:Rocket Raccoon 2.00
45 JBy,A:Razorback 2.00
46 JBy,A:Rocket Raccoon 2.00
47 V:D'Bari 2.00
48 JBy,A:Rocket Raccoon 2.00
49 V:Skrulls,D'Bari 2.00
50 JBy,WS,TA,DGb,AH,HC,
   D:She-Hulk 4.00
51 TMo,V:Savage She-Hulk 2.00
52 D:She-Hulk,A:Thing,Mr.Fantastic,
   I:Rumbler,V:Titania 2.00
53 AH(c),A:Zapper 2.00
54 MGo(c),A:Wonder Man 2.00

55 V:Rumbler 2.00
56 A:War Zone 2.00
57 A:Hulk 2.00
58 V:Electro 2.00
59 V:Various Villains 2.00
60 last issue 2.00
TPB rep. #1–#8 . . . . 12.95

SHE HULK: CEREMONY
1 JBr/SDr 4.00
2 JBr/FS 4.00

SHIELD
February, 1973
1 . . . . 5.00
2 . . . . 3.00
3 . . . . 3.00
4 . . . . 3.00
5 October, 1973 . . . . 3.00

SHOGUN WARRIORS
February, 1979
1 HT,DGr,F:Raydeen, Combatra,
  Dangard Ace 4.00
2 HT,DGr,V:Elementals of Evil . . 2.50
3 AM(c),HT,DGr,V:Elementals
  of Evil 2.50
4 HT,DGr,'Menace of the
  Mech Monsters' 2.50
5 HT,DGr,'Into The Lair
  of Demons' 2.50
6 HT,ME 2.00
7 HT,ME 2.00
8 HT,ME 2.00
9 'War Beneath The Waves' . . . 2.00
10 'Five Heads of Doom' 2.00
11 TA(c) 2.00
12 WS(c) 2.00
13 'Demons on the Moon' 2.00
14 V:Dr. Demonicus 2.00
15 . . . . 2.00
16 . . . . 2.00
17 . . . . 2.00
18 . . . . 2.00
19 A:Fantastic Four 2.50
20 September, 1980 . . . . 2.00

SHROUD
Limited Series
1 B:MiB(s),MCW,A:Spider-Man,
  V:Scorpion 2.00
2 MCW,A:Spider-Man,V:Scorpion 2.00
3 MCW,I:Kali 2.00
4 MCW,Final Issue 2.00

SILVERHAWKS
August, 1987
1 thru 5 . . . . @1.00
6 June, 1988 . . . . 1.00

SILVER SABLE
1 Foil stamped(c),A:Sandman,
  Spider-Man 3.50
2 I:Gattling 2.00
3 V:Gattling,Foreigner 1.75
4 Infinity War,V:Doctor Doom . . 1.75
5 Infinity War,V:Doctor Doom . . 1.50
6 A:Deathlok 1.50
7 A:Deathlok 1.50
8 V:Hydra 1.50
9 O:Silver Sable 1.50
10 A:Punisher,Leviathan 1.50
11 Cyber Warriors,Hydra 1.50

Silver Sable #2
© Marvel Entertainment Group

12 V:Cyberwarriorss,R:Sandman . 1.50
13 For Love Nor Money#3,
  A:Cage,Terror 1.50
14 For Love Nor Money#6,
  A:Cage,Terror 1.50
15 V:Viper,A:Captain America . . . 1.50
16 SBt,Infinty Crusade 1.50
17 Infinity Crusade 1.50
18 A:Venom 1.50
19 Siege of Darkness x-over 1.50
20 GWt(s),StB,BU:Sandman,Fin . 1.50
21 Gang War 1.50
22 . . . . 1.50
23 GWt(s),A:Deadpool,Daredevil,
  BU:Sandman 1.50
24 GWt(s),BU:Crippler,w/card . . . 1.75
25 V:Hydra 2.25
26 F:Sandman 1.75
27 A:Code Blue 1.50
28 F:Chen 1.50
29 A:Wild Pack 1.50
30 problems with law 1.50
31 V:terrorists 1.50
32 A:The Foreigner 1.50
33 V:Hammerhead 1.50
34 . . . . 1.50
35 Li'l Silvie Tale 1.50

SILVER SURFER
[1st Series]
August, 1968
1 B:StL(s),JB,JSr,GC,O:Silver Surfer,
  O:Watcher,I:Shala Bal 410.00
2 JB,JSr,GC,A:Watcher 150.00
3 JB,JSr,GC,I:Mephisto 125.00
4 JB,A:Thor,low distribution
  scarce 385.00
5 JB,A:Fant.Four,V:Stranger . . . 80.00
6 JB,FB,A:Watcher 90.00
7 JB,A:Watcher,I:Frankenstein's
  Monster 80.00
8 JB,DA,A:Mephisto,I:Ghost . . . 60.00
9 JB,DA,A:Mephisto,A:Ghost . . . 60.00
10 JB,DA,South America 60.00
11 JB,DA 50.00

12 JB,DA,V:The Abomination . . . 50.00
13 JB,DA,V:Doomsday Man . . . 50.00
14 JB,DA,A:Spider-Man 70.00
15 JB,DA,A:Human Torch 50.00
16 JB,V:Mephisto 50.00
17 JB,V:Mephisto 50.00
18 E:StL(s),JK,V:Inhumans 50.00
[2nd Regular Series]
1 JBy,TP,Direct Only,V:Mephisto 10.00
[3rd Regular Series]
1 MR,JRu,A:Fantastic Four,
  Galactus,V:Champion 12.00
2 MR,A:Shalla Bal,V:Skrulls 8.00
3 MR,V:Collector & Runner 7.00
4 MR,JRu,A:Elders,I:Obliterator . 7.00
5 MR,JRu,V:Obliterator 6.00
6 MR,JRu,O:Obliterator,A:Kree,
  Skrulls 6.00
7 MR,JRu,V:Supremor,Elders/
  Soul Gems 5.00
8 MR,JRu,V:Supremor 5.00
9 MR,Elders Vs.Galactus 5.00
10 MR,A:Galactus,Eternity 5.00
11 JSon,JRu,V:Reptyl 4.50
12 MR,JRu,V:Reptyl,A:Nova 4.50
13 JSon,DC,V:Ronan 4.50
14 JSon,JRu,V:Skrull Surfer 4.50
15 RLm,JRu,A:Fantastic Four . . 12.00
16 RLm,Inbetweener possesses
  Soul Gem,A:Fantastic Four . . . 6.00
17 RLm,A:Inbetweener,Galactus,
  Fantastic Four,D:Trader,
  Possessor,Astronomer 5.00
18 RLm,Galactus V:Inbetweener . 5.00
19 RLm,MR,V:Firelord 4.50
20 RLm,A:Superskrull,Galactus . 4.50
21 MR,DC,V:Obliterator 4.50
22 RLm,V:Ego 4.50
23 RLm,V:Dragon 4.50
24 RLm,V:G.I.G.O. 4.50
25 RLm,V:Ronan,Kree Skrull War 4.50
26 RLm,V:Nenora 4.50
27 RLm,V:Stranger 4.50
28 RLm,D:Super Skrull,V:Reptyl . 4.50
29 RLm,V:Midnight Sun 4.50
30 RLm,V:Midnight Sun 4.50
31 RLm,O:Living Tribunal &
  Stranger (double size) 5.50
32 RF,JSt,A:Mephisto 4.50
33 Rlm,V:Impossible Man 4.50
34 RLm,(1stJSn),2nd R:Thanos . 14.00
35 RLm,A:Thanos,R:Drax 11.00
36 RLm,V:Impossible Man,A:Warlock
  Capt.Marvel,C:Thanos 8.50
37 RLm,V:Drax,A:Mentor 7.00
38 RLm,V:Thanos(continued in
  Thanos Quest) 10.00
39 JSh,V:Algol 3.50
40 RLm,V:Dynamo City 4.00
41 RLm,V:Dynamo City,A:Thanos 5.00
42 RLm,V:Dynamo City,A:Drax . . 4.00
43 RLm,V:DynamoCity 4.00
44 RLm,R:Thanos,Drax,
  O:Inf.Gems 5.50
45 RLm,Thanos vs. Mephisto . . . 7.00
46 RLm,R:Warlock,A:Thanos . . . 10.00
47 RLm,Warlock V:Drax,
  A:Thanos 9.00
48 RLm,A:Galactus,Thanos 6.00
49 RLm,V:Thanos Monster 5.00
50 RLm,Silver Stamp(D.size),
  V:Thanos Monster 10.00
50a 2nd printing 4.00
50b 3rd printing 2.50
51 RLm,Infinity Gauntlet x-over . . 4.00

All comics prices listed are for *Near Mint* condition.   **CVA Page 221**

52 RLm,Infinity Gauntlet x-over . . 3.00
53 RLm,Infinity Gauntlet x-over . . 2.50
54 RLm,I.Gauntlet x-over,V:Rhino 2.50
55 RLm,I.Gauntlet x-over,Universe
   According to Thanos,pt.1 . . . . 2.50
56 RLm,I.Gauntlet x-over,Universe
   According to Thanos,pt.2 . . . . 2.50
57 RLm,Infinity Gauntlet x-over . . 2.50
58 RLm(c),Infinity Gauntlet x-over,
   A:Hulk,Namor,Dr.Strange 2.50
59 RLm(c),TR,Infinity Gauntlet,
   Thanos V:Silver Surfer 2.50
60 RLm,V:Midnight Sun,
   A:Inhumans 2.00
61 RLm,I:Collection.Agency 2.00
62 RLm,O:Collection Agency 2.00
63 RLm,A:Captain Marvel 2.00
64 RLm,V:Dark Silver Surfer 2.00
65 RLm,R:Reptyl,I:Princess
   Alaisa 2.00
66 RLm,I:Avatar,Love & Hate . . . 2.00
67 RLm(c),KWe,Inf.War,V:Galactus
   A:DrStrange 2.00
68 RLm(c),KWe,Inf.War,O:Nova . . 2.00
69 RLm(c),KWe,Infinity War,
   A:Galactus 2.00
70 RLm(c),Herald War#1,I:Morg . 2.00
71 RLm(c),Herald War#2,V:Morg . 2.00
72 RLm(c),Herald War#3,R:Nova . 2.00

Silver Surfer #5
© *Marvel Entertainment Group*

73 RLm,R:Airwalker 2.00
74 RLm,V:Terrax 2.00
75 RLm,E:Herald Ordeal,V:Morg,
   D:Nova 3.00
76 RLm,A:Jack of Hearts 1.50
77 RLm,A:Jack of Hearts 1.50
78 RLm,R:Morg,V:Nebula 1.50
79 RLm,V:Captain Atlas 1.50
80 RLm,I:Ganymede,Terrax
   Vs.Morg 1.50
81 RLm,O:Ganymedel:Tyrant . . . 1.50
82 RLm,V:Tyrant,double sized . . . 2.50
83 Infinity Crusade 1.50
84 RLm(c),Infinity Crusade 1.50
85 RLm(c),Infinity Crusade 2.50
86 RLm(c), Blood & Thunder,pt.2

V:Thor,A:Beta Ray Bill 1.50
87 RLm(c),Blood & Thunder,pt.7 . 1.50
88 RLm(c),Blood & Thunder,pt.10 1.50
89 RLm(c),CDo,C:Legacy 1.50
90 RLm(c),A:Legacy,C:Avatar . . . 1.50
91 RLm 1.50
92 RLm,V:Avatar 1.75
93 V:Human Torch 1.75
94 A:Fantastic Four, Warlock . . . 1.75
95 SEa,A:Fantastic Four 1.50
96 A:Fantastic Four,Hulk 1.50
97 A:Fantastic Four,R:Nova 1.50
98 R:Champion 1.50
99 A:Nova 1.50
100 V:Mephisto 2.25
100a enhanced ed. 3.95
101 RMz,JoP,A:Shalla Bal 1.50
102 V:Galactus 1.50
103 I:Death quad 1.50
104 Surfer Rampage 1.50
105 V:Super Skrull 1.50
106 A:Legacy,Morg 1.50
Ann.#1 RLm,JSon,Evolution War . 7.00
Ann.#2 RLm,Atlantis Attacks . . . 5.00
Ann.#3 RLm,Lifeform #4 . . . . . . 4.00
Ann.#4 RLm,Korvac Quest #3,A:
   Guardians of Galaxy 3.00
Ann.#5 RLm,Ret.o/Defenders #3 . 2.50
Ann.#6 RLm(c),I:Legacy,w/card . 3.75
GNv The Enslavers,KP 16.95
GNv Homecoming,
   A:Moondragon 12.95
TPB Rebirth of Thanos,reprints
   #34-38 . . . . 12.95
Ashcan .75

SILVER SURFER
Epic
December, 1988
1 Moebius,V:Galactus 3.00
2 Moebius,V:Galactus 3.00
Graphic Novel 14.95

SILVER SURFER
THE ENSLAVERS
1 KP 16.95

SILVER SURFER VS.
DRACULA
1 rep,MWn(s),GC,TP 1.75

SILVER SURFER/
WARLOCK:
RESURRECTION
1 JSn,V:Mephisto,Death 3.50
2 JSn,TA,V:Death 3.00
3 JSn,TA,V:Mephisto 3.00
4 JSn,TA,V:Mephisto 3.00

SISTERHOOD OF STEEL
Epic
December, 1984
1 I:Sisterhood 2.00
2 . . . . 2.00
3 . . . . 2.00
4 thru 8 . . . . @1.50

SIX FROM SIRIUS
Epic
July, 1984
1 PG,limited series 3.00
2 PG 2.00

3 PG 2.00
4 PG 2.00

SIX FROM SIRIUS II
Epic
February, 1986
1 PG 1.75

SIX-GUN WESTERN
Atlas
January, 1957
1 JSe(c),RC,JR,'Kid Yukon
   Gunslinger' 100.00
2 SSh,AW,DAy,JO,'His Guns
   Hang Low' 75.00
3 AW,BP,DAy 75.00
4 JSe(c),JR,GWb 50.00

SKELETON WARRIORS
1 based on cartoon 1.50
2 Legion of Light 1.50
3 V:Grimstar 1.50
4 Grimskull abandons Legion
   of Light 1.50

SKULL, THE SLAYER
August, 1975
1 GK(c),O:Skull the Slayer 2.50
2 GK(c),'Man Against Gods' . . . 1.50
3 'Trapped in the Tower
   of Time' 1.50
4 'Peril of the Pyramids',
   A:Black Knight 1.50
5 A:Black Knight 1.50
6 'The Savage Sea' 1.50
7 'Dungeon of Blood' 1.50
8 JK(c),November, 1976 . . . . . . 1.50

SLAPSTICK
1 TA(i),I:Slapstick 1.50
2 TA(i),A:Spider-Man,V:Overkill . 1.25
3 V:Dr.Denton 1.25
4 A:GR,DD,FF,Cap.America 1.25

SLEDGE HAMMER
February, 1988
1 . . . . 1.25
2 March, 1988 . . . . 1.00

SLEEPWALKER
June, 1991
1 BBI,I:Rick Sheridan,C:8-Ball . . . 5.00
2 BBI,V:8-Ball 4.00
3 BBI,A:Avengers,X-Men,X-Factor,
   FF,I:Cobweb,O:Sleepwalker . . 3.00
4 RL,I:Bookworm 2.00
5 BBI,A:SpM,K.Pin,V:Ringleader . 2.00
6 BBI,A:SpM,Inf.Gauntlet x-over . 2.00
7 BBI,Infinity Gauntlet x-over,
   V:Chain Gang 2.00
8 BBI,A:Deathlok 1.50
9 BBI,I:Lullabye 1.50
10 BBI,MM,I:Dream-Team 1.50
11 BBI,V:Ghost Rider 1.50
12 JQ,A:Nightmare 2.50
13 BBI,MM,I:Spectra 1.50
14 BBI,MM,V:Spectra 1.50
15 BBI,MM,I:Thought Police 1.50
16 BBI,MM,A:Mr.Fantastic,Thing . 1.50
17 BBI,A:Spider-Man,Darkhawk,
   V:Brotherhood o/Evil Mutants . 1.50
18 JQ(c),Inf.War,A:Prof.X 1.50
19 V:Cobweb,w/pop out Halloween

Mask 2.00
20 V:Chain Gang,Cobweb 1.50
21 V:Hobgoblin 1.50
22 V:Hobgoblin,8-Ball 1.50
23 V:Cobweb,Chain Gang 1.50
24 Mindfield#6 . . . . 1.50
25 O:Sleepwalker,Holo-grafx(c) . . 3.50
26 V:Mindspawn 1.50
27 A:Avengers 1.50
28 I:Psyko 1.50
29 DG,V:Psyko 1.50
30 V:Psyko 1.50
31 DG(ci),A:Spectra 1.50
32 V:Psyko 1.50
33 V:Mindspawn,Last issue 1.50
Holiday Spec.#1 JQ(c) 2.25

SLEEZE BROTHERS
August, 1989
1 Private Eyes 1.75
2 thru 6 . . . . @1.75

SMURFS
December, 1982
1 thru 3 . . . . @1.00
Treasury Edition 2.50

SOLARMAN
January, 1989
1 JM 1.25
2 MZ/NR,A:Dr.Doom, May, 1990 . 1.25

SOLO
[Limited Series]
1 RoR,I:Cygnus 1.75
2 RoR,V:A.R.E.S. 1.75
3 RoR,V:Spidey 1.75
4 final issue 1.75

SOLO AVENGERS
December, 1987
1 MBr,JRu,JLe,AW,Hawkeye;
 Mockingbird 6.00
2 MBr,JRu,KD,BMc,Hawkeye;
 Capt.Marvel 1.50
3 MBr,JRu,BH,SDr,Hawkeye;
 Moon Knight 1.50
4 RLm,JRu,PR,BL,Hawkeye;
 Black Knight 2.00
5 MBr,JRu,JRy,Hawkeye;
 Scarlet Witch 1.50
6 MBr,JRu,TGr,Hawkeye;Falcon . 1.25
7 MBr,JG,BL,Hawkeye;Bl.Widow . 1.25
8 MBr,Hawkeye;Dr.Pym 1.25
9 MBr,JBr,SDr,Hawkeye;Hellcat . 1.25
10 MBr,LW,Hawkeye;Dr.Druid . . . 1.25
11 MBr,JG,BL,Hawkeye;Hercules . 1.25
12 RLm,SDr,Hawkeye; New
 Yellow Jacket 2.00
13 RLm,JG,Hawkeye;WonderMan 2.00
14 AM,AD,JRu,Hawkeye;She-Hulk 1.25
15 AM,Hawkeye;Wasp 1.25
16 AM,DP,JA,Hawkeye;
 Moondragon 1.25
17 AM,DH,DC,Hawkeye;
 Sub-Mariner 1.25
18 RW,DH,Hawkeye;Moondragon 1.25
19 RW,DH,Hawkeye,BlackPanther 1.25
20 RW,DH,Hawkeye;Moondragon 1.25
Becomes:
 AVENGERS SPOTLIGHT

SOLOMON KANE
September, 1985
1 F:Solomon Kane 1.50
2 . . . . 1.00
3 BBI,'Blades of the Brotherhood' 1.00
4 MMi 1.00
5 'Hills of the Dead' 1.00
6 . . . . 1.00

SON OF SATAN
December, 1975
1 GK(c),JM,F:Daimon Hellstrom 15.00
2 Demon War,O:Possessor 9.00
3 . . . . 6.00
4 The Faces of Fear 6.00
5 V:Mind Star 6.00
6 A World Gone Mad 6.00
7 Mirror of Judgement 6.00
8 RH,To End in Nightmare
 February, 1977 . . . . 6.00

SOVIET SUPER SOLDIERS
1 AMe,JS,I:Redmont 4 . . . . 2.00

SPACEMAN
Atlas
September, 1953
1 BEv(c),F:Speed Carter and
 the Space Sentinals 350.00
2 JMn,'Trapped in Space' . . . 250.00
3 BEv(c),JMn,V:Ice Monster . 200.00
4 JMn 200.00
5 GT 200.00
6 JMn,'The Thing From Outer
 Space',October, 1954 . . . . 200.00

Space Squadron #4
© Marvel Entertainment Group

SPACE SQUADRON
Atlas
June, 1951
1 F:Capt. Jet Dixon,Blast,Dawn,
 Revere,Rusty Blake 350.00
2 GT(c) 300.00
3 'Planet of Madness',GT 250.00
4 . . . . 250.00
5 . . . . 250.00
Becomes:

SPACE WORLDS
April, 1952
6 'Midnight Horror' 225.00

SPECIAL COLLECTOR'S EDITION
December, 1975
1 Kung-Fu,Iron Fist 6.00

SPECIAL MARVEL EDITION
January, 1971
1 JK,B:Thor,B:Reprints 6.00
2 JK,V:Absorbing Man 5.00
3 JK,'While a Universe
 Trembles' 5.00
4 JK,'Hammer and the Holocaust',
 E:Thor 5.00
5 JSe(c),JK,DAy,B:Sgt. Fury . . . 5.00
6 HT(c),DAy,'Death Ray of
 Dr. Zemo' 4.00
7 DAy,V:Baron Strucker 4.00
8 JSe(c),DAy'On To Okinawa' . . 4.00
9 DAy,'Crackdown of
 Captain Flint 4.00
10 DAy 4.00
11 JK,DAy,A:Captaim
 America & Bucky 4.00
12 DAy,V:Baron Strucker 4.00
13 JK/DAy(c),DAy,SD,'Too Small
 to Fight, Too Young To Die' . 4.00
14 DAy,E:Reprints,Sgt. Fury 4.00
15 JSn,AM,I:Shang-Chi & Master of
 Kung Fu,I&O:Nayland Smith,
 Dr. Petrie 35.00
16 JSn,AM,I&O:Midnight 25.00
KingSz.Ann.#1 A:Iron Fist 7.00
Becomes:
 MASTER OF KUNG FU

SPECTACULAR SPIDER-MAN
July, 1968
(magazine)
1 . . . . 65.00
2 V:Green Goblin,Nov.1968 . . 110.00

SPECTACULAR SPIDER-MAN
December, 1976
Prev: Peter Parker
134 SB,A:Sin-Eater,V:Electro 4.50
135 SB,A:Sin-Eater,V:Electro 3.00
136 SB,D:Sin-Eater,V:Electro 3.00
137 SB,I:Tarantula II 3.00
138 SB,A:Capt.A.,V:TarantulaII . . 3.00
139 SB,O:Tombstone 4.00
140 SB,A:Punisher,V:Tombstone . 5.00
141 SB,A:Punisher,V:Tombstone . 8.00
142 SB,A:Punisher,V:Tombstone . 7.00
143 SB,A:Punisher,D:Persuader,
 I:Lobo Brothers. 7.00
144 SB,V:Boomerang 3.00
145 SB,A:Boomerang 3.00
146 SB,R:Green Goblin 5.00
147 SB,V:Hobgoblin (Demonic
 Power) 17.00
148 SB,Inferno 3.00
149 SB,V:Carrion II 5.00
150 SB,A:Tombstone,Trial
 J.Robertson 3.00
151 SB,V:Tombstone 3.00

---

152 SB,O:Lobo Bros.,A:Punisher,
  Tombstone 4.00
153 SB,V:Hammerhead,A:
  Tombstone 3.00
154 SB,V:Lobo Bros.,Puma 3.00
155 SB,V,Tombstone 3.00
156 SB,V:Banjo,A:Tombstone . . 3.00
157 SB,V:Shocker,Electro,
  A:Tombstone 3.00
158 SB,Super Spider Spec.,
  I:Cosmic Spider-Man 11.00
159 Cosmic Powers,V:Brothers
  Grimm 7.00
160 SB,A:Hydro Man,Shocker,
  Rhino,Dr.Doom 6.00
161 SB,V:Hobgoblin,Hammerhead,
  Tombstone 3.00
162 SB,V:Hobgoblin,Carrion II . . 3.00
163 SB,V:Hobgoblin,D:Carrion II . 3.00
164 SB,V:Beetle 2.75
165 SB,SDr,D:Arranger,I:Knight
  & Fogg 2.50
166 SB,O:Knight & Fogg 2.50
167 SB,D:Knight & Fogg 2.50
168 SB,A:Kingpin,Puma,
  Avengers 2.50
169 SB,I:Outlaws,A:R.Racer,
  Prowler,Puma,Sandman 2.50
170 SB,A:Avengers,Outlaws 2.50
171 SB,V:Puma 2.50
172 SB,V:Puma 2.50
173 SB,V:Puma 2.50
174 SB,A:Dr.Octopus 2.50
175 SB,A:Dr.Octopus 2.50
176 SB,I:Karona 2.50
177 SB,V:Karona,A:Mr.Fantastic . 2.50
178 SB,B:Child Within,V:Green
  Goblin, A:Vermin 3.50
179 SB,V:Green Goblin,Vermin . . 3.00
180 SB,V:Green Goblin,Vermin . . 3.00
181 SB,V:Green Goblin 3.00
182 SB,V:Green Goblin 3.00
183 SB,V:Green Goblin 3.00
184 SB,E:Child Within,V:Green
  Goblin 3.00
185 SB,A:Frogman,White Rabbit . 2.00
186 SB,B:FuneralArrangements
  V:Vulture 2.00
187 SB,V:Vulture 2.00
188 SB,E:Funeral Arrangements
  V:Vulture 2.00
189 SB,30th Ann.,Hologram(c),
  V:Green Goblin 8.00
189a Gold 2nd printing 3.25
190 SB,V:Rhino,Harry Osborn . . 2.00
191 SB,Eye of the Puma 1.75
192 SB,Eye of the Puma 1.75
193 SB,Eye of the Puma 1.75
194 SB,Death of Vermin#1 . . . . . 1.75
195 SB,Death of Vermin#2 . . . . . 1.75
195a Dirtbag Spec,w/Dirt#4 tape . 2.50
196 SB,Death of Vermin#3 . . . . . 1.75
197 SB,A:X-Men,V:Prof.Power . . . 1.75
198 SB,A:X-Men,V:Prof.Power . . . 1.75
199 SB,A:X-Men,Green Goblin . . 2.00
200 SB,V:Green Goblin,D:Harry
  Osborn,Holografx(c) 5.00
201 SB,Total Carnage,V:Carnage,
  Shriek,A:Black Cat,Venom . . . 1.75
202 SB,Total Carnage#9,A:Venom,
  V:Carnage 1.75
203 SB,Maximum Carnage#13 . 1.50
204 SB,A:Tombstone 1.50
205 StG(s),SB,V:Tombstone,
  A:Black Cat 1.50

206 SB,V:Tombstone 1.50
207 SB,A:The Shroud 1.50
208 SB,A:The Shroud 1.50
209 StB,SB,I:Dead Aim,
  BU:Black Cat 1.50
210 StB,SB,V:Dead Aim,
  BU:Black Cat 1.50
211 Pursuit#2,V:Tracer 1.50
212 . . . . 1.50
213 ANo(s),V:Typhiod Mary,w/cel 3.25
213a Newsstand Ed. 1.75
214 V:Bloody Mary 1.75
215 V:Scorpion 1.50
216 V:Scorpion 1.50
217 V:Judas Traveller,clone 1.50
217a Foil(c),bonus stuff 2.95
218 V:Puma 1.50
219 Back from the Edge,pt.2 . . . . 1.50
220 Web of Death,pt.3 . . . . 1.50
221 Web of Death,finale 1.50
222 The Price of Truth 1.50
223 Aftershocks,pt.4 . . . . 1.50
223a enhanced cover 2.95
224 The Mark of Kaine,pt.4 . . . . . 1.50
225 SB,TDF,BSz,I:New Green
  Goblin, 48pg.s 2.95
225a,3-D HoloDisk Cover 3.95
226 SB,BSz,The Trial of Peter
  Parker,pt.4, identity revealed . . 2.95
Ann.#8 MBa,RLm,TD,Evolutionary
  Wars,O:Gwen Stacy Clone . . . 5.00
Ann.#9 DR,MG,DJu,MBa,Atlantis
  Attacks 4.00
Ann.#10 SLi(c),RB,MM,TM,RA . . . 6.00
Ann.#11 EL(c),RWi,Vib.Vendetta . 2.50
Ann.#12 Hero Killers#2,A:New
  Warriors,BU:Venom 4.50
Ann.#13 I:Noctune,w/Card 3.25
Ann.#14 V:Green Goblin 2.95

SPEEDBALL
September, 1988

1 SD,JG,O:Speedball 2.00
2 SD,JG,V:Sticker,Graffiti Gorillas 1.50
3 SD,V:Leaper Logan 1.25
4 SD,DA,Ghost Springdale High . 1.25
5 SD,V:Basher 1.25
6 SD,V:Bug-Eyed Voice 1.25
7 SD,V:Harlequin Hit Man 1.25
8 SD,V:Bonehead Gang 1.25
9 SD,V:Nathan Boder 1.25
10 SD,V:Mutated Pigs,Killer
  Chickens, last issue 1.25

SPELLBOUND
Atlas
March, 1952

1 'Step into my Coffin' 300.00
2 BEv,RH,'Horror Story',
  A:Edgar A. Poe 150.00
3 RH(c),OW 125.00
4 RH,Decapitation story 125.00
5 BEv,JM,'Its in the Bag' 125.00
6 BK,'The Man Who Couldn't
  be Killed' 125.00
7 BEv,JMn,'Don't Close
  the Door' 100.00
8 BEv(c),RH,JSt,DAy,
  'The Operation' 100.00
9 BEv(c),RH,'The Death of
  Agatha Slurl' 100.00
10 JMn(c),BEv,RH,'The Living
  Mummy' 100.00
11 'The Empty Coffin' 80.00

12 RH,'My Friend the Ghost' . . . 80.00
13 JM,'The Dead Men' 80.00
14 BEv(c),RH,JMn,'Close Shave' 80.00
15 'Get Out of my Graveyard' . . 80.00
16 RH,BEv,JF,JSt,'Behind
  the Door' 80.00
17 BEv(c),GC,BK,'Goodbye
  Forever' 100.00
18 BEv(c),JM 80.00
19 BEv(c),BP,'Witch Doctor' . . . 80.00
20 RH(c),BP 80.00
21 RH(c) 75.00
22 . . . . 75.00
23 . . . . 75.00
24 JMn(c),JR 60.00
25 JO,'Look into my Eyes' 60.00
26 JR,'The Things in the Box' . . 60.00
27 JMn,JR,'Trap in the Mirage' . 60.00
28 BEv 60.00
29 JSe(c),SD 75.00
30 BEv(c) 60.00
31 . . . . 60.00
32 BP,'Almost Human' 60.00
33 AT 60.00
34 June, 1957 . . . . 60.00

SPELLBOUND
January, 1988

1 thru 3 . . . . @1.50
4 A:New Mutants 2.00
5 . . . . 1.50
6 double-size 2.25

Spider-Man #14
© Marvel Entertainment Group

SPIDER-MAN
August, 1990

1 TM Purple Web(c),V:Lizard,
  A:Calypso,B:Torment 5.00
1a Silver Web(c) 7.00
1b Bag,Purple Web 10.00
1c Bag,Silver Web 20.00
1d 2nd print,Gold(c) 5.00
1e 2nd print Gold UPC(rare) . . . 25.00
1f Platinum Ed. 250.00
2 TM,V:Lizard,A:Calypso 6.00
3 TM,V:Lizard,A:Calypso 5.00

4 TM,V:Lizard,A:Calypso 5.00
5 TM,V:Lizard,A:Calypso,
  E:Torment 5.00
6 TM,A:Ghost Rider,V:Hobgoblin   6.00
7 TM,A:Ghost Rider,V:Hobgoblin   6.00
8 TM,B:Perceptions,A:Wolverine
  I:Wendigo IV 5.00
9 TM,A:Wolverine,Wendigo 4.00
10 TM,RLd,SW,JLe(i),A:Wolv. .. 4.00
11 TM,A:Wolverine,Wendigo..... 4.00
12 TM,E:Perceptions,A:Wolv.. .. 4.00
13 TM,V:Morbius,R:Black Cost. .. 6.00
14 TM,V:Morbius,A:Black Cost. .. 5.00
15 EL,A:Beast 3.00
16 TM,RLd,A:X-Force,V:Juggernaut,
  Black Tom,cont.in X-Force#4 . 4.00
17 RL,AW,A:Thanos,Death 4.00
18 EL,B:Return of the Sinister Six,
  A:Hulk 3.00
19 EL,A:Hulk,Deathlok 3.00
20 EL,A:Nova 2.50
21 EL,A:Hulk,Deathlok,Solo 2.50
22 EL,A:Ghost Rider,Hulk 2.50
23 EL,E:Return of the Sinister Six,
  A:Hulk,G.Rider,Deathlok,FF .. 2.50
24 Infinity War,V:Hobgoblin,
  Demogoblin 2.25
25 CMa,A:Excalibur,V:Arcade ... 2.25
26 RF,MBa,Hologram(c),30th Anniv.
  I:New Burglar 5.00
27 MR,Handgun issue 2.25
28 MR,Handgun issue 2.25
29 CMa,Ret.to Mad Dog Ward#1 . 2.25
30 CMa,Ret.to Mad Dog Ward#2 . 2.25
31 CMa,Ret.to Mad Dog Ward#3 . 2.25
32 BMc,A:Punisher,V:Master of
  Vengeance 2.25
33 BMc,A:Punisher,V:Master of
  Vengeance. 2.25
34 BMc,A:Punisher,V:Master of
  Vengeance 2.25
35 TL,Total Carnage#4,V:Carnage,
  Shriek,A:Venom,Black Cat .. 2.25
36 TL,Total Carnage#8,V:Carnage,
  A:Venom,Morbius 2.25
37 TL,Total Carnage#12,
  V:Carnage 2.00
38 thru 40 KJ,V:Electro 2.00
41 TKa(s),JaL,I:Platoon,
  A:Iron Fist 2.00
42 TKa(s),JaL,V:Platoon,
  A:Iron Fist 2.00
43 TKa(s),JaL,V:Platoon,
  A:Iron Fist 2.00
44 HMe(s),TL,V:Hobgoblin 2.25
45 HMe(s),TL,SHa,Pursuit#1,
  V:Chameleon 2.00
46 HMe(s),TL,V:Hobgoblin,w/cel . 3.25
46a Newsstand Ed. 1.75
47 TL,SHa,V:Demogoblin 1.95
48 TL,SHa,V:Hobgoblin,
  D:Demogoblin 1.95
49 TL,SHa,I:Coldheart 2.25
50 TL,SHa,I:Grim Hunter,foil(c) .. 4.25
50a newsstand ed. 2.50
51 TL,SHa,Power,pt.3,foil(c) 3.25
51a newsstand ed. 2.25
52 TL,SHa,Spide-clone,V:Venom . 1.95
53 TL,SHa,Clone,V:Venom 2.25
54 Web of Life,pt.3 .... 2.25
55 Web of Life,finale 2.25
56 Smoke and Mirrors 1.95
57 Aftershocks,pt.1 .... 2.50
57a enhanced cover 2.95
58 The Mark of Kaine,pt.3 ...... 1.95

59 F:Travellor,Host 1.95
60 TL,SHa,HMa,The Trial of
  Peter Parker,pt.3 .... 1.95
GN Fear Itself 12.95
GN Nothing Stops Juggernaut ... 3.95
GN Parallel Lives 8.95
GN JMD,MZ,Soul of the Hunter .. 5.95
HC Kraven's Last Hunt 19.95
HC CV,Spirits of the Earth 18.95
Spec. Chaos in Calgary 1.50
Spec. Double Trouble 1.50
Spec. Hit and Run, Canadian ... 1.50
Spec. Skating on Thin Ice 1.50
Spec. Trial of Venom,UNICEF .. 15.00
Sup.Sz.Spec#1 Planet of the
  Symbiotes, pt.2;
  flipbookF:Scarlet Spider 3.95
TPB Assasination Plot 14.95
TPB Carnage 6.95
TPB Cosmic Adventures 19.95
TPB Hooky 6.95
TPB Maximum Carnage 24.95
TPB Origin of the Hobgoblin .. 14.95
TPB Return of the Sinister Six .. 15.95
TPB Round Robin 15.95
TPB Saga of the Alien Costume   14.00
  2nd printing 12.95
TPB Spider-Man vs. Venom ... 9.95
TPB Torment Rep.#1-#5 ..... 12.95
TPB Venom Returns 12.95
TPB Very Best of Spider-Man .. 15.95
TPB The Wedding 12.95
TPB Invasion Spider Slayers ... 15.95

SPIDER-MAN ADVENTURES

1 From animated series 1.50
1a foil (c) 2.95
2 Animated Adventures 1.50
3 V:Spider-Slayer 1.50
4 Animated Adventures 1.50
5 V:Mysterio 1.50
6 V:Kraven 1.50
7 V:Doctor Octopus 1.50
8 O:Venom 1.50

SPIDER-MAN & AMAZING FRIENDS
December, 1981

1 DSp,A:Iceman,I:Firestar 5.50

SPIDER-MAN: ARACHNIS PROJECT

1 Wld, beginnings 1.75
2 Wld,V:Diggers 1.75
3 Wld,V:Jury 1.75
4 Wld,V:Life Foundation 1.75
5 Wld,V:Jury 1.75

SPIDER-MAN CLASSICS

1 rep.Amazing Fantasy#15 ..... 1.75
2 thru 11 rep.Amaz.SpM#1-#10 @1.75
12 rep.Amaz.SpM#11 .... 1.50
13 rep.Amaz.SpM#12 .... 1.50
14 rep.Amaz.SpM#13 .... 1.50
15 rep.Amaz.SpM#14,w/cel 3.25
15a Newsstand Ed. 1.50

SPIDER-MAN: THE CLONE JOURNALS

One-shot 1.95

SPIDER-MAN COMICS MAGAZINE
January, 1987

1 .... 2.50
2 thru 12 .... @1.50
13 1988 .... 1.50

SPIDER-MAN: FRIENDS AND ENEMIES

1 V:Metahumes 1.95
2 A:Nova,Darkhawk,Speedball .. 1.95
3 V:Metahumes 1.95
4 F:Metahumes 1.95

SPIDER-MEN: FUNERAL FOR AN OCTOPUS

1 Doc Oc Dead 1.95
2 A:Sinister Six 1.50
3 Final Issue 1.50

SPIDER-MAN MEGAZINE

1 rep. 2.95
2 rep. 2.95
3 rep. 2.95
4 rep. 2.95
5 Vision rep. 2.95
6 V:Thing & Torch, rep. 2.95

SPIDER-MAN: MUTANT AGENDA

0 thru 2 Paste in Book ...... @1.50
3 Paste in Book 1.50

SPIDER-MAN: POWER OF TERROR

1 R:Silvermane,A:Deathlok 1.95
2 V:Silvermane 1.95
3 New Scorpion 1.95
4 V:Silvermane 1.95

SPIDER-MAN/PUNISHER/ SABERTOOTH: DESIGNER GENES

1 SMc,Foil(c) 9.50

SPIDER-MAN SAGA
November, 1991

1 SLi(c),History from Amazing
  Fantasy #15-Amaz.SpM#100 . 3.25
2 SLi(c),Amaz.SpM#101-#175 .. 3.25
3 Amaz.SpM#176-#238 .... 3.25
4 Amaz.SpM #239-#300 ..... 3.25

SPIDER-MAN 2099

1 RL,AW,I:Spider-Man 2099 ... 6.50
2 RL,AW,O:Spider-Man 2099 ... 5.00
3 RL,AW,V:Venture 3.00
4 RL,AW,I:Specialist,
  A:Doom 2099 .... 2.00
5 RL,AW,V:Specialist 2.00
6 RL,AW,I:New Vulture 2.00
7 RL,AW,Vulture of 2099 ..... 2.00
8 RL,AW,V:New Vulture 2.00
9 KJo,V:Alchemax 2.00
10 RL,AW,O:Wellvale Home 2.00
11 RL,AW,V:S.I.E.G.E. 2.00
12 RL,AW,w/poster 2.00
13 RL,AW,V:Thanatos 1.75
14 PDd(s),RL(c),TGb,Downtown . 1.75
15 PDd(s),RL,I:Thor 2099,

Heimdall 2099 . . . . 1.75
16 PDd(s),RL,Fall of the
   Hammer#1 . . . . 1.75
17 PDd(s),RL,V:Bloodsword 1.75
18 PDd(s),RLm,V:Lyla 1.75
19 PDd(s),RL,w/card 1.75
20 PDd(s),RL,Crash & Burn 1.75
21 V:Gangs 1.75
22 V:Gangs 1.75
23 RL,I:Risque 1.75
24 Kasey 1.75
25 A:Hulk 2099, dbl-size,foil(c) . . 3.25
25a Newsstand ed. 2.25
26 V:Headhunter, Travesty 1.50
27 V:Travesty 1.50
28 V:Travesty 1.50
29 V:Foragers 1.50
30 V:Flipside 1.50
31 I:Dash 1.50

Becomes:

SPIDER-MAN 2099 A.D.
32 I:Morgue 1.95
33 One Nation Under Doom 1.95
Ann.#1 PDd(s),RL 2.95

SPIDER-MAN UNLIMITED
1 RLm,Maximun Carnage#1,I:Shriek,
  R:Carnage 5.00
2 RLm,Maximum Carnage#14 . . 4.50
3 RLm,O:Doctor Octopus 4.50
4 RLm,V:Mysterrio,Rhino 4.25
5 RLm,A:Human Torch,
  I:Steel Spider 4.25
6 RLm,A:Thunderstrike 3.95
7 RLm,A:Clone 3.95
8 Tom Lyle 3.95
9 The Mark of Kaine,pt.5 . . . . . . 3.95

SPIDER-MAN VS. DRACULA
1 rep. 1.75

SPIDER-MAN vs. VENOM
1990
1 TM(c) 8.95

SPIDER-MAN vs. WOLVERINE
1990
1 MBr,AW,D:Ned Leeds(the original
  Hobgoblin),V:Charlie 27.00
1a reprint 5.00

SPIDER-MAN: WEB OF DOOM
1 3-part series 1.75
2 Spidey falsely accused 1.75
3 conclusion 1.75

SPIDER-MAN & X-FACTOR: SHADOW GAMES
1 PB,I:Shadowforce 2.25
2 PB,V:Shadowforce 2.25
3 PB,V:Shadowforce, final issue . 2.25

SPIDER-WOMAN
April, 1978
1 CI,TD,O:Spiderwoman 6.00
2 CI,TD,I:Morgan Le Fey 2.00
3 CI,TD,I:Brother's Grimm 2.00

Spider-Woman #28
© Marvel Entertainment Group

4 CI,TD,V:Hangman 2.00
5 CI,TD,Nightmares 2.00
6 CI,A:Werewolf By Night 2.00
7 CI,SL,AG,V:Magnus 2.00
8 CI,AG,"Man who would not die" 2.00
9 CI,AG,A:Needle,Magnus 2.00
10 CI,AG,I:Gypsy Moth 2.00
11 CI,AG,V:Brothers Grimm 1.50
12 CI,AG,V:Brothers Grimm 1.50
13 CI,AG,A:Shroud 1.50
14 BSz(c),CI,AG,A:Shroud 1.50
15 BSz(c),CI,AG,A:Shroud 1.50
16 BSz(c),CI,AG,V:Nekra 1.50
17 CI,Deathplunge 1.50
18 CI,A:Flesh 1.50
19 CI,A:Werewolf By Night,
  V:Enforcer 1.75
20 FS,A:Spider-Man 1.50
21 FS,A:Bounty Hunter 1.50
22 FS,A:Killer Clown 1.50
23 TVE,V:The Gamesmen 1.50
24 TVE,V:The Gamesmen 1.50
25 SL,Two Spiderwomen 1.50
26 JBy(c),SL,V:White Gardenia . . 1.50
27 BSz(c),JBi,A:Enforcer 1.50
28 BSz(c),SL,A:Enforcer,Spidey . 1.50
29 JR2(c),ECh,FS,A:Enforcer,
  Spider-Man 1.50
30 FM(c),SL,JM,I:Dr.Karl Malus . 1.50
31 FM(c),SL,JM,A:Hornet 1.50
32 FM(c),SL,JM,A:Werewolf 1.75
33 SL,V:Yesterday's Villian 1.50
34 SL,AM,V:Hammer and Anvil . . 1.50
35 SL,AG,V:Angar the Screamer . 1.50
36 SL,Spiderwoman Shot 1.50
37 SL,TA,BWi,AM,FS,A:X-Men,I:
  Siryn,V:Black Tom 3.50
38 SL,BWi,A:X-Men,Siryn 3.00
39 SL,BWi,Shadows 1.50
40 SL,BWi,V:The Flying Tiger 1.50
41 SL,BWi,V:Morgan LeFay 1.50
42 SL,BWi,V:Silver Samurai 1.50
43 SL,V:Silver Samurai 1.50
44 SL,V:Morgan LeFay 1.50
45 SL,Spider-Man Thief Cover . . . 1.50
46 SL,V:Mandroids,A:Kingpin 1.50

47 V:Daddy Longlegs 1.50
48 O:Gypsy Moth 1.50
49 A:Tigra 1.50
50 PH(c),D:Spiderwoman 3.50
[Limited Series]
1 V:Therak 2.00
2 O:Spider-Woman 2.00
3 V:Deathweb 2.00
4 V:Deathweb,Last issue 2.00

SPIDEY SUPER STORIES
October, 1974
1 Younger reader's series in
  association with the Electric
  Company,O:Spider-Man 4.00
2 A:Kraven 3.00
3 A:Ringleader 3.00
4 A:Medusa 3.00
5 A:Shocker 3.00
6 A:Iceman 3.00
7 A:Lizard, Vanisher 3.00
8 A:Dr. Octopus 3.00
9 A:Dr. Doom 3.00
10 A:Green Goblin 3.25
11 A:Dr. Octopus 3.00
12 A:The Cat,V:The Owl 3.00
13 A:Falcon 3.00
14 A:Shanna 3.00
15 A:Storm 3.25
16 . . . . 2.50
17 A:Captain America 2.50
18 A:Kingpin 2.50
19 A:Silver Surfer,Dr. Doom 3.25
20 A;Human Torch,Invisible Girl . 2.50
21 A:Dr. Octopus 2.50
22 A:Ms. Marvel,The Beetle 2.50
23 A:Green Goblin 3.00
24 A:Thundra 2.50
25 A:Dr. Doom 2.50
26 A:Sandman 2.50
27 A:Thor,Loki 2.50
28 A:Medusa 2.50
29 A:Kingpin 2.50
30 A:Kang 2.50
31 A:Moondragon,Dr. Doom 2.50
32 A:Spider-Woman,Dr. Octopus . 2.50
33 . . . . 2.50
34 A:Sub-Mariner 2.50
35 . . . . 2.50
36 A:Lizard 2.50
37 A:White Tiger 2.50
38 A:Fantastic Four 2.50
39 A:Hellcat,Thanos 6.00
40 A:Hawkeye 2.00
41 A:Nova, Dr. Octopus 2.00
42 A:Kingpin 2.00
43 A:Daredevil,Ringmaster 2.00
44 A:Vision 2.00
45 A:Silver Surfer,Dr. Doom 3.25
46 A:Mysterio 2.00
47 A:Spider-Woman,Stilt-Man . . . 2.00
48 A:Green Goblin 2.25
49 Spidey for President 2.00
50 A:She-Hulk 2.00
51 . . . . 2.00
52 . . . . 2.00
53 A:Dr. Doom 2.00
54 'Attack of the Bird-Man' 2.00
55 A:Kingpin 2.00
56 A:Captain Britain,
  Jack O'Lantern 3.00
57 March, 1982 . . . . 2.00

SPITFIRE AND THE TROUBLESHOOTERS
October, 1986
1 HT/JSt 1.00
2 HT 1.00
3 HT,Macs Armor 1.00
4 TM/BMc(Early TM work) 5.00
5 HT/TD,A:StarBrand 1.00
6 HT,Trial 1.00
7 HT 1.00
8 HT,New Armor 1.00
9 . . . . 1.00
Becomes:
CODE NAME: SPITFIRE
10 MR/TD 1.00
11 . . . . 1.00
12 . . . . 1.00
13 . . . . 1.00

SPOOF
October, 1970
1 MSe 3.00
2 MSe,'Brawl in the Family' 2.00
3 MSe,Richard Nixon cover 2.00
4 MSe,'Blechhula' 2.00
5 MSe,May, 1973 . . . . 4.00

Sports Action #2
© Marvel Entertainment Group

SPORT STARS
November, 1949
1 The Life of Knute Rockne . . 200.00
Becomes:
SPORTS ACTION
2 BP(c),The Life of
   George Gipp 200.00
3 BEv,Hack Wilson 150.00
4 Art Houtteman 125.00
5 Nile Kinnick 125.00
6 Warren Gun 125.00
7 Jim Konstanty 125.00
8 Ralph Kiner 135.00
9 Ed "Strangler" Lewis 125.00
10 JMn,'The Yella-Belly' 125.00
11 'The Killers' 125.00
12 'Man Behind the Mask' 125.00
13 Lew Andrews 125.00
14 MWs,Ken Roper,

September, 1952 . . . . 100.00

SPOTLIGHT
September, 1978
1 F:Huckleberry Hound, Yogi Bear 1.25
2 Quick Draw McDraw 1.00
3 The Jetsons 1.00
4 Magilla Gorilla, March, 1979 . . 1.00

SPY CASES
See: KID KOMICS

SPY FIGHTERS
March, 1951
1 GT 100.00
2 GT 50.00
3 . . . . 45.00
4 thru 13 . . . . @40.00
14 thru 15 July, 1953 . . . . . . @45.00

SPYKE
Epic
1 BR,I:Spyke 2.75
2 V:Conita 2.75
3 thru 4 BR . . . . @1.95

SPY THRILLERS
Atlas
November, 1954
1 'The Tickling Death' 100.00
2 V:Communists 50.00
3 . . . . 40.00
4 . . . . 40.00
Becomes:
POLICE BADGE
5 September, 1955 . . . . 30.00

SQUADRON SUPREME
September, 1985
1 BH,L:Nighthawk 3.50
2 BH,F:Nuke,A:Scarlet Centurion 2.50
3 BH,D:Nuke 2.50
4 BH,L:Archer 2.00
5 BH,L:Amphibian 2.00
6 PR,J:Institute of Evil 2.00
7 JB,JG,V:Hyperion 2.00
8 BH,V:Hyperion 2.00
9 BSz(c),PR,D:Tom Thumb 2.00
10 PR,V:Quagmire 2.00
11 PR,V:Redeemers 2.00
12 PR,D:Nighthawk,Foxfire,
   Black Archer 2.50
GN Death of a Universe 9.95

STALKERS
Epic
April, 1990
1 MT 1.50
2 MT 1.50
3 MT 1.50
4 MT 1.50
5 MT 1.50
6 VM,MT 1.50
7 VM,MT 1.50
8 VM,MT 1.50
9 VM 1.50
10 VM 1.50
11 VM 1.50
12 VM, 1991 . . . . 1.50

STARBLAST
1 MGu(s),HT,After the Starbrand 2.25

2 MGu(s),HT,After the Starbrand 2.00
3 MGu(s),HT,After the Starbrand 2.00
4 MGu(s),HT,Final Issue 2.00

STARBRAND
October, 1986
1 JR2,O:Starbrand 1.50
2 JR2/AW 1.00
3 JR2/AW 1.00
4 JR2/AW 1.00
5 JR2/AW 1.00
6 JR2/AW 1.00
7 JR2/AW 1.00
8 JR2/AW 1.00
9 KG/BWi,A:Nightmask 1.00
10 . . . . 1.00
11 JR2,TP 1.00
12 JR2,TP,X-Men X-over 1.25
13 JR2,TP 1.25
14 JR2,TP 1.25
15 . . . . 1.25
16 . . . . 1.25
17 JBy,TP,New Starbrand 1.50
18 JBy/TP 1.50
19 JBy/TP 1.50
Ann.#1 . . . . 1.25

STAR COMICS MAGAZINE
December, 1986
(digest size)
1 F:Heathcliff,Muppet Babies,
   Ewoks 1.50
2 thru 13 1988 . . . . @1.50

STAR-LORD, SPECIAL EDITION
February, 1982
1 JBy reprints 6.00

STARRIORS
August, 1984
1 . . . . 1.50
2 . . . . 1.25
3 . . . . 1.25
4 February, 1982 . . . . 1.25

STARSTRUCK
March, 1985
1 MK 2.00
2 MK 1.75
3 thru 8 MK, Feb. 1986 . . . . . @1.50

STAR TREK
April, 1980
1 DC,KJ,rep.1st movie Adapt. . . . 7.00
2 DC,KJ,rep.1st movie Adapt. . . . 6.00
3 DC,KJ,rep.1st movie Adapt. . . . 5.00
4 DC,KJ,The Weirdest Voyage . . 5.00
5 DC,KJ,Dr.McCoy..Killer 5.00
6 DC,KJ,A:Ambassador Phlu . . . 5.00
7 MN,KJ,Kirk/Spock(c) 5.00
8 DC(p),F:Spock 5.00
9 DC,FS,Trapped in a Web of
   Ghostly Vengeance 5.00
10 KJ(i),Spock the Barbarian . . . 5.00
11 TP(i),Like A Woman Scorned . 5.00
12 TP(i),Trapped in a Starship
   Gone Mad 5.00
13 TP(i),A:Barbara McCoy 5.00
14 LM,GD,We Are Dying,
   Egypt,Dying 5.00
15 GK,The Quality of Mercy 5.00

16 LM,There's no Space
  like Gnomes 5.00
17 EH,TP,The Long Nights Dawn 5.00
18 A Thousand Deaths,last issue . 5.00

STAR WARS
July, 1977

1 HC,30 Cent,movie adaption. . 35.00
1a HC,35 Cent(square Box). . . 400.00
2 HC,movie adaptation 10.00
3 HC,movie adaptation 10.00
4 HC,SL,movie adapt.(low dist.) 13.00
5 HC,SL,movie adaptation 10.00
6 HC,DSt,E:movie adaption . . . 10.00

Star Wars #14
© Marvel Entertainment Group

7 HC,FS,F:Luke&Chewbacca . . . 7.00
8 HC,TD,Eight against a World . . 7.00
9 HC,TP,V:Cloud Riders 7.00
10 HC,TP,Behemoth fr.Below . . . 7.00
11 CI,TP,Fate o/Luke Skywalker . 5.00
12 TA,CI,Doomworld 5.00
13 TA,JBy,CI,Deadly Reunion . . . 5.00
14 TA,CI 5.00
15 CI,V:Crimson Jack 5.00
16 WS,V:The Hunter 5.00
17 Crucible, Low Dist. 6.00
18 CI,Empire Strikes(Low Dist). . . 6.00
19 CI,Ultimate Gamble(Low Dist) 6.00
20 CI,Death Game(Scarce) 6.00
21 TA,CI,Shadow of a Dark
  Lord(Scarce) 6.00
22 CI,Han Solo vs.Chewbacca . . 5.00
23 CI,Flight Into Fury 5.00
24 CI,Ben Kenobi Story 5.00
25 CI,Siege at Yavin 5.00
26 CI,Doom Mission 4.00
27 CI,V:The Hunter 4.00
28 CI,Cavern o/t Crawling Death 4.00
29 CI,Dark Encounter 4.00
30 CI,A Princess Alone 4.00
31 CI,Return to Tatooine 4.00
32 CI,The Jawa Express 4.00
33 CI,GD,V:Baron Tagge 4.00
34 CI,Thunder in the Stars 4.00
35 CI,V:Darth Vader 4.00
36 CI,V:Darth Vader 4.00

37 CI,V:Darth Vader 4.00
38 TA,MG,Riders in the Void 4.00
39 AW,B:Empire Strikes Back . . . 6.00
40 AW,Battleground Hoth 5.00
41 AW,Imperial Pursuit 5.00
42 AW,Bounty Hunters 5.00
43 AW,Betrayal at Bespin 5.00
44 AW,E:Empire Strikes Back . . . 5.00
45 CI,GD,Death Probe 4.00
46 DI,TP,V:Dreamnaut Devourer . 4.00
47 CI,GD,Droid World 4.00
48 CI,Leia vs.Darth Vader 4.00
49 SW,TP,The Last Jedi 4.00
50 WS,AW,TP,G-Size issue 5.00
51 WS,TP,Resurrection of Evil . . . 3.00
52 WS,TP 3.00
53 CI,WS 3.00
54 CI,WS 3.00
55 thru 66 WS,TP . . . . @3.00
67 TP 3.00
68 GD,TP 3.00
69 GD,TP 3.00
70 A:Han Solo 3.00
71 A:Han Solo 2.50
72 . . . . 2.50
73 Secret of Planet Lansbane . . 2.50
74 thru 91 . . . . @2.50
92 BSz(c) 2.50
93 thru 97 . . . . @2.50
98 AW 2.50
99 . . . . 2.50
100 Painted(c),double-size 3.50
101 BSz 2.50
102 KRo's Back 2.50
103 thru 106 . . . . @2.50
107 WPo(i),last issue 3.00
Ann.#1 WS(c),V:Winged Warlords 5.00
Ann.#2 RN 4.00
Ann.#3 RN,Darth Vader(c) 4.00

STEELGRIP STARKEY
Epic
July, 1986

1 . . . . 1.75
2 . . . . 1.75
3 . . . . 1.75
4 . . . . 1.75
5 . . . . 1.75
6 June, 1987 . . . . 1.75

STEELTOWN ROCKERS
April, 1990—Sept., 1990

1 SL 1.50
2 thru 6 SL . . . . @1.50

STRANGE COMBAT TALES

1 thru 2 . . . . 2.75
3 Tiger by the Tail 2.50
4 Midnight Crusade 2.50

STRANGE STORIES OF SUSPENSE
See: RUGGED ACTION

STRANGE TALES
June, 1951
[1st Regular Series]

1 'The Room' 1,600.00
2 'Trapped In A Tomb' 600.00
3 JMn,'Man Who Never Was' 450.00
4 BEv,'Terror in the Morgue' . 500.00
5 'A Room Without A Door' . 500.00

6 RH(c),'The Ugly Man' 300.00
7 'Who Stands Alone' 300.00
8 BEv(c),'Something in the Fog' 300.00
9 'Drink Deep Vampire' 300.00
10 BK,'Hidden Head' 300.00
11 BEv(c),GC,'O'Malley's Friend' 200.00
12 'Graveyard At Midnight' . . . 200.00
13 BEv(c),'Death Makes A Deal' 200.00
14 GT,'Horrible Herman' 200.00
15 BK,'Don't Look Down' 200.00
16 Decapitation cover 200.00
17 DBr,JRo,'Death Feud' 200.00
18 'Witch Hunt' 200.00
19 RH(c),'The Rag Doll' 200.00
20 RH(c),GC,SMo,'Lost World' . 200.00
21 BEv 150.00
22 BK,JF 150.00
23 'The Strangest Tale in
  the World' 150.00
24 'The Thing in the Coffin' . . . 150.00
25 . . . . 150.00
26 . . . . 150.00
27 JF,'The Garden of Death' . . 150.00
28 'Come into my Coffin' 150.00
29 'Witch-Craft' 150.00

Strange Tales #41
© Marvel Entertainment Group

30 'The Thing in the Box' . . . 150.00
31 'The Man Who Played
  with Blocks' 150.00
32 . . . . 150.00
33 JMn(c),'Step Lively Please' . 150.00
34 'Flesh and Blood' 125.00
35 'The Man in the Bottle' 125.00
36 . . . . 125.00
37 'Out of the Storm' 125.00
38 . . . . 125.00
39 'Karnoff's Plan' 125.00
40 BEv,'The Man Who Caught a
  Mermaid' 125.00
41 BEv,'Riddle of the Skull' . . . 135.00
42 DW,BEv,JMn,'Faceless One' 135.00
43 JF,'The Mysterious Machine' 125.00
44 . . . . 125.00
45 JKa,'Land of the
  Vanishing Men' 135.00
46 thru 57 . . . . @90.00
58 AW 100.00
59 BK 125.00
60 . . . . 85.00

61 BK	125.00	140 SD,JK,V:Dormammu	25.00	177 FB,F:Golem	4.00
62	85.00	141 SD,JK,I:Fixer,Mentallo	25.00	178 JSn,B&O:Warlock,I:Magus	27.00
63	125.00	142 SD,JK,I:THEM,V:Hydra	25.00	179 JSn,I:Pip,I&D:Capt.Autolycus	18.00
64 AW	100.00	143 SD,JK,V:Hydra	25.00	180 JSn,I:Gamora,Kray-tor	18.00
65	85.00			181 JSn,E:Warlock	18.00
66	85.00			182 SD,GK,rep Str.Tales	

67 thru 78 .... @100.00
79 SD,JK,Dr.Strange Prototype 105.00
80 thru 83 SD,JK .... @90.00
84 SD,JK,Magneto Prototype .. 125.00
85 SD,JK 100.00
86 SD,JK,'I Who
  Created Mechano' 100.00
87 SD,JK,'Return of Grogg' ... 100.00
88 SD,JK,'Zzutak' 100.00
89 SD,JK,'Fin Fang Foom' 275.00
90 SD,JK,'Orrgo the
  Unconquerable' 90.00
91 SD,JK,'The Sacrifice' 90.00
92 SD,JK,'The Thing That Waits
  For Me' 90.00
93 SD,JK,'The Wax People' 90.00
94 SD,JK,'Pildorr the Plunderer'. 90.00
95 SD,JK,'Two-Headed Thing'. 90.00
96 SD,JK,'I Dream of Doom' .. 90.00
97 SD,JK,'When A Planet Dies' 250.00
98 SD,JK,'No Human Can
  Beat Me' 100.00
99 SD,JK,'Mister Morgan's
  Monster' 100.00
100 SD,JK,'I Was Trapped
  in the Crazy Maze' 100.00
101 B:StL(),SD,JK,
  B:Human Torch 725.00
102 SD,JK,I:Wizard 250.00
103 SD,JK,I:Zemu 200.00
104 SD,JK,I:The Trapster 200.00
105 SD,JK,V:Wizard 200.00
106 SD,A:Fantastic Four 125.00
107 SD,V:Sub-Mariner 155.00
108 SD,JK,A:FF,I:The Painter . 125.00
109 SD,JK,I:Sorcerer 125.00
110 SD,I&B:Dr.Strange,
  Nightmare 1,300.00
111 SD,I:Asbestos,
  Baron Mordo 225.00
112 SD,I:The Eel 95.00
113 SD,I:Plant Man 95.00
114 SD,JK,A:Captain America . 215.00
115 SD,O:Dr.Strange 320.00
116 SD,V:Thing 75.00
117 SD,V:The Eel 65.00
118 SD,V:The Wizard 70.00
119 SD,C:Spider-Man 80.00
120 SD,1st Iceman/Torch T.U. .. 65.00
121 SD,V:Plantman 45.00
122 SD,V:Dr.Doom 40.00
123 SD,A:Thor,I:Beetle 40.00
124 SD,I:Zota 40.00
125 SD,V:Sub-Mariner 40.00
126 SD,I:Dormammu,Clea 45.00
127 SD,V:Dormammu 35.00
128 SD,I:Demon 32.00
129 SD,I:Tiboro 32.00
130 SD,C:Beatles 38.00
131 SD,I:Dr.Vega 32.00
132 SD,I:Orini 32.00
133 SD,I:Shazana 32.00
134 SD,E:Torch,I:Merlin 32.00
135 SD,JK:I:Shield & Hydra
  B:Nick Fury 75.00
136 SD,JK,V:Dormammu 30.00
137 SD,JK,A:Ancient One 35.00
138 SD,JK,I:Eternity 25.00
139 SD,JK,V:Dormammu 25.00

144 SD,JK,V:Druid,I:Jasper
  Sitwell 25.00
145 SD,JK,I:Mr.Rasputin 25.00
146 SD,JK,V:Dormammu,I:AIM. 25.00
147 BEv,JK,F:Wong 25.00
148 BEv,JK,O:Ancient One 27.00
149 BEv,JK,V:Kaluu 23.00
150 BEv,JK,JB(1st Marvel Art)
  I:Baron Strucker,Umar 23.00
151 JK,JSo(1st Marvel Art),
  I:Umar 45.00
152 BEv,JK,JSo,V:Umar 20.00
153 JK,JSo,MSe,V:Hydra 20.00
154 JSo,MSe,I:Dreadnought ... 20.00
155 JSo,MSe,A:L.B.Johnson ... 20.00
156 JSo,MSe,I:Zom 20.00
157 JSo,MSe,A:Zom,C:Living
  Tribunal 20.00
158 JSo,MSe,A:Zom,I:Living
  Tribunal(full story) 24.00
159 JSo,MSe,O:Nick Fury,A:Capt.
  America,I:Val Fontaine 30.00
160 JSo,MSe,A:Captain America
  I:Jimmy Woo 20.00
161 JSo,I:Yellow Claw 20.00
162 JSo,DA,A:Captain America. 20.00
163 JSo,DA,V:Yellow Claw ... 20.00
164 JSo,DA,V:Yellow Claw ... 20.00
165 JSo,DA,V:Yellow Claw ... 20.00
166 DA,GT,JSo,A:AncientOne .. 20.00
167 JSo,DA,V:Doctor Doom ... 30.00
168 JSo,DA,E:Doctor Strange,Nick
  Fury,V:Yandroth 20.00
169 JSo,I&O:Brother Voodoo .. 5.00
170 JSo,O:Brother Voodoo 5.00
171 GC,V:Baron Samed 4.00
172 GC,DG,V:Dark Lord 4.00
173 GC,DG,I:Black Talon 4.00
174 JB,JM,O:Golem 4.00
175 SD,R:Torr 4.00
176 F:Golem 4.00

    #123,124 .... 3.00
183 SD,rep Str.Tales #130,131 .. 3.00
184 SD,rep Str.Tales #132,133 .. 3.00
185 SD,rep Str.Tales #134,135 .. 3.00
186 SD,rep Str.Tales #136,137 .. 3.00
187 SD,rep Str.Tales #138,139 .. 3.00
188 SD,rep Str.Tales #140,141 .. 3.00
Ann.#1 V:Grottu,Diablo 300.00
Ann.#2 A:Spider-Man 355.00

[2nd Regular Series]
1 BBI,CW,B:Cloak&Dagger,Dr.
  Strange,V:Lord of Light 1.50
2 BBI,CW,V:Lord of Light,Demon 1.25
3 BBI,AW,CW,A:Nightmare,Khat. 1.25
4 BBI,CW,V:Nightmare 1.25
5 BBI,V:Rodent,A:Defenders 1.25
6 BBI,BWi,V:Erlik Khan,
  A:Defenders 1.25
7 V:Nightmare,A:Defenders 1.25
8 BBI,BWi,V:Kaluu 1.25
9 BBI,BWi,A:Dazzler,I:Mr.Jip,
  V:Kaluu 1.25
10 BBI,BWi,RCa,A:Black Cat,
  V:Mr.Jip,Kaluu 1.25
11 RCa,BWi,V:Mr.Jip,Kaluu 1.25
12 WPo,BWi,A:Punisher,V:Mr.Jip. 2.00
13 JBr,BWi,RCa,Punisher,
  Power Pack 2.00
14 JBr,BWi,RCa,Punisher,P.Pack 2.00
15 RCa,BMc,A:Mayhem 1.25
16 RCa,BWi,V:Mr.Jip 1.25
17 RCa,BWi,V:Night 1.25
18 RCa,KN,A:X-Factor',V:Night . 1.50
19 MMi(c),EL,TA,RCa,A:Thing . 1.25
TPB Fully painted 6.95

**STRANGE TALES
OF THE UNUSUAL**
Dec., 1955—Aug., 1957
1 JMn(c),BP,DH,JR,'Man Lost' 200.00
2 BEv,'Man Afraid' 100.00
3 AW,'The Invaders' 125.00
4 'The Long Wait' 75.00
5 RC,SD,'The Threat' 100.00
6 BEv 75.00
7 JK,JO 85.00
8 .... 75.00
9 BEv(c),BK 100.00
10 GM,AT 75.00
11 BEv(c),August, 1957 ...... 75.00

STRANGE WORLDS
December, 1958
1 JK,SD 350.00
2 SD 225.00
3 JK 175.00
4 AW 175.00
5 SD 150.00

**STRAWBERRY
SHORTCAKE**
Star
June, 1985—April, 1986
1 .... 1.25
2 thru 7 .... @1.00

Strange Tales #111
© Marvel Entertainment Group

All comics prices listed are for _Near Mint_ condition.

STRAY TOASTERS
Epic
January, 1988

1 BSz	5.00
2 BSz	4.50
3 BSz	4.00
4 BSz,End mini-series	4.00

STRIKEFORCE MORITURI
December, 1986

1 BA,SW,WPo(1st pencils-3 pages),I:Blackwatch	3.25
2 BA,SW,V:The Horde	1.50
3 BA,SW,V:The Horde	1.50
4 BA,SW,WPo,V:The Horde	2.00
5 BA,SW,V:The Horde	1.50
6 BA,SW,V:The Horde	1.25
7 BA,SW,V:The Horde	1.25
8 BA,SW,V:The Horde	1.25
9 BA,SW,V:THe Horde	1.25
10 WPo,(1st pencils-full story),SW,R:Black Watch,O:Horde	4.00
11 BA,SW,V:The Horde	1.25
12 BA,SW,D:Jelene	1.25
13 BA,SW,Old V:NewTeam	1.25
14 BA,AW,V:The Horde	1.25
15 BA,AW,V:The Horde	1.25
16 WPo,SW,V:The Horde	3.00
17 WPo(c),SW,V:The Horde	1.25
18 BA,SW,V:Hammersmith	1.25
19 BA,SW,V:THe Horde,D:Pilar	1.25
20 BA,SW,V:The Horde	1.25
21 MMi(c),TD(i),V:The Horde	1.25
22 TD(i),V:The Horde	1.25
23 MBa,VM,V:The Horde	1.50
24 VM(i),I:Vax,V:The Horde	1.75
25 TD(i),V:The Horde	1.75
26 MBa,VM,V:The Horde	1.75
27 MBa,VM,O:MorituriMaster	1.75
28 MBa,V:The Tiger	1.75
29 MBa,V:Zakir Shastri	1.75
30 MBa,V:Andre Lamont,The Wind	1.75
31 MBa(c),V:The Wind,last issue	1.75

STRYFE'S STRIKE FILE

1 LSn,NKu,GCa,BP,C:Siena Blaze,Holocaust	4.00
1a 2nd Printing	1.75

SUB-MARINER
May, 1968

1 JB,O:Sub-Mariner	140.00
2 JB,A:Triton	48.00
3 JB,A:Triton	25.00
4 JB,V:Attuma	25.00
5 JB,I&O:Tiger Shark	30.00
6 JB,DA,V:Tiger Shark	25.00
7 JB,I:Ikthon	25.00
8 JB,V:Thing	28.00
9 MSe,DA,A:Lady Dorma	25.00
10 GC,DA,O:Lemuria	25.00
11 GC,V:Capt.Barracuda	17.00
12 MSe,I:Lyna	17.00
13 MSe,JS,A:Lady Dorma	17.00
14 MSe,V:Fake Human Torch	36.00
15 MSe,V:Dragon Man	17.00
16 MSe,I:Nekaret,Thakos	12.00
17 MSe,I:Stalker,Kormok	12.00
18 MSe,A:Triton	12.00
19 MSe,I:Stingray	14.00
20 JB,V:Dr.Doom	12.00
21 MSe,D:Lord Seth	12.00

Sub-Mariner #1
© Marvel Entertainment Group

22 MSe,A:Dr.Strange	12.00
23 MSe,I:Orka	9.00
24 JB,JM,V:Tiger Shark	9.00
25 SB,JM,O:Atlantis	9.00
26 SB,A:Red Raven	9.00
27 SB,I:Commander Kraken	10.00
28 SB,V:Brutivae	9.00
29 SB,V:Hercules	9.00
30 SB,A:Captain Marvel	10.00
31 SB,A:Triton	8.00
32 SB,JM,I&O:Llyra	8.00
33 SB,JM,I:Namora	9.00
34 SB,JM,AK,1st Defenders	18.00
35 SB,JM,A:Silver Surfer	18.00
36 BWr,SB,W:Lady Dorma	9.00
37 RA,D:Lady Dorma	8.00
38 RA,JSe,O:Rec,I:Thakorr,Fen	8.00
39 RA,JM,V:Llyra	8.00
40 GC,I:Turalla,A:Spidey	10.00
41 GT,V:Rock	6.00
42 GT,JM,V:House Named Death	6.00
43 GC,V:Tunal	6.00
44 MSe,JM,V:Human Torch	7.00
45 MSe,JM,V:Tiger Shark	6.00
46 GC,D:Namor's Father	6.00
47 GC,A:Stingray,V:Dr.Doom	6.00
48 GC,V:Dr.Doom	6.00
49 GC,V:Dr.Doom	6.00
50 BEv,I:Namorita	9.00
51 BEv,O:Namorita,C:Namora	7.00
52 GK,V:Sunfire	6.00
53 BEv,V:Sunfire	6.00
54 BEv,AW,V:Sunfire,I:Lorvex	6.00
55 BEv,V:Torg	6.00
56 DA,I:Coral	6.00
57 BEv,I:Venus	6.00
58 BEv,I:Tamara	6.00
59 BEv,V:Tamara	6.00
60 BEv,V:Tamara	6.00
61 BEv,JM,V:Dr.Hydro	6.00
62 HC,JSt,I:Tales of Atlantis	6.00
63 HC,JSt,V:Dr.Hydro,I:Arkus	6.00
64 HC,JSe,I:Maddox	6.00
65 DH,DP,V:She-Devil,inc.BEv Eulogy Pin-up	6.00

66 DH,V:Orka,I:Raman	6.00
67 DH,A:FF,V:Triton,N:Namor I&O:Force	6.00
68 DH,O:Force	6.00
69 GT,V:Spider-Man	7.00
70 GT,I:Piranha	6.00
71 GT,V:Piranha	6.00
72 DA,V:Slime/Thing	6.00

[Limited Series]

1 RB,BMc,Namor's Birth	2.50
2 RB,BMc,Namor Kills Humans	2.00
3 RB,BMc,V:Surface Dwellers	2.00
4 RB,BMc,V:Human Torch	2.00
5 RB,BMc,A:Invaders	2.00
6 RB,BMc,V:Destiny	2.00
7 RB,BMc,A:Fantastic Four	2.00
8 RB,BMc,A:Hulk,Avengers	2.00
9 RB,BMc,A:X-Men,Magneto	2.00
10 RB,BMc,V:Thing	2.00
11 RB,BMc,A:Namorita, Defenders	2.00
12 RB,BMc,A:Dr.Doom, AlphaFlight	2.00

(SAGA OF THE) SUB-MARINER
[Mini-Series]
November, 1988

1 RB,BMc,Namor's Birth	2.50
2 RB,BMc,Namor Kills Humans	1.50
3 RB,BMc,V:Surface Dwellers	1.50
4 RB,BMc,V:Human Torch	1.50
5 RB,BMc,A:Invaders	1.50
6 RB,BMc,V:Destiny	1.50
7 RB,BMc,A:Fantastic Four	1.50
8 RB,BMc,A:Hulk,Avengers	1.50
9 RB,BMc,A:X-Men,Magneto	2.00
10 RB,BMc,V:Thing	1.50
11 RB,BMc,A:Namorita,Defenders	1.50
12 RB,BMc,A:Dr.Doom,Alp.Flight	1.50

SUB-MARINER COMICS
Timely
Spring, 1941

1 ASh(c),BEv,PGn,B:Sub-Mariner,The Angel	8,000.00
2 ASh(c),BEv,Nazi Submarine (c)	2,200.00
3 ASh(c),BEv	1,600.00
4 ASh(c),BEv,BW	1,300.00
5	1,000.00
6 ASh(c)	750.00
7	750.00
8 ASh(c)	750.00
9 ASh(c),BW	750.00
10 ASh(c)	750.00
11 ASh(c)	500.00
12 ASh(c)	500.00
13 ASh(c)	500.00
14 ASh(c)	500.00
15 ASh(c)	500.00
16 ASh(c)	500.00
17 ASh(c)	500.00
18 ASh(c)	500.00
19	500.00
20 ASh(c)	500.00
21 SSh(c),BEv	400.00
22 SSh(c),BEv	400.00
23 SSh(c),BEv	400.00
24 MSy(c),BEv,A:Namora, bondage cover	400.00
25 MSy(c),HK,B:The Blonde Phantom, A:Namora, bondage(c)	500.00

26 BEv,A:Namora 400.00
27 DRi(c),BEv,A:Namora 400.00
28 DRi(c),BEv,A:Namora 400.00
29 BEv,A:Namora,Human Torch 400.00
30 DRi(c),BEv,'Slaves Under
  the Sea' 400.00
31 BEv,'The Man Who Grew',
  A:Capt. America,E:Blonde
  Phantom 400.00
32 BEv,O:Sub-Mariner 800.00
33 BEv,O:Sub-Mariner,A:Human
  Torch,B:Namora 400.00
34 BEv,A:Human Torch,bondage
  cover 350.00
35 BEv,A:Human Torch 350.00
36 BEv 350.00
37 JMn(c),BEv 350.00
38 SSh(c),BEv,JMn 400.00
39 JMn(c),BEv 350.00
40 JMn(c),BEv 350.00
41 JMn(c),BEv 350.00
42 BEv,October, 1955 . . . . 400.00

SUBURBAN JERSEY
NINJA SHE-DEVILS
1 I:Ninja She-Devils 1.50

SUPERNATURAL
THRILLERS
December, 1972
1 JSo(c),JSe,FrG,IT! 1.50
2 VM,DA,The Invisible Man 1.50
3 GK,The Valley of the Worm . . 1.25
4 Dr. Jekyll and Mr. Hyde 1.25
5 RB,The Living Mummy 1.25
6 GT,JA,The Headless Horseman 1.25
7 VM,B:The Living Mummy,'
  Back From The Tomb' 1.25
8 VM,'He Stalks Two Worlds' . . 1.25
9 GK/AM(c),VM,DA,'Pyramid of
  the Watery Doom' 1.25
10 VM,'A Choice of Dooms' 1.25
11 VM,'When Strikes the ASP' . . . 1.25
12 VM,KJ,'The War That Shook
  the World' 1.25
13 VM,DGr,'The Tomb of the
  Stalking Dead' 1.25
14 VM,AMc,'All These Deadly
  Pawns' 1.25
15 TS, E:The Living Mummy,'Night
of Armageddon',October, 1975 1.25

SUPER SOLDIERS
1 I:Super Soldier,A:USAgent 2.75
2 A:USAgent 2.00
3 A:USAgent 2.00
4 A:USAgent,Avengers 2.00
5 A:Captain America,AWC 2.00
6 O:Super Soldiers 2.00
7 in Savage Land 2.00

SUPER-VILLAIN
CLASSICS
May, 1983
1 O:Galactus 3.50

SUPER-VILLAIN
TEAM-UP
August, 1975
1 GT/BEv(c),B:Dr.Doom/Sub-
  Mariner,A:Attuma,Tiger Shark 6.00
2 SB,A:Tiger Shark, Attuma 4.00

3 EH(c),JA,V:Attuma 4.00
4 HT,JM,Dr.Doom vs. Namor . . . 4.00
5 RB/JSt(c),HT,DP,A:Fantastic
  Four,I:Shroud 4.00
6 HT,JA,A:Shroud,Fantastic Four 3.00
7 RB/KJ(c),HT,O:Shroud 3.00
8 KG,V:Ringmaster 3.00
9 ST,A:Avengers,Iron Man 3.00
10 BH,DP,A:Capt.America,
  V:Attuma,Red Skull 3.00
11 DC/JSt(c),BH,DP,B:Dr. Doom,
  Red Skull,A:Capt. America . . . 3.00
12 DC/AM(c),BH,DP,Dr.Doom vs.
  Red Skull 3.00
13 KG,DP,Namor vs. Krang 3.00
14 JBy/TA(c),BH,DP,V:Magneto,
  X-over with Champions #15 . . 5.00
15 GT,ME,A:Red Skull 3.00
16 CI,A:Dr. Doom 3.00
17 KP(c),Red Skull Vs.Hatemonger
  June 1976 . . . . 3.00
Giant#1 F:Namor, Dr.Doom 3.00
Giant#2 F:Namor, Dr.Doom 3.00

SUSPENSE
Atlas
December, 1949
1 BP,Ph(c),Sidney Greenstreet/
  Peter Lorne (Maltese Falcon) 300.00
2 Ph(c),Dennis O'Keefe/Gale
  Storm (Abandoned) 175.00
3 B:Horror stories,'The Black
  Pit' 175.00
4 'Thing In Black' 125.00
5 BEv,GT,RH,BK,DBr,'Hangman's
  House' 135.00
6 BEv,GT,PAM,RH,'Madness
  of Scott Mannion' 125.00
7 DBr,GT,DR,'Murder' 125.00
8 GC,DRi,RH,'Don't Open
  the Door' 125.00
9 GC,DRi,'Back From The Dead'125.00
10 JMn(c),WIP,RH,'Trapped
  In Time' 125.00
11 MSy,'The Suitcase' 100.00
12 GT,'Dark Road' 100.00
13 JMn(c),'Strange Man',
  bondage cover 100.00
14 RH,'Death And Doctor Parker'100.00
15 JMn(c),OW,'The Machine' . . 100.00
16 OW,'Horror Backstage' 100.00
17 'Night Of Terror' 100.00
18 BK,'The Cozy Coffin' 100.00
19 BEv,RH 85.00
20 . . . . 85.00
21 BEv(c) 85.00
22 BEv(c),BK,OW 85.00
23 BEv 85.00
24 RH,GT 100.00
25 'I Died At Midnight' 100.00
26 BEv(c) 75.00
27 DBr 80.00
28 BEv 65.00
29 JMn,BF,JRo,April, 1953 . . . . 65.00

SWORDS OF THE
SWASHBUCKLERS
1 JG,Adult theme 2.25
2 JG 1.75
3 JG 1.75
4 JG 1.50
5 JG 1.50
6 JG 1.50
7 JG 1.50

8 . . . . 1.50
9 . . . . 1.50
10 . . . . 1.50
11 . . . . 1.50
12 June, 1987 . . . . 1.50

TALE OF THE MARINES
See: DEVIL-DOG DUGAN

TALES OF ASGARD
October, 1968
1 . . . . 35.00
Vol.2 #1 Feb,1984 . . . . 2.00

TALES OF G.I. JOE
January, 1988
1 reprints,#1 . . . . 2.00
2 #2 . . . . 1.50
3 #3 . . . . 1.50
4 #4 . . . . 1.50
5 #5 . . . . 1.50
6 #6 . . . . 1.50
7 rep. #7 - #16 . . . . 1.50

TALES OF JUSTICE
See: JUSTICE COMICS

TALES OF THE
MARVELS BLOCKBUSTER
Fully Painted 5.95

Tales of Suspense #48
© Marvel Entertainment Group

TALES OF SUSPENSE
January, 1959
1 DH(c),AW,'The Unknown
  Emptiness' 1,200.00
2 SK,'Robot in Hiding' 500.00
3 SD,JK,'The Aliens Who
  Captured Earth' 400.00
4 JK,AW,'One Of Us
  Is A Martian' 450.00
5 JF,'Trapped in the Tunnel
  To Nowhere' 275.00
6 JK(c),'Howl in the Swamp' . 275.00

---

7 SD,JK,'The Molten Man-Thing'275.00
8 BEv,'Monstro' 275.00
9 JK(c),JF,'Diablo' 300.00
10 RH,'I Bought Cyclops Back
   To Life' 275.00
11 JK(c),'I Created Sporr' 200.00
12 RC,'Gorkill The Living Demon'200.00
13 'Elektro' 200.00
14 JK(c),'I Created Colossus' .. 200.00
15 JK/DAy(c),'Behold...Goom' . 200.00
16 JK/DAy(c),'The Thing Called
   Metallo' 250.00
17 JK/DAy(c),'Goo Gam, Son
   of Goom' 200.00
18 JK/DAy(c),'Kraa the Inhuman' 200.00
19 JK,DAy,SD,'The Green Thing' 200.00
20 JK,DAy,SD,'Colossus Lives
   Again' 200.00
21 JK/DAy(c),SD,'This Is Klagg' 150.00
22 JK/DAy(c),SD,'Beware
   Of Bruttu' 150.00
23 JK,DAy,SD,'The Creature
   in the Black Bog' 150.00
24 JK,DAy,SD,'Insect Man' ... 150.00
25 JK,DAy,SD,'The Death of
   Monstrollo' 150.00
26 JK,DAy,SD,'The Thing That
   Crawled By Night' 150.00
27 JK,DAy,SD,'When Oog Lives
   Again' 150.00
28 JK,DAy,SD,'Back From
   the Dead' 150.00
29 JK,DAy,SD,DH,'The Martian
   Who Stole A City' 125.00
30 JK,DAy,SD,DH,'The Haunted
   Roller Coaster' 125.00
31 JK,DAy,SD,DH,'The Monster
   in the Iron Mask' 125.00
32 JK,DAy,SD,DH,'The Man in
   the Bee-Hive' 135.00
33 JK,DAy,SD,DH,'Chamber of
   Fear' 125.00
34 JK,DAy,SD,DH,'Inside The
   Blue Glass Bottle' 125.00
35 JK,DAy,SD,DH,'The Challenge
   of Zarkorr' 125.00
36 SD,'Meet Mr. Meek' 125.00
37 DH,SD,'Hagg' 125.00
38 'The Teenager who ruled
   the World 125.00
39 JK,O&I:Iron Man 2,700.00
39a rep.#39,Marvel Milestone . 2.95
40 JK,C:Iron Man 1,000.00
41 JK 600.00
42 DH,SD,I:Red Pharoah 250.00
43 JK,DH,I:Kala,A:Iron Man ... 250.00
44 DH,SD,V:Mad Pharoah 240.00
45 DH,V:Jack Frost 240.00
46 DH,CR,I:Crimson Dynamo . 160.00
47 SD,V:Melter 160.00
48 SD,N:Iron Man 175.00
49 SD,A:Angel 140.00
50 DH,I:Manderin 90.00
51 DH,I:Scarecrow 80.00
52 DH,I:Black Widow 110.00
53 DH,O:Watcher 100.00
54 DH,V:Mandarin 60.00
55 DH,V:Mandarin 60.00
56 DH,I:Unicorn 60.00
57 DH,I&O:Hawkeye 125.00
58 DH,B:Captain America 225.00
59 DH,1st S.A. Solo Captain America,
   I:Jarvis 225.00
60 DH,JK,V:Assassins 100.00
61 DH,JK,V:Mandarin 60.00

62 DH,JK,O:Mandarin 60.00
63 JK,O:Captain America 150.00
64 DH,JK,A:Black Widow,
   Hawkeye 70.00
65 DH,JK,I:Red Skull 85.00
66 DH,JK,O:Red Skull 80.00
67 DH,JK,V:Adolph Hitler 35.00
68 DH,JK,V:Red Skull 35.00
69 DH,JK,I:Titanium Man 37.00
70 DH,JK,V:Titanium Man 35.00
71 DH,JK,WW,V:Titanium Man . 32.00
72 DH,JK,V:The Sleeper 32.00
73 JK,GT,A:Black Knight 32.00
74 JK,GT,V:The Sleeper 32.00
75 JK,I:Batroc,Sharon Carter ... 35.00
76 JR,V:Mandarin 32.00
77 JK,JR,V:Ultimo,I:Peggy
   Carter 32.00
78 GC,JK,V:Ultimo 32.00
79 GC,JK,V:Red Skull,
   I:Cosmic Cube 45.00
80 GC,JK,V:Red Skull 50.00
81 GC,JK,V:Red Skull 37.00
82 GC,JK,V:The Adaptoid 37.00
83 GC,JK,V:The Adaptoid 37.00
84 GC,JK,V:Mandarin 37.00
85 GC,JK,V:Batroc 37.00
86 GC,JK,V:Mandarin 37.00
87 GC,V:Mole Man 37.00
88 JK,GC,V:Power Man 37.00
89 JK,GC,V:Red Skull 37.00
90 JK,GC,V:Red Skull 37.00
91 GC,JK,V:Crusher 37.00
92 GC,JK,A:Nick Fury 37.00
93 GC,JK,V:Titanium Man 37.00
94 GC,JK,I:Modok 39.00
95 GC,JK,V:Grey Gargoyle,IR:Cap.
   America 37.00
96 GC,JK,V:Grey Gargoyle 37.00
97 GC,JK,I:Whiplash,
   A:Black Panther 37.00
98 GC,JK,I:Whitney Frost
   A:Black Panther 50.00
99 GC,JK,A:Black Panther 60.00
Becomes:

CAPTAIN AMERICA

TALES OF SUSPENSE
MARVEL MILESTONE
1 Metallic(c) rep. Tales 2.95

TALES OF THE ZOMBIE
August, 1973
(black & white magazine)
1 Reprint Menace #5,O:Zombie 18.00
2 GC,GT 10.00
3 .... 10.00
4 'Live and Let Die' 10.00
5 BH 10.00
6 .... 10.00
7 thru 9 AA .... @10.00
10 March, 1975 .... 10.00

TALES TO ASTONISH
[1st Series]
January, 1959
1 JDa,'Ninth Wonder o/t World'1,000.00
2 SD,'Capture A Martian' 500.00
3 SD,JK,'The Giant From
   Outer Space' 350.00
4 SD,JK,'The Day The
   Martians Struck' 350.00
5 SD,AW,'The Things on

Tales to Astonish #31
© Marvel Entertainment Group

   Easter Island' 350.00
6 SD,JK,'Invasion of the
   Stone Men' 300.00
7 SD,JK,'The Thing on Bald
   Mountain' 250.00
8 SD,JK,'Mummex, King of
   the Mummies' 250.00
9 JK(c),SD,'Droom, the
   Living Lizard' 250.00
10 JK,SD,'Titano' 250.00
11 JK,SD,'Monstrom, the Dweller
   in the Black Swamp' 200.00
12 JK/DAy(c),SD,'Gorgilla' 200.00
13 JK,SD,'Groot, the Monster
   From Planet X' 200.00
14 JK,SD,'Krang' 200.00
15 JK/DAy,'The Blip' 200.00
16 JK,SD,'Thorr' 200.00
17 JK,SD,'Vandoom' 200.00
18 JK,SD,'Gorgilla Strikes Again' 200.00
19 JK,SD,'Rommbu' 200.00
20 JK,SD,'X, The Thing
   That Lived' 200.00
21 JK,SD,'Trull the Inhuman' .. 150.00
22 JK,SD,'The Crawling
   Creature' 150.00
23 JK,SD,'Moomba is Here' ... 150.00
24 JK,SD,'The Abominable
   Snowman' 150.00
25 JK,SD,'The Creature From
   Krogarr' 150.00
26 JK,SD,'Four-Armed Things' . 150.00
27 StL(s),SD,JK,I:Antman ... 2,500.00
28 JK,SD,I Am the Gorilla Man 125.00
29 JK,SD,When the Space
   Beasts Attack 125.00
30 JK,SD,Thing From the
   Hidden Swamp 125.00
31 JK,SD,The Mummy's Secret 125.00
32 JK,SD,Quicksand 125.00
33 JK,SD,Dead Storage 125.00
34 JK,SD,Monster at Window . 125.00
35 StL(s),JK,SD, B:Ant Man
   (2nd App.) 1,200.00
36 JK,SD,V:Comrade X 450.00
37 JK,SD,V:The Protector 225.00
38 JK,SD,Betrayed By the Ants 225.00
39 JK,DH,V:Scarlet Beetle 225.00

Tales to Astonish #87
© Marvel Entertainment Group

40 JK,SD,DH,The Day Ant-Man
   Failed 225.00
41 DH,St,SD,V:Kulla 135.00
42 DH,JSe,SD,Voice of Doom . 135.00
43 DH,SD,Master of Time 135.00
44 JK,SD,I&O:Wasp 225.00
45 DH,SD,V:Egghead 100.00
46 DH,SD,I:Cyclops(robot) 100.00
47 DH,SD,V:Trago 100.00
48 DH,SD,I:Porcupine 100.00
49 JK,DH,AM,Ant-Man Becomes
   Giant-Man 135.00
50 JK,SD,I&O:Human Top 72.00
51 JK,V:Human Top 72.00
52 I&O:Black Knight 72.00
53 DH,V:Porcupine 72.00
54 DH,I:El Toro 72.00
55 V:Human Top 72.00
56 V:The Magician 75.00
57 A:Spider-Man 95.00
58 V:Colossus(not X-Men one) . 68.00
59 V:Hulk,Black Knight 110.00
60 SD,B:Hulk,Giant Man 200.00
61 SD,I:Glenn Talbot,
   V:Egghead 60.00
62 I:Leader,N:Wasp 60.00
63 SD,O:Leader(1st full story) . . 60.00
64 SD,V:Leader 60.00
65 DH,SD,N:Giant-Man, ... 60.00
66 JK,SD,V:Leader,Chameleon . 75.00
67 JK,SD,I:Kanga Khan 75.00
68 JK,N:Human Top,V:Leader . . 75.00
69 JK,V:Human Top,Leader,
   E:Giant-Man 75.00
70 JK,B:Sub-Mariner/Hulk,I:
   Neptune 80.00
71 JK,V:Leader,I:Vashti 56.00
72 JK,V:Leader 56.00
73 JK,V:Leader,A:Watcher 56.00
74 JK,V:Leader,A:Watcher 56.00
75 JK,A:Watcher 56.00
76 JK,Atlantis 56.00
77 JK,V:Executioner 56.00
78 GC,JK,Prince and the Puppet 56.00
79 JK,Hulk vs.Hercules 56.00

80 GC,JK,Moleman vs Tyrannus 56.00
81 GC,JK,I:Boomerang,Secret Empire,
   Moleman vs Tyrannus 56.00
82 GC,JK,V:Iron Man 60.00
83 JK,V:Boomerang 50.00
84 GC,JK,Like a Beast at Bay . . 50.00
85 GC,JB,Missile & the Monster 50.00
86 JB,V:Warlord Krang 50.00
87 BEv,IR:Hulk 50.00
88 BEv,GK,V:Boomerang 50.00
89 BEv,GK,V:Stranger 50.00
90 JK,I:Abomination 50.00
91 BEv,DA,V:Abomination 50.00
92 MSe,C:Silver Surfer x-over . 62.00
93 MSe,Silver Surver x-over . 60.00
94 BEv,MSe,V:Dragorr,High
   Evolutionary. 50.00
95 BEv,MSe,V:High Evolutionary 50.00
96 MSe,Skull Island,High Evol. . 50.00
97 MSe,C:Kazar,X-Men 55.00
98 DA,MSe,I:Legion of the Living
   Lightning,I:Seth 50.00
99 DA,MSe,V:Legion of the Living
   Lighting 50.00

Tales to Astonish #100
© Marvel Entertainment Group

100 MSe,DA,Hulk v.SubMariner . 60.00
101 MSe,GC,V:Loki 70.00
Becomes: INCREDIBLE HULK

TALES TO ASTONISH
[2nd Series]
December, 1979

1 JB,rep.Sub-Mariner#1 . . . . . . 1.75
2 JB,rep.Sub-Mariner#2 . . . . . 1.25
3 JB,rep.Sub-Mariner#3 . . . . . 1.25
4 JB,rep.Sub-Mariner#4 . . . . . 1.25
5 JB,rep.Sub-Mariner#5 . . . . . 1.25
6 JB,rep.Sub-Mariner#6 . . . . . 1.25
7 JB,rep.Sub-Mariner#7 . . . . . 1.25
8 JB,rep.Sub-Mariner#8 . . . . . 1.25
9 JB,rep.Sub-Mariner#9 . . . . . 1.25
10 JB,rep.Sub-Mariner#10 . . . . . 1.25
11 JB,rep.Sub-Mariner#11 . . . . . 1.25
12 JB,rep.Sub-Mariner#12 . . . . . 1.25
13 JB,rep.Sub-Mariner#13 . . . . . 1.25
14 JB,rep.Sub-Mariner#14 . . . . . 1.25

Tarzan #23
© Marvel Entertainment Group

TARZAN
June, 1977

1 JB,Edgar Rice Burroughs Adapt. 1.50
2 JB,O:Tarzan 1.25
3 JB,'The Alter of the Flaming
   God',I:LA 1.25
4 JB,TD,V:Leopards 1.25
5 JB,TD,'Vengeance',A:LA . . . 1.25
6 JB,TD,'Rage of Tantor,A:LA . . 1.25
7 JB,TD,'Tarzan Rescues The
   Moon' 1.00
8 JB,'Battle For The Jewel Of
   Opar' 1.00
9 JB,'Histah, the Serpent' 1.00
10 JB,'The Deadly Peril of
   Jane Clayton' 1.00
11 JB 1.00
12 JB,'Fangs of Death' 1.00
13 JB,'Lion-God' 1.00
14 JB,'The Fury of Fang and Claw' 1.00
15 JB,'Sword of the Slaver' 1.00
16 JB,'Death Rides the Jungle
   Winds' 1.00
17 JB,'The Entrance to the
   Earths Core' 1.00
18 JB,'Corsairs of the Earths Core' 1.00
19 'Pursuit' 1.00
20 'Blood Bond' 1.00
21 'Dark and Bloody Sky' 1.00
22 JM,RN,'War In Pellucidar' . . . 1.00
23 'To the Death' 1.00
24 'The Jungle Lord Returns' . . . 1.00
25 RB(c),V:Poachers 1.00
26 RB(c),'Caged' 1.00
27 RB(c),'Chaos in the Caberet' . . 1.00
28 'A Savage Against A City' 1.00
29 October, 1979 . . . . 1.00
Ann.#1 JB 1.50
Ann.#2 'Drums of the
   Death-Dancers' 1.25
Ann.#3 'Ant-Men and the
   She-Devils 1.25

TARZAN OF THE APES
July, 1984

1 (movie adapt.) 1.25
2 . . . . 1.25

All comics prices listed are for *Near Mint* condition.   **CVA Page 233**

TEAM AMERICA
June, 1982
1 O:Team America		2.50
2 V:Marauder		1.25
3 LMc,V:Mr.Mayhem		1.25
4 Lmc,V:Arcade Assassins		1.25
5 A:Marauder		1.25
6 A:R.U. Ready		1.25
7 LMc,V:Emperor of Texas		1.25
8 DP,V:Hydra		1.25
9 A:Iron Man		1.25
10 V:Minister Ashe		1.00
11 A:Marauder,V:GhostRider		5.50
12 DP,Marauder unmasked, May, 1983		2.50

TEAM HELIX
1 A:Wolverine		2.00
2 A:Wolverine		2.00

TEEN COMICS
See: ALL WINNERS COMICS

TEENAGE ROMANCE
See: MY ROMANCE

TERMINATOR 2
September, 1991
1 KJ,movie adaption		1.25
2 KJ,movie adaption		1.25
3 KJ,movie adaption		1.25
Terminator II (bookshelf format)		4.95
Terminator II (B&W mag. size)		2.25

TERRARISTS
Epic
1 thru 4 w/card		@2.50
5 thru 7		@2.50

TERROR INC.
1 JZ,I:Hellfire		3.00
2 JZ,I:Bezeel,Hellfire		2.50
3 JZ,A:Hellfire		2.00
4 JZ,A:Hellfire,V:Barbatos		2.00
5 JZ,V:Hellfire,A:Dr Strange		2.00
6 JZ,MT,A:Punisher		2.00
7 JZ,V:Punisher		2.00
8 Christmas issue		2.00
9 JZ,V:Wolverine		2.25
10 V:Wolverine		2.25
11 A:Silver Sable,Cage		2.00
12 For Love Nor Money#4,A:Cage, Silver Sable		2.00
13 Inf.Crusade,A:Gh.Rider		2.00

TESSIE THE TYPIST
Timely
Summer, 1944
1 BW,'Doc Rockblock'		275.00
2 BW,'Powerhouse Pepper'		200.00
3 Football cover		60.00
4 BW		125.00
5 BW		125.00
6 BW,HK,'Hey Look'		125.00
7 BW		125.00
8 BW		125.00
9 BW,HK,'Powerhouse Pepper'		135.00
10 BW,A:Rusty		135.00
11 BW,A:Rusty		135.00
12 BW,HK		135.00
13 BW,A:Millie The Model,Rusty		110.00
14 BW		80.00

15 HK,A:Millie,Rusty		80.00
16 HK		55.00
17 HK,A:Millie, Rusty		55.00
18 HK		55.00
19 Annie Oakley story		50.00
20		45.00
21 A:Lana, Millie		45.00
22		45.00
23		45.00

Becomes:
TINY TESSIE
24		35.00

Becomes:
REAL EXPERIENCES
25 Ph(c),January, 1950		25.00

TEXAS KID
Atlas
January, 1951
1 GT,JMn,O:Texas Kid		125.00
2 JMn		60.00
3 JMn,'Man Who Didn't Exist'		50.00
4 JMn		50.00
5 JMn		50.00
6 JMn		50.00
7 JMn		50.00
8 JMn		50.00
9 JMn		50.00
10 JMn,July, 1952		50.00

TEX DAWSON, GUNSLINGER
January, 1973
1 JSo(c)		2.00

Becomes:
GUNSLINGER
2		1.25
3 June, 1973		1.25

TEX MORGAN
August, 1948
1		150.00
2 'Boot Hill Welcome For A Bad Man'		100.00
3		75.00
4 'Trapped in the Outlaws Den', A:Arizona Annie		75.00
5 'Valley of Missing Cowboys'		75.00
6 'Never Say Murder', A:Tex Taylor		75.00
7 CCB,Ph(c),'Captain Tootsie', A:Tex Taylor		100.00
8 Ph(c),'Terror Of Rimrock Valley',A:Diablo		100.00
9 Ph(c),'Death to Tex Taylor' February, 1950		100.00

TEX TAYLOR
September, 1948
1 'Boot Hill Showdown'		150.00
2 'When Two-Gun Terror Rides the Range'		90.00
3 'Thundering Hooves and Blazing Guns'		80.00
4 Ph(c),'Draw or Die Cowpoke'		90.00
5 Ph(c),'The Juggler of Yellow Valley',A:Blaze Carson		90.00
6 Ph(c),'Mystery of Howling Gap'		80.00
7 Ph(c),'Trapped in Times' Lost Land',A:Diablo		100.00
8 Ph(c),'The Mystery of Devil-Tree Plateau',A:Diablo		100.00

9 Ph(c),'Guns Along the Border', A:Nimo,March, 1950		100.00

THANOS QUEST
1990
1 JSn,RLm,V:Elders, for Soul Gems		13.00
1a 2nd printing		5.50
2 JSn,RLm,O:SoulGems,I: Infinity Gauntlet (story cont.in SilverSurfer #44)		15.00
2a 2nd printing		5.50

Thing #5
© Marvel Entertainment Group

THING, THE
July, 1983
1 JBy,O:Thing		2.50
2 JBy,Woman from past		1.75
3 JBy,A:Inhumans		1.50
4 JBy,A:Lockjaw		1.50
5 JBy,A:Spider-Man,She-Hulk		1.50
6 JBy,V:Puppet Master		1.25
7 JBy,V:Goody Two Shoes		1.25
8 JBy,V:Egyptian Curse		1.25
9 JBy,F:Alicia Masters		1.25
10 JBy,Secret Wars		1.25
11 JBy,B:Rocky Grimm		1.25
12 JBy,F:Rocky Grimm		1.25
13 JBy,F:Rocky Grimm		1.25
14 F:Rocky Grimm		1.25
15 F:Rocky Grimm		1.25
16 F:Rocky Grimm		1.25
17 F:Rocky Grimm		1.25
18 F:Rocky Grimm		1.25
19 F:Rocky Grimm		1.25
20 F:Rocky Grimm		1.25
21 V:Ultron		1.25
22 V:Ultron		1.25
23 R:Thing to Earth,A:Fant.Four		1.25
24 V:Rhino,A:Miracle Man		1.25
25 V:Shamrock		1.50
26 A:Vance Astro		1.50
27 I:Sharon Ventura		1.25
28 A:Vance Astro		1.25
29 A:Vance Astro		1.25
30 Secret Wars II,A:Vance Astro		1.25

All comics prices listed are for *Near Mint* condition.

31 A:Vance Astro	1.25
32 A:Vance Astro	1.25
33 A:Vance Astro,I:NewGrapplers	1.25
34 V:Titania,Sphinx	1.25
35 I:New Ms.Marvel,PowerBroker	1.25
36 Last Issue,A:She-Hulk	1.25

[Mini-Series]

1 rep.Marvel Two-in-One #50	1.75
2 rep Marvel Two-in-One,V:GR	1.75
3 rep Marvel Two-in-One #51	1.25
4 rep Marvel Two-in-One #43	1.25

THOR, THE MIGHTY

Prev: Journey Into Mystery
March, 1966

126 JK,V:Hercules	125.00
127 JK,I:Pluto,Volla	45.00
128 JK,V:Pluto,A:Hercules	45.00
129 JK,V:Pluto,I:Ares	45.00
130 JK,V:Pluto,A:Hercules	45.00
131 JK,I:Colonizers	45.00
132 JK,A:Colonizers,I:Ego	45.00
133 JK,A:Colonizers,A:Ego	45.00
134 JK,I:High Evolutionary, Man-Beast	55.00
135 JK,O:High Evolutionary	50.00
136 JK,F:Odin	45.00
137 JK,I:Ulik	45.00
138 JK,V:Ulik,A:Sif	45.00
139 JK,V:Ulik	45.00
140 JK,V:Growing Man	45.00
141 JK,V:Replicus	33.00
142 JK,V:Super Skrull	33.00
143 JK,BEv,V:Talisman	33.00
144 JK,V:Talisman	33.00
145 JK,V:Ringmaster	33.00
146 JK,O:Inhumans Part 1	35.00
147 JK,O:Inhumans Part 2	35.00
148 JK,I:Wrecker,O:Black Bolt	35.00
149 JK,O:Black Bolt,Medusa	32.00
150 JK,A:Triton	32.00
151 JK,V:Destroyer	32.00
152 JK,V:Destroyer	32.00
153 JK,F:Dr.Blake	32.00
154 JK,I:Mangog	32.00
155 JK,V:Mangog	32.00

The Mighty Thor #126
© Marvel Entertainment Group

156 JK,V:Mangog	32.00
157 JK,D:Mangog	32.00
158 JK,O:Don Blake Part 1	70.00
159 JK,O:Don Blake Part 2	35.00
160 JK,I:Travrians	32.00
161 JK,Shall a God Prevail	23.00
162 JK,O:Galactus	35.00
163 JK,I:Mutates,A:Pluto	23.00
164 JK,A:Pluto,V:Greek Gods	23.00
165 JK,V:Him/Warlock	60.00
166 JK,V:Him/Warlock	60.00
167 JK,F:Sif	23.00
168 JK,O:Galactus	35.00
169 JK,O:Galactus	35.00
170 JK,BEv,V:Thermal Man	21.00
171 JK,BEv,V:Wrecker	21.00
172 JK,BEv,V:Ulik	21.00
173 JK,BEv,V:Ulik,Ringmaster	21.00
174 JK,BEv,V:Crypto-Man	21.00
175 JK,Fall of Asgard,V:Surtur	21.00
176 JK,V:Surtur	21.00
177 JK,I:Igon,V:Surtur	21.00
178 JK,V:Silver Surfer	24.00
179 JK,MSe,C:Galactus	21.00
180 NA,JSi,V:Loki	15.00
181 NA,JSi,V:Loki	15.00
182 JB,V:Dr.Doom	7.50
183 JB,V:Dr.Doom	7.50
184 JB,I:The Guardian	7.50
185 JB,JSt,V:Silent One	7.50
186 JB,JSt,V:Hela	7.50
187 JB,JSt,V:Odin	7.50
188 JB,JM,F:Odin	7.50
189 JB,JSt,V:Hela	7.50
190 JB,I:Durok	7.50
191 JB,JSt,V:Loki	7.50
192 JB	7.50
193 JB,SB,V:Silver Surfer	45.00
194 JB,SB,V:Loki	7.50
195 JB,JR,V:Mangog	7.50
196 JB,NR,V:Kartag	7.50
197 JB,V:Mangog	7.50
198 JB,V:Pluto	7.50
199 JB,V:Pluto,Hela	7.50
200 JB,Ragnarok	9.00
201 JB,JM,Odin resurrected.	6.00
202 JB,V:Ego-Prime	6.00
203 JB,V:Ego-Prime	6.00
204 JB,JM,Demon from t/Depths	6.00
205 JB,V:Mephisto	6.00
206 JB,V:Absorbing Man	5.00
207 JB,V:Absorbing Man	5.00
208 JB,V:Mercurio	5.00
209 JB,I:Druid	5.00
210 JB,DP,I:Ulla,V:Ulik	5.00
211 JB,DP,V:Ulik	4.00
212 JB,JSt,V:Sssthgar	4.00
213 JB,DP,I:Gregor	4.00
214 SB,JM,V:Dark Nebula	4.00
215 JB,JM,J:Xorr	4.00
216 JB,JM,V:4D-Man	4.00
217 JB,SB,I:Krista,V:Odin	4.00
218 JB,JM,A:Colonizers	4.00
219 JB,I:Protector	4.00
220 JB,V:Avalon	4.00
221 JB,V:Olympus	4.00
222 JB,JSe,A:Hercules,V:Pluto	4.00
223 JB,A:Hercules,V:Pluto	4.00
224 JB,V:Destroyer	4.00
225 JB,JSi,I:Fire Lord	8.00
226 JB,A:Watcher,Galactus	4.00
227 JB,JSi,V:Ego	4.00
228 JB,JSi,A:Galactus,D:Ego	4.00
229 JB,JSi,A:Hercules,I:Dweller	4.00
230 JB,A:Hercules	4.00

The Mighty Thor #148
© Marvel Entertainment Group

231 JB,DG,V:Armak	4.00
232 JB,JSi,A:Firelord	4.00
233 JB,Asgard Invades Earth	4.00
234 JB,V:Loki	4.00
235 JB,JSi,I:Possessor (Kamo Tharnn)	4.00
236 JB,JSi,V:Absorbing Man	3.50
237 JB,JSi,V:Ulik	3.50
238 JB,JSi,V:Ulik	3.50
239 JB,JSi,V:Ulik	3.50
240 SB,KJ,V:Seth	3.50
241 JB,JGi,I:Geb	3.50
242 JB,JSi,V:Servitor	3.50
243 JB,JSt,V:Servitor	3.50
244 JB,JSt,V:Servitor	3.50
245 JB,JSt,V:Servitor	3.50
246 JB,JSt,A:Firelord	3.50
247 JB,JSt,A:Firelord	3.50
248 JB,V:Storm Giant	3.50
249 JB,V:Odin	3.50
250 JB,D:Igron,V:Mangog	3.50
251 JB,A:Sif	3.50
252 JB,V:Ulik	3.50
253 JB,I:Trogg	3.50
254 JK,O:Dr.Blake rep	3.50
255 Stone Men of Saturn Rep.	3.50
256 JB,I:Sporr	3.50
257 JK,JB,I:Fee-Lon	3.50
258 JK,JB,V:Grey Gargoyle	3.50
259 JB,A:Spider-Man	4.00
260 WS,I:Doomsday Star	4.00
261 WS,I:Soul Survivors	3.00
262 WS,Odin Found,I:Odin Force	3.00
263 WS,V:Loki	3.00
264 WS,V:Loki	3.00
265 WS,V:Destroyer	3.00
266 WS,Odin Quest	3.00
267 WS,F:Odin	3.00
268 WS,V:Damocles	3.00
269 WS,V:Stilt-Man	3.00
270 WS,V:Blastaar	3.00
271 Avengers,Iron Man x-over	3.00
272 JB,Day the Thunder Failed	3.00
273 JB,V:Midgard Serpent	3.00
274 JB,D:Balder,I:Hermod,Hoder	3.00
275 JB,V:Loki,I:Sigyn	3.00
276 JB,Trial of Loki	2.50
277 JB,V:Fake Thor	2.50

All comics prices listed are for *Near Mint* condition.

278 JB,V:Fake Thor 2.50
279 A:Pluto,V:Ulik 2.50
280 V:Hyperion 2.50
281 O:Space Phantom 2.50
282 V:Immortus,I:Tempus 2.50
283 JB,V:Celestials 2.50
284 JB,V:Gammenon 2.50
285 JB,R:Karkas 2.50
286 KP,KRo,D:Kro,I:Dragona . . . 2.50
287 KP,2nd App & O:Forgotten
   One(Hero) 2.50
288 KP,V:Forgotten One 2.50
289 KP,V:Destroyer 2.50
290 I:Red Bull(Toro Rojo) 2.50
291 KP,A:Eternals,Zeus 2.50
292 KP,V:Odin 2.50
293 KP,Door to Minds Eye 2.50
294 KP,O:Odin & Asgard,I:Frey . . 2.50
295 KP,I:Fafnir,V:Storm Giants. . . 2.50
296 KP,D:Siegmund 2.50
297 KP,V:Sword of Siegfried 2.50
298 KP,V:Dragon(Fafnir) 2.50
299 KP,A:Valkyrie,I:Hagen 2.50
300 KP,giant,O:Odin & Destroyer,
   Rindgold Ring Quest ends,D:Uni-
   Mind,I:Mother Earth 5.00
301 KP,O:Mother Earth,V:Apollo . 2.50
302 KP,V:Locus 2.50
303 KP,Whatever Gods There Be . 2.50
304 KP,V:Wrecker 2.50
305 KP,R:Gabriel(Air Walker) . . . 2.50
306 KP,O&V:Firelord,O:AirWalker 2.50
307 KP,I:Dream Demon 2.50
308 KP,V:Snow Giants 2.50
309 V:Bomnardiers 2.50
310 KP,V:Mephisto 2.50
311 KP,GD,A:Valkyrie 2.50
312 KP,V:Tyr 2.50
313 KP,Thor Trial 2.50
314 KP,A:Drax,Moondragon 2.50
315 KP,O:Bi-Beast 2.50
316 KP,A:Iron Man,Man Thing,
   V:Man-Beast 2.50
317 KP,V:Man-Beast 2.50
318 GK,V:Fafnir 2.50
319 KP,I&D:Zaniac 2.50
320 KP,V:Rimthursar 2.75
321 I:Menagerie 2.50
322 V:Heimdall 2.50
323 V:Death 2.50
324 V:Graviton 2.50
325 JM,O:Darkoth,V:Mephisto . . 2.75
326 I:New Scarlet Scarab 2.75
327 V:Loki & Tyr 2.50
328 I:Megatak 2.75
329 HT,V:Hrungnir 2.50
330 BH,I:Crusader 2.50
331 Threshold of Death 2.50
332 V:Dracula 2.75
333 BH,V:Dracula 2.75
334 Quest For Rune Staff 2.50
335 V:Possessor 2.50
336 A:Captain Ultra 2.75
337 WS,I:Beta Ray Bill,A:Surtur . 7.00
338 WS,O:Beta Ray Bill,I:Lorelei . 5.00
339 WS,V:Beta Ray Bill 3.50
340 WS,A:Beta Ray Bill 3.00
341 WS,V:Fafnir 2.25
342 WS,V:Fafnir,I:Eilif 2.25
343 WS,V:Fafnir 2.25
344 WS,Balder Vs.Loki,I:Malekith . 2.25
345 WS,V:Malekith 2.25
346 WS,V:Malekith 2.25
347 WS,V:Malekith,I:Algrim
   (Kurse) 2.25

The Mighty Thor #239
© Marvel Entertainment Group

348 WS,V:Malekith 2.25
349 WS,R:Beta Ray Bill,O:Odin,
   I&O:Vili & Ve(Odin's brothers) . 2.50
350 WS,V:Surtur 2.25
351 WS,V:Surtur 2.25
352 WS,V:Surtur 2.25
353 WS,V:Surtur,D:Odin 2.25
354 WS,V:Hela 2.25
355 WS,SB,A:Thor's Great
   Grandfather 2.25
356 BL,BG,V:Hercules 2.25
357 WS,A:Beta Ray Bill 2.50
358 WS,A:Beta Ray Bill 2.50
359 WS,V:Loki 2.25
360 WS,V:Hela 2.25
361 WS,V:Hela 2.25
362 WS,V:Hela 2.25
363 WS,Secret Wars II,V:Kurse . 2.50
364 WS,I:Thunder Frog 2.25
365 WS,A:Thunder Frog 2.25
366 WS,A:Thunder Frog 2.25
367 WS,D:Malekith,A:Kurse 2.25
368 WS,F:Balder t/Brave,Kurse . 2.25
369 WS,F:Balder the Brave 2.25
370 JB,V:Loki 2.25
371 SB,I:Justice Peace,V:Zaniac . 2.25
372 SB,V:Justice Peace 2.25
373 SB,A:X-Factor,(Mut.Mass) . . . 5.00
374 WS,SB,A:X-Factor,(Mut.Mass)
   A:Sabretooth 7.00
375 WS,SB,N:Thor(Exoskeleton) . 2.25
376 WS,SB,V:Absorbing Man . . . 2.25
377 WS,SB,N:Thor,A:Ice Man . . . 2.25
378 WS,SB,V:Frost Giants 2.25
379 WS,V:Midgard Serpent 2.25
380 WS,V:Midgard Serpent 2.25
381 WE,SB,A:Avengers 2.50
382 WS,SB,V:Frost Giants,Loki . 2.50
383 BBr,Secret Wars story 2.50
384 RF,BBr,I:Future Thor(Dargo) . 4.00
385 EL,V:Hulk 2.00
386 RF,BBr,I:Leir 2.00
387 RF,BBr,V:Celestials 2.00
388 RF,BBr,V:Celestials 2.00
389 RF,BBr,V:Celestials 2.00

390 RF,BBr,A:Avengers,V:Seth . . 2.00
391 RF,BBr,I:Mongoose,Eric
   Masterson,A:Spiderman 6.00
392 RF,I:Quicksand 2.00
393 RF,BBr,V:Quicksand,A:DD . . 2.00
394 RF,BBr,V:Earth Force 2.00
395 RF,V:Earth Force 2.00
396 RF,A:Black Knight 2.00
397 RF,A:Loki 2.00
398 RF,DH,R:Odin,V:Seth 2.00
399 RF,RT,R:Surtur,V:Seth 2.00
400 RF,JSt,CV,V:Surtur,Seth 5.00
401 V:Loki 2.00
402 RF,JSt,V:Quicksand 2.00
403 RF,JSt,V:Executioner 2.00
404 RF,JSt,TD,V:Annihilus 2.00
405 RF,JSt,TD,V:Annihilus 2.00
406 RF,JSt,TD,V:Wundagore 2.00
407 RF,JSt,R:Hercules,High Evol. 2.00
408 RF,JSt,I:Eric Masterson/Thor
   V:Mongoose 3.50
409 RF,JSt,V:Dr.Doom 2.00
410 RF,JSt,V:Dr.Doom,She-Hulk . 2.00
411 RF,JSt,C:New Warriors
   V:Juggernaut,A of V 10.00
412 RF,JSt,I:New Warriors
   V:Juggernaut,A of V 15.00
413 RF,JSt,A:Dr.Strange 1.75
414 RF,JSt,V:Ulik 1.75
415 HT,O:Thor 1.75
416 RF,JSt,A:Hercules 1.75
417 RF,JSt,A:High Evolutionary . . 1.75
418 RF,JSt,V:Wrecking Crew 1.75
419 RF,JSt,B:Black Galaxy
   Saga,I:Stellaris 1.75
420 RF,JSt,A:Avengers,V:Stellaris 1.75
421 RF,JSt,V:Stellaris 1.75
422 RF,JSt,V:High Evol.,Nobilus . 1.75
423 RF,JSt,A:High Evol.,Celestials
   Count Tagar 1.75
424 RF,JSt,V:Celestials,E:Black
   Galaxy Saga 1.75
425 RF,AM,V:Surtur,Ymir 1.75
426 RF,JSt,HT,O:Earth Force . . . 1.50
427 RF,JSt,A:Excalibur 1.50
428 RF,JSt,A:Excalibur 1.50
429 RF,JSt,A:Ghost Rider 2.00
430 RF,AM,A:Mephisto,Gh.Rider . 1.75
431 HT,AM,V:Ulik,Loki 1.75
432 RF,D:Loki,Thor Banished,Eric
   Masterson becomes 2nd Thor . 4.00
433 RF,V:Ulik 5.00
434 RF,AM,V:Warriors Three 2.50
435 RF,AM,V:Annihilus 2.50
436 RF,AM,V:Titania,Absorbing
   Man,A:Hercules 1.50
437 RF,AM,V:Quasar 1.50
438 RF,JSt,A:Future Thor(Dargo) . 1.50
439 RF,JSt,A:Drago 1.50
440 RF,AM,I:Thor Corps 2.50
441 RF,AM,Celestials vs.Ego 2.50
442 RF,AM,Don Blake,Beta Ray
   Bill,Mephisto 1.50
443 RF,AM,A:Dr.Strange,Silver
   Surfer,V:Mephisto 1.50
444 RF,AM,Special X-mas tale . . . 1.50
445 AM,Galactic Storm,pt.7
   V:Gladiator 1.50
446 AM,Galactic Storm,pt.14
   A:Avengers 1.50
447 RF,AM,V:Absorbing Man
   A:Spider-Man 1.50
448 RF,AM,V:Titania,A:SpM 1.50
449 RF,AM,V:Ulik 1.50
450 RF,AM,V:Heimdall,A:Code Blue

Double-Sized,Gatefold(c),rep.
Journey Into Mystery#87 . . . . . 3.25
451 RF,AM,I:Bloodaxe 1.50
452 RF,AM,V:Bloodaxe 1.50
453 RF,AM,V:Mephisto 1.50
454 RF,AM,V:Mephisto,Loki,
Karnilla 1.50
455 AM(i),V:Loki,Karnilla,R:Odin,
A:Dr.Strange 1.50
456 RF,AM,V:Bloodaxe 1.50
457 RF,AM,R:1st Thor 1.50
458 RF,AM,Thor vs Eric 1.50
459 RF,AM,C&I:Thunderstrike(Eric
Masterson) 2.00
460 I:New Valkyrie 1.50
461 V:Beta Ray Bill 1.50
462 A:New Valkyrie 1.50
463 Infinity Crusade 1.50
464 Inf.Crusade,V:Loki 1.50
465 Infinity Crusade 1.50
466 Infinity Crusade 1.50
467 Infinity Crusade 1.50
468 RMz(s),Blood & Thunder#1 . . 3.00
469 RMz(s),Blood & Thunder#5 . . 1.50
470 MCW,Blood & Thunder#9 . . . 1.50
471 MCW,E:Blood & Thunder . . . 1.50
472 B:RTs(s),MCW,I:Godling,C:High
Evolutionary 1.50
473 MCW,V:Godling,High Evolutionary
I&C:Karnivore(Man-Beast) 1.75
474 MCW,C:High Evolutionary . . . 1.50
475 MCW,Foil(c),A:Donald Blake,
N:Thor 3.00
475a Newsstand Ed. 2.00
476 V:Destroyer 1.75
477 V:Destroyer,A:Thunderstrike . 1.75
478 V:Norvell Thor 1.75
479 V:Norvell Thor 1.75
480 V:High Evolutionary 1.50
481 V:Grotesk 1.50
482 Don Blake construct 1.50
483 RTs,MCW,V:Loki 1.50
484 Badoy and Soul 1.50
485 V:The Thing 1.50
486 High Evolutionary,Godpack . . 1.50
487 V:Kurse 1.50
488 RTs,MCW,Kurse Saga concl. 1.50
Ann.#2 JK,V:Destroyer 50.00
Ann.#3 JK,rep,Grey Gargoyle. . . 13.00
Ann.#4 JK,rep,TheLivingPlanet. . 11.00
Ann.#5 JK,JB,Hercules,O:Odin . 10.00
Ann.#6 JK,JB,A:Guardians of the
Galaxy,V:Korvac 10.00
Ann.#7 WS,Eternals 9.00
Ann.#8 JB,V:Zeus 8.00
Ann.#9 LMc,Dormammu 7.00
Ann.#10 O:Chthon,Gaea,A:Pluto . 6.00
Ann.#11 O:Odin 6.00
Ann.#12 BH,I:Vidar(Odin's son) . 6.00
Ann.#13 JB,V:Mephisto 6.00
Ann.#14 AM,DH,Atlantis Attacks . 5.00
Ann.#15 HT,Terminus Factor #3 . 4.00
Ann.#16 Korvac Quest,pt.2,
Guardians of Galaxy 2.50
Ann.#17 Citizen Kang#2 . . . . 2.50
Ann.#18 TGr,I:The Flame,w/card . 3.25
Ann.#19 V:Flame 3.25
G-Size.#1 Battles,A:Hercules . . . 12.00
TPB Alone Against the Celestials,
rep.Thor#387-389 . . . . 5.95
TPB Ballad of Beta Ray Bill,rep.
Thor#337-340 . . . . 8.95

THOR CORPS
[Limited Series]
1 TDF(s),PO,V:Demonstaff 2.00
2 TDF(s),PO,A:Invaders 2.00
3 TDF(s),PO,A:Spider-Man 2099 2.00
4 TDF(s),PO,Last Issue 2.00

THREE MUSKETEERS
1 thru 2 movie adapt. 1.25

THUNDERCATS
Star
December, 1985
1 JM,TV tie-in 3.00
1a 2nd printing 1.00
2 JM,A:Berbils,V:Mumm-Ra 2.00
3 . . . . 1.50
4 JM,I:Lynxana 1.50
5 JM 1.50
6 JM 1.50
7 Return to Thundera 1.50
8 V:Monkiang 1.50
9 V:Pekmen 1.00
10 . . . . 1.00
11 I:The Molemen 1.00
12 'The Protectors' 1.00
13 EC/AW,V:Safari Joe 1.00
14 V:Snaf 1.00
15 JM,A:Spidera 1.00
16 'Time Capsule' 1.00
17 . . . . 1.00
18 EC/AW,'Doom Gaze' 1.00
19 . . . . 1.00
20 EC/AW 1.00
21 JM,A:Hercules Baby 1.00
22 I:Devious Duploids 1.00
23 V:Devious Duploids 1.00
24 June, 1988 . . . . 1.00

THUNDERSTRIKE
1 B:TDF(s),RF,Holografx(c),
V:Bloodaxe,I:Car Jack 3.25
2 RF,V:Juggernaut 1.50
3 RF,I:Sangre 1.50
4 RF,A:Spider-Man,I:Pandora . . . 1.50
5 RF,A:Spider-Man,V:Pandora . . 1.50
6 RF,I:Blackwulf,Bristle,Schizo,Lord
Lucian,A:SpM,Code:Blue,Stellaris,
V:SHIELD,Pandora,C:Tantalus 1.50
7 KP,V:Tantalus,D:Jackson 1.75
8 RF,I&V:Officer ZERO 1.75
9 RF,V:Bloodaxe 1.75
10 RF,A:Thor 1.75
11 RF,A:Wildstreak 1.50
12 RF,A:Whyte Out 1.50
13 RF,Inferno 42 . . . . 1.50
13a Double Feature flip book
with Code Blue #1 . . . . 2.50
14 RF, Inferno 42 . . . . 1.50
14a Double Feature flip book
with Code Blue #2 . . . . 2.50
15 RF,V:Methisto 1.50
15a Double Feature flip book
with Code Blue #3 . . . . 2.50
16 . . . . 1.50
17 V:Bloodaxe 1.50
18 V:New Villain 1.50
19 Shopping Network 1.50
20 A: Black Panther 1.50
21 A:War Machine,V:Loki 1.50
22 TDF,AM,RF,Mystery of Bloodaxe
blows open 1.50

TIMESPIRITS
Epic
January, 1985
1 TY 2.00
2 . . . . 1.75
3 . . . . 1.75
4 AW 1.50
5 . . . . 1.50
6 . . . . 1.50
7 . . . . 1.50
8 March, 1986 . . . . 1.50

TIMESTRYKE
1 . . . . 1.95
2 . . . . 1.95

TINY TESSIE
See: TESSIE THE TYPIST

TOMB OF DARKNESS
See: BEWARE

Tomb of Dracula #8
© Marvel Entertainment Group

TOMB OF DRACULA
April, 1972
1 GC,Night of the Vampire 75.00
2 GC,Who Stole My Coffin? . . . 40.00
3 GC,TP,I:Rachel Van Helsing . 25.00
4 GC,TP,Bride of Dracula! 25.00
5 GC,TP,To Slay A Vampire . . . 25.00
6 GC,TP,Monster of the Moors . 20.00
7 GC,TP,Child is Slayer o/t Man 20.00
8 GC(p),The Hell-Crawlers 20.00
9 The Fire Cross 20.00
10 GC,I:Blade Vampire Slayer . . 28.00
11 GC,TP,Master of the Undead
Strikes Again! 15.00
12 GC,TP,House that Screams . 15.00
13 GC,TP,O:Blade 20.00
14 GC,TP,Vampire has Risen
from the Grave 15.00
15 GC,TP,Stay Dead 15.00
16 GC,TP,Back from the Grave . 15.00
17 GC,TP,A Vampire Rides This
Train! 15.00

18 GC,TP,A:Werewolf By Night . 16.00
19 GC,TP,Snowbound in Hell . . 15.00
20 GC,TP,ManhuntForAVampire 15.00
21 GC,TP,A:Blade 16.00
22 GC,TP,V:Gorna 10.00
23 GC,TP,Shadow over Haunted
    Castle 10.00
24 GC,TP,I am your Death 10.00
25 GC,TP,Blood Stalker of Count
    Dracula 10.00
26 GC,TP,A Vampire Stalks the
    Night 10.00
27 GC,TP,..And the Moon Spews
    Death! 10.00
28 GC,TP,Five came to Kill a
    Vampire' 10.00
29 GC,TP,Vampire goes Mad? . 10.00

Tomb of Dracula #40
© Marvel Entertainment Group

30 GC,TP,A:Blade 10.00
31 GC,TP,Child of Blood 10.00
32 GC,TP,The Vampire Walks
    Among Us 10.00
33 GC,TP,Blood on My Hands . . 10.00
34 GC,TP,Bloody Showdown . . . 10.00
35 GC,TP,A:Brother Voodoo . . . 10.00
36 GC,TP,Dracula in America . . 10.00
37 GC,TP,The Vampire Walks
    Among Us 9.00
38 GC,TP,Bloodlust for a Dying
    Vampire 9.00
39 GC,TP,Final Death of Dracula . 9.00
40 GC,TP,Triumph of Dr.Sun 9.00
41 GC,TP,A:Blade 8.00
42 GC,TP,V:Dr.Sun 7.00
43 GC,TP,A:NewYear'sNightmare 7.00
44 GC,TP,A:Dr.Strange 7.00
45 GC,TP,A:Hannibal King 8.00
46 GC,TP,W:Dracula & Domini . . 7.00
47 GC,TP,Death-Bites 7.00
48 GC,TP,A:Hannibal King 8.00
49 GC,TP,A:Robin Hood,
    Frankenstein's Monster 7.00
50 GC,TP,A:Silver Surfer 15.00
51 GC,TP,A:Blade 7.50
52 GC,TP,V:Demon 6.00
53 GC,TP,A:Hannibal King,Blade . 7.50

54 GC,TP,Twas the Night Before
    Christmas 6.00
55 GC,TP,Requiem for a Vampire 6.00
56 GC,TP,A:Harold H. Harold . . . 6.00
57 GC,TP,The Forever Man 6.00
58 GC,TP,A:Blade 7.00
59 GC,TP,The Last Traitor 6.00
60 GC,TP,The Wrath of Dracula . 6.00
61 GC,TP,Resurrection 6.00
62 GC,TP,What Lurks Beneath . . 6.00
63 GC,TP,A:Janus 6.00
64 GC,TP,A:Satan 6.00
65 GC,TP,Where No Vampire
    Has Gone Before 6.00
66 GC,TP,Marked for Death 6.00
67 GC,TP,A:Lilith 6.00
68 GC,TP,Dracula turns Human . . 6.00
69 GC,TP,Cross of Fire 6.00
70 GC,TP,double size,last issue . 8.50
Savage Return of Dracula. rep.
    Tomb of Dracula #1,#2 . . . . . 2.00
Wedding of Dracula. rep.Tomb
    of Dracula #30,#45,#46 . . . . . 2.00
Requiem for Dracula. rep.Tomb
    of Dracula #69,70 . . . . 2.00

TOMB OF DRACULA
[Mini-Series]
November, 1991

1 GC,AW,Day of Blood 6.00
2 GC,AW,Dracula in DC 5.50
3 GC,AW,A:Blade 5.50
4 GC,AW,D:Dracula 5.50

TOMB OF DRACULA
November, 1979
(black & white magazine)

1 . . . . 3.50
2 SD 5.00
3 FM 5.00
4 . . . . 3.00
5 . . . . 3.00
6 September, 1980 . . . . 3.00

TOMORROW KNIGHTS
Epic
June, 1990

1 . . . . 1.95
2 . . . . 1.50
3 . . . . 1.50
4 Origin 1.50
5 . . . . 2.25
6 . . . . 2.25

TOP DOG
Star Comics
April, 1985

1 . . . . 1.25
2 thru 14, June 1987 . . . . @1.00

TOR

1 JKu,R:Tor,Magazine Format . . 6.25
2 JKu 6.25
3 JKu,V:The Iduard Ring 6.25

TOUGH KID
SQUAD COMICS
Timely
March, 1942

1 O:The Human Top,Tough Kid
    Squad,A:The Flying Flame,
    V:Doctor Klutch 5,000.00

Tower of Shadows #8
© Marvel Entertainment Group

TOWER OF SHADOWS
September, 1969

1 JR(c),JSo,JCr,'At The Stroke
    of Midnight' 30.00
2 JR(c),DH,DA,NA,'The Hungry
    One' 15.00
3 GC,BWs,GT,'Midnight in the Wax
    Museum' 16.00
4 DH,'Within The Witching Circle' 8.00
5 DA,BWS,WW,'Demon That Stalks
    Hollywood' 9.00
6 WW,SD,'Pray For the Man in the
    Rat-Hole 12.00
7 BWS,WW,'Titano' 12.00
8 WW,SD,'Demons of
    Dragon-Henge' 9.00
9 BWr(c),TP,Lovecraft story . . . 8.00
Becomes:

CREATURES ON
THE LOOSE
March, 1971

10 BWr,A:King Kull 35.00
11 DAy,rep Moomba is Here 4.00
12 JK,'I Was Captured By Korilla' 4.00
13 RC,'The Creature
    From Krogarr' 4.00
14 MSe,'Dead Storage' 4.00
15 SD,'Spragg the Living Mountain' 2.25
16 GK,BEv,GK,B&O:Gullivar Jones,
    Warrior of Mars 4.00
17 GK,'Slaves o/t Spider Swarm' . 2.25
18 RA,'The Fury of Phra' 4.00
19 WB,JM,GK,'Red Barbarian
    of Mars' 4.00
20 GK(c),GM,SD,'The Monster...
    And the Maiden 4.00
21 JSo(c),GM,'Two Worlds To
    Win',E:Gulliver 4.00
22 JSo(c),SD,VM,B:Thongor,
    Warrior of Lost Lemuria 4.00
23 VM,'The Man-Monster Strikes' 4.00
24 VM,'Attack of the Lizard-Hawks' 2.25
25 VM,GK(c),'Wizard of Lemuria' . 4.00
26 VM,'Doom of the Serpent Gods' 1.75
27 VM,SD,'Demons Dwell in the
    Crypts of Yamath' 3.50
28 SD,'The Hordes of Hell' 3.50

Creatures on the Loose #13
© *Marvel Entertainment Group*

29 GK(c),'Day of the Dragon Wings',
   E:Thongor,Warrior of Lost
   Lemuria 3.50
30 B:Man-Wolf,'Full Moon, Dark
   Fear' 3.50
31 GT,'The Beast Within' 3.50
32 GT,V:Kraven the Hunter 3.50
33 GK(c),GP,'The Name of the
   Game is Death' 3.50
34 GP,'Nightflight to Fear' 3.50
35 GK(c),GP 3.50
36 GK(c),GP,'Murder by Moonlight' 1.75
37 GP,September, 1975 . . . . 3.50

TOXIC AVENGER
March, 1991
1 VM(i)I&O:Toxic Avenger 2.25
2 VM(i) 1.75
3 VM(i)'Night of LivingH.bodies . . 1.50
4 Legend of Sludgeface 1.50
5 I:Biohazard 1.50
6 V:Biohazard 1.50
7 'Sewer of Souviaki' 1.50
8 'Sewer of Souviaki' conc. 1.50
9 Abducted by Aliens 1.50
10 'Die,Yuppie Scum',pt.1 . . . . . . 1.50

TOXIC CRUSADERS
1 F:Toxic Avengers & Crusaders 1.50
2 SK(c),V:Custard-Thing 1.25
3 SK(c),V:Custard-Thing 1.25
4 V:Giant Mutant Rats 1.25
5 V:Dr.Killemoff 1.25
6 V:Dr.Killemoff 1.25
7 F:Yvonne 1.25
8 V:Psycho 1.25
(2nd Series)
1 . . . . 1.25
2 . . . . 1.25

TRANSFORMERS
September, 1984
[1st Regular Series]
1 FS,Toy Comic 3.00
2 FS,OptimusPrime V:Megatron . 2.00
3 FS.A:Spider-Man 2.00
4 MT(c),FS 1.50

5 Transformers Dead? 1.50
6 Autobots vs.Decepticons 1.50
7 KB,V:Megatron 1.50
8 KB,A:Dinobots 1.50
9 MM,A:Circuit Breaker 1.50
10 Dawn of the Devastator 1.50
11 HT 1.50
12 HT,V:Shockwave 1.50
13 DP,Return of Megatron 1.50
14 DP,V:Decepticons 1.50
15 DP 1.50
16 KN,A:Bumblebee 1.50
17 DP,I:New Transformers,pt.1 . . 1.50
18 DP,I:New Transformers,pt.2 . . 1.50
19 DP,I:Omega Supreme 1.50
20 HT,Skid vs.Ravage 1.50
21 DP,I:Aerialbots 1.25
22 DP,I:Stuntacons(Menasor) . . . 1.25
23 DP,Return of Circuit Breaker . . 1.25
24 DP,D:Optimus Prime 1.25
25 DP,Decpticons (full story) 1.25
26 DP 1.25
27 DP,V:Head Hunter 1.25
28 DP 1.25
29 DP,I:Scraplets, Triplechangers 1.25
30 DP,V:Scraplets 1.25
31 DP,Humans vs. Decepticons . . 1.25
32 DP,'Autobots for Sale' 1.25
33 DP,Autobots vs.Decepticons . . 1.25
34 V:Sky Lynx 1.25
35 JRy,I:UK.version Transformers 1.25
36 . . . . 1.00
37 . . . . 1.00
38 . . . . 1.00
39 . . . . 1.00
40 Autobots' New Leader 1.00

Transformers #9
© *Marvel Entertainment Group*

41 . . . . 1.00
42 Return of Optimus Prime 1.00
43 Optimus Prime,Goldbug 1.00
44 FF,Return of Circuit Breaker . . 1.00
45 V:The Jammers 1.00
46 I:New Transformers 1.00
47 B:Underbase saga,I:Seacons . 1.00
48 Optimus Prime/Megatron
   (past story) 1.00

49 Underbase saga Contd. 1.00
50 E:Underbase saga,I:New
   Characters 1.00
51 I:Pretender Decepticon Beasts 1.00
52 I:Mecannibles,pt.1 . . . . 1.00
53 Mecannibles,pt.2 . . . . 1.00
54 I:Micromasters 1.00
55 MG 1.00
56 Return of Megatron 1.00
57 Optimus Prime vs.Scraponok . 1.00
58 V:Megatron 1.00
59 A:Megatron,D:Ratchet 1.00
60 Battle on Cybertron 1.00
61 O:Transformers 1.00
62 B:Matrix Quest,pt.1 . . . . 1.00
63 . . . . 1.00
64 I:The Klud 1.00
65 GSr 1.00
66 E:Matrix Quest,pt.5 . . . . 1.00
67 V:Unicorn,Also Alternative
   World 1.00
68 I:Neoknights 1.00
69 Fate of Ratchet & Megatron
   revealed 1.00
70 Megatron/Ratchet fused
   together 1.00
71 Autobots Surrender to
   Decepticons 1.00
72 Decepticon Civil War,
   I:Gravitron 1.00
73 I:Unicron,A:Neoknights 1.00
74 A:Unicron&Brothers of Chaos . 1.00
75 V:Thunderwing & Dark Matrix . 1.00
76 Aftermath of War 1.00
77 Unholy Alliance 1.00
78 Galvatron vs.Megatron 1.00
79 Decepticons Invade Earth 1.00
80 Return of Optimus Prime,final . 1.00
[2nd Regular Series]
1 Split Foil(c),A:Dinobots 3.50
2 A:G.I.Joe,Cobra 2.00
3 . . . . 2.00
4 MaG,V:Jhiaxus 2.00
5 . . . . 2.00
6 V:Megatron 2.00
7 V:Darkwing 2.00
8 V:Darkwing 2.00
9 . . . . 2.00
10 Total War 2.00
11 . . . . 1.75

TRANSFORMERS COMICS MAGAZINE
October, 1986
1 Digest Size 1.50
2 thru 10 . . . . @1.50
11 1988 . . . . 1.50

TRANSFORMERS, THE MOVIE
December, 1986
1 Animated Movie adapt. 1.25
2 Animated Movie adapt. 1.25
3 Animated Movie adapt,February,
   1987 . . . . 1.25

TRANSFORMERS UNIVERSE
December, 1986
1 . . . . 1.25
2 . . . . 1.25
3 . . . . 1.25
4 March, 1987 . . . . 1.25

All comics prices listed are for *Near Mint* condition.

TRANSMUTATION OF IKE GARAUDA
Epic
1 JSh,I:IkeGaruda 3.95
2 JSh,conclusion 3.95

TROUBLE WITH GIRLS
1 BBl,AW,R:Lester Girls 2.75
2 BBl,AW,V:Lizard Lady 2.25
3 BBl,AW,V:Lizard Lady 2.25
4 BBl,AW,last issue 2.25

TRUE COMPLETE MYSTERY
See: COMPLETE MYSTERY

TRUE SECRETS
See: OUR LOVE

TRUE WESTERN
December, 1949
1 Ph(c),Billy the Kid 80.00
2 Ph(c),Alan Ladd,Badmen vs. Lawmen 90.00
Becomes:
TRUE ADVENTURES
3 BP,MSy,Boss of Black Devil . 70.00
Becomes:
MEN'S ADVENTURES
4 He Called me a Coward . . . 135.00
5 Brother Act 60.00
6 Heat of Battle 50.00
7 The Walking Death 50.00
8 RH,Journey Into Death 50.00
9 Bullets,Blades and Death . . . 35.00
10 BEv,The Education of Thomas Dillon 35.00
11 Death of A Soldier 35.00
12 Firing Squad 35.00
13 RH(c),The Three Stripes 35.00
14 GC,BEv,Steel Coffin 35.00
15 JMn(c) 35.00
16 . . . . 35.00
17 . . . . 35.00
18 . . . . 35.00
19 JRo 35.00
20 RH(c) 35.00
21 BEv(c),JSt,The Eye of Man . . 50.00
22 BEv,JR,Mark of the Witch . . . 50.00
23 BEv(c),RC,The Wrong Body . 50.00
24 RH,JMn,GT,Torture Master . . 50.00
25 SSh(c),Who Shrinks My Head 50.00
26 Midnight in the Morgue 50.00
27 CBu(c),A:Capt.America,Human Torch,Sub-Mariner 400.00
28 BEv,A:Capt.America,Human Torch, Sub-Mariner,July, 1954 . . . . 350.00

TRY-OUT WINNER BOOK
March, 1988
1 Spiderman vs. Doc Octopus . 15.00

TV STARS
August, 1978
1 A:Great Grape Ape 1.25
2 . . . . 1.00
3 . . . . 1.00
4 A:Top Cat,February, 1979 . . . 1.00

2-GUN KID
See: BILLY BUCKSKIN

TWO-GUN KID
Atlas
March, 1948—April, 1977
1 B:Two-Gun Kid,The Sheriff . 500.00
2 Killers of Outlaw City 225.00
3 RH,A:Annie Oakley 175.00
4 RH,A:Black Rider 175.00

Two-Gun Kid #72
© *Marvel Entertainment Group*

5 . . . . 225.00
6 . . . . 150.00
7 RH,Brand of a Killer 150.00
8 The Secret of the Castle of Slaves 150.00
9 JSe,Trapped in Hidden Valley A:Black Rider 150.00
10 JK(c),The Horrible Hermit of Hidden Mesa 150.00
11 JMn(c),GT,A:Black Rider . . 125.00
12 JMn(c),GT,A:Black Rider . . 125.00
13 thru 24 . . . . @100.00
25 AW 100.00
26 . . . . 90.00
27 . . . . 90.00
28 . . . . 90.00
29 . . . . 90.00
30 AW 100.00
31 thru 44 . . . . 50.00
45 . . . . 55.00
46 . . . . 55.00
47 . . . . 35.00
48 . . . . 40.00
49 . . . . 35.00
50 . . . . 30.00
51 . . . . 40.00
52 thru 59 . . . . @20.00
60 DAy,New O:Two Gun Kid . . 20.00
61 JK,DAy,The Killer and The Kid 20.00
62 JK,DAy,At the Mercy of Moose Morgan 20.00
63 DAy,The Guns of Wild Bill Taggert 10.00
64 DAy,Trapped by Grizzly Gordon 10.00
65 DAy,Nothing Can Save Fort Henry 10.00
66 DAy,Ringo's Raiders 10.00
67 DAy,The Fangs of the Fox . . 10.00
68 DAy,The Purple Phantom . . . 10.00

69 DAy,Badman Called Goliath . 10.00
70 DAy,Hurricane 10.00
71 DAy,V:Jesse James 10.00
72 DAy,V:Geronlmo 10.00
73 Guns of the Galloway Gang . 10.00
74 Dakota Thompson 10.00
75 JK,Remember the Alamo . . . 10.00
76 JK,Trapped on the Doom . . . 10.00
77 JK,V:The Panther 10.00
78 V:Jesse James 10.00
79 The River Rats 10.00
80 V:The Billy Kid 10.00
81 The Hidden Gun 5.00
82 BEv,Here Comes the Conchos 5.00
83 Durango,Two-Gun Kid Unmasked 5.00
84 Gunslammer 5.00
85 Fury at Falcon Flats, A:Rawhide Kids 5.00
86 V:Cole Younger 5.00
87 OW,The Sidewinder and the Stallion 5.00
88 thru 100 . . . . @5.00
101 . . . . 5.00
102 thru 136 . . . . @2.00

TWO GUN WESTERN
See: CASEY–CRIME PHOTOGRAPHER

TWO-GUN WESTERN
See: BILLY BUCKSKIN

2001: A SPACE ODYSSEY
October, 1976
1 JK,FRg,Based on Movie 3.00

2001: A SPACE ODYSSEY
Dec., 1976—Sept., 1977
1 JK,Based on Movie 2.50
2 JK,Vira the She-Demon 1.50
3 JK,Marak the Merciless 1.50
4 JK,Wheels of Death 1.50
5 JK,Norton of New York 1.50
6 JK,Immortality ...Death 1.50
7 JK,The New Seed 1.50
8 JK,Capture of X-51,I&O:Mr. Machine(Machine-Man) 4.00
9 JK,A:Mr Machine 1.50
10 Hotline to Hades,A:Mr Machine 1.50

2010
April, 1985
1 TP,movie adapt 1.00
2 TP,movie adapt,May, 1985 . . . 1.00

2099 A.D.
1 Chromium cover 3.95

2099 SPECIAL: THE WORLD OF DOOM
1 The World of Doom 2.25

2099 UNLIMITED
1 DT,I:Hulk 2099,A:Spider-Man 2099, I:Mutagen 4.50
2 DT,F:Hulk 2099,Spider-Man 2099, I:R-Gang 4.25
3 GJ(s),JJB,F:Hulk 2099 . 4.25
4 PR(c),GJ(s),JJB,I:Metalscream 2099,Lachryma 2099 . . . . 4.25
5 GJ(s),I:Vulx,F:Hazarrd 2099 . . . 3.95

6 . . . . 3.95
Becomes:

2099 A.D. UNLIMITED
7 . . . . 3.95
8 F:Public Enemy 3.95
9 One Nation Under Doom 3.95

ULTIMATE AGE OF APOCALYPSE
Rep. #1-#4 Age of Apocalypse stories:
Ultimate Amazing X-Men 8.95
Ultimate Astonishing X-Men 8.95
Ultimate Factor X 8.95
Ultimate Gambit and the X-Ternals 8.95
Ultimate Generation Next 8.95
Ultimate Weapon X 8.95
Ultimate X-Calibre 8.95
Ultimate X-Man 8.95

ULTRA X-MEN COLLECTION
1 Metallic(c), art from cards 2.95
2 thru 5 art from cards . . . . . . @2.95

UNCANNY TALES
Atlas
June, 1952
1 RH,While the City Sleeps . . 350.00
2 JMn,BEv 200.00
3 Escape to What 175.00
4 JMn,Nobody's Fool 175.00
5 Fear 175.00
6 He Lurks in the Shadows . . 175.00
7 BEv,Kill,Clown,Kill 150.00
8 JMn,Bring Back My Face . . . 150.00
9 RC,The Executioner 150.00
10 RH(c),JR,The Man Who Came
Back To Life 150.00
11 GC,The Man Who Changed 125.00
12 BP,BEv,Bertha Gets Buried 125.00
13 RH,Scared Out of His Skin . 125.00
14 RH,The Victims of Vonntor . 125.00
15 JSt,The Man Who Saw Death 125.00
16 JMn,GC,Zombie at Large . . 125.00
17 GC,I Live With Corpses . . . 125.00
18 JF,BP,Clock Face(c) 125.00
19 DBr,RKr,The Man Who Died
Again 125.00
20 DBr,Ted's Head 125.00
21 thru 27 . . . . @100.00
28 . . . . 110.00
29 thru 41 . . . . @60.00
42 . . . . 65.00
43 thru 49 . . . . @55.00
50 . . . . 60.00
51 . . . . 65.00
52 . . . . 55.00
53 . . . . 55.00
54 . . . . 65.00
55 . . . . 55.00
56 September, 1957 . . . . 65.00

UNCANNY TALES FROM THE GRAVE
Dec., 1973—Oct., 1975
1 RC,Room of no Return 3.00
2 DAy,Out of the Swamp 2.00
3 No Way Out 2.00
4 JR,SD,Vampire 2.00
5 GK,GT,Don't Go in the Cellar . 2.00
6 JR,SD,The Last Kkrul 2.00
7 RH,SD,Never Dance With a

Vampire 2.00
8 SD,Escape Into Hell 2.00
9 JA,The Nightmare Men 2.00
10 SD,DH,Beware the Power of
Khan 2.00
11 SD,JF,RH,Dead Don't Sleep . . 2.00
12 SD,Final Issue 2.00

UNCANNY X-MEN
SEE: X-MEN

UNKNOWN WORLDS OF SCIENCE FICTION
January, 1975
(black & white magazine)
1 AW,RKr,AT,FF,GC 4.00
2 FB,GP 3.25
3 GM,AN,GP,GC 3.25
4 . . . . 3.25
5 GM,NC,GC 3.25
6 FB,AN,GC,November, 1975 . . 3.25
Spec.#1 AN,NR,JB 3.50

U.S.A. COMICS
Timely
August, 1941
1 S&K(c),BW,Bondage(c),The
Defender(c) 6,000.00
2 S&K(c),BW,Capt.Terror(c) . 2,000.00
3 S&K(c),Capt.Terror(c) 1,500.00
4 . . . . 1,200.00
5 Hitler(c),O:American Avenger1,000.00
6 ASh(c),Capt.America(c) . . . 1,300.00
7 BW,O:Marvel Boy 1,200.00
8 Capt.America (c) 800.00
9 Bondage(c), Capt.America . . 800.00
10 SSh(c),Bondage(c), Capt.
America 800.00
11 SSh(c),Bondage(c), Capt.
America 700.00
12 ASh(c),Capt.America 700.00
13 ASh(c),Capt.America 700.00
14 Capt.America 500.00
15 Capt.America 500.00
16 ASh(c),Bondage(c),
Capt.America 500.00
17 Bondage(c),Capt.America . . 500.00

U.S. 1
May, 1983
1 AM(c),HT,Trucking Down the
Highway 1.25
2 HT,Midnight 1.00
3 FS,ME,Rhyme of the Ancient
Highwayman 1.00
4 FS,ME 1.00
5 FS,ME,Facing The Maze 1.00
6 FS,ME 1.00
7 FS,ME 1.00
8 FS,ME 1.00
9 FS,ME,Iron Mike-King of the
Bike 1.00
10 FS,ME 1.00
11 FS,ME 1.00
12 FS,ME,Final Issue,Oct.,1984 . . 1.00

U.S. AGENT
1 V:Scourge,O:U.S.Agent 2.00
2 V:Scourge 2.00
3 V:Scourge 2.00
4 last issue 2.00

UNTAMED
1 I:Griffen Palmer 2.75
2 V:Kosansui 2.25
3 V:Kosansui 2.25

VAMPIRE TALES
August, 1973
(black & white magazine)
1 BEv,B:Morbius the Living.
Vampire 25.00
2 JSo,I:Satana 10.00
3 A:Satana 15.00
4 GK 15.00
5 GK,O:Morbius The Living
Vampire 18.00
6 AA,I:Lilith 15.00
7 HC,PG 15.00
8 AA,A:Blade The Vampire
Slayer 15.00
9 RH,AA 15.00
10 . . . . 15.00
11 June, 1975 . . . . 15.00
Ann.#1 . . . . 15.00

Vault of Evil #21
© Marvel Entertainment Group

VAULT OF EVIL
Feb., 1973—Nov., 1975
1 B:1950's reps,Come Midnight,
Come Monster 5.00
2 The Hour of the Witch 3.00
3 The Woman Who Wasn't 3.00
4 Face that Follows 3.00
5 Ghost 3.00
6 The Thing at the Window 3.00
7 Monsters 3.00
8 The Vampire is my Brother . . . 3.00
9 Giant Killer 3.00
10 The Lurkers in the Caves 3.00
11 Two Feasts For a Vampire . . . 3.00
12 Midnight in the
Haunted Mansion 3.00
13 Hot as the Devil 3.00
14 Midnight in the Haunted Manor 3.00
15 Don't Shake Hands with the
Devil 3.00

---

16 A Grave Honeymoon	3.00
17 Grave Undertaking	3.00
18 The Deadly Edge	3.00
19 Vengeance of Ahman Ra	3.00
20	3.00
21 Victim of Valotorr	3.00
22	3.00
23 Black Magician Lives Again	3.00

VENOM
1 MBa,A:Spider-Man.holo-grafx(c)	5.00
1a Gold Ed..	50.00
1b Black Ed..	220.00
2 MBa,A:Spider-Man	3.50
3 MBa,Families of Venom's victims	3.50
4 RLm,A:Spider-Man,V:Life Foundation	3.50
5 RLm,V:Five Symbiotes,A:SpM	3.50
6 RLm,V:Spider-Man	3.50
Venom:Deathtrap:The Vault,RLm, A:Avengers,Freedom Force	6.95
TPB Lethal Protector RLm,DvM	15.95

VENOM: CARNAGE UNLEASHED
1 Venom vs. Carnage	2.95
2 Venom vs. Carnage	2.95
3 No Spider-Help	2.95
4 JRu,Wld,LHa,cardstock(c)	2.95

VENOM: ENEMY WITHIN
1 BMc,Glow-in-the-dark(C), A:Demogoblin,Morbius	3.25
2 BMc,A:Demogoblin,Morbius	3.25
3 BMc,V:Demogoblin,A:Morbius	3.25

VENOM: FUNERAL PYRE
1 TL,JRu,A:Punisher	3.50
2 TL,JRu,AM,V:Gangs	3.50
3 TL,JRu,Last issue	3.50

VENOM: THE MACE
1 Embossed(c),CP(s),LSh,I:Mace	3.25
2 CP(s),LSh,V:Mace	3.25
3 CP(s),LSh,V:Mace,final issue	3.25

VENOM: THE MADNESS
1 B:ANi(s),KJo,V:Juggernaut	3.50
2 KJo,V:Juggernaut	3.25
3 E:ANi(s),KJo,V:Juggernaut	3.25

VENOM: NIGHTS OF VENGEANCE
1 RLm,I:Stalkers,A:Vengeance	3.25
2 RLm,A:Vengeance,V:Stalkers	3.25
3 RLm,V:Stalkers	3.25
4 RLm,final issue	3.25

VENOM: SEPARATION ANXIETY
1 Embossed(c)	2.95
2 V:Symbiotes	2.95
3	2.95

VENUS
Atlas
August, 1948
1 B:Venus,Hedy Devine,HK,Hey Look	650.00
2 Venus(c)	350.00

3 Carnival(c)	300.00
4 Cupid(c).HK,Hey Look	325.00
5 Serenade(c)	325.00
6 Wrath of a Goddess,A:Loki	300.00
7 The Romance That Could Not Be	300.00
8 The Love Trap	300.00
9 Whom the Gods Destroy	300.00
10 B:Scince Fiction/Horror, Trapped On the Moon	300.00
11 The End of the World	350.00
12 GC,The Lost World	250.00
13 BEv,King of the Living Dead	400.00
14 BEv,The Fountain of Death	400.00
15 BEv,The Empty Grave	400.00
16 BEv,Where Gargoyles Dwell	400.00
17 BEv,Tower of Death, Bondage(c)	400.00
18 BEv,Terror in the Tunnel	400.00
19 BEv,THe Kiss Of Death	400.00

VERY BEST OF MARVEL COMICS
One Shot reps Marvel Artists Favorite Stories	12.95

VIDEO JACK
November, 1987
1 KGi,O:Video Jack	2.50
2 KGi	2.00
3 KGi	1.75
4 KGi	1.75
5 KGi	1.75
6 KGi,NA,BWr,AW	1.25

VISION, THE
1 BHs,mini-series	1.75
2 BHs	1.75
3 BHs	1.75

VISION & SCARLET WITCH
[1st Series]
November, 1982
1 RL,V:Halloween	2.00
2 RL,V:Isbisa,D:Whizzer	1.50
3 RL,A:Wonderman,V:GrimReaper	1.50
4 RL,A:Magneto,Inhumans	1.50
[2nd Series]
1 V:Grim Reaper	2.00
2 V:Lethal Legion,D:Grim Reaper	1.75
3 V:Salem's Seven	1.75
4 I:Glamor & Illusion	1.75
5 A:Glamor & Illusion	1.75
6 A:Magneto	1.75
7 V:Toad	1.75
8 A:Powerman	1.75
9 V:Enchantress	1.75
10 A:Inhumans	1.75
11 A:Spider-Man	1.75
12 Birth of V&S's Child	1.25

VISIONARIES
Star
November, 1987
1 thru 5	@1.00
6 September, 1988	1.00

VOID INDIGO
Epic
November, 1984
1 VM,Epic Comics	2.00

2 VM,Epic Comics,March, 1985	2.00

WACKY DUCK
See: DOPEY DUCK

WALLY THE WIZARD
Star
April, 1985
1	1.25
2 thru 11	@1.00
12 March, 1986	1.00

WAR, THE
1989
1 Sequel to The Draft & The Pit	3.50
2	3.50
3	3.50
4 1990	3.50

WAR ACTION
Atlas
April, 1952
1 JMn,RH,War Stories, Six Dead Men	80.00
2	35.00
3 Invasion in Korea	25.00
4 thru 10	@25.00
11	40.00
12	40.00
13 BK	40.00
14 Rangers Strike,June, 1953	25.00

WAR ADVENTURES
Atlas
January, 1952
1 GT,Battle Fatigue	80.00
2 The Story of a Slaughter	30.00
3 JRo	25.00
4 RH(c)	25.00
5 RH,Violent(c)	25.00
6 Stand or Die	25.00
7 JMn(c)	25.00
8 BK	40.00
9 RH(c)	20.00
10 JRo(c),Attack at Dawn	20.00
11 Red Trap	20.00
12	20.00
13 RH(c),The Commies Strike February, 1953	20.00

WAR COMBAT
Atlas
March, 1952
1 JMn,Death of a Platoon Leader	60.00
2	30.00
3 JMn(c)	20.00
4 JMn(c)	20.00
5 The Red Hordes	20.00
Becomes:	

COMBAT CASEY
6 BEv,Combat Casey cont	40.00
7	30.00
8 JMn(c)	22.00
9	20.00
10 RH(c)	30.00
11	15.00
12	15.00
13 thru 19	@30.00
20	15.00
21 thru 33	@12.00
34 July, 1957	12.00

WAR COMICS
Atlas
December, 1950

1 You Only Die Twice	120.00
2 Infantry's War	60.00
3	40.00
4 GC,The General Said Nuts	40.00
5	40.00
6 The Deadly Decision of General Kwang	40.00
7 RH	40.00
8 RH,No Survivors	40.00
9 RH	40.00
10	40.00
11 thru 21	@30.00
22	50.00
23 thru 37	@25.00
38 JKu	40.00
39	25.00
40	25.00
41	25.00
42	25.00
43 AT	35.00
44	25.00
45	25.00
46 RC	40.00
47	25.00
48	25.00
49 September, 1957	35.00

WARHEADS

1 GEr,I:Warheads,A:Wolverine,	2.25
2 GEr,V:Nick Fury	2.00
3 DTy,A:Iron Man	2.00
4 SCy,A:X-Force	2.00
5 A:X-Force,C:Deaths'Head II	2.00
6 SCy,A:Death's Head II	2.00
7 SCy,A:Death's Head II,S.Surfer	2.00
8 SCy,V:Mephisto	2.00
9 SCy,V:Mephisto	2.00
10 JCz,V:Mephisto	2.00
11 A:Death's Head II	2.00
12 V:Mechanix	2.00
13 Xenophiles Reptiles	2.00
14 last issue	2.00

WARHEADS: BLACK DAWN

1 A:Gh.Rider,Morbius	3.25
2 V:Dracula	2.00

WAR IS HELL
Jan., 1973—Oct., 1975

1 B:Reprints,Decision at Dawn	2.00
2 Anytime,Anyplace,War is Hell	1.50
3 Retreat or Die	1.50
4 Live Grenade	1.50
5 Trapped Platoon	1.50
6 We Die at Dawn	1.50
7 While the Jungle Sleeps,A:Sgt Fury	1.50
8 Killed in Action,A;Sgt Fury	1.50
9 B:Supernatural,War Stories	1.50
10 Death is a 30 Ton Tank	1.50
11 thru 15	@1.50

WARLOCK
[1st Regular Series]
August, 1972

1 GK,I:Counter Earth,A:High Evolutionary	30.00
2 JB,TS,V:Man Beast	12.00
3 GK,TS,V:Apollo	11.00
4 JK,TS,V:Triax	10.00
5 GK,TS,V:Dr.Doom	10.00
6 TS(i),O:Brute	10.00
7 TS(i),V:Brute,D:Dr.Doom	10.00
8 TS(i),R:Man-Beast(cont in Hulk #176)	10.00
9 JSn,1st'Rebirth'Thanos,O:Magnus, N:Warlock,I:In-Betweener	18.00
10 JSn,SL,O:Thanos,V:Magus, A:In-Betweener	25.00
11 JSn,SL,D:Magus,A:Thanos, In-Betweener	20.00
12 JSn,SL,O:Pip,V:Pro-Boscis A:Starfox	10.00
13 JSn,SL,I&O:Star-Thief	10.00
14 JSn,SL,V:Star-Thief	10.00
15 JSn,A:Thanos,V:Soul-Gem	25.00

[2nd Regular Series]

1 JSn,rep.Strange Tales #178-180 Baxter Paper	3.00
2 JSn,rep.Strange Tales #180 & Warlock #9	2.50
3 JSn,rep.Warlock #10-#12	2.50
4 JSn,rep.Warlock #13-#15	2.50
5 JSn,rep.Warlock #15	2.50
6 JSn,rep.	2.50

Warlock #5
© *Marvel Entertainment Group*

WARLOCK
(Limited Series)

1 Rep.Warlock Series	3.50
2 Rep.Warlock Series	3.00
3 Rep.Warlock Series	3.00
4 Rep.Warlock Series	3.00
5 Rep.Warlock Series	3.00
6 Rep.Warlock Series	3.00

WARLOCK AND THE INFINITY WATCH

1 AMe,Trial of the Gods(from Infinity Gauntlet)	4.00
2 AMe,I:Infinity Watch(Gamora,Pip, Moondragon,Drax & 1 other)	3.00
3 RL,TA,A:High Evolutionary, Nobilus,I:Omega	3.00
4 RL,TA,V:Omega	2.50
5 AMe,TA,V:Omega	2.50
6 AMe,V:Omega(Man-Beast)	2.50
7 TR,TA,V:Mole Man,A:Thanos	2.50
8 TR,TA,Infinity War,A:Thanos	2.25
9 AMe,TA,Inf.War,O:Gamora	2.00
10 AMe,Inf.War,Thanos vs Doppleganger	2.50
11 O:Pip,Gamora,Drax,M'dragon	2.00
12 TR,Drax Vs.Hulk	2.00
13 TR,Drax vs Hulk	2.00
14 AMe,V:United Nations	2.00
15 AMe,Magnus,Him	2.00
16 TGr,I:Count Abyss	2.00
17 TGr,I:Maxam	2.00
18 AMe,Inf.Crusade,N:Pip	2.00
19 TGr,A:Hulk,Wolverine,Infinity Crusade	2.00
20 AMe,Inf.Crusade	2.00
21 V:Thor	2.00
22 AMe,Infinity Crusade	2.00
23 JSn(s),TGb,Blood & Thunder#4	2.00
24 JSn(s),TGb,V:Geirrodur	2.00
25 JSn(s),AMe,Die-Cut(c),Blood & Thunder #12	3.25
26 A:Avengers	2.00
27 TGb,V:Avengers	2.00
28 TGb,V:Man-Beast	2.00
29 A:Maya	2.25
30 PO	2.25
31	1.95
32 Heart & Soul	1.95
33 V:Count Abyss	1.95
34 V:Count Abyss	1.95
35 V:Tyrannus	1.95
36	1.95
37 A:Zaharius	1.95
38	1.95
39 V:Domitron	1.95
40 A:Thanos	1.95
41 Monster Island	1.95
42 Warlock vs. Maxam, Atlantis Rising, final issue	1.95

WARLOCK CHRONICLES

1 TR,F:Adam Warlock,holo-grafx(c), I:Darklore,Meer'lyn	3.25
2 TR,Infinity Crusade,Thanos revealed to have the Reality Gem	2.25
3 TR,A:Mephisto	2.25
4 TR,A:Magnus	2.25
5 TR(c),Inf.Crusade	2.25
6 TR,Blood & Thunder,pt.#3	2.25
7 TR,Blood & Thunder,pt.#7	2.25
8 TR,Blood & Thunder,pt.#11	2.25
9 TR	2.00
10 TR	2.00
11 TR	2.00

WAR MACHINE

1 GG,Foil Embossed(c),B:LKa&StB, O:War Machine,V:Cable, C:Deathlok	3.25
1a Newstand Ed.	2.25
2 GG,V:Cable,Deathlok,w/card	1.75
3 GG,V:Cable,Deathlok	1.75
4 GG,C:Force Works	1.75
5 GG,I:Deachtoll	1.50
6 GG,V:Deathtoll	1.50
7 GG,A:Hawkeye	1.50
8 reg ed.	1.50
8a neon(c),w/insert print	3.00
9 Hands of Mandarin,pt.2	1.50
10 Hands of Mandarin,pt.5	1.50

---

11 X-Mas Party 1.50
12 V:Terror Device 1.50
13 V:The Rush Team 1.50
14 A:Force Works 1.50
15 In The Past of WWII 2.50
16 DAn,A:Rick Fury,Cap.America . 2.50

WAR MAN
Epic
1 thru 2 CDi(s) 2.50

WEAPON X
1 Wolverine After Xavier 4.00
2 Full Scale War 2.25
3 Jean Leaves 1.95
4 F:Gateway 1.95

WEAVEWORLD
Epic
1 MM, Clive Barker adaptation . . 4.95
2 MM,'Into the Weave' 4.95
3 MM 4.95

Web of Spider-Man #8
© Marvel Entertainment Group

WEB OF SPIDER-MAN
April, 1985
1 JM,V:New Costume 25.00
2 JM,V:Vulture 10.00
3 JM,V:Vulture 8.00
4 JM,JBy,V:Dr.Octopus 7.00
5 JM,JBy,V:Dr.Octopus 7.00
6 MZ,BL,JM,Secret Wars II 7.00
7 SB,A:Hulk,V:Nightmare,
    C:Wolverine 7.00
8 V:Smithville Thunder 7.00
9 V:Smithville Thunder 7.00
10 JM,A:Dominic Fortune,
    V:Shocker 7.00
11 BMc,V:Thugs 7.00
12 BMc,SB,V:Thugs 7.00
13 BMc,V:J.JonahJameson 7.00
14 KB,V:Black Fox 7.00
15 V:Black Fox,I:Chance 8.00
16 MS,KB,V:Magma 5.00
17 MS,V:Magma 5.00

18 MS,KB,Where is Spider-Man? . 8.00
19 MS,BMc,I:Solo,Humbug 6.00
20 MS,V:Terrorists 5.00
21 V:Fake Spider-Man 5.00
22 MS,V:Terrorists 5.00
23 V:Slyde 5.00
24 SB,V:Vulture,Hobgoblin 6.00
25 V:Aliens 5.00
26 V:Thugs 5.00
27 V:Headhunter 5.00
28 BL,V:Thugs 5.00
29 A:Wolverine,2nd App:New
    Hobgoblin 15.00
30 KB,O:Rose,C:Daredevil,Capt.
    America,Wolverine,Punisher . 14.00
31 MZ,BMc,V:Kraven 11.00

Web of Spider-Man #79
© Marvel Entertainment Group

32 MZ,BMc,V:Kraven 10.00
33 BSz(c),SL,V:Kingpin,Mad
    Dog Ward,pt.#1 . . . . 5.00
34 SB,A:Watcher 4.00
35 AS,V:Living Brain 4.00
36 AS,V:Phreak Out,I:Tombstone . 6.00
37 V:Slasher 4.00
38 AS,A:Tombstone,V:Hobgoblin . 6.00
39 AS,V:Looter(Meteor Man) 4.00
40 AS,V:Cult of Love 4.00
41 AS,V:Cult of Love 4.00
42 AS,V:Cult of Love 4.00
43 AS,V:Cult of Love 4.00
44 AS,V:Warzone,A:Hulk 3.00
45 AS,V:Vulture 3.00
46 A:Dr.Pym,V:Nekra 3.00
47 AS,V:Hobgoblin 5.00
48 AS,O:New Hobgoblin's Demonic
    Power 13.00
49 VM,V:Drugs 3.00
50 AS,V:Chameleon(double size) . 5.00
51 MBa,V:Chameleon,Lobo Bros. 4.00
52 FS,JR,O:J.Jonah Jameson
    V:Chameleon 4.00
53 MBa,V:Lobo Bros.,C:Punisher
    A:Chameleon 4.50
54 AS,V:Chameleon,V:Lobo Bros. 4.00
55 AS,V:Chameleon,Hammerhead,
    V:Lobo Bros. 4.00

56 AS,I&O:Skin Head,
    A:Rocket Racer 3.50
57 AS,D:SkinHead,
    A:Rocket Racer 3.00
58 AS,V:Grizzly 3.00
59 AS,Acts of Vengeance,V:Titania
    A:Puma,Cosmic Spider-Man . . 9.00
60 AS,A of V,V:Goliath 5.00
61 AS,A of V,V:Dragon Man 5.00
62 AS,V:Molten Man 3.00
63 AS,V:Mister Fear 3.00
64 AS,V:Graviton,Titania,Trapster 3.00
65 AS,V:Goliath,Trapster,Graviton 3.00
66 AS,V:Tombstone,A:G.Goblin . . 4.00
67 AS,A:GreenGoblin,
    V:Tombstone 4.00
68 AS,A:GreenGoblin,
    V:Tombstone 3.50
69 AS,V:Hulk 5.00
70 AS,I:The Spider/Hulk 3.00
71 A:Silver Sable 2.50
72 AM,A:Silver Sable 2.50
73 AS,A:Human Torch,
    Colossus,Namor 2.50
74 AS,I:Spark,V:Bora 2.50
75 AS,C:New Warriors 2.50
76 AS,Spidey in Ice 2.50
77 AS,V:Firebrand,Inheritor 2.50
78 AS,A:Firebrand,Cloak&Dagger 2.50
79 AS,V:Silvermane 2.50
80 AS,V:Silvermane 2.50
81 I:Bloodshed 2.25
82 V:Man Mountain Marko 2.25
83 V:A.I.M. Supersuit 2.25
84 AS,B:Name of the Rose 3.00
85 AS,Name of the Rose 2.50
86 AS,I:Demogoblin 2.50
87 AS,I:Praetorian Guard 2.50
88 AS,Name of the Rose 2.50
89 AS,E:Name of the Rose,
    I:Bloodrose 2.50
90 AS,30th Ann.,w/hologram,
    polybagged,V:Mysterio 6.00
90a Gold 2nd printing 3.25
91 AS,V:Whisper And Pulse 2.00
92 AS,V:Foreigner 2.00
93 AS,BMc,V:Hobgoblin,A:Moon
    Knight,Foreigner 2.00
94 AS,V:Hobgoblin,A:MoonKnight 2.00
95 AS,Spirits of Venom#1,A:Venom,
    J.Blaze,GR,V:Hag & Troll 4.00
96 AS,Spirits of Venom#3, A:G.R,
    J.Blaze,Venom,Hobgoblin . . . 3.00
97 AS,I:Dr.Trench,V:Bloodrose . . 1.75
98 AS,V:Bloodrose,Foreigner . . . 1.75
99 I:Night Watch,V:New Enforcer . 1.75
100 AS,JRu,V:Enforcers,Bloodrose,
    Kingpin(Alfredo),I:Spider Armor,
    O:Night Watch,Holografx(c) . . . 4.00
101 AS,Total Carnage,V:Carnage,
    Shriek,A:Cloak and Dagger,
    Venom 1.75
102 Total Carnage#6,V:Carnage,
    A:Venom,Morbius 1.75
103 AS,Maximum Carnage#10,
    V:Carnage 1.50
104 AS,Infinity Crusade 1.50
105 AS,Infinity Crusade 1.50
106 AS,Infinity Crusade 1.50
107 AS,A:Sandman,Quicksand . . 1.50
108 B:TKa(s),AS,I:Sandstorm,
    BU:Cardiac 1.50
109 AS,V:Shocker,A:Night Thrasher,
    BU:D:Calypso 1.50
110 AS,I:Warrant,A:Lizard 1.50

Web of Spider-Man #93
© Marvel Entertainment Group

111 AS,V:Warrant,Lizard 1.50
112 AS,Pursuit#3,V:Chameleon,
w/card 1.75
113 AS,A:Gambit,Black Cat,w/cel . 3.25
113a Newsstand Ed. 1.75
114 AS 1.75
115 AS,V:Facade 1.75
116 AS,V:Facade 1.75
117 Foil(c), flip book with
Power & Responsibility #1 . . . 3.25
117a Newsstand ed. 1.75
118 Spider-clone, V:Venom 1.50
119 Clone,V:Venom 1.50
119a bagged with Milestone rep.
Amazing Sp-Man #150,checklist 6.50
120 Web of Life,pt.1 . . . . 1.50
121 Web of Life,pt.3 . . . . 1.50
122 Smoke and Mirrors,pt.1 . . . . . 1.50
123 The Price of Truth,pt.2 . . . . . 1.50
124 The Mark of Kaine,pt.1 . . . . . 1.50
125 R:Gwen Stacy 2.95
125a 3-D Holodisk cover 3.95
126 The Trial of Peter Parker,pt.1 1.50
Ann.#1 V:Future Max 6.00
Ann.#2 AAd,MMi,A:Warlock 8.00
Ann.#3 AS,DP,JRu,JM,BL 4.50
Ann.#4 AS,TM,RLm,Evolutionary
Wars,A:Man Thing,V:Slug 5.00
Ann.#5 AS,SD,JS,Atlantis
Attacks,A:Fantastic Four 3.50
Ann.#6 SD,JBr,SB,A:Punisher . . . 4.50
Ann.#7 Vibranium Vendetta #3 . . 2.50
Ann.#8 Hero Killers#3,A:New
Warriors,BU:Venom,Black Cat . 3.00
Ann.#9 CMa,I:Cadre,w/card 3.25
Ann.#10 V:Shriek 3.75

WEIRD WONDERTALES
December, 1973
1 B:Reprints 5.00
2 I Was Kidnapped by a Flying
Saucer 2.50
3 The Thing in the Bog 2.50
4 It Lurks Behind the Wall 2.50
5 . . . . 2.50

6 The Man Who Owned a Ghost 2.50
7 The Apes That Walked
like Men 2.50
8 Reap A Deadly Harvest 2.50
9 The Murder Mirror 2.50
10 Mister Morgans Monster 2.50
11 Slaughter in Shrangri-La 2.50
12 The Stars Scream Murder . . . 2.50
13 The Totem Strikes 2.50
14 Witching Circle 2.50
15 . . . . 2.50
16 The Shark 2.50
17 Creature From Krogarr 2.50
18 Krang 2.50
19 A:Dr Druid 2.50
20 The Madness 2.50
21 A:Dr Druid 2.50
22 The World Below,May, 1975 . . 2.50

WEREWOLF BY NIGHT
September, 1972
1 MP(cont from Marvel Spotlight)
FullMoonRise..WerewolfKill . . 38.00
2 MP,Like a Wild Beast at Bay . 17.00
3 MP,Mystery of the Mad Monk . 10.00
4 MP,The Danger Game 10.00
5 MP,A Life for a Death 10.00
6 MP,Carnival of Fear 8.00
7 MP,JM,Ritual of Blood 8.00
8 MP,Krogg,Lurker from Beyond . 8.00
9 TS,V:Tatterdemalion 8.00
10 TS,bondage cover 8.00
11 GK,TS,Full Moon..Fear Moon . 6.00
12 GK,Cry Monster 6.00
13 MP,ManMonsterCalledTaboo . 6.00
14 MP,Lo,the Monster Strikes . . . 6.00
15 MP,(new)O:Werewolf,
V:Dracula 7.00
16 MP,TS,A:Hunchback of Notre
Dame 6.00
17 Behold the Behemoth 6.00
18 War of the Werewolves 6.00
19 V:Dracula 7.00
20 The Monster Breaks Free 6.00
21 GK(c),To Cure a Werewolf 5.00
22 GK(c),Face of a Friend 5.00
23 Silver Bullet for a Werewolf . . . 5.00
24 GK(c),V:The Brute 5.00
25 GK(c),Eclipse of Evil 5.00
26 GK(c),A Crusade of Murder . . 5.00
27 GK(c),Scourge o/t Soul-Beast . 5.00
28 GK(c),V:Dr.Glitternight 5.00
29 GK(c),V:Dr.Glitternight 5.00
30 GK(c),Red Slash across
Midnight 5.00
31 Death in White 5.00
32 I&O:Moon Knight 45.00
33 Were-Beast..Moon Knight
A:Moon Knight(2nd App) 25.00
34 GK(c),TS,House of Evil..House
of Death 4.00
35 TS,JS,BWi,Jack Russell vs.
Werewolf 5.00
36 Images of Death 4.00
37 BWr(c),BW,A:Moon Knight,
Hangman,Dr.Glitternight 8.50
38 . . . . 3.50
39 V:Brother Voodoo 3.50
40 A:Brother Voodoo,V:Dr.
Glitternight 3.50
41 V:Fire Eyes 3.50
42 A:IronMan,Birth of a Monster . 3.50
43 Tri-Animal Lives,A:Iron Man . . 3.50
Giant#2,SD,A:Frankenstein
Monster (reprint) 3.00

Giant#3 GK(c),Transylvania 3.50
Giant#4 GK(c),A:Morbius 12.00
Giant#5 GK(c),Peril of
Paingloss 3.00

West Coast Avengers #1
© Marvel Entertainment Group

WEST COAST AVENGERS
[Limited Series]
September, 1984
1 BH,A:Shroud,J:Hawkeye,IronMan,
WonderMan,Mockingbird,Tigra 6.00
2 BH,V:Blank 5.00
3 BH,V:Graviton 4.00
4 BH,V:Graviton 4.00

[Regular Series]
1 AM,JSt,V:Lethal Legion 6.00
2 AM,JSt,V:Lethal Legion 4.00
3 AM,JSt,V:Kraven 3.00
4 AM,JSt,A:Firebird,Thing,I:Master
Pandemonium 3.00
5 AM,JSt,A:Werewolf,Thing 3.00
6 AM,KB,A:Thing 3.00
7 AM,JSt,V:Ultron 3.00
8 AM,JSt,V:Rangers,A:Thing . . . 3.00
9 AM,JSt,V:Master Pandemonium 3.00
10 AM,JSt,V:Headlok,Griffen 3.00
11 AM,JSt,A:Nick Fury 2.50
12 AM,JSt,V:Graviton 2.50
13 AM,JSt,V:Graviton 2.50
14 AM,JSt,V:Pandemonium 2.50
15 AM,JSt,A:Hellcat 2.50
16 AM,JSt,V:Tiger Shark,
Whirlwind 2.50
17 AM,JSt,V:Dominus' Minions . . 2.50
18 AM,JSt,V:The Wild West 2.50
19 AM,JSt,A:Two Gun Kid 2.50
20 AM,JSt,A:Rawhide Kid 2.50
21 AM,JSt,A:Dr.Pym,Moon Knight 2.50
22 AM,JSt,A:Fant.Four,Dr.Strange,
Night Rider 2.00
23 AM,RT,A:Phantom Rider 2.00
24 AM,V:Dominus 2.00
25 AM,V:Abomination 2.00
26 AM,V:Zodiac 2.00
27 AM,V:Zodiac 1.75
28 AM,V:Zodiac 1.75

29	AM,V:Taurus,A:Shroud	1.75
30	AM,C:Composite Avenger	1.75
31	AM,V:Arkon	1.75
32	AM,TD,V:Yetrigar,J:Wasp	1.75
33	AM,O:Ant-Man,Wasp; V:Madam X,El Toro	1.75
34	AM,V:Quicksilver,J:Vision & Scarlet Witch	1.75
35	AM,V:Dr.Doom,Quicksilver	1.75
36	AM,V:The Voice	1.75
37	V:The Voice,A:Mantis	1.75
38	AM,TMo,V:Defiler	1.75
39	AM,V:Swordsman	1.75
40	AM,MGu,V:NightShift, A:Shroud	1.75
41	TMo,I:New Phantom Rider, L:Moon Knight	1.75
42	JBy,Visionquest#1,V:Ultron	3.50
43	JBy,Visionquest#2,	2.50
44	JBy,Visionquest#3,J:USAgent	2.00
45	JBy,Visionquest#4, I:New Vision	2.50
46	JBy,I:Great Lakes Avengers	2.00
Ann. #1	MBr,GI,V:Zodiak	2.25
Ann. #2	AM,A:SilverSurfer,V:Death, Collector,R:Grandmaster	2.00
Ann. #3	AM,RLm,TD,Evolutionary Wars,R:Giant Man	3.50

Becomes:

AVENGERS WEST COAST

Western Gunfighters #9
© Marvel Entertainment Group

WESTERN GUNFIGHTERS
August, 1970
[2nd series]

1	JK,JB,DAy,B:Ghost Rider A:Fort Rango,The Renegades Gunhawk	6.00
2	HT(c),DAy,JMn,O:Nightwind, V:Tarantula	3.50
3	DAy,V:Hurricane(reprint)	3.50
4	HT(c),DAy,TS,B:Gunhawk, Apache Kid,A:Renegades	3.50
5	DAy,FrG,A:Renegades	3.50
6	HT(c),DAy,SSh,Death of Ghost Rider	4.00
7	HT(c),DAy,SSh,O:Ghost Rider retold,E:Ghost Rider,Gunhawk	5.00

8	DAy,SSh,B:Black Rider,Outlaw Kid(rep)	3.00
9	DW,Revenge rides the Range	3.00
10	JK,JMn,O:Black Rider,B:Matt Slade,E:Outlaw Kid	3.00
11	JK,Duel at Dawn	3.00
12	JMn,O:Matt Slade	3.00
13	Save the Gold Coast Expires	3.00
14	JSo(c),Outlaw Town	3.00
15	E:Matt Slade,Showdown in Outlaw Canyon	3.00
16	B:Kid Colt,Shoot-out in Silver City	3.00
17 thru 20		@3.00
21 thru 24		@2.50
25		2.50
26	F:Kid Colt,Gun-Slinger,Apache Kid	2.50
27 thru 32		@2.50
33	November, 1975	2.50

WESTERN KID
December, 1954
[1st Series]

1	JR,B:Western Kid,O:Western Kid (Tex Dawson)	100.00
2	JMn,JR,Western Adventure	50.00
3	JMn(c),JR,Gunfight(c)	40.00
4	JMn(c),JR,The Badlands	40.00
5	JR	40.00
6	JR	40.00
7	JR	40.00
8	JR	40.00
9	JR,AW	50.00
10	JR,AW,Man in the Middle	50.00
11		30.00
12		30.00
13		30.00
14		30.00
15		30.00
16		30.00
17	August, 1957	30.00

WESTERN KID
December, 1971
[2nd Series]

1	Reprints	4.00
2		3.00
3		3.00
4		3.00
5	August, 1972	3.00

WESTERN OUTLAWS
Atlas
Feb., 1954—Aug., 1957

1	JMn(c),RH,BP,The Greenville Gallows,Hanging(c)	100.00
2		50.00
3 thru 10		@40.00
11	AW	45.00
12		30.00
13	MB	35.00
14	AW	45.00
15	AT,GT	40.00
16	BP	30.00
17		35.00
18		30.00
19		40.00
20 and 21		@35.00

WESTERN OUTLAWS
& SHERIFFS
See: BEST WESTERN

WESTERN TALES
OF BLACK RIDER
See: ALL WINNERS COMICS

WESTERN TEAM-UP
November, 1973

1	Rawhide Kid/Dakota Kid	2.00

WESTERN THRILLERS
November, 1954

1	JMn,Western tales	75.00
2		40.00
3		40.00
4		40.00

Becomes:

COWBOY ACTION

5	JMn(c),The Prairie Kid	45.00
6		30.00
7		30.00
9		30.00
10		30.00
11	MN,AW,Ther Manhunter March, 1956	45.00

Becomes:

QUICK-TRIGGER
WESTERN

12	Bill Larson Strikes	55.00
13	The Man From Cheyenne	60.00
14	BEv,RH(c)	50.00
15	AT	40.00
16	JK	35.00
17	GT	35.00
18	GM	35.00
19	JSe	30.00

WESTERN WINNERS
See: ALL WINNERS COMICS

WHAT IF?
[1st Regular Series]
February, 1977

1	Spider-Man joined Fant.Four	20.00
2	GK(c),Hulk had Banner brain	11.00
3	GK,KJ,F:Avengers	7.00
4	GK(c),F:Invaders	7.00
5	F:Captain America	7.00
6	F:Fantastic Four	7.00
7	GK(c),F:Spider-Man	7.00
8	GK(c),F:Daredevil	5.50
9	JK(c),F:Avengers of the '50s	6.00
10	JB,F:Thor	5.00
11	JK,F:FantasticFour	5.00
12	F:Hulk	5.00
13	JB,Conan Alive Today	6.00
14	F:Sgt. Fury	5.00
15	CI,F:Nova	5.00
16	F:Master of Kung Fu	5.00
17	CI,F:Ghost Rider	7.00
18	TS,F:Dr.Strange	4.00
19	PB,F:Spider-Man	5.00
20	F:Avengers	4.00
21	GC,F:Sub-Mariner	4.00
22	F:Dr.Doom	4.00
23	JB,F:Hulk	4.00
24	GK,RB,Gwen Stacy had lived	5.00
25	F:Thor,Avengers,O:Mentor	4.00
26	JBy(c),F:Captain America	4.00
27	FM(c),Phoenix hadn't died	12.00
28	FM,F:Daredevil,Ghost Rider.	10.00
29	MG(c),F:Avengers	4.00
30	RB,F:Spider-Man	11.00
31	Wolverine killed the Hulk	15.00

What If? #9
© Marvel Entertainment Group

32 Avengers lost to Korvac 3.50
33 BL,Dazzler herald of Galactus . 3.50
34 FH,FM,JBy,BSz:Humor issue . 3.50
35 FM,Elektra had lived 6.00
36 JBy,Fant.Four had no powers . 3.00
37 F:Thing,Beast,Silver Surfer ... 3.50
38 F:Daredevil,Captain America .. 3.00
39 Thor had fought Conan 3.00
40 F:Dr.Strange 3.00
41 F:Sub-Mariner 3.50
42 F:Fantastic Four 3.00
43 F:Conan 3.00
44 F:Captain America 3.00
45 F:Hulk,Berserk 3.50
46 Uncle Ben had lived 5.00
47 F:Thor,Loki 3.00
Spec.#1 F:Iron Man,Avengers ... 4.00
Best of What IF? rep.#1,#24,
   #27,#28 .... 12.95
[2nd Regular Series]
1 RWi,MG,The Avengers had lost
   the Evolutionary War 5.00
2 GCa,Daredevil Killed Kingpin,
   A:Hobgoblin, The Rose 4.00
3 Capt.America Hadn't Given Up
   Costume,A:Avengers 3.50
4 MBa,Spider-Man kept Black
   Costume,A:Avengers,Hulk 4.50
5 Vision Destroyed Avengers,
   A:Wonder Man 3.50
6 RLm,X-Men Lost Inferno,
   A:Dr.Strange 6.00
7 RLd,Wolverine Joined Shield,
   A:Nick Fury,Black Widow 7.00
8 Iron Man Lost The Armor Wars,
   A:Ant Man 3.50
9 RB,New X-Men Died 5.00
10 MZ(c),BMc,Punisher's Family
   Didn't Die,A:Kingpin 4.00
11 TM(c),JV,SM,Fant.Four had the
   Same Powers,A:Nick Fury ... 3.50
12 JV,X-Men Stayed in Asgard,
   A:Thor,Hela 3.00
13 JLe(c),Prof.X Became
   Juggernaut,A:X-Men 3.50
14 RLm(c),Capt.Marvel didn't die
   A:Silver Surfer 2.50
15 GCa,Fant.Four Lost Trial of

Galactus,A:Gladiator 2.25
16 Wolverine Battled Conan,
   A:X-Men,Red Sonja 5.00
17 Kraven Killed Spider-Man,
   A:Daredevil,Captain America .. 2.50
18 LMc,Fant.Four fought Dr.Doom
   before they gained powers ... 2.25
19 RW,Vision took over Earth,
   A:Avengers,Dr.Doom 2.25
20 Spider-Man didn't marry Mary
   Jane,A:Venom,Kraven 3.00
21 Spider-Man married Black Cat,
   A:Vulture,Silver Sable 2.50
22 RLm,Silver Surfer didn't escape
   Earth,A:F.F,Mephisto,Thanos . 4.00
23 New X-Men never existed,
   A:Eric the Red,Lilandra 2.50
24 Wolverine Became Lord of
   Vampires,A:Punisher 3.00
25 Marvel Heroes lost Atlantis
   Attacks,double size 3.25
26 LMc,Punisher Killed Daredevil,
   A:Spider-Man 2.50
27 Submariner Joined Fantastic
   Four,A:Dr. Doom 2.00
28 RW,Capt.America led Army of
   Super-Soldiers,A:Submariner . 2.00
29 RW,Capt.America formed the
   Avengers 2.00
30 Inv.Woman's 2nd Child had
   lived,A:Fantastic Four 2.00
31 Spider-Man/Captain Universe
   Powers 2.00
32 Phoenix Rose Again,pt.1 .... 2.00
33 Phoenix Rose Again,pt.2 .... 2.00
34 Humor Issue 1.75
35 B:Time Quake,F.F. vs.Dr.Doom
   & Annihilus 1.75
36 Cosmic Avengers,V:Guardians
   of the Galaxy 1.75
37 X-Vampires,V:Dormammu 1.75
38 Thor was prisoner of Set 1.75
39 E:Time Quake,Watcher saved the
   Universe 1.75
40 Storm remained A thief? 1.75
41 JV,Avengers fought Galactus . 2.00
42 KWe,Spidey kept extra arms .. 1.75
43 Wolverine married Mariko 1.75
44 Punisher possessedby Venom 1.75
45 Barbara Ketch became G.R. .. 1.75
46 Cable Killed Prof.X,Cyclops &
   Jean Grey 1.75
47 Magneto took over USA 1.75
48 Daredevil Saved Nuke 1.50
49 Silver Surfer had Inf.Gauntlet? 1.50
50 Hulk killed Wolverine 4.00
51 PCu,Punisher is Capt.America 1.50
52 BHi,Wolverine led Alpha Flight 1.50
53 F:Iron Man,Hulk 1.50
54 F:Death's Head 1.50
55 LKa(s),Avengers lose G.Storm 1.50
56 Avengers lose G.Storm#2 .... 1.50
57 Punisher a member of SHIELD 1.50
58 Punisher kills SpM 1.50
59 Wolverine lead Alpha Flight .. 2.00
60 RoR,Scott & Jean's Wedding . 1.50
61 Spider-Man's Parents 1.50
62 Woverine vs Weapon X 2.25
63 F:War Machine,Iron Man 1.95
64 Iron Man sold out 2.25
65 Archangel fell from Grace 1.50
66 Rogue and Thor 1.50
67 Cap.America returns 1.50
68 Captain America story 1.50
69 Stryfe Killed X-Men 1.50

What If? #34
© Marvel Entertainment Group

70 Silver Surfer 1.50
71 The Hulk 1.50
72 Parker Killed Burglar 1.50
73 Daredevil,Kingpin 1.50
74 Sinister Formed X-Men 1.50
75 Gen-X's Blink had lived 1.50
TPB Best of What If? 12.95

WHAT THE -?!
[Parodies]
August, 1988

1 .... 6.00
2 JBy,JOy,AW, ... 4.00
3 TM, ... 5.00
4 .... 4.00
5 EL,JLe,WPo,Wolverine 5.00
6 Wolverine,Punisher 4.00
7 .... 2.50
8 DK 2.50
9 .... 1.75
10 JBy,X-Men,Dr.Doom, Cap.
   America 1.75
11 DK,RLd(part) 2.00
12 Conan, F.F.,Wolverine. 1.50
13 Silver Burper,F.F.,Wolverine. .. 1.50
14 Spittle-Man 1.50
15 Capt.Ultra,Wolverina 1.50
16 Ant Man,Watcher 1.25
17 Wulverean/Pulverizer,Hoagg/
   Spider-Ham,SleepGawker,F.F. 1.25
18 .... 1.25
19 .... 1.25
20 Infinity Wart Crossover 1.25
21 Weapon XX,Toast Rider 1.25
22 F:Echs Farce 1.25
23 .... 1.25
24 Halloween issue 1.25
25 .... 1.25
26 Spider-Ham 2099 .... 1.25
Summer Spec. 2.50
Fall Spec. 2.50

WHERE CREATURES ROAM
July, 1970—Sept., 1971
1 JK,SD,DAy,B:Reprints		
The Brute That Walks	4.50
2 JK,SD,Midnight/Monster	2.50
3 JK,SD,DAy,Thorg	2.50
4 JK,SD,Vandoom	2.50
5 JK,SD,Gorgilla	2.50
6 JK,SD,Zog	2.50
7 SD	2.50
8 The Mummy's Secret,E:Reprints	2.50

WHERE MONSTERS DWELL
January, 1970
1 B:Reprints,Cyclops	5.00
2 Sporr	3.50
3 Grottu	3.50
4	3.50
5 Taboo	3.50
6 Groot	3.50
7 Rommbu	3.50
8 The Four-Armed Men	3.50
9 Bumbu	3.50
10 Monster That Walks Like A Man	3.50
11 Gruto	3.00
12 Orogo	3.00
13 The Thing That Crawl	3.00
14 The Green Thing	3.00
15 Kraa- The Inhuman	3.00
16 Beware the Son Of Goom	3.00
17 The Hidden Vampires	3.00
18 The Mask of Morghum	3.00
19 The Insect Man	3.00
20 Klagg	3.00
21 Fin Fang Foom	3.00
22 Elektro	3.00
23 The Monster Waits For Me	3.00
24 The Things on Easter Island	3.00
25 The Ruler of the Earth	3.00
26	3.00
27	3.00
28 Droom,The Living Lizard	3.00
29 thru 37 Reprints	@3.00
38 Reprints,October, 1975	3.00

WHIP WILSON
See: BLAZE CARSON

WILD
Atlas
February, 1954
1 BEv,JMn,Charlie Chan Parody	125.00
2 BEv,RH,JMn,Witches(c)	80.00
3 CBu(c),BEv,RH,JMn,	60.00
4 GC,Didja Ever See a Cannon Brawl	60.00
5 RH,JMn,August, 1954	60.00

WILD CARDS
Epic
September, 1990
1 JG	5.50
2 JG,V:Jokers	4.50
3 A:Turtle	4.50

WILD THING
1 A:Virtual Reality Venom and Carnage	3.00

2 A:VR Venom and Carnage	2.00
3 A:Shield	2.00
4	2.00
5 Virtual Reality Gangs	2.00
6 Virtual Reality Villians	2.00
7 V:Trask	2.00
8	1.75
9	1.75
10	1.75
11	1.75
12	1.75
13	1.75

WILD WEST
Spring, 1948
1 SSh(c),B:Two Gun Kids,Tex Taylor,Arizona Annie	150.00
2 SSh(c),CCb, Captain Tootsie	125.00
Becomes:

WILD WESTERN
3 SSh(c),B:Tex Morgan,Two Gun Kid,Tex Taylor,Arizona Annie	150.00
4 Rh,SSh,CCB,Capt. Tootsie. A:Kid Colt,E:Arizona Annie	125.00
5 RH,CCB,Captain Tootsie A;Black Rider,Blaze Carson	125.00
6 A:Blaze Carson,Kid Colt	75.00
7	75.00
8 RH	75.00
9 Ph(c),B:Black Rider	100.00
10 Ph(c)	125.00
11	75.00
12	60.00
13	60.00
14	60.00
15	65.00
16 thru 20	@55.00
21 thru 29	@50.00
30 JKa	55.00
31 thru 40	@35.00
41 thru 47	@25.00
48	35.00
49 thru 53	@25.00
54 AW	45.00
55 AW	45.00
56	25.00

William Shatner's Tek World #1
© Marvel Entertainment Group

57 September, 1957	25.00

WILLIAM SHATNER'S TEK WORLD
1 LS,Novel adapt.	2.25
2 LS,Novel adapt.cont.	2.00
3 LS,Novel adapt.cont.	2.00
4 LS,Novel adapt.cont.	2.00
5 LS,Novel adapt.concludes	2.00
6 LS,V:TekLords	2.00
7 E:The Angel	2.00
8	2.00
9	2.00
10	2.00
11 thru 17	2.00
18	2.00
19 Sims of the Father#1	1.75
20 Sims of the Father#2	1.75
21 Who aren't in Heaven	1.75
22 Father and Guns	1.75
23 We'll be Right Back	2.00
24	1.75

WILLIE COMICS
See: IDEAL COMICS

WILLOW
August, 1988
1 Movie adapt.	1.00
2 Movie adapt.	1.00
3 Movie adapt,October, 1988.	1.00

WITNESS, THE
September, 1948
1	450.00

WOLFPACK
August, 1988
1 I:Wolfpack	1.00
2 thru 11	@1.00
12 July, 1988	1.00

WOLVERINE
September, 1982
[Limited Series]
1 B:CCl(s),FM,JRu,A:Mariko, I:Shingen	37.00
2 FM,JRu,A:Mariko,I:Yukio	30.00
3 FM,JRu,A:Mariko,Yukio	30.00
4 B:CCl(s),FM,JRu,A:Mariko, D:Shingen	32.00
[Regular Series]
1 JB,AW,V:Banipur	30.00
2 JB,KJ,V:Silver Samurai	17.00
3 JB,AW,V:Silver Samurai	12.00
4 JB,AW,I:Roughouse, Bloodsport	10.00
5 JB,AW,V:Roughouse, Bloodsport	10.00
6 JB,AW,V:Roughouse, Bloodsport	10.00
7 JB,A:Hulk	9.00
8 JB,A:Hulk	9.00
9 GC,Old Wolverine Story	9.00
10 JB,BSz,V:Sabretooth (1st battle)	30.00
11 JB,BSz,B:Gehenna Stone	7.00
12 JB,BSz,Gehenna Stone	7.00
13 JB,BSz,Gehenna Stone	7.00
14 JB,BSz,Gehenna Stone	7.00
15 JB,BSz,Gehenna Stone	7.00
16 JB,BSz,E:Gehenna Stone	7.00
17 JBy,KJ,V:Roughouse	6.00

18 JBy,KJ,V:Roughouse	5.00
19 JBy,KJ,A of V,I:La Bandera	5.00
20 JBy,KJ,A of V,V:Tigershark	5.00
21 JBy,KJ,V:Geist	5.00
22 JBy,KJ,V:Geist,Spore	5.00
23 JBy,KJ,V:Geist,Spore	5.00
24 GC,'Snow Blind'	4.50
25 JB,O:Wolverine(part)	5.00
26 KJ,Return to Japan	5.00
27 thru 30 Lazarus Project	4.50
31 MS,DGr,A:Prince o'Mandripoor	4.50
32 MS,DGr,V:Ninjas	4.50
33 MS,Wolverine in Japan	4.50
34 MS,DGr,Wolverine in Canada	4.50
35 MS,DGr,A:Puck	4.50
36 MS,DGr,A:Puck,Lady D'strike	4.50
37 MS,DGr,V:Lady Deathstrike	4.50
38 MS,DGr,A:Storm,I:Elsie Dee	4.50
39 MS,DGr,Wolverine Vs. Clone	4.50
40 MS,DGr,Wolverine Vs. Clone	4.50

Wolverine #7
© *Marvel Entertainment Group*

41 MS,DGr,R:Sabretooth, A:Cable	10.00
41a 2nd printing	2.25
42 MS,DGr,A:Sabretooth,Cable	8.00
42a 2nd printing	2.00
43 MS,DGr,A:Sabretooth,C:Cable	5.00
44 LSn,DGr	4.00
45 MS,DGr,A:Sabretooth	5.00
46 MS,DGr,A:Sabretooth	4.50
47 V:Tracy	4.00
48 LHa(s),MS,DGr,B:Shiva Scenario	4.00
49 LHa(s),MS,DGr	4.00
50 LHa(s),MS,DGr,A:X-Men,Nick Fury, I:Shiva,Slash-Die Cut(c)	6.00
51 MS,DGr,A:Mystique,X-Men	3.50
52 MS,DGr,A:Mystique,V:Spiral	3.50
53 MS,A:Mystique,V:Spiral,Mojo	3.50
54 A:Shatterstar	3.50
55 MS,V:Cylla,A:Gambit,Sunfire	3.50
56 MS,A:Gambit,Sunfire,V:Hand, Hydra	3.50
57 MS,D:Lady Mariko,A:Gambit	4.00
58 A:Terror	3.00
59 A:Terror	3.00

60 Sabretooth vs.Shiva, I:John Wraith	3.50
61 MT,History of Wolverine and Sabretooth,A:John Wraith	3.50
62 MT,A:Sabretooth,Silver Fox	3.00
63 MT,V:Ferro,D:Silver Fox	3.00
64 MPa,V:Ferro,Sabretooth	3.00
65 MT,A:Professor X	3.00
66 MT,A:X-Men	3.00
67 MT,A:X-Men	3.00
68 MT,V:Epsilon Red	3.00
69 DT,A:Rogue,V:Sauron,tie-in to X-Men#300	2.75
70 DT,Sauron,A:Rogue,Jubilee	2.75
71 DT,V:Sauron,Brain Child,A:Rogue, Jubilee	2.75
72 DT,Sentinels	2.75
73 DT,V:Sentinels	2.75
74 ANi,V:Sentinels	2.50
75 AKu,Hologram(c),Wolv. has Bone Claws,leaves X-Men	12.00
76 DT(c),B:LHa(s),A:Deathstrike, Vindicator,C:Puck	2.25
77 AKu,A:Vindicator,Puck,V:Lady Deathstrike	2.25
78 AKu,V:Cylla,Bloodscream	2.25
79 AKu,V:Cyber,I:Zoe Culloden	2.25
80 IaC,V:Cyber,	2.25
81 IaC,V:Cyber,A:Excalibur	2.25
82 AKu,BMc,A:Yukio,Silver Samurai	2.25
83 AKu,A:Alpha Flight	2.25
84 A:Alpha Flight	1.95
85 Phalanx Covenant, Final Sanction, V:Phalanx,holografx(c)	2.95
85a newsstand ed.	2.00
86 AKu,V:Bloodscream	1.95
87 AKu,deluxe,V:Juggernaut	1.95
87a newsstand ed.	1.50
88 AKu,deluxe ed.	1.95
88a newsstand ed.	1.50
89 deluxe ed.	1.95
89a newsstand ed.	1.50
90 V:Sabretooth, deluxe ed.	1.95
90a newsstand ed.	1.50
91 LHa,Logan's future unravels	1.95
TPB Wolverine rep Marvel Comics Presents #1-#10	2.95
Jungle Adventure MMi,(Deluxe)	5.50
SC Acts of Vengeance, rep.	6.95
Bloodlust (one shot),AD V:Siberian Were-Creatures	6.00
Global Jeapordy,PDd(s)	2.95
Killing, KSW,JNR	5.95
Rahne of Terror, C:Cable	8.00
Save the Tiger,rep.	2.95
GNv Bloody Choices,JB,A:N.Fury	12.95
Typhoid's Kiss,rep.	6.95
Inner Fury,BSz,V:Nanotech Machines	6.25
GN Scorpio Rising, T.U.Fury	5.95
HC Weapon X	19.95

WOLVERINE & PUNISHER: DAMAGING EVIDENCE

1 B:CP(s),GEr,A:Kingpin	2.25
2 GEr,A:Kingpin,Sniper	2.25
3 GEr,Last issue	2.25

WOLVERINE SAGA
September, 1989

1 RLd(c),	6.50
2	5.00
3	5.00

4 December, 1989	5.00

WONDER DUCK
September, 1949

1 Whale(c)	50.00
2	33.00
3 March, 1950	33.00

WONDERMAN
March, 1986

1 KGa,one-shot special	3.00

WONDER MAN
September, 1991

1 B:GJ(s),JJ,V:Goliath	2.25
2 JJ,A:West Coast Avengers	1.50
3 JJ,V:Abominatrix,I:Spider	1.50
4 JJ,I:Splice,A:Spider	1.50
5 JJ,A:Beast,V:Rampage	1.50
6 JJ,A:Beast,V:Rampage	1.50
7 JJ,Galactic Storm	1.50
8 JJ,Galactic Storm,pt.4, A:Hulk & Rich Jones	1.50
9 JJ,GalacticStorm,pt.11,A:Vision	1.50
10 JJ,V:Khmer Rouge	1.50
11 V:Angkor	1.50
12 V:Angkor	1.50
13 Infinity War	1.50
14 Infinity War,V:Warlock	1.50
15 Inf.War,V:Doppleganger	1.50
16 JJ,I:Armed Response, A:Avengers West Coast	1.50
17 JJ,A:Avengers West Coast	1.50
18 V:Avengers West Coast	1.50
19	1.50
20 V:Splice,Rampage	1.50
21 V:Splice,Rampage	1.50
22 JJ,V:Realm of Death	1.50
23 JJ,A:Grim Reaper,Mephisto	1.50
24 JJ,V:Grim Reaper,Goliath	1.50
25 JJ,N:Wonder Man,D:Grim Reaper, V:Mephisto	3.25
26 A:Hulk,C:Furor,Plan Master	1.50
27 A:Hulk	1.50
28 RoR,A:Spider-Man	1.50
29 RoR,A:Spider-Man	1.50
30 V:Hate Monger	1.25
31	1.25
32	1.25
33	1.25
Spec.#1 (1985),KGa	3.00
Ann.#1 System Bytes #3	2.25
Ann.#2 I:Hit-Maker,w/card	2.95

WORLD CHAMPIONSHIP WRESTLING

1 F:Lex Luger,Sting	1.50
2	1.25
3	1.25
4 Luger Vs El Gigante	1.25
5 Rick Rude Vs. Sting	1.25
6 F:Dangerous Alliance,R.Rude	1.25
7 F:Steiner Brothers	1.25
8 F:Sting,Dangerous Alliance	1.25
9 Bunkhouse Brawl	1.25
10 Halloween Havoc	1.25
11 Sting vs Grapplers	1.25
12 F:Ron Simmons	1.25

WORLD OF FANTASY
Atlas
May, 1956

1 The Secret of the Mountain	200.00

All comics prices listed are for *Near Mint* condition.

2 AW,Inside the Tunnel 125.00	
3 DAy,SC, The Man in the Cave 100.00	
4 BEv(c),Back to the Lost City . 75.00	
5 BEv(c),BP,In the Swamp 75.00	
6 BEv(c),The Strange Wife of	
Henry Johnson 75.00	
7 BEv(c),GM,Man in Grey 75.00	
8 GM,JO,MF,The Secret of the	
Black Cloud 100.00	
9 BEv,BK 75.00	
10 . . . . 65.00	
11 AT 75.00	
12 BEv(c) 65.00	
13 BEv,JO 65.00	
14 JMn(c),GM,JO 65.00	
15 JK(c) 65.00	
16 AW,SD,JK 100.00	
17 JK(c),SD 90.00	
18 JK(c) 90.00	
19 JK(c),SD,August, 1959 . . . . . 90.00	

WORLD OF MYSTERY
Atlas
June, 1956

1 BEv(c),AT,JO,The Long Wait 200.00
2 BEv(c),The Man From
   Nowhere 75.00
3 SD,AT,JDa, The Bugs 100.00
4 SD(c),BP,What Happened in the
   Basement 100.00
5 JO,She Stands in the Shadows 75.00
6 AW,SD,Sinking Man 110.00
7 Pick A Door July, 1957 . . . . 75.00

WORLD OF SUSPENSE
Atlas
April, 1956

1 JO,BEv,A Stranger Among Us 165.00
2 SD,When Walks the Scarecrow 90.00
3 AW,The Man Who Couldn't
   Be Touched 100.00
4 Something is in This House . 75.00
5 BEv,DH,JO 75.00
6 BEv(c),BP 75.00
7 AW,The Face 85.00
8 The Prisoner of the Ghost Ship 75.00

WORLDS UNKNOWN
May, 1973

1 GK,AT,The Coming of the
   Martians,Reprints 3.00
2 GK,TS,A Gun For A Dinosaur . 2.00
3 The Day the Earth Stood
   Still 2.00
4 JB,Arena 2.00
5 DA,JM,Black Destroyer 2.00
6 GK(c),The Thing Called It 2.00
7 GT,The Golden Voyage of
   Sinbad,Part 1 . . . . 2.00
8 The Golden Voyage of
   Sinbad,Part 2, August, 1974 . 2.00

WULF THE BARBARIAN
February, 1975

1 O:Wulf 2.00
2 NA,I:Berithe The Swordsman . 1.50
3 . . . . 1.50
4 September, 1975 . . . . 1.50

WYATT EARP
Atlas
November, 1955

1 JMn,F:Wyatt Earp 100.00

---

2 AW,Saloon(c) 60.00
3 JMn(c),The Showdown,
   A:Black Bart 50.00
4 Ph(c),Hugh O'Brian,JSe,
   India Sundown 50.00
5 Ph(c),Hugh O'Brian,DW,
   Gun Wild Fever 50.00
6 . . . . 50.00
7 AW 60.00
8 . . . . 50.00
9 and 10 . . . . @50.00
11 . . . . 60.00
12 AW 50.00
13 thru 20 . . . . @35.00
21 JDa(c) 30.00
22 thru 29 . . . . @25.00
30 Reprints 2.50
31 thru 33 Reprints . . . . @1.25
34 June, 1973 . . . . 1.25

X-CALIBRE

1 Excaliber After Xavier 3.50
2 V:Callisto & Morlock Crew 1.95
3 D:Juggernaut 1.95
4 Secret Weapon 1.95

X-Factor #69
© Marvel Entertainment Group

X-FACTOR
February, 1986

1 WS(c),JG,BL,JRu,I:X-Factor,
   Rusty 16.00
2 JG,BL,I:Tower 8.00
3 JG,BL,V:Tower 7.00
4 KP,JRu,V:Frenzy 5.00
5 JG,JRu,I:Alliance of Evil,
   C:Apocalypse 7.00
6 JG,BMc,I:Apocalypse 10.00
7 JG,JRu,V:Morlocks,I:Skids . 3.50
8 MS,JRu,V:Freedom Force . . . 3.50
9 JRu(i),V:Freedom Force
   (Mutant Massacre) 7.00
10 WS,BWi,V:Marauders(Mut.Mass),
   A:Sabretooth 8.00
11 WS,BWi,A:Thor(Mutant Mass) . 5.00
12 MS,BWi,V:Vanisher 4.00
13 WS,DGr,V:Mastermold 4.00

---

14 WS,BWi,V:Mastermold 4.00
15 WS,BWi,D:Angel 5.00
16 DM,JRu,V:Masque 4.00
17 WS,BWi,I:Rictor 6.00
18 WS,BWi,V:Apocalypse 4.00
19 WS,BWi,V:Horsemen of
   Apocalypse 4.00
20 JBr,A:X-Terminators 3.00
21 WS,BWi,V:The Right 3.00
22 SB,BWi,V:The Right 3.00
23 WS,BWi,C:Archangel 10.00
24 WS,BWi,Fall of Mutants,
   I:Archangel 16.00
25 WS,BWi,Fall of Mutants 5.00
26 WS,BWi,Fall of Mutants,
   N:X-Factor 5.00
27 WS,BWi,Christmas Issue 3.50
28 WS,BWi,V:Ship 3.00
29 WS,BWi,V:Infectia 3.00
30 WS,BWi,V:Infectia,Free.Force . 3.00
31 WS,BWi,V:Infectia,Free.Force . 3.00
32 SLi,A:Avengers 3.00
33 WS,BWi,V:Tower & Frenzy,
   R:Furry Beast 3.00
34 WS,BWi,I:Nanny,
   Orphan Maker 3.00
35 JRu(i),WS(c),V:Nanny,
   Orphan Maker 3.00
36 WS,BWi,Inferno,V:Nastirh . . . 3.50
37 WS,BWi,Inferno,V:Gob.Queen . 3.50
38 WS,AM,Inferno,A:X-Men,D:
   MadelynePryor(GoblinQueen) . 3.50
39 WS,AM,Inferno,A:X-Men,
   V:Mr.Sinister 3.50
40 RLd,AM,O:Nanny,Orphan Maker
   1st Liefeld Marvel work 14.00
41 AAd,AM,I:Alchemy 3.50
42 AAd,AM,A:Alchemy 3.50
43 PS,AM,V:Celestials 3.00
44 PS,AM,V:Rejects 2.50
45 PS,AM,V:Rask 2.50
46 PS,AM,V:Rejects 2.50
47 KD,AM,V:Father 2.50
48 thru 49 PS,AM,V:Rejects 2.50
50 RLd&TM(c),RB,AM,A:Prof.X
   (double sized),BU:Apocalypse . 5.00
51 AM,V:Sabretooth,Caliban . . . 7.00
52 RLd(c),AM,V:Sabretooth,
   Caliban 6.00
53 AM,V:Sabretooth,Caliban 6.00
54 MS,AM,A:Colossus,I:Crimson . 2.00
55 MMi(c),CDo,AM,V:Mesmero . . 2.00
56 AM,V:Crimson 2.00
57 NKu,V:Crimson 2.00
58 JBg,AM,V:Crimson 2.00
59 AM,V:Press Gang 2.00
60 JBg,AM,X-Tinction Agenda#3 20.00
60a 2nd printing(gold) 7.00
61 JBg,AM,X-Tinction Agenda#6 . 8.00
62 JBg,AM,JLe(c),E:X-Agenda . 9.00
63 WPo,I:Cyberpunks 16.00
64 WPo,ATb,V:Cyberpunks 9.00
65 WPo,ATb,V:Apocalypse 7.00
66 WPo,ATb,I:Askani,
   V:Apocalypse 8.00
67 WPo,ATb,V:Apocalypse,I:Shinobi
   Shaw,D:Sebastian Shaw . . . 7.00
68 WPo,ATb,V:Apocalypse,
   L:Nathan,(taken into future) . . 10.00
69 WPo,V:Shadow King 5.00
70 MMi(c),JRu,Last old team . . . 3.50
71 LSn,AM,New Team 4.00
71a 2nd printing 1.50
72 LSn,AM,Who shot Madrox
   revealed 4.00

---

73 LSn,AM,Mob Chaos in D.C. . . . 3.00
74 LSn,AM,I:Slab 2.75
75 LSn,AM,I:Nasty Boys(doub.sz) 3.25
76 LSn,AM,A:Hulk,Pantheon . . . 2.50
77 LSn,AM,V:Mutant Lib. Front. . . 2.25
78 LSn,AM,V:Mutant Lib. Front . . 2.25
79 LSn,AM,V:Helle's Belles 2.25
80 LSn,AM,V:Helle's Belles,
 C:Cyber 2.25
81 LSn,AM,V:Helle's Belles,Cyber 2.25
82 JQ(c),LSn,V:Brotherhood of Evil
 Mutants,I:X-iles 2.25
83 MPa,A:X-Force,X-iles 2.25
84 JaL,X-Cutioners Song #2,
 V:X-Force,A:X-Men 5.00
85 JaL,X-Cutioners Song #6,
 Wolv.& Bishop,V:Cable 7.00
86 JaL,AM,X-Cutioner's Song#10,
 A:X-Men,X-Force,V:Stryfe 5.00
87 JQ,X-Cutioners Song
 Aftermath 3.00
88 JQ,AM,V:2nd Genegineer,
 I:Random 3.00
89 JQ,V:Mutates,Genosha 2.00
90 JQ,AM,Genosha vs. Aznia . . . 2.00
91 AM,V:Armageddon 1.75
92 JQ,AM,V:Fabian Cortez,
 Acolytes,hologram(c) 6.00
93 Magneto Protocols 3.00
94 PR,J:Forge 3.00
95 B:JMD(s),AM,Polaris
 Vs. Random 1.75
96 A:Random 1.75
97 JD,I:Haven,A:Random 1.75
98 GLz,A:Haven,A:Random 1.50
99 JD,A:Haven,Wolfsbane returns
 to human 1.50
100 JD,Red Foil(c),V:Haven,
 D:Madrox 3.25
100a Newstand Ed. 2.00
101 JD,AM,Aftermath 1.50
102 JD,AM,V:Crimson Commando,
 Avalanche 1.50
103 JD,AM,A:Malice 1.75
104 JD,AM,V:Malice,
 C:Mr. Sinister 1.75
105 JD,AM,V:Malice 1.75
106 Phalanx Covenant,Life Signs
 Holografx(c) 3.25
106a newsstand ed 2.00
107 A:Strong Guy 1.50
108 A:Mystique, deluxe ed. 2.50
108a newsstand ed. 1.50
109 A:Mystique,V:Legion, deluxe . 1.95
109a newsstand ed. 1.50
110 Invasion 1.95
110a deluxe ed. 1.95
111 Invasion 1.50
111a deluxe ed. 1.95
112 AM,JFM,SEp,F:Guido,Havok . 1.95
Spec #1 JG,Prisoner of Love . . . 5.00
Ann.#1 BL,BBr,V:CrimsonDynamo 5.00
Ann.#2 TGr,JRu,A:Inhumans 4.00
Ann.#3 WS(c),AM,JRu,PC,TD,
 Evolutionary War 3.50
Ann.#4 JBy,WS,JRu,MBa,Atlantis
 Attacks,BU:Doom & Magneto . 3.50
Ann.#5 JBg,AM,DR,GI,Days of Future
 Present,A:Fant.Four,V:Ahab . 4.00
Ann.#6 Flesh Tears Saga,pt.4,
 A:X-Force, New Warriors 4.00
Ann #7 JQ,JRu,Shattership,pt.3 . . 4.00
Ann.#8 I:Charon,w/card 3.25
Ann.#9 JMD(s),MtB,V:Prof.Power,
 A:Prof.X,O:Haven 3.25

X-Force #8
© Marvel Entertainment Group

X-FORCE
August, 1991

1 RLd,V:Stryfe,Mutant Liberation
 Front,bagged, white on black graphics
 with X-Force Card 6.00
1a with Shatterstar Card 4.50
1b with Deadpool Card 4.50
1c with Sunspot & Gideon Card . 4.50
1d with Cable Card 6.00
1e Unbagged Copy 1.75
1f 2nd Printing 1.75
2 RLd,I:New Weapon X,V:
 Deadpool 4.50
3 RLd,C:Spider-Man,
 V:Juggernaut,Black Tom 4.00
4 RLd,SpM/X-Force team-up,
 V:Juggernaut(cont.from SpM#16)
 Sideways format 4.00
5 RLd,A:Brotherhood Evil Mutants 3.50
6 RLd,V:Bro'hood Evil Mutants . . 3.00
7 RLd,V:Bro'hood Evil Mutants . . 3.00
8 MMi,O:Cable(Part) 3.00
9 RLd,D:Sauron,Masque 2.50
10 MPa,V:Mutant Liberation Front 2.00
11 MPa,Deadpool Vs Domino . . . 2.00
12 MPa,A:Weapon Prime,Gideon . 2.00
13 MPa,V:Weapon Prime 2.00
14 TSr,V:Weapon Prime,Krule . . . 2.00
15 GCa,V:Krule,Deadpool 2.00
16 GCa,X-Cutioners Song #4,
 X-Factor V:X-Force 3.00
17 GCa,X-Cutioners Song#8,
 Apocalypse V:Stryfe 3.00
18 GCa,X-Cutioners Song#12,
 Cable vs Stryfe 3.00
19 GCa,X-Cutioners Song
 Aftermath,N:X-Force 1.75
20 GCa,O:Graymalkin 1.75
21 GCa,V:War Machine,SHIELD . 1.75
22 GCa,V:Externals 1.50
23 GCa,V:Saul,Gigeon,A:Six Pack 1.50
24 GCa,A:Six Pack,A:Deadpool . 1.50
25 GCa,A:Mageneto,Exodus,
 R:Cable 6.00
26 GCa(c),MtB,I:Reignfire 1.50

27 GCa(c),MtB,V:Reignfire,MLF,
 I:Moonstar,Locus 1.50
28 MtB,V:Reignfire,MLF 1.50
29 MtB,V:Arcade,C:X-Treme 1.50
30 TnD,V:Arcade,A:X-Treme 1.50
31 F:Siryn 1.50
32 Child's Play#1,A:New Warriors 1.50
33 Child's Play#3,A:New Warriors,
 V:Upstarts 1.50
34 F:Rictor,Domino,Cable 1.75
35 TnD,R:Nimrod 1.50
36 TnD,V:Nimrod 1.75
37 PaP,I&D:Absalom 1.50
38 TaD,Life Signs,pt.2,I:Generation X
 foil(c) 2.95
38a newsstand ed. 2.00
39 TaD 1.50
40 TaD, deluxe 1.95
40a newsstand ed. 1.50
41 TaD,O:feral,deluxe 1.95
41a newsstand ed. 1.50
42 Emma Frost, deluxe 1.95
42a newsstand ed. 1.50
43 Home is Where Heart 1.50
43a deluxe ed. 1.95
44 AdP,Prof.X,X-Mansion 1.95
Ann.#1 Shattershot,pt1 . . . . 2.75
Ann.#2 JaL,LSn,I:X-Treme,w/card 3.25
Ann.#3 . . . . 2.95

X-FORCE & SPIDER-MAN: SABOTAGE
TPB rep.X-Force #3 & #4 and
 Spider-Man #16 . . . . 6.95

X-MAN
1 Cable after Xavier 3.50
2 Sinister's Plan 1.95
3 V:Domino 1.95
4 V:Sinister 1.95

X-MEN
September, 1963

1 JK,O:X-Men,I:Professor X,Beast
 Cyclops,Marvel Girl,Iceman

X-Men #1
© Marvel Entertainment Group

All comics prices listed are for *Near Mint* condition. **CVA Page 251**

Angel,Magneto 3,800.00	
2 JK,I:Vanisher 1,300.00	
3 JK,I:Blob 550.00	
4 JK,I:Quicksilver,Scarlet Witch	
Mastermind,Toad 600.00	
5 JK,V:Broth. of Evil Mutants . 400.00	
6 JK,V:Sub-Mariner 300.00	
7 JK,V:Broth. of Evil Mutants,	
Blob 250.00	
8 JK,I:Unus,1st Ice covered	
Iceman 250.00	
9 JK,A:Avengers,I:Lucifer 250.00	
10 JK,I:Modern Kazar 250.00	
11 JK,I:Stranger 200.00	
12 JK,O:Prof.X,I:Juggernaut . . 235.00	
13 JK,JSt,V:Juggernaut 175.00	
14 JK,I:Sentinels 175.00	
15 JK,O:Beast,V:Sentinels . . . 175.00	
16 JK,V:Mastermold,Sentinels . 175.00	
17 JK,V:Magneto 125.00	
18 V:Magneto 125.00	
19 I:Mimic 125.00	
20 V:Lucifer 125.00	
21 V:Lucifer,Dominus 100.00	
22 V:Maggia 100.00	
23 V:Maggia 100.00	
24 I:Locust(Prof.Hopper) 100.00	
25 JK,I:El Tigre 100.00	
26 V:El Tigre 85.00	
27 C:Fant.Four,V:Puppet Master . 85.00	
28 I:Banshee 100.00	
29 V:Super-Apaptoid 80.00	

X-Men #100
© *Marvel Entertainment Group*

30 JK,I:The Warlock 80.00	
31 JK,I:Cobalt Man 67.00	
32 V:Juggernaut 67.00	
33 GK,A:Dr.Strange,Juggernaut . 67.00	
34 V:Tyrannus,Mole Man 67.00	
35 JK,A:Spider-Man,Banshee . . 75.00	
36 V:Mekano 58.00	
37 DH,V:Blob,Unus 58.00	
38 DH,A:Banshee,O:Cyclops . . 65.00	
39 DH,GT,A:Banshee,V:Mutant	
Master,O:Cyclops 58.00	
40 DH,GT,V:Frankenstein,	
O:Cyclops 58.00	

41 DH,GT,I:Grotesk,O:Cyclops . 50.00	
42 DH,GT,JB,V:Grotesk,	
O:Cyclops,D:Prof.X 50.00	
43 GT,JB,V:Magneto,Quicksilver,	
Scarlet Witch,C:Avengers . . . 55.00	
44 V:Magneto,Quicksilver,Sc.Witch,	
R:Red Raven,O:Iceman 55.00	
45 PH,JB,V:Magneto,Quicksilver,	
Scarlet Witch,O:Iceman 55.00	
46 DH,V:Juggernaut,O:Iceman . 50.00	
47 DH,I:Maha Yogi 50.00	
48 DH,JR,V:Quasimodo 50.00	
49 JSo,DH,C:Magneto,I:Polaris,	
Mesmero,O:Beast 60.00	
50 JSo,V:Magneto,O:Beast 55.00	
51 JSo,V:Magneto,Polaris,	
Erik the Red,O:Beast 55.00	
52 DH,MSe,JSt,O:Lorna Dane	
V:Magneto,O:Beast 50.00	
53 1st BWS,O:Beast 65.00	
54 BWS,DH,I:Havok,O:Angel . . 70.00	
55 BWS,DH,O:Havok,Angel . . . 60.00	
56 NA,V:LivingMonolith,O:Angel . 56.00	
57 NA,V:Sentinels,A:Havok 56.00	
58 NA,A:Havoc,V:Sentinels 56.00	
59 NA,V:Sentinels,A:Havoc 56.00	
60 NA,I:Sauron 60.00	
61 NA,V:Sauron 56.00	
62 NA,A:Kazar,Sauron,Magneto . 56.00	
63 A:Ka-Zar,V:Magneto 56.00	
64 DH,A:Havok,I:Sunfire 47.00	
65 NA,MSe,A:Havok,Shield,	
Return of Prof.X 56.00	
66 SB,MSe,V:Hulk,A:Havok . . . 40.00	
67 rep.X-Men #12,#13 . . . . 25.00	
68 rep.X-Men #14,#15 . . . . 25.00	
69 rep.X-Men #16,#19 . . . . 25.00	
70 rep.X-Men #17,#18 . . . . 25.00	
71 rep.X-Men #20 . . . . 25.00	
72 rep.X-Men #21,#24 . . . . 25.00	
73 thru 93 rep.X-Men #25-45 . @25.00	
94 GK(c),B:CCl(s),DC,BMc,B:2nd	
X-Men,V:Count Nefaria . . . 300.00	
95 GK(c),DC,V:Count Nefaria,	
Ani-Men,D:Thunderbird 75.00	
96 DC,I:Moira McTaggert,	
Kierrok 56.00	
97 DC,V:Havok,Polaris,Eric	
the Red,I:Lilandra 45.00	
98 DC,V:Sentinels,Stephen Lang 45.00	
99 DC,V:Sentinels,S.Lang 46.00	
100 DC,V:Stephen Lang 50.00	
101 DC,I:Phoenix,Black Tom,	
A:Juggernaut 42.00	
102 DC,O:Storm,V:Juggernaut,	
Black Tom 30.00	
103 DC,V:Juggernaut,Bl.Tom . . 28.00	
104 DC,V:Magneto,I:Star	
Jammers,A:Lilandra 25.00	
105 DC,BL,V:Firelord 25.00	
106 DC,TS,V:Firelord 25.00	
107 DC,DGr,I:Imperial Guard,Star	
Jammers,Gladiator,Corsair . 27.00	
108 JBy,TA,A:Star Jammers,	
C:Fantastic Four,Avengers. . 55.00	
109 JBy,TA,I:Vindicator 40.00	
110 TD,DC,V:Warhawk 25.00	
111 JBy,TA,V:Mesmero,A:Beast,	
Magneto 25.00	
112 GP(c),JBy,TA,V:Magneto,	
A:Beast 25.00	
113 JBy,TA,V:Magneto,A:Beast . 25.00	
114 JBy,TA,A:Beast,R:Sauron . . 25.00	
115 JBy,TA,V:Sauron,Garokk,	
A:Kazar,I:Zaladane 22.00	

116 JBy,TA,V:Sauron,Garokk,	
A:Kazar 22.00	
117 JBy,TA,O:Prof.X,I:Amahl	
Farouk (Shadow King) 25.00	
118 JBy,I:Moses Magnum,A:Sunfire	
C:Iron Fist,I:Mariko 22.00	
119 JBy,TA,V:Moses Magnum,	
A:Sunfire 22.00	
120 JBy,TA,I:AlphaFlight (Shaman,	
Sasquatch,Northstar,Snowbird,	
Aurora) 36.00	
121 JBy,TA,V:Alpha Flight 45.00	
122 JBy,TA,A:Juggernaut,Black	
Tom,Arcade,Power Man . . . 20.00	
123 JBy,TA,V:Arcade,A:SpM . . 17.00	
124 JBy,TA,V:Arcade 17.00	
125 JBy,TA,A:Beast,Madrox the	
Multiple Man,Havok,Polaris . . 18.00	
126 JBy,TA,I:Proteus,	
A:Havok,Madrox 16.00	
127 JBy,TA,V:Proteus,A:Havok,	
Madrox 15.00	
128 GP(c),JBy,TA,V:Proteus,	
A:Havok,Madrox 15.00	
129 JBy,TA,I:Shadow Cat,White	
Queen,C:Hellfire Club 22.00	
130 JR2(c),JBy,TA,I:Dazzler	
V:White Queen 20.00	
131 JBy,TA,V:White Queen,	
A:Dazzler 16.00	
132 JBy,TA,I:Hellfire Club,	
V:Mastermind 16.00	
133 JBy,TA,V:Hellfire Club,	
Mastermind,F:Wolverine . . . 17.00	
134 JBy,TA,V:Hellfire Club,Master	
mind,I:Dark Phoenix,A:Beast . 14.00	
135 JBy,TA,V:Dark Phoenix,C:SpM,	
Fant.Four,Silver Surfer 15.00	
136 JBy,TA,V:Dark Phoenix,	
A:Beast 14.00	
137 JBy,TA,D:Phoenix,V:Imperial	
Guard,A:Beast 17.00	
138 JBy,TA,History of X-Men,	
L:Cyclops,C:Shadow Cat . . . 14.00	
139 JBy,TA,A:Alpha Flight,R:Wendigo,	
N:Wolverine,J:Shadowcat . . 28.00	
140 JBy,TA,V:Wendigo,A:Alpha	
Flight 23.00	
141 JBy,TA,I:2nd Brotherhood of Evil	
Mutants,I:Rachel (Phoenix II) 30.00	

Becomes: UNCANNY X-MEN

142 JBy,TA,V:Evil Mutants,	
A:Rachel (Phoenix II) 25.00	
143 JBy,TA,V:N'Garai,I:Lee	
Forrester 10.00	
144 BA,JRu,A:Man-Thing,	
O:Havok, V:D'Spayre 9.00	
145 DC,JRu,V:Arcade,A:DrDoom . 9.00	
146 DC,JRu,V:Dr.Doom,Arcade . 9.00	
147 DC,JRu,V:Dr.Doom,Arcade . . 9.00	
148 DC,JRu,I:Caliban,A:Dazzler	
Spiderwoman 9.00	
149 DC,JRu,A:Magneto 9.00	
150 DC,JRu,BWi,V:Magneto . . . 13.00	
151 JSh,BMc,JRu,V:Sentinels . . 7.00	
152 BMc,JRu,V:White Queen . . 7.00	
153 DC,JRu,I:Bamf 7.00	
154 DC,JRu,BWi,I:Sidrian Hunters	
A:Corsair,O:Cyclops(part) . . . 7.00	
155 DC,BWi,V:Deathbird,I:Brood . 7.00	
156 DC,BWi,V:Death Bird,	
A:Tigra, Star Jammers 7.00	
157 DC,BWi,V:Deathbird 7.00	
158 DC,BWi,2nd A:Rogue,	
Mystique 10.00	

159 BSz,BWi,V:Dracula 8.00
160 BA,BWi,V:Belasco,I:Magik . . . 8.00
161 DC,BWi,I:Gabrielle Haller,
    O:Magneto,Professor X 10.00
162 DC,BWi,V:Brood 10.00

Uncanny X-Men #143
© Marvel Entertainment Group

163 DC,BWi,V:Brood 7.00
164 DC,BWi,V:Brood,I:Binary 7.00
165 PS,BWi,V:Brood 8.00
166 PS,BWi,V:Brood,A:Binary,
    I:Lockheed 8.00
167 PS,BWi,V:Brood,A:N.Mutants 8.00
168 PS,BWi,I:Madelyne Pryor . . . 7.00
169 PS,BWi,I:Morlocks 7.00
170 PS,BWi,A:Angel,V:Morlocks . 7.00
171 WS,BWi,J:Rogue,V:Binary . 11.00
172 PS,BWi,V:Viper,Silver
    Samurai, ... 9.00
173 PS,BWi,V:Viper,Silver
    Samurai, ... 8.00
174 PS,BWi,A:Mastermind 7.00
175 PS,JR2,BWi,W:Cyclops and
    Madelyne,V:Mastermind 8.00
176 JR2,BWi,I:Val Cooper 7.00
177 JR2,JR,V:Brotherhood of
    Evil Mutants 6.00
178 JR2,BWi,BBr,V:Brotherhood
    of Evil Mutants 6.00
179 JR2,DGr,V:Morlocks 6.00
180 JR2,DGr,BWi,Secret Wars . . 6.00
181 JR2,DGr,A:Sunfire 6.00
182 JR2,DGr,V:S.H.I.E.L.D. 6.00
183 JR2,DGr,V:Juggernaut 6.00
184 JR2,DGr,V:Selene,I:Forge . . . 7.00
185 JR2,DGr,V:Shield,U.S.
    Govt.,Storm loses powers 6.00
186 BWS,TA,Lifedeath,
    V:Dire Wraiths 7.00
187 JR2,DGr,V:Dire Wraiths 6.00
188 JR2,DGr,V:Dire Wraiths 6.00
189 JR2,SL,V:Selene,A:Magma . . 6.00
190 JR2,DGr,V:Kulan Gath,A:SpM,
    Avengers,New Mutants 6.00
191 JR2,DGr,A:Avengers,Spider-Man,
    New Mutants,I:Nimrod 6.00
192 JR2,DGr,V:Magus 6.00
193 JR2,DGr,V:Hellions,I:Firestar
    Warpath,20th Anniv. 8.00
194 JR2,DGr,SL,V:Nimrod 6.00

195 BSz(c),JR2,DGr,A:Power
    Pack,V:Morlocks 6.00
196 JR2,DGr,J:Magneto 7.00
197 JR2,DGr,V:Arcade 6.00
198 BWS,F:Storm,'Lifedeath II' . . 6.00
199 JR2,DGr,I:Freedom Force,
    Rachel becomes 2nd Phoenix . 6.00
200 JR2,DGr,A:Magneto,I:Fenris 10.00
201 RL,WPo(i),I:Nathan
    Christopher (Cyclops son) . . . 25.00
202 JR2,AW,Secret Wars II 5.00
203 JR2,AW,Secret Wars II 5.00
204 JBr,WPo,V:Arcade 6.00
205 BWS,A:Lady Deathstrike . . . 18.00
206 JR2,DGr,V:Freedom Force . . 5.00
207 JR2,DGr,V:Selene 5.00
208 JR2,DGr,V:Nimrod,
    A:Hellfire Club 5.00
209 JR2,CR,V:Nimrod,A:Spiral . . . 5.00
210 JR2,DGr,I:Marauders,
    (Mutant Massacre) 25.00
211 JR2,BBI,AW,V:Marauders,
    (Mutant Massacre) 25.00
212 RL,DGr,V:Sabretooth,
    (Mutant Massacre) 38.00
213 AD,V:Sabretooth (Mut.Mass) 38.00
214 BWS,BWi,V:Malice,A:Dazzler 6.00
215 AD,DGr,I:Stonewall,Super
    Sabre,Crimson Commando . . . 5.00
216 BWS(c),JG,DGr,V:Stonewall . 5.00
217 WS(c),JG,SL,V:Juggernaut . . 5.00
218 AAD(c),MS,DGr,V:Juggernaut 5.00
219 BBI,DGr,V:Marauders,Polaris
    becomes Malice,A:Sabertooth . 7.00
220 MS,DGr,A:Naze 5.00
221 MS,DGr,I:Mr.Sinister,
    V:Maruaders 13.00
222 MS,DGr,V:Marauders,Eye
    Killers,A:Sabertooth 20.00
223 KGa,DGr,A:Freedom Force . . 5.00
224 MS,DGr,V:Adversary 5.00
225 MS,DGr,Fall of Mutants
    I:1st US App Roma 9.00
226 MS,DGr,Fall of Mutants 8.00
227 MS,DGr,Fall of Mutants 8.00
228 RL,TA,A:OZ Chase 5.00
229 MS,DGr,I:Reavers,Gateway . 5.00
230 RL,DGr,Xmas Issue 5.00
231 RL,DGr,V:Limbo 5.00
232 MS,DGr,V:Brood 5.00
233 MS,DGr,V:Brood 5.00
234 MS,JRu,V:Brood 5.00
235 RL,CR,V:Magistrates 5.00
236 MS,DGr,V:Magistrates 5.00
237 RL,TA,V:Magistrates 5.00
238 MS,DGr,V:Magistrates 5.00
239 MS,DGr,Inferno,A:Mr.Sinister 5.50
240 MS,DGr,Inferno,V:Marauders 6.00
241 MS,DGr,Inferno,O:Madeline
    Pryor,V:Marauders 6.00
242 MS,DGr,Inferno,D:N'Astirh,
    A:X-Factor,Double-sized 6.00
243 MS,Inferno,A:X-Factor. 6.00
244 MS,DGr,I:Jubilee 15.00
245 RLd,DGr,Invasion Parody . . . 5.00
246 MS,DGr,V:Mastermold,
    A:Nimrod 5.00
247 MS,DGr,V:Mastermold 5.00
248 JLe(1st X-Men Art),DGr,
    V:Nanny & Orphan Maker . . . 25.00
248a 2nd printing 2.00
249 MS,DGr,C:Zaladane,
    V:Savage Land Mutates. 5.00
250 MS,SL,I:Zaladane. 5.00
251 MS,DGr,V:Reavers 5.00

X-Men #171
© Marvel Entertainment Group

252 JLe,BSz(c),RL,SW,V:Reavers 5.00
253 MS,SL,V:Amahl Farouk 5.00
254 JLe(c),MS,DGr,V:Reavers . . . 5.00
255 MS,DGr,V:Reavers,D:Destiny 5.00
256 JLe,SW,Acts of Vengeance,
    V:Manderin,A:Psylocke 12.00
257 JLe,JRu,AofV,V:Manderin . . 12.00
258 JLe,SW,AofV,V:Manderin . . 13.50
259 MS,DGr,V:Magistrates, ... 4.50
260 JLe(c),MS,DGr,A:Dazzler . . . 4.50
261 JLe(c),MS,DGr,V:Hardcase &
    Harriers 4.50
262 KD,JRu,V:Masque,Morlocks . 4.50
263 JRu(i),O:Forge,V:Morlocks . . 4.50
264 JLe(c),MC,JRu,V:Magistrate . 4.50
265 JRu(i),V:Shadowking 4.50
266 NKu(c),MC,JRu,I:Gambit . . . 40.00
267 JLe,WPo,SW,V:Shadowking 16.00
268 JLe,SW,A:Captain America,
    Black Widow,V:The Hand,
    Baron Strucker 25.00
269 JLe,ATi,Rogue V:Ms.Marvel . 9.00
270 JLe,ATi,SW,X-Tinction Agenda
    #1, A:Cable,New Mutants . . . 12.00
270a 2nd printing(Gold) 4.50
271 JLe,SW,X-Tinction Agenda
    #4,A:Cable,New Mutants 10.00
272 JLe,SW,X-Tinction Agenda
    #7,A:Cable,New Mutants 10.00
273 JLe,WPo,JBy,KJ,RL,MS,MGo,
    LSn,SW,A:Cable,N.Mutants . . 8.50
274 JLe,SW,V:Zaladane,A:Magneto,
    Nick Fury,Kazar 6.00
275 JLe,SW,R:Professor X,A:Star
    Jammers,Imperial Guard 12.00
275a 2nd Printing (Gold) 3.00
276 JLe,SW,V:Skrulls,Shi'ar 6.00
277 JLe,SW,V:Skrulls,Shi'ar 6.00
278 PS,Professor X Returns to
    Earth,V:Shadowking 4.50
279 NKu,SW,V:Shadowking 4.50
280 E:CCl(s),NKu,A:X-Factor,
    D:Shadowking,Prof.X Crippled . 4.50
281 WPo,ATi,new team (From X-Men
    #1),D:Pierce,Hellions,V:Sentinels,
    I:Trevor Fitzroy,Upstarts 6.00
281a 2nd printing,red(c) 1.25
282 WPo,ATi,V:Fitzroy,C:Bishop 14.00

All comics prices listed are for *Near Mint* condition.

282a 2nd printing,gold(c) of #281
   inside 1.25
283 WPo,ATi,I:Bishop,Malcolm,
   Randall 12.00
284 WPo,ATi,SOS from USSR. . . 4.00
285 WPo,I:Mikhail(Colossus'
   brother from Russia) 3.25
286 JLe,WPo,ATi,A:Mikhail 3.25
287 JR2,O:Bishop,
   D:Malcolm,Randall 4.50
288 NKu,BSz,A:Bishop 3.00
289 WPo,ATi,Forge proposes
   to Storm 3.00
290 WPo,SW,V:Cyberpunks,
   L:Forge 3.00
291 TR,V:Morlocks 2.50
292 TR,V:Morlocks 2.50
293 TR,D:Morlocks,Mikhail 2.50
294 BP,TA,X-Cutioner's Song#1,
   Stryfe shoots Prof X,A:X-Force,
   X-Factor,polybag.w/ProfX card   4.50
295 BP,TA,X-Cutioners Song #5,
   V:Apocalypse 3.00
296 BP,TA,X-Cutioners Song #9,
   A:X-Force,X-Factor,V:Stryfe . . 3.00
297 BP,X-Cutioners Song
   Aftermath 2.00
298 BP,TA,V:Acolytes 2.00
299 BP,A:Forge,Acolytes,I:Graydon
   Creed (Sabretooth's son) . . . 2.00
300 JR2,DGr,BP,V:Acolytes,A:Forge,
   Nightcrawler,Holografx(c) 6.50

Uncanny X-Men #243
© Marvel Entertainment Group

301 JR2,DGr,I:Sienna Blaze,
   V:Fitzroy 2.00
302 JR2,V:Fitzroy 2.00
303 JR2,V:Upstarts,D:Illyana 2.00
304 JR2,JaL,PS,L:Colossus,
   V:Magneto,Holo-grafx(c) 5.00
305 JD,F:Rogue,Bishop 2.00
306 JR2,V:Hodge 2.00
307 JR2,Bloodties#4,A:Avengers,
   V:Exodus,Cortez 2.00
308 JR2,Scott & Jean announce
   impending marriage 2.00
309 JR2,O:Professor X & Amelia . 2.00
310 JR2,DG,A:Cable,V:X-Cutioner,
   w/card 4.00
311 JR2,DG,AV,V:Sabretooth,

C:Phalanx 1.75
312 JMd,DG,A:Yukio,I:Phalanx,
   w/card 1.75
313 JMd,DG,V:Phalanx 1.75
314 LW,BSz,R:White Quen 1.75
315 F:Acolytes 1.75
316 V:Phalanx,I:M,Phalanx Covenant
   Generation Next,pt.1, holo(c) . . 3.25
316a newsstand ed. 1.75
317 JMd,V:Phalanx,prism(c) 3.25
317a newsstand ed. 1.75
318 JMd,I:Jubilee, deluxe 2.25
318a newsstand ed. 1.75
319 R:Legion, deluxe 2.25
319a newsstand ed. 1.75
320 deluxe ed. 2.25
320 newsstand ed. 1.75
321 R:Lilandra, deluxe ed. 2.25
321 newsstand ed. 1.50
322 SLo,TGu,Rogue,Iceman run from
   Gambit's Secret 1.95
Ann.#1 rep.#9,#11 . . . . 45.00
Ann.#2 rep.#22,#23 . . . . 35.00
Ann.#3 GK(c),GP,TA,A:Arkon . . 18.00
Ann.#4 JR2,BMc,A:Dr.Strange . . 12.00
Ann.#5 BA,BMc,A:F.F. 10.00
Ann.#6 BSz,BWi,Dracula 11.00
Ann.#7 MGo,TMd,BWi,TA,BBr,BA,JRu,
   BBI,SL,AM,V:Impossible Man . 8.00
Ann.#8 SL,Kitty's story 8.00
Ann.#9 AAd,AG,MMi,Asgard,V:Loki,
   Enchantress,A:New Mutants . 13.00
Ann.#10 AAd,TA,V:Mojo,
   J:Longshot,A:New Mutants . . 13.00
Ann.#11 AD,V:Horde,A:CaptBrit . . 6.00
Ann.#12 AAd,BWi,RLm,TD,Evol.
   War,V:Terminus,Savage Land . 6.00
Ann.#13 MBa,JRu,Atlantis Attacks 5.00
Ann.#14 AAd,DGr,BWi,AM,ATi,
   V:Ahab,A:X-Factor, ... 10.00
Ann.#15,TR,JRu,MMi(c),Flesh Tears,
   Pt.3,A:X-Force,New Warriors . . 4.50
Ann.#16 JaL,JRu,Shattershot
   Part.2 . . . . 8.00
Ann.#17 JPe,MFm,I:X-Cutioner,
   D:Mastermind,w/card 4.00
Ann.#18 JR2,V:Caliban,
   BU:Bishop 3.25
G-Size #1,GK,DC,I:New X-Men
   (Colossus,Storm,Nightcrawler,
   Thunderbird,3rd A:Wolv.) . . 350.00
G-Size #2,rep.#57-59 . . . . 40.00
GNv Pryde of the X-Men 10.95
PF God Loves, Man Kills 6.95
TPB Asgardian Wars 15.95
TPB Bloodties V:Exodus 15.95
TPB Coming of Bishop 12.95
TPB Dark Phoenix Saga 12.95
TPB Day of Future Present 14.95
TPB Days of Future Past 4.95
TPB Fatal Attractions 17.95
TPB From the Ashes 16.95
TPB Greatest Battles 15.95
TPB Savage Land 9.95
TPB X-Cutioner's Song 24.95
TPB X-Tinction Agenda 19.95
X-Men Survival Guide to the Manison
   NKu(c) 6.95

X-MEN
[2nd Regular Series]
October, 1991
1 A(c);Storm,Beast,B:CCI(s),JLe,SW
   I:Fabian Cortez,Acolytes,
   V:Magneto 2.50

1 B(c);Colossus,Psylocke 2.50
1 C(c);Cyclops,Wolverine 2.50
1 D(c);Magneto 2.50
1 E(c);Gatefold w/pin-ups 5.00
2 JLe,SW,V:Magneto Contd. 5.00
3 E:CCI(s),JLe,SW,V:Magneto . . 4.00
4 JBy(s),JLe,SW,I:Omega Red,
   V:Hand 6.00
5 B:SLo(s),JLe,SW,V:Hand,
   Omega Red,I:Maverick 6.00
6 JLe,SW,V:Omega Red, Hand,
   Sabretooth 5.00
7 JLe,SW,V:Omega Red,Hand,
   Sabretooth 5.00
8 JLe,SW,Bishop vs. Gambit 5.00
9 JLe,SW,A:Ghost Rider,V:Brood 5.00
10 JLe,SW,MT,Longshot Vs. Mojo,
   BU:Maverick 5.00
11 E:SLo(s)JLe,MT,V:Mojo,
   BU:Maverick 4.00
12 B:FaN(s),ATb,BWi,I:Hazard . . . 3.00
13 ATb,BWi,V:Hazard 3.00
14 NKu,X-Cutioners Song#3,A:X-Fact.
   X-Force,V:Four Horsemen . . . 3.00
15 NKu,X-Cutioners Song #7,
   V:Mutant Liberation Front . . . 3.00
16 NKu,MPn,X-Cutioners Song #11,
   A:X-Force,X-Factor,V:Dark Riders,
   Apocalypse Vs.Archangel,IR:Stryfe
   is Nathan Summers 4.00
17 NKu,MPn,R:Illyana,A:Darkstar . 2.50
18 NKu,MPn,R:Omega Red,V:Soul
   Skinner 2.50
19 NKu,MPn,V:Soul Skinner,
   Omega Red 2.50
20 NKu,MPn,J.Grey vs Psylocke . 2.00
21 NKu,V:Silver Samurai,Shinobi . 2.00
22 BPe,V:Silver Samurai,Shinobi . 2.00
23 NKu,MPn,V:Dark Riders,
   Mr.Sinister 2.00
24 NKu,BSz,A Day in the Life 2.00
25 NKu,Hologram(c),V:Magneto,Wolv.'s
   Adamantium skel. pulled out . 10.00
26 NKu,Bloodties#2,A:Avengers,
   I:Unforgiven 3.00
27 RiB,I:Threnody 2.50
28 NKu,MRy,F:Sabretooth 2.50
29 NKu,MRy,V:Shinobi 2.50
30 NKu,MRy,W:Cyclops&Jean Grey,
   w/card 6.00
31 NKu,MRy,A:Spiral,Matsuo,
   D:Kwannon 2.25
32 NKu,MRy,A:Spiral,Matsuo 2.25
33 NKu,MRy,F:Gambit &
   Sabretooth 2.25
34 NKu,MRy,A:Riptide 2.25
35 LSh,A:Nick Fury 2.25
36 NKu,MRy,I:Synch, Phalanx Covenant
   Generation Next,pt.2, deluxe . . 3.50
36a Newsstand ed. 1.75
37 NKu,MRy,Generation Next,pt.3
   foil(c) 3.50
37a newsstand ed. 1.75
38 NKu,MRy,F:Psylocke 2.50
38a newsstand ed. 1.50
39 X-Treme, deluxe 2.50
39a newsstand ed. 1.50
40 deluxe 2.50
40a newsstand ed. 1.50
41 V:Legion, deluxe 2.50
41a newsstand ed. 1.50
42 PS,PaN,Mysterious Visitor . . . 1.95
Ann.#1 JLe,Shattershot,pt.1,
   I:Mojo II 3.00
Ann.#2 I:Empyrean,w/card 3.25

Ann.#3 F:Storm 3.50

X-MEN ADVENTURES
[1st Season]
1 V:Sentinals, Based on TV
    Cartoon 6.00
2 V:Sentinals,D:Morph 5.00
3 V:Magneto,A:Sabretooth 4.00
4 V:Magneto 4.00
5 V:Morlocks 4.00
6 V:Sabretooth 3.50
7 V:Cable,Genosha,Sentinels . . . 3.00
8 A:Colossus,A:Juggernaut 3.00
9 I:Colussus(on cartoon),
    V:Juggernaut 3.00
10 A:Angel,V:Mystique 3.00
11 I:Archangel(on cartoon) 2.00
12 V:Horsemen of Apocalypse . . . 2.00
13 RMc(s),I:Bishop(on cartoon) . . 2.00
14 V:Brotherhood of Evil Mutants . 2.00
TPB Vol.1 . . . . 4.95
TPB Vol.2 . . . . 4.95
TPB Vol.3 . . . . 5.95
TPB Vol.4 rep. Days of Future Past
    and Final Conflict 6.95
[2nd Season]
1 R:Morph,I:Mr. Sinister
    (on cartoon) 3.00
2 I:Nasty Boys (on cartoon) 2.00
3 I:Shadow King (on cartoon) . . . 2.00
4 I:Omega Red (on cartoon) 2.00
5 I:Alpha Flight (on cartoon) 2.00
6 F:Gambit 2.00
7 A:Cable,Bishop,Apocalypse . . . 1.25
8 A:Cable,Bisiph,Apocalypse . . . 1.50
9 O:Rogue 1.50
10 . . . . 1.50
11 F:Mojo,Longshot 1.50
12 Reunions,pt.1 . . . . 1.50
13 Reunions,pt.1 . . . . 1.50
[3rd Season]
1 Out of the Past,pt.1 . . . . 1.50
2 V:Spirit Drinker 1.50
3 Phoenix Saga,pt.1 . . . . 1.50
4 Phoenix Saga,pt.2 . . . . 1.50
5 Phoenix Saga,pt.3 . . . . 1.50

X-MEN/ALPHA FLIGHT
January, 1986
1 PS,BWi,V:Loki 5.00
2 PS,BWi,V:Loki 4.00

X-MEN/
ANIMATION SPECIAL
TV Screenplay Adapt 10.95

X-MEN AT STATE FAIR
1 KGa,Dallas Times Herald . . . 35.00

X-MEN CHRONICLES
1 X-Men Unlimited AX 3.95
2 V:Abbatoir 3.95

X-MEN CLASSICS
December, 1983
1 NA,rep. 3.50
2 NA,rep. 3.50
3 NA,rep. 3.50

X-MEN: EARLY YEARS
1 rep. X-Men (first series) #1 . . . 1.75
2 rep. X-Men (first series) #2 . . . 1.75

3 rep. X-Men (first series) #3 . . . 1.75
4 thru 15 rep. X-Men (first series)
    #4 to #15 . . . . @1.50

X-Men Classics #1
© Marvel Entertainment Group

CLASSIC X-MEN
September, 1986
1 AAd(c),JBo,New stories, rep.
    giant size X-Men 1 . . . . 10.00
2 rep.#94,JBo/AAd(c),BU:
    Storm & Marvel Girl 6.00
3 rep.#95,JBo/AAd(c),BU:
    I:Thunderbird II 5.00
4 rep.#96,JBo/AAd(c),BU:
    Wolverine & N.Crawler 4.50
5 rep.#97,JBo/AAd(c),BU:
    Colossus 4.00
6 rep.#98,JBo/AAd(c),BU:
    JeanGrey,I:Seb.Shaw 4.00
7 rep.#99,JBo/AAd(c),BU:
    HellfireClub,W.Queen 4.00
8 rep.#100,JBo/AAd(c),BU:
    O:Jean Grey/Phoenix 4.00
9 rep.#101,JBo/AAd(c),BU:
    Nightcrawler 4.00
10 rep.#102,JBo/AAd(c),BU:
    Wolverine,A:Sabretooth 9.00
11 rep.#103,JBo/BL(c),BU:Storm . 3.50
12 rep.#104,JBo/AAd(c),BU:
    O:Magneto 8.00
13 rep.#105,JBo/AAd(c),BU:
    JeanGrey & Misty Knight 3.50
14 rep.#107,JBo/AAd(c),BU:
    Lilandra 3.50
15 rep.#108,JBo/AAd(c),BU:
    O:Starjammers 3.50
16 rep.#109,JBo/AAd(c),BU:
    Banshee 3.50
17 rep.#111,JBo/TA(c),BU:
    Mesmero 6.50
18 rep.#112,JBo/AAd(c),BU:
    Phoenix 3.00
19 rep.#113,JBo/AAd(c),BU:
    Magneto 6.00
20 rep.#114,JBo/AAd(c),
    BU:Storm 3.00
21 rep.#115,JBo/AAd(c),
    BU:Colossus. 2.75

22 rep.#116,JBo/AAd(c),
    BU:Storm 2.75
23 rep.#117,JBo/KGa(c),BU:
    Nightcrawler 2.75
24 rep.#118,JBo/KGa(c),BU:
    Phoenix 2.75
25 rep.#119,JBo/KGa(c),BU:Wolv. 3.00
26 rep.#120,JBo/KGa(c),BU:Wolv. 5.50
27 rep.#121,JBo/KD(c),BU:
    Wolverine & Phoenix 3.00
28 rep.#122,JBo/KD(c),BU:X-Men 2.50
29 rep.#123,JBo/KD(c),BU:
    Colossus 2.50
30 rep.#124,JBo/SLi(c),BU:
    O:Arcade 2.25
31 rep.#125,JBo/SLi(c),BU:
    Professor.X 2.25
32 rep.#126,JBo/SLi(c),BU:
    Wolverine. 3.00
33 rep.#127,JBo/SLi(c),BU:
    Havok 2.25
34 rep.#128,JBo/SLi(c),BU:
    W.Queen,M.Mind 2.25
35 rep.#129,JBo/SLi(c),BU:
    K.Pryde 2.25
36 rep.#130,MBr/SLi(c),BU:
    Banshee & Moira 2.25
37 rep.#131,RL/SLi(c),BU:
    Dazzler 2.25
38 rep.#132,KB/SLi(c),BU:
    Dazzler 2.25
39 rep.#133,2nd JLe X-Men/SLi(c),
    BU:Storm 8.00
40 rep.#134,SLi(c),BU:N.Crawler . 2.00
41 rep.#135,SLi(c),BU:
    Mr. Sinister,Cyclops 2.00
42 rep.#136,SLi(c),BU:
    Mr. Sinister,Cyclops 2.00
43 rep.#137,JBy(c),BU:
    Phoenix,Death 2.50

Classic X-Men #6
© Marvel Entertainment Group

Becomes:
X-MEN CLASSICS
44 rep.#138,KD/SLi(c) 2.00
45 thru 49 rep.#139-#145,SLi(c) @2.00
50 thru 69 rep.#146-#165 . . . . @1.50
70 rep.#166 . . . . 1.75
71 thru 99 rep.#167-#195 . . . . @1.50

All comics prices listed are for *Near Mint* condition.   **CVA Page 255**

100 thru 105 rep. #196–#201 . . @1.50
106 Phoenix vs. Beyonder 1.50
107 F:Rogue 1.50
108 F:Nightcrawler 1.50
109 rep. #205 . . . . 1.50

X-MEN: DAYS OF FUTURE PAST
1 Rep. X-Men #141-142 . . . . . . 4.00

X-MEN: DAYS OF FUTURE PRESENT
1 MMi(c),Rep.F.F.Ann.#23,X-Men
Ann.#14,X-Factor Ann.#5,
New Mutant Ann.#10 . . . . . 14.95

X-MEN INDEX
SEE: OFFICIAL MARVEL INDEX TO THE X-MEN

X-MEN/MICRONAUTS
January, 1984
1 JG,BWi,Limited Series 3.50
2 JG,BWi,KJo,V:Baron Karza . . . 2.50
3 JG,BWi,V:Baron Karza 2.50
4 JG,BWi,V:Baron Karza,Apr.1984 2.50

X-MEN OMEGA
1 FaN,Slo,After Xavier, concl. . . . 6.00
1a Gold ed. Chromium(c) 48pg. . . 49.95

X-MEN PRIME
1 SLo,FaN,BHi,major plotlines for
all X books begin, chromium(c) 4.95

X-MEN SPOTLIGHT ON STARJAMMERS
1990
1 DC,F:Starjammers,A:Prof.X . . . 5.00
2 DC,F:Starjammers,A:Prof.X . . . 5.00

X-MEN 2099
1 B:JFM(s),RLm,JP,I:X-Men 2099 5.00
1a Gold Ed. 40.00
2 RLm,JP,V:Rat Pack 3.00
3 RLm,JP,D:Serpentina 2.50
4 RLm,JP,I:Theatre of Pain . . . 2.00
5 RLm,JP,Fall of the Hammer#3 . 2.00
6 RLm,JP,I:Freakshow 2.00
7 RLm,JP,V:Freakshow 2.00
8 RLm(c),JS3,JP,N:Metalhead,
I:2nd X-Men 2099 . . . . 2.00
9 RLm,JP,V:2nd X-Men 2099 . . . 2.00
10 RLm,JP,A:La Lunatica 2.00
11 RLm,JP,V:2nd X-Men 2099 . . . 1.75
12 RLm,JP,A:Junkpile 1.75
13 RLm,JP 1.75
14 RLm,JP,R:Loki 1.75
15 RLm,JP,F:Loki,I:Haloween Jack 1.50
16 . . . . 1.50
17 X'ian 1.50
18 Haloween Jack 1.50
19 Conclusion Halloween Jack . . 1.50
Becomes:

X-MEN 2099 A.D.
20 F:Bloodhawk 1.95
21 Doom Factor 1.95
22 One Nation Under Doom 1.95

X-MEN UNLIMITED
1 CBa,BP,O:Siena Blaze 10.00

2 JD,O:Magneto 9.00
3 FaN(s),BSz(c),MMK,Sabretooth
joins X-Men,A:Maverick 8.00
4 SLo(s),RiB,O:Nightcrawler,Rogue,
Mystique,IR:Mystique is
Nightcrawler's mother 8.00
5 JFM(s),LSh,After Shi'ar/
Kree War 6.00
6 JFM(s),PS,Sauron 3.95
7 JR2,HMe,O:Storm 3.95

X-MEN VS. AVENGERS
April, 1987
1 MS,JRu,V:Soviet SuperSoldiers 4.00
2 MS,JRu,V:Sov.Super Soldiers . 3.00
3 MS,JRu,V:Sov.Super Soldiers . 3.00
4 KP,JRu,BMc,AW,AM,V:Magneto
July 1987 . . . . 3.00
TPB 12.95

X-MEN VS. DRACULA
1 rep. X-Men Ann.#6 . . . . 2.00

X-MEN: X-TINCTION AGENDA
TPB,rep.X-Men #270-272,X-Factor
#60-62,New Mutants #95-97 . 19.95

X-TERMINATORS
October, 1988—Jan., 1989
1 JBg,AW,AM,I:N'astirh 4.00
2 JBg,AM,V:N'astirh 3.50
3 JBg,AM,V:N'astirh 2.50
4 JBg,AM,A:New Mutants 2.50

X-UNIVERSE
1 The Other Heroes 3.50
2 F:Ben Grimm,Tony Stark 3.50

YOGI BEAR
November, 1977
1 A:Flintstones 1.25
2 . . . . 1.25
3 . . . . 1.25
4 . . . . 1.25
5 . . . . 1.25
6 . . . . 1.25
7 . . . . 1.25
8 . . . . 1.25
9 March, 1979 . . . . 1.25

YOUNG ALLIES COMICS
Timely
Summer, 1941—Oct., 1946
1 S&K,Hitler(c),I&O:Young Allies
1st meeting Capt. America &
Human Torch,A:Red Skull 6,500.00
2 S&K,A;Capt.America,Human
Torch 1,500.00
3 Remember Pearl Harbor(c) 1,200.00
4 A;Capt. America,Torch,Red Skull
ASh(c),Horror In Hollywood
A:Capt.America,Torch 1,500.00
5 ASh(c) 700.00
6 ASh(c) 500.00
7 ASh(c) 500.00
8 ASh(c) 500.00
9 ASh(c),Axis leaders(c),B:Tommy
Type 500.00
10 ASh(c) 500.00
11 ASh(c) 400.00
12 ASh(c) 400.00
13 ASh(c) 400.00

14 . . . . 400.00
15 ASh(c) 400.00
16 ASh(c) 400.00
17 ASh(c) 400.00

Young Allies #15
© Marvel Entertainment Group

18 ASh(c) 400.00
19 ASh(c),E:Tommy Type 400.00
20 . . . . 400.00

YOUNG HEARTS
Nov., 1949—Feb., 1950
1 . . . . 37.50
2 February, 1950 . . . . 22.00

YOUNG MEN
See: COWBOY ROMANCES

YUPPIES FROM HELL
1989
1 Satire 2.95
2 . . . . 2.95
3 . . . . 2.95

ZORRO
Marvel United Kingdom
1990
1 Don Diego 1.00
2 thru 12 . . . . @1.00

A-1 COMICS
Magazine Enterprises
1944

N# A:Kerry Drake,Johnny
  Devildog & Streamer Kelly . 150.00
1 A:Dotty Driple,Mr. EX,Bush
  Berry and Lew Loyal 90.00
2 A:Texas Slim & Dirty Dalton,
  The Corsair,Teddy Rich,Dotty
  Dripple,IncaDinca,TommyTinker
  Little Mexico and Tugboat . . . 50.00
3 same 30.00
4 same 30.00
5 same 30.00
6 same 28.00
7 same 25.00

A-1 Comics #8
© Magazine Enterprises

8 same 25.00
9 Texas Slim Issue 28.00
10 Same characters as
  issues #2–#8 . . . . 25.00
11 Teena 40.00
12 Teena 30.00
13 JCr,Guns of Fact and Fiction,
  narcotics & junkies featured . 150.00
14 Tim Holt WesternAdventures 325.00
15 Teena 35.00
16 Vacation Comics 28.00
17 Jim Holt #2, E:A-1 on cover 200.00
18 Jimmy Durante, Ph(c) 175.00
19 Tim Holt #3 . . . . 150.00
20 Jimmy Durante Ph(c) 150.00
21 OW,Joan of Arc movie adapt. 135.00
22 Dick Powell (1949) 150.00
23 Cowboys N' Indians #6 . . . . . 35.00
24 FF(c),LbC,Trail Colt #2 . . . . . 250.00
25 Fibber McGee & Molly (1949) 45.00
26 LbC, Trail Colt #2 . . . . 185.00
27 Ghost Rider#1,O:GhostRider 350.00
28 Christmas (Koko & Kola) . . . 20.00
29 FF(c), Ghost Rider #2 . . . . . 325.00
30 BP, Jet Powers #1 . . . . 175.00
31 FF,Ghost Rider#3,O:Ghost
  Rider 300.00
32 AW,GE,Jet Powers #2 . . . . . 125.00
33 Muggsy Mouse #2 . . . . 28.00
34 FF(c),Ghost Rider #4 . . . . . 300.00
35 AW,Jet Powers 190.00

36 Muggsy Mouse 35.00
37 FF(c),Ghost Rider 325.00
38 AW,WW,Jet Powers 200.00
39 Muggsy Mouse 20.00
40 Dogface Dooley 28.00
41 Cowboys N' Indians 22.00
42 BP,Best of the West 250.00
43 Dogface Dooley 20.00
44 Ghost Rider 125.00
45 American Air Forces 25.00
46 Best of the West 100.00
47 FF,Thunda 650.00
48 Cowboys N' Indians 22.00
49 Dogface Dooley 15.00
50 BP,Danger Is Their Busines65 50.00
51 Ghost Rider 125.00
52 Best of the West 100.00
53 Dogface Dooley 15.00
54 BP,American Air Forces 25.00
55 BP,U.S. Marines 25.00
56 BP,Thunda 100.00
57 Ghost Rider 110.00
58 American Air Forces 25.00
59 Best of the West 100.00
60 The U.S. Marines 25.00
61 Space Ace 240.00
62 Starr Flagg 200.00
63 Manhunt 150.00
64 Dogface Dooley 15.00
65 BP,American Air Forces 25.00
66 Best of the West 100.00
67 American Air Forces 25.00
68 U.S. Marines 25.00
69 Ghost Rider 120.00
70 Best of the West 75.00
71 Ghost Rider 110.00
72 U.S. Marines 25.00
73 BP,Thunda 75.00
74 BP,American Air Forces 20.00
75 Ghost Rider 100.00
76 Best of the West 75.00
77 Manhunt 110.00
78 BP,Thunda 80.00
79 American Air Forces 28.00
80 Ghost Rider 100.00
81 Best of the West 75.00
82 BP,Cave Girl 200.00
83 BP,Thunda 75.00
84 Ghost Rider 100.00
85 Best of the West 75.00
86 BP,Thunda 70.00
87 Best of the West 75.00
88 Bobby Benson's B-Bar-B . . . 45.00
89 BP,Home Run,Stan Musial . 150.00
90 Red Hawk 60.00
91 BP,American Air Forces 20.00
92 Dream Book of Romance . . . 30.00
93 BP,Great Western 100.00
94 FF,White Indian 150.00
95 BP,Muggsy Mouse 15.00
96 BP,Cave Girl 175.00
97 Best of the West 70.00
98 Undercover Girl 175.00
99 Muggsy Mouse 12.00
100 Badmen of the West 125.00
101 FF,White Indian 135.00
101(a) FG, Dream Book of
  Romance, Marlon Brando . 100.00
103 BP,Best of the West 75.00
104 FF,White Indian 125.00
105 Great Western 60.00
106 Dream Book of Love 40.00
107 Hot Dog 25.00
108 BP,BC,Red Fox 75.00
109 Dream Book of Romance . . 25.00

110 Dream Book of Romance . . 25.00
111 I'm a Cop 65.00
112 Ghost Rider 90.00
113 BP,Great Western 60.00
114 Dream Book of Love 40.00
115 Hot Dog 18.00
116 BP,Cave Girl 155.00
117 White Indian 55.00
118 BP(c),Undercover Girl 175.00
119 Straight Arrow's Fury 75.00
120 Badmen of the West 75.00
121 Mysteries of the
  Scotland Yard 75.00
122 Black Phantom 200.00
123 Dream Book of Love 25.00
124 Hot Dog 18.00
125 BP,Cave Girl 160.00
126 BP,I'm a Cop 55.00
127 BP,Great Western 60.00
128 BP,I'm a Cop 50.00
129 The Avenger 190.00
130 BP,Strongman 100.00
131 BP,The Avenger 125.00
132 Strongman 80.00
133 BP,The Avenger 125.00
134 Strongman 75.00
135 White Indian 50.00
136 Hot Dog 15.00
137 BP,Africa 125.00
138 BP,Avenger 125.00
139 BP,Strongman, 1955 . . . . . 85.00

ABBIE AN' SLATS
United Features Syndicate
March, 1948

1 RvB(c) 100.00
2 RvB(c) 75.00
3 RvB(c) 55.00
4 August, 1948 . . . . 45.00
N# 1940,Earlier Issue 225.00
N# 175.00

ABBOTT AND COSTELLO
St. John Publishing Co.
February, 1948

1 PP(c), Waltz Time 300.00
2 Jungle Girl and Snake cover 135.00
3 Outer Space cover 85.00
4 MD, Circus cover 60.00
5 MD,Bull Fighting cover 60.00
6 MD,Harem cover 60.00
7 MD,Opera cover 60.00
8 MD,Pirates cover 60.00
9 MD,Polar Bear cover 60.00
10 MD,PP(c),Son of Sinbad tale 125.00
11 MD 55.00
12 PP(c) 50.00
13 Fire fighters cover 50.00
14 Bomb cover 50.00
15 Bubble Bath cover 50.00
16 thru 29 MD . . . . @50.00
30 thru 39 MD . . . . @40.00
40 MD,September, 1956 . . . . . . 40.00

ACE COMICS
David McKay Publications
April, 1937

1 JM, F:Katzenjammer Kids . 1,900.00
2 JM, A:Blondie 550.00
3 JM, A:Believe It Or Not . . . 385.00
4 JM, F:Katzenjammer Kids . . 360.00
5 JM, A:Believe It Or Not . . . 350.00
6 JM, A:Blondie 300.00
7 JM, A:Believe It Or Not . . . 290.00

Ace Comics #30 © David McKay Publ.

8 JM, A:Jungle Jim	285.00
9 JM, A:Blondie	290.00
10 JM, F:Katzenjammer Kids	250.00
11 I:The Phantom series	350.00
12 A:Blondie, Jungle Jim	250.00
13 A:Ripley's Believe It Or Not	225.00
14 A:Blondie, Jungle Jim	225.00
15 A:Blondie	210.00
16 F:Katzenjammer Kids	210.00
17 A:Blondie	210.00
18 A:Ripley's Believe It Or N8t	210.00
19 F:Katzenjammer Kids	200.00
20 A:Jungle Jim	200.00
21 A:Blondie	185.00
22 A:Jungle Jim	175.00
23 F:Katzenjammer Kids	175.00
24 A:Blondie	175.00
25	160.00
26 O:Prince Valiant	525.00
27 thru 36	@150.00
37 Krazy Kat Ends	130.00
38 thru 49	@100.00
50 thru 59	@90.00
60 thru 69	@85.00
70 thru 79	@80.00
80 thru 89	@75.00
90 thru 99	@60.00
100	75.00
101 thru 109	@60.00
110 thru 119	@52.00
120 thru 143	@50.00
144 Beginning of Phantom covers	80.00
145 thru 150	@70.00
151 October-November, 1949	75.00

ACES HIGH
E.C. Comics
March-April, 1955

1 GE(c)	200.00
2 GE(c)	125.00
3 GE(c)	100.00
4 GE(c)	100.00
5 GE(c)Nov.-Dec., 1955	100.00

ADVENTURES INTO DARKNESS
Standard Publications
August, 1952

5 JK(c)	125.00
6 GT, JK	75.00
7 JK(c)	75.00
8 ATh	90.00
9 JK	80.00
10 JK,ATh,MSy	65.00
11 JK,ATh,MSy	65.00
12 JK,ATh,MYs	65.00
13 Cannibalism feature	75.00
14	65.00

ADVENTURES INTO THE UNKNOWN!
American Comics Group
Fall 1948

1 FG, Haunted House cover	800.00
2 Haunted Island cover	350.00
3 AF, Sarcophagus cover	400.00
4 Monsters cover	200.00
5 Monsters cover	200.00
6 Giant Hands cover	155.00
7 Skeleton Pirate cover	140.00
8 Horror	135.00
9 Snow Monster	135.00
10 Red Bats	135.00
11 Death Shadow	135.00
12 OW(c)	110.00
13 OW(c),Dinosaur	120.00
14 OW(c),Cave	120.00
15 Red Demons	120.00
16	110.00
17 OW(c),The Thing Type	130.00

Adventures Into the Unknown! #2 © American Comics Group

18 OW(c),Wolves	120.00
19 OW(c),Graveyard	110.00
20 OW(c),Graveyard	110.00
21 Bats and Dracula	110.00
22 Death	110.00
23 Bats	100.00
24	100.00
25	100.00
26	100.00
27 AW	135.00
28 thru 39	@90.00
40 thru 49	@85.00
50	75.00
51 Lazarus	150.00
52 Lazarus	150.00

53	140.00
54	140.00
55	140.00
56 Lazarus	140.00
57	140.00
58 Lazarus	140.00
59	100.00
60	65.00
61	65.00
62 thru 69	@60.00
70 thru 79	@35.00
80 thru 89	@30.00
90 thru 99	@35.00
100	30.00
101 thru 115	@25.00
116 AW,AT	22.00
117 thru 120	@20.00
121 thru 152	@17.00
153 A:Magic Agent	17.00
154 O:Nemesis	15.00
155	15.00
156 A:Magic Agent	17.00
157 thru 173	@15.00
174 August, 1967	15.00

ADVENTURES IN WONDERLAND
Lev Gleason Publications
April, 1955

1	40.00
2	25.00
3	20.00
4	20.00
5	28.00

ADVENTURES OF MIGHTY MOUSE
St. John Publishing Co.
November, 1951

1 Mighty Mouse Adventures	125.00
2 Menace of the Deep	100.00
3 Storm Clouds of Mystery	75.00
4 Thought Control Machine	60.00

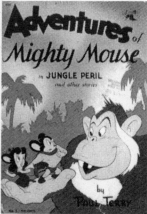

Adventures of Mighty Mouse #5 © St. John Publishing Co.

5 Jungle Peril	60.00
6 'The Vine of Destruction'	60.00
7 Space Ship(c)	60.00

8 Charging Alien(c)	60.00
9 Meteor(c)	50.00
10 Revolt at the Zoo"	50.00
11 Jungle(c)	50.00
12 A:Freezing Terror	50.00
13 A:Visitor from Outer Space	50.00
14 V:Cat	45.00
15	45.00
16	45.00
17	45.00
18 May, 1955	45.00

Aggie Mack #4
© Four Star Comics/Superior Comics

AGGIE MACK
Four Star Comics/ Superior Comics
January, 1948

1 AF,HR(c)	120.00
2 JK(c)	65.00
3 AF,JK(c)	60.00
4 AF	80.00
5 AF,JK(c)	65.00
6 AF,JK(c)	60.00
7 AF,Burt Lancaster on cover	65.00
8 AF,JK(c), August 1949	60.00

BILL BARNES, AMERICA'S AIR ACE
Street and Smith Publications
July, 1940

1 (Bill Barnes Comics)	450.00
2 Second Battle Valley Forge	260.00
3 A:Aviation Cadets	200.00
4 Shotdown(c)	185.00
5 A:Air Warden, Danny Hawk	175.00
6 A:Danny Hawk,RocketRodney	160.00
7 How to defeat the Japanese	160.00
8 Ghost Ship	160.00
9 Flying Tigers, John Wayne	165.00
10 I:Roane Waring	160.00
11 Flying Tigers	160.00
12 War Workers	160.00

Becomes:
AIR ACE

2-1 Invades Germany	120.00
2-2 Jungle Warfare	65.00
2-3 A:The Four Musketeers	60.00

2-4 A:Russell Swann	60.00
2-5 A:The Four Musketeers	60.00
2-6 Raft(c)	55.00
2-7 BP, What's New In Science	55.00
2-8 XP-59	55.00
2-9 The Northrop P-61	55.00
2-10 NCG-14	50.00
2-11 Whip Lanch	50.00
2-12 PP(c)	50.00
3-1	45.00
3-2 Atom and It's Future	45.00
3-3 Flying in the Future	45.00
3-4 How Fast Can We Fly	45.00
3-5 REv(c)	45.00
3-6 V:Wolves	45.00
3-7 BP(c), Vortex of Atom Bomb	90.00
3-8 February-March, 1947	45.00

AIRBOY
(see AIR FIGHTERS COMICS)

AIR FIGHTERS COMICS
Hillman Periodicals
November, 1941

1 I:BlackCommander (only App)	1,150.00
2 O:Airboy A:Sky Wolf	1,750.00
3 O:Sky Wolf and Heap	875.00
4 A:Black Angel, Iron Ace	600.00
5 A:Sky Wolf and Iron Ace	500.00
6 Airboy's Bird Plane	450.00
7 Airboy battles Kultur	375.00
8 A:Skinny McGinty	350.00

Air Fighters Comics #9
© Hillman Periodicals

9 A:Black Prince, Hatchet Man	350.00
10 I:The Stinger	340.00
11 Kida(c)	335.00
12 A:Misery	335.00
2-1 A:Flying Dutchman	325.00
2-2 I:Valkyrie	425.00
2-3 Story Panels cover	325.00
2-4 V:Japanese	325.00
2-5 Air Boy in Tokyo	325.00
2-6 'Dance of Death'	325.00
2-7 A:Valkyrie	325.00
2-8 Airboy Battles Japanese	325.00
2-9 Airboy Battles Japanese	325.00

2-10 O:Skywolf	400.00

Becomes:
AIRBOY

2-11	350.00
2-12 A:Valykrie	250.00
3-1	200.00
3-2	180.00
3-3 Never published	
3-4 I:The Heap	175.00
3-5 Airboy	150.00
3-6 A:Valykrie	150.00
3-7 AMc,Witch Hunt	150.00
3-8 A:Condor	160.00
3-9 O:The Heap	190.00
3-10	150.00
3-11	150.00
3-12 Airboy missing	190.00
4-1 Elephant in chains cover	180.00
4-2 I:Rackman	120.00
4-3 Airboy profits on name	125.00
4-4 S&K	135.00
4-5 S&K,The American Miracle	160.00
4-6 S&K,A:Heap and Flying Fool	160.00
4-7 S&K	160.00
4-8 S&K,Girlfriend captured	160.00
4-9 S&K,Airboy in quick sand	160.00
4-10 S&K,A:Valkyrie	160.00
4-11 S&K,A:Frenchy	160.00
4-12 FBe	120.00
5-1 LSt	75.00
5-2 I:Wild Horse of Calabra	75.00
5-3	75.00
5-4 CI	75.00
5-5 Skull on cover	75.00
5-6	75.00
5-7	75.00
5-8 Bondage Cover	85.00

Airboy #70 (6/11) © Hillman Periodicals

5-9 Zoi,Row	75.00
5-10 A:Valykrie,O:The Heap	85.00
5-11 Airboy vs. The Rats	75.00
5-12 BK,Rat Army captures Airboy	75.00
6-1	75.00
6-2	75.00
6-3	75.00
6-4 Airboy boxes	80.00
6-5 A:The Ice People	75.00
6-6	75.00

All comics prices listed are for *Near Mint* condition.

6-7 Airboy vs. Chemical Giant . 75.00
6-8 O:The Heap 100.00
6-9 .... 75.00
6-10 .... 75.00
6-11 .... 75.00
6-12 .... 75.00
7-1 .... 70.00
7-2 BP 70.00
7-3 BP 70.00
7-4 I:Monsters of the Ice 70.00
7-5 V:Monsters of the Ice 70.00
7-6 .... 70.00
7-7 Mystery of the Sargasso
Sea 70.00
7-8 A:Centaur 70.00
7-9 I:Men of the StarlightRobot . 70.00
7-10 O:The Heap 70.00
7-11 .... 70.00
7-12 Airboy visits India 70.00
8-1 BP,A:Outcast and Polo
Bandits 65.00
8-2 BP,Suicide Dive cover 65.00
8-3 I:The Living Fuse 65.00
8-4 A:Death Merchants of the Air 70.00
8-5 A:Great Plane from Nowhere 65.00
8-6 .... 65.00
8-7 .... 65.00
8-8 .... 65.00
8-9 .... 65.00
8-10 A:Mystery Walkers 65.00
8-11 .... 65.00
8-12 .... 70.00
9-1 .... 65.00
9-2 A:Valkrie 60.00
9-3 A:Heap (cover) 60.00
9-4 A:Water Beast, Frog Headed
Riders 65.00
9-5 A:Heap vs.Man of Moonlight 60.00
9-6 Heap cover 60.00
9-7 Heap cover 60.00
9-8 Heap cover 65.00
9-9 .... 65.00
9-10 Space cover 65.00
9-11 .... 60.00
9-12 Heap cover 60.00
10-1 Heap cover 60.00
10-2 Ships on Space 60.00
10-3 .... 60.00
10-4 May, 1953 .... 60.00

AL CAPP'S
DOG PATCH COMICS
Toby Press
June, 1949
1 .... 175.00
2 A:Daisy 125.00
3 .... 110.00
4 December, 1949 .... 110.00

AL CAPP'S SHMOO
Toby Press
July, 1949
1 100 Trillion Schmoos 235.00
2 Super Shmoo(c) 175.00
3 .... 175.00
4 .... 150.00
5 April, 1950 .... 150.00

AL CAPP'S WOLF GAL
Toby Press
1951
1 Pin-Up 225.00
2 1952 .... 200.00

Al Capp's Wolf Gal #1 © Toby Press

ALL-FAMOUS CRIME
Star Publications
May, 1951
8 LbC(c) 75.00
9 LbC(c) 85.00
10 LbC(c) 60.00
4 LbC(c) 60.00
5 LbC(c) 60.00
Becomes:

ALL-FAMOUS
POLICE CASES
6 LbC(c) 75.00
7 LbC(c) 65.00
8 LbC(c) 60.00
9 LbC(c) 55.00
10 thru 15 LbC(c) .... @50.00
16 September, 1954 ...... 60.00

ALL GOOD COMICS
R. W. Voight/Fox Publ.
/St. John Publ.
1 1944 .... 85.00
1 1946 .... 65.00
N# 1949 .... 350.00

ALL GREAT COMICS
(see DAGGER,
DESERT HAWK)

ALL HERO COMICS
Fawcett Publications
March, 1943
1 A:Capt. Marvel Jr.,Capt.
Midnight,Ibis, Golden Arrow
and Spy Smasher 850.00

ALL HUMOR COMICS
Comic Favorites, Inc.
(Quality Comics)
Spring 1946
1 .... 100.00
2 PG 50.00
3 I:Kelly Poole 25.00
4 thru 7 .... @25.00
8 PG 25.00

All Humor Comics #8
© Comic Favorites, Inc./Quality Comics

9 .... 25.00
10 .... 25.00
11 thru 17 .... @18.00

ALL LOVE ROMANCES
(see SCREAM COMICS)

ALL NEGRO COMICS
1 .... 1,600.00

ALL-NEW COMICS
Family Comics
(Harvey Publ.)
January, 1943
1 A:Steve Case, Johnny Rebel
I:Detective Shane 800.00
2 JKu,O:Scarlet Phantom 400.00
3 .... 300.00
4 AdH 300.00
5 Flash Gordon 275.00
6 I:Boy Heroes and Red Blazer 275.00
7 JKu,AS(c),A:Black Cat &
Zebra 300.00
8 JKu,A:Shock Gibson 300.00
9 JKu,A:Black Cat 300.00
10 JKu,A:Zebra 275.00
11 A:Man in Black, Girl
Commandos 275.00
12 JKu 275.00
13 Stuntman by S&K,
A:Green Hornet&cover 300.00
14 A:Green Hornet 275.00
15 Smaller size, Distributed
by Mail, March-April, 1947 . 325.00

ALL TOP COMICS
William H. Wise Co.
1944
N# 132pgs.,A:Capt.
V,Red Robbins 160.00

ALL TOP COMICS
Fox Features Syndicate
Spring 1946
1 A:Cosmo Cat, Flash Rabbit 100.00

2	50.00
3	40.00
4	40.00
5	40.00
6	40.00
7	40.00
7a	85.00
8 JKa(c),Blue Beetle 1st app	750.00
9 JKa(c),A:Rulah	450.00
10 JKa(c),A:Rulah	475.00
11 A:Rulah,Blue Beetle	350.00
12 A:Rulah,Jo Jo,Blue Beetle	350.00
13 A:Rulah	300.00
14 A:Rulah,Blue Beetle	375.00
15 A:Rulah	300.00
16 A:Rulah,Blue Beetle	325.00
17 A:Rulah,Blue Beetle	325.00
18 A:Dagar,Jo Jo	250.00

Green Publ.

6 1957	20.00
6 1958	20.00
6 1959	20.00
6 1959	20.00
6 Supermouse cover	20.00

ALLEY OOP
Argo Publications
November, 1955

1	85.00
2	65.00
3 March, 1956	65.00

Amazing Adventures #3
© Ziff-Davis Publ. Co.

AMAZING ADVENTURES
Ziff-Davis Publ. Co.
1950

1 WW	325.00
2	135.00
3	135.00
4	135.00
5	135.00
6	175.00

AMAZING GHOST STORIES
(See: WEIRD HORRORS)

AMAZING-MAN COMICS
Centaur Publications
September, 1939

5 BEv,O:Amazing Man	13,000.00
6 BEv,B:The Shark	2,500.00
7 BEv,I:Magician From Mars	1,400.00
8 BEv	1,200.00
9 BEv	1,200.00
10 BEv	900.00
11 BEv,I:Zardi	800.00
12 SG(c)	800.00
13 SG(c)	800.00
14 B:Reef Kinkaid, Dr. Hypo	600.00
15 A:Zardi	500.00
16 Mighty Man's powers revealed	550.00
17 A:Dr. Hypo	500.00
18 BLb(a),SG(c)	500.00
19 BLb(a),SG(c)	500.00
20 BLb(a),SG(c)	500.00
21 O:Dash Dartwell	450.00
22 A:Silver Streak, The Voice	450.00
23 I&O:Tommy the Amazing Kid	500.00
24 B:King of Darkness,Blue Lady	450.00
25 A:Meteor Marvin	800.00
26 A:Meteor Marvin,Electric Ray February, 1942	600.00

Amazing Mystery Funnies #7
© Centaur Publications

AMAZING MYSTERY FUNNIES
Centaur Publications
1938

1 Skyrocket Steele in the Year X	2,500.00
2 WE,Skyrocket Steele	1,100.00
3	500.00
(#4) WE,bondage (c)	550.00
2-1(#5)	475.00
2-2(#6) Drug use	475.00
2-3(#7) Air Sub DX	475.00
2-4(#8)	475.00
2-5(#9)	600.00
2-6(#10)	475.00
2-7(#11) scarce	2,400.00
2-8(#12) Speed Centaur	800.00
2-9(#13)	500.00
2-10(#14)	500.00

2-11(#15)	500.00
2-12(#16) BW,I:Space Patrol	1,250.00
3-1(#17) I:Bullet	450.00
18	425.00
19 BW,Space Patrol	600.00
20	425.00
21 BW,Space Patrol	600.00
22 BW,Space Patrol	600.00
23 BW,Space Patrol	600.00
24 BW,Space Patrol	600.00

AMAZING WILLIE MAYS
Famous Funnies
1954

1 Willie Mays(c)	450.00

American Library # 6
© David McKay Publ.

AMERICAN LIBRARY
David McKay Publ.
1943

(#1) Thirty Seconds Over Tokyo, movie adapt.	225.00
(#2) Guadalcanal Diary	175.00
3 Look to the Mountain	80.00
4 The Case of the Crooked Candle (Perry Mason)	80.00
5 Duel in the Sun	80.00
6 Wingate's Raiders	90.00

AMERICA'S BEST COMICS
Nedor/Better/Standard Publications
February 1942

1 B:Black Terror, Captain Future, The Liberator, Doc Strange	775.00
2 O:American Eagle	400.00
3 B:Pyroman	275.00
4 A:Doc Strange, Jimmy Cole	225.00
5 A:Lone Eagle, Capt. Future	200.00
6 A:American Crusader	190.00
7 A:Hitler,Hirohito	185.00
8 The Liberator ends	150.00
9 ASh(c)	175.00
10 ASh(c)	150.00
11 ASh(c)	150.00
12 Red Cross cover	150.00

All comics prices listed are for _Near Mint_ condition.

13 .... 150.00
14 Last American Eagle app .. 150.00
15 ASh(c) 125.00
16 ASh(c) 130.00
17 Doc Strange carries football 125.00
18 Bondage cover 125.00
19 ASh(c) 125.00
20 vs. the Black Market 125.00
21 Infinity cover 110.00
22 A:Captain Future 110.00
23 B:Miss Masque 150.00
24 Bondage cover 160.00
25 A:Sea Eagle 110.00
26 A:The Phantom Detective .. 145.00
27 ASh(c) 135.00
28 A:Commando Cubs,
   Black Terror 135.00
29 A:Doc Strange 135.00
30 ASh(c) 135.00
31 July, 1949 .... 135.00

AMERICA'S BIGGEST COMICS BOOK
William H. Wise
1944
1 196 pgs. A:Grim Reaper, Zudo,
  Silver Knight, Thunderhoof,
  Jocko and Socko,Barnaby
  Beep,Commando Cubs 225.00

AMERICA'S GREATEST COMICS
Fawcett Publications
Fall 1941
1 MRa(c),A:Capt. Marvel,
  Bulletman,Spy Smasher and
  Minute Man 1,500.00
2 .... 675.00
3 .... 500.00
4 B:Commando Yank 450.00
5 Capt.Marvel in "Lost Lighting" 450.00
6 Capt.Marvel fires Machine
  Gun 350.00
7 A:Balbo the Boy Magician . 325.00
8 A:Capt.Marvel Jr.,Golden
  Arrow Summer 1943 ..... 350.00

AMERICA IN ACTION
Dell Publishing Co.
1942
1 .... 100.00

ANDY COMICS
(see SCREAM COMICS)

ANGEL
Dell Publishing Co.
August, 1954
(1) see Dell Four Color #576
2 .... 15.00
3 thru 16 .... @12.00

ANIMAL ANTICS
Dell Publishing Co.
1946
1 B:Racoon Kids 275.00
2 .... 150.00
3 thru 10 .... @90.00
11 thru 23 .... @50.00

Animal Antics #19
© Dell Publications Co.

ANIMAL COMICS
Dell Publishing Co.
1942
1 WK,Pogo 750.00
2 Uncle Wiggily(c),A:Pogo ... 400.00
3 Muggin's Mouse(c),A:Pogo . 275.00
4 Uncle Wiggily(c) 275.00
5 Uncle Wiggily(c) 250.00
6 Uncle Wiggily 175.00
7 Uncle Wiggily 175.00
8 Pogo 200.00
9 War Bonds(c),A:Pogo 220.00
10 Pogo 175.00
11 Pogo 135.00
12 Pogo 135.00
13 Pogo 135.00
14 Pogo 135.00
15 Pogo 135.00
16 Uncle Wiggily 80.00
17 Pogo(c) 100.00
18 Pogo(c) 85.00
19 Pogo(c) 85.00
20 Pogo 80.00
21 Pogo(c) 85.00
22 Pogo 75.00
23 Pogo 75.00
24 Pogo(c) 85.00
25 Pogo(c) 85.00
26 Pogo(c) 85.00
27 Pogo(c) 65.00
28 Pogo(c) 65.00
29 Pogo(c) 65.00
30 Pogo(c) 65.00

ANIMAL FABLES
E.C. Comics
July-August 1946
1 B:Korky Kangaroo,Freddy Firefly
  Petey Pig and Danny Demon 200.00
2 B:Aesop Fables 140.00
3 .... 125.00
4 .... 125.00
5 Firefly vs. Red Ants 125.00
6 .... 125.00
7 O:Moon Girls,Nov.-Dec.1947 375.00

ANIMAL FAIR
Fawcett Publications
March 1946
1 B:Captain Marvel Bunny,
  Sir Spot 125.00
2 A:Droopy, Colonel Walrus .. 60.00
3 .... 35.00
4 A:Kid Gloves, Cub Reporter . 35.00
5 .... 35.00
6 .... 35.00
7 .... 35.00
8 .... 25.00
9 .... 25.00
10 .... 25.00
11 February 1947 .... 25.00

ANNIE OKLEY & TAGG
Dell Publishing Co.
1953
(1) see Dell Four Color #438
(2) see Dell Four Color #481
(3) see Dell Four Color #575
4 .... 65.00
5 .... 65.00
6 .... 65.00
7 .... 65.00

Animal Fair #2 © Fawcett Publications

8 .... 65.00
9 .... 65.00
10 .... 65.00
11 thru 18 .... @50.00

ARCHIE COMICS
MLJ Magazines
Winter, 1942-43
1 I:Jughead & Veronica ... 7,500.00
2 .... 1,500.00
3 .... 1,000.00
4 .... 700.00
5 .... 700.00
6 .... 450.00
7 thru 11 .... @400.00
12 thru 15 .... @300.00
16 thru 19 .... @275.00
Archie Publications
20 .... 275.00
21 .... 250.00
22 thru 31 .... @150.00

All comics prices listed are for *Near Mint* condition.

32 thru 42	@100.00
43 thru 50	@75.00
51 thru 60	@50.00
61 thru 70	@40.00
71 thru 80	@30.00
81 thru 99	@25.00
100	35.00
101	25.00
102 thru 115	@15.00
116 thru 130	@12.00
131 thru 145	@10.00
146 thru 160	@7.50
161 thru 180	@5.00
181 thru 200	@4.00
201 thru 250	@3.00
251 thru 280	@2.00
281 thru 389	@1.50

ARCHIE'S GIANT SERIES MAGAZINE
Archie Publications
1954

1	650.00

Archie #6 © Archie Publications

2	375.00
3	250.00
4	200.00
5	200.00
6 thru 10	@150.00
11 thru 20	@125.00
21 thru 29	@100.00
30 thru 35	@30.00
136 thru 141	@30.00
142	32.00
143 thru 160	@12.00
161 thru 199	@8.00
200	5.00
201 thru 250	@2.50
251 thru 299	@1.50
300 thru 500	@1.00

ARCHIE'S GIRLS BETTY AND VERONICA
Archie Publications
1950

1	750.00
2	375.00
3	225.00

4	175.00
5	170.00
6 thru 10	@160.00
11 thru 15	@125.00
16 thru 20	@100.00
21	90.00
22 thru 29	@85.00
30 thru 40	@60.00
41 thru 50	@50.00
51 thru 60	@40.00
61 thru 70	@35.00
71 thru 80	@30.00
81 thru 90	@25.00
91 thru 99	@20.00
100	25.00
101 thru 120	@12.00
121 thru 140	@10.00
141 thru 160	@7.00
161 thru 180	@3.00
181 thru 199	@2.00
200	3.00
201 thru 220	@2.00
221 thru 240	@1.50
241 thru 347	@1.00

Archie's Girls Betty and Veronica #27
© Archie Publications

ARCHIE'S JOKE BOOK MAGAZINE
Archie Publications
1953

1	450.00
2	250.00
3	160.00
15 thru 19	@125.00
20 thru 25	@100.00
26 thru 35	@75.00
36 thru 40	@50.00
41	125.00
42 thru 48	@50.00
49 thru 60	@20.00
61 thru 70	@15.00
71 thru 80	@10.00
81 thru 100	@5.00
101 thru 200	@2.50
201 thru 288	@1.00

ARCHIE'S MECHANICS
Archie Publications

September, 1954

September, 1954

1	500.00
2	350.00
3	250.00

ARCHIE'S PAL, JUGHEAD
Archie Publications
1949

1	650.00
2	350.00
3	200.00
4	175.00
5	175.00
6	150.00
7 thru 10	@125.00
11 thru 15	@100.00
16 thru 20	@85.00
21 thru 30	@65.00
31 thru 39	@50.00
40 thru 50	@35.00
51 thru 60	@30.00
61 thru 70	@25.00
71 thru 80	@20.00
81 thru 99	@15.00
100	17.00
101 thru 126	@10.00

Archie's Pals 'n' Gals
© Archie Publications

ARCHIE'S PALS 'N' GALS
Archie Publications
1952 thru 53

1	450.00
2	225.00
3	150.00
4	135.00
5	135.00
6	80.00
7	80.00
8 thru 10	@75.00
11 thru 15	@50.00
16 thru 20	@35.00
21 thru 30	@20.00
31 thru 40	@20.00
41 thru 50	@12.00
51 thru 60	@10.00

61 thru 70 . . . . @7.00
71 thru 80 . . . . @5.00
81 thru 99 . . . . @2.50
100 . . . . 3.00
101 thru 120 . . . . @2.00
121 thru 160 . . . . @1.50
161 thru 224 . . . . @1.00

Archie's Rival Reggie #3
© Archie Publications

ARCHIE'S RIVAL REGGIE
Archie Publications
1950

1 . . . . 400.00
2 . . . . 225.00
3 . . . . 175.00
4 . . . . 150.00
5 . . . . 150.00
6 . . . . 125.00
7 thru 10 . . . . @100.00
11 thru 13 . . . . @75.00
14 thru 15 . . . . @65.00
16 August, 1954 . . . . 70.00

ARMY & NAVY COMICS
(see SUPERSNIPE COMICS)

ARROW, THE
Centaur Publications
October 1940

1 B:Arrow 1,000.00
2 BLB(c) 600.00
3 O:Dash Dartwell,Human
Meteor, Rainbow, Bondage
cover, October, 1941 . . . . . 550.00

ATOMAN
Spark Publications
February 1946

1 JRo,MMe,O:Atoman,A:Kid
Crusaders 275.00
2 JRo,MMe 200.00

ATOMIC COMICS
Green Publishing Co.
January, 1946

1 S&S,A:Radio Squad, Barry
O'Neal 650.00
2 MB,A:Inspector Dayton, Kid
Kane 300.00
3 MB,A:Zero Ghost Detective 175.00
4 JKa(c), July-August, 1946 . . 150.00

ATOMIC COMICS
Daniels Publications
1946 (Reprints)

1 A:Rocketman,Yankee Boy,
Bondage cover,rep. 125.00

ATOMIC MOUSE
Capital Stories/
Charlton Comics
March, 1953

1 AFa,O:Atomic Mouse 110.00
2 AFa,Ice Cream cover 50.00
3 AFa,Genie and Magic
Carpet cover 35.00
4 AFa 35.00
5 AFa,A:Timmy the Timid Ghost 35.00
6 thru 10 Funny Animal . . . . @32.00
11 thru 14 Funny Animal . . . . @20.00
15 A:Happy the Marvel Bunny . 25.00
16 Funny Animal,Giant 27.00
17 thru 30 Funny Animal . . . . @20.00
31 thru 36 Funny Animal . . . . @15.00
37 A:Atom the Cat 15.00
38 thru 40 Funny Animal . . . . @12.00
41 thru 53 Funny Animal . . . . @10.00
54 June, 1963 . . . . 10.00

ATOMIC THUNDER BOLT, THE
Regor Company
February, 1946

1 I:Atomic Thunderbolt,
Mr. Murdo 250.00

Authentic Police Cases #3
© St. John Publ. Co.

AUTHENTIC POLICE CASES
St. John Publ. Co.
1948

1 Hale the Magician 165.00
2 Lady Satan, Johnny Rebel . . 100.00
3 A:Avenger 200.00
4 Masked Black Jack 110.00
5 JCo 110.00
6 JCo,MB(c) 200.00
7 thru 10 . . . . @75.00
11 thru 15 . . . . @70.00
16 thru 23 . . . . @50.00
24 thru 28 . . . . @100.00
29 thru 38 . . . . @35.00

AVIATION AND MODEL BUILDING
(see TRUE AVIATION PICTURE STORIES)

AVON ONE-SHOTS
Avon Periodicals
1949-1953
{Listed in Alphabetical Order}

1 Atomic Spy Cases 150.00

Attack on Planet Mars
© Avon Periodicals

N# WW,Attack on Planet Mars . 475.00
1 Batchelor's Diary 135.00
1 Badmen of the West 150.00
N# Badmen of Tombstone 75.00
1 Behind Prison Bars 140.00
2 Betty and Her Steady 35.00
N# Blackhawk Indian
Tomahawk War 75.00
1 Blazing Sixguns 75.00
1 Butch Cassidy 80.00
N# Chief Crazy Horse 100.00
N# FF,Chief Victorio's
Apache Massacre 250.00
N# City of the Living Dead 250.00
1 Complete Romance 150.00
N# Custer's Last Fight 75.00
1 Dalton Boys 70.00
N# Davy Crockett 70.00
N# The Dead Who Walk 250.00
1 Diary of Horror,Bondage(c) . 200.00
N# WW,An Earth Man on Venus 650.00
1 Eerie, bondage (c) 550.00
1 Escape from Devil's Island . 150.00
N# Fighting Daniel Boone 75.00

N# For a Night of Love 125.00
1 WW,Flying Saucers 350.00
N# Flying Saucers. 320.00
1 Going Steady with Betty 60.00
N# Hooded Menace 250.00
N# King of the Badmen
   of Deadwood 80.00
1 King Solomon's Mines 175.00
N# Kit Carson & the
   Blackfeet Warriors 50.00
N# Last of the Comanches 75.00
N# Masked Bandit 75.00
1 WW,Mask of Dr. Fu Manchu 500.00
N# Night of Mystery 150.00
1 Outlaws of the Wild West . 150.00
1 Out of this World 350.00
N# Pancho Villa 125.00
1 Phantom Witch Doctor 185.00
1 Pixie Puzzle Rocket
   to Adventureland 50.00
1 Prison Riot,drugs 125.00
N# Red Mountain Featuring
   Quantrell's Raiders 125.00
N# Reform School Girl 550.00
1 Robotmen of the Lost Planet 550.00
N# WW(c),Rocket to the Moon 575.00
N# JKu,Secret Diary of
   Eerie Adventures 750.00
1 Sheriff Bob Dixon's
   Chuck Wagon 65.00
1 Sideshow 135.00
1 JKu,Sparkling Love 80.00
N# Speedy Rabbit 30.00
1 Teddy Roosevelt &
   His Rough Riders 100.00
N# The Underworld Story 125.00
N# The Unknown Man 130.00
1 War Dogs of the U.S. Army .. 75.00
N# White Chief of the
   Pawnee Indians 65.00
N# Women to Love 150.00

BABE
Prize/Headline Feature
June-July 1948
1 BRo,A;Boddy Rogers 75.00
2 BRo,same 50.00
3 Bro,same 40.00
4 thru 9 BRo,same .... @35.00

BABE RUTH
SPORTS COMICS
Harvey Publications
April, 1949
1 BP 300.00
2 BP 200.00
3 BP,Joe Dimaggio(c) 185.00
4 BP,Bob Feller(c) 150.00
5 thru 8,BP .... @150.00
9 BP, Stan Musial(c) 125.00
11 February, 1951 .... 100.00

BANNER COMICS
Ace Magazines
September, 1941
3 B:Captain Courageous,
   Lone Warrior 600.00
4 JM(c),Flag(c) 400.00
5 .... 350.00
Becomes:
CAPTAIN COURAGEOUS
COMICS
6 I:The Sword 350.00

BARNYARD COMICS
Animated Cartoons
June, 1944
1 (fa) 80.00
2 (fa) 40.00
3 (fa) 25.00
4 (fa) 25.00
5 (fa) 25.00
6 thru 12 (fa) .... @22.00
13 FF(ti) 30.00
14 FF(ti) 30.00
15 FF(ti) 30.00
16 .... 35.00
17 FF(ti) 30.00
18 FF,FF(ti) 75.00
19 FF,FF(ti) 75.00
20 FF,FF(ti) 75.00
21 FF(ti) 30.00
22 FF,FF(ti) 75.00
23 FF(ti) 30.00
24 FF,FF(ti) 75.00
25 FF,FF(ti) 75.00
26 FF(ti) 30.00
27 FF(ti) 30.00
28 .... 20.00
29 FF(ti) 30.00
30 .... 20.00
31 .... 20.00
Becomes:
DIZZY DUCK
32 thru 39 .... @15.00

BASEBALL COMICS
Will Eisner Productions
Spring, 1949
1 A:Rube Rocky 500.00

BASEBALL HEROS
Fawcett Publications
1952
N# Babe Ruth cover 500.00

BASEBALL THRILLS
Ziff-Davis Publ. Co.
Summer 1951
10 Bob Feller Predicts Pennant
   Winners 275.00
2 BP, Yogi Berra story 200.00
3 EK, Joe DiMaggio story,
   Summer 1952 .... 250.00

BATTLEFIELD ACTION
(see DYNAMITE)

BEANY & CECIL
Dell Publishing Co.
January, 1952
1 .... 125.00
2 .... 100.00
3 .... 100.00
4 .... 100.00
5 .... 100.00

BEN BOWIE & HIS
MOUNTAIN MEN
Dell Publishing Co.
1952
(1) *see Dell Four Color #443*
(2 thru 6) *see Dell Four Color*
7 .... 15.00
8 thru 10 .... @15.00

11 I:Yellow Hair 17.00
12 .... 12.00
13 .... 12.00
14 .... 12.00
15 .... 12.00
16 .... 12.00
17 .... 12.00

BEST COMICS
Better Publications
November, 1939
1 B:Red Mask 400.00
2 A:Red Mask, Silly Willie 250.00
3 A:Red Mask 250.00
4 Cannibalism story,
   February, 1940 .... 300.00

BEWARE
(see CAPTAIN SCIENCE)

BIG CHIEF WAHOO
Eastern Color Printing
July, 1942
1 .... 250.00
2 BWa(c),Three Ring Circus . 125.00
3 BWa(c) 75.00
4 BWa(c) 75.00
5 BWa(c),Wild West Rodeo .. 75.00
6 A:Minnie-Ha-Cha 50.00
7 .... 50.00
8 .... 50.00
9 .... 50.00
10 .... 50.00
11 thru 22 .... @20.00
23 1943 .... 20.00

Big Shot #55 © Columbia Comics

BIG SHOT COMICS
Columbia Comics Group
May, 1940
1 MBi,OW,Skyman,B:The Face,
   Joe Palooka, Rocky Ryan . 1,000.00
2 MBi,OW,Marvelo cover 375.00
3 MBi,Skyman cover 300.00
4 MBi,OW,Joe Palooka cover 250.00
5 MBi,Joe Palooka cover 250.00
6 MBi,Joe Palooka cover 250.00
7 MBi,Elect Joe Palooka

---

and Skyman 225.00
8 MBi,Joe Palooka and Skyman
dress as Santa 225.00
9 MBi,Skyman 235.00
10 MBi,Skyman 235.00
11 MBi 200.00
12 MBi,OW 200.00
13 MBi,OW 200.00
14 MBi,OW,O:Sparky Watts . . . 200.00
15 MBi,OW,O:The Cloak 225.00
16 MBi,OW 150.00
17 MBi(c),OW 150.00
18 MBi,OW 150.00
19 MBi,OW,The Face cover . . . 160.00
20 MBi,OW,OW(c),Skyman cov. 160.00
21 MBi,OW,A:Raja the Arabian
Knight 125.00
22 MBi,OW,Joe Palooka cover 125.00
23 MBi,OW,Sparky Watts cover 110.00
24 MBi,OW,Uncle Sam cover . 125.00
25 MBi,OW,Sparky Watts cover 110.00
26 MBi,OW,Devildog cover . . . 125.00
27 MBi,OW,Skyman cover 130.00
28 MBi,OW,Hitler cover 150.00
29 MBi,OW,I:Captain Yank . . . 130.00
30 MBi,OW,Santa cover 110.00
31 MBi,OW,Sparky Watts cover 100.00
32 MBi,OW,B:Vic Jordan
newspaper reps 110.00
33 MBi,OW,Sparky Watts cover . 90.00
34 MBi,OW 100.00
35 MBi,OW 100.00
36 MBi,OW,Sparky Watts cover . 85.00
37 MBi,OW 100.00
38 MBi,Uncle Slap Happy cover . 85.00
39 MBi,Uncle Slap Happy cover . 85.00
40 MBi,Joe Palooka Happy cover 85.00
41 MBi,Joe Palooka 75.00
42 MBi,Joe Palooka parachutes . 75.00
43 MBi,V:Hitler 85.00
44 MBi,Slap Happy cover 75.00
45 MBi,Slap Happy cover 75.00
46 MBi,Uncle Sam cover,V:Hitler 85.00
47 MBi,Uncle Slap Happy cover . 75.00
48 MBi 75.00
49 MBi 70.00
50 MBi,O:The Face 70.00
51 MBi 60.00
52 MBi,E:Vic Jordan (Hitler cov)
newspaper reps 75.00
53 MBi,Uncle Slap Happy cover . 60.00
54 MBi,Uncle Slap Happy cover . 60.00
55 MBi,Happy Easter cover 60.00
56 MBi 60.00
57 MBi 60.00
58 MBi 60.00
59 MBi,Slap Happy 60.00
60 MBi,Joe Palooka 50.00
61 MBi 45.00
62 MBi 45.00
63 MBi 45.00
64 MBi,Slap Happy 40.00
65 MBi,Slap Happy 40.00
66 MBi,Slap Happy 40.00
67 MBi 40.00
68 MBi,Joe Palooka 40.00
69 MBi 40.00
70 MBi,OW,Joe Palooka cover . 40.00
71 MBi,OW 42.00
72 MBi,OW 42.00
73 MBi,OW,The Face cover 42.00
74 MBi,OW 42.00
75 MBi,OW,Polar Bear swim
club cover 42.00
76 thru 80 MBi,OW . . . . @35.00

81 thru 84 MBi,OW . . . . @30.00
85 MBi,OW,Dixie Dugan cover . . 32.00
86 thru 95 MBi,OW . . . . @25.00
96 MBi,OW,X-Mas cover 25.00
97 thru 99 MBi,OW . . . . @25.00
100 MBi,OW,Special issue 30.00
101 thru 103 MBi,OW . . . . . . @25.00
104 MBi, August, 1949 . . . . 30.00

BIG-3
Fox Features Syndicate
Fall 1940
1 B:Blue Beetle,Flame,Samson 900.00
2 A:Blue Beetle,Flame,Samson 450.00
3 same 325.00
4 same 300.00
5 same 300.00
6 E:Samson, bondage cover . 275.00
7 A:V-Man, January, 1942 . . . 250.00

BILL BARNES,
AMERICA'S AIR ACE
(see AIR ACE)

BILL BOYD WESTERN
Fawcett Publications
February, 1950
1 B:Bill Boyd, MidnitePh(c) . . . 275.00
2 P(c) 150.00
3 B:Ph(c) 125.00
4 . . . . 100.00
5 . . . . 100.00
6 . . . . 100.00
7 . . . . 75.00
8 . . . . 75.00
9 . . . . 75.00
10 . . . . 75.00
11 . . . . 70.00
12 . . . . 70.00
13 . . . . 70.00
14 . . . . 70.00
15 . . . . 65.00
16 . . . . 65.00
17 . . . . 65.00
18 . . . . 65.00
19 . . . . 65.00
20 . . . . 65.00
21 . . . . 65.00
22 E:Ph(c) 65.00
23 June, 1952 . . . . 75.00

BILL STERN'S
SPORTS BOOK
Approved Comics
Spring-Summer, 1951
1 Ewell Blackwell 125.00
2 . . . . 75.00
2-2 EK Giant 100.00

BILLY THE KID
ADVENTURE MAGAZINE
Toby Press
October, 1950
1 AW,FF,AW(c),FF(c) 175.00
2 Photo cover 50.00
3 AW,FF 160.00
4 . . . . 30.00
5 . . . . 30.00
6 Photo cover 30.00
7 Photo cover 30.00
8 . . . . 30.00
9 HK Pot-Shot Pete 60.00

Billy the Kid #10 © Toby Press

10 . . . . 30.00
11 . . . . 30.00
12 . . . . 30.00
13 HK 35.00
14 AW,FF 50.00
15 thru 21 . . . . @25.00
22 AW,FF 30.00
23 thru 29 . . . . @22.00
30 1955 . . . . 25.00

BINGO COMICS
Howard Publications
1945
1 . . . . 125.00

BLACK CAT COMICS
Harvey Publications
(Home Comics)
June-July, 1946
1 JKu 300.00
2 JKu,JSm(c) 150.00
3 JSm(c) 125.00
4 B:Red Demon 125.00
5 S&K 160.00
6 S&K,A:Scarlet Arrow,
O:Red Demon 160.00
7 S&K 160.00
8 S&K,B:Kerry Drake 145.00
9 S&K,O:Stuntman 175.00
10 JK,JSm 110.00
11 . . . . 110.00
12 "Ghost Town Terror" 110.00
13 thru 16 LEI . . . . @100.00
17 A:Mary Worth, Invisible
Scarlet 100.00
18 LEI 100.00
19 LEI 100.00
20 A:Invisible Scarlet 100.00
21 LEI 90.00
22 LEI 90.00
23 LEI 90.00
24 LEI 90.00
25 LEI 90.00
26 LEI 90.00
27 X-Mas issue 100.00
28 I:Kit,A:Crimson Raider 100.00
29 Black Cat bondage cover . . 120.00
Becomes:

BLACK CAT MYSTERY

30 RP,Black Cat(c)	100.00
31 RP	70.00
32 BP,RP,Bondage cover	80.00
33 BP,RP,Electrocution cover	85.00
34 BP,RP	70.00
35 BP,RP,OK	85.00
36 RP	100.00
37 RP	65.00
38 RP	65.00
39 RP	100.00
40 RP	65.00
41	65.00
42	65.00
43 BP	65.00
44 BP,HN,JkS,Oil Burning cover	85.00
45 BP,HN,Classic cover	125.00
46 BP,HN	75.00
47 BP,HN	75.00
48 BP,HN	75.00
49 BP,HN	75.00
50 BP,Rotting Face	125.00
51 BP,HN,MMe	75.00
52 BP	55.00
53 BP	55.00

Becomes:

BLACK CAT WESTERN

54 A:Black Cat & Story	75.00
55 A:Black Cat	50.00
56 same	50.00

Becomes:

BLACK CAT MYSTIC

58 JK,Starts Comic Code	65.00
59 KB	60.00
60 JK	60.00
61 HN	50.00
62	40.00
63 JK	40.00
64 JK	55.00
65 April, 1963	55.00

BLACK DIAMOND WESTERN
(see DESPERADO)

UNCLE SAM QUARTERLY
Quality Comics Group
Fall, 1941

1 BE,LF(c),JCo	1,600.00
2 LG(c),BE	650.00
3 GT,GT(c)	550.00
4 GT,GF(c)	400.00
5 RC,GT	350.00
6 thru 8 GT	@300.00

Becomes:

BLACKHAWK
Comic Magazines
Winter, 1944

9 Bait for a Death Trap	1,900.00
10 RC	700.00
11 RC	400.00
12 Flies to thrilling adventure	375.00
13 Blackhawk Stalks Danger	375.00
14 BWa	350.00
15 Patrols the Universe	350.00
16 RC,BWa,Huddles for Action	325.00
17 BWa,Prepares for Action	325.00
18 RC,RC(c),BWa,One for All and All for One	300.00
19 RC,RC(c),BWa,Calls for Action	300.00
20 RC,RC(c),BWa,Smashes	

Blackhawk #12 © Comic Magazines

Rugoth the ruthless God	300.00
21 BWa,Battles Destiny Written n Blood	250.00
22 RC,RC(c),BWa,Fear battles Death and Destruction	250.00
23 RC,RC(c),BWa,Batters Down Oppression	250.00
24 RC,RC(c),BWa	250.00
25 RC,RC(c),BWa,V:The Evil of Mung	250.00
26 RC,RC(c),V:Menace of a Sunken World	225.00
27 BWa,Destroys a War-Mad Munitions Magnate	225.00
28 BWa,Defies Destruction in the Battle of the Test Tube	225.00
29 BWa,Tale of the Basilisk Supreme Chief	225.00
30 BWa,RC,RC(c),The Menace of the Meteors	225.00
31 BWa,RC,RC(c),JCo,Treachery among the Blackhawks	185.00
32 BWa,RC,RC(c),A:Delya, Flying Fish	185.00
33 RC,RC(c),BWa, A:The Mockers	185.00
34 BWa,A:Tana,Mavis	185.00
35 BWa,I:Atlo,Strongest Man on Earth	185.00
36 RC,RC(c),BWa,V:Tarya	175.00
37 RC,RC(c),BWa,V:Sari,The Rajah of Ramastan	175.00
38 BWa	175.00
39 RC,RC(c),BWa,V:Lilith	175.00
40 RC,RC(c),BWa,Valley of Yesterday	175.00
41 RC,RC(c),BWa	135.00
42 RC,RC(c),BWa, V:Iron Emperor	135.00
43 RC,RC(c),BWa,Terror from the Catacombs	135.00
44 RC,RC(c),BWa,The King of Winds	135.00
45 BWa,The Island of Death	135.00
46 RC,RC(c),BWa,V:DeathPatrol	135.00
47 RC,RC(c),BWa,War!	135.00
48 RC,RC(c),BWa,A:Hawks of Horror,Port of Missing Ships	135.00
49 RC,RC(c),BWa,A:Valkyrie,	

Waters of Terrible Peace	135.00
50 RC,RC(c),BWa,I:Killer Shark, Flying Octopus	150.00
51 BWa,V:The Whip, Whip of Nontelon	125.00
52 RC,RC(c),BWa,Traitor in the Ranks	125.00
53 RC,RC(c),BWa,V:Golden Mummy	125.00
54 RC,RC(c),BWa,V:Dr. Deroski, Circles of Suicide	125.00
55 RC,RC(c),BWa,V:Rocketmen	125.00
56 RC,RC(c),BWa,V:The Instructor, School for Sabotage	125.00
57 RC,RC(c),BWa,Paralyzed City of Armored Men	125.00
58 RC,RC(c),BWa,V:King Cobra, The Spider of Delanza	125.00
59 BWa,V:Sea Devil	125.00
60 RC,RC(c),BWa,V:Dr. Mole and His Devils Squadron	125.00
61 V:John Smith, Stalin's Ambassador of Murder	110.00
62 V:General X, Return of Genghis Kahn	110.00
63 RC,RC(c),The Flying Buzz-Saws	110.00
64 RC,RC(c),V:Zoltan Korvas, Legion of the Damned	110.00
65 Olaf as a Prisoner in Dungeon of Fear	110.00
66 RC,RC(c),V:The Red Executioner, Crawler	110.00
67 RC,RC(c),V:Future Fuehrer	110.00
68 V:Killers of the Kremlin	100.00
69 V:King of the Iron Men, Conference of the Dictators	100.00
70 V:Killer Shark	100.00
71 V:Von Tepp, The Man Who could Defeat Blackhawk O:Blackhawk	135.00
72 V:Death Legion	100.00
73 V:Hangman,The Tyrannical Freaks	100.00
74 Plan of Death	100.00
75 V:The Mad Doctor Baroc, The Z Bomb Menace	100.00
76 The King of Blackhawk Island	100.00
77 V:The Fiendish Electronic Brain	100.00
78 V:The Killer Vulture, Phantom Raider	100.00
79 V:Herman Goering, The Human Bomb	100.00
80 V:Fang, the Merciless, Dr. Death	100.00
81 A:Killer Shark, The Sea Monsters of Killer Shark	100.00
82 V:Sabo Teur, the Ruthless Commie Agent	100.00
83 I:Hammmer & Sickle, V:Madam Double Cross	100.00
84 V:Death Eye,Dr. Genius, The Dreaded Brain Beam	100.00
85 V:The Fiendish Impersonator	100.00
86 V:The Human Torpedoes	100.00
87 A:Red Agent Sovietta,V:Sea Wolf, Le Sabre,Comics Code	80.00
88 V:Thunder the Indestructible, The Phantom Sniper	80.00
89 V:The Super Communists	80.00
90 V:The Storm King, Villainess who smashed the Blackhawk team	80.00
91 Treason in the Underground	80.00

All comics prices listed are for *Near Mint* condition. **CVA Page 267**

92 V:The World Traitor 80.00
93 V:Garg the Destroyer,
   O:Blackhawk 95.00
94 V:Black Widow, Darkk the
   Destroyer 80.00
95 V:Madam Fury, Queen of the
   Pirates 80.00
96 Doom in the Deep 80.00
97 Revolt of the Slave Workers . 80.00
98 Temple of Doom 80.00
99 The War That Never Ended . 80.00
100 The Delphian Machine 85.00
101 Satan's Paymaster 80.00
102 The Doom Cloud 80.00
103 The Super Race 80.00
104 The Jet Menace 80.00
105 The Red Kamikaze Terror . 80.00
106 The Flying Tank Platoon . . 80.00
107 The Winged Menace 80.00
   (Please see DC Listings)

BLACK HOOD
(see LAUGH COMICS)

BLACK TERROR
Better Publications/
Standard
Winter, 1942-43
1 Bombing cover 950.00
2 V:Arabs,Bondage(c) 400.00
3 V:Nazis,Bondage(c) 350.00
4 V:Sub Nazis 250.00
5 V:Japanese 250.00
6 Air Battle 200.00
7 Air Battle,V:Japanese,
   A:Ghost 200.00
8 V:Nazis 200.00
9 V:Japanese,Bondage(c) . . 225.00
10 V:Nazis 200.00
11 thru 16 . . . . @175.00
17 Bondage(c) 200.00
18 ASh 175.00
19 ASh 175.00
20 ASh 175.00
21 ASh 185.00
22 FF,ASh 150.00
23 ASh 150.00
24 Bondgae(c) 175.00
25 ASh 150.00
26 GT,ASh 150.00
27 MME,GT,ASh 150.00

BLAZING COMICS
Enwil Associates/Rural Home
June, 1944
1 B:Green Turtle, Red Hawk,
   Black Buccaneer 250.00
2 Green Turtle cover 150.00
3 Green Turtle cover 145.00
4 Green Turtle cover 145.00
5 March, 1945 . . . . 145.00
5a Black Buccaneer(c),1955 . . . 50.00
6 Indian-Japanese(c), 1955 . . . 50.00

BLONDIE COMICS
David McKay
Spring, 1947
1 . . . . 125.00
2 . . . . 55.00
3 . . . . 50.00
4 . . . . 50.00
5 . . . . 50.00
6 thru 10 . . . . @30.00

11 thru 15 . . . . @20.00
Harvey Publications
16 . . . . 25.00
17 thru 20 . . . . @15.00
21 thru 30 . . . . @12.00
31 thru 50 . . . . @10.00
51 thru 80 . . . . @7.50
81 thru 99 . . . . @6.00
100 . . . . 7.50
101 thru 124 . . . . @6.00
125 Giant 7.00
126 thru 135 . . . . @6.00
136 thru 140 . . . . @5.00
141 thru 163 . . . . @7.00
King Publications
164 thru 167 . . . . @7.00
168 thru 174 . . . . @3.00
Charlton Comics
175 thru 200 . . . . @2.00
201 thru 220 . . . . @1.50

Blue Beetle #25
© Fox Features Syndicate

BLUE BEETLE, THE
Fox Features Syndicate/
Holyoke Publ.
Winter 1939
1 O:Blue Beetle,A:Master
   Magician 2,000.00
2 . . . . 750.00
3 JSm(c) 550.00
4 Mentions marijuana 400.00
5 A:Zanzibar the Magician . . 300.00
6 B:Dynamite Thor,
   O:Blue Beetle 300.00
7 A:Dynamo 275.00
8 E:Thor,A:Dynamo 275.00
9 A:Black Bird,Gorilla 275.00
10 A:Black Bird, bondage cover 275.00
11 A:Gladiator 250.00
12 A:Black Fury 250.00
13 B:V-Man 275.00
14 JKu,I:Sparky 275.00
15 JKu 275.00
16 . . . . 225.00
17 A:Mimic 200.00
18 E:V-Man,A:Red Knight . . . 200.00
19 JKu,A:Dascomb Dinsmore . 250.00
20 I&O:The Flying Tiger

Squadron 250.00
21 . . . . 150.00
22 A:Ali-Baba 150.00
23 A:Jimmy DooLittle 150.00
24 I:The Halo 150.00
25 . . . . 150.00
26 General Patton story 175.00
27 A:Tamoa 135.00
28 . . . . 125.00
29 . . . . 125.00
30 L:Holyoke 125.00
31 F:Fox 110.00
32 Hitler cover 135.00
33 Fight for Freedom 100.00
34 A:Black Terror,Menace of K-4 85.00
35 . . . . 85.00
36 The Runaway House 85.00
37 Inside the House 85.00
38 Revolt of the Zombies 85.00
39 . . . . 85.00
40 . . . . 85.00
41 A:O'Brine Twins 80.00
42 . . . . 80.00
43 . . . . 80.00
44 . . . . 80.00
45 . . . . 80.00
46 A:Puppeteer 100.00
47 JKa,V:Junior Crime Club . . 450.00
48 JKa,A:Black Lace 325.00
49 JKa 325.00
50 JKa,The Ambitious Bride . . 315.00
51 JKa, Shady Lady 300.00
52 JKa(c),Bondage cover . . . 465.00
53 JKa,A:Jack "Legs"
   Diamond,Bondage(c) 325.00
54 JKa,The Vanishing Nude . . 600.00
55 JKa 300.00
56 JKa,Tri-State Terror 300.00
57 JKa,The Feagle Bros. 300.00
58 . . . . 75.00
59 . . . . 75.00
60 August, 1960 . . . . 75.00

BLUE BEETLE
(see THING!, THE)

BLUE BOLT
Funnies, Inc./Novelty Press/
Premium Service Co
June, 1940
1 JSm,PG,O:Blue Bolt 1,500.00
2 JSm 750.00
3 S&K,A:Space Hawk 600.00
4 PG 550.00
5 BEv,B:Sub Zero 500.00
6 JK,JSm 500.00
7 S&K,BEv 550.00
8 S&K(c) 500.00
9 . . . . 400.00
10 S&K(c) 500.00
11 BEv(c) 450.00
12 . . . . 450.00
2-1 BEv(c),PG,O:Dick Cole &
   V:Simba 150.00
2-2 BEv(c),PG 125.00
2-3 PG,Cole vs Simba 100.00
2-4 BD 100.00
2-5 I:Freezum 100.00
2-6 O:Sgt.Spook, Dick Cole . . . 90.00
2-7 BD 75.00
2-8 BD 75.00
2-9 JW 75.00
2-10 JW 75.00
2-11 JW 75.00

Blue Bolt #7
© Funnies, Inc./Novelty Press

2-12 E:Twister	75.00
3-1 A:115th Infantry	60.00
3-2 A:Phantom Sub	60.00
3-3	60.00
3-4 JW(c)	40.00
3-5 Jor	40.00
3-6 Jor	40.00
3-7 X-Mas cover	40.00
3-8	40.00
3-9 A:Phantom Sub	40.00
3-10 DBa	40.00
3-11 April Fools cover	40.00
3-12	40.00
4-1 Hitler,Tojo,Mussolini cover	65.00
4-2 Liberty Bell cover	35.00
4-3 What are You Doing for Your Country	35.00
4-4 I Fly for Vengence	35.00
4-5 TFH(c)	35.00
4-6 HcK	35.00
4-7 JWi(c)	35.00
4-8 E:Sub Zero	35.00
4-9	35.00
4-10	35.00
4-11	35.00
4-12	35.00
5-1 thru 5-12	@25.00
6-1	25.00
6-2 War Bonds (c)	30.00
6-3	20.00
6-4 Racist(c)	50.00
6-5 Soccer cover	25.00
6-6 thru 6-12	@22.00
7-1 thru 7-12	@22.00
8-1 Baseball cover	30.00
8-2 JHa	22.00
8-3 JHe	22.00
8-4 JHa	22.00
8-5 JHe	22.00
8-6 JDo	22.00
8-7 LbC(c).	25.00
8-8	22.00
8-9 AMc(c)	22.00
8-10	22.00
8-11 Basketball cover	25.00
8-12	22.00
9-1 AMc,Baseball cover	25.00
9-2 AMc	22.00

9-3	22.00
9-4 JHe	22.00
9-5 JHe	22.00
9-6 LbC(c),Football cover	25.00
9-7 JHe	22.00
9-8 Hockey cover	30.00
9-9 LbC(c),3-D effect	24.00
9-10	24.00
9-11	24.00
9-12	24.00
10-1 Baseball cover,3-D effect	30.00
10-2 3-D effect	24.00

Star Publications

102 LbC(c),Cameleon	150.00
103 LbC(c),same	125.00
104 LbC(c),same	125.00
105 LbC(c),O:Blue Bolt Space, Drug Story	250.00
106 S&K,LbC(c),A;Space Hawk	200.00
107 S&K,LbC(c),A;Space Hawk	200.00
108 S&K,LbC(c),A:Blue Bolt	200.00
109 BW,LbC(c)	200.00
110 B:Horror covers,A:Target	200.00
111 Weird Tales of Horror, A:Red Rocket	175.00
112 JyD,WiP	190.00
113 BW,JyD,A:Space Hawk	175.00
114 LbC(c),JyD	175.00
115 LbC(c),JyD,A:Sgt.Spook	225.00
116 LbC(c),JyD,A:Jungle Joe	175.00
117 LbC(c),A:Blue Bolt,Jo-Jo	175.00
118 WW,LbC(c),A:White Spirit	200.00
119 LbC(c)	175.00

Becomes:

GHOSTLY WEIRD STORIES
Star Publications
September, 1953

120 LbC,A:Jo-Jo	150.00
121 LbC,A:Jo-Jo	125.00
122 LbC,A:The Mask	125.00
123 LbC,A:Jo-Jo	125.00
124 LbC, September, 1954	125.00

BLUE CIRCLE COMICS
Enwil Associates/Rural Home
June, 1944

1 B:Blue Circle,O:Steel Fist	135.00
2	90.00
3 Hitler parody cover	110.00
4	55.00
5 E:Steel Fist,A:Driftwood Davey	55.00
6	45.00

BLUE RIBBON COMICS
MLJ Magazines
November, 1939

1 JCo,B:Dan Hastings, Richy-Amazing Boy	1,700.00
2 JCo,B:Bob Phantom, Silver Fox	650.00
3 JCo,A:Phantom,Silver Fox	450.00
4 O:Fox,Ty Gor,B:Doc Strong, Hercules	500.00
5 Gattling Gun cover	325.00
6 Amazing Boy Richy cover	300.00
7 A:Fox cover,Corporal Collins V:Nazis	300.00
8 E:Hercules	300.00
9 O&I:Mr. Justice	1,200.00
10 Mr. Justice cover	550.00
11 SCp(c)	550.00
12 E:Doc Strong	550.00

13 B:Inferno	550.00
14 A:Inferno	475.00
15 A:Inferno,E:Green Falcon	475.00
16 O:Captain Flag	850.00
17 Captain Flag V:Black Hand	500.00
18 Captain Flag-Black Hand	450.00
19 Captain Flag cover	425.00
20 Captain Flag V:Nazis cover	425.00
21 Captain Flag V:Death	400.00
22 Circus Cover, March, 1942	400.00

BLUE RIBBON COMICS
St. John Publications
February, 1949

1 Heckle & Jeckle	40.00
2 MB(c),Diary Secrets	55.00
3 MB,MB(c),Heckle & Jeckle	35.00
4 Teen-age Diary Secrets	55.00
5 MB,Teen-age Diary Secrets	65.00
6 Dinky Duck	12.00

BO
Charlton Comics
June, 1955

1	35.00
2	30.00
3 October, 1955	30.00

BOB COLT
Fawcett Publications
November, 1950

1 B:Bob Colt,Buck Skin	250.00
2 Death Round Train	150.00
3 Mysterious Black Knight of the Prairie	125.00
4 Death Goes Downstream	125.00
5 The Mesa of Mystery	125.00
6 The Mysterious Visitors	125.00
7 Dragon of Disaster	100.00
8 Redman's Revenge	100.00
9 Hidden Hacienda	100.00
10 Fiend from Vulture Mountain	100.00

BOLD STORIES
Kirby Publishing Co.
March, 1950

1 WW,Near nudity cover	400.00
2 GI,Cobra's Kiss	300.00
3 WW,Orge of Paris,July, 1950	350.00
4 Case of the Winking Buddha	125.00
5 It Rhymes with Lust	125.00
6 Candid Tales, April 1950	125.00

BOMBER COMICS
Elliot Publishing Co.
March, 1944

1 B:Wonder Boy,Kismet, Eagle Evans	225.00
2 Wonder Boy cover	150.00
3 Wonder Boy-Kismet cover	150.00
4 Hitler,Tojo, Mussolini cover	175.00

BOOK OF ALL COMICS
William H. Wise
1945

1 A:Green Mask,Puppeteer	200.00

BOOK OF COMICS, THE
William H. Wise
1945

N# A:Captain V	200.00

All comics prices listed are for _Near Mint_ condition.

BOY COMICS
Comic House, Inc.
(Lev Gleason Publ.)
April, 1942

3 O:Crimebuster,Bombshell,Young
Robin, B:Yankee Longago,
Swoop Storm 1,500.00
4 Hitler,Tojo,Mussolini cover . 550.00
5 Crimebuster saves day cover 450.00
6 O:Iron Jaw & Death of Son,
B:Little Dynamite 1,000.00
7 Hitler,Tojo,Mussolini cover . 350.00

Boy Comics #8 © Lev Gleason Publ.

8 D:Iron Jaw 400.00
9 I:He-She 350.00
10 Iron Jaw returns 600.00
11 Iron Jaw falls in love ... 275.00
12 Crimebuster V:Japanese ... 275.00
13 V:New,more terrible
Iron Jaw 275.00
14 V:Iron Jaw 275.00
15 I:Rodent,D:Iron Jaw ... 300.00
16 Crimebuster V:Knight 180.00
17 Flag cover,Crimebuster
V:Moth 185.00
18 Smashed car cover 175.00
19 Express train cover 175.00
20 Coffin cover 175.00
21 Boxing cover 125.00
22 Under Sea cover 125.00
23 Golf cover 125.00
24 County insane asylum cover 125.00
25 52 pgs 125.00
26 68 pgs 125.00
27 Express train cover 135.00
28 E:Yankee Longago 135.00
29 Prison break cover 135.00
30 O:Crimebuster,Murder cover 165.00
31 68 pgs 125.00
32 E:Young Robin Hood 125.00
33 .... 125.00
34 Suicide cover & story 100.00
35 .... 85.00
36 .... 85.00
37 .... 85.00
38 .... 85.00
39 E:Little Dynamite 85.00
40 .... 85.00
41 thru 50 .... @75.00

51 thru 56 .... @65.00
57 B:Dilly Duncan 70.00
58 .... 60.00
59 .... 60.00
60 Iron Jaw returns 75.00
61 O:Iron Jaw,Crimebuster 80.00
62 A:Iron Jaw 75.00
63 thru 70 .... @60.00
71 E:Dilly Duncan 60.00
72 .... 60.00
73 .... 60.00
74 thru 79 .... @50.00
80 I:Rocky X 50.00
81 thru 88 .... @50.00
89 A:The Claw 55.00
90 same 55.00
91 same 55.00
92 same 55.00
93 The Claw(c),A:Rocky X 60.00
94 .... 40.00
95 .... 40.00
96 .... 40.00
97 .... 40.00
98 A:Rocky X 50.00
99 .... 40.00
100 .... 50.00
101 thru 118 .... @50.00
119 March, 1956 .... 50.00

BOY EXPLORERS
(see TERRY AND
THE PIRATES)

Brenda Starr #14
© Four Star Comics Corp.

BRENDA STARR
Four Star Comics Corp./
Superior Comics Ltd.
September, 1947

13(1) 400.00
14(2) JKa,Bondage cover 385.00
2-3 .... 300.00
2-4 JKa,Operating table cover . 350.00
2-5 Swimsuit cover 275.00
2-6 .... 275.00
2-7 .... 275.00
2-8 Cosmetic cover 275.00
2-9 Giant Starr cover 275.00
2-10 Wedding cover 275.00

2-11 .... 275.00
2-12 .... 275.00

BRICK BRADFORD
Best Books
(Standard Comics)
July, 1949

5 .... 85.00
6 Robot cover 65.00
7 AS 60.00
8 .... 60.00

BROADWAY ROMANCES
Quality Comics Group
January, 1950

1 PG,BWa&(c) 175.00
2 BWa,Glittering Desire 100.00
3 BL,Stole My Love 45.00
4 Enslaved by My Past 50.00
5 Flame of Passion,Sept.,1950 . 50.00

Bronco Bill #2 © Standard Comics

BRONCHO BILL
Visual Editions
(Standard Comics)
January, 1948

5 .... 55.00
6 AS(c) 35.00
7 AS(c) 28.00
8 ASh 28.00
9 AS(c) 28.00
10 AS(c) 28.00
11 AS(c) 22.00
12 AS(c) 22.00
13 AS(c) 22.00
14 ASh 22.00
15 ASh 22.00
16 AS(c) 22.00

BRUCE GENTRY
Four Star Publ./
Visual Editions/
Superior
January, 1948

1 B:Ray Bailey reprints 200.00
2 Plane crash cover 150.00
3 E:Ray Bailey reprints 135.00
4 Tiger attack cover 100.00

5 . . . . 100.00	
6 Help message cover 100.00	
7 . . . . 100.00	
8 End of Marriage cover,	
July, 1949 . . . . 100.00	

BUCCANEERS
(see KID ETERNITY)

BUCK JONES
Dell Publishing Co.
October, 1950

1 . . . . 120.00
2 . . . . 55.00
3 . . . . 40.00
4 . . . . 40.00
5 . . . . 40.00
6 . . . . 40.00
7 and 8 . . . . @40.00

Buck Rogers #3
© Eastern Color Printing

BUCK ROGERS
Eastern Color Printing
Winter 1940

1 Partial Painted(c) 1,600.00
2 . . . . 850.00
3 Living Corpse from Crimson
Coffin 700.00
4 One man army of greased
lightning 600.00
5 Sky Roads 650.00
6 September, 1943 . . . . 650.00
Toby Press
100 Flying Saucers 150.00
101 . . . . 125.00
9 . . . . 125.00

BUG MOVIES
Dell Publishing Co.
1931

1 . . . . 100.00

BUGS BUNNY
DELL GIANT EDITIONS
Dell Publishing Co.
Christmas

1 Christmas Funnies (1950) . . 250.00
2 Christmas Funnies (1951) . . 175.00
3 Christmas Funnies (1952) . . 150.00
4 Christmas Funnies (1953) . . 150.00
5 Christmas Funnies (1954) . . 150.00
6 Christmas Party (1955) 125.00
7 Christmas Party (1956) 135.00
8 Christmas Funnies (1957) . . 135.00
9 Christmas Funnies (1958) . . 135.00
1 County Fair (1957) 175.00
Halloween
1 Halloween Parade (1953) . . 175.00
2 Halloween Parade (1954) . . 150.00
3 Trick 'N' Treat
Halloween Fun (1955) 160.00
4 Trick 'N' Treat
Halloween Fun (1956) 155.00
Vacation
1 Vacation Funnies (1951) . . . 250.00
2 Vacation Funnies (1952) . . . 225.00
3 Vacation Funnies (1953) . . . 175.00
4 Vacation Funnies (1954) . . . 150.00
5 Vacation Funnies (1955) . . . 150.00
6 Vacation Funnies (1956) . . . 135.00
7 Vacation Funnies (1957) . . . 135.00
8 Vacation Funnies (1958) . . . 135.00
9 Vacation Funnies (1959) . . . 135.00

Bugs Bunny #8 © Dell Publishing Co.

BUGS BUNNY
Dell Publishing Co.
1942
see Four Color for early years

28 thru 30 . . . . @20.00
31 thru 50 . . . . @15.00
51 thru 70 . . . . @12.00
71 thru 85 . . . . @10.00
86 Giant-Show Time 50.00
87 thru 100 . . . . @7.00
101 thru 120 . . . . @5.00
121 thru 140 . . . . @4.00
141 thru 190 . . . . @3.00
191 thru 245 . . . . @2.00

BULLETMAN
Fawcett Publications
Summer, 1941

1 I:Bulletman & Bulletgirl . . . 1,700.00
2 MRa(c) 800.00

3 MRa(c) 550.00
4 V:Headless Horror,
Guillotine cover 500.00
5 Riddle of Dr. Riddle 450.00
6 V:Japanese 400.00
7 V:Revenge Syndicate 375.00
8 V:Mr. Ego 350.00
9 V:Canine Criminals 350.00
10 I:Bullet Dog 375.00

Bulletman #7 © Fawcett Publications

11 V:Fiendish Fiddler 350.00
12 . . . . 325.00
13 . . . . 325.00
14 V:Death the Comedian 325.00
15 V:Professor D 325.00
16 VanishingElephant,Fall 1946 325.00

BUSTER CRABBE
Lev Gleason Pub.
1953

1 Ph(c) 100.00
2 ATh 125.00
3 ATh 125.00
4 F. Gordon(c) 100.00

BUSTER CRABBE
Famous Funnies
November, 1951

1 The Arrow of Death 180.00
2 AW&GE(c) 200.00
3 AW&GE(c) 225.00
4 FF(c) 250.00
5 AW,FF,FF,(c) 700.00
6 Sharks cover 60.00
7 FF 60.00
8 Gorilla cover 60.00
9 FF 60.00
10 . . . . 60.00
11 Snakes cover 50.00
12 September, 1953 . . . . 50.00

BUZ SAWYER
Standard Comics
June, 1948

1 . . . . 120.00
2 I:Sweeney 75.00
3 . . . . 50.00
4 . . . . 50.00
5 June, 1949 . . . . 50.00

CALLING ALL BOYS
Parents Magazine Institute
January, 1946

1 Skiing	50.00
2	30.00
3 Peril Out Post	25.00
4 Model Airplane	25.00
5 Fishing	25.00
6 Swimming	25.00
7 Baseball	25.00
8 School	25.00
9 The Miracle Quarterback	25.00
10 Gary Cooper cover	30.00
11 Rin-Tin-Tin cover	25.00
12 Bob Hope cover	40.00
13 Bing Cosby cover	30.00
14 J. Edgar Hoover cover	25.00
15 Tex Granger cover	18.00
16	18.00
17 Tex Granger cover, May, 1948	18.00

Becomes:

TEX GRANGER

18 Bandits of the Badlands	55.00
19 The Seven Secret Cities	45.00
20 Davey Crockett's Last Fight	35.00
21 Canyon Ambush	35.00
22 V:Hooded Terror	35.00
23 V:Billy the Kid	35.00
24 A:Hector, September, 1949	40.00

CALLING ALL GIRLS
Parent Magazine Press, Inc.
September, 1941

1	65.00
2 Virginia Weidler cover	30.00
3 Shirley Temple cover	50.00
4 Darla Hood cover	25.00
5 Gloria Hood cover	25.00
6	18.00
7	18.00
8	18.00
9 Flag cover	20.00
10	18.00
11 thru 20	@15.00
21 thru 39	@10.00
40 Liz Taylor	45.00
41	7.00
42	7.00
43 October, 1945	7.00

CALLING ALL KIDS
Quality Comics, Inc.
December/January, 1946

1 Funny Animal stories	25.00
2	18.00
3	12.00
4	10.00
5	10.00
6	10.00
7	10.00
8	10.00
9	10.00
10	10.00
11 thru 25	@6.00
26 August, 1949	6.00

CAMERA COMICS
U.S. Camera Publishing Corp.
July-September, 1944

1 Airfighter,Grey Comet	125.00
2 How to Set Up a Darkroom	75.00
3 Linda Lens V:Nazi cover	80.00
4 Linda Lens cover	60.00

5 Diving cover	60.00
6 Jim Lane cover	60.00
7 Linda Lens cover	60.00
8 Linda Lens cover	60.00
9 Summer, 1946	60.00

CAMP COMICS
Dell Publishing Co.
February, 1942

1 Ph(c),WK,A:Bugs Bunny	350.00
2 Ph(c),WK,A:Bugs Bunny	250.00
3 Ph(c),Wk	350.00

CAPTAIN AERO COMICS
Holyoke Publishing Co.
December, 1941

1 B:Flag-Man&Solar,Master of Magic Captain Aero, Captain Stone	650.00
2 A:Pals of Freedom	350.00
3 JKu,B:Alias X,A:Pals of Freedom	350.00
4 JKu,O:Gargoyle, Parachute jump	350.00
5 JKu	275.00
6 JKu,Flagman,A:Miss Victory	275.00
7 Alias X	175.00
8 O:Red Cross,A:Miss Victory	175.00
9 A:Miss Victory,Alias X	150.00
10 A:Miss Victory,Red Cross	100.00
11 A:Miss Victory	75.00
12 same	75.00
13 same	75.00
14 same	75.00
15 AS(c),A:Miss Liberty	75.00
16 AS(c),Leather Face	60.00
17 LbC(c)	60.00
21 LbC(c)	75.00
22 LbC(c),I:Mighty Mite	75.00
23 LbC(c)	75.00
24 American Planes Dive Bombs Japan	80.00
25 LbC(c),Science Fiction(c)	100.00
26 LbC(c)	85.00

CAPTAIN BATTLE
New Friday Publ./
Magazine Press
Summer, 1941

1 B:Captain Battle,O:Blackout	650.00
2 Pirate Ship cover	450.00
3 Dungeon cover	375.00
4	275.00
5 V:Japanese, Summer, 1943	250.00

CAPTAIN BATTLE, Jr.
Comic House
Fall, 1943

1 Claw V:Ghost, A:Sniffer	500.00
2 Man who didn't believe in Ghosts	425.00

CAPTAIN COURAGEOUS
(see BANNER COMICS)

CAPTAIN EASY
Standard Comics
1939

N# Swash Buckler	550.00
10	50.00
11	35.00
12	35.00

13 ASh(c)	35.00
14	35.00
15	35.00
16 ASh(c)	35.00
17 September, 1949	35.00

CAPTAIN FEARLESS COMICS
Helnit Publishing Co.
August, 1941

1 O:Mr. Miracle,A:X,Captain Fearless Citizen Smith, A:Miss Victory	400.00
2 A:Border Patrol, September, 1941	250.00

CAPTAIN FLASH
Sterling Comics
November, 1954

1 O:Captain Flash	150.00
2 V:Black Knight	90.00
3 Beasts from 1,000,000 BC	90.00
4 Flying Saucer Invasion	90.00

CAPTAIN FLEET
Approved Comics
Fall, 1952

1 Storm and Mutiny ...Typhoon	75.00

CAPTAIN FLIGHT COMICS
Four Star Publications
March, 1944

N# B:Captain Flight,Ace Reynolds Dash theAvenger,Professor X	
2	85.00
3	75.00
4 B:Rock Raymond Salutes America's Wartime Heroines	80.00
5 Bondage cover,B:Red Rocket A:The Grenade	100.00
6 Girl tied at the stake	75.00
7 Dog Fight cover	70.00
8 B:Yankee Girl,A:Torpedoman	110.00
9 Dog Fight cover	100.00
10 Bondage cover	120.00
11 LBc(c),Future(c), Feb-March, 1947	110.00

CAPTAIN GALLANT
Charlton Comics
1955

1 Ph(c),Buster Crabbe	55.00
2 and 3	@45.00
4 September, 1956	45.00

CAPTAIN JET
Four Star Publ.
May, 1952

1 Factory bombing cover	75.00
2 Parachute jump cover	50.00
3 Tank bombing cover	30.00
4 Parachute cover	30.00
5	30.00

CAPTAIN KIDD
(see ALL GREAT COMICS)

CAPTAIN MARVEL ADVENTURES
Fawcett Publications
Spring, 1941

N# JK, B:Captain Marvel &
    Sivana 20,000.00
2 GT,JK(c),Billy Batson (c) . . 2,400.00
3 JK(c),Thunderbolt (c) 1,500.00
4 Shazam(c) 900.00
5 V:Nazis 650.00
6 Solomon, Hercules, Atlas, Zeus,
    Achilles & Mercury cover . . 500.00
7 Ghost of the White Room . . 425.00
8 Forward America 425.00
9 A:Ibac the Monster, Nippo
    the Nipponese, Relm of
    the Subconscious 425.00
10 V:Japanese 425.00
11 V:Japanese and Nazis . . . 375.00
12 Joins the Army 375.00
13 V:Diamond-Eyed Idol of
    Doom 375.00
14 Nippo meets his Nemesis . . 375.00
15 Big "Paste the Axis" contest 375.00
16 Uncle Sam cover, Paste
    the Axis 375.00
17 P(c), Paste the Axis 350.00
18 P(c), O:Mary Marvel 600.00
19 Mary Marvel & Santa cover . 350.00
20 Mark of the Black
    Swastika 2,400.00
21 Hitler cover 2,300.00
22 B:Mr. Mind serial,
    Shipyard Sabotage 500.00
23 A:Steamboat 325.00
24 Minneapolis Mystery 325.00
25 Sinister Faces cover 325.00
26 Flag cover 325.00
27 Joins Navy 260.00
28 Uncle Sam cover 275.00
29 Battle at the China Wall . . . 250.00
30 Modern Robinson Crusoe . 250.00
31 Fights his own Conscience . 250.00
32 V:Mole Men, Dallas 250.00
33 Mt. Rushmore parody
    cover, Omaha 240.00
34 Oklahoma City 240.00
35 O:Radar the International

Captain Marvel #17
© Fawcett Publications

Policeman, Indianapolis . . . 200.00
36 Missing face contest,
    St. Louis 200.00
37 V:Block Busting Bubbles,

Cincinnati 200.00
38 V:Chattanooga Ghost,
    Rock Garden City 200.00
39 V:Mr. Mind's Death Ray,
    Pittsburgh 200.00
40 V:Ghost of the Tower, Boston 200.00
41 Runs for President, Dayton . 175.00
42 Christmas special, St. Paul . 175.00
43 V:Mr. Mind,I:Uncle Marvel,
    Chicago 175.00
44 OtherWorlds,Washington,D.C. 175.00
45 V:Blood Bank Robbers 175.00
46 E: Mr. Mind Serial, Tall
    Stories of Jonah Joggins . . . 175.00
47 . . . . 160.00
48 Signs Autographs cover . . . 150.00
49 V: An Unknown Killer 150.00
50 Twisted Powers 150.00
51 Last of the Batsons 125.00
52 O&I:Sivana Jr.,V:Giant
    Earth Dreamer 150.00
53 Gets promoted 125.00
54 Marooned in the Future,
    Kansas City 150.00
55 Endless String, Columbus . . 125.00
56 Goes Crazy, Mobile 125.00
57 A:Haunted Girl, Rochester . 125.00
58 V:Sivana 125.00
59 . . . . 125.00
60 Man who made Earthquakes 125.00
61 I&V: Oggar, the Worlds
    Mightiest Immortal 150.00
62 The Great Harness Race . . 125.00
63 Stuntman 125.00
64 . . . . 125.00
65 V:Invaders from Outer Space 125.00
66 Atomic War cover 150.00
67 Hartford 125.00
68 Scenes from the Past,
    Baltimore 125.00
69 Gets Knighted 125.00
70 Horror in the Box 125.00
71 Wheel of Death 125.00
72 . . . . 125.00
73 Becomes a Petrophile 125.00
74 Who is the 13th Guest 125.00
75 V:Astonishing Yeast Menace 125.00
76 A:Atom Ambassador 125.00
77 The Secret Life 125.00
78 O:Mr. Tawny 150.00
79 O:Atom,A:World's Worst
    Actor 175.00
80 Twice told story 250.00
81 A:Mr. Atom 100.00
82 A:Mr. Tawny 100.00
83 Indian Chief 100.00
84 V:Surrealist Imp 100.00
85 Freedom Train 135.00
86 A:Mr. Tawny 100.00
87 V:Electron Thief 100.00
88 Billy Batson's Boyhood 100.00
89 V:Sivana 100.00
90 A:Mr. Tawny 100.00
91 A:Chameleon Stone 100.00
92 The Land of Limbo 100.00
93 Book of all Knowledge 100.00
94 Battle of Electricity 100.00
95 The Great Ice Cap 100.00
96 V:Automatic Weapon 100.00
97 Wiped Out 100.00
98 United Worlds 100.00
99 Rain of Terror 100.00
100 V:Sivana,Plot against
    the Universe 225.00
101 Invisibility Trap 100.00

102 Magic Mix-up 100.00
103 Ice Covered World of
    1,000,000 AD 100.00
104 Mr. Tawny's Masquerade . 100.00
105 The Dog Catcher 100.00
106 V:Menace of the Moon . . . 100.00
107 V:Space Hunter 100.00
108 V:Terrible Termites 100.00
109 The Invention Inventor . . . 100.00
110 V:Sivana 100.00
111 The Eighth Sea 100.00
112 . . . . 100.00
113 Captain Marvel's Feud . . . 100.00
114 V:The Ogre 100.00
115 . . . . 100.00
116 Flying Saucer 110.00
117 . . . . 90.00
118 V:Weird Water Man 100.00
119 . . . . 100.00
120 . . . . 100.00
121 . . . . 100.00
122 . . . . 100.00
123 . . . . 100.00
124 V:Discarded Instincts 100.00
125 V:Ancient Villain 100.00
126 . . . . 100.00
127 . . . . 100.00
128 . . . . 100.00
129 . . . . 100.00
130 . . . . 100.00
131 . . . . 100.00
132 V:Flood 100.00
133 . . . . 100.00
134 . . . . 100.00
135 Perplexing Past Puzzle . . . 100.00
136 . . . . 100.00
137 . . . . 100.00
138 V:Haunted Horror 100.00
139 . . . . 100.00
140 Hand of Horror 100.00
141 Horror 100.00
142 . . . . 100.00
143 Great Stone Face
    on the Moon 100.00
144 . . . . 100.00
145 . . . . 100.00
146 . . . . 100.00
147 . . . . 100.00
148 V:The World 100.00
149 . . . . 100.00
150 Captains Marvel's Wedding,
    November, 1953 . . . . 150.00

CAPTAIN MARVEL JR.
Fawcett Publications
November, 1952

1 O:Captain Marvel, Jr.,
    A:Capt. Nazi 1,900.00
2 O:Capt.Nippon,V:Capt. Nazi 900.00
3 Parade to Excitement 600.00
4 V:Invisible Nazi 550.00
5 V:Capt. Nazi 500.00
6 Adventure of Sabbac 450.00
7 City under the Sea 450.00
8 Dangerous Double 375.00
9 Independence cover 375.00
10 Hitler cover 400.00
11 . . . . 300.00
12 Scuttles the Axis Isle in the
    Sky 350.00
13 V:The Axis,Hitler,cover 325.00
14 X-Mas cover, Santa wears
    Capt. Marvel uniform 350.00
15 . . . . 250.00
16 A:Capt. Marvel, Sivana, Pogo 275.00

Captain Marvel Jr. #12
© Fawcett Publications

17 Meets his Future self 275.00
18 V:Birds of Doom 275.00
19 A:Capt. Nazi & Capt. Nippon 300.00
20 Goes on the Warpath 275.00
21 Buy War Stamps 200.00
22 Rides World's oldest
    steamboat 200.00
23 . . . . 200.00
24 V:Weather Man 200.00
25 Flag cover 200.00
26 Happy New Year 200.00
27 Jungle Thrills 200.00
28 V:Sivana's Crumbling Crimes 200.00
29 Blazes a Wilderness Trail . . 200.00
30 . . . . 200.00
31 . . . . 150.00
32 Keeper of the Lonely Rock . 150.00
33 . . . . 150.00
34/35 I&O:Sivana Jr. 150.00
36 Underworld Tournament . . . 150.00
37 FreddyFreeman'sNews-stand 150.00
38 A:Arabian Knight 150.00
39 V:Sivana Jr., Headline
    Stealer 150.00
40 Faces Grave Situation 150.00
41 I:The Acrobat 110.00
42 V:Sivana Jr. 110.00
43 V:Beasts on Broadway 110.00
44 Key to the Mystery 110.00
45 A:Icy Fingers 110.00
46 . . . . 110.00
47 V:Giant of the Beanstalk . . 110.00
48 Whale of a Fish Story 110.00
49 V:Dream Recorder 110.00
50 Wanted: Freddy Freeman . 110.00
51 The Island Riddle 100.00
52 A:Flying Postman 100.00
53 Atomic Bomb on the Loose . 125.00
54 V:Man with 100 Heads 100.00
55 Pyramid of Eternity 100.00
56 Blue Boy's Black Eye 100.00
57 Magic Ladder 100.00
58 Amazing Mirror Maze 100.00
59 . . . . 100.00
60 V:Space Menace 100.00
61 V:Himself 90.00
62 . . . . 90.00
63 V:Witch of Winter 90.00

64 thru 70 . . . . @90.00
71 thru 74 . . . . @80.00
75 V:Outlaw of Crooked Creek . 80.00
76 thru 85 . . . . @80.00
86 Defenders of time 80.00
87 thru 89 . . . . @80.00
90 The Magic Trunk 75.00
91 thru 99 . . . . @75.00
100 V:Sivana Jr 80.00
101 thru 106 . . . . @75.00
107 The Horror Dimension 75.00
108 thru 118 . . . . @75.00
119 Condemned to Die,
    June, 1953 . . . . 75.00

CAPTAIN MIDNIGHT
Fawcett Publications
September, 1942

1 O:Captain Midnight,
    Capt. Marvel cover 1,500.00
2 Smashes Jap Juggernaut . . 700.00
3 Battles the Phantom Bomber 500.00
4 Grapples the Gremlins 450.00
5 Double Trouble in Tokyo . . 450.00
6 Blasts the Black Mikado . . . 350.00
7 Newspaper headline cover . 350.00
8 Flying Torpedoes
    Berlin-Bound 350.00
9 MRa(c), Subs in Mississippi 350.00
10 MRa(c), Flag cover 350.00
11 MRa(c), Murder in Mexico . 275.00

Captain Midnight #1
© Fawcett Publications

12 V:Sinister Angels 275.00
13 Non-stop Flight around
    the World 275.00
14 V:King of the Villains 275.00
15 V:Kimberley Killer 275.00
16 Hitler's Fortress Breached . 275.00
17 MRa(c), Hello Adolf 250.00
18 Death from the Skies 250.00
19 Hour of Doom for the Axis . 250.00
20 Brain and Brawn against Axis 250.00
21 Trades with Japanese 200.00
22 Plea for War Stamps 200.00
23 Japanese Prison cover 200.00
24 Rising Sun Flag cover 225.00
25 Amusement Park Murder . . 200.00
26 Hotel of Horror 200.00

27 Death Knell for Tyranny . . . 200.00
28 Gliderchuting to Glory 200.00
29 Bomb over Nippon 200.00
30 . . . . 200.00
31 . . . . 150.00
32 . . . . 150.00
33 V:Shark 150.00
34 . . . . 150.00
35 thru 40 . . . . @135.00
41 thru 50 . . . . @125.00
51 thru 63 . . . . @125.00
64 V:XOG, Ruler of Saturn . . 125.00
65 . . . . 125.00
66 V:XOG 125.00
67 Fall, 1948 . . . . 125.00
Becomes:
SWEET HEART
68 Robert Mitchum 65.00
69 thru 118 . . . . @20.00
111 Ronald Reagan story 30.00
119 Marilyn Monroe 150.00
120 Atomic Bomb story . . . . . @35.00
121 . . . . 15.00
122 1954 . . . . 12.00

CAPTAIN SCIENCE
Youthful Magazines
November, 1950

1 WW,O:Captain Science,
    V:Monster God of Rogor . . . 450.00
2 WW,V:Cat Men of Phoebus,
    Space Pirates 225.00
3 Ghosts from the Underworld 275.00
4 WW,Vampires 275.00
5 WW,V:Shark Pirates of Pisces 275.00
6 WW,V:Invisible Tyrants,
    bondage cover 400.00
7 WW,Bondage cover,
    December, 1951 . . . . 400.00
Becomes:
FANTASTIC
8 Isle of Madness 145.00
9 Octopus cover 90.00
Becomes:
BEWARE
10 SHn,Doll of Death 150.00
11 SHn,Horror Head 125.00
12 SHn,Body Snatchers 125.00
Becomes:
CHILLING TALES
13 MF,Screaming Skull 200.00
14 SHn,Smell of Death 125.00
15 SHn,Curse of the Tomb . . . 150.00
16 HcK,Mark of the Beast
    Bondage(c) 125.00
17 MFc(c),Wandering Willie,
    Oct.,1953 . . . . 150.00

CAPTAIN STEVE SAVAGE
[1st Series]
Avon Periodicals
1950

N# WW 250.00
2 EK(c),The Death Gamble . . 100.00
3 EK(c),Crash Landing in
    Manchuria 35.00
4 EK(c),V:Red Raiders from
    Siang-Po 35.00
5 EK(c),Rockets of Death 35.00
6 Operation Destruction 30.00
7 EK(c),Flight to Kill 30.00
8 EK(c),V:Red Mystery Jet . . . 30.00

9 EK(c) 30.00
10 .... 30.00
11 EK(c) 35.00
12 WW 70.00
13 .... 40.00
[2nd Series]
September/October, 1954
5 .... 35.00
6 WW 50.00
7 thru 13 .... @20.00

CAPTAIN VIDEO
Fawcett Publications
February, 1951
1 GE,Ph(c) 450.00
2 Time when Men could not
    Walk 325.00
3 GE,Indestructible Antagonist 275.00
4 GE,School of Spies 275.00
5 GE,Missiles of Doom,
    Photo cover 275.00
6 GE,Island of Conquerors,
    Photo cover; Dec. 1951 ... 275.00

CASPER, THE
FRIENDLY GHOST
St. John Publishing
September, 1949
1 O:Baby Huey 550.00
2 .... 350.00
3 .... 300.00
4 .... 250.00
5 .... 250.00
Harvey Publications
7 .... 200.00
8 thru 9 .... @100.00
10 I:Spooky 150.00
11 A:Spooky 100.00
12 thru 18 .... @75.00
19 I:Nightmare 85.00
20 I:Wendy the Witch 85.00
21 thru 30 .... @50.00
31 thru 40 .... @40.00
41 thru 50 .... @30.00
51 thru 60 .... @25.00
61 thru 69 .... @20.00
70 July, 1958 .... 22.00

CAT MAN COMICS
Helnit Publ. Co./
Holyoke Publ. Co./
Continental Magazine
May, 1941
1 O:Deacon&Sidekick Mickey,
    Dr. Diamond & Ragman,A:Black
    Widow, B:Blaze Baylor ... 1,200.00
2 Ragman 500.00
3 B:Pied Piper 325.00
4 CQ 300.00
5 I&O: The Kitten 275.00
6 CQ 250.00
7 CQ 250.00
8 JKa, I:Volton 325.00
9 JKa 250.00
10 JKa,O:Blackout,
    B:Phantom Falcon 225.00
11 JKa,DRi,BF 235.00
12 .... 175.00
13 .... 175.00
14 CQ 175.00
15 Rajah of Destruction 175.00
16 Bye-Bye Axis 200.00
17 Buy Bonds and Stamps ... 175.00

Cat Man Comics #9
© Helnit Publ. Co./Holyoke Publ. Co.

18 Buy Bonds and Stamps ... 175.00
19 CQ,Hitler,Tojo and
    Mussolini cover 200.00
20 CQ,Hitler,Tojo and
    Mussolini cover 200.00
21 CQ 175.00
22 CQ 175.00
23 CQ 175.00
N# V:Japanese,Bondage(c) 185.00
N# V:Demon 175.00
N# A:Leather Face 175.00
27 LbC(c),Flag cover,O:Kitten . 200.00
28 LbC(c),Horror cover 225.00
29 LbC(c),BF 225.00
30 LbC(c),Bondage(c) 235.00
31 LbC(c) 225.00
32 August, 1946 .... 225.00

CHALLENGER, THE
Interfaith Publications
1945

Chamber of Chills #23
© Harvey Publications

N# O:The Challenger Club .. 165.00
2 JKa 150.00
3 JKa 150.00
4 JKa,BF 150.00

CHAMBER OF CHILLS
Harvey Publications/
Witches Tales
June, 1951
21 .... 200.00
22 .... 100.00
23 Eyes Ripped Out 100.00
24 Bondage cover 110.00
5 Shrunken Skull,
    Operation Monster 120.00
6 Seven Skulls of Magondi .. 100.00
7 Pit of the Damned 100.00
8 Formula for Death 100.00
9 Bondage cover 85.00
10 Cave of Death 85.00
11 Curse of Morgan Kilgane ... 75.00
12 Swamp Monster 75.00
13 The Lost Race 85.00
14 Down to Death 55.00
15 Nightmare of Doom 80.00
16 Cycle of Horror 80.00
17 Amnesia 80.00
18 Hair cut-Atom Bomb 90.00
19 Happy Anniversary 80.00
20 Shock is Struck 80.00
21 BP,Nose for News 95.00
22 Is Death the End? 80.00
23 BP,Heartline 80.00
24 BP,Bondage(c) 90.00
25 .... 40.00
26 HN,Captains Return 40.00
Becomes:
CHAMBER OF CLUES
27 BP,A:Kerry Drake 50.00
28 A:Kerry Drake 30.00

CHAMPION COMICS
Worth Publishing Co.
December, 1939
2 B:Champ, Blazing Scarab, Neptina,
    Liberty Lads, Jingleman ... 650.00
3 .... 300.00
4 Bailout(c) 325.00
5 Jungleman(c) 325.00
6 MNe 325.00
7 MNe,Human Meteor 350.00
8 .... 300.00
9 .... 300.00
10 Bondage cover 325.00
Becomes:
CHAMP COMICS
11 Human Meteor 400.00
12 Human Heteor 325.00
13 Dragon's Teeth 300.00
14 Liberty Lads 300.00
15 Liberty Lads 300.00
16 Liberty Lads 300.00
17 Liberty Lads 300.00
18 Liberty Lads 300.00
19 A:The Wasp 275.00
20 A:The Green Ghost 300.00
21 .... 275.00
22 A:White Mask 300.00
23 Flag cover 300.00
24 thru 29 .... @275.00

CHARLIE McCARTHY
Dell Publishing Co.
November, 1947

1	120.00
2	45.00
3	45.00
1	45.00
2	45.00
3	45.00
4	45.00
5	45.00
6	45.00
7	45.00
8	45.00
9	45.00

CHIEF, THE
Dell Publishing Co.
August, 1950
(1) see Dell Four Color #290

2	30.00

CHILLING TALES
(see CAPTAIN SCIENCE)

CHUCKLE THE GIGGLY BOOK OF COMIC ANIMALS
R. B. Leffing Well Co.
1944

1	125.00

CINEMA COMICS HERALD
Paramount/Universal/RKO/ 20th Century Fox
Giveaways 1941-43

N# Mr. Bug Goes to Town	40.00
N# Bedtime Story	40.00
N# Lady for a Night,J.Wayne	45.00
N# Reap the Wild Wind	40.00
N# Thunderbirds	40.00
N# They All Kissed Me	40.00
N# Bombardier	40.00
N# Crash Dive	40.00
N# Arabian Nights	40.00

Cisco Kid
© Dell Publishing Co.

CIRCUS THE COMIC RIOT
Globe Syndicate
June, 1938

1 BKa,WE,BW	2,500.00
2 BKa,WE,BW	1,500.00
3 BKa,WE,BW, August, 1938	1,500.00

CISCO KID, THE
Dell Publishing Co.
(1) See Dell Four Color #292

2 January, 1951	150.00
3	75.00
4	75.00
5	75.00
6 thru 10	@60.00
11 thru 20	@50.00
21 thru 36	@40.00
37 thru 41 Ph(c)'s	@75.00

CLAIRE VOYANT
Leader Publ./Visual Ed./ Pentagon Publ.
1946-47

N#	300.00
2 JKa(c)	225.00
3 Case of the Kidnapped Bride	225.00
4 Bondage cover	250.00

CLOAK AND DAGGER
Approved Comics (Ziff-Davis)
Fall, 1952

1 NS(c),Al Kennedy of the Secret Service	90.00

Clue Comics #14 (2/2)
© Hillman Periodicals

CLUE COMICS
Hillman Periodicals
January, 1943

1 O:Boy King,Nightmare,Micro-Face, Twilight,Zippo.	525.00
2	275.00
3 Boy King V:The Crane	225.00
4 V:The Crane	200.00
5 V:The Crane	175.00

6 Hells Kitchen	125.00
7 V:Dr. Plasma,Torture(c)	150.00
8 RP,A:The Gold Mummy King	125.00
9 I:Paris	125.00
10 O:Gun Master	125.00
11 A:Gun Master	90.00
12 O:Rackman	125.00
2-1 S&K,O:Nightro,A:Iron Lady	150.00
2-2 S&K,Bondage(c)	165.00
2-3 S&K	125.00

Becomes:

REAL CLUE CRIME STORIES

2-4 DBw,S&K,True Story of Ma Barker	190.00
2-5 S&K, Newface surgery cover	150.00
2-6 S&K, Breakout cover	135.00
2-7 S&K, Stick up cover	135.00
2-8 Kidnapping cover	35.00
2-9 DBa,Boxing fix cover	35.00
2-10 DBa,Murder cover	35.00
2-11 Attempted bank robbery cover	35.00
2-12 Murder cover	35.00
3-1 thru 3-12	@25.00
4-1 thru 4-12	@45.00
5-1 thru 5-12	@25.00
6-1 thru 6-12	@25.00
6-10 Bondage(c)	45.00
7-1 thru 7-12	@20.00
8-1 thru 8-4	@20.00
8-5 May, 1953	20.00

C-M-O COMICS
Comic Corp. of America (Centaur)
May, 1942

1 Invisible Terror	500.00
2 Super Ann	300.00

COCOMALT BIG BOOK OF COMICS
Harry A. Chesler
1938

1 BoW,PGn,FG,JCo,(Give away) Little Nemo	1,100.00

COLOSSUS COMICS
Sun Publications
March, 1940

1 A:Colossus	1,600.00

COLUMBIA COMICS
William H. Wise Co.
1944

1 Joe Palooka,Charlie Chan	150.00

COMICS, THE
Dell Publishing Co.
March, 1937

1 I:Tom Mix & Arizona Kid	900.00
2 A:Tom Mix & Tom Beaty	450.00
3 A:Alley Oop	350.00
4 same	350.00
5 same	350.00
6 thru 11 same	@350.00

COMICS ON PARADE
United Features Syndicate
April, 1938

1 B:Tarzan,Captain and the Kids,	

Little Mary, Mixup,Abbie & Slats,
Broncho Bill,Li'l Abner ... 1,600.00
2 Circus Parade of all 700.00
3 .... 600.00
4 On Rocket 400.00
5 All at the Store 400.00
6 All at Picnic 300.00
7 Li'l Abner(c) 300.00
8 same 300.00

Comics on Parade #9
© United Features Syndicate

9 same 300.00
10 same 300.00
11 same 250.00
12 same 250.00
13 same 250.00
14 Abbie n' Slats (c) 250.00
15 Li'l Abner(c) 250.00
16 Abbie n' Slats(c) 250.00
17 Tarzan,Abbie n' Slats(c) .. 250.00
18 Li'l Abner(c) 250.00
19 same 250.00
20 same 250.00
21 Li'l Abner(c) 200.00
22 Tail Spin Tommy(c) 200.00
23 Abbie n' Slats(c) 200.00
24 Tail Spin Tommy(c) 200.00
25 Li'l Abner(c) 200.00
26 Abbie n' Slats(c) 200.00
27 Li'l Abner(c) 200.00
28 Tail Spin Tommy(c) 200.00
29 Abbie n' Slats(c) 200.00
30 Li'l Abner(c) 200.00
31 The Captain & the Kids(c) .. 125.00
32 Nancy and Fritzi Ritz(c) 80.00
33 Li'l Abner(c) 125.00
34 The Captain & the Kids(c) ... 90.00
35 Nancy and Fritzi Ritz(c) 70.00
36 Li'l Abner(c) 125.00
37 The Captain & the Kids(c) ... 75.00
38 Nancy and Fritzi Ritz(c) 60.00
39 Li'l Abner(c) 125.00
40 The Captain & the Kids(c) ... 75.00
41 Nancy and Fritzi Ritz(c) 55.00
42 Li'l Abner(c) 90.00
43 The Captain & the Kids(c) ... 75.00
44 Nancy and Fritzi Ritz(c) 50.00
45 Li'l Abner(c) 75.00
46 The Captain & the Kids(c) ... 60.00
47 Nancy and Fritzi Ritz(c) 50.00

48 Li'l Abner(c) 75.00
49 The Captain & the Kids(c) ... 60.00
50 Nancy and Fritzi Ritz(c) 50.00
51 Li'l Abner(c) 65.00
52 The Captain & the Kids(c) ... 45.00
53 Nancy and Fritzi Ritz(c) 40.00
54 Li'l Abner(c) 65.00
55 Nancy and Fritzi Ritz(c) 45.00
56 The Captain & the Kids(c) ... 45.00
57 Nancy and Fritzi Ritz(c) 40.00
58 Li'l Abner(c) 65.00
59 The Captain & the Kids(c) ... 40.00
60 Nancy and Fritzi Ritz(c) 35.00
61 thru 76 same .... @35.00
77 Nancy & Sluggo(c) 25.00
78 thru 103 same .... @25.00
104 same, February, 1955 ..... 25.00

COMPLETE BOOK OF COMICS AND FUNNIES
William H. Wise & Co.
1945
1 Wonderman-Magnet 230.00

CONFESSIONS OF LOVE
Artful Publications
April, 1950
1 .... 150.00
2 July, 1950 .... 80.00

CONFESSIONS OF LOVE
Star Publications
July, 1952
11 AW,LbC(c)Intimate Secrets of
Daring Romance 60.00
12 AW,LbC(c),I Couldn't Say No 60.00
13 AW,LbC(c),Heart Break ... 60.00
14 AW,LbC(c),My Fateful Love 30.00
4 JyD,AW,LbC(c),The Longing
Heart 30.00
5 AW,LbC(c),I Wanted Love ... 30.00
6 AW,LbC(c),My Jealous Heart . 30.00
Becomes:
CONFESSIONS OF ROMANCE
7 LbC(c)Too Good 45.00
8 AW,LbC(c),I Lied About Love 30.00
9 WW,AW,LbC(c),I Paid
Love's Price 60.00
10 JyD,AW,LbC(c),My Heart Cries
for Love 35.00
11 JyD,AW,LbC(c),Intimate
Confessions, November, 1954 35.00

CONFESSIONS OF LOVELORN
(see LOVELORN)

CONQUEROR COMICS
Albrecht Publications
Winter, 1945
1 .... 80.00

CONTACT COMICS
Aviation Press
July, 1944
N# LbC(c),B:Black Venus,
Golden Eagle 200.00
2 LbC(c),Peace Jet 150.00
3 LbC(c),LbC,E:Flamingo .. 125.00
4 LbC(c),LbC 125.00

5 LbC(c),A:Phantom Flyer ... 150.00
6 LbC(c),HK 175.00
7 LbC(c),Flying Tigers 100.00
8 LbC(c),Peace Jet 100.00
9 LbC(c),LbC,A:Marine Flyers 100.00
10 LbC(c),A:Bombers of the AAF 100.00
11 LbC(c),HK,AF,Salutes Naval
Aviation 175.00
12 LbC(c),A:Sky Rangers, Air Kids,
May, 1946 .... 125.00

COO COO COMICS
Nedor/Animated Cartoons (Standard)
October, 1942
1 O&I:Super Mouse 125.00
2 .... 55.00
3 .... 35.00
4 .... 35.00
5 .... 35.00
6 .... 30.00
7 thru 10 .... @30.00
11 thru 33 .... @25.00
34 thru 40 FF illustration ... @35.00
41 FF 75.00
42 FF 75.00
43 FF illustration 45.00
44 FF illustration 45.00
45 FF illustration 45.00
46 FF illustration 45.00
47 FF 75.00
48 FF illustration 35.00
49 FF illustration 35.00
50 FF illustration 35.00
51 thru 61 .... @15.00
62 April, 1952 .... 15.00

"COOKIE"
Michel Publ./Regis Publ.
(American Comics Group)
April, 1946
1 .... 90.00
2 .... 50.00
3 .... 35.00
4 .... 35.00
5 .... 35.00
6 thru 20 .... @25.00
21 thru 30 .... @20.00
31 thru 54 .... @15.00
55 August, 1955 .... 15.00

COSMO CAT
Fox Features Syndicate
July/August, 1946
1 .... 90.00
2 .... 50.00
3 O:Cosmo Cat 65.00
4 thru 10 .... @35.00

COURAGE COMICS
J. Edward Slavin
1945
1 .... 45.00
2 Boxing cover 45.00
77 Naval rescue, PT99 cover .. 45.00

COWBOY COMICS
(see STAR RANGER)

COWBOYS 'N' INJUNS
Compix
(M.E. Enterprises)

All comics prices listed are for *Near Mint* condition.

1946-47

1 Funny Animal Western 40.00
2 thru 8 .... @25.00

COWBOY WESTERN COMICS/HEROES
(see YELLOWJACKET COMICS)

COWGIRL ROMANCES
Fiction House Magazine
1952

1 The Range of Singing Guns   150.00
2 The Lady of Lawless Range . 80.00
3 Daughter of the Devil's Band 70.00
4 Bride Wore Buckskin 65.00
5 Taming of Lone-Star Lou ... 60.00
6 Rose of Mustang Mesa 55.00
7 Nobody Loves a Gun Man .. 55.00
8 Wild Beauty 55.00
9 Gun-Feud Sweethearts 55.00
10 JKa,AW,No Girl of Stampede
   Valley 60.00
11 Love is Where You Find It .. 55.00
12 December, 1952 .... 55.00

COW PUNCHER
Avon Periodicals/ Realistic Publ.
January, 1947

1 JKu 175.00
2 JKu,JKa(c),Bondage cover . 150.00
3 AU(c) 100.00
4 .... 100.00
5 .... 100.00
6 WJo(c),Drug story 100.00
7 .... 100.00
1 JKu 125.00

CRACK COMICS
Comic Magazines
(Quality Comics Group)
May, 1940

1 LF,O:Black Condor,Madame
  Fatal, Red Torpedo, Rock
  Bradden, Space Legion,
  B:The Clock,Wizard Wells . 2,400.00
2 Black Condor cover 1,000.00
3 The Clock cover 750.00
4 Black Condor cover 650.00
5 LF,The Clock cover 550.00
6 PG,Black Condor cover   ... 500.00
7 Clock cover 500.00
8 Black Condor cover   ... 500.00
9 Clock cover 500.00
10 Black Condor cover   ... 500.00
11 LF,PG,Clock cover   .. 450.00
12 LF,PG,Black Condor cover . 450.00
13 LF,PG,Clock cover   ... 450.00
14 AMc,LF,PG,Clack Condor(c) 450.00
15 AMc,LF,PG,Clock cover ... 450.00
16 AMc,LF,PG,Black Condor(c) 450.00
17 FG,AMc,LF,PG,Clock cover 450.00
18 AMc,LF,PG,Black Condor(c) 450.00
19 AMc,LF,PG,Clock cover   ... 450.00
20 AMc,LF,PG,Black Condor(c) 450.00
21 AMc,LF,PG,same 350.00
22 LF,PG,same 350.00
23 AMc,LF,PG,same 350.00
24 AMc,LF,PG,same 350.00
25 AMc,same 250.00
26 AMc,same 250.00
27 AMc,I&O:Captain Triumph . 500.00

Crack Comics #32
© *Quality Comics Group*

28 Captain Triumph cover 250.00
29 A:Spade the Ruthless 250.00
30 I:Biff 225.00
31 Helps Spade Dig His Own
   Grave 125.00
32 Newspaper cover 125.00
33 V:Men of Darkness 125.00
34 .... 125.00
35 V:The Man Who Conquered
   Flame 125.00
36 Good Neighbor Tour 125.00
37 V:The Tyrant of Toar Valley 125.00
38 Castle of Shadows 125.00
39 V:Crime over the City 125.00
40 Thrilling Murder Mystery ... 85.00
41 .... 85.00
42 All that Glitters is Not Gold .. 85.00
43 Smashes the Evil Spell of
   Silent 85.00
44 V:Silver Tip 85.00
45 V:King-The Jack of all Trades 85.00
46 V:Mr. Weary 85.00
47 V:Hypnotic Eyes Khor 85.00
48 Murder in the Sky 85.00
49 .... 85.00
50 A Key to Trouble 85.00
51 V:Werewolf 85.00
52 V:Porcupine 85.00
53 V:Man Who Robbed the Dead 85.00
54 Shoulders the Troubles
   of the World 85.00
55 Brain against Brawn 85.00
56 Gossip leads to Murder 85.00
57 V:Sitok - Green God of Evil .. 85.00
58 V:Targets 85.00
59 A Cargo of Mystery 85.00
60 Trouble is no Picnic 85.00
61 V:Mr. Pointer-Finger of Fear . 85.00
62 V:The Vanishing Vandals ... 85.00

Becomes:

CRACK WESTERN

63 PG, I&O:Two-Gun Lil, B:Frontier
   Marshal,Arizona Ames, ... 120.00
64 RC,Arizona AmesV:Two-
   Legged Coyote 90.00
65 RC,Ames Tramples on Trouble 90.00
66 Arizona Ames Arizona Raines,

Tim Holt,Ph(c) 75.00
67 RC, Ph(c) 85.00
68 .... 75.00
69 RC 75.00
70 O&I:Whip and Diablo 80.00
71 RC(c) 85.00
72 RC,Tim Holt,Ph(c) 72.00
73 Tim Holt,Ph(c) 55.00
74 RC(c) 60.00
75 RC(c) 60.00
76 RC(c),Stage Coach to Oblivion 60.00
77 RC(c),Comanche Terror 60.00
78 RC(c),Killers of Laurel Ridge . 60.00
79 RC(c),Fires of Revenge 60.00
80 RC(c),Mexican Massacre ... 60.00
81 RC(c),Secrets of Terror
   Canyon 60.00
82 The Killer with a Thousand
   Faces 40.00
83 Battlesnake Pete's Revenge . 40.00
84 PG(c),Revolt at Broke Creek
   May,1951 .... 40.00

CRACKAJACK FUNNIES
Dell Publishing Co.
June, 1938

1 AMc,A:Dan Dunn,The Nebbs,
  Don Winslow 1,000.00
2 AMc,same 500.00
3 AMc,same 350.00
4 AMc,same 250.00
5 AMc,Naked Women(c) 300.00
6 AMc,same 200.00
7 AMc,same 200.00
8 AMc,same 200.00
9 AMc,A:Red Ryder 300.00
10 AMc,A:Red Ryder 200.00
11 AMc,A:Red Ryder 190.00
12 AMc,A:Red Ryder 190.00
13 AMc,A:Red Ryder 190.00
14 AMc,A:Red Ryder 190.00
15 AMc,A:Tarzan 225.00
16 AMc 125.00

Crackajack Funnies #12
© *Dell Publishing Co.*

17 AMc 125.00
18 AMc 125.00
19 AMc 125.00
20 AMc 125.00

All comics prices listed are for *Near Mint* condition.

21 AMc	125.00
22 AMc	125.00
23 AMc	125.00
24 AMc	125.00
25 AMc,I:The Owl	325.00
26 AMc	250.00
27 AMc	250.00
28 AMc,A:The Owl	250.00
29 AMc,A:Ellery Queen	250.00
30 AMc,A:Tarzan	250.00
31 AMc,A:Tarzan	250.00
32 AMc,O:Owl Girl	275.00
33 AMc,A:Tarzan	200.00
34 AMc,same	200.00
35 AMc,same	200.00
36 AMc,same	200.00
37 AMc	150.00
38 AMc	150.00
39 AMc,I:Andy Panada	225.00
40 AMc,A:Owl(c)	150.00
41 AMc	150.00
42 AMc	150.00
43 AMc,A:Owl(c)	150.00

Crash Comics #3
© Tem Publishing Co.

CRASH COMICS
Tem Publishing Co.
May, 1940

1 S&K,O:Strongman, B:Blue Streak, Perfect Human, Shangra	1,300.00
2 S&K	700.00
3 S&K	500.00
4 S&K,O&I:Catman	900.00
5 S&K, November, 1940	500.00

CRIME AND PUNISHMENT
Lev Gleason Publications
April, 1948

1 CBi(c),Mr.Crime(c)	125.00
2 CBi(c)	65.00
3 CBi(c),BF	60.00
4 CBi(c),BF	40.00
5 CBi(c)	40.00
6 thru 10 CBi(c)	@35.00
11 thru 15 CBi(c)	@30.00
16 thru 27 CBi(c)	@25.00
28 thru 38	@20.00

39 Drug issue	35.00
40 thru 44	@20.00
45 Drug issue	30.00
46 thru 73	@15.00
66 ATh	175.00
67 Drug Storm	130.00
68 ATh(c)	100.00
69 Drug issue	30.00
74 August, 1955	12.00

CRIME DETECTIVE COMICS
Hillman Publications
March-April, 1948

1 BFc(c),A:Invisible 6	120.00
2 Jewel Robbery cover	45.00
3 Stolen cash cover	35.00
4 Crime Boss Murder cover	35.00
5 BK,Maestro cover	35.00
6 AMc,Gorilla cover	30.00
7 GMc,Wedding cover	30.00
8	30.00
9 Safe Robbery cover (a classic)	150.00
10	35.00
11 BP	35.00
12 BK	35.00
2-1 Bluebird captured	38.00
2-2	25.00
2-3	25.00
2-4 BK	35.00
2-5	25.00
2-6	25.00
2-7 BK,GMc	35.00
2-8	25.00
2-9	25.00
2-10	25.00
2-11	25.00
2-12	25.00
3-1 Drug Story	25.00
3-2 thru 3-7	@24.00
3-8 May/June, 1953	20.00

CRIME DOES NOT PAY
(see SILVER STREAK COMICS)

CRIME ILLUSTRATED
E.C. Comics
November-December, 1955

1 Grl,RC,GE,JO	75.00
2 Grl,RC,JCr,JDa,JO	60.00

CRIME MUST STOP
Hillman Periodicals
October, 1952

1 BK	275.00

CRIME MYSTERIES
Ribage Publishing Corp.
May, 1952

1 Transvestism,Bondage(c)	225.00
2 A:Manhunter, Lance Storm, Drug	150.00
3 FF-one page, A:Dr. Foo	100.00
4 A:Queenie Star, Bondage Star	200.00
5 Claws of the Green Girl	100.00
6	100.00
7 Sons of Satan	100.00
8 Death Stalks the Crown, Bondage(c)	90.00

9 You are the Murderer	85.00
10 The Hoax of the Death	85.00
11 The Strangler	85.00
12 Bondage(c)	90.00
13 AT,6 lives for one	100.00
14 Painted in Blood	80.00
15 Feast of the Dead,Acid Face	150.00

Becomes:

SECRET MYSTERIES

16 Hiding Place,Horror	100.00
17 The Deadly Diamond,Horror	60.00
18 Horror	70.00
19 Horror,July, 1955	70.00

CRIMES ON THE WATERFRONT
(see FAMOUS GANGSTERS)

INTERNATIONAL COMICS
E.C. Publ. Co.
Spring, 1947

1 KS,I:Manhattan's Files	425.00
2 KS,A: Van Manhattan & Madelon	300.00
3 KS,same	250.00
4 KS,same	250.00
5 I:International Crime-Busting Patrol	250.00

Becomes:

INTERNATIONAL CRIME PATROL

6 A:Moon Girl & The Prince	400.00

Becomes:

CRIME PATROL

7 SMo,A:Capt. Crime Jr.,Field Marshall of Murder	350.00
8 JCr,State Prison cover	300.00
9 AF,JCr,Bank Robbery	300.00
10 AF,JCr,Wanted:James Dore	300.00
11 AF,JCr	300.00
12 AF,Grl,JCr,Interrogation(c)	300.00
13 AF,JCr	300.00
14 AF,JCr,Smugglers cover	300.00
15 AF,JCr,Crypt of Terror	1,500.00
16 AF,JCr,Crypt of Terror	1,250.00

Becomes:

CRYPT OF TERROR
E.C. Comics
April, 1950

17 JCr&(c),AF,'Werewolf Strikes Again'	1,700.00
18 JCr&(c),AF,WW,HK 'The Living Corpse'	1,200.00
19 JCr&(c),AF,Grl, 'Voodoo Drums'	1,200.00

Becomes:

TALES FROM THE CRYPT
October, 1950

20 JCr&(c),AF,GI,JKa 'Day of Death'	900.00
21 AF&(c),WW,HK,GI,'Cooper Dies in the Electric Chair	700.00
22 AF, JCr(c)	700.00
23 AF&(c),JCr,JDa,Grl 'Locked in a Mauseleum'	450.00
24 AF(c),WW,JDa,JCr,Grl 'Danger...Quicksand'	450.00
25 AF(c),WW,JDa,JKa,Grl 'Mataud Waxworks'	450.00
26 WW(c),JDa,Grl,	

Tales from the Crypt #23
© E.C. Comics

'Scared Graveyard' 350.00
27 JKa, WW(c), Guillotine cover 350.00
28 AF(c),JDa,JKa,Grl,JO
'Buried Alive' 350.00
29 JDa&(c),JKa,Grl,JO
'Coffin Burier' 350.00
30 JDa&(c),JO,JKa,Grl
'Underwater Death' 350.00
31 JDa&(c),JKa,Grl,AW
'Hand Chopper' 400.00
32 JDa&(c),GE,Grl,'Woman
Crushed by Elephant' 300.00
33 JDa&(c),GE,JKa,Grl,'Lower
Berth',O:Crypt Keeper 500.00
34 JDa&(c),JKa,GE,Grl,'Jack the
Ripper,'Ray Bradbury adapt. 300.00
35 JDa&(c),JKa,JO,Grl,
'Werewolf' 300.00
36 JDa&(c),JKa,GE,Grl, Ray
Bradbury adaptation 300.00
37 JDa(c),JO,BE 300.00
38 JDa(c),BE,RC,Grl,'Axe Man' 300.00
39 JDa&(c),JKa,JO,Grl,'Children
in the Graveyard' 300.00
40 JDa&(c),GE,BK,Grl,
'Underwater Monster' 300.00
41 JDa&(c),JKa,GE,Grl,
'Knife Thrower' 250.00
42 JDa(c),JO,Vampire cover .. 250.00
43 JDa(c),JO,GE 250.00
44 JO,RC,Guillotine cover 250.00
45 JDa&(c),JKa,BK,Gl,'Rat
Takes Over His Life' 250.00
46 JDa&(c),GE,JO,Gl,'Werewolf
man being hunted,Feb.1955 350.00

CRIME REPORTER
St. John Publishing Co.
August, 1948
1 Death Makes a Deadline .. 200.00
2 GT,MB(c),Matinee Murders . 350.00
3 GT,MB(c),December, 1948 . 175.00

CRIMES BY WOMEN
Fox Features Syndicate
June, 1948
1 Bonnie Parker 600.00

2 Vicious Female 325.00
3 Prison break cover 300.00
4 Murder cover 275.00
5 .... 275.00
6 Girl Fight cover 300.00
7 .... 275.00
8 .... 275.00
9 .... 275.00
10 .... 275.00
11 .... 275.00
12 .... 275.00
13 ACME jewelry robbery cover 275.00
14 Prison break cover 275.00
15 August, 1951 .... 275.00

CRIME SMASHER
Fawcett Publications
Summer, 1948
1 The Unlucky Rabbit's Foot . 200.00

CRIME SMASHERS
Ribage Publishing Corp.
October, 1950
1 Girl Rape 375.00
2 JKu,A:Sally the Sleuth, Dan Turner,
Girl Friday, Rat Hale 200.00
3 MFa 135.00
4 Zak(c) 135.00
5 WW 180.00
6 .... 100.00
7 Bondage cover,Drugs 125.00
8 .... 80.00
9 Bondage cover 80.00
10 .... 100.00
11 .... 100.00
12 FF 120.00
13 .... 110.00
14 .... 100.00
15 .... 100.00

CRIME SUSPENSTORIES
L.L. Publishing Co.
(E.C. Comics)
October-November, 1950
1a JCr,Grl 600.00
1 JCr,WW,Grl 450.00
2 JCr,JKa,Grl 350.00
3 JCr,WW,Grl 300.00
4 JCr,Gln,Grl,JDa 275.00
5 JCr,JKa,Grl,JDa 250.00
6 JCr,JDa,Grl 200.00
7 JCr,Grl 200.00
8 JCr,Grl 200.00
9 JCr,Grl 200.00
10 JCr,Grl 200.00
11 JCr,Grl 150.00
12 JCr,Grl 150.00
13 JCr,AW 175.00
14 JCr 150.00
15 JCr 150.00
16 JCr,AW 175.00
17 JCr,FF,AW, Ray Bradbury . 200.00
18 JCr,RC,BE 150.00
19 JCr,RC,GE,AF(c) 150.00
20 RC,JCr, Hanging cover ... 175.00
21 JCr 100.00
22 RC,JO,JCr(c),
Severed head cover 140.00
23 JKa,RC,GE 140.00
24 BK,RC,JO 100.00
25 JKa,(c),RC 100.00
26 JKa,(c),RC,JO 100.00
27 JKa,(c),GE,Grl,March, 1955 100.00

CRIMINALS ON THE RUN
Premium Group of Comics
August, 1948
4-1 LbC(c) 120.00
4-2 LbC(c), A:Young King Cole 80.00
4-3 LbC(c), Rip Roaring Action
in Alps 80.00
4-4 LbC(c), Shark cover 80.00
4-5 AMc 80.00
4-6 LbC 75.00
4-7 LbC 150.00
5-1 LbC 75.00
5-2 LbC 75.00
10 LbC 80.00
Becomes:

CRIME-FIGHTING DETECTIVE
11 LbC, Brodie Gang Captured . 65.00
12 LbC(c), Jail Break Genius .. 50.00
13 .... 40.00
14 LbC(c), A Night of Horror ... 60.00
15 LbC(c) 50.00
16 LbC(c), Wanton Murder 50.00
17 LbC(c), The Framer
was Framed 50.00
18 LbC(c), A Web of Evil 50.00
19 LbC(c), Lesson of the Law .. 50.00
Becomes:

SHOCK DETECTIVE CASE
20 LbC(c), The Strangler 75.00
21 LbC(c), Death Ride 75.00
Becomes:

SPOOK DETECTIVE CASES
22 Headless Horror 130.00

Spook Suspense and Mystery #25
© Premium Group

Becomes:

SPOOK SUSPENSE AND MYSTERY
23 LbC,Weird Picture of Murder . 85.00
24 LbC(c),Mummy's Case 100.00
25 LbC(c),Horror Beyond Door . 75.00
26 LbC(c),JyD,Face of Death ... 75.00

27 LbC(c),Ship of the Dead 75.00
28 LbC(c),JyD,Creeping Death . 75.00
29 LbC(c),Solo for Death 75.00
30 LbC(c),JyD,Nightmare,
  Oct.,1954 .... 75.00

CROWN COMICS
Golfing/McCombs Publ.
Winter 1944
1 Edgar Allen Poe adapt. 250.00
2 MB,I:Mickey Magic 125.00
3 MB,Jungle adventure cover 125.00
4 MB(c) 150.00
5 MB(c),Jungle adventure cover 150.00
6 MB(c),Jungle adventure cover 150.00
7 JKa,AF,MB(c),Race Car driving
  cover 150.00
8 MB 135.00
9 .... 85.00
10 Plane crash cover 85.00
11 LSt 75.00
12 LSt 75.00
13 LSt 75.00
14 .... 95.00
15 FBe 75.00
16 FBe,Jungle adventure(c) 75.00
17 FBe 75.00
18 FBe 75.00
19 BP,July, 1949 .... 75.00

CRUSADER FROM MARS
Approved Publ.
(Ziff-Davis)
January-March, 1952
1 Mission Thru Space, Death in
  the Sai 400.00
2 Beachhead on Saturn's Ring,
  Bondage(c),Fall, 1952 ..... 325.00

CRYIN' LION, THE
William H. Wise Co.
Fall, 1944
1 .... 65.00
2 .... 40.00
3 Spring, 1945 .... 40.00

CRYPT OF TERROR
(see CRIME PATROL)

CYCLONE COMICS
Bibara Publ. Co.
June, 1940
1 O:Tornado Tom 550.00
2 .... 300.00
3 .... 250.00
4 Voltron 250.00
5 A:Mr. Q,October, 1940 .... 250.00

ALL GREAT COMICS
Fox Features Syndicate
October, 1947
12 A:Brenda Starr 225.00
13 JKa,O:Dagger, Desert Hawk 200.00
Becomes:

DAGAR, DESERT HAWK
14 JKa,Monster of Mura 350.00
15 JKa,Curse of the Lost
  Pharaoh 225.00
16 JKa,Wretched Antmen 200.00
19 Pyramid Doom 175.00
20 JKa(c),The Ghost of Fate . 175.00
21 .... 200.00

22 .... 175.00
23 Bondage cover 190.00
Becomes:

CAPTAIN KIDD
24 Blackbeard the Pirate 75.00
25 Sorceress of the Deep 75.00
Becomes:

MY SECRET STORY
26 He Wanted More Than Love . 60.00
27 My Husband Hated Me 40.00
28 I Become a Marked Women . 40.00
29 My Forbidden Rapture,
  April, 1950 .... 40.00

DAFFY
Dell Publishing Co.
March, 1953
(1) see Dell Four Color #457
(2) see Dell Four Color #536
(3) see Dell Four Color #615
4 thru 7 .... @18.00
8 thru 11 .... @15.00
12 thru 17 .... @12.00
Becomes:

DAFFY DUCK
18 .... 12.00
19 .... 12.00
20 .... 12.00
21 thru 30 .... @8.00
Gold Key
31 thru 40 .... @7.00
41 thru 59 .... @5.00
60 B&A:Road Runner 3.00
61 thru 90 same .... @3.00
91 thru 127 .... @2.00
Whitman
128 thru 145 .... @2.00

DAGWOOD
Harvey Publications
September, 1950
1 .... 65.00
2 .... 35.00
3 thru 10 .... @25.00
11 thru 20 .... @20.00
21 thru 30 .... @15.00
31 thru 50 .... @10.00
51 thru 70 .... @8.00
71 thru 109 .... @7.00
110 thru 140 .... @5.00

DANGER AND ADVENTURE
(see THIS MAGAZINE IS HAUNTED)

DANGER IS OUR BUSINESS
Toby Press/ I.W. Enterprises
1953
1 AW,FF,Men who Defy Death
  for a Living 300.00
2 Death Crowds the Cockpit .. 60.00
3 Killer Mountain 50.00
4 .... 50.00
5 thru 9 .... @40.00
10 June, 1955 .... 50.00

DAREDEVIL COMICS

Lev Gleason Publications
July, 1941
1 Daredevil Battles Hitler, A:Silver
  Streak, Lance Hale, Dickey Dean,
  Cloud Curtis,V:The Claw,
  O:Hitler 6,000.00
2 I:The Pioneer, Champion of
  American,B:London,Pat
  Patriot,Pirate Prince 2,000.00
3 CBi(c),O:Thirteen 1,000.00
4 CBi(c),Death is the Refere .. 950.00
5 CBi(c),I:Sniffer&Jinx, Claw
  V:Ghost,Lottery of Doom ... 800.00

Daredevil #33
© *Lev Gleason Publications*

6 CBi(c) 700.00
7 CBi(c), What Ghastly Sight Lies
  within the Mysterious Trunk . 600.00
8 V:Nazis cover, E:Nightro ... 550.00
9 V:Double 550.00
10 America will Remember
  Pearl Harbor 550.00
11 Bondage cover, E:Pat
  Patriot, London 525.00
12 BW,CBi(c), O:The Law 800.00
13 BW,I:Little Wise Guys 750.00
14 BW,CBi(c) 400.00
15 BW,CBi(c), D:Meatball 575.00
16 BW,CBi(c) 375.00
17 BW,CBi(c), Into the Valley
  of Death 350.00
18 BW,CBi(c), O:Daredevil,
  double length story 750.00
19 BW,CBi(c), Buried Alive ... 300.00
20 BW,CBi(c), Boxing cover .. 300.00
21 CBi(c), Can Little Wise Guys
  Survive Blast of Dynamite? . 500.00
22 CBi(c) 200.00
23 CBi(c), I:Pshyco 200.00
24 CBi(c), Punch and Judy
  Murders 200.00
25 CBi(c), baseball cover 225.00
26 CBi(c) 200.00
27 CBi(c), Bondage cover 225.00
28 CBi(c) 200.00
29 CBi(c) 200.00
30 CBi(c), Ann Hubbard White
  1922-1943 .... 200.00
31 CBi(c), D:The Claw 450.00
32 V:Blackmarketeers 165.00

---

33 CBi(c) 165.00
34 CBi(c) 165.00
35 B:Two Daredevil stories
   every issue 150.00
36 CBi(c) 150.00
37 CBi(c) 150.00
38 CBi(c), O:Daredevil 250.00
39 CBi(c) 150.00
40 CBi(c) 150.00
41 .... 150.00
42 thru 50 CBi(c) .... @125.00
51 CBi(c) 100.00
52 CBi(c),Football cover 125.00
53 thru 57 .... @100.00
58 Football cover 125.00
59 .... 100.00
60 .... 100.00
61 thru 68 .... @100.00
69 E:Daredevil 100.00
70 .... 75.00
71 thru 78 .... @55.00
79 B:Daredevil 65.00
80 .... 60.00
81 .... 40.00
82 .... 40.00
83 thru 99 .... @40.00
100 .... 45.00
101 thru 133 .... @35.00
134 September, 1956 .... 35.00

DARING CONFESSIONS
(see YOUTHFUL HEART)

DARING LOVE
(see YOUTHFUL ROMANCES)

DARK MYSTERIES
Merit Publications
June-July, 1951
1 WW, WW(c), Curse of the
  Sea Witch 375.00
2 WW, WW(c), Vampire Fangs
  of Doom 300.00
3 Terror of the Unwilling
  Witch 125.00
4 Corpse that Came Alive 125.00
5 Horror of the Ghostly Crew . 100.00
6 If the Noose Fits Wear It! .. 100.00
7 Terror of the Cards of Death 100.00
8 Terror of the Ghostly Trail . 100.00
9 Witch's Feast at Dawn 100.00
10 Terror of the Burning Witch . 125.00
11 The River of Blood 90.00
12 Horror of the Talking Dead .. 90.00
13 Terror of the Hungry Cats .. 90.00
14 Horror of the Fingers of Doom 95.00
15 Terror of the Vampires Teeth 90.00
16 Horror of the Walking Dead . 90.00
17 Terror of the Mask of Death . 90.00
18 Terror of the Burning Corpse 90.00
19 The Rack of Terror 125.00
20 Burning Executioner 110.00
21 The Sinister Secret 75.00
22 The Hand of Destiny 75.00
23 The Mardenburg Curse 60.00
24 Give A Man enough Rope,
   July, 1955 .... 60.00

DAVY CROCKETT
Avon Periodicals
1951
1 .... 90.00

DEAD END CRIME STORIES
Kirby Publishing Co.
April, 1949
N# BP 300.00

DEAD-EYE WESTERN COMICS
Hillman Periodicals
November-December, 1948
1 BK 80.00
2 .... 45.00
3 .... 45.00
4 thru 12 .... @25.00
2-1 .... 20.00
2-2 .... 20.00
2-3 .... 35.00
2-4 .... 35.00
2-5 thru 2-12 .... @20.00
3-1 .... 20.00

DEADWOOD GULCH
Dell Publishing Co.
1931
1 .... 120.00

DEAR BEATRICE FAIRFAX
Best Books (Standard Comics)
November, 1950
5 .... 40.00
6 thru 9 .... @25.00

DEAR LONELY HEART
Artful Publications
March, 1951
5 .... 75.00
6 .... 35.00
7 MB,Jungle Girl 75.00
8 .... 30.00
9 .... 30.00

DEAR LONELY HEARTS
Comic Media
August, 1953
1 Six Months to Live 38.00
2 Date Hungry, Price of Passion 22.00
3 thru 8 .... @22.00

DEARLY BELOVED
Approved Comics (Ziff-Davis)
Fall, 1952
1 Ph(c) 75.00

DEBBIE DEAN, CAREER GIRL
Civil Service Publishing
April, 1945
1 .... 75.00
2 .... 70.00

DELL GIANT EDITIONS
Dell Publishing Co.
1953-58
Abe Lincoln Life Story 90.00
Cadet Gray of West Point 75.00
Golden West Rodeo Treasury . 100.00
Life Stories of

American Presidents 75.00
Lone Ranger Golden West ... 250.00
Lone Ranger Movie Story 450.00
Lone Ranger Western
  Treasury('53) 250.00
Lone Ranger Western
  Treasury('54) 150.00
Moses & Ten Commandments .. 75.00
Nancy & Sluggo Travel Time .. 100.00
Pogo Parade 400.00
Raggedy Ann & Andy 250.00
Santa Claus Funnies 150.00
Tarzan's Jungle Annual #1 ... 150.00
Tarzan's Jungle Annual #2 ... 100.00
Tarzan's Jungle Annual #3 ... 100.00
Tarzan's Jungle Annual #4 ... 100.00
Tarzan's Jungle Annual #5 ... 100.00
Tarzan's Jungle Annual #6 ... 100.00
Tarzan's Jungle Annual #7 ... 100.00
Treasury of Dogs 75.00
Treasury of Horses 75.00
Universal Presents-Dracula-
  The Mummy & Other Stories 250.00
Western Roundup #1 .... 300.00
Western Roundup #2 .... 200.00
Western Roundup #3 .... 150.00
Western Roundup #4 thru #5 @150.00
Western Roundup #6 thru #10 @140.00
Western Roundup #11 thru #17@135.00
Western Roundup #18 ...... 125.00
Western Roundup #19 thru #25 125.00
Woody Woodpecker Back
  to School #1 .... 125.00
Woody Woodpecker Back
  to School #2 .... 100.00
Woody Woodpecker Back
  to School #3 .... 85.00
Woody Woodpecker Back
  to School #4 .... 85.00
Woody Woodpecker County
  Fair #5 .... 85.00
Woody Woodpecker Back
  to School #6 .... 80.00
Woody Woodpecker County
  Fair #2 .... 75.00
Also See:
Bugs Bunny
Marge's Little Lulu
Tom and Jerry, &
Walt Disney Dell Giant Editions

DELL GIANT COMICS
Dell Publishing Co.
September 1959
21 M.G.M. Tom & Jerry
   Picnic Time 175.00
22 W.Disney's Huey, Dewey & Louie
   Back to School (Oct 1959) . 125.00
23 Marge's Little Lulu &
   Tubby Halloween Fun 175.00
24 Woody Woodpeckers
   Family Fun 120.00
25 Tarzan's Jungle World 160.00
26 W.Disney's Christmas
   Parade,CB 325.00
27 W.Disney's Man in
   Space (1960) 200.00
28 Bugs Bunny's Winter Fun .. 150.00
29 Marge's Little Lulu &
   Tubby in Hawaii 200.00
30 W.Disney's DisneylandU.S.A. 150.00
31 Huckleberry Hound
   Summer Fun 200.00
32 Bugs Bunny Beach Party ... 85.00
33 W.Disney's Daisy Duck &

Uncle Scrooge Picnic Time .	150.00
34 Nancy&SluggoSummerCamp	100.00
35 W.Disney's Huey, Dewey & Louie Back to School	100.00
36 Marge's Little Lulu & Witch Hazel Halloween Fun	200.00
37 Tarzan, King of the Jungle .	150.00
38 W.Disney's Uncle Donald and his Nephews Family Fun . . .	95.00
39 W.Disney's Merry Christmas .	95.00
40 Woody Woodpecker Christmas Parade	85.00
41 Yogi Bear's Winter Sports . .	200.00
42 Marge's Little Lulu & Tubby in Australia	185.00

Dell Giant #43 © Dell Publishing Co.

43 Mighty Mouse in OuterSpace	300.00
44 Around the World with Huckleberry & His Friends .	200.00
45 Nancy&SluggoSummerCamp	90.00
46 Bugs Bunny Beach Party . . .	80.00
47 W.Disney's Mickey and Donald in Vacationland	150.00
48 The Flintstones #1 (Bedrock Bedlam)	250.00
49 W.Disney's Huey, Dewey & Louie Back to School	85.00
50 Marge's Little Lulu & Witch Hazel Trick 'N' Treat .	200.00
51 Tarzan, King of the Jungle .	125.00
52 W.Disney's Uncle Donald & his Nephews Dude Ranch .	120.00
53 W.Disney's Donald Duck Merry Christmas	100.00
54 Woody Woodpecker Christmas Party	100.00
55 W.Disney's Daisy Duck & Uncle Scrooge Show Boat (1961) .	225.00

DELL JUNIOR TREASURY
Dell Publishing Co.
June, 1955

1 Alice in Wonderland	75.00
2 Aladdin	65.00
3 Gulliver's Travels	50.00
4 Adventures of Mr. Frog	55.00
5 Wizard of Oz	60.00
6 Heidi	65.00
7 Santa & the Angel	65.00

8 Raggedy Ann	65.00
9 Clementina the Flying Pig . . .	60.00
10 Adventures of Tom Sawyer . .	60.00

DENNIS THE MENACE
Visual Editions/Literary Ent.
(Standard, Pines)
August, 1953

1	250.00

Dennis the Menace #1
© Visual Editions

2	150.00
3	75.00
4	75.00
5 thru 10	@65.00
11 thru 20	@50.00
21 thru 30	@30.00
31 thru 40	@20.00
41 thru 50	@18.00
51 thru 60	@15.00
61 thru 70	@10.00
71 thru 90	@7.00
91 thru 140	@3.50
141 thru 166	@3.00

DESPERADO
Lev Gleason Publications
June, 1948

1 CBi(c)	65.00
2 CBi(c)	35.00
3 CBi(c)	30.00
4 CBi(c)	25.00
5 CBi(c)	25.00
6 CBi(c)	25.00
7 CBi(c)	25.00
8 CBi(c)	25.00

Becomes:

BLACK DIAMOND WESTERN

9 CBi(c)	90.00
10 CBi(c)	50.00
11 CBi(c)	35.00
12 CBi(c)	35.00
13 CBi(c)	35.00
14 CBi(c)	35.00
15 CBi(c)	35.00
16 thru 28 BW,Big Bang Buster	@50.00
29 thru 40	@25.00

41 thru 52	@20.00
53 3-D	60.00
54 3-D	50.00
55 thru 60	@25.00

DETECTIVE EYE
Centaur Publications
November, 1940

1 B:Air Man, The Eye Sees, A:Masked Marvel	1,000.00
2 O:Don Rance, Mysticape, December, 1940	750.00

DETECTIVE PICTURE STORIES
Comics Magazine Co.
December, 1936

1 The Phantom Killer	1,700.00
2	700.00
3	650.00
4 WE, Muss Em Up	600.00
5 Trouble, April, 1937	550.00

DEXTER COMICS
Dearfield Publications
Summer, 1948

1	35.00
2	25.00
3	15.00
4	15.00
5 July, 1949	15.00

DIARY CONFESSIONS
(see TENDER ROMANCE)

DIARY LOVES
Comic Magazines
(Quality Comics Group)
September, 1949

1 BWa	85.00
2 BWa	70.00
3	28.00
4 RC	40.00
5	20.00
6	20.00
7	20.00
8 BWa	60.00
9 BWa	60.00
10 BWa	60.00
11	20.00
12	20.00
13	20.00
14	20.00
15 BWa	45.00
16 BWa	45.00
17	20.00
18	20.00
19	20.00
20	20.00
21 BWa	35.00
22 thru 31	@15.00

Becomes:

G.I. SWEETHEARTS

32 Love Under Fire	25.00
33	25.00
34	25.00
35	25.00
36 Lend Lease Love Affair	25.00
37 thru 45	@25.00

Becomes:

GIRLS IN LOVE

46 Somewhere I'll Find You	30.00

47 thru 56 . . . . @20.00
57 MB,MB(c), Can Love Really
    Change Him, Dec., 1956 . . . . 40.00

DIARY SECRETS
(see TEEN-AGE DIARY
SECRETS)

DICK COLE
Curtis Publ./
Star Publications
December-January, 1949
1 LbC,LbC(c),CS,All sports cover 100.00
2 LbC 65.00
3 LbC, LbC(c) 50.00
4 LbC, LbC(c),Rowing cover . . 50.00
5 LbC,LbC(c) 50.00
6 LbC,LbC(c), Rodeo cover . . . 40.00
7 LbC,LbC(c) 40.00
8 LbC,LbC(c), Football cover . . 50.00
9 LbC,LbC(c), Basketball cover 50.00
10 Joe Louis 60.00
Becomes:
SPORTS THRILLS
11 Ted Williams & Ty Cobb . . . 250.00
12 LbC, Joe Dimaggio & Phil
    Rizzuto, Boxing cover 100.00
13 LbC(c),Basketball cover 85.00
14 LbC(c),Baseball cover 75.00
15 LbC(c),Baseball cover,
    November, 1951 . . . . 75.00

DICKIE DARE
Eastern Color Printing Co.
1941
1 BEv(c) 225.00
2 . . . . 150.00
3 . . . . 150.00
4 1942 . . . . 165.00

Dick Tracy Monthly #2
© Dell Publishing Co.

DICK TRACY
MONTHLY
Dell Publishing Co.
January, 1948
1 ChG,Dick Tracy & the Mad

Doctor' 350.00
2 ChG,A:MarySteele,BorisArson 200.00
3 ChG,A:Spaldoni,Big Boy . . . 200.00
4 ChG,A:Alderman Zeld 160.00
5 ChG,A:Spaldoni,Mrs.Spaldoni 160.00
6 ChG,A:Steve the Tramp . . . 160.00
7 ChG,A:Boris Arson,Mary
    Steele 160.00
8 ChG,A:Boris & Zora Arson . 160.00
9 ChG,A:Chief Yellowpony . . 160.00
10 ChG,A:Cutie Diamond 160.00
11 ChG,A:Toby Townly,
    Bookie Joe 125.00
12 ChG,A:Toby Townly,
    Bookie Joe 125.00
13 ChG,A:Toby Townly, Blake . 135.00
14 ChG,A:Mayor Waite Wright . 125.00
15 ChG,A:Bowman Basil 125.00
16 ChG,A:Maw,'Muscle'
    & 'Cut' Famon 125.00
17 ChG,A:Jim Trailer,
    Mary Steele 125.00
18 ChG,A:Lips Manlis,
    Anthel Jones 125.00
19 'Golden Heart Mystery' 150.00
20 'Black Cat Mystery' 150.00
21 'Tracy Meets Number One' . 150.00
22 'Tracy and the Alibi Maker' . 125.00
23 'Dick Tracy Meets Jukebox' 125.00
24 'Dick Tracy and Bubbles' . . 125.00
Becomes:

DICK TRACY
COMICS MONTHLY
Harvey
25 ChG,A:Flattop 150.00
26 ChG,A:Vitamin Flintheart . . 125.00
27 ChG,'Flattop Escapes Prision' 125.00
28 ChG,'Case o/t Torture
    Chamber' 135.00
29 ChG,A:Brow,Gravel Gertie . 125.00
30 ChG,'Blackmail Racket' . . . 125.00
31 ChG,A:Snowflake Falls 100.00
32 ChG,A:Shaky,Snowflake Falls 100.00
33 ChG,'Strange Case
    of Measles' 125.00
34 ChG,A:Measles,Paprika . . . 100.00
35 ChG,'Case of Stolen $50,000' 100.00
36 ChG,'Case of the
    Runaway Blonde' 125.00
37 ChG,'Case of Stolen Money' 100.00
38 ChG,A:Breathless Mahoney 100.00
39 ChG,A:Itchy,B.O.Pleanty . . . 100.00
40 ChG,'Case of Atomic Killer' . 100.00
41 ChG,Pt.1'Murder by Mail' . . 80.00
42 ChG,Pt.2'Murder by Mail' . . . 80.00
43 ChG,'Case of the
    Underworld Brat' 80.00
44 ChG,'Case of the Mouthwash
    Murder' 80.00
45 ChG,'Case of the Evil Eyes' . 80.00
46 ChG,'Case of the
    Camera Killers' 80.00
47 ChG,'Case of the
    Bloodthirsty Blonde' 80.00
48 ChG,'Case of the
    Murderous Minstrel' 80.00
49 ChG,Pt.1'Killer Who Returned
    From the Dead 80.00
50 ChG,Pt.2'Killer Who
    Returned From the Dead' . . . 80.00
51 ChG,'Case of the
    High Tension Hijackers' 75.00
52 ChG,'Case of the
    Pipe-Stem Killer 75.00
53 ChG,Pt.1'Dick Tracy Meets

Dick Tracy #41 © Dell Publ. Co.

the Murderous Midget' 75.00
54 ChG,Pt.2'Dick Tracy Meets
    the Murderous Midget' 75.00
55 ChG,Pt.3'Dick Tracy Meets
    the Murderous Midget' 75.00
56 ChG,'Case of the
    Teleguard Terror' 75.00
57 ChG,Pt.1'Case of the
    Ice Cold Killer' 100.00
58 ChG,Pt.2'Case of the
    Ice Cold Killer' 75.00
59 ChG,Pt.1'Case of the
    Million Dollar Murder' 75.00
60 ChG,Pt.2'Case of the
    Million Dollar Murder' 60.00
61 ChG,'Case of the
    Murderers Mask' 60.00
62 ChG,Pt.1'Case of the
    White Rat Robbers' 60.00
63 ChG,Pt.2'Case of the
    White Rat Robbers' 60.00
64 ChG,Pt.1'Case of the
    Interrupted Honeymoon' 60.00
65 ChG,Pt.2'Case of the
    Interrupted Honeymoon' 60.00
66 ChG,Pt.1'Case of the
    Killer's Revenge' 60.00
67 ChG,Pt.2'Case of the
    Killer's Revenge' 60.00
68 ChG,Pt.1'Case of the
    TV Terror' 60.00
69 ChG,Pt.2'Case of the
    TV Terror' 60.00
70 ChG,Pt.3'Case of the
    TV Terror' 60.00
71 ChG,A:Mrs. Forchune,Opal . 60.00
72 ChG,A:Empty Wiliams,Bonny 60.00
73 ChG,A:Bonny Braids 60.00
74 ChG,A:Mr. & Mrs.
    Fortson Knox 60.00
75 ChG,A:Crewy Lou, Sphinx . . 60.00
76 ChG,A:Diet Smith,Brainerd . . 60.00
77 ChG,A:Crewy Lou,
    Bonny Braids 60.00
78 ChG,A:Spinner Records 60.00
79 ChG,A:Model Jones,
    Larry Jones 60.00
80 ChG,A:Tonsils,Dot View 60.00
81 ChG,A:Edward Moppet,Tonsils 60.00

82 ChG,A:Dot View,Mr. Crime . . 60.00
83 ChG,A:Rifle Ruby,Newsuit Nan 60.00
84 ChG,A:Mr. Crime,Newsuit Nan 60.00
85 ChG,A:Newsuit Nan, Mrs.Lava 60.00
86 ChG,A:Mr. Crime, Odds Zonn 60.00
87 ChG,A:Odds Zonn,Wingy . . . 60.00
88 ChG,A:Odds Zonn,Wingy . . . 60.00
89 ChG,Pt.1'Canhead' 60.00
90 ChG,Pt.2'Canhead' 60.00
91 ChG,Pt.3'Canhead' 60.00
92 ChG,Pt.4'Canhead' 60.00
93 ChG,Pt.5'Canhead' 60.00
94 ChG,Pt.6'Canhead' 60.00
95 ChG,A:Mrs. Green,Dewdrop . 60.00
96 ChG,A:Dewdrop,Sticks 60.00
97 ChG,A:Dewdrop,Sticks 60.00
98 ChG,A:Open-Mind Monty,
   Sticks 60.00
99 ChG,A:Open-Mind Monty,
   Sticks 70.00
100 ChG,A:Half-Pint,Dewdrop . . 75.00
101 ChG,A:Open-Mind Monty . . 60.00
102 ChG,A:Rainbow Reiley,Wingy 60.00
103 ChG,A:Happy,Rughead 60.00
104 ChG,A:Rainbow Reiley,Happy 60.00
105 ChG,A:Happy,Rughead 60.00
106 ChG,A:Fence,Corny,Happy . 60.00
107 ChG,A:Rainbow Reiley 60.00
108 ChG,A:Rughead,Corny,Fence 60.00
109 ChG,A:Rughead,Mimi,Herky 60.00
110 ChG,A:Vitamin Flintheart . . . 60.00
111 ChG,A:Shoulders,Roach . . . 60.00
112 ChG,A:Brilliant,Diet Smith . . 60.00
113 ChG,A:Snowflake Falls 60.00
114 ChG,A:'Sketch'Paree, ... 60.00
115 ChG,A:Rod & Nylon Hoze . . 60.00
116 ChG,A:Empty Williams 60.00
117 ChG,A:Spinner Records . . . 60.00
118 ChG,A:Sleet 60.00
119 ChG,A:Coffyhead 60.00
120 ChG,'Case Against
   Mumbles Quartet' 50.00
121 ChG,'Case of the Wild Boys' 50.00
122 ChG,'Case of the
   Poisoned Pellet' 50.00
123 ChG,'Case of the Deadly
   Treasure Hunt' 50.00
124 ChG,'Case of Oodles
   Hears Only Evil 50.00
125 ChG,'Case of the Desparate
   Widow' 50.00
126 ChG,'Case of Oodles'
   Hideout' 50.00
127 ChG,'Case Against
   Joe Period' 50.00
128 ChG,'Case Against Juvenile
   Delinquent' 50.00
129 ChG,'Case of Son of Flattop' 50.00
130 ChG,'Case of Great
   Gang Roundup' 50.00
131 ChG,'Strange Case of
   Flattop's Conscience' 55.00
132 ChG,'Case of Flattop's
   Big Show' 55.00
133 ChG,'Dick Tracy Follows Trail
   of Jewel Thief Gang' 50.00
134 ChG,'Last Stand of
   Jewel Thieves' 50.00
135 ChG,'Case of the
   Rooftop Sniper' 50.00
136 ChG,'Mystery of the
   Iron Room' 50.00
137 ChG,'Law Versus Dick Tracy' 50.00
138 ChG,'Mystery of Mary X' . . . 50.00
139 ChG,'Yogee the Merciless' . 50.00

140 ChG,'The Tunnel Trap' 50.00
141 ChG,'Case of Wormy &
   His Deadly Wagon 50.00
142 ChG,'Case of the
   Killer's Revenge' 50.00
143 ChG,'Strange Case of
   Measles' 50.00
144 ChG,'Strange Case of
   Shoulders' 50.00
145 ChG,'Case of the Feindish
   Photo-graphers';April, 1961 . . 50.00

DIME COMICS
Newsbook Publ. Corp.
1945
1 LbC,A:Silver Streak 150.00

DING DONG
Compix
(Magazine Enterprises)
1947
1 (fa) 50.00
2 (fa) 30.00
3 thru 5 (fa) . . . . @25.00

DINKY DUCK
St. John Publ. Co./Pines
November, 1951
1 . . . . 30.00
2 . . . . 20.00
3 thru 10 . . . . @15.00
11 thru 15 . . . . @10.00
16 thru 18 . . . . @7.00
19 Summer, 1958 . . . . 7.00

DIXIE DUGAN
Columbia Publ./
Publication Enterprises
July, 1942
1 Boxing cover,Joe Palooka . . 150.00
2 . . . . 75.00
3 . . . . 60.00
4 . . . . 45.00
5 . . . . 45.00
6 thru 12 . . . . @28.00
13 1949 . . . . 28.00

DIZZY DAMES
B&M Distribution Co.
(American Comics)
September-October, 1952
1 . . . . 45.00
2 . . . . 30.00
3 thru 6 July-Aug., 1953 . . . @20.00

DIZZY DON COMICS
Howard Publications/
Dizzy Dean Ent.
1943
1 B&W interior 45.00
2 B&W Interior 20.00
3 B&W Interior 15.00
4 B&W Interior 15.00
5 thru 21 . . . . @15.00
22 October, 1946 . . . . 40.00
1a 30.00
2a 30.00
3a 30.00

DIZZY DUCK
(see BARNYARD COMICS)

DOC CARTER
V.D. COMICS
Health Publ. Inst.
1949
N# 125.00
N# 100.00

DOC SAVAGE COMICS
Street & Smith Publications
May, 1940
1 B:Doc Savage, Capt. Fury, Danny
   Garrett, Mark Mallory, Whisperer,
   Capt. Death, Treasure
   Island, A: The Magician . . 2,000.00
2 O:Ajax,The Sun Man,E:The
   Whisperer 750.00
3 Artic Ice Wastes 650.00
4 E:Treasure Island, Saves
   U.S. Navy 500.00

Doc Savage Comics #5
© Street & Smith Publications

5 O:Astron, the Crocodile
   Queen, Sacred Ruby 400.00
6 E: Capt. Fury, O:Red Falcon,
   Murderous Peace Clan . . . 350.00
7 V:Zoombas 350.00
8 Finds the Long Lost Treasure 350.00
9 Smashes Japan's Secret Oil
   Supply 350.00
10 O:Thunder Bolt, The Living
   Dead A:Lord Manhattan . . . 350.00
11 V:Giants of Destruction 275.00
12 Saves Merchant Fleet from
   Complete Destruction 275.00
2-1 The Living Evil 275.00
2-2 V:Beggar King 275.00
2-3 . . . . 275.00
2-4 Fight to Death 275.00
2-5 Saves Panama Canal from
   Blood Raider 275.00
2-6 . . . . 275.00
2-7 V:Black Knight 275.00
2-8 October, 1943 . . . . 275.00

DR. ANTHONY KING
HOLLYWOOD LOVE
DOCTOR

Harvey, Publ.
1952

1	50.00
2	30.00
3	30.00
4 BP,May, 1954	30.00

DOLL MAN
Comic Favorites
(Quality Comics Group)
Fall, 1941

1 RC,B:Doll Man & Justine Wright	1,500.00
2 B:Dragon	650.00
3 Five stories	500.00
4 Dolls of Death, Wanted: The Doll Man	450.00
5 RC,Four stories	350.00
6 Buy War Stamps cover	300.00
7 Four stories	300.00
8 BWa,Three stories,A:Torchy	350.00
9	250.00
10 RC,V:Murder Marionettes, Grim, The Good Sport	200.00
11 Shocks Crime Square in the Eye	200.00
12	200.00
13 RC,Blows Crime Sky High	200.00

Doll Man #45 © Quality Comics Group

14 Spotlight on Comics	200.00
15 Faces Danger	200.00
16	200.00
17 Deals out Punishment for Crime	200.00
18 Redskins Scalp Crime	200.00
19 Fitted for a Cement Coffin	200.00
20 Destroys the Black Heart of Nemo Black	200.00
21 Problem of a Poison Pistol	175.00
22 V:Tom Thumb	175.00
23 V:Minstrel, musician of menace	175.00
24 V:Elixir of Youth	175.00
25 V:Thrawn, Lord of Lightning	175.00
26 V:Sultan of Satarr & Wonderous Runt	175.00
27 Space Conquest	175.00
28 V:The Flame	175.00
29 V:Queen MAB	175.00

30 V:Lord Damion	175.00
31 I:Elmo, the Wonder Dog	150.00
32 A:Jeb Rivers	150.00
33	150.00
34	150.00
35 Prophet of Doom	150.00
36 Death Trap in the Deep	150.00
37 V:The Skull,B:Doll Girl, Bondage(c)	200.00
38 The Cult of Death	150.00
39 V:The Death Drug	165.00
40 Giants of Crime	100.00
41 The Headless Horseman	100.00
42 Tale of the Mind Monster	100.00
43 The Thing that Kills	100.00
44 V:Radioactive Man	100.00
45 What was in the Doom Box?	100.00
46 Monster from Tomorrow	100.00
47 V:Mad Hypnotist, October, 1953	100.00

FAMOUS GANG, BOOK OF COMICS
Firestone Tire & Rubber Co.
1942

N#	700.00

Becomes:

DONALD AND MICKEY MERRY CHRISTMAS

N# (2),CB, 1943	500.00
N# (3),CB, 1944	500.00
N# (4),CB, 1945	650.00
N# (5),CB,1946	550.00
N# (6),CB, 1947	450.00
N# (7),CB, 1948	450.00
N# (8),CB, 1949	500.00

DONALD DUCK
Whitman

W.Disney's Donald Duck ('35)	2,200.00
W.Disney's Donald Duck ('36)	2,000.00
W.Disney's Donald Duck ('38)	2,200.00

DONALD DUCK GIVEAWAYS

Donald Duck Surprise Party (Icy Frost Ice Cream 1948)WK	900.00
Donald Duck (Xmas Giveaway 1944)	350.00
Donald Duck Tells About Kites (P.G.&E., Florida 1954)	2,000.00
Donald Duck Tells About Kites (S.C.Edison 1954)	1,800.00
Donald Duck and the Boys (Whitman 1948)	125.00
Donald Ducks Atom Bomb (Cherrios 1947)	275.00

(WALT DISNEY'S) DONALD DUCK
Dell Publishing Co.
November 1952

(#1-#25) See Dell Four Color

26 CB;"Trick or Treat" (1952)	240.00
27 CB(c);"Flying Horse"('53)	90.00
28 CB(c); Robert the Robot	85.00
29 CB(c)	85.00
30 CB(c)	85.00
31 thru 39	@45.00
40 thru 44	@40.00
45 CB	125.00
46 CB; "Secret of Hondorica"	175.00

Donald Duck #62
© Dell Publishing Co.

47 thru 51	@40.00
52 CB; "Lost Peg-Leg Mine"	125.00
53	30.00
54 CB; "Forbidden Valley"	125.00
55 thru 59	@30.00
60 CB; "Donald Duck & the Titanic Ants"	125.00
61 thru 67	@30.00
68 CB	100.00
69 thru 78	@30.00
79 CB (1 page)	35.00
80	25.00
81 CB (1 page)	30.00
82	25.00
83	25.00
84	25.00

See: Independent Color Listings

DON FORTUNE MAGAZINE
Don Fortune Publ. Co.
August, 1946

1 CCB	100.00
2 CCB	75.00
3 CCB,Bondage(c)	50.00
4 CCB	40.00
5 CCB	40.00
6 CCB, January, 1947	40.00

DON NEWCOMBE
Fawcett Publications
1950

1 Baseball Star	250.00

DON WINSLOW OF THE NAVY
Fawcett Publ./ Charlton Comics
February, 1943

1 Captain Marvel cover	550.00
2 Nips the Nipponese in the Solomons	300.00
3 Single-Handed invasion of the Philippines	225.00
4 Undermines the Nazis!	150.00
5 Stolen Battleship Mystery	150.00

---

6 War Stamps for Victory cover	150.00
7 Coast Guard	125.00
8 U.S. Marines	125.00
9 Fighting Marines	125.00
10 Fighting Seabees	125.00
11	75.00
12 Tuned for Death	75.00
13 Hirohito's Hospitality	80.00
14 Catapults against the Axis	80.00
15 Fighting Merchant Marine	70.00
16 V:The Most Diabolical Villain of all Time	70.00
17 Buy War Stamps cover	70.00
18 The First Underwater Convoy	65.00
19 Bonape Excersion	65.00
20 The Nazi Prison Ship	65.00
21 Prisoner of the Nazis	50.00

Don Winslow of the Navy #6
© Fawcett Publications

22 Suicide Football	50.00
23 Peril on the High Seas	50.00
24 Adventures on the High Seas	50.00
25 Shanghaied Red Cross Ship	50.00
26 V:The Scorpion	50.00
27 Buy War Stamps	50.00
28	50.00
29 Invitation to Trouble	50.00
30	50.00
31 Man or Myth?	45.00
32 Return of the Renegade	45.00
33 Service Ribbons	45.00
34 Log Book	45.00
35	45.00
36	45.00
37 V: Sea Serpent	45.00
38 Climbs Mt. Everest	45.00
39 Scorpion's Death Ledger	45.00
40 Kick Off!	50.00
41 Rides the Skis!	40.00
42 Amazon Island	40.00
43 Ghastly Doll Murder Case	40.00
44 The Scorpions Web	40.00
45 V:Highwaymen of the Seas	40.00
46 Renegades Jailbreak	40.00
47 The Artic Expedition	40.00
48 Maelstrom of the Deep	40.00
49 The Vanishing Ship!	40.00
50 V:The Snake	40.00
51 A:Singapore Sal	35.00
52 Ghost of the Fishing Ships	35.00

53	35.00
54	35.00
55	35.00
56 Far East	35.00
57 A:Singapore Sal	35.00
58	35.00
59	35.00
60	35.00
61	35.00
62	35.00
63	35.00
64 MB	50.00
65 Ph(c)	45.00
66 Ph(c)	45.00
67 Ph(c)	45.00
68 Ph(c)	45.00
69 Ph(c), Jaws of Destruction	45.00
70	35.00
71	35.00
72	35.00
73 September, 1955	35.00

DOPEY DUCK
Non-Pareil Publ. Corp.
Fall, 1945

1 A:Krazy Krow,Casper Cat	70.00
2 same	65.00

Becomes:

WACKY DUCK

3	50.00
4	40.00
5	40.00
6 Summer, 1947	40.00

DOROTHY LAMOUR
(see JUNGLE LIL)

DOTTY DRIPPLE
Magazine Enterprises/
Harvey Publications
1946

1	25.00
2	15.00
3 thru 10	@10.00
11 thru 20	@7.00
21 thru 23	@5.00
24 June, 1952	5.00

Becomes:

HORACE &
DOTTY DRIPPLE

25 thru 42	@6.00
43 October, 1955	6.00

DOUBLE COMICS
Elliot Publications

1 ('40),Masked Marvel	1,350.00
2 ('41),Tornado Tim	900.00
3 ('42)	700.00
4 ('43)	500.00
5 ('44)	500.00

DOUBLE UP
Elliot Publications
1941

1	425.00

DOWN WITH CRIME
Fawcett Publications
November, 1951

1 A:Desarro	100.00
2 BP, A:Scanlon Gang	60.00

3 H-is for Heroin	55.00
4 BP, A:Desarro	50.00
5 No Jail Can Hold Me	55.00
6 The Puncture-Proof Assassin	40.00
7 The Payoff, November, 1952	40.00

DUDLEY
Prize Publications
November-December, 1952

1	65.00
2	40.00
3 March-April, 1950	35.00

DUMBO WEEKLY
The Walt Disney Co.
1942

1 Gas giveaways	200.00
2 thru 16	@90.00

DURANGO KID
Magazine Enterprises
October-November, 1949

1 FF, Charles Starrett photo cover B:Durango Kid & Raider	400.00
2 FF, Charles Starrett Ph(c)	250.00
3 FF, Charles Starrett Ph(c)	225.00
4 FF, Charles Starrett Ph(c), Two-Timing Guns	200.00
5 FF, Charles Starrett Ph(c), Tracks Across the Trail	200.00
6 FF	125.00
7 FF,Atomic(c)	135.00
8 FF	125.00
9 FF	125.00
10 FF	125.00
11 FF	100.00
12 FF	100.00
13 FF	100.00
14 FF	100.00
15 FF	100.00
16 FF	100.00
17 O:Durango Kid	120.00
18 FMe,DAy(c)	55.00
19 FMe,FG	50.00
20 FMe,FG	50.00
21 FMe,FG	50.00
22 FMe,FG	55.00
23 FMe,FG,I:Red Scorpion	55.00
24 thru 30 FMe,FG	@55.00
31 FMe,FG	55.00
32 thru 40 FG	@50.00
41 FG,October, 1941	60.00

DYNAMIC COMICS
Dynamic Publications
(Harry 'A' Chesler)
October, 1941

1 EK,O:Major Victory, Dynamic Man, Hale the Magician, A:Black Cobra	675.00
2 O:Dynamic Boy & Lady Satan,I:Green Knight, Lance Cooper	400.00
3 GT	300.00
8 Horror cover	300.00
9 MRa,GT,B:Mr.E	350.00
10	250.00
11 GT	200.00
12 GT	175.00
13 GT	200.00
14	185.00
15	185.00
16 GT,Bondage(c),Marijuana	225.00

17	300.00
18 Ric	165.00
19 A:Dynamic Man	150.00
20 same,Nude Woman	200.00
21 same	150.00
22 same	150.00
23 A:Yankee Girl,1.0948	150.00

DYNAMITE
Comic Media/Allen Hardy Publ.
May, 1953

1 DH(c),A:Danger#6	90.00
2	45.00
3 PAM,PAM(c),B:Johnny Dynamite,Drug	55.00
4 PAM,PAM(c),Prostitution	75.00
5 PAM,PAM(c)	40.00
6 PAM,PAM(c)	40.00
7 PAM,PAM(c)	40.00
8 PAM,PAM(c)	40.00
9 PAM,PAM(c)	40.00

Becomes:
JOHNNY DYNAMITE
Charlton Comics

10 PAM(c)	35.00
11	30.00
12	35.00

Becomes:
FOREIGN INTRIGUES

13 A:Johnny Dynamite	30.00
14 same	25.00
15 same	25.00

Becomes:
BATTLEFIELD ACTION

16	20.00
17	10.00
18	10.00
19	10.00
20	10.00
21 thru 30	@7.00
31 thru 70	@3.00
71 thru 84 October 1984	@1.00

EAGLE, THE
Fox Features Syndicate
July, 1941

1 B:The Eagle,A:Rex Dexter of Mars	900.00
2 B:Spider Queen	500.00
3 B:Joe Spook	400.00
4 January, 1942	375.00

EAGLE
Rural Home Publ.
February-March, 1945

1 LbC	100.00
2 LbC,April-May, 1945	75.00

EAT RIGHT TO WORK AND WIN
Swift Co.
1942

N# Flash Gordon,Popeye	175.00

EDDIE STANKY
Fawcett Publications
1951

N# New York Giants	150.00

EERIE
Avon Periodicals

May-June, 1951

1 JKa,Horror from the Pit, Bondage(c)	400.00
2 WW,WW(c), Chamber of Death	300.00
3 WW,WW(c),JKa,JO Monster of the Storm	325.00
4 WW(c),Phantom of Reality	250.00
5 WW(c), Operation Horror	250.00
6 Devil Keeps a Date	125.00
7 WW(c),JKa,JO,Blood for the Vampire	200.00
8 EK, Song of the Undead	125.00
9 JKa, Hands of Death	150.00
10 Castle of Terror	125.00
11 Anatomical Monster	110.00
12 Dracula	150.00
13	125.00
14 Master of the Dead	135.00
15	75.00
16 WW, Chamber of Death	100.00
17 WW(c),JO,JKa,August-September,1954	125.00

Eerie #5 © Avon Periodicals

EERIE ADVENTURES
Approved Comics
(Ziff-Davis)
Winter, 1951

1 BP,JKa,Bondage	150.00

EGBERT
Arnold Publications/ Comic Magazine
Spring, 1946

1 I:Egbert & The Count	90.00
2	50.00
3	25.00
4	25.00
5	25.00
6 thru 10	@25.00
11 thru 17	@20.00
18 1950	20.00

EH!
Charlton Comics
December, 1953

1 DAy(c),DG	125.00

2 DAy(c)	80.00
3 DAy(c)	70.00
4 DAy(c)	70.00
5 DAy(c)	70.00
6 DAy(c)	70.00
7 DAy(c),November, 1954	70.00

EL BOMBO COMICS
Frances M. McQueeny
1945

1	50.00

ELLERY QUEEN
Superior Comics
May, 1949

1 LbC(c),JKa,Horror	250.00
2	125.00
3 Drug issue	175.00
4 The Crooked Mile, November, 1949	150.00

ELLERY QUEEN
Approved Comics
(Ziff-Davis)
January-March, 1952

1 NS(c),The Corpse the Killed	250.00
2 NS,Killer's Revenge, Summer, 1952	200.00

ELSIE THE COW
D.S. Publishing Co.
October-November, 1949

1 P(c)	150.00
2 Bondage(c)	175.00
3 July-August, 1950	150.00

ENCHANTING LOVE
Kirby Publishing Co.
October, 1949

1 Branded Guilty, Ph(c)	55.00
2 Ph(c),BP	30.00
3 Ph(c),Utter Defeat was our Victory; Jan.-Feb., 1950	25.00

ETTA KETT
Best Books, Inc.
(Standard Comics)
December, 1948

11	45.00
12	30.00
13	30.00
14 September, 1949	30.00

ERNIE COMICS
(see SCREAM COMICS)

EXCITING COMICS
Better Publ./Visual Editions
(Standard Comics)
April, 1940

1 O:Mask, Jim Hatfield, Dan Williams	750.00
2 B:Sphinx	400.00
3 V:Robot	250.00
4 V:Sea Monster	225.00
5 V:Gargoyle	225.00
6	200.00
7 AS(c)	200.00
8	200.00
9 O:Black Terror & Tim, Bondage(c)	1,200.00

Exciting Comics #3
© Better Publ./Visual Editions

10 A:Black Terror 450.00
11 same 350.00
12 Bondage(c) 350.00
13 Bondage(c) 350.00
14 O:Sphinx 250.00
15 O:Liberator 300.00
16 Black Terror 175.00
17 same 175.00
18 same 175.00
19 same 175.00
20 E:Mask,Bondage(c) 185.00
21 A:Liberator 160.00
22 O:The Eaglet,B:American
     Eagle 200.00
23 Black Terror 150.00
24 Black Terror 150.00
25 Bondage(c) 165.00
26 ASh(c) 150.00
27 ASh(c) 150.00
28 ASh(c) 200.00
29 ASh(c) 200.00
30 ASh(c),Bondage(c) 225.00
31 ASh(c) 175.00
32 ASh(c) 175.00
33 ASh(c) 175.00
34 ASh(c) 175.00
35 ASh(c),E:Liberator 175.00
36 ASh(c) 175.00
37 ASh(c) 175.00
38 ASh(c) 175.00
39 ASh(c)O:Kara, Jungle
     Princess 225.00
40 ASh(c) 200.00
41 ASh(c) 200.00
42 ASh(c),B:Scarab 210.00
43 ASh(c) 200.00
44 ASh(c) 200.00
45 ASh(c),V:Robot 200.00
46 ASh(c) 200.00
47 ASh(c) 200.00
48 ASh(c) 200.00
49 ASh(c),E:Kara &
     American Eagle 200.00
50 ASh(c),E:American Eagle . 200.00
51 ASh(c),B:Miss Masque 235.00
52 ASh(c),Miss Masque 175.00
53 ASh(c),Miss Masque 175.00
54 ASh(c),E:Miss Masque 175.00

55 ASh(c),O&B:Judy o/t Jungle 250.00
56 ASh(c) 225.00
57 ASh(c) 225.00
58 ASh(c) 225.00
59 ASh(c),FF,Bondage(c) 250.00
60 ASh(c),The Mystery Rider . 175.00
61 ASh(c) 150.00
62 ASh(c) 150.00
63 thru 65 ASh(c) .... @175.00
66 .... 100.00
67 GT 110.00
68 .... 100.00
69 September, 1949 .... 100.00

EXCITING ROMANCES
Fawcett Publications
1949
1 Ph(c) 60.00
2 thru 3 .... @30.00
4 Ph(c) 35.00
5 thru 14 .... @25.00

EXOTIC ROMANCE
(see TRUE WAR ROMANCES)

EXPLORER JOE
Approved Comics
(Ziff-Davis)
Winter, 1951
1 NS,The Fire Opal
    of Madagscar 55.00
2 BK, October-November, 1952 75.00

EXPOSED
D.S. Publishing Co.
March-April, 1948
1 Corpses Cash and Carry .. 125.00
2 Giggling Killer 90.00
3 One Bloody Night 40.00
4 JO,Deadly Dummy 40.00
5 Body on the Beach 40.00
6 Grl,The Secret in the Snow 160.00
7 The Gypsy Baron,
    July-August, 1949 ...... 150.00

EXTRA
Magazine Enterprises
1947
1 .... 300.00

EXTRA!
E.C. Comics
March-April, 1955
1 JCr,RC,JSe 100.00
2 JCr,RC,JSe 65.00
3 JCr,RC,JSe 65.00
4 JCr,RC,JSe 65.00
5 November-December, 1955 . 65.00

FACE, THE
Publication Enterprises
(Columbia Comics)
1942
1 MBi(c),The Face 450.00
2 MBi(c) 275.00
Becomes:
TONY TRENT
3 MBi,A:The Face 65.00
4 1949 .... 55.00

FAIRY TALE PARADE

Dell Publishing Co.
1942
1 WK,Giant 800.00
2 WK,Flying Horse 500.00
3 WK 350.00
4 WK 300.00
5 WK 300.00
6 WK 250.00
7 WK 250.00
8 WK 250.00
9 WK 250.00

FAMOUS COMICS
Zain-Eppy Publ.
N# Joe Palooka 275.00

FAMOUS CRIMES
Fox Features Syndicate
June, 1948
1 Cold Blooded Killer 200.00
2 Near Nudity cover 150.00
3 Crime Never Pays 200.00
4 .... 75.00
5 .... 75.00
6 .... 75.00
7 Drug issue 175.00
8 thru 19 .... @65.00
20 August, 1951 .... 50.00
51 1952 .... 35.00

FAMOUS FAIRY TALES
K.K. Publication Co.
1942
N# WK, Giveaway 325.00
N# WK, Giveaway 250.00
N# WK, Giveaway 250.00

FAMOUS FEATURE
STORIES
Dell Publishing Co.
1938
1 A:Tarzan, Terry and the Pirates
    Dick Tracy,Smilin' Jack 475.00

FAMOUS FUNNIES
Eastern Color Printing Co.

Famous Funnies #22
© Eastern Color Printing Co.

1933
N# A Carnival of Comics ... 6,500.00
N# February, 1934,
  1st 10¢ comic 17,000.00
1 July, 1934 .... 12,000.00
2 .... 2,500.00
3 B:Buck Rogers 3,000.00
4 Football cover 800.00
5 .... 650.00
6 .... 600.00
7 .... 600.00
8 .... 600.00
9 .... 600.00
10 .... 600.00
11 Four pages of Buck Rogers 500.00
12 Four pages of Buck Rogers 500.00
13 .... 400.00
14 .... 375.00
15 Football cover 375.00
16 .... 375.00
17 Christmas cover 350.00
18 Four pages of Buck Rogers 500.00
19 .... 375.00
20 .... 350.00
21 Baseball 325.00
22 Buck Rogers 325.00
23 .... 275.00
24 B: War on Crime 275.00
25 .... 275.00
26 .... 275.00
27 G-Men cover 275.00
28 .... 275.00
29 .... 275.00
30 .... 275.00
31 .... 225.00
32 .... 225.00
33 A:Baby Face Nelson &
  John Dillinger 225.00
34 .... 225.00
35 Buck Rogers 225.00
36 .... 225.00
37 .... 225.00
38 Portrait,Buck Rogers ... 250.00
39 .... 225.00
40 .... 225.00
41 thru 50 .... @165.00
51 thru 57 .... @150.00
58 Baseball cover 150.00
59 .... 150.00
60 .... 150.00
61 .... 125.00
62 .... 125.00
63 .... 125.00
64 .... 125.00
65 JK 125.00
66 .... 125.00
67 .... 125.00
68 JK 125.00
69 .... 125.00
70 .... 125.00
71 BEv 100.00
72 BEv,B:Speed Spaulding ... 100.00
73 BEv 100.00
74 BEv 100.00
75 BEv 100.00
76 BEv 100.00
77 BEv,Merry Christmas cover . 100.00
78 BEv 100.00
79 BEv 100.00
80 BEv,Buck Rogers 100.00
81 O:Invisible Scarlet O'Neil ... 75.00
82 Buck Rogers cover 100.00
83 Dickie Dare 75.00
84 Scotty Smith 75.00
85 Eagle Scout,Roy Rogers 75.00

86 Moon Monsters 75.00
87 Scarlet O'Neil 75.00
88 .... 75.00
89 O:Fearless Flint 75.00
90 Bondage cover 80.00
91 .... 60.00
92 .... 60.00
93 .... 60.00
94 War Bonds 70.00
95 Invisible Scarlet O'Neil 65.00
96 .... 65.00
97 War Bonds Promo 65.00
98 .... 65.00
99 .... 65.00
100 Anniversary issue 65.00
101 thru 110 .... @60.00
111 thru 130 .... @50.00
131 thru 150 .... @40.00
151 thru 162 .... @30.00
163 Valentine's Day cover 35.00
164 .... 30.00
165 .... 30.00
166 .... 30.00
167 .... 30.00
168 .... 30.00
169 AW 60.00
170 AW 60.00
171 thru 190 .... @30.00
191 thru 203 .... @25.00
204 War cover 28.00
205 thru 208 .... @25.00
209 FF(c),Buck Rogers 300.00
210 FF(c),Buck Rogers 300.00
211 FF(c),Buck Rogers 300.00
212 FF(c),Buck Rogers 300.00
213 FF(c),Buck Rogers 300.00
214 FF(c),Buck Rogers 300.00
215 FF(c),Buck Rogers 300.00
216 FF(c),Buck Rogers 300.00
217 .... 30.00
218 July, 1955 .... 30.00

FAMOUS GANG, BOOK OF COMICS
(see DONALD AND MICKEY MERRY CHRISTMAS)

FAMOUS GANGSTERS
Avon Periodicals
April, 1951
1 Al Capone, Dillinger,
  Luciano & Shultz 175.00
2 WW(c),Dillinger Machine-
  Gun Killer 175.00
3 Lucky Luciano & Murder Inc. 175.00
Becomes:

CRIME ON THE WATERFRONT
4 Underworld Gangsters who
  Control the Shipment of Drugs!,
  May, 1952 .... 150.00

FAMOUS STARS
Ziff-Davis Publ. Co.
August, 1950
1 OW,Shelley Winter,Susan Peters
  & Shirley Temple 175.00
2 BEv,Betty Hutton, Bing Crosby125.00
3 OW,Judy Garland, Alan Ladd 135.00
4 RC,Jolson, Bob Mitchum .. 125.00
5 BK,Elizabeth Taylor,
  Esther Williams 150.00
6 Gene Kelly, Spring, 1952 .. 125.00

FAMOUS STORIES
Dell Publishing Co.
1942
1 Treasure Island 175.00
2 Tom Sawyer 175.00

FAMOUS WESTERN BADMEN
(see REDSKIN)

FANTASTIC
(see CAPTAIN SCIENCE)

FANTASTIC COMICS
Fox Features Syndicate
December, 1939
1 LFc(c),I&O:Samson,B:Star
  Dust, Super Wizard, Space
  Smith & Capt. Kid 1,850.00
2 BP,LFc(c),Samson destroyed the
  Battery and Routed the Foe 850.00
3 BP,LF(c),Slays the Iron
  Monster 600.00

Fantastic #3 © Fox Features Syndicate

4 GT,LFc(c),Demolishes the
  Closing Torture Walls 575.00
5 GT,LFc(c),Crumbles the
  Mighty War Machine 575.00
6 JSm(c),Bondage(c) 500.00
7 JSm(c) 500.00
8 GT,Destroys the Mask of
  Fire,Bondage(c) 500.00
9 Mighty Muscles saved the
  Drowning Girl 500.00
10 I&O:David 400.00
11 Wrecks the Torture Machine
  to save his fellow American . 350.00
12 Heaved the Huge Ship high
  into the Air 350.00
13 .... 350.00
14 .... 350.00
15 .... 350.00
16 E:Stardust 350.00
17 .... 350.00
18 I:Black Fury & Chuck 400.00
19 .... 350.00
20 .... 350.00
21 B&I: The Banshee,Hitler(c) . 400.00

22 .... 400.00
23 O:The Gladiator, Nov., 1941 400.00

FARGO KID
(see JUSTICE TRAPS OF THE GUILTY)

FAST FICTION
Seaboard Publ./
Famous Author Illustrated
October, 1949

1 Scarlet Pimpernel 225.00
2 HcK,Captain Blood 175.00
3 She 250.00
4 The 39 Steps 165.00
5 HcK,Beau Geste 165.00

Becomes:
STORIES BY FAMOUS AUTHORS ILLUSTRATED

1a Scarlet Pimpernel 200.00
2a Captain Blood 200.00
3a She 250.00
4a The 39 Steps 150.00
5a Beau Geste 135.00
6 HcK,MacBeth 150.00
7 HcK,Window 125.00
8 HcK,Hamlet 150.00
9 Nicholas Nickleby 135.00
10 HcK,Romeo & Juliet 135.00
11 GS,Ben Hur 145.00
12 GS,La Svengali 145.00
13 HcK,Scaramouche 145.00

FAWCETT FUNNY ANIMALS
Fawcett Publications
December, 1942

1 I:Hoppy the Marvel,
  Captain Marvel cover 350.00
2 X-Mas Issue 175.00
3 Spirit of '43 .... 120.00
4 and 5 .... @120.00
6 Buy War Bonds and Stamps . 80.00
7 .... 80.00
8 Flag cover 75.00
9 and 10 .... @70.00
11 thru 20 .... @50.00
21 thru 30 .... @30.00
31 thru 40 .... @25.00
41 thru 83 .... @20.00

Charlton Comics
84 .... 25.00
85 thru 91 Feb. 1956 ...... @20.00

FAWCETT MOVIE COMICS
Fawcett Publications
1949

N# Dakota Lil 220.00
N#a Copper Canyon 200.00
N# Destination the Moon 500.00
N# Montana 150.00
N# Pioneer Marshal 150.00
N# Powder River Rustlers ... 175.00
N# Singing Guns 160.00
7 Gunmen of Abilene 175.00
8 King of the Bull Whip 275.00
9 BP,The Old Frontier 160.00
10 The Missourians 160.00
11 The Thundering Trail 225.00
12 Rustlers on Horseback 165.00
13 Warpath 125.00

14 Last Outpost,RonaldReagan 300.00
15 The Man from Planet-X .. 1,200.00
16 10 Tall Men 100.00
17 Rose Cimarron 55.00
18 The Brigand 65.00
19 Carbine Williams 75.00
20 Ivan hoe, December, 1952 . 125.00

Feature Books #25
© David McKay Publications

FEATURE BOOKS
David McKay Publications
May, 1937

N# Dick Tracy 5,000.00
N# Popeye 5,000.00
1 Zane Grey's King of the
  Royal Mounted 600.00
2 Popeye 600.00
3 Popeye and the "Jeep" 550.00
4 Dick Tracy 900.00
5 Popeye and his Poppa 500.00
6 Dick Tracy 700.00
7 Little Orphan Annie 800.00
8 Secret Agent X-9 .... 350.00
9 Tracy & the Famon Boys ... 700.00
10 Popeye & Susan 500.00
11 Annie Rooney 200.00
12 Blondie 500.00
13 Inspector Wade 175.00
14 Popeye in Wild Oats 600.00
15 Barney Baxter in the Air ... 225.00
16 Red Eagle 150.00
17 Gang Busters 450.00
18 Mandrake the Magician ... 350.00
19 Mandrake 350.00
20 The Phantom 600.00
21 Lone Ranger 500.00
22 The Phantom 500.00
23 Mandrake in Teibe Castle .. 350.00
24 Lone Ranger 550.00
25 Flash Gordon on the
  Planet Mongo 625.00
26 Prince Valiant 675.00
27 Blondie 100.00
28 Blondie and Dagwood 90.00
29 Blondie at the Home
  Sweet Home 90.00
30 Katzenjammer Kids 100.00
31 Blondie Keeps the Home

Fires Burning 85.00
32 Katzenjammer Kids 90.00
33 Romance of Flying 70.00
34 Blondie Home is Our Castle . 80.00
35 Katzenjammer Kids 90.00
36 Blondie on the Home Front .. 85.00
37 Katzenjammer Kids 85.00
38 Blondie the ModelHomemaker 75.00
39 The Phantom 350.00
40 Blondie 75.00
41 Katzenjammer Kids 80.00
42 Blondie in Home-Spun Yarns 75.00
43 Blondie Home-Cooked Scraps 75.00
44 Katzenjammer Kids in
  Monkey Business 75.00
45 Blondie in Home of the Free
  and the Brave 70.00
46 Mandrake in Fire World ... 250.00
47 Blondie in Eaten out of
  House and Home 70.00
48 The Maltese Falcon 400.00
49 Perry Mason - The Case of
  the Lucky Legs 150.00
50 The Shoplifters Shoe,
  P. Mason 150.00
51 Rip Kirby - Mystery of
  the Mangler 200.00
52 Mandrake in the Land of X . 250.00
53 Phantom in Safari Suspense 300.00
54 Rip Kirby - Case of the
  Master Menace 225.00
55 Mandrake in 5-numbers
  Treasue Hunt 250.00
56 Phantom Destroys the
  Sky Band 275.00
57 Phantom in the Blue Gang,
  1948 .... 275.00

Feature Funnies #6
© Harry A. Chesler Publications

FEATURE FUNNIES
Harry A. Chesler Publ./
Comic Favorites
October, 1937

1 RuG,RuG(c),A:Joe Palooka,
  Mickey Finn, Bungles, Dixie
  Dugan, Big Top, Strange as
  It Seems, Off the Record . 1,500.00
2 A: The Hawk 700.00

All comics prices listed are for *Near Mint* condition.

3 WE,Joe Palooka,The Clock . 500.00
4 RuG,WE,RuG(c),Joe Palooka 400.00
5 WE, Joe Palooka drawing . 400.00
6 WE, Joe Palooka cover ... 400.00
7 WE,LLe, Gallant Knight story
   by Vernon Henkel 300.00
8 WE 275.00
9 WE, Joe Palooka story 300.00
10 WE,Micky Finn(c) 275.00
11 WE,LLe,The Bungles(c) ... 275.00
12 WE, Joe Palooka(c) 300.00
13 WE,LLe, World Series(c) .. 300.00
14 WE,Ned Brant(c) 250.00
15 WE,Joe Palooka(c) 275.00
16 Mickey Finn(c) 250.00
17 WE 250.00
18 Joe Palooka cover 265.00
19 WE,LLe,Mickey Finn(c) .. 250.00
20 WE,LLe 250.00
Becomes:

FEATURE COMICS
21 Joe Palooka(c) 350.00
22 LLe(c),Mickey Finn(c) ... 225.00
23 B:Charlie Chan 250.00
24 AAr,Joe Palooka(c) 225.00
25 AAr,The Clock(c) 225.00
26 AAr,The Bundles(c) 225.00
27 WE,AAr,I:Doll Man 1,800.00
28 LF,AAr,The Clock(c) 750.00
29 LF,AAr,The Clock(c) 500.00
30 LF,AAr,Doll Man(c) 500.00
31 LF,AAr,Mickey Finn(c) ... 450.00
32 PGv,LF,GFx,Doll Man(c) . 300.00
33 PGv,LF,GFx,Bundles(c) .. 275.00
34 PGv,LF,GFx,Doll Man(c) . 300.00
35 PGv,LF,GFx,Bundles(c) .. 275.00
36 PGv,LF,GFx,Doll Man(c) . 300.00
37 PGv,LF,GFx,Bundles(c) .. 275.00
38 PGv,GFx,Doll Man(c) 240.00
39 PGv,GFx,Bundles(c) 225.00
40 PGv,GFx,WE(c),Doll Man(c) 240.00
41 PGv,GFx,WE(c),Bundles(c) . 225.00
42 GFx,Doll Man(c) 175.00
43 RC,GFx,Bundles(c) 150.00
44 RC,GFx,Doll Man(c) 250.00
45 RC,GFx,Bundles(c) 150.00
46 RC,PGv,GFx,Doll Man(c) . 175.00
47 RC,GFx,Bundles(c) 150.00
48 RC,GFx,Doll Man(c) 175.00
49 RC,GFx,Bundles(c) 150.00
50 RC,GFx,Doll Man(c) 175.00
51 RC,GFx,Bundles(c) 150.00
52 RC,GFx,Doll Man(c) 150.00
53 RC,GFx,Bundles(c) 125.00
54 RC,GFx,Doll Man(c) 150.00
55 RC,GFx,Bundles(c) 125.00
56 RC,GFx,Doll Man(c) 150.00
57 RC,GFx,Bundles(c) 125.00
58 RC,GFx,Doll Man cover .. 150.00
59 RC,GFx,Mickey Finn(c) .. 125.00
60 RC,GFx,Doll Man(c) 150.00
61 RC,GFx,Bundles(c) 125.00
62 RC,GFx,Doll Man(c) 135.00
63 RC,GFx,Bundles(c) 110.00
64 BP,GFx,Doll Man(c) 135.00
65 BP,GFx(c),Bundles(c) 110.00
66 BP,GFx,Doll Man(c) 135.00
67 BP 110.00
68 BP,Doll Man vs.BeardedLady 135.00
69 BP,GFx(c),Devil cover 110.00
70 BP,Doll Man(c) 135.00
71 BP,GFx(c) 90.00
72 BP,Doll Man(c) 90.00
73 BP,GFx(c),Bundles(c) 80.00
74 Doll Man(c) 90.00

75 GFx(c) 75.00
76 GFx(c) 75.00
77 Doll Man cover until #140 ... 80.00
78 Knows no Fear but the
   Knife Does 75.00
79 Little Luck God 75.00
80 .... 75.00
81 Wanted for Murder 70.00
82 V:Shawunkas the Shaman .. 65.00
83 V:Mechanical Man 65.00
84 V:Masked Rider, Death
   Goes to the Rodeo 65.00
85 V:King of Beasts 65.00
86 Is He A Killer? 65.00
87 The Maze of Murder 65.00
88 V:The Phantom Killer 65.00
89 Crook's Goose 65.00
90 V:Whispering Corpse 65.00
91 V:The Undertaker 65.00
92 V:The Image 65.00
93 .... 65.00
94 V:The Undertaker 65.00
95 Flatten's the Peacock's Pride 65.00
96 Doll Man Proves
   Justice is Blind 65.00
97 V:Peacock 65.00
98 V:Master Diablo 65.00
99 On the Warpath Again! 65.00
100 Crushes the City of Crime . 85.00
101 Land of the Midget Men! .. 50.00
102 The Angle 50.00
103 V:The Queen of Ants 50.00
104 V:The Botanist 50.00
105 Dream of Death 50.00
106 V:The Sword Fish 50.00
107 Hand of Horror! 50.00
108 V:Cateye 50.00
109 V:The Brain 50.00
110 V:Fat Cat 50.00
111 V:The Undertaker 50.00
112 I:Mr. Curio & His Miniatures 50.00
113 V:Highwayman 50.00
114 V:Tom Thumb 50.00
115 V:The Sphinx 50.00
116 V:Elbows 50.00
117 Polka Dot on the Spot ... 50.00
118 thru 143 .... @50.00
144 May, 1950 .... 50.00

FEDERAL MEN COMICS
Gerard Publ. Co.
1942
2 S&S,Spanking 175.00

FELIX THE CAT
Dell Publishing Co.
Feb.-March 1948
1 .... 175.00
2 .... 90.00
3 .... 65.00
4 .... 65.00
5 .... 65.00
6 .... 50.00
7 .... 50.00
8 .... 50.00
9 .... 50.00
10 .... 50.00
11 thru 19 .... @45.00
Toby Press
20 thru 30 .... @75.00
31 .... 25.00
32 .... 60.00
33 .... 60.00
34 .... 25.00

Felix the Cat #5 © Dell Publishing Co

35 .... 25.00
36 thru 59 .... @60.00
60 .... 55.00
61 .... 55.00

Harvey
62 thru 80 .... @18.00
81 thru 99 .... @15.00
100 .... 20.00
101 thru 118 .... @12.00
Spec., 100 pgs, 1952 ..... 150.00
Summer Ann., 100 pgs. 1953 . 125.00
Winter Ann.,#2 100 pgs, 1954.. 100.00

FERDINAND THE BULL
Dell Publishing Co.
1938
1 .... 100.00

FIGHT AGAINST CRIME
Story Comics
May, 1951
1 Scorpion of Crime Inspector
   "Brains" Carroway 150.00
2 Ganglands Double Cross ... 60.00
3 Killer Dolan's Double Cross . 50.00
4 Hopped Up Killers - The
   Con's Slaughter,Drug issue . 65.00
5 Horror of the Avenging Corpse 50.00
6 Terror of the Crazy Killer .. 45.00
7 .... 45.00
8 Killer with the Two-bladed
   Knife 45.00
9 Rats Die by Gas,Horror 100.00
10 Horror of the Con's Revenge 100.00
11 Case of the Crazy Killer ... 100.00
12 Horror,Drug issue 120.00
13 The Bloodless Killer 100.00
14 Electric Chair cover 120.00
15 .... 100.00
16 RA,Bondage(c) 120.00
17 Knife in Neck(c) 110.00
18 Attempted hanging cover . 120.00
19 Bondage(c) 120.00
20 Severed Head cover 200.00
21 .... 90.00
Becomes:

FIGHT AGAINST THE GUILTY
22 RA,Electric Chair 110.00
23 March, 1955 . . . . 60.00

Fight Comics #14
© Fiction House Magazines

FIGHT COMICS
Fight Comics Inc.
(Fiction House Magazines)
January, 1940
1 LF,GT,WE(c),O:Spy Fighter 1,250.00
2 GT,WE(c),Joe Lewis 550.00
3 WE(c),GT,B:Rip Regan,
The Powerman 450.00
4 GT,LF(c) 350.00
5 WE(c) 350.00
6 GT,BP(c) 300.00
7 GT,BP(c),Powerman-Blood
Money 300.00
8 GT,Chip Collins-Lair of
the Vulture 300.00
9 GT,Chip Collins-Prey of the
War Eagle 300.00
10 GT,Wolves of the Yukon . . . 300.00
11 . . . . 250.00
12 RA,Powerman-Monster of
Madness 250.00
13 Shark Broodie-Legion
of Satan 250.00
14 Shark Broodie-Lagoon
of Death 250.00
15 Super-American-Hordes of
the Secret Dicator 350.00
16 B:Capt.Fight,SwastikaPlague 350.00
17 Super-American-Blaster of
the Pig-Boat Pirates 300.00
18 Shark Broodie-Plague of
the Yellow Devils 300.00
19 E:Capt. Fight 300.00
20 . . . . 250.00
21 Rip Carson-Hell's Sky-Riders 150.00
22 Rip Carson-Sky Devil's
Mission 150.00
23 Rip Carson-Angels of
Vengeance 150.00
24 Baynonets for the Banzai
Breed! Bondage(c) 165.00
25 Rip Carson-Samurai

Showdown 135.00
26 Rip Carson-Fury of
the Sky-Brigade 135.00
27 War-Loot for the Mikado,
Bondage(c) 135.00
28 Rip Carson 135.00
29 Rip Carson-Charge of the
Lost Region 135.00
30 Rip Carson-Jeep-Raiders of
the Torture Jungle 135.00
31 Gangway for the Gyrenes,
Decapitation cover 150.00
32 Vengeance of the Hun-
Hunters,Bondage(c) 150.00
33 B:Tiger Girl 125.00
34 Bondage(c) 135.00
35 MB 125.00
36 MB 125.00
37 MB 125.00
38 MB,Bondage(c) 135.00
39 MB,Senorita Rio-Slave Brand
of the Spider Cult 125.00
40 MB,Bondage cover 135.00
41 MB,Bondage cover 135.00
42 MB 125.00
43 MB,Senorita Rio-The Fire-Brides
o/t Lost Atlantis,Bondage(c) 135.00
44 MB,R:Capt. Fight 125.00
45 MB,Tonight Don Diablo Rides 125.00
46 MB 125.00
47 MB,SenoritaRio-Horror's
Hacienda 125.00
48 MB 125.00
49 MB,JKa,B:Tiger Girl(c) 125.00
50 MB 125.00
51 MB,O:Tiger Girl 200.00
52 MB,Winged Demons of Doom 100.00
53 MB,Shadowland Shrine 100.00
54 MB,Flee the Cobra Fury . . . 100.00
55 MB,Jungle Juggernaut 100.00
56 MB 100.00
57 MB,Jewels of Jeopardy 100.00
58 MB 100.00
59 MB,Vampires of CrystalCavern 100.00
60 MB,Kraal of Deadly Diamonds 100.00
61 MB,Seekers of the Sphinx,
O:Tiger Girl 125.00
62 MB,Graveyard if the
Tree Tribe 90.00
63 MB 90.00
64 MB,DawnBeast from
Karama-Zan! 90.00
65 Beware the Congo Girl 90.00
66 Man or Ape! 85.00
67 Head-Hunters of Taboo Trek . 85.00
68 Fangs of Dr. Voodoo 85.00
69 Cage of the Congo Fury . . . 85.00
70 Kraal of Traitor Tusks 85.00
71 Captives for the Golden
Crocodile 85.00
72 Land of the Lost Safaris 85.00
73 War-Gods of the Jungle 85.00
74 Advengers of the Jungle . . . 85.00
75 Perils of Momba-Kzar 85.00
76 Kraal of Zombi-Zaro 85.00
77 Slave-Queen of the Ape Man 85.00
78 Great Congo Diamond
Robbery 100.00
79 A:Space Rangers 100.00
80 . . . . 75.00
81 E:Tiger Girl(c) 75.00
82 RipCarson-CommandoStrike . 75.00
83 NobodyLoves a Minesweeper 75.00
84 Rip Carson-Suicide Patrol . . . 75.00
85 . . . . 75.00

86 GE,Tigerman,Summer,1954 . 85.00

FIGHTING AMERICAN
Headline Publications
(Prize)
April-May, 1954
1 S&K,O:Fighting American &
Speedboy 900.00
2 S&K,S&K(c) 500.00
3 S&K,S&K(c) 400.00
4 S&K,S&K(c) 400.00
5 S&K,S&K(c) 400.00
6 S&K,S&K(c),O:Fighting
American 350.00
7 S&K,S&K(c), April-May, 1955 325.00

FIGHTING DAVY CROCKETT
(see KIT CARSON)

FIGHTING INDIANS OF THE WILD WEST
Avon Periodicals
March, 1952
1 EK,EL,Geronimo, Crazy Horse,
Chief Victorio 75.00
2 EK,Same, November, 1952 . 45.00

FIGHTING LEATHERNECKS
Toby Press
February, 1952
1 JkS,Duke's Diary 65.00
2 . . . . 50.00
3 . . . . 45.00
4 . . . . 45.00
5 . . . . 40.00
6 December, 1952 . . . . 30.00

FIGHTIN' TEXAN
(see TEXAN, THE)

FIGHTING YANK
Nedor Publ./Better Publ.
(Standard Comics)
September, 1942
1 B:Fighting Yank, A:Wonder Man,
Mystico, Bondage cover . . 1,000.00
2 JaB 400.00
3 . . . . 300.00
4 AS(c) 250.00
5 AS(c) 200.00
6 AS(c) 200.00
7 AS(c),A:Fighting Yank 190.00
8 AS(c) 190.00
9 AS(c) 190.00
10 AS(c) 190.00
11 AS(c), A:Grim Reaper, Nazis
bomb Washington cover . . . 175.00
12 AS(c), Hirohito bondage cover 175.00
13 AS(c) 150.00
14 AS(c) 150.00
15 AS(c) 150.00
16 AS(c) 150.00
17 AS(c) 150.00
18 AS(c), A:American Eagle . . 150.00
19 AS(c) 150.00
20 AS(c) 150.00
21 AS(c) A:Kara,Jungle
Princess 200.00
22 AS(c) A:Miss Masque-

cover story 225.00

Fighting Yank #20 © Standard Comics

23 AS(c) Klu Klux Klan
   parody cover 200.00
24 A:Miss Masque 175.00
25 JRo,MMe,A:Cavalier 250.00
26 JRo,MMe,A:Cavalier 175.00
27 JRo,MMe,A:Cavalier 175.00
28 JRo,MMe,AW,A:Cavalier . . . 185.00
29 JRo,MMe,August, 1949 . . . 165.00

FILM STAR ROMANCES
Star Publications
January-February, 1950
1 LbC(c), Rudy Valentino story 175.00
2 Liz Taylor & Robert Taylor,
   photo cover 200.00
3 May-June, 1950, photo cover 150.00

FIREHAIR COMICS
Flying Stories, Inc.
(Fiction House Magazine)
Winter, 1948
1 I:Firehair, Riders on the
   Pony Express 250.00
2 Bride of the Outlaw Guns . . 125.00
3 Kiss of the Six-Gun Siren! . 100.00
4 . . . . 100.00
5 . . . . 100.00
6 . . . . 90.00
7 War Drums at Buffalo Bend . 90.00
8 Raid on the Red Arrows 90.00
9 French Flags and Tomahawks 90.00
10 Slave Maiden of the Crees . . 90.00
11 Wolves of the Overland
   Trail,Spring, 1952 . . . . 90.00

FLAME, THE
Fox Feature Syndicate
Summer, 1940
1 LF,O:The Flame 1,400.00
2 GT,LF 700.00
3 BP 450.00
4 . . . . 400.00
5 GT 400.00
6 GT 400.00
7 A:The Yank 400.00
8 The Finger of the Frozen

Death!, January, 1942 . . . . 400.00

FLAMING LOVE
Comic Magazines
(Quality Comics Group)
December, 1949
1 BWa,BWa(c),The Temptress
   I Feared in His Arms 175.00
2 Torrid Tales of Turbulent
   Passion 75.00
3 BWa,RC,My Heart's at Sea 125.00
4 One Women who made a
   Mockery of Love, Ph(c) 65.00
5 Bridge of Longing, Ph(c) . . . 65.00
6 Men both Loved & Feared Me,
   October, 1950 . . . . 65.00

Flash Gordon #2 © Harvey Publications

FLASH GORDON
Harvey Publications
October, 1950
1 AR,Bondage(c) 175.00
2 AR 150.00
3 AR Bondage(c) 165.00
4 AR, April, 1951 . . . . 150.00

FLIP
Harvey Publications
April, 1954
1 HN 110.00
2 HN,BP,June, 1954 . . . . 100.00

FLY BOY
Approved Comics
(Ziff-Davis)
Spring, 1952
1 NS(c),Angels without Wings . 75.00
2 NS(c),Flyboy's Flame-Out,
   October-November, 1952 . . . 50.00

THE FLYING A'S
RANGE RIDER
Dell Publishing Co.
June-August, 1953
(1) = Dell Four Color #404
2 Ph(c) all 40.00
3 . . . . 35.00

4 . . . . 35.00
5 . . . . 35.00
6 . . . . 35.00
7 . . . . 35.00
8 . . . . 35.00
9 . . . . 35.00
10 . . . . 35.00
11 . . . . 30.00
12 . . . . 30.00
13 . . . . 30.00
14 . . . . 30.00
15 . . . . 30.00
16 . . . . 30.00
17 ATh 40.00
18 thru 24 . . . . @30.00

FOODINI
Continental Publications
March, 1950
1 . . . . 75.00
2 . . . . 40.00
3 . . . . 35.00
4 August, 1950 . . . . 35.00

FOOTBALL THRILLS
Approved Comics
(Ziff-Davis)
Fall-Winter, 1952
1 BP,NS(c),Red Grange story 175.00
2 NS(c),Bronko Nagurski,
   Spring,1952 . . . . 135.00

FORBIDDEN LOVE
Comic Magazine
(Quality Comics Group)
March, 1950
1 RC,Ph(c),Heartbreak Road . 400.00
2 Ph(c),I loved a Gigolo 175.00
3 Kissless Bride 175.00
4 BWa,Brimstone Kisses,
   September, 1950 . . . . 250.00

FORBIDDEN WORLDS
American Comics Group
July-August, 1951
1 AW,FF 750.00

Forbidden Worlds #11
© American Comics Group

2	400.00
3 AW,WW,JD	425.00
4 Werewolf cover	200.00
5 AW	325.00
6 AW,King Kong cover	300.00
7	150.00
8	150.00
9 Atomic Bomb	200.00
10 JyD	135.00
11 The Mummy's Treasure	100.00
12 Chest of Death	100.00
13 Invasion from Hades	100.00
14 Million-Year Monster	100.00
15 The Vampire Cat	100.00
16 The Doll	100.00
17	100.00
18 The Mummy	100.00
19 Pirate and the Voodoo Queen	100.00
20 Terror Island	100.00
21 The Ant Master	75.00
22 The Cursed Casket	75.00
23 Nightmare for Two	75.00
24	75.00
25 Hallahan's Head	75.00
26 The Champ	75.00
27 SMo,The Thing with the Golden Hair	75.00
28 Portrait of Carlotta	75.00
29 The Frogman	75.00
30 The Things on the Beach	75.00
31 SMo,The Circle of the Doomed	70.00
32 The Invasion of the Dead Things	70.00
33	70.00
34 Atomic Bomb	90.00
35 Comics Code	55.00
36 thru 62	@35.00
63 AW	45.00
64	30.00
65	30.00
66	30.00
67	30.00
68 OW(c)	30.00
69 AW	45.00
70	30.00
71	30.00
72 OW,I:Herbie	150.00
73	30.00
74	30.00
75 JB	30.00
76 AW	40.00
77	30.00
78 AW,OW(c)	40.00
79 thru 85 JB	@30.00
86 Flying Saucer	35.00
87	30.00
88	30.00
89	30.00
90	30.00
91	30.00
92	30.00
93	30.00
94 OW(c),A:Herbie	50.00
95	20.00
96 AW	35.00
97 thru 115	@20.00
116 OW(c)A:Herbie	25.00
117	20.00
118	20.00
119	20.00
120	20.00
121	20.00
122	20.00
123	20.00
124	20.00

125 I:O:Magic Man	25.00
126 A:Magic Man	15.00
127 same	15.00
128 same	15.00
129 same	15.00
130 same	15.00
131 same	15.00
132 same	15.00
133 I:O:Dragona	10.00
134 A:Magic Man	15.00
135 A:Magic Man	15.00
136 A:Nemesis	15.00
137 A:Magic Man	15.00
138 A:Magic Man	15.00
139 A:Magic Man	15.00
140 SD,A:Mark Midnight	18.00
141 thru 145	@12.00

FOREIGN INTRIGUES
(see DYNAMITE)

FOUR COLOR
Dell Publishing Co.
1939

N# Dick Tracy	5,000.00
N# Don Winslow of the Navy	1,000.00
N# Myra North	600.00
4 Disney'sDonaldDuck(1940)	7,500.00
5 Smilin' Jack	500.00
6 Dick Tracy	1,000.00
7 Gang Busters	275.00
8 Dick Tracy	575.00
9 Terry and the Pirates	475.00
10 Smilin' Jack	425.00
11 Smitty	275.00
12 Little Orphan Annie	375.00
13 Walt Disney's Reluctant Dragon (1941)	1,000.00
14 Moon Mullins	250.00
15 Tillie the Toiler	250.00
16 W.Disney's Mickey Mouse Outwits the Phantom Blob (1941)	6,500.00
17 W.Disney's Dumbo the Flying Elephant (1941)	1,300.00
18 Jiggs and Maggie	275.00
19 Barney Google and Snuffy Smith	275.00
20 Tiny Tim	225.00
21 Dick Tracy	500.00
22 Don Winslow	250.00
23 Gang Busters	200.00
24 Captain Easy	275.00
25 Popeye	550.00

[Second Series]

1 Little Joe	350.00
2 Harold Teen	200.00
3 Alley Oop	350.00
4 Smilin' Jack	325.00
5 Raggedy Ann and Andy	350.00
6 Smitty	150.00
7 Smokey Stover	250.00
8 Tillie the Toiler	150.00
9 Donald Duck finds Pirate Gold!	6,500.00
10 Flash Gordon	500.00
11 Wash Tubs	225.00
12 Bambi	325.00
13 Mr. District Attorney	225.00
14 Smilin' Jack	250.00
15 Felix the Cat	450.00
16 Porky Pig	350.00
17 Popeye	350.00
18 Little Orphan Annie's Junior Commandos	325.00

Dell Four Color #62
© Dell Publishing Co.

19 W.Disney's Thumper meets the Seven Dwarfs	400.00
20 Barney Baxter	150.00
21 Oswald the Rabbit	250.00
22 Tillie the Toiler	110.00
23 Raggedy Ann and Andy	275.00
24 Gang Busters	200.00
25 Andy Panda	300.00
26 Popeye	325.00
27 Mickey Mouse and the Seven Colored Terror	700.00
28 Wash Tubbs	140.00
29 CB,Donald Duck and the Mummy's Ring	5,500.00
30 Bambi's Children	350.00
31 Moon Mullins	150.00
32 Smitty	150.00
33 Bugs Bunny	400.00
34 Dick Tracy	325.00
35 Smokey Stover	125.00
36 Smilin' Jack	175.00
37 Bringing Up Father	125.00
38 Roy Rogers	650.00
39 Oswald the Rabbit	175.00
40 Barney Google and Snuffy Smith	125.00
41 Mother Goose	175.00
42 Tiny Tim	110.00
43 Popeye	225.00
44 Terry and the Pirates	300.00
45 Raggedy Ann	225.00
46 Felix the Cat and the Haunted House	275.00
47 Gene Autry	300.00
48 CB,Porky Pig of the Mounties	600.00
49 W.Disney's Snow White and the Seven Dwarfs	450.00
50 WK,Fairy Tale Parade	225.00
51 Bugs Bunny Finds the Lost Treasure	250.00
52 Little Orphan Annie	225.00
53 Wash Tubs	100.00
54 Andy Panda	150.00
55 Tillie the Toiler	75.00
56 Dick Tracy	250.00
57 Gene Autry	260.00
58 Smilin' Jack	175.00
59 WK,Mother Goose	150.00

60 Tiny Folks Funnies 75.00
61 Santa Claus Funnies 150.00
62 CB,Donald Duck in
    Frozen Gold 1,400.00
63 Roy Rogers-photo cover ... 350.00
64 Smokey Stover 75.00
65 Smitty 75.00
66 Gene Autry 250.00
67 Oswald the Rabbit 90.00
68 WK,Mother Goose 150.00
69 WK,Fairy Tale Parade ... 175.00
70 Popeye and Wimpy 175.00
71 WK,Walt Disney's
    Three Caballeros 600.00
72 Raggedy Ann 175.00
73 The Grumps 75.00
74 Marge's Little Lulu 750.00
75 Gene Autry and the Wildcat 225.00
76 Little Orphan Annie 175.00
77 Felix the Cat 250.00
78 Porky Pig & the Bandit Twins 150.00
79 Mickey Mouse in the Riddle
    of the Red Hat 900.00
80 Smilin' Jack 125.00
81 Moon Mullins 75.00
82 Lone Ranger 275.00
83 Gene Autry in Outlaw Trail . 250.00
84 Flash Gordon 300.00
85 Andy Panda and the
    Mad Dog Mystery 100.00
86 Roy Rogers-photo cover .. 250.00
87 WK,Fairy Tale Parade 150.00
88 Bugs Bunny 125.00
89 Tillie the Toiler 60.00
90 WK,Christmas with
    Mother Goose 135.00
91 WK,Santa Claus Funnies .. 135.00
92 WK,W.Disney's Pinocchio .. 350.00
93 Gene Autry 175.00
94 Winnie Winkle 75.00
95 Roy Rogers,Ph(c) 225.00
96 Dick Tracy 165.00
97 Marge's Little Lulu 400.00
98 Lone Ranger 250.00
99 Smitty 60.00
100 Gene Autry Comics-photo
    cover 175.00
101 Terry and the Pirates 160.00
102 WK,Oswald the Rabbit ... 110.00
103 WK,Easter with
    Mother Goose 135.00
104 WK,Fairy Tale Parade ... 135.00
105 WK,Albert the Aligator ... 550.00
106 Tillie the Toiler 50.00
107 Little Orphan Annie 150.00
108 Donald Duck in the
    Terror of the River 1,100.00
109 Roy Rogers Comics 175.00
110 Marge's Little Lulu 275.00
111 Captain Easy 75.00
112 Porky Pig's Adventure in
    Gopher Gulch 100.00
113 Popeye 100.00
114 WK,Fairy Tale Parade ... 125.00
115 Marge's Little Lulu 260.00
116 Mickey Mouse and the
    House of Many Mysteries . 200.00
117 Roy Rogers Comics,
    Ph(c) 125.00
118 Lone Ranger 250.00
119 Felix the Cat 225.00
120 Marge's Little Lulu 225.00
121 Fairy Tale Parade 50.00
122 Henry 65.00
123 Bugs Bunny's Dangerous

Venture 100.00
124 Roy Rogers Comics,Ph(c) . 125.00
125 Lone Ranger 165.00
126 WK,Christmas with
    Mother Goose 120.00
127 Popeye 100.00
128 WK,Santa Claus Funnies . 125.00
129 W.Disney's Uncle Remus
    and his tales of Brer Rabbit . 225.00
130 Andy Panda 50.00
131 Marge's Little Lulu 235.00
132 Tillie the Toiler 50.00
133 Dick Tracy 135.00
134 Tarzan and the Devil Ogre 450.00
135 Felix the Cat 150.00
136 Lone Ranger 150.00
137 Roy Rogers Comics 135.00
138 Smitty 50.00
139 Marge's Little Lulu 225.00
140 WK,Easter with
    Mother Goose 120.00
141 Mickey Mouse and the
    Submarine Pirates 175.00
142 Bugs Bunny and the
    Haunted Mountain 100.00
143 Oswald the Rabbit & the
    Prehistoric Egg 40.00
144 Poy Rogers Comics,Ph(c) . 125.00
145 Popeye 100.00
146 Marge's Little Lulu 225.00
147 W.Disney's Donald Duck
    in Volcano Valley 750.00
148 WK,Albert the Aligator
    and Pogo Possum 500.00
149 Smilin' Jack 70.00
150 Tillie the Toiler 40.00
151 Lone Ranger 125.00
152 Little Orphan Annie 100.00
153 Roy Rogers Comics 100.00

Dell Four Color #151
© Dell Publishing Co.

154 Andy Panda 50.00
155 Henry 40.00
156 Porky Pig and the Phantom 75.00
157 W.Disney's Mickey Mouse
    and the Beanstalk 175.00
158 Marge's Little Lulu 225.00
159 CB,W.Disney's Donald Duck
    in the Ghost of the Grotto . 625.00
160 Roy Rogers Comics,Ph(c) . 100.00

161 Tarzan and the Fires
    of Tohr 375.00
162 Felix the Cat 120.00
163 Dick Tracy 120.00
164 Bugs Bunny Finds the
    Frozen Kingdom 100.00
165 Marge's Little Lulu 225.00
166 Roy Rogers Comics,Ph(c) . 100.00
167 Lone Ranger 125.00
168 Popeye 90.00
169 Woody Woodpecker,Drug . 120.00
170 W.Disney's Mickey Mouse
    on Spook's Island 150.00
171 Charlie McCarthy 90.00
172 WK,Christmas with
    Mother Goose 110.00
173 Flash Gordon 110.00
174 Winnie Winkle 40.00
175 WK,Santa Claus Funnies . 120.00
176 Tillie the Toiler 40.00
177 Roy Rogers Comics,Ph(c) . 100.00
178 CB,W.Disney's Donald Duck
    Christmas on Bear Mountain 750.00
179 WK,Uncle Wigglly 120.00
180 Ozark the Ike 50.00
181 W.Disney's Mickey Mouse
    in Jungle Magic 150.00
182 Porky Pig in Never-
    Never Land 75.00
183 Oswald the Rabbit 40.00
184 Tillie the Toiler 40.00
185 WK,Easter with
    Mother Goose 120.00
186 W.Disney's Bambi 100.00
187 Bugs Bunny and the
    Dreadful Bunny 85.00
188 Woody Woodpecker 50.00
189 W.Disney's Donald Duck in
    The Old Castle's Secret . 600.00
190 Flash Gordon 110.00
191 Porky Pig to the Rescue .. 75.00
192 WK,The Brownies 110.00
193 Tom and Jerry 95.00
194 W.Disney's Mickey Mouse
    in the World Under the Sea . 150.00

Dell Four Color #162
© Dell Publishing Co.

195 Tillie the Toiler 30.00
196 Charlie McCarthy in The
    Haunted Hide-Out 75.00

    All comics prices listed are for *Near Mint* condition.

197 Spirit of the Border 65.00
198 Andy Panda 40.00
199 W.Disney's Donald Duck in
   Sheriff of Bullet Valley 600.00
200 Bugs Bunny, Super Sleuth . 75.00
201 WK,Christmas with
   Mother Goose 110.00
202 Woody Woodpecker 45.00
203 CB,W.Disney's Donald Duck in
   The Golden Christmas Tree 450.00
204 Flash Gordon 85.00
205 WK,Santa Claus Funnies . 110.00
206 Little Orphan Funnies 50.00
207 King of the Royal Mounted 125.00
208 W.Disney's Brer Rabbit
   Does It Again 100.00
209 Harold Teen 25.00
210 Tippe and Cap Stubbs 22.00
211 Little Beaver 30.00
212 Dr. Bobbs 20.00
213 Tillie the Toiler 30.00
214 W.Disney's Mickey Mouse
   and his Sky Adventure 125.00
215 Sparkle Plenty 70.00
216 Andy Panda and the
   Police Pup 25.00
217 Bugs Bunny in Court Jester 100.00
218 W.Disney's 3 Little Pigs .. 100.00
219 Swee'pea 50.00
220 WK,Easter with
   Mother Goose 110.00
221 WK,Uncle Wiggly 90.00
222 West of the Pecos 55.00
223 CB,W.Disney's Donald Duck in
   Lost in the Andes 575.00
224 Little Iodine 40.00
225 Oswald the Rabbit 25.00
226 Porky Pig and Spoofy 60.00
227 W.Disney's Seven Dwarfs .. 85.00
228 The Mark of Zorro 165.00
229 Smokey Stover 25.00
230 Sunset Press 40.00
231 W.Disney's Mickey Mouse
   and the Rajah's Treasure .. 120.00
232 Woody Woodpecker 30.00
233 Bugs Bunny 90.00
234 W.Disney's Dumbo in Sky
   Voyage 75.00
235 Tiny Tim 30.00
236 Heritage of the Desert 40.00
237 Tillie the Toiler 30.00
238 CB,W.Disney's Donald Duck
   in Voodoo Hoodoo 450.00
239 Adventure Bound 25.00
240 Andy Panda 25.00
241 Porky Pig 60.00
242 Tippie and Cap Stubbs 20.00
243 W.Disney's Thumper
   Follows His Nose 75.00
244 WK,The Brownies 90.00
245 Dick's Adventures in
   Dreamland 25.00
246 Thunder Mountain 30.00
247 Flash Gordon 85.00
248 W.Disney's Mickey Mouse
   and the Black Sorcerer ./.. 120.00
249 Woody Woodpecker 45.00
250 Bugs Bunny in
   Diamond Daze 90.00
251 Hubert at Camp Moonbeam 30.00
252 W.Disney's Pinocchio 75.00
253 WK,Christmas with
   Mother Goose 100.00
254 WK,Santa Claus Funnies . 110.00
255 The Ranger 30.00

256 CB,W.Disney's Donald Duck in
   Luck of the North 350.00
257 Little Iodine 30.00
258 Andy Panda and the
   Ballon Race 25.00
259 Santa and the Angel 30.00
260 Porky Pig, Hero of the
   Wild West 45.00
261 W.Disney's Mickey Mouse
   and the Missing Key 120.00
262 Raggedy Ann and Andy ... 35.00
263 CB,W.Disney's Donald Duck in
   Land of the Totem Poles ... 350.00
264 Woody Woodpecker in
   the Magic Lantern 30.00
265 King of the Royal Mountain . 65.00
266 Bugs Bunny on the Isle of
   Hercules 90.00
267 Little Beaver 20.00
268 W.Disney's Mickey Mouse's
   Surprise Visitor 120.00
269 Johnny Mack Brown,Ph(c) 150.00
270 Drift Fence 30.00
271 Porky Pig 40.00
272 W.Disney's Cinderella 55.00
273 Oswald the Rabbit 25.00
274 Bugs Bunny 75.00
275 CB,W.Disney's Donald Duck
   in Ancient Persia 325.00
276 Uncle Wiggly 35.00
277 PorkyPig in DesertAdventure 45.00
278 Bill Elliot Comics,Ph(c) 90.00
279 W.Disney's Mickey Mouse &
   Pluto Battle the Giant Ants . 110.00
280 Andy Panda in the Isle
   of the Mechanical Men 25.00
281 Bugs Bunny in The Great
   Circus Mystery 75.00
282 CB,W.Disney's Donald Duck in
   The Pixilated Parrot 325.00
283 King of the Royal Mounted . 75.00

Dell Four Color #339
© Dell Publishing Co.

284 Porky Pig in the Kingdom
   of Nowhere 45.00
285 Bozo the Clown 100.00
286 W.Disney's Mickey Mouse
   and the Uninvited Guest ... 100.00
287 Gene Autry's Champion in the
   Ghost Of Black Mountain,Ph(c) 60.00

288 Woody Woodpecker 30.00
289 Bugs Bunny in'Indian Trouble'75.00
290 The Chief 30.00
291 CB,W.Disney's Donald Duck in
   The Magic Hourglass 325.00
292 The Cisco Kid Comics ... 100.00
293 WK,The Brownies 100.00
294 Little Beaver 30.00
295 Porky Pig in President Pig . 45.00
296 W.Disney's Mickey Mouse
   Private Eye for Hire 100.00
297 Andy Panda in The
   Haunted Inn 25.00
298 Bugs Bunny in Sheik
   for a Day 70.00
299 Buck Jones & the Iron Trail . 90.00
300 CB,W.Disney's Donald Duck in
   Big-Top Bedlam 325.00
301 The Mysterious Rider 30.00
302 Santa Claus Funnies 20.00
303 Porky Pig in The Land of
   the Monstrous Flies 35.00
304 W.Disney's Mickey Mouse
   in Tom-Tom Island 90.00
305 Woody Woodpecker 20.00
306 Raggedy Ann 25.00
307 Bugs Bunny in Lumber
   Jack Rabbit 60.00
308 CB,W.Disney's Donald Duck in
   Dangerous Disguise 300.00
309 Dollface and Her Gang 25.00
310 King of the Rotal Mounted . 40.00
311 Porky Pig in Midget Horses
   of Hidden Valley 35.00
312 Tonto 75.00
313 W.Disney's Mickey Mouse in
   the Mystery of the Double-
   Cross Ranch 80.00
314 Ambush 30.00
315 Oswald Rabbit 15.00
316 Rex Allen,Ph(c) 120.00
317 Bugs Bunny in Hare Today
   Gone Tomorrow 50.00
318 CB,W.Disney's Donald Duck in
   No Such Varmint 300.00
319 Gene Autry's Champion .. 25.00
320 Uncle Wiggly 25.00
321 Little Scouts 10.00
322 Porky Pig in Roaring Rockies 35.00
323 Susie Q. Smith 15.00
324 I Met a Handsome Cowboy . 45.00
325 W.Disney's Mickey Mouse
   in the Haunted Castle 90.00
326 Andy Panda 20.00
327 Bugs Bunny and the
   Rajah's Treasure 50.00
328 CB,W.Disney's Donald Duck
   in Old California 325.00
329 Roy Roger's Trigger,Ph(c) .. 65.00
330 Porky Pig meets the
   Bristled Bruiser 30.00
331 Disney's Alice in
   Wonderland 60.00
332 Little Beaver 20.00
333 Wilderness Trek 30.00
334 W.Disney's Mickey Mouse
   and Yukon Gold 90.00
335 Francis the Famous
   Talking Mule 30.00
336 Woody Woodpecker 20.00
337 The Brownies 25.00
338 Bugs Bunny and the
   Rocking Horse Thieves 50.00
339 W.Disney's Donald Duck
   and the Magic Fountain 65.00

All comics prices listed are for *Near Mint* condition.

Dell Four Color #454
© Dell Publishing Co.

340 King of the Royal Mountain   50.00
341 W.Disney's Unbirthday Party
    with Alice in Wonderland 90.00
342 Porky Pig the Lucky
    Peppermint Mine 30.00
343 W.Disney's Mickey Mouse in
    Ruby Eye of Homar-Guy-Am . 80.00
344 Sergeant Preston from
    Challenge of the Yukon 75.00
345 Andy Panda in Scotland Yard 25.00
346 Hideout 30.00
347 Bugs Bunny the Frigid Hare   45.00
348 CB,W.Disney's Donald Duck
    The Crocodile Collector 90.00
349 Uncle Wiggly 25.00
350 Woody Woodpecker 20.00
351 Porky Pig and the Grand
    Canyon Giant 20.00
352 W.Disney's Mickey Mouse
    Mystery of Painted Valley . . . 70.00
353 CB(c),W.Disney'sDuckAlbum 50.00
354 Raggedy Ann & Andy 25.00
355 Bugs Bunny Hot-Rod Hair . 45.00
356 CB(c),W.Disney's Donald
    Duck in Rags to Riches 85.00
357 Comeback 25.00
358 Andy Panada 20.00
359 Frosty the Snowman 25.00
360 Porky Pig in Tree Fortune . 20.00
361 Santa Claus Funnies 20.00
362 W.Disney's Mickey Mouse &
    the Smuggled Diamonds 70.00
363 King of the Royal Mounted . 35.00
364 Woody Woodpecker 20.00
365 The Brownies 20.00
366 Bugs Bunny Uncle
    Buckskin Comes to Town . . . 45.00
367 CB,W.Disney's Donald Duck in
    A Christmas for Shacktown . 250.00
368 Bob Clampett's
    Beany and Cecil 165.00
369 Lone Ranger's Famous
    Horse Hi-Yo Silver 55.00
370 Porky Pig in Trouble
    in the Big Trees 25.00
371 W.Disney's Mickey Mouse
    the Inca Idol Case 65.00
372 Riders of the Purple Sage . . 25.00

373 Sergeant Preston 45.00
374 Woody Woodpecker 20.00
375 John Carter of Mars 200.00
376 Bugs Bunny 45.00
377 Susie Q. Smith 15.00
378 Tom Corbett, Space Cadet 135.00
379 W.Disney's Donald Duck in
    Southern Hospitality 60.00
380 Raggedy Ann & Andy 25.00
381 Marge's Tubby 100.00
382 W.Disney's Show White and
    the Seven Dwarfs 50.00
383 Andy Panda 15.00
384 King of the Royal Mountain . 35.00
385 Porky Pig 25.00
386 CB,W.Disney's Uncle Scrooge
    in Only A Poor Old Man . . . 750.00
387 W.Disney's Mickey Mouse
    in High Tibet 65.00
388 Oswald the Rabbit 20.00
389 Andy Hardy Comics 20.00
390 Woody Woodpecker 20.00
391 Uncle Wiggly 20.00
392 Hi-Yo Silver 25.00
393 Bugs Bunny 50.00
394 CB(c),W.Disney's Donald Duck
    in Malayalaya 85.00
395 Forlorn River 25.00
396 Tales of the Texas Rangers,
    Ph(c) 65.00
397 Sergeant Preston o/t Yukon 45.00
398 The Brownies 20.00
399 Porky Pig in the Lost
    Gold Mine 25.00

Dell Four Color #408
© Dell Publishing Co.

400 AMc,Tom Corbett 85.00
401 W.Disney's Mickey Mouse &
    Goofy's Mechanical Wizard . . 55.00
402 Mary Jane and Sniffles 55.00
403 W.Disney's Li'l Bad Wolf . . . 40.00
404 The Ranger Rider,Ph(c) . . . 75.00
405 Woody Woodpecker 20.00
406 Tweety and Sylvester 50.00
407 Bugs Bunny, Foreign-
    Legion Hare 50.00
408 CB,W.Disney's Donald Duck
    and the Golden Helmet 275.00
409 Andy Panda 15.00
410 Porky Pig in the

Water Wizard 25.00
411 W.Disney's Mickey Mouse
    and the Old Sea Dog 60.00
412 Nevada 25.00
413 Disney's Robin Hood(movie),
    Ph(c) 50.00
414 Bob Clampett's Beany
    and Cecil 125.00
415 Rootie Kazootie 75.00
416 Woody Woodpecker 20.00
417 Double Trouble with Goober 15.00
418 Rusty Riley 30.00
419 Sergeant Preston 35.00
420 Bugs Bunny 40.00
421 AMc,Tom Corbett 75.00
422 CB,W.Disney's Donald Duck
    and the Gilded Man 275.00
423 Rhubarb 15.00
424 Flash Gordon 60.00
425 Zorro 100.00
426 Porky Pig 20.00
427 W.Disney's Mickey Mouse &
    the Wonderful Whizzix 50.00
428 Uncle Wigglily 20.00
429 W.Disney's Pluto in
    Why Dogs Leave Home 70.00
430 Marge's Tubby 55.00
431 Woody Woodpecker 20.00
432 Bugs Bunny and the
    Rabbit Olympics 50.00
433 Wildfire 25.00
434 Rin Tin Tin,Ph(c) 140.00
435 Frosty the Snowman 20.00
436 The Brownies 20.00
437 John Carter of Mars 150.00
438 W.Disney's Annie
    Oakley (TV) 75.00
439 Little Hiawatha 20.00
440 Black Beauty 20.00
441 Fearless Fagan 15.00

Dell Four Color #462
© Dell Publishing Co.

442 W.Disney's Peter Pan 75.00
443 Ben Bowie and His
    Mountain Men 35.00
444 Marge's Tubby 50.00
445 Charlie McCarthy 15.00
446 Captain Hook and Peter Pan 55.00
447 Andy Hardy Comics 15.00
448 Beany and Cecil 125.00

449 Tappan's Burro 25.00
450 CB(c),W.Disney's DuckAlbum 55.00
451 Rusty Riley 20.00
452 Raggedy Ann and Andy ... 25.00
453 Susie Q. Smith 15.00
454 Krazy Kat Comics 20.00
455 Johnny Mack Brown Comics,
　　Ph(c) 35.00
456 W.Disney's Uncle Scrooge
　　Back to the Klondike 450.00
457 Daffy 20.00
458 Oswald the Rabbit 15.00
459 Rootie Kazootie 50.00
460 Buck Jones 35.00
461 Marge's Tubby 50.00
462 Little Scouts 10.00
463 Petunia 15.00
464 Bozo 65.00
465 Francis the Talking Mule ... 10.00
466 Rhubarb, the Millionaire Cat 10.00
467 Desert Gold 25.00
468 W.Disney's Goofy 50.00
469 Beetle Bailey 50.00
470 Elmer Fudd 15.00
471 Double Trouble with Goober 10.00
472 Wild Bill Elliot,Ph(c) 40.00
473 W.Disney's Li'l Bad Wolf ... 35.00
474 Mary Jane and Sniffles 50.00
475 M.G.M.'s the Two
　　Mouseketeers 25.00
476 Rin Tin Tin,Ph(c) 40.00
477 Bob Clampett's Beany and
　　Cecil 125.00
478 Charlie McCarthy 25.00
479 Queen o/t West Dale Evans 100.00
480 Andy Hardy Comics 15.00
481 Annie Oakley and Tagg ... 45.00
482 Brownies 20.00
483 Little Beaver 20.00
484 River Feud 25.00
485 The Little People 25.00
486 Rusty Riley 20.00
487 Mowgli, the Jungle Book ... 20.00
488 John Carter of Mars 150.00
489 Tweety and Sylvester 15.00
490 Jungle Jim 22.00

491 EK,Silvertip 35.00
492 W.Disney's Duck Album ... 35.00

493 Johnny Mack Brown,Ph(c) . 25.00
494 The Little King 75.00
495 CB, W.Disney's Uncle
　　Scrooge 350.00
496 The Green Hornet 225.00
497 Zorro, (Sword of) 120.00
498 Bugs Bunny's Album 30.00
499 M.G.M.'s Spike and Tyke .. 15.00
500 Buck Jones 30.00
501 Francis the Famous
　　Talking Mule 20.00
502 Rootie Kazootie 40.00
503 Uncle Wiggily 20.00
504 Krazy Kat 25.00
505 W.Disney's the Sword and
　　the Rose (TV),Ph(c) 40.00
506 The Little Scouts 10.00
507 Oswald the Rabbit 15.00
508 Bozo 60.00
509 W.Disney's Pluto 50.00
510 Son of Black Beauty 20.00
511 EK,Outlaw Trail 30.00
512 Flash Gordon 35.00
513 Ben Bowie and His
　　Mountain Men 22.00
514 Frosty the Snowman 20.00
515 Andy Hardy 15.00
516 Double Trouble With Goober 10.00
517 Walt Disney's Chip 'N' Dale . 55.00
518 Rivets 15.00
519 Steve Canyon 55.00
520 Wild Bill Elliot,Ph(c) 40.00
521 Beetle Bailey 25.00
522 The Brownies 15.00
523 Rin Tin Tin,Ph(c) 55.00
524 Tweety and Sylvester 15.00
525 Santa Claus Funnies 20.00
526 Napoleon 15.00
527 Charlie McCarthy 20.00
528 Queen o/t West Dale Evans,
　　Ph(c) 60.00
529 Little Beaver 20.00
530 Bob Clampett's Beany
　　and Cecil 100.00
531 W.Disney's Duck Album ... 40.00
532 The Rustlers 25.00
533 Raggedy Ann and Andy ... 25.00
534 EK,Western Marshal 30.00
535 I Love Lucy,Ph(c) 275.00
536 Daffy 20.00
537 Stormy, the Thoroughbred . 20.00
538 EK,The Mask of Zorro ... 100.00
539 Ben and Me 20.00
540 Knights of the Round Table,
　　Ph(c) 35.00
541 Johnny Mack Brown,Ph(c) . 25.00
542 Super Circus Featuring
　　Mary Hartline 25.00
543 Uncle Wiggly 20.00
544 W.Disney's Rob Roy(Movie),
　　Ph(c) 55.00
545 The Wonderful Adventures
　　of Pinocchio 30.00
546 Buck Jones 40.00
547 Francis the Famous
　　Talking Mule 20.00
548 Krazy Kat 20.00
549 Oswald the Rabbit 15.00
550 The Little Scouts 10.00
551 Bozo 60.00
552 Beetle Bailey 25.00
553 Susie Q. Smith 15.00
554 Rusty Riley 20.00
555 Range War 25.00
556 Double Trouble with Goober 15.00

557 Ben Bowie and His
　　Mountain Men 20.00
558 Elmer Fudd 15.00
559 I Love Lucy,Ph(c) 175.00
560 W.Disney's Duck Album ... 40.00
561 Mr. Magoo 65.00
562 W.Disney's Goofy 60.00
563 Rhubarb, the Millionaire Cat 15.00
564 W.Disney's Li'l Bad Wolf ... 20.00
565 Jungle Jim 20.00
566 Son of Black Beauty 15.00
567 BF,Prince Valiant,Ph(c) ... 100.00
568 Gypsy Cat 18.00
569 Priscilla's Pop 15.00
570 Bob Clampett's Beany
　　and Cecil 65.00
571 Charlie McCarthy 20.00
572 EK,Silvertip 30.00
573 The Little People 20.00
574 The Hand of Zorro 90.00
575 Annie and Oakley and Tagg,
　　Ph(c) 45.00
576 Angel 15.00
577 M.G.M.'s Spike and Tyke .. 15.00
578 Steve Canyon 30.00
579 Francis the Talking Mule ... 20.00

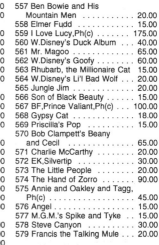

580 Six Gun Ranch 20.00
581 Chip 'N' Dale 15.00
582 Mowgli, the Jungle Book ... 20.00
583 The Lost Wagon Train 25.00
584 Johnny Mack Brown,Ph(c) . 30.00
585 Bugs Bunny's Album 30.00
586 W.Disney's Duck Album ... 35.00
587 The Little Scouts 8.00
588 MB,King Richard and the
　　Crusaders,Ph(c) 70.00
589 Buck Jones 30.00
590 Hansel and Gretel 30.00
591 EK,Western Marshal 30.00
592 Super Circus 25.00
593 Oswald the Rabbit 10.00
594 Bozo 55.00
595 Pluto 20.00
596 Turok, Son of Stone 400.00
597 The Little King 25.00
598 Captain Davy Jones 15.00
599 Ben Bowie and His
　　Mountain Men 20.00

600 Daisy Duck's Diary 30.00
601 Frosty the Snowman 18.00
602 Mr. Magoo and the Gerald
　McBoing-Boing 70.00
603 M.G.M.'s The Two
　Mouseketeers 20.00
604 Shadow on the Trail 25.00
605 The Brownies 20.00
606 Sir Lancelot 50.00
607 Santa Claus Funnies 20.00
608 EK,Silver Tip 30.00
609 The Littlest Outlaw,Ph(c) . . . 25.00
610 Drum Beat,Ph(c) 65.00
611 W.Disney's Duck Album . . . 30.00
612 Little Beaver 15.00
613 EK,Western Marshal 30.00
614 W.Disney's 20,000 Leagues
　Under the Sea (Movie) 65.00
615 Daffy 15.00
616 To The Last Man 25.00
617 The Quest of Zorro 95.00
618 Johnny Mack Brown,Ph(c) . 25.00
619 Krazy Kat 15.00
620 Mowgli, Jungle Book 20.00
621 Francis the Famous
　Talking Mule 20.00
622 Beetle Bailey 25.00
623 Oswald the Rabbit 12.00
624 Treasure Island,Ph(c) 25.00
625 Beaver Valley 15.00
626 Ben Bowie and His
　Mountain Men 20.00
627 Goofy 60.00
628 Elmer Fudd 15.00
629 Lady & The Tramp with Jock 20.00
630 Priscilla's Pop 15.00
631 W.Disney's Davy Crockett
　Indian Fighter (TV),Ph(c) . . . 55.00
632 Fighting Caravans 25.00
633 The Little People 20.00
634 Lady and the Tramp Album . 30.00
635 Bob Clampett's Beany
　and Cecil 100.00
636 Chip 'N' Dale 15.00
637 EK,Silvertip 30.00
638 M.G.M.'s Spike and Tyke . . 12.00
639 W.Disney's Davy Crockett
　at the Alamo (TV),Ph(c) 50.00
640 EK,Western Marshal 30.00
641 Steve Canyon 30.00
642 M.G.M.'s The Two
　Mouseketeers 12.00
643 Wild Bill Elliott,Ph(c) 30.00
644 Sir Walter Raleigh,Ph(c) . . . 40.00
645 Johnny Mack Brown,Ph(c) . 25.00
646 Dotty Dripple and Taffy 15.00
647 Bugs Bunny's Album 30.00
648 Jace Pearson of the
　Texas Rangers,Ph(c) 35.00
649 Duck Album 30.00
650 BF,Prince Valiant 35.00
651 EK,King Colt 25.00
652 Buck Jones 22.00
653 Smokey the Bear 35.00
654 Pluto 35.00
655 Francis the Famous
　Talking Mule 20.00
656 Turok, Son of Stone 225.00
657 Ben Bowie and His
　Mountain Men 20.00
658 Goofy 30.00
659 Daisy Duck's Diary 15.00
660 Little Beaver 12.00
661 Frosty the Snowman 15.00
662 Zoo Parade 25.00

663 Winky Dink 35.00
664 W.Disney's Davy Crockett in
　the Great Keelboat
　Race (TV),Ph(c) 40.00
665 The African Lion 20.00
666 Santa Claus Funnies 15.00
667 EK,Silvertip and the Stolen
　Stallion 30.00
668 W.Disney's Dumbo 50.00
668a W.Disney's Dumbo 50.00
669 W.Disney's Robin Hood
　(Movie),Ph(c) 35.00
669 Robin Hood 20.00
670 M.G.M.'s Mouse Musketeers 12.00
671 W.Disney's Davy Crockett
　and the River Pirates(TV),
　Ph(c) 50.00
672 Quentin Durward,Ph(c) 40.00
673 Buffalo Bill Jr.,Ph(c) 45.00
674 The Little Rascals 50.00
675 EK,Steve Donovan,Ph(c) . . 35.00
676 Will-Yum! 25.00
677 Little King 25.00
678 The Last Hunt,Ph(c) 35.00
679 Gunsmoke 85.00
680 Out Our Way with the
　Worry Wart 12.00
681 Forever, Darling,Ph(c) 75.00
682 When Knighthood Was
　in Flower,Ph(c) 25.00
683 Hi and Lois 12.00
684 SB,Helen of Troy,Ph(c) 75.00
685 Johnny Mack Brown,Ph(c) . 25.00
686 Duck Album 20.00
687 The Indian Fighter,Ph(c) . . . 30.00
688 SB,Alexander the Great,
　Ph(c) 45.00
689 Elmer Fudd 12.00
690 The Conqueror,
　John Wayne Ph(c) 100.00
691 Dotty Dripple and Taffy 12.00
692 The Little People 15.00
693 W.Disney's Brer Rabbit
　Song of the South 75.00
694 Super Circus,Ph(c) 25.00
695 Little Beaver 12.00
696 Krazy Kat 15.00
697 Oswald the Rabbit 12.00
698 Francis the Famous
　Talking Mule 20.00
699 BA,Prince Valiant 40.00
700 Water Birds and the
　Olympic Elk 20.00
701 Jimmy Cricket 30.00
702 The Goofy Success Story . . 55.00
703 Scamp 70.00
704 Priscilla's Pop 12.00
705 Brave Eagle,Ph(c) 25.00
706 Bongo and Lumpjaw 12.00
707 Corky and White Shadow,
　Ph(c) 20.00
708 Smokey the Bear 20.00
709 The Searchers,John
　Wayne Ph(c) 225.00
710 Francis the Famous
　Talking Mule 12.00
711 M.G.M.'s Mouse Musketeers 12.00
712 The Great Locomotive
　Chase, Ph(c) 30.00
713 The Animal World 30.00
714 W.Disney's Spin
　& Marty (TV) 75.00
715 Timmy 12.00
716 Man in Space 65.00
717 Moby Dick,Ph(c) 55.00

718 Dotty Dripple and Taffy 15.00
719 BF,Prince Valiant 40.00
720 Gunsmoke,Ph(c) 90.00
721 Captain Kangaroo,Ph(c) . . . 110.00
722 Johnny Mack Brown,Ph(c) . 25.00
723 EK,Santiago 65.00
724 Bugs Bunny's Album 30.00
725 Elmer Fudd 12.00
726 Duck Album 25.00
727 The Nature of Things 25.00
728 M.G.M.'s Mouse Musketeers 12.00
729 Bob Son of Battle 15.00
730 Smokey Stover 15.00
731 EK,Silvertip and The
　Fighting Four 30.00
732 Zorro, (the Challenge of) . . . 85.00
733 Buck Rogers 25.00
734 Cheyenne,C.Walker Ph(c) . . 70.00
735 Crusader Rabbit 185.00
736 Pluto 35.00

Dell Four Color #737
© Dell Publishing Co.

737 Steve Canyon 30.00
738 Westward Ho, the Wagons,
　Ph(c) 25.00
739 MD,Bounty Guns 20.00
740 Chilly Willy 15.00
741 The Fastest Gun Alive,Ph(c) 35.00
742 Buffalo Bill Jr.,Ph(c) 50.00
743 Daisy Duck's Diary 35.00
744 Little Beaver 12.00
745 Francis the Famous
　Talking Mule 20.00
746 Dotty Dripple and Taffy 10.00
747 Goofy 60.00
748 Frosty the Snowman 15.00
749 Secrets of Life,Ph(c) 30.00
750 The Great Cat 30.00
751 Our Miss Brooks,Ph(c) 40.00
752 Mandrake, the Magician . . . 70.00
753 Walt Scott's Little People . . 15.00
754 Smokey the Bear 25.00
755 The Littlest Snowman 20.00
756 Santa Claus Funnies 15.00
757 The True Story of
　Jesse James,Ph(c) 65.00
758 Bear Country 20.00
759 Circus Boy,Ph(c) 75.00
760 W.Disney's Hardy Boys(TV) 65.00
761 Howdy Doody 70.00

---

762 SB,The Sharkfighters,Ph(c) . 75.00
763 GrandmaDuck'sFarmFriends 55.00
764 M.G.M.'s Mouse Musketeers 12.00
765 Will-Yum! 12.00
766 Buffalo Bill,Ph(c) 25.00
767 Spin and Marty 30.00
768 EK,Steve Donovan, Western
   Marshal,Ph(c) 35.00
769 Gunsmoke 45.00
770 Brave Eagle,Ph(c) 15.00
771 MD,Brand of Empire 20.00
772 Cheyenne,C.Walker Ph(c) . . 50.00
773 The Brave One,Ph(c) 20.00
774 Hi and Lois 8.00
775 SB,Sir Lancelot and
   Brian,Ph(c) 65.00
776 Johnny Mack Brown,Ph(c) . 25.00
777 Scamp 40.00
778 The Little Rascals 25.00
779 Lee Hunter, Indian Fighter . 25.00
780 Captain Kangaroo,Ph(c) . . 100.00
781 Fury,Ph(c) 50.00
782 Duck Album 35.00
783 Elmer Fudd 10.00
784 Around the World in 80
   Days,Ph(c) 45.00
785 Circus Boys,Ph(c) 65.00
786 Cinderella 15.00
787 Little Hiawatha 15.00
788 BF,Prince Valiant 35.00
789 EK,Silvertip-Valley Thieves . 30.00
790 ATh,The Wings of Eagles,
   J.Wayne Ph(c) 125.00
791 The 77th Bengal Lancers,
   Ph(c) 45.00
792 Oswald the Rabbit 12.00
793 Morty Meekle 15.00
794 SB,The Count of Monte
   Cristo 55.00
795 Jiminy Cricket 45.00
796 Ludwig Bemelman's
   Madeleine and Genevieve . . . 20.00
797 Gunsmoke,Ph(c) 45.00
798 Buffalo Bill,Ph(c) 25.00
799 Priscilla's Pop 10.00
800 The Buccaneers,Ph(c) 40.00
801 Dotty Dripple and Taffy . . . 10.00
802 Goofy 60.00
803 Cheyenne,C.Walker Ph(c) . . 35.00
804 Steve Canyon 30.00
805 Crusader Rabbit 100.00
806 Scamp 45.00
807 MB,Savage Range 20.00
808 Spin and Marty,Ph(c) 30.00
809 The Little People 15.00
810 Francis the Famous
   Talking Mule 20.00
811 Howdy Doody 50.00
812 The Big Land,A.Ladd Ph(c) . 60.00
813 Circus Boy,Ph(c) 65.00
814 Covered Wagon,A:Mickey
   Mouse 25.00
815 Dragoon Wells Massacre . . 35.00
816 Brave Eagle,Ph(c) 15.00
817 Little Beaver 15.00
818 Smokey the Bear 20.00
819 Mickey Mouse in Magicland 30.00
820 The Oklahoman,Ph(c) 45.00
821 Wringle Wrangle,Ph(c) 40.00
822 ATh,W.Disney's Paul Revere's
   Ride (TV) 60.00
823 Timmy 15.00
824 The Pride and the Passion,
   Ph(c) 60.00
825 The Little Rascals 25.00

826 Spin and Marty and Annette,
   Ph(c) 75.00
827 Smokey Stover 15.00
828 Buffalo Bill, Jr,Ph(c). 25.00
829 Tales of the Pony Express,
   Ph(c) 25.00
830 The Hardy Boys,Ph(c) 55.00
831 No Sleep 'Til Dawn,Ph(c) . . 35.00
832 Lolly and Pepper 15.00
833 Scamp 50.00
834 Johnny Mack Brown,Ph(c) . 30.00
835 Silvertip- The Fake Rider . . 20.00
836 Man in Fight 25.00
837 All-American Athlete
   Cotton Woods 25.00
838 Bugs Bunny's Life
   Story Album 35.00
839 The Vigilantes 35.00
840 Duck Album 40.00
841 Elmer Fudd 8.00
842 The Nature of Things 25.00
843 The First Americans 25.00
844 Gunsmoke,Ph(c) 40.00
845 ATh,The Land Unknown . . 100.00
846 ATh,Gun Glory 90.00
847 Perri 30.00
848 Marauder's Moon 30.00
849 BF,Prince Valiant 30.00
850 Buck Jones 20.00
851 The Story of Mankind,
   V.Price Ph(c) 30.00
852 Chilly Willy 12.00
853 Pluto 35.00
854 Hunchback of Notre Dame,
   Ph(c) 85.00
855 Broken Arrow,Ph(c) 25.00
856 Buffalo Bill, Jr.,Ph(c) 25.00
857 The Goofy Adventure Story . 20.00
858 Daisy Duck's Diary 30.00
859 Topper and Neil 12.00
860 Wyatt Earp,Ph(c) 80.00
861 Frosty the Snowman 15.00
862 Truth About Mother Goose . 25.00
863 Francis the Famous
   Talking Mule 20.00
864 The Littlest Snowman 15.00
865 Andy Burnett,Ph(c) 50.00
866 Mars and Beyond 70.00
867 Santa Claus Funnies 15.00
868 The Little People 15.00
869 Old Yeller,Ph(c) 25.00
870 Little Beaver 12.00
871 Curly Kayoe 15.00
872 Captain Kangaroo,Ph(c) . . . 75.00
873 Grandma Duck's
   Farm Friends 35.00
874 Old Ironsides 20.00
875 Trumpets West 15.00
876 Tales of Wells Fargo,Ph(c) . 50.00
877 ATh,Frontier Doctor,Ph(c) . . 70.00
878 Peanuts 100.00
879 Brave Eagle,Ph(c) 15.00
880 MD,Steve Donovan,Ph(c) . . 25.00
881 The Captain and the Kids . . 15.00
882 ATh,W.Disney Presents Zorro 75.00
883 The Little Rascals 35.00
884 Hawkeye and the Last
   of the Mohicans,Ph(c) 30.00
885 Fury,Ph(c) 30.00
886 Bongo and Lumpjaw 15.00
887 The Hardy Boys,Ph(c) 45.00
888 Elmer Fudd 10.00
889 ATh,W.Disney's Clint
   & Mac(TV),Ph(c) 65.00
890 Wyatt Earp,Ph(c) 35.00

891 Light in the Forest,
   C.Parker Ph(c) 25.00
892 Maverick,J.Garner Ph(c) . . 120.00
893 Jim Bowie,Ph(c) 30.00
894 Oswald the Rabbit 10.00
895 Wagon Train,Ph(c) 65.00
896 Adventures of Tinker Bell . 25.00
897 Jiminy Cricket 40.00
898 EK,Silvertip 30.00
899 Goofy 50.00
900 BF,Prince Valiant 35.00
901 Little Hiawatha 15.00
902 Will-Yum! 10.00
903 Dotty Dripple and Taffy 10.00
904 Lee Hunter, Indian Fighter . 20.00
905 W.Disney's Annette (TV),
   Ph(c) 120.00
906 Francis the Famous
   Talking Mule 20.00
907 Ath,Sugarfoot,Ph(c) 80.00
908 The Little People
   and the Giant 15.00
909 Smitty 15.00
910 ATh,The Vikings,
   K.Douglas Ph(c) 75.00
911 The Gray Ghost,Ph(c) 50.00
912 Leave it to Beaver,Ph(c) . . 125.00

Dell Four Color #913
© Dell Publishing Co.

913 The Left-Handed Gun,
   Paul Newman Ph(c) 65.00
914 ATh,No Time for Sergeants,
   Ph(c) 60.00
915 Casey Jones,Ph(c) 30.00
916 Red Ryder Ranch Comics . . 15.00
917 The Life of Riley,Ph(c) 75.00
918 Beep Beep, the Roadrunner 60.00
919 Boots and Saddles,Ph(c) . . 50.00
920 Ath,Zorro,Ph(c) 75.00
921 Wyatt Earp.Ph(c) 40.00
922 Johnny Mack Brown,Ph(c) . 35.00
923 Timmy 8.00
924 Colt .45,Ph(c) 52.00
925 Last of the Fast Guns,Ph(c) 35.00
926 Peter Pan 20.00
927 SB,Top Gun 20.00
928 Sea Hunt,L.Bridges Ph(c) . . 75.00
929 Brave Eagle,Ph(c) 15.00
930 Maverick,J. Garner Ph(c) . . 65.00
931 Have Gun, Will Travel,Ph(c) 75.00

All comics prices listed are for *Near Mint* condition.

932 Smokey the Bear 20.00
933 ATh,W.Disney's Zorro 60.00
934 Restless Gun 65.00
935 King of the Royal Mounted . 25.00
936 The Little Rascals 20.00
937 Ruff and Ready 45.00
938 Elmer Fudd 10.00
939 Steve Canyon 27.00
940 Lolly and Pepper 10.00
941 Pluto 25.00
942 Pony Express 18.00
943 White Wilderness 20.00
944 SB,7th Voyage of Sinbad . . 85.00
945 Maverick,J.Garner Ph(c) . . 60.00
946 The Big Country,Ph(c) 30.00
947 Broken Arrow,Ph(c) 25.00
948 Daisy Duck's Diary 40.00
949 High Adventure,Ph(c) 30.00
950 Frosty the Snowman 15.00
951 ATh,Lennon Sisters
    Life Story,Ph(c) 110.00
952 Goofy 40.00
953 Francis the Famous
    Talking Mule 20.00
954 Man in Space 55.00
955 Hi and Lois 8.00
956 Ricky Nelson,Ph(c) 170.00
957 Buffalo Bee 35.00
958 Santa Claus Funnies 15.00
959 Christmas Stories 15.00
960 ATh,W.Disney's Zorro 100.00
961 Jace Pearson's Tales of
    Texas Rangers,Ph(c) 30.00
962 Maverick,J.Garner Ph(c) . . 65.00
963 Johnny Mack Brown,Ph(c) . 30.00
964 The Hardy Boys,Ph(c) 40.00
965 GrandmaDuck'sFarmFriends 40.00
966 Tonka,Ph(c) 25.00
967 Chilly Willy 10.00
968 Tales of Wells Fargo,Ph(c) . 45.00
969 Peanuts 60.00
970 Lawman,Ph(c) 60.00
971 Wagon Train,Ph(c) 40.00
972 Tom Thumb 55.00
973 SleepingBeauty & the Prince 35.00
974 The Little Rascals 20.00
975 Fury,Ph(c) 35.00
976 ATh,W.Disney's Zorro,Ph(c) 90.00
977 Elmer Fudd 8.00
978 Lolly and Pepper 10.00
979 Oswald the Rabbit 8.00
980 Maverick,J.Garner Ph(c) . . 65.00
981 Ruff and Ready 25.00
982 The New Adventures of
    Tinker Bell 25.00
983 Have Gun, Will Travel,Ph(c) 55.00
984 Sleeping Beauty's Fairy
    Godmothers 35.00
985 Shaggy Dog,Ph(c) 25.00
986 Restless Gun,Ph(c) 45.00
987 Goofy 40.00
988 Little Hiawatha 15.00
989 Jimmy Cricket 15.00
990 Huckleberry Hound 40.00
991 Francis the Famous
    Talking Mule 20.00
992 ATh,Sugarfoot,Ph(c) 85.00
993 Jim Bowie,Ph(c) 30.00
994 Sea Hunt,L.Bridges Ph(c) . 45.00
995 Donald Duck Album 40.00
996 Nevada 25.00
997 Walt Disney Presents,Ph(c) . 60.00
998 Ricky Nelson,Ph(c) 160.00
999 Leave It To Beaver,Ph(c) . 125.00
1000 The Gray Ghost,Ph(c) 50.00

Dell Four Color #976
© Dell Publishing Co.

1001 Lowell Thomas' High
    Adventure,Ph(c) 30.00
1002 Buffalo Bee 25.00
1003 ATh,W.Disney's Zorro,Ph(c) 80.00
1004 Colt .45,Ph(c) 40.00
1005 Maverick,J.Garner Ph(c) . . 65.00
1006 SB,Hercules 65.00
1007 John Paul Jones,Ph(c) . . . 30.00
1008 Beep, Beep, the
    Road Runner 35.00
1009 CB,The Rifleman,Ph(c) . 120.00
1010 Grandma Duck's Farm
    Friends 75.00
1011 Buckskin,Ph(c) 45.00
1012 Last Train from Gun
    Hill,Ph(c) 55.00
1013 Bat Masterson,Ph(c) 65.00
1014 ATh,The Lennon Sisters,
    Ph(c) 110.00
1015 Peanuts 65.00
1016 Smokey the Bear 10.00
1017 Chilly Willy 8.00
1018 Rio Bravo,J.Wayne Ph(c) 175.00
1019 Wagoon Train,Ph(c) 40.00
1020 Jungle 15.00
1021 Jace Pearson's Tales of
    the Texas Rangers,Ph(c) . . . 30.00
1022 Timmy 10.00
1023 Tales of Wells Fargo,Ph(c) 45.00
1024 ATh,Darby O'Gill and
    the Little People,Ph(c) 50.00
1025 CB,W.Disney's Vacation in
    Disneyland 175.00
1026 Spin and Marty,Ph(c) 35.00
1027 The Texan,Ph(c) 35.00
1028 Rawhide,
    Clint Eastwood Ph(c) . . . 175.00
1029 Boots and Saddles,Ph(c) . . 30.00
1030 Spanky and Alfalfa, the
    Little Rascals 20.00
1031 Fury,Ph(c) 35.00
1032 Elmer Fudd 10.00
1033 Steve Canyon,Ph(c) 25.00
1034 Nancy and Sluggo
    Summer Camp 15.00
1035 Lawman,Ph(c) 35.00
1036 The Big Circus,Ph(c) 25.00
1037 Zorro,Ph(c) 80.00

1038 Ruff and Ready 25.00
1039 Pluto 25.00
1040 Quick Draw McGraw 55.00
1041 ATh,Sea Hunt,
    L.Bridges Ph(c) 65.00
1042 The Three Chipmunks . . 20.00
1043 The Three Stooges,Ph(c) 145.00
1044 Have Gun, Will Travel,Ph(c) 45.00
1045 Restless Gun,Ph(c) 45.00
1046 Beep Beep, the
    Road Runner 35.00
1047 CB,W.Disney's
    GyroGearloose 150.00
1048 The Horse Soldiers
    J.Wayne Ph(c) 125.00
1049 Don't Give Up the Ship
    J.Lewis Ph(c) 35.00
1050 Huckleberry Hound 25.00
1051 Donald in Mathmagic Land 75.00
1052 RsM,Ben-Hur 70.00
1053 Goofy 40.00
1054 Huckleberry Hound
    Winter Fun 25.00
1055 CB,Daisy Duck's Diary . . 80.00
1056 Yellowstone Kelly,
    C.Walker Ph(c) 30.00
1057 Mickey Mouse Album 20.00
1058 Colt .45,Ph(c) 30.00
1059 Sugarfoot 45.00
1060 Journey to the Center of the
    Earth, P.Boone Ph(c) 80.00
1061 Buffalo Bill 30.00
1062 Christmas Stories 15.00
1063 Santa Claus Funnies 15.00
1064 Bugs Bunny's Merry
    Christmas 25.00
1065 Frosty the Snowman 15.00
1066 ATh,77 Sunset Strip,Ph(c) . 80.00
1067 Yogi Bear 65.00
1068 Francis the Famous
    Talking Mule 20.00
1069 ATh,The FBI Story,Ph(c) . . 65.00
1070 Soloman and Sheba,Ph(c) 55.00
1071 ATh,The Real McCoys,Ph(c)85.00
1072 Blythe 20.00
1073 CB,Grandma Duck's Farm
    Friends 125.00
1074 Chilly Willy 10.00
1075 Tales of Wells Fargo,Ph(c) 40.00
1076 MSy,The Rebel,Ph(c) 75.00
1077 SB,The Deputy,
    H.Fonda Ph(c) 85.00
1078 The Three Stooges,Ph(c) . 65.00
1079 The Little Rascals 25.00
1080 Fury,Ph(c) 35.00
1081 Elmer Fudd 12.00
1082 Spin and Marty 30.00
1083 Men into Space,Ph(c) 50.00
1084 Speedy Gonzales 20.00
1085 ATh,The Time Machine . . 125.00
1086 Lolly and Pepper 10.00
1087 Peter Gunn,Ph(c) 65.00
1088 A Dog of Flanders,Ph(c) . . 20.00
1089 Restless Gun,Ph(c) 50.00
1090 Francis the Famous
    Talking Mule 20.00
1091 Jacky's Diary 20.00
1092 Toby Tyler,Ph(c) 20.00
1093 MacKenzie's Raiders,Ph(c) 35.00
1094 Goofy 50.00
1095 CB,W.Disney's
    GyroGearloose 95.00
1096 The Texan,Ph(c) 40.00
1097 Rawhide,C.Eastwood Ph(c) 125.00
1098 Sugarfoot,Ph(c) 50.00

1099 CB(c),Donald Duck Album . 50.00
1100 W.Disney's Annette's
   Life Story (TV),Ph(c) 125.00
1101 Robert Louis Stevenson's
   Kidnapped,Ph(c) 30.00
1102 Wanted: Dead or Alive,
   Ph(c) 100.00
1103 Leave It To Beaver,Ph(c) 125.00
1104 Yogi Bear Goes to College 30.00
1105 ATh,Gale Storm,Ph(c) . . . 100.00
1106 ATh,77 Sunset Strip,Ph(c) . 65.00
1107 Buckskin,Ph(c) 35.00
1108 The Troubleshooters,Ph(c) 30.00
1109 This Is Your Life, Donald
   Duck,O:Donald Duck 150.00
1110 Bonanza,Ph(c) 220.00
1111 Shotgun Slade 35.00
1112 Pixie and Dixie
   and Mr. Jinks 35.00
1113 Tales of Wells Fargo,Ph(c) 40.00
1114 Huckleberry Finn,Ph(c) . . . 25.00
1115 Ricky Nelson,Ph(c) 125.00
1116 Boots and Saddles,Ph(c) . . 30.00
1117 Boy and the Pirate,Ph(c) . . 35.00
1118 Sword and the Dragon,Ph(c) 40.00
1119 Smokey and the Bear
   Nature Stories 20.00
1120 Dinosaurus,Ph(c) 50.00
1121 RC,GE,Hercules Unchained 65.00
1122 Chilly Willy 10.00
1123 Tombstone Territory,Ph(c) . 45.00
1124 Whirlybirds,Ph(c) 40.00
1125 GK,RH,Laramie,Ph(c) 60.00
1126 Sundance,Ph(c) 55.00
1127 The Three Stooges,Ph(c) . 65.00
1128 Rocky and His Friends . . 200.00
1129 Pollyanna,H.Mills Ph(c) . . . 60.00
1130 SB,The Deputy,
   H.Fonda Ph(c) 65.00
1131 Elmer Fudd 10.00
1132 Space Mouse 20.00
1133 Fury,Ph(c) 35.00
1134 ATh,Real McCoys,Ph(c) . . 75.00
1135 M.G.M.'s Mouse Musketeers 10.00
1136 Jungle Cat,Ph(c) 30.00
1137 The Little Rascals 20.00
1138 The Rebel,Ph(c) 60.00
1139 SB,Spartacus,Ph(c) 75.00
1140 Donald Duck Album 45.00
1141 Huckleberry Hound for
   President 30.00
1142 Johnny Ringo,Ph(c) 50.00
1143 Pluto 30.00
1144 The Story of Ruth,Ph(c) . . 70.00
1145 GK,The Lost World,Ph(c) . . 85.00
1146 Restless Gun,Ph(c) 40.00
1147 Sugarfoot,Ph(c) 50.00
1148 I aim at the Stars,Ph(c) . . . 35.00
1149 Goofy 40.00
1150 CB,Daisy Duck's Diary . . . 80.00
1151 Mickey Mouse Album 20.00
1152 Rocky and His Friends . . 165.00
1153 Frosty the Snowman 15.00
1154 Santa Claus Funnies 15.00
1155 North to Alaska 100.00
1156 Walt Disney Swiss
   Family Robinson 30.00
1157 Master of the World 30.00
1158 Three Worlds of Gulliver . . . 30.00
1159 ATh,77 Sunset Strip 60.00
1160 Rawhide 135.00
1161 CB,Grandma Duck's
   Farm Friends 120.00
1162 Yogi Bera joins the Marines 40.00
1163 Daniel Boone 30.00

1164 Wanted: Dead or Alive . . . 70.00
1165 Ellery Queen 75.00
1166 Rocky and His Friends . . 160.00
1167 Tales of Wells Fargo,Ph(c) 40.00
1168 The Detectives,
   R.Taylor Ph(c) 60.00
1169 New Adventures of
   Sherlock Holmes 125.00
1170 The Three Stooges,Ph(c) . 65.00
1171 Elmer Fudd 10.00
1172 Fury,Ph(c) 35.00
1173 The Twilight Zone 150.00
1174 The Little Rascals 25.00
1175 M.G.M.'s Mouse Musketeers 10.00
1176 Dondi,Ph(c) 25.00
1177 Chilly Willy 10.00
1178 Ten Who Dared 20.00
1179 The Swamp Fox,
   L.Nielson Ph(c) 35.00
1180 The Danny Thomas Show 100.00
1181 Texas John Slaughter,Ph(c) 20.00
1182 Donald Duck Album 30.00
1183 101 Dalmatians 65.00
1184 CB,W.Disney's
   Gyro Gearloose 100.00
1185 Sweetie Pie 15.00
1186 JDa,Yak Yak 50.00
1187 The Three Stooges,Ph(c) . 50.00
1188 Atlantis the Lost
   Continent,Ph(c) 65.00
1189 Greyfriars Bobby,Ph(c) . . . 30.00
1190 CB(c),Donald and
   the Wheel 50.00
1191 Leave It to Beaver,Ph(c) . 125.00
1192 Rocky Nelson,Ph(c) 130.00

Dell Four Color #1184
© Dell Publishing Co.

1193 The Real McCoys,Ph(c) . . 55.00
1194 Pepe,Ph(c) 30.00
1195 National Velvet,Ph(c) 25.00
1196 Pixie and Dixie
   and Mr. Jinks 20.00
1197 The Aquanauts,Ph(c) 35.00
1198 Donald in Mathmagic Land 50.00
1199 Absent-Minded Professor,
   Ph(c) 30.00
1200 Hennessey,Ph(c) 35.00
1201 Goofy 40.00
1202 Rawhide,C.Eastwood Ph(c) 135.00
1203 Pinocchio 35.00

1204 Scamp 25.00
1205 David Goliath,Ph(c) 30.00
1206 Lolly and Pepper 10.00
1207 MSy,The Rebel,Ph(c) 65.00
1208 Rocky and His Friends . . 135.00
1209 Sugarfoot,Ph(c) 50.00
1210 The Parent Trap,
   H.Mills Ph(c) 65.00
1211 RsM,77 Sunset Strip,Ph(c) 50.00
1212 Chilly Willy 10.00
1213 Mysterious Island,Ph(c) . . . 55.00
1214 Smokey the Bear 20.00
1215 Tales of Wells Fargo,Ph(c) 40.00
1216 Whirlybirds,Ph(c) 45.00
1218 Fury,Ph(c) 35.00
1219 The Detectives,
   R Taylor Ph(c) 45.00
1220 Gunslinger,Ph(c) 40.00
1221 Bonanza,Ph(c) 125.00
1222 Elmer Fudd 10.00
1223 GK,Laramie,Ph(c) 40.00
1224 The Little Rascals 25.00
1225 The Deputy,H.Fonda Ph(c) 60.00
1226 Nikki, Wild Dog of the North 15.00
1227 Morgan the Pirate,Ph(c) . . 50.00
1229 Thief of Bagdad,Ph(c) 65.00
1230 Voyage to the Bottom
   of the Sea,Ph(c) 50.00
1231 Danger Man,Ph(c) 50.00
1232 On the Double 20.00
1233 Tammy Tell Me True 30.00
1234 The Phantom Planet 45.00
1235 Mister Magoo 55.00
1236 King of Kings,Ph(c) 60.00
1237 ATh,The Untouchables,
   Ph(c) 110.00
1238 Deputy Dawg 75.00
1239 CB(c),Donald Duck Album . 25.00
1240 The Detectives,
   R.Taylor Ph(c) 40.00
1241 Sweetie Pies 15.00
1242 King Leonardo and
   His Short Subjects 100.00
1243 Ellery Queen 35.00
1244 Space Mouse 20.00
1245 New Adventures of
   Sherlock Holmes 125.00
1246 Mickey Mouse Album . . . 25.00
1247 Daisy Duck's Diary 30.00
1248 Pluto 25.00
1249 The Danny Thomas Show,
   Ph(c) 120.00
1250 Four Horseman of the
   Apocalypse,Ph(c) 45.00
1251 Everything's Ducky 25.00
1252 The Andy Griffith Show,
   Ph(c) 190.00
1253 Spaceman 45.00
1254 "Diver Dan" 35.00
1255 The Wonders of Aladdin . . 30.00
1256 Kona, Monarch of
   Monster Isle 30.00
1257 Car 54, Where Are You?,
   Ph(c) 50.00
1258 GE,The Frogmen 35.00
1259 El Cid,Ph(c) 40.00
1260 The Horsemasters,Ph(c) . . 45.00
1261 Rawhide,C.Eastwood Ph(c) 135.00
1262 The Rebel,Ph(c) 65.00
1263 RsM,77 Sinset Strip,Ph(c) . 50.00
1264 Pixie & Dixie & Mr.Jinks . . 20.00
1265 The Real McCoys,Ph(c) . . 55.00
1266 M.G.M.'s Spike and Tyke . 10.00
1267 CB,GyroGearloose 65.00
1268 Oswald the Rabbit 10.00

1269 Rawhide,C.Eastwood Ph(c) 135.00
1270 Bullwinkle and Rocky ... 110.00
1271 Yogi Bear Birthday Party .. 30.00
1272 Frosty the Snowman 15.00
1273 Hans Brinker,Ph(c) 25.00
1274 Santa Claus Funnies 15.00
1275 Rocky and His Friends .. 100.00
1276 Dondi 20.00
1278 King Leonardo and
    His Short Subjects 100.00
1279 Grandma Duck's Farm
    Friends 40.00
1280 Hennessey,Ph(c) 35.00
1281 Chilly Willy 10.00
1282 Babes in Toyland,Ph(c) .. 65.00
1283 Bonanza,Ph(c) 125.00
1284 RH,Laramie,Ph(c) 50.00
1285 Leave It to Beaver,Ph(c) . 125.00
1286 The Untouchables,Ph(c) . 100.00
1287 Man from Wells Fargo,Ph(c) 30.00
1288 RC,GE,The Twilight Zone 100.00
1289 Ellery Queen 40.00
1290 M.G.M.'s Mouse
    Musketeers 10.00
1291 RsM,77 Sunset Strip,Ph(c) 50.00
1293 Elmer Fudd 10.00
1294 Ripcord 35.00
1295 Mr. Ed, the Talking Horse,
    Ph(c) 50.00
1296 Fury,Ph(c) 35.00
1297 Spanky, Alfalfa and the
    Little Rascals 20.00
1298 The Hathaways,Ph(c) 25.00
1299 Deputy Dawg 50.00
1300 The Comancheros 125.00
1301 Adventures in Paradise .. 25.00
1302 JohnnyJason,TeenReporter 20.00
1303 Lad: A Dog,Ph(c) 20.00
1304 Nellie the Nurse 40.00
1305 Mister Magoo 55.00
1306 Target: The Corruptors,
    Ph(c) 20.00
1307 Margie 20.00
1308 Tales of the Wizard of Oz . 60.00
1309 BK,87th Precinct,Ph(c) .. 60.00
1310 Huck and Yogi Winter
    Sports 20.00
1311 Rocky and His Friends .. 100.00
1312 National Velvet,Ph(c) 20.00
1313 Moon Pilot.Ph(c) 60.00
1328 GE,The Underwater
    City,Ph(c) 40.00
1330 GK,Brain Boy 35.00
1332 Bachelor Father 45.00
1333 Short Ribs 25.00
1335 Aggie Mack 20.00
1336 On Stage 25.00
1337 Dr. Kildare,Ph(c) 35.00
1341 The Andy Griffith Show,
    Ph(c) 185.00
1348 JDa,Yak Yak 50.00
1349 Yogi Berra Visits the U.N. . 40.00
1350 Commanche,Ph(c) 20.00
1354 Calvin and the Colonel ... 35.00

FOUR FAVORITES
Ace Magazines
September, 1941
1 B:Vulcan, Lash Lighting, Magno
    the Magnetic Man, Raven,
    Flag cover,Hitler 650.00
2 A: Black Ace 300.00
3 E:Vulcan 250.00
4 E:Raven,B:Unknown Soldiers 250.00
5 B:Captain Courageous 225.00

6 A: The Flag, B: Mr. Risk ... 225.00
7 JM 200.00
8 .... 200.00
9 RP,HK 200.00
10 HK 300.00
11 HK,LbC,UnKnown Soldier .. 250.00
12 LbC 150.00
13 LbC 125.00
14 Fer 125.00
15 Fer 125.00
16 Bondage(c) 150.00
17 Magno Lighting 125.00
18 Magno Lighting 125.00

4 Favorites #19 © Ace Magazines

19 RP,RP(c) 125.00
20 RP,RP(c) 125.00
21 RP,RP(c) 100.00
22 RP(c) 100.00
23 RP(c) 100.00
24 RP(c) 100.00
25 RP(c) 100.00
26 RP(c) 100.00
27 RP(c) 80.00
28 .... 75.00
29 .... 75.00
30 .... 75.00
31 .... 75.00
32 .... 75.00

FRANKENSTEIN COMICS
Crestwood Publications
(Prize Publ.)
Summer, 1945
1 B:Frankenstein,DBr,DBr(c) . 600.00
2 DBr,DBr(c) 300.00
3 DBr,DBr(c) 200.00
4 DBr,DBr(c) 200.00
5 DBr,DBr(c) 200.00
6 DBr,DBr(c),S&K 175.00
7 DBr,DBr(c),S&K 175.00
8 DBr,DBr(c),S&K 175.00
9 DBr,DBr(c),S&K 175.00
10 DBr,DBr(c),S&K 175.00
11 DBr,DBr(c)A:Boris Karloff .. 150.00
12 DBr,DBr(c) 150.00
13 DBr,DBr(c). 150.00
14 DBr,DBr(c) 150.00
15 DBr,DBr(c) 150.00
16 DBr,DBr(c) 150.00

Frankenstein #10
© Crestwood/Prize Publications

17 DBr,DBr(c) 150.00
18 B:Horror 160.00
19 .... 125.00
3-4 .... 110.00
3-5 .... 110.00
3-6 .... 110.00
4-1 thru 4-6 .... @110.00
5-1 thru 5-4 .... @110.00
5-5 October-November, 1954 . 110.00

FRISKY FABLES
Novelty Press/Premium Group
Spring, 1945
1 AFa 65.00
2 AFa 40.00
3 AFa 35.00
4 AFa 28.00
5 AFa 28.00
6 AFa 28.00
7 AFa,Flag (c) 30.00
2-1 AFa,Rainbow(c) 25.00
2-2 AFa 20.00
2-3 AFa 18.00
2-4 AFa 18.00
2-5 AFa 18.00
2-6 AFa 18.00
2-7 AFa 18.00
2-8 AFa,Halloween (c) 20.00
2-9 AFa,Thanksgiving(c) ... 15.00
2-10 AFa,Christmas cover ... 18.00
2-11 AFa 20.00
2-12 AFa,Valentines Day cover . 15.00
3-1 AFa 12.00
3-2 AFa 12.00
3-3 AFa 15.00
3-4 AFa 12.00
3-5 AFa 12.00
3-6 AFa 12.00
3-7 AFa 12.00
3-8 AFa,Turkey (c) 12.00
3-9 AFa 12.00
3-10 AFa 12.00
3-11 AFa,1948(c) 12.00
3-12 AFa 12.00
4-1 thru 4-7 AFa .... @12.00
5-1 AFa 12.00
5-2 AFa 12.00

5-3	12.00
5-4 Star Publications	12.00
39 LbC(c)	50.00
40 LbC(c)	50.00
41 LbC(c)	50.00
42 LbC(c)	50.00
43 LbC(c)	20.00

Becomes:
FRISKY ANIMALS
Star Publications

44 LbC	70.00
45 LbC	100.00
46 LbC,Baseball	60.00
47 LbC	60.00
48 LbC	60.00
49 LbC	60.00
50 LbC	60.00
51 LbC(c)	60.00
52 LbC(c)	75.00
53 LbC(c)	55.00
54 LbC(c),Supercat(c)	55.00
55 LbC(c),same	55.00
56 LbC(c),same	55.00
57 LbC(c),same	55.00
58 LbC(c),same,July, 1954	55.00

FRITZI RITZ
**United Features Syndicate/
St. John Publications**
Fall, 1948

N# Special issue	75.00
2	35.00
3	30.00
4 thru 7	@25.00
6 A:Abbie & Slats	27.00
8 thru 10	@18.00
11 1958	18.00

FROGMAN COMICS
Hillman Periodicals
January-February, 1952

1	65.00
2	35.00
3	35.00
4 MMe	22.00
5 BK,AT	35.00
6 thru 10	@20.00
11 May, 1953	20.00

FRONTIER ROMANCES
Avon Periodicals
November-December, 1949

1 She Learned to Ride and Shoot, and Kissing Came Natural	275.00
2 Bronc-Busters Sweetheart, January-February, 1950	200.00

FRONTLINE COMBAT
**Tiny Tot Publications
(E.C. Comics)**
July-August, 1951

1 HK(c),WW, JSe,JDa,Hanhung Changjn cover	500.00
2 HK(c),WW,Tank Battle cover	300.00
3 HK(c),WW,Naval Battleship fire cover	275.00
4 HK(c),WW, Bazooka cover	225.00
5 HK(c),JSe	200.00
6 HK(c),WW,JSe	175.00
7 HK(c),WW,JSe,Document of the Action at Iwo Jima	175.00
8 HK(c),WW,ATh	175.00

9 HK(c),WW,JSe,Civil War iss.	175.00
10 GE,HK(c),WW, Crying Child cover	225.00
11 GE	150.00
12 GE,Air Force issue	150.00
13 JSe,GE,WW(c), Bi-Planes cover	150.00
14 JKu,GE,WW(c)	150.00
15 JSe,GE,WW(c), Jan., 1954	150.00

FRONT PAGE COMIC BOOK
Front Page Comics
1945

1 JKu,BP,BF(c),I:Man in Black	200.00

FUGITIVES FROM JUSTICE
St. John Publishing Co.
February, 1952

1	100.00
2 MB, Killer Boomerang	75.00
3 GT	75.00
4	35.00
5 Bondage cover, October, 1952	60.00

FUNNIES, THE
(1ST SERIES)
Dell Publishing Co.
1929-30

1 B:Foxy Grandpa, Sniffy	400.00
2 thru 21	@175.00
N#(22)	150.00
N#(23) thru (36)	@100.00

Funnies #6 © Dell Publishing Co.

FUNNIES, THE
(2ND SERIES)
Dell Publishing Co.
October, 1936

1 Tailspin Tommy,Mutt & Jeff, Capt. Easy,D.Dixon	1,400.00
2 Scribbly	650.00
3	500.00
4 Christmas issue	375.00
5	350.00
6 thru 22	@325.00

23 thru 29	@225.00
30 B:John Carter of Mars	600.00
31 inc. Dick Tracy	375.00
32	375.00
33	375.00
34	375.00
35 John Carter (c)	375.00
36 John Carter (c)	375.00
37 John Carter (c)	375.00
38 Rex King of the Deep (c)	375.00
39 Rex King (c)	375.00
40 John Carter (c)	375.00
41 Sky Ranger (c)	375.00
42 Rex King (c)	375.00
43 Rex King (c)	375.00
44 Rex King (c)	375.00
45 I&O:Phantasmo:Master of the World	300.00
46 Phantasmo (c)	300.00
47 Phantasmo (c)	225.00
48 Phantasmo (c)	200.00
49 Phantasmo (c)	200.00
50 Phantasmo (c)	200.00
51 Phantasmo (c)	200.00
52 Phantasmo (c)	225.00
53 Phantasmo (c)	225.00
54 Phantasmo (c)	225.00
55 Phantasmo (c)	225.00
56 Phantasmo (c) E:John Carter	225.00
57 I&O:Captain Midnight	675.00
58 Captain Midnight (c)	250.00
59 Captain Midnight (c)	250.00
60 Captain Midnight (c)	250.00
61 Captain Midnight (c)	250.00
62 Captain Midnight (c)	250.00
63 Captain Midnight (c)	250.00
64 B: Woody Woodpecker	250.00

Becomes:
NEW FUNNIES
Dell Publishing Co.
July, 1942

65 Andy Panda, Ragady Ann & Andy, Peter Rabbit	450.00

New Funnies #68 © Dell Publishing Co.

66 same	250.00
67 Felix the Cat	250.00
68	250.00
69 WK, The Brownies	250.00
70	250.00

All comics prices listed are for *Near Mint* condition. **CVA Page 305**

71	150.00
72 WK	150.00
73	150.00
74	150.00
75 WK,Brownies	150.00
76 CB,Andy Panda, Woody Woodpecker	750.00
77 same	150.00
78 Andy Panda	150.00
79	100.00
80	100.00
81	100.00
82 WK,Brownies	125.00
83 WK,Brownies	125.00
84 WK,Brownies	100.00
85 WK,Brownies	125.00
86	65.00
87 Woody Woodpecker	60.00
88 same	60.00
89 same	60.00
90 same	60.00
91 thru 99	@45.00
100	50.00
101 thru 110	@25.00
111 thru 118	@20.00
119 Christmas	22.00
120 thru 142	@20.00
143 Christmas cover	25.00
144 thru 149	@15.00
150 thru 154	@10.00
155 Christmas cover	12.00
156 thru 167	@10.00
168 Christmas cover	12.00
169 thru 181	@10.00
182 I&O:Knothead & Splinter	10.00
183 thru 200	@10.00
201 thru 240	@7.00
241 thru 288	@6.00

FUNNY BOOK
Funny Book Publ. Corp.
(Parents Magazine)
December, 1952

1 Alec, the Funny Bunny, Alice in Wonderland	70.00
2 Gulliver in Giant-Land	40.00
3	28.00
4 Adventures of Robin Hood	25.00
5	25.00
6	25.00
7	25.00
8	25.00
9	25.00

FUNNY FILMS
Best Syndicated Features
(American Comics Group)
September-October, 1949

1 B:Puss An' Boots, Blunderbunny	80.00
2	45.00
3	32.00
4	30.00
5	30.00
6	30.00
7	30.00
8	30.00
9	30.00
10	30.00
11 thru 20	@20.00
21 thru 28	@18.00
29 May-June, 1954	18.00

FUNNY FUNNIES

Nedor Publ. Co.
April, 1943

1 Funny Animals	100.00

FUNNYMAN
Magazine Enterprises of Canada
December, 1947

1 S&K,S&K(c)	165.00
2 S&K,S&K(c)	135.00
3 S&K,S&K(c)	100.00
4 S&K,S&K(c)	100.00
5 S&K,S&K(c)	100.00
6 S&K,S&K(c), August, 1948	100.00

FUTURE COMICS
David McKay Publications
June, 1940

1 Lone Ranger,Phantom	1,200.00
2 Lone Ranger	650.00
3 Lone Ranger	475.00
4 Lone Ranger,Sept., 1940	450.00

FUTURE WORLD COMICS
George W. Dougherty
Summer, 1946

1	150.00
2 Fall, 1946	125.00

GABBY HAYES WESTERN
Fawcett Publ./Charlton Comics
November, 1948

1 Ph(c)	250.00
2 Ph(c)	135.00
3 The Rage of the Purple Sage, Ph(c)	90.00
4 Ph(c)	90.00
5 Ph(c)	85.00
6 Ph(c)	85.00
7 Ph(c)	75.00
8 Ph(c)	75.00
9 Ph(c),V:The Kangaroo Crook	75.00
10 Ph(c)	75.00
11 Ph(c), Chariot Race	75.00
12 V:Beaver Ben, The Biting Bandit, Ph(c)	65.00
13 thru 15	@65.00
16	50.00
17	50.00
18 thru 20	@50.00
21 thru 51	@35.00
51 thru 59 December, 1954	@20.00

GANGSTERS AND GUN MOLLS
Realistic Comics
(Avon)
September, 1951

1 WW,A:Big Jim Colosimo, Evelyn Ellis	225.00
2 JKa, A:Bonnie Parker, The Kissing Bandit	165.00
3 EK, A:Juanita Perez, Crimes Homicide Squad	125.00
4 A:Mara Hite, Elkins Boys, June, 1952	125.00

GANGSTERS CAN'T WIN
D.S. Publishing Co.

February-March, 1948

1 Shot Cop cover	150.00
2 A:Eddie Bentz	75.00
3 Twin Trouble Trigger Man	70.00
4 Suicide on SoundStageSeven	70.00
5 Trail of Terror	70.00
6 Mystery at the Circus	70.00
7 Talisman Trail	35.00
8	35.00
9 Suprise at Buoy 13, June-July, 1949	35.00

GANG WORLD
Literary Enterprises
(Standard Comics)
October, 1952

5 Bondage cover	80.00
6 Mob Payoff, January, 1953	50.00

GASOLINE ALLEY
Star Publications
October, 1950

1	125.00
2 LBc	75.00
3 LBc(c), April, 1950	100.00

GEM COMICS
Spotlight Publ.
April, 1945

1 A:Steve Strong,Bondage(c)	125.00

Gene Autry #9 © Fawcett Publications

GENE AUTRY COMICS
Fawcett Publications
January, 1942

1 The Mark of Cloven Hoof	2,200.00
2	575.00
3 Secret of the Aztec Treasure	400.00
4	375.00
5 Mystery of PaintRockCanyon	375.00
6 Outlaw Round-up	350.00
7 Border Bullets	350.00
8 Blazing Guns	325.00
9 Range Robbers	325.00
10 Fightin' Buckaroo, Danger's Trail, Sept., 1943	325.00
11	350.00
12	325.00

All comics prices listed are for _Near Mint_ condition.

GENE AUTRY COMICS
Dell Publishing Co.
May/June 1946

1	325.00
2 Ph(c)	175.00
3 Ph(c)	135.00
4 Ph(c),I:Flap Jack	135.00
5 Ph(c), all	125.00
6 thru 10	@100.00
11 thru 19	@75.00
20	80.00
21 thru 29	@55.00
30 thru 40, B:Giants	@60.00
41 thru 56 E:Giants	@50.00
57	30.00
58 Christmas cover	35.00
59 thru 66	@30.00
67 thru 80, B:Giant	@35.00
81 thru 90, E:Giant	@25.00
91 thru 93	@20.00
94 Christmas cover	22.00
95 thru 99	@20.00
100	25.00
101 thru 111	@20.00
112 thru 121	@15.00

GENE AUTRY'S CHAMPION
Dell Publishing Co.
August, 1950

(1) see Dell Four Color #287	
(2) see Dell Four Color #319	
3 thru 19	@15.00

GEORGE PAL'S PUPPETOON'S
Fawcett Publications
December, 1945

1 Captain Marvel (c)	250.00
2	125.00
3	85.00
4 thru 17	@75.00
18 December, 1947	75.00

GERALD McBOING-BOING AND THE NEARSIGHTED MR. MAGOO
Dell Publishing Co.
August-October, 1952

1	50.00
2	40.00
3	40.00
4	40.00
5	40.00

GERONIMO
Avon Periodicals
1950

1 Massacre at San Pedro Pass	85.00
2 EK(c), Murderous Battle at Kiskayah	50.00
3 EK(c)	50.00
4 EK(c),Apache Death Trap, February, 1952	50.00

GET LOST
Mikeross Publications
February-March, 1954

1	120.00
2	75.00
3 June-July, 1954	65.00

GHOST
Fiction House Magazine
Winter, 1951

1 The Banshee Bells	350.00
2 I Woke In Terror	175.00
3 The Haunted Hand of X	150.00

Ghost Comics #4
© Fiction House Magazine

4 Flee the Mad Furies	150.00
5 The Hex of Ruby Eye	150.00
6 The Sleepers in the Crypt	175.00
7 When Dead Rogues Ride	175.00
8 Curse of the Mist-Thing	175.00
9 It Crawls by Night,Bondage(c)	185.00
10 Halfway to Hades	150.00
11 GE, The Witch's Doll, Summer, 1954	175.00

GHOST BREAKERS
Street & Smith Publications
September, 1948

1 BP,BP(c), A:Dr. Neff	200.00
2 BP,BP(c), Breaks the Voodoo Hoodoo,December, 1948	150.00

GHOSTLY WEIRD STORIES
(see BLUE BOLT)

GIANT BOY BOOK OF COMICS
Newsbook Publ. (Lev Gleason)
1945

1 A:Crime Buster & Young Robin Hood	600.00

GIANT COMICS EDITION
St. John Publ.
1948

1 Mighty Mouse	400.00
2 Abbie and Slats	175.00
3 Terry Toons	300.00
4 Crime Comics	400.00
5 MB, Police Case Book	400.00
6 MB,MB(c), Western Picture Story	400.00

7 May not exist	
8 The Adventures of Mighty Mouse	300.00
9 JKu,MB,Romance & Confession Stories,Ph(c)	400.00
10 Terry Toons	300.00
11 MB,MB(c),JKu,Western Picture Stories	375.00
12 MB,MB(c),Diary Secrets, Prostitute	600.00
13 MB,JKu, Romances	350.00
14 Mighty Mouse Album	350.00
15 MB(c),Romance	350.00
16 Little Audrey	300.00
N#, Mighty Mouse Album	300.00

GIANT COMICS EDITION
United Features Syndicate
1945

1 A:Abbie & Slats, Jim Hardy, Ella Cinders,Iron Vic	225.00
2 Elmo, Jim Hardy, Abbie & Slats, 1945	175.00

G.I. Combat #2
© Quality Comics Group

G.I. COMBAT
Quality Comics Group
October, 1952

1 RC(c), Beyond the Call of Duty	275.00
2 RC(c), Operation Massacre	125.00
3 An Indestructible Marine	120.00
4 Bridge to Blood Hill	120.00
5 Hell Breaks loose on Suicide Hill	120.00
6 Beachhead Inferno	100.00
7 Fire Power Assault	90.00
8 RC(c),Death-trap Hill	90.00
9 Devil Riders	90.00
10 RC(c), Two-Ton Booby Trap	50.00
11 Hell's Heroes	45.00
12 Hand Grenade Hero	45.00
13 Commando Assault	45.00
14 Spear Head Assault	45.00
15 Vengeance Assault	45.00
16 Trapped Under Fire	40.00
17 Attack on Death Mountain	40.00
18 Red Battle Ground	40.00

All comics prices listed are for *Near Mint* condition.   **CVA Page 307**

19 Death on Helicopter Hill	40.00
20 Doomed Legion-Death Trap .	40.00
21 Red Sneak Attack	38.00
22 Vengeance Raid	38.00
23 No Grandstand in Hell	38.00
24 Operation Steel Trap,Comics Code	38.00
25 Charge of the CommieBrigade	35.00
26 Red Guerrilla Trap	35.00

G.I. Combat #25
© Quality Comics Group

27 Trapped Behind Commie Lines	35.00
28 Atomic Battleground	35.00
29 Patrol Ambush	35.00
30 Operation Booby Trap	35.00
31 Human Fly on Heartbreak Hill	35.00
32 Atomic Rocket Assault	70.00
33 Bridge to Oblivion	35.00
34 RC,Desperate Mission	45.00
35 Doom Patrol	35.00
36 Fire Power Assault	35.00
37 Attack at Dawn	35.00
38 Get That Tank	35.00
39 Mystery of No Man's Land ..	35.00
40 Maneuver Battleground	35.00
41 Trumpet of Doom	35.00
42 March of Doom	35.00
43 Operation Showdown	35.00

See DC Comics for 44-120

GIFT COMICS
Fawcett Publications
March, 1942

1 A:Captain Marvel, Bulletman, Golden Arrow,Ibis, the Invincible, Spy Smasher ..	2,000.00
2	1,200.00
3	800.00
4 A:Marvel Family, 1949	600.00

GIGGLE COMICS
Creston Publ./ American Comics Group
October, 1943

1 (fa)same	175.00
2 KHu	90.00
3 KHu	55.00
4 KHu	50.00
5 KHu	50.00

6 KHu	45.00
7 KHu	45.00
8 KHu	45.00
9 I:Super Katt	50.00
10 KHu	45.00
11 thru 20 KHu	@30.00
21 thru 30 KHu	@25.00
31 thru 40 KHu	@20.00
41 thru 94 KHu	@18.00
95 A:Spencer Spook	20.00
96 KHu	18.00
97 KHu	18.00
98 KHu	18.00
99 KHu	18.00
100 and 101 March-April,1955	@18.00

G.I. JANE
Stanhall Publ.
May, 1953

1	55.00
2 thru 6	@25.00
7 thru 9	@20.00
10 December, 1954	18.00

G.I. JOE
Ziff-Davis Publication Co.
1950

10 NS(c),Red Devils of Korea, V:Seoul City Lou	55.00
11 NS(c),The Guerrilla's Lair ...	35.00
12 NS(c)	35.00
13 NS(c),Attack at Dawn	35.00
14 NS(c),Temple of Terror, A:Peanuts the Great	30.00
2-6 It's a Foot Soldiers Job, I:Frankie of the Pump	30.00
2-7 BP,NS(c),The Rout at Sugar Creek	30.00
8 BP,NS(c),Waldo'sSqueezeBox	30.00
9 NS(c),Dear John	30.00
10 NS(c),Joe Flies the Payroll .	30.00
11 NS(c),For the Love of Benny .	30.00
12 NS(c),Patch work Quilt	30.00
13 NS(c)	30.00
14 NS(c),The Wedding Ring ...	30.00
15 The Lacrosse Whoopee	30.00
16 Mamie's Mortar	30.00
17 A Time for Waiting	30.00
18 Giant	80.00
19 Old Army Game..Buck Passer	25.00
20 General Confusion	25.00
21 Save 'Im for Brooklyn	25.00
22 Portrait of a Lady	25.00
23 Take Care of My Little Wagon	25.00
24 Operation 'Operation'	25.00
25 The Two-Leaf Clover	25.00
26 NS(c),Nobody Flies Alone Mud & Wings	25.00
27 "Dear Son...Come Home" ...	25.00
28 They Alway's Come Back Bondage cover	25.00
29 What a Picnic	22.00
30 NS(c),The One-Sleeved Kimono	22.00
31 NS(c),Get a Horse	20.00
32 thru 47	@20.00
48 Atom Bomb	25.00
49 thru 51 June, 1957	@20.00

GINGER
Close-Up Publ.
(Archie Publications)
January, 1951

1 GFs	75.00

2	40.00
3	30.00
4	30.00
5	25.00
6	25.00
7 thru 9	@35.00
10 A:Katy Keene,Summer,1954 .	40.00

GIRLS IN LOVE
Fawcett Publications
May, 1950

1	40.00
2 Ph(c),July, 1950	35.00

GIRLS IN LOVE
(see DIARY LOVES)

G.I. SWEETHEARTS
(see DIARY LOVES)

G.I. WAR BRIDES
Superior Publ. Ltd.
April, 1954

1	25.00
2	12.00
3 thru 7	@10.00
8 June, 1955	10.00

GOING STEADY
(see TEEN-AGE TEMPTATIONS)

GOLDEN ARROW
Fawcett Publications
Spring, 1942

1 B:Golden Arrow	300.00
2	120.00
3	75.00
4	60.00
5 Spring, 1947	50.00
6 BK	60.00
6a 1944 Well Known Comics (Giveaway)	65.00

GOLDEN LAD
Spark Publications

Golden Lad #5 © Spark Publications

July, 1945
1 MMe,MMe(c),A:Kid Wizards,
Swift Arrow,B:Golden Ladd   350.00
2 MMe,MMe(c) 175.00
3 MMe,MMe(c) 175.00
4 MMe,MMe(c), The Menace of
the Minstrel 175.00
5 MMe,MMe(c),O:Golden Girl,
June, 1946 . . . . 175.00

GOLDEN WEST LOVE
Kirby Publishing Co.
September-October, 1949
1 BP,I Rode Heartbreak Hill,
Ph(c) 75.00
2 BP 60.00
3 BP,Ph(c) 60.00
4 BP,April, 1950 . . . . 60.00

GOLD MEDAL COMICS
Cambridge House
1945
N# Captain Truth 135.00

GOOFY COMICS
Nedor Publ. Co./
Animated Cartoons
(Standard Comics)
June, 1943
1 (fa) 110.00
2 . . . . 65.00
3 VP 45.00
4 VP 35.00
5 VP 35.00
6 thru 10 VP . . . . @35.00
11 thru 15 . . . . @30.00
15 thru 19 . . . . @25.00
20 thru 35 FF . . . . @40.00
36 thru 45 . . . . @25.00

GREAT AMERICAN
COMICS PRESENTS–
THE SECRET VOICE
4 Star Publ.
1944
1 Hitler,Secret Weapon 100.00

GREAT COMICS
Novak Publ. Co.
1945
1 LbC(c) 90.00

GREAT COMICS
Great Comics Publications
November, 1941
1 I:The Great Zorro 600.00
2 . . . . 350.00
3 The Lost City, January, 1942 600.00

GREAT LOVER
ROMANCES
Toby Press
March, 1951
1 Jon Juan,A:Dr. King 70.00
2 Hollywood Girl 40.00
3 Love in a Taxi 20.00
4 The Experimental Kiss 20.00
5 After the Honeymoon 20.00
6 HK,The Kid Sister Falls
in Love 35.00
7 Man Crazy 20.00

8 Stand-in Boyfriend 20.00
9 The Cheat 20.00
10 Heart Breaker 20.00
11 . . . . 20.00
12 . . . . 20.00
13 Powerhouse of Deciet 20.00
14 . . . . 20.00
15 Ph(c),Still Undecided,
Liz Taylor 40.00
16 thru 21 . . . . @20.00
22 May, 1955 . . . . 20.00

GREEN GIANT COMICS
Pelican Publications
1941
1 Black Arrow, Dr. Nerod
O:Colossus 6,500.00

GREEN HORNET
COMICS
Helnit Publ. Co./
Family Comics
(Harvey Publ.)
December, 1940
1 B:Green Hornet,P(c) 1,900.00
2 . . . . 750.00
3 BWh(c) 650.00
4 BWh(c) 500.00
5 BWh(c) 500.00
6 . . . . 500.00
7 BP, O:Zebra, B:Robin
Hood & Staff of 76 . . . . . . 475.00
8 BP,Bondage cover 425.00
9 BP, Behind the Cover 400.00
10 BP 400.00
11 Who is Mr. Q? 400.00
12 BP,A:Mr.Q 375.00
13 Hitler cover 325.00
14 BP,Spirit of 76-Twinkle
Twins, Bondage(c) 325.00

Green Hornet #12
© Helnit Publ./Family Comics

15 ASh(c),Nazi Ghost Ship . . . 300.00
16 BP,Prisoner of War 300.00
17 BP,ASh(c),Nazis' Last Stand 300.00
18 BP,ASh(c),Jap's Treacherous
Plot,Bondage cover 325.00
19 BP,ASh(c),Clash with the

Rampaging Japs 300.00
20 BP,ASh(c),Tojo's
Propaganda Hoax 325.00
21 BP,ASh(c),Unwelcome Cargo 250.00
22 ASh(c),Rendezvous with
Jap Saboteurs 250.00
23 BF,ASh(c),Jap's Diabolical
Plot #B2978 . . . . 250.00
24 BF,Science Fiction cover . . 275.00
25 thru 29 . . . . @250.00
30 BP,JKu 250.00
31 BP,JKu 275.00
32 BP,JKu 225.00
33 BP,JKu 225.00
34 BP,JKu 225.00
35 BP,JKu 225.00
36 BP,JKu,Bondage cover 225.00
37 BP,JKu 225.00
38 BP,JKu 225.00
39 S&K 225.00
40 thru 45 . . . . @150.00
46 Drug 160.00
47 September, 1949 . . . . 150.00

GREEN LAMA
Spark Publications/Prize Publ.
December, 1944
1 I:Green Lama, Lt. Hercules
& Boy Champions 750.00
2 MRa,Forward to Victory
in 1945 . . . . 475.00
3 MRa,The Riddles of Toys . . 400.00
4 MRa,Dive Bombs Japan . . . 375.00
5 MRa,MRa(c),Fights for
the Four Freedoms 375.00
6 MRa,Smashes a Plot
against America 375.00
7 MRa,Merry X-Mas 325.00
8 MRa,Smashes Toy Master
of Crime, March, 1946 . . . . 325.00

Green Mask #1
© Fox Features Syndicate

GREEN MASK, THE
Fox Features Syndicate
Summer, 1940
1 O:Green Mask & Domino . 1,200.00
2 A:Zanzibar 600.00
3 BP 350.00

Green–Haunt (column 1)

4 B:Navy Jones 300.00
5 .... 250.00
6 B:Nightbird,E:Navy Jones,
Bondage cover 225.00
7 B:Timothy Smith &
The Tumbler 200.00
8 JSs 175.00
9 E:Nightbird, Death Wields
a Scalpel! 175.00
10 .... 150.00
11 The Banshee of Dead
Man's Hill 150.00
2-1 Election of Skulls 125.00
2-2 Pigeons of Death 100.00
2-3 Wandering Gold Brick ... 100.00
2-4 Time on His Hands 100.00
2-5 JFe,SFd 100.00
2-6 Adventure of the Disappearing
Trains, Oct.-Nov., 1946 .... 100.00

GUMPS, THE
Dell Publishing Co.
1945

1 .... 75.00
2 .... 50.00
3 .... 40.00
4 .... 40.00
5 .... 40.00

GUNS AGAINST GANGSTERS
Curtis Publ./Novelty Press
September-October, 1948

1 LbC,LbC(c),B:Toni Gayle .. 125.00
2 LbC,LbC(c) 75.00
3 LbC,LbC(c) 65.00
4 LbC,LbC(c) 65.00
5 LbC,LbC(c) 65.00
6 LbC,LbC(c),Shark 65.00
2-1 LbC,LbC(c),
September-October, 1949 .. 65.00

GUNSMOKE
Western Comics, Inc.
April-May, 1949

1 GRi,GRi(c),Gunsmoke & Masked
Marvel,Bondage cover 200.00
2 GRi,GRi(c) 120.00
3 GRi,GRi(c) 120.00
4 GRi(c),Bondage(c) 80.00
5 GRi(c) 80.00
6 thru 10 .... @50.00
11 thru 15 .... @35.00
16 January, 1952 .... 35.00

HA HA COMICS
Creston Publ.
(American Comics Group)
October, 1943

1 Funny Animal, all 150.00
2 .... 75.00
3 .... 55.00
4 .... 55.00
5 .... 55.00
6 thru 10 .... @40.00
11 .... 30.00
12 thru 15 KHu .... @30.00
16 thru 20 KHu .... @28.00
21 thru 30 KHu .... @25.00
31 thru 101 .... @20.00
102 February-March, 1955 .... 20.00

MISTER RISK

Humor Publ.
(Ace Magazines)
October, 1950

1 (7) B:Mr. Risk 30.00
2 .... 25.00

Becomes:
MEN AGAINST CRIME

3 A:Mr. Risk, Case of the Carnival
Killer 38.00
4 Murder-And the Crowd Roars 20.00
5 .... 20.00
6 .... 20.00
7 Get Them! 20.00

Becomes:
HAND OF FATE
Ace Magazines

8 .... 175.00
9 LC 80.00
10 LC 75.00
11 Genie(c) 65.00
12 .... 65.00
13 Hanging(c) 70.00
14 .... 65.00
15 .... 65.00
16 .... 60.00
17 .... 60.00
18 .... 60.00
19 Drug issue,Quicksand(c) 80.00
20 .... 60.00
21 Drug issue 80.00
22 .... 60.00
23 Graveyard(c) 60.00
24 LC,Electric Chair 125.00
25 November, 1954 .... 50.00
25a December, 1954 .... 70.00

HANGMAN COMICS
(see LAUGH COMICS)

HAP HAZARD COMICS
A.A. Wyn/Red Seal Publ./
Readers Research
Summer, 1944

1 Funny Teen 60.00
2 Dog Show 30.00
3 Sgr, ... 28.00
4 Sgr, ... 28.00
5 thru 10 Sgr, ... @20.00
11 thru 13 Sgr, ... @15.00
14 AF(c) 35.00
15 thru 24 .... @15.00

Becomes:
REAL LOVE

25 Dangerous Dates 45.00
26 .... 20.00
27 LbC(c), Revenge Conquest .. 32.00
28 thru 40 .... @15.00
41 thru 66 .... @12.00
67 Comics code 10.00
68 thru 76, Nov. 1956 ..... @10.00

HAPPY COMICS
Nedor Publications/
Animated Cartoons
(Standard Comics)
August, 1943

1 Funny Animal in all 110.00
2 .... 75.00
3 .... 45.00
4 .... 40.00
5 thru 10 .... @40.00
11 thru 20 .... @35.00

21 thru 30 .... @30.00
31 and 32 .... @50.00
33 FF 125.00
34 thru 37 FF .... @50.00
38 thru 40 .... @20.00

Becomes:
HAPPY RABBIT

41 Funny Animal in all 25.00
42 thru 50 .... @15.00

Becomes:
HARVEY COMIC HITS

51 Phantom 150.00
52 Steve Canyon's Air Power .. 75.00
53 Mandrake 125.00
54 Tim Tyler's Tales of Jungle
Terror 65.00
55 Love Stories of Mary Worth . 30.00
56 Phantom, Bondage cover .. 130.00
57 Kidnap Racket 110.00
58 Girls in White 25.00
59 Tales of the Invisible 60.00
60 Paramount Animated Comics 225.00
61 Casper the Friendly Ghost . 250.00
62 Paramount Animated Comics,
April, 1953 .... 75.00

HAPPY HOULIHANS
(see SADDLE JUSTICE)

HAUNTED THRILLS
Four Star Publ.
(Ajax/Farrell)
June, 1952

1 Ellery Queen 150.00
2 LbC,Ellery Queen 100.00
3 Drug Story 90.00
4 Ghouls Castle 75.00
5 Fatal Scapel 75.00
6 Pit of Horror 65.00
7 Trail to a Tomb 65.00
8 Vanishing Skull 65.00
9 Madness of Terror 65.00
10 .... 65.00
11 Nazi Concentration Camp .. 80.00
12 RWb 65.00
13 .... 45.00
14 RWb 50.00
15 The Devil Collects 40.00
16 .... 40.00
17 Mirror of Madness 40.00
18 No Place to Go,
November-December, 1954 . 45.00

HAUNT OF FEAR
Fables Publ.
(E.C. Comics)
May-June, 1950

15 JCr,JCr(c),AF,WW 1,600.00
16 JCr,JCr(c),AF,WW 750.00
17 JCr,JCr(c),AF,WW,O:Crypt
of Terror,Vault of Horror
& Haunt of Fear 750.00
4 AF(c),WW,JDa 600.00
5 JCr,JCr(c),WW,JDa,Eye Injury 500.00
6 JCr,JCr(c),WW,JDa 325.00
7 JCr,JCr(c),AF,WW,O:Crypt . 325.00
8 AF(c),JKa,JDa,
Shrunken Head 325.00
9 AF(c),JCr,JDa 325.00
10 AF(c),Grl,JDa 300.00
11 JKa,Grl,JDa 275.00
12 JCr,Grl,JDa 275.00
13 Grl,JDa 275.00

Haunt of Fear #16 © E.C. Comics

14 Grl,Grl(c),JDa,O:Old Witch . 325.00
15 JDa 275.00
16 GRi(c),JDa,Ray Bradbury
   adaptation 275.00
17 JDa,Grl(c),Classic
   Ghastly (c) 275.00
18 JDa,Grl(c),JKa,Ray Bradbury
   adaptation 300.00
19 JDa,Guillotine (c),
   Bondage cover 300.00
20 RC,JDa,Grl,Grl(c) 250.00
21 JDa,Grl,Grl(c) 200.00
22 same 200.00
23 same 200.00
22 same 200.00
23 same 200.00
24 same 200.00
25 same 200.00
26 RC,same 250.00
27 same, Cannibalism 225.00
28 December, 1954 . . . . 225.00

HAWK, THE
Approved Comics
(Ziff-Davis)
Winter, 1951
1 MA,The Law of the Colt,P(c) 120.00
2 JKu,Iron Caravan of the
   Mojave, P(c) 60.00
3 Leverett's Last Stand,P(c) . . 50.00
4 Killer's Town,P(c) 40.00
5 . . . . 35.00
6 . . . . 35.00
7 . . . . 35.00
8 MB(c),Dry River Rampage . . 40.00
9 MB,MB(c),JKu 45.00
10 MB(c) 40.00
11 MB(c) 40.00
12 MB,MB(c), May, 1955 . . . . . 40.00

HEADLINE COMICS
American Boys Comics/
Headline Publ.
(Prize Publ.)
February, 1943
1 B:Jr. Rangers 225.00
2 JaB,JaB(c) 100.00
3 JaB,JaB(c) 80.00

4 . . . . 75.00
5 HcK 75.00
6 HcK 75.00
7 HcK,Jr. Rangers 75.00
8 HcK,Hitler cover 165.00
9 HcK 75.00
10 HcK,Hitler story,Wizard(c) . . 125.00
11 . . . . 40.00
12 HcK,Heroes of Yesterday . . 40.00
13 HcK,A:Blue Streak 45.00
14 HcK,A:Blue Streak 45.00
15 HcK,A:Blue Streak 45.00
16 HcK,O:Atomic Man 125.00
17 Atomic Man(c) 60.00
18 Atomic Man(c) 60.00
19 S&K,Atomic Man(c) 125.00
20 Atomic Man(c) 55.00
21 E:Atomic Man 55.00
22 HcK 35.00
23 S&K,S&K(c),Valentines Day
   Massacre 125.00
24 S&K,S&K(c),You can't Forget
   a Killer 125.00
25 S&K,S&K(c),CrimeNeverPays 110.00
26 S&K,S&K(c),CrimeNeverPays 100.00
27 S&K,S&K(c),CrimeNeverPays 100.00
28 S&K,S&K(c),CrimeNeverPays 100.00
29 S&K,S&K(c),CrimeNeverPays 100.00
30 S&K,S&K(c),CrimeNeverPays 100.00
31 S&K,S&K(c),CrimeNeverPays 100.00
32 S&K,S&K(c),CrimeNeverPays 100.00
33 S&K,S&K(c),Police and FBI
   heroes 100.00
34 S&K,S&K(c),same 100.00
35 S&K,S&K(c),same 100.00
36 S&K,S&K(c),same,Ph(c) 75.00
37 S&K,S&K(c),MvS,same,Ph(c) 45.00
38 S&K,S&K(c),same,Ph(c) 25.00
39 S&K,S&K(c),same,Ph(c) 25.00
40 S&K,S&K(c),Ph(c)Violent
   Crime 25.00
41 Ph(c),J.Edgar Hoover(c) 25.00
42 Ph(c) 18.00
43 Ph(c) 18.00
44 MMe,MvS,WE,S&K 35.00
45 JK 20.00
46 . . . . 15.00
47 . . . . 15.00
48 . . . . 15.00
49 MMe 15.00
50 . . . . 15.00
51 JK 18.00
52 . . . . 15.00
53 . . . . 15.00
54 . . . . 15.00
55 . . . . 15.00
56 S&K 28.00
57 . . . . 15.00
58 . . . . 15.00
59 . . . . 15.00
60 MvS(c) 15.00
61 MMe,MvS(c) 15.00
62 MMe,MMe(c) 15.00
63 MMe,MMe(c) 15.00
64 MMe,MMe(c) 15.00
65 MMe,MMe(c) 15.00
66 MMe,MMe(c) 15.00
67 MMe,MMe(c) 15.00
68 MMe,MMe(c) 15.00
69 MMe,MMe(c) 15.00
70 MMe,MMe(c) 15.00
71 MMe,MMe(c) 15.00
72 MMe,MMe(c) 15.00
73 MMe,MMe(c) 15.00
74 MMe,MMe(c) 15.00

75 MMe,MMe(c) 15.00
76 MMe,MMe(c) 15.00
77 MMe,MMe(c),October, 1956 . 15.00

HEART THROBS
Comics Magazines
(Quality)
August, 1949
1 BWa(c),PG,Spoiled Brat . . . 200.00
2 BWa(c),PG,Siren of
   the Tropics 140.00
3 PG 45.00
4 BWa(c),Greed Turned Me into
   a Scheming Vixen,Ph(c) 60.00
5 Ph(c) 25.00
6 BWa 60.00
7 . . . . 25.00
8 BWa 60.00
9 I Hated Men,Ph(c) 40.00
10 BWa,My Secret Fears 50.00
11 . . . . 18.00
12 . . . . 15.00
13 . . . . 18.00
14 BWa 18.00
15 My Right to Happiness,Ph(c) . 45.00
16 . . . . 16.00
17 . . . . 16.00
18 . . . . 16.00
19 . . . . 16.00
20 . . . . 16.00
21 BWa 35.00
22 BWa 30.00
23 BWa 30.00
24 thru 30 . . . . @15.00
31 thru 33 . . . . @15.00
34 thru 39 . . . . @15.00
40 BWa 25.00
41 . . . . 15.00
42 . . . . 15.00
43 . . . . 15.00
44 . . . . 15.00
45 . . . . 15.00
BECOMES A DC COMIC
(Please see DC listings)

HECKLE AND JECKLE
St. John Publ./Pines

Heckle and Jeckle #9
© St. John Publications

November, 1951

1 Blue Ribbon Comics	175.00
2 Blue Ribbon Comics	100.00
3	75.00
4	60.00
5	60.00
6	60.00
7	55.00
8	50.00
9	50.00
10	50.00
11 thru 15	@35.00
16 thru 20	@30.00
21 thru 33	@24.00
34 June, 1959	25.00

HELLO PAL COMICS
Harvey Publications
January, 1943

1 B:Rocketman & Rocket Girl, Mickey Rooney cover, Ph(c) all	400.00
2 Charlie McCarthy cover	300.00
3 Bob Hope cover, May, 1943	325.00

HENRY
Dell Publishing Co.
October, 1946

1	60.00
2	25.00
3 thru 10	@20.00
11 thru 20	@15.00
21 thru 30	@10.00
31 thru 40	@9.00
41 thru 50	@8.00
51 thru 65	@7.00

HENRY ALDRICH COMICS
Dell Publishing Co.
August-September, 1950

1	60.00
2	30.00
3	25.00
4	25.00
5	25.00
6 thru 10	@22.00
11 thru 22	@16.00

HEROIC COMICS
Eastern Color Printing Co./ Famous Funnies
August, 1940

1 BEv,BEv(c),O:Hydroman,Purple Zombie, B:Man of India	700.00
2 BEv,BEv(c),B:Hydroman covers	350.00
3 BEv,BEv(c)	285.00
4 BEv,BEv(c)	275.00
5 BEv,BEv(c)	225.00
6 BEv,BEv(c)	225.00
7 BEv,BEv(c),O:Man O'Metal	250.00
8 BEv,BEv(c)	150.00
9 BEv	150.00
10 BEv	150.00
11 BEv,E:Hydroman covers	125.00
12 BEv,B&O:Music Master	150.00
13 BEv,RC,LF	125.00
14 BEv	150.00
15 BEv,I:Downbeat	150.00
16 BEv,CCB(c),A:Lieut Nininger, Major Heidger,Lieut Welch,B:P(c)	100.00
17 BEv,A:JohnJames Powers,Hewitt	

Heroic Comics #3
© Eastern Color Printing

T.Wheless, Irving Strobing	100.00
18 HcK,BEv,Pass the Ammunition	100.00
19 HcK,BEv,A:Barney Ross	100.00
20 HcK,BEv	90.00
21 HcK,BEv	75.00
22 HcK,BEv,Howard Gilmore	75.00
23 HcK,BEv	75.00
24 HcK,BEv	75.00
25 HcK,BEv	75.00
26 HcK,BEv	75.00
27 HcK,BEv	75.00
28 HcK,BEv,E:Man O'Metal	75.00
29 HcK,BEv,E:Hydroman	75.00
30 BEv	60.00
31 BEv,CCB,Capt. Tootsie	25.00
32 ATh,CCB,WWII(c), Capt. Tootsie	35.00
33 ATh,	35.00
34 WWII(c)	20.00
35 Ath,B:Rescue(c)	35.00
36 HcK,ATh	35.00
37 same	35.00
38 ATh	35.00
39 HcK,ATh	35.00
40 ATh,Boxing	35.00
41 Grl(c),ATh	35.00
42 ATh	35.00
43 ATh	30.00
44 HcK,ATh	30.00
45 HcK	30.00
46 HcK	30.00
47 HcK	30.00
48 HcK	30.00
49 HcK	30.00
50 HcK	30.00
51 HcK,ATh,AW	32.00
52 HcK,AW	32.00
53 HcK	30.00
54	18.00
55 ATh	18.00
56 ATh(c)	28.00
57 ATh(c)	25.00
58 ATh(c)	25.00
59 ATh(c)	25.00
60 ATh(c)	25.00
61 BEv(c)	20.00
62 BEv(c)	20.00

63 BEv(c)	20.00
64 GE,BEv(c)	22.00
65 HcK(c),FF,ATh,AW,GE	50.00
66 HcK(c),FF	35.00
67 HcK(c),FF,Korean War(c)	35.00
68 HcK(c),Korean War(c)	35.00
69 HcK(c),FF	40.00
70 HcK(c),FF,B:Korean War(c)	35.00
71 HcK(c),FF	35.00
72 HcK(c),FF	40.00
73 HcK(c),FF	35.00
74 HcK(c)	35.00
75 HcK(c),FF	35.00
76 HcK,HcK(c)	12.00
77 same	12.00
78 same	12.00
79 same	12.00
80 same	12.00
81 FF,HcK(c)	15.00
82 FF,HcK(c)	15.00
83 FF,HcK(c)	15.00
84 HcK(c)	15.00
85 HcK(c)	15.00
86 FF,HcK(c)	20.00
87 FF,HcK(c)	20.00
88 HcK(c),E:Korean War covers	12.00
89 HcK(c)	12.00
90 HcK(c)	12.00
91 HcK(c)	12.00
92 HcK(c)	12.00
93 HcK(c)	12.00
94 HcK(c)	12.00
95 HcK(c)	12.00
96 HcK(c)	12.00
97 HcK(c),E:P(c),June, 1955	12.00

HICKORY
Comic Magazine
(Quality Comics Group)
October, 1949

1 ASa,	70.00
2 ASa,	35.00
3 ASa,	25.00
4 ASa,	25.00
5 ASa,	25.00
6 ASa,August, 1950	25.00

HI-HO COMICS
Four Star Publications
1946

1 LbC(c)	90.00
2 LbC(c)	55.00
3 1946	50.00

HI-JINX
B & I Publ. Co.
(American Comics Group)
July-August, 1947

1 (fa) all	65.00
2	42.00
3	40.00
4 thru 7	@38.00
N#	75.00

HI-LITE COMICS
E.R. Ross Publ.
Fall, 1945

1	65.00

HIT COMICS
Comics Magazine
(Quality Comics Group)

All comics prices listed are for *Near Mint* condition.

July, 1940
1 LF(c),O:Neon,Hercules,I:The
  Red Bee, B:Bob & Swab,
  Blaze Barton Strange
  Twins,X-5 Super Agent
  Casey Jones,Jack & Jill . . 2,700.00
2 GT,LF(c),B:Old Witch 1,000.00
3 GT,LF(c),E:Casey Jones . . 900.00
4 GT,LF(c),B:Super Agent &
  Betty Bates,E:X-5 . . . . 800.00
5 GT,LF(c),B:Red Bee cover 1,500.00
6 GT,LF(c) 600.00
7 GT,LF(c),E:Red Bee cover . 625.00
8 GT,LF(c),B:Neon cover . . . 600.00
9 JCo,LF(c),E:Neon cover . . 600.00
10 JCo,RC,LF(c),B:Hercules(c) 600.00
11 JCo,RC,LF(c),A:Hercules . . 550.00
12 JCo,RC,LF(c),A:Hercules . . 550.00
13 JCo,RC,LF(c),A:Hercules . . 550.00
14 JCo,RC,LF(c),A:Hercules . . 550.00
15 JCo,RC,A:Hercules 525.00
16 JCo,RC,LF(c),A:Hercules . . 525.00
17 JCo,RC,LF(c),E:Hercules(c) 525.00
18 JCo,RC,RC(c),O:Stormy
  Foster,B:Ghost of Flanders . 650.00
19 JCo,RC(c),B:StormyFoster(c) 550.00
20 JCo,RC(c),A:Stormy Foster . 550.00
21 JCo,RC(c) 500.00
22 JCo 500.00
23 JCo,RC,RC(c) 450.00
24 JCo,E:Stormy Foster cover . 450.00
25 JCo,RP,O:Kid Eternity 750.00
26 JCo,RP,A:Black Hawk 500.00
27 JCo,RP,B:Kid Eternity covers 300.00
28 JCo,RP,A:Her Highness . . . 300.00
29 JCo,RP 300.00
30 JCo,RP,HK,V:Julius Caesar
  and his Legion of Warriors . 250.00
31 JCo,RP 250.00
32 JCo,RP,V:Merlin the Wizard 150.00
33 JCo,RP 125.00
34 JCo,RP,E:Stormy Foster . . . 125.00
35 JCo,Kid Eternity accused
  of Murder 125.00
36 JCo,The Witch's Curse 125.00
37 JCo,V:Mr. Silence 125.00

Hit Comics #38
© Quality Comics Group

38 JCo 125.00
39 JCo,Runaway River Boat . . 125.00

40 PG,V:Monster from the Past 125.00
41 PG,Did Kid Eternity Lose
  His Power? 100.00
42 PG,Kid Eternity Loses Killer
  Cronson 100.00
43 JCo,PG,V:Modern Bluebeard 100.00
44 JCo,PG,Trips up the Shoe . 100.00
45 JCo,PG,Pancho Villa against
  Don Pablo 100.00
46 JCo,V:Mr. Hardeel 100.00
47 A Polished Diamond can be
  Rough on Rats 100.00
48 EhH,A Treasure Chest
  of Trouble 100.00
49 EhH,V:Monsters from
  the Mirror 100.00
50 EhH,Heads for Trouble . . . 100.00
51 EhH,Enters the Forgotten
  World 75.00
52 EhH,Heroes out of the Past . 75.00
53 EhH,V:Mr. Puny 75.00
54 V:Ghost Town Killer 75.00
55 V:The Brute 75.00
56 V:Big Odds 70.00
57 Solves the Picture in
  a Frame 70.00
58 Destroys Oppression! 70.00
59 Battles Tomorrow's Crimes
  Today! 70.00
60 E:Kid Eternity covers,
  V:The Mummy 70.00
61 RC,RC(c),I:Jeb Rivers 100.00
62 RC(c) 75.00
63 RC(c),A:Jeb Rivers 100.00
64 RC,A:Jeb Rivers 100.00
65 Bondage cover,RC,July, 1950 110.00

HOLIDAY COMICS
Fawcett Publ.
November, 1942
1 Captain Marvel (c) 1,200.00

HOLIDAY COMICS
Star Publ.
January, 1951
1 LbC(c),(fa),Christmas cover . 120.00
2 LbC(c),Parade(c) 130.00
3 LbC(c),July 4th(c) 70.00
4 LbC(c),Vacation(c) 70.00
5 LbC(c),Christmas(c) 70.00
6 LbC(c),Birthday(c) 70.00
7 LbC(c) 65.00
8 LbC(c),Christmas(c) 70.00

HOLLYWOOD COMICS
New Age Publishers
Winter, 1944
1 (fa) 80.00

HOLLYWOOD
CONFESSIONS
St. John Publ. Co.
October, 1949
1 JKu,JKu(c) 120.00
2 JKu,JKu(c), December, 1949 100.00

HOLLYWOOD DIARY
Comics Magazine
(Quality Comics)
December, 1949
1 . . . . 80.00
2 Photo cover 50.00

3 Photo cover 40.00
4 . . . . 40.00
5 Photo cover, August, 1950 . . 40.00

HOLLYWOOD FILM
STORIES
Feature Publications
(Prize)
April, 1950
1 June Allison,Ph(c) 80.00
2 Lizabeth Scott,Ph(c) 55.00
3 Barbara Stanwick,Ph(c) 55.00
4 Beth Hutton, August, 1950 . . 55.00

HOLLYWOOD SECRETS
Comics Magazine
(Quality Comics Group)
November, 1949
1 BWa,BWa(c) 160.00
2 BWa,BWa(c),RC 100.00
3 Ph(c) 50.00
4 Ph(c),May, 1950 . . . . 50.00
5 Ph(c) 50.00
6 Ph(c) 50.00

HOLYOKE ONE-SHOT
Tem Publ.
(Holyoke Publ. Co.)
1944
1 Grit Grady 55.00
2 Rusty Dugan 50.00
3 JK,Miss Victory,O:Cat Woman 130.00
4 Mr. Miracle 55.00
5 U.S. Border Patrol 50.00
6 Capt. Fearless 50.00
7 Strong Man 55.00
8 Blue Streak 50.00
9 S&K, Citizen Smith 80.00
10 S&K, Capt. Stone 75.00

HONEYMOON
ROMANCE
Artful Publications
(Digest Size)
April, 1950
1 . . . . 165.00
2 July, 1950 . . . . 150.00

HOODED HORSEMAN
(see OUT OF THE NIGHT)

HOPALONG CASSIDY
Fawcett Publications
February, 1943
1 B:Hopalong Cassidy & Topper,
  Captain Marvel cover 2,000.00
2 . . . . 400.00
3 Blazing Trails 225.00
4 5-full length story 200.00
5 Death in the Saddle, Ph(c) . 175.00
6 . . . . 150.00
7 . . . . 150.00
8 Phantom Stage Coach 150.00
9 The Last Stockade 150.00
10 4-spine tingling adventures . 150.00
11 Desperate Jetters! Ph(c) . . . 135.00
12 The Mysterious Message . . . 135.00
13 The Human Target, Ph(c) . . 125.00
14 Land of the Lawless, Ph(c) . 125.00
15 Death holds the Reins, Ph(c) 125.00
16 Webfoot's Revenge, Ph(c) . 125.00

17 The Hangman's Noose, Ph(c) 125.00
18 The Ghost of Dude Ranch,
   Ph(c) 125.00
19 A:William Boyd,Ph(c) 125.00
20 The Notorious Nellie Blaine!,
   B:P(c) 100.00
21 V:Arizona Kid 100.00
22 V:Arizona Kid 100.00
23 Hayride Horror 100.00
24 Twin River Giant 100.00
25 On the Trails of the Wild
   and Wooly West 100.00
26 thru 30 .... @90.00
31 52 pages 50.00
32 36 pages 40.00
33 thru 35, 52 pages ...... @50.00
36 36 pages 42.00
37 thru 40, 52 pages ...... @50.00
40 36 pages 42.00
41 E:P(c) 40.00
42 B:Ph(c) 50.00
43 .... 50.00
44 .... 40.00
45 .... 50.00
46 thru 51 .... @40.00
52 .... 35.00
53 .... 40.00
54 .... 40.00
55 .... 35.00
56 .... 40.00
57 .... 40.00
58 thru 70 .... @35.00
71 thru 84 .... @25.00
85 E:Ph(c),January, 1954 ..... 25.00
   (Please see DC listings)

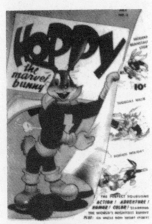

Hoppy the Marvel Bunny #3
© Fawcett Publications

HOPPY THE
MARVEL BUNNY
Fawcett Publications
December, 1945
1 A:Marvel Bunny 125.00
2 .... 65.00
3 .... 50.00
4 .... 50.00
5 .... 50.00
6 thru 14 .... @40.00
15 September, 1947 .... 40.00

HORRIFIC
Artful/Comic Media/
Harwell Publ./Mystery
September, 1952
1 Conductor in Flames(c) 150.00
2 Human Puppets(c) 75.00
3 DH(c),Bullet hole in
  head(c) 125.00
4 DH(c),head on a stick (c) ... 65.00
5 DH(c) 90.00
6 DH(c),Jack the Ripper 60.00
7 DH(c),Shrunken Skulls 55.00
8 DH(c),I:The Teller 65.00
9 DH(c),Claws of Horror, Wolves
  of Midnight 45.00
10 DH(c),The Teller-four
   eerie tales of Horror 45.00
11 DH(c),A:Gary Ghoul,Freddie,
   Demon,Victor Vampire,
   Walter Werewolf 40.00
12 DH(c),A:Gary Ghoul,Freddie
   Demon,Victor Vampire,
   Walter Werewolf 40.00
13 DH(c),A:Gary Ghoul,Freddie
   Demom,Victor Vampire,
   Walter Werewolf 40.00
Becomes:
TERRIFIC COMICS
14 .... 90.00
15 .... 60.00
16 B:Wonderboy 70.00
Becomes:
WONDERBOY
17 The Enemy's Enemy 125.00
18 Success is No Accident,
   July, 1955 .... 110.00

HORROR FROM
THE TOMB
(see MYSTERIOUS STORIES)

HORRORS, THE
Star Publications
January, 1953
11 LbC(c),JyD,of War 100.00
12 LbC(c),of War 100.00
13 LbC(c),of Mystery 90.00
14 LbC(c),of the Underworld .. 100.00
15 LbC(c),of the Underworld,
   April, 1954 .... 100.00

HORSE FEATHER
COMICS
Lev Gleason Publications
November, 1947
1 BW 120.00
2 .... 45.00
3 .... 40.00
4 Summer, 1948 .... 40.00

HOT ROD AND
SPEEDWAY COMICS
Hillman Periodicals
February-March, 1952
1 .... 125.00
2 BK 80.00
3 .... 40.00
4 .... 40.00
5 April-May, 1953 .... 40.00

HOT ROD COMICS

Fawcett Publications
February, 1952
N# BP,BP(c),F:Clint Curtis ... 150.00
2 BP,BP(c),Safety comes in First 85.00
3 BP,BP(c),The Racing Game . 65.00
4 BP,BP(c),Bonneville National
  Championships 65.00
5 BP,BP(c), ... 65.00
6 BP,BP(c),Race to Death,
  February,1953 .... 65.00

HOT ROD KING
Approved Comics
(Ziff-Davis)
Fall, 1952
1 P(c) 120.00

HOWDY DOODY
Dell Publishing Co.
January, 1950
1 Ph(c) 500.00
2 Ph(c) 175.00
3 Ph(c) 125.00
4 Ph(c) 125.00
5 Ph(c) 125.00
6 P(c) 100.00
7 .... 90.00
8 .... 90.00
9 .... 90.00
10 .... 90.00
11 .... 75.00
12 .... 75.00
13 Christmas (c) 75.00
14 thru 20 .... @75.00
21 thru 38 .... @60.00

Howdy Doody Comics #12
© Dell Publishing Co.

HOW STALIN
HOPES WE WILL
DESTROY AMERICA
Pictorial News
1951
N# (Giveaway) 350.00

HUMBUG
Harvey Kurtzman
1957
1 JDa,WW,WE,End of the World 150.00
2 JDa,WE,Radiator 75.00
3 JDa,WE 55.00
4 JDa,WE,Queen Victoria(c) ... 50.00
5 JDa,WE 50.00
6 JDa,WE 50.00
7 JDa,WE,Sputnik(c) 60.00
8 JDa,WE,Elvis/George
  Washington(c) 55.00
9 JDa,WE 50.00
10 JDa,Magazine 75.00
11 JDw,WE,HK,Magazine 75.00

HUMDINGER
Novelty Press/
Premium Service
May-June, 1946
1 B:Jerkwater Line,Dink,
  Mickey Starlight 150.00
2 .... 65.00
3 .... 40.00
4 .... 40.00
5 .... 40.00
6 .... 40.00
2-1 .... 35.00
2-2 July-August, 1947 .... 35.00

HUMPHREY COMICS
Harvey Publications
October, 1948
1 BP,Joe Palooka 70.00
2 BP 35.00
3 BP 30.00
4 BP,A:Boy Heroes 40.00
5 BP 25.00
6 BP 25.00
7 BP,A:Little Dot 25.00
8 BP,O:Humphrey 30.00
9 BP 15.00
10 BP 15.00
11 thru 21 .... @15.00
22 April, 1952 .... 15.00

HYPER MYSTERY
COMICS
Hyper Publications
May, 1940
1 B:Hyper 900.00
2 June, 1940 .... 600.00

IBIS, THE INVINCIBLE
Fawcett Publications
January, 1942
1 MRa(c),O:Ibis 950.00
2 Bondage cover 500.00
3 BW 400.00
4 BW,A:Mystic Snake People 300.00
5 BW,Bondage cover,The
  Devil's Ibistick 350.00
6 BW, The Book of Evil,
  Spring, 1948 .... 300.00

IDEAL ROMANCE
(see TENDER ROMANCE)

IF THE DEVIL
WOULD TALK
Catechetical Guild

1950
N# Rare 500.00
N#, 1958 Very Rare 450.00

ILLUSTRATED STORIES
OF THE OPERA
B. Bailey Publ. Co.
1943
N# Faust 350.00
N# Aida 300.00
N# Carman 325.00
N# Rigoletto 325.00

I LOVED
(see ZOOT COMICS)

I LOVE LUCY COMICS
Dell Publishing Co.
February, 1954
(1) see Dell Four Color #535
(2) see Dell Four Color #559
3 Lucile Ball Ph(c) all 125.00
4 .... 100.00
5 .... 100.00
6 thru 10 .... @85.00
11 thru 20 .... @75.00
21 thru 35 .... @60.00

IMPACT
E.C. Comics
March-April, 1955
1 RC,GE,BK,Grl 125.00
2 RC,JDu,Grl,BK,JO 100.00
3 JO,RC,JDU,Grl,JKa,BK ... 80.00
4 RC,JO,JDa,GE,Grl,BK 80.00
5 November-December, 1955 . 80.00

INCREDIBLE
SCIENCE FANTASY
(see WEIRD SCIENCE)

INCREDIBLE
SCIENCE FICTION
E.C. Comics
July-August, 1955
30 .... 225.00
31 .... 250.00
32 January-February, 1956 . 250.00
33 .... 225.00

INDIAN CHIEF
Dell Publishing Co.
July-September, 1951
3 P(c) all 25.00
4 .... 15.00
5 .... 15.00
6 A:White Eagle 15.00
7 .... 15.00
8 .... 15.00
9 .... 15.00
10 .... 15.00
11 .... 15.00
12 I:White Eagle 25.00
13 thru 29 .... @10.00
30 SB 15.00
31 SB 15.00
32 SB 15.00
33 SB 15.00

INDIAN FIGHTER
Youthful Magazines

May, 1950
1 Revenge of Chief Crazy Horse 55.00
2 Bondage cover 35.00
3 .... 20.00
4 Cheyenne Warpath 20.00
5 .... 20.00
6 Davy Crockett in Death Stalks
  the Alamo 20.00
7 Tom Horn-Bloodshed at
  Massacre Valley 20.00
8 Tales of Wild Bill Hickory,
  January, 1952 .... 20.00

INDIANS
Wings Publ. Co.
(Fiction House)
Spring, 1950
1 B:Long Bow, Manzar, White
  Indian & Orphan 125.00
2 B:Starlight 65.00
3 Longbow(c) 50.00
4 Longbow(c) 50.00
5 Manzar(c) 50.00
6 Captive of the Semecas 40.00
7 Longbow(c) 40.00
8 A:Long Bow 40.00
9 A:Long Bow 40.00
10 Manzar(c) 40.00
11 thru 16 .... @30.00
17 Spring, 1953,Longbow(c) ... 30.00

Indians on the Warpath #1
© St. John Publishing Co.

INDIANS ON
THE WARPATH
St. John Publ. Co.
1950
N# MB(c) 150.00

INFORMER, THE
Feature Television
Productions
April, 1954
1 MSy,The Greatest Social
  Menace of our Time! 45.00
2 MSy 28.00
3 MSy 25.00
4 MSy 25.00

---

5 December, 1954 .... 25.00

IN LOVE
Mainline/Charlton Comics
August, 1954
1 S&K,Bride of the Star 130.00
2 S&K,Marilyn's Men 75.00
3 S&K 60.00
4 S&K,Comics Code 35.00
5 S&K(c) 35.00
6 .... 15.00
Becomes:
I LOVE YOU
7 JK(c),BP 60.00
8 .... 20.00
9 .... 20.00
10 .... 20.00
11 thru 16 .... @15.00
17 .... 12.00
18 .... 9.00
19 .... 9.00
20 .... 9.00
21 thru 50 .... @6.00
51 thru 59 .... @4.00
60 Elvis 75.00
61 thru 100 .... @3.00
101 thru 130 .... @2.00

INTERNATIONAL COMICS
(see CRIME PATROL)

INTERNATIONAL CRIME PATROL
(see CRIME PATROL)

INTIMATE CONFESSIONS
Fawcett Publ./
Realistic Comics
1951
1a P(c) all, Unmarried Bride . 400.00
1 EK,EK(c),Days of Temptation...
 Nights of Desire 150.00
2 Doomed to Silence 100.00
3 EK(c), The Only Man For Me 60.00
3a Robert Briffault 60.00
4 EK(c),Tormented Love 75.00
5 Her Secret Sin 75.00
6 Reckless Pick-up 75.00
7 A Love Like Ours,Spanking . 100.00
8 Fatal Woman, March, 1953 . 75.00

INTIMATE LOVE
Standard Magazines
January, 1950
5 Wings on My Heart,Ph(c) ... 30.00
6 WE,JSe,Ph(c) 35.00
7 WE,JSe,Ph(c),I Toyed
 with Love 35.00
8 WE,JSe,Ph(c) 35.00
9 Ph(c) 25.00
10 Ph(c),My Hopeless Heart ... 35.00
11 thru 18 .... @10.00
19 ATh 35.00
20 .... 10.00
21 ATh 35.00
22 ATh 10.00
23 ATh 10.00
24 ATh 35.00
25 ATh 10.00
26 ATh 35.00
27 ATh 10.00

28 ATh,August, 1954 .... 10.00

INTIMATE SECRETS OF ROMANCE
Star Publications
September, 1953
1 LbC(c) 50.00
2 LbC(c) 45.00

INVISIBLE SCARLET O'NEIL
Harvey Publications
December, 1950
1 .... 75.00
2 .... 55.00
3 April, 1951 .... 50.00

IT REALLY HAPPENED
William H. Wise/
Visual Editions
1945
1 Benjamin Franklin, Kit Carson 120.00
2 The Terrible Tiddlers 60.00
3 Maid of the Margiris 35.00
4 Chaplain Albert J. Hoffman .. 30.00
5 AS(c),Monarchs of the Sea,Lou
 Gehrig, Amelia Earhart 80.00
6 AS(c),Ernie Pyle 30.00
7 FG,Teddy Roosevelt,Jefferson
 Davis, Story of the Helicopter 30.00
8 FG,Man O' War,Roy Rogers . 90.00
9 AS(c),The Story of
 Old Ironsides 30.00
10 AS(c),Honus Wagner, The
 Story of Mark Twain 75.00
11 AS(c),MB,Queen of the Spanish
 Main, October, 1947 .... 50.00

JACK ARMSTRONG
Parents' Institute
November, 1947
1 Artic Mystery 125.00
2 Den of the Golden Dragon .. 75.00
3 Lost Valley of Ice 60.00
4 Land of the Leopard Men ... 60.00
5 Fight against Racketeers of
 the Ring 60.00
6 .... 50.00
7 Baffling Mystery on the
 Diamond 55.00
8 .... 55.00
9 Mystery of the Midgets 55.00
10 Secret Cargo 55.00
11 .... 50.00
12 Madman's Island 50.00
13 September, 1949 .... 50.00

JACE PEARSON OF THE TEXAS RANGERS
Dell Publishing Co.
May, 1952
(1) see Dell Four Color #396
2 Ph(c),Joel McRae 40.00
3 Ph(c),Joel McRae 40.00
4 Ph(c),Joel McRae 40.00
5 Ph(c),Joel McRae 40.00
6 Ph(c),Joel McRae 40.00
7 Ph(c),Joel McRae 40.00
8 Ph(c),Joel McRae 40.00
9 Ph(c),Joel McRae 40.00
(10) see Dell Four Color #648
Becomes:

TALES OF JACE PEARSON OF THE TEXAS RANGERS
11 .... 30.00
12 .... 30.00
13 .... 30.00
14 .... 30.00
15 ATh 40.00
16 ATh 40.00
17 .... 30.00
18 .... 30.00
19 .... 30.00
20 .... 30.00

JACKIE GLEASON
St. John Publishing Co.
September, 1955
1 Ph(c) 500.00
2 .... 400.00
3 .... 300.00
4 December, 1955 .... 275.00

Jackie Robinson #6
© Fawcett Publications

JACKIE ROBINSON
Fawcett Publications
May, 1950
N# Ph(c) all issues 550.00
2 .... 350.00
3 thru 5 .... @300.00
6 May, 1952 .... 300.00

JACK IN THE BOX
(see YELLOW JACKET COMICS)

JACKPOT COMICS
MLJ Magazines
Spring, 1941
1 CBi(c),B:Black Hood,Mr.Justice,
 Steel Sterling,Sgt.Boyle .. 1,500.00
2 SCp(c), ... 650.00
3 Bondage cover 600.00
4 First Archie 1,400.00
5 Hitler(c) 700.00
6 Son of the Skull v:Black
 Hood, Bondage(c) 600.00

7 Bondage (c) 600.00
8 Sal(c), ... 550.00
9 Sal(c), ... 575.00
Becomes:

JOLLY JINGLES
10 Super Duck,(fa) 225.00
11 Super Duck 125.00
12 Hitler parody cover,A:Woody
    Woodpecker 70.00
13 Super Duck 45.00
14 Super Duck 45.00
15 Super Duck 45.00
16 December, 1944 . . . . 45.00

JACK THE GIANT KILLER
Bimfort & Co.
August-September, 1953
1 HcK,HcK(c) 125.00

JAMBOREE
Round Publishing Co.
February, 1946
1 . . . . 90.00
2 March, 1946 . . . . 55.00

JANE ARDEN
St. John Publ. Co.
March, 1948
1 . . . . 100.00
2 June, 1948 . . . . 60.00

JEEP COMICS
R.B. Leffingwell & Co.
Winter, 1944
1 B;Captain Power 150.00
2 . . . . 90.00
3 LbC(c),March-April, 1948 . . . 90.00

JEFF JORDAN, U.S. AGENT
D.S. Publ. Co.
December, 1947
1 . . . . 55.00

JESSE JAMES
**Avon Periodicals/
Realistic Publ.**
August, 1950
1 JKu,The San Antonio Stage
    Robbery 100.00
2 JKu,The Daring Liberty Bank
    Robbery 75.00
3 JKu,The California Stagecoach
    Robberies 65.00
4 EK(c),Deadliest Deed! 25.00
5 JKu,WW,Great Prison Break . 65.00
6 JKu,Wanted Dead or Alive . . 65.00
7 JKu,Six-Gun Slaughter at
    San Romano! 55.00
8 EK,Daring Train Robbery! . . . 40.00
9 EK 25.00
10 thru 14 {Do not exist}
15 . . . . 40.00
16 . . . . 25.00
17 . . . . 18.00
18 JKu 20.00
19 JKu 20.00
20 AW,FF,A:Chief Vic,Kit West . 75.00
21 . . . . 18.00
22 . . . . 15.00

Jesse James #5 © Avon Publications

23 . . . . 15.00
24 EK,B:New McCarty 18.00
25 EK 18.00
26 EK 18.00
27 EK,E:New McCarty 18.00
28 . . . . 18.00
29 August, 1956 . . . . 18.00

JEST
Harry 'A' Chesler
1944
10 J. Rebel,Yankee Boy 75.00
11 1944,Little Nemo 85.00

JET ACES
**Real Adventure Publ. Co.
(Fiction House)**
1952
1 Set 'em up in MIG Alley 75.00
2 Kiss-Off for Moscow Molly . . 40.00
3 Red Task Force Sighted 40.00
4 Death-Date at 40,000, 1953 . 40.00

JET FIGHTERS
Standard Magazines
November, 1953
5 ATh,Korean War Stories 60.00
6 Circus Pilot 25.00
7 ATh, Iron Curtains for Ivan,
    March, 1953 . . . . 45.00

JETTA OF THE 21st CENTURY
Standard Comics
December, 1952
5 Teen Stories 110.00
6 . . . . 65.00
7 April, 1953 . . . . 65.00

JIGGS AND MAGGIE
**Best Books (Standard)/
Harvey Publ.**
June, 1949
11 . . . . 60.00
12 thru 21 . . . . @30.00
22 thru 26 . . . . @22.00

27 February-March, 1954 . . . . . 22.00

JIM HARDY
Spotlight Publ.
1944
N# Dynamite Jim,Mirror Man . 250.00

JIM RAY'S AVIATION SKETCH BOOK
Vital Publishers
February, 1946
1 Radar, the Invisible eye . . . 135.00
2 Gen.Hap Arnold, May, 1946 125.00

JINGLE JANGLE COMICS
Eastern Color Printing Co.
February, 1942
1 B:Benny Bear,Pie Face Prince,
    Jingle Jangle Tales,Hortense 275.00
2 GCn 125.00
3 GCn 110.00
4 GCn,Pie Face cover 110.00
5 GCn,B:Pie Face 100.00
6 GCn, ... 90.00
7 . . . . 85.00
8 . . . . 85.00
9 . . . . 85.00
10 . . . . 85.00
11 thru 15 E:Pie Face . . . . . . @65.00
16 thru 20 . . . . @50.00
21 thru 25 . . . . @40.00
26 thru 30 . . . . @35.00
31 thru 41 . . . . @30.00
42 December, 1949 . . . . 35.00

JING PALS
Victory Publ. Corp.
February, 1946
1 Johnny Rabbit 50.00
2 . . . . 30.00
3 . . . . 30.00
4 August, 1948 . . . . 30.00

JOE COLLEGE
Hillman Periodicals
Fall, 1949
1 BP,DPr 45.00
2 BP, Winter, 1949 . . . . 40.00

JOE LOUIS
Fawcett Periodicals
September, 1950
1 Ph(c),Life Story 375.00
2 Ph(c),November, 1950 . . . . 300.00

JOE PALOOKA
**Publication Enterprises
(Columbia Comics Group)**
1943
1 Lost in the Desert 450.00
2 Hitler cover 300.00
3 KO's the Nazis! 200.00
4 Eiffel tower cover, 1944 . . . 175.00

JOE PALOOKA
Harvey Publications
November, 1954
1 Joe Tells How he became
    World Champ 300.00
2 Skiing cover 150.00

All comics prices listed are for *Near Mint* condition.

Joe Palooka #1 © Columbia Comics

3	90.00
4 Welcome Home Pals!	90.00
5 S&K,The Great Carnival Murder Mystery	125.00
6 Classic Joe Palooka (c)	80.00
7 BP,V:Grumpopski	75.00
8 BP,Mystery of the Ghost Ship	65.00
9 Drooten Island Mystery	65.00
10 BP	60.00
11	50.00
12 BP,Boxing Course	50.00
13	45.00
14 BP,Palooka's Toughest Fight	45.00
15 BP,O:Humphrey	90.00
16 BP,A:Humphrey	45.00
17 BP,A:Humphrey	45.00
18	45.00
19 BP,Freedom Train(c)	50.00
20 Punch Out(c)	45.00
21	40.00
22 V:Assassin	40.00
23 Big Bathing Beauty Issue	40.00
24	40.00
25	40.00
26 BP,Big Prize Fight Robberies	40.00
27 BP,Mystery of Bal Eagle Cabin	40.00
28 BP,Fights out West	40.00
29 BP,Joe Busts Crime Wide Open	40.00
30 BP,V:Hoodlums	35.00
31 BP	35.00
32 BP,Fight Palooka was sure to Lose	35.00
33 BP,Joe finds Ann	35.00
34 BP,How to Box like a Champ	35.00
35 BP,More Adventures of Little Max	35.00
36 BP	35.00
37 BP,Joe as a Boy	35.00
38 BP	35.00
39 BP,Original Hillbillies with Big Leviticus	35.00
40 BP,Joe's Toughest Fight	35.00
41 BP,Humphrey's Grudge Fight	35.00
42 BP	35.00
43 BP	35.00
44 BP,M:Ann Howe	40.00
45 BP	30.00

46 Champ of Champs	30.00
47 BreathtakingUnderwaterBattle	30.00
48 BP,Exciting Indian Adventure	30.00
49 BP	30.00
50 BP,Bondage(c)	30.00
51 BP	30.00
52 BP,V:Balonki	30.00
53 BP	30.00
54 V:Bad Man Trigger McGehee	30.00
55	30.00
56 Foul Play on the High Seas	30.00
57 Curtains for the Champ	30.00
58 V:The Man-Eating Swamp Terror	30.00
59 The Enemy Attacks	30.00
60 Joe Fights Escaped Convict	30.00
61	25.00
62 S&K	35.00
63 thru 68	@25.00
69 A Package from Home	25.00
70 BP	25.00
71	25.00
72	25.00
73 BP	25.00
74 thru 117	@25.00
118 March, 1961	25.00
Giant 1 Body Building	65.00
Giant 2 Fights His Way Back	125.00
Giant 3 Visits Lost City	60.00
Giant 4 All in Family	65.00

JOE YANK
Visual Editions
(Standard Comics)
March, 1952

5 ATh,WE,Korean Jackpot!	60.00
6 Bacon and Bullets, G.I.Renegade	40.00
7 Two-Man War,A:Sgt. Glamour	18.00
8 ATh(c),Miss Foxhole of 1952,	30.00
9 G.I.'s and Dolls,Colonel Blood	15.00
10 A Good Way to Die, A:General Joe	15.00
11	15.00
12 RA	15.00
13	15.00
14	15.00
15	15.00
16 July, 1954	15.00

JOHN HIX SCRAPBOOK
Eastern Color Printing Co.
1937

1 Strange as It Seems	175.00
2 Strange as It Seems	150.00

JOHNNY DANGER
Toby Press
August, 1954

1 Ph(c),Private Detective	75.00

JOHNNY DYNAMITE
(see DYNAMITE)

JOHNNY HAZARD
Best Books
(Standard Comics)
August, 1948

5 FR	75.00
6 FR,FR(c)	55.00
7 FR(c)	50.00
8 FR,FR(c), May, 1949	40.00

JOHNNY LAW, SKY RANGER
Good Comics (Lev Gleason)
April, 1955

1	35.00
2	20.00
3	20.00
4 November, 1955	20.00

JOHN WAYNE ADVENTURE COMICS
Toby Press
Winter, 1949

1 Ph(c),The Mysterious Valley of Violence	500.00
2 AW,FF,Ph(c)	425.00
3 AW,FF,Flying Sheriff	425.00
4 AW,FF,Double-Danger,Ph(c)	425.00
5 Volcano of Death,Ph(c)	400.00
6 AW,FF,Caravan of Doom, Ph(c)	375.00
7 AW,FF,Ph(c)	325.00
8 AW,FF,Duel of Death,Ph(c)	350.00
9 Ghost Guns,Ph(c)	300.00
10 Dangerous Journey,Ph(c)	200.00
11 Manhunt!,Ph(c)	200.00
12 HK,Joins the Marines,Ph(c)	210.00
13 V:Frank Stacy	175.00
14 Operation Peeping John	175.00
15 Bridge Head	200.00
16 AW,FF,Golden Double-Cross	200.00
17 Murderer's Music	200.00
18 AW,FF,Larson's Folly	225.00
19	150.00
20 Whale Cover	150.00
21	150.00
22 Flash Flood!	150.00
23 Death on Two Wheels	150.00
24 Desert	150.00
25 AW,FF,Hondo!,Ph(c)	225.00
26 Ph(c)	175.00
27 Ph(c)	175.00
28 Dead Man's Boots!	175.00
29 AW,FF,Ph(c),Crash in California Desert	225.00
30 The Wild One, Ph(c)	175.00
31 AW,FF,May, 1955	200.00

JO-JO COMICS
Fox Features Syndicate
Spring, 1946

N# (fa)	50.00
2 (fa)	25.00
3 (fa)	25.00
4 (fa)	25.00
5 (fa)	25.00
6 (fa)	25.00
7 B:Jo-Jo Congo King	300.00
8 (7)B:Tanee,V:The Giant Queen	200.00
9 (8)The Mountain of Skulls	200.00
10 (9)Death of the Fanged Lady	160.00
11 (10)	150.00
12 (11)Bondage(c), Water Warriors	150.00
13 (12) Jade Juggernaut	150.00
14 The Leopards of Learda	150.00
15 The Flaming Fiend	150.00
16 Golden Gorilla,bondage(c)	165.00
17 Stark-Mad Thespian, bondage(c)	165.00
18 The Death Traveler	150.00

19 Gladiator of Gore 150.00
20 . . . . 150.00
21 . . . . 150.00
22 . . . . 150.00
23 . . . . 150.00
24 . . . . 150.00
25 Bondage(c) 200.00
26 . . . . 150.00
27 . . . . 150.00
28 . . . . 150.00
29 July, 1949 . . . . 160.00

JOURNEY INTO FEAR
Superior Publications
May, 1951
1 MB,Preview of Chaos 225.00
2 Debt to the Devil 150.00
3 Midnight Prowler 135.00

Journey into Fear #15
© Superior Publications

4 Invisible Terror 125.00
5 Devil Cat 85.00
6 Partners in Blood 85.00
7 The Werewolf Lurks 85.00
8 Bells of the Damned 85.00
9 Masked Death 85.00
10 Gallery of the Dead 85.00
11 Beast of Bedlam 75.00
12 No Rest for the Dead 75.00
13 Cult of the Dead 75.00
14 Jury of the Undead 75.00
15 Corpse in Make-up 80.00
16 Death by Invitation 70.00
17 Deadline for Death 70.00
18 Here's to Horror 70.00
19 This Body is Mine! 70.00
20 Masters of the Dead 70.00
21 Horror in the Clock,
   September, 1954 . . . . 70.00

JUDO JOE
Jay-Jay Corp.
August, 1952
1 Drug 35.00
2 . . . . 25.00
3 Drug, December, 1953 . . . . . 25.00

JUDY CANOVA

Fox Features Syndicate
May, 1950
23 (1)WW,WW(c) 85.00
24 (2)WW,WW(c) 80.00
3 JO,WW,WW(c)
  September, 1950 . . . . 100.00

JUKE BOX
Famous Funnies
March, 1948
1 ATh(c),Spike Jones 250.00
2 Dinah Shore,Transvestitism 150.00
3 Vic Damone 100.00
4 Jimmy Durante 100.00
5 . . . . 90.00
6 January, 1949,Desi Arnaz . 125.00

JUMBO COMICS
Real Adventure Publ. Co.
(Fiction House)
September, 1938
1 LF,BKa,JK,WE,WE(c),B:Sheena
Queen of the Jungle,The Hawk
The Hunchback 11,000.00
2 LF,JK,WE,BKa,BP,
  O:Sheena 3,500.00

Jumbo Comics #7
© Real Adventure Publ./Fiction House

3 JK,WE,WE(c),BP,LF,BKa . 2,500.00
4 WE,WE(c),MMe,LF,BKa,
  O:The Hawk 2,400.00
5 WE,WE(c),BP,BKa 2,000.00
6 WE,WE(c),BP,BKa 1,600.00
7 WE,BKa,BP 1,500.00
8 LF(c),BP,BKa,World of
  Tommorow 1,500.00
9 LF(c),BP 1,600.00
10 WE,LF(c),BKa,Regular size
  issues begin 750.00
11 LF(c),WE&BP,War of the
  Emerald Gas 700.00
12 WE(c),WE&BP,Hawk in Buccaneer
  Vengeance,Bondage(c) 750.00
13 WE(c),BP,Sheena in The
  Thundering Herds 700.00
14 WE(c),LF,BP,Hawk in Siege
  of Thunder Isle,B:Lightning . 800.00
15 BP(c),BP,Sheena(c) 500.00
16 BP(c),BP,The Lightning

Strikes Twice 550.00
17 BP(c), all Sheena covers
  and lead stories 500.00
18 BP 450.00
19 BP(c),BKa,Warriors of
  the Bush 450.00
20 BP,BKa,Spoilers of
  the Wild 450.00
21 BP,BKa,Prey of the
  Giant Killers 350.00
22 BP,BKa,Victims of the
  Super-Ape,O:Hawk 375.00
23 BP,BKa,Swamp of the
  Green Terror 375.00
24 BP,BKa,Curse of the Black
  Venom 375.00
25 BP,BKa,Bait for the Beast . . 350.00
26 BP,BKa,Tiger-Man Terror . . 350.00
27 BP,BKa,Sabre-Tooth Terror . 350.00
28 BKa,RWd,The Devil of
  the Congo 350.00
29 BKa,RWd,Elephant-Scourge 350.00
30 BKa,RWd,Slashing Fangs . 350.00
31 BKa,RWd,Voodoo Treasure
  of Black Slave Lake 300.00
32 BKa,RWd,AB,Captives of
  the Gorilla-Men 300.00
33 BKa,RWd,AB,Stampede
  Tusks 300.00
34 BKa,RWd,AB,Claws of the
  Devil-Cat 300.00
35 BKa,RWd,AB,Hostage of the
  Devil Apes 300.00
36 BKa,RWd,AB,Voodoo Flames 300.00
37 BKa,RWd,AB,Congo Terror . 300.00
38 BKa,RWd,ABDeath-Trap of
  the River Demons 300.00
39 BKa,RWd,AB,Cannibal Bait . 300.00
40 BKa,RWd,AB,
  Assagai Poison 300.00
41 BKa,RWd,AB,Killer's Kraal,
  Bondage(c) 250.00
42 BKa,RWd,AB,Plague of
  Spotted Killers 250.00
43 BKa,RWd,AB,Beasts of the
  Devil Queen 250.00
44 BKa,RWd,AB,Blood-Cult of
  K'Douma 250.00
45 BKa,RWd,AB,Fanged
  Keeper of the Fire-Gem . . . 250.00
46 BKa,RWd,AB,Lair of the
  Armored Monsters 250.00
47 BKa,RWd,AB,The Bantu
  Blood-Monster 250.00
48 BKa,RWd,AB,Red Meat for
  the Cat-Pack 250.00
49 BKa,RWd,AB,Empire of the
  Hairy Ones 250.00
50 BKa,RWd,AB,Eyrie of the
  Leopard Birds 250.00
51 BKa,RWd.AB,Monsters with
  Wings 200.00
52 BKa,RWd,AB,Man-Eaters
  Paradise 200.00
53 RWd,AB,Slaves of the
  Blood Moon 200.00
54 RWd,AB,Congo Kill 200.00
55 RWd,AB,Bait for the Silver
  King Cat 200.00
56 RWd,AB,Sabre Monsters of
  the Aba-Zanzi,Bondage(c) . . 200.00
57 RWd,AB,Arena of Beasts . . 200.00
58 RWd,AB,Sky-Atlas of the
  Thunder-Birds 200.00
59 RWd,AB,Kraal of Shrunken

Heads 200.00
60 RWd,AB,Land of the
　Stalking Death 150.00
61 RWd,AB,King-Beast of
　the Masai 150.00
62 RWd,AB,Valley of Golden
　Death 150.00
63 RWd,AB,The Dwarf Makers　150.00
64 RWd,The Slave-Brand of Ibn
　Ben Satan,Male Bondage . . 150.00
65 RWd,The Man-Eaters of
　Linpopo 150.00
66 RWd,Valley of Monsters . . . 150.00
67 RWd,Land of Feathered Evil 150.00
68 RWd,Spear of Blood Ju-Ju . 150.00
69 RWd,AB,MB,Slaves for the
　White Sheik 150.00
70 RWd,AB,MB,The Rogue
　Beast's Prey 150.00
71 RWd,AB,MB,The Serpent-
　God Speaks 125.00
72 RWd,AB,MB,Curse of the
　Half-Dead 125.00
73 RWd,AB,MB,War Apes of
　the T'Kanis 125.00
74 RWd,AB,MB,Drums of the
　Voodoo God 125.00
75 RWd,AB,MB,Terror Trail of
　the Devil's Horn 125.00
76 RWd,AB,MB,Fire Gems of
　Skull Valley 125.00
77 RWd,AB,MB,Blood Dragons
　from Fire Valley 125.00
78 RWd,AB,MB,Veldt of the
　Vampire Apes 125.00
79 RWd,AB,MB,Dancing
　Skeletons 125.00
80 RWd,AB,MB,Banshee Cats　125.00
81 RWd,MB,AB,JKa,Heads for
　King' Hondo's Harem 110.00
82 RWd,MB,AB,JKa,Ghost Riders
　of the Golden Tuskers 110.00
83 RWd,MB,AB,JKa,Charge of
　the Condo Juggernauts 110.00
84 RWd,MB,AB,JKa,Valley of
　the Whispering Fangs 110.00
85 RWd,MB,AB,JKa,Red Tusks
　of Zulu-Za'an 110.00
86 RWd,MB,AB,JKa,Witch-Maiden
　of the Burning Blade 110.00
87 RWd,AB,MB,JKa,Sargasso of
　Lost Safaris 110.00
88 RWd,AB,MB,JKa,Kill-Quest
　of the Ju-Ju Tusks 110.00
89 RWd,AB,MB,JKa,Ghost Slaves
　of Bwana Rojo 110.00
90 RWd,AB,MB,JKa,Death Kraal
　of the Mastadons 110.00
91 RWd,AB,MB,JKa,Spoor of
　the Sabre-Horn Tiger 100.00
92 RWd,MB,JKa,Pied Piper
　of the Congo 100.00
93 RWd,MB,JKa,The Beasts
　that Dawn Begot 100.00
94 RWd,MB,JKa,Wheel of a
　Thousand Deaths 100.00
95 RWd,MB,JKa,Flame Dance
　of the Ju-Ju Witch 100.00
96 RWd,MB,JKa,Ghost Safari . 100.00
97 RWd,MB,JKa,Banshee Wail
　of the Undead,Bondage(c) . 100.00
98 RWd,MB,JKa,Seekers of
　the Terror Fangs 100.00
99 RWd,MB,JKa,Shrine of
　the Seven Souls 100.00

100 RWd,MB,Slave Brand
　of Hassan Bey 150.00
101 RWd,MB,Quest of the
　Two-Face Ju Ju 100.00
102 RWd,MB,Viper Gods of
　Vengeance Veldt 100.00
103 RWd,MB,Blood for the
　Idol of Blades 100.00
104 RWd,MB,Valley of Eternal
　Sleep 100.00
105 RWd,MB,Man Cubs from
　Momba-Zu 200.00
106 RWd,MB,The River of
　No-Return 200.00
107 RWd,MB,Vandals of
　the Veldt 100.00
108 RWd,MB,The Orphan of
　Vengeance Vale 100.00
109 RWd,MB,The Pygmy's Hiss
　is Poison 100.00
110 RWd,MB,Death Guards the
　Congo Keep 100.00
111 RWd,MB,Beware of the
　Witch-Man's Brew 100.00
112 RWd,MB,The Blood-Mask
　from G'Shinis Grave 95.00
113 RWd,MB,The Mask's of
　Zombi-Zan 95.00
114 RWd,MB, ... 95.00
115 RWd,MB,Svengali of
　the Apes 95.00
116 RWd,MB,The Vessel of
　Marbel Monsters 95.00
117 RWd,MB,Lair of the Half-
　Man King 95.00
118 RWd,MB,Quest of the
　Congo Dwarflings 95.00
119 RWd,MB,King Crocodile's
　Domain 95.00
120 RWd,MB,The Beast-Pack
　Howls the Moon 95.00
121 RWd,MB,The Kraal of
　Evil Ivory 95.00
122 RWd,MB,Castaways of
　the Congo 95.00
123 RWd,MB, ... 95.00
124 RWd,MB,The Voodoo Beasts
　of Changra-Lo 95.00
125 RWd,MB,JKa(c),The Beast-
　Pack Strikes at Dawn 95.00
126 RWd,MB,JKa(c),Lair of the
　Swamp Beast 95.00
127 RWd,MB,JKa(c),The Phantom
　of Lost Lagoon 95.00
128 RWd,MB,JKa(c),Mad Mistress
　of the Congo-Tuskers 95.00
129 RWd,MB,JKa(c),Slaves of
　King Simbas Kraal 95.00
130 RWd,MB,JKa(c),Quest of
　the Pharaoh's Idol 95.00
131 RWd,JKa(c),Congo Giants
　at Bay 90.00
132 RWd,JKa(c),The Doom of
　the Devil's Gorge 90.00
133 RWd,JKa(c),Blaze the
　Pitfall Trail 90.00
134 RWd,JKa(c),Catacombs of
　the Jackal-Men 90.00
135 RWd,JKa(c),The 40 Thieves
　of Ankar-Lo 90.00
136 RWd,JKa(c),The Perils of
　Paradise Lost 90.00
137 RWd,JKa(c),The Kraal of
　Missing Men 90.00
138 RWd,JKa(c),The Panthers

of Kajo-Kazar 90.00
139 RWd,JKa(c),Stampede of
　the Congo Lancers 90.00
140 RWd,JKa(c),The Moon
　Beasts from Vulture Valley . . 90.00
141 RWd,JKa(c),B:Long Bow . . 100.00
142 RWd,JKa(c),Man-Eaters
　of N'Gamba 100.00
143 RWd,JKa(c),The Curse of
　the Cannibal Drum 100.00
144 RWd,JKa(c),The Secrets of
　Killers Cave 100.00
145 RWd,JKa(c),Killers of
　the Crypt 100.00
146 RWd,JKa(c),Sinbad of the
　Lost Lagoon 100.00
147 RWd,JKa(c),The Wizard of
　Gorilla Glade 100.00
148 RWd,JKa(c),Derelict of
　the Slave King 100.00
149 RWd,JKa(c),Lash Lord of
　the Elephants 100.00
150 RWd,JKa(c),Queen of
　the Pharaoh's Idol 90.00
151 RWd,The Voodoo Claws
　of Doomsday Trek 90.00
152 RWd,Red Blades of Africa . 90.00
153 RWd,Lost Legions of the Nile 90.00
154 RWd,The Track of the
　Black Devil 90.00
155 RWd,The Ghosts of
　Blow- Gun Trail 90.00
156 RWd,The Slave-Runners
　of Bambaru 90.00
157 RWd,Cave of the
　Golden Skull 90.00
158 RWd,Gun Trek to
　Panther Valley 90.00
159 RWd,A:Space Scout 85.00
160 RWd,Savage Cargo,
　E:Sheena covers 85.00
161 RWd,Dawns of the Pit 85.00
162 RWd,Hangman's Haunt . . . 85.00
163 RWd,Cagliostro Cursed Thee 85.00
164 RWd,Death Bars the Door . 85.00
165 RWd,Day off from a Corpse　85.00
166 RWd,The Gallows Bird 85.00
167 RWd,Cult of the Clawmen,
　March, 1953 . . . . 85.00

JUNGLE COMICS
Glen Kel Publ./Fiction House
January, 1940

1 HcK,DBr,LF(c),O:The White
　Panther,Kaanga,Tabu, B:The
　Jungle Boy,Camilla, all
　Kaanga covers & stories . . 1,800.00
2 HcK,DBr,WE(c),B:Fantomah　750.00
3 HcK,DBr,GT,The Crocodiles
　of Death River 650.00
4 HcK,DBr,Wambi in
　Thundering Herds 600.00
5 WE(c),GT,HcK,DBr,Empire
　of the Ape Men 500.00
6 WE(c),GT,DBr,HcK,Tigress
　of the Deep Jungle Swamp　475.00
7 BP(c),DBr,GT,HcK,Live
　Sacrifice,Bondage(c) 400.00
8 BP(c),GT,HcK,Safari into
　Shadowland 400.00
9 GT,HcK,Captive of the
　Voodoo Master 400.00
10 GT,HcK,BP,Lair of the
　Renegade Killer 400.00
11 GT,HcK,V:Beasts of Africa's

Ancient Primieval
Swamp Land 300.00
12 GT,HcK,The Devil's
Death-Trap 300.00
13 GT(c),GT,HcK,Stalker of
the Beasts 325.00
14 HcK,Vengeance of the
Gorilla Hordes 300.00
15 HcK,Terror of the Voodoo
Cauldron 300.00
16 HcK,Caveman Killers 300.00
17 HcK,Valley of the Killer-Birds 300.00
18 HcK,Trap of the Tawny
Killer, Bondage(c) 325.00
19 HcK,Revolt of the Man-Apes 300.00
20 HcK,One-offering to
Ju-Ju Demon 300.00
21 HcK,Monster of the Dismal
Swamp, Bondage(c) 275.00
22 HcK,Lair o/t Winged Fiend . 250.00
23 HcK,Man-Eater Jaws 250.00
24 HcK,Battle of the Beasts . . . 250.00
25 HcK,Kaghis the Blood God,
Bondage(c) 275.00
26 HcK,Gorillas of the

Jungle Comics #27
© Glen Kel. Publ./Fiction House

Witch-Queen 250.00
27 HcK,Spore o/t Gold-Raiders 250.00
28 HcK,Vengeance of the Flame
God, Bondage(c) 275.00
29 HcK,Juggernaut of Doom . . 250.00
30 HcK,Claws o/t Black Terror 250.00
31 HcK,Land of Shrunken Skulls 225.00
32 HcK,Curse of the King-Beast 225.00
33 HcK,Scaly Guardians of
Massacre Pool,Bondage(c) . 235.00
34 HcK,Bait of the Spotted
Fury,Bondage(c) 235.00
35 HcK,Stampede of the
Slave-Masters 225.00
36 HcK,GT,The Flame-Death of
Ju Ju Mountain 225.00
37 HcK,GT,Scaly Sentinel of
Taboo Swamp 225.00
38 HcK,GT,Duel of the Congo
Destroyers 225.00
39 HcK,Land of Laughing Bones 225.00
40 HcK,Killer Plague 225.00
41 Hck,The King Ape

Feeds at Dawn 200.00
42 Hck,RC,Master of the
Moon-Beasts 210.00
43 HcK,The White Shiek 200.00
44 HcK,Monster of the
Boiling Pool 200.00
45 HcK,The Bone-Grinders of
B'Zambi, Bondage(c) 210.00
46 HcK,Blood Raiders of
Tree Trail 175.00
47 HcK,GT,Monsters of the Man
Pool, Bondage(c) 200.00
48 HcK,GT,Strangest Congo
Adventure 175.00
49 HcK,GT,Lair of the King
-Serpent 175.00
50 HcK,GT,Juggernaut of
the Bush 175.00
51 HcK,GT,The Golden Lion of
Genghis Kahn 150.00
52 HcK,Feast for the River
Devils, Bondage(c) 200.00
53 HcK,GT,Slaves for Horrors
Harem 200.00
54 HcK,GT,Blood Bride of
the Crocodile 150.00
55 HcK,GT,The Tree Devil . . . 150.00
56 HcK,Bride for the
Rainmaker Raj 150.00
57 HcK,Fire Gems of T'ulaki . . 150.00
58 HcK,Land of the
Cannibal God 150.00
59 HcK,Dwellers of the Mist
Bondage(c) 175.00
60 HcK,Bush Devil's Spoor . . . 150.00
61 HcK,Curse of the Blood
Madness 150.00
62 Bondage(c) 165.00
63 HcK,Fire-Birds for the
Cliff Dwellers 140.00
64 Valley of the Ju-Ju Idols . . . 140.00
65 Shrine of the Seven Ju Jus,
Bondage(c) 150.00
66 Spoor of the Purple Skulls . 140.00
67 Devil Beasts of the Golden
Temple 140.00
68 Satan's Safari 140.00
69 Brides for the Serpent King . 140.00
70 Brides for the King Beast,
Bondage(c) 150.00
71 Congo Prey,Bondage(c) . . . 150.00
72 Blood-Brand o/t Veldt Cats . 125.00
73 The Killer of M'omba Raj,
Bondage(c) 150.00
74 AgF,GoldenJaws,Bondage(c) 150.00
75 AgF,Congo Kill 125.00
76 AgF,Blood Thrist of the
Golden Tusk 125.00
77 AgF,The Golden Gourds
Shriek Blood,Bondage(c) . . 150.00
78 AgF,Bondage(c) 150.00
79 AgF,Death has a
Thousand Fangs 125.00
80 AgF,Salome of the
Devil-Cats Bondage(c) 150.00
81 AgF,Colossus of the Congo 125.00
82 AgF,Blood Jewels of the
Fire-Bird 125.00
83 AgF,Vampire Veldt,
Bondage(c) 150.00
84 AgF,Blood Spoor of the
Faceless Monster 125.00
85 AgF,Brides for the Man-Apes
Bondage(c) 150.00
86 AgF,Firegems of L'hama

Lost, Bondage(c) 150.00
87 AgF,Horror Kraal of the
Legless One,Bondage(c) . . . 125.00
88 AgF,Beyond the Ju-Ju Mists 135.00
89 AgF,Blood-Moon over the
Whispering Veldt 125.00
90 AgF,The Skulls for the
Altar of Doom,Bondage(c) . 135.00
91 AgF,Monsters from the Mist
Lands, Bondage(c) 135.00
92 AgF,Vendetta of the
Tree Tribes 125.00
93 AgF,Witch Queen of the
Hairy Ones 125.00
94 AgF,Terror Raid of
the Congo Caesar 125.00
95 Agf,Flame-Tongues of the
Sky Gods 125.00
96 Agf,Phantom Guardians of the
Enchanted Lake,Bondage(c) 110.00
97 AgF,Wizard of the Whirling
Doom,Bondage(c) 135.00
98 AgF,Ten Tusks of Zulu Ivory 150.00
99 AgF,Cannibal Caravan,
Bondage(c) 125.00
100 AgF,Hate has a
Thousand Claws 125.00
101 AgF,The Blade of
Buddha, Bondage(c) 125.00
102 AgF,Queen of the
Amazon Lancers 110.00
103 AgF,The Phantoms of
Lost Lagoon 110.00
104 AgF 110.00
105 AgF,The Red Witch
of Ubangi-Shan 110.00
106 AgF,Bondage(c) 125.00
107 Banshee Valley 125.00
108 HcK,Merchants of Murder . 125.00
109 HcK,Caravan of the
Golden Bones 110.00
110 HcK,Raid of the Fire-Fangs 110.00
111 HcK,The Trek of the
Terror-Paws 110.00
112 HcK,Morass of the
Mammoths 110.00
113 HcK,Two-Tusked Terror . . 110.00
114 HcK,Mad Jackals Hunt
by Night 110.00
115 HcK,Treasure Trove in
Vulture Sky 110.00
116 HcK,The Banshees of
Voodoo Veldt 110.00
117 HcK,The Fangs of the
Hooded Scorpion 110.00
118 HcK,The Muffled Drums
of Doom 110.00
119 HcK,Fury of the Golden
Doom 110.00
120 HcK,Killer King Domain . . 110.00
121 HcK,Wolves of the
Desert Night 110.00
122 HcK,The Veldt of
Phantom Fangs 110.00
123 HcK,The Ark of the
Mist-Maids 110.00
124 HcK,The Trail of the
Pharaoh's Eye 110.00
125 HcK,Skulls for Sale on
Dismal River 110.00
126 HcK,Safari Sinister 125.00
127 Hck,Bondage(c) 100.00
128 HcK,Dawn-Men of the Congo100.00
129 Hck,The Captives of
Crocodile Swamp 100.00

130 Hck,Phantoms of the Congo 100.00
131 Hck,Treasure-Tomb of the
 Ape-King 100.00
132 Hck,Bondage(c) 125.00
133 Hck,Scourge of the Sudan
 Bondage(c) 125.00
134 Hck,The Black Avengers of
 Kaffir Pass 100.00
135 Hck 100.00
136 Hck,The Death Kraals
 of Kongola 100.00
137 BWg(c),HcK,The Safari of
 Golden Ghosts 100.00
138 BWg(c),HcK,Track of the
 Black Terror Bondage(c) ... 100.00
139 BWg(c),HcK,Captain Kidd
 of the Congo 100.00
140 BWg(c),HcK,The Monsters
 of Kilmanjaro 100.00
141 BWg(c)HcK,The Death Hunt
 of the Man Cubs 100.00
142 BWg(c),Hck,Sheba of the
 Terror Claws,Bondage(c) . 125.00
143 BWg(c)Hck,The Moon of
 Devil Drums 125.00
144 BWg(c)Hck,Quest of the
 Dragon's Claw 125.00
145 BWg(c)Hck,Spawn of the
 Devil's Moon 125.00
146 BWg(c),HcK,Orphans of
 the Congo 125.00
147 BWG(c),HcK,The Treasure
 of Tembo Wanculu 125.00
148 BWg(c),HcK,Caged Beasts
 of Plunder-Men,Bondage(c) . 125.00
149 BWg(c),HcK 100.00
150 BWg(c),HcK,Rhino Rampage,
 Bondage(c) 125.00
151 BWg(c),HcK 100.00
152 BWg(c),HcK,The Rogue of
 Kopje Kull 100.00
153 BWg(c),HcK,The Wild Men
 of N'Gara 100.00
154 BWg(c),HcK,The Fire Wizard 100.00
155 BWg(c),HcK,Swamp of
 the Shrieking Dead 100.00
156 BWg(c),HcK 100.00
157 BWg(c),HcK 100.00
158 BWg(c),HcK,A:Sheena .. 100.00
159 BWg(c),HcK,The Blow-Gun
 Kill 100.00
160 BWg,HcK,King Fang 100.00
161 BWg(c),HcK,The Barbarizi
 Man-Eaters 100.00
162 BWg(c) 100.00
163 BWg(c),Jackals at the
 Kill, Summer,1954 .... 100.00

JUNGLE JIM
Best Books
(Standard Comics)
January, 1949

11 .... 35.00
12 Mystery Island 20.00
13 Flowers of Peril 20.00
14 .... 20.00
15 .... 20.00
16 .... 20.00
17 .... 20.00
18 .... 20.00
19 .... 20.00
20 1951 .... 20.00

JUNGLE JIM

Dell Publishing Co.
August, 1953

(1) see Dell Four Color #490
(1) see Dell Four Color #565
3 P(c) all 20.00
4 .... 20.00
5 .... 20.00
6 .... 15.00
7 .... 15.00
8 .... 15.00
9 .... 15.00
10 .... 15.00
11 .... 15.00
12 .... 15.00
13 'Mystery Island' 15.00
14 'Flowers of Peril' 15.00
15 thru 20 .... @15.00

JUNGLE JO
Hero Books
(Fox Features Syndicate)
March, 1950

N# 165.00
1 Mystery of Doc Jungle ... 175.00
2 .... 135.00
3 The Secret of Youth,
 September, 1950 .... 125.00

JUNGLE LIL
Hero Books
(Fox Features Syndicate)
April, 1950

1 Betrayer of the Kombe Dead 150.00
Becomes:
DOROTHY LAMOUR

2 WW,Ph(c)The Lost Safari .. 125.00
3 WW,Ph(c), August, 1950 .. 100.00

JUNGLE THRILLS
(see TERRORS OF THE JUNGLE)

JUNIE PROM
Dearfield Publishing Co.
Winter, 1947

1 Teenage Stories 50.00
2 .... 25.00
3 .... 20.00
4 .... 20.00
5 .... 20.00
6 June, 1949 .... 20.00

JUNIOR COMICS
Fox Features Syndicate
September, 1947

9 AF,AF(c) ,Teenage Stories . 300.00
10 AF,AF(c) 250.00
11 AF,AF(c) 250.00
12 AF,AF(c) 250.00
13 AF,AF(c) 250.00
14 AF,AF(c) 250.00
15 AF,AF(c) 250.00
16 AF,AF(c),July,1948 ..... 250.00

JUNIOR HOOP COMICS
Stanmor Publications
January, 1952

1 .... 40.00
2 .... 20.00
3 July, 1952 .... 20.00

JUSTICE TRAPS OF THE GUILTY
Headline Publications
(Prize)
October–November, 1947

2-1 S&K,S&K(c),Electric chair
 cover 275.00
2 S&K,S&K(c) 150.00
3 S&K,S&K(c) 135.00
4 S&K,S&K(c),True Confession
 of a Girl Gangleader 125.00
5 S&K,S&K(c) 125.00
6 S&K,S&K(c) 125.00
7 S&K,S&K(c) 125.00
8 S&K,S&K(c) 125.00
9 S&K,S&K(c) 100.00
10 S&K,S&K(c) 125.00
11 S&K,S&K(c) 65.00
12 .... 30.00
13 .... 40.00
14 .... 30.00
15 .... 30.00
16 .... 30.00
17 .... 40.00
18 S&K,S&K(c) 50.00
19 S&K,S&K(c) 50.00
20 .... 30.00
21 S&K 40.00
22 S&K(c) 30.00
23 S&K(c) 30.00
24 .... 20.00
25 .... 25.00
26 .... 20.00
27 S&K 30.00
28 .... 20.00
29 .... 20.00
30 S&K 40.00
31 thru 50 .... @20.00
51 thru 57 .... @15.00
58 Drug 125.00
59 thru 92 .... @15.00
Becomes:

FARGO KID
Headline Publications
(Prize)

93 AW,JSe,O:Kid Fargo 100.00
94 JSe 75.00
95 June-July, 1958,JSe 75.00

KA'A'NGA COMICS
Glen-Kel Publ.
(Fiction House)
Spring, 1949

1 Phantoms of the Congo ... 325.00
2 V:The Jungle Octopus 175.00
3 .... 150.00
4 The Wizard Apes of
 Inkosi-Khan 125.00
5 .... 100.00
6 Captive of the Devil Apes ... 75.00
7 GT,Beast-Men of Mombassa 85.00
8 The Congo Kill-Cry 75.00
9 .... 75.00
10 Stampede for Congo Gold .. 75.00
11 Claws of the Roaring Congo . 60.00
12 Bondage(c) 65.00
13 Death Web of the Amazons . 60.00
14 Slave Galley of the Lost
 Nile Bondage(c) 70.00
15 Crocodile Moon,Bondage(c) . 70.00
16 Valley of Devil-Dwarfs 70.00
17 Tembu of the Elephants ... 50.00
18 The Red Claw of Vengeance 50.00

19 The Devil-Devil Trail	50.00
20 The Cult of the Killer Claws, Summer, 1954	50.00

KASCO COMICS
Kasco Grainfeed
(Giveaway)
1945

1 BWo	85.00
2 1949,BWo	75.00

KATHY
Standard Comics
September, 1949

1 Teen-Age Stories	40.00
2 ASh	22.00
3 thru 6	@15.00
7 thru 17	@12.00

KATY KEENE
Archie Publications/Close-Up
Radio Comics
1949

1 BWo	650.00
2 BWo	350.00
3 BWo	300.00
4 BWo	300.00
5 BWo	275.00
6 BWo	250.00
7 BWo	250.00
8 thru 12 BWo	@225.00
13 thru 20 BWo	@200.00
21 thru 29 BWo	@150.00
30 thru 38 BWo	@125.00
39 thru 62 BWo	@100.00

KEEN DETECTIVE FUNNIES
Centaur Publications
July, 1938

1-8 B:The Clock,	1,000.00
1-9 WE	500.00
1-10	400.00
1-11 Dean Denton	400.00
2-1 The Eye Sees	350.00
2-2 JCo	350.00
2-3 TNT	350.00
2-4 Gabby Flynn	350.00
5	375.00
6	350.00
7 Masked Marvel	650.00
8 PGn,Gabby Flynn,Nudity Expanded 16 pages	400.00
9 Dean Denton	375.00
10	375.00
11 BEv,Sidekick	350.00
12 Masked Marvel(c)	450.00
3-1 Masked Marvel(c)	400.00
3-2 Masked Marvel(c)	400.00
3-3 BEv	400.00
16 BEv	550.00
17 JSm	400.00
18 The Eye Sees,Bondage(c)	425.00
19 LFe	400.00
20 BEv,The Eye Sees	400.00
21 Masked Marvel(c)	375.00
22 Masked Marvel(c)	375.00
23 B:Airman	500.00
24 Airman	500.00

KEEN KOMICS
Centaur Publications

May, 1939

1 Teenage Stories	600.00
2 PGn,JaB,CBu	350.00
3 JCo	350.00

Keen Komics #3 (2/3)
© Centaur Publications

KEEN TEENS
Life's Romances Publ./Leader/
Magazine Enterprises
1945

N# P(c)	125.00
N# Ph(c),Van Johnson	100.00
3 Ph(c),	40.00
4 Ph(c),Glenn Ford	40.00
5 Ph(c),Perry Como	40.00
6	40.00

KEN MAYNARD WESTERN
Fawcett Publications

Ken Maynard Western #3
© Fawcett Publications

September, 1950

1 B:Ken Maynard & Tarzan (horse) The Outlaw Treasure Trail	325.00
2 Invasion of the Badmen	200.00
3 Pied Piper of the West	150.00
4 Outlaw Hoax	150.00
5 Mystery of Badman City	150.00
6 Redwood Robbery	150.00
7 Seven Wonders of the West	150.00
8 Mighty Mountain Menace, Feb.,1952	150.00

KEN SHANNON
Quality Comics Group
October, 1951

1 RC, Evil Eye of Count Ducrie	165.00
2 RC, Cut Rate Corpses	125.00
3 RC, Corpse that Wouldn't Sleep	90.00
4 RC, Stone Hatchet Murder	75.00
5 RC, Case of the Carney Killer	75.00

Ken Shannon #6
© Quality Comics Group

6 Weird Vampire Mob	50.00
7 RC,Ugliest Man in the World	65.00
8 Chinatown Murders,Drug	90.00
9 RC, Necklace of Blood	65.00
10 RC, Shadow of the Chair, Apr. 1953	65.00

KERRY DRAKE DETECTIVE CASES
Life's Romances/M.E./
Harvey Publ.
1944

1	150.00
2 A:The Faceless Horror	100.00
3	75.00
4 A:Squirrel, Dr. Zero, Caresse	75.00
5 Bondage cover	85.00
6 A:Stitches	40.00
7 A:Shuteye	45.00
8 Bondage cover	50.00
9 Drug	75.00
10 BP,A:Meatball,Drug	75.00
11 BP,I:Kid Gloves	40.00
12 BP	40.00

All comics prices listed are for *Near Mint* condition.

13 BP,A:Torso 35.00
14 BP,Bullseye Murder Syndicate 35.00
15 BP,Fake Mystic Racket 35.00
16 BP,A:Vixen 30.00
17 BP,Case of the $50,000
   Robbery 30.00
18 BP,A:Vixen 30.00
19 BP,Case of the Dope
   Smugglers 35.00
20 BP,Secret Treasury Agent .. 30.00
21 BP,Murder on Record 25.00
22 BP,Death Rides the Air Waves 25.00
23 BP,Blackmailer's Secret
   Weapon 25.00
24 Blackmailer's Trap 25.00
25 Pretty Boy Killer 25.00
26 .... 25.00
27 .... 25.00
28 BP 25.00
29 BP 25.00
30 Mystery Mine,Bondage(c) .. 30.00
31 .... 25.00
32 .... 25.00
33 August, 1952 .... 25.00

KEWPIES
Will Eisner Publications
Spring, 1949
1 .... 250.00

KEY COMICS
Consolidated Magazines
January, 1944
1 B:The Key, Will-O-The-Wisp 175.00
2 .... 100.00
3 .... 75.00
4 O:John Quincy,B:The Atom . 80.00
5 HoK,August, 1946 .... 75.00

KID COWBOY
Approved Comics/
St. John Publ. Co.
1950
1 B:Lucy Belle & Red Feather . 65.00
2 Six-Gun Justice 35.00
3 Shadow on Hangman's Bridge 30.00
4 Red Feather V:Eagle of Doom 25.00
5 Killers on the Rampage 25.00
6 The Stovepipe Hat 25.00
7 Ghost Town of Twin Buttes . 25.00
8 Thundering Hoofs 25.00
9 Terror on the Salt Flats 25.00
10 Valley of Death 25.00
11 Vanished Herds,Bondage(c) . 35.00
12 .... 25.00
13 .... 25.00
14 1954 .... 25.00

KIDDIE KARNIVAL
Approved Comics
1952
N# 200.00

KID ETERNITY
Comics Magazine
(Quality Comics Group)
Spring, 1946
1 .... 400.00
2 .... 200.00
3 Follow Him Out of This World 225.00
4 Great Heroes of the Past ... 125.00
5 Don't Kid with Crime 125.00
6 Busy Battling Crime 100.00

7 Protects the World 100.00
8 Fly to the Rescue 100.00
9 Swoop Down on Crime .. 100.00
10 Golden Touch from Mr. Midas 100.00
11 Aid the Living by Calling
   the Dead 80.00
12 Finds Death 80.00
13 Invades General Poschka ... 80.00
14 Battles Double 80.00
15 A: Master Man 80.00
16 Balance Scales of Justice ... 75.00
17 A:Baron Roxx 75.00
18 A:Man with Two Faces ... 75.00
Becomes:
BUCCANEERS
19 RC,Sword Fight(c) 275.00
20 RC,Treasure Chest 200.00
21 RC,Death Trap ... 250.00
22 A:Lady Dolores,Snuff,
   Bondage(c) 150.00
23 RC,V:Treasure Hungry
   Plunderers of the Sea 200.00
24 A:Adam Peril,Black Roger,
   Eric Falcon 125.00

Kid Eternity #15
© Comics Magazine/Quality Comics

25 V:Clews 125.00
26 V:Admiral Blood 125.00
27 RC,RC(c)May, 1951 ...... 200.00

KID ZOO COMICS
Street & Smith Publications
July, 1948
1 (fa) 100.00

KILLERS, THE
Magazine Enterprises
1947
1 LbC(c),Thou Shall Not Kill . 450.00
2 Grl,OW,Assassins Mad Slayers
   of the East,Hanging(c),Drug 450.00

KILROYS, THE
B&L Publishing Co./
American Comics
June-July, 1947
1 Three Girls in Love(c) 125.00
2 Flat Tire(c) 60.00

3 Right to Swear(c) 45.00
4 Kissing Booth(c) 45.00
5 Skiing(c) 45.00
6 Prom(c) 30.00
7 To School 30.00
8 .... 30.00
9 .... 30.00
10 B:Solid Jackson solo 30.00
11 .... 25.00
12 Life Guard(c) 25.00
13 thru 21 .... @25.00
22 thru 30 .... @20.00
31 thru 40 .... @18.00
41 thru 47 .... @15.00
48 3-D effect 100.00
49 3-D effect 100.00
50 thru 54, July 1954 ...... @15.00

KING COMICS
David McKay Publications
April, 1936
1 AR,EC,B:Popeye,Flash Gordon.B:
   Henry,Mandrake 5,000.00
2 AR,EC,Flash Gordon 1,600.00
3 AR,EC,Flash Gordon 1,200.00
4 AR,EC,Flash Gordon 900.00
5 AR,EC,Flash Gordon 650.00
6 AR,EC,Flash Gordon 450.00
7 AR,EC,King Royal Mounties 425.00
8 AR,EC,Thanksgiving(c) ... 400.00

King Comics #44
© David McKay Publications

9 AR,EC,Christmas(c) 400.00
10 AR,EC,Flash Gordon 400.00
11 AR,EC,Flash Gordon 375.00
12 AR,EC,Flash Gordon 375.00
13 AR,EC,Flash Gordon 375.00
14 AR,EC,Flash Gordon 375.00
15 AR,EC,Flash Gordon 375.00
16 AR,EC,Flash Gordon 375.00
17 AR,EC,Flash Gordon 350.00
18 AR,EC,Flash Gordon 350.00
19 AR,EC,Flash Gordon 350.00
20 AR,EC,Football(c) 350.00
21 AR,EC,Flash Gordon 300.00
22 AR,EC,Flash Gordon 300.00
23 AR,EC,Flash Gordon 300.00
24 AR,EC,Flash Gordon 300.00
25 AR,EC,Flash Gordon 300.00

26 AR,EC,Flash Gordon	275.00
27 AR,EC,Flash Gordon	275.00
28 AR,EC,Flash Gordon	275.00
29 AR,EC,Flash Gordon	275.00
30 AR,EC,Flash Gordon	275.00
31 AR,EC,Flash Gordon	275.00
32 AR,EC,Flash Gordon	275.00
33 AR,EC,Skiing(c)	275.00
34 AR,Ping Pong(c)	250.00
35 AR,Flash Gordon	250.00
36 AR,Flash Gordon	250.00
37 AR,Flash Gordon	250.00
38 AR,Flash Gordon	250.00
39 AR,Baseball(c)	250.00
40 AR,Flash Gordon	250.00
41 AR,Flash Gordon	200.00
42 AR,Flash Gordon	200.00
43 AR,Flash Gordon	200.00
44 AR,Popeye golf(c)	200.00
45 AR,Flash Gordon	200.00
46 AR,B:Little Lulu	200.00
47 AR,Flash Gordon	200.00
48 AR,Flash Gordon	200.00
49 AR,Weather Vane	200.00
50 AR,B:Love Ranger	200.00
51 AR,Flash Gordon	200.00
52 AR,Flash Gordon	175.00
53 AR,Flash Gordon	175.00
54 AR,Flash Gordon	175.00
55 AR,Magic Carpet	175.00
56 AR,Flash Gordon	175.00
57 AR,Cows Over Moon(c)	175.00
58 AR,Flash Gordon	175.00
59 AR,Flash Gordon	175.00
60 AR,Flash Gordon	175.00
61 AR,B:Phantom,Baseball(c)	175.00
62 AR,Flash Gordon	175.00
63 AR,Flash Gordon	150.00
64 AR,Flash Gordon	150.00
65 AR,Flash Gordon	150.00
66 AR,Flash Gordon	150.00
67 AR,Sweet Pea	150.00
68 AR,Flash Gordon	150.00
69 AR,Flash Gordon	150.00
70 AR,Flash Gordon	150.00
71 AR,Flash Gordon	150.00
72 AR,Flash Gordon	125.00
73 AR,Flash Gordon	125.00
74 AR,Flash Gordon	125.00
75 AR,Flash Godron	125.00
76 AR,Flag(c)	135.00
77 AR,Flash Gordon	125.00
78 AR,Popeye,Olive Oil(c)	125.00
79 AR,Sweet Pea	125.00
80 AR,Wimpy(c)	125.00
81 AR,B:Blondie(c)	125.00
82 thru 91 AR	@100.00
92 thru 98 AR	@85.00
99 AR,Olive Oil(c)	100.00
100	125.00
101 thru 116 AR	@85.00
117 O:Phantom	75.00
118 Flash Gordon	85.00
119 Flash Gordon	75.00
120 Wimpy(c)	60.00
121 thru 140	@75.00
141 Flash Gordon	60.00
142 Flash Gordon	60.00
143 Flash Gordon	60.00
144 Flash Gordon	60.00
145 Prince Valiant	55.00
146 Prince Valiant	55.00
147 Prince Valiant	55.00
148 thru 154	@45.00
155 E:Flash Gordon	45.00
156 Baseball(c)	45.00
157 thru 159	@35.00

KING OF THE ROYAL MOUNTED
Dell Publishing Co.
December, 1948

(1) *see Dell Four Color #207*	
(2) *see Dell Four Color #265*	
(3) *see Dell Four Color #283*	
(4) *see Dell Four Color #310*	
(5) *see Dell Four Color #340*	
(6) *see Dell Four Color #363*	
(7) *see Dell Four Color #384*	
8	40.00
9	40.00
10	40.00
11 thru 28	@30.00

KIT CARSON
Avon Periodicals
1950

N# EK(c)	65.00
2 EK(c),Kit Carson's Revenge, Doom Trail	40.00
3 EK(c),V:Comanche Raiders	35.00
4	30.00
5 EK(c),Trail of Doom	30.00
6 EK(c)	30.00
7 EK(c)	35.00
8 EK(c)	30.00

Becomes:

FIGHTING DAVY CROCKETT

9 EK(c),October/Nov., 1955	35.00

KOKO AND KOLA
Compix/Magazine Enterprises
Fall, 1946

1 (fa)	40.00
2 X-Mas Issue	20.00
3	15.00
4	15.00
5	15.00
6 May, 1947	15.00

KO KOMICS
Gerona Publications
October, 1945

1	250.00

KOMIK PAGES
Harry 'A' Chestler
April, 1945

1 JK,Duke of Darkness	300.00

KRAZY KAT COMICS
Dell Publishing Co.
May-June, 1951

1	50.00
2	35.00
3	35.00
4	35.00
5	35.00

KRAZY LIFE
(See PHANTOM LADY)

LABOR IS A PARTNER
Catechetical Guild

Educational Society
1949

1	150.00

LAFFY-DAFFY COMICS
Rural Home Publ. Co.
February, 1945

1 (fa)	30.00
2	30.00

Large Feature Comics #3
© Dell Publishing Co.

LARGE FEATURE COMICS
Dell Publishing Co.
1939

1 Dick Tracy vs. the Blank	1,150.00
2 Terry and the Pirates	600.00
3 Lone Ranger—Heigh-Yo Silver	600.00
4 Dick Tracy	625.00
5 Tarzan	1,000.00
6 Terry and the Pirates	500.00
7 Lone Ranger	600.00
8 Dick Tracy,Racket Buster	550.00
9 King of the Royal Mounted	350.00
10 Gang Busters	500.00
11 Dick Tracy	600.00
12 Smilin'Jack	450.00
13 Dick Tracy	650.00
14 Smilin' Jack	500.00
15 Dick Tracy and the Kidnapped Princes	650.00
16 Donald Duck,1st Daisy.	2,700.00
17 Gang Busters	300.00
18 Phantasmo,Master of the World	250.00
19 W.Disney's Dumbo	2,000.00
20 Donald Duck	3,800.00
21 Private Buck	100.00
22 Nuts and Jolts	100.00
23 The Nebbs	125.00
24 Popeye in 'Thimble Theatre'	450.00
25 Smilin'Jack	400.00
26 Smitty	225.00
27 Terry and the Pirates	450.00
28 Grin and Bear It	75.00
29 Moon Mullins	200.00
30 Tillie the Toiler	175.00

[Series 2]

1 Peter Rabbit	350.00
2 Winnie Winkle	150.00
3 Dick Tracy	550.00
4 Tiny Tim	250.00
5 Toots and Casper	100.00
6 Terry and the Pirates	450.00
7 Pluto saves the Ship	1,000.00
8 Bugs Bunny	750.00
9 Bringing Up Father	150.00
10 Popeye	400.00
11 Barney Google&SnuffySmith	200.00
12 Private Buck	100.00
13 1001 Hours of Fun	150.00

**LARRY DOBY,
BASEBALL HERO**
Fawcett Publications
1950

1 Ph(c),BW	500.00

LARS OF MARS
Ziff-Davis Publishing Co.
April-May, 1951

10 MA,'Terror from the Sky'	350.00
11 GC	300.00

LASH LARUE WESTERN
Fawcett Publications
Summer, 1949

1 Ph(c),The Fatal Roundups	600.00
2 Ph(c),Perfect Hide Out	300.00
3 Ph(c),The Suspect	250.00
4 Ph(c),Death on Stage	250.00
5 Ph(c),Rustler's Haven	250.00
6 Ph(c)	225.00
7 Ph(c),Shadow of the Noose	175.00
8 Ph(c),Double Deadline	175.00
9 Ph(c),Generals Last Stand	175.00
10 Ph(c)	175.00
11 Ph(c)	150.00
12 thru 20 Ph(c)	@100.00
21 thru 29 Ph(c)	@90.00
30 thru 46 Ph(c)	@75.00
46 Ph(c),Lost Chance	75.00

LASSIE
(& SEVERAL SPECIAL
ISSUES)
Dell Publishing Co.
October-December, 1950

1 Ph(c) all	100.00
2	45.00
3	28.00
4	28.00
5	28.00
6	28.00
7	28.00
8	28.00
9	28.00
10	28.00
11	20.00
12 Rocky Langford	22.00
13	20.00
14	20.00
15 I:Timbu	22.00
16	20.00
17	20.00
18	20.00
19	20.00
20 MB	25.00
21 MB	25.00
22 MB	25.00

23 thru 38	@15.00
39 I:Timmy	20.00
40 thru 62	@15.00
63 E:Timmy	10.00
64 thru 70	@9.00

LATEST COMICS
Spotlight Publ./
Palace Promotions
March, 1945

1 Funny Animal-Super Duper	60.00
2	40.00

SPECIAL COMICS
MLJ Magazines
(Archie Publ.)
Winter, 1941

1 O:Boy Buddies & Hangman, D:The Comet	1,200.00

Becomes:

HANGMAN COMICS

2 B:Hangman & Boy Buddies	900.00
3 V:Nazis cover,Bondage(c)	500.00
4 V:Nazis cover	450.00
5 Bondage cover	450.00
6	425.00
7 BF,Graveyard cover	425.00
8 BF	425.00

Becomes:

BLACK HOOD

9 BF	500.00
10 BF,A:Dusty, the Boy Detective	300.00
11 Here lies the Black Hood	200.00
12	200.00
13 EK(c)	200.00
14 EK(c)	200.00
15 EK	200.00
16 EK(c)	200.00
17 Bondage cover	225.00
18	200.00
19 I.D. Revealed	250.00

Becomes:

LAUGH COMICS

20 BWo,B:Archie,Katy Keene	400.00
21 BWo	200.00
22 BWo	200.00
23 Bwo	200.00
24 BWo,JK,Pipsy	200.00
25 BWo	200.00
26 BWo	125.00
27 BWo	125.00
28 BWo	125.00
29 BWo	125.00
30 BWo	125.00
31 thru 40 BWo	@75.00
41 thru 50 BWo	@55.00
51 thru 60 BWo	@50.00
61 thru 80 BWo	@25.00
81 thru 99 BWo	@20.00
100 BWo	30.00
101 thru 126 BWo	@20.00
127 A:Jaguar	22.00
128 A:The Fly	22.00
129 A:The Fly	22.00
130 A:Jaguar	22.00
131 A:Jaguar	22.00
132 A:The Fly	22.00
133 A:Jaguar	22.00
134 A:The Fly	22.00
135 A:Jaguar	22.00
136 A:Fly Girl	22.00
137 A:Fly Girl	22.00

138 A:The Fly	22.00
139 A:The Fly	22.00
140 A:Jaguar	22.00
141 A:Jaguar	22.00
142 thru 144	@22.00
145 A:Josie	15.00
146 thru 165	@10.00
166 Beatles cover	15.00
167 thru 220	@5.00
221 thru 250	@2.50
251 thru 300	@2.00
301 thru 400	@1.00

LAUGH COMIX
(see TOP-NOTCH COMICS)

LAUREL AND HARDY
St. John Publishing Co.
March, 1949

1	400.00
2	225.00
3	175.00
26 Rep #1	100.00
27 Rep #2	100.00
28 Rep #3	100.00

LAWBREAKERS
Law & Order Magazines
(Charlton)
March, 1951

1	125.00
2	55.00
3	40.00
4 Drug	55.00
5	40.00
6 LM(c)	55.00
7 Drug	55.00
8	40.00
9 StC(c)	40.00

Becomes:

**LAWBREAKERS
SUSPENSE STORIES**
January, 1953

10 StC(c)	100.00
11 LM(c),Negligee(c)	250.00
12 LM(c)	50.00
13 DG(c)	50.00
14 DG(c),Sharks	55.00
15 DG(c),Acid in Face(c)	150.00

Becomes:

**STRANGE SUSPENSE
STORIES**

16 DG(c); January, 1954	100.00
17 DG(c)	80.00
18 SD,SD(c)	150.00
19 SD,SD(c),Electric Chair	200.00
20 SD,SD(c)	150.00
21 SD,SD(c)	75.00
22 SD,SD(c)	125.00

Becomes:

THIS IS SUSPENSE

23 WW; February, 1955 Comics Code	125.00
24 GE,DG(c)	70.00
25 DG(c)	50.00
26 DG(c)	50.00

Becomes:

**STRANGE SUSPENSE
STORIES**

27 October, 1955	50.00
28	35.00

Strange Suspense Stories #18
© Law & Order Magazines/Charlton

29	35.00
30	35.00
31 SD	90.00
32 SD	90.00
33 SD	90.00
34 SD	90.00
35 SD	90.00
36 SD	90.00
37 SD	90.00
38	35.00
39 SD	100.00
40 SD	100.00
41 SD	100.00
42	30.00
43	30.00
44	30.00
45	30.00
46	30.00
47 SD	75.00
48 SD	75.00
49	30.00
50 SD	75.00
51 SD	75.00
52 SD	75.00
53 SD	75.00
54 thru 60	@25.00
61 thru 74	@15.00
75 SD,SD(c)	100.00
77 Oct 1965	35.00

LAWBREAKERS ALWAYS LOSE
Crime Bureau Stories
Spring, 1948

1 HK; FBI Reward Poster Photo	125.00
2	65.00
3	50.00
4 Vampire	60.00
5	40.00
6 Anti Wertham Edition	50.00
7	125.00
8	40.00
9 Ph(c)	40.00
10 Ph(c), October 1949	40.00

LAW-CRIME
Essenkay Publications

April, 1948

1 LbC,LbC-(c);Raymond Hamilton Dies In The Chair	300.00
2 LbC,LbC-(c);Strangled Beauty Puzzles Police	225.00
3 LbC,LbC-(c);Lipstick Slayer Sought; August '43	275.00

LEROY
Visual Editions (Standard Comics)
November, 1949

1 FunniestTeenager of them All	25.00
2	20.00
3 thru 6	@15.00

LET'S PRETEND
D.S. Publishing Company
May-June, 1950

1 From Radio Nursery Tales	75.00
2	60.00
3 November, 1950	55.00

MISS LIBERTY
Burten/Green Publishing
Circa 1944

1 Reprints-Shield,Wizard	200.00

Becomes:

LIBERTY COMICS

10 Reprints,Hangman	100.00
11	75.00
12 Black Hood	75.00
14	75.00
15	50.00

LIBERTY GUARDS
Chicago Mail Order (Comic Corp of America)
Circa 1942

1 PG(c),Liberty Scouts	175.00

Becomes:

LIBERTY SCOUTS
June, 1941

2 PG,PG(c)O:Fireman,Liberty Scouts	750.00
3 PG,PG(c) August,1941 O:Sentinel	600.00

LIFE STORY
Fawcett Publications
April, 1949

1 Ph(c)	60.00
2 Ph(c)	25.00
3 Ph(c)	22.00
4 Ph(c)	22.00
5 Ph(c)	22.00
6 Ph(c)	22.00
7 Ph(c)	20.00
8 Ph(c)	20.00
9 Ph(c)	20.00
10 Ph(c)	20.00
11	18.00
12	18.00
13 WW,Drug	75.00
14 thru 21	@18.00
22 Drug	25.00
23 thru 35	@18.00
36 Drug	22.00
37 thru 42	@15.00
43 GE	22.00
44	15.00
45 1952	15.00

LIFE WITH SNARKY PARKER
Fox Feature Syndicate
August, 1950

1	125.00

LI'L ABNER
Harvey Publications
December, 1947

61 BP,BW,Sadie Hawkins Day	200.00

Li'l Abner #80 © Harvey Publications

62	125.00
63	125.00
64	125.00
65 BP	125.00
66	90.00
67	90.00
68 FearlessFosdick V:Any Face	100.00
69	90.00
70	90.00

Toby Press

71	80.00
72	75.00
73	75.00
74	75.00
75 HK	90.00
76	75.00
77 HK	90.00
78 HK	90.00
79 HK	90.00
80	55.00
81	55.00
82	55.00
83 Baseball	60.00
84	55.00
85	55.00
86 HK	90.00
87	55.00
88	55.00
89	55.00
90	55.00
91 Rep. #77	60.00
92	54.00
93 Rep. #71	60.00
94	55.00
95 Fearless Fosdick	75.00
96	55.00
97 January, 1955	55.00

All comics prices listed are for *Near Mint* condition.

LI'L GENIUS
Charlton Comics
1955

1	35.00
2	15.00
3 thru 15	@12.00
16 Giants	18.00
17 Giants	18.00
18 Giants,100 pages	22.00
19 thru 40	@8.00
41 thru 54	@5.00
55 1965	5.00

LI'L PAN
Fox Features Syndicate
December-January, 1946-47

6	35.00
7	25.00
8 April-May, 1947	25.00

LINDA
(see PHANTOM LADY)

LITTLE AUDREY
St. John Publ. Co./
Harvey Comics
April, 1948

1	200.00
2	100.00
3 thru 6	@75.00
7 thru 10	@40.00
11 thru 20	@25.00
21 thru 24	@18.00
25 B:Harvey Comics	55.00
26 A: Casper	25.00
27 A: Casper	25.00
28 A: Casper	25.00
29 thru 31	@20.00
32 A: Casper	25.00
33 A: Casper	25.00
34 A: Casper	25.00
35 A: Casper	25.00
36 thru 53	@12.00

Little Bit #2 © Jubilee Publishing Co.

LITTLE BIT
Jubilee Publishing Company
March, 1949

1	20.00
2 June, 1949	20.00

LITTLE DOT
Harvey Publications
September, 1953

1 I: Richie Rich & Little Lotta	450.00
2	250.00
3	150.00
4	125.00
5 O:Dots on Little Dot's Dress	135.00
6 1st Richie Rich(c)	135.00
7	135.00
8	65.00

Little Dot #1 © Harvey Publications

9	65.00
10	65.00
11 thru 20	@45.00
21 thru 30	@22.00
31 thru 38	@20.00
39	50.00
40 thru 50	@12.00
51 thru 60	@10.00
61 thru 70	@8.00
71 thru 80	@6.00
81 thru 100	@5.00
101 thru 130	@3.00
131 thru 140	@3.00
141 thru 145, 52 pages	@3.50
146 thru 163	@1.00

LITTLE EVA
St. John Publishing Co.
May, 1952

1	60.00
2	30.00
3	18.00
4	18.00
5 thru 10	@12.00
11 thru 30	@10.00
31 November, 1956	10.00

LITTLE GIANT COMICS
Centaur Publications
July, 1938

1 PG, B&W with Color(c)	300.00
2 B&W with Color(c)	250.00
3 B&W with Color(c)	275.00
4 B&W with Color(c)	275.00

LITTLE GIANT
DETECTIVE FUNNIES
Centaur Publications
October, 1938

1 B&W	300.00
2 B&W	250.00
3 B&W	250.00
4 January 1939	250.00

LITTLE GIANT
MOVIE FUNNIES
Centaur Publications
August, 1938

1 Ed Wheelan-a	280.00
2 Ed Wheelan-a, Oct., 1938	225.00

LITTLE IKE
St. John Publishing Co.
April, 1953

1	45.00
2	22.00
3	18.00
4 October, 1953	18.00

LITTLE IODINE
Dell Publishing Co.
April, 1949

1	65.00
2	25.00
3	25.00
4	25.00
5	25.00
6 thru 10	@15.00
11 thru 30	@12.00
31 thru 50	@9.00
51 thru 56	@7.00

LITTLE JACK FROST
Avon Periodicals
1951

1	35.00

LITTLE MAX COMICS
Harvey Publications
October, 1949

1 I: Little Dot,Joe Palooka	80.00
2 A: Little Dot	45.00
3 A: Little Dot,Joe Palooka(c)	30.00
4	20.00
5 C: Little Dot	20.00
6 thru 10	@18.00
11 thru 22	@15.00
23 A: Little Dot	10.00
24 thru 37	@8.00
38 Rep. #20	8.00
39 thru 72	@8.00
73 A: Richie Rich; Nov.'61	9.00

LITTLE MISS MUFFET
Best Books
(Standard Comics)
December, 1948

11 Strip Reprints	45.00
12 Strip Reprints	30.00
13 Strip Reprints; Mar.'49	30.00

LITTLE MISS SUNBEAM
COMICS
Magazine Enterprises
June-July, 1950

1	60.00
2	30.00
3	30.00
4 December-January, 1951	30.00

Little Orphan Annie #2
© Dell Publishing Co.

LITTLE ORPHAN ANNIE
Dell Publishing Co.
1941

1	100.00
2 Orphan Annie and the Rescue	65.00
3	65.00

LITTLE ROQUEFORT
St. John Publishing Co.
June,1952

1	40.00
2	20.00
3 thru 9	@15.00
Pines	
10 Summer 1958	18.00

LITTLE SCOUTS
Dell Publishing Co.
March, 1951

(1) *see Dell Four Color #321*

2	10.00
3	10.00
4	10.00
5	10.00
6	10.00

LITTLEST SNOWMAN
Dell Publishing Co.
December, 1956

1	20.00

LIVING BIBLE, THE
Living Bible Corp.
Autumn, 1945

1 LbC-(c) Life of Paul	125.00
2 LbC-(c) Joseph & His Brethern	75.00
3 LbC-(c) Chaplains At War	135.00

LONE EAGLE
Ajax/Farrell

April-May, 1954

1	50.00
2	30.00
3 Bondage(c)	35.00
4 October-November, 1954	30.00

LONE RANGER
Dell Publishing Co.
January-February 1948

1 B:Lone Ranger & Tonto	
B:Strip Reprint	600.00
2	250.00
3	175.00
4	175.00
5	175.00
6	150.00
7	150.00
8 O:Retold	200.00
9	140.00
10	140.00
11 B:Young Hawk	100.00
12 thru 20	@100.00
21	80.00
22	80.00
23 O:Retold	125.00
24 thru 30	@75.00
31 (1st Mask Logo)	80.00
32 thru 36	@65.00
37 (E:Strip reprints)	65.00
38 thru 50	@50.00
51 thru 75	@45.00
76 thru 99	@37.00
100	55.00
101 thru 111	@35.00
112 B:Clayton Moore Ph(c)	125.00
113 thru 117	@65.00
118 O:Lone Ranger & Tonto	
retold, Anniv. issue	125.00
119 thru 144	@60.00
145 final issue,May/July 1962	60.00

THE LONE RANGER'S
COMPANION TONTO
Dell Publishing Co.
January, 1951

(1) *see Dell Four Color #312*

2 P(c) all	50.00
3	50.00
4	28.00
5	28.00
6 thru 10	@25.00
11 thru 20	@22.00
21 thru 25	@18.00
26 thru 33	@15.00

THE LONE RANGER'S
FAMOUS HORSE
HI-YO SILVER
Dell Publishing Co.
January, 1952

(1) *see Dell Four Color #369*
(1) *see Dell Four Color #392*

3 P(c) all	20.00
4	20.00
5	20.00
6 thru 10	@18.00
11 thru 36	@15.00

LONE RIDER
Farrell
(Superior Comics)
April, 1951

1	80.00
2 I&O: Golden Arrow; 52 pgs.	40.00
3	35.00
4	35.00
5	35.00
6 E: Golden Arrow	40.00
7 G. Arrow Becomes Swift Arrow	45.00
8 O: Swift Arrow	55.00
9 thru 14	@25.00
15 O: Golden Arrow Rep. #2	30.00
16 thru 19	@20.00
20	18.00
21 3-D (c)	65.00
22	18.00
23 A: Apache Kid	20.00
24	18.00
25	18.00
26 July, 1955	18.00

LONG BOW
Real Adventures Publ.
(Fiction House)
Winter, 1950

1	75.00
2	40.00
3 "Red Arrows Means War"	35.00
4 "Trial of Tomahawk"	35.00
5	35.00
6 "Rattlesnake Raiders"	30.00
7	30.00
8	30.00
9 Spring, 1953	30.00

LOONEY TUNES AND
MERRIE MELODIES
Dell Publishing Co.
1941

1 B:&1st Comic App.) Bugs Bunny Daffy Duck,Elmer Fudd	5,500.00
2 Bugs/Porky(c)	850.00
3 Bugs/Porky(c) B:WK, Kandi the Cave	700.00
4 Bugs/Porky(c),WK	650.00
5 Bugs/Porky(c),WK, A:Super Rabbit	550.00
6 Bugs/Porky/Elmer(c),E:WK, Kandi the Cave	425.00
7 Bugs/Porky(c)	400.00
8 Bugs/Porky swimming(c),F:WK, Kandi the Cave	425.00
9 Porky/Elmer car painted(c)	375.00
10 Porky/Bugs/Elmer Parade(c)	350.00
11 Bugs/Porky(c),F:WK, Kandi the Cave	325.00
12 Bugs/Porky rollerskating(c)	300.00
13 Bugs/Porky(c)	300.00
14 Bugs/Porky(c)	300.00
15 Bugs/Porky X-Mas(c),F:WK Kandi the Cave	325.00
16 Bugs/Porky ice-skating(c)	275.00
17 Bugs/Petunia Valentines(c)	275.00
18 Sgt.Bugs Marine(c)	275.00
19 Bugs/Painting(c)	275.00
20 Bugs/Porky/ElmerWarBonds(c), B:WK,Pat,Patsy&Pete	300.00
21 Bugs/Porky 4th July(c)	275.00
22 Porky(c)	275.00
23 Bugs/Porky Fishing(c)	275.00
24 Bugs/Porky Football(c)	275.00
25 Bugs/Porky/Petunia Halloween(c),E:WK,Pat, Patsy & Pete	275.00
26 Bugs Thanksgiving(c)	200.00
27 Bugs/Porky New Years(c)	200.00

All comics prices listed are for *Near Mint* condition.

28 Bugs/Porky Ice-Skating(c) . . 200.00
29 Bugs Valentine(c) 200.00
30 Bugs(c) 200.00
31 Bugs(c) 150.00

Looney Tunes & Merrie Melodies #33
© Dell Publ. Co.

32 Bugs/Porky Hot Dogs(c) . . . 150.00
33 Bugs/Porky War Bonds(c) . . 165.00
34 Bugs/Porky Fishing(c) 150.00
35 Bugs/Porky Swimming(c) . . 150.00
36 Bugs/Porky(c) 150.00
37 Bugs Halloween(c) 150.00
38 Bugs Thanksgiving(c) 150.00
39 Bugs X-Mas(c) 150.00
40 Bugs(c) 150.00
41 Bugs Washington's
    Birthday(c) 125.00
42 Bugs Magician(c) 125.00
43 Bugs Dream(c) 125.00
44 Bugs/Porky(c) 125.00
45 Bugs War Bonds(c) 125.00
46 Bugs/Porky(c) 100.00
47 Bugs Beach(c) 100.00
48 Bugs/Porky Picnic(c) 100.00
49 Bugs(c) 100.00
50 Bugs(c) 100.00
51 thru 60 . . . . @75.00
61 thru 80 . . . . @50.00
81 thru 86 . . . . @35.00
87 Bugs X-Mas(c) 40.00
88 thru 99 . . . . @30.00
100 . . . . 40.00
101 thru 110 . . . . @25.00
111 thru 125 . . . . ,. @22.00
126 thru 150 . . . . @20.00
151 thru 165 . . . . @18.00
Becomes:

LOONEY TUNES
August, 1955

166 thru 200 . . . . @12.00
201 thru 245 . . . . @10.00
246 final issue,Sept.1962 . . . . . 10.00

LOST WORLD
**Literacy Enterprises
(Standard Comics)
October, 1952**

5 ATh, Alice in Terrorland . . . 175.00
6 ATh 150.00

LOVE AND MARRIAGE
**Superior Comics Ltd.
March, 1952**

1 . . . . 50.00
2 . . . . 25.00
3 thru 10 . . . . @20.00
11 thru 15 . . . . @20.00
16 September, 1954 . . . . 20.00

LOVE AT FIRST SIGHT
**Periodical House
(Ace Magazines)
October, 1949**

1 P(c) 60.00
2 P(c) 25.00
3 . . . . 15.00
4 P(c) 15.00
5 thru 10 . . . . @15.00
11 thru 33 . . . . @10.00
34 1st Edition Under Code 7.00
35 thru 41 . . . . @7.00
42 1956 . . . . 7.00

LOVE CONFESSIONS
**Comics Magazine
(Quality Comics Group)
October, 1949**

1 PG,BWa(c)& Some-a 150.00
2 PG 50.00
3 . . . . 30.00
4 RC 50.00
5 BWa 55.00
6 Ph(c) 15.00
7 Ph(c) Van Johnson 15.00
8 BWa 50.00
9 Ph(c)Jane Russell/Robert
    Mitchum 15.00
10 BWa 50.00
11 thru 18 Ph(c) . . . . @30.00
19 . . . . 15.00
20 BWa 50.00
21 . . . . 10.00
22 BWa 12.00
23 thru 28 . . . . @12.00
29 BWa 35.00
30 thru 38 . . . . @10.00
39 MB 15.00
40 . . . . 10.00
41 . . . . 10.00
42 . . . . 10.00
43 1st Edition Under Code 8.00
44 thru 46 . . . . @8.00
47 BWa(c) 20.00
48 thru 54 December, 1956 . . . @8.00

LOVE DIARY
**Our Publishing Co./Toytown
July, 1949**

1 BK,Ph(c) 85.00
2 BK,Ph(c) 55.00
3 BK,Ph(c) 55.00
4 thru 9 Ph(c) . . . . @20.00
10 BEv, Ph(c) 25.00
11 thru 24 Ph(c) . . . . @15.00
25 . . . . 12.00
26 . . . . 12.00
27 Ph(c) 15.00
28 . . . . 12.00
29 Ph(c) 15.00
30 . . . . 12.00
31 JB(c) 12.00
32 thru 41 . . . . @12.00
42 MB(c) 12.00

43 thru 47 . . . . @12.00
48 1st Edition Under Code,
    Oct.'55 . . . . 12.00

LOVE DIARY
**Quality Comics Group
September, 1949**

1 BWa(c) 125.00

LOVE LESSONS
**Harvey Publications
October, 1949**

1 . . . . 55.00
2 . . . . 25.00
3 Ph(c) 20.00
4 . . . . 20.00
5 June, 1950 . . . . 20.00

LOVE LETTERS
**Comic Magazines
(Quality Comics Group)
November, 1949**

1 PG,BWa(c) 110.00
2 PG,BWa(c) 100.00
3 PG 60.00
4 BWa 80.00
5 . . . . 20.00
6 . . . . 20.00
7 . . . . 20.00
8 . . . . 20.00
9 Ph(c) of Robert Mitchum . . . 30.00
10 . . . . 20.00
11 BWa 35.00
12 . . . . 15.00
13 . . . . 15.00
14 . . . . 15.00
15 . . . . 15.00
16 Ph(c) of Anthony Quinn . . . 18.00
17 BWa, Ph(c) of Jane Russell . 18.00
18 thru 30 . . . . @12.00
31 BWa 25.00
Becomes:

LOVE SECRETS
32 . . . . 32.00
33 . . . . 15.00
34 BWa 35.00
35 thru 39 . . . . @15.00
40 MB(c)1st Edition Under Code 25.00
41 thru 50 . . . . @12.00
50 MB 12.00
51 MB(c) 12.00
52 thru 56 . . . . @10.00

LOVELORN
**Best Syndicated/Michel Publ.
(American Comics Group)
August-September, 1949**

1 . . . . 65.00
2 . . . . 30.00
3 thru 10 . . . . @22.00
11 thru 17 . . . . @15.00
18 2pgs. MD-a 15.00
19 . . . . 12.00
20 . . . . 12.00
21 Prostitution Story 30.00
22 thru 50 . . . . @12.00
51 July, 1954 3-D 75.00
Becomes:

CONFESSIONS OF LOVELORN
52 3-D 100.00
53 . . . . 30.00

All comics prices listed are for *Near Mint* condition.

54 3-D	100.00
55	20.00
56 Communist Story	35.00
57 Comics Code	15.00
58 thru 90	@15.00
91 AW	35.00
92 thru 105	@10.00
106 P(c)	10.00
107 P(c)	10.00
108 thru 114	@10.00

LOVE MEMORIES
Fawcett Publications
Autumn, 1949

1 Ph(c)	50.00
2 Ph(c)	25.00
3 Ph(c)	25.00
4 Ph(c)	25.00

LOVE MYSTERY
Fawcett Publications
June, 1950

1 GE, Ph(c)	125.00
2 GE, Ph(c)	90.00
3 GE & BP, Ph(c); October, 1950	90.00

Love Problems & Advice #3
© McCombs/Harvey Publ.

LOVE PROBLEMS AND ADVICE ILLUSTRATED
McCombs/Harvey Publications
Home Comics
June, 1949

1 BP	55.00
2 BP	30.00
3	20.00
4	20.00
5 L. Elias(c)	20.00
6	18.00
7 BP	18.00
8 BP	18.00
9 BP	18.00
10 BP	18.00
11 BP	15.00
12 BP	15.00
13 BP	15.00
14 BP	15.00
15	15.00

16	15.00
17 thru 23 BP	@15.00
24 BP, Rape Scene	20.00
25 BP	12.00
26	12.00
27	12.00
28 BP	12.00
29 BP	12.00
30	12.00
31	12.00
32 Comics Code	8.00
33 BP	8.00
34	8.00
35	8.00
36	8.00
37	8.00
38 S&K (c)	8.00
39	8.00
40 BP	8.00
41 BP	8.00
42	8.00
43	8.00
44 March, 1957	8.00

LOVERS LANE
Lev Gleason Publications
October, 1949

1 CBi (c),FG-a	50.00
2 P(c)	35.00
3 P(c)	18.00
4 P(c)	18.00
5 P(c)	18.00
6 GT,P(c), ...	18.00
7 P(c), ...	18.00
8 P(c), ...	18.00
9 P(c), ...	18.00
10 P(c)	18.00
11 thru 19 P(c)	@15.00
20 Ph(c); FF 1 page Ad, ...	15.00
21 Ph(c)	10.00
22 Ph(c)	10.00
23	10.00
24	10.00
25	10.00
26 Ph(c)	10.00
27 Ph(c)	10.00
28 Ph(c)	10.00
29 thru 38	@10.00
39 Story Narrated by	
Frank Sinatra	25.00
40	9.00
41 June, 1954	9.00

LOVE SCANDALS
Comic Magazines
(Quality Comics Group)
February, 1950

1 BW(c)&a	120.00
2 PG-a, Ph(c)	40.00
3 PG-a, Ph(c)	40.00
4 BWa(c)&a 18Pgs.; GFx-a ..	100.00
5 Ph(c), October, 1950	40.00

LOVE STORIES OF MARY WORTH
Harvey Publications
September, 1949

1 Newspaper Reprints	35.00
2 Newspaper Reprints	25.00
3 Newspaper Reprints	20.00
4 Newspaper Reprints, ...	20.00
5 May, 1950	20.00

LUCKY COMICS
Consolidated Magazines
January, 1944

1 Lucky Star	85.00
2 Henry C. Kiefer(c)	50.00
3	50.00
4	50.00
5 Summer, 1946,Devil(c)	50.00

LUCKY DUCK
Standard Comics
(Literary Enterprises)
January, 1953

5 IS (c)&a	35.00
6 IS (c)&a	25.00
7 IS (c)&a	25.00
8 IS (c)&a, September, 1953 ..	25.00

LUCKY FIGHTS IT THROUGH
Educational Comics
1949

N# HK-a, V.D. Prevention ..	1300.00

LUCKY "7" COMICS
Howard Publications
1944

1 Bondage(c) Pioneer	150.00

LUCKY STAR
Nationwide Publications
1950

1 JDa,B:52 pages western ...	65.00
2 JDa	40.00
3 JDa	40.00
4 JDa	35.00
5 JDa	35.00
6 JDa	35.00
7 JDa	35.00
8 thru 13	@25.00
14 1955,E:52 pages western ..	25.00

LUCY, THE REAL GONE GAL
St. John Publishing Co.
June, 1953

1 Negligee Panels,Teenage ...	65.00
2	35.00
3 MD-a	25.00
4 February, 1954	22.00
Becomes:	

MEET MISS PEPPER
St. John Publishing Co.
April, 1954

5 JKu-a	100.00
6 JKu (c)&a, June,1954	90.00

MAD
E.C. Comics
October-November, 1952

1 JSe,HK(c),JDa,WW	3,500.00
2 JSe,JDa(c),JDa,WW	800.00
3 JSe,HK(c),JDa,WW	550.00
4 JSe,HK(c),JDa-Flob Was	
A Slob,JDa,WW	550.00
5 JSe,BE©.JDa,WW	800.00
6 JSe,HK(c),Jda,WW	500.00
7 HK(c),JDa,WW	500.00
8 HK(c),JDa,WW	500.00
9 JSe,HK(c),JDa,WW	500.00
10 JSe,HK(c),JDa,WW	500.00

All comics prices listed are for *Near Mint* condition.

11 BW,BW(c),JDa,WW,Life(c) . 500.00
12 BK,JDa,WW 400.00
13 HK(c),JDa,WW,Red(c) 400.00
14 RH,HK(c),JDa,WW,
   Mona Lisa(c) 400.00
15 JDa,WW,Alice in
   Wonderland(c) 400.00
16 HK(c),JDa,WW,Newspaper(c) 400.00
17 BK,BW,JDa,WW 400.00
18 HK(c),JDa,WW 400.00
19 JDa,WW,Racing Form(c) . . 300.00
20 JDa,WW,Composition(c) . . . 300.00

LOOK GANG! ANOTHER SURPRISE! IN
THIS ISSUE...YOU DRAW THE COVER!

Mad #18 © E.C. Comics

21 JDa,WW,1st A.E.Neuman(c) 300.00
22 BE,JDa,WW,Picasso(c) . . . 300.00
23 Last Comic Format Edition,
   JDa,WW Think(c) 300.00
24 BK,WW, HK Logo & Border;
   1st Magazine Format 650.00
25 WW, Al Jaffee Sterts As Reg. 275.00
26 BK,WW,WW(c) 250.00
27 WWa,RH,JDa(c) 225.00
28 WW,BE(c),RH Back(c) 200.00
29 JKa,BW,WW,WW(c);
   1st Don Martin Artwork 200.00
30 BE,WW,RC; 1st A.E.
   Neuman(c) By Mingo 275.00
31 JDa,WW,BW,Mingo(c) 150.00
32 MD,JO 1st as reg.;Mingo(c);
   WW-Back(c) 150.00
33 WWa,Mingo(c);JO-Back(c) . 150.00
34 WWa,Mingo(c);1st Berg
   as Reg. 125.00
35 WW,RC,Mingo Wraparound(c)125.00
36 WW,BW,Mingo(c),JO,MD . . . 80.00
37 WW,Mingo(c)JO,MD 80.00
38 WW,JO,MD 75.00
39 WW,JO,MD 75.00
40 WW,BW,JO,MD 75.00
41 WW,JO,MD 60.00
42 WW,JO,MD 60.00
43 WW,JO,MD 60.00
44 WW,JO,MD 60.00
45 WW,JO,MD 60.00
46 JO,MD 60.00
47 JO,MD 60.00
48 JO,MD 60.00
49 JO,MD 60.00
50 JO,MD 60.00
51 JO,MD 55.00

52 JO,MD 55.00
53 JO,MD 55.00
54 JO,MD 55.00
55 JO,MD 55.00
56 JO,MD 50.00
57 JO,MD 50.00
58 JO,MD 50.00
59 WW,JO,MD 55.00
60 JO,MD 50.00
61 JO,MD 45.00
62 JO,MD 45.00
63 JO,MD 45.00
64 JO,MD 45.00
65 JO,MD 45.00
66 JO,MD 40.00
67 JO,MD 40.00
68 Don Martin(c),JO,MD 40.00
69 JO,MD 40.00
70 JO,MD 40.00
71 JO,MD 40.00
72 JO,MD 40.00
73 JO,MD 40.00
74 JO,MD 40.00
75 Mingo(c),JO,MD 35.00
76 Mingo(c),SA,JO,MD 35.00
77 Mingo(c),SA,JO,MD 35.00
78 Mingo(c),SA,JO,MD 35.00
79 Mingo(c),SA,JO,MD 35.00
80 Mingo(c),SA,JO,MD 35.00
81 Mingo(c),SA,JO,MD 35.00
82 BW,Mingo(c),SA,JO,MD 35.00
83 Mingo(c),SA,JO,MD 35.00
84 Mingo(c),SA,JO,MD 35.00
85 Mingo(c)SA,JO,MD 35.00
86 Mingo(c);1st Fold-in Back(c),
   SA,JO,MD 35.00
87 Mingo(c),JO,MD 30.00
88 Mingo(c),JO,MD 30.00
89 WK,Mingo(c),JO,MD 35.00
90 Mingo(c); FF-Back(c),JO,MD . 30.00
91 Mingo(c),JO,MD 25.00
92 Mingo(c),JO,MD 25.00
93 Mingo(c),JO,MD 25.00
94 Mingo(c),JO,MD 25.00
95 Mingo(c),JO,MD 25.00
96 Mingo(c),JO,MD 25.00
97 Mingo(c),JO,MD 25.00
98 Mingo(c),JO,MD 25.00
99 JDa,Mingo(c),JO,MD 38.00
100 Mingo(c),JO,MD 25.00
101 Infinity(c) by Mingo,JO,MD . 20.00
102 Mingo(c)JO,MD 20.00
103 Mingo(c)JO,MD 20.00
104 Mingo(c)JO,MD 20.00
105 Mingo(c);Batman TV Spoof
   ,JO,MD 20.00
106 Mingo(c);FF-Back(c),JO,MD 25.00
107 Mingo(c),JO,MD 20.00
108 Mingo(c),JO,MD 20.00
109 Mingo(c),JO,MD 20.00
110 Mingo(c),JO,MD 20.00
111 Mingo(c),JO,MD 20.00
112 JO,MD 20.00
113 JO,MD 20.00
114 JO,MD 20.00
115 JO,MD 20.00
116 JO,MD 20.00
117 JO,MD 20.00
118 JO,MD 20.00
119 JO,MD 20.00
120 JO,MD 20.00
121 Beatles,JO,MD 25.00
122 MD & Mingo(c),JO,MD,
   Reagan 20.00
123 JO,MD 15.00

124 JO,MD 15.00
125 JO,MD 15.00
126 JO,MD 15.00
127 JO,MD 15.00
128 Last JO;MD. 15.00
129 MD 15.00
130 MD 15.00
131 MD 15.00
132 MD 15.00
133 MD 15.00
134 MD 15.00
135 JDa(c),MD 16.00
136 MD 12.00
137 BW,MD 12.00
138 MD 12.00
139 JDa(c),MD 13.00
140 thru 153 MD . . . . @11.00
154 Mineo(c),MD 11.00
155 . . . . 11.00
156 . . . . 11.00
157 . . . . 11.00
158 . . . . 11.00
159 . . . . 11.00
160 Mingo(c),JDa,AT 11.00
161 . . . . 10.00
162 Mingo(c),MD,AT 10.00
163 . . . . 10.00
164 Mingo,PaperMoon(c),AT,
   MD,SA 10.00
165 Don Martin(c),At,MD 10.00
166 . . . . 10.00
167 . . . . 10.00
168 Mingo(c),AT,MD 10.00
169 MD(c) 10.00
170 . . . . 10.00
171 Mingo(c) 8.00
172 Mingo(c) 8.00
173 JDa(c) 8.00
174 . . . . 8.00
175 . . . . 8.00
176 MD(c) 8.00
177 . . . . 8.00
178 JDa(c) 8.00
179 . . . . 8.00
180 Jaws(c),SA,MD,JDA,AT . . . 8.00
181 G.Washington(c),JDa 8.00
182 . . . . 8.00
183 Mingo(c),AT,SA,MD 8.00
184 Mingo(c),Md,AT 8.00
185 . . . . 8.00
186 Star Trek Spoof 10.00
187 . . . . 8.00
188 . . . . 8.00
189 . . . . 8.00
190 . . . . 8.00
191 Clark(c),JDa,MD,AT 8.00
192 . . . . 8.00
193 Charlies Angels(c),
   Rickart,JDa,SA,MD 8.00
194 Rocky(c),Rickart,AT,MD 8.00
195 . . . . 8.00
196 Star Wars Spoof,
   Rickart,AT,JDa 15.00
197 . . . . 8.00
198 UPC(c),AT,MD 8.00
199 Jaffee(c),AT,JDa,SA,MD 8.00
200 Rickart(c),Close Encounters 10.00
201 Rickart(c),Sat.Night Fever . 4.50
202 . . . . 4.50
203 Star Wars Spoof,Rickart(c) . 6.00
204 Hulk TV Spoof,JawsII(c) 5.00
205 Rickart(c),Grease 4.50
206 Mingo,(c),AT,JDa,Md 4.50
207 Jones(c),Animal House(c) . . . 4.50
208 Superman Movie Spoof,

Rickart(c)	5.00
209 Mingo(c),AT,MD	4.50
210 Mingo,Lawn Mower,AT, JDa,MD	4.50
211 Mingo(c)	4.50
212 Jda(c),AT,MD	5.00
213 JDa(c),SA,AT,JDa	5.00
214	4.00
215 Jones(c),MD,AT,JDa	4.00
216	4.00
217 Jaffee(c),For Pres,AT,MD	4.00
218 Martin(c),AT,MD	4.00
219 thru 250	@4.00
251 thru 260	@3.50
261 thru 299	@3.00
300 thru 303	5.00
304 thru 330	2.00

Magic Comics #35
© David McKay Publications

MAGIC COMICS
David McKay Publications
August, 1939

1 Mandrake the Magician, Henry,Popeye,Blondie, Barney Baxter,Secret Agent X-9, Bunky,Henry on(c)	1,350.00
2 Henry on(c)	500.00
3 Henry on(c)	400.00
4 Henry on(c),Mandrake-Logo	325.00
5 Henry on(c),Mandrake-Logo	275.00
6 Henry on(c),Mandrake-Logo	275.00
7 Henry on(c),Mandrake-Logo	275.00
8 B:Inspector Wade,Tippie	225.00
9 Henry-Mandrake Interact(c)	225.00
10 Henry-Mandrake Interact(c)	225.00
11 Henry-Mandrake Interact(c)	200.00
12 Mandrake on(c)	200.00
13 Mandrake on(c)	200.00
14 Mandrake on(c)	200.00
15 Mandrake on(c)	200.00
16 Mandrake on(c)	200.00
17 B:Lone Ranger	225.00
18 Mandrake/Robot on(c)	200.00
19 Mandrake on(c)	200.00
20 Mandrake on(c)	150.00
21 Mandrake on(c)	150.00
22 Mandrake on(c)	150.00
23 Mandrake on(c)	150.00
24 Mandrake on(c)	150.00
25 B:Blondie; Mandrake in Logo for Duration	150.00
26 Blondie (c)	100.00
27 Blondie (c); High School Heroes	100.00
28 Blondie (c); High School Heroes	100.00
29 Blondie (c); High School Heroes	100.00
30 Blondie (c)	100.00
31 Blondie(c);High School Sports Page	85.00
32 Blondie (c);Secret Agent X-9	85.00
33 C. Knight's-Romance of Flying	85.00
34 ClaytonKnight's-War in the Air	85.00
35 Blondie (c)	85.00
36 July'42; Patriotic-(c)	90.00
37 Blondie (c)	85.00
38 ClaytonKnight's-Flying Tigers	85.00
39 Blondie (c)	85.00
40 Jimmie Doolittle Bombs Tokyo	85.00
41 How German Became British Censor	75.00
42 Joe Musial's-Dollar-a-Dither	75.00
43 Clayton Knight's-War in the Air	75.00
44 Flying Fortress in Action	75.00
45 Clayton Knight's-Gremlins	75.00
46 Adventures of Aladdin Jr.	75.00
47 Secret Agent X-9	75.00
48 General Arnold U.S.A.F.	75.00
49 Joe Musial's-Dollar-a-Dither	75.00
50 The Lone Ranger	75.00

Magic Comics #78
© David McKay Publications

51 Joe Musial's-Dollar-a-Dither	65.00
52 C. Knights-Heroes on Wings	65.00
53 C. Knights-Heroes on Wings	65.00
54 High School Heroes	65.00
55 Blondie (c)	70.00
56 High School Heroes	65.00
57 Joe Musial's-Dollar-a-Dither	65.00
58 Private Breger Abroad	65.00
59	65.00
60	65.00
61 Joe Musial's-Dollar-a-Dither	45.00
62	45.00
63 B:Buz Sawyer, Naval Pilot	45.00
64 thru 70	@45.00
71 thru 80	@40.00

80 thru 90	@35.00
91 thru 99	@35.00
100	45.00
101 thru 108	@30.00
108 Flash Gordon	40.00
109 Flash Gordon	40.00
110 thru 113	@30.00
114 The Lone Ranger	30.00
115 thru 119	@30.00
120 Secret Agent X-9	35.00
121 Secret Agent X-9	35.00
122 Secret Agent X-9	35.00
123 Sec. Agent X-9;Nov-Dec.'49	35.00

MAJOR HOOPLE COMICS
Nedor Publications
1942

1 Mary Worth,Phantom Soldier; Buy War Bonds On(c)	200.00

MAJOR VICTORY COMICS
H. Clay Glover Svcs./ Harry A. Chestler
1944

1 O:Major Victory,I:Spider Woman	300.00
2 A: Dynamic Boy	200.00
3 A: Rocket Boy	200.00

MAN HUNT!
Magazine Enterprises
October, 1953

1 LbC,FG,OW(c);B:Red Fox, Undercover Girl, Space Ace	200.00
2 LbC,FG,OW(c); Electrocution(c)	185.00
3 LbC,FG,OW,OW(c)	150.00
4 LbC,FG,OW,OW(c)	150.00
5 LbC,FG,OW,OW(c)	135.00
6 LbC,OW,OW(c)	135.00
7 LbC,OW; E:Space Ace	120.00
8 LbC,OW,FG(c);B:Trail Colt	120.00
9 LbC,OW	120.00
10 LbC,OW,OW(c),GwI	120.00
11 LbC,FF,OW;B:The Duke, Scotland Yard	175.00
12 LbC,OW	90.00
13 LbC,FF,OW;Rep.Trail Colt #1	175.00
14 LbC,OW;Bondage, Hypo-(c);1953	135.00

MAN OF WAR
Comic Corp. of America (Centaur Publ.)
November, 1941

1 PG,PG(c);Flag(c);B:The Fire-Man,Man of War,The Sentinel, Liberty Guards,Vapoman	900.00
2 PG,PG(c);I: The Ferret	800.00

MAN O'MARS
Fiction House/ I.W. Enterprises
1953

1 MA, Space Rangers	200.00
1 MA, Rep. Space Rangers	40.00

All comics prices listed are for *Near Mint* condition.

MARCH OF COMICS
K.K. Publications/
Western Publ.
1946
(All were Giveaways)

N# WK back(c),Goldilocks	250.00
N# WK,How Santa got His Red Suit	250.00
N# WK,Our Gang	350.00
N# CB,Donald Duck; "Maharajah Donald"	6,500.00
5 Andy Panda	150.00
6 WK,Fairy Tales	200.00
7 Oswald the Lucky Rabbit	150.00
8 Mickey Mouse	550.00
9 Gloomey Bunny	75.00
10 Santa Claus	65.00
11 Santa Claus	50.00
12 Santa's Toys	50.00
13 Santa's Suprise	50.00
14 Santa's Kitchen	50.00
15 Hip-It-Ty Hop	75.00
16 Woody Woodpecker	150.00
17 Roy Rogers	175.00
18 Fairy Tales	90.00
19 Uncle Wiggily	75.00
20 CB,Donald Duck	3,750.00
21 Tom and Jerry	75.00
22 Andy Panda	65.00
23 Raggedy Ann and Andy	125.00
24 Felix the Cat; By Otto Messmer	175.00
25 Gene Autrey	175.00
26 Our Gang	175.00
27 Mickey Mouse	400.00
28 Gene Autry	150.00
29 Easter	30.00
30 Santa	25.00
31 Santa	25.00
32 Does Not Exist	
33 A Christmas Carol	25.00
34 Woody Woodpecker	75.00
35 Roy Rogers	160.00
36 Felix the Cat	150.00
37 Popeye	120.00
38 Oswald the Lucky Rabbit	50.00
39 Gene Autry	150.00
40 Andy and Woody	50.00
41 CB,DonaldDuck,SouthSeas	3,600.00
42 Porky Pig	60.00
43 Henry	40.00
44 Bugs Bunny	75.00
45 Mickey Mouse	300.00
46 Tom and Jerry	70.00
47 Roy Rogers	135.00
48 Santa	20.00
49 Santa	20.00
50 Santa	20.00
51 Felix the Cat	125.00
52 Popeye	100.00
53 Oswald the Lucky Rabbit	50.00
54 Gene Autrey	150.00
55 Andy and Woody	45.00
56 CB back(c),Donald Duck	275.00
57 Porky Pig	55.00
58 Henry	30.00
59 Bugs Bunny	70.00
60 Mickey Mouse	275.00
61 Tom and Jerry	45.00
62 Roy Rogers	130.00
63 Santa	20.00
64 Santa	20.00
65 Jingle Bells	20.00
66 Popeye	85.00
67 Oswald the Lucky Rabbit	30.00
68 Roy Rogers	130.00
69 Donald Duck	250.00

70 Tom and Jerry	40.00
71 Porky Pig	55.00
72 Krazy Kat	50.00
73 Roy Rogers	100.00
74 Mickey Mouse	250.00
75 Bugs Bunny	65.00
76 Andy and Woody	35.00
77 Roy Rogers	100.00
78 Gene Autrey; last regular sized issue	100.00

March of Comics
© *K.K./Western Publ.*

79 Andy Panda,5"x7" format	25.00
80 Popeye	65.00
81 Oswald the Lucky Rabbit	22.00
82 Tarzan	125.00
83 Bugs Bunny	50.00
84 Henry	20.00
85 Woody Woodpecker	22.00
86 Roy Rogers	80.00
87 Krazy Kat	25.00
88 Tom and Jerry	20.00
89 Porky Pig	25.00
90 Gene Autrey	80.00
91 Roy Rogers and Santa	80.00
92 Christmas w/Santa	15.00
93 Woody Woodpecker	20.00
94 Indian Chief	50.00
95 Oswald the Lucky Rabbit	18.00
96 Popeye	55.00
97 Bugs Bunny	40.00
98 Tarzan,Lex Barker Ph(c)	120.00
99 Porky Pig	25.00
100 Roy Rogers	75.00
101 Henry	15.00
102 Tom Corbett,P(c)	120.00
103 Tom and Jerry	15.00
104 Gene Autrey	75.00
105 Roy Rogers	75.00
106 Santa's Helpers	15.00
107 Not Published	
108 Fun with Santa	15.00
109 Woody Woodpecker	18.00
110 Indian Chief	30.00
111 Oswald the Lucky Rabbit	15.00
112 Henry	12.00
113 Porky Pig	20.00
114 Tarzan,RsM	120.00
115 Bugs Bunny	40.00
116 Roy Rogers	65.00
117 Popeye	60.00
118 Flash Gordon, P(c)	120.00

119 Tom and Jerry	16.00
120 Gene Autrey	65.00
121 Roy Rogers	65.00
122 Santa's Suprise	12.00
123 Santa's Christmas Book	12.00
124 Woody Woodpecker	15.00
125 Tarzan, Lex Barker Ph(c)	100.00
126 Oswald the Lucky Rabbit	12.00
127 Indian Chief	20.00
128 Tom and Jerry	15.00
129 Henry	12.00
130 Porky Pig	25.00
131 Roy Rogers	65.00
132 Bugs Bunny	30.00
133 Flash Gordon,Ph(c)	90.00
134 Popeye	40.00
135 Gene Autrey	60.00
136 Roy Rogers	60.00
137 Gifts from Santa	10.00
138 Fun at Christmas	10.00
139 Woody Woodpecker	15.00
140 Indian Chief	25.00
141 Oswald the Lucky Rabbit	12.00
142 Flash Gordon	80.00
143 Porky Pig	20.00
144 RsM,Ph(c),Tarzan	100.00
145 Tom and Jerry	15.00
146 Roy Rogers,Ph(c)	60.00
147 Henry	10.00
148 Popeye	30.00
149 Bugs Bunny	25.00
150 Gene Autrey	60.00
151 Roy Rogers	60.00
152 The Night Before Christmas	10.00
153 Merry Christmas	10.00
154 Tom and Jerry	15.00
155 Tarzan,Ph(c)	100.00
156 Oswald the Lucky Rabbit	12.00
157 Popeye	25.00
158 Woody Woodpecker	15.00
159 Indian Chief	20.00
160 Bugs Bunny	20.00
161 Roy Rogers	50.00
162 Henry	10.00
163 Rin Tin Tin	32.00
164 Porky Pig	15.00
165 The Lone Ranger	50.00
166 Santa & His Reindeer	10.00
167 Roy Rogers and Santa	50.00
168 Santa Claus' Workshop	10.00
169 Popeye	25.00
170 Indian Chief	25.00
171 Oswald the Lucky Rabbit	20.00
172 Tarzan	80.00
173 Tom and Jerry	10.00
174 The Lone Ranger	50.00
175 Porky Pig	15.00
176 Roy Rogers	45.00
177 Woody Woodpecker	12.00
178 Henry	10.00
179 Bugs Bunny	20.00
180 Rin Tin Tin	25.00
181 Happy Holiday	8.00
182 Happi Tim	10.00
183 Welcome Santa	8.00
184 Woody Woodpecker	12.00
185 Tarzan, Ph(c)	75.00
186 Oswald the Lucky Rabbit	10.00
187 Indian Chief	20.00
188 Bugs Bunny	25.00
189 Henry	9.00
190 Tom and Jerry	11.00
191 Roy Rogers	45.00
192 Porky Pig	15.00
193 The Lone Ranger	50.00
194 Popeye	25.00
195 Rin Tin Tin	30.00
196 Not Published	

197 Santa is Coming 8.00	274 Popeye 20.00	351 Beep-Beep, The
198 Santa's Helper 8.00	275 Little Lulu 75.00	Road Runner 18.00
199 Huckleberry Hound 40.00	276 The Jetsons 100.00	352 Space Family Robinson . . . 50.00
200 Fury 30.00	277 Daffy Duck 12.00	353 Beep-Beep, The
201 Bugs Bunny 25.00	278 Lassie 18.00	Road Runner 18.00
202 Space Explorer 50.00	279 Yogi Bear 30.00	354 Tarzan 25.00
203 Woody Woodpecker 10.00	280 Ph(c),The Three Stooges . . 65.00	355 Little Lulu 25.00
204 Tarzan 55.00	281 Tom & Jerry 10.00	356 Scooby Doo, Where
205 Mighty Mouse 30.00	282 Mr. Ed 20.00	Are You 22.00
206 Roy Rogers,Ph(c) 45.00	283 Santa's Visit 7.00	357 Daffy Duck & Porky Pig 7.00
207 Tom and Jerry 10.00	284 Christmas Parade 7.00	358 Lassie 10.00
208 The Lone Ranger,Ph(c) 75.00	285 Astro Boy 200.00	359 Baby Snoots 10.00
209 Porky Pig 10.00	286 Tarzan 40.00	360 Ph(c), H.R. Pufnstuf 10.00
210 Lassie 30.00	287 Bugs Bunny 15.00	361 Tom & Jerry 7.00
211 Not Published	288 Daffy Duck 8.00	362 Smokey the Bear 7.00
212 Christmas Eve 8.00	289 The Flintstones 65.00	363 Bugs Bunny & Yosemite Sam 15.00
213 Here Comes Santa 8.00	290 Ph(c), Mr. Ed. 18.00	364 Ph(c), The Banana Splits . . . 7.00
214 Huckleberry Hound 35.00	291 Yogi Bear 25.00	365 Tom & Jerry 7.00
215 Hi Yo Silver 35.00	292 Ph(c), The Three Stooges . . 60.00	366 Tarzan 25.00
216 Rocky & His Friends 75.00	293 Little Lulu 55.00	367 Bugs Bunny & Porky Pig . . . 15.00
217 Lassie 20.00	294 Popeye 20.00	368 Scooby Doo 20.00
218 Porky Pig 15.00	295 Tom & Jerry 7.00	369 Little Lulu 20.00
219 Journey to the Sun 30.00	296 Lassie 15.00	370 Ph(c), Lassie 10.00
220 Bugs Bunny 20.00	297 Christmas Bells 7.00	371 Baby Snoots 7.00
221 Roy and Dale,Ph(c) 40.00	298 Santa's Sleigh 7.00	372 Smokey The Bear 7.00
222 Woody Woodpecker 10.00	299 The Flintstones 60.00	373 The Three Stooges 40.00
223 Tarzan 55.00	300 Tarzan 40.00	374 Wacky Witch 6.00
224 Tom and Jerry 10.00	301 Bugs Bunny 15.00	375 Beep-Beep & Daffy Duck . . . 8.00
225 The Lone Ranger 40.00	302 Ph(c), Laurel & Hardy 30.00	376 The Pink Panther 15.00
226 Christmas Treasury 8.00	303 Daffy Duck 7.00	377 Baby Snoots 7.00
227 Not Published	304 Ph(c), The Three Stooges . . 50.00	378 Turok, Son of Stone 85.00
228 Letters to Santa 8.00	305 Tom & Jerry 7.00	379 Heckle & Jeckle 5.00
229 The Flintstones 100.00	306 Ph(c), Daniel Boone 25.00	380 Bugs Bunny & Yosemite Sam 15.00
230 Lassie 20.00	307 Little Lulu 45.00	381 Lassie 7.00
231 Bugs Bunny 20.00	308 Ph(c), Lassie 15.00	382 Scooby Doo 18.00
232 The Three Stooges 75.00	309 Yogi Bear 20.00	383 Smokey the Bear 5.00
233 Bullwinkle 75.00	310 Ph(c) of Clayton Moore;	384 The Pink Panther 12.00
234 Smokey the Bear 20.00	The Lone Ranger 75.00	385 Little Lulu 15.00
235 Huckleberry Hound 35.00	311 Santa's Show 6.00	386 Wacky Witch 5.00
236 Roy and Dale 30.00	312 Christmas Album 6.00	387 Beep-Beep & Daffy Duck . . . 6.00
237 Mighty Mouse 18.00	313 Daffy Duck 7.00	388 Tom & Jerry 6.00
238 The Lone Ranger 40.00	314 Laurel & Hardy 25.00	389 Little Lulu 15.00
239 Woody Woodpecker 10.00	315 Bugs Bunny 15.00	390 The Pink Panther 12.00
240 Tarzan 45.00	316 The Three Stooges 50.00	391 Scooby Doo 18.00
241 Santa Claus Around the World 8.00	317 The Flintstones 30.00	392 Bugs Bunny & Yosemite Sam 15.00
242 Santa Toyland 8.00	318 Tarzan 35.00	393 Heckle & Jeckle 5.00
243 The Flintstones 100.00	319 Yogi Bear 20.00	394 Lassie 7.00
244 Mr.Ed,Ph(c) 25.00	320 Space Family Robinson . . . 60.00	395 Woodsy the Owl 5.00
245 Bugs Bunny 20.00	321 Tom & Jerry 7.00	396 Baby Snoots 5.00
246 Popeye 20.00	322 The Lone Ranger 35.00	397 Beep-Beep & Daffy Duck . . . 6.00
247 Mighty Mouse 20.00	323 Little Lulu 30.00	398 Wacky Witch 5.00
248 The Three Stooges 70.00	324 Ph(c), Lassie 12.00	399 Turok, Son of Stone 65.00
249 Woody Woodpecker 10.00	325 Fun With Santa 7.00	400 Tom & Jerry 5.00
250 Roy and Dale 30.00	326 Christmas Story 7.00	401 Baby Snoots 5.00
251 Little Lulu & Witch Hazel . . 100.00	327 The Flintstones 55.00	402 Daffy Duck 5.00
252 P(c),Tarzan 45.00	328 Space Family Robinson . . . 55.00	403 Bugs Bunny 10.00
253 Yogi Bear 25.00	329 Bugs Bunny 15.00	404 Space Family Robinson . . . 40.00
254 Lassie 20.00	330 The Jetsons 65.00	405 Cracky 5.00
255 Santa's Christmas List 8.00	331 Daffy Duck 7.00	406 Little Lulu 15.00
256 Christmas Party 8.00	332 Tarzan 30.00	407 Smokey the Bear 5.00
257 Mighty Mouse 20.00	333 Tom & Jerry 7.00	408 Turok, Son of Stone 45.00
258 The Sword in the Stone	334 Lassie 10.00	409 The Pink Panther 10.00
(Disney Version) 35.00	335 Little Lulu 25.00	410 Wacky Witch 5.00
259 Bugs Bunny 20.00	336 The Three Stooges 50.00	411 Lassie 7.00
260 Mr. Ed 20.00	337 Yogi Bear 20.00	412 New Terrytoons 3.00
261 Woody Woodpecker 10.00	338 The Lone Ranger 35.00	413 Daffy Duck 3.00
262 Tarzan 45.00	339 Not Published	414 Space Family Robinson . . . 35.00
263 Donald Duck 75.00	340 Here Comes Santa 7.00	415 Bugs Bunny 10.00
264 Popeye 20.00	341 The Flintstones 55.00	416 The Road Runner 5.00
265 Yogi Bear 20.00	342 Tarzan 30.00	417 Little Lulu 15.00
266 Lassie 18.00	343 Bugs Bunny 15.00	418 The Pink Panther 10.00
267 Little Lulu 90.00	344 Yogi Bear 23.00	419 Baby Snoots 3.00
268 The Three Stooges 60.00	345 Tom & Jerry 7.00	420 Woody Woodpecker 3.00
269 A Jolly Christmas 8.00	346 Lassie 10.00	421 Tweety & Sylvester 3.00
270 Santa's Little Helpers 8.00	347 Daffy Duck 7.00	422 Wacky Witch 3.00
271 The Flintstones 75.00	348 The Jetsons 55.00	423 Little Monsters 3.00
272 Tarzan 45.00	349 Little Lulu 25.00	424 Cracky 3.00
273 Bugs Bunny 20.00	350 The Lone Ranger 30.00	425 Daffy Duck 3.00

All comics prices listed are for *Near Mint* condition.

426 Underdog 18.00	10 . . . . 150.00	198 thru 200 . . . . @15.00
427 Little Lulu 10.00	11 thru 18 . . . . @125.00	201 . . . . 6.00
428 Bugs Bunny 5.00	19 I:Wilbur 125.00	202 . . . . 10.00
429 The Pink Panther 5.00	20 I:Mr.McNabbem 125.00	203 . . . . 6.00
430 The Road Runner 6.00	21 thru 25 . . . . @100.00	204 . . . . 10.00
431 Baby Snoots 3.00	26 rep.Four Color#110 . . . . . . 100.00	205 . . . . 10.00
432 Lassie 5.00	27 thru 29 . . . . @100.00	206 . . . . 6.00
433 Tweety & Sylvester 3.00	30 Christmas cover 100.00	
434 Wacky Witch 3.00	31 thru 34 . . . . @70.00	
435 New Terrytoons 3.00		**MARMADUKE MOUSE**
436 Cracky 3.00		**Quality Comics Group**
437 Daffy Duck 3.00		**(Arnold Publications)**
438 Underdog 10.00		**Spring, 1946**
439 Little Lulu 10.00		1 Funny Animal 65.00
440 Bugs Bunny 7.00		2 Funny Animal 32.00
441 The Pink Panther 5.00		3 thru 8 Funny Animal . . . . @25.00
442 The Road Runner 5.00		9 Funny Animal 22.00
443 Baby Snoots 3.00		10 Funny Animal 22.00
444 Tom & Jerry 3.00		11 thru 20 Funny Animal . . . . @20.00
445 Tweety & Sylvester 3.00		21 thru 30 Funny Animal . . . . @18.00
446 Wacky Witch 2.00		31 thru 40 Funny Animal . . . . @15.00
447 Mighty Mouse 3.00		41 thru 50 Funny Animal . . . . @12.00
448 Cracky 2.00		51 thru 65 Funny Animal . . . . @10.00
449 The Pink Panther 3.00		
450 Baby Snoots 3.00		**MARTIN KANE**
451 Tom & Jerry 3.00		**Hero Books**
452 Bugs Bunny 5.00		**(Fox Features syndicate)**
453 Popeye 3.00		**June, 1950**
454 Woody Woodpecker 3.00		1 WW,WW-(c) 150.00
455 The Road Runner 3.00		2 WW,JO, Auguat, 1950 . . . . 100.00
456 Little Lulu 3.00		

Marge's Little Lulu #9
© Dell Publishing Co.

457 Tweety & Sylvester 3.00	35 B:Mumday Story 70.00	
458 Wacky Witch 2.00	36 thru 38 . . . . @70.00	
459 Mighty Mouse 3.00	39 I:Witch Hazel 80.00	
460 Daffy Duck 3.00	40 Halloween Cover 70.00	
461 The Pink Panther 3.00	41 . . . . 65.00	
462 Baby Snoots 2.00	42 Christmas Cover 65.00	
463 Tom & Jerry 3.00	43 Skiing Cover 65.00	
464 Bugs Bunny 4.00	44 Valentines Day Cover 65.00	
465 Popeye 3.00	45 2nd A:Witch Hazel 65.00	
466 Woody Woodpecker 3.00	46 thru 60 . . . . @65.00	
467 Underdog 8.00	61 . . . . 50.00	
468 Little Lulu 4.00	62 . . . . 50.00	
469 Tweety & Sylvester 3.00	63 I:Chubby 50.00	
470 Wacky Witch 3.00	64 thru 67 . . . . @50.00	
471 Mighty Mouse 3.00	68 I:Professor Cleff 50.00	
472 Heckle & Jeckle 3.00	69 thru 77 . . . . @50.00	
473 The Pink Panther 3.00	78 Christmas Cover 50.00	
474 Baby Snoots 2.00	79 . . . . 50.00	
475 Little Lulu 3.00	80 . . . . 50.00	
476 Bugs Bunny 4.00	81 thru 89 . . . . @35.00	
477 Popeye 3.00	90 Christmas Cover 35.00	
478 Woody Woodpecker 3.00	91 thru 99 . . . . @35.00	
479 Underdog 7.00	100 . . . . 40.00	
480 Tom & Jerry 8.00	101 thru 122 . . . . @30.00	
481 Tweety & Sylvster 3.00	123 I:Fifi 30.00	
482 Wacky Witch 3.00	124 thru 164 . . . . @25.00	
483 Mighty Mouse 3.00	165 giant sized 40.00	
484 Heckle & Jeckle 3.00	166 giant sized 40.00	

Marvel Family #18
© Fawcett Publications

485 Baby Snoots 3.00	167 thru 169 . . . . @20.00	**MARVEL FAMILY, THE**
486 The Pink Panther 3.00	170 . . . . 12.00	**Fawcett Publications**
487 Bugs Bunny 4.00	171 . . . . 10.00	**December, 1945**
488 April, 1982; Little Lulu 3.00	172 . . . . 15.00	1 O:Captain Marvel,Captain Marvel Jr.,
	173 . . . . 10.00	Mary Marvel,Uncle Marvel;
MARGE'S LITTLE LULU	174 . . . . 10.00	V:Black Adam 950.00
Dell Publishing Co.	175 . . . . 15.00	2 . . . . 450.00
1 B:Lulu's Diary 450.00	176 . . . . 15.00	3 . . . . 325.00
2 I:Gloria,Miss Feeny 250.00	177 . . . . 10.00	4 The Witch's Tale 275.00
3 . . . . 200.00	178 thru 196 . . . . @15.00	5 Civilization of a
4 . . . . 200.00	197 . . . . 10.00	Prehistoric Race 250.00
5 . . . . 200.00		6 . . . . 225.00
6 . . . . 150.00		7 The Rock of Eternity 200.00
7 I:Annie,X-Mas Cover 150.00		8 The Marvel Family
8 . . . . 150.00		Round Table 200.00
9 . . . . 150.00		9 V: The Last Vikings 200.00

10 V: The Sivana Family 200.00
11 V: The Well of Evil 165.00
12 V: The Iron Horseman 165.00
13 . . . . 165.00
14 Captain Marvel Invalid 165.00
15 V: Mr. Triangle 150.00
16 World's Mightiest Quarrell . . 150.00
17 . . . . 150.00
18 . . . . 150.00
19 V: The Monster Menace . . . 150.00
20 The Marvel Family Feud . . . 150.00
21 V: The Trio of Terror 125.00
22 V: The Triple Threat 125.00
23 March of Independence (c) . 135.00
24 V: The Fighting Xergos 125.00
25 Trial of the Marvel Family . . 125.00
26 V: Mr. Power 100.00
27 V: The Amoeba Men 100.00
28 . . . . 100.00
29 V: The Monarch of Money . 100.00
30 A:World's Greatest Magician 100.00
31 V:Sivana & The Great Hunger 90.00
32 The Marvel Family Goes
   Into Buisness 90.00
33 I: The Hermit Family 90.00
34 V: Sivana's Miniature Menace 90.00
35 V: The Berzerk Machines . . . 90.00
36 V: The Invaders From Infinity 90.00
37 V: The Earth Changer 90.00
38 V: Sivana's Instinct
   Exterminator Gun 90.00
39 The Legend of Atlantis 90.00
40 Seven Wonders of the
   Modern World 90.00
41 The Great Oxygen Theft 90.00
42 V: The Endless Menace 80.00
43 . . . . 80.00
44 V: The Rust That Menaced
   the World 80.00
45 The Hoax City 80.00
46 The Day Civilization Vanished 80.00
47 V: The Interplanetary Thieves 120.00
48 V: The Four Horsemen 80.00
49 ...Proves Human Hardness . . 80.00
50 The Speech Scrambler
   Machine 80.00
51 The Living Statues 80.00
52 The School of Witches 75.00
53 V: The Man Who Changed
   the World 75.00
54 . . . . 75.00
55 . . . . 75.00
56 The World's Mightiest Project 75.00
57 . . . . 75.00
58 The Triple Time Plot 75.00
59 . . . . 75.00
60 . . . . 75.00
61 . . . . 70.00
62 . . . . 70.00
63 V: The Pirate Planet 70.00
64 . . . . 70.00
65 . . . . 70.00
66 The Miracle Stone 70.00
67 . . . . 70.00
68 . . . . 70.00
69 V: The Menace of Old Age . . 70.00
70 V: The Crusade of Evil 70.00
71 . . . . 70.00
72 . . . . 70.00
73 . . . . 70.00
74 . . . . 70.00
75 The Great Space Struggle . . 70.00
76 . . . . 70.00
77 Anti-Communist 125.00
78 V: The Red Vulture 70.00

79 . . . . 70.00
80 . . . . 70.00
81 . . . . 70.00
82 . . . . 70.00
83 V: The Flying Skull 70.00
84 thru 87 . . . . @70.00
88 Jokes of Jeopardy 70.00
89 And Then There Were None;
   January, 1954 . . . . 70.00

MARVELS OF SCIENCE
Charlton Comics
March, 1946
1 1st Charlton Book; Atomic
   Bomb Story 125.00
2 . . . . 75.00
3 . . . . 75.00

Marvels of Science #1
© Charlton Comics

4 President Truman(c); Jun.'6 . 75.00

MARY MARVEL COMICS
Fawcett Publications/
Charlton Comics
December, 1945
1 Intro: Mary Marvel 750.00
2 . . . . 350.00
3 . . . . 300.00
4 On a Leave of Absence . . . 275.00
5 Butterfly (c) 200.00
6 A:Freckles,Teenager of
   Mischief 200.00
7 The Kingdom Undersea . . . 200.00
8 Holiday Special Issue 200.00
9 Air Race (c) 175.00
10 A: Freckles 175.00
11 A: The Sad Dryads 125.00
12 Red Cross Appeal on(c) . . . 125.00
13 Keep the Homefires Burning 125.00
14 Meets Ghosts (c) 125.00
15 A: Freckles 125.00
16 The Jukebox Menace 100.00
17 Aunt Agatha's Adventures . . 100.00
18 . . . . 100.00
19 Witch (c) 100.00
20 . . . . 100.00
21 V: Dice Head 90.00
22 The Silver Slippers 90.00
23 The Pendulum Strikes 90.00

Mary Marvel #19 © Fawcett
Publications/Charlton Comics

24 V: The Nightowl 90.00
25 A: Freckles 90.00
26 A: Freckles Dressed As Clown 90.00
27 The Floating Oceanliner 90.00
28 September, 1948 . . . . 90.00
Becomes:
MONTE HALE WESTERN
29 Ph(c),B:Monte Hale & His
   Horse Pardner 275.00
30 Ph(c),B:Big Bow-Little
   Arrow; CCB,Captain Tootsie 175.00
31 Ph(c),Giant 125.00
32 Ph(c),Giant 125.00
33 Ph(c),Giant 125.00
34 Ph(c),E:Big Bow-Little
   Arrow;B:Gabby Hayes,Giant 125.00
35 Ph(c),Gabby Hayes, Giant . 125.00
36 Ph(c),Gabby Hayes, Giant . 125.00
37 Ph(c),Gabby Hayes 75.00
38 Ph(c),Gabby Hayes, Giant . 125.00
39 Ph(c);CCB,Captain Tootsie;
   Gabby Hayes, Giant 125.00
40 Ph(c),Gabby Hayes, Giant . 125.00
41 Ph(c),Gabby Hayes 75.00
42 Ph(c),Gabby Hayes, Giant . . 90.00
43 Ph(c),Gabby Hayes, Giant . . 90.00
44 Ph(c),Gabby Hayes, Giant . . 90.00
45 Ph(c),Gabby Hayes 75.00
46 Ph(c),Gabby Hayes, Giant . . 75.00
47 Ph(c),A:Big Bow-Little Arrow;
   Gabby Hayes, Giant 75.00
48 Ph(c),Gabby Hayes, Giant . . 75.00
49 Ph(c),Gabby Hayes 75.00
50 Ph(c),Gabby Hayes, Giant . . 75.00
51 Ph(c),Gabby Hayes, Giant . . 70.00
52 Ph(c),Gabby Hayes, Giant . . 70.00
53 Ph(c),A:Slim Pickens;
   Gabby Hayes 50.00
54 Ph(c),Gabby Hayes, Giant . . 70.00
55 Ph(c),Gabby Hayes, Giant . . 70.00
56 Ph(c),Gabby Hayes, Giant . . 70.00
57 Ph(c),Gabby Hayes 50.00
58 Ph(c),Gabby Hayes, Giant . . 60.00
59 Ph(c),Gabby Hayes, Giant . . 60.00
60 thru 79 Ph(c),Gabby Hayes @45.00
80 Ph(c),E: Gabby Hayes 45.00
81 Ph(c) 45.00

---

82 Final Ph(c), Last Fawcett
Edition 45.00
83 1st Charlton Edition, R:G.
Hayes Back B&W Ph(c) 45.00
84 .... 45.00
85 .... 42.00
86 E: Gabby Hayes 42.00
87 .... 42.00
88 January, 1956 .... 42.00

MASK COMICS
Rural Home Publications
February-March, 1945
1 LbC,LbC-(c), Evil (c) 800.00
2 LbC-(c),A:Black Rider,The
Collector The Boy Magician;
Apr-May'45, Devil (c) 500.00

MASKED MARVEL
Centaur Publications
September, 1940
1 I: The Masked Marvel 950.00
2 PG, ... 650.00
3 December, 1940 .... 600.00

MASKED RANGER
Premier Magazines
April, 1954
1 FF,O&B:The Masked Ranger,
Streak the Horse,The
Crimson Avenger 175.00
2 .... 50.00
3 .... 50.00
4 B: Jessie James,Billy the Kid,
Wild Bill Hickock,
Jim Bowie's Life Story 60.00
5 .... 60.00
6 .... 60.00
7 .... 60.00
8 .... 60.00
9 AT,E:All Features; A:Wyatt
Earp August, 1955 ..... 65.00

MASTER COMICS
Fawcett Publications
March, 1940
1-6 Oversized,7-Normal Format
1 O:Master Man; B:The Devil's
Dagger, El Carin-Master of
Magic, Rick O'Say, Morton
Murch, White Rajah, Shipwreck
Roberts, Frontier Marshall,
Mr. Clue, Streak Sloan .. 5,000.00
2 Master Man (c) 1,200.00
3 Master Man (c) Bondage ... 900.00
4 Master Man (c) 900.00
5 Master Man (c) 900.00
6 E: All Above Features 950.00
7 B:Bulletman,Zorro,The Mystery
Man, Lee Granger, Jungle
King,Buck Jones 1,500.00
8 B:The Red Gaucho,Captain
Venture, Planet Princess .. 800.00
9 Bulletman & Steam Roller .. 650.00
10 E: Lee Granger 650.00
11 O: Minute Man 1,450.00
12 Minute Man (c) 750.00
13 O: Bulletgirl; E: Red Gaucho1,000.00
14 B: The Companions Three . 650.00
15 MRa, Bulletman & Girl (c) .. 650.00
16 MRa, Minute Man (c) 650.00
17 B:MRa on Bulletman 650.00
18 MRa, ... 650.00

Master Comics #33
© Fawcett Publications

19 MRa, Bulletman & Girl (c) .. 650.00
20 MRa,C:Cap.Marvel-Bulletman 650.00
21 MRa-(c),Capt. Marvel in
Bulletman,I&O:CaptainNazi 3,000.00
22 MRa-(c),E:Mystery Man,Captain
Venture; Bondage(c);Capt.
Marvel Jr. X-Over In
Bulletman; A:Capt. Nazi .. 2,700.00
23 MRa,MRa(c),B:Capt.
Marvel Jr. V:Capt. Nazi ... 1,500.00
24 MRa,MRa(c),Death By Radio 575.00
25 MRa,MRa(c),The Jap
Invasion 575.00
26 MRa,MRa(c),Capt. Marvel Jr.
Avenges Pearl Harbor ... 600.00
27 MRa.MRa(c),V For Victory(c) 600.00
28 MRa,MRa(c)Liberty Bell(c) . 600.00
29 MRa,MRa(c),Hitler &
Hirohito(c) 600.00
30 MRa,MRa(c),Flag (c);Capt.
Marvel Jr, V: Capt. Nazi ... 575.00
31 MRa,MRa(c),E:Companions
Three,Capt.Marvel Jr,
V:Mad Dr. Macabre 400.00
32 MRa,MRa(c),E: Buck Jones;
CMJr Strikes Terror Castle . 400.00
33 MRa,MRa(c),B:Balbo the Boy
Magician, Hopalong Cassidy 400.00
34 MRa,MRa(c),Capt.Marvel Jr
V: Capt.Nazi 400.00
35 MRa,MRa(c),CMJr Defies
the Flame 400.00
36 MRa,MRa(c),Statue Of
Liberty(c) 400.00
37 MRa,MRa(c),CMJr Blasts
the Nazi Raiders 350.00
38 MRa,MRa(c),CMJr V:
the Japs 350.00
39 MRa,MRa(c),CMJr Blasts
Nazi Slave Ship 350.00
40 MRa,MRa(c),Flag (c) 350.00
41 MRa,MRa(c),Bulletman,Bulletgirl,
CMJr X-Over In Minuteman . 375.00
42 MRa,MRa(c),CMJr V: Hitler's
Dream Soldier 250.00
43 MRa(c),CMJr Battles For
Stalingrad 250.00
44 MRa(c),CMJr In Crystal City

of the Peculiar Penguins ... 250.00
45 MRa(c), ... 250.00
46 MRa(c) 250.00
47 MRa(c),A:Hitler; E: Balbo .. 275.00
48 MRa(c),I:Bulletboy;Capt.
Marvel A: in Minuteman ... 300.00
49 MRa(c),E: Hopalong Cassidy,
Minuteman 250.00
50 I&O: Radar,A:Capt. Marvel,
B:Nyoka the Jungle Girl ... 200.00
51 MRa(c),CMJr V: Japanese . 150.00
52 MRa(c),CMJr & Radar Pitch
War Stamps on (c) 150.00
53 CMJR V: Dr. Sivana 150.00
54 MRa(c),Capt.Marvel Jr
Your Pin-Up Buddy 150.00
55 .... 150.00
56 MRa(c) 125.00
57 CMJr V: Dr. Sivana 125.00
58 MRA,MRa(c), ... 125.00
59 MRa(c),A:The Upside
Downies 135.00
60 MRa(c) 135.00
61 CMJr Meets Uncle Marvel .. 135.00
62 Uncle Sam on (c) 150.00
63 W/ Radar (c) 100.00
64 W/ Radar (c) 100.00
65 .... 100.00
66 CMJr & Secret Of the Sphinx 100.00
67 Knight (c) 100.00
68 CMJr in the Range of
the Beasts 100.00
69 .... 100.00
70 .... 100.00
71 CMJr V:Man in the MetalMask 90.00
72 CMJr V: Sivana & The Whistle
That Wouldn't Stop 90.00
73 CMJr V: The Ghost of Evil .. 90.00
74 CMJr & The Fountain of Age 90.00
75 CMJr V: The Zombie Master . 90.00
76 .... 90.00
77 Pirate Treasure (c) 90.00
78 CMJr in Death on the Scenic
Railway 90.00
79 CMJr V: The Black Shroud .. 90.00
80 CMJr-The Land of Backwards 90.00
81 CMJr & The Voyage 'Round
the Horn 80.00
82 CMJr,IN,Death at the
Launching 80.00
83 .... 80.00
84 CMJr V: The Human Magnet 80.00
85 CMJr-Crime on the Campus 80.00
86 CMJr & The City of Machines 80.00
87 CMJr & The Root of Evil 80.00
88 CMJr V: The Wreckers;
B: Hopalong Cassidy 80.00
89 .... 80.00
90 CMJr V: The Caveman 80.00
91 CMJr V: The Blockmen 75.00
92 CMJr V: The Space Slavers . 75.00
93 BK,CMJr,V:The Growing Giant 90.00
94 E: Hopalong Cassidy 75.00
95 B: Tom Mix; CMJr Meets
the Skyhawk 75.00
96 CMJr Meets the Worlds
Mightiest Horse 75.00
97 CMJr Faces the Doubting
Thomas 75.00
98 KKK Type 75.00
99 Witch (c) 75.00
100 CMJr V: The Ghost Ship ... 75.00
101 thru 105 .... @70.00
106 E: Bulletman 70.00
107 CMJr Faces the Disappearance

---

of the Statue of Liberty 75.00
108 . . . . 60.00
109 . . . . 60.00
110 CMJr & The Hidden Death . 60.00
111 thru 122 . . . . @60.00
123 CMJr V: The Flying
   Desperado 60.00
124 . . . . 60.00
125 CMJr & The Bed of Mystery 60.00
126 thru 131 . . . . @60.00

Master Comics #113
© Fawcett Publications

132 V: Migs 65.00
133 E: Tom Mix; April, 1953 . . . 60.00

MD
E.C. Comics
April 1955-Jan. 1956
1 RC,GE,Grl,JO,JCr(c) 75.00
2 RC,GE,Grl,JO,JCr(c) 50.00
3 RC,GE,Grl,JO,JCr(c) 50.00
4 RC,GE,Grl,JO,JCr(c) 50.00
5 RC,GE,Grl,JO,JCr(c) 50.00

MEDAL OF HONOR COMICS
Stafford Publication
Spring, 1947
1 True Stories of Medal of Honor
  Recipants 55.00

MEET CORLISS ARCHER
Fox Features Syndicate
March, 1948
1 AF,AF(c), Teenage 250.00
2 AF(c) 200.00
3 . . . . 150.00
Becomes:
MY LIFE
4 JKa,AF, ... 175.00
5 JKa, ... 90.00
6 JKa,AF, ... 90.00
7 Watercolor&Ink Drawing on(c) 50.00
8 . . . . 35.00
9 . . . . 35.00
10 WW, July, 1950 . . . . 75.00

My Life #10 © Fox Features Syndicate

MEET MERTON
Toby Press
December, 1953
1 Dave Berg-a,Teen Stories . . . 30.00
2 Dave Berg-a 15.00
3 Dave Berg-a 12.00
4 Dave Berg-a; June, 1954 . . . 12.00

MEET THE NEW POST GAZETTE SUNDAY FUNNIES
Pitsberg Post Gazette
N# One Shot Insert F: Several
  Syndicated Characters in Stories
  Exclusive to This Edition . . . 550.00

MEL ALLEN SPORTS COMICS
Visual Editions
1949
1 GT 175.00
2 Lou Gehrig 90.00

MEN AGAINST CRIME
(see HAND OF FATE)

MERRY-GO-ROUND COMICS
**LaSalle/Croyden/
Rotary Litho.**
1944
1 LaSalle Publications Edition . 90.00
1a 1946, Croyden Edition 30.00
1b Sept-Oct.'47,Rotary Litho Ed. 40.00
2 . . . . 40.00

MERRY MOUSE
Avon Periodicals
June, 1953
1 (fa),F. Carin (c)&a 35.00
2 (fa),F. Carin (c)&a 20.00
3 (fa),F. Carin (c)&a 20.00
4 (fa),F. Carin (c)&a;Jan.'54 . . 20.00

METEOR COMICS
Croyden Publications
November, 1945
1 Captain Wizard & Baldy Bean 175.00

MICKEY FINN
**Eastern Color/
Columbia Comics Group**
1942
1 . . . . 175.00
2 . . . . 90.00
3 A: Charlie Chan 60.00
4 . . . . 40.00
5 thru 9 . . . . @25.00
10 thru 15 . . . . @20.00

(WALT DISNEY'S) MICKEY MOUSE
Dell Publishing Co.
December 1952
#1-#27 Dell Four Color
28 . . . . 25.00
29 . . . . 20.00
30 . . . . 20.00
31 . . . . 20.00
32 thru 34 . . . . @20.00
35 thru 50 . . . . @15.00
51 thru 73 . . . . @12.00
74 . . . . 15.00
75 thru 99 . . . . @12.00
100 thru 105 rep. . . . . @15.00
106 thru 120 . . . . @10.00
121 thru 130 . . . . @8.00
131 thru 146 . . . . @7.00
147 rep,Phantom Fires 10.00
148 rep. 10.00
149 thru 158 . . . . @6.00
159 rep. 10.00
160 thru 170 . . . . @5.00
171 thru 199 . . . . @2.50
200 rep. 3.00
201 thru 218 . . . . @2.50
See: Independent Color Comics

MICKEY MOUSE MAGAZINE
Kay Kamen
1 (1933) scarce 2,600.00
2 . . . . 850.00
3 thru 8 . . . . @750.00
9 . . . . 700.00

MICKEY MOUSE MAGAZINE
Kay Kamen
1 digest size (1933) 650.00
2 dairy give-away promo(1933) 325.00
3 dairy give-away promo(1934) 200.00
4 dairy give-away promo(1934) 200.00
5 dairy give-away promo(1934) 200.00
6 dairy give-away promo(1934) 200.00
7 dairy give-away promo(1934) 200.00
8 dairy give-away promo(1934) 200.00
9 dairy give-away promo(1934) 200.00
10 dairy give-awaypromo(1934) 200.00
11 dairy give-awaypromo(1934) 200.00
12 dairy give-away promo(1934) 200.00
Volume II
1 dairy give-away promo(1934) 165.00
2 dairy give-away promo(1934) 150.00
3 dairy give-away promo(1935) 150.00
4 dairy give-away promo(1935) 150.00
5 dairy give-away promo(1935) 150.00
6 dairy give-away promo(1935) 150.00
7 dairy give-away promo(1935) 150.00

---

8 dairy give-away promo(1935) 150.00
9 dairy give-away promo(1935) 150.00
10 dairy give-awaypromo(1935) 150.00
11 dairy give-awaypromo(1935) 150.00
12 dairy give-awaypromo(1935) 150.00

MICKEY MOUSE MAGAZINE
K.K. Pub./Westen Pub
1 (1935) 13¼"x10¼" 10,000.00
2 .... 1100.00
3 .... 600.00
4 .... 600.00
5 (1936) Donald Duck solo ... 600.00
6 Donald Duck editor 600.00
7 .... 600.00
8 Donald Duck solo 600.00
9 .... 600.00
10 .... 600.00
11 Mickey Mouse, editor 550.00
12 .... 550.00
Volume II
1 .... 550.00
2 .... 550.00
3 Christmas issue, 100pg ... 1,900.00
4 (1937) Roy Ranger adv.strip 500.00
5 Ted True strip 400.00
6 Mickey Mouse cut-outs 375.00
7 Mickey Mouse cut-outs 375.00
8 Mickey Mouse cut-outs 375.00
9 Mickey Mouse cut-outs 375.00
10 Full color 500.00
11 .... 400.00
12 Hiawatha 400.00

Mickey Mouse Magazine #30 (3/6)
© Kay Kamen

13 .... 400.00
Volume III
2 Big Bad Wolf (c) 375.00
3 First Snow White 750.00
4 (1938) Snow White 600.00
5 Snow White (c) 650.00
6 Snow White ends 500.00
7 7 Dwarfs Easter (c) 375.00
8 .... 350.00
9 Dopey(c) 350.00
10 Goofy(c) 350.00
11 Mickey Mouse Sheriff 350.00
12 A:Snow White 350.00
Volume IV

1 Practile Pig 350.00
2 I:Huey,Louis & Dewey(c) ... 350.00
3 Ferdinand the Bull 350.00
4 (1939),B:Spotty 325.00
5 Pluto solo 350.00
7 Ugly Duckling 325.00
7a Goofy & Wilber 350.00
8 Big Bad Wolf(c) 350.00
9 The Pointer 350.00
10 July 4th 400.00
11 .... 300.00
12 Donald's Penguin 400.00
Volume V
1 Black Pete 400.00
2 Goofy(c) 550.00
3 Pinochio 600.00
4 (1940) 350.00
5 Jimmy Crickett(c) 375.00
6 Tugboat Mickey 375.00
7 Huey, Louis & Dewey(c) ... 400.00
8 Figaro & Cleo 375.00
9 Donald(c),J.Crickett 450.00
10 July 4th 425.00
11 Mickey's Tailor 450.00
12 Change of format 3,000.00
{becomes:
Walt Disney Comics & Stories}

MICKEY MOUSE
Whitman
904 W.Disney's Mickey Mouse
and his friends (1934) 800.00
948 Disney'sMickeyMouse('34) 750.00

MIDGET COMICS
St. John Publishing Co.
February, 1950
1 MB(c),Fighting Indian Stories 70.00
2 April, 1950;Tex West-Cowboy
Marshall 40.00

MIGHTY ATOM, THE
(see PIXIES)

MIGHTY MIDGET
COMICS
Samuel E. Lowe & Co.
1942-43
4"x5" Format
1 Bulletman 75.00
2 Captain Marvel 75.00
3 Captain Marvel Jr. 70.00
4 Golden Arrow 70.00
5 Ibis the Invincible 70.00
6 Spy Smasher 70.00
7 Balbo, The Boy magician .. 25.00
8 Bulletman 60.00
9 Commando Yank 35.00
10 Dr. Voltz, The Human
Generator 30.00
11 Lance O'Casey 25.00
12 Leatherneck the Marine ... 25.00
13 Minute Man 40.00
14 Mister Q 25.00
15 Mr. Scarlet & Pinky 40.00
16 Pat Wilson & His
Flying Fortress 25.00
17 Phantom Eagle 35.00
18 State Trooper Stops Crime .. 25.00
19 Tornado Tom 35.00

MIGHTY MOUSE
Fall, 1946

[1st Series]
1 Terytoons Presents 625.00
2 .... 300.00
3 .... 200.00
4 Summer, 1947 .... 200.00

MIGHTY MOUSE
St. John Publishing
August, 1947
5 .... 200.00
6 thru 10 .... @100.00
11 thru 20 .... @60.00
21 thru 25 .... @50.00
26 thru 30 .... @40.00
31 thru 34 .... @30.00
35 Flying Saucer 40.00
36 .... 35.00
37 .... 35.00
38 thru 45 Giant 100 pgs .... @90.00
46 thru 66 .... @25.00
67 P(c),. 25.00
Pines
68 thru 81 Funny Animal .... @25.00
82 Infinity (c) 25.00
83 June, 1959 .... 25.00

MIGHTY MOUSE
ADVENTURE STORIES
St. John Publishing Co.
1953
N# 384 Pages,Rebound 300.00

MIKE BARNETT,
MAN AGAINST CRIME
Fawcett Publications
December, 1951
1 The Mint of Dionysosi 75.00
2 Mystery of the Blue Madonna 50.00
3 Revenge Holds the Torch ... 40.00
4 Special Delivery 40.00
5 Market For Morphine 50.00
6 October, 1952 .... 40.00

MILITARY COMICS
Comics Magazines
(Quality Comics Group)
August, 1941
1 JCo,CCu,FG,BP,WE(c),O:Blackhawk,
Miss America, Death Patrol,
Blue Tracer; B:X of the Underground, Yankee Eagle,Q-Boat,
Shot & Shell, Archie Atkins,
Loops & Banks 5,500.00
2 JCo,FG,BP,CCu,CCu(c),B:
Secret War News 1,600.00
3 JCo,FG,BP,AMc,CCu,CCu(c),
I&O:Chop Chop 1,300.00
4 FG,BP,AMc,CCu,CCu(c), . 1,000.00
5 FG,BP,AMc,CCu,CCu(c),
B: The Sniper 800.00
6 FG,BP,AMc,CCu,CCu(c) .. 700.00
7 FG,BP,AMc,CCu,CCu(c)
E:Death Patrol 700.00
8 FG,BP,AMc,CCu,CCu(c) .. 700.00
9 FG,BP,AMc,CCu,CCu(c),
B: The Phantom Clipper .. 700.00
10 FG,BP,CCu,AMc,WE(c) ... 800.00
11 FG,BP,CCu,AMc,
WE(c),Flag(c) 600.00
12 FG,BP,AMc,RC,RC(c) 750.00
13 FG,BP,AMc,RC,RC(c),E:X of
the Underground 550.00

14 FG,AMc,RC,RC(c),B:Private
Dogtag 550.00
15 FG,AMc,RC,RC(c), ... 550.00
16 FG,AMc,RC,RC(c),E:The
Phantom Clipper,Blue Tracer 500.00
17 FG,AMc,RC,RC(c),
B:P.T. Boat 500.00
18 FG,AMc,RC,RC(c), V:
The Thunderer 500.00
19 FG,RC,RC(c), V:King Cobra 500.00
20 GFx,RC,RC(c), Death Patrol 500.00
21 FG,GFx 450.00
22 FG,GFx 450.00
23 FG,GFx 450.00
24 FG,GFx,V: Man-Heavy
Glasses 450.00
25 FG,GFx,V: Wang The Tiger 450.00
26 FG,GFx,V: Skull 400.00
27 FG,JCo,R:The Death Patrol 400.00
28 FG,JCo, Dungeon of Doom . 400.00
29 FG,JCo,V: Xanukhara 400.00
30 FG,JCo,BWa,BWa(c),B.Hwk
V: Dr. Koro 400.00
31 FG,JCo,BWa,E:Death
Patrol; I: Captain Hitsu 400.00
32 JCo,A: Captain Hitsu 350.00
33 W/ Civil War Veteran 350.00
34 A: Eve Rice 350.00
35 Shipwreck Island 350.00
36 Cult of the Wailing Tiger ... 350.00
37 Pass of Bloody Peace 350.00
38 B.Hwk Faces Bloody Death 350.00
39 A: Kwan Yin 350.00
40 V: Ratru 325.00
41 W/ Chop Chop (c) 325.00
42 V: Jap Mata Hari 325.00
43 .... 325.00
Becomes:
MODERN COMICS
44 Duel of Honor 350.00
45 V: Sakyo the Madman ... 250.00
46 RC, Soldiers of Fortune .. 250.00
47 RC,PG,V:Count Hokoy 250.00
48 RC,PG,V:Pirates of Perool . 250.00
49 RC,PG,I:Fear,Lady
Adventuress 250.00
50 RC,PG 250.00
51 RC,PG, Ancient City of Evil . 225.00

Modern Comics #63
© Quality Comics Group

52 PG,BWa,V: The Vulture ... 225.00
53 PG,BWa,B: Torchy 275.00
54 PG,RC,RC/CCu,BWa 200.00
55 PG,RC,RC/CCu,BWa 200.00
56 PG,RC/CCu,BWa 200.00
57 PG,RC/CCu,BWa 200.00
58 PG,RC,RC/CCu,BWa,
V:The Grabber 200.00
59 PG,RC/CCu,BWa 200.00
60 PG,RC/CCu,BWa,RC(c),
V:Green Plague 200.00
61 PG,RC/CCu,BWa,RC(c) .. 200.00
62 PG,RC/CCu,BWa,RC(c) .. 200.00
63 PG,RC/CCu,BWa,RC(c) .. 175.00
64 PG,RC/CCu,BWa,RC(c) .. 175.00
65 PG,RC/CCu,BWa,RC(c) .. 175.00
66 PG,RC/CCu,BWa 175.00
67 PG,RC/CCu,BWa,RC(c) .. 175.00
68 PG,RC/CCu,BWa,RC(c);
I:Madame Butterfly 175.00
69 PG,RC/CCu,BWa,RC(c) ... 175.00
70 PG,RC/CCu,BWa,RC(c) ... 175.00
71 PG,RC/CCu,BWa,RC(c) ... 175.00
72 PG,RC/CCu,BWa,RC(c) ... 170.00
73 PG,RC/CCu,BWa,RC(c) ... 170.00
74 PG,RC/CCu,BWa,RC(c) ... 170.00
75 PG,RC/CCu,BWa,RC(c) ... 170.00
76 PG,RC/CCu,BWa,RC(c) ... 170.00
77 PG,RC/CCu,BWa,RC(c) ... 170.00
78 PG,RC/CCu,BWa,JCo,RC(c) 175.00
79 PG,RC/CCu,BWa,JCo,RC(c) 170.00
80 PG,RC/CCu,BWa,JCo,RC(c) 170.00
81 PG,RC/CCu,BWa,JCo,RC(c) 170.00
82 PG,RC/CCu,BWa,JCo,RC(c) 170.00
83 PG,RC/CCu,BWa,JCo,RC(c);
E: Private Dogtag 170.00
84 PG,RC/CCu,BWa,RC(c) ... 170.00
85 PG,RC/CCu,BWa,RC(c) ... 170.00
86 PG,RC/CCu,BWa,RC(c) ... 170.00
87 PG,RC/CCu,BWa,RC(c) ... 170.00
88 PG,RC/CCu,BWa,RC(c) ... 170.00
89 PG,RC/CCu,BWa,RC(c) ... 170.00
90 PG,RC/CCu,GFx,RC(c) ... 170.00
91 RC/CCu,GFx,RC(c) 170.00
92 RC/CCu,GFx,RC(c) 170.00
93 RC/CCu,GFx,RC(c) 170.00
94 RC/CCu,GFx,RC(c) 170.00
95 RC/CCu,GFx,RC(c) 170.00
96 RC/CCu,GFx,RC/CCu(c) ... 170.00
97 RC/CCu,GFx,RC/CCu(c) ... 170.00
98 RC/CCu,GFx,RC/CCu(c) ... 170.00
99 RC/CCu,GFx,JCo,RC/CCu(c) 170.00
100 GFx,JCo,RC/CCu(c) 170.00
101 GFx,JCo,RC/CCu(c) 170.00
102 GFx,JCo,WE,BWa,
RC/CCu(c) 200.00

MILT GROSS FUNNIES
Milt Gross, Inc.
August, 1947
1 Gag Oriented Caricature 50.00
2 Gag Oriented Caricature ... 45.00

MINUTE MAN
Fawcett Publications
Summer, 1941
1 V: The Nazis 850.00
2 V: The Mongol Horde 625.00
3 V: The Black Poet;Spr'42 .. 600.00

MIRACLE COMICS
Hillman Periodicals
February,1940
1 B:Sky Wizard,Master of Space,

Dash Dixon,Man of Might,Dusty
Doyle,Pinkie Parker, The Kid
Cop,K-7 Secret Agent,Scorpion
& Blandu,Jungle Queen ... 900.00
2 .... 450.00
3 B:Bill Colt,The Ghost Rider . 400.00
4 A:The Veiled Prophet,
Bullet Bob; Mar'41 .... 400.00

MISS CAIRO JONES
Croyden Publishers
1944
1 BO,Rep. Newspaper Strip . 125.00

MR. ANTHONY'S
LOVE CLINIC
Hillman Periodicals
1945
1 Ph(c) 60.00
2 .... 35.00
3 .... 30.00
4 .... 30.00
5 Ph(c),Apr/May'50 .... 30.00

MR. MUSCLES
(see THING, THE)

MISTER MYSTERY
Media Publ./SPM Publ./
Aragon Publ.
September, 1951
1 HK,RA,Horror 275.00
2 RA,RA(c) 200.00
3 RA(c) 200.00
4 Bondage(c) 225.00
5 Lingerie(c) 225.00
6 Bondage(c) 225.00
7 BW,Bondage(c);The Brain
Bats of Venus 475.00
8 Lingerie(c) 200.00
9 HN 175.00
10 .... 175.00
11 BW,Robot Woman 275.00
12 Flaming Object to Eye (c) .. 425.00
13 .... 125.00
14 .... 125.00
15 The Coffin & Medusa's Head 150.00
16 Bondage(c) 150.00
17 .... 125.00
18 BW,Bondage(c) 250.00

MISTER RISK
(see HAND OF FATE)

MISTER UNIVERSE
Mr. Publ./Media Publ./
Stanmore
July, 1951
1 .... 100.00
2 RA(c);Jungle That time Forgot 65.00
3 Marijuana Story 70.00
4 Mr. Universe Goes to War ... 35.00
5 Mr. Universe Goes to War;
April, 1952 .... 35.00

MODERN COMICS
(see MILITARY COMICS)

Mister Universe #1
© Mr. Publ./Media Publ.

MODERN LOVE
Tiny Tot Comics
(E.C. Comics)
June-July, 1949
1 Stolen Romance	....	350.00
2 JcR,AF(c),I Craved		
Excitement	....	300.00
3 AF(c);Our Families Clashed		250.00
4 AF(c);I Was a B Girl	......	350.00
5 AF(c);Saved From Shame	.	325.00
6 AF(c);The Love That		
Might Have Been	....	325.00
7 AF(c);They Won't Let Me		
Love Him	....	250.00
8 AF(c);Aug-Sept'50	....	250.00

MOE & SHMOE COMICS
O.S. Publishing Co.
Spring, 1948
1 Gag Oriented Caricature	...	35.00
2 Gag Oriented Caricature	...	25.00

MOLLY O'DAY
Avon Periodicals
February, 1945
1 GT;The Enchanted Dagger	.	275.00

MONKEYSHINES COMICS
Publ. Specialists/Ace/
Summer, 1944
1 (fa),Several Short Features	..	50.00
2 (fa),Same Format Throughout		
Entire Run	....	25.00
3 thru 16 Funny Animal	....	@20.00
Ace		
17 Funny Animal	....	20.00
18 thru 21	....	@15.00
Unity Publ.		
22 (fa)	....	15.00
23 (fa)	....	15.00
24 (fa),AFa,AFa(c)	....	15.00
25 (fa)	....	15.00
26 (fa)	....	15.00
27 (fa),July, 1949	....	15.00

MONSTER
Fiction House Magazines
1953
1 Dr. Drew	....	250.00
2	....	175.00

MONSTER CRIME COMICS
Hillman Periodicals
October, 1952
1 52 Pgs,15 Cent Cover Price	450.00

MONTE HALL WESTERN
(see MARY MARVEL COMICS)

MONTY HALL OF THE U.S. MARINES
Toby Press
August, 1951
1 B:Monty Hall,Pin-Up Pete;		
(All Issues)	....	50.00
2	....	30.00
3 thru 5	....	@25.00
6	....	20.00
7 The Fireball Express	......	20.00
8	....	20.00
9	....	20.00
10 The Vial of Death	.....	20.00
11 Monju Island Prison Break	..	20.00

MOON GIRL AND THE PRINCE
E.C. Comics
Autumn, 1947
1 JCr(c),O:Moon Girl	.....	575.00
2 JCr(c),Battle of the Congo	.	350.00
3	....	300.00
4 V: A Vampire	....	325.00
5 1st E.C. Horror-Zombie Terror	700.00
6	....	325.00
7 O:Star;The Fient Who		
Fights With Fire	....	325.00
8 True Crime Feature	....	325.00
Becomes:		

A MOON, A GIRL ...ROMANCE
9 AF,Grl,AF(c),C:Moon Girl;		
Spanking Panels	....	475.00
10 AF,Grl,WW,AF(c),Suspicious		
of His Intentions	....	400.00
11 AF,Grl,WW,AF(c),Hearts		
Along the Ski Trail	......	400.00
12 AF,Grl,AF(c),		
March-April, 1950	....	500.00

MOPSY
St. John Publishing Co.
February, 1948
1 Paper Dolls Enclosed	.....	100.00
2	....	55.00
3	....	50.00
4 Paper Dolls Enclosed	.....	50.00
5 Paper Dolls Enclosed	.....	50.00
6 Paper Dolls Enclosed	.....	50.00
7	....	40.00
8 Paper Dolls Enclosed;		
Lingerie Panels	....	45.00
9	....	40.00
10	....	40.00

Mopsy #3 © St. John's Publishing Co.
11	....	30.00
12	....	30.00
13 Paper Dolls Enclosed	......	35.00
14 thru 18	....	@30.00
19 Lingerie(c);Paper		
Dolls Enclosed	....	35.00

MORTIE
Magazine Publishers
December, 1952
1 ...Mazie's Friend	....	30.00
2	....	18.00
3	....	15.00

MOTION PICTURE COMICS
Fawcett Publications
November, 1950
101 Ph(c),Monte Hale's-		
Vanishing Westerner	.....	225.00
102 Ph(c),Rocky Lane's-Code		
of the Silver Sage	....	200.00
103 Ph(c),Rocky Lane's-Covered		
Wagon Raid	....	200.00
104 BP,Ph(c),Rocky Lane's-		
Vigilante Hideout	....	200.00
105 BP,Ph(c),Audie Murphy's-		
Red Badge of Courage	....	250.00
106 Ph(c),George Montgomery's-		
The Texas Rangers	.....	200.00
107 Ph(c),Rocky Lane's-Frisco		
Tornado	....	175.00
108 Ph(c),John Derek's-Mask		
of the Avenger	....	125.00
109 Ph(c),Rocky Lane's-Rough		
Rider of Durango	......	175.00
110 GE,Ph(c), When Worlds		
Collide	....	600.00
111 Ph(c),Lash LaRue's-The		
Vanishing Outpost	....	225.00
112 Ph(c),Jay Silverheels'-		
Brave Warrior	....	125.00
113 KS,Ph(c),George Murphy's-		
Walk East on Beacon	....	100.00
114 Ph(c),George Montgomery's-		
Cripple Creek;Jan, 1953	...	100.00

MOTION PICTURES FUNNIES WEEKLY
1st Funnies Incorporated
1939
1 BEv,1st Sub-Mariner ... 20,000.00
2 Cover Only 250.00
3 Cover Only 250.00
4 Cover Only 250.00

MOVIE CLASSICS
(NO #S)
Dell Publishing Co.
January, 1953
1 Around the World Under
  the Sea 20.00
2 Bambi 30.00
3 Battle of the Buldge 20.00
4 Ph(c),Beach Blanket Bingo .. 40.00
5 Ph(c),Bon Voyage 20.00
6 Castilian 25.00
7 Cat 15.00
8 Cheyenne Autumn 40.00
9 Ph(c),Circus World,
  John Wayne (c) 90.00
10 Ph(c),Countdown,J.Caan(c) . 25.00
11 Creature 35.00
12 Ph(c),David Ladd's Life Story 50.00
13 Ph(c),Die Monster Die 40.00
14 Dirty Dozen 35.00
15 Ph(c),Dr. Who & the Daleks 100.00
16 Dracula 35.00
17 El Dorado,J.WaynePh(c) ... 100.00
18 Ensign Pulver 20.00
19 Frankenstein 35.00
20 Ph(c),Great Race 35.00
21 B.LancasterPh(c) 35.00
22 Hatari 60.00
23 Horizontal Lieutenant 20.00
24 Ph(c) Mr. Limpet 20.00
25 Jack the Giant Killer 55.00
26 Ph(c),Jason and the Argonauts 55.00
27 Lancelot & Guinevere 50.00
28 Lawrence 50.00
29 Lion of Sparta 20.00
30 Mad Monster Party 50.00
31 Magic Sword 40.00
32 Ph(c),Masque of the
  Red Death 35.00
33 Maya 30.00
34 McHale's Navy 25.00
35 Ph(c) Merrills' Marauders ... 20.00
36 Ph(c),Mouse on the Moon ... 15.00
37 Mummy 35.00
38 Music Man 25.00
39 Ph(c),Naked Prey 45.00
40 Ph(c),Night of the Grizzly ... 30.00
41 None but the Brave 25.00
42 Ph(c),Operation Bikini 25.00
43 Operation Cross Bold 25.00
44 Prince & the Pauper 25.00
45 Raven,V.Price(c) 40.00
46 Ring of Bright Water 30.00
47 Runaway 15.00
48 Ph(c),Santa Claus Conquers
  the Martians 50.00
49 Ph(c),Six Black Horses 25.00
50 Sky Party 30.00
51 Smoky 20.00
52 Ph(c),Sons of Katie Elder .. 110.00
53 GE,Tales of Terror 25.00
54 Ph(c),3 Stooges meet
  Hercules 60.00
55 Tomb of Legeia 20.00
56 Treasure Island 20.00
57 Twice Told Tales(V.Price) ... 30.00
58 Two on a Guillotine 20.00
59 Valley of Gwangi 40.00
60 War Gods of the Deep 15.00
61 War Wagon (John Wayne) .. 75.00
62 Who's Minding the Mint 20.00
63 Wolfman 30.00
64 Ph(c),Zulu 25.00
65 .... 25.00

MOVIE COMICS
Fiction House Magazines
December, 1946
1 Big Town on(c) 300.00
2 MB,White Tie & Tails 200.00
3 MB,Andy Hardy Laugh Hit . 200.00
4 MB,Slave Girl 225.00

MOVIE LOVE
Famous Funnies Publications
February, 1950
1 Ph(c),Dick Powell(c) 60.00
2 Ph(c),Myrna Loy(c) 30.00
3 Ph(c),Cornell Wilde(c) 25.00
4 Ph(c),Paulette Goddard(c) .. 25.00
5 Ph(c),Joan Fontaine(c) 25.00
6 Ph(c),Ricardo Montalban(c) . 25.00
7 Ph(c),Fred Astaire(c) 30.00
8 AW,FF,Ph(c),Corinne
  Calvert(c) 200.00
9 Ph(c),John Lund(c) 25.00
10 Ph(c),Mona Freeman(c) ... 250.00
11 Ph(c),James Mason(c) 25.00
12 Ph(c),Jerry Lewis &
  Dean Martin(c) 35.00
13 Ph(c),Ronald Reagan(c) ... 125.00
14 Ph(c),Janet Leigh,Gene Kelly 35.00
15 Ph(c), ... 25.00
16 Ph(c),Angela Lansbury 50.00
17 FF,Ph(c),Leslie Caron 25.00
18 Ph(c),Cornel Wilde 25.00
19 Ph(c),John Derek 25.00
20 Ph(c),Debbie Reynolds ... 30.00
21 Ph(c),Patricia Medina 25.00
22 Ph(c),John Payne 25.00

MOVIE THRILLERS
Magazine Enterprises
1949
1 Ph(c),Burt Lancaster's-
  Rope of Sand 185.00

MR. MUSCLES
(see THING!, THE)

MUGGY-DOO, BOY CAT
Stanhall Publications
July, 1953
1 .... 28.00
2 .... 15.00
3 .... 15.00
4 January, 1954 .... 15.00

MURDER, INCORPORATED
Fox Features Incorporated
January, 1948
1 For Adults Only-on(c) 200.00
2 For Adults Only-on(c);Male
  Bondage(c),Electrocution sty 150.00
3 Dutch Schultz-Beast of Evil . 75.00
4 The Ray Hamilton Case,
  Lingerie(c) 85.00
5 thru 8 .... @85.00
9 Bathrobe (c) 90.00
9a Lingerie (c) 100.00
10 .... 75.00
11 .... 65.00
12 .... 65.00
13 .... 75.00
14 Bill Hale-King o/t Murderers . 65.00
15 .... 65.00
16(5),Second Series 50.00
17(2) 50.00
18(3), Bondage(c) w/Lingerie,
  August, 1951 .... 75.00

MURDEROUS GANGSTERS
Avon Periodicals/Realistic
July, 1951
1 WW,Pretty Boy Floyd,
  Leggs Diamond 200.00
2 WW,Baby Face Nelson,Mad
  Dog Esposito 150.00
3 P(c),Tony & Bud Fenner,
  Jed Hawkins 125.00
4 EK(c),Murder By Needle-
  Drug Story, June, 1952 .... 150.00

MUTINY
Aragon Magazines
October, 1954
1 AH(c),Stormy Tales of the
  Seven Seas 75.00
2 AH(c) 45.00
3 Bondage(c),February, '55 ... 50.00

MY CONFESSIONS
(see WESTERN TRUE CRIME)

MY DATE COMICS
Hillman Periodicals
July, 1944
1 S&K,S&K (c), Teenage 150.00
2 S&K,DB,S&K(c) 100.00
3 S&K,DB,S&K(c) 100.00
4 S&K,DB,S&K(c) 100.00

MY DESIRE
Fox Features Syndicate
October, 1949
1 Intimate Confessions 60.00
2 WW,They Called Me Wayward 60.00
3 I Hid My Lover 40.00
4 WW, April, 1950 .... 85.00

MY GREAT LOVE
Fox Features Syndicate
October, 1949
1 Reunion In a Shack 55.00
2 My Crazy Dreams 35.00
3 He Was Ashamed of Me ... 30.00
4 My Two Wedding Rings;Apr'50 40.00

MY INTIMATE AFFAIR
Fox Features Syndicate
March, 1950
1 I Sold My Love 550.00
2 I Married a Jailbird;May'50 .. 30.00

MY LIFE
(see MEET CORLISS ARCHER)

MY LOVE AFFAIR
Fox Features Syndicate
July, 1949
1 Truck Driver's Sweetheart . . 55.00
2 My Dreadful Secret 35.00
3 WW,I'll Make Him Marry Me . 80.00
4 WW,They Called Me Wild . . . 80.00
5 WW,Beauty Was My Bait . . . 80.00
6 WW,The Man Downstairs . . . 80.00

My Love Affair #1
© Fox Features Syndicate

MY LOVE MEMORIES
(see WOMEN OUTLAWS)

MY LOVE LIFE
(see TEGRA, JUNGLE EMPRESS)

MY LOVE STORY
Fox Features Syndicate
September, 1949
1 Men Gave Me Jewels 60.00
2 He Dared Me 40.00
3 WW,I Made Love a Plaything 85.00
4 WW,I Tried to Be Good 85.00

MY PAST CONFESSIONS
(see WESTERN THRILLERS)

MY PRIVATE LIFE
Fox Features Syndicate
February, 1950
16 My Friendship Club Affair . . . 45.00
17 My Guilty Kisses;April'50 . . . 45.00

MY SECRET
Superior Comics
August, 1949
1 True Love Stories 55.00
2 I Was Guilty of Being a
   Cheating Wife 35.00
3 Was I His Second Love?; . . . 35.00
Becomes:

My Private Life #16
© Fox Features Syndicate

OUR SECRET
4 JKa,She Loves Me,She Loves
   Me Not; November, 1949 . . . 50.00
5 . . . . 35.00
6 . . . . 35.00
7 How Do You Fall In Love? . . . 38.00
8 His Kiss Tore At My
   Heart; June, 1950 . . . . 35.00

MY SECRET AFFAIR
Hero Books
(Fox Features Syndicate)
December, 1949
1 WW,SHn,My Stormy
   Love Affair 100.00
2 WW,I Loved a Weakling 65.00
3 WW, April, 1950 . . . . 85.00

MY SECRET LIFE
Fox Features Syndicate
July, 1949
22 WW,I Loved More Than Once 50.00
23 . . . . 75.00
24 Love Was a Habit 30.00
25 . . . . 30.00
Becomes:

ROMEO TUBBS
26 WW,That Lovable Teen-ager 75.00

MY SECRET LOVE
(see PHANTOM LADY)

MY SECRET MARRIAGE
Superior Comics
May, 1953
1 I Was a Cheat 50.00
2 . . . . 25.00
3 We Couldn't Wait 15.00
4 thru 23 . . . . @15.00
24 1956 . . . . 15.00

MY SECRET ROMANCE

Hero Books
(Fox Features Syndicate)
January, 1950
1 WW,They Called Me 'That'
   Woman 85.00
2 WW,They Called Me Cheap . 75.00

MYSTERIES WEIRD AND STRANGE
Superior Comics/
Dynamic Publ.
May, 1953
1 The Stolen Brain 150.00
2 The Screaming Room,
   Atomic Bomb 100.00
3 The Avenging Corpse 60.00
4 Ghost on the Gallows 60.00
5 Horror a la Mode 60.00
6 Howling Horror 60.00
7 Demon in Disguise 60.00
8 The Devil's Birthmark 60.00
9 . . . . 60.00
10 . . . . 75.00
11 . . . . 60.00

MYSTERIOUS ADVENTURES
Story Comics
March, 1951
1 Wild Terror of the
   Vampire Flag 200.00
2 Terror of the Ghoul's Corpse 125.00
3 Terror of the Witche's Curse 100.00
4 The Little Coffin That Grew . 100.00
5 LC,Curse of the Jungle,
   Bondage(c) 125.00
6 LC,Ghostly Terror in the
   Cave 90.00
7 LC,Terror of the Ghostly
   Castle 150.00
8 Terror of the Flowers of Deat 150.00
9 The Ghostly Ghouls-
   Extreme Violence 125.00
10 Extreme Violence 100.00
11 The Trap of Terror 125.00
12 SHn,Vultures of Death-
   Extreme Violence 125.00
13 Extreme Violence 125.00
14 Horror of the Flame Thrower
   Extreme Violence 125.00
15 DW,Ghoul Crazy 150.00
16 Chilling Tales of Horror . . . 150.00
17 DW,Bride of the Dead 150.00
18 Extreme Violence 150.00
19 The Coffin 150.00
20 Horror o/t Avenging Corpse 150.00
21 Mother Ghoul's Nursery
   Tales, Bondage (c) 150.00
22 RA,Insane 100.00
23 RA,Extreme Violence 125.00
24 KS, ... 75.00
25 KS,August, 1955 . . . . 75.00

HORROR FROM THE TOMB
Premier Magazines
September, 1954
1 AT,GWb,The Corpse Returns 150.00
Becomes:

MYSTERIOUS STORIES
2 GWb(c),Eternal Life 135.00
3 GWb,The Witch Doctor . . . 100.00

---

4 That's the Spirit 85.00
5 King Barbarossa 85.00
6 GWb,Strangers in the Night . 100.00

Mysterious Stories #3
© Premier Magazines

7 KS,The Pipes of Pan;Dec'55 . 85.00

MYSTERIOUS TRAVELER COMICS
Trans-World Publications
November, 1948
1 BP,BP(c),Five Miles Down . 275.00

MYSTERY COMICS
William H. Wise & Co.
1944
1 AS(c),B:Brad Spencer-Wonderman, King of Futeria,The Magnet, Zudo-Jungle Boy,The Silver Knight 500.00
2 AS(c),Bondage (c) 300.00
3 AS(c),Robot(c),LanceLewis,B 250.00
4 AS(c),E:All Features, KKK Type(c) 250.00

MYSTERY MEN COMICS
Fox Features Syndicate
August, 1939
1 GT,DBr,LF(c),Bondage(c);I:Blue Beetle,Green Mask,Rex Dexter of Mars,Zanzibar,Lt.Drake,D-13 Secret Agent,Chen Chang, Wing Turner,Capt. Denny   2,400.00
2 GT,BP,DBr,LF(c), Rex Dexter (c) 900.00
3 LF(c) 750.00
4 LF(c),B:Captain Savage ... 700.00
5 GT,BP,LF(c),Green Mask (c) 550.00
6 GT,BP 500.00
7 GT,BP,Bondage(c), Blue Beetle(c) 525.00
8 GT,BP,LF(c),Bondage(c), Blue Beetle 525.00
9 GT,BP,DBr(c),B:The Moth .. 400.00
10 GT,BP,JSm(c),A:Wing Turner; Bondage(c) 425.00
11 GT,BP,JSm(c),I:The Domino 300.00
12 GT,BP,Rex Dexter (c) 275.00
13 GT,I:The Lynx & Blackie ... 300.00

Mystery Men Comics #11
© Fox Features Syndicate

14 GT,Male Bondage (c) 300.00
15 GT,Blue Beetle (c) 275.00
16 GT,Hypo(c),MaleBondage(c) 300.00
17 GT,BP,Blue Beetle (c) 275.00
18 GT,Blue Beetle (c) 275.00
19 GT,I&B:Miss X 325.00
20 GT,DBr,Blue Beetle (c) 250.00
21 GT,E:Miss X 250.00
22 GT,CCu(c),Blue Beetle (c) . 250.00
23 GT,Blue Beetle (c) 250.00
24 GT,BP,DBr, Blue Beetle (c) . 250.00
25 GT,Bondage(c); A:Private O'Hara 275.00
26 GT,Bondage(c);B:The Wraith 275.00
27 GT,Bondage(c),BlueBeetle(c) 275.00
28 GT,Bondage(c);Satan's Private Needlewoman 275.00
29 GT,Bondage(c),Blue Beetle (c) 275.00
30 Holiday of Death 250.00
31 Bondage(c);Feb'42 .... 275.00

MY STORY
(see ZAGO, JUNGLE PRINCE)

NATIONAL COMICS
Comics Magazines
(Quality Comics Group)
July, 1940
1 GT,HcK,LF(c),B:Uncle Sam,Wonder Boy,Merlin the Magician,Cyclone, Kid Patrol,Sally O'Neil-Police-woman, Pen Miller,Prop Powers, Paul Bunyan ... 2,400.00
2 WE,GT,HcK,LF&RC(c) ... 1,000.00
3 GT,HcK,WE&RC(c) 800.00
4 GT,HcK,LF&RC(c),E:Cyclone; Torpedo Islands of Death .. 650.00
5 GT,LF&RC(c),B:Quicksilver; O:Uncle Sam 700.00
6 GT,LF&RC(c) 600.00
7 GT,LF&RC(c) 600.00
8 GT,LF&RC(c) 600.00
9 JCo,LF&RC(c) 600.00
10 RC,JCo,LF&RC(c) 600.00
11 RC,JCo,LF&RC(c) 600.00
12 RC,JCo,LF&RC(c) 450.00

13 RC,JCo,LF,LF&RC(c) 500.00
14 RC,JCo,LF,PG,LF&RC(c) .. 500.00
15 RC,JCo,LF,PG,LF&RC(c) .. 500.00
16 RC,JCo,LF,PG,LF&RC(c) .. 500.00
17 RC,JCo,LF,PG,LF&RC(c) .. 350.00
18 JCo,LF,PG,LF&RC(c), Pearl Harbor 450.00
19 JCo,LF,PG,RC(c),The Black Fog Mystery 350.00
20 JCo,LF,PG,LF&RC(c) ... 350.00
21 LF,JCo,PG,LF(c) 350.00
22 JCo,LF,PG,FG,GFx,LF(c), E:Jack & Jill,Pen Miller, Paul Bunyan 350.00
23 JCo,PG,FG,GFx,AMc,LF & GFx(c),B:The Unknown, Destroyer 171 .... 450.00
24 JCo,PG,RC,AMc,FG, GFx,RC(c) 300.00
25 AMc,RC,JCo,PG,FG, GFx,RC(c) 300.00
26 AMc,Jco,RC,PG,RC(c), E:Prop Powers,WonderBoy . 300.00
27 JCo,AMc 300.00
28 JCo,AMc 300.00
29 JCo,O:The Unknown;U.Sam V:Dr. Dirge 325.00
30 JCo,RC(c) 300.00
31 JCo,RC(c) 275.00
32 JCo,RC(c) 275.00
33 JCo,GFx,RC(c),B:Chic Carter; U.Sam V:Boss Spring 275.00
34 JCo,GFx,U.Sam V:Big John Fales 275.00
35 JCo,GFx,E:Kid Patrol 175.00
36 JCo 175.00
37 JCo,FG,A:The Vagabond .. 175.00
38 JCo,FG,Boat of the Dead .. 175.00

National Comics #54
© Comics Mag./Quality Comics Group

39 JCo,FG,Hitler(c);U.Sam V:The Black Market 200.00
40 JCo,FG,U.Sam V:The Syndicate of Crime 150.00
41 JCo,FG 150.00
42 JCo,FG,JCo(c),B:The Barker 125.00
43 JCo,FG,JCo(c) 125.00
44 JCo,FG 125.00
45 JCo,FG,E:Merlin the Magician 125.00
46 JCo,JCo(c),Murder is no Joke 125.00

47 JCo,JCo(c),E:Chic Carter .. 125.00
48 JCo,O:The Whistler 125.00
49 JCo,JCo(c),A Corpse
   for a Cannonball 125.00
50 JCo,JCo(c),V:Rocks Myzer 125.00
51 JCo,BWa,JCo(c),
   A:Sally O'Neil 175.00
52 JCo,A Carnival of Laughs .. 100.00
53 PG,V:Scramolo 100.00
54 PG,V:Raz-Ma-Taz 100.00
55 JCo,AMc,V:The Hawk 100.00
56 GFx,JCo,AMc,V:The Grifter . 100.00
57 GFX,JCo,AMc,V:Witch Doctor 100.00
58 GFz,JCo,AMc,Talking Animals 100.00
59 GFx,JCo,AMc,V:The Birdman 100.00
60 GFx,JCo,AMc,V:Big Ed Grew 100.00
61 GFx,AMc,Trouble Comes in
   Small Packages 75.00
62 GFx,AMc,V:Crocodile Man . 75.00
63 GFx,AMc,V:Bearded Lady ... 75.00
64 GFx,V:The Human Fly 75.00
65 GFx,GFx(c)V:The King 75.00
66 GFx,GFx(c)V:THe Man Who
   Hates the Circus 75.00
67 GFx,Gfx(c),A:Quicksilver;
   V:Ali Ben Riff Raff 75.00
68 GFx,GFx(c),V:Leo the LionMan 75.00
69 GFx,Gfx(c),A:Percy the
   Powerful 75.00
70 GFx,GFx(c),Barker Tires
   of the Big Top 75.00
71 PG,GFx(c),V:SpellbinderSmith 75.00
72 PG,GFx(c),The Oldest Man
   in the World 75.00
73 PG,GFx(c),V:A CountrySlicker 75.00
74 PG,GFx(c),V:Snake Oil Sam . 75.00
75 PG,GFx(c),Barker Breakes the
   Bank at Monte Marlo;Nov'49 . 75.00

NEBBS, THE
Dell Publishing Co.
1941
1 rep. 60.00

NEGRO ROMANCES
Fawcett Publications
June, 1950
1 GE,Ph(c), Love's Decoy ... 650.00
2 GE,Ph(c), A Tragic Vow ... 500.00
3 GE,Ph(c), My Love
   Betrayed Me 500.00
Charlton Comics
4 Rep.FawcettEd.#2;May,1955 400.00

NEW ROMANCES
Standard Comics
May, 1951
5 Ph(c), The Blame I Bore 45.00
6 Ph(c), No Wife Was I 25.00
7 Ph(c), My Runaway Heart,
   Ray Miland 22.00
8 Ph(c) 22.00
9 Ph(c) 22.00
10 ATh,Ph(c) 50.00
11 ATh,Ph(c) of Elizabeth Taylor 65.00
12 Ph(c) 15.00
13 Ph(c) 15.00
14 ATh,Ph(c) 35.00
15 Ph(c) 15.00
16 ATh,Ph(c) 35.00
17 Ath, ... 35.00
18 and 19 .... @15.00
20 GT, ... 25.00
21 April, 1954 .... 15.00

NICKEL COMICS
Dell Publishing Co.
1938
1 Bobby & Chip 400.00

NICKEL COMICS
Fawcett Publications
May, 1940
1 JaB(c),O&I: Bulletman ... 1,500.00
2 JaB(c), ... 600.00
3 JaB(c), ... 500.00
4 JaB(c), B: Red Gaucho ... 450.00
5 CCB(c),Bondage(c) 450.00
6 and 7 CCB(c) .... @425.00
8 CCB(c),August 23, 1940,
   World's Fair 450.00

NIGHTMARE
(see WEIRD HORRORS)

NIGHTMARE
Ziff-Davis Publishing Co.
1 EK,GT,P(c),The Corpse That
   Wouldn't Stay Dead 250.00
2 EK,P(c),Vampire Mermaid . 175.00
St. John Publishing Co.
3 EK,P(c),The Quivering Brain 150.00
4 P(c),1953 .... 125.00

NORTHWEST MOUNTIES
Jubilee Publications/
St. John Publ. Co.
October, 1948
1 MB,BLb(c),Rose of the Yukon 200.00
2 MB,BLb(c),A:Ventrilo 150.00
3 MB, Bondage(c) 170.00
4 MB(c),A:Blue Monk,July'49 . 165.00

NURSERY RHYMES
Ziff-Davis Publishing Co.
1950
1 How John Came Clean 75.00
2 The Old Woman Who
   Lived in a Shoe 50.00

NUTS!
Premere Comics Group
March, 1954
1 .... 125.00
2 .... 95.00
3 Mention of "Reefers" 100.00
4 .... 90.00
5 Captain Marvel Spoof;Nov.'54 90.00

NUTTY COMICS
Fawcett Publications
Winter, 1946
1 (fa),F:Capt. Kid,Richard Richard,
   Joe Miller...Among others .. 75.00

NUTTY LIFE
(see PHANTOM LADY)

NYOKA THE
JUNGLE GIRL
Fawcett Publications
Winter, 1945
1 Bondage(c);Partial Ph(c) of
   Kay Aldridge as Nyoka ... 325.00
2 .... 200.00

3 .... 175.00
4 Bondage(c) 175.00
5 Barbacosi Madness;
   Bondage(c) 175.00
6 .... 150.00
7 North Pole Jungle;Bondage(c) 165.00
8 Bondage(c) 165.00
9 .... 150.00
10 .... 150.00
11 Danger! Death! in an
   Unexplored Jungle 90.00
12 .... 90.00
13 The Human Leopards 90.00
14 The Mad Witch Doctor;
   Bondage(c) 125.00
15 Sacred Goat of Kristan ... 80.00
16 BK,The Vultures of Kalahari . 90.00
17 BK 90.00
18 BK,The Art of Murder 90.00
19 The Elephant Battle 90.00
20 Explosive Volcano Action ... 90.00
21 .... 65.00
22 The Weird Monsters 65.00
23 Danger in Duplicate 65.00
24 The Human Jaguar;
   Bondage(c) 80.00
25 Hand Colored Ph(c) 50.00
26 A Jungle Stampede 50.00
27 Adventure Laden 50.00
28 The Human Statues of
   the Jungle 50.00

Nyoka the Jungle Girl #5
© Fawcett Publications

29 Ph(c) 50.00
30 Ph(c) 50.00
31 thru 40 Ph(c) .... @40.00
41 thru 50 Ph(c) .... @30.00
51 thru 59 Ph(c) .... @25.00
60 Ph(c) 20.00
61 Ph(c),The Sacred Sword of
   the Jungle 20.00
62 & 63 Ph(c) .... @20.00
64 Ph(c), The Jungle Idol 20.00
65 Ph(c) 20.00
66 Ph(c) 20.00
67 Ph(c), The Sky Man 20.00
68 thru 74 Ph(c) .... @20.00
75 Ph(c), The Jungle Myth
   of Terror 20.00
76 Ph(c) 20.00

77 Ph(c),The Phantoms of the
Elephant Graveyard;Jun'53 . . 20.00

OAKY DOAKS
Eastern Color Printing Co.
July, 1942
1 Humor Oriented 165.00

OH, BROTHER!
Stanhall Publications
January, 1953
1 Bill Williams-a 25.00
2 thru 5 . . . . @15.00

OK COMICS
United Features Syndicate
July, 1940
1 B:Pal Peyton,Little Giant, Phantom
Knight,Sunset Smith,Teller Twins,
Don Ramon, Jerrry Sly,Kip Jaxon,
Leatherneck,Ulysses 375.00
2 October, 1940 . . . . 350.00

100 PAGES OF COMICS
Dell Publishing Co.
1937
101 Alley Oop,OG,Wash Tubbs,
Tom Mix,Dan Dunn 1,000.00

ON THE AIR
NBC Network Comics
1947
1 Giveaway, no cover 150.00

ON THE SPOT
Fawcett Publications
Autumn, 1948
N# Bondage(c),PrettyBoyFloyd 165.00

OPERATION PERIL
American Comics Group
(Michel Publ.)
October-November, 1950
1 LSt,OW,OW(c),B:TyphoonTyler,
DannyDanger,TimeTravellers 200.00
2 OW,OW(c) 125.00
3 OW,OW(c),Horror 100.00
4 OW,OW(c), Flying Saucers . 100.00
5 OW,OW(c), Science Fiction . 100.00
6 OW, Tyr. Rex 100.00
7 OW,OW(c) 85.00
8 OW,OW(c) 85.00
9 OW,OW(c) 85.00
10 OW,OW(c) 85.00
11 OW,OW(c), War 85.00
12 OW,OW(c),E:Time Travellers 85.00
13 OW,OW(c),War Stories 35.00
14 OW,OW(c),War Stories 35.00
15 OW,OW(c),War Stories 35.00
16 OW,OW(c),April-May,1953,
War Stories 35.00

OUR FLAG COMICS
Ace Magazines
August, 1941
1 MA,JM,B:Capt.Victory,Unknown
Soldier,The Three Cheers 1,200.00
2 JM,JM(c),O:The Flag 700.00
3 Tank Battle (c) 550.00
4 MA 550.00
5 I:Mr. Risk;April, 1942,

Male Bondage 575.00

Our Gang #7
© Dell Publishing Co.

OUR GANG COMICS
Dell Publishing Co.
September-October, 1942
1 WK,Barney Bear, Tom & Jerry 700.00
2 WK 350.00
3 WK,Benny Burro 250.00
4 WK 250.00
5 WK 250.00
6 WK 300.00
7 WK 175.00
8 WK,CB,Benny Burro 450.00
9 WK,CB,Benny Burro 400.00
10 WK,CB,Benny Burro 300.00
11 WK,I:Benny Bear 400.00
12 thru 20 WK . . . . @175.00
21 thru 29 WK . . . . @125.00
30 WK,Christmas(c) 100.00
31 thru 34 WK . . . . @85.00
35 WK,CB 85.00
36 WK,CB 85.00
37 thru 40 WK . . . . @50.00
41 thru 50 WK . . . . @30.00
51 thru 56 WK . . . . @20.00
57 . . . . 15.00
58 Our Gang 15.00
59 Our Gang 15.00
Becomes:

TOM AND JERRY
July, 1949
60 . . . . 55.00
61 . . . . 45.00
62 . . . . 40.00
63 . . . . 40.00
64 . . . . 40.00
65 . . . . 40.00
66 Christmas (c) 45.00
67 thru 70 . . . . @40.00
71 thru 76 . . . . @30.00
77 Christmas (c) 35.00
78 thru 80 . . . . @30.00
81 thru 89 . . . . @25.00
90 Christmas (c) 30.00
91 thru 99 . . . . @25.00
100 . . . . 30.00
101 thru 120 . . . . @20.00

121 thru 150 . . . . @15.00
151 thru 212 . . . . @10.00

OUR SECRET
(see MY SECRET)

OUTLAWS
D.S. Publishing Co.
February-March, 1948
1 HcK,Western Crime Stories 150.00
2 Grl,Doc Dawson's Dilema . 150.00
3 Cougar City Cleanup 50.00
4 JO,Death Stakes A Claim . . . 65.00
5 RJ,RJ(c),Man Who Wanted
Mexico 50.00
6 AMc,RJ,RJ(c),The Ghosts of

Outlaws #12 © D.S. Publishing Co.

Crackerbox Hill 50.00
7 Grl,Dynamite For Boss Cavitt 100.00
8 Grl,The Gun & the Pen . . . 100.00
9 FF,Shoot to Kill;June-
July, 1949 . . . . 250.00

WHITE RIDER AND SUPER HORSE
Star Publications
September, 1950
1 LbC(c) 60.00
2 LbC(c) 30.00
3 LbC(c) 30.00
4 LbC(c) 35.00
5 LbC(c),Stampede of Hard
Riding Thrills 35.00
6 LbC(c),Drums of the Sioux . . 35.00
Becomes:

INDIAN WARRIORS
7 LbC(c),Winter on the Great
Plains 40.00
8 LbC(c) 30.00
Becomes:

WESTERN CRIME CASES
9 LbC(c),The Card Sharp Killer 40.00
Becomes:

OUTLAWS, THE
10 LbC(c),Federated Express . . 50.00
11 LbC(c),Frontier Terror!!! 40.00

All comics prices listed are for *Near Mint* condition.

Indian Warriors #7 © Star Publications

12 LbC(c),Ruthless Killer!!! 40.00
13 LbC(c),The Grim Avengers .. 40.00
14 AF,JKa,LbC(c),Trouble in
Dark Canyon,April'54 ...... 40.00

OUT OF THE NIGHT
American Comics Group/ Best Synd. Feature
February-March, 1952
1 AW 300.00
2 AW 250.00
3 .... 110.00
4 AW 250.00
5 .... 100.00
6 The Ghoul's Revenge 100.00
7 .... 100.00
8 The Frozen Ghost 100.00
9 Death Has Wings,
Science Fiction 110.00
10 Ship of Death 100.00
11 .... 85.00
12 Music for the Dead 85.00
13 HN,From the Bottom of
the Well 90.00
14 Out of the Screen 85.00
15 The Little Furry Thing 75.00
16 Nightmare From the Past ... 75.00
17 The Terror of the Labyrinth .. 75.00
Becomes:
HOODED HORSEMAN
18 B: The Hooded Horseman .. 50.00
19 The Horseman's Strangest
Adventure 75.00
20 OW,O:Johnny Injun 50.00
21 OW,OW(c) 40.00
22 OW 40.00
23 .... 40.00
24 .... 40.00
25 .... 40.00
26 O&I:Cowboy Sahib 50.00
27 January-February, 1953 .... 45.00

OUT OF THE SHADOWS
Visual Editions (Standard Comics)
July, 1952
5 ATh,GT,The Shoremouth

Horror 175.00
6 ATh,JKz,Salesman of Death 150.00
7 JK,Plant of Death 100.00
8 Mask of Death 75.00
9 RC,Till Death Do Us Part .. 100.00
10 MS,We Vowed,Till Death
Do Us Part 65.00
11 ATh,Fountain of Fear 100.00
12 ATh,Hand of Death 150.00
13 MS,The Cannibal 120.00
14 ATh,The Werewolf,
August, 1954 .... 125.00

OXYDOL-DREFT
Giveaways
1950
The Set is More Valuable if the
Original Envelope is Present
1 L'il Abner 75.00
2 Daisy Mae 75.00
3 Shmoo 80.00
4 AW&FF(c),John Wayne ... 135.00
5 Archie 65.00
6 Terry Toons Comics 75.00

OZZIE AND BABS
Fawcett Publications
Winter, 1946
1 Humor Oriented, Teenage ... 45.00
2 Humor Oriented 20.00
3 Humor Oriented 15.00
4 Humor Oriented 15.00
5 Humor Oriented 15.00
6 Humor Oriented 15.00
7 Humor Oriented 15.00
8 Humor Oriented 15.00
9 Humor Oriented 15.00
10 Humor Oriented 15.00
11 Humor Oriented 15.00
12 Humor Oriented 15.00
13 Humor Oriented;1949 ...... 15.00

PAGEANT OF COMICS
St. John Publishing Co.
September, 1947
1 Rep. Mopsy 75.00
2 Rep. Jane Arden,Crime
Reporter 75.00

PANHANDLE PETE AND JENNIFER
J. Charles Lave Publishing Co.
July, 1951
1 (fa) 40.00
2 (fa) 30.00
3 (fa),November'51 .... 30.00

PANIC
Tiny Tot Publications (E.C. Comics)
March, 1954
"Humor in a Jugular Vein"
1 BE,JKa,JO,JDa,AF(c) 175.00
2 BE,JO,WW,JDa,A:Bomb ... 125.00
3 BE,JO,BW,WW,JDa,AF(c) . 110.00
4 BE,JO,WW,JDa,BW(c),
Infinity(c) 110.00
5 BE,JO,WW,JDa,AF(c) 90.00
6 BE,JO,WW,JDa,Blank (c) .. 90.00
7 BE,JO,WW,JDa 90.00
8 BE,JO,WW,JDa,Eye Chart (c) 90.00

9 BE,JO,WW,JDa,Ph(c),
Confidential(c) 90.00
10 BE,JDa, Postal Package(c) .. 90.00
11 BE,WW,JDa,Wheaties parody
as Weedies (c) 90.00
12 BE,WW,JDa,JDa(c);
December-January 1955-56 110.00

PARAMOUNT ANIMATED COMICS
Family Publications (Harvey Publ.)
June, 1953
1 (fa),B:Baby Herman & Katnip,
Baby Huey,Buzzy the Crow 110.00
2 (fa) 60.00
3 (fa) 45.00
4 (fa) 45.00
5 (fa) 45.00
6 (fa) 45.00
7 (fa), Baby Huey (c) 120.00
8 (fa), Baby Huey (c) 50.00
9 (fa), Infinity(c),Baby Huey (c) . 50.00
10 thru 21 (fa),Baby Huey(c) . @30.00
22 (fa), July, 1956, Baby Huey (c) 30.00

PAROLE BREAKERS
Avon Periodicals/Realistic
December, 1951
1 P(c),Hellen Willis,Gun
Crazed Gun Moll 200.00
2 JKu,P(c),Vinnie Sherwood,
The Racket King 150.00
3 EK(c),John "Slicer" Berry,
Hatchetman of Crime;
July,1952 .... 125.00

PATCHES
Rural Home Publ./ Patches Publ.
March-April, 1945
1 LbC(c),Imagination In Bed(c) 125.00
2 Dance (c) 60.00
3 Rocking Horse (c) 55.00
4 Music Band (c) 55.00
5 LbC(c),A:Danny Kaye,Football 60.00
6 A: Jackie Kelk 50.00
7 A: Hopalong Cassidy 75.00
8 A: Smiley Burnettte 50.00
9 BK,A: Senator Claghorn 50.00
10 A: Jack Carson 50.00
11 A: Red Skeleton; Dec'47 .... 55.00

PAWNEE BILL
Story Comics
February, 1951
1 A:Bat Masterson,Wyatt Earp,
Indian Massacre
at Devil's Gulch 55.00
2 Blood in Coffin Canyon 35.00
3 LC,O:Golden Warrior,Fiery
Arrows at Apache Pass;
July'51 .... 35.00

PAY-OFF
D.S. Publishing Co.
July-August, 1948
1 .... 120.00
2 The Pennsylvania Blue-Beard 65.00
3 The Forgetful Forger 55.00
4 RJ(c),Lady and the Jewels .. 55.00
5 The Beautiful Embezzeler;

March-April, 1949 .... 55.00

PEDRO
Fox Features Syndicate
January, 1950
1 WW,WW(c),Humor Oriented 150.00
2 August, 1950 .... 85.00

PENNY
Avon Publications
1947
1 The Slickest Chick of 'em All   60.00
2 .... 30.00
3 America's Teen-age
   Sweetheart 30.00
4 .... 30.00
5 .... 30.00
6 Perry Como Ph(c),September-
   October, 1949 .... 35.00

PEP COMICS
MJL Magazines/
Archie Publications
January, 1940
1 IN,JCo,MMe,IN(c),I:Shield,
   O:Comet,Queen of Diamonds,
   B:The Rocket,Press Guardian,
   Sergeant Boyle Chang,Bently
   of Scotland Yard 4,500.00
2 CBi,JCo,IN,IN(c),O:Rocket . 1,000.00
3 JCo,IN,IN(c),Shield (c) 850.00
4 Cbi,JCo,MMe,IN,IN(c),
   C:Wizard(not Gareb) 650.00
5 Cbi,JCo,MMe,IN,IN(c),
   C:Wizard 625.00
6 IN,IN(c), Shield (c) 475.00
7 IN,IN(c),Bondage(c),Shield(c) 475.00
8 JCo,IN, Shield (c) 450.00
9 IN, Shield (c) 450.00
10 IN,IN(c), Shield (c) 450.00
11 MMe,IN,IN(c),I:Dusty ,Boy
   Detective 450.00
12 IN,IN(c),O:Fireball Bondage(c),
   E:Rocket,Queen of Diamonds 650.00
13 IN,IN(c),Bondage(c) 425.00
14 IN,IN(c) 425.00
15 IN,Bondage(c) 425.00
16 IN,O:Madam Satan 650.00
17 IN,IN(c),O:Hangman,
   D:Comet 1,500.00
18 IN,IN(c),Bondage(c) 425.00
19 IN 400.00
20 IN,IN(c),E:Fireball 400.00
21 IN,IN(c),Bondage(c),
   E: Madam Satan 425.00
22 IN,IN(c)I:Archie,
   Jughead, Betty 5,500.00
23 IN,IN(c) 700.00
24 IN,IN(c) 650.00
25 IN,IN(c) 625.00
26 IN,IN(c),I:Veronica 800.00
27 IN,IN(c),Bill of Rights (c) .. 500.00
28 IN,IN(c), V:Capt. Swastika . 500.00
29 ASH (c) 500.00
30 B:Capt.Commando 500.00
31 Bondage(c) 400.00
32 Bondage(c) 400.00
33 .... 375.00
34 Bondage(c) 400.00
35 .... 375.00
36 1st Archie(c) 700.00
37 Bondage(c) 325.00
38 ASH(c) 300.00
39 ASH(c), Human Shield 300.00

Pep Comics #45
© MJL Magazines/Archie Publ.

40 .... 300.00
41 2nd Archie; I:Jughead 275.00
42 F:Archie & Jughead 250.00
43 F:Archie & Jughead 250.00
44 .... 250.00
45 .... 250.00
46 .... 250.00
47 E:Hangman,Infinity(c) 200.00
48 B:Black Hood 200.00
49 .... 200.00
50 .... 200.00
51 .... 175.00
52 B:Suzie 175.00
53 .... 175.00
54 E:Captain Commando 175.00
55 .... 175.00
56 thru 58 .... @150.00
59 E:Suzie 150.00
60 B:Katy Keene 150.00
61 .... 125.00
62 I L'il Jinx 125.00
63 .... 125.00
64 .... 125.00
65 E:Shield 125.00
66 thru 71 .... @85.00
72 thru 80 .... @75.00
81 thru 90 .... @55.00
91 thru 99 .... @45.00
100 .... 75.00
101 thru 110 .... @35.00
111 thru 120 .... @30.00
121 thru 130 .... @25.00
131 thru 140 .... @20.00
141 thru 150 .... @15.00
151 thru 160,A:Super Heroes @15.00
161 thru 200 .... @6.00
201 thru 250 .... @3.00
251 thru 300 .... @2.00
301 thru 350 .... @1.50
351 thru 411 .... @1.00

PERFECT CRIME, THE
Cross Publications
October, 1949
1 BP,DW 125.00
2 BP 65.00
3 .... 50.00

4 BP 50.00
5 DW 50.00
6 .... 50.00
7 B:Steve Duncan 50.00
8 Drug Story 50.00
9 .... 50.00
10 .... 50.00
11 Bondage (c) 65.00
12 .... 40.00
13 .... 40.00
14 Poisoning (c) 40.00
15 "The Most Terrible Menace",
   Drug 50.00
16 .... 30.00
17 .... 30.00
18 Drug (c) 90.00
19 .... 30.00
20 .... 30.00
21 .... 30.00
22 .... 30.00
23 .... 30.00

Perfect Crime #24
© Cross Publications

24 .... 30.00
25 .... 30.00
26 Drug w/ Hypodermic (c) ... 110.00
27 .... 30.00
28 .... 30.00
29 .... 30.00
30 E:Steve Duncan, Rope
   Strangulation (c) 80.00
31 .... 30.00
32 .... 30.00
33 .... 30.00

PERFECT LOVE
Approved Comics(Ziff-Davis)/
St. John Publ. Co.
August-September, 1951
1 (10),P(c),Our Kiss was a
   Prelude to Love Adrift 85.00
2 .... 55.00
3 P(c) 40.00
4 .... 40.00
5 .... 40.00
6 .... 40.00
7 .... 40.00
8 EK 45.00
9 EK,P(c) 35.00

---

10 Ph(c), Dec '53 . . . . 35.00

PERSONAL LOVE
Famous Funnies
January, 1950
1 Ph(c) Are You in Love 80.00
2 Ph(c) Serenade for Suzette
Mario Lanzo 40.00
3 Ph(c) 30.00
4 Ph(c) 30.00
5 Ph(c) 30.00
6 Ph(c) Be Mine Forever 32.00
7 Ph(c) You'll Always Be
Mine, Robert Walker 32.00
8 EK,Ph(c),Esther Williams &
Howard Keel 38.00
9 EK,Ph(c),Debra Paget & Louis
Jordan 38.00
10 Ph(c),Loretta Young
Joseph Cotton 35.00
11 ATh, Ph(c),Gene Tierney &
Glenn Ford 55.00
12 Ph(c) Jane Greer &
William Lundigan 30.00
13 Ph(c) Debra Paget &
Louis Jordan 25.00
14 Ph(c) Kirk Douglas &
Patrice Wymore 40.00
15 Ph(c) Dale Robertson &
Joanne Dru 25.00
16 Ph(c) Take Back Your Love . 25.00
17 Ph(c) My Cruel Deception . . . 25.00
18 Ph(c) Gregory Peck &
Susan Hayward 35.00
19 Ph(c) Anthony Quinn 35.00
20 Ph(c) The Couple in the
Next Apartment, Bob Wagner 30.00
21 Ph(c) I'll Make You Care 25.00
22 Ph(c) Doorway To Heartbreak 25.00
23 Ph(c) SaveMe from that Man 25.00

Personal Love #24 © Famous Funnies

24 FF, Ph(c) Tyrone Power . . . 200.00
25 FF, Ph(c) The Dark Light . . 200.00
26 Ph(c) Love Needs A Break . . 25.00
27 FF, Ph(c) Champ or Chump? 200.00
28 FF, Ph(c) A Past to Forget . 200.00
29 Ph(c) Charlton Heston 35.00
30 Ph(c) The Lady is Lost 25.00
31 Ph(c) Marlon Brando 40.00
32 FF, Ph(c) The Torment,

Kirk Douglas 350.00
33 Ph(c) June ,1955 . . . . 25.00

PETER COTTONTAIL
Key Publications
January, 1954
1 No 3-D (fa) 40.00
1 Feb '54 3-D (fa) 100.00
2 Rep of 3-D #1,not in 3-D 30.00

PETER PAUL'S 4 IN 1 JUMBO COMIC BOOK
Capitol Stories
1953
1 F: Racket Squad in Action,
Space Adventures,Crime &
Justice,Space Western . . . 225.00

PETER PENNY AND HIS MAGIC DOLLAR
American Bakers Association
1947
1 History from Colonial
America to the 1950's 100.00
2 . . . . 50.00

PETER RABBIT
Avon Periodicals
1947
1 H. Cady art 225.00
2 H. Cady art 175.00
3 H. Cady art 150.00
4 H. Cady art 150.00
5 H. Cady art 150.00
6 H. Cady art 150.00
7 thru 10 . . . . @30.00
11 . . . . 15.00

Wotalife
© Fox Feature Syndicate/Green Publ.

KRAZY LIFE
Fox Features Syndicate
1945
1 (fa) 55.00
Becomes:
NUTTY LIFE
2 (fa) 45.00

Becomes:
WOTALIFE
Fox Features Synd./ Green Publ.
August-September, 1946
3 (fa)B:L'il Pan,Cosmo Cat . . . 35.00
4 . . . . 25.00
5 thru 11 . . . . @20.00
12 July, 1947 . . . . 20.00
Becomes:
PHANTOM LADY
Fox Features Syndicate
August, 1947
13(#1) MB,MB(c) Knights of
the Crooked Cross 1,400.00
14(#2) MB,MB(c) Scoundrels
and Scandals 900.00
15 MB,MB(c) The Meanest
Crook In the World 700.00
16 MB,MB(c) Claa Peete The
Beautiful Beast, Negligee . . 700.00
17 MB.MB(c) The Soda Mint
Killer, Bondage (c) 1,600.00
18 MB,MB(c) The Case of
Irene Shroeder 650.00
19 MB,MB(c) The Case of
the Murderous Model 650.00
20 MB,MB(c) Ace of Spades . . 550.00
21 MB,MB(c) 550.00
22 MB,JKa 550.00
23 MB,JKa Bondage (c) 600.00
Becomes:
MY LOVE SECRET
24 JKa, My Love Was For Sale . 75.00
25 Second Hand Love 40.00
26 WW I Wanted Both Men 80.00
27 I Was a Love Cheat 30.00
28 WW, I Gave Him Love 80.00
29 . . . . 30.00
30 Ph(c) 30.00

LINDA
Ajax/Farrell
April-May, 1954
1 . . . . 75.00
2 Lingerie section 55.00
3 . . . . 40.00
4 October-November,1954 . . . 40.00
Becomes:
PHANTOM LADY
5(1) MB,Dec-Jan'54-55 . . . . . 400.00
2 Last Pre-Code Edition 325.00
3 Comics Code 250.00
4 Red Rocket,June, 1955 . . . 250.00

PHIL RIZZUTO
Fawcett Publications
1951
Ph(c) The Sensational Story of
The American Leagues MVP 400.00

PICTORIAL CONFESSIONS
St. John Publishing Co.
September, 1949
1 MB,MB(c),I Threw Away My Repu-
tation on a Worthless Love 125.00
2 MB,Ph(c) I Tried to be a
Hollywood Glamour Girl 75.00
3 JKY,MB,MB(c),They Caught
Me Cheating 75.00

Pictorial Romances #8
© St. John's Publishing Co.

Becomes:
PICTORIAL ROMANCES
4 Ph(c) MB, Trapped By Kisses
  I Couldn't Resist 100.00
5 MB,MB(c) 75.00
6 MB,MB(c) I Was Too Free
  With Boys 50.00
7 MB,MB(c) 50.00
8 MB,MB(c) I Made a
  Sinful Bargain 50.00
9 MB,MB(c) Dishonest Love . . . 50.00
10 MB,MB(c) I Was The
  Other Woman 50.00
11 MB,MB(c) The Worst
  Mistake A Wife Can Make . . . 55.00
12 MB,MB(c) Love Urchin 45.00
13 MB,MB(c) Temptations of a
  Hatcheck Girl 45.00
14 MB,MB(c) I Was A
  Gamblers Wife 45.00
15 MB,MB(c) Wife Without
  Pride or Principles 45.00
16 MB,MB(c) The Truth of My
  Affair With a Farm Boy 45.00
17 MB,MB(c) True Confessions
  of a Girl in Love 100.00
18 MB,MB(c) 100.00
20 MB,MB(c) 100.00
21 MB,MB(c) 40.00
22 MB,MB(c) 40.00
23 MB,MB(c) 40.00
24 MB,MB(c) March,1954 . . . . . 40.00

PICTORIAL LOVE STORIES
St. John Publishing Co.
October, 1952
1 MB,MB(c) I Lost My Head, My
  Heart and My Resistance . . 100.00

PICTURE NEWS
299 Lafayette Street Corp.
January, 1946
1 Will The Atom Blow The
  World Apart 200.00
2 Meet America's 1st Girl Boxing

Expert,Atomic Bomb 100.00
3 Hollywood's June Allison Shows
  You How to be Beautiful,
  Atomic Bomb 80.00
4 Amazing Marine Who Became
  King of 10,000 Voodoos,
  Atomic Bomb 100.00
5 G.I.Babies,Hank Greenberg . . 75.00
6 Joe Louis(c) 100.00
7 Lovely Lady, Englands
  Future Queen 70.00
8 Champion of them All 60.00
9 Bikini Atom Bomb,
  Joe DiMaggio 80.00
10 Dick Quick, Ace Reporter,
  Atomic Bomb
  January/February 1947 . . . . . 65.00

PICTURE STORIES FROM SCIENCE
Educational Comics
Spring, 1947
1 Understanding Air and Water 150.00
2 Fall '47 Amazing Discoveries
  About Food & Health 140.00

PICTURE STORIES FROM WORLD HISTORY
E.C. Comics
Spring, 1947
1 Ancient World to the
  Fall of Rome 150.00
2 Europes Struggle for
  Civilization 125.00

Pinhead and Foodini #4
© Fawcett Publications

PINHEAD AND FOODINI
Fawcett Publications
July, 1951
1 Ph(c) 150.00
2 Ph(c) 75.00
3 Ph(c) Too Many Pinheads . . . 55.00
4 Foodini's Talking Camel
  January, 1952 . . . . 55.00

PIN-UP PETE
Minoan Magazine Publishers
1952
1 Loves of a GI Casanova 85.00

PIONEER PICTURE STORIES
Street & Smith Publications
December, 1941
1 Red Warriors in Blackface . . 150.00
2 Life Story Of Errol Flynn 80.00
3 Success Stories of Brain
  Muscle in Action 60.00
4 Legless Ace & Boy Commando
  Raid Occupied France 60.00
5 How to Tell Uniform and
  Rank of Any Navy Man 60.00
6 General Jimmy Doolittle 70.00
7 Life Story of Admiral Halsey . 70.00
8 Life Story of Timoshenko 60.00
9 Dec. '43,Man Who Conquered
  The Wild Frozen North 60.00

PIRACY
E.C. Comics
October-November, 1954
1 WW,JDa,AW,WW(c),RC,AT   225.00
2 RC,JDa(c),WW,AW,AT 175.00
3 RC,GE, RC(c),Grl 150.00
4 RC,GE,RC(c),Grl 100.00
5 RC,GE,BK(c),Grl 100.00
6 JDa,RC,GE,BK(c),Grl 100.00
7 Oct Nov GE(c),RC,GE,Grl . 100.00

PIRATE COMICS
Hillman Periodicals
February-March, 1950
1 . . . . 125.00
2 . . . . 85.00
3 . . . . 75.00
4 Aug Sept 30 . . . . 70.00

PIXIES, THE
Magazine Enterprises
Winter, 1946
1 Mighty Atom 45.00
2 . . . . 25.00
3 . . . . 20.00
4 . . . . 20.00
5 . . . . 25.00
Becomes:
MIGHTY ATOM, THE
6 . . . . 25.00

PLANET COMICS
Love Romance Publ.
(Fiction House Magazines)
January, 1940
1 AB,DBR,HCK, Planet Comics,
  WE&LF,O:Aura,B:Flint Baker,
  Red Comet,Spurt Hammond,
  Capt. Nelson Cole 7,000.00
2 HcK,LF(c) 2,400.00
3 WE(c),HcK 1,800.00
4 HcK,B:Gale Allan and
  the Girl Squad 1,600.00
5 BP,HcK 1,450.00
6 BP,HcK,BP(c),The Ray
  Pirates of Venus 1,500.00
7 BP,AB,HcK,BP(c) B:Buzz
  Crandall Planet Payson . . 1,200.00
8 BP,AB HcK 1,200.00

All comics prices listed are for *Near Mint* condition.

Planet Comics #58
© *Fiction House Magazines*

9 BP,AB,GT,HcK,B:Don
Granville Cosmo Corrigan . 1,100.00
10 BP,AB,GT HcK 1,100.00
11 HcK, B:Crash Parker 1,100.00
12 Dri,B:Star Fighter 1,100.00
13 Dri,B:Reef Ryan 1,000.00
14 Dri B:Norge Benson 900.00
15 B: Mars,God of War 1,700.00
16 Invasion From The Void ... 900.00
17 Warrior Maid of Mercury ... 900.00
18 Bondage(c) 950.00
19 Monsters of the Inner World 900.00
20 RP, Winged Man Eaters
of the Exile Star 900.00
21 RP,B:Lost World
Hunt Bowman 1,000.00
22 Inferno on the Fifth Moon .. 850.00
23 GT,Lizard Tyrant of
the Twilight World 800.00
24 GT,Grl Raiders From
The Red Moon 800.00
25 Grl,B:Norge Benson 800.00
26 Grl,B:The Space Rangers
Bondage(c) 850.00
27 Grl, The Fire Eaters of
Asteroid Z 650.00
28 Grl, Bondage (c) 675.00
29 Grl,Dragon Raiders of Aztla 650.00
30 GT,Grl City of Lost Souls .. 650.00
31 Grl,Fire Priests of Orbit6X . 550.00
32 Slaver's Planetoid 600.00
33 MA 600.00
34 MA,Bondage 650.00
35 MA B:Mysta of The Moon .. 600.00
36 MA Collosus of the
Blood Moon 600.00
37 MA, Behemoths of the
Purple Void 600.00
38 MA 550.00
39 MA. Death Webs Of Zenith 3 550.00
40 Chameleon Men from
Galaxy 9 .... 550.00
41 MA,Aaf,New O: Auro
Bondage (c) 600.00
42 MA,AaF,E:Gale Allan 550.00
43 MA,AaF Death Rays
From the Sun. 550.00
44 MA,Bbl,B:Futura 550.00

45 Ma,Bbl,Her Evilness
from Xanado 550.00
46 MA,Bbl,GE The Mecho-Men
From Mars 550.00
47 MA,Bbl,GE,The Great
Green Spawn 500.00
48 MA,GE 500.00
49 MA,GE, Werewolves From
Hydra Hell 500.00
50 MA,GE,The Things of Xeves 500.00
51 MA,GE, Mad Mute X-Adapts 450.00
52 GE,Mystery of the Time
Chamber 450.00
53 MB,GE,Bondage(c)
Dwarflings From Oceania .. 450.00
54 MB,GE,Robots From Inferno 450.00
55 MB,GE,Giants of the
Golden Atom 450.00
56 MB,GE,Grl 400.00
57 MB,GE,Grl 400.00
58 MB,GE,Grl 400.00
59 MB,GE,Grl,LSe 400.00
60 GE,Grl,Vassals of Volta ... 400.00
61 GE,Grl, The Brute in the
Bubble 300.00
62 GE,Musta,Moon Goddess .. 300.00
63 GE,Paradise or Inferno ... 300.00
64 GE,Monkeys From the Blue 300.00
65 The Lost World 300.00
66 The Plague of the
Locust Men 300.00
67 The Nymphs of Neptune ... 300.00
68 Synthoids of the 9th Moon . 300.00
69 The Mentalists of Mars ... 300.00
70 Cargo For Amazonia 300.00
71 Sandhogs of Mars 250.00
72 Last Ship to Paradise 250.00
73 The Martian Plague,
Winter 1953 .... 250.00

Plastic Man #34
© *Comics Magazines/Quality Comics*

PLASTIC MAN
Comics Magazines
(Quality Comics Group)
Summer, 1943
1 JCo,JCo(c)Game of Death . 2,000.00
2 JCo,JCo(c)The Gay Nineties
Nightmare 1,000.00

3 JCo,JCo(c) 650.00
4 JCo,JCo(c) 550.00
5 JCo,JCo(c) 450.00
6 JCo,JCo(c) 350.00
7 JCo,JCo(c) 350.00
8 JCo,JCo(c) 350.00
9 JCo,JCo(c) 350.00
10 JCo,JCo(c) 350.00
11 JCo,JCo(c) 300.00
12 JCo,JCo(c),V:Spadehead . 300.00
13 JCo,JCo(c),V:Mr.Hazard ... 300.00
14 JCo,JCo(c),Words,Symbol
of Crime 300.00
15 JCo,JCo(c),V:BeauBrummel 300.00
16 JCo,JCo(c),Money
Means Trouble 300.00
17 JCo,JCo(c),A:The Last
Man on Earth 300.00
18 JCo,JCo(c),Goes Back
to the Farm 300.00
19 JCo,JCo(c),V;Prehistoric
Plunder 300.00
20 JCo,JCo(c),A:Sadly,Sadly .. 300.00
21 JCo,JCo(c),V:Crime Minded
Mind Reader 250.00
22 JCo,JCo(c), Which Twin
is the Phony 250.00
23 JCo,JCo(c),The Fountain
of Age 250.00
24 JCo,JCo(c),The Black Box
of Terror 250.00
25 JCo,JCo(c),A:Angus
MacWhangus 250.00
26 JCo,JCo(c),On the Wrong
Side of the Law? 250.00
27 JCo,JCo(c),V:The Leader . 250.00
28 JCo,JCo(c),V:Shasta 250.00
29 JCo,JCo(c),V:Tricky Toledo . 250.00
30 JCo,JCo(c),V:Weightless
Wiggins 250.00
31 JCo,JCo(c),V:Raka the
Witch Doctor 200.00
32 JCo,JCo(c),V:Mr.Fission ... 200.00
33 JCo,JCo(c),V:The Mad
Professor 200.00
34 JCo,JCo(c),Smuggler'sHaven 200.00
35 JCo,JCo(c),V:The Hypnotist 200.00
36 JCo,JCo(c),The Uranium
Underground 200.00
37 JCo,JCo(c),V:Gigantic Ants . 200.00
38 JCo,JCo(c),The Curse of
Monk Mauley 200.00
39 JCo,JCo(c),The Stairway
to Madness 200.00
40 JCo,JCo(c),The Ghoul of
Ghost Swamp 200.00
41 JCo,JCo(c),The Beast with
the Bloody Claws 175.00
42 JCo,JCo(c),The King of
Thunderbolts 175.00
43 JCo,JCo(c),The Evil Terror . 175.00
44 JCo,JCo(c),The Magic Cup . 175.00
45 The Invisible Raiders 175.00
46 V:The Spider 175.00
47 The Fiend of a
Thousand Faces 175.00
48 Killer Crossbones 175.00
49 JCo,The Weapon for Evil .. 175.00
50 V:Iron Fist 175.00
51 Incredible Sleep Weapon .. 150.00
52 V:Indestructible Wizard 160.00
53 V:Dazzia,Daughter of
Darkness 160.00
54 V:Dr.Quormquat 160.00
55 The Man Below Zero 160.00

56 JCo, The Man Who Broke
the Law of Gravity 160.00
57 The Chemist's Cauldron ... 160.00
58 JCo,The Amazing
Duplicating Machine 160.00
59 JCo,V:The Super Spy 160.00
60 The Man in the Fiery
Disguise 150.00
61 V:King of the Thunderbolts . 150.00
62 V:The Smokeweapon 150.00
63 V:Reflecto 150.00
64 Nov'56 The Invisible
Raiders 150.00

POCAHONTAS
Pocahontas Fuel Co.
October, 1941
N# 65.00
2 .... 50.00

POCKET COMICS
Harvey Publications
August, 1941
1 100 pages,O:Black Cat,Spirit
of '76,Red Blazer Phantom
Sphinx & Zebra,B:Phantom
Ranger,British Agent #99,
Spin Hawkins,Satan 500.00
2 .... 350.00
3 .... 250.00
4 Jan.'42,All Features End ... 225.00

POGO POSSUM
Dell Publishing Co.
1 WK,A:Swamp Land Band .. 445.00
2 WK 350.00

Pogo Possum #5
© Dell Publishing Co.

3 WK 225.00
4 WK 225.00
5 WK 225.00
6 thru 10 WK .... @200.00
11 WK, Christmas cover ... @250.00
12 thru 16 WK .... @150.00

POLICE COMICS
Comic Magazines
(Quality Comics Group)
August, 1941
1 GFx,JCo,WE.PGn,RC,FG,AB,
GFx(c),B&O:Plastic Man
The Human Bomb,#711,I&B,
Chic Canter,The Firebrand
Mouthpiece,Phantom Lady
The Sword 3,500.00
2 JCo,GFx,PGn,WE,RC,FG,
GFx(c) 1,700.00
3 JCo,GFx,PGn,WE,RC,FG,
GFx(c) 1,200.00
4 JCo,GFx,PGn,WE,RC,FG,
GFx&WEC(c) 1,100.00
5 JCo,GFx,PGn,WE,RC,FG,
GFx(c) 1,000.00
6 JCo,GFx,PGn,WE,RC,FG,
GFx(c) 1,000.00
7 JCo,GFx,PGn,WE,RC,FG,
GFx(c) 900.00
8 JCo,GFx,PGn,WE,RC,FG,
GFx(c),B&O:Manhunter .. 1,200.00
9 JCo,GFx,PGn,WE,RC,FG,
GFx(c) 900.00
10 JCo,GFx,PGn,WE,RC,FG,
GFx(c) 800.00
11 JCo,GFx,PGn,WE,RC,FG,
GFx(c),B:Rep:Rep.Spirit
Strips 1,300.00
12 JCo,GFX,PGn,WE,FG,AB,
RC(c) I:Ebony 850.00
13 JCo,GFx,PGn,WE,FG,AB,RC(c)
E:Firebrand,I:Woozy Winks . 850.00
14 JCo,GFx,PGn,WE,Jku,GFX(c) 550.00
15 JCo,GFx,PGn,WE,Jku,GFX(c)
E#711,B:Destiny 550.00
16 JCo,PGn,WE,JKu 550.00
17 JCo,PGn,WE,JKu,JCo(c) .. 550.00
18 JCo,PGn,WE,JCo(c) 550.00
19 JCo,PGn,WE,JCo(c) 550.00
20 JCo,PGn,WE,JCo(c),A:Jack
Cole in Phantom Lady 550.00
21 JCo,PGn,WE,JCo(c) 500.00
22 JCo,PGn,WE,RP,JCo(c)
The Eyes Have it 500.00
23 JCo,WE,RP,JCo(c),E:Phantom
Lady 450.00
24 JCo,WE,HK,JCo(c),B:Flatfoot
Burns 450.00
25 JCo,WE,HK,RP,JCo(c),The
Bookstore Mysrery 450.00
26 JCo,WE,Hk,JCo,(c)E:Flatfoot
Burns 450.00
27 JCo,WE,JCo(c) 450.00
28 JCo,WE,JCo(c) 450.00
29 JCo,WE,JCo(c) 450.00
30 JCo,WE,JCo(c),A Slippery
Racket 450.00
31 JCo,WE,JCo(c),Is Plastic
Man Washed Up? 300.00
32 JCo,WE,JCo(c),Fiesta Turns
Into a Fracas 300.00
33 JCo,WE 300.00
34 JCo,WE,JCO(c) 300.00
35 JCo,WE,JCO(c) 300.00
36 JCo,WE,JCO(c),Rest
In Peace 300.00
37 JCo,PGn,WE,JCo(c),Love
Comes to Woozy 300.00
38 JCo,WE,PGn,JCo(c) 300.00
39 JCo,WE,PGn,JCo(c) 300.00
40 JCo,WE,PGn,JCo(c) 300.00
41 JCo,WE,PGn,JCo(c),E:Reps.

Police Comics #2
© Comics Magazine/Quality Comics

of Spirit Strip 250.00
42 JCo,LF&WE,PGn,JCo(c),
Woozy Cooks with Gas 250.00
43 JCo,LF&WE,PGn,JCo(c) ... 250.00
44 JCo,PGn,LF,JCo(c) 225.00
45 JCo,PGn,LF,JCo(c) 225.00
46 JCo,PGn,LF,JCo(c) 225.00
47 JCo,PGn,LF,JCo(c),
V:Dr.Slicer 225.00
48 JCo,PGn,LF,JCo(c),V:Big
Beaver 225.00
49 JCo,PGn,LF,JCo(c),V:Thelma
Twittle 225.00
50 JCo,PGn,LF,JCo(c) 225.00
51 JCo,PGn,LF,JCo(c),V:The
Granite Lady 175.00
52 JCo,PGn,LF,JCo(c) 175.00
53 JCo,PGn,LF,JCo(c),
V:Dr.Erudite 175.00
54 JCo,PGn,LF,JCo(c) 175.00
55 JCo,PGn,LF,JCo(c),V:The
Sleepy Eyes 175.00
56 JCo,PGn,LF,JCo(c),V:The
Yes Man 175.00
57 JCo,PGn,LF,JCo(c),
V:Mr.Misfit 175.00
58 JCo,PGn,LF,JCo(c),E:The
Human Bomb 175.00
59 JCo,PGn,LF,JCo(c),A:Mr.
Happiness 175.00
60 JCo,PGn,LF,JCo(c) 150.00
61 JCo,PGn,LF,JCo(c) 150.00
62 JCo,PGn,LF,JCo(c) 150.00
63 JCo,PGn,LF,JCo(c),
V:The Crab 150.00
64 JCo,PGn,LF,HK,JCo(c) 150.00
65 JCo,PGn,LF,JCo(c) 150.00
66 JCo,PGn,LF,JCo(c) Love
Can Mean Trouble 150.00
67 JCo,LF,JCo(c),
V:The Gag Man 150.00
68 JCo,LF,JCo(c) 150.00
69 JCo,LF,JCo(c),V:Strecho .. 150.00
70 JCo,LF,JCo(c) 150.00
71 JCo,LF,JCo(c) 150.00
72 JCo,LF,JCo(c),V:Mr.Cat .. 150.00
73 JCo,LF,JCo(c) 150.00
74 JCo,LF,JCo(c),V:Prof.Dimwit 150.00

All comics prices listed are for *Near Mint* condition.

75 JCo,LF,JCo(c) 150.00
76 JCo,LF,JCo(c),V:Mr.Morbid . 150.00
77 JCo,LF,JCo(c),V:Skull Face
    & Eloc 150.00
78 JCo,LF,JCo(c),A Hot Time In
    Dreamland 150.00
79 JCo,LF,JCo(c),V:Eaglebeak . 150.00
80 JCo,LF,JCo(c),V:Penetro . . 150.00
81 JCo,LF,JCo(c),V:A Gorilla . . 150.00
82 JCo,LF,JCo(c) 150.00
83 JCo,LF,JCo(c) 150.00
84 JCo,LF,JCo(c) 150.00
85 JCo,LF,JCo(c),V:Lucky 7 . . 150.00
86 JCo,LF,JCo(c),V:The Baker . 150.00
87 JCo,LF,JCo(c) 150.00
88 JCo,LF,JCo(c),V:The Seen . 150.00
89 JCo,JCo(c),V:The Vanishers . 125.00
90 JCo,LF,JCo(c),V:Capt.Rivers . 125.00
91 JCo,JCo(c),The
    Forest Primeval 135.00
92 JCo,LF,JCo(c),V:Closets
    Kennedy 135.00
93 JCo,JCo(c),V:The Twinning
    Terror 135.00
94 JCo,JCo(c),WE 175.00
95 JCo,JCo(c),WE,V:Scowls . . 175.00
96 JCo,JCo(c),WE,V:Black
    Widow 175.00
97 JCo,JCo(c),WE,V:The Mime . 175.00
98 JCo,JCo(c),WE 175.00
99 JCo,JCo(c),WE 175.00
100 JCo,JCo(c) 200.00
101 JCo,JCo(c) 175.00
102 JCo,JCo(c),E:Plastic Man . 175.00
103 JCo,LF,B&I:Ken Shannon;
    Bondage(c) 125.00
104 The Handsome of Homocide 75.00
105 Invisible Hands of Murder . . 75.00
106 Museum of Murder 75.00
107 Man with the ShrunkenHead 75.00
108 The Headless Horse Player 75.00
109 LF,Bondage(c),Blood on the
    Chinese Fan 85.00
110 Murder with a Bang 75.00
111 Diana the HomocidalHuntress 75.00
112 RC,The Corpse on the
    Sidewalk 75.00
113 RC,RC(c), The Dead Man
    with the Size 13 Shoe . . 75.00
114 The Terrifying Secret of
    the Black Bear 75.00
115 Don't Let Them Kill Me 75.00
116 Stage Was Set For Murder . 75.00
117 Bullet Riddled Bookkeeper . 75.00
118 Case of the Absent Corpse . 75.00
119 A Fast & Bloody Buck 75.00
120 Death & The Derelict 75.00
121 Curse of the Clawed Killer . 75.00
122 The Lonely Hearts Killer . . . 75.00
123 Death Came Screaming . . . 75.00
124 Masin Murder 75.00
125 Bondage(c),The Killer of
    King Arthur's Court 85.00
126 Hit & Run Murders 75.00
127 Oct'53,Death Drivers 75.00

POLICE LINE-UP
Avon Periodicals/
Realistic Comics
August, 1951

1 WW,P(c) 175.00
2 P(c),Drugs 150.00
3 JKu,EK,P(c) 100.00
4 July '52;EK 100.00

POLICE TRAP
Mainline/Charlton Comics
September, 1954

1 S&K(c) 125.00
2 S&K(c) 65.00
3 S&K(c) 65.00
4 S&K(c) 65.00
5 S&K,S&K(c) 100.00
6 S&K,S&K(c) 100.00

POLLY PIGTAILS
Parents' Magazine Institute
January, 1946

1 Ph(c) 55.00
2 Ph(c) 25.00
3 Ph(c) 20.00
4 Ph(c) 20.00
5 Ph(c) 20.00
6 Ph(c) 20.00
7 Ph(c) 15.00
8 . . . . 15.00
9 . . . . 15.00
10 . . . . 15.00
11 thru 22 . . . . @10.00
22 Ph(c) 10.00
23 Ph(c) 10.00
34 thru 43 . . . . @10.00

Popeye #10 © King Features

POPEYE
Dell Publishing Co.
1948

1 . . . . 250.00
2 . . . . 150.00
3 'Welcome to Ghost Island' . . 125.00
4 . . . . 125.00
5 . . . . 125.00
6 . . . . 125.00
7 . . . . 125.00
8 . . . . 125.00
9 . . . . 125.00
10 . . . . 125.00
11 . . . . 100.00
12 . . . . 100.00
13 . . . . 100.00
14 . . . . 100.00
15 . . . . 100.00
16 . . . . 100.00
17 . . . . 100.00

18 . . . . 100.00
19 . . . . 100.00
20 . . . . 100.00
21 thru 30 . . . . @75.00
31 thru 40 . . . . @65.00
41 thru 45 . . . . @50.00
46 O:Sweat Pea 65.00
47 thru 50 . . . . @45.00
51 thru 60 . . . . @35.00
61 thru 65 . . . . @25.00

POPULAR COMICS
Dell Publishing Co.
February, 1936

1 Dick Tracy, Little Orphan
    Annie 2,500.00
2 Terry Pirates 900.00
3 Terry,Annie,Dick Tracy 700.00
4 . . . . 550.00
5 B:Tom Mix 550.00
6 . . . . 450.00
7 . . . . 450.00
8 . . . . 450.00
9 . . . . 450.00
10 Terry,Annie,Tracy 450.00
11 Terry,Annie,Tracy 400.00
12 Christmas(c) 400.00
13 Terry,Annie,Tracy 400.00
14 Terry,Annie,Tracy 400.00
15 same 400.00
16 same 400.00
17 same 400.00
18 same 400.00
19 same 400.00
20 same 400.00
21 same 300.00
22 same 300.00
23 same 300.00
24 same 300.00
25 same 300.00
26 same 300.00
27 E:Terry,Annie,Tracy 300.00
28 A:Gene Autry 250.00
29 . . . . 250.00
30 . . . . 250.00
31 A:Jim McCoy 250.00
32 A:Jim McCoy 250.00
33 . . . . 250.00
34 . . . . 250.00
35 Christmas(c),Tex Ritter 250.00
36 . . . . 250.00
37 . . . . 250.00
38 B:Gang Busters 225.00
39 . . . . 275.00
40 . . . . 275.00
41 . . . . 275.00
42 . . . . 275.00
43 . . . . 285.00
44 . . . . 175.00
45 Tarzan(c) 175.00
46 O:Martan,Marvel Man 265.00
47 . . . . 175.00
48 . . . . 175.00
49 . . . . 175.00
50 . . . . 175.00
51 B&O:Voice 200.00
52 A:Voice 150.00
53 A:Voice 150.00
54 A:Voice 150.00
55 . . . . 165.00
56 . . . . 150.00
57 . . . . 150.00
58 . . . . 150.00
59 . . . . 150.00
60 O:Prof. Supermind 150.00

Popular Comics #3
© Dell Publishing Co.

61	125.00
62	125.00
63 B:Smilin' Jack	125.00
64	125.00
65	125.00
66	125.00
67	125.00
68	125.00
69	125.00
70	125.00
71	125.00
72 B:Owl,Terry & the Pirates	200.00
73	150.00
74	150.00
75 A:Owl	150.00
76 Captain Midnight	200.00
77 Captain Midnight	200.00
78 Captain Midnight	200.00
79 A:Owl	125.00
80 A:Owl	125.00

Popular Comics #81
© Dell Publishing Co.

81 A:Owl	125.00
82 A:Owl	125.00
83 A:Owl	125.00
84 A:Owl	125.00
85 A:Owl	125.00
86	100.00
87	100.00
88	100.00
89	100.00
90	100.00
91	100.00
92	100.00
93	100.00
94	100.00
95	100.00
96	100.00
97	100.00
98 B:Felix Cat	110.00
99	100.00
100	125.00
101 thru 141	60.00
142 E:Terry & the Pirates	55.00
143	55.00
144	55.00
145	55.00

POPULAR ROMANCES
**Better Publications
(Standard Comics)**
December, 1949

5 B:Ph(c)	40.00
6 Ph(c)	25.00
7 RP	25.00
8 Ph(c)	25.00
9 Ph(c)	25.00
10 WW	40.00
11 thru 16	@20.00
17 WE	25.00
18 thru 21	@25.00
22 thru 27 ATh,Ph(c)	@50.00

SCHOOL DAY ROMANCES
Star Publications
November-December, 1949

1 LbC(c),Teen-Age	100.00
2 LbC(c)	75.00
3 LbC(c),Ph(c)	75.00
4 LbC(c),JyD,RonaldReagan	125.00

Becomes:
POPULAR TEEN-AGERS

5 LbC(c),Toni Gay, Eve Adams	125.00
6 LbC(c),Ginger Bunny, Midge Martin	100.00
7 LbC(c)	100.00
8 LbC(c)	100.00
9 LbC(c)	50.00
10 LbC(c)	50.00
11 LbC(c)	40.00
12 LbC(c)	40.00
13 LbC(c),JyD	40.00
14 LbC,WW,Spanking	100.00
15 LbC(c),JyD	40.00
16	35.00
17 LbC(c),JyD	35.00
18 LbC(c)	35.00
19 LbC(c)	35.00
20 LbC(c),JyD	45.00
21 LbC(c),JyD	45.00
22 LbC(c)	30.00
23 LbC(c)	30.00

POWER COMICS
Holyoke/Narrative Publ.
1944

1 LbC(c)	550.00
2 B:Dr.Mephisto,Hitler(c)	575.00
3 LbC(c)	550.00
4 LbC(c)	450.00

PRIDE OF THE YANKEES
Magazine Enterprises
1949

1 N#,OW,Ph(c),The Life of Lou Gehrig	500.00

PRISON BREAK
Avon Periodicals/Realistic
September, 1951

1 WW(c),WW	200.00
2 WW(c),WW,JKu	150.00
3 JD,JO	125.00
4 EK	100.00
5 EK,CI	100.00

PRIZE COMICS
**Feature Publications
(Prize Publ.)**
March, 1940

1 O&B:Power Nelson,Jupiter. B:Ted O'Neil,Jaxon of the Jungle,Bucky Brady, Storm Curtis, Rocket(c)	1,250.00
2 B:The Owl	550.00
3 Power Nelson(c)	450.00
4 Power Nelson(c)	450.00
5 A:Dr.Dekkar	400.00
6 A:Dr.Dekkar	400.00
7 S&K,DBr,JK(c),O&B DR Frost, Frankenstein,B:GreenLama, Capt Gallant,Voodini Twist Turner	1,000.00

Prize Comics #34
© Feature Publications

8 S&K,DBr	500.00
9 S&K,DBr,Black Owl(c)	450.00
10 DBr,Black Owl(c)	400.00
11 DBr,O:Bulldog Denny	375.00

All comics prices listed are for *Near Mint* condition. **CVA Page 355**

12 DBr 375.00
13 DBR,O&B:Yank and
    Doodle,Bondage(c) 400.00
14 DBr,Black Owl(c) 375.00
15 DBr,Black Owl(c) 375.00
16 DBr,JaB,B:Spike Mason . . . 375.00
17 DBr,Black Owl(c) 375.00
18 DBr,Black Owl(c) 375.00
19 DBr,Yank&Doodle(c) 375.00
20 DBr,Yank&Doodle(c) 375.00
21 DBr,JaB(c),Yank&Doodle . . 300.00
22 DBr,Yank&Doodle(c) 300.00
23 DBr,Uncle Sam(c) 300.00
24 DBr,Abe Lincoln(c) 300.00
25 DBr,JaB,Yank&Doodle(c) . . 300.00
26 DBr,JaB,JaB(c),Liberty
    Bell(c) 300.00
27 DBr,Yank&Doodle(c) 200.00
28 DBr,Yank&Doodle(c) 175.00
29 DBr,JaB(c)Yank&Doodle(c) . 175.00
30 DBr,Yank&Doodle(c) 200.00
31 DBr,Yank&Doodle(c) 175.00
32 DBr,Yank&Doodle(c) 175.00
33 DBr,Bondage(c),Yank
    & Doodle 200.00
34 DBr,O:Airmale;New
    Black Owl 200.00
35 DBr,B:Flying Fist & Bingo . . 125.00
36 DBr,Yank&Doodle(c) 125.00
37 DBr,I:Stampy,Hitler(c) 150.00
38 DBr,B.Owl,Yank&Doodle(c) . 125.00
39 DBr,B.Owl,Yank&Doodle(c) . 125.00
40 DBr,B.Owl,Yank&Doodle(c) . 125.00
41 DBr,B.Owl,Yank&Doodle(c) . 125.00
42 DBr,B.Owl,Yank&Doodle(c) . . 90.00
43 DBr,B.Owl,Yank&Doodle(c) . . 90.00
44 DBr, B&I:Boom Boom
    Brannigan 90.00
45 DBr 90.00
46 DBr 90.00
47 DBr 90.00
48 DBr,B:Prince Ra;Bondage(c) 125.00
49 DBr,Boom Boom(c) 75.00
50 DBr,Farnkenstein(c) 90.00
51 DBr 75.00
52 DBr, B:Sir Prize 75.00
53 DBr, The Man Who Could
    Read Features 90.00
54 DBr 75.00
55 DBr,Yank&Doodle(c) 75.00
56 DBr,Boom Boom(c) 75.00
57 DBr,Santa Claus(c) 75.00
58 DBr,The Poisoned Punch . . 75.00
59 DBr,Boom Boom(c) 75.00
60 DBr,Sir Prise(c) 75.00
61 DBr,The Man wih the
    Fighting Feet 75.00
62 DBr,Hck(c),Yank&Doodle(c) . 75.00
63 DBr,S&K,S&K(c),Boom
    Boom(c) 90.00
64 DBr,Blackowl Retires 75.00
65 DBr,DBr(c),Frankenstein . . . 80.00
66 DBr,DBr(c),Frankenstein . . . 80.00
67 DBr,B:Brothers in Crime . . . 75.00
68 DBr,RP(c) 75.00
Becomes:

PRIZE COMICS
WESTERN

69 ACa(c),B:Dusty Ballew 90.00
70 ACa(c) 65.00
71 ACa(c) 65.00
72 ACa(c),JSe 65.00
73 ACa(c) 65.00
74 ACa(c) 65.00

75 JSe,S&K(c),6-Gun Showdown
    at Rattlesnake Gulch 70.00
76 Ph(c),Randolph Scott 85.00
77 Ph(c),JSe,Streets of
    Laredo,movie 65.00
78 Ph(c),JSe,HK,Bullet
    Code, movie 100.00
79 Ph(c),JSe,Stage to
    China, movie 100.00
80 Ph(c),Gunsmoke Justice 75.00
81 Ph(c),The Man Who Shot
    Billy The Kid 75.00
82 Ph(c),MBi,JSe&BE,Death
    Draws a Circle 75.00
83 JSe,S&K(c) 70.00
84 JSe 50.00
85 JSe,B:American Eagle 150.00
86 JSe 60.00
87 JSe&BE 65.00
88 JSe&BE 65.00
89 JSe&BE 65.00
90 JSe&Be 65.00
91 JSe&BE,JSe&BE(c) 65.00
92 JSe,JSe&BE(c) 65.00

Prize Comics Western #93
© Feature Publications

93 JSe,JSe&BE(c), ... 65.00
94 JSe&BE,JSe&BE(c) 65.00
95 JSe,JSe&BE(c) 65.00
96 JSe,JSe&BE,JSe&BE(c) 65.00
97 JSe,JSe&BE,JSeBE(c) 65.00
98 JSe,JSe&BE(c) 65.00
99 JSe&BE,JSe&BE(c) 65.00
100 JSe,JSe(c) 85.00
101 JSe 65.00
102 JSe 65.00
103 JSe 65.00
104 JSe 65.00
105 JSe 65.00
106 JSe 50.00
107 JSe 50.00
108 JSe 70.00
109 JSe&AW 80.00
110 JSe&BE 75.00
111 JSe&BE 75.00
112 . . . . 50.00
113 AW&JSe 75.00
114 MMe,B:The Drifter 35.00
115 MMe 35.00
116 MMe 35.00

117 MMe 35.00
118 MMe,E:The Drifter 35.00
119 Nov/Dec'56 . . . . 35.00

PSYCHOANALYSIS
E.C. Comics
March-April, 1955

1 JKa,JKa(c) 100.00
2 JKa,JKa(c) 75.00
3 JKa,JKa(c) 75.00
4 JKa,JKa(c) Sept.-Oct. 1955 . 75.00

PUBLIC ENEMIES
D.S. Publishing Co.
1948

1 AMc 90.00
2 AMc 100.00
3 AMc 60.00
4 AMc 60.00
5 AMc 60.00
6 AMc 60.00
7 AMc,Eye Injury 75.00
8 . . . . 60.00
9 . . . . 60.00

PUNCH AND JUDY
COMICS
Hillman Periodicals
1944

1 (fa) 75.00
2 . . . . 40.00
3 . . . . 30.00
4 thru 12 . . . . @30.00
2-1 . . . . 25.00
2-2 JK 75.00
2-3 . . . . 25.00
2-4 . . . . 25.00
2-5 . . . . 25.00
2-6 . . . . 25.00
2-7 . . . . 25.00
2-8 . . . . 25.00
2-9 . . . . 25.00
2-10 JK 75.00
2-11 JK 75.00
2-12 JK 75.00
3-1 JK 75.00
3-2 . . . . 65.00
3-3 . . . . 20.00
3-4 . . . . 20.00
3-5 . . . . 20.00
3-6 . . . . 20.00
3-7 . . . . 20.00
3-8 . . . . 20.00
3-9 . . . . 20.00

PUNCH COMICS
Harry 'A' Chesler
December, 1941

1 B:Mr.E,The Sky Chief,Hale
    the Magician,Kitty Kelly 600.00
2 A:Capt.Glory 350.00
3-8 Do Not Exist
9 B:Rocket Man & Rocket
    girl,Master Ken 250.00
10 JCo,A:Sky Chief 200.00
11 JCo,O:Master Key,A:Little
    Nemo 200.00
12 A:Rocket Boy,Capt.Glory . . 175.00
13 Ric(c) 175.00
14 GT 150.00
15 FSm(c) 150.00
16 . . . . 150.00
17 . . . . 150.00

Punch Comics #20 © Harry 'A' Chesler

18 FSm(c),Bondage(c),Drug .. 185.00
19 FSm(c) 150.00
20 Women semi-nude(c) 300.00
21 Drug 175.00
22 I:Baxter,Little Nemo 150.00
23 A:Little Nemo 150.00

PUPPET COMICS
Dougherty, Co.
Spring, 1946
1 Funny Animal 35.00
2 .... 30.00

PURPLE CLAW, THE
Minoan Publishing Co./
Toby Press
January, 1953
1 O:Purple Claw 150.00
2 .... 100.00
3 .... 100.00

PUZZLE FUN COMICS
George W. Dougherty Co.
Spring, 1946
1 PGn 125.00
2 .... 90.00

QUEEN OF THE WEST,
DALE EVANS
Dell Publishing Co.
July, 1953
(1) see Dell Four Color #479
(1) see Dell Four Color #528
3 ATh, Ph(c) all 75.00
4 ATh,RsM 65.00
5 RsM 45.00
6 RsM 45.00
7 RsM 45.00
8 RsM 45.00
9 RsM 45.00
10 RsM 45.00
11 .... 32.00
12 RsM 40.00
13 RsM 40.00
14 RsM 40.00
15 RsM 40.00
16 RsM 40.00

17 RsM 40.00
18 RsM 40.00
19 .... 30.00
20 RsM 40.00
21 .... 30.00
22 RsM 40.00

RACKET SQUAD
IN ACTION
Capitol Stories/
Charlton Comics
May-June, 1952
1 Carnival(c) 125.00
2 .... 60.00
3 Roulette 60.00
4 FFr(c) 60.00
5 Just off the Boat 75.00
6 The Kidnap Racket 55.00
7 .... 45.00
8 .... 45.00
9 2 Fisted fix 45.00
10 .... 45.00
11 SD,SD(c),Racing(c) 125.00
12 JoS,SD(c),Explosion(c) ... 225.00
13 JoS(c),The Notorious Modelling
   Agency Racket,Acid 60.00
14 DG(c),Drug 65.00
15 Photo Extortion Racket 40.00
16 thru 28 .... @40.00
29,March, 1958 .... 45.00

RAGGEDY ANN
AND ANDY
Dell Publishing Co.
1942
1 Billy & Bonnie Bee 200.00
2 .... 100.00
3 DNo,B:Egbert Elephant ... 100.00
4 DNo,WK 120.00
5 DNo 75.00
6 DNo 75.00

Raggedy Ann + Andy #7
© Bobbs & Merrill Co.

7 Little Black Sambo 75.00
8 .... 75.00
9 .... 75.00
10 .... 75.00
11 .... 60.00

12 .... 60.00
13 .... 60.00
14 .... 60.00
15 .... 60.00
16 thru 20 .... @60.00
21 Alice in Wonderland 65.00
22 thru 27 .... @45.00
28 WK 50.00
29 thru 39 .... @45.00

RALPH KINER
HOME RUN KING
Fawcett Publications
1950
1 N#, Life Story of the
   Famous Pittsburgh Slugger . 350.00

RAMAR OF THE
JUNGLE
Toby Press/
Charlton Comics
1954
1 Ph(c),TV Show 90.00
2 Ph(c) 55.00
3 .... 55.00
4 .... 55.00
5 Sept '56 .... 55.00

RANGE ROMANCES
Comics Magazines
(Quality Comics)
December, 1949
1 PGn(c),PGn 125.00
2 RC(c),RC 150.00
3 RC,Ph(c) 90.00
4 RC,Ph(c) 75.00
5 RC,PGn,Ph(c) 75.00

RANGERS OF FREEDOM
Flying Stories, Inc.
(Fiction House)
October, 1941
1 I:Ranger Girl & Rangers
   of Freedom;V:Super-Brain . 1,000.00
2 V:Super -Brain 500.00
3 Bondage(c) The Headsman
   of Hate 400.00
4 Hawaiian Inferno 350.00
5 RP,V:Super-Brain 350.00
6 RP,Bondage(c);Bugles
   of the Damned 350.00
7 RP,Death to Tojo's
   Butchers 300.00
Becomes:
RANGERS COMICS
8 RP,B:US Rangers 300.00
9 GT,BLb,Commando Steel
   for Slant Eyes 300.00
10 BLb,Bondage (c) 325.00
11 Raiders of the
   Purple Death 275.00
12 A:Commando Rangers 275.00
13 Grl,B:Commando Ranger .. 275.00
14 Grl,Bondage(c) 275.00
15 GT,Grl,Bondage(c) 275.00
16 Grl,GT;Burma Raid 300.00
17 GT,GT,Bondage(c),Raiders
   of the Red Dawn 300.00
18 GT 300.00
19 GE,Blb,GT,Bondage(c) ... 250.00
20 GT 200.00
21 GT,Bondage(c) 250.00

22 GT,B&O:Firehair	200.00
23 GT,BLb,B:Kazanda	175.00
24 Bondage(c)	200.00
25 Bondage(c)	200.00
26 Angels From Hell	175.00
27 Bondage(c)	200.00
28 BLb,E:Kazanda;B&O Tiger Man	190.00
29 Bondage(c)	200.00
30 BLb,B:Crusoe Island	210.00
31 BLb,Bondage(c)	175.00
32 BLb	135.00
33 BLb,Drug	150.00
34 BLb	135.00
35 BLB,Bondage(c)	175.00
36 BLb,MB	135.00
37 BLb,Mb	135.00
38 BLb,MB,GE,Bondage(c)	175.00
39 BLb,GE	125.00
40 BLb,GE,BLb(c)	125.00
41 BLb,GE	125.00
42 BLb,GE	125.00
43 BLb,GE	125.00
44 BLb,GE	125.00
45 BLb,GEl	125.00
46 BLb,GE	125.00
47 BLb,JGr	125.00
48 BLb,JGr	125.00
49 BLb,JGr	125.00
50 BLb,JGr,Bondage(c)	125.00
51 BLb,JGr	100.00
52 BLb,JGr,Bondage(c)	125.00
53 BLb,JGr,Prisoners of Devil Pass	100.00
54 JGr,When The Wild Commanches Ride	100.00
55 JGr,Massacre Guns at Pawnee Pass	100.00
56 JGr, Gun Smuggler of Apache Mesa	100.00
57 JGr,Redskins to the Rescue	100.00
58 JGr,Brides of the Buffalo Men	100.00
59 JGr,Plunder Portage	100.00
60 JGr, Buzzards of Bushwack Trail	100.00
61 BWh(c)Devil Smoke at Apache Basin	75.00
62 BWh(c)B:Cowboy Bob	75.00
63 BWh(c)	75.00
64 BWh(c)B:Suicide Smith	75.00
65 BWh(c):Wolves of the Overland Trail,Bondage(c)	75.00
66 BWh(c)	80.00
67 BWh(c)B:Space Rangers	75.00
68 BWh(c);Cargo for Coje	75.00
69 BWh(c);Great Red Death Ray	75.00

REAL CLUE CRIME STORIES
(see CLUE COMICS)

REAL FUNNIES
Nedor Publishing Co.
January, 1943

1 (fa)	135.00
2 and 3 (fa)	@65.00

REAL HEROES COMICS
Parents' Magazine Institiute
September, 1941

1 HcK,Franklin Roosevelt	175.00

2 J, Edgar Hoover	75.00
3 General Wavell	55.00
4 Chiang Kai Shek	55.00
5 Stonewall Jackson	65.00
6 Lou Gehrig	125.00
7 Chennault and his Flying Tigers	55.00
8 Admiral Nimitz	55.00
9 The Panda Man	35.00
10 Carl Akeley-Jungle Adventurer	35.00
11 Wild Jack Howard	32.00
12 General Robert L Eichelberger	30.00
13 HcK,Victory at Climback	30.00
14 Pete Gray	30.00
15 Alexander Mackenzie	30.00
16 Balto of Nome Oct '46	30.00

REAL LIFE STORY OF FESS PARKER
Dell Publishing Co.
1955

1	65.00

REALISTIC ROMANCES
Avon Periodicals/
Realistic Comics
July-August, 1951

1 Ph(c)	90.00
2 Ph(c)	45.00
3 P(c)	30.00
4 P(c)	30.00
5 thru 14	@35.00
15	25.00
16 Drug	50.00
17	25.00

Real Life Comics #12
© Visual Editions/Better/Standard

REAL LIFE COMICS
Visual Editions/Better/
Standard/Nedor
September, 1941

1 ASh(c),Lawrence of Arabia,Uncle Sam(c)	225.00
2 ASh(c),Liberty(c)	100.00
3 Adolph Hitler(c)	175.00

4 ASh(c)Robert Fulton, Charles DeGaulle	75.00
5 ASh(c)Alexander the Great	75.00
6 ASh(c)John Paul Jones,CDR	70.00
7 ASh(c)Thomas Jefferson	70.00
8 Leonardo Da Vinci	70.00
9 US Coast Guard Issue	70.00
10 Sir Hubert Wilkens	70.00
11 Odyssey on a Raft	50.00
12 ImpossibleLeatherneck	50.00
13 ASh(c)The Eternal Yank	50.00
14 Sir Isaac Newton	50.00
15 William Tell	50.00
16 Marco Polo	50.00
17 Albert Einstein	50.00
18 Ponce De Leon	50.00
19 The Fighting Seabees	50.00
20 Joseph Pulitzer	50.00
21 Admiral Farragut	40.00
22 Thomas Paine	40.00
23 Pedro Menendez	40.00
24 Babe Ruth	85.00
25 Marcus Whitman	40.00
26 Benvenuto Cellini	40.00
27 A Bomb Story	75.00
28 Robert Blake	40.00
29 Daniel DeFoe	40.00
30 Baron Robert Clive	40.00
31 Anthony Wayne	40.00
32 Frank Sinatra	45.00
33 Frederick Douglas	40.00
34 Paul Revere,Jimmy Stewart	45.00
35 Rudyard Kipling	40.00
36 Story of the Automobile	40.00
37 Francis Manion	40.00
38 Richard Henry Dana	35.00
39 Samuel FB Morse	30.00
40 FG,ASh(c),Hans Christian Anderson	35.00
41 Abraham Lincoln,Jimmy Foxx	40.00
42 Joseph Conrad,Fred Allen	38.00
43 Louis Braille,O.W.Holmes	35.00
44 Citizens of Tomorrow	35.00
45 ASh(c),Francois Villon	55.00
46 The Pony Express	55.00
47 ASh(c),Montezuma	35.00
48	35.00
49 ASh(c),Gene Bearden, Baseball	40.00
50 FF,ASh(c),Lewis & Clark	125.00
51 GE,ASh(c),Sam Houston	75.00
52 GE,FF,ASh(c),JSe&BE Leif Erickson	135.00
53 JSe&BE,Henry Wells & William Fargo	55.00
54 GT,Alexander Graham Bell	55.00
55 ASh(c),JSe&BE, The James Brothers	55.00
56 JSe&BE	55.00
57 JSe&BE	55.00
58 JSe&BE,Jim Reaves	60.00
59 FF,JSe&BE,Battle Orphan Sept '52	55.00

REAL LOVE
(see HAP HAZARD COMICS)

REAL WEST ROMANCES
Crestwoood Publishing Co./
Prize Publ.
April-May, 1949

1 S&K,Ph(c)	125.00
2 Ph(c),Spanking	90.00
3 JSe,BE,Ph(c)	40.00

4 S&K,JSe,BE,Ph(c) 75.00
5 S&K,MMe,JSe,Audie
   Murphy Ph(c) 65.00
6 S&K,JSe,BE,Ph(c) 50.00

RECORD BOOK OF FAMOUS POLICE CASES
St. John Publishing Co.
1949
1 N#,JKu,MB(c) 200.00

RED ARROW
P.L. Publishing Co.
May,1951
1 Bondage(c) 50.00
2 . . . . 45.00
3 P(c) 35.00

Red Band Comics #3
© Enwil Associates

RED BAND COMICS
Enwil Associates
November, 1944
1 The Bogeyman 150.00
2 O:Bogeyman,same(c)as#1 . . 135.00
3 A:Captain Wizard 125.00
4 May '45,Repof#3,Same(c) . . 125.00

RED CIRCLE COMICS
Enwil Associates
(Rural Home Public)
January, 1945
1 B:Red Riot,The Prankster . . 150.00
2 LSt,A:The Judge 125.00
3 LSt,LSt(c) 100.00
4 LSt,LSt(c) covers of #4
   stapled over other comics . . 100.00

TRAIL BLAZERS
Street & Smith Publications
January, 1942
1 Wright Brothers 175.00
2 Benjamin Franklin,Dodgers . 125.00
3 Red Barber,Yankees 150.00
4 Famous War song 75.00
Becomes:

RED DRAGON COMICS
5 JaB(c),B&O:Red Rover:
   B:Capt.Jack Comkmando
   Rex King&Jet,Minute Man . . 450.00
6 O:Red Dragon 550.00
7 The Curse of the
   Boneless Men 500.00
8 China V:Japan 350.00
9 The Reducing Ray,Jan '44 . 350.00
November, 1947
(2nd Series)
1 B:Red Dragon 450.00
2 BP 350.00
3 BP,BP(c),I:Dr Neff 300.00
4 BP,BP(c) 400.00
5 BP,BP(c) 250.00
6 BP,BP(c) 250.00
7 BP,BP(c),May 49 . . . . 250.00

RED MASK
(see TIM HOLT)

RED RABBIT
Dearfield/
J. Charles Lave Publ. Co.
January, 1941
1 (fa) 55.00
2 . . . . 30.00
3 thru 10 . . . . @20.00
11 thru 22 . . . . @18.00

RED SEAL COMICS
Harry 'A' Chesler, Jr./Superior
October, 1945
14 GT,Bondage(c),Black Dwarf 300.00
15 GT,Torture 225.00
16 GT 300.00
17 GT,Lady Satan,Sky Chief . . 225.00
18 Lady Satan,Sky Chief 225.00
19 Lady Satan,Sky Chief 225.00
20 Lady Satan,Sky Chief 225.00
21 Lady Satan,Sky Chief 225.00
22 Rocketman 150.00

REDSKIN
Youthful Magazines
September, 1950
1 Redskin,Bondage(c) 65.00
2 Apache Dance of Death 45.00
3 Daniel Boone 35.00
4 Sitting Bull- Red Devil
   of the Black Hills 35.00
5 . . . . 35.00
6 Geronimo- Terror of the
   Desert,Bondage 45.00
7 Firebrand of the Sioux 35.00
8 . . . . 35.00
9 . . . . 35.00
10 Dead Man's Magic 35.00
11 . . . . 35.00
12 Quanah Parker,Bondage(c) . . 45.00
Becomes:

FAMOUS WESTERN BADMEN
13 Redskin- Last of the
   Comanches 40.00
14 . . . . 25.00
15 The Dalton Boys Apr '52 . . . 25.00

REMEMBER PEARL HARBOR
Street & Smith Publications
1942
1 N# JaB,Battle of the
   Pacific,Uncle Sam(c) 250.00

RETURN OF THE OUTLAW
Minoan Publishing Co.
February, 1953
1 Billy The Kid 50.00
2 . . . . 30.00
3 thru 11 . . . . @20.00

REVEALING ROMANCES
A.A. Wyn
(Ace Magazines)
September, 1949
1 . . . . 40.00
2 . . . . 20.00
3 thru 6 . . . . @15.00

Rex Allen Comics #2 © Dell Publ. Co.

REX ALLEN COMICS
Dell Publishing Co.
February, 1951
(1) see Dell Four Color #316
2 Ph(c) all 60.00
3 thru 10 . . . . @45.00
11 thru 23 . . . . @35.00
24 ATh 40.00
25 thru 31 . . . . @35.00

REX DEXTER OF MARS
Fox Features Syndicate
Autumn, 1940
1 DBr,DBr(c) Battle of
   Kooba 1,000.00

RIBTICKLER
Fox Features Syndicate
1945
1 . . . . 70.00
2 . . . . 35.00
3 Cosmo Cat 25.00
4 thru 6 . . . . @20.00
7 Cosmo Cat 22.00
8 thru 9 . . . . @20.00

All comics prices listed are for _Near Mint_ condition.

RIN TIN TIN
Dell Publishing Co.
November, 1952
(1) *see Dell Four Color #434*
(1) *see Dell Four Color #476*
(1) *see Dell Four Color #523*
4 thru 10 Ph(c) all .... @50.00
11 thru 20 .... @70.00

ROCKET COMICS
Hillman Periodicals
March, 1940
1 O:Red Roberts;B:Rocket
Riley,Phantom Ranger,Steel
Shank,Buzzard Baynes,Lefty
Larson,The Defender,Man
with 1,000 Faces 1,200.00
2 .... 600.00
3 May '40 E:All Features .. 650.00

ROCKET KELLY
Fox Features Syndicate
Autumn, 1945
N# 150.00
1 .... 150.00
2 A:The Puppeteer 100.00
3 .... 90.00
4 .... 90.00
5 Oct/Nov '46 .... 90.00
6 .... 90.00

ROCKETMAN
Ajax/Farrell Publications
June, 1952
1 Space Stories of the Future . 200.00

ROCKET SHIP X
Fox Features Syndicate
September, 1951
1 .... 350.00
2 N# Variant of Original 250.00

ROCKY LANE WESTERN
Fawcett/Charlton Comics
May, 1949
1 Ph(c)B:Rocky Lane,Slim
Pickins 600.00
2 Ph(c) 250.00
3 Ph(c) 160.00
4 Ph(c)CCB,Rail Riders
Rampage,F Capt Tootsie .. 160.00
5 Ph(c)The Missing
Stagecoaches 160.00
6 Ph(c)Ghost Town Showdown 125.00
7 Ph(c)The Border Revolt 135.00
8 Ph(c)The Sunset Feud 135.00
9 Ph(c)Hermit of the Hills .. 135.00
10 Ph(c)Badman's Reward ... 125.00
11 Ph(c)Fool's Gold Fiasco .. 100.00
12 Ph(c),CCB,Coyote Breed
F:Capt Tootsie,Giant 100.00
13 Ph(c),Giant 100.00
14 Ph(c) 80.00
15 Ph(c)B:Black Jacks
Hitching Post,Giant 85.00
16 Ph(c),Giant 75.00
17 Ph(c),Giant 75.00
18 Ph(c) 80.00
19 Ph(c),Giant 85.00
20 Ph(c)The Rodeo Rustler
E:Slim Pickens 85.00
21 Ph(c)B: Dee Dickens 75.00

22 Ph(c) 65.00
23 thru 30 .... @75.00
31 thru 40 .... @65.00
41 thru 55 .... @65.00
56 .... 60.00
57 thru 60 .... @55.00
61 thru 70 .... @50.00
71 thru 87 .... @45.00

ROD CAMERON WESTERN
Fawcett Publications
February, 1950
1 Ph(c) 350.00
2 Ph(c) 175.00
3 Ph(c),Seven Cities of Cipiola 150.00
4 Ph(c),Rip-Roaring Wild West 125.00
5 Ph(c),Six Gun Sabotage ... 125.00
6 Ph(c),Medicine Bead Murders 125.00
7 Ph(c),Wagon Train Of Death 125.00
8 Ph(c),Bayou Badman 125.00
9 Ph(c),Rustlers Ruse 125.00
10 Ph(c),White Buffalo Trail ... 125.00
11 Ph(c),Lead Poison 100.00
12 thru 19 Ph(c) .... @100.00
20 Phc(c),Great Army Hoax ... 100.00

Roly-Poly Comics #10
© Green Publishing

ROLY-POLY COMICS
Green Publishing Co.
1945
1 B:Red Rube&Steel Sterling . 175.00
6 A:Blue Cycle 90.00
10 A:Red Rube 80.00
11 .... 75.00
12 .... 75.00
13 .... 75.00
14 A:Black Hood 75.00
15 A:Steel Fist;1946 .... 175.00

ROMANCE AND CONFESSION STORIES
St. John Publishing Co.
1949
1 MB(c),MB 200.00

ROMANTIC LOVE
Avon Periodicals/Realistic
September-October, 1949
1 P(c) 120.00
2 P(c) 60.00
3 P(c) 55.00
4 Ph(c) 55.00
5 P(c) 55.00
6 Ph(c),Drug,Thrill Crazy ... 80.00
7 P(c) 55.00
8 P(c) 55.00
9 EK,P(c) 55.00
10 thru 11 P(c) .... @50.00
12 EK 55.00
20 .... 50.00
21 .... 50.00
22 EK 60.00
23 EK 60.00

ROMANTIC MARRIAGE
Ziff-Davis/
St. John Publishing Co.
November-December, 1950
1 Ph(c),Selfish wife 85.00
2 P(c),Mother's Boy 45.00
3 P(c),Hen Peck House 40.00
4 P(c) 40.00
5 Ph(c) 40.00
6 Ph(c) 35.00
7 Ph(c) 35.00
8 P(c) 35.00
9 P(c) 35.00
10 P/PH(c) 75.00
11 .... 32.00
12 .... 32.00
13 Ph(c) 32.00
14 thru 20 .... @32.00
20 Ph(c) 32.00
21 .... 32.00
22 .... 32.00
23 MB 35.00
24 .... 32.00

ROMANTIC PICTURE NOVELETTES
Magazine Enterprises
1946
1 Mary Wothr adventure 75.00

ROMANTIC SECRETS
Fawcett Publ./Charlton Comics
September, 1949
1 Ph(c) 75.00
2 MSy(c) 35.00
3 MSy(c) 35.00
4 GE 45.00
5 BP 40.00
6 .... 22.00
7 BP 22.00
8 .... 22.00
9 GE 30.00
10 BP 25.00
11 .... 22.00
12 BP 25.00
13 .... 22.00
14 .... 22.00
15 .... 22.00
16 BP,MSy 25.00
17 BP 25.00
18 .... 20.00
19 .... 20.00
20 BP.MBi 25.00
21 .... 18.00

22	18.00
23	15.00
24 GE	35.00
25 MSy	15.00
26 BP,MSy	18.00
27 MSy	15.00
28	15.00
29 BP	18.00
30 thru 32	@15.00
33 MSy	18.00
34 BP	18.00
35	12.00
36 BP	18.00
37 BP	18.00
38 thru 52	@15.00

ROMANTIC STORY
Fawcett Publ./Charlton Comics
November, 1949

1 Ph(c)	75.00
2 Ph(c)	40.00
3 Ph(c)	30.00
4 Ph(c)	30.00
5 Ph(c)	30.00
6 Ph(c)	30.00
7 BP,Ph(c)	25.00
8 BP,Ph(c)	25.00
9 Ph(c)	22.00
10 Ph(c)	22.00
11 Ph(c)	22.00
12 Ph(c)	22.00
13 Ph(c)	22.00
14 Ph(c)	22.00
15 GE,Ph(c)	35.00
16 BP,Ph(c)	25.00
17 Ph(c)	20.00
18 Ph(c)	20.00
19 Ph(c)	20.00
20 BP,Ph(c)	22.00
22 ATh,Ph(c)	18.00

Charlton Comics

23	15.00
24 Ph(c)	15.00
25 thru 29	@15.00
30 BP	20.00
31 thru 39	@15.00

ROMANTIC WESTERN
Fawcett Publications
Winter, 1949

1 Ph(c)	90.00
2 Ph(c),AW,AMc	100.00
3 Ph(c)	75.00

ROMEO TUBBS
(see MY SECRET LIFE)

ROUNDUP
D.S. Publishing Co.
July-August, 1948

1 HcK	100.00
2 Drug	75.00
3	50.00
4	50.00
5 Male Bondage	55.00

ROY CAMPANELLA, BASEBALL HERO
Fawcett Publications
1950
N# Ph(c),Life Story of the Battling Dodgers Catcher .. 400.00

Roy Campanella #1 (nn)
© Fawcett Publ.

ROY ROGERS
Dell Publishing Co.

1 photo (c)	400.00
2	175.00
3	160.00
4	150.00
5	10.00
6 thru 10	@125.00
11 thru 20	@75.00
21 thru 30	@65.00
31 thru 46	@50.00
47 thru 50	@40.00
51 thru 56	@35.00
57 Drug	45.00
58 thru 70	@35.00
71 thru 80	@30.00
81 thru 91	@25.00

Becomes:

ROY ROGERS AND TRIGGER

92 thru 99	@25.00
100	40.00
101 thru 118	@25.00
119 thru 125 ATn	@40.00
126 thru 131	@30.00
132 thru 144 RsM	@35.00
145	40.00

ROY ROGER'S TRIGGER
Dell Publishing Co.
May, 1951

(1) *see Dell Four Color #329*	
2 Ph(c)	80.00
3 P(c)	25.00
4 P(c)	25.00
5 P(c)	25.00
6 thru 17 P(c)	@15.00

RULAH, JUNGLE GODDESS
(see ZOOT COMICS)

SAARI, THE JUNGLE GODDESS
P.L. Publishing Co.

November, 1951
1 The Bantu Blood Curse ... 200.00

SABU, ELEPHANT BOY
Fox Features Syndicate
June, 1950

1(30) WW,Ph(c)	125.00
2 JKa,Ph(c),August'50	85.00

Saddle Justice #7
© Fables Publications/E.C. Comics

HAPPY HOULIHANS
Fables Publications
(E.C. Comics)
Autumn, 1947

1 O:Moon Girl	300.00
2	150.00

Becomes:

SADDLE JUSTICE

3 HcK,JCr,AF	300.00
4 AF,JCr	275.00
5 AF,Grl,WI	250.00
6 AF,Grl	250.00
7 AF,Grl	250.00
8 AF,Grl,WI	250.00

Becomes:

SADDLE ROMANCES

9 Grl(c),Grl	300.00
10 AF(c),WW	325.00
11 AF(c),Grl	275.00

SAINT, THE
Avon Periodicals
August, 1947

1 JKa,JKa(c),Bondage(c)	400.00
2	200.00
3 Rolled Stocking Leg(c)	150.00
4 MB(c)	125.00
5 Spanking Panel	200.00
6 B:Miss Fury	250.00
7 P(c),Detective Cases(c)	125.00
8 P(c),Detective Cases"(c)	110.00
9 EK(c),The Notorious Murder Mob	110.00
10 WW,P(c),V:The Communist Menace	125.00
11 P(c),Wanted For Robbery	75.00

All comics prices listed are for *Near Mint* condition.

12 P(c),The Blowpipe Murders
March, 1952 . . . . 110.00

SAM HILL PRIVATE EYE
Close-Up Publications
1950
1 The Double Trouble Caper . . 75.00
2 . . . . 45.00
3 . . . . 40.00
4 Negligee panels 55.00
5 . . . . 35.00
6 . . . . 35.00
7 . . . . 35.00

SAMSON
Fox Features Syndicate
Autumn, 1940
1 BP,GT,A:Wing Turner . . . 1,000.00
2 BP,A:Dr. Fung 450.00
3 JSh(c),A:Navy Jones 350.00
4 WE,B:Yarko 300.00
5 WE 300.00
6 WE,O:The Topper;Sept'41 . 300.00

SAMSON
Ajax Farrell Publ
(Four Star)
April, 1955
12 The Electric Curtain 125.00
13 Assignment Danger 100.00
14 The Red Raider;Aug'55 . . . 100.00

SANDS OF THE
SOUTH PACIFIC
Toby Press
January, 1953
1 2-Fisted Romantic Adventure . 90.00

SCHOOL DAY
ROMANCES
(see POPULAR TEEN-AGERS)

SCIENCE COMICS
Fox Features Syndicate
February, 1940

THE EAGLE • COSMIC CARSON • PERISPHERE PAYNE
Science Comics #3
© Fox Features Syndicate

1 GT,LF(c),O&B:Electro,Perisphere
Payne,The Eagle,Navy Jones;
B:Marga,Cosmic Carson,
Dr. Doom; Bondage(c) . . . 2,000.00
2 GT,LF(c) 900.00
3 GT,LF(c),Dynamo 800.00
4 JK,Cosmic Carson 700.00
5 Giant Comiscope Offer
Eagle(c) 500.00
6 Dynamop(c) 500.00
7 Bondage(c),Dynamo 500.00
8 September, 1940 Eagle(c) . . 475.00

SCIENCE COMICS
Humor Publications
January, 1946
1 RP(c),Story of the A-Bomb . . 75.00
2 RP(c),How Museum Pieces
Are Assembled 35.00
3 AF,RP(c),How Underwater
Tunnels Are Made 75.00
4 RP(c),Behind the Scenes at
A TV Broadcast 25.00
5 The Story of the World's
Bridges; September, 1946 . . 30.00

SCIENCE COMICS
Ziff-Davis Publ. Co.
May, 1946
N# Used For A Mail Order
Test Market 225.00

SCIENCE COMICS
Export Publication Enterprises
March, 1951
1 How to resurrect a dead rat . . 50.00

SCOOP COMICS
Harry 'A' Chesler Jr.
November, 1941
1 I&B:Rocketman&Rocketgirl;B:Dan
Hastings;O&B:Master Key . 550.00
2 A:Rocketboy,Eye Injury . . . 325.00
3 Partial rep. of #2 . . . . 300.00
4 thru 7 do not exist
8 1945 . . . . 200.00

SCREAM COMICS
Humor Publ./Current Books
(Ace Magazines)
Autumn, 1944
1 . . . . 60.00
2 . . . . 30.00
3 . . . . 25.00
4 thru 15 . . . . @25.00
16 I:Lily Belle 28.00
17 . . . . 20.00
18 Drug 35.00
19 . . . . 20.00
Becomes:
ANDY COMICS
20 Teenage 25.00
21 . . . . 25.00
Becomes:
ERNIE COMICS
22 Teenage 30.00
23 thru 25 . . . . @20.00
Becomes:
ALL LOVE ROMANCES
26 Ernie 25.00
27 LbC 32.00

28 thru 32 . . . . @15.00

(Capt. Silvers Log of...)
SEA HOUND, THE
Avon Periodicals
1945
N# The Esmerelda's Treasure . 70.00
2 Adventures in Brazil 50.00
3 Louie the Llama 50.00
4 In Greed & Vengence;
Jan-Feb, 1946 . . . . 50.00

SECRET LOVES
Comics Magazines
(Quality Comics)
November, 1949
1 BWa(c) 100.00
2 BWa(c),Lingerie(c) 90.00
3 RC 60.00
4 . . . . 35.00
5 Boom Town Babe 40.00
6 . . . . 35.00

SECRET MYSTERIES
(see CRIME MYSTERIES)

SELECT DETECTIVE
D.S. Publishing Co.
August-September, 1948
1 MB,Exciting New Mystery
Cases 100.00
2 MB,AMc,Dead Men.... . . . . . 70.00
3 Face in theFrame;Dec-Jan'48 60.00

SERGEANT PRESTON
OF THE YUKON
Dell Publishing Co.
August, 1951
(1 thru 4) see Dell Four Color #344;
#373, 397, 419
5 thru 10 P(c) . . . . @35.00
11 P(c) 30.00
12 P(c) 30.00
13 P(c),O:Sergeant Preston . . 35.00
14 thru 17 P(c) . . . . @30.00

*Seven Seas Comics #6 © Universal
Phoenix Features/Leader Publ*

18 P(c) 35.00
19 thru 29 Ph(c) .... @35.00

SEVEN SEAS COMICS
Universal Phoenix Features/
Leader Publ.
April, 1946
1 MB,RWb(c),B:South Sea
Girl, Captain Cutlass 350.00
2 MB,RWb(c) 300.00
3 MB,AF,MB(c) 275.00
4 MB,MB(c) 275.00
5 MB,MB(c),Hangman's Noose 275.00
6 MB,MB(c);1947 .... 275.00

SHADOW COMICS
Street & Smith Publications
March, 1940
1-1 P(c),B:Shadow,Doc Savage,
Bill Barnes,Nick Carter,
Frank Merriwell,Iron Munro 3,000.00
1-2 P(c),B: The Avenger 1,200.00
1-3 P(c),A: Norgill the
Magician 800.00
1-4 P(c),B:The Three
Musketeers 850.00
1-5 P(c),E: Doc Savage 850.00
1-6 A: Captain Fury 700.00
1-7 O&B: The Wasp 750.00
1-8 A:Doc Savage 550.00
1-9 A:Norgill the Magician ... 550.00
1-10 O:Iron Ghost;B:The Dead
End Kids 550.00
1-11 O:Hooded Wasp 600.00
1-12 Crime Does Not pay 500.00
2-1 .... 500.00
2-2 Shadow Becomes Invisible 500.00
2-3 O&B:supersnipe;
F:Little Nemo 600.00
2-4 F:Little Nemo 500.00
2-5 V:The Ghost Faker 500.00
2-6 A:Blackstone the Magician 400.00
2-7 V:The White Dragon 400.00
2-8 A:Little Nemo 400.00
2-9 The Hand of Death 400.00
2-10 A:Beebo the WonderHorse 400.00
2-11 V:Devil Kyoti 400.00
2-12 V:Devil Kyoti 350.00
3-1 JaB(c),V:Devil Kyoti 350.00
3-2 Red Skeleton Life Story .. 350.00
3-3 V:Monstrodamus 350.00
3-4 V:Monstrodamus 350.00
3-5 V:Monstrodamus 350.00
3-6 V:Devil's of the Deep 350.00
3-7 V: Monstrodamus 350.00
3-8 E: The Wasp 350.00
3-9 The Stolen Lighthouse ... 350.00
3-10 A:Doc Savage 350.00
3-11 P(c),V: Thade 350.00
3-12 V: Thade 350.00
4-1 Red Cross Appeal on (c) . 350.00
4-2 V:The Brain of Nippon ... 350.00
4-3 Little Men in Space 350.00
4-4 ...Mystifies Berlin 350.00
4-5 ...Brings Terror to Tokio .. 350.00
4-6 V:The Tarantula 350.00
4-7 Crypt of the Seven Skulls . 350.00
4-8 V:the Indigo Mob 350.00
4-9 Ghost Guarded Treasure
of the Haunted Glen 350.00
4-10 V:The Hydra 350.00
4-11 V:The Seven Sinners 350.00
4-12 Club Curio 300.00
5-1 A:Flatty Foote 300.00

5-2 Bells of Doom 300.00
5-3 The Circle of Death 300.00
5-4 The Empty Safe Riddle ... 300.00
5-5 The Mighty Master Nomad . 300.00
5-6 ...Fights Piracy Among
the Golden Isles 300.00
5-7 V:The Talon 300.00
5-8 V:The Talon 300.00
5-9 V:The Talon 300.00
5-10 V:The Crime Master 300.00
5-11 The Clutch of the Talon .. 300.00
5-12 Most Dangerous Criminal . 300.00
6-1 Double Z 300.00
6-2 Riddle of Prof.Mentalo ... 300.00
6-3 V:Judge Lawless 300.00
6-4 V:Dr. Zenith 300.00

Shadow Comics #71 (6/11)
© Street & Smith Publications

6-5 .... 300.00
6-6 ...Invades the
Crucible of Death 300.00
6-7 Four Panel Cover 300.00
6-8 Crime Among the Aztecs . 300.00
6-9 I:Shadow Jr. 350.00
6-10 Devil's Passage 300.00
6-11 The Black Pagoda 300.00
6-12 BP,BP(c),Atomic Bomb
Secrets Stolen 325.00
7-1 The Yellow Band 325.00
7-2 A:Shadow Jr. 325.00
7-3 BP,BP(c),Crime Under
the Border 350.00
7-4 BP,BP(c),One Tree Island,
Atomic Bomb 375.00
7-5 A:Shadow Jr. 325.00
7-6 BP,BP(c),The Sacred Sword
of Sanjorojo 350.00
7-7 Crime K.O. 350.00
7-8 ...Raids Crime Harbor 350.00
7-9 BP.BP(c),Kilroy Was Here . 350.00
7-10 BP,BP(c),The Riddle of
the Flying Saucer 400.00
7-11 BP,BP(c),Crime
Doesn't Pay 350.00
7-12 BP,BP(c)Back From
the Grave 350.00
8-1 BP,BP(c),Curse of the Cat 350.00
8-2 BP,BP(c),Decay,Vermin &
Murder in the Bayou 350.00
8-3 BP,BP(c),The Spider Boy . 350.00

8-4 BP,BP(c),Death Rises
Out of the Sea 350.00
8-5 BP,BP(c),Jekyll-
Hyde Murders 350.00
8-6 Secret of Valhalla Hall ... 350.00
8-7 BP,BP(c),Shadow in Danger 350.00
8-8 BP,BP(c),...Solves a
Twenty Year Old Crime ... 350.00
8-9 BP,BP(c),3-D Effect(c) 350.00
8-10 BP,BP(c),Up&Down(c) ... 350.00
8-11 BP,BP(c) 350.00
8-12 BP,BP(c),Arabs,Boat(c) .. 350.00
9-1 Airport(c) 350.00
9-2 BP,BP(c),Flying Cannon(c) 350.00
9-3 BP,BP(c),Shadow's Shadow 350.00
9-4 BP,BP(c) 350.00
9-5 Death in the Stars;Aug'49 . 350.00

SHARP COMICS
H.C. Blackerby
Winter, 1945
1 O:Planetarian(c) 225.00
2 O:The Pioneer 200.00

Sheena Queen of the Jungle #16
© Real Adventures/Fiction House

SHEENA, QUEEN OF
THE JUNGLE
Real Adventures
(Fiction House)
Spring, 1942
1 Blood Hunger 1,200.00
2 Black Orchid of Death 750.00
3 Harem Shackles 450.00
4 The Zebra Raiders 350.00
5 War of the Golden Apes ... 275.00
6 .... 275.00
7 They Claw By Night 250.00
8 The Congo Colossus 250.00
9 and 10 .... @225.00
11 Red Fangs of the Tree Tribe 225.00
12 .... 200.00
13 Veldt o/t Voo Doo Lions ... 200.00
14 The Hoo Doo Beasts of
Mozambique 200.00
15 .... 200.00
16 Black Ivory 200.00
17 Great Congo Treasure Trek 200.00

All comics prices listed are for *Near Mint* condition.

18 Doom of the Elephant Drum
Winter, 1952 . . . . 200.00

SHIELD-WIZARD COMICS
MLJ Magazines
Summer, 1940

1 IN,EA,O:Shield 2,000.00
2 O:Shield;I:Roy 900.00
3 Roy,Child Bondage(c) 550.00
4 Shield,Roy,Wizard 500.00
5 B:Dusty-Boy Dectective,Child
Bondage 500.00
6 B:Roy the Super Boy,Child
Bondage 450.00
7 Shield(c),Roy Bondage(c) . . 450.00
8 Bondage(c) 450.00
9 Shield/Roy(c) 400.00
10 Shield/Roy(c) 400.00
11 Shield/Roy(c) 400.00
12 Shield/Roy(c) 400.00
13 Bondage (c);Spring'44 . . . . 450.00

SHIP AHOY
Spotlight Publishers
November, 1944

1 LbC(c) 75.00

SHOCK DETECTIVE CASE
(see CRIMINALS ON THE RUN)

SHOCK DETECTIVE CASES
(see CRIMINALS ON THE RUN)

SHOCK SUSPENSTORIES
Tiny Tot Comics
(E.C. Comics)
February-March, 1952

1 JDa,JKa,AF(c),ElectricChair . 650.00
2 WW,JDa,Grl,JKa,WW(c) . . . 350.00
3 WW,JDa,JKa,WW(c) 300.00
4 WW,JDa,JKa,WW(c) 300.00
5 WW,JDa,JKa,WW(c),Hanging 250.00
6 WW,AF,JKa,WW(c),
Bondage(c) 300.00
7 JKa,WW,GE,AF(c),Face
Melting 300.00
8 JKa,AF,AW,GE,WW,AF(c) . . 300.00
9 JKa,AF,RC,WW,AF(c) 300.00
10 JKa,WW,RC,JKa(c),Drug . . 300.00
11 JCr,JKa,WW,RC,JCr(c) 275.00
12 AF,JKa,WW,RC,AF(c)Drug 300.00
13 JKa,WW,FF,JKa(c) 350.00
14 JKa,WW,BK,WW(c) 275.00
15 JKa,WW,RC,JDa(c)
Strangulation 225.00
16 GE,RC,JKa,GE(c),Rape . . . 225.00
17 GE,RC,JKa,GE(c) 200.00
18 GE,RC,JKa,GE(c);Jan'55 . . 200.00

SHOCKING MYSTERY CASES
(see THRILLING CRIME CASES)

SILVER STREAK COMICS
Your Guide/New Friday/

Comic House/Newsbrook Publications/Lev Gleason
December, 1939

1 JCo,JCo(c),I&B:The Claw,Red
Reeves Capt.Fearless;B:Mr.
Midnight,Wasp;A:Spiritman 7,000.00
2 JSm,JCo,JSm(c) 2,200.00
3 JaB(c),I&O:Silver Streak;
B:Dickie Dean,Lance Hale,
Ace Powers,Bill Wayne,
Planet Patrol 1,800.00
4 JCo,JaB(c)B:Sky Wolf;
N:Silver Streak,I:Lance
Hale's Sidekick-Jackie 900.00
5 JCo,JCo(c),Dickie Dean
V:The Raging Flood 1,000.00
6 JCo,JaB,JCo(c),O&I:Daredevil
[Blue & Yellow Costume];
R:The Claw 7,000.00
7 JCo,N: Daredevil 4,500.00
8 JCo,JCo(c) 1,400.00
9 JCo,BoW(c) 1,000.00
10 BoW,BoW(c) 900.00
11 DRi(c) I:Mercury 600.00
12 DRi(c) 500.00
13 JaB,JaB(c),O:Thun-Dohr . . . 500.00
14 JaB,JaB(c),A:Nazi
Skull Men 500.00

Silver Streak #14
© *Your Guide/New Friday*

15 JaB,DBr,JaB(c),
B:Bingham Boys 450.00
16 DBr,BoW(c) 450.00
17 DBr,JaB(c),E:Daredevil 450.00
18 DBr,JaB(c),B:The Saint 400.00
19 DBr,EA 300.00
20 BW,BEv,EA 300.00
21 BW,BEv 300.00
Becomes:
CRIME DOES NOT PAY
22(23) CBi(c),The Mad Musician
& Tunes of Doom 1,100.00
23 CBi(c),John Dillinger-One
Man Underworld 600.00
24 CBi(c),The Mystery of the
Indian Dick 500.00
25 CBi(c),Dutch Shultz-King
of the Underworld 350.00
26 CBi(c),Lucky Luciano-The

Deadliest of Crime Rats . . . 350.00
27 CBi(c),Pretty Boy Floyd . . . 350.00
28 CBi(c), ... 350.00
29 CBi(c),Two-Gun Crowley-The
Bad Kid with the Itchy
Trigger Finger 300.00
30 CBi(c),"Monk"Eastman
V:Thompson's Mob 300.00
31 CBi(c) The Million Dollar
Bank Robbery 200.00
32 CBi(c),Seniorita of Sin 200.00
33 CBi(c),Meat Cleaver Murder 200.00
34 CBi(c),Elevator Shaft 200.00
35 CBi(c),Case o/t MissingToe . 200.00
36 CBi(c) 175.00
37 CBi(c) 175.00
38 CBi(c) 175.00
39 FG,CBi(c) 175.00
40 FG,CBi(c) 175.00
41 FG,RP,CBi(c),The Cocksure
Counterfeiter 125.00
42 FG,RP,CBi(c) 150.00
43 FG,RP,CBi(c) 100.00
44 FG,CBi(c),The Most Shot
At Gangster 100.00
45 FG,CBi(c) 100.00
46 FG,CBi(c),ChildKidnapping(c) 110.00
47 FG,CBi(c),ElectricChair 150.00
48 FG,CBi(c) 100.00
49 FG,CBi(c) 100.00
50 FG,CBi(c) 100.00
51 FG,GT,CBi(c),1st Monthly Iss. 75.00
52 FG,GT,CBi(c) 75.00
53 FG,CBi(c) 75.00
54 FG,CBi(c) 75.00

Crime Does Not Pay #55
© *Comic House/Lev Gleason*

55 FG,CBi(c) 75.00
56 FG,GT,CBi(c) 75.00
57 FG,CBi(c) 75.00
58 FG,CBi(c) 75.00
59 FG,Cbi(c) 75.00
60 FG,CBi(c) 75.00
61 FG,GT,CBi(c) 60.00
62 FG,CBi(c),Bondage(c) 85.00
63 FG,GT,CBi(c) 60.00
64 FG,GT,CBi(c) 60.00
65 FG,CBi(c) 60.00
66 FG,GT,CBi(c) 60.00
67 FG,GT,CBi(c) 60.00

68 FG,CBi(c)	60.00
69 FG,CBi(c)	60.00
70 FG,Cbi(c)	60.00
71 FG,CBi(c)	50.00
72 FG,CBi(c)	50.00
73 FG,CBi(c)	50.00
74 FG,CBi(c)	50.00
75 FG,CBi(c)	50.00
76 FG,CBi(c)	50.00
77 FG,CBi(c),The Electrified Safe	55.00
78 FG,CBi(c)	50.00
79 FG	50.00
80 FG	50.00
81 FG	50.00
82 FG	50.00
83 FG	50.00
84 FG	50.00
85 FG	50.00
86 FG	45.00
87 FG,P(c),The Rock-A-Bye Baby Murder	45.00
88 FG,P(c),Death Carries a Torch	45.00
89 FG,BF,BF P(c),The Escort Murder Case	45.00
90 FG,BF P(c),The Alhambra Club Murders	45.00
91 FG,AMc,BF P(c),Death Watches The Clock	45.00
92 BF,FG,BF P(c)	45.00
93 BF,FG,AMc,BF P(c)	45.00
94 BF,FG,BF P(c)	45.00
95 FG,AMc,BF P(c)	45.00
96 BF,FG,BF P(c),The Case of the Movie Star's Double	45.00
97 FG,BF P(c)	45.00
98 BF,FG,BF P(c),Bondage(c)	45.00
99 BF,FG,BF P(c)	45.00
100 FG,BF,AMc,P(c),The Case of the Jittery Patient	60.00
101 FG,BF,AMc,P(c)	35.00
102 FG,BF,AMc,BF P(c)	35.00
103 FG,BF,AMc,BF P(c)	35.00
104 thru 110 FG	@35.00
111 thru 120	@35.00
121 thru 140	@32.00
141 JKu	30.00
142 JKu,CBi(c)	30.00
143 JKu,Comic Code	25.00
144 I Helped Capture"Fat Face" George Klinerz	20.00
145 RP,Double Barrelled Menace	20.00
146 BP,The Con & The Canary	20.00
147 JKu,BP,A Long Shoe On the Highway;July, 1955	25.00

SINGLE SERIES
United Features Syndicate
1938

1 Captain & The Kids	550.00
2 Bronco Bill	300.00
3 Ella Cinders	250.00
4 Li'l Abner	400.00
5 Fritzi Ritz	175.00
6 Jim Hardy	225.00
7 Frankie Doodle	175.00
8 Peter Pat	175.00
9 Strange As it Seems	175.00
10 Little Mary Mixup	165.00
11 Mr. & Mrs. Beans	165.00
12 Joe Jinx	165.00
13 Looy Dot Dope	165.00
14 Billy Make Believe	165.00
15 How It Began	175.00
16 Illustrated Gags	125.00
17 Danny Dingle	125.00

18 Li'l Abner	375.00
19 Broncho Bill	225.00
20 Tarzan	750.00
21 Ella Cinders	200.00
22 Iron Vic	175.00
23 Tailspin Tommy	200.00
24 Alice In Wonderland	250.00
25 Abbie an' Slats	200.00
26 Little Mary Mixup	150.00
27 Jim Hardy	175.00
28 Ella Cinders & Abbie AN' Slats 1942	175.00

SKELETON HAND
American Comics Group
September-October, 1952

1	200.00
2 The Were-Serpent of Karnak	125.00
3 Waters of Doom	100.00
4 Black Dust	100.00
5 The Rise & Fall of the Bogey Man	100.00
6 July-August, 1953	100.00

SKY BLAZERS
Hawley Publications
September, 1940

1 Flying Aces,Sky Pirates	250.00
2 November, 1940	200.00

SKYMAN
Columbia Comics Group
1941

1 OW,OW(c),O:Skyman,Face	450.00
2 OW,OW(c),Yankee Doodle	250.00
3 OW,OW(c)	175.00
4 OW,OW(c),Statue of Liberty(c) 1948	175.00

SKY PILOT
Ziff-Davis Publishing Co.
1950

10 NS P(c),Lumber Pirates	65.00
11 Ns P(c),The 2,00 Foot Drop; April-May, 1951	55.00

SKY ROCKET
Home Guide Publ.
(Harry 'A' Chesler)
1944

1 Alias the Dragon,Skyrocket	125.00

SKY SHERIFF
D.S. Publishing
Summer, 1948

1 I:Breeze Lawson & the Prowl Plane Patrol	65.00

SLAM BANG COMICS
Fawcett Publications
January, 1940

1 B:Diamond Jack,Mark Swift,LeeGranger,JungleKing	800.00
2 F:Jim Dolan Two-Fisted Crime Buster	400.00
3 A: Eric the Talking Lion	500.00
4 F: Hurricane Hansen-Sea Adventurer	350.00
5	350.00
6 I: Zoro the Mystery Man; Bondage(c)	375.00
7 Bondage(c);Sept., 1940	375.00

SLAPSTICK COMICS
Comic Magazine Distrib., Inc.
1945

N# Humorous Parody	125.00

SLAVE GIRL COMICS
Avon Periodicals
February, 1949

1	500.00
2 April, 1949	325.00

SLICK CHICK COMICS
Leader Enterprises, Inc.
1947

1 Teen-Aged Humor	65.00
2 Teen-Aged Humor	45.00
3 1947	45.00

SMASH COMICS
Comics Magazine, Inc.
(Quality Comics Group)
August, 1939

1 WE,O&B:Hugh Hazard, Bozo the Robot,Black X, Invisible Justice: B:Wings Wendall, Chic Carter	1,100.00
2 WE,A:Lone Star Rider	450.00
3 WE,B:Captain Cook,JohnLaw	350.00
4 WE,PGn,B:Flash Fulton	300.00
5 WE,PGn,Bozo Robot	300.00
6 WE,PGn,GFx,Black X(c)	300.00
7 WE,PGn,GFx,Wings Wendell(c)	250.00
8 WE,PGn,GFx,Bozo Robot	250.00
9 WE,PGn,GFx,Black X(c)	250.00
10 WE,PGn,GFx,Bozo robot(c)	250.00
11 WE,PGn,BP,Black X(c)	250.00
12 WE,PGn,GFx,BP,Bozo(c)	250.00
13 WE,PGn,GFx,AB,BP,B:Mango, Purple Trio,BlackX(c)	250.00
14 BP,LF,AB,PGn,I:The Ray	1,200.00
15 BP,LF,AB,PGn,The Ram(c)	600.00

Smash Comics #43
© Comics Magazine/Quality Comics

16 BP,LF,AB,PGn,Bozo(c)	600.00
17 BP,LF,AB,PGn,JCo, The Ram(c)	600.00
18 BP,LF,AB,JCo,PGn,	

B&O:Midnight 700.00
19 BP,LF,AB,JCo,PGn,Bozo(c) 450.00
20 BP,LF,AB,JCo,PGn,
The Ram(c) 450.00
21 BP,LF,AB,JCo,PGn 450.00
22 BP,LF,AB,JCo,PGn,
B:The Jester 450.00
23 BP,AB,JCo,RC,PGn,
The Ram(c) 400.00
24 BP,AB,JCo,RC,PGn,A:Sword,
E:ChicCarter,
N:WingsWendall 400.00
25 AB,JCo,RC,PGn,O:Wildfire . 475.00
26 AB,JCo,RC,PGn,Bozo(c) . . 350.00
27 AB,JCo,RC,PGn,The Ram(c) 350.00
28 AB,JCo,RC,PGn,
1st Midnight (c) 350.00
29 AB,JCo,Rc,PGn,B;Midnight(c) 325.00
30 AB,JCo,PGn 325.00
31 AB,JCo,PGn 300.00
32 AB,JCo,PGn 300.00
33 AB,JCo,PGn,O:Marksman . . 350.00
34 AB,JCo,PGn 300.00
35 AB,JCo,RC,PGn 300.00
36 AB,JCo,RC,PGn,E:Midnight(c)325.00
37 AB,JCo,RC,PGn,Doc
Wacky becomes Fastest
Human on Earth 325.00
38 JCo,RC,PGn,B:Yankee Eagle 300.00
39 PGn,B:Midnight(c) 250.00
40 PGn,E:Ray 250.00
41 PGn 125.00
42 PGn,B:Lady Luck 135.00
43 PGn 150.00
44 PGn 135.00
45 PGn,E:Midnight(c) 135.00
46 RC,Twelve Hours to Live . . 135.00
47 Wanted Midnight,
Dead or Alive 135.00
48 Midnight Meets the
Menace from Mars 135.00
49 PGn,FG,Mass of Muscle . . . 135.00
50 I:Hyram the Hermit 135.00
51 A:Wild Bill Hiccup 100.00
52 PGn,FG,Did Ancient Rome Fall,
or was it Pushed? 100.00
53 Is ThereHonorAmongThieves 100.00
54 A:Smear-Faced Schmaltz . . 100.00
55 Never Trouble Trouble until
Trouble Troubles You 100.00
56 The Laughing Killer 100.00
57 A Dummy that Turns Into
A Curse 100.00
58 . . . . 100.00
59 A Corpse that Comes Alive . 100.00
60 The Swooner & the Trush . . 100.00
61 . . . . 85.00
62 V:The Lorelet 85.00
63 PGn 85.00
64 PGn,In Search of King Zoris . 85.00
65 PGn,V:Cyanide Cindy 85.00
66 Under Circle's Spell 85.00
67 A Living Clue 85.00
68 JCo,Atomic Dice 85.00
69 JCo,V:Sir Nuts 85.00
70 . . . . 85.00
71 . . . . 75.00
72 JCo,Angela,the Beautiful
Bovine 75.00
73 . . . . 75.00
74 . . . . 75.00
75 The Revolution 75.00
76 Bowl Over Crime 75.00
77 Who is Lilli Dilli? 75.00
78 JCo,Win Over Crime 75.00

79 V:The Men From Mars 75.00
80 JCo,V:Big Hearted Bosco . . . 75.00
81 V:Willie the Kid 75.00
82 V:Woodland Boy 75.00
83 JCo,Quizmaster 75.00
84 A Date With Father Time . . . 75.00
85 JCo,A Singing Swindle 75.00

SMASH HITS SPORTS COMICS
Essankay Publications
January, 1949
1 LbC,LbC(c) 125.00

SMILEY BURNETTE WESTERN
Fawcett Publications
March, 1950
1 Ph(c),B:Red Eagle 300.00
2 Ph(c) 200.00
3 Ph(c) 200.00
4 Ph(c) 200.00

Smilin' Jack © Dell Publishing Co.

SMILIN' JACK
Dell Publishing Co.
1940
1 . . . . 75.00
2 . . . . 45.00
3 thru 8 . . . . @35.00

SMITTY
Dell Publishing Co.
1940
1 . . . . 65.00
2 . . . . 40.00
3 . . . . 25.00
4 thru 7 . . . . @20.00

SNAP
Harry 'A' Chesler Jr. Publications
1944
N# Humorous 75.00

SNAPPY COMICS
Cima Publications (Prize)
1945
1 A:Animale 125.00

SNIFFY THE PUP
Animated Cartoons (Standard Comics)
November, 1949
5 FF,Funny Animal 45.00
6 thru 9 Funny Animal . . . . . @20.00
10 thru 17 Funny Animal . . . . @15.00
18 September, 1953 . . . . 15.00

SOLDIER COMICS
Fawcett Publications
January, 1952
1 Fighting Yanks on Flaming
Battlefronts 55.00
2 Blazing Battles Exploding
with Combat 25.00
3 . . . . 25.00
4 A Blow for Freedom 20.00
5 Only The Dead Are Free . . . 20.00
6 Blood & Guts 15.00
7 The Phantom Sub 15.00
8 More Plasma! 15.00
9 Red Artillery 15.00
10 . . . . 15.00
11 September, 1953 . . . . 15.00

SOLDIERS OF FORTUNE
Creston Publications (American Comics Group)
February-March, 1952
1 OW(c),B:Ace Carter,
Crossbones, Lance Larson 125.00
2 OW(c) 75.00
3 OW(c) 60.00
4 . . . . 60.00
5 OW(c) 60.00
6 OW(c),OW,Bondage(c) 65.00
7 . . . . 60.00
8 OW 60.00
9 OW 60.00
10 OW 60.00
11 OW,Format Change to War . 25.00
12 . . . . 25.00
13 OW,February-March, 1953 . . 25.00

SON OF SINBAD
St. John Publishing Co.
February, 1950
1 JKu,JKu(c),The Curse of the
Caliph's Dancer 250.00

SPACE ACTION
Junior Books (Ace Magazines)
June, 1952
1 Invaders from a Lost Galaxy 400.00
2 The Silicon Monster from
Galaxy X 300.00
3 Attack on Ishtar,
October., 1952 . . . . 275.00

SPACE ADVENTURES
Capitol Stories/ Charlton Comics
July, 1952

1 AFa&LM(c) 250.00
2 .... 125.00
3 DG(c) 110.00
4 DG(c) 100.00
5 StC(c) 100.00
6 StC(c),Two Worlds 85.00
7 DG(c),Transformation 100.00
8 DG(c),All For Love 85.00
9 DG(c) 85.00
10 SD,SD(c) 225.00
11 SD,JoS 250.00
12 SD(c) 250.00
13 A:Blue Beetle 100.00
14 A:Blue Beetle 100.00
15 Ph(c) of Rocky Jones 100.00
16 BKa,A:Rocky Jones 125.00
17 A:Rocky Jones 100.00
18 A:Rocky Jones 100.00
19 .... 75.00
20 First Trip to the Moon 150.00
21 .... 75.00
22 Does Not Exist
23 SD,Space Trip to the Moon . 135.00
24 .... 100.00
25 Brontosaurus 100.00
26 SD,Flying Saucers 125.00
27 SD,Flying Saucers 125.00
28 Moon Trap 35.00
29 Captive From Space 35.00
30 Peril in the Sky 35.00
31 SD,SD(c),Enchanted Planet 100.00
32 SD,SD(c),Last Ship
   from Earth 100.00
33 Galactic Scourge,
   I&O:Captain Atom 250.00
34 SD,SD(c),A:Captain Atom .. 110.00
35 thru 40 SD,SD(c),
   A:Captain Atom .... @110.00
41 .... 20.00
42 SD,A:Captain Atom 20.00
43 .... 20.00
44 A:Mercury Man 20.00
45 A:Mercury Man 20.00
46 thru 58 .... @20.00
59 November, 1964 .... 20.00

SPACE BUSTERS
Ziff-Davis Publishing Co.
Spring, 1952

Space Comics #5 © Avon Publications

1 BK,NS(c),Ph(c),Charge of
   the Battle Women 400.00
2 EK,BK,MA,NS(c),
   Bondage(c),Ph(c) 350.00
3 Autumn, 1952 .... 325.00

SPACE COMICS
Avon Periodicals
March-April, 1954

4 (fa),F:Space Mouse 30.00
5 (fa),F:Space Mouse,
   May-June, 1954 .... 25.00

SPACE DETECTIVE
Avon Periodicals
July, 1951

1 WW,WW(c),Opium Smugglers
   of Venus 600.00
2 WW,WW(c),Batwomen of
   Mercury 400.00
3 EK(c),SeaNymphs ofNeptune 225.00
4 EK,Flame Women of Vulcan,
   Bondage(c) 275.00

SPACE MOUSE
Avon Periodicals
April, 1953

1 Funny Animal 45.00
2 Funny Animal 35.00
3 thru 5 Funny Animal .... @20.00

SPACE PATROL
Approved Comics
(Ziff-Davis)
Summer, 1952

1 BK,NS,Ph(c), The Lady of
   Diamonds 500.00
2 BK,NS,Ph(c),Slave King of
   Pluto,Oct.-Nov., 1952 .... 350.00

SPACE THRILLERS
Avon Periodicals
1954

N# Contents May Vary 600.00

SPACE WESTERN
COMICS
(see YELLOWJACKET
COMICS)

SPARKLER COMICS
United Features Syndicate
July, 1940

1 Jim Handy 225.00
2 Frankie Doodle,August, 1940 150.00

SPARKLER COMICS
United Features Syndicate
July, 1941

1 BHg,O:Sparkman;B:Tarzan,Captain
   & the Kids,Ella Cinders,Danny
   Dingle,Dynamite Dunn, Nancy,
   Abbie an' Slats, Frankie
   Doodle,Broncho Bill 1,200.00
2 BHg, The Case of Poisoned
   Fruit 425.00
3 BHg 350.00
4 BHg,Case of Sparkman &
   the Firefly 350.00
5 BHg,Sparkman,Natch 325.00
6 BHg,Case o/t Bronze Bees . 300.00

7 BHg,Case o/t Green Raiders 300.00
8 BHg,V:River Fiddler 300.00
9 BHg,N:Sparkman 300.00
10 BHg,B:Hap Hopper,
   Sparkman's ID revealed ... 300.00
11 BHg,V:Japanese 250.00

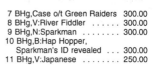

Sparkler Comics #7
© United Features Syndicate

12 BHg,Another N:Sparkman .. 250.00
13 BHg,Hap Hopper Rides
   For Freedom 250.00
14 BHg,BHg(c),Tarzan
   V:Yellow Killer 300.00
15 BHg 250.00
16 BHg,Sparkman V:Japanese 250.00
17 BHg,Nancy(c) 250.00
18 BHg,Sparkman in Crete ... 250.00
19 BHg,I&B:Race Riley
   ,Commandos 250.00
20 BHg,Nancy(c) 225.00
21 BHg,Tarzan(c) 225.00
22 BHg,Nancy(c) 200.00
23 BHg,Capt&Kids(c) 200.00
24 BHg,Nancy(c) 200.00
25 BHg,BHg(c),Tarzan(c) 250.00
26 BHg,Capt&Kids(c) 200.00
27 BHg,Nancy(c) 200.00
28 BHg,BHg(c),Tarzan(c) 250.00
29 BHg,Capt&Kids(c) 200.00
30 BHg,Nancy(c) 200.00
31 BHg,BHg(c),Tarzan(c) 250.00
32 BHg,Capt&Kids(c) 125.00
33 BHg,Nancy(c) 125.00
34 BHg,BHg(c),Tarzan(c) 225.00
35 BHg,Capt&Kids(c) 125.00
36 BHg,Nancy(c) 125.00
37 BHg,BHg(c),Tarzan(c) 225.00
38 BHg,Capt&Kids(c) 125.00
39 BHg,BHg(c),Tarzan(c) 225.00
40 BHg,Nancy(c) 125.00
41 BHg,Capt&Kids(c) 100.00
42 BHg,BHg,Tarzan(c) 175.00
43 BHg,Nancy(c) 100.00
44 BHg,Tarzan(c) 175.00
45 BHg,Capt&Kids(c) 100.00
46 BHg,Nancy(c) 100.00
47 BHg,Tarzan(c) 175.00
48 BHg,Nancy(c) 95.00
49 BHg,Capt&Kids(c) 95.00
50 BHg,BHg(c),Tarzan(c) 165.00

51 BHg,Capt&Kids(c) 75.00
52 BHg,Nancy(c) 75.00
53 BHg,BHg(c),Tarzan(c) .. 150.00
54 BHg,Capt&Kids(c) 65.00
55 BHg,Nancy(c) 65.00
56 BHg,Capt&Kids(c) 65.00
57 BHg,F:Li'l Abner 60.00
58 BHg,A:Fearless Fosdick 70.00
59 BHg,B:Li'l Abner 70.00
60 BHg,Nancy(c) 60.00
61 BHg,Capt&Kids(c) 60.00
62 BHg,Li'L Abner(c) 60.00
63 BHg,Capt&Kids(c) 60.00
64 BHg,Valentines (c) 60.00
65 BHg,Nancy(c) 60.00
66 BHg,Capt&Kids(c) 60.00
67 BHg,Nancy(c) 60.00
68 BHg, ... 60.00
69 BHg,B:Nancy (c) 60.00
70 BHg 60.00
71 thru 80 BHg .... @40.00
81 BHg,E:Nancy(c) 40.00
82 BHg 40.00
83 BHg,Tarzan(c) 30.00
84 BHg 30.00
85 BHg,E:Li'l Abner 30.00
86 BHg 30.00
87 BHg,Nancy(c) 30.00
88 thru 96 BHg .... @30.00
97 BHg,O:Lady Ruggles 50.00
98 BHg 30.00
99 BHg,Nancy(c) 30.00
100 BHg,Nancy(c) 45.00
101 thru 108 BHg .... @25.00
109 BHg,ATh 30.00
110 BHg 25.00
111 BHg 25.00
112 BHg 25.00
113 BHg,ATh 50.00
114 thru 120 BHg .... @25.00

Sparkling Stars #2
© Holyoke Publishing

SPARKLING STARS
Holyoke Publishing Co.
June, 1944
1 B:Hell's Angels,Ali Baba,FBI,
   Boxie Weaver,Petey & Pop . 80.00
2 .... 50.00

3 .... 35.00
4 thru 12 .... @30.00
13 O&I:Jungo, The Man-Beast .. 35.00
14 thru 19 .... @25.00
20 I:Fangs the Wolfboy 30.00
21 thru 28 .... @24.00
29 Bondage(c) 28.00
30 thru 32 .... @25.00
33 March, 1948 .... 25.00

SPARKMAN
Frances M. McQueeny
1944
1 O:Sparkman 200.00

SPARKY WATTS
Columbia Comics Group
1942
1 A:Skyman,Hitler(c) 250.00
2 .... 125.00
3 .... 100.00
4 O:Skyman 90.00
5 A:Skyman 75.00
6 .... 50.00
7 .... 50.00
8 .... 50.00
9 .... 50.00
10 1949 .... 50.00

[STEVE SAUNDERS]
SPECIAL AGENT
Parents Magazine/
Commended Comics
December, 1947
1 J. Edgar Hoover, Ph(c) 60.00
2 .... 30.00
3 thru 7 .... @25.00
8 September, 1949 .... 25.00

SPECIAL COMICS
(see LAUGH COMICS)

SPECIAL EDITION
COMICS
Fawcett Publications
August, 1940
1 CCB,CCB(c),F:Captain
   Marvel 6,500.00

SPEED COMICS
Brookwood/Speed Publ.
Harvey Publications
October, 1939
1 BP,B&O:Shock Gibson,B:Spike
   Marlin,Biff Bannon ... 1,100.00
2 BP ,B:Shock Gibson(c) 500.00
3 BP,GT 300.00
4 BP 275.00
5 BP,DBr 275.00
6 BP,GT 225.00
7 GT,JKu,B:Mars Mason 225.00
8 JKu 200.00
9 JKu 200.00
10 JKu,E:Shock Gibson(c) 200.00
11 JKu,E:Mars Mason 200.00
12 B:The Wasp 250.00
13 I:Captain Freedom;B:Girls
   Commandos,Pat Parker ... 300.00
14 Pocket sized format-100pgs. 250.00
15 Pocket size 250.00
16 JKu,Pocket size 250.00
17 O:Black Cat 400.00

Speed Comics #14
© Brookwood/Speed Publ./Harvey Publ.

18 B:Capt.Freedom,Bondage(c) 225.00
19 .... 190.00
20 .... 190.00
21 JKu(c) 210.00
22 JKu(c) 210.00
23 JKu(c),O:Girl Commandos . 250.00
24 .... 200.00
25 .... 200.00
26 Flag (c) 200.00
27 .... 200.00
28 E:Capt Freedom 200.00
29 Case o/t Black Marketeers . 200.00
30 POW Death Chambers ... 200.00
31 ASh(c),Nazi Thrashing(c) .. 175.00
32 ASh(c) 175.00
33 ASh(c) 175.00
34 ASh(c) 175.00
35 ASh(c),BlackCat'sDeathTrap 200.00
36 ASh(c) 175.00
37 RP(c) 175.00
38 RP(c),War Bond Plea with Iwo
   Jima flag allusion(c) 225.00
39 RP(c),B:Capt Freedom(c) .. 175.00
40 RP(c) 175.00
41 RP(c) 175.00
42 JKu,RP(c) 175.00
43 JKu,E:Capt Freedom(c) ... 175.00
44 BP,JKu,Four Kids on a raft,
   January-February, 1947 ... 175.00

SPEED SMITH THE HOT
ROD KING
Ziff-Davis Publishing Co.
Spring, 1952
1 INS,Ph(c),A:Roscoe
   the Rascal 125.00

All comics prices listed are for *Near Mint* condition.

SPIRIT, THE
Will Eisner
(Weekly Coverless
Comic Book)
June, 1940

WE,O:SPirit	500.00
6/9/40 WE	250.00
6/16/40 WE,Black Queen ..	175.00
6/23/40 WE,Mr Mystic	150.00
6/30/40 WE	150.00
7/7/40 WE,Black Queen ...	150.00
7/14/40 WE	100.00
7/21/40 WE	100.00
7/28/40 WE	100.00
8/4/40 WE	100.00
7/7/40-11/24/40,WE	70.00
12/1/40 WE,Ellen Spanking(c)	100.00
12/8/40-12/29/40	60.00
1941 WE Each	50.00
3/16 WE I:Silk Satin	95.00
6/15 WE I Twilight	60.00
6/22 WE Hitler	60.00
1942 WE Each	40.00
2-1	60.00
2-15	45.00
2-23	65.00
1943 WE Each,LF,WE scripts .	30.00
1944 JCo,LF	15.00
1945 LF Each, ...	15.00
1946 WE Each	30.00
1/13 WE,O:The Spirit	50.00
1/20 WE,Satin	50.00
3/17 WE,I:Nylon	50.00
4/21 WE,I:Mr.Carrion	55.00
7/7 WE,I:Dulcet Tone&Skinny	50.00
10/6 WE,I:F:Gell	60.00
1947 WE Each	30.00
7/13.,WE,Hansel &Gretel ...	45.00
7/20,WE,A:Bomb	50.00
9/28,WE,Flying Saucers	65.00
10/5,WE, Cinderella	32.00
12/7,WE,I:Power Puff	32.00
1948 WE Each	30.00
1/11,WE,Sparrow Fallon ...	35.00
1/25,WE,I:Last A Net	40.00
3/14,WE,A:Kretuama	35.00
4/4,WE,A:Wildrice	35.00
7/25,The Thing	60.00
8/22,Poe Tale,Horror	65.00
9/18, A:Lorelei	35.00
11/7,WE,A:Plaster of Paris ..	40.00
1949 WE Each	30.00
1/23 WE,I:Thorne	40.00
8/21 WE,I:Monica Veto	40.00
9/25 WE,A:Ice	40.00
12/4 WE,I:Flaxen	35.00
1950 WE Each	30.00
1/8 WE,I:Sand Saref	70.00
2/10, Horror Issue	35.00
1951 WE(Last WE 8/12/51) .	@30.00
Non-Eisners	@12.00
1952 Non-Eisners	@12.00
7/27 WW,Denny Colt	350.00
8/3 WW,Moon	350.00
8/10 WW.Moon	350.00
8/17 WW,WE,Heart	300.00
8/24 WW,Rescue	300.00
8/31 WW,Last Man	300.00
9/7 WW,Man Moon	380.00
9/14 WE	80.00
9/21 WE Space	250.00
9/28 WE Moon	300.00
10/5 WE Last Story	125.00

SPIRIT, THE
Quality Comics Group/
Vital Publ.
1944

N# Wanted Dead or Alive! ...	450.00
N# ...in Crime Doesn't Pay ...	275.00
N# ...In Murder Runs Wild ...	200.00
4 ...Flirts with Death	175.00
5 ...Wanted Dead or Alive ...	150.00
6 ...Gives You Triple Value ...	125.00
7 ...Rocks the Underworld ...	125.00
8	125.00
9 ...Throws Fear Into the	
Heart of Crime	125.00
10 ...Stalks Crime	125.00
11 ...America's Greatest	
Crime Buster	125.00
12 WE(c),...The Famous Outlaw	
Who Smashes Crime	200.00
13 WE(c),...and Ebony Cleans Out	
the Underworld;Bondage(c) .	200.00
14 WE(c)	200.00
15 WE(c),Bank Robber at Large	200.00
16 WE(c),The Caase of the	
Uncanny Cat	200.00
17 WE(c),The Organ Grinding	
Bank Robber	200.00
18 WE,WE(c),'The Bucket	
of Blood	250.00
19 WE,WE(c),'The Man Who	
Murdered the Spirit'	250.00
20 WE,WE(c),'The Vortex' ...	250.00
21 WE,WE(c),'P'Gell of Paris' .	250.00
22 WE(c),TheOctopus,Aug.1950	400.00

SPIRIT, THE
Fiction House Magazines
1952

1 Curse of Claymore Castle .	200.00
2 WE,WE(c),Who Says Crime	
Doesn't Pay	250.00
3 WE/JGr(c),League of Lions .	150.00
4 WE,WE&JGr(c),Last Prowl of	
Mr. Mephisto;Bondage (c) .	200.00
5 WE,WE(c),Ph(c)1954	200.00

SPIRITMAN
Will Eisner

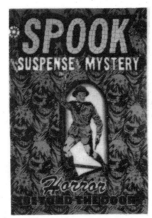

Spook Comics #1 © Baily Publ.

1944

1 3 Spirit Sections from	
1944 Bound Together	125.00
2 LF, 2 Spirit Sections	
from 1944 Bound Together	100.00

SPITFIRE COMICS
Harvey Publ.
August, 1941

1 MKd(c), 100pgs., Pocket size	300.00
2 100 pgs.,Pocket size,	
October, 1941	275.00

SPOOK COMICS
Baily Publications
1946

1 A:Mr. Lucifer	150.00

SPOOK DETECTIVE CASES
(see CRIMINALS ON THE RUN)

SPOOKY
Harvey Publications
November, 1955

1 Funny Apparition	175.00
2 same	75.00
3 thru 10 same	@35.00
11 thru 20 same	@20.00
21 thru 30 same	@15.00
31 thru 40 same	@12.00
41 thru 70 same	@7.00
71 thru 90 same	@4.00
91 thru 120 same	@3.00
121 thru 160 same	@2.50
161 same,September, 1980	2.50

SPOOKY MYSTERIES
Your Guide Publishing Co.
1946

1 Rib-Tickling Horror	75.00

SPORT COMICS
(see TRUE SPORT
PICTURE STORIES)

SPORTS THRILLS
(see DICK COLE)

SPOTLIGHT COMICS
Harry 'A' Chesler Jr.
Publications
November, 1944

1 GT,GT(c),B:Veiled Avenger,	
Black Dwarf,Barry Kuda ...	300.00
2	250.00
3 1945,Eye Injury	250.00

SPUNKY
Standard Comics
April, 1949

1 FF,Adventures of a Junior	
Cowboy	40.00
2 FF	25.00
3	20.00
4	20.00
5	20.00
6	20.00
7 November, 1951	20.00

SPY AND COUNTER SPY
Best Syndicated Features
(American Comics Group)
August-September, 1949

1 I&O:Jonathan Kent		125.00
2		100.00

Becomes:
SPY HUNTERS

3 Jonathan Kent		100.00
4 J.Kent		60.00
5 J.Kent		60.00
6 J.Kent		60.00
7 OW(c),J.Kent		60.00
8 OW(c),J.Kent		60.00
9 OW(c),J.Kent		60.00
10 OW(c),J.Kent		60.00
11		45.00
12 OW(c),MD		45.00
13 and 14		@40.00
15 OW(c)		42.00
16 AW		75.00
17		35.00
18 War (c)		35.00
19 and 20		@35.00
21 B:War Content		35.00
22		35.00
23 Torture		100.00
24 'BlackmailBrigade',July,1953		35.00

SPY SMASHER
Fawcett Publications
Autumn, 1941

1 B;Spy Smasher		1,850.00
2 Mra(c)		900.00
3 Bondage (c)		650.00
4		625.00
5 Mra,Mt. Rushmore(c)		600.00
6 Mra,Mra(c),V:The Sharks of Steel		600.00
7 Mra		600.00
8 AB		450.00
9 AB,Hitler,Tojo, Mussolini(c)		500.00
10 AB,Did Spy Smasher Kill Hitler?		500.00
11 AB,February, 1943		450.00

SQUEEKS
Lev Gleason Publications
October, 1953

1 CBi(c),(fa)		30.00
2 CBi(c),(fa)		15.00
3 CBi(c),(fa)		12.00
4 (fa)		12.00
5 (fa),January, 1954		12.00

STAMP COMICS
Youthful Magazines/Stamp Comics, Inc.
October, 1951

1 HcK,Birth of Liberty		175.00
2 HcK,RP,Battle of White Plains		100.00
3 HcK,DW,RP,Iwo Jima		75.00
4 HcK,DW,RP		75.00
5 HcK,Von Hindenberg disaster		85.00
6 HcK,The Immortal Chaplains		75.00
7 HcK,RKr,RP,B&O:Railroad		125.00

Becomes:
THRILLING ADVENTURES IN STAMPS

8 HcK, 100 Pgs.,Jan.,1953		450.00

Star Comics #17
© Chester Centaur Publications

STAR COMICS
Comic Magazines/Ultem Publ./Chesler
Centaur Publications
February, 1937

1 B:Dan Hastings		800.00
2		425.00
3		350.00
4 WMc(c)		400.00
5 WMc(c),A:Little Nemo		400.00
6 CBi(c),FG		325.00
7 FG		300.00
8 BoW,BoW(c),FG,A:Little Nemo,Horror		350.00
9 FG,CBi(c)		300.00
10 FG,CBi(c),BoW,A:Impyk		450.00
11 FG,BoW,JCo		400.00
12 FG,BoW,B:Riders of the Golden West		325.00
13 FG,BoW		300.00
14 FG,GFx(c)		300.00
15 CBu,B:The Last Pirate		325.00
16 CBu,B:Phantom Rider		325.00
2-1 CBu,B:Phantom Rider(c)		325.00
2-2 CBu,A:Diana Deane		300.00
2-3 GFx(c),CBu		275.00
2-4 CBu		275.00
2-5 CBu		250.00
2-6 CBu,E:Phanton Rider		250.00
2-7 CBu,August, 1939		250.00

STARLET O'HARA IN HOLLYWOOD
Standard Comics
December, 1948

1 The Terrific Tee-Age Comic		100.00
2 Her Romantic Adventures in Movie land		75.00
3 and 4, Sept., 1949		@50.00

STAR RANGER
Comic Magazines/Ultem/ Centaur Publ.
February, 1937

1 FG,I:Western Comic		1,000.00
2		500.00

3 FG		400.00
4		400.00
5		300.00
6 FG		300.00
7 FG		275.00
8 GFx,FG,PGn,BoW		275.00
9 GFx,FG,PGn,BoW		275.00
10 JCo,GFx,FG,PGn,BoW		450.00
11		350.00
12 JCo,JCo(c),FG,PGn		350.00

Becomes:
COWBOY COMICS

13 FG,PGn		650.00
14 FG,PGn		450.00

Becomes:
STAR RANGER FUNNIES

15 WE,PGn		500.00
2-1(16) JCo,JCo(c)		350.00
2-2(17) PGn,JCo,A:Night Hawk		325.00
2-3(18) JCo,FG		325.00
2-4(19) A:Kit Carson		325.00
2-5(20) October, 1939		325.00

STARS AND STRIPES COMICS
Comic Corp of America
(Centaur Publications)
May, 1941

2 PGn,PGn(c),'Called to Colors', The Shark,The Voice		1,250.00
3 PGn,PGn(c),O:Dr.Synthe		750.00
4 PGn,PGn(c),I:The Stars & Stripes		650.00
5		500.00
6(5), December, 1941		500.00

STAR STUDDED
Cambridge House
1945

N# 25 cents (c) price;128 pgs.; 32 F:stories		150.00
N# The Cadet,Hoot Gibson, Blue Beetle,		125.00

STARTLING COMICS
Better Publ./Nedor Publ.
June, 1940

1 WE,LF,B&O:Captain Future, Mystico, Wonder Man; B:Masked Rider		1,000.00
2 Captain Future(c)		375.00
3 same		325.00
4 same		250.00
5 same		200.00
6 same		175.00
7 same		175.00
8 ASh(c)		175.00
9 Bondage(c)		225.00
10 O:Fighting Yank		1,200.00
11 Fighting Yank(c)		350.00
12 Hitler,Mussolini,Tojo cover		250.00
13 JBi		225.00
14 JBi		225.00
15 Fighting Yank (c)		225.00
16 Bondage(c),O:FourComrades		250.00
17 Fighting Yank (c), E:Masked Rider		190.00
18 JBi,B&O:Pyroman		450.00
19 Pyroman(c)		200.00
20 Pyroman(c),B:Oracle		200.00
21 HcK,ASh(c)Bondage(c)O:Ape		200.00

22 HcK,ASh(c),Fighting Yank(c) 175.00
23 HcK,BEv,ASh(c),Pyroman(c) 175.00
24 HcK,BEv,ASh(c),Fighting
   Yank(c) 175.00
25 HcK,BEv,ASh(c),Pyroman(c) 175.00
26 BEv,ASh(c),Fighting Yank(c) 175.00

Startling Comics #27
© Better Publ./Nedor Publ.

27 BEv,ASh(c),Pyroman(c) ... 175.00
28 BEv,ASh(c),Fighting Yank(c) 175.00
29 BEv,ASh(c),Pyroman(c) ... 175.00
30 ASh(c),Fighting Yank(c) ... 175.00
31 ASh(c),Pyroman(c) 175.00
32 ASh(c),Fighting Yank(c) ... 175.00
33 ASh(c),Pyroman(c) 175.00
34 ASh(c),Fighting Yank(c),
   O:Scarab 175.00
35 ASh(c),Pyroman(c) 200.00
36 ASh(c),Fighting Yank(c) ... 175.00
37 ASh(c),Bondage (c) 175.00
38 ASh(c),Bondage(c) 175.00
39 ASh(c),Pyroman(c) 175.00
40 ASh(c),E:Captain Future ... 175.00
41 ASh(c),Pyroman(c) 175.00
42 ASh(c),Fighting Yank(c) ... 175.00
43 ASh(c),Pyroman(c),
   E:Pyroman 175.00
44 Grl(c),Lance Lewis(c) 250.00
45 Grl(c),I:Tygra 250.00
46 Grl,Grl(c),Bondage(c) 250.00
47 ASh(c),Bondage(c) 200.00
48 ASh(c),Lance Lewis(c) 175.00
49 ASh(c),Bondage(c),
   E:Fighting Yank 200.00
50 ASh(c),Lance Lewis(c),
   Sea Eagle 175.00
51 ASh(c),Sea Eagle 175.00
52 ASh(c) 175.00
53 ASh(c),September, 1948 ... 175.00

STARTLING TERROR TALES
Star Publications
May, 1952
10 WW,LbC(c),The Story Starts 300.00
11 LbC(c),The Ghost Spider
   of Death 150.00
12 LbC(c),White Hand Horror .. 75.00
13 JyD,LbC(c),Love From

a Gorgor 75.00
14 LbC(c),Trapped by the
   Color of Blood 75.00
4 LbC(c),Crime at the Carnival 65.00
5 LbC(c),The Gruesome
   Demon of Terror 65.00
6 LbC(c),Footprints of Death .. 65.00

Startling Terror Tales #9
© Star Publications

7 LbC(c),The Case of the
   Strange Murder 75.00
8 RP,LbC(c),Phantom Brigade . 75.00
9 LbC(c),The Forbidden Tomb . 60.00
10 LbC(c),The Horrible Entity ... 75.00
11 RP,LbC(c),The Law Will
   Win, July, 1954 .... 75.00

STEVE CANYON COMICS
Harvey Publications
February, 1948
1 MC,BP,O:Steve Canyon ... 150.00
2 MC,BP 100.00
3 MC,BP,Canyon's Crew 75.00
4 MC,BP,Chase of Death 75.00
5 MC,BP,A:Happy Easter 75.00
6 MC,BP,A:Madame Lynx,
   December, 1948 .... 80.00

STEVE ROPER
Famous Funnies
April, 1948
1 Reprints newspaper strips .. 65.00
2 .... 35.00
3 thru 4 .... @25.00
5 December, 1948 .... 25.00

STORIES BY FAMOUS AUTHORS ILLUSTRATED
(see FAST FICTION)

STORY OF HARRY S. TRUMAN, THE
Democratic National Committee
1948
N# Giveaway-The Life of Our

33rd President 85.00

STRAIGHT ARROW
Magazine Enterprises
February-March, 1950
1 OW,B:Straight Arrow & his
   Horse Fury 250.00
2 BP,B&O:Red Hawk 125.00
3 BP,FF(c) 150.00
4 BP,Cave(c) 75.00
5 BP,StraightArrow'sGreatLeap 75.00
6 BP 60.00
7 BP,The Railroad Invades
   Comanche Country 60.00
8 BP 60.00
9 BP 60.00
10 BP 60.00
11 BP,The Valley of Time 70.00
12 thru 19 BP .... @50.00
20 BP,Straight Arrow's
   Great War Shield 65.00
21 BP,O:Fury 75.00
22 BP,FF(c) 100.00
23 BP 45.00
24 BP,The Dragons of Doom ... 45.00
25 BP 45.00
26 BP 45.00
27 BP 45.00
28 BP,Red Hawk 40.00
29 thru 35 BP .... @40.00
36 BP Drug 45.00
37 BP 35.00
38 BP 35.00
39 BP,The Canyon Beasts 30.00
40 BP,Secret of the
   Spanish Specters 30.00
41 BP 20.00
42 BP 20.00
43 BP,I:Blaze 25.00
44 thru 53 BP .... @20.00
54 BP,March, 1956 .... 20.00

STRANGE CONFESSIONS
Approved Publications (Ziff-Davis)
Spring, 1952
1 EK,Ph(c) 225.00
2 .... 150.00
3 EK,Ph(c),Girls reformatory .. 150.00
4 Girls reformatory 150.00

STRANGE FANTASY
Farrell Publications/ Ajax Comics
August, 1952
(2)1 .... 150.00
2 .... 135.00
3 The Dancing Ghost 125.00
4 Demon in the Dungeon,
   A:Rocketman 110.00
5 Visiting Corpse 80.00
6 .... 75.00
7 A:Madam Satan 110.00
8 A:Black Cat 85.00
9 S&K 100.00
10 .... 85.00
11 Fearful Things Can Happen
   in a Lonely Place 85.00
12 The Undying Fiend 75.00
13 Terror in the Attic,
   Bondage(c) 110.00
14 Monster in the Building,
   October-November, 1954 ... 75.00

UNKNOWN WORLD
Fawcett Publications
June, 1952
1 NS(c),Ph(c),Will You Venture
 to Meet the Unknown 175.00
Becomes:
STRANGE STORIES FROM ANOTHER WORLD
2 NS(c),Ph(c),Will You?
 Dare You 225.00
3 NS(c),Ph(c),The Dark Mirror 175.00
4 NS(c),Ph(c),Monsters of
 the Mind 175.00
5 NS(c),Ph(c),Dance of the
 Doomed February, 1953 .. 175.00

STRANGE SUSPENSE STORIES
Fawcett Publications
June, 1952
1 BP,MSy,MBi 350.00
2 MBi,GE 250.00
3 MBi,GE 200.00
4 BP 200.00
5 MBi(c),Voodoo(c) 200.00
6 BEv 90.00
7 BEv 100.00
8 AW 110.00
9 .... 90.00
10 .... 110.00
11 .... 75.00
12 .... 75.00
13 .... 75.00
14 .... 80.00
15 AW,BEv(c) 75.00
Charlton Comics
16 .... 100.00
17 .... 75.00
18 SD,SD(c) 150.00
19 SD,SD(c) 190.00
20 SD,SD(c) 150.00
21 .... 85.00
22 SD(c) 120.00
Becomes:
THIS IS SUSPENSE!
23 WW 135.00
24 .... 65.00
25 .... 45.00
26 .... 45.00
Becomes:
STRANGE SUSPENSE STORIES
27 .... 45.00
28 .... 35.00
29 .... 35.00
30 .... 35.00
31 SD(c) 85.00
32 SD 85.00
33 SD 85.00
34 SD,SD(c) 85.00
35 SD 85.00
36 SD,SD(c) 85.00
37 SD 90.00
38 .... 85.00
39 SD 30.00
40 SD 85.00
41 SD 75.00
42 .... 25.00
43 .... 25.00
44 .... 25.00
45 SD 65.00

46 .... 25.00
47 SD 65.00
48 SD 65.00
49 .... 25.00
50 SD 75.00
51 thru 53 SD .... @45.00
54 thru 60 .... @25.00
61 thru 74 .... @10.00
75 .... 80.00
76 .... 30.00
77 .... 30.00

STRANGE SUSPENSE STORIES
(see LAWBREAKERS)

STRANGE TERRORS
St. John Publishing Co.
June, 1952
1 The Ghost of Castle
 Karloff, Bondage(c) 200.00
2 UnshackledFlight intoNowhere 125.00
3 JKu,Ph(c),The Ghost Who
 Ruled Crazy Heights 175.00
4 JKu,Ph(c),Terror from
 the Tombs 200.00
5 JKu,Ph(c),No Escaping
 the Pool of Death 150.00
6 LC,PAM,Bondage(c),Giant .. 200.00
7 JKu,JKu(c),Cat's Death,Giant 225.00

STRANGE WORLD OF YOUR DREAMS
Prize Group
August, 1952
1 S&K(c),What Do They Mean–
 Messages Rec'd in Sleep . 350.00
2 MMe,S&K(c),Why did I Dream
 That I Was Being Married
 to a Man without a Face? .. 275.00
3 S&K(c) 250.00
4 MMe,S&K(c),The Story of
 a Man Who Dreamed a Murder
 that Happened 200.00

STRANGE WORLDS
Avon Periodicals

Strange Worlds #5 © Avon Periodicals

November, 1950
1 JKu,Spider God of Akka ... 425.00
2 WW,Dara of the Vikings ... 400.00
3 AW&FF,EK(c),WW,JO 800.00
4 JO,WW,WW(c),The
 Enchanted Dagger 375.00
5 WW,WW(c),JO,Bondage(c);
 Sirens of Space 300.00
6 EK,WW(c),JO,SC,
 Maid o/t Mist 250.00
7 EK, Sabotage on
 Space Station 1 .... 165.00
8 JKu,EK,The Metal Murderer 165.00
9 The Radium Monsters 150.00
18 JKu 150.00
19 Astounding Super
 Science Fantasies 150.00
20 WW(c),Fighting War Stories . 35.00
21 EK(c) 30.00
22 EK(c),Sept.-Oct., 1955 ..... 30.00

STRICTLY PRIVATE
Eastern Color Printing
July, 1942
1 You're in theArmyNow-Humor 125.00
2 F:Peter Plink, 1942 ...... 125.00

STUNTMAN COMICS
Harvey Publications
April-May, 1946
1 S&K,O:Stuntman 550.00
2 S&K,New Champ of Split-
 Second Action 375.00
3 S&K,Digest sized,Mail Order
 Only, B&W interior,
 October-November, 1946 .. 500.00

SUGAR BOWL COMICS
Famous Funnies
May, 1948
1 ATh,ATh(c),The Newest in
 Teen Age! 80.00
2 .... 30.00
3 ATh 60.00
4 .... 30.00
5 January, 1949 .... 30.00

SUN FUN KOMIKS
Sun Publications
1939
1 F:Spineless Sam the
 Sweetheart 150.00

SUNNY, AMERICA'S SWEETHEART
Fox Features Syndicate
December, 1947
11 AF,AF(c) 300.00
12 AF,AF(c) 250.00
13 AF,AF(c) 250.00
14 AF,AF(c) 250.00

SUNSET CARSON
Charlton Comics
February, 1951
1 Painted, Ph(c);Wyoming
 Mail 600.00
2 Kit Carson-Pioneer 400.00
3 .... 300.00
4 Panhandle Trouble,
 August, 1951 .... 300.00

SUPER CIRCUS
Cross Publishing Co.
January, 1951
1 Partial Ph(c)	55.00
2	40.00
3	30.00
4	30.00
5 1951	30.00

SUPER COMICS
Dell Publishing Co.
May 1938
1 Dick Tracy,Terry and the Pirates,Smilin'Jack,Smokey Stover,Orphan Annie,etc.	1,100.00
2	500.00
3	450.00
4	400.00
5 Gumps(c)	375.00
6	300.00
7 Smokey Stover(c)	300.00
8 Dick Tracy(c)	275.00
9	275.00

Super Comics #14
© Dell Publishing Co.

10 Dick Tracy(c)	275.00
11	250.00
12	250.00
13	250.00
14	250.00
15	250.00
16 Terry & the Pirates	225.00
17 Dick Tracy(c)	225.00
18	225.00
19	225.00
20 Smilin'Jack(c)	250.00
21 B:Magic Morro	200.00
22 Magic Morro(c)	210.00
23 all star(c)	200.00
24 Dick Tracy(c)	210.00
25 Magic Morro(c)	200.00
26	190.00
27 Magic Morro(c)	200.00
28 Jim Ellis(c)	210.00
29 Smilin'Jack(c)	200.00
30 inc.The Sea Hawk	210.00
31 Dick Tracy(c)	175.00
32 Smilin' Jack(c)	185.00
33 Jim Ellis(c)	175.00

34 Magic Morro(c)	175.00
35 thru 40 Dick Tracy(c)	@175.00
41 B:Lightning Jim	135.00
42 thru 50 Dick Tracy(c)	@125.00
51 thru 54 Dick Tracy(c)	@110.00
55	100.00
56	100.00
57 Dick Tracy(c)	100.00
58 Smitty(c)	100.00
59	100.00
60 Dick Tracy(c)	120.00
61	85.00
62 Flag(c)	100.00
63 Dick Tracy(c)	100.00
64 Smitty(c)	85.00
65 Dick Tracy(c)	100.00
66 Dick Tracy(c)	100.00
67 Christmas(c)	100.00
68 Dick Tracy(c)	100.00
69 Dick Tracy(c)	100.00
70 Dick Tracy(c)	100.00
71 Dick Tracy(c)	75.00
72 Dick Tracy(c)	75.00
73 Smitty(c)	75.00
74 War Bond(c)	75.00
75 Dick Tracy(c)	75.00
76 Dick Tracy(c)	75.00
77 Dick Tracy(c)	75.00
78 Smitty(c)	60.00
79 Dick Tracy(c)	60.00
80 Smitty(c)	60.00
81 Dick Tracy(c)	60.00
82 Dick Tracy(c)	60.00
83 Smitty(c)	55.00
84 Dick Tracy(c)	60.00
85 Smitty(c)	55.00
86 All on cover	60.00
87 All on cover	60.00
88 Dick Tracy(c)	60.00
89 Smitty(c)	55.00
90 Dick Tracy(c)	60.00
91 Smitty(c)	55.00
92 Dick Tracy(c)	60.00
93 Dick Tracy(c)	60.00
94 Dick Tracy(c)	60.00
95 thru 99	@55.00
100	75.00
101 thru 115	@40.00
116 Smokey Stover(c)	35.00
117 Gasoline Alley(c)	35.00
118 Smokey Stover(c)	35.00
119 Terry and the Pirates(c)	40.00
120	40.00
121	40.00

SUPER-DOOPER COMICS
Able Manufacturing Co.
1946
1 A:Gangbuster	100.00
2	60.00
3 & 4	@45.00
5 A:Captain Freedom,Shock Gibson	50.00
6 & 7 same	@50.00
8 A:Shock Gibson, 1946	50.00

SUPER DUCK COMICS
MLJ Magazines/Close-Up
(Archie Publ.)
Autumn, 1944
1 O:Super Duck	275.00
2	150.00
3 I:Mr. Monster	125.00

4 & 5	@100.00
6 thru 10	@75.00
11 thru 20	@50.00
21 thru 40	@40.00
41 thru 60	@30.00
61 thru 94	@25.00

Super Duck #16
© MLJ Magazines/Archie Publ.

SUPER FUNNIES
Superior Comics Publishers
March, 1954
1 Dopey Duck	250.00
2 Out of the Booby-Hatch	50.00

Becomes:
SUPER WESTERN FUNNIES
3 F:Phantom Ranger	30.00
4 F:Phantom Ranger,Sept. 1954	30.00

Super Magician #46 (4/10)
© Street & Smith Publications

SUPER MAGICIAN COMICS
Street & Smith Publications
May, 1941

1 B:The Mysterious Blackstone	275.00
2 V:Wild Tribes of Africa	200.00
3 V:Oriental Wizard	175.00
4 V:Quetzal Wizard,O:Transo	150.00
5 A:The Moylan Sisters	150.00
6 JaB,JaB(c),The Eddie Cantor story	150.00
7 In the House of Skulls	175.00
8 A:Abbott & Costello	175.00
9 V:Duneen the Man-Ape	150.00
10 V:Pirates o/t Sargasso Sea	150.00
11 JaB(c),V:Fire Wizards	150.00
12 V:Baal	150.00
2-1 A:The Shadow	200.00
2-2 In the Temple of the 10,00 Idols	75.00
2-3 Optical Illusion on (c)-Turn Jap into Monkey	75.00
2-4 V:Cannibal Killers	75.00
2-5 V:The Pygmies of Lemuriai	75.00
2-6 V;Pirates & Indians	75.00
2-7 Can Blackstone Catch the Cannonball?	75.00
2-8 V:Marabout,B:Red Dragon	75.00
2-9	75.00
2-10 Pearl Dives Swallowed By Sea Demons	75.00
2-11 Blackstone Invades Pelican Islands	75.00
2-12 V:Bubbles of Death	75.00
3-1	75.00
3-2 Bondage(c),Midsummers Eve	70.00
3-3 The Enchanted Garden	70.00
3-4 Fabulous Aztec Treasure	70.00
3-5 A:Buffalo Bill	70.00
3-6 Magic Tricks to Mystify	70.00
3-7 V:Guy Fawkes	70.00
3-8 V:Hindu Spook Maker	70.00
3-9	70.00
3-10 V:The Water Wizards	70.00
3-11 V:The Green Goliath	70.00
3-12 Lady in White	70.00
4-1 Cannibal of Crime	65.00
4-2 The Devil's Castle	65.00
4-3 V:Demons of Golden River	65.00
4-4 V:Dr. Zero	65.00
4-5 Bondage(c)	65.00
4-6 V:A Terror Gang	65.00
4-7	65.00
4-8 Mystery of the Disappearing Horse	65.00
4-9 A Floating Light?	65.00
4-10 Levitation	65.00
4-11 Lost, Strange Land of Shangri	65.00
4-12 I:Nigel Elliman	65.00
5-1 V:Voodoo Wizards of the Everglades,Bondage (c)	70.00
5-2 Treasure of the Florida Keys; Bondage (c)	65.00
5-3 Elliman Battles Triple Crime	65.00
5-4 Can A Human Being Really Become Invisible	65.00
5-5 Mystery of the Twin Pools	65.00
5-6 A:Houdini	65.00
5-7 F:Red Dragon	65.00
5-8 F:Red Dragon, Feb.-March, 1947	65.00

SUPERMOUSE
Standard Comics/Pines
December, 1948

1 FF,(fa)	150.00
2 FF,(fa)	85.00
3 FF,(fa)	65.00
4 FF,(fa)	70.00
5 FF,(fa)	65.00
6 FF,(fa)	65.00
7 (fa)	25.00
8 (fa)	25.00
9 (fa)	25.00
10 (fa)	25.00
11 thru 20 (fa)	@20.00
21 thru 44 (fa)	@15.00
45 (fa),Autumn, 1958	15.00

Super-Mystery Comics #23 (4/5)
© Periodical House/Ace Magazines

SUPER-MYSTERY COMICS
Periodical House (Ace Magazines)
July, 1940

1 B:Magno,Vulcan,Q-13,Flint of the Mountes	1,000.00
2 Bondage (c)	500.00
3 JaB,B:Black Spider	400.00
4 O:Davy;A:Captain Gallant	350.00
5 JaB,JM(c),I&B:The Clown	350.00
6 JM,JM(c),V:The Clown	300.00
2-1 JM,JM(c),O:Buckskin, Bondage(c)	300.00
2-2 JM,JM(c),V:The Clown	250.00
2-3 JM,JM(c),V:The Clown	250.00
2-4 JM,JM(c),V:The Nazis	250.00
2-5 JM,JM(c),Bondage(c)	275.00
2-6 JM,JM(c),Bondage(c), 'Foreign Correspondent'	275.00
3-1 B:Black Ace	325.00
3-2 A:Mr, Risk, Bondage(c)	350.00
3-3 HK,HK(c),I:Lancer;B:Dr. Nemesis, The Sword	275.00
3-4 HK	275.00
3-5 HK,LbC,A:Mr. Risk	250.00
3-6 HK,LbC,A:Paul Revere Jr.	250.00
4-1 HK,LbC,A:Twin Must Die	200.00
4-2 A:Mr. Risk	175.00

4-3 Mango out to Kill Davey!	175.00
4-4 Danger Laughs at Mr. Risk	175.00
4-5 A:Mr. Risk	175.00
4-6 RP,A:Mr. Risk	175.00
5-1 RP	150.00
5-2 RP,RP(c),The Riddle of the Swamp-Land Spirit	150.00
5-3 RP,RP(c),The Case of the Whispering Death	150.00
5-4 RP,RP(c)	150.00
5-5 RP,Harry the Hack	150.00
5-6	150.00
6-1	125.00
6-2 RP,A:Mr. Risk	125.00
6-3 Bondage (c)	125.00
6-4 E:Mango;A:Mr. Risk	125.00
6-5 Bondage(c)	125.00
6-6 A:Mr. Risk	125.00
7-1	125.00
7-2 KBa(c)	125.00
7-3 Bondage(c)	125.00
7-4	125.00
7-5	125.00
7-6	125.00
8-1 The Riddle of the Rowboat	100.00
8-2 Death Meets a Train	100.00
8-3 The Man Who Couldn't Die	100.00
8-4 RP(c)	100.00
8-5 GT,MMe,Staged for Murder	100.00
8-6 Unlucky Seven,July, 1949	100.00

ARMY AND NAVY COMICS
Street & Smith Publications
May, 1941

1 Hawaii is Calling You,Capt. Fury,Nick Carter	275.00
2 Private Rock V;Hitler	150.00
3 The Fighting Fourth	100.00
4 The Fighting Irish	100.00
5 I:Super Snipe	250.00

Becomes:

SUPERSNIPE COMICS

6 A "Comic" With A Sense of Humor	450.00
7 A:Wacky, Rex King	300.00
8 Axis Powers & Satan(c), Hitler(c)	325.00
9 Hitler Voodoo Doll (c)	400.00
10 Lighting (c)	300.00
11 A:Little Nemo	300.00
12 Football(c)	300.00
2-1 B:Huck Finn	200.00
2-2 Battles Shark	200.00
2-3 Battles Dinosaur	200.00
2-4 Baseball(c)	200.00
2-5 Battles Dinosaur	200.00
2-6 A:Pochantas	200.00
2-7 A:Wing Woo Woo	200.00
2-8 A:Huck Finn	200.00
2-9 Dotty Loves Trouble	200.00
2-10 Assists Farm Labor Shortage	200.00
2-11 Dotty & the Jelly Beans	200.00
2-12 Statue of Liberty	200.00
3-1 Ice Skating(c)	175.00
3-2 V:Pirates(c)	175.00
3-3 Baseball(c)	175.00
3-4 Jungle(c)	175.00
3-5 Learn Piglatin	175.00
3-6 Football Hero	175.00
3-7 Saves Girl From Grisley	175.00
3-8 Rides a Wild Horse	175.00
3-9 Powers Santa's Sleigh	175.00

3-10 Plays Basketball	175.00
3-11 Is A Baseball Pitcher	175.00
3-12 Flies with the Birds	175.00
4-1 Catches A Whale	125.00
4-2 Track & Field Athlete	125.00
4-3 Think Machine(c)	125.00
4-4 Alpine Skiier	125.00
4-5 Becomes a Boxer	125.00
4-6 Race Car Driver	125.00
4-7 Bomber(c)	125.00
4-8 Baseball Star	125.00
4-9 Football Hero	125.00
4-10 Christmas(c)	125.00
4-11 Artic Adventure	125.00
4-12 The Ghost Remover	125.00
5-1 August-September, 1949	125.00

SUPER SPY
Centaur Publications
October, 1940

1 O:Sparkler	850.00
2 November, 1940,A:Night Hawk, S.S. Swanson the Inner Circle, Drew Ghost,Tim Blain,Gentlemen of Misfortune,Duke Collins	550.00

SUPER WESTERN COMICS
Youthful Magazines
August, 1950

1 BP,BP,(c),B:Buffalo Bill,Wyatt Earp,CalamityJane,SamSlade	55.00
2 thru 4 March, 1951	@35.00

SUPER WESTERN FUNNIES
(see SUPER FUNNIES)

Superworld Comics #3
© Komos Publications

SUPERWORLD COMICS
Komos Publications
(Hugo Gernsback)
April, 1940

1 FP,FP(c),B:Military Powers, Buzz Allen,Smarty Artie, Alibi Alige	2,400.00

2 FP,FP(c),A:Mario	1,400.00
3 FP,FP(c),V:Vest Wearing Giant Grasshoppers	1,000.00

SUSPENSE COMICS
Et Es Go Mag. Inc.
(Continental Magazines)
December, 1945

1 LbC,Bondage(c),B:Grey Mask	100.00
2 DRi,I:The Mask	750.00
3 LbC,ASh(c),Bondage(c)	1,000.00
4 LbC,LbC(c),Bondage(c)	550.00
5 LbC,LbC(c)	550.00
6 LbC,LbC(c),The End of the Road	500.00
7 LbC,LbC(c)	500.00
8 LbC,LbC(c)	750.00
9 LbC,LbC(c)	500.00
10 RP,LbC,LbC(c)	500.00
11 RP,LbC,LbC(c),Satan(c)	750.00
12 LbC,LbC(c),December, 1946	500.00

SUSPENSE DETECTIVE
Fawcett Publications
June, 1952

1 GE,MBi,MBi(c),Death Poised to Strike	200.00
2 GE,MSy	125.00
3 A Furtive Footstep	100.00
4 MBi,MSy,Bondage(c),A Blood Chilling Scream	90.00
5 MSy,MSy(c),MBi,A Hair-Trigger from Death, March, 1953	110.00

SUZIE COMICS
(see TOP-NOTCH COMICS)

SWEENEY
Standard Comics
June, 1949

4 Buzz Sawyer's Pal	45.00
5 September, 1949	40.00

SWEETHEART DIARY
Fawcett
Winter, 1949

1	75.00
2	40.00
3 and 4 WW	@75.00
5 thru 10	@30.00
11 thru 14	@20.00

SWEETHEART DIARY
Charlton Comics
January 1953

32	22.00
33 thru 40	@10.00
41 thru 65	@6.00

SWEET HEART
(see CAPTAIN MIDNIGHT)

SWEET LOVE
Harvey Publications
(Home Comics)
September, 1949

1 Ph(c)	35.00
2 Ph(c)	20.00
3 BP	20.00
4 Ph(c)	15.00
5 BP,JKa,Ph(c)	30.00

SWEET SIXTEEN
Parents' Magazine Group
August-September, 1946

1 Van Johnson story	100.00
2 Alan Ladd story	75.00
3 Rip Taylor	60.00
4 E:Taylor	60.00
5 Gregory Peck story (c)	55.00
6 Dick Hammes(c)	50.00
7 Ronald Reagan(c)	125.00
8 Shirley Jones(c)	50.00
9 William Holden(c)	50.00
10 James Stewart(c)	55.00
11	50.00
12 Bob Cummings(c)	50.00
13 Robert Mitchum(c)	60.00

SWIFT ARROW
Farrell Publications(Ajax)
February-March, 1954

1 Lone Rider's Redskin Brother	60.00
2	35.00
3	30.00
4	30.00
5 October-November, 1954	30.00

2nd Series
April, 1957

1	30.00
2 B:Lone Rider	20.00
3 September, 1957	20.00

TAFFY
Orbit Publications/Rural Home/
Taffy Publications
March-April, 1945

1 LbC(c),(fa),Bondage(c)	100.00
2 LbC(c),(fa)	60.00
3 (fa)	30.00
4 (fa)	25.00
5 LbC(c),A:Van Johnson	50.00
6 A:Perry Como	40.00
7 A:Dave Clark	45.00
8 A:Glen Ford	40.00
9 A:Lon McCallister	40.00
10 A:John Hodiak	40.00
11 A:Mickey Rooney	40.00
12 February, 1948	40.00

Tailspin #1 (nn)
© Spotlight Publications

All comics prices listed are for *Near Mint* condition.

TAILSPIN
Spotlight Publications
November, 1944
N# LbC(c),A:Firebird 90.00

TALES FROM THE CRYPT
(see CRIME PATROL)

TALES FROM THE TOMB
(see Dell Giants)

TALES OF HORROR
Toby Press/Minoan Publ. Corp
June, 1952
1 Demons of the Underworld . 150.00
2 What was the Thing in
  the Pool?,Torture 125.00
3 The Big Snake 75.00
4 The Curse of King Kala! 75.00
5 Hand of Fate 75.00
6 The Fiend of Flame 75.00
7 Beast From The Deep 75.00
8 The Snake that Held A
  City Captive 75.00
9 It Came From the Bottom
  of the World 85.00
10 The Serpent Strikes 85.00
11 Death Flower? 85.00
12 Guaranteed to Make Your
   Hair Stand on End 90.00
13 Ghost with a Torch;
   October, 1954 .... 80.00

Tales of Horror #3
© Toby Press/Minoan Publ.

TALES OF TERROR
Toby Press
1952
1 Just A Bunch of Hokey
  Hogwash 75.00

TALES OF TERROR ANNUAL
E.C. 1951
N# AF 3,000.00

2 AF 1,200.00
3 .... 900.00

TALLY-HO COMICS
Baily Publishing Co.
December, 1944
N# FF,A:Snowman 200.00

TARGET COMICS
Funnies Inc./Novelty Publ./
Premium Group/Curtis
Circulation Co./Star
Publications
February, 1940
1 BEv,JCo,CBu,JSm;B,O&I:Manowar,
  White Streak,Bull's-Eye;B:City
  Editor,High Grass Twins,T-Men,
  Rip Rory,Fantastic Feature
  Films, Calling 2-R 2,200.00
2 BEv,JSm,JCo,CBu,White
  Streak(c) 1,000.00
3 BEv,JSm,JCo,CBu 700.00
4 JSm,JCo 650.00
5 CBu,BW,O:White Streak . 1,800.00
6 CBu,BW,White Streak(c) ... 800.00
7 CBu,BW,BW(c),V:Planetoid
  Stories,Space Hawk(c) ... 2,200.00
8 CBu,BW,White Shark(c) ... 700.00
9 CBu,BW,White Shark(c) ... 700.00
10 CBu,BW,JK(c),The
   Target(c) 1,000.00
11 BW,The Target(c) 950.00
12 BW,same 700.00
2-1 BW,CBu 500.00
2-2 BW,BoW(c) 500.00
2-3 BW,BoW(c),The Target(c) . 450.00
2-4 BW,B:Cadet 450.00
2-5 BW,BoW(c),The Target(c) . 350.00
2-6 BW,The Target(c) 350.00
2-7 BW,The Cadet(c) 350.00
2-8 BW,same 350.00
2-9 BW,The Target(c) 350.00
2-10 BW,same 400.00
2-11 BW,The Cadet(c) 350.00
2-12 BW,same 350.00
3-1 BW,same 325.00
3-2 BW 325.00
3-3 BW,The Target(c) 325.00
3-4 BW,The Cadet(c) 325.00
3-5 BW 325.00
3-6 BW,War Bonds(c) 325.00
3-7 BW 325.00
3-8 BW,War Bonds(c) 325.00
3-9 BW 325.00
3-10 BW 325.00
3-11 .... 75.00
3-12 .... 75.00
4-1 JJo(c) 50.00
4-2 ERy(c) 50.00
4-3 AVi 50.00
4-4 .... 50.00
4-5 API(c),Statue of Liberty(c) .. 55.00
4-6 BW 50.00
4-7 AVi 50.00
4-8,Christmas(c) 50.00
4-9 .... 50.00
4-10 .... 50.00
4-11 .... 50.00
4-12 .... 50.00
5-1 .... 40.00
5-2 The Target 45.00
5-3 Savings Checkers(c) 40.00
5-4 War Bonds Ph(c) 40.00
5-5 thru 5-12 .... @40.00

6-1 The Target(c) 45.00
6-2 .... 40.00
6-3 Red Cross(c) 35.00
6-4 .... 35.00
6-5 Savings Bonds(c) 35.00
6-6 The Target(c) 40.00
6-7 The Cadet(c) 35.00
6-8 AFa 35.00
6-9 The Target(c) 40.00
6-10 .... 35.00
6-11 .... 35.00
6-12 .... 40.00
7-1 .... 35.00
7-2 Bondage(c) 40.00
7-3 The Target(c) 40.00
7-4 DRi,The Cadet(c) 35.00
7-5 .... 35.00
7-6 DRi(c) 35.00
7-7 The Cadet(c) 35.00
7-8 DRi(c) 35.00
7-9 The Cadet(c) 35.00
7-10 DRi,DRi(c) 35.00
7-11 .... 35.00
7-12 JH(c) 35.00

Target #105 (10/3)
© Funnies Inc./Novelty Publ.

8-1 .... 35.00
8-2 DRi,DRi(c),BK 40.00
8-3 DRi,The Cadet(c) 35.00
8-4 DRi,DRi(c) 35.00
8-5 DRi,The Cadet(c) 35.00
8-6 DRi,DRi(c) 35.00
8-7 BK,DRi,DRi(c) 40.00
8-8 DRi,The Cadet(c) 35.00
8-9 DRi,The Cadet(c) 35.00
8-10 DRi,KBa,LbC(c) 100.00
8-11 DRi,The Cadet 35.00
8-12 DRi,The Cadet 35.00
9-1 DRi,LbC(c) 100.00
9-2 DRi 35.00
9-3 DRi,Bondage(c),The Cadet(c) 40.00
9-4 DRi,LbC(c) 100.00
9-5 DRi,Baseball(c) 35.00
9-6 DRi,LbC(c) 100.00
9-7 DRi 35.00
9-8 DRi,LbC(c) 100.00
9-9 DRi,Football(c) 35.00
9-10 DRi,LbC(c) 100.00
9-11,The Cadet 35.00
9-12 LbC(c),Gems(c) 100.00

10-1,The Cadet 35.00
10-2 LbC(c) 100.00
10-3 LbC(c) 100.00
Becomes:

TARGET WESTERN ROMANCES
Star Publications
October-November, 1949
106 LbC(c),The Beauty Scar . . 140.00
107 LbC(c),The Brand Upon His
  Heart 110.00

TARZAN
Dell Publishing Co.
January-February 1948
1 V:White Savages of Vari . . 750.00
2 Captives of Thunder Valley . 400.00
3 Dwarfs of Didona 350.00
4 The Lone Hunter 350.00
5 The Men of Greed 350.00
6 Outlwas of Pal-ul-Don 300.00
7 Valley of the Monsters 300.00
8 The White Pygmies 300.00
9 The Men of A-Lur 300.00
10 Treasure of the Bolgani . . 300.00
11 The Sable Lion 225.00
12 The Price of Peace 225.00
13 B:Lex Barker photo(c) 200.00
14 . . . . 200.00
15 . . . . 200.00
16 . . . . 150.00
17 . . . . 150.00
18 . . . . 150.00
19 . . . . 150.00
20 . . . . 150.00
21 thru 30 . . . . @125.00
31 thru 54 E:L.Barker Ph(c) . . @75.00
55 thru 70 . . . . @55.00
71 thru 79 . . . . @35.00
80 thru 90 B:ScottGordonPh(c) @30.00
91 thru 99 . . . . @28.00
100 . . . . 40.00
101 thru 110 E:S.GordonPh(c) @25.00
111 thru 120 . . . . @20.00
121 thru 131 . . . . @15.00

Teen-Age Diary Secrets #6
© St. John Publishing Co.

TEEN-AGE DIARY SECRETS
St. John Publishing Co.
October, 1949
6 MB,PH(c) 75.00
7 MB,PH(c) 85.00
8 MB,PH(c) 75.00
9 MB,PH(c) 85.00
Becomes:

DIARY SECRETS
10 MB 65.00
11 MB 55.00
12 thru 19 MB . . . . @50.00
20 MB,JKu 55.00
21 thru 28 MB . . . . @30.00
29 MB,Comics Code 25.00
30 MB 25.00

TEEN-AGE ROMANCES
St. John Publishing Co.
January, 1949
1 MB(c),MB 150.00
2 MB(c),MB 85.00
3 MB(c),MB 90.00
4 Ph(c) 75.00
5 MB,Ph(c) 75.00
6 MB,Ph(c) 75.00
7 MB,Ph(c) 75.00
8 MB,Ph(c) 75.00
9 MB,MB(c),JKu 100.00
10 thru 27 MB,MB(c),JKu . . . @60.00
28 thru 30 . . . . @30.00
31 thru 34 MB(c) . . . . @30.00
35 thru 42 MB(c),MB . . . . . . @35.00
43 MB(c),MB,Comics Code 30.00
44 MB(c),MB 30.00
45 MB(c),MB 30.00

TEEN-AGE TEMPTATIONS
St. John Publishing Co.
October, 1952
1 MB(c),MB 175.00
2 MB(c),MB 60.00
3 MB(c),MB 90.00
4 MB(c),MB 90.00
5 MB(c),MB 90.00
6 MB(c),MB 90.00
7 MB(c),MB 90.00
8 MB(c),MB,Drug 100.00
9 MB(c),MB 85.00
Becomes:

GOING STEADY
10 MB(c),MB 75.00
11 MB(c),MB 50.00
12 MB(c),MB 50.00
13 MB(c),MB 50.00
14 MB(c),MB 50.00

TEENIE WEENIES, THE
Ziff-Davis Publishing Co.
1951
10 . . . . 85.00
11 . . . . 80.00

TEEN LIFE
(see YOUNG LIFE)

TEGRA, JUNGLE EMPRESS
(see ZEGRA, JUNGLE EMPRESS)

TELEVISION COMICS
Animated Cartoons
(Standard Comics)
February, 1950
5 Humorous Format,I:Willie Nilly 45.00
6 . . . . 35.00

Television Comics #5
© Standard Comics

7 . . . . 35.00
8 May, 1950 . . . . 35.00

TELEVISION PUPPET SHOW
Avon Periodicals
1950
1 F:Sparky Smith,Spotty,
  Cheeta, Speedy 80.00
2 November, 1950 . . . . 75.00

TELL IT TO THE MARINES
Toby Press
March, 1952
1 I:Spike & Pat 80.00
2 A:Madame Cobra 55.00
3 Spike & Bat on a
  Commando Raid! 35.00
4 Veil Dancing(c) 40.00
5 . . . . 40.00
6 To Paris 35.00
7 Ph(c),The Chinese Bugle . . . 25.00
8 Ph(c),V:Communists in
  South Korea 25.00
9 Ph(c) 25.00
10 . . . . 25.00
11 . . . . 25.00
12 . . . . 25.00
13 John Wayne Ph(c) 50.00
14 Ph(c) 30.00
15 Ph(c),July, 1955 . . . . 30.00

TENDER ROMANCE
Key Publications
December, 1953
1 . . . . 65.00
2 . . . . 35.00
Becomes:

Diary Confessions #9
© Key Publications

IDEAL ROMANCE

3 .... 35.00
4 thru 8 .... @20.00

Becomes:
DIARY CONFESSIONS

9 .... 25.00
10 .... 15.00

TERRIFIC COMICS
(see HORRIFIC)

TERRIFIC COMICS
Et Es Go Mag. Inc./
Continental Magazines
January, 1944

1 LbC,DRi(c),F:Kid
 Terrific Drug 1,000.00
2 LcC,ASh(c),B:Boomerang,
 'Comics' McCormic 750.00
3 LbC,LbC(c) 650.00
4 LbC,RP(c) 700.00
5 LbC,BF,ASh(c),Bondage(c) . 700.00
6 LbC,LbC(c),BF,Nov.,1944 .. 700.00

TERROR ILLUSTRATED
E.C. Comics
November-December, 1955

1 JCr,GE,Grl,JO,RC(c) 75.00
2 Spring, 1956 .... 60.00

TERRIFYING TALES
Star Publications
January, 1953

11 LbC,LbC(c),'TyrantsofTerror' 225.00
12 LbC,LbC(c),'Bondage(c),
 'Jungle Mystery' 175.00
13 LbC(c),Bondage(c),'The
 Death-Fire,Devil Head(c) ... 225.00
14 LbC(c),Bondage(c),'The
 Weird Idol' 175.00
15 LbC(c),'The Grim Secret',
 April, 1954 .... 175.00

Becomes:
JUNGLE THRILLS

Star Publications
February, 1952

16 LbC(c),'Kingdom of Unseen
 Terror' 200.00

Becomes:
TERRORS OF
THE JUNGLE

17 LbC(c),Bondage(c) 200.00
18 LbC(c),Strange Monsters .. 125.00
19 JyD,LbC(c),Bondage(c),The
 Golden Ghost Gorilla 125.00
20 JyD,LbC(c),The Creeping
 Scourge 125.00
21 LbC(c),Evil Eyes of Death! . 150.00
 4 JyD,LbC(c),Morass of Death 110.00
 5 JyD,LbC(c),Bondage(c),
 Savage Train 125.00
 6 JyD,LbC(c),Revolt of the
 Jungle Monsters 120.00
 7 JyD,LbC(c) 110.00
 8 JyD,LbC(c),Death's Grim
 Reflection 110.00
 9 JyD,LbC(c),Doom to
 Evil-Doers 110.00
10 JyD,LbC(c),Black Magic,
 September, 1954 .... 110.00

BOY EXPLORERS

1 S&K(c),S&K,The Cadet 500.00
2 S&K(c),S&K 650.00

Becomes:
TERRY AND THE PIRATES

3 S&K,MC(c),MC,Terry and
 Dragon Lady 225.00
4 S&K,MC(c),MC 125.00
5 S&K,MC(c),MC,BP,
 Chop-Chop(c) 75.00
6 S&K,.MC(c),MC,MC 75.00
7 S&K,MC(c),MC,BP 75.00
8 S&K,MC(c),MC,BP 75.00
9 S&K,MC(c),MC,BP 75.00
10 S&K,MC(c),MC,BP 75.00
11 S&K,MC(c),MC,BP,
 A:Man in Black 60.00
12 S&K,MC(c),MC,BP 60.00
13 S&K,MC(c),MC,Belly Dancers 60.00
14 thru 20 S&K,MC(c),MC ... @50.00
22 thru 26 S&K,MC(c),MC ... @45.00
27 Charlton Comics 40.00
28 .... 40.00

TERRY-BEARS COMICS
St. John Publishing Co.
June, 1952

1 .... 20.00
2 & 3 .... @15.00

TERRY-TOONS COMICS
Select,Timely,Marvel,St. Johns
1942

1 Paul Terry (fa) 650.00
2 .... 320.00
3 thru 6 .... @250.00
7 Hitler,Hirohito,Mussolini(c) .. 165.00
8 thru 20 .... @100.00
21 thru 37 .... @75.00
38 I&(c):Mighty Mouse 750.00
39 Mighty Mouse 175.00
40 thru 49 All Mighty Mouse . @85.00
50 I:Heckle & Jeckle 200.00
51 thru 60 .... @60.00
61 thru 70 .... @45.00
71 thru 86 .... @40.00

TEXAN, THE
St. John Publishing Co.
August, 1948

1 GT,F:Buckskin Belle,The Gay
 Buckaroo,Mustang Jack 80.00
2 GT 40.00
3 BLb(c) 35.00

The Texan #11
© St. John Publishing Co.

4 MB,MB(c) 60.00
5 MB,MB(c),Mystery Rustlers
 of the Rio Grande 60.00
6 MB(c),Death Valley
 Double-Cross 50.00
7 MB,MB(c),Comanche Justice
 Strikes at Midnight 60.00
8 MB,MB(c),Scalp Hunters
 Hide their Tracks 60.00
9 MB(c),Ghost Terror of
 the Blackfeet 60.00
10 MB,MB(c),Treason Rides
 the Warpath 50.00
11 MB,MB(c),Hawk Knife 60.00
12 MB 60.00
13 MB,Doublecross at Devil'sDen 60.00
14 MB,Ambush at Buffalo Trail . 60.00
15 MB,Twirling Blades Tame
 Treachery 60.00

Becomes:
FIGHTIN' TEXAN

16 GT,Wanted Dead or Alive .. 45.00
17 LC,LC(c);Killers Trail,
 December, 1952 .... 40.00

TEX FARRELL
D.S. Publishing Co.
March-April, 1948

1 Pride of the Wild West 75.00

TEX GRANGER
(see CALLING ALL BOYS)

TEX RITTER WESTERN
Fawcett Publications/
Charlton Comics
October, 1950

1 Ph(c),B:Tex Ritter, his Horse

White Flash, his dog Fury, and
his mom Nancy 400.00
2 Ph(c),Vanishing Varmints . . 200.00
3 Ph(c),Blazing Six-Guns . . . 175.00
4 Ph(c),The Jaws of Terror . . 150.00
5 Ph(c),Bullet Trail 150.00
6 Ph(c),Killer Bait 150.00
7 Ph(c),Gunsmoke Revenge . 125.00
8 Ph(c),Lawless Furnace Valley 125.00
9 Ph(c),The Spider's Web . . . 125.00
10 Ph(c),The Ghost Town 125.00
11 Ph(c),Saddle Conquest 125.00
12 Ph(c),Prairie Inferno 75.00
13 Ph(c) 75.00
14 Ph(c) 75.00
15 Ph(c) 75.00
16 thru 19 Ph(c) . . . . @75.00
20 Ph(c),Stagecoach To Danger 75.00
21 . . . . 75.00
22 Panic at Diamond B 60.00
23 A:Young Falcon 50.00
24 A:Young Falcon 50.00
25 A:Young Falcon 50.00
26 thru 38 . . . . @45.00
39 AW,AW(c) 45.00
40 thru 45 . . . . @40.00
46 May, 1959 . . . . 40.00

THING!, THE
Song Hits/Capitol Stories/
Charlton Comics
February, 1952
1 Horror 400.00
2 Crazy King(c) 300.00
3 . . . . 300.00
4 AFa(c),I Was A Zombie 200.00
5 LM(c),Severed Head(c) 225.00
6 . . . . 200.00
7 Fingenail to Eye(c) 350.00
8 . . . . 200.00
9 Severe 375.00
10 Devil(c) 200.00
11 SC,Cleaver 300.00
12 SD,SD(c),Neck Blood
Sucking 375.00
13 SD,SD(c) 375.00
14 SD,SD(c) 375.00
15 SD,SD(c) 375.00
16 Eye Torture 250.00
17 BP,SD(c) 300.00
Becomes:
BLUE BEETLE
18 America's Fastest Moving
Crusader Against Crime 85.00
19 JKa,Lightning Fast 100.00
20 JKa 100.00
21 The Invincible 75.00
Becomes:
MR. MUSCLES
22 World's Most Perfect Man . . . 30.00
23 August, 1956 . . . . 20.00

THIS IS SUSPENSE
(see LAWBREAKERS)

THIS IS WAR
Standard Comics
July, 1952
5 ATh,Show Them How To Die 70.00
6 ATh,Make Him A Soldier . . . 60.00
7 One Man For Himself 20.00
8 Miracle on Massacre Hill . . . 20.00
9 ATh,May, 1953 . . . . 50.00

THIS IS SUSPENSE!
(see STRANGE SUSPENSE
STORIES)

THIS MAGAZINE IS
HAUNTED
Fawcett Publications/
Charlton Comics
October, 1951
1 MBi,F:Doctor Death 300.00
2 GE 200.00
3 MBi,Quest of the Vampire . 100.00
4 BP,The Blind, The Doomed
and the Dead 75.00
5 BP,GE,The Slithering Horror
of Skontong Swamp! 200.00
6 Secret of the Walking Dead . 75.00
7 The Man Who Saw Too Much 75.00
8 The House in the Web 75.00
9 The Witch of Tarlo 75.00
10 I Am Dr Death,
Severed Head(c) 125.00
11 BP,Touch of Death 75.00
12 BP 75.00
13 BP,Severed Head(c) 125.00
14 BP,Horrors of the Damned . . 75.00
15 DG(c) 60.00
16 SD(c) 150.00
17 SD,SD(c) 175.00
18 SD,SD(c) 175.00
19 SD(c) 125.00
20 SMz(c) 75.00
21 SD(c) 125.00
Becomes:
DANGER AND
ADVENTURE
22 The Viking King,F:Ibis the
Invincible 50.00
23 F:Nyoka the Jungle Girl
Comics Code 45.00
24 DG&AA(c) 35.00
25 thru 27 . . . . @30.00
Becomes:
ROBIN HOOD AND HIS
MERRY MEN
28 . . . . 40.00
29 thru 37 . . . . @30.00
38 SD,August, 1958 . . . . 75.00

3-D-ELL
Dell Publishing Co.
1953
1 Rootie Kazootie 250.00
2 Rootie Kazootie 250.00
3 Flunkey Louise 225.00

THREE RING COMICS
Spotlight Publishers
March, 1945
1 Funny Animal 50.00

THREE STOOGES
Jubilee Publ.
February, 1949
1 JKu,Infinity(c) 575.00
2 JKu,On the Set of the
'The Gorilla Girl' 450.00
St. John Publishing Co.
1 JKu,'Bell Bent for
Treasure, Sept., 1953 . . . . 400.00
2 JKu 300.00

Three Stooges #5
© St. John's Publishing Co.

3 JKu,3D 300.00
4 JKu,Medical Mayhem 225.00
5 JKu,Shempador-Matador
Supreme 225.00
6 JKu, ... 225.00
7 JKu,Ocotber, 1954 . . . . 225.00

THRILLING COMICS
Better Publ./Nedor/
Standard Comics
February, 1940
1 B&O:Doc Strange,B:Nickie
Norton 900.00
2 B:Rio Kid,Woman in Red
Pinocchio 400.00
3 B:Lone Eagle,The Ghost . . 300.00
4 Dr Strange(c) 250.00
5 Bondage(c) 225.00
6 Dr Strange(c) 225.00
7 Dr Strange(c) 225.00
8 V:Pirates 225.00
9 Bondage(c) 250.00
10 V:Nazis 250.00
11 ASh(c),V:Nazis 210.00
12 ASh(c) 190.00
13 ASh(c),Bondage(c) 225.00
14 ASh(c) 200.00
15 ASh(c),V:Nazis 200.00
16 Bondage(c) 210.00
17 Dr Strange(c) 210.00
18 Dr Strange(c) 200.00
19 I&O:American Crusader . . . 300.00
20 Bondage(c) 210.00
21 American Crusader(c) 175.00
22 Bondage(c) 200.00
23 American Crusader 175.00
24 I:Mike in Doc Strange 175.00
25 DR Strange(c) 175.00
26 Dr Strange(c) 175.00
27 Bondage(c) 200.00
28 Bondage(c) 200.00
29 E:Rio Kid;Bondage(c) 200.00
30 Bondage(c) 200.00
31 Dr Strange(c) 175.00
32 Dr Strange(c) 150.00
33 Dr Strange(c) 150.00
34 Dr Strange(c) 150.00

---

35 Dr Strange 150.00
36 ASh(c),B:Commando 165.00
37 BO,ASh(c) 150.00
38 ASh(c) 165.00
39 ASh(c),E:American Crusader 150.00
40 ASh(c) 150.00
41 ASh(c),F:American Crusader 165.00

Thrilling Comics #18
© Better Publ./Nedor/Standard Comics

42 ASh(c) 125.00
43 ASh(c) 125.00
44 ASh(c),Hitler(c) 135.00
45 EK,ASh(c) 135.00
46 ASh(c) 135.00
47 ASh(c) 125.00
48 EK,ASh(c) 125.00
49 ASh(c) 125.00
50 ASh(c) 125.00
51 ASh(c) 125.00
52 ASh(c),E:Th Ghost;
   Peto-Bondage(c) 135.00
53 ASh(c),B:Phantom Detective 125.00
54 ASh(c),Bondage(c) 135.00
55 ASh(c),E:Lone Eagle 125.00
56 ASh(c),B:Princess Pantha . . 200.00
57 ASh(c) 175.00
58 ASh(c) 175.00
59 ASh(c) 175.00
60 ASh(c) 175.00
61 ASh(c),GRi,A:Lone Eagle . . 175.00
62 ASh(c) 175.00
63 ASh(c),GT 175.00
64 ASh(c) 175.00
65 ASh(c),E:Commando Cubs,
   Phantom Detective 175.00
66 ASh(c) 175.00
67 FF,ASh(c) 200.00
68 FF,ASh(c) 200.00
69 FF,ASh(c) 200.00
70 FF,ASh(c) 210.00
71 FF,ASh(c) 200.00
72 FF,ASh(c) 200.00
73 FF,ASh(c) 200.00
74 E:Princess Pantha;
   B:Buck Ranger 100.00
75 B:Western Front 50.00
76 . . . . 50.00
77 ASh(c) 50.00
78 Bondage(c) 55.00
79 BK 50.00

80 JSe,BE,April, 1951 . . . . 55.00

THRILLING CRIME CASES
Star Publications
June-July, 1950
41 LbC(c),The Unknowns 75.00
42 LbC(c),The Gunmaster 60.00
43 LbC,LbC(c),The Chameleon . 75.00
44 LbC(c),Sugar Bowl Murder . . 75.00
45 LbC(c),Maze of Murder 75.00

Thrilling Crime Cases #49
© Star Publications

46 LbC,LbC(c),Modern
   Communications 50.00
47 LbC(c),The Careless Killer . . 50.00
48 LbC(c),Road Black 50.00
49 LbC(c),The Poisoner 125.00
Becomes:
SHOCKING MYSTERY CASES
50 JyD,LbC(c),Dead Man's
   Revenge 150.00
51 JyD,LbC(c),A Murderer's
   Reward 75.00
52 LbC(c),The Carnival Killer . . . 65.00
53 LbC(c),The Long Shot of Evil 65.00
54 LbC(c),Double-Cross of Death 65.00
55 LbC(c),Return from Death . . 65.00
56 LbC(c),The Chase 100.00
57 LbC(c),Thrilling Cases 50.00
58 LbC(c),Killer at Large 65.00
59 LbC(c),Relentless Huntdown . 50.00
60 LbC(c),Lesson of the Law,
   October, 1954 . . . . 50.00

THRILLING ROMANCES
Standard Comics
December, 1949
5 Ph(c) 55.00
6 Ph(c) 25.00
7 Ph(c),JSe,BE 35.00
8 Ph(c) 25.00
9 Ph(c),GT 30.00
10 Ph(c),JSe,BE 30.00
11 Ph(c),JSe,BE 30.00
12 Ph(c),WW 45.00
13 Ph(c),JSe 25.00

14 Ph(c),Danny Kaye 18.00
15 Ph(c),Tony Martin,Ph(c) 18.00
16 Ph(c) 15.00
17 Ph(c) 15.00
18 Ph(c) 15.00
19 Ph(c) 15.00
20 Ph(c) 15.00
21 Ph(c) 15.00
22 Ph(c),ATn 35.00
23 Ph(c),ATn 35.00
24 Ph(c),ATn3 . . . . 35.00
25 Ph(c),ATn 35.00

THRILLING TRUE STORY OF THE BASEBALL GIANTS
Fawcett Publications
1952
N# Partial Ph(c),Famous Giants
   of the Past 450.00
2 Yankees Ph(c),Joe DiMaggio,
   Yogi Berra,Mickey Mantle,
   Casey Stengel 500.00

TICK TOCK TALES
Magazine Enterprises
January, 1946
1 (fa) Koko & Kola 65.00
2 (fa) Calender 35.00
3 thru 10 (fa) . . . . @25.00
11 thru 18 (fa) . . . . @20.00
19 (fa),Flag(c) 20.00
20 (fa) 20.00
21 (fa) 15.00
22 (fa) 15.00
23 (fa),Mugsy Mouse 15.00
24 thru 33 (fa) . . . . @15.00
34 (fa), 1951 . . . . 15.00

TIM HOLT
Magazine Enterprises
January-February, 1949
4 FBe,Ph(c) 150.00
5 FBe,Ph(c) 125.00
6 FBe,Ph(c),I:Calico Kid 150.00
7 FBe,Ph(c),Man-Killer Mustang 100.00
8 FBe,Ph(c) 100.00
9 FBe,DAy(c),TerribleTenderfoot 100.00
10 FBe,DAy(c),The Devil Horse 100.00
11 FBe,DAy(c),O&I:Ghost Rider 250.00
12 FBe,DAy(c),Battle at
   Bullock Gap 75.00
13 FBe,DAy(c),Ph(c) 75.00
14 FBe,DAy(c),Ph(c),The
   Honest Bandits 75.00
15 FBe,DAy,Ph(c) 75.00
16 FBe,DAy,Ph(c) 75.00
17 FBe,DAy,Ph(c) 250.00
18 FBe,DAy,Ph(c) 75.00
19 FBe,DAy,They Dig By Night . 60.00
20 FBe,DAy,O:Red Mask 90.00
21 FBe,DAy,FF(c) 225.00
22 FBe,DAy 55.00
23 FF,FBe,DAy 175.00
24 FBe,DAy,FBe(c) 55.00
25 FBe,DAy,FBe(c) 100.00
26 FBe,DAy,FBe(c) 50.00
27 FBe,DAy,FBe(c),V:Straw Man 50.00
28 FBe,DAy,FBe(c),Ph(c) 50.00
29 FBe,DAy,FBe,Ph(c), ... 50.00
30 FBe,DAy,FBe(c),Lady Doom
   & The Death Wheel 45.00
31 FBe,DAy,FBe(c) 45.00

32 FBe,DAy,FBe(c)	45.00
33 FBe,DAy,FBe(c)	45.00
34 FBe,DAy,FBe(c)	60.00
35 FBe,DAy,FBe(c)	60.00
36 FBe,DAy,FBe(c),Drugs	65.00
37 FBe,DAy,FBe(c)	65.00
38 FBe,DAy,FBe(c)	65.00
39 FBe,DAy,FBe(c),3D Effect	70.00
40 FBe,DAy,FBe(c)	70.00
41 FBe,DAy,FBe(c)	70.00

Becomes:

RED MASK

42 FBe,DAy,FBe(c),3D	120.00
43 FBe,DAy,FBe(c),3D	100.00
44 FBe,DAy,FBe(c),Death at Split Mesa,3D	90.00
45 FBe,DAy,FBe(c),V:False Red Mask	90.00
46 FBe,DAy,FBe(c)	90.00
47 FBe,DAy,FBe(c)	90.00
48 FBe,DAy,FBe(c),Comics Code	85.00
49 FBe,DAy,FBe(c)	85.00
50 FBe,DAy	85.00
51 FBe,DAy,The Magic of 'The Presto Kid'	85.00
52 FBe,DAy,O:Presto Kid	90.00
53 FBe,DAy	70.00
54 FBe,DAy,September, 1957	90.00

TIM TYLER COWBOY
Standard Comics
November, 1948

11	40.00
12	30.00
13 The Doll Told the Secret	30.00
14 Danger at Devil's Acres	30.00
15 Secret Treasure	30.00
16	30.00
17	30.00
18 1950	30.00

TINY TOTS COMICS
Dell Publishing Co.
1943

1	250.00

TINY TOTS COMICS
E.C. Comics
March, 1946

N# Your First Comic Book B:Burton Geller(c) and art	175.00
2	125.00
3 Celebrate the 4th	100.00
4 Go Back to School	120.00
5 Celebrate the Winter	100.00
6 Do Their Spring Gardening	90.00
7 On a Thrilling Ride	100.00
8 On a Summer Vacation	100.00
9 On a Plane Ride	100.00
10 Merry X-Mas Tiny Tots E:Burton Geller(c)and art	100.00

TIP TOP COMICS
United Features,St. John,Dell
1930

1 HF,Li'l Abner	4,200.00
2 HF	900.00
3 HF,Tarzan(c)	800.00
4 HF,Li'l Abner(c)	550.00
5 HF,Capt&Kids(c)	475.00
6 HF	450.00
7 HF	450.00
8 HF,Li'l Abner(c)	450.00

9 HF,Tarzan(c)	475.00
10 HF,Li'L Abner(c)	450.00
11 HF,Tarzan(c)	350.00
12 HF,Li'l Abner	325.00
13 HF,Tarzan(c)	350.00
14 HF,Li'L Abner(c)	325.00

Tip Top Comics #33
© United Features/St. John/Dell

15 HF,Capt&kids(c)	325.00
16 HF,Tarzan(c)	350.00
17 HF,Li'L Abner(c)	325.00
18 HF,Tarzan(c)	350.00
19 HF,Football(c)	325.00
20 HF,Capt&Kids(c)	325.00
21 HF,Tarzan(c)	300.00
22 HF,Li'l Abner(c)	250.00
23 HF,Capt&Kids(c)	275.00
24 HF,Tarzan(c)	275.00
25 HF,Capt&Kids(c)	250.00
26 HF,Li'L Abner(c)	250.00
27 HF,Tarzan(c)	275.00
28 HF,Li'l Abner(c)	250.00
29 HF,Capt&Kids(c)	250.00
30 HF,Tarzan(c)	250.00
31 HFCapt&Kids(c)	250.00
32 HF Tarzan(c)	275.00
33 HF,Tarzan(c)	275.00
34 HF,Capt&Kids(c)	275.00
35 HF	250.00
36 HF,HK,Tarzan(c)	275.00
37 HF,Tarzan	275.00
38 HF	250.00
39 HF,Tarzan	275.00
40 HF	250.00
41 Tarzan(c)	250.00
42	225.00
43 Tarzan(c)	275.00
44 HF	225.00
45 HF,Tarzan(c)	250.00
46 HF	225.00
47 HF,Tarzan(c)	250.00
48 HF	225.00
49 HF	200.00
50 HF,Tarzan(c)	225.00
51	200.00
52 Tarzan(c)	225.00
53	200.00
54	250.00
55	200.00
56	200.00

57 BHg	250.00
58	225.00
59 BHg	250.00
60	200.00
61 and 62 BHg	@250.00
63 thru 90	@125.00
91 thru 99	@75.00
100	100.00
101 thru 150	@50.00
151 thru 188	@30.00
189 thru 225	@30.00

T-Man #23
© Comics Magazine/Quality Comics

T-MAN
Comics Magazines
(Quality Comics Group)
September, 1951

1 JCo,Pete Trask-the Treasury Man	200.00
2 RC(c),The Girl with Death in Her Hands	125.00
3 RC,RC(c),Death Trap in Iran	100.00
4 RC,RC(c),Panama Peril	100.00
5 RC,RC(c),Violence in Venice	100.00
6 RC(c),The Man Who Could Be Hitler	90.00
7 RC(c),Mr. Murder & The Black Hand	90.00
8 RC(c),Red Ticket to Hell	90.00
9 RC(c),Trial By Terror	85.00
10	85.00
11 The Voice of Russia	60.00
12 Terror in Tokyo	45.00
13 Mind Assassins	45.00
14 Trouble in Bavaria	45.00
15 The Traitor,Bondage(c)	45.00
16 Hunt For a Hatchetman	45.00
17 Red Triggerman	45.00
18 Death Rides the Rails	45.00
19 Death Ambush	45.00
20 The Fantastic H-Bomb Plot	65.00
21 The Return of Mussolini	45.00
22 Propaganda for Doom	40.00
23 Red Intrigue in Parid,H-Bomb	60.00
24 Red Sabotage	40.00
25 RC,The Ingenious Red Trap	65.00
26 thru 37	@40.00
38 December, 1956	45.00

TNT COMICS
Charles Publishing Co.
February, 1946
1 FBI story,YellowJacket 125.00

TODAY'S BRIDES
Ajax/Farrell Publishing Co.
November, 1955
1	30.00
2	18.00
3	18.00
4 November, 1956	18.00

TODAY'S ROMANCE
Standard Comics
March, 1952
5	30.00
6 ATh	35.00
7	15.00
8	15.00

TOM AND JERRY
see DELL GIANT EDITIONS

Thrills of Tomorrow #17
© Harvey Publications

TOMB OF TERROR
Harvey Publications
June, 1952
1 BP,The Thing From the
  Center of the Earth 125.00
2 RP,The Quagmire Beast ... 75.00
3 BP,RP,Caravan of the
  Doomed, Bondage(c) 85.00
4 RP,I'm Going to Kill You,
  Torture 75.00
5 RP 65.00
6 RP,Return From the Grave .. 65.00
7 RP,Shadow of Death 65.00
8 HN,The Hive 65.00
9 BP,HN,The Tunnel 65.00
10 BP,HN,The Trial 65.00
11 BP,HN,The Closet 65.00
12 BP,HN,Tale of Cain 100.00
13 BP,What Was Out There .. 100.00
14 BP,SC,End Result 85.00
15 BP,HN,Break-up 125.00

16 BP,Going,Going,Gone 100.00
Becomes:

THRILLS OF TOMORROW
17 RP,BP,The World of Mr. Chatt 40.00
18 RP,BP,The Dead Awaken ... 30.00
19 S&K,S&K(c),A:Stuntman ... 160.00
20 S&K,S&K(c),A:Stuntman ... 150.00

TOM CORBETT SPACE CADET
Prize Publications
May-June, 1955
1	125.00
2	100.00
3 September-October, 1955	100.00

TOM MIX
Ralston-Purina Co.
September, 1940
1 O:Tom Mix 1,600.00
2 .... 600.00
3 .... 400.00
4 thru 9 .... @350.00
Becomes:

TOM MIX COMMANDOS COMICS
10 .... 300.00
11 Invisible Invaders 300.00
12 Terrible Talons Of Tokyo .. 300.00

TOM MIX WESTERN
Fawcett Publications
January, 1948
1 Ph(c),Two-Fisted
  Adventures 600.00
2 Ph(c),Hair-Triggered Action 300.00
3 Ph(c),Double Barreled Action 225.00
4 Ph(c),Cowpunching 225.00
5 Ph(c),Two Gun Action ... 225.00
6 CCB,Most Famous Cowboy 175.00
7 CCB,A Tattoo of Thrills ... 175.00
8 EK,Ph(c),Gallant Guns ... 165.00
9 CCB,Song o/t Deadly Spurs 150.00
10 CCB,Crack Shot Western .. 150.00
11 CCB,EK(C),Triple Revenge . 150.00
12 King of the Cowboys 125.00
13 Ph(c),Leather Burns 125.00
14 Ph(c),Brand of Death 125.00
15 Ph(c),Masked Treachery ... 125.00
16 Ph(c),Death Spurting Guns . 125.00
17 Ph(c),Trail of Doom 125.00
18 Ph(c),Reign of Terror 100.00
19 Hand Colored Ph(c) 110.00
20 Ph(c),CCB,F:Capt Tootsie .. 100.00
21 Ph(c) 100.00
22 Ph(c),The Human Beast ... 100.00
23 Ph(c),Return of the Past ... 100.00
24 Hand Colored Ph(c),
  The Lawless City 100.00
25 Hand Colored Ph(c),
  The Signed Death Warrant . 100.00
26 Hand Colored Ph(c),
  Dangerous Escape 100.00
27 Hand Colored Ph(c),
  Hero Without Glory 100.00
28 Ph(c),The Storm Kings ... 100.00
29 Hand Colored Ph(c),The
  Case of the Rustling Rose . 100.00
30 Ph(c),Disappearance
  in the Hills 100.00
31 Ph(c) 80.00

32 Hand Colored Ph(c),
  Mystery of Tremble Mountain 75.00
33 .... 75.00
34 .... 65.00
35 Partial Ph(c),The Hanging
  at Hollow Creek 75.00
36 Ph(c) 75.00
37 Ph(c) 75.00
38 Ph(c),36 pages 65.00
39 Ph(c) 75.00
40 Ph(c) 75.00
41 Ph(c) 70.00
42 Ph(c) 75.00
43 Ph(c) 50.00
44 Ph(c) 50.00
45 Partial Ph(c),The Secret
  Letter 50.00
46 Ph(c) 50.00
47 Ph(c) 50.00
48 Ph(c) 50.00

BLIND DATE WITH DEATH!

Tom Mix Western #49
© Fawcett Publications

49 Partial Ph(c),Blind Date
  With Death 50.00
50 Ph(c) 50.00
51 Ph(c) 50.00
52 Ph(c) 50.00
53 Ph(c) 50.00
54 Ph(c) 50.00
55 Ph(c) 50.00
56 Partial Ph(c),Deadly Spurs .. 50.00
57 Ph(c)5 .... 50.00
58 Ph(c) 50.00
59 Ph(c) 50.00
60 Ph(c) 50.00
61 Partial Ph(c),Lost in the
  Night,May 1953 .... 60.00

TOMMY OF THE BIG TOP
King Features/ Standard Comics
1948
10 Thrilling Circus Adventures .. 30.00
11 .... 20.00
12 March, 1949 .... 20.00

TOM-TOM THE JUNGLE BOY
Magazine Enterprises
1946

1 (fa)	40.00
2 (fa)	30.00
3 Winter 1947,(fa),X-mas issue	15.00
1	15.00

TONTO
(See LONE RANGER'S COMPANION TONTO)

TONY TRENT
(see FACE, THE)

TOP FLIGHT COMICS
Four Star/St. John Publ. Co.
July, 1949

1	50.00
1 Hector the Inspector	35.00

TOP LOVE STORIES
Star Publications
May, 1951

3 LbC(c)	65.00
4 LbC(c)	45.00
5 LbC(c)	45.00
6 LbC(c),WW	80.00
7 thru 16 LbC(c)	@65.00
17 LbC(c),WW	45.00
18 LbC(c)	45.00
19 LbC(c),JyD	45.00

TOP-NOTCH COMICS
MLJ Magazines
December, 1939

1 JaB,JCo,B&O:The Wizard, B:Kandak,Swift of the Secret Service,The Westpointer, Mystic, Air Patrol,Scott Rand, Manhunter	2,800.00

Top-Notch Comics #11
© MLJ Magazines

2 JaB,JCo,B:Dick Storm, E:Mystic, B:Stacy Knight	1,000.00
3 JaB,JCo,EA(c),E:Swift of the Secret Service,Scott Rand	800.00
4 JCo,EA(c),MMe,O&I:Streak, Chandler	650.00
5 Ea(c),MMe,O&I:Galahad, B:Shanghai Sheridan	650.00
6 Ea(c),MMe,A:The Sheild	550.00
7 Ea(c),MMe,N:The Wizard	650.00
8 E:Dick Sorm,B&O:Roy The Super Boy,The Firefly	700.00
9 O&I:Black Hood, B:Fran Frazier	2,500.00
10	800.00
11	450.00
12	450.00
13	450.00
14 Bondage(c)	475.00
15 MMe	450.00
16	450.00
17 Bondage(c)	475.00
18	450.00
19 Bondage(c)	475.00
20	450.00
21	350.00
22	350.00
23 Bondage(c)	375.00
24 Black Hood Smashes Murder Ring	350.00
25 E:Bob Phantom	350.00
26	350.00
27 E:The Firefly	350.00
28 B:Suzie,Pokey Okay, Gag Oriented	350.00
29 E:Kandak	350.00
30	350.00
31	225.00
32	225.00
33 BWo,B:Dotty&Ditto	225.00
34 BWo	225.00

Suzie #100 © Archie Publications

35 BWo	225.00
36 BWo	225.00
37 thru 40 BWo	@225.00
41	225.00
42 BWo	225.00
43	225.00
44 EW:Black Hood,I:Suzie	250.00
45 Suzie(c)	265.00

Becomes:

LAUGH COMIX

46 Suzie & Wilbur	100.00
47 Suzie & Wilbur	85.00
48 Suzie & Wilbur	85.00

Becomes:

SUZIE COMICS

49 B:Ginger	150.00
50 AFy(c)	90.00
51 AFy(c)	90.00
52 AFy(c)	90.00
53 AFy(c)	90.00
54 AFy(c)	100.00
55 AFy(c)	110.00
56 BWo,B;Katie Keene	65.00
57 thru 70 BWo	@65.00
71 thru 79 BWo	@55.00
80 thru 99 BWo	@45.00
100 August, 1954, BWo	45.00

TOPS
Tops Mag. Inc.
(Lev Gleason)
July, 1949

1 RC&BLb,GT,DBa,CBi(c),I'll Buy That Girl,Our Explosive Children	650.00
2 FG,BF,CBi(c),RC&BLb	575.00

TOPS COMICS
Consolidated Book Publishers
1944

2000 Don on the Farm	165.00
2001 The Jack of Spades V:The Hawkman	90.00
2002 Rip Raiders	65.00
2003 Red Birch	20.00

Top Secret #1 © Hillman Publ.

TOP SECRET
Hillman Publications
January, 1952

1 The Tricks of the Secret Agent Revealed	100.00

TOP SECRETS
Street & Smith Publications
November, 1947

1 BP,BP(c),Of the Men Who Guard the U.S. Mail	175.00
2 BP,BP(c),True Story of Jim	

All comics prices listed are for *Near Mint* condition.   **CVA Page 383**

the Penman 125.00
3 BP,BP(c),Crime Solved by
   Mental Telepathy 125.00
4 Highway Pirates 125.00
5 BP,BP(c),Can Music Kill . . . 125.00
6 BP,BP(c),The Clue of the
   Forgotten Film 125.00
7 BP,BP(c),Train For Sale . . . 150.00
8 BP,BP(c) 100.00
9 BP,BP(c) 100.00
10 BP,BP(c),July-August, 1949 100.00

TOPS IN ADVENTURE
**Approved Comics
(Ziff-Davis)
Autumn, 1952**
1 BP,Crusaders From Mars . . 250.00

TOP SPOT COMICS
**Top Spot Publishing Co.
1945**
1 The Duke Of Darkness 150.00

TOPSY-TURVY
**R.B. Leffingwell Publ.
April, 1945**
1 I:Cookie 50.00

TOR
**St. John Publishing Co.
September, 1953**
1 JKu,JKu(c),O:Tor,One Million
   Years Ago 85.00
2 JKu,JKu(c),3-D Issue 75.00
3 JKu,JKu(c),ATh,historic Life . 80.00
4 JKu,JKu(c),ATh 80.00
5 JKu,JKu(c),ATh,October, 1954 80.00

TORCHY
**Quality Comics Group
November, 1949**
1 GFx,BWa(c),The Blonde
   Bombshell 700.00
2 GFx,GFx(c),Beauty at
   its' Best 300.00
3 GFX,GFx(c),You Can't
   Beat Nature 300.00
4 GFx,GFx(c),The Girl to
   Keep Your Eye On 400.00
5 BWa,GFx,BWa(c),At the
   Masquerade Party 450.00
6 September, 1950,BWa,GFx,
   BWa(c),The Libido Driven
   Boy Scout 500.00

TORMENTED, THE
**Sterling Comics
July, 1954**
1 Buried Alive 125.00
2 September, 1954,The Devils
   Circus 100.00

TOYLAND COMICS
**Fiction House Magazines
January, 1947**
1 Wizard of the Moon 125.00
2 Buddy Bruin & Stu Rabbit . . . 70.00
3 GT,The Candy Maker 75.00
4 July, 1947 . . . . 70.00

TOY TOWN COMICS

Toytown Publ./Orbit Publ.
February, 1945
1 LbC,LbC(c)(fa) 90.00
2 LbC,(fa) 50.00
3 LbC,LbC(c),(fa) 45.00
4 LbC,(fa) 45.00

Toy Town Comics #7
© Toytown Publ./Orbit Publ.

5 LbC,(fa) 45.00
6 LbC,(fa) 45.00
7 LbC,(fa),May, 1947 . . . . 45.00

TRAIL BLAZERS
(see RED DRAGON COMICS)

TREASURE COMICS
**Prize Comics Group
1943**
1 S&K,Reprints of Prize Comics
   #7 through #11 . . . . 1,400.00

TREASURE COMICS
**American Boys Comics
(Prize Publications)
June-July, 1945**
1 HcK,B:PaulBunyan,MarcoPolo 150.00
2 HcK,HcK(c),B:Arabian Knight,
   Gorilla King,Dr.Styx 75.00
3 HcK 55.00
4 HcK 55.00
5 HcK,JK 100.00
6 HcK,BK,HcK(c) 85.00
7 HcK,FF,HcK(c) 200.00
8 HcK,FF 200.00
9 HcK,DBa 55.00
10 JK,DBa,JK(c) 125.00
11 BK,HcK,DBa,The Weird
   Adventures of Mr. Bottle . . . 100.00
12 DBa,DBa(c),Autumn, 1947 . . 65.00

TREASURY OF COMICS
**St. John Publishing Co.
1947**
1 RvB,RvB(c),Abbie an' Slats 125.00
2 Jim Hardy 75.00
3 Bill Bimlin 75.00
4 RvB,RvB(c),Abbie an' Slats . 75.00
5 Jim Hardy,January, 1948 . . . 70.00

TRIPLE THREAT
**Gerona Publications
Winter, 1945**
1 F:King O'Leary,The Duke of
   Darkness,Beau Brummell . . . 75.00

TRUE AVIATION PICTURE STORIES
**Parents' Institute/P.M.I.
August, 1942**
1 How Jimmy Doolittle
   Bombed Tokyo 85.00
2 Knight of the Air Mail 45.00
3 The Amazing One-Man
   Air Force 40.00
4 Joe Foss America's No. 1
   Air Force 40.00
5 Bombs over Germany 40.00
6 Flight Lt. Richard
   Hillary R.A.F. 40.00
7 "Fatty" Chow China's
   Sky Champ 40.00
8 Blitz over Burma 40.00
9 Off the Beam 40.00
10 "Pappy" Boyington 40.00
11 Ph(c) 40.00
12 . . . . 40.00
13 Ph(c),Flying Facts 40.00
14 . . . . 40.00
15 . . . . 40.00
Becomes:
AVIATION AND MODEL BUILDING
16 . . . . 45.00
17 February, 1947 . . . . 50.00

True Comics #15
© True Comics/Parents' Magazine

TRUE COMICS
**True Comics/
Parents' Magazine Press
April, 1941**
1 My Greatest Adventure-by
   Lowell Thomas 200.00
2 BEv,The Story of the
   Red Cross 100.00
3 Baseball Hall of Fame 125.00

---

4 Danger in the Artic 90.00
5 Father Duffy-the Fighting
  Chaplin 100.00
6 The Capture of Aquinaldo .. 100.00
7 JKa,Wilderness Adventures of
  George Washington 100.00
8 U.S. Army Wings 55.00
9 A Pig that Made History 55.00
10 Adrift on an Ice Pan 55.00
11 Gen. Douglas MacArthur ... 60.00
12 Mackenzie-King of Cananda . 55.00
13 The Real Robinson Crusoe .. 60.00
14 Australia war base of
   the South Pacific 60.00
15 The Story of West Point 75.00
16 How Jimmy Doolittle
   Bombed Tokyo 70.00
17 The Ghost of Captain Blig,
   B.Feller 75.00
18 Battling Bill of the
   Merchant Marine 80.00
19 Secret Message Codes 45.00
20 The Story of India 40.00
21 Timoshenko the Blitz Buster . 45.00
22 Gen, Bernard L. Montgomery 40.00
23 The Story of Steel 40.00
24 Gen. Henri Giraud-Master
   of Escape 40.00
25 Medicine's Miracle Men 40.00
26 Hero of the Bismarck Sea ... 40.00
27 Leathernecks have Landed .. 45.00
28 The Story of Radar 35.00
29 The Fighting Seabees 35.00
30 Dr. Norman Bethune-Blood
   Bank Founder 35.00
31 Our Good Neighbor Bolivia,
   Red Grange 45.00
32 Men against the Desert 30.00
33 Gen. Clark and his Fighting
   5th 35.00
34 Angel of the Battlefield 30.00
35 Carlson's Marine Raiders ... 30.00
36 Canada's Sub-Busters 30.00
37 Commander of the Crocodile
   Fleet 30.00
38 Oregon Trailblazer 30.00
39 Saved by Sub 30.00
40 Sea Furies 30.00
41 Cavalcade of England 25.00
42 Gen. Jaques Le Clerc-Hero
   of Paris 25.00
43 Unsinkable Ship 30.00
44 El Senor Goofy 25.00
45 Tokyo Express 20.00
46 The Magnificent Runt 25.00
47 Atoms Unleashed,
   Atomic Bomb 55.00
48 Pirate Patriot 25.00
49 Smiking Fists 25.00
50 Lumber Pirates 25.00
51 Exercise Musk-Ox 25.00
52 King of the Buckeneers 25.00
53 Baseline Booby 25.00
54 Santa Fe Sailor 25.00
55 Sea Going Santa 25.00
56 End of a Terror 25.00
57 Newfangled Machines 25.00
58 Leonardo da Vinci-500 years
   too Soon 25.00
59 Pursuit of the Pirates 30.00
60 Emmett Kelly-The World's
   Funniest Clown 25.00
61 Peter Le Grand-
   Bold Buckaneer 25.00
62 Sutter's Gold 25.00

63 Outboard Outcome 25.00
64 Man-Eater at Large 25.00
65 The Story of Scotland Yard .. 25.00
66 Easy Guide to Football
   Formations 30.00

True Confidences #1
© Fawcett Publications

67 The Changing Zebra 25.00
68 Admiral Byrd 22.00
69 FBI Special Agent Steve
   Saunders 30.00
70 The Case of the Seven
   Hunted Men 25.00
71 Story of Joe DiMaggio 150.00
72 FBI,Jackie Robinson 55.00
73 The 26 Mile Dash-Story of
   the Marathon 30.00
74 A Famous Coach's Special
   Football Tips 30.00
75 King of Reporters 30.00
76 The Story of a Buried
   Treasure 30.00
77 France's Greatest Detective . 30.00
78 Cagliostro-Master Rogue ... 50.00
79 Ralph Bunche-Hero of Peace 30.00
80 Rocket Trip to the Moon ... 150.00
81 Red Grange 150.00
82 Marie Celeste Ship of
   Mystery 100.00
83 Bullfighter from Brooklyn ... 100.00
84 King of the Buckaneers,
   August, 1950 .... 100.00

TRUE CONFIDENCES
Fawcett Publications
Autumn, 1949
1 .... 75.00
2 .... 45.00
3 .... 45.00
4 DP 45.00

TRUE CRIME COMICS
Magazine Village, Inc.
May, 1947
2 JCo(c),JCo(c),James Kent-
  Crook,Murderer,Escaped
  Convict; Drug 675.00
3 JCo,JCo(c),Benny Dickson-
  Killer;Drug 500.00

4 JCo,JCo(c),Little Jake-
  Big Shot 475.00
5 JCo(c),The Rat & the Blond
  Gun Moll;Drug 275.00
6 Joseph Metley-Swindler,
  Jailbird, Killer 150.00
2-1(7) ATh,WW,Ph(c),Phil
  Coppolla,September, 1949 . 400.00

TRUE LIFE SECRETS
**Romantic Love Stories/
Charlton Comics
March-April, 1951**
1 .... 60.00
2 .... 30.00
3 .... 25.00
4 .... 25.00
5 thru 20 .... @25.00
21 thru 25 .... @20.00
26 Comics Code 15.00
27 thru 29 .... @15.00

TRUE LIFE ROMANCES
**Ajax/Farrell Publications
December, 1955**
1 .... 45.00
2 .... 25.00
3 August, 1956 .... 30.00

TRUE LOVE PICTORIAL
**St. John Publishing Co.
1952**
1 Ph(c) 70.00
2 MB 35.00
3 MB(c),MB,JKu 150.00
4 MB(c),MB,JKu 150.00
5 MB(c),MB,JKu 150.00
6 MB(c) 60.00
7 MB(c) 60.00
8 MB(c) 50.00
9 MB(c) 40.00
10 MB(c),MB 50.00
11 MB(c),MB 50.00

TRUE MOVIE AND
TELEVISION
Toby Press

True Movie #3 © Toby Press

August, 1950
1 Liz Taylor, Ph(c) 250.00
2 FF,Ph(c),John Wayne,
  L.Taylor 175.00
3 June Allyson,Ph(c) 150.00
4 Jane Powell,Ph(c),Jan.,1951 100.00

SPORT COMICS
Street & Smith Publications
October, 1940
1 F:Lou Gehrig 350.00
2 F:Gene Tunney 200.00
3 F:Phil Rizzuto 250.00
4 F:Frank Leahy 200.00

True Sport #8 © Street & Smith

Becomes:
TRUE SPORT PICTURE
STORIES
5 Joe DiMaggio 250.00
6 Billy Confidence 100.00
7 Mel Ott 150.00
8 Lou Ambers 100.00
9 Pete Reiser 100.00
10 Frankie Sinkwich 100.00
11 Marty Serfo 100.00
12 JaB(c),Jack Dempsey 110.00
2-1 JaB(c),Willie Pep 75.00
2-2 JaB(c) 75.00
2-3 JaB(c),Carl Hubbell 85.00
2-4 Advs. in Football & Battle . 100.00
2-5 Don Hutson 75.00
2-6 Dixie Walker 100.00
2-7 Stan Musial 150.00
2-8 Famous Ring Champions
  of All Time 100.00
2-9 List of War Year Rookies . 150.00
2-10 Connie Mack 100.00
2-11 Winning Basketball Plays . . 75.00
2-12 Eddie Gottlieb 75.00
3-1 Bill Conn 85.00
3-2 The Philadelphia Athletics . . 70.00
3-3 Leo Durocher 100.00
3-4 Rudy Dusek 75.00
3-5 Ernie Pyle 75.00
3-6 Bowling with Ned Day 70.00
3-7 Return of the Mighty (Home
  from War);Joe DiMaggio(c) . 250.00

3-8 Conn V:Louis 200.00
3-9 Reuben Shark 75.00
3-10 BP,BP(c),Don "Dopey"
  Dillock 50.00
3-11 BP,BP(c),Death
  Scores a Touchdown 75.00
3-12 Red Sox V:Senators 75.00
4-1 Spring Training in
  Full Spring 75.00
4-2 BP,BP(c),How to Pitch 'Em
  Where They Can't Hit 'Em . . 35.00
4-3 BP,BP(c),1947 Super Stars . 90.00
4-4 BP,BP(c),Get Ready for
  the Olympics 100.00
4-5 BP,BP,(c),Hugh Casey 75.00
4-6 BP,BP(c),Phantom Phil
  Hergesheimer 75.00
4-7 BP,BP(c),How to Bowl Better 35.00
4-8 Tips on the Big Fight 100.00
4-9 BP,BP(c),Bill McCahan 65.00
4-10 BP,BP(c),Great Football
  Plays 50.00
4-11 BP,BP(c),Football 50.00
4-12 BP,BP(c),Basketball' 50.00
5-1 Satchel Paige 150.00
5-2 History of Boxing,
  July-August, 1949 . . . . 75.00

TRUE SWEETHEART
SECRETS
Fawcett Publications
May, 1950
1 Ph(c) 60.00
2 WW 100.00
3 BD 40.00
4 BD 40.00
5 BD 40.00
6 thru 11 . . . . @35.00

True-To-Life Romances #12
© Star Publications

TRUE-TO-LIFE
ROMANCES
Star Publications
November-December, 1949
3 LbC(c),GlennFord/JanetLeigh 55.00
4 LbC(c) 50.00
5 LbC(c) 50.00

6 LbC(c) 50.00
7 LbC(c) 50.00
8 LbC(c) 50.00
9 LbC(c) 50.00
10 LbC(c) 50.00
11 LbC(c) 45.00
12 LbC(c) 50.00
13 LbC(c),JyD 50.00
14 LbC(c),JyD 50.00
15 LbC(c),WW,JyD 75.00
16 LbC(c),WW,JyD 75.00
17 LbC(c),JyD 55.00
18 LbC(c),JyD 55.00
19 LbC(c),JyD 55.00
20 LbC(c),JyD 55.00
21 LbC(c),JyD 55.00
22 LbC(c) 40.00
23 LbC(c) 40.00

TRUE WAR ROMANCES
Comic Magazines, Inc.
(Quality Comics)
September, 1952
1 Ph(c) 65.00
2 . . . . 30.00
3 thru 10 . . . . @20.00
11 thru 20 . . . . @15.00
21 Comics Code 15.00
Becomes:
EXOTIC ROMANCES
22 . . . . 35.00
23 thru 26 . . . . @20.00
27 MB 35.00
28 MB 35.00
29 . . . . 20.00
30 MB 35.00
31 MB 35.00

TUROK, SON OF STONE
Dell Publishing Co.
December, 1954
(1) see Dell Four Color #596
(2) see Dell Four Color #656
3 . . . . 250.00
4 and 5 . . . . @225.00
6 thru 10 . . . . @150.00
11 thru 20 . . . . @90.00
21 thru 29 . . . . @60.00
See Other Color section

TWEETY AND SYLVESTER
Dell Publishing Co.
June, 1952
(1) see Dell Four Color #406
(2) see Dell Four Color #489
(3) see Dell Four Color #524
4 thru 20 . . . . @15.00
21 thru 37 . . . . @8.00

TWINKLE COMICS
Spotlight Publications
May, 1945
1 Humor Format 70.00

TWO-FISTED TALES
Fables Publications
(E.C. Comics)
November-December, 1950
18 HK,JCr,WW,JSe,HK(c) 750.00
19 HK,JCr,WW,JSe,HK(c) 500.00
20 JDa,HK,WW,JSe,HK(c) 300.00
21 JDa,HK,WW,JSe,HK(c) 250.00

22 JDa,HK,WW,JSe,HK(c) 250.00
23 JDa,HK,WW,JSe,HK(c) 225.00
24 JDa,HK,WW,JSe,HK(c) 200.00
25 JDa,HK,WW,JSe,HK(c) 200.00
26 JDa,JSe,HK(c),Action at
   the Changing Reservoir ... 150.00
27 JDa,JSe,HK(c) 150.00
28 JDa,JSe,HK(c) 150.00
29 JDa,JSe,HK(c) 200.00
30 JDa,JSe,JDa(c) 200.00
31 JDa,JSe,HK(c),Civil
   War Story 160.00
32 JDa,JKu,WW(c) 160.00
33 JDa,JKu,WW(c) 175.00
34 JDa,JSe,JDa(c) 160.00
35 JDa,JSe,JDa(c),Civil
   War Story 175.00
36 JDa,JSe,JSe(c),A
   Difference of Opinion 100.00
37 JSe,JSe(c),Bugles &
   Battle Cries 100.00
38 JSe,JSe(c) 100.00
39 JSe,JSe(c) 100.00
40 JDa,JSe,GE,GE(c) 150.00
41 JSe,GE,JDa(c),March, 1955 100.00

UNCLE CHARLIE'S FABLES
Lev Gleason Publications
January, 1952
1 CBi(c),Ph(c) 55.00
2 BF,CBi(c),Ph(c) 30.00
3 CBi(c),Ph(c) 35.00
4 CBi(c),Ph(c) 35.00
5 CBi,Ph(c),September, 1952 . 30.00

UNCLE SAM
(see BLACKHAWK)

Uncle Scrooge #38
© Dell Publishing Co.

UNCLE SCROOGE
Dell Publishing Co.
March, 1952
(1) *see Dell Four Color #386*
(2) *see Dell Four Color #456*
(3) *see Dell Four Color #495*
4 .... 275.00

5 .... 225.00
6 .... 200.00
7 CB 175.00
8 .... 150.00
9 .... 150.00
10 .... 150.00
11 thru 20 .... @125.00
21 thru 30 .... @100.00
31 thru 39 .... @85.00
See Other Color section

UNDERWORLD
D.S. Publishing Co.
February-March, 1948
1 SMo(c),Violence 200.00
2 SMo(c),Electrocution 225.00
3 AMc,AMc(c),The Ancient Club 175.00
4 Grl,The Beer Baron Murder 150.00
5 Grl,The Postal Clue 90.00
6 The Polka Dot Gang 75.00
7 Mono-The Master 75.00
8 The Double Tenth 75.00
9 Thrilling Stories of the Fight
   Against Crime,June, 1953 .. 75.00

UNDERWORLD CRIME
Fawcett Publications
June, 1952
1 The Crime Army 150.00
2 Jailbreak 75.00
3 Microscope Murder 65.00
4 Death on the Docks 65.00
5 River of Blood 65.00
6 The Sky Pirates 65.00
7 Bondage & Torture(c) 150.00
8 .... 65.00
9 June, 1953 .... 65.00

UNITED COMICS
United Features Syndicate
1950
8 thru 26 Bushmiller(c),
   Fritzi Ritz .... @25.00

UNITED STATES FIGHTING AIR FORCE
Superior Comics, Ltd.
September, 1952
1 Coward's Courage 45.00
2 Clouds that Killed 25.00
3 Operation Decoy 15.00
4 thru 28 .... @15.00
29 October, 1959 .... 15.00

UNITED STATES MARINES
Wm. H. Wise/Magazine Ent/ Toby Press
1943
N# MBi,MBi(c),Hellcat out
   of Heaven 45.00
2 MBi,Drama of Wake Island .. 35.00
3 A Leatherneck Flame Thrower 30.00
4 MBi 30.00
5 BP 25.00
6 BP 25.00
7 BP 20.00
8 .... 20.00
9 .... 20.00
10 .... 20.00
11 1952 .... 20.00

UNKEPT PROMISE
Legion of Truth
1949
1 Anti:Alcoholic Drinking 50.00

UNKNOWN WORLDS
(see STRANGE STORIES FROM ANOTHER WORLD)

UNSEEN, THE
Visual Editions (Standard Comics)
1952
5 ATh,The Hungry Lodger ... 150.00
6 JKa,MSy,Bayou Vengeance 100.00
7 JKz,MSy,Time is the Killer . 100.00
8 JKz,MSy,The Vengance Vat 100.00
9 JKz,MSy,Your Grave is Ready 100.00
10 JKz,MSy 100.00
11 JKz,MSy 100.00
12 ATh,GT,Till Death Do Us Part 125.00
13 .... 65.00
14 .... 65.00
15 ATh,The Curse of the
   Undeadl, July, 1954 ...... 125.00

UNTAMED LOVE
Comic Magazines (Quality Comics Group)
January, 1950
1 BWa(c),PGn 120.00
2 Ph(c) 75.00
3 PGn 80.00
4 .... 75.00
5 PGn 80.00

Untamed Love #4
© Comic Magazines/Quality Comics

USA IS READY
Dell Publishing Co.
1941
1 Propaganda WWII 225.00

U.S. JONES
Fox Features Syndicate
November, 1941
1 Death Over the Airways ... 650.00

2 January, 1942 . . . . 500.00

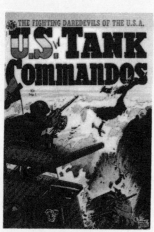

U.S. Tank Commandos #1
© Avon Periodicals

U.S. MARINES IN ACTION!
Avon Periodicals
August, 1952
1 On Land,Sea & in the Air . . . 35.00
2 The Killer Patrol 20.00
3 EK(c),Death Ridge,
December, 1952 . . . . 22.00

U.S. TANK COMMANDOS
Avon Periodicals
June, 1952
1 EK(c),Fighting Daredevils
of the USA 40.00
2 EK(c) 25.00
3 EK,EK(c),Robot Armanda . . . 25.00
4 EK,EK(c),March, 1953 . . . . . 25.00

VALOR
E.C. Comics
March, 1955
1 AW,AT,WW,WW(c),Grl,BK . 250.00
2 AW(c),AW,WWGrl,BK 200.00
3 AW,RC,BK,JOc(c) 150.00
4 WW(c),RC,Grl,BK,JO 150.00
5 WW(c),WW,AW,GE,Grl,BK . 125.00

VARIETY COMICS
Rural Home Publ./
Croyden Publ. Co.
1944
1 MvS,MvS(c),O:Capt, Valiant 100.00
2 MvS,MvS(c) 50.00
3 MvS,MvS(c) 45.00
4 . . . . 35.00
5 1946 . . . . 35.00

VAULT OF HORROR
(see WAR AGAINST CRIME)

V...COMICS
Fox Features Syndicate
January, 1942
1 V:V-Man 650.00
2 The Horror of the
Dungeons, March, 1942 . . . 550.00

VERI BEST SURE SHOT COMICS
Holyoke Publishing Co.
1945
1 reprint Holyoke One-Shots . 175.00

VIC FLINT
St. John Publishing Co.
August, 1948
1 ...Crime Buster 60.00
2 . . . . 40.00
3 . . . . 35.00
4 . . . . 35.00
5 April, 1949 . . . . 35.00

VIC JORDAN
Civil Service Publications
April, 1945
1 Escape From a Nazi Prison . 70.00

VIC TORRY AND HIS FLYING SAUCER
Fawcett Publications
1950
1 Ph(c),Revealed at Last . . . 325.00

VICTORY COMICS
Hillman Periodicals
August, 1941
1 BEv,BEv(c),F:TheConqueror 1,400.00
2 BEv,BEv(c) 650.00
3 The Conqueror(c) 450.00
4 December, 1941 . . . . 450.00

VIC VERITY MAGAZINE
Vic Verity Publications
1945
1 CCB,CCB(c),B:Vic Verity,Hot-

Vic Verity #1
© Vic Verity Publications

Shot Galvan, Tom Travis . . . 85.00
2 CCB,CCB(c),Annual Classic
Dance Recital 45.00
3 CCB 40.00
4 CCB,I:Boomer Young;The
Bee-U-TiFul Weekend 40.00
5 CCB,Championship Baseball
Game 40.00
6 CCB,High School Hero 40.00
7 CCB,CCB(c),F:Rocket Rex . . 40.00

VOODOO
Four Star Publ./Farrell/
Ajax Comics
May, 1952
1 MB,South Sea Girl 225.00
2 MB 175.00
3 Face Stabbing 135.00
4 MB,Rendezvous 125.00
5 Ghoul For A Day,Nazi 100.00
6 The Weird Dead,
Severed Head 110.00
7 Goodbye World 100.00
8 MB, Revenge 135.00
9 Will this thing Never Stew? . . 90.00
10 Land of Shadows & Screams 90.00
11 Human Harvest 85.00
12 The Wazen Taper 85.00
13 Bondage(c),Caskets to
Fit Everybody 100.00
14 Death Judges the
Beauty Contest 85.00
15 Loose their Heads 100.00
16 Fog Was Her Shroud 85.00
17 Apes Laughter,Electric Chair 100.00
18 Astounding Fantasy 85.00
19 MB,Bondage(c);
Destination Congo 120.00

Voodoo Annual #1
© Four Star Publ./Farrell/Ajax Comics

Ann.#1 . . . . 275.00
Becomes:
VOODA
20 MB,MB(c),Echoes of
an A-Bomb 150.00
21 MB,MB(c),Trek of Danger . . 125.00
22 MB,MB(c),The Sun Blew
Away, August, 1955 . . . . . . 125.00

WACKY DUCK
(see DOPEY DUCK)

WALT DISNEY'S
COMICS & STORIES
Dell Publishing Co.

N# 1943 dpt.store giveway	350.00
N# 1945 X-mas giveaway	80.00

WALT DISNEY'S
COMICS & STORIES
Dell Publishing Co.
October, 1940

1 (1940)FG,Donald Duck & Mickey Mouse	10,000.00
2	4,500.00
3	1,500.00
4 Christmas(c)	1,000.00
4a Promo issue	1,400.00
5	800.00
6	700.00
7	650.00
8	650.00
9	650.00
10	650.00
11 1st Huey,Louie,Dewey	550.00
12	600.00

Walt Disney's Comics and Stories #23
© Dell Publ. Co.

13	550.00
14	550.00
15 3 Little Kittens	500.00
16 3 Little Pigs	500.00
17 The Ugly Ducklings	500.00
18	450.00
19	425.00
20	425.00
21	450.00
22	400.00
23	350.00
24	350.00
25	350.00
26	350.00
27	400.00
28	350.00
29	350.00
30	350.00
31 CB; Donald Duck	2,400.00

32 CB	1,100.00
33 CB	800.00
34 CB;WK; Gremlins	650.00
35 CB;WK; Gremlins.	600.00
36 CB;WK; Gremlins	600.00
37 CB;WK; Gremlins	300.00
38 CB;WK; Gremlins	400.00
39 CB;WK; Gremlins	400.00
40 CB;WK; Gremlins	400.00
41 CB;WK; Gremlins	325.00
42 CB	325.00
43 CB	350.00
44 CB	350.00
45 CB	350.00
46 CB	350.00
47 CB	325.00
48 CB	325.00
49 CB	325.00
50 CB	325.00
51 CB	250.00
52 CB; Li'l Bad Wolf begins	250.00
53 CB	250.00
54 CB	250.00
55 CB	250.00
56 CB	250.00
57 CB	250.00
58 CB	250.00
59 CB	250.00
60 CB	250.00
61 CB; Dumbo	200.00
62 CB	200.00
63 CB; Pinocchio	200.00
64 CB; Pinocchio	200.00
65 CB; Pluto	200.00
66 CB	200.00
67 CB	200.00
68 CB	200.00
69 CB	200.00
70 CB	200.00
71 CB	150.00
72 CB	150.00
73 CB	150.00
74 CB	150.00
75 CB; Brer Rabbit	150.00
76 CB; Brer Rabbit	150.00
77 CB; Brer Rabbit	150.00
78 CB	150.00
79 CB	150.00
80 CB	150.00
81 CB	125.00
82 CB;Bongo	135.00
83 CB;Bongo	135.00
84 CB;Bongo	135.00
85 CB	135.00
86 CB;Goofy & Agnes	135.00
87 CB;Goofy & Agnes	125.00
88 CB;Goofy & Agnes, I:Gladstone Gander	150.00
89 CB;Goofy&Agnes,Chip'n'Dale	125.00
90 CB;Goofy & Agnes	125.00
91 CB	100.00
92 CB	100.00
93 CB	100.00
94 CB	100.00
95	100.00
96 Little Toot	100.00
97 CB; Little Toot	100.00
98 CB; Uncle Scrooge	225.00
99 CB	100.00
100 CB	150.00
101 CB	100.00
102 CB	100.00
103 CB	90.00
104	90.00
105 CB	100.00

106 CB	100.00
107 CB	100.00
108	90.00
109	90.00
110 CB	100.00
111 CB	100.00
112 CB; drugs	100.00
113 CB	100.00
114 CB	100.00
115	40.00
116	40.00
117	40.00
118	40.00
119	40.00
120	40.00
121 Grandma Duck begins	40.00
122	40.00
123	40.00
124 CB	75.00
125 CB;I:Junior Woodchucks	100.00
126 CB	75.00
127 CB	75.00
128 CB	75.00
129 CB	75.00
130 CB	75.00
131 CB	75.00
132 CB A:Grandma Duck	75.00
133 CB	75.00
134 I:The Beagle Boys	150.00
135 CB	75.00
136 CB	75.00
137 CB	75.00
138 CB	75.00
139 CB	75.00
140 CB; I:Gyro Gearloose	150.00
141 CB	50.00
142 CB	50.00
143 CB; Little Hiawatha	50.00
144 CB; Little Hiawatha	50.00
145 CB; Little Hiawatha	50.00
146 CB; Little Hiawatha	50.00
147 CB; Little Hiawatha	50.00
148 CB; Little Hiawatha	50.00
149 CB; Little Hiawatha	50.00
150 CB; Little Hiawatha	50.00
151 CB; Little Hiawatha	50.00
152 thru 200 CB	@40.00
201 CB	35.00
202 CB	35.00
203 CB	35.00
204 CB, Chip 'n' Dale & Scamp	35.00
205 thru 240 CB	@35.00
241 CB; Dumbo x-over	30.00
242 CB	30.00
243 CB	30.00
244 CB	30.00
245 CB	30.00
246 CB	30.00
247 thru 255 CB;GyroGearloose	@30.00
256 thru 263 CB;Ludwig Von Drake & Gearloose	@30.00

See: Independent Color Comics

WALT DISNEY ANNUALS
Walt Disney's Autumn Adventure	4.00
Walt Disney's Holiday Parade	3.50
Walt Disney's Spring Fever	3.25
Walt Disney's Summer Fun	3.25

WALT DISNEY
DELL GIANT EDITIONS
Dell Publishing Co.
1 CB,W.Disney'sXmas Parade('49)	900.00

---

2 CB,W.Disney'sXmas
  Parade('50) 700.00
3 W.Disney'sXmas Parade('51) 225.00
4 W.Disney'sXmas Parade('52) 200.00
5 W.Disney'sXmas Parade('53) 200.00
6 W.Disney'sXmas Parade('54) 200.00
7 W.Disney'sXmas Parade('55) 200.00
8 CB,W.Disney'sXmas
  Parade('56) 350.00
9 CB,W.Disney'sXmas
  Parade('57) 300.00
1 CB,W.Disney's Christmas in
  Disneyland (1957) 400.00
1 CB,W.Disney's Disneyland
  Birthday Party (1958) 400.00
1 W.Disney's Donald and Mickey
  in Disneyland (1958) 175.00
1 W.Disney's Donald Duck
  Beach Party (1954) 200.00
2 W.Disney's Donald Duck
  Beach Party (1955) 175.00
3 W.Disney's Donald Duck
  Beach Party (1956) 175.00
4 W.Disney's Donald Duck
  Beach Party (1957) 175.00
5 W.Disney's Donald Duck
  Beach Party (1958) 175.00
6 W.Disney's Donald Duck
  Beach Party (1959) 175.00
1 W.Disney's Donald Duck
  Fun Book (1954) 600.00
2 W.Disney's Donald Duck
  Fun Book (1954) 550.00
1 W.Disney's Donald Duck
  in Disneyland (1955) 200.00
1 W.Disney's Huey, Dewey
  and Louie (1958) 150.00
1 W.Disney's DavyCrockett('55) 135.00
1 W.Disney's Lady and the
  Tramp (1955) 275.00
1 CB,W.Disney's Mickey Mouse
  Almanac (1957) 400.00
1 W.Disney's Mickey Mouse
  Birthday Party (1953) 500.00
1 W.Disney's Mickey Mouse
  Club Parade (1955) 400.00
1 W.Disney's Mickey Mouse
  in Fantasyland (1957) 200.00
1 W.Disney's Mickey Mouse
  in Frontierland (1956) 200.00
1 W.Disney's Summer Fun('58) 200.00
2 CB,W.Disney'sSummer
  Fun('59) 200.00
1 W.Disney's Peter Pan
  Treasure Chest (1953) . . 1,500.00
1 Disney Silly Symphonies('52) 450.00
2 Disney Silly Symphonies('53) 400.00
3 Disney Silly Symphonies('54) 350.00
4 Disney Silly Symphonies('54) 350.00
5 Disney Silly Symphonies('55) 300.00
6 Disney Silly Symphonies('56) 300.00
7 Disney Silly Symphonies('57) 300.00
8 Disney Silly Symphonies('58) 300.00
9 Disney Silly Symphonies('59) 300.00
1 Disney SleepingBeauty('59) . 450.00
1 CB,W.Disney's Uncle Scrooge
  Goes to Disneyland (1957) . 400.00
1 W.Disney's Vacation in
  Disneyland (1958) 175.00
1 CB,Disney's Vacation
  Parade('50) 1,300.00
2 Disney'sVacation Parade('51) 450.00
3 Disney'sVacation Parade('52) 225.00
4 Disney'sVacation Parade('53) 225.00
5 Disney'sVacation Parade('54) 225.00

6 Disney's Picnic Party (1955) 175.00
7 Disney's Picnic Party (1956) 175.00
8 CB,Disney's Picnic
  Party (1957) 350.00

DELL JUNIOR TREASURY
1 W.Disney's Alice in Wonderland
  (1955) 85.00

WALT DISNEY PRESENTS
Dell Publishing Co.
June-August, 1952
1 Ph(c), Four Color 40.00
2 Ph(c) 25.00
3 Ph(c) 25.00
4 Ph(c) 25.00
5 and 6 Ph(c) . . . . @25.00

WAMBI JUNGLE BOY
Fiction House Magazines
Spring, 1942
1 HcK,HcK(c),Vengence of
  the Beasts 400.00
2 HcK,HcK(c),Lair of the
  Killer Rajah 200.00
3 HcK,HcK(c) 150.00
4 HcK,HcK(c),The Valley of
  the Whispering Drums 100.00
5 HcK,HcK(c),Swampland Safari 90.00

Wambi Jungle Boy #6
© Fiction House Magazines

6 Taming of the Tigress 75.00
7 Duel of the Congo Kings . . . 75.00
8 AB(c),Friend of the Animals . 75.00
9 Quest of the Devils Juju . . . 75.00
10 Friend of the Animals 50.00
11 . . . . 50.00
12 Curse of the Jungle Jewels . . 50.00
13 New Adventures of Wambi . . 50.00
14 . . . . 50.00
15 The Leopard Legions 50.00
16 . . . . 50.00
17 Beware Bwana! 50.00
18 Ogg the Great Bull Ape,
  Winter, 1952 . . . . 50.00

WANTED COMICS
Toytown Comics/ Orbit Publications
September-October, 1947
9 Victor Everhart 80.00
10 Carlo Banone 50.00
11 Dwight Band 50.00
12 Ralph Roe 55.00
13 James Spencer;Drug 55.00
14 John "Jiggs" Sullivan;Drug . . 55.00
15 Harry Dunlap;Drug 35.00
16 Jack Parisi;Drug 35.00
17 Herber Ayers;Drug 35.00
18 Satan's Cigarettes;Drug 100.00
19 Jackson Stringer 30.00
20 George Morgan 30.00
21 BK,Paul Wilson 35.00
22 . . . . 30.00
23 George Elmo Wells 20.00
24 BK,Bruce Cornett;Drug 40.00
25 Henry Anger 20.00
26 John Wormly 20.00
27 Death Always Knocks Twice . 20.00
28 Paul H. Payton 20.00
29 Hangmans Holiday 20.00
30 George Lee 20.00
31 M Consolo 20.00
32 William Davis 20.00
33 The Web of Davis 20.00
34 Dead End 20.00
35 Glen Roy Wright 25.00
36 SSh,SSh(c),Bernard Lee
  Thomas 20.00
37 SSh,SSh(c),Joseph M. Moore 20.00
38 SSh,SSh(c) 20.00
39 The Horror Weed;Drug 55.00
40 . . . . 20.00
41 . . . . 20.00

War Against Crime #7
© L.L. Publ./E.C. Comics

42 . . . . 20.00
43 . . . . 20.00
44 . . . . 20.00
45 Killers on the Loose;Drug . . . 45.00
46 Chalres Edward Crews 20.00
47 . . . . 20.00
48 SSh,SSh(c) 20.00
49 . . . . 20.00
50 JB(c),Make Way for Murder . 55.00

51 JB(c),Dope Addict on a
   Holiday of Murder;Drug 35.00
52 The Cult of Killers;
   Classic Drug 35.00
53 April, 1953 .... 20.00

WAR AGAINST CRIME
L.L. Publishing Co.
(E.C. Comics)
Spring, 1948
1 Grl 400.00
2 Grl,Guilty of Murder 250.00
3 JCr(c) 250.00
4 AF,JCr(c) 225.00
5 JCr(c) 225.00
6 AF,JCr(c) 225.00
7 AF,JCr(c) 225.00
8 AF,JCr(c) 225.00
9 AF,JCr(c),The Kid 225.00
10 JCr(c),I:Vault Keeper 1,500.00
11 JCr(c) 1,000.00
Becomes:
VAULT OF HORROR
12 AF,JCr,JCr(c),Wax Museum 3,000.00
13 AF,WW,JCr(c),Grl,Drug ... 800.00
14 AF,WW,JCr(c),Grl 750.00
15 AF,JCr,JCr(c),Grl,JKa 600.00
16 Grl,JKa,JCr,JCr(c) 550.00
17 JDa,Grl,JKa,JCr,JCr(c) 400.00
18 JDa,Grl,JKa,JCr,JCr(c) 400.00
19 JDa,Grl,JKa,JCr,JCr(c) 400.00
20 JDa,Grl,JKa,JCr,JCr(c) 275.00
21 JDa,Grl,JKa,JCr,JCr(c) 275.00
22 JDa,JKa,JCr,JCr(c) 275.00
23 JDa,Grl,JCr,JCr(c) 275.00
24 JDa,Grl,JO,JCr,JCr(c) 275.00
25 JDa,Grl,JKa,JCr,JCr(c) 275.00
26 JDa,Grl,JCr,JCr(c) 275.00
27 JDa,Grl,JCr,GE,JCr(c) 200.00
28 JDa,Grl,JCr,JCr(c) 200.00
29 JDa,Grl,JCr,JKa,JCr(c),
   JDa,Grl,JCr,JCr(c)
   Bradbury Adapt 200.00

Vault of Horror #18 © E.C. Comics

30 JDa,Grl,JCr,JCr(c) 200.00
31 JDa,Grl,JCr,JCr(c),
   Bradbury Adapt 175.00
32 JDa,Grl,JCr,JCr(c) 175.00
33 JDa,Grl,RC,JCr(c) 175.00

34 JDa,Grl,JCr,RC,JCr(c) 175.00
35 JDa,Grl,JCr,JCr(c) 175.00
36 JDa,Grl,JCr,BK,JCr(c),Drug 175.00
37 JDa,Grl,JCr,AW,JCr(c)
   Hanging 175.00
38 JDa,Grl,JCr,BK,JCr(c) 175.00
39 GRi,JCr,BK,RC,JCr(c)
   Bondage(c) 200.00
40 January, 1955, Grl,JCr,BK,JO
   JCr(c) 175.00

WAR BATTLES
Harvey Publications
February, 1952
1 BP,Devils of the Deep 45.00
2 BP,A Present From Benny .. 30.00
3 BP 20.00
4 .... 20.00
5 .... 20.00
6 HN 20.00
7 BP 25.00
8 .... 20.00
9 December, 1953 .... 20.00

WAR BIRDS
Fiction House Magazines
1952
1 Willie the Washout 75.00
2 Mystery MIGs of Kwanjamu . 45.00
3 thru 6 .... @40.00
7 Winter, 1953,Across the
   Wild Yalu 40.00

WAR COMICS
Dell Publishing Co.
May, 1940
1 AMc,Sky Hawk 325.00
2 O:Greg Gildam 175.00
3 .... 125.00
4 O:Night Devils 150.00

WAR HEROES
Dell Publishing Co.
July-September, 1942
1 Gen. Douglas MacArthur (c) 150.00
2 .... 75.00
3 .... 50.00
4 A:Gremlins 100.00
5 .... 45.00
6 thru 11 .... @40.00

WAR HEROES
Ace Magazines
May, 1952
1 Always Comin' 40.00
2 LC,The Last Red Tank 25.00
3 You Got it 20.00
4 A Red Patrol 20.00
5 Hustle it Up 20.00
6 LC,Hang on Pal 25.00
7 .... 25.00
8 LC,April, 1953 .... 25.00

WARPATH
Key Publications/
Stanmore
November, 1954
1 Red Men Raid 50.00
2 AH(c),Braves Battle 30.00
3 April, 1955 .... 30.00

WARRIOR COMICS
H.C. Blackerby
1944
1 Ironman wing Brady 90.00

WAR SHIPS
Dell Publishing Co.
1942
1 AMc 75.00

WAR STORIES
Dell Publishing Co.
1942
5 O:The Whistler 135.00
6 A:Night Devils 100.00
7 A:Night Devils 100.00
8 A:Night Devils 100.00

Wartime Romaces #7
© St. John Publishing Co.

WARTIME ROMANCES
St. John Publishing Co.
July, 1951
1 MB(c),MB 125.00
2 MB(c),MB 75.00
3 MB(c),MB 60.00
4 MB(c),MB 60.00
5 MB(c),MB 50.00
6 MB(c),MB 60.00
7 MB(c),MB 50.00
8 MB(c),MB 50.00
9 MB(c),MB 35.00
10 MB(c),MB 35.00
11 MB(c),MB 35.00
12 Mb(c),MB 35.00
13 MB(c) 30.00
14 MB(c) 30.00
15 MB(c) 30.00
16 MB(c),MB 30.00
17 MB(c) 30.00
18 MB(c),MB 30.00

WAR VICTORY COMICS
U.S. Treasury/War Victory/
Harvey Publ.
Summer, 1942
1 Savings Bond Promo with

Top Syndicated Cartoonists,
benefit USO 225.00
Becomes:

WAR VICTORY ADVENTURES

2 BP,2nd Front Comics 100.00
3 BP,F:Capt Cross of the
Red Cross 90.00

Web of Evil #1
© Comic Magazines/Quality Comics

WEB OF EVIL
Comic Magazines, Inc. (Quality Comics Group)
November, 1952

1 Custodian of the Dead 250.00
2 JCo,Hangmans Horror 150.00
3 JCo 150.00
4 JCo,JCo(c),Monsters of
the Mist 150.00
5 JCo,JCo(c),The Man who Died
Twice,Electric Chair(c) 200.00
6 JCo,JCo(c),Orgy of Death . 150.00
7 JCo,JCo(c),The Strangling
Hands 150.00
8 JCo,Flaming Vengeance .. 125.00
9 JCo,The Monster in Flesh . 125.00
10 JCo,Brain that Wouldn't Die 125.00
11 JCo,Buried Alive 125.00
12 Phantom Killer 60.00
13 Demon Inferno 60.00
14 RC(c),The Monster Genie ... 65.00
15 Crypts of Horror 60.00
16 Hamlet of Horror 60.00
17 Terror in Chinatown 65.00
18 Scared to Death,Acid Face .. 75.00
19 Demon of the Pit 60.00
20 Man Made Terror 60.00
21 December, 1954, Death's
Ambush 60.00

WEB OF MYSTERY
A.A. Wyn Publ. (Ace Magazines)
February, 1951

1 MSy,Venom of the Vampires 200.00
2 MSy,Legacy of the Accursed 125.00
3 MSy,The Violin Curse 100.00

4 GC 100.00
5 .... 100.00
6 LC 100.00
7 MSy 100.00
8 LC,LC(c),MSy,The Haunt of
Death Lake 100.00
9 LC,LC(c) 100.00
10 .... 100.00
11 MSy 100.00
12 LC 80.00
13 LC,LC(c) 80.00
14 MSy 80.00
15 .... 80.00
16 .... 80.00
17 LC,LC(c) 80.00
18 LC 80.00
19 LC 80.00
20 LC 80.00
21 MSy 80.00
22 .... 80.00
23 .... 80.00
24 LC 80.00
25 LC 80.00
26 .... 80.00
27 LC 80.00
28 RP,1st Issue under Comics
Code Authority 60.00
29 MSy,September, 1955 ..... 60.00

WEDDING BELLS
Quality Comics Group
February, 1954

1 OW 70.00
2 .... 45.00
3 .... 25.00
4 .... 25.00
5 .... 25.00
6 .... 25.00
7 .... 25.00
8 .... 25.00
9 Comics Code 25.00
10 BWa 60.00
11 .... 25.00
12 .... 20.00
13 .... 20.00
14 .... 20.00
15 MB(c) 25.00
16 MB(c),MB 35.00
17 .... 20.00
18 MB 25.00
19 MB 25.00

WEEKENDER, THE
Rucker Publishing Co.
September, 1945

3 .... 125.00
4 .... 100.00
2-1(5)JCo,WMc,January, 1946 145.00

WEIRD ADVENTURES
P.L. Publishing
May, 1951

1 MB,Missing Diamonds 200.00
2 Puppet Peril 150.00
3 Blood Vengeance,
October 1951 .... 150.00

WEIRD ADVENTURES
Approved Comics (Ziff-Davis)
July-August, 1951

10 P(c),Seeker from Beyond .. 150.00

WEIRD CHILLS
Key Publications
July, 1954

1 MBi(c),BW 300.00
2 Eye Torture(c) 250.00
3 Bondage(c),November, 1954 150.00

WEIRD COMICS
Fox Features Syndicate
April, 1940

1 LF(c),Bondage(c),B:Birdman,
Thor,Sorceress of Doom,
BlastBennett,Typhon,Voodoo
Man, Dr.Mortal 1,700.00
2 LF(c),Mummy(c) 700.00
3 JSm(c) 500.00
4 JSm(c) 500.00
5 Bondage(c),I:Dart,Ace;E:Thor 500.00
6 Dart & Ace(c) 450.00
7 Battle of Kooba 450.00

Weird Comics #14
© Fox Features Syndicate

8 B:Panther Woman,Dynamo,
The Eagle 450.00
9 V:Pirates 400.00
10 A:Navy Jones 400.00
11 Dart & Ace(c) 300.00
12 Dart & Ace(c) 300.00
13 Dart & Ace(c) 300.00
14 The Rage(c) 300.00
15 Dart & Ace (c) 300.00
16 Flag,The Encore(c) 300.00
17 O:Black Rider 325.00
18 .... 300.00
19 .... 300.00
20 January, 1941,I'm The Master
of Life and Death 300.00

WEIRD FANTASY
I.C. Publishing Co. (E.C. Comics)
May-June, 1950

13(1)AF,HK,JKa,WW,AF(c),
Roger Harvey's Brain 900.00
14(2)AF,HK,JKa,WW,AF(c),
Cosmic Ray Brain Explosion 500.00
15(3)AF,HK,JKa,WW,AF(c),Your
Destination is the Moon ... 450.00

| **All comics prices listed are for *Near Mint* condition.**

16(4)AF,HK,JKa,WW,AF(c) . . . 450.00
17(5)AF,HK,JKa,WW,AF(c),Not
Made by Human Hands . . . 400.00
6 AF,HK,JKa,WW,AF(c) 300.00
7 AF,JKa,WW,AF(c) 300.00
8 AF,JKa,WW,AF(c) 300.00
9 AF,Jka,WW,JO,AF(c) 300.00
10 AF,Jka,WW,JO,AF(c) 350.00
11 AF,Jka,WW,JO,AF(c) 250.00
12 AF,Jka,WW,AF(c) 250.00
13 AF,Jka,WW,JO,AF(c) 250.00
14 AF,JKa,WW,JO,AW&FF,AF(c)350.00
15 AF,JKa,JO,AW&RKr,AF(c),
Bondage(c) 250.00
16 AF,JKa,JO,AW&RKr,AF(c) . 200.00
17 AF,JOP,JKa,AF(c),Bradbury 200.00
18 AF,JO,JKa,AF(c),Bradbury . 200.00
19 JO,JKa,JO(c),Bradbury . . . 200.00
20 JO,JKa,FF,AF(c) 225.00
21 JO,JKa,AW&FF,AF(c) 350.00
22 JO,JKa,JO(c),Nov.,1953 . . . 195.00

WEIRD HORRORS
St. John Publishing Co.
June, 1952
1 GT,Dungeon of the Doomed 200.00
2 Strangest Music Ever 100.00
3 PAM,Strange Fakir From
the Orient 90.00
4 Murderers Knoll 90.00
5 Phantom Bowman 90.00
6 Monsters from Outer Space 165.00
7 LC,Deadly Double 200.00
8 JKu,JKu(c),Bloody Yesterday 135.00
9 JKu,JKu(c),Map Of Doom . . 135.00
Becomes:
NIGHTMARE
10 JKu(c),The Murderer's Mask 250.00
11 BK,Ph(c),Fangs of Death . . 175.00
12 JKu(c),The Forgotten Mask . 150.00
13 BP,Princess of the Sea 125.00
Becomes:
AMAZING GHOST
STORIES
14 EK,MB(c), ... 125.00
15 BP 90.00
16 February, 1955, EK,JKu . . . 100.00

Weird Mysteries #3
© Gilmore Publications

WEIRD MYSTERIES
Gilmore Publications
October, 1952
1 BW(c) 300.00
2 BWi 450.00
3 Severed Heads(c) 200.00
4 BW,Human headed ants(c) . . . 350.00
5 BW,Brains From Head(c) . . . 350.00
6 Severed Head(c) 250.00
7 Used in "Seduction" 300.00
8 The One That Got Away 200.00
9 Epitaph,Cyclops 200.00
10 The Ruby 150.00
11 Voodoo Dolls 150.00
12 September, 1954 . . . . 150.00

WEIRD SCIENCE
E.C. Comics
1950
1 AF(c),AF,JKu,HK,WW 1,000.00
2 AF(c),AF,JKu,HK,WW,Flying
Saucers(c) 600.00
3 AF(c),AF,JKu,HK 550.00
4 AF(c),AF,JKu,HK 550.00
5 AF(c),AF,JKu,HK,WW,
Atomic Bomb(c) 400.00
6 AF(c),AF,JKu,HK 350.00
7 AF(c),AF,JKu,HK,Classic(c) . 400.00
8 AF(c),AF,JKu 350.00
9 WW(c),JKu,Classic(c) 400.00
10 WW(c),JKu,JO,Classic(c) . . 400.00
11 AF,JKu,Space war 275.00
12 WW(c),JKu,JO,Classic(c) . . 275.00
13 WW(c),JKu,JO, ... 300.00
14 WW(c),WW,JO 300.00
15 WW(c),WW,JO,GRi,AW,
RKr,JKa 300.00
16 WW(c),WW,JO,AW,RKr,JKa 300.00
17 WW(c),WW,JO,AW,RKr,JKa 300.00
18 WW(c),WW,JO,AW,RKr,
JKa,Atomic Bomb 250.00
19 WW(c),WW,JO,AW,
FF,Horror(c) 400.00
20 WW(c),WW,JO,AW,FF,JKa . 400.00
21 WW(c),WW,JO,AW,FF,JKa . 400.00
22 WW(c),WW,JO,AW,FF 400.00
Becomes:
WEIRD SCIENCE
FANTASY
23 WW(c),WW,AW,BK 200.00
24 WW,AW,BK,Classic(c) 225.00
25 WW,AW,BK,Classic(c) 250.00
26 AF(c),WW,RC,
Flying Saucer(c) 200.00
27 WW(c),WW,RC 200.00
28 AF(c),WW 250.00
29 AF(c),WW,Classic(c) 400.00
Becomes:
INCREDIBLE SCIENCE
FANTASY
30 WW,JDa(c),BK,AW,RKr,JO 250.00
31 WW,JDa(c),BK,AW,RKr . . . 300.00
32 JDa(c),BK,WW,JO 300.00
33 WW(c),BK,WW,JO 300.00

WEIRD TALES OF
THE FUTURE
S.P.M. Publ./
Aragon Publications
March, 1952
1 RA 325.00
2 BW,BW(c) 550.00

3 BW,BW(c) 500.00
4 BW,BW(c) 300.00
5 BW,BW(c),Jumpin' Jupiter
Lingerie(c) 550.00
6 Bondage(c) 250.00
7 BW,Devil(c) 325.00
8 July-August 1953 . . . . 200.00

WEIRD TERROR
Allen Hardy Associates
(Comic Media)
September, 1952
1 RP,DH,DH(c),Dungeon of the
Doomed;Hitler 175.00
2 HcK(c);PAM 135.00
3 PAM,DH,DH(c) 125.00
4 PAM,DH,DH(c) 150.00
5 PAM,DH,RP,DH(c),Hanging(c) 125.00
6 DH,RP,DH(c),Step into
My Parlour 150.00
7 DH,PAM,DH(c),Blood o/t Bats 100.00
8 DH,RP,DH(c),Step into
My Parlour 125.00
9 DH,PAM,DH(c),The Fleabite 100.00
10 DH,BP,RP,DH(c) 100.00
11 DH,DH(c),Satan's Love Call 125.00
12 DH,DH(c),King Whitey 90.00
13 DH,DH(c),September, 1954,
Wings of Death 100.00

WEIRD THRILLERS
Approved Comics
(Ziff-Davis)
September-October, 1951
1 Ph(c),Monsters & The Model 250.00
2 AW,P(c),The Last Man 200.00
3 AW,P(c),Princess o/t Sea . . 175.00
4 AW,P(c),The Widows Lover . 165.00
5 BP,October, 1952,AW,P(c),
Wings of Death 150.00

WESTERN ACTION
THRILLERS
Dell Publishing Co.
April, 1937
1 . . . . 500.00

WESTERN ADVENTURES
COMICS
A.A. Wyn, Inc.
(Ace Magazines)
October, 1948
N#(1)Injun Gun Bait 125.00
N#(2)Cross-Draw Kid 65.00
N#(3)Outlaw Mesa 65.00
4 Sheriff 45.00
5 . . . . 45.00
6 Rip Roaring Adventure 45.00
Becomes:
WESTERN LOVE TRAILS
7 . . . . 65.00
8 Maverick Love 45.00
9 March, 1950 . . . . 40.00

WESTERN BANDIT
TRAILS
St. John Publishing Co.
January, 1949
1 GT,MB(c) 125.00
2 GT,MB(c) 75.00
3 GT,MB,MB(c),Gingham Fury . 90.00

All comics prices listed are for *Near Mint* condition. **CVA Page 393**

Western Crime-Busters #1
© *Trojan Magazines*

WESTERN CRIME-BUSTERS
Trojan Magazines
September, 1950

1 Gunslingin' Galoots		165.00
2 K-Bar Kate		90.00
3 Wilma West		90.00
4 Bob Dale		90.00
5 Six-Gun Smith		90.00
6 WW		185.00
7 WW,Wells Fargo Robbery		185.00
8		75.00
9 WW,Lariat Lucy		175.00
10 WW,April 1952;Tex Gordon		175.00

WESTERN CRIME CASES
(see WHITE RIDER)

WESTERNER, THE
**Wanted Comics Group/
Toytown Publ.**
June, 1948

14 F:Jack McCall	65.00
15 F:Bill Jarnett	30.00
16 F:Tom McLowery	30.00
17 F:Black Bill Desmond	30.00
18 BK,F:Silver Dollar Dalton	50.00
19 MMe,F:Jess Meeton	30.00
20	25.00
21 BK,MMe	50.00
22 BK,MMe	50.00
23 BK,MMe	50.00
24 BK,MMe	50.00
25 O,I,B:Calamity Jane	50.00
26 BK,F:The Widowmaker	65.00
27	75.00
28	25.00
29	25.00
30	25.00
31	25.00
32 E:Calamity Jane	25.00
33 A:Quest	25.00
34	25.00
35 SSh(c)	25.00
36	25.00
37 Lobo-Wolf Boy	25.00

38	25.00
39	25.00
40 SSh(c)	25.00
41 December, 1951	25.00

WESTERN FIGHTERS
Hillman Periodicals
April-May, 1948

1 S&K(c)	175.00
2 BF(c)	60.00
3 BF(c)	50.00
4 BK,BF	55.00
5	35.00
6	34.00
7 BK	60.00
8	35.00
9	35.00
10 BK	60.00
11 AMC&FF	160.00
2-1 BK	60.00
2-2 BP	40.00
2-3 thru 2-12	@20.00
3-1 thru 3-11	@20.00
3-12 BK	40.00
4-1	20.00
4-2 BK	50.00
4-3 BK	50.00
4-4 BK	50.00
4-5 BK	50.00
4-6 BK	50.00
4-7 March-April 1953	20.00

WESTERN FRONTIER
**P.L. Publishers
(Approved Comics)**
May, 1951

1 Flaming Vengeance	60.00
2	35.00
3 Death Rides the Iron Horse	25.00
4 thru 6	@25.00
7 1952	25.00

WESTERN HEARTS
Standard Magazine, Inc.
December, 1949

1 Ph(c),JSe	100.00
2 Ph(c),AW,FF	150.00
3 Ph(c)	50.00
4 Ph(c),JSe,BE	50.00
5 Ph(c),JSe,BE	50.00
6 Ph(c),JSe,BE	50.00
7 Ph(c),JSe,BE	50.00
8 Ph(c)	55.00
9 Ph(c),JSe,BE	65.00
10 Ph(c),JSe,BE	45.00

WESTERN LOVE
**Feature Publications
(Prize Comics Group)**
July-August, 1949

1 S&K	125.00
2 S&K	100.00
3 JSE,BE	75.00
4 JSE,BE	75.00
5 JSE,BE	75.00

WESTERN PICTURE STORIES
Comics Magazine Co.
February, 1937

1 WE,Treachery Trail, 1st Western	900.00

Whirlwind Comics #2
© *Nita Publications*

2 WE,Weapons of the West	600.00
3 WE,Dragon Pass	450.00
4 June, 1937,CavemanCowboy	450.00

WESTERN THRILLERS
Fox Features Syndicate
August, 1948

1	250.00
2	90.00
3 GT,RH(c)	75.00
4	90.00
5	90.00
6 June, 1949	75.00

Becomes:

MY PAST CONFESSIONS

7	60.00
8	40.00
9	40.00
10	40.00
11	75.00
12	20.00

WESTERN TRUE CRIME
Fox Features Syndicate
August, 1948

1	125.00
2	90.00
3	50.00
4 JCr	125.00
5	50.00
6	50.00

Becomes:

MY CONFESSION

7 WW	100.00
8 WW,My Tarnished Reputation	90.00
9 I:Tormented Men	40.00
10 February, 1950,I Am Damaged Goods	40.00

WHACK
St. John Publishing Co.
December, 1953

1 Steve Crevice,Flush Jordan

V:Bing(Crosby)The Merciful   175.00
2 . . . . 100.00
3 F:Little Awful Fannie 100.00

WHAM COMICS
Centaur Publications
November, 1940
1 PG,The Sparkler & His

Wham Comics #1 © Centaur Publ.

Disappearing Suit 750.00
2 December, 1940,PG,PG(C),
   Men Turn into Icicles 550.00

WHIRLWIND COMICS
Nita Publications
June, 1940
1 F:The Cyclone 550.00
2 A:Scoops Hanlon,Cyclone(c)   450.00
3 September, 1940,A:Magic
   Mandarin,Cyclone(c) 400.00

WHITE PRINCESS OF
THE JUNGLE
Avon Periodicals
July, 1951
1 EK(c),Terror Fangs 225.00
2 EK,EK(c),Jungle Vengeance   175.00
3 EK,EK(c),The Blue Gorilla   . 150.00
4 Fangs of the Swamp Beast   135.00
5 EK,Coils of the Tree Snake
   November, 1952   . . . . 135.00

WHIZ COMICS
Fawcett Publications
February, 1940
1 O:Captain Marvel,B:Spy
   Smasher,Golden Arrow,Dan
   Dare, Scoop Smith,Ibis
   the Invincible, Sivana . . . 45,000.00
2 . . . . 4,500.00
3 Make way for
   Captain Marvel 3,000.00
4 Captain Marvel
   Crashes Through 2,000.00
5 Captain Marvel
   Scores Again! 1,500.00
6 Circus of Death 1,000.00
7 B:Dr Voodoo,Squadron

White Princess of the Jungle #4
© Avon Periodicals

   of Death 1,000.00
8 Saved by Captain Marvel!   . 900.00
9 MRa,Captain Marvel
   on the Job 900.00
10 Battles the Winged Death   . . 900.00
11 Hurray for Captain Marvel . . 750.00
12 Captain Marvel rides
   the Engine of Doom 750.00
13 Worlds Most Powerful Man!   700.00
14 Boomerangs the Torpedo   . . 700.00
15 O:Sivana 800.00
16 . . . . 800.00
17 Knocks out a Tank 800.00
18 V:Spy Smasher 800.00
19 Crushes the Tiger Shark . . . 500.00
20 V:Sivana 500.00
21 O:Lt. Marvels 550.00
22 Mayan Temple 400.00
23 GT,A:Dr. Voodoo 400.00
24 . . . . 400.00
25 O&I:Captain Marvel Jr.,
   Stops the Turbine of Death   2,500.00
26 . . . . 375.00
27 V:Death God of the Katonkas   350.00
28 V:Mad Dervish of Ank-Har   . 350.00
29 Three Lt. Marvels (c), Pan
   American Olympics 350.00
30 . . . . 350.00
31 Douglass MacArthur&Spy
   Smasher(c) 300.00
32 Spy Smasher(c) 300.00
33 Spy Smasher(c) 325.00
34 Three Lt. Marvels (c) 275.00
35 Capt. Marvel and the
   Three Fates 300.00
36 Haunted Hallowe'en Hotel . . 250.00
37 Return of the Trolls 250.00
38 Grand Steeplechase 250.00
39 A Nazi Utopia 250.00
40 A:Three Lt. Marvels, The
   Earth's 4 Corners 250.00
41 Captain Marvel 1,000 years
   from Now 200.00
42 Returns in Time Chair 200.00
43 V:Sinister Spies,
   Spy Smasher(c) 200.00

44 Life Story of Captain Marvel   225.00

Whiz Comics #50
© Fawcett Publications

45 Cures His Critics 200.00
46 . . . . 200.00
47 Captain Marvel needs
   a Birthday 200.00
48 . . . . 200.00
49 Writes a Victory song 200.00
50 Captain Marvel's most
   embarrassing moment 200.00
51 Judges the Ugly-
   Beauty Contest 175.00
52 V:Sivana, Chooses
   His Birthday 175.00
53 Captain Marvel fights
   Billy Batson 175.00
54 Jack of all Trades 175.00
55 Family Tree 175.00
56 Tells what the Future Will Be   175.00
57 A:Spy Smasher,Golden Arrow,
   Ibis 175.00
58 . . . . 175.00
59 V:Sivana's Twin 175.00
60 Missing Person's Machine   . 175.00
61 Gets a first name 150.00
62 Plays in a Band 150.00
63 Great Indian Rope Trick . . . 150.00
64 Suspected of Murder 150.00
65 Lamp of Diogenes 150.00
66 The Trial of Mr. Morris! 150.00
67 . . . . 150.00
68 Laugh Lotion, V:Sivana 150.00
69 Mission to Mercury 150.00
70 Climbs the World's Mightiest
   Mountain 150.00
71 Strange Magician 125.00
72 V:The Man of the Future . . . 125.00
73 In Ogre Land 125.00
74 Old Man River 125.00
75 The City Olympics 125.00
76 Spy Smasher become
   Crime Smasher 125.00
77 . . . . 125.00
78 . . . . 125.00
79 . . . . 125.00
80 . . . . 125.00
81 . . . . 125.00
82 The Atomic Ship 125.00
83 Magic Locket 125.00

All comics prices listed are for *Near Mint* condition.   **CVA Page 395**

84	125.00
85 The Clock of San Lojardo	125.00
86 V:Sinister Sivanas	125.00
87 The War on Olympia	125.00
88 The Wonderful Magic Carpet	125.00
89 Webs of Crime	125.00
90	125.00
91 Infinity (c)	125.00
92	125.00
93 Captain America become a Hobo?	125.00
94 V:Sivana	125.00
95 Captain Marvel is grounded	125.00
96 The Battle Between Buildings	125.00
97 Visits Mirage City	125.00
98	125.00
99 V:Menace in the Mountains	125.00
100	150.00
101	100.00
102 A:Commando Yank	100.00
103	100.00
104	100.00
105	100.00
106 A:Bulletman	100.00
107 The Great Experiment	125.00
108 thru 114	@100.00
115 The Marine Invasion	100.00
116	100.00
117 V:Sivana	100.00
118	100.00
119	100.00
120	100.00
121	100.00
122 V:Sivana	100.00
123	100.00
124	100.00
125 Olympic Games of the Gods	100.00
126	100.00
127	100.00
128	100.00
129	100.00
130	100.00
131 The Television Trap	100.00
132 thru 142	@100.00
143 Mystery of the Flying Studio	100.00
144 V:The Disaster Master	100.00
145	100.00
146	100.00
147	100.00
148	100.00
149	100.00
150 V:Bug Bombs	100.00
151	100.00
152	100.00
153 V:The Death Horror	125.00
154 Horror Tale, I:Dr.Death	125.00
155 V:Legend Horror,Dr.Death	135.00

WHODUNIT?
D.S. Publishing Co.
August-September, 1948

1 MB,Weeping Widow	85.00
2 Diploma For Death	50.00
3 December-January, 1949	50.00

WHO IS NEXT?
Standard Comics
January, 1953

5 ATh,RA,Don't Let Me Kill	100.00

WILD BILL ELLIOT
Dell Publishing Co.
May, 1950

(1) *see Dell Four Color #278*

2	45.00
3 thru 5	@35.00
6 thru 10	@35.00
(11-12) *see Four Color #472, 520*	
13 thru 17	@30.00

WILD BILL HICKOK AND JINGLES
(see YELLOWJACKET COMICS)

WILBUR COMICS
MLJ Magazines
(Archie Publications)
Summer, 1944

1 F:Wilbur Wilkin-America's Song of Fun	300.00
2	150.00
3	125.00
4	100.00
5 I:Katy Keene	400.00
6 thru 10	@125.00
11 thru 20	@70.00
21 thru 30	@45.00
31 thru 40	@35.00
41 thru 50	@25.00
51 thru 89	@20.00
90 October, 1965	20.00

WILD BILL HICKOK
Avon Periodicals
September-October, 1949

1 GRI(c),Frontier Fighter	100.00
2 Ph(c),Gambler's Guns	50.00
3 Ph(c),Great Stage Robbery	25.00
4 Ph(c),Guerilla Gunmen	25.00
5 Ph(c),Return of the Renegade	25.00
6 EK,EK(c),Along the Apache Trail	25.00
7 EK,EK(c)Outlaws of Hell's Bend	25.00
8 Ph(c),The Border Outlaws	25.00
9 PH(c),Killers From Texas	25.00
10 Ph(c)	25.00
11 EK,EK(c),The Hell Riders	25.00
12 EK,EK(c),The Lost Gold MIne	30.00
13 EK,EK(c),Bloody Canyon Massacre	30.00
14	30.00
15	20.00
16 JKa	25.00
17 thru 23	@20.00
24 EK,EK(c)	25.00
25 EK,EK(c)	25.00
26 EK,EK(c)	25.00
27 EK,EK(c)	25.00
28 EK,EK(c),May-June, 1956	25.00

WILD BOY OF THE CONGO
Approved(Ziff-Davis)/ St. John Publ. Co.
February-March, 1951

10(1)NS,PH(c),Bondage(c),The Gorilla God	100.00
11(2)NS,Ph(c),Star of the Jungle	50.00
12(3)NS,Ph(c),Ice-Age Men	50.00
4 NS.Ph(c),Tyrant of the Jungle	55.00
5 NS,Ph(c),The White Robe of Courage	40.00
6 NS,Ph(c)	40.00
7 MB,EK.Ph(c)	45.00

Wild Boy of the Congo #15
© Approved/Ziff-Davis/St. Johns

8 Ph(c),Man-Eater	40.00
9 Ph(c),Killer Leopard	40.00
10	40.00
11 MB(c)	45.00
12 MB(c)	45.00
13 MB(c)	45.00
14 MB(c)	45.00
15 June, 1955	35.00

WINGS COMICS
Wings Publ.
(Fiction House Magazines)
September, 1940

1 HcK,AB,GT,Ph(c), B:Skull Squad, Clipper Kirk,Suicide Smith, War Nurse,Phantom Falcons, GreasemonkeyGriffin,Parachute Patrol,Powder Burns	1,000.00
2 HcK,AB,GT,Bomber Patrol	450.00
3 HcK,AB,GT	350.00
4 HcK,AB,GT,B:Spitfire Ace	325.00
5 HcK,AB,GT,Torpedo Patrol	325.00
6 HcK,AB,GT,Bombs for Berlin	300.00
7 HcK,AB	300.00
8 HcK,AB,The Wings of Doom	300.00
9 Sky-Wolf	275.00
10 The Upside Down	275.00
11	250.00
12 Fury of the fire Boards	250.00
13 Coffin Slugs For The Luftwaffe	250.00
14 Stuka Buster	250.00
15 Boomerang Blitz	250.00
16 O:Capt.Wings	300.00
17 Skyway to Death	225.00
18 Horsemen of the Sky	225.00
19 Nazi Spy Trap	225.00
20 The One Eyed Devil	225.00
21 Chute Troop Tornado	200.00
22 TNT for Tokyo	200.00
23 RP,Battling Eagles of Bataan	200.00
24 RP,The Death of a Hero	200.00
25 RP,Suicide Squeeze	200.00
26 Tojo's Eagle Trap	200.00
27 Blb,Mile High Gauntlet	200.00
28 Blb,Tail Gun Tornado	200.00
29 Blb,Buzzards from Berlin	200.00

30 Blb,Monsters of the
Stratosphere 150.00
31 BLb,Sea Hawks away 150.00
32 BLb,Sky Mammoth 150.00
33 BLb,Roll Call of the Yankee
Eagles 150.00
34 BLb,So Sorry,Mr Tojo 150.00
35 BLb,RWb,Hell's Lightning . . 150.00
36 RWb,The Crash-Master . . . 150.00
37 RWb,Sneak Blitz 150.00
38 RWb,Rescue Raid of the
Yank Eagle 150.00
39 RWb,Sky Hell/Pigboat Patrol 150.00
40 RWb,Luftwaffe Gamble 150.00
41 RWb,.50 Caliber Justice . . . 125.00
42 RWb,PanzerMeat forMosquito 125.00
43 RWb,Suicide Sentinels 125.00
44 RWb,Berlin Bombs Away . . 125.00
45 RWb,Hells Cargo 125.00
46 RWb,Sea-Hawk Patrol 125.00
47 RWb,Tojo's Tin Gibraltar . . . 125.00
48 RWb 125.00
49 RWb,Rockets Away 125.00
50 RWb,Mission For a Madman 125.00
51 RWb,Toll for a Typhoon . . . 110.00
52 MB,Madam Marauder 110.00
53 MB,Robot Death Over
Manhattan 110.00
54 MB,Juggernauts of Death . . 110.00
55 MB 110.00
56 MB,Sea Raiders Grave 110.00

FIGHTING ACES OF WAR SKIES
Wings Comics #28
© *Fiction House Magazines*

57 MB,Yankee Warbirds over
Tokyo 110.00
58 MB 110.00
59 MB,Prey of the Night Hawks 110.00
60 MB,E:Skull Squad,
Hell's Eyes 110.00
61 MB,Raiders o/t Purple Dawn 100.00
62 Twilight of the Gods 100.00
63 Hara Kiri Rides the Skyways 100.00
64 Taps For Tokyo 100.00
65 AB,Warhawk for the Kill . . . 100.00
66 AB,B:Ghost Patrol 100.00
67 AB 85.00
68 AB,ClipperKirkBecomesPhantom
Falcon;O:Phantom Falcon . . . 85.00
69 AB,O:cont,Phantom Falcon . . 85.00
70 AB,N:Phantom Falcon;

O:Final Phantom Falcon 85.00
71 Ghost Patrol becomes
Ghost Squadron 80.00
72 V:Capt. Kamikaze 80.00
73 Hell & Stormoviks 80.00
74 BLb(c),Loot is What She
Lived For 80.00
75 BLb(c),The Sky Hag 80.00
76 BLb(c),Temple of the Dead . . 80.00
77 BLb(c),Sky Express to Hell . . 80.00
78 BLb(c),Loot Queen of
Satan's Skyway 80.00
79 BLb(c),Buzzards of
Plunder Sky 80.00
80 BLb(c),Port of Missing Pilots . 80.00
81 BLb(c),Sky Trail of the
Terror Tong 80.00
82 BLb(c),Bondage(c),Spider &
The Fly Guy 85.00
83 BLb(c),GE,Deep Six For
Capt. Wings 75.00
84 BLb(c),GE,Sky Sharks to
the Kill 75.00
85 BLb(c),GE 75.00
86 BLb(c),GE,Moon Raiders . . . 75.00
87 BLb(c),GE 75.00
88 BLb(c),GE,Madmans Mission 75.00
89 BLb(c),GE,Bondage(c),
Rockets Away 85.00
90 BLb(c),GE,Bondage(c),The
Radar Rocketeers 85.00
91 BLb(c),GE,Bondage(c),V-9 for
Vengeance 85.00
92 BLb(c),GE,Death's red Rocket 80.00
93 BLb(c),GE,Kidnap Cargo . . . 80.00
94 BLb(c),GE,Bondage(c),Ace
of the A-Bomb Patrol 85.00
95 BLb(c),GE,The Ace of
the Assassins 80.00
96 BLb(c),GE 80.00
97 BLb(c),GE,The Sky Octopus . 80.00
98 BLb(c),GE,The Witch Queen
of Satan's Skyways 80.00
99 BLb(c),GE,The Spy Circus . . 80.00
100 BLb(c),GE,King of the Congo 100.00
101 BLb(c),GE,Trator of
the Cockpit 75.00
102 BLb(c),GE,Doves of Doom . 75.00
103 BLb(c),GE 75.00
104 BLb(c),GE,Fireflies of Fury . 75.00
105 BLb(c),GE 75.00
106 BLb(c),GE,Six Aces & A
Firing Squad 75.00
107 BLb(c),GE,Operation Satan . 75.00
108 BLb(c),GE,The Phantom
of Berlin 75.00
109 GE,Vultures of
Vengeance Sky 75.00
110 GE,The Red Ray Vortex . . . 75.00
111 GE,E:Jane Martin 70.00
112 The Flight of the
Silver Saucers 70.00
113 Suicide Skyways 70.00
114 D-Day for Death Rays 70.00
115 Ace of Space 70.00
116 Jet Aces of Korea 70.00
117 Reap the Red Wind 70.00
118 Vengeance Flies Blind 70.00
119 The Whistling Death 70.00
120 Doomsday Mission 70.00
121 Ace of the Spyways 70.00
122 Last Kill Korea 70.00
123 The Cat & the Canaries . . . 70.00
124 Summer, 1954, Death
Below Zero 70.00

WINNIE WINKLE
Dell Publishing Co.
1941

1 . . . . 45.00
2 . . . . 30.00
3 . . . . 20.00
4 thru 7 . . . . @20.00

WITCHCRAFT
Avon Periodicals
March-April, 1952

1 SC,JKu,Heritage of Horror . 300.00
2 SC,JKu,The Death Tattoo . . 225.00
3 EK,Better off Dead 150.00
4 Claws of the Cat,
Boiling Humans 175.00
5 Ph(c),Where Zombies Walk 225.00
6 March, 1953 Mysteries of the
Moaning Statue 150.00

WITCHES TALES
Harvey Publications
January, 1951

1 RP,Bondage(c),Weird Yarns
of Unseen Terror 200.00
2 RP,We Dare You 100.00
3 RP,Bondage(c)Forest of
Skeletons 65.00
4 BP 60.00
5 BP,Bondage(c),Share
My Coffin 75.00
6 BP,Bondage(c),Servants of
the Tomb 75.00
7 BP,Screaming City 75.00
8 Bondage(c) 85.00
9 Fatal Steps 60.00
10 BP,....,IT! 60.00
11 BP,Monster Maker 55.00
12 Bondage(c);The Web
of the Spider 60.00
13 The Torture Jar 55.00
14 Transformation 70.00
15 Drooling Zombie 55.00
16 Revenge of a Witch 55.00

Witches Tales #21
© *Harvey Publications*

17 Dimension IV 75.00
18 HN,Bird of Prey 70.00

---

19 HN,The Pact 70.00
20 HN,Kiss & Tell 70.00
21 HN,The Invasion 70.00
22 HN,A Day of Panic 70.00
23 HN,The Wig Maker 70.00
24 HN,The Undertaker 70.00
25 What Happens at 8:30 PM?
 Severed Heads(c) 70.00
26 Up There 50.00
27 The Thing That Grew 50.00
28 Demon Flies 50.00
Becomes:

WITCHES WESTERN TALES

29 S&K,S&K(c),F:Davy Crockett 100.00
30 S&K.S&K(c) 100.00
Becomes:

WESTERN TALES

31 S&K,S&K(c),F:Davy Crockett 85.00
32 S&K,S&K(c) 85.00
33 S&K,S&K(c),July-Sept.,1956 . 85.00

WITH THE MARINES ON THE BATTLEFRONTS OF THE WORLD
Toby Press
June, 1953
1 Ph(c),Flaming Soul 150.00
2 Ph(c),March, 1954 . . . . 35.00

WITTY COMICS
Irwin H. Rubin/Chicago Nite
Life News
1945
1 . . . . 75.00
2 1945 . . . . 45.00
3 thru 7 . . . . @35.00

WOMEN IN LOVE
Fox Features Synd./
Hero Books/
Ziff-Davis
August, 1949
1 . . . . 250.00

WOMEN OUTLAWS
Fox Features Syndicate
July, 1948
1 . . . . 300.00
2 . . . . 250.00
3 . . . . 225.00
4 thru 8 . . . . @175.00
Becomes:

MY LOVE MEMORIES
9 . . . . 75.00
10 . . . . 35.00
11 . . . . 70.00
12 WW 75.00

WONDERBOY
(see HORRIFIC)

WONDER COMICS
Great Publ./Nedor/
Better Publications
May, 1944
1 SSh(c),B:Grim Reaper,
 Spectro Hitler(c) 450.00
2 ASh(c),O:Grim Reaper,B:Super
 Sleuths,Grim Reaper(c) . . . 275.00

Wonder Comics #16
© Fox Features Syndicate

3 ASh(c),Grim Reaper(c) 225.00
4 ASh(c),Grim Reaper(c) 200.00
5 ASh(c),Grim Reaper(c) 225.00
6 ASh(c),Grim Reaper(c) 200.00
7 ASh(c),Grim Reaper(c) 200.00
8 ASh(c),E:Super Sleuths,
 Spectro 200.00
9 ASh(c),B:Wonderman 200.00
10 ASh(c),Wonderman(c) 225.00
11 Grl(c),B:Dick Devins 225.00
12 Grl(c),Bondage(c) 225.00
13 ASh(c),Bondage(c) 225.00
14 ASh(c),Bondage(c)
 E:Dick Devins 235.00
15 ASh(c),Bondage(c),B:Tara . 275.00
16 ASh(c),A:Spectro,
 E:Grim Reaper 200.00
17 FF,ASh(c),A:Super Sleuth . . 225.00
18 ASh(c),B:Silver Knight 200.00
19 ASh(c),FF 225.00
20 FF,October, 1948 . . . . 275.00

WONDERLAND COMICS
Feature Publications
(Prize Comics Group)
Summer, 1945
1 (fa),B:Alex in Wonderland . . . 50.00
2 . . . . 30.00
3 thru 8 . . . . @20.00
9 1947 . . . . 20.00

WONDER COMICS
Fox Features Syndicate
May, 1930
1 BKa,WE,WE(c),B:Wonderman,
 DR.Kung,K-51 . . . . 6,000.00
2 WE,BKa,LF(c),B:Yarko the
 Great,A:Spark Stevens . . 2,400.00
Becomes:

WONDERWORLD COMICS
3 WE,LF,BP,LF&WE,I:Flame 2,200.00
4 WE,LF,BP,LF(c) 750.00
5 WE,LF,BP,GT,LF(c),Flame . 650.00
6 WE,LF,BP,GT,LF(c),Flame . 650.00
7 WE,LF,BP,GT,LF(c),Flame . 650.00

8 WE,LF,BP,GT,LF(c),Flame . 650.00
9 WE,LF,BP,GT,LF(c),Flame . 650.00
10 WE,LF,BP,LF(c),Flame 650.00
11 WE,LF,BP,LF(c),O:Flame . . 800.00
12 BP,LF(c),Bondage(c),Flame 425.00
13 E:Dr Fung,Flame 400.00
14 JoS,Bondage(c),Flame 425.00
15 JoS&LF(c),Flame 425.00
16 Flame(c) 375.00
17 Flame(c) 375.00
18 Flame(c) 375.00
19 Male Bondage(c),Flame . . . 400.00
20 Flame(c) 375.00
21 O:Black Club &Lion,Flame . 375.00
22 Flame(c) 375.00
23 Flame(c) 300.00
24 Flame(c) 300.00
25 A:Dr Fung,Flame 300.00
26 Flame(c) 300.00
27 Flame(c) 275.00
28 Bondage(c)I&O:US Jones,
 B:Lu-nar,Flame 400.00
29 Bondage(c),Flame 275.00
30 O:Flame(c),Flame 400.00
31 Bondage(c),Flame 275.00
32 Hitler(c),Flame 275.00
33 Male Bondage(c)
 January, 1942 . . . . 275.00

WORLD FAMOUS HEROES MAGAZINE
Comic Corp. of America
(Centaur)
October, 1941
1 BLb,Paul Revere 600.00
2 BLb,Andrew Jackson,V:
 Dickinson 350.00
3 BLb,Juarez-Mexican patriot 250.00
4 BLb,Canadian Mounties . . . 250.00

WORLD'S GREATEST STORIES
Jubilee Publications
January, 1949
1 F:Alice in Wonderland 150.00
2 F:Pinocchio 125.00

World War III #2 © Ace Periodicals

WORLD WAR III
Ace Periodicals
March, 1953
1 Atomic Bomb cover 325.00
2 May, 1953,The War That
  Will Never Happen 275.00

WOTALIFE COMICS
(see PHANTOM LADY)

WOW COMICS
David McKay/Henle Publ.
July, 1936
1 WE,DBr(c),Fu Manchu,
  Buck Jones 1,500.00
2 WE,Little King 1,000.00
3 WE,WE(c) 1,000.00
4 WE,BKa,AR,DBr(c),Popeye,
  Flash Gordon,Nov.,1936 . 1,300.00

Wow Comics #31
© Fawcett Publications

WOW COMICS
Fawcett Publications
Winter, 1940
N#(1)S&K,CCB(c),B&O:Mr Scarlett;
  B:Atom Blake,Jim Dolan,Rick
  O'Shay,Bondage(c) 10,000.00
2 B:Hunchback 1,000.00
3 V:Mummy Ray Gun 550.00
4 O:Pinky 550.00
5 F:Pinky the Whiz Kid 400.00
6 O:Phantom Eagle;
  B:Commando Yank 350.00
7 Spearhead of Invasion 325.00
8 All Three Heroes 325.00
9 A:Capt Marvel,Capt MarvelJr.
  Shazam,B:Mary Marvel . . . 600.00
10 The Sinister Secret of
  Hotel Hideaway 300.00
11 . . . . 225.00
12 Rocketing adventures 225.00
13 Thrill Show 225.00
14 V:Mr Night 225.00
15 The Shazam Girl of America 200.00
16 Ride to the Moon 200.00
17 V:Mary Batson,Alter Ego
  Goes Berserk 200.00

18 I:Uncle Marvel,Infinity(c)
  V is For Victory 200.00
19 A Whirlwind Fantasy 200.00
20 Mary Marvel's Magic Carpet 200.00
21 Word That Shook the World 150.00
22 Come on Boys-
  Everybody Sing 150.00
23 Trapped by the Terror of
  the Future 150.00
24 Mary Marvel 150.00
25 Mary Marvel Crushes Crime 150.00
26 Smashing Star-
  Studded Stories 125.00
27 War Stamp Plea(c) 125.00
28 . . . . 125.00
29 . . . . 125.00
30 In Mirror Land 125.00
31 Stars of Action 100.00
32 The Millinery Marauders . . . 100.00
33 Mary Marvel(c) 100.00
34 A:Uncle Marvel 100.00
35 I:Freckles Marvel 100.00
36 Secret of the Buried City . . . 100.00
37 7th War loan plea 100.00
38 Pictures That Came to Life . 100.00
39 The Perilous Packages 100.00
40 The Quarrel of the Gnomes 100.00
41 Hazardous Adventures 75.00
42 . . . . 75.00
43 Curtain Time 75.00
44 Volcanic Adventure 75.00
45 . . . . 75.00
46 . . . . 75.00
47 . . . . 75.00
48 . . . . 75.00
49 . . . . 75.00
50 Mary Marvel/Commando Yank 75.00
51 . . . . 65.00
52 . . . . 65.00
53 Murder in the Tall Timbers . . 65.00
54 Flaming Adventure 65.00
55 Earthquake! 65.00
56 Sacred Pearls of Comatesh . 65.00
57 . . . . 65.00
58 E:Mary Marvel;The Curse
  of the Keys 65.00
59 B:Ozzie the Hilarious
  Teenager 65.00
60 thru 64 . . . . @50.00
65 A:Tom Mix 55.00
66 A:Tom Mix 55.00
67 A:Tom Mix 55.00
68 A:Tom Mix 55.00
69 A:Tom Mix,Baseball 55.00
Becomes:
REAL WESTERN HERO
70 It's Round-up Time 200.00
71 CCB,P(c),A Rip
  Roaring Rodeo 125.00
72 w/Gabby Hayes 125.00
73 thru 75 . . . . @125.00
Becomes:
WESTERN HERO
76 Partial Ph(c)&P(c) 165.00
77 Partial Ph(c)&P(c) 90.00
78 Partial Ph(c)&P(c) 90.00
79 Partial Ph(c)&P(c),
  Shadow of Death 75.00
80 Partial Ph(c)&P(c) 90.00
81 CCB,Partial Ph(c)&P(c),
  F:Tootsie 90.00
82 Partial Ph(c)&P(c),
  A:Hopalong Cassidy 90.00
83 Partial Ph(c)&P(c) 90.00

84 Ph(c) 80.00
85 Ph(c) 75.00
86 Ph(c),The Case of the
  Extra Buddy, giant 80.00
87 Ph(c),The Strange Lands . . . 80.00
88 Ph(c),A:Senor Diablo 80.00
89 Ph(c),The Hypnotist 80.00
90 Ph(c),The Menace of
  the Cougar, giant 75.00

Western Hero #91 © Fawcett Publ.

91 Ph(c),Song of Death 75.00
92 Ph(c),The Fatal Hide-out,
  giant 75.00
93 Ph(c),Treachery at
  Triple T, giant 75.00
94 Ph(c),Bank Busters,giant . . . 75.00
95 Ph(c),Rampaging River 65.00
96 Ph(c),Range Robbers,giant . . 75.00
97 Ph(c),Death on the
  Hook,giant 75.00
98 Ph(c),Web of Death,giant . . . 75.00
99 Ph(c),The Hidden Evidence . 65.00
100 Ph(c),A:Red Eagle,Giant . . . 75.00
101 Ph(c) 75.00
102 thru 111 Ph(c) . . . . @65.00
112 Ph(c),March, 1952 . . . . 80.00

YANKEE COMICS
Chesler Publications
(Harry A. Chesler)
September, 1941
1 F:Yankee Doodle Jones . . . 500.00
2 The Spirit of '41 . . . . 350.00
3 Yankee Doodle Jones 300.00
4 JCo,Yankee Doodle Jones
  March, 1942 . . . . 300.00

YELLOWJACKET
COMICS
Levy Publ./Frank Comunale/
Charlton
September, 1944
1 O&B:Yellowjackets,B:Diana
  the Huntress 300.00
2 Rosita &The Filipino Kid . . . 175.00
3 . . . . 150.00
4 Fall of the House of Usher . . 175.00
5 King of Beasts 150.00

All comics prices listed are for *Near Mint* condition.   **CVA Page 399**

6	135.00
7 I:Diane Carter;The Lonely Guy	125.00
8 The Buzzing Bee Code	125.00
9	125.00
10 Capt Grim V:The Salvage Pirates	125.00

Becomes:

JACK IN THE BOX

11 Funny Animal,Yellow Jacket	55.00
12 Funny Animal	25.00
13 BW,Funny Animal	80.00
14 thru 16 Funny Animal	@30.00

Becomes:

COWBOY WESTERN COMICS

17 Annie Oakley,Jesse James	75.00
18 JO,JO(c)	50.00
19 JO,JO(c),Legends of Paul Bunyan	50.00
20 JO(c),Jesse James	35.00
21 Annie Oakley VisitsDryGulch	35.00
22 Story of the Texas Rangers	35.00
23	35.00
24 Ph(c),F:James Craig	35.00
25 Ph(c),F:Sunset Carson	35.00
26 Ph(c)	65.00
27 Ph(c),Sunset Carson movie	150.00
28 Ph(c),Sunset Carson movie	100.00
29 Ph(c),Sunset Carson movie	100.00
30 Ph(c),Sunset Carson movie	150.00
31 Ph(c)	30.00
32 thru 34 Ph(c)	@25.00
35 thru 37 Sunset Carson	@75.00
38	25.00
39	25.00

Becomes:

SPACE WESTERN COMICS

40 Spurs Jackson,V:The Saucer Men	300.00
41 StC(c),Space Vigilantes	225.00
42 StC(c)	250.00
43 StC(c),Battle of Spacemans Gulch	225.00
44 StC(c),The Madman of Mars	225.00
45 StC(c),The Moon Bat	225.00

Becomes:

COWBOY WESTERN COMICS

46	70.00

Becomes:

COWBOY WESTERN HEROES

47	25.00
48	25.00

Becomes:

COWBOY WESTERN

49	25.00
50 F:Jesse James	20.00
51 thru 56	@20.00
58, giant	25.00
59 thru 66	@20.00
67 AW&AT	50.00

Becomes:

WILD BILL HICKOK AND JINGLES

68 AW	50.00
69 AW	35.00
70 AW	30.00

71	20.00
72	20.00
73	20.00
74 1960	20.00

YOGI BERRA
Fawcett
1957

1 Ph(c)	400.00

YOUNG BRIDES
Feature Publications
(Prize Comics)
September-October, 1952

1 S&K,Ph(c)	125.00
2 S&K,Ph(c)	60.00
3 S&K,Ph(c)	50.00
4 S&K	50.00
5 S&K	50.00
6 S&K	50.00
2-1 S&K	40.00
2-2 S&K	25.00
2-3 S&K	35.00
2-4 S&K	35.00
2-5 S&K	35.00
2-6 S&K	35.00
2-7 S&K	35.00
2-8 S&K	20.00
2-9 S&K	20.00
2-10 S&K	35.00
2-11 S&K	35.00
2-12 S&K	35.00
3-1	12.00
3-2	15.00
3-3	15.00
3-4	15.00
3-5	15.00
3-6	15.00
4-1	15.00
4-2 S&K	40.00
4-3	15.00
4-4 S&K	35.00
4-5	15.00

YOUNG EAGLE
Fawcett Publications/
Charlton Comics
December, 1950

1 Ph(c)	100.00
2 Ph(c),Mystery of Thunder Canyon	45.00
3 Ph(c),Death at Dawn	40.00
4 Ph(c)	40.00
5 Ph(c),The Golden Flood	40.00
6 Ph(c),The Nightmare Empire	40.00
7 Ph(c),Vigilante Veangeance	40.00
8 Ph(c),The Rogues Rodeo	40.00
9 Ph(c),The Great Railroad Swindle	40.00
10 June, 1952, Ph(c),Thunder Rides the Trail,O:Thunder	25.00

YOUNG KING COLE
Novelty Press/Premium
Svcs. Co.
Autumn, 1945

1-1 Detective Toni Gayle	125.00
1-2	70.00
1-3	60.00
1-4	50.00
2-1	50.00
2-2	40.00
2-3	40.00

2-4	40.00
2-5	40.00
2-6	40.00
2-7	40.00
3-1	35.00
3-2 LbC	35.00
3-3 The Killer With The Hat	30.00
3-4 The Fierce Tiger	30.00
3-5 AMc	30.00
3-6	40.00
3-7 LbC(c),Case of the Devil's Twin	60.00
3-8	50.00
3-9 The Crime Fighting King	50.00
3-10 LbC(c)	50.00
3-11 LbC(c)	50.00
3-12 July, 1948,AMc(c)	35.00

Young King Cole #12 (3/1)
© Novelty Press/Premium Svcs. Co.

YOUNG LIFE
New Age Publications
Summer, 1945

1 Partial Ph(c),Louis Palma	75.00
2 Partial Ph(c),Frank Sinatra	80.00

Becomes:

TEEN LIFE

3 Partial Ph(c),Croon without Tricks,June Allyson(c)	50.00
4 Partial Ph(c),Atom Smasher Blueprints,Duke Ellington(c)	45.00
5 Partial Ph(c), Build Your Own Pocket Radio, Jackie Robinson(c)	60.00

YOUNG LOVE
Feature Publ.
(Prize Comics Group)
February-March, 1949

1 S&K,S&K(c)	200.00
2 S&K,Ph(c)	90.00
3 S&K,JSe,BE,Ph(c)	75.00
4 S&K,Ph(c)	50.00
5 S&K,Ph(c)	50.00
2-1 Ph(c)	60.00
2-2 Ph(c)	30.00
2-3 Ph(c)	30.00
2-4 Ph(c)	30.00

Teen Life #5 © New Age Publications

2-5 Ph(c)	30.00
2-6 S&K(c)	40.00
2-7 S&K(c),S&K	60.00
2-8 S&K	60.00
2-9 S&K(c),S&K	60.00
2-10 S&K(c),S&K	60.00
2-11 S&K(c),S&K	60.00
2-12 S&K(c),S&K	60.00
3-1 S&K(c),S&K	45.00
3-2 S&K(c),S&K	45.00
3-3 S&K(c),S&K	45.00
3-4 S&K(c),S&K	45.00
3-5 Ph(c)	35.00
3-6 BP,Ph(c)	35.00
3-7 Ph(c)	35.00
3-8 Ph(c)	35.00
3-9 MMe,Ph(c)	35.00
3-10 Ph(c)	35.00
3-11 Ph(c)	35.00
3-12 Ph(c)	35.00
4-1 S&K	35.00
4-2 Ph(c)	30.00
4-3 Ph(c)	30.00
4-4 Ph(c)	30.00
4-5 Ph(c)	30.00
4-6 S&K,Ph(c)	30.00
4-7 thru 4-12 Ph(c)	@25.00
5-1 thru 5-12 Ph(c)	@20.00
6-1 thru 6-9	@15.00
6-10 thru 6-12	@15.00
7-1 thru 7-7	@10.00
7-8 thru 7-11	@10.00
7-12 thru 8-5	@12.00
8-6 thru 8-12	@18.00

YOUNG ROMANCE COMICS
**Feature Publ./Headline/
Prize Publ.**
September-October, 1947

1 S&K(c),S&K	200.00
2 S&K(c),S&K	125.00
3 S&K(c),S&K	100.00
4 S&K(c),S&K	100.00
5 S&K(c),S&K	100.00
6 S&K(c),S&K	85.00
2-1 S&K(c),S&K	85.00
2-2 S&K(c),S&K	85.00

2-3 S&K(c),S&K	85.00
2-4 S&K(c),S&K	85.00
2-5 S&K(c),S&K	85.00
2-6 S&K(c),S&K	58.00
3-1 thru 3-12 S&K(c),S&K	@60.00
4-1 thru 4-12 S&K	@50.00
5-1 ATh,S&K	55.00
2	50.00
3	50.00
5-4 thru 5-12 S&K	@50.00
6-1 thru 6-3	@30.00

YOUR UNITED STATES
Lloyd Jacquet Studios
1946

1N# Teeming nation of Nations	150.00

YOUTHFUL HEART
Youthful Magazines
May, 1952

1 Frankie Lane(c)	100.00
2 Vic Damone	75.00
3 Johnnie Ray	75.00

Becomes:

DARING CONFESSIONS

4 DW,Tony Curtis	50.00
5	35.00
6 DW	40.00
7	35.00
8 DW	40.00

*Youthful Romances #8
© Pix Parade/Ribage/Trojan*

YOUTHFUL ROMANCES
**Pix Parade/Ribage/
Trojan**
August-September, 1949

1	100.00
2	55.00
3 Tex Beneke	45.00
4	45.00
5	30.00
6	30.00
7 Tony Martin(c)	35.00
8 WW(c)	90.00
9	30.00
10	30.00
11	30.00
12	30.00

13	30.00
14	30.00

Becomes:

DARLING LOVE

15 WD	40.00
16	30.00
17 DW,Ph(c)	30.00

ZAGO, JUNGLE PRINCE
Fox Features Syndicate
September, 1948

1 A:Blue Beetle	250.00
2 JKa	175.00
3 JKa	175.00
4 MB(c)	175.00

Becomes:

MY STORY

5 JKa,Too Young To Fall in Love	75.00
6 I Was A She-Wolf	35.00
7 I Lost My Reputation	35.00
8 My Words Condemned Me	35.00
9 WW,Wayward Bride	85.00
10 WW,March, 1950,Second Rate Girl	85.00
11	35.00
12	35.00

TEGRA, JUNGLE EMPRESS
Fox Features Syndicate
August, 1948

1 Blue Bettle,Rocket Kelly	225.00

Becomes:

ZEGRA, JUNGLE EMPRESS

2 JKa	275.00
3	225.00
4	225.00
5	225.00

Becomes:

MY LOVE LIFE

6 I Put A Price Tag On Love	65.00
7 An Old Man's Fancy	35.00
8 My Forbidden Affair	35.00
9 I Loved too Often	35.00

*Zip Comics #4
© MLJ Magazines/Archie Comics*

All comics prices listed are for *Near Mint* condition.

10 My Secret Torture 35.00
11 I Broke My Own Heart 35.00
12 I Was An Untamed Filly 35.00
13 I Can Never Marry You,
   August 1950 . . . . 30.00

ZIP COMICS
MLJ Magazines
February, 1940

1 MMe,O&B:Kalathar,The Scarlet
  Avenger,Steel Sterling,B:Mr
  Satan,Nevada Jones,War Eagle
  Captain Valor 2,200.00
2 MMe,CBi(c)B:Steel
  Sterling(c) 1,000.00
3 CBi,MMe,CBi(c) 700.00
4 CBi,MMe,CBi(c) 500.00
5 CBi,MMe,CBi(c) 500.00
6 CBi,MMe,CBi(c) 450.00
7 CBi,MMe,CBi(c) 425.00
8 CBi,MMe,CBi(c),Bondage(c) 450.00
9 CBi,MMe,CBi(c)E:Kalathar,
  Mr Satan;Bondage(c) 450.00
10 CBi,MMe,CBi(c),B:Inferno . . 500.00
11 CBi,MMe,CBi(c) 375.00
12 CBi,MMe,CBi(c),Bondage(c) 375.00
13 CBi,MMe,CBi(c)E:Inferno,
   Bondage(c),Woman in

Zip Comics #19
© MLJ Magazines/Archie Comics

Electric Chair 375.00
14 CBi,MMe,CBi(c),Bondage(c) 375.00
15 CBi,MMe,CBi(c),Bondage(c) 375.00
16 CBi,MMe,CBi(c),Bondage(c) 375.00
17 CBi,CBi(c),E:Scarlet
   Avenger Bondage(c) 400.00
18 IN(c),B:Wilbur 375.00
19 IN(c),Steel Sterling(c) 400.00
20 IN(c),O&I:Black Jack
   Hitler(c) 550.00
21 IN(c),V:Nazis 350.00
22 IN(c) 350.00
23 IN(c),Flying Fortress 350.00
24 IN(c),China Town Exploit . . . 350.00
25 IN(c),E:Nevada Jones 350.00
26 IN(c),B:Black Witch,
   E:Capt Valor 375.00
27 IN(c),I:Web,V:Japanese . . . 550.00
28 IN(C),O:Web,Bondage(c) . . 550.00

29 Steel Sterling & Web 300.00
30 V:Nazis 300.00
31 IN(c) 250.00
32 . . . . 250.00
33 Bondage(c) 265.00
34 I:Applejack;Bondage(c) 265.00
35 E:Zambini 250.00
36 I:Senor Banana 250.00
37 . . . . 250.00
38 E:Web 250.00
39 O&B:Red Rule 250.00
40 . . . . 200.00
41 . . . . 200.00
42 . . . . 200.00
43 . . . . 200.00
44 . . . . 200.00
45 E:Wilbur 200.00
46 . . . . 200.00
47 Crooks Can't Win,
   Summer, 1944 . . . . 200.00

Zip-Jet #2 © St. John Publishing Co.

ZIP-JET
St. John Publishing Co.
February, 1953

1 Rocketman 250.00
2 April,May, 1953, Assassin
  of the Airlanes 225.00

ZOOM COMICS
Carlton Publishing Co.
December, 1945

N# O:Captain Milksop 225.00

ZOOT COMICS
Fox Features Syndicate
Spring, 1946

N#(1)(fa) 100.00
2 A:Jaguar(fa) 85.00
3 (fa) 50.00
4 (fa) 50.00
5 (fa) 35.00
6 (fa) 35.00
7 B:Rulah 400.00
8 JKa(c),Fangs of Stone 300.00
9 JKa(c),Fangs of Black Fury . 300.00
10 JKa(c),Inferno Land 300.00
11 JKa,The Purple Plague,
   Bondage(c) 325.00

Zoot Comics #4
© Fox Features Syndicate

12 JKa(c),The Thirsty Stone,
   Bondage(c) 325.00
13 Bloody Moon 225.00
14 Pearls of Pathos,Woman
   Carried off by Bird 250.00
15 Death Dancers 200.00
16 . . . . 200.00

Becomes:
RULAH, JUNGLE GODDESS

17 JKa(c),Wolf Doctor 400.00
18 JKa(c),Vampire Garden . . . 300.00
19 JKa(c) 300.00
20 . . . . 300.00
21 JKa(c) 300.00
22 JKa(c) 300.00
23 . . . . 235.00
24 . . . . 225.00
25 . . . . 225.00
26 . . . . 225.00
27 . . . . 235.00

Becomes:
I LOVED

28 . . . . 35.00
29 . . . . 25.00
30 . . . . 25.00
31 . . . . 25.00
32 My Poison Love, March, 1950 25.00

ARCHER & ARMSTRONG
Valiant
0 JiS(s),BWS,BL,I&O:Archer,
  I:Armstrong,The Sec 5.00
0 Gold Ed. 5 . . . . 35.00
1 FM(c),B:JiS(s),BWS,BL,Unity #3,
  A:Eternal Warrior 4.00
2 WS(c),E:JiS(s),BWS,BL,Unity
  #11,2nd A:Turok,A:X-O 7.00
3 B:BWS(a&s),BWi,V:Sect
  in Rome 3.00
4 BWS,BWi,V:Sect in Rome 3.00
5 BWS,BWi,I:Andromeda 3.00
6 BWS,BWi,A:Andromeda,
  V:Medoc 3.00
7 BWS,ANi,BWi,V:Sect
  in England 3.00
8 BWS,as Eternal Warrior #8,
  Three Musketeers,I:Ivan 5.00
9 BCh,BWi,in Britain 2.50
10 BWS,A:Ivar 2.50
11 BWS,A:Solar,Ivar 2.50
12 BWS,V:The Avenger 2.50
13 B:MBn(s),RgM,In Los Angeles 2.50
14 In Los Angeles 2.50
15 E:MBn(s),In Las Vegas,
  I:Duerst 2.50
16 V:Sect 2.50
17 B:MBn(s),In Florida 2.50
18 MV,in Heaven 2.50
19 MV,V:MircoboticCult,D:Duerst . 2.50
20 MV,Chrismas Issue 2.50
21 MV,A:Shadowman,Master
  Darque 2.50
22 MV,A:Shadowman,Master
  Darque,w/Valiant Era card . . . 2.50
23 MV, ... 2.50
24 MV, ... 2.50
25 MV,A:Eternal Warrior 2.50
26 Chaos Effect-Gamma #4,
  A:Ivar, Et. Warrior 2.50

Armorines #2 © Valiant

ARMORINES
Valiant
0 (from X-O #25),Card Stock (c),
  Diamond Distributors "Fall
  Fling" Retailer Meeting 7.00
0a Gold Ed. 8.00

1 JGz(s),JCf,B:White Death 2.50
2 JGz(s),JCf,E:White Death 2.50
3 JGz(s),JCf,V:Spider Aliens 2.50
4 JCf, V: Spider Aliens 2.25
5 JCf, Chaos Effect-Delta #2,
  A:H.A.R.D. Corp 2.25
6 Spider Alien Mothership 2.25
7 Rescue 2.25
8 Rescue in Iraq 2.25
9 . . . . 2.25
10 Protect Fidel Castro 2.25
11 V: Spider Super Suit 2.25
12 F: Sirot 2.25
Yearbook I:Linoff 2.95

BAR SINISTER
Windjammer
1 From Shaman's Tears 2.50
2 V:SWAT Team 2.50
3 F: Animus Prime 2.50
4 MGe,RHo,V:Jabbersnatch 2.50

BART SEARS'
X-O MANOWAR
HC Bart Sears' Artwork 17.95

BLOODSHOT
Valiant
0 KVH(a&s),DG(i),Chromium (c),
  O:Bloodshot,A:Eternal Warrior . 3.50
0a Gold Ed.,w/Diamond "Fall
  Fling" logo 20.00
1 BWS(c),B:KVH(s),DP,BWi,I:Carboni,
  V:Mafia,1st Chromium(c) 5.00
2 DP,I:Durkins,V:Ax 3.50
3 DP,V:The Mob 3.00
4 DP,A:Eternal Warrior 2.50
5 DP,A:Eternal Warrior,Rai 2.50
6 DP,I:Ninjak (Not in Costume) . . 4.00
7 DP,JDx,A:Ninjak (1st
  appearance in costume) 3.00
8 DP,JDx,A:Geoff 2.50
9 DP,JDx,V:Slavery Ring 2.50
10 DP,JDx,V:Tunnel Rat 2.50
11 DP,JDx,V:Iwatsu 2.50
12 DP,JDx,Day Off 2.50
13 DP,JDx,V:Webnet 2.50
14 DP,JDx,V:Carboni 2.50
15 DP,JDx,V:Cinder 2.50
16 DP,JDx,w/Valiant Era Card . . . 2.50
17 DP,JDx,A:H.A.R.D.Corps 2.50
18 DP,KVH,After the Missile 2.50
19 DP,KVH,I:Uzzi the Clown 2.25
20 DP,KVH, Chaos Effect-Gamma
  #1, V:Immortal Enemy 2.25
21 DP,V: Immortal Enemy, Ax . . . 2.25
22 Immortal Enemy 2.25
23 Cinder 2.25
24 Geomancer, Immortal Enemy . 2.25
25 V:Uzzi the Clown 2.25
26 V:Uzzi the Clown 2.25
27 Rampage Pt. 1 . . . . 2.25
28 Rampage Pt. 3 . . . . 2.25
29 Rampage Conc. A:Ninjak 2.25
30 V:Shape Shifter 2.25
31 Nanite Killer 2.25
32 KVH,SCh,V: Vampires 2.25
33 KVH,SCh,V: Vampires 2.25
34 NBy,KVH,new villains spawned 2.25
35 NBY,KVH,attempts to control . 2.25
Yearbook #1 KVH,briefcase bomb 4.25
Yearbook 1995 Villagers 2.95

CHAOS EFFECT
Alpha DJ(c), BCh, JOy, A:All
  Valiant Characters 2.25
Alpha Red (c) 5.00
Omega DJ(c), BCh, JOy, A:All
  Valiant Characters 2.25
Epilogue pt.1 . . . . 2.95
Epilogue pt.2 . . . . 2.95

DEATHMATE
Valiant/Image
Preview (Advanced Comics) 4.00
Preview (Previews) 4.00
Preview (Comic Defense Fund) . . 7.00
Prologue BL,JLe,RLd,Solar meets
  Void 3.25
Prologue Gold 15.00
Blue SCh,HSn,F:Solar,Magnus,
  Battlestone,Livewire,Stronghold,
  Impact,Striker,Harbinger,
  Brigade,Supreme 4.00
Blue Gold Ed. 15.00
Yellow BCh,MLe,DP,F:Armstrong,
  H.A.R.D.C.A.T.S.,Ninjak,Zealot,
  Shadowman,Grifter,Ivar 4.00
Yellow Gold Ed. 15.00
Black JLe,MS,F:Warblade,Ripclaw,
  Turok,X-O Manowar 5.25
Black Gold Ed. 15.00
Red RLd,JMs, ... 5.25
Red Gold Ed. 15.00
Epilogue 3.25
Epilogue Gold 15.00

DESTROYER
0 MM 41st Century 2.95

Eternal Warrior #16 © Valiant

ETERNAL WARRIOR
Valiant
1 FM(c),JDx,Unity #2,O:Eternal
  Warrior,Armstrong 5.00
1a Gold Ed. 30.00
1b Gold Foil Logo 40.00
2 WS(c),JDx,Unity #10,A:Solar,
  Harbinger,Eternal Warrior
  of 4001 . . . . 4.00

---

3 JDx,V:Armstrong,I:Astrea 3.00
4 JDx(i),I:Caldone,
C:Bloodshot 7.00
5 JDx,I:Bloodshot,V:Iwatsu's
Men 7.00
6 BWS,JDx,V:Master Darque . . . 3.00
7 BWS,V:Master Darque,
D:Uncle Buck 3.00
8 BWS,as Archer & Armstrong #8
Three Musketeers,I:Ivar 5.00
9 MMo,JDx,B:Book of the
Geomancer 3.00
10 JDx,E:Bk. o/t Geomancer . . . 3.00
11 B:KVH(s),JDx(i),
V:Neo-Nazis 3.00
12 JDx(i),V:Caldone 3.00
13 MMo,JDx(i),V:Caldone,
A:Bloodshot 2.75
14 E:KVH(s),MMo,V:Caldone,
A:Geoff 2.50
15 YG,A:Bloodshot,V:Tanaka . . . 2.50
16 YG,A:Bloodshot 2.50
17 A:Master Darque 2.50
18 C:Doctor Mirage 2.50
19 KVH(s),TeH,A:Doctor Mirage . 2.50
20 KVH(s),Access Denied 2.50
21 KVH(s),TeH,V:Dr. Steiner . . . 2.50
22 V:Master Darque,w/Valiant
Era Card 2.50
23 KVH(s),TeH,Blind Fate 2.50
24 KVH(s),TeH,V:Immortal
Enemy 2.50
25 MBn(s),A:Archer,Armstrong . . 2.25
26 Double(c), Chaos Effect-
Gamma#4, A:Archer, Armstrong,
Ivar 3.00
27 JOs(s) 2.25
28 War on Drugs 2.25
29 Immortal Enemy 2.25
30 Lt. Morgan 2.25
31 JD,JOs 2.25
32 . . . . 2.25
33 Mortal Kin Pt.1 . . . . 2.25
34 Mortal Kin Pt.2 . . . . 2.25
35 Mortal Kin Finale 2.50
36 Fenris League 2.50
37 Youthful Tale 2.50
38 V:Niala, The Dead Queen . . . 2.50
39 JOs,JG,PG(c),V:body thieves . 2.50
40 JOs,JG,PG(c),finds organ farm 2.50
Yearbook #1 . . . . 4.25

FALLEN EMPIRES
MAGIC: THE GATHERING
[Mini-series]
1 with pack of cards 2.75

GEOMANCER
1 RgM, I:Geomancer 3.75
2 RgM, Eternal Warrior 2.25
3 RgM, Darque Elementals 2.25
4 RgM 2.25
5 Riot Gear pt. 1 . . . . 2.25
6 Riot Gear pt. 2 . . . . 2.25
7 F:Zorn 2.25
8 v:Zorn 2.25

HARBINGER
Valiant
0 DL,O:Sting,V:Harada,
from TPB (Blue Bird Ed.) . . . 14.00
0 from coupons 70.00
1 DL,JDx,I:Sting,Torque,
Zeppelin,Flamingo,Kris 30.00

1a w/o coupon 11.00
2 DL,JDx,V:Harbinger Foundation,

Harbinger #6 © Valiant

I:Dr.Heyward 25.00
2a w/o coupon 8.00
3 DL,JDx,I:Ax,Rexo,
V:Spider Aliens 18.00
3a w/o coupon 7.00
4 DL,JDx,V:Ax,I:Fort,
Spikeman,Dog,Bazooka 20.00
4a w/o coupon 8.00
5 DL,JDx,I:Puff,Thumper,
A:Solar,V:Harada 18.00
5a w/o coupon 5.00
6 DL,D:Torque,A:Solar,
V:Harada,Eggbreakers 15.00
6a w/o coupon 5.00
7 DL,Torque's Funeral 8.00
8 FM(c),DL,JDx,Unity#8,
A:Magnus,Eternal Warrior 4.00
9 WS(c),DL,Unity #16,
A:Magnus,Armstrong,Rai,
Archer,Eternal Warrior 4.00
10 DL,I:H.A.R.D.Corps,
Daryl, Shetiqua 7.00
11 DL,V:H.A.R.D.Corps 5.00
12 DL,F:Zeppelin,A:Elfquest 3.00
13 Flamingo Vs. Rock 3.00
14 A:Magnus(Dream Sequence),
C:Stronghold 5.00
15 I:Livewire,Stronghold 5.00
16 A:Livewire,Stronghold 3.00
17 HSn,I:Simon 2.50
18 HSn,I:Screen 2.50
19 HSn,I:Caliph 2.50
20 HSn,V:Caliph 2.50
21 I:Pete's Father 2.50
22 HSn,A:Archer & Armstrong . . . 2.50
23 HSn,B:Twlight of the
Eighth Day 2.50
24 HSn,V:Eggbreakers 2.50
25 HSn,V:Harada,E:Twlight of the
Eighth Day 3.50
26 SCh,AdW,I:Jolt,Amazon,
Mircowave,Anvil,Sonix 2.50
27 SCh,AdW,Chrismas issue 2.50
28 SCh,AdW,O:Sonix,J:Tyger . . . 2.50
29 SCh,AdW,A:Livewire,Stronghold,
w/Valiant Era card 2.50

30 SCh,AdW,A:Livewire,
Stronghold 2.50
31 SCh,AdW,V:H.A.R.D.Corps . . . 2.50
32 SCh,AdW,A:Eternal Warrior . . . 2.50
33 SCh, V:Dr. Eclipse 2.50
34 SCh,Chaos Effect-Delta#1,
A:X-O, Dr. Eclipse 2.50
35 Zephyr 2.50
36 Zephyr, Magnus 2.50
37 Magnus, Harada 2.50
38 A:Spikeman 2.50
39 Zepplin vs. Harada 2.50
40 V:Harbinger 2.50
41 V:Harbinger 2.50
TPB w/#0,rep#1-4 . . . . 25.00
TPB 2nd Printing w/o #0 . . . . . . 9.95
TPB #2, Rep. 6-7,10-11 . . . . . . 9.95

HARBINGER FILES:
HARADA
Valiant
1 BL,DC,O:Harada 2.75
2 Harada's ultimate weapon 2.50

H.A.R.D. Corps #11 © Valiant

H.A.R.D. CORPS
Valiant
1 JLe(c),DL,BL,V:Harbinger Foundation,
I:Flatline, D:Maniac 7.00
1a Gold Ed. 90.00
2 DL,BL,V:Harb.Foundation 4.00
3 DL,BL,J:Flatline 3.50
4 BL 3.50
5 BCh,BL(i),A:Bloodshot 4.00
5a Comic Defense System Ed. . 28.00
6 MLe,A:Spider Aliens 3.50
7 MLe,V:Spider Aliens,I:Hotshot . 4.00
8 MLe,V:Harada,J:Hotshot 3.00
9 MLe,V:Harada,A:Turok 2.75
10 MLe,A:Turok,V:Dinosaurs 2.50
11 YG,I:Otherman 2.50
12 MLe,V:Otherman 2.50
13 YG,D:Superstar 3.00
14 DvM(s),YG,V:Edie Simkus . . . 2.50
15 DvM(s),YG,V:Edie Simkus . . . 2.50
16 DvM(s),YG 2.50
17 DvM(s),RLe,V:Armorines 2.50
18 DvM(s),RLe,V:Armorines,

w/Valiant Era card 2.50	3 ANi,BL,Steel Nation #3 . . . . . 14.00
19 RLe,A:Harada 2.50	3a w/o coupon 4.00
20 RLe,V:Harbingers 2.50	4 ANi,BL,E:Steel Nation 11.00
21 RLe,New Direction 2.25	4a w/o coupon 4.00
22 RLe,V:Midnight Earl 2.25	5 DL,BL(i),I:Rai(#1),V:Slagger
23 RLe,Chaos Effect-Delta #4,	Flipbook format 15.00
A:Armorines, X-O 2.25	5a w/o coupon 4.00
24 Ironhead 2.25	6 DL,A:Solar,V:Grandmother
25 Midnight Earl 2.25	A:Rai(#2) 9.00
26 Heydrich, Omen 2.25	6a w/o coupon 4.00
27 Heydrich shows evil 2.25	7 DL,EC,V:Rai(#3) 8.00
28 New Hardcorps 2.25	7a w/o coupon 4.00
29 V:New Guard 2.25	8 DL,A:Rai(#4),Solar,X-O
30 Final Issue 2.25	Armor.E:Flipbooks 8.00
	8a w/o coupon 4.00

ICE AGE:
MAGIC THE GATHERING
Armada

1 Dominaia, from card game . . . 2.50	9 EC,V:Xyrkol,E-7 . . . . 5.00
2 Ice Age Adventures 2.50	10 V:Xyrkol 5.00
3 CV(c) 2.50	11 V:Xyrkol. 5.00
	12 I:Turok,V:Dr. Noel,

KNIGHTHAWK
Windjammer

1 NA(c&a),I:Knighthawk the	I:Asylum,40pgs 35.00
Protector,V:Nemo 2.50	13 EC,Asylum Pt 1 . . . . 3.50
2 NA(c&a),Birth of Nemo 2.50	14 EC,Asylum Pt2 . . . . 3.50
	15 FM(c),EC,Unity#4,I:Eternal

MAGIC THE GATHERING,
SHADOW MAGE
Armada

1 I:Jared 2.50	Warrior of 4001,O:Unity 3.00
2 F:Hurloon the Minotaur 2.50	16 WS(c),EC,Unity#12,A:Solar,
3 VMk(c&a),V:Ravidel 2.50	Archer,Armstrong,Harbinger,
	X-O,Rai,Eternal Warrior 3.00
	17 JaB,V:Talpa 3.00
	18 SD,R:Mekman,V:E-7 . . . . 3.00
	19 SD,V:Mekmen 3.00
	20 EC,Tale of Magnus' past 3.00
	21 JaB,R:Malevalents,

ROBOT FIGHTER

	Grandmother 5.00
	21a Gold Ed. 25.00
	22 JaB,D:Felina,V:Malevalents,
	Grandmother 3.00
	23 V:Malevolents 2.50
	24 V:Malevolents 2.50
	25 N:Magnus,R:1-A,silver-foil
	(c) 3.00
	26 I:Young Wolves 2.50
	27 V:Dr.Lazlo Noel 2.50
	28 V:The Malevs 2.25
	29 JCf,A:Eternal Warrior 2.25
	30 JCf,V:The Malevs 2.25
	31 JCf,V:The Malevs 2.25
	32 JCf,Battle for South Am 2.25
	33 B:JOs(s),JCf,A:Ivar 2.25
	34 JCf,Captured 2.25
	35 JCf,V:Mekman 2.25
	36 JCf,w/Valiant Era Card 2.25
	37 JCf,A:Starwatchers 2.25
	38 JCf, ... 2.25
	39 JCf,F:Torque 2.25
	40 JCf,F:Torque, A:Rai 2.25
	41 JCf,Chaos Effect-Epsilon#4
	A:Solar, Psi-Lords,Rai 2.50
	42 JCf, F:Torque,A:Takashi 2.25
	43 JCf,F:Torque,Immortal E 2.25
	44 JCf,F:Torque,Stagger 2.25
	45 V:Immortal Enemy 2.25
	46 V:Immortal Enemy 2.25
	47 Cold Blooded,pt.1 . . . . 2.25
	48 Cold Blooded,pt.2 . . . . 2.25
	49 F:Slagger 2.25
	50 V:Invisible Legion 2.25
	51 KoK,RyR,Return of the
	Robots,pt.1 . . . . 2.25
	52 KoK,RyR,Return of the
	Robots,pt.2 . . . . 2.25
	53 KoK,RyR,Return of the
	Robots,pt.3 . . . . 2.25
	54 KoK,RyR,Return of the
	Robots,pt.4 . . . . 2.25
	Yearbook #1 . . . . 3.95

Magnus: Robot Fighter #2
© Voyager Communications, Inc.

MAGNUS:
ROBOT FIGHTER
Valiant

0 PCu,BL,"Emancipator",w/	
BWS card 55.00	
0a PCu,BL,w/o card 22.00	
1 ANi,BL,B:Steel Nation 22.00	
1a w/o coupon 7.00	
2 ANi,BL,Steel Nation #2 . . . . . 18.00	
2a w/o coupon 4.00	

TPB 1-4 . . . . 9.95	

Ninjak #3 © Valiant

NINJAK
Valiant

1 B:MMo(s),JQ,JP,Chromium(c),	
I:Dr.Silk,Webnet 5.00	
1a Gold Ed 35.00	
2 JQ,JP,V:Dr.Silk,Webnet 3.00	
3 JQ,JP,I:Seventh Dragon 2.50	
4 MMo(a&s),V:Seventh Dragon,	
w/Valiant Era card 2.50	
5 MMo(a&s),A:X-O Manowar . . . 2.50	
6 MMo(a&s),A:X-O Manowar,	
V:Dr.Silk,Webnet 2.50	
7 MMo(a&s),I:Rhaman 2.25	
8 MMo(a&s),Chaos Effect-	
Gamma#3,A:Madame Noir . . . 2.50	
9 Dogs of War 2.25	
10 Cantebury Tale #1 . . . . 2.25	
11 Cantebury Tale #2 . . . . 2.25	
12 . . . . 2.25	
13 Mad Dogs and English 2.25	
14 Cry Wolf pt. 1 . . . . 2.25	
15 Cry Wolf pt. 2 . . . . 2.50	
16 Plague Pt. 1 . . . . 2.50	
17 Plague Pt. 2 . . . . 2.50	
18 Computer Virus 2.50	
19 DAn,ALa,MM,Breaking the	
Web,pt.1 . . . . 2.50	
20 DAn,ALa,MM,Breaking the	
Web,pt.2 . . . . 2.50	
21 DAn,ALa,MM,Breaking the	
Web,pt.3 . . . . 2.50	
22 Bitter Wind 2.50	
Yearbook #1, Dr. Silk 3.95	

ORIGINAL CAPTAIN
JOHNAR AND
THE ALIENS

1 Reprint from Magnus 2.95	
2 Russ Manning rep. 2.95	

ORIGINAL DR. SOLAR
MAN OF THE ATOM

1 Reprint 2.95	
2 Reprints 2.95	

---

3 Reprints 2.95

ORIGINAL MAGNUS ROBOT FIGHTER
1 Reprint 2.95
2 Russ Manning Art 2.95
3 Russ Manning 2.95

ORIGINAL TUROK, SON OF STONE
1 Reprint 2.95
2 Alberto Gioletti art 2.95
3 Alberto Gioletti 2.95
4 Reprints 2.95

PSI-LORDS: REIGN OF THE STARWATCHERS
1 MLe,DG,Chromium(c),Valiant
   Vision,V:Spider Aliens 3.75
2 MLe,DG,V:Spider Aliens 2.25
3 MLe,DG,Chaos Effect-Epsilon#2,
   A:Solar 2.25
becomes:

PSI-LORDS
4 V:Ravenrok 2.25
5 V:Ravenrok 2.25
6 . . . . 2.25
7 Micro-Invasion 2.25
8 A:Solar the Destroyer 2.25
9 Frozen Harbingers 2.25
10 F:Ravenrok 2.25

Rai and the Future Force #9
© Voyager Communications

RAI
Valiant
0 DL,O:Bloodshot,I:2nd Rai,D:X-O,
   Archer,Shadowman,F:all Valiant
   heroes,bridges Valiant
   Universe 1992-4001 . . . . 14.00
1 V:Grandmother 18.00
2 V:Icespike 14.00
3 V:Humanists,Makiko 32.00
4 V:Makiko,rarest Valiant 32.00
5 Rai leaves earth,
   C:Eternal Warrior 9.00

6 FM(c),Unity#7,V:Pierce 5.00
7 WS(c),Unity#15,V:Pierce,
   D:Rai,A:Magnus 6.00
8 Epilogue of Unity in 4001 . . . . 5.00
Becomes:

RAI AND THE FUTURE FORCE
9 F:Rai,E.Warrior of 4001,Tekla,
   X-O Commander,Spylocke . . . 2.50
9a Gold Ed. 18.00
10 Rai vs. Malev Emperor 2.50
11 SCh,V:Malevolents 2.50
12 V:Cyber Raiders 2.50
13 Spylocke Revealed 2.50
14 SCh,D:M'Ree 2.50
15 SCh,V:X-O 2.50
16 SCh,V:Malevs 2.50
17 . . . . 2.50
18 JOs(s),Spk,V:Malevs 2.50
19 JCf,V:Malves 2.50
20 JOs(s),DR,V:Malves,Spylocke
   realed to be Spider Alien . . . 2.50
21 DR,I:Starwatchers,b:Torque,
   w/Valiant Era card 2.50
22 DR,D:2nd Rai,
   A:Starwatchers 2.50
23 DR,A:Starwatchers, ... 2.50
24 DR,in Tibet 2.25
25 DR,F:Spylocke 2.25
26 DR,Chaos Effect-Epsilon#3,
   A:Solar Magnus,Psi-Lords . . . 2.25
27 . . . . 2.25
28 V:Takashi 2.25
29 A:Rentaro Nakadai 2.25
30 Splocke 2.25
31 Bad Penny pt. 1 . . . . 2.25
32 Bad Penny pt. 2, F:Axscan . . . 2.25
33 F:Spylocke, Rentaro 2.25
TPB #0-#4 . . . . 11.95
TPB Star System ed. 11.95

SECOND LIFE OF DR. MIRAGE
Valiant
1 B:BL(s),BCh,V:Mast.Darque . . . 3.00
1a Gold Ed. 18.00
2 BCh,V:Master Darque 2.75
3 BCh 2.75
4 BCh,V:Bhrama 2.75
5 BCh,A:Shadowman,V:Master
   Darque 2.75
6 BCh,V:Dr.Eclipse 2.75
7 BCh,V:Dr.Eclipse,w/card 2.75
8 BCh, ... 2.75
9 BCh,A:Otherman 2.75
10 BCh,V:Otherman 2.50
11 BCh,Chaos Effect-Beta#2, . . . 2.75
12 BCh 2.50
13 BCh 2.50
14 . . . . 2.50
15 Chaos Effect 2.50
16 . . . . 2.50
17 . . . . 2.50
18 F:Deathsmith 2.50
19 R:Walt Wiley 2.50

SECRET WEAPONS
Valiant
1 JSP(a&s),BWi(i),I:Dr.Eclipse,
   A:Master Darque,A:Geoff,
   Livewire,Stronghold,Solar,X-O,
   Bloodshot,Shadowman 2.75
1a Gold Ed. 12.00

2 JSP(a&s),V:Master Darque,
   Dr.Eclipse 2.50
3 JSP(a&s),V:Speedshots 2.50
4 JSP(a&s),V:Scatterbrain 2.50
5 JSP(a&s),A:Ninjak 2.50
6 JPS(s),JPh(pl),TeH,
   V:Spider Aliens 2.50
7 JPS(s),V:Spider Aliens 2.50
8 JSP(a&pl),V:Harbingers 2.50
9 JSP(a&s),V:Webnet,
   w/Valiant Era card 2.50
10 JSP(a&s),V:Webnet 2.50
11 PGr,New Line-up 2.75
12 PGr,A:Bloodshot 2.50
13 PGr,Chaos Effect-Gamma#2 . . 2.50
14 PGr,F:Bloodshot 2.25
15 . . . . 2.25
16 . . . . 2.25
17 V:Dr. Silk 2.25
18 Gigo 2.25
19 A:Ninjak 2.25
20 Bloodshot Rampage Pt.2 . . . . 2.25
21 Bloodshot Rampage Pt.4 . . . . 2.25
22 I:Gestalt, Pyroclast 2.25
23 A:Bloodshot 2.25

SECRETS OF THE VALIANT UNIVERSE
1 from Wizard 2.50
2 BH,Chaos Effect-Beta#4,A:Master
   Darque,Dr.Mirage,Max St.James,
   Dr. Eclipse 2.25

Shadow Man #7
© Voyager Communications, Inc.

SHADOW MAN
Valiant
0 BH,TmR,Chromium (c),O:Maxim
   St.James,Shadowman 3.00
0a Newstand ed. 2.50
0b Gold Ed. 18.00
1 DL,JRu,I&O:Shadowman 12.00
2 DL,V:Serial Killer 12.00
3 V:Emil Sosa 9.00
4 DL,FM(c),Unity#6,A:Solar 6.00
5 DL,WS(c),Unity#14,
   A:Archer & Armstrong 5.00
6 SD,L:Lilora 4.00

```
7 DL,V:Creature ............ 4.00
8 JDx(i),I:Master Darque ...... 7.00
9 JDx(i),V:Darque's Minions .... 5.00
10 BH,I:Sandria ............. 4.00
11 BH,N:Shadowman ........ 4.00
12 BH,V:Master Darque ....... 4.00
13 BH,V:Rev.Shadow Man .... 3.00
14 BH,JDx,V:Bikers .......... 3.00
15 BH,JDx,V:JB,Fake
    Shadow Man,C:Turok ...... 3.00
16 BH,JDx,I:Dr.Mirage,
    Carmen ............... 6.00
17 BH,JDx,A:Archer and
    Armstrong ............. 2.75
18 BH,JDx,A:Archer and
    Armstrong ............. 2.75
19 BH,A:Aerosmith .......... 2.50
20 BH,A:Master Darque,
    V:Shadowman's Father ..... 2.50
21 BH,I:Maxim St.James
    (1895 Shadowman) ....... 2.50
22 V:Master Darque ......... 2.50
23 BH(a&s),A:Doctor Mirage,
    V:Master Darque ........ 2.50
24 BH(a&s),V:H.A.T.E. ....... 2.50
25 RgM,w/Valiant Era card .... 2.50
26 w/Valiant Era card ....... 2.75
27 BH,V:Drug Lord .......... 2.50
28 BH,A:Master Darque ...... 2.50
29 Chaos Effect-Beta#1,V:Master
    Darque ............... 2.50
30 R:Rotwak ............... 2.50
31 ..................... 2.50
32 ..................... 2.50
33 ..................... 2.50
34 Voodoo in Carribean ...... 2.50
35 A:Ishmael .............. 2.50
36 F:Ishmael .............. 2.50
37 A:X-O, V:Blister ........ 2.50
38 V:Ishmael, Blister ....... 2.50
39 BH,TmR,Explores Powers ... 2.50
40 BH,TmR,I,Vampire! ....... 2.50
TPB rep.#1-#3,#6 ........... 9.95
```

SOLAR: MAN OF THE ATOM
Valiant

```
1 BWS,DP,BL,B:2nd Death
    B:Alpha & Omega ....... 18.00
2 BWS,DP,BL,V:Dr Solar ..... 14.00
3 BWS,DP,BL,V:Harada
    I:Harbinger Foundation .... 17.00
4 BWS,DP,BL,E:2nd Death
    V:Dr Solar ............ 11.00
5 BWS,EC,V:Alien Armada .... 9.00
6 BWS,DP,SDr,V:Alien Armada
    X-O Armor ............ 8.00
7 BWS,DP,SDr,V:Alien Armada
    X-O Armor ............ 8.00
8 BWS,V:Dragon of Bangkok ... 7.00
9 BWS,DP,SDr, V:Erica's Baby .. 7.00
10 BWS,DP,SDr,JDx,I:Eternal
    Warrior,E:Alpha&Omega .... 28.00
10a 2nd printing ............ 6.00
11 SDr,A:Eternal Warrior,
    Prequel to Unity #0 ....... 5.00
12 SDr,FM(c),Unity#9,O:Pierce,
    Albert ................ 4.00
13 DP,SDr,WS(c),Unity#17,
    V:Pierce ............... 4.00
14 DP,SDr,I:Bender (becomes
    Dr.Eclipse) ........... 10.00
15 SD,V:Bender ............ 6.00
16 Solar moves to California .... 3.00
```

Solar: Man of the Atom #9
© Voyager Communications, Inc.

```
17 SDr(i),V:X-O Manowar ..... 3.00
18 SDr(i),A:X-Manowar ....... 3.00
19 SDr(i),V:Videogame ....... 3.00
20 SDr(i),Dawn of the
    Malevolence ........... 3.00
21 SDr(i),Master Darque ...... 3.00
22 SDr(i),V:Master Darque,A:
    Bender(Dr.Eclipse) ........ 3.00
23 SDr(i),JQ(c),V:Master
    Darque,I:Solar War God .... 3.50
24 SDr(i),A:Solar War God .... 2.75
25 V:Dr.Eclipse ............ 2.50
26 Phil and Gayle on vaction ... 2.50
27 in Austrialia ............ 2.50
28 A:Solar War God ......... 2.50
29 KVH(s),JP(i),Valiant Vision,
    A:Solar War God ......... 3.00
30 KVH(s),JP,V:Energy
    Parasite ............... 2.50
31 KVH(s),JP,Chrismas Issue ... 2.50
32 KVH(s),JP,Parent's Night .... 2.50
33 KVH(s),PGr,JP,B:Solar the
    Destroyer,w/Valiant Era card .. 2.50
34 KVH(s),PGr,V:Spider Alien ... 2.50
35 KVH(s),PGr,E:Solar the
    Destroyer,Valiant Vision ..... 2.50
36 KVH(s),PGr,JP,B:Revenge
    times two,V:Doctor Eclipse,
    Ravenus ............... 2.50
37 PGr,JP,E:Revenge times two,
    V:Doctor Eclipse,Ravenus .... 2.25
38 PGr,JP,Chaos Effect-
    Epsilon#1, .............. 2.25
39 ..................... 2.25
40 ..................... 2.25
41 ..................... 2.25
42 Elements of Evil pt.1 ....... 2.25
43 Elements of Evil pt.2 ....... 2.25
44 I:New Character .......... 2.25
45 Explores Powers .......... 2.25
46 I:The Sentry ............ 2.50
47 DJu,DG,Brave New World,pt.1 2.50
48 DJu,DG,Brave New World,pt.3 2.50
49 DJu,DG,Brave New World,pt.4 2.50
TPB #0 JiS,BWS,BL,Alpha and Omega
    rep. from Solar #1–#10 ...... 9.95
TPB #1 JiS,BWS,GL,V:Doctor Solar
```

```
rep. from Solar #1–#4 ...... 9.95
```

STARSLAYER DIRECTORS CUT
Windjammer

```
1 R:Starslayer, Mike Grell ...... 2.50
2 I:New Star Slayer .......... 2.50
3 Jolly Rodger .............. 2.50
4 V:Battle Droids ............ 2.50
5 I:Baraka Kuhi ............. 2.50
6 V:Valkyrie ............... 2.50
7 MGr(c&a),Can Torin destroy? . 2.50
8 MGr(c&a),JAl, Can Torin live
    with his deeds?,final issue ... 2.50
```

STARWATCHERS
Valiant

```
1 MLe,DG,Chromium(c),Valiant
    Vision, ................ 3.50
```

TIMEWALKER

```
0 BH,DP,O:3 Immortals ....... 2.95
1 DP, BH ................. 2.50
2 DP,BH ................. 2.50
3 DP BH ................. 2.50
4 Ten Commandments ........ 2.50
5 DP,BH ................. 2.50
6 Harbinger Wars Pt.1 ....... 2.50
7 Harbinger Wars Pt.2 ....... 2.50
8 Harbinger Wars Pt.3 ....... 2.50
9 V:Jahk rt ............... 2.50
10 Last God of Dura-Europus,pt.1
    time:260 A.D. ........... 2.50
11 Last God of Dura-Europus,pt.2 2.50
12 3RW,DP,Ashes to Ashes,pt.1 . 2.50
13 3RW,DP,Ashes to Ashes,pt.2 . 2.50
Yearbook F:Harada ........... 2.95
TPB F:Archer & Armstrong ..... 9.95
```

TUROK: DINOSAUR HUNTER
Valiant

```
1 BS,Chromium(c),O:Turok
    retold,V:Monark .......... 4.00
1a Gold Ed. .............. 75.00
2 BS,V:Monark ............ 2.75
```

Turok: Dinosaur Hunter #8 © Valiant

3 BCh,V:Monark 2.75
4 TT(s),RgM,O:Turok 2.75
5 TT(s),RgM,V:Dinosaurs 2.75
6 TT(s),RgM,V:Longhunter 2.75
7 TT(a&s),B:People o/t Spider .. 2.75
8 TT(a&s),V:T-Rex 2.75
9 TT(a&s),E:People o/t Spider .. 2.75
10 MBn,RgM,A:Bile 2.75
11 MBn,RgM,V:Chun Yee,w/
   ValiantEra card 2.75
12 MBn,RgM,V:Dinosaur 2.75
13 B:TT(c&s),RgM, ... 2.75
14 V:Dino-Pirate 2.50
15 RgM,V:Dino-Pirate 2.25
16 Chaos Effect-Beta#3,
   V:Evil Shaman 2.75
17 V:C.I.A. 2.50
18 V:Bionosaurs 2.50
19 A:Manowar 2.50
20 Chichak 2.50
21 Ripsaw 2.50
22 .... 2.50
23 A:Longhunter 2.50
24 R:To The Lost Land 2.50
25 I:Warrior of Mother God 2.50
26 V:Overlord 2.50
27 TT,RgM,Lost Land,pt.4 ..... 2.50
28 MBn,DEA hunts rogue T-Rex . 2.50
29 SFu,Manhunt,pt.1 .... 2.50
30 SFu,Manhunt,pt.2 .... 2.50
Yearbook #1 MBn(s),DC,
   N&V:Mon Ark 4.25
Yearbook 1995 MGr,The Hunted . 2.95

TUROK/SHAMAN'S TEARS
1 MGr,Ghost Dance Pt. 1 ...... 2.50
2 MGr,JAI,White Buffalo
   kidnapped,V:Bar Sinister 2.50

UNITY
Valiant
0 BWS,BL,Chapter#1,A:All
   Valiant Heroes,V:Erica
   Pierce 7.00
0a Red ed.,w/red logo 25.00
1 BWS,BL,Chapter#18,A:All
   Valiant Heroes,D:Erica
   Pierce 6.00
1a Gold logo 30.00
1b Platinum 35.00
TPB Previews Exclusive,Vol.I
   Chap.#1-9 .... 20.00
TPB Previews Exclusive,Vol.II
   Chap.#10-18 .... 20.00
TPB #1 rep Chapters #1-4 ... 10.95
TPB #2 rep Chapters #5-9 ... 9.95
TPB #3 rep Chapters #10-14 . 9.95

VALERIA, THE SHE-BAT
Windjammer
[Mini-series]
1 NA,Valeria & 'Rilla 2.50
2 NA,BSz, final issue 2.50

VALIANT ERA
Valiant
TPB rep.Magnus #12,Shadowman
   #8,Solar #10-11,Eternal
   Warrior#4-5 .... 13.95

VALIANT READER:
GUIDE TO THE VALIANT
UNIVERSE
1 O:Valiant Universe 1.00

VALIANT VISION
STARTER KIT
Valiant
1 w/3-D Glasses 2.95
2 F:Starwatchers 2.95

VINTAGE MAGNUS
ROBOT FIGHTER
Valiant
1 rep. Gold Key Magnus #22
   (which is #1) 6.00
2 rep. Gold Key Magnus #3 .... 4.50
3 rep. Gold Key Magnus #13 ... 3.50
4 rep. Gold Key Magnus #15 ... 3.50

VISITOR
1 New Series 2.50
2 F:The Harbinger 2.50
3 The Bomb 2.50
4 V:F/X Specialists 2.50
5 R:Harbinger 2.50
6 KVH,BS(c),V:Men in Black 2.50
7 KVH,BS(c),V:Men in Black,pt.2 2.50
8 KVH,V:Harbinger identity 2.50
9 KVH,A:Harbinger,Flamingo ... 2.50

VISITOR VS. VALIANT
1 V:Solar 2.95
2 .... 2.95

WWF BATTLEMANIA
Valiant
1 WWF Action 2.50
2 .... 2.50
3 .... 2.50
4 .... 2.50
5 .... 2.50

X-O MANOWAR
Valiant
0 JQ,O:Aric,1st Full
   Chromium(c) 4.00
0a Gold Ed. 30.00
1 BL,BWS,I:Aric,Ken 20.00
2 BL(i),V:Lydia,Wolf-Class
   Armor 18.00
3 I:X-Caliber,A:Solar 15.00
4 MM,A:Harbinger,C:Shadowman
   (Jack Boniface) 18.00
5 BWS(c),V:AX 10.00
5a w/Pink logo 20.00
6 SD,V:Ax(X-O Armor) 8.00
7 FM(c),Unity#5,V:Pierce 5.00
8 WS(c),Unity#13,V:Pierce 5.00
9 Aric in Italy,408 A.D. 4.00
10 N:X-O Armor 4.00
11 V:Spider Aliens 3.50
12 A:Solar 3.50
13 V:Solar 3.50
14 BS,A:Turok,I:Randy Cartier .. 4.00
15 BS,A:Turok 3.00
15a Red Ed. 10.00
16 V:The Mob 3.00
17 BL 3.00
18 JCf,V:CIA,A:Randy,I:Paul 2.75
19 JCf,V:US Government 2.75

X-O Manowar #4
© Voyager Communications, Inc.

20 A:Toyo Harada 2.50
21 V:Ax 2.50
22 Aria in S.America 2.50
23 Aria in S.America 2.50
24 Aria comes back 2.50
25 JCf,JGz,PaK,I:Armories,
   BU:Armories#0 .... 4.00
26 JGz(s),RLv,F:Ken 2.50
27 JGz,RLe,A:Turok,Geomancer,
   Stronghold,Livewire 2.50
28 JGz,RLe,D:X-O,V:Spider
   Aliens,w/Valiant Era card 2.75
29 JGz,RLe,A:Turok,V:Spider
   Aliens 2.50
30 JGz,RLe,A:Solar 2.50
31 JGz,RLe, ... 2.25
32 JGz,RLe,at Orb,Inc. 2.25
33 JGz,RLe,Chaos Effect-Delta#3,
   A:Armorines,H.A.R.D.
   Corps 2.25
34 .... 2.25
35 .... 2.25
36 .... 2.25
37 Wolfbridge Affair pt.1 ..... 2.25
38 Wolfbridge Affair pt.2 ..... 2.25
39 Wolfbridge Affair pt.3 ..... 2.25
40 Wolfbridge Affair pt.4 ..... 2.25
41 Aftermath 2.25
42 A:Shadowman Surprise 2.25
43 Chasitty's Boys 2.25
44 Bart Sears New Direction ... 2.50
45 RMz,V:Crescendo 2.50
46 RMz,V:Crescendo 2.50
47 RMz,V:Crescendo 2.50
48 RMz,BS,A:Turok 2.50
49 RMz,loses control of armor .. 2.50
TPB rep.#1-4,w/X-O Manual ... 11.00

ABYSS, THE
1 MK,Movie Adaptation pt.1 .... 2.50
2 MK,Movie Adaptation pt.2 .... 2.50

ACCIDENT MAN
1 I:Accident Man (B&W) 2.50

AGENTS OF LAW
1 KG, I:Law 2.50
2 A:Barb Wire 2.50
3 KG,DLw,The Judgment Gate .. 2.50

AGE OF REPTILES
1 DRd,Story on Dinosaurs 3.00
2 DRd,Story on Dinosaurs 3.00
3 DRd,Story on Dinosaurs 3.00
4 DRd,Story on Dinosaurs 3.00

Aliens #1 © Dark Horse Comics

ALIENS
(B&W)
1 Movie Sequel,R:Hicks,Newt .. 40.00
1a 2nd printing 4.00
1b 3rd printing 3.00
1c 4th printing 2.50
2 Hicks raids Mental Hospital .. 28.00
2a 2nd printing 3.50
2a 3rd printing 3.00
3 Realize Queen is on Earth ... 15.00
3a 2nd printing 2.50
4 Queen is freed, Newton on
    Aliens World 10.00
5 All out war on Aliens World ... 7.50
6 Hicks & Newt return to Earth .. 6.00
TPB rep.#1-#6 & DHP #24 ..... 11.00
TPB 2nd printing, DvD(c) 11.00
HC rep..#1-#6 & DHP #24 ..... 25.00

ALIENS (II)
[Mini-Series]
1 DB,Hicks,Newt hijack ship ... 12.00
1a 2nd Printing 3.00
2 DB,Crazed general
    training aliens 6.50
2a 2nd Printing 3.00
3 DB,HicksV:General Spears ... 5.00

3a 2nd Printing 2.50
4 DB,Heroes reclaim earth
    from aliens 5.00
HC, 2,500 made 80.00
HC, 1,000 made 100.00

ALIENS: BERSERKER
1 I:Crew of the Nemesis 2.50
2 Terminall 949 .... 2.50
3 Traitor 2.50
4 Finale 2.50

ALIENS: COLONIAL MARINES
1 I: Lt. Joseph Henry 3.00
2 I: Pvt. Carmen Vasquez 2.75
3 V:Aliens 2.75
4 F:Lt.Henry 2.75
5 V:Aliens 2.75
6 F:Herk Mondo 2.75
7 A:Beliveau 2.75
8 F:Lt.Joseph Henry 2.75
9 F:Lt.Joseph Henry 2.75
10 final issue 2.50

ALIENS: EARTH ANGEL
1 JBy 3.00
HC rep. Earth Angel 21.00

Aliens: Hive #1 © Dark Horse

ALIENS: EARTH WAR
1 SK,JBo(c),Renewal of
    Alien's War 10.00
1a 2nd Printing 2.50
2 SK,JBo(c),To trap the Queen .. 7.50
3 SK,JBo(c) Stranded on
    Alien's planet 6.00
4 SK,JBo(c),Resolution,final 6.00
HC Earth War, rep. #1-#4,
    signed and numbered edition 60.00

ALIENS: GENOCIDE
1 Aliens vs. Aliens 4.00
2 Alien Homeworld 3.50
3 Search for Alien Queen 3.00
4 Conclusion, inc. poster 3.00
TPB Genocide rep. #1-#4 ..... 13.95

ALIENS: HIVE
1 KJo,I:Stanislaw Mayakovsky .. 4.00
2 KJo,A:Norbert 3.50
3 KJo,A:Julie,Gill 3.25
4 KJo,A:Stan,Final 3.00
TPB Hive rep. #1-#4 .... 14.00

ALIENS: LABYRINTH
1 F:Captured Alien 3.00
2 .... 2.50
3 O:Dr.Church 2.50
4 D:Everyone 2.50

ALIENS: MONDO PEST
1 I:Herk Mondo 2.50

ALIENS: MUSIC OF THE SPEARS
1 I:Damon Eddington 3.00
2 TBd(c),A:Damon Eddington ... 2.75
3 TBd(c),A:Damon Eddington ... 2.75
4 TBd(c),last issue 2.75

ALIENS: NEWT'S TALE
1 How Newt Survived 5.50
2 JBo(c),Newt's point of view
    on how 'Aliens' ended 4.95

ALIENS: ROGUE
1 F:Mr.Kay 3.00
2 V:Aliens 3.00
3 V:Aliens 3.00
4 V:Aliens King 3.00
TPB Nel(c),rep.#1-#4 .... 14.95

ALIENS: SACRIFICE
1 Rep.Aliens UK 4.95

ALIENS: SALVATION
1 MMi,F:Selkirk 4.95

ALIENS: STRONGHOLD
1 DoM 2.50
2 DoM 2.50
3 DoM 2.50
4 .... 2.50

ALIENS: TRIBES
HC DvD(c) 24.95
TPB 11.95

ALIENS/PREDATOR: DEADLIEST OF THE SPECIES
1 B:CCI(s),JG,F:Caryn Delacroix . 3.75
2 JG,V:Predator 3.00
3 JG,F:Caryn Delacroix 3.00
4 JG,V:Predator 3.00
5 JG,Roadtrip 3.00
6 JG,in Space Station 3.00
7 JG,EB 2.50
8 JG,EB 2.50
9 JG,EB 2.50
10 CCI(s), Human Predators 2.50
11 CCI,EB,JBo(c),Delacroix vs.
    DeMatier 2.50

ALIENS VS. PREDATOR
0 PN,KS,Rep.DHP#34-36,(B&W) 16.00
1 Duel to the Death 12.00
1a 2nd Printing 2.50

2 Dr. Revna missing 7.00
3 Predators attack Aliens 6.00
4 CW,F:Machiko & Predator 5.00
TPB PN,KS,rep.DHP#34-36 . . 19.95
HC PN,KS,rep.DHP#34-36 . . . . 79.95

ALIENS VS. PREDATOR: DUEL
1 Trap, JS 2.50
2 War 2.50

ALIENS VS. PREDATOR: WAR
0 Prelude to New Series 2.50
1 RSd,MM,RCo(c) F:Machiko . . . 2.50

ALIEN 3
1 Movie Adaptation pt.1 . . . . . . 2.50
2 Movie Adaptation pt.2 . . . . . . 2.50
3 Movie Adaptation pt.3 . . . . . . 2.50

AMERICAN, THE
(B&W)
1 CW,'Chinese Boxes,'D:Gleason 8.00
2 CW,'Nightmares 4.50
3 CW,Secrets of the American . . 4.00
4 CW,American vs.Kid America . 4.00
5 A:Kiki the Gorilla 4.00
6 Rashomon-like plot 3.50
7 Pornography business issue . . 3.50
8 Deals with violence issue 3.50
9 American Falls into a cult 3.50

THE AMERICAN: LOST IN AMERICA
1 CMa,American joins a cult 2.50
2 CMa,V:"Feel-Good" cult 2.50
3 CMa,"ApeMask" cult 2.50
4 CMa,Final issue 2.50
ColorSpec.#1 . . . . 2.95

AMERICAN SPLENDOR
1 Letterman 2.95

ANOTHER CHANCE TO GET IT RIGHT
1 . . . . 14.95

APPLESEED DATABOOK
1 Flip Book 3.50
2 Flip Book 3.50

ATLAS
1 BZ,I:Atlas 2.75
2 BZ,V:Sh'en Chui 2.75
3 BZ,V:Sh'en Chui 2.50
4 BZ, final issue 2.50

BABE
1 JBy(a&s) 3.00
2 thru 4 JBy(a&s) . . . . @2.50

BABE 2
1 V:Shrewmanoid 2.50
2 A:Abe Sapien 2.50

BACCHUS COLOR SPECIAL
1 A:Thor 2.95
2 A:Abe Sapien 2.50

BADGER: SHATTERED MIRROR
1 R:Badger 2.50
2 R:Badger 2.50
3 Badger 2.50
4 Phantom, final issue 2.50

BADGER: ZEN POP FUNNY ANIMAL VERSION
1 MBn,R:Badger 2.50
2 Ham 2.50

Badlands #1 © Dark Horse

BADLANDS
(B&W)
1 I:Connie Bremen 3.50
2 Anne Peck, C.I.A. 3.00
3 Assassination Rumor 2.50
4 Connie heads South 2.50
5 November 22, 1963, Dallas . . . 2.25
6 . . . . 2.25

BARB WIRE
Comics' Greatest World
1 Foil(c),I:Deathcard 2.25
2 DLw,I:Hurricane Max 2.25
3 V:Mace Blitzkrieg 2.00
4 Ghost pt.1 . . . . 2.00
5 Ghost pt.2 . . . . 2.00
6 Hardhide, Ignition 2.50
7 A:Motorhead 2.50
8 V:Ignition 2.50
9 A:Mecha, V:Ignition 2.50

BASEBALL GREATS
1 Jimmy Piersall story 3.25

BASIL WOLVERTON'S FANTASIC FABLES
(B&W)
1 BW 2.50
2 BW 2.50

BIG
1 Movie Adaptation 2.00

BILLI 99
(B&W)
1 'Pray for us Sinners' 4.50
2 'Trespasses' 4.00
3 'Daily Bread' 4.00

BLANCHE GOES TO NEW YORK
1 Turn of the Century N.Y. 2.95

BLUE LILY
1 . . . . 4.00
2 . . . . 4.00
3 . . . . 4.00

BOOK OF NIGHT
(B&W)
1 CV 2.50
2 CV 2.00
TPB Children of the Stars 12.95

Boris the Bear #2 © Dark Horse

BORIS THE BEAR
(B&W)
1 V:Funny Animals 3.00
1a 2nd printing 2.00
2 V:Robots 2.00
3 V:Super Heroes 2.00
4 Bear of Steel 2.00
5 Dump Thing 2.00
6 Bat Bear 2.00
7 Elves 2.00
8 LargeSize 2.50
9 Awol 2.00
10 . . . . 2.00
11 Comic Shop 2.00
12 . . . . 2.00
See: Other Pub. B&W section

BORIS THE BEAR
Color Classics
1 thru 7 . . . . @1.95

BUBBLE GUM CRISIS: GRAND MAL
1 . . . . 2.75

2	2.75
3	2.75
4 final issue	2.50

BY BIZARRE HANDS
(B&W)

1 JLd(s)	2.50
2 JLd(s)	2.50
3 JLd(s)	2.50

CARAVAN KIDD
(B&W)

1 thru 10	@2.50
[2nd Series]	
1 thru 9 F:Miam	@2.50
10	2.50
Holiday Spec.	2.50
Valentine's Day Spec.	2.50
[3rd Series]	
1 thru 8	@2.50
Christmas Special	2.50

CATALYST: AGENTS OF CHANGE
Comics' Greatest World

1 JPn(c),V:US Army	2.25
2 JPn(c),I:Grenade	2.25
3 JPn(c),Rebel vs. Titan	2.25
4 JPn(c),Titan vs. Grace	2.00
5 JPn(c),V:Ape	2.00
6	2.00
7	2.00

CHEVAL NOIR
(B&W)

1 DSt(c)	4.00
2 thru 6	@3.50
7 DSt(c)	3.50
8	3.50
9	3.50
10 80 page	4.50
11 80 page	4.50
12 MM(c)	3.95
13 thru 19	@3.95
20 'Great Power o/t Chninkel'	4.50
21 'Great Power o/t Chninkel'	3.95
22 'Great Power o/t Chninkel' concl.	4.50
23 inc."Rork','Forever War' concl.	3.95
24 'In Dreams' Pt.1	3.95
25 'In Dreams' Pt.2	3.95
26 'In Dreams' Pt.3	3.95
27 I:The Man From Ciguri (Airtight Garage Sequel) Dreams Pt.4	2.95
28 Ciguri cont.	2.95
29 Ciguri cont.	2.95
30 Ciguri,cont.	2.95
31 Angriest Dog in the World	2.95
32 thru 38	@2.95
39 In Search of Peter Pan	2.95
40	2.95
41 F:Demon	2.95
42 F:Demon	2.95
43 F:Demon	2.95
44 F:Demon	2.95
45	2.95
46	2.95
47	2.95
48 SwM(c)	2.95
49 F:Rork	2.95
50 F:Rork	2.95

Classic Star Wars #1
© Dark Horse Comics

CLASSIC STAR WARS

1 AW,newspaper strip reps.	14.00
2 AW,newspaper strip reps.	6.00
3 AW,newspaper strip reps.	5.00
4 AW,newspaper strip reps.	4.00
5 AW,newspaper strip reps.	4.00
6 AW,newspaper strip reps.	4.00
7 AW,newspaper reps.	4.00
8 AW,newspaper reps. w/card	4.00
9 AW,newspaper reps.	3.50
10 AW,newspaper reps.	3.50
11 thru 19 AW,newspaper reps.	@3.00
20 AW,newspaper strip reps., with trading card, final issue	4.00
Volume #1 TPB	15.99

CLASSIC STAR WARS: A NEW HOPE

1 AAd(c), rep.	4.25
2 AAd(c), rep.	3.95

CLASSIC STAR WARS: EARLY ADVENTURES

1	3.00
2	2.50
3	2.50
4 RHo(c)	2.50
5 A:Lady Tarkin	2.50
6 Weather Dominator	2.50
7 V:Darth Vader	2.50
8 X-Wing Secrets	2.50
9 A:Boba Fett	2.50

CLASSIC STAR WARS: EMPIRE STRIKES BACK

1 Movie Adaptation	4.00
2 Movie Adaptation	4.00

CLASSIC STAR WARS: RETURN OF THE JEDI

1 Movie Adaptation	4.00
2 Movie Adaptation	3.50

CLASSIC STAR WARS: VANDELHELM MISSION

1 F:Han Solo	3.95

CLONEZONE

Spec #1 B&W	2.00

COLORS IN BLACK
Comics From Spike

1 B:Passion Play	2.95
2 Images	2.95
3 three stories	2.95

Vortex #1 (Division 13)
© Dark Horse Comics

COMICS' GREATEST WORLD
(Arcadia)

1 B:MRi(s),FM(c),B:LW,B:O:Vortex, F:X,I:Seekers	3.00
1a B&W proof ed. (1,500 made)	35.00
1b Hologram(c), with cards	20.00
2 JoP,I:Pit Bulls	1.50
3 AH,I:Ghost	1.50
4 I:Monster	1.50
TPB Arcadia	25.00

(Golden City)

1 B:BKs(s),JOy(c),I:Rebel, Amaz.Grace,V:WarMaker	1.25
1a Gold Ed.	18.00
2 I:Mecha	1.25
3 WS(c),I:Titan	1.25
4 E:BKs(s),GP(c),JD,I:Catalyst	1.25
TBP Golden City	20.00

(Steel Harbor)

1 B:CW(s),PG,I:Barb Wire, V:Ignition	1.25
2 MMi(c),TNa,I:Machine	1.25
3 CW(a&s),I:Wolf Gang	1.25
4 E:CW(s),VGi,I:Motorhead	1.25
TPB Steel Harbor	20.00

(Vortex)

1 B:RSd(s),LW,DoM,I:Division 13	1.25
2 I:Hero Zero	1.25
3 PC,I:King Tiger	1.25
4 B:RSd(s),E:MRi(s)BMc,E:LW, E:O:Vortex,C:Vortex	1.25

All comics prices listed are for *Near Mint* condition.

TPB Vortex 20.00
Sourcebook 10.00

CONCRETE
(B&W)
1 PC,R:Concrete, A Stone among
  Stones 12.50
1a 2nd printing 3.00
2 PC,'Transatlantic Swim' 7.00
3 PC 5.00
4 PC 4.00
5 PC,'An Armchair Stuffed
  with Dynamite' 4.00
6 PC,Concrete works on farm . . . 4.00
7 PC,Concrete grows horns . . . 4.00
8 PC,Climbs Mount Everest . . . 3.50
9 PC,Mount Everest Pt.2 . . . . . 3.50
10 PC,last Issue 3.50
TPB 25.00

CONCRETE
1 PC,ColorSpec. 4.00
EarthDay Spec. PC,Moebius 4.00

Concrete #5 © Dark Horse

CONCRETE, A NEW LIFE
1 . . . . 3.50
Spec.Land & Sea,rep. 3.25

CONCRETE: ECLECTICA
1 PC,The Ugly Boy 3.25
2 PC 3.25

CONCRETE: FRAGILE CREATURE
1 PC,'Rulers o/t Omniverse'Pt.1 . 4.00
2 PC,'Rulers o/t Omniverse'Pt.2 . 3.00
3 PC,'Rulers o/t Omniverse'Pt.3 . 3.00
4 PC,'Rulers o/t Omniverse'Pt.3 . 3.00
TPB 15.95

CONCRETE: KILLER SMILE
1 PC 3.50
2 PC 2.95
3 PC 2.95
4 PC, final issue 2.95

COUTOO
1 Lt. Joe Kraft 3.50

CORMAC MAC ART
1 R.E. Howard adapt. 2.25
2 . . . . 2.25
3 . . . . 2.25

CREEPY
(B&W)
1 KD,TS,GC,SL,Horror 3.95
2 TS,CI,DC,Demonic Baby 3.95
3 JM,TS,JG,V:Killer Clown 3.95
4 TS,Final issue 3.95

CRITICAL ERROR
1 rep.Classic JBy story 2.75

DANGER UNLIMITED
Dark Horse-Legend
1 JBy(a&s),KD,I:Danger Unlimited,
  B:BU:Torch of Liberty 2.50
2 JBy(a&s),KD,O:Danger
  Unlimited 2.25
3 JBy(a&s),KD,O:Torch of
  Liberty 2.25
4 JBy(a&s),KD,Final Issue 2.25
TPB rep. 1-4 . . . . 14.95

DARK HORSE CLASSICS
(B&W)
1 Last of the Mohicans 3.95
2 20,000 Leagues Under the Sea 3.95

DARK HORSE COMICS
1 RL,CW,F:Predator,Robocop,
  I:Renegade,Time Cop,(double
  gatefold cover) 4.00
2 RL,CW,F:Predator,Robocop,
  Renegade,Time Cop 3.00
3 CW,F:Robocop,Time Cop,Aliens,
  Indiana Jones 3.00
4 F:Predator,Aliens,Ind.Jones . . 2.75
5 F:Predator,E:Aliens 2.75
6 F:Robocop,Predator,
  E:Indiana Jones 2.75
7 F:Robocop,Predator,B:StarWars 6.00
8 B&I:X,Robocop 14.00
9 F:Robocop,E:Star Wars 6.00
10 E:X,B:Godzilla,Predator,
  James Bond 5.50
11 F:Godzilla,Predator,James
  Bond,B:Aliens 2.75
12 F:Predator 2.75
13 F:Predator,B:Thing 2.75
14 MiB(s),B:The Mark 2.75
15 MiB(s),E:The Mark,B:Aliens . . 2.75
16 B:Predator,E:Thing,Aliens . . . 2.75
17 B:Aliens,Star Wars:Droids . . . 2.75
18 E:Predator 2.75
19 RL(c),B:X,E:Star Wars:Droids,
  Aliens 2.75
20 B:Predator 2.75
21 F:Mecha 2.75
22 B:Aliens, E:Mecha 2.75
23 B:The Machine 2.50
24 The Machine 2.50
25 Final issue 2.50

DARK HORSE PRESENTS
(B&W)
1 PC,I:Concrete 18.00
1a 2nd printing 3.00
2 PC,Concrete 12.00
3 Boris theBear,Concrete 10.00
4 PC,Concrete 9.00
5 PC,Concrete 8.00
6 PC,Concrete 7.00
7 I:MONQ 5.00
8 PC,Concrete 5.00
9 . . . . 5.00
10 PC,Concrete, I:Masque 15.00
11 Mask 12.00
12 PC,Concrete, Masque 10.00
13 Mask 10.00
14 PC,Concrete, Masque 10.00
15 Mask 10.00
16 PC,Concrete, Masque 10.00
17 Mask 10.00
18 PC,Concrete, Mask 10.00
19 Mask 10.00
20 double,Flaming Carrot 12.00
21 Mask 10.00
22 . . . . 3.00

Dark Horse Presents #14
© Dark Horse

23 . . . . 3.00
24 PC,I:Aliens 30.00
25 thru 31 . . . . @3.00
32 . . . . 4.00
33 . . . . 4.00
34 Aliens 12.00
35 Predator 12.00
36 Aliens vs.Predator 15.00
36a painted cover 18.00
37 . . . . 2.50
38 . . . . 2.50
39 . . . . 2.50
40 I:The Aerialist 2.50
41 . . . . 2.50
42 Aliens 5.00
43 Aliens 4.00
44 . . . . 2.50
45 . . . . 2.50
46 Predator 4.00

47 .... 2.50	86 .... 2.50
48 .... 2.50	87 F:Concrete 2.50
49 .... 2.50	88 Hellboy 2.50
50 inc.'Heartbreakers' 2.50	89 Hellboy 2.50
51 FM(c),inc.'Sin City' 10.00	90 Hellboy 2.50
52 FM,inc. 'Sin City' 7.00	91 Blackheart, Baden 2.50
53 FM,inc. 'Sin City' 7.00	92 Too Much Coffee Man 2.50
54 FM,Sin City;JBy Preview	93 Cud, Blackheart 2.50
of Next Men Pt.1 .... 10.00	94 A:Eyeball Kid 2.50
55 FM,Sin City;JBy Preview	95 Too Much Coffee Man 2.50
of Next Men (JBy) Pt.2 ...... 10.00	96 Kabuli Kid 2.50
56 FM,Sin City,JBy,Next MenPt.3	97 F:Kabuki Kid 2.50
Aliens Genocide(prologue) ... 8.00	Fifth Anniv. Special DGi,PC,
57 FM,SinCity;JBy Next Men	SBi,CW,MW,FM,Sin City,
Pt.4 .... 8.00	Aliens,Give Me Liberty 12.00
58 FM,Sin City,Alien Fire 5.00	Milestone Ed.#1,rep.DHP#1 ..... 2.25
59 FM,Sin City,Alien Fire 5.00	TPB rep.Sin City 15.00
60 FM,Sin City 5.00	

| 61 FM,Sin City .... 3.00 |
| 62 FM,E:Sin City .... 3.00 |
| 63 Moe,Marie Dakar .... 2.50 |
| 64 MWg,R:The Aerialist .... 2.50 |
| 65 B:Accidental Death .... 2.50 |
| 66 PC,inc.Dr.Giggles .... 2.50 |
| 67 B:Predator story(lead in to |
| "Race War"),double size ..... 3.95 |
| 68 F:Predator,Swimming Lessons |

Dark Horse Presents #40
© Dark Horse

| (Nestrobber tie-in) .... 2.50 |
| 69 F:Predator .... 2.50 |
| 70 F:Alec .... 2.50 |
| 71 F:Madwoman .... 2.50 |
| 72 F:Eudaemon .... 2.50 |
| 73 F:Eudaemon .... 2.50 |
| 74 .... 2.50 |
| 75 F:Chairman .... 2.50 |
| 76 F:Hermes Vs.the Eye,Ball Kid . 2.50 |
| 77 F:Hermes Vs.the Eye,Ball Kid . 2.50 |
| 78 F:Hermes Vs.the Eye,Ball Kid . 2.50 |
| 79 B:Shadow Empires Slaves .... 2.50 |
| 80 AAd,I:Monkey Man & O'Brien . 10.00 |
| 81 B:Buoy .... 2.50 |
| 82 B:Just Folks .... 2.50 |
| 83 Last Impression .... 2.50 |
| 84 MBn,F:Nexus,E:Hermes Vs.the |
| Eye Ball Kid .... 2.50 |
| 85 Winner Circle .... 2.50 |

DARK HORSE DOWNUNDER
(B&W)

| 1 F:Australian Writers .... 2.50 |
| 2 Australian Writers .... 2.50 |
| 3 Australian Writers, finale ..... 2.50 |

DEADFACE: DOING ISLANDS WITH BACCHUS
(B&W)

| 1 rep. Bacchus apps. .... 2.95 |
| 2 rep. inc.'Book-Keeper of |
| Atlantis .... 2.95 |

DEADFACE: EARTH, WATER, AIR & FIRE
(B&W)

| 1 Bacchus & Simpson in Sicily .. 2.50 |
| 2 A:Don Skylla .... 2.50 |
| 3 Mafia/Kabeirol-War prep. ..... 2.50 |
| 4 Last issue .... 2.50 |

DEAD IN THE WEST
(B&W)

| 1 TT,Joe Landsdale adapt. ..... 5.00 |
| 2 TT,adapt. .... 5.00 |

DEAD IN THE WEST

| 1 TT(c) .... 3.95 |

DEADLINE USA
(B&W)

| 1 rep. Deadline UK,Inc. Tank Girl |
| Johnny Nemo .... 9.95 |
| 2 inc. Tank Girl,Johnny Nemo ... 9.95 |

DEVIL CHIEF

| 1 I:Devil Chief .... 2.50 |

DIVISION 13

| 1 .... 2.50 |
| 2 .... 2.50 |
| 3 A:Payback .... 2.50 |
| 4 Carnal Genesis .... 2.50 |

DR. GIGGLES

| 1 Horror movie adapt. .... 2.50 |
| 2 Movie adapt.contd. .... 2.50 |

DOMINION
(B&W)

| TPB 1 .... 13.95 |

Dr. Giggles #2 © Dark Horse Comics

DOMU: A CHILD'S DREAMS
B&W, Manga

| 1 Psychic Warfare .... 5.95 |
| 2 Murders Continue .... 5.95 |
| 3 Psychic war conclusion ...... 5.95 |

EDGAR RICE BURROUGHS' TARZAN: THE LOST ADVENTURE

| 1 Lost Manuscript .... 2.95 |
| 2 V:Gorgo the Buffalo .... 2.95 |
| 3 V:Bandits .... 2.95 |
| 4 V:Bandits .... 2.95 |

EDGAR RICE BURROUGHS' TARZAN: MUGAMBI

1-shot, Betrayed by 3 man-beasts 2.95

ENEMY

| 1 MZ(c),StG(s),I:Enemy .... 2.75 |
| 2 MZ(c),StG(s),F:Heller .... 2.75 |
| 3 MZ(c),StG(s),A:Heller .... 2.50 |
| 4 .... 2.50 |
| 5 final issue .... 2.95 |

EUDAEMON, THE

| 1 Nel,I:New Eudaemon .... 3.00 |
| 2 Nel,V:Mordare .... 2.75 |
| 3 Nel,V:Mordare .... 2.75 |

EVIL DEAD III: ARMY OF DARKNESS

| 1 JBo,Movie adaptation .... 4.00 |
| 2 JBo,Movie adaptation .... 3.50 |
| 3 JBo,Movie adaptation .... 3.00 |

EYEBALL KID
(B&W)

| 1 I:Eyeball Kid .... 2.25 |
| 2 V:Stygian Leech .... 2.25 |
| 3 V:Telchines Brothers,last iss. ... 2.25 |

FAT DOG MENDOZA
(B&W)
1 I&O:Fat Dog Mendoza 2.50

Flaming Carrot #25 © Dark Horse

FLAMING CARROT
(B&W)
18 . . . . 3.50
18a Ash-Can-Limited 10.00
19 . . . . 2.00
20 . . . . 2.00
21 . . . . 2.00
22 . . . . 2.00
23 . . . . 2.00
24 . . . . 3.00
25 F:TMNT,Mysterymen,w/card . . 4.00
26 A:TMNT 2.50
27 TM(c),A:TMNT conclusion 2.50
28 . . . . 2.50
29 Man in the Moon,Iron City 2.50
30 V:Man in the Moon 2.50
31 A:Fat Fury 2.50

FLAXEN
1 Based on Model,w/poster 2.95

FLOATERS
(B&W)
1 thru 5 From Spike Lee 2.50

FREAKSHOW
1 JBo,DMc,KB,"Wanda the Worm
Woman","Lillie" 9.95

GHOST
Comics' Greatest World
Spec. AH(c) 3.95

GHOST
1 R:Ghost 2.50
2 AH,MfM,Arcadia Nocturne,pt.2 . 2.50
TPB 8.95

GHOST IN THE SHELL
1 Manga Style 3.95

---

2 Wetware Virus 3.95
3 Killer Robots 3.95
4 Rookie Cop Killed 3.95

GIVE ME LIBERTY
1 FM/DGb, Homes & Gardens . . 9.00
2 FM/DGb 7.00
3 FM/DGb 6.00
4 FM/DGb 6.00
TPB 16.00

GODZILLA
(B&W)
1 Japanese Manga 3.50
2 thru 6 . . . . @2.25
Spec #1 . . . . 1.50
TPB 2nd printing 17.95

GODZILLA
COLOR SPECIAL
1 AAd,R:Godzilla,V:Gekido-Jin . . 4.00

GODZILLA
0 RSd,The King of Monsters
is back! 2.50

GODZILLA VS. BARKLEY
1 MBn(s),JBt,DvD 3.50

GRENDEL TALES:
DEVILS AND DEATHS
1 . . . . 2.95
2 . . . . 2.95

GRENDEL TALES:
DEVIL'S CHOICES
1 F:Goran 2.95
2 Marica 2.95
3 Marica vs. Goran 2.95

GRENDEL TALES:
FOUR DEVILS, ONE HELL
1 MWg(c),F:Four Grendels 3.50
2 MWg(c),F:Four Grendels 3.50
3 MWg(c),F:Four Grendels 3.50
4 MWg(c),F:Four Grendels 3.50
5 MWg(c),F:Four Grendels 3.50
6 MWg(c),last issue 3.25

GRENDEL TALES:
THE DEVIL IN
OUR MIDST
1 MWg(c) 3.50
2 MWg(c) 3.25
3 MWg(c) 2.95
4 . . . . 2.95
5 . . . . 2.95

GRENDEL TALES:
THE DEVIL'S HAMMER
1 MWg(a&s),I:Petrus Christus . . . 3.50
2 MWg(a&s),A:P.Christus 3.25
3 MWg(a&s),last issue 3.25

GRENDEL: DEVIL BY
THE DEED
1 MWg,RRa 3.95

GRENDEL: HOMECOMING
1 Babylon Crash 2.95
2 Babylon Crash pt. 2 . . . . 2.95
3 Too Dead To Die 2.95

*Grendel Tales: The Devil in
Our Midst #2 © Dark Horse Comics*

GRENDEL: WAR CHILD
1 MWg 5.00
2 thru 9 MWg 3.00
10 MWg, final issue, dbl.size 4.00

GUNSMITH CATS
1 I:Rally & Mini May 2.95

HAMMER OF
GOD: PENTATHLON
1 MiB(s),NV 2.50

HAMMER OF GOD:
BUTCH
1 MBn 2.50
2 and 3 MBn . . . . @2.50

HAPPY BIRTHDAY
MARTHA WASHINGTON
1 Frank Miller 2.95

HARD BOILED
1 . . . . 7.50
2 and 3 . . . . @7.00
TPB 14.95

HARD LOOKS
(B&W)
1 thru 10 AVs Adaptations . . . @2.50
Book One 14.95

HARLAN ELLISON'S
DREAM CORRIDOR
1 Various stories 2.95
2 Various stories 2.95
3 JBy, I Have No Mouth and I Must
Scream and other stories 2.95
Spec.1 Various stories 4.95

HELLBOY: SEEDS OF DESTRUCTION
Legend/Dark Horse
1 JBy,MMi,AAd,V:Vampire Frog,
BU:Monkeyman & O'Brien ... 4.00
2 MMi(c),JBy,AAd,BU:Monkeyman
& O'Brien 3.00
3 MMi(c),JBy,AAd,BU:Monkeyman
& O'Brien 3.00
4 MMi(c),JBy,AAd,BU:Monkeyman
& O'Brien 3.00

HELLHOUNDS
(B&W)
1 I:Hellhounds 2.50
2 thru 6 A:Hellhounds ...... @2.50

HERBIE
1 JBy,reps.& new material 2.50
2 Reps.& new material 2.50

HERMES VS. THE EYEBALL KID
1 thru 3 Symphony of Blood 2.95

HERO ZERO
1 First and last issue 2.50

*Indiana Jones and the Fate of
Atlantis #1 © Dark Horse Comics*

INDIANA JONES AND THE ARMS OF GOLD
1 In South America 2.75
2 In South America 2.75
3 V:Incan Gods 2.75
4 .... 2.50

INDIANA JONES AND THE FATE OF ATLANTIS
1 DBa,Search for S.Hapgood
w/card 5.00
1a 2nd printing 3.00
2 DBa,Lost Dialogue of Plato ... 3.00
3 Map Room of Atlantis 3.00
4 Atlantis, Last issue 3.00

INDIANA JONES AND THE GOLDEN FLEECE
1 SnW 2.75
2 SnW 2.50

INDIANA JONES AND THE IRON PHOENIX
1 .... 2.50
2 V:Nazis 2.50
3 A:Nadia Kirov 2.50
4 V:Undead 2.50

INDIANA JONES AND THE SHRINE OF THE SEA DEVIL
1 .... 2.50

INDIANA JONES AND THE SPEAR OF DESTINY
1 I:Spear T/Pierced Christ 2.50
2 DSp, with Henry Jones 2.50

INDIANA JONES: THUNDER IN THE ORIENT
1 DBa(a&s),in Tripoli 2.75
2 DBa(a&s),Muzzad Ram 2.75
3 DBa(a&s),V:Sgt.Itaki 2.75
4 DBa(a&s),In Hindu Kush 2.75
5 DBa(a&s),V:Japanese Army . 2.75
6 DBa(a&s),last issue 2.75

INSTANT PIANO
1 Offbeat humor 3.95
2 .... 3.95
3 Various stories 3.95

IRON HAND OF ALMURIC
(B&W)
1 Robert E. Howard adaption .. 2.00
2 A:Cairn,V:Yagas 2.25
3 V:Yasmeena,The Hive Queen . 2.00
4 Conclusion 2.25

JAMES BOND 007: QUASIMODO GAMBIT
1 I:Maximillion Quasimodo 3.95
2 V:Fanatical Soldiers 3.95
3 V:Steel 3.95

JAMES BOND 007: SERPENT'S TOOTH
1 PG,DgM,V:Indigo 5.50
2 PG,DgM,V:Indigo 5.00
3 PG,DgM 5.25
TPB 15.95

JAMES BOND 007: SHATTERED HELIX
1 V:Cerberus 2.50

JAMES BOND 007: A SILENT ARMAGEDDON
1 V:Troy 3.25
2 V:Omega 3.25
3 V:Omega 3.25

JOHNNY DYNAMITE
1 .... 2.95
2 .... 2.95
3 V:Faust 2.95
4 Last issue 2.95

JONNY DEMON
1 SL(c),KBk,NV 2.75
2 SL(c),KBk,NV 2.75
2 SL(c),KBk,NV, final issue 2.50

JUNIOR CARROT PATROL
(B&W)
1 .... 2.00
2 .... 2.00

KINGS OF THE NIGHT
1 .... 2.25
2 end Mini-Series 2.25

THE LEGEND OF MOTHER SARAH
B&W, Manga
1 I:Mother Sarah 2.50
2 Sarah and Tsutsu 2.50

THE MACHINE
1 (a) The Barb Wire spin 2.50
2 V:Salvage 2.50
3 Freak Show 2.50
4 I:Skion 2.50

MADMAN
Legend
1 MiA(s) 3.50
2 MiA(s) 3.25
3 MiA(s) 2.95
4 MiA(s),Muscleman 2.95
5 MiA(s),I:The Blast 2.95
6 MiA(s),A:Big Guy, Big
Brain-o-rama,pt.1 .... 2.95
7 MiA(s),FM,A:Big Guy, Big
Brain-o-rama,pt.2 .... 2.95

MAGNUS/NEXUS
Dark Horse/Valiant
1 MBn(s), SR 3.25
2 MBn(s), SR 3.25

MARK, THE
1 LSn, in America 1.75
2 LSn 1.95
3 LSn 1.95
4 .... 1.95

MARK, THE
(B&W)
1 .... 1.95
2 thru 7 .... @1.75

MARK, THE
1 MiB(s),V:Archon 2.75
2 MiB(s),V:Archon 2.75
3 MiB(s),V:Archon,A:Pierce 2.75
4 MiB(s),last issue 2.75

MARSHALL LAW: CAPE FEAR
1 KON 2.95

MARSHALL LAW: SECRET TRIBUNAL
1 KON 2.95
2 KON 2.95

MARSHALL LAW: SUPER BABYLON
1 KON 4.95

MARTHA WASHINGTON GOES TO WAR
Dark Horse-Legends
1 FM(s),DGb, V:Fat Boys Corp. . 3.25
2 FM(s),DGb, V:Fat Boys Corp. . 3.25
3 FM(s),DGb, V:Fat Boys Corp. . 3.25
4 FM(s),DGb, V:Fat Boys Corp. . 3.25
5 FM(s),DBb, final issue 3.25

MASK
0 . . . . 4.00
1 I:Lt.Kellaway Mask 11.00
2 V:Rapaz & Walter 9.00
3 O:Mask 8.00
4 final issue 7.50
TPB 14.95

MASK
1 Movie Adaptation 3.00
2 Movie Adaptation 2.50

MASK
(B&W)
0 'Who's Laughing Now' 6.00

MASK RETURNS
1 inc.cut-out Mask 6.00
2 Mask's crime spree 4.00
3 . . . . 4.00
4 . . . . 4.00
TPB 14.95

MASK
[Mini-series]
1 Mask Strikes Back pt.1 . . . . . . 2.50
2 Mask Strikes Back pt.2 . . . . . . 2.50
3 Mask Strikes Back pt.3 . . . . . . 2.50
4 DoM,Mask Strikes Back pt.4 . . 2.50

MAXIMUM OVERLOAD
1 Masque (Mask) 25.00
2 Mask 20.00
3 Mask 20.00
4 Mask 20.00

MECHA
1 color 1.75
2 color 1.75
3 thru 6 B&W . . . . @1.75
Spec.(#1) CW(c),color 2.95

METAL OF HONOR
1 Ace of Aces 2.50
2 . . . . 2.50
3 Andrew's Raid 2.50
4 Frank Miller(c) 2.50
5 final issue 2.50

METAL OF HONOR SPECIAL
1 JKu 2.50

MEZZ GALACTIC TOUR
1 MBn,MV 2.50

MR. MONSTER
(B&W)
1 . . . . 3.50
2 . . . . 2.50
3 Alan Moore story 2.50
4 . . . . 2.50
5 I:Monster Boy 2.00
6 . . . . 2.00
7 . . . . 2.00
8 V:Vampires (giant size) 4.95

MOTORHEAD SPECIAL
1 JLe(c),V:Mace Blitzkrieg 3.95

NEW FRONTIER
(B&W)
1 From series in Heavy Metal . . 2.75
2 Who Killed Ruby Fields? 2.75
3 Conclusion 2.75

NEW TWO FISTED TALES: VOL II
1 War stories 4.95

Next Men #11 © Dark Horse Comics

[JOHN BYRNE'S}
NEXT MEN
0 Rep Next Men from Dark
  Horse Presents 8.00
1 JBy,'Breakout'inc.trading
  card certificate 11.00
1a 2nd Printing Blue 3.00
2 JBy,World View 6.00
3 JBy,A:Sathanis 5.00
4 JBy,A:Sathanis 4.00
5 JBy,A:Sathanis 4.00
6 JBy,O:Senator Hilltop,
  Sathanis,Project Next Men . . 3.50
7 JBy,I:M-4,Next Men Powers
  explained 3.50
8 JBy,I:Omega Project,A:M-4 . . 3.00
9 JBy,A:Omega Project,A:M-4 . 3.00
10 JBy,V:OmegaProject,A:M-4 . 3.00
11 JBy,V:OmegaProject,A:M-4 . 3.00
12 JBy,V:Dr.Jorgenson 3.00

13 JBy,Nathan vs Jack 3.00
14 JBy,I:Speedboy 2.75
15 JBy,in New York 2.75
16 JBy,Jasmine's Pregnant 2.75
17 FM(c),JBy,Arrested 2.75
18 JBy,On Trial 2.75
TPB rep.#1-6 . . . . 16.95
TPB Parallel Collection 16.95

NEXT MEN: FAITH
Dark Horse-Legend
1 JBy(a&s),V:Dr.Trogg,
  Blue Dahlia 3.25
2 JBy,(a&s),F:Jack 2.75
3 MMi(c),JBy(a&s),I:Hellboy . . 3.50
4 JBy(a&s),Last issue 2.75

NEXT MEN: LIES
Dark Horse-Legend
1 JBy 2.50
2 JBy 2.50
3 JBy 2.50
4 JBy 2.50

NEXT MEN: POWER
Dark Horse-Legend
1 JBy(a&s) 2.75
2 JBy(a&s) 2.75
3 JBy(a&s) 2.75
4 JBY(a&s), final issue 2.50

NEXUS: ALIEN JUSTICE
1 . . . . 4.25
2 . . . . 4.25
3 . . . . 3.95

NEXUS: THE LIBERATOR
1 "Waking Dreams" 2.75
2 Civil War,D:Gigo 2.75
3 Civil War contd. 2.75
4 Last issue 2.75

NEXUS: THE ORIGIN
1 SR,O:Nexus 4.95

NEXUS: OUT OF THE VORTEX
1 R:Nexus 2.50
2 Zolot & Nexus Together 2.50
3 O:Vortex 2.50

NEXUS: THE WAGES OF SIN
1 The Client 2.95
2 V:Munson 2.95
3 SR(c&a) Murders in New Eden 2.95

NIGHT BEFORE CHRISTMASK
1 Rick Geary 9.95

NINA'S NEW AND IMPROVED ALL-TIME GREATEST
1 Anthology: Nina Paley 2.50

NOSFERATU
(B&W)
1 The Last Vampire 3.95
2 . . . . 2.95

OH MY GODDESS!
B&W, Manga
1 thru 6 .... @2.50
Part 2
1 thru 4 F:Keiichi .... @2.50

ONE BAD RAT
1 BT 2.95
2 .... 2.95
3 .... 2.95
4 .... 2.95

ORION
(B&W)
1 SF manga-Masamune Shirow . 2.50
2 F:Yamata Empire 2.95

OUTLANDERS
(B&W)
1 .... 3.00
2 .... 2.50
3 thru 7 .... @2.00
8 thru 20 .... @2.25
21 Operation Phoenix 2.25
22 thru 30 .... @2.50
31 Tetsua dying 2.50
32 D:The Emperor 2.50
33 Story finale 2.50
#0 The Key of Graciale 2.75

OUTLANDERS: EPILOGUE
(B&W)
1 .... 2.75

OUT OF THE VORTEX
Comics' Greatest World
1 B:JOs(s),V:Seekers 2.25
2 MMi(c),DaW,A:Seekers 2.25
3 WS(c),E:JOs(s),DaW,A:Seeker,
　C:Hero Zero 2.25
4 DaW,A:Catalyst 2.25
5 V:Destroyers,A:Grace 2.25
6 V:Destroyers,A:Hero Zero ... 2.25
7 AAd(c),DaW,V:Destroyers,
　A:Mecha 2.25
8 DaW,A:Motorhead 2.25
9 DaW,V:Motorhead 2.25
10 MZ(c), A:Division 13 ...... 2.25
11 V:Reaver Swarm 2.50
12 Final issue 2.50

PREDATOR
1 CW,Mini Series 28.00
1a 2ndPrinting 8.00
1b 3rdPrinting 2.50
2 CW 14.00
2a 2ndPrinting 5.00
3 CW 10.00
3a 2ndPrinting 2.50
4 CW 7.00
4a 2ndPrinting 2.50

PREDATOR: BAD BLOOD
1 CW,I:John Pulnick 2.75
2 CW,V:Predator 2.75
3 CW,V:Predator,C.I.A. 2.75
4 Last issue 2.50

PREDATOR: BIG GAME
1 Corp.Nakai Meets Predator ... 4.50
2 Army Base Destroyed 3.50

3 Corp.Nakai Arrested 3.50
4 Nakai vs. Predator 3.50
TPB rep. #1-#4 .... 13.95

PREDATOR: BLOODY SANDS OF TIME
1 DBa,CW,Predator in WWI 4.00
2 DBa,CW, WWII cont'd. 3.25

PREDATOR: COLD WAR
1 Predator in Siberia 4.00
2 U.S. Elite Squad in Siberia ... 3.25
3 U.S. vs. USSR commandos ... 3.25
4 U.S. vs. USSR in Siberia 3.00
TPB 13.95

PREDATOR: INVADERS FROM THE FOURTH DIMENSION
1 .... 3.95

PREDATOR JUNGLE TALES
1 Rite of Passage 2.95

PREDATOR: RACE WAR
0 F:Serial Killer 2.75
1 V:Serial Killer 2.75
2 D:Serial Killer 2.75
3 in Prison 2.75
4 Last Issue 2.75

PREDATOR 2
1 DBy, Movie Adapt Pt1 ...... 3.50
2 MBr, Movie Adapt. Pt2 ..... 3.00

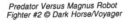

Predator Versus Magnus Robot Fighter #2 © Dark Horse/Voyager

PREDATOR VS. MAGNUS ROBOT FIGHTER
Valiant/Dark Horse
1 LW,A:Tekla 7.00
1a Platinum Ed. 30.00
1b Gold Ed. 15.00
2 LW,Magnus Vs. Predator 4.00

PRIMAL
1 Contd.from Primal:from the
　Cradle to the Grave 2.95
2 A:TJ Cyrus 2.50

Propeller Man #6 © Dark Horse Comics

PROPELLER MAN
1 I:Propeller Man 2.95
2 O:Propeller Man,w/2 card strip . 2.95
3 V:Manipulator 2.95
4 V:State Police,w/2 card strip .. 2.95
5 V:Manipulator 2.95
6 V:Thing, w/2 card strip 2.95
7 .... 2.95
8 Last issue,w/2 card strip 2.95

PUMPKINHEAD
1 Based on the movie 2.50

RACE OF SCORPIONS
(B&W)
1 A:Argos,Dito,Alma,Ka 2.25

RACE OF SCORPIONS
Book 1 short stories 5.00
Book 2 .... 4.95
Book 3 .... 4.95
Book 4 Final issue 2.50

RACK & PAIN
1 GCa(c),I:Rack,Pain 2.50
2 GCa(c),V:Web 2.50
3 GCa(c),V:Web 2.50
4 GCa(c),Final Issue 2.50

RASCALS IN PARADISE
1 I:Spicy Sanders 3.95
2 .... 3.95
3 last issue 3.95

REBEL SWORD
1 B&W 2.50
2 B&W 2.50
3 B&W 2.50
4 V:Ruken 2.50
5 Choice of Jiro 2.50
6 R:Ruken 2.50

REDBLADE
1 V:Demons 2.50
2 V:Tull 2.50
3 Last Issue 2.50

RING OF ROSES
(B&W)
1 Alternate world,1991 . . . . 2.50
2 Plague in London 2.50
3 Plague cont.A:Secret Brotherhood
  of the Rosy Cross 2.50
4 Conclusion 2.50

RIO AT BAY
1 F:Doug Wildey art 2.95
2 F:Doug Wildey art 2.95

ROACHMILL
(B&W)
1 thru 8 . . . . @3.50
9 and 10 . . . . @2.00

ROBOCOP: MORTAL COILS
1 V:Gangs 2.75
2 V:Gangs 2.75
3 V:Coffin,V:Gangs 2.75

Robocop Versus Terminator #4
© Dark Horse Comics

ROBOCOP VERSUS TERMINATOR
1 FM(s),WS,w/Robocop cut-out . 3.50
2 FM(s),WS,w/Terminator cut-out 3.00
3 FM(s),WS,w/cut-out 3.00
4 FM(s),WS,Conclusion 3.00

ROBOCOP: PRIME SUSPECT
1 Robocop framed 2.75
2 thru 4 V:ZED-309s . . . . @2.50
Collected 13.95

ROBOCOP: ROULETTE
1 V:ED-309s 2.75
2 I:Philo Drut 2.75
3 V:Stealthbot 2.75

4 last issue 2.75

ROBOCOP 3
1 B:StG(s),Movie Adapt 2.75
2 V:Aliens,OCP 2.75
3 HNg,ANi(i) 2.75

THE SAFEST PLACE
SC, SD 2.50

SECRET OF THE SALAMANDER
(B&W)
1 Jacquestardi, rep 2.95

SEX WARRIORS
1 I:Dakini 2.50
2 V:Steroids 2.50

THE SHADOW
1 MK 2.75
2 MK 2.50

THE SHADOW: HELL'S HEAT WAVE
1 Racial War 2.95
2 MK,V:ghost 2.95

THE SHADOW: IN THE COILS OF LEVIATHAN
1 MK,V:Monster 3.25
2 MK 3.25
3 MK,w/ GfD poster 3.25
4 MK,Final issue 3.25
TPB, reprints #1–#4 . . . . 13.95

THE SHADOW AND THE MYSTERIOUS THREE
1 Three stories 2.95

SHADOW EMPIRE: FAITH CONQURES
1 CsM 2.95
2 CsM,V:Vaylen 2.95
3 CsM 2.95
4 CsM, final issue 2.95

SIN CITY: A DAME TO KILL FOR
Dark Horse-Legend (B&W)
1 FM(a&s),I:Dwight,Ava 6.00
1a 2nd printing 3.25
2 FM(a&s),A:Ava 5.00
2a 2nd printing 3.25
3 FM(a&s),D:Ava's Husband 5.00
3a 2nd printing 2.95
4 FM(a&s) 4.50
5 FM(a&s) 4.50
6 FM(a&s),Final issue 4.00
TPB rep. #1–#6, new pages . . . 15.00
HC rep. #1–#6, new pages 25.00

SIN CITY: A SMALL KILLING
Dark Horse-Legend
1 GN 14.00

SIN CITY: BABE WORE RED
Dark Horse-Legend
1 PM 2.95

SIN CITY: BIG FAT KILL
Dark Horse-Legend
1 FM 3.50
2 FM 3.25
3 FM, Dump the Stiffs 2.95
4 FM, Town Without Pity 2.95
5 FM, final issue 2.95

SPACEHAWK
(B&W)
1 BW reps. 2.25
2 thru 4 BW . . . . @2.00
5 BW 2.50

STAN SHAW'S BEAUTY & THE BEAST
1 Based on the book 4.95

STARSTRUCK
(B&W)
1 Expanding Universe Pt1 . . . . . 2.95
2 Expanding Universe Pt2 . . . . . 2.95

STAR WARS: DARK EMPIRE
1 CK,Destiny of a Jedi 35.00
1a 2nd Printing 5.00
1b Gold Ed. 50.00
2 CK,Destroyer of worlds,
  very low print run 40.00
2a 2nd Printing 5.00
2b Gold Ed. 50.00
3 CK,V:The Emperor 18.00
3a 2nd printing 4.00
3b Gold Ed. 50.00
4 CK,V:The Emperor 15.00
4a Gold Ed. 50.00
5 CK,V:The Emperor 14.00
5a Gold Ed. 50.00
6 CK,V:Emperor,last issue 12.00
6a Gold Ed. 50.00
TPB rep.#1-6 . . . . 19.95

STAR WARS DARK EMPIRE II
1 2nd chapter 3.25
2 F:Boba Fett 2.95
3 V:Darksiders 2.95
4 Luke Vs. Darksiders 2.95
5 Creatures 2.95
6 CK,DvD(c), save the twins . . . 2.95

STAR WARS: DROIDS
1 F:C-3PO,R2-D2 . . . . 3.25
2 V:Thieves 2.75
3 on the Hosk moon 2.75
4 . . . . 2.75
5 A meeting 2.50
6 final issue 2.50
Spec.#1 I:Olag Greck 2.50

2nd Series
1 Deputized Droids 2.50
2 Marooned on Nar Shaddaa . . . 2.50

Star Wars: Dark Empire #5
© Dark Horse Comics

STAR WARS: JABBA THE HUTT
1 F:Jabba the Hutt 2.50

STAR WARS: RIVER OF CHAOS
1 LSi,JBr,Emperor sends spies . . 2.50

STAR WARS: TALES OF THE JEDI
1 RV,I:Ulic Qel-Droma	5.00
2 RV,A:Ulic Qel-Droma	4.00
3 RV,D:Andur	3.50
4 RV,A:Jabba the Hut	3.00
5 RV,last issue	3.00
TPB	14.95

STAR WARS: TALES OF THE JEDI: DARK LORDS OF THE SITH
1 Bagged with card	2.75
2	2.50
3 Krath Attack	2.50
4 F:Exar Kun	2.50
5 V:TehKrath	2.50
6 Final battle	2.50

STAR WARS: TALES OF THE JEDI: THE FREEDON NADD UPRISING
1	2.75
2	2.50

SUPERMAN VS. ALIENS
DC/Dark Horse
1 DJu,KN 4.95

TALES OF ORDINARY MADNESS
(B&W)
1 JBo(c),Paranoid	3.00
2 JBo(c),Mood	2.50

3 JBo(c),A Little Bit of
Neurosis 2.50

TANK GIRL
(B&W)
1 Rep. from U.K.Deadline Mag. .	5.00
2 V:Indiana Potato Jones	4.00
3 On the Run	3.50
4	3.50
TPB colorized	14.95
[2nd Series]	
1	3.50
2	3.50
3	3.00
4 Last issue	3.00

TANK GIRL
1	3.00
2	3.00

TERMINAL POINT
1	2.50
2	2.50

TERMINATOR
1 CW,Tempest	6.00
2 CW,Tempest	5.00
3 CW	3.00
4 CW, conclusion	3.00

TERMINATOR: END GAME
1 JG,Final *Terminator* series	3.00
2 JG,Cont.last Term.story	2.75
3 JG,(Conclusion of Dark Horse Terminator stories)	2.75

TERMINATOR: ENEMY WITHIN
1 cont. from Sec.Objectives	4.00
2 C890.L.threat contd.	3.00
3 Secrets of Cyberdyne	3.00
4 Conclusion	3.00
SC rep #1-4	13.95

TERMINATOR: HUNTERS & KILLERS
1 V:Russians	3.00
2 V:Russians	2.75
3 V:Russians	2.75

TERMINATOR: ONE SHOT
1 MW,3-D const(c2,pop-up
inside 7.00

TERMINATOR: SECONDARY OBJECTIVES
1 cont. 1st DH mini-series	5.00
2 PG,A:New Female Terminator .	4.00
3 PG,Terminators in L.A.&Mexico	4.00
4 PG,Terminator vs Terminator concl.	4.00

THING, THE
1 JHi, Movie adaptation	5.00
2 JHi, Movie adaptation	3.50

THE THING: COLD FEAR
1 R:Thing	3.00
2	2.75

THING FROM ANOTHER WORLD: CLIMATE OF FEAR
1 Argentinian Military Base (Bahiathetis)	2.75
2 Thing on Base	2.75
3 Thing/takeover	2.75
4 Conclusion	2.75
TPB	15.95

THING FROM ANOTHER WORLD: ETERNAL VOWS
1 PG,I:Sgt. Rowan	2.75
2 PG	2.75
3 PG,in New Zealand	2.75
4 PG,Last issue	2.75

THIRTEEN O'CLOCK
(B&W)
1 Mr.Murmer,from Deadline USA 2.95

TIME COP
1 Movie Adaptation	2.75
2 Movie Adaptation	2.50

TITAN
Spec.#1 BS(c),I:Inhibitors 4.25

TREKKER
(B&W)
1 thru 4	@1.50
5 thru 7	@1.75
8 O:Trekker	1.50
9	1.50

TREKKER
1 . . . . 2.95

TWO FISTED TALES
Spec. WW,WiS 4.95

2112
TPB GNv, JBy,A:Next Men . . .	17.00
2nd printing	9.95
3rd printing	9.95

[ANDREW VACHSS'] UNDERGROUND
(B&W)
1 AVs(s)	4.25
2 AVs(s)	3.95
3 AVs(s)	3.95
4 AVs(s)	3.95

UNIVERSAL MONSTERS
1 AAd,Creature From The Black Lagoon	5.50
2 The Mummy	5.50

VAMPIRELLA
(B&W)
1 'The Lion and the Lizard'Pt.1 . .	4.50
2 'The Lion and the Lizard'Pt.2 . .	3.95
3 'The Lion and the Lizard'Pt.3 . .	3.95
4 'The Lion and the Lizard'Pt.3 . .	3.95

All comics prices listed are for *Near Mint* condition.

Venus Wars II #11
© Dark Horse Comics, Inc.

VENUS WARS
(B&W)

1 Aphrodia V:Ishtar		3.00
2 I: Ken Seno		2.50
3 Aphrodia V:Ishtar		2.50
4 Seno Joins Hound Corps.		2.50
5 SenoV:Octopus Supertanks		2.50
6 Chaos in Aphrodia		2.50
7 All Out Ground War		2.50
8 Ishtar V:Aphrodia contd.		2.50
9 Ishtar V:Aphrodia contd.		2.50
10 Supertanks of Ishtar Advance		2.50
11 Aphrodia Captured		2.50
12 A:Miranda,48pgs		2.75
13 Hound Brigade-Suicide Assault		2.25
14 V:Army		2.50
15		2.50

VENUS WARS II

1 V:Security Police		2.75
2 Political Unrest		2.25
3 Conspiracy		2.25
4 A:Lupica		2.25
5 Love Hotel		2.25
6 Terran Consulate		2.25
7 Doublecross		2.25
8 D:Lupisa		2.95
9 A:Matthew		2.95
10 A:Mad Scientist		2.95
11 thru 15 V:Troopers		@2.95

VIRUS

1 MP(c),F:The Wan Xuan & the crew of the Electra		3.00
2 MP(c),V:Captian Powell		3.00
3 MP(c),V:Virus		3.00
4 MP(c),Last issue		3.00
TPB rep.#1–#4		16.95

VERSION
(B&W)

1.1 thru 2.6 by H. Sakaguchi ... 2.75

2.7 by H. Sakaguchi 2.50

VORTEX, THE
1 .... © 2.00

WARWORLD!
(B&W)
1 .... 1.75

WHITE LIKE SHE
(B&W)

1		2.95
2		2.95
3		2.95

WILL TO POWER
Comics' Greatest World

1 BS, A:X		1.25
2 BS, A:X,Monster		1.25
3 BS, A:X		1.25
4 BS, In Steel Harbor		1.25
5 V:Wolfgang		1.00
6 V:Motorhead		1.00
7 JOy(c),V:Amazing Grace		1.00
8 V:Catalyst		1.00
9 Titan, Grace		1.00
10 Vortex alien, Grace		1.00
11 Vortex alien, King Titan		1.00
12 Vortex alien		1.00

WIZARD OF FOURTH STREET
(B&W)

1 thru 4 .... @1.75

WOLF & RED

1 Looney Tunes		2.50
2 Watchdog Wolf		2.50

X #4 © Dark Horse Comics

X
Comics' Greatest World

1 B:StG(s),DoM,JP,I:X-Killer		3.00
2 DoM,JP,V:X-Killer		2.25
3 DoM,JP,A:Pit Bulls		2.25
4 DoM,JP		2.25
5 DoM,JP,V:Chaos Riders		2.00

6 Cyberassassins		2.00
7 Alamout		2.00
8 A:Ghost		2.50
9 War for Arcadia		2.50
10 War for Arcadia		2.50
11 I:Coffin, War		2.50
12 V:Coffin, A:Monster		2.50
13 D:X		2.50
14 conclusion to War		2.50
15 JS,SiG,war survivors		2.50

X: ONE SHOT TO THE HEAD
1 .... 2.50

XXX

1		3.95
2 V:Dr. Zemph		3.95
3		3.95
4 V:Rhine Lords		3.95
5 I:Klaar		3.95
6 Klaar captured		4.95

YOUNG CYNICS CLUB
(B&W)
1 .... 2.50

Young Indiana Jones #6
© Dark Horse Comics

THE YOUNG INDIANA JONES CHRONICLES

1 DBa,FS,TV Movie Adapt		3.25
2 DBa,TV Movie Adapt		2.75
3 DBa,GM		2.75
4 DBa,GM		2.75
5 DBa,GM		2.75
6 BBa,GM,WW1,French Army		2.75
7 The Congo		2.75
8 Africa,A:A.Schweitzer		2.50
9 Vienna,Sophie-daughter of Arch-Duke Ferdinand		2.50
10 In Vienna continued		2.50
11 Far East		2.50
12 Fever Issue		2.50

All comics prices listed are for *Near Mint* condition.

ANGELA
1 Angela 1.95
2 NGa(s),I:Spawn 2.25
3 NGa(s),In Hell 2.25

ART OF ERIK LARSEN
1 Sketchbook 4.95

ART OF HOMAGE STUDIOS
1 Various Pin-ups,All Homage
    Artists 4.95

BACKLASH
1 Taboo 1.95
2 Savage Dragon 1.95
3 V:Savage Dragon 2.50
4 SRf,A:Wetworks 2.50
5 SRf,A:Dane 2.50
6 BBh,SRf,A:Wetworks 2.50
7 BBh,SRf,A:Bounty Hunters . . . 2.50
8 RMz,BBh,BWS(c),WildStorm
    Rising,pt.8,w/2 cards 2.50
8a Newsstand ed. 1.95

BADROCK
1a RLd(p),TM(c), A:Dragon 1.75
1b SPa(ic),A:Savage Dragon . . . 1.75
1c DF(ic) 1.75
2 RLd,ErS(s),V:Girth,A:Savage
    Dragon 1.75
3 RLd,ErS,V:The Overlord 1.75

BADROCK AND COMPANY
1 KG(s), ... 2.50
1a San Diego Comic Con Ed. . . . 5.00
2 RLd(c),Fuji 2.50
3 Overtkill 2.50
4 A:Velocity 2.50
5 A:Grifter 2.50
6 Finale, A:Shadowhawk 2.50

BATTLESTONE
1 New Series 2.50
2 I&D:Roarke, finale 2.50

BLACK AND WHITE
1 New heroes 1.95
2 ATi(p),apparent death 1.95
3 V:Chang 1.95

BLOODSTRIKE
1 A:Brigade,Rub the Blood(c) . . . 3.50
2 V:Brigade,B:BU:Knight 2.50
3 B:ErS(s),ATi(c),V:Coldsnap . . . 2.25
4 ErS(s), ... 2.25
5 KG,A:Supreme, ... 2.25
6 KG(s),CAx,C&J:Chapel 2.25
7 KG,RHe,A:Badrock 2.25
8 RHe,A:Spawn 2.25
9 RHe,Extreme Prejudice #3, I:Extreme
    Warrior,ATh,BU: Black & White 2.25
10 V:Brigade, B:BU:Knight 1.95
11 ErS(s),ATi(c),V:Coldsnap 1.95
12 ErS(s) 1.95
13 KG,A:Supreme 2.50
14 KG(s),CAx,C&J:Chapel 2.50
15 KG,RHe,A:Badrock 1.95
16 KG,RHe 1.95
17 V:The Horde 2.50
18 Extreme Sacrifice pt. 2 . . . . . 2.50

19 V:The Horde 2.50
20 R:Deadlock New Order 2.50
21 KA,V:Epiphany New Order . . . 2.50

BLOODWULF
[Miniseries]
1 RLd,R:Bloodwulf 2.50
2 A:Hot Blood 2.50
3 Slippery When Wet 2.50
4 final issue 2.50

BOOF
1 . . . . 1.95
2 Meathook 1.95
3 Joyride 1.95
4 Beach 1.95
5 Down on the Farm 1.95
6 V:Gangster Chimps 1.95

BOOF AND THE BRUISE CREW
1 . . . . 1.95
2 . . . . 1.95
3 . . . . 1.95
4 . . . . 1.95
5 Supermarket 1.95
6 I:Mortar, O:Bruise Crew 1.95

Brigade #1 © Rob Liefeld

BRIGADE
[1st Series]
1 RLd(s),MMy,I:Brigade 5.00
1a Gold Ed. 5.00
2 RLd(s),V:Genocide,w/coupon#4 4.00
2a w/o coupon 2.00
3 V:Genocide 2.50
4 CyP,Youngblood#5 flip 2.50
[2nd Series]
0 RLd(s),ATi(c),JMs,NRd,I:Warcry,
    A:Emp,V:Youngblood 2.25
1 V:Bloodstrike 2.75
2 C:Coldsnap 3.50
3 ErS(s),GP(c),MMy,NRd(i),
    V:Bloodstrike 2.25
4 Rip(s),MMy,RHe,I:Roman,
    BU:Lethal 2.25
5 Rip(s),MMy, ... 2.25

6 Rip(s),MMy,I:Coral,BU:Hackers
    Tale 2.25
7 Rip(s),MMy,V:Worlok 2.25
8 ErS(s),MMy,Extreme Prejudice
    #2,BU:Black & White 2.25
9 ErS(s),MMy,Extreme Prejudice
    #6,ATh,BU:Black & White 2.25
25 ErS(s),MMy,D:Kayo,Coldsnap,
    Thermal, ... 2.25
10 Extreme Prejudice 1.95
11 WildC.A.T.S 2.50
12 Battlestone 2.50
13 Thermal 1.95
14 Teamate deaths 1.95
15 R:Roman Birds of Prey 1.95
16 Extreme Sacrifice pt.3 . . . . . . 2.50
17 MWn,I:New Team 2.50
18 I:The Shape New Order 2.50
19 MWn,F:Troll 2.50
20 MWn,alien cult saga,concl. . . . 2.50
Sourcebook 2.95

CHAPEL
1 F:Chapel, BWn 2.50
2 V:Colonel Black 2.50

CODENAME: STYKE FORCE
1 MS(s),BPe,JRu(i), ... 2.25
2 MS(s),BPe,JRu(i), ... 2.25
3 MS(s),BPe,JRu(i), ... 1.95
4 MS(s),BPe,JRu(i), ... 1.95
5 MS(s),BPe,JRu(i), ... 1.95
6 MS(s),BPe,JRu(i), ... 1.95
7 MS(s),BPe,JRu(i), ... 1.95
8 MS(s),BPe,JRu(i), ... 1.95
9 New Teamate 1.95
10 SvG, B:New Adventure 1.95
11 F:Bloodbow 1.95
12 F:Stryker 1.95
13 SvG(s),F:Strkyer 2.25
Spec.#0 O:Stryke Force 2.50

CYBERFORCE
[Limited Series]
0 WS,O:Cyber Force 2.50
1 MS,I:Cyberforce,w/coupon#3 . 10.00
1a w/o coupon 4.00
2 MS,V:C.O.P.S. 4.00
3 MS 2.50
4 MS,V:C.O.P.S,BU:Codename
    Stryke Force. 2.50
[Regular Series]
1 EcS(s),MS,SW, ... 2.25
2 EcS(s),MS,SW,Killer
    Instinct #2,A:Warblade 2.25
3 EcS(s),MS,SW,Killer
    Instinct #4, A:WildC.A.T.S. . . . 2.25
4 EcS(s),MS,Ballistic 1.95
5 EcS(s),MS 1.95
6 EcS(s),MS,Ballistic's Past 1.95
7 S.H.O.C.s 1.95
8 . . . . 1.95
9 A:Huntsman 1.95
10 A:Huntsman 1.95
11 . . . . 1.95
12 T.I.M.M.I.E. goes wild 1.95
13 EcS,MS,O:Cyberdata 2.25
14 EcS,MSI,V:T.I.M.M.I.E. 2.25
Ashcan 1 (San Diego) 25.00
Ashcan 1 (signed) 30.00
Sourcebook 1 . . . . 2.50
Sourcebook 2 I:W.Zero 2.50
Ann.#1 O:Velocity 2.50

TPB new art 12.95
TPB EcS,MS,SW,Assault with a
   Deadly Woman 9.95

CYBERFORCE ORIGINS
1 O:Cyblade 2.50
2 O:Stryker 2.50

DARKER IMAGE
1 BML,BCi(s),RLd,SK,JLe,I:Blood
   Wulf,Deathblow,Maxx 3.00
1a Gold logo(c) 50.00
1b White(c) 30.00
Ashcan 1 . . . . 15.00

DEADLY DUO
1 A:Killcat 2.50
2 A:Pitt, O:Kid Avenger 2.50
3 A:Roman, O:Killcat 2.50
4 A:Savage Dragon 2.50

DEATHBLOW
1 JLe,MN,I:Cybernary 2.75
2 JLe,BU:Cybernary 2.25
3 JLe(a&s),BU:Cybernary 1.95
4 JLe(s),TSe,BU:Cybernary 1.95
5 JLe(s),TSe,BU:Cybernary 1.95
5a different cover 14.00
6 Black Angel 1.95
7 . . . . 1.95
8 Black Angel 1.95
9 The Four Horseman 1.95
10 Michael Cray, Sister Mary 1.95
11 A:Four Horseman 1.95
12 Final Battle 2.50
13 New Story Arc 2.50
14 A:Johnny Savoy 2.50
15 F:Michael Cray 2.50
16 TvS,BWS(c),WildStorm
   Rising,pt.6,w/2 cards 2.50
16a Newsstand ed. 1.95
Ashcan 1 . . . . 16.00

DOOM'S IV
1 I:Doom's IV 2.50
1a Variant(c) 2.50
2 MECH-MAX 2.50
3 Dr. Lychee, Brick 2.50
4 Dr. Lyche, Syber-idol 2.50
Sourcebook 2.50

THE DRAGON
BLOOD AND GUTS
[Miniseries]
1 I:Grip 2.50
2 JPn,KIS 2.50
3 JPn,KIS,finale 2.50

EXTREME
CHRISTMAS SPECIAL
Various artists, new work 2.95

EXTREME SACRIFICE
Prelude A:Everyone 2.50
Epiloque, conclusion 2.50

EXTREME TOUR BOOK
Tour Book 1992 . . . . 3.00
Tour Book 1994 . . . . 25.00

EXTREME ZERO
0 RLd,CYp,ATi(i),I:Cybrid,
   Law&Order,Risk,Code 9,
   Lancers,Black Flag 2.75

Freak Force #7 © Erik Larsen

FREAK FORCE
1 EL(s),KG 2.25
2 EL(s),KG 2.25
3 EL(s),KG 2.25
4 EL(s),KG,A:Vanguard 2.25
5 EL(s),KG 2.25
6 EL(s),KG 2.25
7 EL(s),KG 2.25
8 EL(s),space ants 2.25
9 EL(s),Cyberforce 2.25
10 EL(s),Savage Dragon 2.25
11 EL(s),Invasion pt.1 . . . . 2.50
12 EL(s),Invasion pt.2 . . . . 2.50
13 EL(s),Invasion pt.3 . . . . 2.50
14 EL(s),Team Defeated 2.50
15 EL(s),F:Barbaric 2.50
16 KG,EL(s),V:Chelsea Nirvana . . 2.50
17 EL,KG,major plots converge . . 2.50

GEN¹³
0 . . . . 5.00
1 JLe(s),BCi(s),I:Fairchild,Grunge,
   Freefall,Burnout 40.00
1a 2nd printing 5.00
2 JLe(s),BCi(s), ... 28.00
3 JLe(s),BCi(s),A:Pitt 22.00
4 JLe(s),BCi(s) 12.00
5 Final issue 6.00
5a different cover 13.00
TPB 12.95
Regular Series
1 BCi(s),V:Mercenaries 2.95
2 BCi,BWS(c),WildStorm
   Rising,pt.4, w/2 cards 2.50
2a Newsstand ed. 1.95

GLORY
1 JDy,F:Glory 2.50
2 JDy,V:Demon Father 2.50
3 JDy,A:Rumble & Vandal 2.50

GRIFTER-ONE SHOT
1 SS,DN 1.95

GRIFTER
1 BWS(c), WildStorm
   Rising,pt.5,w/2 cards 2.50
1a Newsstand Ed. 1.95

GROO
1 SA 1.95
2 A:Arba, Dakarba 1.95
3 The Generals Hat 1.95
4 A Drink of Water 1.95
5 SA,A Simple Invasion 1.95
6 SA,A Little Invention 1.95

HELLSHOCK
1 I:Hellshock 1.95
2 Powers & Origin 1.95
3 New foe 1.95
4 . . . . 1.95

HOMAGE STUDIOS
Swimsuit Spec.#1 JLe,WPo,
   MS 2.25

IMAGE ZERO
0 I:Troll,Deathtrap,Pin-ups,rep.
   Savage Dragon #4,O:Stryker,
   F:Shadowhawk 40.00

IMAGES OF
SHADOWHAWK
1 KG,V:Trencher 2.25
2 thru 3 V:Trencher 2.25

KILLER INSTINCT
TOUR BOOK
1 All Homage Artist,I:Crusade . . . 5.00
1a signed 45.00

KINDRED
1 JLe,BCi(s),BBh,I:Knidred 12.00
2 JLe,BCi(s),BBh,V:Kindred 6.00
3 JLe,BCi(s),BBh,V:Kindred 5.00
3a WPo(c),Alternate(c) 11.00
4 JLe,BCi(s),BBh,V:Kindred 3.00
TPB rep. #1–#4 . . . . 9.95

KNIGHTMARE
1 I:Knightmare MMy 2.50
2 I:Caine 2.50
3 RLd,AV,The New Order,
   F:Detective Murtaugh 2.50
4 RLd,AV,MMy,I:Thrillkill 2.50

LEGEND OF SUPREME
1 KG(s),Revelations pt.1 . . . . . . 2.50
2 Revelations pt.2 . . . . 2.50
3 Conclusion 2.50

MAXX
1/2 SK,from Wizard 15.00
1 SK,I:The Maxx 2.25
1a glow in the dark(c) 50.00
2 SK,V:Mr.Gone 2.25
3 SK,V:Mr.Gone 2.25
4 SK, ... 2.25
5 SK, ... 2.25
6 SK, ... 2.25
7 SK,A:Pitt 2.25

8 SK,V:Pitt	1.95
9 SK	1.95
10 SK	1.95
11 SK	1.95
12 SK	1.95
13 Maxx Wanders in Dreams	1.95
14 R:Julie	1.95
15 Julia's Pregnant	1.95
16 SK,Is Maxx in Danger?	1.95
TPB	12.95

MYSTERY, INC.
Ashcan 1	13.50

THE NEW ORDER HANDBOOK
Various artists	1.50

NEWMEN
1 JMs,	2.25
2 JMs,I:Girth	2.25
3 JMs,V:Girth,I:Ikonna	2.25
4 JMs,A:Ripclaw	1.95
5 JMs,Ripclaw,V:Ikonn	2.50
6 JMs	2.50
7 JMs	2.50
8 JMs,Team Youngblood	2.50
9 Kodiak Kidnapped	2.50
10 Extreme Sacrifice pt.4	2.50
11 F:Reign	2.50
12 R:Elemental	2.50
13 ErS,I:Bootleg	2.50
14 ErS,Dominion's Secret	2.50

1963
1 AnM(s),RV,DGb,I:Mystery, Inc.	2.50
1a Gold Ed.	50.00
2 RV,SBi,DGb,JV,I:The Fury	2.25
3 RV,SBi,I:U.S.A.	2.25
4 JV,SBi,I:N-Man, Johnny Beyond	2.25
5 JV,SBi,I:Horus	2.25
6 JV,SBi,I:Tommorrow Synicate, C:Shaft	2.25

NORMAL MAN/ MEGATON MAN SPECIAL
1	2.50

OPERATION KNIGHTSTRIKE
1 RHe,A:Chapel,Bravo, Battlestone	2.50

THE OTHERS
0 JV(s),From Shadowhawk	2.50
1 JV(s)V:Mongrel	2.50
2 JV,Mongrel takes weapons	2.50

PACT
1 JV(s),WMc,I:Pact, C:Youngblood	2.25
2 JV(s),V:Youngblood	1.95
3 JV(s),V:Atrocity	1.95

PHANTOM FORCE
1 RLd,JK,w/card	2.75
2 JK,V:Darkfire	1.95

PITT
1 DK,I:Pitt,Timmy	7.00

2 DK,V:Quagg	4.00
3 DK,V:Zoyvod	3.00
4 DK,V:Zoyvod	2.50
5 DK	2.25
6 DK	2.25
7 DK	2.25
8 Ransom	1.95
9 DK,Artic Adventures	1.95
Ashcan 1	17.00

POWER OF THE MARK
1 I:Ted Miller	2.50
2 V:The Fuse	2.50
3 TMB(s), The Mark	2.50
4 TMB,The Mark's secrets revealed	2.50

PROPHET
0 San Diego Comic-Con Ed.	5.00
1 RLd(s)DPs,O:Prophet	3.50
1a Gold Ed.	15.00
2 RLd(s),DPs,C:Bloodstrike	2.50
3 RLd(s),DPs,V:Bloodstrike, I:Judas	2.50
4 RLd(s),DPs,A:Judas	2.50
4a SPI(c),Limited Ed.	16.00
5 SPI	3.50
6 SPI	2.50
7 SPI War Games pt.1	1.95
8 SPI War Games pt.2	2.50
9 Extreme Sacrifice Prelude	2.50
10 Extreme Sacrifice pt.6	2.50
Sourcebook	2.95

[Regular Series]
1 SPI, New Series	2.50
2 SPL, New Direction	2.50

RIPCLAW
1 A:Killjoy, I:Shadowblade	2.50
2 Cyblade, Heatwave	2.50
3 EcS,BPe,AV,Alliance with S.H.O.C.s	2.50

SAVAGE DRAGON
1 EL,I:Savage Dragon	10.00
2 EL,I:Superpatriot	6.00
3 EL,V:Bedrock,w'coupon#6	6.00
3a EL,w/o coupon	2.50
Savage Dragon Versus Savage Megaton Man 1 EL,DSm,Dragon Vs.Megaton Man	2.50
Gold Ed.	30.00
TBP	9.95

[2nd Series]
1 EL,I:Freaks	2.75
2 EL,V:Teen.Mutant Ninja Turtles, Flip book Vanguard #0	3.50
3 EL,A:Freaks	2.25
4 EL,A:Freaks	2.25
5 EL,Might Man flip book	2.25
6 EL,A:Freaks	2.25
7 EL,Overlord	2.25
8 EL,V:Cutthroat,Hellrazor	2.25
9 thru 10 EL,	2.25
11 EL,A:Overlord	1.95
12 EL	1.95
13 EL,Mighty Man,Star,I:Widow (appeared after issue #20)	2.50
14 Possessed pt.1	2.50
15 Possessed pt.2	2.50
16 Possessed pt.3,V:Mace	2.50
17 V:Dragonslayer	2.50
18 R:The Fiend	2.50
19 V:The Fiend	2.50

Shadowhawk #3 © Jim Valentino

SHADOWHAWK
1 JV,I:Shadowhawk,Black Foil(c), Pin-up of The Others,w/ coupon#1	12.00
1a w/o coupon	6.00
2 JV,V:Arsenal,A:Spawn, I:Infiniti	4.50
3 JV,V:Arsenal,w/glow-in-the-dark(c)	3.00
4 V:Savage Dragon	2.50
TPB rep.#1-4	19.95

[2nd Series]
1 JV,Die Cut(c)	3.50
1a Gold Ed.	25.00
2 JV,Shadowhawk I.D.	4.00
2a Gold Ed.	30.00
3 Poster(c),JV,w/Ash Can	3.25

[3rd Series]
1 JV,CWf,V:Vortex,Hardedge, Red Foil(c)	2.25
1a Gold Ed.	20.00
2 JV,CWf,MA,I:Deadline, BU&I:US Male	2.25
3 JV(a&s),Shadowhawk has AIDS, V:Hardedge,Blackjak	2.50
4 JV(a&s),V:Hardedge,	2.25

Note: #5 thru #11 not used; #12 below is the next issue, and the 12th overall.

12 Monster Within, pt.1	1.95
13 Monster Within, pt.2	1.95
14 Monster Within, pt.3	2.50
15 Monster Within, pt.4	2.50
16 Monster Within, pt.5	2.50
17 Monster Within, pt.6	2.50
18 JV,D:Shadowhawk	2.50

SHADOWHAWK/ VAMPIRELLA
Book 2 V:Kaul	4.95

Note: Book #1: see Vampi/Shadowhawk.

SHAMAN'S TEARS
1 MGr,I:Shaman,B:Origin	4.00
1a Siver Prism Ed.	35.00
2 MGr,Poster(c)	3.50
3 MGr,V:Bar Sinister	2.50
4 MGr,V:Bar Sinister,E:Origin	1.95
5 MGr,R:Jon Sable	1.95

---

6 MGr,V:Jon Sable 1.95
7 MGr,V:Rabids 1.95
8 MGr,A:Sable 1.95
9 MGr,The Becoming of
  Broadarrow 1.95

Spawn #10 © Todd McFarlane

SPAWN

1 TM,I:Spawn,w/GP,DK
  pinups 15.00
2 TM,V:The Violator 13.00
3 TM,V:The Violator 11.00
4 TM,V:The Violator,
  w/coupon #2 . . . . 16.00
4a w/o coupon 6.00
5 TM,O:Billy Kincaid 8.00
6 TM,I:Overt-Kill 7.00
7 TM,V:Overt-Kill 7.00
8 TM,AMo(s),F:Billy Kincaid . . 4.00
9 NGa(s),TM,I:Angela 4.00
10 DS(s),TM,A:Cerebus 3.50
11 FM(s),TM 3.50
12 TM,Chapel killed Spawn 3.00
13 TM,A:Youngblood 3.00
14 TM,A:The Violator 2.75
15 TM 2.75
16 GCa,I:Anti-Spawn 2.50
17 GCa,V:Anti-Spawn 2.50
18 GCa,ATi,D:Anti-Spawn 2.50
19 thru 20 . . . . . **NOT RELEASED**
21 TM 2.50
22 TM 2.25
23 TM 2.25
24 TM 2.25
25 Image X Book 2.25
26 TM 1.95
27 I:The Curse 1.95
28 Faces Wanda 1.95
29 Returns From Angela 1.95
30 A:KKK 1.95
31 R:Redeemer 1.95
32 TM,GCa,New Costume 1.95
TPB Capital Collection rep.#1-3
  limited to 1,200 copies 300.00
TPB TM,rep.#1–#5 . . . . 9.95

SPAWN/BATMAN
Image/DC

1 FM(s),TM, ... 4.50

SPLITTING IMAGE

1 DSm,A:Marginal Seven 2.25
2 DsM,A:Marginal Seven 2.25

STORMWATCH

0 JSc(c),O:Stormwatch,
  V:Terrorists,w/card 2.50
1 JLe(c&s),ScC,TvS(i),
  I:Stormwatch 2.25
1a Gold Ed. 25.00
2 JLe(c&s),ScC,TvS(i),I:Cannon,
  Winter,Fahrenheit,Regent 2.25
3 JLe(c&s),ScC,TvS(i),V:Regent,
  I:Backlash 2.25
4 V:Daemonites 2.25
5 SRf(s),BBh,V:Daemonites 2.25
6 BCi,ScC,TC,A:Mercs 2.25
7 BCi,ScC,TC,A:Mercs 2.25
8 BCi,ScC,TC,A:Mercs 2.25
9 BCi,I:Defile 2.25
25 BCi,A:Spartan 2.50
10 V:Talos 1.95
11 the end? 1.95
12 V:Hellstrike 1.95
13 V:M.A.D.-1 . . . . 1.95
14 Despot 1.95
15 Batallion, Flashpoint 1.95
16 V:Defile 1.95
17 D:Batallion 1.95
18 A:Argos 2.50
19 R:M.A.D.-1,L:Winter 2.50
20 F:Cannon,Winter,Bendix . . . 2.50
21 V:Wildcats 2.50
22 RMz,BWS(c),WildStorm
  Rising,pt.9,w/2 cards 2.50
22a Newsstand ed. 1.95
Sourcebok JLe(s),DT 2.75
Spec.#1 RMz(s),DT, ... 4.25
Spec.#2 F:Fleshpoint 2.50
Ashcan 1 . . . . 14.00

SUPER-PATRIOT

1 N:Super-Patriot 2.25
2 KN(i),O:Super-Patriot 2.25
3 A:Youngblood 2.25
4 . . . . 1.95

SUPREME

1 B:RLd(s&i),BrM,
  V:Youngblood 3.00
1a Gold Ed. 60.00
2 BrM,I:Heavy Mettle 2.50
3 thru 4 BrM 2.50
5 BrM(a&s),Clv(i),I:Thor,
  V:Chrome 2.50
6 BrM,Clv(i),I:Starguard,
  A:Thor,V:Chrome 2.50
7 Rip,ErS(s),SwM,A:Starguard,
  A:Thor, ... 2.50
8 Rip(s),SwM,V:Thor, ... 2.50
9 Rip&KtH(s),BrM,Clv(i),
  V:Thor 2.50
10 KrH(s),BrM,JRu(i),
  BU:I:Black & White 2.50
11 I:Newmen 2.50
12 SPa(c),RLd(s),SwM 2.25
25 SPa(c),RLd(s),SwM,V:Simple
  Simon,Images of Tomorrow . . 1.95
13 B:Supreme Madness 1.95
14 Supreme Madness, pt.2 . . . . 1.95
15 RLd(s)A:Spawn 2.50
16 V:Stormwatch 2.50
17 Supreme Madness, pt.5 . . . . 2.50
18 E:Supreme Madness 2.50

19 V:The Underworld 2.50
20 V:The Unterworld 2.50
21 God Wars 2.50
22 God Wars, V:Thor 2.50
23 Extreme Sacrifice pt.1 . . . . . 2.50
24 Identity Questions 2.50
#25, see above
26 F:Kid Supreme 2.50
27 Rising Son,I:Cortex 2.50
28 Supreme Apocalypse:Prelude . 2.50
Ann.#1 TMB,CAd,KG,I:Vergessen 2.95
Ashcan #1 . . . . 22.00
Ashcan #2 . . . . 15.75

SUPREME: GLORY DAYS

1 Supreme in WWI 2.95
2 Supreme in WWI 2.95

TEAM 7

1 New team 3.50
2 New powers 2.50
3 Members go insane 2.50
4 final issue,V:A Nuke 2.50

TEAM 7
OBJECTIVE: HELL
[Mini-series]

1 CDi,CW,BWS(c),WildStorm
  Rising,Prologue,w/2 cards 2.50
1a Newsstand ed. 1.95

TEAM YOUNGBLOOD

1 B:ErS(s),ATi(c),CYp,NRD(i),
  I:Masada,Dutch,V:Giger 2.25
2 ATi(c),CYp,NRd(i),V:Giger . . . 2.25
3 RLd(s),CYp,NRd(i),C:Spawn,
  V:Giger 2.25
4 ErS(s), ... 2.25
5 ErS(s),CNn,V:Lynx 2.25
6 ErS(s),N:Psi-Fire,
  BU:Black&White 2.25
7 ErS(s),CYp,ATh,Extreme
  Prejudice#1,I:Quantum,
  BU:Black & White 2.25
8 ErS(s),CYp,ATh,Extreme
  Prejudice#5,V:Quantum,
  BU:Black&White 2.25
9 . . . . 1.95
10 ErS(s),CYp,ATh, ... 1.95
11 RLd,ErS,Cyp 1.95
12 RLd,ErS,Cyp 2.50
13 ErS,Cyp 2.50
14 RLd,ErS,Cya 2.50
15 New Blood 2.50
16 I:New Sentinel, Bloodpool . . . 2.50
17 Extreme Sacrifice pt.5 . . . . . 2.50
18 MS, membership drive 2.50

TOP COW/
BALLISTIC STUDIOS

Swimsuit Spec.#1 MS(c) 2.95

TRENCHER

1 KG,I:Trencher 2.25
2 KG, ... 2.25
3 KG,V:Supreme 2.25
4 KG,V:Elvis 2.25

TRIBE

1 TJn(s),LSn,I:The Tribe 2.50
1a Ivory(White) Editon 65.00
Ashcan 1 . . . . 14.00

TROLL
1 RLd(s),JMs,I:Evangeliste,
  V:Katellan Command, ... 2.50

TROLL: ONCE A HERO
1 Troll in WWII 2.50

UNION
0 O:Union 2.50
0a WPo(c), ... 2.50
1 MT,I:Union,A:Stormwatch 2.75
2 MT 2.75
3 MT 2.75
4 MT,Good Intentions 2.75
Regular Series
1 R:Union, Crusade 2.50
2 V:Crusade & Mnemo 2.50
3 A:Savage Dragon 2.50
4 JRo,BWS(c), WildStorm
  Rising,pt.3,w/2 cards 2.50
4a Newsstand ed. 1.95

VANGUARD
1 EL(s),BU:I:Vanguard 2.25
2 EL(s),Roxann, ... 2.25
3 AMe, ... 2.25
4 AMe, ... 2.25
5 AMe,V:Aliens 2.25
6 V:Bank Robber 1.95

VIOLATOR
1 AMo(s),BS,I:Admonisher 2.25
2 AMo(s),BS 1.95
3 AMo(s),BS,last issue 1.95

VIOLATOR/BADROCK
[Mini-series]
1 AMo(s),A:Celestine 2.50

WARBLADE:
ENDANGERED SPECIES
1 I:Pillar 2.95
2 V:Ripclaw 2.50
3 I:Skinner 2.50
4 final issue 2.50

WEAPON ZERO
T-Minus-4 WS 2.50

WETWORKS
1 WPo 4.50
2 WPo,BCi 3.50
3 WPo,BCi,V:Vampire 2.50
4 WPo,BCi,Dozer 2.50
5 WPo,BCi,Pilgrim's Turn 2.50
6 WPo,BCi,Civil War 3.50
7 WPo,BCi,F:Pilgrim 2.50
8 WPo,SW,BWS(c), Wildstorm
  Rising,pt.7,w/2 cards 2.50
8a Newsstand ed. 1.95
Sourcebook 2.50

WILDC.A.T.S.
1 B:BCi(s),JLe,SW(i),
  I:WildC.A.T.S. 8.00
1a Gold Ed. 90.00
1b Gold and Signed 125.00
2 JLe,SW(i),V:Master Gnome,
  I:Wetworks,Prism foil(c),
  w/coupon#5 . . . . 11.00
2a w/o coupon 4.00

3 RLd(c),JLe,SW(i),
  V:Youngblood 5.00
4 E:BCi(s),JLe,LSn,SW(i),w/card,
  A:Youngblood,BU:Tribe 5.00
4a w/red card 50.00
5 BCi(s),JLe,SW,I:Misery 3.00
6 BCi(s),JLe,SW,Killer Instinct,
  A:Misery,C:Ripclaw 3.00
7 BCi(s),JLe,SW,
  A:Cyberforce 3.50
8 BCi(s),JLe,SW, ... 4.50
9 BCi(s),JLe,SW, ... 3.00
10 CCi(s),JLe,SW,I:Huntsman . . . 2.50
11 CCi(s),JLe,SW,V:Triad,
  A:Huntsman 2.50
11a WPo(c) 8.00
12 JLe,CCi,A:Huntsman 2.50
13 JLe,CCi,A:Huntsman 2.50
14 X book 2.50
15 F:Black Razors 2.50
16 Black Razors 2.50
17 A:Stormwatch 2.50
18 R:Hightower 2.50
19 V:Hightower 2.50
20 TC,JeR,BWS(c),WildStorm
  Rising,pt.2,w/2 cards 2.50
20a Newsstand ed. 1.95
Spec.#1 SrG(s),TC,SW,I:Destine,
  Pin-ups 3.50
Spec.#2 . . . . 2.50
TPB rep. #1-4,w/0 . . . . 11.00

Wildstar #1 © Image Comics

WILDC.A.T.S
ADVENTURES
1 From animated TV series 2.50
2 Helspont,Troika 2.00
3 Caught in war 2.00
4 V:The President 2.50
5 I:Lonely 2.50
6 I:Majestics 2.50
7 . . . . 2.50
8 Betrayed 2.50
9 V:Black Razors 2.50
Sourcebook (JS(c) 2.95

WILDC.A.T.S. TRILOGY
1 BCi(s),JaL,V:Artemis 2.50
2 BCi(s),JaL,V:Artemis 2.25

3 BCi(s),JaL,V:Artemis 2.25

WILDSTAR
1 JOy,AG,I:Wildstar 2.25
1a Gold Ed. 50.00
2 JOy,AG 2.25
3 JOy,AG,V:Savage Dragon,
  D:Wildstar 2.25
4 JOy,AG,Last Issue,Pin-ups . . . 2.25
TPB 12.95

WILDSTORM RISING
1 JeR,BWS(c&a) WildStorm Rising,
  pt.1:Tricked by Defile,
  w/2 cards 2.50
1a Newsstand ed. 1.95
2 RMz,BBo,BWS(c) WildStorm
  Rising,pt.10,w/2 cards 2.50
2a Newsstand ed. 1.95
Wildstorm Sourcebook #1 . . . . . 2.50

YOUNGBLOOD
0 RLd,O:Youngblood,w/coupon#7 3.00
0a without coupon 2.50
0b gold coupon 60.00
1 RLd,I:Youngblood(flipbook) . . . 7.00
1a 2nd print.,gold border 3.00
1b RLD,Silent Edition 12.95
2 RLd,I:Shadowhawk 7.50
3 RLd,I:Supreme 3.00
4 RLd,DK,A:Prophet,BU:Pitt 3.00
5 RLd,Flip book,w/Brigade #4 . . . 2.75
6 RLd(a&s),J:Troll,Knight Sabre,
  2nd Die Hard, Proposal to
  Girl friend 3.50
7 Badrock, V:Overkill 2.50
8 Chapel, V:Spawn 2.50
9 . . . . 2.50
10 Bravo, Badrock, Troll 2.50
Yr.Bk.#1 CYp,I:Tyrax 2.75
Ashcan #1 . . . . 35.00
Ashcan #2 . . . . 29.50
TPB rep. #1-#5 . . . . 16.95

YOUNGBLOOD
BATTLEZONE
1 BrM 2.25
2 . . . . 2.95

YOUNGBLOOD
STRIKEFILE
1 JaL,RLd,I:Allies,A:Al
  Simmons (Spawn) 3.00
1a Gold Ed. 30.00
2 JaL,RLd,V:Super Patriot,
  Giger 2.75
2a Gold Ed. 30.00
3 RLd,JaL,DaM(i),
  A:Super Partiot 2.75
4 I:Overkill 2.75
5 . . . . 2.95
6 flip book 2.95
7 flip book 2.95
8 Shaft 2.95
9 Knight Sabre 2.95
10 I:Bloodpool 2.50
11 O:Link Crypt 2.50
TPB rep.#1-#3,sketchbook 12.95

YOUNGBLOOD:
YEAR ONE
1 RLd, the early years 2.50

ARROW
1 V:Dr.Sheldon,A:Man O'War . . . 1.95

BATTLETECH: FALLOUT
1 3 tales, Based on FASA game . 2.95
2 V:Clan Jade Falcon 2.95
3 R:Lea 2.95
4 Conclusion 2.95

BRAVURA PREVIEW BOOK
1995 . . . . 1.50

BREAK-THRU
Ultraverse
1 GJ(s),GP,AV(i),A:All
    Ultraverse Heroes 2.75
2 GJ(s),GP,AV(i),A:All
    Ultraverse Heroes 2.75

'BREED
Bravura
[Limited Series]
1 JSn(a&s),Black (c),I:Stoner . . . 5.00
2 JSn(a&s),I:Rachel 3.00
3 JSn(a&s),V:Rachel 2.75
4 JSn(a&s),I:Stoner's Mom 2.75
5 JSn(a&s),V:Rachel 2.75
6 JSn(a&s),final issue 2.50

'BREED II
Bravura
[Limited Series]
1 JSn,The Book of Revelation . 2.95
1a gold foil edition 17.95
2 JSn,A:Rachel 2.95
3 JSn,V:Actual Demon 2.95
4 JSn,Language of Demons 2.95
5 JSn,R:Rachael 2.95
6 JSn,final issue 2.95

BRUCE LEE
1 MBn(s), Stories of B.Lee 2.95
2 MBn(s), Stories of B.Lee 2.95
3 MBn(s), Stories of B.Lee 2.95
4 . . . . 2.95
5 . . . . 2.95
6 conclusion 2.95

CURSE OF RUNE
1A CU,Rune/Silver Surfer tie-in . . 2.50
1B CU, alternate cover 2.50

DEAD CLOWN
1 I:Force America 2.50
2 I:Sadistic Six 2.50
3 TMs(s),last issue 2.50

DINOSAURS FOR HIRE
1 3-D rep. B&W 3.50
[2nd Series]
1 B:TMs(s),A:Reese,Archie,
    Lorenzo 3.00
2 BU:Dinosaurs 2099 . . . . 2.50
3 A:Ex-Mutants 2.50
4 V:Poacher,Revenue 2.50
5 . . . . 2.50
6 V:Samantha 2.50
7 V:Turret 2.50
8 Genesis#2 . . . . 2.50

9 Genesis#5 . . . . 2.50
10 Flip(c) 2.50
11 V:Tiny Lorenzo 2.50
12 I:Manhatten Bob 2.50
13 I:Lil' Billy Frankenstein 2.50
14 . . . . 2.50

DREADSTAR
Bravura
1 JSn(c),PDd(s),EC,I:New
    Dreadstar (Kalla),w/stamp 2.75
2 JSn(c),PDd(s),EC,w/stamp . . . 2.50
3 JSn(c),PDd(s),EC,w/stamp . . . 2.75
4 PDd,EC,Kalla's origin,w/stamp . 2.50
5 PDd,F:Vanth,w/stamp 2.50
6 PDd,w/stamp 2.50
7 PDd,V:Vanth 2.50

EDGE
Bravura
1 GK,I:Edge 2.50
2 GK,STg,Gold Stamp 2.50
3 GK,The Ultimates 2.50
4 GK,V:Mr. Ultimate 2.50

ELIMINATOR
Ultraverse
0 Man,DJa,MZ,Zothros tries to re-open
    passage to the Godwheel 2.95
1 MZ,Man,DRo, The Search for the
    Missing Infinity Gems,I:Siren . . 2.95
1a Black Cover ed. 3.95

ELVEN
Ultraverse
0 Rep.,double size 2.95
Mini-Series
1 A:Prime, Primevil 2.50
2 AaL,R:Maxi-Man 2.50
3 AaL,V:Duey, Primevil 2.50
4 AaL,F:Primevil 2.50

ETERNITY TRIPLE ACTION
B&W
1 F:Gazonga 1.95
2 F:Gigantor 2.50

EX-MUTANTS
1 I&O:Ex-Mutants 2.25
2 V:El Motho,Beafcake,Brickhouse 2.25
3 A:Sliggo,Zygote 2.25
4 . . . . 2.25
5 Piper Kidnapped 1.95
6 A:Dr.Kildare 1.95
7 V:Dr.Kildare 1.95
8 O:Gelson 1.95
9 F:Dillion 1.95
10 F:Sluggtown 1.95
11 Man(s),Genesis#1,w/card 2.25
12 R0M(s),Genesis#4 . . . . 2.25
13 J:Gravestone,Arc 2.25
14 C:Eye 2.25
15 A:Arrow 2.50
16 A:Arrow,I:KillCorp 2.50
17 A:Arrow,V:KillCorp 2.50
18 A:Arrow,V:KillCorp 2.50

EXILES
Ultraverse
1 TMs(s),PaP,I:Exiles 5.00
1a w/out card 2.25

Exiles #3 © Malibu Comics

1b hologram ed. 40.00
1c Ultra-limited 30.00
2 V:Kort 3.00
3 BWS,Mastodon,BU:Rune 4.00
4 V:Kort 3.00

FERRET
1 (From Protectors),DZ,V:Purple
    Dragon Tong,A:Iron Skull 2.25
[Regular Series]
1 thru 3 . . . . 2.50
4 V:Toxin 2.50
4a Newstand Ed. 2.25
5 SEr,Genesis 2.25
6 SEr,Genesis crossover 2.25
7 V:Airman 2.25
8 I:Posse 2.25
9 DZ,R:Iron Skull,I:Deathsong . . . 2.25
10 DZ 2.25
11 . . . . 2.25

FIREARM
Ultraverse
0 w/video 17.00
1 I:Firearm 3.00
2 BWS,A:Hardcase,BU:Rune . . . 2.75
3 V:Sportsmen 2.25
4 HC,Break-Thru x-over 2.25
5 O:Prime 2.25
6 A:Prime 2.25
7 V:Killer 2.25
8 DIB(c) 2.25
9 at the Rose Bowl 1.95
10 The Lodge 2.25
11 Ultraverse Premier #5,
    BU:Prime 3.50
12 Rafferty Saga,pt.1 . . . . 1.95
13 Rafferty Saga,pt.2 . . . . 1.95
14 Swan 1.95
15 Rafferty Saga,pt.3 . . . . 1.95
16 Rafferty Saga,pt.4 . . . . 1.95
17 Rafferty Saga,pt.5 . . . . 1.95
18 JeR,HC(c),Rafferty Saga,finale 2.50

FLOOD RELIEF
Ultraverse
TPB Ultraverse Heroes 5.00

FRANKENSTEIN

1 movie promo	2.50
2	2.50
3	2.50

FREEX
Ultraverse

1 I:Freex w/Ultraverse card	5.00
1a Ultra-Limited	25.00
1b Full Hologram (c)	45.00
2 L:Valerie,I:Rush	4.00
3 A:Rush	3.00
4 GJ(s),DdW,BWS,BU:Rune	2.75
5 GJ(s),V:Master of the Hunt	2.50
6 GJ(s),BH,Break Thru x-over, A:Night Man	2.25
7 BHr,MZ,O:Hardcase	2.25
8 BHr,V:Lost Angel	2.25
9 BHr,A:Old Man	2.25
10 BHr,V:Ms. Contrary	2.25
11 BHr,E:Origins	2.25
12 GJ,Ultraforce	1.95
13 New look	1.95
14 R:Boomboy	1.95
15 Death of Teamate	3.50
16 Prelude to Godwheel	1.95
17 A:Rune	2.50
18 GJ,A:Contray, Cayman, Juice	2.50
Giant Size#1 A:Prime	2.50

GENESIS

0 GP,w/Pog,F:Widowmaker, A:Arrow	3.50
0a Gold Ed.	15.00

GODWHEEL
Ultraverse

0 R:Argus to Godwheel	2.50
1 I:Primevil	2.50
2 Hardcase new costume	2.50
3 F:Lord Pumpkin	2.50
TPB Wheel of Thunder,rep.#0–#3	9.95

GRAVESTONE

1 D:Gravestone,V:Wisecrack	2.25
1a Newstand Ed.	1.95
2 A:Eternal Man, V:Night Plague	2.25
2a Newstand Ed.	1.95
3 Genesis Tie in,w/skycap	2.25
4 Genesis	2.25
5 V:Scythe	2.25
6 V:Jug	1.95
7 R:Bogg	2.25
8	2.25
9	2.25

HARDCASE
Ultraverse

1 I:Hardcase,D:The Squad	5.00
1a Ultra-Limited	25.00
1b Full Hologram (c)	50.00
2 w/Ultraverse card	4.00
3 Hard decisions	3.00
4 A:Strangers	3.00
5 BWS,V:Hardwire,BU:Rune	3.00
6 V:Hardwire	2.75
7 ScB,Break-Thru x-over, I:Nanotech,A:Solution	2.25
8 GP,O:Solitare	2.25
9 B:O:Choice,I:Turf	2.25
10 O:Choice	2.25
11 ScB,V:Aladdin	2.25
12 AV,A:Choice	1.95

Hardcase #3 © Malibu Comics

13 A:Choice	2.25
14 A:Choice	2.25
15 Hardwires, NIM-E	1.95
16 NIM-E	3.50
17 Prime,NIM-E	1.95
18 V:Nim-E, Battle Royale	1.95
19 Prelude to Godwheel	1.95
20 R:Rex Mindi	2.50
21 Mundiquest prelude	2.50
22 Mundiquest.	2.50
23 A:Loki	2.50

HOSTILE TAKEOVER

1 ashcan Ultraverse x-over	.75

LITA FORD
Rock-It Comix

1 JBa	3.95

LORD PUMPKIN

0 Sludge	2.50

MAN CALLED A-X
Bravura
[Limited Series]

0 1st Puzzle piece	2.95
1 MWn,SwM	2.95
1a Gold foil Edition	18.50
2 MWn,SwM,VLElectobot	2.95
3 MWn,SwM,Mercy Island	2.95
4 MWn,SwM,One Who Came Before	2.95
5 MWn,SwM,Climax	2.95

MAN OF WAR

1 thru 3 V:Lift	2.50
1a thru 5a Newsstand Ed.	1.95
4 w/poster	2.50
5 V:Killinger	2.50
6 KM,Genesis Crossover	2.50
7 DJu,Genesis Crossover	2.50
8 TMs(s),A:Rocket Ranger	2.25
9 thru 12	@2.25

MANTRA
Ultraverse

1 AV,I:Mantra,w/Ultraverse card	5.00
1a Full Hologram (c)	35.00
2 AV,V:Warstrike	3.00
3 AV,V:Kismet Deadly	3.00
4 BWS,Mantra's marriage, BU:Rune	3.00
5 MiB(s),AV(i),V:Wiley Wolf	2.25
6 MiB(s),AV(i),Break Thru x-over	2.25
7 DJu,TA,A:Prime, O:Prototype	2.25
8 B:MiB(s),A:Warstrike	2.25
9 V:Iron Knight,Puppeteer	2.25
10 NBy(c),DaR,B:Archmage Quest, Flip/UltraversePremiere #2	3.75
11 MiB(s),V:Boneyard	1.95
12 MiB(s),A:Strangers	2.25
13 Topaz, Boneyard	2.25
14 Tradesmen, Boneyard	2.25
15 A:Prime,Doc Gross	1.95
16 A:Prime	1.95
17 A:Necromantra	1.95
18 Pregnancy	2.50
19 MiB,Pregnancy	2.50
20 Aftermath of Godwheel	2.50
21 TyD,MiB,Mantra goes bad	2.50
Giant Sized#1 GP(c),I:Topaz	2.50
Ashcan #1	12.00

MANTRA: SPEAR OF DESTINY
Ultraverse

1 Search for Artifact	2.50
2 MiB,Eden vs. Aladdin	2.50

MEGADETH
Rock-it Comix

1	4.25

METALLICA
Rock-it Comix

1	4.25

METAPHYSIQUE
Bravura
[Limited Series]

1 NBy,I:Metaphysique	2.95
1a Gold foil edition	10.50
2 NBy,Mandelbrot malfunctions	2.95
Ashcan NBy,B&W	1.00

MIGHTY MAGNOR

1 thru 5 SA	@1.95
6 SA	1.95

MONSTER POSSE
B&W

1 I:Monster Posse	2.50
2 I:P.O.N.E,Wack Mack Dwac's sister,D-Vicious	2.50

MORTAL KOMBAT

0 Four stories	2.95
1 Based on the Video Game	2.95
1a Foil Ed	14.95
1b with new material	2.95
2 thru 4	@2.95
5 I:Mortal Kombat II	2.95
6 Climax	2.95

All comics prices listed are for *Near Mint* condition.

MORTAL KOMBAT
1 Tournament edition 3.95

MORTAL KOMBAT: BATTLEWAVE
1 New series 2.95
2 Action, Action, Action 2.95
3 The Gathering 2.95
4 F:Goro 2.95

MORTAL KOMBAT: GORO PRINCE OF PAIN
1 Goro 2.95
1a Platinum Edition 6.25
2 Goro, V:Kombatant 2.95
3 Goro, V:God of Pain 2.95

MORTAL KOMBAT: RAYDEN AND KANO
1 J:Rayden Kano 2.95
1a Deluxe Edition 4.95
2 A:Reptile 2.95
3 Kano 2.95

MORTAL KOMBAT: U.S. SPECIAL FORCES
1 V:Black Dragon 3.50
2 V:Black Dragon 2.95

NECROSCOPE
1 Novel adapt., holo(c) 3.25
1a 2nd printing 2.95
2 Adapt.continued 2.95
3 . . . . 2.95
4 . . . . 2.95
Book II
1 thru 5 . . . . 2.95

NECROMANTRA/ LORD PUMPKIN
Ultraverse
1 A:Loki (from Marvel) 2.95
2 MiB,V:Godwheel, flipbook 2.95

NIGHT MAN, THE
Ultraverse
1 I:Night Man,Deathmask 2.75
1a Silver foil (c) 15.00
2 GeH,V:Mangle 2.25
3 SEt,GeH,A:Freex,Mangle 2.25
4 HC,I:Scrapyard,O:Firearm 2.25
5 SEt(s) 2.25
6 V:TNTNT 2.25
7 V:Nick 2.25
8 V:Werewolf 1.95
9 V:Werewolf 2.25
10 . . . . 1.95
11 . . . . 1.95
12 . . . . 1.95
13 . . . . 1.95
14 V:Rafferty 1.95
15 I:Rigoletto 1.95
16 I:Bloodfly 3.50
17 D:Playland 2.50
18 DZ,SEt,V:Bloodfly 2.50
19 DZ,SEt,V:Deathmask 2.50
20 DZ,V:Bloody fly 2.50
Ann.#1 V:Pilgrim, 64pg. 3.95

NOCTURNALS
Bravura
[Limited Series]
1 DIB,I:Nocturnals 2.95
1a Newstand Edition 2.95
2 DIB,I:Komodo, Mister Fane . . . 2.95
3 DIB,F:Raccoon 2.95
4 DIB,I:The Old Wolf 2.95

ORIGINS
Ultraverse
1 O:Ultraverse Heroes 1.25

OZZY OSBORNE
Rock-It Comix
1 w/guitar pick 3.95

PANTERA
Rock-it Comix
1 . . . . 3.95
1a Gold Ed. 19.95

PLAN 9 FROM OUTER SPACE
GNv Movie Adapt. 4.95

POWER & GLORY
Bravura
1A HC(a&s),I:American
   Powerhouse 3.50
1B alternate cover 3.50
1c Blue Foil (c) 10.00
1d w/seirgraph 10.00
1e Newsstand 3.00
2 HC(a&s),O:American
   Powerhouse 2.75
3 HC(a&s) 2.50
4 HC(a&s) 2.50
Winter Special 2.95
TPB Series reprint, w/stamp . . . 12.95

PRIME
Ultraverse
1 B:GJ(s),I:Prime 7.50
1a Ultra-Limited 35.00
1b Full Hologram (c) 60.00
2 V:Organism 8, with
   Ultraverse card 8.00
3 NBy,I:Prototype 5.00
4 NBy,V:Prototype 4.00
5 NBy,BWS,I:Maxi-Man,
   BU:Rune 3.00
6 NBy,A:Pres. Clinton 2.75
7 NBy,Break-Thru x-over 2.25
8 NBy,A:Mantra 2.25
9 NBy,Atomic Lies 2.25
10 NBy,A:Firearm,N:Prime 2.25
11 NBy 2.25
12 NBy,(Ultraverse Premiere#3)
   I:Planet Class 3.50
13 NBy,V:Kutt, Planet Class 2.95
14 DaR,I:Voodoo Master 2.25
15 abused kids 1.95
16 I:Turbo 1.95
17 Atalon 1.95
18 Prime's new partner 1.95
19 Prime accused 1.95
20 GJ,LeS,A:Rafferty 2.50
21 GJ,LeS,World without Prime . . 2.50
22 GJ,LeS,F:Primevil 2.50
Ashcan (first) 16.00
Ashcan #1 BV(c),B&W 75

Ann.#1 R:Doc Gross 3.95
TPB Rep. #1-#4 . . . . 9.95

PROJECT A-KO
1 Based on the Movie 2.95
2 Based on the Movie 2.95
3 Based on the Movie 2.95
4 Based on the Movie 2.95

Protectors #13 © Malibu Comics

PROTECTORS
1 I:Protectors,inc.JBi poster
   (direct) 3.00
1a thru 12a Newsstand . . . . . @1.95
2 V:Mr.Monday,w/poster 2.50
3 V:Steel Army,w/poster 2.50
4 V:Steel Army 2.50
5 Die Cut(c),V:Mr.Monday 2.50
6 V:Mr.Monday 2.50
7 A:Thresher 2.50
8 V:Wisecrack 1.95
9 V:Wisecrack 2.50
10 I:Mantoka 2.50
11 A:Ms.Fury,V:Black Fury 2.50
12 A:Arrow 2.50
13 RAJ(s),Genesis#3 . . . . 2.25
14 RB(c),RAJ(s),Genesis#6 . . . . . 2.25
15 RAJ(s),J:Chalice 2.25
16 So Help Me God 2.25
17 L:Ferret 2.25
18 V:Regulators,BU:Mantako,
   R:Mr. Monday 2.25
19 A:Gravestone,Arc 2.50
20 V:Nowhere Man 2.50
Protectors Handbook 2.50

PROTOTYPE
Ultraverse
1 V:Ultra-Tech,w/card 3.00
1a Ultra-lim. silver foil(c) 12.00
1b Hologram 25.00
2 I:Backstabber 3.00
3 LeS(s),DvA,JmP,BWS,
   V:Ultra-Tech,BU:Rune 3.00
4 TMs(s),V:Wrath 2.25
5 TMs(s),A:Strangers,Break-
   Thru x-over 2.25
6 TMs(s),Origins Month

C:Arena 2.25
7 TMs(s),V:Arena 2.25
8 TMs(s),V:Arena 2.25
9 Prototype Unplugged 2.25
10 TMs(s),V:Prototype 1.95
11 TMs(s),R:Glare 2.25
12 V:Ultratech 1.95
13 Ultraverse Premiere #6 . . . . . . 3.50
14 Jimmy Ruiz, new boss 1.95
15 Techuza, Donoza 1.95
16 New CEO for Terrordy 1.95
17 Ranger Vs. Engine 1.95
18 Turf War 2.50
G-Size, Hostile Takeover 2.50
Spec.#0 LeS,JQ/JP(c) 2.50

PROTOTYPE: TURF WAR
Ultraverse
1 LeS,V:Techuza 2.50
2 LeS,F:Ranger,Arena 2.50

RAFFERTY
1 Ashcan 1.00

Raver #3 © Malibu Comics

RAVER
1 Prism cover 3.00
1a Newsstand 2.25
2 . . . . 1.95
3 Walter Koenig(s) 1.95
4 . . . . 1.95
5 . . . . 1.95

RIPFIRE
0 Prequel to Ripfire Series 2.50

RUNE
Ultraverse
0 BWS(a&s) 10.00
1 BWS(a&s),from Ultraverse 3.00
1a Foil cover 25.00
2 CU(s),BWS,V:Aladdin 2.25
3 DaR,BWS,(Ultraverse Premiere
  #1), Flip book 3.75
4 BWS,V:Twins 2.25
5 BWS 1.95
6 BWS 1.95

7 CU,JS 1.95
8 Rise of Gods,pt.2 . . . . 1.95
9 Prelude to Godwheel 1.95
G-Size #1 . . . . 2.50
TPB BWS(c&a),CU,The Awakening,
  rep.#1–#5 . . . . 12.95

RUNE/SILVER SURFER
Ultravrse
1 BWS(c),A:Adam Warlock 5.95
1a Lim. edition (5,000 made) . . 10.50
1b Standard ed.newsprint 2.95

RUST
1 O:Rust 2.95
2 V:Marion Labs 2.95
3 I:Ashe Sapphire,5th Anniv. . . . 2.95
4 I:Rustmobile 2.95

SANTANA
Rock-it Comix
1 TT(c&s),TY 3.95

SLUDGE
Ultraverse
1 BWS,I:Sludge,BU:I:Rune 2.75
1a Ultra-Limited 30.00
2 AaL,I:Bloodstorm 2.25
3 AaL,V:River Men 2.50
4 AaL,Origins Month,
  V:Alligator 2.25
5 AaL,V:Garret Whale 2.25
6 AaL,A:Dragon Fang,Lord
  Pumpkin 2.25
7 V:Frank Hoag 2.25
8 AaL,V:Monsters 2.25
9 AaL,O:Sludge 2.25
10 AaL,O:Sludge 1.95
11 AaL,V:Bash Brothers 1.95
12 AaL,V:Prime, w/flip book
  w/Ultraverse Premiere #8 . . . . 3.50
13 . . . . 1.95
Red X-Mas 2.50

SOLITAIRE
Ultraverse
1 black baged edition with
  playing card: Ace of Clubs,
  Diamonds, Hearts or Spades . 2.75
1d Newsstand edition,no card . . . 2.25
2 GJ(s),JJ,Break-Thru x-over,
  V:Moon Man 2.25
3 Origins Month,
  I:Monkey-Woman 2.25
4 O:Solitaire 2.25
5 JJ,V:Djinn 2.25
6 JJ,V:Lone 1.95
7 JJ,I:Double Edge 2.25
8 GJ,I:Degenerate 1.95
9 GJ,Degenerate Rafferty 1.95
10 Hostile Takeover #2 . . . . 1.95
11 V:Djinn 1.95
12 V:Anton Lowe 1.95

SOLUTION
Ultraverse
0 DaR,O:Solution 10.00
1 DaR,I:Solution 3.00
1a foil cover 25.00
2 DaR,BWS,V:Rex Mundi,Quatro,
  BU:Rune 3.00
3 DaR,A:Hardcase,Choice 2.50
4 DaR,Break-Thru x-over,

A:Hardcase,Choice 2.50
5 F:Dropkick 2.25
6 B:O:Solution 2.25
7 KM,O:Solution 2.25
8 KM(c),E:O:Solution 2.25
9 F:Shadowmage 2.25
10 V:Vyr 2.25
11 V:Vorlexx 2.25
12 JHi 1.95
13 Hostile Takeover pt.3 . . . . . . 1.95
14 old foes 1.95
15 V:Casino 1.95
16 Flip/UltraverePremiere#10 . . . 3.50
17 F:Casino, Dragons Claws 2.50

THE SQUAD
0-A Hardcase's old team 2.50
0-B 2.50
0-C L.A.Riots 2.50

STAR SLAMMERS
Bravura
1 WS(a&s) 2.75
2 WS(a&s),F:Meredith 2.75
3 WS(a&s) 2.50
4 WS(a&s) 2.50
5 WS,Rojas Choice 2.50

STAR TREK: DEEP SPACE NINE
1 Direct ed. 3.25
1a Photo(c). 3.00
1b Gold foil 28.00
2 w/skycap 3.50
3 Murder on DS9 . . . . 2.75
4 MiB(s),F:Bashir,Dax 2.75
5 MiB(s),V:Slaves 2.75
6 MiB(s),Three Stories 2.75
7 F:Kira 2.75
8 B:Requiem 2.75
9 E:Requiem 2.75
10 Descendants 2.50
11 A Short Fuse 2.75
12 Baby on Board 2.50
13 Problems with Odo 2.75
14 on Bejor 2.75
15 mythologic dilemma 2.75
16 Shangheid 2.50
17 Voyager preview 2.50
18 V:Gwyn 2.50
19 Wormhole Mystery 2.50
20 Sisko Injured 2.50
21 Smugglers attack DS9 . . . . . 2.50
22 Commander Quark 2.50
23 Secret of the Lost Orb,pt.1 . . . 2.50
Ann.#1 Looking Glass 3.95

STAR TREK: DS9 CELEBRITY SERIES: BLOOD AND HONOR
1 Mark Lenard(s) 2.95

STAR TREK: DS9 LIGHTSTORM
1 Direct ed. 3.50
1a Silver foil 20.00

STAR TREK: DS9 HEARTS AND MINDS
[Limited Series]
1 . . . . 3.00

---

2 .... 2.50
3 Into the Abyss,X-over preview . 2.50
4 final issue 2.50

STAR TREK: DS9
THE MAQUIS
[Limited Series]
1 Federation Renegades 2.50
1a Newsstand, photo(c) 2.50
2 Garack 2.50
3 F:Quark, Bashir 2.50

STAR TREK: DS9
TEROK NOR
0 Fully painted by Goring 2.95

STAR TREK: VOYAGER
A V:Maquis 2.75
Aa Newsstand, photo(c) 2.50
B conclusion 2.75
Ba Newsstand, photo(c) 2.50

STRANGERS, THE
Ultraverse
1 I:Strangers 5.00
1a Ultra-Limited 30.00
1b Full Hologram (c) 40.00
2 A:J.D.Hunt,w/Ultraverse card .. 5.00
3 I:TNTNT 3.50
4 A:Hardcase 3.00
5 BWS,BU:Rune 3.00
6 J:Yrial,I:Deathwish 2.25
7 Break-Thru x-over 2.25
8 RHo,ANi,O:Solution 2.25
9 AV(i),I:Ulta Pirates 2.25
10 AV(i),V:Bastinado 2.25
11 in Alderson Disk 2.25
12 O:Yrial 2.25
13 (Ultraverse Premiere#4) 3.50
14 .... 2.25
15 Zip-Zap, Yrail 1.95
16 Ultras, Teknight 1.95
17 Rafferty 1.95
18 Ultra Pirates 1.95
19 V:Pilgrim 1.95
20 Stranger Destroyed 1.95
21 A:Rex Mundi 2.50
22 SEt,V:Guy Hunt 2.50
23 SEt,RHo,V:Tabboo 2.50
24 RHo,SEt,V:Taboo 2.50
Ann.#1 Death 3.95
TPB rep. #1-#4 .... 9.95
Ashcan 1 (signed) 15.00
Ashcan 1 (unsigned) 8.00

STREET FIGHTER
1 Based on Video Game 3.25

STRIKEBACK
Bravura
1 .... 2.95
2 .... 2.95
3 V:Doberman 2.95
4 V:Dragonryder Island 2.95
Spec.#1 KM,JRu,V:Dragon 3.50

TARZAN:
THE BECKONING
1 TY,I:The Spider Man 2.75
2 TY,Going back to Africa 2.50
3 thru 6 .... 2.50

TARZAN THE WARRIOR
1 SBs(c),O:Tarzan 3.50
2 .... 2.75
3 .... 2.75
4 Wom'cha's Ship 2.75

Tarzan the Warrior #1
© Malibu Comics

TARZAN: LOVE, LIES,
AND THE LOST CITY
1 MWg&WS(s),Short Stories 3.95
2 The lost city of Opar 2.50
3 Final issue 2.50

ULTRAFORCE
Ultraverse
1 Prime, Prototype 2.50
2 .... 1.95
3 .... 1.95
4 .... 1.95
5 V:Atalon 1.95
6 V:Atalon 2.50
7 CU,GP(c),F:Ghoul 2.50
8 MWn,CV,GP,F:Black Knight . 2.50
Spec.#0 .... 2.50

ULTRAVERSE
DOUBLE FEATURE
Ultraverse
1 F:Prime, Solitaire 3.95

ULTRAVERSE ORIGINS
Ultraverse
1 O:Ultraverse Heroes 1.25
1a Silver foil cover 12.50

ULTRAVERSE: YEAR
ZERO: THE DEATH
OF THE SQUAD
Ultraverse
1 JHI,A:Squad, Mantra 2.95
2 JHI,DaR(c) prequel to Prime#1 2.95

ULTRAVERSE: YEAR ONE
Ultraverse

1 Handbook, double size 4.95
2 Prime 1.95

WARSTRIKE
Ultraverse
1 HNg,TA,in South America 1.95
2 HNg,TA,Gatefold(c) 1.95
3 in Brazil 1.95
4 HNg,TA,V:Blind Faith 1.95
5 .... 1.95
6 Rafferty 1.95
7 Origin 1.95

WARSTRIKE
Ultraverse
1 Blind Faith/Lord Pumpkin 1.95

WORLD DOMINATION
1 .... 3.95
1a 3.95

Wrath #1 © Malibu Comics

WRATH
Ultraverse
1 B:MiB(s),DvA,JmP,C:Mantra .. 2.25
1a Silver foil 20.00
2 DvA,JmP,V:Hellion 2.25
3 DvA,JmP,V:Radicals,
    I:Slayer 2.25
4 DvA,JmP,V:Freex 2.25
5 DvA,JmP,V:Freex 1.95
6 DvA,JmP 2.25
7 DvA,JmP,I:Pierce,Ogre,
    Doc Virtual 1.95
8 .... 1.95
9 A:Prime 2.25
G-Size #1 .... 2.50

ABBOTT AND COSTELLO
Charlton Comics
February, 1968

1	40.00
2 thru 9	@20.00
10 thru 21	@15.00
22 August, 1971	15.00

ACCIDENT MAN: THE DEATH TOUCH
Apocalypse
One Shot rep.Toxic #10-#16 .... 3.95

ADAM-12
Gold Key
December, 1973

1	22.00
2 thru 9	@12.00
10 February, 1976	12.00

ADAPTERS, THE

1	2.00
2	2.00

ADDAMS FAMILY
Gold Key
October, 1974

1	40.00
2	25.00
3	20.00

ADLAI STEVENSON
Dell Publishing Co.
December, 1966
1 Political Life Story 25.00

ADVENTURES OF BARON MUNCHAUSEN
Now Comics
1 thru 4 Mini-Series .... @1.75

ADVENTURES OF CHRISSIE CLAWS
Hero Graphics
1 Trouble in Toyland 2.95

ADVENTURES OF FELIX THE CAT
Harvey
1 Short Stories 1.25

ADVENTURES OF KUNG FU PIG NINJA FLOUNDER AND 4-D MONKEY

1 thru 6	@1.80
7 thru 10	@2.00

ADVENTURES OF ROBIN HOOD
Gold Key
March, 1974

1	6.00
2 thru 7, January 1975	@3.50

ADVENTURES OF ROGER WILCO

Adventure
1 Based on Space-Quest
Computer games 2.95

ADVENTURES OF THE FLY
Archie Publications/ Radio Comics
August, 1959

1 JSm/JK,O:Fly,I:SpiderSpry A:Lancelot Strong/Shield ...	400.00
2 JSm/JK,DAy,AW	250.00
3 Jack Davis Art, O:Fly	200.00
4 V:Dazzler NA panel	125.00
5 A:Spider Spry	65.00
6 V:Moon Men	60.00
7 A:Black Hood	60.00
8 A:Lancelot Strong/Shield ...	60.00
9 A:Lancelot Strong/Shield I:Cat Girl	60.00
10 A:Spider Spry	60.00
11 V:Rock Men	35.00
12 V:Brute Invaders	35.00
13 I:Kim Brand	40.00
14 I:Fly-Girl(Kim Brand)	50.00
15 A:Spider	35.00
16 A:Fly-Girl	35.00
17 A:Fly-Girl	35.00
18 A:Fly-Girl	35.00
19 A:Fly-Girl	35.00
20 O:Fly-Girl	38.00
21 A:Fly-Girl	25.00
22 A:Fly-Girl	25.00
23 A:Fly-Girl,Jaguar	25.00
24 A:Fly-Girl	25.00
25 A:Fly-Girl	25.00
26 A:Fly-Girl,Black Hood	25.00
27 A:Fly-Girl,Black Hood	25.00
28 A:Black Hood	25.00
29 A:Fly-Girl,Black Hood	25.00
30 A:Fly-Girl,R:Comet	30.00
31 A:Black Hood, Shield, Comet	35.00

ADVENTURES OF THE JAGUAR
Archie Publications/ Radio Comics

Adventures of the Jaguar #4
© Archie Publications

September, 1961

1 I:Ralph Hardy/Jaguar	150.00
2 10 cent cover	65.00
3 Last 10 cent cover	60.00
4 A:Cat-Girl	45.00
5 A:Cat-Girl	45.00
6 A:Cat-Girl	38.00
7	30.00
8	30.00
9	30.00
10	30.00
11	30.00
12 A:Black Hood	30.00
13 A:Cat-Girl,A:Black Hood ...	30.00
14 A:Black Hood	30.00
15 V:Human Octopus,last issue November, 1963	25.00

ADVENTURES OF YOUNG DR. MASTERS
Archie Comics
August, 1964

1	5.00
2 November, 1964	5.00

AGAINST BLACKSHARD
Sirius Comics
1 3-D, August 1986 .... 2.25

AIR FIGHTERS, SGT. STRIKE SPECIAL
Eclipse
1 A:Airboy,Valkyrie 1.95

AIR WAR STORIES
Dell Publishing Co.
September-November, 1964

1	15.00
2	10.00
3 thru 8	@8.00

AIRBOY
Eclipse

1 TT/TY,D:Golden Age Airboy O:New Airboy	3.25
2 TT/TY,I:Marisa,R:SkyWolf	2.25
3 A:The Heap	2.50
4 A:Misery	2.50
5 DSt(c),R:Valkyrie	4.00
6 R:Iron Ace,I:Marlene	3.00
7 PG(c), ...	2.50
8 FH/TT(c)	2.50
9 R:Flying Fool, Riot, O'Hara Cocky, Judge & Turtle	1.75
10 I:Manic,D:Cocky, Judge & Turtle	1.50
11 O:Birdie	1.50
12 R:Flying Fool	1.50
13 I:New Bald Eagle	1.50
14 A:Sky Wolf, Iron Ace	1.50
15 A:Ku Klux Klan	1.50
16 D:Manic,A:Ku Klux Klan	1.50
17 A:HarryS.Truman,Misery	1.75
18 A:Gold.Age Black Angel	1.75
19 A:Gold.Age Rats	1.75
20 Rat storyline	1.75
21 I:Lester Mansfield (rel. of Gold.Age Rackman), Artic Deathzone #1	1.75
22 DSp,Artic Deathzone #2	1.75
23 A:Gold.Age Black Angle, Artic Deathzone #3	1.75

All comics prices listed are for *Near Mint* condition. **CVA Page 431**

Airboy #9 © Eclipse Comics

24 A: Heap 1.75
25 TY,I:Manure Man,A:Heap 1.50
26 R:Flying Dutchman 1.50
27 A:Iron Ace, Heap 1.50
28 A:Heap 1.50
29 . . . . 1.50
30 A:Iron Ace; Sky Wolf story . . . 1.50
31 A:Valkyrie; Sky Wolf story 1.75
32 Hostage Virus, ... 1.75
33 DSp,SkyWolf sty,A:Sgt.Strike . 1.75
34 DSp,A:La Lupina 1.75
35 DSp,A:La Lupina, Sky Wolf . . . 1.75
36 . . . . 1.75
37 DSp 1.75
38 CI, Heap story 1.75
39 CI, Heap story 1.75
40 CI, Heap story 1.75
41 V:Steel Fox, Golden Age rep.
  O:Valkyrie 1.75
42 A:Rackman 1.95
43 Sky Wolf sty, A:Flying Fool . . . 1.95
44 A:Rackman 1.95
45 . . . . 1.95
46 EC,Airboy Diary #1 . . . . 1.95
47 EC,Airboy Diary #2 . . . . 1.95
48 EC,Airboy Diary #3 . . . . 1.95
49 EC,Airboy Diary #4 . . . . 1.95
50 AKu/NKu,double-size 3.95
Meets the Prowler Spec. 1.95
Mr. Monster Spec. 1.75
Vs Airmaidens Spec. 1.95

AIRMAIDENS SPECIAL
Eclipse Comics
1 A:Valkyrie 1.75

ALADDIN
Walt Disney
Prestige. Movie Adapt. 4.95

ALARMING ADVENTURES
Harvey Publications
October, 1962
1 AW,RC,JSe 45.00
2 AW,BP,RC,JSe 30.00
3 JSe,February, 1963 . . . . 30.00

ALARMING TALES
Harvey Publications
September, 1957
1 JK,JK(c) 75.00
2 JK,JK(c) 65.00
3 JK 45.00
4 JK,BP 45.00
5 JK,AW 50.00
6 JK,November, 1958 . . . . 40.00

ALBEDO, VOL. 3
Antartic Press
1 thru 3 Various Artists . . . . . . @2.95

ALIAS
Now Comics
1 . . . . 2.00
2 thru 5 . . . . @1.75

ALIAS: STORMFRONT
Now Comics
1 . . . . 1.75
2 . . . . 1.75

ALIEN ENCOUNTERS
Eclipse Comics
1 . . . . 3.50
2 . . . . 3.00
3 'I Shot the Last Martian' 3.00
4 . . . . 2.00
5 RCo,'Night of the Monkey' 2.00
6 'Now You See It,'Freefall' 2.00
7 . . . . 2.00
8 TY,'Take One Capsule Every
  Million Years,M.Monroe(c) . . . 2.75
9 The Conquered 2.00
10 . . . . 2.00
11 TT,'Old Soldiers' 2.00
12 'What A Relief,''Eyes
  of the Sibyl' 2.00
13 GN,'The Light at the End' 2.00
14 JRy,GN,TL,RT,'Still born' 2.00

ALIEN TERROR
Eclipse
April, 1986
3-D #1 'Standard Procedure' 2.00

ALIEN WORLDS
Pacific
1 AW,VM,NR 4.00
2 DSt 3.50
3 . . . . 3.00
4 DSt(i) 3.00
5 thru 7 . . . . @3.00
3-D #1 AAd,DSt 5.50
Eclipse
8 AW 2.50
9 . . . . 2.50

ALL AMERICAN SPORTS
Charlton
October, 1967
1 . . . . 10.00

ALL HALLOWS EVE
Innovation
1 . . . . 4.95

ALLEY OOP
Dell Publishing Co.
December-February, 1962-63
1 . . . . 50.00
2 . . . . 45.00

ALPHA WAVE
Darkline
1 . . . . 1.75

ALTER EGO
First
1 . . . . 1.75
2 . . . . 1.50
3 . . . . 1.50
4 . . . . 1.25

ALVIN
(& THE CHIPMUNKS)
Dell Publishing Co.
October-December, 1962
1 . . . . 65.00
2 . . . . 40.00
3 . . . . 30.00
4 thru 10 . . . . @25.00
11 thru 20 . . . . @20.00
21 thru 28 . . . . @18.00
1 Alvin for President & his pals
  in Merry Christmas with
  Clyde Crashcup & Leonardo . 15.00

AMAZING CHAN &
THE CHAN CLAN
Gold Key
May, 1973
1 . . . . 9.00
2 . . . . 5.00
3 and 4 . . . . @5.00

AMAZON, THE
Comico
1 . . . . 1.95
2 . . . . 1.95
3 end mini-series 1.95

AMERICAN FLAGG
First
1 HC,I:American Flagg, Hard
  Times Pt.1 . . . . 3.50
2 HC,Hard Times Pt.2 . . . . 2.75
3 HC,Hard Times Pt.3 . . . . 2.75
4 HC,Southern Comfort Pt.1 . . . . 2.75
5 HC,Southern Comfort Pt.2 . . . . 2.75
6 HC,Southern Comfort Pt.3 . . . . 2.75
7 HC,State o/t Union Pt.1 . . . . . . 2.50
8 HC,State o/t Union Pt.2 . . . . . . 2.50
9 HC,State o/t Union Pt.3 . . . . . . 2.50
10 HC,Solidarity-For Now Pt.1
  I:Luthor Ironheart 2.50
11 HC,Solidarity-ForNowPt.2 . . . . 2.50
12 HC,Solidarity-ForNowPt.3 . . . . 2.50
13 HC 2.25
14 PB 2.25
15 HC,AmericanFlagg A Complete
  story Pt.1 . . . . 2.25
16 HC,Complete Story Pt.2 . . . . . 2.00
17 HC,Complete Story Pt.3 . . . . . 2.00
18 HC,Complete Story Pt.4 . . . . . 2.00
19 HC,Bullets&BallotsPt.1 . . . . . 2.00
20 HC,LSn,Bullets&BallotsPt.2 . . . 2.00
21 HC,LSn,Bullets&BallotsPt.3

Alan Moore sty. 2.00
22 HC,LSn,Bullets&BallotsPt.4
Alan Moore sty. 2.00
23 HC,LSn,England Swings Pt.1
Alan Moore sty. 2.00

American Flagg #1 © First Comics

24 HC,England Swings Pt.2,
Alan Moore sty. 2.00
25 HC,England Swings Pt.3,
Alan Moore sty. 2.00
26 HC,England Swings Pt.4,
Alan Moore sty. 2.00
27 Alan Moore sty. with Raul
the Cat 2.00
28 BWg 1.50
29 JSon 1.50
30 JSon 1.50
31 JSon,O:Bob Violence 1.50
32 JSon,A:Bob Violence 1.50
33 A:Bob Violence 1.50
34 A:Bob Violence 1.50
35 A:Bob Violence 1.50
36 A:Bob Violence 1.50
37 A:Bob Violence 1.50
38 New Direction 1.50
39 JSon,A:Bob Violence 1.50
40 A:Bob Violence 1.50
41 . . . . 1.50
42 F:Luther Ironheart 1.50
43 . . . . 1.50
44 . . . . 1.50
45 . . . . 1.50
46 PS 1.75
47 PS 1.75
48 PS 1.75
49 . . . . 1.75
50 HC,last issue 1.75
Special #1 HC,I:Time² 2.50
See Also: Howard Chaykin's
American Flagg

AMERICOMICS
AC Comics
1 GP(c),O:Shade 3.00
2 . . . . 2.00
3 Blue Beetle 2.00
4 O:Dragonfly 2.00

5 . . . . 1.75
6 . . . . 1.75
Spec.#1 Capt.Atom,BlueBeetle . . 1.50

ANDROMEDA
Andromeda
1 I:Andromeda 2.50

ANYTHING GOES
Fantagraphics
1 GK,FlamingCarot,Savage 3.50
2 S:AnM,JK,JSt,SK 3.50
3 DS,NA(c),A:Cerebus 3.00
4 . . . . 2.50
5 A:TMNTurtles 5.00
6 . . . . 2.00

APE NATION
Adventure Comics
1 Aliens land on Planet
of the Apes 4.00
2 General Ollo 3.00
3 V:Gen.Ollo,Danada 2.50
4 D:Danada 2.50

ARACHNAPHOBIA
Walt Disney
1 Movie Adapt 5.95
1a Newsstand 2.95

ARCHIE
See Also:
GOLDEN AGE SECTION

ARCHIE AND FRIENDS
Archie Publications
Dec., 1992
1 thru 10 . . . . @1.50
11 thru 15 . . . . @1.50

ARCHIE AND ME
Archie Publications
October, 1964
1 . . . . 120.00
2 . . . . 60.00
3 . . . . 25.00
4 . . . . 20.00
5 . . . . 20.00
6 thru 10 . . . . @15.00
11 thru 20 . . . . @5.00
21 thru 100 . . . . @3.00
101 thru 162 1987 . . . . @1.50

ARCHIE AS PURE
HEART THE POWERFUL
Archie Publications
September, 1966
1 . . . . 50.00
2 . . . . 30.00
3 thru 6 . . . . @20.00

ARCHIE AT
RIVERDALE HIGH
Archie Publications
August, 1972
1 . . . . 35.00
2 . . . . 15.00
3 . . . . 8.00
4 . . . . 6.00
5 . . . . 6.00

6 thru 10 . . . . @2.50
11 thru 114 . . . . @1.00

ARCHIE COMICS DIGEST
Archie Comics Digest
August, 1973
1 . . . . 35.00
2 . . . . 20.00
3 . . . . 9.00
4 . . . . 6.00
5 thru 10 . . . . @2.00
11 thru 88 . . . . @1.00

ARCHIE MEETS
THE PUNISHER
Archie/Marvel
one-shot crossover, same contents
as Punisher meets Archie 3.00

ARCHIE'S MADHOUSE
Archie Publications
September, 1959
1 . . . . 175.00
2 . . . . 85.00
3 . . . . 60.00
4 . . . . 60.00
5 . . . . 60.00
6 thru 10 . . . . @35.00
11 thru 16 . . . . @25.00
17 thru 21 . . . . @10.00
22 . . . . 40.00
23 thru 30 . . . . @10.00
31 thru 40 . . . . @3.50
41 thru 65 . . . . @1.00
66 February, 1969 . . . . 1.00

ARCHIE'S SUPERHERO
SPECIAL DIGEST
MAGAZINE
Archie Publications
1 JSm/SK,Rept.Double of Capt.Strong
#1,FLy,Black Hood 1.20
2 GM,NA/DG,AMc,I:'70's Black
Hood, Superhero rept. 2.00

ARCHIE'S TV LAUGH-OUT
Archie Publications
December, 1969
1 . . . . 30.00
2 . . . . 12.00
3 . . . . 6.00
4 . . . . 6.00
5 . . . . 6.00
6 thru 10 . . . . @2.00
11 thru 106 1986 . . . . @1.00

ARCHIE 3000
Archie Publications
May, 1989–July, 1991
1 thru 16 . . . . 1.00

ARENA, THE
Alchemy
1 . . . . 1.00
2 . . . . 1.00

ARIANE & BLUEBEARD
Eclipse
Spec. CR 3.95

ARISTOKITTENS, THE
Gold Key
October, 1971
1 Disney	20.00
2	10.00
3	10.00
4 thru 9, Oct. 1975	@10.00

ARMAGEDDON FACTOR
AC Comics
1 Sentinels of Justice	1.95
2	1.95

ARMOR
Continuity
1 TGr,NA,A:Silver Streak, Silver logo	7.00
1a 2nd printing,red logo	2.50
2 TGr,NA(c)	2.50
3 TGr,NA(c)	2.50
4 TGr,NA(c)	2.50

Armor #12 © Continuity Comics

5 BS,NA(c)	2.50
6 TVE,NA(c)	2.50
7 NA(c)	2.50
8 FS,NA(c)	2.50
9 FS,NA&KN(c)	2.50
10 FS,NA&KN(c)	2.50
11 SDr(i),KN(c)	2.50
12 KN(c)	2.50
13 NA(c),direct sales	2.50
14 KN(c), newsstand	2.50

[2nd Series]
1 V:Hellbender,Trading Card	2.50

[3rd Series, Deathwatch 2000]
1 Deathwatch 2000 pt.3,w/card	4.00
2 Deathwatch 2000 pt.9,w/card	2.50
3 Deathwatch 2000 pt.15,w/card	2.50
4	2.50
5 Rise of Magic	2.50
6 Rise of Magic	@2.50

ARMY ATTACK
Charlton
July, 1964
1 SG	12.00
2 SG	8.00

3 SG	5.00
4	5.00
5 thru 47	@5.00

ARMY WAR HEROES
Charlton
December, 1963
1	10.00
2	6.00
3 thru 21	@6.00
22 GS,O&I:Iron Corporal	7.00
23 thru 38, June 1970	5.00

ARTIC COMICS
1	2.00

ART OF ZEN INTER-GALACTIC NINJA
Entity Comics
1 Various artists	2.95

ASH
Event Comics
1 JQ,JP,Fireman with powers	3.50
2 JQ,JP,V:Theresa	2.50
3 JQ,JP,Secret of Origin	2.50

ASSASSIN, INC.
Solson
1 thru 4	@1.95

ASTER
Entity Comics
1 I:Celestial Knight	3.50
1a gold logo	12.00
1b 2nd printing	2.95
2	2.95
3 V:Tolmek	2.95
3a Variant cover	2.95
4 Final Issue	2.95
TPB Rep.#1–#4 + pin-up gallery	12.95

ASTRO BOY
Prev.   Original Astro Boy
18	1.75
19	1.75
20	1.75

ATOM ANT
Gold Key
January, 1966
1	65.00

ATOM-AGE COMBAT
Fago Magazines
November, 1958
1	150.00
2	75.00
3 March, 1959	75.00

ATOMIC RABBIT
Charlton Comics
August, 1955
1	90.00
2	40.00
3 thru 10	@27.00
11 March, 1958	35.00

Becomes:
ATOMIC BUNNY
12	40.00

13 thru 18	@15.00
19 December, 1959	15.00

AVENGERS, THE
Gold Key
November, 1968
1	175.00

AXA
Eclipse
1 'Axa the Adopted'	1.75
2	1.75

AXEL PRESSBUTTON
Eclipse
1 BB(c),Origin	1.75
2	1.75
3 thru 4	@1.75

Becomes:
PRESSBUTTON

AXIS ALPHA
Axis Comics
1 LSn,I:BEASTIES,Dethgrip, Shelter,W	2.75

AZ
Comico
1	4.00
2	2.25

AZTEC ACE
Eclipse
1 NR(i),I:AztecAce	4.00
2 NR(i)	3.50
3 NR(i)	3.00
4 NR(i)	3.00
5 NR(i)	3.00
6 NR(i)	3.00
7 NR(i)	3.00
8 NR(i)	3.00
9 NR(i)	3.00
10 NR(i)	2.00
11	3.50
12	2.50
13	2.50
14	2.50
15 F:Bridget	2.50

BABY HUEY, THE BABY GIANT
Harvey Publications
September, 1956
1	200.00
2	100.00
3	60.00
4	50.00
5	50.00
6 thru 10	@27.00
11 thru 20	@15.00
21 thru 40	@12.00
41 thru 60	@6.00
61 thru 79	@3.00
80	3.50
81 thru 95	@2.00
96 Giant size	4.00
97 Giant size	4.00
98	2.00
99 October, 1980	2.00

BABY HUEY AND PAPA
Harvey Publications
May, 1962

1	100.00
2	40.00
3	20.00
4	20.00
5	20.00
6	12.00
7	12.00
8	12.00
9	12.00
10	12.00
11 thru 20	@5.00
21 thru 33	@3.50
33 January, 1968	3.50

BABY HUEY DUCKLAND
Harvey Publications
November, 1962

1	60.00
2	20.00
3	20.00
4	20.00
5	20.00
6 thru 14	@10.00
15 November, 1966	10.00

BACHELOR FATHER
Dell Publishing Co.
April-June, 1962

1	45.00
2	45.00

BACK TO THE FUTURE
Harvey

1 Chicago 1927	1.25
2 Cretaceous Period	1.25
3 World War I	1.25
4 Doc Retires	1.25

BAD COMPANY
Quality

1 thru 19	@1.50

BADGER
Capital

1 JBt,I:Badger,Ham,Daisy Yak,Yeti	7.00
2 JBt,I:Riley,A:YakYeti	5.00
3 JBt,O:Badger,Ham	4.00
4 JBt,A'Ham	4.00

First

5 BR,DruidTree Pt1	3.50
6 BR,DruidTree Pt2	3.00
7 BR,I:Wonktendonk,Lord Weterlackus	3.00
8 BR,V:Demon	3.00
9 BR,I:Connie,WOatesCbra	2.50
10 BR,A:Wonktendonk, I:Hodag Meldrum	2.50
11 BR,V:Hodag,L.W'lackus	2.50
12 BR,V:Hodag,L.W'lackus	2.50
13 BR,A:L.W'lakus,Clonezone, Judah	2.50
14 BR,I:HerbNg	2.50
15 BR,I:Wombat,JMoranIbob	2.50
16 BR,A:Yak,Yeti	2.50
17 JBt,I:Lamont	3.00
18 BR,I:SpudsGroganA:Cbra	2.50
19 BR,I:Senator1,ClZone	2.50
20 BR,Billionaire'sPicnic	2.50

Badger #3 © Capital Comics

21 BR,I&O:Phantom	2.50
22 BR,I:Dr.BuickRiviera	2.50
23 I:BobDobb,A:Yeti	2.50
24 BR,A:Riley	2.50
25 BR,I:Killdozer	2.50
26 BR,I:RoachWranger	2.50
27 BR,O:RoachWranger	2.50
28 BR,A:Yeti	2.50
29 A:Clonezone,C:GrimJack	2.50
30 BR,I:Dorgan	2.00
31 BR,I:HopLingSung	2.00
32 BR,D:Dorgan,HopLingSng	2.00
33 RLm/AN,I:KidKang	5.00
34 RLm,I:Count Kohler	4.00
35 RLm,I:Count Kohler	4.00
36 RLm,V:Dire Wolf	3.50
37 AMe,A:Lamont	3.50
38 Animal Band	2.00
39 I:Buddy McBride	2.00
40 RLm,I:Sister Twyster	3.50
41 RLm,D:Sister Twyster	3.50
42 RLm,A:Paul Bunyan	3.50
43 RLm,V:Vampires	3.50
44 RLm,V:Vampires	3.50
45 RLm,V:Dr.Buick Riviera	3.50
46 RLm,V:Lort Weterlackus	3.50
47 RLm,Hmds.Sacr.BloodI	3.50
48 RLm,Hmds.Sacr.BloodII	3.50
49 RLm,TRoof off SuckerI	3.50
50 RLm,TRoof off SuckerII	5.00
51 RLm,V:Demon	3.00
52 TV,Tinku	4.00
53 TV,I:Shaza,Badass	4.00
54 TV,D:Shaza	4.00
55 I:Morris Myer	2.00
56 I:Dominance	2.00
57 A:KKang,V:L.W'lackus	2.00
58 A:Lamont,W'bat,V:SpudsJack	2.00
59 Bad Art Issue	2.00
60 I:ChisumBros	2.25
61 V:ChismBros	2.00
62 I:Shanks	2.00
63 V:Shanks	2.00
64 A:Mavis Sykes	2.25
65 A:BruceLee	2.25
66 I:JoeNappleseed	2.25
67 Babysitting	2.25
68 V:GiantFoot	2.25
69 O:Mavis	2.25

70 BR:Klaus(last monthly)	2.25
Graphic Nov.BR,I:Mazis Sykes,D:Hodag	10.00
Badger Bedlam	4.95

BADGER GOES BERSERK
First

1 I:Larry,Jessie	5.00
2 MZ,V:Larry,Jessie	3.50
3 JBt/MZ,V:Larry,Jessie	3.00
4 JBt/MZ,V:Larry,Jessie	3.00

BAD GIRLS OF BLACKOUT
Blackout Comics

1 I:Ms. Cyanide, Ice	3.50

BAKER STREET

1	3.00
2	2.50

BALLAD OF HALO JONES
Quality

1 IG Alan Moore story	2.00
1a IG rep.	2.00
2 thru 12	@1.25

BAMM BAMM & PEBBLES FLINTSTONE
Gold Key
October, 1964

1	30.00

BARBARIANS
Atlas

1	1.50

BARBIE & KEN
Dell Publishing Co.
May-July, 1962

1	140.00
2	125.00
3	125.00
4	125.00
5	125.00

THE BARBIE TWINS ADVENTURES
Topps

1 I:Shane, Sia	2.50

BARNEY AND BETTY RUBBLE
Charlton Comics
January, 1973

1	25.00
2	10.00
3	10.00
4	10.00
5	10.00
6 thru 10	@8.00
11 thru 22	@6.00
23 December, 1976	6.00

BARRY M. GOLDWATER
Dell Publishing Co.
March, 1965

1	20.00

All comics prices listed are for *Near Mint* condition.

BART-MAN
Bongo
1 Foil(c),I:Bart-Man 3.25
2 I:Penalizer 2.25
3 When Bongos Collide,pt.3,
  with card 2.25
4 Crime-Time,pt.1 . . . . 2.25

BASEBALL
Kitchen Sink
1991
1 WE (c) reprint of 1949 orig. . . . 3.95
2 Ray Gotto (c), w/4 BB cards . . 2.95

BAT, THE
Adventure
1 R:The Bat,inspiration for
  Batman says Bob Kane 2.50

BATTLE FORCE
Blackthorne
1 . . . . 1.50
2 . . . . 1.50
3 . . . . 1.75

BATTLE OF
THE PLANETS
Gold Key
June, 1979
1 TV Cartoon 3.50
2 . . . . 2.50
3 . . . . 2.50
4 . . . . 2.50
5 . . . . 2.50
Whitman
6 . . . . 1.50
7 thru 10 . . . . 1.50

BATTLETECH
Blackthorne
1 . . . . 1.50
2 . . . . 1.50
3 . . . . 1.50
4 . . . . 1.75
5 . . . . 1.75
6 . . . . 1.75
(Changed to Black & White)
1 3-D 2.50
2 3-D 2.50

BEAGLE BOYS, THE
Gold Key
November, 1964
1 . . . . 25.00
2 thru 5 . . . . @15.00
6 thru 10 . . . . @10.00
11 thru 20 . . . . @6.00
21 thru 46 . . . . @3.00
47 February, 1979 . . . . 3.00

BEANIE THE MEANIE
Fargo Publications
1958
1 thru 3 . . . . @15.00

B.E.A.S.T.I.E.S.
Axis Comics
1 JS(a&s),I:Beasties 1.95

THE BEATLES,
LIFE STORY
Dell Publishing Co.
September-November, 1964
1 . . . . 475.00

BEAUTY AND THE BEAST
Innovation
1 From TV series 2.50
1a Deluxe 3.95
2 . . . . 2.50
3 . . . . 2.50
4 Siege 2.50
5 Siege 2.50
6 Halloween 2.50
7 . . . . 2.50

BEAUTY AND THE BEAST
PORTRAIT OF LOVE
First
1 WP,TV tie in 12.00
2 . . . . 8.00
Book II:Night of Beauty 5.95

BEAUTY AND THE BEAST
Walt Disney
Movie adapt.(Prestige) 4.95
Movie adapt.(newsstand) 2.50
mini-series
1 Bewitched 1.50
2 Elsewhere 1.50
3 A:Catherine 2.50

BEDLAM!
Eclipse
1 SBi,RV,reprint horror 1.75
2 SBi,RV,reprint horror 1.75

BEETLE BAILEY
Harvey
1 F:Mort Walker's B.Bailey 1.95
2 Beetle builds a bridge 1.25
3 thru 12 . . . . 1.25

BEETLEJUICE
Harvey
1 EC,'This is your lice' 2.00
Holiday Special #1 . . . . 1.25

BEN CASEY
Dell Publishing Co.
June-July, 1962
1 Ph(c) 30.00
2 Ph(c) 20.00
3 Ph(c) 20.00
4 Drug, Ph(c) 22.00
5 Ph(c) 20.00
6 Ph(c) 20.00
7 Ph(c) 20.00
8 Ph(c) 20.00
9 and 10 Ph(c) . . . . @20.00

BERNI WRIGHTSON
MASTER OF
THE MACABRE
Pacific
1 BWr 5.25
2 BWr 3.75
3 BWr 3.50
4 BWr 3.50

Berni Wrightson #1 © Pacific Comics

Eclipse
5 BWr 3.50

BEST FROM BOY'S LIFE
Gilberton Company
October, 1957
1 . . . . 50.00
2 . . . . 25.00
3 . . . . 20.00
4 LbC 30.00
5 . . . . 20.00

BEST OF DONALD DUCK
& UNCLE SCROOGE
Gold Key
November, 1964
1 . . . . 70.00
2 September, 1967 . . . . 65.00

BEST OF DONALD DUCK
Gold Key
November, 1965
1 . . . . 65.00

BEST OF BUGS BUNNY
Gold Key
October, 1966
1 Both Giants 35.00
2 October, 1968 . . . . 25.00

BEST OF DENNIS
THE MENACE, THE
Hallden/Fawcett Publ.
Summer, 1959
1 . . . . 35.00
2 thru 5 Spring, 1961 . . . . 20.00

BETTY
Archie Publications
Sept., 1992
1 thru 27 . . . . @1.50

BETTY AND ME
Archie Publications
August, 1965
1		75.00
2		40.00
3		25.00
4		25.00
5		25.00
6 thru 10	@	12.00
11 thru 30	@	6.00
31 thru 50	@	3.00
51 thru 55	@	2.00
56 thru 199	@	1.50
200 August, 1992		1.50

BETTY & VERONICA
Archie Publications
June, 1987
1 thru 89	@	1.50

BEVERLY HILLBILLYS
Dell Publishing Co.
April-June, 1963
1 Ph(c)		75.00
2 Ph(c)		40.00
3 Ph(c)		30.00
4		15.00
5		25.00
6		25.00
7		25.00
8 Ph(c)		25.00
9 Ph(c)		25.00
10 Ph(c)		25.00
11 Ph(c)		25.00
12 Ph(c)		25.00
13 Ph(c)		25.00
14 Ph(c)		25.00
15		15.00
16		15.00
17 Ph(c)		15.00
18 Ph(c)		15.00
19 Ph(c)		15.00
20 Ph(c)		15.00
21 Ph(c)		15.00

BEWITCHED
Dell Publishing Co.
April-June, 1965
1	75.00
2	40.00
3 Ph(c)	30.00
4 Ph(c)	30.00
5 Ph(c)	30.00
6 Ph(c)	30.00
7 Ph(c)	30.00
8 Ph(c)	30.00
9 Ph(c)	30.00
10 Ph(c)	30.00
11 Ph(c)	30.00
12 Ph(c)	30.00
13 Ph(c)	30.00
14	20.00

BEYOND THE GRAVE
Charlton Comics
July, 1975
1 SD,TS(c),P(c)		5.00
2 thru 5	@	2.00
6 thru 16	@	1.50
17 October, 1984		1.50

BIG BANG
Caliber Press
1 thru 3	@	1.95
4 25 years after #3		1.95

BIG VALLEY, THE
Dell Publishing Co.
June, 1966
1 Ph(c)	30.00
2	15.00
3	15.00
4	15.00
5	15.00
6	15.00

BILL BLACK'S FUN COMICS
AC Comics
1 Cpt.Paragon,B&W		2.50
2 and 3 B&W	@	2.25
4 Color		2.25

BILL THE GALACTIC HERO
Topps
1 thru 3 Harry Harrison adapt.	@	4.95

BILLY NGUYEN
Caliber
1	2.50

BILLY THE KID
Charlton Publ. Co.
November, 1957
9		40.00
10		25.00
11		22.00
12		20.00
13 AW,AT		30.00
14		20.00
15 AW,O:Billy the Kid		30.00
16 AW		30.00
17		20.00
18		20.00
19		20.00
20		30.00
21		30.00
22		30.00
23		10.00
24		30.00
25 JSe		30.00
26 JSe		30.00
27		10.00
28		10.00
29		10.00
30		10.00
31 thru 40	@	7.00
41 thru 60	@	5.00
61 thru 80	@	2.00
81 thru 152	@	1.00
153 March, 1983		1.00

BIONEERS
Mirage/Next
1 New Heroes	2.75
2	2.75
3 All-out War	2.75

BIONIC WOMAN, THE
Charlton
1 Oct, 1977, TV show adapt.		2.00

Bionic Woman #1 © Charlton Comics

2	1.50
3	1.50
4	1.50
5	1.50

BIZARRE 3-D ZONE
Blackthorne
1	2.50

[ORIGINAL] BLACK CAT
1 Reprints	2.00
2 MA(c) rep.	2.00
3 rep.	2.00

BLACK DIAMOND
AC Comics
1 Colt B..U. story	3.00
2 PG(c)	2.00
3 PG(c)	2.00
4 PG(c)	2.00
5 PG(c)	2.00

BLACK ENCHANTRESS
Heroic Publishing
1 and 2 Date Rape issues	@	1.95

BLACK FLAG
Maximum Press
1 Dan Fraga	1.95
2 I:New Character	2.50
3 V:Network, I:Glitz	2.50
4 V:Glitz, Network	2.50

BLACK FURY
Charlton Comics
May, 1955
1		25.00
2		12.00
3 thru 15	@	6.00
16 SD		30.00
17 SD		30.00
18 SD		30.00
19 and 20	@	3.50
21 thru 30	@	1.50
31 thru 56	@	2.00
57 March-April, 1966		2.00

All comics prices listed are for *Near Mint* condition.

BLACK HOOD
Archie Publications
1 ATh,GM,DW 1.00
2 ATh,DSp,A:Fox 1.00
3 ATh,GM 1.00

BLACK JACK
Charlton Comics
November, 1957
20 . . . . 30.00
21 . . . . 15.00
22 . . . . 25.00
23 AW,AT 30.00
24 SD 25.00
25 SD 25.00
26 SD 25.00
27 . . . . 12.00
28 SD 25.00
29 . . . . 10.00
30 November, 1959 . . . . 10.00

BLACK PHANTOM
AC Comics
1 and 2 . . . . @2.50

BLACK RAVEN
Mad Monkey Press
1 Blueprints pt.1 . . . . 2.95
2 Blueprints pt.2 . . . . 2.95
3 V:Temple Assassins 2.95
4 Blueprints pt.4 . . . . 2.95

BLACK TERROR
Eclipse
1 . . . . 3.95
2 . . . . 3.95
3 . . . . 4.95

BLACK WEB
Inks Comics
1 V:Seeker 2.50
2 V:Seeker 2.50
3 V:Seeker 2.50

BLACKBALL COMICS
Blackball Comics
1 KG,A:Trencher 3.25

BLAST-OFF
Harvey Publications
October, 1965
1 JK,AW 25.00

BLAZING COMBAT
Warren Publishing Co.
October, 1965
1 FF(c) 75.00
2 FF(c) 20.00
3 FF(c) 15.00
4 FF(c),July 1966 . . . . 15.00

BLOOD & ROSES
Sky Comics
1 I:Blood,Rose 2.75

BLOOD SWORD DYNASTY
Jademan
1 . . . . 2.25
2 thru 6 . . . . @1.50
7 . . . . 1.95

8 . . . . 1.95
9 . . . . 1.95
10 thru 14 MB . . . . @1.95
15 thru 18 MB . . . . @1.25
19 Kim & Zeo Escape the Crips . . 1.25
20 Skeleton Executioners 1.25
21 Kim,Seeto 1.25
22 Infinite Wounded 1.25
23 Kim vs. Ask me not 1.25
24 . . . . 1.25
25 . . . . 1.25
26 V:Fiery Bird 1.25
27 A:Hero, Shou, Fiery Bird 1.25
28 Hero vs. Fiery Bird 1.25
29 . . . . 1.25
30 . . . . 1.25
31 V:Devil Child 1.25
32 . . . . 1.25
33 . . . . 1.25
34 . . . . 1.25
35 Hero's ancestry 1.25
36 Hero & son in danger 1.25
37 A:Hell Clan,D:North Pole . . . 1.25
38 Fiery Hawk Vs.Inf.Seeto 1.25
39 Hero vs.Infinite seeto 1.25
40 Kim Hung vs.Inf.Seeto 1.25

BLOOD SWORD
Jademan
1 . . . . 3.25
2 . . . . 2.50
3 thru 5 . . . . @2.00
6 thru 9 . . . . @1.75
10 thru 21 . . . . @2.50
22 LW 1.95
23 LW,D:Poisonkiller 1.95
24 LW,A:Hero 1.95
25 . . . . 1.95
26 . . . . 1.95
27 . . . . 1.95
28 V:DevilHeart 1.95
29 . . . . 1.95
30 A:Purgatory 1.95
31 . . . . 1.95
32 V:Mummy 1.95
33 V:Mummy 1.95
34 . . . . 1.95
35 . . . . 1.95
36 A:King Rat 1.95
37 . . . . 1.95
38 Kim Hung in Danger 1.95
39 Masked Men to the Rescue . 1.95
40 . . . . 1.95
41 . . . . 1.95
42 . . . . 1.95
43 A:Russell School Pack 1.95
44 FirefoxV:Tyrant of Venom . . . 1.95
45 A:Yuen Mo 1.95
46 V:Cannibal 2.50
47 . . . . 1.95
48 A:Clairvoyant Assassin 1.95
49 Prophecy of Hero's fate 1.95
50 D:Poison Entity 1.95
51 . . . . 1.95
52 Hero vs.Cannibal 1.95
53 Hero vs.Cannibal 1.95

BLOODBATH
Samson Comics
1 I:Alien 2.50

BLOODCHILDE
Millenium
1 thru 3 Neil Gaiman, Vampires . 2.95

BLOODFIRE
Lightning Comics
0 O:Bloodfire 3.00
1 JZy(s),JJn, red foil 8.00
1a Platinum foil Ed. 35.00
1b B&W Promo Ed. Silver ink . . 25.00
1c B&W Promo Ed. Gold ink . . 75.00
2 JZy(s),JJn,O:Bloodfire 5.00
3 JZy(s),JJn,I:Dreadwolf,
  Judgement Day,Overthrow . . . 4.00
4 JZy(s),JJn,A:Dreadwolf, ... 3.00
5 JZy(s),JJn,I:Bloodstorm, w/card 3.00
6 SZ(s),TLw,V:Storman 3.00
7 SZ(s),TLw,A:Pres.Clinton 3.00
8 SZ(s),TLw,O:Prodigal 3.00
9 SZ(s),TLw,I:Prodigal
  (in Costume) 3.00
10 SZ(s),TLw,B:Rampage,I:Thorpe 3.00
11 . . . . 2.95
12 . . . . 2.95

BLOODLORE
Brave New Worlds
1 Dreamweavers 1.95
2 A Blow to the Crown 1.95

BLOODSCENT
Comico
1 GC 2.00

BLUE BEETLE
Charlton Comics
{1st S.A. Series}
1 O:Dan Garrett/BlueBeetle . . . 60.00
2 . . . . 40.00
3 V:Mr.Thunderbolt 50.00
4 V:Praying Mantis Man 40.00
5 V:Red Knight 40.00
50 V:Scorpion(formerly Unusual
  Tales) 50.00
51 V:Mentor 50.00
52 V:Magno 50.00
53 V:Praying Mantis Man 50.00
54 V:Eye of Horus 50.00
{2nd S.A. Series}
1 SD,I:Question 75.00
2 SD,O:TedKord,D:DanGarrett . 35.00
3 SD,I:Madmen,A:Question . . . 25.00
4 SD,A:Question 25.00
5 SD,VicSage(Question) app. in
  Blue Beetle Story 25.00

BLUE BULLETEER
AC Comics
1 . . . . 2.25

BLUE PHANTOM, THE
Dell Publishing Co.
June-August, 1962
1 . . . . 30.00

BLUE RIBBON
Archie Publications
1 JK,AV,O:Fly rep. 1.50
2 TVe,Mr.Justice 1.50
3 EB/TD,O:Steel Sterling 1.50
4 . . . . 1.00
5 S&K,Shield rep. 1.00
6 DAy/TD,Fox 1.00
7 TD,Fox 1.00
8 NA,GM,Blackhood 1.00
9 thru 11 . . . . @1.00

12 SD,ThunderAgents	1.00
13 Thunderbunny	1.00
14 Web & Jaguar	1.00

BOLD ADVENTURE
Pacific

1	2.00
2	1.50
3 JSe	1.50

BOLT & STARFORCE
AC Comics

1	1.75
Bolt Special #1	1.50

BOMBAST
Topps

1 V:Savage Dragon,Trading Card	3.25

BONANZA
Dell Publishing Co.
June-August, 1960

1	125.00
2	60.00
3	35.00
4	35.00
5	35.00
6	35.00
7	35.00
8	35.00
9	35.00
10	35.00
11	30.00
12	30.00
13	30.00
14	30.00
15	30.00
16	30.00
17	30.00
18	30.00
19	30.00
20	30.00
21	20.00
22	20.00
23	20.00
24	20.00
25	20.00
26	20.00
27	20.00
28	20.00
29	20.00
30	20.00
31	20.00
32	20.00
33	20.00
34	20.00
35	20.00
36	20.00
37	20.00

BORIS KARLOFF TALES OF MYSTERY
Gold Key
April, 1963

1 (Thriller)	70.00
2 (Thriller)	50.00
3 thru 8	@25.00
9 WW	40.00
10	25.00
11 AW,JO	35.00
12 AT,AMc,JO	25.00
13	20.00

14	20.00
15 RC,GE	25.00
16 thru 20	@20.00
21 JJ,Screaming Skull	40.00
22 thru 50	@15.00
51 thru 74	@10.00
75 thru 96	@8.00
97 February, 1980	8.00

BOZO
Innovation

1 1950's reprint stories	6.95

BOZO THE CLOWN
Blackthorne

1 3-D	2.50
2 3-D	2.50

BRADY BUNCH, THE
Dell Publishing Co.
February, 1970

1	30.00
2	30.00

BRAIN BOY
Dell Publishing Co.
April-June, 1962

1	75.00
2	40.00
3	30.00
4	30.00
5	30.00
6	30.00

BREEDING GROUND
Samson Comics

1 I:Mazit, Zero	2.50

BRENDA LEE STORY, THE
Dell Publishing Co.
September, 1962

1	65.00

BRENDA STARR REPORTER
Dell Publishing Co.
October, 1963

1	125.00

BRIAN BOLLAND'S BLACK BOOK
Eclipse

1 BB	2.50

BRIDES IN LOVE
Charlton Comics
August, 1956

1	25.00
2	10.00
3 thru 10	@7.00
11 thru 30	@3.50
31 thru 44	@2.00
45 February, 1965	2.00

BUCK ROGERS
Gold Key
October, 1964

1 P(c)	40.00
2 AMc,FBe,P(c),movie adapt	5.00
3 AMc,FBe,P(c),movie adapt	5.00

4 FBe,P(c)	5.00
5 AMc,P(c)	2.50
6 AMc,P(c)	2.50

Buck Rogers #3 © Whitman

Whitman

7 thru 9 AMc,P(c)	@2.50
10 and 11 AMc,P(c)	@2.00
12 and 13 P(c)	2.00
14 thru 16	2.00

BUCK ROGERS
TSR

1 thru 10	@2.95

BUCKY O'HARE
Continuity

1 MGo	2.75
2	2.00
3	2.00

BUFFALO BILL JR.
Dell Publishing Co.
January, 1956

1	50.00
2	30.00
3	30.00
4	30.00
5	30.00
6	30.00
7 thru 13	@25.00

BUGGED-OUT ADVENTURES OF RALFY ROACH
Bugged Out Comics

1 I: Ralfy Roach	2.95

BULLWINKLE
Gold Key
November, 1962

1 Bullwinkle & Rocky	125.00
2	85.00
3 thru 5	@30.00
6 and 7, rep.	@20.00
8 thru 11	30.00
12 rep.	15.00
13 and 14	@20.00
15 thru 19	@15.00

---

20 thru 24, rep. . . . . @8.00
25 . . . . 15.00

BULLWINKLE
Charlton Comics
July, 1970
1 . . . . 25.00
2 thru 7, July 1971 . . . . @15.00

BULLWINKLE & ROCKY
Eclipse
3-D 12.50

BULLWINKLE FOR PRESIDENT
Blackthorne
1 3-D Special 2.50

BURKE'S LAW
Dell Publishing Co.
January-February, 1964
1 . . . . 25.00
2 . . . . 15.00
3 . . . . 15.00

Cadillacs & Dinosaurs #3
© Topps Comic

CADILLACS & DINOSAURS
Kitchen Sink
1 Rep. from Xenozoic Tales
in 3-D 6.00
Topps
BLOOD & BONES
1 rep. Xenozoic Tales, all covers 2.50
2 rep. Xenozoic Tales, all covers 2.50
3 rep. Xenozoic Tales, all covers 2.50
MAN-EATER
1 thru 3, all covers 2.50
THE WILD ONES
1 thru 3, all covers 2.50

CAGES
Tundra
1 DMc 14.00
2 DMc 11.00

3 DMc 7.50
4 DMc 7.50
5 thru 7 DMc 5.00

CAIN
Harris
1 B:DQ(s),I:Cain,Frenzy 5.00
2 BSz(c),HBk,V:Mortatira 3.25

CAIN'S HUNDRED
Dell Publishing Co.
May-July, 1962
1 . . . . 15.00
2 . . . . 12.00

CALIFORNIA RAISINS
Blackthorne
1 3-D 2.50
2 3-D 2.50
3 3-D 2.50
4 3-D 2.50
5 3-D,O:Calif.Raisins 2.50
6 thru 8 3-D . . . . @2.50

CALVIN & THE COLONEL
Dell Publishing Co.
April-June, 1962
1 . . . . 40.00
2 . . . . 30.00

CAP'N QUICK & FOOZLE
Eclipse
1 . . . . 2.00
2 and 3 . . . . @2.50

CAPT. ELECTRON
Brick Computers Inc.
1 . . . . 2.00
2 . . . . 2.25

CAPTAIN ATOM
See STRANGE SUSPENSE STORIES

CAPTAIN GLORY
Topps
1 A:Bombast,Night Glider,
Trading Card 3.25

CAPTAIN HARLOCK: FALL OF THE EMPIRE
Eternity
1 R:Captain Harlock 2.50
2 V:Tadashi 2.50
3 Bomb on the Arcadia 2.50
4 Final issue 2.50

CAPTAIN NAUTICUS
Entity
1 V:Fathom 2.95
2 V:Fathom's Henchman 2.95
3 Surf's Up 1.95

CAPTAIN NICE
Gold Key
November, 1967
1 Ph(c) 35.00

CAPTAIN PARAGON
Americomics
1 thru 4 . . . . @2.00

CAPTAIN POWER
Continuity
1a NA,TVtie-in(direct sale) 2.00
1b NA,TVtie-in(newsstand) 2.00
2 NA 2.00

CAPTAIN STERN
Kitchen Sink Press
1 BWr,R:Captain Stern 5.25
2 BWr,Running Out of Time 4.95

CAPTAIN THUNDER AND BLUE BOLT
Hero Graphics
1 I:Capt.Thunder & Paul Fremont 1.95
2 Paul becomes Blue Bolt 1.95
3 O:Capt.Thunder 1.95
4 V:Iguana Boys 1.95
5 V:Ian Shriver, in Scotland 1.95
6 V:Krakatoa 1.95
7 V:Krakatoa 1.95
8 A:Sparkplug (from League
of Champions) 1.95
9 A:Sparkplug 1.95
10 A:Sparkplug 1.95

CAPTAIN VENTURE & THE LAND BENEATH THE SEA
Gold Key
October, 1968
1 . . . . 35.00
2 . . . . 30.00

CAPTAIN VICTORY
Pacific
1 JK 2.00
2 JK 1.50
3 NA,JK,I:Ms.Mystic 1.75
4 JK 1.00
5 JK 1.00
6 JK,SD 1.00
7 thru 13 JK . . . . @1.00
Special #1 JK 1.50

CAR 54, WHERE ARE YOU?
Dell Publishing Co.
March-May, 1962
1 Ph(c) 55.00
2 thru 7 Ph(c) . . . . @30.00

CARCA JOU RENAISSANCE
1 and 2 . . . . @1.50

CARNOSAUR CARNAGE
Atomeka
TPB 4.95

CAROLINE KENNEDY
Charlton Comics
1961
1 . . . . 50.00

CASEY JONES & RAPHAEL
Mirage

1 Family War 2.75
2 Johnny Woo Woo 2.75
3 V:Johnny Woo Woo 2.75
4 9mm Raphael 2.75

CASPER ENCHANTED TALES
Harvey

1 short stories 1.25

CASPER
Harvey

1 collection of stories 1.00
2 thru 7 . . . . @1.00
8 thru 14 . . . . @1.25
15 thru 28 . . . . @1.50

CASPER THE FRIENDLY GHOST
Blackthorne

1 3-D 2.50

CASPER & FRIENDS
Harvey

1 thru 4 . . . . @1.00
5 short stories, cont 1.25

CASPER GHOSTLAND
Harvey

1 short stories 1.25

Casper's Ghostland #1
© Harvey Publications

CASPER'S GHOSTLAND
Harvey Publications
Winter, 1958-59

1 . . . . 120.00
2 . . . . 50.00
3 thru 10 . . . . @30.00
11 thru 20 . . . . @15.00

21 thru 40 . . . . @8.00
41 thru 61 . . . . @6.00
62 thru 77 . . . . @3.50
78 thru 97 . . . . @2.50
98 December, 1979 . . . . 2.50

CAT TALES
Eternity

1 3-D 1.95

CAVE GIRL
AC Comics

1 . . . . 2.95

CAVE KIDS
Gold Key
February, 1963

1 . . . . 20.00
2 . . . . 15.00
3 . . . . 15.00
4 . . . . 15.00
5 . . . . 15.00
6 . . . . 8.00
7 A:Pebbles & Bamm Bamm . . 10.00
8 thru 10 . . . . 8.00
11 thru 16 . . . . 8.00

CHAINS OF CHAOS
Harris

1 Vampirella, Rook 2.95
2 V:Chaoschild 2.95
3 Final issue 2.95

CHAMPIONS
Eclipse

1 I:Flare,League of Champions
Foxbat, Dr.Arcane 1.25
2 I:Dark Malice 1.50
3 I:Lady Arcane 1.25
4 O:Dark Malice 2.00
5 O:Flare 1.25
6 D:Giant Demonmaster 1.25

[New Series]
Hero

1 EL,I:Madame Synn,Galloping
Galooper 5.00
2 I:Fat Man, Black Enchantress . 2.25
3 I:Sparkplug&Icicle,O:Flare 2.25
4 I:Exo-Skeleton Man 2.25
5 A:Foxbat 2.25
6 I:Mechanon, C:Foxbat 1.95
7 A:Mechanon,J:Sparkplug,Icicle . 1.95
8 O:Foxbat 1.95
9 Flare #0 (Flare preview) 1.95
10 Olympus Saga #1 . . . . 1.95
11 Olympus Saga #2 . . . . 1.95
12 Olympus Saga #3 . . . . 1.95
Ann.#1 O:Giant & DarkMalice . . . 2.75
Ann.#2 . . . . 3.95

CHAMPIONS CLASSIC
Hero Graphics

1 GP(c),Rep.1st champions
series 1.00

CHARLEMAGNE
Defiant

1 JiS(s),From Hero 2.00
2 JiS(s),I:Charles Smith 2.75
3 JiS(s),A:War Dancer 2.75
4 DGC(s),V:Dark Powers 2.75
5 Schism prequel 2.75

6 V:Wardancer 2.75
7 R:To Vietnam 2.75

CHARLIE CHAN
Dell Publishing Co.
October-December, 1965

1 . . . . 15.00
2 . . . . 10.00

CHARLTON BULLSEYE
Special #1 . . . . 2.00

CHEAP SHODDY ROBOT TOYS
Eclipse

1 A:Ronald Reagan 1.75

CHECKMATE
Gold Key
October, 1962

1 Ph(c) 30.00
2 Ph(c) 25.00

CHEMICAL MAN

1 . . . . 1.75

CHEYENNE
Dell Publishing Co.
October, 1956

1 Ph(c) all 85.00
2 . . . . 45.00
3 . . . . 45.00
4 . . . . 35.00
5 . . . . 35.00
6 . . . . 35.00
7 . . . . 35.00
8 . . . . 35.00
9 . . . . 35.00
10 . . . . 35.00
11 . . . . 35.00
12 . . . . 35.00
13 . . . . 30.00
14 . . . . 30.00
15 . . . . 30.00
16 . . . . 30.00
17 . . . . 30.00
18 . . . . 30.00
19 . . . . 30.00
20 . . . . 30.00
21 . . . . 30.00
22 . . . . 30.00
23 . . . . 30.00
24 . . . . 30.00
25 . . . . 30.00

CHEYENNE KID
(see WILD FRONTIER)

CHILD'S PLAY 2
Innovation

1 Movie Adapt Pt 1 . . . . 2.50
2 Adapt Pt 2 . . . . 2.50
3 Adapt Pt 3 . . . . 2.50

CHILD'S PLAY 3
Innovation

1 Movie Adapt Pt 1 . . . . 2.50
2 Movie Adapt Pt.2 . . . . 2.50

CHILD'S PLAY: THE SERIES
Innovation
1 Chucky's Back		2.50
2 Straight Jacket Blues		2.50
3 M.A.R.K.E.D.		2.50
4 Chucky in Toys 4 You		2.50
5 Chucky in Hollywood		2.50

CHILDREN OF FIRE
• Fantagor
1 RCo		2.00
2 RCo		2.00
3 RCo		2.00

CHIP 'N' DALE
Walt Disney
1		3.50
2		3.00
3		2.50
4		2.50
5		2.50
6		2.50
7		2.50
8 Coast to Coast Pt 1		2.00
9 Coast to Coast Pt 2		2.00
10 Coast to Coast Pt 3		2.00
11 Coast to Coast Pt 4		2.00
12 'Showdown at Hoedown'		1.75
13 Raining Cats & Dogs		1.75
14 'Cobra Kadabra'		1.75
15 I:Techno-Rats,WaspPatrol Fearless Frogs Pt.1		1.75
16 A:Techno-Rats,WaspPatrol, Fearless Frogs Pt.2		1.75
17 'For the Love of Cheese'		1.75
18 'Ghastly Goat of Quiver Moore, Pt.1		1.50

CHOO CHOO CHARLIE
Gold Key
December, 1969
1		32.00

CHOPPER: EARTH, WIND, AND FIRE
Fleetway
1 F:Chopper		2.95

CHRISTMAS PARADE
Gladstone
1 GiantEdition		4.00
2		3.50

CHROMA-TICK SPECIAL EDITION
New England Press
1 Rep.Tick#1,new stories		3.95
2 Rep.Tick#2,new stories		3.95
3 thru 8 Reps.& new stories		@3.50

CHROME
Hot Comics
1 Machine Man		3.50
2 thru 4		@2.00

CHROMIUM MAN, THE
Triumphant Comics
0 Blue Logo		10.00
0		2.50

---

1 I:Chromium Man,Mr.Death		3.50
2 I:Prince Vandal		3.00
3 I:Candi,Breaker,Coil		2.50
4 JnR(s),AdP,Unleashed		2.50
5 JnR(s),AdP,Unleashed		2.50
6 JnR(s),Courier,pt.1		2.50
7 JnR(s),Courier,pt.2		2.50
8 JnR(s),Chromium finds peace		2.50
9 V:Tarsak		2.50
10		2.50
11 Prince Vandal #8		2.50
12 Prince Vandal #9		2.50
13 V:Realm		2.50
14 A:Light		2.50
15		2.50

CHROMIUM MAN: VIOLENT PAST
Triumphant Comics
1 JnR(s),		2.50
2 JnR(s),		2.50
3 JnR(s),		2.50
4 JnR(s),		2.50

CHRONICLES OF CORUM
First
6		2.25
7 thru 12		@2.00

CICERO'S CAT
Dell Publishing Co.
July-August, 1959
1		15.00
2		15.00

CIMMARON STRIP
Dell Publishing Co.
January, 1968
1		25.00

CLASSICS ILLUSTRATED
See Also:
CLASSICS ILLUSTRATED SECTION

CLASSICS ILLUSTRATED
First
1 GW,The Raven		3.75
2 RG,Great Expectations		3.75
3 KB,Thru the Looking Glass		3.75
4 BSz,Moby Dick		3.75
5 SG,TM,KE, Hamlet		3.75
6 PCr,JT, Scarlet Letter		3.75
7 DSp,Count of Monte Cristo		3.75
8 Dr.Jekyll & Mr.Hyde		3.75
9 MP,Tom Sawyer		3.75
10 Call of the Wild		3.75
11 Rip Van Winkle		3.75
12 Dr. Moreau		3.75
13 Wuthering Heights		3.75
14 Fall of House of Usher		3.75
15 Gift of the Magi		3.75
16 A: Christmas Carol		3.75
17 Treasure Island		3.75
18 The Devils Dictionary		3.95
19 The Secret Agent		3.95
20 The Invisible Man		3.95
21 Cyrano de Bergerac		3.95
22 The Jungle Book		3.95
23 Swiss Family Robinson		3.95
24 Rime of Ancient Mariner		3.95
25 Ivanhoe		3.95

---

26 Aesop's Fables		3.95
27 The Jungle		3.95

CLIVE BARKER'S DREAD
Eclipse
Graphic Album		7.95

CLIVE BARKER'S HELLRAISER
Epic Comics
Dark Holiday Spec.#1		4.95

CLIVE BARKER'S TAPPING THE VEIN
Eclipse
1		13.00
2		8.50
3		8.50
4		8.50
5 inc."How Spoilers Breed"		8.50

CLYDE CRASHCUP
Dell Publishing Co.
August-October, 1963
1		65.00
2		50.00
3 thru 5		@50.00

COBALT 60
Innovation
1 reprints		4.95

COBALT BLUE
Innovation
Special #1		1.95
Special #2		1.95
1 and 2		@1.95

Codename: Danger #4 © Lodestone

CODENAME: DANGER
Lodestone
1 RB/BMc,I:Makor		2.50
2 KB,I:Capt.Energy		2.00
3 PS/RB		1.50

All comics prices listed are for *Near Mint* condition.

4 PG 1.50

CODENAME: STRIKEFORCE
Spectrum

1 . . . . 1.00

COLLECTOR'S DRACULA
Millennium

1 . . . . 4.25

COLOSSAL SHOW, THE
Gold Key
October, 1969

1 . . . . 25.00

COLOUR OF MAGIC
Innovation

1 Terry Pratchet novel adapt . . . 3.00
2 'The Sending of Eight' 2.50
3 'Lure of the Worm 2.50
4 final issue 2.50

COLT .45
Dell Publishing Co.
August, 1958

1 Ph(c) all 75.00
2 . . . . 40.00
3 . . . . 40.00
4 . . . . 40.00
5 . . . . 40.00
6 ATh 50.00
7 . . . . 40.00
8 . . . . 40.00
9 . . . . 40.00

COLT SPECIAL
AC Comics

1 . . . . 1.75
2 . . . . 1.75
3 . . . . 1.75

COMBAT
Dell Publishing Co.
Oct.-Nov., 1961

1 SG 35.00
2 SG 15.00
3 SG 15.00
4 JFK cover, Story 2-D 20.00
5 SG 15.00
6 SG 10.00
7 SG 10.00
8 SG 10.00
9 SG 10.00
10 SG 10.00
11 SG 7.00
12 SG 7.00
13 SG 7.00
14 SG 7.00
15 SG 7.00
16 SG 7.00
17 SG 7.00
18 SG 7.00
19 SG 7.00
20 SG 7.00
21 SG 7.00
22 SG 7.00
23 SG 7.00
24 SG 7.00
25 SG 7.00

26 SG 7.00
27 SG 7.00
28 SG 5.00
29 SG 5.00
30 SG 5.00
31 SG 5.00
32 SG 5.00
33 SG 5.00
34 SG 5.00
35 SG 5.00
36 SG 5.00
37 thru 40 SG . . . . @5.00

COMET
Archie Publications

1 CI,O:Comet 1.00
2 CI,D:Hangman 1.00

COMIC ALBUM
Dell Publishing Co.
March-May, 1958

1 Donald Duck 60.00
2 Bugs Bunny 25.00
3 Donald Duck 45.00
4 Tom & Jerry 25.00
5 Woody Woodpecker 25.00
6 Bugs Bunny 25.00
7 Popeye 30.00
8 Tom & Jerry 25.00
9 Woody Woodpecker 25.00
10 Bugs Bunny 25.00
11 Popeye 30.00
12 Tom & Jerry 20.00
13 Woody Woodpecker 20.00
14 Bugs Bunny 20.00
15 Popeye 30.00
16 Flintstones 45.00
17 Space Mouse 25.00
18 3 Stooges,Ph(c) 60.00

COMICO X-MAS SPECIAL
Comico

1 SR/AW/DSt(c) 1.50

COMIX INTERNATIONAL
Warren Magazines
July, 1974

1 . . . . 35.00
2 WW,BW 20.00
3 . . . . 8.00
4 RC 10.00
5 Spring, 1977 . . . . 5.00

COMMANDER BATTLE AND HIS ATOMIC SUB
#20 3-D 2.50

COMMANDOSAURS
1 . . . . 3.50

CONSTRUCT
Mirage

1 I:Constructs 2.75
2 F:Sect.Eight, Armor 2.75

CORBEN SPECIAL
Pacific

1 RCo 1.75

CORUM: THE BULL & THE SPEAR
First

1 thru 4 . . . . @1.95

COSMONEERS SPECIAL
1 . . . . 1.95

COURTSHIP OF EDDIE'S FATHER
Dell Publishing Co.
January, 1970

1 Ph(c) 20.00
2 Ph(c) 18.00

COVER GIRL
1 . . . . 1.95

COWBOY IN AFRICA
Gold Key
March, 1968

1 Chuck Conners,Ph(c) 20.00

CRACKED
Major Magazines
February-March, 1958

1 AW 100.00
2 . . . . 40.00
3 thru 6 . . . . @30.00
7 thru 10 . . . . @18.00
11 thru 20 . . . . @10.00
21 thru 30 . . . . @7.00
31 thru 60 . . . . @3.00
61 thru 252 . . . . @2.50

[THE INCREDIBLE] CRASH DUMMIES
Harvey

1 thru 3, from the toy series . . @1.50

CRAZYMAN
Continuity
[1st Series]

1 Embossed(c),NA/RT(i),

Crazyman #3 © Continuity Comics

O:Crazyman 6.00
2 NA/BB(c) 2.50
3 DBa,V:Terrorists 2.50
[2nd Series]
1 Die Cut(c) 2.50
2 thru 3 . . . . 2.50
4 In Demon World 2.50

CRIME MACHINE
Skywald Publications
February, 1971
1 . . . . 20.00
2 . . . . 15.00

CRIME SUSPENSE STORIES
Russ Cochran
1 Rep. C.S.S. #1 (1950) 1.75
2 Rep. C.S.S. 1.75
3 Rep. C.S.S. 1.75
4 thru 6 Rep. C.S.S 2.00
7 Rep. C.S.S 2.00

CROSSFIRE
Eclipse
1 DSp 3.00
2 DSp 2.50
3 DSp 1.50
4 DSp 1.50
5 DSp 1.50
6 DSp 1.50
7 DSp 2.50
8 DSp 2.50
9 DSp 1.75
10 DSp 1.75
11 DSp 1.75
12 DSp,DSt(c),M.Monroe cover
& story 2.50
13 DSp 1.75
14 DSp 1.75
15 DSp,O:Crossfire 1.75
16 DSp,'The Comedy Place' . . . 1.75
17 DSp,'Comedy Place' Pt.2 . . . 1.75

CROSSFIRE & RAINBOW
Eclipse
1 DSp,V:Marx Brothers 1.75
2 DSp,PG(c),V:Marx Brothers . . 1.50
3 DSp,HC(c),A:Witness 1.50
4 DSp,DSt(c),'This Isn't Elvis' . . 3.50

CROSSROADS
First
1 Sable,Whisper 4.00
2 Sable,Badger 4.00
3 JSon,JAl,Badger/Luther
Ironheart 4.00
4 Grimjack/Judah Macabee 4.00
5 LM,Grimjack/Dreadstar/Nexus . 4.00

CRYING FREEMAN III
Viz
1 A:Dark Eyes,Oshu 6.00
2 A:Dark Eyes, V:Oshu 5.25
3 Freeman vs. Oshu 5.25
4 Freeman Defeated 5.25
5 Freeman clones, A:Nitta 5.25
6 V:Nitta 5.25
7 . . . . 4.95
8 . . . . 4.95
9 . . . . 4.95

CRYING FREEMAN IV
Viz
1 B:The Pomegranate 4.95
2 . . . . 2.75
3 . . . . 2.75
4 . . . . 2.75
5 thru 7 . . . . @2.75
8 E:The Pomegranate 2.75
[2nd Series]
1 The Festival 2.50

CYBERCRUSH: ROBOTS IN REVOLT
Fleetway/Quality
1 inc.Robo-Hunter,Ro-Busters . . 1.95
2 and 3 . . . . @1.95

CYBERPUNK
Innovation
1 . . . . 1.95
2 . . . . 1.95
Bk 2,#1 . . . . 2.25
Bk 2,#2 . . . . 2.25

Cyberrad #6 © Continuity Comics

CYBERRAD
Continuity
1 NA layouts,I:Cyberran 3.00
2 NA I/o 2.50
3 NA I/o 2.50
4 NA I/o 2.50
5 NA I/o Glow in the Dark cov . . 5.00
6 NA I/o,Pullout poster 2.50
7 NA I/o,See-thru(c) 2.50
[2nd Series]
1 Hologram cover 2.00
2 NA(c),'The Disassembled Man' 2.00
[3rd Series]
1 Holo.(c),just say no 3.50
[4th Series, Deathwatch 2000]
1 Deathwatch 2000 pt.8,w/card . . 2.50
2 Deathwatch 2000 pt. w/card . . 2.50

DAGAR THE INVINCIBLE
Gold Key
October, 1972

1 O:Daggar;I:Villians Olstellon
& Scorpio 15.00
2 . . . . 6.00
3 I:Graylon 5.00
4 . . . . 5.00
5 . . . . 5.00
6 1st Dark Gods story 4.00
7 . . . . 4.00
8 . . . . 4.00
9 . . . . 4.00
10 . . . . 4.00
11 thru 19 April, 1982 . . . . @2.00

DAI KAMIKAZE
Now
1 Speed Racer 7.00
1a 2nd printing 1.50
2 . . . . 2.00
3 . . . . 1.50
4 . . . . 1.50
5 . . . . 1.50
6 thru 12 . . . . @1.75

DAKTARI
Dell Publishing Co.
July, 1967
1 . . . . 20.00
2 . . . . 15.00
3 . . . . 15.00
4 . . . . 15.00

DALGODA
Fantagraphics
1 . . . . 3.50
2 KN,I:Grinwood'Daughter 3.00
3 KN 2.50
4 thru 8 . . . . @2.25

DANGER
Charlton Comics
June, 1955
12 . . . . 35.00
13 . . . . 25.00
14 . . . . 25.00
Becomes:
JIM BOWIE
15 . . . . 20.00
16 . . . . 10.00
17 . . . . 10.00
18 . . . . 10.00
19 April, 1957 . . . . 10.00

DANIEL BOONE
Gold Key
January, 1965
1 . . . . 75.00
2 thru 5 . . . . @30.00
6 thru 14 . . . . @20.00
15 April, 1969 . . . . 15.00

DANNY BLAZE
Charlton Comics
August, 1955
1 . . . . 35.00
2 . . . . 30.00
Becomes:
NATURE BOY
3 JB,O:Blue Beetle 125.00
4 . . . . 100.00
5 February, 1957 . . . . 85.00

DARE
Fantagraphics
1 F:Dan Dare 2.75
2 F:Dan Dare 2.75
3 F:Dan Dare 2.50
4 F:Dan Dare 2.50

Dare The Impossible #1
© Fleetway/Quality Comics

DARE THE IMPOSSIBLE
Fleetway/Quality
1 DGb,rep.Dan Dare from 2000AD 1.95
2 DGb, Dare on Waterworld 1.95
3 DGb 1.95
4 DGb 1.95
5 DGb,"The Garden of Eden" . . . 1.95
6 DGb 1.95
7 DGb,V:Deadly Primitives 1.95
8 DGb,The Doomsday Machine . 1.95
9 thru 14 DGb . . . . @1.95

DARK, THE
Continüm
1 LSn(c),MBr,V:Futura 7.50
2 LSn,Shot by Futura 6.00
3 MBr,Dark has amnesia 4.00
4 GT(c),MBr,O:The Dark 4.00
Convention Book 1992 MBr,GP,
  MFm,MMi,VS,LSn,TV 12.00
Convention Book 1993 MBr,PC,
  ECh,BS,BWi,GP(c),Foil(c), . . . 8.00
August House
1 BS(c),Red Foil(c), ... 20.00
1a BS(c),newstand ed. 5.00
1b BS(c),Blue foil 15.00
2 . . . . 4.00
3 BS(c),Foil(c), ... 15.00
4 GP(c),Foil(c),w/cards 12.00
5 thru 9 . . . . @2.50
[2nd Series]
1 Dark Regains Memory 2.50
2 War on Crime 2.50
3 Geoffery Stockton 2.50

DARK ADVENTURES
1 . . . . 1.75

2 . . . . 1.75
3 . . . . 1.75

DARK DOMINION
Defiant
1 SD,I:Michael Alexander 3.25
2 LWn(s),SLi(i), ... 2.75
3 LWn(s),SLi(i), ... 2.75
4 LWn(s),B:Hoxhunt 3.00
5 LWn(s),I:Puritan,Judah 2.75
6 LWn(s),I:Lurk 2.75
7 LWn(s),V:Glimmer 2.75
8 LWn(s),V:Glimmer 2.50
9 LWn(s)V:Puritan 2.50
10 LWn(s),Schism Prequel 2.50
11 LWn(s), X-Over 2.50
12 LWn(s), V:Chasm 2.50

DARK SHADOWS
Gold Key
March, 1969
1 W/Poster,Ph(c) 185.00
2 Ph(c) 70.00
3 W/Poster,Ph(c) 85.00
4 thru 7,Ph(c) . . . . @60.00
8 thru 10 . . . . @50.00
11 thru 20 . . . . @35.00
21 thru 35 . . . . @30.00

DARK SHADOWS
Innovation
1 Based on 1990's TV series . . . 3.50
2 O:Victoria Winters 2.50
3 Barnabus Imprisoned 2.50
4 V: Redmond Swann 2.75
[2nd Series]
1 A:Nathan 2.75
2 thru 4 . . . . 2.75
Dark Shadows:Resurrected 15.95

DARKLON THE MYSTIC
Pacific
1 JSn 1.50

DARKWING DUCK
Walt Disney
1 I:Darkwing Duck 1.75
2 V:Taurus Bulba 1.75
3 'Fowl Play' 1.75
4 'End o/t beginning,'final issue . . 1.75

DARKWOOD
Aircel
1 thru 5 . . . . @2.00

DAUGHTERS OF TIME
3-D
1 I:Kris,Cori,Lhana 3.95

FRONTIER FIGHTER
Charlton Comics
August, 1955
1 . . . . 40.00
2 . . . . 20.00
Becomes:
DAVY CROCKETT
3 thru 7 . . . . @15.00
8 January, 1957 . . . . 10.00
Becomes:
KID MONTANA

9 . . . . 20.00
10 . . . . 9.00
11 . . . . 6.00
12 . . . . 6.00
13 . . . . 14.00
14 thru 20 . . . . @6.00
21 thru 35 . . . . @3.50
36 thru 49 . . . . @2.00
50 March, 1965 . . . . 2.00

DAZEY'S DIARY
Dell Publishing Co.
June-August, 1962
1 . . . . 25.00

DEAMON DREAMS
Pacific
1 . . . . 1.50
2 . . . . 1.50

DEAR NANCY PARKER
Gold Key
June, 1963
1 P(c) 18.00
2 P(c),September, 1963 . . . . . 15.00

DEATHDEALER
Verotika
1 FF(c), I:Deathdealer 4.95

DEATHRACE 2020
1 Pat Mills, Tony Skinner 2.50

DEATH RATTLE
Kitchen Sink
1 thru 5 . . . . @2.00

DEFENDERS, THE
Dell Publishing Co.
September-November, 1962
1 . . . . 20.00
2 . . . . 18.00

DEFIANT:
ORIGIN OF A UNIVERSE
Defiant
1 Giveaway 1.50

DELIVERER
Zion Comics
1 thru 3 . . . . 1.95
4 F:Gabriel 1.95
5 V:Division 1.95

DEMONIC TOYS
Eternity
1 Based on 1992 movie 2.50
2 thru 4 . . . . 2.50

DEN
Fantagor
1 thru 9 RCo . . . . @2.00
10 RCo,Last issue 2.00

DEN SAGA
Tundra/fantagor
1 RCo,O:Den begins 4.95

DEPUTY DAWG
Dell Publishing Co.
August, 1965
1 . . . . 75.00

Destroyer Duck #3 © Eclipse Comics

DESTROYER DUCK
Eclipse
1 JK,AA,SA,I:Groo 12.00
2 JK,AA,Starling 1.50
3 thru 5 JK . . . . @1.50
6 thru 7 JK . . . . @2.00

DETECTIVES, INC.
Eclipse
1 MR,rep.GraphicNovel 3.00
2 MR 2.25
[2nd Series]
1 GC,'A Terror of Dying Dreams' 2.50
2 GC 2.25
3 GC,'Cut to the Bone' 1.50

DETONATOR
Chaos! Comics
1 I:Detonator 2.95
2 V:Messiah & Mindbender 2.75

DEVIL KIDS
STARRING HOT STUFF
Harvey Publications
July, 1962
1 . . . . 80.00
2 . . . . 40.00
3 thru 10 . . . . @20.00
11 thru 20 . . . . @15.00
21 thru 30 . . . . @10.00
31 thru 40 . . . . @7.00
41 thru 50 68 pgs. . . . . @7.00
51 thru 55 62 pgs. . . . . @5.00
56 thru 70 . . . . @3.00
71 thru 100 . . . . @2.00
101 thru 106 . . . . @1.00
107 October, 1981 . . . . 1.00

DICK TRACY
1 3-D 2.50

DICK TRACY:
BIG CITY BLUES
1 Mini Series 3.95
2 Mini Series 5.95
3 Mini Series 5.95

DINO ISLAND
Mirage
1 thru 2 . . . . 2.75

DINOSAUR REX
Fantagraphics
1 thru 3 . . . . @2.00

DINOSAURS
Walt Disney
1 Citizen Robbie(From TV) 2.95

DINOSAURS ATTACK
Eclipse
1 HT,Based on Topps cards 3.50
2 thru 3 HT,Based on cards . . @3.50

DISNEY ADVENTURES
Walt Disney
1 . . . . 2.75
2 . . . . 2.50
3 thru 6 . . . . @2.25
7 Joe Montana 2.25
8 Bronson Pinchot 2.25
9 Hulk Hogan 2.25
10 Mayim Bialik 2.25
11 . . . . 2.25
12 Monsters 2.25
13 A:Darkwing Duck (inc. work
　by DW) 2.25
14 inc. 'Big Top, Big Shot' 1.95
15 . . . . 1.95
16 inc.'Turnabout is Fowl Play' . . 1.95
17 inc.'Kitty Kat Kaper' 1.95
18 Kitty Kat Kaper 1.95
19 The Voice of Wisdom 1.95
20 thru 28 . . . . @1.95

DISNEY COLOSSAL
COMICS COLLECTION
Walt Disney
1 inc.DuckTales, Chip'n'Dale . . . 2.25
2 inc.Tailspin,Duck Tales 1.95
3 inc.Duck Tales 1.95
4 O:Darkwing Duck 1.95
5 Tailspin,Duck Tales 1.95
6 Darkwing Duck,Goofy 1.95
7 inc.Darkwing Duck.Goofy 1.95
8 inc.Little Mermaid 1.95
9 inc.Duck Tales 1.95

DISNEY COMICS IN 3-D
Walt Disney
1 . . . . 2.95

DISNEY COMICS SPEC:
DONALD & SCROOGE
1 inc."Return to Xanadu" 8.95

DISNEYLAND BIRTHDAY
PARTY
Gladstone
1 . . . . 6.00

DIVER DAN
Dell Publishing Co.
February-April, 1962
1 . . . . 30.00
2 . . . . 30.00

DNAgents #2 © Eclipse Comics

DNAGENTS
Eclipse
1 O:DNAgents 4.00
2 . . . . 3.00
3 . . . . 2.50
4 . . . . 2.50
5 . . . . 2.50
6 . . . . 2.50
7 . . . . 2.50
8 . . . . 2.50
9 DSp 2.50
10 . . . . 2.00
11 . . . . 2.00
12 . . . . 2.50
13 . . . . 2.00
14 . . . . 2.00
15 . . . . 2.50
16 . . . . 2.50
17 thru 21 . . . . @2.00
22 . . . . 1.75
23 . . . . 1.75
24 DSt(c) 1.75
25 . . . . 1.75
See also: NEW DNAGENTS

DO YOU BELIEVE
IN NIGHTMARES?
St. John Publishing Co.
November, 1957
1 SD 165.00
2 DAy,January, 1958 . . . . . . 100.00

DOBER-MAN
1 . . . . 2.50

DOC SAVAGE
Millenium
1 V:Russians 2.50

DOC SAVAGE,
THE MAN OF BRONZE
Millenium
1 Monarch of Armageddon,pt.1 . .	3.00
2 Monarch of Armageddon,pt.2 . .	2.75
3 Monarch of Armageddon,pt.3 . .	2.75
4 Monarch of Armageddon,pt.4 . .	2.75

DOC SAVAGE:
THE DEVIL'S THOUGHTS
Millenium
1 V:Hanoi Shan	2.50
2 V:Hanoi Shan	2.50
3 Final issue	2.50

Doc Savage, Doom Dynasty #2
© Millenium

DOC SAVAGE:
DOOM DYNASTY
Millenium
1	2.50
2	2.50

DOC SAVAGE:
MANUAL OF BRONZE
Millenium
1 Fact File	2.50

DOC SAVAGE: REPEL
Innovation
1 DvD(c)	2.50

DOCTOR BOOGIE
Media Arts
1	1.75
2	1.75

DOCTOR CHAOS
Triumphant Comics
1 JnR(s),I:Doctor Chaos	2.50
2 JnR(s), ...	2.50
3 JnR(s),The Coming of the	
Cry,pt.1,I:Cry	2.50
4 JnR(s),The Coming of the	
Cry,pt.2,b:Ky'Li	2.50
5 JnR(s),E:Coming of the	

Cry,pt.3,V:Cry	2.50
6 Recovery	2.50
7 w/coupon	2.50
8 w/coupon	2.50
9 V:Mirth	2.50
10 Co. X #3	2.50
11 Co. X #4	2.50
12 A:Charlotte	2.50

DOCTOR SOLAR
MAN OF THE ATOM
Gold Key
1 BF,I:Dr. Solar	250.00
2 BF,I:Prof.Harbinger	100.00
3 BF,The Hidden Hands	60.00
4 BF,The Deadly Sea	60.00
5 BF,I:Dr.Solar in costume	60.00
6 FBe,I:Nuro	40.00
7 FBe,Vanishing Oceans	40.00
8 FBe,Thought Controller	40.00
9 FBe,Transivac The Energy	
Consuming Computer	40.00
10 FBe,The Sun Giant	40.00
11 FBe,V:Nuro	35.00
12 FBe,The Mystery of the	
Vanishing Silver	35.00
13 FBe,The Meteor from 100	
Million BC	35.00
14 FBe,Solar's Midas Touch . . .	35.00
15 FBe O:Dr.Solar	45.00
16 FBe,V:Nuro	35.00
17 FBe,The Fatal Foe	35.00
18 FBe,The Mind Master	35.00
19 FBe,SolarV:Solar	35.00
20 AMc,Atomic Nightmares	35.00
21 AMc,Challenge from	
Outer Space	25.00
22 AMc,Nuro,I:King	
Cybernoid	25.00
23 AMc,A:King Cybernoid	25.00
24 EC,The Deadly Trio	25.00
25 EC,The Lost Dimension	25.00
26 EC,When Dimensions	
Collide	25.00
27 (1969) The Ladder	
to Mars	25.00
28 (1981),1 pg AMc,The	
Dome of Mystery	12.00
29 DSp,FBe,Magnus	12.00
30 DSp,FBe,Magnus	12.00

DOGHEAD
Tundra
1 Al Columbia,"Poster Child" . . .	4.95

DOGS OF WAR
Defiant
1 F:Shooter,Ironhead	2.75
2	2.50
3 Mouse Deserts	2.50
4 Schism Prequel	2.50
5 X-over	2.50
6 Aftermath	2.50

DOLLMAN
Eternity
1 Movie adapt. sequel	2.50
2 V:Sprug & Braindead Gang . .	2.50
3 Toni Costa Kidnapped	2.50
4	2.50

DONALD DUCK
Dell/Gold Key
December 1962
85 thru 97	25.00
98 rep. #46 CB	25.00
99	22.00
100	20.00
101	18.00
102 A:Super Goog	18.00
103 thru 111	@18.00
112 I:Moby Duck	18.00
113 thru 133	@18.00
134 CB rep.	18.00
135 CB rep.	18.00
136 thru 156	@15.00
157 CB rep.	12.00
158 thru 163	@10.00
164 CB rep.	10.00
165 thru 216	@4.00
Whitman	
217	4.00
218	4.00
219 CB rep.	4.00
220 thru 245	@4.00
Gladstone	
246 CB,Gilded Man	12.00
247 CB	10.00
248 CB,Forbidden Valley	10.00
249 CB	15.00
250 CB,Pirate Gold	15.00
251 CB,Donald's Best Xmas . . .	4.00
252 CB,Trail o/t Unicorn	4.00
253 CB	3.50
254 CB, in old Calif	7.00
255 CB	3.50
256 CB,Volcano Valley	3.50
257 CB,Forest Fire	4.00
258 thru 260 CB	@3.00
261 thru 266 CB	@2.50
267 thru 277 CB	@2.00
278 CB	4.00
279 CB	4.00
280 thru 287 CB rep.	@1.50

DONALD DUCK
ADVENTURES
Gladstone
1 CB,Jungle Hi-Jinks	5.00
2 CB,Dangerous Disquise	4.00
3 CB,Lost in the Andes	5.00
4 CB,Frozen Gold	4.00
5 Rosa Art	3.50
6	2.50
7	2.50
8 Rosa	3.50
9	2.50
10	2.50
11	2.50
12 Giant size,Rosa	3.50
13 Rosa(c)	2.50
14	3.00
15 CB	2.00
16	2.00
17	2.00
18	2.00
19	4.00
20 Giant size	4.00
21 thru 30	@2.95

DONALD DUCK
ADVENTURES
Walt Disney
1 Rosa	5.00

2	3.00
3	2.50
4	2.50
5	2.50
6	2.50
7	2.00
8	2.00
9	2.00
10 'Run-Down Runner'	2.00
11 'Whats for Lunch-Supper'	2.00
12 'Head of Rama Putra'	2.00
13 'JustAHumble,BumblingDuck'	2.00
14 'DayGladstonesLuckRanOut'	1.75
15 'A Tuft Luck Tale'	1.75
16 'Magica's Missin'Magic'	1.75
17 'Secret of Atlantis'	1.75
18 'Crocodile Donald'	1.75
19 'Not So Silent Service'	1.75
20 'Ghost of Kamikaze Ridge'	1.50
21 'The Golden Christmas Tree'	1.50
22 'The Master Landscapist'	1.50
23 'The Lost Peg Leg Mine'	1.50
24 'On Stolen Time'	1.50
25 Sense of Humor	1.50
26 Race to the South Seas	1.50
27 Nap in Nature	1.50
28 Olympic Tryout	1.50
29 rep.March of Comics#20	1.50
30 A:The Vikings	1.50
31 The Sobbing Serpent of Loch McDuck	1.50
32 It Was No Occident	1.50
33 Crazy Christmas on Bear Mountain	1.50
34 Sup.Snooper Strikes Again	1.50
35 CB rep.	1.50
36 CB rep.	1.50
37 CB rep.	1.50

DONALD DUCK ALBUM
Dell Publishing Co.
May-July, 1959

1 CB(c)	40.00
2	25.00

DONATELLO
Mirage

1	10.00

Doomsday Squad #7 © Fantagraphics

DOOMSDAY + 1
Charlton

1 JBy,JBy(c),P(c)	8.00
2	6.00
3 JBy,JBy(c),P(c)	5.00
4 JBy,JBy(c),P(c),I:Lok	5.00
5 and 6 JBy,JBy(c),P(c)	@5.00
7 thru 12 JBy,JBy(c),P(c),rep	2.00

DOOMSDAY SQUAD
Fantagraphics

1 rep. JBy	2.00
2 rep. JBy	2.00
3 rep. SS,A:Usagi Yojimbo	4.00
4 rep. JBy	2.00
5 thru 7, rep. JBy	@2.00

DOUBLE DARE ADVENTURES
Harvey Publications

1 I:B-man,Glowing Gladiator, Magicmaster	22.00
2 AW/RC rep. A:B-Man,Glowing Gladiator, Magicmaster	17.00

DOUBLE IMPACT
High Impact Studios

1 I:China & Jazz	3.95

DOUBLE LIFE OF PRIVATE STRONG
Archie Publications

1 JSm/JK,I:Lancelot Strong/Shield The Fly	275.00
2 JSm/JK,GT A:Fly	200.00

DR. KILDARE
Dell Publishing Co.
April-June, 1962

1	50.00
2	40.00
3	40.00
4	40.00
5	40.00
6	40.00
7	40.00
8	40.00
9	40.00

DRACULA
Dell Publishing Co.
November, 1966

2 O:Dracula	25.00
3	15.00
4	15.00
6	12.00
7	10.00
8	10.00

DRACULA
Topps

1 MMi,Movie adaptation (trading cards in each issue)	5.00
1a Red Foil Logo	65.00
1b 2nd Print	2.95
2 MMi,Movie adapt.contd.	4.00
3 MMi,Movie adapt.contd.	4.00
4 MMi,Movie adapt.concludes	4.00
TPB Collected Album	13.95

DRACULA CHRONICLES
Topps

1 True Story of Dracula	2.50
2 RTs,rep. Vlad #2	2.50

DRACULA VS. ZORRO
Topps

1 DMg(s),TY,Black(c)	2.95
2 DMg(s),TY,w/Zorro #0	2.95
TPB	5.95

DRACULA: VLAD THE IMPALER
Topps

1 EM,I:Vlad Dracua, w/cards	3.25
1a Red Foil	50.00
2 EM, w/cards	3.25

DRAGONCHIANG
Eclipse

1 TT	2.95

DRAGONFLIGHT
Eclipse

1 Anne McCaffrey novel adapt	4.95
2 novel adapt	4.95
3 novel adapt	4.95

DRAGONFLY
AC Comics

1	3.50
2 and 3	@2.00
4 thru 8	@1.75

DRAGONFORCE
Aircel

1 DK	7.50
2 thru 7 DK	@5.00
8 thru 12	@5.00
13	2.00

DRAGONRING
Aircel

1	3.50
2 O:Dragonring	2.50
3 thru 15	@2.00

DREADSTAR
First

27 JSn,from Epic,traitor	2.50
28 JSn	2.25
29 JSn,V:Lord Papal	2.25
30 JSn,D:Lord Papal	2.25
31 JSn,I:The Power	2.25
32 JSn	2.25
33	2.25
34 LM/VM,A:Malchek	2.25
35 LM/VM	2.25
36 LM/VM	2.25
37 LM/VM,A:Last Laugh	2.25
38 LM/VM	2.25
39 AMc,Crossroads tie-in	2.25
40 LM/VM	2.25
41 AMe	2.25
42 JSn,AMe,B.U.Pawns begins	2.25
43 JSn,AMe,Pawns,pt.1	2.25
44 JSn,AMe,Pawns,pt.3	2.25
45 JSn,AMe,Pawns,pt.4	2.25
46 JSn,AMe,Pawns,pt.5	2.25
47 JSn,AMe,Pawns,pt.6	2.25
48 JSn,AMe,Pawns,pt.7	2.25

Dreadstar #51 © First

49 JSn,AMe,Pawns,pt.8 .... 2.25
50 JSn,AMe,Pawns,pt.9
   prestige format 4.25
51 PDd,Woj,Pawns,pt.10,
   Paladox epic begins 2.25
52 AMe 2.25
53 AMe,'Messing with Peoples
   Minds' 2.25
54 JSn,AMe,Pawns ends 2.25
55 AMe,I:Iron Angel 2.25
56 AME,A:Iron Angel 2.25
57 A:Iron Angel 2.25
58 A:Iron Angel 2.25
59 A:Iron Angel 2.25
60 AMe,Paladox epic ends 2.25
61 AME,A:Iron Angel 2.25
62 O:Dreadstar,I:Youngscuz ... 2.25
63 AMe,A:Youngscuz 2.25
64 AMe,A:Youngscuz 2.25

DREDD RULES
Fleetway/Quality
1 SBs(c),JBy,Prev.unpubl.
   in USA 5.00
2 inc.'Eldster Ninja Mud
   Wrestling Vigilantes' 3.50
3 inc.'That Sweet Stuff' 3.50
4 Our Man in Hondo City 3.50
5 .... 3.25
6 BKi,DBw 3.25
7 "Banana City" 3.25
8 "Over the Top" 3.25
9 "Shooting Match" 3.25
10 SBs,inc.Mega-City primer ... 3.25
11 SBs,Legend/Johnny Biker 3.25
12 SBs,Rock on Tommy Who ... 3.25
13 BMy,The Ballad of Toad
   McFarlane 3.25
14 thru 15 .... @3.25
16 A:Russians 3.25
17 F:Young Giant 3.25
18 F:Jonny Cool 2.95
19 V:Hunter's Club 2.95

DRIFT MARLO
Dell Publishing Co.
May–July, 1962
1 .... 18.00

2 .... 15.00

DRUG WARS
Pioneer
1 .... 1.95
2 .... 1.95
3 .... 1.95

DRUNKEN FIST
Jademan
1 .... 3.25
2 .... 2.50
3 .... 2.00
4 thru 9 .... @1.75
10 thru 27 .... @1.95
28 D:Mack 1.95
29 .... 1.95
30 .... 1.95
31 .... 1.95
32 Wong Mo-Gei vs.Swordsman . 1.95
33 Mo-Gei commits suicide 1.95
34 .... 1.95
35 .... 1.95
36 D:Fire Oak 1.95
37 Iron Law Kills Elephant-Man .. 1.95
38 A:Wayne Chan 1.95
39 D:Wayne Chan 1.95
40 D:Toro Yamamoto 1.95
41 Lord Algol vs. Ghing Mob 1.95
42 .... 1.95
43 D:Yamamoto,Swordsman
   in USA 1.95
44 'Cool Hand Wong' 1.95
45 'Black Cult Rising' 1.95
46 .... 1.95
47 .... 1.95
48 Evil Child 1.95
49 I:Hurricane Child 1.95
50 Lord Algol vs.Diabol.Ent. 1.95
51 F:Flying Thunder 1.95
52 Madcap vs.Yama 1.95
53 Swordsman vs.Catman 1.95

DUCKMAN
Topps
1 USA Cartoon 2.50
2 XXX Files 2.50
3 I:King Chicken 2.50
4 V:Toys 2.50
5 F:Cornfed 2.50
6 Star Trek Parody 2.50
7 rep. 1990 B&W 1st app., now
   in color 2.50

DUCKMAN: THE MOB
FROG SAGA
Topps
1 I:Mob Frog 2.50
2 D:Mob Frog 2.50
3 In the Name of the Duck 2.50

DUCK TALES
Gladstone
1 CB(r)I:LaunchpadMcQuck 5.00
2 CB(r) 3.00
3 .... 2.50
4 CB(r) 2.50
5 thru 11 .... @2.25
12 .... 4.00
13 .... 4.00

DUCK TALES
Walt Disney
1 .... 4.00
2 .... 2.50
3 .... 2.25
4 .... 2.25
5 Scrooges'Quest 2.25
6 Scrooges'Quest 2.00
7 Return to Duckburg 2.00
8 .... 2.00
9 7 Sojourns of Scrooge 2.00
10 Moon of Gold 2.00
11 Once & Future Warlock 2.00
12 Lost Beyond the MilkyWay ... 1.75
13 The Doomed of Sarras 1.75
14 Planet Blues 1.75
15 The Odyssey Ends 1.75
16 The Great Chase 1.75
17 Duck in Time Pt.1 .... 1.75
18 Duck in Time Pt.2 .... 1.75
19 Bail Out 1.75

DUDLEY DO-RIGHT
Charlton Comics
August, 1970
1 .... 40.00
2 thru 7 August 1971 ...... @30.00

DUNC & LOO
Dell Publishing Co.
October-December, 1961
1 .... 50.00
2 .... 40.00
3 .... 25.00
4 .... 25.00
5 .... 25.00
6 .... 25.00
7 .... 25.00
8 .... 25.00

DWIGHT D. EISENHOWER
Dell Publishing Co.
December, 1969
1 .... 20.00

DYNAMO
Tower Comics
August, 1966
1 WW,MSy,RC,SD,I:Andor ... 35.00
2 WW,DA,GT,MSy,Weed solo story
   A:Iron Maiden 25.00
3 WW,GT,Weed solo story, A:Iron
   Maiden 25.00
4 WW,DA,A:Iron Maiden,
   June, 1967 .... 25.00

DYNAMO JOE
First
1 .... 3.00
2 .... 3.00
3 thru 14 .... @1.50
Special #1 .... 1.25

EARLY DAYS OF
SOUTHERN KNIGHTS
Vol. 2 Graphic Novel 5.00

EARTH 4
Continuity
[1st Series, Deathwatch 2000]
1 Deathwatch 2000 Pt.6,w/card . 2.50

All comics prices listed are for *Near Mint* condition.

2 Deathwatch 2000 Pt.11,w/card . 2.50
3 V:Hellbenders, w/card 2.50
[2nd Series]
1 WMc, ... 2.50
2 . . . . 2.50
3 . . . . 2.50

EAST MEETS WEST
Innovation
1 . . . . 2.50
2 . . . . 2.50
3 . . . . 2.50

EBONY WARRIOR
Africa Rising
1 I:Ebony Warrior 1.95

ECHO OF FUTURE PAST
Continuity
1 NA,MGo,I:Bucky O'Hare,
Frankenstein 4.00
2 NA,MGo,A:Bucky O'Hare,
Dracula, Werewolf 3.50
3 NA,MGo,A:Bucky 3.50
4 NA,MGo,A:Bucky 3.50
5 NA,MGo,A:Drawla&Bucky 3.50
6 Ath,B:Torpedo 3.50
7 ATh 3.50
8 Ath, ... 3.25
9 Ath,Last issue 3.25

ECLIPSE
GRAPHIC NOVELS
Eclipse
1 Axa 7.00
2 MR,I Am Coyote 7.00
3 DSt,Rocketeer 10.00
3a hard cover 40.00
4 Silver Heels 9.00
4a hard cover 40.00
5 Sisterhood of Steel 10.00
6 Zorro in Old Calif. 8.00

ECLIPSE MONTHLY
Eclipse
1 SD,DW,I:Static&Rio 2.00
2 GC,DW 2.00
3 thru 8 DW . . . . @1.50
9 DW 1.75
10 DW 1.75

EDGE OF CHAOS
Pacific
1 GM 2.00
2 GM 2.00
3 GM 2.00

87th PRECINCT
Dell Publishing Co.
April-June, 1962
1 BK 75.00
2 . . . . 60.00

ELEMENTALS
Comico
1 BWg,I:Destroyers 9.00
2 BWg 5.00
3 BWg 5.00
4 BWg 4.50
5 BWg 4.00
6 BWg 3.00

7 BWg 2.00
8 BWg 2.00
9 BWg 2.00
10 BWg 2.00

Elementals #21 © Comico

11 BWg 1.50
12 BWg 1.50
13 thru 22 . . . . @1.50
23 thru 29 . . . . @1.75
Special #1 . . . . 1.75
Special #2 . . . . 1.95
[Second Series]
1 . . . . 2.25
2 thru 4 . . . . @1.95
5 thru 25 . . . . @2.50
GN Death & Resurrection 12.95

ELFLORD
Aircel
1 Vol.II 3.50
2 . . . . 2.50
3 thru 20 . . . . @2.00
21 double size 4.95
22 thru 24 . . . . @2.00
Special #1 . . . . 2.00

ELFQUEST: BLOOD OF
TEN CHIEFS
Warp Graphics
1 WP 2.25
2 WP 2.25
3 WP,B:Swift Spear pt. 1 . . . . . . 2.25
4 WP,B:Swift Spear pt. 2 . . . . . . 2.25
5 V:Dinosaurs 2.25
6 Snowbeast 2.25
7 . . . . 2.25
8 Spirit Quest 2.25
9 Shadow Shifter 2.25
10 Spheres pt. 1 . . . . 2.25
11 Spheres pt. 2 . . . . 2.25
12 . . . . 2.25
13 Forest 2.25
14 F:Mantricker 2.25
15 F:Bearclaw 2.25
16 Scar Vs. Bearclaw 2.50
17 F:Eldolil,'Howl for Eldolil' 2.50

ELFQUEST:
HIDDEN YEARS
Warp Graphics
1 WP 3.00
2 WP, w/coupon promo. 2.75
3 WP, w/coupon promo.Cont.sty.
previewed in Harbinger#11 . . . 3.25
4 WP,w/coupon 2.50
5 WP,O:Skywise 2.50
6 WP,F:Timmain 2.50
7 F:Timmain 2.50
8 Daughter's Day 2.50
9 WP(s),Enemy Face 2.50
9 1/2 WP,JBy,Holiday Spec. . . . 3.50
10 thru 14 WP . . . . @2.50
15 WP Wolfrider Tribe Splits 3.50
16 thru 18 WP 2.25
19 Mousehunt 2.25
20 F:Recognition 2.25
21 F:Teir, Messenger 2.50
22 F:Embu, Making a Point 2.50

ELFQUEST: JINK
Warp Graphics
1 Future 2.50
2 Future 2.25
3 Neverending Story 2.25
4 Neverending Story 2.25
5 V:True Sons, Hide and Seek . . 2.50
6 V:Truth Holder, Should Auld
Acquaintance 2.50

ELFQUEST:
NEW BLOOD
Warp Graphics
1 JBy,artists try Elfquest 5.00
2 Barry Blair story 3.50
3 thru 5 . . . . @2.50
6 thru 24 . . . . @2.25
25 Forevergreen pt. 13 . . . . 2.25
26 V:Humans 2.25
27 V:Door 2.25
28 I:Windkin, Triompe and Defeat 2.50
Summer Spec.1993 . . . . 4.25

ELFQUEST: THE REBELS
Warp Graphics
1 Aliens, set several hundred
years in future 2.25
2 Escape 2.25
3 He That Goes 2.25
4 Reasons 2.25
5 V:Skyward 2.50
6 F:Shimmer, The Edge 2.50

ELFQUEST: SHARDS
Warp Graphics
1 Division 2.25
2 thru 5 . . . . @2.25
6 F:Two-Edge 2.25
7 F:Shuma 2.25
8 WP,Turnabout,pt.1 . . . . 2.25
9 WP,Turnabout,pt.2,V:Djun 2.50

ELFQUEST:
WAVE DANCERS
Warp Graphics
1 Foil enhanced 3.25
2 thru 6 . . . . @2.25

ELIMINATOR COLOR SPECIAL
Eternity
1 set in the future 2.95

Elric #1 © First Comics

ELRIC
Pacific
1 CR 4.00
2 CR 3.00
3 thru 6 CR .... @2.50

ELRIC, BANE OF THE BLACK SWORD
First
1 Michael Moorcock adapt. 1.75
2 .... 1.75
3 thru 5 .... @1.95

ELRIC, SAILOR ON THE SEVEN SEAS
1 .... 4.00
2 .... 3.00
3 thru 7 .... @2.00

ELRIC, SAILOR ON THE SEVEN SEAS
First
1 Michael Moorcock adapt. 4.00
2 .... 3.00
3 thru 7 .... @2.00

ELRIC–VANISHING TOWER
First
1 Michael Moorcock adapt. 2.50
2 thru 6 .... @2.00

ELRIC, WEIRD OF THE WHITE WOLF
First
1 Michael Moorcock adapt. 3.00
2 .... 2.00
3 .... 2.00
4 .... 2.00

5 .... 2.00
Graphic Novel CR 7.00

E-MAN
Charlton Comics
October, 1973
1 JSon,O:E-Man 20.00
2 SD 8.00
3 .... 8.00
4 SD 8.00
5 SD,Miss Liberty Bell 6.00
6 JBy 8.00
7 JBy 8.00
8 .... 10.00
9 JBy 8.00
10 JBy,September, 1975 ...... 8.00

E-MAN
First
1 JSon,O:E-Man & Nova, A:Rog 2000, 1 pg. JBy 1.75
2 JSon,I:F-Men (X-Men satire) 1 page Mike Mist 1.25
3 JSon, V:F-Men 1.25
4 JSon,Michael Mauser solo 1.25
5 JSon,I:Psychobabbler,A:Omaha, The Cat Dancer 1.25
6 JSon,O:E-Man,V:Feeder 1.25
7 JSon,V:Feeder 1.25
8 JSon,V:HotWax,A:CuteyBunny . 1.25
9 JSon,I:Tyger Lili 1.25
10 JSon,O:Nova Kane pt.1 ..... 1.25
11 JSon,O:Nova Kane pt.2 ..... 1.25
12 JSon,A:Tyger Lili 1.25
13 JSon,V:Warp'sPrinceChaos .. 1.25
14 JSon,V:Randarr 1.25
15 JSon,V:Samuel Boar 1.25
16 JSon,V:Samuel Boar 1.25
17 JSon,'Smeltquest' satire 1.25
18 JSon,'Rosemary..& Time' 1.25
19 JSon, 'Hoodoo Blues' 1.25
20 JSon,A:Donald Duke 1.25
21 JSon,A:B-Team,(satire) 1.25
22 JSon,A:Teddy Q 1.25
23 JSon,A:TygerLili,B-Team 1.25
24 JSon,O:Michael Mauser 1.25
25 JSon,last issue 1.25
Spec #1 .... 2.75

E-MAN
Comico
1 JSon 2.75
2 JSon 2.50
3 JSon 2.50

EMERGENCY
Charlton Comics
June, 1976
1 JSon(c),JBy 10.00
2 JSon 3.00
3 Thru 4 December, 1976 ..... 2.00

ENGIN
Samson Comics
1 I:The Mesh 2.50

ENSIGN O'TOOLE
Dell Publishing Co.
August-October, 1962
1 .... 15.00
2 .... 15.00

EPSILON WAVE
Independent
1 .... 3.00
2 .... 2.50
3 .... 2.25
4 .... 2.00
Elite Comics
5 thru 10 .... @2.00

ESPERS
Eclipse
1 I:ESPers 2.00
2 JBo(c),V:Terrorists 1.50
3 V:Terrorists 1.50
4 Beirut 1.75
5 'The Liquidators' 1.75
6 V:Benito Giovanetti 1.75

ESPIONAGE
Dell Publishing Co.
May-July, 1964
1 .... 20.00
2 .... 18.00

ETERNITY SMITH
Hero
1 .... 1.50
2 .... 1.50
3 .... 1.50
4 Knightshade solo 1.50
5 Knightshade solo 1.50
6 .... 1.50
7 .... 1.95
8 I:Indigo 1.95
9 A:Walter Koenig 1.95
10 .... 1.95
Heroic Publishing
1 Man Vs. Machine 1.95
2 Man Vs. Machine 1.95

EVA THE IMP
Red Top Comic/Decker
1957
1 .... 15.00
2 November, 1957 .... 10.00

Evangeline #12 © First Comics

EVANGELINE
Comico
1	4.00
2	3.00

Lodestone
1	2.50
2	2.50

First
1	3.00
2 thru 9	@1.75
10	1.95
11	1.95
12	1.95

EVERYTHING'S ARCHIE
Archie Publications
May, 1969
1	55.00
2	25.00
3	15.00
4	15.00
5	15.00
6	10.00
7	10.00
8 thru 10	@10.00
11 thru 20	@5.00
21 thru 40	@3.00
41 thru 134	@3.00

EVIL ERNIE
Eternity
1 I:Lady Death	50.00
2 A:Lady Death	35.00
3 A:Lady Death	25.00
4 A:Lady Death	25.00
5 A:Lady Death	22.00

EVIL ERNIE: THE RESURRECTION
Chaos! Comics
1 R:Evil Ernie	5.00
2 Enhanced Cover	4.00
3 Poster Lady Death	4.00
4 Expanded Pages	4.00
TPB	14.95

EVIL ERNIE: REVENGE
Chaos! Comics
1 A:Lady eath	6.00
2 Loses Smiley	3.00
3 V:Dr. Price	3.00
4 Final Issue	3.00

EXECUTIONER
Innovation
1 F:Mack Bolan	3.95
2 War against Mafia	2.75

EXEMPLARS
1	1.95
2	1.95

THE EXODUS
Conquest Comics
1 V:Aliens	2.50

EXO-SQUAD
Topps
[Mini-Series]
1 From Animated Series	2.50
2 F:Nara Burns	2.50

3 V:Neo-Sapiens	2.50

EXTREME VIOLET
Blackout Comics
0 I:Violet	2.95
1 V:Drug Lords	2.95

Becomes:
EXTREMES OF VIOLET
2 A:Matt Chaney	2.95

EYE OF THE STORM
Rival Productions
1 I:Killian, Recon, Finesse, Stray	2.95

FALCON, THE
Aircel
Spec. #1	2.00

FAMILY AFFAIR
Gold Key
February, 1970
1 W/Poster,Ph(c)	25.00
2	15.00
3 Ph(c)	15.00
4 Ph(c)	15.00

FAMOUS INDIAN TRIBES
Dell Publishing Co.
July-September, 1962
1	12.00
2	3.00

FANG
Sirius
1 V:Vampires, I:Fang	2.95

FANTASTIC VOYAGES OF SINBAD, THE
Gold Key
October, 1965
1 Ph(c)	20.00
2 June, 1967	18.00

FANTASY FEATURES
AC
1	1.75
2	1.75

FASHION IN ACTION
Eclipse
Summer Special #1	1.75
Winter Special #1	2.00

FAT ALBERT
Gold Key
March, 1974
1	4.00
2	2.00
3 thru 10	@1.50
11 thru 28	@1.00
29 February, 1979	1.00

FATHOM
Comico
1 thru 3 From Elementals	@2.50

FATMAN, THE HUMAN FLYING SAUCER
Lightning Comics

April, 1967
1 CCB,O:Fatman & Tin Man	45.00
2 CCB	30.00
3 CCB,(Scarce)	45.00

FAZE ONE
AC Comics
1	1.75

FAZE ONE FAZERS
AC Comics
1	5.00
2	3.00
3	2.00
4 thru 6	@1.75

FAZERS SKETCHBOOK
1	1.75

Fearbook #1 © Eclipse Comics

FEARBOOK
Eclipse
1 SBi,RV,'A Dead Ringer'	1.75

FELIX THE CAT
Harvey
1 thru 4	1.25
5 thru 7	1.50

FELIX'S NEPHEWS INKY & DINKY
Harvey Publications
September, 1957
1	45.00
2 thru 7	@20.00

FEMFORCE
AC Comics
1 O:Femforce	5.00
2 A:Captain Paragon	3.50
3 "Skin Game"	2.50
4 "Skin Game"	2.50
5 Back in the Past	2.50
6 EL,Back in the Past	2.50
7 HB,O:Captain Paragon	2.50
8 V:Shade	2.50
9 V:Dr.Rivits	2.50

10 V:Rivits	2.50
11 D:Haunted Horsemen	2.25
12 V:Dr.Rivits	2.25
13 V:She-Cat	2.25
14 V:Alizarin Crimson	2.25
15 V:Alizarin Crimson	2.25
16 thru 56 See Other Publishers	
Black & White	
57 V:Goat God	2.75
58 I:New Sentinels	2.75
59 I:Paragon	2.75
60 V:Sentinels	2.75
61 F:Tara	2.75
62 V:Valkyra	2.75
63 I:Rayda	2.75
64 thru 71	@2.75
72 w/Sentinels of Justice	3.95
72a no extras	2.95
73 w/Compact Comic	3.95
73a Regular edition	2.95
74 Daughter of Darkness	3.95
74a Regular edition	2.95
75 Gorby Poster	4.95
75a Regular edition	2.95
76 Daughters pt. 3	3.95
76a Regular edition	2.95
77 V:Sea Monster	2.95
78 V:Gorgana w/comic	4.95
78a Regular edition	2.95
79 with Index	4.95
79a V:Iron Jaw	2.95
80 with Index	5.90
80a F:Mr. Brimstone, Rad	2.95
81 with Index	5.90
81a Valentines Day Spec.	2.95
82 with Index	5.90
82a F:Ms. Victory	2.95
83 F:Paragon	2.95
84 The Death of Joan Wayne	2.95
84a polybagged with index	5.90
Spec.#1	1.50
Untold Origin Spec #1	4.95

FEMFORCE: UP CLOSE
AC Comics

1 F:Stardust	2.75
2 F:Stardust	2.75
3	2.75
4	2.75
5 with Sticker	3.95
5a Regular Edition	2.95
6 with Sticker	3.95
6a Regular Edition	2.95
7 with Sticker	3.95
7a Regular Edition	2.95
8 with Sticker	3.95
8a Regular Edition	2.95
9	2.95
10	2.95
11	2.95

FENRY
Raven Publications

1	6.95
1a Platinum Ed.	15.00

FIGHT THE ENEMY
Tower Comics
August, 1966

1 BV,Lucky 7	25.00
2 AMc	15.00
3 WW,AMc	15.00

FIGHTING AMERICAN
Harvey

1 SK,Rep Fighting American from 1950's	17.50

FIRST ADVENTURES
First

1 thru 5	@1.25

FIRST GRAPHIC NOVELS
First

1 JBi,Beowolf	8.00
1a 2nd Printing	7.00
2 TT,Time Beavers	6.00
3 HC,American Flag Hard Times	12.00
4 Nexus,SR	8.00
5 Elric,CR	15.00
6 Enchanted Apples of Oz	6.00
7 Secret Island of Oz	8.00
8 HC,Time 2	28.00
9 TMNT	20.00
10 TMNT II	18.00
11 Sailor on the Sea	15.00
12 HC,American Flagg	12.00
13 Ice Ring	8.00
14 TMNT III	14.00
15 Hex Breaker	8.00
16 Forgotten Forest	9.00
17 Mazinger	9.00
18 TMNT IV	13.00
19 O;Nexus	8.00
20 American Flagg	12.00

1st FOLIO
Pacific

1 Joe Kubert School	1.50

FISH POLICE
Comico

Vol 2 #6 thru #15 rep.	@2.50
Vol 2 #16 rep.	3.00
Vol 2 #17 rep.,AuA	3.00
1 Color Special	3.50

FITCH IN TIME

1 and 2	@1.50

FLARE
Hero

1 I:Darkon&Prof.Pomegranite	6.00
2 Blonde Bombshell,A:Galooper	3.25
3 I:Sky Marshall	3.00
Annual #1	4.50
[2nd Series]	
1 A:Galloping Galooper	4.00
2 A:Lady Arcane	3.00
3 I:Britannia	3.00
4 A:Indigo	2.50
5 R:Eternity Smith,O:Die Kriegerin	3.95
6 I:Tigress	3.50
7 V:The Enemies	3.95
8 Morrigan Wars#4,A:Icicle Dragon	3.50
9 Morrigan Wars Pt.7 (B&W)	3.50

FLARE
Hero Graphics

1 I:Darkon&Prof.Pomegranite	6.00
2 Blonde Bombshell,	

A:Galooper	3.25
3 I:Sky Marshall	3.00
Annual #1	4.50
[2nd Series]	
1 A:Galloping Galooper	4.00
2 A:Lady Arcane	3.00
3 I:Britannia	3.00
4 A:Indigo	3.00
5 R:Eternity Smith,O:Die Kriegerin	3.95
6 I:Tigress	3.50
7 V:The Enemies	3.95
8 Morrigan Wars#4,A:Icicle Dragon	3.50
9 Morrigan Wars Pt.7 (B&W)	3.50

FLARE ADVENTURES
Hero Graphics

1 rep.	2.95
2 flipbook w/Champions Classics	2.95
3 flipbook w/Champions Classics	2.95
Becomes B&W	

FLASH GORDON
Gold Key
June, 1965

1	15.00

Flash Gordon #3 © King Comics

FLASH GORDON
King
Sept., 1966

1 AW,DH,A:Mandrake	30.00
1a Complimentary Army giveaway	50.00
2 FBe,A:Mandrake,R:Ming	20.00
3 RE	25.00
4 AW,B:Secret Agent X-9	28.00
5 AW	28.00
6 RC,On the Lost Continent of Mongo	25.00
7 MR, rep.	25.00
8 RC,JAp	25.00
9 AR,rep	30.00
10 AR,rep	30.00
11 RC	20.00
Charlton Sept. 1969	

12 RC	25.00
13 JJ	20.00
14 thru 16	@20.00
17 Brick Bradford story	20.00
18 MK(1970)	20.00

Gold Key Oct.-Nov 1975

19 Flash returns to Mongo	6.00
20 thru 30	@5.00
31 thru 37 AW movie adapt	@3.00

FLATLINE COMICS
Flatline Comics

1 Three stories River Prarie 2.50

FLAXEN: ALTER EGO
Caliber

1 V:Dark Flaxen 2.95

FLESH AND BONES
Fantagraphics

1 Moore	2.50
2 thru 4 Moore	@2.00

FLINTSTONES
Harvey

1	1.25
2 Romeo and Juliet	1.25

FLINTSTONES, THE
Dell Publishing Co.
November-December, 1961

#1 see Dell Giant

2	60.00
3	45.00
4	45.00
5 and 6	@40.00

Gold Key

7	40.00
8 A:Mr.& Mrs. J. Evil Scientists	35.00
9 A:Mr.& Mrs. J. Evil Scientists	35.00
10 A:Mr.& Mrs. J. Evil Scientists	35.00
11 I:Pebbles	50.00
12 'The Too-Old Cowhand'	30.00
13	30.00
14	30.00
15	30.00
16 I:Bamm-Bamm	40.00
17	30.00
18	30.00
19	30.00
20	30.00
21	22.00
22	22.00
23	22.00
24 I:Gruesomes	25.00
25 thru 29	@22.00
30 'Dude Ranch Roundup'	22.00
31 Christmas(c)	22.00
32	20.00
33 A:Dracula & Frankenstein	22.00
34 I:The Great Gazoo	30.00
35	20.00
36 'The Man Called Flintstone'	20.00
37 thru 40	@20.00
41 thru 60	@16.00

FLINTSTONES, THE
Charlton Comics
November, 1970

1	32.00
2	15.00
3 thru 7	@12.00

8	15.00
9	12.00
10	12.00
11 thru 20	@10.00
21 thru 50	@8.00

FLINTSTONES IN 3-D
Blackthorne

1 thru 5 .... @2.50

FLIPPER
Gold Key
April, 1966

1 Ph(c)	35.00
2 and 3 Ph(c)	@25.00

FLY IN MY EYE EXPOSED
Eclipse

1 JJo(c),"Our Visitor" 4.95

FLY, THE
Archie Publications

1 JSn,A:Mr.Justice	1.25
2 thru 9 RB,SD	@1.00

FLYING SAUCERS
Dell
April, 1967

1	15.00
2 thru 5	10.00

FLYMAN
Archie Publications
{Prev: Adventures of the Fly}

31 I:Shield (Bill Higgins), A:Comet, Black Hood	20.00
32 I:Mighty Crusaders	20.00
33 A:Mighty Crusaders, R:Hangman Wizard	20.00
34 MSy,A:Black Hood,Shield,Comet Shield back-up story begins	15.00
35 O:Black Hood	15.00
36 O:Web,A:Hangman in Shield strip	15.00
37 A:Shield	15.00
38 A:Web	14.00
39 A:Steel Sterling	13.00

FOES
Ram Comics

1 TheMaster's Game	1.95
2 TheMaster's Game #2	1.95

FOODANG
August House

1 I:Foodang	1.95
2 I:Maude	2.50
3 V:Undead Clown Man	2.50

FORBIDDEN PLANET
Innovation

1 thru 4 Movie Adapt .... @2.50

FORBIDDEN PLANET
Innovation

1 Movie Adapt	2.50
2 Movie adapt.contd.	2.50
3 Movie adapt.contd.	2.50

Force of the Buddha's Palm #50
© Jademan

FORCE OF THE BUDDHA'S PALM
Jademan

1	3.00
2	2.25
3 thru 10	@1.75
11 thru 24	@1.95
25 V:Maskman	1.95
26 V:Maskman	1.95
27 A:SmilingDemon	1.95
28 Maskman v 10 Demons	1.95
29 Giant Bat	1.95
30	1.95
31	1.95
32 'White Crane Villa'	1.95
33 Devilito defeats White Crane & Giant Bat	1.95
34 Samsun Vs. Devilito	1.95
35 Samsun Vs.Devilito	1.95
36 Samson vs. Devilito	1.95
37 D:Galacial Moon	1.95
38 Persian Elders, Iron Boy	1.95
39 V:Mad Gen.,White Crane, Iron Boy	1.95
40 D:Heaven & Earth Elders	1.95
41 thru 43	@1.95
44 D:White Crane	1.95
45 V:Iron Boy	1.95
46 thru 48	@1.95
49 Iron Boy vs Sainted Jade	1.95
50 Iron Boy & The Holy Blaze	1.95
51 D:Aquarius	1.95
52 V:Son o/t Gemini Lord	1.95
53 Nine Continent's return to full powers	1.95

4-D MONKEY

1 thru 3 .... @1.80

FRANK
Nemesis

1 thru 4 DGc(s),GgP 2.50

FRANK IN THE RIVER
Tundra

1 Avery/Jones style cartoons ... 2.95

FRANK MERRIWELL AT YALE
Charlton Comics
June, 1955

1	25.00
2	15.00
3	15.00
4 January, 1956	15.00

FRANKENSTEIN
Dell Publishing Co.
August-October, 1964

1	20.00
2	15.00
3	10.00
4	10.00

FRANKENSTEIN
Caliber

Novel Adaptation	2.95

FRANKENSTEIN DRACULA WAR
Topps

1 Frank Vs. Drac	2.50
2 F:Saint Germaine	2.50
3 Frank Vs. Drac	2.50

FREDDY
Dell Publishing Co.
May-July, 1963

1	7.00
2 and 3	@5.00

FREDDY'S DEAD

3-D	2.50
1 GN, Movie Adapt	6.95

FREDDY'S DEAD: THE FINAL NIGHTMARE
Innovation

1 Movie adaption, Pt.1	2.50
2 Movie adaption, Pt.2	2.50

FRIDAY FOSTER
Dell Publishing Co.
October, 1972

1	12.00

[CASPER THE] FRIENDLY GHOST
Harvey Publications
August, 1958

1	165.00
2	80.00
3 thru 10	@40.00
11 thru 20	@25.00
21 thru 30	@15.00
31 thru 50	@10.00
51 thru 100	@7.00
101 thru 159	@4.00
160 thru 163 52 pgs.	@3.00
164 thru 238	@2.00

FRIGHT NIGHT
Now

1 thru 22	@1.75

FRIGHT NIGHT
Now

1 Dracula,w/3-D Glasses	2.95

Fright Night II #1 © Now Comics

FRIGHT NIGHT II
Now

Movie Adaptation	3.95

FRISKY ANIMALS ON PARADE
Ajax-Farrell Publ.
September, 1957

1 LbC(c)	60.00
2	20.00
3 LbC(c)	40.00

FROGMEN, THE
Dell Publishing Co.
February-April, 1962

1 GE,Ph(c)	40.00
2 GE,FF	50.00
3 GE,FF	50.00
4	20.00
5 ATh	30.00
6 thru 11	@20.00

FROM HERE TO INSANITY
Charlton Comics
February, 1955

8	75.00
9	60.00
10 SD(c)	110.00
11 JK	125.00
12 JK	125.00
3-1	200.00

F-TROOP
Dell Publishing Co.
August, 1966

1 Ph(c)	45.00
2 Ph(c)	25.00
3 Ph(c)	25.00
4 Ph(c)	25.00
5 Ph(c)	25.00
6 Ph(c)	25.00
7 Ph(c)	25.00

FUN-IN
Gold Key
February, 1970

1	18.00
2 thru 4	@8.00
5	8.00
6	9.00
7 thru 10	@5.00
11 thru 15 December 1974	@5.00

FUNKY PHANTOM
Gold Key
March, 1972

1	15.00
2 thru 5	@5.00
6 thru 12	@3.50
13 March, 1975	3.50

FUTURIANS
Lodestone

1 DC,I:Dr.Zeus	1.00
2 DC,I:MsMercury	1.00
3 DC	1.00
Eternity Graphic Novel, DC,Rep.+new material	9.95

GALL FORCE: ETERNAL STORY
CPM

1 F:Solnoids	2.95

GALLANT MEN, THE
Gold Key
October, 1963

1 RsM	15.00

GALLEGHER BOY REPORTER
Gold Key
May, 1965

1	10.00

GARRISON
Zion Comics

1 I:Wage, Garrison	2.50

GARRISON'S GORRILLAS
Dell Publishing Co.
January, 1968

1 Ph(c)	25.00
2 thru 5 Ph(c)	@15.00

GASP!
American Comics Group
March, 1967

1	25.00
2 thru 4, Aug. 1967	@15.00

G-8 & BATTLE ACES
1 based on '40's pulp characters	3.00

GENE RODDENBERRY'S LOST UNIVERSE
Teckno-Comics

1 Gene Roddenberry's	1.95
2 Grange Discovered	1.95

All comics prices listed are for *Near Mint* condition.

3 Secrets Revealed 1.95
4 F:Penultra 1.95
5 I:New Alien Race 1.95

GENTLE BEN
Dell Publishing Co.
February, 1968

1 Ph(c) 25.00
2 .... 15.00
3 thru 5 .... @15.00

GEORGE OF THE JUNGLE
Gold Key
February, 1969

1 .... 45.00
2 .... 35.00

GET SMART
Dell Publishing Co.
June, 1966

1 Ph(c) all 65.00
2 SD 50.00
3 SD 45.00
4 .... 40.00
5 .... 40.00
6 .... 40.00
7 .... 40.00
8 .... 40.00

GHOST BUSTERS II
Now

1 Mini-series 1.95
2 .... 1.95
3 .... 1.95

GHOST STORIES
Dell Publishing Co.
September-November, 1962

1 .... 35.00
2 .... 20.00
3 .... 15.00
4 .... 15.00
5 .... 15.00
6 .... 15.00
7 .... 15.00
8 .... 15.00
9 .... 15.00
10 .... 15.00
11 .... 10.00
12 .... 10.00
13 .... 10.00
14 .... 10.00
15 .... 10.00
16 .... 10.00
17 .... 10.00
18 .... 10.00
19 .... 10.00
20 .... 10.00
21 .... 5.00
22 .... 5.00
23 .... 5.00
24 .... 5.00
25 .... 5.00
26 .... 5.00
27 .... 5.00
28 .... 5.00
29 .... 5.00
30 .... 5.00
31 .... 5.00
32 .... 5.00
33 .... 5.00
34 rep 5.00
35 rep 8.00
36 rep 5.00
37 rep 5.00

GIANT COMICS
Charlton Comics
Summer, 1957

1 A:Atomic Mouse,Hoppy 60.00
2 A:Atomic Mouse 40.00
3 .... 40.00

GIDGET
Dell Publishing Co.
April, 1966

1 Ph(c),Sally Field 45.00
2 Ph(c),Sally Field 40.00

GIFT, THE
First

Holiday Special 6.00

G.I. JOE 3-D
Blackthorne

1 .... 3.00
2 thru 5 .... @2.50
Annual #1 .... 2.50

GIL THORPE
Dell Publishing Co.
May-July, 1963

1 .... 15.00

GINGER FOX
Comico

1 thru 4 .... @1.75

GIN-RYU
Believe In Yourself

1 F:Japanese Sword 2.75
Ash Can .... .75

G.I. RAMBOT
Wonder Color

1 .... 1.95
2 .... 1.95
3 .... 1.95

G.I. ROBOT
Eternity

1 .... 1.80

GIRL FROM U.N.C.L.E.
Gold Key
January, 1967

1 'The Fatal Accidents Affair' .. 45.00
2 'The Kid Commandos Caper' . 25.00
3 'The Captain Kidd Affair' 25.00
4 'One-Way Tourist Affair' 25.00
5 'The harem-Scarem Affair' ... 25.00

GLOBAL FORCE
Silverline

1 .... 1.95
2 .... 1.95
3 .... 1.95
4 .... 1.95

GO-GO
Charlton Comics
June, 1966

1 Miss Bikini Luv 25.00

2 Beatles 35.00
3 Blooperman 15.00
4 .... 15.00
5 .... 10.00
6 JAp 15.00
7 .... 15.00
8 JAp 15.00
9 Ph(c),October, 1965 ..... 15.00

Gods For Hire #2 © Hot Comics

GODS FOR HIRE
Hot Comics

1 thru 7 .... @1.75

GOLDEN COMICS DIGEST
Gold Key
May, 1969

1 Tom & Jerry,Woody
  Woodpecker, Bugs Bunny ... 15.00
2 Hanna-Barbera TV Fun
  Favorites 20.00
3 Tom & Jerry,Woody
  Woodpecker 7.00
4 Tarzan 20.00
5 Tom & Jerry,Woody
  Woodpecker, Bugs Bunny .. 7.00
6 Bugs Bunny 7.00
7 Hanna-Barbera TV Fun
  Favorites 12.00
8 Tom & Jerry,Woody
  Woodpecker, Bugs Bunny .. 5.00
9 Tarzan 15.00
10 Bugs Bunny 6.00
11 Hanna-Barbera TV Fun
   Favorites 6.00
12 Tom & Jerry,Bugs Bunny 6.00
13 Tom & Jerry 6.00
14 Bugs Bunny Fun Packed
   Funnies 6.00
15 Tom & Jerry,Woody
   Woodpecker, Bugs Bunny 6.00
16 Woody Woodpecker 6.00
17 Bugs Bunny 6.00
18 Tom & Jerry, ... 6.00
19 Little Lulu 15.00
20 Woody Woodpecker 6.00
21 Bugs Bunny Showtime 6.00
22 Tom & Jerry Winter Wingding . 6.00

---

23 Little Lulu & Tubby Fun Fling 14.00
24 Woody Woodpecker Fun
  Festival 6.00
25 Tom & Jerry 6.00
26 Bugs Bunny Halloween Hulla-Boo-
  Loo,Dr. Spektor article 6.00
27 Little Lulu & Tubby in Hawaii . 12.00
28 Tom & Jerry 6.00
29 Little Lulu & Tubby 12.00
30 Bugs Bunny Vacation Funni . 6.00
31 Turk, Son of Stone 15.00
32 Woody Woodpecker
  Summer Fun 6.00
33 Little Lulu & Tubby
  Halloween Fun 12.00
34 Bugs Bunny Winter Funnies . . 6.00
35 Tom & Jerry Snowtime Funtime 6.00
36 Little Lulu & Her Friends 14.00
37 WoodyWoodpecker County Fair 6.00
38 The Pink Panter 6.00
39 Bugs Bunny Summer Fun 6.00
40 Little Lulu 15.00
41 Tom & Jerry Winter Carnival . . 5.00
42 Bugs Bunny 5.00
43 Little Lulu in Paris 14.00
44 Woody Woodpecker Family
  Fun Festival 5.00
45 The Pink Panther 5.00
46 Little Lulu & Tubby 12.00
47 Bugs Bunny 5.00
48 The Lone Ranger,Jan., 1976 . . 5.00

GOLDEN PICTURE STORY BOOK
Racine Press (Western)
December, 1961
1 Huckleberry Hound 125.00
2 Yogi Bear 125.00
3 Babes In Toy Land 150.00
4 Walt Disney 125.00

GOMER PYLE
Gold Key
July, 1966
1 Ph(c) 45.00
2 . . . . 30.00
3 . . . . 30.00

GOOD GUYS
Defiant
1 JiS(s),I:Good Guys 3.75
2 JiS(s),V:Mulchmorg 3.25
3 V:Chasm 2.75
4 Seduction of the Innocent . . 3.25
5 I:Truc 2.75
6 A:Charlemagne 2.75
7 JiS(s),V:Scourge 2.50
8 . . . . 2.50
9 . . . . 2.50
10 . . . . 2.50
11 . . . . 2.50

GOOFY ADVENTURES
Walt Disney
1 . . . . 2.50
2 . . . . 2.00
3 thru 9 . . . . @1.75
10 Samurai 1.75
11 Goofis Khan 1.75
12 'Arizona Goof' Pt. 1 . . . . 1.75
13 'Arizona Goof' Pt. 2 . . . . 1.75
14 'Goofylution' 1.75
15 'Super Goof Vs.Cold Ray' 1.75

16 'Sheerluck Holmes' 1.50
17 GC,TP,'Tomb of Goofula' 1.50

GORGO
Charlton Comics
May, 1961
1 SD 150.00
2 SD,SD(c) 75.00
3 SD,SD(c) 55.00
4 SD(c) 45.00
5 thru 10 . . . . @45.00
11 . . . . 22.00
12 . . . . 10.00
13 thru 15 . . . . @22.00
16 SD 22.00
17 thru 22 . . . . @10.00
23 September, 1965 . . . . 10.00

GORGO'S REVENGE
Charlton Comics
1962
1 . . . . 30.00
Becomes:
RETURN OF GORGO, THE
2 . . . . 25.00
3 . . . . 25.00

GRATEFUL DEAD COMIX
Kitchen Sink
1 TT,inc.DireWolf(large format) . . 5.50
2 TT,inc.Jack Straw 4.95
3 TT,inc. Sugaree 4.95
4 TT,inc. Sugaree 4.95
5 TT,Uncle John's Band 4.95
6 TT,Eagle Mall #1 . . . . 4.95

GREAT AMERICAN WESTERN
AC Comics
1 . . . . 1.75
2 . . . . 2.95
3 . . . . 2.95
4 . . . . 3.50

GREAT EXPLOITS
Decker Publ./Red Top
October, 1957
91 BK 35.00

GREEN HORNET, THE
Gold Key
February, 1967
1 Bruce Lee,Ph(c) 135.00
2 Ph(c) 100.00
3 Ph(c) 100.00

GREEN HORNET
Now
1 O:40's Green Hornet 15.00
1a 2nd Printing 4.00
2 O:60's Green Hornet 9.00
3 . . . . 5.00
4 . . . . 5.00
5 . . . . 5.00
6 . . . . 3.00
7 BSz(c),I:New Kato 3.00
8 . . . . 3.50
9 . . . . 3.50
10 . . . . 3.50

11 . . . . 3.50
12 . . . . 3.50
13 V:Ecoterrorists 3.50
14 V:Ecoterrorists 3.50
Spec #1 . . . . 2.50
Spec #2 . . . . 2.25
[2nd Series]
1 V:Johnny Dollar Pt.1 . . . . 2.25
2 V:Johnny Dollar Pt.2 . . . . 2.25
3 V:Johnny Dollar Pt.3 . . . . 2.25
4 V:Ex-Con/Politician 1.95
5 V:Ex-Con/Politician 1.95
6 Arkansas Vigilante 1.95
7 thru 9 The Beast . . . . @1.95
10 Green Hornet-prey 1.95
11 F:Crimson Wasp 1.95
12 Crimson Wasp/Johnny Dollar
  Pt.1,polybagged w/Button . . 2.50
13 TD(i),Wasp/Dollar Pt.2 . . . . . 2.50
14 TD(i),Wasp/Dollar Pt.3 . . . . . 2.50
15 TD(i),Secondsight 1.95
16 A:Commissioner Hamilton . . . 1.95
17 V:Gunslinger 1.95
18 V:Sister-Hood 1.95
19 V:Jewel Thief 1.95
20 F:Paul's Friend 1.95
21 V:Brick Arcade 1.95
22 V:Animal Testers,
  with Hologravure card 2.95

Green Hornet #25 © Now Comics

23 with Hologravure card 1.95
24 thru 25 Karate Wars . . . . . . @1.95
26 B:City under Siege 1.95
27 with Hologravure card 1.95
28 V:Gangs 1.95
29 V:Gangs 1.95
30 thru 37 . . . . @1.95
38 R:Mei Li 2.50
39 Crimson Wasp 2.50
40 . . . . 2.50
41 . . . . 2.50
42 Baby Killer 2.50
43 Wedding Disasters 2.50
44 F:Amy Hamilton 2.50
45 Plane Hijacking 2.50
Ann.#1 The Blue & the Green . . 2.50
1993 Ann 2.95

All comics prices listed are for *Near Mint* condition.

GREEN HORNET: DARK TOMORROW
Now

1 thru 3 Hornet Vs Kato . . . . . @2.50

GREEN HORNET: SOLITARY SENTINAL
Now

1 Strike Force 2.50
2 thru 3 . . . . 2.50

GREENHAVEN
Aircel

1 . . . . 3.00
2 . . . . 2.50
3 . . . . 2.00

GRENDEL
Comico

1 . . . . 6.00
1a 2nd printing 2.00
2 . . . . 5.00
3 . . . . 4.00
4 . . . . 3.00
5 . . . . 3.00

Grendel #30 © Comico

6 . . . . 3.00
7 MW 2.50
8 . . . . 2.50
9 . . . . 2.50
10 . . . . 2.50
11 . . . . 2.50
12 . . . . 2.50
13 KSy(c) 2.50
14 KSy(c) 2.50
15 KSy(c) 2.50
16 Mage 4.50
17 and 18 . . . . @3.00
19 thru 32 . . . . @2.50
33 . . . . 3.50
34 thru 39 . . . . @2.50
40 . . . . 4.00

GREYLORE
Sirius

1 thru 5 . . . . @2.00

GRIMJACK
First

1 TT Teenage suicide story 3.00
2 TT A:Munden's Bar 2.50
3 TT A:Munden's Bar 2.00
4 TT A:Munden's Bar 2.00
5 TT,JSon,A:Munden's Bar 2.00
6 TT,SR,A:Munden's Bar 2.00
7 TT,A:Munden's Bar 2.00
8 TT,A:Munden's Bar 2.00
9 TT 'My Sins Remembered' . . . 2.00
10 TT,JOy,A:Munden's Bar 2.00
11 TT,A:Munden'sBar 1.75
12 TT,A:Munden'sBar 1.75
13 TT,A:Munden'sBar 1.75
14 TT,A:Munden'sBar 1.75
15 TT,A:Munden'sBar 1.75
16 TT,A:Munden'sBar 1.75
17 TT,A:Munden'sBar 1.75
18 TT,A:Munden'sBar 1.75
19 TT,A:Munden'sBar 1.75
20 TT,A:Munden'sBar 1.75
21 TS,A:Munden's Bar 1.75
22 A:Munden's Bar 1.75
23 TS,A:Munden's Bar 1.75
24 PS,TT,rep.Starslayer10-11 . . 1.75
25 TS,A:Munden's Bar 1.75
26 1st color TMNTurtles 10.00
27 TS,A:Munden's Bar 1.50
28 TS,A:Munden's Bar 1.50
29 A:Munden's Bar 1.50
30 A:Munden's Bar 1.50
31 A:Munden's Bar 1.50
32 A:Spook 1.50
33 JSon,Munden'sBarChristmas
  Tale 1.50
34 V:Spook 1.50
35 A:Munden's Bar 1.50
36 3rd Anniv.IssueD:Grimjack . . . 2.50
37 A:Munden's Bar 1.50
38 A:Munden's Bar 1.50
39 R.Grimjack 1.50
40 . . . . 1.75
41 'Weeping Bride' 1.75
42 'Hardball' 1.75
43 'Beneath the Surface' 1.75
44 Shadow Wars 1.75
45 Shadow Wars 1.75
46 Shadow Wars 1.75
47 Shadow Wars,A:EddyCurrent . 1.75
48 Shadow Wars 1.75
49 Shadow Wars 1.75
50 V:Dancer,ShadowWars ends . . 1.75
51 Crossroads tie-in,A:Judah
  Macabee 2.00
52 . . . . 2.00
53 Time Story 2.00
54 . . . . 2.00
55 FH 2.00
56 FH 2.00
57 FH 2.00
58 FH 2.00
59 FH 2.00
60 FH,Reunion Pt.1 . . . . 2.00
61 FH,Reunion Pt.2 . . . . 2.00
62 FH,Reunion Pt.3 . . . . 2.00
63 FH,A:Justice Drok 2.00
64 FH,O:Multiverse 2.00
65 FH 2.00
66 FH(c),Demon Wars Pt.1 . . . . 2.00
67 FH(c),Demon Wars Pt.2 . . . . . 2.00
68 Demon Wars Pt.3 . . . . 2.00
69 Demon Wars Pt.4 . . . . 2.00
70 FH,I:Youngblood 2.00
71 FH,A:Youngblood 2.00
72 . . . . 2.00
73 FH(c) 2.00
74 FH(c) 2.00
75 FH,TS,V:The Major 2.00
76 FH,A:Youngblood 2.00
77 FH,A:Youngblood 2.25
78 . . . . 2.25
79 FH,Family Business #1 . . . . . 2.25
80 FH,Family Business #2 . . . . . 2.25
81 FH,Family Business #3 . . . . . 2.25

GRIMJACK CASEFILE
First

1 thru 5 rep. . . . . @1.95

GRIMM'S GHOST STORIES
Gold Key/Whitman
January, 1972

1 . . . . 7.00
2 . . . . 4.00
3 . . . . 4.00
4 . . . . 4.00
5 AW 5.00
6 . . . . 4.00
7 . . . . 4.00
8 AW 5.00
9 . . . . 3.00
10 . . . . 3.00
11 thru 16 . . . . @2.00
17 RC 4.00
18 thru 60, June 1982 . . . . @2.00

GROO
Pacific

1 SA,I:Sage,Taranto 20.00
2 SA,A:Sage 10.00
3 SA,C:Taranto 10.00
4 SA,C:Sage 7.50
5 SA,I:Ahax 7.50
6 SA,I:Gratic 7.50
7 SA,I:Chakaal 7.50
8 SA,A:Chakaal 7.50

Eclipse

Spec.#1 SA,O:Groo,rep
  Destroyer Duck #1 . . . . 23.00

GROUND ZERO

1 . . . . 1.35

GROUP LARUE
Innovation

1 . . . . 1.95
2 . . . . 1.95
3 . . . . 1.95

GULLIVER'S TRAVELS
Dell Publishing Co.
September-November, 1965

1 . . . . 20.00
2 and 3 . . . . @15.00

GUMBY
Comico

1 AAd,Summer Fun Special 5.00
1 AAd,Winter Fun Special 3.50

GUMBY IN 3-D

Special #1 . . . . 4.00
2 thru 7 . . . . @2.50

GUNSMOKE
Dell Publishing Co.
February, 1956
1 J.Arness Ph(c) all 100.00
2 . . . . 50.00
3 . . . . 50.00
4 . . . . 50.00
5 . . . . 50.00
6 . . . . 45.00
7 . . . . 45.00
8 . . . . 55.00
9 . . . . 55.00
10 AW,RC 60.00
11 . . . . 55.00
12 AW 60.00
13 . . . . 40.00
14 . . . . 40.00
15 . . . . 40.00
16 . . . . 40.00
17 . . . . 40.00
18 . . . . 40.00
19 . . . . 40.00
20 . . . . 40.00
21 . . . . 40.00
22 . . . . 40.00
23 . . . . 40.00
24 . . . . 40.00
25 . . . . 40.00
26 . . . . 40.00
27 . . . . 40.00

HALL OF FAME
J.C. Productions
1 WW,GK,ThunderAgents 1.00
2 WW,GK,ThunderAgents 1.00
3 WW,Thunder Agents 1.00

HALLOWE'EN HORROR
Eclipse
1 . . . . 1.50

HAMMER OF GOD
First
1 thru 4 . . . . @1.95
Deluxe #1'Sword of Justice Bk#1' 4.95
Deluxe #2'Sword of Justice Bk#2' 4.95

HAMSTER VICE
10 . . . . 2.00
3-D #1 . . . . 2.50

HAND OF FATE
Eclipse
1 I:Artemus Fate 1.75
2 F:Artemis & Alexis 2.00
3 Mystery & Suspense 2.00

HANNA-BARBERA BAND WAGON
Gold Key
October, 1962
1 . . . . 45.00
2 . . . . 40.00
3 April, 1963 . . . . 35.00

HANNA-BARBERA PARADE
Charlton Comics
September, 1971
1 . . . . 60.00
2 thru 10 December 1972 . . . @30.00

HANNA-BARBERA SUPER TV HEROES
Gold Key
April, 1968
1 B:Birdman,Herculiods,Moby Dick,
Young Samson & Goliath . . . 90.00
2 . . . . 85.00
3 thru 7 October 1969 . . . . . @75.00

HARDY BOYS, THE
Gold Key
April, 1970
1 . . . . 10.00
2 thru 4 . . . . @5.00

HARLEM GLOBTROTTERS
Gold Key
April, 1972
1 . . . . 8.00
2 thru 12, Jan. 1975 . . . . @3.00

HARLEY RIDER
1 GM,FS 2.00

HARSH REALM
Harris
1 thru 6 JHi(s), ... @2.95

HARVEY HITS
Harvey Publications
September, 1957
1 The Phantom 150.00
2 Rags Rabbit 12.00
3 Richie Rich 500.00
4 Little Dot's Uncles 80.00
5 Stevie Mazie's Boy Friend . . 10.00
6 JK(c),BP,The Phantom 100.00
7 Wendy the Witch 75.00
8 Sad Sack's Army Life 35.00
9 Richie Rich's Golden Deeds 300.00
10 Little Lotta 60.00
11 Little Audrey Summer Fun . . 50.00
12 The Phantom 100.00
13 Little Dot's Uncles 40.00
14 Herman & Katnip 12.00
15 The Phantom 100.00
16 Wendy the Witch 50.00
17 Sad Sack's Army Life 30.00
18 Buzzy & the Crow 15.00
19 Little Audrey 25.00
20 Casper & Spooky 35.00
21 Wendy the Witch 30.00
22 Sad Sack's Army Life 22.00
23 Wendy the Witch 25.00
24 Little Dot's Uncles 35.00
25 Herman & Katnip 10.00
26 The Phantom 75.00
27 Wendy the Good Little Witch . 25.00
28 Sad Sack's Army Life 12.00
29 Harvey-Toon 18.00
30 Wendy the Witch 20.00
31 Herman & Katnip 5.00
32 Sad Sack's Army Life 10.00
33 Wendy the Witch 25.00
34 Harvey-Toon 10.00
35 Funday Funnies 5.00
36 The Phantom 65.00
37 Casper & Nightmare 14.00
38 Harvey-Toon 9.00
39 Sad Sack's Army Life 6.00
40 Funday Funnies 5.00
41 Herman & Katnip 5.00

Harvey Hits #16 © Harvey Publ.

42 Harvey-Toon 5.00
43 Sad Sack's Army Life 5.00
44 The Phantom 50.00
45 Casper & Nightmare 12.00
46 Harvey-Toon 5.00
47 Sad Sack's Army Life 5.00
48 The Phantom 50.00
49 Harvey-Toon 5.00
50 Harvey-Toon 5.00
51 Sad Sack's Army Life 6.00
52 Casper & Nightmare 15.00
53 Harvey-Toons 5.00
54 Stumbo the Giant 25.00
55 Sad Sack's Army Life 5.00
56 Casper & Nightmare 12.00
57 Stumbo the Giant 25.00
58 Sad Sack's Army Life 5.00
59 Casper & Nightmare 12.00
60 Stumbo the Giant 25.00
61 Sad Sack's Army Life 5.00
62 Casper & Nightmare 12.00
63 Stumbo the Giant 22.00
64 Sad Sack's Army Life 5.00
65 Casper & Nightmare 10.00
66 Stumbo the Giant 22.00
67 Sad Sack's Army Life 5.00
68 Casper & Nightmare 10.00
69 Stumbo the Giant 22.00
70 Sad Sack's Army Life 5.00
71 Casper & Nightmare 4.00
72 Stumbo the Giant 22.00
73 Little Sad Sack 5.00
74 Sad Sack's Muttsy 5.00
75 Casper & Nightmare 7.00
76 Little Sad Sack 5.00
77 Sad Sack's Muttsy 5.00
78 Stumbo the Giant 20.00
79 Little Sad Sack 5.00
80 Sad Sack's Muttsy 5.00
81 Little Sad Sack 5.00
82 Sad Sack's Muttsy 5.00
83 Little Sad Sack 5.00
84 Sad Sack's Muttsy 5.00
85 Gabby Gob 5.00
86 G.I. Juniors 5.00
87 Sad Sack's Muttsy 5.00
88 Stumbo the Giant 20.00
89 Sad Sack's Muttsy 4.00

90 Gabby Goo	4.00
91 G.I. Juniors	4.00
92 Sad Sack's Muttsy	4.00
93 Sadie Sack	4.00
94 Gabby Goo	4.00
95 G.I. Juniors	4.00
96 Sad Sack's Muttsy	4.00
97 Gabby Goo	4.00
98 G.I. Juniors	4.00
99 Sad Sack's Muttsy	4.00
100 Gabby Goo	4.00
101 G.I. Juniors	4.00
102 Sad Sack's Muttsy	4.00
103 Gabby Goo	4.00
104 G.I. Juniors	4.00
105 Sad Sack's Muttsy	4.00
106 Gabby Goo	4.00
107 G.I. Juniors	4.00
108 Sad Sack's Muttsy	4.00
109 Gabby Goo	4.00
110 G.I. Juniors	4.00
111 Sad Sack's Muttsy	4.00
112 G.I. Juniors	4.00
113 Sad Sack's Muttsy	4.00
114 G.I. Juniors	4.00
115 Sad Sack's Muttsy	4.00
116 G.I. Juniors	4.00
117 Sad Sack's Muttsy	4.00
118 G.I. Juniors	4.00
119 Sad Sack's Muttsy	4.00
120 G.I. Juniors	4.00
121 Sad Sack's Muttsy	4.00
122 G.I. Juniors, November, 1967	4.00

HAUNT OF FEAR
Gladstone
1 EC Rep. H of F #17,WS#28	3.00
2 EC Rep. H of F #5,WS #29	2.50

HAUNT OF FEAR
Russ Cochran
1 EC Rep. H of F #15	1.50
2 EC Rep. H of F	1.50

HAUNT OF FEAR
Russ Cochran Publ.
1 EC Rep. H of F #14,WS#13	2.25
2 EC Rep. H of F #18,WF#14	2.00
3 EC Rep. H of F #19,WF#18	2.00
4 EC Rep. H of F #16,WF#15	2.00
5 EC Rep. H of F #5,WF#22	2.00
6 EC Rep. H of F	2.00
7 EC Rep. H of F	2.00

HAVE GUN, WILL TRAVEL
Dell Publishing Co.
August, 1958
1 Richard Boone Ph(c) all	75.00
2	50.00
3	50.00
4	35.00
5	35.00
6	35.00
7	35.00
8	35.00
9	35.00
10	35.00
11	35.00
12	35.00
13	35.00
14	35.00

HAWKMOON, COUNT BRASS
First
1 Michael Moorcock adapt.	1.95
2	1.95
3	1.95
4	1.95

HAWKMOON JEWEL IN THE SKULL
First
1 Michael Moorcock adapt.	3.00
2	2.50
3	2.00
4	2.00

Hawkmoon, Sword of the Dawn #2
© First Comics

HAWKMOON, MAD GOD'S AMULET
First
1 Michael Moorcock adapt.	2.00
2	1.75
3	1.75
4	1.75

HAWKMOON, SWORD OF THE DAWN
First
1 Michael Moorcock adapt.	2.00
2 thru 4	@1.75

HAWKMOON, THE RUNESTAFF
First
1 Michael Moorcock adapt.	2.00
2	2.00
3	1.95
4	1.95

HEADMAN
Innovation
1	2.50
2	2.50

HEARTSTOPPER
Millenium
1 V:Demons	2.95
2 V:Demons	2.95
3 F:Hellfire	2.95

HEAVY METAL MONSTERS
3-D-Zone
1 w/3-D glasses	3.95

HECTOR HEATHCOTE
Gold Key
March, 1964
1	30.00

HERBIE
American Comics Group
April-May, 1964
1	125.00
2	65.00
3	60.00
4	60.00
5 A:Beatles,Dean Martin, Frank Sinatra	80.00
6	50.00
7	50.00
8 O:Fat Fury	60.00
9	50.00
10	50.00
11	30.00
12	30.00
13	30.00
14 A:Nemesis,Magic Man	30.00
15 thru 22	@30.00
23 February, 1967	30.00

HERCULES
Charlton Comics
October, 1967
1	10.00
2 thru 7	@5.00
8 scarce	20.00
9 thru 13 Sept. 1969	4.00

HERETICS
Iquana
1	2.95

HERO ALLIANCE END OF THE GOLDEN AGE
Innovation
1 RLm	5.00
1A 2nd printing	2.50
2 RLm	4.00
3 RLm	3.00

HERO ALLIANCE JUSTICE MACHINE
1	2.50

HERO ALLIANCE Pied Piper
1	4.00
2	3.50
3	3.00
Graphic Novel	10.00

Innovation
1 RLm,BS(c),R:HeroAlliance	6.00

2 RLm,BS(c),Victor vs.Rage 5.00
3 RLm,A:Stargrazers 4.00
4 . . . . 3.00
5 RLm(c) 2.50
6 BS(c),RLm pin-up 3.25
7 V:Magnetron 2.50
8 I:Vector 2.50
9 BS(c),V:Apostate 2.50
10 A:Sentry 2.25
11 . . . . 2.25
12 I:Bombshell 2.25
13 V:Bombshell 2.25
14 Kris Solo Story 2.25
15 JLA Parody Issue 2.25
16 V:Sepulchre 2.25
17 O:Victor,I&D:Misty 2.25
Annual #1 PS,BS,RLm 3.00

HERO ALLIANCE QUARTERLY
Innovation
1 Hero Alliance stories 2.75
2 inc.'Girl Happy' 2.75
3 inc.'Child Engagement' 2.75
4 . . . . 2.75

HERO ALLIANCE SPECIAL
Innovation
1 Hero Alliance update 2.50

HI-SCHOOL ROMANCE DATE BOOK
Harvey Publications
November, 1962
1 BP 18.00
2 . . . . 8.00
3 March, 1963 . . . . 8.00

HIGH CHAPPARAL
Gold Key
August, 1968
1 . . . . 35.00

HIGH SCHOOL CONFIDENTIAL DIARY
Charlton Comics
June, 1960
1 . . . . 15.00
2 thru 11 . . . . @6.00
Becomes:
CONFIDENTIAL DIARY
12 . . . . 5.00
13 thru 17 March, 1963 . . . . . . @3.00

HILLBILLY COMICS
Charlton Comics
August, 1955
1 . . . . 25.00
2 thru 4 July 1956 . . . . @12.00

HIS NAME IS ROG...
ROG 2000
A Plus Comics
1 . . . . 1.75

HOBBIT, THE
Eclipse
1 . . . . 8.00

1a 2ndPrinting 6.00
2 . . . . 7.00
2a 2ndPrinting 5.00
3 . . . . 6.00

HOGAN'S HEROS
Dell Publishing Co.
June, 1966
1 Ph(c) 40.00
2 Ph(c) 25.00
3 JD,Ph(c) 25.00
4 thru 8 Ph(c) . . . . @20.00
8 and 9 . . . . @20.00

HONEY WEST
Gold Key
September, 1966
1 . . . . 75.00

HONEYMOONERS
Lodestone
1 . . . . 4.00
5 Mag. 2.50
Triad
[2nd Series]
1 'They Know What They Like' . . 3.00
2 'The Life You Save' 2.50
3 X-mas special,inc.Art
    Carney interview 3.50
4 'In the Pink' 3.00
5 'Bang, Zoom, To the Moon' . . . 2.00
6 'Everyone Needs a Hero'
    inc. Will Eisner interview 2.00
7 . . . . 2.00
8 . . . . 2.00
9 Jack Davis(c) 4.50
10 thru 13 . . . . @2.00

HOT COMICS PREMIERE
Hot Comics
1 F:Thunderkill, Jacknife 1.95

HOT ROD RACERS
Charlton Comics
December, 1964
1 . . . . 35.00
2 thru 5 . . . . @20.00
6 thru 15 July 1967 . . . . @15.00

HOT STUFF, THE LITTLE DEVIL
Harvey Publications
October, 1967
1 . . . . 175.00
2 1st Stumbo the Giant 100.00
3 thru 5 . . . . @75.00
6 thru 10 . . . . @50.00
11 thru 20 . . . . @30.00
21 thru 40 . . . . @20.00
41 thru 60 . . . . @10.00
61 thru 100 . . . . @5.00
101 thru 105 . . . . @4.00
106 thru 112 52 pg Giants . . . . @5.00
113 thru 172 . . . . @2.00

HOT STUFF SIZZLERS
Harvey Publications
July, 1960
1 B:68 pgs 75.00
2 thru 5 . . . . @30.00
6 thru 10 . . . . @15.00

11 thru 20 . . . . @12.00
21 thru 30 . . . . @10.00
31 thru 44 . . . . @5.00
45 E:68 pgs 4.00
46 thru 50 . . . . @3.00
51 thru 59 . . . . @2.50

HOTSHOTS
1 thru 4 . . . . @1.95

HOTSPUR
Eclipse
1 RT(i),I:Josef Quist 1.75
2 RT(i),Amulet of Kothique Stolen 1.75
3 RT(i),Curse of the SexGoddess 1.75

Howard Chaykin's American Flagg #3
© First

HOWARD CHAYKIN'S AMERICAN FLAGG!
First
1 thru 9 . . . . @1.75
10 thru 12 . . . . @1.95

H.P.LOVECRAFT'S CTHULHU
Millenium
1 I:Miskatonic Project,V:Mi-Go . . 2.50
2 Arkham, trading cards 2.50

HUCK & YOGI JAMBOREE
Dell Publishing Co.
March, 1961
1 . . . . 50.00

HUCKLEBERRY HOUND
Charlton
November, 1970
1 . . . . 15.00
2 thru 7 . . . . @7.50
3 Jan., 1972 . . . . 8.00

HUCKLEBERRY HOUND
Dell Publishing Co.
May-July, 1959

1	50.00
2	35.00
3	35.00
4	35.00
5	35.00
6	35.00
7	35.00
8	25.00
9	25.00
10	25.00
11	20.00
12	20.00
13	20.00
14	20.00
15	20.00
16	20.00
17	20.00

Gold Key

18 Chuckleberry Tales	35.00
19 Chuckleberry Tales	35.00
20 Chuckleberry Tales	12.00
21	12.00
22	12.00
23	12.00
24	12.00
25	12.00
26	12.00
27	12.00
28	12.00
29	12.00
30	12.00
31	10.00
32	10.00
33	10.00
34	10.00
35	10.00
36	10.00
37 rep.	10.00
38	10.00
39	10.00
40	10.00
41	10.00
42	10.00
43	10.00

HUEY, DEWEY & LOUIE JUNIOR WOODCHUCKS
Gold Key
August, 1966

1	40.00
2 thru 5	@25.00
6 thru 17	@20.00
18	10.00
19 thru 25	@12.00
26 thru 30	@10.00
31 thru 57	@10.00
58	12.00
59	12.00
60 thru 80	@8.00
81 1984	8.00

HYBRIDS
Continuity

1	2.50

HYBRIDS
Continuity

0 Deathwatch 2000 prologue	5.00
1 Deathwatch 2000 pt.4,w/card	2.50
2 Deathwatch 2000 pt.13,w/card	2.50
3 Deathwatch 2000 w/card	2.50
4 A:Valeria	2.50
5 O:Valeria	2.50

HYBRIDS: ORIGIN
Continuity

1 thru 5	2.50

HYDE-25
Harris

1 New Drug	2.95

I DREAM OF JEANNIE
Dell Publishing Co.
April, 1965

1 Ph(c),B.Eden	60.00
2 Ph(c),B.Eden	55.00

I SPY
Gold Key
August, 1966

1 Bill Cosby Ph(c)	125.00
2 Ph(c)	75.00
3 thru 4 AMc,Ph(c)	@80.00
5 thru 6 Ph(c) Sept.1968	@75.00

I'M DICKENS – HE'S FENSTER
Dell Publishing Co.
May-July, 1963

1 Ph(c)	25.00
2 Ph(c)	25.00

Icicle #1 © Hero Graphics

ICICLE
Hero Graphics

1 A:Flare,Lady Arcane, V:Eraserhead	4.95

IMP

1	2.25

INNER CIRCLE
Mushroom Comics

1.1 I:Point Blank	2.50
1.2 V:Deathcom	3.50

INNOVATORS
Dark Moon

1 I:Innovator, LeoShan	2.50

INTERVIEW WITH A VAMPIRE
Innovation

1 based on novel,preq.to Vampire Chronicles	3.50
2	3.00
3 Death & Betrayal	3.00
4	3.00
5 D:Lestat	2.50
6 Transylvania Revelation	2.50
7 Louis & Claudia in Paris	2.50
8 thru 10	@2.50
11	2.50

INTERVIEW WITH A VAMPIRE
Innovation

1 based on novel, preq. to Vampire Chronicles	3.50
2	3.00
3 Death & Betrayal	3.00
4	3.00
5 D:Lestat	2.50
6 Transylvania Revelation	2.50
7 Louis & Claudia in Paris	2.50

INTIMATE
Charlton Comics
December, 1957

1	8.00
2 and 3	@8.00

Becomes:
TEEN-AGE LOVE

4	8.00
5 thru 9	@4.00
10 thru 35	@3.00
36 thru 96	@1.00

INTRUDER
TSR

1 thru 8	@2.95

INVADERS FROM HOME
Piranha Press

1 thru 6	@2.50

INVADERS, THE
Gold Key
October, 1967

1 Ph(c),DSp	50.00
2 Ph(c),DSp	30.00
3 Ph(c),DSp	30.00
4 Ph(c),DSp	30.00

INVINCIBLE FOUR OF KUNG FU & NINJA
Victory

1	2.75
2	2.50
3	2.50
4	1.80
5 thru 11	@2.00

IO
Invictus Studios

1 I:IO	2.25
2	2.25
3 V:Major Damage	2.25

IRON HORSE
Dell Publishing Co.
March, 1967

1	12.00
2	12.00

IRON MARSHAL
Jademan

1	2.00
2	1.75
3	1.75
4	1.75
5	1.75
6 V:Bloody Duke	1.75
7	1.75
8	1.75
9 The Unicorn Sword	1.75
10 The Great Thor	1.75
11 A:Exterminator	1.75
12 Bloddy Duke vs. Exterminator	1.75
13 Secret of Unicorn Supreme	1.75
14 A:The Great Thor	1.75
15 A:The Great Thor	1.75
16 V:Tienway Champ	1.75
17 thru 20	1.75
21 Bloody Duke wounded	1.75
22 A:Great Thor	1.75
23	1.75
24	1.75
25	1.75
26 Iron Marshal Betrayed	1.75
27	1.75
28	1.75
29	1.75
30	1.75

IRREGULARS, THE: BATTLETECH Miniseries
Blackthorne

1	1.75
2	1.75
3 B&W	1.75

IRUKASHI

1	1.75

IT! TERROR FROM BEYOND SPACE
Millenium

1	2.50
2	2.50

IT'S ABOUT TIME
Gold Key
January, 1967

1 Ph(c)	25.00

ITCHY & SCRATCHY
Bongo Comics

1 DaC(s),	2.25
2 DaC(s),	2.25

IVANHOE
Dell Publishing Co.
July-September, 1963

1	25.00

JACK HUNTER
Blackthorne

1	1.25
2	1.25

3	1.25

JADEMAN COLLECTION

1	4.50
2	3.00
3	2.50
4	2.50
5	2.50

JADEMAN KUNG FU SPECIAL

1 I:Oriental Heroes, Blood Sword, Drunken Fist	5.00

JAKE TRASH
Aircel

1 thru 3	@2.00

JAMES BOND 007
Eclipse

1 MGr,PerfectBound	5.50
2 MGr	5.00
3 MGr,end series	5.00
GN Licence to Kill, MGr I/o	8.00

JAM SPECIAL
Comico

1	2.50

JAQUAR GOD
Verotika

1 Frazetta, I:Jaquar God	2.95

JASON GOES TO HELL
Topps

1 Movie adapt.,w/3 cards	3.25
2 Movie adapt.,w/3 cards	3.25
3 Movie adapt.,w/3 cards	3.25

JAVERTZ
Firstlight

1 New Series	2.95
2 thru 5 Pieces of an Icon	2.95

JET DREAM
Gold Key
June, 1968

1	20.00

JETSONS, THE
Gold Key
January, 1963

1	175.00
2	100.00
3 thru 10	@75.00
11 thru 20	@50.00
21 thru 36 October 1970	@35.00

JETSONS, THE
Charlton Comics
November, 1970

1	55.00
2	31.00
3 thru 10	@20.00
11 thru 20 December 1973	@15.00

JEZEBEL JADE
Comico

1 AKu,A:Race Bannon	2.00
2 AKu	2.00

3 AKu	2.00

JIGSAW
Harvey Publications
September, 1966

1	6.00
2	3.50

J. N. Williamson's Masques #1
© Innovation

J. N. WILLIAMSON'S MASQUES
Innovation

1 TV,From horror anthology	4.95
2 Olivia(c) inc.Better Than One	4.95

JOHN BOLTON, HALLS OF HORROR
Eclipse

1 JBo	1.75
2 JBo	1.75

JOHN F. KENNEDY LIFE STORY
(WITH 2 REPRINTS)
Dell Publishing Co.
August-October, 1964

1	35.00
2	25.00
3	25.00

JOHN LAW
Eclipse

1 WE	2.00

JOHNNY GAMBIT

1	1.75

JOHNNY JASON TEEN REPORTER
Dell Publishing Co.
February-April, 1962

1	10.00

All comics prices listed are for *Near Mint* condition.

2 . . . . 10.00

JOHNNY NEMO
Eclipse
1 I:Johnny Nemo 2.00
2 . . . . 2.00
3 F:Sindy Shade 2.50

JOHN STEELE SECRET AGENT
Gold Key
December, 1964
1 . . . . 65.00

JONNY QUEST
Gold Key
December, 1964
1 TV show 135.00

JONNY QUEST
Comico
June, 1986
1 DW,SR,A:Dr.Zin 4.50
2 WP/JSon,O:RaceBannon 3.50
3 DSt(c) 3.00
4 TY/AW,DSt(i) 2.50
5 DSt(c)A:JezebelJade 2.50
6 AKu 2.00
7 . . . . 2.00
8 KSy 2.00
9 MA 2.00
10 King Richard III 2.00
11 JSon,BSz(c) 1.50
12 DSp 1.50
12 DSp 1.50
13 CI 1.50
14 . . . . 1.50
15 thru 31 . . . . @1.75
Special #1 . . . . 1.75
Special #2 . . . . 1.75

JONNY QUEST CLASSICS
Comico
1 DW 2.00
2 DW,O:Hadji 2.00
3 DW 2.00

JON SABLE
First
1 MGr,A:President 4.50
2 MGr,Alcohol Issue 3.50
3 MGr,O:Jon Sable 3.00
4 MGr,O:Jon Sable 3.00
5 MGr,O:Jon Sable 3.00
6 MGr,O:Jon Sable 3.00
7 MGr,The Target 2.50
8 MGr,Nuclear Energy 2.50
9 MGr,Nuclear Energy 2.50
10 MGr,Tripitych 2.50
11 MGr,I:Maggie 2.50
12 MGr,Vietnam 2.50
13 MGr,Vietnam 2.50
14 MGr,East Germany 2.50
15 MGr,Nicaragua 2.50
16 MGr,A:Maggie 2.50
17 MGr,1984 Olympics 2.50
18 MGr,1984 Olympics 2.50
19 MGr,,The Widow 2.50
20 MGr,The Rookie 2.50
21 MGr,Africa 2.25
22 MGr,V:Sparrow 2.25

23 MGr,V:Sparrow 2.25
24 MGr,V:Sparrow 2.25
25 MGr,Shatter 3.00
26 MGr,Shatter 3.00
27 MGr,Shatter 3.00
28 MGr,Shatter 3.00
29 MGr,Shatter 3.00
30 MGr,Shatter 2.25

Jon Sable #33 © First Comics

31 MGr,Nicaragua 2.00
32 MGr,Nicaragua 2.00
33 MGr,SA,Leprechauns 2.25
34 MGr,Indians 2.00
35 MGr,Indians 2.00
36 MGr,Africa 2.00
37 MGr,Africa 2.00
38 MGr,Africa 2.00
39 MGr,Africa 2.00
40 MGr,1st Case 2.00
41 MGr,1st Case 2.00
42 MGr,V:Sparrow 2.00
43 MGr,V:Sparrow 2.00
44 Hard Way 2.00
45 Hard Way II 2.00
46 MM,The Tower pt.1 . . . . 2.00
47 MM,The Tower pt.2 . . . . 2.00
48 MM,Prince Charles 2.00
49 MM,Prince Charles 2.00
50 A:Maggie the Cat 2.00
51 Jon Sable,babysitter pt.1 . . . . 2.00
52 Jon Sable,babysitter pt.2 . . . . 2.00
53 MGr. 2.00
54 Jacklight pt.1 . . . . 2.00
55 Jacklight pt.2 . . . . 2.00
56 Jacklight pt.3 . . . . 2.00

JOSIE
Archie Publications
February, 1963
1 . . . . 100.00
2 . . . . 50.00
3 . . . . 25.00
4 . . . . 20.00
5 . . . . 25.00
6 thru 10 . . . . @15.00
11 thru 20 . . . . @12.00
21 thru 30 . . . . @7.00

31 thru 40 . . . . @5.00
41 thru 54 . . . . @4.00
55 thru 74 . . . . @2.00
75 thru 105 . . . . @1.00
106 October, 1962 . . . . 1.00

JUDGE COLT
Gold Key
October, 1969
1 . . . . 8.00
2 . . . . 5.00
3 . . . . 5.00
4 September, 1980 . . . . 5.00

JUDGE DREDD
Eagle
1 BB,I:Judge Death(in USA) . . . 15.00
2 BB(c),V:Perps 11.00
3 BB(c),V:Perps 9.00
4 BB(c),V:Perps 9.00
5 BB(c),V:Perps 8.00
6 BB(c),V:Perps 8.00
7 BB(c),V:Perps 8.00
8 BB(c),V:Perps 8.00
9 BB(c),V:Perps 8.00
10 BB(c),V:Perps 8.00
11 BB(c) 5.00
12 BB(c) 5.00
13 BB(c) 5.00
14 BB(c) 5.00
15 BB(c) 5.00
16 BB(c) 5.00
17 BB(c) 5.00
18 BB(c) 5.00
19 BB(c) 5.00
20 BB(c) 5.00
21 BB(c) 5.00
22 BB(c),V:Perps 4.00
23 BB(c),V:Perps 4.00
24 BB(c),V:Perps 4.00
25 BB(c),V:Perps 4.00
26 BB(c),V:Perps 4.00
27 BB(c),V:Perps 4.00
28 A:Judge Anderson,V:Megaman 5.00
29 A:Monty, the guinea pig 4.00
30 V:Perps 4.00
31 Destiny's Angel, Pt. 1 . . . . . . 4.00
32 Destiny's Angel, Pt. 2 . . . . . . 4.00
33 V:League of Fatties 4.00
34 V:Executioner 4.00

JUDGE DREDD
Quality
1 Cry of the Werewolf Pt.1 . . . 7.00
2 Cry of the Werewolf Pt.2 . . . 5.00
3 Anti-smoking 4.00
4 Wreckers 4.00
5 Highwayman 4.00
6 . . . . 3.00
7 . . . . 3.00
8 . . . . 3.00
9 . . . . 3.00
10 . . . . 3.00
11 . . . . 3.00
12 Starborn Thing, Pt.1 . . . . . . 3.00
13 Starborn Thing, Pt.2 . . . . . . 3.00
14 BB, V:50 foot woman 3.00
15 City of the Damned Pt.1 . . . . 3.00
16 City of the Damned Pt.2 . . . . 3.00
17 City of the Damned conc. . . . 3.00
18 V:Mean Machine Angel 3.00
19 Dredd Angel 3.00
20 V:Perps 3.00
21 V:Perps 3.00

EAGLE COMICS PRESENTS $1.25   No.29

Judge Dredd #29 © Eagle Comics

69	2.50
70 Dinosaurs in Mega City 1	2.50
71	2.50
72 Pirates o/t Black Atlantic	2.50
73	2.50
74	2.50
75	2.50
76 Diary of a Mad Citizen	3.00
TPB:Democracy Now	10.95
TPB:Rapture	12.95
Judge Dredd Special #1	2.50

JUDGE DREDD: AMERICA
Fleetway

1 I:America	3.50

JUDGE DREDD: JUDGE CHILD QUEST
Eagle

1	3.00
2	3.00
3	3.00
4	3.00
5	3.00

22/23 Booby Trap	3.00
24 Junk food fiasco	3.00
25/26 V:Perps	3.00
27 V:Perps	3.00
28 Dredd Syndrome	3.00
29 V:Perps	3.00
30 V:Perps	3.00
31 Hunt Pudge Dempsey's killer .	3.00
32 V:Mutated Sewer Alligator	3.00
33 V:Perps	3.00
34 V:Executioner	3.00
35 V:Shojan	3.00
36 V:Shojan	3.00
37 V:Perps	3.00
38 V:Perps	3.00
39 V:Perps	3.00
40 V:Perps	3.00
41 V:Perps	3.00
42 V:Perps	3.00
43 V:Perps	3.00
44 V:Perps	3.00
45 V:DNA Man	2.50
46 Genie lamp sty	2.50
47 V:Perps	2.50
48 Murder in Mega-City One	2.50
49 V:Perps	2.50
50 V:Perps	2.50
51 V:Perps	2.50
52 V:Perps	2.50
53 V:Perps	2.50
54 V:Perps	2.50
55 V:Perps	2.50
56 inc.JudgeDredd Postcards ...	2.50
57 V:Perps	2.50
58 V:370lb Maniac	2.50
59 V:Perps	2.50
60 Social Misfit	2.50
61 V:Perps	2.50
Becomes:	

JUDGE DREDD CLASSICS

62	2.50
63 Mutants from the Badlands ...	2.50
64	2.50
65	2.50
66 Wit and wisdom of Dredd	2.50
67 V:Otto Sump	2.50
68 V:Otto Sump	2.50

JUDGE DREDD'S CRIME FILE
Eagle

1 JBy	2.50
2	2.50
3	2.50
4	2.50
5	2.50
6	2.50

Quality
(Prestige format)

1 A:Rogue Trooper	6.50
2 IG,V:Fatties, Energy Vampires & Super Fleas	5.95
3 Battles foes from dead A:Judge Anderson	5.95

JUDGE DREDD'S EARLY CASES
Eagle

1 Robot Wars, Pt.1	4.00
2 Robot Wars, Pt.2	3.00
3 V:Perps	3.00
4 IG, Judge Giant	3.00
5 V:Perps	3.00
6 V:Judge killing car Elvis	3.00

JUDGE DREDD'S HARDCASE PAPERS

1 V:The Tarantula	7.50
2 Junkies & Psychos	6.50
3 Crime Call Vid. Show	6.50
4 'Real Coffee',A:Johnny Alpha ..	6.50

JUDGE DREDD: THE MEGAZINE

1 Midnite's Children Pt.1 A:Chopper, Young Death	5.25
2 Midnite's Children Pt.2	4.95

JUDGE PARKER
Argo
February, 1956

1	20.00

2	11.00

JUDGMENT DAY
Lightning Comics

1 B:JZy(s),KIK,V:Razorr,Rift, Nightmare, red prism(c)	5.00
1a Gold Prism(c)	10.00
1b Purple Prism(c)	20.00
1c Misprint,Red Prism(c), Bloodfire Credits inside	30.00
1d Misprint,Gold Prism(c), Bloodfire Credits inside	30.00
1e Misprint,Green Prism(c), Bloodfire Credits inside	30.00
1f B&W promo ed. Gold ink	10.00
1g B&W promo ed. platinum ed.	18.00
2 TLw,I:War Party,BU:Perg, w/card	3.50
3 ErP,O:X-Treme	3.25
4 ErP,In Hell	3.25
5 TLw,In Hell	3.25
6 TLw,I:Red Front,O:Salurio	3.25
7 O:Safeguard	3.25
8	2.95
9	2.95
10	2.95

JUDOMASTER
Charlton Comics
(Special War Series #4)

I:Judomaster	15.00
89 FMc,War stories begin	7.00
89 (90) FMc,A:Thunderbolt	6.00
91 FMc,DG,A:Sarge Steel	6.00
92 FMc,DG,A:Sarge Steel	6.00
93 FMc,DG,I:Tiger	6.00
94 FMc,DG,A:Sarge Steel	6.00
95 FMc,DG,A:Sarge Steel	5.00
96 FMc,DG,A:Sarge Steel	5.00
97 FMc,A:Sarge Steel	4.00
98 FMc,A:Sarge Steel	4.00

JUGHEAD
Archie Publications
Dec., 1965–June, 1987

127 thru 130	@12.00
131 thru 150	@10.00
151 thru 160	@8.00
161 thru 352	1.50

JUGHEAD
Archie Publications
[2nd Series]
Aug., 1987

1 thru 50	@1.25
51 thru 70	@1.50

JUGHEAD AS CAPTAIN HERO
Archie Publications
October, 1966

1	25.00
2	15.00
3 thru 7	@10.00

JUGHEAD'S FANTASY
Archie Publications
August, 1960

1	80.00
2	60.00
3	45.00

JUGHEAD'S JOKES
Archie Publications
August, 1967

1	26.00
2	14.00
3 thru 5	@7.00
6 thru 10	@5.00
11 thru 30	@2.00
31 thru 77	@1.00
78 September, 1982	1.00

JUGHEAD WITH ARCHIE DIGEST
Archie Publications
March, 1974

1	8.00
2	4.00
3 thru 10	@2.00
11 thru 91	1.00

JUNGLE COMICS
Blackthorne

1 DSt(c)	2.00
2	2.00
3	2.00

JUNGLE TALES OF TARZAN
Charlton Comics
December, 1964

1	25.00
2	20.00
3	20.00
4 July, 1965	20.00

JUNGLE WAR STORIES
Dell Publishing Co.
July-September, 1962

1 P(c) all	15.00
2	8.00
3	8.00
4	8.00
5	8.00
6	8.00
7	8.00
8	8.00
9	8.00
10	8.00
11	8.00

Becomes:
GUERRILLA WAR

12	7.00
13	7.00
14	7.00

JUNIOR WOODCHUCKS
Walt Disney

1 CB,'Bubbleweight Champ'	2.00
2 CB,'Swamp of no Return'	2.00
3 'Rescue Run-Around'	2.00
4 'Cave Caper'	2.00

JURASSIC PARK
Topps

1 Movie Adapt.,w/card	6.00
1a Newsstand Ed.	4.00
2 Movie Adapt.,w/card	3.25
2a Newsstand Ed.	2.75
3 Movie Adapt.,w/card	3.25
3a Newsstand Ed.	2.75
4 Movie Adapt.,w/card	3.25

4a Newsstand Ed.	2.75
Ann.#1	3.95

JURASSIC PARK: ADVENTURES
Topps

1 thru 10 reprints titles	@1.95

JURASSIC PARK: RAPTOR
Topps

1 SE w/Zorro #0 ashcan & cards	3.25
2 w/3 cards	2.95

JURASSIC PARK: RAPTORS ATTACK
Topps

1 SEt(s),	2.75
2 SEt(s),	2.75
2 SEt(s),	2.75
3 SEt(s),	2.75

JURASSIC PARK: RAPTOR HIJACK
Topps

1 SEt(s),	2.50
2 SEt(s),	2.50
2 SEt(s),	2.50
3 SEt(s),	2.50

Justice Machine #1 © Comico

JUSTICE MACHINE
Comico

1 MGu	2.50
2 MGu	2.00
3 thru 14 MGu	@1.50
15 thru 27 MGu	@1.75
28 MGu	1.95
29 MGu,IW	1.95
Ann.#1:BWG,I:Elementals, A: Thunder Agents	20.00
Ann.#1	2.50
SummerSpectacular 1	2.75
1 JBy(c) Mag size,B&W	30.00
2 MGu,Mag size,B&W	16.00

3 MGu,Mag size,B&W	10.00
4 MGu,Bluecobalt	8.00
5 MGu	7.00
MINI SERIES	
1 thru 4 F:Elementals	@1.95

JUSTICE MACHINE: CHIMERA CONSPIRACY
Millenium

1 AH,R&N:Justice Machine, wraparound cover	2.50

JUST MARRIED
Charlton Comics
January, 1958

1	25.00
2	15.00
3 thru 10	@10.00
11 thru 30	@8.00
31 thru 113	@4.00
114 December, 1976	4.00

KATO OF THE GREEN HORNET
Now

1 BA,1st Kato solo story	2.50
2 BA,Kato in China contd.	2.50
3 Kato in China contd	2.50
4 Final Issue	2.50

KATO II
Now

1 VM,JSh,A:Karthage	2.50
2 VM,JSh,V:Karthage	2.50
3 VM,JSh,V:Karthage	2.50

KATY KEENE FASHION BOOK MAGAZINE
Archie Publications
1955

1	300.00
2	200.00
3 thru 10 not published	
11 thru 18	@150.00
19	125.00
20	100.00
21	125.00
22	125.00
23 Winter 1958-59	125.00

KATY KEENE PINUP PARADE
Archie Publications
1955

1	300.00
2	200.00
3	150.00
4	150.00
5	150.00
6	125.00
7	125.00
8	125.00
9	125.00
10	165.00
11	125.00
12	125.00
13	125.00
14	125.00
15 September, 1961	300.00

KELLY GREEN
Eclipse
1 SDr,O:Kelly Green	....	2.50
2 SDr,'One,Two,Three'	....	2.00
3 SDr,'Million Dollar Hit'	....	2.00
4 SDr,Rare	....	4.00

KELVIN MACE
Vortex
1	....	6.50
1a 2nd printing	....	1.75
2	....	4.00

KILLER TALES
Eclipse
1	....	1.75

KING LEONARDO AND HIS SHORT SUBJECTS
Dell Publishing Co.
November-January, 1961-62
1	....	75.00
2	....	55.00
3	....	55.00
4	....	55.00

KING LOUIE & MOWGLI
Gold Key
May, 1968
1	....	18.00

KING OF DIAMONDS
Dell Publishing Co.
July-September, 1962
1 Ph(c)	....	30.00

KIT KARTER
Dell Publishing Co.
May-July, 1962
1	....	15.00

KNIGHTS OF THE ROUND TABLE
Dell Publishing Co.
November-January, 1963-4
1 P(c)	....	25.00

KOL MANIQUE RENAISSANCE
1	....	1.50
2	....	1.50

KOMAH
Anubis Press
1 Urban Decay Title	....	2.75

KONA
Dell Publishing Co.
February-April, 1962
1 P(c) all,SG	....	45.00
2 SG	....	20.00
3 SG	....	20.00
4 SG,B:Anak	....	20.00
5 SG	....	20.00
6 SG	....	20.00
7 SG	....	20.00
8 SG	....	20.00
9 SG	....	20.00
10 SG	....	20.00

11 SG	....	15.00
12 SG	....	15.00
13 SG	....	15.00
14 SG	....	15.00
15 SG	....	15.00
16 SG	....	15.00
17 SG	....	15.00
18 SG	....	15.00
19 SG	....	15.00
20 SG	....	15.00
21 SG	....	15.00

KONGA
Charlton Comics
1960
1 SD,DG(c)	....	200.00
2 DG(c)	....	100.00
3 SD	....	75.00
4 SD	....	75.00
5 SD	....	75.00
6 thru 15 SD	....	@55.00
16 thru 22	....	@30.00
23 November, 1965	....	30.00

KONGA'S REVENGE
Charlton Comics
2 Summer, 1962	....	30.00
3 SD,Fall, 1964	....	40.00
1 December, 1968	....	17.00

KOOKIE
Dell Publishing Co.
February-April, 1962
1	....	55.00
2	....	50.00

KORAK, SON OF TARZAN
Gold Key
January, 1964
1	....	40.00
2 thru 11	....	@30.00
12 thru 21	....	@20.00
22 thru 30	....	@10.00
31 thru 40	....	@8.00
41 thru 44	....	@5.00
45 January, 1972	....	5.00

KRUSTY COMICS
Bongo Comics
1 Rise and Fall of Krustyland	...	2.25
2 Rise and Fall of Krustyland	...	2.25
3 Rise and Fall of Krustyland	...	2.25

KULL IN 3-D
Blackthorne
1	....	2.50
2	....	2.50
3	....	2.50

KUNG FU & NINJA
1	....	1.80
2	....	1.80
3	....	1.80
4	....	1.80

LAD: A DOG
Dell Publishing Co.
1961
1	....	30.00
2	....	25.00

LADY ARCANE
Hero Graphics
1 A: Flare,BU:O:Giant	....	4.95
2 thru 3	....	2.95

LADY DEATH
Chaos! Comics
1 BnP, A:Evil Ernie	....	55.00
1a signed gold foil	....	45.00
2 BnP	....	22.00
3 BnP	....	15.00
HC Foil Stamped 1-3	....	24.95
TPB 1-3	....	6.95
1 Swimsuit Edition	....	6.00
1a Velvet Edition	....	30.00

LADY DEATH: BETWEEN HEAVEN & HELL
Chaos! Comics
1 V:Purgatori	....	4.00
1a Limited Edition 5,000c	.....	30.00
2 Lives As Hope	....	2.75

LARS OF MARS
Eclipse
1 3-D MA	....	2.50

LASER ERASER & PRESSBUTTON
Eclipse
1 GL,R:Laser Eraser	....	1.75
2 GL	....	1.75
3 GL,CK,'Tsultrine'	....	1.75
4 MC,'Death'	....	1.75
5 MC,JRy,'Gates of Hell'	....	.95
6 'Corsairs of Illunium'	....	.95
3-D#1 MC,GL(c),'Triple Cross'	...	1.50

LASH LARUE WESTERN
AC Comics
1	....	3.50
Annual	....	2.95

LAST OF THE VIKING HEROES
Genesis West
1 JK	....	4.00
2 JK	....	3.50
3	....	3.00
4	....	2.50
5A sexy cover	....	3.00
5B mild cover	....	2.50
6	....	2.50
7 AA(c)	....	3.50
8	....	2.25
9 Great Battle of Nidhogger	....	2.50
10 'Death Among the Heroes'	....	2.50
Summer Spec.#1 FF,JK	....	3.50
Summer Spec.#2	....	3.00
Summer Spec.#3,A:TMNT	.....	2.50

LAUREL AND HARDY
Dell Publishing Co.
October, 1962
1	....	40.00
2	....	30.00
3	....	30.00
4	....	30.00

LAUREL & HARDY
Gold Key
January, 1967
1		25.00
2 October, 1967		25.00

LAWMAN
Dell Publishing Co.
February, 1959
1 Ph(c) all		75.00
2		40.00
3 ATh		45.00
4		30.00
5		30.00
6		30.00
7		30.00
8		30.00
9		30.00
10		30.00
11		30.00

LAW OF DREDD
Quality
1 V:Perps		5.00
2 BB,Lunar Olympics		4.00
3 BB,V:Judge Death		3.00
4 V:Father Earth		3.00
5 Cursed Earth		3.00
6 V:Perps		3.00
7 V:Perps		3.00

Fleetway
8 Blockmania		3.00
9 BB,DGi,Framed for murders		3.00
10 BB,Day the Law Died Pt.1		2.50
11 BB,Day the Law Died Pt.2		2.50
12 BB,V:Judge Cal		2.50
13 V:Judge Caligula		2.50
14 BB, V:Perps		2.50
15 Under investigation		2.50
16 V:Alien Mercenary		2.50
17 thru 24		@2.50
25 Ugly Clinic		2.50
26 Judge Dredd & Gavel?		2.50
27 Cycles,Lunatics & Graffiti Guerillas		2.50
28 Cadet Training Mission		2.50
29 'Guinea Pig that changed the world		2.50
30 Meka-City,V:Robot		2.50
31 Iso-Block 666		2.50
32 Missing Game Show Hosts		2.50
33 League of Fatties,final issue		3.00

LAZARUS CHURCHYARD
Tundra
1 From UK Blast anthology		4.50
2 Goodnight Ladies		4.50

LEAGUE OF CHAMPIONS
Hero Graphics
{Cont. from Champions #12}
1 Olympus Saga #4		2.95
2 Olympus Saga #5,O:Malice		2.95
3 Olympus Saga ends		2.95

LEATHERFACE
North Star
1		2.75
2		2.75
3		2.75

Legacy #2 © Majestic Comics

LEGACY
Majestic
0 platinum		12.50
1 I:Legacy		2.25
2		2.25

LEGEND OF CUSTER, THE
Dell Publishing Co.
January, 1968
1 Ph(c)		15.00

LEGEND OF SLEEPY HOLLOW
Tundra
One shot.BHa,W.Irving adapt.		6.95

LEGENDS OF JESSE JAMES, THE
Gold Key
February, 1966
1		20.00

LEGENDS OF NASCAR
Vortex
1 HT,Bill Eliott ($1.50 cover Price) 15,000 copies		±25.00
1a ($2.00 cover price) 45,000 copies		±8.00
1b 3rd pr., 80,000 copies		5.00
2 Richard Petty		4.50
3 Ken Schroder		3.50
4 Bob Alison		3.00
5 Bill Elliott		2.50
6 Jr. Johnson		2.50
7 Sterling Marlin		2.25
8		2.00
9 Rusty Wallace		2.00

LEGENDS OF THE STARGRAZERS
Innovation
1		1.95
2		1.95
3		1.95

4		1.95
5		1.95

LEJENTIA
1		1.95
2		2.25

LEMONADE KID
AC Comics
1		2.50

LEONARD NIMOY'S PRIMORTALS
Teckno-Comics
1 I:Primortals		2.50
2 Zeerus Reveals Himself		2.25
3 Contact		1.95
4 Message Deciphered		1.95
5 Place & Time Announced		1.95
6 Zeerus Arrives on Earth		1.95

LEONARDO
Mirage
1 TMNT Character		10.00

LIBERTY PROJECT, THE
Eclipse
1 I:Liberty Project		2.50
2		1.75
3 V:Silver City Wranglers		1.75
4		1.75
5		1.75
6 F:Cimarron,'Misery and Gin'		1.75
7 I:Menace		1.75
8 V:Savage		1.75

LIDSVILLE
Gold Key
October, 1972
1		15.00
2		7.00
3 and 4		@7.00
5 October, 1973		7.00

LIEUTENANT, THE
Dell Publishing Co.
April-June, 1962
1 Ph(c)		15.00

LIFE & ADVENTURES OF SANTA CLAUS
Tundra
GN MP,L.Frank Baum adapt.		24.95

LIFE IN HELL
Blackthorne
1 3-D		2.50

LIFE WITH ARCHIE
Archie Publications
September, 1958
1		225.00
2		100.00
3		60.00
4		60.00
5		60.00
6		30.00
7		30.00
8		30.00
9		30.00

10	30.00
11 thru 20	@20.00
21 thru 30	@15.00
31 thru 40	@10.00
41	7.00
42 B:Pureheart	5.00
43	5.00
44	5.00
45	5.00
46 O:Pureheart	15.00
47 thru 59	@3.50
60 thru 100	@2.50
101 thru 285	@1.00

LIGHT FANTASTIC, THE
Innovation

1 Terry Pratchett adapt.	2.50
2 Adaptation continues	2.50
3 Adaptation continues	2.50
4 Adapt.conclusion	2.50

LIGHTNING COMICS PRESENTS
Lightning Comics

1 B&W Promo Ed.	3.50
1a B&W Promo Ed. Platinum	15.00
1b B&W Promo Ed. Gold	40.00

LINDA LARK
Dell Publishing Co.
October-December, 1961

1	15.00
2	8.00
3	8.00
4	8.00
5	8.00
6	8.00
7	8.00
8	8.00

LINUS, THE LIONHEARTED
Gold Key
September, 1965

1	50.00

LIPPY THE LION AND HARDY HAR HAR
Gold Key
March, 1963

1	50.00

LISA COMICS
Bongo Comics

1 F:Lisa Simpson	2.25

LITTLE AMBROSE
Archie Publications
September, 1958

1	75.00

LITTLE ARCHIE
Archie Publications
1956

1	300.00
2	150.00
3	100.00
4	100.00
5	100.00
6 thru 10	@75.00
11 thru 20	@40.00

21 thru 30	@25.00
31 thru 40	@15.00
41 thru 60	@10.00
61 thru 80	@5.00
81 thru 100	@3.00
101 thru 180	@2.00

LITTLE ARCHIE MYSTERY
Archie Publications
May, 1963

1	75.00
2 October, 1963	40.00

LITTLE AUDREY & MELVIN
Harvey Publications
May, 1962

1	50.00
2 thru 5	@20.00
6 thru 10	@15.00
11 thru 20	@10.00
21 thru 40	@7.00
41 thru 50	@5.00
51 thru 53 52 pgs Giant size	@5.00
54 thru 60	@8.00
61 December, 1973	6.00

LITTLE AUDREY TV FUNTIME
Harvey Publications
September, 1962

1 A:Richie Rich	35.00
2 same	20.00
3 same	15.00
4	15.00
5	15.00
6 thru 10	@6.00
11 thru 20	@5.00
21 thru 32	@3.50
33 October, 1971	3.50

LITTLE DOT DOTLAND
Harvey Publications
July, 1962

1	50.00
2	25.00
3	22.00
4	18.00
5	18.00
6 thru 10	@10.00
11 thru 20	@7.00
21 thru 50	@3.50
51 thru 60	@2.50
61 December, 1973	2.50

LITTLE DOT'S UNCLES & AUNTS
Harvey Enterprises
October, 1961

1	55.00
2	30.00
3	25.00
4	15.00
5	15.00
6 thru 10	@12.00
11 thru 20	@10.00
21 thru 40	@7.00
41 thru 51	@5.00
52 April, 1974	5.00

LITTLE LOTTA
Harvey Publications
November, 1955

1 B:Richie Rich and Little Lotta	225.00
2	125.00
3	100.00
4	60.00
5	60.00
6	45.00
7	45.00
8	45.00
9	45.00
10	45.00
11 thru 20	@30.00
21 thru 40	@20.00
41 thru 60	@15.00
61 thru 80	@7.00
81 thru 99	@5.00
100 thru 103 52 pgs	@3.00
104 thru 120	@2.00
121 May, 1976	2.00

LITTLE LOTTA FOODLAND
Harvey Publications
September, 1963

1 68 pgs	75.00
2	40.00
3	25.00
4	14.00
5	14.00
6 thru 10	@10.00
11 thru 20	@7.00
21 thru 26	@5.50
27	4.50
28	4.50
29 October, 1972	3.50

LITTLE MERMAID
Walt Disney

1 based on movie	1.75
2 'Serpent Teen'	1.50
3 'Guppy Love'	1.50
4	1.50

LITTLE MONSTERS, THE
Gold Key
November, 1964

1	20.00
2	10.00
3 thru 10	@7.00
11 thru 20	@3.00
21 thru 43	@2.00
44 February, 1978	2.00

LITTLE MONSTERS
Now

1 thru 6	@1.75

LITTLE REDBIRDS

1	2.50
2	2.50
3	2.50
4	2.50

LITTLE SAD SACK
Harvey Publications
October, 1964

1 Richie Rich(c)	15.00
2	5.00
3	3.00

---

4 . . . . 3.00
5 . . . . 5.00
6 thru 19 Nov. 1967 . . . . @4.00

LITTLE STOOGES, THE
Gold Key
September, 1972
1 . . . . 10.00
2 . . . . 5.00
3 . . . . 5.00
4 . . . . 5.00
5 . . . . 5.00
6 . . . . 5.00
7 March, 1974 . . . . 5.00

LLOYD LLEWELLYN
1 . . . . 2.00

LOBO
Dell Publishing Co.
December,1965
1 . . . . 10.00
2 . . . . 8.00

LOCKE
Blackthorne
1 PO.Jones 1.75
2 TD 2.25
3 . . . . 1.25
4 . . . . 1.25
5 . . . . 1.25

LONE RANGER, THE
Gold Key
September, 1964
1 . . . . 30.00
2 . . . . 15.00
3 . . . . 10.00
4 . . . . 10.00
5 . . . . 10.00
6 . . . . 8.00
7 . . . . 8.00
8 . . . . 8.00
9 . . . . 8.00
10 . . . . 8.00
11 thru 18 . . . . @7.00
18 thru 27 . . . . @5.00
28 March, 1977 . . . . 5.00

LOST IN SPACE
Innovatiom
{based on TV series}
1 O:Jupiter II Project 3.00
2 'Cavern of IdyllicSummersLost' 2.75
2a Special Edition 2.50
3 Do Not Go Gently into that
   Good Night',Bill Mumy script . . 2.50
4 'People are Strange' 2.50
5 The Perils of Penelope 2.50
6 Time Warp 2.50
7 thru 9 . . . . @2.50
10 inc.Afterthought 2.50
11 F:Judy Robinson 2.50
12 . . . . 2.95
13 Voyage/Bottom Soil 2.95
14 . . . . 2.50
15 . . . . 2.50
16 . . . . 2.50
Project Krell 2.50
Ann.#2 . . . . 2.95
Special- Seduction of the
   Innocent 2.50

Lost in Space #11 © Innovation

LOST PLANET
Eclipse
1 BHa,I:Tyler FLynn 2.00
2 BHa,R:Amelia Earhart 1.75
3 BHa 1.25
4 BHa,'Devil's Eye' 1.25
5 BHa,A:Amelia Earhart 2.00
6 . . . . 2.00

LOVECRAFT
Adventure Comics
1 'The Lurking Fear' adapt. 2.95
2 Beyond the Wall of Sleep . . . 2.95
3 . . . . 2.95
4 . . . . 2.95

LOVE DIARY
Charlton Comics
July, 1958
1 . . . . 30.00
2 . . . . 15.00
3 . . . . 10.00
4 . . . . 10.00
5 . . . . 7.00
6 . . . . 10.00
7 thru 10 . . . . @7.00
11 thru 15 . . . . @3.00
16 thru 20 . . . . @3.00
21 thru 40 . . . . @1.50
41 thru 101 . . . . @1.00
102 December, 1976 . . . . 1.00

LUCY SHOW, THE
Gold Key
June, 1963
1 Ph(c) 65.00
2 Ph(c) 45.00
3 . . . . 40.00
4 . . . . 40.00
5 . . . . 40.00

LUDWIG VON DRAKE
Dell Publishing Co.
November-December, 1961
1 . . . . 25.00

2 . . . . 15.00
3 . . . . 15.00
4 . . . . 15.00

LUGER
Eclipse
1 TY,I:Luger,mini-series 2.00
2 TY 1.75
3 TY,BHa,V:Sharks 1.75

LUNATIC
1 . . . . 1.75
2 . . . . 1.75

LUNATIC FRINGE
Innovation
1 . . . . 1.95
2 . . . . 1.75

LUNATIC FRINGE
Innovation
1 . . . . 1.75

LYNCH MOB
Chaos! Comics
1 GCa(c), I:Mother Mayhem 2.50
2 Lynch Mob Loses 2.50
3 1994 Time Trip 2.50
4 Mother Mayhem at UN 2.50

LYNDON B. JOHNSON
Dell Publishing Co.
March, 1965
1 Ph(c) 15.00

M
Eclipse
1 thru 4 JMu 4.95

MACROSS
Comico
1 . . . . 12.00
Becomes:
Robotech, The Macross Saga

MAD FOLLIES
E.C. Comics
1963
(N#) 150.00
2 1964 . . . . 100.00
3 1965 . . . . 75.00
4 1966 . . . . 85.00
5 1967 . . . . 60.00
6 1968 . . . . 50.00
7 1969 . . . . 50.00

MADMAN
Tundra
1 . . . . 5.00
2 . . . . 5.00
3 . . . . 5.00

MADMAN ADVENTURES
Tundra
1 R & N:Madman 4.50
2 . . . . 3.50
3 thru 4 . . . . 3.25

MAD SPECIAL
E.C. Publications, Inc.
Fall, 1970

1	65.00
2	40.00
3	40.00
4 thru 8	@30.00
9 thru 13	@25.00
14	15.00
15	20.00
16	15.00
17	15.00
18	18.00
19 thru 21	@18.00
22 thru 31	@8.00
32	10.00
33 thru 58	@7.00

MAGE
Comico

1 MWg,I:Kevin Matchstick	13.00
2 MWg,I:Edsel	9.00
3 MWg,V:Umbra Sprite	5.00
4 MWg,V:Umbra Sprite	5.00
5 MWg,I:Sean (Spook)	5.00
6 MWg,Grendel begins	20.00
7 MWg,Grendel	9.00
8 MWg,Grendel	5.00
9 MWg,Grendel	5.00
10 MWg,Grendel,Styx	5.00
11 MWg,Grendel,Styx	5.00
12 MWg,D:Sean,Grendel	5.00
13 MWg,D:Edsel,Grendel	5.00
14 MWg,Grendel,O:Kevin	5.00
15 MWg,D:Umbra Sprite	5.00

MAGEBOOK
Comico

1 rep. Mage #1-4	8.95
2 rep. Mage #5-8	8.95

MAGIC FLUTE
Eclipse

1 CR	4.95

MAGILLA GORILLA
Gold Key
May, 1964

1	25.00
2 thru 10 Dec. 1968	@15.00

MAGILLA GORILLA
Charlton Comics
November, 1970

1	50.00
2 thru 5	@25.00

MAGNUS: ROBOT FIGHTER
Gold Key
February, 1963

1 RM,I:Magnus,Teeja,A-1, I&B:Capt.Johner&aliens	250.00
2 RM,I:Sen.Zeremiah Clane	125.00
3 RM,I:Xyrkol	125.00
4 RM,I:Mekamn,Elzy	75.00
5 RM,The Immortal One	75.00
6 RM,I:Talpa	70.00
7 RM,I:Malev-6,ViXyrkol	85.00
8 RM,I:Outsiders(Chet, Horio, Toun, Malf)	70.00
9 RM, I:Madmot	70.00
10 RM,Mysterious Octo-Rob	70.00
11 RM,I:Danae,Neo-Animals	50.00
12 RM,The Volcano Makers	50.00
13 RM,I:Dr Lazlo Noel	55.00
14 RM,The Monster Robs	50.00
15 RM,I:Mogul Radur	50.00
16 RM,I:Gophs	50.00
17 RM,I:Zypex	50.00
18 RM,I:V'ril Trent	50.00
19 RM,Fear Unlimited	50.00
20 RM,I:Bunda the Great	50.00
21 RM, Space Spectre	50.00
22 Rep. #1	35.00
23 DSp,Mission Disaster	35.00
24 Pied Piper of North Am	35.00
25 The Micro Giants	35.00
26 The Venomous Vaper	35.00
27 Panic in Pacifica	35.00
28 Threats from the Depths	35.00
29 Rep. #7	16.00
30 Rep. #15	16.00
31 Rep. #14	16.00
32 Rep. #2	16.00
33 Rep. #21	16.00
34 Rep. #13	16.00
35 Rep. #6	16.00
36 Rep. #8	16.00
37 Rep. #11	16.00
38 Rep. #12	16.00
39 Rep. #16	16.00
40 Rep. #17	16.00
41 Rep. #18	16.00
42 Rep. #19	16.00
43 Rep. #20	16.00
44 Rep. #23	16.00
45 Rep. #24	16.00
46 Rep. #25	16.00

MAJOR DAMAGE
Invictus Studios

1 I:Major Damage	2.25
2 V:Godkin	2.25
3 First Contact Conclusion	2.25

MAKABRE
Apocalypse

1 Gangsters	3.95

MALICE
Heroic Publishing

1 I:Queen of the Dead	1.95

MAN FROM PLANET X
Planet X Prod.

1	3.00

MAN FROM U.N.C.L.E.
Gold Key
February, 1965

1 'The Explosive Affair'	100.00
2 'The Forthur Cookie Affair'	65.00
3 'The Deadly Devices Affair'	40.00
4 'The Rip Van Solo Affair'	40.00
5 'Ten Little Uncles Affair'	40.00
6 'The Three Blind Mice Affair'	40.00
7 'The Pixilated Puzzle Affair' I:Jet Dream (back-up begins)	45.00
8 'The Floating People Affair'	40.00
9 'Spirit of St.Louis Affair'	40.00
10 'The Trojan Horse Affair'	40.00
11 'Three-Story Giant Affair'	35.00
12 'Dead Man's Diary Affair'	35.00
13 'The Flying Clowns Affair'	35.00
14 'Great Brain Drain Affair'	35.00
15 'The Animal Agents Affair'	35.00
16 'Instant Disaster Affair'	35.00
17 'The Deadly Visions Affair'	35.00
18 'The Alien Affair'	35.00
19 'Knight in Shining Armor Affair'	35.00
20 'Deep Freeze Affair'	35.00
21 rep. #10	30.00
22 rep. #7	30.00

MAN FROM U.N.C.L.E.
Entertainment

1 thru 11	1.50

The Man From U.N.C.L.E. #2
© Millennium

MAN FROM U.N.C.L.E.
Millennium

1 The Birds of Prey Affair,pt.1	2.95
2 The Birds of Prey Affair,pt.2	2.95

MANIFEST DESTINY

1	1.95

MANGLE TANGLE TALES
Innovation

1	2.95

MAN IN BLACK
Harvey Publications
September, 1957

1	75.00
2	45.00
3	45.00
4 March, 1958	45.00

MAN OF WAR
Eclipse

1 thru 3	@1.75

MARKSMAN, THE
Hero

1 O:Marksman, Pt.#1	1.95
2 O:Marksman, Pt.#2	1.95

All comics prices listed are for *Near Mint* condition.

3 O:Marksman ends.I:Basilisk . . . 1.95
4 A:Flare 1.95
5 I:Radar,Sonar . . . . . . : 1.95
Annual #1, A:Champions 1.95

Married with Children #1
© Now Comics

MARRIED... WITH CHILDREN
Now

1 . . . . 6.00
1a 2nd printing 2.00
2 . . . . . . : 4.00
3 . . . . 3.00
4 . . . . 2.50
5 . . . . 2.50
6 . . . . 2.00
7 . . . . 2.50

[2nd Series]
1 Peg-Host of Radio Show 2.25
2 The Bundy Invention 1.95
3 Psychodad,(photo cover) 1.95
4 Mother-In-Law,(photo cover) . . 1.95
5 Bundy the Crusader 1.95
6 Bundy J: The Order of the
 Mighty Warthog 1.95
7 Kelly the VJ 1.95
Spec. 1.95
3-D Spec. 2.50

MARRIED WITH CHILDREN: DYSFUNCTIONAL FAMILY
Now
1 I:The Bundies 2.50
2 TV Appearance 2.50
3 Morally Pure Bundys 2.50

MARRIED WITH CHILDREN: FLASHBACK SPECIAL
Now
1 Peg and Al's first date 1.95
2 and 3 . . . . @1.95

MARRIED WITH CHILDREN: KELLY BUNDY SPECIAL
Now
1 with poster 1.95
2 and 3 with poster . . . . @1.95

MARRIED... WITH CHILDREN: QUANTUM QUARTET
Now
1 thru 4 Fantastic Four parody @1.95
Fall 1994 Spec., flip book 1.95

MARRIED WITH CHILDREN 2099
Mirage
1 thru 3 Cable Parody . . . . @2.50

MARS
First
1 thru 12 . . . . @1.25

MARS ATTACKS
Topps
1 thru 6 KG(s) 2.95

MARSHALL LAW: HATEFUL DEAD
Apocalypse
1 'Rise of the Zombies' 5.95

MARTIANS!!! IN 3-D
1 . . . . 2.00

MARY WORTH
ARGO
March, 1956
1 . . . . 30.00

MASKED MAN
Eclipse
1 . . . . 3.00
2 . . . . 2.00
3 . . . . 2.00
4 . . . . 2.00
5 . . . . 2.00
6 V:Roxie Lamada 2.00
7 . . . . 2.00
8 'Roxy' 1.75
9 W:Dick and Maggie 1.75
10 . . . . 2.00

MASTERWORK SERIES
Seagate DC
1 FFrep.DC,ShiningKnight 1.50
2 FFrep.DC,ShiningKnight 1.50
3 BWr,Horror DC rep. 1.50

MAVERICK
Dell Publishing Co.
April, 1958
1 Ph(c) all 124.00
2 Ph(c) 65.00
3 Ph(c) 65.00
4 Ph(c) 65.00
5 Ph(c) 65.00
6 Ph(c) 55.00

7 Ph(c) 55.00
8 Ph(c) 55.00
9 Ph(c) 55.00
10 Ph(c) 55.00
11 Ph(c) 55.00
12 Ph(c) 55.00
13 Ph(c) 55.00
14 Ph(c) 55.00
15 thru 19 Ph(c) 50.00

MAVERICK MARSHALL
Charlton Comics
November, 1958
1 . . . . 20.00
2 . . . . 15.00
3 . . . . 15.00
4 . . . . 15.00
5 . . . . 15.00
6 . . . . 15.00
7 May, 1960 . . . . 15.00

MAVERICKS
Dagger
1 PuD,RkL, I:Mavericks 2.50
2 PuD,RkL 2.50

MAXIMORTAL
King Hell/Tundra
1 RV,A:True-Man 4.50
2 Crack in the New World 4.25
3 RV,Secret of the Manhattan
 Project revealed 4.25
4 . . . . 4.25
5 A:True Man 3.25
6 A:El Guano 3.25

MAYA
Gold Key
March, 1968
1 . . . . 15.00

MAZE AGENCY
Comico
1 O:Maze Agency 3.00
2 . . . . 2.50
3 . . . . 2.50
4 . . . . 2.50
5 . . . . 2.50
6 . . . . 2.50
7 . . . . 2.75
8 . . . . 1.95
9 . . . . 1.95
10 . . . . 1.95
11 . . . . 1.95
12 . . . . 2.50
13 thru 15 . . . . @1.95
16 thru 23 . . . . @2.50
Spec #1 . . . . 2.75

McHALE'S NAVY
Dell Publishing Co.
May-July, 1963
1 Ph(c) 25.00
2 Ph(c) 20.00
3 Ph(c) 20.00

McKEEVER & THE COLONEL
Dell Publishing Co.
February-April, 1963
1 Ph(c) 35.00
2 Ph(c) 25.00

3 Ph(c) 25.00

MECHANICS
Fantagraphics
1 HB,rep.Love & Rockets 3.00
2 HB,rep.Love & Rockets 2.50
3 HB,rep.Love & Rockets 2.50

MEDIA STARR
Innovation
1 thru 3 .... @1.95

MEGALITH
Continuity
1 MT..................... 6.00
2 MT..................... 4.00
3 MT, Painted issue 2.50
4 NA,TVE 2.50
5 NA,TVE 2.50
6 MN 2.50
7 MN 2.50
8 .... 2.50
9 SDr(i) 2.50
10 .... 2.50
[2nd Series, Deathwatch 2000]
0 Deathwatch 2000 prologue ... 5.00
1 Deathwatch 2000 Pt.5,w/card . 2.50

Megalith #3 © Continuity Comics

2 Deathwatch 2000 Pt.10,w/card . 2.50
3 pt.16,Indestructible(c),w/card .. 2.50
4 Rise of Magic 2.50
5 Rise of Magic 2.50
6 and 7 .... 2.50

MEGATON
1 .... 1.50
Entity Comics
Holiday Spec. w/card 2.95

MEGATON EXPLOSION
1 RLd,AMe,I:Youngblood
preview 25.00

MEGATON MAN
Kitchen Sink
1 Don Simpson art, I:Megaton Man6.00

1a rep. B&W 2.00
2 .... 4.00
3 and 4 .... @3.00
5 .... 2.50
6 Border Worlds 2.50
7 Border Worlds 2.50
8 Border Worlds 2.50
9 Border Worlds 2.50
10 final issue, 1986 .... 2.50

MELTING POT
Mirage
1 .... 3.50
2 .... 3.50

MELVIN MONSTER
Dell Publishing Co.
April-June, 1965
1 .... 100.00
2 .... 75.00
3 .... 75.00
4 .... 75.00
5 .... 75.00
6 .... 75.00
7 .... 75.00
8 .... 75.00
9 .... 75.00
10 .... 75.00

[Katshuiro Otomo's] MEMORIES
Epic
1 .... 2.50

MEN FROM EARTH
Future Fun
1 based on Matt Mason toy 6.50

MERCENARY
NBM
The Voyage 10.95
The Black Globe 9.95
The Fortress 9.95

MERCHANTS OF DEATH
Eclipse
1 King's Castle, The Hero 3.50
2 King's Castle,Soldiers of Fortune 3.50
3 Ransom, Soldier of Fortune ... 3.50
4 ATh(c),Ransom, Men o/t Legion 3.50
5 Ransom,New York City Blues . 3.50

MERLIN REALM
Blackthorne
1 3-D 2.50

META 4
First
1 IG 3.95
2 IG 2.25
3 IG/JSon,FinalMonthly 2.25

MICHAELANGELO
Mirage
1 TMNT Character 15.00

MICKEY & DONALD
Gladstone
1 1449 Firestone 8.00
2 .... 4.00

3 Man of Tomorrow 3.00
4 .... 2.50
5 .... 2.50
6 .... 2.50
7 .... 2.50
8 .... 2.50
9 .... 2.50
10 .... 2.00
11 .... 2.00
12 .... 2.00
13 .... 2.00
14 .... 2.00
15 .... 2.00
16 giant-size 2.50
17 .... 3.00
18 .... 4.00
Becomes:
DONALD AND MICKEY
19 thru 26 .... @1.50

MICKEY MANTLE COMICS
Magnum
1 JSt,Rise to Big Leagues 1.75

MICKEY MOUSE
Gladstone
219 FG,Seven Ghosts 6.00
220 FG,Seven Ghosts 7.00
221 FG,Seven Ghosts 7.00
222 FG,Editor in Grief 5.00
223 FG,Editor in Grief 4.00
224 FG,Crazy Crime Wave 3.00
225 FG,Crazy Crime Wave 3.00
226 FG,Captive Castaways 3.00
227 FG,Captive Castaways 3.00
228 FG,Captive Castaways 3.00
229 FG,Bat Bandit 3.00
230 FG,Bat Bandit 2.50
231 FG,Bobo the Elephant 2.50
232 FG,Bobo the Elephant 2.50
233 FG,Pirate Submarine 2.50
234 FG,Pirate Submarine 2.50
235 FG,Photo Racer 2.50
236 FG,Photo Racer 2.50
237 FG,Race for Riches 2.50
238 FG,Race for Riches 2.50
239 FG,Race for Riches 2.50
240 FG,March of Comics 2.50
241 FG 4.00
242 FG 2.50
243 FG 2.50
244 FG,60th Anniv 5.00
245 FG 2.25
245 FG 2.25
246 FG 2.25
247 FG 2.25
248 FG 2.25
249 FG 5.00
250 FG 2.25
251 FG 2.25
252 FG 2.25
253 FG 2.25
254 FG 2.25
255 FG 4.00
256 FG 4.00

MICKEY MOUSE
Walt Disney
1 .... 3.50
2 .... 3.00
3 .... 2.50
4 .... 2.50
5 .... 2.50

All comics prices listed are for *Near Mint* condition.

Mickey Mouse #1
© Walt Disney Comics

6	. . . .	2.00
7 Phantom Blot	. . . .	2.00
8 Phantom Blot	. . . .	2.00
9	. . . .	2.00
10 Sky Adventure	. . . .	2.00
11 When Mouston Freezes Over	.	2.00
12 Hail & Farewell	. . . .	2.00
13 'What's Shakin''	. . . .	2.00
14 Mouseton,Eagle-Landing	. . .	2.00
15 'Lost Palace of Kashi'	. . . . . .	2.00
16 'Scoundrels in Space'	. . . . .	2.00
17 'Sound of Blunder' Pt.1	. . . . .	1.75
18 'Sound of Blunder' Pt.2	. . . . .	1.75
19 50th Ann. Fantasia Celebration Sorcerer's Apprentice adapt	. .	1.50

MICROBOTS, THE
Gold Key
December, 1971

1	. . . .	1.00

MIDNIGHT EYE: GOKU PRIVATE INVESTIGATOR
Viz

1 A.D. 2014: Tokyo city	. . . . . .	5.25
2 V:Hakuryu,A:Yoko	. . . .	4.95
3 A:Ryoko,Search for Ryu	. . . . .	4.95
4 Goku vs. Ryu	. . . .	4.95
5 Leilah Abducted	. . . .	4.95
6 Lisa's I.D. discovered	. . . . . .	4.95

MIGHTY COMICS
{Prev: Flyman}

40 A:Web	. . . .	12.00
41 A:Shield, Black Hood	. . . . . .	10.00
42 A:Black Hood	. . . .	10.00
43 A:Shield, Black Hood,Web	. .	9.00
44 A:Black Hood, Steel Sterling Shield	. . . .	9.00
45 Shield-Black Hood team-up O:Web	. . . .	9.00
46 A:Steel Sterling, Black Hood, Web	. . . .	9.00
47 A:Black Hood & Mr.Justice	. .	9.00
48 A:Shield & Hangman	. . . . . .	9.00

49 Steel Sterling-Black Hood team up, A:Fox	. . . .	9.00

MIGHTY CRUSADERS
Red Circle
[1st Series]

1 O:Shield (Joe Higgins & Bill Higgins)	. . . .	22.00
2 MSy,O:Comet	. . . .	15.00
3 O:Fly-Man	. . . .	12.50
4 A:Fireball,Jaguar,Web,Fox, Blackjack Hangman & more Golden Age Archie Heroes	. . . .	15.00
5 I:Ultra-Men&TerrificThree	. . . .	11.00

Archie Publications

6 V:Maestro,A:Steel Sterling	. . .	10.00
7 O:Fly-Girl,A:Steel Sterling	. . .	10.00

[2nd Series]

1 RB,R:Joe Higgins & Lancelot Strong as the SHIELD, Mighty Crusaders, A:Mr.Midnight	. . . .	1.50
2 RB,V:Brain Emporer & Eterno	.	1.50
3 RB,I:Darkling	. . . .	1.50
4 DAy,TD	. . . .	1.50
5	. . . .	1.00
6 DAy,TD,Shield	. . . .	1.00
7	. . . .	1.00
8	. . . .	1.00
9	. . . .	1.00
10	. . . .	1.00
11 DAy,D:Gold Age Black Hood, I: Riot Squad, series based on toy lines	. . . .	1.00
12 DAy,I:She-Fox	. . . .	1.00
13 Last issue	. . . .	1.00

MIGHTY HERCULES, THE
Gold Key
July, 1963

1	. . . .	35.00
2	. . . .	35.00

MIGHTY MORPHIN POWER RANGERS
Hamilton

1 From TV Series	. . . .	2.75
2 Switcheroo	. . . .	2.50
3	. . . .	2.25
4 F:White Ranger	. . . .	1.95
5 F:Pink Ranger	. . . .	1.95
6 V:Garganturon	. . . .	1.95

MIGHTY MOUSE
Marvel?
October, 1990

1 EC,Dark Mite Returns	. . . . . .	3.00
2 EC,V:The Glove	. . . .	2.00
3 EC/JBr(c)Prince Say More	. . .	1.50
4 EC/GP(c)Alt.Universe #1	. . . .	1.50
5 EC,Alt.Universe #2	. . . .	1.50
6 'Ferment',A:MacFurline'	. . . . .	1.50
7 EC,V:Viral Worm	. . . .	1.25
8 EC,BAT-BAT:Year One, O:Bug Wonder	. . . .	1.25
9 EC,BAT-BAT:Year One, V:Smoker	. . . .	1.25
10 'Night o/t Rating Lunatics'	. . .	1.25

MIGHTY MOUSE
Spotlight

1 FMc,PC(c)	. . . .	1.50
2 FMc,CS(c)	. . . .	1.50

1 Holiday Special	. . . .	1.75

MIGHTY MUTANIMALS
Archie Publications
[Mini-Series]

1 Cont.from TMNT Adventures#19, A:Raphael, Man Ray, Leatherhead, Mondo Gecko,Deadman, Wingnut & Screwloose	. . . .	1.25
2 V:Mr.Null,Malinga,Soul and Bean and the Malignoid Army	. . . . .	1.25
3 Alien Invasion help off, Raphael returns to Earth	. . . .	1.25
4 "Days of Future Past"	. . . . . .	1.25
5 "Into the Sun"	. . . .	1.25
6 V:Null & 4 Horsemen Pt#2	. . .	1.25
7 Jaws of Doom	. . . .	1.50
Spec#1 rep. all #1-3 +SBi pin-ups	2.95

MIGHTY MUTANIMALS
Archie

1 Quest for Jagwar's Mother	. . .	1.25
2 V:Snake Eyes	. . . .	1.25
3	. . . .	1.25
4 "Days of Future Past"	. . . . . .	1.25
5 "Into the Sun"	. . . .	1.25
6 V:Null & 4 Horsemen Pt#2	. . .	1.25
7 Jaws of Doom	. . . .	1.50

MIGHTY SAMSON
Gold Key
July, 1964

1 O:Mighty Samson	. . . .	35.00
2	. . . .	15.00
3	. . . .	15.00
4	. . . .	15.00
5	. . . .	15.00
6 thru 10	. . . .	@10.00
11 thru 20	. . . .	@8.00
21 thru 31	. . . .	@5.00
32 August, 1982	. . . .	5.00

MIKE GRELL'S SABLE
First

1 thru 8 rep.	. . . .	@1.75
9	. . . .	1.75
10 Triptych	. . . .	1.75

MIKE SHAYNE PRIVATE EYE
Dell Publishing Co.
November-January, 1961-62

1	. . . .	15.00
2	. . . .	12.00
3	. . . .	12.00

MILLENNIUM INDEX
Eclipse

1	. . . .	2.00
2	. . . .	2.00

MILTON THE MONSTER & FEARLESS FLY
Gold Key
May, 1966

1	. . . .	50.00

MIRACLEMAN
Eclipse

1 R:Miracleman	. . . .	3.25
2 AD,Moore,V:Kid Miracleman	. .	2.25

3 AD,Moore,V:Big Ben	2.00
4 AD,Moore,R:Dr.Gargunza	2.00
5 AD,Moore,O:Miracleman	2.00
6 Moore,V:Miracledog, D:Evelyn Cream	2.00
7 Moore,D:Dr.Gargunza	2.00
8 Moore	2.00
9 RV,Moore,Birth of Miraclebaby	2.50
10 JRy,RV,Moore	1.50
11 JTo,Moore,Book III, I:Miraclewoman	1.25
12 Moore	1.25
13 thru 19	@1.75
20 thru 23	@2.50
24 BWS(c),NGa(s),	2.95
25 thru 28	@2.95
3-D Special #1	2.75
Graphic Album Book 1	9.95
Graphic Album Book 2	9.95
Graphic Album Book 3	12.00

MIRACLEMAN APOCRYPHA
Eclipse

1 inc.'Rascal Prince'	2.50
2 Miracleman, Family Stories	2.50
3	2.50

MIRACLEMAN FAMILY
Eclipse

1 British Rep.,A:Kid Miracleman	1.95
2 Alan Moore (s)	1.95

MIRACLE SQUAD
Fantagraphics

1 Hollywood 30's	2.00
2	2.00
3	2.00
4	2.00

MISS FURY
Adventure Comics

1 O:Cat Suit	2.50
2 Miss Fury impersonator	2.50
3 A:Three Miss Fury's	2.50
4 conclusion	2.50

MISSION IMPOSSIBLE
Dell Publishing Co.
May, 1967

1 Ph(c)	50.00
2 Ph(c)	35.00
3 Ph(c)	30.00
4 Ph(c)	30.00
5 Ph(c)	30.00

MISS PEACH
(& SPECIAL ISSUES)
Dell Publishing Co.
October-December, 1963

1	50.00

MR. AND MRS. J. EVIL SCIENTIST
Gold Key
November, 1963

1	40.00
2	25.00
3	25.00
4	25.00

MR. JIGSAW

Special #1	1.75

Mr. Monster © Eclipse Comics

MR. MONSTER
Eclipse

1 I:Mr. Monster	9.00
2 DSt(c)	5.00
3 V:Dr. NoZone	3.50
4	3.00
5 V:Flesh-eating Amoebo	3.00
6 KG,SD,reprints	3.00
7	3.00
8 V:Monster in the Atomic Telling Machine	3.00
9 V:Giant Clams	3.00
10 R:Dr.No Zone, 3-D	2.00

MR. MONSTER ATTACKS
Tundra

1 DGb,SK,short stories	4.25
2 SK,short stories cont.	4.25
3 DGb,last issue	4.25

MR. MONSTER SUPERDUPER SPECIAL
Eclipse

1	2.50
2	2.00
3	2.00
4	2.00
5	2.00
6	2.00
Hi-Voltage Super Science	2.00
3-D Spec. Hi-Octane Horror,JKu, 'Touch of Death' reprint	1.75
Triple Treat	3.95

MR. MONSTER TRUE CRIME
Eclipse

1	1.75
2	1.75
3-D Spec. #1	2.00

MR. MUSCLES
Charlton Comics
March, 1956

22	25.00
23 August, 1956	25.00

MR. MYSTIC
Eclipse

1	2.00
2	2.00
3	2.00

MR. T AND THE T FORCE
Now

1 NA,R:Mr.T,V:Street Gangs	2.50
1a Gold Ed.	40.00
2 NA,V:Demons	2.25
3 NBy,w/card	2.25
4 NBy,In Urban America	2.25
5 thru 10, with card	@2.25

MISTER X
Vortex

1 HB	8.00
2 HB	5.00
3 HB	3.50
4 HB	3.00
5	3.00
6 thru 10	@2.00
11 thru 13	@2.00
14	2.25

MOD SQUAD
Dell Publishing Co.
January, 1969

1	25.00
2	15.00
3	15.00
4	15.00
5 thru 8	@15.00

MOD WHEELS
Gold Key
March, 1971

1	10.00
2 thru 18	@5.00
19 January, 1976	4.00

MONKEE'S, THE
Dell Publishing Co.
March, 1967

1 Ph(c)	80.00
2 Ph(c)	40.00
3 Ph(c)	40.00
4 Ph(c)	40.00
5	30.00
6 Ph(c)	40.00
7 Ph(c)	40.00
8	30.00
9	30.00
10 Ph(c)	40.00
11 thru 17	30.00

MONOLITH
Comico

1 From Elementals	2.50
2 'Seven Levels of Hell'	2.50
3 'Fugue and Variation'	2.50
4 'Fugue and Variation'	2.50

MONROE'S, THE
Dell Publishing Co.
April, 1967
1 Ph(c) 15.00

MONSTER MASSACRE
Atomeka
1 SBs, DBr,DGb 8.50
1a Black Edition 35.00

MOONWALKER IN 3-D
Blackthorne
1 thru 3 .... @2.50

MORNINGSTAR
Special #1 .... 2.50

MOTORBIKE PUPPIES
Dark Zulu Lies
1 I:Motorbike Puppies 2.50

MOVIE COMICS
Gold Key/Whitman
October, 1962
Alice in Wonderland 25.00
Aristocats 55.00
Bambi 1 .... 30.00
Bambi 2 .... 25.00
Beneath the Planet of the Apes . 35.00
Big Red 20.00
Blackbeard's Ghost 22.00
Buck Rogers Giant Movie Edition 22.00
Bullwhip Griffin 30.00
Captain Sinbad 50.00
Chitty, Chitty Bang Bang 40.00
Cinderella 20.00
Darby O'Gill & the Little People . 35.00
Dumbo 20.00
Emil & the Detectives 25.00
Escapade in Florence 50.00
Fall of the Roman Empire 30.00
Fantastic Voyage 40.00
55 Days at Peking 30.00
Fighting Prince of Donegal 25.00
First Men of the Moon 30.00
Gay Purr-ee 30.00
Gnome Mobile 20.00
Goodbye, Mr. Chips 25.00
Happiest Millionaire 20.00
Hey There, It's Yogi Bear 35.00
Horse Without a Head 15.00
How the West Was Won 30.00
In Search of the Castaways 40.00
Jungle Book, The 25.00
Kidnapped 20.00
King Kong 25.00
King Kong N# 8.00
Lady and the Tramp 25.00
Lady and the Tramp 1 .... 40.00
Lady and the Tramp 2 .... 15.00
Legend of Lobo, The 15.00
Lt. Robin Crusoe 15.00
Lion, The 15.00
Lord Jim 20.00
Love Bug, The 22.00
Mary Poppins 40.00
Mary Poppins 1 .... 65.00
McLintock 100.00
Merlin Jones as the Monkey's
  Uncle 40.00
Miracle of the White Stallions .. 15.00
Misadventures of Merlin Jones .. 30.00
Moon-Spinners, The 50.00

Mutiny on the Bounty 25.00
Nikki, Wild Dog of the North ... 15.00
Old Yeller 20.00
One Hundred & One Dalmations 25.00
Peter Pan 1 .... 30.00
Peter Pan 2 .... 25.00
P.T. 109 .... 40.00
Rio Conchos 35.00
Robin Hood 20.00
Shaggy Dog & the Absent-Minded
  Professor 40.00
Snow White & the Seven Dwarfs 22.00
Snow White & the Seven Dwarfs 31.00
Son of Flubber 22.00
Summer Magic 55.00
Swiss Family Robinson 22.00
Sword in the Stone 45.00
That Darn Cat 45.00
Those Magnificent Men in Their
  Flying Machines 25.00
Three Stooges in Orbt 90.00
Tiger Walks, A 35.00
Toby Tyler 15.00
Treasure Island 15.00
20,000 Leagues Under the Sea . 18.00
Wonderful Adventures of
  Pinocchio 18.00
X, the Man with the X-Ray Eyes 50.00
Yellow Submarine 200.00

Ms. Mystic #9 © Pacific Comics

MS. MYSTIC
Pacific
1 NA,Origin 8.00
2 NA,Origin,I:Urth 4 .... 6.00
Continuity
1 NA,Origin rep. 2.00
2 NA,Origin,I:Urth 4 rep 2.00
3 NA,New material 2.00
4 TSh 2.00
5 DT 2.00
6 .... 2.00
7 .... 2.00
8 CH/Sdr,B:Love Story 2.00
9 DB 2.00
9a Newsstand(c) 2.00
[3rd Series]
1 O:Ms.Mystic 2.50

2 A:Hybrid 2.50
3 .... 2.50
4 .... 2.50
[4th Series, Deathwatch 2000]
1 Deathwatch 2000 pt.8,w/card .. 2.50
2 Deathwatch 2000 w/card 2.50
3 Indestructible cover, w/card ... 2.50

MS. TREE
Renegade
1 3-D 2.00

MS. VICTORY
GOLDEN ANNIVERSARY
AC Comics
1 Ms.Victory celebration 5.00

MS. VICTORY SPECIAL
AC Comics
1 .... 1.75

MUMMY: RAMSES
THE DAMNED
Millenium
1 Anne Rice Adapt. 5.00
2 JM,'Mummy in Mayfair' 3.75
3 JM 3.25
4 JM, To Egypt 3.00
5 JM'The Mummy's Hand' 2.50
6 JM 20th Century Egypt 2.50
7 JM,More Ramses Past Revealed 2.50
8 JM,Hunt for Cleopatra 2.50
9 JM,Cleopatra's Wrath contd. .. 2.50
10 JM,Subterranian World 2.50

MUMMY ARCHIVES
Millenium
1.JM,Features,articles 2.50

MUNDEN'S BAR
ANNUAL
First
1 BB,JOy,JSn,SR 2.95

MUNSTERS, THE
Gold Key
January, 1965
1 .... 150.00
2 .... 75.00
3 .... 55.00
4 .... 55.00
5 .... 55.00
6 thru 16 January 1968 .... @50.00

MUPPET BABIES
Harvey
1 Return of Muppet Babies 1.25

MUTANTS & MISFITS
Silverline
1 thru 4 .... @1.95

MY FAVORITE MARTIAN
Gold Key
January, 1964
1 .... 75.00
2 .... 40.00
3 thru 9 October, 1966 .... @40.00

MY LITTLE MARGIE
Charlton Comics
January, 1954

1 Ph(c)	150.00
2 Ph(c)	75.00
3	40.00
4	40.00
5	40.00
6	40.00
7	40.00
8	40.00
9	45.00
10	30.00
11	15.00
12	15.00
13	30.00
14 thru 19	@25.00
20	50.00
21 thru 35	@15.00
36 thru 53	@10.00
54 Beatles (c)November, 1965	100.00

MYSTERIES OF UNEXPLORED WORLDS/ SON OF VULCAN
Charlton Comics
August, 1956

1	175.00
2	55.00
3	100.00
4 SD	110.00
5 SD,SD(c)	125.00
6 SD	125.00
7	135.00
8 SD	125.00
9 SD	125.00
10 SD,SD(c)	135.00
11 SD,SD(c)	135.00
12	75.00
13 thru 18	@20.00
19 SD(c)	50.00
20	25.00
21 thru 24 SD	@75.00
25	75.00
26 SD	75.00
27 thru 30	@20.00
31 thru 45	@15.00
46 I:Son ofVulcan,Dr.Kong(1965)	20.00
47 V:King Midas	12.00
48 V:Captain Tuska	12.00

Becomes:

SON OF VULCAN

49 DC redesigns costume	6.00
50 V:Dr.Kong	5.00

MYSTERIOUS SUSPENSE
1 SD,A:Question	22.00

MYSTERY COMICS DIGEST
Gold Key
March, 1972

1 WW	8.00
2 WW	5.00
3	3.00
4 Ripleys Believe It or Not	2.50
5 Boris Karloff	2.50
6 Twilight Zone	2.50
7 thru 20	@2.50
21 thru 26 Oct., 1975	@1.50

MYSTIC ISLE
1	1.95

Nancy and Sluggo #127
© Dell Publishing Co.

NANCY & SLUGGO
Dell Publishing Co.
September, 1957

146 B:Peanuts	20.00
147	15.00
148	15.00
149	15.00
150 thru 161	15.00
162 thru 165	25.00
166 thru 176 A:OONA	30.00
177 thru 180	25.00
181 thru 187	12.00

NATIONAL VELVET
Dell Publishing Co.
May-July, 1961

1 Ph(c)	22.00
2 Ph(c)	20.00

NEAT STUFF
Fantagraphics

1	4.50
2	3.00
3 thru 5	@2.50
6	2.25
7	2.25

NECROPOLIS
Fleetway

1 SBs(c),CE,A:Dark Judges/ Sisters Of Death	2.95
2	2.95
3 thru 9	@2.95

NEIL GAIMAN'S MR. HERO THE NEWMATIC MAN
Tekno-Comics

1 I:Mr. Hero, Tecknophage	2.50
2 A:Tecknophage	2.25
3 I:Adam Kaine	1.95
4 I:New Body	1.95
5 Earthquake	1.95

6 I:New Character	1.95

NEIL GAIMAN'S TECKNOPHAGE
Teckno-Comics
1 I:Kalighoul, Tom Vietch	1.95

NEIL GAIMAN'S WHEEL OF WORLDS
Teckno-Comics
0 Deluxe Edition w/Posters	2.95
0a I:Lady Justice	1.95

NEMESIS THE WARLOCK
Eagle
1	2.00
2 thru 8	@1.50

NEW ADVENTURES OF FELIX THE CAT
Felix Comics,Inc
1 New stories	2.25
2 "The Magic Paint Brush"	2.25

NEW ADVENTURES OF PINNOCCIO
Dell Publishing Co.
October-December, 1962
1	60.00
2 and 3	@50.00

NEW ADVENTURES OF SPEED RACER
Now
0 Premiere, 3-D cover	1.95
1 thru 11	@1.95

NEW AMERICA
Eclipse
1 A:Scout	1.75
2 A:Scout	1.75
3 A:Roman Catholic Pope	1.75
4 A:Scout	1.75

NEW BREED
Pied Piper
1	2.75
2	2.25

NEW CHAMPIONS
1	2.95
2	2.95

NEW DNAGENTS
Eclipse
1 R:DNAgents	1.50
2 F:Tank	1.00
3 Repopulating the World	1.00
4	1.00
5 'Last Place on Earth'	1.00
6 JOy(c),'Postscript'	1.00
7 V:Venimus	1.00
8 DSp,V:Venimus	1.00
9 V:Venimus,I:New Wave	1.00
10 I:New Airboy	1.00
11 Summer Fun Issue	1.25
12 V:Worm	1.25
13 EL,F:Tank	1.25

---

14 EL,Nudity,'Grounded' 1.25
15 thru 17 . . . . @1.25
3-D #1 . . . . 2.50

NEW JUSTICE MACHINE
Innovation
1 . . . . 1.95
2 . . . . 1.95
3 . . . . 2.50

NEW ORLEANS SAINTS
1 Playoff season(football team) . 6.00

NEW STATESMEN
Fleetway
1 . . . . 4.50
2 thru 5 . . . . @3.95

NEWSTRALIA
Innovation
1 . . . . 1.75
2 . . . . 1.75
3 . . . . 1.95

NEW TERRYTOONS
Dell Publishing Co.
June-August, 1960
1 . . . . 25.00
2 thru 9 . . . . @15.00

NEW WAVE, THE
Eclipse
1 Error Pages 2.00
1a Correction 1.50
2 . . . . 1.00
3 'Space Station Called Hell' . . . 1.00
4 Birth of Megabyte 1.00
5 PG(c),O:Avalon 1.50
6 O:Megabyte 1.50
7 Avalon disappears 1.00
8 V:Heap,V:Druids 1.00
9 . . . . 1.00
10 V:Heap Team 1.00
11 . . . . 1.50
12 . . . . 1.50
13 V:Volunteers 1.50
14 1/3 issue 2.00

NEW WAVE vs.
THE VOLUNTEERS
Eclipse
1 3-D,V:Volunteers 2.50
2 3-D,V:Volunteers 2.50

NEXT MAN
Comico
1 I&O:Next Man 2.50
2 . . . . 1.75
3 . . . . 1.75
4 . . . . 1.50
5 . . . . 1.50

NEXT NEXUS
First
1 SR 1.95
2 SR 1.95
3 SR 1.95
4 SR 1.95

NEXUS

Capital
1 SR 7.00
2 SR,Origin 5.50
3 SR 5.00
4 SR 5.00
5 SR 5.00
6 SR,A:Badger,Trialogue
Trilogy #1 . . . . 4.00

Nexus #8 © First Comics

First
7 SR,A:Badger,Trialogue
Trilogy #2 . . . . 4.00
8 SR,A:Badger,Trialogue
Trilogy #3 . . . . 4.00
9 SR,Teen Angel 2.50
10 SR,BWg,Talking Heads 2.00
11 SR,V:Clausius 2.00
12 SR,V:The Old General 2.00
13 SR,Sundra Peale solo 2.00
14 SR,A:Clonezone,Hilariator . . . 2.00
15 SR,A:Clonezone 2.00
16 SR,A:Clonezone 2.00
17 Judah vs. Jacque,the Anvil . . . 2.00
18 SR,A:Clonezone 2.00
19 SR,A:Clonezone 2.00
20 SR,A:Clonezone 2.00
21 SR,A:Clonezone 2.00
22 KG,A:Badger 2.00
23 SR,A:Clonezone 2.00
24 SR,A:Clonezone 2.00
25 SR,A:Clonezone 2.00
26 SR,A:Clonezone 2.00
27 SR,A:Clonezone 2.00
28 MMi 2.00
29 A:Kreed & Sinclair 2.00
30 JL,C:Badger 2.50
31 Judah solo story 2.00
32 JG,Judah solo story 2.00
33 SR,A:Kreed & Sinclair 2.00
34 SR,Judah solo story 2.00
35 SR,Judah solo story 2.00
36 SR 2.00
37 PS 2.00
38 . . . . 2.00
39 SR, The Boom Search 2.00
40 SR 2.00
41 SR 2.00
42 SR,Bowl-Shaped world 2.00

43 PS 2.00
44 PS 2.00
45 SR,A:Badger Pt.1 . . . . 2.00
46 SR,A:Badger Pt.2 . . . . 2.00
47 SR,A:Badger Pt.3 . . . . 2.00
48 SR,A:Badger Pt.4 . . . . 2.00
49 PS,A:Badger Pt.5 . . . . 2.00
50 SF,double size,A:Badger Pt.6
Crossroads tie-in 3.50
51 PS 2.00
52 PS 2.00
53 PS 2.00
54 PS 2.00
55 PS 1.95
56 . . . . 1.95
57 AH 1.95
58 Sr,I:Stanislaus Korivitsky
as Nexus 1.95
59 SR 1.95
60 SR 1.95
61 . . . . 1.95
62 . . . . 1.95
63 V:Elvonic Order 1.95
64 V:Elvonic Order 1.95
65 V:Elvonic Order 1.95
66 V:Elvonic Order 1.95
67 V:Elvonic Order 1.95
68 LM 1.95
69 . . . . 1.95
70 . . . . 1.95
71 V:Bad Brains 1.95
72 V:Renegade heads 1.95
73 Horatio returns to Ylum 1.95
74 Horatio vs. Stan 1.95
75 Horatio vs. Stan 1.95
76 . . . . 2.25
77 . . . . 2.25
78 O:Nexus,Nexus Files Pt#1 . . . 2.25
79 Nexus Files Pt#2 . . . . 2.25
80 Nexus.Files Pt#3,last iss. . . . 2.25

NEXUS LEGENDS
First
1 thru 13 rep.Nexus . . . . @1.50
14 rep.Nexus 1.75
15 rep.Nexus 1.75
16 rep.Nexus 1.75
17 rep.Nexus 1.75
18 rep.Nexus 1.95
19 rep.Nexus 1.95
20 SR,Sanctuary 1.95
21 thru 23 SR . . . . @1.95

NICK HOLIDAY
Argo
May, 1956
1 Strip reprints 30.00

NIGHT GLIDER
Topps
1 V:Bombast,C:Captain Glory,
Trading Card 3.25

NIGHTMARE
Innovation
1 . . . . 2.50

NIGHTMARE AND
CASPER
Harvey Publications
August, 1963
1 . . . . 40.00
2 . . . . 20.00

| All comics prices listed are for *Near Mint* condition.

3	20.00
4	20.00
5	20.00

Becomes:

CASPER AND NIGHTMARE

6 B:68 pgs	15.00
7	7.00
8	7.00
9	7.00
10	7.00
11 thru 20	@3.50
21 thru 30	@2.50
31	2.50
32 E:68 pgs	2.50
33 thru 45	@2.00
46 August, 1974	2.00

NIGHTMARE ON ELM STREET
Blackthorne

1 3-D	2.50
2 3-D	2.50
3 3-D	2.50

NIGHTMARES ON ELM STREET
Innovation

1 Yours Truly, Freddy Krueger Pt.1	3.00
2 Yours Truly ,Freddy Krueger Pt.2	2.50
3 Loose Ends Pt.1,Return to Springwood	2.50
4 Loose Ends Pt 2	2.50
5	2.50
6	2.50

NIGHTMARES
Eclipse

1	2.50
2	2.00

NIGHT MUSIC
Eclipse

1	2.50
2	2.50
3 CR,JungleBear	3.00
4 Pelias&Melisande	2.00
5 Pelias	2.00
6 Salome	2.00
7 RedDog #1	2.00
Graphic Novel	8.00

NIGHTVEIL
AC Comics

1	3.50
2	2.50
3	2.25
4	2.25
5	2.25
6	1.75
7	1.75
Special #1	1.95

NIGHT WALKER
Fleetway

1 thru 2	2.95

NIGHTWOLF

1	1.75

2	1.75

9 LIVES OF FELIX
Harvey

1 thru 4	@1.25

Ninja High School #8 © Eternity

NINJA HIGH SCHOOL
Eternity

1 Reps.orig.N.H.S.in color	1.95
2 thru 13 reprints	@1.95

NINJA HIGH SCHOOL FEATURING SPEED RACER
Eternity

1B	2.95
2B	2.95

NINJA STAR

1	1.95

NIRA X: CYBERANGEL
Entity

1 From pages of Zen	2.95
2 V:Parradox	2.50
3 In Hydro-Dams	2.50

NOID IN 3-D
Blackthorne

1 thru 3	@2.50

NOMAN
Tower Comics
November, 1966

1 GK,OW	30.00
2 OW,A:Dynamo	20.00

NOOGIE KOOTCH: SECRET AGENT MAN
Hobo Comics

1 I:Noogie Kootch	2.75
2 F:Celutron CIty	2.75

NOSFERATU: PLAGUE OF TERROR
Millenium

1 I:Orlock	2.50
2 19th Century India,A:Sir W. Longsword	2.50
3 WWI/WWII to Viet Nam	2.50
4 O:Orlock,V:Longsword,conc.	2.50

NO TIME FOR SERGEANTS
Dell Publishing Co.
July, 1958

1 Ph(c)	25.00
2 Ph(c)	22.00
3 Ph(c)	22.00

NOVA HUNTER
Ryal Comics

1 thru 3	@2.50
4 Climax	2.50
5 Death and Betrayal	2.50

NUBIAN KNIGHT
Samson Comics

1 I:Shandai	2.50

NURSES, THE
Gold Key
April, 1963

1	20.00
2	15.00
3	15.00

NYOKA, JUNGLE GIRL
Charlton Comics
November, 1955

14	40.00
15	25.00
16	25.00
17	25.00
18	25.00
19	25.00
20	25.00
21	25.00
22 November, 1957	25.00

NYOKA, THE JUNGLE GIRL
AC Comics

1 and 2	@1.95

OCCULT FILES OF DR. SPEKTOR
Gold Key
April, 1973

1 I:Lakot	10.00
2 thru 5	5.00
6 thru 10	3.50
11 I:Spertor as Werewolf	4.00
12 and 13	2.50
14 A:Dr. Solar	15.00
15 thru 24	2.50

Whitman

25 rep	2.00

O.G. WHIZ
Gold Key
February, 1971

1	60.00

All comics prices listed are for *Near Mint* condition.

2	35.00
3	25.00
4	25.00
5	25.00
6	25.00
7	8.00
8	8.00
9	8.00
10	8.00
11 January, 1979	8.00

O'MALLEY AND THE ALLEY CATS
Gold Key
April, 1971

1	15.00
2 thru 9 January, 1974	@10.00

OMEGA 7
Omega 7

1 V:Exterminator X	3.95

OMEGA ELITE
Blackthorne

1	1.50
2	1.50

OMNI MEN
Blackthorne

1	1.25
2	1.25

ON A PALE HORSE
Innovation

1 Piers Anthony adapt	4.95
2 'Magician',I:Kronos	4.95
3	4.95
4 VV,	4.95
5	4.95
6	4.95

ONE-ARM SWORDSMAN

1	2.95
2	2.95
3	2.75
4	1.80
5	1.80
6	1.80
7	1.80
8	1.80
9	2.00
10	2.00
11	2.00

ORBIT
Eclipse

1 DSt(c)	3.95
2	3.95
3	4.95

ORIENTAL HEROES
Jademan

1	2.50
2	2.00
3 thru 13	@1.50
14 thru 27	@1.95
28 V:Skeleton Secretary	1.95
29 Barbarian vs.Lone Kwoon	1.95
30 Barbarian vs.Lone Kwoon	1.95
31 SkeletonSecretaryUprisng	1.95
32 Uprising Continues	1.95

33 Jupiter Kills His Brother	1.95
34 Skeleton Sec. Suicide	1.95
35 Red Sect Vs. Global Cult	1.95
36 A:Tiger	1.95
37 Old Supreme	1.95
38 Tiger vs. 4 Hitmen	1.95
39 D:Infinite White, V:Red Sect.	1.95
40 The Golden Buddhha Temple	1.95
41 thru 43	1.95
44 SilverChime rescue	1.95
45 Global Cult Battle	1.95
46 thru 48	@1.95
49 F:GoldDragon/SilverChime	1.95
50 Return to Global Cult	1.95
51 Gang Of Three Vs.White Beau & Lone Kwoon-Tin	1.95
52 Global Cult vs Red Sect	1.95
53 Global Cult vs.Red Sect	1.95

Original Astro Boy #1 © Now Comics

ORIGINAL ASTRO BOY
Now

1 KSy	3.00
2 KSy	2.00
3 KSy	2.00
4 KSy	2.00
5 KSy	2.00
6 thru 17 KSy	@1.75

ORIGINAL DICK TRACY
Gladestone

1 rep.V:Mrs.Pruneface	1.95
2 rep.V:Influence	1.95
3 rep.V:TheMole	1.95
4 rep.V:ItchyOliver	1.95
5 rep.V:Shoulders	2.00

ORIGINAL E-MAN
First
{rep. Charlton stories}

1 JSon,O:E-Man & Nova	1.75
2 JSon,V:Battery,SamuelBoar	1.75
3 JSon,'City in the Sand'	1.75
4 JSon,A:Brain from Sirius	1.75
5 JSon,V:T.V. Man	1.75
6 JSon,I:Teddy Q	1.75
7 JSon,Vamfire	1.75

ORIGINAL SHIELD
ABC

1 DAy/TD,O:Shield	1.00
2 DAy,O:Dusty	.75
3 DAy	.75
4 DAy	.75

ORIGIN OF THE DEFIANT UNIVERSE
Defiant

1 O:Defiant Characters	1.50

OUTBREED 999
Blackout Comics

1 thru 4	@2.95
5 Search For Daige	2.95

OUTCASTS

1	1.25

OUTER LIMITS, THE
Dell Publishing Co.
January-March, 1964

1 P(c)	45.00
2 P(c)	25.00
3 P(c)	20.00
4 P(c)	20.00
5 P(c)	20.00
6 P(c)	20.00
7 P(c)	20.00
8 P(c)	20.00
9 P(c)	20.00
10 P(c)	20.00
11 thru 18 P(c)	15.00

OUTLAWS OF THE WEST
Charlton Comics
August, 1956

11	40.00
12	20.00
13	20.00
14 Giant	25.00
15	20.00
16	20.00
17	20.00
18 SD	50.00
19	15.00
20	15.00
21 thru 30	@10.00
31 thru 50	@5.00
51 thru 70	@3.00
71 thru 87	@2.00
88 April, 1980	2.00

OUT OF THIS WORLD
Charlton Comics
August, 1956

1	125.00
2	50.00
3 SD	150.00
4 SD	150.00
5 SD	150.00
6 SD	150.00
7 SD,SD(c)	150.00
8 SD	125.00
9 SD	125.00
10 SD	125.00
11 SD	125.00
12 SD	125.00
13	40.00

14 .... 40.00
15 .... 40.00
16 December, 1959 .... 125.00

OUTPOSTS
Blackthorne
1 thru 6 .... @1.25

OWL, THE
Gold Key
April, 1967
1 .... 25.00
2 April, 1968 .... 20.00

PACIFIC PRESENTS
Pacific
1 DSt,Rocketeer,(3rd App.) .. 16.00
2 DSt,Rocketeer,(4th App.) 14.00
3 SD,I:Vanity 2.50
4 .... 2.00
5 .... 2.00

P.A.C.
Artifacts Inc
1 I:P.A.C. 1.95

PALADIN ALPHA
Firstlight
1 I:Paladin Alpha 2.95
2 V:Hellfire Triger 2.95

PARADAX
Eclipes
1 .... 2.25

PARADIGM
Gauntlet
1 A:Predator 2.95

Paragon Dark Apocalypse #1
© AC Comics

PARAGON
DARK APOCALYPSE
AC
1 thru 4, Fem Force crossover .. 2.95

PARANOIA
Adventure Comics
1 (based on video game)'Clone1' 3.25
2 King-R-Thr-2 .... 2.95
3 R:Happy Jack,V:N3F 2.95
4 V:The Computer 2.95
5 V:The Computer 2.95
6 V:Lance-R-Lot,last issue ... 2.95

PARTRIDGE FAMILY, THE
Charlton Comics
March, 1971
1 .... 15.00
2 thru 4 .... @8.00
5 Summer Special 15.00
6 thru 21 .... @7.00
21 December, 1973 .... 7.00

PATHWAYS TO
FANTASY
Pacific
1 BS,JJ art 3.00

PAT SAVAGE: WOMAN
OF BRONZE
Millenium
1 F:Doc Savage's cousin 2.50

PEACEMAKER
Charlton
1 A:Fightin' 5 .... 5.00
2 A:Fightin' 5 .... 3.00
3 A:Fightin' 5 .... 3.00
4 O:Peacemaker,A:Fightin' 5 ... 4.00
5 A:Fightin' 5 .... 2.50

PEANUTS
Dell Publishing Co.
February, 1958
1 .... 85.00
2 .... 65.00
3 .... 65.00
4 .... 45.00
5 .... 30.00
6 .... 30.00
7 .... 30.00
8 .... 30.00
9 .... 30.00
10 .... 30.00
11 .... 30.00
12 .... 30.00
13 .... 30.00

PEANUTS
Gold Key
May, 1963
1 .... 50.00
2 thru 4 .... 30.00

PEBBLES &
BAMM BAMM
Charlton Comics
January, 1972
1 .... 25.00
2 thru 10 .... @12.00
11 thru 35 .... @8.00
36 December, 1976 .... 8.00

PEBBLES FLINTSTONE
Gold Key

September, 1963
1 'A Chip off the old block' 55.00

PELLESTAR
1 .... 1.75

PERG
Lightning Comics
1 Glow in the dark(c),JS(c),
  B:JZy(s),KIK,I:Perg 3.75
1a Platinum Ed. 10.00
1b Gold Ed. 35.00
2 KIK,O:Perg 3.25
2a Platinum Ed. 10.00
3 Flip Book (c), ... 3.25
3a Platinum Ed 10.00
4 TLw,I:Helana 3.25
4a Platinum Ed 10.00
5 A:Helena 3.25
6 PIA,A:Helena 3.25
7 .... 2.95
8 V:Police 2.95

PERRY MASON
MYSTERY MAGAZINE
Dell Publishing Co.
June-August, 1964
1 .... 20.00
2 Ray Burr Ph(c) 20.00

PETER PAN: RETURN
TO NEVERNEVER LAND
1 Peter in Mass. 2.50
2 V:Tiger Lily 2.50

PETER POTAMUS
Gold Key
January, 1965
1 .... 50.00

PETTICOAT JUNCTION
Dell Publishing Co.
October-December, 1964
1 Ph(c) 50.00
2 Ph(c) 35.00
3 Ph(c) 35.00
4 .... 35.00
5 Ph(c) 35.00

PHANTOM, THE
Gold Key
November, 1962
1 RsM 75.00
2 B:King,Queen,Jacks 40.00
3 thru 10 .... @30.00
11 thru 17 .... @25.00
King
18 WW,B:Flash Gordon 30.00
19 .... 20.00
20 .... 20.00
21 thru 29 .... @20.00
Charlton Comics
30 thru 40 .... @15.00
41 thru 50 .... @10.00
46 I:Piranha 15.00
51 thru 70 .... @10.00
71 thru 73 .... @8.00
74 January, 1977 .... 8.00

The Phantom #19 © King Comics

PHANTOM
Wolf Publishing
1 Drug Runners		2.25
2 Mystery Child of the Sea		2.25
3 inc.feature pages on		
Phantom/Merchandise		2.25
4 TV Jungle Crime Buster		2.25
5 Castle Vacula-Transylvania		2.25
6 The Old West		2.25
7 Sercet of Colussus		2.75
8 Temple of the Sun God		2.75

PHANTOM BOLT, THE
Gold Key
October, 1964
1	25.00
2	15.00
3	12.00
4	12.00
5	12.00
6	12.00
7 November, 1966	12.00

PHANTOM FORCE
Genesis West
Previously: Image
0 JK/JLe(c)	2.75
3 thru 10	@2.50

PHAZE
Eclipse
1 BSz(c),Takes place in future	2.25
2 PG(c),V:The Pentagon	1.95
3 Schwieger Vs. Mammoth	1.95

PINK PANTHER, THE
Gold Key
April, 1971
1	20.00
2 thru 10	@10.00
11 thru 30	@7.00
31 thru 60	@4.00
61 thru	4.00

PINOCCHIO
1	1.50

PIRATE CORP.
Eternity
1 thru 5	@1.95

P.I.'S, THE
First
1 JSon,Ms.Tree,M Mauser		1.50
2 JSon,Ms.Tree,M Mauser		1.25
3 JSon,Ms.Tree,M Mauser		1.25

PLANET COMICS
Blackthorne
1 DSt(c)	2.00
2	2.00
3	2.00
4	2.00

POLICE TRAP
Mainline
August-September, 1954
1 S&K(c)	100.00
2 S&K(c)	60.00
3 S&K(c)	60.00
4 S&K(c)	60.00

Charlton Comics
5 S&K,S&K(c)	100.00
6 S&K,S&K(c)	100.00

Becomes:

PUBLIC DEFENDER
IN ACTION
7	40.00
8	30.00
9	30.00
10 thru 12, Oct. 1957	@30.00

POPEYE SPECIAL
Ocean
1	1.75
2	2.00

POWER FACTOR
Pied Piper
1	4.00
2	3.00

POWER FACTOR
Innovation
1 thru 4	@2.25

PRESSBUTTON
Eclipse
(see Axel Pressbutton)
5	1.75
6	1.75

PRIMER
Comico
1 Glow in the Dark (c)	3.75
1a Platinum Edition	15.00
1b Gold Edition	40.00

PRIMUS
Charlton Comics
February, 1972
1	5.00
2	5.00

3 thru 5	@5.00
6 thru 7 October, 1972	@4.00

PRINCE VANDAL
Triumphant
1 JnR(s),	2.50
2 JnR(s),	2.50
3 JnR(s),ShG,I:Claire,V:Nicket,	
Vandal goes to Boviden	2.50
4 JnR(s),ShG,Game's End	2.50
5 JnR(s),ShG,The Sickness,	
the rat appears	2.50
6 JnR(s),ShG,B:Gothic	2.50

PRISON SHIP
1	1.75

PRIVATEERS
Vanguard Graphics
1	1.50
2	1.50

PROFESSIONAL:
GOGOL 13
Viz
1	4.95
2 and 3	@4.95

PROFESSOR OM
Innovation
1	2.50

PROWLER
Eclipse
1 I:Prowler	1.75
2 GN,A:Original Prowler	1.75
3 GN	1.75
4 GN	1.75
5 GN, adaption of 'Vampire Bat'	1.75
6 w/flexi-disk record	1.75

PROWLER IN
'WHITE ZOMBIE'
Eclipse
1	1.75

PRUDENCE AND
CAUTION
1 CCI(s),	3.25
1a Spanish Version	3.25
2 CCI(s),	2.50
2a Spanish Version	2.50
3 CCI(s),	2.50
3a Spanish Version	2.50
4 CCI(s),	2.50
4a Spanish Version	2.50
5 CCI(s),	2.50
5a Spanish Version	2.50

PSYCHO
Innovation
1 Hitchcock movie adapt	2.50
2 continued	2.50
3 continued	2.50

PSYCHOBLAST
First
1 thru 9	@1.75

PUDGE PIG
Charlton Comics
September, 1958
1 .... 8.00
2 .... 8.00

PUPPET MASTER
Eternity
1 Movie Adapt.Andre Toulon ... 2.50
2 Puppets Protecting Diary 2.50
3 R:Andre Toulon 2.50
4 .... 2.50

PUPPET MASTER: CHILDREN OF THE PUPPET MASTER
Eternity
1 Killer Puppets on the loose ... 2.50
2 concl. 2.50

QUANTUM LEAP
Innovation
{based on TV series}
1 1968 Memphis 3.50
1a Special Edition 2.50
2 Ohio 1962,'Freedom of the
Press' 3.00
3 1958 'The $50,000 Quest' 3.00
4 'Small Miracles' 2.50
5 .... 2.50
6 .... 2.50
7 Golf Pro,School Bus Driver ... 2.50
8 1958,Bank Robber 2.50
9 NY 1969,Gay Rights 2.50
10 1960s' Stand-up Comic 2.50
11 1959,Dr.(LSD experiments) ... 2.50
12 .... 2.50

QUEEN OF THE DAMNED
Innovation
1 Anne Rice Adapt.'On the Road
to the Vampire Lestat' 3.50
2 Adapt. continued 2.50
3 The Devils Minion 2.50
4 Adapt.continued 2.50
5 Adapt.continued 2.50
6 Adapt.continued 2.50
7 Adapt.continued 2.50
8 Adapt.continued 2.50

QUICK-DRAW McGRAW
Charlton Comics
November, 1970
1 TV Animated Cartoon 35.00
2 .... 20.00
3 .... 20.00
4 thru 7 .... @20.00
8 January, 1972 .... 20.00

Q-UNIT
Harris
1 I:Q-Unit,w/card 3.25

RACE FOR THE MOON
Harvey Publications
March, 1958
1 BP 80.00
2 JK,AW,JK/AW(c) 150.00
3 JK,AW,JK/AW(c)
November, 1958 .... 150.00

RACER-X
Now
Premire Special 5.00
1 thru 3 .... @2.50
4 thru 11 .... @1.75
[2nd Series]
1 thru 10 .... @1.75

RADICAL DREAMER
Blackball
0 .... 2.00
1 thru 5 V:Jorge Futran ...... @2.50

RADIOACTIVE MAN
Bongo
1 I:Radioactive Man 3.25
88 V:Lava Man 1.95
212 V:Hypno Head 1.95
412 V:Dr. Crab 2.25
679 with card 2.25
1000 Final issue 2.25

RAD PATROL
1 .... 1.95

RADRAX
1 and 2 .... @2.25

RAEL
Eclipse
Vol 1 .... 6.95

RAGAMUFFINS
Eclipse
1 .... 3.00

RALPH SNART ADVENTURES
Now
[Volumes 1 & 2]
see B&W
9 and 10, color 2.50
[Volume 3]

Ralph Snart Adventures #1
© Now Comics

1 .... 4.00
2 thru 10 .... @3.00
11 thru 21 .... @2.00
22 thru 26 .... @1.75
TPB 9.95
[Volume 4]
1 thru 3, with 1 of 2 trading
cards 2.50
[Volume 5]
1 thru 5, with 1 of 2 trading
cards 2.50
3-D Spec.#1 with 3-D glasses and
12 trading cards 3.50

RAMAR OF THE JUNGLE
Toby Press
1954
1 Ph(c), John Hall 65.00
Charlton
2 .... 50.00
3 .... 50.00
4 .... 50.00
5 Sept., 1956 .... 50.00

RAMPANT
Manifest Destiny Comics
1/2 Various Artists 2.50

RANGO
Dell Publishing Co.
August, 1967
1 Tim Conway Ph(c) 18.00

RANMA 1/2
Viz
1 I:Ranma 4.95
2 I:Upperclassmen Kuno 4.95
3 F:Upperclassmen Kuno 4.95
4 Confusion 2.75
5 A:Ryoga 2.95
6 Ryoga plots revenge 2.75
7 Conclusion 2.95
[2nd Series]
1 thru 4 .... @2.95

RAPHAEL
Mirage
1 TMNTurtle characters 15.00

RAT PATROL, THE
Dell Publishing Co.
March, 1967
1 Ph(c) 40.00
2 .... 30.00
3 Ph(c) 25.00
4 Ph(c) 25.00
5 Ph(c) 25.00
6 Ph(c) 25.00

RAVEN
Renaissance Comics
1 I:Raven 2.50
2 V:Macallister 2.50
3 thru 5 .... @2.50
6 V:Nightmare Creatures 2.75

RAVENS AND RAINBOWS
Pacific
1 .... 1.50

All comics prices listed are for *Near Mint* condition.

RAY BRADBURY CHRONICLES
Byron Press
1 short stories	10.00
2 short stories	10.00
3 short stories	10.00

Topps
1 w/Trading Card	3.25
2 w/Trading Card	3.25
3 w/Trading Card	3.25
4 thru 5 w/Trading Card	3.25

R.A.Z.E.
Firstlight
1 I:R.A.Z.E., Secret Weapon	2.95
2 V:Exterminators	2.95

RAZOR
London Night Studios
0	12.00
1	9.00
2 thru 8	@2.95
9 thru 12	@3.00
Annual 1 I:Shi	12.00
Annual 2 O:Razor	3.00

RAZOR BURN
1 V:Styke	3.00
2 Searching for Styke	3.00

SUFFERING
1 thru 3	3.00

REAL GHOSTBUSTERS
Now
1 KSy(c)	4.50
2 thru 7	@2.50
8 thru 24	@1.75

[2nd Series]
1 Halloween Special	1.75
Ann. 3-D w/glasses & pinups	2.95

REAL WAR STORIES
Eclipse
1 BB	3.00
1a 2nd printing	1.50

RE-ANIMATOR
Adventure Comics
1 movie adaption	@2.95
2 movie adaption	@2.95

RE-ANIMATOR
Adventure
1 Prequel to Orig movie	2.50

RE-ANIMATOR: DAWN OF THE RE-ANIMATOR
Adventure
1 Prequel to movie	2.50
2 and 3	@2.50
4 V:Erich Metler	2.50

RE-ANIMATOR: TALES OF HERBERT WEST
Adventure Comics
1 H.P.Lovecraft stories	4.95

RED DOG
Eclipse
1 CR,Mowgli 'Jungle Book' sty	2.00

RED HEAT
1 3-D	2.50

RED SONJA in 3-D
Blackthorne
1	2.50
2	2.50
3	2.50

REESE'S PIECES
Eclipse
1 reprint from Web of Horror	1.50
2 reprint from Web of Horror	1.50

REGGIE
Archie Publications
September, 1963
15	40.00
16	35.00
17	35.00
18	35.00

Becomes:
REGGIE AND ME
19	15.00
20	7.00
21	7.00
22	7.00
23	7.00
24 thru 40	@2.50
41 thru 125	@1.00
126 September, 1980	1.00

REGGIE'S WISE GUY JOKES
Archie Publications
April, 1968
1	15.00
2	6.00
3	6.00
4	6.00
5	2.50
6	2.50
7	2.50
8	2.50
9	2.50
10	2.50
11 thru 60, January 1982	@1.00

REIVERS
Enigma
1 thru 3 Rock 'n' Roll	2.95

REPTILICUS
Charlton Comics
August, 1961
1	85.00
2	60.00

Becomes:
REPTISAURUS
3	35.00
4	30.00
5	30.00
6	30.00
7	30.00
8 Summer, 1963	30.00

RETURN OF KONGA, THE
Charlton Comics
1962
N#	30.00

RETURN OF MEGATON MAN
Kitchen Sink
1 Don Simpson art (1988)	2.00
2 Don Simpson art	2.00
3 Don Simpson art	2.00

RETURN TO JURASSIC PARK
Topps
1 R:Jurassic Park	2.50

REVENGE OF THE PROWLER
Eclipse
1 GN,R:Prowler	1.75
2 GN,A:Fighting Devil Dogs with Flexi-Disk	2.50
3 GN,A:Devil Dogs	1.75
4 GN,V:Pirahna	1.75

REVENGERS
Continuity
1 NA,O:Megalith,I:Crazyman	5.50
2 NA,Megalith meets Armor & Silver Streak,Origin Revengers#1	2.50
3 NA/NR,Origin Revengers #2	2.50
4 NA,Origin Revengers #3	2.50
5 NA,Origin Revengers #4	2.50
6 I:Hybrids	3.00
Special #1 F:Hybrids	4.95

RIBIT
Comico
1 FT,Mini-series	1.95
2 FT,Mini-series	1.95
3 FT,Mini-series	1.95
4 FT,Mini-series	1.95

RICHIE RICH
Harvey Publications
November, 1960
1	550.00
2	300.00
3	200.00
4	200.00
5	200.00
6	100.00
7	100.00
8	100.00
9	100.00
10	100.00
11 thru 20	@45.00
21 thru 40	@30.00
41 thru 60	@20.00
61 thru 80	@15.00
81 thru 99	@7.00
100	7.00
101 thru 111	@4.00
112 thru 116 52 pg Giants	@6.00
117 thru 120	@5.00
121 thru 140	@4.00
141 thru 160	@3.00
161 thru 180	@2.00
181 thru 237	@1.00
238	1.00

RICHIE RICH
Harvey
1 thru 15	@1.25
16 thur 28	@1.50

RICHIE RICH DOLLARS & CENTS
Harvey Publications
August, 1963

1	100.00
2	45.00
3	20.00
4	20.00
5	20.00
6	15.00
7	15.00
8	15.00
9	15.00
10	15.00
11 thru 20	@10.00
21 thru 30	@7.00
31 thru 43	@5.00
44 thru 60	@4.00
61 thru 70	@3.00
71 thru 109	@1.00

RICHIE RICH MILLIONS
Harvey Publications
September, 1961

1	100.00
2	45.00
3 thru 10	@30.00
11 thru 20	@20.00
21 thru 30	@10.00
31 thru 48	@7.00
49 thru 60	@5.00
61 thru 64	@4.00
65 thru 74	@3.00
75 thru 94	@2.50
95 thru 112	@1.00
113 October, 1982	1.00

RICHIE RICH SUCCESS STORIES
Harvey Publications
November, 1964

1	85.00
2	30.00
3	30.00
4	30.00
5	30.00
6	20.00
7	20.00
8	20.00
9 and 10	@20.00
11 thru 30	@10.00
31 thru 38	@7.00
39 thru 55	@5.00
56 thru 66	@3.00
67 thru 104	@1.00
105 September, 1982	1.00

RIOT GEAR
Triumphant

1 JnR(s),I:Riot Gear	2.50
2 JnR(s),I:Rabin	2.50
3 JnR(s),I:Surzar	2.50
4 JnR(s),D:Captain Tich	2.50
5 JnR(s),reactions	2.50
6 JnR(s),Tich avenged	2.50
7 JnR(s),Information Age	2.50
8 JnR(s),	2.50

RIOT GEAR: VIOLENT PAST
Triumphant

1 and 2	@2.50

RIFLEMAN, THE
Dell Publishing Co.
July-September, 1959

1 Chuck Connors Ph(c) all	125.00
2	75.00
3 ATh	65.00
4	55.00
5	55.00
6 ATh	75.00
7	45.00
8	45.00
9	45.00
10	45.00
11	45.00
12	45.00
13	45.00
14	45.00
15	45.00
16	45.00
17	45.00
18	45.00
19	45.00
20	45.00

R.I.P.
TSR

1 thru 8	@2.95

RIPLEY'S BELIEVE IT OR NOT!
Gold Key
April, 1967

4 Ph(c),AMc	35.00
5 GE,JJ	20.00
6 AMc	20.00
7	15.00
8	20.00
9	15.00
10 GE	20.00
11	10.00
12	10.00
13	10.00
14	10.00
15 GE	12.00
16	10.00
17	10.00
18	10.00
19	10.00
20	10.00
21 thru 30	@8.00
31 thru 38	@5.00
39 RC	6.00
40 thru 50	@5.00
51 thru 93	@4.00
94 February, 1980	4.00

ROBIN HOOD
Eclipse

1 TT,Historically accurate series	2.75
2 and 3 TT	@2.75

ROBO HUNTER
Eagle

1	1.50
2 thru 5	@1.00

ROBOTECH: GENESIS
The Legend of Zor
Eternity

1 O:Robotech w/cards	2.95
1a Limited Edition,extra pages with cards #1 & #2	5.95

AN ALL NEW ORIGINAL ROBOTECH ADVENTURE IN FULL COLOR

Robotech Genesis #1 © Eternity

2 thru 6, each with cards	@2.50

ROBOTECH IN 3-D
Comico

1	2.50

ROBOTECH, THE MACROSS SAGA
Comico
(formerly Macross)

2	5.00
3	4.00
4	3.00
5	2.50
6 J:Rick Hunter	2.50
7 V:Zentraedi	2.00
8 A:Rick Hunter	2.00
9 V:Zentraedi	2.00
10 "Blind Game"	2.00
11 V:Zentraedi	2.00
12 V:Zentraedi	2.00
13 V:Zentraedi	2.00
14 "Gloval's Reports"	2.00
15 V:Zentraedi	2.00
16 V:Zentraedi	2.00
17 V:Zentraedi	2.00
18 D:Roy Fokker	2.00
19 V:Khyron	2.00
20 V:Zentraedi	2.00
21 "A New Dawn"	2.00
22 V:Zentraedi	2.00
23 "Reckless"	2.00
24 HB,V:Zentraedi	2.00
25 "Wedding Bells"	2.00
26 "The Messenger"	2.00
27 "Force of Arms"	2.00
28 "Reconstruction Blues"	2.00
29 "Robotech Masters"	2.00
30 "Viva Miriya"	2.00
31 "Khyron's Revenge"	2.00
32 "Broken Heart"	2.00
33 "A Rainy Night"	2.00
34 'Private Time'	2.00
35 'Season's Greetings'	2.00
36 last issue	2.00
Graphic Novel #1	6.00

Robotech, The Macross Saga #3
© *Comico*

ROBOTECH MASTERS
Comico

1	4.00
2	3.00
3 Space Station Liberty	3.00
4 V:Bioroids	2.50
5 V:Flagship	2.50
6 'Prelude to Battle'	2.50
7 'The Trap'	2.50
8 F:Dana Sterling	2.50
9 'Star Dust'	2.50
10 V:Zor	2.50
11 A:De Ja Vu	2.00
12 2OR	2.00
13	2.00
14 "Clone Chamber,"V:Zor	2.00
15 "Love Song"	2.00
16 V:General Emerson	2.00
17 "Mind Games"	2.00
18 "Dana in Wonderland"	2.00
19	2.00
20 A:Zor,Musica	2.00
21 "Final Nightmare"	2.00
22 "The Invid Connection"	2.00
23 "Catastrophe," final issue	2.00

ROBOTECH, NEW GENERATION
Comico

1	4.00
2 'The Lost City'	3.00
3 V:Yellow Dancer	3.00
4 A:Yellow Dancer	3.00
5 SK(i),A:Yellow Dancer	2.50
6 F:Rook Bartley	2.50
7 'Paper Hero'	2.00
8	2.00
9 KSy,"The Genesis Pit"	2.00
10 V:The Invid	2.00
11 F:Scott Bernard	2.00
12 V:The Invid	2.00
13 V:The Invid	2.00
14 "Annie's Wedding"	2.00
15 "Seperate Ways"	2.00
16 "Metamorphosis"	2.00
17 "Midnight Sun"	2.00

18	2.00
19	2.00
20 "Birthday Blues"	2.00
21 "Hired Gun"	2.00
22 "The Big Apple"	2.00
23 Robotech Wars	2.00
24 Robotech Wars	2.00
25 V:Invid, last issue	2.00

ROBOTECH SPECIAL DANA'S STORY
Eclipse

1	5.00

ROBOTECH II: THE SENTINELS
Eternity

Swimsuit Spec.#1	2.95

ROCK & ROLL
Revolutionary
Prev: Black & White

15 Poison	3.50
16 Van Halen	1.95
17 Madonna	2.50
18 AliceCooper	1.95
19 Public Enemy, 2 Live Crew	2.50
20 Queensryche	1.95
21 Prince	1.95
22 AC/DC	1.95
23 Living Color	1.95
24 Anthrax	1.95
25 Z.Z.Top	2.50
26 Doors	2.50
27 Doors	2.50
28 Ozzy Osbourne	2.50
29 The Cure	2.50
30	2.50
31 Vanilla Ice	2.50
32 Frank Zappa	2.50
33 Guns n' Roses	2.50
34 The Black Crowes	2.50
35 R.E.M.	2.50
36 Michael Jackson	2.50
37 Ice T	2.50
38 Rod Stewart	2.50
39	2.50
40 N.W.A./Ice Cube	2.50
41 Paula Abdul	2.50
42 Metallica II	2.50
43 Guns 'N' Roses	2.50
44 Scorpions	2.50
45 Greatful Dead	2.50
46 Grateful Dead	2.50
47 Grateful Dead	2.50
48 (now b/w),Queen	2.50
49 Rush	2.50
50 Bob Dylan Pt.1	2.50
51 Bob Dylan Pt.2	2.50
52 Bob Dylan Pt.3	2.50
53 Bruce Springsteen	2.50
54 U2 Pt.1	2.50
55 U2 Pt.2	2.50
56 thru 72	@2.50

ROCKETEER
Walt Disney

1 DSt(c)RH,MovieAdaptation	7.00
Newsstand Version	3.25

ROCKETEER ADVENTURE MAGAZINE

Comico

1 DSt,MK,Rocketeer(6thApp.)	12.00
2 DSt,MK,Rocketeer(7thApp.)	10.00

ROCKETEER SPECIAL
Eclipse

1 DSt, Rocketeer(5th App.)	26.00

ROCKET MAN: KING OF THE ROCKET MEN
Innovation

1 Adapts movie series	2.50
2 Adapts movie series	2.50
3 Adapts movie series	2.50
4 Adapts movie series	2.50

ROCKET RANGER
Adventure Comics

1 Based on computer game	2.95

ROCKMEEZ
Jzink Comics

1 I:Rockmeez,V:Pyrites	2.50
2 V:Pyrites,Silv.Embos.(c)	2.50

ROCKY HORROR PICTURE SHOW
Calibre/Tome

1	6.00
1a 2nd printing	3.25
2	3.50
3 'The Conclusion'	3.25
Rocky Horror Collection reps.	4.95

ROG 2000
Pacific

1 One-Shot, JBy	2.00

ROGER RABBIT
Walt Disney

1 I:Rick Flint	5.50
2	3.50
3	2.50
4	2.50
5	2.50
6 thru 9	@2.50
10 'Tuned-in-toons'	2.50
11 'Who Framed Rick Flint'	2.00
12 'Somebunny to Love'	2.00
13 'Honey,I Stink with Kids'	2.00
14 'Who Fired Jessica Rabbit'	2.00
15 'The Great Toon Detective'	2.00
16 'See you later Aviator'	2.00
17 Flying Saucers over Toontown	2.00
18 'I Have Seen the Future'	2.00

ROGER RABBIT'S TOONTOWN
Walt Disney

1 (inc.Baby Herman,Jessica stories)	2.00
2 'Pre-Hysterical Roger'	1.75
3 'Lumberjack of tomorrow'	1.75
4 'The Longest Daze'	1.75

ROGUE TROOPER
Quality

1 thru 5	@1.00
6	1.50
7 thru 21	@1.25

22/23	1.50
24	1.50
25/26	1.50
27 thru 35	@1.50
36	1.95
37	1.95
38 thru 40	@1.50
41 thru 43	@1.75

ROGUE TROOPER: THE FINAL WARRIOR
Fleetway

1 RS,Golden Rebellion,pt 1	2.95
2 thru 3	2.95
4 "Saharan Ice-Belt War	2.95

ROMAN HOLIDAYS, THE
Gold Key
February, 1973

1	15.00
2	10.00
3	10.00
4 November, 1973	10.00

ROOM 222
Dell Publishing Co.
January, 1970

1	25.00
2	20.00
3 Drug	25.00
4 Ph(c)	20.00

ROY ROGERS WESTERN CLASSICS
AC Comics

1	2.95
2	2.95
3	2.95
4	3.95

RUFF AND READY
Dell Publishing Co.
September, 1958

1	50.00
2	30.00
3	30.00
4	25.00
5	25.00
6	25.00
7	25.00
8	25.00
9	25.00
10	25.00
11	25.00
12	25.00

RUN, BUDDY, RUN
Gold Key
June, 1967

1	15.00

RUST
Now

1	4.00
2	3.00
3 thru 11	@2.00
12 I:Terminator	10.00
13 thru 15	@1.75
[Volume 2]	
1 thru 10	@1.75

SABLE
First

1 AIDS story	1.75
2 Sable in Iran	1.75
3 Pentathelon	1.75
4	1.75
5 DCw,V:Tong Gangs	1.75
6 In Atlantic City	1.75
7 V:EnvironmentalTerrorists	1.75
8 In Argentina	1.95
9 In Kenya Pt.1	1.95
10 In Kenya Pt.2	1.95
11 Jon Sable bodyguard	1.95
12 In Cambodia Pt.1	1.95
13 In Cambodia Pt.2	1.95
14 Christmas story	1.95
15 A:Ted Koppel	1.95
16 Sable as 'B.B.Flemm' rev.	1.95
17 Turning point issue	1.95
18 Richard Rockwell(i)	1.95
19 A:Maggie the Cat	1.95
20 A:Gary Adler	1.95
21 Richard Rockwell(i)	1.95
22 A:Eden Kendall	1.95
23 TV cover	1.95
24 TV cover	1.95
25 TV cover	1.95
26 TV cover	1.95
27	1.95
28 last issue	1.95

SABRE
Eclipse

1 PG	2.50
2 PG	3.00
3 thru 14	@2.00

SABRINA, THE TEENAGE WITCH
Archie Publications
April, 1971

1	40.00
2	15.00
3	7.00
4	7.00
5	7.00
6 thru 10	@4.00
11 thru 20	@2.00
21 thru 76	@1.00
77 January, 1983	1.00

SAD SACK AND THE SARGE
Harvey Publications
September, 1957

1	80.00
2	35.00
3 thru 10	@25.00
11 thru 20	@15.00
21 thru 40	@6.00
41 thru 50	@5.00
51 thru 90	@2.00
91 thru 96 52 pg Giants	@3.00
97 thru 154	@1.00
155 June, 1982	1.00

SAD SACK'S ARMY LIFE
Harvey Publications
October, 1963

1	35.00
2 thru 10	@20.00
11 thru 20	@10.00

21 thru 30	@7.00
31 thru 50	@3.00
51 thru 60	@2.00
61 May, 1976	2.00

SAD SACK'S FUNNY FRIENDS
Harvey Publications
December, 1955

1	55.00
2 thru 10	@25.00
11 thru 20	@15.00
21 thru 30	@7.00
31 thru 40	@3.00
41 thru 74	@2.00
75 October, 1969	2.00

SAD SACK in 3-D
Blackthorne

1 and 2	@2.50

SALOME
Eclipse

1 CR	2.00

SAM AND MAX, FREE-LANCE POLICE SPECIAL
Comico

1	2.75

Sam Slade RoboHunter #14 © Quality

SAM SLADE ROBOHUNTER
Quality

1	1.00
2	1.00
3 Filby Case	1.00
4	1.00
5	1.00
6 Bax the Burner,Moore	1.00
7	1.00
8 thru 21	@1.25
22/23	1.50
24	1.50
25/26	1.50
27 thru 33	@1.50

All comics prices listed are for *Near Mint* condition.

SAMSONS
Samsons Comics
1/2 Various Artists 2.50

SAMURAI
Eclipse
1 . . . . 2.00
2 . . . . 2.00
3 thru 5 . . . . @2.00

SAMUREE
Continuity
1 NA,A:Revengers 2.00
2 A:Revengers 2.00
3 NA,A:Revengers 2.00
4 A:Revengers 2.00
5 BSz(c),A:Revengers 2.00
6 A:Revengers 2.00
7 . . . . 2.00
8 Drug story 2.00
9 Drug story 2.00
[2nd Series]
1 thru 3 Rise of Magic 2.50

SARGE STEEL/
SECRET AGENT
1 DG,I:SargeSteel & IvanChung . 5.00
2 DG,I:Werner Von Hess 2.50
3 DG,V:Smiling Skull 2.50
4 DG,V:Lynx 2.50
5 FMc,V:Ivan Chung 2.50
6 FMc,A:Judomaster 2.50
7 DG 2.50
8 V:Talon 2.50
Becomes:
SECRET AGENT
9 DG 3.50
10 DG,JAp,A:Tiffany Sinn 3.00

SATAN'S SIX
Topps
1 F:Satan's Six,w/3 cards 3.25
2 V:Kalazarr,w/3 cards 2.95
3 w/3 cards 2.95
4 w/3 cards 2.95

SATURDAY KNIGHTS
Hot
1 . . . . 1.50
2 . . . . 1.50
3 . . . . 1.50
4 . . . . 1.50

SAURAUS FAMILY
Blackthorne
1 3-D 2.00

SAVAGE DRAGON/
TEENAGE MUTANT
NINJA TURLES
CROSSOVER
Mirage
1 EL(s). 2.75

SAVED BY THE BELL
Harvey
1 based on TV series 1.25

SCAVENGERS
Quality
1 thru 7 . . . . @1.25
8 thru 14 . . . . @1.50

SCAVENGERS
Triumphant Comics
0 Fso(c),JnR(s), ... 2.50
0a "Free Copy" 2.50
0b Red Logo 2.50
1 JnR(s),I:Scavengers,Ximos,
   C:Doctor Chaos 2.50
1a 2nd Printing 2.50
2 JnR(s), ... 2.50
3 JnR(s),I:Lurok 2.50
4 JnR(s), ... 2.50
5 Fso(c),JnR(s),D:Jack Hanal . . 2.50
6 JnR(s), ... 2.50
7 JnR(s),I:Zion 2.50
8 JnR(s),Nativity 2.50
9 JnR(s),The Challenge 2.50
10 JnR(s),Snowblind 2.50

SCHISM
Defiant
1 thru 4 Defiant's x-over 3.25

SCION
1 and 2 . . . . @2.00

SCOOBY DOO
Gold Key
March, 1970
1 . . . . 30.00
2 . . . . 20.00
3 . . . . 15.00
4 . . . . 15.00
5 . . . . 15.00
6 . . . . 12.00
7 . . . . 12.00
8 . . . . 12.00
9 . . . . 12.00
10 . . . . 12.00
11 thru 20 . . . . @8.00
21 thru 29 . . . . @5.00
30 February, 1975 . . . . 5.00

SCOOBY DOO
Charlton Comics
April, 1975
1 . . . . 15.00
2 . . . . 6.00
3 . . . . 6.00
4 . . . . 6.00
5 . . . . 6.00
6 . . . . 4.00
7 . . . . 4.00
8 . . . . 4.00
9 . . . . 4.00
10 . . . . 4.00
11 December, 1976 . . . . 4.00

SCORCHED EARTH
Tundra
1 Earth 2025,I:Dr.EliotGodwin . . . 3.50
2 Hunt for Eliot 2.95
3 Mystical Transformation 2.95

SCORPION CORP.
Dagger
1 PuD,JRI,CH, ... 2.75
2 PuD,JRI,CH,V:Victor Kyner . . . 2.75

3 PuD,BIH,V:Victor Kyner 2.75

SCORPIO ROSE
Eclipse
1 MR/TP,I:Dr.Orient 2.00
2 MR/TP 2.00

SCOUT
Eclipse
1 TT,I:Scout,Fash.In Action 6.00
2 TT,V:Buffalo Monster 3.00
3 TT,V:President Grail 2.50
4 TT,V:President Grail 2.50
5 TT,'Killin' Floor' 2.50
6 TT,V:President Grail 2.50
7 TT,TY,Rosanna's Diary 2.50
8 TT,TY 2.50
9 TT,TY,A:Airboy 2.50
10 TT,TY,I:Proj.Mountain Fire . . . 2.00
11 TT,FH,V:Rangers 2.00
12 TT,FH,'Me and the Devil' 2.00
13 TT,FH,Monday:Eliminator 2.00
14 TT,FH,Monday:Eliminator 2.00
15 TT,FH,Monday:Eliminator 2.00
16 TT,3-D issue,F:Santana 2.00
17 TT,A:Beanworld 2.00
18 TT,FH,V:Lex Lucifer 2.00
19 TT,w/Record,V:Lex Lucifer . . . 3.00
20 TT,A:Monday:Eliminator 2.00
21 TT,A:Monday:Eliminator 1.75
22 TT,A:Swords of Texas 1.75
23 TT,A:Swords of Texas 1.75
24 TT, last Issue 1.75

Scout: War Shaman #1
© Eclipse Comics

SCOUT: WAR SHAMAN
Eclipse
1 TT,R:Scout (now a father) . . . 2.25
2 TT,I:Redwire 1.95
3 TT,V:Atuma Yuma 1.95
4 TT,'Rollin' on the River' 1.95
5 TT,Hopi Katchina dieties 1.95
6 TT,Scout vs. Rosa Winter 1.95
7 TT,R:Redwire 1.95
8 TT,R:Beau LaDuke 1.95
9 TT,V:Doodyists 1.95

---

10 TT,TY,V:Redwire	1.95
11 TT,V:Redwire	1.95
12 TT,V:Snow Leopards	1.95
13 TT,F:Beau LaDuke	1.95
14 TT,V:Redwire	1.95
15 TT,V:Redwire	1.95
16 TT,'Wall of Death,'last issue	1.95

SEADRAGON
Elite

1	3.00
1a 2nd printing	1.75
2	2.00
3	2.00
4	2.00
5 thru 8	@1.75

SEA HUNT
Dell Publishing Co.
August, 1958

1 L.BridgesPh(c) all	75.00
2	40.00
3 ATh	65.00
4 RsM	45.00
5 RsM	45.00
6 RsM	45.00
7	40.00
8 RsM	45.00
9 RsM	45.00
10 RsM	45.00
11 RsM	45.00
12	40.00
13 RsM	45.00

SEAQUEST
Nemesis

1 HC(c),DGC,KP,AA,Based on TV Show	2.50

SEBASTIAN
Walt Disney

1 From Little Mermaid	1.50
2 "While da Crab's Away"	1.50

SECRET AGENT
Gold Key
November, 1966

1	75.00
2	50.00

SECRET CITY SAGA
Topps

0 JK	3.25
0 Gold Ed.	40.00
0 Red	25.00
1 w/3 cards	3.25
2 w/3 cards	3.25
3 w/3 cards	3.25
4 w/3 cards	3.25

SECRET SQUIRREL
Gold Key
October, 1966

1	50.00

SEDUCTION OF THE INNOCENT
Eclipse

1 ATh,'Hanged by the Neck' reps.	2.50
2	2.25
3	2.00

4 ATh,NC,'World's Apart'	2.00
5 ATh,'The Phantom Ship'	2.00
6 ATh,RA,'Hands of Don Jose'	2.00
3-D #1 DSt(c)	2.25
3-D #2 ATh,MB,BWr,'Man Who Was Always on Time'	2.00

Seeker #1 © Sky Comics

SEEKER: VENGEANCE
Sky Comics

1 JMt(s),I:Seeker	2.50

SENSEI
First

1 Mini-Series	2.75
2	2.75
3	2.75
4	2.75

SENTINELS OF JUSTICE
AC Comics

1 Capt.Paragon	1.75
2	1.75
3	1.75
4	1.75
5	1.75
6	1.75
7	1.75

SENTRY: SPECIAL
Innovation

1	2.75

SERAPHIM
Innovation

1 and 2	@2.50

77 SUNSET STRIP
Dell Publishing Co.
January-March, 1960

1 Ph(c)	50.00
2 Ph(c),RsM	55.00

SHADE SPECIAL
AC Comics

1	1.50

SHADOW, THE
Archie Comics
August, 1964

1	40.00
2	30.00
3	30.00
4	30.00
5	30.00
6 and 7	@25.00
8 September, 1965	25.00

SHADOW COMICS

1 Guardians of Justice & The O-Force	1.50

SHADOW OF THE TORTURER, THE
Innovation

1 thru 6 Gene Wolfe adapt.	@1.95

SHADOW RAVEN
Poc-It Comics

1 I:Shadow Raven	2.95

SHANGHAI BREEZE

1	1.75

SHAOLIN
Black Tiger Press

1 I:Tiger	2.95
2 I:Crane	2.95

SHATTER
First

1	3.00
2	2.50
3	2.50
4 and 5	@2.00
6 thru 14	@1.75
Special #1 Computer Comic	5.00
#1a 2nd Printing	2.00

SHE-DEVILS ON WHEELS
Aircel

1 V:Man-Eaters	2.95
2 V:Man-Eaters	2.95
3 V:Man-Eaters	2.95

SHERIFF OF TOMBSTONE
Charlton Comics
November, 1958

1 AW,JSe	50.00
2	30.00
3 thru 10	@20.00
11 thru 16	@20.00
17 September, 1961	20.00

SHI
Crusade Comics

1 BiT,HMo,I:Shi	22.00
2 BiT	12.00
3 BiT	7.00
4 BiT	5.00
5 V:Arashi	3.00
6 V:Tomoe	2.50
7 V:Nara Warriors	2.50
TPB Way of the Warrior	12.95

SHIELD
1 A:Steel Sterling 3.50
2 A:Steel Sterling 2.00
3 AN/EB,D:Lancelot Strong 2.00

SHOCK SUSPENSE STORIES
Russ Cochran Press
1 reps.horror stories 1.50
2 inc.Kickback 1.50
3 thru 4 . . . . @2.00
5 thru 7 reps.horror stories 2.00
8 reps.horror stories 2.00

SHOGUNAUT
Firstlight
1 I:Shogunaut 2.95
2 V:Teckno Terror 2.95

SHOOTING STARS
1 . . . . 2.50

SIEGEL & SHUSTER
Eclipse
1 . . . . 1.50
2 . . . . 1.75

SILENT MOBIUS
Viz
1 Katsumi 5.75
2 Katsumi vs. Spirit 5.25
3 Katsumi trapped within entity . . 4.95
4 Nami vs. Dragon 4.95
5 Kiddy vs. Wire 4.95
6 Search for Wire 4.95
GN 14.95

SILENT MOBIUS II
Viz
1 AMP Officers vs. Entities cont . 4.95
2 Entities in Amp H.Q. 4.95
3 V:Entity 4.95
4 The Esper Weapon 4.95
5 Last issue 4.95

SILENT MOBIUS III
Viz
1 F:Lebia/computer network 2.75
2 Lebia/computer link cont. 2.75
3 Lebia in danger 2.75
4 Return to Consciousness 2.75
5 Conclusion 2.75

SILVERBACK
Comico
1 thru 3 . . . . @2.50

SILVERHEELS
Pacific
1 . . . . 2.00
2 and 3 . . . . @1.50

SILVER STAR
Pacific
1 JK 1.00
2 JK 1.00
3 JK 1.00
4 JK 1.00
5 JK 1.00
6 JK 1.00

SILVER STORM
1 . . . . 2.25
2 . . . . 1.95
3 . . . . 1.95
4 . . . . 1.95

SILVER STAR
Topps
1 w/Cards 2.95

SIMPSONS COMICS
Bongo Comics
1 Colossal Horner 5.00
2 A:Sideshow Bob 1.95
3 F:Bart 1.95
4 F:Bart 2.25
5 A:Itchy & Scratchy 2.25
6 F:Lisa 2.25
7 Circus in Town 2.25
8 Mr. Burns Voyage 2.25
9 Autobiographies 2.25
TPB 1-4 . . . . 10.00

SIMPSONS COMICS & STORIES
Welsh Publishing
1 . . . . 4.00
2 R:Sideshow Bob 2.25
3 Stolen Puma 2.25

Six Million Dollar Man #4
© Charlton Comics Group

SIX MILLION DOLLAR MAN, THE
Charlton
1 JSon,Lee Majors Ph(c) 3.00
2 NA(c),JSon,Ph(c) 3.00
3 Ph(c) 1.50
4 Ph(c) 1.50
5 Ph(c) 1.50
6 Ph(c) 1.50
7 Ph(c) 1.50
8 Ph(c) 1.50
9 Ph(c) 1.50

666: MARK OF THE BEAST
Fleetway/Quality
1 I:Fludd, BU:Wolfie Smith 1.95
2 thru 8. . . . . @1.95

SKATEMAN
Pacific
1 NA 1.50

SKY WOLF
Eclipse
1 V:Baron Von Tundra 1.75
2 TL,V:Baron Von Tundra 1.75
3 TL,cont. in Airboy #41 . . . . 1.75

SLAINE THE BERSERKER
Quality
1 thru 14 . . . . @1.25
15/16 . . . . 1.50
17 . . . . 1.50
18/19 . . . . 1.50
20 thru 28 . . . . @1.50
Becomes:

SLAINE THE KING
26 . . . . 1.50

SLAINE
Fleetway
1 thru 4 SBs,From 2000 AD . . @4.95

SLIMER
Now
1 . . . . 2.50
2 thru 15 . . . . @1.75
Becomes:

SLIMER & REAL GHOSTBUSTERS
Now
16 . . . . 1.75
17 . . . . 1.75
18 . . . . 1.75

SNAGGLEPUSS
Gold Key
October, 1962
1 . . . . 35.00
2 . . . . 25.00
3 . . . . 25.00
4 September, 1963 . . . . 25.00

SNOOPER AND BLABBER DETECTIVES
Gold Key
November, 1962
1 . . . . 35.00
2 . . . . 25.00
3 May, 1963 . . . . 25.00

SNOW WHITE & SEVEN DWARVES GOLDEN ANNIVERSARY
Gladstone
1 w/poster & stickers 24.00

SOLDIERS OF FREEDOM
Americomics
1	1.75
2	1.95

SOLOMON KANE
Blackthorne
1 3-D Special	2.50
2 3-D Special	2.50
1 thru 4	@2.50

SOMERSET HOLMES
Pacific
1 BA,AW,I:Cliff Hanger & Somerset Holmes	2.50
2 thru 4 BA,AW	@2.00

Eclipse
5 BA,AW	2.00
6 BA	2.00

SONG OF THE CID
Calibre/Tome
1 Story of El Cid	2.95
2 Story of El Cid concl.	2.95

SONIC THE HEDGEHOG
Archie Publications
Feb., 1993
1 A:Mobius,V:Robotnik	1.50
2 thru 24	@1.50

SON OF MUTANT WORLD
Fantagor
1 BA	2.00
2	2.00

SOULQUEST
Innovation
1 BA	3.95

SOUPY SALES COMIC BOOK
Archie Publications
1965
1	75.00

SPACE ARK
AC Comics
1	3.00
2	2.00

SPACE FAMILY ROBINSON
Gold Key
December, 1962
1 DSp	150.00
2	75.00
3	45.00
4	45.00
5	45.00
6 B:Captain Venture	45.00
7	45.00
8	45.00
9	45.00
10	45.00
11 thru 20	@30.00
21 thru 36 October, 1969	@25.00

SPACE GHOST
Gold Key
March, 1967
1	6.00

SPACE GHOST
Comico
1 SR,V:Robot Master	3.50

SPACE MAN
Dell Publishing Co.
January-March, 1962
1	50.00
2	25.00
3	25.00
4	15.00
5	15.00
6	15.00
7	15.00
8	15.00
9	15.00
10	15.00

SPACE: 1999
A Plus Comics
1 GM,JBy	2.50

Space Usagi #1 © Mirage

SPACE USAGI
Mirage
1 From TMNT	2.75
2 thru 3 From TMNT	2.75

SPACE WAR
Charlton Comics
October, 1959
1	100.00
2	50.00
3	45.00
4 SD,SD(c)	100.00
5 SD,SD(c)	100.00
6 SD	100.00
7	25.00
8 SD,SD(c)	100.00
9	30.00
10 SD,SD(c)	100.00
11	30.00
12	30.00
13	30.00
14	30.00
15	30.00
16 thru 27	@25.00
Becomes:

FIGHTIN' FIVE
28 SD,SD(c)	35.00
29 SD,SD(c)	35.00
30 SD,SD(c)	40.00
31 SD,SD(c)	40.00
32	5.00
33 SD,SD(c)	40.00
34 Sd,SD(c)	40.00

SPECTRUM COMICS PRESENTS
Spectrum
1 I:Survivors	3.50

SPEED RACER
Now
1	3.50
1a 2nd printing	1.50
2 thru 33	@2.00
34 thru 38	@1.75
Special #1	2.50
#1 2nd printing	1.75
Special #2	3.50
Classics, Vol #2	3.95
Classics, Vol #3	3.95

[2nd Series]
1 R:Speed Racer	1.95
2	1.95
3 V:Giant Crab	1.95
4	1.95
5 Racer-X	1.95
6	1.95
7	1.95

SPELLBINDERS
Quality
1 Nemesis the Warlock	1.25
2 Nemesis the Warlock	1.25
3 Nemesis the Warlock	1.25
4 Nemesis the Warlock	1.25
5 Nemesis the Warlock	1.25
6 Nemesis the Warlock	1.25
7 Nemesis the Warlock	1.25
8 Nemesis the Warlock	1.25
9 Nemesis the Warlock	1.25
1O Nemesis the Warlock	1.25
11 Nemesis the Warlock	1.25

SPIDER
Eclipse
1 TT,'Blood Dance'	7.00
2 TT,'Blood Mark'	6.00
3 TT,The Spider Unmasked	5.50

SPIDER: REIGN OF THE VAMPIRE KING
Eclipse
1 TT,I:Legion of Vermin	5.25
2 thru 4 TT	@2.50

SPIDERFEMME
Personality
1 Rep. parody	2.50

All comics prices listed are for *Near Mint* condition.

SPIRAL PATH
Eclipse
1 V:Tairngir	1.75
2 V:King Artuk	1.75

SPIRIT
Harvey
October, 1966
1 WE,O:Spirit	35.00
2 WE,O:The Octopus	35.00

SPIRIT, THE
Kitchen Sink
1 WE(c) (1983)	5.25
2 WE(c)	4.25
3 WE(c) (1984)	4.00
4 WE(c)	4.00
5 WE(c)	3.00
6 WE(c)	3.00
7 WE(c)	3.00
8 thru 11 WE(c) (1985) color	3.00

See: B&W section

SPOOKY HAUNTED HOUSE
Harvey Publications
October, 1972
1	10.00
2	5.00
3	5.00
4	5.00
5	5.00
6 thru 10	@2.50
11 thru 14	@1.00
15 February, 1975	1.00

Spooky #6 © Harvey Publications

SPOOKY SPOOKTOWN
Harvey Publications
June, 1966
1 B:Casper,Spooky,68 pgs	75.00
2	40.00
3	30.00
4	30.00
5	30.00
6 thru 10	@18.00
11 thru 20	@15.00

21 thru 30	@15.00
31 thru 39 E:68 pgs	@4.50
40 thru 45	@2.50
46 thru 65	@1.00
66 December, 1976	1.00

SPYMAN
1 GT,JSo,1st prof work, I:Spyman	15.00
2 DAy,JSo,V:Cyclops	10.00
3	8.00

SQUALOR
First
1	2.75
2	2.75
3	2.75

STAINLESS STEEL RAT
Eagle
1	2.25
2 thru 6	@1.50

STAR BLAZERS
Comico
1	3.00
2	1.75
3	1.75
4	1.75

[2nd Series]
1	1.95
2	1.95
3 thru 5	@2.50

STARBLAZERS
Argo Press
1 F:Dereck Wildstar	2.95

STARFORCE SIX SPECIAL
AC Comics
1	1.50

STARLIGHT
1	1.95

STAR MASTERS
AC Comics
1	1.50

STAR REACH CLASSICS
Eclipse
1 JSn,NA(r)	2.00
2 AN	2.00
3 HC	2.00
4 FB(r)	2.00
5	2.00
6	2.00

STARSLAYER
Pacific
1 MGr,O:Starslayer	3.00
2 MGr,DSt,I:Rocketeer	27.00
3 DSt,MGr,A:Rocketeer(2ndApp.)	20.00
4 MGr,Baraka Kuhr	2.00
5 MGr,SA,A:Groo	17.00
6 MGr.conclusion story	2.00

First
7 MGr layouts	2.00
8 MGr layouts, MG	1.50

9 MGr layouts, MG	2.25
10 TT,MG,I:Grimjack	4.00
11 TT,MG,A:Grimjack	2.00
12 TT,MG,A:Grimjack	2.00
13 TT,MG,A:Grimjack	2.00
14 TT,A:Grimjack	2.00
15 TT,A:Grimjack	2.00
16 TT,A:Grimjack	2.00
17 TT,A:Grimjack	2.00
18 TT,Grimjack x-over	2.00
19 TT,TS,A:Black Flame	1.25
20 TT,TS,A:Black Flame	1.25
21 TT,TS,A:Black Flame	1.25
22 TT,TS,A:Black Flame	1.25
23 TT,TS,A:Black Flame	1.25
24 TT,TS,A:Black Flame	1.25
25 TS,A:Black Flame	1.25
26 TS,Black Flame full story	1.25
27 A:Black Flame	1.25
28 A:Black Flame	1.25
29 TS,A:Black Flame	1.25
30 TS,A:Black Flame	1.25
31 2nd Anniversary Issue	1.25
32 TS,A:Black Flame	1.25
33 TS,A:Black Flame	1.25
34 last issue	1.25
Graphic Novel	9.95

STAR TREK
Gold Key
1 Planet of No Return	400.00
2 Devil's Isle of Space	225.00
3 Invasion of City Builders	175.00
4 Peril of Planet Quick Change	175.00
5 Ghost Planet	175.00
6 When Planets Collide	150.00
7 Voodoo Planet	150.00
8 Youth Trap	130.00
9 Legacy of Lazarus	130.00
10 Sceptre of the Sun	65.00
11 Brain Shockers	65.00
12 Flight of the Buccaneer	56.00
13 Dark Traveler	56.00
14 Enterprise Mutiny	56.00
15 Museum a/t End of Time	56.00
16 Day of the Inquisitors	56.00
17 Cosmic Cavemen	56.00
18 The Hijacked Planet	56.00
19 The Haunted Asteroid	56.00
20 A World Gone Mad	56.00
21 The Mummies of Heitus VII	50.00
22 Siege in Superspace	45.00
23 Child's Play	45.00
24 The Trial of Capt. Kirk	45.00
25 Dwarf Planet	45.00
26 The Perfect Dream	45.00
27 Ice Journey	45.00
28 The Mimicking Menace	45.00
29 rep. Star Trek #1	45.00
30 Death of a Star	42.00
31 'The Final Truth'.	40.00
32 'The Animal People'	40.00
33 'The Choice'	40.00
34 'The Psychocrystals'	40.00
35 rep. Star Trek #4	40.00
36 'A Bomb in Time'	40.00
37 rep. Star Trek #5	40.00
38 'One of our Captains is Missing'	30.00
39 'Prophet of Peace'	30.00
40 AMc,Furlough to Fury, A: Barbara McCoy	30.00
41 AMc,The Evictors	30.00
42 'World Against Time'	30.00
43 'World Beneath the Waves'	30.00

44 'Prince Traitor'	....	30.00
45 rep. Star Trek #7	....	30.00
46 'Mr. Oracle'	....	30.00
47 AMc,'This Tree Bears Bitter Fruit'	....	30.00
48 AMc,Murder on Enterprise	..	30.00
49 AMc,'A Warp in Space'	.....	30.00
50 AMc,'The Planet of No Life'	.	30.00
51 AMc,DestinationAnnihilation6		25.00
52 AMc,'And A Child Shall Lead Them'	....	25.00
53 AMc,'What Fools..Mortals Be'		25.00
54 AMc,'Sport of Knaves'	.....	25.00
55 AMc,A World Against Itself	.	25.00
56 AMc,No Time Like The Past, A:Guardian of Forever	...	25.00
57 AMc,'Spore of the Devil'	....	25.00
58 AMc,'Brain Damaged Planet'	.	25.00
59 AMc,'To Err is Vulcan'	.....	25.00
60 AMc,'The Empire Man'	.....	25.00
61 AMc,'Operation Con Game'	.	25.00

STAR WARS IN 3-D
Blackthorne

1 thru 7	....	@2.50

STARWOLVES: JUPITER RUN

1	....	1.95

S.T.A.T.
Majestic

1 FdS(s),PhH,I:S.T.A.T.	....	2.50

STEALTH SQUAD
Petra Comics

1 I:Stealth Squad	....	2.50

STEED & MRS PEEL
Eclipse

1 IG,The Golden Game	......	4.95
2 IG,The Golden Game	......	4.95
3 IG,The Golden Game	......	4.95

STEEL CLAW
Quality

1 H:Ken Bulmer	....	1.25
2		1.00
3		1.00
4		1.00

STEEL STERLING
Archie Publications
(formerly SHIELD)

4 EB	....	1.00
5 EB	....	1.00
6 EB	....	1.00
7 EB	....	1.00

STEVE CANYON 3-D
Kitchen Sink

Milton Caniff & Peter Poplaski(c), w/glasses (1985)	....	2.00

STEVE ZODIAC & THE FIREBALL XL-5
Gold Key
January, 1964

1	....	50.00

STING OF THE GREEN HORNET
Now

1 Polybagged w/trading card	...	2.75
2 inc.Full color poster	....	2.75
3 inc.Full color poster	....	2.75

STINGER

1	....	1.75

STITCH
Samsons Comics

1 I:Stitch	....	2.50

STORMQUEST
Caliber

1 I:Stormquest	....	1.95
2 Time Stone	....	1.95
3 BU:Seeker	....	1.95
4 F:Shalimar	....	1.95
5 Reunion	....	1.95
6 V:Samuroids	....	1.95

STRANGE DAYS
Eclipse

1	....	2.50
2	....	2.50
3	....	1.50

STRANGE SUSPENSE STORIES/ CAPTAIN ATOM
Charlton Comics

75 SD,O:CaptainAtom,1960Rep.		75.00
76 SD, Capt.Atom,1960Rep.	...	30.00
77 SD, Capt.Atom,1960Rep.	...	30.00

Becomes:

Captain Atom #89 © Charlton Comics

CAPTAIN ATOM
December, 1965

78 SD, new stories begin	.....	65.00
79 SD,I:Dr.Spectro	....	40.00
80 SD	....	40.00
81 SD,V:Dr.Spectro	....	40.00
82 SD,I:Nightshade,Ghost	.....	40.00

83 SD,I:Ted Kord/Blue Beetle	..	35.00
84 SD,N:Captain Atom	....	30.00
85 SD,A:Blue Beetle,I:Punch & Jewelee	....	30.00
86 SD,A:Ghost, Blue Beetle	....	30.00
87 SD,JAp,A:Nightshade	......	30.00
88 SD/FMc,JAp,A:Nightshade	..	30.00
89 SD/FMc,JAp,A:Nightshade, Ghost, last issue Dec.1967	..	30.00

STRAW MEN
Innovation

1	....	1.95
2	....	1.95

STREET FIGHTER
Ocean

1 thru 3	....	@1.75

STRIKE!
Eclipse

1 TL,RT,I&O:New Strike	....	1.75
2 TL,RT		1.25
3 TL,RT		1.25
4 TL,RT,V:Renegade CIA Agents		1.25
5 TL,RT,V:Alien Bugs	....	1.25
6 TL,RT,'Legacy of the Lost'	....	1.75

STRIKER
Viz

1 thru 2	....	2.75

STRIKEFORCE AMERICA
Comico

1 SK(c),I:Strikeforce America	..	2.50

STRIKE! vs. SGT. STRIKE
Eclipse

Spec #1 TL,RT,'The Man'	......	1.95

STRONG MAN
AC Comics

1	....	2.95

STRONTIUM DOG
Eagle

1	....	1.50
2	....	1.25
3	....	1.25
4	....	1.25
5	....	1.25
6	....	1.25
#### Quality		
7	....	1.25
8	....	1.25
9	....	1.25
10	....	1.25
11	....	1.25
12	....	1.25
13	....	1.25
14	....	1.25
15/16	....	1.50
17	....	1.50
18/19	....	1.50
20 thru 29	....	@1.50
#### [2nd Series]		
1	....	1.25
#### Quality		
Spec.#1	....	1.50

STRYKE
London Night Studios
1 I:Stryke 3.00

STUMBO THE GIANT
Blackthorne
1 3-D 2.50

STUMBO TINYTOWN
Harvey Publications
October, 1963
1 .... 75.00
2 .... 40.00
3 .... 25.00
4 .... 25.00
5 .... 25.00
6 thru 12 .... @19.00
13 November, 1966 .... 19.00

STUPID HEROES
Next
1 PeL(s),w/ 2 card-strip 2.75
2 .... 2.75
3 F:Cinder 2.75

STURM THE TROOPER
1 .... 1.95
2 .... 1.95
3 .... 1.95

SUBSPECIES
Eternity
1 Movie Adaptation 3.00
2 Movie Adaptation 2.50
3 Movie Adaptation 2.50
4 Movie Adaptation 2.50

SUN RUNNERS
Pacific
1 .... 2.50
2 .... 2.00
3 .... 2.00
Eclipse
4 .... 2.00
5 .... 2.00
6 'Sins of the Father' 1.75
7 'Dark Side of Mark Dancer' 1.75
Summer Special #1 .... 1.75

SUNSET CARSON
AC Comics
1 Based on Cowboy Star 5.00

SUPERBABES: FEMFORCE
AC Comics
1 Various Artists 5.00

SUPER BOOK OF COMICS
Western Publishing Co.
N# Dick Tracy 225.00
1 Dick Tracy 190.00
2 Smitty,Magic Morro 36.00
3 .... 30.00
4 Red Ryder,Magic Morro 30.00
5 Don Winslow,Magic Morro ... 30.00
5 Don Winslow,Stratosphere Jim 30.00
5 Terry & the Pirates 70.00
6 Don Winslow 38.00

---

7 Little Orphan Annie 38.00
8 .... 72.00
9 Terry & the Pirates 60.00

SUPER-BOOK OF COMICS
Western Publishing Co.
1944
1 Dick Tracy (Omar) 135.00
1 Dick Tracy (Hancock) 100.00
2 Bugs Bunny (Omar) 40.00
2 Bugs Bunny (Hancock) 30.00
3 Terry & the Pirates (Omar) .. 75.00
3 Terry & the Pirates (Hancock) 65.00
4 Andy Panda (Omar) 35.00
4 Andy Panda (Hancock) 30.00
5 Smokey Stover (Omar) 30.00
5 Smokey Stover (Hancock) .. 20.00
6 Porky Pig (Omar) 35.00
6 Porky Pig (Hancock) 30.00
7 Smilin' Jack (Omar) 40.00
7 Smilin' Jack (Hancock) 35.00
8 Oswald the Rabbit (Omar) ... 30.00
8 Oswald the Rabbit (Hancock) 20.00
9 Alley Oop (Omar) 80.00
9 Alley Oop (Hancock) 70.00
10 Elmer Fudd (Omar) 30.00
10 Elmer Fudd (Hancock) 20.00
11 Little Orphan Annie (Omar) .. 45.00
11 Little Orphan Amnie (Hancock) 35.00
12 Woody Woodpecker (Omar) . 35.00
12 WoodyWoodpecker(Hancock) 25.00
13 Dick Tracy (Omar) 80.00
13 Dick Tracy (Hancock) 75.00
14 Bugs Bunny (Omar) 30.00
14 Bugs Bunny (Hanock) 25.00
15 Andy Panda (Omar) 20.00
15 Andy Panda (Hancock) 15.00
16 Terry & the Pirates (Omar) .. 70.00
16 Terry & the Pirates (Hancock) 50.00
17 Smokey Stover (Omar) 30.00
17 Smokey Stover (Hancock) .. 30.00
18 Porky Pig (Omar) 25.00
18 Smokey Stover (Hancock) .. 20.00
19 Smilin' Jack (Omar) 35.00
N# Smilin' Jack (Hancock) 20.00
20 Oswald the Rabbit (Omar) .. 25.00
N# Oswald the Rabbit (Hancock) 15.00
21 Gasoline Alley (Omar) 45.00
N# Gasoline Alley (Hancock) ... 35.00
22 Elmer Fudd (Omar) 25.00
N# Elmer Fudd (Hancock) 30.00
23 Little Orphan Annie (Omar) .. 30.00
N# Little Orphan Annie (Hancock) 25.00
24 Woody Woodpecker (Omar) .. 22.00
N# WoodyWoodpecker(Hancock) 18.00
25 Dick Tracy (Omar) 70.00
N# Dick Tracy (Hancock) 50.00
26 Bugs Bunny (Omar) 25.00
N# Bugs Bunny (Hancock) 20.00
27 Andy Panda (Omar) 20.00
27 Andy Panda (Hancock) 15.00
28 Terry & the Pirates (Omar) .. 70.00
28 Terry & the Pirates (Hancock) 50.00
29 Smokey Stover (Omar) 25.00
29 Smokey Stover (Hancock) .. 20.00
30 Porky Pig (Omar) 25.00
30 Porky Pig (Hancock) 20.00
N# Bugs Bunny (Hancock) 20.00

SUPER CAR
Gold Key
November, 1962
1 .... 150.00

---

2 .... 75.00
3 .... 75.00
4 August, 1963 .... 100.00

SUPERCOPS
Now
1 .... 1.75
2 .... 1.75
3 .... 1.75
4 .... 1.75

SUPER GOOF
Gold Key
October, 1965
1 .... 15.00
2 thru 10 .... @8.00
11 thru 20 .... @5.00
21 thru 30 .... @4.00
31 thru 73 .... @2.00
74 1982 .... 2.00

SUPER HEROES VERSUS SUPERVILLIANS
Archie Publications
July, 1966
1 A:Flyman,Black Hood,The Web,
The Shield 45.00

SUPER MARIO BROS.
1 .... 1.95
2 .... 1.95
3 .... 1.95
4 .... 1.95
5 .... 1.95
6 .... 1.95
Spec #1 .... 1.95

SURGE
Eclipse
1 A:DNAgents 3.00
2 A:DNAgents 2.00
3 A:DNAgents 3.00
4 A:DNAgents 3.00

Survivors #3 © Spectrum Comics

SURVIVORS
Spectrum
1 Mag. size	5.00
2	3.50
3 The Old One	2.50
4	2.50

SURVIVORS
Fantagraphics
1	2.50
2	2.50
3	2.50

SWORDS OF TEXAS
Eclipse
1 FH,New America	2.00
2 FH,V:Baja Badlands	1.75
3 FH,TY(c),V:Dogs of Danger	1.75
4 FH,V:Samurai Master	1.75

SYPHONS
1	1.50
2 thru 7	@1.50

SYPHONS: THE STARGATE STRATAGEM
Now
1 thru 3	@3.95

SYPHONS: COUNTDOWN
Now
1 F:Brigade	2.95
2 Led By Cross	2.95
3 Blown Cover	2.95

TAILSPIN
Walt Disney
[Mini-Series]
1 Take-off Pt.1	3.00
2 Take-off Pt 2	3.00
3 Take-off Pt 3,Khan Job	2.00
4 Take-off pt 4	2.00

TAILSPIN
Walt Disney
[Reg.-Series]
1 Sky-Raker Pt.1	2.50
2 Sky-Raker Pt.2	2.00
3 Idiots Abroad	1.75
4 Contractual Desperation	1.75
5 The Oldman &the Sea Duck	1.75
6 F'reeze a Jolly Good Fellow	1.75

TALES CALCULATED TO DRIVE YOU BATS
Archie Publications
November, 1961
1	45.00
2	20.00
3 thru 6 Nov., 1962	@15.00

TALES FROM THE CRYPT
Gladstone
1 E.C.rep.AW/FF,GS	7.50
2 rep.	4.50
3 rep.	3.50
4 rep.	3.00
5 rep.TFTC #45	3.00
6 rep.TFTC #42	3.00

TALES FROM THE CRYPT
Russ Cochran Publ
1 rep. TFTC #31,CSS#12	2.75
2 rep. TFTC #34,CSS#15	2.50
3 rep. TFTC, CSS	2.50
4 rep. TFTC #43,CSS#18	2.50
5 rep. TFTC,CSS#23	2.00
[2nd Series]
1 rep.horror stories	2.00
2 inc.The Maestro's Hand	2.00
3 thru 6	@2.00
7 thru 8	@2.00

TALES OF TERROR
Eclipse
1	3.00
2 'Claustrophobia'	2.00
3 GM,'Eyes in the Darkness'	2.00
4 TT,TY,JBo(c),'The Slasher'	2.00
5 'Back Forty,''Shoe Button Eyes'	2.00
6 'Good Neighbors'	2.00
7 SBi,JBo,SK(i),'Video'	2.00
8 HB,'Revenant,''Food for Thought'	2.00
9	2.00
10	2.00
11 TT,JBo(c),'Black Cullen'	2.00
12 JBo,FH,'Last of the Vampires'	2.00
13	2.00

TALES OF THE GREEN BERET
Dell Publishing Co.
January, 1967
1 SG	15.00
2	10.00
3	10.00
4	10.00
5	7.00

TALES OF THE GREEN HORNET
Now
1 NA(c),O:Green Hornet Pt.1	3.00
2 O:Green Hornet Pt.2	2.50
3 Gun Metal Green	2.50

Tales of the Mysterious Traveler #2
© Charlton Comics

4 Targets	1.95

TALES OF THE MYSTERIOUS TRAVELER
Charlton Comics
August, 1956
1	200.00
2 SD	175.00
3 SD,SD(c)	175.00
4 SD,SD(c)	225.00
5 SD,SD(c)	225.00
6 SD,SD(c)	225.00
7 SD	175.00
8 SD	175.00
9 SD	175.00
10 SD,SD(c)	200.00
11 SD,SD(c)	200.00
12	65.00
13	65.00
14 (1985)	1.00
15 (1985)	1.00

TALES OF THE SUN RUNNERS
Sirius Comics
1	1.50
2 and 3	@2.00

TALESPIN
Walt Disney
(Mini-Series)
1 Take-off Pt.1	2.75
2 Take-off Pt 2	2.25
3 Take-off Pt 3,Khan Job	2.00
4 Take-off pt 4	1.75

TALESPIN
Walt Disney
(Reg.-Series)
1 'Sky-Raker' Pt.1	2.50
2 'Sky-Raker' Pt.2	2.00
3 'Idiots Abroad'	1.75
4 'Contractual Desperation'	1.75
5 'The Oldman & the Sea Duck'	1.75
6 'F'reeze a Jolly Good Fellow'	1.75

TARGET AIRBOY
Eclipse
1 SK,A:Clint	1.95

TASK FORCE ALPHA
Alpha Productions
1 Forged in Fire	3.50

TASMANIAN DEVIL & HIS TASTY FRIENDS
Gold Key
November, 1962
1	70.00

TASTEE-FREEZ COMICS
Harvey Comics
1957
1 Little Dot	30.00
2 Rags Rabbit	15.00
3 Casper	25.00
4 Sad Sack	15.00
5 Mazie	15.00
6 Dick Tracy	30.00

TEAM ANARCHY
Anarchy
1 I:Team Anarchy	2.75
2 thru 3	2.75
4 PuD,MaS,I:Primal	2.75

TEAM YANKEE
First
1 Harold Coyle novel adapt.	1.95
2 thru 6	@1.95
Trade Paperback	12.95

TEEN-AGE CONFIDENTIAL CONFESSIONS
Charlton Comics
July, 1960
1	9.00
2 thru 5	@5.00
6 thru 10	@3.00
11 thru 21	@2.00
22 1964	2.00

TEENAGE HOTRODDERS
Charlton Comics
April, 1963
1	22.00
2 thru 5	@12.00
6 thru 10	@7.00
11 thru 23	@5.00
24	4.00

Becomes:

TOP ELIMINATOR
25 thru 29	@5.00

Becomes:

DRAG 'N' WHEELS
30	6.00
31 thru 58	@4.00
59 May, 1973	4.00

TEENAGE MUTANT NINJA TURTLES
First
1	6.00
2	4.50
Graphic Novel	17.00

TEENAGE MUTANT NINJA TURTLES
Archie
(From T.V. Series)
1 O:TMNT,April O'Neil,Shredder Krang	6.00
2 V:Shredder,O:Bebop & Rocksteady	4.00
3 V:Shredder & Krang	3.00

TEENAGE MUTANT NINJA TURTLES
Mirage
1 A:Casey Jones	3.00
2 JmL(a&s)	3.00
3 thru 8	@2.75
9 V:Baxter Bot	2.75
10 Mr. Braunze	2.75
11 V:Raphael	2.75
12 V:Darpa	2.75
13 J:Triceraton	2.75

TEENAGE MUTANT NINJA TURTLES ADVENTURES
Archie
[2nd Series]
1 Shredder,Bebop,Rocksteady return to earth	5.00
2 I:Baxter Stockman	3.00
3 'Three Fragments' #1	3.00
4 'Three Fragments' #2	2.50
5 Original adventures begin, I:Man Ray	2.50

*Teenage Mutant Ninja Turtles
Adventures #56 © Archie*

6 I:Leatherhead,Mary Bones	2.50
7 I:Cuddley the Cowlick; Inter-Galactic wrestling issue	2.50
8 I:Wingnut & Screwloose	2.00
9 I:Chameleon	2.00
10 I:Scumbug, Wyrm	2.00
11 I:Rat King & Sons of Silence; Krang returns to earth	2.00
12 Final Conflict #1, A:Leatherhead Wingnut,Screwloose,Trap, I:Malinga	2.00
13 Final Conflict #2	2.00
14 Turtles go to Brazil;I:Jagwar Dreadman	2.00
15 I:Mr. Null	1.50
16 I&D:Bubbla,the Glubbab	1.50
17 Cap'n Mossback	1.25
18 'Man Who Sold World'	1.25
19 I: Mighty Mutanimals	1.25
20 V:Supersoldier,War.Dragon	1.25
21 V:Vid Vicious	1.25
22 GC,Donatello captured	1.50
23 V:Krang,I:Slash,Belly Bomb	1.50
24 V:Krang	1.25
25	1.50
26 I:T'Pau & Keeper	1.50
27 I:Nevermore,Nocturno&Hallocat	1.50
28 Turtle go to Spain, I:Nindar & Chein Klan	1.50
29 Warrior Dragon captured	1.50
30 TMNT/Fox Mutant Ninjara team-up	1.25
31 TMNT/Ninjara team-up cont	1.25
32 A:Sumo Wrestler Tatoo	1.25
33 The Karma of Katmandu	1.25

34 Search For Charlie Llama	1.25
35	1.25
36 V:Shredder	1.25
37 V:Shredder	1.25
38 V:Null & 4 Horsemen Pt.1	1.25
39 V:Null & 4 Horseman Pt.3	1.25
40 1492,A:The Other	1.25
41 And Deliver us from Evil	1.25
42 Time Tripping Trilogy #1	1.25
43 thru 51	@1.25
52 thru 54	@1.50
55 thru 57 Terracide	@1.50
58 thru 70	@1.50
1990 Movie adapt(direct)	5.50
1990 Movie adapt(newsstand)	2.50
1991 TMNT meet Archie	2.50
1991 Movie Adapt II	2.50
Spec.#2 Ghost of 13 Mile Island	2.50
Spec.#3 Night of the Monsterex	2.50
TMNT Mutant Universe Sourcebook	1.95

TEENAGE MUTANT NINJA TURTLES/ FLAMING CARROT
Mirage/Dark Horse
1 JmL	3.00
2 thru 3 JmL	3.00
4 JmL	3.00

TMNT PRESENTS: APRIL O'NEIL
Archie
1 A:Chien Khan,Vid Vicious	1.25
2 V:White Ninja,A:V.Vicious	1.25
3 V:Vhien Khan,concl.	1.25

TMNT: THE MALTESE TURTLE
Mirage
Spec. F:Raphael Detective	2.95

TMNT PRESENTS: DONATELLO AND LEATHERHEAD
1 thru 2	@1.25

TMNT PRESENTS: MERDUDE VS. RAY FILLET
1 thru 3	1.25

TMNT: APRIL O'NEIL THE MAY EAST SAGA
Archie
1 A:TMNT	1.25

TEENAGENTS
Topps
[Mini-Series]
1 WS,AH,w/3 cards	2.95
2 NV,w/3 cards	2.95
3 NV,w/3 cards	2.95
4 NV,w/3 leftover? cards	2.95

TEEN CONFESSIONS
Charlton Comics
August, 1959
1	30.00

2	18.00
3	12.00
4	12.00
5	12.00
6	12.00
7	12.00
8	12.00
9	12.00
10	12.00
11 thru 30	@6.00
31 Beatles cover	35.00
32 thru 36	@2.00
37 Beatles cover,Fan Club story	35.00
38 thru 96	@2.00
97 November, 1976	2.00

TEEN SECRET DIARY
Charlton Comics
October, 1959

1	22.00
2	15.00
3	5.00
4	5.00
5	5.00
6	5.00
7	5.00
8	5.00
9	5.00
10	5.00
11 June, 1961	5.00

TENSE SUSPENSE
Fargo Publications
December, 1958

1	30.00
2 February, 1959	25.00

TERMINATOR
Now

1	25.00
2	12.00
3	7.50
4	5.00
5	4.50
6	4.00
7	4.00
8	4.00
9	4.00
10	4.00
11	4.00
12 I:JohnConnor($1.75cov,dbl.sz)	4.00
13	4.00
14	4.00
15	3.50
16	3.50
17	3.50
Spec. #1	3.50

TERMINATOR:
ALL MY FUTURES PAST
Now

1 Painted Art	4.00
2 Painted Art	4.00

TERMINATOR:
THE BURNING EARTH
Now

1	8.00
2	4.00
3	3.50
4	3.50
5	3.50

TERRAFORMERS
Wonder Comics

1	1.00
2	1.00
3	1.00
4	1.00

TERRANAUTS
Fantasy General

1	1.75
2	1.75

TESS

1	1.95

TEXAS RANGERS
IN ACTION
Charlton Comics
July, 1956

5	30.00
6	15.00
7	15.00
8	15.00
9	15.00
10	15.00
11	35.00
12	8.00
13	30.00
14	8.00
15	8.00
16	8.00
17	8.00
18	8.00
19	8.00
20	8.00
21 thru 30	@6.00
31 thru 59	@2.00
60 B:Riley's Rangers	3.00
61 thru 78	@2.00
79 August, 1970	2.00

THAT WILKIN BOY
Archie Publications
January, 1969

1	15.00
2	7.00
3	7.00
4	7.00
5	7.00
6	7.00
7	7.00
8	7.00
9	7.00
10	7.00
11 thru 20	@3.00
21 thru 26 E:Giant size	@2.00
27 thru 52	@2.00

THESPIAN
Dark Moon

1 I:Thespian	2.50

THING, THE
Darkhorse

1 JHi,From Movie	5.00
2 JHi,Final Issue	3.50

THING: COLD FEAR

1 R:Thing	3.00
2	2.75

THIRD WORLD WAR
Fleet Way

1 HamburgerLady	2.50
2	2.50
3 The Killing Yields	2.50
4 thru 6	@2.50

13: ASSASSIN
TSR

1	2.95
2	2.95
3	2.95
4	2.95
5	2.95
6	2.95
7	2.95
[Mini-series]	
1	2.95

THOSE ANNOYING
POST BROTHERS
Vortex

1	1.75
2	1.75
3	1.75
4	1.75
5	1.75
6	1.75

3-D ZONE PRESENTS
Renegade

1 L.B.Cole(c)	2.00
2	2.00
3	2.00
4	2.00
5	2.00
12 3-D Presidents	2.50
13 Flash Gordon	2.50
14 Tyranostar	2.50
15 Tyranostar	2.50
16 SpaceVixen	2.50

3-D ZONE - 3 DEMENTIA

15	2.50

THREE FACES
OF GNATMAN

1	1.75

THREE STOOGES
Dell Publishing Co.
October-December, 1959

6 Ph(c),B:Prof. Putter	70.00
7 Ph(c)	70.00
8 Ph(c)	70.00
9 Ph(c)	70.00
10 Ph(c)	70.00
11 Ph(c)	50.00
12 Ph(c)	50.00
13 Ph(c)	50.00
14 Ph(c)	50.00
15 Ph(c)	65.00
16 Ph(c),E:Prof. Putter	50.00
17 Ph(c),B:Little Monsters	50.00
18 Ph(c)	50.00
19 Ph(c)	50.00
20 Ph(c)	50.00
21 Ph(c)	50.00
22 Ph(c),Movie Sleeve	50.00
23 Ph(c)	45.00
24 Ph(c)	45.00
25 Ph(c)	45.00

26 Ph(c)	45.00
27 Ph(c)	45.00
28 Ph(c)	45.00
29 Ph(c)	45.00
30 Ph(c)	45.00
31 Ph(c)	40.00
32 Ph(c)	40.00
33 Ph(c)	40.00
34 Ph(c)	40.00
35 Ph(c)	40.00
36 Ph(c)	40.00
37 Ph(c)	40.00
38 Ph(c)	40.00
39 Ph(c)	40.00
40 Ph(c)	40.00
41 Ph(c)	40.00
42 Ph(c)	40.00
43 Ph(c)	40.00
44 Ph(c)	40.00
45 Ph(c)	40.00
46 Ph(c)	40.00
47 Ph(c)	40.00
48 Ph(c)	40.00
49 Ph(c)	40.00
50 Ph(c)	40.00
51	30.00
52 Ph(c)	40.00
53 Ph(c)	40.00
54 Ph(c)	40.00
55 Ph(c)	40.00

THREE STOOGES 3-D
Eclipse

1 thru 3 reprints from 1953	@2.50
4 reprints from 1953	3.50

THRILLING SCIENCE TALES
AC Comics

1	3.50

THRILLOGY
Pacific

1	1.50

THRILL-O-RAMA
Harvey Publications
October, 1965

1 A:Man in Black(Fate),DW,AW	10.00
2 AW,A:Pirana,I:Clawfang,	
The Barbarian	10.00
3 A:Pirana, Fate, December, 1966	7.00

T.H.U.N.D.E.R. AGENTS
Archie Publications

1 WW,RC,GK,MSy,GT,I:Thunder	
Agents,IronMaiden,Warlord	52.00
2 WW,MSy,D:Egghead	33.00
3 WW,DA,MSy,V:Warlords	24.00
4 WW,MSy,RC,I:Lightning	20.00
5 WW,RC,GK,MSy	20.00
6 WW,SD,MSy,I:Warp Wizard	15.00
7 WW,MSy,SD,D:Menthor	15.00
8 WW,MSy,GT,DA,I:Raven	15.00
9 OW,WW,MSy,A:Andor	12.00
10 WW,MSy,OW,A:Andor	12.00
11 WW,DA,MSy	10.00
12 SD,WW,MSy	9.00
13 WW,OW,A:Undersea Agent	10.00
14 SD,WW,GK,N:Raven,A:Andor	10.00
15 WW,OW,GT,A:Andor	9.00
16 SD,GK,A:Andor	9.00
17 WW,OW,GT	8.00

T.H.U.N.D.E.R. Agents #7
© Archie Publications

18 SD,OW,RC	9.00
19 GT,I:Ghost	8.00
20 WW,RC,MSy,all reprints	5.00

T.H.U.N.D.E.R. AGENTS
J.C. Productions

1 MA,Centerfold	2.00
2 I:Vulcan	2.00

THUNDERBOLT
Charlton Comics

1 PAM,O:Thuderbolt	10.00
Prev: Son of Vulcan	
51 PAM,V:Evila	5.00
52 PAM,V:Gore the Monster	3.50
53 PAM,V:The Tong	4.00
54 PAM,I:Sentinels	4.00
55 PAM,V:Sentinels	3.50
56 PAM,A:Sentinels	3.50
57 A:Sentinels	3.50
58 PAM,A:Sentinels	3.50
59 PAM,A:Sentinels	3.50
60 PAM,JAp,I:Prankster	4.00

TIGER GIRL
Gold Key
September, 1968

1	25.00

TIME TUNNEL, THE
Gold Key
February, 1967

1	40.00
2	35.00

TIME TWISTERS
Quality

1 Alan Moore ser.	1.25
2 Alan Moore ser.	1.25
3 Alan Moore ser.	1.25
4 Alan Moore ser.	1.25
5	1.25
6 Alan Moore ser.	1.25
7 Alan Moore ser.	1.25

8	1.25
9	1.25
10	1.25
11	1.25
12	1.25
13 thru 21	@1.50

TIME 2

1 Graphic Novel	8.00

TIPPY'S FRIENDS GO-GO & ANIMAL
Tower Comics
June, 1966

1	10.00
2	4.50
3	4.50
4	4.50
5	4.50
6	4.50
7	4.50
8 Beatles on cover & back	18.00
9 thru 14	@4.50
15 October, 1969	4.50

TIPPY TEEN
Tower Comics
November, 1965

1	8.00
2 thru 26	@3.50
27 February, 1970	3.50

TO DIE FOR

1 3-D	2.50

TOM MIX WESTERN
AC Comics

1	2.95

TOMMY & THE MONSTERS

1	2.00

TOM TERRIFIC!
Pines Comics
Summer, 1957

1	125.00

Tom Terrific #2 © Pines Comics

2	100.00
3	100.00
4	100.00
5	100.00
6 Fall, 1958	100.00

TOP CAT
Charlton Comics
November, 1970

1	30.00
2 thru 10	@20.00
11 thru 19	@12.00
20 November, 1973	12.00

TOR IN 3-D
Eclipse

1 JKu	3.00
1a B&W limited 100 sign	5.00
2 JKu	3.00

TORI-SHI-KITA
Relative Burn

1 Hunter Prey	2.50

TOTAL ECLIPSE
Eclipse

1 BHa,BSz(c),A:Airboy,Skywolf	3.95
2 BHa,BSz(c),A:New Wave, Liberty Project	3.95
3 BHa,BSz(c),A:Scout,Ms.Tree	3.95
4 BHa,BSz(c),A:Miracleman, Prowler	3.95
5 BHa,BSz(c),A:Miracleman, Aztec Ace	3.95

TOTAL ECLIPSE, THE SERAPHIM OBJECTIVE
Eclipse

1 tie-in Total Eclipse #2	1.95

TOTAL WAR
Gold Key
July, 1965

1	35.00
2	35.00

Becomes:
M.A.R.S. PATROL

3 WW	40.00
4	22.00
5	22.00
6	22.00
7	22.00
8	22.00
9	22.00
10	22.00

TOY BOY
Continuity

1 NA.I&O:Toy Boy,A:Megalith	2.00
2 thru 6 TVE	@2.00
7 MG	2.00

TRANCERS: THE ADVENTURES OF JACK DETH
Eternity

1 I:Jack Deth	2.50
2 A:Whistler, final issue	2.50

TRANSFORMERS

1 Robotics	1.50
2	2.00
3	2.50

TRANSFORMERS in 3-D
Blackthorne

1 thru 5	@2.50

TRAVEL OF JAMIE McPHEETERS, THE
Gold Key
December, 1963

1 Kurt Russell	25.00

TRIBE
Axis Comics

2 TJn(s),LSn,V:Alex	2.25
3 TJn(s),LSn,	1.95

TROLL LORDS
Comico

Special #1	1.75
1	1.75
2 and 3	@1.75
4	2.50

Trouble With Girls #2 © Comico

TROUBLE WITH GIRLS
Comico

1	3.00
2	2.50
3	2.50
4	1.95

TRUE LOVE
Eclipse

1 ATh,NC,DSt(c),reprints	2.00
2 ATh,NC,BA(c),reprints	1.50

TUFF GHOSTS STARRING SPOOKY
Harvey Publications
July, 1962

1	50.00
2	30.00

3	30.00
4	30.00
5	30.00
6	20.00
7	20.00
8	20.00
9	20.00
10	20.00
11 thru 20	@10.00
21 thru 30	@7.00
31 thru 39	@3.00
40 thru 42 52 pg. Giants	@3.00
43 October, 1972	3.00

TUROK: SON OF STONE
Dell

1 I&O:Turok,Andar	375.00
2	240.00
3 thru 5	@175.00
6 thru 10	@115.00
11 thru 16	@75.00
17 Prehistoric Pygmies	75.00
18 thru 20	@75.00
21 thr 29	@45.00

Gold Key

30	45.00
31 thru 40	@32.00
41 thru 50	@24.00
51 thru 60	@15.00
61 thru 75	@10.00
76 thru 91	@6.00

Whitman

92 thru 130	@5.00
Giant #1	75.00

TURTLE SOUP
Millenium

1 Book 1, short stories	2.50
2 thru 4	2.50

TV CASPER & COMPANY
Harvey Publications
August, 1963

1 B:68 pg. Giants	55.00
2	30.00
3	30.00
4	30.00
5	30.00
6	25.00
7	25.00
8	25.00
9	25.00
10	25.00
11 thru 20	@7.00
21 thru 31 E:68 pg. Giants	@5.00
32 thru 45	@2.00
46 April, 1974	2.00

TWEETY AND SYLVESTER
Gold Key
November, 1963

1	18.00
2 thru 10	@8.00
11 thru 30	@5.00
31 thru 120	@2.00
121 July, 1984	2.00

TWILIGHT AVENGER
Elite

1 thru 4	@1.75

All comics prices listed are for *Near Mint* condition.

TWILIGHT MAN
First

1 Mini-Series	2.75
2 Mini-Series	2.75
3 Mini-Series	2.75
4 Mini-Series	2.75

TWILIGHT ZONE, THE
Dell Publishing Co.
March-May, 1961

1 RC,FF,GE,P(c) all	75.00
2	50.00
3 ATh,MSy	35.00
4 ATh	35.00
5	30.00
6	30.00
7	30.00
8	30.00
9 ATh	35.00
10	30.00
11	30.00
12 AW	30.00
13 AW,RC,FBe,AMc	30.00
14 RC,JO,RC,AT	30.00
15 RC,JO	30.00
16	25.00
17	25.00
18	25.00
19 JO	25.00
20	20.00
21 RC	25.00
22 JO	25.00
23 JO	25.00
24	20.00
25 GE,RC,ATh	20.00
26 RC,GE	20.00
27 GE	20.00
28	15.00
29	15.00
30	15.00
31	15.00
32 GE	20.00
33	15.00
34	15.00
35	15.00
36	15.00
37	15.00
38	15.00
39 WMc	15.00
40	12.00
41	12.00
42	12.00
43 RC	15.00
44	12.00
45	12.00
46	12.00
47	12.00
48	12.00
49	12.00
50 FBe,WS	12.00
51 AW	15.00
52	12.00
53	12.00
54	12.00
55	12.00
56	12.00
57 FBe	12.00
58	12.00
59 FBe,AMc	15.00
60	10.00
61	10.00
62	10.00
63	10.00
64	10.00
65	10.00
66	10.00
67	10.00
68	10.00
69	10.00
70	10.00
71 rep	8.00
72	10.00
73 rep	8.00
74	10.00
75	10.00
76	10.00
77 FBe	12.00
78 FBe,AMc	12.00
79 rep	8.00
80 FBe,AMc	12.00
81	10.00
82 AMc	12.00
83 FBe,WS	12.00
84 FBe,AMc	12.00
85	10.00
86 rep	8.00
87 thru 91	@10.00

TWILIGHT ZONE
Now

1 NA,BSz(c)	8.00
1a 2nd printing Prestige +Harlan Ellison sty	6.00

[Volume 2]

#1 'The Big Dry' (direct)	2.50
#1a Newsstand	1.95
2 'Blind Alley'	1.95
3 Extraterrestrial	1.95
4 The Mysterious Biker	1.95
5 Queen of the Void	1.95
6 Insecticide	1.95
7 The Outcasts,Ghost Horse	1.95
8 Colonists on Alcor	1.95
9 Dirty Lyle's House of Fun (3-D Holo)	2.95
10 Stairway to Heaven,,Key to Paradise	1.95
11 TD(i),Partial Recall	1.95
3-D Spec.	2.50
Ann. #1	2.75

[Volume 3]

1 thru 2	2.50

Twisted Tales #1 © Pacific Comics

TWISTED TALES
Pacific

1 RCo.AA	3.50
2	2.00
3	2.00
4	2.00
5	2.00
6	2.00
7	2.00
8	2.00

Eclipse

9	2.00
10 GM,BWr	2.00

TWISTED TALES OF BRUCE JONES
Eclipse

1	2.00
2	2.00
3	2.00
4	2.00

TWISTER
Harris

1 inc.Special newspaper/poster, and trading cards	2.95

TWO FISTED TALES
Russ Cochran

1 JSe,HK,WW,JCr,reps	1.50
2 Reps inc.War Story	1.50
3 rep.	1.50
4 thru 6 rep.	2.00
7 thru 8 rep.	2.00

2000 A.D. MONTHLY
Eagle

1 A:JudgeDredd	1.50
2 A:JudgeDredd	1.25
3 A:JudgeDredd	1.25
4 A:JudgeDredd	1.25
5	1.25
6	1.25

[2nd Series]

1	1.25
2	1.25
3	1.25
4	1.25
5	1.25
6	1.25

Quality

7 thru 27	@1.25
28/29	1.50
30	1.50
31/32	1.50
33	1.50
34	1.50
35	1.50
36	1.50
37	1.50

Becomes:

2000 A.D. SHOWCASE

38	1.50
39	1.50
40	1.50
41	1.95
42	1.95
43	1.95
44	1.95
45	1.95
46	1.50
47	1.75

48 . . . . 1.75	
TPB:Killing Time 12.95	

ULTRAMAN
Nemesis

1 EC,O:Ultraman 2.25	
2 . . . . 2.50	
3 . . . . 2.50	
4 V:Blue Ultraman 2.50	

ULTRAMAN
Harvey/Ultracomics

1 w/card 1.50	
2 w/card & virgin cover 1.50	
3 w/card 1.50	

Uncle Scrooge #55 © Dell/Gold Key

UNCLE SCROOGE
Dell/Gold Key

40 . . . . 75.00
41 . . . . 65.00
42 . . . . 65.00
43 . . . . 65.00
44 . . . . 65.00
45 . . . . 65.00
46 Lost Beneath the Sea 65.00
47 . . . . 65.00
48 . . . . 65.00
49 Loony Lunar Gold Rush 65.00
50 Rug Riders in the Sky 65.00
51 How Green Was my Lettuce . . 60.00
52 Great Wig Mystery 60.00
53 Interplanetary Postman 60.00
54 Billion-Dollar Safari! 60.00
55 McDuck of Arabia 60.00
56 Mystery of the Ghost Town
Railroad 60.00
57 Swamp of No Return 60.00
58 Giant Robot Robbers 60.00
59 North of the Yukon 60.00
60 Phantom of Notre Duck 60.00
61 So Far and No Safari 55.00
62 Queen of the Wild Dog Pack . 55.00
63 House of Haunts! 55.00
64 Treasure of Marco Polo! 55.00
65 Micro-Ducks from OuterSpace 55.00
66 Heedless Horseman 55.00
67 CB rep. 55.00
68 Hall of the Mermaid Queen! . 55.00

69 Cattle King! 55.00
70 CB,The Doom Diamond! 55.00
71 . . . . 45.00
72 CB rep. 55.00
73 CB rep. 55.00
74 thru 110 . . . . @40.00
111 thru 148 . . . . @20.00
149 . . . . 15.00
150 thru 168 . . . . @10.00
169 thru 173 . . . . @8.00

Whitman

174 thru 182 . . . . @8.00
183 thru 200 . . . . @6.00
201 thru 209 . . . . @5.00

Gladstone

210 CB 8.00
211 CB,Prize of Pizzaro 6.00
212 CB,city-golden roofs 6.00
213 CB,city-golden roofs 6.00
214 CB 6.00
215 CB, a cold bargain 4.00
216 CB 4.00
217 CB,7 cities of Cibola 5.00
218 CB 4.00
219 Don Rosa,Son of Sun 16.00
220 CB,Don Rosa 4.00
221 CB,A:BeagleBoys 3.00
222 CB,Mysterious Island 3.00
223 CB 3.00
224 CB,Rosa,Cash Flow 6.00
225 CB 2.50
226 CB,Rosa 4.00
227 CB,Rosa 4.00
228 CB 2.50
229 CB 2.50
230 CB 5.00
231 CB,Rosa(c) 2.50
232 CB 2.50
233 CB 2.50
234 CB 2.50
235 Rosa 3.00
236 CB 2.50
237 CB 2.50
238 CB 2.50
239 CB 2.50
240 CB 2.50
241 CB,giant 5.00
242 CB,giant 4.00

Walt Disney

243 CB 3.50
244 . . . . 2.50
245 . . . . 2.50
246 . . . . 2.50
247 . . . . 2.50
248 . . . . 2.50
249 . . . . 2.50
250 CB 3.00
251 . . . . 2.00
252 . . . . 2.00
253 'Fab.Philosophers Stone . . . 2.00
254 The Filling Station 2.00
255 The Flying Dutchman 2.00
256 CB,'Status Seeker' 2.50
257 'Coffee,Louie or Me' 1.75
258 CB,'Swamp of no return' . . . 2.50
259 'The only way to travel' 1.75
260 The Waves Above,
The Gold Below 1.75
261 Rosa,'Return to Zanadu' Pt.1 2.50
262 Rosa,'Return to Zanadu' Pt.2 2.50
263 Rosa,'Treasure Under Glass' 2.50
264 Snobs Club 1.50
265 CB,Ten Cent Valentine 1.50
266 The Money Ocean,Pt.1 . . . . 1.50
267 The Money Ocean,Pt 2 . . . . 1.50

268 CB,Rosa,Island in the Sky . . 2.00
269 The Flowers 1.50
270 V:Magica DeSpell 1.50
271 The Secret o/t Stone 1.50
272 Canute The Brute's
Battle Axe 1.50
273 CB,Uncle Scrooge-Ghost . . . 2.00
274 CB,Hall of the Mermaid
Queen 2.00
275 CB,Rosa,Christmas Cheers,inc.
D.Rosa centerspread 2.50
276 Rosa, thru 277 . . . . @2.00
278 thru 284 . . . . @1.50

Gladstone

285 thru 289 Rosa 2.00
290 thru 293 . . . . @1.50

UNCLE SCROOGE
ADVENTURES
Gladstone

1 CB,McDuck of Arabia 6.00
2 translated from Danish 3.00
3 translated from Danish 3.00
4 CB 3.00
5 Rosa 3.00
6 CB 3.00
7 CB 3.00
8 CB 2.50
9 Rosa 3.00
10 CB 2.50
11 CB 2.50
12 CB 2.50
13 CB 2.50
14 Rosa 2.50
15 CB 2.50
16 CB 2.50
17 CB 2.50
18 CB 2.50
19 CB,Rosa(c) 2.50
20 CB,giant 4.00
21 CB,giant 4.00
22 Rosa(c) 4.00
23 CB,giant 4.00
24 thru 26 . . . . @1.50
27 Rosa,O:Jr. Woodchuck 2.50
28 giant 3.00
29 . . . . 1.50

UNCLE SCROOGE
& DONALD DUCK
Gold Key

1 rep. 60.00

UNCLE SCROOGE GOES
TO DISNEYLAND
Gladstone

1 CB,etc. 100pp 8.00

UNDERDOG
Spotlight

1 FMc,PC(c),The Eredicator 1.50
2 FMc,CS(c), Prisoner of Love/
The Return of Fearo 1.50

UNDERDOG
Charlton
July, 1970

1 Planet Zot 40.00
2 Simon Sez/The Molemen . . . 20.00
3 Whisler's Father 20.00
4 The Witch of Pycoon 20.00
5 The Snowmen 20.00

All comics prices listed are for *Near Mint* condition.   **CVA Page 501**

6 The Big Shrink 20.00
7 The Marbleheads 20.00
8 The Phoney Booths 20.00
9 Tin Man Alley 20.00
10 Be My Valentine (Jan. 1972) . 20.00

UNDERDOG
Gold Key
March, 1975

1 The Big Boom 20.00
2 The Sock Singer Caper 10.00
3 The Ice Cream Scream 8.00
4 . . . . 8.00
5 . . . . 8.00
6 Head in a Cloud 8.00
7 The Cosmic Canine 8.00
8 . . . . 8.00
9 . . . . 8.00
10 Bouble Trouble Gum 8.00
11 The Private Life of
  Shoeshine Boy 4.00
12 The Deadly Fist of Fingers . . . 4.00
13 . . . . 4.00
14 Shrink Shrank Shrunk 4.00
15 Polluter Palooka 4.00
16 The Soda Jerk 4.00
17 Flee For Your Life 4.00
18 Rain Rain Go Away...Okay . . . 4.00
19 Journey To the Center
  of the Earth 4.00
20 The Six Million Dollar Dog . . . 4.00
21 Smell of Success 4.00
22 Antlers Away 4.00
23 Wedding Bells In Outer
  Space (Feb.,1979) 4.00

UNDERDOG IN 3-D
Blackthorne

1 Wanted Dead or Alive 2.50

UNEARTHLY SPECTACULARS

1 DW,AT,I:Tiger Boy 5.00
2 WW,AW,GK,I:Earthman,Miracles,Inc.
  A:Clawfang,TigerBoy 15.00
3 RC,AW,JO,A:Miracles,Inc. . . . 12.00

U.N. FORCE
Gauntlet Comics

0 BDC(s) 2.95
1 B:BDC(s),I:U.N.Force 2.95
2 O:Indigo 2.95
3 . . . . 2.95
4 A:Predator 2.95
5 B:Critial Mass 2.95

U.N. FORCE FILES
Gauntlet Comics

1 KP(c),F:Hunter Seeker,
  Lotus 2.95

UNIVERSAL SOLDIER
Now

1 Based on Movie,Holo.(c) 2.75
2 Luc & Ronnie on the run from
  UniSols 2.50
2a Photo cover 1.95
3 Photo(c) 1.95

UNKNOWN WORLDS OF FRANK BRUNNER

Eclipse

1 FB 2.50
2 FB 2.50

UNLEASHED!
Triumphant

0 JnR(s),I:Skyfire 2.50
1 JnR(s), ... 2.50

UNLV

1 Championship season (basketball
  based on college team) 3.00

UNTAMED LOVE

1 FF 2.00

UNUSUAL TALES
Charlton Comics
November, 1955

1 . . . . 125.00
2 . . . . 60.00
3 . . . . 35.00
4 . . . . 35.00
5 . . . . 35.00
6 SD,SD(c) 110.00
7 SD,SD(c) 110.00
8 SD,SD(c) 110.00
9 SD,SD(c) 125.00
10 SD,SD(c) 120.00
11 SD 120.00
12 SD 85.00
13 . . . . 30.00
14 SD 85.00
15 SD,SD(c) 90.00
16 . . . . 30.00
17 . . . . 30.00
18 . . . . 30.00
19 . . . . 30.00
20 . . . . 30.00
21 . . . . 20.00
22 SD 50.00
23 . . . . 20.00
24 . . . . 20.00
25 SD 55.00
26 SD 55.00
27 SD 55.00
28 . . . . 20.00
29 SD 55.00
30 thru 48 . . . . @20.00
49 March-April, 1965 . . . . 20.00

URI-ON

1 . . . . 1.50
2 . . . . 1.50

URTH 4
Continuity

1 TVE,NA(c) 2.00
2 TVE,NA 2.00
3 TVE,NA 2.00
4 NA,Last issue 2.00

USAGI YOJIMBO
Fantagraphics

1 SS,color Spec 5.00
2 SS,color Spec. 5.00
3 SS,color Spec. 3.00

USAGI YOJIMBO
Mirage

1 thru 4 . . . . 3.00
5 thru 6 . . . . 3.00

Usagi Yojimbo #1
© *Fantagraphics Books*

VALERIA THE SHE BAT
Continuity

1 NA,I:Valeria 20.00
2 thru 4 . . . . . . [NOT RELEASED]
5 Rise of Magic 2.50

VALKYRIE
Eclipse

1 PG,I:Steelfox,C:Airboy,
  Sky Wolf 3.00
2 PG,O:New Black Angel 2.50
3 PG 2.50

[2nd Series]

1 BA,V:Eurasian Slavers 1.95
2 BA,V:Cowgirl 1.95
3 BA,V:Cowgirl 1.95

VAMPIRE LESTAT
Innovation

1 Anne RiceAdap. 26.00
1a 2nd printing 5.00
1b 3rd printing 2.50
2 . . . . 13.00
2a 2nd printing 5.00
2b 3rd printing 2.50
3 . . . . 10.00
3a 2nd printing 2.50
4 . . . . 8.00
4a 2nd printing 2.50
5 . . . . 5.00
6 . . . . 3.50
7 . . . . 3.50
8 . . . . 4.00
9 scarce 4.00
9a 2nd Printing 2.50
10 . . . . 3.00
11 'Those Who Must Be Kept' . . . 2.50
12 conclusion 2.50
Vampire Companion #1 . . . . 4.00
Vampire Companion #2 (preview
  'Interview With The Vampire' . 2.50
Vampire Companion #3 . . . . 2.50
GN rep.#1-#12 (Innovation) 24.95
GN rep.#1-#12 (Ballantine) 25.00

VAMPIRELLA
Warren Publishing Co.
September, 1969

1 I:Vampirella	200.00
2 B:Amazonia	75.00
3	250.00
4	40.00
5	40.00
6	40.00
7	40.00
8	40.00
9	45.00
10	20.00
11 O& 1st app. Pendragon.	30.00
12	25.00
13	25.00
14	25.00
15	25.00
16	20.00
17 B:Tomb of the Gods	20.00
18	20.00
19	25.00
20 thru 25	@20.00
26	10.00
27	12.00
28 thru 36	@10.00
37	8.00
38	7.00
39	7.00
40	7.00
41	6.00
42	6.00
43	6.00
44	6.00
45	6.00
46 O:Vampirella	7.00
47 thru 100	@3.00
101 thru 111	@2.00
112 February, 1983	2.00

VAMPIRELLA
Harris

1 V:Forces of Chaos, w/coupon for DSt poster	40.00
2 AH(c)	30.00
3 A:Dracula	15.00
4 A:Dracula	7.00

VAMPIRELLA CLASSIC
Harris Comics

1 Dark Angel	2.95
2 V:Demogorgon	2.95

VANGUARD

1	1.50

VANGUARD ILLUSTRATED
Pacific

1	1.50
2 DSt(c)	1.50
3 SR	1.50
4 SR	1.50
5 SR	1.50
6 GI	1.50
7 GE,I:Mr.Monster	6.00

VANITY
Pacific

1	1.50
2	1.50

Vault of Horror #1 © Gladstone

VAULT OF HORROR
Gladstone

1 Rep.GS,WW	5.00
2 Rep.VoH #27 & HoF #18	3.50
3 Rep.VoH #13 & HoF #22	3.00
4 Rep.VoH #23 & HoF #13	2.50
5 Rep.VoH #19 & HoF #5	2.50
6 Rep.VoH #32 & WF #6	2.50
7 Rep.VoH #26 & WS #7	2.50

VAULT OF HORROR
Russ Cochran Publ.

1 Rep.VoH #28 & WS #18	2.25
2 Rep.VoH #33 & WS #20	2.25
3 Rep.VoH #26 & WS #7	2.25
4 Rep.VoH #35 & WS #15	2.00
4 Rep.VoH #18 & WS #11	2.00
5 Rep.VoH #18 & WS #11	2.00
2nd Series	
1 thru 7 Rep.VoH	@1.50
8	2.00

VECTOR
Now

1	2.50
2	1.75
3	1.75
4	1.75
5	1.75

VEGAS KNIGHTS
Pioneer

1	1.95
2	1.95
3	1.95

VENGEANCE OF VAMPIRELLA
Harris

1 Hemmorage	25.00
1a Gold Edition	50.00
2 Dervish	15.00
3 On the Hunt	7.00
4 Teenage Vampires	5.00
5 Teenage Vampires	3.50
6	2.95
7	2.95
8 bagged w/card	2.95
9	2.95
10 Bad Jack Rising	2.95
11 Pits of Hell, w/card	2.95
12 V:Passion	2.95
13 V:Passion	2.95
14 Prelude to the Walk,pt.2	2.95
TPB 1-3 Bloodshed	6.95

VENTURE
AC Comics

1	2.00
2 thru 4	@1.75

VERONICA
Archie Publications
April, 1989

1 thru 44	@1.50

VEROTIKA
Verotika

1 thru 3 Jae Lee, Frazetta	2.95

VIC FLINT
Argo Publ.
February, 1956

1	35.00
2	30.00

VILLAINS & VIGILANTES
Eclipse

1 A:Crusaders,Shadowman	2.00
2 A:Condor	2.00
3 V:Crushers	2.00
4 V:Crushers	2.00

VIOLENT CASES
Tundra

1 20's Chicago	11.00

VIRGINIAN, THE
Gold Key
June, 1963

1	30.00

VOLTRON
Solson

1 TV tie-in	2.00
2	1.50
3	1.50

VORTEX
Vortex

1 Peter Hsu art	22.00
2 Mister X on cover	8.00
3	5.00
4	4.00
5	3.00
6 thru 8	@3.00
9 thru 13	@1.75

VORTEX
Comico

1 from Elementals	2.50
2	2.50

VOYAGE TO THE DEEP
Dell Publishing Co.
September-November, 1962
1 P(c)	35.00
2 P(c)	20.00
3 P(c)	20.00
4 P(c)	20.00

WACKY ADVENTURES OF CRACKY
Gold Key
December, 1972
1	10.00
2 thru 11	@5.00
12 September, 1975	3.00

WACKY WITCH
Gold Key
March, 1971
1	18.00
2	10.00
3 thru 20	@6.00
21 December, 1975	4.00

WAGON TRAIN
Gold Key
January, 1964
1	30.00
2	20.00
3	20.00
4 October, 1964	20.00

WALLY
Gold Key
December, 1962
1	18.00
2	15.00
3	15.00
4 September, 1963	15.00

WALLY WOOD'S THUNDER AGENTS
Delux
1 GP,KG,DC,SD,InewMenth	3.00
2 GP,KG,DC,SD	2.50
3 KG,DC,SD	2.00
4 GP,KG,RB,DA	2.00
5 JOy,KG,A:CodenamDangr	2.00

WALT DISNEY ANNUALS
Walt Disney's Autumn Adventure	4.00
Walt Disney's Holiday Parade #1	3.50
Walt Disney's Spring Fever	3.25
Walt Disney's Summer Fun	3.25
Walt Disney's Holiday Parade #2	3.25

WALT DISNEY'S AUTUMN ADVENTURE
1 Rep. CB	4.00

WALT DISNEY'S COMICS AND STORIES
Dell/ Gold Key
264 CB;VonDrake&Gearloose('62)	25.00
265 CB; Von Drake & Gearloose	25.00
266 CB; Von Drake & Gearloose	25.00
267 CB; Von Drake & Gearloose	25.00
268 CB; Von Drake & Gearloose	25.00
269 CB; Von Drake & Gearloose	25.00
270 CB; Von Drake & Gearloose	25.00
271 CB; Von Drake & Gearloose	25.00
272 CB; Von Drake & Gearloose	25.00
273 CB; Von Drake & Gearloose	25.00
274 CB; Von Drake & Gearloose	25.00
275 CB	25.00
276 CB	25.00
277 CB	25.00
278 CB	25.00
279 CB	25.00
280 CB	25.00
281 CB	25.00
282 CB	25.00
283 CB	25.00
284	15.00
285	15.00
286 CB	25.00
287	15.00
288 CB	20.00
289 CB	20.00
290	15.00
291 CB	20.00
292 CB	20.00
293 CB; Grandma Duck's Farm Friends	20.00
294 CB	20.00
295	15.00
296	15.00
297 CB; Gyro Gearloose	20.00
298 CB; Daisy Duck's Dairy	20.00
299 CB rep.	20.00
300 CB rep.	20.00
301 CB rep.	20.00
302 CB rep.	20.00
303 CB rep.	20.00
304 CB rep.	20.00
305 CB rep. Gyro Gearloose	20.00
306 CB rep.	20.00
307 CB rep.	20.00
308 CB	20.00
309 CB	20.00
310 CB	20.00
311 CB	20.00
312 CB	20.00
313 thru 327	@15.00
328 CB rep.	20.00
329	12.00
330	12.00
331	12.00
332	12.00
333	12.00
334	12.00
335 CB rep.	15.00
336	12.00
337	12.00
338	12.00
339	12.00
340	12.00
341	12.00
342 CB rep.	15.00
343 CB rep.	15.00
344 CB rep.	15.00
345 CB rep.	15.00
346 CB rep.	15.00
347 CB rep.	15.00
348 CB rep.	15.00
349 CB rep.	15.00
350 CB rep.	15.00
351 CB rep. with poster	20.00
351a CB rep. without poster	15.00
352 CB rep. with poster12	20.00
352a CB rep. without poster	15.00
353 CB rep. with poster	20.00
353a CB rep. without poster	15.00
354 CB rep. with poster	20.00
354a CB rep. without poster	15.00
355 CB rep. with poster	20.00
355a CB rep. without poster	15.00
356 CB rep. with poster	20.00
356a CB rep. without poster	15.00
357 CB rep. with poster	20.00
357a CB rep. without poster	15.00
358 CB rep. with poster	20.00
358a CB rep. without poster	15.00
359 CB rep. with poster	20.00
359a CB rep. without poster	15.00
360 CB rep. with poster	20.00
360a CB rep. without poster	15.00
361 thru 400 CB rep.	@15.00
401 thru 409 CB rep.	@12.00
410 CB rep. Annette Funichello	12.00
411 thru 429 CB rep.	@12.00
430	8.00
431 CB rep.	10.00
432 CB rep.	10.00
433	8.00
434 CB rep.	10.00
435 CB rep.	10.00
436 CB rep.	10.00
437	5.00
438	5.00
439 CB rep.	8.00
440 CB rep.	8.00
441	5.00
442 CB rep.	8.00
443 CB rep.	8.00
444	5.00
445	5.00
446 thru 465 CB rep.	@8.00
466	8.00
467 thru 473 CB rep.	@8.00

Whitman
474 thru 493 CB rep.	@6.00
494 CB rep.Uncle Scrooge	7.00
495 thru 505 CB rep.	@6.00
506	5.00
507 CB rep.	6.00
508 CB rep.	6.00
509 CB rep.	6.00
510 CB rep.	6.00

Gladstone
511 translation of Dutch	7.00
512 translation of Dutch	8.00
513 translation of Dutch	6.00
514 translation of Dutch	5.00
515 translation of Dutch	4.00
516 translation of Dutch	4.00
517 translation of Dutch	3.50
518 translation of Dutch	3.50
519 CB,Donald Duck	3.50
520 translation of Dutch	3.00
521 Walt Kelly	3.00
522 CB,WK,nephews	3.00
523 Rosa,Donald Duck	3.00
524 Rosa,Donald Duck	3.00
525 translation of Dutch	3.00
526 Rosa,Donald Duck	3.00
527 CB	3.00
528 Rosa,Donald Duck	3.00
529 CB	3.00
530 Rosa,Donald Duck	3.00
531 WK(c)Rosa,CB	3.00
532 CB	2.50
533 CB	2.50
534 CB	2.50
535 CB	2.50
536 CB	2.50
537 CB	2.50
538 CB	2.50
539 CB	2.50

540 CB new art 3.50	
541 double-size,WK(c) 3.00	
542 CB 5.00	
543 CB,WK(c) 2.50	
544 CB,WK(c) 2.50	
545 CB 2.50	
546 CB, WK,giant 4.00	
547 CB,WK,giant 4.00	

Walt Disney

548 CB, WK 3.00
549 CB, ... 2.50
550 CB,prev.unpub.story! 3.50
551 . . . . 2.25
552 . . . . 2.25
553 . . . . 2.25
554 . . . . 2.25
555 . . . . 2.25
556 . . . . 2.25
557 . . . . 2.25
558 'Donald's Fix-it Shop' 2.25
559 'Bugs' 2.25
560 CB,April Fools Story 2.00
561 CB,Donald the 'Flipist' 2.00
562 CB,'3DirtyLittleDucks' 2.00
563 CB,'Donald Camping' 2.00
564 CB,'Dirk the Dinosaur' 2.00
565 CB,DonaldDuck,TruantOfficer 2.00
566 CB,'Will O' the Wisp' 2.00
567 CB,'Turkey Shoot' 2.00
568 CB,'AChristmas Eve Story' . . 2.00
569 CB, New Years Resolutions . 2.00
570 CB,Donald the Mailman
   +Poster 2.00
571 CB,'Atom Bomb' 4.50
572 CB, April Fools 2.00
573 TV Quiz Show 1.50
574 Pinnochio,64pgs 3.50
575 Olympic Torch Bearer,
   Li'l Bad Wolf,64 pgs. 3.50
576 giant 3.50
577 A:Truant Officers,64 pgs. . . . 3.50
578 CB,Old Quacky Manor 2.00
579 CB,Turkey Hunt 2.00
580 CB,The Wise Little Red Hen,
   64 page-Sunday page format . . . 3.50
581 CB,Duck Lake 2.00
582 giant 3.50
583 giant 3.50
584 . . . . 1.75
585 CB, giant 3.00

Gladstone

586 . . . . 1.75
587 thru 598 . . . . @1.75

**WALT DISNEY
COMICS DIGEST
Gold Key
June, 1968
[All done by Carl Barks]**

1 Rep,Uncle Scrooge 40.00
2 . . . . 25.00
3 . . . . 25.00
4 . . . . 25.00
5 . . . . 45.00
6 . . . . 20.00
7 . . . . 20.00
8 . . . . 20.00
9 . . . . 20.00
10 . . . . 20.00
11 . . . . 20.00
12 . . . . 20.00
13 . . . . 20.00
14 . . . . 10.00
15 . . . . 10.00

16 rep.Donald Duck #26 . . . . . 20.00
17 . . . . 15.00
18 . . . . 15.00
19 . . . . 15.00
20 . . . . 15.00
21 . . . . 18.00
22 . . . . 18.00
23 . . . . 18.00
24 . . . . 18.00
25 . . . . 18.00
26 . . . . 18.00
27 . . . . 18.00
28 . . . . 18.00
29 . . . . 18.00
30 . . . . 18.00
31 . . . . 18.00
32 . . . . 8.00
33 . . . . 18.00
34 rep.Four Color #318 . . . . . 15.00
35 . . . . 15.00
36 . . . . 15.00
37 . . . . 15.00
38 rep.Disneyland#1 . . . . 15.00
39 . . . . 15.00
40 . . . . 10.00
41 . . . . 8.00
42 . . . . 8.00
43 . . . . 8.00
44 Rep. Four Color #29 & others 25.00
45 . . . . 6.00
46 CB 8.00
47 . . . . 6.00
48 . . . . 6.00
49 . . . . 6.00
50 CB 8.00
51 rep.Four Color #71 . . . . . . 12.00
52 CB 8.00
53 . . . . 6.00
54 . . . . 6.00
55 . . . . 6.00
56 CB,rep. Uncle Scrooge #32 . 10.00
57 CB,February, 1976 . . . . 8.00

**WALT DISNEY
SHOWCASE
Gold Key**

1 Boatniks (photo cover) 20.00
2 Moby Duck 10.00
3 Bongo & Lumpjaw 8.00
4 Pluto 10.00
5 $1,000,000 Duck (photo cover) 15.00
6 Bedknobs & Broomsticks 12.00
7 Pluto 10.00
8 Daisy & Donald 10.00
9 101 Dalmatians rep. 12.00
10 Napoleon & Samantha 12.00
11 Moby Duck rep. 7.00
12 Dumbo rep. 8.00
13 Pluto rep. 8.00
14 World's Greatest Athlete 12.00
15 3 Little Pigs rep. 12.00
16 Aristocats rep. 12.00
17 Mary Poppins rep. 12.00
18 Gyro Gearloose rep. 12.00
19 That Darn Cat rep. 12.00
20 Pluto rep. 10.00
21 Li'l Bad Wolf & 3 Little Pigs . . 7.00
22 Unbirthday Party rep. 10.00
23 Pluto rep. 10.00
24 Herbie Rides Again rep. 8.00
25 Old Yeller rep. 8.00
26 Lt. Robin Crusoe USN rep. . . . 7.00
27 Island at the Top of the World . 7.00
28 Brer Rabbit, Bucky Bug rep. . 10.00
29 Escape to Witch Mountain . . . 8.00

30 Magica De Spell rep. 15.00
31 Bambi rep. 12.00
32 Spin & Marty rep. 10.00
33 Pluto rep. 10.00
34 Paul Revere's Ride rep. 7.00
35 Goofy rep. 7.00
36 Peter Pan rep. 7.00
37 Tinker Bell & Jiminy
   Cricket rep. 7.00
38 Mickey & the Sleuth, Pt. 1 . . . 8.00
39 Mickey & the Sleuth, Pt. 2 . . . 8.00
40 The Rescuers 8.00
41 Herbie Goes to Monte Carlo . 10.00
42 Mickey & the Sleuth 7.00
43 Pete's Dragon 8.00
44 Return From Witch Mountain &
   In Search of the Castaways . 10.00
45 The Jungle Book rep. 12.00
46 The Cat From Outer Space . . . 7.00
47 Mickey Mouse Surprise Party . 8.00
48 The Wonderful Adventures of
   Pinocchio 7.00
49 North Avenue Irregulars; Zorro 7.00
50 Bedknobs & Broomsticks rep. . 6.00
51 101 Dalmatians 6.00
52 Unidentified Flying Oddball . . 6.00
53 The Scarecrow 6.00
54 The Black Hole 6.00

**WALT KELLY'S
CHRISTMAS CLASSICS
Eclipse**

1 . . . . 2.00

**WALT KELLY'S
SPRINGTIME TALES
Eclipse**

1 . . . . 2.50

**WARCHILD
Maximum Press**

1 I:Sword, Stone 2.50
2 I:Morganna Lefay 2.50
3 V: The Black Knight 2.50
4 Rescue Merlyn 2.50

**WAR DANCER
Defiant**

1 B:JiS(s),I:Ahrq Tsolmec 2.75
2 I:Massakur 2.75
3 V:Massakur 2.75
4 JiS(s),A:Nudge 3.25

**WARHAWKS
TSR**

1 . . . . 2.95
2 . . . . 2.95
3 . . . . 2.95
4 . . . . 2.95
5 . . . . 2.95
6 . . . . 2.95
7 . . . . 2.95

**WARHAWKS 2050
TSR**

1 Pt.1 . . . . 2.95

**WAR HEROES
Charlton Comics
February, 1963**

1 . . . . 3.50

2 . . . . 2.00
3 . . . . 2.00
4 thru 10 . . . . @2.00
11 thru 26 . . . . @1.00
27 November, 1967 . . . . 1.00

WARLASH
CFD
1 Project Hardfire 2.95

WARMASTER
1 . . . . 3.95
2 . . . . 3.95

Warp Special #2 © First Comics

WARP
First
1 FB,JSon,I:Lord Cumulus & Prince
 Chaos, play adapt pt.1 . . . . . . 2.00
2 FB,SD,play adapt pt.2 . . . . 1.50
3 FB,SD,play adapt pt.3 . . . . 1.50
4 FB,SD,I:Xander,play pt.4 . . . . . 1.50
5 FB, play adapt pt.5 . . . . 1.50
6 FB/MG, play adapt pt.6 . . . . . . 1.50
7 FB/MG, play adapt pt.7 . . . . . . 1.50
8 FB/MG,BWg,play adapt pt.8 . . 1.25
9 FB/MG,BWg,play adapt conc. . 1.25
10 JBi/MG,BWg, Second Saga,
 I:Outrider 1.25
11 JBi/MG,A:Outrider 1.25
12 JBi/MG,A:Outrider 1.25
13 JBi/MG,A:Outrider 1.25
14 JBi/MG,A:Outrider 1.25
15 JBi/MG/BWg 1.25
16 BWg/MG,A:Outrider 1.25
17 JBi/MG,A:Outrider 1.25
18 JBi/MG,A:Outrider&Sargon . . 1.25
19 MG,last issue 1.25
Special #1 HC,O:Chaos 1.50
Special #2 MS/MG,V:Ylem 1.50
Special #3 . . . . 1.50

WARRIOR NUN AREALA
Antartic Press
1 V:Lilith 2.95
2 V:Lilith 2.95
3 V:Hellmaster 2.95

WARRIORS OF PLASM
Defiant
1 JiS(s),DL,A:Lorca 3.25
2 JiS(s),DL,Sedition Agenda 3.25
3 JiS(s),DL,Sedition Agenda 3.25
4 JiS(s),DL,Sedition Agenda 3.25
5 JiS(s),B:The Demons of
 Darkedge 2.75
6 JiS(s),The Demons of
 Darkedge,pt.2 . . . . 2.75
7 JiS(s),DL, ... 2.75
8 JiS(s),DL,40pages 3.00
9 JiS(s),LWn(s),DL,40pages 3.00
10 DL, ... 2.50
GN Home for the Holidays 5.95

WART AND THE WIZARD
Gold Key
February, 1964
1 . . . . 14.00

WAVE WARRIORS
1 . . . . 2.00
2 . . . . 2.00

WAXWORK in 3-D
Blackthorne
1 . . . . 2.50

WAYFARERS
Eternity
1 . . . . 1.80
2 . . . . 1.80

WEB-MAN
Argosy
1 flip book with Time Warrior . . . 2.50

WEB OF HORROR
Major Magazines
December, 1969
1 JJ(c),Ph(c),BWr 40.00
2 JJ(c),Ph(c),BWr 25.00
3 BWr,April, 1970 . . . . 25.00

WEIRD FANTASY
Russ Cochran
1 Reps 1.50
2 Reps.inc.The Black Arts 1.50
3 thru 4 rep. . . . . @1.50
5 thru 7 rep. 2.00
8 . . . . 2.00

WEIRD SCIENCE
Gladstone
1 Rep. double size 5.00
2 Rep. #16 . . . . 3.50
3 Rep. #9 . . . . 3.50
4 Rep. 2.00

WEIRD SCIENCE FANTASY
Russ Cochran
1 Rep. W.S.F. #23 (1954) 1.50
2 Rep. Flying Saucer Invasion . . 1.50
3 Rep. 1.50
4 thru 6 Rep. 2.00
7 rep #29 . . . . 2.00
8 . . . . 2.00

WEIRD TALES ILLUSTRATED
Millenium
1 KJo,JBo,PCr,short stories 4.95

WENDY
Blackthorne
1 3-D 2.50

WENDY, THE GOOD LITTLE WITCH
Harvey Publications
August, 1960
1 . . . . 55.00
2 . . . . 26.00
3 . . . . 21.00
4 . . . . 21.00
5 . . . . 21.00
6 . . . . 16.00
7 . . . . 16.00
8 . . . . 16.00
9 . . . . 16.00
10 . . . . 16.00
11 thru 20 . . . . @11.00
21 thru 30 . . . . @6.00
31 thru 50 . . . . @3.50
51 thru 69 . . . . @2.50
70 thru 74 52 pg Giants . . . . . @3.50
75 thru 92 . . . . @1.50
93 April, 1976 . . . . 1.50

WENDY WITCH WORLD
Harvey Publications
October, 1961
1 . . . . 35.00
2 . . . . 17.00
3 . . . . 17.00
4 . . . . 17.00
5 . . . . 17.00
6 . . . . 11.00
7 . . . . 11.00
8 . . . . 11.00
9 . . . . 11.00
10 . . . . 11.00
11 thru 20 . . . . @7.00
21 thru 30 . . . . @3.50
31 thru 39 . . . . @2.50
40 thru 50 . . . . @1.50
51 thru 52 . . . . @1.00
53 September, 1974 . . . . 1.00

WEREWOLF
Blackthorne
1 3-D 3.50

WHAM
1 . . . . 1.75

WHISPER
Capital
1 MG(c) 10.00
2 . . . . 8.00
First
1 . . . . 2.50
2 . . . . 2.00
3 . . . . 2.00
4 . . . . 1.50
5 . . . . 1.50
6 thru 12 . . . . @1.25
13 thru 19 . . . . @1.75
20 O:Whisper 1.95

21 thru 26 . . . . @1.95
27 Ghost Dance #2 . . . . 1.95
28 Ghost Dance #3 . . . . 1.95
29 thru 37 . . . . @1.95
Special #1 . . . . 4.00

WHITE FANG
Walt Disney
1 Movie Adapt. 5.95

WHITE TRASH
Tundra
1 I:Elvis & Dean 3.95
2 Trip to Las Vegas contd. 3.95
3 V:Purple Heart Brigade 3.95

WHODUNNIT
Eclipse
1 DSp,A:Jay Endicott 2.00
2 DSp,'Who Slew Kangaroo?' . . . 2.00
3 DSp,'Who Offed Henry Croft' . . 2.00

WILD ANIMALS
Pacific
1 . . . . 1.50

WILD BILL PECOS
AC Comics
1 . . . . 3.50

WILDFIRE
Zion Comics
1 thru 3 V:Mr. Reeves 1.95
4 Lord D'Rune 1.95

WILD FRONTIER
Charlton Comics
October, 1955
1 Davy Crockett 25.00
2 same 15.00
3 same 15.00
4 same 15.00
5 same 15.00
6 same 15.00
7 O:Cheyenne Kid 15.00
Becomes:
CHEYENNE KID
8 . . . . 20.00
9 . . . . 10.00
10 . . . . 42.00
11 . . . . 42.00
12 . . . . 42.00
13 . . . . 26.00
14 . . . . 26.00
15 . . . . 10.00
16 . . . . 10.00
17 . . . . 10.00
18 . . . . 26.00
19 . . . . 10.00
20 . . . . 13.00
21 . . . . 13.00
22 . . . . 13.00
23 . . . . 6.00
24 . . . . 6.00
25 . . . . 13.00
26 . . . . 8.00
27 . . . . 6.00
28 . . . . 6.00
29 . . . . 6.00
30 . . . . 8.00
31 thru 59 . . . . @2.50
60 thru 98 . . . . @1.00

99 November, 1973 . . . . 1.00

WILD WEST C.O.W.-
BOYS OF MOO MESA
Archie
1 Based on TV cartoon 1.25
2 Cody kidnapped 1.25
3 Law of the Year Parade,
last issue 1.25
(Regular series)
1 Valley o/t Thunder Lizard 1.25
2 Plains, Trains & Dirty Deals . . . 1.25

WILD WILD WEST
Millenium
1 . . . . 2.95
2 thru 4 . . . . @2.95

WILL EISNER'S
3-D CLASSICS
Kitchen Sink
WE art, w/glasses (1985) 2.00

WIN A PRIZE COMICS
Charlton Comics
February, 1955
1 S&K,Edgar Allen adapt. 200.00
2 S&K 150.00
Becomes:
TIMMY THE
TIMID GHOST
3 . . . . 30.00
4 . . . . 20.00
5 . . . . 20.00
6 . . . . 10.00
7 . . . . 10.00
8 . . . . 10.00
9 . . . . 10.00
10 . . . . 10.00
11 . . . . 20.00
12 . . . . 20.00
13 thru 20 . . . . @5.00
21 thru 44 . . . . @4.00
45 1966 . . . . 2.00

WINDRAGE
1 and 2 . . . . @1.25

WINTERWORLD
Eclipse
1 JZ,I:Scully, Wynn 1.75
2 JZ,V:Slave Farmers 1.75
3 JZ,V:Slave Farmers 1.75

WIREHEADS
Fleetway
1 . . . . 2.95

WITCHING HOUR
Millenium/Comico
1 Anne Rice adaptation 2.50
2 & 3 . . . . 2.50

WOODY WOODPECKER
Harvey
1 thru 5 . . . . 1.25

Woody Woodpecker #1
© Harvey Publications

WORLD OF WOOD
Eclipse
1 WW 1.75
2 WW,DSt(i) 1.75
3 WW 1.75
4 WW 1.75

WYATT EARP
Dell Publishing Co.
November, 1957
1 . . . . 30.00
2 . . . . 22.00
3 . . . . 20.00
4 . . . . 20.00
5 . . . . 20.00
6 . . . . 20.00
7 . . . . 20.00
8 . . . . 20.00
9 . . . . 20.00
10 . . . . 20.00
11 . . . . 15.00
12 . . . . 15.00
13 . . . . 15.00

XANADU
Eclipse
1 . . . . 2.00

XENYA
Sanctuary Press
1 thru 3 Hildebrandt Brothers . . . 2.95

XENO MAN
1 . . . . 1.75

XENOTECH
Mirage
1 I:Xenotech 2.75
2 . . . . 2.75
3 w/2 card strip 2.75

X-FILES
Topps
1 From Fox TV Series 15.00

---

2 Aliens Killing Witnesses 8.00
3 The Return 8.00
4 Firebird,pt.1 . . . . 2.50
5 Firebird,pt.2 . . . . 2.50

XIMOS: VIOLENT PAST
Triumphant
1 JnR(s) 2.50
2 JnR(s) 2.50

XL
1 . . . . 1.25

YAKKY DOODLE & CHOPPER
Gold Key
December, 1962
1 . . . . 35.00

YIN FEI
5 . . . . 1.80
6 thru 11 . . . . @2.00

YOGI BEAR
Dell
Feb.-March, 1962
#1 thru #6, See Dell Four Color
7 thru 9 . . . . 30.00
Gold Key
10 . . . . 30.00
11 Jellystone Follies 30.00
12 . . . . 20.00
13 Surprise Party 30.00
14 thru 19 . . . . @20.00
20 thru 29 . . . . @14.00
30 thru 42 . . . . @10.00

YOGI BEAR
Charlton Comics
November, 1970
1 . . . . 25.00
2 thru 10 . . . . @15.00
11 thru 34 . . . . 10.00
35 January, 1976 . . . . 10.00

YOSEMITE SAM
Gold Key/Whitman
December, 1970
1 . . . . 15.00
2 thru 10 . . . . @6.00
11 thru 40 . . . . @3.00
41 thru 80 . . . . @2.00
81 February, 1984 . . . . 2.00

ZEN INTERGALACTIC NINJA
Archie
1 Rumble in the Rain Forest
  prequel,inc.poster 1.25
2 Rumble in Rain Forest #1 . . . . 1.25
3 Rumble in Rain Forest #2 . . . . 1.25
Entity Comics
0 Chromium (c),JaL(c) 3.75
1 Joe Orbeta 2.50
2 Deluxe Edition w/card 4.95
2a V:Rawhead 2.50

ZENITH PHASE II
Fleetway
1 thru 2 . . . . 1.95

Zero Patrol #1 © Continuity Comics

ZERO PATROL
Continuity
1 EM,NA,O&I:Megalith 2.50
2 EM,NA 1.95
3 EM,NA,I:Shaman 1.95
4 EM,NA 1.95
5 EM 1.95
6 thru 8 EM . . . . @2.00

ZERO TOLERANCE
First
1 TV 3.50
2 TV 3.00
3 TV 2.25
4 TV 2.25

Zooniverse #1 © Eclipse

ZOONIVERSE
Eclipse
1 I:Kren Patrol,wrap-around(c) . . 1.25
2 . . . . 1.25

3 . . . . 1.25
4 V:Wedge City 1.25
5 Spak vs. Agent Ty-rote 1.25
6 last issue 1.25

ZORRO
Topps
0 BSf(c),DMG(s), came bagged with
  Jurassic Park Raptor #1 and
  Teenagents #4 . . . . 1.00
1 DMG(s),V:Machete 2.50
2 DMG(s) 2.50
3 DMG(s) I:Lady Rawhide 9.00
4 MGr(c),DMG(s),V:Moonstalker . 2.50
5 . . . . 2.50
6 and 7 A:Lady Rawhide 3.50
8 thru 11 . . . . @2.50

ZOT
Eclipse
1 . . . . 6.00
2 . . . . 3.00
3 . . . . 3.00
4 . . . . 3.00
5 . . . . 3.00
6 . . . . 2.00
7 . . . . 2.50
8 . . . . 2.00
9 . . . . 2.50
10 . . . . 2.00
10a B&W 6.00
10b 2nd printing 25
Original Zot! Book 1 . . . . 9.95
  (Changed to B & W)

A1 #2 © Atomeka Press

A1
Atomeka Press
1 BWs,A:Flaming Carrot,Mr.X.	10.00
2 BWs	9.75
3	9.75
4	5.95
5	6.95
6a	4.95

AARDWOLF
Aardwolf
1 DC,GM(c)	2.95
1a Certificate ed. signed	15.95
2 World Toughest Milkman	2.95
3 R.Block(s),O:Aardwolf	2.95

A.B.C. WARRIORS
Fleetway/Quality
1 thru 8	@1.95

ABUNDI SPECIAL
1	2.50

AC ANNUAL
Aircel
1	3.95
2 Based on 1940's heroes	5.00
3 F:GoldenAge Heroes	3.50
4 F:Sentinels of Justice	3.95

ACE COMICS PRESENTS
1 thru 7	@1.75

ACES
Eclipse
1 thru 5, mag. size	@2.95

ACME
Fandom House
1 thru 9	@1.95

ACTION FORCE
1	1.75

ADAM AND EVE
Bam
1	3.00
2 thru 10	@1.50

ADAM LOGAN
1	1.50

ADOLESCENT RADIOACTIVE BLACK-BELT HAMSTERS
Eclipse
1 I:Bruce,Chuck,Jackie,Clint	2.50
1a 2nd printing	2.00
2 A parody of a parody	2.00
3 I:Bad Gerbil	2.00
4 A:Heap (3-D),Abusement Park	1.50
5 Abusement Park #2	1.50
6 SK,Abusement Park #3	2.00
7 SK,V:Toe-Jam Monsters	2.00
8 SK	2.00
9 All-Jam last issue	2.00

[2nd Series]
Parody Press
1	2.50
2 Hamsters Go Hollywood	2.50

ADVENT
1	1.75

ADVENTURES INTO THE UNKNOWN
A Plus Comics
1 AW	2.95
2 AW	2.95
3 AW	2.95
Halloween Spec. Reps. Charlton & American Comics GroupHorror	2.50

ADVENTURES OF B.O.C.
1	1.50
2	1.50
3	1.50

ADVENTURERS
Aircel/Adventure Publ.
0 Origin Issue	2.50
1 with Skeleton	8.00
1a Revised cover	3.00
1b 2nd printing	2.00
2 Peter Hsu (c)	2.50
3 Peter Hsu (c)	2.50
4 Peter Hsu (c)	2.00
5 Peter Hsu (c)	2.00
6 Peter Hsu (c)	2.00
7	2.00
8	2.00
9	2.00

ADVENTURERS BOOK II
Adventure Publ.
0 O:Man Gods	1.95
1	1.95
2 thru 9	@1.95

ADVENTURERS BOOK III
1A Lim.(c)Ian McCaig	2.25
1B Reg.(c)Mitch Foust	2.25
2 thru 6	@2.25

ADVENTURES IN MYSTWOOD
1	3.00
2 and 3	@2.00

ADVENTURES OF CHRISSY CLAWS, THE
Heroic
1 thru 2	@3.25

Adventures of Chuk the Barbaric #1 © White Wolf

ADVENTURES OF CHUK THE BARBARIC
White Wolf
1	1.25

ADVENTURES OF LUTHER ARKWRIGHT
Valkyrie Press
1	2.25
2	2.25
3	2.25
4	2.25
5	2.25
6	2.25
7	2.25
8	2.25
9	2.25

See Also: Dark Horse seciton

ADVENTURES OF MR. CREAMPUFF
1	1.75

ADVENTURES OF MR. PYRIDINE
Fantagraphics
1	2.25

ADVENTURES OF THE AEROBIC DUO
Lost Cause Productions
1 thru 3	@2.25
4 Gopher Quest	2.25

ADVENTURES OF THEOWN
Pyramid
1 thru 3, Limited series ..... @1.75

AESOP'S FABLES
Fantagraphics
1 Selection of Fables 2.25
2 Selection of Fables 2.25
3 inc. Boy who cried wolf 2.25

AFTERMATH
1 Type a, Partial map 4.50
1a Type b, Full map 2.00

AGENT ORANGE
1 .... 1.75
2 .... 1.75
3 .... 1.75

AGENT UNKNOWN
Renegade
1 thru 3 .... @2.00

AGE OF HEROES
1 .... 1.25
2 .... 1.25
3 .... 1.25

AIRCEL
1 Graphic Novel year 1 .... 6.95

AIRFIGHTERS CLASSICS
Eclipse
1 O:Airboy,rep.Air Fighters#2 .. 3.00
2 rep.Old Airboy appearances .. 3.00
3 thru 6 .... @3.95

AIRMEN
Mansion Comics
1 I:Airmen 2.50

AIRWAVES
Caliber
1 Radio Security 2.50
2 A:Paisley,Ganja 2.50
3 Formation of Rebel Alliance ... 2.50
4 Big Annie,Pt. 1 .... 2.50
5 Big Annie, Pt 2 .... 2.50

A.K.A.: OUTCAST
1 .... 1.75

ALBEDO
Thoughts & Images
0 white cover, yellow drawing table
  Blade Runner 150.00
0a white(c) 85.00
0b blue(c),1st ptg 52.00
0c blue(c),2nd ptg 35.00
0d blue(c),3rd ptg 6.00
0e Photo(c),4th ptg.,inc.
  extra pages 4.00
1 SS,I:Nilson Groundthumper,
  dull red cover 44.00
1a bright red cover 40.00
2 SS,I:Usagi Yojimbo 40.00
3 SS,Erma, Usagi 7.00
4 SS,Usagi 9.00
5 Nelson Groundthumper 8.00

Albedo #5 © Thoughts & Images

6 Erma, High Orbit 7.00
7 .... 4.00
8 Erna Feldna 3.00
9 High Orbit,Harvest Venture .. 2.00
10 .... 2.00
11 .... 2.00
12 .... 2.00
13 .... 2.00
14 .... 2.00

ALBEDO VOL II
Antartic Press
1 New Erma Story 2.50
2 E.D.F. HQ 2.50
3 Birth of Erma's Child 2.50
4 Non action issue 2.50
5 The Outworlds 2.50
6 War preparations 2.50
7 Ekosiak in Anarchy 2.50
8 EDF High Command 2.50

ALIEN DUCKLING
1 .... 2.00
2 thru 4 .... @1.75

ALIEN ENCOUNTERS
Fantagor
1 .... 1.25

ALIEN FIRE
Kitchen Sink Press
1 Eric Vincent art (1987) 3.50
2 Eric Vincent art 2.50
3 Eric Vincent art 2.00

ALIEN MUTANT WAR
1 .... 2.25

ALIEN NATION: A BREED APART
Adventure Comics
1 .... 3.00
2 .... 2.50
3 The 'Vampires' Busted 2.50

4 Final Issue 2.50

ALIEN NATION: THE FIRSTCOMERS
Adventure Comics
1 New Mini-series 2.50
2 Assassin 2.50
3 Search for Saucer 2.50
4 Final Issue 2.50

ALIEN NATION: PUBLIC ENEMY
Adventure Comics
1 'Before the Fall' 2.50
2 Earth & Wehlnistrata 2.50
3 Killer on the Loose 2.50

ALIEN NATION: THE SKIN TRADE
Adventure Comics
1 'Case of the Missing Milksop' .. 2.50
2 'To Live And Die in L.A' 2.50
3 A:Dr. Jekyll 2.50
4 D.Methoraphan Exposed 2.50

Alien Nation: The Spartans #2
© Adventure Comics

ALIEN NATION: THE SPARTANS
Adventure Comics
1 JT/DPo,Yellow wrap 4.00
1a JT/DPo,Green wrap 4.00
1b JT/DPo,Pink wrap 4.00
1c JT/DPo,blue wrap 4.00
1d LTD collectors edition 8.00
2 JT,A:Ruth Lawrence 2.50
3 JT/SM,Spartans 2.50
4 JT/SM,conclusion 2.50

ALIEN4 STRIKE FORCE
1 .... 1.95

ALL-PRO SPORTS
All Pro Sports
1 Unauthorized Bio-Bo Jackson . 2.50
2 Unauthorized Bio-Joe Montana 2.50

ALPHA PREDATOR
1 . . . . 2.00

ALTERNATE HEROES
Prelude Graphics
1 and 2 . . . . @1.95

AMAZING COMICS
Premium
1 thru 9 . . . . @1.95

AMAZING CYNICALMAN
Eclipse
1 . . . . 1.50

AMAZING WAHZOO
1 RB 2.50
2 . . . . 1.75
3 . . . . 1.75

AMAZON WARRIORS
1 rep. 2.50

AMAZONS, THE
1 . . . . 2.95

AMERICAN PRIMITIVE
Spec. #1 . . . . 2.50

AMERICAN SPLENDOR
13 thru 15 . . . . @3.25
16 . . . . 3.95

AMUSING STORIES
Blackthorne
1 thru 3 . . . . @2.00

ANGEL OF DEATH
Innovation
1 thru 4 . . . . @2.25

ANGRY SHADOWS
1 . . . . 4.95

ANIMERICA
(Viz Comics)
1 F:Bubble Gum Crisis 2.95
2 F:Bubble Gum Crisis 2.95
3 F:Bubble Gum Crisis 2.95

ANIVERSE, THE
1 thru 3 . . . . @1.95

ANT BOY
1 . . . . 1.75
1a 2nd Printing 1.75
2 . . . . 1.75

ANTARES CIRCLE
Antarctic Press
1 . . . . 1.75
2 . . . . 1.75

A-OK
Antarctic Press
1 Ninja H.S. spin-off series 2.50
2 F:Paul,Moniko,James 2.50
3 Confrontation 2.50
4 . . . . 2.50

A-OK #3 ©Antarctic Press

APACHE DICK
1 thru 4 . . . . @2.25

APE CITY
Adventure Comics
1 Monkey Business 3.00
2 thru 4 . . . . @2.50

APEX PROJECT
1 . . . . 1.00

APPLESEED
Eclipse
1 MSh,rep. Japanese comic . . . 10.00
2 MSh,arrival in Olympus City . . . 5.00
3 MSh,Olympus City politics 3.00
4 MSh,V:Director 3.00
5 MSh,Deunan vs. Chiffon 3.00
Book Two
1 MSh,AAd(c),Olympus City 3.50
2 MSh,AAd(c),Hitomi vs.EswatUnit 3.00
3 MSh,AAd(c),Deunan vs.Gaia . . 3.00
4 MSh,AAd(c),V:Robot Spiders . . 3.00
5 MSh,AAd(c),Hitome vs.Gaia . . 3.00
Book Three
1 MSh,Brigreos vs.Biodroid 5.00
2 MSh,V:Cuban Navy 3.00
3 MSh,'Benandanti' 3.00
4 MSh,V:Renegade biodroid 3.00
5 . . . . 3.00
Book Four
1 MSh,V:Munma Terrorists 3.50
2 MSh,V:Drug-crazed Munma . . . 3.50
3 MSh,V:Munma Drug Addicts . . 3.50
4 MSh,Deunan vs. Pani 3.50

APPLESEED DATABOOK
Dark-Horse
1 . . . . 3.50
2 . . . . 3.50

ARAMIS WEEKLY
1 mini-series 1.95
2 . . . . 1.95
3 . . . . 1.95

AREA 88
Eclipse
1 I:Shin Kazama 3.00
1a 2nd printing 1.50
2 Dangerous Mission 2.00
2a 2nd printing 1.50
3 O:Shin,Paris '78 . . . . 2.00
4 thru 8 . . . . @2.00
9 thru 39 . . . . @1.50
40 . . . . 1.75
41 . . . . 1.75
42 . . . . 2.00

ARGONAUTS
Eternity
1 thru 5 . . . . @1.95

ARGOSY
Caliber
1 'Walker' vs. Myth Beasts 2.50

ARIK KHAN
A Plus Comics
1 I:Arik Khan 2.50
2 . . . . 2.50

ARISTOCRATIC EXTRA-TERRESTRIAL TIME-TRAVELING THIEVES
Fictioneer Books
1 V:IRS 3.00
2 V:Realty 1.75
3 V:MDM 1.75
4 thru 12 . . . . @1.75

A.R.M.
Adventure Comics
1 Larry Niven adapt.
   Death by Ecstasy,pt.1 . . . . . . 2.50
2 Death by Ecstasy,pt.2 . . . . . . 2.50
3 Death by Ecstasy,pt.3 . . . . . . 2.50

ARMADILLO ANTHOLOGY
1 & 2 . . . . @1.50

ARSENAL
SOL
1 . . . . 2.00

ART D'ECCO
FAN
1 . . . . 2.50

ARTHUR: KING OF BRITAIN
Tome Press
1 Saga of King Arthur Chronicled
   by Geoffrey of Monmouth 2.95

ASHES
Caliber
1 thru 5 . . . . @2.50

ASSASSINETTE
Pocket Change Comics
1 thru 3 . . . . @2.50
4 Psychic Realm 2.50
5 V:Nemesis 2.50

ASTONISH
1 thru 4 . . . . @1.25

ASTRON
1 . . . . 2.00

ASYLUM
1 . . . . 1.75
2 thru 4 . . . . @1.95

ATOMIC COMICS
1 . . . . 1.50
Becomes: MARK I

ATOMIC MAN
1 . . . . 3.00
2 . . . . 2.00
3 . . . . 1.75

ATOMIC MOUSE
A Plus Comics
1 A:Atomic Bunny 2.50

A TRAVELLER'S TALE
Antarctic Press
1 I:Goshin the Traveller 2.50
2 . . . . 2.50

ATTACK OF THE MUTANT MONSTERS
A Plus Comics
1 SD,rep.Gorgo(Kegor) 2.50

AV IN 3D
Aardvark–Vanaheim
1 Color,A:FlamingCarot 6.00

AVENUE X
Innovation
1 Based on NY radio drama 2.50

AWESOME COMICS
1 thru 3 . . . . @2.00

B-Movie Presents #3 © B-Movie Comics

B-MOVIE PRESENTS
B-Movie Comics
1 . . . . 1.70
2 . . . . 1.70
3 Tasma, Queen of the Jungle . . 1.70
4 . . . . 1.70

BACK TO BACK HORROR SPECIAL
1 . . . . 1.50

BAD AXE
1 thru 3 . . . . @2.25

BADEBIKER
1 . . . . 2.50
2 . . . . 2.00
3 thru 5 . . . . @1.50

BAD MOON
1 . . . . 3.00

BAD NEWS
3 . . . . 2.95

BAKER STREET
(Prev. color)
Caliber
3 . . . . 3.25
4 . . . . 1.95
5 Children of the Night Pt.1 . . . . 1.95
6 Children of the Night Pt.2 . . . . 1.95
7 Children of the Night Pt.3 . . . . 2.50
8 Children of the Night Pt.4 . . . . 2.50
9 Children of the Night Pt.5 . . . . 2.50
10 Children of the Night Pt.6 . . . . 2.50

BAKER ST.: GRAPHITTI
Caliber
1 'Elemenary, My Dear' 2.50

BALANCE OF POWER
MU Press
1 thru 4 . . . . @2.50

BANETOWN
1 . . . . 1.50

BANYON OF THE HIGH FORTRESS
1 . . . . 1.95

BAOH
Viz
1 thru 8 . . . . @2.95

BARABBAS
Slave Labor
1 . . . . 4.50
2 thru 4 . . . . @1.50

BARBARIC FANTASY
1 . . . . 1.95
2 . . . . 1.95

BARBARIC TALES
Pyramid
1 . . . . 3.00
2 and 3 . . . . @1.70

BARNEY THE INVISIBLE TURTLE
1 . . . . 1.95

BASEBALL SUPERSTARS
Revolutionary
1 Nolan Ryan 2.50

BAT
1 . . . . 2.25

BATHING MACHINE
1 . . . . 2.50
2 . . . . 2.50
3 . . . . 2.50
4 . . . . 1.50

BATTLE ANGEL ALITA
Viz
1 I:Daisuka,Alita 2.75
2 Alita becomes warrior 2.75
3 A:Daiuke,V:Cyborg 2.75
4 Alita/Cyborg,A:Makaku 2.75
5 The Bounty Hunters Bar 2.75
6 Confrontation 2.75
7 Underground Sewers,A:Fang . . 2.75

BATTLE ANGEL ALITA II
Viz
1 V:Monsters 2.75
2 F:Alita 2.75
Book II
1 V:Zapan 2.95
2 V:Zapan 2.95
3 F:Ido 2.75
4 V:Zapan 2.75
5 V:Zapan 2.75

BATTLE ARMOR
Eternity
1 thru 4 . . . . @1.95

BATTLE AXE
1 . . . . 2.50
2 . . . . 2.95

BATTLE BEASTS
Blackthorne
1 thru 4 . . . . @1.50

BATTLE GROUP PEIPER
Caliber
1 Bio S.S.Lt.Col Peiper 2.95

BATTLETECH
(Prev. Color)
7 thru 12 . . . . @1.75
Ann.#1 . . . . 4.50

BATTLE TO DEATH
1 . . . . 1.80
2 . . . . 1.80
3 . . . . 1.80

BATTRON
NEC
1 WWII story 2.75
2 WWII contd. 2.75

BEACH PARTY
1 .... 2.50

BEAST WARRIOR OF SHAOLIN
1 thru 5 .... @1.95

THE BEATLES EXPERIENCE
Revolutionary
1 Beatles 1960's 3.00
2 Beatles 1964-1966 .... 2.50
3 .... 2.50
4 Abbey Road, Let it be 2.50
5 The Solo Years 2.50
6 Paul McCartney & Wings 2.50
7 The Murder of John Lennon .. 2.50
8 To 1992, final issue 2.50

BECK AND CAUL
Gauntlet
1 I:Beck and Caul 2.95
2 thru 6 .... @2.95

BELLS OF KONGUR
1 .... 2.25

Berzerker #6 © Gauntlet (Caliber)

BERZERKER
Gauntlet (Caliber)
1 thru 6 .... @2.95

BESET BY DEMONS
Tundra
1 Short stories by M.McLester .. 3.50

BEYOND HUMAN
Battlezone Comics
0 .... 3.50

BEYOND MARS
Blackthorne
1 thru 5 .... @2.00

BIG BLACK KISS
Vortex
3 HC some color 3.75

BIG EDSEL BAND
1 FMc 1.75

BIG NUMBERS
1 BSz 6.00
2 BSz 5.50

BIG PRIZE
Eternity
1 .... 1.95

BILL AND MELVIN
Newcomers Publishing
1 O:Bill & Melvin 2.95

BILLY NGUYEN PRIVATE EYE
1 .... 2.00
1a 2nd Printing 2.00
2 thru 6 .... @2.00

BIO-BOOSTER ARMOR GUYVER
Viz
Part II
1 thru 3 F:Sho .... @2.75
4 V:Enzyme II 2.75
5 Sho VS Enzyme II 2.75
6 Final Issue 2.75
Part III
1 Sho Unconscious 2.75

BIRTHRIGHT
1 thru 3 .... @2.00

BIZARRE HEROES
Kitchen Sink
1 DonSimpson art,parody (1990) . 2.50

BLACK BOW
1 .... 1.95

[Original] BLACK CAT
4 rep. 2.00
5 A:Ted Parrish 2.00
6 50th Anniv. Issue 2.00
7 rep. 2.00

BLACK CROSS
Spec #1 .... 2.00
1a 2nd Print 1.75

BLACKENED
Enigma
1 V:Killing Machine 2.95
2 V:Killing Machine 2.95
3 Flaming Altar 2.95

BLACK KISS
Vortex
1 HC,Adult 7.00
1a 2nd printing 4.00
1b 3rd printing 1.25
2 HC 6.00
2a 2nd printing 3.00

3 HC 5.00
4 HC 4.00
5 HC 2.00
6 HC 2.00
7 thru 12 HC .... @1.50

BLACK MAGIC
1 .... 3.50
2 thru 4 .... @2.75

BLACKMASK
Eastern Comics
1 thru 6 .... @1.75

BLACK MOON
1 .... 2.50
2 thru 4 .... @1.50
5 .... 2.00

BLACK PHANTOM
1 .... 2.50

BLACK SCORPION
Special Studio
1 Knight of Justice 2.75
2 A Game for Old Men 2.75
3 Blackmailer's Auction 2.75

BLACK STAR
1 thru 4 .... @1.80

BLACKTHORNE 3 in 1
1 and 2 .... @2.00

BLACK ZEPPLIN
Renegade
1 .... 2.50
2 thru 6 .... @2.00

BLADE OF SHURIKEN
Eternity
1 thru 8 .... @1.95

BLADESMAN
1 .... 2.00

BLANDMAN
Eclipse
1 Sandman parody 2.50

BLAZING WESTERN
1 rep. 2.50

BLIND FEAR
Eternity
1 thru 4 .... @1.95

BLIP AND THE C CADS
1 .... 1.95

BLOOD 'N' GUTS
Aircel
1 .... 2.50
2 .... 2.50
3 .... 2.50

BLOODBROTHERS
Eternity
1 thru 4 .... @1.95

Blood is the Harvest #1 © Eclipse

BLOOD IS THE HARVEST
Eclipse
1 I:Nikita,Milo	4.50
2 V:M'Raud D:Nikita?	2.50
3 Milo captured	2.50
4 F:Nikita/Milo	2.50

BLOOD JUNKIES
Eternity
1 Vampires on Capitol Hill	2.50
2 final issue	2.50

BLOOD OF DRACULA
1 thru 7	@1.75
8 thru 14	@1.95
15 +Record&Mask	3.50
16	1.95
17	2.25

BLOOD OF INNOCENT
Warp Graphics
1 thru 4	@2.50

BLOODSHED
Damage
1 Little Brother	2.95
2 Little Brother	2.95

BLOODWING
Eternity
1 thru 5	@1.95

BLOODY BOHES & BLACK-EYED PEAS
Galaxy
1	2.00

BOB POWELL'S TIMELESS TALES
Eclipse
1	2.00

BODY COUNT
1	2.25
2 and 3	@1.95

4	2.25

BOFFO LAFFS
1 1st hologram	4.00
2 thru 7	@2.00

BOGIE MAN: CHINATOON
Atomeka
1 I:Francis Claine	2.95
2 F:Bogie Man	2.95
3 thr 4 F:Bogie Man	2.95

BOGIE MAN: MANHATTEN PROJECT
Apocalypse
One Shot. D.Quale Assassination Plot	3.95

BOMARC: GUARDIANS OF THE I.F.S. ZONE
Spec.	1.95
Spec. 2	1.95

BONE
Cartoon Books
1 I:Bone	220.00
1a 2nd printing	50.00
1b 3rd Printing	20.00
1c 4th printing	7.00
1d thru 1f 5th-7th printing	@4.00
2	110.00
2a 2nd printing	20.00
2b thru 2e 3rd-6th printing	@3.00
3	85.00
3a 2nd printing	10.00
3b thru 3d 3rd-5th printing	@3.00
4	55.00
4a thru 4c 2nd-4th printing	@3.00
5	45.00
5a thru 5c 2nd-4th printing	@3.00
6	40.00
6a thru 6c 2nd-4th printing	@3.00
7	30.00
7a,7b 2nd,3rd printing	@3.00
8	27.00
8a,8b 2nd,3rd printing	@4.00
9	12.00
9a 2nd printing	4.00
10	8.00
11	6.00
12	4.00
13	3.25
14 thru 17	@2.95
18 V:Bar owner	2.95
19 F:Phoney Bone	2.95
TPB rep.#1-4	14.00

BONES
1 thru 4	@1.95

BONESHAKER
Caliber Press
1 Suicidal Wrestler	3.50

BOOGIE MAN
1 thru 4	@1.95

BOOK OF THE TAROT
Caliber
1 History/Development o/t Tarot	3.95

BORDER GUARD
1	2.00
2	2.00

BORDER WORLDS
Kitchen Sink
1 adult	2.00
2 thru 7	@2.00

BORDER WORLDS: MAROONED
1	2.00

BORIS' ADVENTURE MAGAZINE
1 and 2	@2.00

BORIS THE BEAR
Nikotat
1–12: See Dark Horse section	
13 thru 29	@2.00
30 thru 34	@2.50

BORN TO BE WILD
Eclipse
one shot. Benefit P.E.T.A.	10.95

BORN TO KILL
Aircel
1	2.50
2	2.50
3	2.50

BOSTON BOMBERS
Caliber
1	1.95
2	2.50

BOUNTY
1 'Bounty,"Navarro' Pt.1	2.50
2 'Bounty,"Navarro' Pt.2	2.50
3 'Bounty,"Navarro' Pt.3	2.50

BOY AND HIS BOT
1	2.00

BRAT PACK
King Hell Publications
1	7.00
1a 2nd printing	3.50
2 thru 4	@4.25
5	4.00
Brat Pack Collection	13.00

BRICKMAN
1	2.00

BRIKHAUSS
1	1.75

BRINGERS
Blackthorne
1	3.50

BROID
Eternity
1 thru 4	@2.25

BRONX
Aircel
1 A.Saichann Short Stories 2.50
2 to 3 .... @2.50

BRONX
Aircel
Reprint 2.95

BROTHER MAN
New City Comics
1 .... 5.00
1a...................... 2.00
2 thru 7 .... @2.00

Bruce Jones: Outer Edge #1
© Innovation

BRUCE JONES: OUTER EDGE
Innovation
1 All reprints 2.00

BRUCE JONES: RAZORS EDGE
Innovation
1 All reprints 2.50

BRUTE
1 .... 2.00

BRYMWYCK THE IMP
Planet X Productions
1 .... 1.50

BUCE-N-GAR
RAK
1 .... 1.75
2 .... 1.75
3 .... 1.75

BUCK GODOT
Palliard Press
1 I:Buck Godot 2.95

BUCKWHEAT
1 .... 2.00
2 .... 2.00

BUFFALO WINGS
Antarctic Press
1 .... 2.50

BUG
Planet X Productions
1 .... 1.50
2 .... 1.50

BULLET CROW
Eclipse
1 .... 2.00
2 .... 2.00

BUMBERCOMIC
1 .... 1.00
2 .... 1.00

BURNING KISS
1 with poster 4.95

BUSHIDO
Eternity
1 thru 6 .... @1.95

BUSHIDO BLADE OF ZATSICHI WALRUS
1 .... 3.00
2 .... 2.00

BUZZ
Kitchen Sink
1 Mark Landman (c) (1990) 2.95
2 Mark Landman (c) 2.95
3 Mark Landman (c) (1991) 2.95

CABLE TV
Parody Press
1 Cable Satire 2.50

CAGES
8 Dave McKean art (1993) 3.95

CALIBER PRESENTS
(Prev. High Caliber)
1 TV,I:Crow 85.00
2 Deadworld 6.00
3 Realm 3.00
4 Baker Street 3.00
5 TV,Heart of Darkness,
　Fugitive 2.50
6 TV,Heart of Darkness,
　Fugitive 2.50
7 TV,Heart of Darkness,
　Dragonfeast 2.50
8 TV,Cuda,Fugitive 2.50
9 Baker Street,Sting Inc. 2.00
10 Fugitive, The Edge 2.50
11 Ashes,Random Thoughts 2.50
12 Fugitive,Random Thoughts ... 2.50
13 Random Thoughts,Synergist . 2.50
14 Random Thoughts,Fugitive ... 2.50
15 Random Thoughts,Fringe 2.50
16 Fugitive, The Verdict 3.50
17 Deadworld, The Verdict 3.50
18 Orlak,The Verdict 3.50

---

19 Taken Under,Go-Man 3.50
20 The Verdict,Go-Man 3.50
21 The Verdict,Go-Man 3.50
22 The Verdict,Go-Man 3.50
23 Go-Man,Heat Seeker 3.50
24 Heat Seeker,MacktheKnife ... 3.50
Christmas Spec A:Crow,Deadworld
　Realm,Baker Street 650.00
Summer Spec. inc. the Silencers,
　Swords of Shar-Pei
　(preludes) 3.95

CALIBER PRESENTS
(One Shots)
Hybrid 2.50

CALIFORNIA GIRLS
Eclipse
1 thru 8 .... @2.00

CALIGARI 2050
1 Gothic Horror 2.25
2 Gothic Horror 2.25

CAMELOT ETERNAL
Caliber
1 .... 3.00
2 .... 2.50
3 .... 2.50
4 .... 2.50
5 Mordred Escapes 2.50
6 MorganLeFay returns from dead 2.50
7 Revenge of Morgan 2.50
8 Launcelot flees Camelot 2.50

CANADIAN NINJA
1 .... 1.50
2 .... 1.50

CAPT. CONFEDERACY
1 adult 8.00
2 .... 2.50
3 .... 2.00
4 .... 2.00
4a 1.50
5 thru 8 .... @2.00
9 thru 11 .... @1.75
12 .... 1.95

CAPT. CULT
1 .... 2.00

CAPT. ELECTRON
Brick Computers Inc.
1 .... 2.00
2 .... 2.25

CAPTAIN HARLOCK
Eternity
1 .... 3.00
1a 2nd printing 2.50
2 .... 2.50
3 .... 2.50
4 thru 13 .... @1.95
Christmas special 2.50

CAPTAIN HARLOCK DEATHSHADOW RISING
Eternity
1 .... 2.75
2 .... 2.50

---

3 .... 2.25
4 Harlock/Nevich Truce 2.25
5 Reunited with Arcadia Crew ... 2.25
6 .... 2.95

CAPTAIN HARLOCK:
THE MACHINE PEOPLE
Eternity
1 O:Captain Harlock 2.50

CAPTAIN JACK
Fantagraphics
1 .... 4.00
2 .... 2.50
3 .... 2.50
4 thru 12 .... @2.00

CAPT. OBLIVION
1 .... 1.95

CAPTAIN PHIL
Steel Dragon
1 .... 1.50

CAPTAIN SENTINEL
1 .... 2.00

CAPTAIN STERNN:
RUNNING OUT OF TIME
Kitchen Sink
1 BWr(c) (1993) 4.95
2 BWr(c) 4.95
3 BWr(c) (1994) 4.95
4 BWr(c) 4.95

CAPTAIN THUNDER
AND BLUE BOLT
Hero Graphics
1 New stories 3.50
2 Hard Targets 3.50

CARNIGE
1 .... 1.95
2 .... 1.95

CARTOON HISTORY OF
THE UNIVERSE
Rip Off Press
1 Gonick art 2.50
2 Sticks & Stones 2.50
3 River Realms 2.50
4 Old Testament 2.50
5 Brains & Bronze 2.50
6 These Athenians 2.50
7 All about Athens 2.50

CARTUNE LAND
Magic Carpet Comics
1 .... 1.50

CASES OF
SHERLOCK HOLMES
Renegade
1 thru 18 .... @2.00
19 .... 2.25

CASEY LACE
1 .... 1.50

Cat & Mouse #7 © Aircel

CAT & MOUSE
Aircel
1 .... 4.00
2 .... 3.00
3 thru 8 .... @2.25
9 Cat Reveals Identity 2.25
10 Tooth & Nail 2.25
11 Tooth & Nail 2.25
12 Tooth & Nail, Demon 2.25
13 'Good Times, Bad Times' ... 2.25
14 Mouse Alone 2.25
15 Champion ID revealed 2.25
16 Jerry Critically Ill 2.25
17 Kunoichi vs. Tooth 2.25
18 Search for Organ Donor ... 2.25
Graphic Novel 9.95

CAT CLAW
Eternity
1 O:Cat Claw 2.75
1a 2nd printing 2.50
2 thru 9 .... @2.50

CATFIGHT
Lightning Comics
1 V:Prince Nightmare 2.75
1a Gold Edition 5.75

CAT-KIND
1 .... 2.00

CAT MAN
AC Comics
Ashcan #1 I:Catman & Kitten ... 5.95

CELESTIAL MECHANICS
Innovation
1 .... 2.25
2 .... 2.25
3 .... 2.25

CEMENT SHOOZ
Horse Feathers
1 with color pin-up 2.50

CENOTAPH:
CYBER GODDESS
Northstar
1 I:Cenotaph 3.95

CENTRIFUGAL
BUMBLE-PUPPY
1 Adult 2.25
2 thru 6 .... @2.25
7 .... 2.50

CEREBUS
Aardvark–Vanaheim
0 .... 3.00
0a Gold Ed. 25.00
1 B:DS(s&a),I:Cerebus 250.00
1a Counterfeit 50.00
2 DS,V:Succubus 100.00
3 DS,I:Red Sophia 100.00
4 DS,I:Elrod 75.00
5 DS,A:The Pigts 65.00
6 DS,I:Jaka 65.00
7 DS,R:Elrod 65.00
8 DS,A:Conniptins 35.00
9 DS,I&V:K'cor 35.00
10 DS,R:Red Sophia 35.00
11 DS,I:The Cockroach 35.00
12 DS,R:Elrod 35.00
13 DS,I:Necross 30.00
14 DS,V:Shadow Crawler 30.00
15 DS,V: Shadow Crawler 30.00
16 DS, at the Masque 25.00
17 DS,"Champion" 25.00
18 DS,Fluroc 25.00
19 DS,I:Perce & Greet-a 25.00
20 DS,Mind Game 25.00
21 DS,A:CaptCockroach,rare ... 50.00
22 DS,D:Elrod 25.00
23 DS,DuFort's school 10.00
24 DS,IR:Prof.Clarmont 10.00
25 DS,A:Woman-thing 10.00
26 DS,High Society 10.00
27 DS,Kidnapping of an Avrdvark 10.00
28 DS,Mind Game!! 10.00
29 DS,Reprocussions 10.00
30 DS,Debts 8.00
31 DS,Chasing Cootie 8.00
32 DS 8.00
33 DS,DS,Friction 5.00
34 DS,Three Days Before 5.00
35 thru 50 DS .... @5.00
51 DS,(scarce) 17.00
52 DS 5.00
53 DS,C:Wolveroach 7.00
54 DS,I:Wolveroach 9.00
55 DS,A:Wolveroach 8.00
56 DS,A:Wolveroach 8.00
57 DS 5.00
58 DS 5.00
59 DS,Memories Pt.V 5.00
60 DS,more vignettes 5.00
61 DS,A:Flaming Carrot 6.00
62 DS,A:Flaming Carrot 6.00
63 DS,Mind Game VI 5.00
64 DS,Never Pray for Change .. 5.00
65 DS,Papal Speech 5.00
66 DS,Thrill of Agony 5.00
67 thru 70 DS .... @5.00
71 thru 74 DS .... @4.00
75 DS,Terrible Analogies 4.00
76 DS,D:Weisshaupt 4.00
77 DS,Surreal daydream 4.00
78 DS,Surreal daydream 4.00

79 DS,Spinning Straw	4.00
80 DS,V:Stone Tarim	4.00
81 DS,A:Sacred Wars Roach	4.00
82 DS,A:Tarim	3.50
83 DS,A:Michele	3.50
84 DS,Weisshaupt's Letter	3.50
85 DS,A:Mick Jagger	3.50
86 DS,A:Mick Jagger	3.50
87 DS,Tower Climb	3.50

Cerebus #80 © Aardvark-Vanaheim

88 DS,D:Stone Tarim	3.50
89 DS,A:Cute Elf	3.50
90 DS,Anti-Apartheid(c)	3.50
91 DS	3.50
92 DS,A:Bill & Seth	3.50
93 DS,Astoria in Prison	3.50
94 DS,Rape of Astoria	3.50
95 DS,Sophia-Astoria Dream	3.50
96 DS,Astoria in Prison	3.50
97 DS,Escape Planned	3.50
98 DS,Astoria's Trial	3.50
99 DS,Sorcery in Court	3.50
100 DS,A:Cirin	3.50
101 DS,The Gold Sphere	3.00
102 DS,The Final Ascension	3.00
103 DS,On the Tower	3.00
104 DS,A:Flaming Carrot	3.00
105 DS,V:Fred & Ethel	3.00
106 DS,D:Fred & Ethel	3.00
107 DS,Judge on the Moon	3.00
108 DS,All History	3.00
109 DS,O:Universe	3.00
110 DS,More Universe	3.00
111 DS,Cerebus' Fate	3.00
112 DS,Memories	3.00
113 DS,Memories	3.00
114 DS,I:Rick nash	3.00
115 DS,I:Pud Withers	3.00
116 DS,Rick Meets Cerebus	3.00
117 DS,Young Jaka Injured	3.00
118 DS,Cerebus Apologizes	3.00
119 DS,Jaka Opens Door	3.00
120 DS,I:Oscar	3.00
121 DS,Women Explained	3.00
122 DS,Iest History	3.00
123 DS,Each One's Dream	3.00
124 DS	3.00
125 DS,C:Lord Julius	3.00

126 DS,R:Old Vet'ran	2.50
127 DS,Jaka Dances	2.50
128 DS,L:Cerebus as Fred	2.50
129 DS,Jaka's Story	2.50
130 DS,D:Pud Withers	2.50
131 DS,Jaka Imprisoned	4.00
132 DS,A:Nurse	4.00
133 DS,I:Mrs. Thatcher	4.00
134 DS,Dancing Debate	4.00
135 DS,Jaka Signs	4.00
136 DS,L:Rick	4.00
137 DS,Like-a-Looks	4.00
138 DS,Maids'Gossip	4.00
139 A:Misogynist-roach	4.00
140 I:Old Oscar	4.00
141 A:Cerebus	4.00
142 C:Mick Jagger	4.00
143 DS,Oscars Forboding	4.00
144 DS,I:Doris	4.00
145 thru 150 DS	@4.00
151 DS,B:Mothers & Daughters, Book 1: Flight pt.1	4.00
151a 2nd printing	2.50
152 DS,Flight pt.2	4.00
152a 2nd printing	2.50
153 DS,Flight pt.3	4.00
153a 2nd printing	2.50
154 DS,Flight pt.4	4.00
155 DS,Flight pt.5	4.00
156 DS,Flight pt.6	3.00
157 DS,Flight pt.7	3.00
158 DS,Flight pt.8	3.00
159 DS,Flight pt.9	3.00
160 DS,Flight pt.10	3.00
161 DS,Flight pt.11	3.00
162 DS,E:M&D,Bk.1:Flight pt.12	3.00
163 DS,B:Mothers & Daughters Book 2: Women pt.1	2.75
164 DS,Women pt.2,inc. Tour Momentos	2.50
165 DS,Women pt.3	2.50
166 DS,Women pt.4	2.50
167 DS,Women pt.5	2.50
168 DS,Women pt.6	2.50
169 DS,Women pt.7	2.50
170 DS,Women pt.8	2.50
171 DS,Women pt.9	2.50
172 DS,Women pt.10	2.50
173 DS,Women pt.11	2.50
174 DS,E:M&D,Bk.2:Women pt.12	2.50
175 DS,B:Mothers & Daughters, Book 3: Reads pt.1	2.50
176 DS,Reads pt.2	2.50
177 DS,Reads pt.3	2.50
178 DS,Reads pt.4	2.50
179 DS,Reads pt.5	2.50
180 DS,Reads pt.6	2.50
181 DS,Reads pt.7	2.50
182 DS,Reads pt.8	2.50
183 DS,Reads pt.9	2.50
184 DS,Reads pt.10	2.50
185 DS,Reads pt.11	2.50
186 DS,E:M&D bk.3:Reads pt.12	2.50
187 DS,B:Mothers & Daughters, Book 4:Minds pt.1	2.50
188 DS,Minds pt.2	2.50
189 DS,Minds pt.3	2.50
190 DS,Minds pt.4	2.50
191 DS,Minds pt.5,Apparitions	2.25
192 DS,Minds pt.6	2.25
193 DS,Minds pt.7	2.25
194 DS,Minds pt.8	2.25
Cerebus rep.#1–#25 (500 pgs.)	25.00
High Society rep.#26–#50	25.00
Church & State I rep.#52–#85	30.00

Church & State II rep.#86–#111	30.00
Jaka's Story rep.#114–#136	25.00
Melmoth rep.#139–#150	17.00
Flight rep.#151–#162	17.00
Women rep.#163–#174	17.00
Reads rep.#175–#186	17.00
2nd printing	15.00
Reads, Signed, numbered ed.	28.00

CEREBUS CHURCH & STATE
Aardvark–Vanaheim
1 DS rep #51	2.25
2 thru 30 DS rep #52–#80	@2.00

CEREBUS COMPANION
Aardvark–Vanaheim
1	3.95

CEREBUS HIGH SOCIETY
Aardvark–Vanaheim
1 thru 14 DS (biweekly)	@1.70
15 thru 24 DS rep.	@2.00
25 DS rep. #50, final	2.00

CEREBUSJAM
Aardvark–Vanaheim
1 MA,BHa,TA,WE,A:Spirit	15.00

CEREBUS REPRINTS
Aardvark–Vanaheim
1A thru 28A DS rep	@1.25

See also: Church & State
See also: Swords of Cerebus

CHAINGANG
1	2.50
2	3.50

CHAINSAW VIGILANTE
New England Press
1 Tick Spinoff	3.25

CHAMPION, THE
1	2.50

CHAMPIONS
1	2.25

CHARLIE CHAN
Eternity
1 thru 4	@1.95
5 and 6	@2.25

CHASER PLATOON
Aircel
1 Interstellar War	2.25
2 Ambush	2.25
3 New Weapon	2.25
4 Saringer Battle Robot	2.25
5 Behind Enemy Lines	2.25
6	2.25

CHEERLEADERS FROM HELL
1 and 2	@2.50

CHEMICAL FACTOR
1	1.75

CHICAGO FOLLIES
1 . . . . 2.95

CHIPS & VANILLA
1 Spec. 1.75

CHIRON
1 and 2 . . . . @2.00

CHRONOS CARNIVAL
Fleetway
1 reps. 200 AD stories 7.95

CHUCK CHICKEN AND BRUIN BEAR
Jabberwocky
1 . . . . 3.00

CIRCUS WORLD
1 . . . . 2.50

CLIFFHANGER COMICS
AC Comics
1 rep. 2.50
2 rep. 2.50

CLINT
1 Trigon comics 3.00

CLINT THE HAMSTER
Eclipse
1 . . . . 2.50
2 . . . . 1.50

COBALT BLUE
1 Gustovitch Art 77 . . . . 10.00

COBRA
Viz
1 thru 6 . . . . @2.95
7 . . . . 3.25
8 V:SnowHawks 3.25
9 Zados 3.25
10 thru 12 . . . . @3.25

CODA
1 . . . . 3.00

CODENAME NINJA
1 and 2 . . . . @2.00

COLD BLOODED CHAMELEON COMMANDOS
Blackthorne
1 . . . . 2.00
2 . . . . 1.50
3 . . . . 1.50
4 . . . . 1.75
5 . . . . 1.75
6 . . . . 2.00
7 . . . . 2.00

COLE BLACK
1 Vol.I 15.00
2 Vol.I 10.00
3 Vol.I 10.00
4 Vol.I 10.00
5 Vol.I 12.00

1 Vol.II 3.50
2 Vol.II 2.00
3 Vol.II 1.50

COLONEL KILGORE
Special Studios
1 WWII stories 2.50
2 Command Performance 2.50

COLT
K-Z Comics
1 . . . . 5.00
2 pin-up by Laird 8.00
2 pin-up by Henbeck 2.00
3 . . . . 1.00
4 . . . . 1.00
5 . . . . 1.00

COMICS EXPRESS
1 thru 4 . . . . @2.95
5 thru 11 . . . . @3.95

COMING OF APHRODITE
Hero Graphics
1 Aphrodite/modern day 3.95

COMMAND REVIEW
Thoughts & Images
1 rep. Albedo #1-4 . . . . 6.00
2 rep. Albedo #5-8 . . . . 4.00
3 rep. Albedo #9-13 . . . . 4.00

COMPLETE FLUFFHEAD
1 . . . . 2.00

CONQUEROR
Harrier
1 . . . . 3.50
2 thru 4 . . . . @2.00
5 thru 9 . . . . @1.75

CONQUEROR UNIVERSE
Harrier
1 . . . . 2.75

CONSPIRACY COMICS
Revolutionary
1 Marilyn Monroe 2.50
2 Who Killed JFK 2.50
3 Who Killed RFK 2.50

CONSTELLATION GRAPHICS
STG
1 thru 4 . . . . @1.50

CONTINUM
1 . . . . 1.50
2 . . . . 1.75

CONTRACTORS
Eclipse
1 . . . . 2.25

CORBO
1 . . . . 1.75
2 . . . . 1.75

CORMAC MAC ART
1 thru 4 R.E.Howard adapt. . . @1.95

COSMIC BOOK
1 . . . . 1.95

Cosmic Heroes #7 © Eternity

COSMIC HEROES
Eternity
1 Buck Rogers rep. 1.95
2 thru 6 Buck Rogers rep. . . @1.95
7 thru 9 Buck Rogers rep. . . . @2.25
10 . . . . 3.50
11 . . . . 3.95

COSMIC STELLAR REBELERS
1 thru 4 . . . . @1.50

COSMOS
1 . . . . 1.70
2 . . . . 1.70

COUNTER PARTS
Tundra
1 thru 3 . . . . @2.95

CRAZY MEN GO WILD
1 . . . . 2.00

CREED
Hall of Heroes
1 I:Mark Farley 2.50
2 thru 4 Camping 2.50

CRIME BUSTER
AC Comics
0 from FemForce 2.95

CRIME CLASSICS
Eternity
1 rep Shadow comicstrip 1.95
2 thru 11 . . . . @1.95
12 . . . . 2.25

CRIME SMASHERS
Special Edition
1 . . . . 1.80

CRIMSON DREAMS
Crimson
1 thru 11 . . . . @2.00

CRITTER CORPS
1 . . . . 1.50
2 . . . . 1.50
3 . . . . 1.50

CRITTERS
Fantagraphics Books
1 SS,Usagi Yojimbo,Cutey 7.00
2 Captain Jack,Birthright 4.50
3 SS,Usagi Yojimbo,Gnuff 4.50
4 Gnuff,Birthright 3.00
5 Birthright 3.00
6 SS,Usagi Yojimbo,Birthright . . . 3.00
7 SS,Usagi Yojimbo,Jack Bunny . 3.00
8 SK,Animal Graffiti,Lizards 2.50
9 Animal Graffiti 2.50
10 SS,Usagi Yojimbo 3.00
11 SS,Usagi Yojimbo, ... 4.00
12 Birthright II 2.00
13 Birthright II,Gnuff 2.00
14 SS,Usagi Yojimbo,BirthrightII . 2.50
15 Birthright II,CareBears 2.00
16 SS,Groundthumper,Gnuff 2.00
17 Birthright II,Lionheart 2.00
18 Dragon's 2.00
19 Gnuff,Dragon's 2.00
20 Gnuff 2.00
21 Gnuff 2.00
22 Watchdogs,Gnuff 2.00
23 Flexi-Disc,X-Mas Issue 4.00
24 Angst,Lizards,Gnuff 2.00
25 Lionheart,SBi,Gnuff 2.00
26 Angst,Gnuff 2.00
27 SS,Ground Thumper 2.00
28 Blue Beagle,Lionheart 2.00
29 Lionheart,Gnuff 2.00
30 Radical Dog,Gnuff 2.00
31 SBi,Gnuffs,Lizards 2.00
32 Lizards,Big Sneeze 2.00
33 Gnuff,Angst,Big Sneeze 2.00
34 Blue Beagle vs. Robohop 2.00
35 Lionheart,Fission Chicken 2.00
36 Blue Beagle,Fission Chicken . . 2.00
37 Fission Chicken 2.00
38 SS,double size,Usagi Yojimbo . 2.75
39 Fission Chicken 2.00
40 Gnuff 2.00
41 Duck'Bill Platypus 2.00
42 Glass Onion 2.00
43 Lionheart 2.00
44 Watchdogs 2.00
45 Ambrose the Frog 2.00
46 Lionheart 2.00
47 Birthright 2.00
48 Birthright 2.00
49 Birthright 2.00
50 SS,Neil the Horse,
   UsagiYojimbo 4.95
Spec.1 Albedo,rep+new 10pgStory 2.00

CROSSED SWORDS
1 95
2 95

CROSSFIRE
Eclipse
18 thru 26 DSp . . . . @2.00

CROW, THE
Caliber
1 . . . . 75.00
1a 2nd Printing 20.00
1b 3rd Printing 10.00
2 . . . . 50.00
2a 2nd Printing 15.00
2b 3rd Printing 6.00
3 . . . . 40.00
3a 2nd Printing 10.00
4 . . . . 36.00
Tundra
1 reps. Crow #1, #2 . . . . 35.00
2 and 3 . . . . @8.00
TPB 20.00

Crow of the Bear Clan #1
© Blackthorne

CROW OF
THE BEAR CLAN
Blackthorne
1 . . . . 2.25
2 thru 6 . . . . @1.75

CRUSADERS
Guild
1 Southern Knights 10.00

CRUSADERS
1 . . . . 1.50
2 . . . . 1.50
3 . . . . 1.75
4 . . . . 1.75

CRY FOR DAWN
1 . . . . 70.00
1a 2nd Printing 6.00
1b 3rd Printing 2.50
2 . . . . 40.00
2a 2nd Printing 2.50
3 . . . . 30.00
4 . . . . 25.00

5 . . . . 15.00
6 . . . . 7.00
7 Corporate Ladder,Rock A
   Bye Baby 5.00
8 Decay,This is the Enemy 5.00

CRY FOR DAWN:
SUBTLE VIOLENTS
one shot F:Ryder 2.50

CRYING FREEMAN
Viz
1 . . . . 6.50
2 . . . . 5.50
3 thru 5 . . . . @5.00
6 thru 8 . . . . @4.50

CRYING FREEMAN II
Viz
1 . . . . 4.75
2 . . . . 4.00
3 . . . . 4.00
4 thru 6 . . . . @4.25
7 V:Bugnug 3.95
8 Emu & The Samurai Sword . . . 3.95
9 Final Issue 3.95

CRY FREEMAN V
Viz
1 Return to Japan 2.75
2 A:Tateoka-assassin 2.75
3 . . . . 2.75
4 A:Bagwan 2.75
5 V:Tsunaike 2.75
6 V:Aido Family 2.75
7 V:Tsunaike 2.75
GN:Taste of Revenge 14.95

CRYPT
1 . . . . 1.95

CULTURAL JET LAG
Fantagraphics
1 . . . . 2.50

CURSE OF THE ATOMIC
WRESTLING WOMEN
1 . . . . 1.95

CURSE OF THE SHE-CAT
1 . . . . 2.50

CUTEY BUNNY
1 . . . . 8.00
2 thru 4 . . . . @4.00
Eclipse
5 . . . . 3.00

CYBER 7
Eclipse
1 . . . . 2.50
2 thru 5 . . . . @2.00
Book 2
1 thru 7 . . . . @2.00
8 thru 10 . . . . @2.50

CYBERFROG
Hall of Heroes
1 I:Cyberfrog 2.50
2 V:Ben Riley 2.50

All comics prices listed are for *Near Mint* condition.

CYBERHAWKS
1 . . . . 1.85
2 thru 4 . . . . @1.80

CYBORG GERBELS
1 English comic 4.00

CYCLOPS
Blackthorne
1 Mini-series 1.95
2 . . . . 1.95
3 . . . . 1.95

CYGNUS X-1
Twisted Pearl Press
1 V:Yag'Nost 2.50

CYNDER
Immortelle Studios
1 I:Cynder 2.50

DAEMON MASK
1 . . . . 1.80

DAFFY QADDAFI
Comics Unlimited Ltd.
1 . . . . 2.00

DAIKAZU
1 . . . . 7.00
1a 2nd Printing 1.50
2 . . . . 3.00
2a 2nd Printing 1.50
3 . . . . 4.00
3a 2nd Printing 1.50
4 thru 7 . . . . @1.50
8 . . . . 1.75

DAMLOG
1 . . . . 1.80
1a 2nd printing 1.00
2 thru 5 . . . . @1.80

DAMONSTREIK
Imperial Comics
1 I:Damonstreik 1.95
2 V:Sonix 1.95
3 V:Sonix 1.95
4 J:Ohm 1.95
5 V:Drakkus 1.95

DANGEROUS TIMES
1 MK 2.50
2 MA(c) 2.00
2a 2nd printing 1.75
3 MR(c) 1.95
3a 2nd printing 1.95
4 GP(c) 1.95

DANGERWORLD
1 . . . . 1.00
2 . . . . 1.00
3 . . . . 1.00

DAN TURNER HOLLYWOOD DETECTIVE
Eternity
1 'Darkstar of Death' 2.50

DAN TURNER HOMICIDE HUNCH
Eternity
1 Dan Turner Framed 2.50

DAN TURNER THE STAR CHAMBER
Eternity
1 Death of Folly Hempstead 2.50

DARERAT
1 . . . . 1.95

DARK ADVENTURES
1 . . . . 1.25

DARK ANGEL SPECIAL
1 . . . . 1.75

DARK ASSASSIN
1 thru 3 . . . . @1.50
Vol. 2
1 thru 5 . . . . @2.00

DARK COMICS
1 . . . . 1.80
2 . . . . 1.80

DARK FORCE
Omega 7
1 A:Dark Force 2.00

DARK JUSTICE
IMP Press
1 I:Dark Justice 2.50

DARK LORD
RAK
1 thru 3 . . . . @1.75

DARK REGIONS
1 . . . . 2.50
2 . . . . 2.50
3 Scarce 3.00
4 and 5 . . . . @1.50

Dark Visions #2 © Pyramid Comics

DARK STAR
1 I:Ran 2.25
2 thru 3 . . . . @2.25

DARK VISIONS
Pyramid
1 I:Wasteland Man 1.70
2 thru 4 . . . . @1.70

DARK WOLF
Eternity
1 . . . . 1.95
2 . . . . 1.95
Volume 2
1 thru 14 . . . . @1.95
Annual #1 . . . . 2.25

DATA 6
1 . . . . 1.95
2 . . . . 1.95

DAZE & KNIGHT
1 . . . . 1.80

DAYS OF DARKNESS
Apple
1 From Pearl Harbor
to Midway 2.75
2 Pearl Harbor Attack,cont 2.75
3 Japanese Juggernaut 2.75
4 Bataan Peninsula 2.75

Deadbeats #6 © Claypool Comics

DEADBEATS
Claypool Comics
1 thru 7 . . . . @2.50

DEADFACE
1 . . . . 3.00
2 . . . . 2.50
3 . . . . 1.95

DEADFISH BEDEVILED
1 . . . . 2.25

All comics prices listed are for *Near Mint* condition.

DEAD HEAT
1 .... 1.95

DEADKILLER
Caliber
1 Rep Deadworld 19 thru 21 .... 2.95

DEADTALES
Caliber
1 'When a Body Meets a Body' .. 2.95

DEADTIME STORIES
1 AAd,WS 1.75

DEADWORLD
Arrow
1 Arrow Pyb 6.00
2 .... 4.00
3 V:King Zombie 3.50
4 V:King Zombie 3.50
5 Team Rests 3.50
6 V:King Zombie 3.50
7 F:KZ & Deake, Graphic(c) 3.50
7a Tame cover 2.00
8 V:Living Corpse, Graphic(c) ... 2.50
8a Tame cover 2.00
9 V:Sadistic Punks, Graphic(c) .. 2.50
9a Tame cover 2.00
10 V:King Zombie, Graphic(c) ... 2.50
10a Tame cover 2.00
11 V:King Zombie, Graphic(c) ... 3.00
11a Tame cover 2.50
12 I:Percy, Graphic(c) 3.00
12a Tame cover 2.50
13 V:King Zombie, Graphic(c) ... 3.00
13a Tame cover 2.50
14 V:Voodoo Cult,Graphic(c) 3.00
14a Tame cover 2.50
15 Zombie stories,Graphic(c) 3.00
15a Tame cover 2.50
16 V:'Civilized' Community 2.50
17 V:King Zombie 2.50
18 V:King Zombie 2.50
19 V:Grakken 2.50
20 V:King Zombie 2.50
21 Dead Killer 2.50
22 L:Dan & Joey 2.50
23 V:King Zombie 2.50
24 .... 2.50
25 (R:Vince Locke) 2.50
26 .... 2.50
Caliber
1 thru 11 .... @2.95
12 Death Call 2.95
13 Death Call 2.95
14 Death Call pt. 5 .... 2.95
15 Death Call pt. 6 .... 2.95

DEADWORD ARCHIVES
Caliber
1 Rep.Deadworld series 2.50

DEADWORLD: BITS & PIECES
Caliber
1 Rep.1st Deadworld Story,
Caliber presents #2&#8 ..... 1.60

DEADWORLD: TO KILL A KING
Caliber

1 R:Deadkiller 2.95

DEATHBRINGER
1 thru 4 .... @1.60

DEATHDREAMS OF DRACULA
Apple
1 Selection of short stories 2.50
2 short stories 2.50
3 Inc. Rep. BWr,'Breathless' 2.50
4 short stories 2.50

DEATH HAWK
1 thru 6 .... @1.95

Death Hunt #1 © Eternity

DEATH HUNT
Eternity
1 .... 1.95
2 .... 1.95

DEATHMARK
Lightning Comics
1 O:War Party 2.75

DEATHQUEST
1 .... 1.50

DEATH RATTLE
Kitchen Sink
(Prev. Color)
6 Steve Bissette(c) 2.00
7 Ed Gein 2.00
8 I:Xenozoic Tales 3.00
9 BW,rep. 2.00
10 AW,rep. 2.00
11 thru 15 .... @2.00
16 BW,Spacehawk 2.00
17 Rand Holmes(c) 2.00
18 FMc 2.00

DEATH'S HEAD
Crystal
1 .... 1.95

2 .... 1.95
3 .... 1.95

DEATH WATCH
1 .... 1.75

DEATHWORLD
Adventure Comics
1 Harry Harrison Adapt. 2.50
2 thru 4 .... @2.50

DEATHWORLD II
Adventure Comics
1 Harry Harrison Adapt. 2.50
2 .... 2.50
3 .... 2.50
4 last issue 2.50

DEATHWORLD III
Adventure Comics
1 H.Harrison Adapt.,colonization . 2.50
2 Attack on the Lowlands 2.50
3 Attack on the Lowlands contd. .. 2.50
4 last issue 2.50

DEFENSELESS DEAD
Adventure Comics
1 A:Gil 2.50
2 A:Organlegger 2.50
3 A:Organlegger 2.50

DELIRIUM
1 .... 2.00
2 KG 2.00

DELTA SQUADRON
1 .... 2.00
2 .... 2.00

DELTA TENN
1 thru 11 .... @1.50

DEMON BLADE
1 .... 1.75
2 .... 1.95
3 .... 1.95

DEMON HUNTER
Aircel
1 thru 4 .... @1.95

DEMONIQUE
London Night Studios
1 F:Viper 3.00
2 F:Viper 3.00
3 Mayhem 3.00
4 Final issue 3.00

DEMON'S BLOOD
1 .... 1.70
2 .... 1.85

DEMON'S TAILS
Adventure
1 .... 2.50
2 A:Champion 2.50
3 V:Champion 2.50
4 V:Champion 2.50

DEMON WARRIOR
1 thru 12 . . . . @1.50
13 . . . . 1.75
14 . . . . 1.75

DENIZENS OF DEEP CITY
Jabberwocky
1 thru 8 . . . . @2.00

DERRECK WAYNE'S STRAPPED
Gothic Images
1 Confrontational Factor 2.25
2 Confrontational Factor 2.25

DESCENDING ANGELS
Millenium
1 I:3 Angels 2.00

DESERT PEACH
Thoughts & Images
1 thru 4 . . . . @2.00

DESTROY
Eclipse
1 Large Size 4.95
2 Small Size,3-D 4.95

DIATOM
Photographics
1 Dan Duto Photographic 4.95

DICK TRACY MAGAZINE
1 V:Little Face Finnyo 3.95

DICK TRACY MONTHLY
Blackthorne
1 thru 25 . . . . @2.00

DICK TRACY: THE EARLY YEARS
5 . . . . 2.95
6 . . . . 2.95
7 and 8 . . . . @3.50

DICK TRACY WEEKLY
26 thru 108 . . . . @2.00
Unprinted Stories #3 . . . . 2.95
1 3-D Special 3.00
Spec. #1 . . . . 2.95
Spec. #2 . . . . 2.95
Spec. #3 . . . . 2.95

DIGGERS, THE
C&T
3 . . . . 1.75

DILLINGER
Rip Off Press
1 Outlaw Dillinger 2.50

DINOSAUR REX
1 and 2 . . . . @2.00

DINOSAURS
Caliber
1 History of Dinosaurs 3.00

DINOSAURS FOR HIRE
Eternity
1 . . . . 3.00
1a Rep. 1.95
2 thru 9 . . . . @1.95
Fall Classic #1 . . . . 2.25
Malibu
#1 3-D special 3.50

DIRECTORY TO A NON-EXISTENT UNIVERSE
Eclipse
1 . . . . 1.95

DIRTY-NAIL
1 . . . . 2.00

DIRTY PAIR
1 . . . . 5.00
2 . . . . 4.00
3 . . . . 3.00
4 end mini-series 2.50
Eclipse
reprint 1-3 . . . . 2.50
Vol 2 #1 . . . . 2.25
Vol 2 #2 . . . . 2.25
Vol 2 #3 . . . . 2.00
Vol 2 #4 . . . . 2.00
Vol 2 #5 . . . . 2.00

DIRTY PAIR: PLAGUE OF ANGELS
Eclipse
1 thru 5 . . . . @2.25

DIRTY PAIR: SIM EARTH
Eclipse
1 thru 4 . . . . 2.50

DISQUETTE
1 . . . . 2.50

A DISTANT SOIL
Warp Graphics
1 A:Panda Khan 5.00
2 . . . . 4.00
3 . . . . 3.00
4 . . . . 3.00
5 . . . . 3.00
6 thru 9 . . . . @2.00
Aria Press
1 thru 3 . . . . @2.00

DITKOS WORLD: STATIC
Renegade
1 SD 1.70
2 SD 1.70
3 SD 1.70

DR. GORPON
Eternity
1 I:Dr.Gorpon,V:Demon 2.25
2 A:Doofus,V:ChocolateBunny . . 2.50
3 D:Dr.Gorpon 2.50

DR. RADIUM
Silverline
1 . . . . 3.00
2 . . . . 2.00
3 and 4 . . . . @1.50

DR. RADIUM: MAN OF SCIENCE
Slave Labor
1 And Baby makes 2,BU:Dr.Radiums'
Grim Future 2.50

DOC WEIRD'S THRILL BOOK
1 AW 1.75
2 . . . . 1.75
3 . . . . 1.75

DODEKAIN
Antartic Press
1 and 2 . . . . @2.95
3 Rampage Vs. Zogerians 2.95
4 V:Zogerians 2.95
5 F:Takuma 2.95
6 Dan vs. Takuma 2.75

DOG
1 Military renegade 2.25

Dogaroo #1 © Blackthorne

DOGAROO
Blackthorne
1 . . . . 2.00

DOMETRIUS KUIR
Newcomers Publishing
1 Walt Bayless 2.95

DOMINION
Eclipse
1 . . . . 3.00
2 thru 6 . . . . @2.00

DOMINO CHANCE
Chance
1 1,000 printed 10.00
1a 2nd printing 3.50
2 . . . . 3.00
3 . . . . 3.00
4 . . . . 3.00
5 . . . . 3.00
6 . . . . 3.00

7 I:Gizmo	7.00
8 A:Gizmo	11.00
9	2.50

[2nd Series]

1	3.00
2	1.95
3	1.95

DONATELLO
Mirage

1 A: Turtles	12.00

DON SIMPSON'S BIZARRE HEROES
Fiasco Comics

0 thru 7	2.95
8 V:Darkcease	2.95
9 R:Yan Man	2.95
10 F:Mainstreamers	2.95
TPB Apocalypse Affiliation	12.95

DRACULA

1	3.75
1a 2nd printing	2.50
2	2.50
3	2.50
4	2.50

DRACULA IN HELL
Apple

1 O:Dracula	2.50
2 O:Dracula contd.	2.50

DRACULA: SUICIDE CLUB
Adventure

1 I:Suicide Club in UK	2.50
2 Dracula/Suicide Club cont.	2.50
3 Club raid,A:Insp.Harrison	2.50
4 Vision of Miss Fortune	2.50

DRACULA: THE LADY IN THE TOMB
Eternity

1	2.50

DRAGONFORCE
Aircel
(Prev. Color)

8 thru 13 DK	@2.50

DRAGONFORCE CHRONICLES
Aircel

Vol 1 rep.	2.95
Vol 2 rep.	2.95
Vol 3 rep.	2.95
Vol 4 rep.	2.95
Vol 5 rep	2.95

DRAGON OF THE VALKYR

1	1.75
2 thru 4	@2.00

DRAGON QUEST

1 TV	15.00
2 TV	7.50
3 TV	6.50

Dragonring #1 © Aircel

DRAGONRING
[1st Series]

1 B.Blair,rare	110.00

Aircel

1	3.50
2	2.00
3 thru 6	@1.75

See Also Independent Color

DRAGON'S STAR

1	1.75
2	1.75
3	2.00
4	2.00

DRAGON WEEKLY

1 Southern Knights	1.75
2	1.75
3	1.75

DREAD OF NIGHT
Hamilton

1 Horror story collection	3.95
2 Json, inc.'Genocide'	3.95

DREAMERY
Eclipse

1 thru 13	@2.00

DREAMWOLVES
Dramenon Studios

1	3.00
2	3.00
3 F:Desiree	3.00
4 V:Venefica	3.00
5 V:Venefica	3.00

DRIFTERS AFAR

1	1.70

DUCK & COVER

1	2.00
2	2.00

DUCKBOTS

1	1.75
2	1.75
3	1.75

DUNGEONEERS

1 thru 8	@1.50

DURANGO KID

1	2.50
2	2.50

DUTCH DECKER

1	1.95
2	1.95
3	1.95

DYNAMIC COMICS

1	2.00
2	2.00

EAGLE
Crystal

1	5.00
1a signed & limited	7.00
2 thru 5	@2.75
6 thru 11	@2.25
12	2.50
13 thru 17	@2.00

Apple

18 thru 26	@1.95

EAGLE: DARK MIRROR
Comic Zone

1 A:Eagle, inc reps	2.75
2 In Japan, V:Lord Kagami	2.75
3	2.95
4	2.95

EAGLES DARE
Aager Comics

1 thru 4	1.95
5 V:Dragon	1.95

EARTH LORE: LEGEND OF BEK LARSON
Eternity

1	1.80

EARTH LORE: REIGN OF DRAGON LORD

1	1.80
2	1.75

EARTH: YEAR ZERO
Eclipse

1 thru 4	@2.00

EB'NN THE RAVEN
Now

1	5.00
2	3.00
3	2.50
4	2.00
5 thru 9	@1.50

EDDY CURRENT

1 thru 12	@2.00

All comics prices listed are for *Near Mint* condition.   **CVA Page 523**

EDGAR ALLAN POE
Tell Tale Heart 1.95
Pit & Pendulum 1.95
Masque of the Red Death 1.95
Murder in the Rue Morgue 1.95

EDGE
1 . . . . 3.00
Vol 2 #1 . . . . 3.00
Vol 2 #2 . . . . 3.00
Vol 2 #3 . . . . 3.00
Vol 2 #4 . . . . 2.00
Vol 2 #5 . . . . 2.00
Vol 2 #6 . . . . 2.00

Eightball #7 © Fantagraphics

EIGHTBALL
Fantagraphics
1 . . . . 10.00
2 . . . . 7.00
3 . . . . 6.00
4 . . . . 5.00
5 . . . . 4.00
6 . . . . 4.00
7 . . . . 4.00
8 . . . . 4.00
9 . . . . 4.00
10 . . . . 4.00
11 . . . . 3.50
12 F:Ghost World 3.25
13 . . . . 2.95

ELECTRIC BALLET
Caliber
1 Revisionist History of
  Industrial Revolution 2.50

ELEGANT LADIES
1 . . . . 3.50

ELFLORD
[1st Series]
1 all rare 80.00
2 . . . . 65.00
3 . . . . 60.00
4 . . . . 50.00
5 . . . . 50.00

6 . . . . 80.00
7 . . . . 80.00
8 . . . . 80.00
9 thru 15 . . . . @50.00

ELFLORD
Aircel
1 I:Hawk 5.00
1a 2nd printing 3.50
2 . . . . 3.00
2a 2nd printing 2.00
3 V:Doran 3.00
4 V:Doran 3.00
5 V:Doran 2.00
6 V:Nendo 2.00
7 thru 13 . . . . @2.00
Compilation Book 4.95
  (Vol 2, #1 to #24, see Color)
25 thru 31 . . . . @1.95
32 . . . . 2.50

ELFLORD CHRONICLES
Aircel
1 rep B.Blair 2.50
2 thru 8 rep . . . . @2.50

ELFQUEST
Warp Graphics
1 WP 45.00
1a WP,2nd printing 12.00
1b WP,3rd printing 5.00
1c WP,4th printing 4.00
2 WP 22.00
2a WP,2nd printing 4.00
2b WP,3rd printing 3.00
3 WP 20.00
3a WP,2nd printing 4.00
3b WP,3rd printing 3.00
4 WP 20.00
4a WP,2nd printing 4.00
4b WP,3rd printing 3.00
4c WP,4th printing 2.00
5 WP 20.00
5a WP,2nd printing 4.00
5b WP,3rd printing 3.00
6 WP 20.00
6a WP,2nd printing 4.00
6b WP,3rd printing 3.00
7 WP 14.00
7a WP,2nd printing 3.00
8 WP 14.00
8a WP,2nd printing 3.00
9 WP 14.00
9a WP,2nd printing 3.00
10 thru 15 . . . . @10.00
16 WP,I:DistantSoil 10.00
17 thru 21 WP . . . . @10.00
TPB Gatherum 19.95

ELFQUEST: KINGS OF
THE BROKEN WHEEL
Warp Graphics
1 WP 2.25
2 thru 9 WP . . . . @2.25

ELFQUEST: SEIGE
AT BLUE MOUNTAIN
Warp Graphics/Apple Comics
1 WP,JSo 11.00
1a 2nd printing 3.00
2 WP 6.00
2a 2nd printing 3.00

3 WP 5.00
3a 2nd printing 2.00
4 thru 8 WP . . . . @5.00

ELFTHING
Eclipse
1 . . . . 3.00

ELFTREK
Dimension
1 . . . . 2.00
2 . . . . 1.75

ELF WARRIOR
1 . . . . 3.00
2 . . . . 2.50
3 thru 5 . . . . @1.95

ELIMINATOR
Eternity
1 'Drugs in the Future' 2.50
2 . . . . 2.50

ELVIRA, MISTRESS
OF THE DARK
Claypool Comics
1 thru 13 . . . . @2.50

ELVIRA
Eclipse
1 Rosalind Wyck 2.50

ELVIS: UNDERCOVER
1 . . . . 2.00

EMERALDAS
Eternity
1 thru 4 . . . . @2.25

EMPIRE
Eternity
1 thru 4 . . . . @1.95

EMPIRE LANES
Comico
1 . . . . 2.95

EMPTY BALLOONS
1 . . . . 1.50
2 . . . . 1.50

ENCHANTED VALLEY
Blackthorne
1 . . . . 1.75
2 . . . . 1.75

ENCHANTER
Eclipse
1 thru 3 . . . . @2.00

ENCHANTER:
APOCALYPSE
WIND NOVELLA
Entity
1 Foil Enhanced Cover 2.95

END, THE
1 . . . . 1.95

ENEMY LINES SPECIAL
1 .... 1.75

ENTROPY TALES
1 .... 2.00
2 Domino Chance 1.50
3 thru 5 .... @1.50

EPSILON WAVE
Elite
1 .... 3.00
2 .... 2.00
3 thru 5 .... @1.60

EQUINE THE UNCIVILIZED
Graphspress
1 .... 4.00
2 .... 2.50
3 thru 6 .... @2.00

EQUINOX CHRONICLES
Innovation
1 I:Team Equinox, Black Avatar . 2.25
2 Black Avatar Plans US conquest 2.25

ERADICATORS
1 RLm (1st Work) 5.00
1a 2nd printing 1.50
2 .... 2.50
3 Vigil 2.00
4 thru 8 .... @1.50

ERIC PRESTON IS THE FLAME
B-Movie Comics
1 Son of G.A.Flame .... .95

ERIN
1 .... 1.95

ESCAPE TO THE STARS
Visionary
1 thru 7 .... @1.25
[2nd Series]

Escape Velocity #2
© Escape Velocity Press

1 .... 1.25
2 .... 1.25

ESCAPE VELOCITY
Escape Velocity Press
1 .... 1.50
2 .... 1.50

ESMERALDAS
Eternity
1 thru 4 .... 2.25

ETERNAL THIRST
1 .... 2.00
2 .... 2.00

EVIL ERNIE
Eternity
1 I&O:Evil Ernie (Horror) 5.00
1a Special Edition 2.95
2 Death & Revival of Ernie 4.00
3 Psycho Plague 3.00
4 .... 3.00
5 .... 2.50
TPB rep #1-5 .... 10.95

EX-MUTANTS
Amazing Comics
1 AC/RLm 5.00
1a 2nd printing 2.00
EC
2 .... 3.00
3 .... 2.00
4 .... 2.00
5 .... 2.00
6 PP 1.95
7 .... 1.95
8 .... 1.95
Annual #1 .... 1.95
Pin-Up Spec. #1 .... 1.95

EX-MUTANTS: THE SHATTERED EARTH CHRONICLES
Eternity
1 thru 3 .... @1.95
4 RLd(c) 2.75
5 RLd(c) 2.75
6 thru 14 .... @1.95
Winter Special #1 .... 1.95

EXILE
1 .... 2.00
2 .... 2.00

EXTINCT
NEC
1 Rep Golden age stories 3.50

EXTREMELY SILLY
1 .... 4.00
1 Vol. II 1.25
2 Vol. II 1.25

EYE OF MONGOMBO
1 .... 3.00
2 thru 5 .... @2.00

FAILED UNIVERSE
1 .... 1.75

FANBOYS
Spec #1 .... 2.00

FANGS OF THE WIDOW
Ground Zero
1 I:Emma 2.50

FANTAESCAPE
1 .... 1.75
2 .... 1.75

FANTASCI
Warp Graphics-Apple
1 .... 2.50
2 .... 2.00
3 .... 2.00
4 .... 4.00
5 thru 8 .... @1.75
9 'Apple Turnover' 1.75

FANTASTIC ADVENTURES
1 thru 5 .... @1.75

FANTASTIC FABLES
Silver Wolf
1 .... 1.50
2 .... 1.50

FANTASY QUARTERLY
1 1978 1st Elfquest 65.00

FASTLANE ILLUSTRATED
Fastlane Studios
1 Super Powers & Hot Rods 2.50

FAT NINJA
1 .... 2.50
2 Vigil 2.50
3 thru 8 .... @1.50

FAUNA REBELLION
1 thru 3 .... @2.00

FAUST
North Star
1 Vigil 30.00
1a Vigil,2nd Printing 5.00
1b Vigil,3rd Printing 2.50
1c Tour Edition 50.00
2 Vigil 20.00
2a Vigil,2nd Printing 3.00
2b Vigil,3rd Printing 2.50
3 Vigil 10.00
3a Vigil,2nd Printing 2.50
4 Vigil 5.00
5 Vigil 5.00
6 Vigil 5.00
Rebel Studios
7 Vigil 3.00
8 TV 3.00
9 TV,Love of the Damned 3.00
10 E:DQ(s),TV,Love o/t Damned . 3.00

FAUST VOL. II
REBEL
1 TV,Love of the Damned 2.50

FAUST PREMIERE
North Star
1 Vigil 45.00

FEM FANTASTIQUE
AC Comics
1 .... 1.95

Fem Force #46 © AC Comics

FEM FORCE
AC Comics
(See Color)
16 I:Thunder Fox 2.25
17 F:She-Cat,Ms.Victory, giant .. 2.25
18 double size 2.25
19 .... 2.50
20 Giant,V:RipJaw,
   Black Commando 2.50
21 V:Dr.Pretorius 2.50
22 V:Dr.Pretorius 2.50
23 V:Rad 2.50
24 A:Teen Femforce 2.50
25 V:Madame Boa 2.50
26 V:Black Shroud 2.50
27 V:Black Shroud 2.50
28 A:Arsenio Hall 2.50
29 V:Black Shroud 2.50
30 V:Garganta 2.50
31 I:Kronon Captain Paragon .. 2.75
32 V:Garganta 2.75
33 Personal Lives of team 2.75
34 V:Black Shroud 2.75
35 V:Black Shroud 2.75
36 giant,V:Dragonfly,Shade 2.75
37 A:Blue Bulleteer,She-Cat 2.75
38 V:Lady Luger 2.75
39 F:She-Cat 2.75
40 V:Sehkmet 2.75
41 V:Captain Paragon 2.75
42 V:Alizarin Crimson 2.75
43 V:Glamazons of Galaxy G .. 2.75
44 V:Lady Luger 2.75
45 Nightveil Rescued 2.75
46 V:Lady Luger 2.75
47 V:Alizarin Crimson 2.75
48 .... 2.75
49 I:New Msw.Victory 2.75
50 Ms.Victory Vs.Rad,flexi-disc .. 2.95
51 .... 2.75
52 V:Claw & Clawites 2.75
53 I:Bulldog Deni,V:(Dick
   Briefer's)Frightenstein 2.75

54 The Orb of Bliss 2.75
55 R:Nightveil 2.75
56 V:Alizarin Crimson 2.75

FEMFORCE: FRIGHTBOOK
AC Comics
1 Horror tales by Briefer,Ayers,
   Powell 2.95

FEMME NOIRE
1 .... 2.00
2 .... 2.00

FIFTIES TERROR
Eternity
1 thru 6 .... @1.95

FIGMENTS
1 .... 1.75
2 .... 1.75

FINAL CYCLE
Sirius
Graphic Novel 4.00
1 thru 4 .... @1.50

FINAL MAN
1 .... 1.50
2 .... 1.75
3 .... 1.75

FIRE TEAM
Aircel
1 .... 2.50
2 .... 2.50
3 .... 2.50
4 V:Vietnamese Gangs 2.50
5 Cam in Vietnam 2.50
6 .... 2.50

FISH POLICE
Fishwrap Productions
December 1985
1 1st printing 7.00
1a 2nd printing 3.00
2 .... 5.00
3 thru 5 .... @4.00
Comico Publ.
6 thru 12 .... @3.50
13 thru 17 see Color issues
Apple Publ.
18 thru 24 .... @2.50

FISH SHTICKS
Apple
1 .... 2.75
2 .... 2.75
3 .... 2.50
4 .... 2.50

FISSION CHICKEN
1 thru 5 .... @2.00

FIST OF GOD
Eternity
1 .... 1.95
2 .... 1.95
3 .... 1.95
4 .... 1.95

Fist of the North Star #1
© Viz Comics

FIST OF THE NORTH STAR
Viz Select
1 thru 3 .... @3.25
4 .... 1.95
5 .... 3.25
6 .... 2.95
7 .... 2.95

FITCH IN TIME
Renegade
1 .... 1.50

FLAMING CARROT
Aardvark–Vanaheim
1 1981 Killian Barracks 100.00
1a 1984 .... 45.00
2 .... 25.00
3 .... 15.00
4 thru 6 .... @10.00
Renegade
7 .... 8.00
8 .... 7.00
9 .... 7.00
10 .... 5.00
11 .... 4.00
12 .... 4.00
13 .... 3.00
14 .... 3.00
15 .... 3.00
15a 10.00
16 .... 3.00
17 .... 3.00
See: Dark Horse

FLARE
Hero Graphics
1 thru 8 .... @3.95
9 F:Sparkplug 3.95
10 thru 12 .... 2.95

FLARE ADVENTURES
Hero Graphics
1 Rep 1st issue Flare 1.00

Becomes:
FLARE ADVENTURES/ CHAMPIONS CLASSICS
2 thru 15 . . . . @3.95

FLARE VS. TIGRESS
Hero Graphics
1 . . . . 3.50
2 . . . . 3.50

FLASH MARKS
Fantagraphics
1 . . . . 2.95

FLOYD FARLAND
Eclipse
1 . . . . 2.95

FLYIN RALPH COMICS
1 75

FORBIDDEN KINGDOM
1 thru 11 . . . . @1.95

FORBIDDEN WORLDS
1 SD,JAp,rep. 2.50

FORCE 10
Crow Comics
0 Ash Can Preview 75
1 I:Force 10 . . . . 2.50

FOREVER NOW
1 . . . . 1.50
2 . . . . 1.50

FOTON EFFECT
1 thru 5 . . . . @1.50

FOX COMICS
1 Spec. 2.95
25 . . . . 2.95
26 . . . . 3.50

FRAGMENTS
1 thru 3 . . . . @1.75

FRAN AN' MAABL
1 . . . . 2.50
2 . . . . 2.50

FRANKENSTEIN
Eternity
1 thru 3 . . . . @1.95

FRANKIES FRIGHTMARES
1 Celebrates Frank 60th ann . . . 1.95

FRANK THE UNICORN
Fish Warp
1 thru 7 . . . . @2.00

FREAK-OUT ON INFANT EARTHS
1 Don Chin 1.75
2 Don Chin 1.75

FREAKS
Monster Comics
1 Movie adapt 2.50
2 Movie adapt.cont. 2.50
3 thru 4 Movie adapt. 2.50

FREE FIRE ZONE
1 thru 3 . . . . @1.75

FREE LAUGHS
1 . . . . 1.00

FRENCH ICE
Renegade Press
1 thru 15 . . . . @2.00

FRIENDS
1 thru 5 . . . . @2.00

FRIGHT
Eternity
1 thru 13 . . . . @1.95

FRINGE
1 thru 6 . . . . @2.50

FROM BEYOND
Studio Insidio
1 Short stories-horror 2.25
2 inc.Clara Mutilares 2.50
3 inc.The Experiment 2.50
4 inc.Positive Feedback 2.50

FROM HELL
Tundra
1 . . . . 4.95
Kitchen Sink
Volume Three
1 AMo(s) 3.95

FROM THE DARKNESS
Adventure Comics
1 thru 4 . . . . @2.50

FROM THE DARKNESS II BLOODVOWS
Cry For Dawn
1 R:Ray Thorn,Desnoires 2.50
2 V:Desnoires 2.50
3 . . . . 2.50

FROM THE VOID
1 1st B.Blair,1982 . . . . 75.00

FROST
1 Heart of Darkness 1.95

FROST: THE DYING BREED
Caliber
1 Vietnam Flashbacks 2.95
2 Flashbacks contd. 2.95
3 Flashbacks contd. 2.95

F–III BANDIT
Antarctic Press
1 F:Akira, Yoohoo 2.95
2 F:Yukio 2.95

FUGITOID
Mirage
1 TMNT Tie-in 12.00

FURRLOUGH
Antarctic Press
1 Funny Animal Military stories . . 2.95

FURY
Aircel
1 thru 3 . . . . @1.70

THE FURY OF HELLINA
Lightning Comics
1 V:Luciver 2.75

FUSION
Eclipse
1 . . . . 2.50
2 thru 17 . . . . @2.00

FUTURAMA
Slave Labor
1 thru 4 . . . . @1.75

FUTURE BEAT
1 . . . . 1.50
2 . . . . 1.50
3 . . . . 1.50

FUTURE COURSE
1 . . . . 1.75
2 . . . . 1.75
3 . . . . 1.75

FUTURE CRIME 98
1 . . . . 1.95

FUTURETECH
Mushroom Comics
1 Automotive Hi-Tech 3.50
2 Cyber Trucks 3.50

FUTURIANS
Aardwolf
0 DC R:Futurians 2.95

GAIJIN
1 thru 3 . . . . @1.95

GAJIT GANG
1 . . . . 1.95
2 . . . . 1.95

GAMBIT
1 . . . . 1.95
2 . . . . 1.95

GAMBIT & ASSOCIATES
1 thru 4 . . . . @1.75

GANTAR
1 thru 5 . . . . @1.75

GATEKEEPER
GK Publishing
1 . . . . 2.50
2 and 3 . . . . @2.95

All comics prices listed are for *Near Mint* condition.   **CVA Page 527**

GATES OF THE NIGHT
Jademan
1 thru 4 . . . . @3.50

GATEWAY TO HORROR
1 BW 1.75

GEMS OF THE SAMURAI
Newcomers Publishing
1 I:Master Samurai 2.95

GENOCYBER
Viz
1 I:Genocyber 2.75
2 . . . . 2.75
3 thru 5 ToT 2.75

GERIATRIC GANGRENE JUJITSU GERBILS
Planet X Productions
1 . . . . 2.50
2 . . . . 1.50

GERIATRIC MAN
1 . . . . 1.75

GET LOST
1 . . . . 1.95
1a signed (1200 copies) 6.00
2 . . . . 1.95
3 . . . . 1.95

GHOSTS OF DRACULA
Eternity
1 A:Dracula & Houdini 2.50
2 A:Sherlock Holmes 2.50
3 A:Houdini 2.50
4 Count Dracula's Castle 2.50
5 Houdini, Van Helsing,
   Dracula team-up 2.50

GHOULS
1 . . . . 2.25

GIANT SIZE MINI COMICS
Eclipse
1 thru 4 . . . . @1.50

G.I. CAT
1 . . . . 1.50
2 . . . . 1.50
3 . . . . 1.50

GI GOVERNMENT ISSUED
Paranoid Press
1 thru 7 F:Mac, Jack . . . . @2.00

G.I. MUTANTS
1 and 2 . . . . @1.95

GIDEON HAWK
Big Shot Comics
1 I:Gideon Hawk, Max 9471 . . . . 2.00
2 The Jewel of Shamboli 2.00

GIFT, THE
First
1 . . . . 5.95

GIZMO
Chance
1 . . . . 7.50
Mirage
1 . . . . 5.50
2 . . . . 2.50
3 . . . . 2.00
4 thru 7 . . . . @1.50

GIZMO & THE FUGITOID
1 . . . . 1.75
2 . . . . 1.75

GNATRAT
Prelude
1 . . . . 5.00
2 Early Years 2.00

GNATRAT: THE MOVIE
1 . . . . 2.25

GNOSIS BRIDGE
1 . . . . 1.50

Gobbledygook © Mirage Studios

GOBBLEDYGOOK
Mirage
1 1st series, Rare 275.00
2 1st series, Rare 275.00
1 TMNT series reprint 12.00

GOD'S HAMMER
1 . . . . 2.50
2 . . . . 2.50
3 . . . . 2.50

GOLD DIGGER
Antarctic
[Limited Series]
1 Geena & Cheetah in Peru . . . 2.50
2 Adventures contd. 2.50
3 Adventures contd 2.50
4 Adventures contd 2.50
GN Rep. #1–#4 + new material . . 9.95

[Volume 2]
1 thru 14 by Fred Perry . . . . . @2.50

GOLDEN FEATURES
1 thru 5 . . . . @2.00

GOLDWYN 3-D
Blackthorne
1 . . . . 2.00

GOLGO 13
1 thru 5 . . . . @1.25

GO-MAN
1 thru 4 . . . . @1.50
Graphic Novel 'N' 9.95

GOOD GIRL COMICS
AC
1 F:Tara Fremont 3.95

GOOD GIRLS
Fantagraphics
1 adult 2.00
2 thru 4 . . . . @2.00

GOON PATROL
1 . . . . 1.75

GORE SHRIEK
Fantagor
1 . . . . 2.50
2 . . . . 1.50
3 . . . . 1.50
4 +Mars Attacks 2.95
5 . . . . 2.95
6 . . . . 3.50
Vol 2 #1 . . . . 2.50

GRAPHIC STORY MONTHLY
1 thru 5 . . . . @2.95

GRAPHIQUE MUSIQUE
1 . . . . 2.95
2 . . . . 2.95
3 . . . . 2.95

GRAVE TALES
Hamilton
1 JSon,GM, mag. size 3.95
2 JSon,GM,short stories 3.95
3 JSon,GM, inc.'Stake Out' 3.95

GRENDEL
Comico
1 MW,Rare 60.00
2 MW,Rare 50.00
3 MW,Rare 45.00

GREY
Viz Select
Book 1 . . . . 5.00
Book 2 scarce 5.50
Book 3 . . . . 3.00
Book 4 . . . . 3.00
Book 5 . . . . 3.00
Book 6 . . . . 2.50
Book 7 . . . . 2.50
Book 8 . . . . 2.50

Grey #1 © Viz Select Comics

Book 9 . . . . 2.50

GRIFFIN, THE
Slave Labor
1 . . . . 1.75
1a 2nd printing 1.75
2 thru 4 . . . . @1.75
5 . . . . 1.95

GRINGO
1 . . . . 1.95

GRIPS
Silver Wolf
1 Vigil 20.00
2 Vigil 16.00
3 Vigil 11.00
4 Vigil 9.00
Vol 1 #1 rep 2.50
Volume 2
1 . . . . 2.50
2 . . . . 2.50
3 thru 6 . . . . @2.00
7 . . . . 2.25
8 . . . . 2.25
9 thru 12 . . . . @2.50

GRIPS ADVENTURE
1 double-size 2.50
2 thru 5 . . . . @2.00

GROOTLOTE
1 . . . . 2.00

GROUND POUND
1 JohnPoundArt 2.00

GROUND ZERO
Eternity
1 Science Fiction mini-series . . . 2.50
2 Alien Invasion Aftermath 2.50

GRUN
1 . . . . 1.95
2 . . . . 1.95

GRUNTS
1 . . . . 1.50

GUERRILA GROUNDHOG
Eclipse
1 . . . . 1.50
2 . . . . 1.50

GUILLOTINE
Silver Wolf
1 and 2 . . . . @1.50

GUN FURY
Aircel
1 thru 10 . . . . @1.95

GUN FURY RETURNS
Aircel
1 . . . . 2.95
2 . . . . 2.95
3 V:The Yes Men 2.25
4 . . . . 2.25

GUNS OF SHAR-PEI
Caliber
1 The Good,the Bad & the
Deadly 2.95

HALLOWEEN TERROR
Eternity
1 . . . . 2.50

HALLOWIENERS
Mirage
1 . . . . 1.50
2 . . . . 1.50

HALO BROTHERS
Fantagraphics
Special #1 . . . . 2.25

HAMSTER VICE
Blackthorne
1 . . . . 3.50
2 . . . . 2.50
3 thru 11 . . . . @2.00
New Series
Eternity
1 and 2 . . . . @1.95

HAND SHADOWS
1 . . . . 2.00
2 . . . . 1.50

HARD-BOILED ANIMAL COMICS
1 . . . . 2.50

HARD ROCK COMICS
Revolutionary
1 Metallica-The Early Years 2.50

HAR HAR COMICS
1 . . . . 2.00

HARTE OF HARKNESS
Eternity
1 I:Dennis Harte,Vampire

private-eye 2.50
2 V:Satan's Blitz St.Gang 2.50
3 Jack Grissom/Vampire 2.50
4 V:Jack Grissom, conc. 2.50

HARVEST
Spec. 3.00

HARVY FLIP BOOK
Blackthorne
1 . . . . 2.00
2 . . . . 2.00
3 . . . . 2.00

HATE
Fantagraphics
1 . . . . 20.00
2 . . . . 15.00
3 . . . . 10.00
4 . . . . 8.00
5 . . . . 7.00
6 . . . . 6.00
6a 2nd printing 2.25
7 thru 11 . . . . 5.00
12 . . . . 4.00
13 thru 15 . . . . 3.00

HEAD, THE
1 Old Airboy (1966) 2.00

HEADLESS HORSEMAN
1 . . . . 2.25
2 . . . . 2.25

HEARTBREAK COMICS
Eclipse
1 . . . . 1.50

HEAVY METAL MONSTERS
Revolutionary
1 'Up in Flames' 2.25

HELLBENDER
1 . . . . 2.25

HELL FOR LEATHER
1 and 2 . . . . @1.75

HELLGIRL
Knight Press
1 I:Jazzmine Grayce 2.95

HELLINA TAKING BACK THE NIGHT
Lightning Comics
1 V:Michael Naynar 2.75
1a Nude Cover Variant 9.95

HELLSTALKER
1 . . . . 2.25
2 . . . . 2.25
3 . . . . 2.25

HELLWARRIOR
1 . . . . 2.50
2 . . . . 2.50
3 . . . . 1.95
4 . . . . 1.95

HENRY V
Caliber
1 Play Adaptation 2.95

HEPCATS
Double Diamond
1 . . . . 6.00
2 . . . . 5.00
3 . . . . 4.00
4 . . . . 3.50
5 . . . . 3.50
6 . . . . 3.50
7 thru 10 . . . . @3.00
11 thru 13 . . . . @2.75
14 Chapter 12 . . . . 2.75
15 Snowblind Chp. 13 . . . . 2.75

HERALDS OF CANADA
1 . . . . 1.50
2 . . . . 1.50

HERCULES
A Plus Comics
1 Hercules Saga 2.50

Hercules Project # 1 © Monster Comics

HERCULES PROJECT
Monster Comics
1 Origin issue,V:Mutants 1.95

HEROES
Blackbird
1 . . . . 6.00
2 . . . . 3.00
3 . . . . 2.25
4 comic size 2.00
5 thru 7 . . . . @2.00

HEROES' BLOOD
1 . . . . 1.95

HEROES FROM WORDSMITH
Special Studios
1 WWI,F:Hunter Hawke 2.50

HEROES INCORPORATED
Double Edge Publishing
1 I:Heroes, Inc. 2.95
2 Betrayal 2.95

HEROINES, INC.
1 thru 5 . . . . @1.75

HERO SANDWICH
Slave Labor
1 thru 4 . . . . @1.50
5 thru 8 . . . . @1.75
9 . . . . 1.95
Graphic Novel 7.95

HEY, BOSS
1 . . . . 1.50
2 . . . . 1.50

HIGH CALIBER
1 . . . . 4.00
2 . . . . 3.00
3 . . . . 2.50
4 . . . . 2.50
Becomes:Caliber Presents

High School Agent #4 ©Sun Comics

HIGH SCHOOL AGENT
Sun Comics
1 I:Kohsuke Kanamori 2.50
2 Treasure Hunt at North Pole . . 2.50
3 . . . . 2.50
4 . . . . 2.50

HIGH SHINING BRASS
Apple
1 thru 4 . . . . @2.75

HIGH SOCIETY
Aardvark–Vanaheim
1 DS,Cerebus 25.00

HITOMI
Antarctic Press
1 Shadowhunter,from Ninja HS . . 2.50
2 Synaptic Transducer 2.50

3 Shadowhunter in S.America . . . 2.50
4 V:Mr.Akuma,last issue 2.50

HOLIDAY OUT
1 . . . . 2.00
2 . . . . 2.00
3 . . . . 2.00

HOLO BROTHERS, THE
Monster Comics
1 thru 10 . . . . @1.95

HOLO BROTHERS, THE
Fantagraphics
Spec.#1 . . . . 2.25

HOLY KNIGHT
Pocket Change Comics
1 thru 3 . . . . @2.50
4 V:His Past 2.50
5 V:Souljoiner 2.50
6 V:Demon Priest 2.50

HOMICIDE
1 . . . . 1.95

HONK
Fantagraphics
1 Don Martin 2.75
2 . . . . 2.75
3 . . . . 2.75

HONOR AMONG THIEVES
Gateway Grapnics
1 and 2 . . . . @1.50

HOODOO
Spec. 2.50

HOOHA COMICS
1 Mag. Size Animal
Anthology-500 print 15.00

HORDE
1 . . . . 2.00
2 . . . . 2.00

HORNET SPECIAL
1 . . . . 2.00

HOROBI
Viz
1 . . . . 4.00
2 thru 8 . . . . @3.75
Book 2
1 . . . . 3.50
2 D:Okado,Shoko Kidnapped . . . 4.25
3 Madoka Attacks Zen 4.25
4 D:Abbess Mitsuko 4.25
5 Catharsis! 4.25
6 Shuichi Vs. Zen 4.25
7 Shuichi vs. Zen, conc. 4.25

HORROR
1 . . . . 2.95
2 . . . . 2.95

HORROR IN THE DARK
Fantagor
1 RCo,Inc.Blood Birth 2.00

---

2 RCo,Inc.Bath of Blood 2.00
3 RCo 2.00
4 RCo,Inc.Tales o/tBlackDiamond 2.00

HORROR SHOW
Caliber
1 GD,1977-80 reprint horror . . . 3.50

HORSE
1 . . . . 2.95

HOT SHOTS
1 . . . . 1.95
2 . . . . 1.95

HOUSE OF HORROR
AC Comics
1 . . . . 2.50

HOWL
Eternity
1 . . . . 2.25
2 . . . . 2.25

HOW TO DRAW
ROBOTECH BOOK
1 . . . . 2.00
2 . . . . 2.00

HOW TO DRAW TEENAGE
MUTANT NINJA TURTLES
Solson
1 Lighter cover 15.00
1a Dark cover 5.00

HUGO
Fantagraphics
1 . . . . 4.00
2 . . . . 2.00
3 . . . . 2.00
4 . . . . 2.00

HUMAN GARGOYLES
Eternity
Book one 1.95
Book two 1.95
Book three 1.95
Book four 1.95

HUMAN HEAD
Caliber
1 Alice in Flames 2.50

HUMAN POWERHOUSE
1 and 2 . . . . @1.75
3 . . . . 2.00

HUNT AND
THE HUNTED, THE
Newcomers Publishing
1 I:Aramis Thiron 2.95
2 V:Werewolves 2.95

HURRICANE LEROUX
Inferno Studios
1 I:Deja Vu Jones 2.50

HUZZAH
1 I:Albedo'sErmaFelna 60.00

HY-BREED
Division Publishing
1 thru 3 F:Cen Intel . . . . @2.25

HYPE
1 . . . . 2.00
2 . . . . 2.00

I.F.S. ZONE
1 thru 6 . . . . @1.25

I AM LEGEND
Eclipse
1 Novel Adaptation 5.95
2 Novel Adaptation Cont'd 5.95
3 Novel Adaptation Cont'd 5.95

IAN WARLOCKE
1 . . . . 1.50

ICARUS
1 thru 9 . . . . @1.70

ICON DEVIL
1 . . . . 2.00
2 . . . . 2.00
2nd Series
1 thru 5 . . . . @1.85

IDIOTLAND
Fantagraphic
1 . . . . 2.95

ILIAD II
1 . . . . 3.00
1a 2nd cover variation 3.00
2 . . . . 2.00
3 . . . . 2.00
4 . . . . 1.70

ILLUMINATUS
1 . . . . 2.00
2 . . . . 2.50
3 . . . . 2.50

IN-COUNTRY NAM
1 . . . . 1.75
2 . . . . 1.75
3 . . . . 1.75
4 . . . . 1.95
5 . . . . 1.95

INDEPENDENT COMIC
BOOK SAMPLER
1 . . . . 1.50
2 . . . . 1.50

INK COMICS
1 thru 3 . . . . @2.50

INSANE
1 . . . . 1.75
2 . . . . 1.75

INTERZONE
Brainstorm Comics
1 w/4 cards 2.50
2 w/4 cards 2.50

INVADERS FROM MARS
Eternity
1 . . . . 2.50
2 . . . . 2.50
3 . . . . 2.50
(Book II)
1 Sequel to '50's SF classic 2.50
2 Pact of Tsukus/Humans 2.50
3 Last issue 2.50

INVASION '55
Apple
1 . . . . 2.25
2 . . . . 2.25
3 . . . . 2.25

INVISIBLE PEOPLE
Kitchen Sink
1 WE,I:Peacus Pleatnik 2.95
2 WE,The Power 2.95
3 WE,Final issue 2.95

INVISIOWORLD
1 . . . . 1.95

IRON SAGA'S
ANTHOLOGY
1 thru 3 . . . . @1.75

ISMET
1 Cartoon Dog 12.00
2 . . . . 5.00
3 Rare 5.00
4 . . . . 5.00

IS YOUR BOOGEY-
MAN LOOSE?
1 . . . . 2.95

ITCHY PLANET
3 . . . . 2.25

IT'S SCIENCE
WITH DR. RADIUM
1 thru 7 . . . . @1.50

Jackaroo #1 © Eternity

All comics prices listed are for *Near Mint* condition.   **CVA Page 531**

8 .... 1.75
9 .... 1.95
Spec #1 .... 2.95

JACKAROO
Eternity
1 GCh 2.25
2 GCh 2.25
3 GCh 2.25

J.A.P.A.N.
1 .... 1.80

JACKFROST
1 .... 1.80
2 .... 1.95
3 .... 1.95

JACK HUNTER
Blackthorne
1 .... 3.50
2 .... 3.50
3 .... 3.50

JACK OF NINES
1 .... 1.25
2 thru 4 .... @1.50
5 .... 2.00

JACK THE RIPPER
1 thru 4 .... @2.25

JAKE TRASH
1 .... 3.95

JAM, THE
1 .... 2.00
2 .... 2.00
3 .... 2.25

JAM SPECIAL
1 .... 2.50

JANX
1 and 2 .... @1.00

JASON AND THE ARGONAUTS
Caliber
1 thru 5 .... @2.50

JAX AND THE HELL HOUND
1 thru 4 .... @1.75

JAZZ AGE CHRONICLES
1 thru 6 .... @1.50
7 .... 2.50

JCP FEATURES
1 1st MT;S&K,NA/DG rep.
A:T.H.U.N.D.E.R.Agents,TheFly,
Black Hood Mag.Size 4.50

JEREMIAH: BIRDS OF PREY
Adventure Comics
1 I: Jeremiah,A:Kurdy 2.50
2 conclusion 2.50

JEREMIAH: FIST FULL OF SAND
Adventure Comics
1 A:Captain Kenney 2.50
2 conclusion 2.50

JEREMIAH: THE HEIRS
Adventure Comics
1 Nathanial Bancroft estate 2.50
2 conclusion 2.50

JERRY IGERS FAMOUS FEATURES
Blackthorne
1 .... 3.00
2 thru 4 .... @2.00
Pacific
5 thru 8 .... @2.00

JIM
1 thru 3 .... @2.25
4 .... 2.50

JOE SINN
Caliber
1 I:Joe Sinn,Nikki 2.95
2 .... 2.95

JOHNNY ATOMIC
Eternity
1 I:Johnny A.Tomick 2.50
2 Project X-contingency plan .. 2.50
3 .... 2.50

JOHNNY GAMBIT
4 .... 1.95

JONTAR
1 thru 3 .... @1.75

Journey #4 © Aardvark-Vanaheim

JOURNEY
Aardvark–Vanaheim
1 .... 13.00
2 .... 9.00

3 .... 8.00
4 .... 5.00
5 .... 3.00
6 .... 3.00
7 .... 3.00
8 thru 14 .... @2.50
Fantagraphics
15 .... 2.50
16 thru 28 .... @2.00

JR. JACKALOPE
1 orange cover,1981 .... 8.00
1a Yellow cover,1981 .... 15.00
2 .... 8.00

JUDO JOE
1 and 2 .... @1.75

JUNGLE COMICS
Blackthorne
4 thru 6 .... @2.00

JUNGLE GIRLS
AC Comics
1 incGold.Age reps. 1.95
2 .... 1.95
3 Greed,A:Tara 2.75
4 CaveGirl 2.75
5 Camilla 2.75
6 TigerGirl 2.75
7 CaveGirl 2.75
8 Sheena Queen o/t Jungle .. 2.95
9 Wild Girl,Tiger Girl,Sheena . 2.95
10 F:Tara,Cave Girl,Nyoka ... 2.95
11 F:Sheena,Tiger Girl,Nyoka . 2.95
12 F:Sheena,Camilla,Tig.Girl . 2.95
13 F:Tara, Tiger Girl 2.95

JUSTY
1 thru 9 .... @1.75

KABUKI: CIRCLE OF BLOOD
Caliber Press
1 R:Kabuki 2.95
2 Kabuki Goes Rogue 2.95

KABUKI: DANCE OF DEATH
Caliber Press
1 1st Full series 3.00

KAFKA
1 thru 5 .... @2.00
The Execution Spec. 2.25

KAMIKAZE CAT
1 .... 1.80
2 .... 1.95
3 .... 1.95

KAMUI
Eclipse
1 Sanpei Shirato Art 4.00
1a 2nd printing 2.50
2 Mystery of Hanbie 3.00
2a 2nd printing 1.50
3 V:Ichijiro 2.00
3a 2nd printing 1.50
4 thru 15 .... @1.50
16 thru 19 .... @1.95

Kamui #7 © Eclipse

20 thru 37 . . . . @1.50

KAPTAIN KEEN
1 thru 3 . . . . @1.75
4 and 5 . . . . @1.50
6 and 7 . . . . @1.75

KEIF LLAMA
1 thru 6 . . . . @2.00

KENDOR THE CREON WARRIOR
1 . . . . 1.50
2 . . . . 1.50

KID CANNIBAL
Eternity
1 I:Kid Cannibal 2.50
2 Hunt for Kid Cannibal 2.50
3 A:Janice 2.50
4 final issue 2.50

KID PHOENIX
1 . . . . 1.50

KI-GORR THE KILLER
AC
1 I:Ki-Gorr, Rae 2.95

KIKU SAN
Aircel
1 thru 6 . . . . @1.95

KILGORE
1 thru 5 . . . . @2.00

KILLER OF CROWS
one shot, story of John Johnson . 2.50

KILLING STROKE
Eternity
1 British horror tales 2.50
2 inc.'Blood calls to Blood' 2.50
3 and 4 . . . . @2.50

KIMBER
Antarctic Press
1 I:Kimber 2.50
2 V:Lord Tyrex 2.50

KING KONG
Monster Comics
1 thru 6 . . . . @2.50

KINGS IN DISGUISE
1 thru 5 . . . . @2.00
6 end Mini-series 2.00

KIRBY KING OF THE SERIALS
Blackthorne
1 . . . . 2.00
2 . . . . 2.00
3 . . . . 2.00
4 . . . . 2.00

Kitz 'N' Katz #3 © Eclipse

KITZ 'N' KATZ
1 . . . . 3.50
Eclipse
2 . . . . 2.00
3 . . . . 1.50
4 and 5 . . . . @2.00

KIWANNI
1 . . . . 2.25
2 . . . . 1.75

KLOWN SHOCK
North Star
1 Horror Stories 2.75

KNIGHTMARE
Antarctic Press
1 . . . . 2.75
2 . . . . 2.75
3 Wedding Knight pt.1 . . . . 2.75
4 Wedding Knight pt.2 . . . . 2.75
5 F:Dream Shadow 2.75

KNIGHT MASTERS
1 thru 7 . . . . @1.50

KNIGHT WATCHMAN
Caliber Press
1 Graveyard pt. 1 . . . . 2.95
2 Graveyard pt. 1 . . . . 2.95

KOMODO & THE DEFIANTS
1 thru 6 . . . . @1.50

KUNG FU WARRIORS
(Prev. ROBOWARRIORS)
CFW
12 . . . . 1.95
13 thru 19 . . . . @2.25

KURTZMAN KOMIX
1 . . . . 1.50

KWAR
1 . . . . 1.95

KYRA
1 thru 3 . . . . @1.75
4 . . . . 2.00
5 . . . . 1.75

KZ COMICS
1 I:Colt 1985 . . . . 1.95

L.F.S. ZONE
1 . . . . 1.25

L.I.F.E. BRIGADE
Blue Comet
1 A:Dr. Death 1.50
1a 2nd printing 1.50
2 . . . . 1.50

LABOR FORCE
Blackthorne
1 thru 4 . . . . @1.50
5 thru 8 . . . . @1.75

LADY ARCANE
Heroic Publishing
1 thru 3 . . . . @3.50

LADY CRIME
AC Comics
1 Bob Powell reprints 2.75

LAFFIN GAS
Blackthorne
1 . . . . 2.50
2 thru 12 . . . . @2.00

LANCE STANTON WAYWARD WARRIOR
1 and 2 . . . . @1.50

LANDRA
Polyventura Entertainment Group
1 . . . . 2.50

LAST DITCH
Edge Press
1 CCa(s),THa, ... 2.50

LAST GENERATION
Black Tie Studios
1 . . . . 6.00
2 . . . . 4.00
3 . . . . 2.25
4 . . . . 2.25
5 . . . . 2.25
Book One Rep. 6.95

LAST KISS, THE
Eclipse
Spec. 3.95

LATIGO KID WESTERN
AC Comics
1 . . . . 1.95

LAUGHING TARGET
1 . . . . 3.50
2 . . . . 3.50

LAUNCH
1 . . . . 1.75

LAUREL & HARDY
1 3-D 2.50

LAW
1 . . . . 1.75

LEAGUE OF CHAMPIONS
Hero Comics
(cont. from Innovation L.of C. #3)
1 GP,F:Sparkplug,Icestar 3.50
2 GP(i),F:Marksman,Flare,Icicle . 3.50
3 . . . . 3.50
4 F:Sparkplug,League 3.50
5 Morrigan Wars Pt.#1 . . . . 3.50
6 Morrigan Wars Pt.#3 . . . . 3.50
7 Morrigan Wars Pt.#6 . . . . 3.50
8 Morrigan Wars Conclusion 3.50
9 A:Gargoyle 3.50
10 A:Rose 3.50
11 thru 12 . . . . 3.95
13 V:Malice 3.95
14 V:Olympians 3.95
15 V:Olympians 2.95

LEGEND LORE
1 and 2 . . . . @2.00
combined rep. 8.95

LEGION OF
LUDICROUS HEROES
1 . . . . 2.00

LEGION X-I
1 McKinney 5.00
2 McKinney,rare 15.00
Volume 2
1 thru 4 . . . . @2.00

LEGION X-2
Vol 2 #1 . . . . 2.00
Vol 2 #2 . . . . 2.00
Vol 2 #3 . . . . 2.00

Vol 2 #4 . . . . 2.00

LENSMAN
Eternity
1 E.E.'Doc' Smith adapt. 2.25
2 . . . . 2.25
3 . . . . 2.25
4 . . . . 2.25
5 On Radelix 2.25
6 . . . . 2.25
Collectors Spec #1, 56 pgs. 3.95

LENSMAN:
GALACTIC PATROL
Eternity
1 thru 5 . . . . @2.25

Lensman: War of the Galaxies #5
©*Eternity Comics*

LENSMAN:
WAR OF THE GALAXIES
Eternity
1 thru 7 . . . . @2.25

LEONARDO
1 TMNT 13.00

LIBBY ELLIS
1 . . . . 1.95
2 . . . . 1.95
Eternity
1 thru 4 . . . . @1.95

LIBERATOR
Eternity
1 thru 6 . . . . @1.95

LIBRA
1 . . . . 1.95

LITERACY VOLUNTEERS
1 Word Warriors 1.50
2 Quest for 1.50

LITTLEST NINJA
1 . . . . 1.80

2 . . . . 1.80

LIVINGSTONE MOUNTAIN
Adventure Comics
1 I:Scat,Dragon Rax 2.50
2 Scat & Rax Create Monsters . . 2.50
3 Rax rescue attempt 2.50
4 Final issue 2.50

LLOYD LLEWELLYN
Fantagraphics
1 Mag Size 4.00
2 Mag Size 2.25
3 Mag Size 2.25
4 Mag Size 2.25
5 Mag Size 2.25
6 Mag Size 2.25
7 Regular Size 2.25

LOCKE
1 . . . . 1.25
2 TD 1.25

LOCO VS. PULVERINE
Eclipse
1 Parody 2.50

LOGAN'S RUN
Adventure Comics
1 Novel Adapt 2.25
2 Novel Adapt 2.25
3 Novel Adapt 2.25
4 Novel Adapt 2.25
5 Novel Adapt 2.25
6 Novel Adapt 2.25

LOGAN'S WORLD
Adventure Comics
1 Seq. to Logan's Run 2.50
2 thru 6 . . . . @2.50

LOLLYMARS &
LIGHT LANCERS
1 . . . . 1.75

LONER
Fleetway
1 Pt. 1 of 7 . . . . 1.95
2 Pt. 2 . . . . 1.95
3 Pt. 3 . . . . 1.95
4 Pt. 4 . . . . 1.95
5 Pt. 5 . . . . 1.95
6 Pt. 6 . . . . 1.95

LONE WOLF & CUB
First
1 FM(c) 7.00
1a 2nd printing 2.50
1b 3rd printing 1.50
2 . . . . 4.00
2a 2nd printing 2.00
3 . . . . 3.50
4 thru 10 . . . . @3.00
11 thru 17 . . . . @2.75
18 thru 25 . . . . @2.50
26 thru 36 . . . . @2.95
37 and 38 . . . . @3.25
39 120 Page 5.95
40 . . . . 3.25
41 MP(c), 60 page 3.95
42 MP(c) 3.25

Lone Wolf & Cub #8 © First Publ.

43 MP(c) 3.25
44 MP(c) 3.25
45 MP(c) 3.25

LORD OF THE DEAD
Conquest
1 R.E.Howard adapt. 2.95

LOST ANGEL
Caliber
1 . . . . 3.50

LOST CONTINENT
Eclipse
1 thru 5 . . . . @3.50

LOVE AND ROCKETS
Fantagraphics
1 HB,B&W cover, adult 75.00
1a HB,Color cover 35.00
1b 2nd printing 4.00
2 HB 15.00
3 HB 10.00
4 HB 10.00
5 HB 10.00
6 HB 7.50
7 HB 7.50
8 HB 7.50
9 HB 7.50
10 HB 9.00
11 HB 4.50
12 HB 4.50
13 HB 4.50
14 HB 4.50
15 HB 4.50
16 thru 21 HB . . . . @4.00
22 thru 39 HB . . . . @3.50
40 thru 41 . . . . @3.50
Bonanza rep. 2.95

LOVE FANTASY
1 . . . . 2.00

LUGH, LORD OF LIGHT
1 . . . . 2.50

2 . . . . 1.75

LUM*URUSEI YATSURA
1 Art by Rumiko Takahashi 2.95
2 . . . . 2.95
3 . . . . 2.95
4 . . . . 2.95
5 . . . . 3.25
6 thru 8 . . . . @2.95

M.C. GRIFFIN
1 . . . . 1.95

MACABRE
1 thru 2.00

MACH 1
Fleetway
1 I:John Probe-Secret Agent 1.95

MACK THE KNIFE
1 . . . . 2.50

MACKENZIE QUEEN
1 thru 5 . . . . @3.75

MACROSS II
Viz
1 Macross Saga sequel 2.75
2 A:Ishtar 2.75
3 F:Reporter Hibiki,Ishtar 2.75
4 V:Feff,The Marduk 2.75
5 . . . . 2.75
6 . . . . 2.75
7 Sylvie Confesses 2.75
8 F:Ishtar 2.75
9 V:Marduk Fleet 2.75
10 . . . . 2.75

MACROSS II: THE MICRON CONSPIRACY
1 . . . . 2.75

MAD DOG MAGAZINE
1 thru 3 . . . . @1.75

MAD DOGS
Eclipse
1 I:Mad Dogs(Cops) 2.50
2 V:Chinatown Hood 2.50
3 . . . . 2.50

MAELSTROM
Aircel
1 thru 5 . . . . @1.70
6 thru 13 . . . . @1.50

MAGGOTS
1 JSon, mag size 3.95
2 JSon, mag size 3.95
3 GM/JSon,inc.'Some Kinda
   Beautiful' 3.95

MAGNA-MAN: THE LAST SUPERHERO
1 . . . . 1.95
2 . . . . 1.95
3 . . . . 1.95

Mai, the Psychic Girl #7-#8 © Eclipse

MAI, THE PSYCHIC GIRL
Eclipse
1 I:Mai,Alliance of 13 Sages 3.75
1a 2nd printing 2.00
2 V:Wisdom Alliance 2.00
2a 2nd printing 1.50
3 V:Kaieda,I:Ojii-San 2.00
4 . . . . 2.00
5 thru 19 . . . . @1.75
20 thru 28 . . . . @1.50

MAISON IKKOKY
Viz
1 thru 3 . . . . 2.95

MAN
1 . . . . 2.00
2 . . . . 2.00

MAN EATING COW
1 Spin-off from the Tick 3.25
2 O:Mr.Krinkles,A:Lt.Valentine . . 2.75
3 Final issue 2.75

MAN-ELF
3 A:Jerry Cornelius 2.25

MANDRAKE
1 . . . . 3.95
2 . . . . 3.95
3 . . . . 3.95
Ultimate Mandrake 14.95

MANDRAKE MONTHLY
1 . . . . 3.95
2 . . . . 3.95
3 . . . . 4.95
4 . . . . 4.95
5 . . . . 4.95
6 . . . . 6.95
Special #1 . . . . 6.95

MAN FROM U.N.C.L.E.
Entertainment Publ.
1 'Number One with a Bullet Affair 2.50

2 'Number One with a Bullet Affair 2.00
3 'The E-I-E-I-O Affair' 1.50
4 'The E-I-E-I-O Affair,' concl. . . . 1.50
5 'The Wasp Affair' 1.50
6 'Lost City of THRUSH Affair' . . 1.50
7 'The Wildwater Affair' 1.50
8 'The Wilder West Affair' 1.50
9 'The Cahadian Lightning Affair' 1.75
10 'The Turncoat Affair' 1.75
11 'Craters of the Moon Affair' . . . 1.75

MANGA MONTHLY

0 . . . . 3.00

Mangazine #5 © Antartic Press

MANGAZINE
Antartic Press

1 newsprint cover 7.00
1a reprint 3.00
2 . . . . 5.00
3 . . . . 4.00
4 . . . . 2.00
5 . . . . 1.50
New Series
1 . . . . 3.00
2 . . . . 3.00
3 . . . . 1.75
4 . . . . 1.75
5 thru 7 . . . . @1.95
8 thru 13 . . . . @2.25
14 New Format 2.95
15 . . . . 2.95
16 . . . . 2.95
17 . . . . 2.95

MANIMAL
1 EC,rep. 1.70

MAN IN BLACK
CALLED FATE
1 . . . . 2.00

MAN OF RUST
Blackthorne
1 Cover A 1.50
2 Cover B 1.50

Man of Rust #1 © Blackthorne

MANTUS FILES
Eternity
1 Sidney Williams novel adapt . . 2.50
2 Vampiric Figures 2.50
3 Secarus' Mansion 2.50
4 A:Secarus 2.50

MARAUDERS OF
THE BLACK SUN
1 . . . . 1.75
2 . . . . 1.75

MARCANE
Eclipse
1 Book 1,JMu 5.95

MARIONETTE
1 75

MARK I
(Prev.: Atomic Comics)
2 . . . . 1.50

MARTIANS
1 . . . . 2.00

MARTIAN SUMMERS
1 . . . . 1.75
2 . . . . 1.75

MASKED MAN
Eclipse
12 . . . . 2.00

MASQUERADE
Eclipse
1 . . . . 1.50
2 . . . . 1.95
3 . . . . 1.95

MASTER
1 thru 4 . . . . @1.95

MATT CHAMPION
1 EC 2.00
2 EC 2.00

MAX OF REGULATORS
1 . . . . 5.00
2 . . . . 3.50
3 . . . . 3.50
4 . . . . 3.50

MAX THE MAGNIFICENT
1 . . . . 3.00
2 . . . . 2.00
3 . . . . 2.00

MAXWELL MOUSE
FOLLIES
1 Large format (1981) 5.00
1a Comic Size(1986) 3.00
2 thru 6 . . . . @2.00

MAYHEM
1 thru 6 . . . . @2.50

MECHANOIDS
Caliber
1 . . . . 2.50
2 . . . . 3.50
3 . . . . 3.50

MECHARIDER: THE
REGULAR SERIES
Castle
1 thru 3 F:Winter 2.95

MECHOVERSE
1 . . . . 1.80
2 . . . . 1.50

MECHTHINGS
1 thru 5 . . . . @2.00

MEDUSA
1 . . . . 1.50

MEGATON
Megaton
1 JG(c),EL(1stProWork),GD,MG,
A:Ultragirl,Vanguard 15.00
2 EL,JG(pin-up),A:Vanguard . . . 10.00
3 MG,AMe,JG,EL,I:Savage
Dragon 25.00
4 AMe,EL,2nd A:Savage Dragon
(inc.EL profile) 20.00
5 AMe,RLd(inside front cover) . . 5.00
6 AMe,JG(inside back cover),
EL(Back cover) 5.00
7 AMe 4.00
8 RLd,I:Youngblood(Preview) . . 25.00

MEGATON MAN
1 . . . . 2.00

MEGATON MAN MEETS
THE UNCATEGORIZABLE
X-THEMS
Jabberwocky
1 . . . . 2.00

MENAGERIE
1	1.95
2	1.95
3	2.00

MEN IN BLACK
Aircel
1	2.25
2	2.25
3	2.25
(Book II)	
1	2.50
2	2.50
3 last issue	2.50

MEN IN BLACK: THE ROBORG INCIDENT
Castle
1 thru 3	@2.95

MERCHANTS OF DEATH
Eclipse
1 thru 5	@1.95

Merlin #2 © Adventure Comics

MERLIN
Adventure Comics
1 Merlin's Visions	2.50
2 V:Warlord Carados	2.50
3	2.50
4 Ninevah	2.50
5 D:Hagus	2.50
6 Final Issue	2.50
[2nd Series]	
1 Journey of Rhiannon & Tryon	2.50
2 Conclusion	2.50

MESSENGER 29
1 and 2	@1.50

MESSIAH
1	1.50

METACOPS
Monster Comics
1 and 2	@1.95

METAPHYSIQUE
Eclipse
1 NB,Short Stories	2.50
2 NB,Short Stories	2.50

METAL MEN OF MARS
1	1.95

MIAMI MICE
Rip Off Press
1 1st printing	3.00
1a 2nd printing	2.00
3	2.00
4 Record,A:TMNT	3.00

MICHELANGELO
Mirage
1 TMNT	17.00
1a 2nd Printing	4.50

MICRA
Fictioneer
1	4.00
2	3.00
3	3.00
4	2.00
5 thru 7	@1.75
8	2.25

MIDNIGHT
Blackthorne
1 thru 4	@1.75

MIDNITE SKULKER
1 thru 7	@1.75

MIGHTY GUY
C&T
1 thru 6	@1.50
Summer Fun Spec #1	2.50

MIGHTY MITES
Continüm
1 I:X-Mites	1.95
2	1.95

MIGHTY MOUSE ADVENTURE MAGAZINE
1	2.00

MIGHTY THUN'DA KING OF THE CONGO
1	2.50

MIGHTY TINY
1 thru 4	@1.75
5	2.50
Mouse Marines Collection rep.	7.50

MIKE MIST MINUTE MYSTERIES
Eclipse
1	3.00

MIRACLE SQUAD BLOOD & DUST
Apple
1	1.95

2	1.95
3	1.95

MISSING BEINGS
1 Special	2.25

MISSING LINK
1	1.70
2	1.70

MISTER X
Vortex
Vol 2	
1 thru 11	@2.00

MITES
1	2.50
1a	1.90
2B	1.80
3 and 4	@1.80

MODERN PULP
Special Studio
1 Rep.from January Midnight	2.75

MOGOBI DESERT RATS
Midnight Comics
1 I&O:Desert Rats 'Waste of the World'	2.25

MONSTER BOY
Monster Comics
1 A:Monster Boy	2.25

MONSTER FRAT HOUSE
Eternity
1	2.25

MONSTER POSSE
Adventure
1 thru 3	2.50

MONSTERS ATTACK
1 GM,JSe	2.00

Monsters From Outer Space #2 © Adventure Comics

---

2 GC 1.75
3 ATh,GC 1.49

MONSTERS FROM OUTER SPACE
Adventure
1 thru 3 . . . . @2.50

MOONSTRUCK
1 . . . . 2.00

MOONTRAP
Special #1 . . . . 2.50

MORPHS
1 . . . . 2.00
2 . . . . 2.00
3 . . . . 2.00
4 . . . . 2.00

MORTAR MAN
Marshall Comics
1 I:Mortar Man 1.95
2 thru 3 . . . . @1.95

MORTY THE DOG
1 . . . . 2.00
1 digest size 3.95

MR. CREAM PUFF
1 . . . . 1.75

MR. DOOM
1 . . . . 1.95
2 . . . . 1.95

MR. FIXITT
Apple
1 . . . . 1.95
2 . . . . 1.95

MR. MYSTIC
Eclipse
1 Will Eisner 2.50

Ms. Tree #9 © Eclipse Comics

MS. TREE'S THRILLING DETECTIVE ADVENTURES
Eclipse
1 Miller pin up 4.00
2 . . . . 2.50
3 . . . . 2.00
Becomes:

MS. TREE
4 thru 6 . . . . @2.00
7 . . . . 2.50
8 . . . . 8.00
9 . . . . 2.00
Aardvark–Vanaheim
10 thru 18 . . . . @2.00
Renegade
19 thru 49 . . . . @2.00
50 . . . . 4.50
1 3-D Classic 2.95

MUMMY, THE
Monster Comics
1 A:Dr.Clarke,Prof.Belmore 1.95
2 Mummy's Curse 1.95
3 A:Carloph 1.95
4 V:Carloph, conc. 1.95

MUMMY'S CURSE
Aircel
1 thru 4 . . . . @2.25

MURCIELAGA: SHE-BAT
Hero Graphics
1 Daerick Gross reps. 1.50
2 Reps. contd 2.95

MURDER
Renegade
1 SD 1.70
2 CI(c) 1.70
3 SD 1.70

MURDER (2nd series)
1 . . . . 2.00

MUTANT FORCES
1 . . . . 1.50

MUTANT ZONE
Aircel
1 Future story 2.50
2 F.B.I. Drone Exterminators . . . 2.50
3 conclusion 2.50

MYRON MOOSE FUNNIES
1 thru 3 . . . . @1.75

MYSTERY MAN
Slave Labor
1 thru 5 . . . . @1.75

MYSTICAL NINJA
1 . . . . 1.50

MYTH ADVENTURES
Warp Graphics
1 Mag size 1.50
2 thru 4 . . . . @1.50
5 Comic size 1.50
6 thru 11 . . . . @1.50

12 . . . . 1.75

MYTH CONCEPTIONS
Apple
1 . . . . 1.75
2 . . . . 1.75
3 thru 8 . . . . @1.95

MYTHOS
Wonder Comix
1 and 2 . . . . @1.50

NAIVE INTER-DIMENSIONAL COMMANDO KOALAS
Eclipse
1 . . . . 1.50

NATURE OF THE BEAST
Caliber
1 'The Beast' 2.95

Nausicaä of the Valley of Wind #6
© Viz Comics

NAUSICAÄ OF THE VALLEY OF WIND
Viz Select
Book One 4.50
Book Two 5.50
Book Three 4.00
Book Four 3.00
Book Five 2.50
Book Six 2.95
Book Seven 2.95
[Part 2]
#1 . . . . 2.95
#2 . . . . 2.95
#3 . . . . 2.95
#4 . . . . 2.95
[Part 3]
#1 . . . . 2.95
#2 . . . . 2.95
#3 . . . . 2.95

Naz Rat #4 © Eternity

NAZRAT
Eternity
1	2.50
2	2.00
3 thru 6	@1.80

NEAT STUFF
13	2.50

NEGATIVE BURN
Caliber
1 I:Matrix 7	2.95
2	2.95
3	2.95
4 thru 18 various stories	@2.95
19 Flaming Carrot	2.95
20 In the Park	2.95
21 Trollords	2.95
22 Father the Dryad	2.95
TPB Best of Year One	9.95

NEIL AND BUZZ
1	2.00

NEIL THE HORSE
Aardvark–Vanaheim
1 Art:Arn Sara	6.00
1a 2nd printing	2.00
2	3.00
3	4.00
4	3.00
5 Video Warriors	2.00
6 Video Warriors	2.00
7 Video Warriors	2.00
8 Outer Space	2.00
9 Conan	2.00
10	2.00
Renegade
11 Fred Astair	1.70
12	1.70
13	1.70
14 Special	3.00
15	1.70

NEMESIS
Fleetway
1 thru 16	@1.95

NEO CANTON LEGACY
1	2.00

NEOMAN
1	1.75
2	1.75
3 double-size	3.50

NEON CITY
Innovation
1	2.25

NERVE
1	2.50
2	1.75
3	1.50
4	1.50
5	1.50

NERVOUS REX
1	3.00
1a 2nd printing	2.00
2	3.00
3	3.00
4	2.50
5 thru 10	@2.00
GraphicNovel	3.50

NETHERWORLDS
1	1.50
2	1.50
3	1.95
4	1.95

NEW BEGINNINGS
1 and 2	@1.75

NEWCOMERS ILLUSTRATED
Newcomers Publishing
1 thru 5 various artists	@2.95
6 Science Fiction	2.95
7 thru 8	@2.95

NEW ENGLAND GOTHIC
3	2.00

NEW ERADICATORS
Vol 2 #1 NewBeginnings	2.00
Vol 2 #2 NewBeginnings	2.00
Vol 2 #3 NewFriends	2.00

NEW FRONTIERS
1 CS(c)	3.00
1a 2nd Printing	1.75

NEW FRONTIERS
Evolution
1 A:Action Master, Green Ghost	1.95

NEW GOLDEN AGE
1	1.50

NEW HERO COMICS
Pierce
1 and 2	@1.00

NEW HUMANS
Eternity
1	1.80
2 thru 15	@1.95
Annual #1	2.95

NEW HUMANS
1 Shattered Earth Chron	1.95

NEW KIDS ON THE BLOCK
Harvey
1	1.25

NEW L.I.F.E. BRIGADE
1	1.80
2	1.80
3	1.80

NEW POWER STARS
1	2.00

NEW REALITY
1 thru 6	@1.25

NEWSTRALIA
Innovation
(Prev. Color)
4	2.25
5	2.25

NEW TRIUMPH
Matrix Graphics
1	3.00
1a 2nd printing	1.75
2 thru 4	@1.50

NEW WORLD ORDER
Blazer Studios
1 thru 8	@2.50

NEW YORK CITY OUTLAWS
1 thru 5	@2.50

NEW YORK, YEAR ZERO
Eclipse
1 thru 4	@2.00

NEXUS
Capital
1 SR,I:Nexus,large size	35.00
2 SR,Mag size	15.00
3 SR,Mag size	7.00

NIGHT LIFE
Caliber
1 thru 7	@1.50

NIGHT MASTER
1 Vigil	5.50
2 Vigil	2.50
3	1.50

NIGHT OF THE LIVING DEAD
Fantaco
0 prelude	1.75

1 based on cult classic movie . . . 4.95
2 Movie adapt,continued 4.95
3 Movie adapt,conclusion 4.95
5 . . . . 5.95

NIGHTSTAR
1 . . . . 2.50

NIGHT'S CHILDREN
Fantaco
1 . . . . 3.50
2 . . . . 3.50
3 . . . . 3.50

NIGHT STREETS
Arrow
1 . . . . 2.50
2 thru 4 . . . . @1.50

NIGHT VISITORS
1 . . . . 1.95

NIGHT WOLF
1 thru 4 . . . . @1.75

NIGHTVEIL'S CAULDRON OF HORROR
1 . . . . 2.50

NIGHTWIND
1 & 2 . . . . @1.95

NIGHT ZERO
Fleetway
1 thru 4 . . . . @1.95

NINGA-BOTS
Prelude
1 . . . . 2.00

Ninja #5 © Eternity

NINJA
Eternity
1 . . . . 3.00
2 thru 6 . . . . @1.80

7 thru 13 . . . . @1.95

NINJA ELITE
1 thru 5 . . . . @1.50
6 thru 8 . . . . @1.95

NINJA FUNNIES
Eternity
1 . . . . 1.80
2 . . . . 1.80
3 thru 5 . . . . @1.95

NINJA HIGH SCHOOL
Eternity
1 . . . . 1.75
2 thru 4 . . . . @1.50
5 thru 22 . . . . @1.95
23 Zardon Assassin 2.25
24 . . . . 2.25
25 Return of the Zetramen 2.25
26 Stanley the Demon 2.25
27 Return of the Zetramen 2.25
28 Threat of the super computer . 2.25
29 V:Super Computer 2.25
30 I:Akaru 2.25
31 Jeremy V:Akaru 2.25
32 V:Giant Monsters Pt.1 . . . . . . 2.50
33 V:Giant Monsters Pt.2 . . . . . . 2.50
34 V:Giant Monsters Pt.3 . . . . . . 2.50
35 thru 43 . . . . @2.50
44 Combat Cheerleaders 2.75
45 Cheerleader Competition 2.75
Special #1 . . . . 2.95
Special #2 . . . . 2.95
Special #3 . . . . 2.95
Special #3 1/2 . . . . 2.25
Annual 1989 . . . . 2.95
Annual 3 . . . . 3.95
Volume 15 TPB 3 stories 7.95

NINJA HIGH SCHOOL GIRLS
Antarctic Press
0 . . . . 2.75
1 rep. 2.75
2 rep. 2.75
3 thru 5 rep. 3.95
Yearbook 3.95

NINJA HIGH SCHOOL PERFECT MEMORY
Antarctic Press
1 thru 2 . . . . 4.95

NINJA HIGH SCHOOL SMALL BODIES
Antarctic Press
1 "Monopolize" 2.50
2 thru 4 Omegadon Cannon 2.75

NO COMICS
1 . . . . 2.00
2 . . . . 2.00

NO GUTS, NO GLORY
Fantaco
1 One Shot, K.Eastman's 1st solo
work since TMNT 2.95

NOMADS OF ANTIQUITY
1 thru 6 . . . . @1.50

NORMAL MAN
Aardvark–Vanaheim
1 . . . . 4.00
2 thru 9 . . . . @2.50
Renegade
10 thru 19 . . . . @1.70

NORTHGUARD AND THE MANDES CONCLUSION
1 thru 3 . . . . @1.95

NULL PATROL
1 thru 2 . . . . @1.50

NYOKA THE JUNGLE GIRL
AC Comics
3 . . . . 2.25
4 . . . . 2.25
5 . . . . 2.50

OCTOBERFEST
Now & Then
1 (1976) Dave Sim 15.00

OFFERINGS
Cry For Dawn
1 Sword & Sorcery stories 2.75

OKTOBERFEST
Now & Then
1 (1976) Dave Sim 20.00

OFFICIAL BUZ SAWYER
1 . . . . 2.00
2 . . . . 2.00
3 . . . . 2.00
4 . . . . 1.50
5 . . . . 2.00
6 . . . . 2.00

OFFICIAL HOW TO DRAW G.I. JOE
Blackthorne
1 thru 5 . . . . @2.00

OFFICIAL HOW TO DRAW ROBOTECH
Blackthorne
12 . . . . 2.95
13 thru 16 . . . . @2.00

OFFICIAL HOW TO DRAW TRANSFORMERS
Blackthorne
1 thru 7 . . . . @2.00

OFFICIAL JOHNNY HAZARD
1 . . . . 2.00
2 . . . . 2.00
3 . . . . 2.00
4 . . . . 1.50
5 . . . . 2.00

OFFICIAL JUNGLE JIM
1 thru 5 AR,rep. . . . . @2.00
6 AR,rep. 1.50

7 thru 10 AR,rep.	@2.00
11 thru 20 AR,rep.	@2.50
Annual #1	2.00
Giant Size	3.95

OFFICIAL MANDRAKE

1 thru 5	@2.00
6	1.50
7 thru 10	@2.00
11	2.50
12	2.00
13 thru 17	@2.50
Annual #1	3.95
King Size #1	3.95
Giant Size #1	3.95

Official Modesty Blaize #1
© Solo Syndication

OFFICIAL MODESTY BLAISE
Pioneer

1 thru 4	@2.00
5	1.50
6 thru 14	@2.00
Annual #1	3.95
King Size #1	3.95

OFFICIAL PRINCE VALIANT

1 Hal Foster,rep.	2.00
2 Hal Foster,rep.	2.00
3 Hal Foster,rep.	2.00
4 Hal Foster,rep.	2.00
5 Hal Foster,rep.	2.00
6 Hal Foster,rep.	2.00
7	1.50
8 thru 14	@2.00
15 thru 24	@2.50
Annual #1	3.95
King Size#1	3.95

OFFICIAL RIP KIRBY

1 AR	2.00
2 AR	2.00
3 AR	2.00
4 AR	1.50
5 AR	2.00
6 AR	2.00

OFFICIAL SECRET AGENT

1 thru 5 AW rep	@2.00
6 AW	1.50
7 AW	2.00
8 AW	2.00
9 AW	2.00

OFFWORLDERS' QUARTERLY

1	1.50

OF MYTHS AND MEN

1	1.75
2	1.75

OHM'S LAW
Imperial Comics

1 thru 2	@1.95
3 V:Men in Black	1.95
4 A:Damonstriek	1.95
5 F:Tryst	1.95

OMEGA
North Star

1 1st pr by Rebel,rare	80.00
1a Vigil(Yellow Cov.)	27.00
2	2.00

OMEN
North Star

1	8.00
1a 2nd printing	2.00
2 thru 4	@3.50

OMICRON

1 and 2	@2.25
3	2.50

OMNIMAN

1	2.00

OMNIMEN

1	3.50

ONE SHOT WESTERN
Calibur
One Shot F:Savage Sisters,

Tornpath Outlaw	2.50

ONLY A MATTER OF LIFE AND DEATH

1	3.95

ON THE ROAD WITH GEORGE & BARBARA IN VACATIONLAND

1	2.50

OPEN SEASON
Renegade

1 thru 7	@2.00

OPERATIVE SCORPIO
Blackthorne

1	3.50

ORACLE PRESENTS

1 thru 4	@1.50

ORBIT
Eclipse

1	3.95
2	3.95
3	4.95

ORIGINAL TOM CORBET
Eternity

1 Rep. Newspaper Strips	2.95
2 Rep. Newspaper Strips	2.95
3 Rep. Newspaper Strips	2.95

ORLAK: FLESH & STEEL
Caliber

1 '1991 A.D.'	2.50

ORLAK REDUX
Caliber

1	3.95

The Others #1 © Cormac Publ.

OTHERS, THE
Cormac Publishing

1	1.50

OUT OF THIS WORLD

1	3.50

OUTLANDER

1	4.50
2	3.00
3	2.50
4	2.50
5	2.50
6 and 7	@1.95
8	2.25

OUTLAW OVERDRIVE
Blue Comet Press

1 Red Edition I:Deathrow	2.95
1a Black Edition	2.95

OVERLOAD
Eclipse

1	1.50

All comics prices listed are for *Near Mint* condition.   CVA Page 541

OVERTURE
1	2.25
2	2.25

OZ
Imperial Comics
1 thru 3 Land of Oz Gone Mad	@2.95
4 Tin Woodsmen	2.95
5 F:Pumkinhead	2.95
6 Emerald City	2.95
7 V:Bane Wolves	2.95
Spec.#1	5.95

PAJAMA CHRONICLES
1	1.50
2	1.75
3	1.75

PANDA KHAN
1 thru 4	@2.00

PAPER CUTS
1 E Starzer-1982	17.50
2	2.50
3	2.50

PARTICLE DREAMS
Fantagraphics
1	3.00
2	2.25
3	2.25
4	2.25
5	2.25
6	2.25

PARTNERS IN PANDEMONIUM
Caliber
1 'Hell on Earth'	2.50
2 Sheldon&Murphy become mortal	2.50
3 A:Abra Cadaver	2.50

PARTS OF A HOLE
Caliber
1 Short Stories	2.50

PARTS UNKNOWN
Eclipse
1 I:Spurr,V:Aliens	2.50
2 Aliens on Earth cont.	2.50

PATRICK RABBIT
1	2.00
2	2.00
3	2.00

PAUL THE SAMURAI
New England Comics
1	2.75
2	2.75
3	2.75

PELLESTAR
1	1.95
2	1.95
3	1.95

PENDULUM
Adventure
1 Big Hand,Little Hand	2.50

Pendulum #3 © Adventure Comics

2 The Immortality Formula	2.50
3	2.50

PENGUIN AND PENCILGUIN
1 thru 6	@2.00

PENTACLE: SIGN OF 5
Eternity
1	2.25
2 Det.Sandler,H.Smitts	2.25
3 Det.Sandler => New Warlock	2.25
4 5 warlocks Vs. Kaji	2.50

PETER RISK, MONSTER MASHER
1 thru 4	@2.00
5	1.50

PHANTOM
1	5.95
2	5.95
3	5.95
4 and 5	@6.95

PHANTOM OF FEAR CITY
Claypool
1 thru 7	2.50

PHANTOM OF THE OPERA
Eternity
1	1.95

PHASE ONE
Victory
1	3.00
2	2.00
3 thru 5	@1.50

PHIGMENTS
Eternity
1	5.00
2	2.00
3	1.95

PHONEY PAGES
Renegade
1	1.70
2	1.70

PIED PIPER OF HAMELIN
Tome
1	2.95

PINEAPPLE ARMY
1 thru 10	@1.75

PINK FLOYD EXPERIENCE
Revolutionary
1 based on rock group	2.50
2 Dark Side of the Moon	2.50
3 Dark Side of the Moon, Wish you were here	2.50
4 The Wall	2.50
5 A Momentary lapse of reason	2.50

PIRATE CORPS!
Eternity
6 and 7	@1.95
Spec. #1	1.95

Piranha Is Loose! #1 © Special Studio

PIRANHA! IS LOOSE
Special Studio
1 Drug Runners,F:Piranha	2.95
2 Expedition into Terror	2.95

PIXI JUNKET
Viz
1 thru 6	@2.75

P.J. WARLOCK
Eclipse
1 thru 3	@2.00

PLANET COMICS
Blackthorne
(Prev. Color)
4 and 5	@2.00

PLANET OF TERROR
1 BW 1.75

Planet of the Apes
© Adventure Comics

PLANET OF THE APES
Adventure Comics
1 WD,collect.ed. 7.00
1 2 covers 5.00
1a 2nd printing 2.50
1b 3rd printing 2.25
2 . . . . 3.00
3 . . . . 2.75
4 . . . . 2.75
5 D:Alexander? 2.75
6 Welcome to Ape City 2.75
7 . . . . 2.75
8 Christmas Story 2.50
9 Swamp Ape Village 2.50
10 Swamp Apes in Forbidden City 2.50
11 Ape War continues 2.50
12 W.Alexander/Coure 2.50
13 Planet of Apes/Alien Nation/
   Ape City x-over 2.50
14 Countdown to Zero Pt.1 . . . . 2.50
15 Countdown to Zero Pt.2 . . . . 2.50
16 Countdown to Zero Pt.3 . . . . 2.50
17 Countdown to Zero Pt.4 . . . . 2.50
18 Ape City (after Ape Nation
   mini-series 2.50
19 1991 'Conquest..' tie-in 2.50
20 Return of the Ape Riders 2.50
21 The Terror Beneath,Pt.1 . . . . 2.50
22 The Terror Beneath,Pt.2 . . . . 2.50
23 The Terror Beneath,Pt.3 . . . . 2.50
Ann #1,'Day on Planet o/t Apes' . 3.50
Lim.Ed. #1 . . . . 5.00

PLANET OF THE APES:
BLOOD OF THE APES
Adventure Comics
1 A:Tonus the Butcher 3.00
2 Valia/Taylorite Connection 2.50
3 Ape Army in Phis 2.50
4 . . . . 2.50

PLANET OF THE APES:
FORBIDDEN ZONE
Adventure
1 Battle for the Planet o/t Apes
   & Planet o/t Apes tie-in 2.50
2 A:Juilus 2.50

PLANET OF THE APES:
SINS OF THE FATHER
Adventure Comics
1 Conquest Tie in 2.50

PLANET OF THE APES
URCHAKS' FOLLY
Adventure Comics
1 . . . . 3.00
2 . . . . 2.50
3 'The Taylorites' 2.50
4 Conclusion 2.50

PLANET 29
Caliber
1 A Future Snarl Tale 2.50
2 A:Biff,Squakman 2.50

PLANET-X
Eternity
1 . . . . 2.50

PLAN 9 FROM
OUTER SPACE
Eternity
1 . . . . 2.50
2 . . . . 2.25
3 . . . . 2.25

PLASMA BABY
Caliber
1 'Strange New World' 2.50

PLASTRON CAFE
Mirage
1 Eastman,Laird,RV,inc.North by
   Downeast 2.25

PLAYGROUND 1826
Caliber
1 . . . . 2.50

POINT BLANK
Eclipse
1 thru 5 . . . . @2.95

POLIS
Brave New World
1 I:Polis 2.50

PORK KNIGHT
Silver Snail
1 . . . . 1.75

PORT
Silver Wolf
1 . . . . 1.50
2 . . . . 1.50

PORTABLE LOWLIFE
1 Real life Adventures 4.95

PORTIA PRINZ
Eclipse
1 thru 5 . . . . @2.00

POSSIBLE MAN
1 . . . . 1.75
2 . . . . 1.75

POST BROTHERS
Rip Off Press
15 thru 18 . . . . @2.00
19 . . . . 2.50
20 . . . . 2.50

POWER COMICS
1 Smart-Early Ardvaark 25.00
1a 2nd printing 8.00
2 I:Cobalt Blue 10.00
3 . . . . 3.00
4 . . . . 3.00
5 . . . . 4.00

POWER COMICS
Eclipse
1 BB,DGb,Powerbolt 2.00
2 BB,DGb 2.00
3 BB,DGb . . . . , . . . 2.00

POWER CORPS
1 . . . . , . . 2.50
2 . . . . 2.50

POWER PLAYS
1 . . . . 1.75
2 . . . . 1.75
3 . . . . 1.75

POWER PRINCIPLE
1 thru 3 . . . . @1.95

POWER STATION
1 . . . . 1.75

POWER UNLIMITED
1 . . . . 1.95

PRACTICE IN PAIN
Dramemon Studios
1 I:Queen of the Dead 3.00

PRETEEN DIRTY GENE
KUNG FU KANGAROOS
Blackthorne
1 and 2 . . . . @1.50

PREY
Monster Comics
1 I:Prey,A:Andrina 2.25
2 V:Andrina 2.25
3 conclusion 2.25

PRICE, THE
1 Dreadstar mag. size 20.00

PRIME CUTS
Fantagraphics
1 adult 3.50
2 thru 6 . . . . @3.50
7 thru 12 . . . . @3.95

PRIMER
Comico
1	6.00
2 MW,I:Grendel	100.00
3	5.00
4	5.00
5 SK(1st work)	18.00
6 IN,Evangeline	18.00

PRIME SLIME TALES
Mirage
1	5.00
2	2.50
3 thru 6	@1.50

PRINCE VALIANT
1 thru 4	@4.95
Spec #1	6.95

PRINCE VALIANT MONTHLY
1 thru 6	@3.95
6	4.95
7	4.95
8	4.95
9	6.95

PRIVATE EYES
Eternity
1 Saint rep.	1.95
2	1.95
3	1.95
4	1.95
5	1.95

PROBE
1	1.80
2	1.80

PROGENY
Spec	4.95

PROJECT: HERO
1	1.50
2	1.50
3	1.50

PROTOTYPE
1	1.75

PROWLER IN WHITE
"WHITE ZOMBIE", THE
1	2.00

PRYDERI TERRA
1	1.75
2	1.75

PSI–JUDGE ANDERSON
1 thru 15	@1.95

PSYCHOMAN
Revolutionary
1 I:Psychoman	2.50

PUMA BLUES
Aardvark–Vanaheim
1 10,000 printed	4.50
1a 2nd printing	2.00
2	3.00

Puma Blues #1 © Aardvark Vanaheim

3	2.00
4 thru 19	@1.70
20 Special	2.25

Mirage
21 thru 24	@1.70
25	2.50
26 thru 28	@1.75

PURGATORY USA
1	1.75
2	1.75
3	1.95

QUACK
Star Reach
1	2.00
2	2.00
3	2.00
4 Dave Sim	3.00
5 Dave Sim	3.00
6	2.00

QUADRO GANG
1	1.25

QUAZAR
1	2.00

QUEST PRESENTS
Quest
1 JD	1.75
2 JD	1.75
3 JD	1.75

RADIO BOY
Eclipse
1	2.00

RADREX
1 thru 3	@2.25

RAGNAROK
Sun Comics
1 I:Ragnarok Guy,Honey	2.50
2 The Melder Foundation	2.50

3 Guy/Honey mission contd.	2.50
4 I:Big Gossage	2.50

RAIKA
Sun Comics
1 thru 12	@2.50

RALPH SNART
Now
1	5.00
2	4.00
3	4.00

[Volume 2]
1	3.00
2 thru 8	@1.50
Trade Paperback	2.95

RAMBO
Blackthorne
1 thru 5	@2.00

RAMBO III
Blackthorne
1	2.00

RAMM
Megaton Comics
1 and 2	@1.50

RAMPAGE ALLEY
1	1.75
2	1.75

RANMA 1/2
1 thru 2	2.75

RAPHAEL
1 TMNT	17.50
1a 2nd printing	7.50

RAT FINK
World of Fandom
1 color cover	2.50
2 color cover	2.50

RAW MEDIA MAGS.
Reb
1 TV,SK,short stories	5.00

RAZORGUTS
Monster Comics
1 thru 4	2.25

REACTOMAN
B-Movie Comics
1	1.50
1a signed,numbered	2.75
2 thru 4	@1.50
collection	4.95

REAGAN'S RAIDERS
1 thru 6	@2.50

REAL LIFE
1	2.50

REALM
Arrow
1 Fantasy	7.50

Realm # 18 © Arrow Comics

2	4.00
3	3.00
4 TV,Deadworld	21.00
5 I:L.Kazan	2.00
6 thru 13	@1.50
14 thru 18	@1.95
19	2.50

REAL STUFF
Fantagraphic
1 thru 12	2.50

RED FOX
Harrier
1 scarce	6.00
1a 2nd printing	2.50
2 rare	5.00
3	3.00
4 I:White Fox	3.00
5 I:Red Snail	3.00
6	1.75
7 Wbolton	1.75
8	1.75
9 Demosblurth	1.75

RED & STUMPY
Parody Press
1 Ren & Stimpy parody	2.95

RED HEAT
Blackthorne
1	2.00

REDLAW
Caliber
1 Preview Killer of Crows	2.50

RED SHETLAND
Blackthorne
1	2.00

REID FLEMING
Blackbird-Eclipse
1 I:Reid Fleming	10.00
1a 2nd printing	5.50
1b 3rd printing	2.50

1b 4th printing	2.50

Volume 2
#1 Rogues to Riches Pt.1	6.00
#2 Rogues to Riches Pt.2	4.00
#3 Rogues to Riches Pt.3	3.00
#3a LaterPrinting	2.50
#4 Rogues to Riches Pt.4	3.00
#5 Rogues to Riches Pt.5	2.50

REIGN OF THE DARK LORD
1	1.80
2	1.80
3	1.80
4	1.95

REIVERS
Enigma
1 thru 2 Ch'tocc in Space	2.95

RELENTLESS PURSUIT
1	2.00
2	1.75
3	1.95

RENEGADE
Rip Off Press
1	2.50

RENEGADE RABBIT
1	1.75
2	1.75

RENEGADE ROMANCE
1	2.00
2	3.50

RESISTANCE
1	1.95

RETALIATOR
Eclipse
1 I&O:Retaliator	2.50
2 O:Retaliator cont.	2.50

RETIEF
1 thru 6 Keith Laumer adapt.	@2.00

[New Series]
1 thru 6	@2.25

RETIEF OF THE CDT
1	2.00
2	2.00

RETIEF AND THE WARLORDS
Adventure Comics
1 Keith Laumer Novel Adapt.	2.50
2 Haterakans	2.50
3 Retief Arrested for Treason	2.50
4 Final Battle (last issue)	2.50

RETIEF: DIPLOMATIC IMMUNITY
Adventure Comics
1 Groaci Invasion.	2.50
2 Groaci story cont.	2.50

RETIEF: GARBAGE INVASION
Adventure Comics
1	2.50

RETIEF: THE GIANT KILLER
Adventure Comics
1 V:Giant Dinasaur	2.50

RETIEF: GRIME & PUNISHMENT
Adventure Comics
1 Planet Slunch	2.50

RETROGRADE
Eternity
1 thru 4	@1.95

Return of the Skyman #1 © Ace Comics

RETURN OF THE SKYMAN
Ace Comics
1 SD	1.75

REVOLVER
Renegade
1 SD	1.70
2 thru 6	@1.70
Annual #1	2.00

REVOLVING DOORS
Blackthorne
1	1.75
2	1.75
3	1.75
Graphic Novel	3.95

RHAJ
1	2.00
2	2.00

RHUDIPRRT PRINCE OF FUR
1	2.00

RICK GEARY'S WONDERS & ODDITIES
1 . . . . 2.00

RICK RAYGUN
1 . . . . 2.00
2 thru 8 . . . . @1.75

RIO KID
Eternity
1 I:Rio Kid 2.50
2 V:Blow Torch Killer 2.50
3 . . . . 2.50

RION 2990
Rion
1 . . . . 2.75
2 . . . . 1.50

RIP IN TIME
Fantagor
1 RCo,Limited series 3.00
2 RCo 2.00
3 RCo 2.00
4 RCo 2.00
5 RCo,Last 2.00

RIPLASH: SWEET VENGEANCE
Pocket Change Comics
1 O:Riplash 2.95

RIPPER
1 thru 5 . . . . @2.50

RISING STARS
1 . . . . 1.95

RIVIT: COLD-BLOODED COMMANDO FROG
1 . . . . 1.75

ROACHMILL
1 . . . . 5.50
2 . . . . 3.00
3 . . . . 3.00
4 . . . . 3.00
See: Dark Horse

ROBIN HOOD
1 thru 4 . . . . @2.25

ROBIN RED
1 thru 3 . . . . @1.75

R.O.B.O.T. BATTALION 2050
Eclipse
1 . . . . 2.00

ROBOT COMICS
1 . . . . 1.50

ROBO WARRIORS
CFW
1 thru 11 . . . . @1.95
Becomes:
KUNG FU WARRIORS

ROBOTECH: AFTERMATH
Academy Comics
1 thru 10 R:Bruce Lewis . . . . . @2.95
11 Zentradi Traitor 2.95
12 and 13 . . . . @2.95

ROBOTECH: CLONE
Academy Comics
1 Dialect of Duality 2.95
2 V:Monte Yarrow 2.95
3 Ressurection 2.95
4 Ressurection . . . ./. . . 2.95

ROBOTECH: INVID WAR
Eternity
1 No Man's Land 2.50
2 V:Defoliators 2.50
3 V:The Invid,Reflex Point 2.50
4 V:The Invid 2.50
5 Moonbase Aluce II 2.50
6 Moonbase-Zentraedi plot 2.50
7 Zentraedi plot contd. 2.50
8 A:Lancer 2.50
9 A:Johnathan Wolfe 2.50
10 . . . . 2.50
11 F:Rand 2.50
12 thru 13 . . . . 2.50

ROBOTECH: INVID WAR AFTERMATH
Eternity
1 thru 6 F:Rand 2.75

ROBOTECH: RETURN TO MACROSS
Eternity
1 thru 5 . . . . 2.50

Robotech Return to Macross #20
© Academy Comics

ROBOTECH: RETURN TO MACROSS
Academy Comics
1 thru 17 Roy Fokker 2.75
18 F:The Faithful 2.75
19 F:Lisa 2.75

20 F:Lisa 2.75

ROBOTECH: UNTOLD STORIES
Eternity
1 . . . . 2.50

ROBOTECH: WARRIORS
Academy Comics
1 F:Breetai 2.95
2 F:Mirya 2.95
3 F:Mirya 2.95

ROBOTECH II THE SENTINELS
Eternity
1 . . . . 3.50
1a 2nd printing 1.95
2 . . . . 3.00
2a 2nd printing 1.95
3 . . . . 2.00
3a 2nd printing 1.95
4 thru 16 . . . . @1.95
Book 2
1 thru 12 . . . . @2.25
13 thru 20 . . . . @2.25
Wedding Special #1 . . . . 1.95
Wedding Special #2 . . . . 1.95
Robotech II Handbook 2.50
Book Three
1 thru 8 V:Invid 2.50

ROBOTECH II: THE SENTINELS BOOK
Academy Comics
1 thru 13 F:Tesla . . . . @2.75
14 V:Invid 2.75
15 and 18 . . . . @2.75

ROBOTECH II: THE SENTINELS: CYBERPIRATES
Eternity
1 The Hard Wired Coffin 2.25
2 . . . . 2.25
3 . . . . 2.25
4 finale 2.25

ROBOTECH II: THE SENTINELS: THE MALCONTENT UPRISING
Eternity
1 thru 12 . . . . @1.95

ROCITI'S REVENGE
1 . . . . 1.95

ROCK & ROLL COMICS
Revolutionary
1 Guns & Roses 7.50
1a 2nd printing 3.50
1b 3rd printing 2.00
1c 4th-7th printing 2.00
2 Metalica 5.00
2a 2nd printing 3.00
2b 3rd-5th printing 2.00
3 Bon Jovi 3.50
4 Motley Crue 4.00

5 Def Leppard	2.50
6 RollingStones	4.00
6a 2nd-4th printing	2.00
7 The Who	3.50
7a 2nd-3rd printing	2.00
9 Kiss	8.00
9a 2nd-3rd Printing	2.00
10 Warrant/Whitesnake	2.50
10a 2nd Printing	2.00
11 Aerosmith	2.00
12 New Kids on Block	5.00
12a 2nd Printing	2.00
13 LedZeppelin	3.00
14 Sex Pistols	2.00

See Independent Color

Rocket Ranger #3 © Adventure Comics

ROCKET RANGERS
Adventure
1 thru 3 .... @2.95

ROCKHEADS
1 .... 1.95

ROCKIN ROLLIN MINER ANTS
Fate Comics
1 As seen in TMNT #40	2.25
1a Gold Variant copy	7.50
2 Elephant Hunting, A:Scorn,Blister	2.25
3 V:Scorn, Inc.,K.Eastman Ant pin-up	2.25
4 Animal Experiments,V:Loboto	2.25

ROCKOLA
1 .... 1.50

ROLLING STONES: THE SIXTIES
Personality
1 Regular Version 2.95
1a Deluxe Version,w/cards 6.95

ROSCOE THE DAWG
1 thru 4 .... @2.00

ROSE
Hero Graphics
1 From The Champions 3.50
2 A:Huntsman 3.50
3 thru 5 .... @2.95

ROSE 'N" GUNN
Bishop Pres
1 Deadly Duo 2.95
2 V:Marilyn Monroe 2.95

ROTTWEILER
1 .... 1.50
2 .... 1.50

ROUGH RAIDERS
1 .... 1.80
2 .... 1.80
3 .... 2.00

ROULETTE
1 .... 2.50

ROVERS
Eternity
1 thru 7 .... @1.95

RUBES REVIVED
Fish Warp
1 .... 2.00
2 .... 2.00
3 .... 2.00

RUK BUD WEBSTER
Fish Warp
1 thru 3 .... @1.70

SAGA OF THE MAN-ELF
1 thru 5 .... @2.25

SAGA OF THE VON ERICH WARRIORS
1 .... 2.00

SALIMBA
Blackthorne
1 .... 3.50

SAMURAI (1st series)
1	125.00
2	60.00
3	60.00
4	60.00
5	60.00

SAMURAI
Aircel
1 rare	9.00
1a 2nd printing	3.00
1b 3rd printing	2.00
2	6.00
2a 2nd printing	2.50
3	3.00
4	3.00
5 thru 12	@2.00
13 DK (1st art)	5.00
14 thru 16 DK	@4.00
17 thru 22	@2.00

[3rd series]
#1 .... 1.70

#2	1.70
#3	1.70
#4	1.95
#5	1.95
#6	1.95
#7	1.95
Compilation Book	4.95

SAMURAI FUNNIES
Solson
1 .... 2.00
2 .... 2.00
3 .... 2.00

SAMURAI PENGUIN
Solson
1	3.00
2 I:Dr.Radium	2.00
3	2.00
4	1.50
5 FC	1.50
6 color	2.25
7	2.25
8	1.75
9	1.75

SAMURAI 7
Gauntlet Comics
1 I: Samurai 7 .... 2.50

SAMURAI, SON OF DEATH
Eclipse
1 .... 3.95
1a 2nd printing 3.95

SANCTION 7
1 .... 1.95
2 .... 1.95

SANCTUARY
Viz
1 World of Yakuza 4.95
2 thru 4 .... @4.95
5 thru 9 .... @4.95

SANTA CLAWS
Eternity
1 'Deck the Mall with Blood and Corpses' 2.95

SAVAGE HENRY
Vortex
1 thru 13 .... @1.75
Rip Off Press
14 thru 15 .... @2.00
16 thru 24 .... @2.50

SAVIOR
1 thru 5 .... @1.95

SAX AND COMPANY
1 .... 1.50
2 .... 1.50

SCARAMOUCH
Innovation
1 .... 2.50

SCARLET IN GASLIGHT
1 A:SherlockHolmes 4.00
2 .... 3.00

3	2.50
4	2.50

SCARLET KISS: THE VAMPIRE

1	2.95

SCIMIDAR
Eternity

1	4.25
1a 2nd Printing	2.50
2	3.00
3	3.00
4 HotCover	3.50
4A MildCover	3.00

SCOUT HANDBOOK
Eclipse

1	1.75

SCRATCH
Outside

1	3.00
2	2.00
3	1.75
4	1.75

SCREENPLAY

1	1.75
2 and 3	@1.95

SCROG SPECIAL

1	2.50

SCUD: DISPOSABLE ASSASSIN
Fireman Press

1 thru 6 F:Scud	2.50

SECRET DOORS

1	6.00
1a 2nd printing	2.00

SERPENT RISING
Gauntlet Comics

1	2.95

SENTINEL

1	1.95
2	1.95
3	1.95
4	1.95

SERIUS BOUNTY HUNTER

1 thru 4	@1.75

SHADOWBLADE

1	2.50
2	2.50
3	1.95
4	1.95

SHADOWLAND

1 and 2	@2.25

SHADOWALKER
Aircel

1 thru 4	@1.70

SHADOW LORD

1	1.50

SHADOWMEN

1	2.25

SHADOW OF THE GROUND

1 Groundhog	1.25

SHADOWS FROM THE GRAVE

1	2.00
2	2.00

SHADOW SLASHER
Pocket Change Comics

1 I:Shadow Slasher	2.50
2 V:Riplash	2.50
3 F:Matt Baker	2.50
4 Evolution	2.50

SHADOW SLAYER

0	1.95

SHADOW WARRIOR

1	1.60
2	1.60

SHALOMAN

1 thru 5	@1.75

Shanghaied #2 © Eternity

SHANGHAIED
Eternity

1	1.80
2	1.80
3	1.95
4	1.95

SHAOLIN: 2000

1	1.50

SHARDS
Acension Comics

1 I:Silver, Raptor, Ripple	2.50
2 F:Anomoly	2.50

SHATTERED EARTH
Eternity

1 thru 9	@1.95

Shatterpoint #2 © Eternity Comics

SHATTERPOINT
Eternity

1 thru 4 Broid miniseries	@2.25

SHE-CAT
AC Comics

1 thru 4	@2.50

SHE-DEVILS ON WHEELS
Aircel

1 thru 3	2.95

SHERLOCK HOLMES
Eternity

1 thru 22	@1.95

SHERLOCK HOLMES CASEBOOK
Eternity

1	2.25
2	2.25

SHERLOCK HOLMES: CHRONICLES OF CRIME AND MYSTERY
Northstar

1 'The Speckled Band'	2.25

SHERLOCK HOLMES OF THE '30's
Eternity

1 thru 7	@2.95

SHERLOCK HOLMES: RETURN OF THE DEVIL
Adventure
1 V:Moriarty 2.50
2 V:Moriarty 2.50

SHERLOCK JUNIOR
Eternity
1 Rep.NewspaperStrips 1.95
2 Rep.NewspaperStrips 1.95
3 Rep.NewspaperStrips 1.95

SHOCKWAVES
Knight Press
1 . . . . 2.95

SHRED
CFW
1 thru 10 . . . . @2.25

SHRIEK
1 . . . . 4.95
2 . . . . 4.95
3 . . . . 7.95

SHRIKE
1 thru 6 . . . . @1.50

SHURIKEN
Victory
1 Reggi Byers 6.00
1a 2nd printing 1.50
2 . . . . 3.00
3 . . . . 2.00
4 . . . . 1.75
5 thru 13 . . . . @1.50
Graphic Nov. Reggie Byers 8.00

SHURIKEN
Eternity
1 Shuriken vs. Slate 2.50
2 Neutralizer, Meguomo 2.50
3 R:Slate 2.50
4 Morgan's Bodyguard Serrate . . 2.50
5 Slate as Shuriken & Megumo . 2.50
6 Hunt for Bionauts, final issue . . 2.50

SHURIKEN: COLD STEEL
1 . . . . 1.95
2 . . . . 1.95
3 thru 6 . . . . @1.95

SHURIKEN TEAM-UP
1 thru 3 . . . . @1.95

SIAMESE TWIN COMICS
1 . . . . 2.50

SIDESHOW
7 . . . . 3.50

SIEGEL & SHUSTER
2 . . . . 1.70

SILENT INVASION
Renegade
1 . . . . 4.00
2 thru 12, final issue . . . . @2.00

SILVER FAWN
1 . . . . 1.95

SILVER STORM
Aircel
1 thru 4 . . . . 2.25

SILVER WING
1 . . . . 1.00

SIMON/KIRBY READER
1 . . . . 1.75

SINBAD
1 . . . . 2.25
2 . . . . 2.25
3 . . . . 2.25
4 . . . . 2.25

SINBAD: HOUSE OF GOD
Adventure Comics
1 Caliph's Wife Kidnapped 2.50
2 Magical Genie 2.50
3 Escape From Madhi 2.50
4 A:Genie 2.50

SINNER
4 . . . . 2.75
5 . . . . 2.95
6 . . . . 2.95

SKROG
Comico
1 . . . . 3.00

SKULL
3 No price on cover 3.50

SLAUGHTERMAN
1 . . . . 4.00
2 . . . . 4.00

SLAVE GIRL
1 . . . . 2.25

SNAKE
Special Studio
1 . . . . 3.50

SNARF
Kitchen Sink
1 thru 10 . . . . @2.00
10 (c)BE 2.00
11 thru 13 . . . . @2.00

SNARL
1 and 3 . . . . @2.50

SOCKETEER
Kardia
Rocketeer parody 2.25

SOLDIERS OF FORTUNE
1 . . . . 1.95

SOLD OUT
Fantagor
1 . . . . 1.75
2 . . . . 1.75

SOLO EX-MUTANTS
Eternity
1 thru 6 . . . . @1.95

SOLSON PREVIEW
Solson
1 . . . . 2.00

SOUL
Samson Comics
1 thru 3 F:Sabbeth . . . . @2.50

SOULFIRE
Aircel
1 mini-series 1.70
2 . . . . 1.70
3 . . . . 1.70

SOULSEARCHERS AND CO.
Claypool
1 thru 8 Peter David(s) 3.00

SOUTHERN KNIGHTS
1 See Crusaders
2 . . . . 8.00
3 and 4 . . . . @5.00
5 thru 7 . . . . @4.00
Fictioneer
8 thru 11 . . . . @2.50
12 thru 33 . . . . @2.00
34 . . . . 2.25
35 The Morrigan Wars Pt.#2 . . . 3.50
36 Morrigan Wars Pt.#5 . . . . . . 3.50
Annual #1 . . . . 2.50
DreadHalloweenSpec #1 . . . . . . 2.25
Primer #1 . . . . 2.25

Southern Squadron #1 © Aircel Comics

SOUTHER SQUADRON
Aircel
1 thru 4 . . . . @2.25

SOUTHERN SQUADRON
Eternity
1 I:SQUAD 2.50

All comics prices listed are for *Near Mint* condition.

2 thru 4 . . . . @2.25

SOUTHERN SQUADRON FREEDOM OF INFO. ACT.
Eternity
1 F.F.#1 Parody/Tribute cov. . . 2.50
2 A:Waitangi Rangers 2.50
3 . . . . 2.50

SPACE ARK
Apple
1 . . . . 2.75
2 . . . . 2.50
3 . . . . 1.75
4 . . . . 1.75
5 . . . . 1.75

Space Beaver #3 © Ten-Buck Comics

SPACE BEAVER
Ten-Buck Comics
1 . . . . 2.50
2 . . . . 1.50
3 O&I:Stinger 1.50
4 A:Stinger 1.50
5 . . . . 1.50
6 O:Rodent 1.50
7 thru 12 . . . . @1.50

SPACED
1 I:Zip; 800 printed 40.00
2 . . . . 25.00
3 I:Dark Teddy 15.00
4 . . . . 15.00
5 and 6 . . . . @5.00
7 and 8 . . . . @2.00
Eclipse
9 . . . . 1.75
10 . . . . 1.75
11 thru 13 . . . . @1.50

SPACE GUYS
1 . . . . 2.25

SPACE PATROL
Adventure
1 thru 3 . . . . 2.50

SPACE 34-24-34
1 . . . . 4.50

SPACE USAGI
Mirage Studios
1 Stan Sakai,Future Usagi 2.00
2 Stan Sakai,Future Usagi 2.00
3 Stan Sakai,Future Usagi 2.00

SPACE WOLF
Antarctic Press
1 From Albedo,by Dan Flahive . . 2.50

SPARKPLUG
Hero Graphics
1 From League of Champions . . 2.95

SPARKPLUG SPECIAL
Heroic Publishing
1 V:Overman 2.50

SPATTER
1 . . . . 1.95
2 . . . . 1.95
3 . . . . 1.60
4 . . . . 2.00

SPEED RACER
1 . . . . 3.00
1a 2nd Printing 1.50

SPENCER SPOOK
A.C.E. Comics
1 . . . . 1.95
2 . . . . 1.95
3 thru 8 . . . . @1.75

SPICY TALES
1 thru 13 . . . . @1.95
14 thru 20 . . . . @2.25
Special #2 . . . . 2.25

SPIDER KISS
1 Harlan Ellison 3.95

SPINELESS MAN
Parody Press
1 Spider-Man 2099 spoof 2.50

SPIRAL CAGE
Renegade
Special 3.00

SPIRIT, THE
Kitchen Sink
Note: #1 to #11 are in color
12 thru 86 WE,rep (1986–92) . @2.00

SPIRIT OF THE WIND
1 . . . . 2.00

THE SPIRIT: ORIGIN YEARS
Kitchen Sink
1 I:Denny Colt,Ebony White 2.95
2 I:Commissioner&Ellen Dolan . . 2.95
3 WE,Palyachi,The Killer Clown . 2.95
4 WE,Orphans,Orang t/Ape Man . 2.95
5 WE 2.95

6 WE,Kiss of Death 2.95
7 thru 8 WE 2.95

SPIRIT OF THE DRAGON
Double Edge
0 Dragon Scheme 75

SPITTING IMAGE
Eclipse
1 Marvel & Image parody 2.50

SPLAT
1 thru 4 . . . . @1.75

SPOTLIGHT
1 . . . . 1.50

STAINLESS STEEL ARMIDILLO
Antartic Press
1 I:Saisni, Tania Badan 2.95

STANLEY
1 . . . . 1.50

STAR BLEECH THE GENERATION GAP
Parody Press
1 Parody 3.95

STARCHILD
Taliesin Press
0 . . . . 10.00
1 . . . . 15.00
2 . . . . 6.00
3 . . . . 4.50
4 . . . . 4.00
5 . . . . 3.00
6 . . . . 2.75
7 . . . . 2.75
8 . . . . 2.75
9 . . . . 2.50

STARGATORS
1 . . . . 2.50
2 . . . . 2.50
3 . . . . 2.50

STAR JAM COMICS
Revolutionary
1 F:Hammer 2.50

STARJONGLEUR COLLECTION
1 . . . . 2.50
2 . . . . 2.50
3 . . . . 2.50

STAR BIKERS
1 . . . . 3.95
Special 2.00

STARK FUTURE
Aircel
1 . . . . 2.50
2 thru 7 . . . . @1.75
8 . . . . 2.00
9 thru 14 . . . . @1.70

STAR RANGERS
1 thru 3 . . . . @3.00
4 . . . . 1.95
BOOK II
1 . . . . 1.95
2 . . . . 1.95

STAR REACH
Taliesin Press
1 HC,I:CodyStarbuck 8.00
2 DG,JSn 2.00
3 FB 2.00
4 HC 2.00
5 JSon 2.00
6 GD,Elric 2.00
7 DS 2.00
8 CR,KSy 2.00
9 KSy 2.00
10 KSy 2.00
11 GD 2.00
12 MN,SL 2.00
13 SL,KSy 2.00
14 . . . . 2.00
15 . . . . 2.00
16 . . . . 2.00
17 . . . . 2.00
18 . . . . 2.00

STAR WOLF CONQUEROR
1 . . . . 2.00
2 . . . . 2.00

STARLIGHT
1 . . . . 1.95
2 . . . . 1.95

STARLIGHT AGENCY
Antartic Press
1 I:Starlight Agency 1.95
2 Anderson Kidnapped 1.95
3 . . . . 1.50

STARLIGHT SQUADRON
Blackthorne
1 . . . . 2.00

STATIC
1 SD 1.50
2 SD 1.50
3 SD 1.50

STEALTH FORCE
1 thru 8 . . . . @.95

STEALTH SQUAD
Petra Comics
0 O:Stealth Squad 2.50
1 I:Stealth Squad 2.50
2 I:New Member 2.50
Volume II
1 F:Solar Blade 2.50

STECH
1 and 2 . . . . @1.50

STEEL DRAGON STORIES
Steel Dragon
1 . . . . 1.50

STEPHEN DARKLORD
1 thru 3 . . . . @1.75

STERN WHEELER
Spotlight
1 JA 1.75

STEVE CANYON
Kitchen Sink
1 thru 14 . . . . @5.00

STEVEN
1 . . . . 4.00
1a 2ndPrinting 2.95
2 . . . . 4.00
3 . . . . 2.95
4 and 5 . . . . @3.50

STICKBOY
Revolutionary
1 . . . . 2.00
2 thru 5 . . . . @2.50

STIG'S INFERNO
Vortex
1 . . . . 6.00
2 . . . . 3.50
3 . . . . 3.00
4 . . . . 3.00
5 . . . . 2.00
Eclipse
6 . . . . 1.75
7 . . . . 1.75

STING
Artline
1 . . . . 2.50

STINZ
Fantagraphics
1 . . . . 4.00
2 . . . . 4.00
3 . . . . 4.00
4 . . . . 4.00
[2nd series]
Brave New Words
1 thru 3 . . . . 2.50

STORMBRINGER
Taliesin Press
1 thru 3 . . . . @2.00

STORMWATCHER
Eclipse
1 thru 4 . . . . @2.00

STRAND, THE
Trident
1 . . . . 2.50

STRANGE BEHAVIOR
Twilite Tone Press
1 LSn,MBr,Short Stories 2.95

STRANGE BREW
Aardvark–Vanaheim
1 . . . . 5.00

STRANGE SPORTS STORIES
Adventure
1 w/2 card strip 2.50

2 The Pick-Up Game,w/cards . . . 2.50
3 Spinning Wheels,w/cards 2.50
4 thru 6 w/cards . . . . @2.50

STRANGE WORLDS
1 . . . . 3.95
2 thru 4 . . . . @3.95

STRANGES IN PARADISE
Antarctic Press
1 Terry Moore, I:Katchoo 3.50
1a 2nd printing 2.75
2 and 3 . . . . @2.75

STRATA
Renegade
1 . . . . 3.00
2 . . . . 2.50
3 . . . . 1.70
4 . . . . 1.70
5 . . . . 1.70
6 . . . . 2.00

STRAW MEN
1 thru 5 . . . . @1.95
6 thru 8 . . . . @2.25

Street Fighter #1 © Ocean Comics

STREET FIGHTER
Ocean Comics
1 thru 4 limited series . . . . . . @1.75

STREET HEROES 2005
Eternity
1 thru 3 . . . . @1.95

STREET MUSIC
Fantagraphics
1 . . . . 2.75
2 . . . . 2.75
3 . . . . 2.95
4 . . . . 2.95
5 . . . . 2.50
6 . . . . 3.95

All comics prices listed are for *Near Mint* condition.

STREET POET RAY
Fantagraphics
1	2.50
2	2.00
3	2.95
4	2.95

STREET WOLF
1 limited series	2.00
2 and 3	@2.00
Graphic Novel	6.95

STRIKER: THE ARMORED WARRIOR
Viz
1 Overture	2.75
2 V:Child Esper	2.75
3 Professor taken hostage	2.75

STYGMATA YEARBOOK
Entity
1 V:The Rodent	2.95
TPB Dragon Prophet	6.95

SUBURBAN HIGH LIFE
1 thru 5	@1.75

SUBURBAN NIGHTMARES
1 thru 4	@2.00

SUGAR RAY FINHEAD
Wolf Press
1 I&O Sugar Ray Finhead	2.50
2 I:Bessie & Big-Foot Benny the Pit Bull Man	2.95
3 thru 7 Mardi Gras	@2.95

SULTON
1 thru 3	@1.50

Sultry Teenage Super-Foxes #1
© Solson Comics

SULTRY TEENAGE SUPER-FOXES
Solson
1 thru 4 RB,Woj	@2.00

SUNRISE
1 thru 4	@1.95

SUPERSWINE
Caliber
1 Parody, I:Superswine	2.50

SURVIVALIST CHRONICLES
Survival Art
1	6.50
2	6.50
3 I:Bessie & Big Foot Benny	1.95

SWEET LUCY
Brainstorm Comics
1 w/4 cards	2.50
2	2.50

SWIFTSURE
Harrier Comics
1	2.00
2	2.00
3 thru 8	@1.75
9	9.00
9a 2nd printing	1.75
10	1.75
11	1.95

SWORD OF VALOR
A Plus Comics
1 JAp,rep.Thane of Bagarth	2.50
2 JAp/MK rep	2.50

SWORDS AND SCIENCE
Pyramid
1	1.70
2	1.70
3	1.70

SWORDS OF CEREBUS
Aardvark–Vanaheim
1 rep. Cerebus 1-4	18.00
1a reprint editions	10.00
2 rep. Cerebus 5-8	12.00
2a reprint editions	8.00
3 rep. Cerebus 9-12	12.00
3a reprint editions	8.00
4 rep. Cerebus 13-16	12.00
4a reprint editions	8.00
5 rep. Cerebus 17-20	12.00
5a reprint editions	8.00
6 rep. Cerebus 21-25	12.00
6a reprint editions	8.00

SWORDS OF SHAR-PAI
Caliber
1 Mutant Ninja Dog	2.50
2 Shar-Pei	2.50
3 Final issue	2.50

SWORDS OF VALORS: ROBIN HOOD
A Plus Comics
1 rep. of Charlton comics	2.50

SYSTEM SEVEN
Arrow
1 thru 4	@1.50

T-BIRD CHRONICLES
1	1.50
2	1.50
3	1.50

T-MINUS-ONE
1	2.00
2	2.00

TAKEN UNDER COMPENDIUM
Caliber
1 rep. Cal Presents #19-#22	2.95

TALES FROM THE ANIVERSE
Arrow
1 7,400 printed	10.00
2	4.00
3 10,000 printed	2.50
4	2.50
[2nd series]	
Massive Comics Group	
1 thru 3	1.50

TALES FROM THE HEART
1 thru 5	@1.75
6	1.95
7	1.95

TALES OF BEANWORLD
Eclipse
1	10.00
2	4.00
3	2.50
4 I:Beanish	1.50
5 thru 20	@2.00

TALE OF MYA ROM
Aircel
1	1.70

TALES OF PIRACY SAVING GRACE
1	1.95

TALES OF TEENAGE MUTANT NINJA TURTLES
1	13.00
1B 2nd printing	3.00
2	8.00
3	5.00
4	5.00
5	5.00
6 thru 9	@4.00

TALES OF THE JACKALOPE
BF
1	5.00
2	3.00
3 and 4	@2.50
5 thru 9	@2.00

TALES OF THE NINJA WARRIORS
CFW
1 thru 14	@1.95
15 thru 19	@2.25

All comics prices listed are for *Near Mint* condition.

TALES OF THE PLAGUE
Eclipse
1 RCo 4.00

TALES THE STRIPED MAN KNEW
1 thru 4 . . . . @ 1.50

TALES TOO TERRIBLE TO TELL
1 thru 6 Pre-code horror stories @3.50

TALONZ
1 . . . . 1.75
2 . . . . 1.75

TAMMAS
1 . . . . 1.50

TANTALIZING STORIES
Tundra
1 F:Frank & Montgomery Wart . . 2.25
2 Frank & Mont.stories cont. 2.25

TASK FORCE ALPHA
Academy Comics
1 I:Task Force Alpha 3.50

TATTOOMAN SPECIAL
Fantagraphics
1 . . . . 2.75

TEAM NIPPON
Aircel
1 thru 7 . . . . @1.95

TECHNOPHILIA
Brainstorm Comics
1 w/4 cards 2.50

TEDDY & JOE
1 . . . . 1.50
2 . . . . 1.75

TEENAGE MUTANT NINJA TURTLES*
Mirage Studios
*Counterfeits Exist - Beware
1 I:Turtles 350.00
1a 2nd printing 100.00
1b 3rd printing 35.00
1c 4th printing 20.00
1d 5th printing 4.00
2 . . . . 120.00
2a 2nd printing 18.00
2b 3rd printing 4.00
3 . . . . 45.00
3a 2nd printing 3.50
3b Special printing,rare 75.00
4 . . . . 20.00
4a 2nd printing 3.50
5 A:Fugitoid 15.00
5a 2nd printing 3.50
6 A:Fugitoid 13.00
6a 2nd printing 2.50
7 A:Fugitoid 13.00
7a 2nd printing 2.50
8 A:Cerebus 10.00
9 . . . . 5.50
10 V:Shredder 5.50

11 A:Casey Jones 5.50
12 thru 15 . . . . @5.50
16 thru 18 . . . . @5.50
19 Return to NY 5.00
20 Return to NY 5.00
21 Return to NY,D:Shredder 5.00
22 thru 25 . . . . @5.00
26 . . . . 5.00
27 . . . . 5.00
28 thru 31 . . . . @5.00
32 . . . . 5.00
33 color, Corben 3.25
34 Toytle Anxiety 3.25
35 Souls Withering 3.25
36 Souls Wake 3.25
37 Twilight of the Rings 3.25
38 Spaced Out Pt.1,
   A:President Bush 3.25
39 Spaced Out Pt.2 . . . . 3.25
40 Spaced Out concl.,I:Rockin'
   Rollin' Miner Ants
   (B.U. story) 2.00

Teenage Mutant Ninja Turtles #2
© Mirage Studios

41 Turtle Dreams issue 2.00
42 Juliets Revenge 2.00
43 Halls of Lost Legends 2.00
44 V:Ninjas 2.00
45 A:Leatherhead 2.00
46 V:Samurai Dinosaur 2.00
47 Space Usagi 2.00
48 Shades of Grey Part 1 . . . . . 2.00
49 Shades of Grey Part 2 . . . . . 2.00
50 Eastman/Laird,new direction,
   inc.TM,EL,WS pin-ups 2.00
51 City at War #2 . . . . 2.00
52 City at War #3 . . . . 2.25
53 City at War #4 . . . . 2.25
54 City at War #5 . . . . 2.25
55 thru 65 . . . . @2.25
1990 Movie adaptation 6.50
Spec. The Haunted Pizza 2.25
Volume 2
1 thru 8 . . . . 2.75
9 V:Baxter Bot 2.75
10 Mr. Braunze 2.75
11 F:Raphael 2.75
12 V:DARPA 2.75
13 J:Triceraton 2.75

TEENAGE MUTANT NINJA TURTLES TRAINING MANUAL
1 . . . . 5.00
2 thru 5 . . . . @3.00

TEKQ
Caliber
1 . . . . 2.95

TELL-TALE HEART & OTHER STORIES
1 . . . . 2.50

TEMPEST COMICS PRESENTS
Academy Comics
1 I:Steeple, Nemesis 2.50

TERROR ON THE PLANET OF THE APES
Adventure Comics
1 MP,collectors edition 2.50
2 MP, the Forbidden Zone 2.50
2 and 3 . . . . @2.50

TERROR TALES
Eternity
1 Short stories 2.50

TEX BENSON
Metro Comics
1 thru 3 . . . . @2.00

TEYKWA
1 . . . . 1.75

THIEVES
1 thru 3 . . . . @1.50

39 SCREAMS
1 thru 6 . . . . @2.00

THEY WERE 11
Viz
1 Galactic University 2.75
2 The Accident 2.75
3 Virus 2.75

THIS MAGAZINE IS HAUNTED
A Plus Comics
1 . . . . 1.95

THORR SUERD OR SWORD OF THOR
1 . . . . 3.00
1a 2nd printing 2.00
2 . . . . 1.75
3 . . . . 1.50

THREAT
1 . . . . 5.00
2 . . . . 3.00
3 . . . . 2.00
4 . . . . 2.00
5 thru 10 . . . . @2.25

All comics prices listed are for *Near Mint* condition.

3 X 3 EYES
Innovation
1 Labyrinth o/t DemonsEyePt.1	2.25
2 Labyrinth o/t DemonsEyePt.2	2.25
3 Labyrinth o/t DemonsEyePt.3	2.25
4 Labyrinth o/t DemonsEyePt.4	2.25
5 Labyrinth o/t DemonsEye conc.	2.25

THREE IN ONE
1	1.75

THREE MUSKETEERS
1	1.95
2	1.95
3	1.95

THREE ROCKETEERS
Eclipse
1 JK,AW,rep.	2.00
2 JK,AW,rep.	2.00

THRESHOLD OF REALTY
1 5,000 printed	2.50
2 thru 4	@2.00

THRILLKILL
Caliber
1 rep. Cal.Presents #1-#4	2.50

THUNDERBIRD
Newcomers Publishing
1 thru 2 2 Stories	2.95

THUNDER BUNNY
1 O:Thunder Bunny	2.50
2 VO:Dr.Fog	2.00
3 I:GoldenMan	1.75
4 V:Keeper	1.75
5 I:Moon Mess	1.75
6 V:Mr.Endall	1.75
7 VI:Dr.Fog	1.75
8	1.75
9 VS:Gen. Agents	1.75
10 thru 12	@1.75

THUNDER MACE
1 Proto type-blue & red very rare:1,000 printed	15.00
1a four color cover	3.00
2 thru 5	@1.75
6	2.00
7	2.00
Graphic Novel, rep.1-4	5.00

THUNDER SKULL
1	1.95

TICK
New England Comics
1 BEd	17.00
1a 2nd printing	10.00
1b 3rd printing	6.00
1c 4th printing	2.50
2 BEd	11.00
2a 2nd printing	5.00
2b 3rd printing	4.00
2c 4th printing	2.50
3 BEd	4.00
3a 2nd printing	2.50
4 BEd	4.00
4a 2nd printing	2.50

5 BEd	4.00
6 BEd	4.00
7 BEd	4.00
8 BEd	4.00
8a Spec.No Logo edition	20.00
9 BEd,A:Chainsaw Vigilante, Red Eye	2.75
10 BEd	2.75
11 thru 12 BEd	2.75
Spec. Ed. #1, I:Tick	45.00
Spec. Ed. #2, 2nd App. Tick	40.00

TICK: GIANT CIRCUS OF THE MIGHTY
New England Press
1 A-O	2.75
2 P-Z	2.75
3	2.75

TICK: KARMA TORNADO
New England Press
1	3.25
2 thru 9	2.75

TICK OMNIBUS
New England Press
1 1 to 6 Rep.	14.95

TIGRESS
Hero Graphics
3 A:Lady Arcane	2.95
4 inc. B.U. Mudpie	2.95

TIGERS OF TERRA
Mind-Visions
1 6,000 printed	4.50
1a Signed & Num.	14.00
2	2.00
2a Signed & Num.	11.00
5 thru 7	@3.50
8 thru 10	@3.75
Antarctic	
11 and 12	@3.95
[Vol. 2]	
0 thru 4	@3.75

TIGER-X
Eternity
Special #1	2.50
Spec. #1a 2nd printing	2.25
1 thru 3	@1.95
Book II	
1 thru 4	@1.95

TIME DRIFTERS
Innovation
1 thru 3	@2.25

TIME GATES
Double Edge
1 SF series,The Egg #1	1.95
2 The Egg #2	1.95
3 Spirit of the Dragon #1	1.95
4 Spirit of the Dragon #2	1.95
4a Var.cover	1.95

TIME JUMP WAR
Apple
1 thru 3	@1.95

TIME MACHINE
1 thru 3	@2.50

TIME OUT OF MIND
1 thru 4	@1.85

TIME TRIPPER
1	2.00

TIME WARRIORS
Fantasy General
1 rep.Alpha Track #1	1.50
1a Bi-Weekly	.75
2	.75
3	.75

TO BE ANNOUNCED
1 thru 6	@1.50

TO DIE FOR
Blackthorne
1	2.00

TOM CORBETT SPACE CADET
Eternity
1	2.00
2	2.00
3	2.25
4	2.25

TOM CORBETT II
1 thru 4	@2.25

TOM MIX HOLIDAY ALBUM
Amazing Comics
1	3.50

TOM MIX WESTERN
AC Comics
1	2.50
2	2.50

TOMMY & THE MONSTERS
1 thru 3	@1.95

TOMORROW MAN
Antarctic
1 R:Tommorow Man	2.95
Spec.#1 48 pages	3.95

TONY BRAVADO
1 thru 3	@2.00
4	2.50

TORG
Adventure
1 Based on Role Playing Game	2.50
2 thru 3 Based on Game	@2.50

TOR JOHNSON: HOLLYWOOD STAR
Monster Comics
1 Biographical story	2.50

TORRID AFFAIRS
1	2.25
2	2.25
3 thru 5, 60 pages	@2.95

TOTALLY ALIEN
1	17.00
2	12.00
3	8.00

TOUGH GUYS AND WILD WOMEN
Eternity
1	2.25
2	2.25

TRACKER
Blackthorne
1	2.00
2	1.75
3	2.00
4	2.00

TRANSIT
1	2.00
2 thru 6	@1.75

TRIAD
Blackthorne
1	1.75

TRIAL RUN
1	1.75

TRIARCH
Caliber
1	2.00

TRICKSTER KING MONKEY
1 thru 5	@1.75

TRIDENT
1 thru 7	@3.50
8	4.50

TRIO
1	1.50

TROLLORDS
1 1st printing	6.00
1a 2nd printing	2.00
2	3.00
3	2.00
4 thru 16	@1.50
#1 special	1.75

TROLLORDS: DEATH & KISSES
1	1.95
2 thru 5	@2.25

TROPO
1 and 2	@2.00

TROUBLE SHOOTERS
Nightwolf
1 I:Trouble Shooters	2.50

TROUBLE WITH GIRLS
Eternity
1	3.50
2	2.50
3 thru 14	@1.95
15 thru 21	@2.25
22 Lester's Origin	2.25
Annual #1	2.95
Graphic Novel	7.95
Graphic Novel #2	7.95
Xmas special 'World of Girls'	2.95
NEW SERIES
1 thru 4 see color	
5 thru 11	@1.95

TROUBLE WITH TIGERS
Antartic Press
1 NinjaHighSchool/Tigers x-over	2.00
2	2.00

TRUE CRIME
Eclipse
1 thru 2	2.95

TRUFAN ADVENTURES THEATRE
1	8.00
2 3-D issue	5.00

TRYPTO THE ACID DOG
Renegade
1	2.00

TUNESIA
1	1.50

TURTLE SOUP
1 A:TMNT	6.00

TURTLES TEACH KARATE
Solson
1	4.00
2	3.50

TWILIGHT AVENGER
Eternity
1 thru 18	@1.95

TWIST
Kitchen Sink
1	1.95
2 and 3	@2.00

TWISTED TALES OF THE PURPLE SNIT
Blackthorne
1	2.50
2	2.00

2001 NIGHTS
Viz
1	5.00
2	4.00
3 thru 5	@3.75
6 thru 10	@4.25

TYLOR
Double Edge
0 The Egg	2.95

TYRANNY REX
Fleetway
GN reps. from 2000A.D.	7.95

ULTRA KLUTZ
Onward Comics
1	2.50
2 thru 18	@1.50
19 thru 24	@1.75
25 thru 30	@2.00

UNCANNY MAN-FROG
Mad Dog
1	1.75
2	1.75

UNCENSORED MOUSE
Eternity
1 Mickey Mouse	10.00
2 Mickey Mouse	11.00

UNDERGROUND
1	1.70

UNDIE DOG
1	1.50

UNFORGIVEN, THE
Trinity Comics Ministries
Mission of Tranquility
1 thru 6 V:Dormian Grath	1.95
7 I:Faith	1.95

UNICORN ISLE
Genesis West
1	2.50
2	1.50
3	1.50
Apple
4 thru 6	@1.75

UNICORN KINGS
1	1.00
2	1.00

UNION JACKS
1 thru 3	@2.00

UNSUPERVISED EXISTENCE
1	2.00
2	2.50
3	2.50

UNTOLD ORIGIN OF MS. VICTORY
1	2.50

UNTOUCHABLES
1 thru 20	@.75

USAGI YOJIMBO
Fantagraphics
1 SS	8.00
2 SS,Samurai	6.00
3 SS,Samurai,A:Croakers	4.00
4 SS	4.00
5 thru 7 SS	@4.00
8 SS,A Mother's Love	4.00

All comics prices listed are for *Near Mint* condition.

9 SS 4.00
10 SS,A:Turtles 5.50
11 thru 18 SS . . . . @3.50
19 SS,Frost & Fire,A:Nelson
　Groundthumper 3.50
20 thru 21 SS . . . . @3.50
22 SS,A:Panda Khan 3.50
23 SS,V:Ninja Bats 3.50
24 SS 3.50
25 SS,A:Lionheart 2.50
26 SS,Gambling 2.50
27 SS 2.25
28 thru 31 SS,Circles Pt.1 . . . . @2.25
32 . . . . 2.25
33 SS,Ritual Murder 2.25
34 thru 37 . . . . @2.25
Spec#1 SS,SummerSpec,
　C:Groo 45.00

VAGABONDS
1 thru 3 . . . . @1.75

VALENTINO
Renegade
1 . . . . 1.70
2 . . . . 2.00
3 . . . . 2.00

VALOR THUNDERSTAR
1 and 2 . . . . @1.75

VAMPEROTICA
Brainstorm Comics
1 I:Luxura 2.95
2 . . . . 2.95
3 . . . . 2.95
4 I:Blood Hunterq 2.95

VAMPIRELLA
Harris
1 DC,SL,Summer Nights,48page　3.95

VAMPYRES
Eternity
1 thru 4 . . . . @2.25

VANGUARD: OUTPOST EARTH
1 and 2 . . . . @2.00

VARCEL'S VIXENS
1 thru 3 . . . . @2.50

VAULT OF DOOMNATION
B-Movie Comics
1 . . . . 1.70

VENGEANCE OF DREADWOLF
Lightning Comics
1 O:Dreadwolf 2.75

VERDICT
Eternity
1 thru 4 . . . . @1.95

VIC & BLOOD
Renegade
1 RCo,Ellison 2.00
2 RCo,Ellison 2.00

VICKY VALENTINE
Renegade
1 thru 4 . . . . @1.70

VICTIMS
Silver Wolf
1 . . . . 1.50
2 . . . . 1.50

VICTIMS
Eternity
1 thru 5 . . . . @1.95

VIDEO CLASSICS
1 Mighty Mouse 3.50
2 Mighty Mouse 3.50

VIETNAM JOURNAL
Apple Comics
1 . . . . 5.00
1a 2nd printing 3.00
2 . . . . 3.00
3 thru 5 . . . . @2.50
6 thru 13 . . . . @2.00
14 thru 16 . . . . @2.25

VIGIL: FALL FROM GRACE
Innovation
1 'State of Grace' 2.75
2 The Graceland Hunt 2.50

VIOLET STING ALTERNATE CONCEPTS
1 95

VISION
1 I:Flaming Carrot 150.00
2 Flaming Carrot 50.00
3 Flaming Carrot 20.00
4 Flaming Carrot 15.00

VITAL-MAN
1 thru 3 . . . . @1.70

VITRUVIAM MAN
1 . . . . 2.50

VORTEX
Hall of Heroes
1 thru 5 . . . . @2.50
6 V:The Reverend 2.50

VOX
Apple
1 JBy(c) 1.95
2 thru 3 . . . . @1.95
4 . . . . 2.25
5 . . . . 2.25

WACKY SQUIRREL
1 thru 4 . . . . @1.75
Summer Fun Special #1 . . . . . . 2.00
Christmas Special #1 . . . . 1.75

WALKING DEAD
Aircel
1 thru 4 . . . . @2.25
Zombie Spec. 1 . . . . 2.25

Vox #1 © Apple Comics

WANDER
1 . . . . 1.75

WANDERING STAR
1 . . . . 2.00

WAR
A Plus Comics
1 . . . . 2.50

WARCAT
Alliance Comics
1 thru 7 A:Ebonia 2.50

WARDRUMS
1 Adult 1.75
2 . . . . 1.75
3 . . . . 1.75

WARLOCK 5
Aircel
1 . . . . 6.00
2 . . . . 5.00
3 . . . . 6.00
4 . . . . 5.00
5 . . . . 5.00
6 thru 11 . . . . @4.00
12 . . . . 3.50
13 . . . . 3.50
14 thru 16 . . . . @2.00
17 . . . . 1.70
18 . . . . 1.75
19 thru 22 . . . . @1.95
Book 2 #1 thru #7 . . . . @2.00

WARLOCKS
Aircel
1 thru 3 . . . . @1.70
4 thru 12 . . . . @1.95
Spec #1 Rep. 2.25

WAR OF THE WORLDS
Eternity
1 TV tie-in 1.95
2 thru 6 . . . . @1.95

WAR PARTY
VS. DEATHMARK
Lightning Comics
1 War Party vs. Deathmark 2.75

WARP WALKING
Caliber
1 'Quick and the Dead' 2.50

WARZONE
Entity
1 I:Bella & Supra 2.95
2 F:Bladeback, Alloy, Granite ... 2.95
3 F:Bladeback 2.95

WARRIORS
1 .... 2.50
2 thru 7 .... @1.95

WAVE WARRIORS
1 .... 2.00

WAXWORK
1 .... 2.00

WAYWARD WARRIOR
1 .... 2.00

WEAPON FIVE
Spec. #1 .... 1.95

WEASEL PATROL
Eclipse
Spec. #1 .... 2.00

WEIRD MACABRE
THRILLERS
1 .... 1.95

WEIRD ROMANCE
Eclipse
1 .... 2.00

WEREWOLF
Blackthorne
1 TV tie-in 2.00
2 thru 7 .... @2.00

WEREWOLF AT LARGE
1 thru 3 .... @2.25

WHAT IS THE FACE?
A.C.E. Comics
1 SD/FMc,I:New Face 1.95
2 SD/FMc 1.95
3 SD 1.75

WHISPERS & SHADOWS
1 8 1/2 x 11 .... 2.00
1a Regular size 1.50
2 8 1/2 x 11 .... 1.50
3 8 1/2 x 11 .... 1.50
4 thru 9 .... @1.50

WHITE DEVIL
Eternity
1 thru 8 adult 2.50

White Devil #6 © Eternity Comics

WILD, THE
1 and 2 .... @1.50
3 thru 7 .... @1.75

WILD KNIGHTS
Eternity
1 thru 10 .... @1.95
Shattered Earth Chron. #1 ...... 1.95

WILDMAN
1 and 2 .... @1.50
3 thru 6 .... @1.85

WILD STARS
Vol 2 #1 .... 1.95

WILD THINGS
1 .... 2.00

WILD THINK
2 .... 2.00

WIMMINS' COMIX
13 and 14 .... @2.00

WIND BLADE
1 Elford 1st Blair 60.00

WINDRAVEN
Hero Graphics/Blue comet
1 The Healing,(see
   Rough Raiders) 2.95

WINDRAVEN
Heroic
1 .... 2.95

WITCH
Eternity
1 .... 1.95

WIZARDS OF
LAST RESORT
1 thru 3 .... @1.75
4 .... 2.00

WIZARD OF TIME
David House
1 .... 1.50
1a 2nd printing(blue) 1.50
2 and 3 .... @1.50

WOLF H
Blackthorne
1 and 2 .... @1.75

WORDSMITH
Renegade
1 .... 3.00
2 thru 6 .... @1.70
7 thru 12 .... @2.00

WORLD HARDBALL
LEAGUE
Titus Press
1 F:Big Bat 2.95
2 F:Big Bat 2.95
3 Mount Evrest 2.95
4 Juan Hernandez 2.95

WORLD OF WOOD
Eclipse
5 Flying Saucers 2.00

WORLD OF X-RAY
1 .... 1.80
2 .... 1.80

WRAB
1 .... 2.95

WRAITH
Outlander
1 'Resurrected & the Damned' .. 1.75

WRONG COMIC
1 .... 1.70

WYOMING TERRITORY
1 .... 1.95

XANADU
Thoughts & Images
1 thru 5 .... @2.00

XENA
Brown Study Comics
1 I:Xena 2.95

XENON
Eclipse
1 .... 3.00
2 thru 23 .... @1.50

XENOZOIC TALES
Kitchen Sink
1 .... 5.75
1aRep. 2.00
2 .... 3.50
2a Rep. 2.00
3 .... 3.00
4 .... 2.50
5 thru 7 .... @2.25
8 thru 12 .... @2.00

All comics prices listed are for *Near Mint* condition.

Xenozoic Tales #1 © Kitchen Sink

X-BABES VS. JUSTICE BABES
Personality
1 Spoof/parody 2.95

X-CONS
Parody Press
1 X-Men satire,flip cover 2.50

X-FARCE
Eclipse
One-Shot X-Force parody 3.00

XIOLA
Zion Comics
1 thru 3 F:Kantasia . . . . @1.95
4 Visitor 1.95

X-MAS WITH SUPERSWINE
Spec 2.00

XMEN
1 Parody 1.50

X-THIEVES
1 . . . . 3.00
2 . . . . 1.75
3 . . . . 1.75

YAHOO
1 thru 3 . . . . @2.00

YAKUZA
Eternity
1 thru 5 . . . . @1.95

YARN MAN
1 . . . . 2.00

YAWN
Parody Press
1 Spawn parody 2.50

Enigma
1 Spawn parody rep.? 2.75

YIN-FEI
1 thru 4 . . . . @1.50

YOUNG HERO
1 . . . . 2.50
2 . . . . 2.50

YOUNG MASTERS
1 thru 10 . . . . @1.75

ZELL THE SWORDDANCER
1 Steve Gallacci 5.50
2 and 3 . . . . @2.00

ZEN ILLUSTRATED NOVELLA
Entity
1 thru 4 R:Bruce Lewis . . . . . . @2.95
5 Immortal Combat 2.95
6 Bubble Economy 2.95
7 Zen City 2.95
8 V:Assassins 2.95

ZEN, INTER-GALACTIC NINJA
Entity
1 . . . . 4.00
2 . . . . 3.00
3 thru 9 . . . . @2.50
X-mas Spec #1,V:Black Hole Bob 2.95
[2nd Series]
1 'Down to Earth' 2.25
2 RA, A:Jeremy Baker 2.25
[3rd Series]
0 . . . . 2.95
1 thru 3 A:Niro . . . . @2.95
Sourcebook #1 . . . . 3.50

ZEN INTERGALACTIC NINJA: STARQUEST
Entity
1 thru 6 V:Nolan the Destroyer @2.95
7 V:Dimensional 2.95
8 thru 9 I:New Team . . . . @2.95
TPB 1 thru 4 . . . . @6.95

ZEN INTERGALACTIC NINJA VS. MICHEAL JACK-ZEN
Entity
1 Cameos Galore 2.95

ZENISMS WIT AND WISDOMS
Entity
1 R:Bruce Lewis 2.95

ZEN: MISTRESS OF CHAOS
1 . . . . 2.95

ZENITH: PHASE II
Fleetway
1 GMo(s),SY,Rep.2000 AD 1.95

ZERO & D.D.O.J.
1 . . . . 3.00

ZETRAMAN
Antarctic
1 thru 3 . . . . @1.95
[Vol. 2]
1 and 2 . . . . @2.75

ZIG ZAG
1 . . . . 1.25
2 . . . . 1.25

ZILLION
Eternity
1 thru 4 . . . . @2.50

ZOLASTRAYA AND THE BARD
1 thru 5 . . . . @1.70

ZOMBIE BOY
1 . . . . 1.50

ZOMBIE LOVE
1 . . . . 4.95

ZOMBIE WAR
1 thru 3 . . . . 3.95

ZONE
1 . . . . 1.95

ZONE CONTINUUM
Caliber
1 Master of the Waves 2.95
2 . . . . 2.95

ZORANN: STAR WARRIOR
1 . . . . 2.00

ZOT!
Eclipse
(#1-#10 See: Color)
11 New Series 2.50
12 thru 15 . . . . @2.50
16 A:De-Evolutionaries 2.50
17 thru 36 . . . . @2.00

ZOOT!
Fantagraphics
1 thru 5 . . . . @2.50

Issued As Classic Comics
001-THE THREE MUSKETEERS
By Alexandre Dumas

10/41 **(---)** MKd,MKd(c),
Original,10¢ (c) Price 3,500.00
05/43 **(10)** MKd,MKd(c),
No(c)Price; rep 200.00
11/43 **(15)** MKd,MKd(c),Long
Island Independent Ed; 150.00
6/44 **(18/20)** MKd,MKd(c),
Sunrise Times Edition;rep ... 120.00
7/44 **(21)** MKd,MKd(c),Richmond
Courrier Edition;rep 100.00
6/46 **(28)** MKd,MKd(c);rep 90.00
4/47 **(36)** MKd,MKd(c),
New CILogo;rep 40.00
6/49 **(60)** MKd,MKd(c),CI Logo;rep 25.00
10/49 **(64)** MKd,MKd(c),CI Logo;rep 25.00
12/50 **(78)** MKd,MKd(c),15¢(c)
Price; CI Logo;rep 16.00
03/52 **(93)** MKd,MKd(c),
CI Logo;rep 15.00
11/53 **(114)** CI Logo;rep 12.00
09/56 **(134)** MKd,MKd(c),New
P(c),CI Logo,64 pgs;rep 12.00
03/58 **(143)** MKd,MKd(c),P(c),
CI Logo,64 pgs;rep 11.00
05/59 **(150)** GE&RC New Art,
P(c),CILogo;rep 11.00
03/61 **(149)** GE&RC,P(c),
CI Logo;rep 7.00
62-63 **(167)** GE&RC,P(c),
CI Logo;rep 7.00
04/64 **(167)** GE&RC,P(c),
CI Logo;rep 7.00
01/65 **(167)** GE&RC,P(c),
CI Logo;rep 7.00
03/66 **(167)** GE&RC,P(c),
CI Logo;rep 7.00
11/67 **(166)** GE&RC,P(c),
CI Logo;rep 7.00
Sp/69 **(166)** GE&RC,P(c),25¢(c)
Price,CILogo, Rigid(c);rep 7.00
Sp/71 **(169)** GE&RC,P(c),
CI Logo,Rigid(c);rep 7.00

002-IVANHOE
By Sir Walter Scott

1941 **(---)** EA,MKd(c),Original . 1,300.00
05/43 **(1)** EA,MKd(c),word "Presents"
Removed From(c);rep 175.00
11/43 **(15)** EA,MKd(c),Long Island
Independent Edition;rep 130.00
06/44 **(18/20)** EA,MKd(c),Sunrise
Times Edition;rep 110.00
07/44 **(21)** EA,MKd(c),Richmond
Courrier Edition;rep 100.00
06/46 **(28)** EA,MKd(c);rep 80.00
07/47 **(36)** EA,MKd(c),New
CI Logo; rep 40.00
06/49 **(60)** EA,MKd(c),CI Logo;rep 25.00
10/49 **(64)** EA,MKd(c),CI Logo;rep 20.00
12/50 **(78)** EA,MKd(c),15¢(c)
Price; CI Logo;rep 17.00
11/51 **(89)** EA,MKd(c),CI Logo;rep 16.00
04/53 **(106)** EA,MKd(c),CI
Logo;rep 14.00
07/54 **(121)** EA,MKd(c),CI
Logo;rep 12.00
01/57 **(136)** NN New Art,New
P(c),CI Logo;rep 14.00
01/58 **(142)** NN,P(c),CI Logo;rep .. 6.00
11/59 **(153)** NN,P(c),CI Logo;rep .. 6.00
03/61 **(149)** NN,P(c),CI Logo;rep .. 6.00

62/63 **(167)** NN,P(c),CI Logo;rep . 5.00
05/64 **(167)** NN,P(c),CI Logo;rep .. 6.00
01/65 **(167)** NN,P(c),CI Logo;rep .. 6.00
03/66 **(167)** NN,P(c),CI Logo;rep .. 6.00
09/67 **(166)** NN,P(c),CI Logo;rep .. 6.00
1968 **(166)** NN,P(c),CI Logo;rep .. 6.00
Wr/69 **(169)** NN,P(c),CI
Logo Rigid(c);rep 6.00
Wr/71 **(169)** NN,P(c),CI
Logo,Rigid(c);rep 6.00

CI #4 Last of the Mohicans,
© Gilberton Publications

003-THE COUNT OF MONTE CRISTO
By Alexandre Dumas

03/42 **(---)** ASm,ASm(c),Original 900.00
05/43 **(10)** ASm,ASm(c);rep ... 175.00
11/43 **(15)** ASm,ASm(c),Long Island
Independent Edition;rep 125.00
06/44 **(18/20)** ASm,ASm(c),
Sunrise Times Edition;rep ... 110.00
06/44 **(20)** ASm,ASm(c),Sunrise
Times Edition;rep 100.00
07/44 **(21)** ASm,ASm(c),Richmond
Courrier Edition;rep 80.00
06/46 **(28)** ASm,ASm(c);rep 75.00
04/47 **(36)** ASm,ASm(c),New
CI Logo; rep 40.00
06/49 **(60)** ASm,ASm(c),CI
Logo; rep 25.00
08/49 **(62)** ASm,ASm(c),CI
Logo; rep 35.00
05/50 **(71)** ASm,ASm(c),CI
Logo;rep 20.00
09/51 **(87)** ASm,ASm(c),15¢(c)
Price, CI Logo;rep 14.00
11/53 **(113)** ASm,ASm(c),
CI Logo; rep 12.00
11/56 **(---)** LC New Art,New
P(c), CI Logo;rep 12.00
03/58 **(135)** LC,P(c),CI Logo;rep .. 6.00
11/59 **(153)** LC,P(c),CI Logo;rep .. 6.00
03/61 **(161)** LC,P(c),CI Logo;rep .. 6.00
62/63 **(167)** LC,P(c),CI Logo;rep .. 6.00
07/64 **(167)** LC,P(c),CI Logo;rep .. 6.00
07/65 **(167)** LC,P(c),CI Logo;rep .. 6.00
07/66 **(167)** LC,P(c),CI Logo;rep .. 6.00
1968 **(166)** LC,P(c),25¢(c)
Price, CI Logo;rep 6.00
Wn/69 **(169)** LC,P(c),CI Logo,
Rigid(c);rep 6.00

004-THE LAST OF THE MOHICANS
By James Fenimore Cooper

08/42 **(---)** RR,RR(c),Original ... 850.00
06/43 **(12)** RR,RR(c),Price
Balloon Deleted;rep 175.00
11/43 **(15)** RR,RR(c),Long Island
Independent Edition;rep 150.00
06/44 **(20)** RR,RR(c),Long Island
Independent Edition;rep 125.00
07/44 **(21)** RR,RR(c),Queens
Home News Edition;rep 100.00
06/46 **(28)** RR,RR(c);rep 90.00
04/47 **(36)** RR,RR(c),New
CI Logo; rep 40.00
06/49 **(60)** RR,RR(c),CI Logo;rep . 25.00
10/49 **(64)** RR,RR(c),CI Logo;rep . 20.00
12/50 **(78)** RR,RR(c),15¢(c)
Price,CI Logo rep 17.00
11/51 **(89)** RR,RR(c),CI Logo;rep . 16.00
03/54 **(117)** RR,RR(c),CI Logo;rep 12.00
11/56 **(135)** RR,New P(c),
CI Logo; rep 12.00
11/57 **(141)** RR,P(c),CI Logo;rep . 13.00
05/59 **(150)** JSe&StA New Art;
P(c), CI Logo;rep 12.00
03/61 **(161)** JSe&StA,P(c),CI
Logo; rep 6.00
62/63 **(167)** JSe&StA,P(c),CI
Logo; rep 6.00
06/64 **(167)** JSe&StA,P(c),CI
Logo; rep 6.00
08/65 **(167)** JSe&StA,P(c),CI
Logo; rep 6.00
08/66 **(167)** JSe&StA,P(c),CI
Logo; rep 6.00
1967 **(166)** JSe&StA,P(c),25¢(c)
Price, CI Logo;rep 6.00
Sp/69 **(169)** JSe&StA,P(c),CI
Logo, Rigid(c);rep 6.00

005-MOBY DICK
By Herman Melville

09/42 **(---)** LZ,LZ(c),Original 950.00
05/43 **(10)** LZ,LZ(c),Conray Products
Edition, No(c)Price;rep 175.00
11/43 **(15)** LZ,LZ(c),Long Island
Independent Edition;rep 135.00
06/44 **(18/20)** LZ,LZ(c),Sunrise
Times Edition;rep 125.00
07/44 **(20)** LZ,LZ(c),Sunrise
Times Edition;rep 110.00
07/44 **(21)** LZ,LZ(c),Sunrise
Times Edition;rep 100.00
06/46 **(28)** LZ,LZ(c);rep 80.00
04/47 **(36)** LZ,LZ(c),New
CI Logo;rep 40.00
06/49 **(60)** LZ,LZ(c),CI Logo;rep . 25.00
08/49 **(62)** LZ,LZ(c),CI Logo;rep . 30.00
05/50 **(71)** LZ,LZ(c),CI Logo;rep . 20.00
09/51 **(87)** LZ,LZ(c),15¢(c)
Price, CI Logo;rep 16.00
04/54 **(118)** LZ,LZ(c),CI Logo;rep . 12.00
03/56 **(131)** NN New Art,New
P(c), CI Logo;rep 12.00
05/57 **(138)** NN,P(c),CI Logo;rep .. 6.00
01/59 **(148)** NN,P(c),CI Logo;rep .. 6.00
09/60 **(158)** NN,P(c),CI Logo;rep .. 6.00
62/63 **(167)** NN,P(c),CI Logo;rep .. 6.00
06/64 **(167)** NN,P(c),CI Logo;rep .. 6.00
07/65 **(167)** NN,P(c),CI Logo;rep .. 6.00
03/66 **(167)** NN,P(c),CI Logo;rep .. 6.00
09/67 **(166)** NN,P(c),CI Logo;rep .. 6.00
Wn/69 **(166)** NN,P(c),25¢(c) Price,
CI Logo, Rigid(c);rep 12.00

All comics prices listed are for *Near Mint* condition.

Wn/71 **(169)** NN,P(c),CI Logo;rep   12.00

006-A TALE OF TWO CITIES
By Charles Dickens

11/42 **(---)** StM,StM(c),Original; . 850.00
09/43 **(14)** StM,StM(c),No(c)
Price; rep 165.00
03/44 **(18)** StM,StM(c),Long Island
Independent Edition;rep 135.00
06/44 **(20)** StM,StM(c),Sunrise
Times Edition;rep 125.00
06/46 **(28)** StM,StM(c);rep 75.00
09/48 **(51)** StM,StM(c),New CI
Logo; rep 40.00
10/49 **(64)** StM,StM(c),CI
Logo;rep 25.00
12/50 **(78)** StM,StM(c),15¢(c)
Price, CI Logo; rep 16.00
11/51 **(89)** StM,StM(c),CI Logo;rep 14.00
03/54 **(117)** StM,StM(c),CI
Logo;rep 10.00
05/56 **(132)** JO New Art,New
P(c), CI Logo;rep 14.00
09/57 **(140)** JO,P(c),CI Logo;rep . . 6.00
11/57 **(147)** JO,P(c),CI Logo;rep . . 6.00
09/59 **(152)** JO,P(c),CI Logo;rep . . 90.00
11/59 **(153)** JO,P(c),CI Logo;rep . . 6.00
03/61 **(149)** JO,P(c),CI Logo;rep . . 6.00
62/63 **(167)** JO,P(c),CI Logo;rep . . 6.00
06/64 **(167)** JO,P(c),CI Logo;rep . . 6.00
08/65 **(167)** JO,P(c),CI Logo;rep . . 6.00
05/67 **(166)** JO,P(c),CI Logo;rep . . 6.00
Fl/68 **(166)** JO,NN New P(c),
25¢(c)Price,CI Logo;rep 12.00
Sr/70 **(169)** JO,NN P(c),CI
Logo, Rigid(c);rep 12.00

007-ROBIN HOOD
By Howard Pyle

12/42 **(---)** LZ,LZ(c),Original 650.00
06/43 **(12)** LZ,LZ(c),P.D.C.
on(c) Deleted;rep 150.00
03/44 **(18)** LZ,LZ(c),Long Island
Independent Edition;rep 125.00
06/44 **(20)** LZ,LZ(c),Nassau
Bulletin Edition;rep 120.00
10/44 **(22)** LZ,LZ(c),Queens
City Times Edition;rep 100.00
06/46 **(28)** LZ,LZ(c),rep 75.00
09/48 **(51)** LZ,LZ(c),New CI
Logo;rep 35.00
06/49 **(60)** LZ,LZ(c),CI Logo;rep . 20.00
10/49 **(64)** LZ,LZ(c),CI Logo;rep . 16.00
12/50 **(78)** LZ,LZ(c),CI Logo;rep . 16.00
07/52 **(97)** LZ,LZ(c),CI Logo;rep . 14.00
03/53 **(106)** LZ,LZ(c),CI Logo;rep . 13.00
07/54 **(121)** LZ,LZ(c),CI Logo;rep . 12.00
11/55 **(129)** LZ,New P(c),
CI Logo;rep 12.00
01/57 **(136)** JkS New Art,P(c);rep . 6.00
03/58 **(143)** JkS,P(c),CI Logo;rep . . 6.00
11/59 **(153)** JkS,P(c),CI Logo;rep . . 6.00
10/61 **(164)** JkS,P(c),CI Logo;rep . . 6.00
62/63 **(167)** JkS,P(c),CI Logo;rep . . 6.00
06/64 **(167)** JkS,P(c),CI Logo;rep . . 7.00
05/65 **(167)** JkS,P(c),CI Logo;rep . . 6.00
07/66 **(167)** JkS,P(c),CI Logo;rep . . 6.00
12/67 **(166)** JkS,P(c),CI Logo;rep . . 7.00
Sr/69 **(169)** JkS,P(c),CI
Logo, Rigid(c);rep 6.00

008-ARABIAN KNIGHTS
By Antoine Galland

03/43 **(---)** LCh,LCh(c),Original 1,750.00

09/43 **(14)** LCh,LCh(c);rep 550.00
01/44 **(17)** LCh,LCh(c),Long Island
Independent Edition;rep 850.00
06/44 **(20)** LCh,LCh(c),Nassau
Bulletin Edition,64 pgs;rep . . . 375.00
06/46 **(28)** LCh,LCh(c);rep 225.00
09/48 **(51)** LCh,LCh(c),New CI
Logo; rep 225.00
10/49 **(64)** LCh,LCh(c),CI
Logo;rep 200.00
12/50 **(78)** LCh,LCh(c),CI
Logo;rep 160.00
10/61 **(164)** ChB New Art,P(c),
CI Logo;rep 135.00

CI #7 Robin Hood,
© Gilberton Publications

009-LES MISERABLES
By Victor Hugo

03/43 **(---)** RLv,RLv(c),Original . . 575.00
09/43 **(14)** RLv,RLv(c);rep 175.00
03/44 **(18)** RLv,RLv(c),Nassau
Bulletin Edition;rep 150.00
06/44 **(20)** RLv,RLv(c),Richmond
Courier Edition;rep 125.00
06/46 **(28)** RLv,RLv(c);rep 100.00
09/48 **(51)** RLv,RLv(c),New CI
Logo; rep 40.00
05/50 **(71)** RLv,RLv(c),CI
Logo;rep 30.00
09/51 **(87)** RLv,RLv(c),CI Logo,
15¢(c)Price;rep 25.00
03/61 **(161)** NN New Art,GMc
New P(c), CI Logo;rep 22.00
09/63 **(167)** NN,GMc P(c),CI
Logo; rep 18.00
12/65 **(167)** NN,GMc P(c),CI
Logo; rep 18.00
1968 **(166)** NN,GMc P(c),25¢(c)
Price, CI Logo;rep 25.00

010-ROBINSON CRUSOE
By Daniel Defoe

04/43 **(---)** StM,StM(c),Original . . 550.00
09/43 **(14)** StM,StM(c);rep 175.00
03/44 **(18)** StM,StM(c),Nassau Bulletin
Ed.,'Bill of Rights'Pge.64;rep . 125.00
06/44 **(20)** StM,StM(c),Queens
Home News Edition;rep 100.00
??/45 **(23)** StM,StM(c);rep 75.00
06/46 **(28)** StM,StM(c);rep 75.00
09/48 **(51)** StM,StM(c),New CI
Logo; rep 35.00
10/49 **(64)** StM,StM(c),CI Logo;rep 25.00

12/50 **(78)** StM,StM(c),15¢(c)
Price, CI Logo;rep 20.00
07/52 **(97)** StM,StM(c),CI Logo;rep 15.00
12/53 **(114)** StM,StM(c),CI
Logo;rep 15.00
01/56 **(130)** StM,New P(c),CI
Logo; rep 15.00
09/57 **(140)** SmC New Art,P(c),
CI Logo; rep 12.00
11/59 **(153)** SmC,P(c),CI Logo;rep . 6.00
10/61 **(164)** SmC,P(c),CI Logo;rep . 6.00
62/63 **(167)** SmC,P(c),CI Logo;rep . 6.00
07/64 **(167)** SmC,P(c),CI Logo;rep 10.00
05/65 **(167)** SmC,P(c),CI Logo;rep . 6.00
06/66 **(167)** SmC,P(c),CI Logo;rep . 6.00
Fl/68 **(166)** SmC,P(c),CI Logo,
25¢(c)Price;rep 8.00
1968 **(166)** SmC,P(c),CI Logo,No
Twin Circle Ad;rep 7.00
Sr/70 **(169)** SmC,P(c),CI Logo,
Rigid(c);rep 7.00

011-DON QUIXOTE
By Miguel de Cervantes Saavedra

05/43 **(---)** LZ,LZ(c),Original 600.00
03/44 **(18)** LZ,LZ(c),Nassau
Bulletin Edition;rep 175.00
07/44 **(21)** LZ,LZ(c),Queens
Home News Edition;rep 125.00
06/46 **(28)** LZ,LZ(c);rep 75.00
08/53 **(110)** LZ,TO New P(c),New
CI Logo;rep 22.00
05/60 **(156)** LZ,TO P(c),Pages
Reduced to 48,CI Logo;rep . . . 15.00
1962 **(165)** LZ,TO P(c),CI Logo;rep 8.00
01/64 **(167)** LZ,TO P(c),CI
Logo;rep 8.00
11/65 **(167)** LZ,TO P(c),CI
Logo;rep 8.00
1968 **(166)** LZ,TO P(c),CI Logo,
25¢(c)Price;rep 16.00

012-RIP VAN WINKLE & THE HEADLESS HORSEMAN
By Washington Irving

06/43 **(----)** RLv,RLv(c),Original . 600.00
11/43 **(15)** RLv,RLv(c),Long Island
Independent Edition;rep 175.00
06/44 **(20)** RLv,RLv(c),Long Island
Independent Edition;rep 125.00
10/44 **(22)** RLv,RLv(c),Queens
City Times Edition;rep 110.00
06/46 **(28)** RLv,RLv(c);rep 75.00
06/49 **(60)** RLv,RLv(c),New CI
Logo;rep 25.00
08/49 **(62)** RLv,RLv(c),CI
Logo;rep 23.00
05/50 **(71)** RLv,RLv(c),CI
Logo;rep 20.00
11/51 **(89)** RLv,RLv(c),15¢(c)
Price, CI Logo;rep 11.00
04/54 **(118)** RLv,RLv(c),CI
Logo;rep 11.00
05/56 **(132)** RLv,New P(c),
CI Logo; rep 12.00
05/59 **(150)** NN New Art;P(c),
CI Logo; rep 12.00
09/60 **(158)** NN,P(c),CI Logo;rep . . 6.00
62/63 **(167)** NN,P(c),CI Logo;rep . . 6.00
12/63 **(167)** NN,P(c),CI Logo;rep . . 6.00
04/65 **(167)** NN,P(c),CI Logo;rep . . 7.00
04/66 **(167)** NN,P(c),CI Logo;rep . . 6.00
1969 **(166)** NN,P(c),CI Logo,
25¢(c)Price,Rigid(c);rep 12.00

Sr/70 **(169)** NN,P(c),CI Logo,
Rigid(c);rep 12.00

013-DR. JEKYLL
AND MR.HYDE
By Robert Louis Stevenson
08/43 **(---)** AdH,AdH(c),Original . 750.00
11/43 **(15)** AdH,AdH(c),Long Island
Independent Edition;rep 200.00
06/44 **(20)** AdH,AdH(c),Long Island
Independent Edition;rep 150.00
06/46 **(28)** AdH,AdH(c),No(c)
Price; 110.00
06/49 **(60)** AdH,HcK New(c),New CI
Logo,Pgs.reduced to 48;rep . . . 40.00
08/49 **(62)** AdH,HcK(c),CI
Logo;rep 35.00
05/50 **(71)** AdH,HcK(c),CI
Logo;rep 20.00
09/51 **(87)** AdH,HcK(c),Erroneous Return
of Original Date,CI Logo;rep . . . 18.00
10/53 **(112)** LC New Art,New
P(c), CI Logo;rep 18.00
11/59 **(153)** LC,P(c),CI Logo;rep . . 7.00
03/61 **(161)** LC,P(c),CI Logo;rep . . 7.00
62/63 **(167)** LC,P(c),CI Logo;rep . . 7.00
08/64 **(167)** LC,P(c),CI Logo;rep . . 7.00
11/65 **(167)** LC,P(c),CI Logo;rep . . 7.00
1968 **(166)** LC,P(c),CI Logo,
25¢(c)Price;rep 8.00
Wr/69 **(169)** LC,P(c),CI Logo,
Rigid(c);rep 7.00

014-WESTWARD HO!
By Charles Kingsley
09/43 **(---)** ASm,ASm(c),Original 1,350.00
11/43 **(15)** ASm,ASm(c),Long Island
Independent Edition;rep 550.00
07/44 **(21)** ASm,ASm(c);rep . . . 400.00
06/46 **(28)** ASm,ASm(c),No(c)
Price; rep 350.00
11/48 **(53)** ASm,ASm(c),Pages reduced
to 48, New CI Logo;rep 275.00

015-UNCLE TOM'S CABIN
By Harriet Beecher Stowe
11/43 **(---)** RLv,RLv(c),Original . . 500.00
11/43 **(15)** RLv,RLv(c),Blank
Price Circle, Long Island
Independent Ed.;rep 200.00
07/44 **(21)** RLv,RLv(c),Nassau
Bulliten Edition;rep 150.00
06/46 **(28)** RLv,RLv(c),No(c)
Price; rep 90.00
11/48 **(53)** RLv,RLv(c),Pages Reduced
to 48, New CI Logo;rep 40.00
05/50 **(71)** RLv,RLv(c),CI Logo;rep 22.00
11/51 **(89)** RLv,RLv(c),15¢(c)
Price, CI Logo;rep 22.00
03/54 **(117)** RLv,New P(c),CI
Logo, Lettering Changes;rep . . 12.00
09/55 **(128)** RLv,P(c),"Picture
Progress"Promotion,CI Logo;rep 10.00
03/57 **(137)** RLv,P(c),CI Logo;rep . 6.00
09/58 **(146)** RLv,P(c),CI Logo;rep . 6.00
01/60 **(154)** RLv,P(c),CI Logo;rep . 6.00
03/61 **(161)** RLv,P(c),CI Logo;rep . 6.00
62/63 **(167)** RLv,P(c),CI Logo;rep . 6.00
06/64 **(167)** RLv,P(c),CI Logo;rep . 6.00
05/65 **(167)** RLv,P(c),CI Logo;rep . 6.00
05/67 **(166)** RLv,P(c),CI Logo;rep . 6.00
Wr/69 **(166)** RLv,P(c),CI
Logo, Rigid(c);rep 12.00
Sr/70 **(169)** RLv,P(c),CI
Logo, Rigid(c);rep 12.00

016-GULLIVER'S TRAVELS
By Johnathan Swift
12/43 **(----)** LCh,LCh(c),Original . 450.00
06/44 **(18/20)** LCh,LCh(c),Queen's Home
News Edition,No(c)Price;rep . . 150.00
10/44 **(22)** LCh,LCh(c),Queen's
Home News Editon;rep 125.00
06/46 **(28)** LCh,LCh(c);rep 75.00
06/49 **(60)** LCh,LCh(c),Pgs. Reduced
To 48, New CI Logo;rep 30.00
08/49 **(62)** LCh,LCh(c),CI Logo;rep 19.00
10/49 **(64)** LCh,LCh(c),CI Logo;rep 14.00
12/50 **(78)** LCh,LCh(c),15¢(c)
Price, CI Logo;rep 12.00
11/51 **(89)** LCh,LCh(c),CI Logo;rep 12.00
03/60 **(155)** LCh,New P(c),CI
Logo; rep 6.00
1962 **(165)** LCh,P(c),CI Logo;rep . . 6.00
05/64 **(167)** LCh,P(c),CI Logo;rep . 6.00
11/65 **(167)** LCh,P(c),CI Logo;rep . 6.00
1968 **(166)** LCh,P(c),CI Logo,
25¢(c)Price;rep 6.00
Wr/69 **(169)** LCh,P(c),CI
Logo, Rigid(c);rep 6.00

CI #22 The Pathfinder,
© Gilberton Publications

017-THE DEERSLAYER
By James Fenimore Cooper
01/44 **(----)** LZ,LZ(c),Original . . . 450.00
03/44 **(18)** LZ,LZ(c),No(c)Price;rep 150.00
10/44 **(22)** LZ,LZ(c),Queen's
City Times Edition;rep 110.00
06/46 **(28)** LZ,LZ(c);rep 75.00
06/49 **(60)** LZ,LZ(c),Pgs. Reduced
to 48,New CI Logo;rep 30.00
10/49 **(64)** LZ,LZ(c),CI Logo;rep . 20.00
07/51 **(85)** LZ,LZ(c),15¢(c)
Price, CI Logo;rep 15.00
04/54 **(118)** LZ,LZ(c),CI Logo;rep . 14.00
05/56 **(132)** LZ,LZ(c),CI Logo;rep . 13.00
11/66 **(167)** LZ,LZ(c),CI Logo;rep . 13.00
1968 **(166)** LZ,StA New P(c),CI
Logo, 25¢(c)Price;rep 16.00
Sg/71 **(169)** LZ,StA P(c),CI Logo,
Rigid(c), Letters From Parents
and Educators;rep 14.00

018-THE HUNCHBACK
OF NOTRE DAME
By Victor Hugo
03/44 **(---)** ASm,ASm(c),Original
Gilberton Edition 600.00

03/44 **(---)** ASm,ASm(c),Original
Island Publications Edition . . . 525.00
06/44 **(18/20)** ASm,ASm(c),Queens
Home News Edition;rep 175.00
10/44 **(22)** ASm,ASm(c),Queens
City Times Edition;rep 125.00
06/46 **(28)** ASm,ASm(c);rep . . . 100.00
06/49 **(60)** ASm,HcK New(c)8 Pgs.
Deleted, New CI Logo;rep 30.00
08/49 **(62)** ASm,HcK(c),CI
Logo;rep 20.00
12/50 **(78)** ASm,HcK(c),15¢(c)
Price; CI Logo;rep 16.00
11/51 **(89)** ASm,HcK(c),CI
Logo;rep 12.00
04/54 **(118)** ASm,HcK(c),CI
Logo;rep 21.00
09/57 **(140)** ASm,New P(c),CI
Logo; rep 17.00
09/58 **(146)** ASm,P(c),CI Logo;rep 16.00
09/60 **(158)** GE&RC New Art,GMc
New P(c),CI Logo;rep 7.00
1962 **(165)** GE&RC,GMc P(c),CI
Logo; rep 7.00
09/63 **(167)** GE&RC,GMc P(c),CI
Logo; rep 7.00
10/64 **(167)** GE&RC,GMc P(c),CI
Logo; rep 6.00
04/66 **(167)** GE&RC,GMc P(c),CI
Logo; rep 6.00
1968 **(166)** GE&RC,GMc P(c),CI
Logo, 25¢(c)Price;rep 6.00
Sr/70 **(169)** GE&RC,GMc P(c),CI
Logo, Rigid(c);rep 6.00

019-HUCKLEBERRY FINN
By Mark Twain
04/44 **(---)** LZ,LZ(c),Original
Gilberton Edition 400.00
04/44 **(---)** LZ,LZ(c),Original Island
Publications Company Edition 450.00
03/44 **(18)** LZ,LZ(c),Nassau
Bulliten Editon;rep 175.00
10/44 **(22)** LZ,LZ(c),Queens City
Times Edition;rep 125.00
06/46 **(28)** LZ,LZ(c);rep 85.00
06/49 **(60)** LZ,LZ(c),New CI Logo,
Pgs.Reduced to 48;rep 30.00
08/49 **(62)** LZ,LZ(c),CI Logo;rep . 22.00
12/50 **(78)** LZ,LZ(c),CI Logo;rep . 18.00
11/51 **(89)** LZ,LZ(c),CI Logo;rep . 15.00
03/54 **(117)** LZ,LZ(c),CI Logo;rep . 15.00
03/56 **(131)** FrG New Art,New
P(c), CI Logo; rep 6.00
09/57 **(140)** FrG,P(c),CI Logo;rep . 6.00
05/59 **(150)** FrG,P(c),CI Logo;rep . 6.00
09/60 **(158)** FrG,P(c),CI Logo;rep . 6.00
1962 **(165)** FrG,P(c),CI Logo;rep . 6.00
62/63 **(167)** FrG,P(c),CI Logo;rep . 6.00
06/64 **(167)** FrG,P(c),CI Logo;rep . 6.00
06/65 **(167)** FrG,P(c),CI Logo;rep . 6.00
10/65 **(167)** FrG,P(c),CI Logo;rep . 6.00
09/67 **(166)** FrG,P(c),CI Logo;rep . 6.00
Wr/69 **(166)** FrG,P(c),CI Logo,
25¢(c)Price, Rigid(c);rep 5.00
Sr/70 **(169)** FrG,P(c),CI Logo,
Rigid(c);rep 5.00

020-THE CORSICAN
BROTHERS
By Alexandre Dumas
06/44 **(---)** ASm,ASm(c),Original
Gilberton Edition 450.00
06/44 **(---)** ASm,ASm(c),Original
Courier Edition 400.00

06/44 (---) ASm,ASm(c),Original Long
Island Independent Edition . . . 400.00
10/44 **(22)** ASm,ASm(c),Queens
City Times Edition;rep 175.00
06/46 **(28)** ASm,ASm(c);rep . . . 150.00
06/49 **(60)** ASm,ASm(c),No(c)Price,
New CI Logo,Pgs. Reduced
to 48;rep 125.00
08/49 **(62)** ASm,ASm(c),CI
Logo;rep 115.00
12/50 **(78)** ASm,ASm(c),15¢(c)
Price, CI Logo;rep 100.00
07/52 **(97)** ASm,ASm(c),CI
Logo;rep 90.00

CI #28 Michael Strogoff,
© *Gilberton Publications*

021-FAMOUS MYSTERIES
By Sir Arthur Conan Doyle
Guy de Maupassant
& Edgar Allan Poe
07/44 **(---)** ASm,AdH,LZ,ASm(c),
Original Gilberton Edition 650.00
07/44 **(---)** ASm,AdH,LZ,ASm(c),
Original Island Publications
Edition; No Date or Indicia . . 675.00
07/44 **(---)** ASm,AdH,LZ,ASm(c),Original
Richmond Courier Edition 600.00
10/44 **(22)** ASm,AdH,LZ,ASm(c),
Nassau Bulliten Edition;rep . . . 275.00
09/46 **(30)** ASm,AdH,LZ,ASm(c);
rep 225.00
08/49 **(62)** ASm,AdH,LZ,ASm(c),
New CI Logo;rep 150.00
04/50 **(70)** ASm,AdH,LZ,ASm(c),
CI Logo;rep 135.00
07/51 **(85)** ASm,AdH,LZ,ASm(c),
15¢(c) Price,CI Logo;rep 100.00
12/53 **(114)** ASm,AdH,LZ,New
P(c), CI Logo;rep 100.00

022-THE PATHFINDER
By James Fenimore Cooper
10/44 **(---)** LZ,LZ(c),Original
Gilberton Edition 350.00
10/44 **(---)** LZ,LZ(c),Original
Island Publications Edition; . . . 275.00
10/44 **(---)** LZ,LZ(c),Original
Queens County Times Edition 275.00
09/46 **(30)** LZ,LZ(c),No(c)
Price;rep 90.00
06/49 **(60)** LZ,LZ(c),New CI Logo,
Pgs.Reduced To 48;rep 30.00

08/49 **(62)** LZ,LZ(c),CI Logo;rep . 22.00
04/50 **(70)** LZ,LZ(c),CI Logo;rep . 16.00
07/51 **(85)** LZ,LZ(c),15¢(c)
Price, CI Logo;rep 15.00
04/54 **(118)** LZ,LZ(c),CI Logo;rep . 12.00
05/56 **(132)** LZ,LZ(c),CI Logo;rep . 11.00
09/58 **(146)** LZ,LZ(c),CI Logo;rep . 22.00
11/63 **(167)** LZ,NN New P(c),CI
Logo; rep 17.00
12/65 **(167)** LZ,NN P(c),CI
Logo;rep 17.00
08/67 **(166)** LZ,NN P(c),CI
Logo;rep 17.00

023-OLIVER TWIST
By Charles Dickens
(First Classic produced by
the Iger shop)
07/45 **(---)** AdH,AdH(c),Original . 275.00
09/46 **(30)** AdH,AdH(c),Price
Circle is Blank;rep 200.00
06/49 **(60)** AdH,AdH(c),Pgs. Reduced
To 48, New CI Logo;rep 28.00
08/49 **(62)** AdH,AdH(c),CI
Logo;rep 22.00
05/50 **(71)** AdH,AdH(c),CI
Logo;rep 18.00
07/51 **(85)** AdH,AdH(c),15¢(c)
Price CI Logo;rep 15.00
04/52 **(94)** AdH,AdH(c),CI
Logo;rep 13.00
04/54 **(118)** AdH,AdH(c),CI
Logo; rep 12.00
01/57 **(136)** AdH,New P(c),CI
Logo; rep 13.00
05/59 **(150)** AdH,P(c),CI Logo;rep 10.00
1961 **(164)** AdH,P(c),CI Logo;rep . 10.00
10/61 **(164)** GE&RC New Art,P(c),
CI Logo;rep 16.00
62/63 **(167)** GE&RC,P(c),CI
Logo; rep 6.00
08/64 **(167)** GE&RC,P(c),CI
Logo; rep 6.00
12/65 **(167)** GE&RC,P(c),
CI Logo;rep 6.00
1968 **(166)** GE&RC,P(c),CI
Logo, 25¢(c)Price;rep 6.00
Wr/69 **(169)** GE&RC,P(c),CI
Logo, Rigid(c);rep 6.00

024-A CONNECTICUT
YANKEE IN KING
ARTHUR'S COURT
By Mark Twain
09/45 **(---)** JH,JH(c),Original . . . 300.00
09/46 **(30)** JH,JH(c),Price Circle
Blank;rep 90.00
06/49 **(60)** JH,JH(c),8 Pages
Deleted,New CI Logo;rep 25.00
08/49 **(62)** JH,JH(c),CI Logo;rep . 22.00
05/50 **(71)** JH,JH(c),CI Logo;rep . 14.00
09/51 **(87)** JH,JH(c),15¢(c) Price
CI Logo;rep 12.00
07/54 **(121)** JH,JH(c),CI Logo;rep 11.00
09/57 **(140)** JkS New Art,New
P(c),CI Logo; rep 11.00
11/59 **(153)** JkS,P(c),CI Logo;rep . 6.00
1961 **(164)** JkS,P(c),CI Logo;rep . 6.00
62/63 **(167)** JkS,P(c),CI Logo;rep . 6.00
07/64 **(167)** JkS,P(c),CI Logo;rep . 6.00
06/66 **(167)** JkS,P(c),CI Logo;rep . 6.00
1968 **(166)** JkS,P(c),CI logo,
25¢(c)Price;rep 6.00
Sg/71 **(169)** JkS,P(c),CI Logo,
Rigid(c);rep 64.00

025-TWO YEARS
BEFORE THE MAST
By Richard Henry Dana Jr.
10/45 **(---)** RWb,DvH,Original; . . 300.00
09/46 **(30)** RWb,DvH,Price Circle
Blank;rep 85.00
06/49 **(60)** RWb,DvH,8 Pages
Deleted,New CI Logo;rep 30.00
08/49 **(62)** RWb,DvH,CI Logo;rep 22.00
05/50 **(71)** RWb,DvH,CI Logo;rep 15.00
07/51 **(85)** RWb,DvH,15¢(c) Price
CI Logo;rep 12.00
12/53 **(114)** RWb,DvH,CI Logo;rep 11.00
05/60 **(156)** RWb,DvH,New P(c),CI Logo,
3 Pgs. Replaced By Fillers;rep . 11.00
12/63 **(167)** RWb,DvH,P(c),CI
Logo; rep 6.00
12/65 **(167)** RWb,DvH,P(c),CI
Logo; rep 6.00
09/67 **(166)** RWb,DvH,P(c),CI
Logo; rep 6.00
Wr/69 **(169)** RWb,DvH,P(c),25¢(c)
Price, CI Logo,Rigid(c);rep 6.00

026-FRANKENSTEIN
By Mary Wollstonecraft Shelley
12/45 **(---)** RWb&ABr,RWb
& ABr(c),Original 650.00
09/46 **(30)** RWb&ABr,RWb &ABr(c),
Price Circle Blank;rep 225.00
06/49 **(60)** RWb&ABr,RWb&ABr(c),
New CI Logo;rep 65.00
08/49 **(62)** RWb&ABr,RWb
& ABr(c), CI Logo;rep 75.00
05/50 **(71)** RWb&ABr,RWb
& ABr(c), CI Logo;rep 40.00
04/51 **(82)** RWb&ABr,RWb &ABr(c),
15¢(c) Price,CI Logo;rep 25.00
03/54 **(117)** RWb&ABr,RWb
& ABr(c),CI Logo;rep 15.00
09/58 **(146)** RWb&ABr,NS
New P(c), CI Logo;rep 15.00
11/59 **(153)** RWb&ABr,NS
P(c),CI Logo; rep 25.00
01/61 **(160)** RWb&ABr,NS
P(c),CI Logo; rep 6.00
165 **(1962)** RWb&ABr,NS P(c),
CI Logo; rep 6.00
62/63 **(167)** RWb&ABr,NS P(c),
CI Logo; rep 6.00
06/64 **(167)** RWb&ABr,NS P(c),
CI logo; rep 6.00
06/65 **(167)** RWb&ABr,NS P(c),
CI Logo; rep 6.00
10/65 **(167)** RWb&ABr,NS P(c),
CI Logo; rep 6.00
09/67 **(166)** RWb&ABr,NS P(c),
CI Logo; rep 6.00
Fl/69 **(169)** RWb&ABr,NS P(c),25¢(c)
Price,CI Logo,Rigid(c);rep 6.00
Sg/71 **(169)** RWb&ABr,NS P(c),
CI Logo, Rigid(c);rep 6.00

027-THE ADVENTURES
MARCO POLO
By Marco Polo & Donn Byrne
04/46 **(----)** HFI,HFI(c);Original . . 300.00
09/46 **(30)** HFI,HFI(c);rep 85.00
04/50 **(70)** HFI,HFI(c),8 Pages Deleted,
No(c) Price,New CI Logo;rep . . 25.00
09/51 **(87)** HFI,HFI(c),15¢(c)
Price,CI Logo;rep 17.00
03/54 **(117)** HFI,HFI(c),CILogo;rep 12.00
01/60 **(154)** HFI,New P(c),CI
Logo;rep 11.00

1962 **(165)** HFI,P(c),CI Logo;rep . . 6.00
04/64 **(167)** HFI,P(c),CI Logo;rep . . 6.00
06/66 **(167)** HFI,P(c),CI Logo;rep . . 6.00
Sg/69 **(169)** HFI,P(c),CI Logo,
  25¢(c)Price,Rigid(c);rep 6.00

028-MICHAEL STROGOFF
By Jules Verne
06/46 **(---)** AdH,AdH(c),Original . 300.00
09/48 **(51)** AdH,AdH(c),8 Pages
  Deleted,New CI Logo;rep 90.00
01/54 **(115)** AdH,New P(c),CI
  Logo; rep 15.00
03/60 **(155)** AdH,P(c),CI Logo;rep . 9.00
11/63 **(167)** AdH,P(c),CI Logo;rep . 9.00
07/66 **(167)** AdH,P(c),CI Logo;rep . 9.00
Sr/69 **(169)**AdH,NN,NewP(c),25¢(c)
  Price, CI Logo,Rigid(c);rep 14.00

CI #38 Adventures of Cellini,
© Gilberton Publications

029-THE PRINCE
AND THE PAUPER
By Mark Twain
07/46 **(---)** AdH,AdH(c),Original . 500.00
06/49 **(60)** AdH,New HcK(c),New CI
  Logo,8 Pages Deleted;rep 30.00
08/49 **(62)** AdH,HcK(c),CILogo;rep 25.00
05/50 **(71)** AdH,HcK(c),CILogo;rep 17.00
03/52 **(93)** AdH,HcK(c),CILogo;rep 15.00
12/53 **(114)** AdH,HcK(c),CI
  Logo;rep 12.00
09/55 **(128)** AdH,New P(c),CI
  Logo; rep 12.00
05/57 **(138)** AdH,P(c),CI Logo;rep . 6.00
05/59 **(150)** AdH,P(c),CI Logo;rep . 6.00
1961 **(164)** AdH,P(c),CI Logo;rep . 6.00
62/63 **(167)** AdH,P(c),CI Logo;rep . 6.00
07/64 **(167)** AdH,P(c),CI Logo;rep . 6.00
11/65 **(167)** AdH,P(c),CI Logo;rep . 6.00
1968 **(166)** AdH,P(c),CI Logo,
  25¢(c)Price;rep 6.00
Sr/70 **(169)** AdH,P(c),CI Logo,
  Rigid(c);rep 6.00

030-THE MOONSTONE
By William Wilkie Collins
09/46 **(---)** DRi,DRi(c),Original . . 300.00
06/49 **(60)** DRi,DRi(c),8 Pages
  Deleted,New CI Logo;rep 40.00
04/50 **(70)** DRi,DRi(c),CI Logo;rep 25.00
03/60 **(155)** DRi,LbC New P(c),
  CI Logo;rep 45.00

1962 **(165)** DRi,LbC P(c),CI Logo;
  rep 16.00
01/64 **(167)** DRi,LbC P(c),CI Logo;
  rep 10.00
09/65 **(167)** DRi,LbC P(c),CI Logo;
  rep 7.00
1968 **(166)** DRi,LbC P(c),CI Logo,
  25¢(c)Price;rep 6.00

031-THE BLACK ARROW
By Robert Louis Stevenson
10/46 **(---)** AdH,AdH(c),Original . 275.00
09/48 **(51)** AdH,AdH(c),8 Pages
  Deleted,New CI Logo;rep 35.00
10/49 **(64)** AdH,AdH(c),CI
  Logo;rep 20.00
09/51 **(87)** AdH,AdH(c),15¢(c)
  Price;CI Logo;rep 17.00
06/53 **(108)** AdH,AdH(c),CI
  Logo;rep 15.00
03/55 **(125)** AdH,AdH(c),CI
  Logo;rep 14.00
03/56 **(131)** AdH,New P(c),CI
  Logo; rep 12.00
09/57 **(140)** AdH,P(c),CI Logo;rep . 6.00
01/59 **(148)** AdH,P(c),CI Logo;rep . 6.00
03/61 **(161)** AdH,P(c),CI Logo;rep . 6.00
62/63 **(167)** AdH,P(c),CI Logo;rep . 6.00
07/64 **(167)** AdH,P(c),CI logo;rep . . 6.00
11/65 **(167)** AdH,P(c),CI Logo;rep . 6.00
1968 **(166)** AdH,P(c),CI Logo,
  25¢(c)Price;rep 6.00

032-LORNA DOONE
By Richard Doddridge Blackmore
12/46 **(---)** MB,MB(c),Original . . . 300.00
10/49 **(53/64)** MB,MB(c),8 Pages
  Deleted,New CI Logo;rep 40.00
07/51 **(85)** MB,MB(c),15¢(c)
  Price, CI Logo;rep 26.00
04/54 **(118)** MB,MB(c),CI Logo;rep 16.00
05/57 **(138)** MB,New P(c); Old(c)
  Becomes New Splash Pge.,CI
  Logo;rep 15.00
05/59 **(150)** MB,P(c),CI Logo;rep . 6.00
1962 **(165)** MB,P(c),CI Logo;rep . . 6.00
01/64 **(167)** MB,P(c),CI Logo;rep . 6.00
11/65 **(167)** MB,P(c),CI Logo;rep . 6.00
1968 **(166)** MB,New P(c),CI Logo;
  rep 14.00

033-THE ADVENTURES
OF SHERLOCK HOLMES
By Sir Arthur Conan Doyle
01/47 **(---)** LZ,HcK(c),Original . . 825.00
11/48 **(53)** LZ,HcK(c),"A Study in Scarlet"
  Deleted,New CI Logo;rep 325.00
05/50 **(71)** LZ,HcK(c),CI Logo;rep 275.00
11/51 **(89)** LZ,HcK(c),15¢(c)
  Price,CI Logo;rep 225.00

034-MYSTERIOUS ISLAND
By Jules Verne
Last Classic Comic
02/47 **(---)** RWb&DvH,Original . . 300.00
06/49 **(60)** RWb&DvH,8 Pages
  Deleted,New CI Logo;rep 30.00
08/49 **(62)** RWb&DvH,CI Logo;rep 20.00
05/50 **(71)** RWb&DvH,CI Logo;rep 32.00
12/50 **(78)** RWb&DvH,15¢(c) Price,
  CI Logo;rep 16.00
02/52 **(92)** RWb&DvH,CI Logo;rep 15.00
03/54 **(117)** RWb&DvH,CI Logo;rep 14.00
09/57 **(140)** RWb&DvH,New P(c),CI
  Logo;rep 14.00

05/60 **(156)** RWb&DvH,P(c),CI
  Logo;rep 6.00
10/63 **(167)** RWb&DvH,P(c),CI
  Logo;rep 6.00
05/64 **(167)** RWb&DvH,P(c),CI
  Logo;rep 6.00
06/66 **(167)** RWb&DvH,P(c),CI
  logo;rep 6.00
1968 **(166)** RWb&DvH,P(c),CI Logo,
  25¢(c)Price;rep 6.00

035-LAST DAYS
OF POMPEII
By Lord Edward Bulwer Lytton
First Classics Illustrated
03/47 **(---)** HcK,HcK(c),Original . 300.00
03/61 **(161)** JK,New P(c),
  15¢(c)Price;rep 25.00
01/64 **(167)** JK,P(c);rep 9.00
07/66 **(167)** JK,P(c);rep 9.00
Sg/70 **(169)** JK,P(c),25¢(c)
  Price, Rigid(c);rep 10.00

036-TYPEE
By Herman Melville
04/47 **(---)** EzW,EzW(c),Original . 135.00
10/49 **(64)** EzW,EzW(c),No(c)price,
  8 pages deleted;rep 30.00
03/60 **(155)** EzW,GMc New
  P(c);rep 15.00
09/63 **(167)** EzW,GMc P(c);rep . . . 9.00
07/65 **(167)** EzW,GMc P(c);rep . . . 9.00
Sr/69 **(169)** EzW,GMc P(c),25¢(c)
  Price, Rigid(c);rep 8.00

037-THE PIONEERS
By James Fenimore Cooper
05/47 **(37)** RP,RP(c),Original . . . 135.00
08/49 **(62)** RP,RP(c),8 Pages
  Deleted;rep 25.00
04/50 **(70)** RP,RP(c);rep 75.00
02/52 **(92)** RP,RP(c),15¢(c)Price;rep17.00
04/54 **(118)** RP,RP(c);rep 13.00
03/56 **(131)** RP,RP(c);rep 13.00
05/56 **(132)** RP,RP(c);rep 13.00
11/59 **(153)** RP,RP(c);rep 10.00
05/64 **(167)** RP,RP(c);rep 10.00
06/66 **(167)** RP,RP(c);rep 10.00
1968 **(166)** RP,TO New P(c),
  25¢(c)Price;rep 18.00

038-ADVENTURES
OF CELLINI
By Benvenuto Cellini
06/47 **(---)** AgF,AgF(c),Original . 225.00
1961 **(164)** NN New Art,New P(c);
  rep 15.00
12/63 **(167)** NN,P(c);rep 9.00
07/66 **(167)** NN,P(c);rep 9.00
Sg/70 **(169)** NN,P(c),25¢(c)
  Price, Rigid(c);rep 10.00

039-JANE EYRE
By Charlotte Bronte
07/47 **(---)** HyG,HyG(c),Original . 200.00
06/49 **(60)** HyG,HyG(c),No(c)Price,
  8 pages deleted;rep 30.00
08/49 **(62)** HyG,HyG(c);rep 25.00
05/50 **(71)** HyG,HyG(c);rep 22.00
02/52 **(92)** HyG,HyG(c),15¢(c)
  Price; rep 15.00
04/54 **(118)** HyG,HyG(c);rep 15.00
01/58 **(142)** HyG,New P(c);rep . . 16.00
01/60 **(154)** HyG,P(c);rep 14.00

1962 **(165)** HjK New Art,P(c);rep . 16.00
12/63 **(167)** HjK,P(c);rep 16.00
04/65 **(167)** HjK,P(c);rep 14.00
08/66 **(167)** HjK,P(c);rep 14.00
1968 **(166)** HjK,NN New P(c);rep . 32.00

040-MYSTERIES
(The Pit & the Pendulum, The Adventures of Hans Pfall, Fall of the House of Usher)
By Edgar Allan Poe
08/47 **(---)** HcK,AgF,HyG,HcK(c),
Original 500.00
08/49 **(62)** HcK,AgF,HyG,HcK(c),
8 Pages deleted;rep 225.00
09/50 **(75)** HcK,AgF,HyG,
HcK(c);rep 185.00
02/52 **(92)** HcK,AgF,HyG,HcK(c)
15¢(c) Price;rep 135.00

041-TWENTY YEARS AFTER
By Alexandre Dumas
09/47 **(---)** RBu,RBu(c),Original . 400.00
08/49 **(62)** RBu,HcK New(c),No(c)
Price, 8 Pages Deleted;rep 30.00
12/50 **(78)** RBu,HcK(c),15¢(c)
Price; rep 20.00
05/60 **(156)** RBu,DgR New P(c);rep 14.00
12/63 **(167)** RBu,DgR P(c);rep 8.00
11/66 **(167)** RBu,DgR P(c);rep 6.00
Sg/70 **(169)** RBu,DgR P(c),25¢(c)
Price,Rigid(c);rep 6.00

042-SWISS FAMILY ROBINSON
By Johann Wyss
10/47 **(42)** HcK,HcK(c),Original . 140.00
08/49 **(62)** HcK,HcK(c),No(c)price,
8 Pages Deleted,Not Every Issue
Has 'Gift Box' Ad;rep 30.00
09/50 **(75)** HcK,HcK(c);rep 18.00
03/52 **(93)** HcK,HcK(c);rep 15.00
03/54 **(117)** HcK,HcK(c);rep 12.00
03/56 **(131)** HcK,New P(c);rep . . . 12.00
03/57 **(137)** HcK,P(c);rep 11.00
11/57 **(141)** HcK,P(c);rep 11.00
09/59 **(152)** NN New art,P(c);rep . 11.00
09/60 **(158)** NN,P(c);rep 6.00
12/63 **(165)** NN,P(c);rep 11.00
12/63 **(167)** NN,P(c);rep 7.00
04/65 **(167)** NN,P(c);rep 7.00
05/66 **(167)** NN,P(c);rep 7.00
11/67 **(166)** NN,P(c);rep 6.00
Sg/69 **(169)** NN,P(c);rep 6.00

043-GREAT EXPECTATIONS
By Charles Dickens
11/47 **(---)** HcK,HcK(c),Original . 625.00
08/49 **(62)** HcK,HcK(c),No(c)price;
8 pages deleted;rep 325.00

044-MYSTERIES OF PARIS
By Eugene Sue
12/47 **(44)** HcK,HcK(c),Original . 500.00
08/47 **(62)** HcK,HcK(c),No(c)Price,
8 Pages Deleted,Not Every Issue
Has'Gift Box'Ad;rep 225.00
12/50 **(78)** HcK,HcK(c),15¢(c)
Price; rep 200.00

045-TOM BROWN'S SCHOOL DAYS
By Thomas Hughes
01/48 **(44)** HFl,HFl(c),Original,
1st 48 Pge. Issue 110.00
10/49 **(64)** HFl,HFl(c),No(c)
Price;rep 32.00
03/61 **(161)** JTg New Art,GMc
New P(c);rep 14.00
02/64 **(167)** JTg,GMc P(c);rep . . . 10.00
08/66 **(167)** JTg,GMc P(c);rep . . . 10.00
1968 **(166)** JTg,GMc P(c),
25¢(c)Price;rep 10.00

046-KIDNAPPED
By Robert Louis Stevenson
04/48 **(47)** RWb,RWb(c),Original . 90.00
08/49 **(62)** RWb,RWb(c),Red Circle
Either Blank or With 10¢;rep . . . 62.00
12/50 **(78)** RWb,RWb(c),15¢(c)
Price; rep 16.00
09/51 **(87)** RWb,RWb(c);rep 14.00
04/54 **(118)** RWb,RWb(c);rep . . . 12.00
03/56 **(131)** RWb,New P(c);rep . . . 11.00
09/57 **(140)** RWb,P(c);rep 6.00
05/59 **(150)** RWb,P(c);rep 6.00
05/60 **(156)** RWb,P(c);rep 6.00
1961 **(164)** RWb,P(c),Reduced Pge.
Wdth;rep 6.00
62/63 **(167)** RWb,P(c);rep 6.00
03/64 **(167)** RWb,P(c);rep 6.00
06/65 **(167)** RWb,P(c);rep 6.00
12/65 **(167)** RWb,P(c);rep 6.00
09/67 **(167)** RWb,P(c);rep 6.00
Wr/69 **(166)** RWb,P(c),25¢(c)
Price, Rigid(c);rep 6.00
Sr/70 **(169)** RWb,P(c),Rigid(c);rep . 6.00

047-TWENTY THOUSAND LEAGUES UNDER THE SEA
By Jules Verne
05/58 **(47)** HcK,HcK(c),Original . 110.00
10/49 **(64)** HcK,HcK(c),No(c)
Price; rep 25.00
12/50 **(78)** HcK,HcK(c),15¢(c)
Price; rep 20.00
04/52 **(94)** HcK,HcK(c);rep 18.00
04/54 **(118)** HcK,HcK(c);rep 15.00
09/55 **(128)** HcK,New P(c);rep . . . 12.00
07/56 **(133)** HcK,P(c);rep 12.00
09/57 **(140)** HcK,P(c);rep 6.00
01/59 **(148)** HcK,P(c);rep 6.00
05/60 **(156)** HcK,P(c);rep 6.00
62/63 **(165)** HcK,P(c);rep 6.00
05/48 **(167)** HcK,P(c);rep 6.00
03/64 **(167)** HcK,P(c);rep 6.00
08/65 **(167)** HcK,P(c);rep 6.00
10/66 **(167)** HcK,P(c);rep 6.00
1968 **(166)** HcK,NN New P(c),
25¢(c)Price;rep 12.00
Sg/70 **(169)** HcK,NN P(c),
Rigid(c);rep 12.00

048-DAVID COPPERFIELD
By Charles Dickens
06/48 **(47)** HcK,HcK(c),Original . 110.00
10/49 **(64)** HcK,HcK(c),Price Circle
Replaced By Image of Boy
Reading;rep 25.00
09/51 **(87)** HcK,HcK(c),15¢(c)
Price; rep 18.00
07/54 **(121)** HcK,New P(c);rep . . . 12.00

10/56 **(130)** HcK,P(c);rep 7.00
09/57 **(140)** HcK,P(c);rep 7.00
01/59 **(148)** HcK,P(c);rep 7.00
05/60 **(156)** HcK,P(c);rep 7.00
62/63 **(167)** HcK,P(c);rep 6.00
04/64 **(167)** HcK,P(c);rep 6.00
06/65 **(167)** HcK,P(c);rep 6.00
05/67 **(166)** HcK,P(c);rep 6.00
R/67 **(166)** HcK,P(c);rep 11.00
Sg/69 **(166)** HcK,P(c),25¢(c)
Price, Rigid(c);rep 6.00
Wr/69 **(169)** HcK,P(c),Rigid(c);rep . 6.00

*CI #51 The Spy,
© Gilberton Publications*

049-ALICE IN WONDERLAND
By Lewis Carroll
07/48 **(47)** AB,AB(c),Original . . . 135.00
10/49 **(64)** AB,AB(c),No(c)Price;rep 30.00
07/51 **(85)** AB,AB(c),15¢(c)Price;rep22.00
03/60 **(155)** AB,New P(c);rep . . . 22.00
1962 **(165)** AB,P(c);rep 18.00
03/64 **(167)** AB,P(c);rep 15.00
06/66 **(167)** AB,P(c);rep 15.00
Fl/68 **(166)** AB,TO New P(c),25¢(c)
Price, New Soft(c);rep 25.00
Fl/68 **(166)** AB,P(c),Both Soft &
Rigid(c)s;rep 44.00

050-ADVENTURES OF TOM SAWYER
By Mark Twain
08/48 **(51)** ARu,ARu(c),Original . 110.00
09/48 **(51)** ARu,ARu(c),Original . 130.00
10/49 **(64)** ARu,ARu(c),No(c)
Price; rep 25.00
12/50 **(78)** ARu,ARu(c),15¢(c)
Price; rep 16.00
04/52 **(94)** ARu,ARu(c);rep 14.00
12/53 **(114)** ARu,ARu(c);rep 12.00
03/54 **(117)** ARu,ARu(c);rep 11.00
05/56 **(132)** ARu,ARu(c);rep 11.00
09/57 **(140)** ARu,New P(c);rep 9.00
05/59 **(150)** ARu,P(c);rep 11.00
10/61 **(164)** New Art,P(c);rep 6.00
62/63 **(167)** P(c);rep 6.00
01/65 **(167)** P(c);rep 6.00
05/66 **(167)** P(c);rep 6.00
12/67 **(166)** P(c);rep 6.00
Fl/69 **(169)** P(c),25¢(c) Price,
Rigid(c);rep 6.00
Wr/71 **(169)** P(c);rep 6.00

All comics prices listed are for *Near Mint* condition.

051-THE SPY
By James Fenimore Cooper
09/48 **(51)** AdH,AdH(c),Original,
Maroon(c) 100.00
09/48 **(51)** AdH,AdH(c),Original,
Violet(c) 100.00
11/51 **(89)** AdH,AdH(c),15¢(c)
Price; rep 20.00
07/54 **(121)** AdH,AdH(c);rep . . . 15.00
07/57 **(139)** AdH,New P(c);rep . . 11.00
05/60 **(156)** AdH,P(c);rep 6.00
11/63 **(167)** AdH,P(c);rep 6.00
07/66 **(167)** AdH,P(c);rep 6.00
Wr/69 **(166)** AdH,P(c),25¢(c)Price,
Both Soft & Rigid(c)s;rep 14.00

052-THE HOUSE OF SEVEN GABLES
By Nathaniel Hawthorne
10/48 **(53)** HyG,HyG(c),Original . 100.00
11/51 **(89)** HyG,HyG(c),15¢(c)
Price; rep 20.00
07/54 **(121)** HyG,HyG(c);rep 15.00
01/58 **(142)** GWb New Art,New
P(c); rep 12.00
05/60 **(156)** GWb,P(c);rep 6.00
1962 **(165)** GWb,P(c);rep 6.00
05/64 **(167)** GWb,P(c);rep 6.00
03/66 **(167)** GWb,P(c);rep 6.00
1968 **(166)** GWb,P(c),25¢(c)
Price;rep 6.00
Sg/70 **(169)** GWb,P(c),Rigid(c);rep . 6.00

053-A CHRISTMAS CAROL
By Charles Dickens
11/48 **(53)** HcK,HcK(c),Original . 125.00

054-MAN IN THE IRON MASK
By Alexandre Dumas
12/48 **(55)** AgF,HcK(c),Original . 100.00
03/52 **(93)** AgF,HcK(c),15¢(c)
Price; rep 20.00
09/53 **(111)** AgF,HcK(c);rep 30.00
01/58 **(142)** KBa New Art,New
P(c); rep 12.00
01/60 **(154)** KBa,P(c);rep 6.00
1962 **(165)** KBa,P(c);rep 6.00
05/64 **(167)** KBa,P(c);rep 6.00
04/66 **(167)** KBa,P(c);rep 6.00
Wr/69 **(166)** KBa,P(c),25¢(c)
Price, Rigid(c);rep 6.00

055-SILAS MARINER
By George Eliot
01/49 **(55)** AdH,HcK(c),Original . 100.00
09/50 **(75)** AdH,HcK(c),Price Circle
Blank,'Coming next'Ad(not
usually in reps.);rep 25.00
07/52 **(97)** AdH,HcK(c);rep 15.00
07/54 **(121)** AdH,New P(c);rep . . . 12.00
01/56 **(130)** AdH,P(c);rep 6.00
09/57 **(140)** AdH,P(c);rep 6.00
01/60 **(154)** AdH,P(c);rep 6.00
1962 **(165)** AdH,P(c);rep 6.00
05/64 **(167)** AdH,P(c);rep 6.00
06/65 **(167)** AdH,P(c);rep 6.00
05/67 **(166)** AdH,P(c);rep 6.00
Wr/69 **(166)** AdH,P(c),25¢(c) Price,
Rigid(c);rep,Soft & Stiff 16.00

056-THE TOILERS OF THE SEA
By Victor Hugo
02/49 **(55)** AgF,AgF(c),Original . 135.00
01/62 **(165)** AT New Art,New
P(c); rep 25.00
03/64 **(167)** AT,P(c);rep. 16.00
10/66 **(167)** AT,P(c);rep. 16.00

057-THE SONG OF HIAWATHA
By Henry Wadsworth Longfellow
03/49 **(55)** AB,AB(c),Original . . . 100.00
09/50 **(75)** AB,AB(c),No(c)price,'
Coming Next'Ad(not usually
found in reps.);rep 25.00
04/52 **(94)** AB,AB(c),15¢(c)
Price;rep 16.00
04/54 **(118)** AB,AB(c);rep 15.00
09/56 **(134)** AB,New P(c);rep . . . 12.00
07/57 **(139)** AB,P(c);rep 6.00
01/60 **(154)** AB,P(c);rep 6.00
62/63 **(167)** AB,P(c),Erroneosly
Has Original Date;rep 6.00
09/64 **(167)** AB,P(c);rep 6.00
10/65 **(167)** AB,P(c);rep 6.00
Fl/68 **(166)** AB,P(c),25¢(c) Price;rep 6.00

058-THE PRAIRIE
By James Fenimore Cooper
04/49 **(60)** RP,RP(c),Original . . . 100.00
08/49 **(62)** RP,RP(c);rep 40.00
12/50 **(78)** RP,RP(c),15¢(c) Price
In Double Circle;rep 20.00
12/53 **(114)** RP,RP(c);rep 15.00
03/56 **(131)** RP,RP(c);rep 12.00
05/56 **(132)** RP,RP(c);rep 12.00
09/58 **(146)** RP,New P(c);rep . . . 11.00
03/60 **(155)** RP,P(c);rep 6.00
05/64 **(167)** RP,P(c);rep 6.00
04/66 **(167)** RP,P(c);rep 6.00
Sr/69 **(169)** RP,P(c),25¢(c)
Price; Rigid(c);rep 6.00

059-WUTHERING HEIGHTS
By Emily Bronte
05/49 **(60)** HcK,HcK(c),Original . 105.00
07/51 **(85)** HcK,HcK(c),15¢(c)
Price; rep 26.00
05/60 **(156)** HcK,GB New P(c);rep 14.00
01/64 **(167)** HcK,GB P(c);rep 7.00
10/66 **(167)** HcK,GB P(c);rep 7.00
Sr/69 **(169)** HcK,GBP(c),25¢(c)
Price, Rigid(c);rep 6.00

060-BLACK BEAUTY
By Anna Sewell
06/49 **(62)** AgF,AgF(c),Original . 100.00
08/49 **(62)** AgF,AgF(c);rep 105.00
07/51 **(85)** AgF,AgF(c),15¢(c) Price;
rep 22.00
09/60 **(158)** LbC&NN&StA New
Art, LbC New P(c);rep 22.00
02/64 **(167)** LbC&NN&StA,LbC
P(c); rep 15.00
03/66 **(167)** LbC&NN&StA,LbC
P(c); rep 15.00
03/66 **(167)** LbC&NN&StA,LbC
P(c), 'Open Book'Blank;rep 42.00
1968 **(166)** LbC&NN&StA,AIM New
P(c) 25¢(c) Price;rep 6.00

061-THE WOMAN IN WHITE
By William Wilke Collins
07/49 **(62)** AB,AB(c),Original,
Maroon & Violet(c)s 100.00
05/60 **(156)** AB,DgR New P(c);rep 20.00
01/64 **(167)** AB,DgR P(c);rep 15.00
1968 **(166)** AB,DgR P(c),
25¢(c)Price;rep 15.00

062-WESTERN STORIES
(The Luck of Roaring Camp & The Outcasts of Poker Flat)
By Bret Harte
08/49 **(62)** HcK,HcK(c),Original . 100.00
11/51 **(89)** HcK,HcK(c),15¢(c)
Price; rep 22.00
07/54 **(121)** HcK,HcK(c);rep 16.00
03/57 **(137)** HcK,New P(c);rep . . . 12.00
09/59 **(152)** HcK,P(c);rep 7.00
10/63 **(167)** HcK,P(c);rep 7.00
06/64 **(167)** HcK,P(c);rep 6.00
11/66 **(167)** HcK,P(c);rep 6.00
1968 **(166)** HcK,TO New P(c),
25¢ Price;rep 15.00

063-THE MAN WITHOUT A COUNTRY
By Edward Everett Hale
09/49 **(62)** HcK,HcK(c),Original . 100.00
12/50 **(78)** HcK,HcK(c),15¢(c)Price
In Double Circles;rep 25.00
05/60 **(156)** HcK,GMc New P(c);rep 22.00
01/62 **(165)** AT New Art,GMc P(c),
Added Text Pages;rep 12.00
03/64 **(167)** AT,GMc P(c);rep 6.00
08/66 **(167)** AT,GMc P(c);rep 6.00
Sr/69 **(169)** AT,GMc P(c),25¢(c)
Price, Rigid(c);rep 6.00

064-TREASURE ISLAND
By Robert Louis Stevenson
10/49 **(62)** AB,AB(c),Original 90.00
04/51 **(82)** AB,AB(c),15¢(c)
Price;rep 25.00
03/54 **(117)** AB,AB(c);rep 17.00
03/56 **(131)** AB,New P(c);rep 12.00
05/57 **(138)** AB,P(c);rep 6.00
09/58 **(146)** AB,P(c);rep 6.00
09/60 **(158)** AB,P(c);rep 6.00
1962 **(165)** AB,P(c);rep 6.00
62/63 **(167)** AB,P(c);rep 6.00
06/64 **(167)** AB,P(c);rep 6.00
12/65 **(167)** AB,P(c);rep 6.00
10/67 **(166)** AB,P(c);rep 11.00
10/67 **(166)** AB,P(c),GRIT Ad
Stapled In Book;rep 64.00
Sg/69 **(169)** AB,P(c),25¢(c)
Price, Rigid(c);rep 6.00

065-BENJAMIN FRANKLIN
By Benjamin Franklin
11/49 **(64)** AB,RtH,GS(Iger Shop),
HcK(c),Original 100.00
03/56 **(131)** AB,RtH,GS(Iger Shop),
New P(c) ;rep 15.00
01/60 **(154)** AB,RtH,GS(Iger Shop),
P(c);rep 6.00
02/64 **(167)** AB,RtH,GS(Iger Shop),
P(c);rep 6.00
04/66 **(167)** AB,RtH,GS(Iger Shop),
P(c);rep 6.00
Fl/69 **(169)** AB,RtH,GS(Iger Shop),
P(c), 25¢(c)Price,Rigid(c);rep . . . 5.00

066-THE CLOISTER AND THE HEARTH
By Charles Reade
12/49 **(67)** HcK,HcK(c),Original . 200.00

067-THE SCOTTISH CHIEFS
By Jane Porter
01/50 **(67)** AB,AB(c),Original		90.00
07/51 **(85)** AB,AB(c),15¢(c)		
Price;rep		22.00
04/54 **(118)** AB,AB(c);rep		17.00
01/57 **(136)** AB,New P(c);rep		12.00
01/60 **(154)** AB,P(c);rep		10.00
11/63 **(167)** AB,P(c);rep		10.00
08/65 **(167)** AB,P(c);rep		10.00

CI #68 Julius Caesar,
© Gilberton Publications

068-JULIUS CEASAR
By William Shakespeare
02/50 **(70)** HcK,HcK(c),Original		100.00
07/51 **(85)** HcK,HcK(c),15¢(c)		
Price; rep		22.00
06/53 **(108)** HcK,HcK(c);rep		17.00
05/60 **(156)** HcK,LbC New P(c);rep	20.00
1962 **(165)** GE&RC New Art,		
LbC P(c);rep		20.00
02/64 **(167)** GE&RC,LbC P(c);rep	6.00
10/65 **(167)** GE&RC,LbC P(c),Tarzan	
Books Inside(c);rep		6.00
1967 **(166)** GE&RC,LbC P(c);rep	6.00
Wr/69 **(169)** GE&RC,LbC P(c),		
Rigid(c);rep		6.00

069-AROUND THE WORLD IN 80 DAYS
By Jules Verne
03/50 **(70)** HcK,HcK(c),Original	100.00
09/51 **(87)** HcK,HcK(c),15¢(c)		
Price;rep		22.00
03/55 **(125)** HcK,HcK(c);rep		17.00
01/57 **(136)** HcK,New P(c);rep		12.00
09/58 **(146)** HcK,P(c);rep		6.00
09/59 **(152)** HcK,P(c);rep		6.00
1961 **(164)** HcK,P(c);rep		6.00
62/63 **(167)** HcK,P(c);rep		6.00
07/64 **(167)** HcK,P(c);rep		6.00
11/65 **(167)** HcK,P(c);rep		6.00
07/67 **(166)** HcK,P(c);rep		6.00
Sg/69 **(169)** HcK,P(c),25¢(c)		
Price, Rigid(c);rep		6.00

070-THE PILOT
By James Fenimore Cooper
04/50 **(71)** AB,AB(c),Original		90.00
10/50 **(75)** AB,AB(c),15¢(c)		
Price;rep		22.00
02/52 **(92)** AB,AB(c);rep		17.00
03/55 **(125)** AB,AB(c);rep		12.00
05/60 **(156)** AB,GMc New P(c);rep	8.00
02/64 **(167)** AB,GMc P(c);rep		8.00
05/66 **(167)** AB,GMc P(c);rep		8.00

071-THE MAN WHO LAUGHS
By Victor Hugo
05/50 **(71)** AB,AB(c),Original	125.00
01/62 **(165)** NN,NN New P(c);rep	65.00
04/64 **(167)** NN,NN P(c);rep		60.00

072-THE OREGON TRAIL
By Francis Parkman
06/50 **(73)** HcK,HcK (c),Original	75.00
11/51 **(89)** HcK,HcK (c),15¢(c)		
Price; rep		22.00
07/54 **(121)** HcK,HcK (c);rep		17.00
03/56 **(131)** HcK,New P(c);rep		12.00
09/57 **(140)** HcK,P(c);rep		7.00
05/59 **(150)** HcK,P(c);rep		6.00
01/61 **(164)** HcK,P(c);rep		6.00
62/63 **(167)** HcK,P(c);rep		6.00
08/64 **(167)** HcK,P(c);rep		6.00
10/65 **(167)** HcK,P(c);rep		6.00
1968 **(166)** HcK,P(c),25¢(c)Price;rep	6.00

073-THE BLACK TULIP
By Alexandre Dumas
07/50 **(75)** AB,AB(c),Original . . . 225.00

074-MR. MIDSHIPMAN EASY
By Captain Frederick Marryat
08/50 **(75)** BbL,Original 225.00

075-THE LADY OF THE LAKE
By Sir Walter Scott
09/50 **(75)** HcK,HcK(c),Original	70.00
07/51 **(85)** HcK,HcK(c),15¢(c)		
Price; rep		22.00
04/54 **(118)** HcK,HcK(c);rep		17.00
07/57 **(139)** HcK,New P(c);rep		12.00
01/60 **(154)** HcK,P(c);rep		6.00
1962 **(165)** HcK,P(c);rep		6.00
04/64 **(167)** HcK,P(c);rep		6.00
05/66 **(167)** HcK,P(c);rep		6.00
Sg/69 **(169)** HcK,P(c),25¢(c)		
Price, Rigid(c);rep		6.00

076-THE PRISONER OF ZENDA
By Anthony Hope Hawkins
10/50 **(75)** HcK,HcK(c),Original	60.00
07/51 **(85)** HcK,HcK(c),15¢(c) Price;	
rep		22.00
09/53 **(111)** HcK,HcK(c),rep		17.00
09/55 **(128)** HcK,New P(c);rep		12.00
09/59 **(152)** HcK,P(c);rep		6.00
1962 **(165)** HcK,P(c);rep		6.00
04/64 **(167)** HcK,P(c);rep		6.00
09/66 **(167)** HcK,P(c);rep		6.00
Fl/69 **(169)** HcK,P(c),25¢(c) Price,	
Rigid(c);rep		6.00

077-THE ILLIAD
By Homer
11/50 **(78)** AB,AB(c),Original		60.00
09/51 **(87)** AB,AB(c),15¢(c)		
Price;rep		22.00
07/54 **(121)** AB,AB(c);rep		17.00
07/57 **(139)** AB,New P(c);rep		12.00
05/59 **(150)** AB,P(c);rep		6.00
1962 **(165)** AB,P(c);rep		6.00
10/63 **(167)** AB,P(c);rep		6.00
07/64 **(167)** AB,P(c);rep		6.00
05/66 **(167)** AB,P(c);rep		6.00
1968 **(166)** AB,P(c),25¢(c)Price;rep	6.00

078-JOAN OF ARC
By Frederick Shiller
12/50 **(78)** HcK,HcK(c),Original	60.00
09/51 **(87)** HcK,HcK(c),15¢(c)		
Price; rep		22.00
11/53 **(113)** HcK,HcK(c);rep		17.00
09/55 **(128)** HcK,New P(c);rep		12.00
09/57 **(140)** HcK,P(c);rep		6.00
05/59 **(150)** HcK,P(c);rep		6.00
11/60 **(159)** HcK,P(c);rep		6.00
62/63 **(167)** HcK,P(c);rep		6.00
12/63 **(167)** HcK,P(c);rep		6.00
06/65 **(167)** HcK,P(c);rep		6.00
06/67 **(166)** HcK,P(c);rep		6.00
Wr/69 **(166)** HcK,TO New P(c),		
25¢(c)Price, Rigid(c);rep		14.00

079-CYRANO DE BERGERAC
By Edmond Rostand
01/51 **(78)** AB,AB(c),Original,Movie	
Promo Inside Front(c)		60.00
07/51 **(85)** AB,AB(c),15¢(c)		
Price;rep		22.00
04/54 **(118)** AB,AB(c);rep		17.00
07/56 **(133)** AB,New P(c);rep		15.00
05/60 **(156)** AB,P(c);rep		12.00
08/64 **(167)** AB,P(c);rep		12.00

080-WHITE FANG
By Jack London
(Last Line Drawn (c)
02/51 **(79)** AB,AB(c),Original		60.00
09/51 **(87)** AB,AB(c);rep		22.00
03/55 **(125)** AB,AB(c);rep		17.00
05/56 **(132)** AB,New P(c);rep		15.00
09/57 **(140)** AB,P(c);rep		6.00
11/59 **(153)** AB,P(c);rep		6.00
62/63 **(167)** AB,P(c);rep		6.00
09/64 **(167)** AB,P(c);rep		6.00
07/65 **(167)** AB,P(c);rep		6.00
06/67 **(166)** AB,P(c);rep		6.00
Fl/69 **(169)** AB,P(c),25¢(c)		
Price, Rigid(c);rep		6.00

081-THE ODYSSEY
By Homer
(P(c)s From Now on)
03/51 **(82)** HyG,AB P(c),Original	40.00
08/64 **(167)** HyG,AB P(c);rep		12.00
10/66 **(167)** HyG,AB P(c);rep		12.00
Sg/69 **(169)** HyG,TyT New P(c),		
Rigid(c);rep		12.00

082-THE MASTER OF BALLANTRAE
By Robert Louis Stevenson
04/51 **(82)** LDr,AB P(c),Original	40.00
08/64 **(167)** LDr,AB P(c);rep		14.00

FI/68 **(166)** LDr,Syk New P(c),
Rigid(c);rep 14.00

083-THE JUNGLE BOOK
By Rudyard Kipling
05/51 **(85)** WmB&AB,AB P(c),
Original 35.00
08/53 **(110)** WmB&AB,AB P(c);rep . 7.00
03/55 **(125)** WmB&AB,AB P(c);rep . 6.00
05/56 **(134)** WmB&AB,AB P(c);rep . 6.00
01/58 **(142)** WmB&AB,AB P(c);rep . 6.00
05/59 **(150)** WmB&AB,AB P(c);rep . 6.00
11/60 **(159)** WmB&AB,AB P(c);rep . 6.00
62/63 **(167)** WmB&AB,AB P(c);rep . 6.00
03/65 **(167)** WmB&AB,AB P(c);rep . 6.00
11/65 **(167)** WmB&AB,AB P(c);rep . 6.00
05/66 **(167)** WmB&AB,AB P(c);rep . 6.00
1968 **(166)** NN Art,NN New P(c),
Rigid(c);rep 12.00

084-THE GOLD BUG & OTHER STORIES
(The Gold Bug-The Telltale HeartThe Cask of Amontillado)
By Edgar Allan Poe
06/51 **(85)** AB,RP,JLv,AB P(c),
Original 100.00
07/64 **(167)** AB,RP,JLv,AB P(c);rep 58.00

CI #80 White Fang,
© Gilberton Publications

085-THE SEA WOLF
By Jack London
08/51 **(85)** AB,AB P(c),Original . . 30.00
07/54 **(121)** AB,AB P(c);rep 5.00
05/56 **(132)** AB,AB P(c);rep 5.00
11/57 **(141)** AB,AB P(c);rep 5.00
03/61 **(161)** AB,AB P(c);rep 5.00
02/64 **(167)** AB,AB P(c);rep 5.00
11/65 **(167)** AB,AB P(c);rep 5.00
FI/69 **(169)** AB,AB P(c),25¢(c)
Price, Rigid(c);rep 5.00

086-UNDER TWO FLAGS
By Oiuda
08/51 **(87)** MDb,AB P(c),Original . 30.00
03/54 **(117)** MDb,AB P(c);rep 6.00
07/57 **(139)** MDb,AB P(c);rep 6.00
09/60 **(158)** MDb,AB P(c);rep 6.00
02/64 **(167)** MDb,AB P(c);rep 6.00
08/66 **(167)** MDb,AB P(c);rep 6.00
Sr/69 **(169)** MDb,AB P(c),25¢(c)
Price, Rigid(c);rep 6.00

087-A MIDSUMMER NIGHTS DREAM
By William Shakespeare
09/51 **(87)** AB,AB P(c),Original . . 30.00
03/61 **(161)** AB,AB P(c);rep 6.00
04/64 **(167)** AB,AB P(c);rep 5.00
05/66 **(167)** AB,AB P(c);rep 5.00
Sr/69 **(169)** AB,AB P(c),25¢(c)
Price; rep 5.00

088-MEN OF IRON
By Howard Pyle
10/51 **(89)** HD,LDr,GS,Original . . 30.00
01/60 **(154)** HD,LDr,GS P(c);rep . . 6.00
01/64 **(167)** HD,LDr,GS,P(c);rep . 6.00
1968 **(166)** HD,LDr,GS,P(c),
25¢(c)Price;rep 6.00

089-CRIME AND PUNISHMENT
By Fedor Dostoevsky
11/51 **(89)** RP,AB P(c),Original . . 35.00
09/59 **(152)** RP,AB P(c);rep 6.00
04/64 **(167)** RP,AB P(c);rep 6.00
05/66 **(167)** RP,AB P(c);rep 6.00
FI/69 **(169)** RP,AB P(c),25¢(c)
Price, Rigid(c);rep 6.00

090-GREEN MANSIONS
By William Henry Hudson
12/51 **(89)** AB,AB P(c),Original . . 35.00
01/59 **(148)** AB,New LbC P(c);rep . 11.00
1962 **(165)** AB,LbC P(c);rep 5.00
04/64 **(167)** AB,LbC P(c);rep 5.00
09/66 **(167)** AB,LbC P(c);rep 5.00
Sr/69 **(169)** AB,LbC P(c),25¢(c)
Price, Rigid(c);rep 5.00

091-THE CALL OF THE WILD
By Jack London
01/52 **(92)** MDb,P(c),Original . . 30.00
10/53 **(112)** MDb,P(c);rep 6.00
03/55**(125)**MDb,P(c),'PictureProgress'
Onn. Back(c);rep 5.00
09/56 **(134)** MDb,P(c);rep 5.00
03/58 **(143)** MDb,P(c);rep 5.00
1962 **(165)** MDb,P(c);rep 5.00
1962 **(167)** MDb,P(c);rep 5.00
04/65 **(167)** MDb,P(c);rep 5.00
03/66 **(167)** MDb,P(c);rep 5.00
03/66 **(167)** MDb,P(c),Record
Edition;rep 5.00
11/67 **(166)** MDb,P(c);rep 5.00
Sg/70 **(169)** MDb,P(c),25¢(c)
Price, Rigid(c);rep 5.00

092-THE COURTSHIP OF MILES STANDISH
By Henry Wadsworth Longfellow
02/52 **(92)** AB,AB P(c),Original . . 30.00
1962 **(165)** AB,AB P(c);rep 5.00
03/64 **(167)** AB,AB P(c);rep 5.00
05/67 **(166)** AB,AB P(c);rep 5.00
Wr/69 **(169)** AB,AB P(c),25¢(c)
Price, Rigid(c);rep 5.00

093-PUDD'NHEAD WILSON
By Mark Twain
03/52 **(94)** HcK,HcK P(c),Original 32.00
1962 **(165)** HcK,GMc New P(c);rep 8.00
03/64 **(167)** HcK,GMc P(c);rep . . . 6.00

1968 **(166)** HcK,GMc P(c),25¢(c)
Price, Soft(c);rep 8.00

094-DAVID BALFOUR
By Robert Louis Stevenson
04/52 **(94)** RP,P(c),Original 32.00
05/64 **(167)** RP,P(c);rep 11.00
1968 **(166)** RP,P(c),25¢(c)Price;rep 11.00

095-ALL QUIET ON THE WESTERN FRONT
By Erich Maria Remarque
05/52 **(96)** MDb,P(c),Original 75.00
05/52 **(99)** MDb,P(c),Original 60.00
10/64 **(167)** MDb,P(c);rep 16.00
11/66 **(167)** MDb,P(c);rep 16.00

096-DANIEL BOONE
By John Bakeless
06/52 **(97)** AB,P(c),Original 30.00
03/54 **(117)** AB,P(c);rep 5.00
09/55 **(128)** AB,P(c);rep 5.00
05/56 **(132)** AB,P(c);rep 5.00
----- **(134)** AB,P(c),'Story of
Jesus'on Back(c);rep 5.00
09/60 **(158)** AB,P(c);rep 5.00
01/64 **(167)** AB,P(c);rep 5.00
05/65 **(167)** AB,P(c);rep 5.00
11/66 **(167)** AB,P(c);rep 5.00
Wr/69 **(166)** AB,P(c),25¢(c)
Price, Rigid(c);rep 12.00

097-KING SOLOMON'S MINES
By H. Rider Haggard
07/52 **(96)** HcK,P(c),Original 30.00
04/54 **(118)** HcK,P(c);rep 8.00
03/56 **(131)** HcK,P(c);rep 5.00
09/51 **(141)** HcK,P(c);rep 5.00
09/60 **(158)** HcK,P(c);rep 5.00
02/64 **(167)** HcK,P(c);rep 5.00
09/65 **(167)** HcK,P(c);rep 5.00
Sr/69 **(169)** HcK,P(c),25¢(c)
Price; Rigid(c);rep 6.00

098-THE RED BADGE OF COURAGE
By Stephen Crane
08/52 **(98)** MDb,GS,P(c),Original . 30.00
04/54 **(118)** MDb,GS,P(c);rep 5.00
05/56 **(132)** MDb,GS,P(c);rep 5.00
01/58 **(142)** MDb,GS,P(c);rep 5.00
09/59 **(152)** MDb,GS,P(c);rep 5.00
03/61 **(161)** MDb,GS,P(c);rep 5.00
62/63 **(167)** MDb,GS,P(c),Erronosly
Has Original Date;rep 5.00
09/64 **(167)** MDb,GS,P(c);rep 5.00
10/65 **(167)** MDb,GS,P(c);rep 5.00
1968 **(166)** MDb,GS,P(c),25¢(c)
Price, Rigid(c);rep 15.00

099-HAMLET
By William Shakespeare
09/52 **(98)** AB,P(c),Original 32.00
07/54 **(121)** AB,P(c);rep 5.00
11/57 **(141)** AB,P(c);rep 5.00
09/60 **(158)** AB,P(c);rep 5.00
62/63 **(167)** AB,P(c),Erroneusly
Has Original Date;rep 5.00
07/65 **(167)** AB,P(c);rep 5.00
04/67 **(166)** AB,P(c);rep 5.00
Sg/69 **(169)** AB,EdM New P(c),
25¢(c)Price, Rigid(c);rep 12.00

All comics prices listed are for *Near Mint* condition.

100-MUTINY ON THE BOUNTY
By Charrles Nordhoff

10/52 **(100)** MsW,HcK P(c),Original	28.00
03/54 **(117)** MsW,HcK P(c);rep	5.00
05/56 **(132)** MsW,HcK P(c);rep	5.00
01/58 **(142)** MsW,HcK P(c);rep	5.00
03/60 **(155)** MsW,HcK P(c);rep	5.00
62/63 **(167)** MsW,HcK P(c),Erroneously	
Has Original Date;rep	5.00
05/64 **(167)** MsW,HcK P(c);rep	5.00
03/66 **(167)** MsW,HcK P(c),N#	
or Price;rep	10.00
Sg/70 **(169)** MsW,HcK P(c),	
Rigid(c); rep	4.00

101-WILLIAM TELL
By Frederick Schiller

11/52 **(101)** MDb,HcK P(c),Original	28.00
04/54 **(118)** MDb,HcK P(c);rep	5.00
11/57 **(141)** MDb,HcK P(c);rep	5.00
09/60 **(158)** MDb,HcK P(c);rep	5.00
62/63 **(167)** MDb,HcK P(c),Erroneously	
Has Original Date;rep	5.00
11/64 **(167)** MDb,HcK P(c);rep	5.00
04/67 **(166)** MDb,HcK P(c);rep	5.00
Wr/69 **(169)** MDb,HcK P(c)25¢(c)	
Price, Rigid(c);rep	5.00

102-THE WHITE COMPANY
By Sir Arthur Conan Doyle

12/52 **(101)** AB,P(c),Original	45.00
1962 **(165)** AB,P(c);rep	22.00
04/64 **(167)** AB,P(c);rep	22.00

103-MEN AGAINST THE SEA
By Charles Nordhoff

01/53 **(104)** RP,HcK P(c),Original	32.00
12/53 **(114)** RP,HcK P(c);rep	16.00
03/56 **(131)** RP,New P(c);rep	12.00
03/59 **(149)** RP,P(c);rep	12.00
09/60 **(158)** RP,P(c);rep	21.00
03/64 **(167)** RP,P(c);rep	9.00

104-BRING 'EM BACK ALIVE
By Frank Buck & Edward Anthony

02/53 **(105)** HcK,HcK P(c)Original	27.00
04/54 **(118)** HcK,HcK P(c);rep	5.00
07/56 **(133)** HcK,HcK P(c);rep	5.00
05/59 **(150)** HcK,HcK P(c);rep	5.00
09/60 **(158)** HcK,HcK P(c);rep	5.00
10/63 **(167)** HcK,HcK P(c);rep	5.00
09/65 **(167)** HcK,HcK P(c);rep	5.00
Wr/69 **(169)** HcK,HcK P(c),25¢(c)	
Price, Rigid(c);rep	5.00

105-FROM THE EARTH TO THE MOON
By Jules Verne

03/53 **(106)** AB,P(c),Original	28.00
04/54 **(118)** AB,P(c);rep	5.00
03/56 **(132)** AB,P(c);rep	5.00
11/57 **(141)** AB,P(c);rep	5.00
09/58 **(146)** AB,P(c);rep	5.00
05/60 **(156)** AB,P(c);rep	5.00
62/63 **(167)** AB,P(c),Erroneously	
Has Original Date;rep	5.00
05/64 **(167)** AB,P(c);rep	5.00
05/65 **(167)** AB,P(c);rep	5.00
10/67 **(166)** AB,P(c);rep	5.00

Sr/69 **(169)** AB,P(c),25¢(c)	
Price, Rigid(c);rep	5.00
Sg/71 **(169)** AB,P(c);rep	5.00

CI #105 From the Earth to the Moon,
© Gilberton Publications

106-BUFFALO BILL
By William F. Cody

04/53 **(107)** MDb,P(c),Original	28.00
04/54 **(118)** MDb,P(c);rep	5.00
03/56 **(132)** MDb,P(c);rep	5.00
01/58 **(142)** MDb,P(c);rep	5.00
03/61 **(161)** MDb,P(c);rep	5.00
03/64 **(167)** MDb,P(c);rep	5.00
07/67 **(166)** MDb,P(c);rep	5.00
Fl/69 **(169)** MDb,P(c),Rigid(c);rep	5.00

107-KING OF THE KHYBER RIFLES
By Talbot Mundy

05/53 **(108)** SMz,P(c),Original	30.00
04/54 **(118)** SMz,P(c);rep	5.00
09/58 **(146)** SMz,P(c);rep	5.00
09/60 **(158)** SMz,P(c);rep	5.00
62/63 **(167)** SMz,P(c),Erroneously	
Has Original Date;rep	5.00
62/63 **(167)** SMz,P(c);rep	5.00
10/66 **(167)** SMz,P(c);rep	5.00

108-KNIGHTS OF THE ROUND TABLE
By Howard Pyle?

06/53 **(108)** AB,P(c);rep	30.00
06/53 **(109)** AB,P(c),Original	36.00
03/54 **(117)** AB,P(c);rep	5.00
11/59 **(153)** AB,P(c);rep	5.00
1962 **(165)** AB,P(c);rep	5.00
04/64 **(167)** AB,P(c);rep	5.00
04/67 **(166)** AB,P(c);rep	5.00

109-PITCAIRN'S ISLAND
By Charles Nordhoff

07/53 **(110)** RP,P(c),Original	32.00
1962 **(165)** RP,P(c);rep	9.00
03/64 **(167)** RP,P(c);rep	9.00
06/67 **(166)** RP,P(c);rep	9.00

110-A STUDY IN SCARLET
By Sir Arthur Conan Doyle

08/53 **(111)** SMz,P(c),Original	100.00
1962 **(165)** SMz,P(c);rep	46.00

111-THE TALISMAN
By Sir Walter Scott

09/53 **(112)** HcK,HcK P(c),Original	45.00
1962 **(165)** HcK,HcK P(c);rep	6.00
05/64 **(167)** HcK,HcK P(c);rep	6.00
Fl/68 **(166)** HcK,HcK P(c),	
25¢(c)Price;rep	6.00

112-ADVENTURES OF KIT CARSON
By John S. C. Abbott

10/53 **(113)** RP,P(c),Original	50.00
11/55 **(129)** RP,P(c);rep	6.00
11/57 **(141)** RP,P(c);rep	6.00
09/59 **(152)** RP,P(c);rep	6.00
03/61 **(161)** RP,P(c);rep	6.00
62/63 **(167)** RP,P(c);rep	6.00
02/65 **(167)** RP,P(c);rep	6.00
05/66 **(167)** RP,P(c);rep	6.00
Wr/69 **(166)** RP,EdM New P(c),	
25¢(c)Price, Rigid(c);rep	12.00

113-THE FORTY-FIVE GUARDSMEN
By Alexandre Dumas

11/53 **(114)** MDb,P(c),Original	65.00
07/67 **(166)** MDb,P(c);rep	25.00

114-THE RED ROVER
By James Fenimore Cooper

12/53 **(115)** PrC,JP P(c),Original	65.00
07/67 **(166)** PrC,JP P(c);rep	25.00

115-HOW I FOUND LIVINGSTONE
By Sir Henry Stanley

01/54 **(116)** SF&ST,P(c),Original	65.00
01/67 **(167)** SF&ST,P(c);rep	30.00

116-THE BOTTLE IMP
By Robert Louis Stevenson

02/54 **(117)** LC,P(c),Original	70.00
01/67 **(167)** LC,P(c);rep	25.00

117-CAPTAINS COURAGEOUS
By Rudyard Kipling

03/54 **(118)** PrC,P(c),Original	50.00
02/67 **(167)** PrC,P(c);rep	15.00
Fl/69 **(169)** PrC,P(c),25¢(c)	
Price, Rigid(c);rep	12.00

118-ROB ROY
By Sir Walter Scott

04/54 **(119)** RP,WIP,P(c),Original	65.00
02/67 **(167)** RP,WIP,P(c);rep	25.00

119-SOLDERS OF FORTUNE
By Richard Harding Davis

05/54 **(120)** KS,P(c),Original	65.00
03/67 **(166)** KS,P(c);rep	15.00
Sg/70 **(169)** KS,P(c),25¢(c)	
Price, Rigid(c);rep	12.00

120-THE HURRICANE
By Charles Nordhoff

1954 **(121)** LC,LC P(c),Original	60.00
03/67 **(166)** LC,LC P(c);rep	30.00

121-WILD BILL HICKOCK
Author Unknown
07/54 **(122)** MI,ST,P(c),Original . . 25.00
05/56 **(132)** MI,ST,P(c);rep 6.00
11/57 **(141)** MI,ST,P(c);rep 6.00
01/60 **(154)** MI,ST,P(c);rep 6.00
62/63 **(167)** MI,ST,P(c);rep 6.00
08/64 **(167)** MI,ST,P(c);rep 6.00
04/67 **(166)** MI,ST,P(c);rep 6.00
Wr/69 **(169)** MI,ST,P(c),Rigid(c);rep 6.00

122-THE MUTINEERS
By Charles Boardman Hawes
09/54 **(123)** PrC,P(c),Original . . . 25.00
01/57 **(136)** PrC,P(c);rep 6.00
09/58 **(146)** PrC,P(c);rep 6.00
09/60 **(158)** PrC,P(c);rep 6.00
11/63 **(167)** PrC,P(c);rep 6.00
03/65 **(167)** PrC,P(c);rep 6.00
08/67 **(166)** PrC,P(c);rep 6.00

123-FANG AND CLAW
By Frank Buck
11/54 **(124)** LnS,P(c),Original . . . 25.00
07/56 **(133)** LnS,P(c);rep 6.00
03/58 **(143)** LnS,P(c);rep 6.00
01/60 **(154)** LnS,P(c);rep 6.00
62/63 **(167)** LnS,P(c),Erroneously
Has Original Date;rep 6.00
09/65 **(167)** LnS,P(c);rep 6.00

124-THE WAR OF THE WORLDS
By H. G. Wells
01/55 **(125)** LC,LC P(c),Original . . 45.00
03/56 **(131)** LC,LC P(c);rep 6.00
11/57 **(141)** LC,LC P(c);rep 6.00
01/59 **(148)** LC,LC P(c);rep 6.00
05/60 **(156)** LC,LC P(c);rep 6.00
1962 **(165)** LC,LC P(c);rep 6.00
62/63 **(167)** LC,LC P(c);rep 6.00
11/64 **(167)** LC,LC P(c);rep 6.00
11/65 **(167)** LC,LC P(c);rep 6.00
1968 **(166)** LC,LC P(c),25¢(c)
Price; rep 6.00
Sr/70 **(169)** LC,LC P(c),Rigid(c);rep 6.00

125-THE OX BOW INCIDENT
By Walter Van Tilberg Clark
03/55 **(---)** NN,P(c),Original 30.00
03/58 **(143)** NN,P(c);rep 6.00
09/59 **(152)** NN,P(c);rep 6.00
03/61 **(149)** NN,P(c);rep 6.00
62/63 **(167)** NN,P(c);rep 6.00
11/64 **(167)** NN,P(c);rep 6.00
04/67 **(166)** NN,P(c);rep 6.00
Wr/69 **(169)** NN,P(c),25¢(c)
Price, Rigid(c);rep 6.00

126-THE DOWNFALL
By Emile Zola
05/55 **(---)** LC,LC P(c),Original,'Picture
Progress'Replaces Reorder List 25.00
08/64 **(167)** LC,LC P(c);rep 5.00
1968 **(166)** LC,LC P(c),25¢(c)
Price;rep 9.00

127-THE KING OF THE MOUNTAINS
By Edmond About
07/55 **(128)** NN,P(c),Original 25.00

06/64 **(167)** NN,P(c);rep 9.00
Fl/68 **(166)** NN,P(c),25¢(c)Price;rep 9.00

128-MACBETH
By William Shakespeare
09/55 **(128)** AB,P(c),Original 32.00
03/58 **(143)** AB,P(c);rep 6.00
09/60 **(158)** AB,P(c);rep 6.00
62/63 **(167)** AB,P(c);rep 6.00
06/64 **(167)** AB,P(c);rep 6.00
04/67 **(166)** AB,P(c);rep 6.00
1968 **(166)** AB,P(c),25¢(c)Price;rep 6.00
Sg/70 **(169)** AB,P(c),Rigid(c);rep . . 6.00

CI #133 The Time Machine,
© Gilberton Publications

129-DAVY CROCKETT
Author Unknown
11/55 **(129)** LC,P(c),Original 70.00
09/66 **(167)** LC,P(c);rep 40.00

130-CAESAR'S CONQUESTS
By Julius Caesar
01/56 **(130)** JO,P(c),Original 25.00
01/58 **(142)** JO,P(c);rep 6.00
09/59 **(152)** JO,P(c);rep 6.00
03/61 **(149)** JO,P(c);rep 6.00
62/63 **(167)** JO,P(c);rep 6.00
10/64 **(167)** JO,P(c);rep 6.00
04/66 **(167)** JO,P(c);rep 6.00

131-THE COVERED WAGON
By Emerson Hough
03/56 **(131)** NN,P(c),Original 25.00
03/58 **(143)** NN,P(c);rep 6.00
09/59 **(152)** NN,P(c);rep 6.00
09/60 **(158)** NN,P(c);rep 6.00
62/63 **(167)** NN,P(c);rep 6.00
11/64 **(167)** NN,P(c);rep 6.00
04/66 **(167)** NN,P(c),25¢ 6.00
Wr/69 **(169)** NN,P(c),25¢(c)
Price, Rigid(c);rep 6.00

132-THE DARK FRIGATE
By Charles Boardman Hawes
05/56 **(132)** EW&RWb,P(c),Original 25.00
05/59 **(150)** EW&RWb,P(c);rep . . . 9.00
01/64 **(167)** EW&RWb,P(c);rep . . . 9.00
05/67 **(166)** EW&RWb,P(c);rep . . . 9.00

133-THE TIME MACHINE
By H. G. Wells
07/56 **(132)** LC,P(c),Original 45.00
01/58 **(142)** LC,P(c);rep 8.00
09/59 **(152)** LC,P(c);rep 8.00
09/60 **(158)** LC,P(c);rep 8.00
62/63 **(167)** LC,P(c);rep 8.00
06/64 **(167)** LC,P(c);rep 8.00
03/66 **(167)** LC,P(c);rep 8.00
03/66 **(167)** LC,P(c),N# Or Price;rep 8.00
12/67 **(166)** LC,P(c);rep 8.00
Wr/71 **(169)** LC,P(c),25¢(c)
Price, Rigid(c);rep 10.00

134-ROMEO AND JULIET
By William Shakespeare
09/56 **(134)** GE,P(c),Original 25.00
03/61 **(161)** GE,P(c);rep 6.00
09/63 **(167)** GE,P(c);rep 6.00
05/65 **(167)** GE,P(c);rep 6.00
06/67 **(166)** GE,P(c);rep 6.00
Wr/69 **(166)** GE,EdM New P(c),
25¢(c)Price, Rigid(c);rep 21.00

135-WATERLOO
By Emile Erckmann & Alexandre Chatrian
11/56 **(135)** Grl,AB P(c),Original . 25.00
11/59 **(153)** Grl,AB P(c);rep 5.00
62/63 **(167)** Grl,AB P(c);rep 5.00
09/64 **(167)** Grl,AB P(c);rep 5.00
1968 **(166)** Grl,AB P(c),25¢(c)
Price; rep 5.00

136-LORD JIM
By Joseph Conrad
01/57 **(136)** GE,P(c),Original 25.00
62/63 **(165)** GE,P(c);rep 5.00
03/64 **(167)** GE,P(c);rep 5.00
09/66 **(167)** GE,P(c);rep 5.00
Sr/69 **(169)** GE,P(c),25¢(c)
Price, Rigid(c);rep 5.00

137-THE LITTLE SAVAGE
By Captain Frederick Marryat
03/57 **(136)** GE,P(c),Original 25.00
01/59 **(148)** GE,P(c);rep 5.00
05/60 **(156)** GE,P(c);rep 5.00
62/63 **(167)** GE,P(c);rep 5.00
10/64 **(167)** GE,P(c);rep 5.00
08/67 **(166)** GE,P(c);rep 5.00
Sg/70 **(169)** GE,P(c),25¢(c)
Price, Rigid(c);rep 5.00

138-A JOURNEY TO THE CENTER OF THE EARTH
By Jules Verne
05/57 **(136)** NN,P(c),Original 35.00
09/58 **(146)** NN,P(c);rep 5.00
05/60 **(156)** NN,P(c);rep 5.00
09/60 **(158)** NN,P(c);rep 5.00
62/63 **(167)** NN,P(c);rep 5.00
06/64 **(167)** NN,P(c);rep 5.00
04/66 **(167)** NN,P(c);rep 5.00
1968 **(166)** NN,P(c),25¢(c)Price;rep 5.00

139-IN THE REIGN OF TERROR
By George Alfred Henty
07/57 **(139)** GE,P(c),Original 28.00
01/60 **(154)** GE,P(c);rep 5.00
62/63 **(167)** GE,P(c),Erroneously

All comics prices listed are for *Near Mint* condition.

Has Original Date;rep 5.00
07/64 **(167)** GE,P(c);rep 5.00
1968 **(166)** GE,P(c),25¢(c)Price;rep 5.00

140-ON JUNGLE TRAILS
By Frank Buck
09/57 **(140)** NN,P(c),Original 25.00
05/59 **(150)** NN,P(c);rep 5.00
01/61 **(160)** NN,P(c);rep 5.00
09/63 **(167)** NN,P(c);rep 5.00
09/65 **(167)** NN,P(c);rep 5.00

141-CASTLE DANGEROUS
By Sir Walter Scott
11/57 **(141)** StC,P(c),Original 25.00
09/59 **(152)** StC,P(c);rep 5.00
62/63 **(167)** StC,P(c);rep 5.00
07/67 **(166)** StC,P(c);rep 5.00

142-ABRAHAM LINCOLN
By Benjamin Thomas
01/58 **(142)** NN,P(c),Original 25.00
01/60 **(154)** NN,P(c);rep 5.00
09/60 **(158)** NN,P(c);rep 5.00
10/63 **(167)** NN,P(c);rep 5.00
07/65 **(167)** NN,P(c);rep 5.00
11/67 **(166)** NN,P(c);rep 5.00
Fl/69 **(169)** NN,P(c),25¢(c) Price,
Rigid(c);rep 5.00

143-KIM
By Rudyard Kipling
03/58 **(143)** JO,P(c)Original 25.00
62/63 **(165)** JO,P(c);rep 6.00
11/63 **(167)** JO,P(c);rep 6.00
08/65 **(167)** JO,P(c);rep 6.00
Wr/69 **(169)** JO,P(c),25¢(c) Price,
Rigid(c);rep 6.00

144-THE FIRST MEN IN THE MOON
By H. G. Wells
05/58 **(143)** GWb,AW,AT,RKr,GMC
P(c), Original 32.00
11/59 **(153)** GWb,AW,AT,RKr,GMC
P(c); rep 6.00
03/61 **(161)** GWb,AW,AT,RKr,GMC
P(c); rep 6.00
62/63 **(167)** GWb,AW,AT,RKr,GMC
P(c); rep 6.00
12/65 **(167)** GWb,AW,AT,RKr,GMC
P(c); rep 6.00
Fl/68 **(166)** GWb,AW,AT,RKr,GMC P(c),
25¢(c) Price,Rigid(c);rep .. 6.00
Wr/69 **(169)** GWb,AW,AT,RKr,GMC
P(c), Rigid(c);rep 6.00

145-THE CRISIS
by Winston Churchill
07/58 **(143)** GE,P(c),Original 26.00
05/60 **(156)** GE,P(c);rep 6.00
10/63 **(167)** GE,P(c);rep 6.00
03/65 **(167)** GE,P(c);rep 6.00
1968 **(166)** GE,P(c),25¢(c)Price;rep 6.00

146-WITH FIRE AND SWORD
By Henryk Sienkiewicz
09/58 **(143)** GWb,P(c),Original ... 26.00
05/60 **(156)** GWb,P(c);rep 9.00
11/63 **(167)** GWb,P(c);rep 9.00
03/65 **(167)** GWb,P(c);rep 9.00

147-BEN-HUR
By Lew Wallace
11/58 **(147)** JO,P(c),Original 26.00
11/59 **(153)** JO,P(c);rep 30.00
09/60 **(158)** JO,P(c);rep 6.00
62/63 **(167)** JO,P(c),Has the
Original Date;rep 6.00
----- **(167)** JO,P(c);rep 6.00
02/65 **(167)** JO,P(c);rep 6.00
09/66 **(167)** JO,P(c);rep 6.00
Fl/68 **(166)** JO,P(c),25¢(c)Price,
BothRigid & Soft (c)s;rep 15.00

148-THE BUCKANEER
By Lyle Saxon
01/59 **(148)** GE&RJ,NS P(c),Original25.00
----- **(568)** GE&RJ,NS P(c),Juniors
List Only;rep 9.00
62/63 **(167)** GE&RJ,NS P(c);rep .. 6.00
09/65 **(167)** GE&RJ,NS P(c);rep .. 6.00
Sr/69 **(169)** GE&RJ,NS P(c),25¢(c)
Price, Rigid(c);rep 6.00

149-OFF ON A COMET
By Jules Verne
03/59 **(149)** GMc,P(c),Original ... 25.00
03/60 **(155)** GMc,P(c);rep 6.00
03/61 **(149)** GMc,P(c);rep 6.00
12/63 **(167)** GMc,P(c);rep 6.00
02/65 **(167)** GMc,P(c);rep 6.00
10/66 **(167)** GMc,P(c);rep 6.00
Fl/68 **(166)** GMc,EdM New P(c),
25¢(c)Price;rep 15.00

150-THE VIRGINIAN
By Owen Winster
05/59 **(150)** NN,DrG P(c),Original 40.00
1961 **(164)** NN,DrG P(c);rep 12.00
62/63 **(167)** NN,DrG P(c);rep 11.00
12/65 **(167)** NN,DrG P(c);rep 11.00

151-WON BY THE SWORD
By George Alfred Henty
07/59 **(150)** JTg,P(c),Original 40.00
1961 **(164)** JTg,P(c);rep 11.00
10/63 **(167)** JTg,P(c);rep 11.00
1963 **(167)** JTg,P(c);rep 11.00
07/67 **(166)** JTg,P(c);rep 11.00

152-WILD ANIMALS I HAVE KNOWN
By Ernest Thompson Seton
09/59 **(152)** LbC,LbC P(c),Original 40.00
03/61 **(149)** LbC,LbC P(c),P(c);rep . 6.00
09/63 **(167)** LbC,LbC P(c);rep 5.00
08/65 **(167)** LbC,LbC P(c);rep 5.00
fl/69 **(169)** LbC,LbC P(c),25¢(c)
Price,Rigid(c);rep 5.00

153-THE INVISIBLE MAN
By H. G. Wells
11/59 **(153)** NN,GB P(c),Original . 45.00
03/61 **(149)** NN,GB P(c);rep 7.00
62/63 **(167)** NN,GB P(c);rep 6.00
02/65 **(167)** NN,GB P(c);rep 6.00
09/66 **(167)** NN,GB P(c);rep 6.00
Wr/69 **(166)** NN,GB P(c),25¢(c)
Price,Rigid(c);rep 6.00
Sg/71 **(169)** NN,GB P(c),Rigid(c),
Words Spelling'Invisible Man'
Are' Solid'Not'Invisible';rep 6.00

154-THE CONSPIRACY OF PONTIAC
By Francis Parkman
01/60 **(154)** GMc,GMc P(c),Original 40.00
11/63 **(167)** GMc,GMc P(c);rep .. 15.00
07/64 **(167)** GMc,GMc P(c);rep .. 15.00
12/67 **(166)** GMc,GMc P(c);rep .. 15.00

*CI #160 The Food of the Gods,
© Gilberton Publications*

155-THE LION OF THE NORTH
By George Alfred Henty
03/60 **(154)** NN,GMc P(c),Original 42.00
01/64 **(167)** NN,GMc P(c);rep ... 11.00
1967 **(166)** NN,GMc P(c),25¢(c)
Price; rep 11.00

156-THE CONQUEST OF MEXICO
By Bernal Diaz Del Castillo
05/60 **(156)** BPr,BPr P(c),Original 32.00
01/64 **(167)** BPr,BPr P(c);rep 7.00
08/67 **(166)** BPr,BPr P(c);rep 7.00
Sg/70 **(169)** BPr,BPr P(c),25¢(c)
Price; Rigid(c);rep 6.00

157-LIVES OF THE HUNTED
By Ernest Thompson Seton
07/60 **(156)** NN,LbC P(c),Original 35.00
02/64 **(167)** NN,LbC P(c);rep 14.00
10/67 **(166)** NN,LbC P(c);rep 14.00

158-THE CONSPIRATORS
By Alexandre Dumas
09/60 **(156)** GMc,GMc P(c),Original 35.00
07/64 **(167)** GMc,GMc P(c);rep .. 14.00
10/67 **(166)** GMc,GMc P(c);rep .. 14.00

159-THE OCTOPUS
By Frank Norris
11/60 **(159)** GM&GE,LbC P(c),
Original 32.00
02/64 **(167)** GM&GE,LbC P(c);rep 12.00
166 **(1967)** GM&GE,LbC P(c),25¢(c)
Price;rep 12.00

160-THE FOOD OF THE GODS
By H.G. Wells
01/61 **(159)** TyT,GMc P(c),Original 35.00
01/61 **(160)** TyT,GMc P(c),Original;
Same Except For the HRN# ... 30.00
01/64 **(167)** TyT,GMc P(c);rep ... 12.00
06/67 **(166)** TyT,GMc P(c);rep ... 12.00

161-CLEOPATRA
By H. Rider Haggard
03/61 **(161)** NN,Pch P(c),Original . 45.00
01/64 **(167)** NN,Pch P(c);rep 16.00
08/67 **(166)** NN,Pch P(c);rep 16.00

162-ROBUR THE CONQUEROR
By Jules Verne
05/61 **(162)** GM&DPn,CJ P(c),
Original 32.00
07/64 **(167)** GM&DPn,CJ P(c);rep 12.00
08/67 **(166)** GM&DPn,CJ P(c);rep 12.00

163-MASTER OF THE WORLD
By Jules Verne
07/61 **(163)** GM,P(c),Original 32.00
01/65 **(167)** GM,P(c);rep 12.00
1968 **(166)** GM,P(c),25¢(c)
Price;rep 12.00

164-THE COSSACK CHIEF
By Nicolai Gogol
1961 **(164)** SyM,P(c),Original ... 35.00
04/65 **(167)** SyM,P(c);rep 12.00
Fl/68 **(166)** SyM,P(c),25¢(c)
Price;rep 12.00

165-THE QUEEN'S NECKLACE
by Alexandre Dumas
01/62 **(164)** GM,P(c),Original 35.00
04/65 **(167)** GM,P(c);rep 12.00
Fl/68 **(166)** GM,P(c),25¢(c)
Price;rep 12.00

166-TIGERS AND TRAITORS
By Jules Verne
05/62 **(165)** NN,P(c),Original 60.00
02/64 **(167)** NN,P(c);rep 16.00
11/66 **(167)** NN,P(c);rep 16.00

167-FAUST
By Johann Wolfgang von Goethe
08/62 **(165)** NN,NN P(c),Original . 90.00
02/64 **(167)** NN,NN P(c);rep 50.00
06/67 **(166)** NN,NN P(c);rep 50.00

168-IN FREEDOM'S CAUSE
By George Alfred Henty
Wr/69 **(169)** GE&RC,P(c),
Original, Rigid (c) 80.00

169-NEGRO AMERICANS THE EARLY YEARS
AUTHOR UNKNOWN
Sg/69 **(166)** NN,NN P(c),
Original,Rigid(c) 80.00

Sg/69 **(169)** NN,NN P(c),
Rigid;rep 60.00

See Also:
Independent Color Listings

CLASSICS ILLUSTRATED GIANTS
An Illustrated Library of Great
Adventure Stories
-(reps. of Issues 6,7,8,10) ... 800.00
An Illustrated Library of Exciting
Mystery Stories
-(reps. of Issues 30,21,40,13) . 850.00
An Illustrated Library of Great
Indian Stories
-(reps. of Issues 4,17,22,37) .. 725.00

CI Jr. #502, The Ugly Duckling,
© Gilberton Publications

CLASSICS ILLUSTRATED JUNIOR
501-Snow White and the
Seven Dwarves 70.00
502-The Ugly Duckling 40.00
503-Cinderella 24.00
504-The Pied Piper 16.00
505-The Sleeping Beauty 16.00
506-The Three Little Pigs 16.00
507-Jack and the Beanstalk 16.00
508-Goldilocks and the Three Bears 16.00
509-Beauty and the Beast 16.00
510-Little Red Riding Hood 16.00
511-Puss-N-Boots 16.00
512-Rumpelstilskin 16.00
513-Pinnochio 24.00
514-The Steadfast Tin Soldier ... 32.00
515-Johnny Appleseed 16.00
516-Alladin and His Lamp 24.00
517-The Emperor's New Clothes . 16.00
518-The Golden Goose 16.00
519-Paul Bunyan 16.00
520-Thumbelina 24.00
521-King of the golden River ... 16.00
522-The Nightingale 11.00
523-The Gallant Tailor 11.00
524-The Wild Swans 11.00
525-The Little Mermaid 11.00
526-The Frog Prince 11.00
527-The Golden-Haired Giant ... 11.00
528-The Penny Prince 11.00
529-The Magic Servants 11.00
530-The Golden Bird 11.00
531-Rapunzel 16.00
532-The Dancing Princesses 11.00
533-The Magic Fountain 11.00
534-The Golden Touch 11.00
535-The Wizard of Oz 32.00
536-The Chimney Sweep 11.00
537-The Three Faires 11.00
538-Silly Hans 11.00
539-The Enchanted Fish 24.00
540-The Tinder-Box 24.00
541-Snow White and Rose Red .. 16.00
542-The Donkey's Tail 16.00
543-The House in the Woods ... 11.00
544-The Golden Fleece 32.00
545-The Glass Mountain 16.00
546-The Elves and the Shoemaker 11.00
547-The Wishing Table 11.00
548-The Magic Pitcher 11.00
549-Simple Kate 11.00
550-The Singing Donkey 11.00
551-The Queen Bee 11.00
552-The Three Little Dwarves ... 16.00
553-King Thrushbeard 11.00
554-The Enchanted Deer 11.00
555-The Three Golden Apples ... 11.00
556-The Elf Mound 11.00
557-Silly Willy 28.00
558-The Magic Dish 28.00
559-The Japanese Lantern 28.00
560-The Doll Princess 28.00
561-Hans Humdrum 11.00
562-The Enchanted Pony 24.00
563-The Wishing Well 11.00
564-The Salt Mountain 11.00
565-The Silly Princess 11.00
566-Clumsy Hans 11.00
567-The Bearskin Soldier 11.00
568-The Happy Hedgehog 11.00
569-The Three Giants 11.00
570-The Pearl Princess 7.00
571-How Fire Came to the Indians 9.00
572-The Drummer Boy 14.00
573-The Crystal Ball 14.00
574-Brightboots 14.00
575-The Fearless Prince 16.00
576-The Princess Who Saw
Everything 24.00
577-The Runaway Dumpling 32.00

CLASSICS ILLLUSTRATED SPECIAL ISSUE
N# United Nations 225.00
129-The Story of Jesus 40.00
132A-The Story of America 35.00
135A-The Ten Commandments .. 40.00
138A-Adventures in Science 32.00
141A-The Rough Rider 32.00
144A-Blazing the Trails 32.00
147A-Crossing the Rockies 40.00
150A-Royal Canadian Police ... 35.00
153A-Men, Guns, and Cattle 35.00
156A-The Atomic Age 35.00
159A-Rockets, Jets and Missles . 35.00
162A-War Between the States ... 75.00
165A-To the Stars 40.00
166A-World War II 45.00
167A-Prehistoric World 45.00

All comics prices listed are for *Near Mint* condition.

AMAZING DOPE TALES
Greg Shaw
1 Untrimmed black and white pages, out of order;artist unknown . 110.00
2 Trimmed and proper pages . . . 95.00

AMERICAN SPLENDOR
Harvey Pekar
May, 1976
1 B:Harvey Pekar Stories, HP,RCr,GDu,GBu 12.00
2 HP,RCr,GDu,GBu 6.50
3 HP,RCr,GDu,GBu 6.00
4 HP,RCr,GDu,GBu 5.50
5 HP,RCr,GDu,GBu 5.00
6 HP,RCr,GDu,GBu,GSh 4.50
7 HP,GSh,GDu,GBu 2.50
8 HP,GSh,GDu,GBu 2.00
9 HP,GSh,GDu,GBu 2.75
10 HP,GSh,GDu,GBu 2.75
11 . . . . 3.00
12 . . . . 4.50
13 . . . . 3.25
14-19 . . . . 3.50
20 E:Harvey Pekar Stories 4.00

ANTHOLOGY OF SLOW DEATH
Wingnut Press/Last Gasp
1 140 pgs, RCr,RCo, GiS, DSh,Harlan Ellison VB,RTu 37.00

APEX TREASURY OF UNDERGROUND COMICS, THE
Links Books Inc.
October, 1974
1 . . . . 35.00

APEX TREASURY OF UNDERGROUND COMICS –BEST OF BIJOU FUNNIES
Quick Fox
1981
1 Paperback,comix,various artists 21.00

ARCADE THE COMICS REVUE
Print Mint Inc.
Spring, 1975
1 ASp,BG,RCr,SRo,SCW 16.50
2 ASp,BG,RCr,SRo 12.00
3 ASp,BG,RCr,RW,SCW 8.50
4 ASp,BG,RCr,WBu,RW,SCW . . 8.50
5 ASp,BG,SRo,RW,SCW 7.50
6 ASp,BG,SRo,RCr,SCW 7.50
7 ASp,BG,SRo,RCr,SCW 7.50

BABYFAT
Comix World/Clay Geerdes
1978
1 B:8pg news parodies, one page comix by various artists 4.50
2 same 3.00
3 same 3.00
4 same 3.00
5-9 same 3.00

10 thru 26 same . . . . @2.00

BATTLE OF THE TITANS
University of Illinois
SF Society
1972
1 Sci-Fi;VB,JGa 42.50

BEST BUY COMICS
Last Gasp Eco-Funnies
1 Rep Whole Earth Review;RCr . . 3.50

BEST OF BIJOU FUNNIES, THE
Links Books Inc.
1975
1 164 pgs,paperback 235.00

BEST OF RIP-OFF PRESS
Rip Off Press Inc.
1973
1 132 pgs paperback,SCW, RCr,SRo,RW 24.00
2 100 pgs,GS,FT 27.50
3 100 pgs,FS 10.75
4 132 pgs,GiS,DSh 13.00

BIG ASS
Rip Off Press
1969-1971
1 28 pgs,RCr 75.00
2 RCr 42.00

Bijou Funnies #1
© Bijou Publ. Empire

BIJOU FUNNIES
Bijou Publishing Empire
1968
1 B:JLy,editor;RCr,GS SW 285.00
2 RCr,GS,SW 85.50
3 RCr,SWi,JsG 52.00
4 SWi,JsG 30.00
5 SWi,JsG 33.50
6 E:JLy,editor,SWi,RCr,JsG . . . 27.00
7-8 . . . . 26.00

BINKY BROWN MEETS THE HOLY VIRGIN MARY
March, 1972
Last Gasp Eco-Funnies
N# Autobiography about Growing up w/a Catholic Neurosis,JsG . 22.50
2nd Printing:only text in bottom left panel 12.00

BIZARRE SEX
Kitchen Sink Komix
May, 1972
1 B:DKi,editor,various artists 27.00
2 . . . . 22.00
3 . . . . 16.00
4-6 . . . . @11.00
7 . . . . 4.00
8 . . . . 3.50
9 Omaha the Cat Dancer,RW . 16.50

BLACK LAUGHTER
Black Laughter Publishing Co
Nov 1972
1 James Dixon art 64.00

BLOOD FROM A STONE (GUIDE TO TAX REFORM)
New York Public Interest Research Group Inc.
1977
1 Tax reform proposals 8.50

BOBBY LONDON RETROSPECTIVE AND ART PORTFOLIO
Cartoonist Representatives
1 . . . . 19.50

BOBMAN AND TEDDY
Parrallax Comic Books Inc
1966
1 RFK & Ted Kennedy's struggle to control Democratic party 35.50

BODE'S CARTOON CONCERT
Dell
Sept, 1973
1 132 pgs; VB 27.50

BOGEYMAN COMICS
San Fransisco Comic Book Co., 1969
1 Horror,RHa 55.00
2 Horror,RHa 42.00
The Company & Sons
3 . . . . 31.00

BUFFALO RAG/THE DEAD CONCERT COMIX
Kenny Laramey
Dec 1973
1 Alice in Wonderland parody . 55.00

CAPTAIN GUTS
The Print Mint
1969
1 Super patriotV:Counter

culture 26.50
2 V:Black Panthers 19.00
3 V:Dope Smugglers 19.00

CAPTAIN STICKY
Captain Sticky
1974-75
1 Super lawyer V:Social
Injustice 17.50

CARTOON HISTORY OF THE UNIVERSE
Rip Off Press
September, 1978
1 Evolution of Everything;
B:Larry Gonick 6.50
2 Sticks and Stones 6.50
3 River Realms-Sumer & Egypt . 6.50
4 Part of the Old Testament . . . 4.50
5 Brains and Bronze 4.50
6 Who are these Athenians 3.75

CASCADE COMIX MONTHLY
Everyman Studios
March, 1978
1 Interviews,articles about
comix & comix artists 6.50
2 same 6.50
3 same 6.50
4 thru 11 . . . . @3.00
12 thru 23 . . . . @2.25

CHECKERED DEMON
Last Gasp
July, 1977
1 SCW 13.00
2 SCW 8.50
3 SCW 6.50

CHEECH WIZARD
Office of Student Publications,
Syracuse U
1967
n/n VB 120.00

CHICAGO MIRROR
Jay Lynch/Mirror
Publishing Empire
Autumn, 1967
1 B:Bijou Funnies 45.00
2 same 35.00
3 same 115.00

COLLECTED CHEECH WIZARD, THE
Company & Sons
1972
n/n VB 55.00

COLLECTED TRASHMAN #1, THE
Fat City & The Red Mountain
Tribe Productions
n/n SRo 32.50

COMICS & COMIX
October, 1975
1 . . . . 12.00

COMIX BOOK
Magazine Management Co., Inc.
October, 1974
1 Compilation for newsstand
distribution 14.50
2 . . . . 9.00
3 . . . . 9.00
Kitchen Sink Enterprises
4 . . . . 14.50
5 . . . . 8.50

COMIX COLLECTOR, THE
Archival Press Inc.
December, 1979
1 Fanzine 5.00
2-3 Fanzine 4.00

COMMIES FROM MARS
Kitchen Sink Enterprises
March, 1973
1 TB 32.50
Last Gasp
2 thru 5 TB . . . . @9.50

COMPLETE FRITZ THE CAT
Belier Press
1978
n/n RCr,SRo,DSh 49.50

CONSPIRACY CAPERS
The Conspiracy
1969
1 Benefit Legal Defense of the
Chicago-8 . . . . 79.00

DAN O'NEIL'S COMICS & STORIES
VOL.1 1-3
Company & Sons
1 B:Dan O'Neill 45.00
2-3 . . . . 30.00
1971
VOL.2 1-3
1 . . . . 6.50
2 . . . . 4.50
3 E:Dan O'Neill 4.50

DAS KAMPF
Vaughn Bode
May, 1963
N# 100 Loose pgs. 750.00
2nd Printing 52pgs.-produced by
Walter Bachner&Bagginer,1977 9.50

DEADBONE EROTICA
Bantam Books Inc.
April, 1971
n/n 132 pgs VB 42.50

DEADCENTER CLEAVAGE
April, 1971
1 14 pgs 38.00

DEATH RATTLE
Kitchen Sink Enterprises
June, 1972
1 RCo,TB 25.00
2 TB 19.00
3 TB 16.00

DESPAIR
The Print Mint
1969
1 RCr 33.00

DIRTY DUCK BOOK, THE
Company & Sons
March, 1972
1 Bobby London 25.00

The Fabulous Furry Freak Brothers #1
© Gilbert Shelton

DISNEY RAPES THE 1st AMENDMENT
Dan O'Neil
1974
1 Benefit Air Pirates V:Disney
Law suit; Dan O'Neill 8.50

DOPE COMIX
Kitchen Sink Enterprises
February, 1978
1 Drugs comix;various
artists 7.50
2 same 5.75
3-4 LSD issue 4.00

DOPIN DAN
Last Gasp Eco-Funnies
April, 1972
1 TR 12.00
2 TR 8.50
3 TR 8.50
4 Todays Army,TR 7.50

DR. ATOMIC
Last Gasp Eco-Funnies
September, 1972
1 B:Larry S. Todd 12.00
2 and 3 . . . . @10.00
4 . . . . 7.50
5 E:Larry S. Todd 4.75

DR. ATOMIC'S MARIJUANA MULTIPLIER
Kistone Press
1974

---

1 How to grow great pot 7.50

DRAWINGS BY
S. CLAY WILSON
San Francisco Graphics
1 28 pgs 185.00

DYING DOLPHIN
The Print Mint
1970
n/n 14.50

EBON
San Francisco Comic Book Company
1 Comix version; RCr 20.00
1 Tabloid version 18.00

EL PERFECTO COMICS
The Print Mint
1973
N# Benefit Timothy Leary 27.00
2nd Printing-1975 . . . . 4.00

ETERNAL TRUTH
Sunday Funnies Comic Corp
1 Christian Comix 19.50

EVERMUCH WAVE
Atlantis Distributors
1 Nunzio the Narc; Adventures
   of God 60.00

FABULOUS FURRY
FREAK BROTHERS, THE
COLLECTED ADVENTURES OF
Rip Off Press #1
February, 1971
1 GiS 70.00

FURTHER ADVENTURES OF
Rip Off Press #2
1 GiS,DSh 47.50

A YEAR PASSES LIKE
NOTHING WITH
Rip Off Press #3
1 GiS 17.00

BROTHER CAN YOU
SPARE $.75 FOR
Rip Off Press #4
1 GiS,DSh 12.00

FABULOUS FURRY
FREAK BROTHERS, THE
Rip Off Press #5
1 GiS,DSh 9.50

SIX SNAPPY SOCKERS
FROM THE ARCHIVES OF
Rip Off Press #6
1 GiS 5.25

FANTAGOR
1970
1 (Corben), fanzine 90.00
1a (Last Gasp) 22.00
2-3 . . . . 20.00
4 . . . . 30.00

THE ADVENTURES OF
FAT FREDDY'S CAT,
Rip Off Press
February, 1977
1 . . . . 14.00
2 . . . . 4.50
3 . . . . 6.00
4 . . . . 5.00
5 . . . . 2.50

FEDS 'N' HEADS
COMICS
Gilbert Shelton/Print Mint
1968
N# I:Fabulous Furry Freak Bros.;
Has no 'Print Mint' Address
24 pgs. 350.00
2nd printing,28 pgs. 55.00
3rd printing,May, 1969 . . . . . . 45.00
4th printing,Says 'Forth
  Printing' 17.50
5th-12th printings . . . . @8.00
13th printing 6.50
14th printing 4.75

FELCH
Keith Green
1 RW,SCW,RCr 40.00

FEVER PITCH
Kitchen Sink Enterprises
July, 1976
1 RCo 20.00
Jabberwocky Graphix
2 250 signed & numbered 14.50
3 400 signed & numbered 13.50
4 . . . . 8.50

50'S FUNNIES
Kitchen Sink Enterprises
1980
1 Larry Shell, editor,various
   artists 5.00

FLAMING CARROT
COMICS
Kilian Barracks Free Press
Summer/Autumn, 1981
1 Bob Budden,various artists . . . 8.50

FLASH THEATRE
Oogle Productions
1970
1 44 pgs 37.50

FLESHAPOIDS FROM
EARTH
Popular Culture Exploitation Press
December, 1974
1 36 pgs 33.00

THE COMPLETE FOO!
Bijou Publishing
September, 1980
1 RCr, Charles Crumb, r:Crumb brothers
fanzines 30.00

FRITZ BUGS OUT
Ballentine Books
1972
n/n RCr 50.50

Fantagor #4 © Fantagor

FRITZ THE CAT
Ballentine Books
1969
n/n RCr 100.00

FRITZ THE NO-GOOD
Ballentine Books
1972
n/n RCr 45.00

FRITZ: SECRET AGENT
FOR THE CIA
Ballentine Books
1972
n/n RCr 39.00

FUNNY AMINALS
Apex Novelties/Don Donahue
1972
1 RCr 50.00

GAY COMIX
Kitchen Sink Enterprises
September, 1981
1 36 pgs 7.50
2 36 pgs 5.00

GEN OF HIROSHIMA
Educomics/Leonard Rifas
January, 1980
1 Antiwar comix by Hiroshima
   survivor Keiji Nakawaza 9.50
2 same 6.50

GHOST MOTHER COMICS
John "Mad" Peck
1969
1 SCw,JsG 47.50

GIMMEABREAK COMIX
Rhuta Press
February, 1971
2 48 pgs, #0 & #1 were advertised,but
    may not have been printed . . 95.00

GIRLS & BOYS
Lynda J. Barry
1980
1 B:12 pgs with every other page
    blank, all Barry art 8.00
2 thru 10 same . . . . @6.50
11 thru 20 same . . . . @4.50
20 thru 25 same . . . . @3.50

GOD NOSE
Jack Jackson/
Rip Off Press
1964
N# 42 pgs. 995.00
2nd printing,Pinkish(c);44p 60.00
3rd printing,Blue Border(c) 30.00
4th printing,Red Border(c) 15.00

GOTHIC BLIMP WORKS LTD.
East Village Other/
Peter Leggieri
1969
1 VB,Editor,various artists . . . 185.00
2 same 145.00
3 KDe,editor 135.00
4 KDe,editor 130.00
5-7 KDe,editor . . . . @125.00
8 various artists 185.00

GREASER COMICS
Half-Ass Press
September 1971
1 28 pgs, George DiCaprio 17.50
Rip Off Press
July 1972
2 George DiCaprio 10.00

GRIM WIT
Last Gasp
1972
1 RCo 35.00
2 RCo 25.00

HAROLD HEAD, THE COLLECTED ADVENTURES OF
Georgia Straight
1972
1 . . . . 45.00
2 . . . . 10.00

HARRY CHESS THAT MAN FROM A.U.N.T.I.E.
The Uncensored Adventures
Trojan Book Service
1966
N# 1st Comix By & For Gay
    Community 100.00

HEAR THE SOUND OF MY FEET WALKING....
Glide Urban Center
1969
1 Dan O'Neill, 128 pgs 65.00

HISTORY OF UNDERGROUND COMIX
Straight Arrow Books
1974
1 Book by Mark James Estren about
    Underground Comix 30.00

HOMEGROWN FUNNIES
Kitchen Sink
1971
1 RCr 39.00

HONKYTONK SUE, THE QUEEN OF COUNTRY SWING
Bob Boze Bell
February, 1979
1 BBB 7.00
2-3 BBB 5.00

IKE LIVES
Warm Neck Funnies
1973
1 20 pgs,Mark Fisher 10.00

INSECT FEAR
Last Gasp
1970
1 SRo,GiS,RHa,JsG 75.00
Print Mint
1970-1972
2 . . . . 30.00
3 . . . . 20.00

IT AIN'T ME BABE
Last Gasp Eco-Funnies
July. 1970
n/n First all women comix
    Womens Liberation theme . . 32.50

JAPANESE MONSTER
Carol Lay
July, 1979
1 8pgs, Carol Lay 5.00

JESUS LOVES YOU
Zondervan Books/Craig Yoe
1972
1 Christian, RCr 29.50

THE NEW ADVENTURES OF JESUS
Rip Off Press
November 1971
1 44 pgs, FSt 50.00

JIZ
Apex Novelty
1969
1 36 pgs; RCr, SRo, VMo, SCW; hand
trimmed and unevenly stapled . . 45.00

JUNKWAFFEL
The Print Mint
1971
1 VB 30.00
2 VB 25.00
3 VB 22.00
4 VB,JJ 18.00

KANNED KORN KOMIX
Canned Heat Fan Club
1969
1 20pgs 8.00

KAPTAIN AMERIKA KOMIX
Brief Candle Comix
March 1970
1 anti U.S. involvement in Laos . 27.50

KING BEE
Apex/Don Donahue & Kerry Clark
1969
1 RCr,SCW 100.00

KURTZMAN COMIX
Kitchen Sink Enterprises
September, 1976
1 HK,RCr,GiS,DKi,WE 12.50

LAUGH IN THE DARK
Last Gasp
n/n KDe,RHa,SRo,SCW 14.00

LENNY OF LAVEDO
Sunbury Productions/Print Mint
1965
N# Green(c);1st Joel Beck-a . . 545.00
2nd printing, Orange(c) 390.00
3rd printing, White(c) 195.00

THE MACHINES
Office of Student Publications
Syracuse University
1967
1 VB 125.00

THE MAN
Office of Student Publications
Syracuse University
1966
1 VB 155.00

MAGGOTZINE
Charles Schneider
May, 1981
1 Various Artists,conceptual
    maggot stuff 3.50

MANTICORE
Joe Kubert School of
Cartooning & Graphic Arts Inc.
Autumn, 1976
1 Fanzine,various artists 7.50

MEAN BITCH THRILLS
The Print Mint
1971
1 SRO 7.00

All comics prices listed are for *Near Mint* condition.

MICKEY RAT
Los Angeles Comic Book Co.
May, 1972
1 Robert Armstrong 32.50
2 same 29.00
3 same 9.50

MOM'S HOMEMADE COMICS
Kitchen Sink Enterprises
June 1969
1 DKi, RCr 125.00
The Print Mint
2 DKi 35.00
Kitchen Sink Enterprises
3 DKi,RCr 17.00

MONDAY FUNNIES, THE
Monday Funnies
1977
1 8pgs,various artists 6.50
2 16pgs,various artists 9.00
3 16pgs,various artists 6.50
4 16pgs,various artists 5.50

MONDAY FUNNIES, THE
Passtime Publications
July-August, 1980
1 thru 8 Marc L.Reed .... @4.00

MOUSE LIBERATION FRONT
COMMUNIQUE #2
August, 1979
1 SRo, SCW, VMo,DKi; Disney's suit
against Dan O'Neil's Air Pirates .. 9.50

MOONCHILD COMICS
Nicola Cuti
1968
0 Nicola Cuti 27.00
2 Nicola Cuti 27.00
3 Nicola Cuti 75.00

MOONDOG
The Print Mint
March, 1970
1 All George Metzer 11.00
2 same 6.50
3 same 3.75
4 same 3.75

MORE ADVENTURES OF FAT FREDDY'S CAT
Rip Off Press
January, 1981
1 GiS 14.00

MOTOR CITY COMICS
Rip Off Press
April, 1969
1 RCr 155.00
2 RCr 110.00

MR. NATURAL
San Fransisco Comic Book Co.
August, 1970
1 RCr 85.00
2 RCr 40.00

NARD 'N' PAT, JAYZEY LYNCH'S
Cartoonists Cooperative Press
March, 1974
1 Jay Lynch 7.00
2 Jay Lynch 4.50
Kitchen Sink Press
1972
3 .... 10.00

NEVERWHERE
Ariel Inc.
February 1978
1 RCo 17.50

NICKEL LIBRARY SERIES
Gary Arlington
1 1 pg heavy stock colored
  paper, Reed Crandall 5.00
2 Kim Deitch 1.50
3 Harrison Cady 1.50
4 Frank Frazetta 3.00
5 Will Eisner 3.00
6 Justin Green 1.50
7 C.C. Beck 3.00
8 Wally Wood 3.00
9 Winsor McCay 1.50
10 Jim Osborne 1.50
11 Don Towlley 1.50
12 Frank Frazetta 3.00
13 Will Eisner 3.00
14 Bill Griffith 1.50
15 George Herriman 1.50
16 Cliff Sterrett 1.50
17 George Herriman 1.50
18 Rory Hayes & Simon Deitch .. 1.50
19 Disney Studios 1.50
20 Alex Toth 1.50
21 Will Eisner 1.50
22 Jack Davis 1.00
23 Alex Toth 1.50
24 Michele Brand 1.50
25 Roger Brand 1.50
26 Arnold Roth 1.50
27 Murphy Anderson 2.00
28 Wally Wood 3.00
29 Jack Kirby 4.00
30 Harvey Kurtzman 3.00
31 Jay Kinney 1.50
32 Bill Plimpton 1.50
33 .... 1.50
34 Charles Dallas 1.50
35 thru 39 .... @1.50
40 Bill Edwards 1.50
41 Larry S. Todd 1.50
42 Charles Dallas 1.50
43 Jim Osborne 1.50
43 1/2 Larry S. Todd 1.50
44 Jack Jackson 1.50
45 Rick Griffin 1.50
46 Justin Green 1.50
47 Larry S. Todd 1.50
48 Larry S. Todd 1.50
49 Charles Dallas 1.50
50 Robert Crumb 3.00
51 Wally Wood 3.00
52 Charles Dallas 3.00
53 Larry S. Todd 1.50
54 Larry S. Todd 1.50
55 Charles Dallas 1.50
56 Jim Chase 1.50

57 Charles Dallas 1.50
58 Larry S. Todd 1.50
59 Dave Geiser 1.50
60 Charles Dallas 1.50

ODD WORLD OF RICHARD CORBEN
Warren Publishing
1977
1 84pgs paperback 20.00

O.K. COMICS
Kitchen Sink Enterprises
June, 1972
1 Bruce Walthers 7.00
2 Bruce Walthers 7.00

O.K. Comics #12 © O.K. Comics

O.K. COMICS
O.K. Comic Company
1972
1 Tabloid with comix,
  articles,reviews,nudie
  cuties photos 27.50
2 thru 18 .... @18.75

ORACLE COMIX
Thru Black Holes
Comix Productions
October, 1980
1 Michael Roden 2.50
2 Michael Roden 2.50

PENGUINS IN BONDAGE
Sorcerer Studio/
Wayne Gibson
July, 1981
1 8pgs,Wayne Gibson 2.75

PHANTOM LADY
Randy Crawford
June, 1978
1 Sex funnies 4.50

PHUCKED UP FUNNIES
Suny Binghamton
1969
1 ASp; bound insert in
  yearbook 400.00

PINK FLOYD, THE
October, 1974
1 sold at concerts 27.50

PLASTIC MAN
Randy Crawford
May, 1977
1 Sex funnies,RandyCrawford . . 4.00

PORK
Co-op Press
May, 1974
1 SCW 11.00

PORTFOLIO OF UNDERGROUND ART
Schanes & Schanes
1980
1 SRo,SCW,VMo,RW and many others
13 loose sheets in folder,
32pg book, 1200 signed
and numbered 75.00

POWERMAN AND POWER MOWER SAFETY
Frank Burgmeir, Co.
Outdoor Power Equipment
1 VB; educational comic about power
mower safety 185.00

PROMETHIAN ENTERPRISES
Promethian Enterprises
Memorial Day, 1969
1 B:Jim Vadeboncuor editor . . 72.00
2 same 60.00
3 thru 5 . . . . @25.00

PURE ART QUARTERLY
John A. Adams
July, 1976
1 16pgs, All John A.Adams 8.50
2 thru 5 same . . . . @8.50
6 thru 10 same . . . . @5.00
11 thru 14 same . . . . @3.50

QUAGMIRE COMICS
Kitchen Sink Enterprises
Summer, 1970
1 DKi,Peter Poplaski 11.00

RAW
Raw Books
1980
1 36pgs,10pgs insert 310.00
2 36pgs,20pgs insert 185.00
3 52pgs,16pgs insert 155.00
4 44pgs,32pgs insert,Flexi
disk record 125.00

R. CRUMB'S COMICS AND STORIES
Rip Off Press
1969
1 RCr 75.00

RAWARARAWAR
Rip Off Press
1969
1 GSh 55.00

RED SONJA & CONAN "HOT AND DRY"
Randy Crawford
May, 1977
1 Sex funnies,Randy Crawford . . 3.50

REID FLEMING WORLD'S TOUGHEST MILKMAN
David E. Boswell
December, 1980
1 . . . . 6.00

RIP OFF COMIX
Rip Off Press
April, 1977
1 GiS,FSt,JsG,DSh 17.50
2-5 GiS,FSt . . . . @6.00
6 thru 10 . . . . @4.25

ROWLF
Rip Off Press
July, 1971
1 RCo 55.00

RUBBER DUCK TALES
The Print Mint
March, 1971
1 Michael J Becker 12.00
2 Michael J Becker 11.00

S. CLAY WILSON TWENTY DRAWINGS
Abington Book Shop Inc.
1967
N# (a),Cowboy(c) 460.00
    (b),Pirate(c) 460.00
    (c),Motorcyclist(c) 460.00
    (d),Demon(c) 460.00
    (e),Deluxe with all 4
    variations on same(c) with
    Gold Embossed
    Lettering 675.00

SAN FRANCISCO COMIC BOOK
San Francisco Comic Book Co.
January-February, 1970
1 . . . . 120.00
2 . . . . 20.00
3 . . . . 17.50
4 thru 6 . . . . @12.00

SAVAGE HUMOR
The Print Mint
1973
1 . . . . 4.00

SAY WHAT?
Loring Park Shelter
Community Cartooning Workshop
April, 1979
1 B:Charles T. Smith,editor,
various artists 7.00
2-6 same 6.50

SCHIZOPHRENIA, CHEECH WIZARD
Last Gasp Eco-Funnies
January, 1974
1 VB 30.00

SEX AND AFFECTION
C.P. Family Publishers
1974
1 Sex Education for Children . . . 5.50

SHORT ORDER COMIX
Head Press/Family Fun
1973
1 50 cents,36pgs. 8.50
2 75 cents,44pgs 2.25

SKULL COMICS
Last Gasp
March, 1970
1 Horror,RHa 47.00
2 GiS,DSh,RCo 25.50
3 SRo,DSh,RCo 14.00
4 DSh,Lovecraft issue 14.00
5 SRo,RCo,Lovecraft issue . . . 14.00
6 RCo,Herman Hesse 14.00

SLOW DEATH FUNNIES
Last Gasp
April 1970
1 Ecological Awarness & Red
Border on (c) 47.00
2nd-4th Printings White
Border(c) 10.00
2 Silver(c);1st edition'
pgs 34 . . . . 85.00
2b Non Silver(c);Says 1st
Edition pgs 34 . . . . 20.00
2nd Amorphia Ad on pg 34 . . . . 6.75
3rd Yellow Skull on (c) 5.00
4th 'Mind Candy For the Masses'
Ad on pg. 34 . . . . 5.00
5th $1.00(c) price 3.50
3 thru 5 . . . . @12.00
6 thru 10 . . . . @4.50

SMILE
Kitchen Sink Enterprises
Summer, 1970
1 Jim Mitchell 13.50
2 Jim Mitchell 12.00
3 Jim Mitchell 11.00

SNARF
Kitchen Sink Enterprises
February, 1972
1 DKi,editor,various artists . . . 24.50
2-5 same . . . . @15.00
6 thru 9 same . . . . @6.50

SNATCH COMICS
Apex Novelties
1968
1 RCr,SCW 295.00
2 RCr,SCW 145.00
3 RCr,SCW,RW 65.00

SNATCH SAMPLER
Keith Green
1979

All comics prices listed are for *Near Mint* condition.

n/n RCr,SCw,RW,RHa 32.00

SPACE INVADERS COMICS, DON CHIN'S
Comix World/Clay Geerdes
April, 1972
1 8pgs 4.00

SPASM!
Last Gasp Eco-Funnies
April, 1973
1 JJ 15.00

STONED PICTURE PARADE
San Francisco Comic Book Co., 1975
1 RCr,SRo,SCW,WE 20.00

SUBVERT COMICS
Rip Off Press
November, 1970
1 SRo 25.00
2 SRo 20.00
3 SRo 12.00

TALES OF SEX & DEATH
Print Mint
1971
1 JsG,KDe.RHa,SRo 32.50
2 JsG,KDe.RHa,SRo 19.50

THRILLING MURDER COMICS
San Francisco Comic Book Co., 1971
1   SCW,KDe,RCr,SRo,Jim
   Arlington,editor 24.50

2 (TWO)
Keith Green
February, 1975
1 SCW 7.00

VAMPIRELLA
Randy Crawford
June, 1978
1 Sex Funnies 3.50

VAUGHN BODE THE PORTFOLIO
Northern Comfort Communications
1976
1 VB,16pgs 125.00

VAUGHN BODE PRODUCTIONS PORTFOLIO #1
Vaughn Bode Productions
1978
1 VB,10 pgs 35.00

VAUGHN BODE'S CHEECH WIZARD, THE COLLECTED ADVENTURES OF THE CARTOON MESSIAH
Northern Comfort Communications
1976

1 VB,88pgs 55.00

VAUGHN BODE'S DEADBONE, THE FIRST TESTAMENT OF CHEECH WIZARD
Northern Comfort Communications
1975
1   VB 65.00

VIETNAM
N# 20pgs. Role of Blacks in
the War,TG Lewis 125.00

WEIRDO
Last Gasp Eco-Funnies
March, 1981
1 RCr 10.00
2 RCr 10.00
3 RCr 10.00

WEIRDO, THE
Rodney Schroeter
October, 1977
1 B:Rodney Schroezer,1pg 4.50
2 88pgs 4.50
3 44pgs 4.50

WIMMEN'S COMIX
Last Gasp Eco-Funnies
November, 1972
1   All women artists&comix 10.75
2   same 10.75
3   same 10.00
4-7 same .... @6.75

WONDER WART-HOG AND THE NURDS OF NOVEMBER
Rip Off Press
September, 1980
1 GiS 15.00

WONDER WART-HOG, CAPTAIN CRUD & OTHER SUPER STUFF
Fawcett Publications
1967
1 GiS,VB 22.00

YELLOW DOG
The Print Mint
May, 1968
1   4pgs,RCr 30.00
2   8pgs,RCr 25.00
3   8pgs,RCr 25.00
4   8pgs,RCr,SCW 25.00
5   8pgs,RCr,SCW,KDe 25.00
6 thru 12 .... @25.00
13/14 52pgs RCr,Jay Lynch ... 12.00
15 Don Scheneker,editor 59.00
16 .... 55.00
17 thru 24 .... @15.00

YOUNG AND LUSTLESS
San Francisco Comic Book Co., 1972
1   BG 15.50

YOUNG LUST
Company & Sons
October, 1970
1 BG,ASp 27.00
2   BG 15.00
3 BG,JsG,RCr,ASp 12.00
4 KDe,BG,SRo 10.50
5 BG,SRo 7.50
6 SRo,KDe 5.50

Yow #2 © Last Gasp

YOW
Last Gasp
April, 1978
1   BG 5.75
2   BG 4.75
Becomes:

ZIPPY
3 BG 6.50

ZAP COMIX
Apex Novelties
October, 1967
0   RCr 325.00
1   RCr 325.00
2   RCr,SCW 90.00
3   RCr,SCW,VMo,SRo 55.00
4   VMo,RW,RCr,SCW.SRo,GiS   55.00
5   RW,GiS,RCr,SCW,SRo 50.00
6   RW,GiS,RCr,SCW,SRo 25.00
7   RW,GiS,RCr,SCW,SRo 18.50
8   RW,GiS,RCr,SCW,SRo 10.00
9   RW,GiS,RCr,SCW,SRo 12.00

BIBLIOGRAPHY

Daniels, Les. *Comix: A History of Comic Books in America.* New York, NY: Bonanza Books, 1971.

Gerber, Ernst. *The Photo Journal Guide to Comic Books.* Minden, NV: Gerber Publishing, 1989. Vols. 1 & 2.

Gerber, Ernst. *The Photo Journal Guide to Marvel Comics.* Minden, NV: Gerber Publishing, 1991. Vols. 3 & 4.

Goulart, Ron. *The Adventurous Decade.* New Rochelle, NY: Arlington House, 1975.

Goulart, Ron. *The Encyclopedia of American Comics.* New York, NY. Facts on File Publications, 1990.

Goulart, Ron. *Over 50 Years of American Comic Books.* Lincolnwood, IL: Mallard Press, 1991.

Hegenburger, John. *Collectors Guide to Comic Books.* Radnor, PA: Wallace Homestead Book Company, 1990.

Kennedy, Jay. *The Official Underground and Newave Price Guide.* Cambridge, MA: Boatner Norton Press, 1982.

Malan, Dan. *The Complete Guide to Classics Collectibles.* St. Louis, MO: Malan Classical Enterprises, 1991.

O'Neil, Dennis. *Secret Origins of DC Super Heroes.* New York, NY: Warner Books, 1976.

Overstreet, Robert. *The Overstreet Comic Book Price Guide (25th Edition).* New York, NY. Avon Books, 1995

Rovin, Jeff. *The Encyclopedia of Super Heroes.* New York, NY: Facts on File Publications, 1985.

Rovin, Jeff. *The Encyclopedia of Super Villians.* New York, NY: Facts on File Publications, 1987.

Thompson, Don & Maggie. 7he *Golden Age of Comics, Summer 1982.* Tainpa, FL: New Media Publishing, 1982.

CVA GRADING/PRICE CHART

Grading comics is an objective art. This grading guide outlines the many conditions you should look for when purchasing comics, from the highest grade and top condition to the lowest collectible grade and condition. Your own comics will fall into one of these categories. A more complete description and our comments on comics grades can be found inside. We would like to point out, however, that no reader or advertiser is required to follow this or any other standard. All prices in Comics Values Annual are for comics in Near Mint condition. Happy collecting!

Mint: Perfect, pristine, devoid of any trace of wear or printing or handling flaws. Covers must be fully lustrous with sharply pointed corners. No color fading. Must be well centered. Many "rack" comics are not "Mint" even when new.

Near Mint: Almost perfect with virtually no wear. No significant printing flaws. Covers must be essentially lustrous with sharp corners. Spine is a tight as new. In older comics, minimal color fading is acceptable, as is slight aging of the paper. Most price guides, including CVA, quote prices in this grade.

Very Fine: Well preserved, still pleasing in appearance. Small signs of wear, most particularly around the staples. Most luster is readily visible. Corners may no longer be sharp, but are not rounded. Typical of a comic read only a few times and then properly stored.

Fine: Clean, presentable, with noticeable signs of wear. Some white may show through enamel around staples, and moderate rounding of corners. No tape or writing damage. Book still lies flat.

Very Good: A well worn reading copy with some minor damage such as creasing, small tears or cover flaking. Some discoloration may be evident, with obvious wear around the staples. Little luster remains, and some rolling of the spine may be seen when comic is laid flat on the table.

Good: A fully intact comic with very heavy wear. Tears, cover creases and flaking, and rolled spine will all be evident. No tape repairs present. Only very scarce or valuable issues are collected in this state.

The adjoining price table shows the prices for the other collectible grades which correspond to any "near mint" price given in this book.

Mint	Near Mint	Very Fine	Fine	Very Good
$6,000	$5,000	$3,500	$2,000	$1,000
4,800	4,000	2,800	1,600	800
3,600	3,000	2,100	1,200	600
2,400	2,000	1,400	800	400
1,800	1,500	1,050	600	300
1,200	1,000	700	400	200
1,080	900	630	360	180
960	800	560	320	160
900	750	525	300	150
840	700	490	280	140
780	650	455	260	130
720	600	420	240	120
660	550	385	220	110
600	500	350	200	100
570	475	332	190	95
540	450	315	180	90
510	425	297	170	85
480	400	280	160	80
450	375	262	150	75
420	350	245	140	70
390	325	227	130	65
360	300	210	120	60
330	275	192	110	55
300	250	175	100	50
270	225	157	90	45
240	200	140	80	40
210	175	122	70	35
180	150	105	60	30
150	125	87	50	25
120	100	70	40	20
114	95	66	38	19
108	90	63	36	18
102	85	59	32	17
96	80	56	32	16
90	75	52	30	15
84	70	49	28	14
78	65	45	26	13
72	60	42	24	12
66	55	38	22	11
60	50	35	2	10
54	45	31	18	9
48	40	28	16	8
42	35	24	14	7
36	30	21	12	6
30	25	17	10	5
24	20	14	8	4
22	18	12	7	4
21	17	11	7	4
18	15	10	6	3
17	14	9	5	3
16	13	9	5	3
15	12	8	5	2
14	11	7	4	2
12	10	7	4	2
11	9	6	4	2
10	8	5	3	1
9	7	5	3	1
7	6	4	3	1
6	5	4	2	1
5	4	3	2	0
4	3	2	1	0
3	2	2	0	0
2	1	1	0	0

Antique Trader Publications

BUSINESS REPLY MAIL
FIRST CLASS MAIL   PERMIT NO.50   DUBUQUE, IA

POSTAGE WILL BE PAID BY ADDRESSEE

Antique Trader Publications
PO BOX 1050
DUBUQUE   IA 52004-9969

Antique Trader Publications

NO POSTAGE
NECESSARY
IF MAILED
IN THE
UNITED STATES

BUSINESS REPLY MAIL
FIRST CLASS MAIL   PERMIT NO.50   DUBUQUE, IA

POSTAGE WILL BE PAID BY ADDRESSEE

Antique Trader Publications
PO BOX 1050
DUBUQUE   IA 52004-9969